Property of
FAMILY OF FAITH
LIBRARY

W9-BJD-957

Family of Faith Library

THE EMC MASTERPIECE SERIES

LITERATURE AND THE LANGUAGE ARTS

GRADES 9–12

A truly integrated literature and language arts program

THE EMC MASTERPIECE SERIES

LITERATURE AND THE LANGUAGE ARTS

- Integrates literature and language arts more thoroughly than any other series.
- Contains the most extensive collection of classic literary works available in any series today, as well as engaging contemporary selections.
- Emphasizes reader response, relating literature to student experiences while enabling the teacher to guide responses to ensure cultural transmission.
- Offers the most comprehensive portfolio assessment program available.
- Includes abundant teacher resources: Essential Skills Practice Books in five language arts subject areas; Assessment Portfolio; Reader's Guides and Activity Workbooks; Transparencies; and exciting, motivational multimedia components such as Audiocassettes, a Videocassette, Computer Software, a Video Laser Disc, and two CD-ROM Programs.

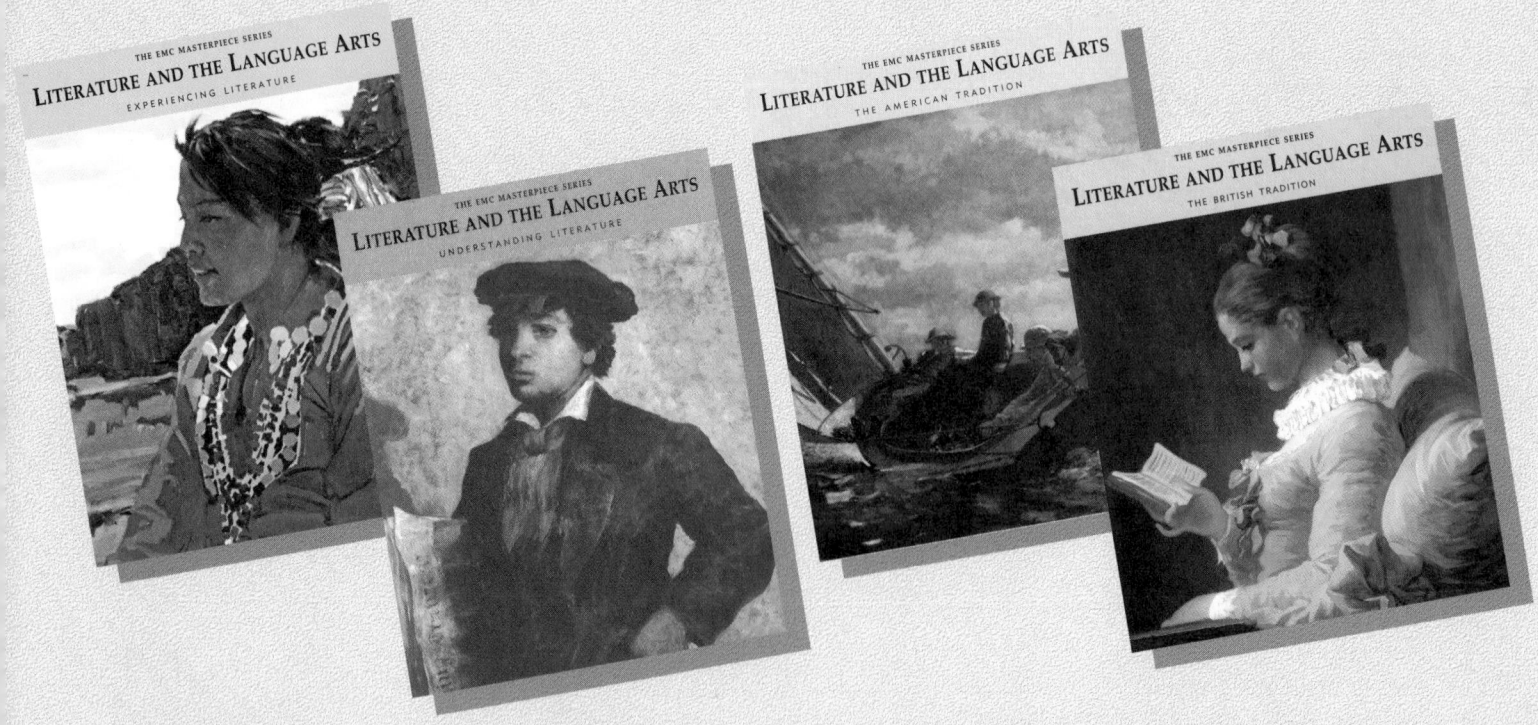

The EMC Masterpiece Series LITERATURE AND THE LANGUAGE ARTS contains the most comprehensive collection of classic literary works available in any series today, as well as current multicultural selections, to captivate your students. In addition, this series thoroughly models the complete range of literary types and genres: poetry, fiction, nonfiction, drama, myth, fairy tale, fable, parable, legend, tall tale, and folk song.

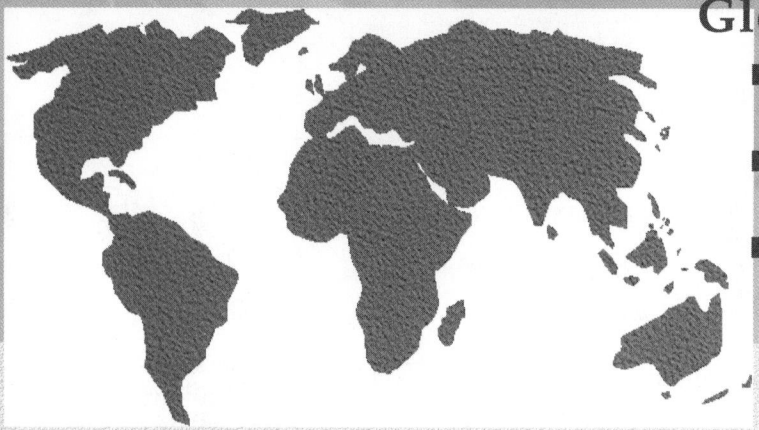

Global Representation of Authors

- Gabriela Mistral (Chile) "Dusk"
- Kamala Markandaya (India) from *Nectar in a Sieve*
- Maya Angelou (United States) "On the Pulse of Morning"
- Wole Solyinka (Nigeria) "Telephone Conversation"
- Julia Alvarez (Dominican Republic) "Dusting"
- Le Ly Hayslip (Vietnam) from *When Heaven and Earth Changed Places*

Strong Representation of Culturally Diverse Authors

The EMC Masterpiece Series contains an unequaled representation of works by authors from various cultural backgrounds. The series provides a well-rounded view of literary activity in cultural contexts around the corner and around the world.

Flexible Organization

The EMC Masterpiece Series provides a flexible organization allowing varied approaches to the literature, so teachers can readily adapt the materials to their individual teaching styles and to their students' needs.

Experiencing Literature and *Understanding Literature*
Grades 9 and 10

These levels are organized into separate sections presenting genres and techniques, themes, and modes (science fiction, fantasy, adventure, romance, mystery, and detective fiction). No other series covers all three in a single volume.

The American Tradition and *The British Tradition*
Grades 11 and 12

These levels have a chronological organization. Additional materials in the Annotated Teacher's Editions facilitate thematic, skill, and genre approaches. Each text begins with a high-interest, thorough review of basic literary types and techniques.

STUDENT TEXTBOOK

PREREADING

"The Conversion of King Edwin"
from *Ecclesiastical History of the English People*
by Saint Bede the Venerable

ABOUT THE AUTHOR

A page from the Grimbald Gospels. British Library, MS Add. 34890 fol. IOV. Courtesy of the British Library

Saint Bede the Venerable (AD 672– or 673–735) was born in Jarrow, in the kingdom of Northumbria. He entered the Monastery of St. Peter in nearby Wearmouth at the age of seven. At nineteen, he was ordained a deacon; at thirty, a priest. Like other monastics of his time, Bede wrote in Latin. He traveled very little, but his fame spread throughout Europe due to his writings on subjects as varied as history, poetry, grammar, mathematics, science, the scriptures, and lives of the saints. Bede's histories make fascinating reading not only for the light that they shed on the distant Anglo-Saxon past but also for their engaging accounts of miraculous and legendary events. In his histories, Bede introduced the practice of dating events from the birth of Christ (i.e., from AD 0, where AD is an abbreviation for the Latin *Anno Domini*, meaning "the year of our Lord"). This method of dating was adopted throughout Europe and is still in use today. Bede was canonized (made a saint of the Roman Catholic Church) in 1899, eleven hundred years after his death.

ABOUT THE SELECTION

Most notable among Bede's works is the *Historia ecclesiastica gentis Anglorum*, or ***Ecclesiastical History of the English People***. Bede's five-book Latin history of the Church in England covers the period from Cæsar's invasion of Britain (55–54 BC) to his own time (the history was finished around AD 731). King Alfred considered the book important enough to have it translated into Old English, the language of the common people. **"The Conversion of King Edwin"** comes from *Book II* of Bede's history and relates the process by which Christian missionaries converted the Anglo-Saxon kings. The selection shows the dramatic contrast between the Anglo-Saxons' grim view of the afterlife and the positive alternative offered by the missionaries. The pre-Christian, or pagan, Anglo-Saxons believed that a warrior who died bravely in battle would go after death to a land reserved for heroes, Valhalla. For others, the future after death was uncertain. The final paragraph of the selection, which compares the time before, during, and after life to the flight of a sparrow, is one of the most famous in all of English literature.

76 UNIT TWO / THE ANGLO-SAXON PERIOD

The British Museum

READER'S JOURNAL

Have you ever changed your mind about something important? Do you find change to be difficult or easy? Freewrite about change in your journal. You might write about personal change or about change that has occurred in your country or in your community.

RESEARCH SKILLS

Read the Language Arts Survey, 4.22, "Using the Card Catalog." Then use the card catalog in a library to find books with information about Saint Bede the Venerable. For each book, list the title, the author's name, the year of publication, the call number, and the kind of information given.

"The Conversion of King Edwin"

FROM *Ecclesiastical History of the English People*

SAINT BEDE THE VENERABLE

At this time the nation of the Northumbrians, that is, the nation of the Angles that live on the north side of the river Humber, with their king, Edwin, received the faith through the preaching of Paulinus.[1] This Edwin, as a reward of his receiving the faith, and as an earnest of his share in the heavenly kingdom, received an increase of that which he enjoyed on earth, for he reduced under his dominion all the borders of Britain that were provinces either of the aforesaid nation, or of the Britons, a thing which no British king had ever done before. . . .

For some time he delayed to receive the word of God at the preaching of Paulinus, and used to sit several hours alone, and seriously to ponder with himself what he was to do, and what religion he was to follow. Then the man of God came to him, laid his right hand on his head, and asked whether he knew that sign.[2] The king in a trembling condition, was ready to fall down at his feet, but he raised him up, and in a familiar manner said to him, "Behold, by the help of God you have escaped the hands of the enemies whom you feared. Behold you have of His gift obtained the kingdom which you desired. Take heed not to delay that which you promised to perform; embrace the faith, and keep the precepts of Him who, delivering you from temporal adversity, has raised you to the honor of

According to Bede, what reward does Edwin receive for converting to Christianity?

1. **Paulinus.** Pope Gregory I sent Paulinus as a missionary to Northumbria in AD 601.
2. **that sign.** The laying on of hands is a ceremony for transmitting spiritual grace to the recipient.

WORDS FOR EVERYDAY USE: **ec • cle • si • as • tic • cal** (e klē' zē as' ti kəl) *adj.*, having to do with the church; **tem • po • ral** (tem' pe rəl) *adj.*, lasting only for a time, limited; of this world, not spiritual; **ad • ver • si • ty** (ad vur' sə tē) *n.*, misfortune, trouble

"THE CONVERSION OF KING EDWIN" 77

- **About the Author** gives background on the author of the selection.
- **About the Selection** provides a background of when and why the selection was written.
- **Reader's Journal** activities relate the literature to students' feelings and experiences.
- **Language Arts Skills** activities referenced at the beginning of each selection are keyed to the Language Arts Survey. No other literature program has such strong integration of literature and language arts skills.
- **Words for Everyday Use** sections provide the definitions for vocabulary that is underlined in the selection.

- **Responding to the Selection** activities relate the literature to students' lives and experiences to spark their interest and to stimulate classroom discussion.
- The unique pedagogical design of this series virtually guarantees close reading. The novel organization of the **Reviewing the Selection** questions ensures that interpretations of the literature will be based on evidence from the selections.
- The **Recalling** questions ask about facts in the selection. Paired with each Recalling question is an **Interpreting** question that uses these facts as a basis for critical analysis and interpretation. **Synthesizing** questions pull together particular parts of the analysis just conducted, enabling students to arrive at a general understanding of each piece. This is the only series that keys all of its Interpreting questions to facts in the selections.
- **Guided Reading Questions** for each selection point out key elements and encourage critical response reading. This series alone provides such a tool for every selection.
- **Understanding Literature** questions provide instruction in literary movements, types, and techniques.

a temporal kingdom; and if, from this time forward, you shall be obedient to His will, which through me He signifies to you, He will not only deliver you from the everlasting torments of the wicked, but also make you partaker with Him of His eternal kingdom in Heaven."

The king, hearing these words, answered, that he was both willing and bound to receive the faith which he taught; but that he would confer about it with his principal friends and counselors, to the end that if they also were of his opinion, they might all together be cleansed in Christ the Fountain of Life. Paulinus consenting, the king did as he said; for, holding a council with the wise men,[3] he asked of every one in particular what he thought of the new doctrine, and the new worship that was preached. To which the chief of his own priests, Coifi, immediately answered, "O king, consider what this is which is now preached to us; for I verily declare to you, that the religion which we have hitherto professed has, as far as I can learn, no virtue in it. For none of your people has applied himself more diligently to the worship of our gods than I; and yet there are many who receive greater favors from you, and are more preferred than I, and are more prosperous in all their undertakings. Now if the gods were good for any thing, they would rather forward me, who have been more careful to serve them. It remains, therefore, that if upon examination you find those new doctrines, which are now preached to us, better and more efficacious, we immediately receive them without any delay."

Another of the king's chief men, approving of his words and exhortations, presently added: "The present life of man, O king, seems to me, in comparison to that time which is unknown to us, like to the swift flight of a sparrow through the room wherein you sit at supper in winter, with your commanders and ministers, and a good fire in the midst, whilst the storms of rain and snow prevail abroad; the sparrow, flying in at one door, and immediately out at another, whilst he is within, is safe from the wintry storm; but after a short space of fair weather, he immediately vanishes out of your sight, into the dark winter from which he had emerged. So this life of man appears for a short space, but of what went before, or what is to follow, we are utterly ignorant. If, therefore, this new doctrine contains something more certain, it seems justly to deserve to be followed." The other elders and king's counselors, by Divine inspiration, spoke to the same effect. ■

To what does the wise counselor compare life on the Anglo-Saxons knew it?

Why does the king's chief priest reject the old gods?

3. **wise men.** These wise men are the Anglo-Saxon *Witenagemot*, or council of elders. From the Old English *witen*, "to know," comes our modern word *wit*.

WORDS FOR EVERYDAY USE: **sig • ni • fy** (sig' nə fī') *vt.*, show by means of words or a sign; **ef • fi • ca • cious** (ef' i kā' shəs) *adj.*, effective, producing the desired result; **dil • i • gent • ly** (dil' ə jənt lē) *adv.*, with great care and attention

78 UNIT TWO / THE ANGLO-SAXON PERIOD

Responding to the Selection

Do the arguments advanced by Edwin's counselors seem reasonable to you? Do you feel that Edwin had reason to forsake his old beliefs and embrace these new ones? Why, or why not? Answer these questions in your journal.

Reviewing the Selection

RECALLING

1. Who is Paulinus? What does he ask of King Edwin? What does Paulinus promise?
2. With whom does King Edwin meet?
3. Who is Coifi? What does he think of the old religion?
4. To what does the king's advisor compare the swift flight of a sparrow?

INTERPRETING

5. Why does Paulinus believe Edwin has a responsibility to "embrace the faith"?
6. Why does King Edwin hold a meeting?
7. What reason does Coifi give for forsaking the old religion?
8. What view of life and of the afterlife is implicit in the counselor's story of the sparrow?

SYNTHESIZING

9. In what ways does the new religion differ from the old religion? What makes the new religion appealing to the elders and to the king's counselors?
10. According to King Edwin's advisors, what is the purpose of religion? In what ways are their views similar to or different from your own?

Understanding Literature (Questions for Discussion)

1. **Narration. Narration,** one of the modes of writing, tells a story. Normally, stories are told by beginning with what happens first and continuing chronologically (through time) toward what happens last. Is Bede's story of Edwin's conversion told chronologically? Where does Bede deviate from a strict chronological ordering? Why do you think he does this? Is the technique effective? Can you think of a story that you have told nonchronologically? Why did you tell it so?

"THE CONVERSION OF KING EDWIN" 79

UNIT 2 THE ANGLO-SAXON PERIOD (449–1066)

King Alfre's Messengers before Ragnar Lodbrok's Sons. J. A. Malmström, 1857. Nordiska Museet, Sweden

68 UNIT TWO / THE ANGLO-SAXON PERIOD

Y

ou each have something divine in your soul, namely Reason and Memory and a discerning will to make choices in life.

—Alfred the Great
King of the West Saxons

69

■ **Unit Openers** feature fine art from the period covered in the unit.

■ Creative, literature-based **Responding in Writing** activities provide opportunities for students to apply the process of writing and develop their writing skills.

■ **Language Labs** develop students' language arts skills in the context of literary study. Additional practice can be found in the Essential Skills Practice Books.

2. **Allegory.** An **allegory** is a work in which each element **symbolizes,** or represents, something else. The last paragraph of the selection contains an allegory comparing human life to the flight of a sparrow. To understand the allegory you need to determine what the characters and objects in the story symbolize. The story speaks of a sparrow, a dining room with a door, supper, winter storms, commanders and ministers, a fire, and our sight. What do these elements in the story symbolize?

3. **Purpose or Aim.** A writer's **aim** is the primary **purpose** that his or her work is meant to achieve. One purpose of "The Conversion of King Edwin" is to teach a lesson. What lesson does the selection teach? From reading the selection, can you tell whether Bede was a Christian or a pagan? How can you tell? How might the purpose be different if Bede were of a different religion?

Responding in Writing

1. **An Allegory.** Think of the story of the sparrow flying through the warm room and then out into the cold. Bede presents this story as an allegory for the life of an individual. An **allegory** is a story that seems simple but has another meaning altogether. What might be an allegory for working hard to accomplish a difficult task—perhaps running a marathon or climbing a tall mountain? Choose one of the following topics or one of your own. Then write an allegory to describe it.

   Possible topics:
   - saying goodbye to a friend
   - leaving home to go to college
   - studying for an important test

2. **A Persuasive Paragraph.** In order to convert King Edwin and his counsel, the missionary Paulinus had to be quite persuasive. What arguments did he use to convince them? How might you convince someone of something you feel strongly about? Maybe you have read a great book, and you are trying to convince a friend to read it. Maybe you are trying to change someone's mind about a political issue. Choose a topic for a persuasive paragraph. In a sentence, describe your position or stand on the topic. Then give two or three arguments to support your position.

Language Lab

Correcting Run-ons. Read the Language Arts Survey, 2.62, "Correcting Run-ons." Then revise the sentences below by changing punctuation and capitalization and adding words, as necessary.

1. Bede's history of Britain was not the first, it was partly based on *On the Fall of Britain,* written by Gildas, a Welshman, in AD 550.

80 UNIT TWO / THE ANGLO-SAXON PERIOD

2. According to stories told by early Welsh historians, one of the soldiers who fought against the Anglo-Saxons was named Arthur such stories gave rise to legends about King Arthur and the knights of the round table.
3. The early Germanic peoples, including the Anglo-Saxons, used alphabetic characters called *runes* to write inscriptions on stones, the runic alphabet is known as *futhark.*
4. The treasure of Sutton Hoo was found in 1939, at Sutton Hoo a seventh-century Anglo-Saxon king had been buried with a large number of jewels, coins, weapons, and tools he was entombed in a ninety-foot-long ship that had been hauled to the top of a one-hundred-foot-high cliff.
5. Our knowledge of the Anglo-Saxons comes from many sources these sources include inscriptions, histories, literature, and archeological finds like Sutton Hoo.

PROJECTS

1. **Improvisation.** Take a few moments to think about what it was like to be one of King Edwin's counselors. Try to imagine other meetings that might have taken place. Then form groups of four to six students. Take turns acting out one of the scenes listed below, with one person playing King Edwin and the others playing the counselors. Use your imagination as you think about the issue that is up for discussion.
   - Discuss adding other lands to the kingdom. The group can discuss whether this will happen as a result of peaceful negotiation or of battle.
   - Discuss a dispute between two earls over the possession of a sword taken from an enemy warrior. Decide who should receive the sword and why.
2. **Community Involvement.** When someone enters a community and tries to make change, sometimes the change is positive, and sometimes the change is negative. In either case, asking people to think in new ways is rarely easy. How might you and your classmates try to make positive change in your community? You might want to change how people feel about litter and the environment, or you might want to make people more excited about becoming involved in town issues or school events. Work with other students to organize a convincing campaign.

"THE CONVERSION OF KING EDWIN" 81

■ The hands-on **Projects** section allows students to perform multimodel, cross-curricular exercises based on the literature, further connecting it to students' actual lives.

Reader Response Emphasis
The *EMC Masterpiece Series* motivates students through high-interest affective and cognitive activities that relate literature to students' experiences, followed by teacher-directed activities to ensure cultural transmission.

Reader Response Activities:
- Reader's Journal
- Guided Reading Questions
- Responding to the Selection

Teacher-Directed Activities:
- Reviewing the Selection
- Responding in Writing
- Understanding Literature

Other Student Textbook Features:

- **Historical Introductions** in Grade 11, *The American Tradition,* and Grade 12, *The British Tradition,* provide thorough, stimulating discussions of historical figures and events, literary and artistic movements, genre and techniques, and major historical and literary figures.
- **Unit Reviews** reinforce major concepts from the unit and provide Synthesizing questions for writing, discussion, and research.
- **Multicultural Extensions** allow for comparative study of British and world literature.
- **Additional Readings** at the ends of units allow students to read extra selections from the authors. No other series offers this feature!
- The **Handbook of Literary Terms** contains twice as many terms as any other textbook program to promote students' understanding of literary movements, types, and techniques.

LANGUAGE ARTS SURVEY

Stimulating, literature-based activities in this series cover the full range of language arts skills:

- Emotional and critical responses to literature
- The process of writing
- Grammar, usage, mechanics, spelling, and vocabulary
- Varieties of English
- Speaking and listening
- Test-taking
- Critical thinking
- Study and research
- Applied English/ Tech prep

ESSENTIAL SKILLS:
Writing

INTRODUCTION TO WRITING

Students sometimes think of writing as a mysterious talent that some people are born with and others aren't. That just isn't so. The ability to write is learned through practice and through reading. If you keep writing, as much as you can, as often as you can, eventually you, too, will be one of those mysteriously talented people who can make written words do wonders.

1.1 THE PROCESS OF WRITING

No two people write exactly alike. Some people get everything down on paper quickly and in rough form. Then they rewrite, over and over, until they get it right. Other people work slowly, refining their ideas and expression as they go.

Despite the differences among writers, for purposes of instruction the writing process can be conveniently divided into six stages:

SIX STAGES IN THE PROCESS OF WRITING	
1. **Prewriting**	Choose a topic, audience, purpose, and form. Then gather ideas and organize these in a reasonable way.
2. **Drafting**	Get your ideas down on paper in rough form without worrying about perfecting spelling, grammar, usage, and mechanics.
3. **Peer and Self-Evaluation**	Study your draft by yourself or with one or more of your peers to find ways to improve it.
4. **Revising**	Revise your draft to improve its content, organization, and style.
5. **Proofreading**	Check your revised draft for errors in spelling, grammar, usage, and mechanics (including punctuation and capitalization). Then prepare a final copy in an appropriate manuscript form and proofread again.
6. **Publishing and Presenting**	Share your work with an audience.

1066 LANGUAGE ARTS SURVEY

ESSENTIAL SKILLS: WRITING

ACTIVITY 1.1

Take some time to examine your past experiences as a writer. On a sheet of paper or in your journal, answer the following questions:

1. Do you enjoy writing? Do you think of yourself as a good writer? Are there any writers—famous or not—whose work you admire? What good and bad experiences have you had as a writer? What are your strengths and weaknesses as a writer?
2. What kind of writing do you most enjoy doing? (Consult the list of Forms of Writing on page 1077.) Do you like writing poems, stories, humorous pieces, or reports? Why do you enjoy this kind of writing? What kinds of writing would you like to learn more about? What kinds of writing would you like to master?
3. Many writers are particular about the tools they use. What writing materials do you prefer? Do you like writing in a spiral notebook? on blank pages in a record book? on loose-leaf pages in a ring binder? on a typewriter or computer? with a pencil or a felt-tip pen?
4. When you have written in the past, did you devote a lot of time to prewriting? What sorts of prewriting activities did you do? Which of these activities were most helpful?
5. Are you the kind of writer who works slowly, perfecting each part as you go, or do you prefer to get a lot of material onto the page and then rework it?
6. In what stages of the writing process do you have the most trouble?
7. How do you feel about having other people read or listen to your writing? What can other people, including your classmates and your teacher, do to help you become a better writer?

1.2 KEEPING A WRITER'S JOURNAL

Think of a **writer's journal** as a storehouse of ideas for use in later writing. Keep your journal in a spiral notebook, a loose-leaf binder, a composition book, a scrapbook, or a bound record book of the kind sold in stationery stores. You'll get more out of a journal if you keep it separate from your other notebooks and write in it every day. The following ideas for journal entries will help you to get started.

IDEAS FOR JOURNAL ENTRIES	
The Journal as Diary	Record the observations and experiences from your daily life. Explore your feelings about people and events.
The Journal as Commonplace Book	Record interesting phrases or ideas that you hear from others or that you encounter in your reading.
The Journal as Writer's Lab	Record your ideas for pieces of writing to do in the future. Do freewriting on subjects of interest to you. Try out different kinds of writing, such as monologues, dialogues, song lyrics, concrete poetry, and riddles.

CONTINUED

ESSENTIAL SKILLS: WRITING 1067

- The **Essential Skills: Writing** section surveys the entire process of writing.

ESSENTIAL SKILLS:
Language

GRAMMAR HANDBOOK

INTRODUCTION TO GRAMMAR

2.1 THE GRAMMAR YOU ALREADY KNOW

Grammar is something you know, even if you have never studied it. Inside the head of every person is a sophisticated device that works, all by itself, to learn how to put words and phrases together grammatically. Even if you don't know an adverb from an aardvark, you know, if you are a speaker of English, that

the little leaf-eating bug

is grammatical and that

the bug little leaf-eating

is not. You can tell that one string of words is grammatical and the other isn't because you have learned, unconsciously, many thousands of rules governing how words can be put together and how they can't.

When you study a grammar textbook, therefore, what you are really learning is not the grammar of the language—for the most part, that's something you already know. What you are learning is terminology for describing what you know so that you can use that terminology when discussing language. Incidentally, as you study textbook grammar, you will also learn a few rules that you never quite learned unconsciously. Remember, however, that most of the grammar is already inside your head. Learning to describe that grammar can therefore be viewed as learning more about yourself and your amazing unconscious abilities.

2.2 THE USES OF GRAMMAR

Why study grammar? After all, no amount of grammar study can match the value of hands-on reading and writing. Grammar is useful, however. It gives you a way to speak about and understand your own writing and that of others. Contrast the following examples:

1106 LANGUAGE ARTS SURVEY

When the Roman general, sitting at supper with a plate of turnips before him, was solicited by large presents to betray his trust, he asked the messengers whether he that could sup on turnips was a man likely to sell his own country. Upon him who has reduced his sense to obedience, temptation has lost its power; he is able to attend impartially to virtue, and execute her commands without hesitation.

—Samuel Johnson, *The Idler* No. 52

Now what's this? What's the object of all this darkness all over me? They haven't gone and buried me alive while my back was turned, have they? Ah, now would you think they'd do a thing like that! Oh, no, I know what it is. I'm awake. That's it. I've waked up in the middle of the night. Well, isn't that nice. Isn't that simply ideal.

—Dorothy Parker, "The Little Hours"

If you had to describe the difference between these two passages, you would find it useful to have precise grammatical terms at your command. The first sentence in the passage by Johnson is composed of an adverbial clause interrupted by a participial phrase, followed by a sentence with an indirect question containing a subjunctive. The sentences in the passage from Parker's story have few of these devices. They are short, casual, and full of contractions. They consist mostly of simple subjects, verbs, and predicates. You may *sense* the differences in these two styles of writing instinctively, but grammar gives you a way to *understand* and *communicate* those differences.

THE PARTS OF SPEECH

2.3 COMMON AND PROPER NOUNS

A **noun** is a word used to refer to a person, place, thing, or idea.

NOUNS Virginia Woolf, England, stone, beauty

A **common noun** is a name that belongs to (is *common* to) all the persons, places, or things in a group. A **proper noun** refers to a *particular* person, place, or thing and begins with a capital letter.

COMMON NOUNS woman, state, religion
PROPER NOUNS Queen Elizabeth I, California, Catholicism

2.4 CONCRETE AND ABSTRACT NOUNS

A **concrete noun** refers to an object that you can perceive by hearing, seeing, smelling, tasting, or touching. An **abstract noun** names a quality, characteristic, or idea.

CONCRETE NOUNS music, light, smoke, honey, silk
ABSTRACT NOUNS difficulty, bravery, evil

ESSENTIAL SKILLS: LANGUAGE 1106

- The **Essential Skills: Language** section surveys key concepts in grammar, usage, mechanics, spelling, vocabulary development, and language variety. Grammar usage and mechanics instruction focuses on editing and proofreading applications.

■ The **Essential Skills: Speaking and Listening** section surveys verbal and nonverbal communication, active listening, interpersonal communication, discussion, public speaking, and oral interpretation.

ESSENTIAL SKILLS:
Speaking and Listening

3.1 A Communication Model

When you ask a friend if you can borrow a pencil, you are operating an extremely complex system that no computer can yet operate. Here's the way the system works: A **sender encodes** a **message** using **symbols.** This message is transmitted along some **channel** to a **recipient** who **decodes** it and provides **feedback.** The following chart describes this communication model:

COMMUNICATION MODEL	
Sender	You
Message	"May I borrow a pencil from you?"
Symbols Used	Words in the English language
Channel	Speech
Recipient	Your friend
Feedback	"Sure, I have an extra one."

For complete communication, encoding must be correct, the channel must be clear, and decoding must be correct. So, for example, if a loud stereo were in the room and your friend didn't hear you, the communication would not be complete. You would need to modify the system by adding a tap on your friend's shoulder or perhaps a repetition of the message in a slightly louder voice.

▸▸▸ ACTIVITY 3.1

Answer the following questions:

1. What are some different symbol systems used to encode messages? Think of both nonverbal and verbal means of communication. (Hint: Street signs are one common nonverbal means for encoding messages.)
2. A space probe on Mars takes a picture of a crater on Mars and transmits this picture by radio to NASA scientists on Earth. The scientists look at the picture and send a command back to the probe telling it to move a bit to the left and take another picture. Describe the sender, the message, the channel, the recipient, and the feedback in this communication situation.

CONTINUED

3. Using terminology from the communication model given above, describe what interferes with communication in each of the following examples:
   a. An American tourist in Rome stops a young man on the street to ask directions. The American asks, "Can you tell me how to get to the Forum?" The Italian answers, "Non parlo inglese."
   b. A ship has run into an iceberg and is sinking. Another ship is passing in the distance. A crew member on the first ship attempts to signal the second ship using flags. The people on the second ship can't see the flags because too much fog is in the air.
   c. A student with a stomachache enters class, wearing a grimace. The student's teacher asks, "Would you like to lead the discussion today, Gloria?" Gloria answers, "Sure." However, the teacher looks at the grimace on Gloria's face and concludes that Gloria doesn't really want to lead the discussion. The teacher asks another student to lead the discussion but fails to tell Gloria why he has made this decision.
4. Why is feedback important to good communication? What kind of feedback does an audience give to an actor or to a speaker? How can people in conversation ensure that they have understood one another correctly? How do newspapers receive feedback from their readers?

3.2 Elements of Verbal Communication

Communication can be verbal or nonverbal. **Verbal communication** is done by means of words and other sounds uttered by speakers. **Nonverbal communication** is done by other means. The following chart describes the most important elements of verbal communication:

ELEMENTS OF VERBAL COMMUNICATION		
ELEMENT	**DESCRIPTION**	**GUIDELINES FOR SPEAKERS**
Volume	The loudness or softness of the voice	Speak loudly enough to be heard, but not so loudly as to make your audience uncomfortable.
Pitch, or Intonation	The highness or lowness of the voice	Vary your pitch to give your expressions a musical quality and to communicate meaning (for example, a rising pitch at the end of a sentence indicates a question). Avoid using a single pitch, or **monotone.**
Enunciation	The clearness with which syllables are spoken	Slightly exaggerate the clearness of your syllables to ensure that you are understood. Do not drop or clip the ends of words or sentences.

CONTINUED

ESSENTIAL SKILLS:
Study and Research

THINKING SKILLS

All human beings have a great number of thinking skills and perform astonishing feats of thinking every day, but often people get set in thinking habits and patterns that aren't very efficient. Learning a few simple thinking strategies can improve dramatically anyone's ability to learn, to solve problems, and to make decisions.

4.1 Strategies for Problem Solving I

All problem solving involves four steps.

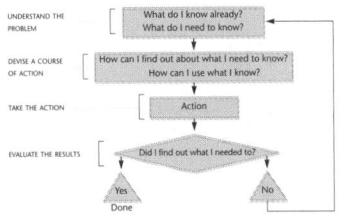

Within this **general problem-solving framework**, there are many particular strategies you can use. A guaranteed strategy for solving a problem is called an **algorithm.** A less than sure-fire strategy is called a **heuristic** or, if the strategy is very simple and straightfo

■ The **Essential Skills: Study and Research** section surveys thinking, reading, research, and test-taking skills, including skills for taking standardized tests.

■ The **Essential Skills: Applied English/Tech Prep** section surveys applications of English skills to the world of work.

ESSENTIAL SKILLS:
Applied English/Tech Prep

LETTERS AND FORMS

Long after you've written your last high-school essay or college term paper, you'll be using your writing skills in a variety of day-to-day situations. Whether you're corresponding with a loan officer at the bank, writing to a friend across the country, communicating via electronic mail with a co-worker, or penning a thank-you note to a thoughtful aunt, you'll want to take care to ensure that your writing reflects your intentions precisely, conveying your thoughts or feelings or any pertinent information.

Familiarizing yourself with the conventions of letter-writing can help you achieve a positive outcome, particularly when addressing correspondence to individuals or groups who don't know you personally.

5.1 Filling Out Forms and Applications

In our information-based society, forms and applications are ubiquitous. Because they're such efficient mechanisms for collecting data, you can expect to encounter them regularly, in such diverse locations as the doctor's office, the bank, your local dry-cleaning establishment, or a favorite mail-order catalog.

When completing a form or application, you should have two objectives: to provide the information requested and to make a positive impression.

Guidelines for completing forms:

- If possible, obtain an extra copy of the form or application.
- Gather any information you will need to complete the form.
- Read all the directions before you begin to enter your data.
- Be neat. Type or print your responses legibly, in pencil or ink, as directed. Avoid smudges or cross-outs.
- Write "N.A." or "not applicable," rather than leave a space blank, if a section of the form or application does not apply to you.
- Proofread. When you've completed the form, check your spelling, grammar, and punctuation, and review the information you've provided.
- If the form is messy or inaccurate, discard it and complete the extra form or application if you have one.
- When you've completed the form to your satisfaction, submit it to the appropriate person, or mail it to the correct address.

Application for Employment
Brennan's Book Emporium

Position Desired: Sales Clerk

Personal Data

Applicant's Name: Mello (*Last name*) Jennifer (*First Name*) M. (*Middle Initial*)

Address: 55 Dartmouth St. (*Street*) Brobdingnag (*City*) Ohio (*State*) 00703 (*Zip*)

Phone: (586) 555-3250 Date of Birth: 5/10/78

Previous Work Experience
(List last two positions held, beginning with the most recent.)

Employer: Ms. Janice Ingram (*Name*) 17 Howe St., Brobdingnag, Ohio 00703 (*Address*)
Phone: (586) 555-8020
Employment Period: 1/95–present
Job Title: Tutor
Hours worked: Flexible, 5–10 hrs./wk.
Salary: $5.00/hr.
Description: Help employer's ten-year-old daughter improve her math skills
Reason for leaving: N.A.

Employer: John and Sandra Neils (*Name*) 48 Dart St., Brobdingnag, Ohio 00703 (*Address*)
Phone: (586) 555-5440
Employment Period: 7/95–9/95
Job Title: Nanny
Hours Worked: 8:30–4:30, Monday–Friday
Salary: $4.50/hr.
Description: Cared for two children, ages 4 and 6, in their home
Reason for Leaving: Returned to school following summer vacation

CONTINUED

The EMC Masterpiece Series has the **most extensive language arts skills coverage of any program.** The coverage of English skills is so comprehensive that an additional English skills textbook isn't needed. The Language Arts Survey sections may be taught as separate units, using the student textbook and ancillary worksheets, or may be taught incidentally in conjunction with study of the literature.

Annotated Teacher's Edition

The Annotated Teacher's Edition contains a wealth of materials to enrich your teaching.

UNIT SKILLS OUTLINE

Literary Skills and Concepts
- Allegory, 80
- Alliteration, 86
- Description, 98
- Epic, 115
- Foil, 93
- Image, 93
- Metaphor, 93
- Narrative, 79
- Oral Tradition, 114
- Personification, 97
- Purpose, 80
- Speaker, 92
- Symbol, 93
- Translation, 86

Writing Skills and Concepts
- Allegory, 80
- Anglo-Saxon Poem, 115
- Critical Essay, 115
- Descriptive Writing, 98
- Dream Record, 87
- Hymn in an Old English Verse Form, 86
- Kenning, 115
- Personal Letter, 93
- Persuasive Paragraph, 80
- Riddle, 98

Grammar, Usage, and Mechanics Skills and Concepts
- Capitalization: Sacred Beings and Writings, 87
- Compound and Collective Nouns, 102, 116
- Correcting Run-ons, 80
- End Marks, 98
- Using the Active Voice, 83
- Using Precise Nouns, 95
- Using Vivid Verbs, 95

Other Language Arts Skills and Concepts
- Interpersonal Communication, 89
- Using the Card Catalog, 77

UNIT 2 THE ANGLO-SAXON PERIOD (449–1066)

King Ælla's Messengers before Ragnar Lodbroke's Sons. J. A. Malmström, 1857. Norrköping Art Museum, Sweden

68 UNIT TWO / THE ANGLO-SAXON PERIOD

GOALS/OBJECTIVES

Studying this unit will enable students to
- interpret and appreciate Anglo-Saxon literature
- summarize the history of pre-Christian England and its literature
- name the sources and tell the history of Old English
- relate themes common in Anglo-Saxon literature to characteristics of Anglo-Saxon society
- describe the achievements of Boadicea, Bede, and Alfred
- describe and explain the influence of Christianity on Anglo-Saxon literature and culture
- identify and give examples of the major characteristics of Anglo-Saxon verse

68 TEACHER'S EDITION

Y

ou each have something divine in your soul, namely Reason and Memory and a discerning will to make choices in life.

—Alfred the Great
King of the West Saxons

69

HISTORICAL NOTE

Alfred the Great (849–899) became king of Wessex, one of the seven Anglo-Saxon kingdoms, in 871. His military exploits contained Danish invaders to the northern part of England and thus made possible the emergence of England as a nation. His commitment to learning did much to further the creation of a native English literature. Alfred subsidized the creation of works in the Old English language and himself translated many Latin works into Old English. These works included Boethius's *Consolation of Philosophy* and, some believe, the *Ecclesiastical History* of the Venerable Bede.

TEACHER'S EDITION 69

CONNECTIONS ACROSS THE CURRICULUM

Arts and Humanities
- Illustrating Grendel, 104
- Inconsistencies in Translation, 86

Mathematics and Sciences
- How Swords Produce Sound, 108

Social Studies
- Community Involvement, 81
- Planning a Celebration, 93

Applied Arts
- Anglo-Saxon Eating Habits, 87
- Technology in Beowulf, 99

TEACHING THE MULTIPLE INTELLIGENCES

Logical-Mathematical
- Survey, 116

Spatial
- Drawing the Wife's Site of Lamentation, 91
- Illustrating Grendel, 104
- Mapping Beowulf, 116

Musical
- The Medieval Harp, 87

Interpersonal
- Community Involvement, 81
- Improvisation, 81
- Losing Opportunities, 91
- Survey, 116

Kinesthetic
- Improvisation, 81

- A list of cross-curricular activities
- A list of activities to exercise multiple intelligences
- Historical and Art Notes providing information on artists, schools, periods, and techniques
- Icons identifying SCANS activities that will help your students reach Goals 2000
- A list of concepts and skills taught in the unit
- A list of suggested affective and cognitive goals for the unit
- A list of worksheets, assessment materials, and multimedia materials to use in teaching the unit
- Additional activities designed with gifted students in mind but also useful for challenging all students
- Notes on syntax and semantics plus lists of idioms, colloquialisms, and additional vocabulary for students needing extra help
- A list of suggested affective and cognitive goals for the selection

ADDITIONAL RESOURCES

Reader's Guide
- Selection Worksheet, 2.1

Assessment Portfolio
- Selection Check Test, 4.2.1
- Selection Test, 4.2.2

Essential Skills Practice Books
- *Writing*, 1.9
- *Language*, 2.62

ENRICHMENT ACTIVITIES

Students can write about or discuss the ways in which a political leader's religion can be significant for his or her country. (This can be linked to current events.)

SUPPORT FOR LEP STUDENTS

Explain that Old English and Modern English are different and separate languages and that students are not expected to know or to learn Old English.

Idioms

shed light on—reveal information that helps one to understand something

fair weather—good weather

Additional Vocabulary

earnest—something given as a pledge or token
aforesaid—mentioned before
partaker—one who participates
confer—speak with
verily—truly
hitherto—until now
forward—help or advance
exhortation—urging
emerge—come into view

PREREADING

"The Conversion of King Edwin"
from *Ecclesiastical History of the English People*
by Saint Bede the Venerable

ABOUT THE AUTHOR

A page from the Grimbald Gospels. British Library, MS Add. 34890 fol. 3OV. Courtesy of the British Library

Saint Bede the Venerable (AD 672– or 673–735) was born in Jarrow, in the kingdom of Northumbria. He entered the Monastery of St. Peter in nearby Wearmouth at the age of seven. At nineteen, he was ordained a deacon; at thirty, a priest. Like other monastics of his time, Bede wrote in Latin. He traveled very little, but his fame spread throughout Europe due to his writings on subjects as varied as history, poetry, grammar, mathematics, science, the scriptures, and lives of the saints. Bede's histories make fascinating reading not only for the light that they shed on the distant Anglo-Saxon past but also for their engaging accounts of miraculous and legendary events. In his histories, Bede introduced the practice of dating events from the birth of Christ (i.e., from AD 0, where AD is an abbreviation for the Latin *Anno Domini*, meaning "the year of our Lord"). This method of dating was adopted throughout Europe and is still in use today. Bede was canonized (made a saint of the Roman Catholic Church) in 1899, eleven hundred years after his death.

ABOUT THE SELECTION

Most notable among Bede's works is the *Historia ecclesiastica gentis Anglorum*, or *Ecclesiastical History of the English People*. Bede's five-book Latin history of the Church in England covers the period from Caesar's invasion of Britain (55–54 BC) to his own time (the history was finished around AD 731). King Alfred considered the book important enough to have it translated into Old English, the language of the common people. **"The Conversion of King Edwin"** comes from *Book II* of Bede's history and relates the process by which Christian missionaries converted the Anglo-Saxon kings. The selection shows the dramatic contrast between the Anglo-Saxons' grim view of the afterlife and the positive alternative offered by the missionaries. The pre-Christian, or pagan, Anglo-Saxons believed that a warrior who died bravely in battle would go after death to a land reserved for heroes, Valhalla. For others, the future after death was uncertain. The final paragraph of the selection, which compares the time before, during, and after life to the flight of a sparrow, is one of the most famous in all of English literature.

76 UNIT TWO / THE ANGLO-SAXON PERIOD

GOALS/OBJECTIVES

Studying this lesson will enable students to
- empathize with Edwin's uncertainties about the afterlife
- describe Bede's accomplishments and explain the historical significance of Bede's writings
- describe some key differences between Anglo-Saxon paganism and Christianity
- explain what an allegory is and recognize allegories as they encounter them in their reading
- use a card catalog to find books on specific topics
- recognize and correct run-ons

76 TEACHER'S EDITION

The British Museum

READER'S JOURNAL

Have you ever changed your mind about something important? Do you find change to be difficult or easy? Freewrite about change in your journal. You might write about personal change or about change that has occurred in your country or in your community.

RESEARCH SKILLS

Read the Language Arts Survey, 4.22, "Using the Card Catalog." Then use the card catalog in a library to find books with information about Saint Bede the Venerable. For each book, list the title, the author's name, the year of publication, the call number, and the kind of information given.

"The Conversion of King Edwin"

FROM *Ecclesiastical History of the English People*

SAINT BEDE THE VENERABLE

At this time the nation of the Northumbrians, that is, the nation of the Angles that live on the north side of the river Humber, with their king, Edwin, received the faith through the preaching of Paulinus.[1] This Edwin, as a reward of his receiving the faith, and as an earnest of his share in the heavenly kingdom, received an increase of that which he enjoyed on earth, for he reduced under his dominion all the borders of Britain that were provinces either of the aforesaid nation, or of the Britons, a thing which no British king had ever done before. . . .

For some time he delayed to receive the word of God at the preaching of Paulinus, and used to sit several hours alone, and seriously to ponder with himself what he was to do, and what religion he was to follow. Then the man of God came to him, laid his right hand on his head, and asked whether he knew that sign.[2] The king in a trembling condition, was ready to fall down at his feet, but he raised him up, and in a familiar manner said to him, "Behold, by the help of God you have escaped the hands of the enemies whom you feared. Behold you have of His gift obtained the kingdom which you desired. Take heed not to delay that which you promised to perform; embrace the faith, and keep the precepts of Him who, delivering you from temporal adversity, has raised you to the honor of

According to Bede, what reward does Edwin receive for converting to Christianity?

1. **Paulinus**. Pope Gregory I sent Paulinus as a missionary to Northumbria in AD 601.
2. **that sign**. The laying on of hands is a ceremony for transmitting spiritual grace to the recipient.

WORDS FOR EXTENSIVE USE

ex • **ch** • **u** • **es** • **ti** • **cal** (e kiz' ch e s' t i kel) *adj.*, having to do with the church

tem • **po** • **ral** (tem' pe rel) *adj.*, lasting only for a time, limited; of this world, not spiritual

ad • **ver** • **si** • **ty** (ad ver' se tē) *n.*, misfortune, trouble

"THE CONVERSION OF KING EDWIN" 77

PREREADING NOTES

Reader's Journal

Suggest that students think about the kind of change that Edwin's conversion involves.

Research Skills

- Students might imagine that they are research assistants for an Anglo-Saxon scholar.
- Inform students about which library or libraries they might visit.
- You may want to combine this activity with a lesson on proper bibliography form. Refer students to the Language Arts Survey, 4.33, "Documenting Sources in a Report."

Answer to Guided Reading Question

Edwin receives an increase of that which he had on earth (an enlarged domain).

VOCABULARY FROM THE SELECTION

adversity
diligently
ecclesiastical
efficacious
signify
temporal

Vocabulary in Context
- The cardinal needed his ecclesiastical robes for the service on Sunday.
- The minister said that solving our temporal troubles is less important than caring for our immortal souls.
- Do you admire someone who deals with adversity by working harder instead of giving in?

TEACHER'S EDITION 77

Historical Note

From AD 616 to 632, Edwin was king of Northumbria and was recognized across England as overlord. Edwin married the princess Aethelburth of Kent, a Christian. She was responsible for bringing Paulinus to Northumbria because she wanted to convert Edwin and his subjects. In 632, Northumbria was invaded by the united armies of King Cadwallon of Gwynedd and King Penda of Mercia. Edwin was killed and his army defeated. Aethelburth and Paulinus fled, and Christianity was suppressed for a time.

Answers to Guided Reading Questions

- The counselor compares life to the flight of a sparrow.
- The priest rejects the old gods because his faith in them has not brought him wealth or influence.

Answers to Selection Check Test 4.2.1

EX. Who wrote "The Conversion of King Edwin"?
The selection was written by Saint Bede the Venerable.

1. What kingdom was ruled by Edwin?
Edwin ruled Northumbria.
2. Who was Paulinus?
He was a Catholic priest and missionary.
3. What did Paulinus want Edwin to do? Did Edwin do it?
Paulinus wanted Edwin to convert to Christianity, which he did.
4. Why did Edwin meet with his friends and counselors?
Edwin wanted his friends and counselors to convert also.
5. What opinion was offered by Edwin's friends and counselors?
They agreed that Christianity was preferable to the old religion.

a temporal kingdom; and if, from this time forward, you shall be obedient to His will, which through me He signifies to you, He will not only deliver you from the everlasting torments of the wicked, but also make you partaker with Him of His eternal kingdom in Heaven."

The king, hearing these words, answered, that he was both willing and bound to receive the faith which he taught; but that he would confer about it with his principal friends and counselors, to the end that if they also were of his opinion, they might all together be cleansed in Christ the Fountain of Life. Paulinus consenting, the king did as he said; for, holding a council with the wise men,[1] he asked of every one in particular what he thought of the new doctrine, and the new worship that was preached. To which the chief of his own priests, Coifi, immediately answered, "O king, consider what this is which is now preached to us; for I verily declare to you, that the religion which we have hitherto professed has, as far as I can learn, no virtue in it. For none of your people has applied himself more diligently to the worship of our gods than I; and yet there are many who receive greater favors from you, and are more preferred than I, and are more prosperous in all their undertakings. Now if the gods were good for any thing, they would rather forward me, who have been more careful to serve them. It remains, therefore, that if upon examination you find those new doctrines, which are now preached to us, better and more efficacious, we immediately receive them without any delay."

Another of the king's chief men, approving of his words and exhortations, presently added: "The present life of man, O king, seems to me, in comparison to that time which is unknown to us, like to the swift flight of a sparrow through the room wherein you sit at supper in winter, with your commanders and ministers, and a good fire in the midst, whilst the storms of rain and snow prevail abroad; the sparrow, flying in at one door, and immediately out at another, whilst he is within, is safe from the wintry storm; but after a short space of fair weather, he immediately vanishes out of your sight, into the dark winter from which he had emerged. So this life of man appears for a short space, but of what went before, or what is to follow, we are utterly ignorant. If, therefore, this new doctrine contains something more certain, it seems justly to deserve to be followed." The other elders and king's counselors, by Divine inspiration, spoke to the same effect. ■

To what does the wise counselor compare life as the Anglo-Saxons know it?

Why does the king's chief priest reject the old gods?

1. **wise men.** These wise men are the Anglo-Saxon *Witenagemot*, or council of elders. From the Old English *witen*, "to know," comes our modern word *wit*.

Words for Everyday Use

dig • nē • fy (nij′ nə fī′) vt., show by means of words or a sign
dil • i • gent • ly (dil′ ə jənt lē) adv. with great care and attention
ef • fē • ca • cious (ef′ i kā′ shəs) adj., effective, producing the desired result

Vocabulary in Context

- Being named captain of the team signifies more than just popularity.
- We all worked diligently throughout the day, and the project was completed on time.

Responding to the Selection

Do the arguments advanced by Edwin's counselors seem reasonable to you? Do you feel that Edwin had reason to forsake his old beliefs and embrace these new ones? Why, or why not? Answer these questions in your journal.

Reviewing the Selection

Recalling

1. Who is Paulinus? What does he ask of King Edwin? What does Paulinus promise?
2. With whom does King Edwin meet?
3. Who is Coifi? What does he think of the old religion?
4. To what does the king's advisor compare the swift flight of a sparrow?

Interpreting

5. Why does Paulinus believe Edwin has a responsibility to "embrace the faith"?
6. Why does King Edwin hold a meeting?
7. What reason does Coifi give for forsaking the old religion?
8. What view of life and of the afterlife is implicit in the counselor's story of the sparrow?

Synthesizing

9. In what ways does the new religion differ from the old religion? What makes the new religion appealing to the elders and to the king's counselors?
10. According to King Edwin's advisors, what is the purpose of religion? In what ways are their views similar to or different from your own?

Understanding Literature (Questions for Discussion)

1. **Narration. Narration,** one of the modes of writing, tells a story. Normally, stories are told by beginning with what happens first and continuing chronologically (through time) toward what happens last. Is Bede's story of Edwin's conversion told chronologically? Where does Bede deviate from a strict chronological ordering? Why do you think he does this? Is the technique effective? Can you think of a story that you have told nonchronologically? Why did you tell it so?

Answers for Understanding Literature

- See the evaluation forms for discussion, active listening, and oral communication, *Assessment Portfolio*, 7.11–7.14.
- **Teaching Note:** The technique of hinting at or telling about something that will occur later in the chronology of a story is called *foreshadowing*. Foreshadowing is often [illegible]owever, telling [illegible]cceptable in [illegible]tive.

[illegible]ice Book: [illegible] (cont.)

Responding to the Selection

Encourage students to consider not only religious beliefs but also beliefs about morals, politics, friendship, technology, etc.

Answers for Reviewing the Selection

Recalling

1. Paulinus is a Catholic priest and missionary. He asks Edwin to convert to Christianity. He promises Edwin internal peace and eternal life.
2. Edwin meets with his friends and closest advisors.
3. Coifi is the king's advisor and chief priest. He thinks the old religion is inferior to the new.
4. The flight of the sparrow is compared to a human life.

Interpreting

5. Paulinus thinks Edwin had a responsibility to convert because he had made a promise to do so.
6. Edwin wants his friends and advisors to convert also.
7. Although Coifi was the most faithful follower of the old religion, he achieved little wealth, influence, or power.
8. *Responses will vary.* Students may say that the story of the sparrow's flight implies the view that human life is brief and insignificant and that what, if anything, comes after life is completely unknown.

Synthesizing

Responses will vary. Possible responses are given.

9. The new religion promises the certainty of an afterlife of eternal happiness, whereas the old religion promises only death and uncertainty. The elders are attracted to the new religion because they think it offers more spiritual certainty and more worldly advantage.
10. The advisors believe that the purpose of religion is worldly success. Student beliefs about the purpose of religion will vary.

Answers for Understanding Literature (cont.)

2. **Allegory.** The sparrow symbolizes life; its brief flight in the dining room symbolizes our short life on earth; the people and comforts in the room symbolize the pleasures of our lives on earth; sight symbolizes our knowledge, and so the room also symbolizes the limits of human knowledge; the winter storms outdoors symbolize the unknown periods before and after our lives. The allegory helps explain Bede's story because it makes more vivid the differences between paganism and Christianity.
- **Teaching Note:** Students might want to discuss the meanings of and differences among the terms *allegory, analogy, metaphor,* and *symbolism*. Refer to the Handbook of Literary Terms.

3. **Purpose.** The selection teaches the value of Christianity. Students may think that the author appears to be a Christian because his discussion is one-sided. If he had been a pagan, he might also have found something good to say about the old religion.
- **Teaching Note:** Students should find evidence that Bede was a Christian in the selection rather than in the instructional apparatus.

Analytic Scales for Responding in Writing

Assign a score from 1 to 25 for each grading criterion below. (For more detailed evaluation, see the evaluation forms for writing, revising, and proofreading, *Assessment Portfolio*, 7.1–7.10.)

1. **An Allegory**
- **Content/Unity.** The allegory presents a sensible extended comparison between two things.
- **Organization/Coherence.** The allegory is clearly organized, presenting both topics and several points of comparison.
- **Language/Style.** The allegory uses vivid, concrete, and precise nouns, verbs, and modifiers.
- **Conventions.** The allegory avoids errors in spelling, grammar, usage, mechanics, and manuscript form.

(cont.)

2. **Allegory.** An **allegory** is a work in which each element **symbolizes,** or represents, something else. The last paragraph of the selection contains an allegory comparing human life to the flight of a sparrow. To understand the allegory you need to determine what the characters and objects in the story symbolize. The story speaks of a sparrow, a dining room with a door, supper, winter storms, commanders and ministers, a fire, and our sight. What do these elements in the story symbolize?

3. **Purpose or Aim.** A writer's **aim** is the primary **purpose** that his or her work is meant to achieve. One purpose of "The Conversion of King Edwin" is to teach a lesson. What lesson does the selection teach? From reading the selection, can you tell whether Bede was a Christian or a pagan? How can you tell? How might the purpose be different if Bede were of a different religion?

Responding in Writing

1. **An Allegory.** Think of the story of the sparrow flying through the warm room and then out into the cold. Bede presents this story as an allegory for the life of an individual. An **allegory** is a story that seems simple but has another meaning altogether. What might be an allegory for working hard to accomplish a difficult task—perhaps running a marathon or climbing a tall mountain? Choose one of the following topics or one of your own. Then write an allegory to describe it.

Possible topics:
- saying goodbye to a friend
- leaving home to go to college
- studying for an important test

2. **A Persuasive Paragraph.** In order to convert King Edwin and his counsel, the missionary Paulinus had to be quite persuasive. What arguments did he use to convince them? How might you convince someone of something you feel strongly about? Maybe you have read a great book, and you are trying to convince a friend to read it. Maybe you are trying to change someone's mind about a political issue. Choose a topic for a persuasive paragraph. In a sentence, describe your position or stand on the topic. Then give two or three arguments to support your position.

Language Lab

Correcting Run-ons. Read the Language Arts Survey, 2.62, "Correcting Run-ons." Then revise the sentences below by changing punctuation and capitalization and adding words, as necessary.

1. Bede's history of Britain was not the first, it was partly based on *On the Fall of Britain,* written by Gildas, a Welshman, in AD 550.

Analytic Scales for Responding in Writing (cont.)

2. **A Persuasive Paragraph**
- **Content/Unity.** The paragraph presents a position and two or three strong arguments to support it.
- **Organization/Coherence.** The paragraph begins with a topic sentence that presents the writer's position. It then presents two or three arguments in a logical order (possibly from most important to least important or vice versa).
- **Language/Style.** The writer has made a clear argument using language that will move the reader intellectually and/or emotionally.
- **Conventions.** The paragraph avoids errors in spelling, grammar, usage, mechanics, and manuscript form.

2. According to stories told by early Welsh historians, one of the soldiers who fought against the Anglo-Saxons was named Arthur such stories gave rise to legends about King Arthur and the knights of the round table.
3. The early Germanic peoples, including the Anglo-Saxons, used alphabetic characters called *runes* to write inscriptions on stones, the runic alphabet is known as *futhark*.
4. The treasure of Sutton Hoo was found in 1939, at Sutton Hoo a seventh-century Anglo-Saxon king had been buried with a large number of jewels, coins, weapons, and tools he was entombed in a ninety-foot-long ship that had been hauled to the top of a one-hundred-foot-high cliff.
5. Our knowledge of the Anglo-Saxons comes from many sources these sources include inscriptions, histories, literature, and archeological finds like Sutton Hoo.

Projects

1. **Improvisation.** Take a few moments to think about what it was like to be one of King Edwin's counselors. Try to imagine other meetings that might have taken place. Then form groups of four to six students. Take turns acting out one of the scenes listed below, with one person playing King Edwin and the others playing the counselors. Use your imagination as you think about the issue that is up for discussion.
- Discuss adding other lands to the kingdom. The group can discuss whether this will happen as a result of peaceful negotiation or of battle.
- Discuss a dispute between two earls over the possession of a sword taken from an enemy warrior. Decide who should receive the sword and why.

2. **Community Involvement.** When someone enters a community and tries to make change, sometimes the change is positive, and sometimes the change is negative. In either case, asking people to think in new ways is rarely easy. How might you and your classmates try to make positive change in your community? You might want to change how people feel about litter and the environment, or you might want to make people more excited about becoming involved in town issues or school events. Work with other students to organize a convincing campaign.

Answers for Language Lab

1. Bede's history of Britain was not the first. It was partly based on *On the Fall of Britain,* written by Gildas, a Welshman, in AD 550.
2. According to early Welsh historians, one of the soldiers who fought against the Anglo-Saxons was named Arthur. Such stories gave rise to legends about King Arthur and the knights of the Round Table.
3. The early Germanic peoples, including the Anglo-Saxons, used alphabetic characters called *runes* to write inscriptions on stones. The *runic* alphabet is known as *futhark*.
4. The treasure of Sutton Hoo was found in 1939. At Sutton Hoo, a seventh-century Anglo-Saxon king had been buried with a large number of jewels, coins, weapons, and tools. He was entombed in a ninety-foot-long ship that had been hauled to the top of a one-hundred-foot-high cliff.
5. Our knowledge of the Anglo-Saxons comes from many sources. These sources include inscriptions, histories, literature, and archaeological finds like Sutton Hoo.

- Additional practice is provided in the *Essential Skills Practice Book: Language,* 2.62.

Project Notes

1. **Improvisation**
- Besides the two stated topics, groups can also discuss issues that they think of themselves.
- Group members may be encouraged to adopt particular characters, real or imaginary.

2. **Community Involvement.** Students should concentrate on presenting reasons that people in the community will find persuasive.

- Color-coded answers for exercises are provided on the same pages as the exercises themselves
- Activities for each of the five nonlinguistic intelligences (musical, logical-mathematical, spatial, kinesthetic, and interpersonal/intrapersonal) facilitate tailoring instruction to individual students' abilities

Also included in the Annotated Teacher's Edition:

- Practical advice and strategies for reader response and portfolio-based language arts instruction
- Sample lesson cycles
- Information on thematic and genre approaches
- Additional resources for language arts teachers

Annotated Teacher's Edition also available on CD-ROM

Assessment Portfolio

The EMC Masterpiece Series has the most comprehensive assessment portfolio available today. This ancillary package contains blackline master materials for:

- Unit Study Guides and Tests, including Vocabula Worksheets
- Selection Check Tests and Comprehensive Tests
- Writing Skills Study Guides and Post-tests
- Other Language Arts Skills Study Guides and Tests
- Worksheets and Forms for Portfolio Assessment
  - Forms for Analytic and Holistic Evaluation for Other Language Arts Activities and Projects
- Worksheets and Forms
- Answer Keys

- **Holistic Evaluation Forms** allow for "total effect" peer, self-, and teacher evaluation of student writing.

Name _____ Class _____ Date _____

Writing Evaluation Form: Holistic Response 7.5

Short Story

CONTENT AND COHERENCE		
The short story…	(Circle one.)	The short story…
• does not have a central conflict • does not develop and resolve the conflict • does not depict the setting vividly • does not develop main character(s) amply •does not develop theme clearly	1 2 3 4 5 6 7 8 9 10 × 7 = _____	• has a central conflict • develops and resolves the conflict • depicts the setting vividly • develops main character(s) amply • develops theme clearly
CONVENTIONS		
The short story…	(Circle one.)	The short story…
• makes errors in spelling • makes errors in grammar • makes errors in usage • makes errors in punctuation • does not follow proper manuscript form	1 2 3 4 5 6 7 8 9 10 × 3 = _____	• uses proper spelling • uses good grammar • avoids errors in usage • uses proper punctuation and capitalization • follows proper manuscript form

CONTENT AND COHERENCE _____ + CONVENTIONS _____ = TOTAL _____

What I like most about this short story is…

What I like least about this short story is…

What I would do to improve this short story is…

STUDENT'S SIGNATURE _____
PEER EVALUATOR'S SIGNATURE _____
TEACHER'S SIGNATURE _____

© 1996 EMC Corporation

- **Analytic Evaluation Forms** allow for part-by-part, criteria-based peer, self-, and teacher evaluation of student writing.

Name _____ Class _____ Date _____

Writing Evaluation Form: Analytic Scale 7.4

Short Story

CONTENT/UNITY	CIRCLE ONE	
A. Introduces, develops, and resolves a central conflict COMMENTS: _____	1 2 3 4	× 4 = _____
B. Presents a vivid setting and develops a mood COMMENTS: _____	1 2 3 4	× 4 = _____
ORGANIZATION/COHERENCE		
C. Presents events in chronological order COMMENTS: _____	1 2 3 4	× 4 = _____
D. Uses flashbacks and foreshadowing appropriately COMMENTS: _____	1 2 3 4	× 4 = _____
LANGUAGE/STYLE		
E. Uses believable dialogue COMMENTS: _____	1 2 3 4	× 2 = _____
F. Uses vivid imagery COMMENTS: _____	1 2 3 4	× 2 = _____
CONVENTIONS		
G. Avoids spelling errors COMMENTS: _____	1 2 3 4	× 1 = _____
H. Avoids grammar errors COMMENTS: _____	1 2 3 4	× 1 = _____
I. Avoids usage errors COMMENTS: _____	1 2 3 4	× 1 = _____
J. Avoids punctuation and capitalization errors COMMENTS: _____	1 2 3 4	× 1 = _____
K. Avoids errors in manuscript form COMMENTS: _____	1 2 3 4	× 1 = _____
	TOTAL	

Key: 1 = needs substantial improvement 2 = needs improvement 3 = good 4 = outstanding

STUDENT'S SIGNATURE _____
PEER EVALUATOR'S SIGNATURE _____
TEACHER'S SIGNATURE _____

© 1996 Prentice-Hall Publishing

- **Portfolio Evaluation Forms** allow students and teachers to monitor the development of student writing over time.

The writer has (Check all that apply.)
- ❑ met or surpassed all of these goals
- ❑ met or surpassed some of these goals
- ❑ made progress toward all of these goals
- ❑ made progress toward some of these goals

(comments) _____

The Portfolio sho
- ❑ trying new p
- ❑ trying new p
- ❑ trying new m
- ❑ using expand
- ❑ trying new t
- ❑ revising for s
- ❑ revising for c
- ❑ revising to a
- ❑ revising for c
- ❑ proofreading

© 1996 EMC Corporation

Name _____ Class _____ Date _____

Comprehensive Portfolio Evaluation Form 6.10

Teacher

Date of last review _____

The portfolio contains ____ pieces of writing.

The special strengths of the pieces of writing in the portfolio are
- ❑ interest/creativity
- ❑ clarity
- ❑ organization
- ❑ unity
- ❑ use of support and details
- ❑ use of vivid words
- ❑ sentence structure
- ❑ use of appropriate conventions

The portfolio shows the writer's improvement in the areas of
- ❑ Process (comments) _____
- ❑ Content (comments) _____
- ❑ Conventions (comments) _____

The writer has previously set the following goals

Process: _____

Content: _____

Conventions: _____

© 1996 EMC Corporation

Additional Components

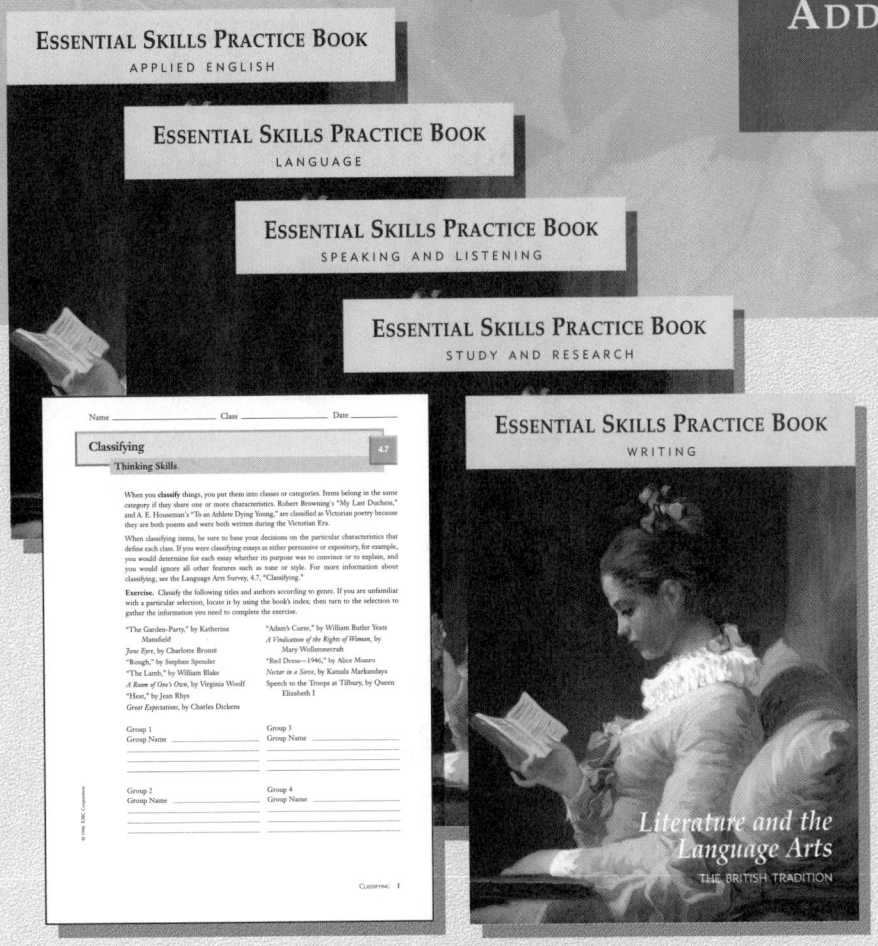

- **Essential Skills Practice Books**—The five Essential Skills Practice Books—Applied English, Language, Speaking and Listening, Study and Research, and Writing—contain blackline masters of exercises keyed to the Language Arts Survey sections of the student textbooks.

- **Transparency Set**—Transparencies guide students through preparation of reader's journals, use of writing portfolios, and peer and self-evaluation of writing.

Multimedia Components

- Four, sixty-minute audiocassettes of songs and dramatic readings from the series
- A videocassette and video laser disc of dramatic performances from the series
- A CD-ROM containing an idea generator for prewriting and a test generator for creating tests appropriate for six-week, nine-week, twelve-week, and semester-long schedules
- Test generators also available on IBM and Macintosh computer disks
- The Annotated Teacher's Edition is available on CD-ROM for random access to the selections

- **Reader's Guide**—The Reader's Guide and Activity Workbook consists of blackline master worksheets that provide a step-by-step process for completing the student textbook activities.

A Truly Integrated Literature and Language Arts Program

EMC Paradigm Publishing
300 York Avenue
St. Paul, MN 55101

Call 800-328-1452
Fax 800-328-4564

Contents

Overview T2
- Program Philosophy T2
- Program Components T7
- Organization of the Text T9
- Lesson Design and Teaching Strategies T11
- Teacher's Edition Annotations T18

Using *Literature and the Language Arts* for Writing Instruction T24

Instructional Options T29
- Approaches to *Literature and the Language Arts* T29
- Teaching Strategies T30
  - Teaching to Develop Students' Multiple Intelligences and to Accommodate Diverse Learning Styles T30
  - Teaching Students Whose Native Language Is Not English T30
  - Teaching Students with Diverse Cultural Backgrounds T30
  - Teaching Students with Learning Disabilities T30
  - Teaching Students with Special Academic Gifts and Talents T31
  - Achieving Gender Equity T31
  - Teaching Students to Work Cooperatively T33
  - Planning for Conferences and Portfolio Evaluation T34

Additional Resources for Language Arts Teachers T35

Key to Icons in the Annotated Teacher's Edition T36

Thematic Organization Chart T37

Selections by Genre Chart T43

Overview

PROGRAM PHILOSOPHY

The Cognitive Revolution and the Teaching of Literature

Through the 1960s, psychology in America was dominated by behaviorism, a theoretical methodology popularized by the brilliant and irascible B. F. Skinner. Skinner and other behaviorists argued that because we cannot observe mental phenomena directly, we cannot speak scientifically (i.e., intelligibly) of such matters as sensations, intuitions, feelings, thoughts, reasons, motives, imaginings, wishes, beliefs, and dreams. Oddly, some behaviorists went so far as to claim that mental phenomena did not exist. Such peculiar notions were positively reinforced by government grants and academic appointments and found expression in several generations of programmed learning textbooks designed to meet behavioral objectives. Learning theorists working within the behaviorist model encouraged educators to consider their students' observable behaviors without regard to, and indeed in scorn of, underlying mental processes.[1]

Of course, most English teachers knew that something was radically wrong with the behaviorist model of learning. They knew all along that they were teaching young *people*, not young bundles of behaviors, that those "mythical" realms of thought and feeling pooh-poohed by the behaviorists were, in fact, the quite real places that they explored daily with students in discussions of works of literature. In the 1960s and '70s, a revolution occurred in American psychology that brought psychologists to an understanding of what teachers had sensed all along. That revolution was the emergence of the field of cognitive science.[2]

One consequence of the cognitive revolution in psychology is that education theorists now widely accept the idea, advanced by psychologist Lev Vygotsky and championed by Jerome Bruner, that **teaching must begin with what students already know and feel and must build on that foundation.** This idea has often been presented as something altogether new. However, it is something that good English teachers have known all along. To help students to understand and to appreciate literature, one must first

> provide opportunities for students to connect with the literature on their own terms

and then

> build from that place toward higher levels of understanding and appreciation.

***EMC's* Literature and the Language Arts** *is the first literature textbook series specifically designed to accomplish both of those higher-order goals. Each lesson in this series first provides opportunities for*

1. According to the behaviorist theory, learning results from the differential positive or negative reinforcement of spontaneously occurring, pre-existing behaviors. A rat turns randomly this way or that way in a maze. By means of positive or negative reinforcements (e.g., food and mild electric shocks), the researcher/teacher reinforces turning one way instead of another, and thus learning takes place.

2. As Thomas Kuhn points out in *The Structure of Scientific Revolutions* (1962), when scientists working in a particular field discover phenomena that cannot be accounted for by extending or modifying the prevailing theoretical paradigm, they are forced to revise that paradigm to come up with a new theory. Kuhn calls the intractable phenomena that force scientists to rethink their theories "anomalies."

The twin anomalies that dealt the death blow to behaviorism were commonplace human behaviors: musical improvisation and speech. Neither could be adequately accounted for by behaviorist theory. Karl Lashley pointed out in a famous paper that musical improvisation, like many other human serial behaviors, cannot be explained without reference to what goes on inside people's minds. Improvisation simply happens too quickly to be explicable as a connected sequence of stimuli and responses. It must involve learned mental constructs, or structures, that are played out. Noam Chomsky, in his review of Skinner's *Verbal Behavior* (1957), explained that stimulus/response or imitation models cannot account for readily observable facts about language such as the production of sentences that, while entirely consistent with the rest of the grammar of the language, are utterly novel in structure (not to mention content).

Cognitive science is a cross-disciplinary study involving work in such fields as artificial intelligence, linguistics, psychology, and neuroscience. The cognitive scientist constructs models of mental processes and then tests these models to see that they yield all the outputs produced by minds and only those outputs. For example, a cognitive scientist might be interested in constructing a model of the mechanism for short-term storage and retrieval of information such as the telephone number of a taxi service. One famous paper in cognitive psychology describes the neurological mechanism for pattern recognition that enables frogs to detect bugs moving across their field of vision. The essential or defining attribute of such studies is that they posit processes that are functionally, or operationally, equivalent to mental processes. See Farnham-Diggory, S. *Cognitive Processes in Education.* New York: Harper, 1992; Bourne, L. E. et al. *Cognitive Processes.* Englewood Cliffs, NJ: Prentice, 1986; and Lindsay, P. H., and D. A. Norman, *Human Information Processing.* New York: Academic Press, 1977.

students to connect to literature through ***reader response*** *activities and then provides materials that teachers can use to assist students in elaborating and refining their responses.*

Reader Response Theory

The Theoretical Foundations of Reader Response Theory. Reader response theory offers a theoretical framework for teaching that enables students to connect to literature on their own terms. The theory springs from a simple observation about the relationship between a literary text and its meaning, or interpretation: this relationship is not as direct as the relationship between text and meaning in, say, a train schedule. Suppose, for example, that a train schedule reads as follows:

> The B train from Marston arrives at Holyoke Station at 12:45.

That statement has one acceptable and correct interpretation. Differing interpretations (e.g., "The B train arrives at 12:55") are simply wrong (and can lead to pointless standing around on railway platforms).

One cannot make such statements about the rightness or wrongness of a literary judgment because literary texts do not function as train schedules do. A literary text provides much more than a report of observable facts about the world: It provides an opportunity for an imaginary experience. If one is reading well, that imaginary experience is every bit as vivid as an actual experience, such as trekking up a mountainside in the Peruvian Andes or shopping in the Ginza district of Tokyo.

When one reads a work of literature, one does not *read about the world,* one *enters a world,* and not *the world as it is,* but *the world as it might be.* That world is an imaginative construct formed partly on the basis of the text and partly on the basis of experiences that the reader brings to the reading.

Imagine, for a moment, that you and some other travelers have just returned from a real-life excursion. There will doubtless be aspects of the trip that you can agree upon (e.g., "The Ginza is crowded"; "The air at high elevations in the Andes is quite thin."). However, the real meaning, or significance, of the trip will differ for each of you depending on what you brought to the journey. The same is true of the journeys that people take when they read. Your experience of Hughes's "The Negro Speaks of Rivers" or Porter's "The Jilting of Granny Weatherall" will differ from another person's depending on what you brought (and continue to bring) to the text.

Literary Works as Worlds. The idea that a literary text offers the reader (or listener) an opportunity to create a world into which he or she can travel is not new. When the Nobel Prize-winning poet Derek Walcott writes

> At the end of this sentence, rain
> will begin.
> At the end of the rain, a sail.

he evokes the ancient, shamanistic power of the poet to call a world into existence. This power connects Walcott in an unbroken line through Shelley and Shakespeare and Homer to the first unknown poet who enthralled an audience with the pre-proto-Indo-European equivalent of "Once upon a time. . . ."

In the early twentieth century, the idea that a literary text creates a world of its own was eloquently advanced by the so-called "New Critics," such as Cleanth Brooks writing in *The Well-Wrought Urn.* The New Critics insisted on close reading of texts, and this insistence led some to think that the New Criticism was about arriving, through analysis, at some one acceptable meaning; however, that is a misinterpretation of New Critical theory. Brooks, Warren, Empson, and other New Critics advanced a much more subtle and powerful idea. They believed that literary texts created worlds and that one had to attend closely to the texts in order to distinguish the nuances of those worlds. In the words of that masterpiece of New Critical theory, Archibald MacLeish's poem "Ars Poetica,"

> A poem should not mean
> But be.

Reader response theory extends this formulation by acknowledging the large role played by the reader, as well as by the text, in the creation of "the world of a reading."

The world of a literary work, like the real world, provides an opportunity to have an experience. Critical faculties and concepts, like a tourist's guidebook, will help to make that experience valuable, but the experience itself has no one meaning, any more than a waterfall or a revolution or any other real-life experience does.

The Construction of Meaning. Different readers will read and interpret a text differently, depending on

what they bring to it. Suppose, for example, that a story begins as follows:

> Isaac opened his lunch box. It contained the usual sandwich wrapped in brown paper (his father, who made his lunches, thought that plastic wrap constituted a sin against the environment). It also contained what seemed to him an ordinary apple.

If you are reading well, then you will give yourself over imaginatively to the story, creating the scene in your mind's eye. Of course, the scene that you create will depend partly on the text and partly on your experiences. When you read about lunch boxes, perhaps you think of the metal variety found beside construction workers perched on girders, or perhaps you think of the plastic variety decorated with Simbas or Power Rangers. When you think of ordinary apples, you might picture a green Granny Smith or a Golden Delicious or a red Winesap. If you are an environmentalist, you might wonder whether Isaac's observation about his father means that the boy is insensitive about environmental issues. You might recall that a certain famous Isaac is popularly associated with apples and might begin wondering whether the juxtaposition of Isaac and apples in this story constitutes some sort of significant allusion. Perhaps this Isaac is going to make a discovery. The point is that as you begin reading the story, you begin constructing the world of the story based on clues in the text and on your own experience. That world will have its similarities to the world constructed by another reader, but it will have its differences, too. To some extent, large or small, your interpretation, your sense of the meaning of the text, will be unique.

Furthermore, the meaning of a text does not remain the same even for a single person. Robert Frost wrote eloquently about the evolution of his understanding of Emerson's poem "Brahma," advising readers not to be too anxious to come to a single, final interpretation of a poem but rather to carry the poem around in their heads so that its meaning would become enlarged and enriched (and, indeed, changed) by experience.

Reader Response or Cultural Transmission?

Relativism and Reader Response. A text comes to have meaning through a complex transaction between the text and the reader. This idea that the reader helps to create meaning can be dated to Louise Rosenblatt's seminal work *Literature as Exploration.* Recent developments of that idea owe much to Post-Modernist critical theory, in particular to Jacques Derrida's Deconstructionism. The same criticisms that have been directed at Derrida can also be directed against the extreme form of reader response theory that holds that a literary text can mean anything.

One such criticism of reader response theory asks: If literary texts mean different things to different people, what happens to the whole concept of cultural transmission through literature? Surely, the skeptic says, the idea that texts have different meanings for different persons is equivalent to Humpty Dumpty's position on the meanings of words, familiar to readers of *Through the Looking Glass:*

> "I don't know what you mean by 'glory'," Alice said.
>
> Humpty Dumpty smiled contemptuously. "Of course you don't—till I tell you. I meant 'there's a nice knock-down argument for you!'"
>
> "But 'glory' doesn't mean 'a nice knock-down argument'," Alice objected.
>
> "When I use a word," Humpty Dumpty said, in a rather scornful tone, "it means just what I choose it to mean—neither more nor less."
>
> "The question is," said Alice, "whether you can make words mean so many different things."
>
> "The question is," said Humpty Dumpty, "which is to be master—that's all."

Some have charged that both Deconstructionism and reader response theory are instances of a Humpty Dumptyish "relativism." Surely, critics of such theories say, "Auld Lang Syne" has a meaning that all Western speakers of English understand. Its meaning is part of the common cultural heritage of English speakers in the West. To deny that Burns's poem has a consensus meaning or interpretation is to ignore that it has become a popular New Year's Eve tune with a cultural significance that is passed from generation to generation in the West. To fail to

teach this meaning to students is to deny them access to their cultural heritage, to deprive them of a small portion of the legacy that binds them to others, making them part of a cultural entity rather than alienated individuals. This attitude forms the core of the argument made eloquently and popularly by E. D. Hirsch and Alan Bloom, among others.[3]

A Nonrelativistic Theory of Reader Response. The charge of relativism holds up only against the radical form of reader response theory that holds that a text can mean anything. To understand what shape a nonrelativistic reader response theory might take, let us return to our guiding metaphor, that of reading as a journey into another place (a journey made possible, as Coleridge pointed out in his *Biographia Literaria*, by "a willing suspension of disbelief"). Imagine that a child from the United States, having learned nothing of ancient Rome, were to stroll through the ruins of the Forum. Most likely, that child would make little sense of the experience, if we read "making sense" as interpreting the experience in grown-up terms. The Forum would be, for the child, a mere pile of rocks. The child's sense of wonder might be aroused by the occasional stray or feral cat or by various trinkets dropped on the ground by tourists. Now imagine that you yourself are walking through the Forum. To make the experience all the more exciting, imagine that you have with you a guide versed in Roman history (Livy or Gibbon would be nice). You wouldn't need a stray cat to arouse your sense of wonder. You are an educated person. You know about ancient Rome (and much of what you don't know can be supplied by your guide).

Reader response theory says that literary texts mean different things to different people, but it does not deny that some readings, like some walks through the Forum, are more informed than others. If one is in the process of becoming educated (and most of us are most of the time), then one's readings will not simply change over time, they will deepen. Furthermore, the process of becoming informed or educated about a text will include coming to understand the consensus interpretations of that text—the interpretations that have become part of our common cultural heritage.

Consider, for example, a line from another famous poem by Burns: "My love is like a red, red rose." One leading reader-response-based literature anthology, after asking students what this comparison might mean, suggests as an answer simply that "answers will vary." However, a red rose, in the context of a love poem, has a definite meaning in a Western cultural context. In the West, a rose is a conventional symbol of beauty and romantic love. Much of the work of a teacher is to pass on the accumulated knowledge, traditions, and symbols of a culture, and any textbook that does not assist teachers in that job does teachers and students a disservice. Such a text undermines the role of the teacher in the transmission of culture and ignores a rather fundamental fact: **the teacher is there because he or she knows much that the students do not as yet know.**

Interpreting literature involves achieving a sort of "equilibrium" among three factors: the reader's background knowledge, experience, and attitudes; the historically developed and culturally recognized canons of meaning; and the text itself.

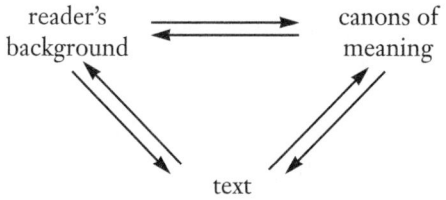

These canons of meaning are part of cultural literacy and include knowledge of literary genres, movements, and techniques as well as familiarity with history, authors' lives, other literary works, and some literary criticism, all part of the special knowledge the professional teacher of literature brings to the classroom. While respecting the student's responses and recognizing that those responses will always be to some large extent unique to that student, the teacher can still guide the student toward fuller, more sophisticated, more informed responses, ones that attend more closely to texts and to culturally transmitted aspects of texts such as conventional symbolism.

3. Preservation of students' unique cultural backgrounds and promotion of a shared cultural literacy need not be, as is often supposed, mutually exclusive goals. To achieve both, educators must expand their definitions of what constitutes the larger shared culture. Long ago, Jean de Crèvecoeur and Alexis de Tocqueville observed that America is strong because that country draws upon its diversity to create a new, larger union. *E pluribus unum*, says the motto on United States coins. The tension, the paradox, in that motto is one that those with literary education will appreciate. Out of such creative tensions new and wonderful syntheses are born.

Reader Response and Cultural Transmission in *Literature and the Language Arts*

What makes *Literature and the Language Arts* unique among available literature programs is that it does not offer teachers an unacceptable choice between reader response and cultural transmission. Instead, it provides ample reader response materials for engaging students on their own terms and then builds on what students already know, refining those responses in light of literary conventions and traditions. The unique design of the study materials in this series enables students to encounter the literature on their own and connect it to their lives and then enables teachers to correct their students' discoveries to the mainstreams of literary tradition.

The psychologist Lev Vygotsky pointed out that at the outset of any learning situation, the learner has already reached a certain stage in his or her understanding. This stage really has two parts: what the learner can do on his or her own and what the learner can do with some assistance. The area between these two points is what Vygotsky called the **zone of proximal development,** or **ZPD.** The teacher's role is to assign the learner tasks that are within the ZPD and to provide the assistance that the learner needs while allowing the learner to do on his or her own as much as he or she is able. The teacher provides **scaffolding** that supports the learner until he or she reaches a new level. Then the old scaffolding is unnecessary and the learner is ready to move on to new learning.

The study materials in *Literature and the Language Arts* make it possible for students to begin with what they already know—their own lives—and connect what they know to the literature. Once that connection is made, students then explore the literature independently and in collaborative activities that provide a foundation for the teacher-assisted instruction, or scaffolding, that follows.

Partial Bibliography

Bloom, A. *The Closing of the American Mind.* New York: Simon and Schuster, 1987.

Brooks, C. *The Well-Wrought Urn.* New York: Renal and Hitchcock, 1947.

Bruner, J. *Toward a Theory of Instruction.* New York: Norton, 1966.

———. *On Knowing: Essays for the Left Hand.* Expanded ed. Cambridge: Belknap/Harvard UP, 1979.

Chomsky, N. *Language and Mind.* New York: Harcourt, 1968.

———. Review of B. F. Skinner's *Verbal Behavior. Language*, 35 (1959), 26–58.

Derrida, J. *Of Grammatology.* Trans. C. Spivak. Baltimore: Johns Hopkins UP, 1976.

Donaldson, M. *Children's Minds.* New York: Norton, 1978.

Eisner, E. *The Educational Imagination.* 2nd ed. New York: Macmillan, 1985.

Farrell, E. J. *Deciding the Future.* Research Rep. No. 12. Urbana, IL: NCTE, 1971.

Flower, L. S. *Problem-Solving Strategies in Writing.* 2nd ed. Orlando, FL: Harcourt, 1985.

Hirsch, E. D. *Cultural Literacy: What Every American Needs to Know.* New York: Houghton, 1987.

Kempson, R. M. *Semantic Theory.* Cambridge: Cambridge UP, 1977.

Kuhn, T. S. *The Structure of Scientific Revolutions.* 2nd ed. Chicago: U of Chicago P, 1970.

Lashley, K. "The Problem of Serial Order in Behavior." L. Jeffries, ed. *Cerebral Mechanisms in Behavior.*

Lindemann, E. *A Rhetoric for Writing Teachers.* 3rd ed. New York: Oxford UP, 1995.

Novak, J. D. *A Theory of Education.* Ithaca, NY: Cornell UP, 1984.

Resnick, L., and L. Klopfer. *Toward the Thinking Curriculum: Current Cognitive Research.* Alexandria, VA: ASCD, 1989.

Rosenblatt, L. *Literature as Exploration.* 4th ed. New York: MLA, 1983.

———. *The Reader, the Text, the Poem: The Transactional Theory of the Literary Work.* Carbondale, IL: Southern Illinois UP, 1978.

Skinner, B. F. *Science and Human Behavior.* New York: Macmillan. 1953.

———. *Verbal Behavior.* New York: Appleton, 1957.

Strike, K. A. "On the Expressive Potential of Behaviorist Language." *American Educational Research Journal,* 11 (1974), 103–20.

Thorndike, E. L. *The Fundamentals of Learning.* New York: Teacher's College, 1932.

Vygotsky, L. S. *Mind in Society.* Cambridge: Harvard UP, 1978.

———. *Thought and Language.* New York: Wiley, 1962.

Watson, J. B. *Behaviorism.* New York: Norton, 1925.

Weaver, C. *Grammar for Teachers.* Urbana, IL: NCTE, 1979.

Wimsatt, W. K. *The Verbal Icon: Studies in the Meaning of Poetry.* UP of Kentucky, 1954.

Program Components

Student Edition

Twelve Units per Book
- Historical Introductions
- Superlative Texts
- Fine Art and Photographs
- Development of the English Language
- Unit Reviews

Selections
- About the Author
- About the Selection
- Guided Reading Questions
- Words for Everyday Use
- Notes

Additional Readings

Selection Study Materials
- Prereading
- Responding to the Selection (Reader Response)
- Reviewing the Selection
- Recalling
- Interpreting
- Synthesizing
- Understanding Literature
- Responding in Writing
- Language Lab
- Additional Language Arts Skills Activities
- Projects

Language Arts Survey
- Writing
- Language
- Speaking and Listening
- Study and Research
- Applied English/Tech Prep

Handbook of Literary Terms

Reader's Guide and Activity Book*

Selection worksheets providing a step-by-step reader response guide for each selection and prewriting assistance for all writing assignments in the text

Essential Skills Practice Books*

Blackline masters for additional practice

Writing

Language

Speaking and Listening

Study, Research, Thinking, and Test-taking

Applied English

Assessment Portfolio*

Unit Study Guides and Tests
- Including vocabulary worksheets

Selection Tests
- Check tests
- Comprehensive tests

Writing Skills Pretests and Post-tests

Other Language Arts Skills Study Guides and Tests

Worksheets and Forms for Writing Evaluation and Portfolio Assessment

Additional Worksheets and Forms

Answer Keys

Scope and Sequence Charts

Transparency Set*

*Contained in the Teacher's Resource Kit

Multimedia Kit

Audiocassette
- Selections from the program

Videocassette
- Selections from the program

CD/ROM
- Idea generator
- Test generator

Diskettes (IBM and Macintosh)
- Test generators

Laser Disc
- Selections from the program

Annotated Teacher's Edition

For Units
- List of skills taught
- List of cross-curricular activities
- List of multiple intelligences
- List of major themes
- List of central literary techniques
- Additional historical and biographical background
- Information on art and artists

For Selections
- List of additional resources
- Enrichment activities
- Support for limited English proficiency students
  - Teaching tips
  - Vocabulary help
- List of goals/objectives
- List of introduced vocabulary words
- Vocabulary words used in sample sentences
- Additional activities
- Discussion prompts
- Historical and literary background notes
- Quotable quotations

Answer Keys
- Selection Check Tests with answers
- Answers for all exercises
- Analytic evaluation scales for writing projects
- Cross-references to additional exercises
- Cross-references to assessment instruments

Teaching Notes and Background Notes
- Additional problems with answers

Identifiers for Cross-curricular Activities, Activities using Multiple Intelligences, and Activities Using SCANS Skills

Themes and Genres Charts

Teaching Strategies and Options

Additional Resources for Language Arts Teachers

Organization of the Text

Textbooks presenting surveys of American literature often begin with selections from the pre-Colonial and Puritan Eras, thus confronting students at the beginning of the course with some of the most challenging work. The editors and authors of this text feel that before beginning a survey of American literature, students should review basic literary types and techniques in connection with readily accessible, high-interest selections. *Literature and the Language Arts: The American Tradition* has been designed to offer just such review of literary concepts in preparation for the historical survey that follows.

The text is organized into three parts:

Part One: Understanding Literature consists of a single unit that reviews the five genres of literature—the oral tradition, poetry, fiction, drama, and nonfiction—and provides an overview of the writing process. The unit is divided into five sections. Each section presents a model work in a particular literary genre. A brief essay at the beginning of each section gives a history and taxonomy of the genre. This essay is followed by a thorough presentation of terminology and techniques of particular relevance to that genre. The model work in each section contains passages set in blue ink and keyed to marginal notes that identify characteristics and techniques typical of works in that genre. Thus the model fictional work contains highlighted passages identifying such elements as setting, character, theme, and the components of the plot. The selections in Unit 1 include ample reader response and teacher-assisted activities.

Part One also leads students through six steps of the writing process: prewriting, drafting, evaluating, revising, proofreading, and sharing or presenting. The writing exercises are cumulative throughout the unit. After completing the unit, each student will have published a piece of his or her own creation. If you do not wish to teach the materials on genre, use the writing activities independently.

Part Two: The American Tradition presents American literature using a historical approach (to use other approaches, see the notes on page T29 of this *Annotated Teacher's Edition*). Units 2–7 begin with historical essays covering major social, political, and intellectual trends associated with the literature of each period from the pre-Colonial Era to the Frontier Era. The "Echoes" page that follows each unit introduction offers intriguing quotations chosen to capture the spirit of the age. Units 8–11 present twentieth-century poetry, prose, drama, and nonfiction respectively. Contemporary literature is treated in Unit 12.

The selections within each unit have been chosen carefully to meet a number of criteria:

- To provide students with engaging, stimulating reading experiences
- To provide outstanding representative examples of each period
- To provide examples of the major genres of literature in each period
- To provoke interesting discussions of significant themes
- To represent major writers in the American literary tradition
- To represent more fully than in the past women's contributions to the historical development of American literature

Following most of the units are **Selections for Additional Reading.** These selections are not accompanied by the usual teaching apparatus, for the editors and authors of this series feel that students should have some "pure" reading experiences, unburdened by exercises and exegeses. Of course, students can use these selections for research when preparing critical papers on literary movements or trends. The Selections for Additional Reading include many classics as well as many remarkable works not normally found in high school anthologies.

Each unit also teaches English vocabulary with Words for Everyday Use and concludes with a Unit Review that offers Synthesis questions for discussion or writing. An extended **Language Lab** at the end of each unit presents instruction and practice in grammar, usage, mechanics, spelling, and the varieties of English.

Part Three of this text contains four sections. **The Language Arts Survey** offers comprehensive instruction in the complete range of language arts skills. (Each lesson in the Language Arts Survey is keyed to a worksheet in one of the five *Essential Skills Practice Books* in the Teacher's Resource Kit.) The **Handbook of Literary Terms** defines and provides examples of terms for literary movements and schools of thought, literary techniques, genres of literature, and common allusions. The **Glossary** collects all the Words for Everyday Use and provides both pronunciations and definitions. The text ends with indexes of titles and authors, skills, and fine art.

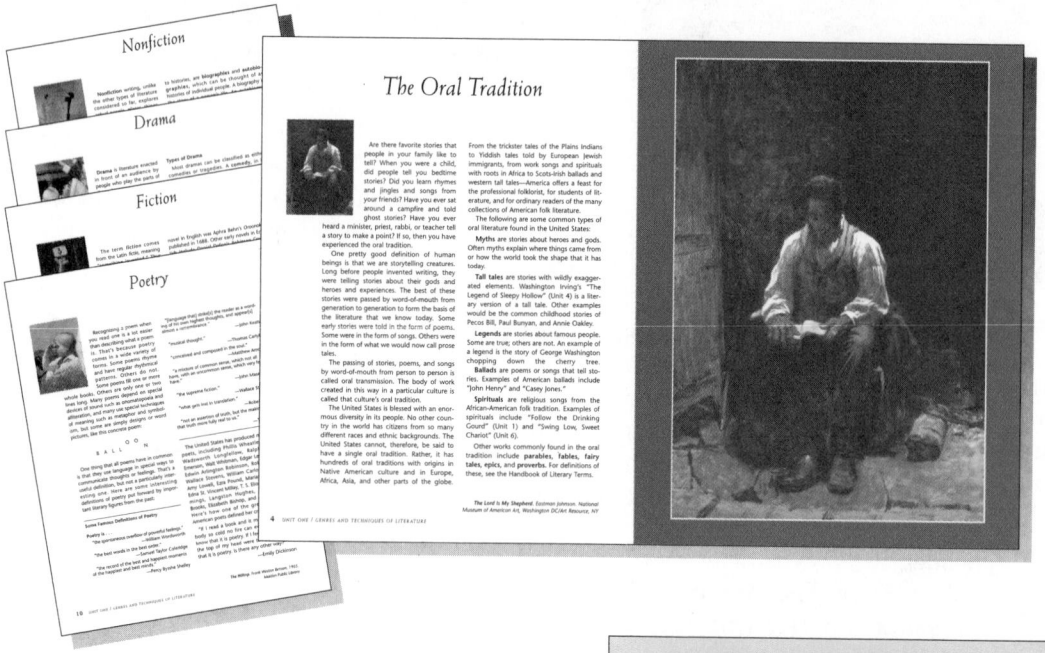

Part One: Understanding Literature *reviews basic literary types and techniques in connection with readily accessible, high-interest selections. This part of the text prepares students for the survey to come.*

Part Two: The American Tradition *surveys American literature from the pre-Colonial Era to the present.*

Part Three *contains*

- *A comprehensive* ***Language Arts Survey***
- *A thorough* ***Handbook of Literary Terms***
- *A* ***Glossary*** *of Words for Everyday Use*
- ***Indexes*** *of Titles and Authors, Skills, and Fine Art*

Lesson Design and Teaching Strategies

Literature Instruction

A typical lesson in *Literature and the Language Arts* contains materials for two phases of instruction, the Reader Response phase and the Teacher-Assisted phase.

The Reader Response Phase. Cognitive theory and common sense tell us that learning is more likely to occur when students are first provided with a context for what they are to learn. As the proverb says, a seed will grow in prepared ground. Each lesson in this book begins with a **Prereading** page that provides essential information about the author and the selection. The precise content of the entries **About the Author** and **About the Selection** varies according to the demands of the work to be read. If basic comprehension of the work requires understanding of an historical allusion, then that allusion is explained. If comprehension requires understanding of a literary technique, then that technique is described. In addition, the Prereading page provides information about the author and selection designed to arouse student interest.

The selection page itself begins with a writing activity to be done in the student's **Reader's Journal.** The Reader's Journal activity raises a central theme from the selection and asks the student to relate that theme to his or her own life. If, for example, a selection deals with a character who fails to exhibit courage, the student might be asked to write about a time when he or she acted courageously or wanted to act courageously but could not. After completing this activity, the student will be thinking about courage in relation to his or her own life and

PREREADING

"Mending Wall"
"Home Burial"
by Robert Frost

ABOUT THE AUTHOR

Robert Frost (1874–1963) was without question the most popular American poet of the twentieth century. He was born in San Francisco and lived there until the age of eleven, when his father died. After that, Frost and his mother moved to New England. Frost graduated at the top of his high school class, sharing the position of valedictorian with Elinor White, whom he later married. At the age of seventeen, he published his first poem. After marrying Elinor, he continued to hold miscellaneous jobs and to write poetry, briefly going to Harvard as a special student before settling as a teacher at Pinkerton Academy in 1906. In 1912, Frost took his family to England, and it was there that his poetry first found a major audience with the publication of *A Boy's Will* (1913) and *North of Boston* (1914). Frost returned to the United States and began to achieve financial stability from the sale of his books. He taught and lectured at various colleges, including Dartmouth, Amherst, and Harvard. He was awarded Pulitzer Prizes in 1924, 1931, 1937, and 1943 and received honorary degrees from many universities. In 1961, he was invited to read a poem at the inauguration of John F. Kennedy, thirty-fifth president of the United States. Frost's many popular works, most of which deal with New England subject matter, include *Mountain Interval* (1916), *New Hampshire* (1923), *West-Running Brook* (1928), *A Way Out* (1929), *A Witness Tree* (1942), and *In the Clearing* (1962).

ABOUT THE SELECTIONS

Robert Frost had a rare talent that enabled him to produce poetry simple and clear enough to appeal to a large audience and yet intellectually rich enough to appeal to sophisticated literary critics. Frost wrote often of the nature and people of his adopted home of New England. He wrote in the language of ordinary speech and didn't care for modern free verse, which he likened to "playing tennis without a net." Instead, he wrote in conventional forms, including **rhymed verse,** as in **"Mending Wall,"** and **blank verse** made up of unrhymed iambic pentameter lines, as in **"Home Burial."** (An iambic pentameter line has ten alternating weakly stressed and strongly stressed syllables.) Many of Frost's finest poems such as "Home Burial," and "The Death of the Hired Man" in the Selections for Additional Reading on page 602, are **dramatic monologues** or **dramatic dialogues.** Such poems present a dramatic interaction in which one or two people speak.

524 UNIT EIGHT / MODERN POETRY

Sample Prereading Page

About the Author *provides contextual information about the author's life and the period in which he or she lived.*

About the Selection *provides keys to comprehension of the selection; this covers literary movements, genres, techniques, or themes, depending upon the demands of the selection and its place in literary history.*

therefore be more likely to relate the selection to himself or herself and so become emotionally invested in it. This emotional investment in the literature is, of course, key, and that is why the Reader's Journal activities are primarily affective in nature. Responses to these Reader's Journal activities can be made on the **Selection Worksheets** found in the ***Reader's Guide and Activity Book,*** or they can be made in the student's notebook.

Once the student begins reading the selection, he or she can then take advantage of the **Guided Reading Questions** that appear in the margins. These questions are designed to bring to the student's attention key passages in the selection and issues raised by those passages. Like a guide taking a tourist through the Roman Forum and pointing out important or interesting landmarks, these questions take the student through the selection, ensuring that the most important or interesting aspects of the selection will not be missed. (It would be wonderful if every student could have his or her own private guide to literature. These questions provide the next best thing.)

Again, the student can answer these questions on the Selection Worksheets or in his or her notebook.

After reading the selection, the student can then meet with other students in small **collaborative learning groups** to share responses to the Reader's Journal activity and Guided Reading Questions. In these groups, students can also discuss the questions raised in the **Responding to the Selection** activity that follows the selection. Again, this is an affective-response activity, one designed to connect the student emotionally to the literature.

These three components of the instructional apparatus, the Reader's Journal activity, the Guided Reading questions, and the Responding to the

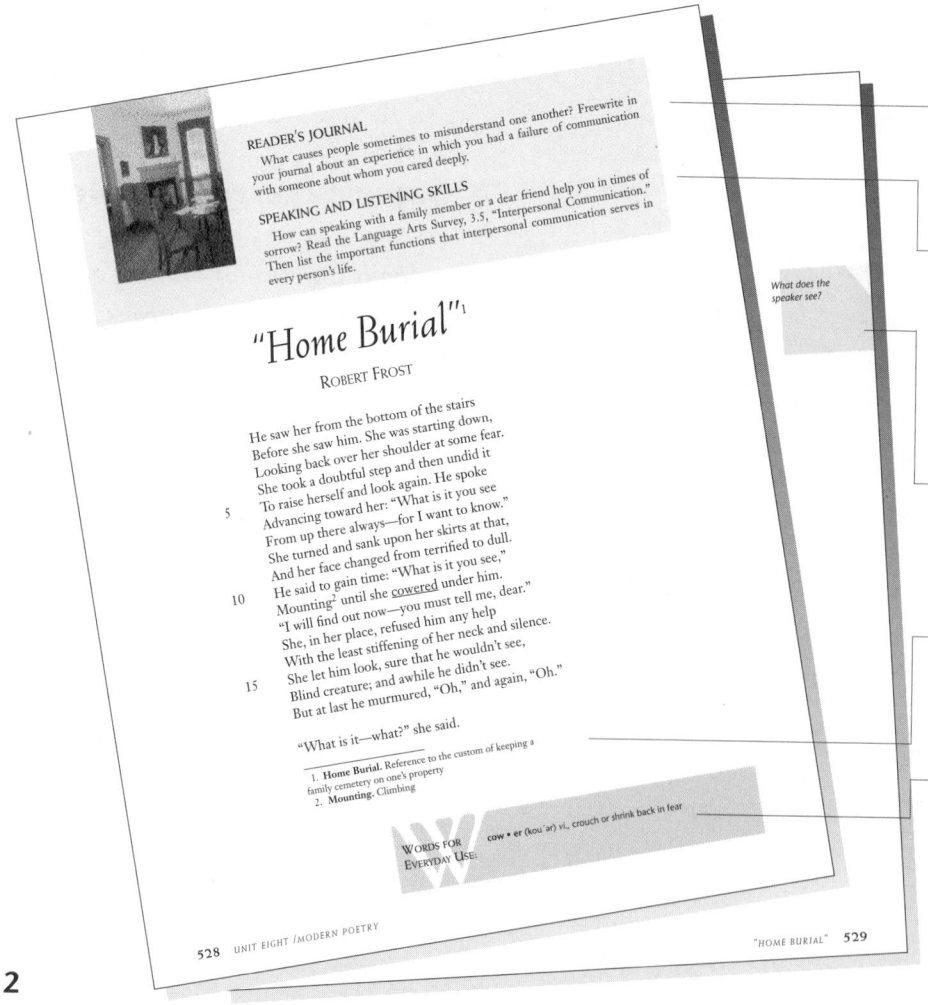

READER'S JOURNAL

What causes people sometimes to misunderstand one another? Freewrite in your journal about an experience in which you had a failure of communication with someone about whom you cared deeply.

SPEAKING AND LISTENING SKILLS

How can speaking with a family member or a dear friend help you in times of sorrow? Read the Language Arts Survey, 3.5, "Interpersonal Communication." Then list the important functions that interpersonal communication serves in every person's life.

"Home Burial"[1]

ROBERT FROST

He saw her from the bottom of the stairs
Before she saw him. She was starting down,
Looking back over her shoulder at some fear.
She took a doubtful step and then undid it
To raise herself and look again. He spoke
Advancing toward her: "What is it you see
From up there always—for I want to know."
She turned and sank upon her skirts at that,
And her face changed from terrified to dull.
He said to gain time: "What is it you see,"
Mounting[2] until she cowered under him.
"I will find out now—you must tell me, dear."
She, in her place, refused him any help
With the least stiffening of her neck and silence.
She let him look, sure that he wouldn't see,
Blind creature; and awhile he didn't see.
But at last he murmured, "Oh," and again, "Oh."

"What is it—what?" she said.

1. **Home Burial.** Reference to the custom of keeping a family cemetery on one's property
2. **Mounting.** Climbing

WORDS FOR EVERYDAY USE: cow • er (kou´ ər) vi., crouch or shrink back in fear

What does the speaker see?

528 UNIT EIGHT /MODERN POETRY

"HOME BURIAL" 529

Sample Selection Pages

*The **Reader's Journal** activity raises an important theme from the selection and connects that theme to the student's life.*

*A variable **Language Arts Skills** activity, keyed to the Language Arts Survey at the back of the book, provides integrated practice in Speaking and Listening, Study and Research, Thinking, or Applied English.*

***Guided Reading Questions** relate important aspects of the selection to the student's own thoughts, feelings, and experiences.*

***Footnotes** explain obscure references, unusual usages, and terms meant to enter students' passive vocabularies.*

***Words for Everyday Use notes** define and give pronunciations for difficult terms meant to enter students' active vocabularies.*

Selection activity, connect the student to the selection, guide him or her through it, and then make it possible for the student to share his or her responses with others. Together, these activities ensure that once the teacher-assisted phase of the instruction begins, the student will have a wealth of responses to share in discussions with the whole class.

Additional teaching suggestions for the Reader's Journal, Guided Reading, and Responding to the Selection activities are provided in the ***Annotated Teacher's Edition.***

The Teacher-Assisted Phase. The **Reviewing the Selection** questions that follow the Responding to the Selection activity are designed to take the student through the selection, step-by-step, building upon his or her responses and refining those through questions of successive complexity. These questions are organized by level of cognitive sophistication into three sections:

The **Recalling** questions ensure basic comprehension of key facts from the selection.

The **Interpreting** questions ask students to make interpretations or critical evaluations based on facts from the selection.

The **Synthesizing** questions ask students to draw together what they have gathered through recall and interpretation to make generalizations about the meaning, significance, or value of the selection. Often these questions ask the student to apply what he or she has learned from the selection to some larger context (to larger trends or themes in literature, for example, or to some larger social, cultural, ethical, or political context).

Uniquely, each Interpreting question in Reviewing the Selection is keyed by means of an arrow to a Recalling question that provides the facts on which the interpretation can be based. **This keying of interpretation to facts from the selection ensures that student responses will be based on evidence from the selection. No other text now available offers this feature.**

Because students often are not readily familiar with literary terminology and its applications, such terminology does not appear in the questions for Reviewing the Selection. Literary terminology and techniques are covered in the next part of the instructional apparatus, which is called **Understanding Literature.** Each Understanding Literature activity begins with a boldfaced term that names a literary movement, genre, or technique. The term is followed by its definition and by one or more questions that apply the concept to the selection. Having responded to the selection and having reviewed it in detail, the student can now learn some of the technical details about how the selection worked to achieve its effects. Students needing or desiring additional information about a term introduced in the Understanding Literature activity can refer to the discussion of that term in the **Handbook of Literary Terms** at the back of the book.

Approaches to the teacher-assisted phase of the literature instruction can vary, depending on your teaching style and the needs of your students. Some teachers will prefer to have students answer questions on Reviewing the Selection and Understanding Literature individually or in small groups and then will hold whole-class discussions of these questions. Others will prefer to treat these questions as prompts for whole-class, teacher-directed discussions. Another alternative, especially appropriate in advanced classes, is to assign students to conduct whole-class discussions of these questions.

Reviewing the Selection

RECALLING

1. What does he see "Before she saw him"?
2. What kind of "creature" does the wife think her husband is?
3. What are the husband's words "nearly always" to his wife?
4. What does the wife "carry to someone else"?

INTERPRETING

5. How might the wife's actions have been different if she had seen her husband watching her?
6. Why does the wife challenge the husband to tell her what he sees?
7. With what does the husband ask for his wife's help?
8. What is the husband's defense against his grief?

SYNTHESIZING

9. What is the husband desperately trying to avoid?
10. What differences exist in how the husband and wife express their grief about the death of their infant son? How has the death of their child ruptured their marriage?

Understanding Literature (Questions for Discussion)

1. **Metaphor. A metaphor** is a figure of speech in which one thing is spoken or written about as if it were another. Consider the following lines in the poem: "I can repeat the very words you were saying:/'Three foggy mornings and one rainy day/Will rot the best birch fence a man can build.'" How are these lines an expression of the man's sense of loss? Does his wife understand that they are such an expression? What does she think that they mean? What has happened to the communication between this man and woman? If you were a therapist attempting to help this couple to deal with the death of their child, what advice would you give each person about communicating effectively with the other?
2. **Diction and Tone. Diction,** when applied to writing, refers to word choice. Much of a writer's style or voice is determined by his or her diction, the types of words that are chosen, whether formal or informal, simple or complex, contemporary or archaic, ordinary or unusual, standard or dialectical. **Tone** is the emotional attitude toward the reader or toward the subject implied by a literary work. Consider the following lines from the poem: "I saw you from that very window there,/Making the gravel leap and leap in air,/Leap up, like that, like that, and land so lightly/And roll back down the mound beside the hole." How would you describe the diction in these lines? How does the diction match with the character of the wife? What tone or emotional attitude toward the husband does the wife express in these lines? What effect do the repetitions within these lines have on the tone?

Why does the speaker feel bitter?

Why does Amy think friends might as well not go?

Where does the speaker think his wife is going? Why?

Responding to the Selection

Imagine that you are either the wife or husband in this poem. Why would you be unable to understand your spouse's way of expressing his or her grief? What comfort or consolation would you seek from your spouse? Write an entry in your journal expressing your feelings about the death of your child.

Sample Literary Skills Pages

Reviewing the Selection *takes students through the work step-by-step, building from their individual responses a complete interpretation of the work.*

Recalling *questions address comprehension of key facts from the selection.*

Interpreting *questions, keyed to the Recalling questions by arrows, evoke interpretations based on evidence from the selection.*

Synthesizing *questions tie together interpretations of parts of the selection and prompt students to make informed generalizations that relate the selection to larger themes or literary trends.*

Understanding Literature *questions provide selection-related study of literary movements, genres, and techniques.*

Responding to the Selection *is a* ***reader response*** *activity designed to elicit an affective response to the selection.*

Instruction in Other Language Arts Skills: An Integrated Approach

It has been shown that a student may demonstrate knowledge in a classroom but be unable to use that knowledge in "real-life" situations. Grammar, usage, mechanics, spelling, and vocabulary skills have traditionally been taught in isolation as independent skills, but just as instruction in the separate concepts of physiology does not make us healthier, neither does instruction in the abstract concepts of speech or grammar make us speak or write better (Hillocks; Braddock). Skills must be taught in ways that enable students to "transfer" them to real contexts, i.e., to use them in their lives. The transferability of knowledge is a function of meaningfulness (Prawat). Teachers can promote meaningfulness by providing (1) a wide variety of examples, (2) practice in a wide variety of contexts, (3) an explanation of the value or uses of the learning, (4) an advance organizer at the beginning of the lesson, and (5) reviews. These five tasks have served as guideposts in the planning and writing of *Literature and the Language Arts.*

The exercises in this text are organized so that instruction in essential skills—those for writing, language, speaking and listening, study and research, thinking, test-taking, and applied English—develops in the context of literature appreciation activities. The study of engaging literature can provide motivation and context for teaching these practical skills.

The **Prereading** activities in this text include, in addition to a journal activity, a variable **Language Arts Skills** activity that relates to and prepares the student for reading the selection. For instance, before students read William

Responding in Writing

Critical Analysis. The two characters in this poem have very different ways of responding to grief and consequently fail to understand one another. Write a critical analysis contrasting the ways in which these characters deal with their grief and explaining why they do not understand one another.

Language Lab

Building Sentences. Read the Language Arts Survey, 2.36, "The Functions of Sentences." Then, decide what the function is of each of the following sentences from the selection. Write the classification of each sentence.

1. He saw her from the bottom of the stairs/Before she saw him.
2. "Tell me what it is."
3. "Can't a man speak of his own child he's lost?"
4. "I don't know how to speak of anything/So as to please you."
5. "There you go sneering now!"

Speaking and Listening Skills

Nonverbal Communication. Read the Language Arts Survey, 3.3, "Elements of Nonverbal Communication." Then, describe how each emotion listed below might be communicated through eye contact, facial expressions, gestures, body language, or proximity.

1. loneliness
2. grief
3. frustration
4. alienation

PROJECT

Dramatic Skit. Collaborate with one other student to write a dramatic scene based on this poem. In your scene, portray the characters of the husband and wife (and the failed communication between them) as they are portrayed in the poem. Write two parts and have one person play the husband and the other play the wife. Rehearse your skit and present it to the rest of the class.

"HOME BURIAL" 533

Sample Language Arts Skills Activities Page

Responding in Writing *activities use the selection as a springboard for engaging writing assignments.*

Integrated ***Language Lab*** *activities provide practice in essential language skills.*

A second variable ***Language Arts Skills*** *activity provides integrated practice in Speaking and Listening, Study and Research, Thinking, or Applied English.*

Many lessons end with special ***Projects*** *that extend your teaching beyond immediate language arts applications and that call upon multiple intelligences.*

Carlos Williams's poem "The Red Wheelbarrow," they receive a lesson on prepositions, which are the key relational words in the poem.

Most skills activities come after the selection.

The **Responding in Writing** activities use the selection as a springboard for creative, interesting writing assignments. **Language Labs** give students practice in essential grammar, usage, and mechanics skills; explore applications of grammar skills to writing; and present key concepts related to varieties of English. A second variable **Language Arts Skills** activity provides more integrated practice in Speaking and Listening, Study and Research, Thinking, or Applied English.

A typical skills activity asks students to read a section of the Language Arts Survey and then complete the exercise. The exercises concern the literature students have just studied. For instance, the Language Lab exercise that follows the selection from Frederick Douglass's *Autobiography* provides additional information about Douglass and about another great crusader against slavery, Harriet Tubman.

Most lessons in the student edition end with one or more **Projects** related to the selection. These projects extend the instruction in the lesson in ways that call upon students' multiple intelligences.

Because language arts skills traditionally have been taught independently, and because conceptual knowledge of grammar, usage, and mechanics is part of cultural literacy, independent Language Labs are also offered at the end of each unit. The twelve end-of-unit Language Labs cover the most essential concepts in grammar, usage, mechanics, spelling, and the varieties of English.

The **Language Arts Survey** at the back of the book provides a comprehensive overview of the complete range of language arts skills. The survey is divided into five sections, as follows:

- Essential Skills: Writing
- Essential Skills: Language
- Essential Skills: Speaking and Listening
- Essential Skills: Study and Research
- Essential Skills: Applied English/ Tech Prep

Students may refer to these sections when doing writing or skills activities. Teachers wishing to give their students additional practice in any of these skills areas will find, for each lesson in the Language Arts Survey, a corresponding worksheet in one of the five ***Essential Skills Practice Books*** found in the Teacher's Resource Kit. Teachers wishing to present whole units related to specific skills can have students work through parts of the Language Arts Survey, doing the activities found there and in the *Essential Skills Practice Books*.

Partial Bibliography

Ausubel, D. *Educational Psychology.* 2nd ed. New York: Holt, 1978.

Braddock, R., R. Lloyd-Jones, and L. Schoer. *Research in Written Composition.* Champaign, IL: NCTE, 1963. (ED 003 374)

Bruner, J. *Toward a Theory of Instruction.* New York: Norton, 1966.

Eggen, P., and D. Kauchak. *Educational Psychology: Classroom Connections.* 2nd ed. New York: Merrill, 1994.

Eisner, E. *The Educational Imagination.* 2nd ed. New York: Macmillan, 1985.

Hillocks, G., Jr. *Research on Written Composition: New Directions for Teaching.* Urbana, IL: Natl. Conference on Research in English and ERIC/CRCS, 1986.

Prawat, R. "Promoting Access to Knowledge, Strategy, and Disposition in Students: A Research Synthesis." *Review of Educational Research*, 59 (1989), 1–41.

Novak, J. D. *A Theory of Education.* Ithaca, NY: Cornell UP, 1984.

END-OF-UNIT EXERCISES

LANGUAGE LAB PROOFREADING FOR OTHER PUNCTUATION ERRORS

When proofreading your writing, check carefully for correct use of semicolons, colons, dashes, hyphens, apostrophes, quotation marks, parentheses, brackets, and ellipses.

LANGUAGE ARTS SURVEY
For additional help, see the Language Arts Survey, 2.97–2.106.

COMMON PUNCTUATION ERRORS

Semicolons. A semicolon is used in the following situations: between closely related independent clauses that are not joined by *and, but, for, nor, or, so,* or *yet;* between independent clauses joined by a conjunctive adverb or transitional expression that is followed by a comma; and between linked independent clauses or items in a list if the clauses or items already contain commas.
EXAMPLES: Sandburg depicts scenes from the Midwest; his verse duplicates the cadences of Midwestern speech.
Many people associate Sandburg with Chicago; however, the poet lived in several cities across the country during his lifetime.
"Chicago" immortalizes the city's noisy, bustling freight yards; hardworking, downtrodden citizens; and legendary spirit.

Colons. A colon introduces a long statement or quotation or a list of items.
EXAMPLE: Stock the icebox with the following: plums, milk, cheese, and grapes.

Dashes. A dash is used to show an abrupt break in thought or to replace an expression such as *in other words, that is,* or *namely.*
EXAMPLE: Do you remember who wrote "The Love Song"—oh, I remember now!

Hyphens. A hyphen is used to link words in a compound adjective, adverb, or noun.
EXAMPLES: flower-fed buffaloes, well-known book, self-knowledge

Apostrophes. An apostrophe is used to form the possessive of nouns and some pronouns. See the Language Arts Survey, 2.102, for complete rules about using apostrophes.
SINGULAR WITH ADDED *S*: Mr. Flood's party, Whiteside's daughter, winter's cold
SINGULAR WITHOUT ADDED *S*: goodness' sake
PLURAL ENDING WITH *S*: tropics' heat, bells' ringing, buffaloes' pelts
PLURAL ENDING WITHOUT *S*: women's conversation, geese's honking, mice's nests

Underlining and Italics. Italics are a type of slanted printing used to show emphasis. (**Underlining** is used when italics are not available.) Some words that receive italics are works of art, books, plays, films, television programs, periodicals, and long musical compositions. Words used as words, letters used as letters, and words from foreign languages also receive italics.
EXAMPLES: *Spoon River Anthology, O'Keeffe's New York Night, Consumer Reports, et tu Brute*

Quotation Marks. Quotation marks are used for a variety of purposes.
DIRECT QUOTATION: "Welcome home!" Mr. Flood cries.
DIRECT WITH PERIOD: Mr. Flood wears "valiant armor of scarred hopes outworn."
DIRECT WITH COMMA: "Drink to the bird," said Mr. Flood.
DIRECT WITH SEMICOLON: Mr. Flood drinks "for auld lang syne"; he seems weary of the world.
TITLES OF SHORT WORKS: "Mr. Flood's Party"

610 UNIT EIGHT / MODERN POETRY

*Extended **Language Labs** at the end of each unit in the student edition treat the most essential skills in grammar, usage, mechanics, spelling, and the varieties of English.*

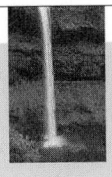

ESSENTIAL SKILLS: *Writing*

INTRODUCTION TO WRITING

For writers of all ages and abilities, writing can sometimes seem a daunting task. The key to writing with confidence and pleasure, though, is simple: just keep writing as much as you can, as often as you can. Like any other skill, writing will improve with practice. Reading will also improve your writing, for reading can expose you to the full range and power of the written word.

1.1 THE PROCESS OF WRITING

Any writing task is much more manageable if you think of it as a process. Each person's writing process is a little different. Some people prefer to get everything down on paper quickly in rough form. Then they rewrite many times to "boil down" and refine what they have written. Other people work slowly and carefully, refining their thoughts and words as they go. For the purpose of instruction, the writing process is often divided into six stages:

SIX STAGES IN THE PROCESS OF WRITING	
1. **Prewriting**	Choose a topic, audience, purpose, and form. Then gather ideas and organize these in a reasonable way.
2. **Drafting**	Get your ideas down on paper in rough form without worrying about perfecting spelling, grammar, usage, and mechanics.
3. **Peer and Self-Evaluation**	Study your draft by yourself or with one or more of your peers to find ways to improve it.
4. **Revising**	Revise your draft to improve its content, organization, and style.
5. **Proofreading**	Check your revised draft for errors in spelling, grammar, usage, and mechanics (including punctuation and capitalization). Then prepare a final copy in an appropriate manuscript form and proofread again.
6. **Publishing and Presenting**	Share your work with an audience.

866 LANGUAGE ARTS SURVEY

*The **Language Arts Survey** at the end of the student edition provides a comprehensive overview of the complete range of language arts skills.*

Essential Skills Practice Books *found in the Teacher's Resource Kit provide activities keyed to each lesson in the Language Arts Survey.*

Teacher's Edition Annotations

The ***Annotated Teacher's Edition*** is designed for your convenience.

Answers for exercises are usually provided on the same pages as the exercises themselves. All items are color-coded: answers to student edition exercises are on white backgrounds, supplementary notes and activities are on yellow backgrounds, and special items, such as lists of goals, enrichment and remedial notes, and selection check test answers, use distinguishing colors.

Sample Unit Opening Pages

Teaching the Multiple Intelligences *lists activities from the unit that call for the exercise of students' multiple intelligences.*

Connections Across the Curriculum *lists the cross-curricular activities from the unit.*

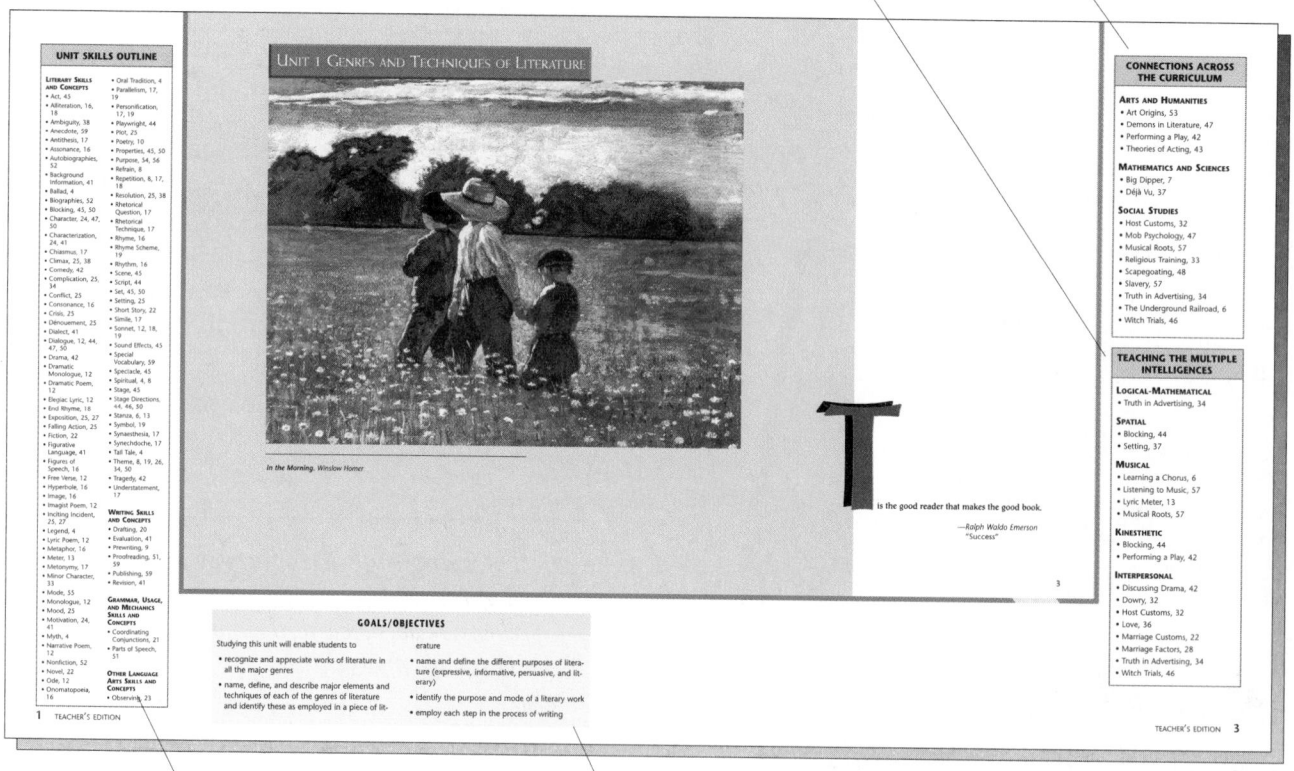

UNIT SKILLS OUTLINE

Literary Skills and Concepts
- Act, 43
- Alliteration, 16, 18
- Ambiguity, 38
- Anecdote, 59
- Antithesis, 17
- Assonance, 16
- Autobiographies, 52
- Background Information, 41
- Ballad, 4
- Biographies, 52
- Blocking, 45, 50
- Character, 24, 47, 50
- Characterization, 24, 41
- Chiasmus, 17
- Climax, 25, 38
- Comedy, 42
- Complication, 25, 34
- Conflict, 25
- Consonance, 16
- Crisis, 25
- Dénouement, 25
- Dialect, 41
- Dialogue, 12, 44, 47, 50
- Drama, 42
- Dramatic Monologue, 12
- Dramatic Poem, 12
- Elegiac Lyric, 12
- End Rhyme, 18
- Exposition, 25, 27
- Falling Action, 25
- Fiction, 22
- Figurative Language, 41
- Figures of Speech, 16
- Free Verse, 12
- Hyperbole, 16
- Image, 16
- Imagist Poem, 12
- Inciting Incident, 25, 27
- Legend, 4
- Lyric Poem, 12
- Metaphor, 16
- Meter, 13
- Metonymy, 17
- Minor Character, 33
- Mode, 55
- Monologue, 12
- Mood, 25
- Motivation, 24, 41
- Myth, 4
- Narrative Poem, 12
- Nonfiction, 52
- Novel, 22
- Ode, 12
- Onomatopoeia, 16
- Oral Tradition, 4
- Parallelism, 17, 19
- Personification, 17, 19
- Playwright, 44
- Plot, 25
- Poetry, 10
- Properties, 45, 50
- Purpose, 34, 56
- Refrain, 8
- Repetition, 8, 17, 18
- Resolution, 25, 38
- Rhetorical Question, 17
- Rhetorical Technique, 17
- Rhyme, 16
- Rhyme Scheme, 19
- Rhythm, 16
- Scene, 45
- Script, 44
- Set, 45, 50
- Setting, 25
- Short Story, 22
- Simile, 17
- Sonnet, 12, 18, 19
- Sound Effects, 45
- Special Vocabulary, 59
- Spectacle, 45
- Spiritual, 4, 6
- Stage, 45
- Stage Directions, 44, 46, 50
- Stanza, 6, 13
- Symbol, 19
- Synaesthesia, 17
- Synechdoche, 17
- Tall Tale, 4
- Theme, 8, 19, 26, 34, 50
- Tragedy, 42
- Understatement, 17

Writing Skills and Concepts
- Drafting, 20
- Evaluation, 41
- Prewriting, 9
- Proofreading, 51, 59
- Publishing, 59
- Revision, 41

Grammar, Usage, and Mechanics Skills and Concepts
- Coordinating Conjunctions, 21
- Parts of Speech, 51

Other Language Arts Skills and Concepts
- Observing, 23

1 TEACHER'S EDITION

UNIT 1 GENRES AND TECHNIQUES OF LITERATURE

In the Morning. Winslow Homer

T

is the good reader that makes the good book.

—Ralph Waldo Emerson
"Success"

3

GOALS/OBJECTIVES

Studying this unit will enable students to
- recognize and appreciate works of literature in all the major genres
- name, define, and describe major elements and techniques of each of the genres of literature and identify these as employed in a piece of literature
- name and define the different purposes of literature (expressive, informative, persuasive, and literary)
- identify the purpose and mode of a literary work
- employ each step in the process of writing

CONNECTIONS ACROSS THE CURRICULUM

Arts and Humanities
- Art Origins, 53
- Demons in Literature, 47
- Performing a Play, 42
- Theories of Acting, 43

Mathematics and Sciences
- Big Dipper, 7
- Déjà Vu, 37

Social Studies
- Host Customs, 32
- Mob Psychology, 47
- Musical Roots, 57
- Religious Training, 33
- Scapegoating, 48
- Slavery, 57
- Truth in Advertising, 34
- The Underground Railroad, 6
- Witch Trials, 46

TEACHING THE MULTIPLE INTELLIGENCES

Logical-Mathematical
- Truth in Advertising, 34

Spatial
- Blocking, 44
- Setting, 37

Musical
- Learning a Chorus, 6
- Listening to Music, 57
- Lyric Meter, 13
- Musical Roots, 57

Kinesthetic
- Blocking, 44
- Performing a Play, 42

Interpersonal
- Discussing Drama, 42
- Dowry, 32
- Host Customs, 32
- Love, 36
- Marriage Customs, 22
- Marriage Factors, 28
- Truth in Advertising, 34
- Witch Trials, 46

TEACHER'S EDITION 3

The ***Unit Skills Outline*** *lists the skills taught in the student edition. This list is particularly useful for planning if you do not take an historical approach.*

A list of ***Goals/Objectives*** *helps you plan overall intended learning outcomes for teaching the unit. Affective goals are consistent with the philosophy of the program and its emphasis on reader involvement. Cognitive goals encompass content, literary technique, and interpretation in historical context.*

Art Notes *(not shown) provide historical background for works and biographical information about artists, relate works to themes in the unit, and describe important artistic trends and techniques.*

Supplementary ***Vocabulary Development Exercises*** *help diversify your teaching.*

VOCABULARY DEVELOPMENT EXERCISES

► Give students the following exercise.

Have students identify at least ten words on page 284 with positive connotations, that is, that refer to positive experiences or things, and at least ten others with negative connotations or meanings. Then have them write ten sentences about the authors or selections in this unit, using ten words from the two lists they have created. Five of the sentences should use words drawn from the "positive connotations" group and five should use words drawn from the "negative connotations" group.

UNIT REVIEW

New England Renaissance Prose

VOCABULARY FROM THE SELECTIONS

abstraction, 236
abyss, 230
accentuation, 226
affinity, 207
ague, 237
analogy, 205
anointed, 235
aperture, 236
arduous, 254
aspect, 200
aspiration, 263
assuage, 208
august, 243
aversion, 254
avert, 237
avidity, 229
balm, 237
baneful, 207
benignity, 243
cadence, 227
cessation, 235, 264
cognizance, 232
conjecture, 236
conjure, 227
connoisseur, 211
consternation, 224
convolution, 231
cordiality, 203
craven, 247
dally, 237
deleterious, 204
delusory, 210
demeanor, 201
depraved, 210
diffuse, 236
discordant, 237
earnest, 260
ebullition, 209
elucidate, 247
emaciated, 213
encompass, 228
encumbrance, 262
endeavor, 264
envoy, 243
ethereal, 261
evanescent, 211
fervor, 211
festooned, 248
fissure, 236
fluctuate, 266
gaudiest, 245
gauntleted, 244
illuminate, 236
imbue, 215
impede, 228
impend, 237
inanition, 233
incantation, 248
indeterminate, 266
ineffable, 242
ingenuity, 232
inquisitorial, 226
insinuate, 217
insuperable, 229
interminable, 227
irrespective, 245
laxly, 268
locution, 226
lozenge, 237
lurid, 208
malignant, 201
moiety, 235
palsied, 248
paltry, 264
perennial, 261
pertinacity, 209, 234
phenomenon, 205
portal, 205
portentous, 248
posterity, 262
predominate, 253
primeval, 244
pungently, 232
recompense, 206
reminiscence, 199
resplendent, 200
reverie, 213
resignation, 259
riband, 236
saturated, 260
speculative, 208
squalid, 254
sublime, 243
superfluous, 265
surmise, 216
supervene, 227
terminate, 202
testily, 204
transcendent, 243
trepidation, 244
undulation, 263
unintelligible, 206
untoward, 209
unwieldy, 266
vengeance, 237
verdure, 206
vermin, 235
viand, 235
volatile, 268
voracity, 235
writhe, 226

284 UNIT FOUR / NEW ENGLAND RENAISSANCE PROSE

LITERARY TERMS

allusion, 222, 250, 270
aphorism, 256, 270
elaboration, 250
essay, 256
fantasy, 222
metaphor, 256
mood, 238
onomatopoeia, 250
point of view, 238
romance, 238
symbol, 222
theme, 256
tone, 270

SYNTHESIS: QUESTIONS FOR WRITING, RESEARCH, OR DISCUSSION

GENRE STUDIES

1. **Short Story.** The work of Washington Irving, Nathaniel Hawthorne, and Edgar Allan Poe contributed to the development of the short story as a literary form. From Poe came the definition that all aspects of the short story combine to create one dominant impression. Examine two short stories from this unit. What dominant impression is created in each one? What details create this impression?

THEMATIC STUDIES

2. **Appearance and Reality.** Sometimes a fine line separates the credible from the incredible. Examine this theme in the excerpt from *Moby-Dick* and in one short story in the unit.
3. **Transcendentalism.** Transcendentalism in New England was an outgrowth of the Romantic Era in Europe. Review the definition of Transcendentalism in the unit introduction and select passages from Emerson and Thoreau that illustrate Transcendental philosophy.

HISTORICAL/BIOGRAPHICAL STUDIES

4. **Copyright Laws.** The lack of an international copyright law until 1891 meant many writers could not support themselves by their writing. Yet, they continued to write and to create. Discuss the creative process, the impulse to write, regardless of monetary gain.

UNIT FOUR / REVIEW 285

►These prompts are suitable as topics for research papers. Refer to the Language Arts Survey, 4.20–4.34, "Research Skills." (To evaluate research papers, see the evaluation forms for writing, revising, and proofreading, *Assessment Portfolio,* 7.1–7.10.)

►These prompts can be adapted for use as topics for oral reports or debates. (To evaluate these projects, see the evaluation forms in the *Assessment Portfolio,* 7.17–7.19.)

ADDITIONAL RESOURCES

ASSESSMENT PORTFOLIO

- Vocabulary Worksheet, 4.4.11
- Study Guide: Unit 4 Test, 4.4.12
- Unit 4 Test, 4.4.13

ESSENTIAL SKILLS PRACTICE BOOKS

- *Language,* 2.20, 2.27, 2.43–2.45, 2.50, 2.62, 2.71, 2.76–2.84, 2.86, 2.116, 2.138
- *Speaking and Listening,* 3.6
- *Study and Research,* 4.1, 4.3, 4.16, 4.30, 4.31

TEACHER'S EDITION 285

Sample Unit Review Pages

Additional Resources notes *identify assessment materials for the unit and study guides and worksheets for student review and practice.*

Sample Prereading Page

Additional Resources *notes identify materials from the Teacher's Resource Kit to use in teaching the selection: worksheets from the Reader's Guide and from the* Essential Skills Practice Books, *recordings from the audiocassette and videocassette, and selection check tests and tests from the* Assessment Portfolio.

Enrichment Activities *provide stimulation and challenge for gifted and high-achieving students, but most are accessible to students of all abilities. These activities call for intellectual creativity, synthetic thinking, and multiple intelligences and often require additional resources and work outside of class.*

Color-coded ***icons*** *identify at a glance* ***cross-curricular*** *activities (brown),* ***multiple intelligences*** *activities (green), and* ***SCANS*** *activities (blue). A key to these icons is provided on page T36 of this* Annotated Teacher's Edition.

Support for LEP Students *teaching notes identify potential trouble spots and offer strategies for helping nonnative speakers of English and other limited English proficiency students. Lists and definitions of potentially troublesome* ***Idioms, Colloquialisms,*** *and* ***Additional Vocabulary*** *help you offer instruction before students encounter difficulties in reading.*

ADDITIONAL RESOURCES

READER'S GUIDE
- Selection Worksheets, 8.5, 8.6

ASSESSMENT PORTFOLIO
- Selection Check Tests, 4.8.9, 4.8.11
- Selection Tests, 4.8.10, 4.8.12

ESSENTIAL SKILLS PRACTICE BOOKS
- *Language,* 2.6, 2.36
- *Speaking and Listening,* 3.3, 3.5

ENRICHMENT ACTIVITIES

Due to the beautiful musical qualities of Frost's poems, they are excellent poems for reading aloud. Have students read the Language Arts Survey, 3.8, "Oral Interpretation." Then students can read other poems by Robert Frost and after they have carefully selected cuttings, perform an oral interpretation of some of Frost's work. Frost gave many creative readings of his poems during his lifetime, and recordings of some readings are available from Cædmon Records. Students might also include a poem read by Frost himself in their interpretation.

SUPPORT FOR LEP STUDENTS

You might have students read the Language Arts Survey, 2.64, "Inverting Sentences for Emphasis." Explain to students that Frost frequently inverts conventional sentence order in his poetry. Have students put sentences that are in inverted order into regular order. For example, "Something there is that doesn't love a wall" reads "There is something that doesn't love a wall" in regular order.

ADDITIONAL VOCABULARY

abreast—side by side
mischief—tendency or disposition to annoy or vex with playful tricks
notion—general idea; vague thought

524 TEACHER'S EDITION

PREREADING

"Mending Wall"
"Home Burial"
by Robert Frost

ABOUT THE AUTHOR

Robert Frost (1874–1963) was without question the most popular American poet of the twentieth century. He was born in San Francisco and lived there until the age of eleven, when his father died. After that, Frost and his mother moved to New England. Frost graduated at the top of his high school class, sharing the position of valedictorian with Elinor White, whom he later married. At the age of seventeen, he published his first poem. After marrying Elinor, he continued to hold miscellaneous jobs and to write poetry, briefly going to Harvard as a special student before settling as a teacher at Pinkerton Academy in 1906. In 1912, Frost took his family to England, and it was there that his poetry first found a major audience with the publication of *A Boy's Will* (1913) and *North of Boston* (1914). Frost returned to the United States and began to achieve financial stability from the sale of his books. He taught and lectured at various colleges, including Dartmouth, Amherst, and Harvard. He was awarded Pulitzer Prizes in 1924, 1931, 1937, and 1943 and received honorary degrees from many universities. In 1961, he was invited to read a poem at the inauguration of John F. Kennedy, thirty-fifth president of the United States. Frost's many popular works, most of which deal with New England subject matter, include *Mountain Interval* (1916), *New Hampshire* (1923), *West-Running Brook* (1928), *A Way Out* (1929), *A Witness Tree* (1942), and *In the Clearing* (1962).

ABOUT THE SELECTIONS

Robert Frost had a rare talent that enabled him to produce poetry simple and clear enough to appeal to a large audience and yet intellectually rich enough to appeal to sophisticated literary critics. Frost wrote often of the nature and people of his adopted home of New England. He wrote in the language of ordinary speech and didn't care for modern free verse, which he likened to "playing tennis without a net." Instead, he wrote in conventional forms, including **rhymed verse**, as in **"Mending Wall,"** and **blank verse** made up of unrhymed iambic pentameter lines, as in **"Home Burial."** (An iambic pentameter line has ten alternating weakly stressed and strongly stressed syllables.) Many of Frost's finest poems such as "Home Burial," and "The Death of the Hired Man" in the Selections for Additional Reading on page 602, are **dramatic monologues** or **dramatic dialogues.** Such poems present a dramatic interaction in which one or two people speak.

524 UNIT EIGHT / MODERN POETRY

GOALS/OBJECTIVES

Studying this lesson will enable students to
- have a positive experience reading free verse and blank verse poems
- understand the life and work of Robert Frost
- identify personal pronouns
- understand symbols they encounter in their reading
- explain a pun
- write a dialogue and debate
- define *diction* and *tone*
- identify and understand metaphors they encounter in their reading

A list of ***Goals/Objectives*** *helps you plan intended learning outcomes for teaching the selection. Affective goals are consistent with the philosophy of the program and its emphasis on reader involvement. Cognitive goals encompass content, literary technique, interpretation of the selection in historical context, and language arts skills taught in the student text.*

Cross-curricular Activities *(not shown) are supplementary activities that involve knowledge, skills, research, and resources from disciplines other than language arts.*

Sample Selection Pages

***Prereading Notes** for the **Reader's Journal** and **Variable Skills** activities give suggestions for helping students relate the topic to their experience, anticipate questions or difficulties students may have, or provide additional prompts for students who have trouble starting. Special attention is given to problems that may arise from student diversity.*

***Cross-references** to additional instruction, worksheets, and assessment materials are provided throughout the annotations.*

***Vocabulary in Context** provides sample sentences using the target vocabulary words from Words for Everyday Use. For selections of more than one page, a list of all target vocabulary words in the selection is given in **Vocabulary from the Selection** on the first page of the selection.*

*Possible **Answers to Guided Reading Questions** are keyed to questions in the student edition.*

***Answers to Selection Check Test** includes the questions and an example and appears on or near the last page of each selection. You can photocopy the test from the* Assessment Portfolio *and distribute it, or you can present the questions orally.*

PREREADING NOTES

READER'S JOURNAL

You might ask students to describe the different ways people express grief. Why might people have a particularly difficult time understanding those who grieve in a different way?

SPEAKING AND LISTENING SKILLS

Students might also list the techniques, both positive and negative, that the couple in the poem use to communicate with each other. Ask students the following questions about the couple to generate ideas: When do they give each other feedback to show that they are listening? When do they fail to listen? Are they thinking before speaking? Are they keeping their emotions under control? What do their gestures and body language reveal?

SUPPORT FOR LEP STUDENTS

ADDITIONAL VOCABULARY

murmured—made a low, indistinct sound
inconsolably—brokenheartedly
sneering—expressing derision, scorn, or contempt
spade—heavy, flat-bladed, long-handled tool for digging

READER'S JOURNAL

What causes people sometimes to misunderstand one another? Freewrite in your journal about an experience in which you had a failure of communication with someone about whom you cared deeply.

SPEAKING AND LISTENING SKILLS

How can speaking with a family member or a dear friend help you in times of sorrow? Read the Language Arts Survey, 3.5, "Interpersonal Communication." Then list the important functions that interpersonal communication serves in every person's life.

"Home Burial"[1]

ROBERT FROST

He saw her from the bottom of the stairs
Before she saw him. She was starting down,
Looking back over her shoulder at some fear.
She took a doubtful step and then undid it
5 To raise herself and look again. He spoke
Advancing toward her: "What is it you see
From up there always—for I want to know."
She turned and sank upon her skirts at that,
And her face changed from terrified to dull.
10 He said to gain time: "What is it you see,"
Mounting[2] until she cowered under him.
"I will find out now—you must tell me, dear."
She, in her place, refused him any help
With the least stiffening of her neck and silence.
15 She let him look, sure that he wouldn't see,
Blind creature; and awhile he didn't see.
But at last he murmured, "Oh," and again, "Oh."

"What is it—what?" she said.

1. **Home Burial.** Reference to the custom of keeping a family cemetery on one's property
2. **Mounting.** Climbing

WORDS FOR EVERYDAY USE: cow • er (kou′ ər) vi., crouch or shrink back in fear

528 UNIT EIGHT / MODERN POETRY

VOCABULARY IN CONTEXT

• The toy poodle cowered in fear before the snarling, wolflike mutt.

528 TEACHER'S EDITION

ANSWER TO GUIDED READING QUESTION

The speaker is willing to agree not to speak about some things but does not believe it is right for a couple who love to have such restrictions.

QUOTABLES

"Howl, howl, howl! O, you are men of stones!/Had I your tongues and eyes, I'd use them so/That heaven's vault should crack. She's gone for ever!"

—King Lear on the death of his daughter Cordelia in William Shakespeare's *The Tragedy of King Lear*

ANSWERS TO SELECTION CHECK TEST 4.8.11

EX. Who is having a conversation in this poem?
A husband and wife are having a conversation.

1. What is the woman doing at the top of the stairs?
She is looking out a window "at some fear."

2. What does the man discover she has been looking at?
The man discovers she has been looking at the family cemetery.

3. Whose death upsets the couple?
The death of their child upsets the couple.

4. What does the husband ask his wife not to do?
He asks his wife not to bring her grief to someone else.

5. What made the woman angry with her husband?
The fact that her husband could dig his child's grave and then talk about "everyday concerns" made her angry.

Let me into your grief. I'm not so much
Unlike other folks as your standing there
Apart would make me out. Give me my chance.
65 I do think, though, you overdo it a little.
What was it brought you up to think it the thing
To take your mother-loss of a first child
So inconsolably—in the face of love.
You'd think his memory might be satisfied—"

70 "There you go sneering now!"

"I'm not, I'm not!
You make me angry. I'll come down to you.
God, what a woman! And it's come to this,
A man can't speak of his own child that's dead."

75 "You can't because you don't know how to speak.
If you had any feelings, you that dug
With your own hand—how could you?—his little grave;
I saw you from that very window there,
Making the gravel leap and leap in air,
80 Leap up, like that, like that, and land so lightly
And roll back down the mound beside the hole.
I thought, Who is that man? I didn't know you.
And I crept down the stairs and up the stairs
To look again, and still your spade kept lifting.
85 Then you came in. I heard your rumbling voice
Out in the kitchen, and I don't know why,
But I went near to see with my own eyes.
You could sit there with the stains on your shoes
Of the fresh earth from your own baby's grave
90 And talk about your everyday concerns.
You had stood the spade up against the wall
Outside there in the entry, for I saw it."

530 UNIT EIGHT / MODERN POETRY

530 TEACHER'S EDITION

Sample Selection Activity Pages

Answers for Reviewing the Selection *give sample responses to Recalling, Interpreting, and Synthesizing questions.*

Answers for Understanding Literature *are supplemented by* ***Teaching Notes*** *that help you to extend the discussion in depth, scope, or both.*

ANSWERS FOR REVIEWING THE SELECTION

RECALLING

1. The speaker sees his wife at the top of the stairs, staring at "some fear."
2. The wife thinks her husband is a "blind creature."
3. The husband's words to his wife are "nearly always an offense."
4. The wife carries her grief to someone else.

INTERPRETING

Responses will vary. Possible responses are given.

5. If the wife had seen her husband watching her, she probably would not have been as open about expressing her distress at seeing the grave through the window.
6. The wife challenges the husband to tell her what he sees because she doesn't believe that he is sensitive enough to see the same thing she sees through the window.
7. The husband asks the wife to help him learn how to better communicate with her.
8. Students might say the husband's defense against grief is to continue to fulfill his responsibilities as best he can without dwelling on his grief.

SYNTHESIZING

Responses will vary. Possible responses are given.

9. The husband is desperately trying to avoid a permanent rupture in the marriage and the departure of his wife.
10. The wife dwells on her grief, while the husband attempts to put it behind him. Neither understands the other's method of expressing grief, and their inability to communicate their grief to one another has damaged their marriage.

Reviewing the Selection

RECALLING

1. What does he see "Before she saw him"?
2. What kind of "creature" does the wife think her husband is?
3. What are the husband's words "nearly always" to his wife?
4. What does the wife "carry to someone else"?

INTERPRETING

5. How might the wife's actions have been different if she had seen her husband watching her?
6. Why does the wife challenge the husband to tell her what he sees?
7. With what does the husband ask for his wife's help?
8. What is the husband's defense against his grief?

SYNTHESIZING

9. What is the husband desperately trying to avoid?
10. What differences exist in how the husband and wife express their grief about the death of their infant son? How has the death of their child ruptured their marriage?

Understanding Literature (Questions for Discussion)

1. **Metaphor. A metaphor** is a figure of speech in which one thing is spoken or written about as if it were another. Consider the following lines in the poem: "I can repeat the very words you were saying:/'Three foggy mornings and one rainy day/Will rot the best birch fence a man can build.'" How are these lines an expression of the man's sense of loss? Does his wife understand that they are such an expression? What does she think that they mean? What has happened to the communication between this man and woman? If you were a therapist attempting to help this couple to deal with the death of their child, what advice would you give each person about communicating effectively with the other?
2. **Diction and Tone. Diction,** when applied to writing, refers to word choice. Much of a writer's style or voice is determined by his or her diction, the types of words that are chosen, whether formal or informal, simple or complex, contemporary or archaic, ordinary or unusual, standard or dialectical. **Tone** is the emotional attitude toward the reader or toward the subject implied by a literary work. Consider the following lines from the poem: "I saw you from that very window there,/Making the gravel leap and leap in air,/Leap up, like that, like that, and land so lightly/And roll back down the mound beside the hole." How would you describe the diction in these lines? How does the diction match with the character of the wife? What tone or emotional attitude toward the husband does the wife express in these lines? What effect do the repetitions within these lines have on the tone?

532 UNIT EIGHT / MODERN POETRY

ANSWERS FOR UNDERSTANDING LITERATURE

► See the evaluation form for discussion, active listening, and oral communication, *Assessment Portfolio,* 7.11–7.14.

1. **Metaphor.** The lines the husband says after digging the child's grave can be read as a metaphoric expression of his grief. He is comparing his child to a sturdy birch fence and the unpredictability of life to the vagaries of weather that can destroy a fence. The wife cannot see the metaphoric meaning of his words; she believes he has already finished grieving for the child. Communication between the two people has broken down. Students' advice to the couple will vary but may include telling the husband to express himself more directly and telling the wife to listen to her husband with a more open mind.
2. **Diction and Tone.** The diction in the description of the husband digging is simple, informal, and contemporary. The wife is excited and upset, and the diction of these lines reflects that mood. The wife is impatient and upset with her husband, and the repetition in these lines intensifies the reader's experience of that attitude.

(cont.)

532 TEACHER'S EDITION

"I shall laugh the worst laugh I ever laughed.
I'm cursed. God, if I don't believe I'm cursed."

95 "I can repeat the very words you were saying:
'Three foggy mornings and one rainy day
Will rot the best birch fence a man can build.'
Think of it, talk like that at such a time!
What had how long it takes a birch to rot
100 To do with what was in the darkened parlor?
You *couldn't* care! The nearest friends can go
With anyone to death, comes so far short
They might as well not try to go at all.
No, from the time when one is sick to death,
105 One is alone, and he dies more alone.
Friends make pretense of following to the grave,
But before one is in it, their minds are turned
And making the best of their way back to life
And living people, and things they understand.
110 But the world's evil. I won't have grief so
If I can change it. Oh, I won't, I won't!"

"There, you have said it all and you feel better.
You won't go now. You're crying. Close the door.
The heart's gone out of it: why keep it up?
115 Amy! There's someone coming down the road!"

"*You*—oh, you think the talk is all. I must go—
Somewhere out of this house. How can I make you—"

"If—you—do!" She was opening the door wider.
"Where do you mean to go? First tell me that.
120 I'll follow and bring you back by force. I *will!*—"

Why does the speaker feel better?

Why does she think friends might as well not go?

Where does the speaker think his wife is going? Why?

Responding to the Selection

Imagine that you are either the wife or husband in this poem. Why would you be unable to understand your spouse's way of expressing his or her grief? What comfort or consolation would you seek from your spouse? Write an entry in your journal expressing your feelings about the death of your child.

"HOME BURIAL" 531

of grief and believes that he is hard-hearted.

ADDITIONAL QUESTIONS AND ACTIVITIES

Have students discuss their feelings about the sentence that ruined this couple's relationship: "Three foggy mornings and one rainy day/Will rot the best birch fence a man can build." Ask students whether they believe that the speaker was just making idle small talk or whether the speaker was expressing his grief metaphorically. Was the speaker talking about fences or about the human condition in general?

RESPONDING TO THE SELECTION

Students may discuss which reaction to the child's death they most identify with. They might wish to debate whether a more stoical attitude signifies a lack of feeling.

TEACHER'S EDITION 531

Notes on presenting and facilitating the ***Responding to the Selection*** *assignment help you help students relate the topic to their experience, anticipate questions or difficulties students might have, or suggest alternative formats (such as large or small group discussion, role playing, etc.). These notes give special attention to concerns of diversity.*

Responding in Writing

Critical Analysis. The two characters in this poem have very different ways of responding to grief and consequently fail to understand one another. Write a critical analysis contrasting the ways in which these characters deal with their grief and explaining why they do not understand one another.

Language Lab

Building Sentences. Read the Language Arts Survey, 2.36, "The Functions of Sentences." Then, decide what the function is of each of the following sentences from the selection. Write the classification of each sentence.

1. He saw her from the bottom of the stairs/Before she saw him.
2. "Tell me what it is."
3. "Can't a man speak of his own child he's lost?"
4. "I don't know how to speak of anything/So as to please you."
5. "There you go sneering now!"

Speaking and Listening Skills

Nonverbal Communication. Read the Language Arts Survey, 3.3, "Elements of Nonverbal Communication." Then, describe how each emotion listed below might be communicated through eye contact, facial expressions, gestures, body language, or proximity.

1. loneliness
2. grief
3. frustration
4. alienation

PROJECT

Dramatic Skit. Collaborate with one other student to write a dramatic scene based on this poem. In your scene, portray the characters of the husband and wife (and the failed communication between them) as they are portrayed in the poem. Write two parts and have one person play the husband and the other play the wife. Rehearse your skit and present it to the rest of the class.

ANALYTIC SCALES FOR RESPONDING IN WRITING

Assign a score from 1 to 25 for each grading criterion below. (For more detailed evaluation, see the evaluation forms for writing, revising, and proofreading, *Assessment Portfolio,* 7.1–7.10.)

Critical Analysis

- **Content/Unity.** The analysis contrasts the characters' methods and provides a clear explanation for their inability to understand one another.
- **Organization/Coherence.** The analysis is organized in a logical manner.
- **Language/Style.** The analysis uses an appropriate tone and precise noun, verbs, and modifiers.
- **Conventions.** The analysis avoids errors in spelling, grammar, usage, mechanics, and manuscript form.

ANSWERS TO LANGUAGE LAB

1. declarative
2. imperative
3. interrogative
4. declarative
5. exclamatory

ANSWERS FOR SPEAKING AND LISTENING SKILLS

Responses will vary. Possible responses are given.

1. Students may respond that loneliness is communicated through hunched shoulders, a downturned head, downturned eyes and mouth, and a physical distancing from others.
2. Students may respond that grief is communicated through tears and crying, by separating oneself from others or clinging to others, by a stoical expression, or by stiff and awkward movements.
3. Students may respond that frustration is communicated by glaring at others right in the eye, by sighs and rolling of the eyes, by flinging one's limbs and/or objects about, or by withdrawal from others' company.
4. Students may say that alienation is communicated by a placid or blank expression, an inability to maintain eye contact, and a physical withdrawal from others.

PROJECT NOTES

▶ See the worksheets and evaluation forms for projects, *Assessment Portfolio,* 7.20–7.23.

Dramatic Skit. Students should avoid repeating the dialogue presented in the poem verbatim. Students should imagine ways in which the conversation can be continued, discover other unresolved issues, or even pose a resolution of the conflict. Then students can improvise and express how they feel about the conflict in their performances.

Sample Selection Activity Page

Analytic Scales for Responding in Writing *provide straightforward analytic criteria for evaluating student writing. Cross-references direct you to more elaborate evaluation instruments should you desire them.*

Answers for Language Lab *often includes* ***For More Practice,*** *which provides an additional item you can use after instruction to verify mastery.*

Answers for Variable Skills *provide model answers for Language Skills, Speaking Skills, Listening Skills, Thinking Skills, Study Skills, Research Skills, Test-taking Skills, Applied English Skills, and Vocabulary Skills activities.*

Project Notes *provide suggestions and caveats for introducing, supporting, and monitoring student work on projects. These notes identify additional resources or persons that may be needed or useful and opportunities for enlarging or limiting the scope and duration of the project.*

Using Literature and the Language Arts *for Writing Instruction*

Recent Advances in the Theory of Writing Instruction

Let's face it. Learning to write well isn't easy. Simply mastering the conventions of spelling, grammar, usage, and mechanics takes years. Learning to write elegant, balanced sentences takes years more. Then there are all those tricks of the writer's craft—the forms or genres, the methods of organization, the rhetorical techniques and figures of speech, the modulations of tone and register, the subtleties of connotation—all these must be learned and then, in a sense, forgotten so that the writer's words flow from some deep, authentic place, from some uncommon spring, to produce a voice, a style. Little wonder it is then that Yeats should write, "there is no fine thing/Since Adam's fall but needs much laboring," or that Chaucer should remind us of the Latin adage *Ars longa; vita brevis:* "Art is long; life, short."

Given the time and effort that it takes to become even reasonably competent as a writer, it follows that no one would do so without some powerful motive. Fortunately for English teachers, children come into the world with such a motive. The child, newly arrived, cries out, trying to communicate: it's cold out here, and strange. As children grow, they keep trying to communicate and will keep trying so long as the will to do so isn't drowned in a sea of criticism. Unfortunately, some well-intentioned but unreflective teachers did, in the past, drown their students' attempts to communicate through writing in red ink that would, taken *in toto*, the multitudinous seas incarnadine (to borrow a phrase from *Macbeth*).

One of the most exciting things that has happened in English education in the past few years is that a new model of writing instruction that respects the student's voice and effort has come to the fore. That model is the process and portfolio approach. Process and portfolio instruction breaks individual acts of writing and the overall business of learning to write into manageable steps, with guidance and feedback at each step. Today, when students are given writing assignments, they no longer have to figure out on their own how to get from the assignment to the completed piece of writing. Instead, they are trained in techniques for prewriting, drafting, evaluating their drafts by themselves and with peers, revising, and publishing. Writing portfolios and evaluation forms are used to track development of pieces of writing over time. Assessment has been expanded from simple marking of papers to include self-evaluation, peer evaluation, and a variety of approaches to assessment by teachers that avoid turning teachers into copyeditors. The result of these changes in writing instruction has been that student writing has improved dramatically in recent years.

Literature and the Language Arts contains comprehensive materials for integrated instruction in the process of writing and for management of writing portfolios. The notes that follow describe those materials and how they can be used.

Pretesting and Post-testing

Before beginning instruction in the process of writing, you may wish to have students do the Pretest: Writing Terminology and Techniques, 3.1.1, in the *Assessment Portfolio* contained in the Teacher's Resource Kit. This test is designed to assess students' familiarity with basic writing concepts and skills. A Post-test: Writing Terminology and Techniques, 3.1.2, in the *Assessment Portfolio*, can be given at the end of the course to assess students' overall progress in basic writing concepts and skills.

Introducing the Writing Process

Section 1 of the Language Arts Survey, which is called Essential Skills: Writing and begins on page 866, surveys the entire writing process from prewriting through publishing. This section of the Survey is

divided into forty-nine lessons, each containing instructional material and a writing activity. Additional practice activities for each lesson in the Language Arts Survey can be found in the *Essential Skills Practice Book: Writing* in the Teacher's Resource Kit.

Teachers who wish to do so can teach the Essential Skills: Writing section of the Language Arts Survey in its entirety as a separate composition unit. Alternatively, teachers can have students refer to the writing section of the Language Arts Survey on an as-needed basis as they complete the composition assignments in the main body of the text.

Unit 1 of the student edition is divided into five sections. The study apparatuses following the selections in Unit 1 contain a single cumulative writing assignment (writing a narrative message) designed to introduce students to the process of writing. Teachers may introduce the writing process by having their students do this cumulative writing assignment. Before beginning the assignment, students should read sections 1.1 through 1.4 of Essential Skills: Writing, pages 866–871. These pages briefly survey the steps in the writing process and teach students how to use writers' journals, writers' portfolios, and computer hardware and software for writing. Each part of the cumulative writing assignment in Unit 1 asks students to complete a step in the writing process and refers them to lessons in the Essential Skills: Writing section for additional information. It is recommended that students review the relevant Essential Skills: Writing sections before doing each part of the assignment.

After students have finished the cumulative writing assignment, distribute copies of the Study Guide: The Process of Writing, 5.1.1, in the *Assessment Portfolio.* This guide will help students to review what they have learned about the writing process in preparation for taking the Test: The Process of Writing, 5.1.2, in the *Assessment Portfolio.*

As students complete their first writing assignment and all subsequent writing assignments in the text, they can make use of the following general evaluation forms and checklists found in the *Assessment Portfolio:*

- Writing Summary Form, 6.11
- Writing Evaluation Form: Process, 7.1
- Writing Evaluation Form: The Writing Plan, 7.2
- Writing Evaluation Form: Structural Evaluation, 7.3
- Writing Evaluation Form: Analytic Scale, 7.4
- Writing Evaluation Form: Holistic Response, 7.5
- Peer and Self-Evaluation Form: Writing, 7.6
- Revision Assessment Form, 7.7
- Revision Checklist, 7.8
- Proofreading Checklist, 7.9
- Proofreading Record, 7.10

Teaching the Writing Assignments in the Text

Following most selections in this text are activities called Responding in Writing. These activities use the literature selections as springboards for an enormous variety of engaging writing assignments. A glance at the writing section of the Index of Skills on page 1071 will give you an idea of just how varied and interesting the types of writing covered in this text are. In most cases, two Responding in Writing activities are given after each selection. You can choose to assign one or both, or you can give students the option of doing either of the two assignments.

As students complete these assignments, they can refer to relevant sections of the Essential Skills: Writing section of the Language Arts Survey. They can also make use of the many evaluation forms and checklists in the *Assessment Portfolio.*

The writing assignments in the text consist of prompts. Complete prewriting guidance for each writing assignment can be found on the Selection Worksheet that corresponds to any given selection. Selection Worksheets can be found in the *Reader's Guide and Activity Book* in the Teacher's Resource Kit.

For each writing assignment in the student edition, there is in this *Annotated Teacher's Edition* an Analytic Scale for Evaluation presenting assessment criteria for content, organization, style, and conventions of grammar, usage, mechanics, spelling, and manuscript form. The editors and authors of this text strongly suggest that these evaluation scales be given to students when they receive the initial writing prompts so that they can keep the eventual evaluation criteria in mind as they work through the writing process. These scales can also be used by students for peer evaluation and self-evaluation. Alternatively, or in addition, students can do peer

evaluation and self-evaluation using the evaluation forms in the *Assessment Portfolio.*

Process for Writing Assignments

The editors and authors recommend the sequence of activities in the chart at the right for each writing assignment in the main body of the text:

Steps 1–11 may be repeated for each writing assignment. Then, periodically, step 12 should also be completed.

Using Writing Portfolios

The student's Writing Portfolio is a folder in which he or she stores drafts and finished pieces of writing. You can ask your students to keep a portfolio to enable you and the students to assess their progress over time. Portfolios show students' capabilities and progress better than any test or single writing assignment can.

You may wish to ask your students to keep **comprehensive portfolios** that contain all the writing that they do for class, along with Writing Summary Forms and/or evaluation forms for each piece of writing. Alternatively, you can ask your students to keep **selected portfolios** that contain pieces of writing chosen by the students as representative of their best work. Students should be encouraged to choose for their selected portfolios pieces that show the various skills they have developed and the various types of writing that they have done (informative, persuasive, creative, etc.).

When students place works in their portfolios, make sure that they attach

Process for Writing Assignments

1. WHOLE CLASS: Study of the literature selection in the student edition textbook, along with its corresponding instructional apparatus
2. TEACHER: Introduction of the writing prompt from the student text
3. STUDENT: Prewriting (with reference to any applicable prewriting lessons in the Essential Skills: Writing section of the Language Arts Survey, pages 871–894 of the student text)
4. STUDENT: Drafting (with reference to the drafting lessons in the Essential Skills: Writing section of the Language Arts Survey, pages 894–898 of the student text)
5. STUDENT: Sharing of draft with one or more peers
6. STUDENT and PEER(S): Evaluation of the draft and conferencing with one another and with the teacher if necessary (with reference to the Analytic Scale for Evaluation from the *Annotated Teacher's Edition* and/or the general evaluation forms and revision checklists, 7.1–7.8, in the *Assessment Portfolio*)
7. STUDENT: Revising (with reference to the Revision Assessment Form and Revision Checklist, 7.7 and 7.8, in the *Assessment Portfolio,* and to the revision sections of the Essential Skills: Writing section of the Language Arts Survey, pages 898–901 of the student text)
8. STUDENT: Proofreading and preparation of the final manuscript (with reference to the Proofreading Checklist and Proofreading Record, 7.9 and 7.10, in the *Assessment Portfolio,* and to the proofreading and manuscript preparation sections of the Essential Skills: Writing section of the Language Arts Survey, pages 901–902 of the student text) and completion of the Writing Survey Form, 6.11, in the *Assessment Portfolio*
9. STUDENT and PEER(S): Publishing and/or presenting of the completed draft (with reference to the lesson on publishing and presenting in the Essential Skills: Writing section of the Language Arts Survey, pages 902–903 of the student text)
10. STUDENT and TEACHER: Assessment and/or conferencing with regard to the completed work
11. STUDENT: Decision as to whether to place the completed work in the student's Writing Portfolio
12. STUDENT and TEACHER: Evaluate the student's Writing Portfolio (using the Comprehensive Portfolio Evaluation Form: Student and the Comprehensive Portfolio Evaluation Form: Teacher, 6.9 and 6.10, in the *Assessment Portfolio*) and hold a teacher-student conference to discuss the evaluation and to set goals for future writing improvement

their notes and drafts behind these works so that you will be able to see at a glance how each piece of writing was developed. Also have students attach to their works any evaluation forms they have used.

From time to time, you will want to do a comprehensive evaluation of the students' portfolios. A Comprehensive Evaluation Form: Teacher, 6.10, in the *Assessment Portfolio*, has been provided for this purpose. You should also have each student do his or her own comprehensive evaluation using the Comprehensive Evaluation Form: Student, 6.11, in the *Assessment Portfolio*. Once these evaluations are complete, you can meet in a conference with each student to discuss his or her progress, provide praise for work well done, and make plans for improvement in the future.

Assessing Student Writing

(For a more complete treatment of assessment, see the introduction to the *Assessment Portfolio* in the Teacher's Resource Kit.)

Assessment of student writing should not have as its primary purpose meting out rewards or punishments. Instead, assessment should be seen as a development tool allowing the teacher and the student, working in collaboration, to monitor the student's progress toward achieving his or her goals.

Approaches to assessment vary. Two common approaches to assessing writing are analytic evaluation and holistic evaluation.

Analytic Evaluation. An analytic evaluation of a piece of writing begins with an analysis of the several features or qualities desired in the writing. These desired features or qualities are then used as standards or criteria against which the piece is compared. The evaluator merely goes down the list of criteria, giving the piece of writing a score for each criterion. A summary evaluation of the writing is obtained by combining these several scores.

Analytic evaluation is particularly valuable for formative evaluation. A general judgment of a student's work may be daunting, especially for students who do not do as well as they expect to do. Likewise, students who perform well, if given general comments about the writing, find in such general judgments little specific guidance telling them what they might do to write better. An analytic evaluation can show students exactly what their strengths and weaknesses are and where they should concentrate their efforts.

Analytic evaluation is valuable as a measure of either progress or achievement. To evaluate progress, you can evaluate the student's progress in each area by comparing the current work with previous similar writing assignments. To measure raw achievement, you can compare the student's product against some imagined ideal. Of course, in either case you must make sure that your students are aware of the criteria on which they are being graded.

The Analytic Evaluation Scales provided next to the writing assignments in this *Annotated Teacher's Edition* provide lists of appropriate criteria for analytic evaluation, along with simple procedures for scoring. In addition, a general Writing Evaluation Form: Analytic Scale is provided as item 7.4 of the *Assessment Portfolio*.

Holistic Evaluation. Holistic evaluation of a piece of writing calls for an overall judgment. Holistic evaluation is most useful as a measure of achievement. It is difficult to score holistic evaluations according to a student's progress. To do a holistic evaluation, simply look over the general analytic criteria and then assign a score that reflects how well the student met those criteria taken as a whole.

Holistic evaluation takes less time than analytic evaluation and in most cases results in the same score. The saved time can be used to make encouraging written comments to the student, pointing out features of the writing that you admire and features of the writing that you would like to see improve in later work by the student. A general Writing Evaluation Form: Holistic Response is provided in the *Assessment Portfolio* as item 7.5.

Grading. Some teachers prefer to grade each writing assignment. Others feel that grading selected assignments chosen by the teacher and student to reflect the student's best work provides a more realistic assessment of the student's optimal capabilities. If the latter option is chosen, you may wish to provide credit for completion of assignments that are not graded.

Marking Student Papers. A student who receives back from a teacher a paper covered with corrections in red ink is not likely to be encouraged to do more and better writing. Furthermore, such marking of student papers is enormously time consuming and discourages frequent writing practice. A more encouraging approach is to mark one or two

consistent problems and to mark three or four successes in each paper or, better yet, to allow students and their peers to do such marking and then to review these evaluations in conferences. Such marking can be done in conjunction with the completion of evaluation forms and/or analytic scales.

Reports and Research Papers

Literature and the Language Arts contains complete materials for instruction in the preparation of reports and research papers. The Research Skills section of Essential Skills: Study and Research in the Language Arts Survey, pages 987–1009 of the student text, contains a complete overview of research procedures from using the library through documenting sources. The Synthesis questions that appear at the end of each Unit Review make excellent topics for extended reports or research papers. Further instruction on preparing longer papers can be found in the section on Drafting Compositions in Essential Skills: Writing in the Language Arts Survey, pages 897–898 of the student text. Of course, these sections of the Language Arts Survey are accompanied by worksheets in the corresponding *Essential Skills Practice Books* in the Teacher's Resource Kit.

Remedial Exercises in Specific Writing Skills

During your evaluations of students' writing, either of individual pieces or of entire portfolios, you will doubtless discover consistent areas of weakness. One student may have trouble with using transitions, another may consistently use serial commas incorrectly, and another may rely too heavily on the passive voice. The Language Arts Survey in the student edition and the accompanying *Essential Skills Practice Book* worksheets provide ample activities for remediation of particular recurring problems. Most of the instruction and activities in the writing and language sections of the Language Arts Survey are useful for this purpose. Thus if a student has a tendency to write sentence fragments, you can have him or her read the Language Arts Survey, 2.61, "Correcting Sentence Fragments," on page 922 of the student text. Then you can have that student do the corresponding worksheet in the *Essential Skills Practice Book: Language.* If a student has problems organizing his or her ideas, you can have him or her read the Language Arts Survey, 1.34, "Organizing Ideas," and do the corresponding worksheet in the *Essential Skills Practice Book: Writing.* Thus the Language Arts Survey and the *Essential Skills Practice Books* can be used to individualize your writing instruction and to target it to remediation of particular writing problems encountered by your students.

Instructional Options

Approaches to Literature and the Language Arts

Literature and the Language Arts contains a number of features that allow you the flexibility to organize your instruction as best suits you and your district's requirements. The following chart offers some tips for using the text in your chosen way.

Features of the Program, by Approach

Historical Approach

- The Unit Introductions tie literary developments to influential intellectual currents and political events, providing historical contexts for the selections.
- About the Author and About the Selection prereading notes provide additional historical background and context.
- Time lines in the introduction provide a spatial representation of watershed events and developments.

Thematic Approach

- The Selections by Theme chart on pages T37–T42 lists all the selections in the book under forty-seven major themes.
- Thematic Currents notes in the *Annotated Teacher's Edition* identify three major themes for each unit.
- Responding in Writing prompts following selections ask students to explore and develop their thoughts about thematic topics.
- Synthesis questions in the Unit Review help students explore thematic relations among selections.

Writing Approach

- The activities in Unit 1 lead students through the writing process in a series of carefully sequenced exercises.
- The Selections by Genre chart on page T43 lists all the selections in the book under five genres of writing. Use the chart to find examples of the types of writing you wish to teach.
- The Language Arts Survey, Essential Skills: Writing, following Unit 12, provides instruction in all the phases and forms of writing, editing, and proofreading.
- The *Essential Skills Practice Book: Writing* provides guided exercises in all the phases and forms of writing, editing, and proofreading. These worksheets are keyed to the instructional text in the Language Arts Survey.

Genre Approach

- The Selections by Genre chart on page T43 lists all the selections in the book under five genres of writing. Use the chart to find examples of the types of writing you wish to teach. The selections are arranged in chronological order to help your class trace the historical development of the several genres.
- Unit Introductions and About the Selection prereading notes help your class trace the historical development of the major genres of literature in English.
- Thematic Currents notes in the *Annotated Teacher's Edition* identify two to four major literary concepts or techniques for each unit.
- The Language Arts Survey, Essential Skills: Writing, following Unit 12, provides instruction in techniques that are characteristic of the various genres of writing.
- Questions for Understanding Literature following selections help students understand the use of literary techniques.
- Synthesis questions in the Unit Review relate matters of genre and literary technique to thematic issues.

Skills Approach

- The Language Arts Survey, following Unit 12, provides instruction in the range of language arts skills and concepts, including writing, grammar, usage, mechanics, speaking and listening, study and research, and thinking.
- Use the Scope and Sequence Charts in the *Assessment Portfolio* to locate additional exercises in specific language arts skills.
- The *Essential Skills Practice Books* provide guided exercises in the range of language arts skills: writing, editing, proofreading, grammar, usage, mechanics, speaking and listening, study and research, testing, and thinking. These worksheets are coordinated with the instructional text in the Language Arts Survey.
- The *Assessment Portfolio* contains tests, study guides, and evaluation forms for language arts skills in writing, editing, proofreading, grammar, usage, mechanics, speaking and listening, study and research, testing, and thinking (5.1–5.10). These materials are coordinated with the instructional text in the Language Arts Survey and with the worksheets in the *Essential Skills Practice Books*.
- The *Assessment Portfolio* also contains comprehensive pretests, post-tests, study guides, and analytic evaluation forms for skills in reading literature (2.1–2.2), and for skills in writing, language, speaking and listening, and study and research (3.1–3.4).
- The *Essential Skills Practice Book: Applied English* contains coordinated instructional text, worksheets, and assessment materials, including pretests, post-tests, study guides, and analytic evaluation forms; and coordinated skills tests and study guides.

Teaching Strategies

Teaching to Develop Students' Multiple Intelligences and to Accommodate Diverse Learning Styles

Activities using multiple intelligences are identified by green icons. See the legend on page T36.

Use the techniques in the chart at right to teach and encourage students with diverse intellectual strengths and learning styles and to help all students use and develop the full range of their abilities.

Teaching Students Whose Native Language Is Not English

Use the techniques in the chart at right to facilitate learning and participation for students whose native language is not English.

Teaching Students with Diverse Cultural Backgrounds

Use the techniques in the chart at right to facilitate learning and participation for students with diverse cultural backgrounds.

Teaching Multiple Intelligences

- Use multiple modes of expression: e.g., read aloud selections; read aloud questions; use visual aids—charts, graphs, tables, or other graphics, art, and films; play songs; and perform demonstrations.
- Encourage students to use multiple modes of expression, including nonverbal expressions and performances such as drawing, painting, collage, sculpture, dance and choreography, acting and oral interpretation, photography, filmmaking, video production, and musicianship and singing.
- Ask students to read aloud.
- Precede written work with a related oral activity.
- Teach students to use graphic aids for understanding and for studying.
- Facilitate group work.
- Use cooperative learning.
- Allow students ample thinking time.

Teaching Students Whose Native Language Is Not English

- Ask students to read aloud.
- Precede written work with a related oral activity.
- Use cooperative learning.
- Allow ample thinking time.
- When using small groups, pair with English-proficient students.
- Provide ample opportunity for nongraded, even nonevaluated, writing in English.
- Use multiple modes of expression: e.g., read aloud selections; read aloud questions; use visual aids—charts, graphs, tables, or other graphics, art, and films; play songs; and perform demonstrations.
- Encourage students to use multiple modes of expression, including nonverbal expressions and performances such as drawing, painting, collage, sculpture, dance and choreography, acting and oral interpretation, photography, filmmaking, video production, and musicianship and singing.

Teaching Students with Diverse Cultural Backgrounds

- Encourage discussion of cultural differences; invite students to share contrasting experiences; invite them to share events and characters that strike them as odd. Rely on students for your cultural information; be aware that you are liable to overlook differences unless you can take up a different point of view.
- Use multiple modes of expression: e.g., read aloud selections; read aloud questions; use visual aids—charts, graphs, tables, or other graphics, art, and films; play songs; and perform demonstrations.
- Encourage students to use multiple modes of expression, including nonverbal expressions and performances such as drawing, painting, collage, sculpture, dance and choreography, acting and oral interpretation, photography, filmmaking, video production, and musicianship and singing.
- Ask students to read aloud.
- Precede written work with a related oral activity.
- Use cooperative learning.
- Allow ample thinking time.
- When using small groups, pair with English-proficient students.
- Preview/explain culturally loaded terms and names.
- Discuss idioms and word origins.
- Discuss topics with universal appeal and relevance—for instance, independence versus family ties; independence versus friendship; identity.
- Discuss literature from both an "insider" and an "outsider" perspective.

Teaching Students with Learning Disabilities

Learning disabilities are physical conditions that make it difficult to complete certain types of tasks. Students with learning disabilities are often highly intelligent but lack specific abilities; for instance, one person may lack the ability to discriminate certain sounds, while another person who has that discrimination may be unable to remember certain auditory messages. Use the techniques in the chart at right to help students with learning disabilities succeed in your classroom.

Teaching Students with Learning Disabilities

- Discover the particular effects of each individual's disability and try to fill gaps.
- Allow ample thinking time.
- Seat students in front.
- Repeat important ideas frequently.
- Summarize and check students' bearings frequently.
- Monitor progress frequently.
- On larger projects, provide step-by-step guidance.
- Precede written work with a related oral activity.
- Use cooperative learning.
- Use multiple modes of expression: e.g., read aloud selections; read aloud questions; use visual aids—charts, graphs, tables, or other graphics, art, and films; play songs; and perform demonstrations.
- Encourage students to use multiple modes of expression, including nonverbal expressions and performances such as drawing, painting, collage, sculpture, dance and choreography, acting and oral interpretation, photography, filmmaking, video production, and musicianship and singing.

Teaching Students with Special Academic Gifts and Talents

Just as students who work below grade level may lose interest because tasks are too difficult, students with special academic gifts and talents may lose interest because they complete work quickly or because they are not sufficiently challenged.

Activities involving other curricular areas are identified by red icons. See the legend on page T36.

Teaching Students with Special Academic Gifts and Talents

- Encourage students to use multiple modes of expression, including nonverbal expressions and performances such as drawing, painting, collage, sculpture, dance and choreography, acting and oral interpretation, photography, filmmaking, video production, and musicianship and singing.
- Use cooperative learning.
- Allow ample thinking time.
- Involve students in the planning, preparation, and presentation or conduct of lessons.
- Provide or encourage extension activities once mastery is demonstrated.
- Provide or encourage self-guided activities and independent research.

"[C]hildren come to school with misconceptions about outside ethnic groups and with a white bias. However, . . . students' racial attitudes can be modified and made more democratic and . . . the racial attitudes of young children are much more easily modified than the attitudes of older students and adults. . . . If we are to help students acquire the attitudes needed to survive in a multicultural and diverse world, we must start early. . . .

A school experience that is multicultural includes content, examples, and realistic images of diverse racial and ethnic groups. Cooperative learning activities in which students from diverse groups work to attain shared goals is also a feature of the school, as well as simulated images of ethnic groups that present them in positive and realistic ways. Also essential within such a school are adults who model the attitudes and behaviors they are trying to teach. Actions speak much louder than words."

—James A. Banks
"Multicultural Education:
Historical Development, Dimensions, and Practice"
Review of Research in Education
19 (1993): 37–38.

Achieving Gender Equity

Sexism cannot be combatted subtly (Sadker and Sadker 123). In addition to using the techniques listed at right, make a directed effort to combat gender stereotypes and to treat all students as valued learners.

Achieving Gender Equity

Facts: Boys call out answers eight times as frequently as do girls (Sadker and Sadker 43). Boys receive more evaluative feedback—both positive and negative (Sadker, Sadker, and Klein 300; Sadker and Sadker 55).

Responses:

- Make a special effort to call on girls and to give them specific feedback, both positive and negative. (Note: if you give more than one-third of your attention to girls you may be accused of favoring girls; see Sadker and Sadker 266–267.)
- When intervening in student-student interactions, concentrate on raising girls' confidence rather than criticizing boys' behavior.

Fact: Exposure to gender-biased materials appears to increase gender stereotypes (Sadker, Sadker, and Klein 279; Sadker and Sadker 73–75, 128–135, 266).

Responses:

- Be aware of biases in literature and point them out.
- When appropriate, provide historical context for stereotyping by explaining older attitudes and practices.
- Provide direct lessons about gender stereotypes and gender-related communication styles.

Facts: Girls are more likely than boys to attribute their successes to luck and less likely than boys to attribute their successes to ability (Sadker, Sadker, and Klein 303). Girls are more likely than boys to attribute their failures to lack of ability and less likely than boys to attribute their failures to lack of effort (303). Teachers are more likely to comment on girls' appearance and the neatness of their work, and more likely to comment on the intellectual qualities of boys' work (Sadker and Sadker 57).

Responses:

- Make an effort to avoid commenting on students', especially girls', appearance.
- Make an effort to attribute all success to effort and ability.
- Make an effort to rebut forcefully students' self-deprecating comments.

Facts: Girls have lower expectations of success (Sadker, Sadker, and Klein 302) and are more likely to display signs of "learned helplessness" (303). Teachers are more likely to help boys solve their own problems but to solve problems for girls (Sadker and Sadker 81–83).

Responses:

- Fear of being "too tough" on girls is patronizing and hinders them from developing independence and confidence. Don't be afraid to criticize girls' work and don't let them off easy (Holt; Sizer).
- Make an effort to rebut forcefully students' self-deprecating comments.

Teaching Students to Work Cooperatively

Prepare your students for work in cooperative learning groups by teaching them how to listen actively, how to participate fully in discussions, and how to give one another positive feedback. Refer students to the lessons on listening, interpersonal communication, and discussion, sections 3.4–3.6 of the Language Arts Survey.

Uses for Small Groups. Use these task and project ideas to direct the work of collaborative learning groups.

- brainstorming
- peer tutorial sessions
- learning partners for practice or review and for all stages of the writing process
- inquiry-based concept learning
- multimedia and community-based projects
- topical symposia
- panel discussions
- mock jury trials
- role playing
- dramatizations
- simulations
- Reader's Theater

Teaching Students to Work Cooperatively

Preparing Students for Small Group Work

PARTICIPATION

- Review/preteach vocabulary and cultural concepts for nonnative speakers.
- Begin with a nongraded, fun, get-to-know-one-another activity.
- Take steps to ensure that group members know each other's names.
- Assign tasks that call on multiple intelligences.
- Ask questions that call for personal response and interpretation.
- Value interpretations that differ from your own.
- Have students determine the wording of their topics or questions.
- Don't talk too much.
- Model tentativeness and openness.
- Model courtesy and respect for all.
- Respond only holistically and orally to early drafts and initial products.
- Avoid judging early drafts; discuss ideas rather than expression.
- Discuss anonymous samples.
- Praise students for taking risks.
- Require (only) positive feedback from peers.
- Use joint grading for group work: (1) everyone in the group receives the average among the group; (2) everyone receives the lowest grade among the group; (3) a final product is graded and everyone receives that grade.

LEADERSHIP

- Ask students to conduct lessons.
- Rotate leadership assignments in groups.
- Appoint two group leaders—one to learn from the other.
- Model and give direct instruction and practice in asking questions.
- Model and give direct instruction and practice in reporting a summary.
- Model and give direct instruction and practice in involving nonparticipants.
- Model and give direct instruction and practice in restraining dominators.
- Model and give direct instruction and practice in providing positive feedback.
- Model and give direct instruction and practice in providing constructive feedback.

LISTENING/DISCUSSING

- Model, explain, and encourage attentive listening, eye contact, and not interrupting.
- Give practice in paraphrasing students' words and your own.
- Ask students to identify good speaking and listening habits and skills.
- Ask students to evaluate group processes and their roles in their groups (use the forms in the *Assessment Portfolio,* 7.13, 7.14, 7.22).

Forming Groups

- Groups should contain a maximum of six students for a complex task, a maximum of four otherwise.
- For peer writing groups, two may be the ideal size. Require periodically that students change partners.
- In the prewriting stage, it can be good to match those who share a primary language other than English.
- Working groups should contain students of varied abilities.
- Allow groups to vary their seating arrangements (suggest possibilities).

Guiding and Monitoring

- Give specific tasks.
- Explain criteria for success.
- Assign roles in group, or assign groups to distribute roles.
- When assigning roles in groups, divide responsibilities to assure interdependence and cooperation. One workable division of responsibilities is among (1) a discussion leader/facilitator; (2) a recorder; (3) a reporter; (4) a materials manager.
- Specify desired behaviors (see "Preparing Students for Small Group Work," above).
- Monitor group interactions and advise when appropriate.
- Intervene to diffuse conflict and to foster collaborative skills.
- When intervening in group work, ask a question rather than giving advice directly.
- If multiple groups have the same problem, interrupt the process and clarify or reteach.

Closure and Assessment

- Ask for sharing of a product.
- Both students and teacher should assess the quality of the product. Assessment can be among the entire class or only within groups.
- Both students and teacher should assess the quality of the group processes and communication.

Planning for Conferences and Portfolio Evaluation

As a teacher you have a number of distinguishable evaluative roles as outlined in the charts at right. Of course, you will not take on all of these roles at once. Make sure that students know which role to expect *before* they receive feedback.

References

Herman, J., P. Aschbacher, and L. Winters. *A Practical Guide to Alternative Assessment.* Alexandria, VA: ASCD, 1992.

Eggen, P., and D. Kauchak. *Educational Psychology.* 2nd ed. New York: Merrill, 1994.

Gardner, H. *Frames of Mind: The Theory of Multiple Intelligences.* New York: Basic, 1985.

———. *The Unschooled Mind: How Children Think and How Schools Should Teach.* New York: Basic, 1991.

Holt, J. *How Children Learn.* New York: Putnam, 1967.

Ohrlich, D., et al. *Teaching Strategies.* 4th ed. Lexington, MA: Heath, 1994.

Sadker, M., and D. Sadker. *Failing at Fairness.* New York: Scribner's, 1993.

Sadker, M., D. Sadker, and S. Klein. "The Issue of Gender in Elementary and Secondary Education." *Review of Research in Education,* 17 (1991), 269–334.

Sizer, T. *Horace's Compromise.* Boston: Houghton, 1984.

Slavin, R. *Cooperative Learning: Theory, Research, and Practice.* Englewood Cliffs, NJ: Prentice, 1990.

———. *Educational Psychology.* 3rd ed. Englewood Cliffs, NJ: Prentice, 1991.

Understanding the Roles of Evaluators

ROLE	FUNCTION
AUDIENCE	to take up ideas, to challenge, to question, to enlarge perspective
PROOFREADER	to correct grammar, usage, and mechanics
GRADER	to judge against external, more or less objective, and more or less arbitrary standards
ADVISOR	to prod to solve problems, to encourage, to give suggestions, to remind of objectives

ROLE	TEACHING TIPS
AUDIENCE	Act exclusively as audience when you read and comment on drafts. Comments on drafts should avoid direct criticism and should aim at raising the student's excitement about further writing and revising.
PROOFREADER	Overemphasis on proofreading and points of grammar, usage, and mechanics can drain students' interest in and enthusiasm for writing as well as their self-confidence. Use proofreading as a peer function, and allow students to learn from reading and proofreading each other's papers.
GRADER	Avoiding grading as much as possible allows both you and students to concentrate on clear and honest expression and to preserve intrinsic motivation.
ADVISOR	Because the advising function requires one-on-one interchange, you should reserve for it as much of the precious evaluation time as you can.

Conducting Conferences

- Examine the portfolio before conferencing. Make sure it contains all required material, including the student's evaluations of each piece of writing (*Assessment Portfolio,* 6.11) and of the portfolio as a whole (*Assessment Portfolio,* 6.9).
- Evaluate the portfolio before conferencing. Complete the portfolio evaluation form (*Assessment Portfolio,* 6.9b), making special note of any discrepancies between your and the student's evaluations.
- Do not attempt to discuss all aspects of the portfolio or the student's class performance. Choose two or three broad, major points and one or two specific problems to focus on in the conference. If students are asked to complete the Skills Self-Assessment Forms (*Assessment Portfolio,* 6.3 and 6.5), this may make it easier to pinpoint areas in which the student already recognizes a need for effort.
- As an alternative to conferencing, you may sometimes complete and hand to students a Portfolio Evaluation Form and additional writing and language skills evaluation forms (*Assessment Portfolio,* 6.4, 6.6–6.8). You will still need to allow time for students to respond to and ask questions about their evaluations, and to hold conferences with students who need special help or encouragement.
- To allow ample class time for conferences, you must assign sufficient work that students can do independently to keep them busy on conference days. Thus, you must establish the writing process and the peer groups early in the term.
- In addition, to allow yourself ample time to evaluate portfolios you must involve students in ongoing self- and peer evaluation.

Additional Resources for Language Arts Teachers

TEACHING LITERATURE

Applebee, A. N. *Tradition and Reform in the Teaching of English: A History.* Urbana, IL: NCTE, 1974.

Atwell, N. *In the Middle: Writing, Reading, and Learning with Adolescents.* Portsmouth, NH: Heinemann, 1987.

Beach, R., and J. Marshall. *Teaching Literature in the Secondary School.* Orlando, FL: Harcourt, 1991.

Becoming a Nation of Readers: The Report of the Commission on Reading. Washington, DC: NIE, 1984.

Buck, C., ed. *The Bloomsbury Guide to Women's Literature.* New York: Prentice, 1992.

Bushman, J., and K. Bushman. *Using Young Adult Literature in the Classroom.* New York: Macmillan, 1992.

Cooper, C. R., ed. *Researching Response to Literature and the Teaching of Literature.* Norwood, NJ: Ablex, 1988.

Farrell, E. J., and J. Squire, eds. *Transactions with Literature: A Fifty-Year Perspective.* Urbana, IL: NCTE, 1990.

Flood, J., et al., eds. *Handbook of Research on Teaching the English Language Arts.* New York: Macmillan, 1991.

Glazer, S. *Reading Comprehension: Self-monitoring Strategies That Create Independent Readers.* New York: Scholastic, 1992.

Langer, J. A., ed. *Literature Instruction: A Focus on Student Response.* Urbana, IL: NCTE, 1992.

Lee, C., and T. Gura. *Oral Interpretation.* 8th ed. Boston: Houghton, 1992.

Marzano, R. *Cultivating Thinking English and the Language Arts.* Urbana, IL: NCTE, 1991.

Newell, G. E., and R. K. Durst. *Exploring Texts: The Roles of Discussion and Writing in the Teaching and Learning of Literature.* Norwood, MA: Christopher-Gorden, 1993.

Probst, R. E. *Response and Analysis: Teaching Literature in Junior and Senior High School.* Portsmouth, NH: Boynton/Cook, 1988.

Rosenblatt, L. *Literature as Exploration.* 4th ed. New York: MLA, 1983.

———. *The Reader, the Text, the Poem: The Transactional Theory of the Literary Work.* Carbondale, IL: Southern Illinois UP, 1978.

Wagner, B. J., and M. Larson. *Situations: A Casebook of Virtual Realities for the English Teacher.* Portsmouth, NH: Boynton/Cook, 1994.

Widdowson, P., ed. *Re-reading English.* London: Routledge, 1982.

TEACHING WRITING

Bogel, F. V., and K. K. Gottschalk, eds. *Teaching Prose.* New York: Norton, 1988.

Dellinger, D. G. *Out of the Heart: How to Design Writing Assignments for High School Courses.* Berkeley, CA: Bay Area Writing Project.

Elbow, P. *Writing with Power: Techniques for Mastering the Writing Process.* New York: Oxford UP, 1981.

Flower, L. S. *Problem-Solving Strategies in Writing.* 2nd ed. Orlando, FL: Harcourt, 1985.

Fulwiler, T., ed. *The Journal Book.* Portsmouth, NH: Heinemann, 1987.

Handa, C., ed. *Computers and Community: Teaching Composition in the Twenty-First Century.* Portsmouth, NH: Boynton/Cook, 1990.

Harris, M. *Teaching One-to-One: The Writing Conference.* Urbana, IL: NCTE, 1986.

Hawisher, G. E. "Research and Recommendations for Computers and Composition." *Critical Perspectives on Computers and Composition Instruction.* Ed. G. E. Hawisher and C. L. Selfe. New York: Teacher's Coll. P, 1989: 44–69.

Irmscher, W. *Teaching Expository Writing.* New York: Holt, 1979.

Kirby, D., and T. Liner. *Inside Out: Developmental Strategies for Teaching Writing.* Upper Montclair, NJ: Boynton/Cook, 1981.

Langer, J. A., and A. N. Applebee. *How Writing Shapes Thinking: A Study of Teaching and Learning.* NCTE Research Rept. No. 22. Urbana, IL: NCTE, 1987.

Lindemann, E. *A Rhetoric for Writing Teachers.* New York: Oxford UP, 1982.

Moffett, J., and B. J. Wagner. *Student-Centered Language Arts, K–12.* 4th ed. Portsmouth, NH: Boynton/Cook, 1992.

Murray, D. *Write to Learn.* New York: Holt, 1984.

Rodrigues, D., and R. Rodrigues. *Teaching Writing with Word Processors, Grades 1–13.* Urbana, IL: NCTE, 1987.

Romano, T. *Clearing the Way: Working with Teenage Writers.* Portsmouth, NH: Heinemann, 1987.

Ross, M., D. Brackett, and A. Maxon. *Assessment and Management of Mainstreamed Hearing-Impaired Children.* Austin, TX: Pro-Ed, 1991.

Shaughnessy, M. *Errors and Expectations.* New York: Oxford UP, 1977.

Spear, K. *Sharing Writing.* Upper Montclair, NJ: Boynton/Cook, 1988.

Tate, G., and E. Corbett, eds. *The Writing Teacher's Sourcebook.* New York: Oxford UP, 1981.

Weaver, Constance. *Grammar for Teachers.* Urbana, IL: NCTE, 1979.

TEACHING GRAMMAR

Elley, W. B., et al. "The Role of Grammar in a Secondary School English Curriculum." *Research in the Teaching of English,* 10 (1976), 5–21.

Hillocks, G., Jr. *Research on Written Composition.* Urbana, IL: Natl. Conference on Research in English and ERIC/CRCS, 1986.

TEACHING THINKING SKILLS

Ausubel, D. P. *Educational Psychology.* 2nd ed. New York: Holt, 1978.

Chance, P. *Thinking in the Classroom: A Survey of Programs.* New York: Teacher's Coll. P, 1986.

Costa, A. L. *Developing Minds: A Resource Book for Teaching Thinking.* Rev. ed. 2 Vols. Alexandria, VA: ASCD, 1991.

Gardner, H. *The Unschooled Mind.* New York: Basic, 1991.

Horton, S. *Thinking through Writing.* Baltimore: Johns Hopkins UP, 1982.

Lazear, D. G. *Teaching for Multiple Intelligences.* Fastback No. 342. Bloomington, IN: Phi Delta Kappa Educ. Foundation, 1992.

Nickerson, R. S., D. N. Perkins, and E. E. Smith. *The Teaching of Thinking.* Hillsdale, NJ: Erlbaum, 1985.

Novak, J. D., and D. B. Gowin. *Learning How to Learn.* New York: Cambridge UP, 1984.

Pressley, M., et al. *Cognitive Strategy Instruction That Really Improves Children's Academic Performance.* Cambridge, MA: Brookline, 1990.

Resnick, L. B. *Education and Learning to Think.* Washington, DC: Natl. Academy P, 1987.

Resnick, L. B., and L. E. Klopfer, eds. *Toward the Thinking Curriculum: Current Cognitive Research.* Alexandria, VA: ASCD, 1989.

Rogoff, B. *Apprenticeship in Thinking.* New York: Cambridge UP, 1989.

Sternberg, R. J. "How Can We Teach Intelligence?" *Educational Leadership,* 42 (1984), 38–50.

Sternberg, R. J., and T. I. Lubart. "Creating Creative Minds." *Phi Delta Kappan,* 72 (1991), 608–614.

Sternberg, R. J., and R. Wagner. *Practical Intelligence.* New York: Cambridge UP, 1985.

ASSESSMENT

California Assessment Program. *The California Assessment Program: A Position Paper on Testing and Instruction.* Sacramento, CA: CAP, 1990.

Cambourne, B., and J. Turbil. "Assessment in Whole-Language Classrooms: Theory into Practice." *Elementary School Journal*, 90 (1991), 337–49.

García, G. E., and P. D. Pearson. "Assessment and Diversity." *Review of Research in Education*, 20 (1994), 337–91.

Gronlund, N. E., and R. L. Linn. *Measurement and Evaluation in Teaching.* 6th ed. New York: Macmillan, 1990.

Herman, J. L., P. R. Aschbacher, and L. Winters. *A Practical Guide to Alternative Assessment.* Alexandria, VA: ASCD, 1992.

Johnston, P. H. *Constructive Evaluation of Literate Activity.* White Plains, NY: Longman, 1992.

Smith, M. A., and M. Ylvisaker, eds. *Teacher's Voices: Portfolios in the Classroom.* Berkeley, CA: Natl. Writing Project, 1994.

Wolf, D., et al. "To Use Their Minds Well: Investigating New Forms of Student Assessment." *Review of Research in Education*, 17 (1991), 31–74.

Yancey, K. B., ed. *Portfolios in the Writing Classroom.* Urbana, IL: NCTE, 1992

TEACHING SPECIAL POPULATIONS

Banks, J., and C. M. Banks, eds. *Multicultural Education: Issues and Perspectives.* 2nd ed. Boston: Allyn, 1993.

Brooks, C., ed. *Tapping Potential: English and the Language Arts for the Black Learner.* Urbana, IL: NCTE, 1985.

Cummins, J. *Empowering Minority Students.* Sacramento, CA: CA Assoc. for Bilingual Education, 1989.

Farr, M., and H. Daniels. *Language Diversity and Writing Instruction.* New York: ERIC Clearinghouse on Urban Education/Columbia UP, 1986.

Garcia, E. E. "Language, Culture, and Education." *Review of Research in Education*, 19 (1993), 51–98.

Haberman, M. "The Pedagogy of Poverty versus Good Teaching." *Phi Delta Kappan* (1991), 290–94.

Hernandez, H. *Multicultural Education: A Teacher's Guide to Content and Process.* Columbus, OH: Merrill, 1989.

Kronick, D. *New Approaches to Learning Disabilities.* Philadelphia, PA: Grune & Stratton, 1988.

Marik, R. *Special Education Students Write: Classroom Activities and Assignments.* Berkeley, CA: Bay Area Writing Project, 1982.

Shade, B. J. *Culture, Style, and the Educative Process.* Springfield, IL: Charles Thomas, 1989.

Slavin, R., N. Karweit, and N. Madden, eds. *Effective Programs for Students at Risk.* Boston: Allyn, 1989.

West, W. W. *Teaching the Gifted and Talented in the English Classroom.* Washington, DC: NEA, 1980.

GENDER ISSUES

Brown, L. M., and C. Gilligan. *Meeting at the Crossroads: Women's Psychology and Girls' Development.* Cambridge: Harvard UP, 1992.

Gilbert, P. *Gender, Literacy, and the Classroom.* Carlton South, Victoria: Austral. Reading Assn., 1989.

Sadker, M., and D. Sadker. *Failing at Fairness: How Schools Cheat Girls.* New York: Scribner's, 1994.

Sadker, M., D. Sadker, and S. Klein. "The Issue of Gender in Elementary and Secondary Education." *Review of Research in Education*, 17 (1991), 269–334.

Wellesley College Center for Research on Women. *How Schools Shortchange Girls: The AAUW Report.* Washington, DC: American Assn. of Univ. Women, 1992.

TEACHING HIGH SCHOOL-AGE STUDENTS

Applebee, A. N. *The Child's Concept of Story: Ages Two to Seventeen.* Chicago: U of Chicago P, 1978.

Flavell, J. *Cognitive Development.* 2nd ed. Englewood Cliffs, NJ: Prentice, 1985.

Kohlberg, L. "Education for Justice: A Modern Statement of the Platonic View." *Five Lectures on Moral Education.* Ed. N. F. Sizer and T. R. Sizer. Cambridge: Harvard UP, 1970.

Key to Icons

Cross-curriculum Icons

- Arts and Humanities
- Mathematics and Sciences
- Social Studies
- Applied Arts

Multiple Intelligence Icons

- Musical Intelligence
- Logical-Mathematical Intelligence
- Spatial Intelligence
- Kinesthetic Intelligence
- Interpersonal/ Intrapersonal Intelligence

SCANS Icons

- Managing Resources
- Interpersonal Skills
- Information Skills
- Systems Skills
- Technology Skills
- Basic Skills
- Thinking Skills
- Personal Qualities

Thematic Organization Chart

The chart on these pages lists forty-seven common literary themes and identifies the selections in this book that deal with these themes. Choose the themes you wish to teach in your course, and use the chart to identify selections that deal with those themes.

	AGE	ALIENATION	ART AND ARTISTRY	BEAUTY	BIRTH	CONFUSION	COURAGE AND FEAR	DEATH	DISCOVERING AND LEARNING	DIVERSITY AND PLURALISM	DRAMA AND ACTING	EXILE	FAITH	FAMILY	FREEDOM	FRIENDSHIP	THE FUTURE	GIVING	GOD	GREED AND AMBITION	GROWTH/GROWING UP	HERO/HEROISM	HOME AND COUNTRY	HONESTY	HOPE	IDENTITY	IMAGINATION	INDEPENDENCE	JUSTICE	KNOWLEDGE/WISDOM	LAW AND CUSTOM	LEADERSHIP AND AUTHORITY	LOSS AND REMEMBRANCE	LOVE	NATURE	ORDER/DISORDER	PARENTS AND CHILDREN	PEACE	PRIDE AND VANITY	RELIGION	SCIENCE	STRUGGLE	TECHNOLOGY	TRUTH/REALITY	WAR	WORK	WRITING AND BOOKS
UNIT 1																																															
"Follow the Drinking Gourd," 8												•			•										•										•												
"Sonnet XXX," 18																																		•				•									
"The Magic Barrel," 27		•											•										•		•				•				•					•					•				
from *The Crucible*, 46						•	•			•			•										•					•		•	•								•		•		•				
from *Blues People*, 56			•						•																																		•		•		
UNIT 2																																															
from the Iroquois Constitution, 76							•								•					•			•				•			•	•			•	•		•						•				
"Song of the Sky Loom," 83			•																															•					•								
from *The Very Brief Relation of the Devastation of the Indies*, 88							•		•		•									•		•							•												•			•			
from *The General History of Virginia, New England, and the Summer Isles*, 94							•		•	•																															•				•		
from *Of Plymouth Plantation*, 101							•					•	•						•				•								•	•														•	
from *The New England Primer*, 109								•											•											•																	•
"To My Dear and Loving Husband," 114																																		•													
from "Sinners in the Hands of an Angry God," 118								•					•						•																			•	•		•		•				
"Some Verses upon the Burning of Our House," 125																							•										•														
"Huswifery," 125																			•																				•								
from *The Wonders of the Invisible World*, 126																													•		•								•				•				
UNIT 3																																															
from *The Autobiography of Benjamin Franklin*, 140														•													•										•			•				•	•
from "Remarks Concerning the Natives of North America," 147									•	•																				•																	
Speech in the Virginia Convention, 152							•								•								•				•					•												•			
from *Crisis, No. 1*, 159							•								•								•																					•			
"To S. M., a Young African Painter, on Seeing His Works," 165			•	•																						•													•								•
Declaration of Independence, 171															•								•				•	•		•	•				•						•						
Letter to John Adams, May 7, 1776, 179									•					•	•								•				•	•		•	•				•						•						
from *Letters from an American Farmer*, 184									•						•								•																								

	AGE	ALIENATION	ART AND ARTISTRY	BEAUTY	BIRTH	CONFUSION	COURAGE AND FEAR	DEATH	DISCOVERING AND LEARNING	DIVERSITY AND PLURALISM	DRAMA AND ACTING	EXILE	FAITH	FAMILY	FREEDOM	FRIENDSHIP	THE FUTURE	GIVING	GOD	GREED AND AMBITION	GROWTH/GROWING UP	HERO/HEROISM	HOME AND COUNTRY	HONESTY	HOPE	IDENTITY	IMAGINATION	INDEPENDENCE	JUSTICE	KNOWLEDGE/WISDOM	LAW AND CUSTOM	LEADERSHIP AND AUTHORITY	LOSS AND REMEMBRANCE	LOVE	NATURE	ORDER/DISORDER	PARENTS AND CHILDREN	PEACE	PRIDE AND VANITY	RELIGION	SCIENCE	STRUGGLE	TECHNOLOGY	TRUTH/REALITY	WAR	WORK	WRITING AND BOOKS
"To the Right Honorable William, Earl of Dartmouth," 185									●						●																																
from *Common Sense*, 185															●																										●				●		
UNIT 4																																															
"Rappaccini's Daughter," 198		●																															●	●	●			●		●			●				
"The Pit and the Pendulum," 225						●	●	●			●															●								●							●		●				
from *Moby-Dick*, "On the Whiteness of the Whale," 241		●		●			●																																								
from *Self-Reliance*, 252									●	●															●		●														●		●				
from *Walden*, 258	●	●							●	●															●		●		●					●									●				
"The Legend of Sleepy Hollow," 272				●			●													●						●							●										●				
from "The Fall of the House of Usher," 283								●	●																	●																					
UNIT 5																																															
"Thanatopsis," 290				●				●																										●													
"The Chambered Nautilus," 296				●				●																										●													
"Stanzas on Freedom," 301									●						●													●																			
"The Village Blacksmith," 306								●						●																																●	
"Telling the Bees," 311								●						●																																	
"Concord Hymn," 317															●						●	●												●													
"The Rhodora," 321		●		●				●																										●													
"This is my letter to the World," 326																									●																						●
"The Soul selects her own Society—," 329																●									●																						
"Because I could not stop for Death—," 332								●																																			●				
"I heard a Fly buzz—when I died—," 335								●																																							
"The Raven," 338							●	●																								●	●														
"Old Ironsides," 346																					●	●																●									
"Each and All," 346																									●		●							●													
"Brahma," 346							●																											●					●								
"There's a certain Slant of light," 347		●		●				●																		●																					
"I never saw a Moor—," 347																		●								●													●								
"'Hope' is the thing with feathers—," 347																								●																							
"Much Madness is divinest Sense—," 347																									●																						
"If you were coming in the fall," 347																																●	●														
"After great pain a formal feeling comes—," 348								●																								●															
"Alone," 348		●																							●	●						●															
"To Helen," 348				●																																											
"Annabel Lee," 348																																●	●														
"The Arsenal at Springfield," 349																																		●			●							●			

	AGE	ALIENATION	ART AND ARTISTRY	BEAUTY	BIRTH	CONFUSION	COURAGE AND FEAR	DEATH	DISCOVERING AND LEARNING	DIVERSITY AND PLURALISM	DRAMA AND ACTING	EXILE	FAITH	FAMILY	FREEDOM	FRIENDSHIP	THE FUTURE	GIVING	GOD	GREED AND AMBITION	GROWTH/GROWING UP	HERO/HEROISM	HOME AND COUNTRY	HONESTY	HOPE	IDENTITY	IMAGINATION	INDEPENDENCE	JUSTICE	KNOWLEDGE/WISDOM	LAW AND CUSTOM	LEADERSHIP AND AUTHORITY	LOSS AND REMEMBRANCE	LOVE	NATURE	ORDER/DISORDER	PARENTS AND CHILDREN	PEACE	PRIDE AND VANITY	RELIGION	SCIENCE	STRUGGLE	TECHNOLOGY	TRUTH/REALITY	WAR	WORK	WRITING AND BOOKS
"A Plan of Life," 350			•					•									•															•		•													
"Ichabod!," 350															•																																
from *Snow-Bound: A Winter Idyl*, 351																																•		•													•
UNIT 6																																															
from *Narrative of the Life of Frederick Douglass, an American Slave, Written by Himself*, 364										•					•										•	•															•		•			•	
"Swing Low, Sweet Chariot," 370								•					•	•	•	•			•			•		•																	•						
The Gettysburg Address, 374								•							•						•	•										•												•			
"An Occurrence at Owl Creek Bridge," 380						•	•	•														•				•				•					•								•	•			
"A Mystery of Heroism," 391							•														•																							•			
"Do not weep, maiden, for war is kind," 402								•						•																		•	•			•							•	•			
from "A House Divided," 404															•							•																			•						
Letter to Mrs. Bixby, 404								•						•							•																							•			
from the Second Inaugural Address, 404																			•			•															•				•			•			
Farewell Address, 405																					•										•													•			
"O Captain! My Captain!," 405								•																							•	•									•						
"When Lilacs Last in the Dooryard Bloom'd," 406								•																							•	•															
"Boyhood Days" from *Up from Slavery*, 406									•					•	•					•						•										•					•					•	
from *An Appeal in Favor of That Class of Americans called Africans*, 410										•					•																										•						
from *Freedom Journal* March 16, 1827, 410									•	•					•																										•						
from Editorial in *The Liberator*, January 1, 1831, 410										•					•																										•						
from "Appeal to the Christian Women of the Southern States," 411										•					•																										•						
from *Slavery*, 411										•					•																										•						
from Argument before the Supreme Court in the Case of Wharton Jones v. John Vanzandt, 1846, 411										•					•														•		•										•						
UNIT 7																																															
"The Outcasts of Poker Flat," 426								•				•																			•																
"A White Heron," 438																																		•							•						
"The Story of an Hour," 450								•						•										•	•							•	•													
"The Notorious Jumping Frog of Calaveras County," 455																				•																								•			

	AGE	ALIENATION	ART AND ARTISTRY	BEAUTY	BIRTH	CONFUSION	COURAGE AND FEAR	DEATH	DISCOVERING AND LEARNING	DIVERSITY AND PLURALISM	DRAMA AND ACTING	EXILE	FAITH	FAMILY	FREEDOM	FRIENDSHIP	THE FUTURE	GIVING	GOD	GREED AND AMBITION	GROWTH/GROWING UP	HERO/HEROISM	HOME AND COUNTRY	HONESTY	HOPE	IDENTITY	IMAGINATION	INDEPENDENCE	JUSTICE	KNOWLEDGE/WISDOM	LAW AND CUSTOM	LEADERSHIP AND AUTHORITY	LOSS AND REMEMBRANCE	LOVE	NATURE	ORDER/DISORDER	PARENTS AND CHILDREN	PEACE	PRIDE AND VANITY	RELIGION	SCIENCE	STRUGGLE	TECHNOLOGY	TRUTH/REALITY	WAR	WORK	WRITING AND BOOKS
"I Will Fight No More Forever," 464								•	•														•									•	•				•				•				•		
"A Man Said to the Universe," 468																																		•					•	•							
from "Song of Myself," 471									•																•	•								•													
"We Wear the Mask," 480																								•		•																	•				
"I Am Alone," 483		•						•	•		•												•									•					•				•						
from *Life on the Mississippi*, 483																				•	•																					•						
"The Revolt of 'Mother'," 485							•							•									•		•			•				•									•						
from *The Age of Innocence*, 491	•																																														
"When I Heard the Learn'd Astronomer," 491																																		•						•							
from *The Souls of Black Folk*, 491									•																							•									•						
from *The Art of Fiction*, 496																											•																				•
UNIT 8																																															
from *Spoon River Anthology*, "Lucinda Matlock," 510							•	•						•											•	•	•					•	•			•					•			•			•
"Petit, the Poet," 513								•																	•							•	•	•							•			•			•
"Mr. Flood's Party," 516	•	•														•																															
"Grass," 521								•																								•		•													
"Mending Wall," 524																						•																							•		
"Home Burial," 528		•						•					•																			•	•			•											
"The Snow Man," 534		•																																•													
"Anecdote of the Jar," 537			•																															•	•												
"Thirteen Ways of Looking at a Blackbird," 539																										•								•	•												
"This Is Just to Say," 545																							•																								
"The Red Wheelbarrow," 548																																		•	•												
"The Dance," 550			•																																												
"Patterns," 553							•																									•	•		•									•			
"In a Station of the Metro," 560				•																																											
"Poetry," 563																																															•
"The Love Song of J. Alfred Prufrock," 567		•																															•														
"Bells for John Whiteside's Daughter," 575								•					•																			•	•			•											
"Ars Poetica," 579																																		•													•
"somewhere i have never travelled, gladly beyond," 584								•																									•														
"Yet Do I Marvel," 588									•									•																							•						
"The Tropics in New York," 591		•																														•															
"The Negro Speaks of Rivers," 594									•												•			•	•																•						
"A Black Man Talks of Reaping," 598									•																•																•				•		
"Miniver Cheevy," 601																										•	•					•												•			

	AGE	ALIENATION	ART AND ARTISTRY	BEAUTY	BIRTH	CONFUSION	COURAGE AND FEAR	DEATH	DISCOVERING AND LEARNING	DIVERSITY AND PLURALISM	DRAMA AND ACTING	EXILE	FAITH	FAMILY	FREEDOM	FRIENDSHIP	THE FUTURE	GIVING	GOD	GREED AND AMBITION	GROWTH/GROWING UP	HERO/HEROISM	HOME AND COUNTRY	HONESTY	HOPE	IDENTITY	IMAGINATION	INDEPENDENCE	JUSTICE	KNOWLEDGE/WISDOM	LAW AND CUSTOM	LEADERSHIP AND AUTHORITY	LOSS AND REMEMBRANCE	LOVE	NATURE	ORDER/DISORDER	PARENTS AND CHILDREN	PEACE	PRIDE AND VANITY	RELIGION	SCIENCE	STRUGGLE	TECHNOLOGY	TRUTH/REALITY	WAR	WORK	WRITING AND BOOKS
"Richard Cory," 601								●																																		●					
"The Flower-Fed Buffaloes," 601								●																									●		●								●				
"The Death of the Hired Man," 602								●														●											●													●	
"An Old Man's Winter Night," 604	●	●																																													
"Disillusionment of Ten O'Clock," 604																										●																	●				
"Wind and Silver," 604																										●									●												
"A Lover," 604																																		●	●												
"The River-Merchant's Wife: A Letter," 604																				●					●								●														
"Euclid Alone Has Looked on Beauty Bare," 605				●																																											
"anyone lived in a pretty how town," 605	●				●															●													●														
"Any Human to Another," 605		●			●																												●								●						
"Storm Ending," 606																																			●												
"For the Union Dead," 606																					●														●	●							●				
"The Geranium," 607		●		●																															●												
"The Death of the Ball Turret Gunner," 607								●																																				●			
UNIT 9																																															
"To Build a Fire," 614							●	●	●																				●						●												
"A Wagner Matinee," 630		●	●	●										●								●			●	●							●														
"The Jilting of Granny Weatherall," 640	●	●				●		●					●	●					●						●	●	●	●					●	●			●						●				
"A Clean, Well-Lighted Place," 650	●	●																	●																												
"The Devil and Daniel Webster," 656																			●	●								●		●										●				●			
from *Winesburg, Ohio*, 662	●																																											●			●
from *The Grapes of Wrath*, 663																				●								●							●												
from *Invisible Man*, 665										●														●	●	●		●													●		●			●	
from *Their Eyes Were Watching God*, 671																										●									●												
from *The Great Gatsby*, 671																																	●														
from *Tell Me How Long the Train's Been Gone*, 672							●		●	●				●						●						●		●									●										
UNIT 10																																															
The Glass Menagerie, 682		●		●			●				●			●												●	●						●	●			●						●				
UNIT 11																																															
"Newsreel LXVII," from *The Big Money*, the third volume in the trilogy *U. S. A.* , 746																				●									●		●	●									●	●	●	●	●		
"The Night the Bed Fell," 752						●								●																																	
Letter to *The Amherst Student*, 759	●																													●																	
Nobel Prize Acceptance Speech, 764																																				●		●			●	●	●	●			●
"Walden," 769																											●								●								●				

UNIT 12

	AGE	ALIENATION	ART AND ARTISTRY	BEAUTY	BIRTH	CONFUSION	COURAGE AND FEAR	DEATH	DISCOVERING AND LEARNING	DIVERSITY AND PLURALISM	DRAMA AND ACTING	EXILE	FAITH	FAMILY	FREEDOM	FRIENDSHIP	THE FUTURE	GIVING	GOD	GREED AND AMBITION	GROWTH/GROWING UP	HERO/HEROISM	HOME AND COUNTRY	HONESTY	HOPE	IDENTITY	IMAGINATION	INDEPENDENCE	JUSTICE	KNOWLEDGE/WISDOM	LAW AND CUSTOM	LEADERSHIP AND AUTHORITY	LOSS AND REMEMBRANCE	LOVE	NATURE	ORDER/DISORDER	PARENTS AND CHILDREN	PEACE	PRIDE AND VANITY	RELIGION	SCIENCE	STRUGGLE	TECHNOLOGY	TRUTH/REALITY	WAR	WORK	WRITING AND BOOKS
"Auto Wreck," 788								●																											●								●				
"Those Winter Sundays," 793														●				●			●															●											
"A Story That Could Be True," 797		●																								●	●									●								●			
"House Guest," 801	●	●																								●																					
"The Secret," 806																									●																						●
"The Starry Night," 810		●	●					●																																							
"Winter Poem," 814				●																												●	●	●													
Selected Poems, 818				●				●						●																																	●
"To Black Women," 824									●																	●															●						
Inaugural Address, 829							●		●						●		●					●					●				●											●					
"Everyday Use," 834			●						●					●				●		●						●										●											
"I Stand Here Ironing," 844														●											●	●										●					●						
"For the Last Wolverine," 855																																●		●													
"A Story," 856																				●												●				●											
"The Lesson of Walls," 856		●																								●																					
"Traveling Through the Dark," 856					●			●																										●													
"Song of Solomon," 857														●											●	●	●						●			●					●						

Selections by Genre

These pages list all the selections in this book, organized by genre. Choose the genres you wish to teach in your course, and use the list to identify selections that represent those genres.

THE ORAL TRADITION

FROM UNIT 1
spiritual—"Follow the Drinking Gourd," 8

FROM UNIT 2
song—"Song of the Sky Loom," 83

FROM UNIT 6
spiritual—"Swing Low, Sweet Chariot," 370

POETRY

FROM UNIT 1
sonnet—"Sonnet XXX," 18

FROM UNIT 2
couplets—from *The New England Primer*, 109
lyric—"To My Dear and Loving Husband," 114
lyric—"Some Verses upon the Burning of Our House," 125
lyric—"Huswifery," 125

FROM UNIT 3
lyric—"To S. M., a Young African Painter, on Seeing His Works," 165
lyric—"To the Right Honorable William, Earl of Dartmouth," 185

FROM UNIT 5
lyric—"Thanatopsis," 290
lyric—"The Chambered Nautilus," 296
lyric—"Stanzas on Freedom," 301
lyric—"The Village Blacksmith," 306
lyric—"Telling the Bees," 311
lyric—"Concord Hymn," 317
lyric—"The Rhodora," 321
lyric—"This is my letter to the World," 326
lyric—"The Soul selects her own Society—," 329
lyric—"Because I could not stop for Death—," 332
lyric—"I heard a Fly buzz—when I died—," 335
lyric—"The Raven," 338
lyric—"Old Ironsides," 346
lyric—"Each and All," 346
lyric—"Brahma," 346
lyric—"There's a certain Slant of light," 347
lyric—"I never saw a Moor—," 347
lyric—"'Hope' is the thing with feathers—," 347
lyric—"Much Madness is divinest Sense—," 347
lyric—"If you were coming in the fall," 347
lyric—"After great pain a formal feeling comes—," 348
lyric—"Alone," 348
lyric—"To Helen," 348
lyric—"Annabel Lee," 348
lyric—"The Arsenal at Springfield," 349
lyric—"A Plan of Life," 350
lyric—"Ichabod!," 350
lyric—from *Snow-Bound: A Winter Idyl*, 351

FROM UNIT 6
lyric—"Do not weep, maiden, for war is kind," 402
lyric—"O Captain! My Captain!," 405
lyric—"When Lilacs Last in the Dooryard Bloom'd," 406

FROM UNIT 7
lyric—"A Man Said to the Universe," 468
lyric—from "Song of Myself," 471
lyric—"We Wear the Mask," 480
lyric—"When I Heard the Learn'd Astronomer," 491

FROM UNIT 8
epitaph—"Lucinda Matlock," 510
epitaph—"Petit, the Poet," 513
narrative—"Mr. Flood's Party," 516
lyric—"Grass," 521
narrative—"Mending Wall," 524
narrative—"Home Burial," 528
lyric—"The Snow Man," 534
lyric—"Anecdote of the Jar," 537
lyric—"Thirteen Ways of Looking at a Blackbird," 539
lyric—"This Is Just to Say," 545
lyric—"The Red Wheelbarrow," 548
lyric—"The Dance," 550
narrative—"Patterns," 553
lyric—"In a Station of the Metro," 560
lyric—"Poetry," 563
dramatic monologue—"The Love Song of J. Alfred Prufrock," 567
lyric—"Bells for John Whiteside's Daughter," 575
lyric—"Ars Poetica," 579
lyric—"somewhere i have never travelled,gladly beyond," 584
lyric—"Yet Do I Marvel," 588
lyric—"The Tropics in New York," 591
lyric—"The Negro Speaks of Rivers," 594
lyric—"A Black Man Talks of Reaping," 598
lyric—"Miniver Cheevy," 601
lyric—"Richard Cory," 601
lyric—"The Flower-Fed Buffaloes," 601
narrative—"The Death of the Hired Man," 602
narrative—"An Old Man's Winter Night," 604
lyric—"Disillusionment of Ten O'Clock," 604
lyric—"Wind and Silver," 604
lyric—"A Lover," 604
lyric—"The River-Merchant's Wife: A Letter," 604
sonnet—"Euclid Alone Has Looked on Beauty Bare," 605
lyric—"anyone lived in a pretty how town," 605
lyric—"Any Human to Another," 605
lyric—"Storm Ending," 606
lyric—"For the Union Dead," 606
lyric—"The Geranium," 607
lyric—"The Death of the Ball Turret Gunner," 607

FROM UNIT 12
lyric—"Auto Wreck," 788
lyric—"Winter Sundays," 793
lyric—"A Story That Could Be True," 797
lyric—"House Guest," 801
lyric—"The Secret," 806
lyric—"The Starry Night," 810
lyric—"Winter Poem," 814
lyric—Selected poems by James Worley, 818
lyric—"To Black Women," 824
lyric—"For the Last Wolverine," 855
lyric—"A Story," 856
lyric—"The Lesson of Walls," 856
lyric—"Traveling Through the Dark," 856

FICTION

FROM UNIT 1
short story—"The Magic Barrel," 27

FROM UNIT 4
short story—"Rappaccini's Daughter," 198
short story—"The Pit and the Pendulum," 225
novel—from *Moby-Dick*, 241
short story—"The Legend of Sleepy Hollow," 272
short story—from "The Fall of the House of Usher, "283

FROM UNIT 6
short story—"An Occurence at Owl Creek Bridge," 380
short story—"A Mystery of Heroism," 391

FROM UNIT 7
short story—"The Outcasts of Poker Flat," 426
short story—"A White Heron," 438
short story—"The Story of an Hour," 450
short story—"The Notorious Jumping Frog of Calaveras County," 455
short story—"The Revolt of 'Mother'," 485
novel—from *The Age of Innocence*, 491

FROM UNIT 9
short story—"To Build a Fire," 614
short story—"A Wagner Matinee," 630
short story—"The Jilting of Granny Weatherall," 640
short story—"A Clean, Well-Lighted Place," 650
short story—"The Devil and Daniel Webster," 656
short story—from *Winesburg, Ohio*, 662
novel—from *The Grapes of Wrath*, 663
novel—from *Invisible Man*, 665
novel—from *Their Eyes Were Watching God*, 671
novel—from *The Great Gatsby*, 671
novel—from *Tell Me How Long the Train's Been Gone*, 672

FROM UNIT 12
short story—"Everyday Use," 834
short story—"I Stand Here Ironing," 844
short story—"Song of Solomon," 857

DRAMA

FROM UNIT 1
from *The Crucible*, 46

FROM UNIT 10
The Glass Menagerie, 682

NONFICTION

FROM UNIT 1
history—from *Blues People*, 56

FROM UNIT 2
document—from the Iroquois Constitution, 76
history—from *The Very Brief Relation of the Devastation of the Indies*, 88
history—from *The General History of Virginia, New England, and the Summer Isles*, 94
history—from *Of Plymouth Plantation*, 101
textbook—from *The New England Primer*, 109
sermon—"Sinners in the Hands of an Angry God," 118
history—from *The Wonders of the Invisible World*, 126

FROM UNIT 3
autobiography—from *The Autobiography of Benjamin Franklin*, 140
essay—"Remarks Concerning the Natives of North America," 147
speech—Speech in the Virginia Convetion, 152
pamphlet—from *Crisis, No. 1*, 159
document—Declaration of Independence, 171
letter—Letter to John Adams, May 7, 1776, 179
essay—from *Letters from an American Farmer*, 184
essay—from *Common Sense*, 185

FROM UNIT 4
essay—from *Self-Reliance*, 252
essay—from *Walden*, 258

FROM UNIT 6
autobiography—from *Narrative of the Life of Frederick Douglass, an American Slave, Written by Himself*, 364
speech—The Gettysburg Address, 374
speech—from "A House Divided," 404
letter—Letter to Mrs. Bixby, 404
speech—from the Second Inaugural Address, 404
speech—Farewell Address, 405
autobiography—from *Up from Slavery*, 406
essay—from *An Appeal in Favor of That Class of Americans Called Africans*, 410
editorial—from *Freedom Journal*, March 16, 1827, 410
editorial—from Editorial in *The Liberator*, January 1, 1831, 411
essay—from "Appeal to the Christian Women of the Southern States," 411
essay—from *Slavery*, 411
court argument—from Argument before the Supreme Court in the Case of Wharton Jones v. John Vanzandt, 1846, 411

FROM UNIT 7
speech—"I Will Fight No More Forever," 464
speech—"I Am Alone," 483
autobiography—from *Life on the Mississippi*, 483
essay—from *The Souls of Black Folk*, 491
essay—from *The Art of Fiction*, 491

FROM UNIT 11
collage—"Newsreel LXVII," 746
essay—"The Night the Bed Fell," 752
letter—Letter to the *Amherst Student*, 759
speech—Nobel Prize Acceptance Speech, 764
essay—"Walden," 769

FROM UNIT 12
speech—Inaugural Address, 829

THE EMC MASTERPIECE SERIES

LITERATURE AND THE LANGUAGE ARTS

The American Tradition

EMC/Paradigm Publishing
St. Paul, Minnesota

Staff Credits:

For **EMC/Paradigm Publishing,** St. Paul, Minnesota

Eileen Slater
Editor

Christine Gensmer
Associate Editor

For **Penobscot School Publishing, Inc.,** Danvers, Massachusetts

Robert D. Shepherd
Executive Editor

Kimberly M. Leahy
Managing Editor

Sara Hyry
Christina Kolb
Associate Editors

Camilla Ayers
Sybil Fetter
Sheila Neylon
Copyeditors

Charles Q. Bent
Production Manager

Sara Day
Art Director

Heath P. O'Leary
Compositor

ISBN 0-8219-1270-4

© 1996 by EMC Corporation

All rights reserved. No part of this publication may be adapted, reproduced, stored in a retrieval system, or transmitted in any form or by any means, electronic, mechanical, photocopying, recording, or otherwise without permission from the publisher.

Published by EMC/Paradigm Publishing
300 York Avenue
St. Paul, Minnesota 55101

Printed in the United States of America.
10 9 8 7 6 5 4 3 2 1 XXX 01 00 99 98 97 96

Acknowledgments:

Alfred A. Knopf, Inc.
From OF PLYMOUTH PLANTATION 1620–1647 by William Bradford, edit., Samuel Eliot Morison. Copyright 1952 by Samuel Eliot Morison and renewed 1980 by Emily M Beck. Reprinted by permission of Alfred A Knopf Inc. "The Negro Speaks of Rivers" From SELECTED POEMS by Langston Hughes. Copyright 1926 by Alfred A Knopf Inc and renewed 1954 by Langston Hughes. Reprinted by permission of the publisher. "Disillusionment of Ten O'Clock," "The Snow Man," "Anecdote of the Jar," and "Thirteen Ways of Looking at a Blackbird," From COLLECTED POEMS by Wallace Stevens. Copyright 1923 and renewed 1951 by Wallace Stevens. Reprinted by permission of Alfred A Knopf Inc."Bells for John Whiteside's Daughter" From SELECTED POEMS by John Crowe Ransom. Copyright 1924 by Alfred A Knopf Inc and renewed 1952 by John Crowe Ransom. Reprinted by permission of the publisher.

The Archives of Claude McKay
"The Tropics in New York" by Claude McKay. Used by permission of The Archives of Claude McKay, Carl Cowl, Administrator.

Bantam Doubleday Dell Publishing Group, Inc.
"Pride and the Proudhammers", from TELL ME HOW LONG THE TRAIN'S BEEN GONE by James Baldwin. Copyright © 1968 by James Baldwin. Used by permission of Doubleday, a division of Bantam Doubleday Dell Publishing Group, Inc. "An Occurrence at Owl Creek Bridge" from *The Complete Stories of Ambrose Bierce,* published by Doubleday & Company, Inc. "I Stand Here Ironing", copyright © 1956, 1957, 1960, 1961 by Tillie Olsen. From TELL ME A RIDDLE by Tillie Olsen. Introduction by John Leonard. Used by permission of Delacorte Press/Seymour Lawrence, a division of Bantam Doubleday Dell Publishing Group, Inc. "The Geranium," copyright 1963 by Beatrice Roethke, Administratrix of the Estate of Theodore Roethke. From THE COLLECTED POEMS OF THEODORE ROETHKE by Theodore Roethke. Used by permission of Doubleday, a division of Bantam Doubleday Dell Publishing Group, Inc.

(continued on page 1083)

LITERATURE AND THE LANGUAGE ARTS

MAPLE LEVEL
THE BRITISH TRADITION

PINE LEVEL
THE AMERICAN TRADITION

WILLOW LEVEL
UNDERSTANDING LITERATURE

BIRCH LEVEL
EXPERIENCING LITERATURE

Consultants and Writers

Edmund J. Farrell, Ph.D.
Emeritus Professor of English Education
University of Texas at Austin

Roger Dick
Teacher of English and Humanities
Brooklyn Center High School
Brooklyn Center, Minnesota

David England, Ph.D.
Associate Dean for Teacher Education
Louisiana State University

Ellen Gabin
Consultant, Hispanic Literature
Rockport, Massachusetts

Donald Gray, Ph.D.
Professor of English
Indiana University

Susan Gubar, Ph.D.
Professor of English
Indiana University

Dael Angelico-Hart
Director of Language Arts
Danvers Public Schools
Danvers, Massachusetts

Gail Ross Hatcher
English Department Chairperson
T. Wingate Andrews High School
High Point, North Carolina

Jim O'Laughlin
Lecturer
University College
Northwestern University

Jane S. Shoaf, Ph.D.
Instructional Specialist for Communication Skills (retired)
North Carolina Department of Public Instruction

Kendra Sisserson
Language Arts Curriculum Facilitator
Academy for Aerospace Technology
Cocoa, Florida

Donald L. Stephan
English Department Chair
Sidney High School
Sidney, Ohio

James W. Swanson
English Instructor
Robbinsdale Armstrong High School
Plymouth, Minnesota

Jill Triplett
Special Collections Librarian
Wellesley College

Hope Vasholz
Teacher of English
Hammond High School
Columbia, Maryland

Arlette Ingram Willis, Ph.D.
Assistant Professor in the Department of Curriculum and Instruction
University of Illinois at Urbana-Champaign

Contents

PART 1 UNDERSTANDING LITERATURE 1

UNIT 1 GENRES AND TECHNIQUES OF LITERATURE 2

The Oral Tradition 4
"Follow the Drinking Gourd," Anonymous Spiritual 8

Poetry 10
"Sonnet XXX," by Edna St. Vincent Millay 18

Fiction 22
"The Magic Barrel," by Bernard Malamud 27

Drama 42
from *The Crucible*, by Arthur Miller 46

Nonfiction
from *Blues People*, by Imamu Amiri Baraka (LeRoi Jones) 56

■ Unit Review 60

■ Language Lab: The Parts of Speech 62

PART 2 THE AMERICAN TRADITION 64

UNIT 2 ORIGINS OF THE AMERICAN TRADITION (TO 1750) 66

Iroquois
from the Iroquois Constitution 76

Tewa
"Song of the Sky Loom" 83

Bartolomé de las Casas
from *The Very Brief Relation of the Devastation of the Indies* 88

John Smith
from *The General History of Virginia, New England, and the Summer Isles* 94

William Bradford
from *Of Plymouth Plantation* 101

Anonymous
from *The New England Primer* 109

Anne Bradstreet
"To My Dear and Loving Husband" 114

Jonathan Edwards
from "Sinners in the Hands of an Angry God" 118

SELECTIONS FOR ADDITIONAL READING: ORIGINS OF THE AMERICAN TRADITION

Anne Bradstreet
"Some Verses upon the Burning of Our House" 125

Edward Taylor
"Huswifery" 125

Cotton Mather
from *The Wonders of the Invisible World* 126

■ Unit Review 128

■ Language Lab: The Sentence 130

UNIT 3 THE AMERICAN REVOLUTION (1750–1800) 132

■ Introduction 134

Benjamin Franklin
from *The Autobiography of Benjamin Franklin* 140
from "Remarks Concerning the Natives of North America" 147

Patrick Henry
Speech in the Virginia Convention 152

Thomas Paine
from *Crisis, No. 1* 159

Phillis Wheatley
"To S. M., a Young African Painter, on Seeing His Works" 165

Thomas Jefferson
Declaration of Independence 171

Abigail Adams
Letter to John Adams, May 7, 1776 179

SELECTIONS FOR ADDITIONAL READING: THE AMERICAN REVOLUTION

J. Hector St. Jean de Crèvecoeur
from "Letters from an American Farmer" 184

Phillis Wheatley
"To the Right Honorable William, Earl of Dartmouth" 185

Thomas Paine
from *Common Sense* 185

■ Unit Review 186

■ Language Lab: Editing for Errors in Verbs 188

UNIT 4 NEW ENGLAND RENAISSANCE PROSE (1800–1860) 190

■ Introduction 192

SHORT STORY

Nathaniel Hawthorne
"Rappacini's Daughter" 198

Edgar Allan Poe
"The Pit and the Pendulum" 225

NOVEL

Herman Melville
from *Moby-Dick*
"On the Whiteness of the Whale" 241

NONFICTION

Ralph Waldo Emerson
from *Self-Reliance* 252

Henry David Thoreau
from *Walden* 258

SELECTIONS FOR ADDITIONAL READING: NEW ENGLAND RENAISSANCE PROSE

Washington Irving
"The Legend of Sleepy Hollow" 272

Edgar Allan Poe
"The Fall of the House of Usher" 283

■ Unit Review 284

■ Language Lab: Editing for Errors in Pronouns 286

UNIT 5 NEW ENGLAND RENAISSANCE POETRY (1800–1860) 288

William Cullen Bryant
"Thanatopsis" 290

Oliver Wendell Holmes
"The Chambered Nautilus" 296

James Russell Lowell
"Stanzas on Freedom" 301

Henry Wadsworth Longfellow
"The Village Blacksmith" 306

John Greenleaf Whittier
"Telling the Bees" 311

Ralph Waldo Emerson
"Concord Hymn" 317
"The Rhodora" 321

Emily Dickinson
"This is my letter to the World" 326
"The Soul selects her own Society—" 329
"Because I could not stop for Death—" 332
"I heard a Fly buzz—when I died—" 335

Edgar Allan Poe
"The Raven" 338

SELECTIONS FOR ADDITIONAL READING: NEW ENGLAND RENAISSANCE POETRY

Oliver Wendell Holmes
"Old Ironsides" 346

Ralph Waldo Emerson
"Each and All" 346
"Brahma" 346

Emily Dickinson
"There's a certain Slant of light" 347
"I never saw a Moor—" 347
"'Hope' is the thing with feathers—" 347
"Much Madness is divinest Sense—" 347
"If you were coming in the fall" 347
"After great pain a formal feeling comes—" 348

Edgar Allan Poe
"Alone" 348

"To Helen" 348
"Annabel Lee" 348

Henry Wadsworth Longfellow
"The Arsenal at Springfield" 349
"A Plan of Life" 350

John Greenleaf Whittier
"Ichabod!" 350
from *Snow-Bound: A Winter Idyl* 351

■ Unit Review 352

■ Language Lab: Editing for Errors in Modifiers 354

UNIT 6 SLAVERY AND THE CIVIL WAR (1860–1865) 356

■ Introduction 358

Frederick Douglass
from *Narrative of the Life of Frederick Douglass, an American Slave, Written by Himself* 364

Spiritual
"Swing Low, Sweet Chariot" 370

Abraham Lincoln
The Gettysburg Address 374

Ambrose Bierce
"An Occurrence at Owl Creek Bridge" 380

Stephen Crane
"A Mystery of Heroism" 391
"Do not weep, maiden, for war is kind" 402

SELECTIONS FOR ADDITIONAL READING: SLAVERY AND THE CIVIL WAR

Abraham Lincoln
from "A House Divided" 404
Letter to Mrs. Bixby 404
from the Second Inaugural Address 404

Robert E. Lee
Farewell Address 405

Walt Whitman
"O Captain! My Captain!" 405
"When Lilacs Last in the Dooryard Bloom'd" 406

Booker T. Washington
"Boyhood Days" from *Up from Slavery* 406

ABOLITIONIST VOICES

Lydia Marie Child
from *An Appeal in Favor of That Class of Americans called Africans* 410

John B. Russwurm
from *Freedom Journal* March 16, 1827 410

William Lloyd Garrison
from Editorial in *The Liberator*, January 1, 1831 410

Angelina Grimké
from "Appeal to the Christian Women of the Southern States" 411

William Ellery Channing
from *Slavery* 411

Salmon P. Chase
from Argument before the Supreme Court in the Case of Wharton Jones v. John Vanzandt, 1846 411

■ Unit Review 412

■ Language Lab: Editing for Errors in Usage 414

UNIT 7 FRONTIERS (1860–1900) 416

■ Introduction 418

SHORT STORY

Bret Harte
"The Outcasts of Poker Flat" 426

Sarah Orne Jewett
"A White Heron" 438

Kate Chopin
"The Story of an Hour" 450

Mark Twain
"The Notorious Jumping Frog of Calaveras County" 455

NONFICTION

Chief Joseph of the Nez Percé
"I Will Fight No More Forever" 464

POETRY

Stephen Crane
"A Man Said to the Universe" 468

Walt Whitman
from "Song of Myself" 471

Paul Laurence Dunbar
"We Wear the Mask" 480

SELECTIONS FOR ADDITIONAL READING: FRONTIERS

Cochise of the Apache
"I Am Alone" 483

Mark Twain
from *Life on the Mississippi* 483

Mary E. Wilkins Freeman
"The Revolt of 'Mother'" 485

Edith Wharton
from *The Age of Innocence* 491

Walt Whitman
"When I Heard the Learn'd Astronomer" 491

W. E. B. Du Bois
from *The Souls of Black Folk* 491

Henry James
from *The Art of Fiction* 496

■ Unit Review 497

■ Language Lab: Proofreading for Comma Errors 499

UNIT 8 MODERN POETRY (1900–1960) 500

■ Introduction 502

Edgar Lee Masters
from *Spoon River Anthology*
"Lucinda Matlock" 510
"Petit, the Poet" 513

Edwin Arlington Robinson
"Mr. Flood's Party" 516

Carl Sandburg
"Grass" 521

Robert Frost
"Mending Wall" 524
"Home Burial" 528

Wallace Stevens
"The Snow Man" 534
"Anecdote of the Jar" 537
"Thirteen Ways of Looking at a Blackbird" 539

William Carlos Williams
"This Is Just to Say" 545
"The Red Wheelbarrow" 548
"The Dance" 550

Amy Lowell
"Patterns" 553

Ezra Pound
"In a Station of the Metro" 560

Marianne Moore
"Poetry" 563

T. S. Eliot
"The Love Song of J. Alfred Prufrock" 567

John Crowe Ransom
"Bells for John Whiteside's Daughter" 575

Archibald MacLeish
"Ars Poetica" 579

E. E. Cummings
"somewhere i have never travelled, gladly beyond" 584

POETRY OF THE HARLEM RENAISSANCE

Countee Cullen
"Yet Do I Marvel" 588

Claude McKay
"The Tropics in New York" 591

Langston Hughes
"The Negro Speaks of Rivers" 594

Arna Bontemps
"A Black Man Talks of Reaping" 598

SELECTIONS FOR ADDITIONAL READING: MODERN POETRY

Edwin Arlington Robinson
"Miniver Cheevy" 601
"Richard Cory" 601

Vachel Lindsay
"The Flower-Fed Buffaloes" 601

Robert Frost
"The Death of the Hired Man" 602
"An Old Man's Winter Night" 604

Wallace Stevens
"Disillusionment of Ten O'Clock" 604

Amy Lowell
"Wind and Silver" 604
"A Lover" 604

Ezra Pound
"The River-Merchant's Wife: A Letter" 604

Edna St. Vincent Millay
"Euclid Alone Has Looked on Beauty Bare" 605

E. E. Cummings
"anyone lived in a pretty how town" 605

Countee Cullen
"Any Human to Another" 605

Jean Toomer
"Storm Ending" 606

Robert Lowell
"For the Union Dead" 606

Theodore Roethke
"The Geranium" 607

Randall Jarrell
"The Death of the Ball Turret Gunner" 607

■ Unit Review 608

■ Language Lab: Proofreading for Other Punctuation Errors 610

UNIT 9 MODERN FICTION (1900–1960) 612

Jack London
"To Build a Fire" 614

Willa Cather
"A Wagner Matinee" 630

Katherine Anne Porter
"The Jilting of Granny Weatherall" 640

Ernest Hemingway
"A Clean, Well-Lighted Place" 650

SELECTIONS FOR ADDITIONAL READING: MODERN FICTION

Stephen Vincent Benét
"The Devil and Daniel Webster" 656

Sherwood Anderson
from *Winesburg, Ohio* 662

John Steinbeck
from *The Grapes of Wrath* 663

Ralph Ellison
from *Invisible Man* 665

Zora Neale Hurston
from *Their Eyes Were Watching God* 671

F. Scott Fitzgerald
from *The Great Gatsby* 671

James Baldwin
from *Tell Me How Long the Train's Been Gone* 672

■ Unit Review 676

■ Language Lab: Proofreading for Capitalization Errors 678

UNIT 10 MODERN DRAMA (1900–1960) 680

Tennessee Williams
The Glass Menagerie 682

■ Unit Review 741

■ Language Lab: Proofreading for Spelling Errors 742

UNIT 11 MODERN NONFICTION (1900–1960) 744

John Dos Passos
"Newsreel LXVII," from *The Big Money*, the third volume in the trilogy *U. S. A.* 746

James Thurber
"The Night the Bed Fell" 752

Robert Frost
Letter to *The Amherst Student* 759

William Faulkner
Nobel Prize Acceptance Speech 764

E. B. White
"Walden" 769

■ Unit Review 777

■ Language Lab: Vocabulary Development 778

UNIT 12 CONTEMPORARY LITERATURE (1960–PRESENT) 780

■ Introduction 782

POETRY

Karl Shapiro
"Auto Wreck" 788

Robert Hayden
"Those Winter Sundays" 793

William Stafford
"A Story That Could Be True" 797

Elizabeth Bishop
"House Guest" 801

Denise Levertov
"The Secret" 806

Anne Sexton
"The Starry Night" 810

Nikki Giovanni
"Winter Poem" 814

James Worley
Selected Poems 818

Gwendolyn Brooks
"To Black Women" 824

NONFICTION

John F. Kennedy
Inaugural Address 829

FICTION

Alice Walker
"Everyday Use" 834

Tillie Olsen
"I Stand Here Ironing" 844

SELECTIONS FOR ADDITIONAL READING: CONTEMPORARY LITERATURE

James Dickey
"For the Last Wolverine" 855

Li-Young Lee
"A Story" 856

Alberto Ríos
"The Lesson of Walls" 856

William Stafford
"Traveling Through the Dark" 856

Amy Bloom
"Song of Solomon" 857

■ Unit Review 860

■ Language Lab: Varieties of English 862

LANGUAGE ARTS SURVEY

1 ESSENTIAL SKILLS: WRITING

Introduction to Writing 866

1.1 The Process of Writing 866
Prewriting
Drafting
Peer and Self-Evaluation
Revising
Proofreading
Publishing and Presenting

1.2 Keeping a Writer's Journal 867
1.3 Keeping a Writer's Portfolio 868
1.4 Using Computers for Writing 868

Prewriting: Developing a Plan for Writing 871

1.5 Choosing and Focusing a Topic 871
1.6 Choosing a Purpose or Aim 873
Expressive Writing
Informative Writing
Persuasive Writing
Literary Writing

1.7 Choosing and Analyzing an Audience 875
1.8 Choosing a Form 876
1.9 Modes of Writing 878

Prewriting: Exploring Ideas on Your Own 879

1.10 Recalling 879
1.11 Observing 880
1.12 Freewriting 881
1.13 Questioning 883
Who, What, Where, When, Why, and How
"What if" Questions

1.14 Analyzing 883
1.15 Imagining 884
1.16 Role Playing 885
1.17 Clustering 885
1.18 Sensory Detail Charts 886
1.19 Time Lines 886
1.20 Flow Charts 886
1.21 Story Maps 887
1.22 Pro and Con Charts 888
1.23 Analysis Charts 888
1.24 Venn Diagrams 888

Prewriting: Using Outside Sources 889

1.25 Brainstorming 889
1.26 Discussion 889
1.27 Interviewing 890
1.28 Using Print Sources 890
1.29 Using Nonprint Sources 891

Prewriting: Organizing Your Ideas 891

1.30 Revising Your Writing Plan 891
1.31 Identifying Main Ideas and Supporting Details 891
1.32 Making a Rough Outline 892
1.33 Making a Formal Outline 892
1.34 Organizing Ideas 893
Chronological Order
Spatial Order
Degree Order
Comparison-and-Contrast Order
Cause-and-Effect Order
Classification Order
Part-by-Part Order

Drafting: Approaches to Writing a Draft 894

1.35 Writing a Discovery Draft 894
1.36 Writing a Careful Draft 894
1.37 The Prewriting, Drafting, and Revising Cycle 895

Drafting: Paragraphs 895

1.38 Paragraphs with Topic Sentences 895
1.39 Paragraphs without Topic Sentences 896
1.40 Elaboration: Types of Supporting Details 896

Drafting: Compositions 897

1.41 Writing a Thesis Statement and Topic Sentences 897
1.42 Organizing a Composition 897

Revising: Approaches to Revision 898

1.43 Self-Evaluation 898
1.44 Peer Evaluation 899
1.45 Four Types of Revision 899
Adding or Expanding
Deleting
Replacing
Moving
1.46 Marking a Manuscript 900

Proofreading and Publishing 901

1.47 Proofreading Checklist 901
Spelling
Grammar
Usage
Mechanics
1.48 Preparing Your Manuscript 901
1.49 Publishing or Presenting Your Work 902

2 ESSENTIAL SKILLS: LANGUAGE

GRAMMAR HANDBOOK

Introduction to Grammar

2.1 The Grammar You Already Know 904
2.2 The Uses of Grammar 904

The Parts of Speech

2.3 Common and Proper Nouns 905
2.4 Concrete and Abstract Nouns 905
2.5 Compound and Collective Nouns 905
2.6 Personal Pronouns 906
2.7 Reflexive and Intensive Pronouns 906
2.8 Demonstrative Pronouns 906
2.9 Indefinite Pronouns 906

2.10 Interrogative Pronouns 907
2.11 Relative Pronouns 907
2.12 Action Verbs 907
2.13 Linking Verbs 907
2.14 Auxiliary Verbs 907
2.15 Transitive and Intransitive Verbs 908
2.16 Verbals: Participles 908
2.17 Verbals: Gerunds 908
2.18 Verbals: Infinitives 908
2.19 Adjectives and Articles 908
2.20 Proper Adjectives 909
2.21 Predicate Adjectives 909
2.22 Adverbs 909
2.23 Adjective or Adverb? 909
2.24 Prepositions 910
2.25 Coordinating Conjunctions 910
2.26 Correlative Conjunctions 910
2.27 Subordinating Conjunctions 910
2.28 Conjunctive Adverbs 911
2.29 Interjections 911
2.30 Words as Other Parts of Speech I 911
2.31 Words as Other Parts of Speech II 911

Using the Parts of Speech in Writing

2.32 Using Precise Nouns 912
2.33 Using Vivid Verbs 912
2.34 Replacing Linking Verbs with Action Verbs 912
2.35 Using Colorful Modifiers 913

Building Sentences

2.36 The Functions of Sentences 913
Declarative Sentences
Interrogative Sentences
Imperative Sentences
Exclamatory Sentences
2.37 Substantives 914
2.38 Simple Sentences: SUB + V 914
2.39 Simple Sentences: SUB + AV + SUB 914
2.40 Simple Sentences: SUB + LV + SUB or ADJ 915
2.41 Simple Sentences: SUB + AV + SUB + SUB 915
2.42 Independent Clauses 916
2.43 Compound Sentences 916
2.44 Complex Sentences 916
2.45 Compound-Complex Sentences 916

Expanding Sentences

2.46 Adding Modifiers 917
2.47 Adding Prepositional Phrases 917
2.48 Adding Appositives and Appositive Phrases 917
2.49 Adding Predicates 917
2.50 Adding Subordinate Clauses 918

Combining Sentences

2.51 Combining Sentences Using Single Words 918
2.52 Combining Sentences Using Phrases 918
2.53 Combining Sentences Using Clauses 919

Editing Sentences

2.54 Varying Sentence Openings 919
2.55 Varying Sentence Length and Structure 920
2.56 Using the Active Voice 920
2.57 Achieving Parallelism 921
2.58 Deleting Repeated or Unnecessary Ideas 921
2.59 Reducing Wordiness 921
2.60 Correcting Sentence Strings 922
2.61 Correcting Sentence Fragments 922
2.62 Correcting Run-ons 923
2.63 Correcting Dangling or Misplaced Modifiers 923
2.64 Inverting Sentences for Emphasis 923

Editing for Errors in Verb Tense

2.65 Improper Shifts in Verb Tense 924
2.66 Irregular Verbs I 924
2.67 Irregular Verbs II 924
2.68 Split Infinitives 925
2.69 Voice and Mood 925

Editing for Errors in Subject/Verb Agreement

2.70 Agreement of Subject and Verb 926
2.71 Agreement with Compound Subjects 927
2.72 Agreement with Indefinite Pronouns 927
2.73 Agreement in Inverted Sentences 928
2.74 Agreement with *Doesn't* and *Don't* 928
2.75 Other Problems in Subject/Verb Agreement 928
Inverted Sentences
Sentences with Predicate Nominatives
Collective Nouns as Subjects
Singular Nouns with Plural Forms
Titles and Groups of Words as Subjects
Words of Amount and Time as Subjects

Editing for Errors in Pronoun Usage

2.76 Pronoun Case I 929
2.77 Pronoun Case II 930
2.78 *Who* and *Whom* 931
2.79 Pronouns with Appositives 931
2.80 Pronouns as Appositives 931
2.81 Pronouns in Comparisons 932
2.82 Agreement of Pronouns and Antecedents 932
2.83 Reference of Pronouns to Antecedents I 932
2.84 Reference of Pronouns to Antecedents II 933

Editing for Errors in Modifier Usage

2.85 Modifiers with Action and Linking Verbs 933
2.86 Comparison of Adjectives and Adverbs 934
2.87 Illogical and Double Comparisons 935
2.88 Double Negatives 935
2.89 Other Problems with Modifiers 935
This and *These; That* and *Those*
Them and *Those*
Bad and *Badly*
Good and *Well*

Usage Handbook

2.90 Usage Problems I 936
2.91 Usage Problems II 937
2.92 Usage Problems III 937

Mechanics Handbook

Proofreading for Errors in End Marks and Commas

2.93 End Marks 938
2.94 Commas I 938
2.95 Commas II 939
2.96 Commas III 940

Proofreading for Other Punctuation Errors

2.97 Semicolons 940
2.98 Colons 941
2.99 Dashes 941
2.100 Hyphens 941
2.101 Parentheses and Brackets 942
2.102 Apostrophes 942
2.103 Underlining and Italics 943
2.104 Quotation Marks I 944
2.105 Quotation Marks II 944
2.106 Ellipses 944

Proofreading for Errors in Capitalization

2.107 Astronomical Terms 945
2.108 Awards 945
2.109 Brand and Trade Names 945
2.110 Buildings and Structures 945
2.111 Days, Months, Years, and Holidays 946
2.112 Directions and Regions 946
2.113 Events and Periods 946
2.114 Family Relationships 946
2.115 First Words 947
2.116 Interjections 947
2.117 Letters 947
2.118 Organizations and Institutions 947
2.119 Outlines 948
2.120 Personal Names 948
2.121 Place Names 948
2.122 Poetry 949
2.123 Proper Nouns and Adjectives 949

2.124 Quotations 950
2.125 Sacred Beings and Writings 950
2.126 School Subjects, Courses, Grades, and Years 950
2.127 The Pronoun *I* 950
2.128 Titles of Artworks 951
2.129 Titles of Literary Works 951
2.130 Titles of Musical Works 951
2.131 Titles of Persons and Occupations 951
2.132 Units of Time 952
2.133 Vehicles 952

SPELLING HANDBOOK

2.134 Proofreading for Spelling Errors 952
2.135 Using Spelling Rules I 952
2.136 Using Spelling Rules II 953

VOCABULARY DEVELOPMENT

2.137 Making a Plan for Vocabulary Development 954
2.138 Using Context Clues I 954
2.139 Using Context Clues II 955
2.140 Base Words and Prefixes 955
2.141 Suffixes 955
2.142 Greek and Latin Roots 955
2.143 Word Origins I 956
2.144 Word Origins II 957
2.145 Words from Other Curricular Areas I 957
2.146 Words from Other Curricular Areas II 958

VARIETIES OF ENGLISH

2.147 Formal and Informal English 958
2.148 Register 959
2.149 Tone and Voice 959
2.150 Dialects of English 960
2.151 Jargon and Gobbledygook 960
2.152 Clichés and Euphemisms 961
2.153 Connotation and Denotation 961

3 ESSENTIAL SKILLS: SPEAKING AND LISTENING

3.1 A Communication Model 962
3.2 Elements of Verbal Communication 963
3.3 Elements of Nonverbal Communication 964
3.4 Active Listening 965
3.5 Interpersonal Communication 966
3.6 Discussion 967
3.7 Public Speaking 967
3.8 Oral Interpretation 968

4 ESSENTIAL SKILLS: STUDY AND RESEARCH

THINKING SKILLS

4.1 Strategies for Problem Solving I 970
4.2 Strategies for Problem Solving II 971
4.3 Strategies for Decision Making 972
4.4 Memorizing 972
4.5 Remembering and Visualizing 973
4.6 Observing 974
4.7 Classifying 974
4.8 Comparing and Contrasting 975
4.9 Estimating and Quantifying 975
4.10 Analyzing 975
4.11 Generalizing 976
4.12 Deducing 976
4.13 Making Hypotheses 977
4.14 Avoiding Faulty Arguments 977
4.15 Understanding Propaganda Techniques 980

READING SKILLS

4.16 Reading Rates 982
Scanning
Skimming
Slow and Careful Reading
4.17 Previewing Your Reading 983
4.18 Reading Actively 984
Responding to Your Reading
Questioning
Predicting

Summarizing
Identifying Main Ideas
Identifying Relationships
Making Inferences
4.19 Reading Charts and Graphs 986

RESEARCH SKILLS
4.20 The Classification of Library Materials 987
4.21 Using Searching Tools 990
4.22 Using the Card Catalog 991
4.23 Using Reference Works 993
4.24 Using Dictionaries 995
4.25 Using Thesauruses 996
4.26 Computer-assisted Research 996
On-line Research
CD/ROM and Other Computer Media
4.27 Other Sources of Information 997
4.28 Evaluating Sources 997
4.29 Bibliographies and Bibliography Cards 998
4.30 Paraphrasing and Summarizing 1004
4.31 Informal Note-taking 1005
4.32 Formal Note-taking 1005
4.33 Documenting Sources in a Report 1007
4.34 Footnotes and Endnotes 1009

TEST-TAKING SKILLS
Objective Tests
4.35 Strategies for Taking Objective Tests 1009
4.36 True/False Questions 1010
4.37 Multiple-choice Questions 1010
4.38 Short-answer Questions 1011

Standardized Tests
4.39 Strategies for Taking Standardized Tests 1011
4.40 Analogy Questions 1012
4.41 Sentence-completion Questions 1012
4.42 Grammar, Usage, and Mechanics Questions 1013
4.43 Reading Comprehension Questions 1014
4.44 Synonym and Antonym Questions 1014

Strategies for Taking Essay Tests
4.45 Analyzing an Essay Question 1014
4.46 Organizing an Answer to an Essay Question 1015
4.47 Reviewing an Answer to an Essay Question 1016

5 ESSENTIAL SKILLS: APPLIED ENGLISH/TECH PREP

LETTERS AND FORMS 1017
5.1 Filling Out Forms and Applications 1017
5.2 The Form of a Personal Letter 1019
5.3 The Form of a Business Letter 1020
5.4 Types of Business Letters I 1021
5.5 Types of Business Letters II 1022

WRITING ON THE JOB 1025
5.6 Writing Memoranda 1025
5.7 Technical Writing 1026
5.8 Writing Promotional and Public Relations Copy 1026

HANDBOOK OF LITERARY TERMS 1028

GLOSSARY OF WORDS FOR EVERYDAY USE 1058

INDEX OF TITLES AND AUTHORS 1067

INDEX OF SKILLS 1071

INDEX OF FINE ART 1080

To the Student

Reading Literature

Have you ever become so wrapped up in a movie that when the credits started to roll and the lights came up, you felt a kind of shock? One moment you were in the world on the screen, perhaps identifying with some hero and feeling her joys and sorrows. The next moment you were back in your own world again. The art of the filmmaker transported you from your time and place into another and back again.

When you read a good story, poem, or play, the same sort of transport should take place. The key to reading literature is to use your imagination to take the journey planned for you by the writer. This willingness to extend yourself imaginatively is the most important characteristic that you can have as a reader. Suppose, for example, that you read the following passage in a story:

> Three lions, a male and two females, lay sunning beside what remained of a kill—an eland, perhaps. We approached in the Range Rover. They ignored us. Chico stopped about fifty meters away, and we both took out binoculars for a closer look. The lions lay heavily, dreamily, sated, self-satisfied. A slight breeze ruffled their fur, yellow-brown like the savannah grass in this season between the rains. It was Chico who noticed that the kill wasn't an eland at all, for attached to part of it was, unmistakably, a large black boot.

It is possible to read that passage and comprehend it, intellectually, without having experienced it. However, reading literature is all about having experiences. To read the passage well, you need to picture three lions, to imagine what it might be like to approach them, to see in your mind's eye the yellow grass, to feel the slight breeze, to notice the boot. If you have done that—if you have imagined the scene vividly—then it will have an impact on you. That impact will be its significance—its meaning for you.

Imagine that you have taken a journey. You have hiked up a mountainside in Peru or have wandered though the Valley of the Kings in Egypt. You have gone shopping in the Ginza district of Tokyo or have bounced in a spacesuit over the surface of the moon. After such an experience, you return home a different person. You think about the experience and what it meant to you.

A work of literature is an opportunity to take just such an exotic journey. Using your imagination, you take the writer's trip. You have an experience. Then you reflect on the experience that you had. You think about what you thought and felt, about what the experience meant to you. That reflection is called **reader response.**

When you sit down to read a literary work, remember that your task, at that moment, is not to prepare for a quiz or to get ready for a class discussion. Your task is to use your imagination to have the experience that the writer has prepared for you. Think of the writer as a tour guide to interesting times and places. In those times and places, you will meet fascinating people and have powerful, moving experiences, ones that will enrich your life immeasurably.

Sharing Your Responses with Others

No two people are exactly alike. Because of this wonderful fact, the experience that you have when reading a particular story, poem, or play will be different from the experience had by the student who sits next to you. That's what makes discussing literature with other students interesting. You can share your experiences with others and learn from them. In this course you will have many opportunities to share responses in class discussion and in collaborative projects.

Educating Your Imagination

You might naturally ask, at the beginning of a course such as this, what you stand to gain from it. Two answers to that question have already been suggested: First, reading literature will provide you with many fascinating imaginative experiences. Second, discussing that literature and doing collaborative projects will provide opportunities for sharing with others. A third answer is implicit in the first two: Reading literature and sharing responses with others will educate your imagination. It will train you to think and feel in new ways.

Life is short, opportunities for real-life experience are limited, and events often happen only once, without your having had the chance to practice, first, how you might react to them. Reading literature is a way around all those difficulties. Through reading, you can find out what it might be like to sail around the globe, to march into battle, to fall in love, to lose a friend, to win a great prize, to live in the rain forest, to be faced with a moral dilemma, to confront your greatest fear, to travel backward in time or forward into the future. Writers write because they want to share interesting, valuable experiences with you—the reader. In the process of reading literary works and thinking about your own and others' responses to them, you will exercise your imaginative faculties and grow in ways that might otherwise have been impossible.

Using this Text

This text is first and foremost a literature anthology. The selections in units 1–12 have been chosen both for their historical importance and for their current relevance to the interests of students like you. To assist you in understanding the selections, the authors and editors have created activities that appear before and after the selections. These activities will also help you to develop your abilities in many language arts areas. Most of these activities ask you to refer to the section at the back of the book called the Language Arts Survey. Before doing the activity, you will read a section of the Survey, which will introduce you to some key concepts. Then you will apply what you have learned from the Survey when doing the activity.

Part One

Understanding Literature

UNIT SKILLS OUTLINE

LITERARY SKILLS AND CONCEPTS

- Act, 45
- Alliteration, 16, 18
- Ambiguity, 38
- Anecdote, 59
- Antithesis, 17
- Assonance, 16
- Autobiographies, 52
- Background Information, 41
- Ballad, 4
- Biographies, 52
- Blocking, 45, 50
- Character, 24, 47, 50
- Characterization, 24, 41
- Chiasmus, 17
- Climax, 25, 38
- Comedy, 42
- Complication, 25, 34
- Conflict, 25
- Consonance, 16
- Crisis, 25
- Dénouement, 25
- Dialect, 41
- Dialogue, 12, 44, 47, 50
- Drama, 42
- Dramatic Monologue, 12
- Dramatic Poem, 12
- Elegiac Lyric, 12
- End Rhyme, 18
- Exposition, 25, 27
- Falling Action, 25
- Fiction, 22
- Figurative Language, 41
- Figures of Speech, 16
- Free Verse, 12
- Hyperbole, 16
- Image, 16
- Imagist Poem, 12
- Inciting Incident, 25, 27
- Legend, 4
- Lyric Poem, 12
- Metaphor, 16
- Meter, 13
- Metonymy, 17
- Minor Character, 33
- Mode, 55
- Monologue, 12
- Mood, 25
- Motivation, 24, 41
- Myth, 4
- Narrative Poem, 12
- Nonfiction, 52
- Novel, 22
- Ode, 12
- Onomatopoeia, 16
- Oral Tradition, 4
- Parallelism, 17, 19
- Personification, 17, 19
- Playwright, 44
- Plot, 25
- Poetry, 10
- Properties, 45, 50
- Purpose, 54, 56
- Refrain, 8
- Repetition, 8, 17, 18
- Resolution, 25, 38
- Rhetorical Question, 17
- Rhetorical Technique, 17
- Rhyme, 16
- Rhyme Scheme, 19
- Rhythm, 16
- Scene, 45
- Script, 44
- Set, 45, 50
- Setting, 25
- Short Story, 22
- Simile, 17
- Sonnet, 12, 18, 19
- Sound Effects, 45
- Special Vocabulary, 59
- Spectacle, 45
- Spiritual, 4, 8
- Stage, 45
- Stage Directions, 44, 46, 50
- Stanza, 6, 13
- Symbol, 19
- Synaesthesia, 17
- Synechdoche, 17
- Tall Tale, 4
- Theme, 8, 19, 26, 34, 50
- Tragedy, 42
- Understatement, 17

WRITING SKILLS AND CONCEPTS

- Drafting, 20
- Evaluation, 41
- Prewriting, 9
- Proofreading, 51, 59
- Publishing, 59
- Revision, 41

GRAMMAR, USAGE, AND MECHANICS SKILLS AND CONCEPTS

- Coordinating Conjunctions, 21
- Parts of Speech, 51

OTHER LANGUAGE ARTS SKILLS AND CONCEPTS

- Observing, 23

UNIT 1 GENRES AND TECHNIQUES OF LITERATURE

In the Morning. *Winslow Homer*

GOALS/OBJECTIVES

Studying this unit will enable students to

- recognize and appreciate works of literature in all the major genres
- name, define, and describe major elements and techniques of each of the genres of literature and identify these as employed in a piece of literature
- name and define the different purposes of literature (expressive, informative, persuasive, and literary)
- identify the purpose and mode of a literary work
- employ each step in the process of writing

T is the good reader that makes the good book.

—*Ralph Waldo Emerson*
"Success"

CONNECTIONS ACROSS THE CURRICULUM

Arts and Humanities

- Art Origins, 53
- Demons in Literature, 47
- Performing a Play, 42
- Theories of Acting, 43

Mathematics and Sciences

- Big Dipper, 7
- Déjà Vu, 37

Social Studies

- Host Customs, 32
- Mob Psychology, 47
- Musical Roots, 57
- Religious Training, 33
- Scapegoating, 48
- Slavery, 57
- Truth in Advertising, 34
- The Underground Railroad, 6
- Witch Trials, 46

TEACHING THE MULTIPLE INTELLIGENCES

Logical-Mathematical

- Truth in Advertising, 34

Spatial

- Blocking, 44
- Setting, 37

Musical

- Learning a Chorus, 6
- Listening to Music, 57
- Lyric Meter, 13
- Musical Roots, 57

Kinesthetic

- Blocking, 44
- Performing a Play, 42

Interpersonal

- Discussing Drama, 42
- Dowry, 32
- Host Customs, 32
- Love, 36
- Marriage Customs, 22
- Marriage Factors, 28
- Truth in Advertising, 34
- Witch Trials, 46

ADDITIONAL RESOURCES

READER'S GUIDE
- Selection Worksheet, 1.1

ASSESSMENT PORTFOLIO
- Selection Check Test, 4.1.1
- Selection Test, 4.1.2

ESSENTIAL SKILLS PRACTICE BOOKS
- *Writing,* 1.1–1.34

AUDIOCASSETTE
- "Follow the Drinking Gourd," Track 1

ENRICHMENT ACTIVITIES

- Ask students the following questions: Does anyone in your family tell stories? Does anyone sing songs? What kinds of stories or songs does that person recite? Do the stories or songs have a particular purpose? Do they express a message? If so, what is that purpose or message? Students might collect stories and songs traditionally told in their families to share with the class. Students can then compare the stories from their families to "Follow the Drinking Gourd." In what ways are their purposes and messages different?
- Each student should think of contemporary popular songs that he or she likes. Does the song tell a story? What message does the singer wish to express? Does the singer address one person or a larger audience? Students can work in groups to discuss popular songs that they all know. What kinds of songs do they all know? What do these songs teach or express? In what ways does this group of songs function as an oral tradition?

The Oral Tradition

Are there favorite stories that people in your family like to tell? When you were a child, did people tell you bedtime stories? Did you learn rhymes and jingles and songs from your friends? Have you ever sat around a campfire and told ghost stories? Have you ever heard a minister, priest, rabbi, or teacher tell a story to make a point? If so, then you have experienced the oral tradition.

One pretty good definition of human beings is that we are storytelling creatures. Long before people invented writing, they were telling stories about their gods and heroes and experiences. The best of these stories were passed by word-of-mouth from generation to generation to form the basis of the literature that we know today. Some early stories were told in the form of poems. Some were in the form of songs. Others were in the form of what we would now call prose tales.

The passing of stories, poems, and songs by word-of-mouth from person to person is called oral transmission. The body of work created in this way in a particular culture is called that culture's oral tradition.

The United States is blessed with an enormous diversity in its people. No other country in the world has citizens from so many different races and ethnic backgrounds. The United States cannot, therefore, be said to have a single oral tradition. Rather, it has hundreds of oral traditions with origins in Native American culture and in Europe, Africa, Asia, and other parts of the globe. From the trickster tales of the Plains Indians to Yiddish tales told by European Jewish immigrants, from work songs and spirituals with roots in Africa to Scots-Irish ballads and western tall tales—America offers a feast for the professional folklorist, for students of literature, and for ordinary readers of the many collections of American folk literature.

The following are some common types of oral literature found in the United States:

Myths are stories about heroes and gods. Often myths explain where things came from or how the world took the shape that it has today.

Tall tales are stories with wildly exaggerated elements. Washington Irving's "The Legend of Sleepy Hollow" (Unit 4) is a literary version of a tall tale. Other examples would be the common childhood stories of Pecos Bill, Paul Bunyan, and Annie Oakley.

Legends are stories about famous people. Some are true; others are not. An example of a legend is the story of George Washington chopping down the cherry tree.

Ballads are poems or songs that tell stories. Examples of American ballads include "John Henry" and "Casey Jones."

Spirituals are religious songs from the African-American folk tradition. Examples of spirituals include "Follow the Drinking Gourd" (Unit 1) and "Swing Low, Sweet Chariot" (Unit 6).

Other works commonly found in the oral tradition include **parables, fables, fairy tales, epics,** and **proverbs.** For definitions of these, see the Handbook of Literary Terms.

The Lord Is My Shepherd. *Eastman Johnson. National Museum of American Art, Washington DC/Art Resource, NY*

GOALS/OBJECTIVES

Studying this lesson will enable students to

- enjoy a spiritual
- explain what oral tradition is and what types of literature are commonly transmitted orally
- define the origins and style of a spiritual
- identify the theme of a literary work
- understand the use of repetition and of a refrain in a song
- use prewriting techniques to choose and focus a topic, analyze an intended audience, and gather and organize ideas

Historical Note

The Underground Railroad was a term that referred to a system that helped fugitive slaves reach safety. Many people traveled the routes or lines of the Underground Railroad. Although it was not an actual railroad, it used railroad terminology such as *station* for a stopping place and *conductor* for people who helped the escaping slaves. Many members of the free African-American community, including escaped slave Harriet Tubman, worked diligently for the Underground Railroad.

The Underground Railroad extended throughout fourteen northern states from Maine to Nebraska with its heaviest activities concentrated in Pennsylvania, Ohio, Indiana, New York, and the New England states. It extended into Canada as well, where slaves were safe from fugitive slave hunters. Estimates of the number of fugitive slaves aided by the Underground Railroad range from forty thousand to one hundred thousand.

Cross-curricular Activities

Mathematics and Sciences. The coded message of "Follow the Drinking Gourd" depends upon a basic understanding of using the stars to navigate. Have students investigate how the Big Dipper is employed as a navigational aid in place of a compass. How are the stars in the Big Dipper interpreted to indicate a particular direction ?

Oral Transmission
For African-American slaves in the 1850s, oral transmission was the dominant method for communicating literature. Works were passed from one person to the next by word-of-mouth rather than in written form. Lack of formal education and the need for secrecy were factors in this particular oral tradition.

"Follow the Drinking Gourd"[1]

Anonymous African-American Song of the Underground Railroad

When the sun comes back and the first quail calls,
  Follow the drinking gourd,
For the old man is a-waiting for to carry you to freedom
  If you follow the drinking gourd.

Stanza Form
The chorus, or refrain, is a part of a song that is repeated, usually at regular intervals. Here, the chorus recurs after each verse of the song, reiterating its main idea.

Chorus

Follow the drinking gourd,
  Follow the drinking gourd,
For the old man is a-waiting for to carry you to freedom
  If you follow the drinking gourd.

The river bank will make a very good road,
  The dead trees show you the way,
Left foot, peg foot[2] traveling on
  Follow the drinking gourd.

Repeat **Chorus**

Stanza Form
Sometimes called a stanza, a verse is a division within a poem or song consisting of several lines. Verses often share a common structure, as with the repeated words follow the drinking gourd.

The river ends between two hills,
  Follow the drinking gourd.
There's another river on the other side,
  Follow the drinking gourd.

Repeat **Chorus**

Where the little river meets the great big river,
  Follow the drinking gourd.
The old man is a-waiting for to carry you to freedom
  If you follow the drinking gourd. ■

1. **Drinking Gourd.** Dried, hollowed-out shell of a fruit (a melon or pumpkin, for example) used for dipping water to drink. In this selection, the speaker is using *drinking gourd* as code words for the Big Dipper, a constellation that served as a guide for escaping slaves.
2. **peg foot.** Wooden foot (replacement for a person's foot)

Literary Technique

Poetry was often chanted or sung by a bard to an audience: the bard told a story, and the audience listened. By contrast, a spiritual song often employed a form of call-and-response chant derived from the African musical heritage. Play the recording of "Follow the Drinking Gourd" (Audiocassette, Track 1). Ask your students to listen to the song with their books closed. Ask them to join in by speaking the chorus whenever it appears. It may be necessary to repeat the song two or three times before students can accurately recall the words of the chorus. Discuss with them the process of memorizing the chorus. How did they learn it? How did they know when to join in? Did they also memorize other parts of the song in the process of memorizing the chorus?

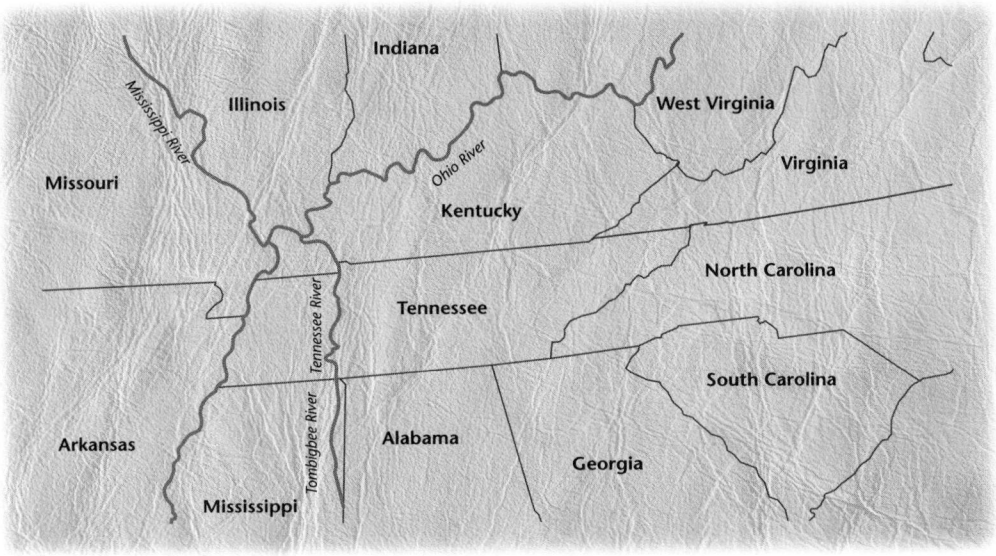

Responding to the Selection

What do you think it would be like to run for your life and for your freedom? How might communicating through songs help you cope with the stresses of your journey? Conversely, how might the need to communicate in code, for example by calling the guiding Big Dipper a "drinking gourd," burden you?

Answers to Selection Check Test 4.1.1

EX. Who is the author of "Follow the Drinking Gourd"?
The author is unknown.

1. What does the "drinking gourd" signify in this song?
The drinking gourd is a constellation, the Big Dipper.

2. How does the singer indicate the time of year for following the drinking gourd?
The singer uses the phrase, "When the sun comes back and the first quail calls."

3. Who will help the fugitive slaves to escape?
The "old man" will help them to escape.

4. What is the road that the escaping slaves should follow?
The slaves should follow the riverbank.

5. Where does the river end?
The river ends "between two hills."

Responding to the Selection

If students have difficulty imagining how songs affected the experiences of escaping slaves, suggest that they reflect upon the role popular music plays in their own lives. Ask them to consider what effects the music they share with their peers has on them.

Answers for Reviewing the Selection

RECALLING

1. African-American slaves are singing this song. They are traveling northward to escape slavery. The slaves are supposed to go when "the sun comes back and the first quail calls." They should travel at night when they can follow the "drinking gourd," or the Big Dipper.

2. The "old man" waits for the travelers.

3. The escaping slaves can use the Big Dipper to guide them northward. The "dead trees" and the rivers help show them the way.

4. The rivers lead the travelers to freedom in the northern states.

INTERPRETING

Responses will vary. Possible responses are given.

5. The image of the "drinking gourd," meaning the Big Dipper, is repeated numerous times in the song (lines 2, 4, 5, 6; 8, 12, 14, 16, 18, 20) as the means by which the escaping slaves can find their way northward. The Big Dipper is referred to in code so that the slaves can hide from their owners both their intentions to escape and the route they will follow. Spring is suggested by the opening line, "When the sun comes back and the first quail calls."

6. The "old man" who is waiting to help the escaped slaves may guide the slaves through unfamiliar territory. He could be a former slave himself, or an abolitionist who helps slaves find their way to freedom in the North.

(cont.)

ANSWERS FOR REVIEWING THE SELECTION (CONT.)

7. The journey undertaken by the escaping slaves is influenced by various natural events or elements, including the time of year (" When the sun comes back," line 1), the time of day (the Big Dipper appears at night), and the landscape ("The river bank," line 9; "The dead trees," line 10; "two hills," line 13; and "the great big river," line 17). They must keep "traveling on" (line 11) because the journey on foot from the South to the free North is a long, arduous one.

8. The "other side" may refer directly to the "two hills" (line 13) or metaphorically to the free North. The "great big river" (line 17) may refer to the Ohio River or the Mississippi River.

SYNTHESIZING

Responses will vary. Possible responses are given.

9. As suggested by the song, the challenges facing escaping slaves are numerous. The escaping slaves must contend with the difficulties of following an unfamiliar trail through the wilderness under cover of darkness. In addition, the song implies that the journey to freedom will be long and arduous, requiring patience, strength, and endurance. While facing these physical trials, the escaping slaves must also live with the constant fear of possible recapture and of the punishment that would ensue.

10. Slaves escaping from Mississippi or Alabama may have followed the Tombigbee and Tennessee Rivers northward, then continued along the Ohio River westward until it met the Mississippi River, which they could follow north into states without slavery. Seeing the "drinking gourd" in the sky may have helped escaping slaves visualize a path to freedom as a constant presence in the night sky. During a journey fraught with uncertainty, physical hardship, and constant danger, the "drinking gourd" may have served as a continual reminder that freedom was possible if they managed to endure.

Reviewing the Selection

RECALLING

1. Who is singing this song? Where are they going and why? When are the travelers supposed to journey?
2. Who waits for the travelers?
3. How can the travelers use natural elements to help them find the way? What element recurs to guide them?
4. Where do the rivers lead the travelers?

INTERPRETING

5. What overriding image is used to guide the travelers toward their destination? Why is this signpost not openly identified? What time of year might be suggested by these natural events?
6. How will the person who waits help the travelers? Who might he be?
7. What forces influence the journey of the travelers? Why must they keep "traveling on"?
8. What might "the other side" refer to? What might the "great big river" be?

SYNTHESIZING

9. What can you infer about the challenges facing escaping slaves from your reading of "Follow the Drinking Gourd"?
10. How does the map accompanying the selection help you visualize the path taken by the travelers? In what ways do you think seeing the "drinking gourd" in the sky helped the travelers visualize their path to freedom?

Understanding Literature (Questions for Discussion)

1. **Theme.** A **theme** is a central idea in a literary work. What do you think is the theme of "Follow the Drinking Gourd"?
2. **Repetition. Repetition** is the use, again, of a sound, word, phrase, sentence, or other element. Through repetition writers return to or focus on their main points. What phrase is repeated again and again in "Follow the Drinking Gourd"?
3. **Spiritual.** A **spiritual** is a song, often but not always religious in context. The style originated in the South, among slaves who needed to express their sorrow and frustration in a nonthreatening forum. Like many ballads, spirituals may tell a story or contain a message. "Follow the Drinking Gourd" is no exception. Taught to slaves by a one-legged sailor named Peg Leg Joe, the song had a message for freedom hidden in its words. What is the message of "Follow the Drinking Gourd"?
4. **Refrain.** A **refrain,** or **chorus,** is a line or group of lines repeated in a poem or song. A refrain may emphasize an important idea. What is the refrain in "Follow the Drinking Gourd"? In what two ways is it used throughout the song?

ANSWERS FOR UNDERSTANDING LITERATURE

▶ See the evaluation forms for discussion, active listening, and oral communication, *Assessment Portfolio,* 7.11–7.14.

Responses will vary. Possible responses are given.

1. Theme. One theme of this song is that through endurance and constant focus on a single objective, escaping slaves can succeed in overcoming obstacles and find their way to freedom against overwhelming odds.

2. Repetition. The phrase "Follow the drinking gourd" is repeated throughout the song. The repetition of this phrase reinforces the song's theme: in order to achieve the goal of freedom, escaping slaves must channel all of their energies into the journey northward.

3. Spiritual. The song hides a dual message about escape. It offers hope and encouragement to those who choose to attempt the escape to the North, but more importantly, it conceals directions for the fugitive slaves to follow to the free lands.

(cont.)

The Process of Writing: Prewriting

A Narrative Message. In addition to entertaining readers, a work of literature may include a message from the writer. In a persuasive or explanatory essay, that message may be openly stated and argued. In a fictional work, such as a short story or poem, the message may be primarily implied or suggested.

Think about a message you would like to share with readers. Then consider what literary form might be most effective for communicating that message. Some possibilities are

- a critical essay
- a concrete poem
- a morality play
- a ballad or folk song
- an epic

Read about these forms, and others that you may consider, in the Handbook of Literary Terms.

Before beginning, obtain a general introduction to the writing process by reading the Language Arts Survey, 1.1–1.34. Then use the following steps to guide you through the planning and prewriting process.

STEP 1 Reread the Language Arts Survey, 1.5, "Choosing and Focusing a Topic." Use the techniques discussed to focus in on your desired message. What is it you want to say in your literary work? Reflect on the literary forms you explored above. Make a final choice that suits your message.

STEP 2 Using the strategies suggested in the Language Arts Survey, 1.7, "Choosing and Analyzing an Audience," shape your theme to the level of knowledge and interest you expect to find in your audience. You might want to work with a peer to test your assumptions about your audience. Refer to the Language Arts Survey, 1.26, "Discussion," for guidance in your conversation.

STEP 3

Fiction Forms

- If you have chosen a form of fiction, consider who your characters will be. After reading the Language Arts Survey, 1.17, "Clustering," create a character cluster in which you show all the important characters and their relationships to one another. In each cell of the diagram, list three types of character attributes: physical appearance, actions, and words.

  With the characters in place, you need to track the narrative events. Consider using a story map to block out important story events. Such a map enables you to experiment with your story's plot before beginning to write. See the Language Arts Survey, 1.21, "Story Maps," for more information.
- For fiction, chronological order is often the clearest sequence. This is discussed in the Language Arts Survey, 1.34, "Organizing Ideas: Chronological Order." If you have any questions about the sequence, use your story map to explore the impact of rearranging story events.

Nonfiction Forms

- If your form is nonfiction, such as an essay, you may want to create an outline of your major ideas. Read the Language Arts Survey, 1.32–1.33, on outlining before you begin.
- Essays often lend themselves to classification or cause-and-effect organization. If these are appropriate to your theme and audience, study the Language Arts Survey, 1.34, "Organizing Ideas," on these organizational approaches.

STEP 4 Review your prewriting notes and confirm the decisions you have made. Save all your notes for later reference in a writing assignment.

Answers for Understanding Literature (cont.)

4. Refrain. The refrain of the song (lines 5–8) is used both to give slaves directions for the path to escape and to convey the message that if they do escape, they will find help from abolitionists along the way.

The Process of Writing: Prewriting

Unit 1 contains a long writing assignment designed to introduce students to the process of writing. The assignment is divided into separate lessons, as follows:

- Prewriting: page 9
- Drafting: page 20
- Evaluating and Revising: page 41
- Proofreading and Publishing: page 59

If the various parts of the assignment are done as encountered in the unit, they will be properly spaced to give students time to reflect on each stage in the writing process before going on to the next.

Many students will balk at so large an undertaking as writing a narrative message. However, the task is well within most students' reach if sufficient guidance is given for each step in the process. With thorough prewriting notes, students will be surprised at their own ability to produce substantial narratives.

Have students do the prewriting steps one at a time. You may choose to have them do these steps in collaboration with their classmates.

Step 1: Students might experiment with different techniques described in the Language Arts Survey, 1.5, "Choosing and Focusing a Topic." When students have sufficiently narrowed their topics, you may wish to discuss the forms of writing listed on page 9 as well as other forms in which students are interested to help them choose appropriate forms.

Step 2: Suggest that students complete the activity in the Language Arts Survey, 1.7, "Choosing and Analyzing an Audience," to help them understand the differences in audiences and the importance of properly assessing an audience.

(cont.)

The Process of Writing: Prewriting (cont.)

Step 3: After students complete Step 3, you may wish to schedule conferences with them to discuss their writing plans. At this stage you can review their prewriting materials and make suggestions that will save them time and effort during the drafting stage.

Evaluating and Prewriting: At all times when evaluating writing, and especially for this first assignment, it is important to be encouraging to students. Do not worry at this stage about spelling, grammar, usage, and mechanics, and do not penalize students for ideas that are as yet derivative or underdeveloped. Instead, evaluate on the basis of whether the prewriting was done and offer helpful suggestions when appropriate.

ADDITIONAL RESOURCES

READER'S GUIDE
- Selection Worksheet, 1.2

ASSESSMENT PORTFOLIO
- Selection Check Test, 4.1.3
- Selection Test, 4.1.4

ESSENTIAL SKILLS PRACTICE BOOKS
- *Writing,* 1.35–1.42

ENRICHMENT ACTIVITIES

Ask students to work in groups and consider the various definitions of poetry offered on page 10. Have them use these definitions to formulate their own, more elaborate definitions of poetry. Which examples do they consider essential to the definition of poetry? Which strike them as unnecessary? Encourage them to add their own ideas about poetry to these definitions. Have each group present its collective definition to the class.

SUPPORT FOR LEP STUDENTS

You may wish to discuss the form of a sonnet with students before they read this poem. A review of the following literary techniques may also be helpful: rhyme, parallelism, personification, symbol, theme, repetition, and alliteration.

Poetry

Recognizing a poem when you read one is a lot easier than describing what a poem is. That's because poetry comes in a wide variety of forms. Some poems rhyme and have regular rhythmical patterns. Others do not. Some poems fill one or more whole books. Others are only one or two lines long. Many poems depend on special devices of sound such as onomatopoeia and alliteration, and many use special techniques of meaning such as metaphor and symbolism, but some are simply designs or word pictures, like this concrete poem:

O O
B A L L N

One thing that all poems have in common is that they use language in special ways to communicate thoughts or feelings. That's a useful definition, but not a particularly interesting one. Here are some interesting definitions of poetry put forward by important literary figures from the past:

Some Famous Definitions of Poetry

Poetry is . . .

"the spontaneous overflow of powerful feelings."
—William Wordsworth

"the best words in the best order."
—Samuel Taylor Coleridge

"the record of the best and happiest moments of the happiest and best minds."
—Percy Bysshe Shelley

"[language that] strike[s] the reader as a wording of his own highest thoughts, and appear[s] almost a remembrance."
—John Keats

"musical thought."
—Thomas Carlyle

"conceived and composed in the soul."
—Matthew Arnold

"a mixture of common sense, which not all have, with an uncommon sense, which very few have."
—John Masefield

"the supreme fiction."
—Wallace Stevens

"what gets lost in translation."
—Robert Frost

"not an assertion of truth, but the making of that truth more fully real to us."
—T. S. Eliot

The United States has produced many fine poets, including Phillis Wheatley, Henry Wadsworth Longfellow, Ralph Waldo Emerson, Walt Whitman, Edgar Lee Masters, Edwin Arlington Robinson, Robert Frost, Wallace Stevens, William Carlos Williams, Amy Lowell, Ezra Pound, Marianne Moore, Edna St. Vincent Millay, T. S. Eliot, E. E. Cummings, Langston Hughes, Gwendolyn Brooks, Elizabeth Bishop, and many others. Here's how one of the greatest of the American poets defined her craft:

"If I read a book and it makes my whole body so cold no fire can ever warm me, I know that it is poetry. If I feel physically as if the top of my head were taken off, I know that it is poetry. Is there any other way?"
—Emily Dickinson

The Hilltop. *Frank Weston Benson, 1905. Malden Public Library*

GOALS/OBJECTIVES

Studying this lesson will enable students to

- enjoy and appreciate a poem
- describe some characteristics of poetry
- use drafting techniques to develop prewriting notes into a coherent narrative
- determine rhyme scheme
- identify examples of parallelism and explain the purpose of the technique
- define *personification* and *symbol* and identify the use of each technique in writing
- use coordinating conjunctions correctly

Art Note

Frank Weston Benson (1862–1951) was a painter and a pioneer of American Impressionism. Benson was born in Salem, Massachusetts, to a prominent seafaring family. He received his formal training at the Museum School in Boston and at the Académie Julian in Paris. Many of his paintings are outdoor, sun-filled portraits of his family as well as coastal, fishing, and hunting scenes. *The Hilltop* garnered Benson a gold prize for painting at the St. Louis Exposition of 1904. The painting depicts two of Benson's children, Eleanor and George, on a hill in North Haven above the ocean. The dazzling portrait captures the youthful exuberance of many of Benson's works.

Additional Questions and Activities

The following suggestions will help students to explore different types of poetry or different poets.

- Students may wish to page through poetry anthologies noting poems that they enjoy. Ask students if they prefer a particular style or form of poetry.
- Students might focus on United States poets and begin by researching the ones cited on page 10.
- Students may wish to work in groups to discuss several poems. Each student can select a poem and read it to the group. Suggest that students refer to pages 12–17 for terminology to use in their discussion.

LITERARY GENRES

Other examples found in the text include the following:

NARRATIVE POEM

"Home Burial," 528
"The Death of the Hired Man," 602

SONNET

"Euclid Alone Has Looked on Beauty Bare," page 605
"Yet Do I Marvel," 588

FREE VERSE LYRIC

"The Secret," 806
"To Black Women," 824

ELEGIAC LYRIC

"After great pain, a formal feeling comes—," page 348
"Annabel Lee," 348

IMAGIST POEM

"Ars Poetica," 579
"Storm Ending," 606

ADDITIONAL QUESTIONS AND ACTIVITIES

Students can host a poetry reading of their favorite poems by other writers or original poems written by the students. Students should practice reading their poems before the actual presentation. Students may also wish to discuss the reasons for their selections.

Elements of Poetry

GENRES, OR TYPES, OF POETRY

Narrative Poetry. A **narrative poem** is a verse that tells a story. Examples of narrative poems include Edgar Allan Poe's "The Raven" (unit 5), and Edwin Arlington Robinson's "Mr. Flood's Party" (unit 8).

Dramatic Poetry. A **dramatic poem** is a verse that relies heavily on dramatic elements such as **monologue** (speech by a single character) or **dialogue** (conversation involving two or more characters). Often dramatic poems are narratives as well. In other words, they often tell stories. A **dramatic monologue** is a poem that presents the speech of a single character in a dramatic situation, often a moment of crisis or self-revelation. The speech is one side of an imagined conversation. See Edgar Lee Masters's "Lucinda Matlock" (unit 8), Edwin Arlington Robinson's "Mr. Flood's Party" (unit 8), and Robert Frost's "Home Burial" (unit 8).

Lyric Poetry. A **lyric poem** is a highly musical verse that expresses the emotions of a speaker. There are many types of lyric poems. Among the most common types are the following:

Sonnet. A **sonnet** is a fourteen-line poem that follows one of a number of different rhyme schemes. Many sonnets deal with the subject of love. See Edna St. Vincent Millay's "Sonnet XXX" (unit 1).

Ode. An **ode** is a lofty lyric poem on a serious theme. William Cullen Bryant's "Thanatopsis" (unit 5) is an ode.

Free Verse Lyric. Free verse, or *vers libre*, is poetry that avoids use of regular rhyme, rhythm, meter, or division into stanzas. The first great writer of free verse in the United States was Walt Whitman. See his "Song of Myself" (unit 7). See also T. S. Eliot's "The Love Song of J. Alfred Prufrock" (unit 8), Langston Hughes's "The Negro Speaks of Rivers" (unit 8), and Li-Young Lee's "A Story" (unit 12).

Elegiac Lyric. An **elegiac lyric** expresses a speaker's feelings of loss, often because of the death of a loved one or friend. See Walt Whitman's "When Lilacs Last in the Dooryard Bloom'd" (unit 6) and John Crowe Ransom's "Bells for John Whiteside's Daughter" (unit 8).

Imagist Poem. An **imagist poem** is a lyric that presents a single vivid picture in words. See Ezra Pound's "In a Station of the Metro" (unit 8), William Carlos Williams's "The Red Wheelbarrow" (unit 8), and Amy Lowell's "A Lover" (unit 8).

Techniques of Poetry: Meter and Stanza Form

Metrical verse follows a set rhythmical pattern. **Free verse**, or *vers libre*, does not. Instead, it follows the rhythms of ordinary speech.

Meter. The **meter** of a poem is its rhythmical pattern. English verse usually is described as being made up of rhythmical units called **feet.** A **foot** consists of some combination of **weakly stressed** (⏑) and **strongly stressed** (/) syllables, as follows:

TYPE OF FOOT	PATTERN	EXAMPLE
iamb, or **iambic foot**	⏑ /	⏑ / afraid
trochee, or **trochaic foot**	/ ⏑	/ ⏑ freedom
anapest, or **anapestic foot**	⏑ ⏑ /	⏑ ⏑ / in a flash
dactyl, or **dactylic foot**	/ ⏑ ⏑	/ ⏑ ⏑ feverish
spondee, or **spondaic foot**	/ /	/ / baseball

Some writers on meter also use the term **pyrrhee**, or **pyrrhic foot**, to describe a foot with two weak stresses, as follows:

anapest				**pyrrhee**	
⏑	⏑	/	|	⏑	⏑
un	re	li	|	a	ble

Additional Questions and Activities

- Ask students to find examples of free verse and metrical verse poems. Students can then analyze the meter of the poems. Students might prefer to analyze and describe the meter of the lyrics of a favorite song.
- Students can analyze the meter of their names, the name of the town or city in which they live, and the name of their school. Then have students think of their own examples of the different types of metrical feet.

The following terms are used to describe the number of feet in a line of poetry:

TERM	NUMBER OF FEET	EXAMPLE
monometer	one foot	⏑ / Today ⏑ / We play
dimeter	two feet	/ ⏑ ⏑ / ⏑ Following | closely / ⏑ / ⏑ Through the | forest
trimeter	three feet	⏑ / ⏑ / ⏑ / God shed | His light | on thee
tetrameter	four feet	/ ⏑ / ⏑ / ⏑ / ⏑ In the | greenest | of our | valleys
pentameter	five feet	⏑ / ⏑ / ⏑ / ⏑ / A vast | re pub | lic famed| through ev | ⏑ / ry clime
hexameter or Alexandrine	six feet	⏑ / ⏑ / ⏑ / ⏑ / In o | ther's eyes | we see | ourselves | ⏑ / ⏑ / the truth | to tell

A complete description of the meter of a line includes both the term for the type of foot that predominates in the line and the term for the number of feet in the line. The most common meters in English are **iambic tetrameter** and **iambic pentameter**.

Stanza Form. A **stanza** is a group of lines in a poem. The following are some common types of stanza:

COUPLET
(two lines)

We dance round in a ring and suppose,
But the Secret sits in the middle and knows.

—Robert Frost, "The Secret Sits"

TRIPLET OR TERCET
(three lines)

Children picking up our bones
Will never know that these were once
As quick as foxes on the hill;

—Wallace Stevens, "A Postcard from the Volcano"

QUATRAIN
(four lines)

By the rude bridge that arched the flood,
Their flag to April's breeze unfurl'd,
Here once the embattled farmers stood,
And fired the shot heard round the world.

—Ralph Waldo Emerson, "Hymn Sung at the Completion of the Concord Monument, April 19, 1836"

QUINTAIN
(five lines)

Gaunt the shadow on your green,
Shenandoah!
The cut is on the crown
(Lo, John Brown),
And the stabs shall heal no more.

—Herman Melville, "The Portent"

SESTET
(six lines)

Once upon a midnight dreary, while I pondered, weak and weary,
Over many a quaint and curious volume of forgotten lore,
While I nodded, nearly napping, suddenly there came a tapping,
As of someone gently rapping, rapping at my chamber door.
"'Tis some visitor," I muttered, "tapping at my chamber door—
Only this, and nothing more."

—Edgar Allan Poe, "The Raven"

HEPTASTICH
(seven lines)

In Heaven a spirit doth dwell
"Whose heart-strings are a lute;"
None sing so wildly well
As the angel Israfel,
And the giddy stars (so legends tell)
Ceasing their hymns, attend the spell
Of his voice, all mute.

—Edgar Allan Poe, "Israfel"

OCTAVE
(eight lines)

The God who made New Hampshire
Taunted the lofty land
With little men;—
Small bat and wren
House in the oak:—
If earth-fire cleave
The upheaved land, and bury the folk,
The southern crocodile would grieve.

—Ralph Waldo Emerson, "Ode, Inscribed to W. H. Channing"

LITERARY TECHNIQUE

Stanza. Ask students to find other examples of these stanza forms in this book.

- Other poems containing **couplets** include Phillis Wheatley's "To S. M., a Young African Painter, on Seeing His Works" (page 165), William Carlos Williams's "The Red Wheelbarrow" (page 548), and Archibald MacLeish's "Ars Poetica" (page 579).
- Wallace Stevens's "The Snow Man" (page 534) contains **triplets.**
- Other poems containing **quatrains** include John Greenleaf Whittier's "Telling the Bees" (page 312), Ralph Waldo Emerson's "Concord Hymn" (page 317) and "Brahma" (page 346); Emily Dickinson's "This is my letter to the World," "The Soul selects her own Society—," "Because I could not stop for Death," and "I heard a Fly buzz—when I died—" (page 326); E. E. Cummings's "somewhere i have never travelled,gladly beyond" (page 584); and Arna Bontemps's "A Black Man Talks of Reaping" (page 599).
- Edgar Allan Poe's "To Helen" (page 348) contains **quintains.**
- Other poems containing **sestets** include Edward Taylor's "Huswifery" (page 125), Henry Wadsworth Longfellow's "The Village Blacksmith" (page 306), Edgar Allan Poe's "The Raven" (page 338) and "Annabel Lee" (page 348), and Countee Cullen's "Any Human to Another" (page 605).
- Other poems containing **hepastichs** include Oliver Wendell Holmes's "The Chambered Nautilus" (page 296) and William Stafford's "A Story That Could Be True" (page 797).
- Other poems containing **octaves** include James Russell Lowell's "Stanzas on Freedom" (page 301), Oliver Wendell Holmes's "Old Ironsides" (page 346), Walt Whitman's "O Captain! My Captain!" (page 405), and Edwin Arlington Robinson's "Mr. Flood's Party" (page 516).

Literary Techniques

Internal Rhyme. Internal rhyme is used in Edgar Allan Poe's "The Raven," line 61, page 341 ("Wondering at the stillness **broken** by reply so aptly **spoken**").

Slant Rhyme. Slant rhyme is used in Emily Dickinson's "The Soul selects her own Society—," lines 6 and 8 ("**Gate**" and "**mat**").

Alliteration. Alliteration is used in Henry Wadsworth Longfellow's "The Village Blacksmith," line 27, page 308 ("**He h**ears the **p**arson **p**ray and **p**reach").

Assonance. Assonance is used in Emily Dickinson's "Because I could not stop for Death—," line 5, page 332 ("We slowly drove—He knew no haste") and in line 11 ("Gazing Grain").

Consonance. Consonance is used in Robert Hayden's "Those Winter Sundays," line 3, page 794 ("then with cra**cked** hands that a**ched**").

Onomatopoeia. Onomatopoeia is used in Edgar Lee Masters's "Petit the Poet," line 1, page 513 ("Seeds in a dry pod, **tick, tick, tick**").

Hyperbole. Hyperbole is used in Anne Bradstreet's "To My Dear and Loving Husband," lines 5–7, page 115 ("I prize thy love more than whole mines of gold/Or all the riches that the East doth hold,/My love is such that rivers cannot quench").

Techniques of Poetry: Sound*

Rhythm. The **rhythm** is the pattern of beats or stresses in a line of verse or prose. A regular rhythmic pattern is called a **meter.**

Rhyme. Rhyme is the repetition of sounds at the ends of words. The following are some types of rhyme:

> **End Rhyme. End rhyme** is rhyme that occurs at the ends of lines.
>
> **Internal Rhyme. Internal rhyme** is the use of rhyming words within lines.
>
> **Slant Rhyme.** A **slant rhyme**, half rhyme, near rhyme, or off rhyme is the substitution of assonance or consonance for true rhyme. The pairs *world/boiled* and *bear/bore* are examples.

Alliteration. Alliteration is the repetition of initial consonant sounds. Edgar Allan Poe's "The Raven" contains the following example of alliteration: "And the silken sad uncertain rustling of each purple curtain."

Assonance. Assonance is the repetition of vowel sounds in stressed syllables that end with different consonant sounds, as in "weak and weary," also in "The Raven."

Consonance. Consonance is the repetition of a consonant sound preceded by a different vowel sound, as in *wind* and *sound.* This technique is also known as **slant rhyme.**

Onomatopoeia. Onomatopoeia is the use of words or phrases that sound like the things to which they refer. Examples include the words *pow, caw, clink,* and *murmur.*

Techniques of Poetry: Meaning*

Image. An **image** is a word or phrase that names something that can be seen, heard, touched, tasted, or smelled. A group of images that together create a given emotion in a reader or listener is called, in a phrase coined by T. S. Eliot, an **objective correlative.**

Figures of Speech. Figures of speech, or **tropes,** are expressions that have more than a literal meaning. The following are examples of common figures of speech:

> **Hyperbole.** A **hyperbole** is an exaggeration made for rhetorical effect.
>
> **Metaphor.** A **metaphor** is a figure of speech in which one thing is spoken or written about as if it were another. This figure of speech invites the reader to make a comparison between the two things: the writer's actual subject, the **tenor** of the metaphor, and another thing to which the subject is likened, the **vehicle** of the metaphor. In

*Note: These techniques are used commonly, but not exclusively, in poetry.

Emily Dickinson's metaphor "'Hope' is the thing with feathers—/That perches in the soul" the tenor is hope. The vehicle is a bird. **Personification** and **simile** are types of metaphor.

Metonymy. Metonymy is the naming of an object associated with a thing in place of the name of the thing itself. Speaking of *the White House* when one means *the president of the United States* is an example.

Personification. Personification is a figure of speech in which an idea, animal, or thing is described as if it were a person. *Night embraces us* is an example.

Simile. A **simile** is a comparison using *like* or *as*. T. S. Eliot's description of evening "spread out against the sky/Like a patient etherized upon a table" is an example.

Synaesthesia. Synaesthesia is a figure of speech that combines in a single expression images related to two or more different senses. Archibald MacLeish's line "Dumb/As old medallions to the thumb," which combines the senses of sound and touch, is an example of synaesthesia.

Synechdoche. A **synechdoche** is a figure of speech in which the name of part of something is used in place of the name of the whole, or vice versa. The use of *hired hands* for *laborers* is an example.

Understatement. An **understatement** is an ironic expression in which something of importance is emphasized by being spoken of as though it were not important.

Rhetorical Techniques. A **rhetorical technique** is an extraordinary but literal use of language to achieve a particular effect. The following rhetorical techniques are commonly used in poetry:

Antithesis. Antithesis is a rhetorical technique in which words, phrases, or ideas are strongly contrasted, often by means of repetition of grammatical structures. An example is Ralph Waldo Emerson's description of the taunting of "lofty land/With little men."

Chiasmus. A **chiasmus** is a rhetorical technique in which the order of occurrence of words or phrases is reversed, as in the traditional line "We can weather changes, but we can't change the weather."

Parallelism. Parallelism is a rhetorical technique in which a writer emphasizes the equal value or weight of two or more ideas by expressing them in the same grammatical form, as in Abraham Lincoln's phrase "of the people, by the people, for the people."

Repetition. Repetition is the use, again, of a sound, word, phrase, sentence, or other element. Walt Whitman used repetition in the line "I celebrate myself, and sing myself,/And what I assume, you shall assume."

Rhetorical Question. A **rhetorical question** is one asked for effect but not meant to be answered because the answer is clear from the context, as in Walt Whitman's "Has any one supposed it lucky to be born?"

Additional Questions and Activities

- **Image.** Have students work in small groups to formulate images that correspond to each of the five senses. Remind them that an image need only be presented in a word or a short phrase, not a complete sentence. Encourage them to generate four to five images for each sense, and have them keep a list of these images.
- **Simile** and **Metaphor.** Have students take the list of images that they have generated and transform each image into a simile and a metaphor. Explain the term *dead metaphor* (see the entry on *dead metaphor* in the Handbook of Literary Terms) to students, and encourage them to come up with both original similes and metaphors as well as dead metaphors. Have each group present its favorite similes and metaphors and discuss how these similes and metaphors transform the meaning of the original image. Elicit discussion comparing the dead metaphors and original metaphors suggested by the students, asking them to consider which are more powerful and why.
- **Metonymy, Synaesthesia,** and **Synechdoche.** Have students perform the same exercise with these figures of speech using their original lists of images.

Historical Note

Point out to students that many sonnets, especially those concerned with a romantic theme, are structured so as to first of all present an argument or an apparently irresolvable difficulty and then, beginning somewhere in the second part of the poem, to resolve the dilemma put forth in the first part. The shift from the argument to the resolution is sometimes called the turn. The Petrarchan sonnet consists of an octave (eight lines) composed of two quatrains (four lines each) followed by a sestet (six lines). The Elizabethan or Shakespearean sonnet consists of three quatrains and a concluding couplet (two lines). Often, the turn in a Petrarchan sonnet comes between the octave and the sestet, the argument established in the first eight lines being resolved in the final six. By contrast, the turn in a Shakespearean sonnet often occurs between the third quatrain and the concluding couplet. Discuss with students the argument formulated in the first part of Millay's sonnet, and ask them to identify where the turn takes place in this poem. How does Millay develop her argument from one quatrain to the next? Does the argumentative development of her sonnet follow Shakespearean structure, or does a turn occur in line 9 as well as in line 13? What rhetorical techniques does Millay use to signal the turn from her argument to the resolution? What effect does she achieve by shifting from the general to the personal? How does the rhyme scheme, and especially the use of a closing couplet, add to the force of her message?

Vocabulary in Context

• Mary's resolution to continue despite her pain was an indication of her courage.

Sonnet

A sonnet is a fourteen-line rhyming poem, often on the subject of love.

End Rhyme

The words drink, *and* sink *are examples of end rhymes, rhymes that appear at the ends of lines.*

Repetition

The repetition of the words rise and sink *emphasizes a drowning person's continual struggles and, possibly, the rise and fall of anyone's fortunes in life.*

Alliteration

The repetition of p *and* r *sounds at the beginnings of words are examples of alliteration.*

"Sonnet XXX"

Edna St. Vincent Millay

Love is not all: it is not meat nor drink
Nor slumber nor a roof against the rain;
Nor yet a floating spar[1] to men that sink
And rise and sink and rise and sink and sink again;
Love can not fill the thickened lung with breath,
Nor clean the blood, nor set the fractured bone;
Yet many a man is making friends with death
Even as I speak, for lack of love alone.
It well may be that in a difficult hour,
Pinned down by pain and moaning for release,
Or nagged by want[2] past resolution's power,
I might be driven to sell your love for peace,
Or trade the memory of this night for food.
It well may be. I do not think I would. ■

1. **spar.** Any pole supporting or extending the sail of a ship; here, the parts of a ship that can be used to keep sailors afloat after the ship has wrecked
2. **want.** Physical need

Edna St. Vincent Millay

Words for Everyday Use: **res • o • lu • tion** (rez´ə lōō´ shən) *n.,* determined state of mind; faithfulness to some person or idea

Answers to Selection Check Test 4.1.3

EX. How many lines does a sonnet have?
A sonnet has fourteen lines.

1. What does the speaker say is not all?
Love is not all.

2. What is love not to men that sink?
Love is not a floating spar.

3. What are many men doing for lack of love?
Many men are "making friends with death."

4. What might cause the speaker to forsake love?
Pain or want might cause the speaker to forsake love.

5. What might the speaker be driven to do?
The speaker might be driven to sell love for peace or the memory of the night with his or her beloved for food.

Responding to the Selection

Do you believe that love is as important as food for a hungry person or release for a person in pain? Discuss this question with your classmates.

Reviewing the Selection

RECALLING

1. In lines 1–4, what does the speaker say that love is not?
2. According to lines 5 and 6, what can love not do?
3. According to lines 7 and 8, what are many men doing?
4. According to lines 9–13, what might move the speaker to sell his or her love for peace? to trade the memory of that love for food?

INTERPRETING

5. According to lines 1 and 2, what other things does a person need besides love? In what ways do people, in the course of their lives, "rise and sink and rise and sink and sink again"?
6. What do the circumstances mentioned in lines 5 and 6 have in common? What needs do people sometimes have that cannot be met by love?
7. According to line 8, what might drive a person to "make friends with death"?
8. What question does the speaker consider in lines 9–14 of the poem? How does he or she answer that question?

SYNTHESIZING

9. Does the speaker believe that love is a fundamental need? Support your answer with evidence from the poem.
10. What do you think are people's most basic needs? Make a list of these. Is your list the same as the speaker's? How does it differ?

Understanding Literature (Questions for Discussion)

1. **Sonnet.** A **sonnet** is a fourteen-line poem that follows one of a number of different rhyme schemes. The **English, Elizabethan,** or **Shakespearean sonnet** can be divided into four parts: three quatrains, or four-line sections, and a final couplet, or two-line section. What is the subject of the first quatrain of "Sonnet XXX"? of the second quatrain? of the third quatrain? of the concluding couplet? Paraphrase each of these sections of the poem by stating their main ideas in your own words.

RESPONDING TO THE SELECTION

If students have difficulty assessing the importance of love, have them begin by listing the things that their loved ones do for them or provide for them, and then ask them to imagine how their lives would be different without these kinds of material and emotional supports.

ANSWERS FOR REVIEWING THE SELECTION

RECALLING

1. The speaker declares that love is not one of the traditional necessities of life: food, sleep, or shelter; nor is it something that can rescue a person in a time of great peril.
2. Love cannot fill a person's lungs with air, cannot remove disease or impurities from a person's blood, and cannot heal a person's injuries.
3. Many men are in the process of dying because they do not have love in their lives.
4. Pain or want might move the speaker to sell his or her love for peace or to trade the memory of that love for food.

INTERPRETING

Responses will vary. Possible responses are given.

5. In addition to love, people need food, drink, sleep, and shelter from the elements. People "rise and sink and rise and sink and sink again" as they alternately experience success and failure in their lives.
6. These circumstances all relate to physical needs or difficulties. People sometimes need medicines or the assistance of doctors to heal their bodies.
7. The absence of love might lead a person to "make friends with death."
8. The speaker wonders if he or she would be willing to sell or trade either a beloved's love or the memory of that love in exchange for release from physical pain or hardship. The final sentence of the poem suggests that the speaker would not do so.

(cont.)

ANSWERS FOR REVIEWING THE SELECTION (CONT.)

SYNTHESIZING

Responses will vary. Possible responses are given.

9. The speaker suggests that love is indeed a fundamental need, as necessary to life as food, sleep, and shelter. Lines 7–8 offer an example of the importance of love in a person's life, implying that without it, a person will die. Lines 9–14 show the speaker pondering how essential love is to his or her own life, and deciding in the end that it is not something he or she would readily give up.
10. Some basic physical needs are food, drink, clothing, and adequate shelter from harsh elements. Emotional needs may include friendship, love, and a sense of security. Additional needs may include such things as money, leisure time, employment, intellectual stimulation, and a sense of social justice.

ANSWERS FOR UNDERSTANDING LITERATURE

▶ See the evaluation forms for discussion, active listening, and oral communication, *Assessment Portfolio,* 7.11–7.14.

Responses will vary. Possible responses are given.

1. Sonnet. The first quatrain declares that love, unlike food, sleep, or shelter, is not a basic necessity of life. The second quatrain asserts that love cannot nourish the body nor heal it when it is ill or injured, but also claims that many people are dying from lack of love. In the third quatrain, the speaker imagines a future time of pain or great physical need, and suggests he or she might sell love for relief. In the concluding couplet, the speaker continues the imaginary situation by suggesting he or she might trade the memory of a night of love for food, but rejects both exchanges in the last line of the poem.

2. Rhyme Scheme. The rhyme scheme for the rest of the poem is *cdcd efef gg.*

3. Parallelism. In lines 1–3, a parallel is drawn between love and meat, drink, slumber, a roof, and a floating spar. In lines 5–6, Millay lists filling lungs with breath, cleaning the blood, and setting a fractured bone as three things love is unable to do. In lines 10–11, the speaker's being "Pinned down by pain" is equated with being "nagged by want." In lines 12–13, the actions the speaker might be driven to, "sell your love for peace" or "trade the memory of this night for food," are expressed in parallel forms.

4. Personification. In line 7, Millay personifies death as somebody who can be befriended. In line 11, she personifies want as something that nags.

5. Symbol. The speaker suggests that love cannot either prevent personal failure nor rescue a person who is experiencing personal misfortune. Students might agree that personal success or failure comes and goes regardless of love.

6. Theme. The theme of "Sonnet XXX" is that although love may not be a fundamental physical necessity, it is nevertheless equally essential to life.

2. **Rhyme Scheme.** A **rhyme scheme** is a pattern of rhymes in a poem. To determine the rhyme scheme of a poem, assign letters of the alphabet to each of the sounds that appear at the ends of lines. The end rhymes of the first four lines of "Sonnet XXX" have the rhyme scheme *abab,* as follows:

drink	*a*
rain	*b*
sink	*a*
again	*b*

What is the rhyme scheme of the rest of the poem?

3. **Parallelism. Parallelism** is a rhetorical technique in which a writer emphasizes the equal value or weight of two or more ideas by expressing them in the same grammatical form. Find three examples of parallelism in "Sonnet XXX." What ideas of equal value are expressed in each example?

4. **Personification. Personification** is a figure of speech in which an idea, animal, or thing is described as if it were a person. What does Millay personify in line 7 of her poem? in line 11?

5. **Symbol.** A **symbol** is a thing that stands for or represents both itself and something else. Common symbols include doves for peace, roses for love or beauty, the color green for jealousy, the color red for anger, spring for youth, and winter or fall for age. In most people's lives, there are good times and bad times, times when their spirits rise and times when they sink. Lines 3 and 4 of this poem can be read as presenting a symbol of such a rise and fall of personal fortunes. If so, what is the speaker saying about the role of love in life? Does the speaker believe that love can be counted on to balance out good and bad fortune? Do you agree with the speaker?

6. **Theme.** A **theme** is a central idea in a literary work. What is the theme, or main idea, of "Sonnet XXX"?

The Process of Writing: Drafting

Drafting. Read the Language Arts Survey, 1.35–1.42, on drafting. Pay particular attention to section 1.42, "Organizing a Composition." Using the notes you created in the prewriting lesson in this unit, write a draft of your personal essay. Save your draft for later revision.

THE PROCESS OF WRITING: DRAFTING

▶ See the Writing Evaluation Form: Process, *Assessment Portfolio,* 7.1.

▶ For detailed evaluation of drafts, see the evaluation forms for writing and drafting, *Assessment Portfolio,* 7.1–7.6.

• You may want to avoid evaluating drafts until students develop receptive attitudes toward critical evaluation and revising. You may want to not read these drafts at all and to encourage students to view writing as something that can be valuable and enjoyable in itself.

• Rather than scoring or critiquing these drafts, discuss with students what is interesting about the theme, development, and examples or plot and character. Allow students to discover, through the discussion, places where each piece of writing could have benefited from additional detail, where it is unclear, and so forth.

TERARY TECHNIQUE

aracter. Have students work in all groups to analyze character. ing as a model a film that is miliar to the students in each roup, have students categorize e different characters in the film cording to the definitions on age 24. Who is the protagonist? Who is the antagonist? Who are the major and minor characters? What are the traits exhibited by the major characters? Which characters are one-dimensional, and what is the dominant quality of each of these caricatures? Which characters are static and which are dynamic? What changes do the dynamic characters undergo? What motivates the different characters, both major and minor?

Elements of Fiction

CHARACTER

A **character** is a person (or sometimes an animal or even a personified thing) who figures in the action of a story. The following are some useful terms for describing characters:

A **protagonist**, or **main character**, is the central figure in a story.

An **antagonist** is a character who is pitted against a protagonist.

A **major character** is one with a significant role in the action of a story. A **minor character** is one who plays a lesser role. Because of limitations of length and focus, most short stories have, at most, one or two major characters.

A **one-dimensional character, flat character,** or **caricature** is one who exhibits a single dominant quality, or **character trait.**

A **three-dimensional, full,** or **rounded character** is one who exhibits the complexity of traits associated with actual human beings.

A **static character** is one who does not change during the course of the story.

A **dynamic character** is one who does change during the course of the story.

A **stock character** is one found again and again in different literary works. Examples of stock characters include the mad scientist and the absent-minded professor.

Motivation is the needs or desires felt by a character, impelling him or her to act or think in certain ways. For example, a character may be **motivated** by greed, love, or friendship. The particular reasons or causes behind a character's actions are his or her **motives.**

CHARACTERIZATION

Characterization is the use of literary techniques to create a character. Three major techniques of characterization used by fiction writers include the following: 1. direct description by a narrator or character, 2. portrayal of a character's words and behavior, and 3. representations of a character's internal states.

Direct description of a character includes what other characters say or think about that character. Skillful writers are able to create characterizations through a few well-chosen, significant details.

Language Lab

Coordinating Conjunctions. After reading the Language Arts Survey, 2.25, "Coordinating Conjunctions," rewrite the sentences below, adding coordinating conjunctions to link the sentence parts.

1. Edna St. Vincent Millay was born _____ raised in Maine in a family with a great interest in literature.
2. She enjoyed reading _____ , while still quite young, wrote poetry for a magazine called *St. Nicholas.*
3. Millay did not expect to attend college, _____ a family friend sponsored her studies at Barnard _____ Vassar.
4. Although she struggled with poverty, Millay also achieved literary _____ popular recognition with her second book, *A Few Figs from Thistles.*
5. Do you remember her best for winning the Pulitzer Prize _____ for her poetic figure of speech about burning the candle at both ends?

ABOUT THE AUTHOR

Edna St. Vincent Millay (1892–1950) was born in Rockland, Maine, and began to write poetry at an early age. In 1912, her poem "Renascence" was published in a collection called *The Lyric Year.* After attending Barnard and Vassar, she published a book of verse, *Renascence and Other Poems,* and moved to Greenwich Village in New York City. There she refined her poetic talents and worked as both an actor and playwright for the Provincetown Players, which produced her plays *The Princess Marries the Page, Aria da Capo,* and *Two Slatterns and a King.* Millay became a master of the sonnet, one of the most difficult of English poetic forms, and her poetry reached a large and enthusiastic audience. In 1923, she received a Pulitzer Prize for *The Ballad of the Harp-Weaver.* In that same year she married and bought a farm in upstate New York, where she continued her writing, including a sonnet cycle, or group of related sonnets, called *Fatal Interview.* Many of her later works dealt with social and political issues. Works by Millay include *Collected Sonnets* (1941), *Collected Lyrics* (1943), and *Collected Poems* (1953).

ANSWERS FOR LANGUAGE LAB

Responses will vary. Possible responses are given.

1. Edna St. Vincent Millay was born and raised in Maine in a family with a great interest in literature.
2. She enjoyed reading and, while still quite young, wrote poetry for a magazine called *St. Nicholas.*
3. Millay did not expect to attend college, but a family friend sponsored her studies at Barnard and Vassar.
4. Although she struggled with poverty, Millay also achieved literary and popular recognition with her second book, *A Few Figs from Thistles.*
5. Do you remember her best for winning the Pulitzer Prize or for her poetic figure of speech about burning the candle at both ends?

ADDITIONAL RESOURCES

READER'S GUIDE
- Selection Worksheet, 1.3

ASSESSMENT PORTFOLIO
- Selection Check Test, 4.1.5
- Selection Test, 4.1.6

ESSENTIAL SKILLS PRACTICE BOOKS
- *Writing,* 1.43–1.45

ENRICHMENT ACTIVITIES

One of the central internal conflicts faced by the protagonist of "The Magic Barrel" involves choosing between his instinct to follow a traditional form of marriage practice involving a matchmaker and his desire to marry a woman he loves. Have students research the marriage practices employed in different cultures. As marriage practices vary widely from culture to culture, separate groups of students might investigate the forms that these practices take in particular cultures. Have each group of students present its findings so that the class as a whole can discuss the differences and similarities between cultural practices. Elicit responses to each type of marriage practice discussed, asking students to consider how their own ideas of love and marriage might appear to in other cultures.

SUPPORT FOR LEP STUDENTS

Explain to students that a matchmaker is a person who arranges marriages for other people. The term is often used today for a person who unofficially tries to bring two people together. In the story, matchmaking is Salzman's profession.

ADDITIONAL VOCABULARY

guffaw—laugh loudly and suddenly
cupid—matchmaker, after Cupid, the god of love
sanctified—purified
semimystical—highly spiritual

Fiction

The term ***fiction*** comes from the Latin *fictio,* meaning "something invented." Thus fiction is any prose writing that tells an invented or imaginary story. Some fiction, the historical novel, for example, is based on fact, while other forms, such as the fantasy tale, are highly unrealistic. Fictional works also vary in structure and length, from the newly recognized **short short** (a very brief short story) to the book-length **novel.** Other forms include the traditional **short story** and the **novella,** a fictional work of intermediate length.

The Development of Fiction

The oldest fictions are the prose stories told in the oral tradition, which include myths, legends, and fables. Early written prose fictions include Petronius's *Satyricon* and Apuleius's *The Golden Ass,* written by Romans in the first and second centuries. The first novel, *The Tale of Genji,* was written by a Japanese woman, Lady Murasaki Shikibu, in the eleventh century. Early fictions from Europe include Boccaccio's *Decameron,* a collection of short prose tales written in the mid-fourteenth century, and Cervantes's *Don Quixote,* a satire of medieval romance tales written in the early seventeenth century.

The Novel

The novel developed from various kinds of nonfictional writing, including autobiographies, biographies, travel sketches, journals, and letters. Arguably the first full-fledged novel in English was Aphra Behn's *Oroonoko,* published in 1688. Other early novels in English include Daniel Defoe's *Robinson Crusoe* (1719) and *Moll Flanders* (1722), and Samuel Richardson's *Pamela* (1740) and *Clarissa* (1747–1748). By the mid-1800s, the novel had become a popular form in the United States. Important American novelists include Nathaniel Hawthorne (1804–1864), Herman Melville (1819–1891), Mark Twain (1835–1910), Henry James (1843–1916), Kate Chopin (1850–1904), Edith Wharton (1862–1937), Stephen Crane (1871–1945), Theodore Dreiser (1871–1945), Willa Cather (1873–1947), Sherwood Anderson (1876–1941), Katherine Anne Porter (1890–1980), Zora Neale Hurston (1891–1960), F. Scott Fitzgerald (1896–1940), William Faulkner (1897–1962), Ernest Hemingway (1899–1961), Richard Wright (1908–1960), John Steinbeck (1902–1968), Eudora Welty (1909–), Saul Bellow (1915–), James Baldwin (1924–), Philip Roth (1933–), and Alice Walker (1944–).

The Short Story

The short story genre, or type, originated in the United States. Important American figures in the development of the short story include Washington Irving (1783–1859), Nathaniel Hawthorne, and Edgar Allan Poe (1809–1849). Poe was instrumental in defining the genre, which he described as a short work that creates a single dominant impression or effect on the reader. According to Poe, every detail in a short story should contribute to creating that overall impression or effect.

The Poor Man's Store. *John Frederick Peto. 1885. Courtesy of Museum of Fine Arts, Boston. Gift of Maxim Karolik to the M. and M. Karolik Collection of American Paintings, 1815–1865*

GOALS/OBJECTIVES

Studying this lesson will enable students to

- empathize with the feelings of Leo Finkle
- understand character motivation
- identify background information in a story
- explain the use of literary techniques to create a character
- recognize dialect and its purpose in a story
- identify figurative language and explain its effect on a reader
- evaluate and revise a piece of writing

ADDITIONAL QU AND ACTIVITIES

- Students can test observation by exan on page 23. (Refer st the Language Arts Su "Observing.") Then w ing at the picture, stu as many items from th they can remember. St then look at the picture create a more detailed d of the picture.
- Have students create a c ing list. Each student can i one or more novels or shor that he or she enjoyed. Eac should include the author's n the title of the work, and a b description of the work inclu its genre and a blurb about th plot. Students might also note thing they particularly enjoyed about the novel or short story.

Language Lab

Coordinating Conjunctions. After reading the Language Arts Survey, 2.25, "Coordinating Conjunctions," rewrite the sentences below, adding coordinating conjunctions to link the sentence parts.

1. Edna St. Vincent Millay was born _____ raised in Maine in a family with a great interest in literature.
2. She enjoyed reading _____ , while still quite young, wrote poetry for a magazine called *St. Nicholas.*
3. Millay did not expect to attend college, _____ a family friend sponsored her studies at Barnard _____ Vassar.
4. Although she struggled with poverty, Millay also achieved literary _____ popular recognition with her second book, *A Few Figs from Thistles.*
5. Do you remember her best for winning the Pulitzer Prize _____ for her poetic figure of speech about burning the candle at both ends?

About the Author

Edna St. Vincent Millay (1892–1950) was born in Rockland, Maine, and began to write poetry at an early age. In 1912, her poem "Renascence" was published in a collection called *The Lyric Year.* After attending Barnard and Vassar, she published a book of verse, *Renascence and Other Poems,* and moved to Greenwich Village in New York City. There she refined her poetic talents and worked as both an actor and playwright for the Provincetown Players, which produced her plays *The Princess Marries the Page, Aria da Capo,* and *Two Slatterns and a King.* Millay became a master of the sonnet, one of the most difficult of English poetic forms, and her poetry reached a large and enthusiastic audience. In 1923, she received a Pulitzer Prize for *The Ballad of the Harp-Weaver.* In that same year she married and bought a farm in upstate New York, where she continued her writing, including a sonnet cycle, or group of related sonnets, called *Fatal Interview.* Many of her later works dealt with social and political issues. Works by Millay include *Collected Sonnets* (1941), *Collected Lyrics* (1943), and *Collected Poems* (1953).

Answers for Language Lab

Responses will vary. Possible responses are given.

1. Edna St. Vincent Millay was born and raised in Maine in a family with a great interest in literature.
2. She enjoyed reading and, while still quite young, wrote poetry for a magazine called *St. Nicholas.*
3. Millay did not expect to attend college, but a family friend sponsored her studies at Barnard and Vassar.
4. Although she struggled with poverty, Millay also achieved literary and popular recognition with her second book, *A Few Figs from Thistles.*
5. Do you remember her best for winning the Pulitzer Prize or for her poetic figure of speech about burning the candle at both ends?

ADDITIONAL RESOURCES

READER'S GUIDE
- Selection Worksheet, 1.3

ASSESSMENT PORTFOLIO
- Selection Check Test, 4.1.5
- Selection Test, 4.1.6

ESSENTIAL SKILLS PRACTICE BOOKS
- *Writing,* 1.43–1.45

ENRICHMENT ACTIVITIES

One of the central internal conflicts faced by the protagonist of "The Magic Barrel" involves choosing between his instinct to follow a traditional form of marriage practice involving a matchmaker and his desire to marry a woman he loves. Have students research the marriage practices employed in different cultures. As marriage practices vary widely from culture to culture, separate groups of students might investigate the forms that these practices take in particular cultures. Have each group of students present its findings so that the class as a whole can discuss the differences and similarities between cultural practices. Elicit responses to each type of marriage practice discussed, asking students to consider how their own ideas of love and marriage might appear to in other cultures.

SUPPORT FOR LEP STUDENTS

Explain to students that a matchmaker is a person who arranges marriages for other people. The term is often used today for a person who unofficially tries to bring two people together. In the story, matchmaking is Salzman's profession.

ADDITIONAL VOCABULARY

guffaw—laugh loudly and suddenly
cupid—matchmaker, after Cupid, the god of love
sanctified—purified
semimystical—highly spiritual

Fiction

The term ***fiction*** comes from the Latin *fictio,* meaning "something invented." Thus fiction is any prose writing that tells an invented or imaginary story. Some fiction, the historical novel, for example, is based on fact, while other forms, such as the fantasy tale, are highly unrealistic. Fictional works also vary in structure and length, from the newly recognized **short short** (a very brief short story) to the book-length **novel.** Other forms include the traditional **short story** and the **novella,** a fictional work of intermediate length.

The Development of Fiction

The oldest fictions are the prose stories told in the oral tradition, which include myths, legends, and fables. Early written prose fictions include Petronius's *Satyricon* and Apuleius's *The Golden Ass,* written by Romans in the first and second centuries. The first novel, *The Tale of Genji,* was written by a Japanese woman, Lady Murasaki Shikibu, in the eleventh century. Early fictions from Europe include Boccaccio's *Decameron,* a collection of short prose tales written in the mid-fourteenth century, and Cervantes's *Don Quixote,* a satire of medieval romance tales written in the early seventeenth century.

The Novel

The novel developed from various kinds of nonfictional writing, including autobiographies, biographies, travel sketches, journals, and letters. Arguably the first full-fledged novel in English was Aphra Behn's *Oroonoko,* published in 1688. Other early novels in English include Daniel Defoe's *Robinson Crusoe* (1719) and *Moll Flanders* (1722), and Samuel Richardson's *Pamela* (1740) and *Clarissa* (1747–1748). By the mid-1800s, the novel had become a popular form in the United States. Important American novelists include Nathaniel Hawthorne (1804–1864), Herman Melville (1819–1891), Mark Twain (1835–1910), Henry James (1843–1916), Kate Chopin (1850–1904), Edith Wharton (1862–1937), Stephen Crane (1871–1945), Theodore Dreiser (1871–1945), Willa Cather (1873–1947), Sherwood Anderson (1876–1941), Katherine Anne Porter (1890–1980), Zora Neale Hurston (1891–1960), F. Scott Fitzgerald (1896–1940), William Faulkner (1897–1962), Ernest Hemingway (1899–1961), Richard Wright (1908–1960), John Steinbeck (1902–1968), Eudora Welty (1909–), Saul Bellow (1915–), James Baldwin (1924–), Philip Roth (1933–), and Alice Walker (1944–).

The Short Story

The short story genre, or type, originated in the United States. Important American figures in the development of the short story include Washington Irving (1783–1859), Nathaniel Hawthorne, and Edgar Allan Poe (1809–1849). Poe was instrumental in defining the genre, which he described as a short work that creates a single dominant impression or effect on the reader. According to Poe, every detail in a short story should contribute to creating that overall impression or effect.

The Poor Man's Store. *John Frederick Peto. 1885. Courtesy of Museum of Fine Arts, Boston. Gift of Maxim Karolik to the M. and M. Karolik Collection of American Paintings, 1815–1865*

GOALS/OBJECTIVES

Studying this lesson will enable students to

- empathize with the feelings of Leo Finkle
- understand character motivation
- identify background information in a story
- explain the use of literary techniques to create a character
- recognize dialect and its purpose in a story
- identify figurative language and explain its effect on a reader
- evaluate and revise a piece of writing

Additional Questions and Activities

- Students can test their powers of observation by examining the art on page 23. (Refer students to the Language Arts Survey, 4.6, "Observing.") Then without looking at the picture, students can list as many items from the picture as they can remember. Students can then look at the picture again and create a more detailed description of the picture.
- Have students create a class reading list. Each student can include one or more novels or short stories that he or she enjoyed. Each entry should include the author's name, the title of the work, and a brief description of the work including its genre and a blurb about the plot. Students might also note anything they particularly enjoyed about the novel or short story.

LITERARY TECHNIQUE

Character. Have students work in small groups to analyze character. Using as a model a film that is familiar to the students in each group, have students categorize the different characters in the film according to the definitions on page 24. Who is the protagonist? Who is the antagonist? Who are the major and minor characters? What are the traits exhibited by the major characters? Which characters are one-dimensional, and what is the dominant quality of each of these caricatures? Which characters are static and which are dynamic? What changes do the dynamic characters undergo? What motivates the different characters, both major and minor?

Elements of Fiction

CHARACTER

A **character** is a person (or sometimes an animal or even a personified thing) who figures in the action of a story. The following are some useful terms for describing characters:

A **protagonist**, or **main character**, is the central figure in a story.

An **antagonist** is a character who is pitted against a protagonist.

A **major character** is one with a significant role in the action of a story. A **minor character** is one who plays a lesser role. Because of limitations of length and focus, most short stories have, at most, one or two major characters.

A **one-dimensional character, flat character,** or **caricature** is one who exhibits a single dominant quality, or **character trait.**

A **three-dimensional, full,** or **rounded character** is one who exhibits the complexity of traits associated with actual human beings.

A **static character** is one who does not change during the course of the story.

A **dynamic character** is one who does change during the course of the story.

A **stock character** is one found again and again in different literary works. Examples of stock characters include the mad scientist and the absent-minded professor.

Motivation is the needs or desires felt by a character, impelling him or her to act or think in certain ways. For example, a character may be **motivated** by greed, love, or friendship. The particular reasons or causes behind a character's actions are his or her **motives.**

CHARACTERIZATION

Characterization is the use of literary techniques to create a character. Three major techniques of characterization used by fiction writers include the following: 1. direct description by a narrator or character, 2. portrayal of a character's words and behavior, and 3. representations of a character's internal states.

Direct description of a character includes what other characters say or think about that character. Skillful writers are able to create characterizations through a few well-chosen, significant details.

Setting and Mood

The **setting** is the time and place in which a story occurs, together with all the details used to create a sense of a particular time and place. The **mood** is the emotion created in the reader by descriptions of the setting, of characters, and of events. In fiction, setting is most often revealed by means of description of such elements as landscape, scenery, buildings, furniture, clothing, weather, and seasons. It also can be revealed by how characters talk and behave. In its widest sense, setting includes the general social, political, moral, and psychological conditions in which characters find themselves. Many American novels and short stories deal with particular regions of the country (New York City, the western frontier, small towns in the South or Midwest, and so on). Writing in which particular settings play an important role is called **regional fiction.** The details used to create a particular regional setting are called **local color.**

Conflict

A **conflict** is a struggle between two forces in a literary work. A plot involves the introduction, development, and, often, the resolution, or ending, of a conflict. One side of the central conflict in a work of fiction usually is taken by the main character. That character may struggle against another character, against the forces of nature, against society or social norms, against fate, or against some element within himself or herself. A struggle that takes place between a character and some outside force is called an **external conflict.** A struggle that takes place within a character is called an **internal conflict.**

Plot

A **plot** is a series of causally connected events in a literary work. The English novelist E. M. Forster explained, famously, that if the king dies and then the queen dies, that is a story, but if the king dies and then the queen dies of grief, that is a plot. A typical plot involves the following elements:

The **exposition,** or **introduction,** sets the tone and mood, introduces the characters and the setting, and provides necessary background information.

The **inciting incident** is the event that introduces the central conflict.

The **rising action,** or **complication,** develops the conflict to a high point of intensity.

The **climax** is the high point of interest or suspense.

The **crisis,** or **turning point,** often the same event as the climax, is the point in the plot where something decisive happens to determine the future course of events and the eventual working out of the conflict.

The **falling action** is all the events that follow the climax.

The **resolution** is the point at which the central conflict is ended, or resolved.

The **dénouement** is any material that follows the resolution and that ties up loose ends.

Literary Technique

Setting and Mood. Ask students as a class to generate a list of details they feel would be essential to a work of regional fiction that takes place in their area. What descriptive elements would be necessary to the work in order to convey the local color of their region? List these elements on the board, encouraging students to come up with as many aspects of setting as they can. Then suggest different moods for this work of regional fiction, such as suspenseful, romantic, or comic, and ask students which elements of the setting would be most appropriate for each mood.

Literary Technique

Plot. In order to help students distinguish between a story and a plot, have students write brief and simple accounts of a recent event, such as going to the movies or doing homework. Ask them to describe what happened or what they did without offering reasons, explanations, or feelings about the subject. Then ask them to rewrite this account, or short story, using different elements of plot structure. Encourage them to use their imaginations in coming up with an inciting incident, a complication, a climax, and a resolution to the conflict. Finally, ask students to consider how the plots that they have developed differ from their original stories.

QUOTABLES

"Anything whatsoever may become the subject of a novel, provided only that it happens in this mundane life and not in some fairyland beyond our human ken."

—Murasaki Shikibu

ADDITIONAL QUESTIONS AND ACTIVITIES

Have students draw Freytag's Pyramid on a piece of paper. As they read "The Magic Barrel," have them identify parts of the plot and fill them in on the diagram.

Plots are often illustrated using the following diagram, known as Freytag's Pyramid for its creator, Gustav Freytag:

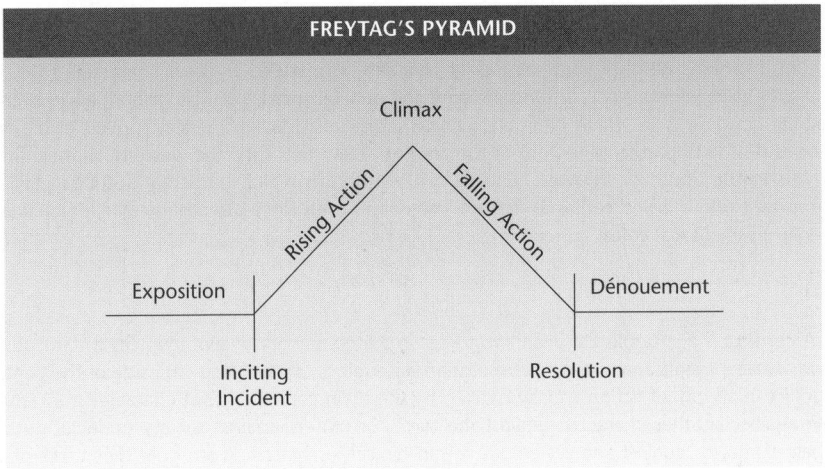

THEME

A **theme** is a central idea in a literary work. A long work such as a novel may deal with several interrelated themes.

> *"[The short story writer] having conceived with deliberate care a certain unique or single effect to be wrought out . . . then invents . . . as may best aid him in establishing his preconceived effects. . . . In the whole composition there should be no word written, of which the tendency, direct or indirect, is not to the one pre-established design."*
>
> *—Edgar Allan Poe*

"The Magic Barrel"

BERNARD MALAMUD

Not long ago there lived in uptown New York, in a small, almost meager room, though crowded with books, Leo Finkle, a rabbinical student at the Yeshiva University.[1] Finkle, after six years of study, was to be ordained in June and had been advised by an acquaintance that he might find it easier to win himself a congregation if he were married. Since he had no present prospects of marriage, after two tormented days of turning it over in his mind, he called in Pinye Salzman, a marriage broker whose two-line advertisement he had read in the *Forward*.[2]

The matchmaker appeared one night out of the dark fourth-floor hallway of the graystone rooming house where Finkle lived, grasping a black, strapped portfolio that had been worn thin with use. Salzman, who had been long in the business, was of slight but dignified build, wearing an old hat, and an overcoat too short and tight for him. He smelled frankly of fish, which he loved to eat, and although he was missing a few teeth, his presence was not displeasing, because of an amiable manner curiously contrasted with mournful eyes. His voice, his lips, his wisp of beard, his bony fingers were animated, but give him a moment of repose and his mild blue eyes revealed a depth of sadness, a characteristic that put Leo a little at ease although the situation, for him, was inherently tense.

He at once informed Salzman why he had asked him to come, explaining that his home was in Cleveland, and that but for his parents, who had married comparatively late in life, he was alone in the world. He had for six years devoted himself almost entirely to his studies, as a result of which, understandably, he had found himself without time for a social life and the company of young women. Therefore he thought it the better part of trial and error—of embarrassing fumbling—to call in an experienced person to advise him on these matters. He remarked in passing that the function of the marriage broker was ancient and honorable, highly approved in the Jewish community, because it made practical the necessary without hindering joy. Moreover, his own parents had been brought together by a matchmaker. They had made, if not a financially profitable marriage—since neither had possessed any worldly goods to speak of—at least a successful one in the sense of their everlasting devotion to each other. Salzman listened

EXPOSITION

The exposition introduces the setting and the main character, or protagonist, Leo Finkle.

INCITING INCIDENT

The inciting incident introduces the central conflict, or struggle, in the story, in this case Leo Finkle's search, through a matchmaker, for an appropriate mate.

1. **Yeshiva University.** University in New York City offering both theological and secular courses
2. **Forward.** *The Jewish Daily Forward*, New York City newspaper written in the Yiddish language

WORDS FOR EVERYDAY USE:

mea • ger (mē´ gər) *adj.*, not rich or bountiful; inadequate

or • dain (ôr dān´) *vt.*, officially give someone the authority and duties of a minister, priest, or rabbi

in • her • ent • ly (in hir´ ənt lē) *adv.*, characteristically; naturally

LITERARY TECHNIQUE

Setting and Mood. What details does the author provide in the opening paragraph of this story to establish a setting and a mood? In what way does he enhance the setting and mood on page 28? *Answers.* The general setting is a Jewish cultural milieu almost contemporary with our own time; the more specific setting is a tiny, cramped, sparsely furnished apartment in uptown New York City: "Not long ago there lived in uptown New York, in a small, almost meager room, though crowded with books, Leo Finkle, a rabbinical student." A claustrophobic and anxious mood is created by describing Leo's apartment as "small" and "crowded," and by mentioning that he has spent the previous two days "tormented" by a decision. The setting and mood are enhanced on page 28 when the author names the month and season ("February, winter") and indicates that Leo has not noticed the change of seasons for a long time ("winter was on its last legs, signs of which he had for the first time in years begun to notice").

VOCABULARY FROM THE SELECTION

abjectly
apparatus
ascetic
avow
exasperating
haggard
imperceptible
inherently
machination
meager
menagerie
nuptial
ordain
profusion
ravenously
refrain
relentless
trepidation
vestibule

VOCABULARY IN CONTEXT

- While the food itself was delicious, the portions were so meager that we left the restaurant almost as hungry as when we had arrived.
- Marla was ecstatic when, after years of study at divinity school, she achieved her goal of being ordained a minister.
- In many foreign countries, Americans enjoy a reputation as an inherently friendly and welcoming people.

Literary Technique

Characterization. What techniques of characterization does the author employ on page 28 to depict Leo Finkle? What details are used in the description of Leo?

Answers. The author portrays Leo through his behavior ("attempting by an act of will to suppress the unpleasant tickle in his throat," "the student pretended not to see and gazed steadfastly out the window," and "Leo blushed"); his words ("'So few?' he asked in disappointment," and "Call me Mr. Finkle. I'm not yet a rabbi"); and through a description from Salzman's point of view ("noting with pleasure the long, severe scholar's nose, brown eyes heavy with learning, sensitive yet ascetic lips, and a certain, almost hollow quality of the dark cheeks").

Additional Questions and Activities

Ask students how individuals from their cultural heritages decide to get married. What are considered important factors in choosing a spouse? Is love a critical factor? finances? previous marital status? family background? What do the students themselves believe are appropriate criteria for deciding whom to marry?

in embarrassed surprise, sensing a sort of apology. Later, however, he experienced a glow of pride in his work, an emotion that had left him years ago, and he heartily approved of Finkle.

The two went to their business. Leo had led Salzman to the only clear place in the room, a table near a window that overlooked the lamp-lit city. He seated himself at the matchmaker's side but facing him, attempting by an act of will to suppress the unpleasant tickle in his throat. Salzman eagerly unstrapped his portfolio and removed a loose rubber band from a thin packet of much-handled cards. As he flipped through them, a gesture and sound that physically hurt Leo, the student pretended not to see and gazed steadfastly out the window. Although it was still February, winter was on its last legs, signs of which he had for the first time in years begun to notice. He now observed the round white moon, moving high in the sky through a cloud menagerie, and watched with half-open mouth as it penetrated a huge hen, and dropped out of her like an egg laying itself. Salzman, though pretending through eyeglasses he had just slipped on, to be engaged in scanning the writing on the cards, stole occasional glances at the young man's distinguished face, noting with pleasure the long, severe scholar's nose, brown eyes heavy with learning, sensitive yet ascetic lips, and a certain, almost hollow quality of the dark cheeks. He gazed around at shelves upon shelves of books and let out a soft, contented sigh.

When Leo's eyes fell upon the cards, he counted six spread out in Salzman's hand.

"So few?" he asked in disappointment.

"You wouldn't believe me how much cards I got in my office," Salzman replied. "The drawers are already filled to the top, so I keep them now in a barrel, but is every girl good for a new rabbi?"

Leo blushed at this, regretting all he had revealed of himself in a curriculum vitae[3] he had sent to Salzman. He had thought it best to acquaint him with his strict standards and specifications, but in having done so, he felt he had told the marriage broker more than was absolutely necessary.

He hesitantly inquired, "Do you keep photographs of your clients on file?"

"First comes family, amount of dowry, also what kind promises," Salzman replied, unbuttoning his tight coat and settling himself in the chair. "After come pictures, rabbi."

"Call me Mr. Finkle. I'm not yet a rabbi."

Salzman said he would, but instead called him doctor, which he changed to rabbi when Leo was not listening too attentively.

Salzman adjusted his horn-rimmed spectacles, gently cleared his throat and read in an eager voice the contents of the top card:

"Sophie P. Twenty four years. Widow one year. No children. Educated high school and two years college. Father promises eight thousand dollars. Has wonderful wholesale business. Also real estate. On the mother's side comes teach-

3. **curriculum vitae.** Summary of one's personal history and professional qualifications

Words for Everyday Use:

me • nag • er • ie (mə naj´ ər ē) *n.,* collection of wild or exotic animals

as • cet • ic (ə set´ ik) *adj.,* self-denying; austere

Vocabulary in Context

- As a child, the writer and zoologist Gerald Durrell transformed his family's house into a veritab menagerie with his collection of insects, exotic birds, and wild animals.
- Many marathon runners follow an ascetic lifestyle in the months before a race in order to achi peak physical condition, denying themselves candy, excess fat, and red meat.
- Adam's reaction to the news was so imperceptible that his friends could not tell if he was elate disappointed.

ers, also one actor. Well known on Second Avenue."

Leo gazed up in surprise. "Did you say a widow?"

"A widow don't mean spoiled, rabbi. She lived with her husband maybe four months. He was a sick boy she made a mistake to marry him."

"Marrying a widow has never entered my mind."

"This is because you have no experience. A widow, especially if she is young and healthy like this girl, is a wonderful person to marry. She will be thankful to you the rest of her life. Believe me, if I was looking now for a bride, I would marry a widow."

Leo reflected, then shook his head.

Salzman hunched his shoulders in an almost imperceptible gesture of disappointment. He placed the card down on the wooden table and began to read another:

"Lily H. High school teacher. Regular. Not a substitute. Has savings and new Dodge car. Lived in Paris one year. Father is successful dentist thirty-five years. Interested in professional man. Well Americanized family. Wonderful opportunity."

"I knew her personally," said Salzman. "I wish you could see this girl. She is a doll. Also very intelligent. All day you could talk to her about books and theater and what not. She also knows current events."

"I don't believe you mentioned her age?"

"Her age?" Salzman said, raising his brows. "Her age is thirty-two years."

Leo said after a while, "I'm afraid that seems a little too old."

Salzman let out a laugh. "So how old are you, rabbi?"

"Twenty-seven."

"So what is the difference, tell me, between twenty-seven and thirty-two? My own wife is seven years older than me. So what did I suffer?—Nothing. If Rothschild's[4] daughter wants to marry you, would you say on account her age, no?"

"Yes," Leo said dryly.

Salzman shook off the no in the yes. "Five years don't mean a thing. I give you my word that when you will live with her for one week you will forget her age. What does it mean five years—that she lived more and knows more than somebody who is younger? On this girl, God bless her, years are not wasted. Each one that it comes makes better the bargain."

"What subjects does she teach in high school?"

"Languages. If you heard the way she speaks French, you will think it is music. I am in the business twenty-five years, and I recommend her with my whole heart. Believe me, I know what I'm talking, rabbi."

"What's on the next card?" Leo said abruptly.

Salzman reluctantly turned up the third card:

"Ruth K. Nineteen years. Honor student. Father offers thirteen thousand cash to the right bridegroom. He is a medical doctor. Stomach specialist with marvelous

4. **Rothschild's.** The Rothschilds were once a very wealthy Jewish family of international bankers and business leaders.

WORDS FOR EVERYDAY USE: **im • per • cep • ti • ble** (im´ pər sep´ tə bəl) *adj.,* not able to be detected by the senses or the mind

ADDITIONAL QUESTIONS AND ACTIVITIES

Ask students why Leo rejects each of the first three potential brides suggested by Salzman. What does Leo seem to expect his wife to be? How does this meeting with Salzman affect the way Leo views the process of finding a wife? How do students feel about this matchmaking process? How would they feel participating in this kind of marriage brokering, either as the seeker or as the potential spouse?

Answers. Leo rejects Sophie P. because she has been married once before. He rejects Lily H. because she is older than he is, and he rejects Ruth K. because she has been in an accident. Leo seems to unrealistically expect his wife to be young, never married, and flawlessly beautiful, as evidenced by his rejection of the potential brides for such petty reasons. The meeting with Salzman discourages Leo; he is no longer confident that the matchmaking process is a good idea.

Additional Questions and Activities

• Leo says of Ruth K., "'I don't understand why an American girl her age should go to a marriage broker." Ask students about the judgment implied in this remark. Why does Leo believe that something must be wrong with Ruth if she is going to a marriage broker?

• Ask students why Leo rejects Ruth K. as a possible wife. In what way does the author suggest that Leo is not being honest when he offers his reason to Salzman? Have students discuss the reason why Leo rejects Ruth. How does this detail contribute to the characterization of Leo?

Answers. Leo thinks that Ruth must have something terribly wrong with her if she is so young and seeks the services of the marriage broker, implying that any young, pretty girl should be able to find a husband on her own. Leo's judgment is hypocritical (as Salzman points out) because Leo himself has sought the services of the marriage broker. Students might take Leo's curses and the implausible reason he offers for rejecting Ruth ("Because I detest stomach specialists") as an indication that Leo rejects Ruth because "she is a little lame on her right foot." Students might say that Leo's prejudicial attitude makes them unsympathetic toward his character.

practice. Brother in law owns own garment business. Particular people."

Salzman looked as if he had read his trump card.

"Did you say nineteen?" Leo asked with interest.

"On the dot."

"Is she attractive?" He blushed. "Pretty?"

Salzman kissed his finger tips. "A little doll. On this I give you my word. Let me call the father tonight and you will see what means pretty."

But Leo was troubled. "You're sure she's that young?"

"This I am positive. The father will show you the birth certificate."

"Are you positive there isn't something wrong with her?" Leo insisted.

"Who says there is wrong?"

"I don't understand why an American girl her age should go to a marriage broker."

A smile spread over Salzman's face.

"So for the same reason you went, she comes."

Leo flushed. "I am pressed for time."

Salzman, realizing he had been tactless, quickly explained. "The father came, not her. He wants she should have the best, so he looks around himself. When we will locate the right boy he will introduce him and encourage. This makes a better marriage than if a young girl without experience takes for herself. I don't have to tell you this."

"But don't you think this young girl believes in love?" Leo spoke uneasily.

Salzman was about to guffaw but caught himself and said soberly, "Love comes with the right person, not before."

Leo parted dry lips but did not speak. Noticing that Salzman had snatched a glance at the next card, he cleverly asked, "How is her health?"

"Perfect," Salzman said, breathing with difficulty. "Of course, she is a little lame on her right foot from an auto accident that it happened to her when she was twelve years, but nobody notices on account she is so brilliant and also beautiful."

Leo got up heavily and went to the window. He felt curiously bitter and upbraided himself for having called in the marriage broker. Finally, he shook his head.

"Why not?" Salzman persisted, the pitch of his voice rising.

"Because I detest stomach specialists."

"So what do you care what is his business? After you marry her do you need him? Who says he must come every Friday night in your house?"

Ashamed of the way the talk was going, Leo dismissed Salzman, who went home with heavy, melancholy eyes.

Though he had felt only relief at the marriage broker's departure, Leo was in low spirits the next day. He explained it as arising from Salzman's failure to produce a suitable bride for him. He did not care for his type of clientele. But when Leo found himself hesitating whether to seek out another matchmaker, one more polished than Pinye, he wondered if it could be—his protestations to the contrary, and although he honored his father and mother—that he did not, in essence, care for the match-making institution? This thought he quickly put out of mind yet found himself still upset. All day he ran around in the woods—missed an important appointment, forgot to give out his laundry, walked out of a Broadway cafeteria without paying and had to run back with the ticket in his hand; had even not recognized his landlady in the street when she passed with a friend and courteously called out, "A good evening to you, Doctor Finkle." By nightfall, however, he had regained sufficient calm to sink his nose into a book and there found peace from his thoughts.

Almost at once there came a knock on the door. Before Leo could say enter, Salzman, commercial cupid, was standing in the room. His face was gray and meager, his expression hungry, and he looked as if he would expire on his feet. Yet the marriage broker managed, by some trick of the muscles, to display a broad smile.

"So good evening. I am invited?"

Leo nodded, disturbed to see him again, yet unwilling to ask the man to leave.

Beaming still, Salzman laid his portfolio on the table. "Rabbi, I got for you tonight good news."

"I've asked you not to call me rabbi. I'm still a student."

"Your worries are finished. I have for you a first-class bride."

"Leave me in peace concerning this subject," Leo pretended lack of interest.

"The world will dance at your wedding."

"Please, Mr. Salzman, no more."

"But first must come back my strength," Salzman said weakly. He fumbled with the portfolio straps and took out of the leather case an oily paper bag, from which he extracted a hard, seeded roll and a small, smoked white fish. With a quick motion of his hand he stripped the fish out of its skin and began ravenously to chew. "All day in a rush," he muttered.

Leo watched him eat.

"A sliced tomato you have maybe?" Salzman hesitantly inquired.

"No."

The marriage broker shut his eyes and ate. When he had finished he carefully cleaned up the crumbs and rolled up the remains of the fish, in the paper bag. His spectacled eyes roamed the room until he

ADDITIONAL QUESTIONS AND ACTIVITIES

Leo "found peace from his thoughts" by reading a book. Ask students how they relax when they are anxious or upset. What strategies do they use to manage stress? Do they read? exercise? go out with friends? Have students discuss both healthy and unhealthy ways to respond to stress. Some students may have ideas about activities that can help other students handle everyday stresses.

WORDS FOR EVERYDAY USE: **rav • e • nous • ly** (rav´ ə nəs lē) *adv.,* in a greedy or wildly hungry manner

VOCABULARY IN CONTEXT

- After finishing *Emma,* Sheila became so enamored of Jane Austen's writing that she read all of Austen's other novels ravenously.

Cross-curricular Activities

Social Studies. In many cultures, a host must follow a traditional code of behavior when entertaining a guest. In some cultures, the host may only be obligated to offer a drink of some kind, while in others the host may be obliged to provide the guest with an elaborate meal. In ancient Greece, for example, a host was expected to give an unexpected guest both food and drink before asking the guest's name and questioning him or her about his or her background. Discuss with students their experiences as guests in the homes of others, as well as how a guest could expect to be treated in their homes. Students may wish to research the hospitality practices of various cultures and present their findings to the class.

Social Studies. For Salzman, one important point about each of the women he suggests to Leo as a wife is the size of the dowry her father will provide. Explain to the students that a dowry is the money, goods, or estate that a woman brings to her husband when she is married. Have students research dowry practices, both past and present. What were/are the reasons that dowries are given? Why were/are dowries given by the bride's family and not the groom's?

discovered, amid some piles of books, a one-burner gas stove. Lifting his hat he humbly asked, "A glass tea you got, rabbi?"

Conscience-stricken, Leo rose and brewed the tea. He served it with a chunk of lemon and two cubes of lump sugar, delighting Salzman.

After he had drunk his tea, Salzman's strength and good spirits were restored.

"So tell me, rabbi," he said amiably, "you considered some more the three clients I mentioned yesterday?"

"There was no need to consider."

"Why not?"

"None of them suits me."

"What then suits you?"

Leo let it pass because he could give only a confused answer.

Without waiting for a reply, Salzman asked, "You remember this girl I talked to you—the high school teacher?"

"Age thirty-two?"

But, surprisingly, Salzman's face lit in a smile. "Age twenty-nine."

Leo shot him a look. "Reduced from thirty-two?"

"A mistake," Salzman avowed. "I talked today with the dentist. He took me to his safety deposit box and showed me the birth certificate. She was twenty-nine years last August. They made her a party in the mountains where she went for her vacation. When her father spoke to me the first time I forgot to write the age and I told you thirty-two, but now I remember this was a different client, a widow."

"The same one you told me about? I thought she was twenty-four?"

"A different. Am I responsible that the world is filled with widows?"

"No, but I'm not interested in them, nor for that matter, in school teachers."

Salzman pulled his clasped hands to his breast. Looking at the ceiling he devoutly exclaimed, "Yiddishe kinder,[5] what can I say to somebody that he is not interested in high school teachers? So what then you are interested?"

Leo flushed but controlled himself.

"In what else will you be interested," Salzman went on, "if you not interested in this fine girl that she speaks four languages and has personally in the bank ten thousand dollars? Also her father guarantees further twelve thousand. Also she has a new car, wonderful clothes, talks on all subjects, and she will give you a first-class home and children. How near do we come in our life to paradise?"

"If she's so wonderful, why wasn't she married ten years ago?"

"Why?" said Salzman with a heavy laugh. "—Why? Because she is *partikiler*.[6] This is why. She wants the *best*."

Leo was silent, amused at how he had entangled himself. But Salzman had aroused his interest in Lily H., and he began seriously to consider calling on her. When the marriage broker observed how intently Leo's mind was at work on the facts he had supplied, he felt certain they would soon come to an agreement.

5. **Yiddishe kinder.** Jewish children (Yiddish); Salzman is both calling Leo a child and lamenting the loss of the more traditional values Leo's parents' generation held.
6. **partikiler.** Particular; having high standards

Words for Everyday Use: a • **vow** (ə vou´) *vt.*, admit frankly

Vocabulary in Context

- "I made a mistake," Frank avowed, "but I learned my lesson and will not cheat on a test again."
- People often approach the unknown with a vague but palpable trepidation; once something is familiar, however, they often laugh at how ill-founded their earlier fears were.
- Everyone at the wedding reception agreed that the nuptial vows exchanged by the bride and groom were the most beautiful they had ever heard.

Late Saturday afternoon, conscious of Salzman, Leo Finkle walked with Lily Hirschorn along Riverside Drive. He walked briskly and erectly, wearing with distinction the black fedora he had that morning taken with trepidation out of the dusty hat box on his closet shelf, and the heavy black Saturday coat he had thoroughly whisked clean. Leo also owned a walking stick, a present from a distant relative, but quickly put temptation aside and did not use it. Lily, petite and not unpretty, had on something signifying the approach of spring. She was au courant,[7] animatedly, with all sorts of subjects, and he weighed her words and found her surprisingly sound—score another for Salzman, whom he uneasily sensed to be somewhere around, hiding perhaps high in a tree along the street, flashing the lady signals with a pocket mirror; or perhaps a cloven-hoofed Pan,[8] piping nuptial ditties as he danced his invisible way before them, strewing wild buds on the walk and purple grapes in their path, symbolizing fruit of a union, though there was of course still none.

Lily startled Leo by remarking, "I was thinking of Mr. Salzman, a curious figure, wouldn't you say?"

Not certain what to answer, he nodded.

She bravely went on, blushing, "I for one am grateful for his introducing us. Aren't you?"

He courteously replied, "I am."

"I mean," she said with a little laugh—and it was all in good taste, or at least gave the effect of being not in bad—"do you mind that we came together so?"

He was not displeased with her honesty, recognizing that she meant to set the relationship aright, and understanding that it took a certain amount of experience in life, and courage, to want to do it quite that way. One had to have some sort of past to make that kind of beginning.

He said that he did not mind. Salzman's function was traditional and honorable—valuable for what it might achieve, which, he pointed out, was frequently nothing.

Lily agreed with a sigh. They walked on for a while and she said after a long silence, again with a nervous laugh, "Would you mind if I asked you something a little bit personal? Frankly, I find the subject fascinating." Although Leo shrugged, she went on half embarrassedly, "How was it that you came to your calling? I mean was it a sudden passionate inspiration?"

Leo, after a time, slowly replied, "I was always interested in the Law."

"You saw revealed in it the presence of the Highest?"

He nodded and changed the subject. "I understand that you spent a little time in Paris, Miss Hirschorn?"

"Oh, did Mr. Salzman tell you, Rabbi Finkle?" Leo winced but she went on, "It was ages ago and almost forgotten. I remember I had to return for my sister's wedding."

And Lily would not be put off. "When," she asked in a trembly voice, "did you become enamored of God?"

Minor Character

A minor character may be introduced, as Lily Hirschorn is, to bring out some aspect of the protagonist's character.

7. **au courant.** In keeping with the times; up-to-date (French)

8. **Pan.** Greek god of fields, forests, wild animals, flocks, and shepherds, represented as a man with the legs of a goat who plays a flutelike instrument

Words for Everyday Use:

trep • i • da • tion (trep´ ə dā´ shən) *n.,* anxiety; nervousness

nup • tial (nup´ shəl) *adj.,* concerning marriage or a wedding

Additional Questions and Activities

Ask students why they think the author chose to make Leo Finkle a rabbinical student. In what way does Leo's occupation complicate the plot of "The Magic Barrel"? In what way does it contribute to the theme of the story? Would the story be as effective if Leo were a factory worker, a police officer, or a young lawyer instead?

Cross-curricular Activities

Social Studies. Training to become a rabbi, a priest, or a minister can be an arduous, complex process. Have students investigate the ordination process of different religions. What are the study requirements? What are the personal restrictions? In what way do different religions view the role of someone who leads a congregation?

Cross-curricular Activities

Social Studies. Many private organizations and government agencies, most notably the Food and Drug Administration and the Consumer Protection Agency, have worked in recent decades to ensure truth in advertising. Two assumptions underlying this movement are that advertisers will mislead or deceive consumers if they can, and that consumers are unable to distinguish false advertising claims from true ones. Divide students into two groups, asking one group to represent the interests of consumers and the other group to argue in behalf of advertisers. Have them debate the following proposition: The only rule of the marketplace should be *caveat emptor*, or "Let the buyer beware." Students may wish to research the topic beforehand in order to support their arguments with concrete evidence.

Literary Technique

Epiphany. When applied to literature, the term *epiphany* refers to a moment of sudden insight in which the essence, or nature, of a person, thing, or situation is revealed. The use of the term in this sense was introduced by James Joyce. In a short story, an epiphany often coincides with the crisis or turning point of the plot. On page 34, Leo experiences an epiphany that culminates with the sentence "It seemed to Leo that his whole life stood starkly revealed and he saw himself for the first time as he truly was—unloved and loveless."

He stared at her. Then it came to him that she was talking not about Leo Finkle, but of a total stranger, some mystical figure, perhaps even passionate prophet that Salzman had dreamed up for her—no relation to the living or dead. Leo trembled with rage and weakness. The trickster had obviously sold her a bill of goods, just as he had him, who'd expected to become acquainted with a young lady of twenty-nine, only to behold, the moment he laid eyes upon her strained and anxious face, a woman past thirty-five and aging rapidly. Only his self control had kept him this long in her presence.

Complication and Theme

Most of the plot of the story is taken up by the complication—the development of the central conflict. This revelation by Finkle deepens the conflict for we learn that in religious matters, as in choosing a mate, Finkle has not acted from love but from a sense of duty.

Most stories present some learning or growth on the part of the protagonist. The necessity of this growth is often the story's main idea, or theme.

"I am not," he said gravely, "a talented religious person," and in seeking words to go on, found himself possessed by shame and fear. "I think," he said in a strained manner, "that I came to God not because I loved Him, but because I did not."

This confession he spoke harshly because its unexpectedness shook him.

Lily wilted. Leo saw a profusion of loaves of bread go flying like ducks high over his head, not unlike the winged loaves by which he had counted himself to sleep last night. Mercifully, then, it snowed, which he would not put past Salzman's machinations.

He was infuriated with the marriage broker and swore he would throw him out of the room the minute he reappeared. But Salzman did not come that night, and when Leo's anger had subsided, an unaccountable despair grew in its place. At first he thought this was caused by his disappointment in Lily, but before long it became evident that he had involved himself with Salzman without a true knowledge of his own intent. He gradually realized—with an emptiness that seized him with six hands—that he had called in the broker to find him a bride because he was incapable of doing it himself. This terrifying insight he had derived as a result of his meeting and conversation with Lily Hirschorn. Her probing questions had somehow irritated him into revealing—to himself more than her—the true nature of his relationship to God, and from that it had come upon him, with shocking force, that apart from his parents, he had never loved anyone. Or perhaps it went the other way, that he did not love God so well as he might, because he had not loved man. It seemed to Leo that his whole life stood starkly revealed and he saw himself for the first time as he truly was—unloved and loveless. This bitter but somehow not fully unexpected revelation brought him to a point of panic, controlled only by extraordinary effort. He covered his face with his hands and cried.

The week that followed was the worst of his life. He did not eat and lost weight. His beard darkened and grew ragged. He stopped attending seminars and almost never opened a book. He seriously considering leaving the Yeshiva, although he was deeply troubled at the thought of the loss of all his years of study—saw them like pages torn from a book, strewn over the city—and at the devastating effect of this decision upon

Words for Everyday Use:

pro • fu • sion (prō fyōō´ zhən) *n.*, large number; abundance

mach • i • na • tion (mak ə nā´ shən) *n.*, clever plot or scheme

Vocabulary in Context

- The dandelions were growing in such profusion in Howard's yard that his lawn resembled a huge yellow blanket.
- Niccolò Machiavelli wrote so persuasively about the art of political machination in his book, *The Prince*, that his last name has come to symbolize anyone who skillfully manipulates others to achieve power.
- The knight begged his captors profusely and abjectly for mercy, throwing aside his sense of honor in the hopes of saving his life.

his parents. But he had lived without knowledge of himself, and never in the Five Books[9] and all the Commentaries—mea culpa[10]—had the truth been revealed to him. He did not know where to turn, and in all this desolating loneliness there was no *to whom*, although he often thought of Lily but not once could bring himself to go downstairs and make the call. He became touchy and irritable, especially with his landlady, who asked him all manner of personal questions; on the other hand, sensing his own disagreeableness, he waylaid her on the stairs and apologized abjectly, until mortified, she ran from him. Out of this, however, he drew the consolation that he was a Jew and that a Jew suffered. But gradually, as the long and terrible week drew to a close, he regained his composure and some idea of purpose in life: to go on as planned. Although he was imperfect, the ideal was not. As for his quest of a bride, the thought of continuing afflicted him with anxiety and heartburn, yet perhaps with this new knowledge of himself he would be more successful than in the past. Perhaps love would now come to him and a bride to that love. And for this sanctified seeking who needed a Salzman?

The marriage broker, a skeleton with haunted eyes, returned that very night. He looked, withal, the picture of frustrated expectancy—as if he had steadfastly waited the week at Miss Lily Hirschorn's side for a telephone call that never came.

Casually coughing, Salzman came immediately to the point: "So how did you like her?

Leo's anger rose and he could not refrain from chiding the matchmaker: "Why did you lie to me, Salzman?"

Salzman's pale face went dead white, the world had snowed on him.

"Did you not state that she was twenty-nine?" Leo insisted.

"I gave you my word—"

"She was thirty-five, if a day. *At least* thirty-five."

"Of this don't be too sure. Her father told me—"

"Never mind. The worst of it was that you lied to her."

"How did I lie to her, tell me?"

"You told her things about me that weren't true. You made me out to be more, consequently less than I am. She had in mind a totally different person, a sort of semimystical Wonder Rabbi."

"All I said, you was a religious man."

"I can imagine."

Salzman sighed. "This is my weakness that I have," he confessed. "My wife says to me I shouldn't be a salesman, but when I have two fine people that they would be wonderful to be married, I am so happy that I talk too much." He smiled wanly. "This is why Salzman is a poor man."

Leo's anger left him. "Well, Salzman, I'm afraid that's all."

The marriage broker fastened hungry eyes on him.

"You don't want any more a bride?"

"I do," said Leo, "but I have decided to seek her in a different way. I am no longer

9. **Five Books.** The Pentateuch, or Five Books of Moses, consists of Genesis, Exodus, Leviticus, Numbers, and Deuteronomy.

10. **mea culpa.** I am to blame' (Latin).

WORDS FOR EVERYDAY USE: **ab • ject • ly** (ab´ jekt´ lē) *adv., miserably;* in a manner that suggests a lack of self-respect

ADDITIONAL QUESTIONS AND ACTIVITIES

Ask students the following questions: What causes Leo's crisis? What roles do Lily and Salzman play in this crisis? How does it affect Leo's behavior and his thoughts? How does Leo finally resolve his crisis?

Answers. The fact that both Lily and he have been lied to causes Leo's crisis. When Lily shows marked interest in Leo's religious convictions, Leo knows that Salzman has been exaggerating not only Lily's qualities but his own. Leo decides after experiencing this crisis to look for a bride "in a different way." He now desires to marry for love, not convenience.

Additional Questions and Activities

Leo states that "Love . . . should be a by-product of living and worship rather than its own end." Ask students to define the distinction that Leo is making in this sentence. Divide the class into small groups and have students discuss the pros and cons of each of the following positions: "Love should be the goal of life" and "Love should be a by-product of life." Have each group make a list of its arguments and present the most persuasive ones to the class as a whole.

Additional Questions and Activities

In order to have a more active social life, Leo is prepared to cut corners financially. Ask students what might motivate them to cut corners financially. Would they cut corners to save for college expenses? a vacation? a particular product they consider a luxury? How would they go about cutting corners? What daily or weekly expenses would they cut down on or eliminate in order to achieve their goals? How long would they be willing to make such sacrifices? What expenses do they consider absolutely essential? Would they take on an extra job to earn money instead of cutting corners? Students may wish to keep a precise record of their expenses for a week, noting how much money they spend and the items or services purchased in order to make informed decisions about cutting corners.

interested in an arranged marriage. To be frank, I now admit the necessity of premarital love. That is, I want to be in love with the one I marry."

"Love?" said Salzman, astounded. After a moment he remarked, "For us, our love is our life, not for the ladies. In the ghetto they—"

"I know, I know," said Leo. "I've thought of it often. Love, I have said to myself, should be a by-product of living and worship rather than its own end. Yet for myself I find it necessary to establish the level of my need and fulfill it."

Salzman shrugged but answered, "Listen, rabbi, if you want love, this I can find for you also. I have such beautiful clients that you will love them the minute your eyes will see them."

Leo smiled unhappily. "I'm afraid you don't understand."

But Salzman hastily unstrapped his portfolio and withdrew a manila packet from it.

"Pictures," he said, quickly laying the envelope on the table.

Leo called after him to take the pictures away, but as if on the wings of the wind, Salzman had disappeared.

March came. Leo had returned to his regular routine. Although he felt not quite himself yet—lacked energy—he was making plans for a more active social life. Of course it would cost something, but he was an expert in cutting corners; and when there were no corners left he would make circles rounder. All the while Salzman's pictures had lain on the table, gathering dust. Occasionally as Leo sat studying, or enjoying a cup of tea, his eyes fell on the manila envelope, but he never opened it.

The days went by and no social life to speak of developed with a member of the opposite sex—it was difficult, given the circumstances of his situation. One morning Leo toiled up the stairs to his room and stared out the window at the city. Although the day was bright his view of it was dark. For some time he watched people in the street below hurrying along and then turned with a heavy heart to his little room. On the table was the packet. With a sudden relentless gesture he tore it open. For a half-hour he stood by the table in a state of excitement, examining the photographs of the ladies Salzman had included. Finally, with a deep sigh he put them down. There were six, of varying degrees of attractiveness, but look at them long enough and they all became Lily Hirschorn: all past their prime, all starved behind bright smiles, not a true personality in the lot. Life, despite their frantic yoohooings, had passed them by; they were pictures in a briefcase that stank of fish. After a while, however, as Leo attempted to return the photographs into the envelope, he found in it another, a snapshot of the type taken by a machine for a quarter. He gazed at it a moment and let out a cry.

Her face deeply moved him. Why, he could at first not say. It gave him the impression of youth—spring flowers, yet age—a sense of having been used to the bone, wasted; this came from the eyes, which were hauntingly familiar yet absolutely strange. He had a vivid impression that he had met her before,

Words for Everyday Use: **re • lent • less** (ri lent´ lis) *adj.,* harsh; pitiless

Vocabulary in Context

- The pirates subjected their prisoner to a relentless barrage of questions, hoping to wear him down and discover where the treasure lay buried.
- Training a new pet can be an exasperating experience, for rarely will a young animal do precisely what its owner demands.
- While observing Ramadan, practicing Muslims refrain from eating during daylight hours and only break their fast once the sun has set.

but try as he might he could not place her although he could almost recall her name, as if he had read it in her own handwriting. No, this couldn't be; he would have remembered her. It was not, he affirmed, that she had an extraordinary beauty—no, though her face was attractive enough; it was that *something* about her moved him. Feature for feature, even some of the ladies of the photographs could do better; but she leaped forth to his heart—had *lived*, or wanted to—more than just wanted, perhaps regretted how she had lived—had somehow deeply suffered: it could be seen in the depths of those reluctant eyes, and from the way the light enclosed and shone from her, and within her, opening realms of possibility: this was her own. Her he desired. His head ached and eyes narrowed with the intensity of his gazing, then as if an obscure fog had blown up in the mind, he experienced fear of her and was aware that he had received an impression, somehow, of evil. He shuddered, saying softly, it is thus with us all. Leo brewed some tea in a small pot and sat sipping it without sugar, to calm himself. But before he had finished drinking, again with excitement he examined the face and found it good: good for Leo Finkle. Only such a one could understand him and help him seek whatever he was seeking. She might, perhaps, love him. How she had happened to be among the discards in Salzman's barrel he could never guess, but he knew he must urgently go find her.

Leo rushed downstairs, grabbed up the Bronx telephone book, and searched for Salzman's home address. He was not listed, nor was his office. Neither was he in the Manhattan book. But Leo remembered having written down the address on a slip of paper after he had read Salzman's advertisement in the "personals" column of the *Forward*. He ran up to his room and tore through his papers, without luck. It was exasperating. Just when he needed the matchmaker he was nowhere to be found. Fortunately Leo remembered to look in his wallet. There on a card he found his name written and a Bronx address. No phone number was listed, the reason—Leo now recalled—he had originally communicated with Salzman by letter. He got on his coat, put a hat on over his skull cap and hurried to the subway station. All the way to the far end of the Bronx he sat on the edge of his seat. He was more than once tempted to take out the picture and see if the girl's face was as he remembered it, but he refrained, allowing the snapshot to remain in his inside coat pocket, content to have her so close. When the train pulled into the station he was waiting at the door and bolted out. He quickly located the street Salzman had advertised.

The building he sought was less than a block from the subway, but it was not an office building, nor even a loft, nor a store in which one could rent office space. It was a very old tenement house. Leo found Salzman's name in pencil on a soiled tag under the bell and climbed three dark flights to his apartment. When he knocked, the door was opened by a thin, asthmatic, gray-haired woman, in felt slippers.

Words for Everyday Use:

ex • as • per • a • ting (eg zas´pər āt iŋ) *part.*, irritating, annoying

re • frain (ri frān´) *vi.*, hold back; keep oneself from doing something

Cross-curricular Activities

Mathematics and Sciences. When he discovers the photograph of Stella, Leo experiences a kind of *déjà vu*, having "a vivid impression that he had met her before," although he is sure he has never laid eyes on her. The psychological phenomenon of *déjà vu* is common, yet poorly understood by medical science. Some neurophysiologists suggest that it results from minor biomechanical malfunctions in the brain. On the other hand, other people see it as evidence of a spiritual dimension beyond the scope of normal human perception. Have students investigate both the scientific and the nonscientific theories offered to explain this phenomenon.

Additional Questions and Activities

Ask students in what way the author uses the geographical setting of his story, New York City, both to increase the tension of the plot and to contribute to the characterization of Leo. Why does the author make it difficult for Leo to find Salzman? Why does the author have Salzman live a train ride away from Leo rather than in his immediate neighborhood? Students may wish to look at a map of New York City to appreciate more fully how geography contributes to the story and to appreciate how a knowledge of that geography can expand their understanding of Leo's character and the story as a whole.

Literary Technique

Allegory. An allegory is a work in which each element symbolizes, or represents, something else. Historically, allegory has frequently been a vehicle in literature for religious themes. On page 38, the author allows an allegorical reading of the story by suggesting through the words of Salzman's wife that Salzman has godlike qualities (she tells Leo that Salzman's office is "in the air," and she replies "who knows where he is? . . . he will find you" to Leo's questions about Salzman's whereabouts). Ask students to consider "The Magic Barrel" in terms of its possible allegorical significance. If Salzman is a symbol of the divine, what new meaning does the story take on?

Answer. If Salzman is a symbolic representation of God, Leo can be seen as a lost soul in need of divine guidance. The truth to which Leo is guided, however, must be earned through an arduous trial. Before Leo can find what he is looking for, he must first reach an understanding of what it is he is truly seeking. Salzman first leads Leo to comprehend that what he seeks is not a wife, but to love and be loved, and then Salzman offers him the opportunity to fulfill this newly understood desire. Since Stella represents the difficulties of enduring love and faith, Leo's ultimate salvation will depend upon his ability to sustain both his love and faith (in Stella and therefore in God) through great trials.

"Yes?" she said, expecting nothing. She listened without listening. He could have sworn he had seen her, too, before but knew it was an illusion.

"Salzman—does he live here? Pinye Salzman," he said, "the matchmaker?"

She stared at him a long minute. "Of course."

He felt embarrassed. "Is he in?"

"No." Her mouth, though left open, offered nothing more.

Ambiguity

An ambiguity is an intentional double meaning. Of whom besides Salzman might it be said that his office is "In the air" and "who knows where he is? . . . he will find you"?

"The matter is urgent. Can you tell me where his office is?"

"In the air." She pointed upward.

"You mean he has no office?" Leo asked.

"In his socks."

He peered into the apartment. It was sunless and dingy, one large room divided by a half-open curtain, beyond which he could see a sagging metal bed. The near side of a room was crowded with rickety chairs, old bureaus, a three-legged table, racks of cooking utensils, and all the apparatus of a kitchen. But there was no sign of Salzman or his magic barrel, probably also a figment of the imagination. An odor of frying fish made Leo weak to the knees.

Climax

The climax is the high point of interest or suspense in a story. At this point, Finkle, having finally discovered the match that he wants, learns that he might not be able to have that match.

"Where is he?" he insisted. "I've got to see your husband."

At length she answered, "So who knows where he is? Every time he thinks a new thought he runs to a different place. Go home, he will find you."

"Tell him Leo Finkle."

She gave no sign she had heard.

He walked downstairs, depressed.

But Salzman, breathless, stood waiting at his door.

Leo was astounded and overjoyed. "How did you get here before me?"

"I rushed."

"Come inside."

They entered. Leo fixed tea, and a sardine sandwich for Salzman. As they were drinking he reached behind him for the packet of pictures and handed them to the marriage broker.

Salzman put down his glass and said expectantly, "You found somebody you like?"

"Not among these."

The marriage broker turned away.

"Here is the one I want." Leo held forth the snapshot.

Salzman slipped on his glasses and took the picture into his trembling hand. He turned ghastly and let out a groan.

"What's the matter?" cried Leo.

"Excuse me. Was an accident this picture. She isn't for you."

Salzman frantically shoved the manila packet into his portfolio. He thrust the snapshot into his pocket and fled down the stairs.

Leo, after momentary paralysis, gave chase and cornered the marriage broker in the vestibule. The landlady made hysterical outcries but neither of them listened.

"Give me back the picture, Salzman."

"No." The pain in his eyes was terrible.

"Tell me who she is then."

"This I can't tell you. Excuse me."

He made to depart, but Leo, forgetting himself, seized the matchmaker by his tight coat and shook him frenziedly.

"Please," sighed Salzman. "*Please.*"

Leo ashamedly let him go. "Tell me

Words for Everyday Use:

ap • pa • ra • tus (ap´ ə rat´ əs) *n.,* materials and tools needed for a specific purpose

ves • ti • bule (ves´ tə byōōl´) *n.,* hallway or small room at the entrance of a building

Vocabulary in Context

- Rube Goldberg was a cartoonist famous for designing comically complex apparatuses, devices whose obvious impracticality made them all the more amusing.
- The movers had piled so many cartons in the vestibule that the postman could not get to the mailboxes to deliver mail to the residents of the apartment building.
- Elwood looked so haggard after three days without sleep that his boss gave him the day off and told him to get some rest.

who she is," he begged. "It's very important for me to know."

"She is not for you. She is a wild one—wild, without shame. This is not a bride for a rabbi."

"What do you mean wild?"

"Like an animal. Like a dog. For her to be poor was a sin. This is why to me she is dead now."

"In God's name, what do you mean?"

"Her I can't introduce to you," Salzman said.

"Why are you so excited?"

"Why, he asks," Salzman said, bursting into tears. "This is my baby, my Stella, she should burn in hell."

Leo hurried up to bed and hid under the covers. Under the covers he thought his life through. Although he soon fell asleep he could not sleep her out of his mind. He woke, beating his breast. Though he prayed to be rid of her, his prayers went unanswered. Through days of torment he endlessly struggled not to love her; fearing success, he escaped it. He then concluded to convert her to goodness, himself to God. The idea alternately nauseated and exalted him.

He perhaps did not know that he had come to a final decision until he encountered Salzman in a Broadway cafeteria. He was sitting alone at a rear table, sucking the bony remains of a fish. The marriage broker appeared haggard, and transparent to the point of vanishing.

Salzman looked up at first without recognizing him. Leo had grown a pointed beard and his eyes were weighted with wisdom.

"Salzman," he said, "love has at last come to my heart."

"Who can love from a picture?" mocked the marriage broker.

"It is not impossible."

"If you can love her, then you can love anybody. Let me show you some new clients that they just sent me their photographs. One is a little doll."

"Just her I want," Leo murmured.

"Don't be a fool, doctor. Don't bother with her."

"Put me in touch with her, Salzman," Leo said humbly. "Perhaps I can be of service."

Salzman had stopped eating and Leo understood with emotion that it was now arranged.

Leaving the cafeteria, he was, however, afflicted by a tormenting suspicion that Salzman had planned it all to happen this way.

Leo was informed by letter that she would meet him on a certain corner, and she was there one spring night, waiting under a street lamp. He appeared, carrying a small bouquet of violets and rosebuds. Stella stood by the lamppost, smoking. She wore white with red shoes, which fitted his expectations, although in a troubled moment he had imagined the dress red, and only the shoes white. She waited uneasily and shyly. From afar he saw that her eyes—clearly her father's—were filled with desperate innocence. He pictured, in her, his own redemption. Violins and lit candles revolved in the sky. Leo ran forward with flowers outthrust.

Around the corner, Salzman, leaning against a wall, chanted prayers for the dead. ■

RESOLUTION

The resolution ends the central conflict, or struggle, in the story.

DÉNOUEMENT

The dénouement presents the consequences of the resolution and ties up loose ends.

WORDS FOR EVERYDAY USE: **hag • gard** (hag´ərd) *adj.,* having a wasted or exhausted look

ADDITIONAL QUESTIONS AND ACTIVITIES

Ask students why the colors of Stella's shoes and dress are important. What do the colors red and white frequently symbolize? Why did Leo, "in a troubled moment," imagine Stella in a red dress with white shoes? What is the significance of having her wearing, instead, a white dress with red shoes? What other images and phrases contribute to the overall impression the reader has of the meeting between Leo and Stella?

ANSWERS TO SELECTION CHECK TEST 4.1.5

EX. Who is the protagonist of "The Magic Barrel"?
Leo Finkle is the protagonist of "The Magic Barrel."

1. What is Leo Finkle's occupation?
He is a rabbinical student at Yeshiva University.

2. What food does Pinye Salzman love to eat?
He loves to eat fish.

3. Where does Leo Finkle meet Lily Hirschorn?
He meets her on Riverside Drive, in New York City.

4. How does Leo Finkle react after his meeting with Lily?
He becomes depressed for a week.

5. Who is Stella?
Stella is Pinye Salzman's daughter.

RESPONDING TO THE SELECTION

If students have difficulty imagining the use of a marriage broker, have them discuss their notions of love and marriage and where they have derived these ideas. Have them list stories, movies, songs, or television shows that represent for them the most powerful conceptions of love and marriage. Ask them to talk about other models for love and marriage, such as family and friends, and to consider how their own ideas are influenced or determined by these cultural models.

THE PROCESS OF WRITING: EVALUATING AND REVISING

▶ See the Writing Evaluation Form: Process, *Assessment Portfolio,* 7.1.

▶ For detailed evaluation, see the checklists and evaluation forms for revisions, *Assessment Portfolio,* 7.7–7.8.

Rather than scoring or critiquing these revisions, discuss with students in small groups what you and others find interesting about their writing. Allow the author to explain what improvements he or she was trying to make. Comment on the writer's successes in making these improvements. Encourage students to continue to revise their drafts. This may be a good time to encourage students to view their writing as a means of self-expression and a source of enjoyment.

▶ Additional practice in revising is provided in the *Essential Skills Practice Book: Writing,* 1.49–1.58.

Answers for Reviewing the Selection

RECALLING

1. Salzman is a marriage broker who arranges marriages. Finkle employs Salzman to help him find a bride.

2. Salzman first suggests Sophie P., a childless widow with two years of college education; Lily H., a high school teacher with a new car who lived in Paris; and Ruth K., a nineteen-year-old honor student who is slightly lame.

3. Leo is angry at Salzman for having lied both to him and to Lily, and he scolds the matchmaker for having misrepresented each potential partner to the other. Before Salzman departs, he leaves an envelope with pictures of available marriage partners on Leo's table.

4. Leo discovers a photograph of a woman whose face deeply moves him. He falls in love with the woman in the photograph and desperately seeks Salzman in order to discover her identity.

INTERPRETING

Responses will vary. Possible responses are given.

5. Finkle wants Salzman's help because he feels an ordained rabbi has a better chance of securing a congregation if married.

6. Leo offers various reasons: he does not wish to marry a widow; he does not wish to marry a woman older than he; and he does not like the profession of one woman's father. After Salzman leaves, Leo begins to have doubts about the matchmaking process, wondering if he dislikes it as an institution.

7. At first, Leo seems disappointed with something particular about each of the women Salzman suggests, but then he seems to become bitter at feeling compelled to employ a marriage broker and ashamed that he has done so. Leo's actions suggest that he is in the process of realizing that he finds the matchmaking process distasteful and contrary to his personal beliefs. After his meeting with Lily Hirschorn, he is especially upset by the false por-

(cont.)

Responding to the Selection

How do you think love and marriage should be related? What is your reaction to Leo Finkle's use of a marriage broker? How did you feel when he rejected the idea and pursued a love based on instinct instead? Explain your thinking.

Reviewing the Selection

Recalling

1. What kind of services does Pinye Salzman sell? What is the nature of Leo Finkle's business with Pinye Salzman?

2. Who are the women Salzman initially suggests as potential brides? What characteristics do they have?

3. When Pinye Salzman reappears at Finkle's apartment after Leo's meeting with Lily Hirschorn, how does Leo react? What does Salzman do?

4. What does Leo find in the photographs Salzman leaves behind? How does he behave after his discovery?

Interpreting

5. Why does Leo Finkle want to buy Pinye Salzman's help? On what important reason has he based his decision to contact Salzman?

6. Why does Leo reject the first batch of women? How does he feel about the matchmaking process now?

7. How do you explain Leo's actions at this meeting? In what ways do they suggest the change in his feelings about the marriage process?

8. The photograph Leo finds touches important emotions inside him. What are these feelings? What elements in the photograph contribute to the effect?

Synthesizing

9. What suspicion torments Leo at the end of the story? What would this interpretation of the events suggest about Pinye Salzman's character?

10. What inference does Salzman invite through his description of Stella? Identify some clues to support your answer.

Answers for Reviewing the Selection (cont.)

trayal of potential mates by Salzman.

8. The photograph inspires in Leo a sense of familiarity, a feeling of sympathy for the suffering he sees in the woman's eyes and face, and an intense desire to meet her; however, he also experiences a sudden fear because of a vague impression of evil he receives from the picture, particularly from the woman's eyes and the way the light shines on her face.

SYNTHESIZING

Responses will vary. Possible responses are given.

9. At the end of the story, Leo is haunted by the thought that Salzman had planned from the beginning to manipulate Leo into falling in love with Stella. If true, Salzman would not be the awkward, hapless, and almost inept old man that he seemed to be, but rather a clever, resourceful, though deceptive, matchmaker who

(cont.)

Understanding Literature (Questions for Discussion)

1. **Motivation.** A **motivation** is a force that moves a character to think, feel, or behave in a certain way. Think about Leo Finkle's actions throughout "The Magic Barrel." How do you think his motivations change as the story progresses?

2. **Background Information.** Often part of the exposition or introduction to a literary work, **background information** orients readers to important details about major characters. These details might include family background, opinions, physical traits, strengths and weaknesses, or anything the writer feels readers must know in order to understand the story. Find three facts from "The Magic Barrel" that provide background information.

3. **Characterization. Characterization** is the use of literary techniques to create a character. These techniques may include description of the character's appearance, insight into the character's thinking processes, and observation of the character's actions. What techniques does Bernard Malamud use to portray Leo Finkle and Pinye Salzman?

4. **Dialect. Dialect** is a version of a language spoken by the people of a particular place, time, or social group. The use of dialect helps writers create vivid characters by placing those characters in a social, temporal, or geographic context. Find some examples of dialect in "The Magic Barrel." From what context do they originate? What do they tell you about the characters in the story?

5. **Figurative Language. Figurative language** is language that suggests something more than the literal meanings of the words. For example, "winter was on its last legs," suggests that winter is almost dead, or over. What other examples of figurative language can you find in "The Magic Barrel"? How do they affect your experience as a reader of the story?

The Process of Writing: Evaluating and Revising

Evaluation and Revision. Read the Language Arts Survey, 1.43–1.45, on different methods of evaluating and revising. Using the writing assignment you began on page 9, exchange papers with a classmate for peer evaluation. Then consider your peer's comments as you complete a self-evaluation. Employ the four types of revision—adding or expanding, deleting, replacing, and moving—in response to both evaluations.

Answers for Reviewing the Selection (cont.)

employed great insight into human character in order to achieve his goal of finding someone to love his daughter.

10. By describing Stella as "wild, without shame"; "not a bride for a rabbi"; "dead" to him; and someone who "should burn in hell," Salzman suggests that Stella has rebelled against her parents and refused to obey their wishes. His description of Stella also reinforces Leo's impression that she has suffered and that she might possess a certain kind of "evil." This description seems also to suggest to Leo that Stella is a misunderstood and unappreciated person, someone as needful of love as Leo is himself.

Answers for Understanding Literature

1. Motivation. At first, Leo's motive is unsentimentally professional: he believes a wife will further his career as a rabbi. Later, his motivation transforms into an emotional need to give and receive love.

2. Background Information. Leo grew up within a traditional, conservative Jewish culture that believed love was a product of marriage rather than its foundation. The most influential model for marriage in his life was his parents' marriage, which had been arranged by a matchmaker. Leo had devoted the previous six years of his life to his studies and lacked a circle of social acquaintances in which to find a wife.

3. Characterization. Leo's character is revealed through his initial desire to employ a marriage broker to find a wife, his responses to the women proposed by Salzman, his encounter with Lily and his subsequent reaction to this meeting, and through the insight Malamud gives the reader into Leo's thoughts. Salzman's character is revealed through physical description, the almost magical way that he appears and disappears during the course of the story, the description of his apartment, and through his response to Leo's wish to meet Stella.

(cont.)

Answers for Understanding Literature (cont.)

4. Dialect. Salzman frequently speaks in grammatically incorrect English, as in the phrase, "You wouldn't believe me how much cards I got in my office" (page 28). He also employs Yiddish phrases, such as *Yiddishe kinder* (page 32). While Salzman's English follows the grammatical rules of Yiddish, Leo's English is more standard, emphasizing the fact that Salzman is more closely connected to traditional Jewish culture.

5. Figurative Language. Salzman sees Leo's eyes as "heavy with learning"(page 28), emphasizing the marriage broker's reverent approval of Leo as a potential husband. During his encounter with Lily, Leo imagines Salzman to be nearby like "a cloven-hoofed Pan" (page 33), stressing Malamud's portrayal of Salzman throughout the story as possessing some vague magical powers. Such phrases serve to deepen and to emphasize the impression that the reader already has at these particular moments in the story.

ADDITIONAL RESOURCES

READER'S GUIDE
- Selection Worksheet, 1.4

ASSESSMENT PORTFOLIO
- Selection Check Test, 4.1.7
- Selection Test, 4.1.8

ESSENTIAL SKILLS PRACTICE BOOKS
- *Writing,* 1.47
- *Language,* 2.3–2.29

ENRICHMENT ACTIVITIES

- Students can discuss how reading a drama differs from reading other works of literature. Ask students to consider how ideas are presented, how characterization is portrayed, and how the work is interpreted. What effect does seeing a drama performed have on interpreting a play?

- A selection from "The Crucible" is given in this unit. Some students may wish to read the whole play. Interested students might then practice and perform the play or give a dramatic reading of it. Other students might benefit from observing such a presentation.

SUPPORT FOR LEP STUDENTS

Read the background note on page 46 with students and make sure they understand the historical background to the play before they begin reading the selection.

ADDTIONAL VOCABULARY

agape—open mouthed in surprise or wonder
unperturbed—unbothered
sporting—pretending, playing

Drama

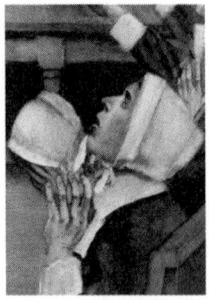

Drama is literature enacted in front of an audience by people who play the parts of the characters. No one knows for certain how drama originated, but we do know that ritual performances have been held by people around the globe since long before the beginning of recorded history.

The first literary dramas were created long ago in ancient Greece and may have developed from reenactments of ritual sacrifices. In fact, the ancient Greek word *tragōidia,* from which our word *tragedy* derives, meant "song of the goats." According to one theory, people in ancient Greece would come together to sacrifice an animal to win a god's favor. Eventually, that sacrifice developed into an elaborate show involving an actor, a priest, and a chorus with whom the priest interacted. In the fifth century BC, the Greek playwright Aeschylus added a second actor, and drama as we know it was born.

Types of Stages

In classical times, dramas were performed in open-air amphitheaters, or **arena stages.** In the Middle Ages, plays were often produced on the backs of wagons in the courtyards of inns. From these developed the **thrust stage** used in Elizabethan England, a platform that jutted into an area open to the sky. In the nineteenth and twentieth centuries, the **proscenium stage,** or **picture stage,** became common. Such a stage is a box-like area with three walls (or curtains) and a removed "fourth wall" through which the audience views the action.

Types of Drama

Most dramas can be classified as either comedies or tragedies. A **comedy,** in its original sense, was any work with a happy ending. The term is widely used today to refer to any humorous work, especially one prepared for the stage or the screen. A **tragedy** initially was a drama that told the story of the fall of a person of high status, though in recent years the word has been used to describe any play about the downfall of a central character, or protagonist, who wins the audience's sympathies in some way.

Drama in the United States

The United States has produced many of the world's finest dramatists. Important figures in the history of American drama include Eugene O'Neill (1888–1953), Elmer Rice (1892–1967), Thornton Wilder (1897–1975), Lillian Hellman (1905–1984), Tennessee Williams (1911–1983), Arthur Miller (1915–), Edward Albee (1928–), Lanford Wilson (1937–), August Wilson (1945–), David Mamet (1947–), and Beth Henley (1952–).

The earliest American theatrical productions were vaudeville shows and **melodramas,** plays with exaggerated characters, scenes, and situations. From the 1920s through the 1950s, American **Realist theater** blossomed in the work of O'Neill, Hellman, and Miller. Williams and Albee introduced to American theater many experimental elements, extending and enriching the Realist tradition.

The trial of two "witches" at Salem, Massachusetts, in 1692.
Illustration by Howard Pyle.
The Granger Collection, New York

GOALS/OBJECTIVES

Studying this lesson will enable students to

- enjoy reading a drama
- recognize the elements of drama
- identify and explain the purpose of stage directions
- describe a set and identify properties needed for a play
- understand and discuss the theme of a drama
- proofread an essay
- identify parts of speech

Cross-curricular Activities

Arts and Humanities. Students can research different theories of acting, such as method acting (also known as the Method or the Stanislavski Method), a theory and technique that requires the actor to identify with the character being played and to render his or her performance in a naturalistic, individualized manner.

Additional Questions and Activities

As students read the selection, have them look again at the illustration on page 43. They can try to identify characters in the illustration and explain what the characters are doing based on the selection from the play.

Quotables

"All theories of what a good play is, or how a good play should be written, are futile. A good play is a play which when acted upon the boards makes an audience interested and pleased. A play that fails in this is a bad play."

—Maurice Baring

Historical Note

In Elizabethan England, a theater stage projected out into the pit, where lower-paying customers stood to watch the play. In some instances, spectators were allowed to sit on the apron of the stage. At the same time, in Renaissance France, the nobility who attended plays were often seated on the stage itself, becoming, in a way, part of the entire spectacle available to the theatergoer.

Additional Questions and Activities

On a stage, if one is available, or in the classroom itself, have students who have been assigned the various roles in the selection from *The Crucible* block out the stage directions from the scene. Have them decide where each character must be situated at the opening of the scene and then ask them to walk through the action. Have students alternate roles so that they can all get a sense of how actors must learn to move on stage.

Additional Questions and Activities

Dialogue. To introduce students to the ways in which the dialogue of a play often conveys information that in fiction is furnished by the narrator, have students transform the opening paragraphs of the previous selection (Bernard Malamud's "The Magic Barrel") into dramatic form. Ask students to consider what information is essential for the audience and decide how best to put it into dramatic form. Encourage them to add monologues and/or dialogues that do not appear in the original selection.

Elements of Drama

The Playwright and the Script

Playwright. The author of a play is the **playwright.** The relationship between a playwright and the play is more tenuous that that of an ordinary author to his or her text. A novelist or poet has enormous control over the form in which his or her work will be presented to its audience, the reader. A playwright, in contrast, must depend upon the interpretations given his or her work by producers, directors, set designers, actors, and other persons involved in producing the work for the stage. The playwright's art is collaborative.

Script. A **script** is the written work from which a drama is produced. It contains stage directions and dialogue and may be divided into acts and scenes.

Stage Directions. Stage directions are notes provided by the playwright to describe how something should be presented or performed on the stage. Stage directions often describe elements of the **spectacle,** such as lighting, music, sound effects, costumes, properties, and set design. They also may describe entrances and exits, the movements of characters, facial expressions, gestures, body language, tone of voice, or other elements related to the acting of the play. Sometimes, especially in reading versions of plays, stage directions provide historical or background information. Stage directions usually are printed in italics and enclosed in brackets or parentheses. In stage directions, the parts of the stage are often described using the terms *up, down, right, left,* and *center,* which describe stage areas from the point of view of the actors.

Stage Areas

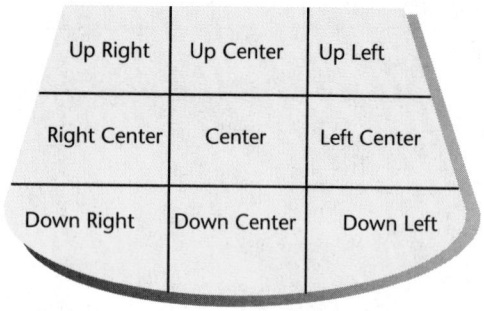

Dialogue. Dialogue is the term used to describe the speech of actors in a play. The dialogue usually consists of the characters' names and the words and other utterances to be spoken by the actors. The dialogue of a play may contain many **monologues,** or long speeches given by actors. A speech given by a lone character on stage is called a **soliloquy.** A statement intended to be heard by the audience or by a single other character but not by other characters on the stage is called an **aside.**

Acts and Scenes. An **act** is a major division of a drama. The plays of ancient Rome and of Elizabethan England were typically divided into **five acts.** In the Modern Era, **three-act** and **one-act plays** are quite common. The acts may be divided into scenes. Typically, a **scene** begins with the entrance of one or more characters and ends with the exit of one or more characters. The time and place of acts or scenes may change from one to the next.

The Spectacle

Spectacle. The **spectacle** is all the elements of the drama presented to the senses of the audience—the lights, sets, curtains, costumes, makeup, music, sound effects, properties, and movements of the actors, including any special movement such as pantomime or dance. Spectacle is one major feature that differentiates dramatic from nondramatic works. The following chart describes common parts of the spectacle.

ELEMENT OF SPECTACLE	DESCRIPTION
Stage	This is the area in which the action is performed. An **arena stage,** or **theater in the round,** is one in which the audience stands or sits around a circular or semicircular open space. A **thrust stage** is one that extends into the audience, which is situated on three sides of the playing area. A **proscenium,** or **picture stage,** is one that has an arch around an opening that acts as a removed "fourth wall."
Set	The set is everything placed upon the stage to give the impression of a particular setting, or time and place. Sets often include walls, furnishings, and painted backdrops.
Properties	Properties are items that can be carried on and off the stage by actors or manipulated by actors during scenes. Examples of properties include books, fans, gavels, and walking sticks.
Sound effects	These are sounds introduced to create mood or to indicate the presence of something. Common sound effects include thunder, ringing telephones, and police sirens.
Blocking	This is the act of determining how actors will move on a stage. Blocking is almost always done by the director of the play.

Additional Questions and Activities

Acts and Scenes. Have students take notes while watching television shows at home in order to keep track of the scenes in each show. Ask them to write a brief summary of each scene, noting the time, setting, characters, action, and content of the dialogue. Have students watch both half-hour sitcoms and hour-long dramatic series so that they can compare the structure of each format. Can these shows be easily divided into acts? How many scenes and acts are there in a typical half-hour sitcom? in a typical one-hour drama? Students might perform the same exercise while watching a movie.

Additional Questions and Activities

Spectacle. Arrange to screen (on video) portions of two plays that make very different use of the elements of spectacle. For example, many productions of Shakespeare's plays attempt to reproduce the locations and costumes appropriate to the plays' settings and periods. In contrast, productions of such minimalist dramas as Samuel Beckett's *Waiting for Godot* and *End Game* make limited use of properties, scenery, and costumes. For each video, have students note the sets, properties, and costumes employed by the directors. How do the different uses of these elements of theater drastically alter the play-going experience?

Cross-curricular Activities

Social Studies. Divide students into two groups and have one group of students research the Salem witch trials of 1692 while the other group researches the McCarthy hearings of the early 1950s. Ask them to consider the following questions while researching: What were the origins of each event? How many people initiated each event? What motivated the instigators as well as those who subsequently supported the trials and hearings? Did anyone speak out against these crusaders? What happened to them? Why? Have each group of students present their findings in class. Then hold a class discussion about the similarities and differences between these two historical moments.

Additional Questions and Activities

Ask students to consider how the thematic content of Miller's play (that is, a witch hunt and the mob psychology it produces) might have compelled the playwright to set his play in the seventeenth century. Why did Miller not simply write a drama set in the 1950s that dealt directly with the McCarthy hearings in Congress? How did the nature of the McCarthy "witch hunt," and Miller's position in the entertainment field prevent Miller from dealing with his subject matter openly? Is the play more or less effective as a result of its setting in seventeenth-century New England?

FROM

The Crucible

ARTHUR MILLER

Background Note: In 1692, a series of trials was held in Salem, Massachusetts, of persons accused of witchcraft. Many people in the community and in surrounding areas had developed a disease resembling epilepsy, and suspicions arose that the afflictions might be the work of witches. The governor of the colony of Massachusetts, Sir William Phips, instituted court proceedings. The proceedings were inflamed by accusations made by the daughters of a Salem minister named Parris. These daughters, including Abigail Parris, pretended to be possessed by spirits and made spectacles in the courtroom during examinations of the accused witches. In all, nineteen persons were hanged as a result of the trials, and one person was pressed to death. Many others were imprisoned and tortured.

Arthur Miller became interested in the Salem witch trials during the McCarthy Era of the 1950s, a time when a similar "witch hunt" occurred in the United States, this one for suspected communists and other radicals in public office and the entertainment industry. Miller's play explores the psychology of mob hysteria and guilt by association. In this scene from the play, John Proctor, whose wife, Elizabeth, has been arrested as a witch, has brought to the court Mary Warren, who has evidence that Abigail and the other afflicted girls have been pretending. As the scene opens, Abigail interrupts an interrogation of John Proctor by the prosecutor, Danforth.

Stage Directions

Stage directions are notes that tell about the movements and ways of speaking of characters, about the setting, or about such elements of the spectacle as lighting, costumes, properties, and sound effects.

Abigail, with a weird, wild, chilling cry, screams up to the ceiling.

ABIGAIL. You will not! Begone! Begone, I say!

DANFORTH. What is it, child? (*But Abigail, pointing with fear, is now raising up her frightened eyes, her awed face, toward the ceiling—the girls are doing the same—and now Hawthorne, Haler, Putnam, Cheever, Herrick, and Danforth do the same.*) What's there? (*He lowers his eyes from the ceiling, and now he is frightened; there is real tension in his voice.*) Child! (*She is transfixed—with all the girls, she is whimpering open-mouthed, agape at the ceiling.*) Girls! Why do you—?

MERCY LEWIS. (*pointing*) It's on the beam! Behind the rafter!

DANFORTH. (*looking up*) Where!

ABIGAIL. Why—? (*She gulps.*) Why do you come, yellow bird?

PROCTOR. Where's a bird? I see no bird!

ABIGAIL. (*to the ceiling*) My face? My face?

PROCTOR. Mr. Hale—

DANFORTH. Be quiet!

PROCTOR. (*to Hale*) Do you see a bird?

DANFORTH. Be quiet!!

ABIGAIL. (*to the ceiling, in a genuine conversation with the "bird," as though trying to talk* *it out of attacking her*) But God made my face; you cannot want to tear my face. Envy is a deadly sin, Mary.

Mary Warren. (*on her feet with a spring, and horrified, pleading*) Abby!

Abigail. (*unperturbed, continuing to the "bird"*) Oh, Mary, this is a black art[1] to change your shape. No, I cannot, I cannot stop my mouth; it's God's work I do.

Mary Warren. Abbey, I'm *here!*

Proctor. (*frantically*) They're pretending, Mr. Danforth!

Abigail. (*Now she takes a backward step, as though in fear the bird will swoop down momentarily.*) Oh, please, Mary! Don't come down.

Susanna Walcott. Her claws, she's stretching her claws!

Proctor. Lies, lies.

Abigail. (*backing further, eyes still fixed above*) Mary, please don't hurt me!

Mary Warren. (*to Danforth*) I'm not hurting her!

Danforth. (*to Mary Warren*) Why does she see this vision?

Mary Warren. She sees nothin'!

Abigail. (*now staring full front as though hypnotized, and mimicking the exact tone of Mary Warren's cry*) She sees nothin'!

Mary Warren. (*pleading*) Abby, you mustn't!

Abigail and All the Girls. (*all transfixed*) Abby, you mustn't!

Mary Warren. (*to all the girls*) I'm here, I'm here!

Girls. I'm here, I'm here!

Danforth. (*horrified*) Mary Warren! Draw back your spirit out of them!

Mary Warren. Mr. Danforth!

Girls. (*cutting her off*) Mr. Danforth!

Danforth. Have you compacted with the devil? Have you?

Mary Warren. Never, never!

Girls. Never, never!

Danforth. (*growing hysterical*) Why can they only repeat you?

Proctor. Give me a whip—I'll stop it!

Mary Warren. They're sporting, They—!

Girls. They're sporting!

Mary Warren. (*turning on them all hysterically and stamping her feet*) Abby, stop it!

Girls. (*stamping their feet*) Abby, stop it!

Mary Warren. Stop it!

Girls. Stop it!

Mary Warren. (*screaming it out at the top of her lungs, and raising her fists*) Stop it!!

Girls. (*raising their fists*) Stop it!!

Mary Warren, utterly confounded, and becoming overwhelmed by Abigail's—and the girls'—utter conviction, starts to whimper, hands half raised, powerless, and all the girls begin whimpering exactly as she does.

Danforth. A little while ago you were afflicted. Now it seems you afflict others; where did you find this power?

Mary Warren. (*staring at Abigail*) I—have no power.

Girls. I have no power.

Proctor. They're gulling you, Mister!

1. **black art.** Evil magic

Characters

The people in a play are its characters. Names of characters are given before the words that they speak.

Dialogue

In a play, the dialogue is the speech of the characters. In a play, dialogue is not placed in quotation marks.

Words for Everyday Use:

con • found (kən found´) *vt.*, confuse, bewilder

gull (gul) *vt.*, trick; dupe

Cross-curricular Activities

Arts and Humanities. Students may wish to research the topic of devils, demons, and monsters, particularly their representation in literature, drama, and film. What different forms do these embodiments of evil take? What various kinds of roles do they play?

Social Studies. Have students investigate the psychological phenomenon of mob hysteria. What are the different theories of its origins? Why does it become difficult, if not impossible, for one individual to oppose a mass of people fixed on a single objective? How do instances of mob hysteria usually terminate? Can students offer examples of recent instances of mob hysteria (e.g., celebrations taking place after sporting events such as the World Series and the Super Bowl)?

Vocabulary in Context

- The data that the physicists received from their tests confounded them at first because they appeared to contradict the known laws of physics.
- It is a tradition on the first day of April to attempt to gull others into believing the most outlandish stories.

Cross-curricular Activities

Social Studies. Scapegoating is a cultural phenomenon that can be traced at least as far back as ancient Greek culture. In religious contexts, the designation of one individual to serve as a scapegoat is often a ritual act intended to appease a god or gods for a sacrilege that the community has committed or believes it has committed. Have students investigate the phenomenon of scapegoating in different cultural and religious contexts. In what ways are the events depicted in this scene from *The Crucible* an example of cultural scapegoating? Why does this New England community perceive a need for a scapegoat? Why did the United States in the 1950s seem to need scapegoats? Is scapegoating still practiced in some form in contemporary cultures? Can students offer examples of scapegoating in their own lives?

Answers to Selection Check Test 4.1.7

EX. What is the setting of the play?
The play takes place in Salem, Massachusetts, in 1692.

1. What does Abigail do at the opening of the scene?
She screams wildly up at the ceiling.

2. How does Proctor respond to the claims of the girls?
He tells the court the girls are pretending.

3. How does Proctor encourage Mary to tell the truth?
He tells her that "God damns liars."

4. Of what crime does Danforth accuse Mary?
He accuses her of making a pact with the devil.

5. What does Mary claim the devil wants from her?
She says he wants her to sign her name in his book.

DANFORTH. Why did you turn about this past two weeks? You have seen the Devil, have you not?

HALE. (*indicating Abigail and the girls*) You cannot believe them!

MARY WARREN. I—

PROCTOR. (*sensing her weakening*) Mary, God damns all liars!

DANFORTH. (*pounding it into her*) You have seen the Devil, you have made compact with Lucifer,[2] have you not?

Mary utters something unintelligible, staring at Abigail, who keeps watching the "bird" above.

PROCTOR. God damns liars, Mary!

DANFORTH. I cannot hear you. What do you say? (*Mary utters again unintelligibly.*) You will confess yourself or you will hang! (*He turns her roughly to face him.*) Do you know who I am? I say you will hang if you do not open with me!

PROCTOR. Mary, remember the angel Raphael—do that which is good and—

ABIGAIL. (*pointing upward*) The wings! Her wings are spreading! Mary, please, don't, don't—!

HALE. I see nothing, Your Honor!

DANFORTH. Do you confess this power! (*He is an inch from her face.*) Speak!

ABIGAIL. She's going to come down! She's walking the beam!

DANFORTH. Will you speak!

MARY WARRREN. (*staring in horror*) I cannot!

GIRLS. I cannot!

PARRIS. Cast the Devil out! Look him in the face! Trample him! We'll save you, Mary, only stand fast against him and—

ABIGAIL. (*looking up*) Look out! She's coming down!

She and all the girls run to one wall, shielding their eyes. And now, as though cornered, they let out a gigantic scream, and Mary, as though infected, opens her mouth and screams with them. Gradually Abigail and the girls leave off, until only Mary is left there, staring up at the "bird," screaming madly. All watch her, horrified by this evident fit. Proctor strides to her.

PROCTOR. Mary, tell the Governor what they— (*He has hardly got a word out, when seeing him coming for her, she rushes out of his reach, screaming in horror.*)

MARY WARREN. Don't touch me—don't touch me! (*At which the girls halt at the door.*)

PROCTOR. (*astonished*) Mary!

MARY WARREN. (*pointing at Proctor*) You're the Devil's man!

He is stopped in his tracks.

PARRIS. Praise God!

GIRLS. Praise God!

PROCTOR. (*numbed*) Mary, how—?

MARY WARREN. I'll not hang with you! I love God, I love God.

DANFORTH. (*to Mary*) He bid you do the Devil's work?

MARY WARREN. (*hysterically, indicating Proctor*) He come at me by night and every day to sign, to sign, to—

DANFORTH. Sign what?

PARRIS. The Devil's book? He come with a book?

MARY WARREN. (*hysterically, pointing at Proctor, fearful of him*) My name, he want my name. "I'll murder you," he says, "if my wife hangs! We must go and overthrow the court," he says!

Danforth's head jerks toward Proctor, shock and horror in his face.

PROCTOR. (*turning, appealing to Hale*) Mr. Hale!

2. **Lucifer.** Name for the devil

Additional Questions and Activities

Have students rewrite the final two pages of this scene (pages 48–49) so that Mary opposes Abigail and the girls while supporting Proctor instead. Encourage students to adhere as closely as possible to the characterizations presented in the original scene.

MARY WARREN. (*her sobs beginning*) He wake me every night, his eyes were like coals and his fingers claw my neck, and I sign, I sign . . .

HALE. Excellency, this child's gone wild!

PROCTOR (*as Danforth's wide eyes pour on him*) Mary, Mary!

MARY WARREN, (*screaming at him*) No, I love God; I go your way no more. I love God, I bless God. (*Sobbing, she rushes to Abigail.*) Abby, Abby, I'll never hurt you more! (*They all watch, as Abigail, out of her infinite charity, reaches out and draws the sobbing Mary to her, and then looks up to Danforth.*) ■

Responding to the Selection

Why does Mary Warren turn on Proctor and make an accusation against him? What pressures lead her to do this? Discuss social pressure with your classmates. Why is it important to stand up for what you believe in the face of such pressure?

Reviewing the Selection

RECALLING

1. What does Abigail claim to see on the beam, behind the rafter? What does Abigail say is "a deadly sin"?
2. What question does Danforth ask Mary after she says, "I'm not hurting her"?
3. What does Mary mean when she says that the girls are "sporting"?
4. Of what does Mary accuse Proctor? To whom does Mary rush at the end of the selection?

INTERPRETING

5. According to Abigail, who is making the bird appear? What is the bird?
6. What pressure does Danforth's question put on Mary? What might happen to Mary if the court believes Abigail and the girls?
7. Does Mary see the bird? What explanation for the bird does she offer at first?
8. Why does Mary change her mind and accuse Proctor?

RESPONDING TO THE SELECTION

Have students offer examples of social pressure from their own lives, asking them to cite instances of both positive influence and negative pressure. Invite them to formulate strategies for countering unwelcome social pressure and consider how Mary Warren might have withstood the influence of the other girls.

ANSWERS FOR REVIEWING THE SELECTION

RECALLING

1. She claims to see a yellow bird. Abigail says that "Envy is a deadly sin."
2. He asks her why Abigail is seeing the vision of the yellow bird.
3. She means that the girls are only pretending to be possessed.
4. Mary accuses Proctor of being "the Devil's man" and of trying to get her to sign her name in the devil's book. At the end of the scene, Mary rushes over to Abigail.

INTERPRETING

Responses will vary. Possible responses are given.

5. Abigail claims that Mary is making the bird appear and that the bird is, in fact, Mary herself.
6. He pressures her to decide if she will agree with the girls or contradict their story. Mary might be hanged for witchcraft if the court believes Abigail and the girls.
7. She does not see the bird and tells Danforth that Abigail does not really see it, either.
8. She is afraid that the court will believe the girls and that she will be sentenced to hang if she does not side with them against Proctor.

SYNTHESIZING

Responses will vary. Possible responses are given.

9. The "spectral evidence" depicted in this scene is the yellow bird that Abigail and the girls claim to see in the rafters. Such evidence is no longer admissible in courts because it is considered unscientific and cannot be demonstrated to be

(cont.)

ANSWERS FOR REVIEWING THE SELECTION (CONT.)

true beyond a reasonable doubt.

10. Danforth threatens to hang Mary if she does not confess herself and admit that she has been possessed by the devil. In addition, Parris pressures Mary to contradict Proctor when he assures her that they will "save" her if she resists the devil's temptations. Mary's decision to denounce Proctor and side with the girls is understandable in the context of the trial and of the Salem witch hunt in general, for anyone who contradicted the prevailing belief that the devil had taken possession of many citizens risked being ostracized or hanged. Mary's actions may be seen as excusable if it is accepted that an adolescent lacks the strength of character necessary to withstand such enormous social pressures. However, her actions must be seen as immoral if it is understood that she knew the truth and refused to declare it to the court.

ANSWERS FOR UNDERSTANDING LITERATURE

► See the evaluation forms for discussion, active listening, and oral communication, *Assessment Portfolio,* 7.11–7.14.

Responses will vary. Possible responses are given.

1. Stage Directions. The scene opens with a stage direction that indicates both part of the setting and how Abigail is to speak: "Abigail, with a weird, wild, chilling cry, screams up to the ceiling." The stage direction for Mary, "(on her feet with a spring, and horrified, pleading)" indicates how she should move and speak. Similarly, when Proctor advances toward Mary, stage directions indicate that "she rushes out of his reach, screaming in horror." The setting is further indicated by the directions, "She and all the girls run to one wall," and "the girls halt at the door."

2. Character. The major characters in this scene are Mary Warren, Proctor, Danforth, and Abigail. The minor characters include Hale, Parris, Mercy Lewis, and Susanna Walcott. Mary seems to be virtuous and honest at heart but timid and easily swayed by the influence of others. Proctor appears as a devout, moral individual willing to stand up for his beliefs despite overwhelming odds against him. Danforth is portrayed as a single-minded zealot who is less concerned with the truth than he is with exercising his authority and making others conform to his will. Abigail seems to thrive on being the center of a spectacle, on exploiting her prominence, and on employing fear to make others follow her lead. Proctor and Hale seem the only admirable characters in this scene, for they are the only ones who refuse to submit to the mob hysteria incited by Abigail and the girls. Mary Warren evokes sympathy because at first she attempts to expose the fictional vision concocted by Abigail and the girls, yet when she finally breaks down under pressure, denounces Proctor, and joins with the girls, she evokes outrage and disappointment. Danforth and Abigail are presented as detestable characters who derive

(cont.)

SYNTHESIZING

9. In Puritan New England, debate raged over the admissibility in court of "spectral evidence," the evidence of spirits seen by some people but not by others. What example of such "spectral evidence" appears in this selection? Why isn't such evidence now admissible in courts of law?

10. What pressures are put on Mary to denounce Proctor? Is what Mary does understandable? excusable? moral? Why, or why not?

Understanding Literature (Questions for Discussion)

1. **Stage Directions. Stage directions** are notes included in a play in addition to the dialogue for the purpose of describing how something should be performed on stage. Stage directions describe movements and ways of speaking of characters, the setting, and such elements of the spectacle as lighting, costumes, properties, and sound effects. Find examples in this scene of stage directions that indicate parts of the setting and stage directions that indicate how characters are to speak or move.

2. **Character. Characters** are the people (or sometimes animals) who figure in the action of a literary work. In a play, the names of characters are given before the words that they speak. Who are the major characters in this scene from *The Crucible*? Who are the minor characters? Briefly describe the personalities of the major characters, based on their words and actions in this scene. Which characters do you admire? Which do you not admire? Why?

3. **Dialogue. Dialogue** is conversation involving two or more characters. In a play, dialogue appears after the characters' names and is not placed in quotation marks, as it would be in a novel or short story. Find examples in this scene of dialogue that would probably not be spoken by characters in a modern setting but that is appropriate to Miller's setting of the play in colonial New England.

4. **Set and Properties.** In a drama, the **set** is the physical area of the stage, along with any backdrops, curtains, walls, or fixed pieces of scenery or furniture. **Properties** are small objects that can be carried on and off the stage. If you were designing a set for this scene from *The Crucible,* what elements would you have to include? What properties might you have the actors use?

5. **Blocking. Blocking** is the process of planning the movements of actors on a stage. What movements described in the stage directions for this scene would have to be taken into account by the person, such as the director, who was planning the blocking of the scene?

6. **Theme.** A **theme** is a central idea in a literary work. What do you think is the theme of this scene from the play? What does the scene reveal about the forces that cause people to give in to mob hysteria? Why do some people foresake their convictions in situations like the one described in this scene?

ANSWERS FOR UNDERSTANDING LITERATURE (CONT.)

great pleasure in wielding authority.

3. Dialogue. Examples of dialogue that is more appropriate to a colonial New England setting than a modern one include, "Begone! Begone, I say!" (page 46); "Why do you come, yellow bird?" (page 46); "I cannot stop my mouth" (page 47); "Have you compacted with the devil?" (page 47); "They're sporting" (page 47); "They're gulling you, Mister!" (page 47); "Why did you turn about this past two weeks?" (page 48); "you will hang if you do not open with me!" (page 48); "I'll not hang with you!" (page 48); "He bid you do the Devil's work?" (page 48); and "He come with a book?" (page 48).

4. Set and Properties. The set for this scene might include a desk or table with a chair for the judge, a table and chair for the prosecutor, seats for a jury and specta-

(cont.)

The Process of Writing: Proofreading

Proofreading. Read the Language Arts Survey, 1.47, "Proofreading Checklist," and 1.48, "Preparing Your Manuscript." Proofread the personal essay that you revised for the revision lesson on page 41. Then prepare a clean, final copy of your essay and proofread it once more. When preparing your final copy, follow proper manuscript form as described in the Language Arts Survey or by your teacher.

Language Lab

The Parts of Speech. Review the Language Arts Survey, 2.3–2.29, "The Parts of Speech." Then identify the part of speech of each italicized word in the paragraph below.

[1] *Joseph Raymond McCarthy* entered the United States Senate in 1946. [2] *After* two undistinguished years in the Senate, [3] *he* gained national recognition in 1950 by charging that over two hundred communists [4] *had infiltrated* the State Department, that part of the government that oversees foreign relations. At the time, the United States was at war with the communist government in North Korea, and many citizens of the country were [5] *deeply* fearful about communist advances in Europe and China. McCarthy's charges struck a chord with the people, and for several years thereafter, [6] *innocent* people were hounded from their jobs in government and in the entertainment industry because of "suspected" communist activities and "associations" with communists. Targets [7] *of* McCarthyism included such well-known literary figures as Ring Lardner, Jr., and Lillian Hellman. McCarthy went too far, however, when he made accusations against such popular figures as President Dwight D. Eisenhower. In 1954, the Senate formally voted to condemn McCarthy for his [8] *conduct,* and the McCarthy Era came to an end. Did anything positive come out of the McCarthy Era? [9] *Yes,* this period in American history gave people a new understanding of the dangers of character assassination, guilt by association, [10] *and* mass hysteria. It also gave us Arthur Miller's fine play, The Crucible.

Arthur Miller (1915–) was born in New York City. During his youth, his father's business failed as part of the general economic downturn known as the Great Depression. This failure had a permanent impact on Miller, who went on to write great plays on themes related to social and political justice. After graduating from high school, Miller worked and raised money to attend the University of Michigan. There he began writing plays. His most famous work, *Death of a Salesman* (1949), tells the story of the tragic downfall of its title character, partially as a result of his willingness to do anything for the "almighty dollar." Miller's play is a classic exposé of the consequences of hypocrisy and greed. When Miller was called before the House Un-American Activities Committee and asked to name suspected communists whom he had met ten years before at a writer's meeting, he refused to do so. He was cited for contempt but overturned the citation on appeal. Miller's other plays included *The Crucible* (1953) and *A View from the Bridge* (1955). In addition to his plays for the stage, Miller wrote screenplays, including the script for *The Misfits,* a film that starred his second wife, Marilyn Monroe.

ANSWERS FOR UNDERSTANDING LITERATURE (CONT.)

tors, at least one wall with a door in it, and rafters supporting a ceiling. Appropriate properties might include a gavel for the judge, a whip hanging on the wall, a Bible on the prosecutor's table, and small crosses carried by the girls and by Danforth.

5. Blocking. Movements that would have to be taken into account when blocking the play include Mary springing to her feet (page 47), Abigail taking a backward step and then backing up further (page 47), Danforth turning Mary roughly to face him (page 48), Abigail and the girls running to one wall (page 48), Proctor advancing toward Mary and then Mary rushing away out of his reach (page 48), the girls halting at the door (page 48), and Mary rushing over to Abigail at the end of the scene (page 49).

6. Theme. A major theme of this scene is how even an individual who wishes to be honest and true to her moral convictions can be overwhelmed by the extraordinary pressures of misguided authority and of mass prejudice into acting dishonestly and contrary to her beliefs. This scene suggests the ways in which people in positions of power can abuse their authority through the use of fear and by condemning anyone who disagrees with them. Regardless of their convictions, some people will submit to mob hysteria out of fear of standing apart or from fear of the personal harm that might result from defying authority.

ANSWERS FOR LANGUAGE LAB

1. *Joseph Raymond McCarthy*—n.
2. *After*—prep.
3. *he*—pro.
4. *had infiltrated*—v.
5. *deeply*—adv.
6. *innocent*—adj.
7. *of*—prep.
8. *conduct*—n.
9. *Yes*—int.
10. *and*—conj.

►Additional practice is provided in the *Essential Skills Practice Book: Language,* 2.3–2.29.

THE PROCESS OF WRITING: PROOFREADING

► See the Proofreading Checklist and Proofreading Record, *Assessment Portfolio,* 7.9–7.10. Use this as an opportunity to make sure students understand the manuscript form you require. Students might find it useful to proofread one another's papers as well as their own.

► Additional practice is provided in the *Essential Skills Practice Book: Writing,* 1.47 and 1.48.

ADDITIONAL RESOURCES

READER'S GUIDE
- Selection Worksheet, 1.5

ASSESSMENT PORTFOLIO
- Selection Check Test, 4.1.9
- Selection Test, 4.1.10

ESSENTIAL SKILLS PRACTICE BOOKS
- *Writing,* 1.47

ENRICHMENT ACTIVITIES

Literary criticism of the past thirty years has focused attention on the extent to which such nonfiction genres as histories, biographies, and autobiographies are just as much products of the imagination as novels, poetry, and drama. Invite students to consider how nonfiction can be viewed as imaginative writing. What similarities of composition, structure, and purpose exist between fiction and nonfiction?

SUPPORT FOR LEP STUDENTS

You may wish to play some of the various types of music discussed (work songs, blues, spirituals, and jazz) to help students distinguish between the forms and to better understand and enjoy the writer's analysis.

ADDITIONAL VOCABULARY

flyleaves—pages at the beginning of a book

Nonfiction

Nonfiction writing, unlike the other types of literature considered so far, explores actual people, places, things, events, and ideas. Types of nonfiction writing include the following:

Histories, such as the selections from Imamu Baraka's *Blues People* (unit 1), Bartolomé de las Casas's *The Very Brief Relation of the Devastation of the Indies* (unit 2), John Smith's *The General History of Virginia* (unit 2), William Bradford's *Of Plymouth Plantation* (unit 2), and W. E. B. Du Bois's *The Souls of Black Folk* (unit 7), provide accounts of past events.

Of importance to historians in preparing their works are many types of public records, such as **speeches, sermons, contracts, deeds, constitutions, laws,** and **political tracts.** Examples in this text include the selection from the Iroquois Constitution (unit 2), Jonathan Edwards's "Sinners in the Hands of an Angry God" (unit 2), Patrick Henry's Speech in the Virginia Convention (unit 3), Thomas Paine's *Crisis No. 1* (unit 3), the Declaration of Independence (unit 3), Abraham Lincoln's "A House Divided" (unit 6), and Gettysburg Address (unit 6), Robert E. Lee's Farewell Address (unit 6), Chief Joseph's "I Will Fight No More Forever" (unit 7), Cochise's "I Am Alone" (unit 7), William Faulkner's Address upon Receiving the Nobel Prize for Literature (unit 11), and John F. Kennedy's Inaugural Address (unit 12).

Other types of nonfiction, closely related to histories, are **biographies** and **autobiographies,** which can be thought of as histories of individual people. A biography is the story of a person's life. An autobiography is the story of a person's life, written by that person. John Smith's *The General History of Virginia* is an interesting example of an autobiography because, although it is the history of his own life, Smith chose to write from the third-person point of view, typical of the biography. Other examples of autobiographies in this text include the selections from *The Autobiography of Benjamin Franklin* (unit 3), *Narrative of the Life of Frederick Douglass* (unit 6), and Booker T. Washington's *Up from Slavery* (unit 6).

Biographers often work from the **letters, diaries,** and **journals** of their subjects. Examples of letters in this text are Abigail Adams's Letter to John Adams (unit 3), and Abraham Lincoln's Letter to Mrs. Bixby (unit 6). Henry David Thoreau's *Walden* and Ralph Waldo Emerson's "Self-Reliance," selections from which appear (unit 4), were developed from journals or diaries kept by their authors.

Emerson's "Self-Reliance" and the chapters in Thoreau's *Walden* are examples of a form of nonfiction known as the **essay.** The word *essay* originally meant a "trial or attempt." In an essay, a writer does not attempt an exhaustive treatment of a topic but rather presents a single main idea, or thesis, about the topic.

Share Croppers. *Robert Gwathmey, 1941, 17 3/4" × 12 3/4", watercolor. Courtesy of San Diego Museum of Art. Museum purchase with funds provided by Mrs. Leon D. Bonnet.*

GOALS/OBJECTIVES

Studying this lesson will enable students to
- interpret and appreciate a piece of nonfiction writing
- identify and describe forms of nonfiction writing
- describe modes of writing and modes of exposition
- define *anecdote* and identify anecdotes in their reading
- explain the purpose of the use of special vocabulary
- proofread and publish their writing

©1995 Estate of Robert Gwathmy/Licensed by VAGA, New York, NY

Cross-curricular Activities

Arts and Humanities. Students may wish to investigate other forms of art that had their origins in, or were shaped by, the period of slavery in the United States. How, for example, did slavery influence the form and content of writings or visual arts by African Americans in the decades after its abolition?

LITERARY TECHNIQUE

Purpose. Have students look at several magazines. Ask them to identify the purpose(s) of several pieces in the magazine. Ask students what the type of writing (expressive, expository, persuasive, literary) seems to be most common in each magazine. Examples of magazines that often contain writing that encompasses all four purposes are *New Yorker, The Atlantic Monthly,* and *Harper's.*

ADDITIONAL QUESTIONS AND ACTIVITIES

Explain to students that writing most commonly expresses more than a single purpose. Invite them to consider, for instance, how a piece of literary writing (Malamud's "The Magic Barrel" might be used as an example) works to persuade its reader, how it conveys particular information to the reader, and how the writer expresses emotions, beliefs, and values.

Purpose and Mode in Nonfiction

THE PURPOSES OF WRITING

Purpose. A writer's **purpose,** or **aim,** is what he or she wants a work to accomplish. Nonfiction writing generally is produced with some overall purpose in mind. The following chart classifies types of writing by purpose.

TYPE OF WRITING	PURPOSE
Expressive Writing	The writer expresses himself or herself, describing personal feelings, attitudes, ideas, values, or beliefs.
Expository or Informative Writing	The writer attempts to inform others about a subject.
Persuasive Writing	The writer attempts to persuade others to adopt some belief or to take some course of action.
Literary Writing	The writer creates an imaginary world to entertain and, sometimes, to instruct.

This classification system derives from the work of James Kinneavy, who, in *A Theory of Discourse,* bases his classification of writing on an analysis of the standard "communication model." According to this model, a sender encodes a message about some subject in a set of symbols and then transmits that message to a recipient. In **expressive writing,** the emphasis is on the sender of the message, the writer. The major purpose is to express the writer's state of mind. In **expository writing,** the emphasis is on the subject. The major purpose is to provide information about that subject. In **persuasive writing,** the emphasis is on the recipient. The major purpose is to change the recipient's mind or to move the recipient to action. In **literary writing,** the emphasis is on the symbols—the words themselves and the form into which they are organized. The major purpose is to create an imaginary world by which to entertain or instruct.

The Modes of Writing

Mode. Another common classification system divides various types of writing according to the method of treatment of the subject. The following chart describes methods of treating subjects, or **modes** of writing, that are commonly used in nonfiction.

MODE OF WRITING	DESCRIPTION
Narration	Writing in this mode describes events. Histories, biographies, autobiographies, and news reports all make extensive use of narration.
Dialogue	Writing in this mode presents words as they were actually spoken by people.
Description	Writing in this mode portrays in words how things look, sound, smell, taste, or feel.
Exposition	Writing in this mode presents facts or opinions in an organized manner.

Types of Exposition. There are many modes of expository writing used in nonfiction works. The following chart describes some of the most common.

MODE OF EXPOSITION	DESCRIPTION
Analysis	Writing in this mode breaks something into its parts and shows how the parts are related.
Classification	Writing in this mode places subjects into categories, or classes, according to their properties or characteristics.
Comparison and Contrast	Writing in this mode presents similarities and differences.
Process/How to	Writing in this mode presents the steps in a process.

Additional Questions and Activities

Mode. Refer students to the Language Arts Survey, 1.9, "Modes of Writing." The following activities should help students understand the different modes of writing.

- Have students write a paragraph giving an account of some recent event in their lives. Ask them to identify the mode(s) of writing they used to formulate their accounts. Students could also attempt to write the same account four times, employing each time one of the different modes of writing (narration, dialogue, description, and exposition).
- Ask students to examine their textbook and find examples of the different modes of writing and exposition.

► Additional practice is provided in the *Essential Skills Practice Book: Writing*, 1.9.

About the Author

Imamu Amiri Baraka (1934–) was born as Everett LeRoy Jones in Newark, New Jersey. He later changed his name to reflect his African roots. Baraka attended Rutgers University and received his Bachelor's degree from Howard University. He earned Master's degrees from Columbia University and the New School for Social Research. Baraka's work as a writer, playwright, music critic, and black activist has been as dynamic as the evolution of his ideas. His early works were influenced by his friendships with Beat poets. With the rise of the Civil Rights movement and his exposure to writers from developing countries, Baraka began to use his writing to express his changing political views and his anger against racism. In 1964, his play *Dutchman* won the *Village Voice* Obie Award. Baraka became a black nationalist in 1965 and completely withdrew from white society. Later, Baraka renounced these views. He now writes poetry and plays that express his revolutionary ideals. Baraka has also published studies of the evolution of jazz and blues music and has been an important supporter of African-American artists.

Additional Questions and Activities

Have students rewrite the first paragraph of the selection from *Blues People* in the form of an interview. What questions must they ask in order to evoke the information provided by the author?

Vocabulary from the Selection

catalyst	formidable
conceivably	impetus
conjunction	metrical
eerie	predominantly
formalize	

FROM

Blues People

IMAMU AMIRI BARAKA

Purpose
While the purpose is not directly stated, the kind of information Baraka includes suggests an ***expository*** *or* ***informative*** *purpose.*

Parenthetical Statement
A parenthetical statement is one not directly related to the point of the discussion but included nonetheless because of its interest.

Since most Negroes before and after slavery were agricultural laborers, the corn songs and arwhoolies,[1] the shouts and hollers, issued from one kind of work. Some of the work songs, for instance, use as their measure[2] the grunt of a man pushing a heavy weight or the blow of a hammer against a stone to provide the metrical precision and rhythmical impetus behind the singer. ("Take this hammer, uh,/Take it to the captain, uh,/Take it to the captain, uh,/Tell him I'm gone.") Contemporary work songs, for example, songs recorded by Negro convicts working in the South—laying railroad ties, felling trees, breaking rocks, take their impetus from the work being done, and the form of the singing itself is dictated by the work. These workers for the most part do not sing blues. The labor is central to the song: not only is the recurring grunt or moan of these work songs some kind of metrical and rhythmical insistence,[3] it is the very catalyst for the song. On one recent record, the Louisiana Folklore Society's, *Prison Worksongs* recorded in Angola, Louisiana, at the Louisiana State Penitentiary there, one song listed as *Take This Hammer* begins as that song, but lasts as that for only about three "bars" (three strokes of the hammer) and then wanders irresolutely[4] into *Alberta, Berta*, several blues verses, and a few lines from a spiritual. The point is that the primitive blues was at once a more formal music since the three-line, twelve-bar song became rapidly standardized, and was also a more liberated music since there was literally *more* to sing about. In one's leisure one can begin to formalize a method of singing as well as find new things to sing about. (It is an interesting thought that perhaps all the music that Negroes in America have made might have been quite different if the work that they were brought here to do had been different. Suppose Negroes had been brought to this country to make vases or play basketball. How might the blues have developed then from the impetus of work songs geared to those occupations?)

Work songs and shouts were, of course, almost always *a capella*.[5] It would have been extremely difficult for a man to pick cotton or shuck corn and play an instrument at the same time. For this reason pre-blues secular singing[6] did not have

1. **arwhoolies.** Field hollers
2. **as their measure.** As a way of marking the regular pattern of rhythm
3. **insistence.** Demand
4. **irresolutely.** Hesitantly
5. **a capella.** Without instrumental accompaniment
6. **secular singing.** Singing not related to religious practice

Words for Everyday Use:

met • ri • cal (me´ tri kəl) *adj.,* related to the number of beats in each line of a verse or song
im • pe • tus (im´pə təs) *n.,* driving force behind an activity
cat • a • lyst (kat´ ə list´) *n.,* something that stimulates or hastens a result
for • mal • ize (fôr´ mə līz´) *vt.,* give definite form to

Vocabulary in Context

- Those who find the metrical simplicity of rock and roll music monotonous fail to appreciate its appeal.
- Once the senator withdrew his powerful support, the impetus behind the act of legislation disappeared, and it failed to pass.
- Some credit John F. Kennedy as being the catalyst behind the successful efforts of the United States to put a human on the moon.
- By making the regular effort to formalize her reactions to literature in a journal, Liza discovered the complex emotions literature evoked in her.

the discipline or strict formality that a kind of singing employing instruments must have. But it is obvious from the very earliest form of the blues that instrumental accompaniment was beginning to be taken into consideration. The twelve-bar blues[7]—the more or less final form of blues—is constructed so that each verse is of three lines, each line about four bars long. The words of the song usually occupy about one-half of each line, leaving a space of two bars for either a sung answer or an instrumental response.

It may seem strange that the formal blues should evolve *after* slavery, after so many years of bondage and exposure by the slaves to the larger Western cultural unit,[8] into a form that is patently non-Western;[9] the three-line verse form of the blues springs from no readily apparent Western source. But the use of instruments on a large scale was also something that happened after the Emancipation;[10] the very possession of instruments, except those few made from African models, was rare in the early days of slavery. The stereotyped pictures that many of the apologists[11] for the Southern way of life used as flyleaves for their numerous novels after the Civil War, depicting a happy-go-lucky black existentialist[12] strumming merrily on his banjo while sitting on a bale of cotton, were, I'm sure, more romantic fiction than fact. The slave would hardly have had the time to sit on his master's bale of cotton during the work day, and the only instruments that were in common usage among the slaves were drums, rattles, tambourines,

Folksinger. *Charles White. Collection of Harry Belafonte. Courtesy Heritage Gallery, Los Angeles, CA*

scrapers (the jawbone of a horse over which a piece of wood was scraped), and the like; even such an African instrument as the banjo was very scarce. The guitar was not commonly played by Negroes until much after the Civil War. An instrument like the harmonica grew in popularity among a great many Negroes simply because it took up almost no space and was so easy to carry around. But even the harmonica did not come into common use until after slavery, and certainly the possession and mastery[13] of European instruments did not occur until much later.

7. **twelve-bar blues.** Music in which each verse consists of twelve units, marked by twelve accented beats
8. **Western cultural unit.** Customs and values of the West, mainly of European Americans who controlled the lives of African-American slaves for four hundred years
9. **patently non-Western.** Uniquely and definitely outside the Western tradition
10. **the Emancipation.** President Abraham Lincoln signed the Emancipation Proclamation in 1862, legally freeing all African Americans from slavery.
11. **apologists.** People who try to rationalize or explain an unpopular political position, such as the idea that slavery was good for the slaves
12. **existentialist.** Someone who takes the philosophical point of view that actuality is better than possibility
13. **mastery.** Ability to use properly

Cross-curricular Activities

Social Studies. Ask groups of students to research the origins of other musical genres (e.g., reggae, salsa, samba, bluegrass, country & western, and classical). Do other musical genres derive, as do the blues, from particular historical events or situations? Have each group present its findings to the class and discuss both similarities and differences between musical types. Suggest that students find recordings of selections of the musical genres they research to play in class.

Social Studies. Have students research the working lives of slaves. What kind of work were slaves required to perform? How many hours a day did they have to work? What was their typical living situation like? What opportunities, if any, did they have for leisure and entertainment? How does this compare to stereotyped pictures of slaves? You might refer students to the selection from *Narrative of the Life of Frederick Douglass, an American Slave, Written by Himself,* found on page 364, which discusses the theme of slave music and its misinterpretation.

Additional Questions and Activities

Arrange to play several examples of traditional blues music. Ask students to take notes, as they are listening, about the lyrical content of these songs. What themes are expressed? In what ways do these songs clearly belong to a musical history having its roots in slavery? Invite students to comment on the interrelationship of the music and the lyrics. How do they complement each other?

Answers to Selection Check Test 4.1.9

EX. What is the subject of *Blues People?*
It is about the origins of the blues.

1. What kind of work did most African Americans perform as slaves?
Most African-American slaves were agricultural laborers.

2. What influence did physical labor have on early African-American music?
It dictated the rhythm and meter of the music.

3. When did the use of instruments in the blues begin?
It began after the Emancipation Proclamation in 1862.

4. Why was the harmonica a common instrument for early blues musicians?
It was small and easy to carry around.

5. What later form of music had its origins in the blues?
Jazz music evolved from the early blues.

Responding to the Selection

Have students list what they like and dislike about nonfiction in general, asking them to be precise about what they do and do not find interesting. Invite them to make comparisons with forms of writings that they especially like or dislike, such as novels, poetry, drama, and short stories. How are the reader's efforts different when reading nonfiction as opposed to other forms of literature?

Answers for Reviewing the Selection

RECALLING

1. Work songs are a predominant source of early African-American music.

2. They are still sung by prison workers in the South.

3. They originated in field hollers, the grunts of men working, and the rhythmic blows of hammers against stone.

(cont.)

When primitive or country blues did begin to be influenced by instruments, it was the guitar that had the most effect on the singers. And when the great masses of Negroes were just beginning to learn the instrument, the relatively simple chords of the country blues were probably what they learned. Conceivably, this also brought about another change: blues, a vocal music, was made to conform to an instrument's range. But, of course, the blues widened the range of the instrument, too. Blues guitar was not the same as classical or "legitimate"[14] guitar: the strings had to make vocal sounds, to imitate the human voice and its eerie cacophonies.[15] Perhaps the reason why the guitar was at once so popular was not only because it was much like the African instrument, the banjo (or *banjor*), but because it was an instrument that still permitted the performer to *sing*.

ORGANIZATION

Though various organization strategies are used by Baraka throughout this piece, the overall pattern is ***chronological****, in order of the occurrence of events in time.*

When the Negro finally did take up the brass instruments for strictly instrumental blues or jazz, the players still persisted in singing in the "breaks."[16] This could be done easily in the blues tradition with the call-and-response form of blues. Even much later in the jazz tradition, not only were instruments made to sound like the human voice but a great many of the predominantly instrumental songs were still partially sung. The first great soloist of jazz, Louis Armstrong,[17] was a formidable blues singer, as was the great jazz pianist Jelly Roll Morton.[18] Both men sang blues almost as beautifully as they played their instruments.

CLASSIFICATION

Classification divides a subject or subjects into categories according to particular features. While not rigidly structured, Baraka's discussion of African-American music looks at three musical styles: work songs, blues, and jazz.

The primitive blues was still very much a vocal music; the singers relied on the unpredictability and mobility of the human voice for their imaginative catalysts. But the growing use of European instruments such as brass and reeds almost precluded song, except as accompaniment or as an interlude.[19] When Negroes began to master more and more "European" instruments and began to think musically in terms of their timbres,[20] as opposed to, or in conjunction with, the voice, blues began to change, and the era of jazz was at hand. ■

14. **legitimate.** Conventional
15. **cacophonies.** Loud, unharmonious sounds
16. **breaks.** Pauses in the music, for example, in the two-bar, half-line break in each line of twelve-bar blues
17. **Louis Armstrong.** (1900–1971) Jazz musician famous for his singing voice
18. **Jelly Roll Morton.** (1885–1941) Famed for his trumpet playing and his distinctive scat, or improvisational, singing style
19. **precluded . . . interlude.** Replaced song except as a break in the vocal music
20. **timbres.** Tonal quality of sounds

Responding to the Selection

In general, do you enjoy reading historical analysis? Did you find this selection from *Blues People* interesting? What, if any, topics from the selection would you like to learn more about?

WORDS FOR EVERYDAY USE:

con • ceiv • a • bly (kən sēv´ə blē) *adv.,* in a manner that can be understood or imagined
ee • rie (ir´ē) *adj.,* mysterious; weird
pre • dom • i • nant • ly (prē däm´ə nənt lē) *adv.,* mostly; prevailingly
for • mi • da • ble (fôr´mə də bəl) *adj.,* strikingly impressive
con • junc • tion (kən juŋk´shən) *n.,* association; combination

Vocabulary in Context

- While the general's battle plan could have conceivably succeeded, the probability of victory seemed so low that he abandoned it in favor of a surer alternative.
- John longed for company as the eerie shriek of the wind called about the house.
- While the autumn foliage of the hills was predominantly orange, there were splotches of red, yellow, and brown mixed in as well.
- It is thrilling to watch an underdog defy the odds and triumph over a formidable opponent.
- The unusual conjunction of a full moon, high tides, and strong winds resulted in severe flooding.

Reviewing the Selection

RECALLING

1. What kinds of songs are central to early African-American music?
2. In what current circumstances do work songs still appear?
3. From what musical source did the sounds of early African-American work songs primarily come?
4. When did formal blues music evolve? What instrument had the most effect on blues singers?

INTERPRETING

5. What situation led to the creation of African-American music?
6. How are work songs related to their source?
7. Why were most work songs primarily vocal?
8. What additional element influenced the development of formal blues? Which instrument fit the blues singers' goals?

SYNTHESIZING

9. How was African-American music changed by musicians' growing expertise with "European" instruments?
10. How would you characterize the relationship between African-American music and the expanding opportunity and skills of its musicians?

Understanding Literature (Questions for Discussion)

1. **Anecdote.** An **anecdote** is a brief story, usually one that serves a specific purpose of the author. Find an example of an anecdote in the selection from *Blues People.* What purpose does it serve?
2. **Special Vocabulary. Special vocabulary** includes words from other languages and/or from particular fields, such as science or the arts. Find an example of special vocabulary in this selection. Use a dictionary to learn the meaning and origins of the term. Why do you think Baraka chose to use this word in his writing? How does it enrich his exposition?

The Process of Writing: Proofreading and Publishing

Proofreading and Publishing. Proofread your most recent draft from the writing assignment in this unit. Refer to the Language Arts Survey, 1.47, "Proofreading Checklist," as you work. Using a clean, final copy of your manuscript, read your work to a small group of peers. Then, after all students have read their work, divide the manuscripts into groups related by theme. Create a table of contents listing all the works and titling the thematic sections. Compile your group's work into a pamphlet and share it with other groups in the class.

ANSWERS FOR REVIEWING THE SELECTION (CONT).

4. Formal blues evolved after the abolition of slavery. The guitar had the greatest effect on early blues singers.

INTERPRETING

Responses will vary. Possible responses are given.

5. The forced labor of slavery was at the root of African-American music.

6. Work songs derive their meter, rhythm, and content from manual labor.

7. Singers were unable to play instruments while they worked.

8. The use of instruments as accompaniment greatly influenced the development of the blues. The guitar fit the blues singers' goals because it could both imitate the human voice and allow the player to sing while playing.

SYNTHESIZING

Responses will vary. Possible responses are given.

9. Blues music was made to conform to the range of European instruments. As African-American musicians began to focus on the music of the instruments instead of the human voice, jazz emerged as a musical genre.

10. As African-American musicians molded traditional, vocal songs to the range of their musical instruments, they also broadened the range of those instruments beyond their classical uses. The more opportunities musicians had and the greater their skills became, the more they were able to expand both traditional African-American music and the music produced by European instruments.

ANSWERS TO UNDERSTANDING LITERATURE

► See the evaluation forms for discussion, active listening, and oral communication, *Assessment Portfolio,* 7.11–7.14.

Responses will vary. Possible responses are given.

1. Anecdote. The author refers to the "stereotyped pictures" found in many novels after the Civil War that depicted "a happy-go-lucky black existentialist strumming merrily on his banjo." He employs this image to debunk the "romantic fiction" that slaves had the time to become accomplished at the use of musical instruments before the abolition of slavery and to support his argument that formal blues did not evolve until the end of the Civil War.

2. Special Vocabulary. Examples of special vocabulary in *Blues People* include *arwhoolies, bar, a capella, banjo, cacophonies, breaks, interlude,* and *timbres.* Baraka uses these musical terms to enrich and add authenticity to his writing about the blues.

THE PROCESS OF WRITING: PROOFREADING AND PUBLISHING

If these are students' first completed pieces of writing, consider not assigning grades. Instead, make positive written evaluative comments on the students' papers or hold conferences to discuss each student's paper individually.

► Additional practice is provided in the *Essential Skills Practice Book: Writing,* 1.47–1.49.

VOCABULARY DEVELOPMENT EXERCISES

► Give students the following exercise.

Read the Language Arts Survey, 2.138 and 2.139, "Using Context Clues I and II." Then choose twenty words from the list on page 60 that you would like to incorporate into your everyday vocabulary. Write a sentence containing a context clue for each word you chose. Use more than one type of context clue in your sentences.

ADDITIONAL RESOURCES

ASSESSMENT PORTFOLIO

- Vocabulary Worksheet, 4.1.11
- Study Guide, Unit 1 Test, 4.1.12
- Unit 1 Test, 4.1.13

ESSENTIAL SKILLS PRACTICE BOOKS

Writing

- Drafting, 1.35–1.42
- Evaluating and Revising, 1.43–1.46
- Prewriting, 1.1–1.34
- Proofreading and Publishing, 1.47–1.49

Language

- Parts of Speech, 2.3–2.29

UNIT REVIEW

Genres and Techniques of Literature

VOCABULARY FROM THE SELECTIONS

abjectly, 35
apparatus, 38
ascetic, 28
avow, 32
catalyst, 56
conceivably, 58
confound, 47
conjunction, 58
eerie, 58
exasperating, 37
formalize, 56
formidable, 58
gull, 47
haggard, 39
imperceptible, 29
impetus, 56
inherently, 27
machination, 34
meager, 27
menagerie, 28
metrical, 56
nuptial, 33
ordain, 27
predominantly, 58
profusion, 34
ravenously, 31
refrain, 37
relentless, 36
resolution, 18
trepidation, 33
vestibule, 38

LITERARY TERMS

anecdote, 59
background information, 41
blocking, 50
character, 50
characterization, 41
dialect, 41
dialogue, 50
figurative language, 41
motivation, 41
parallelism, 20
personification, 20
properties, 50
refrain, 8
repetition, 8
rhyme scheme, 20
sonnet, 19
set, 50
special vocabulary, 59
spiritual, 8
stage directions, 50
symbol, 20
theme, 8, 20, 50

SYNTHESIS: QUESTIONS FOR WRITING, RESEARCH, OR DISCUSSION

THE ORAL TRADITION

1. **Spirituals and the Oral Tradition.** Why were the spirituals transmitted orally instead of being written down? What special historical circumstance made oral transmission of the spirituals necessary? What messages did the spirituals convey?

POETRY

2. **Lyric Poetry.** How do lyric poems differ from narrative and dramatic ones? What special poetic devices, including devices of sound and rhetorical techniques, are used in "Sonnet XXX"? What characteristics make this poem a sonnet?

FICTION

3. **Short Story Structure.** Into what parts is a typical plot divided? What events in "The Magic Barrel" correspond to these parts?

DRAMA

4. **The Spectacle in Drama.** Imagine that you will be directing a production of the scene from *The Crucible* given in this unit. Make a complete list, with descriptions, of the following elements of the spectacle in your production: the stage set, the lighting, the properties, and the costumes.

NONFICTION

5. **Purpose and Organization in Nonfiction.** What is the main purpose of the selection in this unit from *Blues People*? What method of organization does the selection use?

▶ These prompts are suitable as topics for research papers. Refer to the Language Arts Survey, 4.20–4.34, "Research Skills." (To evaluate research papers, see the evaluation forms for writing, revising, and proofreading, *Assessment Portfolio,* 7.1–7.10.)

▶ These prompts can be adapted for use as topics for oral reports or debates. (To evaluate these projects, see the evaluation forms in the *Assessment Portfolio,* 7.17–7.19.)

ADDITIONAL QUESTIONS AND ACTIVITIES

Have students identify the part of speech of the underlined words in the following sentences from "The Magic Barrel."

1. Leo trembled with rage and weakness.
   with—preposition,
   weakness—noun

2. Salzman pulled his clasped hands to his breast.
   pulled—verb,
   clasped—adjective

3. Her face deeply moved him.
   deeply—adverb,
   him—pronoun

4. Leo ran forward with flowers outthrust.
   Leo—noun,
   forward—adverb

LANGUAGE LAB THE PARTS OF SPEECH

Thousands of years ago in ancient India, grammarians developed a method for classifying words in categories or types. These types are known as the **parts of speech.** The eight parts of speech are shown on the following chart.

THE EIGHT PARTS OF SPEECH	
1	A **noun** is the name of a person, place, thing, or idea. *Tennessee Williams, Laura, Africa, New York City, barrel, people, poetry, sadness*
2	A **pronoun** is a word that stands for or refers to a noun. *she, it, them, anything, someone, which, that, whose*
3	A **verb** is a word that describes an action or a state of being. *tell, disappoint, were singing, drink, is, are, were, be, appear, grow*
4	An **adjective** is a word that modifies a noun or a pronoun. *magic, shy, pale, confused, resourceful, courageous*
5	An **adverb** is a word that modifies a verb, an adjective, or another adverb. *quietly, insistently, extremely, very, only, later*
6	A **preposition** is a word that shows a relationship between a noun or a pronoun and some other word in a sentence. *about, against, around, as, between, down, for, from, in, of, off, outside, through, under*
7	A **conjunction** is a word that is used to join words, groups of words, or complete sentences. *and, or, nor, for, but, so, yet, because, since, unless, when, but also*
8	An **interjection** is a word used to express an emotion or to indicate a pause in speech or writing. *wow, oh, yes, yikes, well, hey, oh my, hi*

SENTENCE MODEL

INT	ADV	ADJ	N	V	ADJ	CONJ	ADJ	PREP	PRO	N
Oh,	painfully	shy	Laura	feels	rejected	and	humiliated	by	her	caller.

LANGUAGE ARTS SURVEY

For additional help, see the Language Arts Survey, 2.3–2.31.

Exercise A Identifying the Parts of Speech

Identify the part of speech of each italicized word in the following paragraph. Use *n.* for noun, *pro.* for pronoun, *v.* for verb, *adj.* for adjective, *adv.* for adverb, *prep.* for preposition, *conj.* for conjunction, and *int.* for interjection.

v. *conj.*

EXAMPLE: Tennessee Williams *enjoyed* a long *and* productive career.

Williams revised some of [1] *his* one-act plays and short stories to create many of his full-length plays. Was The Glass Menagerie a [2] *revision* of an earlier work? [3] *Yes,* says a scholar who has traced its origins. Before it came to Broadway in 1945, The Glass Menagerie had been through [4] *several* revisions. Sometime before 1943, Williams wrote "Portrait of a Girl in Glass," a short story that he had also adapted [5] *into* a one-act play. While working for MGM studios in 1943, Williams [6] *wrote* a movie treatment for the story, entitled "The Gentleman Caller." Working with the script [7] *later* that year, he expanded the play to seven scenes, [8] *and* it is this version that appears in most literary anthologies. During rehearsals for the play, [9] *Williams* revised the script once more, adding an eighth scene; this version of the play is the one that [10] *usually* is performed.

Exercise B Using the Parts of Speech in Writing

Many words in English can be used as more than one part of speech. Identify the part of speech of each italicized word below. Then, write a new sentence using each word as the part of speech given in parentheses.

EXAMPLE: The gentleman caller, Jim, will *call* on Laura in the next scene. (Use as a noun.)

The director has announced a casting call for the part of Laura.

1. The main *character* in Bernard Malamud's "The Magic Barrel" is Leo Finkle. (Use as an adjective.)
2. Although he is best known for his poetry, Imamu Amiri Baraka also has written essays, short stories, *plays,* a novel, and an autobiography. (Use as a verb.)
3. Williams built his reputation on the plays he wrote between 1945 and 1961; his *later* plays received less favorable reviews. (Use as an adverb.)
4. "*Wow,* that was a powerful production of The Glass Menagerie!" exclaimed one of the theatergoers. (Use as a verb.)
5. The drinking gourd has been worn smooth from *age* and use. (Use as a verb.)
6. We attended the cast party *after* we saw the play's final performance. (Use as a preposition.)
7. While living in Greenwich Village in the late 1950s, Baraka associated with such *Beat* poets as Allen Ginsberg and Frank O'Hara. (Use as a verb.)
8. Laura's unicorn is made of *glass.* (Use as an adjective.)
9. Bernard Malamud's stories often *blend* reality with fantasy. (Use as a noun.)
10. Some people transmit stories of the *past* orally. (Use as a preposition.)

LANGUAGE ARTS SURVEY

For additional help, see the Language Arts Survey, 2.30–2.31.

ANSWERS FOR LANGUAGE LAB

Exercise A

1. pro.
2. n.
3. int.
4. adj.
5. prep.
6. v.
7. adv.
8. conj.
9. n.
10. adv.

Exercise B

Responses will vary. Possible sentences are given.

1. *character*—n.

Bernard Malamud's "The Magic Barrel" is a character study of a young man at a crucial moment in his life.

2. *plays*—n.

In his poetry and his fiction, Imamu Amiri Baraka plays with language in surprising ways.

3. *later*—adj.

Despite setbacks early in his career, Williams later wrote many plays that achieved both critical and popular acclaim.

4. *Wow*—int.

The entire audience was wowed by the original and forceful production of "The Glass Menagerie."

5. *age*—n. Many cheeses must age before they can be eaten.

6. *after*—adv.

When John called, I asked if I could call him back after supper.

7. *Beat*—adj.

As the plot of the film thickened, my heart beat faster and faster.

8. *glass*—n.

Jennifer saves her pennies in a glass jar.

9. *blend*—v.

Many contemporary songs represent a blend of different styles ranging from jazz to classical.

10. *past*—n.

She told the man asking for directions that the post office was the building just past the bank on the left.

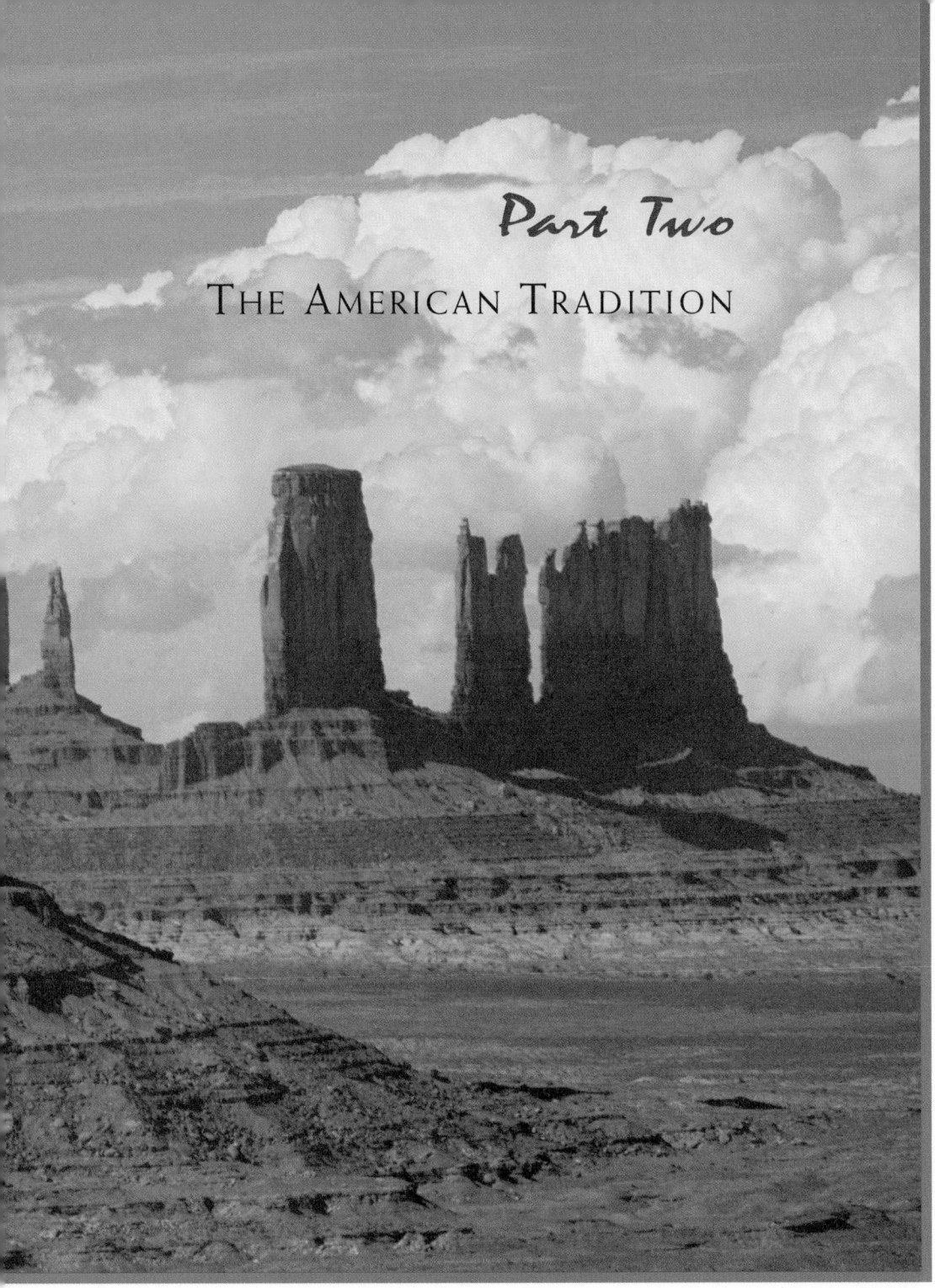

Part Two

The American Tradition

UNIT SKILLS OUTLINE

Literary Skills and Concepts

- Aim, 112
- Allusion, 112
- Chronological Order, 108
- Couplet, 112
- Effect, 123
- Emphasis, 123
- Hyperbole, 117
- Irony, 108
- Metaphor, 85
- Mood, 93
- Myth, 85
- Oxymoron, 117
- Parallelism, 85
- Point of View, 93
- Sight Rhyme, 117
- Symbol, 80
- Tone, 86

Writing Skills and Concepts

- Annotations, 112
- Children's Lesson Story, 112
- Comparison and Contrast, 123
- Curriculum, 112
- Hymn, 86
- Lyric Poem, 108
- Memoir, 108
- Speech, 81

Grammar, Usage, and Mechanics Skills and Concepts

- Achieving Parallelism, 85, 115
- Action Verbs, 89
- Adding Appositives or Appositive Phrases, 119
- Auxiliary Verbs, 86
- Concrete and Abstract Nouns, 124
- Formal and Informal English, 87
- Interjections, 86
- Inverting Sentences, 86, 117
- Linking Verbs, 86, 113
- Organizations and Institutions, 77
- Proofreading for Spelling Errors, 110
- Register, 87
- Sacred Beings and Writings, 77
- Simple Sentences, 86
- Using Precise Nouns, 82
- Using the Active Voice, 95
- Verbals: Gerunds, 86
- Verbals: Participles, 86

Other Language Arts Skills and Concepts

- Active Listening, 84
- Choosing and Analyzing an Audience, 81
- Classifying, 113
- Clustering, 86
- A Communication Model, 124
- Formal Note-taking, 117
- Making Hypotheses, 102
- Memorizing, 84
- Sensory Detail Charts, 86

Unit 2 Origins of the American Tradition (to 1750)

Quaker Meeting. *Courtesy of Museum of Fine Arts, Boston. Bequest of Maxim Karolik*

GOALS/OBJECTIVES

Studying this unit will enable students to

- appreciate the origins of the American literary tradition
- recognize the effects of nature on life and its portrayal in literature
- explain the religious background of many early American writings
- describe education in the American colonies during the 1600s and 1700s
- understand parallelism, aim, and irony
- identify point of view, mood, and hyperboles
- explain symbols and allusions
- write a speech, a hymn, and a comparison-and-contrast essay

Here individuals of all nations are melted into a new race . . . whose labors and posterity will one day cause great changes in the world.

—J. Hector St. Jean de Crèvecoeur, "What Is an American?"

CONNECTIONS ACROSS THE CURRICULUM

Arts and Humanities

- Lament of the Last Survivor, 88
- Native American Art and Architecture, 87
- Pop Culture Alphabet Book, 113
- Researching Weaving, 83

Mathematics and Sciences

- Compasses, 98

Social Studies

- Exploring the Protestant Reformation and the Puritan Movement, 124
- Maps of the New World, 97
- The *Mayflower*, 103
- Mayflower Compact, 101
- Native American Art and Architecture, 87
- Peoples of the Six Nations, 76
- Pocahontas, 98
- Pre-Columbian Cultures, 68
- Researching Explorers, 90
- Virginia Colonies, 94
- The Wampanoag, 71

TEACHING THE MULTIPLE INTELLIGENCES

Logical-Mathematical

- Compasses, 98

Spatial

- Maps of the New World, 97
- Researching Explorers, 90
- Researching Weaving, 83

Kinesthetic

- Memory Bee, 113
- Role Play, 92

Interpersonal

- Discussing Art, 84
- Exploring the Protestant Reformation and the Puritan Movement, 124
- Historical Portrayals, 95
- Maps of the New World, 97
- The Mayflower, 103
- Memory Bee, 113
- Native American Art and Architecture, 87
- Peoples of the Six Nations, 76
- Pop Culture Alphabet Book, 113
- Pre-Columbian Cultures, 68
- The Wampanoag, 71

Historical Note

You might inform students that from about 90,000 BC to 8,000 BC the world experienced one of several glaciations, or periods in which the polar ice caps spread. Because much of the planet's water was in ice form, the oceans were significantly lower, making a land bridge across the Bering Strait highly probable. The migration of peoples across this land bridge did not occur en masse over a short period of time; on the contrary, straggling groups of hunters probably followed game into the Americas over a period of thousands of years, their journeys spanning many generations, until the groups reached their final destinations in the Americas.

Cross-curricular Activities

Social Studies. Students might research pre-Columbian cultures that flourished long before Europeans set foot in the Americas. Divide students into small groups, each of which should research one of the following cultures: the Olmec, Maya, Toltec, or Aztec of Mesoamerica; or the Mogollon, Hohokam, Anasazi, Mound Builder, or Temple Mound Builder of North America. Students in each group should present what they have learned about the culture to the class. Presentations may be brief, but students should try to portray something of the culture's achievements and beliefs. You should emphasize to students that a variety of rich and vital cultures existed in the Americas before European settlement.

Buffalo Bull's Back Fat, head chief, Blood Tribe (Blackfoot). *George Catlin, 1832. National Museum of American Art, Washington, DC/Art Resource, NY*

The First Americans

Long before the first Europeans set foot on American soil, peoples from Asia came to the Americas, crossing a land bridge now submerged beneath the Bering Strait. The date of the arrival of the first humans in America is unknown, with estimates ranging from twenty thousand to fifty thousand years ago. Other people may have arrived in South America via sea routes from the South Pacific, though that theory remains controversial.

The Pre-Columbian Cultures of North America

Descendants of the first Americans populated North, Central, and South America, creating an extraordinary variety of cultures. When Europeans arrived in the late fifteenth century, there were perhaps 240 distinct Native American cultures in North America alone and a population variously estimated at between one million and two million people. Historians, archaeologists, and anthropologists divide these cultures into eight major groups, those of the Northwest Coast, California, the Northern Plateau, the Great Basin, the Southwest, the Plains, the Eastern Woodlands, and the Southeast. Although these cultures varied widely in their social customs, modes of government, economic systems, dress, religions, architecture, and languages, they shared a common reverence for and connection with the natural world. Europeans, in contrast, tended to see the natural world as something to be subdued, owned, and turned to human ends.

Literary Events

► = American Events

1517. Martin Luther posts his 95 Theses, beginning the Protestant Reformation
1516. Ludovico Ariosto's *Orlando Furioso* published
1515. Sir Thomas More's *Utopia* published
1513. Niccolo Machiavelli writes *The Prince*
1510. *Everyman,* English morality play, performed

1475 **1500** **1525**

►1492. Christopher Columbus crosses the Atlantic and lands in the Bahamas
►1502. Amerigo Vespucci returns from the New World; his account of the voyage led to his name being given to the New World
►1521. Aztec capital of Tenochtitlán falls to Hernando Cortés of Spain

Historical Events

THEMATIC CURRENTS

Use the following selections to explore these themes with your students.

Views of the Natural World
- from the Iroquois Constitution, 76
- "Song of the Sky Loom," 83

Life in the New World
- from *The General History of Virginia,* 94
- from *Of Plymouth Plantation,* 101
- from *The Very Brief Relation of the Devastation of the Indies,* 88

Puritanism
- from *The New England Primer,* 10
- from "Sinners in the Hands of ar Angry God," 118
- "Huswifery," 125

The Arrival of the Europeans

Historians today believe that the first Europeans to arrive in North America were Norse sailors. In 1001, **Leif Ericsson** established a very brief settlement in Labrador, which he called **Vinland**, or "Land of Wine." However, the Norse soon withdrew from the Americas, and it was almost five hundred years before Europeans returned. They did so as the result of a misguided attempt by the Italian sailor **Christopher Columbus** to find a route from Europe via the Atlantic to Japan and China. Funded by the king and queen of Spain, Columbus's expedition set sail on August 3, 1492. After months of fear and upset among the crew, the sailors arrived on October 12 at an island in the present-day Bahamas that Columbus named San Salvador. Thinking that he had reached India, Columbus called the natives whom he met "Indians." Although he made two subsequent voyages across the Atlantic Ocean, Columbus died without realizing that he had "discovered" two continents. These continents were called by Europeans **"the Americas"** because of a mistake made by a German mapmaker who believed, erroneously, that the continents had been discovered by the Portuguese explorer Amerigo Vespucci.

Reconstructions of Columbus's ships, the Nina, Pinta, and Santa Maria

After Columbus's initial voyage, European powers competed with one another to seize the opportunity that they imagined the "New World" offered them. Throughout the next two hundred years, many European explorers set sail for the Americas, including Juan Ponce de León, Vasco Nuñez de Balboa, Ferdinand Magellan, Hernando Cortés, Francisco Pizarro, Hernando de Soto, Cabeza de Vaca, Giovanni da Verrazano, Jacques Cartier, Samuel de Champlain, Father Jacques Marquette, Louis Joliet, Robert de La Salle, John Cabot, Francis Drake, Humphrey Gilbert, Walter Ralegh, Martin Frobisher, and Henry Hudson. The Spanish, Dutch, French, and English all established colonies in North America.

1591. William Shakespeare's *The Comedy of Errors* produced

1578. Holinshed's *Chronicles of English History to 1575* published

1550 **1575** **1600**

1534. Henry VIII breaks with the Church of Rome, founds the Church of England

►1541. Hernando de Soto discovers the Mississippi River

►1558. Queen Elizabeth crowned

1565. Spanish found first permanent North American settlement in St. Augustine, Florida

►1584. Sir Walter Ralegh founds the colony at Roanoke

1588. England defeats the Spanish Armada

LITERARY CURRENTS

Use the following selections to explore these techniques with your students.

Historical Accounts

- from *The General History of Virginia,* 94
- from *Of Plymouth Plantation,* 101
- from *The Very Brief Relation of the Devastation of the Indies,* 88

Extended Metaphors

- "Huswifery," 125
- "Song of the Sky Loom," 83

Cross-curricular Activities

Social Studies. Divide students into two groups. The first group should research European explorers and their accomplishments. A list of these explorers is provided on page 69. The second group should research the effects of European colonialism upon the indigenous populations of the Americas. Students might research Hernando Cortés's treatment of the Aztecs, Hernando de Soto's interactions with the natives of southeastern North America, Richard Grenville and Walter Ralegh's interactions with the natives of Roanoke Island, Samuel de Champlain's conflicts with the Iroquois, the Powhatan wars in the Virginia colony, or the Pequot war of the Connecticut River Valley. Then engage the two groups in a discussion about the moral and ethical implications of the Europeans' actions in the Americas. Encourage students who have researched European explorers to emphasize the daring of the explorers and the value of their explorations to the European community. Encourage students who have researched the interaction between Native Americans and European explorers and colonists to emphasize the brutal treatment of the native population and the destruction of their advanced civilizations.

► **Teaching Note:** The conflict between European settlers and Native American populations is a sensitive issue that may raise strong feelings in students. In the early twentieth century, the effects of colonization upon Native Americans were simply ignored and figures such as Christopher Columbus were idolized; Americans now have a different understanding of colonization and better realize the horrors Native Americans underwent. However, it is not illuminating to discuss European contact with the Americas in terms of generalizations such as "The explorers destroyed the native populations because they were evil, brutal, and greedy." To label all explorers as evil is to overlook the socioeconomic pressures and religious beliefs that led the colonists to feel they had the right to treat native populations as they did. Encourage students' discussions to move beyond the level of finding fault with European colonists and toward a discussion of why the Europeans believed they had the right to act as they did. Remind students that understanding the Europeans' behavior does not mean they are condoning it.

BIOGRAPHICAL NOTE

Sir Walter Ralegh (1552–1618) led an astonishingly full and varied life as a soldier, explorer, courtier, philosopher, colonist, poet, student of science, and historian. In addition to establishing the Roanoke Colony in Virginia, Ralegh imported the potato to Ireland and introduced the poet Edmund Spenser to the English court. Ralegh was always a favorite of Queen Elizabeth, and he was known at court for his flamboyant dress, his enthusiasm for life, and his quick temper. Ralegh did not find favor with Elizabeth's successor, King James, who sent him to the Tower of London, where he was imprisoned until his execution for treason in 1618. While incarcerated, Ralegh wrote his unfinished *History of the World,* which begins with the creation of the world and breaks off at 168 BC.

For the native population of the Americas, the arrival of Europeans spelled disaster. Millions of Native Americans in North, Central, and South America died as a result of European diseases, to which they had no natural immunities. Millions more were enslaved or driven from their ancestral lands. An account of the devastation of the first Native Americans to come in contact with Europeans is given in the selection from **Bartolomé de las Casas** in this unit.

JAMESTOWN AND THE ORIGINS OF THE PLANTATION SYSTEM

In 1587, a group of 117 English settlers led by **Sir Walter Ralegh** and **John White** founded a colony on **Roanoke Island,** off the coast of what is now North Carolina. After going back to England for supplies, John White returned to Roanoke in 1590 to find no trace of the colony that he left behind. The fate of the Roanoke colonists remains a mystery.

Settled in 1607, **Jamestown, Virginia,** was the first English colony to survive. The colonists hoped to establish a self-sustaining community, but because they knew little of the new land, they were not successful at first. They endured uncertainty and almost unimaginable hardship, facing fierce weather with little food and, for the most part, hastily fashioned holes in the ground for shelter. The numbers tell the grim story: of the 104 Jamestown colonists who survived the ocean voyage, only 38 lived through the first winter. In the face of such conditions, and with a community made up mostly of upper-class men unaccustomed to manual labor, **John Smith,** a natural leader among the colonists, was forced to proclaim that "he who does not work shall not eat," and to institute a rigorous, organized schedule of planting and working. In his *General History of Virginia, New England, and the Summer Isles,* an excerpt from which appears in this unit, Smith tells the story of being captured by Native Americans and rescued by the young daughter of **Powhatan,** their chief. The story of Smith's rescue by this girl, whose nickname was **Pocahantas,** may or may not be true, but it has captured the imaginations of Americans and contains, at least, a symbolic truth: only with the assistance of native peoples were the colonists able to survive. Native Americans taught the colonists how to build adequate shelters and how to cultivate crops such as corn and tobacco for food and export.

LITERARY EVENTS

►1624. John Smith's *The General History of Virginia* published
1623. Shakespeare's First Folio is published posthumously
1615. Miguel de Cervantes's *Don Quixote* published
1668. John Dryden becomes first English poet laureate
1655. Molière's first play performed
►1650. Anne Bradstreet's *The Tenth Muse Lately Sprung Up* published
►1638. The Bay Psalm Book becomes the first printed in New England

► = American Events

1625 **1650** **1675**

HISTORICAL EVENTS

1603. Elizabeth I dies; James VII of Scotland crowned James I
►1607. Jamestown settlement founded by Virginia company
1608. French found Quebec
►1625. Dutch found New Amsterdam settlement (later New York) on Manhattan Island
►1620. Pilgrims establish Plymouth settlement; Mayflower Compact
►1621. Pilgrims and Native Americans celebrate first Thanksgiving
1642. Civil War in England
►1643. The New England Confederation formed of Massachusetts, Plymouth, Connecticut, and New Haven colonies
1648. Oliver Cromwell and the Roundheads defeat the royalists
1660. English Civil War ends

Jamestown did not develop into a community of small family farms, like those soon to be established in New England. Instead, it turned tobacco into a profitable export crop, creating large plantations and importing slaves to do the work. Thus developed the plantation system and the slave trade that would have a dramatic effect on the subsequent course of North American history.

Belle Grove Plantation, Virginia

New England Colonization and the Puritan Era

Two other settlements begun in the early colonial years played a decisive role in North American history and literature. The **Plymouth Colony,** founded in 1620, and **The Massachusetts Bay Colony,** founded in 1630, were Puritan settlements. The New England colonists, like the Jamestown settlers, endured great difficulties and depended for their survival on the assistance of Native Americans. The core group of the Plymouth colonists, often referred to as the **Pilgrims,** were **Separatist Puritans,** so called because they had separated from the Church of England after giving up hope of "purifying" that church of what they considered to be Popish, or Catholic, tendencies. After moving from England to Holland to escape religious persecution, the Pilgrims set sail for North America on the ***Mayflower*** in 1620. They landed on Cape Cod and established their colony by means of the **Mayflower Compact** in what is now the town of Plymouth, Massachusetts. After a difficult winter, the colonists learned from native peoples, particularly **Squanto,** a member of the **Wampanoag** group, how to plant native crops. Under the direction of governor **William Bradford,** the colony flourished.

In 1691, Plymouth incorporated with a much larger settlement of Puritans, the Massachusetts Bay Colony. This group was made up of Congregationalist Puritans who did not separate entirely from the Church of England, believing it could be reformed from within.

Cross-curricular Activities

Social Studies. Students might learn more about the Pilgrim's interactions with the Wampanoag people. Two major points of interest are Squanto's interactions with the first settlers and King Philip's War. Students might then discuss their findings as a class. Students should focus on how and why the relationship between the settlers and the natives deteriorated. What was the result of the conflict between the natives and the settlers? What happened to the Wampanoag people?

►1704. America's first newspaper, the *News-Letter,* appears in Boston

►1702. Cotton Mather's *Magnolia Christi Americana* published

►1693. Cotton Mather's *The Wonders of the Invisible World* published

►1688. Aphra Behn writes *Oroonoko,* the first novel in English

►1683. William Penn's *A General Description of Pennsylvania* published

1678. John Bunyan's *Pilgrim's Progress* published

►1741. Jonathan Edwards delivers "Sinners in the Hands of an Angry God"

►1731. Benjamin Franklin founds first public library company in Philadelphia

►1729. Benjamin Franklin purchases *The Pennsylvania Gazette*

1700 **1725** **1750**

►1682. William Penn founds Philadelphia; Louisiana territory and the Mississippi Valley claimed by the Sieur de La Salle for the French

1685. James II succeeds Charles II

1688. Willam and Mary of Orange assume throne

►1692. Salem Witch Trials begin

1702. Anne succeeds William

1714. George I succeeds Anne

1715. Louis XIV dies in France after a seventy-two year reign

1727. George I succeeded by George II

►1737. First city-paid police force founded by Benjamin Franklin in Philadelphia

►1739. French explorers Pierre and Paul Mallet become first Europeans to view the Rocky Mountains

►1744. King George's War with France breaks out in North America and the Caribbean

QUOTABLES

"To the Puritan all things are impure, as somebody says."

—D. H. Lawrence

ADDITIONAL QUESTIONS AND ACTIVITIES

Have students discuss the Puritan beliefs described on page 72. What do they find attractive or unattractive about these beliefs? Do they think that the Puritans' beliefs enabled them to be successful colonists? Why, or why not?

They found inspiration for their early struggles in America in the belief that their actions were divinely guided. Their governor, **John Winthrop,** would write in his ***A Model of Christian Charity*** that they were about the business of building, as described in the New Testament, a "city upon a hill" in the new land.

PURITAN BELIEFS

The first Puritans in these settlements shared several basic religious and social beliefs. First, they had a remarkably strong belief in the importance of the community as a whole. Their belief that they were on a grand historical and religious mission formed a common purpose and sense of support, and they imagined the destiny of the community as everyone's responsibility. Various consent agreements or compacts, such as the Mayflower Compact mentioned previously, reflected and formalized this communal orientation. John Winthrop envisioned the Puritans bound together in a selfless, harmonious community directed by God. Second, the Puritans believed in **original sin,** the idea that because of the transgression of Adam and Eve, all people were born sinful and could be saved only by divine grace. Third, although they thought they were a chosen people, they did not believe that all souls among them were chosen. They adopted the French theologian **John Calvin's** theory of **predestination,** holding that God has chosen in advance which souls are to be saved and which are not. They understood this to mean they could not change their individual fates directly, by force of will. Since none could be sure of having been saved, however, they maintained a steady and humble watch over their lives for proof that they were among the **elect,** those chosen for salvation by God at the beginning of time. Finally, the Puritans shared a belief in hard work, thinking that material and social successes were signs of God's providence and that such work, though it could not win salvation, was nonetheless a sign of salvation. This complex belief in strict moral propriety, community service, and hard work is today referred to as the **Puritan Ethic.**

POLITICS, SOCIETY, AND THE PROBLEM OF ORTHODOXY

Despite these shared beliefs, a notable though subdued tension existed in Puritan society and politics between its official, orthodox beliefs and the beliefs of some colonists. Puritan communities functioned as **theocracies,** societies guided by religious law, and early Puritan leaders were largely intolerant of any opposition, religious or political. When **Roger Williams** voiced his objections in 1635 about what he saw as the Puritans' arrogant intolerance of diversity and about the taking of lands from the Native Americans, he was banished from Massachusetts. He went on to found the colony of Rhode Island and to espouse principles of religious freedom. In 1637, when **Anne Hutchinson** bypassed the official church and began teaching her own theories in home Bible classes with other women and their husbands, she was accused of threatening the religion and of being more a "husband than a wife." She was banished from Massachusetts as well. Although advanced among colonies of the time in supporting education for women, Massachusetts was not necessarily interested in being educated by women on matters of church doctrine. Its leaders retained an Old Testament model of patriarchal authority.

Even though pressures from progressive elements led in 1662 to the **Half-Way Covenant,** which relaxed old rules and allowed more people direct membership in the church, tensions remained. Some saw the relaxing of orthodoxy as a sign of weakness, and their concerns surfaced dramatically in the belief that Satan had infiltrated the town of Salem and nearby

A witch trial at Salem, Massachusetts, in 1692. The Granger Collection, NY

communities. The **Salem Witch Trials,** begun in 1692, resulted in the execution of twenty people and the imprisonment and torture of many more. Followed by embarrassment and recanting, the trials further diminished the Puritan hold on New England. In 1692, a new Massachusetts charter changed the colony's government from a theocratic one to a secular one in which voting was no longer restricted by religious requirements.

Religion and Allegory in Early Puritan Writing

Religion was a dominant influence and presence in the works of early Puritan writers. In sermons, colonial histories, personal diaries, and devotional poetry, Puritan writers often explored the story of spiritual struggles in personal and public life, interpreting or portraying events as emblems, or **allegories,** of the progress of souls or of God's design. In diaries, writers would record their thoughts from day to day and chart their individual spiritual development, often reading seemingly trivial everyday events or conflicts as signs of God's will working itself out in the world. Puritan writers of history sought to find Biblical precedents in current events and in the various travails of their communities as a whole.

Puritan literature was not entirely an expression of official views and beliefs, however, and in it we can find examples of the struggle with orthodoxy and conformity mentioned earlier. For example, in her "Prologue," the poet **Anne Bradstreet** asserted that her male critics' judgment was distorted by their views of women: "For such despite they cast on female wits:/If what I do prove well, it won't advance,/They'll say it's stol'n, or else it was by chance."

Although not all Puritans in seventeenth-century New England were educated, they nonetheless valued and promoted education and reading. They founded **Harvard College** in 1636 and began the first colonial printing press two years later. Writers of this era were influenced by their European counterparts, and some of their works, including the poems of Bradstreet, reveal a familiarity with the styles, themes, and figures of the newly available literature of classical Greece and Rome.

Literary Note

You might inform students that during the Renaissance and the Enlightenment the literature being produced in Europe was very different from the literature being produced in and about the Americas. In England, dramatists such as Shakespeare were producing masterpieces, sonnets, and other lyrical forms of poetry, were gaining increasing popularity, and the novel was being developed. In America, the dominant forms of literature were historical accounts, political treatises, and religious allegories. (The Native Americans, however, continued to produce traditional myths and songs in addition to political treatises like the highly poetical Iroquois Constitution.) Explain to students that historical accounts, political treatises, and religious allegories are typical works of newcomers to an unfamiliar land. Poetry, drama, and prose are more often produced by those with more leisure time and who are more firmly established in a land.

QUOTABLES

"No man's knowledge here can go beyond his experience."

—John Locke

"If I have seen further it is by standing on the shoulders of giants."

—Sir Isaac Newton

THE EUROPEAN ENLIGHTENMENT AND THE GREAT AWAKENING

The emergence in mid-seventeenth-century England of scientific and empirical thinking, legitimated and encouraged by the formation in 1660 of a science academy called **The Royal Society,** was to have a significant effect on later Puritan intellectuals such as **Cotton Mather** and **Jonathan Edwards.** English Enlightenment thinkers such as **John Locke** and **Isaac Newton** believed that **empirical inquiry,** the study of human experience and the natural world, was the proper approach for achieving true knowledge. In opposition to medieval theories of innate knowledge derived from God, Locke held that people begin life as blank slates and must slowly build up their knowledge from sense impressions. Similarly for Newton, the proper focus of study was nature, the analysis of which, he believed, supported religious belief by revealing the orderly plan of God's design.

In the preachings and writings of Jonathan Edwards, this Enlightenment emphasis on empirical evidence and human experience gave rise to the claim that one needed to feel or experience God, not just intuit his existence from one's belief or from the Bible. Such experiences, or **awakenings,** as they came to be called, formed the basis for a religious revival, called the **Great Awakening,** which from its beginnings in 1734 in Edwards's Northampton congregation quickly spread to Boston and then throughout the colonies. Edwards's eventual call for a return to stricter church membership requirements and his demand for proof of an awakening and conversion were ultimately unpopular, however, and he was removed from his pulpit in 1750.

Echoes:

Origins of the American Tradition

"Where today are the Pequot? Where are the Narragansett, the Mohican, the Pokanoket, and many other once powerful tribes of our people? They have vanished . . . as snow before a summer sun."

— Tecumseh, Shawnee chief, on the destruction of Native American peoples and ways of life

"The earth receives my body . . .
Each in its own turn so that
The circle of life is never broken."

— Anonymous Taos Pueblo saying on the interconnectedness of people and nature

"He shall make us a praise and glory that men shall say of succeeding plantations, 'the lord make it like that of NEW ENGLAND.' For we must consider that we shall be as a city upon a hill. The eyes of all people are upon us, so that if we shall deal falsely with our God in this work we have undertaken, and so cause Him to withdraw His present help from us, we shall be made a story and a by-word through the world."

— John Winthrop on the creation of the Massachusetts Bay Colony

"I will fear GOD, and honor the KING.
I will honor my Father & Mother.
I will Obey my Superiors.
I will Submit to my Elders.
I will Love my Friends.
I will hate no Man.
I will forgive my Enemies, and pray to God for them.
I will as much as in me lies keen all God's Holy Commandments."

— "The Dutiful Child's Promises," from *The New England Primer*

"I am obnoxious to each carping tongue
Who says my hand a needle better fits,
A poet's pen all scorn I should thus wrong,
For such despite they cast on female wits:
If what I do prove well, it won't advance,
They'll say it's stol'n, or else it was by chance.

— Anne Bradstreet on men's responses to women writers in the Puritan Era

"Unclean, unclean: my Lord, undone, all vile,
Yea, all defiled: what shall Thy servant do?
Unfit for Thee: not fit for holy soil,
Nor for communion of saints below.
A bag of botches, lump of loathsomeness:
Defiled by touch, by issue: Leproused flesh."

— Edward Taylor, Puritan minister, on the unredeemed state of humankind

ADDITIONAL RESOURCES

READER'S GUIDE
- Selection Worksheet, 2.1

ASSESSMENT PORTFOLIO
- Selection Check Test, 4.2.1
- Selection Test, 4.2.2

ESSENTIAL SKILLS PRACTICE BOOKS
- *Writing,* 1.7, 1.9, 1.24, 1.38–1.40
- *Language,* 2.32, 2.118, 2.125

ENRICHMENT ACTIVITIES

Students can work in small groups to research the Mohawk, Oneida, Onondaga, Cayuga, Seneca, and Tuscarora. Each group can then share what they have learned with the rest of the class. In what ways were the groups of Native Americans similar? In what ways were they different? Why might they have joined together as a confederacy? Students can discuss these questions after each group has made its presentation.

SUPPORT FOR LEP STUDENTS

Some students may have difficulty understanding the symbolism in this selection. Discuss the meanings of roots, the shade of a tree, and the eagle that sits atop the tree. Students can brainstorm ideas about what these items might symbolize. Then, as they read the selection, students can apply their ideas to the text to see what symbol makes sense in the context of the work.

ADDITIONAL VOCABULARY
ascend—travel upward
trivial—unimportant
chide—scold

PREREADING

from the Iroquois Constitution

ABOUT THE SELECTION

The **Iroquois Constitution**, dating from the fifteenth or sixteenth century, joined together several peoples who lived on the shores of the Great Lakes into the Iroquois League, or Iroquois Confederacy. Initially, the Iroquois League included the Mohawk, Oneida, Onondaga, Cayuga, and Seneca. In the 1700s, however, the Tuscarora joined the Confederacy, making it the League of Six Nations. Tradition holds that the league was begun by Dekanawidah, a Huron whose words open the constitution, and by Hiawatha, an Onondaga who lived among the Mohawks. Each brought to the league his own special talents. Dekanawidah was a diplomat who envisioned the many branches of the Iroquois people united under his Tree of Great Peace. Hiawatha brought this message of unity—the Great Law of Peace—to the Iroquois people as he traveled the country.

The Iroquois lived by hunting, trading, and raising crops such as corn, beans, and squash. For shelter, they built magnificent long houses, covered with elm bark, that housed several families. Kinship groups, or clans, many named after totem, or symbolic, animals such as the beaver or hawk, were united into half tribes, or moieties. These were united into tribes, and the tribes into the league. Decisions of the league were made in great council meetings. Each member of the league had one vote, and all member nations had to agree before any action was taken. The league was ruled by fifty male peace chiefs, or sachems, who were chosen by the Iroquois women. The political system of the Iroquois was well known to the Founding Fathers of the United States, including Benjamin Franklin, who saw in the Iroquois Constitution a model for representative government.

After the coming of Europeans, many Native American populations were decimated by epidemics of diseases such as smallpox. During the Colonial Period, the total Iroquois population numbered only about twelve thousand, and the total number of Iroquois warriors at any time numbered only a little over two thousand. Despite these small numbers, the Iroquois waged successful war against neighboring groups and held both British and French invaders at bay. Particularly impressive was the ability of the Iroquois to battle successfully against the French, who were allied with the the Huron. During the American Revolution, two Iroquois groups sided with the colonists. The rest, led by Chief Joseph Brant, sided with the British, leading George Washington to send troops in retaliation to destroy Iroquois settlements, fields, and stores of food. Later treaties set aside reservation lands for the Onondaga, Seneca, and Tuscarora in New York. The Mohawks and Cayuga settled in Canada, and the Oneida in Wisconsin.

GOALS/OBJECTIVES

Studying this lesson will enable students to
- appreciate the constitution and beliefs of the Iroquois people
- explain the historical circumstances of the Iroquois people
- interpret symbols in their reading
- write a speech
- create a Venn diagram and use it to organize information
- use precise nouns

READER'S JOURNAL

What do you consider to be the ideal form of government? If you were going to design a constitution for a new country, what elements would that constitution have? Write about these questions in your journal.

LANGUAGE SKILLS

Read the Language Arts Survey, 2.118, "Organizations and Institutions," and 2.125, "Sacred Beings and Writings." As you read the following selection, find examples of each type of capitalization and copy them into your journal. Also see if you can find in the selection an example of the capitalization of the name of a legal work.

FROM THE

Iroquois Constitution

I am Dekanawidah and with the Five Nations[1] confederate lords I plant the Tree of the Great Peace. I name the tree the Tree of the Great Long Leaves. Under the shade of this Tree of the Great Peace we spread the soft white feathery down of the globe thistle as seats for you, Adodarhoh, and your cousin lords.

We place you upon those seats, spread soft with the feathery down of the globe thistle, there beneath the shade of the spreading branches of the Tree of Peace. There shall you sit and watch the council fire of the confederacy of the Five Nations, and all the affairs of the Five Nations shall be transacted at this place before you.

Roots have spread out from the Tree of the Great Peace, one to the north, one to the east, one to the south, and one to the west. The name of these roots is the Great White Roots and their nature is peace and strength.

If any man or any nation outside the Five Nations shall obey the laws of the Great Peace and make known their disposition to the lords of the confederacy, they may trace the roots to the tree and if their minds are clean and they are obedient and promise to obey the wishes of the confederate council, they shall be welcomed[2] to take shelter beneath the Tree of the Long Leaves.

We place at the top of the Tree of the Long Leaves an eagle who is able to see afar.

If he sees in the distance any evil approaching or any danger threatening he will at once warn the people of the confederacy.

1. **Five Nations.** The Mohawk, Oneida, Onondaga, Cayuga, and Seneca tribes. These tribes formed the Iroquois Confederacy.
2. **they shall be welcomed.** The Tuscarora tribe joined the Confederacy in 1722.

❶ *On what terms would someone outside the Five Nations gain acceptance?*

WORDS FOR EVERYDAY USE:

con • fed • er • a • cy (kən fed´ ər ə sē) *n.,* people or groups united for common purpose

dis • po • si • tion (dis´ pə zish´ ən¯) *n.,* state of mind; general nature

PREREADING NOTES

READER'S JOURNAL

Students may want to consider the different forms of government of which they are aware. What aspects of these governments do they admire? What aspects would they like to avoid? These questions may help students begin to think about different forms of government.

LANGUAGE SKILLS

Examples of capitalization of sacred beings and writings are Creator and Great Creator; examples of capitalization of organizations and institutions include Five Nations, Tree of the Long Leaves, and Great Peace.

▶Additional practice is provided in the *Essential Skills Practice Book: Language,* 2.118 and 2.125.

ANSWER TO GUIDED READING QUESTION

❶ An outsider would gain acceptance to the Five Nations by obeying the laws of the Great Peace, letting the lords of the confederacy know their disposition, having a clean mind, and promising to obey the wishes of the confederate council.

VOCABULARY FROM THE SELECTION

confederacy	estimation
disposition	furnish

VOCABULARY IN CONTEXT

- The Balloos, the Ursas, and the Yogis stopped feuding and formed a confederacy to save their vanishing homeland in the mountains.
- Angelica is a pleasure to be around due to her sunny disposition.

Answer to Guided Reading Question

❶ The following acknowledgements were made at the opening of a council meeting: thanks to the earth for being a place to live; to the streams, pools, springs, and lakes; to maize and fruits; to medicinal herbs and trees; to forest trees for their usefulness; to animals for serving as food and clothing; to the winds, thunders, sun, and moon; to the messengers of the Creator; and to the Great Creator, who creates and rules health and life.

The smoke of the confederate council fire shall ever ascend and pierce the sky so that other nations who may be allies may see the council fire of the Great Peace. . . .

Whenever the confederate lords shall assemble for the purpose of holding a council, the Onondaga lords shall open it by expressing their gratitude to their cousin lords and greeting them, and they shall make an address and offer thanks to the earth where men dwell, to the streams of water, the pools, the springs and the lakes, to the maize and the fruits, to the medicinal herbs and trees, to the forest trees for their usefulness, to the animals that serve as food and give their pelts for clothing, to the great winds and the lesser winds, to the thunderers, to the sun, the mighty warrior, to the moon, to the messengers of the Creator who reveal his wishes and to the Great Creator who dwells in the heavens above, who gives all the things useful to men, and who is the source and the ruler of health and life.

What acknowledgments occurred at the opening of a council meeting? ❶

Then shall the Onondaga lords declare the council open. . . .

All lords of the Five Nations' Confederacy must be honest in all things. . . . It shall be a serious wrong for anyone to lead a lord into trivial affairs, for the people must ever hold their lords high in estimation out of respect to their honorable positions.

When a candidate lord is to be installed he shall furnish four strings of shells (or wampum)[3] one span in length bound together at one end. Such will constitute the evidence of his pledge to the confederate lords that he will live according to the constitution of the Great Peace and exercise justice in all affairs.

When the pledge is furnished the speaker of the council must hold the shell strings in his hand and address the opposite side of the council fire and he shall commence his address saying: "Now behold him. He has now become a confederate lord. See how splendid he looks." An address may then follow. At the end of it he shall send the bunch of shell strings to the opposite side and they shall be received as evidence of the pledge. Then shall the opposite side say:

3. **wampum.** Small beads made of shell, usually white or dark purple in color

Words for Everyday Use: **es • ti • ma • tion** (es´ tə mā´ shən) *n.,* respect; value
fur • nish (fur´ nish) *vt.,* supply or provide

Vocabulary in Context

- At the end of the year the students honored Ms. Leopold, a teacher they held in high estimation.
- The clues he found along with the information furnished by a witness helped Larry solve the crime.

"We now do crown you with the sacred emblem of the deer's antlers, the emblem of your lordship. You shall now become a mentor of the people of the Five Nations. The thickness of your skin shall be seven spans—which is to say that you shall be proof against anger, offensive actions and criticism. Your heart shall be filled with peace and good will and your mind filled with a yearning for the welfare of the people of the confederacy. With endless patience you shall carry out your duty and your firmness shall be tempered with tenderness for your people. Neither anger nor fury shall find lodgement in your mind and all your words and actions shall be marked with calm deliberation. In all of your deliberations in the confederate council, in your efforts at law making, in all your official acts, self-interest shall be cast into oblivion. Cast not over your shoulder behind you the warnings of the nephews and nieces should they chide you for any error or wrong you may do, but return to the way of the Great Law which is just and right. Look and listen for the welfare of the whole people and have always in view not only the present but also the coming generations, even those whose faces are yet beneath the surface of the ground—the unborn of the future nation." ■

Illustration by Helen Abraham

❶ *What view should a lord take?*

Responding to the Selection

Think about the way in which the Iroquois began their council meetings. To whom or what did they offer thanks before proceeding? What is the relationship between these nations and the land? Are people today as connected to the natural environment? Discuss these questions with your classmates.

Responding to the Selection

Ask students to invent their own ways of praising or thanking the earth, the waters, and other natural elements. Students may want to consider activities such as recycling or cleaning up a park or forest as part of their praise.

Answer to Guided Reading Question

❶ A lord should "look and listen for the welfare of the people" and always consider future generations.

Answers to Selection Check Test 4.2.1

EX. Which peoples formed the Iroquois Confederacy?
The Mohawk, Oneida, Onondaga, Cayuga, and Seneca formed the Iroquois Confederacy.

1. What is the nature of the Great White Roots?
The nature of the Great White Roots is peace and strength.

2. Who is placed at the top of the tree and what is he able to do?
The eagle is placed at the top of the tree. He is able to see far.

3. What must the Onondaga lords do to open a council?
They must offer gratitude to their cousins and thank the many aspects of nature and the Great Creator.

4. What must a candidate lord offer as evidence of his pledge to the Confederacy?
He must offer four strings of shells (or wampum).

5. Whose welfare concerns a mentor of the people of the Five Nations?
The welfare of the whole people, present and future, concerns the mentor.

Reviewing the Selection

Recalling

1. Who plants and names the Tree of Great Peace with Dekanawidah?
2. To whom is Dekanawidah speaking? Who do you think Adodarhoh is?
3. What rituals begin each Iroquois council meeting?
4. How does a candidate lord show his pledge to the council? What does his offering symbolize?

Interpreting

5. What is the purpose of the meeting at which Dekanawidah speaks? Why do you think oratory skills were prized by the Iroquois?
6. Why do you think Dekanawidah refers to the assembled lords as "cousins"? Are they literally related to one another?
7. What relationship exists between the Iroquois and the natural environment?
8. According to the constitution, what qualities should a leader have? What qualities should a leader put aside?

Synthesizing

9. In what ways is framing a constitution like planting a tree? In what ways are the spread-out roots of a tree like a confederacy of nations?
10. What special ceremony did the Iroquois hold for the installation of a new "confederate lord"? In what ways is this ceremony similar to and different from the inauguration of a United States president or the swearing in of a United States senator or representative?

Understanding Literature (Questions for Discussion)

Symbol. A **symbol** is a thing that stands for or represents both itself and something else. The chart below lists some common symbols used in literary works. In the Iroquois Constitution, what does the tree symbolize? its roots? What does it mean to take shelter under the leaves of this tree? What does the eagle perched in the top of the tree symbolize?

SYMBOL	CONVENTIONAL INTERPRETATION
wind	change, inspiration
rainbow	hope
rose	beauty, love
moon	fickleness, inconstancy
roads, paths	the journey through life
spring	youth

CONTINUED

Answers for Reviewing the Selection

RECALLING

1. The Five Nations confederate lords plant the Tree of Great Peace with Dekanawidah.

2. Dekanawidah is speaking to his assembled people. Students may think that Adodarhoh is an important Iroquois leader or a god.

3. Onondaga lords must offer gratitude to their cousins and thank the many aspects of nature, including the earth and water, and the Great Creator before opening the council.

4. A candidate lord shows his pledge by offering four strings of shells (or wampum) that are "one span in length and bound together at one end." This offering symbolizes that he "will live according to the constitution of the Great Peace."

INTERPRETING

Responses will vary. Possible responses are given.

5. The purpose of the meeting was to plant the Tree of Great Peace and establish some of the guidelines of the confederacy. Oratory skills may have been highly valued because communication skills were necessary for deciding upon actions in council.

6. Although many may not be literally related to one another, Dekanawidah refers to the lords as cousins because they are related in their cause, their quest for peace, and their concern for the welfare of their people.

7. The Iroquois seem to have a very close, respectful relationship with nature, as demonstrated by the offering of thanks they give before opening the council meeting and the many references to council creations as natural items, such as the Tree of Great Peace.

8. A leader should be full of peace and good will, patience, and calm deliberation. A leader's mind should be turned away from himself or herself and toward the welfare of the people. A leader must cast aside anger, offensive actions, and criticism.

(cont.)

Answers for Reviewing the Selection (cont.)

SYNTHESIZING

Responses will vary. Possible responses are given.

9. Framing a constitution is the beginning of a government that will hopefully grow and flourish. It allows the laws of the people to take root. A confederacy of nations is far-reaching with different needs and different things to offer. A confederacy, or group joined for a common purpose, is like the roots of a tree that come from many directions to one place where they all join.

10. When a candidate was to become lord, he had to offer wampum strings as a pledge of his commitment to the confederacy and to exercising justice in all affairs. At an inauguration a president also swears an oath to uphold the office. In both cases, the swearing in is often followed by an address to the people.

fall, winter	age
woods, darkness	spiritual or moral confusion
storm	trouble, confusion, anger
thorns	trouble, pain, suffering
stars	unchangeableness, constancy
mirror	vanity, introspection
snake	evil, duplicity
owl	wisdom
fox	craftiness

Responding in Writing

Speech. According to the Iroquois Constitution, a newly accepted candidate lord may make an address to his fellow council lords. Imagine you are such a lord and write the text of your acceptance speech. Try to use the speaking style exemplified by the selection. Refer to the Language Arts Survey, 1.7, "Choosing and Analyzing an Audience."

Writing Skills

Venn Diagram. Read the Language Arts Survey, 1.24, "Venn Diagrams." Then consider the goals and overall structure of the Iroquois form of government as described on page 68 and in the selection. How is that form of government similar to and different from the government of the United States? To organize your thoughts, create a Venn diagram similar to the one shown here:

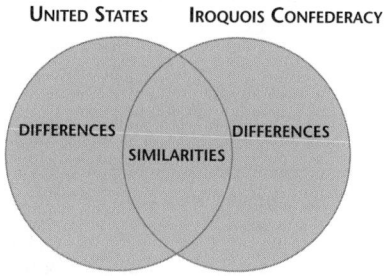

Use the information in your diagram to write a brief comparison-contrast paragraph explaining your ideas. Refer to the Language Arts Survey, 1.9, "Modes of Writing," and 1.38–1.40, "Drafting: Paragraphs."

Answers for Understanding Literature

►See the evaluation forms for discussion, active listening, and oral communication, *Assessment Portfolio,* 7.11–7.14.

Responses will vary. Possible responses are given.

Symbol. The tree symbolizes the interconnectedness of the nations that are part of the confederacy. The roots might symbolize the nations that make up the confederacy. The roots might also symbolize the constitution that deeply anchors the tree of peace. Taking shelter under the leaves means enjoying the peace of the nations or the security brought through the work of the council. The eagle perched in the tree symbolizes foresight to protect the people from evil or danger.

Analytic Scales for Responding in Writing

Assign a score from 1 to 25 for each grading criterion below. (For more detailed evaluation, see the evaluation forms for writing, revising, and proofreading, *Assessment Portfolio,* 7.1–7.10.)

Speech

- **Content/Unity.** The speech expresses acceptance of the position. It may suggest how the speaker will serve the people or indicate the speaker's feelings about the confederacy and the constitution.
- **Organization/Coherence.** The speech has a definite introduction, body, and conclusion. The speech is written in a logical and sensible order.
- **Language/Style.** The speech is in a style appropriate for a formal occasion and may be similar to the style of speech in the constitution. The speech employs vivid and precise nouns, verbs, and modifiers.
- **Conventions.** The speech avoids errors in spelling, grammar, usage, mechanics, and manuscript form.

Answers for Writing Skills

Students' Venn diagrams should show the similarities and differences they address in their paragraph. Paragraphs should both compare and contrast the two forms of government.

►Additional practice is provided in the *Essential Skills Practice Book: Writing,* 1.9 and 1.38–1.40.

ANSWERS FOR LANGUAGE LAB

Responses will vary. Possible responses are given.

1. Hiawatha is a famous, fifteenth-century hero of Iroquois legend.
2. The name Hiawatha, in Onondaga, means "He Makes Rivers."
3. According to tradition, Hiawatha helped form the League of Five Nations and became chief of the Onondaga.
4. Legend holds that Dekanawidah convinced Hiawatha of the importance of planting the Tree of the Great Peace.
5. One of the most famous lyrics of the American poet Henry Wadsworth Longfellow is his "Song of Hiawatha," written in 1855.

►Additional practice is provided in the *Essential Skills Practice Book: Language,* 2.32.

PROJECT NOTES

►See the worksheets and evaluation forms for projects, *Assessment Portfolio,* 7.20–7.23.

Constitution. Students might begin by brainstorming the basic rights people have, what they expect leaders to do, how they think leaders should be chosen, etc. Students should then think of problems that might arise on the island and think of laws or political structures that might eliminate these problems.

Language Lab

Using Precise Nouns. Read the Language Arts Survey, 2.32, "Using Precise Nouns." Then rewrite the sentences below using precise nouns. Don't worry about whether your new sentences are factually correct.

1. Hiawatha, who may have lived in the fifteenth century, is a famous figure in Iroquois legend.
2. The name Hiawatha, in a Native American language, means "He Makes Rivers."
3. According to tradition, Hiawatha helped to form a political body and became a chief of a Native American group.
4. Legend holds that it was another respected chief who convinced Hiawatha of the importance of establishing peace among the nations.
5. One of the most famous works of the American poet Henry Wadsworth Longfellow is his "Song of Hiawatha," written in 1855.

PROJECT

Constitution. Imagine that you and your classmates win a trip to the South Seas. On the way there, you are shipwrecked on an island with no means of contacting the outside world. On the island, you find plenty of natural shelter, fruit to eat, and other necessities of life. After living on the island for some time, you decide that you need to create a constitution for your new island government. Work with other students to write such a constitution establishing the basic laws and political structure of your new country. Do not refer to any existing constitutions as you are writing yours. When you are finished, you may wish to compare your constitution to actual constitutions such as that of the United States of America.

FROM *The Song of Hiawatha*

You shall hear how Hiawatha
Prayed and fasted in the forest,
Not for greater skill in hunting,
Not for greater craft in fishing,
Not for triumphs in the battle,
And renown among the warriors,
But for profit of the people,
For advantage of the nations.

Henry Wadsworth Longfellow

PREREADING

"Song of the Sky Loom"

Tewa Tribal Song

About the Selection

The language of **"Song of the Sky Loom"** is taken directly from weaving. The Tewa, a Pueblo people of the Southwest, are accomplished weavers. They, in their turn, passed the art on to the Navajo, now renowned weavers of blankets and rugs. In addition to weaving, the Tewa make intricately decorated pottery and elaborate baskets. They live in multilevel, multiunit adobe structures often built into the hard mesas of the Southwest. Like other Pueblo peoples, the Tewa have a vital interdependence with nature, performing various rituals and ceremonies related to nature, especially to bringing much-needed rain.

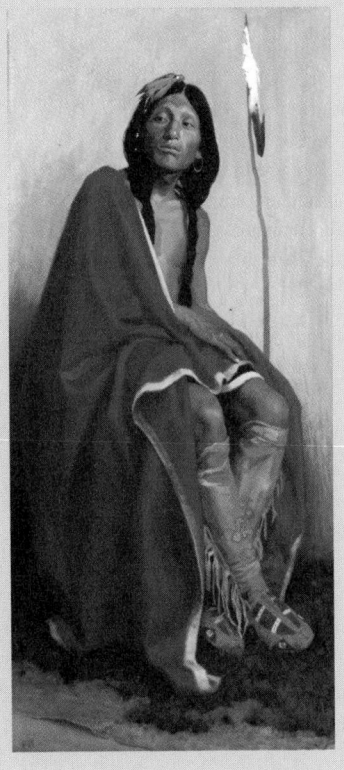

Elk-Foot of the Taos Tribe. *Eanger Irving Couse, circa 1909. National Museum of American Art, Washington, DC/Art Resource, NY*

GOALS/OBJECTIVES

Studying this lesson will enable students to

- appreciate an extended metaphor based on traditional art
- understand a speaker's feelings about religion, art, work, and nature
- identify, define, and illustrate with examples the terms *parallelism, metaphor,* and *myth*
- write a hymn
- explain the differences between formal and informal English

ADDITIONAL RESOURCES

Reader's Guide

- Selection Worksheet, 2.2

Assessment Portfolio

- Selection Check Test, 4.2.3
- Selection Test, 4.2.4

Essential Skills Practice Books

- *Writing,* 1.17, 1.18
- *Language,* 2.13, 2.14, 2.16, 2.17, 2.19, 2.40, 2.57, 2.64, 2.147, 2.148
- *Speaking and Listening,* 3.4
- *Study and Research,* 4.20–4.27

ENRICHMENT ACTIVITIES

Students can learn more about weaving in one or more of the following ways: researching and finding photographs of the weavings of Tewa, Navajo, and other Pueblo peoples; trying their own hands at weaving on a small hand loom; or arranging a demonstration by a local weaver.

SUPPORT FOR LEP STUDENTS

While the vocabulary of the song is fairly simple, some students may have difficulty understanding some of the terms from the art of weaving used in the selection. In addition to encouraging students to pay careful attention to the footnotes, you may wish to review with students the additional vocabulary below before they read the selection.

Additional Vocabulary

garment—piece of clothing
fringes—threads or strips of fabric hanging from the edges of a weaving
border—ornamental design at the edges of a weaving

PREREADING NOTES

READER'S JOURNAL

Students can discuss with others the art forms they chose to describe themselves and why they feel the art forms are appropriate. Ask students why these forms of art appeal to them. What makes these forms different or special to them?

SPEAKING AND LISTENING SKILLS

Because of the repetition and the simplicity of the language, this song is an excellent piece for memorization. Refer students to the Language Arts Survey, 4.4, "Memorizing." Because this song has more than one speaker and is written in the first person plural, groups of students might memorize the poem and recite it together, or pairs of students might recite alternate lines.

▶Additional practice is provided in the *Essential Skills Practice Books: Speaking and Listening,* 3.4, and *Study and Research,* 4.4.

ANSWERS TO GUIDED READING QUESTIONS

❶ "Our Mother the Earth" and "our Father the Sky" are addressed in this song.

❷ The garment will be woven of brightness, the white light of morning, the red light of evening, the falling rain, and the standing rainbow.

READER'S JOURNAL

Think of an art form to describe yourself. Are you a painting? a sculpture? musical work? a ceramic pot? a patchwork quilt? Write a short paragraph in your journal identifying the art form and explaining why you chose it.

SPEAKING AND LISTENING SKILLS

"Song of the Sky Loom" can be experienced more fully as a spoken work of literature. Read the Language Arts Survey, 3.4, "Active Listening." Then listen as a classmate reads the poem aloud.

"Song of the Sky Loom"

TEWA TRIBAL SONG

❶ Who is addressed in this song?

❷ Of what will the garment be woven?

O our Mother the Earth, O our Father the Sky,
Your children are we, and with tired backs
We bring you the gifts you love.
Then weave for us a garment of brightness;
May the warp[1] be the white light of morning,
May the weft[2] be the red light of evening,
May the fringes be the falling rain,
May the border be the standing rainbow.
Thus weave for us a garment of brightness,
That we may walk fittingly where birds sing,
That we may walk fittingly where grass is green,
O our Mother the Earth, O our Father the Sky. ■

1. **warp.** Threads in a loom that run lengthwise
2. **weft.** Horizontal threads in a loom. The weft crosses the warp to make a woven fabric.

ANSWERS TO SELECTION CHECK TEST 4.2.3

EX. To whom is the song addressed?
The song is addressed to Mother Earth and Father Sky.
1. With what do the speakers bring their gifts?
They bring their gifts "with tired backs."
2. To what two parts of a loom do the speakers refer?
The speakers refer to the warp and the weft.
3. What should be the falling rain?
The fringes should be the falling rain.
4. What kind of garment do the speakers ask for twice?
The speakers ask twice for "a garment of brightness."
5. Where do the speakers wish to walk "fittingly"?
The speakers wish to walk "fittingly" where birds sing and where the grass is green.

Responding to the Selection

How does "Song of the Sky Loom" make you feel? What images does it create in your mind?

Reviewing the Selection

RECALLING

1. To whom is "Song of the Sky Loom" addressed? How do the speakers name themselves?
2. What elements of nature are described in the poem?

INTERPRETING

3. What is the speakers' message? What do "we" offer, and what do "we" ask in return?
4. What role does each element of nature play in the tapestry woven by Mother Earth and Father Sky? How are the elements linked to one another?

SYNTHESIZING

5. What is the central comparison in "Song of the Sky Loom"? What relationship does the poem suggest exists between humans and the divine?

Understanding Literature (Questions for Discussion)

1. **Parallelism. Parallelism** is a rhetorical technique in which a writer emphasizes the equal value or weight of two or more ideas by expressing them in the same grammatical form. What examples of parallelism can you identify in "Song of the Sky Loom"? What is the common link between the several ideas named? (Refer to the Language Arts Survey, 2.57, "Achieving Parallelism.")

2. **Metaphor.** A **metaphor** is a figure of speech in which one thing is spoken or written about as if it were another, thus encouraging a comparison between features of the two things. The writer's, or speaker's, actual subject is called the *tenor* of the metaphor, while the thing to which it is likened is called the *vehicle*. What are the tenor and vehicle of the central metaphor the "Song of the Sky Loom"? What is the "garment of brightness"?

3. **Myth.** A **myth** is a story that explains objects or events in the natural world as resulting from the action of some supernatural force or entity. Every early culture around the globe has produced its own myths, or supernatural explanations of natural phenomena. What mythical elements appear in "Song of the Sky Loom"? What can you infer about Tewa religious beliefs and practices based on this poem?

RESPONDING TO THE SELECTION

Students might discuss their own visions of a beautiful world. Ask students what kind of world they think they could walk in "fittingly." To what kind of world do they feel they most belong?

ANSWERS FOR REVIEWING THE SELECTION

RECALLING

1. The song addresses "our Mother the Earth" and "our Father the Sky." The speakers call themselves "the children" of these two deities or forces.

2. The speakers describe the light of morning and evening, rain, the rainbow, birds' songs, and green grass.

INTERPRETING

Responses will vary. Possible responses are given.

3. The speakers' message is that "we" are the children of the Earth and sky. "We" offer gifts brought "with tired backs" and ask for "a garment of brightness," or the creative weaving of nature, in return.

4. The white light of morning is the warp; the red light of evening is the weft. The rain is the fringe and the border is a rainbow. These are all linked as elements of nature. In the poem, these elements become bound together as a weaving. In nature, light and rain combine to create a rainbow as in the poem the warp and weft are woven into the border.

SYNTHESIZING

Responses will vary. Possible responses are given.

5. The central comparison is between the creative work of nature and the creative work of humans, in this case, weaving. Humans and the divine are connected and dependent upon one another.

ANSWERS FOR UNDERSTANDING LITERATURE

▶ See the evaluation forms for discussion, active listening, and oral communication, *Assessment Portfolio,* 7.11–7.14.

Responses will vary. Possible responses are given.

1. Parallelism. Some examples of parallelism are "O our Mother the Earth" and "O our Father the Sky"; "May the warp be," "May the weft be," "May the fringes be," and "May the border be"; and "That we may walk fittingly where birds sing" and "That we may walk fittingly where grass is green." The link between the first set of examples is the vocative used with two opposite but complementary forces—Mother Earth and Father Sky. The link between the second set of examples is the phrase "May . . . be," followed by a natural description. The link between the third set of examples is the idea of walking "fittingly" in natural surroundings.

(cont.)

ANSWERS FOR UNDERSTANDING LITERATURE (CONT.)

2. Metaphor. The tenor of the central metaphor is the work of Mother Earth and Father Sky, or nature; the vehicle of the metaphor is a woven garment. "The garment of brightness" is the beautiful and vibrant natural world.

3. Myth. One mythical element is the explanation of the natural world as being something woven by Mother Earth and Father Sky. The poem suggests that the beautiful natural things we enjoy are gifts from the gods. Nature seems to be very important in Tewa religion, and the poem suggests that offerings are made to the earth and sky and that such gifts accompany requests of the deities.

4. Tone. The poem honors and celebrates the natural world. Students might say that the tone is reverent, sincere, respectful, and joyous.

ANALYTIC SCALES FOR RESPONDING IN WRITING

Assign a score from 1 to 25 for each grading criterion below. (For more detailed evaluation, see the evaluation forms for writing, revising, and proofreading, *Assessment Portfolio,* 7.1–7.10.)

Hymn

- **Content/Unity.** The hymn praises or offers thanks for some aspect of the natural world.
- **Organization/Coherence.** The hymn is written in a clear and sensible order.
- **Language/Style.** The hymn uses vivid and precise nouns, verbs, and modifiers.
- **Conventions.** The hymn avoids errors in spelling, grammar, usage, mechanics, and manuscript form.

4. **Tone. Tone** is the emotional attitude toward the reader or toward the subject implied by a literary work. What attitude toward the natural world does this poem express? What adjectives could you use to name this tone?

Responding in Writing

Hymn. A **hymn** is a song of praise or thanksgiving. Imagine that you have been invited to speak at an Earth Day celebration in your community. Write a brief hymn praising or offering thanks for some aspect of the natural world. If you wish to do so, you can model your hymn on "Song of the Sky Loom," using parallelism and unrhymed lines to express your thoughts and feelings. To gather ideas for writing, try creating a cluster chart or sensory detail chart. Refer to the Language Arts Survey, 1.17, "Clustering," and 1.18, "Sensory Detail Charts."

Language Lab

Grammar. Answer the following questions, referring to "Song of Sky Loom" and to the parts of the Language Arts Survey indicated in parentheses.

1. What interjections are used in the first and last lines of this poem? (See the Language Arts Survey, 2.29, "Interjections.")
2. In what line of this poem does the subject come before the main verb? (See the Language Arts Survey, 2.64, "Inverting Sentences for Emphasis," and 2.40, "Simple Sentences: SUB + LV + SUB or ADJ.")
3. What linking verb is used in each line from line 5 through line 8? What auxiliary verb is used in each line? (See the Language Arts Survey, 2.13, "Linking Verbs," and 2.14, "Auxiliary Verbs.")
4. In what lines of this poem is the usual order of subject + auxiliary verb + main verb varied so that the auxiliary verb comes first? How would the meanings of these lines change if the subject came first? (See the Language Arts Survey, 2.64, "Inverting Sentences for Emphasis.")
5. Are the words *falling* and *standing,* in lines 7 and 8, gerunds or participles? What about the word *fittingly,* in lines 10 and 11? Explain your answer. (See the Language Arts Survey, 2.16, "Verbals: Participles," and 2.17, "Verbals: Gerunds.")

ANSWERS FOR LANGUAGE LAB

1. The interjection *O* is used.
2. The subject comes before the main verb in line 3.
3. The linking verb *be* is used. The auxiliary verb *may* is used.
4. The usual order is varied in lines 5–8. If the order were reversed, the lines would be statements rather than requests.
5. *Falling* and *standing* are participles that modify the nouns *rain* and *rainbow. Fittingly* is used as an adverb.

Language Skills

Formal English, Informal English, and Register. Read the Language Arts Survey, 2.147, "Formal and Informal English," and 2.148, "Register." Is the language of "Song of the Sky Loom" formal or informal? Explain. What is the register of the language used in the poem? For what sort of occasion would such language be appropriate? Many people associate formal language with big words and complicated sentence structures. Can language be formal without being complicated or stuffy? Explain.

PROJECT

Early Native American Art and Architecture. The hundreds of different Native American cultures that existed before the coming of the Europeans created a wide variety of exquisite types of art and architecture. Working in a small group, research the early Native American art and architecture of one of the following cultural groups of North, Central, or South America:

the Penobscot, Algonquin, Iroquois, Ojibway, or Delaware (eastern North America)

the Cherokee, Creek, Chickasaw, Alabama, Choctaw, Apalachee, Timucua, or Catawba (southeastern United States)

the Blackfoot, Crow, Sioux, Cheyenne, Pawnee, Arapaho, Kiowa, or Comanche (western plains of North America)

the Anasazi, Hopi, Navaho, Apache, Zuni, or Pima (southwestern North America)

the Coast Salish or Wenatchee (northwestern coast of North America)

the Olmec, Aztec, or Maya (Central America)

the Inca, Chimú, or Nazca (South America)

Refer to the Language Arts Survey, 4.20–4.27, for information on conducting research. Present the results of your research in an oral report to your classmates. Use visual aids such as maps and pictures from books to make your report vivid and interesting.

ANSWERS FOR LANGUAGE SKILLS

Responses will vary. Possible responses are given.

The language of the song is formal because it does not use slang or colloquialisms. The register is firm and respectful such as that of a human talking to a deity. The language is appropriate for a ceremonial request. Language does not need to be complicated or stuffy to be formal. Simple grammatical techniques along with easily understandable words can be used; if the grammar and diction is standard, it will be appropriate for formal use. Formal English may seem stuffier than informal English because it excludes many words and grammatical constructions we are used to hearing daily.

PROJECT NOTES

Early Native American Art and Architecture. After each group has made its presentation, students might discuss the effects of geography and natural resources on the arts of different peoples.

ADDITIONAL RESOURCES

READER'S GUIDE
- Selection Worksheet, 2.3

ASSESSMENT PORTFOLIO
- Selection Check Test, 4.2.5
- Selection Test, 4.2.6

ESSENTIAL SKILLS PRACTICE BOOKS
- *Language,* 2.12

ENRICHMENT ACTIVITIES

Encourage students to imagine that they are one of the last survivors of the Arawaks and are writing a lament for their people. Students might want to read some of the excellent speeches by Native American survivors of the westward expansion in Dee Brown's *Bury My Heart at Wounded Knee.* Then students should write their lament, either in prose or in verse, exploring what it would be like to be the last survivor of the Arawak people and to have witnessed the atrocities of the Spanish conquistadors.

SUPPORT FOR LEP STUDENTS

Some students may have difficulty with the vocabulary de las Casas uses. In addition to encouraging students to pay careful attention to the Words for Everyday Use, you may wish to review with students the additional vocabulary below before they read the selection. Point out to students that de las Casas uses the terms *Christians* and *Spaniards* interchangeably. He often uses the term *Christian* to point out the great difference between the beliefs and practices of the Spaniards.

ADDITIONAL VOCABULARY

inhabited—lived in
transaction—act

PREREADING

from *The Very Brief Relation of the Devastation of the Indies*
by Bartolomé de las Casas

ABOUT THE AUTHOR

Bartolomé de las Casas (1474–1566) first voyaged to the Caribbean in 1502 with his father. He soon found himself taking part in Spanish attacks on the Taino people in response to a rebellion. Such attacks were common and exceedingly brutal. De las Casas was rewarded with a group of Native American slaves for his work in the attacks. He continued to receive such benefits even after becoming a priest in 1512 or 1513.

In 1515 de las Casas realized the cruelty and inhumanity that surrounded him and in which he participated. De las Casas became a spokesperson for rights of the native peoples of the New World. He gave up all of his slaves and urged other slaveholders to do the same. Returning to Spain to plead his case, he was appointed protector of the indigenous peoples. With the permission of the Spanish government, de las Casas began a colony on the coast of Venezuela. The peaceful settlement did not last long because the Spanish continued to raid the coast for slaves, rousing the anger of the native Cumaná.

Despite the growing existence of slavery and the lack of success of his colony, de las Casas continued to strive for the end of enslavement, working both in the colonies and in Europe. He used oral arguments, writings including *The Very Brief Relation of the Devastation of the Indies,* and his own example to argue his case. In the 1530s, laws were passed that banned further enslavement and gave native people the protection of the courts. De las Casas tried to enforce the laws in Mexico where he was serving as bishop, but firm resistance by the colonists led to the repeal of the laws.

ABOUT THE SELECTION

The Very Brief Relation of the Devastation of the Indies, or the *Relation,* as it is sometimes called, exposed the grievous behavior of Spanish explorers in the New World. The excerpt included here focuses on Spanish actions at Hispaniola. Hispaniola, an island in the Caribbean Sea, is thought to be one of Christopher Columbus's first landing sites. Certainly, it is where he began his first colonies. The island, which is now divided between the countries of Haiti and the Dominican Republic, was occupied by the Arawak. While the first exchanges between Columbus and the Arawak were relatively friendly, this situation soon changed. Columbus's later voyages, and the voyages of the explorers who followed him over the years, produced savage treatment of the native people. In combination with European diseases against which the native people had no resistance, Spanish cruelty killed most of the native people of the Caribbean Islands. There are no pure Arawaks living in the Caribbean today.

GOALS/OBJECTIVES

Studying this lesson will enable students to

- identify with the speaker's feelings of outrage at witnessing the destruction of a people
- explain the literary and historical significance of de las Casas's writing
- describe the effects of European contact upon the indigenous population of the Caribbean
- identify, define, and illustrate with examples the terms *mood* and *point of view*

READER'S JOURNAL

Why do you think human beings so often mistreat those over whom they have power? Think about situations you know from history or your own experience. Then write a brief paragraph in your journal that attempts to explain this unfortunate part of human nature.

LANGUAGE SKILLS

Read the Language Arts Survey, 2.12, "Action Verbs." Then identify some action verbs from the selection. Group the verbs into physical and mental actions.

FROM

The Very Brief Relation of the Devastation of the Indies

BARTOLOMÉ DE LAS CASAS

From *Hispaniola*

This was the first land in the New World to be destroyed and depopulated by the Christians, and here they began their subjection of the women and children, taking them away from the Indians to use them and ill use them, eating the food they provided with their sweat and toil. The Spaniards did not content themselves with what the Indians gave them of their own free will, according to their ability, which was always too little to satisfy enormous appetites, for a Christian eats and consumes in one day an amount of food that would suffice to feed three houses inhabited by ten Indians for one month. And they committed other acts of force and violence and oppression which made the Indians realize that these men had not come from Heaven.[1] And some of the Indians concealed their foods while others concealed their wives and children and still others fled to the mountains to avoid the terrible transactions of the Christians.

And the Christians attacked them with buffets and beatings, until finally they laid hands on the nobles of the villages. . . . From that time onward the Indians began to seek ways to throw the Christians out of their lands. They took up arms, but their weapons were very weak and of little service

1. **realize . . . Heaven.** Columbus and other early European voyagers reported that the natives took them to be gods who had come from the heavens.

❶ *According to de las Casas, how much did Christians eat?*

❷ *What did the native people begin to seek?*

WORDS FOR EVERYDAY USE:

de • pop • u • late (dē päp´yə lāt´) *vt.,* reduce the population of, especially by violence or disease

sub • jec • tion (sub jek´shən) *n.,* bringing under control or dominion

suf • fice (sə fīs´) *vi.,* be enough

op • pres • sion (ə prəsh´ən) *n.,* keeping down by cruel or unjust use of authority

buf • fet (buf´it) *n.,* blow with the hand or fist

PREREADING NOTES

READER'S JOURNAL

As an alternate activity, students might write about historical figures or people they know who have supported others who were being persecuted. What makes one person stand up against injustice when others are afraid to voice their opinions? What can students do to stand up for others?

LANGUAGE SKILLS

Students might also compare the verbs de las Casas uses to describe the actions of the Europeans to the verbs he uses to describe the actions of the natives. Why might he have used such vivid action verbs to describe the situation in the Caribbean?

▶Additional practice is provided in the *Essential Skills Practice Book: Language,* 2.12.

ANSWERS TO GUIDED READING QUESTIONS

❶ De las Casas says that one Christian ate enough in a single day to feed thirty natives for a month.

❷ The native people began to seek ways of removing the Christians from their land.

VOCABULARY FROM THE SELECTION

buffet	oppression
burnish	ruffian
depopulate	subjection
flourish	suffice
infest	vestige
inhuman	

VOCABULARY IN CONTEXT

- Because of plagues and famines, much of Europe was depopulated during the Medieval Period.
- The subjection of the American colonists by the British crown sparked the American Revolution.
- One small salad per day will not suffice to nourish a growing adolescent.
- "We must rise up from under this oppression," Zenethia cried, rallying the support of the crowd.
- Unable to strike a blow or avoid the buffets of his opponent, the boxer was soon knocked out.

Answers to Guided Reading Questions

❶ The Spaniards said that for every Christian slain they would kill one hundred natives.

❷ The native people were famished, fainting, and falling down.

Cross-curricular Activities

Social Studies. Students can research Christopher Columbus and other explorers who landed in the New World. They can chart the routes of various explorers, labeling points of departure and landing or settlement areas such as Hispaniola, the Lucayos Islands (now the Bahamas), Puerto Rico, and so on.

in offense and still less in defense. (Because of this, the wars of the Indians against each other are little more than games played by children.) And the Christians, with their horses and swords and pikes began to carry out massacres and strange cruelties against them. . . .

And because all the people who could do so fled to the mountains to escape these inhuman, ruthless, and ferocious acts, the Spanish captains, enemies of the human race, pursued them with the fierce dogs they kept which attacked the Indians, tearing them to pieces and devouring them. And because on few and far between occasions, the Indians justifiably killed some Christians, the Spaniards made a rule among themselves that for every Christian slain by the Indians, they would slay a hundred Indians.

❶ *In what way did the Spaniards say they would retaliate for each Christian slain?*

❷ *What condition were the native people in when they arrived at Hispaniola?*

From *The Coast of Pearls, Paria, and the Island of Trinidad*

[The Spaniards] have brought to the island of Hispaniola and the island of San Juan[2] more than two million souls taken captive, and have sent them to do hard labor in the mines, labors that caused many of them to die. And it is a great sorrow and heartbreak to see this coastal land which was so flourishing, now a depopulated desert.

This is truth that can be verified, for no more do they bring ships loaded with Indians that have been thus attacked and captured as I have related. No more do they cast overboard into the sea the third part of the numerous Indians they stow on their vessels, these dead being added to those they have killed in their native lands, the captives crowded into the holds of their ships, without food or water, or with very little, so as not to deprive the Spanish tyrants who call themselves ship owners and who carry enough food for themselves on their voyages of attack. And for the pitiful Indians who died of hunger and thirst, there is no remedy but to cast them into the sea. And verily, as a Spaniard told me, their ships in these regions could voyage without compass or chart, merely by following for the distance between the Lucayos Islands[3] and Hispaniola, which is sixty or seventy leagues,[4] the trace of those Indian corpses floating in the sea, corpses that had been cast overboard by earlier ships.

Afterward, when they disembark on the island of Hispaniola, it is heartbreaking to see those naked Indians, heartbreaking for anyone with a vestige of piety, the famished state they are in, fainting and falling down, weak from hunger, men, women, old people, and children.

Then, like sheep, they are sorted out into flocks of ten or twenty persons, separating fathers from sons, wives from husbands, and the Spaniards draw lots, the ship owners carrying off their share, the best flock, to compensate them for the moneys they have invested in their fleet of two or three ships, the ruffian tyrants getting their share of captives who will be house slaves, and when in this "*repartimiento*"[5] a tyrant gets an old person or an invalid, he says, "Why do you give me this

2. **San Juan.** Puerto Rico
3. **Lucayos Islands.** The Bahamas
4. **leagues.** Linear unit of measure that varies in different periods of time; usually equal to about three miles
5. **repartimiento.** Distribution (Spanish). A royal decree in 1503 ordered masters of native persons to try to convert them to Christianity and hold their property. In reality it was a system of slavery.

Words for Everyday Use:

in • hu • man (in hyōō´mən) *adj.*, unfeeling; cruel; barbarous
flour • ish (flur´ish) *vi.*, grow vigorously; thrive; prosper
ves • tige (ves´tij) *n.*, trace; bit
ruf • fi • an (ruf´ē an) *adj.*, brutal; violent; lawless

Vocabulary in Context

- Many might call the brutal actions of the Spanish conquistadors inhuman.
- Because of the adequate rain and sunshine, their garden flourished and produced a variety of vegetables.
- The Roanoke colony disappeared and not a vestige remained of its former settlers.
- People called Steve a ruffian because he was always picking on younger children.
- The Bonadio home was infested with termites that gnawed upon the wood.

one? To bury him? And this sick one, do you give him to me to make him well?" See by such remarks in what esteem the Spaniards hold the Indians and judge if they are accomplishing the divine concepts of love for our fellow man, as laid down by the prophets.

The tyranny exercised by the Spaniards against the Indians in the work of pearl fishing is one of the most cruel that can be imagined. There is no life as infernal and desperate in this century that can be compared with it, although the mining of gold is a dangerous and burdensome way of life. The pearl fishers dive into the sea at a depth of five fathoms, and do this from sunrise to sunset, and remain for many minutes without breathing, tearing the oysters out of their rocky beds where the pearls are formed. They come to the surface with a netted bag of these oysters where a Spanish torturer is waiting in a canoe or skiff, and if the pearl diver shows signs of wanting to rest, he is showered with blows, his hair is pulled, and he is thrown back into the water, obliged to continue the hard work of tearing out the oysters and bringing them again to the surface.

The food given the pearl divers is codfish, not very nourishing, and the bread made of maize, the bread of the Indies. At night the pearl divers are chained so they cannot escape.

Often a pearl diver does not return to the surface, for these waters are infested with man-eating sharks of two kinds, both vicious marine animals that can kill, eat, and swallow a whole man.

In this harvesting of pearls let us again consider whether the Spaniards preserve the divine concepts of love for their fellow men, when they place the bodies of the Indians in such mortal danger, and their

❶ *What happened if a pearl diver wanted to rest?*

WORDS FOR EVERYDAY USE: **in • fest** (in fest´) *vt.,* overrun or inhabit in large numbers

ANSWER TO GUIDED READING QUESTION

❶ If a pearl diver wanted to rest, he was beaten, his hair was pulled, and he was thrown back into the water.

ANSWERS TO SELECTION CHECK TEST 4.2.5

EX. What was the first land in the New World to be destroyed and depopulated?
Hispaniola was the first land in the New World to be destroyed and depopulated.

1. What did acts of force and violence make the native people realize?
These acts made the native people realize that the Spanish had not come from heaven.

2. What rule did the Spaniards make regarding slain Christians?
The Spaniards agreed that for every Christian killed they would kill one hundred native people.

3. According to one Spaniard, how was the death of slaves aboard ship related to charting a course?
One Spaniard said that a map was not needed between the Lucayos Islands and Hispaniola because one could just follow the trail of corpses.

4. Why did some pearl divers not return to the surface?
Some pearl divers did not return to the surface because they were probably eaten by sharks.

5. Why didn't Spanish judges do anything about the terrible treatment of the native people?
The judges ignored the treatment because the native people were so good at getting pearls.

Answer to Guided Reading Question

❶ The judges didn't stop the enslavement and the mistreatment of the native population because they wanted the pearls that the skilled native swimmers were able to get.

Responding to the Selection

Based on de las Casas's tone in his writing and the actions he undertook in his life, he was appalled and dismayed by the cruelty of his people. Students may wish to role play a situation in which one of their friends is behaving cruelly in order to explore different ways of handling such a situation.

souls, too, for these pearl divers perish without the holy sacraments.[6] And it is solely because of the Spaniards' greed for gold that they force the Indians to lead such a life, often a brief life, for it is impossible to continue for long diving into the cold water and holding the breath for minutes at a time, repeating this hour after hour, day after day; the continual cold penetrates them, constricts the chest, and they die spitting blood, or weakened by diarrhea.

Why didn't the judges stop the enslavement and mistreatment of the native population? ❶

The hair of these pearl divers, naturally black, is as if burnished by the saltpeter in the water, and hangs down their backs making them look like sea dogs or monsters of another species. And in this extraordinary labor, or, better put, in this infernal labor, the Lucayan Indians are finally consumed, as are captive Indians from other provinces. And all of them were publicly sold for one hundred and fifty castellanos,[7] these Indians who had lived happily on their islands until the Spaniards came, although such a thing was against the law. But the unjust judges did nothing to stop it. For all the Indians of these islands are known to be great swimmers.[8] ■

6. **sacraments.** Certain rites believed to be means of grace: baptism, confirmation, the Eucharist, penance, holy orders, matrimony, and Anointing of the Sick in Roman and Eastern Orthodox churches; baptism and the Lord's Supper in Protestant churches

7. **castellanos.** Spanish gold coin bearing the arms of Castile

8. **But the unjust . . . great swimmers.** Spanish judges ignored the mistreatment of the native peoples because their abilities at pearl diving were impressive.

Responding to the Selection

How do you think Bartolomé de las Casas felt when he witnessed his own people behaving so abominably? How would you feel if you saw a friend behave cruelly? What might you do or say in response?

Words for Everyday Use: **bur • nish** (bur´nish) *vt.,* make shiny by rubbing

Vocabulary in Context

• The burnished candlesticks glowed dully in the dim light.

Reviewing the Selection

RECALLING

1. What did the Spaniards make native women and children do?
2. How did the Spanish react to native efforts at self-defense?
3. How were pearl divers treated by the Spaniards?
4. Did the judges stop the illegal sale of natives?

INTERPRETING

5. Why, according to de las Casas, did the Spaniards want so much food?
6. Why did they punish the natives so severely?
7. What was the inevitable fate of the pearl divers? What word does de las Casas use to describe their labor?
8. Why didn't the judges stop the sale of natives? What motivated the Spaniards in their relations with the natives?

SYNTHESIZING

9. Why do you think Bartolomé de las Casas risked everything, even incurring a charge of treason against Spain, to write the *Relation*?
10. Why do you think the natives continued to resist, hiding in the mountains and sometimes killing Christians?

Understanding Literature (Questions for Discussion)

1. **Mood. Mood,** or atmosphere, is the emotion created in the reader by part or all of a literary work. Whether sadness, suspense, or humor, mood provides writers with an important tool to engage the reader's attention. Describe the mood of the *Relation.* Find four examples of concrete details that you feel support that mood.

2. **Point of View. Point of view** is the vantage point from which a story, whether fiction or nonfiction, is told. A story may be told by one of the participants, who uses *I* to refer to himself or herself or by an outsider who avoids the use of *I*. From what point of view is the *Relation* told? How can you tell?

ANSWERS FOR REVIEWING THE SELECTION

RECALLING

1. The Spaniards made native women and children prepare food for them.

2. The Spaniards were angered by native efforts at self-defense and agreed amongst themselves to kill one hundred natives for every Christian killed.

3. Pearl divers were not treated as humans. They were beaten and forced continuously to risk their lives for the financial benefit of the Spaniards.

4. No, the judges ignored the illegal sale of the natives.

INTERPRETING

Responses will vary. Possible responses are given.

5. According to de las Casas, one Christian ate more food in a day than thirty natives needed in a month.

6. The natives were punished so severely to stop them from rebelling. The Spaniards hoped to kill the strength and spirit of the native people.

7. The pearl divers dove to their deaths. They were either eaten by sharks, beaten to death, or worked to exhaustion and death. De las Casas calls the work "infernal labor."

8. The judges didn't stop the sale of natives because it was lucrative to them. The Spaniards were motivated by greed.

SYNTHESIZING

Responses will vary. Possible responses are given.

9. De las Casas risked everything because he truly believed in what he was doing. He realized that the actions of the Spaniards, some of which he had taken part in, were cruel, unjust, and inhuman.

10. The natives hoped to survive the Spaniards and to overcome them. They occasionally killed a Spaniard, perhaps in revenge or as a message to the Spaniards that they had not ceased to fight.

ANSWERS FOR UNDERSTANDING LITERATURE

▶ See the evaluation forms for discussion, active listening, and oral communication, *Assessment Portfolio,* 7.11–7.14.

Responses will vary. Possible responses are given.

1. Mood. The selection has a mood of outrage and abhorrence at the actions of the Spaniards. The horrors listed, such as the setting of dogs upon the natives, the beatings of pearl divers, the shark attacks on the pearl divers, and the rule made by the Spaniards that for every Christian killed they would kill one hundred natives, create this mood.

2. Point of View. *The Relation* is told in the third person from de las Casas's point of view. He does not claim to be one of either the natives or the Spaniards. He uses *they* to refer to the Spaniards, or Christians, and the natives. He refers to himself as the narrator of the story he relates. He also draws in the reader through phrases such as "let us."

ADDITIONAL RESOURCES

READER'S GUIDE
- Selection Worksheet, 2.4

ASSESSMENT PORTFOLIO
- Selection Check Test, 4.2.7
- Selection Test, 4.2.8

ESSENTIAL SKILLS PRACTICE BOOKS
- *Language,* 2.56

ENRICHMENT ACTIVITIES

Students might learn more about the Virginia Colony, the founding of Jamestown, or the lost colony of Roanoke. After conducting research and reading accounts of settlers, students might present their findings in the form of journals or letters written from the perspective of settlers in the colony they researched. Students might imagine themselves as colonists or write from the viewpoint of an imaginary or historical character.

SUPPORT FOR LEP STUDENTS

You may wish to point out to students that Smith begins the account in the third person, then switches to the first person, referring to himself and the people with him as *we,* and later returns to the use of the third person, refering to himself as *Captain Smith* and *he.*

Students who have difficulty with Smith's constructions can work with a partner to summarize each paragraph.

ADDITIONAL VOCABULARY

victual—food and provisions
demeaned—humbled; behaved
slain—killed

PREREADING

from *The General History of Virginia, New England, and the Summer Isles*
by John Smith

ABOUT THE AUTHOR

John Smith (1580–1631) was born in Willoughby, England. As a youth, he worked on his father's farm and was apprenticed to a shopkeeper. At the age of twenty, he went to Hungary to fight against the Turks, was taken captive, escaped to Russia, and then returned to England. In 1606, he joined a group of about one hundred people and set sail for the New World. There, on the Chesapeake Bay, he helped to found the first permanent English colony in America, Jamestown. Smith explored Virginia, making maps of the land and its waterways. In 1607, he was captured by Powhatan, chief of one of the native peoples of Chesapeake Bay. In later writings, he claimed to have been saved from execution by the chief's young daughter, known to history by her nickname, Pocahontas. Smith served as governor of the Jamestown Colony from 1608 to 1609, at which time he returned to England. Smith returned to America in 1614, this time to a part of the continent that he called New England. There he made maps of the coastline. In 1615, Smith was captured by pirates but managed to escape. Smith published several maps and accounts of his explorations, including *Map of Virginia* (1612), *A Description of New England* (1616), and *The True Travels, Adventures, and Observations of Captain John Smith in Europe, Asia, Africa, and America* (1630).

ABOUT THE SELECTION

In ***The General History of Virginia, New England, and the Summer Isles,*** John Smith presents a detailed and often exciting account of the events in the early years of the Virginia Colony from 1607, the year of its founding at Jamestown, to 1609, the year when Smith departed Virginia never to return. *The General History of Virginia* was completed in 1624, fifteen years after Smith's return to England. The book includes writings by other colonists as well as by Smith and covers events in both British colonies in America at that time—Plymouth Plantation in New England and the Jamestown Colony in Virginia. In this part of the account, Smith describes how he was saved from death by Pocahontas, the sixteen-year-old daughter of Chief Powhatan.

GOALS/OBJECTIVES

Studying this lesson will enable students to

- have a positive experience reading a historical account
- discuss the relationship between Smith and the colonists and Powhatan and the Native Americans
- recognize the active and passive voices

READER'S JOURNAL

Before you begin to read John Smith's history, think for a moment about stories you may have heard about the early colonial period in North America. In what way are the colonists typically presented? the Native Americans? To what extent do you believe the portrayals of colonists and Native Americans, given that most accounts came from the colonial perspective?

LANGUAGE SKILLS

Read the Language Arts Survey, 2.56, "Using the Active Voice." As you read the selection, make two lists of verbs that are used—active voice and passive voice. Which type of verb is used more often?

FROM

The General History of Virginia

JOHN SMITH

What Happened Till the First Supply

Being thus left to our fortunes, it fortuned[1] that within ten days, scarce ten amongst us could either go[2] or well stand, such extreme weakness and sickness oppressed us. And thereat none need marvel if they consider the cause and reason, which was this: While the ships stayed, our allowance was somewhat bettered by a daily proportion of biscuit which the sailors would pilfer to sell, give, or exchange with us for money, sassafras,[3] or furs. But when they departed, there remained neither tavern, beer house, nor place of relief but the common kettle.[4] Had we been as free from all sins as gluttony and drunkenness we might have been canonized for saints, but our President[5] would never have been admitted for engrossing to his private,[6] oatmeal, sack,[7] oil, aqua vitae,[8] beef, eggs, or what not but the kettle: that indeed he allowed equally to be distributed, and that was half a pint of wheat and as much barley boiled with water for a man a day, and this, having fried some twenty-six weeks in the ship's hold, contained as many worms as grains so that we might truly call it rather so much bran than corn; our drink was water, our lodgings castles in the air.

❶ *Why might the colonists have been canonized as saints? Why wouldn't the president have been included as a saint?*

1. **fortuned.** Happened
2. **go.** Go about; walk
3. **sassafras.** Tree with aromatic bark, the root bark of which was valued for its supposed medicinal qualities
4. **common kettle.** Public or general cooking pot
5. **President.** Edward Maria Wingfield (*circa* 1560–1613), first president of Virginia colony
6. **private.** Private or personal stock
7. **sack.** Dry, Spanish white wine, popular in England during the sixteenth and seventeenth centuries
8. **aqua vitae.** Brandy

WORDS FOR EVERYDAY USE:

pil • fer (pil´fər) *vt.,* steal
glut • ton • y (glut´'n ē) *n.,* habit or act of eating too much
can • on • ize (kan´ən īz´) *vt.,* declare a deceased person a saint in formal church procedure

VOCABULARY IN CONTEXT

- In the drawer we found Jerry's notebook, Shelly's compass, Adam's jackknife, Lila's keys, and many other items John had pilfered.
- Gladys was sickened by the gluttony she witnessed when Manny attacked the pies, puddings, pork chops, pot roast, and pickled herring.
- Mandy said that Louise was a saint, but she didn't mean that Louise had actually been canonized.

PREREADING NOTES

READER'S JOURNAL

Students might want to write an account of the colonists from the point of view of a Native American.

After writing, students can discuss their ideas about portrayals of historical people.

LANGUAGE SKILLS

Examples of active voice include "they tied him to a tree," "they quartered in the woods," and "Pocahontas with her attendants brought him so much provisions." Examples of passive voice include "our allowance was somewhat bettered" and "now was all our provision spent."

For practice in using the active voice, students can rewrite in the active voice sentences that Smith cast in the passive voice. Students should refer to the Language Arts Survey, 2.56, "Using the Active Voice."

▶Additional practice is provided in the *Essential Skills Practice Book: Language,* 2.56.

ANSWER TO GUIDED READING QUESTION

❶ The colonists might have been canonized as saints if they had been "as free from all sins as gluttony and drunkenness." The president wouldn't have been considered a saint because he had his own store of food and drink.

VOCABULARY FROM THE SELECTION

canonize	entreaty
conceit	extremity
conjuration	gluttony
diversity	mollify
doleful	pilfer
ensue	presumption

Answers to Guided Reading Questions

❶ The speaker says that everything of worth comes only with great difficulty.

❷ Captain Smith was a man of "good words" and fair promise who took on large shares of work himself to help provide for others, or so he says of himself. Others writing about Smith might have seen him in a different light.

Additional Questions and Activities

You might ask students how they feel about Captain Smith praising himself so highly on page 96 of the selection. Why might Smith have been motivated to praise himself in the third person? Does this praise affect Smith's reliability in any way? Do students trust him as a narrator?

Answers. Students might say that Captain Smith's praise is self-serving and makes him seem a little too proud of himself. Smith might have written his praise for himself in the third person so that he would seem more humble. Students may say that Smith's extreme self-glorification ("himself always bearing the greatest task for his own share" and "neglecting any for himself") makes his account of events seem biased. Students may either trust or distrust Smith as a narrator but should support their reasoning with evidence from the selection.

What did the speaker feel about the difficulties the colonists had undergone? ❶

What type of person was Captain Smith? Does the fact that the author described himself in this passage influence your description? ❷

With this lodging and diet, our extreme toil in bearing and planting palisades[9] so strained and bruised us and our continual labor in the extremity of the heat had so weakened us, as were cause sufficient to have made us as miserable in our native country or any other place in the world.

From May to September, those that escaped lived upon sturgeon[10] and sea crabs. Fifty in this time we buried: the rest seeing the President's projects to escape these miseries in our pinnace[11] by flight (who all this time had neither felt want nor sickness) so moved our dead spirits as we deposed him and established Ratcliffe in his place . . .

But now was all our provision spent, the sturgeon gone, all helps abandoned, each hour expecting the fury of the savages; when God, the patron of all good endeavors, in that desperate extremity so changed the hearts of the savages that they brought such plenty of their fruits and provision as no man wanted.

And now where some affirmed it was ill done of the Council[12] to send forth men so badly provided, this incontradictable reason will show them plainly they are too ill advised to nourish such ill conceits: First, the fault of our going was our own: what could be thought fitting or necessary we had, but what we should find, or want, or where we should be, we were all ignorant and supposing to make our passage in two months, with victual to live and the advantage of the spring to work; we were at sea five months where we both spent our victual and lost the opportunity of the time and season to plant, by the unskillful presumption of our ignorant transporters that understood not at all what they undertook.

Such actions have ever since the world's beginning been subject to such accidents, and everything of worth is found full of difficulties, but nothing so difficult as to establish a commonwealth so far remote from men and means and where men's minds are so untoward[13] as neither do well themselves nor suffer others. But to proceed.

The new President and Martin, being little beloved, of weak judgment in dangers, and less industry in peace, committed the managing of all things abroad[14] to Captain Smith, who, by his own example, good words, and fair promises set some to mow, others to bind thatch, some to build houses, others to thatch them, himself always bearing the greatest task for his own share, so that in short time he provided most of them lodgings, neglecting any for himself . . .

Leading an expedition on the Chickahominy River, Captain Smith and his men are attacked by Indians, and Smith is taken prisoner.

When this news came to Jamestown, much was their sorrow for his loss, few expecting what ensued.

Six or seven weeks those barbarians kept him prisoner, many strange triumphs and

9. **palisades.** Pointed stakes set in the ground to form a fence for fortification or defense
10. **sturgeon.** Large, edible, bony fish
11. **pinnace.** Small sailing ship
12. **Council.** Group in charge of the Virginia experiment
13. **untoward.** Stubborn
14. **abroad.** Outside of the enclosed camp

Words for Everyday Use:

ex • trem • i • ty (ek strem´ə tē) *n.,* state of extreme necessity, danger, etc.

con • ceit (kən sēt´) *n.,* idea, thought; personal opinion

pre • sump • tion (prē zump´shən) *n.,* overstepping of proper bounds or the taking of something for granted

en • sue (en sōō) *vi.,* come afterward; follow immediately

Vocabulary in Context

- The extremity of the situation facing the skiers trapped in the blizzard instilled fear into every heart in the party.
- Hakim never shares his thoughts so it is impossible to know what conceits arise in his mind.
- When Jen returned home to find her belongings moved to the hallway, she was shocked by her new roommate's presumption.
- After Rodney's antagonistic speech, a scuffle ensued.
- Through a strange conjuration the cow appeared to vanish into thin air.

conjurations they made of him, yet he so demeaned himself amongst them, as he not only diverted them from surprising the fort, but procured his own liberty, and got himself and his company such estimation amongst them, that those savages admired him.

The manner how they used and delivered him is as followeth:

The savages having drawn from George Cassen whither Captain Smith was gone, prosecuting[15] that opportunity they followed him with three hundred bowmen, conducted by the King of Pamunkee, who in divisions searching the turnings of the river found Robinson and Emry by the fireside; those they shot full of arrows and slew. Then finding the Captain, as is said, that used the savage that was his guide as his shield (three of them being slain and divers[16] others so galled),[17] all the rest would not come near him. Thinking thus to have returned to his boat, regarding them, as he marched, more than his way, slipped up to the middle in an oozy creek and his savage with him; yet dared they not come to him till being near dead with cold he threw away his arms. Then according to their composition[18] they drew him forth and led him to the fire where his men were slain. Diligently they chafed his benumbed limbs.

15. **prosecuting.** Following up or pursuing
16. **divers.** Several
17. **galled.** Wounded
18. **composition.** Habits; customary manners

WORDS FOR EVERYDAY USE: **con • jur • a • tion** (kän´joo rā´shən) *n.,* magic; sorcery

CROSS-CURRICULAR ACTIVITIES

Geography. John Smith explored and mapped the coastlines of Virginia and New England. Students can create maps of these areas, marking early settlements. In groups, students can research these areas, including the terrain, climate, and native flora and fauna. Students can discuss the effects of these aspects of the land upon settlers.

LITERARY TECHNIQUE

The **action** is the sequence of events that actually occurs in a literary work, as opposed to those that occur off-scene or that precede or follow the events in the work itself. Students might make a list of all the events that occur during Smith's encounter with the Native Americans on pages 97 and 98 in order to get a sense of how action-packed Smith's narrative is. Then ask students the following questions: In what way would you characterize the action in these scenes? Why might this particular story have fascinated Americans for so many hundreds of years?

Answers. The action in these scenes is dramatic and thrilling. This story may have fascinated Americans because it is exciting and because it is one of the few positive episodes in the history of relations between European colonists and Native Americans.

Answers to Guided Reading Questions

❶ Smith gave Opechancanough a round ivory double compass dial.

❷ Smith says he demonstrated the roundness of the earth and skies; the sphere of the sun, moon, and stars; how the sun went about world; the greatness of the land and sea; the diversity of nations; and other like matters.

❸ Smith's head was placed on two great stones to be beaten by clubs. Pocahontas saved him by placing her head over his.

Cross-curricular Activities

• **Mathematics and Sciences.** Students might research the advent of the compass. Why was this such an important invention? Is it really possible to demonstrate with a compass all the things Smith claims he demonstrated? If not, why might Smith have claimed he demonstrated these things? Why might a compass have been particularly important to Smith as an explorer?

• **Social Studies.** Students may wish to research what is known about the life of Pocahontas. As students research her life, they should consider the following questions: What role did Pocahontas play in establishing relations between Virginian colonists and the Native Americans? What sort of life did Pocahontas lead? Why do most Americans know about her saving Smith but are unaware of her being kidnapped and her dying of smallpox in England while awaiting return to her native land? Is the story of Pocahontas's relations with Europeans as mutually good-natured and beneficial as Smith would have it seem?

❶ *What did Smith give to Opechancanough?*

❷ *What did Smith say he demonstrated with the compass?*

❸ *What happened to Smith despite his demonstration? Who saved him? How did this person save him?*

He demanding for their captain, they showed him Opechancanough, King of Pamunkee, to whom he gave a round ivory double compass dial. Much they marveled at the playing of the fly and needle,[19] which they could see so plainly and yet not touch it because of the glass that covered them. But when he demonstrated by that globe-like jewel the roundness of the earth and skies, the sphere of the sun, moon, and stars, and how the sun did chase the night round about the world continually, the greatness of the land and sea, the diversity of nations, variety of complexions, and how we were to them antipodes[20] and many other such like matters, they all stood as amazed with admiration.

Notwithstanding, within an hour after, they tied him to a tree, and as many as could stand about him prepared to shoot him, but the King holding up the compass in his hand, they all laid down their bows and arrows and in a triumphant manner led him to Orapaks where he was after their manner kindly feasted and well used. . . .

At last they brought him to Werowocomoco, where was Powhatan, their Emperor. Here more than two hundred of those grim courtiers stood wondering at him, as he had been a monster, till Powhatan and his train had put themselves in their greatest braveries. Before a fire upon a seat like a bedstead, he sat covered with a great robe made of raccoon skins and all the tails hanging by. On either hand did sit a young wench of sixteen or eighteen years and along on each side the house, two rows of men and behind them as many women, with all their heads and shoulders painted red, many of their heads bedecked with the white down of birds, but every one with something, and a great chain of white beads about their necks.

At his entrance before the King, all the people gave a great shout. The Queen of Appomattoc was appointed to bring him water to wash his hands, and another brought him a bunch of feathers, instead of a towel, to dry them; having feasted him after their best barbarous manner they could, a long consultation was held, but the conclusion was, two great stones were brought before Powhatan; then as many as could, laid hands on him, dragged him to them, and thereon laid his head and being ready with their clubs to beat out his brains, Pocahontas, the King's dearest daughter, when no entreaty could prevail, got his head in her arms and laid her own upon his to save him from death; whereat the Emperor was contented he should live to make him hatchets, and her bells, beads, and copper, for they thought him as well of all occupations as themselves.[21] For the King himself will make his own robes, shoes, bows, arrows, pots; plant, hunt, or do anything so well as the rest.

Two days after, Powhatan, having disguised himself in the most fearfulest manner he could, caused Captain Smith to be brought forth to a great house in the woods and there upon a mat by the fire to be left alone. Not long after, from behind a mat that divided the house, was made

19. **fly and needle.** Parts of a compass
20. **antipodes.** On opposite sides of the earth
21. **him as well . . . as themselves.** He had as much

Words for Everyday Use:
di • ver • si • ty (də vur´sə tē) *n.,* variety
en • treat • y (en trēt´ē) *n.,* earnest request

Vocabulary in Context

- The diversity of the museum's collection made it fascinating to people with far-reaching interests.
- Once Doug has made up his mind, no entreaty will make him change it.
- Cleo's joyful cry was halted by the doleful look on the messenger's face.
- As Antonio began to rant about the fiasco, Carmen tried to mollify him with soothing words of encouragement.

the most dolefulest noise he ever heard; then Powhatan more like a devil than a man, with some two hundred more as black as himself, came unto him and told him now they were friends, and presently he should go to Jamestown to send him two great guns and a grindstone for which he would give him the country of Capahowasic and forever esteem him as his son Nantaquond.

So to Jamestown with twelve guides Powhatan sent him. That night they quartered in the woods, he still expecting (as he had done all this long time of his imprisonment) every hour to be put to one death or other, for all their feasting. But almighty God (by His divine providence) had mollified the hearts of those stern barbarians with compassion. The next morning betimes[22] they came to the fort, where Smith having used the savages with what kindness he could, he showed Rawhunt, Powhatan's trusty servant, two demiculverins[23] and a millstone to carry Powhatan: they found them somewhat too heavy, but when they did see him discharge them, being loaded with stones, among the boughs of a great tree loaded with icicles, the ice and branches came so tumbling down that the poor savages ran away half dead with fear. But at last we regained some conference with them and gave them such toys and sent to Powhatan, his women, and children such presents as gave them in general full content.

Now in Jamestown they were all in combustion, the strongest preparing once more to run away with the pinnace; which, with the hazard of his life, with saker falcon[24] and musket shot, Smith forced now the third time to stay or sink.

Some, no better than they should be, had plotted with the President the next day to have him put to death by the Levitical law,[25] for the lives of Robinson and Emry; pretending the fault was his that had led them to their ends; but he quickly took such order with such lawyers that he laid them by their heels till he sent some of them prisoners for England.

Now every once in four or five days, Pocahontas with her attendants brought him so much provision that saved many of their lives, that else for all this had starved with hunger.

His relation of the plenty he had seen, especially at Werowocomoco, and of the state and bounty of Powhatan (which till that time was unknown), so revived their dead spirits (especially the love of Pocahontas) as all men's fear was abandoned.

Thus you may see what difficulties still crossed any good endeavor; and the good success of the business being thus oft brought to the very period of destruction: yet you see by what strange means God hath still delivered it. ■

❶ *What did some of the colonists wish to do with Smith? Why did they wish to do this?*

❷ *Who saved the colonists?*

22. **betimes.** Early
23. **demiculverins.** Large cannons
24. **saker falcon.** Small cannon
25. **Levitical law.** Biblical law from the Old Testament that states "He that killeth man shall surely be put to death" (Leviticus 24:17).

WORDS FOR EVERYDAY USE: **dole • ful** (dōl´fəl) *adj.,* full of or causing sorrow or sadness **mol • li • fy** (mäl´ə fī´) *vt.,* soothe the temper of

ANSWERS TO GUIDED READING QUESTIONS

❶ Some of the colonists wished to put Smith to death under right of Biblical law for the deaths of Robinson and Emry.

❷ Pocahontas and her attendants saved the colonists by bringing them provisions.

ANSWERS TO SELECTION CHECK TEST 4.2.7

EX. What benefit did the colonists receive while the ship remained?

The colonists were able to get biscuits from the sailors.

1. Why were the colonists miserable?

They had poor lodging and diet and they had to work very hard in extreme heat just to survive.

2. What was Smith doing when he was captured by the Native Americans?

Smith was leading a round expedition on the Chickahominy River.

3. What happened to Robinson and Emry?

They were shot full of arrows.

4. What did Smith give to Opechancanough, King of Pamunkee?

Smith gave him a round ivory double compass dial.

5. According to Smith, in what two ways did Pocahontas save his life?

Pocahontas saved him from being beaten to death. She also saved him by bringing provisions to the settlers.

RESPONDING TO THE SELECTION

Students might like to discuss cultural misunderstandings they have experienced. Might there have been misunderstandings on either side of the meeting between Smith and Powhatan? What might these misunderstandings have been?

ANSWERS FOR REVIEWING THE SELECTION

RECALLING

1. Powhatan wears a robe of raccoon skins and tails. The native people around him have their heads and shoulders painted red and their heads bedecked in white bird down. Each person also wears a chain of white beads around his or her neck.
2. Powhatan orders Smith's execution. Smith is to have his head beaten until he is dead, but Powhatan's daughter, Pocahontas, saves Smith by putting her head on his before the beating can begin.
3. Pocahontas brings food regularly to the colonists. Without her gifts, the colonists will likely starve to death.
4. Knowledge of Powhatan's plenty brings new hope to the colonists whose spirits have been dashed by the difficulties they face in the new land.

INTERPRETING

Responses will vary. Possible responses are given.

5. Powhatan is probably trying to impress Smith and put fear into him. The courtiers are probably wary of Smith, who has killed some of their people. His appearance may make the Native Americans wonder about him as well.
6. Students may say Pocahontas saves Smith's life out of sympathy.
7. The meeting with Powhatan saves the colony of Jamestown in two ways. It saves its residents from starving because after the meeting Pocahontas brings them food. Second, it saves them from despair because the knowledge of Powhatan's bounty restores their spirits.

(cont.)

Responding to the Selection

Entering a foreign or unfamiliar culture can be both fascinating and frightening. If you had been in Smith's place in Powhatan's village, what emotions might you have been feeling? Would you ever like to visit a place where the customs are different from your own? Where would you like to go?

Reviewing the Selection

RECALLING

1. Describe the people present at the event that Smith relates. What people are there, and what do they look like?
2. Who orders Smith's execution? Who saves Smith from death? How does she save him?
3. What does Pocahontas bring to Smith and his fellow colonists regularly after the rescue? How do her gifts help the colonists?
4. What effect does the knowledge of Powhatan's wealth, power, and plenty have upon the colonists?

INTERPRETING

5. Why do you think Powhatan dresses himself in his "greatest braveries" to speak with John Smith? Why does Smith feel that the courtiers treat him "as if he had been a monster"? Explain why this is a natural reaction to Smith's presence in the village.
6. Smith's account explains very little about Pocahontas. Therefore, the reader is free to build a story around the bare facts that Smith presents. Why do you think Pocahontas saves Smith's life?
7. Why is the meeting with Powhatan crucial to the survival of the colony of Jamestown?
8. Why does the knowledge that Powhatan has all the food and goods that he needs encourage the colonists? How do you think they expect to benefit from his good fortune?

SYNTHESIZING

9. It is possible that Smith was never in danger from Powhatan at all, that he misunderstood a custom of Powhatan's people and mistakenly assumed he was in mortal danger. Why do you think Smith told this story over and over again and included it in his history fifteen years later? Do you think Smith believed his interpretation of the events fifteen years later, or might he have had other reasons for telling the story?
10. What qualities did it take to be an early colonist in America? What qualities of character did Powhatan and Pocahontas show in their first meeting with a European?

ANSWERS FOR REVIEWING THE SELECTION (CONT.)

8. The colonists may be encouraged by Powhatan's good fortune because it provides them with hope about their own survival. They may hope to learn or receive aid from Powhatan, or they may think they can trade manufactured goods for food, or that they can force him to provide food.

SYNTHESIZING

Responses will vary. Possible responses are given.

9. Smith might have misunderstood the experience because of his fear. He may have presented the story in this way to make a point about colonial relationships with Native Americans. Smith might also have told the story many times because he thought it was an exciting and entertaining story.
10. Determination and creativity were essential qualities for early colonists. They had to work hard, make do without things, and find new foods and ways of doing things in the new land they inhabited. Powhatan and Pocahontas both showed themselves to be generous to Smith.

PREREADING

from *Of Plymouth Plantation*
by William Bradford

About the Author

William Bradford (1590–1657) was born in Austerfield in Yorkshire, England, and was educated in the arts of farming. Bradford joined the community of Separatists, Puritans who had left the Church of England. To escape persecution, the Separatists fled to Holland, where Bradford joined them in 1609. The group was later granted land in the New World and sailed across the Atlantic on the *Mayflower,* landing in Plymouth, Massachusetts, in 1620. Despite initial hardships, the colonists survived and they elected Bradford their governor, a position he held for over thirty years. Bradford wrote a history of the founding of Plymouth Colony, including the history of the Puritan and Separatist movements. Bradford's descriptions of the voyage of the Mayflower, the writing of the Mayflower Compact, and the Pilgrims' and Native Americans' celebration of Thanksgiving have become a vital part of American culture as an example of freedom won through courage and determination.

About the Selection

William Bradford began writing ***Of Plymouth Plantation*** in 1630, ten years after the settlement of the colony. He continued this work until 1650, covering events through 1646. The manuscript was in two parts, the first part of which was copied into the Plymouth church records by the time of the American Revolution. After the revolution, the manuscript disappeared, and the second part was lost for almost a century. Then the entire manuscript was discovered in the residence of the bishop of London and was published, finally, in 1856. In 1897, the manuscript was returned to America to be kept in the State House in Boston.

ADDITIONAL RESOURCES

Reader's Guide
- Selection Worksheet, 2.5

Assessment Portfolio
- Selection Check Test, 4.2.9
- Selection Test, 4.2.10

Essential Skills Practice Books
- *Writing,* 1.19
- *Study and Research,* 4.13

ENRICHMENT ACTIVITIES

The Mayflower Compact was one of the earliest foundations of government in the colonies. Interested students can do further research on the compact and the effect it had on the colonies. What are the basic beliefs on which the compact was created? Is the governing power created by the compact similar in any way to the current American system of government? Explain.

SUPPORT FOR LEP STUDENTS

Point out to students that although Bradford himself was a Pilgrim, he refers to the Pilgrims as *they* and refers to himself, as the narrator, in the first person.

Additional Vocabulary

divers—several
providence—guidance of God
omit—leave out
habitation—place to live

GOALS/OBJECTIVES

Studying this lesson will enable students to

- empathize with the colonists of New England
- interpret or create hypotheses
- understand chronological order and order events chronologically
- make a time line
- define *irony of situation* and identify it in their reading
- write a lyric poem or a memoir

PREREADING NOTES

READER'S JOURNAL

As an alternate activity, students might imagine how they would feel as Native Americans, watching strange new people with unfamiliar customs arrive upon their land. Would they feel frightened? angry? curious? Would they try to help the colonists survive in their land or would they try to expel the colonists?

THINKING SKILLS

You might ask students to make some hypotheses about the selection based on their knowledge from the prereading page and other background they may have read or heard about the Pilgrims.

►Additional practice is provided in the *Essential Skills Practice Book: Study and Research,* 4.13.

ANSWER TO GUIDED READING QUESTION

❶ The haughty young man wants to throw the sick off the ship once they have died. The haughty young man becomes ill, dies, and is thrown overboard.

VOCABULARY FROM THE SELECTION

calamity	mutinous
commendation	ordinance
consultation	profane
deliberation	prosperous
feign	recompense
inevitable	reprove
light	sundry
loath	

READER'S JOURNAL

What would make you leave your home and travel to a strange, unsettled land? profit? hopes for better lives for your children? How do you think the Pilgrims must have felt on leaving Europe? What fears might they have had? what hopes and dreams?

THINKING SKILLS

Read the Language Arts Survey, 4.13, "Making Hypotheses." Then, as you read this selection, decide what hypotheses William Bradford presents to explain the causes of the events he reports.

FROM

Of Plymouth Plantation

WILLIAM BRADFORD

Book I, Chapter IX. Of Their Voyage and How They Passed the Sea; and of Their Safe Arrival at Cape Cod

❶ *What does the haughty young man want to do? What happens to him during the trip?*

September 6. These troubles[1] being blown over, and now all being compact together in one ship, they put to sea again with a prosperous wind, which continued divers days together, which was some encouragement unto them; yet, according to the usual manner, many were afflicted with seasickness. And I may not omit here a special work of God's providence. There was a proud and very profane young man, one of the seamen, of a lusty,[2] able body, which made him the more haughty; he would always be condemning the poor people in their sickness and cursing them daily with grievous execrations;[3] and did not let[4] to tell them that he hoped to help to cast half of them overboard before they came to their journey's end, and to make merry with what they had; and if he were by any gently reproved, he would curse and swear most bitterly. But it pleased God before they came half seas over, to smite this young man with a grievous disease, of which he died in a desperate manner, and so was himself the first that was thrown overboard. Thus his curses light on his own head, and it was an astonishment to all his fellows for they noted it to be the just hand of God upon him.

After they had enjoyed fair winds and weather for a season, they were encountered

1. **troubles.** Another vessel, the *Speedwell,* had proved unseaworthy and everything was transferred to the *Mayflower.*
2. **lusty.** Strong; energetic
3. **execrations.** Curses
4. **let.** Hesitate

WORDS FOR EVERYDAY USE:

pros • per • ous (präs´ pər əs) *adj.,* conducive to success; favorable

pro • fane (prō fān´) *adj.,* showing disrespect for sacred things

re • prove (ri prōōv´) *vt.,* speak to in disapproval

light (līt) *vi.,* fall or strike suddenly

VOCABULARY IN CONTEXT

- The prosperous land yielded far more than the settlers could eat.
- Liddy's profane language shocked her pious brother.
- Jordi was reproved by Ms. Lyon for letting out a yawn during her lecture.
- I see the cardinal every morning when it lights on the branch outside my window.
- After the free consultation, Gloria decided she did not need to cover her house in vinyl siding.
- The dark storm clouds signified that an afternoon shower was inevitable.
- With the championship on the line, Hank was loath to give up even one point.

The Beginning of New England: after the painting by Clyde O. Deland. *The Granger Collection, NY*

many times with cross winds and met with many fierce storms with which the ship was shroudly[5] shaken, and her upper works made very leaky; and one of the main beams in the midships was bowed and cracked, which put them in some fear that the ship could not be able to perform the voyage. So some of the chief of the company, perceiving the mariners to fear the sufficiency of the ship as appeared by their mutterings, they entered into serious consultation with the master and other officers of the ship, to consider in time of the danger, and rather to return than to cast themselves into a desperate and inevitable peril. And truly there was great distraction and difference of opinion amongst the mariners themselves; fain[6] would they do what could be done for their wages' sake (being now near half the seas over) and on the other hand they were loath to hazard their lives too desperately. But in examining of all opinions, the master and others affirmed they knew the ship to be strong and firm under water; and for the buckling of the main beam, there was a great iron screw the passengers brought out of Holland, which would raise the beam into his place; the which being done, the carpenter and master affirmed that with a post put under it, set firm in the lower deck and otherways bound, he would make it sufficient. And as for the decks and upper works, they would caulk them as well as they could, and though with the working of the ship they would not long keep staunch,[7] yet there would otherwise be no great danger, if they did not overpress her with sails. So they committed themselves to the will of God and resolved to proceed.

❶ *What made the people on the ship worry about their voyage?*

❷ *Why did the people decide to continue with their voyage?*

5. **shroudly.** Shrewdly, meaning wickedly
6. **fain.** Gladly
7. **staunch.** Watertight

WORDS FOR EVERYDAY USE:

con • sul • ta • tion (kän´səl tā´ shən) *n.,* meeting to discuss, decide, or plan something

in • ev • i • ta • ble (in ev´ i tə bəl) *adj.,* that cannot be avoided or evaded

loath (lōth) *adj.,* unwilling, reluctant

ART NOTE

Ask students to look at the picture on page 103. What do they see in it? What can they learn about colonial life from this picture? Have students write a one- or two-paragraph description of life in colonial America.

ANSWERS TO GUIDED READING QUESTIONS

❶ The people on the ship worried about their voyage because the ship was in bad condition. The upper works were leaky and one of the main beams was bowed and cracked.

❷ The master and others on the ship agreed it would be safe enough to continue. They were able to raise the beam into its place and caulk the decks and works. Having bested the danger, the Pilgrims committed themselves to the will of God and continued on their voyage.

CROSS-CURRICULAR ACTIVITIES

Social Studies. Students might research, both by closely examining more of Bradford's work and by exploring other sources, what living conditions were like on the *Mayflower.* (Some students may have even visited the replica of the *Mayflower* in Plymouth, Massachusetts, or know others who have done so.) Students should discover how large the *Mayflower* was and how many people traveled to Massachusetts aboard the ship. Were the living conditions close or comfortable? How long did the voyage last? How much and what type of provisions did the Pilgrims bring with them for the journey? Students can form groups to complete their research and then discuss what it would have been like to have traveled to the Americas aboard the *Mayflower.*

Answer to Guided Reading Question

❶ Some of the "strangers" on the ship suggested that they would live under their own liberty on Cape Cod since the patent the colonists had was for Virginia, not for New England.

Additional Questions and Activities

Students might enjoy learning more about life in Plymouth Colony. In Plymouth, Massachusetts, there is an excellent reenactment of the Pilgrims' lives and living conditions at Plimoth Plantation. Students might try to locate the plantation's guidebook, *Plimoth Plantation: A Pictorial Guidebook,* in order to see what the costumes, homes, and working conditions of the Pilgrims were like.

In sundry of these storms the winds were so fierce and the seas so high, as they could not bear a knot of sail, but were forced to hull[8] for divers days together. And in one of them, as they thus lay at hull in a mighty storm, a lusty young man called John Howland, coming upon some occasion above the gratings was, with a seele[9] of the ship, thrown into sea; but it pleased God that he caught hold of the topsail halyards[10] which hung overboard and ran out at length. Yet he held his hold (though he was sundry fathoms under water) till he was hauled up by the same rope to the brim of the water, and then with a boat hook and other means got into the ship again and his life saved. And though he was something ill with it, yet he lived many years after and became a profitable member both in church and commonwealth. In all this voyage there died but one of the passengers, which was William Butten, a youth, servant to Samuel Fuller, when they drew near the coast.

What reasons led to the creation of the Mayflower Compact? ❶

But to omit other things (that I may be brief) after long beating at sea they fell with that land which is called Cape Cod; the which being made and certainly known to be it, they were not a little joyful. After some deliberation had amongst themselves and with the master of the ship, they tacked[11] about and resolved to stand for the southward (the wind and weather being fair) to find some place about Hudson's River for their habitation. But after they had sailed that course about half the day, they fell amongst dangerous shoals and roaring breakers, and they were so far entangled therewith as they conceived themselves in great danger; and the wind shrinking upon them withal, they resolved to bear up again for the Cape and thought themselves happy to get out of those dangers before night overtook them, as by God's good providence they did. And the next day they got into Cape Harbor[12] where they rid in safety.

From *Book II, Chapter XI. The Remainder of Anno 1620*

THE MAYFLOWER COMPACT

I shall a little return back, and begin with a combination[13] made by them before they came ashore; being the first foundation of their government in this place. Occasioned partly by the discontented and mutinous speeches that some of the strangers[14] amongst them had let fall from them in the ship: That when they came ashore they would use their own liberty, for none had power to command them, the patent[15] they had being for Virginia and not for New England, which belonged to another government, with which the Virginia Company had nothing to do. And partly that such an act by them done, this their condition considered, might be as firm as any patent, and in some respects more sure.

---

8. **hull.** Drift with the wind with short sails
9. **seele.** Roll
10. **halyards.** Rope for raising and lowering a sail
11. **tacked.** Change course against the wind
12. **Cape Harbor.** The ship arrived in Cape Harbor, now known as Provincetown Harbor, on November 11, 1620, sixty-five days after leaving England.
13. **combination.** Union
14. **strangers.** Those outside the Puritan church
15. **patent.** Document granting a right or privilege

Words for Everyday Use:

sun • dry (sun´drē) *adj.,* various; miscellaneous

de • lib • er • a • tion (di lib´ər ā´shən) *n.,* discussion; consideration of alternatives

mu • ti • nous (myōōt´ᵊn əs) *adj.,* inclined to revolt against authority

Vocabulary in Context

- Mello's Mercantile sells film, batteries, figurines, stamps, and other sundry items.
- After four days of deliberation, the jury made a decision.
- The mutinous crew tied their captain to the mast and turned the ship around.
- A city ordinance forbids walking dogs on the beach.
- Inez received a medal of commendation for saving the children from the burning building.
- "Harriet is a calamity waiting to happen," muttered Ben as Harriet tripped into the pond.

The form was as followeth:
IN THE NAME OF GOD, AMEN.

We whose names are underwritten, the loyal subjects of our dread Sovereign Lord King James, by the Grace of God of Great Britain, France, and Ireland King, Defender of the Faith, etc.

Having undertaken, for the Glory of God and advancement of the Christian Faith and Honor of our King and Country, a Voyage to plant the First Colony in the Northern Parts of Virginia, do by these presents solemnly and mutually in the presence of God and one of another, Covenant and Combine ourselves together into a Civil Body Politic, for our better ordering and preservation and furtherance of the ends aforesaid; and by virtue hereof to enact, constitute and frame such just and equal Laws, Ordinances, Acts, Constitutions and Offices, from time to time, as shall be thought most meet[16] and convenient for the general good of the Colony, unto which we promise all due submission and obedience. In witness whereof we have hereunder subscribed our names at Cape Cod, the 11th of November, in the year of the reign of our Sovereign Lord King James, of England, France and Ireland the eighteenth, and of Scotland the fifty-fourth. Anno Domini 1620.

THE STARVING TIME

But that which was most sad and lamentable was, that in two or three months' time half of their company died, especially in January and February, being the depth of winter, and wanting houses and other comforts; being infected with the scurvy[17] and other diseases which this long voyage and their inaccommodate[18] condition had brought upon them. So as there died some times two or three of a day in the foresaid time, that of 100 and odd persons, scarce fifty remained. And of these, in the time of most distress, there was but six or seven persons who to their great commendations, be it spoken, spared no pains night nor day, but with abundance of toil and hazard of their own health, fetched them wood, made them fires, dressed them meat, made their beds, washed their loathsome clothes, clothed and unclothed them. In a word, did all the homely[19] and necessary offices for them which dainty and queasy stomachs cannot endure to hear named; and all this willingly and cheerfully, without any grudging in the least, showing herein their true love unto their friends and brethren; a rare example and worthy to be remembered. Two of these seven were Mr. William Brewster, their reverend Elder, and Myles Standish, their Captain and military commander, unto whom myself and many others were much beholden in our low and sick condition. And yet the Lord so upheld these persons as in this general calamity they were not at all infected either with sickness or lameness. And what I have said of these I may say of many others who died in this general visitation, and others yet living; that whilst they had health, yea, or

16. **meet.** Suitable, fit
17. **scurvy.** Disease characterized by weakness and bleeding gums
18. **inaccommodate.** Lacking adequate housing
19. **homely.** Intimate

❶ *For what purpose is the Civil Body Politic formed? For what does the compact provide?*

❷ *How many people died? Why was the death rate so high?*

WORDS FOR EVERYDAY USE:
or • di • nance (ôrd´n əns) *n.,* regulation; direction, command
com • men • da • tion (käm´ən dā´shən) *n.,* praise
ca • lam • i • ty (kə lam´ə tē) *n.,* deep trouble or misery

ANSWERS TO GUIDED READING QUESTIONS

❶ The Civil Body Politic is formed for the better ordering and preserving of the people. The compact provides for the making of laws and calling of meetings of the people.

❷ Half of the people died during January and February because the winter was harsh, they did not have adequate housing, and they were sick with scurvy and other diseases from their voyage.

ADDITIONAL QUESTIONS AND ACTIVITIES

Ask students to compare the experiences of the colonists described by Bradford and those described by John Smith in *The General History of Virginia, New England, and the Summer Isles.* What difficulties did colonists in both places face? Which experiences were unique to one colony or the other? Students may also want to read Smith's account of the New England colonies to compare to Bradford's.

Answer to Guided Reading Question

❶ Reports were made to people in England of the abundance of food in the New World.

Answers to Selection Check Test 4.2.9

EX. What was the name of the first ship on which the Pilgrims were to voyage?

The ship was the *Speedwell.*

1. What happened to the haughty young seaman?

He became ill, died, and was thrown overboard.

2. What difference of opinion was there among the mariners when the ship seemed to be of questionable seaworthiness?

Some of the sailors wanted to turn around because they feared for the safety of the ship. Others wanted to continue because they had come so far and they did not want to lose their wages.

3. How many passengers died during the voyage?

One passenger died during the voyage.

4. What did all the men sign before going ashore?

They signed the Mayflower Compact.

5. When was the first Thanksgiving?

The first Thanksgiving was in the fall of 1621.

Responding to the Selection

Students can discuss the things for which they are willing to take risks or face danger. Is freedom worth the difficulties the Pilgrims faced? is adventure? is anything?

any strength continuing, they were not wanting[20] to any they had need of them. And I doubt not but their recompense is with the Lord.

From *Book II, Chapter XII. Anno 1621*

FIRST THANKSGIVING

What reports were made to people in England? ❶

They began now to gather in the small harvest they had, and to fit up their houses and dwellings against winter, being all well recovered in health and strength and had all things in good plenty. For as some were thus employed in affairs abroad, others were exercised in fishing, about cod and bass and other fish, of which they took good store, of which every family had their portion. All the summer there was no want; and now began to come in store of fowl,[21] as winter approached, of which this place did abound when they came first (but afterward decreased by degrees). And besides waterfowl there was great store of wild turkeys, of which they took many, besides venison, etc. Besides they had about a peck a meal a week to a person, or now since harvest, Indian corn to that proportion. Which made many afterwards write so largely of their plenty here to their friends in England, which were not feigned but true reports.

20. **wanting.** Lacking in attention
21. **fowl.** Birds

Words for Everyday Use: **rec • om • pense** (rek´əm pens´) *n.,* repayment or reward
feign (fān) *vt.,* make up, invent

Vocabulary in Context

- Cathy received a sizable reward as recompense for her role in catching the bandit.
- Kiki was bored silly but she feigned interest in Lyle's endless chatter.

Responding to the Selection

After reading about the Pilgrims' troubles, would you have been willing to join the expedition? Why, or why not?

Reviewing the Selection

Recalling

1. When the Pilgrims' ship began to look unseaworthy, why were the sailors reluctant to turn around and go back to England?
2. How many of the passengers died during the trip?
3. What did the "strangers" aboard ship threaten to do when they went ashore?
4. Compare the events of January and February 1621 with the events of the fall of 1621.

Interpreting

5. Bradford does not explicitly record the Pilgrims' response to the news that the ship might lack seaworthiness. How willing do you suppose they were to return to Europe? Why might they have resisted that possibility?
6. Why did the Pilgrims stop their travels near Cape Cod rather than go further south, where their charter gave them permission to land? Do you think they were right to do so?
7. Why did the leaders of the Pilgrims insist that every man who was going ashore first sign the Mayflower Compact? How would the compact help the Pilgrims?
8. What were some of the indications that the Pilgrims formed a close, sharing community, where everyone depended on everyone else?

Synthesizing

9. Bradford does not mention the "discontented and mutinous" strangers in his reports of what happened after everyone went ashore. Do you suppose they gave no further trouble? What do you suppose they were doing by the end of the first year in America?
10. In what ways were Bradford and the other Pilgrims sustained by their religious faith? Why was this faith particularly important to them in the New World?

Answers for Reviewing the Selection

RECALLING

1. The sailors were reluctant to turn back because they were halfway there and did not want to lose their wages.
2. Only one of the Pilgrims died during the journey.
3. Some of the "strangers" claimed they would live under their own authority since the document of commanding privilege was for Virginia, not for New England.
4. In January and February 1621, many people died of hunger and illness for they had neither homes nor adequate food. The fall of 1621 was a happier time. People had gathered a small harvest and recovered from earlier illnesses. The bounty of food made many of the colonists write to their friends in England about the abundance of food in the New World.

INTERPRETING

Responses will vary. Possible responses are given.

5. Despite the danger, the Pilgrims might have been very reluctant to return to Europe where they had been persecuted. They may also have felt that because they were on a voyage to escape religious persecution, God would oversee their difficult and dangerous journey.
6. They attempted to go further south but ran into dangerous waters. Having sailed through many difficulties already, they feared this last danger and decided to go ashore where they might.
7. The leaders insisted that every man going ashore sign the Mayflower Compact to prevent mutiny. The Mayflower Compact was written in part in response to the mutinous talk of some of the strangers and in part to replace the patent that they had for Virginia. The compact stated that all who signed it agreed to combine as a political body for the better government of all.
8. The people who were well did all they could for the sick, even risking their own health. The

(cont.)

Answers for Reviewing the Selection (cont.)

weakened and depleted group made homes and soon grew a small harvest to sustain themselves.

SYNTHESIZING

Responses will vary. Possible responses are given.

9. Most likely the mutinous people had to join the group or go off on their own. In light of the dangers and hardships in the new land, they may have decided to stay and work with the group. They may also have succumbed to illness, lack of housing, and the hard winter.

10. God is seen as the reason for the Pilgrims landing safely, and as the power who saved the young man who was almost thrown off the ship. The Pilgrims left Europe to seek religious freedom, survived many difficulties, and attributed their success to their religious convictions. Faith was a sustaining and motivating force for the Pilgrims.

ANSWERS FOR UNDERSTANDING LITERATURE

See the evaluation forms for discussion, active listening, and oral communication, *Assessment Portfolio,* 7.11–7.14.)

1. Chronological Order. Bradford is accounting a voyage and the beginning of a new way of life. It is logical to arrange the events he discusses in chronological order because it is a historical narrative. These are some major events to be included on student time lines: *Speedwell* proves unseaworthy; Pilgrims transfer to *Mayflower;* Pilgrims fear that ship won't make it; John Howland almost lost at sea; William Butten, only passenger fatality, dies; Pilgrims find Cape Cod; Pilgrims sail south until dangerous waters change plans; Pilgrims return to Cape Cod; Pilgrims sign Mayflower Compact; half of company dies; Pilgrims gather small harvest; remaining members healthy. Students should insert these events and others on a time line, using exact dates when possible.

►Additional practice is provided in the *Essential Skills Practice Book: Writing,* 1.19.

2. Irony. The haughty young man expected that he would throw many of the passengers overboard after they died. It is ironic that he was the first to die and be thrown overboard.

Understanding Literature (Questions for Discussion)

1. **Chronological Order. Chronological order** is the arrangement of details in order of their occurrence. Why does chronological order suit Bradford's purpose? Make a time line of the events related in this selection.

2. **Irony. Irony** is a difference between appearance and reality. In *irony of situation* an event occurs that violates the expectations of the characters, the reader, or the audience. What did the haughty young man expect at the beginning of the selection? What was ironic about his demise?

Responding in Writing

Lyric Poem or Memoir. In *Of Plymouth Plantation,* Bradford describes the first Thanksgiving, which occurred in the fall of 1621. The first Thanksgiving was a three-day feast held by the Pilgrims to celebrate the bounty of the autumn harvest, the survival of the colony, and the aid given the Pilgrims by neighboring Native Americans. By the mid-nineteenth century, Thanksgiving Day had become a traditional holiday in New England, and it was proclaimed an official national holiday in 1863 by President Abraham Lincoln. Write a lyric poem of thanksgiving appropriate for reading on Thanksgiving Day. Your poem can be about the first Thanksgiving or about something for which you personally are thankful. If you prefer to do so, write a brief memoir, or autobiographical account, describing a Thanksgiving celebration in which you participated. Whether you decide to write a lyric poem or a memoir, use concrete sensory details to make your subject vivid for your readers. If you decide to write a lyric poem, you may wish to do some library research on the first Thanksgiving or some freewriting about things for which you are thankful. If you decide to write a memoir, begin by making a time line listing the events that occurred on the day that you will be describing. Refer to the Language Arts Survey, 1.12, "Freewriting"; 1.19, "Time Lines"; and 4.20–4.28, on research techniques.

ANALYTIC SCALES FOR RESPONDING IN WRITING

Assign a score from 1 to 25 for each grading criterion below. (For more detailed evaluation, see the evaluation forms for writing, revising, and proofreading, *Assessment Portfolio,* 7.1–7.10.)

Lyric Poem or Memoir

- **Content/Unity.** The lyric poem is about either the first Thanksgiving or something for which the speaker is thankful, or the memoir is based on a Thanksgiving memory of the writer.
- **Organization/Coherence.** The poem or memoir is written in a logical and sensible order.
- **Language/Style.** The poem or memoir uses concrete sensory details and employs vivid and precise nouns, verbs, and modifiers.
- **Conventions.** The poem or memoir avoids errors in spelling, grammar, usage, mechanics, and manuscript form.

PREREADING

from *The New England Primer*

Anonymous

About the Selection

The New England Primer was the first textbook produced in America to teach reading. Evidence places publication of the first edition between 1687 and 1690. Since the New England colonies were founded for religious reasons, it was only natural that religion formed the basis of all education and therefore dominated the book. Its contents included the Lord's Prayer and the Apostles' Creed, a series of moral and instructive sentences from the Bible, and an illustrated alphabet. The *Primer* was popular throughout the English colonies and was sold in the United States until the nineteenth century. The excerpt here is the alphabet from the 1727 edition of the *Primer.*

a b c d e f g h i j k l m
n o p q r ſ s t v u w x
y z &
Vowels.
A E I O U Y a e i o u y
Conſonants,
b c d f g h i k l m n p q r ſ t v w x z
Double Letters,
ff ff ſt ſi ſi ſh ſl ſl ffi ffl ffl ct
Italick Letters.
Aa Bb Cc Dd Ee Ff Gg Hh
Ii Kk Ll Mm Nn Oo Pp Qq
Rr Sſ Tt Uu Ww Xx Yy Zz
Italick Double Letters
ff ſſ ſt ſi ſh ſl ſl ſſl ffi ffl ct

GOALS/OBJECTIVES

Studying this lesson will enable students to

- appreciate a learning tool from an earlier time
- compare and contrast current educational styles with those of the 1600s and 1700s
- identify the aim of a piece of writing
- identify and explain biblical and historical allusions
- define *couplet* and identify couplets in their reading
- develop and implement a classification system

ADDITIONAL RESOURCES

Reader's Guide

- Selection Worksheet, 2.6

Assessment Portfolio

- Selection Check Test, 4.2.11
- Selection Test, 4.2.12

Essential Skills Practice Books

- *Language,* 2.13, 2.134, 2.148
- *Study and Research,* 4.7

ENRICHMENT ACTIVITIES

The art on page 109 is representative of a sampler, a small piece of cloth displaying samples of needlework. Samplers were made for practice or to demonstrate skill. They often included letters, numbers, and a verse. Students might research samplers to discover who made them, more about why they were created, and what popular verses were used on samplers. Students might also consider the intricate skill needed to create a sampler and discuss why samplers are now cherished as folk art.

SUPPORT FOR LEP STUDENTS

Some students may find the use of an *f* instead of an *s*, as in *finned* for *sinned* and *glafs* for *glass,* confusing. Suggest that if a line seems to make little sense, they might try replacing an *f* with an *s*.

Additional Vocabulary

glass—hourglass, a time-telling device

anoints—rubs with oil

beauteous—beautiful

PREREADING NOTES

READER'S JOURNAL

Students might consider how easily rhymes and jingles are remembered. They might refer to other things they have learned through rhyme, or they might consider the way advertising jingles can get stuck in their heads. They then might write about why rhyme can be a good learning tool.

LANGUAGE SKILLS

Changed words include *whipt* to *whipped* and *majestie* to *majesty.* Students may also list many of the words that include the letter *f* instead of *s,* such as *glafs, bleffes,* and *difmal.* Students may also recognize the verb form *doth,* an archaic form of the verb *do.*

▶Additional practice is provided in the *Essential Skills Practice Book: Language,* 2.134.

ANSWERS TO GUIDED READING QUESTIONS

❶ A student should pay attention to this book so he or she can mend his or her life.

❷ "No man of blood" might mean that the king does not often engage in warfare, that he is not quick to impose death sentences on his people, or that he is not an earthly man and possesses some immortal qualities.

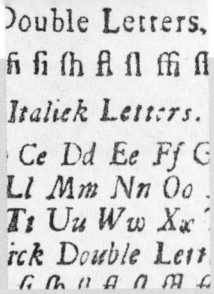
Double Letters.
Italick Letters.

READER'S JOURNAL

You have probably seen illustrated alphabet books published in recent years. Perhaps you even remember some of the pictures or rhymes in these books. What makes this approach to learning the alphabet more enjoyable than mere memorization? Jot down your ideas in your journal.

LANGUAGE SKILLS

Read the Language Arts Survey, 2.134, "Proofreading for Spelling Errors." Then examine this selection for words whose spelling has changed since publication of the *Primer.* List the words as they are spelled in the text and as they are spelled today.

FROM

The New England Primer

ANONYMOUS

Why should a student pay close attention to this book? ❶

What might the description "No man of blood" mean? ❷

A

In *Adam's* Fall
We finned[1] all.

B

Thy Life to mend
This *Book* attend.

C

The *Cat* doth play
And after flay.

D

A *Dog* will bite
A Thief at Night.

E

An *Eagles* Flight
Is out of Sight.

F

An idle *Fool*
Is whipt at School.

G

As runs the *Glafs*
Man's life doth pafs.

H

My *Book* and *Heart*
Shall never part.

J

Job feels the Rod
Yet bleffes GOD.

K

Our *K I N G* the
good
No man of blood.

L

The *Lion* bold
The *Lamb* doth hold.

M

The *Moon* gives light
In time of night.

1. **finned.** Sinned. The letter *s* often appears as an *f* in the early print style of the *Primer.*

N

O

P

Q

R

S

Nightingales fing
In Time of Spring.

The *Royal Oak*
it was the Tree
That fav'd His
Royal Majeftie.

Peter denies
His Lord and cries

Queen *Efther* comes
in Royal State
To Save the Jews
from difmal Fate

Rachol doth mourn
For her firft born.

Samuel anoints
Whom God appoints:

T

U

W

X

Y

Z

Time cuts down all
Both great and fmall.

Uriah's beauteous Wife
Made *David* feek his
Life.

Whales in the Sea
God's Voice obey.

Xerxes the great did
die,
And fo muft you & I.

Youth forward flips
Death fooneft nips.

Zacheus he
Did climb the Tree
His Lord to Fee.

❶ *What attitude toward death is expressed in this passage?*

Responding to the Selection

Which—if any—of the rhymes in this alphabet might appear in a modern alphabet book? Why would others among these rhymes be unsuitable for a modern American book? How have ideas about child rearing changed since the Puritan Era?

Reviewing the Selection

Recalling

1. What animals appear in the rhyme for the letter *L*?
2. Which letters have rhymes that might refer to the *Primer* itself?
3. During an era of political chaos and revolution in seventeenth-century England, the king saved himself from enemies by hiding in a tree. Which letter has a rhyme referring to this incident?
4. To what kind of glass does the rhyme for the letter *G* refer to?

Interpreting

5. What two qualities might the animals referred to in the rhyme for the letter *L* represent?
6. Explain the couplet for the letter *B*. To what book does it refer?
7. Which couplet tells how New Englanders felt about the king during the seventeenth century?
8. What does the rhyme for the letter *F* tell about the treatment of school children during the time the *Primer* was in use?

Answer to Guided Reading Question

❶ Death is presented as an inevitable part of life that comes quickly to all.

Responding to the Selection

Rhymes that might appear in a modern alphabet book include "An *Eagles* Flight/Is out of Sight," "The *Lion* bold/The *Lamb* doth hold," "The Moon gives light/In time of night," and "Nightingales sing/ In Time of Spring." Many of the other rhymes would be unsuitable because of their preoccupation with death. Historical references and changing ideas on education would make other rhymes unsuitable. Most alphabet books today focus on subjects that children enjoy rather than trying to teach them a moral lesson along with the alphabet.

Answers for Reviewing the Selection

RECALLING

1. A lion and a lamb appear in the rhyme for *L*.
2. *B* and *H* have rhymes that might refer to the *Primer* itself.
3. The rhyme for *O* refers to the oak in which the king hid.
4. The rhyme refers to an hourglass, a time-telling device.

INTERPRETING

Responses will vary. Possible responses are given.

5. The lion might represent pride or ferociousness. The lamb might represent gentleness or compassion.
6. The couplet for *B* suggests that to live a good life one should follow the moral lessons presented in the *Primer* or, perhaps, in the Bible from which many of the lessons of the *Primer* are taken.
7. The couplet for *K* says that the king is "good/No man of blood."
8. The couplet indicates that corporal punishment was common and acceptable.

(cont.)

Answers for Reviewing the Selection (cont.)

SYNTHESIZING

Responses will vary. Possible responses are given.

9. The rhymes for *G, R, T, X,* and *Y* refer to death or aging. While many children will face the death of somebody they know, there are other means for discussing such issues. The repetition of the theme of death in a rhyme created to teach the alphabet is not appropriate. Also, the manner in which death is presented gives a grim picture of both life and death.

10. Education in the 1600s and 1700s had a strong religious base that is not present today. Much of this verse seems intent on teaching not only the alphabet but fear of death as well. The other major difference demonstrated is the means of punishment. The rhyme for *F* suggests that whipping was a common means of punishment in the 1600s and 1700s.

Answers to Selection Check Test 4.2.1

EX. What kind of book was *The New England Primer?*
***The New England Primer* was a textbook.**

1. What will a dog do according to the rhyme for *D?*
A dog will bite a thief at night.

2. What happens to an idle fool?
An idle fool is whipped at school.

3. The rhymes for which two letters refer to the king?
The rhymes for *K* and *O* refer to the king.

4. The rhymes for which two letters refer to the swift passage of life?
The rhymes for *G* and *Y* refer to the swift passage of life.

5. What message do the lines for *T* and *X* share?
They share the message that everyone, powerful or not, must die.

Answers for Understanding Literature

See the evaluation forms for discussion, active listening, and oral communication, *Assessment Portfolio,* 7.11–7.14.

1. Aim. The *Primer* teaches moral lessons and reminds us that life is short and death comes to all. The rhymes contain biblical references and reminders that sinners will be punished.

2. Allusion. Biblical allusions include the rhymes for *A,* Adam and the fall of humankind; *J,* Job, who blesses God despite the hardships he must endure; *P,* Peter, who denies his Lord three times; *Q,* the story of Esther saving the Jews; *R,* the story of Rachel; *S,* the story of Samuel; *U,* the story of Uriah and David; and *Z,* Zacheus, who climbed a tree to better see Jesus.

3. Couplet. The rhyme for *Z* is not written in couplet form. Instead, it is a rhyming tercet. The couplets for *K, O, Q, U,* and *X* are printed in more than two lines for space reasons.

SYNTHESIZING

9. At least three rhymes warn of age and death. Identify the letters with these rhymes. Do you think that these are appropriate rhymes for children? Why, or why not?

10. After reading the selection, what can you tell about the differences between education and culture in the 1600s and 1700s and education and culture today?

Understanding Literature (Questions for Discussion)

1. **Aim.** A writer's **aim** is the primary purpose that his or her work is meant to achieve. The aim of the *Primer* was education, but education in what? What characteristics of the alphabet support your answer?

2. **Allusion.** An **allusion** is a figure of speech in which a reference is made to a person, event, object, or work from history or literature. Identify three allusions in this alphabet to the Bible.

3. **Couplet.** A **couplet** is a pair of rhyming lines that express a complete thought. Which letter is given a verse that is not a couplet? How would you describe that particular verse? Several of the couplets are written in four lines of type simply because the width of the page limits the number of characters on a line. Identify one of those couplets, writing it in couplet form.

Responding in Writing

1. **Annotations.** An **annotation** for a literary work is an explanatory note for some part of that work. For example, annotations often explain difficult vocabulary and obscure references. If you are unfamiliar with the references in this selection, do some research to familiarize yourself with them. Write two annotations for the section of the alphabet from *O* through *S.*

2. **Children's Lesson Story.** Write a lesson story for an audience of young children, with the aim not merely of entertaining your audience but also of educating the children about good behavior. Choose a behavior you wish to promote. Then write a short story that demonstrates why this behavior is desired. You may wish to demonstrate rewards for following the behavior and punishments for deviating from such behavior. Refer to the Language Arts Survey, 2.148, "Register."

3. **Curriculum.** A **curriculum** consists of the courses provided by a school. What courses would you need to understand all the historical and biblical references in the *Primer* alphabet? Write a curriculum for your studies, with a short description of each course.

Analytic Scales for Responding in Writing

Assign a score from 1 to 25 for each grading criterion below. (For more detailed evaluation, see the evaluation forms for writing, revising, and proofreading, *Assessment Portfolio,* 7.1–7.10.)

1. Annotations

- **Content/Unity.** The annotations demonstrate an understanding of the reference and explain how the reference is used within the *Primer* text.
- **Organization/Coherence.** The annotations present the reference in a logical manner.
- **Language/Style.** The annotations use vivid and precise nouns, verbs, and modifiers.
- **Conventions.** The annotations avoid errors in spelling, grammar, usage, mechanics, and manuscript form.

2. Children's Lesson Story

- **Content/Unity.** The story should entertain as well as teach a lesson about a particular behavior.
- **Organization/Coherence.** The story should present a

(cont.)

Language Lab

Linking Verbs. Read the Language Arts Survey, 2.13, "Linking Verbs." On a separate sheet of paper, write each verb from the following sentences. Underline each linking verb.

1. Some modern people feel ignorant when they read Puritan writings.
2. Although the language looks familiar, its meaning is sometimes obscure because of historical and religious references with which modern-day people are often unfamiliar.
3. Footnotes are one means of providing information about obscure references in literary works and other written materials.
4. Religion was the central force within the Puritan community, and all aspects of life felt its influence.
5. That is why Puritan writings were full of religious references.

Thinking Skills

Classifying. Read the Language Arts Survey, 4.7, "Classifying." Then create a system for classifying the verses in this selection. Identify each class, and list the letters whose verses share the characteristics of that class.

PROJECTS

1. **Pop Culture Alphabet Book.** With a small group, create an original alphabet book in which you associate the letters with elements of pop culture (Example: *R* is for rap). Begin with a brainstorming session during which all suggestions are listed. Next, vote on the best word for each letter, and decide what form to use—phrases, couplets, or another form. Divide the alphabet among the group members, and write the entries. Illustrate them as your group chooses. Finally, assemble the pages, and add a title page and cover.

2. **Memory Bee.** Try playing the game known as a Memory Bee. Two teams are needed. After no more than five minutes of memorizing the *Primer* alphabet, each team chooses a representative to run the contest. The leaders make out a card for each letter of the alphabet and mix the cards. Then they take turns drawing letters and challenging the opposing team with them, spelling-bee style. If a team member can name the person or thing associated with the letter, the team gets one point. If the member can recite the entire couplet, the team gets three points. The team with the most points after twelve turns wins.

ANSWERS FOR LANGUAGE LAB

1. feel, read
2. looks, is, are
3. are
4. was, felt
5. is, were

ANSWERS FOR THINKING SKILLS

Possible categories for classification include biblical reference, historical reference, suitable for a modern alphabet book, and unsuitable for a modern alphabet book.

PROJECT NOTES

►See the worksheets and evaluation forms for projects, *Assessment Portfolio,* 7.20–7.23.

1. Pop Culture Alphabet Book. Students may wish to share their books with younger students in an elementary school or through the children's room of a local library.

2. Memory Bee. After playing the game, students might discuss strategies for memorization and which parts of the *Primer* they had the most difficulty recalling.

ANALYTIC SCALES FOR RESPONDING IN WRITING (CONT.)

behavior and through an illustrative example teach a lesson. It should be written in a clear and sensible order.
• **Language/Style.** The story should use vivid and precise nouns, verbs, and modifiers.
• **Conventions.** The story avoids errors in spelling, grammar, usage, mechanics, and manuscript form.

3. Curriculum
• **Content/Unity.** The curriculum should include several courses needed for understanding the references in the *Primer.* Course descriptions should demonstrate why the course is included.
• **Organization/Coherence.** The curriculum should include concise course descriptions organized in a logical manner.
• **Language/Style.** The curriculum uses vivid and precise nouns, verbs, and modifiers.
• **Conventions.** The curriculum avoids errors in spelling, grammar, usage, mechanics, and manuscript form.

ADDITIONAL RESOURCES

READER'S GUIDE
- Selection Worksheet, 2.7

ASSESSMENT PORTFOLIO
- Selection Check Test, 4.2.13
- Selection Test, 4.2.14

ESSENTIAL SKILLS PRACTICE BOOKS
- *Language,* 2.56, 2.63
- *Study and Research,* 4.37

ENRICHMENT ACTIVITIES

Anne Bradstreet's education was unusual for a woman living in the 1600s. Students can do further research on Bradstreet's education and life. They may also wish to explore the typical level of education and the role of women in society at the time during which Bradstreet lived.

SUPPORT FOR LEP STUDENTS

In this poem, Bradstreet often uses inverted sentence structures that may prove challenging to some students. Students can work in pairs to rewrite each sentence in a more standard order.

ADDITIONAL VOCABULARY

quench—extinguish; overcome; subdue

PREREADING

"To My Dear and Loving Husband"

by Anne Bradstreet

ABOUT THE AUTHOR

Anne Bradstreet (*circa* 1612–1672) had the advantage of an education unusual fo women of her time and began writing poetry as a child. She married Simon Bradstreet, graduate of Cambridge University and an associate of her father, when she was only sixteen A year after marriage to Anne, Simon was appointed to assist in the preparations of th Massachusetts Bay Company, and the Bradstreets sailed to the New World. Life in the nev world was hard, especially for Anne, who had been weakened by a childhood illness. Whe her husband became governor of the Bay Colony, Anne's duties increased as well. Despit her many obligations, Bradstreet found time to continue writing poetry, as she had when sh was a young girl. Unknown to Anne, her brother-in-law had a collection of her poetry printe in London in 1650—the first published volume of poems by a New World resident.

ABOUT THE SELECTION

The date of composition of **"To My Dear and Loving Husband,"** like most of Anne Bradstreet's work, is unknown. Originally, she distributed her writings only among family anc friends, but after publication of some poems, she then decided to put out a second, authorized edition. That second edition did not appear until after her death, being publishec in Boston in 1678. "To My Dear and Loving Husband" appeared in the second edition. The poem remains a noble expression of the sustaining and transforming power of love.

GOALS/OBJECTIVES

Studying this lesson will enable students to

- empathize with the feelings of love expressed by the speaker
- identify parallelism and oxymorons in their reading
- define *hyperbole* and identify the use of hyperbole in their reading
- identify sight rhymes in their reading
- understand inverted sentences and recast them in standard word order
- take formal notes

READER'S JOURNAL

When you choose greeting cards for birthdays or special events, what sorts of messages do you prefer? For whom might you buy a poem? for what occasion? Write about these questions in your journal.

LANGUAGE SKILLS

Read the Language Arts Survey, 2.56, "Achieving Parallelism." Then identify two or more instances of parallelism in this selection.

"To My Dear and Loving Husband"

ANNE BRADSTREET

If ever two were one, then surely we.
If ever man were loved by wife, then thee;
If ever wife was happy in a man,
Compare with me, ye women, if you can.
5 I prize thy love more than whole mines of gold
Or all the riches that the East doth hold.
My love is such that rivers cannot quench,
Nor ought but love from thee, give recompense.
Thy love is such I can no way repay,
10 The heavens reward thee manifold, I pray.
Then while we live, in love let's so persevere
That when we live no more, we may live ever. ■

❶ *How much does the speaker prize her husband's love?*

❷ *If the couple perseveres in their love, what will be the consequences?*

Responding to the Selection

What is special about the marriage that Anne Bradstreet describes? What must happen for people to develop the sort of relationship indicated by this poem? Discuss these questions with your classmates.

WORDS FOR EVERYDAY USE:

rec • om • pense (rek´əm pens´) *n.*, reward; compensation, payment
man • i • fold (man´ə fōld´) *adv.*, in many forms or ways
per • se • vere (pər´sə vir´) *vi.*, continue in spite of difficulty; persist

VOCABULARY IN CONTEXT

- The only recompense the volunteers received was the thanks of the people they had helped.
- Maggie spent hours searching for the manifold appearances of the hidden troll throughout the story.
- After the battle, the general shouted, "We must persevere! Onward, troops!"

PREREADING NOTES

READER'S JOURNAL

Students might write their own greeting card message, either in the style they are used to reading in greeting cards or in a more personal style such as they might write in a blank card to a friend or family member.

LANGUAGE SKILLS

Parallelism is used in the beginning of the first three lines; in lines 1 and 2 it is carried throughout the line.

▶Additional practice is provided in the *Essential Skills Practice Book: Language,* 2.56.

ANSWERS TO GUIDED READING QUESTIONS

❶ The speaker prizes her husband's love more than gold and more than all the riches of the East.

❷ If the couple perseveres in their love, they will continue to live in love even after they have died.

RESPONDING TO THE SELECTION

Students may want to freewrite about marriage and relationships before the discussion. Students should note that Bradstreet describes a profound, strong love for her husband and, with the last line, creates a sense of the timelessness of this love.

Answers for Reviewing the Selection

RECALLING

1. If two people were ever one person, then surely we are. If ever a man were loved by his wife, then you are.
2. *Prize* means "to treasure or cherish."
3. Only the return of love can be proper recompense for the love she gives.
4. Persevering in love while they live will allow the speaker and her beloved to live forever.

INTERPRETING

Responses will vary. Possible responses are given.

5. Bradstreet may have used elliptical sentences because the missing words were not necessary to the meaning of the lines; also, leaving them out fits the meter of the line better.
6. My love is like an insatiable thirst. My love is like a fire that not even a river could extinguish. My love is so strong that a river cannot destroy it.
7. I pray that heaven will reward you in many ways for your love.
8. *Answers will vary.*

SYNTHESIZING

Responses will vary. Possible responses are given.

9. The speaker and her husband seem to have a very loving relationship. The speaker indicates that she both loves deeply and is loved as well. She says that they are happy together.
10. The speaker has a hopeful view of the afterlife. She suggests that if she and her husband persevere in the difficulties of love in this life, they will be rewarded in their next life.

Elizabeth Freake and Baby Mary. *Artist unknown,* circa *1671–74. Worcester Art Museum, Worcester, MA. Gift of Mr. and Mrs. Albert W. Rice.*

Reviewing the Selection

RECALLING

1. Both lines 1 and 2 consist of elliptical sentences—that is, not all the words are provided; some are understood. Write out the complete sentences, supplying the understood words. (If you like, use *you* instead of *thee.*)
2. What is the sense, or meaning, of *prize* in line 5?
3. *Recompense* means "payment." What is the one thing that can be recompense for the speaker's love?
4. According to lines 11 and 12, what will help the speaker and her beloved to live forever?

INTERPRETING

5. Why did Bradstreet use elliptical sentences? What effect do they have on the poem?
6. Complete the comparison suggested in line 7 by the use of the word *quenched:* My love is like _____.
7. Restate line 10 in your own words.
8. What sorts of difficulties might these people or any married people face? Why is it important to any relationship to be willing to persevere in spite of difficulties?

Answers to Selection Check Test 4.2.13

EX. To whom is this poem addressed?
The poem is addressed to the speaker's "dear and loving husband."

1. What challenge does the speaker offer to other women?
She challenges them to compare her happiness with her husband to their happiness with their husbands.

2. How much does the speaker prize her husband's love?
The speaker prizes her husband's love more than whole mines of gold or all the riches of the East.

3. What are rivers unable to do?
Rivers are unable to quench the love of the speaker.

4. What does the speaker pray will compensate for her inability to repay love?
She hopes heaven will reward her husband.

5. What result does the speaker hope to achieve by persevering in love?
The speaker hopes to continue living in love even after death.

SYNTHESIZING

9. In your own words, how would you describe the relationship between the speaker and her husband?

10. In lines 11–12, the speaker suggests that if the two persevere in their love while living, they will live forever. What does the speaker believe about the afterlife? about the consequences of being, in this life, someone who perseveres in love despite its difficulties?

Understanding Literature (Questions for Discussion)

1. **Hyperbole**. A **hyperbole** is an exaggeration made for rhetorical effect. Find an instance of hyperbole in this poem.

2. **Oxymoron**. An **oxymoron** is a statement that contradicts itself. What oxymoron appears in the final lines of this poem? Why do you suppose the poet chose to use this technique? What is its effect?

3. **Sight rhyme**. **Sight rhyme**, or **eye rhyme**, is a pair of words, generally at the ends of lines of verse, that are spelled similarly but pronounced differently. In which lines of the selection is sight rhyme used?

Language Lab

Inverting Sentences for Emphasis. Read the Language Arts Survey, 2.63, "Inverting Sentences for Emphasis." Then rewrite these lines in usual word order, that is, *subject-verb-object.*

1. My love I have not confessed.
2. Not to keep secrets, it's best.
3. Thy love I cannot repay.
4. The heavens reward thee, I pray.
5. My future in your hands I rest.

Study and Research Skills

Formal Note-taking. Read the Language Arts Survey, 4.37, "Formal Note-taking." Then look up Anne Bradstreet in two library reference books. Take one or more notes from each reference book, using the note form recommended in the Language Arts Survey.

ANSWERS FOR UNDERSTANDING LITERATURE

► See the evaluation forms for discussion, active listening, and oral communication, *Assessment Portfolio,* 7.11–7.14.

Responses will vary. Possible responses are given.

1. Hyperbole. Bradstreet uses hyperbole to express the depth and strength of her love as in "I prize thy love more than whole mines of gold/Or all the riches that the East doth hold" or "My love is such that rivers cannot quench."

2. Oxymoron. Bradstreet uses the oxymoron "that when we live no more, we may live ever." This oxymoron indicates the speaker's belief in an afterlife that is affected by the actions of this life. The phrase "when we live no more" preceding "we may live ever" adds to the power of the timelessness of the speaker's love.

3. Sight Rhyme. Sight rhyme is used in the last lines with *persevere* and *ever.*

ANSWERS FOR LANGUAGE LAB

1. I have not confessed my love.
2. It's best not to keep secrets.
3. I cannot repay thy love.
4. I pray that the heavens reward thee.
5. I rest my future in your hands.

►Additional practice is provided in the *Essential Skills Practice Book: Language,* 2.63.

ANSWERS FOR STUDY AND RESEARCH SKILLS

Students should follow the proper form when taking their notes. After researching Anne Bradstreet, students can share the information they uncover.

►Additional practice is provided in the *Essential Skills Practice Book: Study and Research,* 4.37.

ADDITIONAL RESOURCES

READER'S GUIDE
- Selection Worksheet, 2.8

ASSESSMENT PORTFOLIO
- Selection Check Test, 4.2.15
- Selection Test, 4.2.16

ESSENTIAL SKILLS PRACTICE BOOKS
- *Language,* 2.4, 2.48
- *Speaking and Listening,* 3.1

AUDIOCASSETTE
- "Sinners in the Hands of an Angry God," Track 2

ENRICHMENT ACTIVITIES

Students can compare Edwards's religious beliefs with those of William Bradford and the opinions expressed in *The New England Primer.* Ask students the following questions to stimulate their thinking: Are any of these views similar? If so, in what ways? What differences do you see? How do you think the differing views were treated in the early days of the colonies? When was each of these works written? Do you think the time period affected the attitudes and beliefs expressed in each piece?

SUPPORT FOR LEP STUDENTS

Point out to students that this selection was delivered as a sermon. It contains many elements common to speeches such as repetition and elaboration. Students may find it helpful to hear the selection read aloud to hear how these techniques work. Students might make a list of the main ideas Edwards is trying to convey and examine the way in which he elaborates on or repeats each idea.

ADDITIONAL VOCABULARY

prudence—wisdom
wrath—anger
obligation—duty
abominable—nasty and disgusting

PREREADING

from "Sinners in the Hands of an Angry God"

by Jonathan Edwards

ABOUT THE AUTHOR

Jonathan Edwards (1703–1758) was born in East Windsor, Connecticut. He was a dedicated scholar even as a child and was admitted to Yale College when he was only thirteen. Edwards flourished in the rigorous academic setting and devoted himself to the study of theology. Edwards came from a line of noteworthy ministers and was determined to carry on his family's tradition. Edwards moved to Northampton, Massachusetts, where he succeeded his grandfather as minister of the local church, married, and raised a family. Edwards's goal as a minister was not only to heighten his followers' commitment to religion, but to enrich their religious experience. Known for his vivid and fiery sermons, Edwards sought to make religion so moving and real that it was almost a physical experience. Edwards's religious views gained great popularity and began the Great Awakening, a religious revival that swept across the colonies in the 1730s. When he decided, however, to actually name prestigious members of the clergy who were not expressing the proper devotion and reinstate the rite of communion, he was dismissed from his church. Edwards then served as a missionary to the Housatonic Indians and was elected president of the College of New Jersey (now Princeton).

ABOUT THE SELECTION

The following excerpt is from **"Sinners in the Hands of an Angry God,"** a sermon Edwards delivered in Enfield, Connecticut, on Sunday, July 8, 1741. Another minister who was present reported that Edwards spoke with calm dignity, yet the effect was highly emotional, with "such a breathing of distress, and weeping, that the preacher was obliged to speak to the people and desire silence, that he might be heard." The text of the sermon was published over eighty years later, in 1829–1830, in a multivolume edition of Edwards's works.

GOALS/OBJECTIVES

Studying this lesson will enable students to

- appreciate a vivid and fiery sermon
- describe the effect of a piece of writing
- recognize emphasis achieved through repetition and elaboration
- write an essay comparing and contrasting two views
- identify appositives and appositive phrases
- identify concrete and abstract nouns
- interpret nonverbal signs

READER'S JOURNAL

What does the word *grace* mean to you? In what ways can people extend grace to other people around them? Write your thoughts on these questions in your journal.

LANGUAGE SKILLS

Read the Language Arts Survey, 2.48, "Adding Appositives and Appositive Phrases." Then identify sentences in this selection that include one or more appositives or appositive phrases. Be able to point out both the appositive and the word or phrase to which it is in apposition.

FROM

"Sinners in the Hands of an Angry God"

JONATHAN EDWARDS

You probably are not sensible[1] of this; you find you are kept out of hell, but do not see the hand of God in it; but look at other things, as the good state of your bodily constitution, your care of your own life, and the means you use for your own preservation. But indeed these things are nothing; if God should withdraw His hand, they would avail no more to keep you from falling, than the thin air to hold up a person that is suspended in it.

Your wickedness makes you as it were heavy as lead, and to tend downwards with great weight and pressure towards hell; and if God should let you go, you would immediately sink and swiftly descend and plunge into the bottomless gulf, and your healthy constitution, and your own care and prudence, and best contrivance, and all your righteousness, would have no more influence to uphold you and keep you out of hell, than a spider's web would have to stop a fallen rock. Were it not for the sovereign pleasure of God, the earth would not bear you one moment; for you are a burden to it; the creation groans with you; the creature is made subject to the bondage of your corruption, not willingly; the sun does not willingly shine upon you to give you light to serve sin and Satan; the earth does not willingly yield her increase[2] to satisfy your lusts; nor is it willingly a stage for your wickedness to be acted upon; the air does not willingly

1. **sensible.** Aware
2. **increase.** Harvest

❶ *According to Edwards, what would happen to people if God withdrew his hand? What would fail to save them?*

❷ *To what are people a burden, according to Edwards?*

WORDS FOR EVERYDAY USE:

con • sti • tu • tion (kän´stə tōō´shən) *n.,* physical makeup of a person

a • vail (ə vāl´) *vi.,* be of use or advantage

gulf (gulf) *n.,* wide, deep gap or separation

con • triv • ance (kən trī´vəns) *n.,* invention; ingenious plan

sov • er • eign (säv´rən) *adj.,* above or superior to all others

PREREADING NOTES

READER'S JOURNAL

As an alternate activity, students might write in their journals about the effect of public speakers on listeners. Students should consider a speaker who evoked particularly strong feelings in them. Why was the speaker so powerful? What reaction did the student have while listening to the speaker? What reaction did other listeners have?

LANGUAGE SKILLS

One example is "look at other things, as the good state of your bodily constitution, your care of your own life, and the means you use for your own preservation" in which "the good state of your bodily constitution, your care of your own life, and the means you use for your own preservation" are appositives to "other things." Students may want to work in pairs to identify other appositives in the selection.

►Additional practice is provided in the *Essential Skills Practice Book: Language,* 2.48.

ANSWERS TO GUIDED READING QUESTIONS

❶ According to Edwards, if God withdrew his hand, people would fall into hell. Their constitution, care of life, and means of self-preservation would not save them.

❷ People are a burden to the Earth, according to Edwards.

VOCABULARY FROM THE SELECTION

abhor	incense
ascribe	induce
avail	loathsome
constitution	provoke
contrivance	sovereign
gulf	subserve

VOCABULARY IN CONTEXT

- Fran's constitution suffered from sitting at a desk for hours with no time to exercise.
- Maurice tried to get tickets to the concert, but to no avail, for they sold out in the first hour.
- People cross gulfs upon fallen trees in movies, but when I got to the edge of that cavernous drop, I was determined to go no further.
- I thought we'd be trapped in the pit for days, but Connie's clever contrivance got us out in no time.
- The sovereign looked out over the land and chortled with glee, "It's mine! All mine!"

Answers to Guided Reading Questions

❶ A black cloud of God's wrath is hanging over the heads of people.

❷ Edwards reminds those who doubt his words of people whose lives were suddenly snuffed out by the whim of God.

❸ Everyone who hasn't passed under a mighty change of heart by the power of the Spirit of God is in the hands of an angry God.

Historical Note

The Great Awakening was a religious revival that occurred primarily among Baptists, Congregationalists, Dutch Reformed, and Presbyterians. It was the American counterpart of the Evangelical movement in England led by John Wesley. Influenced by Wesley, George Whitefield first preached in the colonies in 1739–1740 and emphasized the unworthiness of sinners and the anger of God. Whitefield's sermons drew such large crowds that he could only preach outdoors. Jonathan Edwards followed in Whitefield's wake but applied a more academic and psychological approach to his preaching. The Great Awakening can be seen as a reaction to the rationalism of the Enlightenment, although Edwards did try to incorporate empiricism in his sermons by emphasizing the need to directly feel and experience God.

serve you for breath to maintain the flame of life in your vitals,[3] while you spend your life in the service of God's enemies. God's creatures are good, and were made for men to serve God with, and do not willingly subserve to any other purpose, and groan when they are abused to purposes so directly contrary to their nature and end. And the world would spew[4] you out, were it not for the sovereign hand of Him who hath subjected it in hope. There are black clouds of God's wrath now hanging directly over your heads, full of the dreadful storm, and big with thunder; and were it not for the restraining hand of God, it would immediately burst forth upon you. The sovereign pleasure of God, for the present, stays His rough wind; otherwise it would come with fury, and your destruction would come like a whirlwind, and you would be like the chaff of the summer threshing floor. . . .[5]

❶ *What is hanging directly over the heads of people?*

❷ *How does Edwards address those who may doubt his words?*

The bow of God's wrath is bent, and the arrow made ready on the string, and justice bends the arrow at your heart, and strains the bow, and it is nothing but the mere pleasure of God, and that of an angry God, without any promise or obligation at all, that keeps the arrow one moment from being made drunk with your blood. Thus all you that never passed under a great change of heart, by the mighty power of the Spirit of God upon your souls, all you that were never born again, and made new creatures, and raised from being dead in sin, to a state of new, and before altogether unexperienced light and life, are in the hands of an angry God. However you may have reformed your life in many things, and may have had religious affections,[6] and may keep up a form of religion in your families and closets,[7] and in the house of God, it is nothing but His mere pleasure that keeps you from being this moment swallowed up in everlasting destruction. However unconvinced you may now be of the truth of what you hear, by and by you will be fully convinced of it. Those that are gone from being in the like circumstances with you see that it was so with them; for destruction came suddenly upon most of them; when they expected nothing of it and while they were saying, peace and safety: now they see that those things on which they depended for peace and safety, were nothing but thin air and empty shadows.

❸ *Which people are in the hands of an angry God?*

The God that holds you over the pit of hell, much as one holds a spider or some loathsome insect over the fire, abhors you, and is dreadfully provoked: His wrath towards you burns like fire; He looks upon you as worthy of nothing else but to be cast into the fire; He is of purer eyes than to bear to have you in His sight; you are ten thousand times more abominable in His eyes than the most hateful venomous serpent is in ours. You have offended Him infinitely more than ever a stubborn rebel did his prince; and yet it is nothing but His hand that holds you from falling into the fire every moment. It is to be ascribed to nothing else, that you did not go to hell the last night; that you was suffered to

3. **vitals.** Necessary organs
4. **spew.** Throw up; eject
5. **chaff . . . threshing floor.** *Chaff*—husks of wheat that are left behind; *threshing floor*—place where grain is separated from its husks
6. **affections.** Feelings
7. **closets.** Studies; meditations

Words for Everyday Use:

sub • serve (səb sûrv´) *vt.*, be useful or helpful; serve
loath • some (lōth´səm) *adj.*, disgusting
ab • hor (ab hôr´) *vt.*, shrink from in disgust
pro • voke (prō vōk´) *vt.*, anger, irritate, annoy
as • cribe (ə skrīb´) *vt.*, assign; attribute

Vocabulary in Context

- The pious nun subserved her God.
- The loathsome beast left a trail of slime in the wake of its destruction.
- "Nature abhors a vacuum," Shirley said when Lennie noticed her rug was grungy and suggested she clean it.
- "Don't poke the ill-tempered dog with that stick. You'll only provoke him," Buck said.
- Glenda ascribed her success at basketball to her mother's coaching.

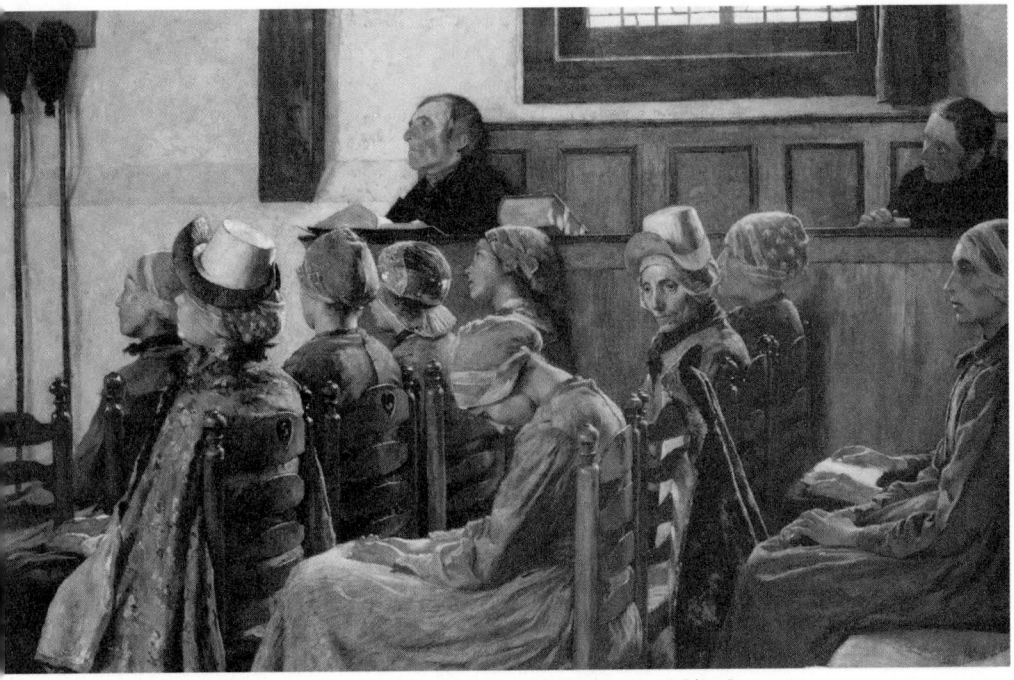

The Sermon. Gari Melchers, 1886. National Museum of American Art, Washington, DC/Art Resource

awake again in this world, after you closed your eyes to sleep. And there is no other reason to be given, why you have not dropped into hell since you arose in the morning, but that God's hand has held you up. There is no other reason to be given why you have not gone to hell, since you have sat here in the house of God, provoking His pure eyes by your sinful wicked manner of attending His solemn worship. Yea, there is nothing else that is to be given as a reason why you do not this very moment drop down into hell.

O sinner! Consider the fearful danger you are in: it is a great furnace of wrath, a wide and bottomless pit, full of the fire of wrath, that you are held over in the hand of that God, whose wrath is provoked and incensed as much against you, as against many of the damned in hell. You hang by a slender thread, with the flames of divine wrath flashing about it, and ready every moment to singe it, and burn it asunder; and you have no interest in any Mediator, and nothing to lay hold of to save yourself, nothing to keep off the flames of wrath, nothing of your own, nothing that you have done, nothing that you can do, to induce God to spare you one moment. ■

❶ *According to Edwards, how much control do people who are sinful in the eyes of God have over their destinies?*

WORDS FOR EVERYDAY USE: **in • cense** (in sens´) *vt.*, make very angry
in • duce (in dōōs) *vt.*, persuade; prevail on

ANSWER TO GUIDED READING QUESTION

❶ People who are sinful in the eyes of God have no control over their destinies.

ANSWERS TO SELECTION CHECK TEST 4.2.15

EX. What does Edwards say is responsible for keeping people out of hell?

The hand of God keeps people out of hell.

1. What does your wickedness make you resemble, according to Edwards?

Edwards says your wickedness makes you heavy as lead.

2. Edwards says the Earth would not bear you for a moment if it were not for what?

The Earth would not bear you for a moment if not for God's sovereign pleasure.

3. According to Edwards, what would happen if the violence of God's anger exploded like a wind?

People would be swept away like the chaff of the summer threshing floor.

4. How much does a sinner offend God, according to Edwards?

The sinner offends God more than a rebel offends a prince.

5. In what danger does Edwards say the sinner is in the last paragraph?

The sinner is held over a great furnace of fire and wrath.

VOCABULARY IN CONTEXT

- Muriel was incensed when she found out Myron had stolen her idea for the science fair.
- Despite the rising flood waters, rescue workers were unable to induce Otto to leave.

RESPONDING TO THE SELECTION

Fear and despair are emotions this sermon might prompt. Students can discuss which of these emotions, or perhaps another emotion, is most strongly appealed to by this sermon.

ANSWERS FOR REVIEWING THE SELECTION

RECALLING

1. According to Edwards, the average person thinks that a healthy body, taking care of oneself, and the means of self-preservation are what keeps him or her alive. Edwards gives complete credit to God's will.

2. Edwards says that the Sun does not willingly shine to give people light to serve sin, the Earth does not yield a harvest to satisfy human lusts, the Earth is not a stage for human wickedness, nor is the air meant to be breathed by those serving God's enemies.

3. Sinners can only change by having a great change of heart caused by the Spirit of God upon their souls.

4. They both build up the image of the burning pit of hell over which the sinner precariously balances.

INTERPRETING

Responses will vary. Possible responses are given.

5. The first simile suggests that the sinner's soul is heavy as a rock and would plummet to the depths of hell if not held by the hand of God. The second simile suggests the transitory state of life that could blow away in a moment if God so chose.

6. Edwards describes God's wrath as black storm clouds full of thunder. He says God's will is like a rough and furious wind that is stayed only for the moment. These elements are threatening and ready to strike out violently and unexpectedly at any moment.

7. Justice is personified. Justice bends an arrow on your heart and at any moment might choose to let that arrow pierce you. It is frightening to think that one is so endangered.

(cont.)

Responding to the Selection

Can you sympathize with the members of Edwards's congregation who reacted to this sermon with weeping? What two emotions might be involved? Which emotion do you think this sermon appeals to most?

Reviewing the Selection

RECALLING

1. According to Edwards, what does the average person think keeps him or her alive? To what does Edwards give complete credit?

2. What are some of the elements of creation that Edwards lists as "not willingly" serving the sinner?

3. What does Edwards claim is required to take a person out of the sinner classification?

4. Paragraphs 4 and 5 both build up the same image. What is this image?

INTERPRETING

5. In paragraph 2, Edwards compares the sinner first with a fallen rock and later with chaff on a threshing floor. What does he mean by each of these similes?

6. Which elements of nature does Edwards use in paragraph 2 to represent God's anger? What qualities do these elements have in common with anger?

7. What abstract ideal is personified—described as a person—in paragraph 3? In what action is this personified ideal occupied? Why is this comparison frightening?

8. In paragraph 4, Edwards traces the threat to the sinner's continued existence from the previous night, through rising in the morning, to sitting in church as Edwards speaks. Why might this progression be particularly effective in arousing fear?

SYNTHESIZING

9. Which of the images in this sermon is the most memorable? Why?

10. Do you think that this sermon could be influential, on a short-term basis, in inspiring listeners to throw themselves on the mercy of an angry God? What would you expect would be its long-term impact? Why?

ANSWERS FOR REVIEWING THE SELECTION (CONT.)

8. The speaker takes his listeners back to the previous night and brings them forward in small increments, telling them that at each of those points they could have been cast into hell by God. That Edwards's progression leads to the listeners' positions sitting in church is terrifying because it implies that the listeners could be cast into hell at this very moment. The incremental effect heaps more and more fear and apprehension on the listener and adds to the power of the speaker's words.

SYNTHESIZING

Responses will vary. Possible responses are given.

9. Students may say that the sinner being held over the pit of hell by the gossamer thread of a spider is most memorable. It is vividly described, it is reiterated twice, and the apprehension attached to it lends it even greater power as an image.

10. The sermon might be influential on a short-term basis

(cont.)

Understanding Literature (Questions for Discussion)

1. **Effect.** The **effect** of a literary work is the general impression or emotional impact that it achieves. Describe the effect of this sermon.

2. **Emphasis. Emphasis** is the importance placed on an element in a literary work. Repetition and elaboration are two of the techniques used to produce emphasis. Identify a paragraph in which Edwards uses both techniques to emphasize an important concept. State the concept being emphasized. Then identify the repeated words or phrases, and list some additions or changes that elaborate on the original statement.

Responding in Writing

Comparison and Contrast. Read the following speech from William Shakespeare's play *The Merchant of Venice.* Write a brief essay comparing and contrasting the view of God presented in this speech with that presented in Edwards's sermon.

> PORTIA: The quality of mercy is not strain'd,
> It droppeth as the gentle rain from heaven
> Upon the place beneath. It is twice blessed:
> It blesseth him that gives and him that takes.
> 'Tis mightiest in the mightiest, it becomes
> The throned monarch better than his crown.
> His scepter shows the force of temporal power,
> The attribute to awe and majesty,
> Wherein doth sit the dread and fear of kings;
> But mercy is above this sceptered sway,
> It is enthroned in the hearts of kings,
> It is an attribute to God himself;
> And earthly power doth then show likest God's
> When mercy seasons justice.
>
> —act IV, scene i, *The Merchant of Venice*

Answers for Reviewing the Selection (cont.)

by instilling fear. For some people the effect of fear would continue on a long-term basis. Others might begin to doubt after some time passed and the listeners began to feel comfortable again, forgetting Edwards's message about the tenuousness of this comfort.

Answers for Understanding Literature

► See the evaluation forms for discussion, active listening, and oral communication, *Assessment Portfolio,* 7.11–7.14.

Responses will vary. Possible responses are given.

1. Effect. The effect of the sermon is fear because Edwards convincingly portrays humans as bad, lowly creatures who only sin and do evil. They are not fit to live on the Earth and it is only the hand of God that keeps them from being rejected into hell.

2. Emphasis. In paragraph 4, Edwards uses both repetition and elaboration to emphasize that it is only the hand of God that holds his listeners out of hell. He elaborates on the ideas that the listener is a loathsome spider that God hates to look upon and that the listener deserves to be tossed into the flames. The idea that God's hand holds you up is repeated in this paragraph. Edwards's litany of times during which the listener was held out of the fiery depths of hell by God emphasizes that the listener is only tenuously avoiding that fate.

Analytic Scales for Responding in Writing

Assign a score from 1 to 25 for each grading criterion below. (For more detailed evaluation, see the evaluation forms for writing, revising, and proofreading, *Assessment Portfolio,* 7.1–7.10.)

Comparison and Contrast

- **Content/Unity.** The essay offers both similarities and differences between the view of God in the speech from *The Merchant of Venice* and in the selection from "Sinners in the Hands of an Angry God."
- **Organization/Coherence.** The essay is organized in a logical manner, such as comparison-and-contrast order.
- **Language/Style.** The essay employs vivid and precise nouns, verbs, and modifiers.
- **Conventions.** The essay avoids errors in spelling, grammar, usage, mechanics, and manuscript form.

ANSWERS FOR LANGUAGE LAB

1. Jonathan Edwards, spokesperson, Puritanism
2. concept, omnipotence, God, unworthiness, humans
3. power, congregations, emotion
4. years, words, era, belief, Awakening
5. inability, downfall

▶Additional practice is provided in the *Essential Skills Practice Book: Language,* 2.4.

ANSWERS FOR SPEAKING AND LISTENING SKILLS

Responses will vary. Possible responses are provided.

The tone of Edwards's work suggests anger and perhaps that Edwards might glare, pound his fist on a table or shake it at the congregation, or that he might point accusingly at different individuals throughout the sermon. It is reported, however, that Edwards spoke with calm dignity, so his gestures and facial features may have been more subtle.

▶Additional practice is provided in the *Essential Skills Practice Book: Speaking and Listening,* 3.1.

PROJECT NOTES

▶See the worksheets and evaluation forms for projects, *Assessment Portfolio,* 7.20–7.23.

Exploring the Protestant Reformation and the Puritan Movement.

Students should work in groups to research one of the religious leaders. Students should discuss their findings among their groups before discussing each religious leader's goals and beliefs as a class. After they role play discussions, students can discuss what they learned about all four leaders and their views.

Language Lab

Concrete and Abstract Nouns. Read the Language Arts Survey, 2.4, "Concrete and Abstra Nouns." On a separate sheet of paper, write each of the nouns in these sentences. Underlir the concrete nouns once. Underline the abstract ones twice.

1. Jonathan Edwards was the last great spokesperson for Puritanism.
2. His concept of the omnipotence of God and the unworthiness of humans was uncompromising.
3. He wrote and spoke with such power that congregations reacted with barely controllable emotion.
4. For years, his words inspired an era of belief called "The Great Awakening."
5. Eventually, however, his inability to compromise ended in his downfall.

Speaking and Listening Skills

A Communication Model. Read the Language Arts Survey, 3.1, "A Communication Model. What are some of the nonverbal signs that a speaker such as Edwards might employ delivering a sermon? Describe these signs.

PROJECT

Exploring the Protestant Reformation and the Puritan Movement. In small groups, d library research on the life and work of Martin Luther, John Calvin, and John Knox. On person from each group might represent Luther, Calvin, Knox, and Edwards in a discussio of their religious goals.

"Upon the Burning of Our House" by Anne Bradstreet

In silent night when rest I took
For sorrow near I did not look
I wakened was with thund'ring noise
And piteous shrieks of dreadful voice.
5 That fearful sound of "Fire!" and "Fire!"
Let no man know is my desire.
I, starting up, the light did spy,
And to my God my heart did cry
To strengthen me in my distress
10 And not to leave me succorless.[1]
Then, coming out, beheld a space
The flame consume my dwelling place.
And when I could no longer look,
I blest His name that gave and took,
15 That laid my goods now in the dust.
Yea, so it was, and so 'twas just.
It was His own, it was not mine,
Far be it that I should repine;[2]
He might of all justly bereft
20 But yet sufficient for us left.
When by the ruins oft I past
My sorrowing eyes aside did cast,
And here and there the places spy
Where oft I sat and long did lie:
25 Here stood that trunk, and there that chest,
There lay that store I counted best.
My pleasant things in ashes lie,
And them behold no more shall I.
Under thy roof no guest shall sit,
30 Nor at thy table eat a bit.
No pleasant tale shall e'er be told,
Nor things recounted done of old.
No candle e'er shall shine in thee,
Nor bridegroom's voice e'er heard shall be.
35 In silence ever shall thou lie,
Adieu,[3] Adieu, all's vanity.
Then straight I 'gin my heart to chide,[4]
And did thy wealth on earth abide?[5]
Didst fix thy hope on mold'ring dust?
40 The arm of flesh didst make thy trust?
Raise up thy thoughts above the sky
That dunghill mists away may fly.
Thou hast an house on high erect,
Framed by that mighty Architect,
45 With glory richly furnished,
Stands permanent though this be fled.
It's purchased and paid for too
By Him who hath enough to do.
A price so vast as is unknown
50 Yet by His gift is made thine own;
There's wealth enough, I need no more,
Farewell, my pelf,[6] farewell my store.
The world no longer let me love,
My hope and treasure lies above.

1. **succorless.** Helpless
2. **repine.** Complain; worry
3. **adieu.** Farewell (French)
4. **chide.** Scold
5. **abide.** Stay; remain
6. **pelf.** Money or wealth regarded with contempt

"Huswifery"[7] by Edward Taylor

Make me, O Lord, Thy Spinning Wheel complete.
Thy Holy Word my Distaff[8] make for me.
Make mine Affections Thy Swift Flyers[9] neat
And make my Soul thy holy Spool[10] to be.
5 My conversation make to be Thy Reel[11]
And reel the yarn thereon spun of Thy Wheel.

Make me Thy Loom then, knit therein this Twine:
And make Thy Holy Spirit, Lord, wind quills:
Then weave the Web Thyself. The yarn is fine.
10 Thine Ordinances make my Fulling Mills.[12]
Then dye the same in Heavenly Colors Choice,
All pinked[13] with Varnished Flowers of Paradise.

Then clothe therewith mine Understanding, Will,
Affections, Judgment, Conscience, Memory,
15 My Words, and Actions, that their shine may fill
My ways with glory and Thee glorify.
Then mine apparel shall display before Ye
That I am Clothed in Holy robes for glory.

7. **Huswifery.** Housekeeping, here specifically weaving
8. **Distaff.** Tool that holds the raw wool
9. **Flyers.** Parts that regulate the spinning
10. **Spool.** Part on which yarn is wound
11. **Reel.** Part that takes up the finished thread
12. **Fulling Mills.** Where cloth is beaten and cleansed
13. **pinked.** Adorned

"Upon the Burning of Our House

About the Author. A biography of **Anne Bradstreet** appears on page 144.

About the Selection. The selection is written about the actual burning of the Bradstreet home in 1666. The full title of the selection is "Here Follows Some Verses upon the Burning of Our House July 10th, 1666. Copied out of a Loose Paper."

"Huswifery"

About the Author. Edward Taylor (1642–1729) was born in England but emigrated to New England at age twenty-six rather than sign a loyalty oath to the Church of England. An ardent Puritan, Taylor studied theology at Harvard College and later became minister at the then-remote town of Westfield, Massachusetts. Taylor's religious poetry was not discovered until the twentieth century.

About the Selection. The selection is an extended metaphor in which the creations of God are compared to weaving. Students might compare this work with "Song of the Sky Loom" on page 83.

FROM *THE WONDERS OF THE INVISIBLE WORLD*

About the Author. Cotton Mather (1663–1728) came from a prominent New England family. He studied theology at Harvard College and succeeded his father, Increase Mather, as pastor of a Boston church. He is renowned as a historian of the Puritan period.

About the Selection. Mather wrote the selection at the request of the judges of Salem's witch trials, describing the case against the accused.

from *The Wonders of the Invisible World*
by Cotton Mather

But I shall no longer detain my reader from his expected entertainment, in a brief account of the trials which have passed upon some of the malefactors[1] lately executed at Salem, for the witchcrafts whereof they stood convicted. For my own part, I was not present at any of them; nor ever had I any personal prejudice at the persons thus brought upon the stage; much less at the surviving relations of those persons, with and for whom I would be as hearty a mourner as any man living in the world: The Lord comfort them! But having received a command[2] so to do, I can do no other than shortly relate the chief matters of fact, which occurred in the trials of some that were executed, in an abridgment collected out of the court papers on this occasion put into my hands. You are to take the truth, just as it was; and the truth will hurt no good man. There might have been more of these, if my book would not thereby have swollen too big; and if some other worthy hands did not perhaps intend something further in these collections; for which cause I have only singled out four or five, which may serve to illustrate the way of dealing, wherein witchcrafts use to be concerned; and I report matters not as an advocate, but as an historian.

The Trial of Martha Carrier

AT THE COURT OF OYER AND TERMINER,[3] HELD BY ADJOURNMENT AT SALEM, AUGUST 2, 1692.

I. Martha Carrier was indicted for the bewitching certain persons, according to the form usual in such cases, pleading not guilty to her indictment; there were first brought in a considerable number of the bewitched persons who not only made the court sensible[4] of an horrid witchcraft committed upon them, but also deposed that it was Martha Carrier, or her shape, that grievously tormented them, by biting, pricking, pinching and choking of them. It was further deposed that while this Carrier was on her examination before the magistrates, the poor people were so tortured that every one expected their death upon the very spot, but that upon the binding of Carrier they were eased. Moreover the look of Carrier then laid the afflicted people for dead; and her touch, if her eye at the same time were off them, raised them again: which things were also now seen upon her trial. And it was testified that upon the mention of some having their necks twisted almost round, by the shape of this Carrier, she replied, "It's no matter though their necks had been twisted quite off."

II. Before the trial of this prisoner, several of her own children had frankly and fully confessed not only that they were witches themselves, but that this their mother had made them so. This confession they made with great shows of repentance, and with much demonstration of truth. They related place, time, occasion; they gave an account of journeys, meetings and mischiefs by them performed, and were very credible in what they said. Nevertheless, this evidence was not produced against the prisoner at the bar,[5] inasmuch as there was other evidence enough to proceed upon.

III. Benjamin Abbot gave his testimony that last March was a twelvemonth, this Carrier was very angry with him, upon laying out some land near her husband's: her expressions in this anger were that she would stick as close to Abbot as the bark stuck to the tree; and that he should repent of it afore seven years came to an end, so as Doctor Prescot should never cure him. These words were heard by others besides Abbot himself; who also heard her say, she would hold his nose as close to the grindstone as ever it was held since his name was Abbot. Presently after this, he was taken with a swelling in his foot, and then with a pain in his side, and exceedingly tormented. It bred into a sore, which was lanced[6] by Doctor Prescot, and several gallons of corruption[7] ran out of it. For six weeks it continued very bad, and then another sore bred in the groin, which was also lanced by Doctor Prescot. Another sore then bred in his groin which was likewise cut, and put him to very great misery: he was brought unto death's door, and so remained until Carrier was taken, and carried away by the constable from which very day he began to mend, and so grew better every day, and is well ever since.

Sarah Abbot also, his wife, testified that her husband was not only all this while afflicted in his body, but also that strange, extraordinary and unaccountable calamities befell his cattle; their death being such as they could guess at no natural reason for.

IV. Allin Toothaker testified that Richard, the son of Martha Carrier, having some difference with him, pulled him down by the hair of the head. When he rose again he was going to strike at Richard Carrier but fell down flat on his back to the ground and had not power to stir hand or foot, until he told Carrier he yielded; and then he saw the shape of Martha Carrier go off his breast.

This Toothaker had received a wound in the wars; and he now testified that Martha Carrier told him he should

1. **malefactors.** Wrongdoers
2. **command.** Request by the judges to explain the sentencing of those convicted in the Salem witch trials
3. **of oyer and terminer.** To hear and determine
4. **sensible.** Aware
5. **bar.** Court
6. **lanced.** Cut open
7. **corruption.** Infected fluid

never be cured. Just afore the apprehending of Carrier, he could thrust a knitting needle into his wound four inches deep; but presently after her being seized, he was thoroughly healed.

He further testified that when Carrier and he some times were at variance she would clap her hands at him, and say he should get nothing by it; whereupon he several times lost his cattle, by strange deaths, whereof no natural causes could be given.

V. John Rogger also testified that upon the threatening words of this malicious Carrier, his cattle would be strangely bewitched; as was more particularly then described.

VI. Samuel Preston testified that about two years ago, having some difference with Martha Carrier, he lost a cow in a strange, preternatural,[1] unusual manner; and about a month after this, the said Carrier, having again some difference with him she told him he had lately lost a cow, and it should not be long before he lost another; which accordingly came to pass, for he had a thriving and well-kept cow, which without any known cause quickly fell down and died.

VII. Phebe Chandler testified that about a fortnight before the apprehension of Martha Carrier, on a Lordsday, while the Psalm was singing in the Church this Carrier then took her by the shoulder and shaking her, asked her, where she lived: she made her no answer, although as Carrier, who lived next door to her father's house, could not in reason but know who she was. Quickly after this, as she was at several times crossing the fields, she heard a voice, that she took to be Martha Carrier's, and it seemed as if it was over her head. The voice told her she should within two or three days be poisoned. Accordingly, within such a little time, one half of her right hand became greatly swollen and very painful; as also part of her face: whereof she can give no account how it came. It continued very bad for some days; and several times since she has had a great pain in her breast; and been so seized on her legs that she has hardly been able to go. She added that lately, going well to the house of God, Richard, the son of Martha Carrier, looked very earnestly upon her, and immediately her hand, which had formerly been poisoned, as is abovesaid, began to pain her greatly, and she had a strange burning at her stomach; but was then struck deaf, so that she could not hear any of the prayer, or singing, till the two or three last words of the Psalm.

VIII. One Foster, who confessed her own share in the witchcraft for which the prisoner stood indicted, affirmed that she had seen the prisoner at some of their witch-meetings, and that it was this Carrier, who persuaded her to be a witch. She confessed that the devil carried them on a pole to a witch-meeting; but the pole broke, and she hanging about Carrier's neck, they both fell down, and she then received an hurt by the fall, whereof she was not at this very time recovered.

IX. One Lacy, who likewise confessed her share in this witchcraft, now testified, that she and the prisoner were once bodily present at a witch-meeting in Salem Village; and that she knew the prisoner to be a witch, and to have been at a diabolical sacrament, and that the prisoner was the undoing of her and her children by enticing them into the snare of the devil.

X. Another Lacy, who also confessed her share in this witchcraft, now testified, that the prisoner was at the witch-meeting, in Salem Village, where they had bread and wine administered unto them.

XI. In the time of this prisoner's trial, one Susanna Sheldon in open court had her hands unaccountably tied together with a wheel-band so fast that without cutting, it could not be loosed: it was done by a specter; and the sufferer affirmed it was the prisoner's.

Memorandum. This rampant hag, Martha Carrier, was the person of whom the confessions of the witches, and of her own children among the rest, agreed that the devil had promised her she should be Queen of Hebrews.

1. **preternatural.** Abnormal

Additional Questions and Activities

Encourage students to discuss how they feel about the "evidence" presented at this trial. Would this evidence be admissible today? Why, or why not?

Answers. Students might say that the "evidence" seems like over-imaginative nonsense. This evidence would not be admissible today because most of it is hearsay and "spectral" evidence.

VOCABULARY DEVELOPMENT EXERCISES

► Give students the following exercise.

For each word in the vocabulary list on page 128, write its part of speech and a brief definition. Then write a different form of the word, its part of speech, and a brief definition.

Example.

gluttony—n., act of eating too much

glutton—n., person who greedily eats too much

ADDITIONAL RESOURCES

ASSESSMENT PORTFOLIO

- Vocabulary Worksheet, 4.2.17
- Study Guide: Unit 2 Test, 4.2.18
- Unit 2 Test, 4.2.19

ESSENTIAL SKILLS PRACTICE BOOKS

Writing

- Choosing and Analyzing an Audience, 1.7
- Sensory Detail Charts, 1.18
- Venn Diagrams, 1.24

Language

- Achieving Parallelism, 2.57
- Action Verbs, 2.12
- Adding Appositives or Appositive Phrases, 2.48
- Auxiliary Verbs, 2.14
- Concrete and Abstract Nouns, 2.4
- Formal and Informal English, 2.147
- Interjections, 2.29
- Inverting Sentences, 2.64
- Linking Verbs, 2.13
- Organizations and Institutions, 2.118
- Proofreading for Spelling Errors, 2.134
- Register, 2.148
- Sacred Beings and Writings, 2.125
- Simple Sentences, 2.38
- Using Precise Nouns, 2.32
- Using the Active Voice, 2.56
- Verbals: Gerunds, 2.17
- Verbals: Participles, 2.16

Speaking and Listening

- Active Listening, 3.4
- A Communication Model, 3.1

Study and Research

- Classifying, 4.7
- Formal Note-taking, 4.32
- Making Hypotheses, 4.13
- Memorizing, 4.4

UNIT REVIEW

Origins of the American Tradition

VOCABULARY FROM THE SELECTIONS

abhor, 120
ascribe, 120
avail, 119
buffet, 89
burnish, 92
calamity, 105
canonize, 95
commendation, 105
conceit, 96
confederacy, 77
conjuration, 97
constitution, 119
consultation, 103
contrivance, 119
deliberation, 104
depopulate, 89
disposition, 77
diversity, 98
doleful, 99
ensue, 96
entreaty, 98
estimation, 78
extremity, 96
feign, 106
flourish, 90
furnish, 78
gluttony, 95
gulf, 119
incense, 121
induce, 121
inevitable, 103
infest, 91
inhuman, 90
light, 102
loath, 103
loathsome, 120
manifold, 115
mollify, 99
mutinous, 104
oppression, 89
ordinance, 105
persevere, 115
pilfer, 95
presumption, 96
profane, 102
prosperous, 102
provoke, 120
recompense, 106, 115
reprove, 102
ruffian, 90
sovereign, 119
subjection, 89
subserve, 120
suffice, 89
sundry, 104
vestige, 90

LITERARY TERMS

aim, 112
allusion, 112
chronological order, 108
couplet, 112
effect, 123
emphasis, 123
hyperbole, 117
irony, 108
metaphor, 85
mood, 93
myth, 85
oxymoron, 117
parallelism, 85
point of view, 93
sight rhyme, 117
symbol, 80
tone, 86

SYNTHESIS: QUESTIONS FOR WRITING, RESEARCH, OR DISCUSSION

GENRE STUDIES

1. **Poetry.** Bradstreet's poem "To My Dear and Loving Husband" is built on couplets. A couplet is a pair of rhyming lines expressing a complete thought. Each couplet expands her notion of love. Examine each couplet and give its central thought.

THEMATIC STUDIES

2. **Order, Harmony, and Judgment.** Edwards, the Tewa, and the framers of the Iroquois Constitution use extended metaphors to express their themes. What theme does each selection convey? How does the metaphor in each fit the theme? Refer to the definition of *extended metaphor* in the Handbook of Literary Terms.

HISTORICAL/BIOGRAPHICAL STUDIES

3. **Political Thought and Education.** *The New England Primer* was a vehicle for evolving political thought. What view of the English king is evident in the selection printed in this text? Research subsequent editions of the *Primer* and see how this view changed as the colonists headed toward revolution.

4. **Settlers' Goals.** Compare the goals of the settlers of Virginia with the goals of the Puritan settlers of Massachusetts. Refer to the introduction to this unit and to the writings of Smith, Bradford, and Edwards.

▶ These prompts are suitable as topics for research papers. Refer to the Language Arts Survey, 4.20–4.34, "Research Skills." (To evaluate research papers, see the evaluation forms for writing, revising, and proofreading, in the *Assessment Portfolio,* 7.1–7.10.)

▶ These prompts can be adapted for use as topics for oral reports or debates. To evaluate these projects, see the evaluation forms in the *Assessment Portfolio,* 7.17–7.19.

LANGUAGE LAB THE SENTENCE

A **sentence** contains a subject and a verb and expresses a complete idea. A group of words that does not contain both a subject and a verb and that does not express a complete idea is a **sentence fragment.**

LANGUAGE ARTS SURVEY

For additional help, see the Language Arts Survey, 2.61.

CORRECTING SENTENCE FRAGMENTS
SENTENCE FRAGMENT: Among friends. *(does not express a complete idea)* COMPLETE SENTENCE: Anne Bradstreet often distributed her work among friends.
SENTENCE FRAGMENT: Wrote poetry as a child. *(does not contain a subject)* COMPLETE SENTENCE: Bradstreet wrote poetry as a child.
SENTENCE FRAGMENT: In 1650, a collection of Bradstreet's poetry. *(does not contain a verb)* COMPLETE SENTENCE: In 1650, a collection of Bradstreet's poetry was published.

When two sentences are run together without proper punctuation or conjunctions, they are called a **run-on.** The following chart shows ways to correct run-ons.

LANGUAGE ARTS SURVEY

For additional help, see the Language Arts Survey, 2.62.

CORRECTING RUN-ONS	
RUN-ON:	The Five Nations of the Iroquois Confederation agreed to keep peace among themselves, they made war on enemy nations.
CORRECTED USING A COMMA AND A COORDINATING CONJUNCTION:	The Five Nations of the Iroquois Confederation agreed to keep peace among themselves, but they made war on enemy nations.
CORRECTED BY TURNING ONE SENTENCE INTO A SUBORDINATE CLAUSE:	Although the Five Nations of the Iroquois Confederation agreed to keep peace among themselves, they made war on enemy nations.
CORRECTED BY ADDING A SEMICOLON AND A CONJUNCTIVE ADVERB:	The Five Nations of the Iroquois Confederation agreed to keep peace among themselves; however, they made war on enemy nations.

To add variety, interest, and clarity to your writing, combine sentences by adding words, phrases, and clauses. Use the methods described in the following chart.

Exercise Correcting Fragments and Run-ons

Rewrite the following paragraph, correcting all sentence fragments and run-ons.

EXAMPLE: Many native peoples lost their lands to Europeans, the nations of the Iroquois Confederation kept their territory for almost two hundred years.

While many native peoples lost their lands to Europeans, the nations of the Iroquois Confederation kept their territory for almost two hundred years.

Around 1570, the Mohawk, Oneida, Onondaga, Cayuga, and Seneca peoples. Formed the Iroquois Confederation, or Five Nations. Before this time, the five groups often had warred against each other, their agreement to keep peace among themselves strengthened them. Against their enemies who included other Native Americans and, later, Europeans. Their Algonquian-speaking enemies called them Iroquois, or "real adders," the Iroquois called themselves We Who Are of the Extended Lodge. Representatives from each nation formed a governing council, the women of the respective groups elected men to serve on the council. In 1715, the Tuscarora joined the confederation. Which was then known as the Six Nations.

LANGUAGE ARTS SURVEY

For additional help, see the Language Arts Survey, 2.61–2.62.

ANSWERS FOR LANGUAGE LAB

Exercise

Responses will vary. Possible responses are given.

Around 1570, the Mohawk, Oneida, Onondaga, Cayuga, and Seneca peoples formed the Iroquois Confederation, or Five Nations. Before this time, the five groups often had warred against each other, so their agreement to keep peace among themselves strengthened them against their enemies, who included other Native Americans and, later, Europeans. Their Algonquian-speaking enemies called them Iroquois, or "real adders"; the Iroquois, however, called themselves We Who Are of the Extended Lodge. Representatives from each nation, elected by the women of the respective groups, formed a governing council. In 1715, the Tuscarora joined the confederation, which was then known as the Six Nations.

UNIT SKILLS OUTLINE

Literary Skills and Concepts

- Age of Reason, 137
- Aim, 183
- Alliteration, 177
- Allusion, 169
- Aphorism, 145, 155
- Argumentation, 164
- Assonance, 164
- Autobiography, 145
- Chiasmus, 150
- Enlightenment, 137, 157
- Heroic Couplet, 169
- Metaphor, 155
- Neoclassicism, 150
- Parallelism, 157, 177
- Persona, 144
- Poetry, 187
- Proverb, 145
- Rhetorical Question, 155, 156, 164
- Stereotype, 150
- Style, 144

Writing Skills and Concepts

- Abstract, 170
- Agenda, 150
- Captions, 170
- Cartoon, 150
- Credo, 177
- Letter, 183
- Memoranda, 170
- Minutes, 157
- Nomination Speech, 157
- Pamphlet, 151
- Petition, 157

Grammar, Usage, and Mechanics Skills and Concepts

- Agreement of Pronouns and Antecedents, 164
- Agreement of Subject and Verb, 188
- Combining Sentences Using Clauses, 180
- Common and Proper Nouns, 170
- Coordinating Conjunctions, 153
- Functions of Sentences, 158
- Gerunds, 141, 146
- Infinitives, 166
- Irregular Verbs I, 188
- Irregular Verbs II, 188
- Participles, 146
- Parts of Speech, 151
- Split Infinitives, 188
- Verb Tense, 188

Other Language Arts Skills and Concepts

- Analyzing, 172
- Comparing and Contrasting, 147, 160
- Freewriting, 141
- Paraphrasing and Summarizing, 183
- Public Speaking, 158
- Reading Actively, 172
- Synonym and Antonym Questions, 186
- Understanding Propaganda Techniques, 164

UNIT 3 THE AMERICAN REVOLUTION (1750–1800)

Midnight Ride of Paul Revere. *Grant Wood, 1931. The Metropolitan Museum of Art. Arthur Hoppock Hearn Fund, 1950. (50.117)*

GOALS/OBJECTIVES

Studying this unit will enable students to

- understand and appreciate the principles that shaped the American Revolution, including the ideas of natural and inalienable rights, representative government, and government by consent of the governed
- become familiar with major writings by the most prominent American figures of the Revolutionary War Era
- understand that the ideas that influenced the American Revolution derived from an Enlightenment Era belief in the perfectibility of the social and political orders

©1950 by the Metropolitan Museum of Art
ate of Grant Wood/Licensed by VAGA, NY

To secure these rights, governments are instituted among men, deriving their just powers from the consent of the governed.

—Thomas Jefferson
The Declaration of Independence

ART NOTE

Grant Wood (1892–1942) was born near Anamosa, Iowa, and lived for most of his life in that state. His early work was in an Impressionist style. However, after traveling to Germany and becoming acquainted with the works of the Old Masters, he abandoned Impressionism in favor of the stylized realism with which he is generally associated today. His best-known paintings are *American Gothic* (1930), a portrait of two midwestern farm people, and *Daughters of Revolution* (1932). Both works combine a satirical eye with sympathy toward their subjects. Known primarily as a midwestern regionalist, Wood nonetheless did paint works on other subjects, including his well-known *Midnight Ride of Paul Revere* (1931). This painting is interesting for its high degree of stylization and for its *chiarascuro*, or contrast between darkness and light, which heightens the drama of the depicted ride.

CONNECTIONS ACROSS THE CURRICULUM

ARTS AND HUMANITIES
- Analyzing the Bill of Rights, 177

SOCIAL STUDIES
- Analyzing the Bill of Rights, 177
- Revision of Declaration of Independence, 173
- Royal Television Commercial, 158

APPLIED ARTS AND SCIENCES
- Multimedia Show, 170
- Royal Television Commercial, 158

TEACHING THE MULTIPLE INTELLIGENCES

KINESTHETIC
- Pre-Revolutionary Twenty Questions, 158

Historical Note

The Quakers. *Quaker* is the common name given to members of the Christian church known as the Society of Friends or Friends Church. This church, founded by George Fox, stresses the role of the Holy Spirit in people's lives, favors simplicity in worship, and conducts its affairs without ordained ministers. The name Quaker, like the name Puritan, was originally used in derision because the intensity of the religious zeal of members of the Society of Friends led them to quake, or tremble, at the contemplation of God. Quakers were considered a heretical group by colonial Puritans.

THEMATIC CURRENTS

Use the following selections to explore these themes with your students.

Independence

- from *The Autobiography of Benjamin Franklin,* 140
- Speech in the Virginia Convention, 152
- from *Crisis, No. 1,* 159
- Declaration of Independence, 171

Diversity

- "Remarks Concerning the Natives of North America," 147
- "To S. M., a Young African Painter, on Seeing His Works," 165
- Letter to John Adams, May 7, 1776, 179

Self-Improvement, Moral Aspiration

- from *The Autobiography of Benjamin Franklin,* 140
- "To S. M., a Young African Painter, on Seeing His Works," 165
- Declaration of Independence, 171

Portrait of Benjamin Franklin. *Robert Feke,* circa *1746. Harvard University, Portrait Collection. Bequest of Dr. John Collins Warren, 1856*

The Emergence of American Diversity

During the Colonial Period, New England remained relatively homogenous, populated primarily by Puritans of British descent. However, the Mid-Atlantic and the South saw rapid growth and an influx of different peoples, religions, and ways of life. Indeed, by the time of the **American Revolution,** the colonies had achieved a great deal of the social diversity that we now think of as distinctively American.

In the colony of Pennsylvania, **Quakers** of English and Welsh descent established a community based on equality for all citizens and tolerance of religious diversity, for the Quakers believed people to have within them a divine spark that could be demonstrated through love for "all in God's world." In the 1680s, the Quakers became the first group in America to advocate the abolition of slavery, and, unlike the Puritans, they allowed women a voice in religious affairs. As a result of tolerant Quaker attitudes, Pennsylvania by the 1750s had attracted people from a wide variety of ethnic and religious groups, including Native Americans and free persons of African descent. It had also become a center for progressive thinking. **Benjamin Franklin** himself, though he had earlier mocked Quaker meetings in his writings, adopted the Quaker rhetoric of equality and went on to play important roles in the American Revolution, which included helping to establish the terms of the **Treaty of Paris** that ended the war.

In other parts of the Mid-Atlantic such as New York, New Jersey, and Delaware, which saw new arrivals of Jewish, German, and Irish immigrants, the communal social and economic relations practiced by the Puritans and the Quakers were supplanted by an emerging **Capitalist** ethic of individual profit-making. One result was that in these places land came to be viewed more as a commodity than as part of a homestead or as a source of a community's sustenance. Many middle-sized farms emerged on which owners used wage-laborers, indentured servants, and slaves.

Literary Events

► = American Events

1751. Denis Diderot's *Encyclopedie* published

►1752. George Berkeley's *On the Prospect of Planting Arts and Learning in America* published

1755. Samuel Johnson's *A Dictionary of the English Language* published

►1755. Benjamin Franklin's "Observations Concerning the Increase of Mankind" published

1759. Voltaire's *Candide* published

1760. Laurence Sterne's *The Life and Opinions of Tristram Shandy* published

1750 **1755** **1760**

Historical Events

1750. British pass the Iron Act, prohibiting colonies from producing iron products

►1751. Benjamin Franklin experiments with electricity

►1752. Philadelphia's Liberty Bell is cast

►1754. The French and Indian War begins

1759. British win decisive victory over French outside Quebec City

1760. George III succeeds George II

By the mid-eighteenth century the economies of the Southern colonies were centered primarily on commercial agriculture, particularly on the cultivation of cotton and tobacco. The heavy reliance of commercial **plantations** on slave labor had a number of social consequences of concern during and after the revolutionary period, not the least of which was that in many areas (and in some entire states such as South Carolina), the majority of the population consisted of enslaved African Americans.

The overall sense of dynamism and opportunity that the colonies, rural and urban, were coming to represent can perhaps be seen best in the growth of the population itself. In 1650, the total population of the colonies was almost 60,000; by the 1790s, it was 3,500,000. Infant mortality rates were down, fertility rates were up, and many more children were surviving into adulthood. The young country had a young populace; in 1776, the year of independence from Britain, roughly half of the people were twenty-one or younger. Benjamin Franklin and others extolled abroad the virtues of America's healthy environment, as well as the many opportunities that the colonies offered for economic advancement through hard work. Europeans, increasingly non-English ones, heeded the call, often fleeing economic hardship and overcrowding at home.

Rebellion Against Great Britain

The diverse and growing population of the colonies, bound to provide supplies and soldiers for English wars and to help pay for those wars afterward, found subservience to distant England increasingly irksome. In 1763, after the **French and Indian War**, England imposed, through the Stamp Act, the first in a series of heavy taxes that would prove unpopular in the colonies and serve as a focal point of colonial resentment. The colonists began boycotting British goods, leading the British to repeal the Stamp Act. Then, in March 1770, British soldiers and colonial citizens skirmished in Boston, resulting in the deaths of five colonists. Among the colonists killed in this so-called **Boston Massacre** was **Crispus Attucks**, the first African American to die in the Revolutionary cause. In 1773, when England imposed a new tax on tea, colonial patriots held what is known as the **Boston Tea Party**, dumping tea from British ships into Boston Harbor. The British

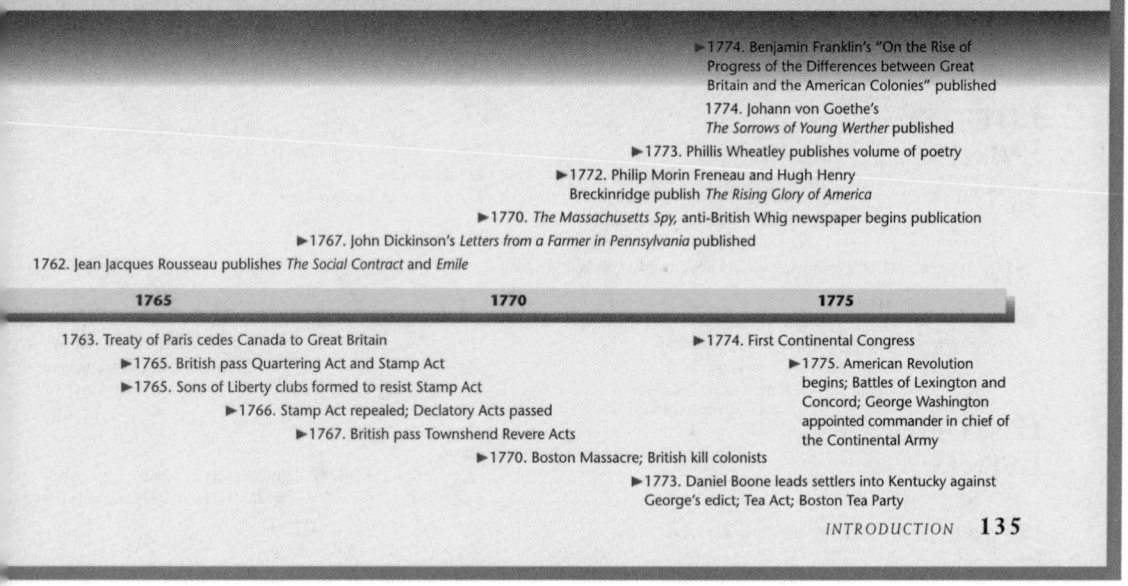

Historical Note

The British Argument for Taxation. The French and Indian War, fought to solidify English colonial interests in North America, was extremely costly to the British government, and after the war, Britain provided large sums to Massachusetts in compensation for its wartime expenditures. The British therefore felt that they had a right to levy taxes on the colonies to recover some of these losses. However, the colonists felt, with justification, that taxation should be accompanied by equal representation in the British Parliament. "No Taxation without Representation" became a rallying cry of the American Revolutionaries.

Historical Note

The Boston Tea Party. In 1773, Britain passed the Tea Act, which gave the East India Company a monopoly on the sale of tea in the colonies. This tea would be taxed by the British government under an existing tax law that was largely ignored by colonial purchasers and sellers of illegal, smuggled tea. On December 16, 1773, a group of men from Boston, disguised as Mohawks, climbed aboard British ships in Boston Harbor and dumped tea worth £18,000 into the water. In response, Britain closed the port of Boston and reorganized the government of Massachusetts, doing away with the town meetings that fomented rebellion. Although the Boston Tea Party was controversial even in the colonies, it ultimately served its radical purpose, for it led Britain to repressive measures that further increased colonial feeling that their interests were not represented by the British government.

LITERARY CURRENTS

Use the following selections to explore these techniques with your students.

The Enlightenment
- from *The Autobiography of Benjamin Franklin,* 140
- Declaration of Independence, 171

The Essay
- "Remarks Concerning the Natives of North America," 147
- Speech in the Virginia Convention, 152
- from *Crisis, No. 1,* 159

Argumentation, Persuasion
- Speech in the Virginia Convention, 152
- from *Crisis, No. 1,* 159
- Declaration of Independence, 171
- Letter to John Adams, May 7, 1776, 179

QUOTABLES

"We must all hang together, or assuredly we shall all hang separately."

—Benjamin Franklin on the Signing of the Declaration of Independence

George Washington

Parliament responded with severe restrictions on the self-government of Massachusetts, known as the **Intolerable Acts.** In counterresponse, representatives from the colonies met in Philadelphia in 1774 for the **First Continental Congress.** There they vented their outrage in letters of protest to King George, asked citizens to boycott British goods, and called for the organization of militia, or armed citizens, to defend against British aggression throughout the colonies.

In April 1775, British General Thomas Gage moved troops toward Concord, Massachusetts, with the aim of capturing rebel arms and leaders, but the rebels had been forewarned, thanks to **Paul Revere, William Dawes,** and **Samuel Prescott.** On Concord Bridge, on the morning of April 19, thirty-five militiamen blocked the path of seven hundred British troops. After a brief standoff, a shot was fired, and the American Revolution had begun. That day, fighting between British troops and colonial militiamen in Concord and Lexington left almost three hundred British soldiers and one hundred colonials dead or wounded.

The **Second Continental Congress,** meeting in Philadelphia in May 1775, organized an army under **General George Washington.** In June, after the **Battle of Bunker Hill,** near Boston, King George officially declared the colonies in rebellion against the crown. Early in 1776, Thomas Paine, recently arrived in America from Great Britain, published his pamphlet ***Common Sense,*** the first work to call for the colonies' independence. In June of that year, acting on resolutions introduced by Richard Henry Lee, a delegate from Virginia, the Continental Congress voted in favor of independence and appointed a committee, which included **Thomas Jefferson,** Benjamin Franklin, and **John Adams,** to draft a **Declaration of Independence.** Jefferson wrote a draft of that declaration which, with some changes, was adopted on July 4, thereafter known in the United States as **Independence Day.**

LITERARY EVENTS

► = American Events

►1776. Declaration of Independence; Thomas Paine publishes *Common Sense* and *Crisis*

1778. Fanny Burney's *Evelina* introduces the novel of manners

1781. L. Immanuel Kant's *Critique of Pure Reason*

1782. J. Hector St. Jean de Crèvecoeur's *Letters from an American Farmer* published

►1783. Noah Webster's *Spelling Book* published

►1787. James Madison and Alexander Hamilton publish *The Federalist Papers*

1780 **1785** **1790**

HISTORICAL EVENTS

►1778. France recognizes America's independence

1779. Spain declares war on Britain

►1781. General Cornwallis of Britain surrenders at Yorktown

►1783. Treaty of Paris recognizes independence of the thirteen colonies

►1787. Constitutional Convention

►1788. United States Constitution ratified

1789. French Revolution

►1789. George Washington becomes the first president

The Philosophical Background of the Revolution

Paul Revere. *John Singleton Copley*

The Declaration of Independence was a bold document, for it declared that "all men are created equal," that people have certain "inalienable rights" that cannot be taken from them, that governments derive their right to rule from the consent of the governed, and that when a government fails to protect the natural rights of its citizens, those citizens have not only a right but a duty to rebel. The theories that informed the Declaration of Independence had their origins in the European **Enlightenment,** or **Age of Reason,** and in European **Romanticism.** Thinkers of the Enlightenment, encouraged by discoveries in the natural sciences such as those made by **Sir Isaac Newton,** believed that through reason people could discover principles that would guarantee social and political harmony. The English philosopher **Thomas Hobbes,** though a monarchist, argued that certain natural rights existed that no individual could turn over to a sovereign. Another English philosopher, **John Locke,** reasoned that to ensure the preservation of their natural rights, a people should balance the power of the sovereign against the power of Parliament and retain the right to rebel against oppression. The French philosopher **Jean-Jacques Rousseau** argued that governments are instituted as a **social contract** made by the people for their mutual benefit. Rousseau was one of the foremost thinkers of the **Romantic Movement,** which began in the eighteenth century and continued into the nineteenth century. Among other goals, this movement championed democratic ideals and the rights of the individual, rights that were to be enshrined in the **Bill of Rights**—the first ten Amendments to the United States Constitution.

1798. Samuel Taylor Coleridge and William Wordsworth publish *Lyrical Ballads;* Thomas Robert Malthus publishes "Essay on the Principles of Population"

►1798. Charles Brockden Brown's *Alcuin: A Dialogue on the Rights of Women* and *Wieland, or the Transformation*

►1793. Joel Barlow's *Advice to the Privileged Orders* published

1792. Mary Wollstonecraft's *Vindication of the Rights of Woman* published

1790 **1795** **1800**

►1791. The Bill of Rights becomes United States law

1793. Reign of Terror begins; Louis XVI and Marie Antoinette guillotined

►1793. Fugitive Slave Act passed

1795. Napoleon Bonaparte named commander of the Armée d'Interieur

►1796. John Adams becomes president, Thomas Jefferson vice president

1799. Napoleon Bonaparte becomes first consul of France; Rosetta Stone

Literary Note

The **Enlightenment**, also known as the **Age of Reason** and as the **Neoclassical Era,** was that period in European and American culture that saw the revival of ideals of art and literature derived from the Greek and Roman classics. These ideals included respect for authority and tradition, austerity, clarity, conservatism, decorum, economy, grace, imitation of the natural order, harmony, moderation, proportion, reason, restraint, self-control, simplicity, tradition, wit, and unity. Neoclassical literature was witty and socially astute but tended toward excessive didacticism and an excessive distrust of invention and imagination. Popular forms of Neoclassical writing included the essay, the epistle, the satire, the parody, poems in rhymed couplets, and the earliest novels. As if in response to Pope's dictum that "The proper study of man is man," Neoclassical writers wrote primarily about social life and social interactions.

The **Romantic Era** followed the Enlightenment and was a reaction against it. **Romanticism** was a literary and artistic movement of the eighteenth and nineteenth centuries that placed value on emotion and imagination over reason, the individual over society, nature and wildness over human works, the country over the town, common people over aristocrats, and freedom over control or authority.

Literary/Historical Note

Rousseau and the Social Contract. Jean-Jacques Rousseau's greatest work, *The Social Contract* (*Du contrat social, ou Principes du droit politique*) begins with the famous words "Man is born free, and he is everywhere in chains." The importance of Rousseau's work lies in his conception of the origins of legitimate government. Rousseau argued that in the natural state there is no government at all. People are born free, but they agree, in what he termed "a social contract," to surrender to government some of their natural freedoms or rights in exchange for protection by that government of other rights. Thus fundamental sovereignty lies not in the hands of a leader or king but rather in the general will of the people. This principle of a government deriving its right to exist from the consent of the governed was to be enshrined in the Preamble to the Declaration of Independence of the American colonies.

Additional Questions and Activities

You may wish to have your students research the following topics related to the history of the American Revolution:

- The Battle of Bunker Hill
- The Battles of Concord and Lexington
- Benedict Arnold
- The Boston Massacre
- The Boston Tea Party
- Crispus Attucks
- George Washington at Valley Forge
- The Intolerable Acts
- John Paul Jones
- The New York–New Jersey Campaign
- Paul Revere's Ride
- The Role of France in the War
- The Role of the Iroquois in the War
- The Surrender of General Burgoyne at Saratoga
- The Surrender of General Cornwallis at Yorktown
- Ticonderoga
- The Trenton-Princeton Campaign

Quotables

"My lords, you cannot conquer America. . . . You may swell every expense and every effort still more extravagantly; pile and accumulate every assistance you can buy or borrow; traffic and barter with every little pitiful German prince that sells and sends his subjects to the shambles [Britain was making use of German mercenary soliders in their war with the colonies]; your efforts are forever vain and impotent—doubly so from this mercenary aid on which you rely, for it irritates, to an incurable resentment, the minds of your enemies. . . . If I were an American, as I am an Englishman, while a foreign troop was landed in my country, I never would lay down my arms,—never!—never!—never!"

—The Earl of Chatham, addressing the British Parliament on November 18, 1777

Phillis Wheatley

The New Nation

In 1777, Congress adopted the **Articles of Confederation,** which created a weak central government and left most power to the former colonies, now sovereign states. In 1781, the British, under General George Cornwallis, suffered a decisive defeat at Yorktown, Virginia, effectively ending the war, despite sporadic fighting over the next one and a half years. In 1783, the American Revolution officially ended with the signing of the Treaty of Paris, in which Great Britain gave up its claims on the colonies. In 1787, delegates in Philadelphia adopted a new Constitution, beginning with these stirring words:

> We, the people of the United States, in order to form a more perfect Union, establish justice, insure domestic tranquility, provide for the common defense, promote the general welfare, and secure the blessings of liberty to ourselves and our posterity do ordain and establish this Constitution for the United States of America.

The task of establishing "a more perfect union" from the diverse peoples of the United States would prove challenging in years to come, but the very diversity that would create tensions in the young country would also be its greatest strength. By the time of the Revolution, America had already produced the first of its great African-American poets in the person of **Phillis Wheatley.** In the years since, its diversity has made American literature one of the finest the world has ever seen.

A Nation of Readers

As the population of the young country grew and standards of living climbed, literacy increased dramatically. By the end of the eighteenth century, most of the white population could read, and literacy was blossoming among free African Americans in the North. This burst of literacy created a demand for more and more literature of various kinds, a demand met by technological developments in printing that brought into full flower the "reading revolution." One critical factor underlying the increased demand for printed works was the heightened value that "print culture" (as opposed to spoken or oral culture) was coming to play in shaping the ideals of the emerging nation. Print came to be seen not merely as a means of transmitting information but as a new way of conducting public discourse on important issues. People were beginning to associate print with public debate held without regard to distinctions of status or person. Through the printed word, one might present arguments, as Thomas Paine did in *Common Sense,* and have those arguments stand or fall solely on their merit. Print became, therefore, a vehicle for the new nation's democratic identity and principles.

Historical Note

The Treaty of Paris. This treaty, negotiated with Great Britain by Benjamin Franklin, John Adams, John Jay, and Henry Laurens, not only granted independence to the colonies but also ceded Britain's right to the territory between the Alleghenies, Florida, the Mississippi River, and the Great Lakes.

Echoes:

The American Revolution

"In reality there is perhaps no one of our natural Passions so hard to subdue as *Pride*. . . . For even if I could conceive that I had completely overcome it, I should probably be proud of my Humility."

—Benjamin Franklin, on pride

"Here [in America] individuals of all nations are melted into a new race of men, whose labors and posterity will one day cause great changes in the world."

—J. Hector St. Jean de Crèvecoeur, on American diversity

"Strange order of things! Oh, Nature, where are thou?—Are not these blacks thy children as well as we?"

—J. Hector St. John de Crèvecoeur, on slavery

"These are the times that try men's souls. The summer soldier and the sunshine patriot will, in this crisis, shrink from the service of their country; but he that stands it now, deserves the love and thanks of man and woman."

—Thomas Paine, in *Crisis, No. 1,* on the American Revolution

"A little rebellion now and then is a good thing."

—Thomas Jefferson, writing about Shay's Rebellion in a letter to James Madison

"The tree of liberty must be refreshed from time to time with the blood of patriots and tyrants."

—Thomas Jefferson, in a letter to W. S. Smith

"In framing a government which is to be administered by men over men, the great difficulty lies in this: you must first enable the government to control the governed; and in the next place oblige it to control itself."

—James Madison, *The Federalist Papers, No. 51,* on control of government

ADDITIONAL QUESTIONS AND ACTIVITIES

Ask students to think about the ideas of liberty and government. Students might reflect on the ideals expressed on page 139 and on their experiences. Students can discuss or write about their definition of liberty, how it is gained and maintained, and the role of government.

ADDITIONAL RESOURCES

READER'S GUIDE

- Selection Worksheets, 3.1, 3.2

ASSESSMENT PORTFOLIO

- Selection Check Tests, 4.3.1, 4.3.3
- Selection Tests, 4.3.2, 4.3.4

ENRICHMENT ACTIVITIES

Motivated students might attempt a brief autobiographical essay about a formative event or influential person in their childhood.

Suggest that they begin by freewriting. Refer students to the Language Arts Survey, 1.12, "Freewriting."

SUPPORT FOR LEP STUDENTS

The selections may be challenging because Franklin uses sophisticated vocabulary and an elegant, formal tone. Encourage students to pause after each paragraph and paraphrase the main ideas that have been presented.

ADDITIONAL VOCABULARY

rude—uncultured or uncivilized
compel—force
transactions—interactions between or among people
abundance—plenty
leisure—rest, relaxation
laborious—having to do with work
slavish—in a manner like that of a slave
frivolous—petty, unimportant, silly
principal—primary or most important
proposition—a statement or idea for consideration or debate
defer—put off, delay
maintenance—act of taking care of
amiss—wrong
formerly—in past times

PREREADING

from *The Autobiography of Benjamin Franklin*
From "Remarks Concerning the Natives of North America"
by Benjamin Franklin

ABOUT THE AUTHOR

Benjamin Franklin (1706–1790) was a writer, scientist, inventor, and diplomat. Born the tenth child in a large Boston family, he left school to work for his father, a maker of soap and candles. Unsatisfied with his father's profession, Franklin entered the printing trade as his brother's apprentice and had his first essay published under the name "Silence Dogood." At the age of sixteen, Franklin undertook the responsibility of running his brother's paper while his brother was imprisoned for an article he printed. At seventeen, Franklin moved to Philadelphia where he started a printing shop that produced paper currency for the Pennsylvania colony as well as a newspaper, the *Pennsylvania Gazette.* His *Poor Richard's Almanac,* known for its witty sayings and practical good sense, was enormously successful and was published annually for twenty-five years. These enterprises helped to make Franklin quite wealthy. A man of many talents with a keen intelligence and a passion for science, Franklin experimented with electricity and invented both a cookstove and bifocal glasses. He also started a library and was instrumental in the founding of the University of Pennsylvania. Respected for his insight and wisdom, Franklin represented the colonies in England, served on the committee that drafted the Declaration of Independence, signed the treaty that ended the American Revolution, and was a delegate to the Constitutional Convention.

ABOUT THE SELECTIONS

Benjamin Franklin wrote ***The Autobiography of Benjamin Franklin*** over a period of twenty years. It covers his life only until 1758, before his career as a diplomat. He began writing in 1771 and wrote the last two sections between 1788 and 1790, when illness forced him to put the work aside. Although the first part of the book was published in 1791, the entire work was not published until 1868. Franklin's writing style was developed, he noted, by imitation of great models, primarily of such Neoclassical masters as Joseph Addison. (The Neoclassicists of the eighteenth century valued reason and sought to discover orderly principles, or natural laws, by which the life of an individual or of a nation could be conducted in order to achieve relative harmony and tranquility. For more information on Neoclassicism, see the introduction to this unit and the entry on *Neoclassicism* in the Handbook of Literary Terms.)

During his stay in France from 1776 to 1785 as the United States' ambassador, Franklin had his own press with which he printed several pamphlets, mostly on light topics. The selection from **"Remarks Concerning the Natives of North America"** comes from one of the essays he produced at that time. The essay was published in 1784.

GOALS/OBJECTIVES

Studying this lesson will enable students to

- enjoy Franklin's prose style in an autobiography and in a pamphlet
- identify gerunds and participles
- compare the author's styles
- apply aphorisms to their own lives
- make a compare-and-contrast chart
- define *chiasmus* and identify examples of chiasmus in their reading
- write an agenda
- identify words used as different parts of speech
- create a pamphlet

READER'S JOURNAL

In the following selection, Franklin discusses a time in his youth when he was first establishing himself as a writer and printer. As you will see from the selection, Franklin had tremendous drive and worked hard to achieve his goals. What goals do you want to achieve in your youth? What do you hope to accomplish by the time you are twenty-five? Write about these questions in your journal.

LANGUAGE SKILLS

Read the Language Arts Survey, 2.17, "Verbals: Gerunds." Then examine the selection to find examples of gerunds. Note each gerund and how it is used, for example, as subject or object of a verb (identify the verb), or object of a preposition (identify the preposition).

FROM

The Autobiography of Benjamin Franklin

BENJAMIN FRANKLIN

My Brother had in 1720 or '21, begun to print a Newspaper. It was the second that appeared in America and was called the *New England Courant.*[1] The only one before it was *The Boston News Letter.* I remember his being dissuaded by some of his Friends from the Undertaking, as not likely to succeed, one Newspaper being in their Judgment enough for America. At this time (1771) there are not less than five-and-twenty. He went on, however, with the Undertaking, and after having worked in composing the Types and printing off the Sheets, I was employed to carry the Papers through the Streets to the Customers. He had some ingenious Men among his Friends who amused themselves by writing little Pieces for this Paper, which gained it Credit and made it more in Demand, and these Gentlemen often visited us. Hearing their Conversations and their Accounts of the Approbation[2] their Papers were received with, I was excited to try my Hand among them. But being still a Boy, and suspecting that my Brother would object to printing any Thing of mine in his Paper if he knew it to be mine, I contrived to disguise my Hand, and writing an anonymous Paper, I put it

1 *What was Benjamin Franklin excited to try? Why was he excited? What was his one worry?*

1. **It was . . . New England Courant.** James Franklin's paper was actually the fifth American paper.
2. **Approbation.** Approval or commendation

WORDS FOR EVERYDAY USE: **in • gen • ious** (in jēn´yəs) *adj.,* having great mental ability

PREREADING NOTES

READER'S JOURNAL

Students might begin by freewriting about their goals or by making a list of things that they want to accomplish by the time they are twenty-five. They can then transfer goals from their freewriting or list to a time line. For more information on time lines, refer students to the Language Arts Survey, 1.19, "Adjectives and Articles."

LANGUAGE SKILLS

The italicized words from the following sentences in the selection are gerunds. Their uses are described in parentheses.

1. "I remember his being dissuaded by some of his Friends from the *Undertaking."* (*Undertaking* is the object of the preposition *from.*)
2. ". . . after having worked in *composing* the Types and *printing* off the Sheets, I was employed to carry the Papers through the Streets to the Customers." (*Composing* and *printing* are both objects of the preposition *in.*)
3. "He had some ingenious Men among his Friends who amused themselves by writing little Pieces for this Paper." (*Writing* is the object of the preposition *by.*)

ANSWER TO GUIDED READING QUESTION

1 Franklin was excited to try his hand at writing something for the paper because he had heard people talk about the commendation they received for their pieces. He was worried that his brother would object to printing it.

VOCABULARY IN CONTEXT

- A truly ingenious fellow, Henry Ford not only perfected the automobile but also invented the assembly line.

VOCABULARY FROM THE SELECTION

admonish	indulgence
consultation	ingenious
evade	venture

Answers to Guided Reading Questions

❶ James Franklin was imprisoned for including a piece in his newspaper that offended the Assembly. This was in the days before the American Revolution and before the guarantee in the Bill of Rights of freedom of the press.

❷ James Franklin's friends started to think highly of Benjamin's work, and James felt that their praise made his younger brother too vain.

Historical Note

Apprenticeship is a legal arrangement under which a person goes into the service of a master in order to be trained in an art, craft, or trade. In the days before mechanization, skilled craftspeople and artisans were extremely important, and apprenticeship provided a method for training new generations of workers. Apprenticeship has a long history. It was practiced in ancient Babylon, Egypt, and Rome. In medieval Europe, most job training was done by means of apprenticeship supervised by guilds, or professional associations. The "indentures" referred to by Franklin are the terms of the contract that binds the apprentice to his or her master for a specified period. The industrial revolution created many new unskilled and semiskilled jobs and thus made apprenticeship less important as a method for training workers. In addition, especially in the twentieth century, the importance of apprenticeship diminished because people often received their training for work in school or on the job. In the United States today, entry into many skilled trades (plumbing, electrical work, and carpentry are examples) still requires a period of apprenticeship. To become an apprentice in the United States, one generally needs a high school diploma. The period of apprenticeship varies from two to five years and usually involves both work and study at a vocational or technical school.

in at Night under the Door of the Printing-House.

It was found in the Morning and communicated to his Writing Friends when they called in as Usual. They read it, commented on it in my Hearing, and I had the exquisite Pleasure of finding it met with their Approbation, and that, in their different Guesses at the Author, none were named but Men of some Character among us for Learning and Ingenuity. I suppose now that I was rather lucky in my Judges, and that perhaps they were not really so very good ones as I then esteemed them. Encouraged however by this, I wrote and conveyed in the same Way to the Press several more Papers, which were equally approved, and I kept my Secret till my small Fund of Sense for such Performances was pretty well exhausted, and then I discovered[3] it, when I began to be considered a little more by my Brother's Acquaintance, and in a manner that did not quite please him, as he thought, probably with reason, that it tended to make me too vain. And perhaps this might be one Occasion of the Differences that we began to have about this Time. Though a Brother, he considered himself as my Master, and me as his Apprentice,[4] and accordingly expected the same Services from me as he would from another; while I thought he demeaned me too much in some he required of me, who from a Brother expected more Indulgence. Our Disputes were often brought before our Father, and I fancy I was either generally in the right or else a better Pleader, because the Judgment was generally in my favor. But my Brother was passionate and had often beaten me, which I took extremely amiss; and, thinking my Apprenticeship very tedious, I was continually wishing for some Opportunity of shortening it, which at length offered in a manner unexpected.

❶ *Why was James Franklin imprisoned?*

❷ *What was one cause of the differences between Franklin and his brother?*

One of the Pieces in our Newspaper, on some political Point which I have now forgotten, gave Offense to the Assembly. He was taken up, censured, and imprisoned[5] for a Month by the Speaker's Warrant. I suppose because he would not discover his Author. I too was taken up and examined before the Council; but though I did not give them any Satisfaction, they contented themselves with admonishing me, and dismissed me, considering me perhaps as an Apprentice who was bound to keep his Master's Secrets. During my Brother's Confinement, which I resented a good deal, notwithstanding our private Differences, I had the Management of the Paper, and I made bold to give our Rulers some Rubs[6] in it, which my Brother took very kindly, while others began to consider me in an unfavorable Light, as a young Genius that had a Turn for Libeling and Satire.[7] My Brother's Discharge was accompanied with an Order of the House (a very odd one) "that James Franklin should no longer print the paper called the *New England Courant.*" There was a Consultation held in our Printing-House among his Friends what he should do in this Case. Some pro-

3. **discovered.** Revealed
4. **Apprentice.** Person under legal agreement to work a specified length of time for a master craftsman in return for instruction and, formerly, support
5. **imprisoned.** James Franklin was charged with libel in 1722 because his paper linked local officials to pirates who were raiding outside Boston Harbor.
6. **Rubs.** Insults
7. **Libeling and Satire.** *Libeling*—making false public accusation; *satire*—humorous but critical portrayal

Words for Everyday Use:

in • dul • gence (in dul´jəns) *n.,* favor or privilege

ad • mon • ish (ad män´ish) *vt.,* caution against specific faults

con • sul • ta • tion (kän´səl tā´shən) *n.,* meeting to discuss, decide, or plan something

Vocabulary in Context

- The librarian allowed us to hold our meetings in the stacks, and we were grateful for his indulgence.
- Please admonish your sister not to put the gerbils in her pockets.
- After a brief consultation, the toddlers decided that Marvin would play the schoolteacher, and Chico would play the student.
- Vera tried to evade Mel's wrath by telling him that Alice had spilled a bowl of grits in the customer's lap.
- Shayna had no idea what the answer was but she ventured a guess.

posed to evade the Order by changing the Name of the Paper; but my Brother seeing Inconveniences in that, it was finally concluded on as a better Way to let it be printed for the future under the Name of Benjamin Franklin. And to avoid the Censure of the Assembly that might fall on him as still printing it by his Apprentice, the Contrivance was that my old Indenture[8] should be returned to me with a full Discharge on the Back[9] of it, to be shown on Occasion; but to secure to him the Benefit of my Service, I was to sign new Indentures for the Remainder of the Term, which were to be kept private. A very flimsy Scheme it was; but however, it was immediately executed, and the Paper went on accordingly under my Name for several Months.[10] At length a fresh Difference arising beween my Brother and me, I took upon me to assert my Freedom, presuming that he would not venture to produce the new Indentures. It was not fair in me to take this Advantage, and this I therefore reckon one of the first Errata[11] of my Life; but the Unfairness of it weighed little with me, when under the Impressions of Resentment, for the Blows his Passion too often urged him to bestow upon me. Though he was otherwise not an ill-natured Man: perhaps I was too saucy and provoking. ■

8. **Indenture.** Contract binding a person to work for another for a given length of time
9. **Discharge on the Back.** Release of the remainder
10. **Paper . . . several Months.** Actually, the paper remained in Franklin's name until 1726, nearly three years after he left Boston.
11. **Errata.** Printer's term for errors

❶ *How did the newspaper come to be published under Franklin's name?*

❷ *In what way did Franklin take advantage of his brother? Why might the "Unfairness of it" weigh little with him?*

Responding to the Selection

If you had a chance to read more of the *Autobiography,* what would attract you to do so? curiosity about the adventures in which Franklin was involved? appreciation for his humor? interest in the character of the man himself? What do you find most appealing about this work?

Words for Everyday Use:

e • vade (ē vād´) *vt.,* avoid or escape from by deceit or cleverness
ven • ture (ven´chər) *vt.,* undertake the risk of

Answers to Guided Reading Questions

❶ James Franklin was ordered by the government to stop publishing his newspaper. Therefore, he decided to print the paper, in the future, under the name of Benjamin Franklin.

❷ Franklin took advantage of his brother by asserting his freedom (perhaps to control the paper), knowing that James would not risk producing the "indentures" that bound him. Franklin was little bothered by the unfairness of this because James sometimes hit him.

Responding to the Selection

Ask students to consider how reading about Franklin in another source, such as an encyclopedia article, a history book, or a recent biography, might differ from reading Franklin's autobiography. Students should consider the style as well as content of the different writings.

Answers to Selection Check Test 4.3.1

EX. What kind of business did Franklin's brother run?
Franklin's brother ran a newspaper.

1. What work did Franklin do for his brother?
Franklin set type, printed pages, and delivered the newspapers.

2. What did Franklin want to do after hearing the conversations of his brother's friends?
He wanted to write a piece for the paper.

3. What reason did Franklin's brother give for his anger when Franklin's secret was revealed?
His brother said it made Franklin too vain.

4. Who ran the paper while James Franklin was imprisoned?
Benjamin Franklin ran the paper.

5. Why does Franklin later think that perhaps his brother was not wrong for his treatment of Franklin?
Franklin says that perhaps he provoked his brother by being too "saucy."

Reviewing the Selection

RECALLING

1. What tasks did Benjamin Franklin perform for his brother as his apprentice?
2. How did Franklin trick his brother into publishing his writing?
3. How did James Franklin offend the Assembly? What was his punishment for the offense?
4. What finally led to Franklin's leaving the newspaper and his job as apprentice?

INTERPRETING

5. Franklin and his brother often had disagreements. Explain why Franklin often felt misused and wished to end the apprenticeship.
6. Why did Franklin resort to trickery in order to get his work printed? Why did he finally reveal that he was the author?
7. How did Franklin benefit from the Assembly's restrictions on his brother's printing?
8. How did Franklin feel about abandoning his apprenticeship at the time he left? How had his attitude concerning the incident and his actions changed by the time he wrote his autobiography? Why had it changed?

SYNTHESIZING

9. Franklin had signed the new indenture that secretly made him his brother's apprentice for the remainder of the previously agreed-upon term, but he eventually left the job knowing his brother could not publicly prosecute him. Do you think Franklin acted fairly? Was he justified in leaving his brother? Explain why, or why not.
10. Franklin published the newspaper by himself during his brother's absence. What do you think he might have learned about himself and the newspaper business during that time? How do you think that experience affected his decision to leave his brother later?

Understanding Literature (Questions for Discussion)

1. **Style. Style** is the manner in which something is said or written. Any recurring feature that distinguishes one writer's work from another can be said to be part of that writer's style. Franklin's style includes many of the qualities of Neoclassicism. (See the definition of Neoclassicism in the Handbook of Literary Terms.) What characteristics of the *Autobiography* do you notice that set off Franklin's work from that of other prose writers you have read?
2. **Persona.** A **persona** consists of the qualities of a person or character that are shown through speech or actions. What qualities does Franklin wish the reader to perceive in

ANSWERS FOR REVIEWING THE SELECTION

RECALLING

1. Franklin composed the type, printed the sheets of the paper, and carried the papers to the customers.

2. Franklin disguised his handwriting and slipped an anonymous piece for the paper under the door of the printing house.

3. James published something in the paper that the Assembly found objectionable for political reasons. He was jailed and then ordered to stop publishing the paper.

4. Franklin was led to "assert his freedom" (i.e., to leave his apprenticeship) by disagreements with his brother, James.

INTERPRETING

Responses will vary. Possible responses are given.

5. Franklin felt misused because his brother gave him tedious, demeaning tasks to do and treated him like a subordinate. James also beat him.

6. Franklin resorted to trickery because he believed that James would not publish something by his younger brother. He finally revealed his authorship of the pieces because he grew tired of the imposture.

7. Franklin benefited in two ways from the Assembly's restrictions on James. First, Franklin became the publisher of the newspaper. Second, he was able to get out of his indentured apprenticeship, which he found onerous, because James did not dare reveal that the publisher of the paper was legally his apprentice.

8. At the time, Franklin was happy to leave. Afterward, at the time of the writing of the *Autobiography,* he felt that perhaps he deserved some of his brother's ill feeling.

SYNTHESIZING

Responses will vary. Possible responses are given.

9. Some students may feel that having signed the document making himself an indentured apprentice, Franklin was bound to keep

(cont.)

ANSWERS FOR REVIEWING THE SELECTION (CONT.)

his word. Others may feel that by mistreating his brother physically, James invalidated the agreement. Certainly, no one should be required by any law, contract, or agreement to submit to physical abuse.

10. One never learns as much about any enterprise or undertaking as one does through actually doing it. Running the newspaper by himself would have given Franklin an opportunity to learn the business inside out, from making editorial decisions to setting type, from gathering advertising to selling the product. The experience of running the paper by himself might have taught Franklin that he had the capability of functioning on his own, without his brother's guidance.

him? How does he show these qualities in his account? How accurately do you suppose the persona in his work reflects Franklin's character?

3. **Autobiography.** An **autobiography** is the story of a person's life, written by that person. Name some advantages that an autobiography has over a biography—that is, an account of a person's life written by someone else. Name some advantages a biography has over an autobiography. From this excerpt, do you feel you can trust Franklin's account? Why, or why not?

4. **Proverb, or Aphorism.** A **proverb,** or **aphorism,** is a short saying or pointed statement. The following is a list of aphorisms from the writings of Benjamin Franklin. Many come from Franklin's *Poor Richard's Almanac,* which he edited under the pseudonym of Richard Saunders. Discuss the meanings of these aphorisms with your classmates. Paraphrase them, and identify those that offer advice about living a good life. Discuss how this advice might be applied to your own lives.

Aphorisms from *Poor Richard's Almanac* and Other Writings by Benjamin Franklin

"A learned blockhead is a greater blockhead than an ignorant one."

"A penny saved is a penny earned."

"A plowman on his legs is higher than a gentleman on his knees."

"A word to the wise is enough and many words won't fill a bushel."

"At the workingman's house hunger looks in, but dares not enter."

"Beware of little expenses; a small leak will sink a great ship."

"Creditors have better memories than debtors."

"Early to bed, and early to rise, makes a man healthy, wealthy, and wise."

"Experience keeps a dear school, but fools will learn in no other, and scarce in that."

"God heals, and the doctor takes the fee."

"God helps them that help themselves."

"Have you somewhat to do tomorrow, do it today."

"He that falls in love with himself, will have no rivals."

"He that goes a-borrowing goes a-sorrowing."

"I should have no objection to a repetition of the same life from its beginning, only asking the advantages authors have in a second edition to correct some faults of the first."

"If you will not hear reason, she'll surely rap your knuckles."

"If you would like to know the value of money, go and try to borrow some."

"If you would not be forgotten as soon as you are dead, either write things worth reading or do things worth writing."

"In this world nothing can be said to be certain except death and taxes."

"Keep your eyes wide open before marriage and half-shut afterwards."

"Little strokes fell great oaks."

"Lost time is never found again."

"Necessity never made a good bargain."

"Plow deep, while sluggards sleep, and you shall have corn to sell and to keep."

ANSWERS FOR UNDERSTANDING LITERATURE

► See the evaluation forms for discussion, active listening, and oral communication, *Assessment Portfolio,* 7.11–7.14.

Responses will vary. Possible responses are given.

1. Style. Characteristics of Franklin's writing include clarity of thought and expression, a tendency toward generalization and moral instruction, and egotism (or, more sympathetically, enlightened self-interest tempered by a willingness to question his own actions). These characteristics are common among the writers of the Neoclassical Era.

2. Persona. Franklin doubtless wishes to present himself as a talented, astute character with a keen interest in self-advancement and self-improvement. Unsympathetic readers of the *Autobiography* might view Franklin as a smug, self-centered man willing to take every advantage that promotes his own interests. However, such a reading of Franklin judges a person of one age by the standards of another. Franklin was, by any account, an exceptional human being—an inventor, diplomat, revolutionary, publisher, philosopher, and scientist. A sympathetic account of his character would present him as a man of irrepressible talent.

3. Autobiography. A biography, if written by a disinterested party, is usually more objective and less self-serving than an autobiography. An autobiography, however, usually contains more concrete detail. Franklin does not present a lot of colorful, realistic detail, but this defect in the work (from a modern point of view) is made up for by his wit, especially by his aphoristic ability to distill characters and events into wise, general commentaries. Some students might feel that Franklin's desire to write for the newspaper was motivated by vanity and that he was less than honest in his dealings with his brother. They also might wonder whether Franklin suffers from false modesty.

(cont.)

ANSWERS FOR UNDERSTANDING LITERATURE (CONT.)

4. Proverb, or Aphorism. The following are some sample paraphrases:
"A learned blockhead is a greater blockhead than an ignorant one." (Possible paraphrase: An educated fool is more foolish than an uneducated one is. Analysis: Sometimes people concentrate on narrow specialities and view everything through distorted lenses. Thus an evolutionary biologist might be tempted to view all interactions as involving struggles for existence among autonomous entities motivated by self-interest, or a football player might view all interactions as games to be won or lost. These are extreme examples, and certainly are not true of all biologists or all football players.) "A penny saved is a penny earned." (Possible paraphrase: Money is not really earned until an effort is made to save it. Analysis: In a very real sense, money

(cont.)

ANSWERS FOR UNDERSTANDING LITERATURE (CONT.)

that is squandered as soon as it comes into one's possession has not been earned, for part of the work of earning money is involved in hanging on to it.) "A plowman on his legs is higher than a gentleman on his knees." (Possible paraphrase: Independence and integrity are more important than social status. Analysis: One can be a well-to-do person and still not have any independence or autonomy. Franklin is saying that it is better to be of modest status and independent than to be of high status and subservient. "A word to the wise is enough and many words won't fill a bushel." (Possible paraphrase: Be concise or frugal with your words, and intelligent people will get what you are saying. Wordiness will get you nowhere because verbiage has no substance. Analysis: When it comes to words, less often is more. A point made economically is much more likely to register and be remembered.)

ANSWERS FOR LANGUAGE LAB

1. Gerund: publishing; participles: challenging, rewarding
2. Participles: annoying, printing; gerund: running
3. Participle: joining; gerunds: writing, publishing
4. Gerunds: experimenting, inventing; participle: used
5. Participles: retired, serving

"snug/as a bug/in a rug"

"The early bird catches the worm."

"There never was a good war, or a bad peace."

"Time is money."

"We must indeed all hang together, or, most assuredly, we shall all hang separately."

"What maintains one vice would bring up two children."

Language Lab

Verbals. Read the Language Arts Survey, 2.16 and 2.17, "Verbals: Gerunds and Participles." Then find the gerunds and participles in these sentences. On your own paper, identify each gerund and each participle.

1. To young Franklin, publishing was a challenging and rewarding career.
2. Even though annoying disagreements with his brother drove him into running away to Philadelphia, the printing skills he acquired gave him valuable experience.
3. Joining his abilities in writing and publishing with keen business sense, Franklin gained success quickly.
4. Then he enjoyed experimenting with electricity and inventing useful tools, such as the bifocals used by many people today.
5. Retired from business at age forty-two, Franklin spent most of the rest of his life as a diplomat, serving his country as ambassador to France.

The body of
Benjamin Franklin, printer,
(Like the cover of an old book,
Its contents worn out,
And stript of its lettering and gilding)
Lies here, food for worms!
Yet the work itself shall not be lost,
For it will, as he believed, appear once more
In a new
And more beautiful edition,
Corrected and amended
By its Author!

READER'S JOURNAL

Imagine that you have been asked to come up with a plan for the ideal education for a young person in your society. What would your plan be? What do you think young people should learn? What subjects should they study? What skills should they develop? Write about these questions in your journal.

THINKING SKILLS

Read the Language Arts Survey, 4.8, "Comparing and Contrasting." Then, as you read the selection, make a chart to compare and contrast the colonists' and the Native Americans' ideas about education.

FROM

"Remarks Concerning the Natives of North America"

BENJAMIN FRANKLIN

Savages we call them, because their manners differ from ours, which we think the perfection of civility; they think the same of theirs.

Perhaps, if we could examine the manners of different nations with impartiality, we should find no people so rude, as to be without any rules of politeness; nor any so polite, as not to have some remains of rudeness.

The Indian men, when young, are hunters and warriors; when old, counselors; for all their government is by counsel of the sages;[1] there is no force, there are no prisons, no officers to compel obedience, or inflict punishment. Hence they generally study oratory, the best speaker having the most influence. The Indian women till the ground, dress the food, nurse and bring up the children, and preserve and hand down to posterity the memory of public transactions. These employments of men and women are accounted natural and honorable. Having few artificial wants, they have abundance of leisure for improvement by conversation. Our laborious manner of life, compared with theirs, they esteem[2] slavish and base; and the learning, on which we value ourselves, they regard as frivolous and useless. An instance of this occurred at the Treaty of Lancaster, in Pennsylvania, *anno* 1744, between the government of Virginia and the Six Nations.[3] After the

❶ *How do the Native Americans regard the white people's learning?*

1. **sages.** Very wise people, widely respected for their wisdom, experience, and judgment
2. **esteem.** Consider; hold to be
3. **Six Nations.** Confederation of Iroquoian peoples, comprising the Mohawk, Oneida, Onondaga, Cayuga, Seneca, and Tuscarora

WORDS FOR EVERYDAY USE:

ci • vil • i • ty (sə vil´ə tē) *n.,* politeness

im • par • ti • al • i • ty (im pär´shē al´ i tē) *n.,* free of bias

or • a • to • ry (ôr´ə tôr´ē) *n.,* art of public speaking

pos • ter • i • ty (päs ter´ə tē) *n.,* all of a person's descendants

PREREADING NOTES

READER'S JOURNAL

Students might approach this activity by considering what skills a person needs to function in contemporary society. You may wish to have students debate in class the merits of study of such subjects as the arts, computer science, intermediate mathematics, physical education, vocational education, grammar, literature, and writing.

THINKING SKILLS

Students can set up their comparisons and contrasts in the form of a chart with the headings "Colonists' Views" and "Native Americans' Views." As they read, they can fill in their charts. Then they can study the charts to find similarities and differences in these views.

ANSWER TO GUIDED READING QUESTION

❶ According to Franklin, the Native Americans regarded the white people's learning as "frivolous and useless."

ENRICHMENT ACTIVITIES

Have students research various Native American groups of the Eastern Woodlands area. Possible subjects for research include the Abnaki, Beothuk, Cayuga, Chickahominy, Delaware, Erie, Huron, Illinois, Kickapoo, Mahican, Malecite, Massachuset, Mattapony, Menominee, Miami, Micmac, Mohawk, Mohican, Nanticoke, Narraganset, Ojibwa (Chippewa), Oneida, Onondaga, Ottawa, Pamlico, Passamaquoddy, Pennacook, Penobscot, Peoria, Pequot, Piankasaw, Potawatomi, Powhatan, Seneca, Shawnee, Susquehanna, Wampanoag, Wappinger, Wea, and Winnebago.

VOCABULARY IN CONTEXT

- Chandra was impressed by the civility of the people of Minneapolis; everyone she met seemed very friendly and polite.
- The prosecuting attorney questioned the witness's impartiality because the witness was the defendant's cousin.
- Lincoln's "Gettysburg Address" is one of the most famous examples of American oratory.
- We have a responsibility to leave a clean, safe environment to posterity.

Answers to Guided Reading Questions

❶ The commissioners offer to educate six Native American youths at the college at Williamsburg.

❷ The speaker says that different nations have different conceptions of things, including education.

Answers to Selection Check Test 4.3.3

EX. According to Franklin, what do the colonists call the native peoples of the Americas?
They call them savages.

1. According to Franklin, what occupations do Native American men have when they are young?
They are hunters and warriors.

2. According to Franklin, what occupations do Native American men have when they are old?
They are counselors.

3. How do the Native Americans regard the colonists' learning?
They regard it as frivolous and useless.

4. What offer is made to the Six Nations by the commissioners of Virginia?
They offer to educate six Native American young men at the college at Williamsburg.

5. What counteroffer is made by the Six Nations?
They offer to instruct a dozen sons of Virginia gentlemen, teaching them all that they know and thus making men of them.

VOCABULARY FROM THE SELECTION

civility
heartily
impartial
oratory
posterity

Vocabulary in Context

• The president heartily thanked her supporters for helping her to win reelection.

The Twin, Wife of Bloody Hand. *George Catlin, 1832. National Museum of American Art, Washington, DC/Art Resource, NY*

principal business was settled, the commissioners from Virginia acquainted the Indians by a speech, that there was at Williamsburg a college, with a fund for educating Indian youth; and that, if the Six Nations would send down half a dozen of their young lads to that college, the government would take care that they should be well provided for, and instructed in all the learning of the white people. It is one of the Indian rules of politeness not to answer a public proposition the same day that it is made; they think it would be treating it as a light matter, and that they show it respect by taking time to consider it, as of a matter important. They therefore deferred their answer till the day following; when their speaker began, by expressing their deep sense of the kindness of the Virginia government, in making them that offer; "for we know," says he, "that you highly esteem the kind of learning taught in those Colleges, and that the maintenance of our young men, while with you, would be very expensive to you. We are convinced, therefore, that you mean to do us good by your proposal; and we thank you heartily. But you, who are wise, must know that different nations have different conceptions of things; and you will therefore not take it amiss, if our ideas of this kind of education happen not to be the same with yours. We have had some experience of it; several of our young people were formerly brought up at the colleges of the northern provinces; they

❶ *What offers do the commissioners make to the Native Americans?*

❶ *What does the speaker for the six nations say about different nations' conceptions of things?*

Words for Everyday Use: **heart • i • ly** (härt ´l ē) *adv.,* in a friendly, sincere way

Historical Note

The Iroquois are one of the great native peoples of the Americas. In the late sixteenth century, five groups of the Iroquois—the Mohawk, Onondaga, Oneida, Cayuga, and Seneca—formed what is variously known as the Iroqouis League, the Iroquois Confederacy, or the Five Nations. Then, in the early eighteenth century, the Tuscaroras of North Carolina joined the confederacy. The territory of the Iroquois covered the area near the St. Lawrence River and the Great Lakes. For many years, the Iroquois were allies of the British and bitter enemies of the French. The Iroquois played an important role in helping the British to consolidate their control over North America east of the Mississippi River. During the American Revolution, they continued their support of the British. Henry Wadsworth Longfellow's poem "Song of Hiawatha," an excerpt from which appears on page 82 of this text, is about one of the two legendary founders of the Iroquois Confederacy.

were instructed in all your sciences; but, when they came back to us, they were bad runners, ignorant of every means of living in the woods, unable to bear either cold or hunger, knew neither how to build a cabin, take a deer, or kill an enemy, spoke our language imperfectly, were therefore neither fit for hunters, warriors, nor counselors; they were totally good for nothing. We are however not the less obliged by your kind offer, though we decline accepting it; and, to show our grateful sense of it, if the gentlemen of Virginia will send us a dozen of their sons, we will take great care of their education, instruct them in all we know, and make *men* of them." ■

❶ *What reasons does the speaker give for declining the offer?*

❷ *What offer does the speaker make in return?*

Responding to the Selection

The Native Americans and the colonists in this selection have very different ideas about an appropriate education for a young person. What are those ideas? What do they reveal about the cultures of these people? If you could redesign the curriculum, or program of study, at your school, what changes would you make? What do you think young people should study today? Discuss these questions with your classmates.

Reviewing the Selection

Recalling

1. According to Franklin, how did the colonists often refer to the natives of North America? Why did the colonists call them that?
2. Explain the offer the commissioners of Virginia made to the Six Nations.
3. What were the Native Americans' reasons for refusing the offer?
4. What counteroffer did the speaker for the Six Nations make in response to the commissioners' offer?

Interpreting

5. What is the definition of the word *savage?* Why could the term be considered negative and insulting? What does the term suggest about the self-image of the people who use the term?
6. How do you think the commissioners expected their offer to be received? What response do you think they expected from the Native Americans?
7. Summarize the reasons why the representatives of the Six Nations thought that their college-educated sons were "good for nothing."
8. Do you think the Six Nations' offer was well received? Based on what you know about relations between the white people and the natives of North America, what might have been the reaction of the commissioners to the speaker's suggestion?

Answers to Guided Reading Questions

❶ The speaker says that when young men educated at the white man's college returned, they didn't have the skills that Iroquois men needed. They were poor runners, ignorant of life in the woods, unable to stand cold or hunger, unable to build a cabin, incapable of killing a deer or an enemy, poor speakers of the language, and bad counselors.

❷ The Native American speaker offers to take a dozen white young men and instruct them in order to "make *men* of them."

Responding to the Selection

The Native American who speaks at the end of the selection tells of the importance of the following skills: running, living in the woods, withstanding cold and hunger, building a cabin, hunting deer, killing enemies, speaking the language, and serving as a counselor. The selection does not specifically address the skills taught in white universities, although one would expect those skills to have been less practical. For example, in those days university students typically learned a great deal of Latin and Greek.

When students discuss the redesign of the curriculum, have them refer to their Reader's Journal entries.

Answers for Reviewing the Selection

RECALLING

1. Franklin says that the colonists often referred to the natives as "savages" because their manners were different from those of the colonists.

2. The commissioners of Virginia offered to pay for the education of six Native American youths at Williamsburg College.

3. The Native Americans refused the offer because they believed that the young men would be educated in white ways instead of learning the essential skills that they needed in order to take their

(cont.)

Answers for Reviewing the Selection (cont.)

places in the Native American culture.

4. The speaker for the Six Nations offered to take a dozen young sons of the white people of Virginia and educate them in Native American ways.

INTERPRETING

Responses will vary. Possible responses are given.

5. The word *savage* is used derogatorily to refer to people whom the speaker or writer believes to be animalistic, wild, barbarous, and without cultural refinements. The term is negative and insulting because it dismisses the real cultural attainments of the people to whom it is applied. People who use this term to refer to other peoples think of themselves and their culture as superior.

6. The commissioners probably expected their offer to be received with gratitude. They probably

(cont.)

ANSWERS FOR REVIEWING THE SELECTION (CONT.)

thought of it as extremely generous and expected the Native Americans to be thankful.

7. They thought that their college-educated sons were "good for nothing" because they had few or none of the skills essential to life in the Six Nations.

8. The commissioners might have reacted in several ways—with surprise, bewilderment, incredulity, or hostility. They would not have taken the Native Americans up on their offer. One can only hope that they would have realized that the people of the Six Nations had turned the tables on them, and that like Franklin they would have reflected on the situation and become less complacent or smug about the superiority of their own culture.

SYNTHESIZING

Responses will vary. Possible responses are given.

9. At a minimum, people from different cultures need an openness and an interest in learning about different ways of life. They must realize that misunderstandings and differences will be inevitable and must look for commonalities beneath the differences. They must develop a "live and let live" attitude of tolerance and respect for differences.

10. The speaker for the Six Nations was extremely diplomatic. He expressed the Nations' refusal of the offer in gentle but firm words after having first thanked the Virginia commissioners heartily for their offer. The relationship represented is therefore one of cautious diplomacy practiced between two peoples who do not understand one another, but who are willing to attempt to communicate.

SYNTHESIZING

9. In your opinion, what are the best methods by which two cultures can learn about each other? What attitudes must both cultures demonstrate in order to get along?

10. Read the Six Nations' speaker's words carefully. From this speech, how would you describe the relationship between the tribes he represented and colonial society at that time?

Understanding Literature (Questions for Discussion)

1. **Chiasmus.** A **chiasmus** is a rhetorical technique in which the order of occurrence of words or phrases is reversed, as in the line "We can weather changes, but we can't change the weather." Identify an example of chiasmus within the first third of this excerpt. Which words (in slightly varied forms) are reversed?

2. **Neoclassicism. Neoclassicism** is the term used to describe the revival during the English Enlightenment or Restoration Era of ideals of art and literature derived from the Greek and Roman classics. Critical among these ideals were reason and civility; the Neoclassicists cherished in art and life such characteristics as balance, proportion, restraint, and wit. How do these ideals influence Franklin's remarks? Point out passages in which Franklin balances ideas or phrases, where he points out uncivil or irrational attitudes, where he recommends restraint, and/or where he is witty or shows an appreciation for wit.

3. **Stereotype.** A **stereotype** is an uncritically accepted fixed or conventional idea, particularly such an idea held about whole groups of people. Against what stereotype does Franklin's essay present an argument? Why might the Native Americans have been justified in considering the colonists "savages"? Why might people think that a civilization is savage or uncivilized simply because it is very different from their own? Why is it so difficult for people from very different cultures to accept one another's ways of life as equally advanced, despite the differences?

Responding in Writing

1. **Agenda.** An **agenda** is a list of the topics or items of business to be discussed in a meeting. Write an agenda for a meeting of Ambassador Franklin with representatives of King Louis XVI of France to raise support for the United States in its war with Britain. List specific topics that either side might want to consider. (Refer to the Language Arts Survey, 3.6, "Discussion.")

2. **Cartoon.** Draw a one- to four-panel cartoon, with speech balloons or captions, that points out the ridiculousness of a widely accepted belief or practice, just as "Remarks Concerning the Natives of North America" challenges the white person's assumption that college learning would benefit eighteenth-century Native Americans.

ANSWERS FOR UNDERSTANDING LITERATURE

►See the evaluation forms for discussion, active listening, and oral communication, *Assessment Portfolio,* 7.11–7.14.

Responses will vary. Possible responses are given.

1. Chiasmus. Franklin's "we should find no people so rude, as to be without any rules of politeness; nor any so polite, as not to have some remains of rudeness" is a an example of chiasmus. The reversed words are *rude/rudeness* and *politeness/polite.*

2. Neoclassicism. The purpose or aim of Franklin's essay is to persuade people away from an extreme, uncivil, irrational point of view about the differences between and relative value of cultures toward a view that is more balanced and restrained. In sharing the Six Nations' reply at the end of his piece, Franklin shows a wit's appreciation for irony.

(cont.)

Language Lab

Words as Other Parts of Speech. Read the Language Arts Survey, 2.31–2.32, "Words Used as Other Parts of Speech I and II." Then find the single word used as two different parts of speech in each pair of sentences below. Copy the word and identify the part of speech it is used as in each sentence.

1. Did his apprentice's departure cause James Franklin's newspaper to go under?

   No; in fact, for three more years the paper was printed under Benjamin Franklin's name.

2. Franklin achieved great business success in Philadelphia, Pennsylvania.

   With part of the money that he earned from his business, Franklin funded public works.

3. One of Franklin's most famous inventions, a free-standing stove, successfully countered the drafts that usually chilled colonists in their poorly insulated homes.

   Franklin helped draft the Declaration of Independence, and he was one of its signers.

4. Franklin made more than one trip across the Atlantic Ocean.

   As ambassador, he rarely tripped in his dealings with the French court.

5. While in France, Franklin frequently appeared at great events wearing a fur cap.

   Franklin's participation in the Constitutional Convention capped a long career of public service.

Projects

1. **Pamphlet.** Try your hand at some Franklinesque writing and printing. Choose a topic that is light and entertaining, such as silly dog tricks or outdated clothing styles. Write an essay on the topic in a style imitating Benjamin Franklin's. Type your essay, or input it on a computer, and lay it out in the form of a four-page pamphlet. Print or duplicate several copies for distribution.

2. **Invention.** Review the inventions credited to Benjamin Franklin. Then, with one or more classmates, brainstorm ideas for a new invention. Begin by choosing some currently unmet need, such as organizing all the papers for your classes or keeping your textbooks from becoming worn and tattered. Then brainstorm possible solutions to that problem. Select the best approach and refine it. Then draw plans for, or make a model of, your invention. Be sure to provide captions or notes to indicate how the invention might work.

3. **Humor Calendar.** With several co-editors, collect jokes and funny anecdotes from your friends. Then create a calendar with a joke or story for each week of the year.

Project Notes

►See the worksheets and evaluation forms for projects, *Assessment Portfolio,* 7.20–7.23.

1. Pamphlet. Have students prepare a layout based on a newspaper or magazine design that contains a masthead and columns.

2. Invention. You may wish to give students a specific format for reporting their invention ideas.

3. Humor Calendar. Encourage students to review humorous calendars available commercially. Make sure students credit the sources of the material that they use.

Answers for Understanding Literature (cont.)

3. Stereotype. Franklin's essay is an argument against the stereotype of the ignorant, uncultured savage. Franklin shows that the Native Americans might just as easily have considered the white Europeans savages because of the whites' lack of cultural attainments. Thinking of people from a different culture as savage comes from not understanding those people and their way of life and thus dismissing as unimportant the real cultural attainments that they have.

Answers for Language Lab

1. *under:* adverb, preposition
2. *business:* adjective, noun
3. *draft(s):* noun, verb
4. *trip/tripped:* noun, verb
5. *cap/capped:* noun, verb

Analytic Scales for Responding in Writing

Assign a score from 1 to 25 for each grading criterion below. (For more detailed evaluation, see the evaluation forms for writing, revising, and proofreading, *Assessment Portfolio,* 7.1–7.10.)

1. Agenda

- **Content/Unity.** The agenda lists items for discussion, all of which are related to the topic.
- **Organization/Coherence.** The agenda presents a list of points for discussion in a logical order.
- **Language/Style.** The agenda is clear and diplomatic.
- **Conventions.** The agenda avoids errors in spelling, grammar, usage, mechanics, and manuscript form.

2. Cartoon

- **Content/Unity.** The cartoon satirizes a widely accepted belief or practice.
- **Organization/Coherence.** The cartoon consists of panels with captions and/or speech balloons.
- **Language/Style.** The captions and/or speech balloons are clear and colloquial.
- **Conventions.** The captions and/or speech balloons avoid errors in spelling, grammar, usage, and mechanics.

ADDITIONAL RESOURCES

READER'S GUIDE
- Selection Worksheet, 3.3

ASSESSMENT PORTFOLIO
- Selection Check Test, 4.3.5
- Selection Test, 4.3.6

ESSENTIAL SKILLS PRACTICE BOOKS
- *Language,* 2.25, 2.36
- *Speaking and Listening,* 3.7

AUDIOCASSETTE
- from Speech in the Virginia Convention, Track 3

ENRICHMENT ACTIVITIES

Have students review the Language Arts Survey, 3.2, "Elements of Verbal Communication"; 3.3, "Elements of Nonverbal Communication"; and 3.7, "Public Speaking." Then have them analyze the speech and make notes about what techniques they would use to deliver the speech forcefully. Ask them to identify the various emotions that the speaker should express through his or her tone and the places where the speaker might emphasize a point through increased or lowered volume, facial expressions, body language, and gestures.

SUPPORT FOR LEP STUDENTS

Make sure that students understand, before reading the selection, the issue with which the selection deals. Britain had sent additional troops and naval forces to the colonies to maintain order in reaction to protests against taxes. The question at hand was whether to attempt reconciliation with Britain or to risk open warfare. You may wish to play the recording of the speech, Audiocassette Track 3.

ADDITIONAL VOCABULARY

patriotism—positive feeling for one's country and one's people

reserve—hesitation, holding back

PREREADING

Speech in the Virginia Convention
by Patrick Henry

ABOUT THE AUTHOR

Patrick Henry (1736–1799) was a distinguished statesman and orator during the American Revolution. Born in Hanover County, Virginia, Henry's public schooling was brief, for his education was taken over by his father, a well-educated gentleman. Henry first tried his hand as a storekeeper but proved to be a poor businessman. He then turned to law and received his license in 1760. Gaining fame as an orator, he was elected to the Virginia House of Burgesses, where he became a leader. His speech against the Stamp Act in 1765 is considered one of his finest, and who can forget the words he uttered in the Virginia Convention on March 23, 1775: "I know not what course others may take, but as for me, give me liberty or give me death!" He served as governor of Virginia, became a conservative member of the Federalist party, and declined membership in the Constitutional Convention and the U.S. Senate. He refused George Washington's offers of appointment as secretary of state and chief justice of the Supreme Court. He was chiefly responsible for the drafting of the Bill of Rights. In 1796, Henry was elected governor of Virginia for the sixth time but refused to take office. His last campaign was for the office of representative in the Virginia state legislature. He won the election but died before taking office.

ABOUT THE SELECTION

The **Speech in the Virginia Convention,** probably Patrick Henry's best-known oration, was not written down until years after its delivery on March 23, 1775. It had so captured the attention of its listeners that they were able to recall it for Henry's biographer, William Wirt. The speech was delivered to the Virginia Convention during a time of growing political unrest. Over a year before, on December 16, 1773, disguised men had defied the British Parliament by dumping imported tea into Boston Harbor to avoid paying the taxes on it. In retaliation, Parliament had passed harsh measures in 1774 that became known as the Intolerable Acts. British soldiers were sent to the colonies to enforce the acts and were lodged in Massachusetts homes. Despite the British presence, colonists in Massachusetts, as in other colonies, were stockpiling arms and ammunition, and their militia—the Minutemen—were drilling in anticipation of clashes with the soldiers. Henry referred to these preparations in his line "Our brethren are already in the field!" Less than a month after Henry's speech, his prediction of open battle in the North was fulfilled in the opening skirmishes of the American Revolution at Lexington and Concord on April 19, 1775.

GOALS/OBJECTIVES

Studying this lesson will enable students to

- appreciate a famous piece of American political oratory
- understand some of the causes that moved the American colonies to armed rebellion
- understand such literary and rhetorical techniques as allusion, parallelism, and the use of rhetorical questions
- relate the rhetoric of an American Revolution-era speech to general principles or tendencies of the Enlightenment
- understand the functions of sentences (declarative, interrogative, and exclamatory)
- deliver an extemporaneous speech

READER'S JOURNAL

Recall what you know of the events that led to the American Revolution. Try to put yourself in those times, unable to predict the outcome of a war, knowing only that the forces of England were much larger than those of the colonies. If you had been a colonist, would you have favored war or tried to settle the differences peacefully? In your journal, write about the stand you would have taken, and why.

LANGUAGE SKILLS

Read the Language Arts Survey, 2.25, "Coordinating Conjunctions." Then examine this selection for examples of coordinating conjunctions between words, phrases, and clauses. List at least three examples.

Speech in the Virginia Convention

PATRICK HENRY

Mr. President:[1] No man thinks more highly than I do of the patriotism, as well as abilities, of the very worthy gentlemen who have just addressed the house. But different men often see the same subject in different lights: and, therefore, I hope it will not be thought disrespectful to those gentlemen, if, entertaining, as I do, opinions of a character very opposite to theirs, I shall speak forth my sentiments freely and without reserve. This is no time for ceremony. The question before the house is one of awful moment to this country. For my own part, I consider it as nothing less than a question of freedom or slavery. And in proportion to the magnitude of the subject ought to be the freedom of the debate. It is only in this way that we can hope to arrive at truth, and fulfill the great responsibility which we hold to God and our country. Should I keep back my opinions at such a time, through fear of giving offense, I should consider myself as guilty of treason toward my country, and of an act of disloyalty toward the Majesty of Heaven, which I revere above all earthly kings.

Mr. President, it is natural to man to indulge in the illusions of hope. We are apt to shut our eyes against a painful truth, and listen to the song of that siren till she transforms us into beasts. Is this the part of wise men, engaged in a great and arduous struggle for liberty? Are we disposed to be of the number of those who having eyes see not, and having ears hear not, the things which so nearly concern their temporal salvation? For my part, whatever anguish of spirit it may cost, I am willing to know the whole truth; to know the worst and to provide for it.

1. **Mr. President.** President of the Virginia Convention

WORDS FOR EVERYDAY USE: **tem • po • ral** (tem´pə rəl) *adj.*, lasting only for a time; temporary

PREREADING NOTES

READER'S JOURNAL

In preparation for doing this journal activity, have students review the background material in the introduction to the unit, pages 134–137.

LANGUAGE SKILLS

The following are examples of coordinating conjunctions from the selection:

1. I have but one lamp by which my feet are guided, *and* that is the lamp of experience. (Page 154, paragraph 1)
2. We have held the subject up in every light of which it is capable; *but* it has been all in vain. (Page 154, paragraph 3)
3. I know not what course others may take; *but* as for me, give me liberty *or* give me death! (Page 155, last line)

LITERARY NOTE

Allusion. An **allusion** is a reference in a work of art to some well-known aspect of history or culture. Henry's line "listen to the song of that siren till she transforms us into beasts" is a conflation, or running together, of two allusions to Homer's epic poem, *The Odyssey.* The sirens were creatures, half bird and half woman, whose beautiful singing lured sailors to their deaths. Odysseus, the hero of Homer's poem, managed to hear the siren's song without being lured to his death by plugging the ears of his sailors and having himself lashed to the mast of his ship. The reference to transformation into beasts might be to Circe, the temptress from *The Odyssey* who transformed Odysseus's men into pigs. The essence of Henry's comment is that hope can be a dangerous siren's song, luring people to disaster.

VOCABULARY IN CONTEXT

- Slim's anger was temporal, and soon his good-natured grin returned.

VOCABULARY FROM THE SELECTION

avert	inviolate	submission
comport	martial	supinely
effectual	prostrate	temporal
formidable	remonstrate	
inestimable	solace	
insidious	subjugation	

Answers to Guided Reading Questions

❶ Experience guides the speaker.

❷ The colonists have responded to British threats with entreaties and supplications, petitions, remonstrations, and prostrations.

Literary Note

Allusion. An **allusion** is a reference in a work of art to some well-known aspect of history or culture. When Henry tells the Virginia Burgesses, "Suffer not yourselves to be betrayed with a kiss," he is alluding to the kiss that Judas gave to Christ when betraying the latter to Roman soldiers. The allusion reveals Henry's feeling that the English king cannot be trusted.

Aphorism. An **aphorism** is a brief, memorable statement. "I know of no way of judging the future but by the past" is an example of an aphorism.

Answers to Selection Check Test 4.3.5

EX. To whom does Patrick Henry address his remarks?
He addresses them to the Virginia House of Burgesses.

1. What does Henry describe as "illusions" and as a "delusive phantom"?
He describes hope as "illusions" and as a "delusive phantom."

2. By what means does Henry say one should judge the future?
He says that one should judge the future by the past.

3. Of what are the British fleets and armies sent to the colonies a sign?
They are a sign of the intention of Britain to subjugate the colonies.

4. According to Henry, who is "already in the field"?
Henry says, "Our brethren are already in the field," meaning members of the colonial militia.

5. What counsel does Henry give for dealing with Great Britain?
He urges warfare with Great Britain.

Patrick Henry speaking against the Stamp Act in the Virginia House of Burgesses in 1765. *Nineteenth-century colored engraving. The Granger Collection, NY*

What guides the speaker? ❶

I have but one lamp by which my feet are guided, and that is the lamp of experience. I know of no way of judging of the future but by the past. And judging by the past, I wish to know what there has been in the conduct of the British ministry for the last ten years to justify those hopes with which gentlemen have been pleased to solace themselves and the house? Is it that insidious smile with which our petition[2] has been lately received? Trust it not, sir: it will prove a snare to your feet. Suffer not yourselves to be betrayed with a kiss. Ask yourselves how this gracious reception of our petition comports with those warlike preparations which cover our waters and darken our land. Are fleets and armies necessary to a work of love and reconciliation? Have we shown ourselves so unwilling to be reconciled that force must be called in to win back our love? Let us not deceive ourselves, sir. These are the implements of war and subjugation—the last arguments to which kings resort.

How have the colonists responded to British threats? ❷

I ask gentlemen, sir, what means this martial array,[3] if its purpose be not to force us to submission? Can gentlemen assign any other possible motive for it? Has Great Britain any enemy in this quarter of the world, to call for all this accumulation of navies and armies? No, sir, she has none. They are meant for us: they can be meant for no other. They are sent over to bind and rivet upon us those chains which the British ministry have been so long forging.

And what have we to oppose to them? Shall we try argument? Sir, we have been trying that for the last ten years. Have we anything new to offer upon the subject? Nothing. We have held the subject up in every light of which it is capable; but it has been all in vain. Shall we resort to entreaty and humble supplication? What terms shall we find which have not been already exhausted? Let us not, I beseech[4] you, sir, deceive ourselves longer.

Sir, we have done everything that could be done to avert the storm which is now coming on. We have petitioned; we have

2. **petition.** "Olive Branch Petition," in which the king was asked to intercede between Parliament and the colonies

3. **array.** Display; assembly

Words for Everyday Use:

so • lace (säl´is) *vt.*, comfort, relieve
in • sid • i • ous (in sid´ē əs) *adj.*, sly; crafty
com • port (kəm pôrt´) *vi.*, agree; go along
sub • ju • ga • tion (sub´jə gā´shen) *n.*, takeover; enslavement
mar • tial (mär´shəl) *adj.*, warlike; of the military
sub • mis • sion (sub mish´ən) *n.*, act of yielding; surrendering
a • vert (ə vurt´) *vt.*, prevent

Vocabulary in Context

- Emily's mother solaced her with a hug and a smile.
- I refuse to go along with your insidious plan, Edgar!
- Her actions do not comport with her stated ideals.
- I saw this great science fiction movie about the subjugation of Earth by fifty-foot ants from outer space.
- "The Battle Hymn of the Republic" is a martial song.
- The puppy showed his submission by dropping the stick and wagging his tail.
- Even storm clouds could not avert the delivery of the mail.

remonstrated; we have supplicated; we have prostrated ourselves before the throne, and have implored its interposition[5] to arrest the tyrannical hands of the ministry and Parliament. Our petitions have been slighted; our remonstrances have produced additional violence and insult; our supplications have been disregarded; and we have been spurned with contempt from the foot of the throne! In vain, after these things, may we indulge the fond[6] hope of peace and reconciliation. There is no longer any room for hope. If we wish to be free, if we mean to preserve inviolate those inestimable privileges for which we have been so long contending, if we mean not basely to abandon the noble struggle in which we have been so long engaged, and which we have pledged ourselves never to abandon until the glorious object of our contest shall be obtained—we must fight! I repeat it, sir, we must fight! An appeal to arms and to the God of Hosts is all that is left us!

They tell us, sir, that we are weak—unable to cope with so formidable an adversary. But when shall we be stronger? Will it be the next week, or the next year? Will it be when we are totally disarmed, and when a British guard shall be stationed in every house? Shall we gather strength by irresolution and inaction? Shall we acquire the means of effectual resistance by lying supinely on our backs and hugging the delusive phantom of hope until our enemies shall have bound us hand and foot? Sir, we are not weak, if we make a proper use of those means which the God of nature hath placed in our power. Three millions of people, armed in the holy cause of liberty, and in such a country as that which we possess, are invincible by any force which our enemy can send against us. Besides, sir, we shall not fight our battles alone. There is a just God who presides over the destinies of nations and who will raise up friends to fight our battles for us. The battle, sir, is not to the strong alone; it is to the vigilant, the active, the brave. Besides, sir, we have no election.[7] If we were base enough to desire it, it is now too late to retire from the contest. There is no retreat but in submission and slavery! Our chains are forged! Their clanging may be heard on the plains of Boston! The war is inevitable—and let it come! I repeat it, sir, let it come![8]

It is in vain, sir, to extenuate the matter. Gentlemen may cry, "Peace, peace"—but there is no peace. The war is actually begun! The next gale that sweeps from the north will bring to our ears the clash of resounding arms! Our brethren are already in the field! Why stand we here idle? What is it that gentlemen wish? What would they have? Is life so dear, or peace so sweet, as to be purchased at the price of chains and slavery? Forbid it, Almighty God! I know not what course others may take; but as for me, give me liberty or give me death! ■

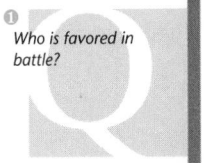

❶ *Who is favored in battle?*

4. **beseech.** Beg; plead
5. **interposition.** Intervention
6. **fond.** Foolish
7. **election.** Choice
8. **the war . . . come.** Boston had recently been occupied by British troops under the leadership of General Howe.

WORDS FOR EVERYDAY USE:

re • mon • strate (ri män´strāt´) *vt.,* demonstrate
pros • trate (präs´trāt´) *vt.,* bow down
in • vi • o • late (in vī´ə lit) *adj.,* sacred
in • es • ti • ma • ble (in es´tə mə bəl) *adj.,* too great to be measured
for • mi • da • ble (fôr´mə de bəl) *adj.,* overwhelming
ef • fec • tu • al (e fek´chōō əl) *adj.,* effective
su • pine • ly (sōō´pīn´lə) *adv.,* passively

ANSWER TO GUIDED READING QUESTION

❶ In battle, the vigilant, the active, and the brave are favored.

LITERARY NOTE

Metaphor. A **metaphor** is a figure of speech in which one thing is written or spoken about as if it were another. The figure of speech invites the listener or reader to make a comparison between the two things. Henry's speech is full of metaphors. For example, Henry calls hope "a delusive phantom." He describes the attempts by Britain to subjugate the colonies as the forging of chains.

Aphorism. An **aphorism** is a brief, memorable statement. Examples of aphorisms on this page include "There is no retreat but in submission and slavery!" and "As for me, give me liberty or give me death!"

Rhetorical Question. A **rhetorical question** is one that is asked in order to make a point, not in order to receive an answer. Speakers use rhetorical questions as a means for reinforcing a point that they have already made or that should, from the speaker's point of view, be obvious to the audience. Henry asks several rhetorical questions in the last paragraph, including, "Is life so dear, or peace so sweet, as to be purchased at the price of chains and slavery?"

RESPONDING TO THE SELECTION

The last sentence can be quoted outside the speech and often is. It is applicable, generally, to situations that are completely intolerable. Students are likely to know the quotation already but to be unfamiliar with its context. Learning about this context should deepen their appreciation of the meaning of the sentence.

VOCABULARY IN CONTEXT

- Daniel remonstrated his objections with a lengthy argument.
- The people of the court prostrated themselves before the king.
- Wilma's Sunday morning with the comics and a doughnut is inviolate.
- You have my inestimable gratitude for doing the dishes.
- Washing the pile of dirty dishes was quite a formidable task.
- A simple "No" was effectual in quieting the dog.
- I cannot sit supinely by while you shirk your responsibilities this way.

Answers for Reviewing the Selection

RECALLING

1. According to Henry, the only way to arrive at truth is to engage in free and honest debate.
2. British warships standing off the coastline and British soldiers camped in Massachusetts convince Henry that England means to wage war.
3. Colonists have petitioned, entreated, and prostrated themselves before the throne. Their efforts have been disregarded or spurned.
4. Henry welcomes war and the chance for the colonists to fight back.

INTERPRETING

Responses will vary. Possible responses are given.

5. Henry feels he must speak out in opposition to the previous speakers who urged moderation and a peaceful attitude toward the British because such peaceful attempts had had little effect on Britain's attitude toward the colonies. Further, it was apparent Britain was readying a military intervention in the colonies.
6. Henry distrusts "The insidious smile with which" their latest petition was received because prior petitions had been similarly received and ignored.
7. Henry feels fighting now is wiser than waiting because the colonists are as strong an opponent as they will ever be; they have not yet been totally disarmed, the British have not yet stationed a soldier in every house.
8. The alternative to war, according to Henry, is "submission and slavery" to Britain.

SYNTHESIZING

Responses will vary. Possible responses are given.

9. *Students should explain their responses.*
10. Students might mention that the reaction of the Massachusetts colonists to Henry's speech could be one of gratitude and relief, and that the reaction of the British government to Henry's speech might be one of smug indifference.

Responding to the Selection

You are probably familiar with the final sentence of this speech. Why can it be quoted outside of this speech? Was it more meaningful to you in the context of the speech? Why, why not?

Reviewing the Selection

RECALLING

1. According to Henry, what is the only way to arrive at truth?
2. What evidence suggests strongly to Henry that Britain means to wage war "to force us to submission"?
3. What efforts have the colonists made to maintain peace? How have their efforts been received by the British government?
4. What is Henry's response to the possibility that war may break out soon?

INTERPRETING

5. Why does Henry feel he must speak out in opposition to the previous speakers who urged moderation and the maintenance of a peaceful attitude toward Britain?
6. Why does Henry distrust "the insidious smile with which our petition has been lately received"?
7. Henry argues that peaceful options have been exhausted and that war will come sooner or later. Summarize the argument Henry makes for fighting now instead of waiting.
8. What does Henry see as the alternative to war? Why is that alternative so unthinkable?

SYNTHESIZING

9. If you had been a representative to the Virginia Convention, would Henry's words have persuaded you to take up arms against Britain? In your opinion, which of his arguments are most convincing?
10. Describe the probable reaction of the Massachusetts colonists to Henry's speech. Describe the probable reaction of the British government to his speech.

Understanding Literature (Questions for Discussion)

1. **Rhetorical Question.** A rhetorical question is one asked for effect but not meant to be answered because the answer is clear from the context. Paragraph 2 contains this example: "Are we disposed to be of the number of those who having eyes see not, and

Answers for Understanding Literature

▶ See the evaluation forms for discussion, active listening, and oral communication, *Assessment Portfolio,* 7.11–7.14.

Responses will vary. Possible responses are given.

1. Rhetorical Question. Three examples of rhetorical questions follow. "Is this the part of wise men, engaged in a great and arduous struggle for liberty?"; "Is it that insidious smile with which our petition has been lately received?"; and "Are fleets and armies necessary to a work of love and reconciliation?"

2. Enlightenment. (a) Henry supports the importance of using reason as a guide to action when he points out the war preparations made by the British. (b) The hypothesis presented by the previous speakers was that "entreaty and humble supplication" would convince the British to respect the colonists' desire for self-determination. The "experimental results" that Henry reports are

(cont.)

having ears hear not, the things which so nearly concern their temporal salvation?" Identify three more passages in which the speaker poses rhetorical questions.

2. **Enlightenment.** The **Enlightenment** was an eighteenth-century philosophical movement characterized by belief in reason, the scientific method, and the perfectibility of people and society. Look for indications in this speech that Patrick Henry participated in this movement. (a) Where does he support the importance of using reason as a guide to action? (b) The scientific method calls for hypothesizing and predicting, experimenting to test the hypothesis, and basing further action on the results of the experiments. What hypothesis have the previous speakers presented with regard to the political situation? What "experimental results" does Henry report? What prediction does he make based on observable phenomena? (c) Does Henry accept the idea that people and society are perfectible—or, at least, that they can be improved? What passages support your answer?

3. **Parallelism. Parallelism** is a rhetorical technique in which a writer emphasizes the equal value or weight of two or more ideas by expressing them in the same grammatical form. For example, in the phrase "freedom or slavery" (paragraph 1, sentence 5), Henry balances two nouns; in "the magnitude of the subject" and "the freedom of the debate" (paragraph 1, sentence 6), he balances two noun phrases; and in "Should I keep back my opinions" and "I should consider myself as guilty of treason" (paragraph 1, sentence 8), he equates two predicates. Find at least four other instances of parallelism. For each, identify the grammatical form used.

Responding in Writing

1. **Nomination Speech.** Select a character from a book, play, or movie to run for election to your state legislature. Write a brief nomination speech, presenting the character's credentials and calling on your audience to support the nomination. Use rhetorical techniques, such as those in Henry's speech to the Virginia Convention to excite your audience about your candidate.

2. **Minutes.** In the minutes of a meeting, the secretary of an organization summarizes the discussion on each item of business and records formal movements and decisions. Imagine that you are the secretary for the Virginia Convention. Write a brief passage for the minutes, covering Patrick Henry's speech.

3. **Petition.** Patrick Henry referred to the petitions that his countrymen had sent to the king of England, seeking what they perceived as their rights as English citizens. Consider your various roles, as family member, student, citizen, and so on. What rights do you feel belong to a role, but have not been open to you? Who might be able to improve this situation? Write a petition to the authority figure you choose, identifying the rights that you seek and explaining why you deserve them.

Answers for Understanding Literature (cont.)

that their entreaties and humble supplications have not borne any results. Based on observable phenomena of British warships off their coast and British troops in Boston, he predicts the British will completely subjugate the colonists unless the colonists fight for their rights. (c) Henry does not accept the idea that people and society are perfectible because he points out all of the avenues pursued by the colonists in their quest for self-determination from British rule and how the British have completely ignored all such requests.

3. Parallelism. Following are four examples of parallelism from Henry's speech: "having eyes see not, and having ears hear not (participial phrases); "to know the whole truth; to know the worst and to provide for it" (infinitive phrases); "They are meant for us. . . they can be meant . . They are sent over . . ." (independent clauses); "If we wish to be free, if we mean to preserve. . . if we mean" (dependent clauses).

Analytic Scales for Responding in Writing

Assign a score from 1 to 25 for each grading criterion below. (For more detailed evaluation, see the evaluation forms for writing, revising, and proofreading, *Assessment Portfolio,* 7.1–7.10.)

1. Nomination Speech

- **Content/Unity.** The speech presents the character's credentials and calls upon the audience to support the nomination.
- **Organization/Coherence.** The speech is brief and follows a logical progression.
- **Language/Style.** The speech is persuasive and makes use of rhetorical techniques.
- **Conventions.** The speech avoids errors in spelling, grammar, usage, mechanics, and manuscript form.

2. Minutes

- **Content/Unity.** The minutes accurately summarize the content of Henry's speech.
- **Organization/Coherence.** The minutes are in note form.

(cont.)

Analytic Scales for Responding in Writing (cont.)

- **Language/Style.** The minutes are brief and to the point.
- **Conventions.** The minutes avoid errors in spelling, grammar, usage, mechanics, and manuscript form.

3. Petition

- **Content/Unity.** The petition makes a request related to rights and presents a case supporting the request.
- **Organization/Coherence.** The petition uses proper paragraph form.
- **Language/Style.** The language is polite and persuasive.
- **Conventions.** The petition avoid errors in spelling, grammar, usage, mechanics, and manuscript form.

ANSWERS FOR LANGUAGE LAB

1. Declarative
2. Declarative
3. Interrogative
4. Exclamatory
5. Declarative

ANSWERS FOR SPEAKING AND LISTENING SKILLS

▶ **Teaching Note:** The activity calls for extemporaneous speeches. Remind students that an extemporaneous speech is one that has had thorough preparation beforehand and that is delivered from notes rather than memorized. If you do not wish to take the time to have students do prewriting and prepare notes for their speeches, you can have them do impromptu speeches instead. If you decide to do this, make sure to inform students that you are changing the activity from one on extemporaneous speaking to one on impromptu speaking.

PROJECT NOTES

▶ See the worksheets and evaluation forms for projects, *Assessment Portfolio,* 7.20–7.23.

1. Royal Television Commercial. Make sure students understand that preparing a television commercial for King George is an example of anachronism—that television was a much later invention. Possible arguments that students might present in support of the king include the following:
a. that, in keeping with tradition, the colonists, as British subjects, owe allegiance to their king.
b. that the unpopular taxes imposed by Britain help to pay for expenses from the French and Indian War, which benefited the British colonists.
c. that many of the rebellious actions of the revolutionaries involve what is (from the loyalist point of view) an insupportable and wanton destruction of property.

(cont.)

Language Lab

Functions of Sentences. Read the Language Arts Survey, 2.36, "The Functions of Sentences." Then identify the functions of each of the following sentences from Patrick Henry's speech.

1. Let us not deceive ourselves, sir.
2. This is no time for ceremony.
3. And what have we to oppose to them?
4. There is no retreat but in submission and slavery!
5. Sir, we are not weak, if we make a proper use of those means which the God of nature hath placed in our power.

Speaking and Listening Skills

Public Speaking. Read the Language Arts Survey, 3.7, "Public Speaking." Then join with a small group of classmates. Take two to three minutes to brainstorm topics for extemporaneous speeches explaining, supporting, or attacking objects, practices, or ideas. Then each group member should write two topics on a slip of paper. After the slips are mixed up in a container, each member should draw one, choose one of the two suggested topics, and give an extemporaneous one- to two-minute speech on the topic.

PROJECTS

1. **Royal Television Commercial.** King George III needs to make his case to the American colonists. Write a television commercial to arouse support for him. Write the text and describe the audiovisual techniques to be used, including still photographs, animated sequences, and music.

2. **Pre-Revolutionary Twenty Questions.** Each person in the class should select a known or anonymous person from pre-Revolutionary America, for example, George Washington or one of the accusers in the Salem witch trials, and do any necessary research to represent that person. Then the class should play a game of Twenty Questions. Each player takes a turn representing his or her selected person, and the rest of the class may ask up to twenty questions to determine the person's identity. All questions must have yes or no answers.

PROJECT NOTES (CONT.)

2. Pre-Revolutionary Twenty Questions. Possible subjects for research include the following: Sam Adams, Vasco Núñez de Balboa, William Bradford, John Cabot, Chief Powhatan, Christopher Columbus; Hernando Cortés; Benjamin Franklin; King George III, Patrick Henry, Anne Hutchinson, Thomas Jefferson, Ponce de León, Ferdinand Magellan, Montezuma, Thomas Paine, William Penn, Pocohantas, Sir Walter Ralegh, Paul Revere, John Smith, Amerigo Vespucci, George Washington, and Roger Williams.

PREREADING

from *Crisis, No. 1*
by Thomas Paine

About the Author

Thomas Paine (1737–1809) was born in the village of Thetford, in Norfolk, England, the son of a Quaker father and an Anglican mother. He received little formal education. He attended grammar school until he was thirteen and then worked as an apprentice in the shop belonging to his father, a corset maker. Benjamin Franklin, who met Paine in London, recognized the younger man's potential and supplied him with letters of introduction when he sailed for Philadelphia. There Paine became a spokesperson against slavery and the author of a pamphlet entitled *Common Sense,* the first published work in the colonies to call for independence from Great Britain. Paine helped to raise money for weapons to be used by the American revolutionaries, and wrote sixteen pamphlets, the *Crisis* papers, to lift the morale of the troops. While he received numerous political appointments, he found public office confining. He returned to England, where his *Rights of Man,* a condemnation of hereditary monarchy, led to charges of treason. He fled to France where, ironically for this supporter of both the American and the French Revolutions, he was arrested for expressing the view that the French king should be exiled instead of executed. With the help of the American ambassador, Paine won release from prison, left France, and returned to America. On his return, he wrote *The Age of Reason,* the title of which is often taken to describe the entire period of the eighteenth century in Europe. During the last part of his life, Paine lived on land granted to him by the state of New York for his service during the Revolution. Unfortunately, few people remembered Paine's important contributions, and many disliked him because of his unorthodox religious views. This champion of freedom, whose words helped to forge the American experiment in democracy, spent his last years in poverty and obscurity.

About the Selection

The following selection is from the first of a series of sixteen pamphlets published from 1776 to 1783 entitled ***Crisis.*** In December 1776, when the first pamphlet appeared, the American cause was at low ebb. Washington and his troops had just retreated to Trenton, and support for the revolution was wavering. The rebels welcomed Paine's words of encouragement and inspiration; in fact, Washington immediately read them to his troops to lift their morale. Paine tried to conceal his identity by signing his pamphlets "Common Sense" instead of using his own name because the sentiments he expressed in them were clearly treasonous, but the identity of the author was soon common knowledge.

GOALS/OBJECTIVES

Studying this lesson will enable students to

- appreciate a pamplet from the American Revolution
- analyze comparisons and contrasts in their reading
- summarize an argument
- define *assonance* and recognize assonance that they encounter in their reading
- understand the effect of rhetorical questions
- correct agreement between pronouns and antecedents
- understand propaganda techniques

ADDITIONAL RESOURCES

Reader's Guide
- Selection Worksheet, 3.4

Assessment Portfolio
- Selection Check Test, 4.3.7
- Selection Test, 4.3.8

ENRICHMENT ACTIVITIES

Have students read the selection from Paine's *Common Sense* in the Selections for Additional Reading on page 185. Share with students the following text of the title page from Paine's *Common Sense:*

COMMON SENSE;
addressed to the
INHABITANTS
of
AMERICA,
On the following interesting
SUBJECTS.

I. Of the Origin and Design of Government in General, with Concise Remarks on the English Constitution.
II. Of Monarchy and Hereditary Succession.
III. Thoughts on the present State of American Affairs.
IV. Of the present Ability of America; with some Miscellaneous Reflections.

Discuss with students how titles and title pages have changed since Paine's days and the relative advantages and disadvantages of creating title pages that are primarily outlines of the work.

SUPPORT FOR LEP STUDENTS

Additional Vocabulary

crisis—difficult or demanding situation
esteem—judge well of
dearness—expense
celestial—having to do with the heavens
ravage—take extreme liberties with
perish—end, die

PREREADING NOTES

READER'S JOURNAL

Encourage students to think about the differences between communication via television and via pamphlets. Television is a pictorial medium in which the presentation of ideas tends to be very brief and, as a result, simplistic. A pamphlet, in contrast, provides the author and the reader with an opportunity to think about an issue in depth, to weigh the pros and cons of an issue carefully.

THINKING SKILLS

Students can analyze the comparison by making a chart with the headings "The Colonial Situation" and "A Burglary by an Intruder." Have them list the similarities on the chart.

ANSWER TO GUIDED READING QUESTION

❶ Summer soldiers and sunshine patriots—people without firm loyalties or resolve—may fail to respond to the needs of the country.

VOCABULARY FROM THE SELECTION

calamity	offensive
consolation	penitentially
duration	reflection
hypocrisy	repulse
impious	resolution
induce	sottish

READER'S JOURNAL

In colonial days and the early days of the American Revolution, pamphlets and newspapers were the only ways to spread ideas among the colonies. Today, television is the medium through which many people air their views. Have you ever seen a television show in which someone presented a strongly held point of view? Freewrite in your journal about such a person whom you have seen on TV and explain the cause he or she was supporting. Was the speaker convincing enough to change your mind?

THINKING SKILLS

Read the Language Arts Survey, 4.8, "Comparing and Contrasting." Then, as you read Paine's essay, identify the part in which he compares the actions of the colonists to those of a person defending his or her house against an intruder. Consider these questions: Why does Paine make this comparison? What point does he wish to make by means of this comparison? Is the comparison effective? Why, or why not?

Crisis, No. 1

THOMAS PAINE

Who may fail to respond to the needs of the country? ❶

These are the times that try men's souls. The summer soldier and the sunshine patriot will, in this crisis, shrink from the service of their country, but he that stands it now, deserves the love and thanks of man and woman. Tyranny like hell, is not easily conquered; yet we have this consolation with us, that the harder the conflict, the more glorious the triumph. What we obtain too cheap, we esteem too lightly: it is dearness only that gives everything its value. Heaven knows how to put a proper price upon its goods; and it would be strange indeed if so celestial an article as freedom should not be highly rated. Britain, with an army to enforce her tyranny, has declared that she has a right (not only to tax) but "to bind us in all cases whatsoever," and if being bound in that manner is not slavery, then is there not such a thing as slavery upon earth. Even the expression is impious; for so unlimited a power can belong only to God.

Whether the independence of the continent was declared too soon, or delayed too long, I will not now enter into as an argument; my own simple opinion is, that had it been eight months earlier, it would have been much better. We did not make a proper use of last winter, neither could we, while we were in a dependent state. However, the fault, if it were one, was all our own;[1] we have none to blame but

1. **own.** Paine wanted an immediate declaration of independence uniting the colonies.

WORDS FOR EVERYDAY USE:

con • so • la • tion (kän´sə lā´shən) *n.,* comfort

im • pi • ous (im´pē əs) *adj.,* lacking reverence for God

VOCABULARY IN CONTEXT

- Knowing that they had tried their best was some consolation to the losing hockey team.
- Orthodox Hindus consider disturbing cattle an impious act.

ourselves. But no great deal is lost yet. All that Howe[2] has been doing for this month past is rather a ravage than a conquest, which the spirit of the Jerseys,[3] a year ago, would have quickly repulsed, and which time and a little resolution will soon recover.

I have as little superstition in me as any man living, but my secret opinion has ever been, and still is, that God Almighty will not give up a people to military destruction, or leave them unsupportedly to perish, who have so earnestly and so repeatedly sought to avoid the calamities of war, by every decent method which wisdom could invent. Neither have I so much of the infidel[4] in me as to suppose that He has relinquished the government of the world, and given us up to the care of devils; and as I do not, I cannot see on what grounds the King of Britain can look up to heaven for help against us: a common murderer, a highwayman, or a housebreaker has as good a pretense as he.

'Tis surprising to see how rapidly a panic will sometimes run through a country. All nations and ages have been subject to them: Britain has trembled like an ague[5] at the report of a French fleet of flat-bottomed boats, and in the fourteenth century[6] the whole English army, after ravaging the kingdom of France, was driven back like men petrified with fear; and this brave exploit was performed by a few broken forces collected and headed by a woman, Joan of Arc. Would that heaven might inspire some Jersey maid to spirit up her countrymen, and save her fair fellow sufferers from ravage and ravishment! Yet panics, in some cases, have their uses; they produce as much good as hurt. Their duration is always short; the mind soon grows through them, and acquires a firmer habit than before. But their peculiar advantage is that they are the touchstones[7] of sincerity and hypocrisy, and bring things and men to light, which might otherwise have lain forever undiscovered. In fact, they have the same effect on secret traitors, which an imaginary apparition would have upon a private murderer. They sift out the hidden thoughts of man, and hold them up in public to the world. Many a disguised tory[8] has lately shown his head, that shall penitentially solemnize with curses the day on which Howe arrived upon the Delaware. . . .

The far and the near, the home counties and the back,[9] the rich and poor will suffer or rejoice alike. The heart that feels not now is dead: the blood of his children will curse his cowardice who shrinks back at a time when a little might have saved the whole, and made them happy. I love the man that can smile in trouble, that can gather strength from distress, and grow

❶ *What benefits arise from panic?*

❷ *Whom does Paine admire?*

2. **Howe.** Lord William Howe was commander of the British Army in America from 1775 to 1778.
3. **Jerseys.** East and West Jersey were separate colonies.
4. **infidel.** Person who does not accept some particular theory, belief, etc.; used derogatorily
5. **ague.** Chill; fit of shivering
6. **fourteenth century.** Actually the fifteenth; Joan of Arc triumphed over the English in 1429.
7. **touchstones.** Types of stone formerly used to test the purity of gold or silver; hence, any test for determining genuineness or value
8. **tory.** Supporter of continued allegiance to Great Britain
9. **back.** Backwoods

WORDS FOR EVERYDAY USE:

re • pulse (ri puls´) *vt.,* drive back
res • o • lu • tion (rez´ə lōō´shən) *n.,* determination
ca • lam • i • ty (kə lam´ə tē) *n.,* deep trouble or misery
du • ra • tion (dōō rā´shən) *n.,* continuance in time
hy • poc • ri • sy (hi päk´rə sē) *n.,* pretending to be what one is not, or to feel what one does not feel
pen • i • ten • tial • ly (pen´i ten´shəl lē) *adv.,* in a manner suggesting regret for wrongdoing

VOCABULARY IN CONTEXT

- A small band of Pawnee warriors repulsed the cavalry, sending them scurrying back to the fort.
- Mark made a resolution to try to remember his friend's birthday in the future.
- The fire at the Library of Alexandria, which destroyed many of the books of the ancient world, was a great calamity.
- The duration of the drought was about three months.
- Pretending to be a friend while secretly harboring ill will is a kind of hypocrisy.
- After knocking over the vase, the dog penitentially lowered its head and tail, as though it were saying, "Please forgive me."

ANSWERS TO GUIDED READING QUESTIONS

❶ People soon get over panic and acquire, as a result of the experience, more firmness than they had before. Furthermore, panic reveals people's true natures—whether they are sincere or hypocritical.

❷ Paine admires people who can smile when there is trouble and who gather strength from distress.

LITERARY TECHNIQUE

Aphorism. An **aphorism** is a brief, memorable statement. This selection from Paine's work is full of aphorisms. These are some examples:

"These are the times that try men's souls."

"Tyranny, like hell, is not easily conquered."

"[W]e have none to blame but ourselves."

"The heart that feels not now is dead."

"I love the man that can smile in trouble, that can gather strength from distress, and grow brave by reflection."

"Not all the treasures of the world . . . could have induced me to support an offensive war."

ANSWERS FOR LANGUAGE LAB

Responses will vary. Possible responses are given.

1. The summer soldier will, in this crisis, shrink from the service of *his or her* country. The antecedent of *his or her* is *soldier.*

2. God will not give up a people to military destruction or leave *them* to perish. The antecedent of *them* is *people.*

3. Would that heaven might inspire some Jersey maid to spirit up *her* countrymen. The antecedent of *her* is *maid.*

4. Many a disguised Tory has lately shown *his or her* head. The antecedent of *his or her* is *Tory.*

5. The man whose heart is firm, and whose conscience approves his conduct, will pursue *his* principles unto death. The antecedent of *his* is *man.*

ANSWERS TO SELECTION CHECK TEST 4.3.7

EX. How does Paine characterize the times in the famous opening statement of *Crisis, No. 1*?

He says that "These are the times that try men's souls."

1. According to Paine, what will a "summer soldier" and "sunshine patriot" do?

They will "shrink from the service of their country."

2. According to Paine, why is it "impious" for Britain to declare that it has the right "to bind us in all cases whatsoever"?

Paine says that such a claim is impious because only God has such unlimited power.

3. To whom does Paine compare "a common murderer, a highwayman, or a housebreaker"?

He compares the British king to these people.

4. According to Paine, what kind of circumstance makes the mind "acquire a firmer habit than before" and shows the truth about the sincerity or hypocrisy of people?

Panic does these things.

5. According to Paine, who will, at the last day, be "shrieking to the rocks and mountains to cover him, and fleeting with terror from the orphan, the widow, and the slain of America"?

The British king will do these things.

brave by reflection. 'Tis the business of little minds to shrink; but he whose heart is firm, and whose conscience approves his conduct, will pursue his principles unto death. My own line of reasoning is to myself as straight and clear as a ray of light. Not all the treasures of the world, so far as I believe, could have induced me to support an offensive war, for I think it murder; but if a thief breaks into my house, burns and destroys my property, and kills or threatens to kill me, or those that are in it, and to "bind me in all cases whatsoever"[10] to his absolute will, am I to suffer it? What signifies it to me, whether he who does it is a king or a common man; my countryman or not my countryman; whether it be done by an individual villain, or an army of them? If we reason to the root of things we shall find no difference; neither can any just cause be assigned why we should punish in the one case and pardon in the other. Let them call me rebel, and welcome, I feel no concern from it; but I should suffer the misery of devils were I to make a whore of my soul by swearing allegiance to one whose character is that of a sottish, stupid, stubborn, worthless, brutish man. I conceive likewise a horrid idea in receiving mercy from a being, who at the last day shall be shrieking to the rocks and mountains to cover him, and fleeing with terror from the orphan, the widow, and the slain of America. ■

10. **"bind me . . . whatsoever."** On February 24, 1776, the Declaratory Act of Parliament established British authority over the American colonies.

WORDS FOR EVERYDAY USE:

re • flec • tion (ri flek´shən) *n.*, serious thought; contemplation
in • duce (in dōōs´) *vt.*, lead on to some action, condition, or belief
of • fen • sive (ə fen´siv) *adj.*, attacking; aggressive
sot • tish (sät´ish) *adj.*, foolish

VOCABULARY IN CONTEXT

- On further reflection, young Christopher decided that the world must be round.
- "Nothing could induce me to betray our friendship," Yolanda told Martin.
- In the third inning, the White Sox went on the offensive, scoring four runs.
- The congressman was censured by his colleagues for his sottish behavior.

Responding to the Selection

If you had been an American soldier at this time, would *Crisis, No. 1* have inspired you to carry on? What phrases or sentences do you find most effective and memorable? Which arguments do you find most persuasive?

Reviewing the Selection

RECALLING

1. How does Paine describe the time in which his pamphlet is written? What does he fear some supporters of the revolution might do?

2. According to Paine, God will help and protect the Americans. Why is God on the revolutionary side? Why would God not support the king of Britain?

3. What example of panic from history does Paine cite? What happened as a result of panic? Is panic always harmful?

4. Why would Paine refuse to support what he calls an offensive war?

INTERPRETING

5. Why does Paine entitle his pamphlet *Crisis?* Restate in your own words what is meant by the phrase "the summer soldier and the sunshine patriot."

6. Why does Paine mention God in this essay? How do you think Paine's assurance of God's endorsement of the American Revolution affected the pamphlet's American readers?

7. Why are panics sometimes useful? How has the present panic helped the revolution?

8. Does Paine consider the American Revolution to be an offensive war? What is his justification for waging war against England?

SYNTHESIZING

9. Why does Paine find the phrase "to bind [us or me] in all cases whatsoever" so objectionable? Find the two places where he uses the phrase. How does it contribute to his argument with the king of England?

10. Paine's demand for independence from the English monarchy was considered treasonous by the English. Imagine if Paine were alive today and criticizing the United States government the way he criticized the English government. How do you think his opinions would be received in modern America if they were so openly antigovernment? Would he be protected by freedom of speech or would he be in trouble? In your opinion, should his freedom of speech be protected?

RESPONDING TO THE SELECTION

Students may wish to write their own persuasive pieces alluding to or quoting from Paine to help achieve their desired effect.

ANSWERS FOR REVIEWING THE SELECTION

RECALLING

1. "These are the times that try men's souls" is how Paine describes the time in which his pamphlet is written. He fears some supporters of the revolution might lose their resolve and withdraw support from the rebels.

2. According to Paine, God is on the revolutionary side because he believes God will not allow the military destruction of peace-seeking people; furthermore, God will not allow the world to be ruled by evil people. Paine argues that God would not support a British king because he is no better than a murderer or a highwayman.

3. The example of panic from history that Paine cites is the defeat of the British by Joan of Arc. As the result of panic, the British retreated from France. Paine believes panic is not always harmful.

4. Paine would refuse to support an offensive war because he equates that with murder.

INTERPRETING

Responses will vary. Possible responses are given.

5. Paine entitles his pamphlet *Crisis* because he believes the colonies face a crisis with the British from which the colonies cannot afford to retreat. "The summer soldier and the sunshine patriot" refers to individuals who are willing to drill and train during peacetime but who would shirk their duties when and if war actually occurred.

6. Paine mentions God in this essay because most, if not all, of the colonists were deeply religious. Paine's assurance of God's endorsement of the American Revolution gave the pamphlet's American readers more resolve, more faith, and more courage to continue the revolution.

7. Panics are sometimes useful

(cont.)

ANSWERS FOR REVIEWING THE SELECTION (CONT.)

because they can result in greater firmness of resolution and they reveal sincerity and hypocrisy. The present panic helped the revolution by identifying secret traitors.

8. Paine does not believe the American Revolution to be an offensive war. Rather he likens it to defending one's home against a thief.

SYNTHESIZING

Responses will vary. Possible responses are given.

9. Paine says that being bound by Britain is slavery and that in binding the colonists in this way, Britain takes on a power that belongs only to God. Paine uses the argument that the king does not have the rights he is claiming. He later uses the phrase in his thief analogy and argues that he is not to bear such actions against himself.

10. Paine would not be in trouble because he has the right to speak his mind. Students should explain their opinions about free speech.

Understanding Literature (Questions for Discussion)

1. **Argumentation. Argumentation** presents reasons or arguments for accepting a position or for adopting a course of action. Summarize the arguments Paine gives for continuing to wage war against England.
2. **Assonance. Assonance** is the repetition of vowel sounds in stressed syllables that end with different consonant sounds. Read these lines from the opening paragraph: "These are the times that try men's souls. The sunshine soldier and the summer patriot will, in this crisis, shrink from the service of their country." What vowel sound is repeated in the first sentence? in the second sentence? Notice how the repetition of sounds makes the lines more memorable.
3. **Rhetorical Question.** A **rhetorical question** is one asked for effect but not meant to be answered because the answer is clear from context. Find a rhetorical question in *Crisis, No. 1.* What answer does the author make clear?

Language Lab

Agreement of Pronouns and Antecedents. Read the Language Arts Survey, 2.83, "Agreement of Pronouns and Antecedents I." Rewrite each sentence below to make every italicized pronoun agree with its antecedent. Circle the antecedent.

1. The summer soldier will, in this crisis, shrink from the service of *their* country.
2. God will not give up a people to military destruction, or leave *her* to perish.
3. Would that heaven might inspire some Jersey maid to spirit up *his* countrymen.
4. Many a disguised Tory has lately shown *their* head.
5. The man whose heart is firm, and whose conscience approves his conduct, will pursue *their* principles unto death.

Thinking Skills

Propaganda. Read the Language Arts Survey, 4.15, "Understanding Propaganda Techniques." Identify propaganda techniques that are used in *Crisis, No.1.* Do you believe that propaganda is justifiable depending on why it is used, or do you feel that it is unfair under any circumstances? Explain your answer.

Answers for Understanding Literature

▶See the evaluation forms for discussion, active listening, and oral communication, *Assessment Portfolio,* 7.11–7.14.

1. Argumentation. Paine presents the following arguments: (1) those who shrink from this crisis are traitors, summer soldiers, and sunshine patriots; (2) Britain is impious in declaring that it has the right "to bind us in all cases whatsoever"; (3) the cause is not lost even though independence should have been declared sooner; (4) God is on the colonists' side because the British king is behaving like a common murderer, a highwayman, or a housebreaker; (5) good will come of the current panic; (6) many loyalists, or Tories, will change their minds in the course of coming events; (7) the colonists' cause is just; and (8) the welfare and future opinion of children is at stake.

2. Assonance. The long *i* sound is repeated in stressed syllables with different consonant sounds in the words *times, try, shine,* and *crisis.* The long *o* sound is repeated in the words *souls* and *soldier.*

▶Teaching Note: Point out to students that the lines also contain **alliteration,** or repetition of initial consonant sounds, such as the *t* sound in *times* and *try* and the *s* sound in *souls, sunshine, soldier, summer, shrink,* and *service.*

3. Rhetorical Question. Paine asks, "If a thief breaks into my house, burns and destroys my property, and ills or threatens to kill me, or those that are in it, and to 'bind me in all cases whatsoever' to his absolute will, am I to suffer it?" The answer to this question, which Paine believes to be analogous to the question of suffering the British presence in America, is clearly "no."

Answers for Language Lab

Answers for Language Lab appear on page 161.

Answers for Thinking Skills

In this essay, Paine makes extensive use of the *argumentum ad hominem,* also known as character assassination. He attacks "summer soldiers" and "sunshine patriots" and heaps invective on King George of Great Britain, comparing him to a murderer, a highwayman, and a burglar and claiming that he has taken to himself prerogatives given only to God. Paine also makes use of many loaded words, such as *impious* and *murderer.* Paine also uses transfer, hoping to transfer people's feelings about thieves and murderers onto the British. One could argue that the invocation of God's opinion is an example of testimonial.

The question of whether propaganda techniques are justified in a good cause is a variety of the larger question of whether proper ends justify improper means. Doubtless there is a proper place for strong rhetoric in political debate, and good causes sometimes fail because of the superior propaganda of the other side, but one would hope that reason would be, itself, enough to prevail over falsehood.

PREREADING

"To S. M., a Young African Painter, on Seeing His Works"
by Phillis Wheatley

About the Author

Phillis Wheatley (*circa* 1753–1784) was born in West Africa, captured as a child, and brought on a slave ship to Boston in 1761. There John Wheatley, a Boston tailor, purchased the girl to work for his wife, Susannah, who provided an education for Wheatley. A child prodigy, Wheatley rapidly learned to read both English and Latin. By the age of fourteen, she was writing poetry. She achieved fame early for a poem that she wrote about an evangelical preacher named George Whitefield. In 1773, she went to London with the Wheatleys' son, Nathaniel, partly to seek support for her first book, *Poems on Various Subjects, Religions and Morals.* She returned to Boston before the publication of her work, having received news that Susannah Wheatley was dying. Before Susannah's death in 1774, the family released Wheatley from slavery. In 1776, the year in which America declared its independence from Britain, Wheatley met General George Washington after she had written a poem dedicated to him. In 1778, Wheatley married John Peters, a freedman. Her later life was one of grief as she endured poverty and the loss of two children. Her third child, ill when Phillis Wheatley died, passed away shortly afterward and was buried with her in an unmarked grave. Rediscovered in the 1830s, Wheatley's poetry shows her to have been an eloquent spokesperson for her faith, for American independence, and for the abolition of slavery.

About the Selection

Phillis Wheatley wrote **"To S. M., a Young African Painter, on Seeing His Works"** in praise of the work of Scipio Moorhead, a servant to the Reverend John Moorhead of Boston. It was published in her volume of 1773.

ADDITIONAL RESOURCES

Reader's Guide
- Selection Worksheet, 3.5

Assessment Portfolio
- Selection Check Test, 4.3.9
- Selection Test, 4.3.10

Essential Skills Practice Books
- *Language,* 2.18

Audiocassette
- "To S. M., a Young African Painter, . . ." Track 4

ENRICHMENT ACTIVITIES

Have students read and discuss Wheatley's "To the Right Honorable William, Earl of Dartmouth" in the Selections for Additional Reading on page 185.

SUPPORT FOR LEP STUDENTS

Explain to students that this poem is written as encouragement to a fellow African-American artist and poet. Also explain that when reading poetry, one should not stop at the ends of lines but rather should read whole sentences.

Additional Vocabulary

intent—desire, want, goal
prospects—views, scenes
exalted—raised up
radiant—shining, giving off light
serene—peaceful
invest—fill
realms—countries, places, kingdoms

GOALS/OBJECTIVES

Studying this lesson will enable students to

- appreciate one of the earliest published works by an African American
- appreciate the obstacles that Phillis Wheatley overcame to become a famous poet
- recognize the use of heroic couplets in a poem
- understand and identify allusions in a poem
- write abstracts, captions, and memoranda
- differentiate between common and proper nouns
- develop a multimedia show

PREREADING NOTES

READER'S JOURNAL

To prepare students for this activity, you may wish to discuss elements of painting such as line, form, color, hue, saturation, and value, and some major schools of painting, including Classicism, Romanticism, Realism, Surrealism, Impressionism, and Abstract Expressionism.

LANGUAGE SKILLS

The italicized words in the following lines from the selection are examples of infinitives:

1. *To show* the laboring bosom's deep intent, (line 1)
2. And thought in living characters *to paint,* (line 2)
3. And breathing figures learnt from thee *to live,* (line 4)
4. *To aid* thy pencil, and thy verse conspire! (line 10)
5. Thrice happy, when exalted *to survey* (line 15)
6. No more *to tell* of Damon's tender sighs, (line 29)

ANSWER TO GUIDED READING QUESTION

❶ The speaker hopes that the subject of the poem will be inspired and will achieve fame.

VOCABULARY FROM THE SELECTION

ardent	elate
balmy	ethereal
contemplation	transport

READER'S JOURNAL

Think about a painting or other work of art that you find particularly moving or interesting. If you cannot think of one, look through this textbook until you find one that you like. In your journal, freewrite about the work, explaining what attracts you to it.

LANGUAGE SKILLS

Read the Language Arts Survey, 2.18, "Verbals: Infinitives." Then look for examples of infinitives as you read the selection.

"To S. M.,[1] a Young African Painter, on Seeing His Works"

PHILLIS WHEATLEY

To show the laboring bosom's deep intent,
And thought in living characters to paint,
When first thy pencil did those beauties give,
And breathing figures learnt from thee to live,
5 How did those prospects give my soul delight,
A new creation rushing on my sight?
Still, wond'rous youth! each noble path pursue,
On deathless glories fix thine ardent view:
Still may the painter's and the poet's fire
10 To aid thy pencil, and thy verse conspire!
And may the charms of each seraphic[2] theme
Conduct thy footsteps to immortal fame!
High to the blissful wonders of the skies
Elate thy soul, and raise thy wishful eyes.
15 Thrice[3] happy, when exalted to survey
That splendid city, crowned with endless day,

What does the speaker hope for the subject of the poem? ❶

1. **S. M.** Scipio Moorhead, servant to a Boston minister
2. **seraphic.** Angelic
3. **Thrice.** Triple (extremely)

WORDS FOR EVERYDAY USE:
ar • dent (ärd´ ´nt) *adj.,* intensely enthusiastic or devoted
e • late (ē lāt´) *vt.,* raise the spirits of

VOCABULARY IN CONTEXT

- Phil, an ardent animal lover, volunteers at the animal shelter.
- After weeks of rain, Louisa was elated by the warm, sunny day.
- The dog was engaged in rapt contemplation of its own tail.
- On a balmy day in May, Piglet decided to fly a kite.
- What transport Yolanda felt when first she heard the music of Bach!
- New Age music often attempts to create an ethereal, elevated, unearthly mood.

Whose twice six gates[4] on radiant hinges ring:
Celestial Salem[5] blooms in endless spring.

Calm and serene thy moments glide along,
And may the muse[6] inspire each future song!
Still, with the sweets of contemplation blest,
May peace with balmy wings your soul invest!
But when these shades of time are chased away,
And darkness ends in everlasting day,
On what seraphic pinions[7] shall we move,
And view the landscape in the realms above?
There shall thy tongue in heavenly murmurs flow,
And there my muse with heavenly transport glow:
No more to tell of Damon's[8] tender sighs,
Or rising radiance of Aurora's[9] eyes,
For nobler themes demand a nobler strain,
And purer language on the ethereal plain.
Cease, gentle muse! the solemn gloom of night
Now seals the fair creation from my sight. ■

❶ *What words are used to describe the artist's movements? Who inspires him?*

❷ *What event does the speaker describe in the last lines of the poem? Why, in the last line, is she unable to see the creation?*

4. **twice six gates.** Twelve gates to heaven
5. **Salem.** Jerusalem
6. **muse.** Any of the nine goddesses who preside over literature and the arts in Greek mythology
7. **pinions.** Wings
8. **Damon.** Mythical hero and loyal friend (to Pythias)
9. **Aurora.** Mythical goddess of dawn

Responding to the Selection

Wheatley advises the young painter as follows: "High to the blissful wonders of the skies/Elate thy soul, and raise thy wishful eyes." What conditions at the time of the writing of this poem would have made it difficult for an African-American artist or writer to have such a positive vision? What makes Wheatley's optimism and positive spirit so remarkable?

Words for Everyday Use:

con • tem • pla • tion (kän´ təm plā´ shən) *n.*, thoughtful inspection, study, or meditation
balm • y (bäm´ ē) *adj.*, soothing, mild, or pleasant
trans • port (trans´ pôrt) *n.*, strong emotion; rapture
e • the • re • al (ē thir´ ē əl) *adj.*, not earthly; heavenly, celestial

Answers to Guided Reading Questions

❶ The artist's movements are described as *calm* and *serene*. He is inspired by the muse.

❷ The speaker describes death. The speaker is unable to see the creation because her vision has found new, ethereal sights.

Answers to Selection Check Test 4.3.9

EX. What is the race of the person to whom this poem is addressed?
The person is African or African American.

1. What arts are practiced by the person to whom this poem is addressed?
The person is a painter and a poet.

2. What gave the speaker's soul delight?
Seeing the painter's works gave the speaker's soul delight.

3. On what does the speaker urge the painter to fix his "ardent view"?
The speaker urges the painter to fix his "ardent view" on "deathless glories," that is, on noble, probably religious, subjects.

4. What name does the speaker give to "that splendid city, crowned with endless day" (i.e., the celestial city)?
The speaker calls the celestial city Salem.

5. According to the speaker, what will happen when "these shades of time are chased away"?
The speaker and the painter will travel on "seraphic pinions" to view the landscape of heaven and will create art "on nobler themes" and in a "purer language."

Responding to the Selection

Most African Americans of the time lived in slavery or in servitude, conditions that would make it difficult for anyone to have a positive vision. That Wheatley could have such a positive attitude given such conditions is remarkable. The theme of escape into the blissfulness of heaven is a common theme in early African-American song and poetry.

ART NOTE

Palmer Hayden's *The Janitor Who Paints* is a complex work, one that bears considerable analysis. It is paired with Wheatley's poem because of a thematic similarity between the poem and the painting. Both deal with higher aspirations expressed through art. Although he is nominally a janitor, and although the tools of his janitorial trade are fully in evidence around him (the feather duster, the broom, the trash can lid), the central figure in this painting clearly has another, more important calling—his art. He stares intently at his work and is wearing the French beret associated with artists and bohemia at the time when the painting was created.

It is possible that the members of this family—one assumes that one is viewing a husband, wife, and child—have been out or are going out, for they are dressed formally. She is wearing a corsage and heels. He is wearing a tie. But whether they are coming in or going out, they have stopped to allow him to work for a moment at his canvas, an indication that when the Muse makes her presence known, one must heed the call. This shows the importance of the work to this artist. The woman seems to understand the importance of her husband's work, for she gazes into space serenely as though seeing some better future that is taking shape in the midst of this squalor (note the bare pipes and lightbulb—the family is poor; however, these people are not desperate or downtrodden; there are signs here of gentle domesticity—the upright piano and the comfortably sleeping cat). The child stares intently at the father, further emphasizing the importance of what the father is doing. In this way, the child learns of the importance of art.

The painting is replete with possible symbolic interpretations—the light representing inspiration, the woman and her child representing the Madonna and child (note the child's swaddling clothes). The pose of the painter suggests that of a drummer—the palette and trash can lid suggesting cymbals and the

(cont.)

The Janitor Who Paints. *Palmer Hayden,* circa *1937. National Museum of American Art, Washington, DC/Art Resource*

ART NOTE (CONT.)

painter's brushes suggesting the drumsticks and brushes of a jazz musician. The pose of the woman and child suggest that they might be the subjects of the painting within this painting. However, if they are the subjects, then the painter definitely is at the avant-garde, for he transforms his subject into the colorful swirls on the piece of the painting that we can see. The avant-garde nature of the work is consistent with the jazz drummer stance and with the bohemian look of the painter's attire and his apartment/studio.

Reviewing the Selection

RECALLING

1. What is the speaker's emotional response to the painter's work?
2. What advice does the speaker give the painter for selecting subjects and themes for his paintings?
3. What does the speaker hope will aid the painter in the creation of his work?
4. The speaker refers to the time of death as "when these shades of time are chased away,/And darkness ends in everlasting day." What does the speaker picture as happening to the artist after death?

INTERPRETING

5. What does the speaker mean when she says that the painter creates "breathing figures"? What does she mean by "a new creation"?
6. Why might the speaker suggest that the painter try different themes for his work? What does she suggest may be his reward for painting "each seraphic theme"?
7. What might the speaker mean by the phrase: "Still may the painter's and the poet's fire/To aid thy pencil, and thy verse conspire!"?
8. How should the poet's and the painter's work change after they die and "view the landscape in the realms above"?

SYNTHESIZING

9. The speaker wishes the painter peace and the blessing of "sweets of contemplation." Why is time for contemplation necessary for artists such as painters and writers?
10. Why do you think Wheatley responded to the young man's painting with a poem instead of a letter of encouragement? What message could a poem send that a letter might not communicate?

Understanding Literature (Questions for Discussion)

1. **Heroic Couplet.** A **heroic couplet** is a pair of rhyming iambic pentameter lines. An iambic foot contains one weakly stressed syllable followed by a strongly stressed syllable. A pentameter line has five iambic feet. Which pairs of lines in this poem are heroic couplets?
2. **Allusion.** An **allusion** is a rhetorical technique in which reference is made to a person, event, object, or work from history or literature. Identify two or three allusions in this poem, and explain their meanings.

Answers for Reviewing the Selection

RECALLING

1. The speaker's emotional response to the painter's work is one of delight.
2. The speaker advises the painter to consider other painters and poets to help him select subjects and themes for his paintings.
3. The speaker hopes that angelic forces will aid the painter in his painting.
4. After his death, the artist will paint more noble and more pure works, according to the speaker.

INTERPRETING

Responses will vary. Possible responses are given.

5. When the speaker states that the painter creates "breathing figures," she means his paintings are so lifelike they appear to breathe. By "a new creation," she means that a work of beauty exists where none previously existed.
6. The speaker might suggest that the painter try different themes for his work as a means of expanding his talent or creating a variety of beauty. She suggests his reward for painting "each seraphic theme" might be immortal fame.
7. By the phrase, "Still may . . . conspire," the speaker might mean that the work of other artists might assist the painter in expanding his own creativity and creative output.
8. After the poet and the painter die, their works should reflect nobler themes and purer language and images as a result of the heavenly glories they will experience.

SYNTHESIZING

Responses will vary. Possible responses are given.

9. Contemplation allows painters and writers to reflect on and to improve their art. An artist needs to consider new subject matter, new themes, and new techniques so that he or she can grow as an artist and not stagnate by merely imitating himself or herself.
10. Wheatley responded to the young man's painting with a poem instead of a letter of encouragement because a poem, with its compression of emotion, can state much more in fewer words. Responding in a poem also reflects her understanding of being an artist.

Answers for Understanding Literature

► See the evaluation forms for discussion, active listening, and oral communication, *Assessment Portfolio,* 7.11–7.14.

Responses will vary. Possible responses are given.

1. **Heroic Couplet.** The entire poem is composed of heroic couplets.
2. **Allusion.** Following are allusions from the selection:

Line 20: "And may the muse inspire each future song" (an allusion to the mythological Greek goddess, or Muse, who presided over poetry).

Line 29: "No more to tell of Damon's tender sighs" (an allusion to the mythical Greek hero and loyal friend of Pythias).

Line 30: "Or rising radiance of Aurora's eyes" (an allusion to the Greek goddess of dawn).

Responding in Writing

1. **Abstract.** An **abstract** is a brief account of the main ideas or arguments presented in a work. Write an abstract of the Wheatley poem or of another selection in this unit.
2. **Captions.** Collect prints or other copies of about six pieces of art or fine photography by African Americans. Write an imaginative caption for each, to explain its origins or to highlight its features.

Language Lab

Common and Proper Nouns. Read the Language Arts Survey, 2.3, "Common and Proper Nouns." Then make two lists of the nouns in the sentences below, one headed *Common Nouns* and the other *Proper Nouns*.

1. The origins of Phillis Wheatley are still a mystery.
2. Records of the time suggest that the ship that brought her to North America came from an area called Senegambia, near the west coast of Africa.
3. Today the nations of Senegal and Gambia occupy much of that territory.
4. That Phillis was given an education was extraordinary, even for a white woman of the time.
5. Wheatley became a firm advocate of freedom for the colonies, a fact that may be related to her own lack of personal freedom.

Applied English/Tech Prep Skills

Writing Memoranda. Read the Language Arts Survey, 5.6, "Writing Memoranda." Imagine that you are the president of a Fortune 500 company called American Amalgamated Motors. Your board of directors has approved a donation of $1,250,000 to the Emerson Institute of American Arts and Crafts to begin a collection of works by famous African-American artists, to be called the "Scipio Moorhead Collection" in honor of the artist to whom Wheatley's poem is addressed. Write a memo to Ms. Paula Palette, director of the museum, announcing your company's decision. Follow proper memo form.

PROJECT

Multimedia Show. Work with a group to develop a multimedia show about elements of modern American culture that are products of African or African-American artists and performers. Your show can include live demonstrations, as of dance or poetry; audiotapes, as of jazz or popular music; videotapes, as of political speeches or dramatic performances; and such visual media as sculpture, painting, and photography. Your show must include commentary and transitional material that holds the elements together.

ANALYTIC SCALES FOR RESPONDING IN WRITING

Assign a score from 1 to 25 for each grading criterion below. (For more detailed evaluation, see the evaluation forms for writing, revising, and proofreading, *Assessment Portfolio,* 7.1–7.10.)

1. Abstract

- **Content/Unity.** The abstract accurately summarizes the main ideas or arguments of the work.
- **Organization/Coherence.** The abstract is brief and contains no extraneous, unnecessary material.
- **Language/Style.** The abstract is clear and reflects the tone of the original work.
- **Conventions.** The abstract avoids errors in spelling, grammar, usage, mechanics, and manuscript form.

2. Captions

- **Content/Unity.** The captions are imaginative and say something interesting or insightful about each work.
- **Organization/Coherence.** The captions are brief.
- **Language/Style.** The captions are clearly expressed.
- **Conventions.** The captions avoid errors in spelling, grammar, usage, and mechanics.

ANSWERS FOR LANGUAGE LAB

Common Nouns	Proper Nouns
1. origins mystery	1. Phillis Wheatley
2. records time ship area west coast	2. North America Senegambia Africa
3. nations territory	3. Senegal Gambia
4. education woman time	4. Phillis
5. advocate freedom colonies fact lack freedom	5. Wheatley

ANSWERS FOR APPLIED ENGLISH/TECH PREP SKILLS

Memos should be clear, concise, and appropriate in tone.

PROJECT NOTES

► See the worksheets and evaluation forms for projects, *Assessment Portfolio,* 7.20–7.23.

Multimedia Show. You may wish to divide the class into groups and to ask each group to choose a fairly specific topic. Examples of possible topics include

- contemporary African-American dance troupes
- great African-American playwrights
- important African-American political figures
- famous African-American actors
- the origins or development of various types of music (gospel, ragtime, blues, jazz, rock and roll, soul, rap)

PREREADING

Declaration of Independence
by Thomas Jefferson

About the Author

Thomas Jefferson (1743–1826) was a man of many talents and achievements. Born in 1743 in Albemarle County, Virginia, Jefferson attended William and Mary College in Williamsburg, studied law, and was admitted to the bar. He kept up his studies, mastering law, political philosophy, architecture, and a number of foreign languages.

Jefferson's political career began after college when he was elected to the Virginia House of Burgesses. In 1774, he wrote a pamphlet denying British authority over America. In 1775, he was sent as a delegate to the Second Continental Congress, where he drafted, with input from Benjamin Franklin, John Adams, and others, the Declaration of Independence. Jefferson then returned to the Virginia legislature, and drafted a statute guaranteeing religious freedom. In 1779, he became governor of Virginia. In 1789, he became the first secretary of state under the new Constitution. During that time, he became embroiled in a controversy with Alexander Hamilton that resulted in the formation of the American two-party political system.

In 1779, Jefferson became vice president under John Adams. Then, in 1800, he was elected president. As president, he more than doubled the size of the country through the Louisiana Purchase, an acquisition of North American lands owned by France. After his retirement from public life, Jefferson devoted himself to planning the buildings and curriculum of the new University of Virginia, believing that education was key to the survival of democratic ideals. The Library of Congress was founded with some ten thousand volumes from Jefferson's private library. He died a few hours before John Adams on the fourth of July, fifty years after the signing of the Declaration of Independence.

About the Selection

In June of 1776, Richard Lee, a delegate from Virginia, brought before the Continental Congress two resolutions, one calling for separation from Great Britain and the other calling for formation of a new government. After much debate, Congress decided to accept the resolutions and set up a committee to draft a declaration of independence. Jefferson drafted the document, adding a strong statement against slavery that was deleted from the version adopted on July 4, 1776. The **Declaration of Independence** is unique in its insistence on inalienable rights, rights that cannot be taken away from the people, and on the notion that government derives its legitimacy from the consent of the governed. The Declaration of Independence is divided into three parts: the basic argument of the Declaration, a list of grievances against Great Britain, and the formal declaration of independence and nationhood. The original document is on display at the National Archives in Washington, DC.

GOALS/OBJECTIVES

Studying this lesson will enable students to

- appreciate and understand the principles that make the Declaration of Independence one of the most important political documents of all time
- identify examples of alliteration and parallelism
- write a credo
- paraphrase the articles of the Bill of Rights

ADDITIONAL RESOURCES

Reader's Guide
- Selection Worksheet, 3.6

Assessment Portfolio
- Selection Check Test, 4.3.11
- Selection Test, 4.3.12

Essential Skills Practice Books
- *Study and Research,* 4.10, 4.18

Audiocassette
- Declaration of Independence, Track 5

ENRICHMENT ACTIVITIES

Share with students these lines from Jefferson's letter to John Adams, October 28, 1813:

"I agree with you that there is a natural aristocracy among men. . . . I consider [it] the most precious gift of nature for the instruction, the trusts, and government of society. . . . May we not even say that that form of government is the best which provides the most effectually for a pure selection of these natural aristoi into the offices of government?"

Ask students the following question: the Declaration states "All men are created equal." This letter states "there is a natural aristocracy among men." Did Jefferson contradict himself on this point?

SUPPORT FOR LEP STUDENTS

The following outline may help students follow the text.

Paragraphs 1 and 2 state the purpose of the Declaration: dissolving the bonds with Great Britain. These paragraphs also provide reasons for the necessity of this dissolution: people have rights that cannot be taken away; governments are created to protect these rights; governments derive their right to exist from the people; and when a government does not respect these rights, the people have a right to rebel.

Paragraphs 3–31 list grievances against King George and describe the attempts of the colonies to address those grievances.

Paragraph 32 is the official declaration of the independence of the colonies.

PREREADING NOTES

READER'S JOURNAL

Refer students to the Bill of Rights, reprinted on page 178.

STUDY AND RESEARCH SKILLS

For an outline of the Declaration, see the Support for LEP Students note on page 171.

ANSWER TO GUIDED READING QUESTION

❶ The purpose of the Declaration is to dissolve the bonds of one people with another.

VOCABULARY FROM THE SELECTION

abdicate	naturalization
acquiesce	rectitude
assent	redress
compliance	sufferance
convulsion	tenure
evince	transient
inestimable	unalienable
insurrection	usurpation
magnanimity	

READER'S JOURNAL

Do you believe that people have basic rights that should not be taken away from them by any government? If so, what do you think that these rights are? Write about these questions in your journal.

STUDY AND RESEARCH SKILLS

Read the Language Arts Survey, 4.18, "Reading Actively," and 4.10, "Analyzing." Then, as you read the Declaration of Independence, analyze it, making notes of key points, or main ideas, in each of its three major sections.

Declaration of Independence

THOMAS JEFFERSON

IN CONGRESS, JULY 4, 1776

What is the reason for the drafting of the Declaration as stated in its opening paragraph? ❶

When in the course of human events, it becomes necessary for one people to dissolve the political bands which have connected them with another, and to assume, among the powers of the earth, the separate and equal station to which the laws of nature and of nature's God entitle them, a decent respect to the opinions of mankind requires that they should declare the causes which impel them to the separation.

We hold these truths to be self-evident: —that all men are created equal; that they are endowed by their Creator with certain unalienable rights; that among these are life, liberty, and the pursuit of happiness. That, to secure these rights, governments are instituted among men, deriving their just powers from the consent of the governed; that, whenever any form of government becomes destructive of these ends, it is the right of the people to alter or to abolish it, and to institute a new government, laying its foundation on such principles, and organizing its powers in such form, as to them shall seem most likely to effect their safety and happiness. Prudence, indeed, will dictate that governments long established should not be changed for light and transient causes; and, accordingly, all experience hath shown that mankind are more disposed to suffer, while evils are sufferable, than to right themselves by abolishing the forms to which they are accustomed. But, when a long train of abuses and usurpations, pursuing invariably the same object, evinces a design to reduce them under absolute despotism,[1] it is their right, it is their duty, to throw off such government,

1. **despotism.** Government by a tyrant

WORDS FOR EVERYDAY USE:

un • al • ien • a • ble (un āl´ yən ə bəl) *adj.,* that which may not be taken away

tran • si • ent (tran´ sē ənt) *adj.,* not permanent; temporary

u • sur • pa • tion (yōō zər pā´ shən) *n.,* unlawful or violent taking of power

e • vince (ē vins´) *vt.,* show plainly

VOCABULARY IN CONTEXT

- Her parents laughted when Melody claimed that staying up late was an unalienable right.
- Fortunately, colds are transient; they go away after a week or so.
- The prime minister was accused of usurpation of rights belonging to the king.
- The server's scowl evinced his displeasure at the small size of the tip.

IN CONGRESS, JULY 4, 1776.

A DECLARATION

BY THE REPRESENTATIVES OF THE

UNITED STATES OF AMERICA,

IN GENERAL CONGRESS ASSEMBLED.

WHEN in the Course of human Events, it becomes necessary for one People to dissolve the Political Bands which have connected them with another, and to assume among the Powers of the Earth, the separate and equal Station to which the Laws of Nature and of Nature's God entitle them, a decent Respect to the Opinions of Mankind requires that they should declare the causes which impel them to the Separation.

We hold these Truths to be self-evident, that all Men are created equal, that they are endowed by their Creator with certain unalienable Rights, that among these are Life, Liberty, and the Pursuit of Happiness—That to secure these Rights, Governments are instituted among Men, deriving their just Powers from the Consent of the Governed, that whenever any Form of Government becomes destructive of these Ends, it is the Right of the People to alter or to abolish it, and to institute new Government, laying its Foundation on such Principles, and organizing its Powers in such Form, as to them shall seem most likely to effect their Safety and Happiness. Prudence, indeed, will dictate that Governments long established should not be changed for light and transient Causes; and accordingly all Experience hath shewn, that Mankind are more disposed to suffer, while Evils are sufferable, than to right themselves by abolishing the Forms to which they are accustomed. But when a long Train of Abuses and Usurpations, pursuing invariably the same Object, evinces a Design to reduce them under absolute Despotism, it is their Right, it is their Duty, to throw off such Government, and to provide new Guards for their future Security. Such has been the patient Sufferance of these Colonies; and such is now the Necessity which constrains them to alter their former Systems of Government. The History of the present King of Great-Britain is a History of repeated Injuries and Usurpations, all having in direct Object the Establishment of an absolute Tyranny over these States. To prove this, let Facts be submitted to a candid World.

He has refused his Assent to Laws, the most wholesome and necessary for the public Good.

He has forbidden his Governors to pass Laws of immediate and pressing Importance, unless suspended in their Operation till his Assent should be obtained; and when so suspended, he has utterly neglected to attend to them.

He has refused to pass other Laws for the Accommodation of large Districts of People, unless those People would relinquish the Right of Representation in the Legislature, a Right inestimable to them, and formidable to Tyrants only.

He has called together Legislative Bodies at Places unusual, uncomfortable, and distant from the Depository of their public Records, for the sole Purpose of fatiguing them into Compliance with his Measures.

He has dissolved Representative Houses repeatedly, for opposing with manly Firmness his Invasions on the Rights of the People.

He has refused for a long Time, after such Dissolutions, to cause others to be elected, whereby the Legislative Powers, incapable of Annihilation, have returned to the People at large for their exercise; the State remaining in the mean time exposed to all the Dangers of Invasion from without, and Convulsions within.

He has endeavoured to prevent the Population of these States; for that Purpose obstructing the Laws for Naturalization of Foreigners; refusing to pass others to encourage their Migrations hither, and raising the Conditions of new Appropriations of Lands.

He has obstructed the Administration of Justice, by refusing his Assent to Laws for establishing Judiciary Powers.

He has made Judges dependent on his Will alone, for the Tenure of their Offices, and the Amount and Payment of their Salaries.

He has erected a Multitude of new Offices, and sent hither Swarms of Officers to harass our People, and eat out their Substance.

He has kept among us, in Times of Peace, Standing Armies, without the Consent of our Legislatures.

He has affected to render the Military independent of and superior to the Civil Power.

and to provide new guards for their future security. Such has been the patient sufferance of these colonies; and such is now the necessity that constrains them to alter their former systems of government. The history of the present King of Great Britain[2] is a history of repeated injuries and usurpations, all having, in direct object, the establishment of an absolute tyranny over these States. To prove this, let facts be submitted to a candid world.

He has refused his assent to laws the most wholesome and necessary for the public good.

He has forbidden his Governors to pass laws of immediate and pressing importance, unless suspended in their operation till his assent should be obtained; and when so suspended, he has utterly neglected to attend to them.

He has refused to pass other laws for the accommodation of large districts of people, unless these people would relinquish the right of representation in the legislature—a right inestimable to them, and formidable to tyrants only.

He has called together legislative bodies at places unusual, uncomfortable, and distant from the depository of their public

❶ *What had the king asked the people to relinquish? What did this right mean to them? Why is such a right formidable to tyrants?*

2. **present King of Great Britain.** King George III (1760–1820)

WORDS FOR EVERYDAY USE:

suf • fer • ance (suf´ ər əns) *n.*, power to tolerate pain

as • sent (ə sent´) *n.*, agreement

in • es • ti • ma • ble (in es´ tə mə bəl) *adj.*, that which cannot be measured

VOCABULARY IN CONTEXT

- The workers tired of their long sufferance of poor working conditions; they demanded improvements.
- Marge nodded in assent.
- Da Vinci's paintings are of inestimable value.

ANSWER TO GUIDED READING QUESTION

❶ According to the selection, the king had asked the people of the colonies to relinquish their right to representation in the government. The value of this right was unmeasurable to the people. Such a right is formidable to tyrants because people ruled by representatives will oppose a tyrant's wishes.

HISTORICAL NOTE

The Declaration of Independence was written by Jefferson but revised in committee before it was adopted by the delegates. The following lines contained a strong statement opposing slavery and appeared in the original document but were deleted from the final version:

He [King George] has waged cruel war against human nature itself, violating its most sacred rights of life and liberty in the persons of a distant people who never offended him, captivating and carrying them into slavery in another hemisphere, or to incur miserable death in their transportation thither. This piratical warfare, the opprobrium of INFIDEL powers, is the warfare of the CHRISTIAN king of Great Britain. Determined to keep open a market where MEN should be bought and sold, he has prostituted his negative for suppressing every legislative attempt to prohibit or to restrain this execrable commerce. And that this assemblage of horrors might want no fact of distinguished die, he is now exciting those very people to rise in arms among us, and to purchase that liberty of which he has deprived them, by murdering the people on whom he also obtruded them: thus paying off former crimes committed against the LIBERTIES of one people, with crimes which he urges them to commit against the LIVES of another.

Answers to Guided Reading Questions

❶ The king has dissolved representative houses in the colonies. The Declaration claims that when a leader dissolves a representative body, then the legislative powers that were invested in that body return to the people themselves.

❷ The king has declared the colonies outside his protection. He has waged war against them, plundered their seas, ravaged their coasts, burned their towns, and destroyed lives.

Answers to Selection Check Test 4.3.11

EX. What is the purpose of the Declaration?
The purpose of the Declaration is to declare independence from Britain and to explain why the colonists feel that such independence is necessary.

1. On what date was the Declaration adopted?
The Declaration was adopted on July 4, 1776.

2. What unalienable rights are specifically mentioned in the Declaration?
The Declaration specifically mentions the unalienable rights to life, liberty, and the pursuit of happiness.

3. What right does a people have when it has been reduced "under absolute despotism"?
It has the right to throw off that government and provide for its future security.

4. Against whom does the Declaration contain a long list of grievances?
It contains a long list of grievances against King George.

5. What status does the final paragraph claim for the colonies?
It claims that they are free and independent states.

records, for the sole purpose of fatiguing them into compliance with his measure.

He has dissolved representative houses repeatedly, for opposing, with manly firmness, his invasions on the rights of the people.

❶ *What has the king dissolved? What effect has this had on the people?*

He has refused, for a long time after such dissolutions, to cause others to be elected; whereby the legislative powers, incapable of annihilation, have returned to the people at large for their exercise; the State remaining, in the meantime, exposed to all dangers of invasion from without, and convulsions within.

He has endeavored to prevent the population of these States; for that purpose obstructing the laws for the naturalization of foreigners; refusing to pass others to encourage their migration hither, and raising the conditions of new appropriations of lands.

He has obstructed the administration of justice, by refusing his assent to laws for establishing judiciary powers.

He has made judges dependent on his will alone for the tenure of their offices, and the amount and payment of their salaries.

He has erected a multitude of new offices, and sent hither swarms of officers to harass our people and eat out their substance.

❷ *What has the king declared? What destructive things has he done?*

He has kept among us in times of peace, standing armies, without the consent of our legislatures.

He has affected to render the military independent of, and superior to, the civil power.

He has combined with others to subject us to a jurisdiction foreign to our constitutions, and unacknowledged by our laws; giving his assent to their acts of pretended legislation:

For quartering large bodies of armed troops among us;

For protecting them, by a mock trial, from punishment for any murders which they should commit on the inhabitants of these States;

For cutting off our trade with all parts of the world;

For imposing taxes on us without our consent;

For depriving us, in many cases, of the benefits of trial by jury;

For transporting us beyond the seas, to be tried for pretended offences;

For abolishing the free system of English laws in a neighboring province, establishing there an arbitrary government, and enlarging its boundaries, so as to render it at once an example and fit instrument for introducing the same absolute rule into these colonies;

For taking away our charters, abolishing our most valuable laws, and altering, fundamentally, the forms of our governments;

For suspending our own legislatures, and declaring themselves invested with power to legislate for us in all cases whatsoever.

He has abdicated government here, by declaring us out of his protection, and waging war against us.

He has plundered our seas, ravaged our coasts, burnt our towns, and destroyed the lives of our people.

He is at this time transporting large armies of foreign mercenaries[3] to complete the works of death, desolation, and tyranny,

3. **mercenaries.** Hired soldiers

Words for Everyday Use:

com • pli • ance (kəm plī´əns) *n.,* act of giving in to wishes or demands
con • vul • sion (kən vul´ shən) *n.,* sudden, violent disturbance
nat • u • ral • i • za • tion (nach´ər əl iz´ā shən) *n.,* bestowal of the rights of citizenship
ten • ure (ten´yər) *n.,* right to hold a position permanently
ab • di • cate (ab´di kāt´) *vt.,* give up a right or a responsibility

Vocabulary in Context

- Compliance with the tax laws is not voluntary; it is required.
- The feverish patient was shaken by convulsions.
- Through the naturalization process, an immigrant becomes a citizen of his or her new country.
- The governor's tenure in office is four years.
- The powerful barons forced the king to abdicate his throne.

already begun with circumstances of cruelty and perfidy[4] scarcely paralleled in the most barbarous ages, and totally unworthy the head of a civilized nation.

He has constrained our fellow-citizens, taken captive on the high seas, to bear arms against their country, to become the executioners of their friends and brethren, or to fall themselves by their hands.

He has excited domestic insurrection amongst us, and has endeavored to bring on the inhabitants of our frontiers the merciless Indian savages, whose known rule of warfare is an undistinguished destruction of all ages, sexes, and conditions.

In every state of these oppressions we have petitioned for redress, in the most humble terms; our repeated petitions have been answered only by repeated injury. A prince whose character is thus marked by every act which may define a tyrant is unfit to be the ruler of a free people.

Nor have we been wanting in our attentions to our British brethren. We have warned them, from time to time, of attempts by their legislature to extend an unwarrantable jurisdiction over us. We have reminded them of the circumstances of our emigration and settlement here. We have appealed to their native justice and magnanimity; and we have conjured them, by the ties of our common kindred, to disavow these usurpations, which would inevitably interrupt our connections and correspondence. They, too, have been deaf to the voice of justice and of consanguinity.[5] We must, therefore, acquiesce in the necessity which denounces our separation; and hold them, as we hold the rest of mankind, enemies in war, in peace friends.

WE, THEREFORE, THE REPRESENTATIVES OF THE UNITED STATES OF AMERICA, in General Congress assembled, appealing to the Supreme Judge of the world for the rectitude of our intentions, do, in the name and by the authority of the good people of these colonies, solemnly publish and declare, That these United Colonies are, and of right ought to be, FREE AND INDEPENDENT STATES; that they are absolved from all allegiance to the British crown, and that all political connection between them and the state of Great Britain is, and ought to be, totally dissolved; and that, as free and independent states, they have full power to levy war, conclude peace, contract alliances, establish commerce, and to do all other acts and things which independent states may of right do. And, for the support of this declaration, with a firm reliance on the protection of Divine Providence, we mutually pledge to each other our lives, our fortunes, and our sacred honor. ■

❶ *What powers do the united colonies have?*

4. **perfidy.** Betrayal of trust
5. **consanguinity.** Close connection; relatedness

ANSWER TO GUIDED READING QUESTION

❶ The united colonies have full power to make war, to make peace, to form alliances, to conduct trade, and to do anything else that independent countries do.

WORDS FOR EVERYDAY USE:

in • sur • rec • tion (in´sə rek´shən) *n.,* uprising
re • dress (rē´dres´) *n.,* compensation
mag • na • nim • i • ty (mag´nə nim´ə tē) *n.,* state of being above pettiness
ac • qui • esce (ak´wē es´) *vi.,* agree without protest
rec • ti • tude (rek´tə tōōd´) *n.,* correctness

VOCABULARY IN CONTEXT

- In 1913, Irish patriots took over the Dublin Post Office, but British troops put down the insurrection.
- The weary housekeeper demanded generous redress for her day's toil.
- A good leader does not seek to serve himself or herself but rather treats the people with magnanimity.
- We asked the people next door to turn down their music, but they would not acquiesce to our request.
- The judge will determine the rectitude of your case.

RESPONDING TO THE SELECTION

Answers will vary.

ANSWERS FOR REVIEWING THE SELECTION

RECALLING

1. According to Jefferson, all men are created equal.

2. An "unalienable" right is one that is not capable of being taken away or transferred. Jefferson considers life, liberty, and the pursuit of happiness as being "unalienable" rights.

3. Specific grievences the colonists had against the British monarch included refusing to let the colonists establish their own judiciary system, keeping a standing army on American soil, cutting off American trade with other countries, imposing taxes without colonists' consent, abolishing trial by jury, and suspending the colonists' legislatures.

4. In the last paragraph, the colonies "solemnly publish and declare" that the United Colonies are free and independent states and absolved from all allegiance to the British crown.

INTERPRETING

Responses will vary. Possible responses are given.

5. All people are "equal" under the law. Identity concerns individual differences in appearances, social status, education, and so on. Equality concerns equal treatment within a social-political-economic system.

6. Governments are "instituted among" people to give them the right to life, liberty, and the pursuit of happiness. When a government "becomes destructive," people have the right to overthrow it.

7. *Answers will vary.*

8. After declaring their independence, the colonists could govern themselves as they saw fit, with their own elected leaders, lawmakers, and judges. They could establish their own economic system, including trade with other countries.

SYNTHESIZING

Responses will vary. Possible responses are given.

(cont.)

Responding to the Selection

What do you think Jefferson meant when he wrote that "all men are created equal"? when he wrote of the rights to "life, liberty, and the pursuit of happiness"? Discuss these questions with your classmates.

Reviewing the Selection

RECALLING

1. In what state, according to Jefferson, are all men created?

2. What is an "unalienable" right? What rights does Jefferson list as being unalienable?

3. What specific grievances did the colonists have against the British monarch?

4. What does the last paragraph of the selection "solemnly publish and declare"?

INTERPRETING

5. In what sense are all people "equal"? What is the difference between equality and identity?

6. According to the Declaration, why are governments "instituted among" people? What right does a people have when its government "becomes destructive" of the ends of securing the rights to life, liberty, and the pursuit of happiness?

7. Which of the offenses attributed to the British crown do you find most offensive? Why?

8. What could the colonies do on their own after declaring independence that they could not do on their own before making that declaration?

SYNTHESIZING

9. The eighteenth-century English philosopher John Locke held that people are born with "natural rights" that cannot be taken from them. The eighteenth-century French philosopher Jean-Jacques Rousseau believed that government is a social contract entered into by the people for their mutual protection and well-being. In what ways are these ideas reflected in the Declaration of Independence?

10. The Declaration ends with a personal statement made by its signers: "[F]or the support of this declaration, . . . we mutually pledge to each other our lives, our fortunes, and our sacred honor." What risks were the signers of the Declaration taking upon themselves? In what way does their willingness to take on this risk show their commitment to liberty?

ANSWERS FOR REVIEWING THE SELECTION (CONT.)

9. Locke's idea that people are born with "natural rights" that cannot be taken from them is reflected by Jefferson in the Declaration of Independence when he writes that all men are created equal with certain "unalienable rights." Rousseau's idea that government is a social contract entered into by people for their mutual protection and well-being is reflected by Jefferson in the Declaration of Independence when he writes that governments are instituted among men to secure life, liberty, and the pursuit of happiness.

10. The signers were taking upon themselves many risks. Had the revolution failed, their property would have been confiscated, and they would have been tried and then imprisoned or executed. They realized the risks they were taking; that they took those risks indicates their commitment to liberty.

Understanding Literature (Questions for Discussion)

1. **Alliteration. Alliteration** is the repetition of initial consonant sounds. In addition to his many other talents, Thomas Jefferson was known as a great prose stylist. Reread the sentence that begins with the words "We hold these truths to be self-evident." What makes this sentence so memorable? What examples of alliteration can you find in the sentence?

2. **Parallelism. Parallelism** is a rhetorical technique in which a writer emphasizes the equal value or weight of two or more ideas by expressing them in the same grammatical form. How does Jefferson use parallelism in his presentation of the grievances against King George?

Responding in Writing

Credo. Thomas Jefferson was a great defender of individual liberty, of the rights of people to speak their minds freely and openly, to express their beliefs without fear. Take advantage of this freedom to write your own credo, or statement of belief, expressing your own most strongly held opinions and values. Follow Jefferson's model and use parallelism to express your beliefs effectively. Refer to the Language Arts Survey, 2.57, "Achieving Parallelism."

PROJECT

Analyzing the Bill of Rights. The first ten amendments to the Constitution of the United States, ratified in 1791 and known collectively as the Bill of Rights, are printed on the next page. Working with other students in a small group, paraphrase each of these amendments (that is, put them into your own words). Then discuss situations to which the amendments, which have the force of law, might be applied.

ANSWERS FOR UNDERSTANDING LITERATURE

► See the evaluation forms for discussion, active listening, and oral communication, *Assessment Portfolio,* 7.11–7.14.

Responses will vary. Possible responses are given.

1. Alliteration. The first sentence of the second paragraph, "We hold these truths to be self-evident," is memorable because it contains the entire premise upon which a new nation, the United States of America, was founded. Following are examples of alliteration in this sentence:

". . . **th**ese . . .; **th**at **th**ey . . . **th**eir; **th**at . . . **th**ese . . . **th**e . . ."; ". . . tru**th**s to . . . "; ". . . **l**ife . . . **l**iberty. . . ."

2. Parallelism. Jefferson uses parallelism in his presentation of the grievances against King George as follows: "He has refused . . . He has called . . . He has disolved . . . He has refused . . . He has endeavored . . . He has obstructed . . . He has made . . . He has erected. . . ." Jefferson continues using parallelism when he accuses King George of lending his weight to unlawful jurisdiction by the British as follows: "For quartering . . . For protecting them . . . For cutting off . . . For imposing taxes . . . For depriving . . . For transporting. . . ."

ANALYTIC SCALES FOR RESPONDING IN WRITING

Assign a score from 1 to 25 for each grading criterion below. (For more detailed evaluation, see the evaluation forms for writing, revising, and proofreading, *Assessment Portfolio,* 7.1–7.10.)

Credo

- **Content/Unity.** The credo presents the author's beliefs.
- **Organization/Coherence.** The credo makes use of proper paragraph form.
- **Language/Style.** The credo is in formal language and uses parallelism to express its ideas memorably.
- **Conventions.** The credo avoids errors in spelling, grammar, usage, mechanics, and manuscript form.

PROJECT NOTES

► See the worksheets and evaluation forms for projects, *Assessment Portfolio,* 7.20–7.23.

Analyzing the Bill of Rights. You may wish to refer students to an American history or government textbook for more background information on the Bill of Rights. Give students the following example of a situation to which the Bill of Rights might apply:

A newspaper in a small town publishes an article criticizing the mayor. The mayor orders the local police to confiscate copies of the newspaper.

This would be a clear violation of the First Amendment guarantee of freedom of the press.

Historical Note

The Bill of Rights, ratified in 1791, consists of the first ten amendments to the Constitution. All of these amendments limit in some way the powers of the federal government. The issues addressed by the Bill of Rights are ones that were hotly debated during the ratification of the Constitution of the United States. The Federalist Party managed to convince people to ratify the Constitution only by promising that such a Bill of Rights would be added to it. Interpretation of the exact meanings of the amendments in the Bill of Rights has been one of the most important functions of the courts since that time.

The Bill of Rights

Amendment 1

Congress shall make no law respecting an establishment of religion, or prohibiting the free exercise thereof; or abridging the freedom of speech, or of the press; or the right of the people peaceably to assemble, and to petition the Government for a redress of grievances.

Amendment 2

A well-regulated militia, being necessary to the security of a free State, the right of the people to keep and bear arms shall not be infringed.

Amendment 3

No soldier shall, in time of peace, be quartered in any house, without the consent of the owner, nor in time of war, but in a manner to be prescribed by law.

Amendment 4

The right of the people to be secure in their persons, houses, papers, and effects, against unreasonable searches and seizures, shall not be violated, and no warrants shall issue, but upon probable cause, supported by oath or affirmation, and particularly describing the place to be searched, and the persons or things to be seized.

Amendment 5

No person shall be held to answer for a capital, or otherwise infamous crime, unless on a presentment or indictment of a Grand Jury, except in cases arising in the land or naval forces, or in the militia, when in actual service in time of war or public danger; nor shall any person be subject for the same offense to be twice put in jeopardy of life or limb; nor shall be compelled in any criminal case to be a witness against himself, nor be deprived of life, liberty, or property, without due process of law; nor shall private property be taken for public use without just compensation.

Amendment 6

In all criminal prosecutions, the accused shall enjoy the right to a speedy and public trial, by an impartial jury of the State and district wherein the crime shall have been committed, which district shall have been previously ascertained by law, and to be informed of the nature and cause of the accusation; to be confronted with the witnesses against him; to have compulsory process for obtaining witnesses in his favor, and to have the assistance of counsel for his defense.

Amendment 7

In suits at common law, where the value in controversy shall exceed twenty dollars, the right of trial by jury shall be preserved, and no fact tried by a jury shall be otherwise reexamined in any court of the United States, than according to the rules of the common law.

Amendment 8

Excessive bail shall not be required, nor excessive fines imposed, nor cruel and unusual punishments inflicted.

Amendment 9

The enumeration in the Constitution, of certain rights, shall not be construed to deny or disparage others retained by the people.

Amendment 10

The powers not delegated to the United States by the Constitution, nor prohibited by it to the States, are reserved to the States respectively, or to the people.

PREREADING

Letter to John Adams, May 7, 1776

by Abigail Adams

About the Author

Abigail Adams (1744–1818) was born in Weymouth, Massachusetts, the daughter of a minister. At the age of twenty, she married John Adams, a Boston lawyer who played important roles in the founding and governing of the United States. An ardent supporter of the American Revolution, Adams began a remarkable correspondence with her husband when, in 1774, he became a delegate to the First Continental Congress (a federal parliamentary body established by the British colonies in America). From 1774 to 1783 (the year in which a peace treaty was signed with England), John Adams was often away from home, involved in work that included the drafting of the Declaration of Independence, the conduct of the American Revolution and the formation of the new nation. During this time, Adams kept up a lively, fascinating correspondence with him. This correspondence offers many insights into the revolution and into daily life during the period. In her letters, Adams proved to be one of the first American champions of women's rights. She was particularly interested in expanding educational opportunities for women, which at that time were few. Adams was also an ardent opponent of slavery. After the American Revolution, John Adams served as a diplomat in Europe, and she traveled with him, living at various times in Paris, The Hague, and London. John Adams served as the first vice president of the new nation and then as its second president, and during this period, Adams divided her time between the family residence in Massachusetts and the temporary capital in Philadelphia. In 1800, Adams became the first First Lady to live in the new White House in Washington, DC. Her son John Quincy Adams became the sixth president of the United States.

About the Selection

Abigail Adams wrote the following letter to her husband, John, then a delegate to the First Continental Congress. The letter was written shortly before the drafting of the Declaration of Independence, at a time when members of the Congress were debating whether to declare the colonies' independence from Britain.

ADDITIONAL RESOURCES

Reader's Guide
- Selection Worksheet, 3.7

Assessment Portfolio
- Selection Check Test, 4.3.13
- Selection Test, 4.3.14

Essential Skills Practice Books
- *Language,* 2.53

ENRICHMENT ACTIVITIES

In 1972, the required two-thirds majority in the House and the Senate approved the following amendment to the Constitution:

"Equality of rights under the law shall not be denied or abridged by the United States or any state on account of sex."

For an amendment to become law, it must be ratified by three-quarters of the states. This Equal Rights Amendment was ratified in twenty-two states but then ran into stiff opposition. Some people argued that the amendment would do away with necessary or positive distinctions between men and women that are made by current law. Others argued that the amendment was unnecessary because the law already applied equally to men and to women. The Equal Rights Amendment was not ratified and so did not become part of United States constitutional law. Have students research and hold a debate on the question of whether an Equal Rights Amendment to the Constitution is necessary or desirable.

SUPPORT FOR LEP STUDENTS

Make sure that your students understand the situation in which the letter from Adams was written. Her husband, John, was a delegate to the Second Continental Congress at the time and was involved in the debate over breaking with Great Britain. Both Adams

(cont.)

GOALS/OBJECTIVES

Studying this lesson will enable students to

- appreciate the behind-the-scenes role of a woman in the making of the American Revolution
- understand that the issue of gender equality is not recent but was being discussed as far back as the period of the American Revolution
- understand the concept of aim and identify the aim in a piece of nonfiction writing
- write a paraphrase and a letter of opinion on a political topic

PREREADING NOTES

READER'S JOURNAL

You might suggest that students think about issues that might have been addressed at the time in order to avoid latter controversy. Slavery is one such issue. Gender equality is another.

LANGUAGE SKILLS

The following is an example of a compound-complex sentence from the selection broken into separate simple sentences:

Original sentence: "If I had taken up my pen, perhaps some unbecoming invective might have fallen from it; the eyes of our rulers have been closed and a lethargy has seized almost every member."

Separate sentences: I didn't take up my pen. Some unbecoming invective might have fallen from it. The eyes of our rulers have been closed. A lethargy has seized almost every member.

ANSWER TO GUIDED READING QUESTION

❶ The good of the country must come before the needs of individuals because the ultimate fate of the individuals depends upon the fate of the country.

SUPPORT FOR LEP STUDENTS (CONT.)

and her husband strongly supported independence. Adams wrote this letter from her home in Braintree, near Boston. At that time, Boston was in turmoil due to the presence of British troops and the mustering of colonial arms.

ADDITIONAL VOCABULARY

solitary—alone
domestic—having to do with the home
mortified—dead
acquiesce—give up, agree to
invective—verbal assault, insult
lethargy—weariness
quench—douse with water

READER'S JOURNAL

If you could have given the Continental Congress one piece of advice about what laws to establish for the new country, what would that advice have been? Write this advice in your journal.

LANGUAGE SKILLS

In her letter, Abigail Adams uses fairly long, complex sentences made up of several clauses. (A clause is a group of words that contains a verb and its subject.) Read the Language Arts Survey, 2.53, "Combining Sentences Using Clauses." Then choose one long, complex sentence from the letter and rewrite it as two or more shorter independent sentences.

Letter to John Adams, May 7, 1776

ABIGAIL ADAMS

Braintree[1]

How many are the solitary hours I spend, ruminating upon the past and anticipating the future whilst you, overwhelmed with the cares of state, have but few moments you can devote to any individual. All domestic pleasures and enjoyments are absorbed in the great and important duty you owe your country "for our country is, as it were, a secondary god and the first and greatest parent. It is to be preferred to parents, wives, children, friends and all things; the gods only excepted. For if our country perishes, it is as impossible to save an individual as to preserve one of the fingers of a mortified hand." Thus do I suppress every wish and silence every murmur, acquiescing in a painful separation from the companion of my youth and the friend of my heart.

Why must the good of the country come before the needs of individuals? ❶

I believe it is near ten days since I wrote you a line. I have not felt in a humor to entertain you. If I had taken up my pen, perhaps some unbecoming invective might have fallen from it; the eyes of our rulers have been closed and a lethargy has seized almost every member. I fear a fatal security has taken possession of them. Whilst the building is in flame, they tremble at the expense of water to quench it. In short, two months have elapsed since the evacuation of Boston and very little has been done in that time to secure it or the harbor from future invasion until the people are all in a flame, and no one among us that I have heard of even mentions expense. They think universally that there has been an amazing neglect somewhere. Many have turned out as volunteers to work upon

1. **Braintree.** Town south of Boston

WORDS FOR EVERYDAY USE: **ru • mi • nate** (rōō´mə nāt´) *vt.,* turn over in one's mind

VOCABULARY IN CONTEXT

- Ms. Sandoz would often ruminate about the shortness of life and the many wonderful things we have to do and see during our allotted time.

Nodles Island, and many more would go upon Nantasket if it was once set on foot. "It is a maxim of state that power and liberty are like heat and moisture; where they are well mixed everything prospers; where they are single, they are destructive."

A government of more stability is much wanted in this colony, and they are ready to receive it from the hands of the Congress, and since I have begun with maxims of state, I will add another: A people may let a king fall, yet still remain a people, but if a king lets his people slip from him, he is no longer a king. And as this is most certainly our case, why not proclaim to the world in decisive terms your own importance?

Shall we not be despised by foreign powers for hesitating so long at a word?

I cannot say that I think you very generous to the ladies, for whilst you are proclaiming peace and good will to men, emancipating all nations, you insist upon retaining an absolute power over wives. But you must remember that arbitrary power is like most other things which are very hard, very liable to be broken—and notwithstanding all your wise laws and maxims, we have it in our power not only to free ourselves but to subdue our masters, and without violence throw both your natural and legal authority at our feet—

Charm by accepting, by submitting sway
Yet have our humor most when we obey.

I thank you for several letters which I have received since I wrote last. They alleviate a tedious absence, and I long earnestly for a Saturday evening and experience a similar pleasure to that which I used to find in the return of my friend upon that day after a week's absence. The idea of a year dissolves all my philosophy.

John Adams. *Gilbert Stuart, 1826. National Museum of American Art, Washington DC/Art Resource, NY*

Our little ones, whom you so often recommend to my care and instruction, shall not be deficient in virtue or probity[2] if the precepts of a mother have their desired effect, but they would be doubly enforced could they be indulged with the example of a father constantly before them; I often point them to their sire

Engaged in a corrupted state
Wrestling with vice and faction. ■

2. **probity.** Integrity

❶ *If people lose faith in their leader, what happens?*

Answer to Guided Reading Question

❶ If the people lose faith in their leader, then he or she no longer is their leader.

Historical Note

John Adams did not heed his wife's advice about being "generous to the ladies." In fact, he wrote, "Depend on it. We know better than to repeal our masculine systems." The American Revolution did little to bring women into the political process. It wasn't until 1920, when the Nineteenth Amendment to the Constitution was ratified, that women were guaranteed the right to vote by federal law.

Answers to Selection Check Test 4.3.13

EX. Why does Abigail Adams spend so many solitary hours "ruminating upon the past and anticipating the future"?
Her husband is away on political business. He is a delegate to the Second Continental Congress.

1. What, according to Adams, is "a secondary god and the first and greatest parent"?
According to Adams, "your country is . . . a secondary god and the first and greatest parent."

2. What event has recently occurred in Boston?
The city has been evacuated.

3. According to Adams, what can make a person "no longer a king"?
She says that a person is no longer a king when his people slip from him.

4. To whom does Abigail Adams say that her husband is not being generous?
She says that he is not being "generous to the ladies."

5. According to Adams, what would doubly enforce virtue and probity in her children?
Having the example of a father constantly before them would doubly enforce virtue and probity in the children.

RESPONDING TO THE SELECTION

If students have difficulty getting started, suggest that each student pick one issue and outline his or her views to prepare for discussion.

ANSWERS FOR REVIEWING THE SELECTION

RECALLING

1. According to the opening of her letter, Adams spends her time thinking about the past and anticipating the future. Her husband is overwhelmed with helping to establish a new nation.

2. According to Adams, the eyes of the leaders of the upcoming revolution have been closed. These leaders are suffering a "fatal security."

3. Adams writes that a king is no longer a king if he lets his people "slip from him."

4. Adams writes that her husband and the other delegates have proclaimed "peace and good will" to other men and nations, but that they failed to give that consideration to women.

INTERPRETING

Responses will vary. Possible responses are given.

5. Although Adams misses her husband's company and help in raising their children, she recognizes the importance of what he is doing and does not resent his absence.

6. The metaphor Adams uses to describe the reluctance of some members of Congress to take the necessary actions to create an army and to petition for independence is their reluctance to incur the expense of water to quench a burning building.

7. Adams does not believe in the divine right of kings. People are justified in saying their king is no longer their king when he has let his people slip from him.

8. Adams wanted her husband and the other delegates to grant women equal rights.

SYNTHESIZING

Responses will vary. Possible responses are given.

9. That government derives its rights from "the consent of the governed" and is justified in exercising those rights only as long as the gov-

(cont.)

Responding to the Selection

In her letter, Abigail Adams shows a sense of high moral purpose. Discuss with your classmates the issues that Adams raises: the relative importance of personal and political duties, the need for stable government, the duties owed by a king to his subjects, equality of political rights for women, and the moral education of children. What are Adams's views on these issues? What are your own?

Reviewing the Selection

RECALLING

1. According to the opening of the letter, how does Adams spend her time? With what duties is her husband "overwhelmed"?

2. According to Adams, whose "eyes . . . have been closed"? Who is suffering from a "fatal security"?

3. According to Adams, when is a king no longer a king?

4. To whom, according to Adams, have her husband and the other delegates proclaimed "peace and good will"? To whom have they failed to give just consideration?

INTERPRETING

5. Does Adams resent her husband's absence? Why, or why not?

6. What metaphor does Adams use in the second paragraph of her letter to describe the reluctance of some members of the Congress to take the necessary actions to create an army and to petition for independence?

7. For centuries, most British subjects believed that kings were divinely appointed, that their will was supreme and beyond any earthly challenge. Does Adams subscribe to such a view? Under what circumstances, according to Adams, are people justified in saying that their king is no longer their king?

8. What might Adams have wanted her husband and the other delegates to do with regard to women?

ANSWERS FOR REVIEWING THE SELECTION (CONT.)

erned continue in their consent was an extremely radical idea at the time because no other country in the world was governed by such a philosophy. Adams's letter shows that she believes government not consented to by the governed to be illegitimate when she states the maxim "power and liberty." She further shows this when she explains that a king who lets his people slip is no longer a king.

10. Adams would agree with Hobbes that a strong central authority is necessary to maintain order and ensure self-preservation so that everyone can enjoy the freedom of life, liberty, and the pursuit of happiness without infringing on the rights of others to do the same. She would disagree with Hobbes if that strong central authority restricted or interfered with an individual's right to life, liberty, and the pursuit of happiness.

SYNTHESIZING

9. The United States was the first country in the world founded on the principle that government derives its rights from "the consent of the governed" and is justified in exercising those rights only as long as the governed continue in their consent. Why might this have seemed like an extremely radical idea at the time? What passages in Adams's letter show that she believes government not consented to by the governed to be illegitimate?

10. The seventeenth-century philosopher Thomas Hobbes argued that life in the "state of nature" is "solitary, poor, nasty, brutish, and short" and that a strong central authority, a sovereign or king, is necessary to maintain order and ensure self-preservation. In what respect would Adams have agreed with Hobbes? In what respect would she have disagreed?

Understanding Literature (Questions for Discussion)

Aim. A writer's **aim** is the primary purpose that his or her work is meant to accomplish. Reread paragraph 5 of Adams's letter. What might have been her purpose for including this paragraph in the letter? What might she have hoped that her husband and the other delegates might do?

Thinking Skills

Paraphrase. Read the Language Arts Survey, 4.30, "Paraphrasing and Summarizing." Then paraphrase, or put into your own words, paragraph 5 of Adams's letter.

Responding in Writing

Letter. Choose some political issue of interest to you and write a letter to a political figure, such as your town's mayor, your congressperson, or one of your senators, regarding that issue. Refer to the Language Arts Survey, 5.3, "The Form of a Business Letter," and write your letter in proper business letter form. (Note: A reference librarian in your community will be able to help you to identify the names and titles of political figures at the local, state, and national levels.)

ANSWERS FOR UNDERSTANDING LITERATURE

▶See the evaluation forms for discussion, active listening, and oral communication, *Assessment Portfolio,* 7.11–7.14.

Responses will vary. Possible responses are given.

Aim. Adams might have included paragraph 5 of her letter to remind her husband that the new nation he and others were creating had much to say about the rights of men, but little or nothing to say about the rights of women. It might have been her hope that her husband and the other delegates would include specific references to the rights of women in the new nation.

ANSWERS FOR THINKING SKILLS

The paraphrase should contain the most important ideas of the original, presented in the same order but in different words.

ANALYTIC SCALES FOR RESPONDING IN WRITING

Assign a score from 1 to 25 for each grading criterion below. (For more detailed evaluation, see the evaluation forms for writing, revising, and proofreading, *Assessment Portfolio,* 7.1–7.10.)

Letter

- **Content/Unity.** The letter states and supports a position on a political issue.
- **Organization/Coherence.** The letter is in proper business letter form.
- **Language/Style.** The letter is in formal English appropriate for addressing an elected official.
- **Conventions.** The letter avoids errors in spelling, grammar, usage, mechanics, and manuscript form.

FROM *LETTERS FROM AN AMERICAN FARMER*

About the Author. J. Hector St. Jean de Crèvecoeur (1735–1813) was born in France. At the age of nineteen, he moved to England. When his fiancée died, he traveled to Canada. He then traveled throughout the colonies and settled in New York. He supported the British during the American Revolution and returned to France. While he was gone, his home was destroyed, and his wife was killed.

About the Selection. ***Letters from an American Farmer,*** published in London in 1782, and 1784 in France, was quite successful because of the interest that the revolution had created with regard to America and Americans. Two sections of de Crèvecoeur's collection of essays and observations are particularly interesting—his celebration of American diversity and his condemnation of slavery.

from *Letters from an American Farmer*
by J. Hector St. Jean de Crèvecoeur

I wish I could be acquainted with the feelings and thoughts which must agitate the heart and present themselves to the mind of an enlightened[1] Englishman, when he first lands on this continent. He must greatly rejoice that he lived at a time to see this fair country discovered and settled; he must necessarily feel a share of national pride, when he views the chain of settlements which embellishes these extended shores. When he says to himself, this is the work of my countrymen, who, when convulsed by factions,[2] afflicted by a variety of miseries and wants, restless and impatient, took refuge here. They brought along with them their national genius, to which they principally owe what liberty they enjoy, and what substance they possess. Here he sees the industry of his native country displayed in a new manner, and traces in their works the embryos of all the arts, sciences, and ingenuity which flourish in Europe. Here he beholds fair cities, substantial villages, extensive fields, an immense country filled with decent houses, good roads, orchards, meadows, and bridges, where an hundred years ago all was wild, woody, and uncultivated! What a train of pleasing ideas this fair spectacle must suggest; it is a prospect which must inspire a good citizen with the most heartfelt pleasure. The difficulty consists in the manner of viewing so extensive a scene. He is arrived on a new continent; a modern society offers itself to his contemplation, different from what he had hitherto seen. It is not composed, as in Europe, of great lords who possess everything, and of a herd of people who have nothing. Here are no aristocratical families, no courts, no kings, no bishops, no ecclesiastical dominion,[3] no invisible power giving to a few a very visible one; no great manufacturers employing thousands, no great refinements of luxury. The rich and the poor are not so far removed from each other as they are in Europe. Some few towns excepted, we are all tillers of the earth, from Nova Scotia to West Florida. We are a people of cultivators, scattered over an immense territory, communicating with each other by means of good roads and navigable rivers, united by the silken bands of mild government, all respecting the laws, without dreading their power, because they are equitable. We are all animated with the spirit of an industry which is unfettered and unrestrained, because each person works for himself. If he travels through our rural districts he views not the hostile castle, and the haughty mansion, contrasted with the clay-built hut and miserable cabin, where cattle and men help to keep each other warm, and dwell in meanness, smoke, and indigence.[4] A pleasing uniformity of decent competence appears throughout our habitations. The meanest of our log-houses is a dry and comfortable habitation. Lawyer or merchant are the fairest titles our towns afford; that of a farmer is the only appellation of the rural inhabitants of our country. It must take some time ere he can reconcile himself to our dictionary, which is but short in words of dignity, and names of honor. There, on a Sunday, he sees a congregation of respectable farmers and their wives, all clad in neat homespun, well mounted, or riding in their own humble wagons. There is not among them an esquire, saving the unlettered[5] magistrate. There he sees a parson as simple as his flock, a farmer who does not riot on the labor of others. We have no princes, for whom we toil, starve, and bleed; we are the most perfect society now existing in the world. Here man is free as he ought to be; nor is this pleasing equality so transitory as many others are. Many ages will not see the shores of our great lakes replenished with inland nations, nor the unknown bounds of North America entirely peopled. Who can tell how far it extends? Who can tell the millions of men whom it will feed and contain? for no European foot has as yet traveled half the extent of this mighty continent!

The next wish of this traveler will be to know whence[6] came all these people? They are a mixture of English, Scotch, Irish, French, Dutch, Germans and Swedes. From this promiscuous breed, that race now called Americans have arisen. The eastern provinces must indeed be excepted,[7] as being the unmixed descendants of Englishmen. I have heard many wish that they had been more intermixed also: for my part, I am no wisher, and think it much better as it has happened. They exhibit a most conspicuous figure in this great and variegated picture; they too enter for a great share in the pleasing perspective displayed in these thirteen provinces.[8] I know it is fashionable to reflect on them, but respect them for what they have done; for the accuracy and wisdom with which they have settled their territory; for the decency of their manners; for their early love of letters; their ancient college,[9] the first in this hemisphere; for their industry, which to me who am but a farmer is the criterion of everything. There never was a people, situated as they are, who with so ungrateful a soil have done more in so short a time.

1. **enlightened.** Knowledgeable; full of understanding
2. **convulsed by factions.** Upset by disagreement among groups of citizens
3. **ecclesiastical dominion.** Religious authority over a state
4. **indigence.** Poverty
5. **unlettered.** Uneducated
6. **whence.** From where
7. **excepted.** Excluded
8. **provinces.** Colonies
9. **college.** Harvard College (founded in 1636) in Cambridge, Massachusetts

"To the Right Honorable William, Earl of Dartmouth"
by Phillis Wheatley

Hail, happy day, when, smiling like the morn,
Fair *Freedom* rose *New-England* to adorn:
The northern clime[1] beneath her genial[2] ray,
Dartmouth, congratulates thy blissful sway:
5 Elate with hope her race no longer mourns,
Each soul expands, each grateful bosom burns,
While in thine hand with pleasure we behold
The silken reins, and *Freedom's* charms unfold.
Long lost to realms beneath the northern skies
10 She shines supreme, while hated *faction* dies:
Soon as appear'd the *Goddess* long desir'd;
Sick at the view, she languish'd and expir'd;[3]
Thus from the splendors of the morning light
The owl in sadness seeks the caves of night.

15 No more, *America*, in mournful strain
Of wrongs, and grievance unredress'd complain,
No longer shalt thou dread the iron chain,
Which wanton *Tyranny* with lawless hand
Had made, and with it meant t' enslave the land.

20 Should you, my lord, while you peruse my song,
Wonder from whence my love of *Freedom* sprung,
Whence flow these wishes for the common good,
By feeling hearts alone best understood,
I, young in life, by seeming cruel fate
25 Was snatch'd from *Afric's* fancy'd happy seat:
What pangs excruciating must molest,
What sorrows labor in my parent's breast?
Steel'd was that soul and by no misery mov'd
That from a father seiz'd his babe belov'd:
30 Such, such my case. And can I then but pray
Others may never feel tyrannic sway?

For favors past, great Sir, our thanks are due,
And thee we ask thy favors to renew,
Since in thy pow'r, as in thy will before,
35 To sooth the griefs, which thou did'st once deplore.
May heav'nly grace the sacred sanction give
To all thy works, and thou forever live
Not only on the wings of fleeting *Fame*,
Though praise immortal crowns the patriot's name,
40 But to conduct to heav'ns refulgent fane,[4]
May fiery coursers sweep th' ethereal plain,
And bear thee upwards to that blest abode,
Where, like the prophet, thou shalt find thy God.

1. **clime.** Region
2. **genial.** Warm and friendly
5. **languish'd and expir'd.** Suffered and died
4. **refulgent fane.** Radiant, glowing temple or church

from *Common Sense*
by Thomas Paine

From *III. Thoughts on the Present State of American Affairs*

In the following pages I offer nothing more than simple facts, plain arguments, and common sense: and have no other preliminaries to settle with the reader, than that he will divest himself of prejudice and prepossession, and suffer his reason and his feelings to determine for themselves: that he will put on, or rather that he will not put off, the true character of a man, and generously enlarge his views beyond the present day.

Volumes have been written on the subject of the struggle between England and America. Men of all ranks have embarked in the controversy, from different motives, and with various designs; but all have been ineffectual, and the period of debate is closed. Arms as the last resource decide the contest; the appeal was the choice of the King, and the continent has accepted the challenge.

♦ ♦ ♦

A government of our own is our natural right: and when a man seriously reflects on the precariousness of human affairs, he will become convinced that it is infinitely wiser and safer to form a constitution of our own in a cool deliberate manner, while we have it in our power, than to trust such an interesting event to time and chance. If we omit it now, some Massanello[5] may hereafter arise, who, laying hold of popular disquietudes, may collect together the desperate and the discontented, and by assuming to themselves the powers of government, finally sweep away the liberties of the continent like a deluge. Should the government of America return again into the hands of Britain, the tottering situation of things will be a temptation for some desperate adventurer to try his fortune; and in such a case, what relief can Britain give? Ere she could hear the news, the fatal business might be done; and ourselves suffering like the wretched Britons under the oppression of the conqueror. Ye that oppose independence now, ye know not what ye do: ye are opening a door to eternal tyranny by keeping vacant the seat of government. There are thousands and tens of thousands, who would think it glorious to expel from the continent that barbarous and hellish power.

5. **Massanello.** Thomas Anello, or Massanello, a fisherman, became king for a day after inciting a revolt against the Spanish who were occupying his city of Naples.

"To the Right Honorable William, Earl of Dartmouth"

A biography of **Phillis Wheatley** appears on page 165.

from *Common Sense*

About the Author. A biography of **Thomas Paine** appears on page 159.

About the Selection. Thomas Paine's ***Common Sense*** has been called the most influential essay ever written because it galvanized public opinion in favor of independence from Britain. Published anonymously, *Common Sense* was the first publication to call for independence. It rapidly sold over one hundred thousand copies and eventually sold almost five hundred thousand copies. At the time of its publication, the Second Continental Congress was meeting in Philadelphia, and Boston was being attacked by the British. Paine wrote plainly what was in many people's minds and hearts and so earned his place as one of the fathers of the revolution.

Vocabulary Development Exercises

▶ Give students the following exercise.

Read the Language Arts Survey, 4.44, "Synonym and Antonym Questions." Using the vocabulary words on page 186, write a test containing five synonym and antonym questions. Write three answer choices for each problem. When you are done, exchange tests with a partner.

Example.

Write the letter of the word that is most nearly *opposite* in meaning to the word in capital letters.

1. IMPIOUS

(A) reverent
(B) impractical
(C) ebulliant

Answer: (A) reverent

ADDITIONAL RESOURCES

Assessment Portfolio

- Vocabulary Worksheet, 4.3.15
- Study Guide: Unit 3 Test, 4.3.16
- Unit 3 Test, 4.3.17

Essential Skills Practice Books

Writing

- Freewriting, 1.12

Language

- Agreement of Pronouns and Antecedents, 2.83
- Agreement of Subject and Verb, 2.70
- Combining Sentences Using Clauses, 2.53
- Common and Proper Nouns, 2.3
- Functions of Sentences, 2.36
- Improper Shifts in Verb Tense, 2.65
- Irregular Verbs I, 2.66
- Split Infinitives, 2.68
- Using Words as Other Parts of Speech I, 2.30
- Using Words as Other Parts of Speech II, 2.31

(cont.)

Unit Review

The American Revolution

VOCABULARY FROM THE SELECTIONS

abdicate, 174
acquiesce, 175
admonish, 142
ardent, 166
assent, 173
avert, 154
balmy, 167
calamity, 161
civility, 147
compliance, 174
comport, 154
consolation, 160
consultation, 142
contemplation, 167
convulsion, 174
duration, 161
effectual, 155
elate, 166
ethereal, 167
evade, 143
evince, 172
formidable, 155
heartily, 148
hypocrisy, 161
impartiality, 147
impious, 160
induce, 162
indulgence, 142
inestimable, 155, 173
ingenious, 141
insidious, 154
insurrection, 175
inviolate, 155
magnanimity, 175
martial, 154
naturalization, 174
offensive, 162
oratory, 147
penitentially, 161
posterity, 147
prostrate, 155
rectitude, 175
redress, 175
reflection, 162
remonstrate, 166
repulse, 161
resolution, 161
ruminate, 180
solace, 154
sottish, 162
subjugation, 154
submission, 154
sufferance, 173
supinely, 155
temporal, 153
tenure, 174
transient, 172
transport, 167
unalienable, 172
usurpation, 172
venture, 143

LITERARY TERMS

aim, 183
alliteration, 177
allusion, 169
aphorism, 145
argumentation, 164
assonance, 164
autobiography, 145
chiasmus, 150
Enlightenment, 157
heroic couplet, 169
Neoclassicism, 150
parallelism, 157, 177
persona, 144
proverb, 145
rhetorical question, 156, 164
stereotype, 150
style, 144

ADDITIONAL RESOURCES (CONT.)

- Verbals: Gerunds, 2.17
- Verbals: Infinitives, 2.18
- Verbals: Participles, 2.16

Study and Research

- Analyzing, 4.10
- Comparing and Contrasting, 4.8
- Paraphrasing and Summarizing, 4.30
- Reading Actively, 4.18
- Synonym and Antonym Questions, 4.44
- Understanding Propaganda Techniques, 4.15

SYNTHESIS: QUESTIONS FOR WRITING, RESEARCH, OR DISCUSSION

GENRE STUDIES

1. **Poetry.** Interestingly, Phillis Wheatley achieves with her poem what the subject of her poem achieves with his painting. In some ways her poem is a treatise on what an artist or poet can do. Discuss Wheatley's view of art and what an artist does.

THEMATIC STUDIES

2. **The Search for Freedom.** Examine the writings of Henry, Paine, and Jefferson. Their words were important tools in the American Revolution. Each makes a clear statement of case followed by a rallying cry. How does each define freedom? What price is it sometimes necessary to pay for freedom? Which expressions from their works would have had an emotional impact: Discuss their statements of situation, their concept of the nature of freedom, and the power of their language.
3. **Future Rebellions.** Even as most of America moved toward independence, some groups were overlooked. Examine Franklin's "Remarks Concerning the Natives of North America" and Adams's letter to her husband. What seeds of future conflict do you find? What appeals by the representatives of the two minorities are given? How would you characterize their presentations?

HISTORICAL/BIOGRAPHICAL STUDIES

4. **The Emerging Nation.** Economic factors play an important role in history and politics. What economic factors in the Mid-Atlantic and Southern colonies made independence feasible? What other growth factors strengthened the colonies?
5. **European Roots.** The Declaration of Independence can trace its roots to the European Age of Reason and Romanticism. Name three or four philosophers, writers, or scientists whose work in Europe had influence on the colonists. Briefly describe their work and explain how it is related to the thinking of the colonists.

▶ These prompts are suitable as topics for research papers. Refer to the Language Arts Survey, 4.20–4.34, "Research Skills." (To evaluate research papers, see the evaluation forms for writing, revising, and proofreading, *Assessment Portfolio,* 7.1–7.10.)

▶ These prompts can be adapted for use as topics for oral reports or debates. To evaluate these projects, see the evaluation forms in the *Assessment Portfolio,* 7.17–7.19.

LANGUAGE LAB EDITING FOR ERRORS IN VERBS

During the editing or proofreading stage of the writing process, check your work to make sure that it is free of errors in the use of verbs. The following chart describes common errors in verb usage.

COMMON ERRORS IN VERB USAGE

LANGUAGE ARTS SURVEY

For additional help, see the Language Arts Survey, 2.65.

Improper Shifts in Verb Tense. Throughout a passage, the tenses, or times, of verbs should be consistent.

IMPROPER SHIFT FROM PAST TO PRESENT TENSE: As the young country grew, literacy increases dramatically.
CORRECTED SENTENCE: As the young country grew, literacy increased dramatically.

LANGUAGE ARTS SURVEY

For additional help, see the Language Arts Survey, 2.66–2.67.

Misuse of Irregular Verb Forms. Many verbs, such as *swim, go, bring, bite, buy, fight,* and *see,* have irregular past tense forms. Make sure to use the proper verb form in the past tense. If you are unsure about the proper form, check a dictionary.

MISUSE OF IRREGULAR VERB FORM: Franklin had went to Philadelphia to start a printing shop.
CORRECTED SENTENCE: Franklin had gone to Philadelphia to start a printing shop.

LANGUAGE ARTS SURVEY

For additional help, see the Language Arts Survey, 2.68.

Split Infinitives. An **infinitive** is a verb form made up of the word *to* and the base form of the verb, as in *to play* or *to suggest.* In formal speech and writing, try to avoid placing a modifier between *to* and the verb.

SPLIT INFINITIVE: Paine had to quickly flee to France.
CORRECTED SENTENCE: Paine had to flee quickly to France.

LANGUAGE ARTS SURVEY

For additional help, see the Language Arts Survey, 2.70.

Agreement of Subject and Verb. A verb should agree in number with its subject. If the subject is a compound joined by *and,* the verb should be plural. If the subject is a compound joined by *or, either . . . or,* or *neither . . . nor,* the verb should agree with the nearer subject.

AGREEMENT ERROR: Phillis Wheatley and Nathaniel was seeking support for publishing Wheatley's poems.
CORRECTED SENTENCE: Phillis Wheatley and Nathaniel were seeking support for publishing Wheatley's poems.
AGREEMENT ERROR: Neither Thomas Jefferson nor the other delegates was sure how successful their efforts would be.
CORRECTED SENTENCE: Neither Thomas Jefferson nor the other delegates were sure how successful their efforts would be.

EXERCISE A Correcting Errors in Verb Usage

Rewrite the following sentences, correcting the errors in verb usage.

EXAMPLE: America was to quite rapidly become a nation of readers.
America was to become quite rapidly a nation of readers.

1. Print became a vehicle to indelibly forge the nation's identity.
2. Franklin enters the printing trade and had his first essay published.
3. Neither Franklin nor his father and brother was above disputes.
4. People neither remembered nor like Paine in his later years.
5. Adams believed that to foolishly suffer from false security was unwise.

LANGUAGE ARTS SURVEY

For additional help, see the Language Arts Survey, 2.65–2.75.

EXERCISE B Revising for Errors in Verb Usage

Rewrite the following paragraphs, correcting the errors in verb usage.

EXAMPLE: Phillis was buyed by John and Susannah Wheatley.
Phillis was bought by John and Susannah Wheatley.

A. [1] Phillis Wheatley is born in West Africa and was captured as a child. [2] John and Susannah Wheatley provides the young slave girl with an education. [3] Wheatley had to abruptly return home from London when she heard of Susannah's death. [4] Wheatley meets George Washington after having dedicated a poem to him.

B. [1] Neither Paine nor the other revolutionists is properly respected today for their courageous stand against tyranny. [2] They chose to decisively act for the good of the people despite great potential danger to themselves. [3] They could have been throwed into prison or executed for treason against Great Britain. [4] They fighted for freedom, knowing that by so doing they make their own lives precarious. [5] Americans and other citizens of democratic states around the world owes the revolutionists a great debt of thanks.

ANSWERS FOR LANGUAGE LAB

Exercise A

1. Print became a vehicle to forge indelibly the nation's identity.

2. Franklin entered the printing trade and had his first essay published.

3. Neither Franklin nor his father and brother were above disputes.

4. People neither remembered nor liked Paine in his later years.

5. Adams believed that to suffer foolishly from false security was unwise.

Exercise B

A. [1] Phillis Wheatley was born in West Africa and was captured as a child. [2] John and Susannah Wheatley provided the young slave girl with an education. [3] Wheatley had to return home abruptly from London when she heard of Susannah's death. [4] Wheatley met George Washington after having dedicated a poem to him.

B. [1] Neither Paine nor the other revolutionists are properly respected today for their courageous stand against tyranny. [2] They chose to act decisively for the good of the people despite great potential danger to themselves. [3] They could have been thrown into prison or executed for treason against Great Britain. [4] They fought for freedom and knew that by so doing they made their own lives precarious. [5] Americans and other citizens of democratic states around the world owe the revolutionists a great debt of thanks.

UNIT SKILLS OUTLINE

LITERARY SKILLS AND CONCEPTS

- Allusion, 222, 250, 270
- Aphorism, 256, 270
- Elaboration, 250
- Essay, 256
- Fantasy, 222
- Metaphor, 256
- Mood, 239
- Onomatopoeia, 250
- Point of View, 238
- Romance, 239
- Symbol, 222
- Theme, 256
- Tone, 270

WRITING SKILLS AND CONCEPTS

- Advice Column, 256
- Billboard Ad, 256
- Biography, 256
- Blues, 270
- Descriptive Paragraph, 250
- Diary Entries, 223
- Epitaph, 270
- Gothic Tale, 239
- News Story, 223
- Obituary, 250
- Press Release, 239
- Real Estate Ad, 270
- Recommendations, 222
- Slogan, 250
- Storyboard, 239

GRAMMAR, USAGE, AND MECHANICS

- Adding Subordinate Clauses, 199
- Comparison of Adjectives and Adverbs, 250
- Compound Sentences, 259
- Correcting Run-ons, 257
- Deleting Repeated or Unnecessary Ideas, 271
- Editing for Errors in Pronoun Usage, 287
- Interjections, 226
- Proper Adjectives, 242
- Relative Pronouns, 223
- Subordinating Conjunctions, 199, 223
- Using Context Clues I, 239

OTHER LANGUAGE ARTS SKILLS AND CONCEPTS

- Discussion, 251
- Informal Note-taking, 240
- Paraphrasing and Summarizing, 257
- Reading Rate: Slow and Careful Reading, 253
- Strategies for Decision Making, 224
- Strategies for Problem Solving I, 271

UNIT 4 NEW ENGLAND RENAISSANCE PROSE

Watson and the Shark. *John Singleton Copley. Courtesy of Museum of Fine Arts, Boston. Gift of Mr. George von Lengerke Meyer*

GOALS/OBJECTIVES

Studying this unit will enable students to

- appreciate the contributions of Hawthorne, Poe, and Irving in the development of the short story
- recognize and understand Transcendentalism, the major literary movement of American literature in the first half of the nineteenth century, and identify its leaders
- understand the impact of social and political events of the early nineteenth century on American literature
- interpret the impact of Transcendentalist philosophy on contemporary American culture and thought

But oh! shipmates! on the starboard hand of every woe, there is a sure delight; and higher the top of that delight, than the bottom of the woe is deep.

—Herman Melville
Moby-Dick

CONNECTIONS ACROSS THE CURRICULUM

Arts and Humanities
- Drawing Comparisons, 283
- Fantasy Garden Catalog, 222
- Obscure Allusions, 251
- Painting Lima, Peru, 247
- Scene Painting, 261
- A Slanted Perception, 275
- Story Comparison, 225
- Transcendental Art, 253
- Collage, 251

Mathematics and Sciences
- Calculating Dimensions, 229
- Fantasy Garden Catalog, 222
- Geometric Morphing, 237
- Nature Study, 271
- Pendulums, 232
- Physics of Color, 248
- Strange Plants, 211
- Taking a Survey, 240

Social Studies
- Alexander the Great, 214
- Changing High Tech, 259
- Continents, 245
- Obscure Allusions, 251
- Role Playing a Trial, 240
- Social Standing, 279
- Spanish Inquisition, 240
- Symbols of State, 250

Applied Arts
- Thoreau and Pop Culture, 261

TEACHING THE MULTIPLE INTELLIGENCES

Logical-Mathematical
- Contrasting Views, 203
- Identifying Organization, 243
- Problem Solving, 224
- Setting the Mood, 212
- Story Comparison, 225

Spatial
- Calculating Dimensions, 229
- Drawing Comparisons, 283
- Map of Garden, 201
- Painting Lima, Peru, 229
- Reading Area Map, 265
- Set Design, 220

Musical
- Mood Music, 283
- Movie Score, 219

Kinesthetic
- Attracting Followers, 258
- Characterization through Mime, 209
- Proverb Charades, 257
- Role Playing, 198

(cont.)

TEACHING THE MULTIPLE INTELLIGENCES (CONT.)

Interpersonal
- Advice Booklet, 257
- Effect of Isolation, 236
- Evaluating Characteristics, 198
- Paraphrasing, 224
- Persuasive Speech, 258
- Recording Interjections, 226
- Standards of Behavior, 207
- Thoreau at School, 258

ART NOTE

John Singleton Copley (1738–1815), born in Boston, was a successful portrait painter by 1766, when he sent *Boy with a Squirrel* to a London exhibition. Praising that work, British painters Joshua Reynolds and Benjamin West recommended that Copley study in Europe. However, he did not act on their suggestion for several years. During this time he produced many fine portraits that present Americans in settings of everyday life. Critics especially appreciate his rich use of color, texture, light, and shade. In 1774, Copley moved to England permanently, and his work gradually took on some of the characteristics of British painting. In 1778, Copley began painting historical subjects. *Watson and the Shark* is one of the most successful of these paintings.

Andrew Jackson

THE NEW ENGLAND RENAISSANCE (1800–1860)

SOCIAL EXPANSION AND DEMOCRATIZATION

After the **Louisiana Purchase** of 1803, which doubled the size of the country, the United States expanded rapidly across the continent. By 1836, the original thirteen colonies had grown into twenty-five states, stretching as far west as Arkansas. Two important technological developments helped to make that expansion seem less daunting. The invention of the telegraph by **Samuel Morse** in 1838 made it possible to communicate across distances instantly. The introduction of the steam locomotive by **John Stephens** in 1825 made possible the development of a railway system to connect towns and cities across the vast country. By the 1850s, the East Coast was connected to Chicago by rail and beyond that to the western side of the Mississippi. Still, while industrial transformation was well underway in various part of the East, the rest of the country remained predominantly agricultural, with many new farms springing up in the new territories.

The 1820s, culminating in the presidency of **Andrew Jackson**, saw an ideological shift to the "common people." In many states, voting rights, which the wealthy property owners who framed the Constitution had not granted, were extended to all free men. This shift was also felt in an emerging local and national interest in the public's cultural and educational life. In the mid-1830s, **Horace Mann** of Massachusetts undertook studies that would eventually lead to more systematic methods for public education throughout the North. Many states, beginning with Massachusetts, began to offer free public education at the primary and secondary levels; by 1850, free education was widespread in the North. In addition, the **Lyceum Movement** emerged. Begun in 1826, lyceums were institutions that offered educational and inspirational lectures, debates, and entertainments in large public halls. These presentations covered a wide range of subject matters, from philosophy

LITERARY EVENTS

► = American Events

►1800. Library of Congress established

►1800. Mason Locke Weems's *The Life and Memorable Actions of George Washington* published

1804. Johann Christoph Friedrich von Schiller's *Wilhelm Tell* published

►1806. Noah Webster's *Compendious Dictionary of the English Language* published

1807. William Wordsworth's *Poetry in Two Volumes* published

►1809. Washington Irving's *Rip van Winkle* published

1800 **1805** **1810**

HISTORICAL EVENTS

►1800. Thomas Jefferson elected president

►1803. Louisiana Purchase

1804. Napoleon declared emperor of France; sets up Napoleonic Code

►1804. Alexander Hamilton, Secretary of the Treasury, killed in a duel with Aaron Burr

►1804. Thomas Jefferson reelected

►1804. Lewis and Clarke expedition

►1807. Chesapeake incident; British impress United States sailors

►1808. James Madison elected president

THEMATIC CURRENTS

Use the following selections to explore these themes with your students.

THE INDIVIDUAL AND PERSONAL RESPONSIBILITY

- "Rappaccini's Daughter," 198
- from *Self-Reliance*, 252
- from *Walden*, 258

TRANSCENDENTALISM

- from *Self-Reliance*, 252
- from *Walden*, 258

THE NATURE OF REALITY

- "Rappaccini's Daughter," 198
- "The Pit and the Pendulum," 225
- from *Moby-Dick*, 241
- from *Walden*, 258
- "The Legend of Sleepy Hollow," 272

to anthropology to the questions of slavery and women's rights. By 1860, there were more than 3000 lyceums in the United States serving as focal points for the transmission of ideas and culture.

Horace Mann

Romanticism and Transcendentalism

In Europe, the cultural and political era of the Enlightenment was superseded by **Romanticism.** Enlightenment thinkers of the eighteenth century had stressed objectivity and the power of reason to discover the laws of the universe in an objective, scientific, systematic fashion. To the young writers of the Romantic Period, the Enlightenment emphasis on reason undervalued private, subjective experience, including human emotions and the creative imagination. The English poet and essayist Samuel Taylor Coleridge, building on his reading of German writers such as Immanuel Kant, argued that there was a higher form of reason, to be distinguished from the ordinary "understanding" by which we know things in the physical world of sense perception. This higher reason was an intuitive capacity to grasp "metaphysical" truths in the physical world, to see in nature more than the mere operation of regularity and laws, and to see in life more than the practical advancement of social systems of organization. Nature was a repository of and stimulus for such intuitions, which might transform the individual by granting him or her access to higher truths than ordinary experience and social interaction could afford. British writers of the **Romantic Era,** including Coleridge; William Wordsworth; John Keats; Percy Shelley; Mary Shelley; and George Gordon, Lord Byron, praised the natural over the artificial, emotion over reason, and the individual conscience over all types of authority and external control.

European Romanticism had a profound impact on American literature. By the first decades of the nineteenth century, its influence could already be seen in the works of the American "Knickerbocker" writers such as **Washington Irving.** Centered around New York City, these writers had begun to turn their attention toward nature and to critique the ethic of material

1811. Jane Austen's *Sense and Sensibility* published
►1814. Francis Scott Key's "Star Spangled Banner" published
1816. Georg Hegel completes third volume of philosophy
►1817. William Cullen Bryant's "Thanatopsis" published
1818. Mary Shelley's *Frankenstein* published
1819. Arthur Schopenhauer's *The World as Will and Idea* published
►1820. Washington Irving's *The Sketch Book* published
►1826. James Fenimore Cooper's *The Last of the Mohicans* published
►1827. *The Freeman's Journal,* first African-American newspaper
►1828. Noah Webster's *An American Dictionary of the English Language* published
►1830. Oliver Wendell Holmes's "Old Ironsides" published

1815 **1820** **1825** **1830**

►1812. War of 1812 against Britain
►1812. James Madison reelected
►1814. Bombing of Fort McHenry
►1814. Treaty of Ghent ends War of 1812
►1815. Battle of New Orleans; United States defeats Britain, both armies unaware of the Treaty of Ghent
1815. Battle of Waterloo; Napolean defeated
►1816. James Monroe elected president
►1817. First Seminole War
1819. Florida purchased from Spain
►1820. James Monroe reelected
►1820. Missouri Compromise
►1823. The Monroe Doctrine
►1825. John Quincy Adams elected president
1825. Decembrist Revolution quelled in Russia
►1828. Andrew Jackson elected president
►1830. President Jackson signs Indian Removal Act

Quotables

"Lost, yesterday, somewhere between sunrise and sunset, two golden hours, each set with sixty diamond minutes. No reward is offered, for they are gone forever."

—Horace Mann

Additional Questions and Activities

Students may wish to read works of some of the British writers of the Romantic Era listed on page 193 to better understand Romanticism. Students can discuss how the ideas of nature over the artificial, emotion over reason, and the individual conscience over authority are expressed in the works they read. Students can keep these ideas in mind as they read American Transcendental writers.

LITERARY CURRENTS

Use the following selections to explore these techniques with your students.

Short Story
- "Rappaccini's Daughter," 198
- "The Pit and the Pendulum," 225
- "The Legend of Sleepy Hollow," 272

Essay
- from *Self-Reliance,* 252
- from *Walden,* 258

Aphorism
- from *Self-Reliance,* 252
- from *Walden,* 258

Symbol
- "Rappaccini's Daughter," 198

Allusion
- "Rappaccini's Daughter," 198
- from *Moby-Dick,* 241
- from *Self-Reliance,* 252
- from *Walden,* 258
- "The Legend of Sleepy Hollow," 272

Historical/Literary Note

An informal group called the Transcendental Club, whose members included Ralph Waldo Emerson, Henry David Thoreau, Nathaniel Hawthorne, Bronson Alcott, W. E. Channing, and Margaret Fuller, began meeting in 1836 and continued to meet, often at Emerson's house, for the next eight years. The group, which discussed literature, theology, and philosophy, called itself the Symposium or the Hedge Club because the members often met when F. H. Hedge made a trip to Boston. A quarterly magazine, which Bronson Alcott named *The Dial,* sprang out of the group's meetings and was published from July 1840 through April 1844.

Washington Irving

success and social advancement espoused by writers like Benjamin Franklin in the post-Revolutionary years.

The real flowering of Romanticism in American literature came in the New England literary movement called **Transcendentalism,** which gave its own distinctive inflection and variation to European Romanticism and put the United States on the world literary map to stay. At the core of Transcendentalism was a belief in a realm of spiritual or transcendent truths beyond sense perception and material existence. These truths could be intuited by humans in heightened moments of contemplation or under the influence of natural environs. Though quite abstract, the Transcendentalist philosophy had a number of quite practical implications. The Transcendentalists valued spiritual over material success, and so opposed the materialism, or desire for increased wealth, that was present in the American psyche since the time of the Puritans and that was elevated to an ideal in the writings of Benjamin Franklin. Contrast, for example, the Transcendentalist Ralph Waldo Emerson's "Things are in the saddle/And ride mankind" with Benjamin Franklin's "Get what you can, and what you get hold; 'Tis the stone that will turn all your lead into gold." Because they believed each person capable of intuiting truths directly, the Transcendentalists also dismissed tradition and social convention—any authority beyond that of the individual conscience. Emerson wrote, for example, that "Nothing is at last sacred but the integrity of our own mind. . . . The only right is what is after my constitution, the only wrong what is against it." Emerson's friend **Henry David Thoreau** carried out an experiment in self-reliance, in keeping with Transcendentalist philosophy, building for himself a small cabin in the woods near Walden Pond in order to live simply and in closer contact with nature. Thoreau's ***Walden,*** a record of this experience, tells us, "If a man does not keep pace with his companions, perhaps it is because he hears a different drummer. Let him step to the music which he hears, however measured or far away." Thoreau's keen observations of nature have made his book a source of inspiration to environmentalists around the world, in addition to being one of the definitive statements of American individualism.

Literary Events

► = American Events

►1831. William Lloyd Garrison's *The Liberator* published

►1831. John Greenleaf Whittier's *Legends of New England in Prose and Verse* published

►1835. Alexis de Tocqueville's *Democracy in America* published

►1837. Ralph Waldo Emerson's "The American Scholar" and "Concord Hymn" published

►1837. Nathaniel Hawthorne's *Twice-Told Tales* published

►1839. Edgar Allan Poe's "The Fall of the House of Usher" published

►1841. Ralph Waldo Emerson's *Self-Reliance* published

►1841. Henry Wadsworth Longfellow's *Ballads and Other Poems* published

►1842. Edgar Allan Poe's "The Raven" published

1843. Søren Kierkegaard's *Either-Or* published

►1843. Edgar Allan Poe's "The Pit and the Pendulum" published

1843. Charles Dickens's *A Christmas Carol* published

1835 **1840** **1845**

Historical Events

►1831. Nat Turner's rebellion

►1832. Andrew Jackson reelected

►1835. Second Seminole War

►1835. Texas secedes from Mexico

►1836. Texas wins independence, becomes a republic

►1836. Martin Van Buren elected president

1837. Queen Victoria becomes monarch in Britain

►1838. Underground Railroad begins

►1838. Trail of Tears; Cherokee forced to march; thousands die

►1840. William Henry Harrison elected president

►1841. President Harrison dies; John Tyler succeeds

►1843. Dorothea Dix begins humanitarian reforms

►1844. James Knox Polk elected president

1845. Potato famine in Ireland; immigration to United States increases

Emerson was an eternal optimist in his view of nature's goodness; in the midst of the 1837 economic panic and subsequent nationwide depression, he could blithely remark that "on the bosom of this vast (natural) plenty the blight of trade & manufacture seems to me a momentary mischance." Thoreau was capable of similar optimism, though he generally was much more socially reclusive and skeptical of his peers.

Several other major writers of the period, though influenced by Transcendentalism, did not take so sanguine a view of nature. In short stories such as "Rappacini's Daughter" and in the brilliant allegorical novel *The Scarlet Letter,* **Nathaniel Hawthorne** dealt with the darker aspects of human nature, specifically with sin and the ways in which humans deal with temptation and guilt. Hawthorne joined a Boston-area Transcendentalist utopian community called **Brook Farm** in 1840, but left a year later in disgust, and wrote a satire about it called *The Blithedale Romance.* **Herman Melville** explored the forces of evil and obsession in his masterpiece, *Moby-Dick.* **Edgar Allan Poe** brought the horror story to its zenith, exploring the psychology of madness and terror in such works as "The Pit and the Pendulum" and "The Fall of the House of Usher." Irving, Hawthorne, and Poe were collectively responsible for the development of the modern short story, a form that Poe defined as a brief fictional work designed to create in the reader a single dominant impression or effect.

Nathaniel Hawthorne.
Peabody Essex Museum

The Writing Profession and Social Purpose

Despite their recognition by some important figures abroad, the Transcendentalists were not popular writers. Of the seven hundred copies of Thoreau's *Walden* printed in the first edition, most were eventually returned to him, unsold, by the publisher. Thoreau eventually filled orders himself by mail. It remained for later generations to recognize the quintessentially American genius that informed Transcendentalism.

Biographical Note

Nathaniel Hawthorne and Washington Irving both enjoyed using pseudonyms so that they could comment in a lighthearted way on their own work. In his introduction to "Rappaccini's Daughter" in its original publication, Hawthorne criticized several of the techniques supposedly used by the obscure French author of the piece. Irving's first huge success was published under the name of Diedrich Knickerbocker, and several of his later books used the name of Geoffrey Crayon, Esquire. For a taste of his comments on his alter ego, see the postscript to "The Legend of Sleepy Hollow" found on page 283.

►1846. Henry Wadsworth Longfellow's *The Belfry of Bruges and Other Poems* published
1847. Charlotte Brontë's *Jane Eyre* published
1847. Emily Brontë's *Wuthering Heights* published
1848. William Makepeace Thackeray's *Vanity Fair*
►1850. Nathaniel Hawthorne's *The Scarlet Letter*
►1851. Herman Melville's *Moby-Dick* published
►1851. Nathaniel Hawthorne's *The House of the Seven Gables*
►1852. Harriet Beecher Stowe's *Uncle Tom's Cabin* published
►1854. Henry David Thoreau's *Walden* published
►1855. Walt Whitman's *Leaves of Grass* published
1857. Gustave Flaubert's *Madame Bovary*
1859. Charles Dickens's *A Tale of Two Cities* published

1850 **1855** **1860**

►1846. Mexican War; United States annexes New Mexico
►1848. Zachary Taylor elected president
►1849. First gold rush
►1849. Harriet Tubman escapes from slavery
►1850. President Taylor dies; Millard Fillmore succeeds
►1852. Franklin Pierce elected president
►1854. Kansas-Nebraska Act repeals Missouri Compromise
►1856. James Buchanan elected president
►1856. "Bleeding Kansas"
►1857. Dred Scott decision

BIOGRAPHICAL NOTE

James Fenimore Cooper (1789–1851), best known as the author of the *Leather-Stocking Tales,* became an author on a dare. After serving in the United States Navy from 1806 to 1811, Cooper settled in upstate New York, intending to become a farmer. When he told his wife he could write a better novel than the one he had just read, she challenged him to do so. His first novel was not successful, but his second one, *The Spy* (1821), was, and he went on to a full-time writing career. His best-known novels tell about the vanishing American frontier as they follow a highly individualistic hero, Natty Bumppo, from the forests of New York to the prairies of the West, trying to outrun civilization. The books, in the order of Bumppo's life, are *The Deerslayer* (1841), *The Last of the Mohicans* (1826), *The Pathfinder* (1840), *The Pioneers* (1823), and *The Prairie* (1823). Cooper also wrote the first American novel about the sea, *The Pilot* (1824), and several nonfiction works critical of American society.

Some American writers were popular, however, and there were American bestsellers in this era, notably the historical novels of **James Fenimore Cooper** and Herman Melville's tales of seafaring adventure such as *Typee* and *Omoo.* The economics of publication, however, did not yet favor writing as a source of income, even if a work was popular. It was not yet possible to make a living in America as a professional writer because, though United States Copyright laws were enacted in the states in 1841, there was no international copyright protection until 1891. American books could be sold legally in England without paying royalties to the American author, and English books could be sold in America without paying royalties to the English author. The cost of publishing a book from abroad was therefore less than the cost of publishing a work by an American. To get their books published under such circumstances, American writers usually had to sell their books without any claim to royalties.

Why, then, did these individuals write? One answer is that they were committed to effecting change and believed in the power of literature to shape society. Thoreau's *Walden,* for example, is a kind of guide for living a simple life characterized by a fundamental relation to the natural world. Emerson, too, sought to change how people live and think, to teach people how to trust their own better natures.

NEW ENGLAND RENAISSANCE POETRY

Other writers of the period also had social purpose in their writing; for example, **Henry Wadsworth Longfellow, James Russell Lowell, John Greenleaf Whittier,** and **Oliver Wendell Holmes** wrote poems on various social and political issues of the time such as slavery. These men were not social rebels, however; they were models of the respectable citizen-poet, and their poetry was highly popular. They were part of a group now known alternately as the **Fireside,** or **Schoolroom, Poets** because their work was quite popular among families reading in the evening around the fire and because their work came to be recited and memorized widely in American schoolrooms. Their most popular poems were songlike, containing regular rhythms and rhymes that made the poems easy to recite and remember. These poets offered mostly idealized, romantic, morally uplifting views of the nation and its past, in lyric and narrative verse. Though the work of the Fireside Poets has often been denigrated by twentieth-century critics as unchallenging, their works helped to create greater popular interest in poetry and to elevate the status of the poet in the national imagination; indeed, Longfellow's seventy-fifth birthday was an occasion for a national celebration. The work of another poet of this era, **Edgar Allan Poe,** was similarly straightforward in its rhymes and rhythms but explored elements of the gothic, the macabre, and the mysterious.

Completely different from the Fireside or Schoolroom Poetry in almost every respect was the poetry of **Emily Dickinson,** which is generally more highly regarded by critics today. Dickinson called her poems her "letter to the world," but of the hundreds that she wrote, only a handful were read by the world in her lifetime; the rest were discovered in a storage trunk by her sister and later published by a friend. Dickinson's poetry does not follow the regular rhythmic patterns of the Schoolroom poets; it is full of interrupted thoughts and sudden bursts of awareness, often jarring the reader through irony and paradox into a wholly different, more unsettling view of the world. Dickinson often treats not an idealized past but a vivid present or an uncertain future, addressing time, isolation, and death from a surprising number of perspectives. Though she seems not to have directly registered the social issues of the day in her poetry, her work does reflect an awareness of some issues being treated by her contemporaries.

Echoes:

New England Renaissance Prose

Quotations from Ralph Waldo Emerson

On accomplishment: "If a man write a better book, preach a better sermon, or make a better mouse-trap than his neighbor, tho' he build his house in the woods, the world will make a beaten path to his door."

On ambition: "Hitch your wagon to a star."

On consistency: "A foolish consistency is the hobgoblin of little minds."

On enthusiasm: "Nothing great was ever achieved without enthusiasm."

On history: "There is properly no history, only biography."

On individuality: "Whoso would be a man must be a nonconformist."

On individuality: "To believe your own thought, to believe that what is true for you in your private heart is true for all men,—that is genius."

On rewards for actions: "The reward of a thing well done, is to have done it."

On society: "Society everywhere is in conspiracy against the manhood of every one of its members."

On the histories of words: "Language is fossil poetry."

On writing: "The art of writing consists in putting two things together that are unlike and that belong together like a horse & cart."

Quotations from Henry David Thoreau

On economics: "For more than five years I maintained myself thus solely by the labor of my hands, and I found, that by working about six weeks in a year, I could meet all the expenses of living."

On government: "I heartily accept the motto, 'That government is best which governs least.' "

On individuality: "If a man does not keep pace with his companions, perhaps it is because he hears a different drummer. Let him step to the music which he hears, however measured or far away."

On nature: "I frequently tramped eight or ten miles through the deepest snow to keep an appointment with a beech-tree, or a yellow birch, or an old acquaintance among the pines."

On nature: "I once had a sparrow alight on my shoulder for a moment while I was hoeing in a village garden, and I felt that I was more distinguished by that circumstance than I should have been by any epaulet I could have worn."

On solitude: "I never found the companion that was so companionable as solitude."

On technology: "Men have become the tools of their tools."

On the failure to follow one's dreams: "The mass of men live lives of quiet desperation."

On travel: "I have traveled a good deal in Concord."

ADDITIONAL QUESTIONS AND ACTIVITIES

- In small groups students can discuss the quotations from Emerson and Thoreau on page 197. Then, each student can choose one quotation and use it as the beginning of a personal or persuasive essay. Students may wish to examine other aphorisms of the two writers to use in their essay, or students might choose a subject and use quotations from both Emerson and Thoreau.
- Ask students to brainstorm other aphorisms about one of the following topics: accomplishment, ambition, dreams, individuality, society, and solitude. Students can discuss which aphorisms best reflect their own ideas and experiences.

ADDITIONAL RESOURCES

READER'S GUIDE
- Selection Worksheet, 4.1

ASSESSMENT PORTFOLIO
- Selection Check Test, 4.4.1
- Selection Test, 4.4.2

ESSENTIAL SKILLS PRACTICE BOOKS
- *Language,* 2.11, 2.27, 2.50
- *Study and Research,* 4.3

ENRICHMENT ACTIVITIES

- Students might write an essay exploring Puritan themes such as sin and salvation present in "Rappaccini's Daughter," drawing on the knowledge they gained in Unit 3.
- Students could also write a comparison and contrast essay, comparing and contrasting this piece to the story of Adam and Eve in Genesis.

SUPPORT FOR LEP STUDENTS

Have students look for common themes in the vocabulary of the story and list words, both new and familiar, under topics to which they refer, such as "Smells" *(inhaling, fragrance, odor, perfume)*, "Medicine/Drugs/Poisons" *(herbs, distil, medicines, apothecary, disease)*, "Richness" *(mansion, opulent, resplendent, magnificent)*, and "Evil or Unpleasantness" *(strange, ruin, malignant, license, fatality, dangerous)*.

IDIOMS

armorial bearings—family crest

ADDITIONAL VOCABULARY

malice—evil intent
luxuriant—growing with vigor and great abundance
delectable—delicious; delightful

PREREADING

SHORT STORY

"Rappaccini's Daughter"
by Nathaniel Hawthorne

ABOUT THE AUTHOR

Nathaniel Hawthorne (1804–1864) was born in Salem, Massachusetts. His ancestors took part in the Salem witch trials and the Quaker persecution. He studied at Bowdoin College where he met Franklin Pierce and Henry Wadsworth Longfellow. For over a decade after graduation, he studied the Puritans and wrote, anonymously publishing his first novel, *Fanshawe.* Then he directed his efforts to short stories and published *Twice-Told Tales.* His next collection, *Mosses from an Old Manse,* received a glowing review by Herman Melville. After leaving employment as a surveyor at the Salem Customs House, Hawthorne published *The Scarlet Letter.* From 1850 on, Hawthorne concentrated on writing for children, notably *The House of Seven Gables* and *The Blithedale Romance.* Hawthorne was named American consul at Liverpool and Manchester, England (1853–1855) by President Franklin Pierce. When he left this post, he traveled through Europe and published *The Marble Faun.* When he died, he left several unfinished works.

ABOUT THE SELECTION

In 1842, Nathaniel Hawthorne and his wife moved to Emerson's former home, The Old Manse, in Concord, Massachusetts. During the following four years, Hawthorne produced many of his finest stories, publishing them individually in magazines or in the collections *Twice-Told Tales* and *Mosses from an Old Manse.* **"Rappaccini's Daughter"** was first published in December 1844, in the *Democratic Review,* with a mock-autobiographical introduction. The story shows many of Hawthorne's characteristic traits, including strong use of symbolism, a psychological approach, and a focus on the Puritan preoccupation with evil.

GOALS/OBJECTIVES

Studying this lesson will enable students to

- interpret and appreciate a short story
- identify, define, and illustrate with examples the terms *fantasy, symbol,* and *allusion*
- write a recommendation, a diary entry, and a news story
- use subordinate clauses properly

READER'S JOURNAL

Have you ever had a friend who was a bad influence on you or who eventually proved to be hurtful? Have you disliked or feared someone and later learned that this person had helped you? Think of friends and acquaintances who seemed to be one way but turned out to be quite different. Freewrite in your journal about the difficulty of recognizing a person's true nature.

LANGUAGE SKILLS

Read the Language Arts Survey, 2.27, "Subordinating Conjunctions," and 2.50, "Adding Subordinate Clauses." Then list several subordinate clauses you find in "Rappaccini's Daughter." Briefly identify how each clause adds to the meaning of the sentence (for example, "describes the stranger") or how it is used in the sentence (for example, "the object of the verb *recollected*").

"Rappaccini's Daughter"

NATHANIEL HAWTHORNE

A young man, named Giovanni Guasconti, came, very long ago, from the more southern region of Italy, to pursue his studies at the University of Padua. Giovanni, who had but a scanty supply of gold ducats in his pocket, took lodgings in a high and gloomy chamber of an old edifice,[1] which looked not unworthy to have been the palace of a Paduan[2] noble, and which, in fact, exhibited over its entrance the armorial bearings of a family long since extinct. The young stranger, who was not unstudied in the great poem of his country, recollected that one of the ancestors of this family, and perhaps an occupant of this very mansion, had been pictured by Dante as a partaker of the immortal agonies of his Inferno.[3] These reminiscences and associations, together with the tendency to heartbreak natural to a young man for the first time out of his native sphere, caused Giovanni to sigh heavily, as he looked around the desolate and ill-furnished apartment.

"Holy Virgin, signor,[4]" cried old dame Lisabetta, who, won by the youth's remarkable beauty of person, was kindly endeavoring to give the chamber a habitable air, "what a sigh was that to come out of a young man's heart! Do you find this old mansion gloomy? For the love of heaven, then, put your head out of the window, and you will see as bright sunshine as you have left in Naples."

❶ *What causes Giovanni to sigh?*

1. **edifice.** Building
2. **Paduan.** From Padua, Italy
3. **Dante . . . his Inferno.** Dante Alighieri (1265–1321), Italian poet who wrote *The Divine Comedy;* "Inferno" is that section of *The Divine Comedy* which describes hell and the suffering of the damned.
4. **signor.** Sir (Italian)

WORDS FOR EVERYDAY USE: **rem • i • nis • cence** (rəm´ə nis´əns) *n.,* memory or something remembered

PREREADING NOTES

READER'S JOURNAL

You might ask students to describe the problems that can result from prejudging a person's character.

LANGUAGE SKILLS

Students might try writing subordinate clauses that could be used to replace the subordinate clauses from "Rappaccini's Daughter." Students' clauses should be creative, yet should make sense within the context of the story.

▶ Additional practice is provided in the *Essential Skills Practice Book: Language,* 2.27 and 2.50.

ANSWER TO GUIDED READING QUESTION

❶ Giovanni's mental associations with Dante's "Inferno" and the "tendency to heartbreak" caused by being out of his "natural sphere" make him sigh.

VOCABULARY FROM THE SELECTION

affinity
analogy
articulated
aspect
assuage
baneful
connoisseur
cordiality
deleterious
delusory
demeanor
deportment
depraved
ebullition
efficacious
emaciated
equanimity
erroneous
evanescent
evince
fervor
imbue
imperturbable
infringing
insinuate
lurid
malignant
opulent
pertinacity
phenomenon
portal
recompense
reminiscence
resplendent
reverie
sophistry
speculative
surmise
terminate
testily
transmute
unintelligible
untoward
vacuity
vagary
verdure

VOCABULARY IN CONTEXT

- As an adult writer, Proust described his reminiscences of his youth.

Answer to Guided Reading Question

❶ He finds a particular shrub with beautiful, purple flowers eye-catching.

Historical Note

At the time during which the story is set, what is now Italy was an array of independent city-states, some of which ranked among the most important powers in Europe. These states often warred against each other. Students can locate on a map the different regions of Italy mentioned.

Guasconti mechanically did as the old woman advised, but could not quite agree with her that the Lombard[5] sunshine was as cheerful as that of southern Italy. Such as it was, however, it fell upon a garden beneath the window, and expended its fostering influences on a variety of plants, which seemed to have been cultivated with exceeding care.

"Does this garden belong to the house?" asked Giovanni.

"Heaven forbid, signor!—unless it were fruitful of better pot-herbs than any that grow there now," answered old Lisabetta. "No: that garden is cultivated by the own hands of Signor Giacomo Rappaccini, the famous Doctor, who, I warrant him, has been heard of as far as Naples. It is said he distils these plants into medicines that are as potent as a charm. Oftentimes you may see the signor Doctor at work, and perchance the signora[6] his daughter, too, gathering the strange flowers that grow in the garden."

What does Giovanni find particularly eye-catching in the garden? ❶

The old woman had now done what she could for the aspect of the chamber, and, commending the young man to the protection of the saints, took her departure.

Giovanni still found no better occupation than to look down into the garden beneath his window. From its appearance, he judged it to be one of those botanic gardens, which were of earlier date in Padua than elsewhere in Italy, or in the world. Or, not improbably, it might once have been the pleasure place of an opulent family; for there was the ruin of a marble fountain in the center, sculptured with rare art, but so woefully shattered that it was impossible to trace the original design from the chaos of remaining fragments. The water, however, continued to gush and sparkle into the sunbeams as cheerfully as ever. A little gurgling sound ascended to the young man's window, and made him feel as if the fountain were an immortal spirit, that sung its song unceasingly, and without heeding the vicissitudes[7] around it; while one century embodied it in marble, and another scattered the garniture[8] on the soil. All about the pool into which the water subsided, grew various plants, that seemed to require a plentiful supply of moisture for the nourishment of gigantic leaves, and, in some instances, flowers gorgeously magnificent. There was one shrub in particular, set in a marble vase in the midst of the pool, that bore a profusion of purple blossoms, each of which had the luster and richness of a gem; and the whole together made a show so resplendent that it seemed enough to illuminate the garden, even had there been no sunshine. Every portion of the soil was peopled with plants and herbs, which, if less beautiful, still bore tokens of assiduous[9] care; as if all had their individual virtues, known to the scientific mind that fostered them. Some were placed in urns, rich with old carving, and others in common garden-pots; some crept serpent-like along the ground, or climbed on high, using whatever means of ascent was offered them. One plant had wreathed itself round

5. **Lombard.** Lombardy, region of northern Italy on the border of Switzerland
6. **signora.** Mrs., Madam; Italian title of respect
7. **vicissitudes.** Changes
8. **garniture.** Decoration, ornament
9. **assiduous.** Done with constant and careful attention

Words for Everyday Use:
as • pect (as´ pekt´) *n.,* appearance
op • u • lent (äp´yōō lənt) *adj.,* very wealthy or rich
re • splend • ent (ri splen´dənt) *adj.,* shining brightly

Vocabulary in Context

- The aspect of a panther is beautiful; its temper, however, can be ferocious.
- The showy mansion belongs to an opulent family.
- The queen put on so many diamonds that she was positively resplendent.
- Bill does not have the most pleasant demeanor; in fact, most people say he is very obnoxious.
- The wicked witch was malignant in her desire to harm Hansel and Gretel.

a statue of Vertumnus,[10] which was thus quite veiled and shrouded in a drapery of hanging foliage, so happily arranged that it might have served a sculptor for a study.

While Giovanni stood at the window, he heard a rustling behind a screen of leaves, and became aware that a person was at work in the garden. His figure soon emerged into view, and showed itself to be that of no common laborer, but a tall, emaciated, sallow, and sickly looking man, dressed in a scholar's garb[11] of black. He was beyond the middle term of life, with grey hair, a thin grey beard, and a face singularly marked with intellect and cultivation, but which could never, even in his more youthful days, have expressed much warmth of heart.

Nothing could exceed the intentness with which this scientific gardener examined every shrub which grew in his path; it seemed as if he was looking into their inmost nature, making observations in regard to their creative essence, and discovering why one leaf grew in this shape, and another in that, and wherefore such and such flowers differed among themselves in hue and perfume. Nevertheless, in spite of the deep intelligence on his part, there was no approach to intimacy between himself and these vegetable existences. On the contrary, he avoided their actual touch, or the direct inhaling of their odors, with a caution that impressed Giovanni most disagreeably; for the man's demeanor was that of one walking among malignant influences, such as savage beasts, or deadly snakes, or evil spirits, which, should he allow them one moment of license, would wreak upon him some terrible fatality. It was strangely frightful to the young man's imagination, to see this air of insecurity in a person cultivating a garden, that most simple and innocent of human toils, and which had been alike the joy and labor of the unfallen parents of the race. Was this garden, then, the Eden of the present world?—and this man, with such a perception of harm in what his own hands caused to grow, was he the Adam?[12]

❶ *To what is the garden compared? the gardener?*

The distrustful gardener, while plucking away the dead leaves or pruning the too luxuriant growth of the shrubs, defended his hands with a pair of thick gloves. Nor were these his only armor. When, in his walk through the garden, he came to the magnificent plant that hung its purple gems beside the marble fountain, he placed a kind of mask over his mouth and nostrils, as if all this beauty did but conceal a deadlier malice. But finding his task still too dangerous, he drew back, removed the mask, and called loudly, but in the infirm voice of a person affected with inward disease:

❷ *What does the gardener do when examining the plant that Giovanni noticed?*

"Beatrice!—Beatrice!"

"Here am I, my father! What would you?" cried a rich and youthful voice from the window of the opposite house; a voice as rich as a tropical sunset, and which made Giovanni, though he knew not why, think of deep hues of purple or crimson, and of perfumes heavily delectable.—"Are you in the garden?"

❸ *What images does the voice suggest to Giovanni?*

"Yes, Beatrice," answered the gardener, "and I need your help."

10. **Vertumnus.** Roman god of the changing seasons
11. **garb.** Attire; manner of dress
12. **Adam.** Name of the first man created, according to the book of Genesis in the Bible

WORDS FOR EVERYDAY USE:

de • mean • or (di mēn´ər) *n.,* way of behaving; manner

ma • lig • nant (mə lig´nənt) *adj.,* wishing evil

ANSWERS TO GUIDED READING QUESTIONS

❶ The garden is compared to Eden. The gardener is compared to Adam.

❷ The gardener places a mask upon his face.

❸ The voice suggests a tropical sunset and makes Giovanni think of deep purple or crimson and heavy perfume.

ADDITIONAL QUESTIONS AND ACTIVITIES

Students can supplement the description in the text with their own imagination to map Rappaccini's garden. Students may wish to create sketches of the garden as they imagine it, including details of the fountain, carved flower pots and urns, strange plants, or Rappaccini tending his garden.

Answers to Guided Reading Questions

❶ Giovanni dreams of a rich flower and a beautiful girl filled with peril.

❷ Beatrice handles and inhales the odor of several of the plants her father avoids.

Additional Questions and Activities

What is Giovanni's first impression of Beatrice? What change in his impression occurred as he watched her on the first day? To what is Beatrice compared? Ask students to look for other examples of this comparison in the text.

Answers. Giovanni first thinks that Beatrice is full of life, health, and energy. As he watches her, he begins to think that she appears as another flower to be handled only with another glove and mask. Later Beatrice refers to the flower as her sister whom she will tend and who gives her the breath of life.

Quotables

"Sleeping or waking, we hear not the airy footsteps of the strange things that almost happen."

—Nathaniel Hawthorne

Soon there emerged from under a sculptured portal the figure of a young girl, arrayed with as much richness of taste as the most splendid of the flowers, beautiful as the day, and with a bloom so deep and vivid that one shade more would have been too much. She looked redundant[13] with life, health, and energy; all of which attributes were bound down and compressed, as it were, and girdled tensely, in their luxuriance, by her virgin zone. Yet Giovanni's fancy must have grown morbid, while he looked down into the garden; for the impression which the fair stranger made upon him was as if here were another flower, the human sister of those vegetable ones, as beautiful as they—more beautiful than the richest of them—but still to be touched only with a glove, nor to be approached without a mask. As Beatrice came down the garden path, it was observable that she handled and inhaled the odor of several of the plants, which her father had most sedulously[14] avoided.

❶ *What does Giovanni dream?*

❷ *What does Beatrice do that her father does not?*

"Here, Beatrice," said the latter,—"see how many needful offices require to be done to our chief treasure. Yet, shattered as I am, my life might pay the penalty of approaching it so closely as circumstances demand. Henceforth, I fear, this plant must be consigned to your sole charge."

"And gladly will I undertake it," cried again the rich tones of the young lady, as she bent toward the magnificent plant, and opened her arms as if to embrace it. "Yes, my sister, my splendor, it shall be Beatrice's task to nurse and serve thee; and thou shalt reward her with thy kisses and perfumed breath, which to her is as the breath of life!"

Then, with all the tenderness in her manner that was so strikingly expressed in her words, she busied herself with such attentions as the plant seemed to require; and Giovanni, at his lofty window, rubbed his eyes, and almost doubted whether it were a girl tending her favorite flower, or one sister performing the duties of affection to another. The scene soon terminated. Whether Doctor Rappaccini had finished his labors in the garden, or that his watchful eye had caught the stranger's face, he now took his daughter's arm and retired. Night was already closing in; oppressive exhalations seemed to proceed from the plants, and steal upward past the open window; and Giovanni, closing the lattice, went to his couch, and dreamed of a rich flower and beautiful girl. Flower and maiden were different and yet the same, and fraught[15] with some strange peril in either shape.

But there is an influence in the light of morning that tends to rectify whatever errors of fancy, or even of judgment, we may have incurred during the sun's decline, or among the shadows of the night, or in the less wholesome glow of moonshine. Giovanni's first movement on starting from sleep, was to throw open the window, and gaze down into the garden which his dreams had made so fertile of mysteries. He was surprised, and a little ashamed, to find how real and matter-of-fact an affair it proved to be, in the first rays of the sun, which gilded the dewdrops that hung upon

13. **redundant.** Overfull, as though having more than one's share of life
14. **sedulously.** Diligently; persistently
15. **fraught.** Filled

Words for Everyday Use: **ter • mi • nate** (tʉr´ mə nāt´) *vi.,* end, stop, cease leaf and blossom, and, while giving a brighter beauty to each rare flower, brought everything within the limits of ordinary experience. The young man rejoiced, that, in the heart of the barren city, he had the privilege of overlooking this spot of lovely and luxuriant vegetation. It would serve, he said to himself, as a symbolic language, to keep him in communion with nature. Neither the sickly and thought-worn Doctor Giocomo Rappaccini, it is true, nor his brilliant daughter were now visible; so that Giovanni could not determine how much of the singularity which he attributed to both, was due to their own qualities, and how much to his wonder-working fancy. But he was inclined to take a most rational view of the whole matter.

In the course of the day, he paid his respects to Signor Pietro Baglioni, professor of medicine in the University, a physician of eminent repute, to whom Giovanni had brought a letter of introduction. The professor was an elderly personage, apparently of genial nature, and habits that might almost be called jovial; he kept the young man to dinner, and made himself very agreeable by the freedom and liveliness of his conversation, especially when warmed by a flask or two of Tuscan wine. Giovanni, conceiving that men of science, inhabitants of the same city, must needs be on familiar terms with one another, took an opportunity to mention the name of Dr. Rappaccini. But the professor did not respond with so much cordiality as he had anticipated.

"Ill would it become a teacher of the divine art of medicine," said Professor Pietro Baglioni, in answer to a question of Giovanni, "to withhold due and well-considered praise of a physician so eminently skilled as Rappaccini. But, on the other hand, I should answer it but scantily to my conscience, were I to permit a worthy youth like yourself, Signor Giovanni, the son of an ancient friend, to imbibe erroneous ideas respecting a man who might hereafter chance to hold your life and death in his hands. The truth is, our worshipful Doctor Rappaccini has as much science as any member of the faculty—with perhaps one single exception—in Padua, or all Italy. But there are certain grave objections to his professional character."

"And what are they?" asked the young man.

"Has my friend Giovanni any disease of body or heart, that he is so inquisitive about physicians?" said the Professor, with a smile. "But as for Rappaccini, it is said of him—and I, who know the man well, can answer for its truth—that he cares infinitely more for science than for mankind. His patients are interesting to him only as subjects for some new experiment. He would sacrifice human life, his own among the rest, or whatever else was dearest to him, for the sake of adding so much as a grain of mustard-seed to the great heap of his accumulated knowledge."

"Methinks he is an awful[16] man, indeed," remarked Guasconti, mentally recalling the cold and purely intellectual aspect of Rappaccini. "And yet, worshipful Professor, is it not a noble spirit? Are there many men capable of so spiritual a love of science?"

16. **awful.** Awe-inspiring

❶ *What does Baglioni find objectionable about Rappaccini?*

ANSWER TO GUIDED READING QUESTION

❶ Baglioni thinks the fact that Rappaccini is willing to sacrifice human life is objectionable.

LITERARY TECHNIQUE

Hawthorne presents a strong contrast between Giovanni's first view of Dr. Rappaccini's garden by night and his second view by day. Encourage students to look for differences in descriptive words, sentence structure, mood, tone, or other characteristics that bring out the changes in Giovanni's perceptions.

WORDS FOR EVERYDAY USE:

cor • di • al • i • ty (kôr´jē al´ə tē) *n.,* warm, friendly act or remark

er • ro • ne • ous (ər rō´ nē əs) *adj.,* mistaken, wrong

VOCABULARY IN CONTEXT

- I wish you two boys would terminate this petty feud.
- Mrs. Rogers was a woman of great cordiality, always welcoming people to her home with a smile.
- The man was convicted, but it was later revealed that certain evidence was erroneous, and he was released.

Answers to Guided Reading Questions

❶ Rappaccini's interest is in poison.

❷ There has long been professional rivalry between Rappaccini and Baglioni, and Rappaccini is generally acknowledged as the better scientist.

Literary Technique

An author gives a story verisimilitude, or the appearance of truth, by including realistic details, actions that seem natural under the given circumstances, and actual or imaginary references to outside sources. Point out the assertion that a rivalry between Rappaccini and Baglioni is recorded in "certain black-letter tracts . . . preserved in the medical department of the University of Padua." Have students examine the selection for other similar statements that claim a connection between the characters of the story and other sources.

"God forbid," answered the Professor, somewhat testily—"at least, unless they take sounder views of the healing art than those adopted by Rappaccini. It is his theory, that all medicinal virtues are comprised within those substances which we term vegetable poisons. These he cultivates with his own hands, and is said even to have produced new varieties of poison, more horribly deleterious than Nature, without the assistance of this learned person, would ever have plagued the world with. That the signor Doctor does less mischief than might be expected, with such dangerous substances, is undeniable. Now and then, it must be owned, he has effected—or seemed to effect—a marvelous cure. But, to tell you my private mind, Signor Giovanni, he should receive little credit for such instances of success—they being probably the work of chance—but should be held strictly accountable for his failures, which may justly be considered his own work."

❶ *What is Rappaccini's particular interest?*

The youth might have taken Baglioni's opinions with many grains of allowance, had he known that there was a professional warfare of long continuance between him and Doctor Rappaccini, in which the latter was generally thought to have gained the advantage. If the reader be inclined to judge for himself, we refer him to certain black-letter tracts on both sides, preserved in the medical department of the University of Padua.

❷ *Why might Baglioni have a motivation to lie about Rappaccini?*

"I know not, most learned Professor," returned Giovanni, after musing on what had been said of Rappaccini's exclusive zeal for science—"I know not how dearly this physician may love his art; but surely there is one object more dear to him. He has a daughter."

"Aha!" cries the Professor with a laugh. "So now our friend Giovanni's secret is out. You have heard of this daughter, whom all the young men in Padua are wild about, though not half a dozen have ever had the good hap to see her face. I know little of the Signora Beatrice, save that Rappaccini is said to have instructed her deeply in his science, and that, young and beautiful as fame reports her, she is already qualified to fill a professor's chair. Perchance her father destines her for mine! Other absurd rumors there be, not worth talking about, or listening to. So now, Signor Giovanni, drink off your glass of Lacryma."

Guasconti returned to his lodgings somewhat heated with the wine he had quaffed,[17] and which caused his brain to swim with strange fantasies in reference to Doctor Rappaccini and the beautiful Beatrice. On his way, happening to pass by a florist's, he bought a fresh bouquet of flowers.

Ascending to his chamber, he seated himself near the window, but within the shadow thrown by the depth of the wall, so that he could look down into the garden with little risk of being discovered. All beneath his eye was a solitude. The strange plants were basking in the sunshine, and now and then nodding gently to one another, as if in acknowledgment of sympathy and kindred. In the midst, by the shattered fountain, grew the magnificent shrub, with its purple gems clustering

17. **quaffed.** Drunk

Words for Everyday Use: **tes • ti • ly** (tes´tə lē) *adv.,* in an irritable manner; **del • e • te • ri • ous** (del´ə tir´ ē əs) *adj.,* harmful to health or well-being

Vocabulary in Context

- "I will not go to bed!" said the overly tired child testily.
- It has been proven that asbestos is deleterious to human health.
- The portal to the castle was heavily barred and the drawbridge across the moat was up, so there was no way to enter the castle.
- You could draw a definite analogy between her treatment as a child and her behavior as an adult.
- A total eclipse is a rare phenomenon.

all over it; they glowed in the air, and gleamed back again out of the depths of the pool, which thus seemed to overflow with colored radiance from the rich reflection that was steeped in it. At first, as we have said, the garden was a solitude. Soon, however,—as Giovanni had half-hoped, half-feared, would be the case,—a figure appeared beneath the antique sculptured portal, and came down between the rows of plants, inhaling their various perfumes, as if she were one of those beings of old classic fable, that lived upon sweet odors. On again beholding Beatrice, the young man was even startled to perceive how much her beauty exceeded his recollection of it; so brilliant, so vivid in its character, that she glowed amid the sunlight, and, as Giovanni whispered to himself, positively illuminated the more shadowy intervals of the garden path. Her face being now more revealed than on the former occasion, he was struck by its expression of simplicity and sweetness; qualities that had not entered into his idea of her character, and which made him ask anew, what manner of mortal she might be. Nor did he fail again to observe, or imagine, an analogy between the beautiful girl and the gorgeous shrub that hung its gem-like flowers over the fountain; a resemblance which Beatrice seemed to have indulged a fantastic humor in heightening, both by the arrangement of her dress and the selection of its hues.

Approaching the shrub, she threw open her arms, as with a passionate ardor, and drew its branches into an intimate embrace; so intimate, that her features were hidden in its leafy bosom, and her glistening ringlets all intermingled with the flowers.

"Give me thy breath, my sister," exclaimed Beatrice; "for I am faint with common air! And give me this flower of thine, which I separate with gentlest fingers from the stem, and place it close beside my heart."

With these words, the beautiful daughter of Rappaccini plucked one of the richest blossoms of the shrub, and was about to fasten it in her bosom. But now, unless Giovanni's draughts of wine had bewildered his senses, a singular incident occurred. A small orange-colored reptile of the lizard or chameleon species, chanced to be creeping along the path, just at the feet of Beatrice. It appeared to Giovanni—but, at the distance from which he gazed, he could scarcely have seen anything so minute—it appeared to him, however, that a drop or two of moisture from the broken stem of the flower descended upon the lizard's head. For an instant, the reptile contorted itself violently, and then lay motionless in the sunshine. Beatrice observed this remarkable phenomenon, and crossed herself, sadly, but without surprise; nor did she therefore hesitate to arrange the fatal flower in her bosom. There it blushed, and almost glimmered with the dazzling effect of a precious stone, adding to her dress and aspect the one appropriate charm, which nothing else in the world could have supplied. But Giovanni, out of the shadow of his window bent forward and shrank back, and murmured and trembled.

❶ *What shocking incident occurs?*

ANSWER TO GUIDED READING QUESTION

❶ A drop of moisture from the flower kills a lizard.

WORDS FOR EVERYDAY USE:

por • tal (pôrt´l) *n.,* doorway, gate, or entrance
a • nal • o • gy (ə nal´ə jē) *n.,* similarity in some respects between things otherwise unlike
phe • nom • e • non (fə näm´ə nən´) *n.,* extremely unusual or extraordinary thing or occurrence

Answers to Guided Reading Questions

❶ She says she would like to give him the purple flower but doesn't because Giovanni's window is too far up.

❷ The bouquet withers in her grasp.

Additional Questions and Activities

What is lured into the garden by the perfumes of the shrubs? What happens to this creature as it flutters about Beatrice? What does Beatrice do in response?

Answers. A beautiful insect is attracted by the scent and enters the garden. The creature falls down dead. Beatrice crosses herself and sighs.

"Am I awake? Have I my senses?" said he to himself. "What is this being?—beautiful, shall I call her?—or inexpressibly terrible?"

Beatrice now strayed carelessly through the garden, approaching closer beneath Giovanni's window, so that he was compelled to thrust his head quite out of its concealment in order to gratify the intense and painful curiosity which she excited. At this moment, there came a beautiful insect over the garden wall; it had perhaps wandered through the city and found no flowers nor verdure among those antique haunts of men, until the heavy perfumes of Doctor Rappaccini's shrubs had lured it from afar. Without alighting on the flowers, this winged brightness seemed to be attracted by Beatrice, and lingered in the air and fluttered about her head. Now here it could not be but that Giovanni Guasconti's eyes deceived him. Be that as it might, he fancied that while Beatrice was gazing at the insect with childish delight, it grew faint and fell at her feet!—its bright wings shivered! it was dead!—from no cause that he could discern, unless it were the atmosphere of her breath. Again Beatrice crossed herself and sighed heavily, as she bent over the dead insect.

❶ *What does Beatrice say she would like to give Giovanni in return? Why doesn't she?*

❷ *What happens to the bouquet Giovanni gives to Beatrice?*

An impulsive movement of Giovanni drew her eyes to the window. There she beheld the beautiful head of the young man—rather a Grecian than an Italian head, with fair, regular features, and a glistening of gold among his ringlets—gazing down upon her like a being that hovered in mid-air. Scarcely knowing what he did, Giovanni threw down the bouquet which he had hitherto held in his hand.

"Signora," said he, "there are pure and healthful flowers. Wear them for the sake of Giovanni Guasconti!"

"Thanks, Signor," replied Beatrice, with her rich voice, that came forth as it were like a gush of music; and with a mirthful expression half childish and half womanlike. "I accept your gift, and would fain[18] recompense it with this precious purple flower; but if I toss it into the air, it will not reach you. So Signor Guasconti must even content himself with my thanks."

She lifted the bouquet from the ground, and then as if inwardly ashamed at having stepped aside from her maidenly reserve to respond to a stranger's greeting, passed swiftly homeward through the garden. But, few as the moments were, it seemed to Giovanni when she was on the point of vanishing beneath the sculptured portal, that his beautiful bouquet was already beginning to wither in her grasp. It was an idle thought; there could be no possibility of distinguishing a faded flower from a fresh one at so great a distance.

For many days after the incident, the young man avoided the window that looked into Doctor Rappaccini's garden, as if something ugly and monstrous would have blasted his eyesight, had he been betrayed into a glance. He felt conscious of having put himself, to a certain extent, within the influence of an unintelligible power, by the communication which he had opened with Beatrice. The wisest course would have been, if his heart were in any real danger, to quit his lodgings and Padua itself, at once; the next wiser, to

18. **fain.** With eagerness; gladly

Words for Everyday Use:

ver • dure (vur´jər) *n.,* green growing plants and trees

rec • om • pense (rek´ əm pens´) *vt.,* repay; reward

un • in • tel • li • gi • ble (un in tel´i jə bəl) *adj.,* that cannot be understood

Vocabulary in Context

- Autumn is lovely and colorful in New England, but I prefer the green verdure of the spring.
- "To recompense your hard work, we will take a vacation," said their employer.
- The radio picked up so much static that the announcer's voice was unintelligible.
- One of his vagaries was that he planned to take a hot-air balloon around the world.
- One of the affinities between amphibians and fish is that both can live in water.
- Hemlock is a baneful substance, as Socrates would attest.

Carnival Evening. *Henri Rousseau, 1886. Philadelphia Museum of Art, Louis E. Stern Collection*

have accustomed himself, as far as possible, to the familiar and day-light view of Beatrice; thus bringing her rigidly and systematically within the limits of ordinary experience. Least of all, while avoiding her sight, should Giovanni have remained so near this extraordinary being, that the proximity and possibility even of intercourse, should give a kind of substance and reality to the wild vagaries which his imagination ran riot continually in producing. Guasconti had not a deep heart—or at all events, its depths were not sounded now—but he had a quick fancy, and an ardent southern temperament, which rose every instant to a higher fever-pitch. Whether or no Beatrice possessed those terrible attributes—that fatal breath—the affinity with those so beautiful and deadly flowers—which were indicated by what Giovanni had witnessed, she had at least instilled a fierce and subtle poison into his system. It was not love, although her rich beauty was a madness to him; nor horror, even while he fancied her spirit to be imbued with the same baneful essence that seemed to pervade her physical frame; but a wild offspring of both love and horror that had each parent in it, and burned like one and shivered like the other. Giovanni knew not what to dread; still less did he know

❶ *What poison has Beatrice unwittingly instilled in Giovanni?*

WORDS FOR EVERYDAY USE:

va • ga • ry (və ger´ ē) *n.,* odd, whimsical, or freakish idea or notion
af • fin • i • ty (ə fin´i tē) *n.,* close relationship; connection
bane • ful (bān´ fəl) *adj.,* causing distress, death, or ruin

ART NOTE

French artist **Henri Rousseau** (1844–1910) had no professional training, but his works strongly influenced a major school of modern painting, Surrealism. Born in Laval, France, Rousseau worked as a customs official in Paris until he retired in 1885 to paint full time. His work is noted for its bold colors and patterns, with each detail noted and the whole canvas given a polished look. Many of his works show realistic figures in fantastic or mysterious settings. In *Carnival Evening,* the two human figures are dwarfed by the moody landscape behind them.

ANSWER TO GUIDED READING QUESTION

❶ The poison she has instilled is a mixture of love and horror.

Answers to Guided Reading Questions

❶ Rappaccini looks at Giovanni speculatively, as if he were the subject of an experiment.

❷ Baglioni warns Giovanni that he may be the subject of one of Rappaccini's experiments.

what to hope; *hope* and *dread* kept a continual warfare in his breast, alternately vanquishing one another and starting up afresh to renew the contest. Blessed are all simple emotions, be they dark or bright! It is the lurid intermixture of the two that produces the illuminating blaze of the infernal regions.

Sometimes he endeavored to assuage the fever of his spirit by a rapid walk through the streets of Padua, or beyond its gates; his footsteps kept time with the throbbings of his brain, so that the walk was apt to accelerate itself to a race. One day, he found himself arrested; his arm was seized by a portly personage who had turned back on recognizing the young man, and expended much breath in overtaking him.

❶ *What sort of look does Rappaccini give Giovanni?*

"Signor Giovanni!—stay, my young friend!" cried he. "Have you forgotten me? That might well be the case, if I were as much altered as yourself."

It was Baglioni, whom Giovanni had avoided, ever since their first meeting, from a doubt that the professor's sagacity would look too deeply into his secrets. Endeavoring to recover himself, he stared forth wildly from his inner world into the outer one, and spoke like a man in a dream.

"Yes; I am Giovanni Guasconti. You are Professor Pietro Baglioni. Now let me pass!"

❷ *What warning does Baglioni give Giovanni?*

"Not yet—not yet, Signor Giovanni Guasconti," said the Professor, smiling, but at the same time scrutinizing the youth with an earnest glance.—"What; did I grow up side by side with your father, and shall his son pass me like a stranger, in these old streets of Padua? Stand still, Signor Giovanni; for we must have a word or two, before we part."

"Speedily, then, most worshipful Professor, speedily!" said Giovanni, with feverish impatience. "Does not your worship see that I am in haste?"

Now, while he was speaking, there came a man in black along the street, stooping and moving feebly, like a person in inferior health. His face was all overspread with a most sickly and sallow hue, but yet so pervaded with an expression of piercing and active intellect, that an observer might easily have overlooked the merely physical attributes, and have seen only this wonderful energy. As he passed, this person exchanged a cold and distant salutation with Baglioni, but fixed his eyes upon Giovanni with an intentness that seemed to bring out whatever was within him worthy of notice. Nevertheless, there was a peculiar quietness in the look, as if taking merely a speculative, not a human interest, in the young man.

"It is Doctor Rappaccini!" whispered the Professor, when the stranger had passed.—"Has he ever seen your face before?"

"Not that I know," answered Giovanni starting at the name.

"He *has* seen you!—he must have seen you!" said Baglioni, hastily. "For some purpose or other, this man of science is making a study of you. I know that look of his! It is the same that coldly illuminates his face, as he bends over a bird, a mouse, or a butterfly, which, in pursuance of some experiment, he has killed by the perfume of a flower;—a look as deep as nature

Words for Everyday Use:
lu • rid (loor´id) *adj.,* vivid in a harsh or shocking way
as • suage (ə swāj´) *vt.,* lessen; calm; pacify
spec • u • la • tive (spek´ yōō lāt´ iv) *adj.,* theoretical

Vocabulary in Context

- The bright lights of the casinos and dance halls cast a lurid glow over the city.
- To assuage his guilt, he told his sister that he had lost her favorite compact disc.
- This branch of science is still speculative; it hasn't been put into practice yet.

itself, but without nature's warmth of love. Signor Giovanni, I will stake my life upon it, you are the subject of one of Rappaccini's experiments!"

"Will you make a fool of me?" cried Giovanni, passionately. "*That*, Signor Professor, were an untoward experiment."

"Patience, patience!" replied the imperturbable Professor.—"I tell thee, my poor Giovanni, that Rappaccini has a scientific interest in thee. Thou hast fallen into fearful hands! And the Signora Beatrice? What part does she act in this mystery?"

But Guasconti, finding Baglioni's pertinacity intolerable, here broke away and was gone before the Professor could again seize his arm. He looked after the young man intently, and shook his head.

"This must not be," said Baglioni to himself. "The youth is the son of my old friend, and should not come to any harm from which the arcana[19] of medical science can preserve him. Besides, it is too insufferable an impertinence in Rappaccini, thus to snatch the bud out of my own hands, as I may say, and make use of him for his infernal experiments. This daughter of his! It shall be looked to. Perchance, most learned Rappaccini, I may foil you where you little dream of it!"

Meanwhile, Giovanni had pursued a circuitous route, and at length found himself at the door of his lodgings. As he crossed the threshold, he was met by old Lisabetta, who smirked and smiled, and was evidently desirous to attract his attention; vainly, however, as the ebullition of his feelings had momentarily subsided into a cold and dull vacuity. He turned his eyes full upon the withered face that was puckering itself into a smile, but seemed to behold it not. The old dame, therefore, laid her grasp upon his cloak.

"Signor!—Signor!" whispered she, still with a smile over the whole breadth of her visage, so that it looked not unlike a grotesque carving in wood, darkened by centuries—"Listen, Signor! There is a private entrance into the garden!"

"What do you say?" exclaimed Giovanni, turning quickly about, as if an inanimate thing should start into feverish life.—"A private entrance into Doctor Rappaccini's garden!"

"Hush! hush!—not so loud!" whispered Lisabetta, putting her hand over his mouth. "Yes; into the worshipful Doctor's garden, where you may see all his fine shrubbery. Many a young man in Padua would give gold to be admitted among those flowers."

Giovanni put a piece of gold into her hand.

"Show me the way," said he.

A surmise, probably excited by his conversation with Baglioni, crossed his mind, that this interposition of old Lisabetta might perchance be connected with the intrigue, whatever were its nature, in which the Professor seemed to suppose that Doctor Rappaccini was involving him. But such a suspicion, though it disturbed Giovanni, was inadequate to restrain him. The instant he was aware of the possibility of approaching Beatrice, it seemed an absolute necessity of his existence to do so. It mattered not whether she were angel or demon; he was irrevocably within her sphere, and must obey the law that whirled

19. **arcana.** Secrets or mysteries

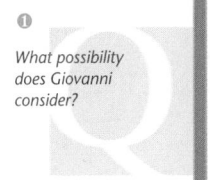

What possibility does Giovanni consider?

WORDS FOR EVERYDAY USE:

un • to • ward (un tô´ərd) *adj.*, improper, unseemly; not favorable

im • per • turb • a • ble (im´pər tur´ bə bəl) *adj.*, that cannot be disconnected or disturbed

per • ti • nac • i • ty (pur´tə nas´ə tē) *n.*, stubborn persistence; obstinacy

eb • ul • li • tion (eb´ə lish´ən) *n.*, boiling or bubbling up

va • cu • i • ty (va kōō´ə tē) *n.*, empty space, void, or vacuum

ANSWER TO GUIDED READING QUESTION

❶ Giovanni considers that Lisabetta may be involved in Rappaccini's scheme.

LITERARY TECHNIQUE

Encourage students to discuss the minor character Lisabetta, identifying her function(s) in the story and the techniques used to give her character believability. What purpose does she serve in the story?

ADDITIONAL QUESTIONS AND ACTIVITIES

Have students mime the chance encounter on the street of Giovanni, Professor Baglioni, and Rappaccini, showing by body language the different personalities of the three characters.

VOCABULARY IN CONTEXT

- Such untoward and improper behavior will not be tolerated.
- Jeff was imperturbable; nothing could ruffle him.
- Because of her pertinacity she would not give up until she reached the top of the mountain.
- Jamie's ebullition was the result of her winning the tennis match.
- When I am tired, my head feels empty, like a dark vacuity.

Answer to Guided Reading Question

❶ The flowers do not look like the natural work of God but the "monstrous offspring" of humanity.

him onward, in ever lessening circles, towards a result which he did not attempt to foreshadow. And yet, strange to say, there came across him a sudden doubt, whether this intense interest on his part were not delusory— whether it were really of so deep and positive a nature as to justify him in now thrusting himself into an incalculable position—whether it were not merely the fantasy of a young man's brain, only slightly, or not at all, connected with his heart!

He paused—hesitated—turned half about—but again went on. His withered guide led him along several obscure passages, and finally undid a door, through which, as it was opened, there came the sight and sound of rustling leaves, with the broken sunshine glimmering among them. Giovanni stepped forth, and forcing himself through the entanglement of a shrub that wreathed its tendrils over the hidden entrance, he stood beneath his own window, in the open area of Doctor Rappaccini's garden.

❶ *What is shocking or objectionable about the flowers' appearance?*

How often is it the case, that, when impossibilities have come to pass, and dreams have condensed their misty substance into tangible realities, we find ourselves calm, and even coldly self-possessed, amid circumstances which it would have been a delirium of joy or agony to anticipate! Fate delights to thwart us thus. Passion will choose his own time to rush upon the scene, and lingers sluggishly behind, when an appropriate adjustment of events would seem to summon his appearance. So was it now with Giovanni. Day after day, his pulses had throbbed with feverish blood, at the improbable idea of an interview with Beatrice, and of standing with her, face to face, in this very garden, basking in the oriental sunshine of her beauty, and snatching from her full gaze the mystery which he deemed the riddle of his own existence. But now there was a singular and untimely equanimity within his breast. He threw a glance around the garden to discover if Beatrice or her father were present, and perceiving that he was alone, began a critical observation of the plants.

The aspect of one and all of them dissatisfied him; their gorgeousness seemed fierce, passionate, and even unnatural. There was hardly an individual shrub which a wanderer, straying by himself through a forest, would not have been startled to find growing wild, as if an unearthly face had glared at him out of the thicket. Several, also, would have shocked a delicate instinct by an appearance of artificialness, indicating that there had been such commixture, and, as it were, adultery of various vegetable species, that the production was no longer of God's making, but the monstrous offspring of man's depraved fancy, glowing with only an evil mockery of beauty. They were probably the result of experiment, which, in one or two cases, had succeeded in mingling plants individually lovely into a compound possessing the questionable and ominous character that distinguished the whole growth of the garden. In fine, Giovanni recognized but two or three plants in the collection, and those of a kind that he well knew to be poisonous. While busy with these contemplations, he

Words for Everyday Use:

de • lu • so • ry (di lōō´sə rē) *adj.,* quality of seeming unreal
e • qua • nim • i • ty (ek´wə nim´ ə tē) *n.,* evenness of mind or temper
de • praved (dē prāvd´) *adj.,* morally bad; corrupt

Vocabulary in Context

- He thought he saw a pool of water in the desert, but it proved to be a delusory fantasy.
- John never seemed overly upset or excited as he was a person of great equanimity.
- Lucille considered any but the most upright behavior to be depraved.
- Etiquette is concern for the proper deportment of individuals.
- She was a regular apple connoisseur; she knew her pippins from her Granny Smiths.
- Alex had a fervor for life; he tried to live his life to its fullest potential.
- Dreams are evanescent; they vanish with the dawn.

heard the rustling of a silken garment, and turning, beheld Beatrice emerging from beneath the sculptured portal.

Giovanni had not considered with himself what should be his deportment; whether he should apologize for his intrusion into the garden, or assume that he was there with the privity, at least, if not the desire of Doctor Rappaccini or his daughter. But Beatrice's manner placed him at his ease, though leaving him still in doubt by what agency he had gained admittance. She came lightly along the path, and met him near the broken fountain. There was surprise in her face, but brightened by a simple and kind expression of pleasure.

"You are a connoisseur in flowers, Signor," said Beatrice with a smile, alluding to the bouquet which he had flung her from the window. "It is no marvel, therefore, if the sight of my father's rare collection has tempted you to take a nearer view. If he were here, he could tell you many strange and interesting facts as to the nature and habits of these shrubs, for he has spent a lifetime in such studies, and this garden is his world."

"And yourself, lady"—observed Giovanni—"if fame says true—you, likewise, are deeply skilled in the virtues indicated by these rich blossoms, and these spicy perfumes. Would you deign[20] to be my instructress, I should prove an apter scholar than under Signor Rappaccini himself."

"Are there such idle rumors?" asked Beatrice, with the music of a pleasant laugh. "Do people say that I am skilled in my father's science of plants? What a jest is there! No; though I have grown up among these flowers, I know no more of them than their hues and perfume; and sometimes, methinks I would fain rid myself of even that small knowledge. There are many flowers here, and those not the least brilliant, that shock and offend me, when they meet my eye. But, pray, Signor, do not believe these stories about my science. Believe nothing of me save what you see with your own eyes."

"And must I believe all that I have seen with my own eyes?" asked Giovanni pointedly, while the recollection of former scenes made him shrink. "No, Signora, you demand too little of me. Bid me believe nothing, save what comes from your own lips."

It would appear that Beatrice understood him. There came a deep flush to her cheek; but she looked full into Giovanni's eyes, and responded to his gaze of uneasy suspicion with a queen-like haughtiness.

"I do so bid you, Signor!" she replied. "Forget whatever you may have fancied in regard to me. If true to the outward senses, still it may be false in its essence. But the words of Beatrice Rappaccini's lips are true from the heart outward. Those you may believe!"

A fervor glowed in her whole aspect, and beamed upon Giovanni's consciousness like the light of truth itself. But while she spoke, there was a fragrance in the atmosphere around her, rich and delightful, though evanescent, yet which the young man, from an indefinable reluctance, scarcely dared to draw into his

20. **deign.** Condescend to do something slightly beneath one's dignity

❶ *What does Beatrice ask Giovanni to do?*

❷ *Why does Beatrice blush?*

WORDS FOR EVERYDAY USE:

de • port • ment (dē pôrt´mənt) *n.,* manner of conducting or bearing oneself

con • nois • seur (kän´ə sur´) *n.,* person who has expert knowledge in some field

fer • vor (fur´vər) *n.,* great warmth or emotion

ev • a • nes • cent (ev´ə nes´ənt) *adj.,* tending to fade; vanishing

ANSWERS TO GUIDED READING QUESTIONS

❶ Beatrice asks Giovanni to believe only what he sees with his own eyes.

❷ Beatrice blushes because she realizes that Giovanni may be falling in love with her.

CROSS-CURRICULAR ACTIVITIES

Encourage students to investigate and report on strange plants, poisonous or not, with unusual characteristics, such as insect-eaters, tubelike plants that live at great ocean depths, and rare species in the rain forests.

Answers to Guided Reading Questions

❶ Beatrice has forgotten the flowering shrub.

❷ Giovanni frightens Beatrice by approaching the plant as if to touch it.

Literary Technique

Point out the passage on page 212 describing Giovanni and Beatrice's discussion next to the purple-blossomed shrub. Have students compare and contrast the vocabulary, sentence length, and sentence structure of this passage with the same elements in passages discussing Giovanni's internal thoughts. Ask them to summarize how the differences affect the mood of the passages.

Answer. Shorter, simpler words and sentences give a suggestion of fast action to the description of the encounter; multisyllabic, difficult words and complex sentences give a slower, thoughtful tone to the other passages.

lungs. It might be the odor of the flowers. Could it be Beatrice's breath, which thus embalmed her words with a strange richness, as if by steeping them in her heart? A faintness passed like a shadow over Giovanni, and flitted away; he seemed to gaze through the beautiful girl's eyes into her transparent soul, and felt no more doubt or fear.

The tinge of passion that had colored Beatrice's manner vanished; she became gay, and appeared to derive a pure delight from her communion with the youth, not unlike what the maiden of a lonely island might have felt, conversing with a voyager from the civilized world. Evidently her experience of life had been confined within the limits of that garden. She talked now about matters as simple as the daylight or summer clouds, and now asked questions in reference to the city, or Giovanni's distant home, his friends, his mother, and his sisters; questions indicating such seclusion, and such lack of familiarity with modes and forms, that Giovanni responded as if to an infant. Her spirit gushed out before him like a fresh rill,[21] that was just catching its first glimpse of the sunlight, and wondering at the reflections of earth and sky which were flung into its bosom. There came thoughts, too, from a deep source, and fantasies of a gem-like brilliancy, as if diamonds and rubies sparkled upward among the bubbles of the fountain. Ever and anon, there gleamed across the young man's mind a sense of wonder, that he should be walking side by side with the being who had so wrought upon his imagination—whom he had idealized in such hues of terror—in whom he had positively witnessed such manifestations of dreadful attributes—that he should be conversing with Beatrice like a brother, and should find her so human and so maiden-like. But such reflections were only momentary; the effect of her character was too real, not to make itself familiar at once.

❶ *What has Beatrice forgotten for the first time in her life?*

❷ *What does Giovanni do that frightens Beatrice?*

In this free intercourse, they had strayed through the garden, and now, after many turns among its avenues, were come to the shattered fountain, beside which grew the magnificent shrub with its treasury of glowing blossoms. A fragrance was diffused from it, which Giovanni recognized as identical with that which he had attributed to Beatrice's breath, but incomparably more powerful. As her eyes fell upon it, Giovanni beheld her press her hand to her bosom, as if her heart were throbbing suddenly and painfully.

"For the first time in my life," murmured she, addressing the shrub, "I had forgotten thee!"

"I remember, Signora," said Giovanni, "that you once promised to reward me with one of these living gems for the bouquet, which I had the happy boldness to fling to your feet. Permit me now to pluck it as a memorial of this interview."

He made a step towards the shrub, with extended hand. But Beatrice darted forward, uttering a shriek that went through his heart like a dagger. She caught his hand, and drew it back with the whole force of her slender figure. Giovanni felt her touch thrilling through his fibres.

"Touch it not!" exclaimed she, in a voice of agony. "Not for thy life! It is fatal!"

Then, hiding her face, she fled from him, and vanished beneath the sculptured portal. As Giovanni followed her with his

21. **rill.** Little brook or stream

eyes, he beheld the emaciated figure and pale intelligence of Doctor Rappaccini, who had been watching the scene, he knew not how long, within the shadow of the entrance.

No sooner was Guasconti alone in his chamber, than the image of Beatrice came back to his passionate musings, invested with all the witchery that had been gathering around it ever since his first glimpse of her, and now likewise imbued with a tender warmth of girlish womanhood. She was human: her nature was endowed with all gentle and feminine qualities; she was worthiest to be worshiped; she was capable, surely, on her part, of the height and heroism of love. Those tokens, which he had hitherto considered as proofs of a frightful peculiarity in her physical and moral system, were now either forgotten, or, by the subtle sophistry of passion, transmuted into a golden crown of enchantment, rendering Beatrice the more admirable, by so much as she was the more unique. Whatever had looked ugly, was now beautiful; or, if incapable of such a change, it stole away and hid itself among those shapeless half-ideas, which throng the dim region beyond the daylight of our perfect consciousness. Thus did Giovanni spend the night, nor fell asleep, until the dawn had begun to awake the slumbering flowers in Doctor Rappaccini's garden, whither his dreams doubtless led him. Up rose the sun in his due season, and flinging his beams upon the young man's eyelids, awoke him to a sense of pain. When thoroughly aroused, he became sensible of a burning and tingling agony in his hand—in his right hand—the very hand which Beatrice had grasped in her own, when he was on the point of plucking one of the gem-like flowers. On the back of that hand there was now a purple print, like that of four small fingers, and the likeness of a slender thumb upon his wrist.

Oh, how stubbornly does love—or even that cunning semblance of love which flourishes in the imagination, but strikes no depth of root into the heart—how stubbornly does it hold its faith, until the moment come, when it is doomed to vanish into thin mist! Giovanni wrapt a handkerchief about his hand, and wondered what evil thing had stung him, and soon forgot his pain in a reverie of Beatrice.

After the first interview, a second was in the inevitable course of what we call fate. A third; a fourth; and a meeting with Beatrice in the garden was no longer an incident in Giovanni's daily life, but the whole space in which he might be said to live; for the anticipation and memory of that ecstatic hour made up the remainder. Nor was it otherwise with the daughter of Rappaccini. She watched for the youth's appearance, and flew to his side with confidence as unreserved as if they had been playmates from early infancy—as if they were such playmates still. If, by any unwonted[22] chance, he failed to come at the appointed moment, she stood beneath the window, and sent up the rich sweetness of her tones to float around him in his chamber, and echo and reverberate throughout his heart— "Giovanni! Giovanni! Why tarriest thou? Come

❶ *What has happened to Giovanni's hand?*

❷ *How do Giovanni and Beatrice feel about each other?*

22. **unwonted.** Not common or usual

WORDS FOR EVERYDAY USE:

e • ma • ci • at • ed (ē mā´shē āt əd) *part.*, abnormally thin

soph • ist • ry (säf´is trē) *n.*, unsound or misleading but clever, plausible, and subtle argument or reasoning

trans • mute (trans myōōt´) *vt.*, change from one form, species, or condition into another

rev • er • ie (rev´ər ē) *n.*, dreamy thinking

ANSWERS TO GUIDED READING QUESTIONS

❶ Giovanni's hand is marked with a purple handprint.

❷ Beatrice and Giovanni are in love with each other.

VOCABULARY IN CONTEXT

- After being ill, I had lost so much weight that I appeared emaciated.
- It sounded like a no-risk plan, but I realized the salesperson's money-making scheme was just a clever bit of sophistry.
- The caterpillar was once an ugly wormlike creature, but it has transmuted itself into a gorgeous butterfly.
- The bus driver woke me from my reverie by saying, "Hey, dreamy, isn't this your stop?"

Answer to Guided Reading Question

❶ In the book, Alexander the Great discovers that the beautiful woman has been nourished with poisons all her life. Baglioni tells this story to warn Giovanni about Beatrice.

Cross-curricular Activities

Social Studies. Encourage students to research the life and accomplishments of Alexander the Great. Students may wish to share with each other information or anecdotes that they uncover about Alexander.

down!"—And down he hastened into that Eden of poisonous flowers.

But, with all this intimate familiarity, there was still a reserve in Beatrice's demeanor, so rigidly and invariably sustained, that the idea of infringing it scarcely occurred to his imagination. By all appreciable signs, they loved; they had looked love, with eyes that conveyed the holy secret from the depths of one soul into the depths of the other, as if it were too sacred to be whispered by the way; they had even spoken love, in those gushes of passion when their spirits darted forth in articulated breath, like tongues of long-hidden flame; and yet there had been no seal of lips, no clasp of hands, nor any slightest caress, such as love claims and hallows. He had never touched one of the gleaming ringlets of her hair; her garment—so marked was the physical barrier between them—had never been waved against him by a breeze. On the few occasions when Giovanni had seemed tempted to overstep the limit, Beatrice grew so sad, so stern, and withal wore such a look of desolate separation, shuddering at itself, that not a spoken word was requisite to repel him. At such times, he was startled at the horrible suspicions that rose, monster-like, out of the caverns of his heart, and stared him in the face; his love grew thin and faint as the morning mist; his doubts alone had substance. But when Beatrice's face brightened again, after the momentary shadow, she was transformed at once from the mysterious, questionable being, whom he had watched with so much awe and horror; she was now the beautiful and unsophisticated girl, whom he felt that his spirit knew with a certainty beyond all other knowledge.

❶ *What happens in the classic book Baglioni has been reading? Why does he relate this story to Giovanni?*

A considerable time had now passed since Giovanni's last meeting with Baglioni. One morning, however, he was disagreeably surprised by a visit from the Professor, whom he had scarcely thought of for whole weeks, and would willingly have forgotten still longer. Given up, as he had long been, to a pervading excitement, he could tolerate no companions, except upon condition of their perfect sympathy with his present state of feeling. Such sympathy was not to be expected from Professor Baglioni.

The visitor chatted carelessly, for a few moments, about the gossip of the city and the University, and then took up another topic.

"I have been reading an old classic author lately," said he, "and met with a story that strangely interested me. Possibly you may remember it. It is of an Indian prince, who sent a beautiful woman as a present to Alexander the Great. She was as lovely as the dawn, and gorgeous as the sunset; but what especially distinguished her was a certain rich perfume in her breath—richer than a garden of Persian roses. Alexander, as was natural to a youthful conqueror, fell in love at first sight with this magnificent stranger. But a certain sage physician, happening to be present, discovered a terrible secret in regard to her."

"And what was that?" asked Giovanni, turning his eyes downward to avoid those of the Professor.

"That this lovely woman," continued Baglioni, with emphasis, "had been nour-

Words for Everyday Use:

in • fring • ing (in frinj´ iŋ) *part.,* violating; trespassing

ar • tic • u • lat • ed (ar tik´ yōō lāt´əd) *adj.,* made up of distinct syllables or words, as human speech

Vocabulary in Context

- By restricting our voting rights, you are infringing on our rights as citizens.
- The first speaker was excellent, but the second was superior; her speech was very well articulated.
- Francine was imbued with an inner strength that would carry her through many difficult situations.
- Although Lawrence said he did not mind helping with the dishes, his face evinced his displeasure.

ished with poisons from her birth upward, until her whole nature was so imbued with them, that she herself had become the deadliest poison in existence. Poison was her element of life. With that rich perfume of her breath, she blasted the very air. Her love would have been poison!—her embrace death! Is not this a marvelous tale?"

"A childish fable," answered Giovanni, nervously starting from his chair. "I marvel how your worship finds time to read such nonsense, among your graver studies."

"By the by," said the Professor, looking uneasily about him, "what singular fragrance is this in your apartment? Is it the perfume of your gloves? It is faint, but delicious, and yet, after all, by no means agreeable. Were I to breathe it long, methinks it would make me ill. It is like the breath of a flower—but I see no flowers in the chamber."

"Nor are there any," replied Giovanni, who had turned pale as the Professor spoke; "nor, I think, is there any fragrance, except in your worship's imagination. Odors, being a sort of element combined of the sensual and the spiritual, are apt to deceive us in this manner. The recollection of a perfume—the bare idea of it—may easily be mistaken for a present reality."

"Aye; but my sober imagination does not often play such tricks," said Baglioni; "and were I to fancy any kind of odor, it would be that of some vile apothecary[23] drug, wherewith my fingers are likely enough to be imbued. Our worshipful friend Rappaccini, as I have heard, tinctures his medicaments with odors richer than those of Araby. Doubtless, likewise, the fair and learned Signora Beatrice would minister to her patients with draughts as sweet as a maiden's breath. But woe to him that sips them!"

Giovanni's face evinced many contending emotions. The tone in which the Professor alluded to the pure and lovely daughter of Rappaccini was a torture to his soul; and yet, the intimation of a view of her character, opposite to his own, gave instantaneous distinctness to a thousand dim suspicions, which now grinned at him like so many demons. But he strove hard to quell them, and to respond to Baglioni with a true lover's perfect faith.

"Signor Professor," said he, "you were my father's friend—perchance, too, it is your purpose to act a friendly part towards his son. I would fain feel nothing towards you, save respect and deference. But I pray you to observe, Signor, that there is one subject on which we must not speak. You know not the Signora Beatrice. You cannot, therefore, estimate the wrong—the blasphemy, I may even say—that is offered to her character by a light or injurious word."

"Giovanni!—my poor Giovanni!" answered the Professor, with a calm expression of pity "I know this wretched girl far better than yourself. You shall hear the truth in respect to the poisoner Rappaccini, and his poisonous daughter. Yes; poisonous as she is beautiful! Listen; for even should you do violence to my gray hairs, it shall not silence me. That old fable of the Indian

23. **apothecary.** Druggist or pharmacist

❶ *How does Giovanni respond to Baglioni's tale? Which of his actions reveal that he believes the professor's story?*

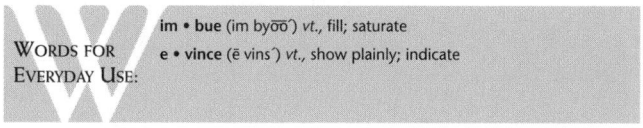

ANSWER TO GUIDED READING QUESTION

❶ Giovanni calls it a "childish fable," but he nervously gets up from his chair, revealing that he believes the professor's story.

Answer to Guided Reading Question

❶ Baglioni gives Giovanni an antidote that will render the most potent poison harmless.

Additional Questions and Activities

What recollections does Giovanni have of the darker side of Beatrice's character? What is his overall image of her character? Why is he unable to believe otherwise about her?

Answers. Giovanni remembers the flowers and the insect that seemed to wither and die for no other reason than her breath. He thinks she is affectionate, natural, simple, and guileless. She had shown her character to him in the way he now sees her, and the glimpses of her darker side cannot be substantiated.

woman has become a truth, by the deep and deadly science of Rappaccini, and in the person of the lovely Beatrice!"

Giovanni groaned and hid his face.

"Her father," continued Baglioni, "was not restrained by natural affection from offering up his child, in this horrible manner, as the victim of his insane zeal for science. For—let us do him justice—he is as true a man of science as ever distilled his own heart in an alembic.[24] What, then, will be your fate? Beyond a doubt, you are selected as the material of some new experiment. Perhaps the result is to be death—perhaps a fate more awful still! Rappaccini, with what he calls the interest of science before his eyes, will hesitate at nothing."

"It is a dream!" muttered Giovanni to himself, "surely it is a dream!"

"But," resumed the professor, "be of good cheer, son of my friend! It is not yet too late for the rescue. Possibly, we may even succeed in bringing back this miserable child within the limits of ordinary nature, from which her father's madness has estranged her. Behold this little silver vase! It was wrought by the hands of the renowned Benvenuto Cellini,[25] and is well worthy to be a lovegift to the fairest dame in Italy. But its contents are invaluable. One little sip of this antidote would have rendered the most virulent poisons of the Borgias[26] innocuous. Doubt not that it will be as efficacious against those of Rappaccini. Bestow the vase, and the precious liquid within it, on your Beatrice, and hopefully await the result."

❶ *What does Baglioni give to Giovanni? What is it supposed to do?*

Baglioni laid a small, exquisitely wrought silver phial[27] on the table, and withdrew, leaving what he had said to produce its effect upon the young man's mind.

"We will thwart Rappaccini yet!" thought he, chuckling to himself, as he descended the stairs. "But, let us confess the truth of him, he is a wonderful man!—a wonderful man indeed! A vile empiric,[28] however, in his practice, and therefore not to be tolerated by those who respect the good old rules of the medical profession!"

Throughout Giovanni's whole acquaintance with Beatrice, he had occasionally, as we have said, been haunted by dark surmises as to her character. Yet, so thoroughly had she made herself felt by him as a simple, natural, most affectionate and guileless creature, that the image now held up by Professor Baglioni, looked as strange and incredible, as if it were not in accordance with his own original conception. True, there were ugly recollections connected with his first glimpses of the beautiful girl; he could not quite forget the bouquet that withered in her grasp, and the insect that perished amid the sunny air, by no ostensible agency, save the fragrance of her breath. These incidents, however, dissolving in the pure light of her character, had no longer the efficacy of facts, but were acknowledged as mistaken fantasies, by whatever testimony of the senses they might appear to be substantiated. There is

24. **alembic.** Apparatus used for distilling
25. **Benvenuto Cellini.** (1500–1578) Italian goldsmith and sculptor
26. **Borgias.** Italian family, religiously and politically influential during the Renaissance, but also known for cruelty
27. **phial.** Small bottle
28. **empiric.** Person who relies on practical experiences rather than on scientific principles

Words for Everyday Use:
ef • fi • ca • cious (ef´ i kā´ shəs) *adj.,* producing or capable of producing the desired effect
sur • mise (sər mīz´) *n.,* conjecture; guess

Vocabulary in Context

- It made no sense to repair the computer myself, so I called an expert who would be more efficacious in achieving the desired results.
- From Laura's strange behavior, I surmised that she was upset about something.
- Helene had always been jealous of Lucy and Kelly's friendship, so she gradually tried to insinuate herself between the two friends.

something truer and more real, than what we can see with the eyes, and touch with the finger. On such better evidence, had Giovanni founded his confidence in Beatrice, though rather by the necessary force of her high attributes, than by any deep and generous faith, on his part. But, now, his spirit was incapable of sustaining itself at the height to which the early enthusiasm of passion had exalted it; he fell down, grovelling among earthly doubts, and defiled therewith the pure whiteness of Beatrice's image. Not that he gave her up; he did but distrust. He resolved to institute some decisive test that should satisfy him, once for all, whether there were those dreadful peculiarities in her physical nature, which could not be supposed to exist without some corresponding monstrosity of soul. His eyes, gazing down afar, might have deceived him as to the lizard, the insect, and the flowers. But if he could witness, at the distance of a few paces, the sudden blight of one fresh and healthful flower in Beatrice's hand, there would be room for no further question. With this idea, he hastened to the florist's, and purchased a bouquet that was still gemmed with the morning dewdrops.

It was now the customary hour of his daily interview with Beatrice. Before descending into the garden, Giovanni failed not to look at his figure in the mirror; a vanity to be expected in a beautiful young man, yet, as displaying itself at that troubled and feverish moment, the token of a certain shallowness of feeling and insincerity of character. He did gaze, however, and said to himself, that his features had never before possessed so rich a grace, nor his eyes such vivacity, nor his cheeks so warm a hue of superabundant life.

"At least," thought he, "her poison has not yet insinuated itself into my system. I am no flower to perish in her grasp!"

With that thought, he turned his eyes on the bouquet, which he had never once laid aside from his hand. A thrill of indefinable horror shot through his frame, on perceiving that those dewy flowers were already beginning to droop; they wore the aspect of things that had been fresh and lovely, yesterday. Giovanni grew white as marble, and stood motionless before the mirror, staring at his own reflection there, as at the likeness of something frightful. He remembered Baglioni's remark about the fragrance that seemed to pervade the chamber. It must have been the poison in his breath! Then he shuddered—shuddered at himself! Recovering from his stupor, he began to watch, with curious eye, a spider that was busily at work, hanging its web from the antique cornice of the apartment, crossing and recrossing the artful system of interwoven lines, as vigorous and active a spider as ever dangled from an old ceiling. Giovanni bent towards the insect, and emitted a deep, long breath. The spider suddenly ceased its toil; the web vibrated with a tremor originating in the body of the small artisan. Again Giovanni sent forth a breath, deeper, longer, and imbued with a venomous feeling out of his heart; he knew not whether he were wicked or only desperate. The spider made a convulsive gripe with his limbs, and hung dead across the window.

❶ *What does Giovanni assume about Beatrice's outer and inner nature?*

❷ *What does Giovanni realize about himself?*

WORDS FOR EVERYDAY USE: **in • sin • u • ate** (in sin´yōō āt´) *vt.,* introduce or work into gradually

ANSWERS TO GUIDED READING QUESTIONS

❶ Giovanni assumes that Beatrice's outer and inner nature must be identical.

❷ Giovanni realizes that his breath is poison to other creatures.

Answers to Guided Reading Questions

❶ The plant sprang from the soil the moment that Beatrice was born. Beatrice has been nourished by the poisonous flower.

❷ Giovanni is unable to estimate her nature because he assumes her to be either a heavenly angel or a vile monster but never anything in between.

Bibliographical Note

Students may wish to read other works by Hawthorne. The following list offers suggestions for interested students.

Short Stories

"The Maypole of Merrymount"
"The Minister's Black Veil"
"Mr. Higginbotham's Catastrophe"
"Dr. Heidegger's Experiment"
"The Gray Champion"
"The Celestial Railroad"
"The Birthmark"

Novels

The Scarlet Letter
The House of Seven Gables

"Accursed! Accursed!" muttered Giovanni, addressing himself. "Hast thou grown so poisonous, that this deadly insect perishes by the breath?"

At that moment, a rich, sweet voice came floating up from the garden:—

"Giovanni! Giovanni! It is past the hour! Why tarriest thou! Come down!"

"Yes," muttered Giovanni again. "She is the only being whom my breath may not slay! Would that it might!"

He rushed down, and in an instant, was standing before the bright and loving eyes of Beatrice. A moment ago, his wrath and despair had been so fierce that he could have desired nothing so much as to wither her by a glance. But, with her actual presence, there came influences which had too real an existence to be at once shaken off; recollections of the delicate and benign power of her feminine nature, which had so often enveloped him in a religious calm; recollections of many a holy and passionate outgush of her heart, when the pure fountain had been unsealed from its depths, and made visible in its transparency to his mental eye; recollections which, had Giovanni known how to estimate them, would have assured him that all this ugly mystery was but an earthly illusion, and that, whatever mist of evil might seem to have gathered over her, the real Beatrice was a heavenly angel. Incapable as he was of such high faith, still her presence had not utterly lost its magic. Giovanni's rage was quelled into an aspect of sullen insensibility. Beatrice, with a quick spiritual sense, immediately felt that there was a gulf of blackness between them, which neither he nor she could pass. They walked on together, sad and silent, and came thus to the marble fountain, and to its pool of water on the ground, in the midst of which grew the shrub that bore gem-like blossoms. Giovanni was affrighted at the eager enjoyment—the appetite, as it were—with which he found himself inhaling the fragrance of the flowers.

❶ *How did the plant come into being? What is its relation to Beatrice?*

❷ *Why is Giovanni incapable of seeing Beatrice's true nature?*

"Beatrice," asked he abruptly, "whence came this shrub?"

"My father created it," answered she, with simplicity.

"Created it! created it!" repeated Giovanni. "What mean you, Beatrice?"

"He is a man fearfully acquainted with the secrets of nature," replied Beatrice; "and, at the hour when I first drew breath, this plant sprang from the soil, the offspring of his science, of his intellect, while I was but his earthly child. "Approach it not!" continued she, observing with terror that Giovanni was drawing nearer to the shrub. "It has qualities that you little dream of. But I, dearest Giovanni,—I grew up and blossomed with the plant, and was nourished with its breath. It was my sister, and I loved it with a human affection: for—alas! hast thou not suspected it? there was an awful doom."

Here Giovanni frowned so darkly upon her that Beatrice paused and trembled. But her faith in his tenderness reassured her, and made her blush that she had doubted for an instant.

"There was an awful doom," she continued,—"the effect of my father's fatal love of science—which estranged me from all society of any kind. Until Heaven sent thee, dearest Giovanni, Oh! how lonely was thy poor Beatrice!"

"Was it a hard doom?" asked Giovanni, fixing his eyes upon her.

"Only of late have I known how hard it was," answered she tenderly. "Oh, yes; but my heart was torpid,[29] and therefore quiet."

29. **torpid.** Dormant; sluggish

Giovanni's rage broke forth from his sullen gloom like a lightning flash out of a dark cloud.

"Accursed one!" cried he, with venomous scorn and anger. "And finding thy solitude wearisome, thou hast severed me, likewise, from all the warmth of life, and enticed me into thy region of unspeakable horror!"

"Giovanni!" exclaimed Beatrice, turning her large bright eyes upon his face. The force of his words had not found its way into her mind; she was merely wonder-struck.

"Yes, poisonous thing!" repeated Giovanni, beside himself with passion. "Thou has done it! Thou has blasted me! Thou hast filled my veins with poison! Thou hast made me as hateful, as ugly, as loathsome and deadly a creature as thyself,—a world's wonder of hideous monstrosity! Now—if our breath be happily as fatal to ourselves as to all others—let us join our lips in one kiss of unutterable hatred, and so die!"

"What has befallen me?" murmured Beatrice, with a low moan out of her heart. "Holy Virgin pity me, a poor heart-broken child!"

"Thou! Dost thou pray?" cried Giovanni, still with the same fiendish scorn. "Thy very prayers, as they come from thy lips, taint the atmosphere with death. Yes, yes; let us pray! Let us to church, and dip our fingers in the holy water at the portal! They that come after us will perish as by a pestilence. Let us sign crosses in the air! It will be scattering curses abroad in the likeness of holy symbols!"

"Giovanni," said Beatrice calmly, for her grief was beyond passion, "why dost thou join thyself with me thus in those terrible words? I, it is true, am the horrible thing thou namest me. But thou!—what hast thou to do, save with one other shudder at my hideous misery, to go forth out of the garden and mingle with thy race, and forget that there ever crawled on earth such a monster as poor Beatrice?"

"Dost thou pretend ignorance?" asked Giovanni, scowling upon her. "Behold! This power have I gained from the pure daughter of Rappaccini!"

There was a swarm of summer-insects flitting through the air, in search of the food promised by the flower-odors of the fatal garden. They circled round Giovanni's head, and were evidently attracted towards him by the same influence which had drawn them, for an instant, within the sphere of several of the shrubs. He sent forth a breath among them, and smiled bitterly at Beatrice, as at least a score of the insects fell dead upon the ground.

"I see it! I see it!" shrieked Beatrice. "It is my father's fatal science! No, no, Giovanni; it was not I! Never, never! I dreamed only to love thee, and be with thee a little time, and so to let thee pass away, leaving but thine image in mine heart. For, Giovanni—believe it—though my body be nourished with poison, my spirit is God's creature, and craves love as its daily food. But my father!—he has united us in this fearful sympathy. Yes; spurn me!—tread upon me!—kill me! Oh, what is death, after such words as thine? But it was not I! Not for a world of bliss would I have done it!"

Giovanni's passion had exhausted itself in its outburst from his lips. There now came across a sense, mournful, and not without tenderness, of the intimate and peculiar relationship between Beatrice and himself. They stood, as it were, in an utter solitude, which would be made none the less solitary by the densest throng of human life. Ought not, then, the desert of humanity around them to press this insulated pair close together? If they should be cruel to one

❶ *How does Giovanni behave toward Beatrice?*

❷ *What does Beatrice say her intentions were? Does she resemble in any way the woman Giovanni has accused her of being?*

Answers to Guided Reading Questions

❶ Giovanni is irate with Beatrice and accuses her of knowingly poisoning him.

❷ Beatrice says she only wanted to love Giovanni and then let him pass away from her. She is not the woman Giovanni accuses her of being.

Additional Questions and Activities

Ask students to identify several major scenes that would be included in a movie version of the story and to choose background music for each one. Students might play samples of the music they select and discuss the mood created by each piece.

Answers to Guided Reading Questions

❶ Giovanni realizes he should have loved and had sympathy for Beatrice rather than despise and curse her.

❷ Beatrice shrinks from Giovanni because he has hurt her deeply.

Answers to Selection Check Test 4.4.1

EX. What catches Giovanni's eye immediately?
A beautiful purple flower catches his eye immediately.

1. What does the gardener wear when tending the flowering plant?
The gardener wears a mask.

2. What can Beatrice do with the plant that is unusual?
She can handle it and breathe its scent.

3. What does Baglioni give to Giovanni?
Baglioni gives Giovanni an antidote.

4. What does Giovanni's breath do?
It kills a spider.

5. What effect does the antidote have on Beatrice?
The antidote kills her.

Additional Questions and Activities

If students were in charge of set design for a play version of this story, how would they arrange the stage? How would they show the parts of the garden, the balcony from which Baglioni calls, and the interior of Giovanni's room? In particular, how would they stage the final scene so as to present all three centers of action—Giovanni and Beatrice at the fountain inside the garden, Rappaccini at the portal, and Baglioni on the balcony? Encourage them to sketch one or more set designs and to indicate the characters' positions for the final scene.

❶ *What does Giovanni realize? Why is it too late?*

❷ *Why is Beatrice shrinking from Giovanni now?*

another, who was there to be kind to them? Besides, thought Giovanni, might there not still be a hope of his returning within the limits of ordinary nature, and leading Beatrice—the redeemed Beatrice—by the hand? Oh, weak, and selfish, and unworthy spirit, that could dream of an earthly union and earthly happiness as possible, after such deep love had been so bitterly wronged as was Beatrice's love by Giovanni's blighting words! No, no; there could be no such hope. She must pass heavily, with that broken heart, across the borders—she must bathe her hurts in some fount of Paradise, and forget her grief in the light of immortality—and *there* be well!

But Giovanni did not know it.

"Dear Beatrice," said he, approaching her, while she shrank away, as always at his approach, but now with a different impulse—"dearest Beatrice, our fate is not yet so desperate. Behold! There is a medicine, potent, as a wise physician has assured me, and almost divine in its efficacy. It is composed of ingredients the most opposite to those by which thy awful father has brought this calamity upon thee and me. It is distilled of blessed herbs. Shall we not quaff it together and thus be purified from evil?"

"Give it me!" said Beatrice, extending her hand to receive the little silver phial which Giovanni took from his bosom. She added, with a peculiar emphasis; "I will drink—but do thou await the result."

She put Baglioni's antidote to her lips; and, at the same moment, the figure of Rappaccini emerged from the portal, and came slowly towards the marble fountain. As he drew near, the pale man of science seemed to gaze with a triumphant expression at the beautiful youth and maiden, as might an artist who should spend his life in achieving a picture or a group of statuary, and finally be satisfied with his success. He paused—his bent form grew erect with conscious power, he spread out his hand over them, in the attitude of a father imploring a blessing upon his children. But those were the same hands that had thrown poison into the stream of their lives! Giovanni trembled. Beatrice shuddered nervously, and pressed her hand upon her heart.

"My daughter," said Rappaccini, "thou art no longer lonely in the world! Pluck one of those precious gems from thy sister shrub, and bid thy bridegroom wear it in his bosom. It will not harm him now! My science, and the sympathy between thee and him, have so wrought within his system, that he now stands apart from common men, as thou dost, daughter of my pride and triumph, from ordinary women. Pass on, then, through the world, most dear to one another, and dreadful to all besides!"

"My father," said Beatrice, feebly—and still, as she spoke, she kept her hand upon her heart—"wherefore didst thou inflict this miserable doom upon thy child?"

"Miserable!" exclaimed Rappaccini. "What mean you, foolish girl? Dost thou deem it misery to be endowed with[30] marvelous gifts, against which no power nor strength could avail an enemy? Misery, to be able to quell the mightiest with a breath? Misery, to be as terrible as thou art beautiful? Wouldst thou, then, have preferred the condition of a weak woman, exposed to all evil, and capable of none?"

"I would fain have been loved, not feared," murmured Beatrice, sinking down upon the ground.—"But now it matters not; I am going, father, where the evil, which thou hast striven to mingle with my being, will pass away like a dream—like the fragrance of these poisonous flowers,

30. **endowed with.** Given

which will no longer taint my breath among the flowers of Eden. Farewell, Giovanni! Thy words of hatred are like lead within my heart—but they, too, will fall away as I ascend. Oh, was there not, from the first, more poison in thy nature than in mine?"

To Beatrice—so radically had her earthly part been wrought upon by Rappaccini's skill—as poison had been life, so the powerful antidote was death. And thus the poor victim of man's ingenuity and of thwarted nature, and of the fatality that attends all such efforts of perverted wisdom, perished there, at the feet of her father and Giovanni. Just at that moment, Professor Pietro Baglioni looked forth from the window, and called loudly, in a tone of triumph mixed with horror, to the thunderstricken man of science:

"Rappaccini! Rappaccini! And is *this* the upshot of your experiment?" ■

❶ *What does Beatrice ask Giovanni?*

Responding to the Selection

How do you think Rappaccini felt at the end of the story? Do you suppose he blamed himself for what happened? or Giovanni? or Baglioni? Which of the three would you hold responsible for Beatrice's death? Why?

Reviewing the Selection

Recalling

1. When and in what city does the story take place? How does Giovanni Guasconti happen to be on the scene?
2. What color links the spectacular shrub in the garden with Beatrice? Name at least one other characteristic common to the two.
3. Who is Baglioni? What is his relationship with Rappaccini?
4. Before Giovanni meets Beatrice, what does he see, or think he sees, that makes him fear her? After he meets her, what makes him ignore his fears until Baglioni's visit?

Interpreting

5. Giovanni suspects that Rappaccini has arranged for him to visit the garden. Why does he think so? What might be Rappaccini's reasons for allowing a man to visit Beatrice? for choosing Giovanni to be that man?
6. During their first meeting in the garden, why does Beatrice stop Giovanni from plucking a blossom from her "sister" plant? What causes her to hide her face and run away?
7. Could Giovanni trust Baglioni's opinion of Rappaccini? Why, or why not? At the tale's end, why does Baglioni's voice suggest triumph as well as horror?
8. When Giovanni suggests that both he and Beatrice drink Baglioni's antidote, why does she say, "I will drink—but do thou await the result"?

Answer to Guided Reading Question

❶ Beatrice asks Giovanni if, from the first, there was not more poison in his nature than in hers.

Responding to the Selection

Ask students to compare how they felt about Giovanni in the story's beginning to how they felt about him after Beatrice's death. Were their sympathies meant to change during the course of the story?

Answers for Reviewing the Selection

RECALLING

1. The story takes place "long ago" in Padua, Italy. Giovanni is pursuing his studies at the University of Padua.

2. The color purple links the two, as does their beauty.

3. Baglioni, like Rappaccini, is a teacher of medicine. Rappaccini is Baglioni's rival.

4. He thinks he sees liquid from the flower she loves kill a lizard. After their meeting, Giovanni is too enthralled by Beatrice to fear her.

INTERPRETING

Responses will vary. Possible responses are given.

5. He thinks Rappaccini has arranged a visit because Lisabetta suddenly shows him the entrance. Rappaccini might allow a man to visit Beatrice to see if he will become poisonous as well. Rappaccini may have chosen Giovanni because he sensed Giovanni had an interest in Beatrice.

6. Beatrice stops Giovanni so that he will not be poisoned. She turns away because she is ashamed of her poisonous nature.

(cont.)

Answers for Reviewing the Selection (cont.)

7. Giovanni could not trust Baglioni's opinion because Baglioni and Rappaccini were rivals. His voice has a tone of triumph because he has seen Rappaccini's experiment fail.

8. Beatrice says this to test the results of the antidote for Giovanni, which further emphasizes her good nature.

9. Giovanni is not truly in love with Beatrice. She is truly in love with him. This is revealed in the fact that he acts selfishly and she acts unselfishly.

10. Students may tend to agree with Beatrice. Although Beatrice's body was full of poison, her spirit was not.

SYNTHESIZING

Responses will vary. Possible responses are given.

Answers for Understanding Literature

► See the evaluation forms for discussion, active listening, and oral communication, *Assessment Portfolio*, 7.11–7.14.

1. Fantasy. Some fantastic elements include the garden itself, the poisonous flower, the poisonous Beatrice, and the "antidote."

2. Symbol. The cheerful fountain may represent the good in the midst of evil. Beatrice represents the complex mingling of good and evil that exists in all people. Rappaccini represents evil, or man's vanity in trying to equal the works of God.

3. Allusion. Rappaccini, like God, is trying to create a mate for his creation. Rappaccini is motivated solely by pride; he wants to prove the vast extent of his power. Evil is revealed as not a part of a human's body but as part of a human's spirit.

Analytic Scales for Responding in Writing

Assign a score from 1 to 25 for each grading criterion below. (For more detailed evaluation, see the evaluation forms for writing, revising, and proofreading, *Assessment Portfolio*, 7.1–7.10.)

1. Recommendations

- **Content/Unity.** The writing presents two recommendations of Giovanni from two different points of view.
- **Organization/Coherence.** Each of the recommendations is written in a logical and sensible order.
- **Language/Style.** The recommendations use vivid and precise nouns, verbs, and modifiers.
- **Conventions.** The recommendations avoid errors in spelling, grammar, usage, mechanics, and manuscript form.

2. Diary Entries

- **Content/Unity.** The diary entries describe Beatrice's feelings during three specific moments.

(cont.)

SYNTHESIZING

9. Is Giovanni truly in love with Beatrice? Is she truly in love with him? Give reasons for your answers.

10. Giovanni called Beatrice a "poisonous thing"; she claimed that there was more poison in his nature than in hers. With whom do you agree?

Understanding Literature (Questions for Discussion)

1. **Fantasy.** A **fantasy** is a literary work that contains highly unrealistic elements. Identify some of the fantastic elements in "Rappaccini's Daughter."

2. **Symbol.** A **symbol** is a thing that stands for or represents both itself and something else. For example, the lush, poisonous foliage in Rappaccini's garden probably represents temptation or evil. If so, what does the fountain that flows "cheerfully" into the garden pool symbolize? Does Beatrice also represent evil, or something more complex? What might Rappaccini himself symbolize?

3. **Allusion.** An **allusion** is a figure of speech in which a reference is made to a person, event, object, or work from history or literature. According to the Bible, God declared that "It is not good for man to be alone" and therefore created Eve to be Adam's partner in the Garden of Eden. In the final scene of "Rappaccini's Daughter," set in the poisonous garden, Rappaccini tells Beatrice that, due to his science, Giovanni is a fit partner and "thou art no longer lonely." How does this allusion to the Biblical story of creation demonstrate Rappaccini's pride? What light does it throw on the nature of the evil in Rappaccini and his garden?

Responding in Writing

1. **Recommendations.** Frequently, students and job-seekers must submit recommendations from teachers, former employers, or others who can attest to their abilities and habits. What sort of recommendation might Baglioni write for Giovanni on the basis of their first meeting? Which of Giovanni's qualities—both good and bad—would seem important to him and worth mentioning? Would Rappaccini's opinion at the time Giovanni began to visit Beatrice be similar, or would he emphasize different qualities in the young man? Take the role of each of these learned men; for each, write a short recommendation for Giovanni for admission to graduate school.

Analytic Scales for Responding in Writing (cont.)

- **Organization/Coherence.** Each of the entries is written in a logical and sensible order.
- **Language/Style.** The entries use vivid and precise nouns, verbs, and modifiers.
- **Conventions.** The entries avoid errors in spelling, grammar, usage, mechanics, and manuscript form.

3. News Story

- **Content/Unity.** The news story presents information about Beatrice.
- **Organization/Coherence.** The news story is written in a logical and sensible order.
- **Language/Style.** The news story uses vivid and precise nouns, verbs, and modifiers.
- **Conventions.** The news story avoids errors in spelling, grammar, usage, mechanics, and manuscript form.

2. **Diary Entries.** In his conversations with Beatrice, Giovanni discovered that she had little, if any, experience with the world outside her father's garden. What topics, then, might she discuss in her diary? Write three diary entries in Beatrice's style of speaking: the first preceding Giovanni's moving in next door, the second following his first words to her from the upper-floor window, and the third about his visits to the garden.

3. **News Story.** Write one of these news stories about Beatrice Rappaccini: (1) a factual, objective report on her death and the coroner's decision blaming it on natural causes; (2) a sensational, tabloid-style report on her ability to kill small animals with her breath, and humans with her kiss.

Language Lab

Subordinate Clauses. Read the material about subordinate clauses and their introductory words in the Language Arts Survey, 2.11, "Relative Pronouns," and 2.27, "Subordinating Conjunctions." Then find the subordinate clause or clauses in each of these sentences. Write out each subordinate clause, draw one line under any relative pronoun that connects the clause, and draw two lines under any introductory subordinating conjunction.

1. Nathaniel Hawthorne, who died over a century ago, still ranks as one of the greatest of American authors.
2. His most important work, *The Scarlet Letter*, examines the effects on a sinner of guilt that is hidden.
3. The setting of this novel, like that of many other tales by Hawthorne, is Puritan New England, where one of Hawthorne's ancestors served as a judge in witch trials.
4. Although Nathaniel Hawthorne did not accept the optimism of the Transcendentalists, he befriended many members of the movement, including Ralph Waldo Emerson and Henry Thoreau, with whom he enjoyed conversations and ice-skating.
5. Another activity that Hawthorne enjoyed was gardening, as readers will discover when they read his introduction to *Mosses from an Old Manse,* a collection of short stories that Hawthorne wrote while he lived in the house named in the title.

Answers for Language Lab

1. who died over a century ago
2. that is hidden
3. like that of many other tales by Hawthorne

where one of Hawthorne's ancestors served as a judge in witch trials

4. Although Nathaniel Hawthorne did not accept the optimism of the Transcendentalists

with whom he enjoyed conversations and ice-skating

5. that Hawthorne enjoyed

as readers will discover

when they read his introduction to *Mosses from an Old Manse,*

that Hawthorne wrote

while he lived in the house named in the title

For More Practice

► *Problem.* Today, travelers who come to visit the bridge over the Concord River where American patriots fought British troops on April 19, 1775, often stop to tour the nearby Old Manse.

Answer. who come to visit the bridge over the Concord River where American patriots fought British troops on April 19, 1775

► Additional practice is provided in the *Essential Skills Practice Book: Language,* 2.11 and 2.27.

ANSWERS FOR THINKING SKILLS

Responses will vary. Possible responses are given.

Possible approaches might include the following: Leave the Rappaccinis and their garden immediately to see if a changed environment will correct his condition or ask Baglioni for help. Students should apply one decision-making technique to the two approaches they choose. If students have difficulty reaching a decision using one method, suggest that they try the other.

▶ Additional practice is provided in the *Essential Skills Practice Book: Study and Research,* 4.3.

PROJECT NOTES

▶ See the worksheets and evaluation forms for projects, *Assessment Portfolio,* 7.20–7.23.

1. Fantasy Garden Catalog. Students should refer to catalogs of plants or other merchandise to become familiar with the types of information needed.

2. Paraphrasing. This activity may be especially helpful to students who have difficulty with the dialogue in the text. Ask students if their paraphrased dialogues would work in the story or if other language would need to be changed as well.

Thinking Skills

Decision Making. Read the Language Arts Survey, 4.3, "Strategies for Decision Making." Then think about Giovanni's predicament when he discovers that his breath is poisonous. Develop at least two different approaches to resolving the problem, besides confronting and accusing Beatrice. Apply either of the strategies described in the survey to select the best approach—one that, if possible, will avoid Beatrice's death.

PROJECTS

1. **Fantasy Garden Catalog.** Work with a partner to create a two- to four-page catalog advertising fantastic plants such as those in Rappaccini's garden. Brainstorm possible variations on existing plants, or combinations of two or more species. Use your imagination to produce frightening, mysterious, or comical plants. Develop illustrations of the plants by drawing, using computer art programs, or splicing together pieces of pictures of real plants. Write a description of each plant, keeping a consistent tone, which may be academic, attention-getting, or tongue-in-cheek. Lay out the pages, pasting art and text in place.

2. **Paraphrasing.** Work with a small group of students to translate some of the dialogue in "Rappaccini's Daughter" into modern English, either formal or informal. Refer to the Language Arts Survey, 2.147, "Formal and Informal English." Take turns reading the speeches aloud and restating the ideas in language more natural to your group. Try not to change the thoughts as you change words or word order. (Of course, any translation will necessarily change the meaning somewhat. Robert Frost once wrote that "Poetry is what gets lost in the translation." You may find it interesting to discuss with your classmates the differences between some of the "translations" and the original passages.)

PREREADING

SHORT STORY

"The Pit and the Pendulum"
by Edgar Allan Poe

ABOUT THE AUTHOR

Edgar Allan Poe (1809–1849) led a short, troubled life but managed in his forty years to make major contributions to literary form and to criticism. Considered to be one of the two creators of the modern short story (the other being Nathaniel Hawthorne), Poe also invented detective fiction, wrote lyric poetry, and pioneered the psychological horror story. Poe's major innovation in the last of these literary forms was to use a technique of double meaning, whereby a tale could be read as being either about the supernatural or about the imaginings of a madman. Few writers have had such enduring popularity and influence as Poe. As a critic, Poe offered a superb definition of the short story, which he thought of as a brief fictional work, the details of which are carefully chosen to create in the reader a single dominant impression.

Poe's father deserted the family when Edgar was a year old. His mother died at the age of twenty-four, and Poe, two years old, was taken in by John Allan, a prosperous Richmond, Virginia, merchant. Poe attended the University of Virginia and did well in his studies. He joined the army after writing *Tamerlane and Other Poems* and was appointed to West Point, but poor class attendance led to his expulsion from the academy. Poe later held various editorial jobs, reviewed literary works, and wrote one novel, *The Narrative of Arthur Gordon Pym,* in addition to producing numerous short stories and poems. Briefly famous and successful after the publication of his poem "The Raven" (Unit 5), Poe nonetheless spent most of his adult life in poverty, losing one job after another due to drinking and quarrelsomeness. After his death, he was hailed as a genius, particularly in France, where he greatly influenced the Symbolist poets Paul Valéry and Charles Baudelaire.

ABOUT THE SELECTION

"The Pit and the Pendulum" is a tale of terror, a short story nightmare. The Spanish Inquisition, which lasted from the 1400s to the 1800s, provides a fitting setting for this story of a man who finds himself imprisoned for reasons he cannot understand and becomes the helpless victim of unknowable and cruel torturers. The Inquisition began as an attempt by the Catholic Church to identify and punish heretics, those who refused to believe in the church's teachings. However, it degenerated into an excuse for those in power to persecute their enemies, as was the case with the prisoner in this tale. Poe's stories often were set in foreign locales, rarely in familiar American locations. Removed from familiar settings, the stories take on romantic, exotic overtones that add to their overall mood of strangeness and suspense.

GOALS/OBJECTIVES

Studying this lesson will enable students to

- enjoy and appreciate a psychological horror story
- recognize elements of the psychological horror story
- describe Edgar Allan Poe's contribution to American literature
- define *romance* and identify a romance
- define *mood* and analyze how a mood is created in the literature they read
- write a press release, a storyboard, and a Gothic tale
- recognize and use context clues to figure out the meaning of unfamiliar words
- use note-taking skills to produce an oral report

ADDITIONAL RESOURCES

READER'S GUIDE
- Selection Worksheet, 4.2

ASSESSMENT PORTFOLIO
- Selection Check Test, 4.4.3
- Selection Test, 4.4.4

ESSENTIAL SKILLS PRACTICE BOOKS
- *Language,* 2.116, 2.138
- *Study and Research,* 4.31

ENRICHMENT ACTIVITIES

- Ask students if they have ever read any horror stories by modern authors. Have them describe briefly the characters, settings, and problems presented in the stories. Then ask students to compare those modern stories with "The Pit and the Pendulum."
- Invite students to select portions of the story to read aloud and record. Encourage students to read the chosen portions with the intensity that the words suggest. Allow time for the class to hear the taped readings.

SUPPORT FOR LEP STUDENTS

Explain that the story is written in a relatively high style, which has the effect of making the story both more unusual and more difficult to understand. Often, understanding the meanings of individual words and phrases is not essential to following the plot of the story. Even so, encourage students to reread parts of the story that confuse them during the first reading. Point out that most people did not use this style in everyday speech during Poe's time.

(cont.)

PREREADING NOTES

Reader's Journal

Have students jot down adjectives and adverbs that describe their feelings as they participate in thrilling or frightening activities. Explain that by analyzing their feelings, they may better understand the appeal of the activities.

Language Skills

Some students may enjoy reading the interjections they have recorded aloud, using the voice of the speaker as they imagine he would sound.

▶ Additional practice is provided in the *Essential Skills Practice Book: Language,* 2.116.

Answer to Guided Reading Question

❶ The judges' lips seem as white as paper and grotesquely thin. The prisoner sees Fate in the judges' moving lips.

SUPPORT FOR LEP STUDENTS (CONT.)

Idioms

my teeth were on edge—I was extremely nervous and agitated
took to heart—considered carefully

Additional Vocabulary

grotesque—distorted or bizarre
specters—ghosts
swoon—faint
tumultuous—wild, disorderly, or noisy
insensibility—unconsciousness
subterranean—below ground
treacherous—dangerous
ascertain—find out

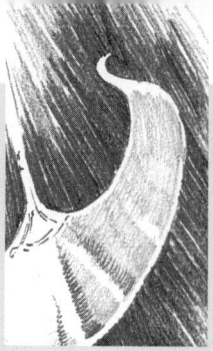

READER'S JOURNAL

Why do people enjoy taking carnival rides, going to "haunted houses," and watching or reading thrillers and horror stories? Freewrite in your journal about the common characteristics of these activities and what their appeal might be. Then, as you read Poe's story, consider the question of why his stories are so immensely popular.

LANGUAGE SKILLS

Read the Language Arts Survey, 2.116, "Interjections." Then, as you read the story, make a list of all the interjections that the speaker uses. Note how Poe capitalizes and punctuates the interjections.

"The Pit and the Pendulum"

EDGAR ALLAN POE

I was sick—sick unto death with that long agony; and when they at length unbound me, and I was permitted to sit, I felt that my senses were leaving me. The sentence—the dread sentence of death—was the last of distinct accentuation which reached my ears. After that, the sound of the inquisitorial voices seemed merged in one dreamy indeterminate hum. It conveyed to my soul the idea of *revolution*—perhaps from its association in fancy with the burr of a mill wheel. This only for a brief period; for presently I heard no more. Yet, for a while, I saw; but with how terrible an exaggeration! I saw the lips of the black-robed judges. They appeared to me white—whiter than the sheet upon which I trace these words—and thin even to grotesqueness; thin with the intensity of their expression of firmness—of immovable resolution—of stern contempt of human torture. I saw that the decrees of what to me was Fate were still issuing from those lips. I saw them writhe with a deadly locution. I saw them fashion the syllables of my name; and I shuddered because no sound succeeded. I saw, too, for a few moments of delirious horror, the soft and nearly imperceptible waving of the sable draperies which enwrapped the walls of the apartment. And then my vision fell upon the seven tall candles upon the table. At first they wore the aspect of charity, and seemed white slender angels who would save me; but then, all at once, there came a most deadly nausea over my spirit, and I felt every fiber in my frame thrill as if I had touched the wire of a galvanic[1] battery, while the angel forms became meaningless specters, with heads of flame, and I saw that from them there would be no help. And then there

What exaggerations does the prisoner see? ❶

1. **galvanic.** Producing an electric current

WORDS FOR EVERYDAY USE:

ac • cen • tu • a • tion (ak sen´chōō ā´ shən) *n.,* emphasis; clear pronunciation
in • quis • i • to • ri • al (in kwiz´ə tôr´ē əl) *adj.,* prying
in • de • ter • mi • nate (in´dē tur´mi´nit) *adj.,* unspecific; unsettled
writhe (rīth) *vt.,* make twisting movements
lo • cu • tion (lō kyōō´shən) *n.,* word; phrase

VOCABULARY IN CONTEXT

- The speaker prided herself on her clear accentuation.
- "That's none of your business!" Cole snapped at his inquisitorial neighbor.
- Our vacation will last an indeterminate number of days.
- After being hit by the pitch, the batter writhed on the ground in pain.
- The receptionist smiled and beckoned me into the office, intoning the dreaded locution, "Next."

stole into my fancy, like a rich musical note, the thought of what sweet rest there must be in the grave. The thought came gently and stealthily, and it seemed long before it attained full appreciation; but just as my spirit came at length properly to feel and entertain it, the figures of the judges vanished, as if magically, from before me; the tall candles sank into nothingness; their flames went out utterly; the blackness of darkness supervened; all sensations appeared swallowed up in a mad rushing descent as of the soul into Hades.[2] Then silence, and stillness, and night were the universe.

I had swooned; but still will not say that all of consciousness was lost. What of it there remained I will not attempt to define, or even to describe; yet all was not lost. In the deepest slumber—no! In delirium—no! In a swoon—no! In death—no! even in the grave all is *not* lost. Else there is no immortality for man. Arousing from the most profound of slumbers, we break the gossamer web of *some* dream. Yet in a second afterward (so frail may that web have been), we remember not that we have dreamed. In the return to life from the swoon there are two stages; first, that of the sense of mental or spiritual; secondly, that of the sense of physical, existence. It seems probable that if, upon reaching the second stage, we could recall the impressions of the first, we should find these impressions eloquent in memories of the gulf beyond. And that gulf is—what? How at least shall we distinguish its shadows from those of the tomb? But if the impressions of what I have termed the first stage, are not, at will, recalled, yet, after long interval, do they not come unbidden, while we marvel whence they come? He who has never swooned is not he who finds strange palaces and wildly familiar faces in coals that glow; is not he who beholds floating in midair the sad visions that the many may not view; is not he who ponders over the perfume of some novel flower—is not he whose brain grows bewildered with the meaning of some musical cadence which has never before arrested his attention.

❶ *What sorts of visions has the prisoner experienced?*

Amid frequent and thoughtful endeavors to remember; amid earnest struggles to regather some token of the state of seeming nothingness into which my soul had lapsed, there have been moments when I have dreamed of success; there have been brief, very brief periods when I have conjured up remembrances which the lucid reason of a later epoch assures me could have had reference only to that condition of seeming unconsciousness. These shadows of memory tell, indistinctly, of tall figures that lifted and bore me in silence down—down—still down—till a hideous dizziness oppressed me at the mere idea of the interminableness of the descent. They tell also of a vague horror at my heart, on account of that heart's unnatural stillness. Then comes a sense of sudden motionlessness throughout all things; as if those who bore me (a ghastly train!) had outrun, in their descent, the limits of the limitless, and paused from the wearisomeness of their toil. After this I call to mind flatness and dampness; and then all is madness—the madness of a

2. **Hades.** In Greek mythology, home of the dead; underground

Words for Everyday Use:

su • per • vene (sōō´pər vēn´) *vi.*, happen unexpectedly
ca • dence (kād´´ns) *n.*, rhythmic flow of sound or tone
ear • nest (ŭr´nist) *adj.*, serious; intense
con • jure (kun´jər) *vt.*, call
in • ter • mi • na • ble (in tŭr´mi nə bəl) *adj.*, without, or seemingly without, end

Answer to Guided Reading Question

❶ The prisoner has seen palaces and familiar faces in glowing coals and strange visions floating in midair, smelled the perfume of a new flower, and heard a musical cadence he never noticed before.

Biographical Note

Poe's preoccupation with death is understandable, considering that his young wife Virginia was gravely ill at the time Poe wrote this story. She eventually died in poverty at the age of twenty-four.

Literary Technique

Both Poe in this story and Hawthorne in "Rappaccini's Daughter" deal with death, either actual or imagined. Compare and contrast their views on death and their treatment of the death of a main character.

Vocabulary from the Selection

abstraction	illuminate
abyss	impede
accentuation	impend
ague	inanition
anointed	indeterminate
aperture	ingenuity
avert	inquisitorial
avidity	insuperable
balm	interminable
cadence	locution
cessation	lozenge
cognizance	moiety
conjecture	pertinacity
conjure	pungently
convolution	riband
dally	supervene
diffuse	vengeance
discordant	vermin
earnest	viand
encompass	voracity
fissure	writhe

Vocabulary in Context

- The runner intended to enter the race, but her leg injury supervened.
- The sergeant shouted a familiar cadence as the soldiers marched across the field.
- Despite his earnest efforts to understand, he could not agree with her point of view.
- The words *ski lodge* conjured up images of roaring fires, hot chocolate, and good friends.
- The hour-long speech seemed interminable.

ANSWER TO GUIDED READING QUESTION

❶ He fears he is in a tomb.

QUOTABLES

"The boundaries which divide Life and Death are at best shadowy and vague. Who shall say where the one ends, and where the other begins?"

—Edgar Allan Poe

memory which busies itself among forbidden things.

Very suddenly there came back to my soul motion and sound—the tumultuous motion of the heart, and, in my ears, the sound of its beating. Then a pause in which all is blank. Then again sound, and motion, and touch—a tingling sensation pervading my frame. Then the mere consciousness of existence, without thought—a condition which lasted long. Then, very suddenly, *thought*, and shuddering terror, and earnest endeavor to comprehend my true state. Then a strong desire to lapse into insensibility. Then a rushing revival of soul and a successful effort to move. And now a full memory of the trial, of the judges, of the sable draperies, of the sentence, of the sickness, of the swoon. Then entire forgetfulness of all that followed; of all that a later day and much earnestness of endeavor have enabled me vaguely to recall.

So far, I had not opened my eyes. I felt that I lay upon my back, unbound. I reached out my hand, and it fell heavily upon something damp and hard. There I suffered it to remain for many minutes, while I strove to imagine where and *what* I could be. I longed, yet dared not to employ my vision. I dreaded the first glance at objects around me. It was not that I feared to look upon things horrible, but that I grew aghast lest there should be *nothing* to see. At length, with a wild desperation at heart, I quickly unclosed my eyes. My worst thoughts, then, were confirmed. The blackness of eternal night encompassed me. I struggled for breath. The intensity of the darkness seemed to oppress and stifle me. The atmosphere was intolerably close. I still lay quietly, and made effort to exercise my reason. I brought to mind the inquisitorial proceedings, and attempted from that point to deduce my real condition. The sentence had passed; and it appeared to me that a very long interval of time had since elapsed. Yet not for a moment did I suppose myself actually dead. Such a supposition, notwithstanding what we read in fiction, is altogether inconsistent with real existence;—but where and in what state was I? The condemned to death, I knew, perished usually at the autos-da-fe,[3] and one of these had been held on the very night of the day of my trial. Had I been remanded to my dungeon, to await the next sacrifice, which would not take place for many months? This I at once saw could not be. Victims had been in immediate demand. Moreover, my dungeon, as well as all the condemned cells at Toledo,[4] had stone floors, and light was not altogether excluded.

Where does the prisoner fear he is? ❶

A fearful idea now suddenly drove the blood in torrents upon my heart, and for a brief period, I once more relapsed into insensibility. Upon recovering, I at once started to my feet, trembling convulsively in every fiber. I thrust my arms wildly above and around me in all directions. I felt nothing; yet dreaded to move a step, lest I should be impeded by the walls of a *tomb*. Perspiration burst from every pore, and stood in cold big beads upon my forehead. The agony of suspense grew at length intolerable, and I cautiously moved

3. **autos-da-fe.** Public ceremonies in which the inquisitors pronounced judgment and passed sentences on heretics

4. **Toledo.** Spanish city

WORDS FOR EVERYDAY USE:

en • com • pass (en kum´pəs) *vt.,* surround

im • pede (im pēd´) *vt.,* obstruct; hinder

VOCABULARY IN CONTEXT

- The small sailboat was unexpectedly encompassed by a thick fog.
- Sandbags were used to impede the floodwaters.
- Its financial difficulties proved insuperable, and the company went bankrupt.
- Now that her goals were clear, the student attacked her studies with avidity.

forward, with my arms extended, and my eyes straining from their sockets, in the hope of catching some faint ray of light. I proceeded for many paces; but still all was blackness and vacancy. I breathed more freely. It seemed evident that mine was not, at least, the most hideous of fates.

And now, as I still continued to step cautiously onward, there came thronging upon my recollection, a thousand vague rumors of the horrors of Toledo. Of the dungeons there had been strange things narrated—fables I had always deemed them—but yet strange, and too ghastly to repeat, save in a whisper. Was I left to perish of starvation in this subterranean world of darkness; or what fate, perhaps even more fearful, awaited me? That the result would be death, and a death of more than customary bitterness, I knew too well the character of my judges to doubt. The mode and the hour were all that occupied or distracted me.

My outstretched hands at length encountered some solid obstruction. It was a wall, seemingly of stone masonry—very smooth, slimy, and cold. I followed it up; stepping with all the careful distrust with which certain antique narratives had inspired me. This process, however, afforded me no means of ascertaining the dimensions of my dungeon; as I might make its circuit, and return to the point whence I set out, without being aware of the fact; so perfectly uniform seemed the wall. I therefore sought the knife which had been in my pocket, when led into the inquisitorial chamber; but it was gone; my clothes had been exchanged for a wrapper of coarse serge.[5] I had thought of forcing the blade in some minute crevice of the masonry, so as to identify my point of departure. The difficulty, nevertheless, was but trivial; although, in the disorder of my fancy, it seemed at first insuperable. I tore a part of the hem from the robe and placed the fragment at full length, and at right angles to the wall. In groping my way around the prison, I could not fail to encounter this rag upon completing the circuit. So, at least I thought; but I had not counted upon the extent of the dungeon, or upon my own weakness. The ground was moist and slippery. I staggered onward for some time, when I stumbled and fell. My excessive fatigue induced me to remain prostrate; and sleep soon overtook me as I lay.

Upon awaking, and stretching forth an arm, I found beside me a loaf and a pitcher with water. I was too much exhausted to reflect upon this circumstance, but ate and drank with avidity. Shortly afterward, I resumed my tour around the prison, and with much toil, came at last upon the fragment of the serge. Up to the period when I fell I had counted fifty-two paces, and upon resuming my walk, I had counted forty-eight more;—when I arrived at the rag. There were in all, then, a hundred paces; and, admitting two paces to the yard, I presumed the dungeon to be fifty yards in circuit. I had met, however, with many angles in the wall, and thus I could form no guess at the shape of the vault; for vault I could not help supposing it to be.

I had little object—certainly no hope—in these researches; but a vague curiosity

5. **serge.** Sturdy fabric

❶ *What were the rumors about Toledo?*

❷ *How does the prisoner measure his cell?*

WORDS FOR EVERYDAY USE:

in • su • per• a • ble (in sōō´pər ə bəl) *adj.,* insurmountable

a • vid • i • ty (ə vid´ə tē) *n.,* eagerness; enthusiasm

ANSWERS TO GUIDED READING QUESTIONS

❶ The rumors spoke of dungeons in which ghastly things happened such as allowing prisoners to starve or worse.

❷ He sets a piece of his robe at right angles to the wall and then walks next to the wall, counting his steps. When he circles back to the scrap of robe, he knows how many steps it takes to walk the perimeter of his cell. He then calculates that two steps represent a yard, so one hundred steps represent fifty yards.

CROSS-CURRICULAR ACTIVITIES

Mathematics and Sciences. Have students figure how long each side of the room would have been if the prisoner's pacing had been accurate and the room had been square. Ask volunteers to measure the dimensions in a large area in the school, such as a hall. Later, when the prisoner finds that the room is half that size, students should recalculate the wall sizes, again assuming that the room is square.

Answers to Guided Reading Questions

❶ He trips on the hem of his robe and falls. As he lies on the floor, he notices that his lips and upper head touch nothing and his forehead feels a clammy vapor rising onto it. He reaches out with his arm and discovers the circular pit of unknown depth.

❷ He falls asleep, perhaps because of the effect of drugs in the water.

Literary Technique

Sensory details are words and phrases that describe how things look, sound, smell, taste, and feel. At this point in the story, the prisoner cannot use his sense of sight and must rely on his other senses. Ask students to look for sensory details that describe the prisoner's situation without using any visual details.

Additional Questions and Activities

Have students write a description of a place without using any visual details. Without the sense of sight, the other senses will become the only ways to learn about the surroundings.

prompted me to continue them. Quitting the wall, I resolved to cross the area of the enclosure. At first I proceeded with extreme caution, for the floor, although seemingly of solid material, was treacherous with slime. At length, however, I took courage, and did not hesitate to step firmly; endeavoring to cross in as direct a line as possible. I had advanced some ten or twelve paces in this manner, when the remnant of the torn hem of my robe became entangled between my legs. I stepped on it, and fell violently on my face.

In the confusion attending my fall, I did not immediately apprehend a somewhat startling circumstance, which yet, in a few seconds afterward, and while I still lay prostrate, arrested my attention. It was this—my chin rested upon the floor of the prison, but my lips and the upper portion of my head, although seemingly at a less elevation than the chin, touched nothing. At the same time my forehead seemed bathed in a clammy vapor, and the peculiar smell of decayed fungus arose to my nostrils. I put forward my arm, and shuddered to find that I had fallen at the very brink of a circular pit, whose extent, of course, I had no means of ascertaining at the moment. Groping about the masonry just below the margin, I succeeded in dislodging a small fragment, and let it fall into the abyss. For many seconds I hearkened to its reverberations as it dashed against the sides of the chasm in its descent; at length there was a sullen plunge into water, succeeded by loud echoes. At the same moment there came a sound resembling the quick opening, and as rapid closing of a door overhead, while a faint gleam of light flashed suddenly through the gloom, and as suddenly faded away.

❶ *How does the prisoner discover the pit?*

❷ *What condition follows the prisoner's quenching his thirst?*

I saw clearly the doom which had been prepared for me, and congratulated myself upon the timely accident by which I had escaped. Another step before my fall, and the world had seen me no more. And the death just avoided, was of that very character which I had regarded as fabulous and frivolous in the tales respecting the Inquisition. To the victims of its tyranny, there was the choice of death with its direst physical agonies, or death with its most hideous moral horrors. I had been reserved for the latter. By long suffering my nerves had been unstrung, until I trembled at the sound of my own voice, and had become in every respect a fitting subject for the species of torture which awaited me.

Shaking in every limb, I groped my way back to the wall; resolving there to perish rather than risk the terrors of the wells, of which my imagination now pictured many in various positions about the dungeon. In other conditions of mind I might have had courage to end my misery at once by a plunge into one of these abysses; but now I was the veriest of cowards. Neither could I forget what I had read of these pits—that the *sudden* extinction of life formed no part of their most horrible plan.

Agitation of spirit kept me awake for many long hours; but at length I again slumbered. Upon arousing, I found by my side, as before, a loaf and a pitcher of water. A burning thirst consumed me, and I emptied the vessel at a draught. It must have been drugged; for scarcely had I drunk, before I became irresistibly drowsy.

Words for Everyday Use: **a • byss** (ə bis´) *n.,* bottomless hole

Vocabulary in Context

- Because of its incredible depth, the Grand Canyon is sometimes called the "Divine Abyss."
- The snake handler reached fearlessly into a convolution of poisonous snakes.

A deep sleep fell upon me—a sleep like that of death. How long it lasted of course, I know not; but when, once again, I unclosed my eyes, the objects around me were visible. By a wild sulphurous[6] luster, the origin of which I could not at first determine, I was enabled to see the extent and aspect of the prison.

In its size I had been greatly mistaken. The whole circuit of its walls did not exceed twenty-five yards. For some minutes this fact occasioned me a world of vain trouble; vain indeed! for what could be of less importance, under the terrible circumstances which environed me, than the mere dimensions of my dungeon? But my soul took a wild interest in trifles, and I busied myself in endeavors to account for the error I had committed in my measurement. The truth at length flashed upon me. In my first attempt at exploration I had counted fifty-two paces, up to the period when I fell; I must then have been within a pace or two of the fragment of serge; in fact, I had nearly performed the circuit of the vault. I then slept, and upon awaking, I must have returned upon my steps—thus supposing the circuit nearly double what it actually was. My confusion of mind prevented me from observing that I began my tour with the wall to the left; and ended it with the wall to the right.

I had been deceived, too, in respect to the shape of the enclosure. In feeling my way I had found many angles, and thus deduced an idea of great irregularity; so potent is the effect of total darkness upon one arousing from lethargy or sleep! The angles were simply those of a few slight depressions, or niches, at odd intervals. The general shape of the prison was square. What I had taken for masonry seemed now to be iron, or some other metal, in huge plates, whose sutures or joints occasioned the depression. The entire surface of this metallic enclosure was rudely daubed in all the hideous and repulsive devices to which the charnel[7] superstition of the monks has given rise. The figures of fiends in aspects of menace, with skeleton forms, and other more really fearful images, overspread and disfigured the walls. I observed that the outlines of these monstrosities were sufficiently distinct, but that the colors seemed faded and blurred, as if from the effects of a damp atmosphere. I now noticed the floor, too, which was of stone. In the center yawned the circular pit from whose jaws I had escaped; but it was the only one in the dungeon.

All this I saw indistinctly and by much effort: for my personal condition had been greatly changed during slumber. I now lay upon my back, and at full length, on a species of low framework of wood. To this I was securely bound by a long strap resembling a surcingle.[8] It passed in many convolutions about my limbs and body, leaving at liberty only my head, and my left arm to such extent that I could, by dint of much exertion, supply myself with food from an earthen dish which lay by my side on the floor. I saw, to my horror, that the pitcher had been removed. I say

6. **sulphurous.** Similar to the color of burning sulphur, suggesting the fires of hell
7. **charnel.** Building where bodies and bones are placed
8. **surcingle.** Strap passed around a horse's body to hold on a saddle

❶ *What absorbs the prisoner's interest?*

❷ *What change has taken place?*

WORDS FOR EVERYDAY USE: **con • vo • lu • tion** (kän´və lo̅o´ shən) *n.,* twist, coil, fold

ANSWERS TO GUIDED READING QUESTIONS

❶ He tries to figure out why his estimate of the room size was so inaccurate.

❷ The prisoner is lying on his back, tied to a frame of wood. Only his head and his left arm can move.

Answers to Guided Reading Questions

❶ The pendulum has descended.

❷ The rats are attracted by the scent of the meat.

Cross-curricular Activities

Mathematics and Sciences. Interested students might choose to research pendulums. How is the movement of a pendulum affected by variations in its height/length?

Students can learn about the principles behind the actions of the pendulum in Poe's story and report to the class.

to my horror, for I was consumed with intolerable thirst. This thirst it appeared to be the design of my persecutors to stimulate, for the food in the dish was meat pungently seasoned.

What is most frightening about the pendulum? ❶

Looking upward, I surveyed the ceiling of my prison. It was some thirty or forty feet overhead, and constructed much as the side walls. In one of its panels a very singular figure riveted my whole attention. It was the painted figure of Time as he is commonly represented, save that, in lieu of a scythe, he held what, at a casual glance, I supposed to be the pictured image of a huge pendulum such as we see on antique clocks. There was something, however, in the appearance of this machine which caused me to regard it more attentively. While I gazed directly upward at it (for its position was immediately over my own) I fancied that I saw it in motion. In an instant afterward the fancy was confirmed. Its sweep was brief, and of course slow. I watched it for some minutes, somewhat in fear, but more in wonder. Wearied at length with observing its dull movement, I turned my eyes upon the other objects in the cell.

A slight noise attracted my notice, and, looking to the floor, I saw several enormous rats traversing it. They had issued from the well, which lay just within view to my right. Even then, while I gazed, they came up in troops, hurriedly, with ravenous eyes, allured by the scent of the meat. From this it required much effort and attention to scare them away.

What attracts the rats? ❷

It might have been half an hour, perhaps even an hour (for I could take but imperfect note of time), before I again cast my eyes upward. What I then saw confounded and amazed me. The sweep of the pendulum had increased in extent by nearly a yard. As a natural consequence, its velocity was also much greater. But what mainly disturbed me was the idea that it had perceptibly *descended.* I now observed—with what horror it is needless to say—that its nether extremity was formed of a crescent of glittering steel, about a foot in length from horn to horn; the horns upward, and the under edge evidently as keen as that of a razor. Like a razor also, it seemed massy and heavy, tapering from the edge into a solid and broad structure above. It was appended to a weighty rod of brass, and the whole *hissed* as it swung through the air.

I could no longer doubt the doom prepared for me by monkish ingenuity in torture. My cognizance of the pit had become known to the inquisitorial agents—*the pit,* whose horrors had been destined for so bold a recusant[9] as myself—*the pit,* typical of hell, and regarded by rumor as the Ultima Thule[10] of all their punishments. The plunge into this pit I had avoided by the merest of accidents, and I knew that surprise, or entrapment into torment, formed an important portion of all the grotesquerie of these dungeon deaths. Having failed to fall, it was no part of the demon plan to hurl me into the abyss; and thus (there being no alternative) a different and a milder destruction awaited me. Milder! I half smiled in my agony as I thought of such application of such a term.

9. **recusant.** Person who refuses to obey an established authority
10. **Ultima Thule.** Farthest limit

Words for Everyday Use:
pun • gent • ly (pun´jənt lē) *adv.,* sharply, strongly
in • ge • nu • i • ty (in´jə nōō´ə tē) *n.,* cleverness
cog • ni • zance (käg´nə zəns) *n.,* knowledge

Vocabulary in Context

- The skunk pungently scented the air, causing its enemies to flee.
- The ingenuity of inventors always amazes me.
- The speaker's cognizance of the skill level of her listeners led her to alter her presentation.
- After his long ordeal, the lost hiker could barely speak due to inanition.

What boots it[11] to tell of the long, long hours of horror more than mortal, during which I counted the rushing oscillations of the steel! Inch by inch—line by line—with a descent only appreciable at intervals that seemed ages—down and still down it came! Days passed—it might have been that many days passed—ere it swept so closely over me as to fan me with its acrid breath. The odor of the sharp steel forced itself into my nostrils. I prayed—I wearied heaven with my prayer for its more speedy descent. I grew frantically mad, and struggled to force myself upward against the sweep of the fearful scimitar.[12] And then I fell suddenly calm, and lay smiling at the glittering death, as a child at some rare bauble.

There was another interval of utter insensibility; it was brief; for, upon again lapsing into life there had been no perceptible descent in the pendulum. But it might have been long; for I knew there were demons who took note of my swoon, and who could have arrested the vibration at pleasure. Upon my recovery, too, I felt very—oh, inexpressibly sick and weak, as if through long inanition. Even amid the

❶ *For what does the prisoner pray?*

11. **What boots it.** What good is it
12. **scimitar.** Curved sword

WORDS FOR EVERYDAY USE: **in • a • ni • tion** (in´ə nish´ən) *n.,* lack of strength due to lack of food

ANSWER TO GUIDED READING QUESTION

❶ He prays that the pendulum will descend more quickly and kill him.

LITERARY TECHNIQUE

Explain that **alliteration** is the repetition of initial consonant sounds. Have students identify the alliteration in the first sentence on this page. Then have them look for more examples of alliteration in the story.

Answers to Guided Reading Questions

❶ He cannot think straight anymore.

❷ Hope lives even in the dungeon.

Analytic Scales for Responding in Writing

Assign a score from 1 to 25 for each grading criterion below. (For more detailed evaluation, see the evaluation forms for writing, revising, and proofreading, *Assessment Portfolio*, 7.1–7.10.)

1. Press Release

- **Content/Unity.** The press release presents facts about an event in a simple, objective style.
- **Organization/Coherence.** The press release is clearly organized, usually in an inverted pyramid; that is, the most essential facts are presented first, followed by smaller, less important details.
- **Language/Style.** The press release uses vivid and precise nouns, verbs, and modifiers.
- **Conventions.** The press release avoids errors in spelling, grammar, usage, mechanics, and manuscript form.

2. Storyboard

- **Content/Unity.** The storyboard describes and pictures the series of events that create the plot of "The Pit and the Pendulum."
- **Organization/Coherence.** The storyboard presents the plot events in chronological order. It may include the thoughts of the character and descriptive details about character and setting.
- **Language/Style.** The storyboard uses vivid and precise nouns,verbs, and modifiers.
- **Conventions.** The storyboard avoids errors in spelling, grammar, usage, mechanics, and manuscript form.

3. Gothic Tale

- **Content/Unity.** The Gothic tale tells a story of characters in strange settings facing mysterious or horrible conflicts.
- **Organization/Coherence.** The Gothic tale builds suspense up to an exciting climax.
- **Language/Style.** The Gothic tale uses vivid and precise nouns, verbs, and modifiers.
- **Conventions.** The Gothic tale avoids errors in spelling, grammar, usage, mechanics, and manuscript form.

agonies of that period, the human nature craved food. With painful effort I outstretched my left arm as far as my bonds permitted, and took possession of the small remnant which had been spared me by the rats. As I put a portion of it within my lips, there rushed to my mind a half-formed thought of joy—of hope. Yet what business had *I* with hope? It was, as I say, a half-formed thought—man has many such which are never completed. I felt that it was of joy—of hope; but I felt also that it had perished in its formation. In vain I struggled to perfect—to regain it. Long suffering had nearly annihilated all my ordinary powers of mind. I was an imbecile—an idiot.

❶ *What is happening to the prisoner's mind?*

The vibration of the pendulum was at right angles to my length. I saw that the crescent was designed to cross the region of the heart. It would fray the serge of my robe—it would return and repeat its operations—again—and again. Notwithstanding its terrifically wide sweep (some thirty feet or more) and the hissing vigor of its descent sufficient to sunder these very walls of iron, still the fraying of my robe would be all that, for several minutes, it would accomplish. And at this thought I paused. I dared not go further than this reflection. I dwelt upon it with a pertinacity of attention—as if, in so dwelling, I could arrest *here* the descent of the steel. I forced myself to ponder upon the sound of the crescent as it should pass across the garment—upon the peculiar thrilling sensation which friction of cloth produces on the nerves. I pondered upon all this frivolity until my teeth were on edge.

❷ *What lives even in the dungeon?*

Down—steadily down it crept. I took a frenzied pleasure in contrasting its downward with its lateral velocity. To the right—to the left—far and wide—with the shriek of a damned spirit; to my heart with the stealthy pace of the tiger! I alternately laughed and howled as the one or the other idea grew predominant.

Down—certainly, relentlessly down! It vibrated within three inches of my bosom! I struggled violently, furiously, to free my left arm. This was free only from the elbow to the hand. I could reach the latter, from the platter beside me, to my mouth, with great effort, but no farther. Could I have broken the fastenings above the elbow I would have seized and attempted to arrest the pendulum. I might as well have attempted to arrest an avalanche!

Down—still unceasingly—still inevitably down! I gasped and struggled at each vibration. I shrunk convulsively at its every sweep. My eyes followed its outward or upward whirls with the eagerness of the most unmeaning despair; they closed themselves spasmodically at the descent, although death would have been a relief, oh! how unspeakable! Still I quivered in every nerve to think how slight a sinking of the machinery would precipitate that keen, glistening ax upon my bosom. It was *hope* that prompted the nerve to quiver—the frame to shrink. It was *hope*—the hope that triumphs on the rack—that whispers to the death-condemned even in the dungeons of the Inquisition.

I saw that some ten or twelve vibrations would bring the steel in actual contact with my robe, and with this observation there suddenly came over my spirit all the keen, collected calmness of despair. For the first time during many hours—or perhaps

Words for Everyday Use: **per • ti • nac • i • ty** (pur´tə nas´ə tē) *n.*, stubbornness

Vocabulary in Context

- In the light of many previous failures, it took real pertinacity to try again.
- If only a moiety of what you say is true, you were lucky to survive that accident.
- Vermin are often attracted by garbage.
- The hikers packed enough viands for a five-day journey.
- The sudden cessation of the sound of the fan woke me up.
- I was surprised by my own voracity at the salad bar.
- The priest anointed the forehead of the dying man with holy oil.

days—I *thought*. It now occurred to me that the bandage, or surcingle, which enveloped me, was *unique*. I was tied by no separate cord. The first stroke of the razorlike crescent athwart any portion of the band, would so detach it that it might be unwound from my person by means of my left hand. But how fearful, in that case, the proximity of the steel! the result of the slightest struggle, how deadly! Was it likely, moreover, that the minions of the torturer had not foreseen and provided for this possibility? Was it probable that the bandage crossed my bosom in the track of the pendulum? Dreading to find my faint, and, as it seemed, my last hope frustrated, I so far elevated my head as to obtain a distinct view of my breast. The surcingle enveloped my limbs and body close in all directions—*save in the path of the destroying crescent.*

Scarcely had I dropped my head back into its original position, when there flashed upon my mind what I cannot better describe than as the unformed half of that idea of deliverance to which I have previously alluded, and of which a moiety only floated indeterminately through my brain when I raised food to my burning lips. The whole thought was now present—feeble, scarcely sane, scarcely definite—but still entire. I proceeded at once, with the nervous energy of despair, to attempt its execution.

For many hours the immediate vicinity of the low framework upon which I lay, had been literally swarming with rats. They were wild, bold, ravenous; their red eyes glaring upon me as if they waited but for motionlessness on my part to make me their prey. "To what food," I thought, "have they been accustomed in the well?"

They had devoured, in spite of all my efforts to prevent them, all but a small remnant of the contents of the dish. I had fallen into an habitual seesaw, or wave of the hand about the platter; and, at length, the unconscious uniformity of the movement deprived it of effect. In their voracity the vermin frequently fastened their sharp fangs in my fingers. With the particles of the oily and spicy viand which now remained, I thoroughly rubbed the bandage wherever I could reach it; then, raising my hand from the floor, I lay breathlessly still.

❶ *What actions are part of the prisoner's plan?*

At first the ravenous animals were startled and terrified at the change—at the cessation of movement. They shrank alarmedly back; many sought the well. But this was only for a moment. I had not counted in vain upon their voracity. Observing that I remained without motion, one or two of the boldest leaped upon the framework and smelt at the surcingle. This seemed the signal for a general rush. Forth from the well they hurried in fresh troops. They clung to the wood—they overran it, and leaped in hundreds upon my person. The measured movement of the pendulum disturbed them not at all. Avoiding its strokes, they busied themselves with the anointed bandage. They pressed—they swarmed upon me in ever accumulating heaps. They writhed upon my throat; their cold lips sought my own; I was half stifled by their

❷ *What do the rats do?*

WORDS FOR EVERYDAY USE:

moi • e • ty (moi ə tē) *n.*, half
ver • min (vur´mən) *n.*, small animals regarded as pests
vi • and (vī´ənd) *n.*, article of food
ces • sa • tion (se sā´shən) *n.*, ceasing or stopping
vo • rac • i • ty (vô ras´ə tē) *n.*, greediness
a • noint • ed (ə noint´əd) *part.*, rubbed with the oil from the meat

ANSWERS TO GUIDED READING QUESTIONS

❶ The prisoner rubs the oily, spicy food on his bandage and then lies still.

❷ The hungry rats swarm over the prisoner and gnaw through the bandage in their attempt to eat the remains of the food.

Answers to Guided Reading Questions

❶ The prisoner is no longer bound but is still controlled by his persecutors.

Additional Questions and Activities

A large part of the horror of the prisoner's situation came from his isolation. Discuss how the story would have been different if the prisoner had not been alone.

thronging pressure; disgust, for which the world has no name, swelled my bosom and chilled, with a heavy clamminess, my heart. Yet one minute, and I felt that the struggle would be over. Plainly I perceived the loosening of the bandage. I knew that in more than one place it must be already severed. With a more than human resolution I lay *still.*

Nor had I erred in my calculations—nor had I endured in vain. I at length felt that I was *free.* The surcingle hung in ribands from my body. But the stroke of the pendulum already pressed upon my bosom. It had divided the serge of the robe. It had cut through the linen beneath. Twice again it swung, and a sharp sense of pain shot through every nerve. But the moment of escape had arrived. At a wave of my hand my deliverers hurried tumultuously away. With a steady movement—cautious, sidelong, shrinking, and slow—I slid from the embrace of the bandage and beyond the reach of the scimitar. For the moment, at least, *I was free.*

Why is the prisoner free but not free? ❶

Free!—and in the grasp of the Inquisition! I had scarcely stepped from my wooden bed of horror upon the stone floor of the prison, when the motion of the hellish machine ceased and I beheld it drawn up, by some invisible force, through the ceiling. This was a lesson which I took desperately to heart. My every motion was undoubtedly watched. Free!—I had but escaped death in one form of agony, to be delivered unto worse than death in some other. With that thought I rolled my eyes nervously around on the barriers of iron that hemmed me in. Something unusual—some change which, at first, I could not appreciate distinctly—it was obvious, had taken place in the apartment. For many minutes of a dreamy and trembling abstraction, I busied myself in vain, unconnected conjecture. During this period, I became aware, for the first time, of the origin of the sulphurous light which illuminated the cell. It proceeded from a fissure, about half an inch in width, extending entirely around the prison at the base of the walls, which thus appeared, and were, completely separated from the floor. I endeavored, but of course in vain, to look through the aperture.

As I arose from the attempt, the mystery of the alteration in the chamber broke at once upon my understanding. I have observed that, although the outlines of the figures upon the walls were sufficiently distinct, yet the colors seemed blurred and indefinite. These colors had now assumed, and were momentarily assuming, a startling and most intense brilliancy, that gave to the spectral and fiendish portraitures an aspect that might have thrilled even firmer nerves than my own. Demon eyes, of a wild and ghastly vivacity, glared upon me in a thousand directions where none had been visible before, and gleamed with the lurid luster of a fire that I could not force my imagination to regard as unreal.

Unreal!—Even while I breathed there came to my nostrils the breath of the vapor of the heated iron! A suffocating odor pervaded the prison! A deeper glow settled each moment in the eyes that glared at my agonies! A richer tint of crimson diffused itself over the pictured horrors of blood. I panted! I gasped for breath! There could

Words for Everyday Use:

rib • and (rib´ənd) *n.,* ribbon
ab • strac • tion (ab strak´shən) *n.,* mental withdrawal; absent-mindedness
con • jec • ture (kən jek´chər) *n.,* speculation
il • lu • mi • nate (i lo̅o̅´mə nāt´) *vt.,* light up
fis • sure (fish´ər) *n.,* deep crack
ap • er • ture (ap´ər cher) *n.,* opening; hole
dif • fuse (di fyo̅o̅s´) *vt.,* spread out; pour out

Vocabulary in Context

- To show their support for the soldiers, civilians decorated their homes with yellow ribands.
- The psychiatrist noticed with alarm that the patient's periods of abstraction were becoming more frequent.
- My certainty that I would be selected was based purely on conjecture, not facts.
- Some people like to illuminate their homes during the holidays.
- The rock climber looked for a fissure in the rock face where she could get a good grip.
- Light enters the camera through an aperture that can be increased or decreased in size.
- We hurriedly opened the windows to diffuse the natural gas concentration.

be no doubt of the design of my tormentors—oh! most unrelenting! oh! most demoniac of men! I shrank from the glowing metal to the center of the cell. Amid the thought of the fiery destruction that impended, the idea of the coolness of the well came over my soul like balm. I rushed to its deadly brink. I threw my straining vision below. The glare from the enkindled roof illumined its inmost recesses. Yet, for a wild moment, did my spirit refuse to comprehend the meaning of what I saw. At length it forced—it wrestled its way into my soul—it burned itself in upon my shuddering reason.—Oh! for a voice to speak!—oh! horror!—oh! any horror but this! With a shriek, I rushed from the margin, and buried my face in my hands—weeping bitterly.

The heat rapidly increased, and once again I looked up, shuddering as with a fit of the ague. There had been a second change in the cell—and now the change was obviously in the *form*. As before, it was in vain that I, at first, endeavored to appreciate or understand what was taking place. But not long was I left in doubt. The inquisitorial vengeance had been hurried by my twofold escape, and there was to be no more dallying with the King of Terrors. The room had been square. I saw that two of its iron angles were now acute—two, consequently, obtuse. The fearful difference quickly increased with a low rumbling or moaning sound. In an instant the apartment had shifted its form into that of a lozenge. But the alteration stopped not here—I neither hoped nor desired it to stop. I could have clasped the red walls to my bosom as a garment of eternal peace. "Death," I said, "any death but that of the pit!" Fool! might I have not known that *into the pit* it was the object of the burning iron to urge me? Could I resist its glow? or, if even that, could I withstand its pressure? And now, flatter and flatter grew the lozenge, with a rapidity that left me no time for contemplation. Its center, and of course, its greatest width, came just over the yawning gulf. I shrank back—but the closing walls pressed me resistlessly onward. At length for my seared and writhing body there was no longer an inch of foothold on the firm floor of the prison. I struggled no more, but the agony of my soul found vent in one loud, long, and final scream of despair. I felt that I tottered upon the brink—I averted my eyes—.

There was a discordant hum of human voices! There was a loud blast as of many trumpets! There was a harsh grating as of a thousand thunders! The fiery walls rushed back! An outstretched arm caught my own as I fell, fainting, into the abyss. It was that of General Lasalle. The French army had entered Toledo. The Inquisition was in the hands of its enemies. ■

❶ *What form does the rescue take?*

WORDS FOR EVERYDAY USE:

im • pend (im pend´) *vi.*, be about to happen
balm (bäm) *n.*, anything healing or soothing
a • gue (a´gyōō) *n.*, fever with chills
venge • ance (ven´jəns) *n.*, revenge
dal • ly (dal´ē) *vi.*, waste time
loz • enge (läz´ənj) *n.*, diamond shape
a • vert (ə vurt´) *vt.*, turn away
dis • cord • ant (dis kōrd´nt) *adj.*, disagreeing; conflicting

ANSWER TO GUIDED READING QUESTION

❶ The French army has taken over Toledo, and a general catches the prisoner as he is about to fall into the pit.

CROSS-CURRICULAR ACTIVITIES

Mathematics and Sciences. Have students demonstrate how the room was changing by drawing the shapes leading to the transformation of the cell on the board, e.g., square to rhomboidal. Have them point out the acute and obtuse angles referred to in the story.

ANSWERS TO SELECTION CHECK TEST 4.4.3

EX. Who jailed the prisoner?
Judges of the Inquisition put the prisoner in jail.

1. What danger is hidden in the darkness of the cell?
At the center of the cell is a deep pit into which the prisoner may fall.

2. Why is the prisoner afraid of the pendulum?
The pendulum is as sharp as a razor and it is descending. Eventually it would run across his chest.

3. How does the prisoner make use of the rats?
He smears his bonds with food and the rats eat through them, freeing him.

4. What is unusual about the walls of the cell?
The walls are made of metal and are movable.

5. Why are the moving walls dangerous?
The walls can force the prisoner into the pit.

VOCABULARY IN CONTEXT

- The yellow sky and strange calm should have warned the crew of the storm that impended.
- I spread a cooling balm over my sunburn.
- Is the ague ever fatal?
- The invading army took out its vengeance on innocent civilians.
- You have no time to dally finishing your breakfast.
- The kite was the shape of a lozenge.
- I always avert my eyes when movies show violent scenes.
- Neighbors called the police when they head loud, discordant voices coming from the house.

RESPONDING TO THE SELECTION

Review the three ways that the prisoner faces and escapes death before asking students to choose the most terrifying one.

ANSWERS FOR REVIEWING THE SELECTION

RECALLING

1. The reason for his imprisonment is not made clear. The prisoner remembers only the appearance of the judges and his own feelings as he is sentenced to death.

2. The cell is, at first, absolutely dark. The square cell has a perimeter of about twenty-five yards, it is made of metal, and it has a circular pit at its center.

3. He smears the bandage that binds him with food and lets the rats eat their way through the cloth, thus freeing him.

4. The French army takes over Toledo and General Lasalle catches him as he begins to fall into the pit.

INTERPRETING

Responses will vary. Possible responses are given.

5. The prisoner may have been so exhausted that he could not remember, or he could have been mistreated or drugged.

6. The torturers' intention is to have the prisoner fall into the pit and die slowly. Considering the cruelty of the torturers, it is possible that they preferred to inflict a slow, painful death upon the prisoner rather than a quick, relatively painless death.

7. He is resourceful and intelligent. He was too frightened and possibly drugged at first to think straight.

8. The prisoner despairs when the walls have pushed him to the brink of the pit. He must feel intense relief and gratitude to be saved from a hideous death.

(cont.)

Responding to the Selection

The main character in this tale escapes death three times. Of the three methods of death, which would have been most terrifying to you? Why? Answer these questions in your journal.

Reviewing the Selection

RECALLING

1. What causes the prisoner to be confined to his cell? What does he remember about the reason why he is imprisoned?
2. Describe the cell where the prisoner is kept.
3. How does the prisoner escape the descending pendulum?
4. How is the prisoner saved at the end of the story?

INTERPRETING

5. What could account for the speaker's fuzzy memory of the events that led to his imprisonment?
6. Why is there a pit in the center of the cell? Why wasn't the prisoner executed immediately?
7. What does the prisoner's plan for escape tell you about his character? Why did it take so long for him to devise his plan for escape from the swinging blade?
8. When does the prisoner scream out in despair? How does he feel when he hears the voices and feels the arm catching his arm?

SYNTHESIZING

9. What does the reader understand about why the prisoner is arrested and condemned? Why do you think the writer is ambiguous about this information?
10. Tales of terror, or horror stories, force readers to confront their deepest fears. Why do you think that stories such as this one are still popular with modern readers?

Understanding Literature (Questions for Discussion)

1. **Point of View. Point of view** is the vantage point from which a story is told. This story is written from a first-person point of view, in which the narrator uses words such as *I* and *me*. The point of view is also classified as limited, meaning that the narrator can reveal only his private, internal thoughts. How does the first-person limited point of view add to the suspense in the story?

ANSWERS FOR REVIEWING THE SELECTION (CONT.)

SYNTHESIZING

Responses will vary. Possible responses are given.

9. The reader does not know why the prisoner has been arrested. Because the reader does not know the reasons and there is a possibility that the prisoner has done nothing wrong, the torture seems even less understandable and more cruel, increasing the reader's identification with the prisoner.

10. Horror stories let people face their deepest fears in a risk-free, safe way. They let readers know that the ultimate fear can be faced and overcome.

2. **Romance.** In the nineteenth century, fictional adventures that took place in exotic locations and involved extraordinary or mysterious events and characters were called **romances.** What is the location in which this story takes place? Can the story be categorized as an adventure? Do you think that the setting and the plot are exotic enough to consider this story a romance? Why, or why not?

3. **Mood. Mood,** or **atmosphere,** is the emotion created in the reader by part or all of a literary work. How would you describe the mood of "The Pit and the Pendulum"? What details does Poe use to create the mood?

Responding in Writing

1. **Press Release.** The lifesaving event at the end of the story, the conquest of the tormentors by the French army, and the release of the prisoner would be covered as a major news story if it happened today. Write a press release describing the events leading up to the prisoner's rescue from his cell. The press release should offer facts and should avoid opinion.

2. **Storyboard.** When writers and directors imagine a play or movie, they often describe and picture the major events of the story in a **storyboard.** Decide on the major events of "The Pit and the Pendulum." Then make a storyboard with descriptions of scenes accompanied by drawings of the main character in the settings where he finds himself.

3. **Gothic Tale.** A **Gothic tale** is a story containing elements of horror, suspense, mystery, and magic. Try your hand at writing a Gothic tale. Choose characters, settings, and plot events that evoke terror or suspense. Include details that add to the dark, brooding feeling.

Language Lab

Using Context Clues. Read the Language Arts Survey, 2.138, "Using Context Clues I." Then read each of the following sentences. Write the definition of each underlined word, using context clues to deduce its meaning.

1. The prisoner searched frantically for a crevice in the masonry but could find no such crack or opening.
2. He had been remanded, or sent back, to his dungeon after the sentence was passed.
3. Pictures of monstrosities such as fiends, leering skeletons, and evil spirits covered the wall.

ANALYTIC SCALES FOR RESPONDING IN WRITING

Grading scales appear on page 234.

ANSWERS FOR UNDERSTANDING LITERATURE

►See the evaluation forms for discussion, active listening, and oral communication, *Assessment Portfolio,* 7.11–7.14.

Responses will vary. Possible responses are given.

1. Point of View. Because the story is written in first-person limited point of view, the reader is unaware of events that are going on around the character except for what that character perceives. The reader feels he or she is in the same fearful situation as that of the main character.

►**Teaching Note:** Point out specific instances in which the speaker leads the reader to incorrect conclusions. Discuss how the reader comes to see the truth of the situation along with the speaker.

2. Romance. The story takes place in a dungeon in Spain. It could be considered an adventure since unusual and exciting events are taking place. Because it is set in a time and place that are foreign to the modern reader, it can be considered a romance.

►**Teaching Note:** Make sure students understand that the nineteenth-century romance did not necessarily involve romantic love.

3. Mood. The mood created by certain details is frightening and suspenseful. Some details describe the attitude and psychological state of the speaker: the vision of candles as angels; the visions of strange palaces and familiar faces, scents of perfume, and the sounds of a strange cadence that the speaker sees, smells and hears during his swoon; and the unstrung nerves and agitation of spirit.

(cont.)

ANSWERS FOR UNDERSTANDING LITERATURE (CONT.)

Some details describe the cruel tortures he is put through and the weird setting of the story: the darkness and slimy walls of the dungeon, the plunge and echo of the rock into the abyss, the light that appears above the prisoner after he discovers the pit, and the crescent of glittering steel attached to the end of the descending pendulum.

ANSWERS FOR STUDY AND RESEARCH SKILLS

Responses will vary. Possible responses are given.

Students' notes need not be understandable to anyone but the note-taker. Urge students to rewrite the notes later in more detail if necessary to ensure comprehensibility in the future.

For More Practice

To practice informal note-taking, ask students to take notes during a television newscast. Then have students check how understandable their notes are by repeating the top news stories to a friend or family member.

►Additional practice is provided in the *Essential Skills Practice Book: Study and Research,* 4.31.

PROJECT NOTES

►See the worksheets and evaluation forms for projects, *Assessment Portfolio,* 7.20–7.23.

1. Role Playing a Trial. You may wish to show a film or video about trials before assigning this project. Remind students that the Inquisition's trials only loosely resembled American court trials.

2. Taking a Survey. Suggest that students use a computer spreadsheet for recording their results. The spreadsheet program can then produce the required graphs and charts.

4. The prisoner was horrified to see several rats traversing, or traveling across, the floor.
5. The prisoner went through a period of insensibility, and remembered nothing that happened during this time of unconsciousness.

Study and Research Skills

Informal Note-taking. Read the Language Arts Survey, 4.31, "Informal Note-taking." Then look up the Spanish Inquisition in an encyclopedia and take notes for a brief oral report on it.

PROJECTS

1. **Role Playing a Trial.** After doing research on the Inquisition, role play an Inquisition trial. Try to imagine what the inquisitors might ask and how the defendant might respond. Enact the trial from the reading of the charges through the defense and the prosecution to the eventual sentencing.

2. **Taking a Survey.** Many people enjoy tales of horror and suspense while others find them distasteful. Take a survey of various groups of people concerning their reaction to horror stories. The results of the survey will be more interesting if you categorize your interviewees by age, sex, or some other criterion. Publish the results of your survey in a graph or chart.

ANSWERS FOR LANGUAGE LAB

1. crack or opening
2. sent back
3. monsters and fearful creatures
4. traveling across
5. unconsciousness

FOR MORE PRACTICE

Problem. The angles were simply those of a few slight depressions, or niches, at odd intervals.

Answer. depressions

►Additional practice is provided in the *Essential Skills Practice Book: Language,* 2.138.

PREREADING

NOVEL

from *Moby-Dick*
"The Whiteness of the Whale"
by Herman Melville

ABOUT THE AUTHOR

Herman Melville (1819–1891) was born into a relatively wealthy family, whose fortune declined. Melville had a variety of jobs until he sailed on a whaler for the South Seas. Jumping ship in the Marquesas, he lived with a tribe of natives, was picked up by an Australian whaler, took part in a mutiny, and was imprisoned. He was twenty-five when he returned home and began writing *Typee,* a story about his South Sea adventures. Published in 1846, *Typee* was a tremendous success and was soon followed by another South Seas adventure, *Omoo.* His next two books, *Mardi* and *Pierre,* were poorly received. His reputation tarnished, Melville wrote anonymous short stories for magazines and sought political appointments. Before his death, a revival of his fame began, leaving Melville with the hope that his reputation as a writer would be reestablished. Today, that reputation rests largely on his masterwork, *Moby-Dick,* a work of genius little understood until the twentieth century.

ABOUT THE SELECTION

Although not well received at the time it was published and almost forgotten by the public at the time of Melville's death, ***Moby-Dick*** is today seen as one of the greatest American novels. It begins as a narrative about a whaling expedition and turns into a metaphorical study of the nature of good, evil, and reality. It includes detailed descriptions of the adventure and drudgery of whaling, varied and sharp characterization, and philosophical discussions on God, man, and the universe. The narrator is a sailor, Ishmael. The main character is his ship's captain, Ahab, who sees the great white whale, Moby-Dick, as a symbol of all that challenges his being and who pursues the beast with a single-minded intensity that eventually destroys his entire ship and crew, save Ishmael. In the chapter **"The Whiteness of the Whale,"** the narrator ponders the question of what makes this whale so threatening, not only to the mad Ahab but even to a fairly reasonable person like himself.

When *Moby-Dick* was published in 1851, most of Melville's audience, hoping for more of the straightforward adventure and romantic settings of his earliest books, *Typee* and *Omoo,* did not appreciate the book, and the reviews were derogatory. In the 1920s, the book received critical acclaim as a masterpiece.

GOALS/OBJECTIVES

Studying this lesson will enable students to

- appreciate a prose discussion of abstract concepts
- understand the thoughts of the narrator
- recognize allusions
- understand the purpose of elaboration
- define and identify examples of onomatopoeia
- write a descriptive paragraph, obituary, or slogan
- participate in an effective discussion as a group project

ADDITIONAL RESOURCES

READER'S GUIDE
- Selection Worksheet, 4.3

ASSESSMENT PORTFOLIO
- Selection Check Test, 4.4.5
- Selection Test, 4.4.6

ESSENTIAL SKILLS PRACTICE BOOKS
- *Language,* 2.20, 2.86
- *Speaking and Listening,* 3.6

ENRICHMENT ACTIVITIES

- Point out the information in About the Author and About the Selection concerning Melville's adventures as a young man and his use of those experiences in his writing. Encourage students to consider which modern occupations Melville might have chosen.
- Have students research the whaling industry and report on its importance to Americans at the time of Melville's novel.

SUPPORT FOR LEP STUDENTS

Have students keep a running list of all words and phrases that refer to whiteness or colorlessness. Point out that many clauses refer to little-known facts that the author used to add weight to his statements, and that they need only understand the main point he is trying to illustrate with all these details. Advise them to write a single phrase, such as "good things about the color white" or "an example of white being scary," that summarizes the point of each paragraph.

ADDITIONAL VOCABULARY

intensity—force, energy
appalled—discouraged with fear
enhance—add to, increase
elusive—difficult to understand or grasp
accessory—contributing, aiding
malicious—acting from hatred or ill will
annihilate—destroy
mariner—sailor

PREREADING NOTES

READER'S JOURNAL

Invite students to consider the possible effects of changing the colors of grass and leaves to bright orange, of wood to blue, and of sky to pink. This may help them become conscious of the effects of familiar colors.

LANGUAGE SKILLS

If the exercise is done as a group activity, have students identify the proper noun from which the proper adjective is derived.

Proper adjectives: Hanoverian, Austrian, Cæsarian, Persian, Latin, Christian, Romish, Western, Indian, American, Antarctic

► Additional practice is provided in the *Essential Skills Practice Book: Language,* 2.20.

ANSWERS TO GUIDED READING QUESTIONS

❶ Whiteness enhances beauty in many natural objects, such as marbles, japonicas, and pearls.

❷ The whiteness of the whale was its most appalling characteristic.

VOCABULARY FROM THE SELECTION

august	incantation
benignity	ineffable
consternation	irrespective
craven	palsied
elucidate	portentous
envoy	primeval
festooned	sublime
gaudiest	transcendent
gauntleted	trepidation

READER'S JOURNAL

Do you associate certain colors with different moods or feelings? For example, to some people red is an exciting color; to some, it symbolizes good luck, while to others, it stands for danger. Choose one or more colors, and explain in your journal their meanings for you.

LANGUAGE SKILLS

Read the Language Arts Survey, 2.20, "Proper Adjectives." Then find at least five proper adjectives in this excerpt.

FROM

Moby-Dick

HERMAN MELVILLE

CHAPTER XXXII

"The Whiteness of the Whale"

In what things does whiteness add to beauty? ❶

What the white whale was to Ahab, has been hinted; what, at times, he was to me, as yet remains unsaid.

Aside from those more obvious considerations touching Moby Dick, which could not but occasionally awaken in any man's soul some alarm, there was another thought, or rather vague, nameless horror concerning him, which at times by its intensity completely overpowered all the rest; and yet so mystical and well nigh ineffable was it, that I almost despair of putting it in a comprehensible form. It was the whiteness of the whale that above all things appalled me. But how can I hope to explain myself here; and yet, in some dim, random way, explain myself I must, else all these chapters might be naught.

What was the most appalling thing about the whale? ❷

Though in many natural objects, whiteness refiningly enhances beauty, as if imparting some special virtue of its own, as in marbles, japonicas,[1] and pearls; and though various nations have in some way recognized a certain royal pre-eminence in this hue, even the barbaric, grand old king of Pegu[2] placing the title "Lord of the White Elephants" above all their other magniloquent ascriptions of dominion; and the modern kings of Siam[3] unfurling the same snow-white quadruped

1. **japonicas.** Any of various trees, shrubs, or plants associated with the Far East
2. **Pegu.** City in southern Mayanmar, formerly Burma, for centuries the capital of Burma but now a shadow of its former splendor
3. **Siam.** Former name of Thailand

WORDS FOR EVERYDAY USE: **in • ef • fa • ble** (in ef´ə bəl) *adj.,* too overwhelming to be expressed in words; awesome

VOCABULARY IN CONTEXT

- Even the most practical scientist aboard the rocket found the view of Earth from space too ineffable to enter into the daily reports.

in the royal standard; and the Hanoverian flag bearing the one figure of a snow-white charger; and the great Austrian Empire, Cæsarian, heir to overlording Rome, having for the imperial color the same imperial hue; . . . and though, besides, all this, whiteness has been even made significant of gladness, for among the Romans a white stone marked a joyful day; and though in other mortal sympathies and symbolizings, this same hue is made the emblem of many touching, noble things—the innocence of brides, the benignity of age; though among the native people of America the giving of the white belt of wampum was the deepest pledge of honor; though in many climes, whiteness typifies the majesty of Justice in the ermine[4] of the Judge, and contributes to the daily state of kings and queens drawn by milk-white steeds; though even in the higher mysteries of the most august religions it has been made the symbol of the divine spotlessness and power; by the Persian fire worshippers, the white forked flame being held the holiest on the altar; and in the Greek mythologies, Great Jove himself being made incarnate in a snow-white bull; and though to the noble Iroquois, the midwinter sacrifice of the sacred White Dog was by far the holiest festival of their theology, that spotless, faithful creature being held the purest envoy they could send to the Great Spirit with the annual tidings of their own fidelity; and though directly from the Latin word for white, all Christian priests derive the name of one part of their sacred vesture, the alb or tunic, worn beneath the cassock;[5] and though among the holy pomps[6] of the Romish faith, white is specially employed in the celebration of the Passion of our Lord; though in the Vision of St. John, white robes are given to the redeemed, and the four-and-twenty elders stand clothed in white before the great white throne, and the Holy One that sitteth there white like wool; yet for all these accumulated associations, with whatever is sweet, and honorable, and sublime, there yet lurks an elusive something in the innermost idea of this hue, which strikes more of panic to the soul than that redness which affrights in blood.

This elusive quality it is, which causes the thought of whiteness, when divorced from more kindly associations, and coupled with any object terrible in itself, to heighten that terror to the furthest bounds. Witness the white bear of the poles, and the white shark of the tropics; what but their smooth, flaky whiteness makes them the transcendent horrors they are? That ghastly whiteness it is which imparts such an abhorrent mildness, even more loathsome than terrific, to the dumb gloating of their aspect. So that not the fierce-fanged tiger in his heraldic coat can so stagger courage as the white-shrouded bear or shark.

Bethink thee of the albatross,[7] whence come those clouds of spiritual wonderment and pale dread, in which that white

❶ What are some of the symbols of honor associated with the color white?

❷ What other emotion does the color white arouse? What animals impart this feeling?

4. **ermine.** Weasel that turns white in winter; has highly prized fur
5. **alb . . . cassock.** *Alb* (from Latin *alba*, "white")—white linen garment worn by priests. *Cassock*—outer garment, generally black
6. **pomps.** Religious pageants
7. **albatross.** Large white bird found chiefly in the South Seas; used as a symbol of guilt in a poem by Samuel Taylor Coleridge

WORDS FOR EVERYDAY USE:

be • nig • ni • ty (bi nig´nə tē) *n.,* kindliness
au • gust (ô gust´) *adj.,* magnificent; worthy of respect
en • voy (än´voi) *n.,* messenger; agent
sub • lime (sə blīm´) *adj.,* noble; majestic
tran • scend • ent (tran sen´dənt) *adj.,* beyond the limits of knowledge or experience

ANSWERS TO GUIDED READING QUESTIONS

❶ Symbols of honor associated with the color white include the following: a white charger on the Hanoverian flag; white as the imperial color of the Austrian Empire; the white belt of wampum as a pledge of honor among Native Americans; the white ermine of judges; the white forked flame of Persian fire worshippers; the sacrifice of the sacred White Dog by the Iroquois, to be their envoy to the Great Spirit; the white alb worn by Christian priests; and, in the Vision of St. John, the white robes given to the redeemed, those worn by the elders, and the whiteness of the Holy One (God) and his throne.

❷ White also arouses terror; white animals that support this statement are the white bear of the poles and the white shark of the tropics.

ADDITIONAL QUESTIONS AND ACTIVITIES

Have students summarize each of the first four paragraphs of the selection in a phrase or sentence to clarify the pattern of organization of the argument.

VOCABULARY IN CONTEXT

- All the children in the neighborhood call Mr. and Mrs. Smith "Grandpa" and "Grandma" because of the couple's benignity toward them.
- The tourists fell silent in awe as they entered the august chamber of the Supreme Court.
- The envoy delivered the message to the governor and waited for his reply.
- The author felt that having her work chosen for a Nobel Prize was a sublime experience that would never be equaled.
- The guru promised that he could lead his followers to a transcendent truth.

Answers to Guided Reading Questions

❶ The White Steed evoked both reverence and terror.

❷ The skin of a dead person is pale and whitish; the shroud wrapped around a dead person is also white.

Literary Technique

Simile. A **simile** is a comparison using *like* or *as*. In the description of the White Steed and his followers is the simile "the countless cohorts that endlessly streamed it over the plains, like an Ohio." Have students identify what two things are being compared and how they are alike.

What two feelings did the White Steed evoke? ❶

phantom sails in all imaginations? Not Coleridge first threw that spell; but God's great, unflattering laureate,[8] Nature.

Most famous in our Western annals and Indian traditions is that of the White Steed of the Prairies; a magnificent milk-white charger, large-eyed, small-headed, bluff-chested, and with the dignity of a thousand monarchs in his lofty, overscorning carriage. He was the elected Xerxes[9] of vast herds of wild horses, whose pastures in those days were only fenced by the Rocky Mountains and the Alleghanies. At their flaming head he westward trooped it like that chosen star which every evening leads on the hosts of light. The flashing cascade of his mane, the curving comet of his tail, invested him with housings more resplendent than gold and silver-beaters could have furnished him. A most imperial and archangelical apparition of that unfallen, western world, which to the eyes of the old trappers and hunters revived the glories of those primeval times when Adam walked majestic as a god, bluff-browed and fearless as this mighty steed. Whether marching amid his aides and marshals in the van of countless cohorts that endlessly streamed it over the plains, like an Ohio; or whether with his circumambient[10] subjects browsing all around at the horizon, the White Steed gallopingly reviewed them with warm nostrils reddening through his cool milkiness; in whatever aspect he presented himself, always to the bravest Indians he was the object of trembling reverence and awe. Nor can it be questioned from what stands on legendary record of this noble horse, that it was his spiritual whiteness chiefly, which so clothed him with divineness; and that this divineness had that in it which, though commanding worship, at the same time enforced a certain nameless terror.

But there are other instances where this whiteness loses all that accessory and strange glory which invests it in the White Steed and Albatross. . . .

Nor, in quite other aspects, does Nature in her least palpable but not the less malicious agencies, fail to enlist among her forces this crowning attribute of the terrible. From its snowy aspect, the gauntleted ghost of the Southern Seas has been denominated the White Squall. Nor, in some historic instances, has the art of human malice omitted so potent an auxiliary. How wildly it heightens the effect of that passage in Froissart,[11] when, masked in the snowy symbol of their faction, the desperate White Hoods of Ghent murder their bailiff in the market-place!

In what two ways is the color white related to death? ❷

Nor, in some things, does the common, hereditary experience of all mankind fail to bear witness to the supernaturalism of this hue. It cannot well be doubted, that the one visible quality in the aspect of the dead which most appals the gazer, is the marble pallor lingering there; as if indeed that pallor were as much like the badge of consternation in the other world, as of mortal trepidation here. And from that pallor of the dead, we borrow the expressive hue of the shroud in which we wrap them. Nor even in our superstitions do we

8. **laureate.** One to whom honor is given
9. **Xerxes.** (*circa* 519–465 BC) King of Persia
10. **circumambient.** Extending all around
11. **Froissart.** Jean Froissart (*circa* 1337–1410), French chronicler and poet

Words for Everyday Use:

pri • me • val (prī mē´ vəl) *adj.*, of the earliest times or ages

gaunt • let • ed (gônt´lit id) *adj.*, wearing a gauntlet, or glove; figuratively, combative

con • ster • na • tion (kän´stər nā´shən) *n.*, dismay; great fear

trep • i • da • tion (trep´ə dā´shən) *n.*, fearful uncertainty

Vocabulary in Context

- This huge sequoia looks old enough to be from a primeval forest.
- The knight wore armor and was helmeted and gauntleted, ready for battle.
- The player returned from his turn at bat with an expression of consternation—he had struck out!
- Although she claimed she would be cleared of all charges, the suspect waited for her trial in trepidation.
- Death comes to everyone, irrespective of wealth or position.
- Circus tents are the gaudiest enclosures I've ever seen.

fail to throw the same snowy mantle round our phantoms; all ghosts rising in a milk-white fog—Yea, while these terrors seize us, let us add, that even the king of terrors, when personified by the evangelists, rides on his pallid horse.[12]

Therefore, in his other moods, symbolize whatever grand or gracious thing he will by whiteness, no man can deny that in its profoundest idealized significance it calls up a peculiar apparition to the soul.

But though without dissent this point be fixed, how is mortal man to account for it? To analyze it, would seem impossible. Can we, then, by the citation of some of those instances wherein this thing of whiteness—though for the time either wholly or in great part stripped of all direct associations calculated to import to it aught fearful, but nevertheless, is found to exert over us the same sorcery, however modified;—can we thus hope to light upon some chance clue to conduct us to the hidden cause we seek ?

Let us try. But in a matter like this, subtlety appeals to subtlety; and without imagination no man can follow another into these halls. And though, doubtless, some at least of the imaginative impressions about to be presented may have been shared by most men, yet few perhaps were entirely conscious of them at the time, and therefore may not be able to recall them now.

Why to the man of untutored ideality, who happens to be but loosely acquainted with the peculiar character of the day, does the bare mention of Whitsuntide[13] marshal in the fancy such long, dreary, speechless processions of slow-pacing pilgrims, down-cast and hooded with newfallen snow? Or to the unread, unsophisticated Protestant of the Middle American States, why does the passing mention of a White Friar or a White Nun, evoke such an eyeless statue in the soul?

Or what is there apart from the traditions of dungeoned warriors and kings (which will not wholly account for it) that makes the White Tower of London tell so much more strongly on the imagination of an untravelled American, than those other storied structures, its neighbors—the Byward Tower, or even the Bloody? And those sublimer towers, the White Mountains of New Hampshire, whence, in peculiar moods, comes that gigantic ghostliness over the soul at the bare mention of that name, while the thought of Virginia's Blue Ridge is full of a soft, dewy, distant dreaminess? Or why, irrespective of all latitudes and longitudes, does the name of the White Sea exert such a spectralness over the fancy, while that of the Yellow Sea lulls us with mortal thoughts of long lacquered mild afternoons on the waves, followed by the gaudiest and yet sleepiest of sunsets? Or, to choose a wholly unsubstantial instance, purely addressed to the fancy, why, in reading the old fairy tales of Central Europe, does "the tall pale man" of the Hartz forests, whose changeless pallor unrustlingly glides through the green of the groves—why is this phantom

❶ *What does the color white call up?*

❷ *What natural things are noted for their whiteness? How do they differ from things named with different colors?*

12. **king . . . horse.** Death is depicted in the Bible as riding on a pale horse.
13. **Whitsuntide.** Week beginning with Whitsunday (White Sunday) on Pentecost (seventh Sunday after Easter), marked by ceremonies and processions

WORDS FOR EVERYDAY USE:

ir • re • spec • tive (ir´ri spek´tiv) *adj.*, regardless

gaud • i • est (göd´ē əst) *adj.*, brightest and showiest, but lacking good taste

ANSWERS TO GUIDED READING QUESTIONS

❶ White calls up "a peculiar apparition" to the soul.

❷ Two natural things noted for their whiteness are the White Mountains of New Hampshire and the White Sea. They seem ghostly and unnatural when compared with natural things named with such colors as blue and yellow.

CROSS-CURRICULAR ACTIVITIES

Social Studies. Have students review the selection to this point to identify place names and begin a list of them according to the continents on which they are found. As they continue reading, they should add to the list. At the end of the selection, have them determine which continents are best represented and which are poorly represented or not mentioned at all. Encourage them to come up with possible reasons for the distribution, keeping in mind both Melville's personal travels and the types of books available while he was working on his novel.

ART NOTE

Lithographs produced by **Nathaniel Currier** (1813–1888) and **James Merritt Ives** (1824–1895) provide a pictorial record of the history and daily life of the United States in the 1800s. Currier, at age fifteen an apprentice to the country's first lithographers, William S. and John B. Pendleton of Boston, opened his own shop in 1834 in New York City. He issued his first two prints in 1835, concerning events in the news. During the following years, he produced color prints of both specific events and typical moments in daily life. In 1852 Currier took on Ives as a bookkeeper; Ives's eye for technical perfection and sense of what the public wanted made him so valuable that he became Currier's partner in 1857. The firm of Currier and Ives produced thousands of different prints on a remarkable range of topics, making use of many important artists, including George Catlin. Both the quantity and quality of the Currier and Ives lithographs made the firm stand out from the hundreds of other lithographers of the time. Although many Currier and Ives prints were originally produced in volume and sold for pennies, they have become favorites with collectors and are now rare and costly.

The Whale Fishery, The Sperm Whale in a Flurry shows a dangerous moment in the business of whaling, one of the major industries of America through most of the nineteenth century.

ANSWER TO GUIDED READING QUESTION

❶ Lima appears to be a sad city because it is so white.

The Whale Fishery, The Sperm Whale in a Flurry. *Lithograph by Currier & Ives. The Granger Collection, NY*

more terrible than all the whooping imps of the Blocksburg?

Nor is it, altogether, the remembrance of her cathedral-toppling earthquakes; nor the stampedoes of her frantic seas; nor the tearlessness of arid skies that never rain; nor the sight of her wide field of leaning spires, wrenched cope-stones,[14] and crosses all adroop (like canted yards[15] of anchored fleets); and her suburban avenues of housewalls lying over upon each other, as a tossed pack of cards;—it is not these things alone which make tearless Lima, the strangest, saddest city thou can'st see. For Lima has taken the white veil; and there is a higher horror in this whiteness of her woe. Old as Pizarro,[16] this whiteness keeps her ruins for ever new; admits not the cheerful greenness of complete decay; spreads over her broken ramparts the rigid pallor of an apoplexy[17] that fixes its own distortions.

What makes Lima the saddest city you can see? ❶

I know that, to the common apprehension, this phenomenon of whiteness is not confessed to be the prime agent in exaggerating the terror of objects otherwise terrible; nor to the unimaginative mind is there aught of terror in those appearances whose awfulness to another mind almost solely consists in this one phenomenon, especially when exhibited under any form at all approaching to muteness or universality. What I mean by these two

14. **cope-stones.** Uppermost stone in a structure
15. **canted yards.** Tilted masts on a ship
16. **Pizarro.** Francisco Pizarro (*circa* 1474–1541), Spanish conqueror of Peru
17. **apoplexy.** Loss of the power to feel, think, or move

statements may perhaps be respectively elucidated by the following examples.

First: The mariner, when drawing nigh the coasts of foreign lands, if by night he hear the roar of breakers, starts to vigilance, and feels just enough of trepidation to sharpen all his faculties; but under precisely similar circumstances, let him be called from his hammock to view his ship sailing through a midnight sea of milky whiteness—as if from encircling headlands[18] shoals of combed white bears were swimming round him, then he feels a silent, superstitious dread; the shrouded phantom of the whitened waters is horrible to him as a real ghost; in vain the lead assures him he is still off soundings;[19] heart and helm they both go down; he never rests till blue water is under him again. Yet where is the mariner who will tell thee, "Sir, it was not so much the fear of striking hidden rocks, as the fear of that hideous whiteness that so stirred me?"

Second: To the native Indian of Peru, the continual sight of the snow-howdahed Andes conveys naught of dread, except, perhaps, in the mere fancying of the eternal frosted desolateness reigning at such vast altitudes, and the natural conceit of what a fearfulness it would be to lose oneself in such inhuman solitude. Much the same is it with the backwoodsman of the West, who with comparative indifference views an unbound prairie sheeted with driven snow, no shadow of tree or twig to break the fixed trance of whiteness. Not so the sailor, beholding the scenery of the Antarctic seas; where at times, by some infernal trick of legerdemain[20] in the powers of frost and air, he shivering and half shipwrecked, instead of rainbows speaking hope and solace to his misery, views what seems a boundless churchyard grinning upon him with its lean ice monuments and splintered crosses.

But thou sayest, methinks this white-lead chapter about whiteness is but a white flag hung out from a craven soul; thou surrenderest to a hypo,[21] Ishmael.

Tell me, why this strong young colt, foaled in some peaceful valley of Vermont, far removed from all beasts of prey—why is it that upon the sunniest day, if you but shake a fresh buffalo robe behind him, so that he cannot even see it, but only smells its wild animal muskiness—why will he start, snort, and with bursting eyes paw the ground in phrensies of affright? There is no remembrance in him of any gorings of wild creatures in his green northern home, so that the strange muskiness he smells cannot recall to him anything associated with the experience of former perils; for what knows he, this New England colt, of the black bisons of distant Oregon?

No; but here thou beholdest even in a dumb brute, the instinct of the knowledge of the demonism in the world. Though thousands of miles from Oregon, still when he smells that savage musk, the rending, goring bison herds are as present as to the deserted wild foal of the prairies, which this instant they may be trampling into dust.

❶ *What frightens the colt? Why?*

❷ *What is more horrible to the sailor than the dangerous rocks?*

18. **headlands.** Points of land reaching out into the water
19. **lead . . . soundings.** A weight attached to a line and tossed over the side of the ship is used to determine depth. Here the depth is still greater than the length of the sounding line.
20. **legerdemain.** Sleight of hand, deception; trickery
21. **hypo.** Morbid depression of spirits

WORDS FOR EVERYDAY USE:

e • lu • ci • date (ə lōō´ sə dāt´) *vt.,* make clear

cra • ven (krā´vən) *adj.,* very cowardly

HISTORICAL NOTE

The city of Lima, Peru, was founded in 1535 by the Spanish conquistador Francisco Pizarro. It was one of the most important of the Spanish colonial capitals, with an aristocracy enriched by gold and silver mining. The city remained a stronghold of the Spanish colonial empire until 1821. Throughout its history it has been subject to earthquakes, the most powerful of which struck in 1746. Almost every building now standing in the city was built or rebuilt after that quake.

ANSWERS TO GUIDED READING QUESTIONS

❶ Shaking a fresh buffalo robe behind the colt frightens him because the colt has an instinctive knowledge of the danger that a buffalo would present to a colt on the prairie.

❷ The sailor considers the hideous whiteness of the fog more horrible than the rocks.

CROSS-CURRICULAR ACTIVITIES

Arts and Humanities. Have students paint the city of Lima according to Melville's description and their own imagination. Students should try to capture the mood of Lima as described by Melville in their painting.

VOCABULARY IN CONTEXT

- The math students hoped that the difficult chapter in their textbook would be elucidated by the teacher's lecture.
- Our troops easily won the battle against the craven quitters on the enemy side.

Answers to Guided Reading Questions

❶ The sea is called milky, the mountains have festooned frosts, and the prairies have windrowed snows. These scenes are compared to the shaking of the buffalo robe near the frightened colt because they are as frightening to Ishmael as the robe is to the colt.

❷ The narrator asks if whiteness indicates the "heartless voids" of the universe and suggests to mankind thoughts of nothingness. He asks if a possible explanation is that, since whiteness is the absence of color at the same time as it is "the concrete of all colors," it suggests atheism.

Answers to Selection Check Test 4.4.5

EX. What effect did the whiteness of the whale have on the speaker?

The whale's whiteness appalled the speaker.

1. What is one of the good qualities that whiteness can symbolize?

Whiteness can symbolize any of these: gladness, honor, power, innocence, kindness, majesty, purity, and holiness.

2. What is most frightening about a polar bear, according to the speaker?

The polar bear's most frightening aspect is its whiteness.

3. What animal in America was said to have a unique power and majesty?

The White Steed of the Prairies had special honor in Native American traditions.

4. What color is linked with both death and ghosts?

The color white has connections with death, and it is the color of ghosts.

5. What color does light itself have?

Light itself is white.

What words are used to describe the sea, the mountains, and the prairies? To what are all of these things compared? ❶

Thus, then, the muffled rollings of a milky-sea; the bleak rustlings of the festooned frosts of mountains; the desolate shiftings of the windrowed snows of prairies; all these, to Ishmael, are as the shaking of that buffalo robe to the frightened colt!

Though neither knows where lie the nameless things of which the mystic sign gives forth such hints; yet with me, as with the colt, somewhere those things must exist. Though in many of its aspects this visible world seems formed in love, the invisible spheres were formed in fright.

But not yet have we solved the incantation of this whiteness, and learned why it appeals with such power to the soul; and more strange and far more portentous—why, as we have seen, it is at once the most meaning symbol of spiritual things, nay, the very veil of the Christian's Deity; and yet should be as it is, the intensifying agent in things the most appalling to mankind.

What question does the narrator ask about whiteness? What explanations might there be for fear or horror caused by whiteness? ❷

Is it that by its indefiniteness it shadows forth the heartless voids and immensities of the universe, and thus stabs us from behind with the thought of annihilation, when beholding the white depths of the milky way? Or is it, that as in essence whiteness is not so much a color as the visible absence of color; and at the same time the concrete of all colors; is it for these reasons that there is such a dumb blankness, full of meaning, in a wide landscape of snows—a colorless, all-color of atheism from which we shrink? And when we consider that other theory of the natural philosophers, that all other earthly hues—every stately or lovely emblazoning—the sweet tinges of sunset skies and woods; yea, and the gilded velvets of butterflies, and the butterfly cheeks of young girls; all these are but subtile deceits, not actually inherent in substances, but only laid on from without; so that all deified Nature absolutely paints like the harlot, whose allurements cover nothing but the charnel-house[22] within; and when we proceed further, and consider that the mystical cosmetic which produces every one of her hues, the great principle of light, for ever remains white or colorless in itself, and if operating without medium upon matter, would touch all objects, even tulips and roses, with its own blank tinge—pondering all this, the palsied universe lies before us a leper;[23] and like wilful travellers in Lapland,[24] who refuse to wear colored and coloring glasses upon their eyes, so the wretched infidel gazes himself blind at the monumental white shroud that wraps all the prospect around him. And of all these things Albino whale was the symbol. Wonder ye then at the fiery hunt? ■

22. **charnel-house.** Place where corpses or bones are deposited
23. **leper.** One suffering from leprosy, a disease that attacks the skin and nerves causing white scaly scabs, deformities, and loss of sensation
24. **Lapland.** Extreme northern region of Europe

Words for Everyday Use:

fes • tooned (fes tōōnd´) *part.*, adorned with curving decorations

in • can • ta • tion (in´kan tā´shən) *n.*, chanting of magical words; spell

por • ten • tous (pôr ten´təs) *adj.*, ominous; warning of evil

pal • sied (pôl´ zēd) *part.*, paralyzed

Vocabulary in Context

- The fancy hat was festooned with plumes.
- Perhaps the Puritans mistook the old woman's thoughtless mumbling for the incantation of a witch.
- Stockholders considered the unexpected change of interest rates portentous, and the stock market fell sharply.
- Is the man in that hospital bed palsied by disease or injury?

Responding to the Selection

Did the narrator convince you that there is something threatening in the whiteness of the whale? With which of his statements about white being a scary color did you agree?

Reviewing the Selection

Recalling

1. Early in the excerpt, the narrator notes many situations in which whiteness is associated with respected and honorable people, events, and ideas. List three of these situations.
2. The narrator claims that some animals automatically become more impressive and feared because of their whiteness. Name three of them.
3. What is the attitude of a sailor when approaching an unknown coast in the darkness of night? What is a sailor's attitude approaching such a coast in the whiteness of fog?
4. What does the narrator say can scare a Vermont-bred colt? Why is it so remarkable that this object has an effect on the colt?

Interpreting

5. Find the fifth sentence of the chapter, beginning with the words "Though in many natural objects." With which words does the sentence end? Summarize the main idea of the sentence in your own words.
6. According to the narrator, in what ways is whiteness associated with death?
7. Does the typical sailor admit that he fears the whiteness of fog? What point is the narrator making by mentioning this?
8. According to the narrator, how is he like the frightened colt?

Synthesizing

9. The narrator claims, "Though in many of its aspects this visible world seems formed in love, the invisible spheres were formed in fright." What does this observation have to do with whiteness?
10. Do you suppose that the complete novel *Moby-Dick* gives a more specific statement of what the whiteness of the whale represents? Give a reason for your answer.

Responding to the Selection

Students might want to conduct the role playing activity as an improvisational activity, picking up cues from each other's lines to determine the relationship between the two characters.

Answers for Reviewing the Selection

RECALLING

1. *Responses will vary.* Possible responses include the white charger on the Hanoverian flag, white as the imperial color of the Austrian Empire, the honorable white belt of wampum, and the white forked flame of Persian fire worshippers.

2. *Responses will vary.* Possible responses include the polar bear, the white shark, the albatross, and the legendary White Steed of the Prairies.

3. A sailor approaching an unknown coast at night is cautious but calm; one who approaches in fog is full of dread and fear.

4. The aromas from a buffalo robe can scare a colt, which is odd when the colt has no experience with buffalo to cause such a fear.

INTERPRETING

Responses will vary. Possible responses are given.

5. The fifth sentence ends with the words "than that redness which affrights in blood." The main idea is that although white is often associated with noble things such as royalty, joy, and innocence, there is still something frightening about the color.

6. The skin of the dead grows pale, the shroud wrapped around a dead person is white, ghosts are traditionally thought of as white, and even Death, when personified in the New Testament, rides a pale horse.

7. The typical sailor won't admit that he fears a powerless color, and he may not even be aware of the color as the cause of his fear. In the same way, the average person may not recognize or allow himself or herself to admit fear of a color which would explain why the reader resists the narrator's insistence on white being a threatening color.

(cont.)

Answers for Reviewing the Selection (cont.)

8. The narrator is like the frightened colt in that his fear doesn't come from his own experience, and yet he is confident that there is good reason for it.

SYNTHESIZING

Responses will vary. Possible responses are given.

9. White is associated with invisible things, therefore with those parts of the world that were "formed in fright."

10. Students might suspect that the rest of the novel is just as ambiguous as this excerpt; reasons will vary, but students might note that the meaning of the whiteness of the whale has only been hinted at, according to the opening sentence of the chapter.

ANSWERS FOR UNDERSTANDING LITERATURE

► See the evaluation forms for discussion, active listening, and oral communication, *Assessment Portfolio*, 7.11–7.14.

Responses will vary. Possible responses are given.

1. Allusion. Possible answers include royal titles or flags of various nations; symbolism of ancient Rome; traditional symbols, as of brides; Native American ceremonies; and religious symbolism or ceremonies of Persian fire-worshippers, ancient Greeks, the Iroquois, and Christians.

► **Teaching Note:** Direct students to the first project, Background Report.

2. Elaboration. Another example of elaboration is found in the first paragraph of page 244 in which the qualities of the White Steed are elaborated.

► **Teaching Note:** Invite students to justify their answers by identifying the idea of the chosen passage and the technique(s) used to amplify the original statement.

3. Onomatopoeia. Sounds that suggest gliding are the *l, s,* and *r* sounds. Sounds that suggest noise-making are the *p* and *b* sounds.

ANALYTIC SCALES FOR RESPONDING IN WRITING

Assign a score from 1 to 25 for each grading criterion below. (For more detailed evaluation, see the evaluation forms for writing, revising, and proofreading, *Assessment Portfolio*, 7.1–7.10.)

1. Descriptive Paragraph

- **Content/Unity.** The descriptive paragraph identifies a specific situation and provides sensory details to enable the reader to picture it.
- **Organization/Coherence.** Details are presented in a logical order such as spatial or chronological.
- **Language/Style.** The paragraph uses vivid and precise nouns, verbs, and modifiers.
- **Conventions.** The paragraph avoids errors in spelling, grammar, usage, mechanics, and manuscript form.

2. Obituary

- **Content/Unity.** Each obituary presents a selection of facts about

(cont.)

Understanding Literature (Questions for Discussion)

1. **Allusion.** An **allusion** is a rhetorical technique in which reference is made to a person, event, object, or work from history or literature. The narrator alludes to historical events, religious practices, and other practices and writings to support his arguments that white is revered but too complex to be trusted. List at least five allusions in the selection to people or events outside the novel.

2. **Elaboration. Elaboration,** or **amplification,** is a writing technique in which a subject is introduced and then expanded upon by means of repetition with slight changes, the addition of details, or similar devices. An example of this device is found in the fifth sentence of this selection. Find another example of this device in the selection.

3. **Onomatopoeia. Onomatopoeia** is the use of words or phrases that sound like the things to which they refer. Here is an example of onomatopoeia found in the selection: "why . . . does 'the tall pale man' of the Hartz forests, whose changeless pallor unrustlingly glides through the green of the groves—why is this phantom more terrible than all the whooping imps of the Blocksburg?" Which sounds suggest gliding? Which suggest "whooping" or, at least, excited noisemaking?

Responding in Writing

1. **Descriptive Paragraph.** Think of a situation that always makes your adrenaline rise and your heart beat faster, as the shaking of the buffalo robe frightened the colt. Describe the situation so as to suggest what aspects of it, harmless as they may seem, panic you.

2. **Obituary.** Write two obituaries for Herman Melville—the first presenting the attitude toward the writer that existed at the time of his death, and the second presenting the attitude that came into being in the 1920s. The selection of facts should vary between the two obituaries, reflecting the opinions of each time.

3. **Slogan.** The main ideas of many ad campaigns and political movements have been popularized by short, stirring, and easy-to-remember slogans. Examples are "Taxation without representation is tyranny," "Remember the Alamo," and "We shall overcome." Come up with a slogan that summarizes this excerpt's attitude toward whiteness.

Language Lab

Comparison of Adjectives and Adverbs. Read the Language Arts Survey, 2.86, "Comparison of Adjectives and Adverbs." Then use that information to correct the following sentences.

1. What could be more friendlier than the color green?

ANALYTIC SCALES FOR RESPONDING IN WRITING (CONT.)

the life of Herman Melville consistent with the opinion of the era.

- **Organization/Coherence.** The obituaries arrange the events in either chronological order or order of importance.
- **Language/Style.** The obituaries use vivid and precise nouns, verbs, and modifiers.
- **Conventions.** The obituaries avoid errors in spelling, grammar, usage, mechanics, and manuscript form.

3. Slogan

- **Content/Unity.** The slogan presents a single, easily understood concept.
- **Organization/Coherence.** The slogan consists of a simple sentence.
- **Language/Style.** The slogan uses vivid and precise language.
- **Conventions.** The slogan avoids errors in spelling, grammar, usage, and mechanics.

2. Of all the seasons of the year, spring is the more encouraging, and I believe strongliest that this effect is due to the arrival of green leaves.
3. Even the most rainiest of spring days is enjoyabler than a temperate winter day.
4. Nature skillfulliest uses an extraordinarily rich palette of greens to paint the grasses, trees, bushes, and other plants that appear at this most welcomest time of year.
5. Of course, I admit that green is also most unfortunate the color of many molds that grow in my refrigerator abundantlier than flowers in my garden.

Speaking and Listening Skills

Discussion. Read the Language Arts Survey, 3.6, "Discussion." Then join a small group of classmates to discuss whether any colors have inherent meanings for all people. Report your conclusions to the class.

PROJECTS

1. **Background Report.** Many of the allusions in the chapter "The Whiteness of the Whale" are obscure and confusing. Work with a group to develop a background report that clarifies as many of these allusions as possible. Each member of the group is to select one or more of the allusions and research them, producing short explanations and illustrations, where possible. Together, assemble the individual reports on a bulletin board or poster or as separate pages of a book. As the heading for each report, use the quotation from the chapter that includes the allusion.

2. **Collage.** Collect scraps of white materials having different tints and textures. Combine them in a flat or three-dimensional collage that brings out the contrasts in shade and feel.

3. **A Focused Thesaurus.** Develop a thesaurus that lists nouns and adjectives related to the concept of whiteness. Begin by identifying all the words in the excerpt from *Moby-Dick* that touch on this concept, such as *pallid, milk,* and *snowy,* and add as many as you can. Indicate how the meaning of each word is differentiated from the others. Refer to the Language Arts Survey, 4.25, "Using Thesauruses."

ANSWERS FOR LANGUAGE LAB

Responses will vary. Possible responses are given.

1. What could be friendlier than the color green?
2. Of all the seasons of the year, spring is the most encouraging, and I believe most strongly that this effect is due to the arrival of green leaves.
3. Even the rainiest of spring days is more enjoyable than a temperate winter day.
4. Nature most skillfully uses an extraordinarily rich palette of greens to paint the grasses, trees, bushes, and other plants that appear at this most welcome time of year.
5. Of course, I admit that green is also most unfortunately the color of many molds that grow in my refrigerator more abundantly than flowers in my garden.

► Additional practice is provided in the *Essential Skills Practice Book: Language,* 2.86.

SPEAKING AND LISTENING SKILLS

Students can write short essays about the meaning of colors based on their group discussions and on class conclusions.

► Additional practice is provided in the *Essential Skills Practice Book: Speaking and Listening,* 3.6.

PROJECT NOTES

► See the worksheets and evaluation forms for projects, *Assessment Portfolio,* 7.20-7.23.

1. Background Report. Before students begin this assignment, review relevant source books likely to be found in the collections of the libraries the students will use. Encourage students to use both texts and on-line

(cont.)

PROJECT NOTES (CONT.)

reference sources, and to compare the strengths of various resources in different content areas.

2. Collage. Request all class members to contribute to the collection of materials, even though only a few students will work with the scraps, in order to provide a wide variety of materials in a short time. Provide display space for the product(s) of this project.

3. A Focused Thesaurus. Students can brainstorm a list of words and then refer to thesauruses for others. Suggest that students use more than one thesaurus for research and as models for a usable format. Students might discuss the connotations of the different words they use.

ADDITIONAL RESOURCES

READER'S GUIDE
- Selection Worksheet, 4.4

ASSESSMENT PORTFOLIO
- Selection Check Test, 4.4.7
- Selection Test, 4.4.8

ESSENTIAL SKILLS PRACTICE BOOKS
- *Language,* 2.62
- *Study and Research,* 4.30

ENRICHMENT ACTIVITIES

- Discuss the meaning and importance of self-reliance. Why was self-reliance so attractive during the early years of the country?
- Have students research Emerson's life to find out which other writers and thinkers were part of Emerson's circle of friends. How did the location of their homes in New England affect the strength of their national influence?

SUPPORT FOR LEP STUDENTS

Point out that every word in this essay is carefully chosen and full of meaning. Before students begin to read, review the meanings of the words below. Encourage students to look up each unfamiliar word they encounter as they read.

COLLOQUIALISMS

live after the world's opinion—make your decisions based on the opinions of others

Out upon your guarded lips!—Do not be overly careful of what you say!

ADDITIONAL VOCABULARY

Providence—God

genius—main spirit of a place or time

betray—reveal

conspiracy—agreement to perform an evil deed

conformity—action that agrees with customs or rules

consistency—agreement between past and present thoughts and acts

PREREADING

NONFICTION

from *Self-Reliance*
by Ralph Waldo Emerson

ABOUT THE AUTHOR

Ralph Waldo Emerson (1803–1882) grew up in Boston and became the greatest American thinker of his day. At the age of fourteen, he entered Harvard, graduating with honors in 1821. Thereafter, he taught school and then studied for the ministry. In 1829, he was ordained as junior pastor of Boston's Second Church, and in the same year, he married Ellen Tucker, who died sixteen months later of tuberculosis. With literary friends from Boston, Emerson founded a magazine, *The Dial,* which became an important vehicle for the **Transcendentalist Movement,** of which Emerson was a leader. The Transcendentalist, like the English Romantics, believed in a deep spiritual connection between people and nature. Emerson also believed that by attending closely to one's innermost thoughts and feelings, one could glimpse the great spirit of the universe, what Emerson called the "Over-Soul." Such beliefs led Emerson to a radical individualism that helped to shape the American spirit. The finest expression of this individualism is, perhaps, his essay "Self-Reliance." Emerson traveled in Europe and, on returning, moved to Concord, Massachusetts and married Lydia Jackson, with whom he had four children. During their fifty years of marriage, the Emersons entertained at home many of the leading intellectuals of the day, including their neighbors the Alcotts and Henry David Thoreau. Today, Emerson's house in Concord remains a place of literary pilgrimage in America. Emerson himself has become a symbol of American optimism and independent thinking.

ABOUT THE SELECTION

Self-Reliance was first published in 1841 as part of the book *Essays.* It is a combination of different ideas from a journal in which Emerson recorded his thoughts for years. Emerson used his journal as a source of ideas for his frequent lectures. He would test and perfect his style and wording before audiences, noting their reactions. He would then condense his ideas into essay form, as he does here in *Self-Reliance,* for a wider audience to read and reread.

GOALS/OBJECTIVES

Studying this lesson will enable students to

- understand the importance and benefits of self-reliance
- describe Ralph Waldo Emerson's contribution to American literature
- define *essay* and identify the theme of an essay
- define and identify an *aphorism*
- research and write a biography
- apply the skills of paraphrasing and summarizing

READER'S JOURNAL

Have you ever been in a situation where you had to choose between what you thought was the right course of action and the course that others thought you should take? What was your final decision? Did you think for yourself or were you swayed by the opinions of others? Were you satisfied with the outcome? Freewrite in your journal about such an incident.

READING SKILLS

Read the Language Arts Survey, 4.16, "Reading Rate: Slow and Careful Reading." As you read, take a few moments to think about the ideas in Emerson's essay and how they apply to situations in your own life.

FROM

Self-Reliance

RALPH WALDO EMERSON

There is a time in every man's education when he arrives at the conviction that envy is ignorance; that imitation is suicide; that he must take himself for better, for worse, as his portion; that though the wide universe is full of good, no kernel of nourishing corn can come to him but through his toil bestowed on that plot of ground which is given to him to till.

♦ ♦ ♦

Trust thyself: every heart vibrates to that iron string. Accept the place the divine Providence has found for you; the society of your contemporaries, the connexion of events. Great men have always done so and confided themselves childlike to the genius of their age, betraying their perception that the Eternal was stirring at their heart, working through their hands, predominating in all their being.

♦ ♦ ♦

Society everywhere is in conspiracy against the manhood of every one of its members. Society is a joint-stock company[1] in which the members agree for the better securing of his bread to each shareholder, to surrender the liberty and culture of the eater. The virtue in most

1. **joint-stock company.** Company in which joint owners hold the capital

❶ *Whom should you trust? What should you accept?*

WORDS FOR EVERYDAY USE: **pre • dom • i • nate** (prē dŏm´ ə nāt´) *vi.,* have authority or influence over others

PREREADING NOTES

READER'S JOURNAL

Suggest that students explain the situation and then outline the various options and their potential consequences. Remind them to decide whether their eventual course of action was determined solely by others' opinions.

READING SKILLS

You might also refer students to the Lanaguage Arts Survey, 4.18, "Reading Actively." Ask students to use one or more of the techniques described.

ANSWER TO GUIDED READING QUESTION

❶ Trust yourself. Accept the place the divine Providence has found for you.

VOCABULARY FROM THE SELECTION

arduous	predominate
aversion	squalid

CROSS-CURRICULAR ACTIVITIES

Arts and Humanities. Have students research the American painters who were producing works during the 1830s and 1840s. Did these artists show the influence of the Transcendentalists? If so, explain how.

VOCABULARY IN CONTEXT

- The sound of the carousel's pipe organ predominated over all the other sounds at the amusement park.

HISTORICAL NOTE

Beginning in the 1830s, the lyceum system began to flourish in New England and the Middle Atlantic states. To educate and entertain their citizens, villages and towns set up lecture series to be held during the winter months. Speakers were paid a small fee for their presentations. Emerson earned a modest income by participating in these lecture series.

Answers to Guided Reading Questions

❶ The speaker points out that many of the people who accomplished the most throughout history were once misunderstood.

❷ It is easy to live paying attention to the world's opinion. You should follow your own inner opinion.

Answers to Selection Check Test 4.4.7

EX. What does Emerson say imitation is?
Imitation is suicide.

1. What is the virtue requested most often in society?
The virtue most requested is conformity.

2. How does Emerson describe "a foolish consistency"?
A foolish consistency is the hobgoblin of little minds.

3. Name three of the people Emerson identifies as misunderstood by society.
Correct answers include three of the following: Pythagoras, Socrates, Jesus, Luther, Copernicus, Galileo, and Newton.

4. Of what two things does Emerson hope we have heard the last?
Emerson hopes we have heard the last of conformity and consistency.

5. What does Emerson say is "the lengthened shadow of one man"?
An institution is the lengthened shadow of one man.

Literary Technique

Syntax is the pattern of arrangement of words in a statement. Analyze Emerson's syntax in this essay. Have students decide whether Emerson uses a simple, conventional syntax or one that is surprising and unusual. Then discuss why that syntax is appropriate for his message.

Answer. Emerson's syntax is usually a straightforward subject-predicate arrangement. This syntax is most conducive to communicating a clear message.

request is conformity. Self-reliance is its aversion. It loves not realities and creators, but names and customs.

Whoso would be a man must be a nonconformist. He who would gather immortal palms must not be hindered by the name of goodness, but must explore if it be goodness. Nothing is at last sacred but the integrity of our own mind.

What evidence does the speaker offer to suggest that being misunderstood is not bad? ❶

◆ ◆ ◆

What I must do, is all that concerns me, not what the people think. This rule, equally arduous in actual and in intellectual life, may serve for the whole distinction between greatness and meanness. It is the harder, because you will always find those who think they know what is your duty better than you know it. It is easy in the world to live after the world's opinion; it is easy in solitude to live after our own; but the great man is he who in the midst of the crowd keeps with perfect sweetness the independence of solitude.

By what opinion is it easy to live? Whose opinion should you follow? ❷

◆ ◆ ◆

A foolish consistency is the hobgoblin of little minds, adored by little statesmen and philosophers and divines. With consistency a great soul has simply nothing to do. He may as well concern himself with his shadow on the wall. Out upon your guarded lips! Sew them up with packthread, do. Else, if you would be a man, speak what you think today in words as hard as cannon balls, and tomorrow speak what tomorrow thinks in hard words again, though it contradict every thing you said today. Ah, then, exclaim the aged ladies, you shall be sure to be misunderstood. Misunderstood! It is a right fool's word. Is it so bad then to be misunderstood? Pythagoras was misunderstood, and Socrates, and Jesus, and Luther, and Copernicus, and Galileo, and Newton, and every pure and wise spirit that ever took flesh. To be great is to be misunderstood.

◆ ◆ ◆

I hope in these days we have heard the last of conformity and consistency. Let the words be gazetted and ridiculous henceforward.[2] Instead of the gong for dinner, let us hear a whistle from the Spartan fife.[3] Let us bow and apologize never more. A great man is coming to eat at my house. I do not wish to please him: I wish that he should wish to please me. I will stand here for humanity, and though I would make it kind, I would made it true. Let us affront and reprimand the smooth mediocrity and squalid contentment of the times, and hurl in the face of custom, and trade, and office, the fact which is the upshot of all history, that there is a great responsible Thinker and Actor moving wherever moves a man; that a true man belongs to no other time or place, but is the center of things. Where he is, there is nature. . . . Every true man is a cause, a country, and an age; requires infinite spaces and numbers and time fully to accomplish his thought;—and posterity seem to follow his steps as a procession. A

2. **gazetted and ridiculous henceforward.** Labeled and not used from now on

3. **gong . . . fife.** The gong stands for ease and leisure, and the fife represents disciplined, alert life.

Words for Everyday Use:
a • ver • sion (ə vur´zhən) *n.,* definite dislike
ar • du • ous (är´jōō əs) *adj.,* difficult
squal • id (skwäl´id) *adj.,* wretched, miserable

Vocabulary in Context

- Many people feel an aversion to spiders.
- The arduous journey across the mountains took several weeks.
- Children were dying of disease and starvation in the squalid temporary settlement.

man Cæsar is born, and for ages after, we have a Roman Empire. Christ is born, and millions of minds so grow and cleave[4] to his genius, that he is confounded with virtue and the possible of man. An institution is the lengthened shadow of one man; as, the Reformation, of Luther; Quakerism, of Fox; Methodism, of Wesley; Abolition, of Clarkson.[5] Scipio,[6] Milton called, "the height of Rome;" and all history resolves itself very easily into the biography of a few stout and earnest persons. ■

4. **cleave.** Cling; adhere
5. **Reformation . . . Clarkson.** Martin Luther (1483–1546), founder of the Reformation; George Fox (1624–1691), founder of Quakerism; John Wesley (1703–1791), founder of Methodism; and Thomas Clarkson (1760–1846), abolitionist
6. **Scipio.** (237-183 BC) Roman conqueror of Carthage, a city-state of ancient Africa

Responding to the Selection

Choose a quote from *Self-Reliance* that you agree with strongly. Why did you choose that one? What about it makes sense to you? Why is it important to remember that idea? Discuss with your classmates the quote you chose and your response to it.

Reviewing the Selection

Recalling

1. According to Emerson, what does each person come to realize at a certain point in education?
2. What is the virtue that society asks of each person? Does Emerson believe that people should fulfill that request? If not, what should people strive for instead?
3. Emerson says that it is easy to live your life doing what other people think is appropriate and it is also easy to act on your own beliefs when you are alone. What type of behavior does he say is difficult but essential for greatness?
4. Name some of the people Emerson says were misunderstood in their time. What qualities do these people have in common?

Interpreting

5. Why does Emerson say that imitation is suicide? What is the alternative to imitation that Emerson recommends?
6. Why does Emerson advocate nonconformity? What does he mean by nonconformity?
7. What does Emerson mean by the phrase "the independence of solitude"? Why is it something for which to strive?
8. Why might great people sometimes be inconsistent? Why does Emerson feel that consistency is unimportant?

Responding to the Selection

Have students work in small groups to share their quotes and the reasons why they chose them.

Answers for Reviewing the Selection

RECALLING

1. Each person eventually comes to realize that envy is ignorance and that imitation is suicide.
2. Society asks for conformity from its members. Emerson advocates nonconformity instead.
3. Emerson says that great people are those who keep independent attitudes even though they live and work with other people. They don't let other people dictate their actions.
4. Pythagoras, Socrates, Jesus, Luther, Copernicus, Galileo, and Newton were all great thinkers who acted on their beliefs and left a lasting mark on the world. None of them allowed the opinions of others to keep them from doing what they thought was right.

INTERPRETING

Responses will vary. Possible responses are given.

5. Constant imitation can mean that the real person eventually disappears. When you never think and act for yourself, you no longer know what you stand for. Emerson recommends that people accept and trust themselves.
6. Emerson advocates nonconformity, meaning deciding for oneself what the right course of action or thought is and then following the voice within, because he believes that it is the only way to live a life that is true and real.
7. The independence of solitude is the type of freethinking that one is forced to do when there is no one else to ask for advice. He believes that the conclusions you come to by yourself are most likely to be correct.

(cont.)

Answers for Reviewing the Selection (cont.)

8. Great people are not afraid to change their minds because they are always open to new ideas. Being consistent can mean closing your mind and refusing to rethink decisions that have already been made; that can lead to maintaining ideas that are incorrect.

SYNTHESIZING

Responses will vary. Possible responses are given.

9. When you rely on yourself, your life makes sense to you; you can justify your actions because you act upon what you believe. Your life has integrity.
10. Nonconformists can change society because they refuse to fit in. Society must either get rid of them or adapt to them, and often adapting to them is easier to do.

Answers for Understanding Literature

► See the evaluation forms for discussion, active listening, and oral communication, *Assessment Portfolio,* 7.11-7.14.

Responses will vary. Possible responses are given.

1. Essay and Theme. People must work hard and think and act for themselves if they ever hope to be great. Individuals must learn to rely on their own good sense and integrity.

► **Teaching Note:** Several themes are possible for this selection. Make sure that students can support their themes with evidence from the essay.

2. Aphorism. Chosen quotations should be fairly short and easy to understand and remember. The following are examples:

Imitation is suicide.
Trust thyself.
Nothing is at last sacred but the integrity of our own mind.
A foolish consistency is the hobgoblin of little minds.
To be great is to be misunderstood.

Reasons for choosing the quotes could refer to their truth and applicability to many kinds of people.

3. Metaphor. Society and a company are similar because people belong to both for their own welfare. Like those who give up money in a company in return for economic opportunity, people are willing to surrender some of their liberty in return for the security that society can offer.

Analytic Scales for Responding in Writing

Assign a score from 1 to 25 for each grading criterion below. (For more detailed evaluation, see the evaluation forms for writing, revising, and proofreading, *Assessment Portfolio,* 7.1–7.10.)

1. Biography

- **Content/Unity.** The biography presents a description of the major events in the life of the subject.

(cont.)

SYNTHESIZING

9. What are some of the benefits of relying on yourself rather than upon others for your values and your principles?

10. In your opinion, if society values conformity over individualism, why do nonconformists seem to have the greatest impact on society? Why can nonconformists change society so radically, as Cæsar, Jesus, and Martin Luther did?

Understanding Literature (Questions for Discussion)

1. **Essay and Theme.** An **essay** is a brief work of prose nonfiction. A good essay develops a single idea. A **theme** is a central idea in a literary work. Identify at least one theme that runs through *Self-Reliance.*

2. **Aphorism.** An **aphorism** is a short saying or pointed statement. An aphorism that gains currency and is passed from generation to generation is called a proverb or adage. Select two quotations from Emerson that could be considered to be aphorisms and that you believe have the potential of becoming proverbs. Explain why you chose them and why you think they will speak to many generations.

3. **Metaphor.** A **metaphor** is a figure of speech in which one thing is spoken or written about as if it were another. In the metaphor "Society is a joint-stock company," how are society and a company similar?

Responding in Writing

1. **Biography.** A **biography** is the story of a person's life, told by someone other than that person. Read about the life of one of the people that Emerson mentions in his essay: Scipio, Pythagoras, Socrates, Jesus, Luther, Copernicus, Galileo, Newton, Cæsar, Fox, Wesley, Clarkson. Write a brief biography about that person, including the most memorable events in his life.

2. **Advice Column.** Imagine that Emerson were the writer of an advice column. What kinds of questions might he be asked? What might his advice be? Compose an appropriate question to pose to Emerson and then write an answer in the style of Emerson.

3. **Billboard Ad.** Emerson often gave lectures to groups to supplement his income. Create a billboard advertising an upcoming lecture. Include what his topics would be. Give the potential audience good reasons for paying to see and hear him.

Analytic Scales for Responding in Writing (cont.)

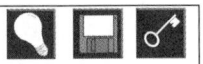

- **Organization/Coherence.** The biography is organized in chronological order or other logical order.
- **Language/Style.** The biography uses vivid and precise nouns, verbs, and modifiers.
- **Conventions.** The biography avoids errors in spelling, grammar, usage, mechanics, and manuscript form.

2. Advice Column

- **Content/Unity.** The advice column presents questions and answers about an appropriate topic.
- **Organization/Coherence.** Questions are followed by answers or advice.
- **Language/Style.** The column uses vivid and precise nouns, verbs, and modifiers.
- **Conventions.** The advice column avoids errors in

(cont.)

Language Lab

Correcting Run-ons. Read the Language Arts Survey, 2.62, "Correcting Run-ons." Then read each of the following sentences. If it is a run-on, rewrite it correctly.

1. Emerson trained to be a minister for years when he began his ministry he found that it had lost its meaning.
2. After visiting Europe, Emerson's spirits were revived, and he was inspired to write his first book.
3. Emerson lectured on many topics he always included a discussion of the moral principles that underlay his thinking.
4. Believing that slavery was an abomination, Emerson delivered lectures against it even when he was emotionally involved with his subject he kept his dignity.
5. Emerson's optimism is obvious in most of his works he believed that people have within themselves everything they need to know about the meaning of their own existence.

Study and Research Skills

Paraphrasing and Summarizing. Read the Language Arts Survey, 4.30, "Paraphrasing and Summarizing." Then choose two of the passages from *Self-Reliance* and rewrite them in your own words.

PROJECTS

1. **Advice Booklet.** Everyone has been given advice from his or her parents, relatives, and friends while growing up. Have everyone in your class ask friends and family for advice or rules by which to live that he or she was given as a child. Assemble and organize all the advice in a booklet, perhaps even including illustrations.

2. **Proverb Charades.** Write proverbs on slips of paper, one to a slip. You may wish to include aphorisms from writers such as Emerson, Henry David Thoreau, or Benjamin Franklin. Divide your class into two teams and have team members take turns selecting proverbs and pantomiming them for the rest of the team. See how long it takes each team to guess the proverb that is written on the sheet.

ANALYTIC SCALES FOR RESPONDING IN WRITING (CONT.)

spelling, grammar, usage, mechanics, and manuscript form.

3. Billboard Ad

- **Content/Unity.** The billboard ad presents pertinent facts about an upcoming lecture and attempts to convince readers to attend.
- **Organization/Coherence.** The billboard ad communicates a single, forceful message that can be grasped quickly and easily.
- **Language/Style.** The billboard ad uses vivid and connotative, nouns, verbs, and modifiers.
- **Conventions.** The billboard avoids errors in spelling, grammar, usage, mechanics, and manuscript form.

ANSWERS FOR LANGUAGE LAB

Responses may vary. Possible responses are given.

1. Emerson trained to be a minister for years, but when he began his ministry, he found that it had lost its meaning.
2. Correct
3. Emerson lectured on many topics, and he always included a discussion of the moral principles that underlay his thinking.
4. Believing that slavery was an abomination, Emerson delivered lectures against it. Even when he was emotionally involved with his subject he kept his dignity.
5. Emerson's optimism is obvious in most of his works. He believed that people have within themselves everything they need to know about the meaning of their own existence.

► Additional practice is provided in the *Essential Skills Practice Book: Language,* 2.62.

PROJECT NOTES

1. Advice Booklet. Students may want to identify the source of the advice, for example, mother, brother, or friend, and organize the booklet by the sources. Advice might also be arranged by topic.

2. Proverb Charades. Have students work in small groups to concentrate on one of the writers mentioned. Each group could then submit several proverbs or adages by their author for the others to act out.

ANSWERS FOR STUDY AND RESEARCH SKILLS

Paraphrases should indicate comprehension of the selections chosen.

►Additional practice is provided in the *Essential Skills Practice Book: Study and Research,* 4.30.

ADDITIONAL RESOURCES

READER'S GUIDE
- Selection Worksheet, 4.5

ASSESSMENT PORTFOLIO
- Selection Check Test, 4.4.9
- Selection Test, 4.4.10

ESSENTIAL SKILLS PRACTICE BOOKS
- *Language,* 2.43–2.45, 2.58
- *Study and Research,* 4.1

ENRICHMENT ACTIVITIES

- After students have read the selection, have them discuss whether a student with Thoreau's attitudes would get along well in their school with either administration or students, providing reasons for their opinions.

- Invite students to select either the passage on page 263 about the importance of morning and taking a conscious role in affecting the quality of one's life or the passage on page 264 about the need for simplification and present it as a persuasive speech.

SUPPORT FOR LEP STUDENTS

Alert students that the various sections of this selection are not closely connected and that they should expect new topics to be introduced at each break indicated by bullets. Explain that some passages are description, while others compare the author's experiences with events in ancient literature, and still others are primarily discussions of Thoreau's ideas about correct behavior.

IDIOMS

apple of one's eye—one's favorite

ADDITIONAL VOCABULARY

anticipate—expect
contemplation—serious thought
conformity—sameness
perception–understanding

PREREADING

NONFICTION

from *Walden*
by Henry David Thoreau

ABOUT THE AUTHOR

Henry David Thoreau (1817–1862) lived in Concord, Massachusetts, most of his life. He won his place in American literature by, as he put it, traveling a good deal in Concord. He made numerous trips to Maine, Cape Cod, and New Hampshire, and also traveled to Quebec, Canada, and Minnesota in an unsuccessful attempt to strengthen his tubercular lungs. Thoreau never married. He read widely and wrote constantly in his journals, using them as sources for lectures, essays, and his books *A Week on the Concord and Merrimack Rivers* (1849) and *Walden* (1854). His neighbors knew him as an educated man without an occupation. He worked as a school teacher, a handyman at Ralph Waldo Emerson's house, and a tutor. Thoreau lived for two years in a cabin he built on Emerson's property at Walden Pond. During that time, he also surveyed property, wrote magazine articles, and worked in his father's pencil factory. Sections of his books *The Maine Woods* and *Cape Cod* were published after his death. His most popular books during his lifetime were *Slavery in Massachusetts* and *A Plea for Captain John Brown.* A naturalist and social philosopher, he was forty-four when he died at his mother's house in Concord.

ABOUT THE SELECTION

One of the two books that Thoreau published during his lifetime, ***Walden*** is drawn from the journals he kept before, during, and after his stay on Emerson's property at Walden Pond from July 4, 1845, to September 6, 1847. His first book, *A Week on the Concord and Merrimack Rivers,* was published in 1849 but did not sell well. The unpopularity of his first book caused Thoreau to hold back his *Walden* manuscript for five years. During that time he revised and reworked the text numerous times, enriching and perfecting the work. The book firmly established his reputation as a writer as well an an outspoken individualist.

GOALS/OBJECTIVES

Studying this lesson will enable students to

- appreciate an extended essay
- understand the importance of Henry David Thoreau in forming the social conscience of modern society
- discuss the advantages of nonconformity
- identify allusions to Greek mythology
- interpret aphorisms
- recognize the author's tone in nonfiction writing
- write a real estate ad, a blues song, and an epitaph
- apply a problem-solving strategy

READER'S JOURNAL

What do you, personally, need in order to be happy? How could you test your answer? Think about these questions for several minutes and write your responses in your journal.

LANGUAGE SKILLS

Read the Language Arts Survey, 2.43–2.45, "Compound Sentences," "Complex Sentences," and "Compound-Complex Sentences." Then find two or more examples of each kind of sentence in this selection.

FROM

Walden

HENRY DAVID THOREAU

FROM "ECONOMY"

The mass of men lead lives of quiet desperation. What is called resignation is confirmed desperation. From the desperate city you go into the desperate country, and have to console yourself with the bravery of minks and muskrats. A stereotyped but unconscious despair is concealed even under what are called the games and amusements of mankind. There is no play in them, for this comes after work. But it is a characteristic of wisdom not to do desperate things.

When we consider what, to use the words of the catechism, is the chief end of man,[1] and what are the true necessaries and means of life, it appears as if men had deliberately chosen the common mode of living because they preferred it to any other. Yet they honestly think there is no choice left. But alert and healthy natures remember that the sun rose clear. It is never too late to give up our prejudices. No way of thinking or doing, however ancient, can be trusted without proof. What every body echoes or in silence passes by as true today may turn out to be falsehood tomorrow, mere smoke of opinion, which some had trusted for a cloud that would sprinkle fertilizing rain on their fields. What old people say you cannot do you try and find that you can. Old deeds for old people, and new deeds for new. Old people did not know enough once, perchance, to fetch fresh fuel to keep the fire a-going; new people put a little dry wood under a pot, and are whirled

1. **When . . . man.** Refers to a line from the shorter Catechism in the *New England Primer*, "What is the chief end of man? Man's chief end is to glorify God and enjoy him forever."

❶ *What kind of lives do most people lead? What does Thoreau call resignation?*

❷ *What happens to things people believe to be true?*

WORDS FOR EVERYDAY USE: **res • ig • na • tion** (rez´ig nā´shən) *n.*, submission, patient acceptance

PREREADING NOTES

READER'S JOURNAL

Students should consider both material and psychological needs. Ask students to consider what life would be like without some of the things they think they need.

LANGUAGE SKILLS

Students should be able to identify the subject and predicate of each clause, and point out conjunctions or punctuation linking clauses.

► Additional practice is provided in the *Essential Skills Practice Book: Language*, 2.43–2.45.

ANSWERS TO GUIDED READING QUESTIONS

❶ Most people lead lives of quiet desperation. Thoreau says resignation is confirmed desperation.

❷ What everybody accepts as true today may turn out to be falsehood tomorrow.

VOCABULARY FROM THE SELECTION

aspiration	perennial
cessation	posterity
earnest	resignation
encumbrance	saturated
endeavor	superfluous
ethereal	undulation
fluctuate	unwieldy
laxly	volatile
paltry	

VOCABULARY IN CONTEXT

- The farmers had to accept the drought with resignation, for they could not change the weather.

ADDITIONAL QUESTIONS AND ACTIVITIES

Have students identify the invention to which Thoreau refers in the passage "new people put a little dry wood under a pot, and are whirled round the globe with the speed of birds" (the steam engine-powered railway system). Encourage them to compare transportation, technology, and popular attitudes of Thoreau's era to ours.

Answers to Guided Reading Questions

❶ Thoreau does not believe in the wisdom of old age because old people have not gained as much as they have lost. He questions whether anyone learns anything valuable by living.

❷ Thoreau compares humans, who make little effort to leave uncomfortable conditions, to the striped snake he saw that had not completely warmed up after going into a "torpid state" to survive the cold of winter.

Does Thoreau believe in the wisdom of old age? Why, or why not? ❶

round the globe with the speed of birds, in a way to kill old people, as the phrase is. Age is no better, hardly so well, qualified for an instructor as youth, for it has not profited so much as it has lost. One may almost doubt if the wisest man has learned any thing of absolute value by living. Practically, the old have no very important advice to give the young, their own experience has been so partial, and their lives have been such miserable failures, for private reasons, as they must believe; and it may be that they have some faith left which belies that experience, and they are only less young than they were. I have lived some thirty years on this planet and I have yet to hear the first syllable of valuable or even earnest advice from my seniors. They have told me nothing, and probably cannot tell me any thing, to the purpose. Here is life, an experiment to a great extent untried by me; but it does not avail me that they have tried it. If I have any experience which I think valuable, I am sure to reflect that this my Mentors[2] said nothing about.

◆ ◆ ◆

To what does Thoreau compare the condition of humans? ❷

Near the end of March, 1845, I borrowed an axe and went down to the woods by Walden Pond, nearest to where I intended to build my house, and began to cut down some tall arrowy white pines, still in their youth, for timber. It is difficult to begin without borrowing, but perhaps it is the most generous course thus to permit your fellow-men to have an interest in your enterprise. The owner of the axe, as he released his hold on it, said that it was the apple of his eye; but I returned it sharper than I received it. It was a pleasant hillside where I worked, covered with pine woods, through which I looked out on the pond, and a small open field in the woods where pines and hickories were springing up. The ice in the pond was not yet dissolved, though there were some open spaces, and it was all dark colored and saturated with water. There were some slight flurries of snow during the days that I worked there, but for the most part when I came out on to the railroad, on my way home, its yellow sand heap stretched away gleaming in the hazy atmosphere, and the rails shone in the spring sun, and I heard the lark and pewee and other birds already come to commence another year with us. They were pleasant spring days, in which the winter of man's discontent was thawing as well as the earth, and the life that had lain torpid began to stretch itself. One day, when my axe had come off and I had cut a green hickory for a wedge, driving it with a stone and had placed the whole to soak in a pond hole in order to swell the wood, I saw a striped snake run into the water, and he lay on the bottom, apparently without inconvenience, as long as I staid there, or more than a quarter of an hour; perhaps because he had not yet fairly come out of the torpid state. It appeared to me that for a like reason men remain in their present low and primitive condition; but if they should feel the influence of the spring of springs arousing them, they would of necessity rise to a higher and

2. **Mentors.** Wise advisors; from Mentor, the friend of Odysseus in Homer's *Odyssey* who educated his son

Words for Everyday Use:
ear • nest (ŭr´nist) *adj.,* serious; sincere
sat • u • rat • ed (sach´ə rāt´əd) *adj.,* thoroughly soaked

Vocabulary in Context

- If you are earnest about wanting to get a job, you must try every means of finding out what jobs are available.
- When the sponge is saturated, it weighs about twice as much as it does when it is dry.
- Many listeners feel that a harp sounds ethereal, and angels are often shown playing small harps.
- People who use glasses only for reading have the perennial problem of recalling where they last left them.

more ethereal life. I had previously seen the snakes in frosty mornings in my path with portions of their bodies still numb and inflexible, waiting for the sun to thaw them. On the 1st of April it rained and melted the ice, and in the early part of the day, which was very foggy, I heard a stray goose groping about over the pond and cackling as if lost, or like the spirit of the fog.

So I went on for some days cutting and hewing timber, and also studs and rafters, all with my narrow axe, not having many communicable or scholarlike thoughts, singing to myself,—

> Men say they know many things;
> But lo! they have taken wings,—
> The arts and sciences
> And a thousand appliances
> The wind that blows
> Is all that any body knows.

I hewed the main timbers six inches square, most of the studs on two sides only, and the rafters and floor timbers on one side, leaving the rest of the bark on, so that they were just as straight and much stronger than sawed ones. Each stick was carefully mortised or tenoned[3] by its stump, for I had borrowed other tools by this time. My days in the woods were not very long ones, yet I usually carried my dinner of bread and butter, and read the newspaper in which it was wrapped, at noon, sitting amid the green pine boughs which I had cut off, and to my bread was imparted some of their fragrance, for my hands were covered with a thick coat of pitch. Before I had done I was more the friend than the foe of the pine tree, though I had cut down some of them, having become better acquainted with it. Sometimes a rambler in the wood was attracted by the sound of my axe, and we chatted pleasantly over the chips which I had made.

By the middle of April, for I made no haste in my work, but rather made the most of it, my house was framed and ready for the raising. I had already bought the shanty of James Collins, an Irishman who worked on the Fitchburg Railroad, for boards. James Collins' shanty was considered an uncommonly fine one. When I called to see it he was not at home. I walked about the outside, at first unobserved from within, the window was so deep and high. It was of small dimensions, with a peaked cottage roof, and not much else to be seen, the dirt being raised five feet all around as if it were a compost heap. The roof was the soundest part, though a good deal warped and made brittle by the sun. Door-sill there was none, but a perennial passage for the hens under the door board. Mrs. C. came to the door and asked me to view it from the inside. The hens were driven in by my approach. It was dark, and had a dirt floor for the most part, dank, clammy, and aguish, only here a board and there a board which would not bear removal. She lighted a lamp to show me the inside of the roof and the walls, and also that the board floor extended under the bed, warning me not to step into the cellar, a sort of dust hole two feet deep. In her own words, they

❶ *What is the shanty like?*

3. **mortised or tenoned.** Joined or fastened

WORDS FOR EVERYDAY USE:

e • the • re • al (ē thir´ē əl) *adj.,* heavenly

per • en • ni • al (pər en´ē əl) *adj.,* throughout the year; perpetual

ANSWER TO GUIDED READING QUESTION

❶ The shanty is small, with a floor mainly of dirt but with a few boards that can't be moved. The peaked roof is the soundest part but is warped. There is a single window, no door-sill, and just a door board.

CROSS-CURRICULAR ACTIVITIES

Arts and Humanities. Have students draw or paint one of the scenes described by Thoreau on these pages—the site of his cabin as he started construction, his path homeward, or the shanty of Mr. and Mrs. Collins.

ADDITIONAL QUESTIONS AND ACTIVITIES

Challenge students to name a currently popular song, movie, poem, story, television program, or other element of pop culture with which Thoreau would agree, or which he might appreciate. Encourage discussion of how Thoreau would react to modern life. Some specific topics to discuss might be numerous newscasts, supermarkets, the "information superhighway," and leisure activities such as video games.

Answers to Guided Reading Questions

❶ An Irish neighbor named Seeley watches Thoreau. Thoreau feels that having an audience raises his activity to a memorable occasion, like the removal of household gods by the mythological hero Aeneas.

❷ The cellar of a house is important because it is useful as a storage area, it lasts even longer than the house, and it is like a burrow into the earth to which the house provides a porch.

Who watches Thoreau? What effect does the spectator have on the occasion? ❶

were "good boards overhead, good boards all around, and a good window,"—of two whole squares originally, only the cat had passed out that way lately. There was a stove, a bed, and a place to sit, an infant in the house where it was born, a silk parasol, gilt-framed looking-glass, and a patent new coffee mill nailed to an oak sapling, all told. The bargain was soon concluded, for James had in the mean while returned. I to pay four dollars and twenty-five cents tonight, he to vacate at five tomorrow morning, selling to nobody else meanwhile: I to take possession at six. It were well, he said, to be there early, and anticipate certain indistinct but wholly unjust claims on the score of ground rent and fuel. This he assured me was the only encumbrance. At six I passed him and his family on the road. One large bundle held their all,— bed, coffee-mill, looking-glass, hens, all but the cat, she took to the woods and became a wild cat, and, as I learned afterward, trod in a trap set for woodchucks, and so became a dead cat at last.

Why is the cellar of a house so important? ❷

I took down this dwelling the same morning, drawing the nails, and removed it to the pond side by small cartloads, spreading the boards on the grass there to bleach and warp back again in the sun. One early thrush gave me a note or two as I drove along the woodland path. I was informed treacherously by a young Patrick that neighbor Seeley, an Irishman, in the intervals of the carting, transferred the still tolerable, straight, and drivable nails, staples, and spikes to his pocket, and then stood when I came back to pass the time of day, and look freshly up, unconcerned, with spring thoughts, at the devastation; there being a dearth[4] of work, as he said. He was there to represent spectatordom, and help make this seemingly insignificant event one with the removal of the gods of Troy.[5]

I dug my cellar in the side of a hill sloping to the south, where a woodchuck had formerly dug his burrow, down through sumach and blackberry roots, and the lowest stain of vegetation, six feet square by seven deep, to a fine sand where potatoes would not freeze in any winter. The sides were left shelving, and not stoned; but the sun having never shone on them, the sand still keeps its place. It was but two hours' work. I took particular pleasure in this breaking of ground, for in almost all latitudes men dig into the earth for an equable temperature. Under the most splendid house in the city is still to be found the cellar where they store their roots as of old, and long after the superstructure has disappeared posterity remark its dent in the earth. The house is still but a sort of porch at the entrance of a burrow.

At length, in the beginning of May, with the help of some of my acquaintances, rather to improve so good an occasion for neighborliness than from any necessity, I set up the frame of my house. No man was ever more honored in the character of his raisers than I. They are destined, I trust, to assist at the raising of loftier structures one day. I began to occupy my house on the 4th of July, as soon as it was boarded and roofed, for the boards were carefully feather-edged and lapped, so that

4. **dearth.** Scarcity
5. **gods of Troy.** Reference to Virgil's *Aeneid* in which Aeneas escapes with his household gods

Words for Everyday Use: **en • cum • brance** (en kum´brəns) *n.,* hindrance
pos • ter • i • ty (päs ter´ə tē) *n.,* succeeding generations

Vocabulary in Context

- Although John is eager to suit up and play with his team, the cast on his arm is too great an encumbrance to overcome.
- Often an author honored during his or her lifetime is judged insignificant by posterity.
- Many young guitar players practice willingly because they have aspirations of becoming famous.
- The snake slithered across the road in smooth undulations of its long body.

it was perfectly impervious to rain;[6] but before boarding I laid the foundation of a chimney at one end, bringing two cartloads of stones up the hill from the pond in my arms. I built the chimney after my hoeing in the fall, before a fire became necessary for warmth, doing my cooking in the mean while out of doors on the ground, early in the morning: which mode I still think is in some respects more convenient and agreeable than the usual one. When it stormed before my bread was baked, I fixed a few boards over the fire, and sat under them to watch my loaf, and passed some pleasant hours in that way. In those days, when my hands were much employed, I read but little, but the least scraps of paper which lay on the ground, my holder, or table-cloth, afforded me as much entertainment, in fact answered the same purpose as the Iliad.[7]

♦ ♦ ♦

FROM "WHERE I LIVED AND WHAT I LIVED FOR"

Every morning was a cheerful invitation to make my life of equal simplicity, and I may say innocence, with Nature herself. I have been as sincere a worshipper of Aurora[8] as the Greeks. I got up early and bathed in the pond; that was a religious exercise, and one of the best things which I did. They say that characters were engraven on the bathing tub of king Tching-thang to this effect: "Renew thyself completely each day; do it again, and again, and forever again."[9] I can understand that. Morning brings back the heroic ages. I was as much affected by the faint hum of a mosquito making its invisible and unimaginable tour through my apartment at earliest dawn, when I was sitting with door and windows open, as I could be by any trumpet that ever sang of fame. It was Homer's requiem; itself an Iliad and Odyssey in the air, singing its own wrath and wanderings. There was something cosmical about it, a standing advertisement, till forbidden,[10] of the everlasting vigor and fertility of the world. The morning, which is the most memorable season of the day, is the awakening hour. Then there is least somnolence in us; and for an hour, at least, some part of us awakes which slumbers all the rest of the day and night. Little is to be expected of that day, if it can be called a day, to which we are not awakened by our Genius, but by the mechanical nudgings of some servitor, are not awakened by our own newly-acquired force and aspirations from within, accompanied by the undulations of celestial music, instead of factory bells and a fragrance filling the air—to a higher life than we fell asleep from; and thus the darkness bear its fruit, and prove itself to be good, no less than the light. That man who does not believe that each day contains an earlier, more sacred, and auroral hour than he has yet profaned, has despaired of life, and is pursuing a descending and darkening way. After a

6. **feather-edged . . . rain.** The boards' thin edges overlapped, making the roof watertight.
7. **Iliad.** Greek epic by Homer
8. **Aurora.** Goddess of dawn
9. **"Renew . . . again."** From Confucius, Chinese philosopher
10. **standing . . . forbidden.** Advertisement that was to be run "till forbidden" or stopped by the advertiser

WORDS FOR EVERYDAY USE:

as • pi • ra • tion (as´pə rā´shən) *n.,* strong ambition

un • du • la • tion (un´dyōō lā´shən) *n.,* act of moving in waves

HISTORICAL NOTE

Thoreau mentions his Irish neighbors Collins, Seeley, and young Patrick. All of them were probably recent additions to the neighborhood. From 1845 to 1847 a disastrous plant disease destroyed Ireland's potato crop, upon which half the nation's population depended for food. About 750,000 people died of starvation and sickness, and hundreds of thousands more emigrated to other lands to survive. A large proportion of those emigrants came to the United States, many getting jobs on the railroads. Because of their willingness to work for low wages at difficult jobs, Irish laborers were looked down on by both the business people who took advantage of them and the local workers who had to compete for the same jobs.

Answers to Guided Reading Questions

❶ The "highest of arts" is to affect the quality of the day.

❷ Thoreau went into the woods because he wished to live deliberately, to face only the essential facts of life, and to see if he could learn what life had to teach.

❸ Thoreau defines being awake as being fully alive.

Additional Questions and Activities

Ask students to consider Thoreau's life and the ideas he had about simplification in the context of today's world. Then have students read E. B. White's essay "Walden" on page 769 of this text. Are the ideas expressed in White's "Walden" consistent with their own ideas regarding implementing Thoreau's experiences and philosophies in the world today? Have students discuss their own ideas and the ideas expressed by White. How could students live their lives more "deliberately"?

partial cessation of his sensuous life, the soul of man, or its organs rather, are reinvigorated each day, and his Genius tries again what noble life it can make. All memorable events, I should say, transpire in morning time and in a morning atmosphere. The Vedas[11] say, "All intelligences awake with the morning." Poetry and art, and the fairest and most memorable of the actions of men, date from such an hour. All poets and heroes, like Memnon,[12] are the children of Aurora, and emit their music at sunrise. To him whose elastic and vigorous thought keeps pace with the sun, the day is a perpetual morning. It matters not what the clocks say or the attitudes and labors of men. Morning is when I am awake and there is a dawn in me. Moral reform is the effort to throw off sleep. Why is it that men give so poor an account of their day if they have not been slumbering? They are not such poor calculators. If they had not been overcome with drowsiness they would have performed something. The millions are awake enough for physical labor; but only one in a million is awake enough for effective intellectual exertion, only one in a hundred millions to a poetic or divine life. To be awake is to be alive. I have never yet met a man who was quite awake. How could I have looked him in the face?

❶ *What is the "highest of arts"?*

❷ *Why did Thoreau go to the woods?*

❸ *What meaning does Thoreau give to the word* awake?

We must learn to reawaken and keep ourselves awake, not by mechanical aids, but by an infinite expectation of the dawn, which does not forsake us in our soundest sleep. I know of no more encouraging fact than the unquestionable ability of man to elevate his life by a conscious endeavor. It is something to be able to paint a particular picture, or to carve a statue, and so to make a few objects beautiful; but it is far more glorious to carve and paint the very atmosphere and medium through which we look, which morally we can do. To affect the quality of the day, that is the highest of arts. Every man is tasked to make his life, even in its details, worthy of the contemplation of his most elevated and critical hour. If we refused, or rather used up, such paltry information as we get, the oracles[13] would distinctly inform us how this might be done.

I went to the woods because I wished to live deliberately, to front only the essential facts of life, and see if I could not learn what it had to teach, and not, when I came to die, discover that I had not lived. I did not wish to live what was not life, living is so dear; nor did I wish to practice resignation, unless it was quite necessary. I wanted to live deep and suck out all the marrow of life, to live so sturdily and Spartan-like[14] as to put to rout all that was not life, to cut a broad swath and shave close, to drive life into a corner, and reduce it to its lowest terms, and, if it proved to be mean, why then to get the whole and genuine meanness of it, and publish its meanness to the world; or if it were sublime, to know it by experience, and be able to give a true account of it in my next excursion. For most men, it appears to me, are in a strange uncertainty about it, whether it is of the devil or of God, and have somewhat hastily concluded

11. **Vedas.** Hindu scriptures
12. **Memnon.** King killed by Achilles in the Trojan War
13. **oracles.** People in communication with the gods
14. **Spartan-like.** Without excess comforts

Words for Everyday Use:
ces • sa • tion (se sā´shən) *n.,* stopping
en • deav • or (en dev´ər) *n.,* effort, attempt
pal • try (pôl´trē) *adj.,* insignificant

Vocabulary in Context

- No one in the building could hear anything until the cessation of drilling on the street outside.
- Serious work has been done in the endeavor to make contact with intelligent life somewhere else in the universe.
- The magician told Jack he would sell the magic beans for a paltry amount.
- Sprinkling your lawn after a rainstorm just adds superfluous water.

Walden Pond. *Concord, Massachusetts*

that it is the chief end of man here to "glorify God and enjoy him forever."[15]

Still we live meanly, like ants; though the fable tells us that we were long ago changed into men;[16] like pygmies we fight with cranes; it is error upon error, and clout upon clout, and our best virtue has for its occasion a superfluous and evitable wretchedness. Our life is frittered away by detail. An honest man has hardly need to count more than his ten fingers, or in extreme cases he may add his ten toes, and lump the rest. Simplicity, simplicity, simplicity! I say, let your affairs be as two or three, and not a hundred or a thousand; instead of a million count half a dozen, and keep your accounts on your thumb nail. In the midst of this chopping sea of civilized life, such are the clouds and storms and quicksands and thousand-and-one items to be allowed for, that a man has to live, if he would not founder and go to the bottom and not make his port at all, by dead reckoning, and he must be a great calculator indeed who succeeds. Simplify, simplify. Instead of three

❶ *What does Thoreau recommend?*

15. **"glorify . . . forever."** Reference to the *New England Primer*
16. **fable . . . men.** Refers to a Greek fable in which Zeus turns ants into men

WORDS FOR EVERYDAY USE: **su • per • flu • ous** (sə pur´flōō əs) *adj.,* excessive

HISTORICAL NOTE

Walden Pond is still in existence, as shown in the photograph on page 265. Have students locate a map of the area around Concord, Massachusetts, and identify where the pond lies in relation to the center of town and to historical sites in the area.

ANSWER TO GUIDED READING QUESTION

❶ Thoreau recommends that people simplify their affairs.

ANALYTIC SCALES FOR RESPONDING IN WRITING

Assign a score from 1 to 25 for each grading criterion below. (For more detailed evaluation, see the evaluation forms for writing, revising, and proofreading, *Assessment Portfolio,* 7.1–7.10.)

1. Real Estate Ad

- **Content/Unity.** The real estate ad includes the facts listed by Thoreau but in words with more appealing connotations.
- **Organization/Coherence.** Details in the ad are organized either in order of importance or spatial order.
- **Language/Style.** The ad uses vivid and precise nouns, verbs, and modifiers.
- **Conventions.** The ad avoids errors in spelling, grammar, usage, mechanics, and manuscript form.

2. Blues

- **Content/Unity.** The blues song expresses feelings of sadness or melancholy based on desperation.
- **Organization/Coherence.** The blues song follows a stanza structure. There may be a repeated refrain.
- **Language/Style.** The song uses vivid and precise nouns, verbs, and modifiers.
- **Conventions.** The blues song avoids errors in spelling, but may use colloquialisms and informal grammar, usage, and mechanics.

(cont.)

ANALYTIC SCALES FOR RESPONDING IN WRITING (CONT.)

3. Epitaph

- **Content/Unity.** The epitaph lists one or more of the admirable characteristics of Thoreau. It may include his birth and death dates.
- **Organization/Coherence.** The epitaph may be arranged in parallel phrases or clauses, or may be in one or more complete sentences. It must be short, and must focus on highlights of Thoreau's life and/or character.
- **Language/Style.** The epitaph uses vivid and precise nouns, verbs, and modifiers.
- **Conventions.** The epitaph avoids errors in spelling, grammar, usage, and mechanics.

Answers to Guided Reading Questions

❶ Thoreau advises everyone to simplify and to reduce consumption, first of food and then of everything else in proportion.

❷ Thoreau feels that progress doesn't help people; it simply distracts them from important matters and, in effect, uses people instead of the other way around.

Literary Technique

A **pun** is a play on words, one that wittily exploits a double meaning. Invite students to discuss Thoreau's pun about sleepers. What two meanings does the word have? What point is Thoreau making by using this pun?

Quotables

"The world is too much with us; late and soon,
Getting and spending, we lay waste our powers:
Little we see in Nature that is ours."

—William Wordsworth

What advice does Thoreau give? ❶

meals a day, if it be necessary eat but one, instead of a hundred dishes, five; and reduce other things in proportion. Our life is like a German Confederacy, made up of petty states, with its boundary forever fluctuating, so that even a German cannot tell you how it is bounded at any moment. The nation itself, with all its so called internal improvements, which, by the way, are all external and superficial, is just such an unwieldy and overgrown establishment, cluttered with furniture and tripped up by its own traps, ruined by luxury and heedless expense, by want of calculation and a worthy aim, as the million households in the land; and the only cure for it as for them is in a rigid economy, a stern and more than Spartan simplicity of life and elevation of purpose. It lives too fast. Men think that it is essential that the Nation have commerce, and export ice, and talk through a telegraph, and ride thirty miles an hour, without a doubt, whether they do or not; but whether we should live like baboons or like men, is a little uncertain. If we do not get out sleepers,[17] and forge rails, and devote days and nights to the work, but go to tinkering upon our lives to improve them, who will build railroads? And if railroads are not built, how shall we get to heaven in season? But if we stay at home and mind our business, who will want railroads? We do not ride on the railroad; it rides upon us. Did you ever think what those sleepers are that underlie the railroad? Each one is a man, an Irish-man, or a Yankee man. The rails are laid on them, and they are covered with sand, and the cars run smoothly over them. They are sound sleepers, I assure you. And every few years a new lot is laid down and run over; so that, if some have the pleasure of riding on a rail, others have the misfortune to be ridden upon. And when they run over a man that is walking in his sleep, a supernumerary[18] sleeper in the wrong position, and wake him up, they suddenly stop the cars, and make a hue and cry about it, as if this were an exception. I am glad to know that it takes a gang of men for every five miles to keep the sleepers down and level in their beds as it is, for this is a sign that they may sometime get up again.

What does Thoreau think of "progress"? ❷

Why should we live with such hurry and waste of life? We are determined to be starved before we are hungry. Men say that a stitch in time saves nine, and so they take a thousand stitches today to save nine tomorrow. As for work, we haven't any of any consequence. We have the Saint Vitus' dance[19] and cannot possibly keep our heads still. If I should only give a few pulls at the parish bell-rope, as for a fire, that is, without setting the bell, there is hardly a man on his farm in the outskirts of Concord, notwithstanding that press of engagements which was his excuse so many times this morning, nor a boy, nor a woman, I might almost say, but would forsake all and follow that sound, not mainly to save property from the flames, but, if we will confess the truth, much more to see it burn, since burn it must, and we, be it known, did not set it on fire,—or to see it put out, and have a hand in it, if that is

17. **sleepers.** Railroad ties
18. **supernumerary.** Extra
19. **Saint Vitus' dance.** Refers to a nervous disorder with symptoms of jerky motions

Words for Everyday Use:
fluc • tu • ate (fluk´chōō āt´) *vi.,* change or vary continuously
un • wield • y (un wēl´dē) *adj.,* hard to manage

Vocabulary in Context

- There is no way to predict the stock market because its value fluctuates from minute to minute.
- That large box is light but too unwieldy to move up the stairs.

done as handsomely; yes, even if it were the parish church itself. Hardly a man takes a half hour's nap after dinner, but when he wakes he holds up his head and asks "What's the news?" as if the rest of mankind had stood his sentinels. Some give directions to be waked every half hour, doubtless for no other purpose; and then, to pay for it, they tell what they have dreamed. After a night's sleep the news is as indispensable as the breakfast. "Pray tell me any thing new that has happened to a man any where on this globe",—and he reads it over his coffee and rolls, that a man had had his eyes gouged out this morning on the Wachito River; never dreaming the while that he lives in the dark unfathomed mammoth cave of this world, and has but the rudiment of an eye himself.[20]

♦ ♦ ♦

I left the woods for as good a reason as I went there. Perhaps it seemed to me that I had several more lives to live, and could not spare any more time for that one. It is remarkable how easily and insensibly we fall into a particular route, and make a beaten track for ourselves. I had not lived there a week before my feet wore a path from my door to the pond-side; and though it is five or six years since I trod it, it is still quite distinct. It is true, I fear that others may have fallen into it, and so helped to keep it open. The surface of the earth is soft and impressible by the feet of men; and so with the paths which the mind travels. How worn and dusty, then, must be the highways of the world, how deep the ruts of tradition and conformity! I did not wish to take a cabin passage, but rather to go before the mast and on the deck of the world, for there I could best see the moonlight amid the mountains. I do not wish to go below now.

I learned this, at least, by my experiment; that if one advances confidently in the direction of his dreams, and endeavors to live the life which he has imagined, he will meet with a success unexpected in common hours. He will put some things behind, will pass an invisible boundary; new, universal, and more liberal laws will begin to establish themselves around and within him; or old laws be expanded, and interpreted in his favor in a more liberal sense, and he will live with the license of a higher order of beings. In proportion as he simplifies his life, the laws of the universe will appear less complex, and solitude will not be solitude, nor poverty poverty, nor weakness weakness. If you have built castles in the air, your work need not be lost; that is where they should be. Now put the foundations under them.

It is a ridiculous demand which England and America make, that you shall speak so that they can understand you. Neither men nor toadstools grow so. As if that were important, and there were not enough to understand you without them. As if Nature could support but one order of understandings, could not sustain birds as well as quadrupeds, flying as well as creeping things, and *hush* and *who*, which Bright[21] can understand, were the best English. As if there were safety in stupidity alone. I fear chiefly lest my expression may not be *extra-vagant* enough, may not wander far enough beyond the narrow limits of my daily experience, so as to be adequate to the truth of which I have been convinced. *Extra vagance!* it depends on how you are yarded. The migrating buffalo, which seeks new pastures in another latitude, is not extravagant like the cow which kicks over the pail, leaps the cow-yard

❶ *What did Thoreau learn?*

❷ *Why did Thoreau leave the woods? What easily happens to people?*

20. **dark . . . himself.** Reference to sightless fish found in Mammoth Cave
21. **Bright.** Name for an ox

Answers to Guided Reading Questions

❶ Thoreau learned that if a person moves confidently in the direction of his or her dreams and tries to live life according to his or her own plan, he or she will meet with unexpected success.

❷ Thoreau left the woods because he felt he had given enough time to that endeavor. He saw how easy it is for people to fall into routines.

Additional Questions and Activities

To what does Thoreau compare a person who wakes up with a demand for news?

Answer. The person is like a creature living in an uncharted cave with little, if any, sight.

Additional Questions and Activities

What is meant by "castles in the air"? Does the image have positive or negative connotations? Why? How does Thoreau build on and alter the saying?

Answers. The phrase refers to dreaming about things that can never come true, and has a negative connotation because it accuses the dreamer of not being intelligent enough to face facts. Thoreau says that building castles in the air is good, as long as the dreamer will then "put the foundation under them."

Answer to Guided Reading Question

❶ Thoreau rejects conformity, advocating instead that each person be his or her own distinct self.

Additional Questions and Activities

Students can discuss what Thoreau means by this statement: "Who that has heard a strain of music feared then lest he should speak extravagantly any more forever?"

Answers to Selection Check Test 4.4.9

EX. According to Thoreau, what kind of lives do most people lead?
Most people lead lives of quiet desperation.

1. Where did Thoreau go in March of 1845?
Thoreau went to the woods by Walden Pond.

2. What purpose did morning serve for Thoreau?
Morning served as an invitation to make his life innocent and simple.

3. What did Thoreau hope to avoid by going into the woods?
He hoped that when he died, he would not find that he had not lived.

4. By what are our lives frittered away?
Our lives are frittered away by detail.

5. What is the commonest sense?
The commonest sense is the sense of men sleeping.

fence, and runs after her calf, in milking time. I desire to speak somewhere *without* bounds; like a man in a waking moment, to men in their waking moments; for I am convinced that I cannot exaggerate enough even to lay the foundation of a true expression. Who that has heard a strain of music feared then lest he should speak extravagantly any more forever? In view of the future or possible, we should live quite laxly and undefined in front, our outlines dim and misty on that side; as our shadows reveal an insensible perspiration toward the sun. The volatile truth of our words should continually betray the inadequacy of the residual statement. Their truth is instantly *translated;* its literal monument alone remains. The words which express our faith and piety are not definite; yet they are significant and fragrant like frankincense[22] to superior natures.

Why level downward to our dullest perception always, and praise that as common sense? The commonest sense is the sense of men asleep, which they express by snoring. Sometimes we are inclined to class those who are once-and-a-half witted with the half-witted, because we appreciate only a third part of their wit. Some would find fault with the morning-red, if they ever got up early enough. "They pretend," as I hear, "that the verses of Kabir have four different senses; illusion, spirit, intellect, and the exoteric doctrine of the Vedas;" but in this part of the world it is considered a ground for complaint if a man's writings admit of more than one interpretation. While England endeavors to cure the potato-rot, will not any endeavor to cure the brain-rot, which prevails so much more widely and fatally?

I do not suppose that I have attained to obscurity, but I should be proud if no more fatal fault were found with my pages on this score than was found with the Walden ice. Southern customers objected to its blue color, which is the evidence of its purity, as if it were muddy, and preferred the Cambridge ice, which is white, but tastes of weeds. The purity men love is like the mists which envelop the earth, and not like the azure ether beyond.

Some are dinning in our ears that we Americans, and moderns generally, are intellectual dwarfs compared with the ancients, or even the Elizabethan[23] men. But what is that to the purpose? A living dog is better than a dead lion.[24] Shall a man go and hang himself because he belongs to the race of pygmies, and not be the biggest pygmy that he can? Let every one mind his own business, and endeavor to be what he was made.

Why should we be in such desperate haste to succeed, and in such desperate enterprises? If a man does not keep pace with his companions, perhaps it is because he hears a different drummer. Let him step to the music which he hears, however measured or far away. It is not important that he should mature as soon as an apple-tree or an oak. Shall he turn his spring into summer? If the condition of things which we were made for is not yet, what were any reality which we can substi-

Does Thoreau advocate conformity? ❶

22. **frankincense.** Type of incense
23. **Elizabethan.** From the time of Queen Elizabeth I (1533–1603)
24. **A living . . . lion.** Ecclesiastes 9:4

Words for Everyday Use:
lax • ly (laks´lē) *adv.,* loosely, not strictly
vol • a • tile (väl´ə təl) *adj.,* unstable; fleeting

Vocabulary in Context

- After the fifth inning, the ticket takers guarded the entrances rather laxly, and late fans entered the stadium without paying.
- Mixing these chemicals creates a volatile substance that can explode at the slightest disturbance.

tute? We will not be shipwrecked on a vain reality. Shall we with pains erect a heaven of blue glass over ourselves, though when it is done we shall be sure to gaze still at the true ethereal heaven far above, as if the former were not? ■

Responding to the Selection

Basing your answer on what you learned of Thoreau in this excerpt, do you think you would get along with the author? Give reasons.

Reviewing the Selection

RECALLING

1. According to Thoreau, age alone does not qualify people to be teachers of the young. Why not?
2. Describe the area in which Thoreau built his home.
3. Why did Thoreau decide to live in the woods for a while? What did he hope to learn from his experience?
4. Name one thing Thoreau learned from his experiment of life in the woods.

INTERPRETING

5. Explain why Thoreau encourages us to examine our assumptions and "to give up our prejudices." Describe his attitudes toward what older people consider to be conventional wisdom.
6. What evidence suggests that Thoreau was not interested in expending a lot of money or time in building a home that others would admire?
7. What does Thoreau mean when he urges us to "Simplify, simplify"?
8. Do you believe that Thoreau "heard a different drummer"? Explain your answer.

RESPONDING TO THE SELECTION

Encourage students to find specific passages in the selection to support their claims about what Thoreau thought or might have thought about various topics.

ANSWERS FOR REVIEWING THE SELECTION

RECALLING

1. Thoreau believes that living a long time doesn't prove that the person has learned more, only that he or she has lost more. Old people may have no good advice to give young people because their experiences were limited and they may not have learned from their life.

2. His home was on a wooded hillside near a pond and a small open field in a wood of pine and hickory.

3. He wanted to "live deliberately," to strip away the nonessentials and confront life simply. He hoped that by doing so, he would learn what it meant to be truly alive.

4. *Responses will vary. Possible responses are given.* He learned that if you follow your dreams, you will be successful. By simplifying your life, you will see that "the laws of the universe will appear less complex" and life will seem more manageable.

INTERPRETING

Responses will vary. Possible responses are given.

5. Thoreau is skeptical of every piece of so-called wisdom and advice passed on to us because some of it may not be true. Things that were thought to be fact in the past have turned out to be only opinion. That which was at one time considered impossible has been accomplished.

6. Thoreau did most of the work of digging a foundation, felling the trees, and erecting his house himself. He borrowed tools, bought a cheap shanty and reconstructed it, and didn't bother to put in a fireplace for warmth until much later. His emphasis was on usefulness, not necessarily beauty.

(cont.)

ANSWERS FOR REVIEWING THE SELECTION (CONT.)

7. Thoreau believes that most people never understand the underlying realities of life because they are so consumed with unimportant daily details. When he urges us to simplify, he is asking that we rid our lives of unnecessary details that distract us from confronting life.

8. Thoreau seems to have heard and followed "a different drummer" because his lifestyle was so unconventional. He chose to turn his back on normal society and live alone in a house that many others would have found intolerable. He ridiculed many aspects of society and wrote in opposition of practices and traditions that had been valued for years.

SYNTHESIZING

Responses will vary. Possible responses are given.

9. Students might suggest that they would need to go to a place that was relatively uninhabited.

(cont.)

ANSWERS FOR REVIEWING THE SELECTION (CONT.)

They might consider living without cars, televisions, computers, electricity, or newspapers. Stepping back for a short period of time might be a refreshing change of pace that allows a person to reevaluate what is important in life.

10. *Responses will vary.* Students should clearly summarize the meaning of the passage they have chosen and explain why they feel strongly about the ideas expressed.

ANSWERS FOR UNDERSTANDING LITERATURE

► See the evaluation forms for discussion, active listening, and oral communication, *Assessment Portfolio,* 7.11–7.14.

Responses will vary. Possible responses are given.

1. Allusion. In discussing carrying off the boards from the Collins shanty, Thoreau compares the event to "the removal of the gods of Troy." When discussing morning, he calls himself "as sincere a worshipper of Aurora as the Greeks." The mosquito's hum was "Homer's requiem . . . an Iliad and Odyssey in the air." He states, "All poets and heroes, like Memnon, are the children of Aurora."

►**Teaching Note:** If possible, have available a reference book defining names and terms from mythology.

2. Aphorism. Both of these statements reflect a truth that many people recognize in their own experiences. The first aphorism suggests that many people are not living the lives they would like to lead. The second aphorism reflects an acceptance of nonconformity and suggests that we should all follow our own "drummer," or lead the life we choose although it may be different and not understood by others.

3. Tone. Thoreau's tone is challenging. He expects his reader to be a person concerned with the idea of worthwhile life and tries to get that person to think seriously about

(cont.)

SYNTHESIZING

9. If you wanted to withdraw from modern society for a while, where would you go? What would you do? Does stepping back from normal life seem like a good idea? Why, or why not?

10. Choose a passage or paragraph that strikes a chord in you. Explain why you agree with the sentiments Thoreau has expressed in that passage.

Understanding Literature (Questions for Discussion)

1. **Allusion.** An **allusion** is a rhetorical technique in which a reference is made to a person, event, object, or work from history or literature. In the second paragraph of the excerpt is an allusion to Mentor, a character in Homer's *Odyssey* who taught Odysseus's son. (Today the proper noun *Mentor* has become the common noun *mentor,* meaning *guide.*) Find at least two other references to Greek mythology or literature in the selection.

2. **Aphorism.** An **aphorism** is a short saying or pointed statement. This excerpt begins with a famous aphorism, "The mass of men lead lives of quiet desperation." The final paragraph includes what may be Thoreau's best-known statement, "If a man does not keep pace with his companions, perhaps it is because he hears a different drummer." Select one of these aphorisms and suggest an explanation for its popularity.

3. **Tone. Tone** is the emotional attitude toward the reader or toward the subject implied by a literary work. Consider such statements in this excerpt as these: "I have lived some thirty years on this planet, and I have yet to hear the first syllable of valuable or even earnest advice from my seniors"; "I have never yet met a man who was quite awake"; "Our life is frittered away by detail." How would you describe the attitude toward the reader implied in these statements? Whom does Thoreau expect to be his reader? How does he expect his reader to react to these statements?

Responding in Writing

1. **Real Estate Ad.** Thoreau has "left the woods" and wants to sell his small house there. Write a newspaper ad accurately describing the building and highlighting its advantages.

2. **Blues.** The **blues** are a style of music that expresses sadness; a song or composition in this style has melancholy words. Write a blues song in response to Thoreau's statement that "The mass of men lead lives of quiet desperation."

3. **Epitaph.** An **epitaph** is an inscription on a tomb or gravestone in memory of the person buried there. Write an epitaph for Henry David Thoreau.

ANSWERS FOR UNDERSTANDING LITERATURE (CONT.)

what must be done to improve the quality of life. By these bold statements, he hopes to wake up the reader to possibilities ignored by traditional attitudes.

ANALYTIC SCALES FOR RESPONDING IN WRITING

Grading scales appear on page 265.

Language Lab

Editing Sentences. Read the Language Arts Survey, 2.58, "Deleting Repeated or Unnecessary Ideas." Then revise these sentences, following Thoreau's edict to "Simplify, simplify."

1. The usual picture we get from *Walden* is that Thoreau lived a rather solitary life by himself.
2. However, many sequences show how the neighbors who lived around Walden Pond were an important part of the writer's life.
3. For example, one neighbor lent Thoreau an axe, and he was careful to sharpen that axe before he returned the tool when he was finished with it.
4. Thoreau also notes that he had pleasant chats when he talked with people who were taking walks in his woods.
5. The passage about his contract with James Collins, in which he made a bargain with Collins to buy the boards of the Irishman's shanty, is amusing and makes the reader laugh.

Thinking Skills

Problem Solving. Read the Language Arts Survey, 4.1, "Strategies for Problem Solving I." Then analyze the selection as an example of problem solving as outlined in the diagram. If going into the woods was the action, what was the problem? What did Thoreau expect to gain from the action? How did he evaluate and apply the results?

PROJECT

Nature Study. While at Walden, Thoreau observed nature closely, taking notes on the activities of ants as well as the beauty of the scenery. Create a display on topics of nature of interest to you. Try to select items that work together to develop a theme, or an appreciation of some particular aspect of nature. Possible highlights could include audiotapes of bird songs, photographs of trees, weather charts, videotapes of tornadoes, or even an ant colony. Each item should have both a label and a short essay explaining its presence in the display.

ANSWERS FOR LANGUAGE LAB

Responses will vary. Possible responses are given.

1. The usual picture we get from *Walden* is that Thoreau lived a rather solitary life.
2. However, many sequences show how neighbors were an important part of the writer's life.
3. For example, one neighbor lent Thoreau an axe, and he was careful to sharpen the tool before he returned it.
4. Thoreau also notes that he had pleasant chats with people taking walks in his woods.
5. The passage about his contract with James Collins to buy the boards of his shanty is amusing.

FOR MORE PRACTICE

Problem. Not many modern people of today would choose to go and live in the woods, away from the conveniences of modern life.

Answer. Today, not many people would choose to live in the woods, away from modern conveniences.

► Additional practice is provided in the *Essential Skills Practice Book: Language*, 2.58.

ANSWERS FOR THINKING SKILLS

Responses will vary. Possible responses are given.

The problem: To find out what is truly necessary to a life worth living.

The expectation: To get a clearer view of the essentials of life.

Evaluation: Thoreau considered his experiment useful and summarized his findings in these words: "In proportion as [a person] simplifies his life, the laws of the universe will appear less complex."

► Additional practice is provided in the *Essential Skills Practice Book: Study and Research*, 4.1.

PROJECT NOTES

► See the worksheets and evaluation forms for projects, *Assessment Portfolio*, 7.20–7.23.

Nature Study.

- If possible, when assigning this activity, set up an area in the classroom for display of the projects, or post a sign-up schedule so students can bring in their work in small groups for a single period.
- Students with shared interest should work together to research and create display items. Suggest that students use their own observations of nature if possible. Students might contact conservation or nature-related organizations as well as use library sources for their research.

"The Legend of Sleepy Hollow"

About the Author. Washington Irving (1783–1859), born in New York City and trained to be a lawyer, was the first American writer to gain favorable attention in Europe. He began writing as a teenager, contributing satirical letters and essays to newspapers and magazines. In 1809, he dropped his law practice to become a writer. That same year he published his first book, a humorous history of his hometown, told in the person of Diedrich Knickerbocker, and familiarly called *Knickerbocker's History of New York*. It was a comic masterpiece. In 1810, Irving moved to Europe to work in a family business; when it failed, he stayed on to travel and write. His book of short stories and other pieces, *The Sketch Book of Geoffrey Crayon, Gent.*, in 1819, established him as a respected writer in Europe. He produced a number of other works while in Europe, mostly based on German, British, and, later, Spanish folk tales and themes. His later work was seen as too much influenced by European literature and lacking the originality of his early writing. In 1826, Irving became a United States diplomat, first in Spain and then, in 1829, in London. In 1832, he returned to the United States and wrote about travel, history, and biography. He returned to Spain from 1842 to 1846 as the United States minister, and then settled in his home near Tarrytown, New York, for the remainder of his life. He died just after completing a five-volume biography of George Washington. Irving's influence on American literature was strongest in his use of folklore, his imaginative treatment of history, and his contribution to establishing the short story as a popular literary form.

About the Selection. "The Legend of Sleepy Hollow" was one of the most important tales in *The Sketch Book of Geoffrey Crayon, Gent.*, Irving's first book published in Europe. Although set in New York, the story is based on a German folk tale. Irving's comic descriptions make it distinctly American in flavor.

"The Legend of Sleepy Hollow"
by Washington Irving

(Found among the Papers of the Late Diedrich Knickerbocker)

A pleasing land of drowsy head it was,
Of dreams that wave before the half-shut eye;
And of gay castles in the clouds that pass,
Forever flushing round a summer sky.
—*Castle of Indolence*[1]

In the bosom of one of the spacious coves which indent the eastern shore of the Hudson, at that broad expansion of the river denominated by the ancient Dutch navigators the Tappaan Zee, and where they always prudently shortened sail, and implored the protection of St. Nicholas when they crossed, there lies a small market town or rural port, which by some is called Greensburgh, but which is more universally and properly known by the name of Tarry Town. This name was given it, we are told, in former days, by the good housewives of the adjacent country, from the inveterate propensity of their husbands to linger about the village tavern on market days. Be that as it may, I do not vouch for the fact, but merely advert to it, for the sake of being precise and authentic. Not far from this village, perhaps about three miles, there is a little valley, or rather lap of land among high hills, which is one of the quietest places in the whole world. A small brook glides through it, with just murmur enough to lull you to repose, and the occasional whistle of a quail, or tapping of a woodpecker, is almost the only sound that ever breaks in upon the uniform tranquillity.

I recollect that when a stripling, my first exploit in squirrel shooting was in a grove of tall walnut trees that shades one side of the valley. I had wandered into it at noon time, when all nature is peculiarly quiet, and was startled by the roar of my own gun, as it broke the sabbath stillness around, and was prolonged and reverberated by the angry echoes. If ever I should wish for a retreat, whither I might steal from the world and its distractions, and dream quietly away the remnant of a troubled life, I know of none more promising than this little valley.

From the listless repose of the place, and the peculiar character of its inhabitants, who are descendants from the original Dutch settlers, this sequestered glen has long been known by the name of SLEEPY HOLLOW, and its rustic lads are called the Sleepy Hollow Boys throughout all the neighboring country. A drowsy, dreamy influence seems to hang over the land, and pervade the very atmosphere. Some say that the place was bewitched by a high German[2] doctor during the early days of the settlement; others, that an old Indian chief, the prophet or wizard of his tribe, held his powwows there before the country was discovered by Master Hendrick Hudson.[3] Certain it is, the place still continues under the sway of some witching power, that holds a spell over the minds of the good people, causing them to walk in a continual reverie. They are given to all kinds of marvelous beliefs; have trances and visions, and see strange sights, and hear music and voices in the air. The whole neighborhood abounds with local tales, haunted spots, and twilight superstitions; stars shoot and meteors glare oftener across the valley than in any other part of the country, and the night-mare, with her whole nine fold,[4] seems to make it the favorite scene of her gambols.

The dominant spirit, however, that haunts this enchanted region, and seems to be commander of all the powers of the air, is the apparition of a figure on horseback without a head. It is said by some to be the ghost of a Hessian trooper,[5] whose head had been carried away by a cannon-ball, in some nameless battle during the revolutionary war, and who is ever and anon seen by various of the country people, hurrying along in the gloom of night, as if on the wings of the wind. His haunts are not confined to the valley, but extend at times to the adjacent roads, and especially to the vicinity of a church that is at no great distance. Indeed, certain of the most authentic historians of those parts, who have been careful in collecting and collating the floating facts concerning this specter, allege, that the body of the trooper having been buried in the churchyard, the ghost rides forth to the scene of battle in nightly quest of his head, and the rushing speed with which he sometimes passes along the hollow, like a midnight blast, is owing to his being belated, and in a hurry to get back to the churchyard before daybreak.

Such is the general purport of this legendary superstition, which has furnished materials for many a wild story in that region of shadows; and the specter is known, at all the country firesides, by the name of The Headless Horseman of Sleepy Hollow.

It is remarkable that the visionary turn I have mentioned is not confined to the native inhabitants of the valley, but is imperceptibly acquired by every one who resides there for a time. However wide awake they may have been before they entered that sleepy region, they are sure, in a little time, to imbibe the witching influence of the air, and begin to grow

1. **Castle of Indolence.** Poem by James Thomson (1700–1748)
2. **high German.** From southern Germany
3. **Hendrick Hudson.** English navigator who worked for the Dutch
4. **night-mare, . . . fold.** Demon and her nine offspring who tormented sleepers
5. **Hessian trooper.** German mercenary soldier hired by the British to fight in the American Revolution

ADDITIONAL QUESTIONS AND ACTIVITIES

- Where is the story set?

Answer. The setting is an isolated glen called Sleepy Hollow, near the small town of Tarry Town, New York.

- Who was the Headless Horseman of Sleepy Hollow?

Answer. The Headless Horseman was a ghost that was said to haunt the area of Sleepy Hollow, riding on horseback through the valley and on adjacent roads as far as the nearby church. He was said to be the ghost of a Hessian trooper killed in the Revolutionary War.

imaginative—to dream dreams, and see apparitions.

I mention this peaceful spot with all possible laud; for it is in such little retired Dutch valleys, found here and there embosomed in the great state of New York, that populations, manners, and customs, remained fixed, while the great torrent of emigration and improvement, which is making such incessant changes in other parts of this restless country, sweeps by them unobserved. They are like those little nooks of still water, which border a rapid stream, where we may see the straw and bubble riding quietly at anchor, or slowly revolving in their mimic harbor, undisturbed by the rushing of the passing current. Though many years have elapsed since I trod the drowsy shades of Sleepy Hollow, yet I question whether I should not still find the same trees and the same families vegetating in its sheltered bosom.

In this by-place of nature there abode, in a remote period of American history, that is to say, some thirty years since, a worthy wight[1] of the name of Ichabod Crane, who sojourned, or, as he expressed it, "tarried," in Sleepy Hollow, for the purpose of instructing the children of the vicinity. He was a native of Connecticut, a state which supplies the Union with pioneers for the mind as well as the forest, and sends forth yearly its legions of frontier woodmen and country schoolmasters. The cognomen[2] of Crane was not inapplicable to his person. He was tall, but exceedingly lank, with narrow shoulders, long arms and legs, hands that dangled a mile out of his sleeves, feet that might have served for shovels, and his whole frame most loosely hung together. His head was small, and flat at top, with huge ears, large green glassy eyes, and a long snipe nose, so that it might have been mistaken for a weathercock perched upon his spindle neck, to tell which way the wind blew. To see him striding along the profile of a hill on a windy day, with his clothes bagging and fluttering about him, one might have mistaken him for the genius[3] of famine descending upon the earth, or some scarecrow eloped from a cornfield.

His schoolhouse was a low building of one large room rudely constructed of logs; the windows partly glazed, and partly patched with leaves of old copy books. It was most ingeniously secured at vacant hours, by a withe[4] twisted in the handle of the door, and stakes set against the window shutters; so that though a thief might get in with perfect ease, he would find some embarrassment in getting out; an idea most probably borrowed by the architect, Yost Van Houten, from the mystery of an eelpot. The school-house stood in rather a lonely but a pleasant situation, just at the foot of a woody hill, with a brook running close by, and a formidable birch tree growing at one end of it. From hence the low murmur of his pupils' voices conning over their lessons, might be heard of a drowsy summer's day, like the hum of a bee-hive; interrupted now and then by the authoritative voice of the master, giving menace or command, or, peradventure, the appalling sound of the birch, as he urged some tardy loiterer along the flowery path of knowledge. Truth to say, he was a conscientious man, that ever bore in mind the golden maxim, "spare the rod and spoil the child."—Ichabod Crane's scholars certainly were not spoiled.

I would not have it imagined, however, that he was one of those cruel potentates of the school, who joy in the smart[5] of their subjects, on the contrary, he administered justice with discrimination rather than severity; taking the burthen off the backs of the weak, and laying it on those of the strong. Your mere puny stripling, that winced at the least flourish of the rod, was passed by with indulgence; but the claims of justice were satisfied, by giving a double portion to some little, tough, wrong-headed, broad-skirted Dutch urchin, who sulked and swelled and grew dogged and sullen beneath the birch. All this he called "doing his duty by their parents;" and he never inflicted a chastisement without following it by the assurance, so consolatory to the smarting urchin, that he would remember it and thank him for it the longest day he had to live.

When school hours were over, he was even the companion and playmate of his larger boys; and would convoy some of the smaller ones home of a holyday, who happened to have pretty sisters, or good housewives for mothers, noted for the comforts of the cupboard. Indeed, it behooved him to keep on good terms with his pupils. The revenue arising from his school was small, and would have been scarcely sufficient to furnish him with daily bread, for he was a huge feeder, and though lank, had the dilating powers of an Anaconda; but to help out his maintenance, he was, according to country custom in those parts, boarded and lodged at the houses of the farmers, whose children he instructed. With these he lived alternately a week at a time, thus going the rounds of the neighborhood, with all his worldly effects tied up in a cotton handkerchief.

That all this might not be too onerous on the purses of his rustic patrons, who are apt to consider the costs of schooling a grievous burthen, and schoolmasters mere drones, he had various ways of rendering himself both useful and agreeable. He assisted the farmers occasionally in the light labors of their farms, helped to make hay, mended the fences, took the horses to water, drove the cows from pasture, and cut wood for the winter fire. He laid aside, too, all the dominant dignity and absolute sway, with which he lorded it in his little empire, the school, and became wonderfully gentle and ingratiating. He found favor in the eyes of the mothers, by petting the children, particularly the youngest, and like the lion bold, which whilome[6] so magnanimously the lamb did hold,[7] he would sit with a child on one knee, and rock a cradle with his foot, for whole hours together.

In addition to his other vocations, he was the singing-master of the neighborhood, and picked up many

1. **wight.** Person
2. **cognomen.** Last name
3. **genius.** Image
4. **withe.** Flexible branch used as a rope
5. **smart.** Pain
6. **whilome.** Formerly
7. **lion . . . hold.** Reference to the *New England Primer* in which the verse for *L* is "The lion bold/The lamb doth hold."

LITERARY TECHNIQUE

Irving uses many metaphors, similes, and other comparisons, including three in the description of Ichabod Crane: his feet "might have served for shovels"; his nose "might have been mistaken for a weathercock . . . to tell which way the wind blows"; and his whole body looked like "some scarecrow eloped from a cornfield." Have students identify the two things being compared in each of these passages and decide which of the comparisons, if any, are metaphors or similes.

ADDITIONAL QUESTIONS AND ACTIVITIES

- Why was Crane popular with the women of the neighborhood?

Answer. He was appreciated as a man of learning but also as a messenger who brought the gossip of the area along with him when he came to stay at a home.

- What was Crane's attitude toward tales of witchcraft and spirits?

Answer. Crane believed in witchcraft, loved to read about it, and listened to tales of local sightings of unnatural beings.

bright shillings by instructing the young folks in psalmody.[1] It was a matter of no little vanity to him on Sundays, to take his station in front of the church gallery, with a band of chosen singers; where, in his own mind, he completely carried away the palm from the parson. Certain it is, his voice resounded far above all the rest of the congregation, and there are peculiar quavers still to be heard in that church, and which may even be heard half-a-mile off, quite to the opposite side of the mill-pond, of a still Sunday morning, which are said to be legitimately descended from the nose of Ichabod Crane. Thus, by diverse little make shifts, in that ingenious way which is commonly denominated "by hook and by crook," the worthy pedagogue got on tolerably enough, and was thought, by all those who understood nothing of the labor of headwork, to have a wonderful easy life of it.

The schoolmaster is generally a man of some importance in the female circle of a rural neighborhood, being considered a kind of idle gentlemanlike personage, of vastly superior taste and accomplishments to the rough country swains, and, indeed, inferior in learning only to the parson. His appearance, therefore, is apt to occasion some little stir at the tea-table of a farmhouse, and the addition of a supernumerary dish of cakes or sweetmeats, or, peradventure, the parade of a silver tea-pot. Our man of letters, therefore, was peculiarly happy in the smiles of all the country damsels. How he would figure among them in the churchyard, between services on Sundays; gathering grapes for them from the wild vines that overrun the surrounding trees; reciting for them all the epitaphs on the tombstones, or sauntering, with a whole bevy of them, along the banks of the adjacent mill-pond; while the more bashful country bumpkins hung sheepishly back, envying his superior elegance and address.

From his half itinerant life, also he was a kind of traveling gazette, carrying the whole budget of local gossip from house to house; so that his appearance was always greeted with satisfaction. He was, moreover, esteemed by the women as a man of great erudition, for he had read several books quite through, and was a perfect master of Cotton Mather's History of New-England Witchcraft, in which, by the way, he most firmly and potently believed.

He was, in fact, an odd mixture of small shrewdness and simple credulity. His appetite for the marvelous, and his powers of digesting it, were equally extraordinary; and both had been increased by his residence in this spell-bound region. No tale was too gross or monstrous for his capacious swallow. It was often his delight, after his school was dismissed of an afternoon, to stretch himself on the rich bed of clover, bordering the little brook that whimpered past his schoolhouse, and there con over old Mather's direful tales, until the gathering dusk of evening made the printed page a mere mist before his eyes. Then, as he wended his way, by swamp and stream and awful[2] woodland, to the farmhouse where he happened to be quartered, every sound of nature, at that witching hour, fluttered his excited imagination: the moan of the whip-poor-will from the hillside; the boding cry of the tree-toad, that harbinger of storm; the dreary hooting of the screech-owl; or the sudden rustling in the thicket, of birds frightened from their roost. The fire-flies, too, which sparkled most vividly in the darkest places, now and then startled him, as one of uncommon brightness would stream across his path; and if, by chance, a huge blockhead of a beetle came winging his blundering flight against him, the poor varlet was ready to give up the ghost, with the idea that he was struck with a witch's token. His only resource on such occasions, either to drown thought, or drive away evil spirits, was to sing psalm tunes;—and the good people of Sleepy Hollow, as they sat by their doors of an evening, were often filled with awe, at hearing his nasal melody, "in linked sweetness long drawn out," floating from the distant hill, or along the dusky road.

Another of his sources of fearful pleasure was, to pass long winter evenings with the old Dutch wives, as they sat spinning by the fire, with a row of apples roasting and sputtering along the hearth, and listen to their marvelous tales of ghosts and goblins, and haunted fields and haunted brooks, and haunted bridges and haunted houses, and particularly of the headless horseman, or galloping Hessian of the Hollow, as they sometimes called him. He would delight them equally by his anecdotes of witchcraft, and of the direful omens and portentous sights and sounds in the air, which prevailed in the earlier times of Connecticut; and would frighten them woefully with speculations upon comets and shooting stars, and with the alarming fact that the world did absolutely turn round, and that they were half the time topsy-turvy!

But if there was a pleasure in all this, while snugly cuddling in the chimney corner of a chamber that was all of a ruddy glow from the crackling wood fire, and where, of course, no specter dare to show its face, it was dearly purchased by the terrors of his subsequent walk homewards. What fearful shapes and shadows beset his path, amidst the dim and ghostly glare of a snowy night!—With what wistful look did he eye every trembling ray of light streaming across the waste fields from some distant window!—How often was he appalled by some shrub covered with snow, which like sheeted specter beset his very path!—How often did he shrink with curdling awe at the sound of his own steps on the frosty crust beneath his feet; and dread to look over his shoulder, lest he should behold some uncouth being tramping close behind him!—and how often was he thrown into complete dismay by some rushing blast, howling among the trees, in the idea that it was the galloping Hessian on one of his nightly scourings.

All these, however, were mere terrors of the night, phantoms of the mind, that walk in darkness; and though he had seen many specters in his time, and been more than once beset by Satan in diverse shapes, in his lonely perambula-

1. **psalmody.** Singing versions of the psalms
2. **awful.** Terrifying

tions, yet daylight put an end to all these evils; and he would have passed a pleasant life of it, in despite of the Devil and all his works, if his path had not been crossed by a being that causes more perplexity to mortal man, than ghosts, goblins, and the whole race of witches put together, and that was—a woman.

Among the musical disciples who assembled, one evening in each week, to receive his instructions in psalmody, was Katrina Van Tassel, the daughter and only child of a substantial Dutch farmer. She was a blooming lass of fresh eighteen; plump as a partridge; ripe and melting and rosy-cheeked as one of her father's peaches, and universally famed, not merely for her beauty, but her vast expectations. She was withal a little of a coquette, as might be perceived even in her dress, which was a mixture of ancient and modern fashions, as most suited to set off her charms. She wore the ornaments of pure yellow gold, which her great-great-grandmother had brought over from Saardam;[1] the tempting stomacher[2] of the olden time, and withal a provokingly short petticoat, to display the prettiest foot and ankle in the country round.

Ichabod Crane had a soft and foolish heart toward the sex; and it is not to be wondered at, that so tempting a morsel soon found favor in his eyes, more especially after he had visited her in her paternal mansion. Old Baltus Van Tassel was a perfect picture of a thriving, contented, liberal-hearted farmer. He seldom, it is true, sent either his eyes or his thoughts beyond the boundaries of his own farm; but within those every thing was snug, happy, and well-conditioned. He was satisfied with his wealth, but not proud of it, and piqued himself upon the hearty abundance, rather than the style in which he lived. His strong hold was situated on the banks of the Hudson, in one of those green, sheltered, fertile nooks, into which the Dutch farmers are so fond of nestling. A great elm tree spread its broad branches over it, at the foot of which bubbled up a spring of the softest and sweetest water, in a little kind of well, formed of a barrel, and then stole sparkling away through the grass, to a neighboring brook, that babbled along among elders and dwarf willows. Hard by the farmhouse was a vast barn, that might have served for a church; every window and crevice of which seemed bursting forth with the treasures of the farm; the flail was busily resounding within it; swallows and martins skimmed twittering about the eaves, and rows of pigeons, some with one eye turned up, as if watching the weather, some with their heads under their wings, or buried in their bosoms, and others, swelling, and cooing, and bowing about their dames, were enjoying the sunshine on the roof. Sleek unwieldy porkers were grunting in the repose and abundance of their pens, from whence sallied forth, now and then, troops of sucking pigs, as if to snuff the air. A stately squadron of snowy geese were riding in an adjoining pond, convoying whole fleets of ducks; regiments of turkeys were gobbling about the farm yard, and guinea fowls fretting like ill-tempered housewives, with their peevish discontented cry. Before the barn door strutted the gallant cock, that pattern of a husband, a warrior, and a fine gentleman, clapping his burnished wings, and crowing in the pride and gladness of his heart—sometimes tearing up the earth with his feet, and then generously calling his ever-hungry family of wives and children to enjoy the rich morsel he had discovered.

The pedagogue's mouth watered, as he looked upon this sumptuous promise of luxurious winter fare. In his devouring mind's eye, he pictured to himself every roasting pig running about with a pudding in its belly, and an apple in its mouth; the pigeons were snugly put to bed in a comfortable pie, and tucked in with a coverlet of crust; the geese were swimming in their own gravy; and the ducks pairing cosily in dishes, like snug married couples, with a decent competency of onion sauce; in the porkers he saw carved out the future sleek side of bacon, and juicy relishing ham; not a turkey, but he beheld daintily trussed up, with its gizzard under its wing, and, peradventure, a necklace of savory sausages; and even bright chanticleer[3] himself lay sprawling on his back, in a side dish, with uplifted claws, as if craving that quarter, which his chivalrous spirit disdained to ask while living.

As the enraptured Ichabod fancied all this, and as he rolled his great green eyes over the fat meadow lands, the rich fields of wheat, of rye, of buckwheat, and Indian corn and the orchards burthened with rudely fruit, which surrounded the warm tenement[4] of Van Tassel, his heart yearned after the damsel who was to inherit these domains, and his imagination expanded with the idea, how they might be readily turned into cash, and the money invested in immense tracts of wild land, and shingle palaces in the wilderness. Nay, his busy fancy already put him in possession of his hopes, and presented to him the blooming Katrina, with a whole family of children, mounted on the top of a wagon loaded with household trumpery, with pots and kettles dangling beneath; and he beheld himself bestriding a pacing mare, with a colt at her heels, setting out for Kentucky, Tennessee, or the Lord knows where!

When he entered the house, the conquest of his heart was complete. It was one of those spacious farm houses, with high-ridged, but lowly-sloping roofs, built in the style handed down from the first Dutch settlers. The low, projecting eaves formed a piazza along the front, capable of being closed up in bad weather. Under this were hung flails, harness, various utensils of husbandry, and nets for fishing in the neighboring river. Benches were built along the sides for summer use; and a great spinning wheel at one end, and a churn at the other, showed the various uses to which this important porch might be devoted. From this piazza the wondering Ichabod entered the hall, which formed the center of the mansion, and the place of usual residence. Here,

1. **Saardam.** Now Zaandam, a city near Amsterdam
2. **stomacher.** Decorative waistband worn over a dress
3. **chanticleer.** Rooster
4. **tenement.** Residence

Additional Questions and Activities

- In the paragraph that introduces the character of Katrina Van Tassel, identify two similes.

Answer. Katrina was "as plump as a partridge" and "ripe and melting and rosy-cheeked as one of her father's peaches."

- How did a visit to Katrina's home convince Ichabod that he wanted to marry her, even before he entered the house?

Answer. As soon as he saw how rich Katrina's father was, Crane hoped to share in that wealth by gaining Katrina's hand.

Additional Questions and Activities

Washington uses many interesting images in this story. Invite students to select the funniest comparisons that can be illustrated. Students can create a collage of silly drawings, for example, of Ichabod with shovels for feet and a flat weathervane for a head, and Katrina as an animated peach.

Cross-curricular Activities

Arts and Humanities. Have students draw or paint what Ichabod imagined as he looked at the animals on the Van Tassel farm.

Additional Questions and Activities

• Who was Ichabod Crane's rival for Katrina? Describe his appearance and behavior.

Answer. Crane's rival was Abraham Van Brunt, called Brom Bones. Brom was a large, strong man and a natural leader who was first in all contests. He was always ready for "a fight or a frolick." He and his friends often rode about the countryside making noise.

• What does the reader learn about Katrina's father from the line "he loved his daughter better even than his pipe"?

Answer. Her father seems shallow or stupid, not able to recognize or value his daughter as an independent person.

rows of resplendent pewter, ranged on a long dresser, dazzled his eyes. In one corner stood a huge bag of wool ready to be spun; in another a quantity of linsey-woolsey just from the loom; ears of Indian corn, and strings of dried apples and peaches, hung in gay festoons along the walls, mingled with the gaud of red peppers; and a door left ajar, gave him a peep into the best parlor, where the claw-footed chairs, and dark mahogany tables, shone like mirrors; andirons, with their accompanying shovel and tongs, glistened from their covert of asparagus tops; mock oranges and conch shells decorated the mantlepiece; strings of various colored birds' eggs were suspended above it; a great ostrich egg was hung from the center of the room, and a corner cupboard, knowingly left open, displayed immense treasures of old silver and well-mended china.

From the moment Ichabod laid his eyes upon these regions of delight, the peace of his mind was at an end, and his only study was how to gain the affections of the peerless daughter of Van Tassel. In this enterprise, however, he had more real difficulties than generally fell to the lot of a knight-errant of yore, who seldom had any thing but giants, enchanters, fiery dragons, and such like easily conquered adversaries, to contend with; and had to make his way merely through gates of iron and brass, and walls of adamant,[1] to the castle keep, where the lady of his heart was confined; all which he achieved as easily as a man would carve his way to the center of a Christmas pie, and then the lady gave him her hand as a matter of course. Ichabod, on the contrary, had to win his way to the heart of a country coquette, beset with a labyrinth of whims and caprices, which were for ever presenting new difficulties and impediments, and he had to encounter a host of fearful adversaries of real flesh and blood, the numerous rustic admirers, who beset every portal to her heart, keeping a watchful and angry eye upon each other, but ready to fly out in the common cause against any new competitor.

Among these, the most formidable, was a burley, roaring, roystering blade, of the name of Abraham, or, according to the Dutch abbreviation, Brom Van Brunt, the hero of the country round, which rung with his feats of strength and hardihood. He was broad shouldered and double jointed, with short curly black hair, and a bluff, but not unpleasant countenance, having a mingled air of fun and arrogance. From his Herculean frame and great powers of limb, he had received the nick-name of BROM BONES, by which he was universally known. He was famed for great knowledge and skill in horsemanship, being as dexterous on horseback as a Tartar. He was foremost at all races and cockfights, and with the ascendancy which bodily strength always acquires in rustic life, was the umpire in all disputes, setting his hat on one side, and giving his decisions with an air and tone that admitted of no gainsay or appeal. He was always ready for either a fight or a frolick; had more mischief than ill-will in his composition; and with all his overbearing roughness, there was a strong dash of waggish good humor at bottom. He had three or four boon companions of his own stamp, who regarded him as their model, and at the head of whom he scoured the country, attending every scene of feud or merriment for miles round. In cold weather he was distinguished by a fur cap, surmounted with a flaunting fox's tail, and when the folks at a country gathering descried this well-known crest at a distance, whisking about among a squad of hard riders, they always stood by for a squall. Sometimes his crew would be heard dashing along past the farm-houses at midnight, with whoop and halloo, like a troop of Don Cossacks,[2] and the old dames, startled out of their sleep, would listen for a moment till the hurry scurry had clattered by, and then exclaim, "aye, there goes Brom Bones and his gang!" The neighbors looked upon him with a mixture of awe, admiration, and good-will; and when any mad-cap prank, or rustic brawl, occurred in the vicinity, always shook their heads, and warranted Brom Bones was at the bottom of it.

This rantipole[3] hero had for some time singled out the blooming Katrina for the object of his uncouth gallantries, and though his amorous toyings were something like the gentle caresses and endearments of a bear, yet it was whispered that she did not altogether discourage his hopes. Certain it is, his advances were signals for rival candidates to retire, who felt no inclination to cross a lion in his amours; insomuch, that when his horse was seen tied to Van Tassel's paling,[4] of a Sunday night, (a sure sign that his master was courting, or, as it is termed, "sparking," within,) all other suitors passed by in despair, and carried the war into other quarters.

Such was the formidable rival with whom Ichabod Crane had to contend and, considering all things, a stouter man than he would have shrunk from the competition, and a wiser man would have despaired. He had, however, a happy mixture of pliability and perseverance in his nature; he was in form and spirit like a supple jack—yielding, but tough; though he bent, he never broke; and though he bowed beneath the slightest pressure, yet, the moment it was away—jerk!—he was as erect, and carried his head as high as ever.

To have taken the field openly against his rival, would have been madness; for he was not a man to be thwarted in his amours, any more than that stormy lover, Achilles.[5] Ichabod, therefore, made his advances in a quiet and gently-insinuating manner. Under cover of his character of singing master, he made frequent visits at the farm-house; not that he had any thing to apprehend from the meddlesome interference of parents, which is so often a stumbling block in the path of lovers. Balt Van Tassel was an easy indulgent soul; he loved his daughter better even than his pipe, and like a reasonable man, and an excellent father, let her have her way in every thing. His notable little wife too, had enough to do to attend

1. **adamant.** Impenetrable stone of fable and legend
2. **Don Cossacks.** Russian Cavalry
3. **rantipole.** Unruly
4. **paling.** Fence
5. **Achilles.** Legendary warrior Achilles sulks over a lost love until he is roused to fight in anger.

to her housekeeping and manage the poultry, for, as she sagely observed, ducks and geese are foolish things, and must be looked after, but girls can take care of themselves. Thus while the busy dame bustled about the house, or plied her spinning wheel at one end of the piazza, honest Balt would sit smoking his evening pipe at the other, watching the achievements of a little wooden warrior, who, armed with a sword in each hand, was most valiantly fighting the wind on the pinnacle of the barn. In the mean time, Ichabod would carry on his suit with the daughter by the side of the spring under the great elm, or sauntering along in the twilight, that hour so favorable to the lover's eloquence.

I profess not to know how women's hearts are wooed and won. To me they have always been matters of riddle and admiration. Some seem to have but one vulnerable point, or door of access; while others have a thousand avenues, and may be captured a thousand different ways. It is a great triumph of skill to gain the former, but a still greater proof of generalship to maintain possession of the latter, for a man must battle for his fortress at every door and window. He that wins a thousand common hearts, is therefore entitled to some renown; but he who keeps undisputed sway over the heart of a coquette, is indeed a hero. Certain it is, this was not the case with the redoutable Brom Bones; and from the moment Ichabod Crane made his advances, the interests of the former evidently declined; his horse was no longer seen tied at the palings on Sunday nights, and a deadly feud gradually arose between him and the preceptor of Sleepy Hollow.

Brom, who had a degree of rough chivalry in his nature, would fain have carried matters to open warfare, and settled their pretensions to the lady, according to the mode of those most concise and simple reasoners, the knights-errant of yore—by single combat: but Ichabod was too conscious of the superior might of his adversary to enter the lists against him; he had overheard the boast of Bones, that he would "double the schoolmaster up, and put him on a shelf;" and he was too wary to give him an opportunity. There was something extremely provoking in this obstinately pacific system; it left Brom no alternative but to draw upon the funds of rustic waggery in his disposition, and play off boorish practical jokes upon his rival. Ichabod became the object of whimsical persecution to Bones, and his gang of rough riders. They harried his hitherto peaceful domains; smoked out his singing school, by stopping up the chimney; broke into the school-house at night, in spite of its formidable fastenings of withe and window stakes, and turned every thing topsy-turvy, so that the poor schoolmaster began to think all the witches in the country held their meetings there. But what was still more annoying, Brom took all opportunities of turning him into ridicule in presence of his mistress, and had a scoundrel dog, whom he taught to whine in the most ludicrous manner, and introduced as a rival of Ichabod's, to instruct her in psalmody.

In this way, matters went on for some time, without producing any material effect on the relative situations of the contending powers. On a fine autumnal afternoon, Ichabod, in pensive mood, sat enthroned on the lofty stool from whence he usually watched all the concerns of his little literary realm. In his hand he swayed a ferule, that scepter of despotic power; the birch of justice reposed on three nails, behind the throne a constant terror to evil doers; while on the desk before him might be seen sundry contraband articles and prohibited weapons, detected upon the persons of idle urchins, such as half-munched apples, popguns, whirligigs, fly-cages, and whole legions of rampant little paper game cocks. Apparently there had been some appalling act of justice recently inflicted, for his scholars were all busily intent upon their books, or slyly whispering behind them with one eye kept upon the master; and a kind of buzzing stillness reigned throughout the school-room. It was suddenly interrupted by the appearance of a negro in tow-cloth jacket and trousers, a round crowned fragment of a hat, like the cap of Mercury,[1] and mounted on the back of a ragged, wild, half-broken colt, which he managed with a rope by way of halter. He came clattering up to the school door with an invitation to Ichabod to attend a merry-making, or "quilting frolick," to be held that evening at Mynheer Van Tassel's, and having delivered his message with that air of importance, and effort at fine language, which a negro is apt to display on petty embassies of the kind, he dashed over the brook, and was seen scampering away up the hollow, full of the importance and hurry of his mission.

All was now bustle and hubbub in the late quiet school room. The scholars were hurried through their lessons, without stopping at trifles; those who were nimble, skipped over half with impunity, and those who were tardy, had a smart application now and then in the rear, to quicken their speed, or help them over a tall word. Books were flung aside, without being put away on the shelves; inkstands were overturned, benches thrown down, and the whole school turned loose an hour before the usual time; bursting forth like a legion of young imps, yelping and racketing about the green, in joy at their early emancipation.

The gallant Ichabod now spent at least an extra half hour at his toilet, brushing and furbishing up his best, and indeed only suit of rusty black, and arranging his looks by a bit of broken looking glass, that hung up in the school house. That he might make his appearance before his mistress in the true style of a cavalier, he borrowed a horse from the farmer with whom he was domiciliated, a choleric old Dutchman, of the name of Hans Van Ripper, and thus gallantly mounted, issued forth like a knight-errant in quest of adventures. But it is meet I should, in the true spirit of romantic story, give some account of the looks and equipments of my hero and his steed. The animal he bestrode was a broken-down plough horse, that had outlived almost every thing but his viciousness. He was gaunt and shagged, with a ewe neck and hammer head; his rusty mane and tail were tangled and knotted

1. **cap of Mercury.** Winged cap like that worn by Mercury, the messenger of the gods

ADDITIONAL QUESTIONS AND ACTIVITIES

- Why did Brom Bones and his friends begin to play tricks on Ichabod Crane?

Answer. Katrina seemed to prefer Ichabod to Brom.

- Why did Ichabod borrow a horse from the farmer with whom he was staying?

Answer. He was invited to a party at the Van Tassels, and he wanted to impress Katrina.

ADDITIONAL QUESTIONS AND ACTIVITIES

• Describe the sight of Ichabod on the horse in a single word.

Answer. Possible choices include *comical, ridiculous, awkward,* and *absurd.*

• What sort of horse did Brom Bones ride?

Answer. Brom rode a mischief-filled horse named Daredevil that only he could manage.

with burrs, one eye had lost its pupil, and was glaring and spectral, but the other had the gleam of a genuine devil in it. Still he must have had fire and mettle in his day, if we may judge from his name, which was Gunpowder. He had, in fact, been a favorite steed of his master's, the choleric Van Ripper, who was a furious rider, and had infused, very probably, some of his own spirit into the animal, for, old and broken-down as he looked, there was more lurking deviltry in him than in any young filly in the country.

Ichabod was a suitable figure for such a steed. He rode with short stirrups, which brought his knees nearly up to the pommel of the saddle; his sharp elbows stuck out like grasshoppers'; he carried his whip perpendicularly in his hand, like a scepter, and as the horse jogged on, the motion of his arms was not unlike the flapping of a pair of wings. A small wool hat rested on the top of his nose, for so his scanty strip of forehead might be called, and the skirts of his black coat fluttered out almost to the horse's tail. Such was the appearance of Ichabod and his steed, as they shambled out of the gate of Hans Van Ripper, and it was altogether such an apparition as is seldom to be met with in broad day light.

It was, as I have said, a fine autumnal day, the sky was clear and serene, and nature wore that rich and golden livery which we always associate with the idea of abundance. The forests had put on their sober brown and yellow, while some trees of the tenderer kind had been nipped by the frosts into brilliant dyes of orange, purple, and scarlet. Streaming files of wild ducks began to make their appearance high in the air; the bark of the squirrel might be heard from the groves of beech and hickory nuts, and the pensive whistle of the quail at intervals from the neighboring stubble field.

The small birds were taking their farewell banquets. In the fullness of their revelry, they fluttered, chirping and frolicking, from bush to bush, and tree to tree, capricious from the very profusion and variety around them. There was the honest cock-robin, the favorite game of stripling sportsmen, with its loud querulous note; and the twittering blackbirds flying in sable clouds; and the golden winged woodpecker, with his crimson crest, his broad black gorget, and splendid plumage; and the cedar bird, with its red tipt wings and yellow tipt tail, and its little monteiro cap[1] of feathers; and the blue jay, that noisy coxcomb, in his gay light blue coat and white under clothes, screaming and chattering, nodding, and bobbing, and bowing, and pretending to be on good terms with every songster of the grove.

As Ichabod jogged slowly on his way, his eye, ever open to every symptom of culinary abundance, ranged with delight over the treasures of jolly autumn. On all sides he beheld vast store of apples, some hanging in oppressive opulence on the trees, some gathered into baskets and barrels for the market, others heaped up in rich piles for the cider-press. Further on he beheld great fields of Indian corn, with its golden ears peeping from their leafy coverts, and holding out the promise of cakes and hasty pudding; and the yellow pumpkins lying beneath them, turning up their fair round bellies to the sun, and giving ample prospects of the most luxurious of pies; and anon he passed the fragrant buckwheat fields, breathing the odor of the bee-hive, and as he beheld them, soft anticipations stole over his mind of dainty slap-jacks, well buttered, and garnished with honey or treacle,[2] by the delicate little dimpled hand of Katrina Van Tassel.

Thus feeding his mind with many sweet thoughts and "sugared suppositions," he journeyed along the sides of a range of hills which look out upon some of the goodliest scenes of the mighty Hudson. The sun gradually wheeled his broad disk down into the west. The wide bosom of the Tappaan Zee lay motionless and glassy, excepting that here and there a gentle undulation waved and prolonged the blue shadow of the distant mountain: a few amber clouds floated in the sky, without a breath of air to move them. The horizon was of a fine golden tint, changing gradually into a pure apple green, and from that into a deep blue of the mid-heaven. A slanting ray lingered on the woody crests of the precipices that overhung some parts of the river, giving greater depth to the dark grey and purple of their rocky sides. A sloop was loitering in the distance, dropping slowly down with the tide, her sail hanging uselessly against the mast, and as the reflection of the sky gleamed along the still water, it seemed as if the vessel was suspended in the air.

It was toward evening that Ichabod arrived at the castle of the Heer Van Tassel, which he found thronged with the pride and flower of the adjacent country. Old farmers, a spare, leathern-faced race, in homespun coats and small clothes, blue stockings, huge shoes and magnificent pewter buckles. Their brisk withered little dames in close crimped caps, long waisted short gowns, homespun petticoats, with scissors and pincushions, and gay calico pockets, hanging on the outside. Buxom lasses, almost as antiquated as their mothers, excepting where a straw hat, a fine riband, or perhaps a white frock, gave symptoms of city innovations. The sons, in short square-skirted coats with rows of stupendous brass buttons, and their hair generally queued in the fashion of the times, especially if they could procure an eel-skin for the purpose, it being esteemed throughout the country as a potent nourisher and strengthener of the hair.

Brom Bones, however, was the hero of the scene, having come to the gathering on his favorite steed Daredevil, a creature, like himself, full of mettle and mischief, and which no one but himself could manage. He was in fact noted for preferring vicious animals, given to all kinds of tricks, which kept the rider in constant risk of his neck, and held a tractable well-broken horse as unworthy a lad of spirit.

Fain would I pause to dwell upon the world of charms that burst upon the enraptured gaze of my hero, as he entered the state parlor of Van Tassel's mansion. Not those of the bevy of buxom lasses, with their luxurious display of red and white: but the ample charms of a genuine Dutch country tea-table, in the sumptuous time of autumn. Such heaped up platters of cakes of various and almost indescrib-

1. **monteiro cap.** Hunting cap
2. **treacle.** Molasses

able kinds, known only to experienced Dutch housewives. There was the doughty dough-nut, the tenderer oly koek,[1] and the crisp and crumbling cruller; sweet cakes and short cakes, ginger cakes and honey cakes, and the whole family of cakes. And then there were apple pies and peach pies and pumpkin pies; not to mention slices of ham and smoked beef, together with broiled shad and roasted chickens; besides delectable dishes of preserved plums, and peaches, and pears, and quinces; with bowls of milk and cream, all mingled higgledy-piggledy, pretty much as I have enumerated them, with the motherly tea-pot sending up its clouds of vapor from the midst—Heaven bless the mark! I want breath and time to discuss this banquet as it deserves, and am too eager to get on with my story. Happily, Ichabod Crane was not in so great a hurry as his historian, but did ample justice to every dainty.

He was a kind and thankful toad, whose heart dilated in proportion as his skin was filled with good cheer, and whose spirits rose with eating, as some men's do with drink. He could not help, too, rolling his large eyes round him as he eat, and chuckling with the possibility that he might one day be lord of all this scene of almost unimaginable luxury and splendor. Then, he thought, how soon he'd turn his back upon the old school house; snap his fingers in the face of Hans Van Ripper, and every other niggardly patron, and kick any itinerant pedagogue out of doors that dared to call him comrade!

Old Baltus Van Tassel moved about among his guests with a face dilated with content and good humour, round and jolly as the harvest moon. His hospitable attentions were brief, but expressive, being confined to a shake of the hand, a slap on the shoulder, a loud laugh, and a pressing invitation to "reach to, and help themselves."

And now the sound of the music from the common room or hall, summoned to the dance. The musician was an old grey-headed negro, who had been the itinerant orchestra of the neighborhood for more than half a century. His instrument was as old and battered as himself. The greater part of the time he scraped away on two or three strings, accompanying every movement of the bow with a motion of the head; bowing almost to the ground, and stamping with his foot whenever a fresh couple were to start.

Ichabod prided himself upon his dancing as much as upon his vocal powers. Not a limb, not a fibre about him was idle, and to have seen his loosely hung frame in full motion, and clattering about the room, you would have thought Saint Vitus[2] himself, that blessed patron of the dance, was figuring before you in person. He was the admiration of all the negroes, who, having gathered, of all ages and sizes, from the farm and the neighborhood, stood forming a pyramid of shining black faces at every door and window, gazing with delight at the scene, rolling their white eye-balls, and showing grinning rows of ivory from ear to ear. How could the flogger of urchins be otherwise than animated and joyous; the lady of his heart was his partner in the dance; she smiled graciously in reply to all his amorous oglings, while Brom Bones, sorely smitten with love and jealousy, sat brooding by himself in one corner.

When the dance was at an end, Ichabod was attracted to a knot of the sager folks, who, with old Van Tassel, sat smoking at one end of the piazza, gossiping over former times, and drawling out long stories about the war.

This neighborhood, at the time of which I am speaking, was one of those highly favored places which abound with chronicle and great men. The British and American line had run near it during the war; it had, therefore, been the scene of marauding, and been infested with refugees, cow boys,[3] and all kind of border chivalry. Just sufficient time had elapsed to enable each story teller to dress up his tale with a little becoming fiction, and in the indistinctness of his recollection, to make himself the hero of every exploit.

There was the story of Doffue Martling, a large, blue-bearded Dutchman, who had nearly taken a British frigate with an old iron nine-pounder from a mud breastwork,[4] only that his gun burst at the sixth discharge. And there was an old gentleman who shall be nameless, being too rich a mynheer to be lightly mentioned, who in the battle of Whiteplains, being an excellent master of defense, parried a musket ball with a small sword, insomuch that he absolutely felt it whiz round the blade, and glance off at the hilt: in proof of which, he was ready at any time to show the sword, with the hilt a little bent. There were several more who had been equally great in the field, not one of whom but was persuaded that he had a considerable hand in bringing the war to a happy termination.

But all these were nothing to the tales of ghosts and apparitions that succeeded. The neighborhood is rich in legendary treasures of the kind. Local tales and superstitions thrive best in these sheltered, long settled retreats; but they are trampled under foot, by the shifting throng that forms the population of most of our country places. Besides, there is no encouragement for ghosts in the generality of our villages, for they have scarce had time to take their first nap, and turn themselves in their graves, before their surviving friends have traveled away from the neighborhood, so that when they turn out of a night to walk the rounds, they have no acquaintance left to call upon. This is perhaps the reason why we so seldom hear of ghosts excepting in our long-established Dutch communities.

The immediate cause, however, of the prevalence of supernatural stories in these parts, was doubtless owing to the vicinity of Sleepy Hollow. There was a contagion in the very air that blew from that haunted region; it breathed forth an atmosphere of dreams and fancies infecting all the land. Several of the Sleepy Hollow people were present at Van Tassel's, and, as usual, were doling out their wild and

1. **oly koek.** Type of doughnut
2. **Saint Vitus.** Christian martyr prayed to by Catholics for relief from nervous disorders
3. **cow boys.** Tory, or British, supporting raiders
4. **breastwork.** Fortification

Additional Questions and Activities

• Was Ichabod really in love with Katrina? Give a reason for your answer.

Answer. No, because whenever he considered being married to her he had material possessions, food, and status in mind, not Katrina herself.

• How gifted was Ichabod as a dancer?

Answer. He was not at all gifted; he looked ridiculous, with his arms and legs in almost uncontrolled motion.

• Why are there so few ghosts outside long-established Dutch communities?

Answer. In other communities, people move so quickly that when people die, their surviving friends leave town before the dead can return as ghosts to visit them.

Cross-curricular Activities

Social Studies. Have students use hints in the story to determine the social standing of schoolteachers and free African Americans in the New York community during the era of the selection.

Additional Questions and Activities

• Where did the guests at the party say the Headless Horseman was seen?

Answer. They said that the Headless Horseman was often seen at a bridge over the brook that ran near the church.

• Why did Ichabod stay at the Van Tassel home later than other guests? In what mood did he leave?

Answers. He stayed late to have a private conversation with Katrina, and he left in an unhappy mood.

Historical Note

Major John André (1751–1780), an aide to the British general Sir Henry Clinton, was hanged as a spy by American forces during the American Revolution. André was sent by Clinton to receive secret plans from American traitor Benedict Arnold for a British takeover of the American fort at West Point, New York. On the night of September 21, 1780, after André had received papers concerning the plot, the boat that was carrying him back to the British lines was fired on, and he tried to return by foot. However, he made a mistake by changing into civilian clothes, for when he was stopped by American militia, he was charged with spying, tried by a military court, and sentenced to death. He was hanged on October 2, 1780. He was charming and courageous, popular with his troops, and mourned even by his American captors.

wonderful legends. Many dismal tales were told about funeral trains, and mournful cries and wailings heard and seen about the great tree where the unfortunate Major André[1] was taken, and which stood in the neighborhood. Some mention was made also of the woman in white, that haunted the dark glen at Raven Rock, and was often heard to shriek on winter nights before a storm, having perished there in the snow. The chief part of the stories, however, turned upon the favorite specter of Sleepy Hollow, the headless horseman, who had been heard several times of late, patroling the country; and it was said, tethered his horse nightly among the graves in the churchyard.

The sequestered situation of this church seems always to have made it a favorite haunt of troubled spirits. It stands on a knoll, surrounded by locust trees and lofty elms, from among which its decent, whitewashed walls shine modestly forth, like Christian purity, beaming through the shades of retirement. A gentle slope descends from it to a silver sheet of water, bordered by high trees, between which, peeps may be caught at the blue hills of the Hudson. To look upon its grass-grown yard, where the sunbeams seem to sleep so quietly, one would think that here at least the dead might rest in peace. On one side of the church extends a wide woody dell, along which raves a large brook among broken rocks and trunks of fallen trees. Over a deep black part of the stream, not far from the church, was formerly thrown a wooden bridge; the road that led to it, and the bridge itself, were thickly shaded by overhanging trees, which cast a gloom about it, even in the day time; but occasioned a fearful darkness at night. Such was one of the favorite haunts of the headless horseman, and the place where he was most frequently encountered. The tale was told of old Brouwer, a most heretical disbeliever in ghosts, that he met the horseman returning from his foray into Sleepy Hollow, and was obliged to get up behind him; that they galloped over bush and brake, over hill and swamp, until they reached the bridge, when the horseman suddenly turned into a skeleton, threw old Brouwer into the brook, and sprang away over the treetops with a clap of thunder.

This story was immediately matched by a thrice marvelous adventure of Brom Bones, who made light of the galloping Hessian as an errant jockey. He affirmed, that on returning one night from the neighborhood village of Sing-Sing, he had been overtaken by this midnight trooper; that he had offered to race with him for a bowl of punch, and would have won it too, for Daredevil beat the goblin horse all hollow, but just as they came to the church bridge, the Hessian bolted, and vanished in a flash of fire.

All these tales, told in that drowsy under tone with which men talk in the dark, the countenances of the listeners only now and then receiving a casual gleam from the glare of a pipe, sunk deep in the mind of Ichabod. He repaid them in kind with large extracts from his invaluable author, Cotton Mather, and added many very marvellous events that had taken place in his native state of Connecticut, and fearful sights which he had seen in his nightly walks about Sleepy Hollow.

The revel now gradually broke up. The old farmers gathered together their families in their wagons, and were heard for some time rattling along the hollow roads, and over the distant hills. Some of the damsels, mounted on pillions[2] behind their favorite swains, and their light-hearted laughter mingling with the clatter of hoofs, echoed along the silent woodlands, sounding fainter and fainter until they gradually died away—and the late scene of noise and frolic was all silent and deserted. Ichabod only lingered behind, according to the custom of country lovers, to have a tête-a-tête[3] with the heiress; fully convinced that he was now on the high road to success. What passed at this interview I will not pretend to say, for in fact I do not know. Something, however, I fear me, must have gone wrong, for he certainly sallied forth, after no very great interval, with an air quite desolate and chopfallen—Oh these women! these women! Could that girl have been playing off any of her coquettish tricks?—Was her encouragement of the poor pedagogue all a mere sham to secure her conquest of his rival?—Heaven only knows, not I!—Let it suffice to say, Ichabod stole forth with the air of one who had been sacking a hen roost, rather than a fair lady's heart. Without looking to the right or left to notice the scene of rural wealth, on which he had so often gloated, he went straight to the stable, and with several hearty cuffs and kicks, roused his steed most uncourteously from the comfortable quarters in which he was soundly sleeping, dreaming of mountains of corn and oats, and whole valleys of timothy and clover.

It was the very witching time of night that Ichabod, heavyhearted and bedrooped, pursued his travel homewards, along the sides of the lofty hills which rise above Tarry Town, and which he had traversed so cheerily in the afternoon. The hour was as dismal as himself. Far below him the Tappaan Zee spread its dusky and indistinct waste of waters, with here and there the tall mast of a sloop, riding quietly at anchor under the land. In the dead hush of midnight, he could even hear the barking of the watch-dog from the opposite shore of the Hudson; but it was so vague and faint as only to give an idea of his distance from this faithful companion of man. Now and then, too, the long-drawn crowing of a cock, accidentally awakened, would sound far, far off, from some farm house away among the hills—but it was like a dreaming sound in his ear. No signs of life occurred near him, but occasionally the melancholy chirp of a cricket, or perhaps the gutteral twang of a bullfrog, from a neighboring marsh, as if sleeping uncomfortably and turning suddenly in his bed.

All the stories of ghosts and goblins that Ichabod had heard in the afternoon, now came crowding upon his recollection. The night grew darker and darker; the stars seemed to sink deeper in the sky, and driving clouds occasionally hid them from his sight. He had never felt so lonely and dismal. He was, more-

1. **Major André.** British spy arrested in Tarrytown
2. **pillions.** Pads that allow a second rider to sit behind a saddled rider
3. **tête-a-tête.** French for "head-to-head," meaning a private conversation

over, approaching the very place where many of the scenes of the ghost stories had been laid. In the center of the road stood an enormous tulip tree, which towered like a giant above all the other trees of the neighborhood, and formed a kind of landmark. Its limbs were vast, gnarled, and fantastic, twisting down almost to the earth, and rising again into the air, and they would have formed trunks for ordinary trees. It was connected with the tragical story of the unfortunate André, who had been taken prisoner hard by it, and it was universally known by the name of Major André's tree. The common people regarded it with a mixture of respect and superstition, partly out of sympathy for the memory of its ill-starred namesake, and partly from the tales, strange sights, and doleful lamentations, told concerning it.

As Ichabod approached this fearful tree, he began to whistle; he thought his whistle was answered: it was but a blast sweeping sharply through the dry branches. As he approached a little nearer, he thought he saw something white, hanging in the midst of the tree: he paused and ceased whistling; but on looking more narrowly, perceived that it was a place where the tree had been scathed by lightning, and the white wood laid bare. Suddenly he heard a groan—his teeth chattered, and his knees smote against the saddle: it was but the rubbing of one huge bough upon another, as they were swayed about by the breeze. He passed the tree in safety, but new perils lay still before him.

About two hundred yards from the tree, a small brook crossed the road, and ran into a marshy and thickly wooded glen, known by the name of Wiley's Swamp. A few rough logs, laid side by side, served for a bridge over this stream. On that side of the road where the brook entered the wood, a group of oaks and chestnuts, matted thick with wild grape vines, threw a cavernous gloom over it. To pass this bridge, was the severest trial. It was at this identical spot that the unfortunate André was captured, and under the covert of those chestnuts and vines were the sturdy yeomen concealed who surprised him. This has ever since been considered a haunted stream, and fearful are the feelings of the schoolboy who has to pass it alone after dark.

As he approached the stream, his heart began to thump; he, however, summoned up all his resolution, gave his horse half a score of kicks in the ribs, and attempted to dash briskly across the bridge; but instead of starting forward, the perverse old animal made a lateral movement, and ran broadside against the fence. Ichabod, whose fears increased with the delay, jerked the reins on the other side, and kicked lustily with the contrary foot: it was all in vain; his steed started, it is true, but it was only to plunge to the opposite side of the road into a thicket of brambles and alder bushes. The schoolmaster now bestowed both whip and heel upon the starvelling ribs of old Gunpowder, who dashed forward, snuffling and snorting, but came to a stand just by the bridge with a suddenness that had nearly sent his rider sprawling over his head. Just at this moment a plashy tramp by the side of the bridge caught the sensitive ear of Ichabod. In the dark shadow of the grove, on the margin of the brook, he beheld something huge, misshapen, black and towering. It stirred not, but seemed gathered up in the gloom, like some gigantic monster ready to spring upon the traveler.

The hair of the affrighted pedagogue rose upon his head with terror. What was to be done? To turn and fly was now too late; and besides, what chance was there of escaping ghost or goblin, if such it was, which can ride upon the wings of the wind? Summoning up, therefore, a show of courage, he demanded in stammering accents—"who are you?" He received no reply. He repeated his demand in a still more agitated voice.—Still there was no answer. Once more he cudgelled the sides of the inflexible Gunpowder, and shuttering his eyes, broke forth with involuntary fervor into a psalm tune. Just then the shadowy object of alarm put itself in motion, and with a scramble and a bound, stood at once in the middle of the road. Though the night was dark and dismal, yet the form of the unknown might now in some degree be ascertained. He appeared to be a horseman of large dimensions, and mounted on a black horse of powerful frame. He made no offer of molestation or sociability, but kept aloof on one side of the road, jogging along on the blind side of old Gunpowder, who had now got over his fright and waywardness.

Ichabod, who had no relish for this strange midnight companion, and bethought himself of the adventure of Brom Bones with the galloping Hessian, now quickened his steed, in hopes of leaving him behind. The stranger, however, quickened his horse to an equal pace; Ichabod pulled up, and fell into a walk, thinking to lag behind—the other did the same. His heart began to sink within him; he endeavored to resume his psalm tune, but his parched tongue clove to the roof of his mouth, and he could not utter a stave.[1] There was something in the moody and dogged silence of this pertinacious companion, that was mysterious and appalling. It was soon fearfully accounted for. On mounting a rising ground, which brought the figure of his fellow traveller in relief against the sky, gigantic in height, and muffled in a cloak, Ichabod was horror-struck, on perceiving that he was headless! but his horror was still more increased, on observing, that the head, which should have rested on his shoulders, was carried before him on the pommel of the saddle! His terror rose to desperation; he rained a shower of kicks and blows upon Gunpowder, hoping, by a sudden movement, to give his companion the slip—but the specter started full jump with him. Away, then, they dashed, through thick and thin; stones flying, and sparks flashing, at every bound. Ichabod's flimsy garments fluttered in the air, as he stretched his long lank body away over his horse's head, in the eagerness of his flight.

They had now reached the road which turns off to Sleepy Hollow; but Gunpowder, who seemed possessed with a demon, instead of keeping up it, made an opposite turn, and plunged headlong down hill to the left. This road leads through a sandy hollow shaded by trees for about a quarter of a mile, where it crosses the bridge famous in goblin story,

1. **stave.** Line or verse

Additional Questions and Activities

- When Ichabod encountered a horseman on his way home, how did the horseman behave at first?

Answer. The horseman jogged along on the other side of the road, keeping up with Ichabod.

- What caused Ichabod to flee from the horseman?

Answer. When the horseman was at the top of a rise, Ichabod saw that the figure was headless and, further, that he carried his head before him on the pommel of his saddle.

- To what location did Gunpowder run? What is significant about this location?

Answers. Gunpowder left the road and plunged through the brush toward the bridge near the church. The location to which Gunpowder runs is the place famous in goblin stories.

Additional Questions and Activities

• What caused Ichabod to almost fall from his horse?

Answer. As old Gunpowder ran, the saddle fell off, and Ichabod had to grab the horse's mane to stay on.

• What finally caused him to fall? Where did this happen?

Answer. Ichabod fell off when he was struck in the head by the horseman's head, which the horseman threw just as Gunpowder carried Crane to the opposite side of the bridge.

• After Ichabod's disappearance, what did the local people think happened to him?

Answer. Local people thought that the Headless Horseman had carried him away.

• How did Brom Bones hint that he knew more about Ichabod's disappearance than others?

Answer. Brom always looked knowing when Ichabod's story was told, and he burst out laughing at the mention of the pumpkin found smashed on the ground near the bridge the morning after Ichabod's disappearance.

Quotables

"I am always at a loss to know how much to believe of my own stories."

—Washington Irving

and just beyond swells the green knoll on which stands the whitewashed church.

As yet the panic of the steed had given his unskillful rider an apparent advantage in the chase, but just as he had got half way through the hollow, the girths of the saddle gave way, and he felt it slipping from under him; he seized it by the pommel, and endeavored to hold it firm, but in vain; and had just time to save himself by clasping old Gunpowder round the neck, when the saddle fell to the earth, and he heard it trampled under foot by his pursuer. For a moment of terror of Hans Van Ripper's wrath passed across his mind—for it was his Sunday saddle; but this was no time for petty fears: the goblin was hard on his haunches; and, unskillful rider that he was! he had much-ado to maintain his seat; sometimes slipping on one side, sometimes on another, and sometimes jolted on the high ridge of his horse's back bone, with a violence that he verily feared would cleave him asunder.

An opening in the trees now cheered him with the hopes that the Church Bridge was at hand. The wavering reflection of a silver star in the bosom of the brook told him that he was not mistaken. He saw the walls of the church dimly glaring under the trees beyond. He recollected the place where Brom Bones's ghostly competitor had disappeared. "If I can but reach that bridge," thought Ichabod, "I am safe."[2] Just then he heard the black steed panting and blowing close behind him; he fancied he felt his hot breath. Another convulsive kick in the ribs, and old Gunpowder sprung upon the bridge; he thundered over the resounding planks; he gained the opposite side, and now Ichabod cast a look behind to see if his pursuer should vanish, according to rule, in a flash of fire and brimstone. Just then he saw the goblin rising in his stirrups, and in the very act of hurling his head at him. Ichabod endeavored to dodge the horrible missile, but too late. It encountered his cranium with a tremendous crash—he was tumbled headlong into the dust, and Gunpowder, the black steed, and the goblin rider, passed by like a whirlwind—

The next morning the old horse was found without his saddle, and the bridle under his feet, soberly cropping the grass at his master's gate. Ichabod did not make his appearance at breakfast—dinner-hour came, but no Ichabod. The boys assembled at the schoolhouse, and strolled idly about the banks of the brook; but no schoolmaster. Hans Van Ripper now began to feel some uneasiness about the fate of poor Ichabod, and his saddle. An inquiry was set on foot, and after diligent investigation they came upon his traces. In one part of the road leading to the church, was found the saddle trampled in the dirt; the tracks of horses' hoofs deeply dented in the road, and evidently at furious speed, were traced to the bridge, beyond which, on the bank of a broad part of the brook, where the water ran deep and black, was found the hat of the unfortunate Ichabod, and close beside it a shattered pumpkin.

The brook was searched, but the body of the schoolmaster was not to be discovered. Hans Van Ripper, as executor of his estate, examined the bundle which contained all his worldly effects. They consisted of two old shirts and a half; two stocks for the neck; a pair of worsted stockings with holes in them; an old pair of corduroy small-clothes; a book of psalm tunes full of dog's ears; a pitch pipe out of order; a rusty razor; a small pot of bear's grease for the hair, and a cast-iron comb. As to the books and furniture of the schoolhouse, they belonged to the community, excepting Cotton Mather's History of Witchcraft, a New-England Almanac, and a book of dreams and fortune telling, in which last was a sheet of foolscap much scribbled and blotted by several fruitless attempts to make a copy of verses in honor of the heiress of Van Tassel. These magic books and the poetic scrawl were forthwith consigned to the flames by Hans Van Ripper, who from that time forward determined to send his children no more to school, observing, that he never knew any good come of this same reading and writing. Whatever money the schoolmaster possessed, and he had received his quarter's pay but a day or two before, he must have had about his person at the time of his disappearance.

The mysterious event caused much speculation at the Church on the following Sunday. Knots of gazers and gossips were collected in the church-yard at the bridge, and at the spot where the hat and pumpkin had been found. The stories of Brouwer, of Bones, and a whole budget of others, were called to mind; and when they had diligently considered them all, and compared them with the symptoms of the present case, they shook their heads, and came to the conclusion, that Ichabod had been carried off by the galloping Hessian. As he was a bachelor, and in nobody's debt, nobody troubled his head any more about him, the school was removed to a different quarter of the hollow, and another pedagogue reigned in his stead.

It is true, an old farmer, who had been down to New York on a visit several years after, and from whom this account of the ghostly adventure was received, brought home the intelligence that Ichabod Crane was still alive; that he had left the neighborhood partly through fear of the goblin and Hans Van Ripper, and partly in mortification at having been suddenly dismissed by the heiress; that he had changed his quarters to a distant part of the country; had kept school and studied law at the same time; had been admitted to the bar, turned politician, electioneered, written for the newspapers, and finally had been made a Justice of the Ten Pound Court.[1] Brom Bones too, who, shortly after his rival's disappearance, conducted the blooming Katrina in triumph to the altar, was observed to look exceedingly knowing whenever the story of Ichabod was related, and always burst into a hearty laugh at the mention of the pumpkin; which led some to suspect that he knew more about the matter than he chose to tell.

The old country wives, however, who are the best judges

1. **I am safe.** Crane believed the superstition that spirits could not cross water.

2. **Ten Pound Court.** Small-claims court

of these matters maintain to this day, that Ichabod was spirited away by supernatural means; and it is a favorite story often told about the neighborhood round the winter evening fire. The bridge became more than ever an object of superstitious awe, and that may be the reason why the road has been altered of late years, so as to approach the church by the border of the millpond. The schoolhouse being deserted, soon fell to decay, and was reported to be haunted by the ghost of the unfortunate pedagogue; and the plough boy, loitering homeward of a still summer evening, has often fancied his voice at a distance, chanting a melancholy psalm tune among the tranquil solitudes of Sleepy Hollow.

POSTSCRIPT, FOUND IN THE HANDWRITTING OF MR. KNICKERBOCKER

The preceding Tale is given, almost in the precise words in which I heard it related at the corporation meeting of the ancient city of the Manhattoes, at which were present many of its sagest and most illustrious burghers. The narrator was a pleasant, shabby, gentlemanly old fellow, in pepper and salt clothes, with a sadly humorous face, and one whom I strongly suspected of being poor, he made such efforts to be entertaining. When his story was concluded, there was much laughter and approbation, particularly from two or three deputy aldermen, who had been asleep the greater part of the time. There was, however, one tall, dry-looking old gentleman, with beetling eyebrows, who maintained a grave and rather severe face throughout; now and then folding his arms, inclining his head, and looking down upon the floor, as if turning a doubt over in his mind. He was one of your wary men, who never laugh but upon good grounds—when they have reason and the law on their side. When the mirth of the rest of the company had subsided, and silence was restored, he leaned one arm on the elbow of his chair, and sticking the other a-kimbo, demanded, with a slight, but exceedingly sage motion of the head, and contraction of the brow, what was the moral of the story, and what it went to prove.

The story-teller, who was just putting a glass of wine to his lips, as a refreshment after his toils, paused for a moment, looked at his inquirer with an air of infinite deference, and lowering the glass slowly to the table, observed, that the story was intended most logically to prove,

"That there is no situation in life but has its advantages and pleasures, provided we will but take a joke as we find it:

"That, therefore, he that runs races with goblin troopers, is likely to have rough riding of it:

"Ergo, for a country schoolmaster to be refused the hand of a Dutch heiress, is a certain step to high preferment in the state."

The cautious old gentleman knit his brows tenfold closer after this explanation, being sorely puzzled by the ratiocination of the syllogism; while me thought the one in pepper and salt eyed him with something of a triumphant leer. At length he observed, that all this was very well, but still he thought the story a little on the extravagant—there were one or two points on which he had his doubts.

"Faith, sir," replied the story-teller, "as to that matter, I don't believe one half of it myself."

from "The Fall of the House of Usher"
by Edgar Allan Poe

During the whole of a dull, dark, and soundless day in the autumn of the year, when the clouds hung oppressively low in the heavens, I had been passing alone, on horseback, through a singularly dreary tract of country; and at length found myself, as the shades of the evening drew on, within view of the melancholy House of Usher. I know not how it was—but, with the first glimpse of the building, a sense of insufferable gloom pervaded my spirit. I say insufferable; for the feeling was unrelieved by any of that half-pleasurable, because poetic, sentiment, with which the mind usually receives even the sternest natural images of the desolate or terrible. I looked upon the scene before me—upon the mere house, and the simple landscape features of the domain—upon the bleak walls—upon the vacant eye-like windows—upon a few rank sedges—and upon a few white trunks of decayed trees—with an utter depression of soul which I can compare to no earthly sensation more properly than to the after-dream of the reveler upon opium—the bitter lapse into common life—the hideous dropping off of the veil. There was an iciness, a sinking, a sickening of the heart—an unredeemed dreariness of thought which no goading of the imagination could torture into aught of the sublime. What was it—I paused to think—what was it that so unnerved me in the contemplation of the House of Usher? It was a mystery all insoluble; nor could I grapple with the shadowy fancies that crowded upon me as I pondered. I was forced to fall back upon the unsatisfactory conclusion, that while, beyond doubt, there *are* combinations of very simple natural objects which have the power of thus affecting us, still the reason, and the analysis, of this power, lie among considerations beyond our depth. It was possible, I reflected, that a mere different arrangement of the particulars of the scene, of the details of this picture, would be sufficient to modify, or perhaps to annihilate its capacity for sorrowful impression; and, acting upon this idea, I reined my horse to the precipitous brink of a black and lurid tarn[1] that lay in unruffled luster by the dwelling, and gazed down—but with a shudder even more thrilling than before—upon the remodeled and inverted images of the gray sedge, and the ghastly tree-stems, and the vacant and eye-like windows.

1. **tarn.** Small lake

Literary Technique

Point out the postscript and the parenthetical note at the beginning of the story. Have students discuss what effect these elements have on the story and its impact on the reader. (The frame distances the story from the reader and lets the reader know that even the storyteller thinks the tale is absurd. The postscript adds more absurdity.)

from "The Fall of the House of Usher"

About the Author. A biography of **Edgar Allan Poe** appears on page 225.

About the Selection. The short story **"The Fall of the House of Usher"** was first printed in 1839 in *Burton's Gentleman's Magazine* where Poe worked as an assistant editor for less than a year. Like other Poe stories, it is obsessed with decay, madness, death, and a world that seems out of control. The narrator is summoned to the home of an old friend and finds that he arrives just in time to witness his friend's death along with the total destruction of his family and his gloomy mansion.

Additional Questions and Activities

• Describe the mansion as the narrator first sees it. Which details reveal the state of decay in the scene?

Answer. The house seems incredibly gloomy. It has bleak walls and vacant eye-like windows. Positioned around it are a few rank sedges and a few white trunks of decayed trees. Near the house is a black, motionless lake.

• How does the narrator explain the sense of melancholy he feels as he looks at the House of Usher? What does he do to try to lessen the gloomy impression?

Answers. The narrator believes that certain arrangements of details are responsible for the sense of gloom that he feels. In an attempt to alter his impression, he rides closer to

(cont.)

Additional Questions and Activities (cont.)

the mansion to get a different perspective on it.

• What words and phrases contribute to the melancholy mood of the selection?

Answer. Words such as *oppressively, dreary, melancholy,* and *desolate* and phrases such as *dark, dull and soundless day* and *a sense of insufferable gloom pervaded my spirit, an iciness, a sinking, a sickening of the heart* all contribute to the melancholy mood.

VOCABULARY DEVELOPMENT EXERCISES

►Give students the following exercise.

Have students identify at least ten words on page 284 with positive connotations, that is, that refer to positive experiences or things, and at least ten others with negative connotations or meanings. Then have them write ten sentences about the authors or selections in this unit, using ten words from the two lists they have created. Five of the sentences should use words drawn from the "positive connotations" group and five should use words drawn from the "negative connotations" group.

ADDITIONAL RESOURCES

ASSESSMENT PORTFOLIO

- Vocabulary Worksheet, 4.4.11
- Study Guide: Unit 4 Test, 4.4.12
- Unit 4 Test, 4.4.13

ESSENTIAL SKILLS PRACTICE BOOKS

- *Language,* 2.20, 2.27, 2.43–2.45, 2.50, 2.62, 2.71, 2.76–2.84, 2.86, 2.116, 2.138
- *Speaking and Listening,* 3.6
- *Study and Research,* 4.1, 4.3, 4.16, 4.30, 4.31

UNIT REVIEW

New England Renaissance Prose

VOCABULARY FROM THE SELECTIONS

abstraction, 236
abyss, 230
accentuation, 226
affinity, 207
ague, 237
analogy, 205
anointed, 235
aperture, 236
arduous, 254
aspect, 200
aspiration, 263
assuage, 208
august, 243
aversion, 254
avert, 237
avidity, 229
balm, 237
baneful, 207
benignity, 243
cadence, 227
cessation, 235, 264
cognizance, 232
conjecture, 236
conjure, 227
connoisseur, 211
consternation, 224
convolution, 231
cordiality, 203
craven, 247
dally, 237
deleterious, 204
delusory, 210
demeanor, 201
depraved, 210
diffuse, 236
discordant, 237
earnest, 260
ebullition, 209
elucidate, 247
emaciated, 213
encompass, 228
encumbrance, 262
endeavor, 264
envoy, 243
ethereal, 261
evanescent, 211
fervor, 211
festooned, 248
fissure, 236
fluctuate, 266
gaudiest, 245
gauntleted, 244
illuminate, 236
imbue, 215
impede, 228
impend, 237
inanition, 233
incantation, 248
indeterminate, 266
ineffable, 242
ingenuity, 232
inquisitorial, 226
insinuate, 217
insuperable, 229
interminable, 227
irrespective, 245
laxly, 268
locution, 226
lozenge, 237
lurid, 208
malignant, 201
moiety, 235
palsied, 248
paltry, 264
perennial, 261
pertinacity, 209, 234
phenomenon, 205
portal, 205
portentous, 248
posterity, 262
predominate, 253
primeval, 244
pungently, 232
recompense, 206
reminiscence, 199
resplendent, 200
reverie, 213
resignation, 259
riband, 236
saturated, 260
speculative, 208
squalid, 254
sublime, 243
superfluous, 265
surmise, 216
supervene, 227
terminate, 202
testily, 204
transcendent, 243
trepidation, 244
undulation, 263
unintelligible, 206
untoward, 209
unwieldy, 266
vengeance, 237
verdure, 206
vermin, 235
viand, 235
volatile, 268
voracity, 235
writhe, 226

LITERARY TERMS

allusion, 222, 250, 270
aphorism, 256, 270
elaboration, 250
essay, 256
fantasy, 222
metaphor, 256
mood, 238
onomatopoeia, 250
point of view, 238
romance, 238
symbol, 222
theme, 256
tone, 270

SYNTHESIS: QUESTIONS FOR WRITING, RESEARCH, OR DISCUSSION

GENRE STUDIES

1. **Short Story.** The work of Washington Irving, Nathaniel Hawthorne, and Edgar Allan Poe contributed to the development of the short story as a literary form. From Poe came the definition that all aspects of the short story combine to create one dominant impression. Examine two short stories from this unit. What dominant impression is created in each one? What details create this impression?

THEMATIC STUDIES

2. **Appearance and Reality.** Sometimes a fine line separates the credible from the incredible. Examine this theme in the excerpt from *Moby-Dick* and in one short story in the unit.
3. **Transcendentalism.** Transcendentalism in New England was an outgrowth of the Romantic Era in Europe. Review the definition of Transcendentalism in the unit introduction and select passages from Emerson and Thoreau that illustrate Transcendental philosophy.

HISTORICAL/BIOGRAPHICAL STUDIES

4. **Copyright Laws.** The lack of an international copyright law until 1891 meant many writers could not support themselves by their writing. Yet, they continued to write and to create. Discuss the creative process, the impulse to write, regardless of monetary gain.

▶These prompts are suitable as topics for research papers. Refer to the Language Arts Survey, 4.20–4.34, "Research Skills." (To evaluate research papers, see the evaluation forms for writing, revising, and proofreading, *Assessment Portfolio,* 7.1–7.10.)

▶These prompts can be adapted for use as topics for oral reports or debates. (To evaluate these projects, see the evaluation forms in the *Assessment Portfolio,* 7.17–7.19.)

LANGUAGE LAB EDITING FOR ERRORS IN PRONOUNS

Case is the form that a noun or a pronoun takes to indicate its use in a sentence: nominative, objective, or possessive. The nominative case is used for the subject of a verb or for a predicate nominative. The objective case is used for a direct object, an indirect object, or the object of a preposition. The possessive case is used to show possession. For additional help, see the Language Arts Survey, 2.76–2.77. The following chart lists common errors in pronoun usage.

PRONOUN USAGE

***Who* and *Whom*.** The pronoun *who* is referred to as an interrogative pronoun when it is used to form a question. When it is used to introduce a subordinate clause, it is referred to as a relative pronoun. In both cases, the nominative is *who,* the objective is *whom,* and the possessive is *whose.*

SUBJECT: *Who* designed Monticello?
DIRECT OBJECT: *Whom* did Jefferson hire to construct his home?
OBJECT OF PREPOSITION: *To whom* did Jefferson give the plans?

Pronouns in Comparisons. The ends of sentences that compare people or things are often left unexpressed. Pronouns in such sentences should be the same case as they would have been if the sentence had been completed.

EXAMPLE: Referring to Thomas Jefferson, the guide said that no revolutionary had done as much to shape the United States as *he* [had done].

Agreement of Pronouns and Antecedents. Check the pronouns in your writing to be sure they agree in **number, person,** and **gender** with their antecedents.

INCORRECT NUMBER: The guide spoke about several architectural landmarks on the campus and *its* historical significance.
CORRECT NUMBER: The guide spoke about several architectural landmarks on the campus and *their* historical significance.

Reference of Pronouns to Antecedents. Avoid weak, ambiguous, indefinite, and general references between pronouns and antecedents.

WEAK REFERENCE: During the prospective-students tour, they asked many questions.
CLEAR ANTECEDENT: During their tour, the prospective students asked many questions.
AMBIGUOUS REFERENCE: As the tour guide spoke of Jefferson, he seemed to come to life.
CLEAR REFERENCE: As the tour guide spoke of him, Jefferson seemed to come to life.
INDEFINITE REFERENCE: Since Jefferson's death, they have grouped his writings into four categories.
PRONOUN ELIMINATED: Since Jefferson's death, scholars have grouped his writings into four categories.
GENERAL REFERENCE: In the informational brochure, it had a complete biography of Jefferson.
SENTENCE REWORDED: The informational brochure had a complete biography of Jefferson.

EXERCISE A Avoiding Errors in Pronoun Usage

In each sentence below, choose the correct word from within the parentheses.

EXAMPLE: The writer of the New England Renaissance (who, whom) I most admire is Ralph Waldo Emerson.
whom

1. The scholar believed that no one had researched the life of Nathaniel Hawthorne more thoroughly than (her, she).
2. Melville's early writings were well received by (his, their) audience.
3. Tina thinks that the short stories of Poe are the best ever written and none can compare to (them, they).
4. (Who, whom) wrote "The Legend of Sleepy Hollow"?
5. Both Thoreau and Emerson printed works based on (his, their) journals.
6. To (who, whom) did you lend my copy of *Moby-Dick?*
7. Emerson said that people must be nonconformists and that nothing is sacred but the integrity of (our, their) minds.
8. Did the end of "The Pit and the Pendulum" surprise you as much as it did (I, me)?
9. Dr. Heideigger offered his friends water from the fountain of youth, and he watched the effects on (him, them).
10. Thoreau's advice to "simplify, simplify" is difficult for Alana to follow but nobody needs to simplify as much as (her, she).

LANGUAGE ARTS SURVEY

For additional help, see the Language Arts Survey, 2.78–2.82.

Exercise B Correcting Errors in Pronoun Usage

Rewrite the following sentences, correcting the errors in pronoun usage.

EXAMPLE: The University of Virginia seal says that it was founded in 1819.
The University of Virginia seal reads, "Founded 1819."

1. Thomas Jefferson founded the University of Virginia. He considered this one of his three greatest accomplishments.
2. As the whale watch began, they read a segment from *Moby-Dick.*
3. In *Poor Richard's Almanack*, they convey Franklin's common-sense philosophy.
4. Tony, a fan of Thoreau, went to visit Walden Pond because he had lived there.
5. When Patrick Henry delivered speeches, it often created an impassioned response from his audience.

LANGUAGE ARTS SURVEY

For additional help, see the Language Arts Survey, 2.83–2.84

ANSWERS FOR LANGUAGE LAB

Exercise A

1. she
2. his
3. them
4. Who
5. their
6. whom
7. their
8. me
9. them
10. she

Exercise B

Responses will vary. Possible responses are given.

1. Thomas Jefferson considered founding the University of Virginia one of his three greatest accomplishments.
2. A segment from *Moby-Dick* was read as the whale watch began.
3. The advice and aphorisms in *Poor Richard's Almanack* convey Franklin's common-sense philosophy.
4. Tony, a fan of Thoreau, went to visit Walden Pond because his favorite author had lived there.
5. Patrick Henry's delivery of his speeches often created an impassioned response from his audience.

UNIT SKILLS OUTLINE

LITERARY SKILLS AND CONCEPTS

- Alliteration, 310, 320, 344
- Apology, 327
- Apostrophe, 300, 305, 320
- Assonance, 334
- Blank Verse, 295
- Couplet, 305
- Elaboration, 295
- Euphony, 300
- Extended Metaphor, 334
- Image, 310
- Irony, 334
- Meter, 319, 327
- Mood, 315
- Narrative Poem, 310
- Onomatopoeia, 337
- Personification, 327
- Point of View, 315, 334
- Repetition, 331
- Rhetorical Question, 305
- Rhyme, 323, 344
- Romanticism, 323
- Run-on Line, 344
- Sight Rhyme, 331
- Slant Rhyme, 331
- Stanza, 300, 305, 334
- Symbol, 337
- Synaesthesia, 336
- Tone, 315

WRITING SKILLS AND CONCEPTS

- Character Sketch, 310
- Comic Strip, 344
- Description, 337
- Diary Entry, 316
- Editorial, 323
- Fantasy, 344
- Original Lyric Poem, 328
- Obituary, 316
- Stream of Consciousness, 323

GRAMMAR, USAGE, AND MECHANICS SKILLS AND CONCEPTS

- Adding Prepositional Phrases, 310
- Adjectives and Articles, 307
- Agreement of Pronouns and Adjectives I, 300
- Agreement of Pronouns and Adjectives II, 300
- Capitalization, 291, 329
- Correcting Dangling or Misplaced Modifiers, 323
- Dashes, 328, 332
- Double Negatives, 305
- Improper Shifts in Verb Tense, 316
- Inverting Sentences for Emphasis, 321
- Irregular Verbs I, 312
- Prepositions, 295
- Quotation Marks I, 345
- Semicolons, 320, 328
- Voice and Mood, 331

OTHER LANGUAGE ARTS SKILLS AND CONCEPTS

- Bibliographies and Bibliography Cards, 326
- Choosing an Audience, 302
- Comparing and Contrasting, 297
- Elaboration: Types of Supporting Details, 335
- Elements of Verbal Communication, 318
- The Form of a Personal Letter, 328
- Making Hypotheses, 316
- Public Speaking, 339
- Sensory Detail Charts, 321
- Using Dictionaries, 331
- Using Reference Works, 30
- Using Searching Tools, 305

UNIT 5 NEW ENGLAND RENAISSANCE POETRY (1800–1860)

Still Life with Copper Tankard. William M. Harnett

GOALS/OBJECTIVES

Studying this unit will enable students to

- enjoy reading the poetry of the New England Renaissance
- describe the influence of Romanticism on New England Renaissance poets
- describe the political sentiments of certain New England Renaissance poets
- analyze the expression of Transcendentalism in literature
- identify a variety of literary and rhetorical techniques as they are used in the poetry of the New England Renaissance
- edit for errors in modifiers

Our day of dependence, our long apprenticeship to the learning of other lands, draws to a close. . . . Events, actions arise, that must be sung, that will sing themselves. Who can doubt that poetry will revive and lead in a new age?

—Ralph Waldo Emerson
"The American Scholar"

ART NOTE

William M. Harnett (1848–1892) immigrated to the United States from Ireland and became known as a master of trompe l'oeil painting, or painting that captures the realism of a photograph. Harnett's still life is a visual statement of the transition from colonial America to independent America. Parlor contents typical of seventeenth-century Europe (the copper tankard, drinking gourd, and hookah) nestle among early American pantry items on a kitchen table.

LITERARY CURRENTS

Use the following selections to explore these concepts and techniques with your students.

ELEGIAC VERSE

- "Thanatopsis," 290
- "Telling the Bees," 311
- "The Raven," 338

EXTENDED METAPHOR

- "The Chambered Nautilus," 296
- "Because I could not stop for Death—," 332

RHETORICAL QUESTION

- "Stanzas on Freedom," 301

NARRATIVE POEM

- "The Village Blacksmith," 306

ROMANTIC VERSE

- "Thanatopsis," 290
- "The Chambered Nautilus," 296
- "The Rhodora," 321

PERSONIFICATION

- "The Chambered Nautilus," 296
- "This is my letter to the World," 326

► Note: Lists for Connections across The Curriculum and Teaching the Multiple Intelligences appear on page 353.

THEMATIC CURRENTS

Use the following selections to explore these themes with your students.

INDIVIDUALISM

- "This is my letter to the World," 326
- "The Soul selects her own Society—," 329

COMMON BONDS

- "Stanzas on Freedom," 301
- "The Village Blacksmith," 306
- "Concord Hymn," 318

FACING DEATH

- "Thanatopsis," 290
- "The Village Blacksmith," 306
- "Telling the Bees," 311
- "Because I could not stop for Death—," 332
- "I heard a Fly buzz—when I died—," 335
- "The Raven," 338

THE NATURAL WORLD

- "The Chambered Nautilus," 296
- "Telling the Bees," 311
- "The Rhodora," 321

ADDITIONAL RESOURCES

READER'S GUIDE
- Selection Worksheet, 5.1

ASSESSMENT PORTFOLIO
- Selection Check Test, 4.5.1
- Selection Test, 4.5.2

ESSENTIAL SKILLS PRACTICE BOOKS
- *Language,* 2.24, 2.119–2.121

ENRICHMENT ACTIVITIES

Students can research the personal history of Abraham Lincoln and compare it to that of William Cullen Bryant. Encourage students to discuss parallels in the lives of the two men such as the way in which their families' economic limitations affected them, their shared interest in law and involvement in politics, and their sense of personal responsibility for inspiring and protecting the working people of America.

SUPPORT FOR LEP STUDENTS

Some students may have difficulty with Bryant's vocabulary. You may wish to review the additional vocabulary below with students before they read the selection.

IDIOMS

brood of care—gathering of worried individuals
quarry-slave—miner
rude swain—careless youth

ADDITIONAL VOCABULARY

various—varied, changing
musings—views and thoughts
ere—before
resolv'd—reconnected, returned
vales—valleys
abodes—homes
scourged—driven with force (whipped)

PREREADING

"Thanatopsis"
by William Cullen Bryant

ABOUT THE AUTHOR

William Cullen Bryant (1794–1878), born in rural Cummington, Massachusetts, had an abiding love for nature. He briefly attended Williams College in 1810 but dropped out, hoping to go to Yale. Because his father could not afford that expense, Bryant read for the law and was admitted to practice in 1815. Heavily influenced by the English Romantic poets Thomas Gray and William Wordsworth, Bryant began to write poetry at a young age but realized that he could not afford to pursue a full-time career as a poet. Appointed justice of the peace in Great Barrington in 1820, the following year Bryant married Frances Fairchild and published a volume entitled *Poems.* The Bryants moved to New York City, where he worked as an editor of the *New York Review* and *Atheneum Magazine.* Thereafter, he became editor-in-chief and part owner of the *Evening Post,* a position that brought him wealth, fame, and influence. Bryant championed humanitarian causes, including the abolition of slavery and of debtors' prisons. He also became a key figure in American political life, helping to form the Republican Party and to get both Andrew Jackson and Abraham Lincoln elected president. He traveled widely in Europe and in the Middle East and published letters about his experiences. Bryant continued writing into his seventies, translating Homer's epics, *The Odyssey* and *The Iliad,* and writing poems.

ABOUT THE SELECTION

Bryant probably began **"Thanatopsis"** in 1811, when he was only sixteen years old. The subject and moral outlook of the poem owe much to Thomas Gray's "Elegy Written in a Country Churchyard." The first version of the poem consisted of the present poem's lines 18–66. Bryant's father submitted this poem and another on the subject of death to the *North American Review* in 1817, and the two were mistakenly published as a single work. In 1821, Bryant completed "Thanatopsis," framing the original lines with an introduction (lines 1–17) and a conclusion (lines 66–82). In the earlier version, the central lines had been in the poet's own voice; in the later version, the speaker is a romanticized and personified Nature. The ideas in the three parts of the poem betray the changes in the poet's thinking over the ten years of its composition. Nevertheless, the beauty of the poem's language and the grandeur of its images immediately established Bryant's literary reputation and helped to create pride in the ability of Americans to match the literary creations of the British Romantic school.

GOALS/OBJECTIVES

Studying this lesson will enable students to
- empathize with a speaker's feelings about nature and death
- describe Bryant's literary accomplishments and explain the historical significance of his writing
- recognize and explain the characteristics of blank verse
- define *elaboration* and identify the use of this technique in their reading
- identify prepositions
- compare Thomas Gray's "Elegy Written in a Country Churchyard" to this selection

READER'S JOURNAL

Some people perceive nature as violent and cruel, while others see it as beautiful and inspirational. Write briefly in your journal about your attitude toward nature. Support your opinion with specific observations.

LANGUAGE SKILLS

Read about particular uses of capitalization in the Language Arts Survey, 2.119–2.121, "Personal Names," "Place Names," and "Poetry." Then find examples in the poem of all three types of capitalization.

"Thanatopsis[1]"

WILLIAM CULLEN BRYANT

To him who in the love of Nature holds
Communion with her visible forms, she speaks
A various language; for his gayer hours
She has a voice of gladness, and a smile
5 And eloquence of beauty, and she glides
Into his darker musings, with a mild
And gentle sympathy, that steals away
Their sharpness, ere he is aware. When thoughts
Of the last bitter hour come like a blight
10 Over thy spirit, and sad images
Of the stern agony, and shroud, and pall,
And breathless darkness, and the narrow house,[2]
Make thee to shudder, and grow sick at heart,—
Go forth under the open sky, and list[3]
15 To Nature's teachings, while from all around—
Earth and her waters, and the depths of air,—
Comes a still voice—Yet a few days, and thee
The all-beholding sun shall see no more

❶ *What effect can thoughts of death have?*

❷ *Where should the reader seek comfort?*

1. **Thanatopsis.** This word, coined by Bryant, means "views and thoughts on death."
2. **shroud . . . narrow house.** *Shroud*—cloth used to wrap a corpse for burial; *pall*—cloth draped over a coffin; *narrow house*—grave
3. **list.** Listen

WORDS FOR EVERYDAY USE:

com • mun • ion (kə myōōn´yən) *n.,* act of sharing thoughts and actions

blight (blīt) *n.,* anything that destroys or prevents growth

PREREADING NOTES

READER'S JOURNAL

Students may perceive both the cruel and the beautiful aspects of nature in their journal entries. Encourage students to describe the changeable temperament of nature—the way it can seem serene and lovely one moment and threatening and volatile the next.

LANGUAGE SKILLS

In the three categories of capitalization, students may list *Nature* under "Personal Names"; and *Barcan desert, Oregan,* and *Earth* under "Place Names." Students will list first word capitalizations under "Poetry."

ANSWERS TO GUIDED READING QUESTIONS

❶ Thoughts of death can terrify and even sicken the thinker.

❷ The reader should seek comfort under the open sky, listening to nature's sounds.

VOCABULARY FROM THE SELECTION

blight	lapse
clods	patriarch
communion	pensive
hoary	sepulcher
insensible	venerable

LITERARY NOTE

Bryant's "Thanatopsis" eventually earned him his literary reputation. The poem also strengthened the belief of American poets that they could stand on equal ground with the British Romantic school of poets.

VOCABULARY IN CONTEXT

- The boy stared into the gray stallion's eyes in silent communion with the horse.
- All the chestnut trees fell to the ground during the season of the blight.

Art Note

Albert Bierstadt (1830–1902) was an extremely popular American landscape painter. He explored the American West, searching for interesting subject matter. His paintings capture the magnificence of the American countryside.

Historical Note

The original version of the poem began at line 18 of the selection given here and ended with the full stop in line 66. Bryant began the poem in 1811, and his father submitted it for publication in 1817. During this period, the United States was at war with Great Britain (War of 1812). Perhaps speaking for his fellow citizens who were at war with their colonial oppressor, Bryant was struggling with the dilemma of choosing between death and liberty.

Additional Questions and Activities

Bryant was sixteen when he wrote "Thanatopsis." Have students discuss in small groups this young man's idea that communion with nature strengthens us in the face of death. Ask students how and why nature soothes us in our fears. Students may identify with the image of this adolescent alone grappling with the hugeness of death. Help them to envision the speaker of the poem, who feels small as one of a few living humans, yet feels powerful as one of many mortal beings on the Earth.

Among the Sierra Nevada Mountains, California. *Albert Bierstadt, 1868. National Museum of American Art, Washington, DC/Art Resource, NY*

In all his course; nor yet in the cold ground,
20 Where thy pale form was laid, with many tears,
Nor in the embrace of ocean shall exist
Thy image. Earth, that nourished thee, shall claim
Thy growth, to be resolv'd to earth again;
And, lost each human trace, surrend'ring up
25 Thine individual being, shalt thou go
To mix forever with the elements,
To be a brother to th' insensible rock
And to the sluggish clod, which the rude swain
Turns with his share,[4] and treads upon. The oak
30 Shall send his roots abroad, and pierce thy mould.[5]
Yet not to thy eternal resting place
Shalt thou retire alone—nor couldst thou wish

4. **share.** Plough
5. **mould.** Form or body

Words for Everyday Use:
in • sen • si • ble (in sen´sə bəl) *adj.*, lacking sensation; unaware
clod (kläd) *n.*, lump, such as lump of earth or clay

Vocabulary in Context

- The marathon runners seemed insensible to thirst, exhaustion, and pain.
- A clod of curds floated in the butter churn.

Couch more magnificent. Thou shalt lie down
With patriarchs of the infant world—with kings
35 The powerful of the earth—the wise, the good,
Fair forms, and hoary seers of ages past,
All in one mighty sepulcher.—The hills
Rock-ribb'd and ancient as the sun,—the vales
Stretching in pensive quietness between;
40 The venerable woods—rivers that move
In majesty, and the complaining brooks
That make the meadows green; and pour'd round all,
Old ocean's grey and melancholy waste,—
Are but the solemn decorations all
45 Of the great tomb of man. The golden sun,
The planets, all the infinite host of heaven,
Are shining on the sad abodes of death,
Through the still lapse of ages. All that tread
The globe are but a handful to the tribes
50 That slumber in its bosom.—Take the wings
Of morning—and the Barcan desert[6] pierce,
Or lose thyself in the continuous woods
Where rolls the Oregan,[7] and hears no sound,
Save his own dashings—yet—the dead are there,
55 And millions in those solitudes, since first
The flight of years begin, have laid them down
In their last sleep—the dead reign there alone.—
So shalt thou rest—and what if thou shalt fall
Unnoticed by the living—and no friend
60 Take note of thy departure? All that breathe
Will share thy destiny. The gay will laugh
When thou art gone, the solemn brood of care
Plod on, and each one as before will chase
His favorite phantom; yet all these shall leave
65 Their mirth and their employments, and shall come,
And make their bed with thee. As the long train
Of ages glide away, the sons of men,
The youth in life's green spring, and he who goes
In the full strength of years, matron, and maid,
70 The bow'd with age, the infant in the smiles

6. **Barcan desert.** Desert in northeast Libya
7. **Oregan.** Early spelling of Oregon

❶ *With whom will the reader share the grave?*

❷ *What is the ratio of living to deceased?*

❸ *What happens after a single death?*

WORDS FOR EVERYDAY USE:

pa • tri • arch (pā´ trē ärk´) *n.,* father, ruler; founder
hoar • y (hôr´ē) *adj.,* having white or gray hair
sep • ul • cher (sep´əl kər) *n.,* vault for burial
pen • sive (pen´siv) *adj.,* expressing deep thoughtfulness, often with some sadness
ven • er • a • ble (ven´ər ə bəl) *adj.,* worthy of respect by reason of age and dignity
lapse (laps) *n.,* gliding or passing away

ANSWERS TO GUIDED READING QUESTIONS

❶ The reader will lie with patriarchs, kings, the wise, the good, the fair, and white-haired prophets.

❷ The living are a handful in comparison to all the tribes of the deceased on Earth.

❸ Life goes on as usual for the joyful and the mourners alike.

LITERARY NOTE

You might inform students that Bryant's brooding upon the transitory nature of life and the swift approach of death is not unique but rather a common theme in literature. The *contemptu mundi* theme (which lamented that the world is fallen and full of woe) and the *memento mori* theme (which warned that death comes quickly and unexpectedly) have appeared in the very first examples of English poetry, and these themes continued to emerge in English and American literature throughout the centuries. However, rather than expressing that the world is fallen and woeful, Bryant celebrates the magnificence and beauty of the world. Bryant adapts the *memento mori* theme by infusing it with the Romantic school's love of the natural world. Rather than something to be dreaded, swiftly approaching death is instead part of the natural order. Bryant compares death to a "magnificent" couch where the dead lie down "to pleasant dreams." The entire natural world is seen as "solemn decoration" for "the great tomb of man."

VOCABULARY IN CONTEXT

- Johnny Carson, former *Tonight Show* host, is the patriarch of late-night talk shows.
- Noah is often shown on his ark with hoary hair blowing in the salt breeze.
- The king was laid to rest in the sepulcher with great honor.
- Turning her head to face the new highway, the farmer looked pensive.
- Miguel Antonio said that he would give his venerable grandfather the first piece of cake.
- Danielle was an alert equestrian, but one lapse in judgment left her in the brook next to the first fence on the course.

ANSWER TO GUIDED READING QUESTION

❶ The reader is counseled to be trusting, calm, and dignified.

RESPONDING TO THE SELECTION

Students will react to the speaker's attitude toward death in various ways. They may disagree or agree with the speaker. Comments should include ideas related to the poem's major themes—life cycles, condolence, grief, and common destiny.

ANSWERS FOR REVIEWING THE SELECTION

RECALLING

1. For gayer voices, Nature answers with a voice of gladness; for darker musings, Nature answers with mild and gentle sympathy.

2. The speaker is the lover of Nature up through line 17; from the end of line 17 on, the speaker is Nature itself.

3. Some of the people the speaker lists are "patriarchs of the infant world," "powerful kings," "the wise, the good," "fair forms," and "hoary seers of ages past."

4. The speaker advises the listener to go not like a "quarry-slave at night" but strong and calm in trust like someone going to rest on a soft couch to have pleasant dreams.

INTERPRETING

Responses will vary. Possible responses are given.

5. *Wording will vary.*

6. Every human's remains will return to the earth and become unfeeling like rock.

7. No, lines that describe elements of Nature covering the millions of people who once lived support the answer.

8. Students might say that the

(cont.)

And beauty of its innocent age cut off,—
Shall one by one be gathered to thy side,
By those, who in their turn shall follow them.
So live, that when thy summons comes to join
75 The innumerable caravan, that moves
To the pale realms of shade, where each shall take
His chamber in the silent halls of death,
Thou go not, like the quarry-slave at night,
Scourged to his dungeon, but sustain'd and sooth'd
80 By an unfaltering trust, approach thy grave,
Like one who wraps the drapery of his couch
About him, and lies down to pleasant dreams. ■

What should be the reader's attitude approaching the grave? ❶

Responding to the Selection

How does thinking about the earth as one great, common grave make you feel? Is the fact that you share this fate with all humanity comforting? Do you agree that the poem's attitude gives death dignity?

Reviewing the Selection

RECALLING

1. The introduction (lines 1–17) describes various moods of a person. Identify two of these moods, which draw different responses from Nature.

2. Who is the speaker up to line 17 of the poem? Who begins to speak in line 17?

3. Who are some of the people the speaker lists as lying down in "one mighty sepulcher"?

4. How does the speaker advise the listener to go to the grave?

INTERPRETING

5. In your own words, explain each of the "sad images" of lines 11 and 12: the "stern agony," the "shroud," the "pall," the "breathless darkness," and the "narrow house."

6. In what way will every human become "a brother to the insensible rock" (line 27)?

7. Does the speaker feel that a dignified funeral is important? Cite lines of the poem that support your answer.

8. The speaker does not explicitly identify in whom or what the listener is to place an "unfaltering trust" (line 80). What or whom do you suppose the speaker had in mind?

ANSWERS FOR REVIEWING THE SELECTION (CONT.)

speaker had in mind a greater power, such as God or the spiritual connection among all members of the human community.

SYNTHESIZING

Responses will vary. Possible responses are given.

9. Students may say that Nature is personified as a goddess. Other students may answer that Nature is the earth or that Nature is every being in the universe that is not created by humans.

10. Students may answer that questions about life, death, and nature are as relevant today as they were in 1811; thus, the poem is meaningful today. Students may comment that the allusions and language of the poem could be a barrier to understanding for some individuals today.

SYNTHESIZING

9. In this poem, is Nature the same as the planet Earth? If not, how would you describe it?

10. If this poem were published today, do you think it would become as popular as it did with the people of 175 years ago? Why, or why not?

Understanding Literature (Questions for Discussion)

1. **Blank Verse. Blank verse** is unrhymed poetry written in iambic pentameter. (An iambic pentameter line consists of five feet, each containing two syllables, the first weakly stressed and the second strongly stressed.) Copy the first five lines of "Thanatopsis" and mark the strongly stressed syllables with accent marks. Which line is least regular?

2. **Elaboration. Elaboration**, or **amplification**, is a writing technique in which a subject is introduced and then expanded upon by means of repetition with slight changes, the addition of details, or similar devices. How does this poem make use of the technique of elaboration? What is the idea that is elaborated?

Language Lab

Prepositions. Read the Language Arts Survey, 2.24, "Prepositions." Then write out these sentences. Underline each prepositional phrase with a single underscore and each preposition with a double underscore.

1. "Thanatopsis," the best-known poem by William Cullen Bryant, draws its title from the Greek language.
2. In Greek, *thanatopsis* means "view of death"; no one could object to this phrase as a summary of the poem.
3. Despite Bryant's upbringing in the Calvinistic tradition, the poem reflects toward its topic a Wordsworthian pantheism, or nature worship.
4. Bryant seems to have been strongly impressed by the ideas of several English poets grouped by the title "graveyard school."
5. Clearly, however, the major influence on Bryant was William Wordsworth, one of the greatest English Romantic poets, who wrote about Nature as a loving friend to humanity.

ANSWERS FOR UNDERSTANDING LITERATURE

► See the evaluation forms for discussion, active listening, and oral communication, *Assessment Portfolio,* 7.11–7.14.

Responses will vary. Possible responses are given.

1. Blank Verse. Teachers should encourage students to read aloud the five lines as well as marking the accents on their transcription. This will help them decide which of the five lines is least regular (line 2).

2. Elaboration. The idea of the earth as a tomb is elaborated by descriptions of the world that follow the lines "Thou shalt" and "Thou go."

ANSWERS TO SELECTION CHECK TEST 4.5.1

EX. Who is speaking at the beginning of the poem?
A lover of nature is speaking.

1. In what way does Nature answer humans' "darker musings"?
Nature answers "with a mild/And gentle sympathy."

2. What effect can thoughts of death evoke in people?
Thoughts of death can make people "shudder" and "grow sick at heart."

3. To whom does the "still voice" that speaks belong?
The "still voice" belongs to Nature.

4. With whom does the speaker say the reader will share a grave?
The speaker says the reader will share a grave with patriarchs, kings, the wise, the good, the fair, and "hoary seers."

5. In what way does the speaker say the reader should approach death?
The speaker says the reader should approach death as if he or she were about to sleep on a couch and have pleasant dreams.

ANSWERS FOR LANGUAGE LAB

1. "Thanatopsis," the best-known poem by William Cullen Bryant, draws its title from the Greek language.

2. In Greek, *thanatopsis* means "view of death"; no one could object to this phrase as a summary of the poem.

3. Despite Bryant's upbringing in the Calvinistic tradition, the poem reflects toward its topic a Wordsworthian pantheism, or nature worship.

4. Bryant seems to have been strongly impressed by the ideas of several English poets grouped by the title "graveyard school."

5. Clearly, however, the major influence on Bryant was William Wordsworth, one of the greatest English Romantic poets, who wrote about Nature as a loving friend to humanity.

ADDITIONAL RESOURCES

READER'S GUIDE
- Selection Worksheet, 5.2

ASSESSMENT PORTFOLIO
- Selection Check Test, 4.5.3
- Selection Test, 4.5.4

ESSENTIAL SKILLS PRACTICE BOOKS
- *Language,* 2.81, 2.82
- *Study and Research,* 4.8, 4.28

ENRICHMENT ACTIVITIES

Students might write their own creative piece, either in prose or verse, about a specific natural object or animal from which they have learned or can learn a lesson. Students should describe the appearance and/or actions of their subject using vivid sensory details and then explain the lesson that can be learned from the appearance and/or actions of their subject.

SUPPORT FOR LEP STUDENTS

Students may be unfamiliar with the sirens of Greek and Roman mythology. Inform students that the sirens were sea nymphs, part bird and part woman, who lured sailors to their untimely deaths on rocky coasts with their beautiful singing. You might also review the additional vocabulary below with students before they read the selection.

ADDITIONAL VOCABULARY

feign—pretend; imagine
venturous—inclined to take chances
bark—any boat, especially a small sailing vessel
unfurl—open or spread out
tenant—occupant or dweller in a specified place
irised—rainbowlike
forlorn—abandoned or deserted
low-vaulted—having a low arch

PREREADING

"The Chambered Nautilus"

by Oliver Wendell Holmes

ABOUT THE AUTHOR

Oliver Wendell Holmes (1809–1894) was born in Cambridge, Massachusetts, and was class poet at Harvard in 1829. After first studying law, he then went to Paris to study medicine. He was awarded his M.D. degree from Harvard in 1836, the year his *Poems* was published. After serving as professor of anatomy at Dartmouth from 1839 to 1840, he moved to Boston, where he wrote medical treatises. He married Amelia Lee Jackson in 1840, and the couple raised three children, the first of whom, Oliver Wendell Holmes, Jr., became a famous Supreme Court justice. From 1847 until 1882, Holmes was a professor of anatomy at Harvard, writing several important scientific papers, including one that demonstrated that childhood fevers, a common cause of death, were spread by contact with infected persons. He became known as an essayist and poet in the late 1850s when the *Atlantic Monthly,* which he helped found, serialized his humorous essays and printed his poems, including "The Chambered Nautilus" and "The Deacon's Masterpiece." Of his four volumes of essays, the most famous is *The Autocrat at the Breakfast Table,* which presents the reflections of an imaginary cultured man who lives in a boarding house and entertains other guests with his lively conversation. Holmes also wrote three novels—"medicated novels" was his term for them—that dealt with genetic and psychological determinism. (Determinism is the belief that people's ideas, thoughts, feelings, and actions are caused by outside hereditary and environmental forces. From the 1860s through the 1880s, Holmes published volumes of poems and essays, as well as a biography of Ralph Waldo Emerson. Holmes was the most famous after-dinner speaker of his time, a leading figure in literary circles, and a witty writer of occasional verse.

ABOUT THE SELECTION

"The Chambered Nautilus" was published in the February 1858 issue of the *Atlantic Monthly* in one of Holmes's *Autocrat of the Breakfast Table* essays. The creature of the title is a mollusk, related to clams and octopi, that gradually builds a spiral, pearly-lined shell with a series of air-filled chambers. The creature acquired the name *nautilus,* from the Greek word for "sailor," because of the belief that it had a membrane that served as a sail, by means of which it navigated the waters of the Indian and Pacific oceans. Triton, referred to in line 26, was a Greek god of the sea, often pictured as blowing a horn made of a spirally twisted seashell. Holmes may have conceived the idea for the poem when reading the essay "Compensation," by Ralph Waldo Emerson, which compares human development to that of a shellfish.

GOALS/OBJECTIVES

Studying this lesson will enable students to

- enjoy a lyric poem that celebrates an aspect of nature
- describe Holmes's literary accomplishments and explain the historical significance of his writing
- identify the message the speaker sees in the chambered nautilus
- define *stanza, apostrophe,* and *euphony* and identify stanzas, apostrophes, and euphony in their reading
- use pronouns correctly
- locate and use reference works

READER'S JOURNAL

Have you ever put a curving seashell to your ear to hear the ocean's roar? What do people like about the look and feel of shells? Think about how shells affect your senses. Write about what makes handling seashells so satisfying.

THINKING SKILLS

Read the Language Arts Survey, 4.8, "Comparing and Contrasting." Then, as you read the poem, think about the two things that are being compared in it and what they have in common.

"The Chambered Nautilus"

OLIVER WENDELL HOLMES

This is the ship of pearl, which, poets feign,
Sails the unshadowed main,—
The venturous bark that flings
On the sweet summer wind its purpled wings
In gulfs enchanted, where the siren sings,
And coral reefs lie bare,
Where the cold sea-maids rise to sun their streaming hair.

Its webs of living gauze no more unfurl;
Wrecked is the ship of pearl!
And every chambered cell,
Where its dim dreaming life was wont to dwell,
As the frail tenant shaped his growing shell,
Before thee lies revealed,—
Its irised ceiling rent, its sunless crypt unsealed!

Year after year beheld the silent toil
That spread his lustrous coil;
Still, as the spiral grew,
He left the past year's dwelling for the new,
Stole with soft step its shining archway through,
Built up its idle door,
Stretched in his last-found home, and knew the old no more.

PREREADING NOTES

READER'S JOURNAL

As an alternate activity, students might write about the lessons they see in the natural world. Why might people search for messages in nature? Do students think that people look for specific messages in nature to comfort them or make them feel a certain way, or are the lessons already present, waiting to be discovered?

THINKING SKILLS

Students should compare the nautilus that abandons its shells periodically to humans who should build "more stately mansions" for their souls. Students might also compare the different aspects of the nautilus described in the poem—its personification as a sailor and its identity as a unique form in nature.

HISTORICAL NOTE

Holmes called his fiction "medicated novels." In his essays and speeches, the former anatomy professor wove into one strand both scientific and literary principles. Upper-class men in nineteenth-century America were encouraged to express all of their intellectual energy. They often practiced law or medicine as graduates. Then as they matured, they often sought involvement in creative avocations—in the arts, in new technologies, or in politics.

Upper-class men in nineteenth-century Europe were similarly encouraged. English mathematician Lewis Carroll was the author of the children's classic *Alice in Wonderland*. French mathematician and World War I aviator Antoine de Saint-Exupéry was the author of the pacifist allegory *Le Petit Prince* (*The Little Prince*).

QUOTABLES

"A moment's insight is sometimes worth a life's experience."

—Oliver Wendell Holmes

ANSWERS TO SELECTION CHECK TEST 4.5.3

EX. What is a chambered nautilus?
A chambered nautilus is the pearly, spiral shell of a mollusk.

1. What do poets feign or imagine?
Poets feign that the shell is a pearl sailing vessel.

2. Who sings in enchanted gulfs?
Sirens sing in enchanted gulfs.

3. Where is the creature that lived in the shell?
The creature has abandoned his shell, or home, for another one.

4. What does the shell of the nautilus bring the speaker?
The shell brings the speaker a "heavenly message."

5. What does the speaker want his or her soul to build?
The speaker wants his or her soul to build "more stately mansions."

CROSS-CURRICULAR ACTIVITIES

Mathematics and Sciences. Students might research the many different types of mollusks. There are eight major groups of mollusks, and you might break students into eight groups to research each one. (The groupings are Tryblidia, Gastropoda, Bivalvia, Scaphopoda, Solenogastres, Cephalopoda, Caudofoveata, and Placophora.) Students should discover the origins of mollusks, the different species in their groups, and the appearances and major characteristics of these species. Some mollusks are quite beautiful, and students may try to locate actual empty shells or pictures of shells to share with the class.

Illustration by Rodney Busch

Thanks for the heavenly message brought by thee,
    Child of the wandering sea,
    Cast from her lap, forlorn!
From thy dead lips a clearer note is born
Than ever Triton blew from wreathéd horn!
    While on mine ear it rings,
Through the deep caves of thought I hear a voice that sings:—

Build thee more stately mansions, O my soul,
    As the swift seasons roll!
    Leave thy low-vaulted past!
Let each new temple, nobler than the last,
Shut thee from heaven with a dome more vast,
    Till thou at length art free,
Leaving thine outgrown shell by life's unresting sea! ■

Responding to the Selection

Did the poet's link between the development of a shell and that of a person seem natural to you? How does referring to a picture of the shell aid in understanding and appreciating the poem?

Reviewing the Selection

Recalling

1. What fantastic details does the speaker provide about the life of the nautilus?
2. Review lines 10 through 14. What do they tell you about the present physical condition of the shell that is being described?
3. To whom are stanzas 1 to 3 addressed? stanza 4? stanza 5?
4. What does the singing voice of stanza 4 tell its listener to build? What might these structures represent?

Interpreting

5. Remember that Holmes was a scientific person, a trained physician. Why do you suppose the speaker in Holmes's poem introduces the shellfish with imagined details instead of using a scientifically accurate description?
6. In the first three stanzas, how does the speaker give the shellfish a personality? What are some of the details that make the audience more sympathetic toward it?
7. In stanza 4, the speaker credits the nautilus for bringing a message, but whose voice is singing?
8. From what do the soul's mansions, temples, and domes separate the soul? When does the separation end?

Synthesizing

9. Which do you think was more important to Holmes in choosing this particular shellfish—its name and related myth of being able to sail the waters, or its compartmented shape and pearly walls? How would the message of the poem be affected if either of these sets of characteristics was lacking?
10. Review the poem for instances of alliteration, assonance, or other sound effects. Which phrases seemed most melodious or striking to you? Explain why.

Responding to the Selection

Students may have difficulty understanding the leap the author makes when he moves from discussing the shell to discussing the human soul and human development. Stress that the nautilus leaves its shell behind when it becomes too small just as people must move on when they have developed past a certain stage.

Answers for Reviewing the Selection

RECALLING

1. The speaker marvels at the nautilus's ability to grow and inhabit a new shell at the same time that it disengages itself from its old shell; during the process, the shellfish travels long distances on the open ocean.

2. The shell's interior is luminous and iridescent; the empty shell reveals numerous chambered cells where the animal grew and transformed.

3. Stanzas 1 and 3 are addressed to the reader. Stanza 4 is addressed to the nautilus. Stanza 5 is addressed to the speaker's soul.

4. The singing voice of stanza 4 advises the listener to build stronger dwellings for its soul as the seasons pass, to leave the cumbersome entrappings behind, and to let each home grow larger and closer to heaven until the dweller is free.

INTERPRETING

Responses will vary. Possible responses are given.

5. The speaker may introduce the shellfish with imagined details to make the nautilus seem magical, awe-inspiring, and wonderful—a worthy thing to be compared to the development of the human soul.

6. The speaker gives the shellfish a personality by calling it "venturous," describing the creature within the shell as "dreaming," and finally by using the pronoun *he* when referring to the creature within the shell. The audience is sympathetic to the "silent toil" of the creature and its leaving the old home for the new and seeing the old home "no more."

(cont.)

Answers for Reviewing the Selection (cont.)

7. The voice singing is that of the speaker's soul.

8. The soul's mansions, temples, and domes separate it from heaven. The separation ends when the speaker dies.

SYNTHESIZING

Responses will vary. Possible responses are given.

9. Both the myth and physical characteristics of the shellfish were important to Holmes. If the related myth were missing, the romantic and magical quality of the shellfish would be lost. If the shape and pearly walls were missing, the comparison to the shell and to the mansions of the soul would be lost.

10. Students might say the line "Where the cold sea-maids rise to sun their streaming hair" is striking because of the alliteration, as is "Where its dim dreaming life was wont to dwell."

Understanding Literature (Questions for Discussion)

1. **Stanza.** A **stanza** is a recurring pattern of grouped lines in a poem. How many stanzas are in this poem? How many lines are in each stanza? What rhyme pattern do you find in each stanza?

2. **Apostrophe.** An **apostrophe** is a rhetorical technique in which an object or person is directly addressed. Identify an example of apostrophe in the fourth stanza. Who or what is being addressed? The apostrophe signals a development in the content of the poem. How do the lines that follow the apostrophe differ from those before it?

3. **Euphony. Euphony** is pleasing sound. Listen carefully to the sounds in the first half of stanza 5. How does the repeated sound of *l* suggest a steady forward movement at the same time as it contributes strongly to the euphony of the lines?

Language Lab

Pronouns and Antecedents. Read the Language Arts Survey, 2.81–2.82. "Agreement of Pronouns and Antecedents I and II." Then rewrite these sentences, using pronouns correctly.

1. Long ago, people really believed in myths, but today we see it simply as literature.
2. Still, mythology says something about human nature that makes him more than just old stories.
3. In the Greek myths, sirens are "cold sea-maids," as the poem says, but to us she stands for all sorts of temptations, such as the temptation to seek dangerous adventure or to act in a greedy manner in order to become wealthy.
4. Everybody knows that they can blame Pandora for the world's problems, for according to Greek myth, she was the one who let all the evils of the world out of a box.
5. Though different cultures call their gods of war by different names, he represents the same weaknesses in all of us, distrust and hostility toward people who are not like ourselves.

Study and Research Skills

Reference Works. Read the material about specialized encyclopedias in the Language Arts Survey, 4.28, "Using Reference Works." Then investigate a library to find out which encyclopedias of literature, mythology, literary terms, authors, and the like are available in the reference department. List the title and the particular focus of each. Look up Triton in two of these encyclopedias and compare the amount and type of information provided.

Answers for Understanding Literature

► See the evaluation forms for discussion, active listening, and oral communication, *Assessment Portfolio,* 7.11–7.14.

Responses will vary. Possible responses are given.

1. Stanza. Students should identify the five recurring patterns of grouped lines, the number of lines in each stanza (7), and the rhyme patterns of the stanzas (*aabbbcc*).

2. Apostrophe. Students should recognize that the apostrophe "thee,/Child of the wandering sea. . . " addresses the nautilus. Discussion should center on the change in the speaker's attitude as he moves from describing the nautilus to praising the nautilus directly.

3. Euphony. One comment might be that the *l* gives the stanza a joyful wavelike feeling. The language seems to roll forward melodically as the waves did.

Answers for Language Lab

Responses will vary. Possible responses are given.

1. Long ago, people really believed in myths, but today we see them simply as literature.
2. Still, mythology says something about human nature that makes it more than just old stories.
3. In the Greek myths, sirens are "cold sea-maids," as the poem says, but to us they stand for all sorts of temptations, such as the temptation to seek dangerous adventure or to act in a greedy manner in order to become wealthy.
4. Everybody knows that he or she can blame Pandora for the world's problems, for according to Greek myth, she was the one who let all the evils of the world out of a box.
5. Though different cultures call their gods of war by different names, they represent the same weaknesses in all of us, distrust and hostility toward people who are not like ourselves.

Answers for Study and Research Skills

Students should describe the types of information available on Triton in at least two general reference works at their library.

PREREADING

"Stanzas on Freedom"

by James Russell Lowell

About the Author

James Russell Lowell (1819–1891) was born in Cambridge, Massachusetts, and educated at Harvard. He studied law, but never practiced it, choosing a literary and academic life instead. Lowell was an idealist who devoted himself to a number of causes, including women's rights; temperance, or abstinence from alcohol; and abolition. In 1844, he married Maria White, also a writer and dedicated abolitionist. Lowell contributed to antislavery papers, including the *National Anti-Slavery Standard* and the *Pennsylvania Freeman*. He became recognized nationally in 1848 upon the publication of *Second Series, A Fable for Critics,* the first series of *The Bigelow Papers,* and *The Vision of Sir Launfal.* After the death of three of his children and his wife, a distraught Lowell continued to publish his work in magazines. In 1855 he became professor of modern languages at Harvard. He turned his writing mainly to criticism and essays. In 1857, he became the editor of the *Atlantic Monthly,* and later became coeditor of the *North American Review.* He used his magazines to promote the Union cause during the Civil War in which he lost many friends and family members. He served as United States ambassador to Spain from 1877 to 1880 and as ambassador to England from 1880 to 1885. Some of Lowell's poems remain popular, but his main literary influence was as a critic and an editor.

About the Selection

Before the Civil War, a strong abolitionist movement flourished among the writers of New England. An ardent abolitionist himself, Lowell wrote a number of poems and prose selections in support of his views. He contributed regularly to abolitionist publications, including the *National Anti-Slavery Standard,* which he also edited. In **"Stanzas on Freedom,"** Lowell pleads with his fellow citizens to recognize the horrors of slavery and the necessity of eradicating it.

ADDITIONAL RESOURCES

Reader's Guide
- Selection Worksheet, 5.3

Assessment Portfolio
- Selection Check Test, 4.5.5
- Selection Test, 4.5.6

Essential Skills Practice Books
- *Writing,* 1.7
- *Language,* 2.88
- *Study and Research,* 4.21

ENRICHMENT ACTIVITIES

Students might try writing their own answers to Lowell's rhetorical questions. Encourage students to try to write their answers in simple rhyming verse (*aabb*), but students may also write in prose if they feel more comfortable doing so. Students might then have a class discussion in which they compare their answers to the answer Lowell gives in the poem. In what ways are students' answers different from Lowell's? In what ways are they similar?

SUPPORT FOR LEP STUDENTS

Review with students the additional vocabulary below before they read the selection.

Archaic Language

ye—you

Additional Vocabulary

base—having or showing little or no honor, courage, or decency

lava—melted rock issuing from a volcano

scoffing—mocking contempt, scorn, derision, or jeering

GOALS/OBJECTIVES

Studying this lesson will enable students to

- empathize with a speaker's feelings about slavery
- describe Lowell's literary accomplishments and explain the historical significance of his writing
- define *stanzas, couplets, apostrophes,* and *rhetorical questions* and identify these techniques in their reading
- avoid double negatives
- use searching tools

PREREADING NOTES

READER'S JOURNAL

Students should clearly state the social issue, their point of view on the issue, and their ideas for working toward resolution of the issue.

WRITING SKILLS

Students should describe Lowell's audience, American people of the pre-Civil War era. Students might suggest that Lowell is encouraging his audience to take a public stand against slavery. Students should list points that Lowell makes in his argument against slavery.

ANSWER TO GUIDED READING QUESTION

❶ No one can be "truly free and brave" while anyone alive is still a slave.

READER'S JOURNAL

Is there any social problem you feel strongly about, such as gang conflicts, drug abuse, or discrimination based on race or gender? What would be an effective way to make your point of view known? Freewrite in your journal about how you could advertise your stand on one major social issue; then explain your point of view regarding the problem and your thoughts on how to work toward its solution.

WRITING SKILLS

Read the Language Arts Survey, 1.7, "Choosing an Audience." Then, as you read the poem, decide who the intended audience for this poem is and what the speaker wants to convince that audience to think and do.

"Stanzas on Freedom"

JAMES RUSSELL LOWELL

According to Lowell, why are people not "truly free and brave"? ❶

Men! whose boast it is that ye
Come of fathers brave and free,
If there breathe on earth a slave,
Are ye truly free and brave?
If ye do not feel the chain,
When it works a brother's pain,
Are ye not base slaves indeed,
Slaves unworthy to be freed?

Women! who shall one day bear
Sons to breathe New England air,
If ye hear, without blush,
Deeds to make the roused blood rush
Like red lava through your veins,
For your sisters now in chains—
Answer! are ye fit to be
Mothers of the brave and free?

Is true freedom but to break
Fetters for our own dear sake,
And, with leathern[1] hearts, forget

1. **leathern.** Like leather; tough, hard

WORDS FOR EVERYDAY USE: **fet • ter** (fet´ər) *n.,* shackle or chain for the feet

VOCABULARY IN CONTEXT

- The prisoners wore heavy iron fetters to prevent their escape.
- Brian was earnest about his studies, and he quietly worked while the crew celebrated.

Last Sale of Slaves on the Courthouse Steps. T. Satterwhite Noble, 1860. Missouri Historical Society

20 That we owe mankind a debt?
No! true freedom is to share
All the chains our brothers wear,
And, with heart and hand, to be
Earnest to make others free!

❶ *What is true freedom?*

25 They are slaves who fear to speak
For the fallen and the weak;
They are slaves who will not choose
Hatred, scoffing, and abuse,
Rather than in silence shrink
30 From the truth they needs must think;
They are slaves who dare not be
In the right with two or three. ■

WORDS FOR EVERYDAY USE: **ear • nest** (ur´nist) *adj.*, zealous and sincere

ANSWER TO GUIDED READING QUESTION

❶ True freedom is sharing the pain of all who are enslaved and striving to achieve freedom for all.

CROSS-CURRICULAR ACTIVITIES

Arts and Humanities. Students might be moved by the artwork on page 303. There are many other such poignant representations of the plight of the slaves. Encourage students who enjoy art to locate some of these representations. Students should select one piece of artwork and then write brief essays (one or two pages) about the way the artwork succeeds in portraying the plight of slaves and the evils of slavery.

Social Studies. Lowell believed that the Mexican War (1846–1848) was waged by the United States in an attempt to extend the area of slavery. Have students research the Mexican War and then write brief essays (one or two pages) either supporting or refuting Lowell's position on the Mexican War.

ANSWERS TO SELECTION CHECK TEST 4.5.5

EX. What is the subject of Lowell's stanzas?
The subject of Lowell's stanzas is freedom.

1. What is the first question that the speaker asks of men?
The speaker asks whether they are truly brave and free.

2. What question does the speaker ask of women?
The speaker asks if they are fit to be the mothers of the free and brave.

3. What kind of hearts forget they owe mankind a debt?
Leathern hearts forget they owe mankind a debt.

4. What is the definition of "true freedom"?
The definition of "true freedom" is to wear our brothers' chains and strive to set others free.

5. What does the speaker call those who fear to speak out for "the fallen and the weak"?
The speaker calls those who fear to speak out "slaves."

RESPONDING TO THE SELECTION

Students should support their viewpoints. To stimulate discussion, ask students the following questions: Why might someone feel it is impossible to be free when others are enslaved? Why might freedom for all be such an important part of the speaker's definition of freedom?

ANSWERS FOR REVIEWING THE SELECTION

RECALLING

1. Slavery prevents people from being truly free and brave.

2. He asks women if they are fit to be mothers of the brave and free; he asks men if they can be brave and free people. The speaker does not seem to consider women brave and free people in their own right.

3. True freedom is sharing the chains of slaves and committing oneself to freeing them. True freedom is not breaking our own chains and forgetting the plight of others

4. He says that they are slaves themselves and urges them to speak out against slavery even if they are in the minority.

INTERPRETING

Responses will vary. Possible responses are given.

5. People who knew that slavery was wrong but still tolerated it showed a lack of courage. They became slaves to other people's opinions.

6. The speaker means that they are uncaring if they ignore injustice.

7. The debt all people owe humanity is concern over the well-being and freedom of their fellow humans. To care only about one's own problems is selfish.

8. The speaker believes that such people are cowards—afraid of retaliation or afraid of standing alone. *Students' answers will vary.*

SYNTHESIZING

Responses will vary. Possible responses are given.

9. An abolitionist might become

(cont.)

Responding to the Selection

The speaker maintains that those who tolerate injustice and cruelty to others are not free themselves. Do you agree with the speaker? Explain why, or why not.

Reviewing the Selection

RECALLING

1. According to the speaker, what social injustice prevents people from being truly free and brave?
2. What question does the speaker ask the women of New England? Is this question the same as the one that he asks the men? If not, how is it different?
3. According to the speaker, what is true freedom? What does he say true freedom is not?
4. What does the speaker call "those who fear to speak/For the fallen and the weak"? What does he recommend that they do?

INTERPRETING

5. In what sense did the existence of slavery diminish the freedom and courage of everyone?
6. What does the speaker mean when he asks women if they can hear about injustice "without a blush"?
7. What is the debt all people owe humanity? Why is simply taking care of one's own problems not enough to pay the debt?
8. Why does the speaker scold those who believe slavery is wrong and yet choose not to speak out about it? Explain some reasons why someone might choose not to act on his or her principles.

SYNTHESIZING

9. How might an abolitionist react to this poem? On the other hand, how might a slaveholder react? Describe the probable effect of such a poem on relations between the North and the South.
10. The speaker has slightly different messages for the men and the women. Why do you think he varied his message for each gender? What might a modern woman find objectionable in Lowell's approach?

ANSWERS FOR REVIEWING THE SELECTION (CONT.)

enthused to continue or extend the fight against slavery. A slaveholder might feel angry or guilty. Relations between the North and the South would probably deteriorate because of a poem such as this one.

10. The poet may have wanted to add variety to his questions, or he may have viewed women's ability to bear children as their most valuable aspect. A modern woman might find objectionable the speaker's implication that men have their own power, while women have power only in their ability to bear and raise children.

Understanding Literature (Questions for Discussion)

1. **Stanza.** A **stanza** is a recurring pattern of grouped lines in a poem. How many stanzas are there in this poem? To whom is the first stanza addressed? the second?
2. **Couplet.** A **couplet** is a pair of rhyming lines that expresses a complete thought. Identify five examples of couplets from the poem. Couplets are often easy to memorize. Why would ease of recall make couplets an appropriate choice for use in a poem such as this?
3. **Apostrophe.** An **apostrophe** is a rhetorical technique in which an object or person is directly addressed. Whom does the speaker address in "Stanzas on Freedom"? Considering the poet's purpose in writing, why do you think he speaks so directly to his audience?
4. **Rhetorical Question.** A **rhetorical question** is one asked for effect but not meant to be answered because the answer is clear from the context. What rhetorical questions does the speaker ask in this poem? What point does the speaker wish to make by means of each of these rhetorical questions?

Language Lab

Double Negatives. Read the Language Arts Survey, 2.88, "Double Negatives." Then read each of the following sentences. If you find a double negative, rewrite the sentence correctly.

1. If you allow others to be enslaved, you cannot hardly be called free yourself.
2. Women who don't care not at all for the suffering of their sisters are not fit to be the mothers of the free and brave.
3. If you don't work for the freedom of all, you aren't fulfilling your responsibility to mankind.
4. You can't scarcely in good conscience feel like a decent person when you ignore your responsibilities.
5. You are a slave if you can't never think for yourself and you let others control your actions.

Study and Research Skills

Using Searching Tools. Read the Language Arts Survey, 4.21, "Using Searching Tools." Visit your school or local library and search the card catalog or the computerized catalog for materials relating to slavery. Record the title, author, and call number of five books that you turn up in your search.

Answers for Understanding Literature

►See the evaluation forms for discussion, active listening, and oral communication, *Assessment Portfolio,* 7.11–7.14

Responses will vary. Possible Responses are given.

1. Stanza. There are four stanzas. Stanza 1, addressed to men, asks if they can be free when others are enslaved; stanza 2, addressed to women, asks if they can be mothers of brave people while ignoring the suffering of slaves.

2. Couplet. Couplets can be found throughout the poem. The poet may have wanted the words to sound over and over in people's thoughts so they could be repeated to others. This way the sentiments in the poem would be shared and spread among the reading population quickly.

3. Apostrophe. The speaker addresses the men and women of New England. He speaks directly to them because he is urging them to take immediate action against slavery.

4. Rhetorical Question. The speaker asks, "Are ye truly free and brave?/If ye do not feel the chain,/When it works a brother's pain,/Are ye not base slaves indeed,/Slaves unworthy to be freed?"; "are ye fit to be/Mothers of the brave and free?"; and "Is true freedom but to break/Fetters for our own dear sake,/And, with leathern hearts, forget/That we owe mankind a debt?" The speaker means to point out that the truly brave and free are interested in actively working to achieve freedom for others.

Answers for Study and Research Skills

Students should record the authors, titles, and call numbers of at least five books.

Answers for Language Lab

1. If you allow others to be enslaved, you cannot be called free yourself.
2. Women who don't care for the suffering of their sisters are not fit to be the mothers of the free and brave.
3. Correct
4. You can't in good conscience feel like a decent person when you ignore your responsibilities.
5. You are a slave if you can't think for yourself and you let others control your actions.

ADDITIONAL RESOURCES

READER'S GUIDE
- Selection Worksheet, 5.4

ASSESSMENT PORTFOLIO
- Selection Check Test, 4.5.7
- Selection Test, 4.5.8

ESSENTIAL SKILLS PRACTICE BOOKS
- *Writing,* 1.17
- *Language,* 2.19, 2.47

ENRICHMENT ACTIVITIES

Students might write about a modern occupation that requires the same industry and hard work as the blacksmith's occupation. To begin, students might pick an occupation that is seldom glamorized in literature or the media, then research trade journals or interview people to learn more about the profession. Students should make a list of the qualities a person must have to succeed in this occupation. Finally, students should write a descriptive paragraph or two about a fictional character who practices this profession. Encourage students to use their imaginations to create a vivid and compelling character who is employed in an occupation that is not often praised.

SUPPORT FOR LEP STUDENTS

Students may need help in understanding the tasks a village blacksmith performed and how essential a blacksmith was to the community. Inform students that metal goods such as horseshoes, farming implements, and household tools were all obtained through the services of the town blacksmith.

ADDITIONAL VOCABULARY

brawny—muscular
sledge—heavy, long-handled hammer
forge—furnace or fire for melting and forming metals
threshing—separating grain from husk
toiling—laboring
repose—rest

PREREADING

"The Village Blacksmith"
by Henry Wadsworth Longfellow

ABOUT THE AUTHOR

Henry Wadsworth Longfellow (1807–1882) was the most popular of the so-called "Fireside Poets," a group that included Ralph Waldo Emerson, John Greenleaf Whittier, James Russell Lowell, and Oliver Wendell Holmes. The name of the group derived from the fact that people often entertained one another in the evening by reading aloud by the fireside. Longfellow was born in Portland, Maine, and attended Bowdoin College there. Following graduation and language study in Europe, Longfellow taught foreign languages first at Bowdoin and then at Harvard. Well-known works by Longfellow include "A Psalm of Life," "The Wreck of the Hesperus," "Excelsior," "The Arsenal at Springfield," *Evangeline, Song of Hiawatha,* "The Children's Hour," *The Courtship of Miles Standish,* and "Paul Revere's Ride" (one of the *Tales of a Wayside Inn*). Longfellow also edited an important anthology, *The Poets and Poetry of Europe.* As famous in Britain as in the United States, he received honorary degrees from Oxford and Cambridge and was given a private audience with Queen Victoria. After his death, a bust of Longfellow was installed in the Poet's Corner of Westminster Abbey, making him the only American poet to be so honored.

ABOUT THE SELECTION

"The Village Blacksmith" was first published in an 1841 collection called *Ballads and Other Poems.* At the time of the poem's publication, Longfellow was a professor at Harvard. His poetry collections had begun to make him famous, not only in America but also in England. Sweet, romantic, didactic, and occasionally gripping in their retellings of stories from history or legend, Longfellow's poems appealed greatly to the tastes of the day. This poem focuses on a common man, honest and hard-working, whose strength and positive attitude matched the popular notion of the ideal citizen of the young, unsophisticated country.

GOALS/OBJECTIVES

Studying this lesson will enable students to

- enjoy a poem that praises a common nineteenth-century occupation
- discuss the universality of work, joy, and sorrow in communities throughout history
- recognize and explain the characteristics of a narrative poem
- define *image* and *alliteration* and identify the use of these techniques in their reading
- recognize prepositional phrases

READER'S JOURNAL

Every day you see workers performing their jobs with dedication. Think about a worker whom you admire. Picture him or her on the job, and then freewrite in your journal about what that person might do on a typical day.

LANGUAGE SKILLS

Read the Language Arts Survey, 2.19, "Adjectives and Articles." As you read "The Village Blacksmith," make a running list of the adjectives you encounter. Which of these questions do most of the adjectives answer: What kind? Which ones? How many?

"The Village Blacksmith"

HENRY WADSWORTH LONGFELLOW

Under a spreading chestnut tree
The village smithy[1] stands:
The smith, a mighty man is he,
With large and sinewy hands,
And the muscles of his brawny arms
Are strong as iron bands.

His hair is crisp,[2] and black, and long,
His face is like the tan;
His brow is wet with honest sweat,
He earns whate'er he can,
And looks the whole world in the face,
For he owes not any man.

Week in, week out, from morn till night,
You can hear his bellows[3] blow,
You can hear him swing his heavy sledge,
With measured beat and slow,
Like a sexton[4] ringing the village bell,
When the evening sun is low.

1. **smithy.** Blacksmith shop
2. **crisp.** Curly and wiry
3. **bellows.** Fan for keeping a fire going
4. **sexton.** Church official who rings the bells

❶ *What words are used to describe the strength of the smith?*

❷ *To what is the smith swinging his sledge compared?*

WORDS FOR EVERYDAY USE: **sin • ew • y** (sin´yōō ē) *adj.,* muscular; strong

PREREADING NOTES

READER'S JOURNAL

As an alternate activity, students might write about the professions they imagine themselves practicing as adults. What would they enjoy about the occupations? What do they imagine they would do on a typical day?

LANGUAGE SKILLS

Students should list most of the adjectives in the selection. They should categorize the adjectives by the questions they answer. Most of the adjectives will answer the question "What kind?"

ANSWERS TO GUIDED READING QUESTIONS

❶ The modifiers used are *mighty, sinewy, brawny,* and *strong.*

❷ The smith is compared to a church sexton ringing the village church bells.

VOCABULARY FROM THE SELECTION

sinewy
wrought

VOCABULARY IN CONTEXT

- After a summer of gardening, her upper arms were hard and sinewy.

Answers to Guided Reading Questions

❶ He goes to church with his family and hears his daughter's voice in the choir and the sound of prayers. He feels joy.

❷ His daughter's singing voice reminds him of his dead wife's singing voice. He feels sorrow.

Additional Questions and Activities

Ask students the following questions: In what manner does the blacksmith go through life? What earns him a night's repose? To what is life compared? Do you agree that life is like this thing?

Answers. The blacksmith goes through life "Toiling—rejoicing—working." "Something attempted, something done" earns the blacksmith a night's repose. Life is compared to a "flaming forge." Students might agree that life is like a forge because people are tempered and wrought by their experiences.

Answers to Selection Check Test 4.5.7

EX. What is the profession of the character described in the poem?
The character described in the poem is a blacksmith.

1. Where does the blacksmith stand?
The blacksmith stands under a spreading chestnut tree.

2. What can you hear "week in, week out"?
You can hear the bellows blow and the blacksmith swinging his sledge.

3. What do the children love to do?
They love to visit the blacksmith at work, see the forge, and hear the bellows roar.

4. Of what does his daughter's voice in the church choir remind the blacksmith?
His daughter's voice reminds the blacksmith of his dead wife's voice.

5. Why does the speaker thank the blacksmith?
The speaker thanks the blacksmith for teaching him or her a lesson.

Pat Lyon at the Forge. *John Neagle, 1826–7. Courtesy of the Museum of Fine Arts, Boston. Herman and Zoe Oliver Sherman Fund, 1975*

And children coming home from school
20 Look in at the open door;
They love to see the flaming forge,
And hear the bellows roar,
And catch the burning sparks that fly
Like chaff[5] from a threshing floor.

25 He goes on Sunday to the church,
And sits among his boys;
He hears the parson pray and preach,
He hears his daughter's voice
Singing in the village choir,
30 And it makes his heart rejoice.

It sounds to him like her mother's voice,
Singing in Paradise!
He needs must think of her once more,
How in the grave she lies;
35 And with his hard, rough hand he wipes
A tear out of his eyes.

Toiling—rejoicing—sorrowing,
Onward through life he goes;
Each morning sees some task begin,
40 Each evening sees it close;
Something attempted, something done,
Has earned a night's repose.

Thanks, thanks to thee, my worthy friend.
For the lesson thou hast taught!
45 Thus at the flaming forge of life
Our fortunes must be wrought;
Thus on its sounding anvil shaped
Each burning deed and thought. ■

5. **chaff.** Husks of grain separated during threshing

❶ *What does the smith do on Sundays? What does he hear? How does he feel?*

❷ *Of what does the smith's daughter's voice remind him? What effect does it have on him?*

Words for Everyday Use: **wrought** (rôt) *alt. pp. of* work, worked; made

Vocabulary in Context

- The activists wrought change by transforming their ideals into realities.

Responding to the Selection

The blacksmith is probably not a wealthy man. What gifts that are more important than money does life offer him? Which aspects of his life, if any, seem attractive to you? With which aspects of his life, if any, would you have difficulty coping?

Reviewing the Selection

RECALLING

1. What does the village blacksmith look like?
2. What evidence does the poem provide that the blacksmith is hard-working?
3. What has happened to the blacksmith's wife? What details show you how he feels about this?
4. According to the speaker, what lesson can be learned from the life of the blacksmith?

INTERPRETING

5. How would you describe the character of the blacksmith? Cite details from the poem that support your answer.
6. Do you think that the blacksmith's job gives him high prestige in the village? Compare his job with a modern job, such as car mechanic or truck driver. How are they similar or different?
7. What is the blacksmith's relationship with his children? How do you know?
8. Restate the lesson the blacksmith teaches in your own words. How does his life teach that lesson?

SYNTHESIZING

9. What qualities made the blacksmith a popular character in American culture in the nineteenth century? Are those qualities still considered desirable in the United States today? If not, what other qualities are now more important?
10. Some critics think that this poem is overly sentimental and preachy. Tell why you agree or disagree with their point of view.

RESPONDING TO THE SELECTION

Encourage students to consider the elements of the blacksmith's life with which they can identify. What experiences are common to all humans?

ANSWERS FOR REVIEWING THE SELECTION

RECALLING

1. He looks strong and healthy; he is tan and black-haired.
2. His arms are muscular; his brow is covered with sweat; he earns what he can and owes no man; his bellows and hammering are heard from morning until night all week and every week.
3. His wife has died. He cries when he hears his daughter's singing voice, which is like her mother's.
4. The lesson is that our deeds and thoughts are shaped by our daily work.

INTERPRETING

Responses will vary. Possible responses are given.

5. The blacksmith is honorable, kind, and hard-working. Students might mention his constant work and the way he is loved by children.
6. The blacksmith probably does not have high prestige, but his position in the community is essential to its well-being, as are the jobs of mechanics and truck drivers. He has probably been the town's only blacksmith for many years, and his family is actively involved in the church.
7. He loves and trusts them, and they love and honor him. They enjoy coming to the forge every day after school. They sit with their father in church every Sunday.
8. An individual makes his fortune, or fate, through dedication to the community; honest, hard work; and family support.

(cont.)

ANSWERS FOR REVIEWING THE SELECTION (CONT.)

SYNTHESIZING

Responses will vary. Possible responses are given.

9. The blacksmith was independent, self-supporting, and necessary to a thriving community. These qualities are still important.
10. Judgments about the poem's sentimental or didactic nature will differ. Students should support their assertions with evidence from the text.

ANSWERS FOR UNDERSTANDING LITERATURE

▶ See the evaluation forms for discussion, active listening, and oral communication, *Assessment Portfolio,* 7.11–7.14.

Responses will vary. Possible responses are given.

1. Image. Images that describe the blacksmith include his brow wet with sweat, the blows of his sledge, and his weeping at his daughter's singing voice.

2. Alliteration. In lines 1 through 4, the initial *s* sound is repeated, as is the *th* sound in line 43.

3. Narrative Poem. The poem is narrative in that it describes a series of sequential events, beginning with the daily work, moving to the Sunday worship, and ending with the "night's repose."

ANALYTIC SCALES FOR RESPONDING IN WRITING

Assign a score from 1 to 25 for each grading criterion below. (For more detailed evaluation, see the evaluation forms for writing, revising, and proofreading, *Assessment Portfolio,* 7.1–7.10.)

Character Sketch

- **Content/Unity.** The character sketch describes how a person looks, sounds, and acts.
- **Organization/Coherence.** The character sketch is written in a clear and sensible order.
- **Language/Style.** The character sketch uses vivid and precise nouns, verbs, and modifiers.
- **Conventions.** The character sketch avoids errors in spelling, grammar, usage, mechanics, and manuscript form.

Understanding Literature (Questions for Discussion)

1. **Image.** An **image** is a word or phrase that names something that can be seen, heard, touched, tasted, or smelled. What images does Longfellow use to describe the blacksmith?

2. **Alliteration. Alliteration** is the repetition of initial consonant sounds. Find two examples of alliteration in the poem.

3. **Narrative Poem.** A **narrative poem** is a verse that tells a story. Do you think that "The Village Blacksmith" is a narrative poem? Why, or why not?

Responding in Writing

Character Sketch. Read the Language Arts Survey, 1.17, "Clustering." Then make a cluster chart about a person you know well. Circle your topic in the center of the page and connect associated ideas to the topic and to each other. Include details about how the person looks, sounds, and acts. Use the information in your chart to write a brief description, or character sketch, of your subject.

Language Lab

Adding Prepositional Phrases. Read the Language Arts Survey, 2.47, "Adding Prepositional Phrases." Then read each sentence below. Underline each prepositional phrase and circle the word it modifies. Draw an arrow connecting the word and its modifying phrase. Finally, tell whether the phrase is adjectival or adverbial.

1. Under the spreading chestnut tree the village smithy stands.
2. The smith is a mighty man with large and sinewy hands.
3. On Sunday, he goes to church and sits among his boys.
4. The mother of his children is now dead and he remembers her with sadness.
5. Each deed and thought must be shaped on the sounding anvil.

ANSWERS FOR LANGUAGE LAB

Boldfaced words are modified by the underlined prepositional phrases.

1. Under the spreading chestnut tree the village smithy **stands.** (adverbial)
2. The smith is a mighty **man** with large and sinewy hands. (adjectival)
3. On Sunday, he **goes** to church and sits among his boys. (adverbial)
4. The **mother** of his children is now dead and he **remembers** her with sadness. (adjectival; adverbial)
5. Each deed and thought must be **shaped** on the sounding anvil. (adverbial)

PREREADING

"Telling the Bees"
by John Greenleaf Whittier

About the Author

John Greenleaf Whittier (1807–92), one of the so-called schoolroom or fireside poets, is known for his simple, lovely poems about life in rural New England, such as "Telling the Bees" and *Snow-Bound,* and for such politically oriented verse as "Barbara Fritchie" and "Icabod." Whittier was raised a Quaker in Massachusetts. His early religious training, with its emphasis on the brotherhood of all people, deeply influenced the course of his life and of his work. His poems were also strongly influenced by the work of Robert Burns, the pre-Romantic Scottish poet who wrote in rural dialect about rustic subjects. Whittier published his first poems in the newspaper published by William Lloyd Garrison, *The Abolitionist Leader.* Because of his religious beliefs and the influence of Garrison, Whittier himself became a strong advocate of abolition, speaking at antislavery meetings, editing antislavery newspapers, and writing both prose and verse in opposition to slavery. Whittier also served as a Massachusetts state legislator. Works by Whittier include *Legends of New-England in Prose and Verse* (1829), *Poems Written During the Progress of the Abolition Question* (1835), *Voices of Freedom* (1846), *Home Ballads, Poems and Lyrics* (1860), and *Snow-Bound* (1866).

About the Selection

A year after the death of his mother, Whittier wrote this simple poem about the death of a loved one, "**Telling the Bees.**" Whittier was deeply affected by his mother's death; he had never married and had supported his mother and two sisters most of his life. To explain his poem, Whittier wrote this note when he submitted it for publication in the *Atlantic Monthly* magazine (which he cofounded with Oliver Wendell Holmes): "A remarkable custom, brought from the Old Country, formerly prevailed in the rural district of New England. On the death of a member of the family, the bees were at once informed of the event, and their hives dressed in mourning. This ceremonial was supposed to be necessary to prevent the swarms from leaving their hives and seeking a new home."

ADDITIONAL RESOURCES

Reader's Guide
- Selection Worksheet, 5.5

Assessment Portfolio
- Selection Check Test, 4.5.9
- Selection Test, 4.5.10

Essential Skills Practice Books
- *Language,* 2.65, 2.66
- *Study and Research,* 4.13

ENRICHMENT ACTIVITIES

Encourage students to write a short prelude to Whittier's poem. Students should give an explanation of what transpired between the speaker and Mary, why they parted a month ago, and what happened to Mary after the speaker left.

SUPPORT FOR LEP STUDENTS

You might check students' understanding of the poem to be sure they realize the speaker is talking about the death of his beloved.

Idiom

mind me—remind myself; remember

Additional Vocabulary

ranged—spread out

gable—peaked roof over a windowed room

fret—worry

GOALS/OBJECTIVES

Studying this lesson will enable students to

- create a mental picture of a place described in concrete sensory images
- describe in detail the mood created by a literary work
- deduce a series of past events from allusions in a poem
- describe the tone and point of view of a literary work
- write an obituary
- correct shifts in verb tense

PREREADING NOTES

READER'S JOURNAL

Encourage students to freewrite sensory details of the memory using concrete nouns, colorful adjectives, and vivid verbs.

LANGUAGE SKILLS

Students should list ten irregular verbs from the selection. They should create a three-column chart headed *Base, Past,* and *Past Participle.* In each column, students should list the appropriate form of each irregular verb from the selection.

ANSWER TO GUIDED READING QUESTION

❶ The speaker says the year has gone by like a tortoise. The time has gone by slowly and heavily during the past year.

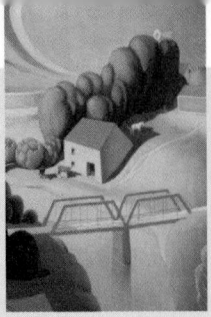

READER'S JOURNAL

Have you ever had an experience that was so clear and vibrant that you can remember it perfectly, even years later? Perhaps it was a time of great happiness, excitement, or sadness. Freewrite about such a memorable experience in your journal.

LANGUAGE SKILLS

Read the Language Arts Survey, 2.66, "Irregular Verbs I." Then choose ten verbs from the poem. Make a chart presenting the base form, the past, and the past participle of each verb. Identify each verb as regular or irregular.

"Telling the Bees"

JOHN GREENLEAF WHITTIER

Here is the place; right over the hill
  Runs the path I took;
You can see the gap in the old wall still,
  And the steppingstones in the shallow brook.

5 There is the house, with the gate red-barred,
  And the poplars[1] tall;
And the barn's brown length, and the cattle yard,
  And the white horns tossing above the wall.

There are the beehives ranged in the sun;
10 And down by the brink
Of the brook are her poor flowers, weed-o'errun,[2]
  Pansy and daffodil, rose and pink.

A year has gone, as the tortoise goes,
  Heavy and slow;
15 And the same rose blows, and the same sun glows,
  And the same brook sings of a year ago.

What has the year been like according to the speaker? What do you think the speaker means by making this comparison? ❶

1. **poplars.** Trees of the willow family with soft wood, rapid growth, and spikes of flowers without petals
2. **weed-o'errun.** Taken over by weeds

WORDS FOR EVERYDAY USE: **brink** (brĭŋk) *n.,* edge, especially at the top of a steep place

VOCABULARY IN CONTEXT

- Looking over the brink of the cliff, Marta saw the city spread out below her in miniature.

Stone City Iowa. *Grant Wood. Joslyn Art Museum, Omaha, NE*

There's the same sweet clover smell in the breeze;
And the June sun warm
Tangles his wings of fire in the trees,
20 Setting, as then, over Fernside farm.

I mind me how with a lover's care
From my Sunday coat
I brushed off the burrs,[3] and smoothed my hair,
And cooled at the brookside my brow and throat.

25 Since we parted, a month had passed,—
To love, a year;
Down through the beeches[4] I looked at last
On the little red gate and the well sweep[5] near.

❶ *What did the speaker do "with a lover's care"?*

❷ *What other sign of love is used?*

3. **burrs.** Rough, prickly seedcases of certain plants
4. **beeches.** Trees with smooth, gray bark; hard wood; dark green leaves; and edible nuts; classical symbol of romantic couple
5. **sweep.** Long pole mounted on a pivot with a bucket at one end; used for raising water

Answers to Guided Reading Questions

❶ The speaker brushed burrs off his Sunday coat "with a lover's care."

❷ The speaker uses the word "love" and mentions beeches, a classical symbol of a romantic couple.

Quotables

"For all sad words of tongue or pen,
The saddest are these: 'It might have been!'"

—John Greenleaf Whittier

Answers to Selection Check Test 4.5.9

EX. Where is the path the speaker took?
The path is "right over the hill."

1. What is "ranged in the sun"?
The beehives are "ranged in the sun."

2. What did the speaker do "with a lover's care"?
The speaker brushed burrs from his Sunday coat.

3. How much time has passed since the speaker and his beloved have parted?
One month has passed.

4. What is the chore-girl doing?
The chore-girl is draping the hives with black fabric.

5. Who has died?
Mistress Mary has died.

Answers to Guided Reading Questions

❶ The speaker refers to the journey from life to death. The chore-girl was telling the bees about Mary and her death.

❷ He learns that Mary is dead.

Responding to the Selection

Students might imagine that they would react more emotionally to the death of a loved one. However, you should point out to students that the speaker is describing how he found out about Mary's death and how strange it is that the countryside remains beautiful without her, not describing his reaction to her death. The speaker's response to her death is not overt, but his sadness and grief can be inferred.

Answers for Reviewing the Selection

RECALLING

1. A month has passed since the speaker last saw Mary here.
2. He was expecting to see Mary, his beloved.
3. He thought Mary's grandfather had died.
4. He heard the chore-girl sing, "Mistress Mary is dead and gone."

INTERPRETING

Responses will vary. Possible responses are given.

5. The speaker has been melancholy.
6. He was expecting to see his dear friend and beloved, Mary.
7. The speaker knew that there had been death in the house.
8. The impact of the chore-girl's words about Mary's death changed the speaker's life in that moment.

SYNTHESIZING

Responses will vary. Possible responses are given.

9. He wants to share his feelings of grief with a friend. The speaker

(cont.)

I can see it all now,—the slantwise rain
30 Of light through the leaves,
The sundown's blaze on her windowpane,
The bloom of her roses under the eaves.

Just the same as a month before,—
The house and the trees,
35 The barn's brown gable, the vine by the door,—
Nothing changed but the hives of bees.

Before them, under the garden wall,
Forward and back,
Went drearily singing the chore-girl small,
40 Draping each hive with a shred of black.

To what journey does the speaker refer? What was the chore-girl telling the bees? ❶

Trembling, I listened: the summer sun
Had the chill of snow;
For I knew she was telling the bees of one
Gone on the journey all must go!

45 Then I said to myself, "My Mary weeps
For the dead today:
Haply[6] her blind old grandsire sleeps
The fret and the pain of his age away."

But her dog whined low; on the doorway sill,
50 With his cane to his chin,
The old man sat; and the chore-girl still
Sung to the bees stealing out and in.

What does the speaker learn from the chore-girl's song? ❷

And the song she was singing ever since
In my ear sounds on:—
55 "Stay at home, pretty bees, fly not hence!
Mistress Mary is dead and gone!" ■

6. **Haply.** Perhaps

Responding to the Selection

The speaker in the poem looks back on this experience with a combination of sadness and peace. How do people usually respond to the death of a loved one? What stages of feeling do they go through? Does the speaker's response in this poem seem like a realistic, reasonable response to the death of a loved one? Do you imagine it would be similar to your response a year after the death of someone close to you?

Answers for Reviewing the Selection (cont.)

might feel the need to share the story of that particular day because it was one of the most significant days of his life—the day his beloved died.

10. He wants to reassure himself that even though time has passed, the country setting remains as beautiful as it was when Mary was alive.

Reviewing the Selection

RECALLING

1. The speaker in the poem seems to be walking with a friend and describing a past event. How long has it been since the event the speaker is describing?
2. Whom was the speaker expecting to see at the house? What was his relationship with that person?
3. Who did the speaker first think had died?
4. How did the speaker discover who had really died?

INTERPRETING

5. Describe the speaker's mood for the past year.
6. Why did the speaker brush the burrs from his coat and smooth his hair? Why was he dressed in a "Sunday suit"?
7. Why did the summer sun suddenly have "the chill of snow" when the speaker saw the chore-girl draping the hives in black?
8. The speaker still hears the song the chore-girl sang on that day. What does his persistent memory of the song suggest about the importance of the event?

SYNTHESIZING

9. The speaker seems to be talking to someone as the poem opens. Why do you think he has brought someone to the house he visited one year ago? Why might he share the story of that day?
10. The speaker mentions all the things that are the same as they were last year. Why does he emphasize the permanence of the country setting?

Understanding Literature (Questions for Discussion)

1. **Point of View. Point of view** is the vantage point from which a story is told. Identify the point of view—first-person or third-person—from which this story of this poem is told. Why is this point of view especially effective in such a personal poem?
2. **Tone. Tone** is the emotional attitude toward the reader or toward the subject implied by a literary work. Would you describe the tone of this poem as conversational or dramatic? Explain your choice.
3. **Mood. Mood** is the emotion created in the reader by part or all of a literary work. How would you describe the mood of this poem? Explain your answer.

ANSWERS FOR UNDERSTANDING LITERATURE

► See the evaluation forms for discussion, active listening, and oral communication, *Assessment Portfolio,* 7.11–7.14.

Responses will vary. Possible responses are given.

1. Point of View. This poem is told from the first-person point of view, which is effective because the poem describes the personal feelings and thoughts of the speaker.

2. Tone. The tone of the poem is at first conversational and then dramatic. The speaker describes everyday things in a rural setting, becoming more emotional as he describes himself arriving at Mary's gate and discovering that she has died.

3. Mood. The mood created in the reader is melancholy, somber, and sorrowful.

ANALYTIC SCALES FOR RESPONDING IN WRITING

Assign a score from 1 to 25 for each grading criterion below. (For more detailed evaluation, see the evaluation forms for writing, revising, and proofreading, *Assessment Portfolio,* 7.1–7.10.)

1. Obituary

- **Content/Unity.** The obituary describes real or imagined details about Mary's life and death.
- **Organization/Coherence.** The obituary is written in a clear and sensible order.
- **Language/Style.** The obituary uses vivid and precise nouns, verbs, and modifiers.
- **Conventions.** The obituary avoids errors in spelling, grammar, usage, mechanics, and manuscript form.

2. Diary Entry

- **Content/Unity.** The diary entry reveals the actions, words, and feelings of the speaker on the day of Mary's death.

(cont.)

ANALYTIC SCALES FOR RESPONDING IN WRITING (CONT.)

- **Organization/Coherence.** The diary entry is written in a clear and sensible order.
- **Language/Style.** The diary entry uses vivid and precise nouns, verbs, and modifiers.
- **Conventions.** The diary entry avoids errors in spelling, grammar, usage, mechanics, and manuscript form.

ANSWERS FOR LANGUAGE LAB

1. I showed my companion the path over the hill that I took last year.
2. I brushed the burrs off my Sunday coat and smoothed my hair.
3. After we parted, a month passed before I returned.
4. The brook still sings and the sun glows the same as before.
5. The chore-girl sings a song and is draping black mourning cloth on the hives.

ANSWERS FOR THINKING SKILLS

The speaker assumed that Mary was inside the house, grieving over the death of her grandfather. It was a logical hypothesis because the speaker had just seen Mary alive a month ago and knew that her grandfather felt "the fret and the pain of his age." The chore-girl's song disproved the hypothesis.

PROJECT NOTES

1. Customs and Superstitions. Encourage a class discussion on superstitions and whether or not students believe in superstition.

2. Cemetery Visit. Teachers may want to suggest that students go in small groups to a local church or burial place. There they can arrange to meet with someone who officiates at funerals and perhaps interview that person about either customs and superstitions or the difference between nineteenth-century and twentieth-century inscriptions in American cemeteries.

Responding in Writing

1. **Obituary**. An **obituary** is a brief description of someone who died, meant to be printed publicly to inform readers of a death. Using what you know about Mary in the poem, write an obituary for her. You may add details that are not mentioned in the poem.
2. **Diary Entry.** Write a diary entry for the speaker telling how he reacted to the news of his loved one's death. What did he do, say, and think on that day after he heard the bad news?

Language Lab

Shifts in Verb Tense. Read the Language Arts Survey, 2.65, "Improper Shifts in Verb Tense." Rewrite the following sentences, correcting the verb tense shift in each.

1. I showed my companion the path over the hill that I take last year.
2. I brushed the burrs off my Sunday coat and smooth my hair.
3. After we parted, a month passed before I return.
4. The brook still sings and the sun glowed the same as before.
5. The chore-girl sang a song and is draping black mourning cloth on the hives.

Thinking Skills

Making Hypotheses. Read the Language Arts Survey, 4.13, "Making Hypotheses." What hypothesis did the speaker in this poem make when he saw the chore-girl draping black on the bee hives? Was it a logical hypothesis? Why, or why not? What discovery disproved the hypothesis?

PROJECTS

1. **Customs and Superstitions**. Together with other members of the class, survey friends and family about their customs and superstitions. Assemble the information you gather into a classroom booklet. You may wish to categorize your findings in some way, such as by country of origin, purpose, or occasion for use.
2. **Cemetery Visit**. Visit a cemetery and read some of the tombstones there. If possible, find tombstones from the nineteenth century and record what was written on them. How are those tombstones and their inscriptions different from modern ones? Present your findings to the class.

PREREADING

"Concord Hymn"
"The Rhodora"

by Ralph Waldo Emerson

About the Author

A biography of **Ralph Waldo Emerson** appears on page 252.

About the Selections

On April 18, 1775, British soldiers marched out of Boston, intent on destroying colonial supplies of powder and guns in nearby Lexington and Concord. The next morning, the soldiers met opposition from American volunteer militia, or Minutemen, who confronted them by the bridge over the Concord River. After a brief exchange of gunfire that resulted in casualties on both sides, the British were turned back and the American Revolution began in earnest. Sixty-two years later, grateful citizens erected a monument to commemorate the heroism of the Americans on that day. Emerson, a local resident, contributed his **"Concord Hymn"** as part of the celebration. On July 4, 1837, at the dedication of the monument, celebrants first read aloud Emerson's "Concord Hymn" and then sang it to the tune of a traditional church hymn, "Old Hundred." Today, stanza 1 of this poem is engraved on the base of the statue of a Minuteman that stands at the site of the historic confrontation.

The ideas presented in **"The Rhodora"** are extensions of thoughts expressed in the long essay *Nature,* Emerson's first published book. In *Nature,* published in 1836, Emerson maintains that all natural forms, such as "a leaf, sunbeam, a landscape, the ocean," are harmonious and always beautiful. They work together to express a universal beauty and truth that transcend the beauty and truth of the natural world. Humans can understand absolute, or universal, beauty and truth only through what can be experienced through our senses. "The Rhodora," written in 1847, is an eloquent statement of Emerson's belief in the value of each of nature's creations, including every individual.

ADDITIONAL RESOURCES

Reader's Guide
- Selection Worksheets, 5.6, 5.7

Assessment Portfolio
- Selection Check Tests, 4.5.11, 4.5.13
- Selection Tests, 4.5.12, 4.5.14

Essential Skills Practice Books
- *Language,* 2.63, 2.97
- *Study and Research,* 3.2, 2.64

ENRICHMENT ACTIVITIES

Students may benefit from reading an account of the American Revolution battle at Lexington and Concord, which occurred on April 19, 1775. Inform students that in Massachusetts, April 19 is called Patriot's Day and is a statewide holiday. Ask students to discuss why this day is so important. Do students believe this day changed the course of history?

SUPPORT FOR LEP STUDENTS

Review with students the additional vocabulary below before they read the selection.

Additional Vocabulary

unfurled—unfolded, floating on the breeze

embattled—oppressed by military forces

redeem—save

shaft—tall, narrow monument

GOALS/OBJECTIVES

Studying this lesson will enable students to

- empathize with a speaker's feelings about a historical event
- appreciate a speaker's feelings about nature
- describe Emerson's literary accomplishments and explain the historical significance of his writing
- identify the meter of a poem
- define *apostrophe, alliteration,* and *rhyme* and recognize these techniques in their reading
- define *Romanticism* and understand its influence on New England Renaissance poets
- use semicolons properly and correct dangling or misplaced modifiers

PREREADING NOTES

READER'S JOURNAL

Students should freewrite and explore the idea of a tribute to someone using original phrases and concrete description. The action that benefited the student, the reason for the student's appreciation, and the receiver of the tribute should be clearly defined.

THINKING SKILLS

Students should practice reciting the hymn in various voices and tones. Point out that there is a difference between the way a speaker in 1836 would have read the poem and the way a speaker would read the poem today.

ANSWERS TO GUIDED READING QUESTIONS

❶ Over time, the bridge disintegrated.

❷ They fought so that their children would be free from allegiance to the British monarchy.

ANSWERS TO SELECTION CHECK TEST 4.5.11

EX. When was this hymn sung?
This hymn was sung at the completion of the battle monument on April 19, 1836.

1. Who stood "embattled"?
Farmers stood "embattled."

2. Where was the first shot heard?
The first shot was heard around the world.

3. What has happened to the foe, the conqueror, and the bridge?
The foe and conqueror sleep "in silence" and the bridge has disintegrated over time.

4. What are the speakers setting by "this soft stream"?
The speakers are setting "a votive stone," or monument.

5. Why did the heroes dare to die?
The heroes dared to die to set their children free.

READER'S JOURNAL

Has anyone ever done something for which you are grateful? How has that person's kindness, intelligence, or courage affected your life? In your journal, freewrite about a situation in which someone's actions benefited you and how you feel toward that person now.

THINKING SKILLS

Read the Language Arts Survey, 3.2, "Elements of Verbal Communication." Then, as you read the poem, imagine how it would have sounded when it was read aloud the first time. Practice reading it aloud yourself, following the guidelines in the Language Arts Survey.

"Concord Hymn"

RALPH WALDO EMERSON

Sung at the Completion of the Battle Monument, April 19, 1836

By the rude bridge that arched[1] the flood,
Their flag to April's breeze unfurled,
Here once the embattled farmers stood,
And fired the shot heard round the world.

What happened to the bridge that was the site of the battle? ❶

The foe[2] long since in silence slept;
Alike the conqueror silent sleeps;
And Time the ruined bridge has swept
Down the dark stream which seaward creeps.

On this green bank, by this soft stream,
We set today a votive[3] stone;
That memory may their deed redeem,
When, like our sires,[4] our sons are gone.

For what did they fight? ❷

Spirit, that made those heroes dare
To die, and leave their children free,
Bid Time and Nature gently spare
The shaft we raise to them and thee. ■

1. **rude . . . arched.** Lexington–Concord Bridge; stone bridge across the Concord River
2. **foe.** England
3. **votive.** Expressing thanks or devotion
4. **sires.** Fathers

Responding to the Selection

How does the speaker feel toward the colonists who fought for independence? What are your feelings toward them? What would you say to these people if you could speak to them today? Write about these questions in your journal.

Reviewing the Selection

RECALLING

1. Who fired the "shot heard round the world"?
2. What happened at the Concord Bridge in 1775?
3. How is the historic event being commemorated?
4. How long does the speaker hope the memory of the battle will last?

INTERPRETING

5. Why does the speaker call the first shot fired at Concord "the shot heard round the world"? What is the significance of this shot?
6. Why did the heroes risk their lives? What was their goal?
7. What is the purpose of the monument at the Concord Bridge?
8. Find clues that make clear how the speaker feels about the event that took place here.

SYNTHESIZING

9. Do you think that this poem was well received at the dedication ceremony? If the dedication were held today, why would modern listeners like or dislike the poem?
10. Why do people erect monuments? What feelings are monuments meant to produce? Do you believe that monuments are worthwhile? Why, or why not?

Understanding Literature (Questions for Discussion)

1. **Meter.** The **meter** of a poem is its rhythmical pattern. A line of poetry can be described as being made up of rhythmical units called *feet*. A foot is a unit of rhythm consisting of strongly and weakly stressed syllables. How many feet are there in this line?

   And fired | the shot | heard round | the world.

   Now read the poem again. This time count the number of feet in each line. Is the number of feet consistent throughout the poem? Why is that pattern appropriate for a hymn?

RESPONDING TO THE SELECTION

Students may note questions they would have for the colonists at the Concord Bridge. They should recognize that the speaker of the poem has great respect for the American revolutionaries.

ANSWERS FOR REVIEWING THE SELECTION

RECALLING

1. One of the farmers fired "the shot heard round the world."
2. The British troops and American militia fired upon each other in the opening shots of the American Revolution.
3. Celebrants are setting a "votive stone" at the site of the battle.
4. The speaker hopes the memory will last beyond the lifespans of the grandchildren of the celebrants.

INTERPRETING

Responses will vary. Possible responses are given.

5. The first shot may be called "the shot heard round the world" because it represents a revolution against tyranny and a breaking away from old ways of governing. It is the first time that Americans and British fired upon one another.
6. They risked their lives to ensure freedom for themselves and their children. Their goal was to create a new nation, independent of England.
7. The monument was erected to perpetuate the memory of the brave deeds of the Minutemen who fought for independence at the bridge.
8. The speaker is proud of the events that took place at the bridge and grateful to the farmers who risked and gave their lives in the battle. He asks nature to spare the monument and keep the memory of the battle alive.

(cont.)

ANSWERS FOR REVIEWING THE SELECTION (CONT.)

SYNTHESIZING

Responses will vary. Possible responses are given.

9. Answers should include an opinion about the popularity of the poem in modern times and reasons for the opinion.
10. Monuments are erected to bring significant events or people to mind. They are usually meant to engender pride, gratitude, admiration, awe, or sorrow.

ANSWERS FOR UNDERSTANDING LITERATURE

► See the evaluation forms for discussion, active listening, and oral communication, *Assessment Portfolio,* 7.11–7.14.

Responses will vary. Possible responses are given.

1. Meter. There are four feet in the line. The number of feet is consistent throughout the poem. If a poem is to be sung to the tune of a hymn, it should have a consistent pattern to coincide with the consistent rhythm of the song.

2. Apostrophe. The speaker calls upon the "Spirit" that inspired the heroes to ask time and nature to care for the monument that is being raised.

3. Alliteration. In stanza 2, examples of alliteration include **s**ilence, **s**lept, **s**wept, **s**tream, and **s**eaward. Examples of alliteration in stanza 3 include **s**oft **s**tream, **s**tone, **s**ires, and **s**ons.

ANSWERS FOR LANGUAGE LAB

1. The American farmers decided to take a stand against what they considered to be British tyranny; they would not retreat from the oncoming battle.

2. The heroes of Concord had passed away years ago; however, their deeds were recalled with gratitude by their descendants.

3. They read the poem, loudly and with emotion; they sang the song, replacing the traditional lyrics with new words; and they dedicated the monument, hoping that the heroes would be remembered.

4. The setting is deceptively peaceful; yet, sixty years ago upon this site a historic battle was fought.

5. The statue of the Minuteman still stands beside the Concord Bridge; it commemorates the courage of the men who fought there in 1775.

2. **Apostrophe.** An **apostrophe** is a rhetorical technique in which an object or person is directly addressed. Identify the use of apostrophe in the poem. Whom or what does the speaker address? What does the speaker ask of that person or thing?

3. **Alliteration. Alliteration** is the repetition of initial consonant sounds. Find examples of alliteration in stanzas 2 and 3 of this poem.

Language Lab

Semicolons. Read the Language Arts Survey, 2.97, "Semicolons." Then correctly add a semicolon to each sentence below.

1. The American farmers decided to take a stand against what they considered to be British tyranny they would not retreat from the oncoming battle.
2. The heroes of Concord had passed away years ago however, their deeds were recalled with gratitude by their descendants.
3. They read the poem, loudly and with emotion they sang the song, replacing the traditional lyrics with new words and they dedicated the monument, hoping that the heroes would be remembered for generations.
4. The setting is deceptively peaceful yet, sixty years ago upon this site a historic battle was fought.
5. The statue of the Minuteman still stands beside the Concord Bridge it commemorates the courage of the men who fought there in 1775.

READER'S JOURNAL

For many people, experiences in nature are particularly satisfying and uplifting. Have you ever experienced a special moment in nature, for example, when you were hiking or bicycling? Try to recreate that moment in your mind, and jot down in your journal a few notes about the sights you saw, the sounds you heard, and the emotions you felt.

LANGUAGE SKILLS

Read the Language Arts Survey, 2.64, "Inverting Sentences for Emphasis." Find at least two instances in this poem in which the usual order of subject + verb + predicate has been changed. Rewrite the sentences in the usual order.

"The Rhodora[1]"

RALPH WALDO EMERSON

On Being Asked, Whence[2] Is the Flower?

In May, when sea-winds pierced our solitudes,
I found the fresh Rhodora in the woods,
Spreading its leafless blooms in a damp nook,
To please the desert and the sluggish brook.
5 The purple petals, fallen in the pool,
Made the black water with their beauty gay;
Here might the red-bird come his plumes to cool,
And court the flower that cheapens his array.
Rhodora! if the sages[3] ask thee why
10 This charm is wasted on the earth and sky,
Tell them, dear, that if eyes were made for seeing,
Then Beauty is its own excuse for being:
Why thou wert there,[4] O rival of the rose!
I never thought to ask, I never knew;
15 But, in my simple ignorance, suppose
The self-same Power that brought me there brought you. ■

1. **Rhodora.** Deciduous plant, native to northeastern United States, that bears pink flowers in spring
2. **Whence.** From where
3. **sages.** Wise older people
4. **thou wert there.** You were there

❶ *Who enjoys what the flower offers?*

PREREADING NOTES

READER'S JOURNAL

Students should use sensory details in describing their experience in nature. Encourage students to make a sensory detail chart about their experience. Refer them to the *Language Arts Survey,* 1.18, "Sensory Detail Charts."

LANGUAGE SKILLS

The following is an example of an inverted form from the selection.

(line 7) Here might the red-bird come his plumes to cool,

Rewritten, the sentence would appear

The red-bird might come here to cool his plumes.

SUPPORT FOR LEP STUDENTS

Review with students the additional vocabulary below before they read the selection.

ADDITIONAL VOCABULARY

solitude—quality of being alone
nook—secluded or sheltered place
sluggish—slow
plume—feather
array—clothing

ANSWER TO GUIDED READING QUESTION

❶ The red-bird and the speaker enjoy the flower.

ANSWERS TO SELECTION CHECK TEST 4.5.13

EX. What flower does the speaker find?
The speaker finds the rhodora.
1. In what month does the speaker find the rhodora?
The speaker finds the rhodora in May.
2. Where does the speaker find the rhodora?
The speaker finds the rhodora in a "damp nook."
3. Why might the red-bird come?
The red-bird might come to cool his plumes and court the rhodora.
4. What is the rhodora's excuse for being?
The rhodora's beauty itself is its excuse for being.
5. What does the speaker suppose in "simple ignorance"?
The speaker supposes that the rhodora and he or she were brought into being by the same power.

RESPONDING TO THE SELECTION

The two natural objects can relate to the students' interests, personal experiences, or sense of beauty.

ANSWERS FOR REVIEWING THE SELECTION

RECALLING

1. He finds it in May.
2. It is growing in a dark corner near a pool of water. The rhodora brightens and makes beautiful the area in which it blooms.
3. Sages might ask the rhodora why it is hidden from human eyes. The speaker answers, "Beauty is its own excuse for being."
4. The speaker was brought by the same power that brought the rhodora.

INTERPRETING

Responses will vary. Possible responses are given.

5. It is especially beautiful because most of the plants around it have not bloomed yet. The rhodora and the rose are both red and full.
6. The speaker believes the rhodora is his or her secret, that the flower has a special message for him or her alone.
7. No, the speaker believes that the sages do not understand the true nature of beauty.
8. Yes, he may believe that nature has offered him a gift of understanding through the flower.

SYNTHESIZING

Responses will vary. Possible responses are given.

9. The rhodora is vibrant and full of life and color. Students will favor different springtime sights.
10. The speaker prefers the wildflowers. He appreciates the mystery of nature recreating itself rather than humanity attempting to recreate nature.

Responding to the Selection

The speaker in this poem focuses on a flower that holds special meaning for him. What natural objects found in the woods, on the mountains, at the beach, or in the meadow do you find particularly beautiful or affecting? Choose two of these objects and explain why you chose them.

Reviewing the Selection

RECALLING

1. At what time of year does the speaker find the rhodora in the woods?
2. Where is the rhodora growing? What is the rhodora's effect on the area in which it is blooming?
3. What might "sages" ask the rhodora? According to the speaker, how can the rhodora justify its blooming alone in the woods when usually no one sees it?
4. What brought the speaker to the same place as the rhodora?

INTERPRETING

5. Why is the rhodora especially beautiful at this time of year? Why do you think the speaker compares the rhodora to a rose?
6. Does the speaker believe that any other person besides himself has appreciated the rhodora's beauty? Why is the isolated location of the rhodora significant to the speaker?
7. Does the speaker really believe that the sages are wise? Explain why, or why not.
8. Do you think that the speaker is glad that he happened upon the rhodora in the woods? What do you think he gained through this encounter?

SYNTHESIZING

9. Winter in New England is long and cold, and spring is always welcome. Why does the sight of the rhodora delight the speaker so? What springtime sight gives you the most pleasure?
10. Which flower do you think the speaker would find more pleasing—the rhodora blooming alone in the woods or the pampered orchid blooming in a greenhouse? Would the speaker find them equally pleasing? Explain your answer.

Understanding Literature (Questions for Discussion)

1. **Rhyme. Rhyme** is the repetition of sounds at the ends of words. Identify the rhyme scheme of "The Rhodora," labeling the sound at the end of each line with a letter of the alphabet. If the sound is the same as one that came before, label it with the same letter. If it is a different sound, assign it a new letter. When you are done, look for the pattern or rhyme scheme.

2. **Romanticism. Romanticism** was a literary and artistic movement of the eighteenth and nineteenth centuries that placed value on emotion or imagination over realism, and on nature and wildness over human works. Explain why this poem may be categorized as Romantic.

Responding in Writing

1. **Stream of Consciousness. Stream-of-consciousness writing** attempts to render the flow of feelings, thoughts, and impressions within the minds of characters. Imagine that you are walking in the woods on that May day with the speaker. Write a long paragraph that describes what you would be experiencing and thinking as you hike along. Include your thoughts on finding the rhodora by the stream.

2. **Editorial.** Write an editorial in which you state your point of view on the desirability of preserving wilderness areas in the United States. Begin by explaining the issue you will be discussing; then give at least three reasons why you feel as you do. Conclude with a recommendation about what you believe is the correct course of action.

Language Lab

Correcting Modifiers. Read the Language Arts Survey, 2.63, "Correcting Dangling or Misplaced Modifiers." Then correctly rewrite each sentence below.

1. While blooming by a quiet stream, the speaker discovered a hidden rhodora.
2. Fallen into the water, the river washed the petals downstream.
3. Cooling his plumes at the brook, the rhodora's purple petals contrasted with the bird's red feathers.
4. The Transcendentalists had a lasting effect on American literature who believed that through intuition humans can know truth.
5. Even more useful than the teachings of organized religion, Emerson believed that the most direct way to enlightenment was an openness to nature.

Answers for Understanding Literature

► See the evaluation forms for discussion, active listening, and oral communication, *Assessment Portfolio,* 7.11–7.14.

Responses will vary. Possible responses are given.

1. Rhyme. The rhyme scheme of this poem is *aabbcdcd.*

2. Romanticism. Students should point out aspects of Romanticism in the poem—reverence for wildness and imagination, and disdain for human works and realism.

Analytic Scales for Responding in Writing

Assign a score from 1 to 25 for each grading criterion below. (For more detailed evaluation, see the evaluation forms for writing, revising, and proofreading, *Assessment Portfolio,* 7.1–7.10.)

1. Stream of Consciousness

- **Content/Unity.** The stream-of-consciousness writing presents a description of the student's thoughts and feelings as he or she accompanies the speaker.
- **Organization/Coherence.** The paragraph is written in a clear and sensible order.
- **Language/Style.** The paragraph uses vivid and precise nouns, verbs, and modifiers.
- **Conventions.** The paragraph avoids errors in spelling, grammar, usage, mechanics, and manuscript form.

2. Editorial

- **Content/Unity.** The editorial provides a point of view on preserving wilderness areas.
- **Organization/Coherence.** The editorial is written in a clear and sensible order.
- **Language/Style.** The editorial uses vivid and precise nouns, verbs, and modifiers.
- **Conventions.** The editorial avoids errors in spelling, grammar, usage, mechanics, and manuscript form.

Answers for Language Lab

1. The speaker discovered a hidden rhodora blooming by a quiet stream.
2. The river washed downstream the petals that had fallen into the water.
3. The rhodora's purple petals contrasted with the red feathers of the bird, cooling his plumes at the brook.
4. The Transcendentalists, who believed that through intuition humans can know truth, had a lasting effect on American literature.
5. Emerson believed that an openness to nature, more than the teachings of organized religion, was the most direct way to enlightenment.

ADDITIONAL RESOURCES

READER'S GUIDE
- Selection Worksheets, 5.8, 5.9, 5.10, 5.11

ASSESSMENT PORTFOLIO
- Selection Check Tests, 4.5.15, 4.5.17, 4.5.19, 4.5.21
- Selection Tests, 4.5.16, 4.5.18, 4.5.20, 4.5.22

ESSENTIAL SKILLS PRACTICE BOOKS
- *Writing,* 1.40
- *Language,* 2.69, 2.96, 2.98, 2.99, 2.107–2.133
- *Study and Research,* 4.24, 4.29, 5.2

ENRICHMENT ACTIVITIES

Imagine yourself to be someone who lives in the center of New England politics and culture in 1863, a year in which the United States was embroiled in civil war. Write a response to Dickinson's poem, thanking her for the letter, which you view as a gift from an innocent countrywoman. Your letter can be factual or emotional. Give yourself an identity and an address for future correspondence.

SUPPORT FOR LEP STUDENTS

Students may have difficulty understanding Dickinson's sentence structure and unique use of punctuation. You may wish to paraphrase the poems for students.

ADDITIONAL VOCABULARY

majesty—sovereign power, authority, or dignity

PREREADING

"This is my letter to the World"
"The Soul selects her own Society—"
"Because I could not stop for Death—"
"I heard a Fly buzz—when I died—"

by Emily Dickinson

ABOUT THE AUTHOR

Emily Dickinson (1830–1886) lived a private life, rarely venturing beyond her home and her close circle of family and friends, but she lived that life intensely, in vivid moments of observation and reflection captured in astonishingly original verse. Considered by many critics and writers to be the greatest of American lyric poets, she did not seek fame, for which she had considerable contempt, but rather kept her writing to herself, sharing small portions of it with her intimates. Only seven of her poems were published during her lifetime, all anonymously and without her full consent. The first volumes of her poetry, published after her death, mangled the work by "correcting" her unconventional punctuation and her purposeful deviations from grammatical propriety. Only in 1955, with the publication of *The Poems of Emily Dickinson,* edited by T. H. Johnson, did the full extent of her achievement become known.

At her death, which occurred in the house in Amherst, Massachusetts, where she was born, Dickinson had produced well over one thousand lyrics. These explored a tremendous range of subjects in language remarkable for its wit, inventiveness, and economy of expression. Taken as a whole, her verses, most of them quite brief, present a complex self-portrait, a sort of spiritual autobiography. Her voice is alternately humble and proud, intimate and aloof, ecstatic and sorrowful, but always questioning, reflective, and intensely alive. She was a keen observer of particulars—capable of sudden, breathtaking generalizations that synthesized these particulars into truths.

Much nonsense has been made of the few details known of her life, which because of its outward meagerness has invited much speculation. This speculation has centered on her various male friends and on her famed reclusiveness. She was born to a prominent Amherst family. Her closest friends were her brother, William Austin, and her sister, Lavinia. Neither Emily nor Lavinia married. Emily seldom left Amherst, although she did spend one year at Mt. Holyoke Female Seminary, ten miles away, and took a trip to Washington and Philadelphia with her father. Her grandfather was one of the founders of Amherst College. Her father, Edward, served as treasurer of Amherst College, a state representative, and a state senator.

GOALS/OBJECTIVES

Studying this lesson will enable students to
- have a positive experience reading the unique lyrical poetry of Emily Dickinson
- describe Dickinson's literary accomplishments and explain the historical significance of her writing
- write an original lyric poem, a personal letter, and a description
- define *personification, apology, meter, sight rhyme, slant rhyme, repetition, stanza, extended metaphor, assonance, irony, point of view, synaesthesia, onomatopoeia,* and *symbol* and recognize the use of these literary techniques in their reading
- correctly use semicolons and dashes

Dickinson attended Amherst Academy before spending her year at Mt. Holyoke. At home again, she delighted in reading books that might "joggle the Mind." She read a few books very deeply, especially the Bible, the plays of Shakespeare, and the works of such contemporary writers as Emerson, Keats, Tennyson, and George Eliot. Early on, she was befriended by Benjamin Newton, a law student who encouraged her writing. His early death led to a period of spiritual crisis during which she turned for advice to a well-known minister from Philadelphia, Charles Wadsworth, who became a close friend. In the late 1850s, she wrote drafts of love letters to an unknown person identified in the letters as "Master," and some of her poems of the period reflect the frustrations and tensions of thwarted romantic feeling.

She corresponded with the critic Thomas Wentworth Higginson, who encouraged but failed to understand her work, and she was courted by a family friend, Judge Otis P. Lord. Perhaps because of physical problems, her last twenty-five years were spent in seclusion from all but the closest of friends and family members.

About the Selections

When T. H. Johnson numbered all Dickinson's known poems for his three-volume edition of *The Poems of Emily Dickinson* (1955), he used such clues as handwriting differences to infer the order of composition. **"This is my letter to the World"** was assigned number 441. It was written in the early 1860s, probably in 1862, when Dickinson was most prolific, averaging a poem a day.

In **"The Soul selects her own Society,"** written in about 1862, Dickinson might be speaking about herself. Contemporary scholars have offered various explanations for Dickinson's withdrawal from society, including thwarted love and physical disabilities. The poems themselves support the theory that her reclusiveness was the determined, willful act of someone who wished to encounter life on her own terms. This view is supported, for example, by the affirmation in "The Soul selects her own Society" of an individual's freedom to choose associates.

Most critics agree that **"Because I could not stop for Death"** is one of Dickinson's best poems. The writer and critic Allen Tate has written that it is "one of the greatest in the English language; it is flawless to the last detail. . . . Every image is precise and . . . fused with the central idea." The poem was written in 1863 and published in 1890 in the first collection of Dickinson's work.

As a member of a solid New England family, Emily Dickinson was immersed in the Puritan tradition, and for many years she attended church services twice each Sunday. Many of her poems deal with religious subjects, often with questions about the relationship of the individual soul to God and about immortality and the afterlife. In **"I heard a Fly buzz—when I died—,"** the speaker imagines her own death, expressing with brilliant irony her fears about the transition from this life to the next.

Quotables

"The artist, like the God of the creation, remains within or behind or beyond or above his handiwork, invisible, refined out of existence, indifferent, paring his fingernails."

—James Joyce

"Every artist writes his own autobiography."

—Havelock Ellis

Additional Questions and Activities

You might encourage students to have a discussion on the nature of the artist before they read the Dickinson selections. Ask students to discuss the following questions: Must the artist experience a variety of people, cultures, and situations in order to produce art, or does art spring from the solitary power of human imagination? What can we tell about the artist from his or her work? Should we see the artist as removed from his or her work as Joyce suggests, or should we see every work of the artist as part of his or her autobiography, as revealing something about his or her individual experience? Students might then discuss these same questions again after they have read the selections to see if their perceptions have changed in any way.

PREREADING NOTES

READER'S JOURNAL

Students should write letters as though the reader will be someone who knows very little about life in the United States at the close of the twentieth century. The ideas expressed should be those students feel are important to convey to future generations—about the student and about the world as experienced by the student.

RESEARCH SKILLS

Students' bibliography cards should follow the guidelines given in the Language Arts Survey, 4.29, "Bibiographies and Bibliography Cards."

ANSWER TO GUIDED READING QUESTION

❶ Her subject matter is found in "The simple News that Nature told—/With tender Majesty."

ANSWERS TO SELECTION CHECK TEST 4.5.15

EX. As what literary form does the speaker describe her poem?
The speaker describes her poem as a letter.

1. To whom is the letter addressed?
The letter is addressed to the world.

2. What has the world never done?
The world has never written to the speaker.

3. What is written in the speaker's letter?
"The simple News that Nature told—/With tender Majesty" is written in the letter.

4. To whom is nature's message committed?
Nature's message is committed to hands the speaker cannot see.

5. What does the speaker ask of her countrymen?
The speaker asks her countrymen to judge her tenderly.

READER'S JOURNAL

If you were to write a "letter to the world" that would be read by others after your death, what would that letter say? Write such a letter, to be placed in a time capsule to be opened sometime late in the next century.

RESEARCH SKILLS

Read the Language Arts Survey, 4.29, "Bibliographies and Bibliography Cards." Then use the card catalog in a library to find at least four books with information about Emily Dickinson and her work. Make bibliography cards for these books, following proper form as described in the Language Arts Survey.

"This is my letter to the World"

EMILY DICKINSON

Where does the poet find her subject matter? ❶

This is my letter to the World
That never wrote to Me—
The simple News that Nature told—
With tender Majesty

5 Her Message is committed
To Hands I cannot see—
For love of Her—Sweet—countrymen—
Judge tenderly—of Me ■

Responding to the Selection

What does the speaker of this poem ask of you, her reader? What reason does the speaker give for judging her work tenderly? Do you find this reason persuasive? Why, or why not?

RESPONDING TO THE SELECTION

Students may find the writer's reasoning either faulty or persuasive and should give explanations for their judgments.

Reviewing the Selection

RECALLING

1. What does the speaker call her poem, or her poetry in general?
2. Which line of stanza 1 describes the content of the speaker's "letter"?
3. Which lines of the poem describe those to whom the speaker's work "is committed"?
4. Whom or what is referred to by the word "Her" in line 7?

INTERPRETING

5. Why does the speaker say that her writing is intended for others who "never wrote to Me"?
6. Is the poet being sincere or ironic—or both—in describing nature's "News" as "simple"?
7. Which word in stanza 2 suggests that a poem is incomplete without a reader?
8. What benefit does the speaker suggest is possible for the reader who judges her work "tenderly"? What information or understanding might the reader gain?

SYNTHESIZING

9. Why does the poet request that she be judged "tenderly"? What fears might she have about her audience?
10. During her lifetime, Dickinson intentionally kept her poetry from being published. What light does this poem shed on her motives? Is it likely that she meant never to share her work with an audience?

Understanding Literature (Questions for Discussion)

1. **Personification. Personification** is a figure of speech in which an idea, animal, or thing is described as if it were a person. What force is personified in this poem? What qualities of humans are given to the force?
2. **Apology.** An **apology** is a literary defense. Explain how this poem can be seen as an apology. What does it defend?
3. **Meter.** The **meter** of a poem is its rhythmical pattern. How many feet, or beats, are used in most of the lines of this poem? The even-numbered lines are the most regular. Describe these lines completely, telling both the type of foot (for example, iambic or trochaic) and the number of feet per line. Refer to the section on *meter* in the Handbook of Literary Terms.

ANSWERS FOR REVIEWING THE SELECTION

RECALLING

1. She calls them messages from nature.
2. Line 3 describes the content of the "letter."
3. Lines 5 and 6 say the work is committed "To hands I cannot see—."
4. In line 7, "Her" refers to nature.

INTERPRETING

Responses will vary. Possible responses are given.

5. She has not shared her writing with the public, and she has few friends outside her family.
6. She is being sincere; nature has many expressions, but its message to humanity can be read easily by the speaker.
7. The word *committed* shows the poet's sense of connection to the reader.
8. The reader who judges the poet's work tenderly might learn something about nature's message.

SYNTHESIZING

Responses will vary. Possible responses are given.

9. The poet may request that she be judged "tenderly" because she has never shown an audience her work. She might fear that her audience will not understand her work or her unique view of life.
10. It is likely that Dickinson meant never to share her work with an audience. She seems to have believed that her understanding was a delicate, mysterious gift from nature that did not belong to her in a commercial or public sense.

ANSWERS FOR UNDERSTANDING LITERATURE

See the evaluation forms for discussion, active listening, and oral communication, *Assessment Portfolio,* 7.11–7.14.

Responses will vary. Possible responses are given.

1. Personification. The force of nature is personified in this poem. The ability and will to communicate a subtle idea are given to nature by the poet.

2. Apology. The poem defends itself against harsh judgment, saying that it came through the poet but not directly from her.

3. Meter. Students should refer to the section on meter in the Handbook of Literary Terms. Lines 2, 4, 5, and 6 have three feet; lines 1, 3, 7, and 8 have four feet. The poem includes iambs and trochees.

ANALYTIC SCALES FOR RESPONDING IN WRITING

Assign a score from 1 to 25 for each grading criterion below. (For more detailed evaluation, see the evaluation forms for writing, revising, and proofreading, *Assessment Portfolio,* 7.1–7.10.)

Original Lyric Poem

- **Content/Unity.** The lyric poem presents a description of a meaningful moment.
- **Organization/Coherence.** The lyric poem is written in a clear and sensible order.
- **Language/Style.** The lyric poem uses vivid and precise nouns, verbs, and modifiers.
- **Conventions.** The lyric poem avoids errors in spelling, grammar, usage, mechanics, and manuscript form.

ANSWERS FOR LANGUAGE LAB

1. I toured New England recently—did I tell you that I visited three very old graveyards?
2. There's a big difference between the old tombstones and modern ones; the old ones have much more personality.
3. On many old stones, the writing has worn off; however, the pictures are still visible.
4. The old stones have carvings of skulls, skeletons, and grieving mourners—our ancestors faced death more directly, I think.
5. I made several rubbings of the old tombstones; here are two of them.

Responding in Writing

Original Lyric Poem. Choose a scene in nature or a particularly meaningful moment for you, and write an original lyric poem about your topic. Use short lines and verses, in the style of Emily Dickinson. Be sure to focus on a single image or moment.

Language Lab

Semicolons and Dashes. Read the Language Arts Survey, 2.96, "Semicolons," and 2.98, "Dashes." Then rewrite the following sentences, inserting semicolons or dashes where they are needed.

1. I toured New England recently did I tell you that I visited three very old graveyards?
2. There's a big difference between the old tombstones and modern ones the old ones have much more personality.
3. On many old stones, the writing has worn off however, the pictures are still visible.
4. The old stones have carvings of skulls, skeletons, and grieving mourners our ancestors faced death more directly, I think.
5. I made several rubbings of the old tombstones here are two of them.

Applied English/Tech Prep Skills

Personal Letters. Read the Language Arts Survey, 5.2, "The Form of a Personal Letter." Choose a writer, either living or past, whose work you enjoy. Write a letter to that writer, discussing such topics as the writer's works, attitudes or experiences that you and the writer share, and ideas for new works by either the writer or you. Follow the correct form for a personal letter.

ANSWERS FOR APPLIED ENGLISH/TECH PREP SKILLS

The letter should be to a writer whose work the student enjoys. Topics should include the writer's works, attitudes, or experiences that the student and writer share, and ideas for new works. The guidelines explained in the Language Arts Survey, 5.2, "The Form of a Personal Letter," should be followed.

READER'S JOURNAL

Who are your closest friends? Did you choose them, or have you just been thrown together by chance? Do you expect them to be close friends two years from now? Why, or why not? Write about how friendships form—and about how you believe they *should* form.

LANGUAGE SKILLS

Review the guidelines for using capitalization in the Language Arts Survey, 2.107–2.133. As you read the poem, note the places where Dickinson uses irregular capitalization. Consider why she might have chosen to emphasize these particular words by capitalizing them.

"The Soul selects her own Society—"

EMILY DICKINSON

The Soul selects her own Society—
Then—shuts the Door—
To her divine Majority—
Present no more—

5 Unmoved—she notes the Chariots—pausing—
At her low Gate—
Unmoved—an Emperor be kneeling
Upon her Mat—

I've known her—from an ample nation—
10 Choose One—
Then—close the Valves of her attention—
Like Stone— ■

QUOTABLES

"Great souls by instinct to each other turn,
demand alliance, and in friendship burn."

—Joseph Addison

PREREADING NOTES

READER'S JOURNAL

You might also ask students to consider what qualities they look for in friends. Do they look for the same basic qualities in every friend or do they enjoy the varying qualities of many individuals?

LANGUAGE SKILLS

Students should discuss why Dickinson capitalized the following words in the selection: *Soul, Society, Door, Majority, Chariots, Gate, Emperor, Mat, One, Valves,* and *Stone.*

SUPPORT FOR LEP STUDENTS

Review with students the additional vocabulary below before they read the selection.

ADDITIONAL VOCABULARY

present—bring a person into the presence of, and introduce formally to, another

ample—more than enough; abundant

ANSWERS TO SELECTION CHECK TEST 4.5.17

EX. What does the soul do?
The soul selects her own society.

1. What does the soul do after she selects her own society?
The soul then shuts the door.

2. What does the soul note outside her "low Gate" and "Upon her Mat—"?
The soul notes the waiting chariots and the kneeling emperor.

3. How does the soul feel when she notes these things?
The soul remains "unmoved."

4. What has the speaker known the soul to choose?
The speaker has known the soul to choose one "from an ample nation."

5. In what way does the soul close "the Valves of her attention"?
The soul closes "the Valves of her attention—/Like Stone—."

RESPONDING TO THE SELECTION

Students should explain the way they think good friendships are best formed and nurtured.

ANSWERS FOR REVIEWING THE SELECTION

RECALLING

1. The verbs in stanza 1 are *selects, shuts,* and *present.* To conform with standard grammar, the break should be after "Door":

The Soul selects her own Society,
Then shuts the Door.

2. The soul and her select companions are "her divine Majority."

3. The unsuccessful attractions are "Chariots" and "an Emperor."

4. The soul "closes the Valves of her attention."

INTERPRETING

Responses will vary. Possible responses are given.

5. The verb *present* appears in the command "Present no more," in which the speaker orders everyone not to bother the soul by introducing anyone new. The command sounds like it might be delivered in a royal court.

6. The poet suggests that in a democracy, the majority has the same divine right to vote as a king does in an absolute monarchy. The poet is also suggesting that the individual soul is a majority of one and has the right to determine rules for itself.

7. The "Chariots" might stand for large numbers of people, such as the community as a whole. The "Emperor" might symbolize a significant individual, such as a social leader or an influential acquaintance.

8. "Ample nation" probably refers to a large number of people. The poem is not concerned with any particular political groupings; it is about the human condition in general.

(cont.)

Responding to the Selection

Does a person have a right to choose his or her own friends and acquaintances? Is your own experience of choosing friends and acquaintances similar to or different from the experience of the speaker in the poem? Discuss these questions with your classmates.

Reviewing the Selection

RECALLING

1. What three verbs appear in stanza 1? If you were to write stanza 1 using commas, periods, or no punctuation in place of the dashes, where would you place a sentence break?
2. Who or what is "her divine Majority"?
3. Identify two attractions that fail to tempt the interest of the soul.
4. In the final stanza, how does the soul block off access by anyone or anything other than the one she has chosen?

INTERPRETING

5. Which of the three verbs in stanza 1 expresses a command? Explain the command.
6. Before the creation of such democracies as the United States, where the vote of the majority rules, kings were thought to rule by divine right. When the poet substitutes the words "divine Majority" for the phrase "divine Majesty," what attitude toward groups of people, or majorities, does she suggest?
7. What real-life attractions might be symbolized by the "Chariots" and the "Emperor"?
8. Do you suppose that the phrase "ample nation" in the final stanza refers to the United States, another country, or simply to a large number of people? Explain your answer.

SYNTHESIZING

9. Until the final stanza, every line of the poem has four or more syllables. The second and final lines of the last stanza, however, have only two syllables each. How does this abruptness contribute to the meaning of the stanza?
10. What good qualities or advantages do you see in this description of an individual's selection of friends? What possible drawbacks might the speaker's actions have?

ANSWERS FOR REVIEWING THE SELECTION (CONT.)

SYNTHESIZING

Responses will vary. Possible responses are given.

9. The last stanza discusses how the soul cuts itself off from everyone except its chosen acquaintance, and the abruptness of the meter reinforces that concept of closure.

10. Good qualities include devotion and loyalty to the chosen friends. Drawbacks include lack of sympathy or interest for other individuals outside the select circle of friends.

Understanding Literature (Questions for Discussion)

1. **Sight Rhyme.** A **sight rhyme,** or **eye rhyme,** is a pair of words, generally at the ends of lines of verse, that are spelled similarly but pronounced differently. Find an example of sight rhyme in this poem.

2. **Slant Rhyme.** A **slant rhyme** is one in which the rhyming sounds are similar but not exact. Identify examples of slant rhyme in this poem.

3. **Repetition. Repetition** is the use, again, of a sound, word, phrase, sentence, or other element. Where is repetition of a word used in this poem? What is its effect? Where is the strongest use of repetition of a sound? For what purpose?

Language Lab

Voice and Mood. Read the Language Arts Survey, 2.69, on the subjunctive mood and the past subjunctive. Then write these sentences and underline each verb that is used in the subjunctive mood.

1. To understand Dickinson's work, it is important that the reader remember the pressures on women of her day.
2. Society required that a single woman marry in order to be respected.
3. Certainly, friends would suggest that a girl accept almost any proposal, no matter how undesirable.
4. Were I a woman in Dickinson's era, I would not have been able to plan a career of my own.
5. Can you imagine Dickinson's surprise and pleasure if she were to see the great number of modern women, both single and married, with important careers in business, science, and the arts?

Study and Research Skills

Etymology. Read the information about etymologies in the Language Arts Survey, 4.24, "Using Dictionaries." The word *majority* comes from the Latin word *maior,* meaning "greater." The Latin word for "great" is *magnus.* Using a dictionary that gives etymologies, identify at least four other English words that are drawn from either *maior* or *magnus.*

Answers for Understanding Literature

See the evaluation forms for discussion, active listening, and oral communication, *Assessment Portfolio,* 7.11–7.14.

Responses will vary. Possible responses are given.

1. Sight Rhyme. Sight rhyme is found in stanza 3 in the words *one* and *stone.*

2. Slant Rhyme. Examples of slant rhyme are "Society/Majority," "Gate/Mat," and "nation/attention."

3. Repetition. Repetion of complete words is used in stanza 2, where "Unmoved" appears twice. This emphasizes the adamant stand of the soul against outside appeals for attention. In line 1, the *s* sound occurs five times, which gives special emphasis to the line.

Answers for Language Lab

1. To understand Dickinson's work, it is important that the reader remember the pressures on women of her day.
2. Society required that a single woman marry in order to be respected.
3. Certainly, friends would suggest that a girl accept almost any proposal, no matter how undesirable.
4. Were I a woman in Dickinson's era, I would not have been able to plan a career of my own.
5. Can you imagine Dickinson's surprise and pleasure if she were to see the great number of modern women, both single and married, with important careers in business, science, and the arts?

Answers for Study and Research Skills

Four other words that are drawn from *maior* or *magnus* are *major, major-domo, mayor, magnate, magnitude, magnanimous, magnificent,* and *magnify.*

PREREADING NOTES

READER'S JOURNAL

Students may have various ideas about existence beyond physical death. Encourage them to draw on their religious and cultural backgrounds and to use their imaginations as well.

LANGUAGE SKILLS

Students should list places where dashes are consistent with the guidelines in the Language Arts Survey, 2.99, "Dashes." Dashes are used correctly in lines 5, 14, and 19.

ANSWER TO GUIDED READING QUESTION

❶ The carriage passes a school playground, fields of grain, and a setting sun.

SUPPORT FOR LEP STUDENTS

Review with students the additional vocabulary below before they read the selection.

ADDITIONAL VOCABULARY

strove—tried very hard; struggled; fought

gossamer—very thin, soft, filmy cloth

LITERARY NOTE

The concept of meeting and being carried off by Death is a common one in literature. Perhaps one of the earliest and most famous parallels to the journey Dickinson describes is that of Persephone in Greek mythology. Persephone was the daughter of Demeter and Zeus who was abducted and carried to the underworld by Hades, god of the dead, to be his wife. Demeter, goddess of the grains, made the earth barren after Persephone was abducted. Persephone was eventually allowed to return to her mother for nine months of the year but had

(cont.)

READER'S JOURNAL

What are your beliefs about life after death? What sort of existence might that be? Write briefly about what you expect to happen to you after your death.

LANGUAGE SKILLS

Read the Language Arts Survey, 2.99, "Dashes." Then compare the guidelines for using dashes with Dickinson's creative use of this punctuation mark. Then analyze this poem as if it were in prose sentences, and find a place where the poet's dashes are consistent with the guidelines.

"Because I could not stop for Death—"

EMILY DICKINSON

Because I could not stop for Death—
He kindly stopped for me—
The Carriage held but just Ourselves—
And Immortality.

5 We slowly drove—He knew no haste
And I had put away
My labor and my leisure too,
For His Civility—

What three things does the carriage pass? ❶

We passed the School, where Children strove
10 At recess—in the Ring—
We passed the Fields of Gazing Grain—
We passed the Setting Sun—

Or rather—He passed Us—
The Dews drew quivering and Chill—
15 For only Gossamer, my Gown—
My Tippet[1]—only Tulle[2]—

1. **Tippet.** Short cape worn over the shoulders
2. **Tulle.** Thin netting

WORDS FOR EVERYDAY USE: **ci • vil • i • ty** (sə vil´ə tē) *n.*, gentleness; a civilized manner

LITERARY NOTE (CONT.)

to remain in Hades for the other three months. Dickinson was conscious of this myth as she was writing her poem; she writes that Death acts with "civility," almost like a bridegroom, and the speaker and Death pass "Fields of Gazing Grain" on their way to Death's "House."

VOCABULARY IN CONTEXT

- She longed for a world of civility in which gentleness, cooperation, and manners would be prized.

Winter Sunday in Norway, Maine. *Artist unknown,* circa *1860. New York State Historical Association, Cooperstown, NY*

We paused before a House that seemed
A Swelling of the Ground—
The Roof was scarcely visible—
20 The Cornice[1]—in the Ground

Since then—'tis Centuries—and yet
Feels shorter than the Day
I first surmised the Horses Heads
Were toward Eternity— ■

1. **Cornice.** Molded projection at the top of a building

❶ *What is this house?*

Responding to the Selection

What sort of attitude toward death is reflected in this poem? How is Death portrayed? Do you share the speaker's conception of death? Why, or why not?

Answer to Guided Reading Question

❶ The house may be a grave with a tombstone.

Answers to Selection Check Test 4.5.19

EX. For whom could the speaker not stop?
The speaker could not stop for Death.

1. What did Death do for the speaker?
Death "kindly stopped" for the speaker.

2. Who are the passengers in Death's carriage?
Death, the speaker, and "Immortality" are the passengers in the carriage.

3. What do Death and the speaker pass?
They pass a school playground, a field of grain, and the setting sun.

4. Where do the speaker and Death pause?
They pause before a house that seems "A Swelling of the Ground," or a grave.

5. Where did the speaker surmise the horses' heads were turned?
The speaker surmised the horses' heads were turned toward eternity.

Responding to the Selection

Some students will find the poet's portrayal of Death as a gentle and a civilized person comforting, while others may strongly disagree with this portrayal. It might be interesting to read to students Dylan Thomas's "Do Not Go Gentle into That Good Night" in which a very different attitude toward death is described. Ask students whether they believe that death is something that should be raged against, as Thomas suggests, or accepted with quiet civility, as Dickinson suggests.

Answers for Reviewing the Selection

RECALLING

1. Stanza 1 pictures Death as a gentleman who invites the speaker for a ride in a carriage.

2. The three visual images are the school, the fields of grain, and the setting sun.

3. Stanza 4 relates to the sense of touch—"quivering," "chill," "dew," and thin clothing. The stanza makes the reader feel cold with apprehension for what is happening to the speaker.

4. Stanza 6 tells the reader that the speaker has been dead for centuries.

INTERPRETING

Responses will vary. Possible responses are given.

5. During life, the speaker was too concerned with daily events to consider stopping.

(cont.)

ANSWERS FOR REVIEWING THE SELECTION (CONT.)

6. The school suggests childhood, the grain suggests maturity, and the setting sun suggests age. The speaker suggests that death is as much a part of a person's life as any other stage in his or her development.

7. Stanza 5 describes the grave or mausoleum that houses the speaker now that she has died.

8. The speaker seems comfortable with death, as with an old acquaintance.

SYNTHESIZING

Responses will vary. Possible responses are given.

9. At first, the speaker is too busy and does not have time for Death. But she is joined in the carriage by another rider, who is immortality, or timelessness. The drive is slow; the speaker has stopped being concerned about time. The speaker decides that the sun has passed the carriage rather than the other way around. Therefore, the sun is moving faster than Death's carriage. The centuries since her death seem shorter than the day of her death. These examples indicate a development in the speaker's understanding of time.

10. Some students will believe the speaker passes from life to death on the journey, while others will believe the speaker has died at the beginning of the poem. Students should support their answers with evidence from the text.

ANSWERS FOR UNDERSTANDING LITERATURE

▶ See the evaluation forms for discussion, active listening, and oral communication, *Assessment Portfolio,* 7.11–7.14.

1. Stanza. There are six stanzas in the poem. Stanza 1: Death, like a gentleman caller, takes the speaker for a carriage ride. Stanza 2: The drive is slow; neither Death nor the speaker is hurried. Stanza 3: The carriage passes a school, fields of grain, and the setting sun. Stanza 4: The speaker grows chilly. Stanza 5: The carriage reaches its destination, a house in the ground. Stanza 6: The speaker reflects on the centuries since the ride.

2. Extended Metaphor. The carriage ride is an extended metaphor for a

(cont.)

Reviewing the Selection

RECALLING

1. How does stanza 1 picture Death?
2. Identify the three visual images the speaker notes during the carriage ride.
3. To which sense does most of stanza 4 relate? How does this stanza make you feel?
4. What do you learn in stanza 6 about the speaker?

INTERPRETING

5. Why do you think that the speaker could not stop for Death?
6. In what way do the three images reflect stages of life? What is the speaker saying about the presence of death as a factor in all of a person's life?
7. What "House" is described in stanza 5?
8. What is the speaker's attitude toward death?

SYNTHESIZING

9. Review the poem for references to time. Do these references present a single concept or a development in the speaker's understanding of time? Discuss your findings.
10. Do you suppose the speaker is dead at the beginning of the poem or passes from life to death at some point during the journey? Give a reason for your answer.

Understanding Literature (Questions for Discussion)

1. **Stanza.** A **stanza** is a recurring pattern of grouped lines in a poem. How many stanzas form this poem? Describe the development of the poem's story, stanza by stanza.
2. **Extended Metaphor.** An **extended metaphor** is a point-by-point presentation of one thing as though it were another. For what is the carriage ride in this poem an extended metaphor? Explain several of the points it mentions.
3. **Assonance. Assonance** is the repetition of vowel sounds in stressed syllables that end with different consonant sounds. Find at least two examples of assonance in this poem.
4. **Irony. Irony** is a contradiction between appearance and reality. What makes the speaker's comments about death in stanza 1 of the poem witty and ironic? How do the speaker's feelings about death progress throughout the poem?
5. **Point of View. Point of view** is the vantage point from which a literary work is told. This poem is told from the first-person point of view by a speaker who uses the words *I, me,* and *ourselves.* What is unusual about this speaker? From what perspective does she view the events that she relates? What might account for the calmness and humor of her description of her experience of death?

ANSWERS FOR UNDERSTANDING LITERATURE (CONT.)

funeral procession. Death, personified, is in control of the carriage (stanzas 1–3). The rider grows cold, just as the body of a dead person grows cold (stanza 4). The destination of the trip is a "House" in the ground—the grave (stanza 5).

3. Assonance. Examples of assonance include line 5: "slowly drove/no"; line 11: "gazing grain"; line 14: "dews drew"; and line 15: "first surmised."

4. Irony. The speaker says because she could not stop for Death, he "kindly" stopped for her. She describes Death as if it were a courtly gentleman who kindly offers her a ride, rather than an inevitable and often dreaded part of all people's lives. The speaker experiences more apprehension when she grows chill.

5. Point of View. The point of view is first person; the speaker is the dead person who is looking back on her death and passage through life. She views death with calmness and humor because she has experienced it; death is no longer unknowable and dreaded.

READER'S JOURNAL

Have you ever tried to meditate? Is it easy to concentrate on a single thought? How can you eliminate distractions? Set aside a quiet time to try to limit your thoughts to a topic meaningful to you. Then rate how successful you were. Record difficulties you encountered.

WRITING SKILLS

Review the nature and purpose of sensory details by reading the Language Arts Survey, 1.40, "Elaboration: Types of Supporting Details." Then find at least three sensory details in this poem. Be ready to discuss which sense(s) each detail appeals to.

"I heard a Fly buzz—when I died—"

EMILY DICKINSON

I heard a Fly buzz—when I died—
The Stillness in the Room
Was like the Stillness in the Air—
Between the Heaves of Storm—

5 The Eyes around—had wrung them dry—
and Breaths were gathering firm
For that last Onset—when the King
Be witnessed—in the Room

I willed my Keepsakes[1]—Signed away
10 What portion of me be
Assignable—and then it was
There interposed[2] a Fly—

With Blue—uncertain stumbling Buzz—
Between the light—and me—
15 And then the Windows failed—and then
I could not see to see— ■

1. **Keepsakes.** Personal items that are treasured
2. **interposed.** Appeared suddenly

❶ *Who else is in the room besides the speaker?*

PREREADING NOTES

READER'S JOURNAL

Students' journal entries should include ratings of their success with meditation. They should discuss difficulties or distractions that interfered and ways they tried to eliminate these distractions. If the students encountered difficulty with this exercise, suggest that they try other meditation practices or other environments that will be more likely to support peaceful contemplation.

WRITING SKILLS

Students should list three sensory details in this poem. Possibilities include eyes sore from crying (sense of touch), intermittent buzzing from a fly (hearing), heavy stillness (touch and hearing), and faint light from a window (sight).

SUPPORT FOR LEP STUDENTS

Review with students the additional vocabulary below before they read the selection.

ADDITIONAL VOCABULARY

heave—act of rising or swelling
onset—attack; assault

ANSWER TO GUIDED READING QUESTION

❶ The others are probably relatives and friends of the dying speaker.

ANSWERS TO SELECTION CHECK TEST 4.5.21

EX. What happens to the speaker in this poem?
The speaker dies.

1. What does the speaker hear when she dies?
The speaker hears a fly buzz.

2. What was the stillness of the room like?
The stillness of the room was like the stillness of the air "Between the Heaves of Storm."

3. Who is witnessed at the "last Onset"?
The "King" is witnessed at the "last Onset."

4. What "interposed" between the light and the speaker?
A fly "with Blue—uncertain stumbling Buzz—" interposed between the light and the speaker.

5. What happened after "the Windows failed"?
After "the Windows failed," the speaker "could not see to see—."

RESPONDING TO THE SELECTION

Encourage students to explain what makes the deathbed scene seem realistic or unrealistic. Students may find the deathbed scene frightening and sad, as it describes the loss of both the senses and contact with the material world.

ANSWERS FOR REVIEWING THE SELECTION

RECALLING

1. In a very quiet room lies a dying person with friends and family attending her.

2. The eyes of those attending are already cried out, and the breathing of the weepers is steadying; those upset have had time to react to the news.

3. The verb is before the subject in line 12.

4. The speaker notices the buzzing of the fly; then she senses that the fly has come between her and the windows' light. After the fly enters, the speaker cannot concentrate on the rest of the room.

INTERPRETING

Responses will vary. Possible responses are given.

5. The comparison of the stillness in the room with the lull in a storm suggests that, like a storm returning, something dramatic (the speaker's death) will soon occur.

6. At the time of death, the dying person expects to see God, the king of heaven. The king's arrival may signify that the speaker has passed from this life to the hereafter.

7. The sudden change in sentence pattern makes the clause more noticeable; it puts more emphasis on the words *interposed* and *fly*. In addition, it produces a break between the first part of the poem and the last stanza, where the mood changes.

8. The poem seems to stop at the moment of death. The speaker is unable to see beyond the windows, perhaps to God. The speaker's mood might be described as

(cont.)

Responding to the Selection

Did the deathbed scene pictured in this poem seem believable to you? Did it surprise you? Did it sadden or frighten you? Why, or why not?

Reviewing the Selection

RECALLING

1. In your own words, describe the scene at the beginning of the poem.
2. What sensory details tell you that the speaker's death is not sudden or unexpected?
3. All the sentences and clauses in the poem except one follow the subject-verb pattern. Identify the clause that breaks away from that pattern. What pattern does it use?
4. What does the speaker notice about the fly? What does she notice about the rest of the room after the fly enters?

INTERPRETING

5. How does stanza 1 suggest that something momentous is about to happen?
6. Who is the "King" whose arrival is expected? What will his arrival signify?
7. Why did the poet vary the sentence pattern in the single clause? What effect does the unusual word order produce?
8. At what moment does the action stop? What is the speaker's mood at that point? Why?

SYNTHESIZING

9. What fear(s) about death—and life—does this poem explore?
10. What is surprising about the ending of this poem? How does the speaker's actual experience contradict the expectations of the people gathered around her deathbed?

Understanding Literature (Questions for Discussion)

1. **Synaesthesia. Synaesthesia** is a figure of speech that combines in a single expression images related to two or more different senses. Find an example of synaesthesia in stanza 4. To what two senses does the expression relate?

ANSWERS FOR REVIEWING THE SELECTION (CONT.)

disappointed. She was expecting death to be a great event, and now something as trivial as a fly dominates it.

SYNTHESIZING

Responses will vary. Possible responses are given.

9. The poem focuses on our inability to know anything about the afterlife with certainty. It presents graphically the possibility that, despite believers' hopes for eternal happiness, death may be a total end to one's consciousness.

10. The ending of the poem is surprising because a moment that is expected to be dramatic and uplifting is interrupted by a mundane fly. People are expecting the speaker to meet "the King" after death and instead she only experiences the presence of a buzzing fly.

2. **Onomatopoeia. Onomatopoeia** is the use of words or phrases that sound like the things to which they refer. Read line 13 aloud. What is described? What repeated sounds in the words suggest the thing described?

3. **Symbol.** A **symbol** is a thing that stands for or represents both itself and something else. For example, a dove is a traditional symbol of peace. Of what is light a traditional symbol? (Think, for example, of conventional expressions such as "a sudden illumination" and "to shed light on a problem.") What literal interpretation might be given to the light in the last stanza? What symbolic interpretation might it be given? In the Middle Ages, one of the demons of hell was considered to be Beelzebub, the so-called "Lord of the Flies." What literal interpretation might be given to what the speaker sees at the end of the stanza? What symbolic interpretation might it be given? What various interpretations might be given of the speaker's inability to see at the end of the poem?

Responding in Writing

Description. Read the Language Arts Survey, 1.18, "Sensory Detail Charts," paying particular attention to the sample sensory detail chart. Then select an object or room with which you are familiar, and create a sensory detail chart for that subject. List at least two details in each column, in other words, for each sense. Use the information in your chart to write a description of the object or room.

PROJECTS

1. **Assembling an Anthology.** With a small group of students who enjoy writing poetry, work together to assemble an anthology of original poems. Begin by sharing poems all of you have written and selecting a reasonable number to represent each member of the group. Split up the tasks of designing the cover and any artwork, typing or inputting the manuscript, laying out pages, and duplicating and assembling pages. Use desktop publishing methods, if possible. Make your anthology available to classmates, teachers, and parents.

2. **Community Survey.** Work with a large group, such as your whole class, to collect data for a community survey concerning the arts. Draw up a small number of specific questions concerning community attitudes toward the arts, artists, and/or community resources in the arts (museums, theaters, libraries, etc.). After every group member has interviewed three or more different community members, tabulate your results. Look for generalizations you can justifiably draw from the results. Announce your findings through a classroom display, letter to the editor of the local paper, or some other means.

3. **Historical Research/Women's Studies.** Do independent research on the roles and rights of women in the United States in the mid-1800s. If you like, focus on individuals whose unusual accomplishments throw the usual lot of women into stronger contrast. Present your findings in a paper or multimedia presentation.

ANSWERS FOR UNDERSTANDING LITERATURE

1. Synaesthesia. Line 13—"With blue uncertain stumbling Buzz"—relates to both sight and sound, giving the sound of the buzzing the color blue.

2. Onomatopoeia. Examples of words that sound like their meanings are *buzz, heaves,* and *stumbling.*

3. Symbol. Literally, the speaker is dying and can no longer see the light. The light in stanza 4 could symbolize the ruling life force in the speaker; the fly could symbolize impending death and possible damnation.

ANALYTIC SCALES FOR RESPONDING IN WRITING

Assign a score from 1 to 25 for each grading criterion below. (For more detailed evaluation, see the evaluation forms for writing, revising, and proofreading, *Assessment Portfolio,* 7.1–7.10.)

Description

- **Content/Unity.** The description provides the sensory details of an object or room with which the student is familiar.
- **Organization/Coherence.** The description is written in a clear and sensible order.
- **Language/Style.** The description uses vivid and precise nouns, verbs, and modifiers.
- **Conventions.** The description avoids errors in spelling, grammar, usage, mechanics, and manuscript form.

PROJECT NOTES

▶ See the worksheets and evaluation forms for projects, *Assessment Portfolio,* 7.20–7.23.

1. Assembling an Anthology. Students who enjoy poetry may wish to write the majority of the poems,

(cont.)

PROJECT NOTES (CONT.)

while students who are more comfortable with other forms of literature might focus on the artwork and publishing tasks.

2. Community Survey. Students should make sure they choose appropriate questions that will elicit information before they survey members of the community.

3. Historical Research/Women's Studies. Students might focus on Nelly Bly (the first female reporter); Amelia Bloomer, Elizabeth Cady Stanton, or Susan B. Anthony (feminists); Harriet Tubman (civil rights leader); or Florence Nightingale (founder of the Red Cross).

ADDITIONAL RESOURCES

READER'S GUIDE
- Selection Worksheet, 5.12

ASSESSMENT PORTFOLIO
- Selection Check Test, 4.5.23
- Selection Test, 4.5.24

ESSENTIAL SKILLS PRACTICE BOOKS
- *Language,* 2.103
- *Speaking and Listening,* 3.7
- *Study and Research,* 4.28

ENRICHMENT ACTIVITIES

Inform students that birds have been associated with messages from the spirit world in various cultures. The raven is a large dark bird of prey. Poe's speaker views the bird as both wise and terrifying. Ask students to write a descriptive paragraph about another animal or bird that might serve as a spiritual messenger. Students should explain their choices. What about the creature's appearance or actions makes the creature seem like it could be a spiritual messenger? They might also like to consider what message they imagine the creature bearing. To whom is the message sent? Why?

SUPPORT FOR LEP STUDENTS

Students may have difficulty with Poe's language. Review the additional vocabulary below with students before they read the selection.

ADDITIONAL VOCABULARY

chamber—bedroom
peering—staring intently
decorum—attitude
discourse—speak
placid—calm, still
aptly—ably
respite—rest; release from hard work
pallid—pale

PREREADING

"The Raven"
by Edgar Allan Poe

ABOUT THE AUTHOR

A biography of **Edgar Allan Poe** appears on page 225.

ABOUT THE SELECTION

"The Raven" was Edgar Allan Poe's first international success. When it was published in 1845 in the *New York Evening Mirror,* the editor warned readers that "it would stick to the memory of everybody who reads it." It seems that this prophecy came true, because soon after the poem's publication, "The Raven" was read and reread by critics, poets, and students all over the world. To this day, "The Raven" is included in many anthologies; it has become a staple in the education of many American students. Poe himself considered it to be one of his finest works. In 1846, he claimed that "future generations will be able to sift the gold from the dross, and 'The Raven' will be beheld, shining above them all as a diamond of purest water."

GOALS/OBJECTIVES

Studying this lesson will enable students to

- enjoy and appreciate a lyric poem
- define *internal rhyme* and identify examples of it in a poem
- find examples of alliteration in a poem
- understand run-on lines and end-stopped lines
- write a comic strip and a fantasy
- use quotation marks correctly
- use reference works
- prepare an oral presentation of a poem

READER'S JOURNAL

Have you ever had the feeling that an animal, such as a pet cat or dog, knew something important but couldn't tell it to you? What might a pet say if it could talk? Write down your ideas about these questions in your journal.

SPEAKING AND LISTENING SKILLS

Read the Language Arts Survey, 3.7, "Public Speaking." Because this poem is so musical, it is especially appropriate to be read aloud. After reading the poem, choose a few stanzas and prepare an oral reading of them, following the guidelines in the Language Arts Survey.

The Raven

EDGAR ALLAN POE

Once upon a midnight dreary, while I pondered, weak and weary,
Over many a quaint and curious volume of forgotten lore,
While I nodded, nearly napping, suddenly there came a tapping,
As of some one gently rapping, rapping at my chamber door.
5 " 'Tis some visiter," I muttered, "tapping at my chamber door—
Only this, and nothing more."

Ah, distinctly I remember it was in the bleak December,
And each separate dying ember wrought its ghost upon the floor.
Eagerly I wished the morrow;—vainly I had tried to borrow
10 From my books surcease of sorrow—sorrow for the lost Lenore—
For the rare and radiant maiden whom the angels name Lenore—
Nameless here for evermore.

❶ *What is the cause of the speaker's sorrow?*

And the silken sad uncertain rustling of each purple curtain
Thrilled me—filled me with fantastic terrors never felt before;
15 So that now, to still the beating of my heart, I stood repeating
" 'Tis some visiter entreating entrance at my chamber door—
Some late visiter entreating entrance at my chamber door;—
This it is, and nothing more."

Presently my soul grew stronger; hesitating then no longer,
20 "Sir," said I, "or Madam, truly your forgiveness I implore;

WORDS FOR EVERYDAY USE:

sur • cease (sur sēs´) *n.,* respite; end
en • treat (en trēt´) *vt.,* beg; implore; ask earnestly

PREREADING NOTES

READER'S JOURNAL

You might ask students to think about whether pets would talk about the same things that people do. Would their conversations focus on other issues? What subjects might pets find interesting?

SPEAKING AND LISTENING SKILLS

Students' recitations can be either memorized or extemporaneous (using written note cards). Students should try to recite the poem vividly and dramatically.

ANSWER TO GUIDED READING QUESTION

❶ The speaker is sorrowful because his beloved Lenore has died.

VOCABULARY FROM THE SELECTION

adjure	morrow
beguiling	obeisance
censer	ominous
craven	quaff
entreat	surcease
lattice	tempest
mien	undaunted

VOCABULARY IN CONTEXT

- The ice pack was the only thing that brought surcease to the throbbing pain in her sprained ankle.
- I entreat you not to divulge my secret to anyone.

Answers to Guided Reading Questions

❶ The raven steps in through the open window.

❷ The visitor sits on the bust of Pallas, the Greek goddess of wisdom.

❸ No, the speaker doesn't find the bird's response meaningful.

Additional Questions and Activities

What does the speaker see when he opens the door? What word does the speaker whisper after he opens the door? Why does the speaker whisper this word? What is revealed about the speaker's mental state by this whisper?

Answers. The speaker sees darkness and "nothing more" when he opens the door. The speaker whispers the word *Lenore* into the darkness. The speaker seems surprised to find he has whispered this word; however, he has probably whispered his beloved's name because he misses her and longs to have her back in the world of the living. The speaker is in an anguished and tormented mental state because of his grief; he whispers his beloved's name when he opens the door even though he knows she is dead.

But the fact is I was napping, and so gently you came rapping,
And so faintly you came tapping, tapping at my chamber door,
That I scarce was sure I heard you"—here I opened wide the door,—
Darkness there, and nothing more.

Deep into that darkness peering, long I stood there wondering, fearing,
Doubting dreaming dreams no mortal ever dared to dream before;
But the silence was unbroken, and the darkness gave no token,
And the only word there spoken was the whispered word, "Lenore!"
This *I* whispered, and an echo murmured back the word, "Lenore!"
Merely this, and nothing more.

Then into the chamber turning, all my soul within me burning,
Soon I heard again a tapping somewhat louder than before.
"Surely," said I, "surely that is something at my window lattice;
Let me see, then, what thereat is, and this mystery explore—
Let my heart be still a moment and this mystery explore;—
'Tis the wind, and nothing more!"

❶ *Who enters through the open window?*

Open here I flung the shutter, when, with many a flirt and flutter,
In there stepped a stately raven of the saintly days of yore;
Not the least obeisance made he; not an instant stopped or stayed he;
But, with mien of lord or lady, perched above my chamber door—
Perched upon a bust of Pallas[1] just above my chamber door—
Perched, and sat, and nothing more.

❷ *Where does the visitor sit?*

Then this ebony bird beguiling my sad fancy into smiling,
By the grave and stern decorum of the countenance it wore,
"Though thy crest be shorn and shaven, thou," I said, "art sure no craven,
Ghastly grim and ancient raven wandering from the Nightly shore—
Tell me what thy lordly name is on the Night's Plutonian[2] shore!"
Quoth the raven, "Nevermore."

❸ *Does the speaker find the visitor's response meaningful?*

Much I marvelled this ungainly fowl to hear discourse so plainly,
Though its answer little meaning—little relevancy bore;
For we cannot help agreeing that no sublunary[3] being
Ever yet was blessed with seeing bird above his chamber door—
Bird or beast upon the sculptured bust above his chamber door,
With such name as "Nevermore."

1. **Pallas.** Greek goddess of wisdom
2. **Plutonian.** Black; relating to the underworld
3. **sublunary.** Earthly

Words for Everyday Use:
lat • tice (lat´is) *n.,* shutter; openwork structure used as a screen
o • bei • sance (ō bā´səns) *n.,* gesture of respect
mien (mēn) *n.,* manner; appearance
cra • ven (krā´vən) *n.,* coward

Vocabulary in Context

- The window lattice, covered with ivy and morning glories, opened out onto a view of a garden.
- The young man knelt before the king as a sign of obeisance.
- With the mien of a warrior, the young girl showed her determination to stand up to the bully.
- A peacemaker must not be a craven when needed to step in and stop a fight.
- On the night before a journey, the morrow has infinite possibility.
- The minister adjured him to do so, but the condemned prisoner would not admit his guilt.

Illustration to Edgar Allan Poe's Le Corbeau (The Raven). *Edouard Manet, 1875. Courtesy, Museum of Fine Arts, Boston*

But the raven, sitting lonely on the placid bust, spoke only
That one word, as if his soul in that one word he did outpour.
Nothing farther then he uttered—not a feather then he fluttered—
Till I scarcely more than muttered, "Other friends have flown before—
On the morrow *he* will leave me, as my hopes have flown before."
Quoth the raven, "Nevermore."

Wondering at the stillness broken by reply so aptly spoken,
"Doubtless," said I, "what it utters is its only stock and store,
Caught from some unhappy master whom unmerciful Disaster
Followed fast and followed faster—so, when Hope he would adjure,
Stern Despair returned, instead of the sweet Hope he dared adjure—
That sad answer, "Nevermore!"

WORDS FOR EVERYDAY USE:
mor • row (mär´ō) *n.,* next day
ad • jure (ə jer´) *vt.,* urge; beg

ART NOTE

Edouard Manet (1832–1883) produced illustrations (such as that on page 341) and prints but is primarily known for his paintings. The French artist displayed his "Luncheon on the Grass" at the Salon des Refusés and helped spark the movement known as Impressionism. Manet was a part of an elite, artistic society then flourishing in Europe that included fellow painters Edgar Degas and Claude Monet, poet Charles Baudelaire, novelist Emile Zola, and others. Poe's work was appreciated by many French artists, including Baudelaire, while it remained underrated in the United States for many years.

CROSS-CURRICULAR ACTIVITIES

Mathematics and Sciences. Encourage students as a group to research and discuss ravens. Questions to consider are the following: What do ravens look like? In what ways are ravens commonly described in literature? What do ravens feed on? What do ravens sound like? Then, encourage students to discuss why Poe chose this particular bird as an ominous messenger in this poem.

Answers. Ravens are larger than crows and have lustrous blue-black feathers. Ravens are often symbols of death and disease in literature. Ravens feed on rodents, insects, and grain, but often live on carrion and garbage in the winter. Ravens have a rasping croak. Poe may have chosen a raven to be an ominous messenger because of its dramatic appearance and rasping voice as well as the fact that it feeds on dead animals and is a classical symbol of death and disease.

LITERARY TECHINIQUE

A **refrain** is a line or a group of lines repeated in a poem or song. Students should easily recognize that the sixth line of each stanza ends in the refrain "Nevermore." The poet varies this refrain, especially at the beginning of the poem, using the phrases "nothing more" and "evermore." Ask students to describe the effect of the refrain. What mood does the refrain set?

Answers. The refrain emphasizes the hopeless state of the speaker and his desperation. The refrain casts a gloomy mood.

Answers to Guided Reading Questions

❶ The spectator sits on a velvet-cushioned seat.

❷ The speaker is thinking of Lenore.

❸ While at first the speaker saw "little meaning" in the bird's words, now the speaker becomes agitated, fearful, and angry when the bird speaks.

Literary Technique

A **symbol** is something that stands for or represents both itself and something else. You might encourage students to discuss the symbolism of the raven's taking up residence on the bust of Pallas in the speaker's room. Point out that the bird says it will leave "Nevermore," and that the speaker says that his soul will never escape the shadow of the bird. What might the bird represent for the speaker?

Answer. The bird might represent the gloom and depression that has become a permanent part of the speaker's life since the passing of his beloved Lenore.

Answers to Selection Check Test 4.5.23

EX. What is the speaker's visitor?
The speaker's visitor is a raven.

1. What does the speaker hear that wakes him when he is "nearly napping"?
The speaker hears a "rapping" and a "tapping" at his chamber door.

2. Why does the speaker feel sorrowful?
The speaker feels sorrowful because he has lost his beloved Lenore.

3. What is the raven's one reply to every question?
The raven's reply to every question is "Nevermore."

4. Why does the speaker become angry with the raven?
The speaker becomes angry with the raven because it says he will never forget Lenore or his sorrow and will never see Lenore again in "the distant Aidenn."

5. Where does the bird remain?
The bird remains on a bust of Pallas above the speaker's door.

Where does the speaker sit? ❶

But the raven still beguiling all my sad soul into smiling,
Straight I wheeled a cushioned seat in front of bird, and bust, and door;
Then upon the velvet sinking, I betook myself to linking
70 Fancy unto fancy thinking what this ominous bird of yore—

What this grim, ungainly, ghastly, gaunt, and ominous bird of yore
Meant in croaking "Nevermore."

This I sat engaged in guessing, but no syllable expressing
To the fowl whose fiery eyes now burned into my bosom's core;
75 This and more I sat divining, with my head at ease reclining
On the cushion's velvet lining that the lamplight gloated o'er,
But whose velvet violet lining with the lamplight gloating o'er,
She shall press, ah, nevermore!

Of whom is the speaker thinking? ❷

Then, methought, the air grew denser, perfumed from an unseen censer
80 Swung by angels whose faint foot-falls tinkled on the tufted floor.
"Wretch," I cried, "thy God hath lent thee—by these angels he hath sent thee
Respite—respite and Nepenthe[4] from thy memories of Lenore!
Let me quaff this kind Nepenthe and forget this lost Lenore!"
Quoth the raven, "Nevermore."

85 "Prophet!" said I, "thing of evil!—prophet still, if bird or devil!—
Whether Tempter sent, or whether tempest tossed thee here ashore,
Desolate, yet all undaunted, on this desert land enchanted—
On this home by Horror haunted—tell me truly, I implore—
Is there—*is* there balm in Gilead?[5]—tell me—tell me, I implore!"
90 Quoth the raven, "Nevermore."

How has the speaker's attitude toward the raven's answers changed? ❸

"Prophet!" said I, "thing of evil!—prophet still, if bird or devil!
By that Heaven that bends above us—by that God we both adore—
Tell this soul with sorrow laden if, within the distant Aidenn,[6]
It shall clasp a sainted maiden whom the angels name Lenore—
95 Clasp a rare and radiant maiden whom the angels name Lenore."
Quoth the raven, "Nevermore."

---

4. **Nepenthe.** Potion used to induce forgetfulness of pain or sorrow

5. **balm in Gilead.** Gilead is a mountainous area in the Middle East where evergreens provide medicinal resins. The question echoes Jeremiah 8:22, "Is there no balm in Gilead?"

6. **Aidenn.** Name created by Poe to suggest Eden

Words for Everyday Use:

be • guil • ing (bē gīl´iŋ) *part.,* charming; leading by deception
om • i • nous (äm´ə nəs) *adj.,* forewarning evil
cen • ser (sen´sər) *n.,* container for burning incense
quaff (kwäf) *vi.,* drink deeply
tem • pest (tem´pəst) *n.,* violent storm
un • daunt • ed (ən dônt´əd) *adj.,* resolute in the face of danger

Vocabulary in Context

- The sailor's songs were beguiling, and he gathered crowds wherever he traveled.
- An ominous creak woke the campers from their bunks in the old cabin.
- There was a marble censer at the foot of the Buddha, and each monk knelt to breathe its incense.
- The thirsty traveler quaffed deeply from the clear brook.
- After the late summer tempest, seven of the smaller fishing boats were missing from the harbor.
- Undaunted despite the icy slopes, the skier bvreathed deeply and began his descent.
- Freida admired the beautiful plumes of the peacock.

"Be that word our sign of parting, bird or fiend!" I shrieked, upstarting—
Get thee back into the tempest and the Night's Plutonian shore!
Leave no black plume as a token of that lie thy soul hath spoken!
100 Leave my loneliness unbroken—quit the bust above my door!
Take thy beak from out my heart, and take thy form from off my door!"
Quoth the raven, "Nevermore."

And the raven, never flitting, still is sitting, still is sitting
On the pallid bust of Pallas just above my chamber door;
105 And his eyes have all the seeming of a demon that is dreaming,
And the lamp-light o'er him streaming throws his shadow on the floor;
And my soul from out that shadow that lies floating on the floor
Shall be lifted—nevermore! ■

Responding to the Selection

How does the appearance of the raven affect the speaker's mood? Do you think that the raven is real or is it simply imagined by the speaker? If imagined, what does the raven reveal about the speaker's frame of mind? Answer these questions in your journal.

Reviewing the Selection

Recalling

1. What is the speaker doing when he first hears the rapping at his door?
2. Who or what enters the room through the open window?
3. What is the raven's single-word answer to every question?
4. How does the raven react to the speaker's anger?

Interpreting

5. Why does the speaker hesitate before answering the door?
6. Describe the raven. How is it different from normal birds? What is the speaker's reaction to it?
7. The speaker soon knows how the raven will respond to his questions and commands. Why does he continue to talk to it and ask it questions?
8. Why does the speaker become so angry at the raven that he orders it to leave his room?

Words for Everyday Use: **plume** (plüm) *n.*, feather

Responding to the Selection

Students should consider what the raven represents and why its appearance is significant. Have students discuss the questions they explored in their journals.

Answers for Reviewing the Selection

RECALLING

1. The speaker is napping.
2. A raven enters the room.
3. The raven's answer is "Nevermore."
4. The raven does not show any reaction to the speaker's anger.

INTERPRETING

Responses will vary. Possible responses are given.

5. The speaker is not sure he heard a knock because the tapping is so faint.
6. The raven is "stately" and has the "mien of lord or lady"; the bird appears to be communicating to the speaker from the moment it appears at the window.
7. The speaker becomes more and more concerned about the subject of his questioning, Lenore.
8. The speaker becomes angry because the raven will not change its answer, nor will it leave the speaker's chamber door.

SYNTHESIZING

Responses will vary. Possible responses are given.

9. Poe could have chosen a chimpanzee or a parakeet. The raven's appearance is dignified, mysterious, and awe-inspiring. Also, since the raven can fly, it seems more likely to be able to carry messages from distant lands, even from beyond mortal existence. Chosing a different animal would have given the poem a less somber feeling.
10. *Nevermore* creates a feeling of overwhelming sadness and hopelessness. It is an absolute and negative word.

ANSWERS FOR UNDERSTANDING LITERATURE

► See the evaluation forms for discussion, active listening, and oral communication, *Assessment Portfolio,* 7.11–7.14.

Responses will vary. Possible responses are given.

1. Rhyme. Students should list five examples of internal rhyme (for example, the first line of each stanza contains internal rhyme). Answers about the internal rhyming's contribution to student's enjoyment of the poem will vary.

2. Alliteration. Students should find the following alliterative consonant sounds: *n* in stanza 3, *s* in stanza 5, and *d* in stanza 12. Other examples of alliteration in the selection include the use of *m* in stanzas 6 and 9, of *f* in stanzas 11 and 13, and *p* in stanza 17.

3. Run-on Line. Students can find many examples of run-on lines, including lines 1 and 3 of stanza 3, line 1 of stanza 7, and line 3 of stanza 9. Two examples of end-stopped lines are line 5 of stanza 14 and line 1 of stanza 15. Including a variety of lines rather than relying on one or the other keeps the poem from sounding stilted.

ANALYTIC SCALES FOR RESPONDING IN WRITING

Assign a score from 1 to 25 for each grading criterion below. (For more detailed evaluation, see the evaluation forms for writing, revising, and proofreading, *Assessment Portfolio,* 7.1–7.10.)

1. Comic Strip

- **Content/Unity.** The comic strip retells the story of "The Raven."
- **Organization/Coherence.** The comic strip follows the order of the poem.
- **Language/Style.** The comic strip uses vivid and precise nouns, verbs, and modifiers.
- **Conventions.** The comic strip avoids errors in spelling, grammar, usage, mechanics, and manuscript form.

(cont.)

9. Other birds, such as the parrot, also can be trained to speak. Why do you think Poe chose the raven to visit the despondent speaker? What other animal could he have chosen? How would a different animal have changed the poem?
10. What feelings does the word *nevermore* create in you? Why is it such a sorrowful word?

Understanding Literature (Questions for Discussion)

1. **Rhyme. Rhyme** is the repetition of sounds at the ends of words. A particular kind of rhyme called *internal rhyme,* in which rhyming words appear within lines of verse, can be found in "The Raven," for example, "Wondering at the stillness broken by reply so aptly spoken." Find at least five other examples of internal rhyme in the poem. Does the internal rhyme add to your enjoyment of the poem? Why, or why not?

2. **Alliteration. Alliteration** is the repetition of initial consonant sounds. Find examples of the use of alliteration in stanzas 3, 5, and 12. Find at least one other example of alliteration in another stanza.

3. **Run-on Line.** A **run-on line** is a line of verse in which the sense or the grammatical structure does not end with the end of the line but rather is continued on one or more subsequent lines. Find two examples of run-on lines in "The Raven." Then identify two examples of the opposite of run-on lines, that is, **end-stopped lines** in which both the sense and the grammar are complete at the end of the line. What is the effect of including a variety of lines in a poem rather than only one or the other?

Responding in Writing

1. **Comic Strip.** The intense emotions and strange events of "The Raven" could make an interesting comic strip. Draw a comic strip telling the story of "The Raven." Include details about the changing appearance and emotions of the speaker, as well as details about the setting, such as the speaker's lonely, gloomy room.

2. **Fantasy.** Talking animals have appeared in folk tales, myths, children's stories, and fantasies for centuries. Write an original fantasy in which an animal that repeats a word or phrase plays a major role. First, decide on the characters and setting and make preliminary notes. Then map out the story events. Finally, write the story, including dialect from all characters.

ANALYTIC SCALES FOR RESPONDING IN WRITING (CONT.)

2. Fantasy

- **Content/Unity.** The fantasy tells a story about an animal that repeats a word or a phrase.
- **Organization/Coherence.** The fantasy is written in a clear sensible order.
- **Language/Style.** The fantasy uses vivid and precise nouns, verbs, and modifiers.
- **Conventions.** The fantasy avoids errors in spelling, grammar, usage, mechanics, and manuscript form.

Language Lab

Quotation Marks. Read the Language Arts Survey, 2.103, "Quotation Marks I." For each quotation below, add the correct punctuation.

1. It is a visitor tapping at my door I said.
2. Nevermore said the enigmatic raven.
3. I said that others had left me and that the raven would soon leave, too.
4. I pleaded Tell me if I shall ever escape from my memories of Lenore.
5. Take thy beak from out my heart, and take thy form from off my door I shrieked.

Study and Research Skills

Reference Works. Read the Language Arts Survey, 4.28, "Using Reference Works." Find at least two types of references that contain information about Edgar Allan Poe. List the names of the sources in which you found the information you were seeking.

PROJECTS

1. **Interview.** After researching Edgar Allan Poe, choose a critical point in his life and stage an interview with him. Work with a partner; one person should play Poe, and the other the interviewer. Have significant people from Poe's life appear with him on stage and review their relationships. Discuss the major events in Poe's life and his plans for the future.

2. **1840s Diorama.** In "The Raven," Poe refers to his chamber, in particular to its doorway, its shutters, and its furnishings. Find out how a typical parlor or bedroom of the 1840s would have been arranged and furnished. Construct a diorama, or model, of the room in which the events of the poem could have taken place.

ANSWERS FOR LANGUAGE LAB

1. "It is a visitor tapping at my door," I said.
2. "Nevermore," said the enigmatic raven.
3. Correct
4. I pleaded, "Tell me if I shall ever escape from my memories of Lenore."
5. "Take thy beak from out my heart, and take thy form from off my door," I shrieked.

ANSWERS FOR STUDY AND RESEARCH SKILLS

Students should list at least two references that include information about Poe. Ask students to look for a particular piece of information about the author. Then students can give the references for the information in addition to presenting it.

PROJECT NOTES

▶See the worksheets and evaluation forms for projects, *Assessment Portfolio,* 7.20–7.23.

1. Interview. The staged interview will require some class time for performance and perhaps some costumes and/or props. Some students will benefit from having note cards for some of the interview questions and answers.

2. 1840s Diorama. Students may want to find pictures of mid-nineteenth century bedrooms in a community library. If a nearby city or town has historic houses open to the public, a field trip could be arranged. Materials that could be useful in making the diorama are leftover fabrics, cotton wadding or newspapers; and cardboard. The diorama can be built in any square or rectangular container.

"Old Ironsides"

About the Author. A biography of **Oliver Wendell Holmes** appears on page 296.

About the Selection. This poem was written in response to a newspaper article that called for the dismantling of the ship popularly known as *Old Ironsides*, which was used to fend off the British in the War of 1812. The poem is credited with saving the ship, which is now on display in Charlestown, Massachusetts.

"Each and All"

"Brahma"

About the Author. A biography of **Ralph Waldo Emerson** appears on page 252.

About the Selections. **"Each and All"** and **"Brahma"** are poems, which like "The Rhodora," were clearly influenced by the Romantic movement. "Each and All" contains many beautiful elements of nature, and like many Romantics, Emerson shows his interest in Eastern culture and religion in "Brahma."

Historical Note

Hinduism is a religion with social, economic, and artistic aspects practiced in India, Pakistan, Bangladesh, Sri Lanka, Nepal, and Sikkim. It stems from Vedism, a religion of early Indo-European people. There are three main branches of Hinduism; each focuses on one of the following deities: Vishnu, god of extension and pervasiveness; Siva, creator, preserver, and destroyer of the universe; and Sakti, goddess of creative energies. Central to Hinduism is the belief in the Brahman, the individual or "self" of all forms of life. The final religious goal is commune between the "self" and the cosmic principle.

Selections for Additional Reading: New England Renaissance Poetry

"Old Ironsides"[1]
by Oliver Wendell Holmes

Ay, tear her tattered ensign[2] down!
Long has it waved on high,
And many an eye has danced to see
That banner in the sky;
Beneath it rung the battle shout,
And burst the cannon's roar;—
The meteor of the ocean air
Shall sweep the clouds no more!

Her deck, once red with heroes' blood
Where knelt the vanquished foe,
When winds were hurrying o'er the flood
And waves were white below,
No more shall feel the victor's tread,
Or know the conquered knee;—
The harpies[3] of the shore shall pluck
The eagle of the sea!

O better that her shattered hulk
Should sink beneath the wave;
Her thunders shook the mighty deep
And there should be her grave;
Nail to the mast her holy flag,
Set every thread-bare sail,
And give her to the god of storms,—
The lightning and the gale!

"Each and All"
by Ralph Waldo Emerson

Little thinks, in the field, yon red-cloaked clown,[4]
Of thee from the hill-top looking down;
The heifer that lows in the upland farm,
Far-heard, lows not thine ear to charm;
The sexton, tolling his bell at noon,
Deems not that great Napoleon
Stops his horse, and lists with delight,
Whilst his files sweep round yon Alpine height;
Nor knowest thou what argument
Thy life to thy neighbor's creed has lent.
All are needed by each one;
Nothing is fair or good alone.
I thought the sparrow's note from heaven,
Singing at dawn on the alder bough;
I brought him home, in his nest, at even;
He sings the song, but it cheers not now,
For I did not bring home the river and sky;—
He sang to my ear,—they sang to my eye.
The delicate shells lay on the shore;
The bubbles of the latest wave
Fresh pearls to their enamel gave;
And the bellowing of the savage sea
Greeted their safe escape to me.
I wiped away the weeds and foam,
I fetched my sea-born treasures home;
But the poor, unsightly, noisome things
Had left their beauty on the shore,
With the sun, and the sand, and the wild uproar.
The lover watched his graceful maid,
As 'mid the virgin train she strayed,
Nor knew her beauty's best attire
Was woven still by the snow-white choir.
At last she came to his hermitage,
Like the bird from the woodlands to the cage;—
The gay enchantment was undone,
A gentle wife, but fairy none.
Then I said, "I covet truth;
Beauty is unripe childhood's cheat;
I leave it behind with the games of youth."—
As I spoke, beneath my feet
The ground-pine curled its pretty wreath,
Running over the club-moss burrs;
I inhaled the violet's breath;
Around me stood the oaks and firs;
Pine-cones and acorns lay on the ground,
Over me soared the eternal sky,
Full of light and of deity;
Again I saw, again I heard,
The rolling river, the morning bird;—
Beauty through my senses stole;
I yielded myself to the perfect whole.

"Brahma"[5]
by Ralph Waldo Emerson

If the red slayer think he slays,
Or if the slain think he is slain,
They know not well the subtle ways
I keep, and pass, and turn again.

---

1. **Old Ironsides.** USS *Constitution*, oldest warship in U.S. Navy
2. **ensign.** Flag
3. **harpies.** In Greek mythology, harpies were voracious monsters.
4. **clown.** Peasant
5. **Brahma.** Supreme spirit of the universe in the Hindu religion

5 Far or forgot to me is near;
Shadow and sunlight are the same;
The vanished gods to me appear;
And one to me are shame and fame.

They reckon ill who leave me out;
10 When me they fly, I am the wings;
I am the doubter and the doubt,
And I the hymn the Brahmin[1] sings.

The strong gods pine for my abode,
And pine in vain the sacred Seven;[2]
15 But thou, meek lover of the good!
Find me, and turn thy back on heaven.

"There's a certain Slant of light"
by Emily Dickinson

There's a certain Slant of light,
Winter Afternoons—
That oppresses, like the Heft
Of Cathedral Tunes—

5 Heavenly Hurt, it gives us—
We can find no scar,
But internal difference,
Where the Meanings, are—

None may teach it—Any—
10 'Tis the Seal Despair—
An imperial affliction
Sent us of the Air—

When it comes, the Landscape listens—
Shadows—hold their breath—
15 When it goes, 'tis like the Distance
On the look of Death—

"I never saw a Moor"
by Emily Dickinson

I never saw a Moor—
I never saw the Sea—
Yet know I how the heather looks
And what a Billow be.

5 I never spoke with God
Nor visited in Heaven—
Yet certain am I of the spot
As if the Checks[3] were given—

"'Hope' is the thing with feathers"
by Emily Dickinson

"Hope" is the thing with feathers—
That perches in the soul—
And sings the tune without the words—
And never stops—at all—

5 And sweetest—in the Gale—is heard—
And sore must be the storm—
That could abash the little Bird
That kept so many warm—

I've heard it in the chilliest land—
10 And on the strangest Sea—
Yet, never, in Extremity,
It asked a crumb—of Me.

"Much Madness is divinest Sense"
by Emily Dickinson

Much Madness is divinest Sense—
To a discerning Eye—
Much Sense—the starkest Madness—
'Tis the Majority
5 In this, as All, prevail—
Assent—and you are sane—
Demur—you're straightway dangerous—
And handled with a Chain—

"If you were coming in the Fall"
by Emily Dickinson

If you were coming in the Fall,
I'd brush the Summer by
With half a smile and half a spurn,
As Housewives do, a Fly.

5 If I could see you in a year,
I'd wind the months in balls—
And put them each in separate Drawers,
For fear the numbers fuse—

If only Centuries, delayed,
10 I'd count them in my Hand,

1. **Brahmin.** Hindu priest
2. **sacred Seven.** Most sacred of the Hindu saints
3. **Checks.** Tickets on seats to mark the destination of passengers whose tickets have been collected

"THERE'S A CERTAIN SLANT OF LIGHT"

"I NEVER SAW A MOOR"

"'HOPE' IS THE THING WITH FEATHERS"

"MUCH MADNESS IS DIVINEST SENSE"

"IF YOU WERE COMING IN THE FALL"

"AFTER GREAT PAIN, A FORMAL FEELING COMES"

About the Author. A biography of **Emily Dickinson** appears on page 324.

About the Selections. These selections can be linked to "This is my letter to the World," "The Soul selects her own Society—," "Because I could not stop for Death—," and "I heard a Fly buzz—when I died—" as they further explore the powers of the individual imagination when faced with issues such as death, loneliness, and loss.

"ALONE"

"TO HELEN"

"ANNABEL LEE"

About the Author. A biography of **Edgar Allan Poe** appears on page 225.

About the Selections. Students might enjoy reading **"Alone"** as an account of Poe's own feelings about being an artist and having a different view of the world than others. **"To Helen"** is a lyric peom about the transformative power of love. **"Annabel Lee"** is probably Poe's most recognized poem, other than "The Raven." This poem is also about lost love, but while "The Raven" has supernatural elements and an ominous mood, "Annabel Lee" is reminiscent, sentimental elegiac verse.

Subtracting, till my fingers dropped
Into Van Diemen's land.[1]

If certain, when this life was out—
That yours and mine, should be
15 I'd toss it yonder, like a Rind,
And take Eternity—

But, now, uncertain of the length
Of this, that is between,
It goads me, like the Goblin Bee—
20 That will not state—its sting.

"After great pain, a formal feeling comes"
by Emily Dickinson

After great pain, a formal feeling comes—
The Nerves sit ceremonious, like Tombs—
The stiff Heart questions was it He, that bore,
And Yesterday, or Centuries before?

5 The Feet, mechanical, go round—
Of Ground, or Air, or Ought—
A Wooden way
Regardless grown,
A Quartz contentment, like a stone—

10 This is the Hour of Lead—
Remembered, if outlived,
As Freezing persons, recollect the Snow—
First—Chill—then Stupor—then the letting go—

"Alone"
by Edgar Allan Poe

From childhood's hour I have not been
As others were—I have not seen
As others saw—I could not bring
My passions from a common spring—
5 From the same source I have not taken
My sorrow—I could not awaken
My heart to joy at the same tone—
And all I lov'd—*I* lov'd alone—
Then—in my childhood—in the dawn
10 Of a most stormy life—was drawn
From ev'ry depth of good and ill
The mystery which binds me still—
From the torrent, or the fountain—
From the red cliff of the mountain—
15 From the sun that round me roll'd
In its autumn tint of gold—
From the lightning in the sky
As it pass'd me flying by—
From the thunder, and the storm—
20 And the cloud that took the form
(When the rest of Heaven was blue)
Of a demon in my view—

"To Helen"
by Edgar Allan Poe

Helen, thy beauty is to me
Like those Nicéan barks[2] of yore,
That gently, o'er a perfumed sea,
The weary, way-worn wanderer bore
5 To his own native shore.

On desperate seas long wont to roam,
Thy hyacinth hair, thy classic face,
Thy Naiad[3] airs have brought me home
To the glory that was Greece,
10 And the grandeur that was Rome.

Lo! in yon brilliant window-niche
How statue-like I see thee stand,
The agate lamp within thy hand!
Ah, Psyche,[4] from the regions which
15 Are Holy-Land!

"Annabel Lee"
by Edgar Allan Poe

It was many and many a year ago,
In a kingdom by the sea
That a maiden there lived whom you may know,
By the name of ANNABEL LEE;
5 And this maiden she lived with no other thought
Than to love and be loved by me.

I was a child and *she* was a child,
In this kingdom by the sea;
But we loved with a love that was more than love—
10 I and my ANNABEL LEE—
With a love that the wingèd seraphs[5] of heaven
Coveted her and me.

---

1. **Van Diemen's land.** Tasmania; island south of Australia discovered by the Dutch; once named for Van Diemen, the Dutch governor
2. **Nicéan barks.** Boats of Nice, France
3. **Naiad.** Fairylike
4. **Psyche.** Goddess of the soul
5. **seraphs.** Highest order of angels

And this was the reason that, long ago,
In this kingdom by the sea,
15 A wind blew out of a cloud, chilling
My beautiful ANNABEL LEE;
So that her highborn kinsmen came
And bore her away from me,
To shut her up in a sepulchre
20 In this kingdom by the sea.

The angels, not half so happy in heaven,
Went envying her and me—
Yes!—that was the reason (as all men know,
In this kingdom by the sea)
25 That the wind came out of the cloud by night,
Chilling and killing my ANNABEL LEE.

But our love it was stronger by far than the love
Of those who were older than we—
Of many far wiser than we—
30 And neither the angels in heaven above,
Nor the demons down under the sea,
Can ever dissever my soul from the soul
Of the beautiful ANNABEL LEE:

For the moon never beams, without bringing me dreams
35 Of the beautiful ANNABEL LEE;
And the stars never rise, but I feel the bright eyes
Of the beautiful ANNABEL LEE:
And so, all the night tide, I lie down by the side
Of my darling—my darling—my life and my bride,
40 In her sepulchre there by the sea—
In her tomb by the sounding sea.

"The Arsenal at Springfield"
by Henry Wadsworth Longfellow

This is the Arsenal. From floor to ceiling,
Like a huge organ, rise the burnished arms:
But from their silent pipes no anthem pealing
Startles the villages with strange alarms.

5 Ah! what a sound will rise, how wild and dreary,
When the death angel touches those swift keys!
What loud lament and dismal Miserere[1]
Will mingle with their awful symphonies!

I hear even now the infinite fierce chorus,
10 The cries of agony, the endless groan,
Which, through the ages that have gone before us,
In long reverberations reach our own.

On helm and harness rings the Saxon hammer,
Through Cimbric[2] forest roars the Norseman's song,
15 And loud, amid the universal clamor,

O'er distant deserts sounds the Tartar[3] gong.
I hear the Florentine, who from his palace
Wheels out his battle bell with dreadful din,
And Aztec priests upon their teocallis[4]
20 Beat the wild war drums made of serpent's skin;

The tumult of each sacked and burning village;
The shout that every prayer for mercy drowns;
The soldiers' revels in the midst of pillage;
The wail of famine in beleaguered towns;

25 The bursting shell, the gateway wrenched asunder,
The rattling musketry, the clashing blade;
And ever and anon, in tones of thunder
The diapason[5] of the cannonade,

Is it, O man, with such discordant noises,
30 With such accursed instruments as these,
Thou drownest Nature's sweet and kindly voices,
And jarrest the celestial harmonies?

Were half the power that fills the world with terror,
Were half the wealth bestowed on camps and courts,
35 Given to redeem the human mind from error;
There were no need of arsenals or forts:

The warrior's name would be a name abhorred!
And every nation, that should lift again
Its hand against a brother, on its forehead
40 Would wear forevermore the curse of Cain![6]

Down the dark future, through long generations,
The echoing sounds grow fainter and then cease:
And like a bell, with solemn, sweet vibrations,
I hear once more the voice of Christ say, "Peace!"

45 Peace! and no longer from its brazen portals
The blast of War's great organ shakes the skies!
But beautiful as songs of the immortals,
The holy melodies of love arise.

---

1. **Miserere.** Biblical reference to Psalm 51, which begins "Have mercy upon me, O God."
2. **Cimbric.** Of a Germanic people from central Europe
3. **Tartar.** The Tartars ruled parts of Asia and Eastern Europe in the fourteenth and fifteenth centuries.
4. **teocallis.** Temples erected by the Aztecs in Mexico and Central America
5. **diapason.** Entire range of an activity
6. **Cain.** According to the Bible, Cain was the first murderer.

"THE ARSENAL AT SPRINGFIELD"

"A PSALM OF LIFE"

About the Author. A biography of **Henry Wadsworth Longfellow** appears on page 306.

About the Selections. "The Arsenal at Springfield" is a moving antiwar poem. **"A Psalm of Life"** is inspirational verse meant to evoke appreciation of the gift of life. Both poems display the sentimental and sympathetic view that made Longfellow the most renowned poet of his age.

"ICHABOD!"

FROM *SNOW-BOUND: A WINTER IDYL*

About the Author. A biography of **John Greenleaf Whittier** appears on page 311.

About the Selections. "Ichabod!" laments statesman Daniel Webster's decision to support the Fugitive Slave Act that was part of the Compromise of 1850. (See the Biographical Note on page 351.) The selection from ***Snow-Bound: A Winter Idyl*** is similar to "Telling the Bees" in that both share the beautiful natural descriptions that typify the works of those poets with Romantic sensibilities.

"A Psalm of Life"
by Henry Wadsworth Longfellow

"Life that shall send
A challenge to its end,
And when it comes, say, 'Welcome, friend.'"

What the Heart of the Young Man Said to the Psalmist

I

Tell me not, in mournful numbers,
  Life is but an empty dream!
For the soul is dead that slumbers,
  And things are not what they seem.

II

Life is real—life is earnest—
  And the grave is not its goal:
Dust thou art, to dust returnest,
  Was not spoken of the soul.

III

Not enjoyment, and not sorrow,
  Is our destin'd end or way;
But to act, that each to-morrow
  Find us farther than to-day.

IV

Art is long, and time is fleeting,
  And our hearts, though stout and brave,
Still, like muffled drums, are beating
  Funeral marches to the grave.

V

In the world's broad field of battle,
  In the bivouac of Life,
Be not like dumb, driven cattle!
  Be a hero in the strife!

VI

Trust not Future, howe'er pleasant!
  Let the dead Past bury its dead!
Act—act in the glorious Present!
  Heart within, and God o'er head!

VII

Lives of great men all remind us
  We can make our lives sublime,
And, departing, leave behind us
  Footsteps on the sands of time.

VIII

Footsteps, that, perhaps another,
  Sailing o'er life's solemn main,
A forlorn and shipwreck'd brother,
  Seeing, shall take heart again.

IX

Let us then be up and doing,
  With a heart for any fate;
Still achieving, still pursuing,
  Learn to labor and to wait.

"Ichabod!"[1]
by John Greenleaf Whittier

So fallen! so lost! the light withdrawn
  Which once he wore!
The glory from his gray hairs gone
  Forevermore!

5 Revile him not—the Tempter hath
  A snare for all;
And pitying tears, not scorn and wrath,
  Befit his fall!

Oh! dumb be passion's stormy rage,
10 When he who might
Have lighted up and led his age,
  Falls back in night.

Scorn! would the angels laugh, to mark
  A bright soul driven,
15 Fiend-goaded, down the endless dark,
  From hope and heaven!

Let not the land, once proud of him,
  Insult him now,
Nor brand with deeper shame his dim,
20 Dishonored brow.

But let its humbled sons, instead,
  From sea to lake,
A long lament, as for the dead,
  In sadness make.

25 Of all we loved and honored, nought
  Save power remains—
A fallen angel's pride of thought,
  Still strong in chains.

All else is gone; from those great eyes
30 The soul has fled:
When faith is lost, when honor dies,
  The man is dead!

Then, pay the reverence of old days
  To his dead fame;
35 Walk backward, with averted gaze,
  And hide the shame!

---

1. **Icabod!** The title of the poem refers to 1 Samuel 4:21, which reads, "And she named the child Ichabod, saying, The glory is departed from Israel." Icabod here refers to Daniel Webster, Senator from Massachusetts, whose support of the Fugitive Slave Act led Whittier, a staunch abolitionist, to write this work.

from *Snow-Bound: A Winter Idyl*
by John Greenleaf Whittier

The sun that brief December day
Rose cheerless over hills of gray,
And, darkly circled, gave at noon
A sadder light than waning moon
Slow tracing down the thickening sky
Its mute and ominous prophecy,
A portent seeming less than threat,
It sank from sight before it set.
A chill no coat, however stout,
Of homespun stuff could quite shut out,
A hard, dull bitterness of cold,
That checked, mid-vein, the circling race
Of life-blood in the sharpened face,
The coming of the snow-storm told.

The wind blew east: we heard the roar
Of Ocean on his wintry shore,
And felt the strong pulse throbbing there
Beat with low rhythm our inland air.

Meanwhile we did our nightly chores,—
Brought in the wood from out of doors,
Littered the stalls, and from the mows
Raked down the herd's-grass for the cows;
Heard the horse whinnying for his corn;
And, sharply clashing horn on horn,
Impatient down the stanchion rows
The cattle shake their walnut bows;
While, peering from his early perch
Upon the scaffold's pole of birch,
The cock his crested helmet bent
And down his querulous challenge sent.

Unwarmed by any sunset light
The gray day darkened into night,
A night made hoary with the swarm
And whirl-dance of the blinding storm,
As zigzag wavering to and fro
Crossed and recrossed the winged snow:
And ere the early bed-time came
The white drift piled the window-frame,
And through the glass the clothes-line posts
Looked in like tall and sheeted ghosts.
So all night long the storm roared on:
The morning broke without a sun;
In tiny spherule traced with lines
Of Nature's geometric signs,
In starry flake, and pellicle,
All day the hoary meteor fell;
And, when the second morning shone,
We looked upon a world unknown,
On nothing we could call our own.
Around the glistening wonder bent
The blue walls of the firmament,
No cloud above, no earth below,—
A universe of sky and snow!
The old familiar sights of ours
Took marvellous shapes, strange domes and towers
Rose up where sty or corn-crib stood,
Or garden wall, or belt of wood;
A smooth white mound the brush-pile showed,
A fenceless drift what once was road;
The bridle-post an old man sat
With loose-flung coat and high cocked hat;
The well-curb had a Chinese roof
And even the long sweep, high aloof,
In its slant splendor, seemed to tell
Of Pisa's leaning miracle.

◆ ◆ ◆

Yet, haply, in some lull of life,
Some Truce of God which breaks its strife,
The worldling's eyes shall gather dew,
Dreaming in throngful city ways
Of winter joys his boyhood knew
And dear and early friends—the few
Who yet remain—shall pause to view
These Flemish pictures of old days;
Sit with me by the homestead hearth,
And stretch the hands of memory forth
To warm them at the wood-fire's blaze!
And thanks untraced to lips unknown
Shall greet me like the odors blown
From unseen meadows newly mown,
Or lilies floating in some pond,
Wood-fringed, the wayside gaze beyond;
The traveller owns the grateful sense
Of sweetness near, he knows not whence,
And, pausing, takes with forehead bare
The benediction of the air.

Biographical Note

Daniel Webster (1782–1852) was an American orator and politician who served as secretary of state and a congressman. His rebuttal to John C. Calhoun and Robert Y. Hayne's theory that states could secede from the Union in response to tariffs that threatened Southern slave owners is particularly memorable: "Liberty *and* Union, now and forever, one and inseparable." However, in an effort to placate the South, Webster chose to support the Fugitive Slave Act, which called for the return of runaway slaves who sought refuge in the North. His efforts to appease both North and South were the "snare" to which Whittier refers.

VOCABULARY DEVELOPMENT EXERCISES

▶ Give students the following exercise.

Read the Language Arts Survey, 4.41, "Sentence-Completion Questions." Using the vocabulary words on page 352, write a test containing five sentence-completion questions. Write three answer choices for each problem. Vary the forms of the words as necessary. When you are done, exchange tests with a partner.

Example.

1. Aliya searched for a _____ from the _____ wind.

(A) cairn . . . incomprehensible
(B) refuge . . . remorseless
(C) compromise . . . fruitless

Answer: B

ADDITIONAL RESOURCES

ASSESSMENT PORTFOLIO

- Vocabulary Worksheet, 4.5.25
- Study Guide: Unit 5 Test, 4.5.26
- Unit 5 Test, 4.5.27

ESSENTIAL SKILLS PRACTICE BOOKS

Writing

- Choosing an Audience, 1.7
- Elaboration: Types of Supporting Details, 1.40
- Sensory Detail Charts, 1.18

Language

- Adding Prepositional Phrases, 2.47
- Adjectives and Articles, 2.19
- Agreement of Pronouns and Antecedents, 2.82
- Capitalization, 2.107–2.133
- Correcting Dangling or Misplaced Modifiers, 2.63
- Dashes, 2.99
- Double Negatives, 2.88
- Improper Shifts in Verb Tense, 2.65
- Inverting Sentences for Emphasis, 2.64
- Irregular Verbs I, 2.66
- Prepositions, 2.24
- Quotation Marks I, 2.104
- Semicolons, 2.97
- Voice and Mood, 2.69

(cont.)

UNIT REVIEW

New England Renaissance Poetry

VOCABULARY FROM THE SELECTIONS

adjure, 341
beguiling, 342
blight, 291
brink, 312
censer, 342
civility, 332
clod, 292
communion, 291
cornice, 354
craven, 340
earnest, 303
entreat, 339
fetter, 302
hoary, 293
insensible, 292
lapse, 293
lattice, 340
mien, 340
morrow, 341
obeisance, 340
ominous, 342
patriarch, 293
pensive, 293
plume, 343
quaff, 342
sepulcher, 293
sinewy, 307
surcease, 339
tempest, 342
undaunted, 342
venerable, 293
wrought, 308

LITERARY TERMS

alliteration, 310, 319, 344
apology, 327
apostrophe, 300, 305, 319
assonance, 334
blank verse, 295
couplet, 305
elaboration, 295
euphony, 300
extended metaphor, 334
image, 310
irony, 334
meter, 319, 327
mood, 315
narrative poem, 310
onomatopoeia, 337
personification, 327
point of view, 315, 334
repetition, 331
rhetorical question, 305
rhyme, 323, 344
Romanticism, 323
run-on line, 344
sight rhyme, 331
slant rhyme, 331
stanza, 300, 305, 334
symbol, 337
synaesthesia, 336
tone, 315

ADDITIONAL RESOURCES (CONT.)

Speaking and Listening

- Elements of Verbal Communication, 3.2
- Public Speaking, 3.7

Study and Research

- Bibliographies and Bibliography Cards, 4.29
- Comparing and Contrasting, 4.8
- Making Hypotheses, 4.13
- Using Dictionaries, 4.24
- Using Reference Works, 4.23
- Using Searching Tools, 4.21

Applied English/Tech Prep

- The Form of a Personal Letter, 5.2

SYNTHESIS: QUESTIONS FOR WRITING, RESEARCH, OR DISCUSSION

GENRE STUDIES

1. Romantic Poetry. Romantic poetry celebrates the value of the common person, individual liberty, the common bonds of all people, emotion over reason, and the connection of human beings to the natural world. Think about these poems: "Thanatopsis" by William Cullen Bryant; "Stanzas on Freedom," by James Russell Lowell; "The Village Blacksmith," by Henry Wadsworth Longfellow; ""Telling the Bees" and Snow-Bound: A Winter Idyl," by John Greenleaf Whittier; and "The Raven," "Alone," and "Annabel Lee," by Edgar Allan Poe. What makes each of these a fine example of a Romantic poem?

2. Didacticism. A work of **didactic literature** has as its primary purpose teaching a moral lesson. In the nineteenth century, didactic literature was quite popular. What qualities make "Thanatopsis," by Bryant; "The Chambered Nautilus," by Holmes, "The Village Blacksmith" and "A Psalm of Life" by Longfellow; and "The Rhodora" and "Each and All" by Emerson examples of didactic poetry? What lesson does each of these poems teach?

THEMATIC STUDIES

3. Individualism. Much of American literature celebrates the values of individualism and self-reliance. How is the theme of individualism treated in "The Soul selects her own Society" and "This is my letter to the World," by Dickinson? in "Alone," by Poe?

HISTORICAL/BIOGRAPHICAL STUDIES

4. Occasional Verse. Occasional verse is poetry written for a specific occasion. What occasions prompted the writing of Emerson's "Concord Hymn," Whittier's "Icabod!," and Holmes's "Old Ironsides"? Do some research on these occasions and describe each occasion and the poet's response to it.

5. Slavery. Many of the poets of the New England Renaissance were vehemently opposed to the institution of slavery. What abolitionist sentiments are expressed in Whittier's "Icabod!" and Lowell's "Stanzas on Freedom"? What message does each poet have for the proponents of slavery?

►These prompts are suitable as topics for research papers. Refer to the Language Arts Survey, 4.20–4.34, "Research Skills." (To evaluate research papers, see the evaluation forms for writing, revising, and proofreading, *Assessment Portfolio,* 7.1–7.10.)

►These prompts can be adapted for use as topics for oral reports or debates. (To evaluate these projects, see the evaluation forms in the *Assessment Portfolio,* 7.17–7.19.)

CONNECTIONS ACROSS THE CURRICULUM

ARTS AND HUMANITIES
- Assembling an Anthology, 337
- Cemetery Visit, 316
- Community Survey, 337
- Interview, 345
- Role of the Artist, 325

MATHEMATICS AND SCIENCES
- Mollusks, 298
- Ravens, 341

SOCIAL STUDIES
- Community Survey, 337
- Customs and Superstitions, 316
- 1840s Diorama, 345
- Historical Research/Women's Studies, 337
- Researching Abraham Lincoln, 290
- Response to Emily Dickinson, 324
- Role of the Artist, 325

APPLIED ARTS
- Assembling an Anthology, 337
- 1840s Diorama, 345

TEACHING THE MULTIPLE INTELLIGENCES

SPATIAL
- 1840s Diorama, 345

KINESTHETIC
- Interview, 345

INTERPERSONAL
- Answering Rhetorical Questions, 301
- Assembling an Anthology, 337
- Cemetery Visit, 316
- Community Survey, 337
- Customs and Superstitions, 316
- Discussion, 292
- Interview, 345
- Mollusks, 298
- Ravens, 341

LANGUAGE LAB

EDITING FOR ERRORS IN MODIFIERS

A **modifier** is a word that modifies—that is, changes or explains—the meaning of another word. When editing your writing, you should watch carefully for these errors in modifier usage.

MODIFIER USAGE

Modifiers with Action and Linking Verbs

To modify the subject of a **linking verb,** use an **adjective.** To modify an **action verb,** use an **adverb.**

LINKING VERB AND ADJECTIVE: By the 1820s, Washington Irving's reputation *was established* both in the United States and in Europe.

ACTION VERB AND ADVERB: Throughout his early adulthood, Irving *lived mostly* in England.

LANGUAGE ARTS SURVEY

For additional help, see the Language Arts Survey, 2.85.

Comparison of Adjectives and Adverbs

Each modifier has three forms of comparison: **positive, comparative,** and **superlative.** Most one-syllable modifiers and some two-syllable modifiers form the comparative and superlative degrees by adding *–er* and *–est.* Other two-syllable modifiers, and all modifiers of more than two syllables, use *more* and *most* to form these degrees. To show a decrease in the quality of any modifier, form the comparative and superlative degrees by using *less* and *least.*

EXAMPLES: *sturdy, sturdier, sturdiest*
popular, more popular, most popular
successful, less successful, least successful

LANGUAGE ARTS SURVEY

For additional help, see the Language Arts Survey, 2.86.

Illogical and Double Comparisons

An **illogical comparison** occurs when one member of a group is compared with the group of which it is a part. Clarify an illogical comparison by including the word *other* or *else* in the sentence. A **double comparison** occurs when two comparative forms or two superlative forms are used to modify the same word. Correct a double comparison by editing out one of the comparative or superlative forms.

ILLOGICAL: Ralph Waldo Emerson embodied Transcendentalism more than nineteenth-century American writers.

LOGICAL: Ralph Waldo Emerson embodied Transcendentalism more than any other nineteenth-century American writer.

DOUBLE COMPARISON: From his most youngest days, William Cullen Bryant wanted to be a poet.

SINGLE COMPARISON: From his youngest days, William Cullen Bryant wanted to be a poet.

LANGUAGE ARTS SURVEY

For additional help, see the Language Arts Survey, 2.87.

Double Negatives

A **double negative** is a construction in which two negative words are used instead of one. Do not use more than one negative word, such as *no, none, not* (and its contraction, *–n't*), *nothing, barely, hardly,* or *scarcely,* in the same sentence.

DOUBLE NEGATIVE: Transcendentalists didn't adhere to none of the laws of eighteenth-century philosophy.

SINGLE NEGATIVE: Transcendentalists didn't adhere to the laws of eighteenth-century philosophy.

LANGUAGE ARTS SURVEY

For additional help, see the Language Arts Survey, 2.88.

Other Problems with Modifiers
Distinguish between the following modifiers: *this* and *these, that* and *those, those* and *them, bad* and *badly,* and *good* and *well.*

LANGUAGE ARTS SURVEY

For additional help, see the Language Arts Survey, 2.89.

Exercise A Correcting Errors in Modifier Usage

Rewrite the following sentences, correcting the errors in modifier usage.

EXAMPLE: William Cullen Bryant held steady to his Unitarian beliefs.
William Cullen Bryant held steadily to his Unitarian beliefs.

LANGUAGE ARTS

For additional help, see the Language Arts Survey, 2.85–2.89

1. Captain Ahab can't think of nothing but the White Whale.
2. Emerson's hymn commemorates the many soldiers who died heroic at the battles of Lexington and Concord.
3. Rappaccini's daughter felt herself growing more weaker.
4. Before her death, the woman willed them keepsakes to her relatives.
5. The fly sounded more louder than anything in the room.
6. The prisoner edged careful away from the deep pit.
7. Thoreau's experiment at Walden Pond went good.
8. The young student felt badly for the poisoned girl and tried to cure her.
9. Emily Dickinson seems to have thought good of death.
10. I was so frightened by them scenes of suspense that I couldn't hardly finish "The Pit and the Pendulum."

Exercise B Avoiding Errors in Modifier Usage

In each sentence below, choose the correct word from within the parentheses.

EXAMPLE: After they worked in the garden, a dip in Walden Pond felt (good, well).
good

LANGUAGE ARTS SURVEY

For additional help, see the Language Arts Survey, 2.85–2.89

1. After many battles, the *Constitution,* nicknamed "Old Ironsides," was damaged (bad, badly) and scheduled for destruction.
2. Oliver Wendell Holmes (could, couldn't) hardly believe the news of the *Constitution's* fate.
3. Holmes wrote (eloquent, eloquently) in the ship's defense in his poem "Old Ironsides."
4. Holmes's poem received such a (good, well) response that the destruction plans were canceled and the ship was rebuilt.
5. Today, the reconstructed *Constitution* stands (majestic, majestically) on exhibit in Charlestown, Massachusetts.

ANSWERS FOR LANGUAGE LAB

Exercise A

1. Captain Ahab can't think of anything but the White Whale.
2. Emerson's hymn commemorates the many soldiers who died heroically at the battles of Lexington and Concord.
3. Rappaccini's daughter felt herself growing weaker.
4. Before her death, the woman willed those keepsakes to her relatives.
5. The fly sounded louder than anything in the room.
6. The prisoner edged carefully away from the deep pit.
7. Thoreau's experiment at Walden Pond went well.
8. The young student felt bad for the poisoned girl and tried to cure her.
9. Emily Dickinson seems to have thought well of death.
10. I was so frightened by those scenes of suspense that I could hardly finish "The Pit and the Pendulum."

Exercise B

1. badly
2. could
3. eloquently
4. good
5. majestically

UNIT SKILLS OUTLINE

LITERARY SKILLS AND CONCEPTS

- Alliteration, 403
- Allusion, 373
- Antithesis, 378
- Climax, 390
- Flashback, 389
- Free Verse, 403
- Irony, 403
- Metaphor, 400
- Naturalism, 389, 400
- Parallelism, 378, 403
- Psychological Fiction, 389, 400
- Refrain, 373
- Simile, 400
- Spiritual, 373
- Stereotype, 369
- Syntax, 378
- Theme, 373, 400
- Thesis, 369
- Tone, 369

WRITING SKILLS AND CONCEPTS

- Citation for Bravery, 401
- Daydream, 390
- Directions, 390
- News Story, 378

GRAMMAR, USAGE, AND MECHANICS SKILLS AND CONCEPTS

- Appositives, 369
- Auxiliary Verbs, 390
- Dialects of English, 392
- Intransitive Verbs, 376
- Transitive Verbs, 376
- Usage Problems, 414

OTHER LANGUAGE ARTS SKILLS AND CONCEPTS

- Achieving Parallelism, 379
- Choosing a Purpose or Aim, 365
- Elements of Verbal Communication, 402
- Memorizing, 379
- Remembering and Visualizing, 390
- Sensory Detail Charts, 381
- Strategies for Taking Essay Tests, 371

UNIT 6 SLAVERY AND THE CIVIL WAR (1860–1865)

Rainy Day in Camp. *Winslow Homer, 1871. The Metropolitan Museum of Art. Gift of Mrs. William F. Milton, 1923 (23.77.1)*

GOALS/OBJECTIVES

Studying this unit will enable students to

- interpret and appreciate prose and poetry of the Civil War period
- identify the major literary movements of the mid-nineteenth century, including Naturalism and American Realism
- identify the theme of literature they read
- understand the impact of slavery and the Civil War on American literature during the nineteenth century
- describe the technique of parallelism and identify it in literature they read
- correct errors in usage

We here highly resolve that these dead shall not have died in vain, that this nation, under God, shall have a new birth of freedom.

—Abraham Lincoln
The Gettysburg Address

CONNECTIONS ACROSS THE CURRICULUM

Arts and Humanities

- Choral Reading, 379
- Visual Representation of Spiritual, 371

Mathematics and Sciences

- Memorizing Periodic Table, 379

Social Studies

- Abolitionists, 359
- Battle of Gettysburg, 379
- Civil War Weapons, 393
- Diagram Plantation, 383
- Gettysburg Cemetery, 375
- Lives of Freed African Americans, 367
- Mapping Battles, 360
- Politics of Slavery, 360
- Researching Civil War Battles, 401

TEACHING THE MULTIPLE INTELLIGENCES

Logical-Mathematical

- Arguments Against War, 403
- Identifying a Thesis, 368
- Interpreting a Phrase, 367

Musical

- Bugle Calls and Drum Signals, 402
- Civil War Music, 376
- Researching and Presenting Spirituals, 373
- Singing Spirituals, 370

Kinesthetic

- Reenactment of Speech, 376
- Relaxing to Music, 372
- Role Play, 397
- Tableau of a Scene, 382

Interpersonal

- Discussing Images, 370
- Imagined Impact of Speech, 377
- Politics of Slavery, 360

Spatial

- Diagram Plantation, 383
- Mapping Slavery, 364
- Tableau of a Scene, 382

Historical Note

Unlike any war before it in history, the American Civil War was recorded in photographs. Mathew Brady (*circa* 1823–1896), a portrait photographer from New York, recognized in the battles and camp scenes of the war a unique opportunity to record history. He hired a team of photographers to cover the war and they produced thousands of pictures, from grisly post-battle scenes to on-the-spot portraits of generals and enlisted men. Through these photos, the realities and horrors of war were brought home even to nonparticipants.

Farm, Massanutten Mountains

A House Divided

In the early years of the nineteenth century, the new nation developed in two different directions. The North became a center for industrial manufacturing and the export of finished goods. The South, in contrast, was almost entirely agricultural, producing rice, tobacco, cotton, and sugar and exporting many of these goods to Great Britain. To protect its export business, the North favored high tariffs on imported goods. The South, which depended on imports for finished products, naturally opposed high tariffs. The economic differences between the North and the South created enormous tensions, exacerbated by fundamental differences in lifestyle. Many people in the North lived in cities and towns and worked in factories, in mills, or on small farms. Most of the people in the South worked the land, some on small farms and some on large rice, tobacco, cotton, and sugar plantations.

The Issue of Slavery

At the very inception of the United States, differences arose between Northerners and Southerners over the issue of slavery. Thomas Jefferson had included a strong antislavery statement in his draft of the Declaration of Independence, but pressure from Southern delegates led to its deletion from the declaration in its final form. As the **plantation system** developed, the South began to depend more and more on imported slaves to carry out the work of its large "factory farms." While some Southerners opposed slavery, most saw it as a necessary part of the Southern economy. The slave trade was ended by law in 1808, but smuggling of slaves into the United States continued until the outbreak of the Civil War in 1860. By 1830, there were approximately three million slaves of African descent in the United States. About 2,500,000 of these people were forced agricultural laborers. By 1860,

Literary Events

► = American Events

1860	1861	1862
►1860. Nathaniel Hawthorne publishes *The Marble Faun*		►1862. Julia Ward Howe writes the lyrics of "The Battle Hymn of the Republic"
1860. George Eliot publishes *The Mill on the Floss*	1861. Charles Dickens publishes *Great Expectations*	1862. Christina Rossetti publishes *Goblin Market and Other Poems*
		1862. Ivan Turgenev publishes *Fathers and Sons*
		1862. Victor Hugo publishes *Les Misérables*

Historical Events

1860	1861	1862
►1860. Abraham Lincoln elected president	►1861. Kansas enters Union as free state	►1862. Battle of Shiloh
►1860. South Carolina's Ordinance of Secession	►1861. Mississippi, Florida, Alabama, Georgia, Louisiana, Texas, Virginia, Tennessee, Arkansas, and North Carolina secede from the Union	►1862. London refuses to recognize Confederacy
►1860. Elizabeth Cady Stanton urges women's suffrage to New York State Legislature	►1861. The Confederate States of America formed; Jefferson Davis named president	►1862. Lincoln delivers Emancipation Proclamation
	►1861. Civil War begins; Confederates attack Fort Sumter	►1862. First regiment of former slaves formed
	►1861. Trent affair, British/United States crisis	

THEMATIC CURRENTS

Use the following selections to explore these themes with your students.

Struggling Against Slavery

- from *Narrative of the Life of Frederick Douglass,* 364
- "Swing Low, Sweet Chariot," 370
- from "A House Divided," 404
- from *Up from Slavery,* 406
- Abolitionist Voices, 410

The Individual and War

- The Gettysburg Address, 374
- "An Occurrence at Owl Creek Bridge," 380
- "A Mystery of Heroism," 391
- "Do not weep, maiden, for war is kind," 402

Reflecting on Death

- "An Occurrence at Owl Creek Bridge," 380
- "Do not weep, maiden, for war is kind," 402
- "O Captain! My Captain!," 405
- from "When Lilacs Last in the Dooryard Bloom'd," 406

the number of enslaved blacks in the country had reached almost four million.

Apologists for slavery in America have often argued that the institution was benign because owners treated their "valuable property" well; however, the truth is slavery was brutal. Slaves typically worked hard, from sunup to sundown. They were fed meagerly; lived in squalid, flea-infested shacks; were often whipped for minor "offenses" by cruel overseers; were forbidden by law to learn to read and write; were sold away from their wives, husbands, or children; and suffered the basic indignity of continual subservience to others. Thousands of slaves ran away to freedom or to find family members from whom they had been separated, and hundreds revolted against their owners. In 1800, the Virginia militia put down a revolt of over a thousand slaves near Richmond. In 1822, a free black organizer named **Denmark Vesey** was hanged for attempting to organize a slave revolt in Charleston. In 1831, **Nat Turner** succeeded in organizing a revolt that led to bloody fighting and the deaths of 160 people.

Illustration from abolitionist literature

In the North, a strong movement emerged for the abolition, or ending by law, of slavery. The leader of the Northern abolitionists was **William Lloyd Garrison,** whose newspaper, *The Liberator,* called for an immediate end to the South's "peculiar institution." Other important antislavery publications included the first black-owned newspaper, **John Russwurm** and **Samuel Cornish's** *Freedom's Journal,* and **Frederick Douglass's** *The North Star.* The New England Anti-Slavery Society, based in Massachusetts, and the Free African Society of Philadelphia became important voices in the antislavery movement. Some abolitionists, such as **Elijah P. Lovejoy** and **Charles T. Torrey,** both Protestant ministers, died for the cause. Other abolitionists organized what became known as the **Underground Railroad,** a system of safe houses and guides for leading runaways from slave states in the South to free states in the North. The most famous conductor on the Underground Railroad was **Harriet Tubman,** herself a runaway slave.

1863	1864	1865
►1863. Henry Wadsworth Longfellow publishes *Tales of a Wayside Inn* ►1863. Edward Everett Hale publishes "The Man Without a Country"	►1864. John Greenleaf Whittier publishes *In War Time*	1865. Lewis Carroll publishes *Alice's Adventures in Wonderland* ►1865. Mark Twain publishes "The Celebrated Jumping Frog of Calaveras County" ►1865. Walt Whitman publishes "When Lilacs Last in the Dooryard Bloom'd"
►1863. The Battle of Gettysburg ►1863. West Virginia secedes from Virginia to join Union ►1863. Draft riots in Northern cities ►1863. Lincoln delivers Gettysburg Address	►1864. General Sherman leads march to the sea, leveling a path through Georgia ►1864. Lincoln reelected ►1864. Geneva Conventions signed	►1865. General Lee surrenders at Appamattox Court House ►1865. President Lincoln assassinated by John Wilkes Booth; vice president Andrew Johnson becomes president ►1865. Thirteenth Amendment, prohibiting slavery, ratified

QUOTABLES

"Wherever there is a human being, I see God-given rights inherent in that being, whatever may be the sex or complexion."

—William Lloyd Garrison

CROSS-CURRICULAR ACTIVITIES

Social Studies. Students might research the abolitionist movement. To begin, students should read the selections in the section Abolitionist Voices that appears on pages 410 and 411 in the Selections for Additional Reading. Students might then choose one of the writers or selections presented for further research. Other students might research the Underground Railroad, the New England Anti-Slavery Society, or the Free African Society of Philadelphia. Students can work in small groups and present their findings to the class.

LITERARY CURRENTS

Use the following selections to explore these techniques with your students.

NATURALISM
- "An Occurrence at Owl Creek Bridge," 380
- "A Mystery of Heroism," 391

IRONY
- "A Mystery of Heroism," 391
- "Do not weep, maiden, for war is kind," 402

THEME
- "Swing Low, Sweet Chariot," 370
- "A Mystery of Heroism," 391
- from *Up from Slavery,* 406

POINT OF VIEW
- from *Narrative of the Life of Frederick Douglass,* 364
- from *Up from Slavery,* 406

ESSAY OR EDITORIAL
- "A Letter to Mrs. Bixby," 404

Cross-curricular Activities

• Students can trace the debates about slavery that divided the United States in the years preceding the Civil War. Interested students might research and discuss the impact of the debates surrounding the following acts and decisions: the Fugitive Slave Act, the Missouri Compromise, the Kansas-Nebraska Act, and the Dred Scott decision. Some students may wish to focus their research on a particular person who felt strongly about these issues, such as Henry Clay, Daniel Webster, John Brown, Abraham Lincoln, or Stephen Douglas.

• Students can make a map of the United States that shows which states belonged to the Union and which to the Confederacy. Students can also mark Fort Sumter and other battle sites such as Shiloh, Gettysburg, New Orleans, Antietam, Fredericksburg, Chancellorsville, and Vicksburg.

Quotables

"Slavery is founded on the selfishness of man's nature—opposition to it on his love of justice. These principles are in eternal antagonism; and when brought into collision so fiercely as slavery extension brings them, shocks and throes and convulsions must ceaselessly follow."

—Abraham Lincoln

Robert E. Lee

Ulysses S. Grant

By the 1850s, a great deal of national energy, both political and literary, was focused on the question of slavery. At the center of concern were two issues: fugitive slave laws and the status of slavery in new territories. The **Fugitive Slave Act** of 1850 established that "good citizens" in free states could be deputized to assist federal marshals in the capture of runaway slaves. The act also imposed heavy fines for anyone assisting a runaway, a provision that greatly heightened tensions in the North, where many prominent people were involved directly or indirectly in the abolitionist movement and in the Underground Railroad. One such Northerner, **Henry David Thoreau**, in a speech called "Slavery in Massachusetts," spoke out publicly after a famous local case about the enforcement of the act, asserting that he had "lost his country." In 1852, **Harriet Beecher Stowe's** antislavery novel *Uncle Tom's Cabin* became a bestseller, helping to turn the tide of opinion in the North against slavery.

In the years preceding the Civil War, the country debated the question of whether slavery would be allowed in newly added territories such as California, New Mexico, Utah, Kansas, and Nebraska. The **Missouri Compromise** of 1820 allowed slavery only south of the 36°30′ parallel. A second compromise, put forward by Senator **Henry Clay** of Kentucky in 1850, called for California to be a free state, for new territories to decide on their own whether to be free or slave, and provided protections for slavery as it already existed in the South. This compromise was supported by **Daniel Webster** of Massachusetts, who believed it necessary in order to preserve the Union. In 1854, after much debate, the **Kansas-Nebraska Act** was passed, allowing voters in these new states to decide the issue of slavery for themselves. There followed bitter, bloody fighting in Kansas between proslavery and antislavery forces. Among the latter was a fiery militant named **John Brown.** In 1857, the Supreme Court's **Dred Scott decision** upheld the right of a slave owner to continue to own a slave, even if he moved into free territory. In the presidential election of 1857 and in the debates between senatorial candidates **Stephen Douglas** and **Abraham Lincoln** in 1858, the issue of slavery in new territories and states was paramount. Then, in 1859, John Brown led a raid on the government arsenal at **Harpers Ferry,** Virginia, hoping to capture weapons and to turn those over to slaves, thus beginning a slave revolt throughout the South. Brown was hanged and became a martyr to the antislavery cause, celebrated in "The Battle Hymn of the Republic."

Secession and Civil War

When Abraham Lincoln became president in 1860, seven states—South Carolina, Mississippi, Florida, Alabama, Georgia, Louisiana, and Texas—had already voted to secede from the Union. In 1861, delegates from throughout the South met in Montgomery, Alabama, and formed the **Confederate States of America,** choosing **Jefferson Davis** of Mississippi as their new president. On April 12, 1861, Confederate troops fired on the federal stronghold at **Fort Sumter,** on Charleston Harbor, thus beginning the most troubled period in American history. Lincoln offered to put Virginian **Robert E. Lee** in charge of the Union

Ulysses S. Grant

army, but Lee, who was initially opposed to secession, declined, not wishing to fight against the people of his own state. When Virginia seceded from the Union, Lee took command of the Grand Army of the Confederacy.

Many people on both sides expected the **Civil War** to be over in a month, but it lasted five years. Union troops lost the first major campaign of the war, suffering defeat at the First Battle of Bull Run by troops under **Stonewall Jackson** and **P. G. T. Beauregard.** That defeat moved the Union to action. The Grand Army of the Potomac was organized under **George B. McClellan.** In the fighting that followed at Shiloh, New Orleans, Bull Run, Antietam, Fredericksburg, Chancellorsville, Gettysburg, Vicksburg, and Petersburg, among other places, 360,000 Union soldiers and 329,000 Confederate soldiers lost their lives, many more from disease than from battle. Union forces were at first plagued by poor leadership, but eventually, under the able direction of **Ulysses S. Grant,** the hero of the Battle of Vicksburg, they were able to bring the war to an end, invading the Confederate capital of Richmond, Virginia, in April 1865. General Robert E. Lee surrendered to Grant at **Appomattox Court House** in Virginia on April 9.

The Literature of Abolition and Protest

Well before the war there was a large and substantial body of abolitionist writing, including the work of several of the writers of the New England Renaissance such as Emerson, Thoreau, Whittier, and Lowell. Abolitionist societies, like the New England Anti-Slavery Society, sprang up as networks for support; by 1850 there were about two thousand of these. Publishers such as William Lloyd Garrison and Frederick Douglass made important contributions to the cause, as did novelists such as Harriet Beecher Stowe.

Though some of this literature was written by Northern whites, especially women, who were attempting in part to appeal to the family concerns of their Southern female counterparts, African Americans in the South developed two original forms of literature that played an important role in the abolitionist movement. First was the **spiritual,** which combined

Quotables

"I do not see how a barbarous community and a civilized community can constitute a state. I think we must get rid of slavery or we must get rid of freedom."

—Ralph Waldo Emerson

"Once to every man and nation comes the moment to decide,
In the strife of Truth and Falsehood, for the good or evil side."

—James Russell Lowell

"Our fellow-countrymen in chains!
Slaves—in a land of light and law!
Slaves—crouching on the very plains
Where rolled the storm of Freedom's war!"

—John Greenleaf Whittier

Walt Whitman

African and European music and a poetic text using religious images from the Bible to create dramatic symbols of the suffering of slaves and their hopes for deliverance. Second was the **slave narrative,** an autobiographical account of the life of a former slave, chronicling the extraordinary conditions under which he or she had lived. Ranging in length from a few pages to an entire book, hundreds of slave narratives were published in the decades before the war. These narratives were remarkable for a number of reasons, not least of which was that most of their authors had come from Southern states that by law prohibited teaching blacks to read or write. They deployed various literary strategies designed to gain sympathy without offending their primarily white audiences, many of whom were unschooled in the gorier details and horrors of slavery and not anxious to see evil in their Southern Christian counterparts. For example, Frederick Douglass's narrative, excerpted in this unit, tries repeatedly to put blame on the institution of slavery rather than on individual owners; of one owner's wife Douglass noted, "When I went there, she was a pious, warm, and tender-hearted woman. . . . Slavery soon proved its ability to divest her of these heavenly qualities."

The Literature of the War

Much of the literature during and immediately after the war addressed itself to a concern with restoring a national identity, hoping to find threads of unity amid the horrific bloodletting, and often doing this by appealing to and honoring the courage and heroism of those who had fought. Lincoln, in the speeches excerpted in this unit, Lee, and **Walt Whitman,** in his elegy to Lincoln, honor the efforts of those in the war while insisting in various ways on a national identity and on reconciliation. As Whitman expressed it in one poem, "For my enemy is dead, a man divine as myself is dead."

In the first decades after the war, writings about the war became vehicles for achieving that reconciliation and reshaping the nation's self-image or identity. Much of this writing romanticized the war and the contributions of those who participated in it, glorifying the United States itself in the process; however, there also emerged a contrary voice in the works of **Ambrose Bierce** and **Stephen Crane.** These writers explored the darker aspects of the war, portraying courage and heroism as myths, seeing actions as the result of accident or panic under environmental pressures rather than as reflections of human strength and triumph.

Echoes:

Slavery and the Civil War

"'A house divided against itself cannot stand.' I believe this government cannot endure, permanently half slave and half free."

—Abraham Lincoln, in a speech delivered in 1858

"In thinking of America, I sometimes find myself admiring her bright blue sky—her grand old woods—her fertile fields—her beautiful rivers—her mighty lakes and star-crowned mountains. But my rapture is soon checked when I remember that all is cursed with the infernal spirit of slave-holding and wrong; When I remember that with the waters of her noblest rivers, the tears of my brethren are borne to the ocean, disregarded and forgotten; That her most fertile fields drink daily of the warm blood of my outraged sisters, I am filled with unutterable loathing."

—Frederick Douglass,
former slave, editor of The North Star, *and crusader against slavery*

"I can anticipate no greater calamity for the country than a dissolution of the Union. It would be an accumulation of all the evils we complain of, and I am willing to sacrifice everything but honor for its preservation. . . . Secession is nothing but revolution."

—Robert E. Lee, later leader of the Confederate forces, writing about secession in a letter to his son dated January 1861

"My paramount object in this struggle is to save the Union. . . . If I could save the Union without freeing any slave, I would do it; and if I could save it by freeing all the slaves, I would do it; and if I could save it by freeing some and leaving others alone, I would also do that. . . . I have here stated my purpose according to my views of official duty and I intend no modification of my oft-expressed personal wish that all men everywhere could be free."

—Abraham Lincoln,
in a letter to Horace Greeley, dated August 22, 1862

ADDITIONAL QUESTIONS AND ACTIVITIES

In small groups students can discuss each of the quotes found on page 363. Students should consider the issues of slavery and the dissolution of the Union and keep these ideas in mind as they read the selections in Unit 6.

ADDITIONAL RESOURCES

READER'S GUIDE
- Selection Worksheet, 6.1

ASSESSMENT PORTFOLIO
- Selection Check Test, 4.6.1
- Selection Test, 4.6.2

ESSENTIAL SKILLS PRACTICE BOOKS
- *Writing,* 1.6

ENRICHMENT ACTIVITIES

Suggest that students create maps of the North American continent in 1820, 1840, and 1860 that indicate areas where slavery was legal and where it was illegal. Encourage them to indicate also the numbers of slaves in each state or territory, and to identify patterns regarding where slavery flourished.

SUPPORT FOR LEP STUDENTS

Alert students to the fact that many of the expressions used by Douglass are considered old-fashioned or more elaborate than in contemporary English.

IDIOM

expression of feeling—a tear

ADDITIONAL VOCABULARY

plantation—large farm where crops are raised
overseer—person who watches over and directs the work of others
privilege—special advantage, right, or benefit granted to a person or group
reverberate—echo
consult—refer to
pathetic—causing or able to cause sadness
sentiment—thought or attitude
testimony—evidence, proof
ineffable—not capable of being expressed

PREREADING

from *Narrative of the Life of Frederick Douglass, an American Slave, Written by Himself*

by Frederick Douglass

ABOUT THE AUTHOR

Frederick Douglass (1818–1895) was an eloquent speaker, a tireless campaigner against slavery, and a champion of civil rights for women and for persons of African descent. Born a slave in Maryland, Douglass was taught to read and write in violation of a Maryland state law prohibiting the education of African Americans. After escaping to Massachusetts in 1838, he associated with such prominent abolitionists as William Lloyd Garrison, J. G. Birney, and John Brown, and he became an influential force in the fight to end slavery. In 1845, he published the first of three autobiographies, *Narrative of the Life of Frederick Douglass, an American Slave,* in which he told of his childhood, his youth, and his escape to freedom. After traveling in Britain and Ireland, where he lectured for the abolitionist cause, Douglass returned to America. Friends helped him to buy his freedom, and he moved to Rochester, New York, where he began publishing an abolitionist newspaper, *The North Star,* later called *Frederick Douglass's Weekly* and *Frederick Douglass's Monthly.* In 1855, he published an expanded, updated version of his autobiography, *My Bondage and My Freedom,* which was followed in 1881 by a final autobiographical volume, *The Life and Times of Frederick Douglass.* Unjustly implicated in John Brown's attack on the arsenal at Harpers Ferry, West Virginia, which Brown had hoped would instigate a slave revolt, Douglass fled to Canada and England before the Civil War. During the war, he returned to the United States where he helped to organize regiments of African-American soldiers to fight for the Northern cause, and he personally called on Abraham Lincoln, sixteenth president of the United States, to secure fair compensation for those soldiers. He also worked as a conductor on the Underground Railroad. After the war, Douglass held a number of political offices, including United States marshall and recorder of deeds for the District of Columbia, minister to Haiti, and chargé d'affaires to Santo Domingo. He also continued his political activities, lobbying for legislation to prevent discrimination of all kinds.

ABOUT THE SELECTION

Frederick Douglass had already established himself as an orator of exceptional ability when he determined to commit the heart of his speeches, that is, his experiences under slavery, to writing in ***Narrative of the Life of Frederick Douglass, an American Slave, Written by Himself.*** Knowing that publication of the book would reveal his identity and make him a target for slave-catchers, he went to England until money could be raised to buy his freedom.

GOALS/OBJECTIVES

Studying this lesson will enable students to

- comprehend the significance of song to an oppressed people
- recognize Frederick Douglass's contribution to the antislavery movement
- recognize the tone of a nonfiction selection
- become alert to stereotypes
- identify appositives and appositive phrases, and use them in writing

READER'S JOURNAL

What is your favorite song? What feelings do you usually have when you hear it or sing it? Write in your journal about how music makes you feel and about how your feelings affect your choices of music.

WRITING SKILLS

Read the Language Arts Survey, 1.6, "Choosing a Purpose or Aim." Then identify the mode of Douglass's writing and the reasons it was so well suited for his purpose.

FROM

Narrative of the Life of Frederick Douglass, an American Slave, Written by Himself

FREDERICK DOUGLASS

Colonel Lloyd[1] kept from three to four hundred slaves on his home plantation, and owned a large number more on the neighboring farms belonging to him. The names of the farms nearest to the home plantation were Wye Town and New Design. Wye Town was under the overseership of a man named Noah Willis. New Design was under the overseership of a Mr. Townsend. The overseers of these, and all the rest of the farms, numbering over twenty, received advice and direction from the managers of the home plantation. This was the great business place. It was the seat of government for the whole twenty farms.[2] All disputes among the overseers were settled here. . . .

Here, too, the slaves of all the other farms received their monthly allowance of food, and their yearly clothing. The men and women slaves received, as their monthly allowance of food, eight pounds of pork, or its equivalent in fish, and one bushel of corn meal. Their yearly clothing consisted of two coarse linen shirts, one pair of linen trousers, like the shirts, one jacket, one pair of trousers for winter, made of coarse negro cloth, one pair of stockings, and one pair of shoes; the whole of which could not have cost more

❶ *How many slaves did Colonel Lloyd own?*

❷ *What happened at the "home plantation"?*

1. **Colonel Lloyd.** Owner of the large plantation in Maryland where Douglass was born
2. **twenty farms.** Lloyd family papers indicate only thirteen farms.

PREREADING NOTES

READER'S JOURNAL

Have students respond in writing to the prompt before discussing it in order to avoid letting others' opinions influence answers. However, encourage students to add comments to their journal afterward to incorporate ideas that come to light during the discussion.

WRITING SKILLS

Ask students to consider and evaluate nonprint forms that might be used effectively to tell Douglass's life story.

▶ Additional practice is provided in the *Essential Skills Practice Book:* Writing, 1.6.

ANSWERS TO GUIDED READING QUESTIONS

❶ Colonel Lloyd owned from three to four hundred slaves on his home plantation, and a large number of others on neighboring farms.

❷ The "home plantation" was the "seat of government" of Colonel Lloyd's farms, where all the overseers received advice and direction and all disputes were settled.

VOCABULARY FROM THE SELECTION

diligently
obdurate
rapturous

HISTORICAL NOTE

As the owner of hundreds of slaves, Colonel Lloyd was quite unusual. In 1808, ten years before Douglass's birth, the importation of slaves into the United States was made illegal. By then most northern states had passed laws against slavery, but there were more than 700,000 slaves in the South. Although the total number of slaves rose in following years, the percentage of slaveholders dropped. By 1860, fewer than 5 percent of whites in the South owned slaves and only about half of those owners had more than five.

Answers to Guided Reading Questions

❶ Douglass was separated from his mother while he was an infant. Usually children were raised by old women no longer fit for field labor.

❷ Many slaves from the neighboring farms felt privileged when they were sent on errands at the Great House Farm because the farm was associated with greatness, and being given such an assignment was a sign of the overseer's confidence in the chosen worker. Besides, while a slave was doing the errand, he or she was excused from field labor.

Answers to Selection Check Test 4.6.1

EX. What were the names of the neighboring farms closest to Colonel Lloyd's home plantation?

The farms were Wye Town and New Design.

1. On the Lloyd plantations, what was an adult slave's monthly allotment of food?

Each month, an adult slave was given eight pounds of pork, or its equivalent in fish, and one bushel of corn meal.

2. What job was often given to slave women too old for field work?

Older women were given the job of raising children.

3. What assignment did the slaves on the out-farms consider as a privilege?

The slaves regarded being sent on errands at the Great House Farm to be a great honor.

4. Who made up the songs that the slaves sang on their way to the Great House Farm?

The slaves made up their songs as they went on the errands.

5. According to Douglass, why did slaves sing?

The slaves sang to relieve their sorrow.

❶ *When was Douglass separated from his mother? What happened to children who were separated from their mothers in this way?*

❷ *How did some slaves feel about doing errands at the Great House Farm? Why?*

than seven dollars. The allowance of the slave children was given to their mothers, or the old women having the care of them. My mother and I were separated when I was but an infant—before I knew her as my mother. It is a common custom, in the part of Maryland from which I ran away, to part children from their mothers at a very early age. Frequently, before the child has reached its twelfth month, its mother is taken from it, and hired out on some farm a considerable distance off, and the child is placed under the care of an old woman, too old for field labor. The children unable to work in the field had neither shoes, stockings, jackets, nor trousers, given to them; their clothing consisted of two coarse linen shirts per year. When these failed them, they went naked until the next allowance-day. Children from seven to ten years old, of both sexes, almost naked, might be seen at all seasons of the year.

The home plantation of Colonel Lloyd wore the appearance of a country village. All the mechanical operations for all the farms were performed here. The shoemaking and mending, the blacksmithing, cartwrighting, coopering,[3] weaving, and grain-grinding, were all performed by the slaves on the home plantation. The whole place wore a businesslike aspect very unlike the neighboring farms. The number of houses, too, conspired to give it advantage over the neighboring farms. It was called by the slaves the *Great House Farm*. Few privileges were esteemed higher, by the slaves of the out-farms, than that of being selected to do errands at the Great House Farm. It was associated in their minds with greatness. A representative could not be prouder of his election to a seat in the American Congress, than a slave on one of the out-farms would be of his election to do errands at the Great House Farm. They regarded it as evidence of great confidence reposed in them by their overseers; and it was on this account, as well as a constant desire to be out of the field from under the driver's lash, that they esteemed it a high privilege, one worth careful living for. He was called the smartest and most trusty fellow, who had this honor conferred upon him the most frequently. The competitors for this office sought as diligently to please their overseers, as the office-seekers in the political parties seek to please and deceive the people. The same traits of character might be seen in Colonel Lloyd's slaves, as are seen in the slaves of the political parties.

The slaves selected to go to the Great House Farm, for the monthly allowance for themselves and their fellow slaves, were peculiarly enthusiastic. While on their way, they would make the dense old woods, for miles around, reverberate with their wild songs, revealing at once the highest joy and the deepest sadness. They would compose and sing as they went along, consulting neither time nor tune. The thought that came up, came out—if not in the word, in the sound—and as frequently in the one as in the other. They would sometimes sing the most pathetic sentiment in the most rapturous tone, and the most rapturous sentiment in the most pathetic tone. Into all of their songs they

3. **cartwrighting, coopering.** *Cartwrighting*—building carts; *coopering*—making barrels

Words for Everyday Use: **dil • i • gent • ly** (dil´ə jənt lē) *adv.* painstakingly, industriously; **rap • tur • ous** (rap´ chər əs) *adj.* full of joy or pleasure

Vocabulary in Context

- The cook's helper peeled potatoes diligently for hours before the banquet.
- When the man saw his sister, from whom he had been separated for twenty years, he yelled a rapturous greeting.
- Although the little girl begged and cried to stay up late, her mother was obdurate in declaring it was bedtime.

would manage to weave something of the Great House Farm. Especially would they do this when leaving home. They would then sing most exultingly the following words:

I am going away to the Great House Farm!
O, yea! O, yea! O!

This they would sing, as a chorus, to words which to many would seem unmeaning jargon, but which, nevertheless, were full of meaning to themselves. I have sometimes thought that the mere hearing of those songs would do more to impress some minds with the horrible character of slavery, than the reading of whole volumes of philosophy on the subject could do.

I did not, when a slave, understand the deep meaning of those rude and apparently incoherent songs. I was myself within the circle; so that I neither saw nor heard as those without might see and hear. They told a tale of woe which was then altogether beyond my feeble comprehension; they were tones loud, long, and deep; they breathed the prayer and complaint of souls boiling over with the bitterest anguish. Every tone was a testimony against slavery, and a prayer to God for deliverance from chains. The hearing of those wild notes always depressed my spirit, and filled me with ineffable sadness. I have frequently found myself in tears while hearing them. The mere recurrence to those songs, even now, afflicts me; and while I am writing these lines, an expression of feeling has already found its way down my cheek. To those songs I trace my first glimmering conception of the dehumanizing character of slavery. I can never get rid of that conception. Those songs still follow me, to deepen my hatred of slavery, and quicken my sympathies for my brethren in bonds. If any one wishes to be impressed with the soul-killing effects of slavery, let him go to Colonel Lloyd's plantation, and, on allowance-day, place himself in the deep pine woods; and there let him, in silence, analyze the sounds that shall pass through the chambers of his soul, and if he is not thus impressed, it will only be because "there is no flesh in his obdurate heart."

I have often been utterly astonished, since I came to the north, to find persons who could speak of the singing, among slaves, as evidence of their contentment and happiness. It is impossible to conceive of a greater mistake. Slaves sing most when they are most unhappy. The songs of the slave represent the sorrows of his heart; and he is relieved by them, only as an aching heart is relieved by its tears. At least, such is my experience. I have often sung to drown my sorrow, but seldom to express my happiness. Crying for joy, and singing for joy, were alike uncommon to me while in the jaws of slavery. The singing of a man cast away upon a desolate island might be as appropriately considered as evidence of contentment and happiness, as the singing of a slave; the songs of the one and of the other are prompted by the same emotion. ■

❶ *According to Douglass, what might some songs by slaves tell people about the character of slavery?*

❷ *What astonished Douglass? According to him, when did slaves sing? What did their songs represent?*

WORDS FOR EVERYDAY USE: **ob • dur • ate** (äb´door it) *adj.,* unsympathetic; hardened

ANSWERS TO GUIDED READING QUESTIONS

❶ Slave songs, Douglass says, can tell volumes about "the horrible character" of slavery.

❷ Douglass was astonished to learn that some Northerners thought that the songs of slaves were proof of their happiness. It was his experience that slaves sang most when they were very unhappy. Their songs represented the sorrows of their hearts.

ADDITIONAL QUESTIONS AND ACTIVITIES

What does Douglass mean by the phrase "while in the jaws of slavery"? What comparison is he suggesting? Why is it appropriate?

Answers. The phrase refers to time endured as a slave. It suggests a comparison between the institution of slavery and a strong, flesh-eating animal such as a bear or lion. The comparison is appropriate because slavery ate away at the souls of its victims and destroyed people as surely as a human-eating beast could.

CROSS-CURRICULAR ACTIVITIES

Social Studies. Have students investigate the careers of other free (or freed) African Americans before and during the Civil War, such as Richard Allen, Benjamin Banneker, Paul Cuffe, Samuel Cornish, Jean Baptiste Point du Sable, James Forten, John Russwurm, Peter Salem, and Sojourner Truth.

RESPONDING TO THE SELECTION

Encourage students to identify specific songs that have helped them over rough periods or that suggest to them the sadness of the singer or composer.

ANSWERS FOR REVIEWING THE SELECTION

RECALLING

1. Colonel Lloyd owned approximately four hundred slaves.

2. Children were taken from their mothers at about one year of age and brought up by women who were too old for field labor. Until the children were old enough to work in the fields, they were given no clothes other than two shirts a year, and when those were not usable, they went naked.

3. He compares them with political office-seekers who "seek to please and deceive the people."

4. The songs were made up as the people sang, without concern for rhythm, melody, or words, simply expressing their emotions, especially their sorrows and their desire for freedom.

INTERPRETING

Responses will vary. Possible responses are given.

5. All the overseers from the different farms were brought to a central, home plantation for direction and settlement of differences.

6. Many children didn't even know who their mothers were, and even those who recognized their mothers didn't spend enough time with them to develop close relationships. If slaves didn't know who was related to them, they might be less concerned about other slaves, raise fewer objections to mistreatment of others, and be more easily controlled by the slaveholder.

7. He could logically hold against politicians the laws that enforced slavery and even required the return of escaped slaves who lived in free states.

8. The beatings and other mistreatment were external; the

(cont.)

The Slave Narrative

Narrative of the Life of Frederick Douglass, an American Slave, was perhaps the greatest of a series of autobiographical accounts by escaped slaves that helped to turn the tide of opinion against the institution of slavery. Other important slave narratives include the following:

A Narrative of the Uncommon Sufferings and Surprising Deliverance of Briton Hammon, a Negro Man (1760)

A Narrative of the Lord's Wonderful Dealings with J. Murrant, a Black, Taken Down from His Own Relation (1784)

The Interesting Narrative of Olaudah Equiano, or Gustavus Vassa, the African (1789)

Scenes in the Life of Harriet Tubman (1869)

Responding to the Selection

What did you learn from this selection? Had you ever thought of music in this way before? Do you think this will affect the way you listen to some songs in the future?

Reviewing the Selection

RECALLING

1. Approximately how many slaves did Colonel Lloyd own?
2. What were the lives of slave children like?
3. With what group outside of slavery does Douglass compare the slaves chosen to run errands to the Great House Farm?
4. Describe the "songs" sung by the slaves sent for supplies on allowance-day.

INTERPRETING

5. How did Colonel Lloyd coordinate the management of his many farms?
6. What effect would you expect the separation of children from their mothers to have on family relationships? Why would this effect be desirable to the slaveholder?
7. Why do you suppose Douglass had such a low opinion of many politicians?
8. How could listening to slaves' singing, rather than seeing them being sold, beaten, or otherwise mistreated, teach most clearly the "dehumanizing character" and "soul-killing effects" of slavery?

ANSWERS FOR REVIEWING THE SELECTION (CONT.)

singing came from an internal anguish that could not be ended under slavery.

SYNTHESIZING

Responses will vary. Possible responses are given.

9. Both types of music relieve sorrow by expressing it in song.

10. Southerners wanted to justify their treatment of slaves; if the slaves were so happy that they were always singing, then slavery must be acceptable to them. Northerners didn't want to get involved if they could avoid it, so seeing the slaves as content relieved them of any responsibility for ending slavery. The unfortunate result of such thinking was lack of effort, on the part of the majority, to end slavery.

SYNTHESIZING

9. In what ways is the music we now call the blues similar to the singing Douglass describes?

10. Why do you suppose some people of the time chose to interpret the slaves' singing as a sign of happiness? What was wrong with this interpretation?

Understanding Literature (Questions for Discussion)

1. **Tone. Tone** is the emotional attitude toward the idea or toward the subject implied by a literary work. It may be expressed by word choice, imagery, and other techniques. What is Douglass's attitude toward slavery? toward enslaved people? How does his word choice express his tone? Find specific examples from the text to support your answer.

2. **Thesis.** A **thesis** is a main idea that is supported in a work of nonfictional prose. From what you have read in this excerpt, state a thesis of Douglass's autobiography as a whole.

3. **Stereotype.** A **stereotype** is an uncritically accepted fixed or conventional idea, particularly such an idea held about whole groups of people. What stereotype did Douglass argue against in this excerpt? What was his nonstereotypical interpretation of the situation under discussion? How did his analogy with "a man cast away upon a desolate island" reinforce his interpretation?

Language Lab

Appositives. Read the Language Arts Survey, 2.48, "Adding Appositives and Appositive Phrases." Then revise these sentences, adding to each a word or phrase in apposition to the italicized word(s). Use the information provided in parentheses following each sentence.

1. *Frederick Douglass* worked to free slaves by speaking, writing, and serving as a conductor on the Underground Railroad. (Douglass was a famous autobiographer, speaker, and newspaper publisher.)
2. *Harriet Tubman* chose another route. (Tubman was known as the Moses of her people.)
3. After escaping from a Maryland plantation in 1849, Tubman worked with the *Underground Railroad.* (The Underground Railroad was a series of safe houses between slave states and free states.)
4. Acting as a *conductor,* Tubman was responsible for liberating about three hundred people from slavery. (A conductor was a guide.)
5. After the war, both Tubman and Douglass strongly supported the civil rights struggle and the *women's suffrage movement.* (The women's suffrage movement was an attempt to secure voting rights for women.)

ANSWERS FOR UNDERSTANDING LITERATURE

▶ See the evaluation forms for discussion, active listening, and oral communication, *Assessment Portfolio,* 7.11–7.14.

Responses will vary. Possible responses are given.

1. Tone. Douglass's tone of deep anger and hatred toward slavery is suggested by such phrases as "the horrible character of slavery" and "the soul-killing effects of slavery." When discussing the enslaved people and their songs, his tone is one of sorrow and sympathy, suggested by such phrases as "bitterest anguish," "ineffable sadness," "sorrows of his heart," and "aching heart."

2. Thesis. A central thesis of the autobiography is that slavery is wrong and must be brought to an end.

▶**Teaching Note:** Encourage students to read the the entire *Narrative,* a relatively short book, and report back on additional theses they identify in other passages.

3. Stereotype. Douglass rejects the idea of contented slaves who are satisfied with their lot. He insists that the singing of the slave is not from happiness but from sorrow, a means of hanging on to life when life is unbearable. The analogy with the cast-away stresses the thought that the slave had absolutely nothing else to work with but inner resources.

▶**Teaching Note:** Ask students to cite other stereotypes about slaves that Douglass's life and writings disproved.

ANSWERS FOR LANGUAGE LAB

Responses will vary. Possible responses are given.

1. Frederick Douglass, a famous autobiographer, speaker, and newspaper publisher, worked to free slaves by speaking, writing, and serving as a conductor on the Underground Railroad.

2. Harriet Tubman, an African American known as the Moses of her people, chose another route.

3. After escaping from a Maryland plantation in 1849, Tubman worked with the Underground Railroad, a series of safe houses between slave states and free states.

4. Acting as a conductor, or guide, Tubman was responsible for liberating about three hundred people from slavery.

5. After the war, both Tubman and Douglass strongly supported the civil rights struggle and the women's suffrage movement, an attempt to secure voting rights for women.

ADDITIONAL RESOURCES

READER'S GUIDE
- Selection Worksheet, 6.2

ASSESSMENT PORTFOLIO
- Selection Check Test, 6.4.3
- Selection Test, 6.4.4

ESSENTIAL SKILLS PRACTICE BOOKS
- *Study and Research,* 4.45–4.47

AUDIOCASSETTE
- "Swing Low, Sweet Chariot," Track 12

ENRICHMENT ACTIVITIES

Students can write about or discuss stories and images from the Bible or other religious traditions with which they are familiar and that have meaning to them, as the image of the Jordan River and Elijah's chariot were meaningful to the writer of this spiritual.

Invite students to prepare and sing this or other spirituals of their choice, either as soloists or in choruses.

SUPPORT FOR LEP STUDENTS

Provide students unfamiliar with this song the opportunity to hear it performed, to give them a more complete understanding and better appreciation of the spiritual.

COLLOQUIALISMS

coming for to—coming in order to

ADDITIONAL VOCABULARY

chariot—horse-drawn, two-wheeled vehicle used in ancient times

PREREADING

"Swing Low, Sweet Chariot"

Anonymous African-American Spiritual

ABOUT THE SELECTION

By the middle of the nineteenth century, there were more than four million slaves in the United States. Most came from the west coast of Africa. As explained in Imamu Amiri Baraka's *Blues People,* an excerpt from which appears on page 56, West Africans lived in closely knit communities and often engaged in communal labor accompanied by song. In America, such traditional songs developed into the work songs and calls of laborers on plantations. These work songs typically contained repeated lines or phrases and were sung in unison by the workers or in an answer-response format.

Kept from practicing their traditional religions, many African Americans adopted Christianity. Slave owners actively encouraged the Christianizing of the slaves, some because of concern for their slaves' immortal souls, but many more out of hope that people who look for rewards in the next life might be happier with a terrible lot in this one. Combining elements of traditional African music, work songs, and Christian hymns, African Americans created a new kind of music known as the spiritual, a forerunner of many modern musical styles, including gospel and blues. Spirituals such as **"Swing Low, Sweet Chariot"** had Christian themes. They often retold stories from the Bible or dealt with subjects such as salvation and the afterlife. Their form was that of the traditional folk hymn, with repeated elements of the kind found in work songs. They were often sung by groups, with rhythmical accompaniments like those found in African music. Interestingly, many of the spirituals, such as "Swing Low, Sweet Chariot," were intentionally ambiguous, or allegorical, dealing on one level with deliverance from earthly toil into a pleasant afterlife in heaven and on another level with deliverance from slavery.

GOALS/OBJECTIVES

Studying this lesson will enable students to

- enjoy and appreciate a spiritual
- recognize allusions to Biblical passages in African-American compositions
- identify layers of meaning in an ambiguous piece of literature
- define characteristics of the spiritual, and identify the refrain in a spiritual

READER'S JOURNAL

Do you ever dream of escaping to some pleasant, faraway place? Write about such a place in your journal. Use your imagination to describe your idea of paradise.

TEST-TAKING SKILLS

Read the Language Arts Survey, 4.45–4.47, "Strategies for Taking Essay Tests." Then, as you read the spiritual, think about how you might answer this essay question: What figurative, or nonliteral, interpretation related to slavery can be given to "Swing Low, Sweet Chariot"? Identify possible interpretations of the following elements in the spiritual: the chariot, home, the Jordan River, and the band of angels.

"Swing Low, Sweet Chariot"

ANONYMOUS AFRICAN-AMERICAN SPIRITUAL

Swing low, sweet chariot,
Coming for to carry me home,
Swing low, sweet chariot,
Coming for to carry me home.

I looked over Jordan[1] and what did I see
Coming for to carry me home,
A band of angels coming after me,
Coming for to carry me home.

If you get there before I do,
Coming for to carry me home,
Tell all my friends I'm coming too,
Coming for to carry me home.

Swing low, sweet chariot,
Coming for to carry me home,
Swing low, sweet chariot,
Coming for to carry me home. ■

1. **Jordan.** According to a biblical story, the Israelites in exile had to cross the Jordan River to reach the Promised Land of Canaan.

❶ *Where does the speaker want to go?*

❷ *What does the speaker want his or her friends to know?*

PREREADING NOTES

READER'S JOURNAL

Suggest that students consider each of the senses in responding to this prompt. What will they see, hear, smell, taste, and touch in their "paradise"? Suggest, also, that they list actions they will do, and what others will do with or for them.

TEST-TAKING SKILLS

After reading and discussing the selection, ask students to put their responses to this essay question in writing. Remind them that a superior essay answer includes an introduction and a conclusion, as well as the body of the answer. Take time to discuss several responses, evaluating them for completeness and consistency.

►Additional practice is provided in the *Essential Skills Practice Book: Study and Research,* 4.45–4.47.

ANSWERS TO GUIDED READING QUESTIONS

❶ The speaker wants to go home to the Promised Land.

❷ The speaker wants his or her friends who have already reached the Promised Land to know that he or she is coming, too.

CROSS-CURRICULAR ACTIVITIES

Arts and Humanities. Students can translate the spiritual into a visual medium, presenting their interpretations in either representational or abstract approaches.

ANSWERS TO SELECTION CHECK TEST 4.6.3

EX. What is coming for the speaker?
A "sweet chariot" is coming.

1. Where will the chariot take the speaker?
It will take the speaker home to heaven.

2. Who is coming for the speaker?
A band of angels is coming.

3. Where is the person addressed by the speaker going?
That person is also going to heaven.

4. What message does the speaker entrust to the person addressed?
The person is to tell the speaker's friends in heaven that he or she is coming, too.

5. Why does the speaker give the message to the other person?
The other person might get to heaven first.

RESPONDING TO THE SELECTION

Students might consider why they find certain types of music relaxing. Does the music serve as a distraction from troubles? Do the words affect the students' mood? Does the music? What other things offer this type of escape?

ANSWERS FOR REVIEWING THE SELECTION

RECALLING

1. In the first stanza, a "sweet chariot" is coming for the speaker. In the second stanza, a band of angels is also coming.

2. The singer looks over the Jordan River and sees a band of angels coming.

3. The singer seems to be addressing a fellow-believer, probably a friend, because the other person seems to know who the singer's friends are.

4. The singer feels bound toward heaven, his or her spiritual home.

INTERPRETING

Responses will vary. Possible responses are given.

5. The chariot could be a conductor on the Underground Railroad, coming into the South to help slaves escape to the North, the "Promised Land," or the Underground Railroad itself.

6. The Ohio River separated the slaveholding states of Kentucky and Virginia from the states of Ohio, Indiana, and Illinois, in which abolitionist feeling was strong and there were many stations on the Underground Railroad.

7. The singer might be addressing an accomplice in a plan to escape to the North.

8. The home that a slave would hope for here on Earth would be either a free state of the North or, better yet, Canada, where the Fugitive Slave Law had no effect.

(cont.)

Responding to the Selection

How does this singer feel about being taken away to another place? Why might this song be comforting? Do you have any favorite songs or stories that help you to "escape" temporarily and relax?

Reviewing the Selection

RECALLING

1. What is coming to carry the singer home?
2. Over what river does the singer look? What does the singer see?
3. Who, according to stanza 3, is being addressed by the singer?
4. Toward what does the singer feel that he or she is bound?

INTERPRETING

5. If this song is interpreted as being about escape from slavery, what might the "sweet chariot" be? (Hint: See the introduction to this unit.)
6. If this song deals with slavery, what actual river in the United States might be represented?
7. If this song deals with slavery, whom might the singer be addressing in stanza 3? What plan is shared by the singer and the person being addressed?
8. If this song deals with slavery, what might be the "home" referred to throughout the song?

SYNTHESIZING

9. Why might this song have been comforting to the person singing it? What feelings does the song express?
10. "Swing Low, Sweet Chariot" is written in a kind of code. What intention does it reveal? Under what circumstances did it acquire such a meaning? What reason might a singer have had to express his or her real intention symbolically rather than explicitly?

ANSWERS FOR REVIEWING THE SELECTION (CONT.)

SYNTHESIZING

Responses will vary. Possible responses are given.

9. The comparison the song presents between the Israelites, who eventually reached the Promised Land, and the slaves longing for a better place to live must have offered hope of success. The song expresses trust in God, conviction that the speaker would survive the present bad situation, and a reliance on friends and friendship.

10. The spiritual reveals the speaker's intention to escape from slavery to freedom. This concept of heaven was a natural outgrowth of the conditions under which the singer lived, in which heaven on Earth was any place where a person was free. The singer had to conceal the desire to escape to avoid punishment and tight surveillance by his or her owner.

Understanding Literature (Questions for Discussion)

1. **Theme.** A **theme** is a central idea in a literary work. What is the theme of "Swing Low, Sweet Chariot"?

2. **Allusion.** An **allusion** is a reference in a literary work to another literary work or to some other part of history or culture. In II Kings 2:11, the prophet Elijah is described as being carried into heaven after the appearance of a fiery chariot:

   > And it came to pass, as they still went on, and talked, that, behold, there appeared a chariot of fire, and horses of fire, and parted them both asunder; and Elijah went up by a whirlwind into heaven.

   See footnote 1 on page 391, which describes the Jordan River. Then explain the two biblical allusions in the song and how they are related to escape from slavery.

3. **Spiritual.** A **spiritual** is a type of religious song that originated in the African-American folk tradition. Many spirituals are ambiguous (in other words, they have double meanings). The spiritual "Go Down, Moses," for example, describes the captivity of the Israelites in Egypt, but it can also be read as describing the captivity of the slaves in America:

   > When Israel was in Egypt land
   > Let my people go
   > Oppressed so hard they could not stand
   > Let my people go.

   What is the symbolic interpretation of "Swing Low, Sweet Chariot"?

4. **Refrain.** A **refrain** is a repeated line or group of words in a song or poem. Often spirituals were sung by a lone singer, with a group of people joining in for the refrain. What is the refrain in "Swing Low, Sweet Chariot"? To what does the word "home" in this refrain refer?

Answers for Understanding Literature

► See the evaluation forms for discussion, active listening, and oral communication, *Assessment Portfolio,* 7.11–7.14.

Responses will vary. Possible responses are given.

1. Theme. The theme of the spiritual is the hope and expectation of reaching heaven or freedom.

2. Allusion. In the Bible, the chariot took the prophet Elijah from Earth into heaven; to the slave, it symbolized any force that would take the enslaved person out of slavery in the South and into freedom in the North, such as the Underground Railroad and its conductors. In the Bible, the Jordan River was the boundary that separated the Israelites in exile from their home in the land of Canaan, promised to them by God. To the slave, the Jordan River represented physical boundaries between slave and free territories, such as the Ohio River.

3. Spiritual. The symbolic interpretation of this spiritual is that the speaker has confidence that, with the help of God and friends, he or she will escape from slavery to the Promised Land of freedom.

4. Refrain. The refrain is the line "Coming for to carry me home." The word *home* refers either to heaven, in the surface meaning of the song, or to free territory, in the symbolic interpretation.

Additional Questions and Activities

Students can do further research on the nature of the spiritual and/or its development into gospel music. Reports could be presented on audiotape, with excerpts from illustrative recordings.

ADDITIONAL RESOURCES

READER'S GUIDE
- Selection Worksheet, 6.3

ASSESSMENT PORTFOLIO
- Selection Check Test, 4.6.5
- Selection Test, 4.6.6

ESSENTIAL SKILLS PRACTICE BOOKS
- *Language,* 2.15, 2.57
- *Study and Research,* 4.4

AUDIOCASSETTE
- *"The Gettysburg Address,"* Track 13

ENRICHMENT ACTIVITIES

Lincoln was largely self-taught but seemed to have mastered the art of oral speaking. Discuss with students how they could teach themselves to become effective speakers. Whom would they consult? Whom would they imitate? Where would they go for help in learning the art of both writing and delivering speeches?

Have students find speeches by other famous Americans, for example, John F. Kennedy, Franklin Roosevelt, or Martin Luther King, Jr., and practice reciting parts of them. Have them research the style of the speaker and try to recreate that style.

SUPPORT FOR LEP STUDENTS

Remind students to pause at the commas and dashes in this speech. The frequent pauses will give them a chance to think carefully about the words and will make the meaning of the speech clearer and more accessible.

ADDITIONAL VOCABULARY

dedicate—set apart for a special use

proposition—plan or idea that is not yet accepted

PREREADING

The Gettysburg Address
by Abraham Lincoln

ABOUT THE AUTHOR

Abraham Lincoln (1809–1865), known to history as the Great Emancipator and responsible for preserving the Union during the Civil War, rose from obscurity to a place of reverence in the annals of American history. Born to frontier parents in a backwoods cabin in Kentucky, he nonetheless managed to school himself through voracious reading. In fact, the figure of the young Lincoln reading by candlelight in the evening has become a part of American legend. Lincoln's mother died when he was nine. His father remarried a woman who singled out Abraham for special attention and was later referred to by him as his "angel mother." A strong, lanky youth, Lincoln split rails to fence in the family farm when they moved to Illinois, and then held a succession of jobs as a flatboatman, storekeeper, postmaster, and surveyor. He served as a captain in the Black Hawk War and decided to prepare himself for a career in law. Again, he schooled himself, reading law books and passing the bar exam in 1836. Moving to the Illinois capital of Springfield, he was elected to the state legislature, where he served four terms. His romance with Ann Rutledge was cut short by her death at age nineteen, and he married Mary Todd in 1842. In 1858, Lincoln entered the state senatorial race against Stephen A. Douglas. Lincoln lost that election, but the Lincoln-Douglas Debates showed the losing candidate to be a brilliant speaker, combining learned references with homespun witticisms and steeltrap logic. In 1860, running as the candidate of the newly formed Republican party, Lincoln was elected the sixteenth president of the United States. Perhaps no other president has faced such a crisis on taking office, for immediately he was embroiled in the Civil War, brought about by the succession of Southern states from the Union to form the Confederacy. After many false starts and mistakes, Lincoln finally installed the proper leadership to lead his Union troops to victory. During the war, Lincoln issued the Emancipation Proclamation, freeing slaves in states then in rebellion. After the war he worked for passage of the Thirteenth Amendment, which ended slavery in the United States once and for all. In April 1865, shortly after being reelected for a second term as president, Lincoln was assassinated while watching a play at Ford's Theater in Washington.

GOALS/OBJECTIVES

Studying this lesson will enable students to

- appreciate the sacrifice of the soldiers who fought and died at Gettysburg
- describe the contributions of Abraham Lincoln to American literature and history
- define *parallelism* and recognize its use in a speech
- define *antithesis* and identify examples of it in a speech
- write a news story
- apply skills in memorizing

About the Selection

On November 19, 1863, Lincoln delivered his famous address at the dedication of the national cemetery at Gettysburg. Gettysburg had been the site of one of the bloodiest battles in the Civil War; in July 1863, Union and Confederate troops fought for a grueling three days on the usually peaceful farmlands of Pennsylvania. Many historians feel that this battle signified the turning point of the Civil War. However, at the time that Lincoln gave his speech, the war was still unfinished. In light of the bitterness of the conflict, one of the most remarkable aspects of **The Gettysburg Address** is its avoidance of angry or inflammatory rhetoric that would incite listeners to further hostility against the enemy. Instead, the speech focuses on the sacrifice of the participants in the battle and the need for rededication to the principles of the nation's founders. There was a sharp contrast between this simple three-paragraph speech and the two-hour address by well-known orator Edward Everett that preceded it. In fact, Lincoln's speech was considered unimportant at the time of its delivery.

The Wit and Wisdom of Abraham Lincoln

On a book: "People who like this sort of thing will find this the sort of thing they like."

On being asked to replace a general: "It is best not to swap horses while crossing the river."

On charity toward one's enemies: "Am I not destroying my enemies when I make friends of them?"

On deception: "You can fool all the people some of the time, and some of the people all the time, but you cannot fool all the people all of the time."

On economy in speech: "He can compress the most words into the smallest ideas, of any man I ever met."

On government: "No man is good enough to govern another man without that other's consent."

On justice: "He reminds me of the man who murdered both his parents, and then, when sentence was about to be pronounced, pleaded for mercy on the grounds that he was an orphan."

On personal appearance: "The Lord prefers common-looking people. That is the reason He makes so many of them."

On slavery: "I intend no modification of my oft-expressed personal wish that all men everywhere should be free."

On slavery: "In giving freedom to the slave, we assure freedom to the free,—honorable alike in what we give and what we preserve."

On slavery: "Slavery is founded on the selfishness of man's nature—opposition to it on his love of justice."

On the conduct of the war: "Now, gentlemen, we have got our harpoon into the monster, but we must still take uncommon care, or else by a single flop of his tail he will send us all into eternity."

On the Union: "A house divided against itself cannot stand. I believe this government cannot endure permanently, half slave and half free."

On voting: "The ballot is stronger than the bullet."

To Harriet Beecher Stowe, author of the popular antislavery novel *Uncle Tom's Cabin:* "So you're the little woman who wrote the book that made this great war!"

Answers to Selection Check Test 4.6.5

EX. Why are the people gathered?

They are gathered to dedicate a cemetery at Gettysburg.

1. According to Lincoln, what is the Civil War testing?

The Civil War is testing whether a nation "conceived in Liberty and dedicated to the proposition that all men are created equal" can survive.

2. Why did the soldiers give their lives, according to Lincoln?

They gave their lives so that the nation might live.

3. What task do the living have?

The living must be dedicated to the unfinished work the dead advanced.

4. What does Lincoln urge his audience to resolve?

He urges them to resolve that the dead shall not have died in vain.

5. What does Lincoln hope will happen to the nation?

He hopes that the nation will have a new birth of freedom and will not die.

Biographical Note

According to popular tradition, Lincoln wrote the Gettysburg Address on the back of an envelope while riding on a train on the way to the cemetery, although this story has never been proved.

Cross-curricular Activities

Social Studies. Have interested students research the reasons why Gettysburg was chosen as the site for the national cemetery. This research may lead to additional research on the Battle of Gettysburg itself.

PREREADING NOTES

READER'S JOURNAL

To make the assignment more concrete, have students discuss reasons why a specific group might become discouraged. By analyzing the problems the group is facing, a speaker may be better able to encourage group members in a realistic way. Then, discuss whether a logical approach or an emotional approach would be more effective or if the approach would depend on the characteristics of the group or the severity of problems that must be faced.

LANGUAGE SKILLS

Give students several examples of transitive and intransitive verbs in everyday speech before assigning this task.

▶Additional practice is provided in the *Essential Skills Practice Book: Language,* 2.15.

ANSWERS TO GUIDED READING QUESTIONS

❶ The Civil War is being fought. The participants in the war are testing whether the nation, conceived in liberty and dedicated to the proposition that all men are equal, can endure.

❷ To honor the dead, people can devote themselves more intensely to preserving the Union and supporting the war effort.

VOCABULARY FROM THE SELECTION

consecrate score

LITERARY TECHNIQUE

Repetition is the use again, of a sound, word, phrase, sentence, or other element. Have students analyze the first sentence in the third paragraph. What is repeated? What is the effect of the repetition?

READER'S JOURNAL

Imagine you are a leader responsible for encouraging a discouraged group. Perhaps you are the coach of a football team that is losing at halftime, or the head of an environmental organization that has just learned about a major oil spill on a nearby beach. How would you inspire your subordinates? What arguments might induce your listeners to continue their struggle? In your journal, write the words and methods you might use to inspire your listeners.

LANGUAGE SKILLS

Read the Language Arts Survey, 2.15, "Transitive and Intransitive Verbs." Find five transitive and five intransitive verbs in The Gettysburg Address. For each transitive verb, identify the direct object.

The Gettysburg Address

ABRAHAM LINCOLN

What event is taking place at the time this speech is delivered? What is being tested by this event? ❶

What should people do to honor the dead? ❷

Four score and seven years ago our fathers brought forth on this continent, a new nation, conceived in Liberty, and dedicated to the proposition that all men are created equal.

Now we are engaged in a great civil war, testing whether that nation, or any nation so conceived and so dedicated, can long endure. We are met on a great battlefield of that war. We have come to dedicate a portion of that field, as a final resting place for those who here gave their lives that that nation might live. It is altogether fitting and proper that we should do this.

But, in a larger sense, we can not dedicate—we can not consecrate—we can not hallow—this ground. The brave men, living and dead, who struggled here, have consecrated it, far above our poor power to add or detract. The world will little note, nor long remember what we say here, but it can never forget what they did here. It is for us the living, rather, to be dedicated here to the unfinished work which they who fought here have thus far so nobly advanced. It is rather for us to be here dedicated to the great task remaining before us—that from these honored dead we take increased devotion to that cause for which they gave the last full measure of devotion—that we here highly resolve that these dead shall not have died in vain—that this nation, under God, shall have a new birth of freedom—and that government of the people, by the people, for the people, shall not perish from the earth. ■

WORDS FOR EVERYDAY USE:
score (skôr) *n.,* set of twenty
con • se • crate (kan´si krāt´) *vt.,* make or declare sacred

VOCABULARY IN CONTEXT

- "We don't need one hundred eggs!" Corky exclaimed when she heard Lou order five score.
- The bishop will consecrate the church before its first service.

Responding to the Selection

Audience members were probably expecting a long speech from the president. How might they have reacted to this short address? How would you have responded to this speech? Do you think it should have been longer? Why, or why not?

Reviewing the Selection

RECALLING

1. Lincoln refers to an event "four score and seven years ago." To what date and event is he referring?
2. Lincoln uses the word "dedicate" six times in the course of this brief speech. Look up the word and decide which of its meanings were intended by Lincoln.
3. Why does Lincoln say that, in a larger sense, he cannot consecrate the cemetery? Who has consecrated it better than he can?
4. To what cause does Lincoln ask that his listeners dedicate themselves?

INTERPRETING

5. Why does Lincoln begin by referring to the principles of the founders of the United States? What emotions does he hope to evoke in his listeners?
6. Keeping in mind that the Emancipation Proclamation was issued in January 1863, why do you think Lincoln emphasized that the nation was "dedicated to the proposition that all men are created equal"?
7. What does Lincoln mean by the phrase, "the last full measure of devotion"? How did the soldiers show this devotion? To what were they devoted?
8. Under what circumstances would the dead be considered to have died in vain? What can the listeners do to ensure that the deaths were not futile?

RESPONDING TO THE SELECTION

Try to impress upon students the gravity and importance of this event. Have them try to imagine themselves as members of the audience who had lost a loved one recently and were hoping to gain some consolation or strength from the ceremony. Would the speech have fulfilled those needs?

ANSWERS FOR REVIEWING THE SELECTION

RECALLING

1. Lincoln is referring to the signing of the Declaration of Independence on July 4, 1776, eighty-seven years before the dedication ceremony.

2. Among meanings used are the following: to consecrate, to set aside for a particular purpose, to commit to a course of action, and to open for public use in a ceremony.

3. The ground has already been consecrated by the soldiers who fought at the site who made the ground holy by their bravery and dedication to principles.

4. He asks that they dedicate themselves to preserving the United States.

INTERPRETING

Responses will vary. Possible responses are given.

5. Lincoln wants to remind his listeners of the principles for which the soldiers fought and died. He may want to evoke pride in their history and a desire to maintain the founders' principles.

6. Lincoln may want to build support for the Emancipation Proclamation and to remind his listeners that equality is promised to all people, without regard to race.

7. The "last full measure of devotion" refers to the willingness to give everything, even one's life, for a cause. The soldiers gave their lives to preserve the United States and its principles.

8. The dead would have died in vain if the cause were ultimately lost and the nation fell apart. Lincoln urges listeners to support efforts to preserve the nation.

(cont.)

ANSWERS FOR REVIEWING THE SELECTION (CONT.)

SYNTHESIZING

Responses will vary. Possible responses are given.

9. The speech is significant because it quotes words that are central to the national philosophy from the Declaration of Independence and the Constitution. It is simple and easy to understand and its words and phrases are almost poetic. Because it is short and logical, it is easy to memorize.

10. With the families and friends of the fallen soldiers in attendance, it would have been inappropriate to make a long speech about the war effort in which the dead can no longer participate. Maybe Lincoln wanted to speak to these people as friends, so he chose simple words that would reach their hearts.

ANSWERS FOR UNDERSTANDING LITERATURE

Responses will vary. Possible responses are given.

► See the evaluation forms for discussion, active listening, and oral communication, *Assessment Portfolio,* 7.11–7.14.

Responses will vary. Possible responses are given.

1. Parallelism. A possible paraphrasing would be that the dead may inspire us to continue the struggle for which they gave their lives; that we solemnly decide to work for the preservation of the Union so that their lives were not wasted; that the United States will be born again in freedom, that the democratic government will not disappear.

Parts of speech: *people*—noun; *of, by, for*—prepositions; *the*—article; all the phrases are prepositional phrases.

The phrase "of the people" describes all governments. The phrase "by the people" describes only democratic governments. The phrase "for the people" describes all governments that have the people's welfare at heart.

2. Antithesis. Examples of antithesis are the following: "as a final resting place for those who here gave their lives that that nation might live," "The world will little note, nor long remember what we say here, but it can never forget what they did here," "that from these honored dead we take increased devotion to that cause for which they gave the last full measure of devotion," "that we here highly resolve that these dead shall not have died in vain—that this nation, under God, shall have a new birth of freedom." The use of antithesis gives unity and organization to the speech. It allows the speaker to say a lot in a few words and still be clear.

3. Syntax. Make sure that the new sentence preserves the meaning of Lincoln's original sentence.

SYNTHESIZING

9. Lincoln said, "The world will little note, nor long remember what we say here." However, this speech has been repeated for over one hundred years, and has even been memorized by admirers and students during that time. Why do you think this speech has touched Americans so deeply since 1863? What qualities make it memorable?

10. Why is this simple speech so appropriate to the dedication of a cemetery in which thousands of people have been buried? Why do you think Lincoln chose to speak simply and avoided long sentences and fancy phrases at this time?

Understanding Literature (Questions for Discussion)

1. **Parallelism. Parallelism** is a rhetorical technique in which a writer emphasizes the equal value or weight of two or more ideas by expressing them in the same grammatical form. Lincoln uses parallelism extensively in the final sentence of this selection. Notice, for example, that the sentence contains a number of clauses beginning with the word *that.* (A **clause** is a group of words containing a subject and a verb.) Paraphrase each of these clauses. Then examine the series of phrases *of the people, by the people, for the people* near the end of the speech. Identify the parts of speech used in this series of phrases. (Refer to the Language Arts Survey, 2.3, "Common and Proper Nouns"; 2.24, "Prepositions"; and 2.47, "Adding Prepositional Phrases.") Then explain the difference in meaning of each phrase. Which phrase describes all governments? Which describes all governments that have the people's welfare at heart? Which describes only democratic governments?

2. **Antithesis. Antithesis** is a rhetorical technique in which words, phrases, or ideas are strongly contrasted, often by means of a repetition of grammatical structure. Find an example of the use of antithesis in The Gettysburg Address. What is the effect of this use of antithesis? How does it strengthen the speech?

3. **Syntax. Syntax** is the pattern of arrangement of words in a statement. Many people enjoy the unusual syntax that Lincoln uses in The Gettysburg Address. Choose one of the ten sentences in this speech and reword it in a more normal, everyday kind of language, paying special attention to changing the order of the words whenever possible. Then decide which sentence you like better—Lincoln's or your own. Explain your choice.

Responding in Writing

News Story. Imagine that you were a member of the audience at the dedication of the national cemetery at Gettysburg. How might you have reported the proceedings? Write a short news article in which you describe the scene and review Lincoln's speech.

ANALYTIC SCALES FOR RESPONDING IN WRITING

Assign a score from 1 to 25 for each grading criterion below. (For more detailed evaluation, see the evaluation forms for writing, revising, and proofreading, *Assessment Portfolio,* 7.1–7.10.)

News Story

- **Content/Unity.** The news story presents a factual reporting of events, including audience reaction, and summarizes the content of the speech.
- **Organization/Coherence.** The news story presents the most essential information first and then presents the less important details.
- **Language/Style.** The news story uses vivid and precise nouns, verbs, and modifiers.
- **Conventions.** The news story avoids errors in spelling, grammar, usage, mechanics, and manuscript form.

Language Lab

Achieving Parallelism. Read the Language Arts Survey, 2.57, "Achieving Parallelism." Then rewrite each of the following sentences below to achieve parallelism.

1. Our ancestors brought forth a new nation conceived in liberty and it was also being dedicated to the principle of equality for all people.
2. It is fitting and proper to dedicate the cemetery and setting aside a portion of the cemetery to the fallen soldiers.
3. The brave men who were fighting and died here consecrated the ground better than we can.
4. The world does not note nor will it remember what we say here.
5. We must resolve that these dead shall not have died in vain and to dedicate ourselves to the preservation of the nation.

Thinking Skills

Memorizing. Read the Language Arts Survey, 4.4, "Memorizing." Then choose and practice a method for memorizing items in a series, such as the last ten presidents of the United States or the names of important battles in the Civil War. Be ready to display your memorization skills and explain which method of memorization you used.

PROJECTS

1. **Report on the Battle of Gettysburg.** The Battle of Gettysburg is a rich topic for study and analysis. Research the events and strategies of the battle and write a report that describes some of its major skirmishes, efforts, and errors.
2. **Choral Reading.** Work with a group to research speeches, sayings, and jokes attributed to Abraham Lincoln. Practice reading these works aloud, and then present them to an audience. Works may be read by individuals or by groups of two or three taking turns or speaking in unison.

ANSWERS FOR LANGUAGE LAB

Responses will vary. Possible responses are given.

1. Our ancestors brought forth a new nation conceived in liberty and dedicated to the principle of equality for all people.
2. It is fitting and proper to dedicate the cemetery and to set aside a portion of the cemetery to the fallen soldiers.
3. The brave men who fought and died here consecrated the ground better than we can.
4. The world will neither note nor remember what we say here.
5. We must resolve that these dead shall not have died in vain and must dedicate ourselves to the preservation of the nation.

For More Practice

Problem. We are testing whether any nation so conceived and has been so dedicated can long endure.

Answer. We are testing whether any nation so conceived and so dedicated can long endure.

►Additional practice is provided in the *Essential Skills Practice Book: Language,* 2.00.

ANSWERS FOR THINKING SKILLS

Responses will vary. Possible responses are given.

Students may choose any of the mnemonics methods or may devise a method of their own. The method of loci may be most appropriate for remembering a series of items.

For More Practice

Problem. Choose a method for remembering the first ten elements in the periodic table.

Answer. An appropriate method for remembering the names of elements might be an embellished letter or a sentence made up of words whose initial letters correspond to the initial letters of the names of the elements.

►Additional practice is provided in the *Essential Skills Practice Book: Study and Research,* 4.4.

PROJECT NOTES

►See the worksheets and evaluation forms for projects, *Assessment Portfolio,* 7.20–7.23.

1. Report on the Battle of Gettysburg. It is easy to become overwhelmed by the amount of information available about the Battle of Gettysburg. Suggest that students begin their research with an encyclopedia and supplement that information with a few interesting books.

2. Choral Reading. Some students may enjoy trying to imitate Lincoln's characteristic way of speaking, for example, his high-pitched voice and his homespun, ready sense of humor. Suggest that students include a variety of selections, both serious and humorous.

ADDITIONAL RESOURCES

READER'S GUIDE
- Selection Worksheet, 6.4

ASSESSMENT PORTFOLIO
- Selection Check Test, 4.6.7
- Selection Test, 4.6.8

ESSENTIAL SKILLS PRACTICE BOOKS
- *Writing,* 1.18
- *Language,* 2.14
- *Study and Research,* 4.5

ENRICHMENT ACTIVITIES

Have students locate a copy of *The Devil's Dictionary* and ask them to select their ten favorite definitions. Set aside time for the students to read their selections aloud to the class.

SUPPORT FOR LEP STUDENTS

Explain that students will encounter many unfamiliar words in this selection. Encourage them to jot down the unfamiliar words in a journal and look them up later. In the meantime, have them use context clues to help them figure out the meanings of the new words without interrupting the flow of the story. Refer to the Language Arts Survey, 2.137 and 2.138, "Using Context Clues I" and "Using Context Clues II."

COLLOQUIALISMS

get the better of—outwit or fool

ADDITIONAL VOCABULARY

dignitary—person of importance
deference—respect
apprehension—fear or dread
evade—avoid through cleverness
evolve—develop gradually
agony—intense pain
chafe—become irritated or annoyed
inaccessible—not reachable
apprise—inform
preternaturally—beyond usual natural bounds; exceptionally

PREREADING

"An Occurrence at Owl Creek Bridge"

by Ambrose Bierce

ABOUT THE AUTHOR

Ambrose Bierce (1842–*circa* 1914), known as "Bitter Bierce," was a cynical, unhappy man with a sharp, satirical wit. Born in Ohio, he grew up in a large, poor family. An unhappy childhood followed by exposure to unimaginable brutality during the Civil War combined to create in Bierce the pessimism that became the dominant trait of his character and his fiction. After spending a year at a military academy, Bierce joined the Union army, rising to the rank of lieutenant. He was a distinguished soldier and participated in a number of major battles. His war experiences provided material for some of his best stories, including "An Occurrence at Owl Creek Bridge" and "Chickamauga." After the war he moved to San Francisco and worked as a journalist, establishing himself through witty, satirical columns as a major literary figure in that rough-and-tumble frontier city. There Bierce counted among his friends such major writers as Mark Twain and Bret Harte. In 1872 he married, moving with his wife to England, where he continued his journalistic work. The relationship with Mrs. Bierce was not a happy one. In *The Cynic's Word Book* (1906), later retitled as *The Devil's Dictionary,* Bierce defined love as "a temporary insanity, curable by marriage." Returning to San Francisco, Bierce worked for many years for *The San Francisco Examiner,* published by William Randolph Hearst. Disaster plagued him: his marriage ended in divorce, one son was killed in a fight, and another son died of alcoholism. In 1913, Bierce traveled to Mexico, which was then in the throes of a civil war. There he disappeared without a trace. His greatest legacy, besides his humorous, if grotesque, *The Devil's Dictionary,* was a handful of stories acclaimed today for their suspensefulness and their psychological realism.

ABOUT THE SELECTION

Bierce, a Civil War veteran who had served with distinction, uses details about military customs and regulations to lend authenticity to this strange tale. In its use of authentic, precisely observed details, the story is a fine early example of American Realism. The story is also an early example of Naturalism, a type of writing that reveals the forces beyond people's control that determine not only their circumstances and fate but also their characters, personalities, and subjective experiences. Unlike traditional straightforward narratives that present plot events chronologically, this story relies on flashbacks and journeys into the mind of the main character. Bierce's stories paved the way for much modern fiction with portrayals of the private psychological states of characters. Although Bierce is often remembered for his bitter and caustic wit, in "**An Occurrence at Owl Creek Bridge**" he concentrates on telling a good story with enough twists and turns to keep the reader guessing until the last sentence.

GOALS/OBJECTIVES

Studying this lesson will enable students to
- enjoy a suspenseful, psychological story
- recognize elements of Naturalism and American Realism
- describe Ambrose Bierce's contributions to American literature
- define *flashback* and explain its function in a short story
- define *psychological fiction* and identify its elements in a short story
- write clear directions and a descriptive paragraph
- identify auxiliary verbs in sentences
- recall and describe a vivid sensory experience

READER'S JOURNAL

If you had only one day left to live, where would you go? What would you do? With whom would you spend your time? Freewrite about your choices in your journal.

WRITING SKILLS

Read the Language Arts Survey, 1.18, "Sensory Detail Charts." Create a blank chart before you begin to read the story and, as you read, fill in each section with details from the story. See whether every sense is represented in the work.

"An Occurrence at Owl Creek Bridge"

AMBROSE BIERCE

I

A man stood upon a railroad bridge in northern Alabama, looking down into the swift water twenty feet below. The man's hands were behind his back, the wrists bound with a cord. A rope closely encircled his neck. It was attached to a stout cross timber above his head and the slack fell to the level of his knees. Some loose boards laid upon the sleepers[1] supporting the metals of the railway supplied a footing for him and his executioners—two private soldiers of the Federal army, directed by a sergeant who in civil life may have been a deputy sheriff. At a short remove upon the same temporary platform was an officer in the uniform of his rank, armed. He was a captain. A sentinel at each end of the bridge stood with his rifle in the position known as "support," that is to say, vertical in front of the left shoulder, the hammer resting on the forearm thrown straight across the chest—a formal and unnatural position, enforcing an erect carriage of the body. It did not appear to be the duty of these two men to know what was occurring at the center of the bridge; they merely blockaded the two ends of the foot planking that traversed it.

Beyond one of the sentinels nobody was in sight; the railroad ran straight away into a forest for a hundred yards, then, curving, was lost to view. Doubtless there was

1. **sleepers.** Ties that support railroad tracks

❶ *What is about to happen to the man?*

WORDS FOR EVERYDAY USE: **sen • ti • nel** (sen´ti nəl) *n.,* person acting as a guard

PREREADING NOTES

READER'S JOURNAL

Suggest that some individuals might choose to spend their time doing things they have never done before while others might choose to spend the time with the people who mean the most to them. Ask for other suggestions from the class before allowing them to write their own ideas.

WRITING SKILLS

Students may compare their charts in small groups and then share the details that each group decides are most vivid and realistic with the whole class.

▶ Additional practice is provided in the *Essential Skills Practice Book: Writing,* 1.18

ANSWER TO GUIDED READING QUESTION

❶ The man is about to be hanged.

VOCABULARY FROM THE SELECTION

acclivity	ludicrous
aspirated	malign
efface	oscillation
embrasure	sentinel
gesticulate	

VOCABULARY IN CONTEXT

- The sentinel chose a spot on a high cliff where he could see the surrounding countryside.

Answers to Guided Reading Questions

❶ Death is a dignitary, or a person of importance. Death should be received with respect.

❷ The man has a straight nose; firm mouth; broad forehead; long, dark hair; a mustache and beard; and large, dark gray eyes. His clothes fit him well and mark him as a civilian and a planter. The kind expression in his eyes is surprising to find in a person who is about to be hanged.

Additional Questions and Activities

Have the students recreate the scene on the bridge as it is described on pages 381 and 382. Some students may enjoy drawing or painting a picture of the tableau.

Literary Technique

Realism is the attempt to render in art an accurate portrayal of reality. Have students identify the elements of realism in this story. Remind them to analyze both the plot and the style of writing.

an outpost farther along. The other bank of the stream was open ground—a gentle acclivity topped with a stockade of vertical tree trunks, loopholed for rifles with a single embrasure through which protruded the muzzle of a brass cannon commanding the bridge. Midway of the slope between bridge and fort were the spectators—a single company of infantry in line, at "parade rest," the butts of the rifles on the ground, the barrels inclining slightly backward against the right shoulder, the hands crossed upon the stock. A lieutenant stood at the right of the line, the point of his sword upon the ground, his left hand resting upon his right. Excepting the group of four at the center of the bridge, not a man moved. The company faced the bridge, staring stonily, motionless. The sentinels, facing the banks of the stream, might have been statues to adorn the bridge. The captain stood with folded arms, silent, observing the work of his subordinates, but making no sign. Death is a dignitary who when he comes announced is to be received with formal manifestations of respect, even by those most familiar with him. In the code of military etiquette silence and fixity are forms of deference.

What is Death? How should Death be received? ❶

The man who was engaged in being hanged was apparently about thirty-five years of age. He was a civilian, if one might judge from his habit, which was that of a planter. His features were good—a straight nose, firm mouth, broad forehead, from which his long, dark hair was combed straight back, falling behind his ears to the collar of his well-fitting frock coat. He wore a mustache and pointed beard, but no whiskers; his eyes were large and dark gray, and had a kindly expression which one would hardly have expected in one whose neck was in the hemp.[2] Evidently this was no vulgar assassin. The liberal military code makes provision for hanging many kinds of persons, and gentlemen are not excluded.

What does the man who is about to be hanged look like? What do his clothes reveal about him? What aspect of his appearance is surprising? ❷

The preparations being complete, the two private soldiers stepped aside and each drew away the plank upon which he had been standing. The sergeant turned to the captain, saluted and placed himself immediately behind that officer, who in turn moved apart one pace. These movements left the condemned man and the sergeant standing on the two ends of the same plank, which spanned three of the crossties of the bridge. The end upon which the civilian stood almost, but not quite, reached a fourth. This plank had been held in place by the weight of the captain; it was now held by that of the sergeant. At a signal from the former the latter would step aside, the plank would tilt and the condemned man go down between two ties. The arrangement commended itself to his judgment as simple and effective. His face had not been covered nor his eyes bandaged. He looked a moment at his "unsteadfast footing," then let his gaze wander to the swirling water of the stream racing madly beneath his feet. A piece of dancing driftwood caught his attention and his eyes followed it down the current. How slowly it appeared to move! What a sluggish stream!

He closed his eyes in order to fix his last thoughts upon his wife and children. The

2. **hemp.** Rope made of hemp

Words for Everyday Use:

ac • cliv • i • ty (ə kliv´ə tē) *n.,* upward slope

em • bra • sure (em brā´zhər) *n.,* slanted opening in a wall that increases the firing angle of a gun

Vocabulary in Context

- The house plans accommodated for the slight acclivity on the homesite.
- Firing though the embrasure, the soldiers were protected from enemy fire.

water, touched to gold by the early sun, the brooding mists under the banks at some distance down the stream, the fort, the soldiers, the piece of drift—all had distracted him. And now he became conscious of a new disturbance. Striking through the thought of his dear ones was a sound which he could neither ignore nor understand, a sharp, distinct, metallic percussion like the stroke of a blacksmith's hammer upon the anvil; it had the same ringing quality. He wondered what it was, and whether immeasurably distant or near by—it seemed both. Its recurrence was regular, but as slow as the tolling of a death knell. He awaited each stroke with impatience and—he knew not why—apprehension. The intervals of silence grew progressively longer; the delays became maddening. With their greater infrequency the sounds increased in strength and sharpness. They hurt his ear like the thrust of a knife; he feared he would shriek. What he heard was the ticking of his watch.

He unclosed his eyes and saw again the water below him. "If I could free my hands," he thought, "I might throw off the noose and spring into the stream. By diving I could evade the bullets and, swimming vigorously, reach the bank, take to the woods and get away home. My home, thank God, is as yet outside their lines; my wife and little ones are still beyond the invader's farthest advance."

As these thoughts, which have here to be set down in words, were flashed into the doomed man's brain rather than evolved from it the captain nodded to the sergeant. The sergeant stepped aside.

II

Peyton Farquhar was a well-to-do planter, of an old and highly respected Alabama family. Being a slave owner and like other slave owners a politician he was naturally an original secessionist and ardently devoted to the Southern cause. Circumstances of an imperious nature, which it is unnecessary to relate here, had prevented him from taking service with the gallant army that had fought the disastrous campaigns ending with the fall of Corinth, and he chafed under the inglorious restraint, longing for the release of his energies, the larger life of the soldier, the opportunity for distinction. That opportunity, he felt, would come, as it comes to all in war time. Meanwhile he did what he could. No service was too humble for him to perform in aid of the South, no adventure too perilous for him to undertake if consistent with the character of a civilian who was at heart a soldier, and who in good faith and without too much qualification assented to at least a part of the frankly villainous dictum that all is fair in love and war.

One evening while Farquhar and his wife were sitting on a rustic bench near the entrance to his grounds, a gray-clad soldier rode up to the gate and asked for a drink of water. Mrs. Farquhar was only too happy to serve him with her own white hands. While she was fetching the water her husband approached the dusty horseman and inquired eagerly for news from the front.

"The Yanks are repairing the railroads," said the man, "and are getting ready for another advance. They have reached the Owl Creek bridge, put it in order and built a stockade on the north bank. The commandant has issued an order, which is posted everywhere, declaring that any civilian caught interfering with the railroad, its bridges, tunnels or trains will be summarily hanged. I saw the order."

"How far is it to the Owl Creek bridge?" Farquhar asked.

❶ *What was the man unable to do? What did he long to do?*

❷ *What sound did the man seem to hear? What effect did the sound have on him? What was he actually hearing?*

Answers to Guided Reading Questions

❶ The man was unable to join the army. He longed to be a soldier who could prove his courage and could serve with distinction.

❷ The sound, which is like a death knell, reminds him of a blacksmith's hammer striking the anvil. The sound makes him impatient and nervous. He is really hearing his watch tick.

Literary Technique

Foreshadowing is the act of presenting materials that hint at events to occur much later in the story. How do Farquhar's escape plans foreshadow later story events?

Cross-curricular Activities

Social Studies. Have students research the appearance and functioning of an antebellum plantation in the South. They might draw a diagram of the various buildings in the typical plantation and may outline the assignment of the tasks that made a plantation run.

Answers to Guided Reading Questions

❶ Farquhar is planning a way to destroy the bridge.

❷ The soldier in gray is really a Federal scout. He has set a trap for Farquhar; if Farquhar tries to destroy the bridge, the Union soldiers will be ready for him.

❸ Farquhar does not wish to be shot.

Additional Questions and Activities

Does the reader know the exact sequence of events that have led Farquhar to his present dangerous situation? Is it necessary to know exactly what happened? Why do you think the author omitted that information?

Answer. The reader does not know exactly what action Farquhar took to put himself in this situation. The author gives only hints to suggest that Farquhar tried to destroy the bridge. The author may have omitted the information because he felt that the consequences of his action are more important than the details describing the action.

"About thirty miles."

"Is there no force on this side the creek?"

"Only a picket post[3] half a mile out, on the railroad, and a single sentinel at this end of the bridge."

❶ *What does Farquhar have in mind?*

"Suppose a man—a civilian and student of hanging—should elude the picket post and perhaps get the better of the sentinel," said Farquhar, smiling, "what could he accomplish?"

The soldier reflected. "I was there a month ago," he replied. "I observed that the flood of last winter had lodged a great quantity of driftwood against the wooden pier at this end of the bridge. It is now dry and would burn like tow."[4]

The lady had now brought the water, which the soldier drank. He thanked her ceremoniously, bowed to her husband and rode away. An hour later, after nightfall, he repassed the plantation, going northward in the direction from which he had come. He was a Federal scout.

❷ *Who is the soldier in the gray uniform? What is the importance of the revelation of his identity?*

III

As Peyton Farquhar fell straight downward through the bridge he lost consciousness and was as one already dead. From this state he was awakened—ages later, it seemed to him—by the pain of a sharp pressure upon his throat, followed by a sense of suffocation. Keen, poignant agonies seemed to shoot from his neck downward through every fiber of his body and limbs. These pains appeared to flash along well defined lines of ramification and to beat with an inconceivably rapid periodicity. They seemed like streams of pulsating fire heating him to an intolerable temperature. As to his head, he was conscious of nothing but a feeling of fullness—of congestion. These sensations were unaccompanied by thought. The intellectual part of his nature was already effaced; he had power only to feel, and feeling was torment. He was conscious of motion. Encompassed in a luminous cloud, of which he was now merely the fiery heart, without material substance, he swung through unthinkable arcs of oscillation, like a vast pendulum. Then all at once, with terrible suddenness, the light about him shot upward with the noise of a loud splash; a frightful roaring was in his ears, and all was cold and dark. The power of thought was restored; he knew that the rope had broken and he had fallen into the stream. There was no additional strangulation; the noose about his neck was already suffocating him and kept the water from his lungs. To die of hanging at the bottom of a river!—the idea seemed to him ludicrous. He opened his eyes in the darkness and saw above him a gleam of light, but how distant, how inaccessible! He was still sinking, for the light became fainter and fainter until it was a mere glimmer. Then it began to grow and brighten, and he knew that he was rising toward the surface—knew it with reluctance, for he was now very comfortable. "To be hanged and drowned," he thought, "that is not so bad; but I do not wish to be shot. No; I will not be shot; that is not fair."

❸ *What thought does Farquhar have as he rises to the surface of the water?*

3. **picket post.** Troops that protect an army from a surprise attack
4. **tow.** Flammable fibers of hemp or flax

Words for Everyday Use:
ef • face (ə fās´) *vt.,* erase, wipe out
os • cil • la • tion (äs´ə lā´shən) *n.,* act of swinging back and forth
lu • di • crous (lōō´di krəs) *adj.,* absurd, ridiculous

Vocabulary in Context

- The inscription on the old tombstone had been effaced by time and weather so that it was barely readable.
- The oscillation of the hypnotist's watch soon put the audience volunteer in a trance.
- The thought of a huge elephant being afraid of a tiny mouse is ludicrous.
- Late for her appointment, the woman wildly gesticulated to the cab driver to stop.

He was not conscious of an effort, but a sharp pain in his wrist apprised him that he was trying to free his hands. He gave the struggle his attention, as an idler might observe the feat of a juggler, without interest in the outcome. What splendid effort!—what magnificent, what superhuman strength! Ah, that was a fine endeavor! Bravo! The cord fell away; his arms parted and floated upward, the hands dimly seen on each side in the growing light. He watched them with a new interest as first one and then the other pounced upon the noose at his neck. They tore it away and thrust it fiercely aside, its undulations resembling those of a watersnake. "Put it back, put it back!" He thought he shouted these words to his hands, for the undoing of the noose had been succeeded by the direst pang that he had yet experienced. His neck ached horribly; his brain was on fire; his heart, which had been fluttering faintly, gave a great leap, trying to force itself out at his mouth. His whole body was racked and wrenched with an insupportable anguish! But his disobedient hands gave no heed to the command. They beat the water vigorously with quick, downward strokes, forcing him to the surface. He felt his head emerge; his eyes were blinded by the sunlight; his chest expanded convulsively, and with a supreme and crowning agony his lungs engulfed a great draft of air, which instantly he expelled in a shriek!

He was now in full possession of his physical senses. They were, indeed, preternaturally keen and alert. Something in the awful disturbance of his organic system had so exalted and refined them that they made record of things never before perceived. He felt the ripples upon his face and heard their separate sounds as they struck. He looked at the forest on the bank of the stream, saw the individual trees, the leaves and the veining of each leaf—saw the very insects upon them: the locusts, the brilliant-bodied flies, the gray spiders stretching their webs from twig to twig. He noted the prismatic colors in all the dewdrops upon a million blades of grass. The humming of the gnats that danced above the eddies of the stream, the beating of the dragonflies' wings, the strokes of the water spiders' legs, like oars which had lifted their boat—all these made audible music. A fish slid along beneath his eyes and he heard the rush of its body parting the water.

❶ *In what state are Farquhar's senses? What sensory details does he notice?*

He had come to the surface facing down the stream; in a moment the visible world seemed to wheel slowly round, himself the pivotal point, and he saw the bridge, the fort, the soldiers upon the bridge, the captain, the sergeant, the two privates, his executioners. They were in silhouette against the blue sky. They shouted and gesticulated, pointing at him. The captain had drawn his pistol, but did not fire; the others were unarmed. Their movements were grotesque and horrible, their forms gigantic.

Suddenly he heard a sharp report and something struck the water smartly within a few inches of his head, spattering his face with spray. He heard a second report, and saw one of the sentinels with his rifle at his shoulder, a light cloud of blue smoke rising from the muzzle. The man in the water saw the eye of the man on the

WORDS FOR EVERYDAY USE: **ges • tic • u • late** (jes tik´yōō lat´) *vi.,* make gestures with hands or arms

ANSWER TO GUIDED READING QUESTION

❶ Farquhar's senses are extraordinarily keen and alert. He feels the river's ripples on his face and hears the sounds as they struck. He sees individual trees, leaves and their veins, and locusts, flies, and spiders. He sees prismatic colors in the dewdrops on the blades of grass. He hears the humming of gnats, the beating of dragonflies' wings, and the strokes of water spiders' legs. He sees a fish and hears the sound of its body parting the water.

Answers to Guided Reading Questions

❶ The marksman's eyes are gray and Farquhar has heard that the best and most accurate marksman always have gray eyes. He fears that this marksman will hit him, but he misses, proving the superstition false.

❷ He hears the sound of the lieutenant's voice ordering his troops to fire. He believes that they will soon be shooting at him.

Analytic Scales for Responding in Writing

Assign a score from 1 to 25 for each grading criterion below. (For more detailed evaluation, see the evaluation forms for writing, revising, and proofreading, *Assessment Portfolio,* 7.1–7.10.)

1. Directions

- **Content/Unity.** Directions present a series of detailed steps for completing a simple, familiar task or process.
- **Organization/Coherence.** Directions should begin with a statement of their overall goal. The individual steps should be written in logical or chronological order.
- **Language/Style.** Directions use precise nouns, verbs, and modifiers.
- **Conventions.** Directions avoid errors in spelling, grammar, usage, mechanics, and manuscript form.

2. Daydream

- **Content/Unity.** The daydream presents an imaginative description of unusual or fantastic events.
- **Organization/Coherence.** The daydream may use dialogue, descriptive details, or action to describe the daydreamer's experience.
- **Language/Style.** The daydream uses vivid and precise nouns, verbs, and modifiers.
- **Conventions.** The daydream avoids unintended errors in spelling, grammar, usage, mechanics, and manuscript form. The writer may wish to introduce some unconventional elements for effect.

❶ *What does Farquhar notice about the marksman? What does he fear this means? Is the superstition he had heard true?*

bridge gazing into his own through the sights of the rifle. He observed that it was a gray eye and remembered having read that gray eyes were keenest, and that all famous marksmen had them. Nevertheless, this one had missed.

A counterswirl had caught Farquhar and turned him half round; he was again looking into the forest on the bank opposite the fort. The sound of a clear, high voice in a monotonous singsong now rang out behind him and came across the water with a distinctness that pierced and subdued all other sounds, even the beating of the ripples in his ears. Although no soldier, he had frequented camps enough to know the dread significance of that deliberate, drawling, aspirated chant; the lieutenant on shore was taking a part in the morning's work. How coldly and pitilessly—with what an even, calm intonation, presaging, and enforcing tranquillity in the men—with what accurately measured intervals fell those cruel words:

❷ *What sound does Farquhar hear? What does he take it to mean?*

"Attention, company! . . . Shoulder arms! . . . Ready! . . . Aim! . . . fire!"

Farquhar dived—dived as deeply as he could. The water roared in his ears like the voice of Niagara, yet he heard the dulled thunder of the volley and, rising again toward the surface, met shining bits of metal, singularly flattened, oscillating slowly downward. Some of them touched him on the face and hands, then fell away, continuing their descent. One lodged between his collar and neck; it was uncomfortably warm and he snatched it out.

As he rose to the surface, gasping for breath, he saw that he had been a long time under water; he was perceptibly farther down stream—nearer to safety. The soldiers had almost finished reloading; the metal ramrods flashed all at once in the sunshine as they were drawn from the barrels, turned in the air, and thrust into their sockets. The two sentinels fired again, independently and ineffectually.

The hunted man saw all this over his shoulder; he was now swimming vigorously with the current. His brain was as energetic as his arms and legs; he thought with the rapidity of lightning.

"The officer," he reasoned, "will not make that martinet's[5] error a second time. It is as easy to dodge a volley as a single shot. He has probably already given the command to fire at will. God help me, I cannot dodge them all!"

An appalling splash within two yards of him was followed by a loud, rushing sound, *diminuendo,*[6] which seemed to travel back through the air to the fort and died in an explosion which stirred the very river to its deeps! A rising sheet of water curved over him, fell down upon him, blinded him, strangled him! The cannon had taken a hand in the game. As he shook his head free from the commotion of the smitten water he heard the deflected shot humming through the air ahead, and in an instant it was cracking and smashing the branches in the forest beyond.

"They will not do that again," he thought; "the next time they will use a charge of grape.[7] I must keep my eye

5. **martinet's.** Of a strict disciplinarian
6. **diminuendo.** Musical term meaning a reduction in volume
7. **grape.** Cluster of small iron balls fired from a cannon

Words for Everyday Use: **as • pi • rat • ed** (as´pə rāt´əd) *adj.,* articulated with a puff of breath before or after

Vocabulary in Context

- Is the *h* in the word *herb* aspirated or not?

upon the gun; the smoke will apprise me—the report arrives too late; it lags behind the missile. That is a good gun."

Suddenly he felt himself whirled round and round—spinning like a top. The water, the banks, the forests, the now distant bridge, fort and men—all were commingled and blurred. Objects were represented by their colors only; circular horizontal streaks of color—that was all he saw. He had been caught in a vortex and was being whirled on with a velocity of advance and gyration that made him giddy and sick. In a few moments he was flung upon the gravel at the foot of the left bank of the stream—the southern bank—and behind a projecting point which concealed him from his enemies. The sudden arrest of his motion, the abrasion of one of his hands on the gravel, restored him, and he wept with delight. He dug his fingers into the sand, threw it over himself in handfuls and audibly blessed it. It looked like diamonds, rubies, emeralds; he could think of nothing beautiful which it did not resemble. The trees upon the bank were giant garden plants; he noted a definite order in their arrangement, inhaled the fragrance of their blooms. A strange, roseate light shone through the spaces among their trunks and the wind made in their branches the music of aeolian harps.[8] He had no wish to perfect his escape—was content to remain in that enchanting spot until retaken.

A whiz and rattle of grapeshot among the branches high above his head roused him from his dream. The baffled cannoneer had fired him a random farewell. He sprang to his feet, rushed up the sloping bank, and plunged into the forest.

All that day he traveled, laying his course by the rounding sun. The forest seemed interminable; nowhere did he discover a break in it, not even a woodman's road. He had not known that he lived in so wild a region. There was something uncanny in the revelation.

Photograph: Ken Pelka

Young Soldier. *Separate study of a soldier giving water to a wounded companion. Winslow Homer, 1861. Cooper-Hewitt, National Design Museum, Smithsonian Inst./Art Resource, NY*

❶ *What causes Farquhar's delight and contentment?*

8. **aeolian harps.** Harps that produce music when air blows over the strings

Answer to Guided Reading Question

❶ Farquhar is happy because everything seems so beautiful and precious, now that he has been released from the sickening whirlpool.

Answers to Selection Check Test 4.6.7

EX. In what state is Owl Creek bridge located?

The bridge is in northern Alabama.

1. Why were the soldiers assembled at the bridge?

They were there to witness an official hanging of a civilian gentleman.

2. What was the man's plan for escape, provided he could free his hands?

He planned to take off the noose, dive into the stream, evade the bullets by swimming to the bank, set off into the woods, and go home.

3. What about the bridge would make it easy to destroy, according to the gray-clad traveler?

He said there was a collection of dry, easy-to-burn driftwood piled up against the pier at the end of the bridge.

4. What was unusual about the forest into which Farquhar escaped?

The forest was huge and wild; it had no breaks or even small roads cut into it.

5. What happens to Farquhar as he reaches for his wife?

He feels a blow to the back of his head, sees a blinding light, and hears a sound like the roar of a cannon; then he feels, sees, and hears nothing. He is dead.

Art Note

Winslow Homer (1836–1910) was born in Boston. He did not receive a formal education in art, but instead learned his techniques when he was apprenticed to a lithographer and during his early career as a magazine illustrator. As pictorial reporter during the Civil War, Homer produced oil paintings that were objective and realistic, a style that he would maintain throughout his career. Have the students study the face and posture of the *Young Soldier* and write a short paragraph in which they imagine what his thoughts may be at that moment.

Answers to Guided Reading Questions

❶ The description brings to mind the details usually associated with death by hanging.

❷ His actions were only in his mind. None of them had actually taken place.

Responding to the Selection

Allow time for students to reread sections of the story, looking for details that seemed out of place or unusual. Discuss the devices that often let movie or television viewers know that the characters are imagining or dreaming.

Answers for Reviewing the Selection

RECALLING

1. The man is a civilian, about thirty-five years old, good-looking and probably rich. He has long, dark hair; a mustache and a pointed beard; and grey eyes. His tied hands and the armed soldiers guarding him indicate that he is a prisoner. The noose around his neck shows he is about to be hanged.

2. The man tells Farquhar and his wife that the Yanks have taken over the Owl Creek bridge and fortified it. He also says that anyone who is caught interfering with the use of the railroad will be hanged. Finally he gives Farquhar an idea of how to sabotage the bridge by burning it.

3. The rope breaks and Farquhar falls into the stream and swims away. When he reaches the shore, he begins to run through the forest.

4. Farquhar is hanged and dies.

INTERPRETING

Responses will vary. Possible responses are given.

5. The reason the man is being hanged is not revealed immediately, but later it is revealed that the man is a Southern sympathizer who has attempted to destroy a

(cont.)

By night fall he was fatigued, footsore, famishing. The thought of his wife and children urged him on. At last he found a road which led him in what he knew to be the right direction. It was as wide and straight as a city street, yet it seemed untraveled. No fields bordered it, no dwelling anywhere. Not so much as the barking of a dog suggested human habitation. The black bodies of the trees formed a straight wall on both sides, terminating on the horizon in a point, like a diagram in a lesson in perspective. Overhead, as he looked up through this rift in the wood, shone great golden stars looking unfamiliar and grouped in strange constellations. He was sure they were arranged in some order which had a secret and malign significance. The wood on either side was full of singular noises, among which—once, twice, and again, he distinctly heard whispers in an unknown tongue.

What description is given of Farquhar? What image does this description bring to mind? ❶

His neck was in pain and lifting his hand to it he found it horribly swollen. He knew that it had a circle of black where the rope had bruised it. His eyes felt congested; he could no longer close them. His tongue was swollen with thirst; he relieved its fever by thrusting it forward from between his teeth into the cold air. How softly the turf had carpeted the untraveled avenue—he could no longer feel the roadway beneath his feet!

What is revealed in the last paragraph about Farquhar's actions? ❷

Doubtless, despite his suffering, he had fallen asleep while walking, for now he sees another scene—perhaps he has merely recovered from a delirium. He stands at the gate of his own home. All is as he left it, and all bright and beautiful in the morning sunshine. He must have traveled the entire night. As he pushes open the gate and passes up the wide white walk, he sees a flutter of female garments; his wife, looking fresh and cool and sweet, steps down from the veranda to meet him. At the bottom of the steps she stands waiting, with a smile of ineffable joy, an attitude of matchless grace and dignity. Ah, how beautiful she is! He springs forward with extended arms. As he is about to clasp her he feels a stunning blow upon the back of the neck; a blinding white light blazes all about him with a sound like the shock of a cannon—then all is darkness and silence!

Peyton Farquhar was dead; his body, with a broken neck, swung gently from side to side beneath the timbers of the Owl Creek bridge. ■

Responding to the Selection

At what point did you begin to suspect that things were not as they seemed in this story? Did the imaginary or dream sequence remind you of other stories you have read or seen enacted at the movies or on television? How were those other stories similar to this one?

Words for Everyday Use: **ma • lign** (mə līn´) *adj.,* malicious, evil

Vocabulary in Context

- The dictator's malign intention was to silence all opposition.

Reviewing the Selection

RECALLING

1. Describe the man on the railroad bridge and explain his situation. What is about to happen to him? How do you know?
2. What does the gray-clad soldier tell Farquhar and his wife when he stops by their home?
3. What prevents Farquhar from being killed by hanging? How does he escape the soldiers?
4. What happens to Farquhar at the end of the story?

INTERPRETING

5. How did the man get into this predicament? What was his crime and who is punishing him?
6. What details suggest that Farquhar might attempt to destroy the railroad bridge?
7. As Farquhar continues his escape, he begins to experience strange occurrences. Which sights and experiences seem strange to you?
8. How could Farquhar have dreamed or thought all these experiences so quickly? Does this story seem plausible to you?

SYNTHESIZING

9. Do you agree that "all is fair in love and war," as Farquhar believes? Do you feel that Farquhar's punishment was deserved and justified because it was an act of war?
10. Do you enjoy stories in which the characters are really dreaming or imagining much of the action? Give reasons why, or why not.

Understanding Literature (Questions for Discussion)

1. **Flashback.** A **flashback** is a section of a literary work that presents an event or series of events that occurred earlier than the current time in the work. How does the flashback in this story advance the story's plot? What necessary information does the flashback provide?
2. **Psychological Fiction. Psychological fiction** is fiction that emphasizes the interior, subjective experiences of its characters, and especially such fiction when it deals with emotional or mental disturbance or anguish. What parts of the story qualify it as psychological fiction?
3. **Naturalism. Naturalism** was a literary movement of the late nineteenth and early twentieth centuries that portrayed the lives of characters as being determined, or caused, by outside events beyond their control. What elements of this story make it an example of Naturalism?

ANSWERS FOR REVIEWING THE SELECTION (CONT.)

railroad bridge that the Union army has taken over. The Union army is hanging him for interfering with their war effort.

6. Although Farquhar has been forced to stay at home instead of joining the army, he longs "for the release of his energies, the larger life of the soldier, the opportunity for distinction." He asks the passing soldier for suggestions about how the bridge can be destroyed.

7. The following sights and experiences seem strange: no break in the "interminable" forest; the wildness of the forest; the wide, straight road with no one on it; no fields or dwellings bordering the road; the wall of black trees on either side of the road; golden stars in strange constellations; voices speaking in unknown languages; his inability to feel the roadway beneath his feet; and the ease with which he arrives at his house to meet his smiling wife.

8. It is possible to think thoughts very quickly. The mind has amazing powers that we scarcely understand. Students might suggest that the ending of the story makes it seem more plausible because it explains the strange details of the rest of the story.

SYNTHESIZING

Responses will vary. Possible responses are given.

9. If students believe "all is fair in love and war" they should see his punishment as justified. Some students may think that even in wartime taking another person's life as punishment is not justifiable.

10. Some students may say they enjoy such stories because they have a surprise ending. Other students may dislike stories in which most of the action is dreamed or imagined because they seem unrealistic.

ANSWERS FOR UNDERSTANDING LITERATURE

▶ See the evaluation forms for discussion, active listening, and oral communication, *Assessment Portfolio,* 7.11–7.14.

Responses will vary. Possible responses are given.

1. Flashback. In the flashback, the reader learns the reason why Farquhar is being hanged. It also introduces the reader to Farquhar, showing how he thinks, acts, and feels.

▶**Teaching Note:** Ask the class to imagine the story if it had been written in the more conventional chronological order. Discuss the order in which events occurred and why the use of a flashback was the better choice for this story.

2 Psychological Fiction. The story qualifies as psychological fiction because it delves into the mind of the main character, Farquhar, at the most critical point in

(cont.)

ANALYTIC SCALES FOR RESPONDING IN WRITING

Grading scales appear on page 386.

ANSWERS FOR UNDERSTANDING LITERATURE (CONT.)

his life. The section of the story that describes Farquhar's thoughts and experiences from a first-person limited point of view, that is, from the time when he hears the watch ticking loudly and slowly until the point when "all is darkness and silence" is imaginary and found only in Farquhar's mind.

3. Naturalism. Chance events determine Farquhar's fate. Farquhar is caught up in a war and is tricked into committing an act of war by a scout who just happens to be passing when he and his wife are enjoying a quiet evening on their grounds. Despite Farquhar's intentions to stay away from the fighting, he is pulled into the action unknowingly.

▶ **Teaching Note:** Suggest that students read the discussion of Naturalism in the Handbook of Literary Terms. Then ask them if the story displays additional elements of Naturalism.

4. Climax. The climax occurs when Farquhar, reaching for his beloved wife, feels a blow at the back of his neck, sees a blinding light, hears a sound like the shock of a cannon, and descends into silence and darkness. The falling action is the description of Farquhar swinging from the bridge, dead of a broken neck.

▶ **Teaching Note:** Students can compare the placement and length of the falling action to the falling action of other short stories they have read. Discuss why the brief falling action is appropriate for this story.

ANSWERS FOR LANGUAGE LAB

1. It did not appear to be the duty of these two men to know what was occurring at the center of the bridge.
2. The sentinels, facing the banks of the stream, might have been statues to adorn the bridge.
3. This plank had been held in place by the weight of the captain.
4. "The Yanks are repairing the railroads," said the man, "and are getting ready for another advance."
5. The captain had drawn his pistol, but did not fire.

4. **Climax.** The **climax** is the point of highest interest and suspense in a literary work. The term is sometimes also used to describe the turning point of the action in a story or play, the point at which the rising action ends and the falling action begins. See the Handbook of Literary Terms for more information on these elements of plot. Identify the climax in this story. Then describe the falling action.

Responding in Writing

1. **Directions.** Bierce gives specific details about the way each soldier is standing and holding his rifle. His description is so exact that a reader could duplicate the position of the rifle after a careful reading. Write directions for a simple action that you know well. Include specific details so the reader can carry out your instructions after a careful reading. Refer to the Language Arts Survey, 1.40, "Elaboration: Types of Supporting Details."
2. **Daydream.** Everyone daydreams occasionally. Like the main character in "An Occurrence at Owl Creek Bridge," you can feel as if you were somewhere else when you daydream. Write a descriptive paragraph about a daydream you had or that you could have. Let your imagination go.

Language Lab

Auxiliary Verbs. Read the Language Arts Survey, 2.14, "Auxiliary Verbs." Underline the auxiliary verbs in the following sentences.

1. It did not appear to be the duty of these two men to know what was occurring at the center of the bridge.
2. The sentinels, facing the banks of the stream, might have been statues to adorn the bridge.
3. This plank had been held in place by the weight of the captain.
4. "The Yanks are repairing the railroads," said the man, "and are getting ready for another advance."
5. The captain had drawn his pistol, but did not fire.

Thinking Skills

Remembering and Visualizing. Read the Language Arts Survey, 4.5, "Remembering and Visualizing." Then take a few moments to remember and visualize an incident in which your senses came alive, for example, when you jumped into cold water, when you descended into a damp basement, or when you sat by a roaring bonfire. Jot down some notes on what your senses experienced at that time.

ANSWERS FOR THINKING SKILLS

Responses will vary.

Students should include sensory details about more than one sense to visualize and remember the experience more completely.

For More Practice

Problem. Have students visualize an event they have never experienced, such as skydiving or working in a steel factory. Have them jot down ideas about how the experience would affect all their senses.

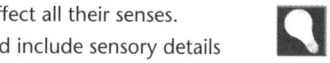

Answer. Notes should include sensory details from all senses.

▶ **Teaching Note:** Students might find it helpful to organize their ideas in a sensory detail chart. Refer them to the Language Arts Survey, 1.18, "Sensory Detail Charts."

PREREADING

"A Mystery of Heroism"
"Do not weep, maiden, for war is kind"
by Stephen Crane

About the Author

Stephen Crane (1871–1900) lived only twenty-eight years, but in that time he established himself as a great American fiction writer and poet. A literary pioneer, Crane applied to fiction his belief that human beings are pawns, moved by forces beyond their control to take actions beyond their understanding. This idea that nature—the forces of heredity and environment—causes humans to think, believe, feel, and act as they do is known in philosophy as Determinism and in literary theory as Naturalism. To the Determinist or Naturalist, free will is an illusion, because the decisions that people believe they are making freely are in fact the inevitable consequences of the forces acting upon them.

Crane was born in Newark, New Jersey, the youngest of fourteen children. His father, a Methodist minister, died when Crane was nine years old. Crane attended Syracuse University but left after one semester. In 1893, Crane finished revising his novel *Maggie: A Girl of the Streets,* the draft of which he had finished while at Syracuse. Shocked by the novel's grim realism, publishers rejected the book, and Crane was forced to pay for its publication. In 1894, Crane's masterful novel about the Civil War, *The Red Badge of Courage,* was published serially in a magazine, and Crane began work as a reporter. In 1895, the novel was released in book form, and Crane's reputation was established. That same year, Crane issued the first volume of his experimental free verse, *The Black Rider.* This was followed by another volume of poetry, *War Is Kind,* in 1899. Crane's experiences as a reporter in Mexico, the American West, and Florida provided material for a number of short stories, including "The Blue Hotel" and "The Open Boat." As a reporter, Crane covered the Greco-Turkish War and the Spanish-American War, seeing firsthand, the cruelties of battle about which he had written so eloquently. Before his death, Crane spent some time in England, where he met many famous writers, including H. G. Wells, Joseph Conrad, and Henry James. By that time, he was severely ill with tuberculosis. He died at a health spa in Badenweiler, Germany.

About the Selections

Readers of *The Red Badge of Courage* and the other war stories and poems of Stephen Crane are often surprised to learn that Crane did not experience the Civil War firsthand. The astonishingly realistic details of these works are tributes to what a writer can do through careful, exhaustive research. **"A Mystery of Heroism"** is a definitive example of both Realism and Naturalism in American fiction. **"Do not weep, maiden, for war is kind"** illustrates typical characteristics of Crane's poetry—irony, realistic details, and a conversational tone, all expressed in free verse void of traditional patterns of rhyme, rhythm, and stanza form.

GOALS/OBJECTIVES

Studying this lesson will enable students to

- empathize with the feelings of soldiers caught up in the confusion and excitement of war
- reflect on the uselessness of war
- describe the contributions of Stephen Crane to American literature
- recognize elements of Naturalism
- define *simile* and *metaphor* and identify examples of each in the literature they read
- write a citation for bravery

ADDITIONAL RESOURCES

Reader's Guide
- Selection Worksheets, 6.5, 6.6

Assessment Portfolio
- Selection Check Tests, 4.6.9, 4.6.11
- Selection Tests, 4.6.10, 4.6.12

Essential Skills Practice Books
- *Language,* 2.150
- *Speaking and Listening,* 3.2

ENRICHMENT ACTIVITIES

- Point out that Crane had never experienced a war before he wrote most of his stories about the Civil War. Discuss the personal qualities Crane must have possessed to recreate the battle scenes so convincingly.
- Have a group of students research the recruiting methods and advertisements that were used during the Civil War and compare them to the methods used now.

SUPPORT FOR LEP STUDENTS

Some students may be confused by the dialect in which much of the dialogue is written. Explain that some of the words may be spelled incorrectly to simulate the way they sound. Have students who need extra help work with others who have a strong understanding of the dialect.

Colloquialisms

over yonder—over there
had the blood in him—had the courage
if that ain't th' derndest thing—that is hard to believe

Additional Vocabulary

conflagration—fire
demeanor—way of behaving
falsetto—having a high male voice
calamity—disaster
carnage—widespread death, slaughter

PREREADING NOTES

READER'S JOURNAL

Have students think particularly of times when they were urged by friends to do something they probably would not have done alone.

LANGUAGE SKILLS

Ask students to speculate as to why Crane used dialect instead of translating the soldiers' words into standard English. What purpose does the dialect serve?

ANSWER TO GUIDED READING QUESTION

❶ The bugler is hit by an exploding shell.

BIOGRAPHICAL NOTE

Stephen Crane's name became linked with war stories in the public mind after the success of *The Red Badge of Courage.* Like that novel, the short story collection *The Little Regiment* (1896), in which "A Mystery of Heroism" appears, was written before Crane had witnessed or participated in a war himself. A later collection, *Wounded in the Rain,* reflects his actual war experiences.

VOCABULARY FROM THE SELECTION

convulsive	indolent
furtive	obliterate
gesticulating	provisional
imprecation	stolidity
incessant	

READER'S JOURNAL

Have you ever done something and later wondered why you did it? Have you ever felt swept along by events and not really in control of what was happening? Write about such an experience in your journal.

LANGUAGE SKILLS

"A Mystery of Heroism" contains some examples of dialect spoken by soldiers during the time of the Civil War. Read the Language Arts Survey, 2.150, "Dialects of English." Then, as you read the story, copy three examples of dialect into your journal and translate them into contemporary English of the kind spoken in your community.

"A Mystery of Heroism"

STEPHEN CRANE

What happens to the bugler? ❶

The dark uniforms of the men were so coated with dust from the incessant wrestling of the two armies that the regiment almost seemed a part of the clay bank which shielded them from the shells. On the top of the hill a battery[1] was arguing in tremendous roars with some other guns, and to the eye of the infantry the artillerymen, the guns, the caissons,[2] the horses, were distinctly outlined upon the blue sky. When a piece was fired, a red streak as round as a log flashed low in the heavens, like a monstrous bolt of lightning. The men of the battery wore white duck trousers, which somehow emphasized their legs; and when they ran and crowded in little groups at the bidding of the shouting officers, it was more impressive than usual to the infantry.

Fred Collins, of A Company, was saying, "Thunder! I wisht I had a drink. Ain't there any water round here?" Then somebody yelled, "There goes th' bugler!"

As the eyes of half the regiment swept in one machine-like movement, there was an instant's picture of a horse in a great convulsive leap of a death-wound and a rider leaning back with a crooked arm and spread fingers before his face. On the ground was the crimson terror of an exploding shell, with fibers of flame that seemed like lances.[3] A glittering bugle swung clear of the rider's back as fell headlong the horse and the man. In the air was an odor as from a conflagration.

Sometimes they of the infantry looked down at a fair little meadow which spread at their feet. Its long green grass was

1. **battery.** Place equipped with heavy guns
2. **caissons.** Two-wheeled carts for carrying ammunition and supplies
3. **lances.** Long, sharp weapons

WORDS FOR EVERYDAY USE:

in • ces • sant (in ses´ant) *adj.,* not ceasing or stopping

con • vul • sive (kən vul´siv) *adj.,* marked by violent contractions or spasms

VOCABULARY IN CONTEXT

- The incessant barking of the neighbor's dog kept me awake all night.
- The strange new dance had violent, almost convulsive movements.
- The old man's constant stolidity, even during a quarrel, was a source of frustration for his wife.
- The waves obliterated the footprints on the beach, leaving no trace of the many people who had walked there.
- The fighters were pulled apart, but they still assaulted each other with imprecations.

rippling gently in a breeze. Beyond it was the gray form of a house half torn to pieces by shells and by the busy axes of soldiers who had pursued firewood. The line of an old fence was now dimly marked by long weeds and by an occasional post. A shell had blown the well-house to fragments. Little lines of gray smoke ribboning upward from some embers indicated the place where had stood the barn.

From beyond a curtain of green woods there came the sound of some stupendous scuffle, as if two animals of the size of islands were fighting. At a distance there were occasional appearances of swift-moving men, horses, batteries, flags; and with the crashing of infantry volleys were heard, often, wild and frenzied cheers. In the midst of it all Smith and Ferguson, two privates of A Company, were engaged in a heated discussion which involved the greatest questions of the national existence.

The battery on the hill presently engaged in a frightful duel. The white legs of the gunners scampered this way and that way, and the officers redoubled their shouts. The guns, with their demeanors of stolidity and courage, were typical of something infinitely self-possessed in this clamor of death that swirled around the hill.

One of a "swing" team[4] was suddenly smitten quivering to the ground, and his maddened brethren dragged his torn body in their struggle to escape from this turmoil and danger. A young soldier astride one of the leaders swore and fumed in his saddle and furiously jerked at the bridle. An officer screamed out an order so violently that his voice broke and ended the sentence in a falsetto shriek. The leading company of the infantry regiment was somewhat exposed, and the colonel ordered it moved more fully under the shelter of the hill. There was the clank of steel against steel.

A lieutenant of the battery rode down and passed them, holding his right arm carefully in his left hand. And it was as if this arm was not at all a part of him, but belonged to another man. His sober and reflective charger[5] went slowly. The officer's face was grimy and perspiring, and his uniform was tousled as if he had been in direct grapple with an enemy. He smiled grimly when the men stared at him. He turned his horse toward the meadow.

Collins, of A Company, said, "I wisht I had a drink. I bet there's water in that there ol' well yonder!"

"Yes; but how you goin' to git it?"

For the little meadow which intervened was now suffering a terrible onslaught of shells. Its green and beautiful calm had vanished utterly. Brown earth was being flung in monstrous handfuls. And there was a massacre of the young blades of grass. They were being torn, burned, obliterated. Some curious fortune of the battle had made this gentle little meadow the object of the red hate of the shells, and each one as it exploded seemed like an imprecation in the face of a maiden.

The wounded officer who was riding across this expanse said to himself: "Why, they couldn't shoot any harder if the whole army was massed here!"

A shell struck the gray ruins of the house, and as, after the roar, the shattered

❶ *In what ways does the description of the guns differ from the description of the soldiers?*

4. **"swing" team.** Middle team of a group of six soldiers on horseback
5. **charger.** War horse

WORDS FOR EVERYDAY USE:

sto • lid • i • ty (stə lid´ə tē´) *n.,* display of little or no emotion

ob • lit • er • ate (ə blit´ər āt´) *vt.,* do away with entirely, leaving no trace

im • pre • ca • tion (im´pri kā´shən) *n.,* curse

LITERARY TECHNIQUE

The **short story** is a narrative literary work that focuses on one central idea or theme. Crane's strength was the short story in which he presents a "slice of life"—a brief episode or story fragment, unconnected to any other events. The short story format reflects Crane's philosophy that the world is ruled by unconnected chaotic events, and there can be no purposeful rules by which humans can live.

CROSS-CURRICULAR ACTIVITIES

Social Studies. Have the students research the weapons that were used during the Civil War. Were any new weapons introduced? If so, which ones?

ANSWER TO GUIDED READING QUESTION

❶ The guns seem calm and in control while the soldiers are running around in confusion.

Additional Questions and Activities

What is happening as Collins and his comrades begin quarreling? What other reactions to the battle scene are noted? Does Collins seem to be connected with the carnage happening around him?

Answers. A bloody battle is taking place as Collins and his comrades begin to quarrel. People are being injured and killed all around them. A fat major notes that a hurrying, angry lieutenant wants to get back with orders quickly before there are no soldiers left. A captain suggests that the infantry will soon attack the hill. Somebody notices a wounded officer spread over his fallen horse. None of these people seems especially concerned about what is happening around them or what is likely to happen to them.

wall fell in fragments, there was a noise which resembled the flapping of shutters during a wild gale of winter. Indeed, the infantry paused in the shelter of the bank appeared as men standing upon a shore contemplating a madness of the sea. The angel of calamity had under its glance the battery upon the hill. Fewer white-legged men labored about the guns. A shell had smitten one of the pieces, and after the flare, the smoke, the dust, the wrath of this blow were gone, it was possible to see white legs stretched horizontally upon the ground. And at that interval to the rear where it is the business of battery horses to stand with their noses to the fight, awaiting the command to drag their guns out of the destruction, or into it, or wheresoever these incomprehensible humans demanded with whip and spur—in this line of passive and dumb spectators, whose fluttering hearts yet would not let them forget the iron laws of man's control of them—in this rank of brute-soldiers there had been relentless and hideous carnage. From the ruck[6] of bleeding and prostrate horses, the men of the infantry could see one animal raising its stricken body with its forelegs and turning its nose with mystic and profound eloquence toward the sky.

Some comrades joked Collins about his thirst. "Well, if yeh want a drink so bad, why don't yeh go git it?"

"Well, I will in a minnet, if yeh don't shut up!"

A lieutenant of artillery floundered his horse straight down the hill with as little concern as if it were level ground. As he galloped past the colonel of the infantry, he threw up his hand in swift salute. "We've got to get out of that," he roared angrily. He was a black-bearded officer, and his eyes, which resembled beads, sparkled like those of an insane man. His jumping horse sped along the column of infantry.

The fat major, standing carelessly with his sword held horizontally behind him and with his legs far apart, looked after the receding horseman and laughed. "He wants to get back with orders pretty quick, or there'll be no batt'ry left," he observed.

The wise young captain of the second company hazarded to the lieutenant-colonel that the enemy's infantry would probably soon attack the hill, and the lieutenant-colonel snubbed him.

A private in one of the rear companies looked out over the meadow, and then turned to a companion and said, "Look there, Jim!" It was the wounded officer from the battery, who some time before had started to ride across the meadow, supporting his right arm carefully with his left hand. This man had encountered a shell, apparently, at a time when no one perceived him, and he could now be seen lying face downward with a stirruped foot stretched across the body of his dead horse. A leg of the charger extended slantingly upward, precisely as stiff as a stake. Around this motionless pair the shells still howled.

There was a quarrel in A Company. Collins was shaking his fist in the faces of some laughing comrades. "Dern yeh! I ain't afraid t' go. If yeh say much, I will go!"

"Of course, yeh will! You'll run through that there medder, won't yeh?"

Collins said, in a terrible voice: "You see now!"

At this ominous threat his comrades broke into renewed jeers.

Collins gave them a dark scowl, and went to find his captain. The latter was conversing with the colonel of the regiment.

"Captain," said Collins, saluting and standing at attention—in those days all trousers bagged at the knees—"Captain, I

6. **ruck.** Mass, collection, heap

want t' get permission to go git some water from that there well over yonder!"

The colonel and the captain swung about simultaneously and stared across the meadow. The captain laughed. "You must be pretty thirsty, Collins?"

"Yes, sir, I am."

"Well—ah," said the captain. After a moment, he asked, "Can't you wait?"

"No, sir."

The colonel was watching Collins's face. "Look here, my lad," he said, in a pious sort of voice—"Look here, my lad"—Collins was not a lad—"don't you think that's taking pretty big risks for a little drink of water?"

"I dunno," said Collins uncomfortably. Some of the resentment toward his companions, which perhaps had forced him into this affair, was beginning to fade. "I dunno w'ether 'tis."

The colonel and the captain contemplated him for a time.

"Well," said the captain finally.

"Well," said the colonel, "if you want to go, why, go."

Collins saluted. "Much obliged t' yeh."

As he moved away the colonel called after him. "Take some of the other boys' canteens[7] with you, an' hurry back, now."

"Yes, sir, I will."

The colonel and the captain looked at each other then, for it had suddenly occurred that they could not for the life of them tell whether Collins wanted to go or whether he did not.

They turned to regard Collins, and as they perceived him surrounded by gesticulating comrades, the colonel said, "Well, by thunder! I guess he's going."

Collins appeared as a man dreaming. In the midst of the questions, the advice, the warnings, all the excited talk of his company mates, he maintained a curious silence.

❶ *Why might Collins be silent?*

They were very busy in preparing him for his ordeal. When they inspected him carefully, it was somewhat like the examination that grooms give a horse before a race; and they were amazed, staggered, by the whole affair. Their astonishment found vent in strange repetitions.

"Are yeh sure a-goin'?" they demanded again and again.

"Certainly I am," cried Collins at last, furiously.

He strode sullenly away from them. He was swinging five or six canteens by their cords. It seemed that his cap would not remain firmly on his head, and often he reached and pulled it down over his brow.

There was a general movement in the compact column. The long animal-like thing moved slightly. Its four hundred eyes were turned upon the figure of Collins.

"Well, sir, if that ain't th' derndest thing! I never thought Fred Collins had the blood in him for that kind of business."

"What's he goin' to do, anyhow?"

"He's goin' to that well there after water."

"We ain't dyin' of thirst, are we? That's foolishness."

❷ *Why might the colonel and the captain be unsure whether Collins wants to cross the meadow?*

"Well, somebody put him up to it, an' he's doin' it."

"Say, he must be a desperate cuss."

When Collins faced the meadow and walked away from the regiment, he was

7. **canteens.** Containers for holding water

WORDS FOR EVERYDAY USE: **ges • tic • u • lat • ing** (jes tik´yōō lāt´iŋ) *part.,* making gestures

ANSWERS TO GUIDED READING QUESTIONS

❶ Collins may be beginning to understand the danger into which he has placed himself. He may be struggling with fear.

❷ Collins does not offer any good reason why he should risk his life for the water. He seems unsure about the risk he is running and the worth of the deed.

LITERARY TECHNIQUE

An **antihero** is a central character who lacks all the qualities traditionally associated with heroes. Antiheroes are common figures in modern fiction. How does Collins qualify as an antihero?

VOCABULARY IN CONTEXT

- The gesticulating third-base coach communicated a message to the batter.

Answers to Guided Reading Questions

❶ Collins realizes that he has been talked into going to the well needlessly. Even so, he does not want to back out, and not simply because he wants to avoid the shame of backing out. He is willing to go through with his boast, but he doesn't really know why.

❷ Collins does not feel like a hero. He feels that he is an imposter, "an intruder in the land of fine deeds."

Literary Technique

Irony is a difference between appearance and reality. The irony in this story is that Collins, who in reality has succumbed to pride and is not sensible enough to think through his situation, appears to be a hero. Have students read the entry on *irony* in the Handbook of Literary Terms and decide whether this irony is dramatic irony, verbal irony, or irony of situation.

Answer. This is an example of irony of situation.

Additional Questions and Activities

Do you think Collins's reaction to the turn of events is realistic? Why, or why not?

Collins reflects on what a hero is and whether or not he is one. Do you think Collins is a hero? Why, or why not?

Does Collins want to go to the well? Why, or why not? ❶

Does Collins feel like a hero? Why, or why not? ❷

vaguely conscious that a chasm, the deep valley of all prides, was suddenly between him and his comrades. It was provisional, but the provision was that he return as a victor. He had blindly been led by quaint emotions, and laid himself under an obligation to walk squarely up to the face of death.

But he was not sure that he wished to make a retraction, even if he could do so without shame. As a matter of truth, he was sure of very little. He was mainly surprised.

It seemed to him supernaturally strange that he had allowed his mind to maneuver his body into such a situation. He understood that it might be called dramatically great.

However, he had no full appreciation of anything, excepting that he was actually conscious of being dazed. He could feel his dulled mind groping after the form and color of this incident. He wondered why he did not feel some keen agony of fear cutting his sense like a knife. He wondered at this, because human expression had said loudly for centuries that men should feel afraid of certain things, and that all men who did not feel this fear were phenomena—heroes.

He was, then, a hero. He suffered that disappointment which we would all have if we discovered that we were ourselves capable of those deeds which we most admire in history and legend. This, then, was a hero. After all, heroes were not much.

No, it could not be true. He was not a hero. Heroes had no shames in their lives, and, as for him, he remembered borrowing fifteen dollars from a friend and promising to pay it back the next day, and then avoiding that friend for ten months. When, at home, his mother had aroused him for the early labor of his life on the farm, it had often been his fashion to be irritable, childish, diabolical; and his mother had died since he had come to the war.

He saw that, in this matter of the well, the canteens, the shells, he was an intruder in the land of fine deeds.

He was now about thirty paces from his comrades. The regiment had just turned its many faces toward him.

From the forest of terrific noises there suddenly emerged a little uneven line of men. They fired fiercely and rapidly at distant foliage on which appeared little puffs of white smoke. The spatter of skirmish firing was added to the thunder of the guns on the hill. The little line of men ran forward. A color-sergeant fell flat with his flag as if he had slipped on ice. There was hoarse cheering from this distant field.

Collins suddenly felt that two demon fingers were pressed into his ears. He could see nothing but flying arrows, flaming red. He lurched from the shock of this explosion, but he made a mad rush for the house, which he viewed as a man submerged to the neck in a boiling surf might view the shore. In the air little pieces of shell howled, and the earthquake explosions drove him insane with the menace of their roar. As he ran the canteens knocked together with a rhythmical tinkling.

As he neared the house, each detail of the scene became vivid to him. He was

Words for Everyday Use: **pro • vi • sion • al** (prō vizh´ə nəl) *adj.,* lasting for a short while, not permanent

Vocabulary in Context

- A provisional agreement for a two-week cease-fire was reached in talks yesterday.
- The child flashed a furtive glance toward his mother before he stole his sister's cookie.
- In the old fable, the indolent grasshopper did not prepare for the winter.

aware of some bricks of the vanished chimney lying on the sod. There was a door which hung by one hinge.

Rifle bullets called forth by the insistent skirmishers came from the far-off bank of foliage. They mingled with the shells and the pieces of shells until the air was torn in all directions by hootings, yells, howls. The sky was full of fiends who directed all their wild rage at his head.

When he came to the well, he flung himself face downward and peered into its darkness. There were furtive silver glintings some feet from the surface. He grabbled one of the canteens and, unfastening its cap, swung it down by the cord. The water flowed slowly in with an indolent gurgle.

And now, as he lay with his face turned away, he was suddenly smitten with the terror. It came upon his heart like the grasp of claws. All the power faded from his muscles. For an instant he was no more than a dead man.

The canteen filled with a maddening slowness, in the manner of all bottles. Presently he recovered his strength and addressed a screaming oath to it. He leaned over until it seemed as if he intended to try to push water into it with his hands.

❶ *What does Collins begin to feel as he fills the canteen?*

Words for Everyday Use:

fur • tive (fur´tiv) *adj.,* secretive, stealthy

in • do • lent (in´də lənt) *adj.,* lazy or inactive

Answer to Guided Reading Question

❶ Collins begins to feel terror and powerlessness.

Additional Questions and Activities

Students can role play Collins's comrades as he crosses the meadow. Their dialogue should indicate what they think of Collins and how they feel about their role in urging him to go get the water.

Answer to Guided Reading Question

❶ Collins may feel that this is his last chance to become a real hero. He has so far risked his life for no reason, but giving water to the dying soldier might make it worthwhile after all.

Additional Questions and Activities

Have the students write a diary entry of a soldier who observes Collins's desperate act. What is his reaction to it? Is he impressed or does he consider it a foolish, unnecessary risk?

Answers to Selection Check Test 6.4.9

EX. What has happened to the well-house?
It has been blown into fragments by a shell.

1. Why does Collins want to go to the well?
He feels thirsty.

2. What is the officers' response to Collins's request to go to the well?
The officers suggest that it is a foolish risk, but they agree to let him go if that is what he wants to do.

3. Why does Collins believe that he cannot be a hero?
He knows that heroes have no shame in their lives, and he has done things for which he feels ashamed.

4. Whom does Collins meet as he runs back from the well?
Collins meets a dying soldier who asks for a drink of water.

5. Who gets the water bucket first when Collins returns?
Two young lieutenants take it first.

His eyes as he gazed down into the well shone like two pieces of metal, and in their expression was a great appeal and a great curse. The stupid water derided him.

There was the blaring thunder of a shell. Crimson light shone through the swift-boiling smoke, and made a pink reflection on part of the wall of the well. Collins jerked out his arm and canteen with the same motion that a man would use in withdrawing his head from a furnace.

He scrambled erect and glared and hesitated. On the ground near him lay the old well bucket, with a length of rusty chain. He lowered it swiftly into the well. The bucket struck the water and then, turning lazily over, sank. When, with hand reaching tremblingly over hand, he hauled it out, it knocked often against the walls of the well and spilled some of its contents.

Why might Collins change his mind and return to the dying soldier? ❶

In running with a filled bucket, a man can adopt but one kind of gait. So, through this terrible field over which screamed practical angels of death, Collins ran in the manner of a farmer chased out of a dairy by a bull.

His face went staring white with anticipating—anticipation of a blow that would whirl him around and down. He would fall as he had seen other men fall, the life knocked out of them so suddenly that their knees were no more quick to touch the ground than their heads. He saw the long blue line of the regiment, but his comrades were standing looking at him from the edge of an impossible star. He was aware of some deep wheel ruts and hoofprints in the sod beneath his feet.

The artillery officer who had fallen in this meadow had been making groans in the teeth of the tempest of sound. These futile cries, wrenched from him by his agony, were heard only by shells, bullets. When wild-eyed Collins came running, this officer raised himself. His face contorted and blanched from pain, he was about to utter some great beseeching cry. But suddenly his face straightened, and he called: "Say, young man, give me a drink of water, will you?"

Collins had no room amid his emotions for surprise. He was mad from the threats of destruction.

"I can't!" he screamed, and in his reply was a full description of his quaking apprehension. His cap was gone and his hair was riotous. His clothes made it appear that he had been dragged over the ground by the heels. He ran on.

The officer's head sank down, and one elbow crooked. His foot in its brass-bound stirrup still stretched over the body of his horse and the other leg was under the steed.

But Collins turned. He came dashing back. His face had now turned gray, and in his eyes was all terror. "Here it is! here it is!"

The officer was as a man gone in drink. His arm bent like a twig. His head drooped as if his neck were of willow. He was sinking to the ground, to lie face downward.

Collins grabbed him by the shoulder. "Here it is. Here's your drink. Turn over. Turn over, man, for God's sake!"

With Collins hauling at his shoulder, the officer twisted his body and fell with his face turned toward that region where lived the unspeakable noises of the swirling missiles. There was the faintest shadow of a smile on his lips as he looked at Collins. He gave a sigh, a little primitive breath like that from a child.

Collins tried to hold the bucket steadily, but his shaking hands caused the water to splash all over the face of the dying man. Then he jerked it away and ran on.

The regiment gave him a welcoming roar. The grimed faces were wrinkled in laughter.

His captain waved the bucket away. "Give it to the men!"

The two genial, skylarking young lieutenants were the first to gain possession of it. They played over it in their fashion.

When one tried to drink, the other teasingly knocked his elbow. "Don't Billie! You'll make me spill it," said the one. The other laughed.

Suddenly there was an oath, the thud of wood on the ground, and a swift murmur of astonishment among the ranks. The two lieutenants glared at each other. The bucket lay on the ground, empty. ■

❶ *What happens to the water Collins brings from the well?*

Responding to the Selection

Do you think that the actions of the main character, or protagonist, in this story are heroic? Does the character think that his own actions are heroic? Why, or why not? Did reading this story give you any insights into what sometimes causes people to act heroically? Discuss these questions with your classmates.

Reviewing the Selection

RECALLING

1. Of what does Collins complain at the beginning of the story? Why do the other members of the regiment taunt him?
2. What does Collins decide to do?
3. What does Collins decide that he is as he heads toward the well?
4. Who stops Collins as he is returning from the well with the bucket? What does this person request? What is Collins's initial reaction? What does he then decide to do?

INTERPRETING

5. How does Collins feel as a result of the other soldiers' taunts?
6. What makes going to the well a very dangerous action to undertake? Why does Collins decide to go?
7. How would you describe Collins's state of mind as he heads toward the well? Does he act as the result of a conscious, free decision? What discovery does Collins make about heroism as he considers his own actions?
8. What makes it dangerous for Collins to bring the dying soldier a drink of water? Why does Collins do this despite the danger?

ANSWER TO GUIDED READING QUESTION

❶ The water spills on the ground before anyone gets a chance to drink any of it.

RESPONDING TO THE SELECTION

Before you assign this question, ask students to identify some heroes they have heard of or known. Discuss what qualities a hero displays.

ANSWERS FOR REVIEWING THE SELECTION

RECALLING

1. Collins complains that he is thirsty. Other members of the regiment taunt him because he boasts that he is willing to cross the meadow that is being shelled just to get some water.
2. Collins decides to make good on his boast and get water from the well.
3. Collins decides that because he feels no fear and is doing a brave deed, he must be a hero. He immediately rethinks his decision and decides that he cannot be a hero because he has done shameful things. He decides he is just an impostor.
4. A dying soldier stops Collins and asks for a drink of water. At first, Collins says that he can't stop, but then he returns and gives the man a drink.

INTERPRETING

Responses will vary. Possible responses are given.

5. Collins feels angry that anyone would doubt his word or his courage.
6. The well is in the middle of an area that is being shelled heavily. Collins decides to go because he boasted that he would and he sees no reason to decide otherwise.

(cont.)

ANSWERS FOR REVIEWING THE SELECTION (CONT.)

7. Collins is confused and not thinking clearly as he heads toward the well. He is surprised to find himself undertaking such a dangerous act for no good reason. He feels that he has somehow been tricked into doing this. He discovers that anyone can be a hero and that heroism is not that special. He feels that he is in some way a fraud or impostor because he had done shameful things that he thinks a hero would have avoided.
8. The area in which the soldier lies is being shelled heavily. Both the soldier and Collins may be hit at any moment. Collins may return to give the soldier a drink because he feels that it is his last chance to perform a truly heroic act.

(cont.)

ANSWERS FOR REVIEWING THE SELECTION (CONT.)

SYNTHESIZING

Responses will vary. Possible responses are given.

9. Collins realizes that his motives were not particularly heroic. He suspects now that other people who appear to be heroes may not be entirely selfless in their motivations either. They, too, may have performed their heroic deeds almost by accident.

10. The men cheer and laugh when Collins returns. The bucket of water is spilled almost immediately. Collins's act of heroism has been worthless. Crane may be trying to say that people who are considered to be heroes do not always deserve the glory or that heroes are often people simply reacting mindlessly to chance situations.

ANSWERS FOR UNDERSTANDING LITERATURE

▶ See the evaluation forms for discussion, active listening, and oral communication, *Assessment Portfolio,* 7.11–7.14.

Responses will vary. Possible responses are given.

1. **Psychological Fiction.** Collins decides to go to the well because he feels anger at his fellow soldiers for doubting that he would go through with his boast. It is desperate because it is dangerous and yet it is the only course of action that Collins can take without losing his pride. Collins notes a feeling of surprise but no fear.

2. **Naturalism.** Collins does not choose freely, understanding all the consequences of his decision, but instead is swept along by chance events. The sentence might be paraphrased as "He couldn't believe that he had let himself be talked into this." Crane may be saying that heroes are often created by accident.

▶ **Teaching Note:** Ask students if Crane's attitude toward heroes has affected how they themselves feel about heroism and the opportunities for heroism that war can offer.

3. **Theme.** The more heroic act is bringing water to a dying man. It

(cont.)

SYNTHESIZING

9. On the way to the well, Collins thinks, "This, then, was a hero. After all, heroes were not much." Why does he think this? Do you agree with Collins? Why, or why not?

10. When Collins returns with the water, how do the men react to him? What happens to the bucket of water? What purpose has Collins's heroism served? What point do you think the author is making about heroism by ending the story in this way?

Understanding Literature (Questions for Discussion)

1. **Psychological Fiction. Psychological fiction** is fiction that emphasizes the interior, subjective experiences of its characters, and especially such fiction when it deals with emotional or mental disturbance or anguish. What feelings cause Collins to decide to go to the well? What makes this a "desperate" thing to do? What feelings does Collins note in himself as he makes his perilous walk?

2. **Naturalism. Naturalism** was a literary movement of the late nineteenth and early twentieth centuries that saw actions and events as resulting inevitably from biological or natural forces or from forces in the environment. Does Collins in this story act heroically as a result of a free, conscious, well-thought-out decision? How would you paraphrase this thought of Collins's: "It seemed to him supernaturally strange that he had allowed his mind to maneuver his body into such a situation"? What do you think the author is saying about the forces that impel people to heroic actions? Explain.

3. **Theme.** A **theme** is a central idea in a work of literature. Which is the more heroic act, going for the water or bringing the water to the dying man? Why?

4. **Simile and Metaphor.** A **simile** is a comparison using *like* or *as.* A **metaphor** is a description of one thing as if it were another. The description invites the reader to make a comparison between two things. Read the following similes and metaphors from the story. Explain what things are being compared in each case and what these two things have in common.
   - "When a piece was fired, a red streak as round as a log flashed low in the heavens, like a monstrous bolt of lightning."
   - "From beyond a curtain of green woods there came the sound of some stupendous scuffle, as if two animals of the size of islands were fighting."
   - ". . . the red hate of the shells . . ."
   - "A leg of the charger extended slantingly upward, precisely as stiff as a stake."
   - ". . . the shells still howled."
   - "There was a general movement in the compact column. The long animal-like thing moved slightly. Its four hundred eyes were turned upon the figure of Collins."
   - ". . . he was vaguely conscious that a chasm, the deep valley of all prides, was suddenly between him and his comrades."

ANSWERS FOR UNDERSTANDING LITERATURE (CONT.)

is a conscious decision to risk one's life to help another person.

4. **Simile and Metaphor.**

- The streak and the log are both round. The streak is like lightning because it is fast, it is bright, and it is dangerous.
- The armies are like large animals because they share similiar screeching, thrashing, and trampling sounds.
- Shells are like red hate because they carry intense suffering and violence.
- The leg of the horse and a stake are both stiff and stand upright from the ground.
- The shells are like animals that howl because they make the same frightening sound.
- The column is like an animal because all the people in it move together, as is they were one being.

(cont.)

- ". . . some keen agony of fear cutting his sense like a knife."
- ". . . he made a mad rush for the house, which he viewed as a man submerged to the neck in a boiling surf might view the shore."
- "The sky was full of fiends who directed all their wild rage at his head."
- ". . . his comrades were standing looking at him from the edge of an impossible star."
- "His arm bent like a twig. His head drooped as if his neck were of willow."

Responding in Writing

Citation for Bravery. Imagine that you are one of the commanders in charge of Collins's regiment. Write a brief statement commending him for his actions during the battle.

PROJECT

Battles of the Civil War. Working with other students in a small group, choose a famous battle of the Civil War, research that battle, and report on it to your class. Possible battles to consider include the following:

Fort Sumter	Shiloh	Vicksburg	Petersburg
Bull Run	New Orleans	Fort Wagner	The *Merrimack* and the *Monitor*
Fredericksburg	Sharpsburg	Gettysburg	
Chancellorsville	Antietam	Chickamauga	

ANSWERS FOR UNDERSTANDING LITERATURE (CONT.)

- Pride is like a deep valley separating Collins from his comrades.
- Fear is like a knife because it cuts through his feelings.
- The house and the shore are both places of safety to a person in extreme danger.
- The bullets and shells are like angry monsters because they both have the power to kill him.
- Both his comrades and an impossible star seem unreachable.
- The fallen soldier is like any other natural thing such as a tree at the mercy of a huge force.

►**Teaching Note:** You may wish to divide these similes and metaphors and assign them to small groups of students. Have students find each quotation in the story, so they can use hints from the story to understand the simile or metaphor.

ANALYTIC SCALES FOR RESPONDING IN WRITING

Assign a score from 1 to 25 for each grading criterion below. (For more detailed evaluation, see the evaluation forms for writing, revising, and proofreading, *Assessment Portfolio,* 7.1–7.10.)

Citation for Bravery

- **Content/Unity.** The citation for bravery commends an individual for a heroic act.
- **Organization/Coherence.** The citation for bravery presents the reasons for special commendation and describes the gratitude of those who benefit from the heroic act.
- **Language/Style.** The citation for bravery uses vivid and precise nouns, verbs, and modifiers.
- **Conventions.** The citation for bravery avoids errors in spelling, grammar, usage, mechanics, and manuscript form.

PROJECT NOTES

►See the worksheets and evaluation forms for projects, *Assessment Portfolio,* 7.20–7.23.

Battles of the Civil War

- There are many excellent books and videos about the Civil War. Schedule a trip to the library to find materials on the topic. Depending on your location, you may be able to schedule a field trip to one of the battlefields for a first-hand look at the site.
- Students may wish to use models, diagrams, or pictures to supplement their reports.

PREREADING NOTES

READER'S JOURNAL

Before students write their notes on the question, read aloud Abraham Lincoln's "Letter to Mrs. Bixby" on page 404 to see how he approached this difficult task.

SPEAKING AND LISTENING SKILLS

Discuss why the poem is divided in this way and the emotions that each stanza conveys.

ANSWERS TO GUIDED READING QUESTIONS

❶ The lover is hit by a bullet or a shell, and he falls from his horse.

❷ The speaker does not believe in the "virtue of slaughter" or the "excellence of killing." If the speaker really believed in them he would choose different words than *slaughter, killing,* and *corpses* to describe the scene of battle.

ANSWERS TO SELECTION CHECK TEST 4.6.11

EX. What happens to the horse?
The horse runs on alone.

1. What were "these men" born to do?
They were born to drill and die.

2. Where is the Kingdom of the Battle-God?
The Battle-God's Kingdom is the field where a thousand corpses lie.

3. What happens to the father?
The father dies in the trenches.

4. What can be found on the flag of the regiment?
The flag shows an eagle with a crest of red and gold.

5. Where is the mother's heart hung?
The mother's heart hangs on her son's shroud.

READER'S JOURNAL

What can one possibly say to the parent or spouse of a person who dies in battle? If you were given the task of comforting someone who had lost a loved one in a war, what words would you choose? What would be your message? Write a few of your ideas in your journal.

SPEAKING AND LISTENING SKILLS

Read the Language Arts Survey, 3.2, "Elements of Verbal Communication." Then after you read the poem, practice presenting the poem with another reader. One person should read aloud stanzas 1, 3, and 5, and the other should read aloud stanzas 2 and 4.

"Do not weep, maiden, for war is kind"

STEPHEN CRANE

What happens to the lover? ❶

Do not weep, maiden, for war is kind.
Because your lover threw wild hands toward the sky
And the affrighted steed ran on alone,
Do not weep.
War is kind.

Hoarse, booming drums of the regiment,
Little souls who thirst for fight,
These men were born to drill and die.
The unexplained glory flies above them,
Great is the Battle-God, great, and his Kingdom—
A field where a thousand corpses lie.

Do not weep, babe, for war is kind.
Because your father tumbled in the yellow trenches,
Raged at his breast, gulped and died,
Do not weep.
War is kind.

Does the speaker believe in the "virtue of slaughter" and the "excellence of killing"? What makes you think so? ❷

Swift blazing flag of the regiment,
Eagle with crest of red and gold,
These men were born to drill and die.
Point for them the virtue of slaughter,
Make plain to them the excellence of killing
And a field where a thousand corpses lie.

Mother whose heart hung humble as a button
On the bright splendid shroud of your son,
Do not weep.
War is kind. ■

ADDITIONAL QUESTIONS AND ACTIVITIES

Have students locate military bugle, drum, or bagpipe music played to communicate to troops, for example, to warn of a call to action or to signal lights out. Allow them to play recordings of the music or encourage them to recreate the music or rhythms using their own instruments.

LITERARY TECHNIQUE

An **image** is a word or phrase that names something that can be seen, heard, touched, tasted, or smelled. Have students choose the image in "Do not weep, maiden, for war is kind" that they find most affecting and memorable. Ask students to share their chosen images with the class and explain why they selected them.

Responding to the Selection

In what ways is war not kind? Discuss this question with your classmates.

Reviewing the Selection

RECALLING

1. What three people are addressed by the speaker of the poem? What does the speaker say to each of these people?
2. What happens to the lover, the father, and the son?

INTERPRETING

3. Does the speaker mean literally what he says to the three people he addressed? Explain.
4. What emotional effect does the description of what happens to the lover, the father, and the son have on the reader?

SYNTHESIZING

5. This poem is written in mock heroic language. What phrases in the two indented stanzas of the poem suggest that the speaker does not, in fact, believe that war is kind?

Understanding Literature (Questions for Discussion)

1. **Irony. Irony** is a difference between appearance and reality. In **verbal irony,** something is said that implies its opposite. What examples of verbal irony can you find in this poem?
2. **Free Verse. Free verse** is poetry that does not employ traditional patterns of rhyme, rhythm, or stanza form. Free verse tends to sound a lot more like ordinary speech than traditional verse does. What elements in this poem show that it is intended as speech, or one side of an imaginary conversation?

   When writing free verse, poets often invent their own unique structures, or organizational patterns, to replace traditional rhyming stanzas. What is the structure of this poem? Into how many stanzas is it divided? What do stanzas 1, 3, and 5 have in common? What kind of language is being mocked in stanzas 2 and 4? Why might stanzas 2 and 4 be more traditional in their use of poetic devices, such as a regular meter and rhyme, than stanzas 1, 3, and 5?
3. **Parallelism and Alliteration. Parallelism** is a rhetorical technique in which a writer emphasizes the equal value or weight of two or more ideas by expressing them in the same grammatical form. **Alliteration** is the repetition of initial consonant sounds. When writing free verse, poets often make use of devices such as parallelism and alliteration, in place of traditional rhymes, to give their work a poetic quality. What examples of parallelism and alliteration can you find in the poem?

RESPONDING TO THE SELECTION

Record students' suggestions on the board. Ask students to consider the ways war affects those who fight and those who don't. Students might also consider lingering effects of war.

ANSWERS FOR REVIEWING THE SELECTION

RECALLING

1. The speaker addresses the maiden, the babe, and the mother. He assures them that war is kind and tells them not to weep.

2. The lover, the father, and the son are all killed in the war.

INTERPRETING

Responses will vary. Possible responses are given.

3. He cannot really mean that war is kind because it has taken away the people that the maiden, the babe, and the mother love and need.

4. The descriptions shock and sadden the reader.

SYNTHESIZING

Responses will vary. Possible responses are given.

5. The phrases "little souls who thirst for fight," "the virtue of slaughter," "the excellence of killing," and "a field where a thousand corpses lie" evoke feelings of horror, not kindness.

ANSWERS FOR UNDERSTANDING LITERATURE

▶ See the evaluation forms for discussion, active listening, and oral communication, *Assessment Portfolio,* 7.11–7.14.

Responses will vary. Possible responses are given.

1. Irony. "War is kind" is ironic because war is so clearly unkind. Slaughter can never be a virtue, and killing can never be excellent. The son's shroud would not normally be described as "bright splendid."

2. Free Verse. The speaker is addressing real people who would be affected by the deaths described in the poem so it makes sense that the tone would be conversational.

(cont.)

ANSWERS FOR UNDERSTANDING LITERATURE (CONT.)

The poem is divided into 5 stanzas. Stanzas 1, 3, and 5 are addressed to the grieving families of the dead soldiers. Stanzas 2 and 4 mock the high-flown language of those who encourage others to fight and advertise the glory of war. Those stanzas may be more traditional because war is an institution that depends on traditional support systems.

3. Parallelism and Alliteration. Stanzas 1 and 3 begin with "Do not weep, (maiden, babe), for war is kind." Stanzas 1, 3, and 5 all end with the same two lines. Stanzas 2 and 4 share these phrases: "of the regiment," "These men were born to drill and die," and "a field where a thousand corpses lie." Alliteration of ***w*** is used in *weep, war* in stanzas 1, 3, and 5. In stanza 1 *wild* is also alliterative. In stanza 5 alliteration is used in line 1: "**W**hose **h**eart **h**ung **h**umble."

FROM "A HOUSE DIVIDED"

LETTER TO MRS. BIXBY

FROM THE SECOND INAUGURAL ADDRESS

About the Author. A biography of **Abraham Lincoln** appears on page 374.

About the Selections. Lincoln believed that slavery should not be allowed in the territories. He was convinced that the government could not continue to be half slave and half free, an idea expressed in his **"A House Divided"** speech.

Lincoln wrote a letter of condolence to Mrs. Bixby whose five sons were reported to have been killed in battle. Later it was learned that only two had died. Nonetheless, Lincoln's letter eloquently offers condolence and gratitude to a grieving victim of war.

Lincoln's **Second Inaugural Address** reflects upon his first inauguration, at which time the country was trying to avoid war. He also looks ahead to the healing process the country must undergo. The address was delivered on March 4, 1865, little more than a month before Lincoln was assassinated.

QUOTABLES

"To set the stones back in the wall

Lest the divided house should fall

The beams of peace he laid,

While kings looked on afraid."

—John Vance Cheney

from "A House Divided"
by Abraham Lincoln

SPEECH DELIVERED AT SPRINGFIELD, ILLINOIS, AT THE CLOSE OF THE REPUBLICAN STATE CONVENTION. JUNE 16, 1858

If we could first know *where* we are, and *whither* we are tending, we could better judge *what* to do, and *how* to do it.

We are now far into the *fifth* year, since a policy was initiated, with the *avowed* object, and *confident* promise, of putting an end to slavery agitation.

Under the operation of that policy, that agitation has not only, *not ceased*, but has *constantly augmented*.

In my opinion, it *will* not cease, until a *crisis* shall have been reached, and passed—

"A house divided against itself cannot stand."[1]

I believe this government cannot endure, permanently half *slave* and half *free*.

I do not expect the Union to be *dissolved*—I do not expect the house to *fall*—but I *do* expect it will cease to be divided.

It will become *all* one thing, or *all* the other.

Either the *opponents* of slavery, will arrest the further spread of it, and place it where the public mind shall rest in the belief that it is in course of ultimate extinction; or its *advocates* will push it forward, till it shall become alike lawful in *all* the States, *old* as well as *new*—*North* as well as *South*.

Letter to Mrs. Bixby
by Abraham Lincoln

Executive Mansion, Washington,
November 21, 1864

Mrs. Bixby, Boston, Massachusetts:

Dear Madam:

I have been shown in the files of the War Department a statement of the Adjutant-General of Massachusetts that you are the mother of five sons who have died gloriously on the field of battle. I feel how weak and fruitless must be any words of mine which should attempt to beguile you from the grief of a loss so overwhelming. But I cannot refrain from tendering to you the consolation that may be found in the thanks of the Republic they died to save. I pray that our Heavenly Father may assuage the anguish of your bereavement, and leave you only the cherished memory of the loved and lost, and the solemn pride that must be yours to have laid so costly a sacrifice upon the altar of freedom.

Yours very sincerely and respectfully,

Abraham Lincoln

from the Second Inaugural Address
by Abraham Lincoln

On the occasion corresponding to this four years ago, all thoughts were anxiously directed to an impending civil war. All dreaded it—all sought to avert it. While the inaugural address was being delivered from this place, devoted altogether to *saving* the Union without war, insurgent agents were in the city seeking to *destroy* it without war—seeking to dissol[v]e the Union, and divide effects, by negotiation. Both parties deprecated war; but one of them would *make* war rather than let the nation survive; and the other would *accept* war rather than let it perish. And the war came.

One eighth of the whole population were colored slaves, not distributed generally over the Union, but localized in the Southern part of it. These slaves constituted a peculiar and powerful interest. All knew that this interest was, somehow, the cause of the war. To strengthen, perpetuate, and extend this interest was the object for which the insurgents would rend the Union, even by war; while the government claimed no right to do more than to restrict the territorial enlargement of it. Neither party expected for the war, the magnitude, or the duration, which it has already attained. Neither anticipated that the *cause* of the conflict might cease with, or even before, the conflict itself should cease. Each looked for an easier triumph, and a result less fundamental and astounding. Both read the same Bible, and pray to the same God; and each invokes His aid against the other. It may seem strange that any men should dare to ask a just God's assistance in wringing their bread from the sweat of other men's faces; but let us judge not that we be not judged. The prayers of both could not be answered; that

1. **"A house . . . stand."** Biblical reference to Mark 3:25, "If a house be divided against itself, that house cannot stand."

of neither has been answered fully. The Almighty has his own purposes. "Woe unto the world because of offenses! for it must needs be that offenses come; but woe to that man by whom the offense cometh!" If we shall suppose that American Slavery is one of those offenses which, in the providence of God, must needs come, but which, having continued through His appointed time, He now wills to remove, and that He gives to both North and South, this terrible war, as the woe due to those by whom the offense came, shall we discern therein any departure from those divine attributes which the believers in a Living God always ascribe to Him? Fondly do we hope—fervently do we pray—that this mighty scourge of war may speedily pass away. Yet, if God wills that it continue, until all the wealth piled by the bond-man's two hundred and fifty years of unrequited toil[1] shall be sunk, and until every drop of blood drawn with the lash, shall be paid by another drawn with the sword, as was said three thousand years ago, so still it must be said "the judgments of the Lord, are true and righteous altogether."

With malice toward none; with charity for all; with firmness in the right, as God gives us to see the right, let us strive on to finish the work we are in; to bind up the nation's wounds; to care for him who shall have borne the battle, and for his widow, and his orphan—to do all which may achieve and cherish a just and lasting peace, among ourselves, and with all nations.

"Farewell to His Army"
by Robert E. Lee

Headquarters, Army Northern Virginia,
April 10, 1865

After four years of arduous service, marked by unsurpassed courage and fortitude, the Army of Northern Virginia has been compelled to yield to overwhelming numbers and resources. I need not tell the survivors of so many hard-fought battles, who have remained steadfast to the last, that I have consented to this result from no distrust of them; but, feeling that valor and devotion could accomplish nothing that could compensate for the loss that would have attended the continuation of the contest, I have determined to avoid the useless sacrifice of those whose past services have endeared them to their countrymen. By the terms of the agreement, officers and men can return to their homes, and remain there until exchanged.[2]

You will take with you *the satisfaction that proceeds from the consciousness of duty faithfully performed;* and I earnestly pray that a merciful God will extend to you his blessing and protection. With an unceasing admiration of your constancy and devotion to your country, and a grateful remembrance of your kind and generous consideration of myself, I bid you an affectionate farewell.

"O Captain! My Captain!"
by Walt Whitman

O Captain! my Captain! our fearful trip is done,
The ship has weather'd every rack,[3] the prize we sought is won,
The port is near, the bells I hear, the people all exulting,
While follow eyes the steady keel,[4] the vessel grim and daring;
But O heart! heart! heart!
O the bleeding drops of red,
Where on the deck my Captain lies,
Fallen cold and dead.

O Captain! my Captain! rise up and hear the bells;
Rise up—for you the flag is flung—for you the bugle trills,
For you bouquets and ribbon'd wreaths—for you the shores a-crowding,
For you they call, the swaying mass, their eager faces turning;
Here Captain! dear father!
This arm beneath your head!
It is some dream that on the deck,
You've fallen cold and dead.

My Captain does not answer, his lips are pale and still,
My father does not feel my arm, he has no pulse nor will,
The ship is anchor'd safe and sound, its voyage closed and done,
From fearful trip the victor ship comes in with object won;
Exult O shores, and ring O bells!
But I with mournful tread,
Walk the deck my Captain lies,
Fallen cold and dead.

1. **bond-man's . . . toil.** Refers to the period of slavery in which the slaves were not requited or paid for their labor
2. **exchanged.** Discharged from military service
3. **rack.** Upheaval; torment
4. **keel.** Beam along the bottom of a boat that supports the frame

"Farewell to His Army"

About the Author. Robert E. Lee (1807–1870), the Confederacy's greatest soldier, was a lieutenant colonel with the United States Army when his home state, Virginia, joined other Southern states in seceding from the Union. At that time, President Lincoln offered him command of the Union forces. Lee did not favor secession, and had shown his disapproval of slavery by freeing his own slaves years earlier. Yet, to defend his state, he declined Lincoln's offer and joined the Confederate Army instead. As commander of the Army of Northern Virginia from 1862 to the end of the war, he made brilliant use of his limited manpower and supplies. Nevertheless, Union forces were not seriously weakened by the loss of many battles and thousands of men, while Lee's forces dwindled. Named general in chief of all Confederate forces early in 1865, Lee recognized that the South could not win the war. When Union forces surrounded Lee's troops at Appomattox Court House, in Virginia, Lee surrendered to the Union commander, Ulysses S. Grant, on April 9, 1865. After the war, Lee became president of Washington College in Lexington, Virginia. He took a strong stand against the bitterness that continued to divide the nation, working peaceably to restore the South.

About the Selection. In this letter, dated the day after his surrender to Union forces, Lee officially announces his action to his men.

ADDITIONAL RESOURCES

AUDIOCASSETTE

- "Farewell to His Army," Track 14

Additional Questions and Activities

- What "useless sacrifice" does Lee avoid by surrendering?

Answer. Because the North has "overwhelming numbers and resources," Lee is sure that further resistance by his small army would result, inevitably, in the death of all his men.

- Why does Lee stress his appreciation of the courage and devotion of his men?

Answer. He wants his men to know that the surrender was not their fault and not due to any distrust of them on Lee's part.

- How did Lee's men feel toward him? What phrases in the letter suggest their attitude?

Answer: Lee's reference to the men's "kind and generous consideration of myself" suggests that they held him in extremely high regard.

"O Captain! My Captain!"

from "When Lilacs Last in the Dooryard Bloom'd"

About the Author. Walt Whitman (1819–1892) was born on Long Island and grew up in the city of Brooklyn. Although he dropped out of school at age eleven, he became an itinerant country school teacher six years later. From 1841 until 1862, he worked as a printer, journalist, newspaper editor, book store owner, and poet. His first collection of twelve poems, *Leaves of Grass*, was so unusual that he couldn't find a publisher, so he published it himself in 1855. Critics ignored the volume, but Emerson wrote him, "I greet you at the beginning of a great career." Whitman revised and added to *Leaves of Grass* in eight more editions during his life.

During the Civil War, Whitman worked as a government clerk in Washington, DC, volunteered much of his time as a nurse in the military hospitals, and wrote. Fired from one clerkship because a supervisor considered his poetry indecent, he held other government positions until 1873, when he suffered a stroke. He moved to Camden, New Jersey, where he continued to write poetry, essays, and other articles until his death.

Whitman is considered the last great Romantic because of his response to nature, love of the common person, and emphasis on feelings and imagination. Other aspects of his work were later characteristic of Realism, such as a concentration on the commonplace. He developed an original, free verse form to reflect what he saw as a new American literature. His poetic technique had a great influence on many twentieth-century poets.

About the Selections. "O Captain! My Captain!" is probably Whitman's most popular poem, but its use of formal patterns of rhyme and rhythm is not characteristic of his style. Like **"When Lilacs Last in the Dooryard Bloom'd,"** "O Captain! My Captain!" reflects on Abraham Lincoln's death.

(cont.)

from "When Lilacs Last in the Dooryard Bloom'd" by Walt Whitman

1

When lilacs last in the dooryard bloom'd,
And the great star[1] early droop'd in the western sky in the night,
I mourn'd, and yet shall mourn with ever-returning spring.
Ever-returning spring, trinity sure to me you bring,
5 Lilac blooming perennial and drooping star in the west,
And thought of him I love.

2

O powerful western fallen star!
O shades of night—O moody, tearful night!
O great star disappear'd—O the black murk that hides the star!
10 O cruel hands that hold me powerless—O helpless soul of me!
O harsh surrounding cloud that will not free my soul.

6

Coffin that passes through lanes and streets,
Through day and night with the great cloud darkening the land,
35 With the pomp of the inloop'd flags with the cities draped in black,
With the show of the States themselves as of crape-veil'd women standing,
With processions long and winding and the flambeaus[2] of the night,
With the countless torches lit, with the silent sea of faces and the unbared heads,
With the waiting depot, the arriving coffin, and the sombre faces,
40 With dirges through the night, with the thousand voices rising strong and solemn,
With all the mournful voices of the dirges pour'd around the coffin,
The dim-lit churches and the shuddering organs—where amid these you journey,
With the tolling tolling bells' perpetual clang,
Here, coffin that slowly passes,
45 I give you my sprig of lilac.

7

(Nor for you, for one alone,
Blossoms and branches green to coffins all I bring,
For fresh as the morning, thus would I chant a song for you O sane and sacred death.

All over bouquets of roses,
50 O death, I cover you over with roses and early lilies,
But mostly and now the lilac that blooms the first,
Copious I break, I break the sprigs from the bushes,
With loaded arms I come, pouring for you,
For you and the coffins all of you O death.)

from *Up From Slavery* by Booker T. Washington

After the coming of freedom there were two points upon which practically all the people on our place were agreed, and I find that this was generally true throughout the South: that they must change their names, and that they must leave the old plantation for at least a few days or weeks in order that they might really feel sure that they were free.

In some way a feeling got among the colored people that it was far from proper for them to bear the surname of their former owners, and a great many of them took other surnames. This was one of the first signs of freedom. When they were slaves, a colored person was simply called "John" or "Susan." There was seldom occasion for more than the use of one name. If "John" or "Susan" belonged to a white man by the name of "Hatcher," sometimes he was called "John Hatcher," or as often "Hatcher's John." But there was a feeling that "John Hatcher" or "Hatcher's John" was not the proper title by which to denote a freeman; and so in many cases "John Hatcher" was changed to "John S. Lincoln" or "John S. Sherman," the initial "S" standing for no name, it being simply a part of what the colored man proudly called his "entitles."[3]

As I have stated, most of the colored people left the old plantation for a short while at least, so as to be sure, it seemed, that they could leave and try their freedom on to see how it felt. After they had remained away for a time, many of the older slaves, especially, returned to their old homes and made some kind of contract with their former owners by which they remained on the estate.

My mother's husband, who was the stepfather of my brother John and myself, did not belong to the same owners as did my mother. In fact, he seldom came to our plantation. I remember seeing him there perhaps once a

1. **great star.** Refers to Venus but comes to be associated with Lincoln
2. **flambeaus.** Torches
3. **entitles.** That to which one has a right; also implies giving a title or name to oneself

from "When Lilacs Last in the Dooryard Bloom'd" (cont.)

President Abraham Lincoln was shot on April 14, 1865, barely a week after the end of the Civil War, and died early the next morning. A week later, on April 21, a funeral train began its journey with his coffin from Washington, DC, to his hometown of Springfield, Illinois. The train made numerous stops along the way so that the grief-stricken people could show their respects. Walt Whitman had seen the president frequently on the streets of Washington, DC, and noted at the time, "We have got so that we exchange bows." He was home in Brooklyn, at lilac time, when he heard the news of the assassination. During the next few months, he wrote "When Lilacs Last in the Dooryard Boom'd" in tribute to the slain president, and he published it that fall. "When Lilacs Last in the Courtyard Bloom'd" tells not only

(cont.)

year, that being about Christmas time. In some way, during the war, by running away and following the Federal soldiers, it seems, he found his way into the new state of West Virginia.[1] As soon as freedom was declared, he sent for my mother to come to the Kanawha Valley, in West Virginia. At that time a journey from Virginia over the mountains to West Virginia was rather a tedious and in some cases a painful undertaking. What little clothing and few household goods we had were placed in a cart, but the children walked the greater portion of the distance, which was several hundred miles.

I do not think any of us had been very far from the plantation, and the taking of a long journey into another state was quite an event. The parting from our former owners and the members of our own race on the plantation was a serious occasion. From the time of our parting till their death we kept up a correspondence with the older members of the family, and in later years we have kept in touch with those who were the younger members. We were several weeks making the trip, and most of the time we slept in the open air and did our cooking over a log fire out of doors. One night I recall that we camped near an abandoned log cabin, and my mother decided to build a fire in that for cooking, and afterward to make a "pallet"[2] on the floor for our sleeping. Just as the fire had gotten well started a large black snake fully a yard and a half long dropped down the chimney and ran out on the floor. Of course we at once abandoned that cabin. Finally we reached our destination—a little town called Malden, which is about five miles from Charleston, the present capital of the state.

At that time salt-mining was the great industry in that part of West Virginia, and the little town of Malden was right in the middle of the salt-furnaces. My stepfather had already secured a job at a salt-furnace, and he had also secured a little cabin for us to live in. Our new house was no better than the one we had left on the old plantation in Virginia. In fact, in one respect it was worse. Notwithstanding the poor condition of our plantation cabin, we were at all times sure of pure air. Our new home was in the midst of a cluster of cabins crowded closely together, and as there were no sanitary regulations, the filth about the cabins was often intolerable. Some of our neighbors were colored people, and some were the poorest and most ignorant and degraded white people. It was a motley mixture. Drinking, gambling, quarrels, fights, and shockingly immoral practices were frequent. All who lived in the little town were in one way or another connected with the salt business. Though I was a mere child, my stepfather put me and my brother at work in one of the furnaces. Often I began work as early as four o'clock in the morning.

The first thing I ever learned in the way of book knowledge was while working in this salt-furnace. Each salt-packer had his barrels marked with a certain number. The number allotted to my stepfather was "18." At the close of the day's work the boss of the packers would come around and put "18" on each of our barrels, and I soon learned to recognize that figure wherever I saw it, and after a while got to the point where I could make that figure, though I knew nothing about any other figures or letters.

From the time that I can remember having any thoughts about anything, I recall that I had an intense longing to learn to read. I determined, when quite a small child, that, if I accomplished nothing else in life, I would in some way get enough education to enable me to read common books and newspapers. Soon after we got settled in some manner in our new cabin in West Virginia, I induced my mother to get hold of a book for me. How or where she got it I do not know, but in some way she procured an old copy of Webster's "blue-back" spelling-book, which contained the alphabet, followed by such meaningless words as "ab," "ba," "ca," "da." I began at once to devour this book, and I think that it was the first one I ever had in my hands. I had learned from somebody that the way to begin to read was to learn the alphabet, so I tried in all the ways I could think of to learn it—all of course without a teacher, for I could find no one to teach me. At that time there was not a single member of my race anywhere near us who could read, and I was too timid to approach any of the white people. In some way, within a few weeks, I mastered the greater portion of the alphabet. In all my efforts to learn to read my mother shared fully my ambition, and sympathized with me and aided me in every way that she could. Though she was totally ignorant, so far as mere book knowledge was concerned, she had high ambitions for her children, and a large fund of good, hard, common sense which seemed to enable her to meet and master every situation. If I have done anything in life worth attention, I feel sure that I inherited the disposition from my mother.

In the midst of my struggles and longing for an education, a young colored boy who had learned to read in the state of Ohio came to Malden. As soon as the colored people found out that he could read, a newspaper was secured, and at the close of nearly every day's work this young man would be surrounded by a group of men and women who were anxious to hear him read the news contained in the papers. How I used to envy this man! He seemed to me to be the one young man in all the world who ought to be satisfied with his attainments.

About this time the question of having some kind of a school opened for the colored children in the village began to be discussed by members of the race. As it would be the first school for Negro children that had

1. **new state of West Virginia.** West Virginia became a state in 1863.

2. **pallet.** Small bed or a pad filled with straw and used directly on the floor

Additional Questions and Activities

• In section 1 of "When Lilacs Last in the Dooryard Boom'd," what three things does the speaker connect as a "trinity"? In what way are they linked?
Answers. He links the lilac in bloom, a star low in the west, and "thought of him I love"—President Lincoln. All three things came to the speaker in the spring.

• In section 2, what does the western star symbolize? In what way is the star like what it stands for?
Answers. The star symbolizes Lincoln. Like Lincoln, the speaker says, the star is powerful but now fallen; it is from the west (Lincoln was from Illinois, in the western half of the United States of that era); and it has disappeared.

• What event is described in section 6?
Answer. The section describes how people mourned in each town where the train carrying Lincoln's coffin stopped.

• According to section 7, for whom does the speaker mourn?
Answer. He states that he brings his symbols of mourning not only to Lincoln but to all the dead—probably with special regard for all those killed in the Civil War.

Literary Technique

Explain that **repetition** is the use, again, of a sound, word, phrase, sentence or other element, and that it was a favorite technique of Whitman. Have students examine section 6 to find answers to these questions:

• How many times are these words repeated: *coffin, with, dirges, voices, tolling*?

• Which phrases combine two or more of the repeated words?
Answers. Repetitions: *coffin*—4, *with*—12, *dirges*—2, *voices*—2, *tolling*—2. One sample phrase combining repeated words is "With all the mournful voices of the dirges pour'd around the coffin."

From "When Lilacs Last in the Dooryard Bloom'd" (cont.)

of the president and the country's grief at his death, but also of the process the poet experienced in turning his emotional response into poetry. Among the many poems written on the death of Abraham Lincoln, this poem is considered the best.

FROM *UP FROM SLAVERY*

About the Author. Booker T. Washington (*circa* 1856–1915), whose birth date is uncertain (he chose April 5, 1856), was born to a mother who was a slave in Hale's Ford, Virginia. The identity of his father, a white man, is unknown. Like most slaves, Booker had only a first name; when he attended school he adopted his stepfather's first name as his last name. At the end of the Civil War he went with his mother to Malden, West Virginia, to join his stepfather, who was working in a salt furnace there. While attending makeshift schools in odd hours, he worked as a salt packer, coal miner, and houseboy. Filled with the desire to learn to read and write, he earned his way through Hampton Normal and Agricultural Institute in Virginia by working as a janitor. He graduated with honors and a certificate to teach trade school and, in 1881, became first principal of what is now Tuskegee Institute. He became a national figure as a result of a short address, Chapter 14 of *Up from Slavery*, at the Atlanta Exposition of 1895. The address seemed to offer up black rights for low-income opportunity and nonviolent relations with whites. Known as the "Moses of his Race," he received an honorary degree from Harvard University, was invited to dine with President Theodore Roosevelt, and advised politicians and business leaders—a major power broker of his time.

About the Selection. ***Up from Slavery*** first appeared in weekly serials in the magazine *Outlook* from November 3, 1900, to February 23, 1901, and was published in book form in March 1901, when Booker T. Washington was forty-five years old. It is actually Washington's second autobiography, the first being *The Story of My Life and Work*. Washington had entrusted much of the writing of that earlier book to a ghostwriter and was reportedly disappointed with the result. He became much more involved with his second autobiography. Although he worked with a ghostwriter again, this time the

(cont.)

ever been opened in that part of Virginia, it was, of course, to be a great event, and the discussion excited the widest interest. The most perplexing question was where to find a teacher. The young man from Ohio who had learned to read the papers was considered, but his age was against him. In the midst of the discussion about a teacher, another young colored man from Ohio, who had been a soldier, in some way found his way into town. It was soon learned that he possessed considerable education, and he was engaged by the colored people to teach their first school. As yet no free schools[1] had been started for colored people in that section, hence each family agreed to pay a certain amount per month, with the understanding that the teacher was to "board 'round"—that is, spend a day with each family. This was not bad for the teacher, for each family tried to provide the very best on the day the teacher was to be its guest. I recall that I looked forward with an anxious appetite to the "teacher's day" at our little cabin.

This experience of a whole race beginning to go to school for the first time, presents one of the most interesting studies that has ever occurred in connection with the development of any race. Few people who were not right in the midst of the scenes can form any exact idea of the intense desire which the people of my race showed for an education. As I have stated, it was a whole race trying to go to school. Few were too young, and none too old, to make the attempt to learn. As fast as any kind of teachers could be secured, not only were day-schools filled, but night-schools as well. The great ambition of the older people was to try to learn to read the Bible before they died. With this end in view, men and women who were fifty or seventy-five years old would often be found in the night-school. Sunday-schools were formed soon after freedom, but the principal book studied in the Sunday- school was the spelling-book. Day-school, night-school, Sunday-school, were always crowded, and often many had to be turned away for want of room.

The opening of the school in the Kanawha Valley, however, brought to me one of the keenest disappointments that I ever experienced. I had been working in a salt-furnace for several months, and my stepfather had discovered that I had a financial value, and so, when the school opened, he decided that he could not spare me from my work. This decision seemed to cloud my every ambition. The disappointment was made all the more severe by reason of the fact that my place of work was where I could see the happy children passing to and from school, mornings and afternoons. Despite this disappointment, however, I determined that I would learn something, anyway. I applied myself with greater earnestness than ever to the mastering of what was in the "blue-back" speller.

My mother sympathized with me in my disappointment, and sought to comfort me in all the ways she could, and to help me find a way to learn. After a while I succeeded in making arrangements with the teacher to give me some lessons at night, after the day's work was done. These night lessons were so welcome that I think I learned more at night than the other children did during the day. My own experiences in the night-school gave me faith in the night-school idea, with which, in after years, I had to do both at Hampton and Tuskegee. But my boyish heart was still set upon going to the day-school, and I let no opportunity slip to push my ease. Finally I won, and was permitted to go to the school in the day for a few months, with the understanding that I was to rise early in the morning and work in the furnace till nine o'clock, and return immediately after school closed in the afternoon for at least two more hours of work.

The schoolhouse was some distance from the furnace, and as I had to work till nine o'clock, and the school opened at nine, I found myself in a difficulty. School would always be begun before I reached it, and sometimes my class had recited. To get around this difficulty I yielded to a temptation for which most people, I suppose, will condemn me; but since it is a fact, I might as well state it. I have great faith in the power and influence of facts. It is seldom that anything is permanently gained by holding back a fact. There was a large clock in a little office in the furnace. This clock, of course, all the hundred or more workmen depended upon to regulate their hours of beginning and ending the day's work. I got the idea that the way for me to reach school on time was to move the clock hands from half-past eight up to the nine o'clock mark. This I found myself doing morning after morning till the furnace "boss" discovered that something was wrong, and locked the clock in a case. I did not mean to inconvenience any body. I simply meant to reach that schoolhouse in time.

When, however, I found myself at the school for the first time, I also found myself confronted with two other difficulties. In the first place, I found that all of the other children wore hats or caps on their heads, and I had neither hat nor cap. In fact, I do not remember that up to the time of going to school I had ever worn any kind of covering upon my head, nor do I recall that either I or anybody else had even thought anything about the need of covering for my head. But, of course, when I saw how all the other boys were dressed, I began to feel quite uncomfortable. As usual, I put the case before my mother, and she explained to me that she had no money with which to buy a "store hat," which was a rather new institution at that time among the members of my race and was considered quite the thing for young and old to own, but that she would find a way to help me out of the difficulty. She accordingly got two pieces of "homespun"[2]

1. **free schools.** Schools set up and supervised by the Freedmen's Bureau, an agency set up after the Civil War to aid African Americans in transition from slavery to freedom
2. **homespun.** Coarse, loosely woven cloth spun at home

FROM *UP FROM SLAVERY* (CONT.)

writer merely transcribed Washington's words; the ideas, organization, style, and message were Washington's own. *Up from Slavery* focuses on the personal experiences that shaped Washington's life as well as the convictions that grew out of those experiences. Washington described his goals for the book in this way: "My general plan is to give the first place to facts and incidents and to hang the generalizations on to these facts—taking for granted that the average reader is more interested in an interesting fact than in a generalization based on that fact, and for this reason I have sought not to use too many generalizations and when they are used to have them well sugar-coated with some interesting incident."

and sewed them together, and I was soon the proud possessor of my first cap.

The lesson that my mother taught me in this has always remained with me, and I have tried as best I could to teach it to others. I have always felt proud, whenever I think of the incident, that my mother had strength of character enough not to be led into the temptation of seeming to be that which she was not—of trying to impress my schoolmates and others with the fact that she was able to buy me a "store hat" when she was not. I have always felt proud that she refused to go into debt for that which she did not have the money to pay for. Since that time I have owned many kinds of caps and hats, but never one of which I have felt so proud as of the cap made of the two pieces of cloth sewed together by my mother. I have noted the fact, but without satisfaction, I need not add, that several of the boys who began their careers with "store hats" and who were my schoolmates and used to join in the sport that was made of me because I had only a "homespun" cap, have ended their careers in the penitentiary, while others are not able now buy any kind of hat.

My second difficulty was with regard to my name, or rather *a* name. From the time when I could remember anything, I had been called simply "Booker." Before going to school it had never occurred to me that it was needful or appropriate to have an additional name. When I heard the school-roll called, I noticed that all of the children had at least two names, and some of them indulged in what seemed to me the extravagance of having three. I was in deep perplexity, because I knew that the teacher would demand of me at least two names, and I had only one. By the time the occasion came for the enrolling of my name, an idea occurred to me which I thought would make me equal to the situation; and so, when the teacher asked me what my full name was, I calmly told him "Booker Washington,"[1] as if I had been called by that name all my life; and by that name I have since been known. Later in life I found that my mother had given me the name of "Booker Taliaferro" soon after I was born, but in some way that part of my name seemed to disappear, and for a long while was forgotten, but as soon as I found out about it I revived it, and made my full name "Booker Taliaferro Washington." I think there are not many men in our country who have had the privilege of naming themselves in the way that I have.

More than once I have tried to picture myself in the position of a boy or man with an honored and distinguished ancestry which I could trace back through a period of hundreds of years, and who had not only inherited a name, but fortune and a proud family homestead; and yet I have sometimes had the feeling that if I had inherited these, and had been a member of a more popular race, I should have been inclined to yield to the temptation of depending upon my ancestry and my color to do that for me which I should do for myself. Years ago I resolved that because I had no ancestry myself I would leave a record of which my children would be proud, and which might encourage them to still higher effort.

The world should not pass judgment upon the Negro, and especially the Negro youth, too quickly or too harshly. The Negro boy has obstacles, discouragements, and temptations to battle with that are little known to those not situated as he is. When a white boy undertakes a task, it is taken for granted that he will succeed. On the other hand, people are usually surprised if the Negro boy does not fail. In a word, the Negro youth starts out with the presumption against him.

The influence of ancestry, however, is important in helping forward any individual or race, if too much reliance is not placed upon it. Those who constantly direct attention to the Negro youth's moral weaknesses, and compare his advancement with that of white youths, do not consider the influence of the memories which cling about the old family homesteads. I have no idea, as I have stated elsewhere, who my grandmother was. I have, or have had, uncles and aunts and cousins, but I have no knowledge as to what most of them are. My case will illustrate that of hundreds of thousands of black people in every part of our country. The very fact that the white boy is conscious that, if he fails in life, he will disgrace the whole family record, extending back through many generations, is of tremendous value in helping him to resist temptations. The fact that the individual has behind and surrounding him proud family history and connection serves as a stimulus to help him to overcome obstacles when striving for success.

The time that I was permitted to attend school during the day was short, and my attendance was irregular. It was not long before I had to stop attending day-school altogether, and devote all of my time again to work. I resorted to the night-school again. In fact, the greater part of the education I secured in my boyhood was gathered through the night-school after my day's work was done. I had difficulty often in securing a satisfactory teacher. Sometimes, after I had secured some one to teach me at night, I would find, much to my disappointment, that the teacher knew but little more than I did. Often I would have to walk several miles at night in order to recite my night-school lessons. There was never a time in my youth, no matter how dark and discouraging the days might be, when one resolve did not continually remain with me, and that was a determination to secure an education at any cost.

Soon after we moved to West Virginia, my mother adopted into our family, notwithstanding our poverty, an orphan boy, to whom afterward we gave the name of James B. Washington. He has ever since remained a member of the family.

1. **Booker Washington.** Washington was his stepfather's first name.

Additional Questions and Activities

• Where did Booker and his family move after freedom was declared?

Answer. Booker and his family moved to West Virginia after freedom was declared.

• When Washington thinks of what he wanted as a child, he remembers a longing to learn how to do one thing. What was that thing? Why was the entire African-American community intent on becoming educated?

Answers. Washington was very interested in learning to read. The African-American community had not had a chance to receive an education. Now that there was the opportunity to learn to read, all ages wished to learn.

• How did the family's financial situation affect Booker's education? How did his difficulties in attending school affect his attitude toward the importance of education?

Answers. Booker was unable to attend school because he had to work, but he was intent on getting an education and studied dilligently on his own and with a teacher at night.

FROM *AN APPEAL IN FAVOR OF THAT CLASS OF AMERICANS CALLED AFRICANS*

About the Author. Lydia Maria Child (1802–1880) was born in Medford, Massachusetts, and at eighteen became a teacher. At twenty-two, she wrote her first novel, *Hobomok*, which gained immediate success. A second novel and a succession of books on home management and history, primarily biographies of women, quickly made her one of the most popular female authors in the United States. In 1826, she founded the first children's magazine in America, *Juvenile Miscellany*. In 1828, she married David Child, a Boston lawyer and abolitionist, and the couple's friendship with William Lloyd Garrison caused Child to take up the abolitionist cause. In 1833, she wrote the first antislavery volume published in the United States, *An Appeal in Favor of That Class of Americans Called Africans*. Widely read and almost as widely attacked, the work caused an immediate and thirty-year-long boycott of her writings in the South, bringing an end to *Juvenile Miscellany* in 1834. Until emancipation, Child was a major spokesperson for abolition, producing numerous pamphlets and books and countless letters to individuals, lawmaking bodies, and newspapers. From 1841 to 1843, she was editor of a weekly newspaper, the *National Anti-Slavery Standard*. When the abolitionist cause was finally won, she fought for just treatment of Native Americans, for equal rights for African Americans, and for women's suffrage.

About the Selection. About 1830, Lydia Maria Child was honored with an invitation to use the private library of the Boston Athenaeum; she was only the second woman to receive this privilege. She used the library's resources to research the history of slavery in America and to find proof against excuses for racial discrimination in the accomplishments of African nations and the lives of successful African Americans. When ***An Appeal*** was published, she sent the Athenaeum a copy. Antiabolitionist feeling was so

(cont.)

After I had worked in the salt-furnace for some time, work was secured for me in a coal mine which was operated mainly for the purpose of securing fuel for the salt-furnace. Work in the coal mine I always dreaded. One reason for this was that any one who worked in a coal mine was always unclean, at least while at work, and it was a very hard job to get one's skin clean after the day's work was over. Then it was fully a mile from the opening of the coal mine to the face of the coal, and all, of course, was in the blackest darkness. I do not believe that one ever experiences anywhere else such darkness as he does in a coal mine. The mine was divided into a large number of different "rooms" or departments, and, as I never was able to learn the location of all these "rooms," I many times found myself lost in the mine. To add to the horror of being lost, sometimes my light would go out, and then, if I did not happen to have a match, I would wander about in the darkness until by chance I found some one to give me a light. The work was not only hard, but it was dangerous. There was always the danger of being blown to pieces by a premature explosion of powder, or of being crushed by falling slate.[1] Accidents from one or the other of these causes were frequently occurring, and this kept me in constant fear. Many children of the tenderest years were compelled then, as is now true I fear, in most coal mining districts, to spend a large part of their lives in these coal mines, with little opportunity to get an education; and, what is worse, I have often noted that, as a rule, young boys who begin life in a coal mine are often physically and mentally dwarfed. They soon lose ambition to do anything else than to continue as a coal miner.

In those days, and later as a young man, I used to try to picture in my imagination the feelings and ambitions of a white boy with absolutely no limit placed upon his aspirations and activities. I used to envy the white boy who had no obstacles placed in the way of his becoming a Congressman, Governor, Bishop, or President by reason of the accident of his birth or race. I used to picture the way that I would act under such circumstances; how I would begin at the bottom and keep rising until I reached the highest round of success.

In later years, I confess that I do not envy the white boy as I once did. I have learned that success is to be measured not so much by the position that one has reached in life as by the obstacles which he has overcome while trying to succeed. Looked at from this standpoint, I almost reach the conclusion that often the Negro boy's birth and connection with an unpopular race is an advantage, so far as real life is concerned. With few exceptions, the Negro youth must work harder and must perform his task even better than a white youth in order to secure recognition. But out of the hard and unusual struggle which he is compelled to pass, he gets a strength, a confidence, that one misses whose pathway is comparatively smooth by reason of birth and race.

From any point of view, I had rather be what I am, a member of the Negro race, than be able to claim membership with the most favored of any other race. I have always been made sad when I have heard members of any race claiming rights and privileges, or certain badges of distinction, on the ground simply that they were members of this or that race, regardless of their own individual worth or attainments. I have been made to feel sad for such persons because I am conscious of the fact that mere connection with what is known as a superior race will not permanently carry an individual forward unless he has individual worth, and mere connection with what is regarded as an inferior race will not finally hold an individual back if he possesses intrinsic, individual merit. Every persecuted individual and race should get much consolation out of the great human law, which is universal and eternal, that merit, no matter under what skin found, is in the long run, recognized and rewarded. This I have said here, not to call attention to myself as an individual, but to the race to which I am proud to belong.

ABOLITIONIST VOICES

from *An Appeal in Favor of That Class of Americans Called Africans*
by Lydia Maria Child

We first debase the nature of man by making him a slave, and then very coolly tell him that he must always remain a slave because he does not know how to use freedom. We first crush people to the earth, and then claim the right of trampling on them forever, because they are prostrate. Truly, human selfishness never invented a rule which worked out so charmingly both ways!

from *Freedom Journal* March 16, 1827
by John B. Russwurm

Education being an object of the highest importance to the welfare of society, we shall endeavor to present just and adequate views of it, and to urge upon our brethren the necessity and expediency of training their children . . . It is surely time that we should awake from this lethargy of years, and make a concentrated effort for the education of our youth. We form a spoke in the human wheel, and it is necessary that we should understand our dependence on the different parts, and their on us, in order to perform our part with propriety.

1. **slate.** Hard, fine-grained rock

FROM *AN APPEAL IN FAVOR OF THAT CLASS OF AMERICANS CALLED AFRICANS* (CONT.)

strong, even in Boston, that she was promptly asked not to return to the library. However, the book's powerful arguments won many to abolitionism, including William Ellery Channing and Wendell Phillips, who took leading roles in the cause.

FROM *FREEDOM JOURNAL* MARCH 16, 1827

About the Author. John B. Russwurm (1799–1851) was born in Jamaica, but moved to Canada and then to Maine. At twenty, Russwurm moved to Boston to teach. When he found a college that would accept him, he entered Bowdoin College in Brunswick, Maine. In the fall of 1826, he became the second African American to graduate from college. He then moved to New York to join the struggle for emancipation and

(cont.)

The interesting fact that there are *five hundred thousand* free persons of color, one half of whom might peruse, and the whole benefitted by the publication of the Journal; that no publication, as yet, has been devoted exclusively to their improvement—that many selections from approved standard authors, which are within the reach of few, may occasionally be made—and more important still, that this large body of our citizens have no public channel—all serve to prove the real necessity, at present, for the appearance of the FREEDOM'S JOURNAL.

from Editorial in *The Liberator*, January 1, 1831
by William Lloyd Garrison

I am aware that many object to the severity of my language, but is there not cause for severity? I will be harsh as truth, and as uncompromising as justice. On this subject, I do not wish to think, or speak, or write, with moderation. No! No! Tell a man whose house in on fire to sound a moderate alarm . . . but urge me not to use moderation in cause like the present . . .

I am in earnest—I will not equivocate—I will not excuse—I will not retreat a single inch—AND I WILL BE HEARD.

from "Appeal to the Christian Women of the Southern States"
by Angelina Grimké

Man, who was created in the image of his Maker, never can properly be termed a thing, though the laws of the Slave States do call him a "chattel personal"[1]; Man, I assert, never was put under the feet of men by the first charter of human rights which was given by God . . . It has been justly remarked that "God never made a slave," he made man upright, his back was not made to carry burdens, nor his neck to wear a yoke, and the man must be crushed within him, before his back can be fitted to the burden of perpetual slavery; and that his back is not fitted to it, is manifest by the insurrections that so often disturb the peace and security of slaveholding countries . . . Slavery always has, and always will produce insurrections wherever it exists, because it is a violation of the natural order of things, and no human power can much longer perpetuate it.

from *Slavery*
by William Ellery Channing

I come now to what is to my own mind the great argument against seizing and using a man as property. He cannot be property in the sight of God and justice, because his a Rational, Moral, Immortal Being; because created in God's image, and therefore in the highest sense his child; because created to unfold godlike faculties, and to govern himself by a Divine Law written on his heart, and republished in God's Word. His whole nature forbids that he should be seized as property. From his very nature it follows, that so to seize him is to offer an insult to his Maker, and to inflict aggravated social wrong. . . .

No man, who seriously considers what human nature is, and what it was made for, can think of setting up a claim to a fellow-creature. What! own a spiritual being, a being made to know and adore God, and who is to outlive the sun and stars? What! chain to our lowest uses a being made for truth and virtue? convert into a brute instrument that intelligent nature, on which the idea of Duty has dawned, and which is a nobler type of God than all outward creation! Should we not deem it a wrong which no punishment could expiate, were one of our children seized as property, and driven by the ship to toil? And shall God's child, dearer to him than an only son to a human parent, be thus degraded?

from Argument before the Supreme Court in the Case of Wharton Jones v. John Vanzandt, 1846
by Salmon P. Chase

The law of the Creator, which invests every human being with an inalienable title to freedom, cannot be repealed by any inferior law, which asserts that man is property. Such a law may be enforced by power; but the exercise of the power must be confined within the jurisdiction of the state, which establishes the law. It cannot be enforced—it can have no operation whatever—in any other jurisdiction. The very moment a slave passes beyond the jurisdiction of the state, in which he is held as such, he ceases to be a slave; not because any law or regulation of the state which he enters confers freedom upon him, but because he continues to be a man and leaves behind him the law of force, which made him a slave.

1. **chattel personal.** Movable item of personal property

FROM *FREEDOM JOURNAL* MARCH 16, 1827 (CONT.)

equal rights. Within months he was asked to co-edit a weekly newspaper, *Freedom Journal*, the first newspaper in the United States owned and published by African Americans. Russwurm soon lost hope of seeing an end to slavery in America. In 1829, he resigned from *Freedom Journal* and joined the movement to establish colonies of free African Americans in western Africa. He migrated to the colony of Liberia, where he held various administrative posts, and then, in 1836, to the nearby Maryland Colony, to become governor. He served there until his death in 1851.

About the Selection. The article from which the excerpt comes appeared in the first edition of ***Freedom Journal***, wherein Russwurm and his co-editor, Samuel Cornish, discussed the role of the publication.

FROM EDITORIAL IN *THE LIBERATOR*, JANUARY 1, 1831

About the Author. William Lloyd Garrison (1805–1879) was born and raised in Massachusetts, where he became a printer's apprentice at age thirteen and was editor of a Boston pro-temperance journal at twenty-two. In 1828, he met Benjamin Lundy, a Quaker antislavery advocate, and took up his cause. Unlike other abolitionists of the time, who believed in gradual emancipation, Garrison demanded an immediate end to slavery. Because of his attacks on slave trading, he was convicted of libel in 1830 and spent seven weeks in jail. From 1831 until passage of the Thirteenth Amendment, ending slavery, in 1865, he edited *The Liberator*, an aggressive antislavery paper with an influence far wider than its paid circulation. Around 1832 he founded the New England Anti-Slavery Society in Boston and the American Anti-Slavery Society in Philadelphia. His antislavery writing, speeches, and organizing caused his life to be threatened by a Boston mob during a riot against abolitionists in 1835. Garrison insisted on abolition as a

(cont.)

FROM EDITORIAL IN *THE LIBERATOR*, JANUARY 1, 1831 (CONT.)

moral cause, rejecting political action, but eventually approved of Abraham Lincoln and accepted the Civil War as necessary. At the end of the war, he took up the causes of women's suffrage, prohibition, and rights of Native Americans.

About the Selection. The circulation of *The Liberator* never went above three thousand subscribers (mostly free African Americans), but its effect was far-reaching. Many blamed it, at least in part, for the Nat Turner uprising in August 1831, and Southern states outlawed circulation of the paper and tried to prosecute its editor.

VOCABULARY DEVELOPMENT EXERCISES

▶ Give students the following exercise.

Read the Language Arts Survey, 2.153, "Connotation and Denotation." For each of the vocabulary words on page 412, write the word, and next to the word, identify its connotation as either positive, negative, or neutral. Then write a word that has a similar denotation but a different connotation, and identify the connotation of this word.

Example.

work—neutral
toil—negative

ADDITIONAL RESOURCES

ASSESSMENT PORTFOLIO

- Vocabulary Worksheet, 4.6.11
- Study Guide: Unit 6 Test, 4.6.12
- Unit 6 Test, 4.6.13

ESSENTIAL SKILLS PRACTICE BOOKS

Writing

- Choosing a Purpose or Aim, 1.6
- Sensory Detail Charts, 1.8

Language

- Achieving Parallelism, 2.57
- Adding Appositives and Appositive Phrases, 2.48
- Dialects of English, 2.150
- Transitive and Intransitive Verbs, 2.15
- Usage Problems I, II, and III, 2.90–2.92

Speaking and Listening

- Elements of Verbal Communication, 3.2

Study and Research

- Memorizing, 4.4
- Strategies for Taking Essay Tests, 4.45–4.47

UNIT REVIEW

Slavery and the Civil War

VOCABULARY FROM THE SELECTIONS

acclivity, 382
aspirated, 386
consecrate, 376
convulsive, 392
diligently, 366
efface, 384
embrasure, 382
furtive, 397
gesticulate, 385, 395
imprecation, 393
incessant, 392
indolent, 397
ludicrous, 384
malign, 388
obdurate, 367
obliterate, 393
oscillation, 384
provisional, 396
rapturous, 366
score, 376
sentinel, 381
stolidity, 393

LITERARY TERMS

alliteration, 403
allusion, 373
antithesis, 378
climax, 390
flashback, 389
free verse, 403
irony, 403
metaphor, 400
Naturalism, 389, 400
parallelism, 378, 403
psychological fiction, 389, 400
refrain, 373
simile, 400
spiritual, 361, 373
stereotype, 369
syntax, 378
theme, 373, 400
thesis, 369
tone, 369

SYNTHESIS: QUESTIONS FOR WRITING, RESEARCH, OR DISCUSSION

GENRE STUDIES

1. **Speeches.** A good speech is written in simple, direct language that appeals to the emotions and interests of its audience. With these criteria in mind, answer the following question: What qualities make The Gettysburg Address, "A House Divided," Lincoln's Second Inaugural Address, and Lee's Farewell Address excellent speeches? Why are these speeches so often remembered and quoted?
2. **Spirituals.** Many spirituals were ambiguous. Explain what ambiguity is. Then explain how and why ambiguity was used in spirituals such as "Swing Low, Sweet Chariot" in this unit and "Follow the Drinking Gourd" in Unit 1.

THEMATIC STUDIES

3. **Naturalism.** Naturalism is the philosophical belief that people's actions, thoughts, feelings, and values result not from the free action of the will but rather are caused, or determined, by external forces or by heredity. What makes Ambrose Bierce's "An Occurrence at Owl Creek Bridge" and Stephen Crane's "A Mystery of Heroism" examples of Naturalism?

HISTORICAL/BIOGRAPHICAL STUDIES

4. **Abraham Lincoln.** Study the selections by Lincoln in this unit, the quotations from Lincoln on the "Echoes" page at the end of the unit introduction, and the two poems about Lincoln by Whitman ("O Captain! My Captain" and "When Lilacs Last in the Dooryard Bloom'd"). What sort of person do you think Lincoln was, based on these materials? What were his concerns, both moral and political? Why is Lincoln so greatly revered today?
5. **Slavery and Its Aftermath.** Based on the unit introduction, the selection from Douglass's *Narrative*, and the spiritual "Swing Low, Sweet Chariot," answer the following questions: What was the institution of slavery like for the enslaved? What hardships did it impose? How did enslaved people feel about the institution of slavery? Why was it important for ex-slaves to become educated? What difficulties did ex-slaves encounter?

▶ These prompts are suitable as topics for research papers. Refer to the Language Arts Survey, 4.20–4.34, "Research Skills." (To evaluate research papers, see the evaluation forms for writing, revising, and proofreading, *Assessment Portfolio,* 7.1–7.10.)

▶ These prompts can be adapted for use as topics for oral reports or debates. To evaluate these projects, see the evaluation forms in the *Assessment Portfolio,* 7.17–7.19.

LANGUAGE LAB EDITING FOR ERRORS IN USAGE

There are some words that are often misused. When editing your writing, you should watch carefully for these usage problems.

COMMON USAGE ERRORS

LANGUAGE ARTS SURVEY

For additional help, see the Language Arts Survey, 2.90.

adapt, adopt. *Adapt* means to modify something to fit a specific use or situation. *Adopt* means to make something one's own.

EXAMPLES: Some soldiers could not *adapt* to the harsh realities of war.
Some soldiers *adopted* an attitude of bravado to survive their experiences.

affect, effect. If you wish to use a verb meaning "have an effect on," use *affect*. If you wish to use a noun meaning "the result of an action," use *effect*.

EXAMPLES: The Civil War *affected* the entire country.
The *effects* of the war would be felt by generations to come.

LANGUAGE ARTS SURVEY

For additional help, see the Language Arts Survey, 2.91.

imply, infer. *Imply* means "to express indirectly rather than openly." *Infer* means "to arrive at a conclusion by reasoning from evidence."

EXAMPLES: Your silence *implies* that you were very moved by Whitman's poem.
What can you *infer* from the poem about the emotional scars left by the Civil War?

like, as, as if. *Like* is a preposition, not a conjunction, and should not be used in place of *as* or *as if* in your writing.

EXAMPLE: The lilacs returned *as if* they had no knowledge of death and suffering.

literally. Use *literally* in the sense "actually," not in the sense "not actually, but in effect, or for all practical purposes."

EXAMPLE: A successful and accomplished orator, Frederick Douglass would *literally* speak for hours.
Douglass was a *virtually* tireless speaker.

LANGUAGE ARTS SURVEY

For additional help, see the Language Arts Survey, 2.92.

of. The preposition *of* should not be used in place of *have* after verbs such as *could, should, would, might, must,* and *ought*.

EXAMPLE: Abraham Lincoln must *have* experienced an enormous amount of stress as president.

than, then. Use *than* as a conjunction in comparisons. Use *then* as an adverb that tells when something occurred.

EXAMPLES: Stephen Crane wrote more in his short life *than* other writers write in a lifetime.
Crane wrote *The Red Badge of Courage,* and *then* got his first view of war as a correspondent in Greece.

Exercise A Avoiding Usage Problems

In each sentence below, choose the correct word from within the parentheses.

EXAMPLE: I enjoy Stephen Crane's fiction more (than, then) his poetry.
than

1. The title of Booker T. Washington's autobiography, *Up from Slavery,* (implies, infers) the struggles and triumphs of Washington's life.
2. Lincoln wrote more (than, then) one version of the Gettysburg Address; he penned one at the White House, revised it on the train, and (than, then) delivered a slightly different version at the ceremony.
3. Many spirituals were (adapted, adopted) from Methodist hymns.
4. In "An Occurrence at Owl Creek Bridge," it seems (as if, like) the spy is making a daring escape from his executors.
5. The reader can (imply, infer) Whitman's sorrow over Lincoln's death from "When Lilacs Last in the Dooryard Bloom'd."
6. The news of Stephen Crane's early death from tuberculosis must (have, of) been shocking and saddening.
7. During his accomplished lifetime, Booker T. Washington served (as, like) an educator and lecturer.
8. More (than, then) 214,900 men, both Union and Confederate, died in Civil War battles.
9. The rhyme and meter of "Oh Captain! My Captain!" have a highly emotional (affect, effect).
10. Who could (have, of) predicted Lincoln's assassination?

LANGUAGE ARTS SURVEY

For additional help, see the Language Arts Survey, 2.90–2.92.

Exercise B Proofreading for Usage Errors

Proofread the following paragraph for usage errors and correct any improperly used words.

In the twentieth century, Abraham Lincoln's Gettysburg Address is more revered then almost any other speech in United States history. However, it had a quite different affect when Lincoln first delivered it. The main speaker at the Gettysburg Cemetery dedication ceremony was not Lincoln, but well-known orator Edward Everett. To an audience that had just listened to Everett's two-hour speech, it must of seemed like Lincoln spoke for only a brief moment. In fact, Lincoln's speech was virtually just ten sentences long. Unused to such brevity, some people thought Lincoln's speech should of been longer and more grandiose; perhaps they believed that length and complexity inferred greatness. However, Everett's recognition of the speech's impact can be implied in his comment to Lincoln: "I should be glad if I could flatter myself that I came as near to the central idea of the occasion in two hours as you did in two minutes."

LANGUAGE ARTS SURVEY

For additional help, see the Language Arts Survey, 2.90–2.92

ANSWERS FOR LANGUAGE LAB

Exercise A

1. implies
2. than; then
3. adapted
4. as if
5. infer
6. have
7. as
8. than
9. effect
10. have

Exercise B

In the twentieth century, Abraham Lincoln's Gettysburg Address is more revered *than* almost any other speech in United States history. However, it had a quite different *effect* when Lincoln first delivered it. The main speaker at the Gettysburg Cemetery dedication ceremony was not Lincoln but well-known orator Edward Everett. To an audience that had just listened to Everett's two-hour speech, it must *have* seemed *as if* Lincoln spoke for only a brief moment. In fact, Lincoln's speech was *actually* just ten sentences long. Unused to such brevity, some people thought Lincoln's speech should *have* been longer and more grandiose; perhaps they believed that length and complexity *implied* greatness. However, Everett's recognition of the speech's impact can be *inferred* in his comment to Lincoln: "I should be glad if I could flatter myself that I came as near to the central idea of the occasion in two hours as you did in two minutes."

UNIT SKILLS OUTLINE

Literary Skills and Concepts

- Catalog, 479
- Conflicts, 448
- Dialect, 461
- Dialogue, 470
- Elaboration, 479
- Frame Tale, 462
- Irony, 454, 470
- Motif, 448
- Oral Tradition, 467
- Parallelism, 479
- Personification, 470
- Point of View, 441
- Reversal, 454
- Rhyme, 482
- Sentimentality, 437
- Speaker, 482
- Stereotype, 437
- Stock Character, 437
- Symbol, 479

Writing Skills and Concepts

- Character Sketch, 448
- Comparison, 467
- Dialogue, 470, 482
- Diary Entry, 454
- Essay, 462
- Free Verse, 479
- Paragraph, 454
- Parody, 437
- Tall Tale, 462
- Wanted Poster, 479

Grammar, Usage, and Mechanics Skills and Concepts

- Capitalization, 427
- Combining Sentences, 454
- Correcting Run-ons, 449
- Dialects of English, 439
- Editing for Errors in Modifier Usage, 456
- End Marks, 469
- Formal and Informal Language, 481
- Linking Verbs, 472
- Pronouns, 451
- Quotation Marks I, 469
- Quotation Marks II, 469
- Varieties of English, 463

Other Language Arts Skills and Concepts

- Elements of Verbal Communication, 465
- Public Speaking, 465

UNIT 7 FRONTIERS (1860–1900)

Photograph ©1994, The Art Institute of Chicago, All Rights Reserved

American Gothic. *Grant Wood, American, 1891–1942. Oil on beaver board, 1930, 74.3 x 62.4 cm. Friends of the American Art Collection, 1930.934*

GOALS/OBJECTIVES

Studying this unit will enable students to

- understand selected works of American Frontier literature
- name the main reasons for America's Westward Expansion in the nineteenth century
- identify the differences between early and late nineteenth-century American literature
- define Realism, Naturalism, and regionalism and identify the main practitioners of these literary modes in late nineteenth-century America
- describe the ways the displacement of Native Americans was accomplished, what its effects were, and some key moments in its history

CONNECTIONS ACROSS THE CURRICULUM

ARTS AND HUMANITIES
- Oral Interpretation, 463

SOCIAL STUDIES
- History of Indian Wars, 464
- Andrew Jackson and Daniel Webster, 458
- Early American Cities, 440
- Amateur Naturalists, 442
- Treatment of Animals, 442
- Forestation, 444
- Women's Rights, 452

TEACHING THE MULTIPLE INTELLIGENCES

INTERPERSONAL
- Oral Interpretation, 463
- Telling a Tall Tale, 463

Every part of this soil is sacred in the estimation of my people. Every hillside, every valley, every plain and grove, has been hallowed by some sad or happy event in days long vanished. Even the rocks, which seem to be dumb and dead as they swelter in the sun along the silent shore, thrill with memories of stirring events connected with the lives of my people, and the very dust upon which you now stand responds more lovingly to their footsteps than to yours.

—Chief Seattle of the
Suquamish and Duwamish

ART NOTE

Painter and printmaker **Grant Wood** (1891–1942) founded the regionalist movement in late nineteenth- and early twentieth-century American art. Like the regionalist writers of the period, Wood and artists such as Thomas Hart Benton and John Steuart Curry believed that artists should portray the people and land of their home communities. All of his life Wood lived and worked in Iowa, but he admired and emulated the realism, precise detail, and enamel-like surface of fifteenth- and sixteenth-century German and Flemish art. In his most famous painting, of a midwestern farmer and his daughter, Wood explores midwestern rigidity and conformity.

Historical Note

In his famous **frontier thesis**, historian Frederick Jackson Turner claimed that the Westward Expansion recapitulated the development of human civilization from primitive society to European civilization. According to Turner, the settling of the West involved a "natural" progression from Indian to hunter, pioneer, homesteader, and city-dweller. He claimed that the Europeans' encounter with the frontier was the source of the energy, individualism, and democracy that defined the character of the United States.

THEMATIC CURRENTS

Use the following selections to explore these themes with your students.

People and Nature
- "A White Heron," 438
- "A Man Said to the Universe," 468
- from "Song of Myself," 471
- "I Am Alone," 483
- "When I Heard the Learn'd Astronomer," 491

Definitions of Self
- "The Outcasts of Poker Flat," 426
- "The Story of an Hour," 450
- from "Song of Myself," 471
- "A Man Said to the Universe," 468
- "We Wear the Mask," 480
- from *Life on the Mississippi,* 483

Women Writers
- "A White Heron," 438
- "The Story of an Hour," 450
- "The Revolt of 'Mother,'" 485
- from *The Age of Innocence,* 491

Interior Frontiers
- "A White Heron," 438
- "The Story of an Hour," 450
- from "Song of Myself," 471

(cont.)

Wagon train

An Expanding Nation

Without doubt, the Civil War was the most costly event in the history of the United States. Fought on American soil between Americans, it wrought destruction throughout the South, cost the federal government more than fifteen billion dollars, and resulted in an estimated 618,000 deaths of Union and Confederate soldiers. In five years' time, the country lost an entire generation of its male youth. After the war, an exhausted nation set about the painful business of **Reconstruction**, setting the conditions under which rebellious states would be readmitted to the Union.

Many Civil War veterans, having traveled away from home for the first time in their lives, developed a taste for freewheeling adventure, a willingness to strike out for places unknown. Some headed west to homestead or to seek their fortunes. They were joined by thousands of settlers moving from lands along the Mississippi River and by recent European immigrants who, finding little hope in the increasingly crowded cities of the East, looked to the frontier for a better life. In a few decades, people of European descent had established homes across the American West, from the prairie lands of Nebraska to the coasts of California. In the course of this **Westward Expansion**, Americans developed a self-reliance that gave substance to what might otherwise have been a merely theoretical belief in freedom and democracy. By the end of the century, most of the United States territories from the Atlantic to the Pacific had become states with the exceptions of Oklahoma, New Mexico, and Arizona.

Literary Events

► = American Events

►1870. Ralph Waldo Emerson's "Civilization" published

►1869. Louisa May Alcott's *Little Women* and Bret Harte's "The Outcasts of Poker Flat" published

►1868. Bret Harte's "The Luck of Roaring Camp" published

►1866. Walt Whitman's "O Captain! My Captain!" published

1866. Feodor Dostoyevsky's *Crime and Punishment* published

1860 **1865** **1870**

Historical Events

►1860. Navajos attack Fort Defiance, New Mexico; Pony Express begins

►1861. Kansas enters Union

►1862. Cochise leads Apaches in raids; Sioux uprising under Little Crow; Homestead Act; Congress funds construction of transcontinental railroads

►1863. Nez Percé forced to sign treaty and give up land; Kit Carson resettles Navajos and Apaches

►1864. Navajos set off on "long walk" to Bosque Redondo concentration camp; Cheyenne, Arapahoe, Apache, Comanche, and Kiawa massacred at Sand Creek

►1866. Reconstruction begins in South

►1867. Alaska purchased, Nebraska admitted to Union

►1868. Attempt to impeach President Johnson; Ulysses S. Grant elected president

►1869. Union Pacific and Central Pacific Railroads link

►1870. First African-American legislators take seats at Washington, DC

THEMATIC CURRENTS (CONT.)

Rites of Passage
- "The Outcasts of Poker Flat," 426
- "A White Heron," 438
- from *Life on the Mississippi,* 483

The Native American Experience
- "I Will Fight No More Forever," 464
- "I Am Alone," 483

Politics and Discrimination
- "I Will Fight No More Forever," 464
- "We Wear the Mask," 480
- "I Am Alone," 483
- from *The Souls of Black Folk,* 491

Pioneers, Prospectors, and Ranchers

The Westward Expansion, begun early in the century, was encouraged by the **Homestead Act** of 1862, which, for a fee of ten dollars, granted 160 acres of federal land in the Western Territories to anyone who would live on that land for five years. This expansion was a continuation of efforts begun in the 1820s by adventurous settlers following the routes carved out by traders and trappers. Throughout the period from the 1820s to the 1870s, pioneers loaded their belongings and their dreams onto covered wagons and headed west along the Mormon, Oregon, California, Santa Fe, and Old Spanish trails. By the 1840s, many Americans had come to believe that it was their **"Manifest Destiny,"** in the words of one newspaperman, to cover the continent from coast to coast. The expansion was fueled, as well, by dreams of striking it rich prospecting for gold and silver. The discovery of gold in 1848 at Sutter's Mill, on California's Sacramento River, was the first of many **"gold rushes"** that led to the building of boom towns—Sacramento, San Francisco, Boise, Silver City, Virginia City, Carson City, Denver, Pueblo, Tuscon, Tombstone, Custer City, and Deadwood. These towns became legendary for their rough-and-tumble lawlessness, giving rise to the legends of the **"Wild West,"** with its gamblers, gunfighters, prospectors, and other colorful characters, including Calamity Jane, Deadwood Dick, Wild Bill Hickock, Annie Oakley, Billy the Kid, and Jesse James.

Jesse James

Cattle ranching, begun in Texas, became a big business throughout the Western Plains. Ranchers would herd their cattle together and drive them over great distances to new railway stops that would take the cattle back east, to Chicago, the center of the developing stockyard and meatpacking industry. The ranch owner and the cowboy drover were added to the West's long list of colorful stock characters. Ellsworth, Dodge City, and Abilene were among the greatest of the western cattle towns.

►1883. James Whitcomb Riley's *The Old Swimmin' Hole and 'Leven More Poems* published

►1881. Helen Maria Fiske Hunt Jackson's *A Century of Dishonor* published

1879. Henrik Ibsen's *A Doll's House* published

►1879. Henry James's *Daisy Miller* published

1885. Émile Zola's *Germinal* published

1877. Leo Tolstoy's *Anna Karenina* published

►1876. Mark Twain's *Tom Sawyer* published

► 1884. Mark Twain's *The Adventures of Huckleberry Finn* published

1872. George Eliot's *Middlemarch* published

1875 **1880** **1885**

►1871. Indian Appropriation Act makes Native Americans wards of the federal government; Cochise forced to surrender; Chicago fire

►1876. Colorado admitted to Union; Chiricahua leader Geronimo terrorizes white settlers; Battle of Little Big Horn

►1880. James Abram Garfield elected president

►1884. Grover Cleveland elected president

►1881. Garfield assassinated; Chester Alan Arthur succeeds as president

►1872. Ulysses S. Grant reelected president; Victoria Woodhull runs for president; Susan B. Anthony arrested for trying to vote

►1877. Electoral commission appoints Rutherford B. Hayes president; Nez Percé captured fleeing to Canada

►1882. Chinese Exclusion Act; first immigration restrictions

►1875. Comanche chief Quanah Parker ends his resistance; Tennessee enacts first "Jim Crow" law

Biographical Note

Jesse James was the most famous outlaw on the American frontier and robbed about twenty-five banks and trains in Missouri and other states. The son of a Baptist minister, James was described by some as a hero who robbed from the rich and gave to the poor, and by others as a vicious murderer and thief. Hoping to win the reward offered for his capture, one of his gang members, Robert Fort, shot him in the head in 1882.

LITERARY CURRENTS

Use the following selections to explore these techniques with your students.

Dialect
- "The Outcasts of Poker Flat," 426
- "A White Heron," 438
- "The Notorious Jumping Frog of Calaveras County," 455
- "The Revolt of 'Mother,'" 485

Characterization
- "The Outcasts of Poker Flat," 426
- "A White Heron," 438
- "The Story of an Hour," 450
- "The Notorious Jumping Frog of Calaveras County," 455
- from *Life on the Mississippi*, 483
- from *The Age of Innocence*, 491

Short Story
- "The Outcasts of Poker Flat," 426
- "A White Heron," 438
- "The Story of an Hour," 450
- "The Notorious Jumping Frog of Calaveras County," 455

Poetry
- "A Man Said to the Universe," 468
- from "Song of Myself," 471
- "We Wear the Mask," 480
- "When I Heard the Learn'd Astronomer," 491

(cont.)

LITERARY CURRENTS (CONT.)

Free Verse
- "A Man Said to the Universe," 468
- from "Song of Myself," 471
- "When I Heard the Learn'd Astronomer," 491

Nonfiction
- "I Will Fight No More Forever," 464
- "I Am Alone," 483
- from *Life on the Mississippi*, 483
- from *The Souls of Black Folk*, 491
- from *The Art of Fiction*, 496

Historical Note

Chicago, the frontier's main urban center for grain, lumber, and meat trade, derived its name from the numerous wild garlic plants growing among the wetlands and prairie grass. Native Americans called the place Chigagou, "the land of the wild onion." They had been using the land around the Chicago River for centuries, but under the pressure of white development, the Potawatomis signed away their last rights to the land in 1833.

Historical Note

The history of America's Westward Expansion began with Christopher Columbus, who gave the people he met, the Tainos of San Salvador, the name **Indios**, which some pronounced as **Indien, Indianer, or Indian.**

Biographical Note

Crazy Horse, leader of the Ogalalas, believed that men lived in a shadow world and could enter the real world only through dreams. When he visited the real world, everything, even his horse, floated and danced as if it were wild or crazy. This is why he called himself Crazy Horse.

Four Young Ilte Indians

The Displacement of Native Americans

While the nineteenth century was one of new frontiers for settlers of European descent, it was one of heartbreak and trial for Native Americans, who were forced from their ancestral lands, killed in numerous "Indian Wars," and confined to reservations, often undesirable sections of the country far from their original homes. The **Indian Removal Act** passed by Congress in 1830 gave the president of the United States the power to require that all native peoples east of the Mississippi move west. This power was used by President Andrew Jackson, over the objections of the Supreme Court, to remove Cherokee peoples from Georgia and Tennessee to the newly established Indian Territory in what is now Oklahoma. Escorted by federal troops, thirteen thousand Cherokee were put on a forced march, now known as the **"Trail of Tears"** because of the deaths of some four thousand of their number en route. The Cherokee were one of many peoples who had either to fight or to submit to being moved to reservations.

The building of railroads led to widespread slaughter of the herds of Great Plains buffalo that provided sustenance to the Native Americans of that region. As new settlers moved westward, they continually revised their ideas about what lands would belong to Native Americans "for as long as the waters run," breaking numerous treaties and promises. Some Native American groups fought back. The 1860s and 1870s saw warfare between United States troops and native groups throughout the West, with much brutality and carnage on both sides. In 1864, a massacre of over four hundred Cheyenne men, women, and children led to all-out war between the United States government and the combined forces of the Cheyenne, the Sioux, and other Plains peoples. In 1876, the Sioux defeated Lieutenant George Armstrong Custer at the **Battle of Little Big Horn**, killing the 264 men in his company. In 1886, federal troops overpowered and captured **Geronimo**, the leader of the Chiricahua Apaches, who had fought

Literary Events

► = American Events

►1891. Ambrose Bierce's *Tales of Soldiers and Civilians* published
1891. Thomas Hardy's *Tess of the d'Urbervilles,* and Oscar Wilde's *The Picture of Dorian Gray* published

►1890. *Poems by Emily Dickinson* published posthumously

►1896. Sarah Orne Jewett's "Country of the Pointed Firs" published

►1895. Stephen Crane's *The Red Badge of Courage* published

►1899. Kate Chopin's *The Awakening* published

►1894. Mark Twain's *Pudd'nhead Wilson* published

►1886. William Dean Howells's *Indian Summer* published
1886. Robert Louis Stevenson's *The Strange Case of Dr. Jekyll and Mr. Hyde* published

►1893. Frederick Jackson Turner's "The Significance of the Frontier in American History" published

1890 **1895** **1900**

Historical Events

►1886. Haymarket riots; Geronimo captured

►1889. North Dakota, South Dakota, Montana, and Washington admitted to Union

►1890. Battle of Wounded Knee ends Native American resistance; Sherman Anti-Trust Act

►1892. Grover Cleveland elected

►1893. Hawaii annexationists overthrow Queen Liliuokalani

►1895. Booker T. Washington's Atlanta Compromise

►1896. Utah admitted to Union; William McKinley elected president

►1897. United States annexes Hawaii

►1898. Spanish-American War; Louisiana adopts "grandfather clause," restricting African-American voters

1899. Great Britain begins the Boer War; Philippine insurrection

Wagons approach a challenging crossing.

long and successfully against the invaders of his people's land in the Southwest. In 1887, they captured **Chief Joseph** of the Nez Percé after his people's long flight, punctuated by fighting. That same year, Congress passed the **Dawes Act,** which granted citizenship to Native Americans after twenty-five years but took away Native American reservation lands for use by settlers, offering in exchange small plots for heads of families. In 1889, in another of a string of broken promises, the United States Congress opened up much of Indian Territory to new settlement. In a single day, the entire territory was settled. In 1890, at **Wounded Knee,** South Dakota, federal troops massacred over two hundred mostly unarmed Sioux in what was to be the last action of the Indian Wars.

Immigration, the Growth of Cities, and Industrialism

The last forty years of the nineteenth century was a time of unprecedented change in American cities. Between 1880 and 1900, nine million immigrants arrived in the United States from Europe. Previous immigration had been made up for the most part of northern Europeans. The new wave of immigration brought southern and eastern Europeans, as well as Asians, thus greatly diversifying the United States population. This trend would continue and expand in the first two decades of the next century.

Another important trend during these years was the growth of cities. By 1900, fully 40 percent of the United States population lived in urban centers. Many of these people were recent immigrants, many were newly free African Americans from rural areas of the South, and many more were white citizens moving from farms to find jobs in America's booming industrial centers. American industry had benefited from technological developments made during the Civil War era, and a class of millionaire industrialists had emerged with monopolistic control of meatpacking, railroads, and the production of oil and steel. The fabulous wealth

Historical Note

Toward the end of the Indian wars, the Ghost Dance religion began to spread to every Native American reservation in the West. Founded by the Paiute messiah, Wovoka, the religion claimed that if Native Americans danced the ghost dance, the Great Spirit would return in the spring, bring back the game, raise Native American warriors from the dead, and drown all the settlers in a great flood.

Historical Note

In 1860, the population of Chicago was 109,000; in 1910, it was 2.2 million. In 1870, less than 20 percent of United States citizens lived in a town with a population greater than 8,000.

ART NOTE

The term **local color** implies a comparison to seventeenth-century Dutch painters of "genre" scenes, realistic pictures of everyday, middle-class life in a particular locale.

HISTORICAL NOTE

The regional writing of Sarah Orne Jewett, Kate Chopin, and Mary Wilkins Freeman represents a form of early feminist fiction. These women, along with Harriet Beecher Stowe, Charlotte Perkins Gilman, Alice Brown, Rose Terry Cook, and others, wrote in protest against a world dominated by men and the nineteenth-century male preoccupation with progress, conquering nature, and material prosperity.

HISTORICAL NOTE

Regionalism can be seen as a recurring attempt to preserve a diversity of lifestyles in the face of the uniformity of life in an industrial society. Examples of contemporary American regionalists include poets such as Gary Snyder of northern California and Wendell Berry of Kentucky.

Mark Twain

of these often unscrupulous industrialists, satirized in Mark Twain's ***The Gilded Age,*** which he coauthored with Charles Dudley Warner, stood in sharp contrast with the poverty and terrible working conditions of the average laborer. At the turn of the century, the so-called **"muckraker"** journalists Ida Tarbell and Lincoln Steffans would make careers of exposing unscrupulous practices among business people and corrupt political officials.

THE EXPANDING LITERARY FRONTIER

The literature of the early nineteenth century in America was dominated by Romanticism and concentrated in New England. The great authors of the period were primarily scholarly, moralistic gentlemen, and public tastes ran to the sentimental and nostalgic. Expansion across the frontier in the late nineteenth century was accompanied by an equally dramatic expansion of literary frontiers. Significant writers appeared across the breadth of the nation, in the Midwest, the South, and the West. Many of these writers were women, such as **Sarah Orne Jewett, Kate Chopin,** and **Mary Wilkins Freeman.** Many were journalists and adventurers, such as **Mark Twain, Bret Harte, Ambrose Bierce,** and **Stephen Crane.** One of the greatest writers of the period, **Henry James,** spent much of his life in Europe, chronicling the lives of newly wealthy Americans living abroad. The characters in the fiction of the day became correspondingly diverse, including gunfighters and ranchers, runaway slaves and Civil War soldiers, steamboat captains and con artists, Cajuns and Creoles, pioneer women and children, millionaire tycoons and the desperate urban poor. The literature of the period fulfilled the vision of Walt Whitman: "I hear America singing, the varied carols I hear."

REGIONALISM AND LOCAL COLOR

One outgrowth of this diversity was **Regionalism,** or **local color** writing. The mostly female readers of the many new magazines in the East developed an intense interest in the lives and lifestyles of persons living in such faraway, exotic parts of the country as the Louisiana bayou, the Mississippi River valley, and the western boom towns. Journalists and others rushed to fill the demand. Soon, most regions of the country were represented by local colorists who created often humorous pieces about the odd characters scattered across the newly conquered continent. One of the first of these local color writers was Bret Harte, who wrote stories from San Francisco such as "The Luck of Roaring Camp" and "The Outcasts of Poker Flat," beginning a fascination with the West in American popular culture. **Samuel Clemens,** who took the pseudonym Mark Twain, traveled widely throughout the country, posting short stories and humorous sketches about peoples and places as diverse as the con artists, steamboat captains, and riverboat gamblers of the Mississippi River, the natives and missionaries of the Sandwich Islands (later Hawaii), and the denizens of western mining camps, as in his tall tale "The Notorious Jumping Frog of Calaveras County." Kate Chopin and **George Washington Cable** wrote of the people of the Louisiana bayou country. **Joel Chandler Harris** wrote dialectical pieces based on the oral traditions of African Americans in the South. **Edward Eggleston** and **James Whitcomb Riley** wrote of the Hoosiers of backwoods Indiana. Sarah Orne Jewett and Mary Wilkins Freeman wrote of backwoods New England.

Original wagon wheel from Oregon Trail carriage

The Emergence of Realism

The presentation in fiction of local dialect and varied, unsavory characters were two expressions of a new and dominant mode in American fiction of the late nineteenth century—**Realism.** The early nineteenth-century Romantics of New England had tended to present idealized materials designed to inspire lofty emotions. The Realists, in contrast, drew portraits from life, often shocking more sensitive readers with their grim depictions of realities, as the country itself had been shocked by the grim realities of the Civil War. Ambrose Bierce wrote devastatingly bitter, unsentimental portrayals of the horrors of the war, including such masterful short stories as "Chickamauga" and "An Occurrence at Owl Creek Bridge." Twain, widely known for his satirical humor, often involving exaggerated, colorful characters, also showed elements of Realism. Because of its realistic use of a variety of dialects and its quintessentially American theme of the individual's quest for freedom, Twain's *Adventures of Huckleberry Finn* is often considered the greatest of American novels. Ernest Hemingway wrote, for example, that "All modern American literature comes from one book by Mark Twain called *Huckleberry Finn.*" The great champion of Realism was the novelist **William Dean Howells,** who, as editor of *Harper's Weekly, Harper's Monthly,* and the *North American Review,* promoted the works of Twain and James. In novels such as *The Rise of Silas Lapham, Annie Kilburn, A Hazard of New Fortunes,* and *Quality of Mercy,* Howells presented the breakdown of traditional values and the misery of the poor that he observed in urban America. Several authors applied the penetrating accuracy of Realism to the interior lives of their characters, pioneering what became known as **Psychological Realism.** Among these, though very different in attitude, experience, style, and subject matter, are Ambrose Bierce in stories such as "An Occurrence at Owl Creek Bridge," Kate Chopin in works such as "The

Additional Questions and Activities

Literary critics traditionally contrast Realism, which is said to portray life as it is, with Romanticism, which is said to present life as we would like it to be. Have students make a list of their favorite novels or films. Then ask them to categorize each as Realistic or Romantic and to defend their opinion.

Historical Note

The literary movement known as Realism was not limited to the United States. Its practitioners included George Eliot (1819–1880) in England, Honoré de Balzac (1799–1850) in France, and Leo Tolstoy (1828–1910) in Russia.

Additional Questions and Activities

Realist novelists create an illusion of real life by choosing an ordinary, average citizen as a protagonist; by presenting the story in a reportorial manner; by grounding the story in a particular social setting through the use of numerous particular details; and by organizing their plots according to the law of cause and effect. Have students begin to outline a realistic short story using the principles mentioned above.

Biographical Note

Born to poor parents, Jack London (1876–1916) became a criminal by the age of fifteen, specializing in stealing oysters in San Francisco Bay. After a thirty-day jail sentence, he vowed to avoid the fate of the poor by using his mind. By the time he died at the age of forty, he had written fifty books and had become an internationally recognized author.

Selected Bibliographies

Jack London

The Call of the Wild, 1903
The Sea-Wolf, 1904
White Fang, 1906
The Iron Heel, 1908
Martin Eden, 1909

Theodore Dreiser

Sister Carrie, 1900
The Financier, 1912
The Titan, 1914
The Genius, 1915
An American Tragedy, 1925

Jack London

Story of an Hour" and *The Awakening,* **Charlotte Perkins Gilman** in her feminist horror tale "The Yellow Wallpaper," and **Henry James** in novels such as *Portrait of a Lady* and *The Turn of the Screw.*

The Rise of Naturalism

Naturalism was an extension and refinement of Realism, based on the theories of the French novelist **Émile Zola.** Inspired by nineteenth-century naturalists such as Charles Darwin and Thomas Huxley, Zola held that people's actions and beliefs resulted not from free will but from the arbitrary, outside forces of heredity and environment. He believed that, like a naturalist studying the causes of behavior in animals, the novelist could write "scientific" fiction that demonstrated the exact causes of human behavior. In the United States, Naturalism found its champion in Stephen Crane. In novels like *The Red Badge of Courage* and stories like "The Open Boat," "The Blue Hotel," and "A Mystery of Heroism," Crane showed human beings to be pawns manipulated by the cruel, indifferent forces of nature and society, a philosophy expressed succinctly in his poem "A Man Said to the Universe." Crane's Naturalism, however, was tempered by his belief that in such an indifferent universe, people must stick together with acts of kindness and compassion to counter the terrible forces to which they are subjected. At the turn of the century, Naturalism was to become a dominant mode in American fiction, realized in the works of such writers as **Frank Norris,** author of *McTeague* and *The Octopus;* **Jack London,** author of "To Build a Fire" and *The Call of the Wild,* and **Theodore Dreiser,** author of *Sister Carrie* and *An American Tragedy.*

Echoes:

Frontiers

Quotations from Mark Twain

On flattery: "I can live for two months on a good compliment."

On golf: "Golf is good walk spoiled."

On grief and joy: "Grief can take care of itself, but to get the full value from joy you must have somebody to divide it with."

On his own writing: "You don't know about me without you have read a book by the name of *The Adventures of Tom Sawyer;* but that ain't no matter. That book was made by Mr. Mark Twain, and he told the truth, mainly."

On humans: "Man is the only animal that blushes. Or needs to."

On the desire to teach others to be good: "To be good is noble, but to teach others how to be good is nobler—and less trouble."

On obedience: "Of all God's creatures there is only one that cannot be made the slave of the lash. That one is the cat. If man could be crossed with the cat it would improve man, but it would deteriorate the cat."

On parents: "When I was a boy of fourteen, my father was so ignorant I could hardly stand to have the old man around. But when I got to be twenty-one, I was astonished at how much he had learned in seven years."

On politeness: "Good breeding consists in concealing how much we think of ourselves and how little we think of the other person."

On school: "I have never let my schooling interfere with my education."

On success: "All you need in this life is ignorance and confidence, and then success is sure."

QUOTABLES

"What oft was thought, but ne'er so well expressed."

— Alexander Pope's definition of "true wit."

LITERARY TECHNIQUE

Twain was a master of the **epigram**, a short, often witty saying. Epigrams can be written in either prose or verse. **Wit** is a brief verbal statement that concludes with a comic surprise. Some wit is harmless and makes us laugh without malice, but wit can also be aggressive, an attempt to ridicule people, ideas, and customs. What is the meaning of the Twain epigrams? If they are aggressive, what or whom is Twain ridiculing? Do students find these epigrams witty? Why, or why not?

ADDITIONAL QUESTIONS AND ACTIVITIES

Ask students to write their own epigrams on the topic of parents, school, obedience, or a favorite sport. Students may want to create posters to display their epigrams in the classroom.

ADDITIONAL RESOURCES

READER'S GUIDE
- Selection Worksheet, 7.1

ASSESSMENT PORTFOLIO
- Selection Check Test, 4.7.1
- Selection Test, 4.7.2

ESSENTIAL SKILLS PRACTICE BOOKS
- *Language,* 2.107–2.133

ENRICHMENT ACTIVITIES

Students can role play interesting characters of their own creation, each character narrating his or her life story to the class. Students should aim to enter sympathetically into a totally different person's mind and situation. Presentations can be followed by a question-and-answer period.

SUPPORT FOR LEP STUDENTS

Harte displays a preference for indirect, understated, or ironic phrases. As they read, students should underline these difficult phrases. Discuss these phrases in small groups or with the class.

ADDITIONAL VOCABULARY

impropriety—improper act
expletives—curses
regenerate—restore one's strength
emigrant—one who leaves a country
prescience—knowing beforehand
admonish—criticize or correct
amicable—friendly
commiseration—sympathy
vernacular—native language
denominate—name or call

PREREADING

SHORT STORY

"The Outcasts of Poker Flat"
by Bret Harte

ABOUT THE AUTHOR

Bret Harte (1836–1902) was the pen name of Francis Brett Harte, who gave many Easterners their first glimpse of the Old West in his amusing stories, full of local color and characterized by unusual juxtapositions of characters and surprise endings. Though associated with the West, Harte was born in Albany, New York. After his father died, he moved in 1854 to California, where he married and gathered the material he would later use in his stories, riding shotgun on Wells Fargo stagecoaches and prospecting like so many other Californians in those days of the Gold Rush. Settling in San Francisco, he worked as a typesetter and then as a writer for the *Californian.* In 1861, he took a job as editor of the *Overland Monthly,* in which he published the work that would make him famous, including the stories "The Luck of Roaring Camp" and "The Outcasts of Poker Flat" and the poem "Plain Language from Truthful James." Becoming well known in literary circles, he socialized with such San Francisco luminaries as Ambrose Bierce and Mark Twain. Harte's regionalism met with an eager audience back East, so eager that the *Atlantic Monthly* in Boston offered him the then astronomical sum of ten thousand dollars to write twelve pieces for the magazine. Harte left for Boston, but the pieces that he produced under his contract were mediocre, and his fame subsided. Thereafter, Harte produced several collections of stories, two novels, and two plays, but none equaled his earlier work. He served as a United States diplomat in Prussia and in Scotland and then settled in London, England, where he lived for the rest of his life.

ABOUT THE SELECTION

"The Outcasts of Poker Flat" is an example of nineteenth-century regional literature. Regional writers portray what is special about a particular part of the country. They write about the specific landscape, people, values, and modes of life of a region. Regionalists explore issues that are common to all human beings, but they do so only by way of writing about a particular time and place. Harte is known for his stories about life on America's Western frontier, especially his amusing explorations of the people and the landscape of northern California's High Sierras, the Gold Rush region. In "The Outcasts of Poker Flat," Harte treats the conflict between a society and its "outcasts," those people whose behavior is unacceptable to the moral values that the majority at least pretend to uphold. Harte explores this timeless conflict, however, by describing the fate of some typical characters from the American frontier. Today these characters are familiar to anyone who watches Western movies, but in the nineteenth century they were still new, and Harte was one of the first to describe them.

GOALS/OBJECTIVES

Studying this lesson will enable students to

- appreciate regionalist or local-color fiction, recognizing that it treats issues common to all human beings through representations of particular times and places
- identify Bret Harte as a nineteenth-century regionalist and briefly describe the region he portrayed
- describe Harte's treatment of the conflict between society and its "outcasts"
- define *stereotype* and *sentimentality* using examples from the selection
- write a parody of a piece of Western fiction

READER'S JOURNAL

What types of people are outcasts in our society? What do they wear? What kinds of activities do they engage in? How do others treat them? How do the outcasts respond? Write in your journal about what makes people outcasts.

LANGUAGE SKILLS

Skim the Language Arts Survey, 2.107–2.133, on capitalization. As you read the selection, copy onto a piece of paper the capitalized words that you encounter. Then, referring to the Language Arts Survey, explain why each word is capitalized.

"The Outcasts of Poker Flat"

BRET HARTE

As Mr. John Oakhurst, gambler, stepped into the main street of Poker Flat on the morning of the twenty-third of November, 1850, he was conscious of a change in its moral atmosphere from the preceding night. Two or three men, conversing earnestly together, ceased as he approached, and exchanged significant glances. There was a Sabbath lull in the air, which, in a settlement unused to Sabbath influences, looked ominous.

Mr. Oakhurst's calm, handsome face betrayed small concern of these indications. Whether he was conscious of any predisposing cause, was another question. "I reckon they're after somebody," he reflected; "likely it's me." He returned to his pocket the handkerchief with which he had been whipping away the red dust of Poker Flat from his neat boots, and quietly discharged his mind of any further conjecture.

In point of fact, Poker Flat was "after somebody." It had lately suffered the loss of several thousand dollars, two valuable horses, and a prominent citizen. It was experiencing a spasm of virtuous reaction, quite as lawless and ungovernable as any of the acts that had provoked it. A secret committee[1] had determined to rid the town of all improper persons. This was done permanently in regard of two men who were then hanging from the boughs of a sycamore in the gulch, and temporarily in the banishment of certain other objectionable characters. I regret to say that some of these were ladies. It is but due

❶ *To what are the citizens of Poker Flat reacting?*

1. **secret committee.** Vigilance committee; group that helps maintain order and punish crime when processes of law are not effective

WORDS FOR EVERYDAY USE: **om • i • nous** (äm´ə nəs) *adj.,* threatening; **pre • dis • pos • ing** (prē dis pō´ziŋ) *part.,* giving previous tendency; **con • jec • ture** (kən jek´chər) *n.,* prediction based on guesswork

PREREADING NOTES

READER'S JOURNAL

Ask students to note their own attitudes toward "outcasts." Do their attitudes change as they become older and more mature?

LANGUAGE SKILLS

Students might want to exchange lists of capitalized words and check each other's answers.

ANSWER TO GUIDED READING QUESTION

❶ In casting out all improper persons from the town, the citizens of Poker Flat are reacting to a recent robbery and murder.

VOCABULARY FROM THE SELECTION

anathema	guileless
bellicose	infelicitous
cavalcade	jocular
conjecture	ominous
contortion	ostentatiously
coquetry	precipitous
dissuade	predisposing
equanimity	querulous
expatriated	remonstrance
extemporize	vociferation
felonious	vituperative

VOCABULARY IN CONTEXT

- The dark clouds in the sky looked ominous.
- Black leather and tatoos are not necessarily predisposing characteristics of a violent person.
- The detective's conjecture regarding the murderer's identity threw everyone into confusion.

Answers to Guided Reading Questions

❶ The vigilantes resent him because he won their money in a poker game.

❷ The other deportees are the Duchess, Mother Shipton, and Uncle Billy.

to the sex, however, to state that their impropriety was professional, and it was only in such easily established standards of evil that Poker Flat ventured to sit in judgment.

Why do vigilantes resent Oakhurst? ❶

Mr. Oakhurst was right in supposing that he was included in this category. A few of the committee had urged hanging him as a possible example, and a sure method of reimbursing themselves from his pockets of the sums he had won from them. "It's agin justice," said Jim Wheeler, "to let this yer young man from Roaring Camp—an entire stranger—carry away our money." But a crude sentiment of equity residing in the breasts of those who had been fortunate enough to win from Mr. Oakhurst, overruled this narrower local prejudice.

Mr. Oakhurst received his sentence with philosophic calmness, none the less coolly, that he was aware of the hesitation of his judges. He was too much of a gambler not to accept Fate. With him life was at best an uncertain game, and he recognized the usual percentage in favor of the dealer.

A body of armed men accompanied the deported wickedness of Poker Flat to the outskirts of the settlement. Besides Mr. Oakhurst, who was known to be a coolly desperate man, and for whose intimidation the armed escort was intended, the expatriated party consisted of a young woman familiarly known as "The Duchess"; another, who had gained the infelicitous title of "Mother Shipton,"[2] and "Uncle Billy," a suspected sluice[3] robber and confirmed drunkard. The cavalcade provoked no comments from the spectators, nor was any word uttered by the escort. Only when the gulch which marked the uttermost limit of Poker Flat was reached, the leader spoke briefly and to the point. The exiles were forbidden to return at the peril of their lives.

Who are the other deportees? ❷

As the escort disappeared, their pent-up feelings found vent in a few hysterical tears from "The Duchess," some bad language from Mother Shipton, and a Partheian[4] volley of expletives from Uncle Billy. The philosophic Oakhurst alone remained silent. He listened calmly to Mother Shipton's desire to cut somebody's heart out, to the repeated statements of "The Duchess" that she would die in the road, and to the alarming oaths that seemed to be bumped out of Uncle Billy as he rode forward. With the easy good-humor characteristic of his class, he insisted upon exchanging his own riding-horse, "Five Spot," for the sorry mule which the Duchess rode. But even this act did not draw the party into any closer sympathy. The young woman readjusted her somewhat draggled plumes with a feeble, faded coquetry; Mother Shipton eyed the possessor of "Five Spot" with malevolence, and Uncle Billy included the whole party in one sweeping anathema.

The road to Sandy Bar—a camp that not having as yet experienced the regenerating influences of Poker Flat, consequently seemed to offer some invitation to the emigrants—lay over a steep mountain

2. **Mother Shipton.** (1488–1560) Known as a witch and believed to have been taken by the devil and to have born him an imp

3. **sluice.** Trough used to separate gold from other materials

4. **Partheian.** Like the Partheians, an ancient people from Asia known for firing shots while in retreat

Words for Everyday Use:

ex • pa • tri • at • ed (eks pā´trē āt´id) *part.*, driven from one's land

in • fe • lic • i • tous (in fə lis´ə təs) *adj.*, unfortunate, unsuitable

cav • al • cade (kav´əl kād´) *n.*, procession (of horses)

co • quet • ry (kō´kə trē) *n.*, flirting

a • nath • e • ma (ə nath´ə mə) *n.*, curse

Vocabulary in Context

- The expatriated writer longed for his homeland.
- Calamity Jane was born under an infelicitous star.
- The king's cavalcade filled the village children with wonder.
- A pretty girl's coquetry threw the shy boy into confusion.
- The angry workers cast anathemas upon their boss.

range. It was distant a day's severe journey. In that advanced season, the party soon passed out of the moist, temperate regions of the foot-hills, into the dry, cold, bracing air of the Sierras.[5] The trail was narrow and difficult. At noon the Duchess, rolling out of her saddle upon the ground, declared her intention of going no further, and the party halted.

The spot was singularly wild and impressive. A wooded amphitheater, surrounded on three sides by precipitous cliffs of naked granite, sloped gently toward the crest of another precipice that overlooked the valley. It was undoubtedly the most suitable spot for a camp, had camping been advisable. But Mr. Oakhurst knew that scarcely half the journey to Sandy Bar was accomplished, and the party were not equipped or provisioned for delay. This fact he pointed out to his companions curtly, with a philosophic commentary on the folly of "throwing up their hand before the game was played out." But they were furnished with liquor, which in this emergency stood them in place of food, fuel, rest and prescience. In spite of his remonstrances, it was not long before they were more or less under its influence. Uncle Billy passed rapidly from a bellicose state into one of stupor, the Duchess became maudlin, and Mother Shipton snored. Mr. Oakhurst alone remained erect, leaning against a rock, calmly surveying them.

Mr. Oakhurst did not drink. It interfered with a profession which required coolness, impassiveness and presence of mind, and, in his own language, he "couldn't afford it." As he gazed at his recumbent fellow-exiles, the loneliness begotten of his pariah-trade,[6] his habits of life, his very vices, for the first time seriously oppressed him. He bestirred himself in dusting his black clothes, washing his hands and face, and other acts characteristic of his studiously neat habits, and for a moment forgot his annoyance. The thought of deserting his weaker and more pitiable companions never perhaps occurred to him. Yet he could not help feeling the want of that excitement, which singularly enough was most conducive to that calm equanimity for which he was notorious. He looked at the gloomy walls that rose a thousand feet sheer above the circling pines around him; at the sky, ominously clouded; at the valley below, already deepening into shadow. And doing so, suddenly he heard his own name called.

A horseman slowly ascended the trail. In the fresh, open face of the newcomer, Mr. Oakhurst recognized Tom Simson, otherwise known as "The Innocent" of Sandy Bar. He had met him some months before over a "little game," and had, with perfect equanimity, won the entire fortune—amounting to some forty dollars—of that guileless youth. After the game was finished, Mr. Oakhurst drew the youthful speculator behind the door and thus addressed him: "Tommy, you're a good little man, but you can't gamble worth a cent. Don't try it over again." He then handed him his money back, pushed him gently from the room, and so made a devoted slave of Tom Simson.

5. **Sierras.** Mountains in California
6. **pariah-trade.** Profession scorned by others

❶ *Why is it unwise to halt the journey?*

❷ *Why does Oakhurst not drink?*

WORDS FOR EVERYDAY USE:

pre • cip • i • tous (prē sip´ə təs) *adj.*, steep
re • mon • strance (ri män strə´ns) *n.*, protest, objection
bel • li • cose (bel´i kōs) *adj.*, hostile, eager to fight
e • qua • nim • i • ty (ek´wə nim´ə tē) *n.*, evenness of temper; quality of remaining calm
guile • less (gīl´lis) *adj.*, without deceit

ANSWERS TO GUIDED READING QUESTIONS

❶ It is unwise to halt the journey because the outcasts do not have enough equipment or provisions.

❷ Oakhurst does not drink because it interferes with his gambling.

HISTORICAL NOTE

The outcasts of Poker Flat are **scapegoats**, people who take on the sins of others. The practice is as old as human society itself, but the word originates in the early Israelite practice of symbolically placing the community's sins on the head of a goat and sending it into the wilderness. Scapegoating tries to change an internal conflict within the community into an external conflict between the community and something outside of it.

VOCABULARY IN CONTEXT

- The children rode their sleds down the precipitous hillside.
- Despite the remonstrances of the striking workers, people crossed the picket line.
- The bellicose customer demanded to speak with the manager.
- A good soldier retains his equanimity under the stress of battle.
- The guileless child softened the heart of the cynical man.

Answers to Guided Reading Questions

❶ Tom and Piney are going to Poker Flat to be married.

❷ Oakhurst urges Simson not to delay because the outcasts are not good company for Tom and Piney.

Literary Technique

In the meeting between the outcasts and the young people, Harte juxtaposes a **naive** or innocent character, one who interprets the actions of others with childlike simplicity, and **ironic** or experienced characters who know the true meaning of events. Other literary works that make use of this technique include John Steinbeck's *Of Mice and Men*, William Blake's *Songs of Innocence and Experience*, and Shakespeare's *As You Like It*.

There was a remembrance of this in his boyish and enthusiastic greeting of Mr. Oakhurst. He had started, he said, to go to Poker Flat to seek his fortune. "Alone?" No, not exactly alone; in fact—a giggle—he had run away with Piney Woods. Didn't Mr. Oakhurst remember Piney? She that used to wait on the table at the Temperance House? They had been engaged a long time, but old Jake Woods had objected, and so they had run away, and were going to Poker Flat to be married, and here they were. And they were tired out, and how lucky it was they had found a place to camp and company. All this The Innocent delivered rapidly, while Piney—a stout, comely damsel of fifteen—emerged from behind the pine tree, where she had been blushing unseen, and rode to the side of her lover.

Where are Tom Simson and Piney Woods going? ❶

Mr. Oakhurst seldom troubled himself with sentiment. Still less with propriety. But he had a vague idea that the situation was not felicitous. He retained, however, his presence of mind sufficiently to kick Uncle Billy, who was about to say something, and Uncle Billy was sober enough to recognize in Mr. Oakhurst's kick a superior power that would not bear trifling. He then endeavored to dissuade Tom Simson from delaying further, but in vain. He even pointed out the fact that there was no provision, nor means of making a camp. But, unluckily, "The Innocent" met this objection by assuring the party that he was provided with an extra mule loaded with provisions, and by the discovery of a rude attempt at a log-house near the trail. "Piney can stay with Mrs. Oakhurst," said The Innocent, pointing to the Duchess, "and I can shift for myself."

Why does Oakhurst urge Simson not to delay? ❷

Nothing but Mr. Oakhurst's admonishing foot saved Uncle Billy from bursting into a roar of laughter. As it was, he felt compelled to retire up the canyon until he could recover his gravity. There he confided the joke to the tall pine trees, with many slaps of his leg, contortions of his face, and the usual profanity. But when he returned to the party, he found them seated by a fire—for the air had grown strangely chill and the sky overcast—in apparently amicable conversation. Piney was actually talking in an impulsive, girlish fashion to the Duchess, who was listening with an interest and animation she had not shown for many days. The Innocent was holding forth, apparently with equal effect, to Mr. Oakhurst and Mother Shipton, who was actually relaxing into amiability. "Is this yer a d——d picnic?" said Uncle Billy, with inward scorn, as he surveyed the sylvan group, the glancing fire-light and the tethered animals in the foreground. Suddenly an idea mingled with the alcoholic fumes that disturbed his brain. It was apparently of a jocular nature, for he felt impelled to slap his leg again and cram his fist into his mouth.

As the shadows crept slowly up the mountain, a slight breeze rocked the tops of the pine trees, and moaned through their long and gloomy aisles. The ruined cabin, patched and covered with pine boughs, was set apart for the ladies. As the lovers parted, they unaffectedly exchanged a parting kiss, so honest and sincere that it might have been heard above the swaying pines. The frail Duchess and the malevolent Mother

Words for Everyday Use:

dis • suade (di swād´) *vt.*, talk out of

con • tor • tion (kən tôr´shən) *n.*, twisting out of shape

joc • u • lar (jäk´yoo lər) *adj.*, humorous

Vocabulary in Context

- The man tried to dissuade the boys from swimming in the dangerous waters.
- The circus clown performed amazing bodily contortions.
- Only a person with a jocular temperament could keep a positive outlook in such trying circumstances.

Shipton were probably too stunned to remark upon this last evidence of simplicity, and so turned without a word to the hut. The fire was replenished, the men lay down before the door, and in a few minutes were asleep.

Mr. Oakhurst was a light sleeper. Toward morning he awoke benumbed and cold. As he stirred the dying fire, the wind, which was now blowing strongly, brought to his cheek that which caused the blood to leave it—snow!

He started to his feet with the intention of awakening the sleepers, for there was no time to lose. But turning to where Uncle Billy had been lying he found him gone. A suspicion leaped to his brain and a curse to his lips. He ran to the spot where the mules had been tethered; they were no longer there. The tracks were already rapidly disappearing in the snow.

The momentary excitement brought Mr. Oakhurst back to the fire with his usual calm. He did not waken the sleepers. The Innocent slumbered peacefully, with a smile on his good-humored, freckled face; the virgin Piney slept beside her frailer sisters as sweetly as though attended by celestial guardians, and Mr. Oakhurst, drawing his blanket over his shoulders, stroked his mustachios and waited for the dawn. It came slowly in a whirling mist of snowflakes, that dazzled and confused the eye. What could be seen of the landscape appeared magically changed. He looked over the valley, and summed up the present and future in two words—"Snowed in!"

A careful inventory of the provisions, which, fortunately for the party, had been stored within the hut, and so escaped the felonious fingers of Uncle Billy, disclosed the fact that with care and prudence they might last ten days longer. "That is," said Mr. Oakhurst, *sotto voce*[7] to The Innocent, "if you're willing to board us. If you ain't—and perhaps you'd better not—you can wait till Uncle Billy gets back with provisions." For some occult reason, Mr. Oakhurst could not bring himself to disclose Uncle Billy's rascality, and so offered the hypothesis that he had wandered from the camp and had accidentally stampeded the animals. He dropped a warning to the Duchess and Mother Shipton, who of course knew the facts of their associate's defection. "They'll find out the truth about us all, when they find out anything," he added, significantly, "and there's no good frightening them now."

❶ *Who departs from the camp? What does he take?*

Tom Simson not only put all his worldly store at the disposal of Mr. Oakhurst, but seemed to enjoy the prospect of their enforced seclusion. "We'll have a good camp for a week, and then the snow'll melt, and we'll all go back together." The cheerful gayety of the young man and Mr. Oakhurst's calm infected the others. The Innocent, with the aid of pine boughs, extemporized a thatch for the roofless cabin, and the Duchess directed Piney in the rearrangement of the interior with a taste and tact that opened the blue eyes of that provincial maiden to their fullest extent. "I reckon now you're used to fine things at Poker Flat," said Piney. The Duchess turned away sharply to conceal something that reddened her cheeks

❷ *What kind of outlook does Simson have?*

7. **sotto voce.** In an undertone, so as not to be overheard

WORDS FOR EVERYDAY USE:

fe • lo • ni • ous (fə lō´nē əs) *adj.*, of a criminal

ex • tem • po • rize (eks tem´pə rīz´) *vt.*, contrive in a makeshift way to meet a pressing need

ANSWERS TO GUIDED READING QUESTIONS

❶ Uncle Billy departs from the camp with the mules.

❷ Simson has a completely optimistic outlook.

BIOGRAPHICAL NOTE

The struggle to survive in a harsh, natural world is a favorite theme of nineteenth-century American practitioners of Naturalism. Students interested in Naturalism should be encouraged to read Jack London's *The Call of the Wild.*

VOCABULARY IN CONTEXT

- The judge could not let the felonious action go unpunished.
- The volunteers extemporized a puppet show to cheer the children at the shelter.

Answer to Guided Reading Question

❶ The snowbound campers pass the time by singing songs and telling stories.

Additional Questions and Activities

Have students discuss the role of luck in Harte's story. How does each outcast deal with his or her streak of bad luck? Does anyone run into good luck in the story?

Answers. Mr. Oakhurst faces his bad luck coolly because he saw life as a game in which the dealer had better odds. The outcasts take their bad luck as it comes, perhaps believing as Oakhurst does that the only thing certain about luck is that it is bound to change. None of the outcasts enjoys good luck.

through its professional tint, and Mother Shipton requested Piney not to "chatter." But when Mr. Oakhurst returned from a weary search for the trail, he heard the sound of happy laughter echoed from the rocks. He stopped in some alarm, and his thoughts first naturally reverted to the whiskey—which he had prudently *cachéd.*[8] "And yet it don't somehow sound like whiskey," said the gambler. It was not until he caught sight of the blazing fire through the still blinding storm, and the group around it, that he settled to the conviction that it was "square fun."

Whether Mr. Oakhurst had *cachéd* his cards with the whiskey as something debarred the free access of the community, I cannot say. It was certain that, in Mother Shipton's words, he "didn't say cards once" during that evening. Haply the time was beguiled by an accordion, produced somewhat ostentatiously by Tom Simson, from his pack. Notwithstanding some difficulties attending the manipulation of this instrument, Piney Woods managed to pluck several reluctant melodies from its keys, to an accompaniment by The Innocent on a pair of bone castanets. But the crowning festivity of the evening was reached in a rude camp-meeting hymn, which the lovers, joining hands, sang with great earnestness and vociferation. I fear that a certain defiant tone and Covenanter's swing[9] to its chorus, rather than any devotional quality, caused it to speedily infect the others, who at last joined in the refrain:

How do the snowbound campers pass the time? ❶

"I'm proud to live in the service of the Lord

And I'm bound to die in His army."[10]

The pines rocked, the storm eddied and whirled above the miserable group, and the flames of their altar leaped heavenward, as if in token of the vow.

At midnight the storm abated, the rolling clouds parted, and the stars glittered keenly above the sleeping camp. Mr. Oakhurst, whose professional habits had enabled him to live on the smallest possible amount of sleep, in dividing the watch with Tom Simson, somehow managed to take upon himself the greater part of that duty. He excused himself to The Innocent, by saying that he had "often been a week without sleep." "Doing what?" asked Tom. "Poker!" replied Oakhurst, sententiously; "when a man gets a streak of luck—he don't get tired. The luck gives in first. Luck," continued the gambler, reflectively, "is a mighty queer thing. All you know about it for certain is that it's bound to change. And it's finding out when it's going to change that makes you. We've had a streak of bad luck since we left Poker Flat—you come along and slap you get into it, too. If you can hold your cards right along you're all right. For," added the gambler, with cheerful irrelevance,

"I'm proud to live in the service of the Lord,

And I'm bound to die in His army."

The third day came, and the sun, looking through the white-curtained valley,

8. **cachéd.** Hidden
9. **Covenanter's swing.** Sung with a vigorous rhythm with a martial beat, as done by the covenanters, a group of Scottish Presbyterians who wished to separate from the Church of England
10. **"I'm proud . . . His army."** Refrain of the early American spiritual "Service of the Lord"

Words for Everyday Use: **os • ten • ta • tious • ly** (äs ten tā´shəs lē) *adv.,* so as to attract attention
vo • cif • er • a • tion (vō sif´ər ā´shən) *n.,* shouting

Vocabulary in Context

- The rich man ostentatiously decorated his home with antique furniture and paintings by famous artists.
- The protesters outside the White House chanted their slogans with angry vociferation.

saw the outcasts divide their slowly decreasing store of provisions for the morning meal. It was one of the peculiarities of that mountain climate that its rays diffused a kindly warmth over the wintry landscape, as if in regretful commiseration of the past. But it revealed drift on drift of snow piled high around the hut; a hopeless, uncharted, trackless sea of white lying below the rocky shores to which the castaways still clung. Through the marvelously clear air, the smoke of the pastoral village of Poker Flat rose miles away. Mother Shipton saw it, and from a remote pinnacle of her rocky fastness, hurled in that direction a final malediction. It was her last vituperative attempt, and perhaps for that reason was invested with a certain degree of sublimity. It did her good, she privately informed the Duchess. "Just you go out there and cuss, and see." She then set herself to the task of amusing "the child," as she and the Duchess were pleased to call Piney. Piney was no chicken, but it was a soothing and ingenious theory of the pair to thus account for the fact that she didn't swear and wasn't improper.

When night crept up again through the gorges, the reedy notes of the accordion rose and fell in fitful spasms and long-drawn gasps by the flickering campfire. But music failed to fill entirely the aching void left by insufficient food, and a new diversion was proposed by Piney—story-telling. Neither Mr. Oakhurst nor his female companions caring to relate their personal experiences, this plan would have failed, too, but for The Innocent. Some months before he had chanced upon a stray copy of Mr. Pope's[11] ingenious translation of the Iliad. He now proposed to narrate the principal incidents of that poem—having thoroughly mastered the argument and fairly forgotten the words—in the current vernacular of Sandy Bar. And so for the rest of that night the Homeric demi-gods again walked the earth. Trojan bully and wily Greek wrestled in the winds, and the great pines in the canyon seemed to bow to the wrath of the son of Peleus.[12] Mr. Oakhurst listened with quiet satisfaction. Most especially was he interested in the fate of "Ash-heels,"[13] as The Innocent persisted in denominating the "swift-footed Achilles."

So with small food and much of Homer and the accordion, a week passed over the heads of the outcasts. The sun again forsook them, and again from leaden skies the snow-flakes were sifted over the land. Day by day closer around them drew the snowy circle, until at last they looked from their prison over drifted walls of dazzling white, that towered twenty feet above their heads. It became more and more difficult to replenish their fires, even from the fallen trees beside them, now half-hidden in the drifts. And yet no one complained. The lovers turned from the dreary prospect and looked into each other's eyes, and were happy. Mr. Oakhurst settled himself coolly to the losing game before him. The Duchess, more

❶ *How does Simson distract the outcasts' attention?*

❷ *What do the outcasts need?*

11. **Alexander Pope.** (1688–1744) English poet. His translation of Homer's *Iliad* was written in heroic couplets.
12. **son of Peleus.** Achilles, chief hero on the Greek side of the Trojan War
13. **Ash-heels.** The speaker means Achilles (ak il´ēz), whose only vulnerable spot was his heel, a fact emphasized by the mispronunciation

WORDS FOR EVERYDAY USE: **vi • tu • per • a • tive** (vī tōō´ pə rā´tiv) *adj.,* abusive; viciously fault-finding

ANSWERS TO GUIDED READING QUESTIONS

❶ Simson distracts the hungry outcasts by telling the story of the *Iliad.*

❷ The outcasts need food.

LITERARY TECHNIQUE

An **allusion** is a rhetorical technique in which reference is made to a person, event, object, or work from history or literature. An allusion invites a reader to compare the characters, setting, or action of one story to another story, whether true or imaginary.

ADDITIONAL QUESTIONS AND ACTIVITIES

Harte's allusion to Achilles, the hero of Homer's *Iliad,* invites the reader to compare the outcasts of Poker Flat to the heroes of ancient epics. Students might define a hero or heroine, describe the idea of heroism, and discuss the heroism displayed by the outcasts of Poker Flat.

What is Oakhurst's "Achilles heel," his vulnerable or weak spot? *Answer.* Oakhurst has a weak spot for innocence that leads him to return the money he wins from Tom Simson and protect Tom and Piney Woods from Uncle Billy.

VOCABULARY IN CONTEXT

- No one visited the vituperative man because he made people feel bad.

Answer to Guided Reading Question

❶ Mother Shipton is starving to death. She has been saving her rations for Piney.

Additional Questions and Activities

Have students research frontier settlements, analyze the frontier town as presented in Westerns, and make scale models of a typical frontier community.

Answers to Selection Check Test 4.7.1

EX. What did a committee in Poker Flat decide to do to prevent more crime in the town?
The committee decided to rid the town of people judged to be improper or objectionable.

1. What were the outcasts told when they were brought to the outskirts of Poker Flat?
They were told that their lives would be in danger if they tried to return.

2. Where does the group of outcasts plan to go?
They plan to go to a settlement known as Sandy Bar.

3. Where were Tom Simson, "The Innocent," and Piney Woods going?
They were sneaking to Poker Flat to get married.

4. Why does the group become stranded?
A snowstorm hits the group, and Uncle Billy leaves with the horses.

5. What happens to Mother Shipton? to the Duchess and Piney? to John Oakhurst?
Mother Shipton dies of starvation, the Duchess and Piney freeze to death, and John Oakhurst shoots himself.

cheerful than she had been, assumed the care of Piney. Only Mother Shipton—once the strongest of the party—seemed to sicken and fade. At midnight on the tenth day she called Oakhurst to her side. "I'm going," she said, in a voice of querulous weakness, "but don't say anything about it. Don't waken the kids. Take the bundle from under my head and open it." Mr. Oakhurst did so. It contained Mother Shipton's rations for the last week, untouched. "Give 'em to the child," she said, pointing to the sleeping Piney. "You've starved yourself," said the gambler. "That's what they call it," said the woman querulously, as she lay down again, and turning her face to the wall, passed quietly away.

What is happening to Mother Shipton? What has she been doing? Why? ❶

The accordion and the bones were put aside that day, and Homer was forgotten. When the body of Mother Shipton had been committed to the snow, Mr. Oakhurst took The Innocent aside, and showed him a pair of snow-shoes, which he had fashioned from the old pack-saddle. "There's one chance in a hundred to save her yet," he said, pointing to Piney; "but it's there," he added pointing toward Poker Flat. "If you can reach there in two days she's safe." "And you?" asked Tom Simson. "I'll stay here," was the curt reply.

The lovers parted with a long embrace. "You are not going, too," said the Duchess, as she saw Mr. Oakhurst apparently waiting to accompany him. "As far as the canyon." he replied. He turned suddenly, and kissed the Duchess, leaving her pallid face aflame, and her trembling limbs rigid with amazement.

Night came, but not Mr. Oakhurst. It brought the storm again and the whirling snow. Then the Duchess, feeding the fire,

Words for Everyday Use: **quer • u • lous** (kwer´yōō ləs) *adj.*, full of complaint

Vocabulary in Context

- A querulous patron asked for faster service.

found that some one had quietly piled beside the hut enough fuel to last a few days longer. The tears rose to her eyes, but she hid them from Piney.

The women slept but little. In the morning, looking into each other's faces, they read their fate. Neither spoke; but Piney, accepting the position of the stronger, drew near and placed her arm around the Duchess's waist. They kept this attitude for the rest of the day. That night the storm reached its greatest fury, and rending asunder the protecting pines, invaded the very hut.

Toward morning they found themselves unable to feed the fire, which gradually died away. As the embers slowly blackened, the Duchess crept closer to Piney, and broke the silence of many hours: "Piney, can you pray?" "No, dear," said Piney, simply. The Duchess, without knowing exactly why, felt relieved, and putting her head upon Piney's shoulder, spoke no more. And so reclining, the younger and purer pillowing the head of her soiled sister upon her virgin breast, they fell asleep.

The wind lulled as if it feared to waken them. Feathery drifts of snow, shaken from the long pine boughs, flew like white-winged birds, and settled about them as they slept. The moon through the rifted clouds looked down upon what had been the camp. But all human stain, all trace of earthly travail, was hidden beneath the spotless mantle mercifully flung from above.

They slept all that day and the next, nor did they waken when voices and footsteps broke the silence of the camp. And when pitying fingers brushed the snow from their wan faces, you could scarcely have told from the equal peace that dwelt upon them, which was she that had sinned. Even the Law of Poker Flat recognized this, and turned away, leaving them still locked in each other's arms.

❶ *What do Piney and the Duchess understand?*

But at the head of the gulch, on one of the largest pine trees, they found the deuce of clubs pinned to the bark with a bowie knife. It bore the following, written in pencil, in a firm hand:

†
BENEATH THIS TREE
LIES THE BODY
OF
JOHN OAKHURST,
WHO STRUCK A STREAK OF BAD LUCK
ON THE 23D OF NOVEMBER, 1850,
AND
HANDED IN HIS CHECKS
ON THE 7TH DECEMBER, 1850
†

And pulseless and cold, with a Derringer[14] by his side and a bullet in his heart, though still calm as in life, beneath the snow, lay he who was at once the strongest and yet the weakest of the outcasts of Poker Flat. ■

❷ *What has Oakhurst done?*

14. **Derringer.** Short-barreled pocket pistol, invented by Henry Derringer

Answers to Guided Reading Questions

❶ Piney and the Duchess know that they are going to die.

❷ Oakhurst has committed suicide.

Literary Technique

An **epitaph** is an inscription or verse written to be used on a tomb or written in commemoration of someone who has died. It memorializes what is distinctive about the deceased. Have students create epitaphs for the other outcasts of Poker Flat. Students should use the style, lettering, and arrangement of words used on a tombstone, as in Oakhurst's epitaph.

Additional Questions and Activities

If life is a poker game to Oakhurst, what might it be for the other outcasts of Poker Flat?

Answers. Answers will vary. To the Duchess and Mother Shipton life is an evening with a client. To Tom Simson and Piney Woods life is a bowl of cherries. To Uncle Billy life is a gold robbery.

RESPONDING TO THE SELECTION

Students might assume the role of spokesperson for the group with whom they sympathize. They can describe events from their group's point of view, defend their group's actions, or explain their group's view of the other groups.

ANSWERS FOR REVIEWING THE SELECTION

RECALLING

1. A vigilance committee in Poker Flat exile the outcasts in reaction to a recent robbery and murder.

2. The outcasts meet Tom Simson, the Innocent from Sandy Bar, and Piney Woods, his fiance. Their names tell the reader that they are young, inexperienced, and naive.

3. Oakhurst discovers that Uncle Billy has stolen the mules and departed and that the rest of the outcasts are snowed in.

4. The young people sing the hymn with "earnestness" and "vociferation." Their action tells us they are religious. The outcasts join in not because they are religious but because the song is rhythmical.

INTERPRETING

Responses will vary. Possible responses are given.

5. The people of Poker Flat are justified in that they have the right to punish those who break the law. However, they are simply using the outcasts as scapegoats, and their reaction, as the narrator says, is itself "lawless and ungovernable."

6. The two young people are running away to Poker Flat to be married. The town is dangerous and corrupt, so their journey is unwise.

7. Oakhurst wants to preserve the young people's innocence. The young people might be frightened to learn that the people they have met are outlaws.

(cont.)

Responding to the Selection

In Harte's story there are three main groups of characters: the townspeople of Poker Flat, the outcasts, and the two young people from Sandy Bar. With whom do you sympathize most, the people who want to rid their town of immoral and suspicious characters, the outcasts, or the young couple? Why?

Reviewing the Selection

RECALLING

1. Why are the outcasts thrown out of Poker Flat?

2. Whom do the outcasts meet on the road to Sandy Bar? What do the names of these two people tell the reader about them?

3. What does Oakhurst discover has happened in the middle of the night?

4. How do the young people sing the hymn around the campfire? What does this tell us about them? Why do the outcasts join in the singing?

INTERPRETING

5. Do you believe that the people of Poker Flat are justified in throwing out some of the community's members? Why, or why not?

6. Why are the two young people traveling to Poker Flat? What kind of town is Poker Flat? Is the elopement of the young people wise or unwise?

7. Why does Oakhurst lie to the young people about Uncle Billy's theft? Why might the truth frighten the young people?

8. The narrator says that Oakhurst is "at once the strongest and yet the weakest of the outcasts of Poker Flat." In what way is he strong and in what way is he weak?

SYNTHESIZING

9. When they find Piney and the Duchess dead, the people of Poker Flat can't tell the difference between the two. The "human stain" of the Duchess is "hidden beneath the spotless mantle" of snow, and the narrator says that "you could scarcely have told from the equal peace that dwelt upon them, which was she that had sinned." What comment is the narrator making here about outcasts and ordinary people?

10. How do the various characters in the story respond to their streak of bad luck? In your opinion, which characters are the most admirable?

ANSWERS FOR REVIEWING THE SELECTION (CONT.)

8. Oakhurst is strong in that he realizes he is not going to survive, and yet he remains calm and detached. He is weak in that he cannot face dying of hunger and cold.

SYNTHESIZING

Responses will vary. Possible responses are given.

9. Harte is saying that all people, moral and immoral, ordinary people and outcasts, are equal in the face of death.

10. Uncle Billy saves himself. Mother Shipton sacrifices herself for Piney Woods. The Duchess becomes weak and frightened. Piney Woods is strong and comforts the Duchess. Tom Simson, the Innocent, tries to save them all by trying to make it to Poker Flat on foot. Oakhurst remains calm and detached but ultimately kills himself.

Understanding Literature (Questions for Discussion)

1. **Stereotype or Stock Character.** A **stereotypical,** or **stock, character** is one who does not deviate from conventional expectations of such a character. Who are the stock characters in Bret Harte's story about the American frontier? In what ways is their behavior predictable? In what ways is their behavior unpredictable? What are some other stock characters in stories of the American West? How do we expect them to behave?

2. **Sentimentality. Sentimentality** is an excessive expression of emotion. What one generation of readers thinks of as a normal amount of emotion in a story, another generation of readers finds excessive. Do you think Bret Harte's story is sentimental? What are the moments in the story when the reader is meant to feel the greatest emotion? What makes those moments emotional? What are some of the most sentimental moments in other stories you have read in books or seen at the movies? Do you like sentimental stories or not? Why?

Responding in Writing

Parody. A **parody** is a literary work that imitates another work for humorous, often satirical, purposes. Work with other students to plan a parody of a piece of Western fiction. Begin by coming up with a list of stock characters from Westerns, such as the straight-shooting, straight-talking, fearless lawman; the sharp-shooting, reckless young gunfighter; the kindly, honest owner of the general store; the discontented Eastern lady transplanted to the lawless, uncomfortable frontier; the sunburned old prospector certain that he will hit the mother lode any day, and so on. After creating a list of such characters, make up humorous names, dress, and habits for them. Then work on creating a setting. Name the town in which these people live. Draw a map of Main Street. Name the businesses and other places there. Again, strive to create names that are humorous. Next, create a plot by thinking of a conflict, or struggle, that might arise in the town. Here are some possibilities:

1. A mysterious Man in Black arrives in town, walks into the local watering hole, and challenges any and all comers to a pea-shooting contest

2. The cattlemen of the town become angry when a flamingo rancher starts buying up range land and fencing it in to create preserves for his birds

3. The Jones Brothers—five strapping sons of a local rancher whose collective I.Q. equals that of a cabbage—all fall in love with the lovely Miss Elvira Hornswaggle

Finally, brainstorm a list of events involving your characters that show the conflict being introduced, developed, and resolved. See if you can come up with a humorous, surprise ending for your story.

Answers for Understanding Literature

► See the evaluation forms for discussion, active listening, and oral communication, *Assessment Portfolio,* 7.11–7.14.

Responses will vary. Possible responses are given.

1. Stereotype or Stock Character. Oakhurst, the Gambler, behaves with calm, cool detachment, though his farewell kiss of the Duchess and his suicide are uncharacteristic actions. The Duchess and Mother Shipton, the Harlots, display the profanity and rough, uncouth behavior of their type, though the Duchess reveals a gentle and childlike dependency upon Piney Woods while Mother Shipton heroically sacrifices herself for Piney. Uncle Billy, the Drunkard and Thief, behaves strictly according to character by stealing the mules and abandoning the others. Tom Simson and Piney Woods, the Innocents, display the naive heroism of their type. Other stock characters of the West include the fearless Sheriff, the Prospector, the sophisticated Eastern Lady, the independent and lonesome Cowboy, the silent Gunslinger, the timid Proprietor of the General Store, and the prim and proper School Marm.

2. Sentimentality. The sentimental moments occur at the end of the story when the outcasts die. Mother Shipton's death is emotionally charged by her heroic self-sacrifice, her deliberate decision to starve herself for Piney. The death of the Duchess and Piney Woods reaches its sentimental climax when the snow buries them, wiping away the difference between the harlot and the maiden. Some of the most sentimental moments occur when Oakhurst, the calm, cool, and detached gambler, reveals his tender side when he kisses the Duchess farewell, when he leaves wood for the women, and when he commits suicide.

Analytic Scales for Responding in Writing

Assign a score from 1 to 25 for each grading criterion below. (For more detailed evaluation, see the evaluation forms for writing, revising, and proofreading, *Assessment Portfolio,* 7.1–7.10.)

Parody

- **Content/Unity.** The parody presents a set of well-developed stock characters from Western fiction, a vivid setting, and a plot with fully imagined events. All these elements of the parody use an ample number of particular details.
- **Organization/Coherence.** The parody relates a story, a series of scenes arranged in sequential, chronological order. The scenes should introduce, develop, and resolve a single, central conflict between two characters, groups, or forces.
- **Language/Style.** The parody uses vivid and precise nouns, verbs, and modifiers, and well-developed and coherent paragraphs.
- **Conventions.** The parody avoids errors in spelling, grammar, usage, mechanics, and manuscript form.

ADDITIONAL RESOURCES

READER'S GUIDE
- Selection Worksheet, 7.2

ASSESSMENT PORTFOLIO
- Selection Check Test, 4.7.3
- Selection Test, 4.7.4

ESSENTIAL SKILLS PRACTICE BOOKS
- *Language,* 2.62, 2.150

ENRICHMENT ACTIVITIES

Have students stage a New England town meeting in nineteenth- or twentieth-century America. The topic to be discussed is whether an industrialist should be allowed to build a factory in a rural community. Each student should play a role during the meeting. Elect one person to play the industrialist and one person to play a naturalist. Students should be city councilors, farmers, unemployed shopkeepers, and librarians.

SUPPORT FOR LEP STUDENTS

Some students might have difficulty understanding the dialect of Jewett's rural characters. These students can be paired up with English-proficient students to translate the passages of dialect into standard English.

PREREADING

SHORT STORY

"A White Heron"
by Sarah Orne Jewett

ABOUT THE AUTHOR

Sarah Orne Jewett (1849–1909) was born in South Berwick, Maine, the daughter of a small-town country doctor. When she was young she often traveled with her father when he made house calls to his patients in the country. Inspired by the work of Harriet Beecher Stowe, as a teenager she published her first short story in the *Atlantic Monthly*, a well-known national magazine. In the fiction she wrote when she grew older, she described and celebrated rural Maine and its people. Her novel *A Country Doctor* tells of a young woman from New England who takes the then unheard-of step of refusing to marry to pursue a career in medicine. Jewett is best known for her collections of short stories, including *Deephaven* (1877), *A White Heron* (1886), *The King of Folly Island* (1888), *A Native of Winby* (1893), and her finest work, *The County of the Pointed Firs* (1896).

ABOUT THE SELECTION

"A White Heron," which appeared in a collection by the same name, is an example of regional literature. The nineteenth-century regionalists wrote at a time when the United States was being rapidly industrialized, when the production of material goods was being taken from people in their homes and transferred to machines in factories. Industrialization was accompanied by the movement of large numbers of people from the country to the city, where they could find work. Ancient, old-growth forests were being cut down to plant farms to feed city dwellers, and the wild animals that inhabited these places were losing their natural habitats. Like much regional literature, "A White Heron" can be seen as a protest against these events. It encourages the reader to develop an intimate relationship with a place. Above all, it describes a conflict felt during frontier days by people who lived off the land: the conflict between a desire to conquer the natural world and the need to relate to it on its own terms. This conflict is still being worked out in our own time.

GOALS/OBJECTIVES

Studying this lesson will enable students to

- empathize with the protagonist's inner conflicts
- relate American regionalist fiction of the nineteenth century to industrialization
- identify Sarah Orne Jewett as a nineteenth-century regionalist and briefly describe the region she portrayed
- define the literary concepts of *motif* and *conflict* using examples from the selection
- write a sketch of a character from the selection
- recognize and correct run-on sentences

READER'S JOURNAL

Have you ever known something that somebody else wanted to know? Did you keep it a secret, or did you tell someone? Why, or why not? If you don't mind telling it, what was the secret? If you did tell the secret, to whom did you tell it? Why? Were you happy that you told the secret? Why, or why not?

LANGUAGE SKILLS

Read the Language Arts Survey, 2.150, "Dialects of English." Then find a sentence in the selection in which a character speaks in a regional dialect. Rewrite the sentence in standard English. What differences does the sentence that you chose show between the regional dialect and standard English?

"A White Heron"

SARAH ORNE JEWETT

I

The woods were already filled with shadows one June evening, just before eight o'clock, though a bright sunset still glimmered faintly among the trunks of the trees. A little girl was driving home her cow, a plodding, dilatory, provoking creature in her behavior, but a valued companion for all that. They were going away from whatever light there was, and striking deep into the woods, but their feet were familiar with the path, and it was no matter whether their eyes could see it or not.

There was hardly a night the summer through when the old cow could be found waiting at the pasture bars; on the contrary, it was her greatest pleasure to hide herself away among the high huckleberry bushes, and though she wore a loud bell she had made the discovery that if one stood perfectly still it would not ring. So Sylvia had to hunt for her until she found her, and call Co'! Co'! with never an answering Moo, until her childish patience was quite spent. If the creature had not given good milk and plenty of it, the case would have seemed very different to her owners. Besides, Sylvia had all the time there was, and very little use to make of it. Sometimes in pleasant weather it was a consolation to look upon the cow's pranks as an intelligent attempt to play hide and seek, and as the child had no playmates she lent herself to this amusement with a good deal of zest. Though this chase had been so long that the wary animal herself had given an unusual signal of her whereabouts, Sylvia had only laughed when she came upon Mistress Moolly at the swamp-side, and urged her affectionately homeward with a twig of birch leaves. The old cow was not inclined to wander farther, she even turned in the

❶ *Why might Sylvia look upon the cow as a playmate?*

WORDS FOR EVERYDAY USE: **dil • a • to • ry** (dil´ə tôr´ē) *adj.,* causing delay

VOCABULARY IN CONTEXT

- The child used many dilatory tactics to avoid going to bed.

PREREADING NOTES

READER'S JOURNAL

Ask students to reflect on secrecy in their journals. When is secrecy appropriate? reprehensible? fun? dangerous? nasty? interesting? childish?

RESEARCH SKILLS

Have students show on the board the differences between the regional dialect and the standard English version of their chosen sentence.

ANSWER TO GUIDED READING QUESTION

❶ Sylvia might look upon the cow as a playmate because she has no human playmates.

VOCABULARY FROM THE SELECTION

course	ponderous
demure	premonition
dilatory	proffer
gallantly	rebuke
gravity	shoal
hermitage	squalor
inaudibly	vex
ornithologist	wretched
pinion	

Answers to Guided Reading Questions

❶ Sylvia loves living on the farm where she has plenty of room to wander.

❷ Sylvia is surprised by a whistle. She is "horror-stricken" because it is a boy's whistle.

Historical Note

By the end of World War I one-half of the people in the United States lived in twelve major cities, and 8.5 million of these people were factory workers. Life in manufacturing towns was marked by low wages, dangerous working conditions, and overcrowded and filthy living quarters. Students interested in early-American cities should be encouraged to read Upton Sinclair's *The Jungle*.

right direction for once as they left the pasture, and stepped along the road at a good pace. She was quite ready to be milked now, and seldom stopped to browse. Sylvia wondered what her grandmother would say because they were so late. It was a great while since she had left home at half past five o'clock, but everybody knew the difficulty of making this errand a short one. Mrs. Tilley had chased the hornéd torment[1] too many summer evenings herself to blame anyone else for lingering, and was only thankful as she waited that she had Sylvia, nowadays, to give such valuable assistance. The good woman suspected that Sylvia loitered occasionally on her own account; there never was such a child for straying about out-of-doors since the world was made! Everybody said that it was a good change for a little maid who had tried to grow for eight years in a crowded manufacturing town, but, as for Sylvia herself, it seemed as if she never had been alive at all before she came to live at the farm. She thought often with wistful compassion of a wretched geranium that belonged to a town neighbor.

How does Sylvia feel about living on the farm? ❶

"'Afraid of folks,'" old Mrs. Tilley said to herself, with a smile, after she had made the unlikely choice of Sylvia from her daughter's houseful of children, and was returning to the farm. "'Afraid of folks,' they said! I guess she won't be troubled no great with 'em up to the old place!" When they reached the door of the lonely house and stopped to unlock it, and the cat came to purr loudly, and rub against them, a deserted pussy, indeed, but fat with young robins, Sylvia whispered that this was a beautiful place to live in, and she never should wish to go home.

What sound surprises Sylvia in the woods? Why is she "horror-stricken" to hear this sound? ❷

The companions followed the shady woodroad, the cow taking slow steps, and the child very fast ones. The cow stopped long at the brook to drink, as if the pasture were not half a swamp, and Sylvia stood still and waited, letting her bare feet cool themselves in the shoal water, while the great twilight moths struck softly against her. She waded on through the brook as the cow moved away, and listened to the thrushes with a heart that beat fast with pleasure. There was a stirring in the great boughs overhead. They were full of little birds and beasts that seemed to be wide awake, and going about their world, or else saying good-night to each other in sleepy twitters. Sylvia herself felt sleepy as she walked along. However, it was not much farther to the house, and the air was soft and sweet. She was not often in the woods so late as this, and it made her feel as if she were a part of the gray shadows and the moving leaves. She was just thinking how long it seemed since she first came to the farm a year ago, and wondering if everything went on in the noisy town just the same as when she was there; the thought of the great red-faced boy who used to chase and frighten her made her hurry along the path to escape from the shadow of the trees.

Suddenly this little woods-girl is horror-stricken to hear a clear whistle not very far away. Not a bird's whistle, which would have a sort of friendliness, but a boy's whistle, determined, and somewhat

1. **hornéd torment.** Exasperating cow

Words for Everyday Use: **wretch • ed** (rech´id) *adj.,* miserable
shoal (shōl) *adj.,* shallow

Vocabulary in Context

- Cold, hunger, thirst, and lack of sleep made the man feel wretched.
- Hunting for frogs, the heron walked the shoal pond.

aggressive. Sylvia left the cow to whatever sad fate might await her, and stepped discreetly aside into the bushes, but she was just too late. The enemy had discovered her, and called out in a very cheerful and persuasive tone, "Halloa, little girl, how far is it to the road?" and trembling Sylvia answered almost inaudibly, "A good ways."

She did not dare to look boldly at the tall young man, who carried a gun over his shoulder, but she came out of her bush and again followed the cow, while he walked alongside.

"I have been hunting for some birds," the stranger said kindly, "and I have lost my way, and need a friend very much. Don't be afraid," he added gallantly. "Speak up and tell me what your name is, and whether you think I can spend the night at your house, and go out gunning early in the morning."

Sylvia was more alarmed than before. Would not her grandmother consider her much to blame? But who could have foreseen such an accident as this? It did not seem to be her fault, and she hung her head as if the stem of it were broken, but managed to answer "Sylvy," with much effort when her companion again asked her name.

Mrs. Tilley was standing in the doorway when the trio came into view. The cow gave a loud moo by way of explanation.

"Yes, you'd better speak up for yourself, you old trial! Where'd she tucked herself away this time, Sylvy?" But Sylvia kept an awed silence; she knew by instinct that her grandmother did not comprehend the gravity of the situation. She must be mistaking the stranger for one of the farmer-lads of the region.

The young man stood his gun beside the door, and dropped a lumpy gamebag beside it; then he bade Mrs. Tilley good-evening, and repeated his wayfarer's story, and asked if he could have a night's lodging

"Put me anywhere you like," he said. "I must be off early in the morning, before day; but I am very hungry, indeed. You can give me some milk at any rate, that's plain."

"Dear sakes, yes," responded the hostess, whose long slumbering hospitality seemed to be easily awakened. "You might fare better if you went out to the main road a mile or so, but you're welcome to what we've got. I'll milk right off, and you make yourself at home. You can sleep on husks or feathers," she proffered graciously. "I raised them all myself. There's good pasturing for geese just below here towards the ma'sh. Now step round and set a plate for the gentleman, Sylvy!" And Sylvia promptly stepped. She was glad to have something to do, and she was hungry herself.

It was a surprise to find so clean and comfortable a little dwelling in this New England wilderness. The young man had known the horrors of its most primitive housekeeping, and the dreary squalor of that level of society which does not rebel at the companionship of hens. This was the best thrift of an old-fashioned farmstead, though on such a small scale that it seemed like a hermitage. He listened eagerly to the old woman's quaint talk, he watched Sylvia's pale face and shining gray

❶ *Why might Sylvia be alarmed?*

WORDS FOR EVERYDAY USE:

in • au • di • bly (in ô´də blē) *adv.,* not loudly enough to be heard
gal • lant • ly (gal´ənt lē) *adv.,* politely, nobly
grav • i • ty (grav´i tē) *n.,* seriousness
prof • fer (präf´ər) *vt.,* offer
squal • or (skwäl´ər) *n.,* filth and misery
her • mi • tage (hər´mi tij) *n.,* place where a person can live away from others

ANSWER TO GUIDED READING QUESTION

❶ Sylvia might be alarmed because she believes her grandmother will be angry at her for bringing a strange boy home.

LITERARY TECHNIQUE

The **point of view** is the vantage point from which a story is told. "A White Heron" is a **third-person, limited narrative**, which means that the narrator is not a character in the story but someone outside it, someone who refers to the characters as "he," "she," and "they"; the narrator limits herself to what one character (in this case, Sylvia) experiences, thinks, and feels.

ADDITIONAL QUESTIONS AND ACTIVITIES

Ask students to identify and discuss those moments when it is especially clear that the reader is seeing events through Sylvia's eyes.

VOCABULARY IN CONTEXT

- The small child spoke inaudibly, so we had difficulty hearing him.
- The prince gallantly threw down his cloak for the princess to sit upon.
- The gravity of the speech created silence in the auditorium.
- Proffering food to the poor made the rich man happy.
- The squalor in that city made its mayor feel shame.
- Withdrawing to his hermitage was the monk's solution to his problems.

Answers to Guided Reading Questions

❶ The guest is interested in Sylvia and her knowledge of birds.

❷ The young man has come in Sylvia's direction in search of a white heron. He is an amateur ornithologist collecting specimens of rare birds.

Historical Note

The nineteenth century was the heyday of the amateur naturalist. The young ornithologist in "A White Heron" has modeled himself upon eighteenth- and nineteenth-century naturalists like Carl von Linne, or Linnaeus. In his *Systema Naturae*, Linneaus set out to catalogue and systematically classify the world's plant and animal species. A correct identification of a particular animal or plant demanded a close examination of a specimen, which could be conducted only after killing it.

Additional Questions and Activities

Have students discuss the different ways that animals are treated in nature parks, zoos, biology labs, suburban neighborhoods, and hunting areas. Then ask them to identify the different types of people and activities associated with these practices and to debate the pros and cons of these activities.

In what is the guest interested? ❶

eyes with ever growing enthusiasm, and insisted that this was the best supper he had eaten for a month, and afterward the new-made friends sat down in the doorway together while the moon came up.

Soon it would be berry-time, and Sylvia was a great help at picking. The cow was a good milker, though a plaguy thing to keep track of, the hostess gossiped frankly, adding presently that she had buried four children, so Sylvia's mother, and a son (who might be dead) in California were all the children she had left. "Dan, my boy, was a great hand to go gunning," she explained sadly. "I never wanted for pa'tridges or gray squer'ls while he was to home. He's been a great wand'rer, I expect, and he's no hand to write letters. There, I don't blame him, I'd ha' seen the world myself if it had been so I could.

Why has the young man come in Sylvia's direction? ❷

"Sylvia takes after him," the grandmother continued affectionately, after a minute's pause. "There ain't a foot o' ground she don't know her way over, and the wild creaturs counts her one o' themselves. Squer'ls she'll tame to come an' feed right out o' her hands, and all sorts o' birds. Last winter she got the jay-birds to bangeing[2] here, and I believe she'd 'a' scanted herself[3] of her own meals to have plenty to throw out amongst 'em, if I hadn't kep' watch. Anything but crows, I tell her, I'm willin' to help support—though Dan he had a tamed one o' them that did seem to have reason same as folks. It was round here a good spell after he went away. Dan an' his father they didn't hitch,—but he never held up his head ag'in after Dan had dared him an' gone off."

The guest did not notice this hint of family sorrows in his eager interest in something else.

"So Sylvy knows all about birds, does she?" he exclaimed, as he looked round at the little girl who sat, very demure but increasingly sleepy, in the moonlight. "I am making a collection of birds myself. I have been at it ever since I was a boy." (Mrs. Tilley smiled.) "There are two or three very rare ones I have been hunting for these five years. I mean to get them on my own ground if they can be found."

"Do you cage 'em up?" asked Mrs. Tilley doubtfully, in response to this enthusiastic announcement.

"Oh, no, they're stuffed and preserved, dozens and dozens of them," said the ornithologist, "and I have shot or snared every one myself. I caught a glimpse of a white heron three miles from here on Saturday, and I have followed it in this direction. They have never been found in this district at all. The little white heron, it is," and he turned again to look at Sylvia with the hope of discovering that the rare bird was one of her acquaintances.

But Sylvia was watching a hop-toad in the narrow footpath.

"You would know the heron if you saw it," the stranger continued eagerly. "A queer tall white bird with soft feathers and long thin legs. And it would have a nest perhaps in the top of a high tree, made of sticks, something like a hawk's nest."

Sylvia's heart gave a wild beat; she knew that strange white bird, and had once stolen softly near where it stood in some

2. **bangeing.** Hanging around
3. **'a' scanted herself.** Would have deprived herself

Words for Everyday Use:

de • mure (di myoor´) *adj.*, modest; shy

or • ni • thol • o • gist (ôr´nə thäl´ə jist) *n.*, one who studies birds

Vocabulary in Context

- They were too polite and demure to ask the celebrity for his autograph.
- Ornithologists gathered at the convention to discuss the loss of species habitat.
- The old woman's premonitions of disaster have usually turned out to be true.

bright green swamp grass, away over at the other side of the woods. There was an open place where the sunshine always seemed strangely yellow and hot, where tall, nodding rushes grew, and her grandmother had warned her that she might sink in the soft black mud underneath and never be heard of more. Not far beyond were the salt marshes just this side the sea itself, which Sylvia wondered and dreamed about, but never had seen, whose great voice could sometimes be heard above the noise of the woods on stormy nights.

"I can't think of anything I should like so much as to find that heron's nest," the handsome stranger was saying. "I would give ten dollars to anybody who could show it to me," he added desperately, "and I mean to spend my whole vacation hunting for it if need be. Perhaps it was only migrating, or had been chased out of its own region by some bird of prey."

Mrs. Tilley gave amazed attention to all this, but Sylvia still watched the toad, not divining, as she might have done at some calmer time, that the creature wished to get to its hole under the doorstep, and was much hindered by the unusual spectators at that hour of the evening. No amount of thought, that night, could decide how many wished-for treasures the ten dollars, so lightly spoken of, would buy.

The next day the young sportsman hovered about the woods, and Sylvia kept him company, having lost her first fear of the friendly lad, who proved to be most kind and sympathetic. He told her many things about the birds and what they knew and where they lived and what they did with themselves. And he gave her a jackknife, which she thought as great a treasure as if she were a desert-islander. All day long he did not once make her troubled or afraid except when he brought down some unsuspecting singing creature from its bough. Sylvia would have liked him vastly better without his gun; she could not understand why he killed the very birds he seemed to like so much. But as the day waned, Sylvia still watched the young man with loving admiration. She had never seen anybody so charming and delightful; the woman's heart, asleep in the child, was vaguely thrilled by a dream of love. Some premonition of that great power stirred and swayed these young creatures who traversed the solemn woodlands with soft-footed silent care. They stopped to listen to a

Louisiana Heron. *Rodney Busch. Private collection*

❶ *How does Sylvia feel about the young man killing birds?*

WORDS FOR EVERYDAY USE: **prem • o • ni • tion** (prēm´ə nish´ən) *n.,* feeling that something will happen

ANSWER TO GUIDED READING QUESTION

❶ Sylvia does not understand why the young man kills the birds that he likes so much.

ADDITIONAL QUESTIONS AND ACTIVITIES

What might be the "bird of prey" who has chased the heron out of its own region?

Answer. The "bird of prey" might be hunters like the young sportsman.

Answers to Guided Reading Questions

❶ Yes, Sylvia is hoping to help find the white heron.

❷ Sylvia is kept awake by her plan to find the white heron.

Historical Note

At the dawn of the colonial era, 95 percent of the New England landscape was forested. In the nineteenth century, 90 percent of the woodlots were cleared in pioneer settlement, the great white pines being used for the masts of ships. As a result of a decline in farming and the use of fossil fuels, 80 percent of the land is once again forested.

Answers to Selection Check Test 4.7.3

EX. What is Sylvia doing when she hears a whistle?
Sylvia is driving home the cow.

1. What does the guest do with the birds he collects?
He stuffs and preserves them.

2. What is the hunter's special interest while on this particular trip?
He would like to find a white heron.

3. How does Sylvia feel about the guest and his hunting?
She does not understand how he can shoot the birds that he admires so much, but she likes and admires him because he is so kind to her.

4. Why does bringing the hunter to the heron appeal to Sylvia?
She would like to have the money the hunter is offering, and she would like to please the hunter.

5. What does Sylvia finally decide to do?
She decides to keep the heron's whereabouts a secret.

bird's song; they pressed forward again eagerly, parting the branches,—speaking to each other rarely and in whispers; the young man going first and Sylvia following, fascinated, a few steps behind, with her gray eyes dark with excitement.

Is Sylvia hoping to help find the white heron? ❶

She grieved because the longed-for white heron was elusive, but she did not lead the guest, she only followed, and there was no such thing as speaking first. The sound of her own unquestioned voice would have terrified her,—it was hard enough to answer yes or no when there was need of that. At last evening began to fall, and they drove the cow home together, and Sylvia smiled with pleasure when they came to the place where she heard the whistle and was afraid only the night before.

What keeps Sylvia awake? ❷

II

Half a mile from home, at the farther edge of the woods, where the land was highest, a great pine tree stood, the last of its generation. Whether it was left for a boundary mark, or for what reason, no one could say; the woodchoppers who had felled its mates were dead and gone long ago, and a whole forest of sturdy trees, pines and oaks and maples, had grown again. But the stately head of this old pine towered above them all and made a landmark for sea and shore miles and miles away. Sylvia knew it well. She had always believed that whoever climbed to the top of it could see the ocean; and the little girl had often laid her hand on the great rough trunk and looked up wistfully at those dark boughs that the wind always stirred, no matter how hot and still the air might be below. Now she thought of the tree with a new excitement, for why, if one climbed it at break of day, could not one see all the world, and easily discover from whence the white heron flew, and mark the place, and find the hidden nest?

What a spirit of adventure, what wild ambition! What fancied triumph and delight and glory for the later morning when she could make known the secret! It was almost too real and too great for the childish heart to bear.

All night the door of the little house stood open and the whippoorwills came and sang upon the very step. The young sportsman and his old hostess were sound asleep, but Sylvia's great design kept her broad awake and watching. She forgot to think of sleep. The short summer night seemed as long as the winter darkness, and at last when the whippoorwills ceased, and she was afraid the morning would after all come too soon, she stole out of the house and followed the pasture path through the woods, hastening toward the open ground beyond, listening with a sense of comfort and companionship to the drowsy twitter of a half-awakened bird, whose perch she had jarred in passing. Alas, if the great wave of human interest which flooded for the first time this dull little life should sweep away the satisfactions of an existence heart to heart with nature and the dumb life of the forest!

There was the huge tree asleep yet in the paling moonlight, and small and silly Sylvia began with utmost bravery to mount to the top of it, with tingling, eager blood coursing the channels of her whole frame, with her bare feet and fingers, that pinched and held like bird's claws to the

Words for Everyday Use: **course** (kôrs) *vi.,* move swiftly; flow through

Vocabulary in Context

- The overflowing river coursed through the streets of the town.
- The ponderous elephant walked through the jungle.
- Clipping the hawk's pinions kept it from flying away.

monstrous ladder reaching up, up, almost to the sky itself. First she must mount the white oak tree that grew alongside, where she was almost lost among the dark branches and the green leaves heavy and wet with dew; a bird fluttered off its nest, and a red squirrel ran to and fro and scolded pettishly at the harmless housebreaker. Sylvia felt her way easily. She had often climbed there, and knew that higher still one of the oak's upper branches chafed against the pine trunk, just where its lower boughs were set close together. There, when she made the dangerous pass from one tree to the other, the great enterprise would really begin.

She crept out along the swaying oak limb at last, and took the daring step across into the old pine tree. The way was harder than she thought; she must reach far and hold fast, the sharp dry twigs caught and held her and scratched her like angry talons, the pitch made her thin little fingers clumsy and stiff as she went round and round the tree's great stem, higher and higher upward. The sparrows and robins in the woods below were beginning to wake and twitter to the dawn, yet it seemed much lighter there aloft in the pine tree, and the child knew that she must hurry if her project were to be of any use.

The tree seemed to lengthen itself out as she went up, and to reach farther and farther upward. It was like a great main-mast to the voyaging earth; it must truly have been amazed that morning through all its ponderous frame as it felt this determined spark of human spirit winding its way from higher branch to branch. Who knows how steadily the least twigs held themselves to advantage this light, weak creature on her way! The old pine must have loved his new dependent. More than all the hawks, and bats, and moths, and even the sweet-voiced thrushes, was the brave, beating heart of the solitary gray-eyed child. And the tree stood still and frowned away the winds that June morning while the dawn grew bright in the east.

Sylvia's face was like a pale star, if one had seen it from the ground, when the last thorny bough was past, and she stood trembling and tired but wholly triumphant, high in the treetop. Yes, there was the sea with the dawning sun making a golden dazzle over it, and toward that glorious east flew two hawks with slow-moving pinions. How low they looked in the air from that height when one had only seen them before far up, and dark against the blue sky. Their gray feathers were as soft as moths; they seemed only a little way from the tree, and Sylvia felt as if she too could go flying away among the clouds. Westward, the woodlands and farms reached miles and miles into the distance; here and there were church steeples, and white villages; truly it was a vast and awesome world!

The birds sang louder and louder. At last the sun came up bewilderingly bright. Sylvia could see the white sails of ships out at sea, and the clouds that were purple and rose-colored and yellow at first began to fade away. Where was the white heron's nest in the sea of green branches, and was this wonderful sight and pageant of the world the only reward for having climbed

WORDS FOR EVERYDAY USE:

pon • der • ous (pän´dər əs) *adj.*, very heavy

pin • ion (pin´yən) *n.*, part of a bird's wing

LITERARY TECHNIQUE

An **archetype** is an inherited, often unconscious, ancestral memory or motif that recurs throughout history and literature. The landmark pine in "A White Heron" can be seen as an archetype. Like Jacob's ladder in Genesis, the pine is an image of the universal pillar, or *axis mundi,* that connects heaven and earth. Other examples include the Babylonian ziggurat, the Egyptian pyramid, and the New England church steeple.

ADDITIONAL QUESTIONS AND ACTIVITIES

Ask students to develop a list of archetypes and then find examples of those archetypes in literature, movies, television, comic strips, magazines, and fairy tales. Some archetypes they might include in their list are the journey to the underworld, the heavenly ascent, the scapegoat, the image of paradise, the wicked stepmother, and the heavenly messenger.

Answers to Guided Reading Questions

❶ The young man is anticipating the pleasure of searching for and finding the white heron.

❷ Sylvia does not tell the location of the heron's nest because the young man will kill it even though she has developed a special relationship with the bird.

Literary Technique

A **reversal** is a dramatic change in the direction of events in a drama or narrative, especially a change in the fortunes of the protagonist. This change usually stems from the protagonist's recognition of something previously unrecognized.

Additional Questions and Activities

What is the reversal that occurs at the end of "A White Heron"?

Answer. The reversal that occurs is Sylvia's decision not to tell the young man the location of the heron's nest.

Have students form small groups and identify those moments in the story in which Sylvia forms and develops her plan to discover and reveal the nest's location.

What "day's pleasure" is the young man anticipating? ❶

to such a giddy height? Now look down again, Sylvia, where the green marsh is set among the shining birches and dark hemlocks; there where you saw the white heron once you will see him again; look, look! a white spot of him like a single floating feather comes up from the dead hemlock and grows larger, and rises, and comes close at last, and goes by the landmark pine with steady sweep of wing and outstretched slender neck and crested head. And wait! wait! do not move a foot or a finger, little girl, do not send an arrow of light and consciousness from your two eager eyes, for the heron has perched on a pine bough not far beyond yours, and cries back to his mate on the nest, and plumes his feathers for the new day!

The child gives a long sigh a minute later when a company of shouting catbirds comes also to the tree, and vexed by their fluttering and lawlessness the solemn heron goes away. She knows his secret now, the wild, light, slender bird that floats and wavers, and goes back like an arrow presently to his home in the green world beneath. Then Sylvia, well satisfied, makes her perilous way down again, not daring to look far below the branch she stands on, ready to cry sometimes because her fingers ache and her lamed feet slip. Wondering over and over again what the stranger would say to her, and what he would think when she told him how to find his way straight to the heron's nest.

Does Sylvia tell the location of the white heron's nest? Why, or why not? ❷

"Sylvy, Sylvy!" called the busy old grandmother again and again, but nobody answered, and the small husk bed was empty and Sylvia had disappeared.

The guest waked from a dream, and remembering his day's pleasure hurried to dress himself that might it sooner begin. He was sure from the way the shy little girl looked once or twice yesterday that she had at least seen the white heron, and now she must really be made to tell. Here she comes now, paler than ever, and her worn old frock is torn and tattered, and smeared with pine pitch. The grandmother and the sportsman stand in the door together and question her, and the splendid moment has come to speak of the dead hemlock tree by the green marsh.

But Sylvia does not speak after all, though the old grandmother fretfully rebukes her, and the young man's kind, appealing eyes are looking straight in her own. He can make them rich with money; he has promised it, and they are poor now. He is so well worth making happy, and he waits to hear the story she can tell.

No, she must keep silence! What is it that suddenly forbids her and makes her dumb? Has she been nine years growing and now, when the great world for the first time puts out a hand to her, must she thrust it aside for a bird's sake? The murmur of the pine's green branches is in her ears, she remembers how the white heron came flying through the golden air and how they watched the sea and the morning together, and Sylvia cannot speak; she cannot tell the heron's secret and give its life away.

Dear loyalty, that suffered a sharp pang as the guest went away disappointed later in the day, that could have served and followed him and loved him as a dog loves!

Words for Everyday Use: **vex** (veks) *vt.,* annoy
re • buke (ri byōōk´) *vt.,* blame or scold in a sharp way

Vocabulary in Context

- The hungry moles vexed the gardener who was trying to grow turnips.
- The teacher rebuked the students for not doing their homework.

Many a night Sylvia heard the echo of his whistle haunting the pasture path as she came home with the loitering cow. She forgot even her sorrow at the sharp report of his gun and the sight of thrushes and sparrows dropping silent to the ground, their songs hushed and their pretty feathers stained and wet with blood. Were the birds better friends than their hunter might have been,—who can tell? Whatever treasures were lost to her, woodlands and summertime, remember! Bring your gifts and graces and tell your secrets to this lonely country child! ■

Responding to the Selection

At the end of the story, Sylvia does not tell the young man where the white heron nests. Were you glad that she did not tell, or did you think she should have told him? Why?

Reviewing the Selection

Recalling

1. Why is Sylvia usually late in getting home when she goes to fetch the cow from the pasture? How is the cow similar to Sylvia?
2. Why does Sylvia's grandmother, Mrs. Tilley, bring Sylvia rather than one of Sylvia's brothers or sisters to the farm?
3. Whom does Sylvia meet on the way home? What is he doing on the road?
4. Why is Sylvia at first afraid of the young man? How does Sylvia's attitude toward him change in the course of the story?

Interpreting

5. What does the young man want to know about the white heron? Why does he want to know it? What does he offer Sylvia in return for this knowledge?
6. Why does Sylvia want the money that the young man offers in return for knowledge of where the white heron nests?
7. What does Sylvia do to find out what the young man wants to know?
8. Why does Sylvia decide not to tell the young man the secret?

Responding to the Selection

Students can divide into two groups, one that favors keeping the secret and another that favors telling it. Students should be encouraged to recognize what Sylvia both loses and gains in keeping the secret, and to imagine the good as well as the bad things that might have happened if Sylvia had told the young man the location of the nest.

Answers for Reviewing the Selection

RECALLING

1. Sylvia usually is late in getting home because the cow is difficult to find. It likes to hide itself in the huckleberry bushes. Both Sylvia and the cow like to stray and wander.

2. Mrs. Tilley brings Sylvia to the farm because she is "afraid of people." She knows that Sylvia will like the farm because there are few people in the area.

3. Sylvia meets a young man, an amateur ornithologist who is hunting for birds to add to his collection of stuffed and preserved specimens.

4. Sylvia is afraid of him at first because he reminds her of a boy who used to chase her when she lived in the city and because he carries a gun. She grows to like the young man because he tells her about the birds and he gives her a knife.

INTERPRETING

Responses will vary. Possible responses are given.

5. He wants to know where the white heron nests so he can kill it and add it to his collection of specimens. He offers her money in return for the secret.

6. Sylvia wants the money so that she and her grandmother can buy the things that they desire.

7. To discover the nest Sylvia wakes early and climbs to the top of the landmark pine tree from which she can see where the

(cont.)

Answers for Reviewing the Selection (cont.)

heron nests.

8. Sylvia does not tell the secret because she loves the heron. By watching the sunrise and seeing the sea together from the top of the pine tree, they have established a friendship.

SYNTHESIZING

Responses will vary. Possible responses are given.

9. Mrs. Tilley could not see the world because she is both poor and a woman. Unlike the women in the story, the men wander far from home in pursuit of knowledge and wealth. The young man is described as a "gentleman" because he is well mannered; an "ornithologist" because he studies and collects specimens of birds; a "sportsman" because he hunts and kills the birds with a gun; and a "stranger," a "guest," and a "wayfarer"

(cont.)

ANSWERS FOR REVIEWING THE SELECTION (CONT.)

because he travels far from his home to pursue the birds. The fact that he has many names suggests that he, unlike the women in the story, can be many things. He is similar to Dan in that he wanders far from his home.

10. Sylvia resolves her conflict beween her love of nature and her attraction to the young man by abandoning her interest in the young man entirely. Sylvia loses his companionship. It is not a great loss, however, because in the relationship he offers, Sylvia would have been the submissive follower. She would have "loved him as a dog loves!" The narrator asks the woods to give Sylvia knowledge about the lives of the animals and wonderful moments like those she had in the pine tree watching the sunrise with the heron.

ANSWERS FOR UNDERSTANDING LITERATURE

▶ See the evaluation forms for discussion, active listening, and oral communication, *Assessment Portfolio,* 7.11–7.14.

Responses will vary. Possible responses are given.

1. Motif. The motif of the birds appears in the following places: Like the birds, who make "sleepy twitters," Sylvia is sleepy. The description emphasizes that Sylvia is at one with nature, one of its creatures (page 440); Sylvia's habit of feeding the birds displays the love and responsibility she feels for them (page 442); the young man's bird collection shows that he treats the birds as objects to be studied rather than creatures to love (page 442); in order to study them, the young man must kill the birds he loves (page 443); Sylvia is described as a creature in a hawk's "talons," which emphasizes the danger of her undertaking (page 445).

2. Conflict. Sylvia's close relation-

(cont.)

SYNTHESIZING

9. At one point in the story, Mrs. Tilley says to the young wanderer, "I'd ha' seen the world myself if it had been so I could." Why is it that Mrs. Tilley cannot go and see the world? How do the men in the story, the young man and Mrs. Tilley's son Dan differ from the women? The narrator of "A White Heron" calls the young man by many different names. What are these names? Why is he called by them? What does the fact that he has so many names tell us about him? How is he similar to Mrs. Tilley's son Dan?

10. When the story begins, Sylvia is a shy country girl, a companion to all the creatures in the natural world. With the arrival of the strange young man, however, she begins to take an interest in people. "A great wave of human interest," the narrator says, "flooded for the first time this dull little life." How does Sylvia resolve this conflict between her love for nature and her interest in the young man? Besides the money he was going to give her, what does Sylvia lose by not telling the young man about the heron? Is this a great loss? What are the "gifts," "graces," and "secrets" that the narrator asks the woodlands to give her in return?

Understanding Literature (Questions for Discussion)

1. **Motif.** A **motif** is any element that recurs in one or more works of literature. Each time the motif occurs it means something slightly different because it occurs in different moments in the story. In "A White Heron," for example, images of birds occur repeatedly. Find all the moments in the story in which birds are mentioned. What does each occurrence of this motif teach us about Sylvia's or the young man's relationship to birds? What does each one teach us about their relationship to nature?

2. **Conflict.** A **conflict** is a struggle between two forces in a literary work. In "A White Heron," the central conflict is **internal.** It occurs within Sylvia, who is the main character, or **protagonist.** Sylvia's love of the creatures in the woods conflicts with her desire to help the young man find the heron. What are examples of Sylvia's close relationship with the animals? Why does she want to help the young man find the heron? What are some other conflicts or struggles within the story? What is the relation between these minor conflicts and the main conflict?

Responding in Writing

Character Sketch. Choose a character from the story: the grandmother, Sylvia, or the young man. Write a character sketch of this person. A **character sketch** is a description of a person that reveals such details as the person's appearance, habits, occupation, background, beliefs, values, attitudes, and personality. You can write a character sketch by answering the following questions:

ANSWERS FOR UNDERSTANDING LITERATURE (CONT.)

ship with animals is exemplified in her companionship with the cow and her feeding of and friendship with the birds. She wants to help the young man find the heron even though he is going to kill it because she likes him and he has promised her money. Other conflicts in the story include Sylvia's struggle to find the cow and her struggle to climb the landmark pine. The first conflict sets up her meeting with the young man whose arrival inaugurates her conflict between nature and human society. The second is an effort to resolve her conflict by helping the young man find the heron, which in the end she decides against doing.

1. What does the character look like? What does the character wear?
2. What does the character do for work and for play?
3. How does the character speak? Use examples from the story.
4. What are the major personality traits of the character? The character, for instance, might be shy, playful, aggressive, simple-minded, or serious. For each trait, provide an illustration from the story.
5. How do the other characters in the story view the character you have chosen?
6. What is a quotation from the character that illustrates his or her personality or beliefs? Write it down and describe what it illustrates about the character.
7. How is your character different from the other characters in the story?
8. Do you like the character? Why, or why not?
9. If you were the character, what would you want out of life? What plans or goals would you have for the future?
10. If you had to compare the character to an animal, which animal would you choose. Why?

Language Lab

Correcting Run-ons. Read the Language Arts Survey, 2.62, "Correcting Run-ons." Then rewrite the following run-ons. Correct each one either by making it into two or three separate sentences or by adding a comma and a coordinating conjunction. If the sentence is not a run-on, copy it as it is.

1. Regional writers write about a particular part of the country they write about what makes the region special.
2. Sarah Orne Jewett wrote about rural Maine, she was brought up in the area.
3. The story "A White Heron" is about a shy young country girl who loves the creatures in the woods because they are the companions with whom she plays, these creatures bring her great happiness.
4. The young man in "A White Heron" treats the creatures of the woods as something to study, Sylvia treats them as companions.
5. Sarah Orne Jewett was a nineteenth-century "feminist" writer, other nineteenth-century feminists include Kate Chopin and Mary E. Wilkins Freeman.

Analytic Scales for Responding in Writing

Assign a score from 1 to 25 for each grading criterion below. (For more detailed evaluation, see the evaluation forms for writing, revising, and proofreading, *Assessment Portfolio,* 7.1–7.10.)

Character Sketch

- **Content/Unity.** The character sketch answers all the listed questions using specific details from the story.
- **Organization/Coherence.** The character sketch is organized in an essay format with an introduction; well-developed, coherent paragraphs; smooth transitions; and a concluding paragraph.
- **Language/Style.** The character sketch uses vivid and precise nouns, verbs, and modifiers.
- **Conventions.** The character sketch avoids errors in spelling, grammar, usage, mechanics, and manuscript form.

Answers for Language Lab

1. Regional writers write about a particular part of the country. They write about what makes the region special.
2. Sarah Orne Jewett wrote about rural Maine, for she was brought up in the area.
3. The story "A White Heron" is about a shy young country girl who loves the creatures in the woods. They are the companions with whom she plays, and they bring her great happiness.
4. The young man in "A White Heron" treats the creatures of the woods as something to study, but Sylvia treats them as companions.
5. Sarah Orne Jewett was a nineteenth-century "feminist" writer. Other nineteenth-century feminists include Kate Chopin and Mary E. Wilkins Freeman.

ADDITIONAL RESOURCES

READER'S GUIDE
- Selection Worksheet, 7.3

ASSESSMENT PORTFOLIO
- Selection Check Test, 4.7.5
- Selection Test, 4.7.6

ESSENTIAL SKILLS PRACTICE BOOKS
- *Language,* 2.51–2.53, 2.76–2.77

ENRICHMENT ACTIVITIES

Ask students to spend time in small groups discussing the facts of Chopin's life. Encourage them to go to the library and research more details about her life and work. Then ask them to write short papers in which they discuss the ways in which the details of Chopin's life might have affected the attitudes expressed in her work.

SUPPORT FOR LEP STUDENTS

Some students might have difficulty understanding Chopin's passages of psychological analysis. Have students reread those passages as a class or one-on-one with an English-proficient student. Be sure that all students understand the irony of the story's ending. You might want to hold a discussion focusing on the ending.

ADDITIONAL VOCABULARY

afflicted—bothered or tormented
forestall—prevent or hinder
significance—extreme importance
repression—holding back or controlling of thoughts and feelings
perception—observation and understanding
illumination—realization; understanding
unwittingly—in a manner that is unaware of unknowing
composedly—calmly

PREREADING

SHORT STORY

"The Story of an Hour"
by Kate Chopin

ABOUT THE AUTHOR

Kate Chopin (1851–1904), born Kate O'Flaherty, was raised in St. Louis. When she was four years old, her father died in a train wreck. She was brought up by her French-speaking Creole mother, her grandmother, and her great-grandmother, who was a fine storyteller. Until the age of seventeen, she attended a Catholic school called the St. Louis Academy of the Sacred Heart. At eighteen, she met a twenty-five-year-old banker named Oscar Chopin, whom she married. The Chopins moved to New Orleans, her husband's hometown, and before she was thirty years old, Kate Chopin gave birth to six children. When her husband's cotton business failed, the couple moved to Cloutierville in Natchitoches Parish, Louisiana. Her family physician in St. Louis recognized the quality of the writing in Chopin's letters from Louisiana and urged her to write as an outlet for her emotions. Many of the stories that Chopin was to write in later years dealt with the lives of the Creoles and Cajuns whom she came to know in Louisiana. When her husband suddenly died of swamp fever, Chopin moved back to St. Louis and began her literary career. She wrote two novels, over one hundred short stories, poetry, book reviews, and literary criticism, all while raising her six children. Chopin's second novel, *The Awakening* (1899), met with much censorship in its time but is today considered a masterpiece, having received renewed critical attention in the twentieth century because of its strong feminist message.

ABOUT THE SELECTION

Kate Chopin began her career as a regional writer, like Bret Harte and Sarah Orne Jewett. In her fiction, she carefully portrayed the landscape of the Gulf Islands and the people of Louisiana—the French Creoles of New Orleans and the rural Cajuns of Natchitoches. Besides being a regionalist, however, Kate Chopin was a pioneering feminist writer. Her most famous novel, *The Awakening*, tells the story of the intellectual and emotional development of a young woman. The novel scandalized Chopin's contemporaries, partially because it depicts the woman's rebellion against her husband's authority. **"The Story of an Hour"** is another fine example of Chopin's feminist fiction.

GOALS/OBJECTIVES

Studying this lesson will enable students to
- identify Kate Chopin as a nineteenth-century regionalist and briefly describe the region she portrayed
- use the selection to illustrate Kate Chopin's pioneering feminism
- define *reversal* and *irony* using examples from the selection
- compose a paragraph with specific details that support a topic sentence
- combine sentences using single words, phrases, or clauses

READER'S JOURNAL

Think of a time when you felt happy but were supposed to feel sad or a time when you were sad but were supposed to feel happy. Describe the experience. How were you supposed to feel? Why did you feel differently? Did you express or hide your feelings? Why? How did other people respond? Write about these questions in your journal.

LANGUAGE SKILLS

Read the Language Arts Survey, 2.76–2.77, on the cases of pronouns. Then find nine sentences in the selection: three that include a nominative case pronoun, three that include an objective case pronoun, and three that include a possessive case pronoun.

"The Story of an Hour"

KATE CHOPIN

Knowing that Mrs. Mallard was afflicted with a heart trouble, great care was taken to break to her as gently as possible the news of her husband's death.

It was her sister Josephine who told her, in broken sentences; veiled hints that revealed in half concealing. Her husband's friend Richards was there, too, near her. It was he who had been in the newspaper office when intelligence of the railroad disaster was received, with Brently Mallard's name leading the list of "killed." He had only taken the time to assure himself of its truth by a second telegram, and had hastened to forestall any less careful, less tender friend in bearing the sad message.

She did not hear the story as many women have heard the same, with a paralyzed inability to accept its significance. She wept at once, with sudden, wild abandonment, in her sister's arms. When the storm of grief had spent itself she went away to her room alone. She would have no one follow her.

There stood, facing the open window, a comfortable, roomy armchair. Into this she sank, pressed down by a physical exhaustion that haunted her body and seemed to reach into her soul.

She could see in the open square before her house the tops of trees that were all aquiver with the new spring life. The delicious breath of rain was in the air. In the street below a peddler was crying his wares. The notes of a distant song which someone was singing reached her faintly, and countless sparrows were twittering in the eaves.

There were patches of blue sky showing here and there through the clouds that had met and piled one above the other in the west facing her window.

She sat with her head thrown back upon the cushion of the chair, quite motionless except when a sob came up into her throat and shook her, as a child who has cried itself, to sleep continues to sob in its dreams.

She was young, with a fair, calm face, whose lines bespoke repression and even a certain strength. But now there was a dull stare in her eyes, whose gaze was fixed away off yonder on one of those patches

❶ *What is Mrs. Mallard's immediate reaction to news of her husband's death?*

PREREADING NOTES

READER'S JOURNAL

Give students ample time to freewrite about these questions in their journals. Encourage students to explore the nature and source of standards in society and in their own lives. Ask them to analyze why they have been expected to act and feel in certain ways. Some students might want to discuss their ideas in class.

LANGUAGE SKILLS

Have students exchange and correct one another's sentences. Ask them to explain why a particular pronoun takes the case or form that it does.

ANSWER TO GUIDED READING QUESTION

❶ Mrs. Mallard immediately reacts with unrestrained grief, weeping uncontrollably, then secluding herself in her room.

ANSWERS TO SELECTION CHECK TEST 4.7.5

EX. With what is Mrs. Mallard afflicted?
Mrs. Mallard is afflicted with heart trouble.

1. What has apparently happened to Mrs. Mallard's husband?
He has been killed in a train wreck.

2. What is Mrs. Mallard's first reaction to the news about her husband?
Mrs. Mallard weeps loudly in her sister's arms.

3. What does Mrs. Mallard say over and over under her breath in the privacy of her room?
Mrs. Mallard says, "free, free, free!" under her breath.

4. Who enters the house as Mrs. Mallard descends the stairs?
Mrs. Mallard's husband enters the house.

5. What happens to Mrs. Mallard at the end of the story?
She dies of "heart disease."

LITERARY TECHNIQUE

An **objective correlative** is a group of images that together create a particular emotion in the reader. Explain to students that Chopin's description of the view from Mrs. Mallard's window is an example of an objective correlative.

ADDITIONAL QUESTIONS AND ACTIVITIES

Ask students to rewrite Chopin's description of the view from Mrs. Mallard's window using a different objective correlative, or set of images. What different images might they use to express the emotions Mrs. Mallard is feeling? Discuss in class the differences between the students' images and Chopin's images.

Answer to Guided Reading Question

❶ The thought that possesses Mrs. Mallard is that she is now free. She realizes that now she can "live for herself."

Historical Note

After seventy years of activism, women gained the right to vote in 1920. Up until this time, women were largely confined to housekeeping and factory work, and it was considered indecent for young women to walk the streets without a male or female companion.

Additional Questions and Activities

How does Mrs. Mallard define freedom?

Answer. Mrs. Mallard defines freedom as the right to determine one's own life, without other people imposing their will.

Students can discuss this definition of freedom. Is it correct? Are there any circumstances under which it might be legitimate to impose one's will on another? What might those circumstances be?

Responding to the Selection

Some students might not be able to relate to the social circumstances that lead to Mrs. Mallard's sense of release at the death of her husband. You might have to explain that in the nineteenth century, women's lives were often quite restricted. Also point out to students that Mrs. Mallard's responses to her husband's death are mixed.

of blue sky. It was not a glance of reflection but rather indicated a suspension of intelligent thought.

There was something coming to her and she was waiting for it, fearfully. What was it? She did not know: it was too subtle and elusive to name. But she felt it, creeping out of the sky, reaching toward her through the sounds, the scents, the color that filled the air.

Now her bosom rose and fell tumultuously. She was beginning to recognize this thing that was approaching to possess her, and she was striving to beat it back with her will—as powerless as her two white slender hands would have been.

What is the thought that possesses her? ❶

When she abandoned herself, a little whispered word escaped her slightly parted lips. She said it over and over under her breath: "free, free, free! The vacant stare and the look of terror that had followed it went from her eyes. They stayed keen and bright. Her pulses beat fast, and the coursing blood warmed and relaxed every inch of her body.

She did not stop to ask if it were or were not a monstrous joy that held her. A clear and exalted perception enabled her to dismiss the suggestion as trivial.

She knew that she would weep again when she saw the kind, tender hands folded in death; the face that had never looked save with love upon her, fixed and gray and dead. But she saw beyond that bitter moment a long procession of years to come that would belong to her absolutely. And she opened and spread her arms out to them in welcome.

There would be no one to live for her during those coming years; she would live for herself. There would be no powerful will bending hers in that blind persistence with which men and women believe they have a right to impose a private will upon a fellow creature. A kind intention or a cruel intention made the act seem no less a crime as she looked upon it in that brief moment of illumination.

And yet she had loved him—sometimes. Often she had not. What did it matter! What could love, the unsolved mystery, count for in face of this possession of self-assertion which she suddenly recognized as the strongest impulse of her being!

"Free! Body and soul free!" she kept whispering.

Josephine was kneeling before the closed door with her lips to the keyhole, imploring for admission. "Louise, open the door! I beg; open the door—you will make yourself ill. What are you doing, Louise? For heaven's sake open the door."

"Go away. I am not making myself ill." No; she was drinking in a very elixir of life[1] through that open window.

Her fancy was running riot along those days ahead of her. Spring days, and summer days, and all sorts of days that would be her own. She breathed a quick prayer that life might be long. It was only yesterday she had thought with a shudder that life might be long.

She arose at length and opened the door to her sister's importunities. There was a feverish triumph in her eyes, and she carried herself unwittingly like a goddess of Victory. She clasped her sister's waist, and

1. **elixir of life.** Substance sought by medieval alchemists to prolong life indefinitely

Words for Everyday Use:
tu • mul • tu • ous • ly (tōō mul´ chōō əs lē) *adv.,* wildly
im • por • tu • ni • ty (im´por tōōn´ i tē) *n.,* persistent demand

Vocabulary in Context

- The hurricane made the sea rage tumultuously.
- The child's importunity persuaded her parents to stay at the park.

together they descended the stairs. Richards stood waiting for them at the bottom.

Someone was opening the front door with a latchkey. It was Brently Mallard who entered, a little travel-stained, composedly carrying his gripsack[2] and umbrella. He had been far from the scene of accident, and did not know there had been one. He stood amazed at Josephine's piercing cry; at Richards's quick motion to screen him from the view of his wife.

But Richards was too late.

When the doctors came they said she had died of heart disease—of joy that kills. ■

Is it really joy that kills Mrs. Mallard?

2. **gripsack.** Small bag for traveling clothes

Responding to the Selection

Do you approve or disapprove of Mrs. Mallard's response to her husband's "death"? Why?

Reviewing the Selection

Recalling

1. What does Mrs. Mallard learn from her sister Josephine at the beginning of the story? Why does Josephine have to break this news gently?
2. What does Mrs. Mallard do when she hears the news? What appears to be Mrs. Mallard's reaction to the news?
3. What is Mrs. Mallard's second response to the news?
4. Who enters the house just as Josephine and Mrs. Mallard are descending the stairs? What happens to Mrs. Mallard?

Interpreting

5. How well does Mr. Mallard's friend Richards check the truth of the news? Why does he want to be the first person to break the news to Mrs. Mallard?
6. What sights and smells does Mrs. Mallard experience at the open window in her room? What do these sights and smells represent to her?
7. How did Mr. Mallard treat Mrs. Mallard in their marriage? What are Mrs. Mallard's feelings about Mr. Mallard?
8. How does Mrs. Mallard appear as she walks down the stairs? What does her appearance reveal?

Synthesizing

9. Why is the story called "The Story of an Hour"? What hour does the story describe? Is this a happy and fulfilling hour, a disappointing hour, or both? Explain.
10. To what does Mrs. Mallard look forward? What happens to her at the end of the story? Why?

Answer to Guided Reading Question

❶ It appears to be not joy but pain and sorrow at the loss of freedom that kills Mrs. Mallard.

Answers for Reviewing the Selection

RECALLING

1. Mrs. Mallard learns that her husband has died. Josephine has to break this news gently for fear of how it might affect Mrs. Mallard, who has a heart condition.
2. She goes away to her room alone. She appears to be grief-stricken.
3. Her second response is one of exhilaration and release because she is free.
4. Mr. Mallard enters the house, and Mrs. Mallard has a heart attack.

INTERPRETING

Responses will vary. Possible responses are given.

5. The friend pauses only long enough to confirm the news by means of a second telegram. He wants to ensure that the news is broken sensitively to Mrs. Mallard.
6. She experiences, at the window, the new spring growth, the breath of rain, and the blue sky, among other things that are, for her, the very elixir of life.
7. There is no indication in the story that Mr. Mallard's treatment of Mrs. Mallard was particularly horrible. The reader is simply told that married people make impositions on one another and that Mrs. Mallard feels freed from those impositions.
8. As Mrs. Mallard comes down the stairs, she has a feverish look of triumph in her eyes. Her appearance reveals that her major response to her husband's death is one of relief.

SYNTHESIZING

Responses will vary. Possible responses are given.

9. The story's title derives from the short period of time in which it

(cont.)

Answers for Reviewing the Selection (cont.)

takes place. The story is an example of an epiphany, or sudden revelation, that takes place within a single hour, from the time that Richards hears the news of Mr. Mallard's "death" to the time that Mr. Mallard arrives home, quite alive. In the course of this hour, Mrs. Mallard learns the shocking truth about her feelings about her husband and her marriage. It is a happy hour in that she feels the exhilaration of freedom and a disappointing hour because she learns that she doesn't have her freedom after all.

10. She looks forward to days that will be her own. At the end of the story, she has a heart attack and dies. People believe that her death is due to joy, but it is actually due to shock over the sudden loss of her freedom.

Understanding Literature (Questions for Discussion)

1. **Reversal.** A **reversal** is a dramatic change in the direction of events in a narrative, especially a change in the fortunes of the protagonist. There are two major reversals in "The Story of an Hour." The first occurs when Mrs. Mallard's sadness about her husband's death turns to joy at the freedom she feels. The second occurs when her husband opens the door and everyone learns that he has not died. Does your response to Mrs. Mallard change when her sadness turns to joy? How do you feel when you learn that Mrs. Mallard's husband is dead?

2. **Irony. Irony** is a difference between appearance and reality. **Dramatic irony** occurs when a situation appears one way to the reader of the story and another way to the characters in the story. At the end of the selection, the doctors say that Mrs. Mallard died of "joy that kills." How is this an example of dramatic irony? What do the doctors believe to be the cause of Mrs. Mallard's death? What actually caused her death? How does it feel to realize that you know the truth and the doctors in the story do not?

Responding in Writing

1. **Paragraph.** A **paragraph** is a group of sentences that develops one main idea or that serves a single purpose. A paragraph often consists of a topic sentence that states the main idea and several sentences that explain and support the main idea with specific details. Choose one of the following topic sentences. Then write a paragraph in support of that sentence using details from the story.
   - Kate Chopin's short story, "The Story of an Hour," has a surprising plot.
   - Mrs. Mallard, the main character of "The Story of an Hour," has a love-hate relationship with her husband.
   - "The Story of an Hour" is a feminist story.

2. **Diary Entry.** Imagine that you are Mrs. Mallard and that you are sitting in the room alone, thinking about the death of your husband and about your future life. Write a diary entry that she might have written at that time.

Language Lab

Combining Sentences. Read the Language Arts Survey, 2.51–2.53, on combining sentences. Then combine the following pairs of sentences using single words, phrases, or clauses.

1. She sank into the armchair. She was pressed down by a physical exhaustion that haunted her body and seemed to reach into her soul.
2. She sat with her head thrown back upon the cushion of the chair. She was quite motionless.
3. There was something coming to her. She was waiting for it.
4. Her pulse beat fast. The coursing blood warmed and relaxed every inch of her body.

Answers for Understanding Literature

► See the evaluation forms for discussion, active listening, and oral communication, *Assessment Portfolio,* 7.11–7.14.

1. Reversal. *Answers will vary.* Most students will be surprised and a bit shocked at Mrs. Mallard's sudden sense of joy. They will be surprised again by the double irony at the end of the story—that Mr. Mallard is not really dead and that Mrs. Mallard's death should be taken as resulting from joy.

2. Irony. The ending is an example of dramatic irony because the reader knows that Mrs. Mallard actually dies from shock at the negative realization that her new-found freedom was illusory.

Analytic Scales for Responding in Writing

Assign a score from 1 to 25 for each grading criterion below. (For more detailed evaluation, see the evaluation forms for writing, revising, and proofreading, *Assessment Portfolio,* 7.1–7.10.)

1. Paragraph

- **Content/Unity.** The paragraph presents a single main idea and supports that idea with details from the selection.
- **Organization/Coherence.** The paragraph is organized in a logical manner, using transitions to connect the ideas.
- **Language/Style.** The paragraph uses vivid and precise nouns, verbs, and modifiers.
- **Conventions.** The paragraph avoids errors in spelling, grammar, usage, mechanics, and manuscript form.

2. Diary Entry

- **Content/Unity.** The diary entry contains details consistent with those presented in the story.
- **Organization/Coherence.** The entry does not stray from topics that would be of concern to Mrs. Mallard.

(cont.)

Analytic Scales for Responding in Writing (cont.)

- **Language/Style.** The voice is consistent with the character as presented in the story.
- **Conventions.** The diary entry avoids errors in spelling, grammar, usage, mechanics, and manuscript form, except where these are introduced for purposes of faithfulness to the character or to the period.

Answers for Language Lab

1. She sank into the armchair, pressed down by a physical exhaustion that haunted her body and seemed to reach into her soul.
2. She sat motionless with her head thrown back upon the cushion of the chair.
3. There was something coming to her, and she was waiting for it.
4. Her pulse beat fast, and the coursing blood warmed and relaxed every inch of her body.

PREREADING

SHORT STORY

"The Notorious Jumping Frog of Calaveras County"
by Mark Twain

ABOUT THE AUTHOR

Mark Twain (1835–1910) was the pseudonym of Samuel Langhorne Clemens. Clemens took the name from a term for "the second mark," referring to water that was two fathoms deep, or a safe depth for a boat, a term that he encountered as a riverboat pilot. Born in Florida, Missouri, Twain grew up in the nearby river town of Hannibal. At the age of twenty-one, he headed to New Orleans to depart for a trip to the Amazon. The plan fell apart, but Twain found a position as an apprentice riverboat pilot, a prestigious job that fulfilled a childhood dream. Before the Civil War, a lucrative trade was done on the Mississippi. When the war interrupted that trade, and Twain was forced to find another job, he went west and took a job as a reporter for the *Sacramento Union.* He began to write his most famous books in 1870. *The Adventures of Tom Sawyer* (1876), *Life on the Mississippi* (1883), and *The Adventures of Huckleberry Finn* (1883) all draw from his experiences on the Mississippi River. *Huckleberry Finn,* often referred to as the great American novel, tells the story of a boy named Huck who, together with an escaped slave named Jim, travels down the Mississippi on a raft. Alternately funny and serious, the book is an implicit indictment of racism, showing that beneath outward differences, people have similar feelings and dreams. In the 1890s, Twain suffered a series of misfortunes, including the death of a daughter, the illness of another daughter and of his wife, and monetary loss due to failed speculative investments. The writings of Twain's last years contain a great deal of bitterness directed at the hypocrisies of his fellow human beings. Twain's severest criticisms, included in *The War Prayer* and *Letters from Earth,* were not published until long after his death. Born on the day of the appearance of Halley's comet, Twain died on the day of its reappearance seventy-two years later.

ABOUT THE SELECTION

"The Notorious Jumping Frog of Calaveras County" is Twain's retelling of a popular nineteenth-century tall tale. A **tall tale** is a lighthearted and humorous story that contains highly exaggerated, unrealistic events. Twain first became known nationally when the story was published in the *Saturday Press* in 1865. The story is also an outstanding example of regional writing. It portrays the entertainments of simple, uneducated men living in a frontier mining camp. The setting is a perfect arena for Twain to display his gift for capturing regional dialects.

GOALS/OBJECTIVES

Studying this lesson will enable students to

- name Mark Twain's most significant works and describe the special place Twain has in American literature
- identify Twain as a humorous novelist and regionalist writer of the Mississippi River valley
- understand the conflict in the Twain selection between the lofty and educated and the lowly and uneducated
- define *dialect* and *frame tale* using examples from the selection
- write a tall tale and an essay on the selection
- rewrite informal, nonstandard English sentences into standard, formal English

ADDITIONAL RESOURCES

READER'S GUIDE
- Selection Worksheet, 7.4

ASSESSMENT PORTFOLIO
- Selection Check Test, 4.7.7
- Selection Test, 4.7.8

ESSENTIAL SKILLS PRACTICE BOOKS
- *Language,* 2.85–2.89, 2.147–2.150

ENRICHMENT ACTIVITIES

Ask students to look in a library for collections of folklore and tall tales. Encourage them to locate one or two tales that represent a particular place and time. Students should work individually or in small groups to learn the tales and then prepare to present them to the class. If some students know tales passed down through their own families, towns, or neighborhoods, they may use these in their presentations. Ask the class to address the following questions: Why do legends and tall tales appeal to people? Why might they exist and continue to get passed down from generation to generation?

SUPPORT FOR LEP STUDENTS

Have students work with an English-proficient student to understand the elevated language of Twain's narrator and Simon Wheeler's colloquial speech.

ADDITIONAL VOCABULARY

hereunto—a variation on *hereto,* which means "to this point"
infamous—having a bad reputation
exasperating—annoying
reminiscence—remembrance
tedious—long and boring
countenance—face
commissioned—ordered

QUOTABLES

"Persons attempting to find a motive in this narrative will be prosecuted; persons attempting to find a moral in it will be banished; persons attempting to find a plot in it will be shot."

—Mark Twain
Adventures of Huckleberry Finn

PREREADING NOTES

READER'S JOURNAL

Students should express what was humorous about all aspects of the situation: what was said, what was done, and how everyone appeared.

LANGUAGE SKILLS

Students can work in small groups to locate the errors and then compare their findings with those of the rest of the class. They might identify some of the following words and phrases as errors: *curiousest, uncommon lucky, he most always come out a winner, anywheres, dangdest, little small,* and *heart was broke.*

ANSWERS TO GUIDED READING QUESTIONS

❶ A friend from the East has written to the narrator, asking him to visit Simon Wheeler to inquire about a mutual friend, Leonidas W. Smiley.

❷ The narrator suspects that Smiley is a myth.

LITERARY TECHNIQUE

The psychoanalyst Sigmund Freud distinguished between *tendency wit,* humor that is meant to ridicule a person, an idea, or a social practice, and *harmless wit,* humor that is meant simply to be enjoyed. Twain's tall tale is an example of harmless wit.

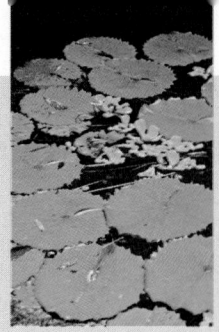

READER'S JOURNAL

Think of a time when something humorous happened to you, your friends, or your family. Write the story of what happened. Try exaggerating to make the story even funnier than it was in reality.

LANGUAGE SKILLS

Read the Language Arts Survey, 2.85–2.89, "Editing for Errors in Modifier Usage." Then read the story within a story told by Sam Wheeler in "The Notorious Jumping Frog of Calaveras County," and look for errors in Sam's modifier usage. Think about how the intentional use of errors in dialogue can contribute to the realism and humor of a work.

"The Notorious Jumping Frog of Calaveras County"

MARK TWAIN

Why does the narrator visit Simon Wheeler? ❶

What does the narrator suspect about Leonidas W. Smiley? ❷

In compliance with the request of a friend of mine, who wrote me from the East, I called on good-natured, garrulous old Simon Wheeler, and inquired after my friend's friend, Leonidas W. Smiley, as requested to do, and I hereunto append the result. I have a lurking suspicion that *Leonidas W.* Smiley is a myth; that my friend never knew such a personage; and that he only conjectured that if I asked old Wheeler about him, it would remind him of his infamous *Jim* Smiley, and he would go to work and bore me to death with some exasperating reminiscence of him as long and as tedious as it should be useless to me. If that was the design, it succeeded.

I found Simon Wheeler dozing comfortably by the barroom stove of the dilapidated tavern in the decayed mining camp of Angel's, and I noticed that he was fat and bald-headed, and had an expression of winning gentleness and simplicity upon his tranquil countenance. He roused up, and gave me good-day. I told him a friend of mine had commissioned me to make some inquiries about a cherished companion of his boyhood named *Leonidas* W. Smiley—*Rev. Leonidas W.* Smiley, a young minister of the Gospel, who he had heard was at one time a resident of Angel's Camp. I added that if Mr. Wheeler could tell me anything about this

WORDS FOR EVERYDAY USE:

gar • ru • lous (gar´ə ləs) *adj.,* talking much or too much

ap • pend (ə pend´) *vt.,* attach or affix

con • jec • ture (kən jek´chər) *vi.,* guess

di • lap • i • dat • ed (də lap´ ə dāt´ id) *adj.,* falling to pieces or into disrepair

VOCABULARY IN CONTEXT

- The garrulous shopkeeper told us his entire life story.
- I will append the note from my mother to the refrigerator.
- My conjecture is that the rain will eventually subside.
- The dilapidated fishing shack out on the pier was finally torn down.
- The couple had to wait on line for what seemed like an interminable period of time.
- To the devout congregation, the preacher was a great exhorter.

Rev. Leonidas W. Smiley, I would feel under many obligations to him.

Simon Wheeler backed me into a corner and blockaded me there with his chair, and then sat down and reeled off the monotonous narrative which follows this paragraph. He never smiled, he never frowned, he never changed his voice from the gentle-flowing key to which he tuned his initial sentence, he never betrayed the slightest suspicion of enthusiasm; but all through the interminable narrative there ran a vein of impressive earnestness and sincerity, which showed me plainly that, so far from his imagining that there was anything ridiculous or funny about his story, he regarded it as a really important matter, and admired its two heroes as men of transcendent genius in *finesse*.[1] I let him go on in his own way, and never interrupted him once.

Rev. Leonidas W. H'm, Reverend Le—well, there was a feller here once by the name of *Jim* Smiley, in the winter of '49—or maybe it was the spring of '50—I don't recollect exactly, somehow, though what makes me think it was one or the other is because I remember the big flume[2] warn't finished when he first come to the camp; but any way, he was the curiousest man about always betting on anything that turned up you ever see, if he could get anybody to bet on the other side; and if he couldn't he'd change sides. Any way that suited the other man would suit *him*—any way just so's he got a bet, *he* was satisfied. But still he was lucky, uncommon lucky; he most always come out winner. He was always ready and laying for a chance; there couldn't be no solit'ry thing mentioned but that feller'd offer to bet on it, and take ary side you please, as I was just telling you. If there was a horse-race, you'd find him flush[3] or you'd find him busted[4] at the end of it; if there was a dog-fight, he'd bet on it; if there was a cat-fight, he'd bet on it; if there was a chicken-fight, he'd bet on it; why, if there was two birds setting on a fence, he would bet you which one would fly first, or if there was a camp-meeting,[5] he would be there reg'lar to bet on Parson Walker, which he judged to be the best exhorter about here, and so he was too, and a good man. If he even see a straddle-bug[6] start to go anywheres, he would bet you how long it would take him to get to—to wherever he was going to, and if you took him up, he would foller that straddle-bug to Mexico but what he would find out where he was bound for and how long he was on the road. Lots of the boys here has seen that Smiley, and can tell you about him. Why, it never made no difference to *him*—he'd bet on *any* thing—the dangdest feller. Parson Walker's wife laid very sick once, for a good while, and it seemed as if they warn't going to save her; but one morning he come in, and Smiley up and asked him how she was, and he said she was considable better—thank the Lord for his inf'nite mercy—and coming on so smart that with the blessing of Prov'dence she'd

1. **transcendent . . . finesse.** Extraordinary skill, cunning, or artfulness
2. **flume.** Artificial channel for carrying water to furnish power or transport objects
3. **flush.** Well supplied with money
4. **busted.** Penniless
5. **camp-meeting.** Religious gathering at the camp, or mining community
6. **straddle-bug.** Long-legged insect

❶ *What is curious about Jim Smiley?*

WORDS FOR EVERYDAY USE:

in • ter • mi • na • ble (in tur´mi nə bel) *adj.*, without, or apparently without, end

ex • hor • ter (eg zôrt´ər) *n.*, one who urges earnestly, by advice or warning

ANSWER TO GUIDED READING QUESTION

❶ Jim Smiley is curious in that he bets on anything and everything, and he will do anything to enter a bet, even change sides.

LITERARY TECHNIQUE

Characters in fiction can be divided into two types. A one-dimensional character, flat character, or caricature is one who exhibits a single dominant quality. A three-dimensional, full, or rounded character is one who exhibits the complexity of traits associated with actual human beings. Explain to students that characters in myths, legends, or tall tales are often one dimensional. This is because in these types of stories, more than in others, the characters are often merely vehicles for the plot or theme.

ADDITIONAL QUESTIONS AND ACTIVITIES

Have students identify the characters in Twain's story as either flat or rounded. Then ask them to write character sketches rounding out the story's flat characters. Students will need to use their imaginations, but their ideas about the characters' lives and personalities should be based on information provided in the story.

Answer to Guided Reading Question

❶ The dog without hind legs has the advantage because Andrew Jackson's favorite trick is to grab hold of one of the other dog's hind legs.

Historical Note

Andrew Jackson (1767–1845), the seventh president of the United States, was a famous general and political leader of the late eighteenth and early nineteenth centuries. Nicknamed Old Hickory, Jackson served as a general in the War of 1812. Jackson is also known for leading the political movement known as Jacksonian democracy. This movement called for equality in government and greater rights for the common man. Daniel Webster (1782–1852) was a nineteenth-century political leader and diplomat. A renowned orator and a fierce debater, he served as a senator from Massachusetts through most of the 1830s and 1840s.

Literary Technique

A fallible or unreliable narrator is a storyteller whom the reader cannot trust for one reason or another. This type of narrator generally distorts the nature of things, so the reader cannot believe that he or she is telling the story in a truthful or objective way.

Additional Questions and Activities

What makes Simon Wheeler an unreliable narrator?

Answer. Simon Wheeler thinks that the story is genuinely important, that Jim Smiley is really a hero, and that his animals are really geniuses.

get well yet; and Smiley, before he thought says, "Well, I'll resk two-and-a-half she don't anyway."

Thish-yer Smiley had a mare—the boys called her the fifteen-minute nag, but that was only in fun, you know, because of course she was faster than that—and he used to win money on that horse, for all she was so slow and always had the asthma, or the distemper, or the consumption, or something of that kind. They used to give her two or three hundred yards start, and then pass her under way; but always at the fag end[7] of the race she'd get excited and desperate-like, and come cavorting and straddling up, and scattering her legs around limber, sometimes in the air, and sometimes out to one side among the fences, and kicking up m-o-r-e dust and raising m-o-r-e racket with her coughing and sneezing and blowing her nose—and *always* fetch up at the stand just about a neck ahead, as near as you could cipher it down.

In what way does the dog without hind legs have an advantage over Andrew Jackson? ❶

And he had a little small bull-pup, that to look at him you'd think he warn't worth a cent but to set around and look ornery and lay for a chance to steal something. But as soon as money was up on him he was a different dog; his underjaw'd begin to stick out like the fo'castle[8] of a steamboat, and his teeth would uncover and shine like the furnaces. And a dog might tackle him and bully-rag him, and bite him, and throw him over his shoulder two or three times, and Andrew Jackson—which was the name of the pup—Andrew Jackson would never let on but what *he* was satisfied, and hadn't expected nothing else—and the bets being doubled and doubled on the other side all the time, till the money was all up; and then all of a sudden he would grab that other dog jest by the j'int of his hind leg and freeze to it—not chaw, you understand, but only just grip and hang on till they throwed up the sponge, if it was a year. Smiley always come out winner on that pup, till he harnessed a dog once that didn't have no hind legs, because they'd been sawed off in a circular saw, and when the thing had gone along far enough, and the money was all up, and he come to make a snatch for his pet holt[9] he see in a minute how he's been imposed on, and how the other dog had him in the door, so to speak, and he 'peared surprised, and then he looked sorter discouraged-like, and didn't try no more to win the fight, and so he got shucked out bad. He give Smiley a look, as much as to say his heart was broke, and it was *his* fault, for putting up a dog that hadn't no hind legs for him to take holt of, which was his main dependence in a fight, and then he limped off a piece and laid down and died. It was a good pup, was that Andrew Jackson, and would have made a name for hisself if he'd lived, for the stuff was in him and he had genius—I know it, because he hadn't no opportunities to speak of, and it don't stand to reason that a dog could make such a fight as he could under them circumstances if he hadn't no talent. It always makes me feel sorry when I think of that last fight of his'n, and the way it turned out.

7. **fag end.** Last part
8. **fo'castle.** Upper deck of a boat; part of a bow that protrudes
9. **pet holt.** Favorite hold

Words for Everyday Use:
ca • vort (kə vôrt´) *vi.,* leap about, prance
or • ner • y (ôr´nər ē) *adj.,* having an ugly or mean disposition

Vocabulary in Context

- The children love to watch the newborn lamb cavort in the green field.
- It is difficult to be with ornery people in school or in the workplace.

Well, thish-yer Smiley had rat-terriers[10] and chicken cocks,[11] and tomcats and all them kind of things, till you couldn't rest, and you couldn't fetch nothing for him to bet on but he'd match you. He ketched a frog one day, and took him home, and said he cal'lated to educate him; and so he never done nothing for three months but set in his back yard and learn that frog to jump. And you bet you he *did* learn him, too. He'd give him a little punch behind, and the next minute you'd see that frog whirling in the air like a doughnut—see him turn one summerset, or maybe a couple, if he got a good start, and come down flat-footed and all right, like a cat. He got him up so in the matter of ketching flies, and kep' him in practice so constant, that he'd nail a fly every time as fur as he could see him. Smiley said all a frog wanted was education, and he could do 'most anything—and I believe him. Why, I've seen him set Dan'l Webster down here on this floor—Dan'l Webster was the name of the frog—and sing out, "Flies, Dan'l, flies!" and quicker'n you could wink he'd spring straight up and snake a fly off'n the counter there, and flop down on the floor ag'in as solid as a gob of mud, and fall to scratching the side of his head with his hind foot as indifferent as if he hadn't no idea he'd been doin' any more'n any frog might do. You never see a frog so modest and straightfor'ard as he was, for all he was so gifted. And when it come to fair and square jumping on a dead level, he could get over more ground at one straddle than any animal of his breed you ever see. Jumping on a dead level was his strong suit, you understand; and when it come to that, Smiley would ante up money on him as long as he had a red.[12] Smiley was monstrous proud of his frog, and well he might be, for fellers that had traveled and been everywheres all said he laid over any frog that ever *they* see.

Well, Smiley kep' the beast in a little lattice box, and he used to fetch him down-town sometimes and lay for a bet. One day a feller—a stranger in the camp, he was—come acrost him with his box, and says:

"What might it be that you've got in the box?"

And Smiley says, sorter indifferent-like. "It might be a parrot, or it might be a canary, maybe, but it ain't—it's only just a frog."

And the feller took it, and looked at it careful, and turned it round this way and that, and says. "H'm—so 'tis. Well, what's *he* good for?"

"Well," Smiley says, easy and careless, "he's good enough for *one* thing, I should judge—he can outjump any frog in Calaveras county."

The feller took the box again, and took another long, particular look, and give it back to Smiley, and says, very deliberate, "Well," he says, "I don't see no p'ints about that frog that's any better'n any other frog."

"Maybe you don't," Smiley says. "Maybe you understand frogs and maybe you don't understand em; maybe you've had experience, and maybe you ain't only a amature, as it were. Anyways, I've got *my* opinion, and I'll resk forty dollars that he can outjump any frog in Calaveras county."

And the feller studied a minute, and then says, kinder sad like, "Well, I'm only a stranger here, and I ain't got no frog; but if I had a frog, I'd bet you."

And then Smiley says. "That's all right—that's all right—if you'll hold my box a

❶ *What is amusing or ironic about calling a frog modest?*

10. **rat-terriers.** Small, aggressive dogs
11. **chicken cocks.** Roosters trained to fight each other
12. **red.** Red cent; a very small amount of money

Answer to Guided Reading Question

❶ It is amusing to call a frog modest because it assumes that a frog understands what it is doing in the same way that a human understands.

Additional Questions and Activities

Smiley says that "all a frog wanted was education, and he could do 'most anything." Why might one call Twain's story a frog with education?

Answer. Twain's story can be called a frog with education because it combines the unsophisticated perspective of Simon Wheeler with the educated perspective of the frame narrator.

Have students adopt an educated, sophisticated narrative voice to present a lowly, uneducated, and unsophisticated character from any piece of American literature. They may also reverse the process and adopt an unsophisticated narrative voice to present a lofty, educated, and sophisticated character.

Quotables

"I reckon I got to light out for the territory ahead of the rest, because Aunt Sally she's going to adopt me and sivilize me, and I can't stant it. I been there before."

—Huck Finn

Answer to Guided Reading Question

❶ The stranger fills the frog's mouth full of quail shot so that it cannot jump.

Biographical Note

Mark Twain first went west, to the Nevada Territory, in 1861, with his brother Orion. In *Roughing It*, he recounted the adventures they had together on the way and their various, unsuccessful attempts to get rich quick.

Answers to Selection Check Test 4.7.7

EX. Whom does the narrator visit?
The narrator visits Simon Wheeler.

1. For whom is the narrator looking?
The narrator is looking for Leonidas W. Smiley, a friend of his friend.

2. What had Jim Smiley always liked to do?
He had always liked to bet on everything.

3. How does Jim Smiley's dog Andrew Jackson always win over other dogs?
He grabs them by one of their hind legs.

4. What does the stranger do to Dan'l Webster the frog?
The stranger fills Dan'l Webster with quail shot so he can't jump.

5. What does Simon Wheeler start to do as the narrator tries to leave?
Simon tries to begin another story.

minute, I'll go and get you a frog." And so the feller took the box. and put up his forty dollars along with Smiley's, and set down to wait.

So he set there a good while thinking and thinking to hisself, and then he got the frog out and prized his mouth open and took a teaspoon and filled him full of quailshot[13]—filled him pretty near up to his chin—and set him on the floor. Smiley he went to the swamp and slopped around in the mud for a long time, and finally he ketched a frog, and fetched him in, and give him to this feller, and says:

What does the stranger do to the frog, Dan'l Webster? ❶

"Now, if you're ready, set him alongside of Dan'l, with his forepaws just even with Dan'l's, and I'll give the word." Then he says, "One—two—three—*git!*" and him and the feller touched up the frogs from behind, and the new frog hopped off lively, but Dan'l give a heave, and hysted up his shoulders—so—like a Frenchman, but it warn't no use—he couldn't budge; he was planted as solid as a church, and he couldn't no more stir than if he was anchored out. Smiley was a good deal surprised, and he was disgusted too, but he didn't have no idea what the matter was, of course.

The feller took the money and started away; and when he was going out at the door, he sorter jerked his thumb over his shoulder—so—at Dan'l, and says, again very deliberate, "Well," he says, "*I* don't see no p'ints about that frog that's any better'n any other frog."

Smiley he stood scratching his head and looking down at Dan'l a long time, and at last he says, "I do wonder what in the nation that frog throw'd off for—I wonder if there ain't something the matter with him—he 'pears to look mighty baggy, somehow." And he ketched Dan'l by the nap of the neck, and hefted him, and says, "Why blame my cats if he don't weigh five pound!" and turned him upside down and he belched out a double handful of shot. And then he see how it was, and he was the maddest man—he set the frog down and took out after that feller, but he never ketched him. And—"

Here Simon Wheeler heard his name called from the front yard, and got up to see what was wanted. And turning to me as he moved away, he said: "Just set where you are, stranger, and rest easy—I ain't going to be gone a second."

But, by your leave, I did not think that a continuation of the history of the enterprising vagabond *Jim* Smiley would be likely to afford me much information concerning the *Rev. Leonidas W.* Smiley, and so I started away.

At the door I met the sociable Wheeler returning, and he button-holed[14] me and recommenced;

"Well, thish-yer Smiley had a yaller one-eyed cow that didn't have no tail, only jest a short stump like a bannanner, and—"

However, lacking both time and inclination, I did not wait to hear about the afflicted cow, but took my leave. ■

13. **quailshot.** Lead pellets used for hunting quail
14. **button-holed.** Made a person listen to one, as if by grabbing his or her coat by a buttonhole

Words for Everyday Use:
vag • a • bond (vag´ ə bänd´) *n.*, wandering, idle, disreputable, or shiftless person
af • flic • ted (ə flikt´ əd) *part.*, having a physical condition, usually painful or distressing

Vocabulary in Context

- People are sometimes suspicious and afraid of vagabonds.
- The old man was afflicted with a strange and rare disease.

Responding to the Selection

Do you find Simon Wheeler's story as boring, tedious, and monotonous as the narrator finds it, or do you find it as interesting as Simon finds it?

Reviewing the Selection

RECALLING

1. Where does the story take place?
2. Why does the narrator go to see Simon Wheeler? About whom does Simon Wheeler tell his story?
3. What two animals besides the frog does Jim Smiley use for gambling?
4. What does Smiley bet the stranger?

INTERPRETING

5. Think about what the men at the camp do. Why is it funny that this place is called Angel's Camp?
6. What is the narrator's response to Wheeler's story? Why might the narrator have this response?
7. Why do Smiley's animals always win?
8. Which frog wins the contest? Why?

SYNTHESIZING

9. The tale ends when Wheeler tries to trap the narrator into listening to another story about one of Jim Smiley's animals, "a yaller one-eyed cow that didn't have no tail, only jest a short stump like a bannanner." How does the narrator respond when Wheeler starts to tell the second story? What makes this response humorous?
10. Throughout his story of "The Notorious Jumping Frog of Calaveras County," Twain draws a contrast between things that are lowly and uneducated and things that are lofty and educated. What are some examples of this contrast?

Understanding Literature (Questions for Discussion)

1. **Dialect.** A **dialect** is a version of a language spoken by the people of a particular place, time, or social group. In "The Notorious Jumping Frog of Calaveras County," Simon Wheeler speaks an uneducated Western dialect, and the narrator speaks an educated Eastern dialect. What are the differences between the narrator's language and Simon Wheeler's language? Use particular examples from the selection to show how they differ.

RESPONDING TO THE SELECTION

Students can be encouraged to see the story from both perspectives. Ask students why the tale might be boring to one person and interesting to another person.

ANSWERS FOR REVIEWING THE SELECTION

RECALLING

1. The story takes place in a Western mining camp called Angel's.

2. A friend asks the narrator to see if Simon Wheeler knows anything about a childhood companion, the Reverend Leonidas W. Smiley. Simon tells a story about Jim Smiley, a notorious gambler.

3. Smiley also owns a dog named Andrew Jackson and a horse.

4. Smiley bets that his frog, Dan'l Webster, can "outjump any frog in Calaveras County."

INTERPRETING

Responses will vary. Possible responses are given.

5. The fact that the camp is called Angel's is funny because the men are less than angelic. They like to drink, gamble, race horses, and hold dogfights.

6. The narrator finds the tale boring, tedious, and monotonous. The narrator might have this response because he is sophisticated and educated, while Wheeler thinks of Jim Smiley and the stranger as heroes of extraordinary talents.

7. Smiley's animals always win because they appear to be worthless but are in fact worth their weight in gold.

8. The stranger's frog wins the contest. While Smiley goes to the swamp to find a frog for the stranger, the stranger fills Smiley's frog with quail shot.

(cont.)

ANSWERS FOR REVIEWING THE SELECTION (CONT.)

SYNTHESIZING

Responses will vary. Possible responses are given.

9. The last scene shows us that Twain's story "The Notorious Jumping Frog of Calaveras County" is less about Jim Smiley's frog than it is about Simon Wheeler's love of telling tall tales.

10. Some examples of Twain's contrast between the high and the low are the stranger's uneducated frog and Smiley's educated frog; Jim Smiley the gambler and Leonidas W. Smiley the Reverend; and Simon Wheeler's attitude toward his story and uneducated use of language and the narrator's educated perspective and language.

ANSWERS FOR UNDERSTANDING LITERATURE

► See the evaluation forms for discussion, active listening, and oral communication, *Assessment Portfolio,* 7.11–7.14.

Responses will vary. Possible responses are given.

1. **Dialect.** The narrator uses formal English, elegant diction, and sophisticated sentence structure such as "in compliance with a request of a friend" and "I hereunto append the result." He speaks politely, as when he says that he would "feel under many obligations to" Wheeler if Wheeler tells him about Leonidas Smiley. Simon Wheeler uses colloquial diction and inelegant phrases such as "he was the curiousest man about always betting on anything that turned up you ever see."

2. **Frame Tale.** As the frame narrator says, Simon Wheeler tells his tale with "impressive earnestness and sincerity" that show he thinks the tale is "a really important matter" and he "admired its two heroes as men of transcendent genius in *finesse.*" The frame narrator finds the tale "monotonous" and boring. Twain finds both Wheeler's tale of Jim Smiley's frog and the frame narrator's tale of his visit to Wheeler hilarious.

ANALYTIC SCALES FOR RESPONDING IN WRITING

Assign a score from 1 to 25 for each grading criterion below. (For more detailed evaluation, see the evaluation forms for writing, revising, and proofreading, *Assessment Portfolio,* 7.1–7.10.)

1. Tall Tale

- **Content/Unity.** The tall tale humorously describes the animal and its history, some anecdotes that illustrate its uniqueness, and its final competition.
- **Organization/Coherence.** The tall tale is related as a sequence of events revolving around the animal's extraordinary feats.

(cont.)

2. **Frame Tale.** A **frame tale** is a story that itself provides a vehicle for the telling of other stories. In "The Notorious Jumping Frog of Calaveras County," the frame tale is the narrator's story of his visit to Simon Wheeler. It is a vehicle for another story, Simon Wheeler's tale of Jim Smiley's frog. What is Simon Wheeler's attitude toward his story about Jim Smiley? What is the frame narrator's attitude toward Wheeler's story? What do you think is Twain's attitude toward Jim Smiley's story?

Responding in Writing

1. **Tall Tale.** A **tall tale** is a story, often lighthearted or humorous, that contains highly exaggerated, unrealistic events. Write a tall tale modeled on Simon Wheeler's story of Jim Smiley's frog in "The Notorious Jumping Frog of Calaveras County." First choose an animal, perhaps a pet dog, cat, or rabbit. Give the animal a name and some extraordinary talent or ability. Begin by describing the animal and its history: where your narrator acquired it, how it was trained, and how it became famous. Tell some anecdotes that illustrate its uniqueness. End the tale by telling the story of the animal's final performance or the story of its death or retirement. Feel free to exaggerate when describing the animal's good or bad qualities and when relating the incidents of its past.

2. **Essay.** An **essay** is a brief work of prose nonfiction. Write a five-paragraph essay in support of one of the following theses about "The Notorious Jumping Frog of Calaveras County." Your essay should include an introduction to the thesis, three paragraphs that support the thesis, and a conclusion. To aid you in your writing, each of the following theses includes an italicized plural noun. This noun can be elaborated into three main ideas that can be developed into the body of your essay. For example, if you choose to support the first thesis, each paragraph in the body of your essay could describe and illustrate a different technique that Twain used to make his story funny.

   1. In "The Notorious Jumping Frog of Calaveras County," Twain uses three main *techniques* to make the story humorous.

   2. There are at least three major *differences* between the narrator's language and the language of Simon Wheeler.

   3. In "The Notorious Jumping Frog of Calaveras County," Twain makes use of three *types* of exaggeration.

   4. In Mark Twain's "The Notorious Jumping Frog of Calaveras County," Simon Wheeler, the narrator of the story within the story, displays three primary character *traits.*

ANALYTIC SCALES FOR RESPONDING IN WRITING (CONT.)

- **Language/Style.** The tall tale uses complete sentences with vivid and precise nouns, verbs, and modifiers but may use nonstandard language for humorous effect.
- **Conventions.** The tall tale avoids errors in spelling, grammar, usage, mechanics, and manuscript form but uses them for humorous effect when appropriate.

2. Essay

- **Content/Unity.** The essay supports the chosen thesis using specific details from the selection.
- **Organization/Coherence.** The essay is organized into five well-developed paragraphs.
- **Language/Style.** The essay uses complete sentences with vivid and precise nouns, verbs, and modifiers.
- **Conventions.** The essay avoids errors in spelling, grammar, usage, mechanics, and manuscript form.

Language Lab

Varieties of English. Read the Language Arts Survey, 2.147–2.150, on the varieties of English. Then rewrite the following sentences in standard, formal English.

1. He most always come out a winner.
2. There couldn't be no solit'ry thing mentioned but that feller'd offer to bet on it, and take ary side you please.
3. Smiley always come out a winner on that pup, till he harnessed a dog once that didn't have no hind legs.
4. He give Smiley a look, as much as to say his heart was broke, and it was his fault, for putting up a dog that hadn't no hind legs for him to take holt of.
5. So he set there a good while thinking and thinking to hisself.

Projects

1. **Oral Interpretation.** Find a recording or videotape of actor Hal Holbrook's brilliant one-person stage show *Mark Twain Tonight* and listen to or view it with your class. After doing this, discuss with your classmates which of Holbrook's selections from Twain's writing you most enjoyed and how Holbrook's acting contributed to making those selections come alive. Refer to the Language Arts Survey, 3.8, "Oral Interpetation."

2. **Telling a Tall Tale.** Here's a very short tall tale that has been part of the American oral tradition for years:

> A fellow was camping up in Maine during mosquito season. One night as he was getting ready to bed down, he saw against the outside of his tent, illuminated by a lantern he'd left sitting outside, the shadows of two mosquitoes. From the size of their shadows, the mosquitoes appeared to be six, maybe seven feet tall. These were Maine mosquitoes, after all. The man lay still, listening as one of them whispered to the other, "Well, shall we eat 'im here, or carry 'im back to camp?" The other mosquito answered, "I say we eat 'im here. If we carry 'im back, the big ones are liable to steal 'im from us."

Think up your own brief tall tale. Then sit with some other students and tell your tales. Try to outdo one another in your use of wild exaggerations, or hyperboles. Why do you think that telling such stories was a popular entertainment in the Old West?

Answers for Language Lab

1. He almost always wins.
2. There was nothing about which the fellow would not offer a bet, and he would take any side you wanted him to take.
3. Smiley always won with that dog, until he challenged a man whose dog had no hind legs.
4. He glanced at Smiley as if to say that his heart was broken and that it was all Smiley's fault because Smiley had put him up against a dog with no hind legs to grab.
5. So he sat there awhile thinking to himself.

Project Notes

►See the evaluation forms for projects, *Assessment Portfolio,* 7.20–7.23.

1. Oral Interpretation. Help students to locate the Holbrook show on video- or audiotape at a store or local library. You might want to have the class read other selections by Twain before they watch *Mark Twain Tonight.* Encourage discussion about Twain's work and about the Holbrook presentation.

2. Telling a Tall Tale. Give students time to freewrite about their ideas for tales. Encourage them to think of traditions, funny personal experiences, or lessons they've learned as seeds for their tall tales.

ADDITIONAL RESOURCES

READER'S GUIDE
- Selection Worksheet, 7.5

ASSESSMENT PORTFOLIO
- Selection Check Test, 4.7.9
- Selection Test, 4.7.10

ESSENTIAL SKILLS PRACTICE BOOKS
- *Speaking and Listening,* 3.2, 3.7

AUDIOCASSETTE
- "I Will Fight No More Forever," Track 15

ENRICHMENT ACTIVITIES

Students might research how nineteenth-century European settlers viewed Native American people and their way of life, and conversely, how Native American people viewed European settlers and their lifestyle. You might also ask students to write original letters or speeches from the point of view of each side.

SUPPORT FOR LEP STUDENTS

Students can pair up with English-proficient students to paraphrase the speech and to outline the main points made in the postscript.

ADDITIONAL VOCABULARY

overrun—invaded and completely taken over

HISTORICAL NOTE

Students interested in the history of the Indian wars from the Native American perspective should be encouraged to read Dee Brown's *Bury My Heart at Wounded Knee.*

PREREADING

NONFICTION

"I Will Fight No More Forever"

by In-mut-too-yah-lat-lat, Chief Joseph of the Nez Percé

ABOUT THE AUTHOR

In-mut-too-yah-lat-lat (*circa* 1840–1904), or Thunder Traveling over the Mountains, known in English as **Chief Joseph,** is remembered as a valiant leader who attempted to preserve the way of life of his people, the Nez Percé, in the face of overwhelming odds. He was born in Wallowa Valley, the ancestral home of the Nez Percé, in what the United States government then called Oregon Territory. His father, a Nez Percé chief, had been converted to Christianity, and Joseph himself attended a school run by missionaries. In the first part of the nineteenth century, relations between the Nez Percé and the persons of European descent in their midst were fairly good. However, relations became strained with increasing white settlement. At that time, the United States government negotiated treaties with some Nez Percé to obtain land rights for the settlers, but the Nez Percé did not consider the negotiators to be their legitimate representatives. In 1877, Chief Joseph was preparing to move with his people to a reservation in Idaho when he learned of an attack that had been made by three Native Americans on some settlers. Fearing reprisals, Joseph decided to flee with his people to Canada. Pursued by troops of the United States Army, this group of men, women, and children traveled over a thousand miles, often meeting and defeating their pursuers in combat. Surrounded by United States troops and recognizing that his weakened, small band had the means neither to escape nor to continue fighting, Chief Joseph surrendered in October of 1877, only forty miles from the Canadian border and freedom. The Nez Percé under Chief Joseph were further decimated by sickness after their removal to a temporary reservation in what is now Oklahoma. In 1885, those who remained were sent to the Colville Indian Reservation in Washington State.

ABOUT THE SELECTION

"I Will Fight No More Forever" is the surrender speech of In-mut-too-yah-lat-lat, known to persons of European descent as Chief Joseph. In-mut-too-yah-lat-lat was chief of the Wallam-wat-kin band of the Chute-pa-lu. To the French who first encountered them, the Chute-pa-lu were known as the "Nez Percé," a name that refers to the custom of piercing the nose for personal adornment. The speech was delivered on October 5, 1877, when Chief Joseph surrendered to General Nelson Miles. Chief Joseph was told that, after the surrender, his people would be returned to their homeland. That promise, like so many others made to Native Americans, was not kept.

GOALS/OBJECTIVES

Studying this lesson will enable students to

- identify Chief Joseph and describe key events in his people's struggle to preserve their way of life during the Westward Expansion
- understand the conditions of the Nez Percé as described in Chief Joseph's surrender speech
- define *oral tradition* and describe Chief Joseph's view of the relation between words and action
- write a comparison between the postscript to Chief Joseph's speech and the opening of the Declaration of Independence

READER'S JOURNAL

How would you feel if you were forced to give up your homeland and to move to a place where no one wanted to live? Would you be willing to fight for your homeland? How would it feel to surrender to those who would take that homeland away? Write about these questions in your journal.

SPEAKING AND LISTENING SKILLS

Read the Language Arts Survey, 3.2, "Elements of Verbal Communication," and 3.7, "Public Speaking." Then practice delivering the surrender speech of Chief Joseph. What tone is appropriate for this speech?

"I Will Fight No More Forever"

CHIEF JOSEPH

Tell General Howard[1] I know his heart. What he told me before, I have in my heart. I am tired of fighting. Our chiefs are killed. Looking Glass is dead. Toohoolhoolzote[2] is dead. The old men are all dead. It is the young men who say yes and no. He who led on the young men is dead. It is cold and we have no blankets. The little children are freezing to death. My people, some of them, have run away to the hills and have no blankets, no food; no one knows where they are—perhaps freezing to death. I want to have time to look for my children and see how many I can find. Maybe I shall find them among the dead. Hear me, my chiefs. I am tired; my heart is sick and sad. From where the sun now stands I will fight no more forever. ■

❶ *What does Chief Joseph want time to do? What does he expect to find?*

1. **General Howard.** Oliver Howard (1830–1909), who conducted the operation against Chief Joseph and the Nez Percé (1877)
2. **Looking Glass . . . Toohoolhoolzote.** Two Nez Percé leaders

Postscript

In April of 1879, Chief Joseph provided the following account of his attempt to achieve justice for his people by political means: "At last I was granted permission to come to Washington. . . . I am glad we came. I have shaken hands with a great many friends, but there are some things I want to know which no one seems able to explain. . . . I cannot understand why so many chiefs are allowed to talk in so many different ways, and promise so many different

(cont.)

PREREADING NOTES

READER'S JOURNAL

Students might begin by describing the things with which they would have most difficulty parting: their friends and family, their home, their school, and their room and their possessions. Encourage students to be specific about both the objects and people they would miss and the feelings that losing them would evoke.

SPEAKING AND LISTENING SKILLS

Students should also practice listening to the speeches of other students. Direct their attention to the effects brought about by varying their speech patterns, their volume, pitch, enunciation, pace, stress, and tone.

ANSWER TO GUIDED READING QUESTION

❶ Chief Joseph wants time to search for his children, though he expects to find them dead.

HISTORICAL NOTE

A white commissioner once asked Chief Joseph if his people wanted churches. Chief Joseph replied, "No. They will teach us to quarrel about God. We do not want to learn that. We may quarrel with men sometimes about things on this earth, but we never quarrel about God. We do not want to learn that."

QUOTABLES

"The country was made without lines of demarcation, and it is no man's business to divide it."

—Chief Joseph

RESPONDING TO THE SELECTION

Students might think about whether their race, gender, nationality, and age affect their response.

ANSWERS FOR REVIEWING THE SELECTION

RECALLING

1. He is tired of fighting, and he feels terrible about the toll the fighting has taken on his people.
2. The leaders, chiefs, and old men have been killed in battle. The young men have taken their place.
3. The children are either lost, dead, or freezing to death.
4. Some of the people have run up into the hills. They have no food or blankets to keep them warm, and are in danger of starving and freezing to death.

INTERPRETING

Responses will vary. Possible responses are given.

5. Chief Joseph surrenders because he is sick of fighting, and he wants to look for his children, who are lost and probably dead.
6. It is dangerous to have the young men in charge because they have little experience.
7. If all the children die, the tribe will be extinguished.
8. Chief Joseph wants time to look for his children, but he fears that they are dead.

SYNTHESIZING

Responses will vary. Possible responses are given.

9. Chief Joseph addresses his speech to General Nelson Miles. He asks him for time to look for his children. He is sick and tired, and he pledges that he will fight no more.
10. The phrase means not just that he is laying down his weapons for a little while or for the time being, but that he is giving up fighting altogether. The sun probably stands in the west, which means that the sun is setting. Chief Joseph's fighting days have come to an end just as the day has come to an end.

things. I have seen the Great Father Chief, the next Great Chief, the Commissioner Chief, the Law Chief, and many other law chiefs,[1] and they all say they are my friends and that I shall have justice; but while their mouths all talk right, I do not understand why nothing is done for my people. I have heard talk and talk, but nothing is done. Good words do not last long unless they amount to something. Words do not pay for my dead people. They do not pay for my country, now overrun by white men. They do not protect my father's grave. They do not pay for all my horses and cattle. Good words will not give me back my children. . . . It makes my heart sick when I remember all the good words and all the broken promises. . . . All men were made by the same Great Spirit Chief. They are all brothers. The earth is the mother of all people, and all people should have equal rights upon it." ■

1. **Great Father Chief . . . other law chiefs.** President Theodore Roosevelt, various members of his administration, and various members of Congress

Responding to the Selection

How did reading Chief Joseph's speech make you feel? Why might this speech be quoted often? What qualities make it moving and memorable?

Reviewing the Selection

RECALLING

1. How does Chief Joseph feel at the time of his surrender?
2. What has happened to all of the peoples' leaders, the chiefs and the old men? Who has taken their place?
3. What is the condition of the children?
4. Where have some of Chief Joseph's people run to after the defeat? What might be their condition?

INTERPRETING

5. Why does Chief Joseph surrender?
6. What is dangerous about having the chiefs dead and the young men in charge?
7. What might happen to the people if all the children die?
8. What does Chief Joseph want time to do? What does he fear?

SYNTHESIZING

9. To whom does Chief Joseph address his surrender speech? What does he ask of these people? What does he pledge to them? Why?

10. The most famous line from Chief Joseph's surrender speech is the last: "From where the sun now stands I will fight no more forever." What does this sentence mean? What does it mean for him to say that he will fight "no more forever"? How does that differ from simply saying that he will fight "no more"? What does the position of the sun mark? Why does he say that he will not fight "from where the sun now stands"?

Understanding Literature (Questions for Discussion)

Oral Tradition. The body of work passed down by word-of-mouth from generation to generation within a culture is known as that culture's **oral tradition.** To appreciate fully the words of Chief Joseph, it helps to remember that his was an oral society. The knowledge, laws, history, and customs of his people were passed down orally rather than in writing. Simplicity, directness, and honesty in speech are prized in many oral societies, for these qualities ensure that the speech will be remembered and can be trusted. What puzzled Chief Joseph about his dealings with politicians on the subject of an appropriate homeland for his people?

Responding in Writing

Comparison. Reread the concluding lines of the Postscript to Chief Joseph's surrender speech. Then read the opening lines of the Declaration of Independence in Unit Three. Write a paragraph comparing the ideas expressed in these two documents. What similarity exists between Chief Joseph's beliefs and those expressed by Thomas Jefferson in the Declaration?

ANSWERS TO SELECTION CHECK TEST 4.7.9

EX. To what group does Chief Joseph direct his speech?
He directs his speech to settlers of European descent.

1. In the speech, how does Chief Joseph feel about fighting?
He is tired of fighting.

2. What has happened to the chiefs and the people who led the young men?
They are dead.

3. What has happened to the children?
The children are freezing to death.

4. What does Chief Joseph not understand about people in Washington?
He does not understand why so many different people seem to be in charge, and why people seem to make so many different promises.

5. How does Chief Joseph view the earth and how people should interact while living on the earth?
He views the earth as the mother of all people, and he believes that all people should have equal rights while living on the earth.

ANSWERS FOR UNDERSTANDING LITERATURE

► See the evaluation forms for discussion, active listening, and oral communication, *Assessment Portfolio,* 7.11–7.14.

Responses will vary. Possible responses are given.

Oral Tradition. Chief Joseph was puzzled by who in Washington was in authority, because he spoke to many different men in positions of power who promised him many different things. He is especially puzzled about why the white leaders merely talk about giving the Nez Percé justice but actually do nothing to see justice carried out.

ANALYTIC SCALES FOR RESPONDING IN WRITING

Assign a score from 1 to 25 for each grading criterion below. (For more detailed evaluation, see the evaluation forms for writing, revising, and proofreading, *Assessment Portfolio,* 7.1–7.10.)

Comparison

- **Content/Unity.** The comparison identifies both similarities and differences between the two documents.
- **Organization/Coherence.** The comparison is written in the form of a paragraph and includes a topic sentence and a point-by-point comparison and contrast of ideas.
- **Language/Style.** The comparison uses vivid and precise nouns, verbs, and modifiers.
- **Conventions.** The comparison avoids errors in spelling, grammar, usage, mechanics, and manuscript form.

ADDITIONAL RESOURCES

READER'S GUIDE
- Selection Worksheet, 7.6

ASSESSMENT PORTFOLIO
- Selection Check Test, 4.7.11
- Selection Test, 4.7.12

ESSENTIAL SKILLS PRACTICE BOOKS
- *Language,* 2.93, 2.104–2.105

ENRICHMENT ACTIVITIES

Students in pairs can enact the dialogue in Crane's poem. Class discussion can focus on differences between interpretations.

SUPPORT FOR LEP STUDENTS

Because this poem is so brief and subtle, some students might struggle with its meaning. Read, as a class, About the Selection on page 468. Spend some time discussing Naturalism before asking students to read the poem.

ADDITIONAL VOCABULARY

obligation—responsibility, something one is supposed to do

HISTORICAL NOTE

Students interested in Naturalism in nineteenth-century American literature should be encouraged to read the works of Frank Norris, Theodore Dreiser, and James Farrell.

PREREADING

POETRY

"A Man Said to the Universe"
by Stephen Crane

ABOUT THE AUTHOR

See the biography of Stephen Crane on page 391.

ABOUT THE SELECTION

The poetry of Stephen Crane was influenced by late nineteenth- and early twentieth-century **Naturalism**, a philosophical perspective and literary movement that viewed human action as strictly determined by biological and environmental forces. In **"A Man Said to the Universe,"** Crane presents an imaginary dialogue that perfectly illustrates the world view of the Naturalists. The universe is not so much antagonistic as indifferent to human endeavor. Much of Crane's work emphasizes that in a world governed by natural laws indifferent to human life, compassion and solidarity are of the utmost importance.

GOALS/OBJECTIVES

Studying this lesson will enable students to

- define late nineteenth- and early twentieth-century Naturalism
- explain how Crane's poetry embodies the principle tenets of Naturalism
- define *personification, irony,* and *dialogue* and illustrate examples of these techniques using Crane's poem
- write a dialogue modeled on Crane's poem

READER'S JOURNAL

Think of a time when the environment in which you found yourself was particularly indifferent to your comfort and well-being. For instance, you might have been caught in a rainstorm or a blizzard, or you might have had to endure a seemingly unbearable heat wave or cold spell. In your journal, describe the situation. How did you respond to it?

LANGUAGE SKILLS

Read the Language Arts Survey, 2.104–2.105, "Quotation Marks I and II." Then read 2.93, "End Marks," paying particular attention to the discussion of the exclamation point. Using the correct form for quotation marks, write a dialogue between two people in which the first person exclaims something and the second answers the exclamation calmly.

"A Man Said to the Universe"

STEPHEN CRANE

A man said to the universe,
"Sir, I exist!"
"However," replied the universe,
"The fact has not created in me
A sense of obligation." ■

Responding to the Selection

How do you feel about the man's exclamation to the universe? If you were the man, how would you respond in turn to the universe's reply? What else might the man say to the universe? What are some other ways that the universe might respond to the man's exclamation?

PREREADING NOTES

READER'S JOURNAL

Students might compare this time to a time when the environment was especially congenial to their well-being and comfort, perhaps a warm spring day when they wanted to take a bike ride.

LANGUAGE SKILLS

Students can exchange dialogues and check them for correct use of quotation and exclamation marks.

ANSWERS TO SELECTION CHECK TEST 4.7.11

EX. What literary movement is reflected in "A Man Said to the Universe"?
The literary movement known as Naturalism is reflected in "A Man Said to the Universe."

1. To whom is the man speaking?
The man is speaking to the universe.
2. What does the man tell the universe?
The man tells the universe that he does exist.
3. What tone of voice does the man use when he speaks to the universe?
The man shouts when he speaks to the universe.
4. What has the fact of the man's existence not created in the universe?
The fact of the man's existence has not created a sense of obligation in the universe.
5. How does the universe appear to feel toward the man?
The universe appears to feel indifferent.

ANSWERS FOR REVIEWING THE SELECTION

RECALLING

1. The two participants in the dialogue are a man and the universe.
2. The man says that he exists, and the universe says that fact does not make it feel obligated to the man.

INTERPRETING

Responses will vary. Possible responses are given.

3. A person would proclaim his or her existence so

(cont.)

LITERARY TECHNIQUE

The **pathetic fallacy** is the tendency to attribute human emotions to nonhuman things, particularly to things in the natural world. The derogatory term was coined by Victorian critic John Ruskin to describe the false appearances of natural objects when under the influence of strong emotional or imaginative moods. This term is usually used when dealing with overly sentimental verse.

RESPONDING TO THE SELECTION

Students might assume the role of a person who has just experienced a life-threatening situation in nature, such as a victim of a natural disaster or a shipwreck survivor.

ANSWERS FOR REVIEWING THE SELECTION (CONT.)

passionately when feeling threatened. One can infer that the man is suffering.

4. The universe expresses indifference.

SYNTHESIZING

Responses will vary. Possible responses are given.

5. According to the poem, the universe is essentially separate from human beings and uninterested in their fate.

ANALYTIC SCALES FOR RESPONDING IN WRITING

Assign a score from 1 to 25 for each grading criterion below. (For more detailed evaluation, see the evaluation forms for writing, revising, and proofreading, *Assessment Portfolio,* 7.1–7.10.)

Dialogue

- **Content/Unity.** The dialogue raises other issues of man's place in the universe and remains consistent with Crane's poem.
- **Organization/Coherence.** The dialogue is written as a conversation between the man and the universe with the narrator providing explanation and commentary.
- **Language/Style.** The dialogue uses vivid and precise nouns, verbs, and modifiers.
- **Conventions.** The dialogue avoids errors in spelling, grammar, usage, mechanics, and manuscript form.

ANSWERS FOR UNDERSTANDING LITERATURE

► See the evaluation forms for discussion, active listening, and oral communication, *Assessment Portfolio,* 7.11–7.14.

Responses will vary. Possible responses are given.

1. **Personification.** We might give the universe emotions such as anger, joy, melancholy, boredom, excitement, and bliss; endowments such as intelligence, logic, creativity, analytic skills, and intuition; or physical capabilities such as strength, endurance, and flexibility. We might endow the universe with human characteristics: a face, a body, a home, a childhood, a job, (cont.)

Reviewing the Selection

RECALLING

1. Who are the two participants in the dialogue?
2. What does each participant say to the other?

INTERPRETING

3. Under what circumstance might a person proclaim his or her existence so passionately? What can you infer about the life of the man who speaks in this poem?
4. What attitude is expressed by the universe in its reply to the man?

SYNTHESIZING

5. According to this poem, what relationship exists between the universe and human beings?

Understanding Literature (Questions for Discussion)

1. **Personification. Personification** is a figure of speech in which an idea, animal, or thing is described as if it were a person. Crane personifies the universe by having the man address it as "Sir" and by imagining that the universe can speak. What other human attributes might we give to Crane's universe? What human traits, both physical and emotional, would you ascribe to the universe?
2. **Irony. Irony** is a difference between appearance and reality. What attitude does the universe in this poem have toward the man? What statement is being made about the universe? Given this statement, why is it ironic that Crane has personified the universe in the poem?
3. **Dialogue.** A **dialogue** is a conversation involving two or more people or characters. What is the topic of the conversation between the man and the universe? What other topics of conversation might arise between a person and the universe? What is the tone of the conversation in this poem—serious or idle? playful or angry? polite or impolite? What would the conversation be like if it continued? What might the man and the universe argue about? What questions might the universe put to the man? What questions might the man put to the universe? On what points would they disagree? On what would they agree? What would it be like if there were other characters involved? Who would the other characters be, and what would they say?

Responding in Writing

Dialogue. Write a continuation of the dialogue between the man and the universe begun by Crane. See question 3 in the Understanding Literature section for ideas.

ANSWERS FOR UNDERSTANDING LITERATURE (CONT.)

hobbies, a family and friends, a car, a favorite color, a CD collection, and a boyfriend or girlfriend.

2. **Irony.** The universe adopts an attitude of indifference to the man. Crane is suggesting that the universe is inhuman, which is ironic because to personify the universe as he does is to give it human characteristics.

3. **Dialogue.** The implicit topic of the conversation is human suffering. In such a conversation many other topics might arise, like human love, the beauty of nature, or the meaning of life. The tone of the conversation is serious; the man is indignant and the universe is aloof. They might argue about whether the universe should feel a sense of obligation to the man. The universe might ask why he should feel an obligation, and the man might reply that he has been created by or out of the materials of the universe. Other characters might be trees, mountains, planets, stars, comets, animals, rocks, and water.

PREREADING

POETRY

from "Song of Myself"
by Walt Whitman

ABOUT THE AUTHOR

Walt Whitman (1819–1892) was the son of a Long Island farmer who turned carpenter and moved his family to Brooklyn in 1823. Whitman left school at age eleven, became an office boy in a law firm, then worked for a doctor. By twelve he was working in the printing office of a newspaper. By fifteen he was on his own. In his midteens he contributed pieces to a Manhattan newspaper and attended debating societies. After working as a journeyman printer for a time, Whitman returned home where he taught school and continued to work on newspapers. Later in his life, Whitman held various newspaper positions in Manhattan and Brooklyn, including reviewer of books, musicals, and theater events. He attended many operas and claimed that they inspired him to write *Leaves of Grass*. Sometime in 1851 or 1852 he became a house builder, making friends with the working class as well as the upper class. Always self-taught, Whitman began to write full time, later combining that career with his job as a clerk in the attorney general's office. Whitman's rise to fame was slow and at times his poetry drew harsh criticism. He suffered a paralytic stroke in 1873 and lost his job but continued writing. Of all American writers of his period, Whitman was the best example of fidelity to his art.

ABOUT THE SELECTION

Whitman writes within the tradition of **Romanticism,** a literary and artistic movement of the eighteenth and nineteenth centuries that placed value on emotion and imagination rather than reason. The Romantics elevated the individual over society, nature over human works, country life over city life, common people over aristocrats, and freedom over control or authority. "**Song of Myself**" is the first poem of *Leaves of Grass*, a single volume that Whitman spent his life writing. The poem is Whitman's effort to describe his personality, or as he put it: "one man's—the author's—identity, ardors, observations, faiths, and thoughts." The selection that follows exemplifies all the themes for which Whitman is best known: his belief that small, insignificant, lowly subjects are in fact worthy of poetry; his democratic celebration of the common people; and his love of natural and animal pleasure. All of these themes are summed up in the grass, the symbol central to his life work. Like all the poems in *Leaves of Grass*, "Song of Myself" is written in **free verse:** the poem does not fit into any planned form, and it has no regular pattern of rhyme, meter, or stanza length. To Whitman, a poem is like an acorn that grows into an oak. It has a life of its own. The poet provides the energy necessary to its growth, but it develops spontaneously, in largely unpredictable ways.

GOALS/OBJECTIVES

Studying this lesson will enable students to

- illustrate the main tenets of Romanticism using passages from Whitman's "Song of Myself"
- describe the autobiographical aim of *Leaves of Grass*
- name the most common themes of Whitman's poetry using examples from the selection
- explain the significance of the symbol of the grass in Whitman's poems
- define *free verse, elaboration, symbol, parallelism,* and *catalog* using examples from the selection
- write a free verse poem and create a wanted poster

ADDITIONAL RESOURCES

READER'S GUIDE
- Selection Worksheet, 7.7

ASSESSMENT PORTFOLIO
- Selection Check Test, 4.7.13
- Selection Test, 4.7.14

ESSENTIAL SKILLS PRACTICE BOOKS
- *Language,* 2.13

AUDIOCASSETTE
- from "Song of Myself," Track 16

ENRICHMENT ACTIVITIES

Whitman printed the first edition of *Leaves of Grass* privately and anonymously on July 4, 1855. The poem was a complete commercial failure but was immediately praised by Ralph Waldo Emerson, to whom Whitman sent a copy. Ask interested students to read other pieces in *Leaves of Grass* and then to refer to the work of Emerson on pages 252, 317, 321, and 346 of their textbook. Ask them to then research the styles, attitudes, and values of the mid-1800s. Ask students to write about and discuss why *Leaves of Grass* might have been a commercial failure. Did this fact have anything to do with particular values or styles of the time? Why, or why not? Why might Emerson have enjoyed Whitman's work? Do the men share any common ideas, themes, or styles?

SUPPORT FOR LEP STUDENTS

Have students highlight particularly difficult passages from the selection and then put their problem with the passage into the form of a specific question.

ADDITIONAL VOCABULARY

assume—to suppose without evidence

hazard—danger

designedly—purposely uniform, unchanging

PREREADING NOTES

READER'S JOURNAL

Before explaining its importance or interest, students might first describe the lowly person, place, or thing in detail and tell how other people commonly react to it. Students can celebrate the object by comparing it to something that is normally considered lofty, uncommon, and significant.

LANGUAGE SKILLS

Have students read the Language Arts Survey, 2.12 and 2.14, and ask them to distinguish linking verbs from action and auxiliary verbs using examples from the selection.

ANSWER TO GUIDED READING QUESTION

❶ The speaker celebrates himself and identifies himself with the reader.

HISTORICAL NOTE

Whitman's "Song of Myself" participates in a Romantic tradition of autobiographical verse that begins in William Wordsworth's *The Prelude*. Similarly, Whitman's love of common speech and exaltation of lowly objects into poetic subjects was a doctrine first voiced in Wordsworth's Preface to *Lyrical Ballads*.

ADDITIONAL QUESTIONS AND ACTIVITIES

Have students compare and contrast Whitman's sense of place as it is illustrated in lines 6–9 of "Song of Myself" and the sense of place of nineteenth-century regionalists like Bret Harte, Sarah Orne Jewett, and Kate Chopin.

READER'S JOURNAL

Think of some person, place, or thing that people in general consider lowly, common, insignificant, or unworthy of attention but that you find fascinating. What is interesting about it? Why is it important? What makes it wonderful in your eyes? Write an entry in your journal celebrating it.

LANGUAGE SKILLS

Read the Language Arts Survey, 2.13, "Linking Verbs." Then make a three-columned chart using sentences from the selection that use linking verbs. In the columns of your chart, list (1) the noun; (2) the noun, pronoun, or adjective that describes or identifies the first noun; and (3) the linking verb that connects the two.

FROM

"Song of Myself"

WALT WHITMAN

1

What does the speaker celebrate? In what way is the speaker connected to the reader? ❶

I celebrate myself, and sing myself,
And what I assume you shall assume,
For every atom belonging to me as good belongs to you.

I loafe and invite my soul,
5 I lean and loafe at my ease observing a spear of summer grass.

My tongue, every atom of my blood, form'd from this soil, this air,
Born here of parents born here from parents the same, and their parents the same,
I, now thirty-seven years old in perfect health begin,
Hoping to cease not till death.

10 Creeds and schools in abeyance,
Retiring back a while sufficed at what they are, but never forgotten,
I harbor for good or bad, I permit to speak at every hazard,

WORDS FOR EVERYDAY USE:

creed (krēd) *n.*, statement of belief, principles, or opinions on any subject

a • bey • ance (ə bā´əns) *n.*, temporary suspension, as of an activity or function

suf • fice (sə fīs´) *vt.*, be enough; be sufficient or adequate

har • bor (här´bər) *vt.*, serve as, or provide, a place of protection

VOCABULARY IN CONTEXT

- The creed of the organization centered around helping others and the environment.
- Work on the highway was put in abeyance until the city could raise funds to pay the workers.
- The five-course meal sufficed the hungry guests.
- Harboring runaway criminals is a capital offense in this state.

Nature without check with original energy.
Looks down, is erect, or bends an arm on an impalpable certain rest,
15 Looking with side-curved head curious what will come next,
Both in and out of the game and watching and wondering at it.

Backward I see in my own days where I sweated through fog with linguists and contenders,
I have no mockings or arguments, I witness and wait.

♦ ♦ ♦

6

A child said *What is the grass?* fetching it to me with full hands;
20 How could I answer the child? I do not know what it is any more than he.

I guess it must be the flag of my disposition, out of hopeful green stuff woven.

Or I guess it is the handkerchief of the Lord,
A scented gift and remembrancer designedly dropt,
Bearing the owner's name someway in the corners, that we may see and remark, and say *Whose?*

25 Or I guess the grass is itself a child, the produced babe of the vegetation.

Or I guess it is a uniform hieroglyphic,[1]
And it means, Sprouting alike in broad zones and narrow zones,
Growing among black folks as among white,

❶ *What question does the child ask? What is the speaker's first response?*

❷ *What does the speaker say the grass is?*

1. **hieroglyphic.** Picture or symbol representing a word, syllable, or sound, used by the ancient Egyptians and others instead of alphabetical letters

WORDS FOR EVERYDAY USE:

im • pal • pa • ble (im pal´pə bəl) *adj.,* that which cannot be felt by touching

lin • guist (liŋ´gwist) *n.,* specialist in the science of language

con • tend • er (kən ten´dər) *n.,* one who strives or fights in competition

dis • po • si • tion (dis´pə zis´hən) *n.,* one's customary frame of mind

ANSWERS TO GUIDED READING QUESTIONS

❶ The child asks, "What is the grass?" The speaker's first response is that he does not know what it is.

❷ The speaker says the grass is a sign of his temperament; a "handkerchief of the Lord"; a child; and a hieroglyphic.

HISTORICAL NOTE

In the Romantic tradition of which Whitman is a part, the figure of the child is a model of the human capacity to experience objects freshly, without intellectual preconceptions and perceptual habits. The true Romantic returns to childhood only in order to bring its innocence into his or her adult life.

ADDITIONAL QUESTIONS AND ACTIVITIES

Students might write personal essays describing some particularly wondrous or interesting childhood experiences of their own. Ask students to share their essays in small groups. Then, in groups, students should discuss why childhood is considered to be such a special and magical time. What is positive and magical about being a child? What are the negative aspects of childhood?

LITERARY TECHNIQUE

A **metaphor** is a figure of speech in which one thing is spoken or written about as if it were another. The two "things" involved are the writer's actual subject, the *tenor,* and the thing to which the subject is likened, the *vehicle.*

VOCABULARY IN CONTEXT

- Impalpable things like emotions often confuse people.
- The linguist has written many books about language and how it changes over time.
- At one time the boxer had been a contender for the heavyweight title.
- Although the young child often has a sunny and content disposition, today he seems slightly sad and restless.

Answers to Guided Reading Questions

❶ The speaker hears the voices of the dead. He cannot understand the "hints" about the dead.

❷ The smallest sprout shows that there is no death or that death is always a prelude to life.

Additional Questions and Activities

- An **elegy** is a long formal poem about death or loss. Lines 30–50 of "Song of Myself" can be read as a meditation on the death of loved ones.
- Have students read "When Lilacs Last in the Dooryard Bloom'd," Whitman's elegy to Lincoln. Students can then write free verse elegies to deceased or lost loved ones of their own, or to deceased public figures whom they've admired.
- Students may compare Whitman's attitude toward death to the attitude toward death expressed by Bret Harte in "The Outcasts of Poker Flat" or by a Naturalist like Stephen Crane or Jack London.

Historical Note

Students interested in the elegy as a poetic form should be encouraged to read such classics as Tennyson's *In Memoriam*, W. H. Auden's "In Memory of W. B. Yeats," and Gray's "Elegy Written in a Country Churchyard."

Kanuck, Tuckahoe, Congressman, Cuff,[2] I give them the same, I receive them the same.

30 And now it seems to me the beautiful uncut hair of graves.

Tenderly will I use you curling grass,
It may be you transpire from the breasts of young men,
It may be if I had known them I would have loved them,
It may be you are from old people, or from offspring taken soon out of their mothers' laps,
35 And here you are the mothers' laps.

This grass is very dark to be from the white heads of old mothers,
Darker than the colorless beards of old men,
Dark to come from under the faint red roofs of mouths.

O I perceive after all so many uttering tongues,
40 And I perceive they do not come from the roofs of mouths for nothing.

What does the speaker hear? What hints does the speaker not understand? ❶

I wish I could translate the hints about the dead young men and women,
And the hints about old men and mothers, and the offspring taken soon out of their laps.

What do you think has become of the young and old men?
And what do you think has become of the women and children?

What does the smallest sprout show? ❷

45 They are alive and well somewhere,
The smallest sprout shows there is really no death,
And if ever there was it led forward life, and does not wait at the end to arrest it,
And ceas'd the moment life appear'd.

All goes onward and outward, nothing collapses,
50 And to die is different from what any one supposed, and luckier.

♦ ♦ ♦

2. **Kanuck, Tuckahoe, Congressman, Cuff.** *Kanuck*—French Canadian; *Tuckahoe*— Virginian; *Cuff*—from the African word *cuffee*, refers to African Americans.

7

Has any one supposed it lucky to be born?
I hasten to inform him or her it is just as lucky to die, and I know it.

I pass death with the dying and birth with the new-wash'd babe, and am not contain'd between my hat and boots,

And peruse manifold objects, no two alike and every one good,
55 The earth good and the stars good, and their adjuncts all good.

I am not an earth nor an adjunct of an earth,
I am the mate and companion of people, all just as immortal and fathomless as myself,
(They do not know how immortal, but I know.)

Every kind for itself and its own, for me mine male and female,
60 For me those that have been boys and that love women,
For me the man that is proud and feels how it stings to be slighted,
For me the sweet-heart and the old maid, for me mothers and the mothers of mothers,
For me lips that have smiled, eyes that have shed tears,
For me children and the begetters of children.

65 Undrape! you are not guilty to me, nor stale nor discarded,
I see through the broadcloth and gingham[3] whether or no,
And am around, tenacious, acquisitive, tireless, and cannot be shaken away.

◆ ◆ ◆

31

I believe a leaf of grass is no less than the journey-work of the stars,
And the pismire[4] is equally perfect, and a grain of sand, and the egg of the wren,

3. **broadcloth and gingham.** *Broadcloth*—fine wool; *gingham*—cotton cloth that is woven in checks or plaids
4. **Pismire.** Ant

❶ *What attitude does the speaker have toward death? Why might the speaker feel this way?*

❷ *What does the speaker say he is not? What does the speaker claim to be?*

Answers to Guided Reading Questions

❶ The speaker thinks that one is lucky to die. He feels this way because he has experienced both and seen them as equally marvelous.

❷ The speaker is not "an earth or an adjunct of an earth" but a "companion" of people.

Literary Technique

An **allusion** is a figure of speech in which a reference is made to a person, event, object, or work from history or literature. Lines 54 and 55 of Whitman's "Song of Myself" allude to a refrain from the first chapter of Genesis, the lines that describe God's response to his creation: "And God saw that it was good."

Additional Questions and Activities

An allusion invites the reader to compare the work he or she is reading to another work. For example, Whitman's allusion to Genesis invites the reader to compare Whitman to a creator. Ask students to find and describe the significance of other allusions in Whitman's poems.

Quotables

"To articulate and faithfully express in literary or poetic form, and uncompromisingly, my own physical, emotional, moral, intellectual, and aesthetic Personality."

—Walt Whitman
on the aim of *Leaves of Grass*

Historical Note

Romantics like Whitman often translate traditional religious ideas of the supernatural into naturalistic terms. Judeo-Christian religious traditions generally define a miracle as a suspension of natural law, or a supernatural event. In lines 68–74, Whitman suggests that miracles occur every day in the most insignificant natural objects.

Additional Questions and Activities

Have students describe some ordinary, natural object that they see as miraculous. The focus of the description should be the object's strange or wondrous quality.

And the tree-toad is a chief-d'oeuvre[5] for the highest,
And the running blackberry would adorn the parlors of heaven,
And the narrowest hinge in my hand puts to scorn all machinery,
And the cow crunching with depress'd head surpasses any statue,
And a mouse is miracle enough to stagger sextillions[6] of infidels.

I find I incorporate gneiss,[7] coal, long-threaded moss, fruits, grains, esculent roots,
And am stucco'd with quadrupeds and birds all over,
And have distanced what is behind me for good reasons,
But call any thing back again when I desire it.

In vain the speeding or shyness,
In vain the plutonic rocks[8] send their old heat against my approach,
In vain the mastodon retreats beneath its own powder'd bones,
In vain objects stand leagues off and assume manifold shapes,
In vain the ocean settling in hollows and the great monsters lying low,

5. **chief-d'oeuvre.** Master or culminating work
6. **sextillions.** Number represented by one followed by twenty-one zeros
7. **gneiss.** Metamorphic rock with minerals arranged in layers
8. **plutonic rocks.** Rocks formed far below the surface of the earth

Words for Everyday Use:

in • fi • del (in´fə del´) *n.,* person who does not believe in a particular religion

es • cu • lent (es´kyōō lənt) *adj.,* fit for food, edible

quad • ru • ped (kwä´drōō ped´) *n.,* animal, especially a mammal, with four feet

Vocabulary in Context

- The crusaders set off to convert the infidels to their religion.
- The berries we found in the woods were esculent, and so we enjoyed them as an afternoon snack.
- In science class we completed a unit on quadrupeds, and tomorrow we'll complete a unit on bipeds.
- The rock climber ascended the mountain by way of the fissures in the rocks.
- Most businesses do not appreciate loitering on their front steps.
- The crowd at that concert was too barbaric, so the musical group will not be invited to return.
- The jags on the saw were sharp and dangerous.

In vain the buzzard houses herself with the sky,
85 In vain the snake slides through the creepers and logs,
In vain the elk takes to the inner passes of the woods,
In vain the razor-bill'd auk[9] sails far north to Labrador,[10]
I follow quickly, I ascend to the nest in the fissure of the cliff.

◆ ◆ ◆

32

I think I could turn and live with animals, they are so placid and self-contain'd,
90 I stand and look at them long and long.

They do not sweat and whine about their condition,
They do not lie awake in the dark and weep for their sins,
They do not make me sick discussing their duty to God,
Not one is dissatisfied, not one is demented with the mania of owning things,
95 Not one kneels to another, nor to his kind that lived thousands of years ago,
Not one is respectable or unhappy over the whole earth.

Why would the speaker like to live with the animals? In what ways are they different from humans?

◆ ◆ ◆

52

The spotted hawk swoops by and accuses me, he complains of my gab and my loitering.

I too am not a bit tamed, I too am untranslatable,
I sound my barbaric yawp[11] over the roofs of the world.

100 The last scud of day holds back for me,
It flings my likeness after the rest and true as any on the shadow'd wilds,
It coaxes me to the vapor and the dusk.

I depart as air, I shake my white locks at the runaway sun,
I effuse my flesh in eddies, and drift it in lacy jags.

9. **auk.** Shore bird of northern seas with a heavy body, a short tail, and short wings used as paddles
10. **Labrador.** Region along the Atlantic coast of northeastern Canada
11. **yawp.** Loud, harsh cry or call

Words for Everyday Use:

fis • sure (fish´ər) *n.,* long, narrow, deep cleft or crack
loi • ter (loi´tər) *vi.,* linger in an aimless way
bar • bar • ic (bär ber´ik) *adj.,* wild, crude, and unrestrained
jag (jag) *n.,* sharp, toothlike projection

Answer to Guided Reading Question

❶ The speaker would like to live with the animals because they are not unhappy with their lot on earth, tortured by guilt, perpetually dissatisfied, materialistic, or superstitious as human beings are.

Answers to Selection Check Test 4.7.13

EX. What does the narrator celebrate in the poem?
The narrator celebrates himself.

1. What does the speaker observe in the opening lines of the poem?
The speaker observes a blade of grass.

2. Who first asks the question, "What is the grass?"
A child asks the question, "What is the grass?"

3. What is "no less than the journey work of the stars"?
A leaf of grass is no less than the journey work of the stars.

4. Why does the speaker want to live with animals?
According to the speaker, animals are placid and self-contained.

5. Where should people look for the speaker after his death?
People should look for the speaker within the grass, "under [their] boot-soles."

Analytic Scales for Responding in Writing

Assign a score from 1 to 25 for each grading criterion below. (For more detailed evaluation, see the evaluation forms for writing, revising, and proofreading, *Assessment Portfolio,* 7.1–7.10.)

1. Free Verse

- **Content/Unity.** The writer chose a natural object around which to create a poem in the style of "Song of Myself."
- **Organization/Coherence.** The free verse poem is organized in a way that makes sense to the reader but avoids the use of regular rhyme, rhythm, or stanzas.

(cont.)

Analytic Scales for Responding in Writing (cont.)

- **Language/Style.** The poem uses vivid and precise language.
- **Conventions.** The poem avoids errors in spelling, grammar, usage, and mechanics.

2. Wanted Poster

- **Content/Unity.** The wanted poster is based on details from Whitman's life.
- **Organization/Coherence.** The poster is organized in a way that would make sense to readers.
- **Language/Style.** The poster is creative and makes good use of vivid details.
- **Conventions.** The poster avoids errors in spelling, grammar, usage, and mechanics.

ANSWER TO GUIDED READING QUESTION

❶ To see the speaker one should look under one's feet, in the grass. By listening to the speaker one will gain health.

RESPONDING TO THE SELECTION

Give students time to freewrite about these issues. You might also allow them to gather in small groups to discuss the poem.

ANSWERS FOR REVIEWING THE SELECTION

RECALLING

1. Whitman first says he does not know what it is, but then he says that it is the "flag of his disposition," the "handkerchief of the Lord," "a child," and a "uniform hieroglyphic."

2. Whitman says that death does not exist, or that if it does exist, it is always a prelude to life. He says that to die is lucky, and dying, like the giving of birth, is a miracle to behold.

3. Whitman compares a leaf of grass to the work of the stars, a tree-toad to a chef-d'oeuvre, a blackberry bush to a heavenly parlor decoration, a hinge in his hand to machinery, a cow eating grass to a statue, and a mouse to a miracle.

4. According to Whitman the animal's lives are placid and self-contained.

INTERPRETING

Responses will vary. Possible responses are given.

5. He wants to treat the grass tenderly because it could be that somebody has died nearby and their spirit has entered the grass. A sprout of vegetation proves that there is no death or that death is only a prelude to more life.

6. Perhaps Whitman feels this way about death because he has experienced the spring or other instances when new life rose from

(cont.)

Where should you look to see the speaker? What will the speaker do for the people he is addressing? ❶

105 I bequeath myself to the dirt to grow from the grass I love,
If you want me again look for me under your boot-soles.

You will hardly know who I am or what I mean,
But I shall be good health to you nevertheless,
And filter and fibre your blood.

110 Failing to fetch me at first keep encouraged,
Missing me one place search another,
I stop somewhere waiting for you. ■

Responding to the Selection

In "Song of Myself," Whitman views death as a force that unites him with both nature and other human beings. How do you feel about Whitman's views? Do you find Whitman's views comforting and hopeful or unrealistic and unsatisfying?

Reviewing the Selection

RECALLING

1. What answer does Whitman give in response to the question "What is the grass?"
2. What does Whitman say about dying in sections 6 and 7?
3. What are the small, commonplace, and insignificant things that Whitman describes in section 31? To what does he compare each of these "lowly" things?
4. What are the lives of animals like according to Whitman in section 32?

INTERPRETING

5. Why does he want to treat the grass tenderly? According to Whitman, what does a sprout of vegetation prove about life and death?
6. What reasons does Whitman give for that view of death? Why might he feel that way?
7. What do Whitman's comparisons indicate about his feelings for commonplace things?
8. Why could Whitman "turn and live with" the animals? What view does he express about humans in contrast to animals?

ANSWERS FOR REVIEWING THE SELECTION (CONT.)

the ashes of the old.

7. Whitman's comparisons indicate that he celebrates commonplace things.

8. Whitman could live with the animals because he is sick of human beings who complain about their human condition, feel guilt, argue endlessly about their duty to God, and worship superstitiously.

SYNTHESIZING

Responses will vary. Possible responses are given.

9. Whitman's message is, among other things, that ordinary objects are worthy, even superior subjects for poetry, and free verse approximates the rhythms of ordinary speech.

10. By examining death Whitman affirms his position as part of the cycle of life and nature. He talks about how he will "grow from the grass I love."

SYNTHESIZING

9. Why is the free verse form a good vehicle for Whitman's message?

10. In this poem Whitman both sounds his "barbaric yawp," proclaiming his existence, and reconciles himself to death. In what way is examining death an affirmation of life for Whitman?

Understanding Literature (Questions for Discussion)

1. **Elaboration. Elaboration,** or amplification, is a writing technique in which a subject is introduced and then expanded upon by means of repetition with slight changes, the addition of details, or similar devices. For instance, in section 6 the child asks, "What is the grass?" The speaker responds with a series of possibilities, each of which begins with the same phrase: "I guess it is . . ." Find other examples of elaboration in the selection. What is its effect in each case? What is its effect in general?

2. **Symbol.** A **symbol** is a thing that stands for or represents both itself and something else. In Whitman's poem, the grass is both a conventional symbol, one with widely recognized associations, and an idiosyncratic symbol, one that assumes secondary meanings because of the special uses to which it is put by the writer. Find all the passages in which the symbol of the grass occurs. What does the grass symbolize in each of these instances?

3. **Parallelism. Parallelism** is a rhetorical technique in which a writer emphasizes the equal value or weight of two or more ideas by expressing them in the same grammatical form. Find examples of parallelism in "Song of Myself." What ideas are being emphasized by the speaker?

4. **Catalog.** A **catalog** is a list of people or things. What is cataloged in this poem? Why do you think Whitman used this list? What else might he have included?

Responding in Writing

1. **Free Verse. Free verse** is poetry that avoids the use of regular rhyme, rhythm, meter, or division into stanzas. Write a free verse poem using section 6 of Whitman's "Song of Myself" as a model. For the symbol of the grass, however, substitute some other natural object: a river, mountain, bird, or rock. Begin the poem with a line similar to Whitman's: "A child said *What is the . . . ?*" Write the rest of the poem by elaborating upon the answer in the way Whitman does. Begin each stanza with the phrase, "I guess it is . . ."

2. **Wanted Poster.** Whitman celebrated behavior that was "lawless as snowflakes." His disregard for conventional poetic subjects and forms made him unacceptable to genteel society in his day. Create a wanted poster for Walt Whitman. Include a picture, a description of his appearance, and a list of the crimes for which the authorities want to imprison him.

ANSWERS FOR UNDERSTANDING LITERATURE

► See the evaluation forms for discussion, active listening, and oral communication, *Assessment Portfolio,* 7.11–7.14.

Responses will vary. Possible responses are given.

1. Elaboration. Students will find a good example of elaboration in section 32: "I think I could turn and live with animals, they are so placid and self-contain'd." He then lists several attributes of animals, each line beginning with "They do not. . . ." The effect of the elaboration is to illustrate the differences between the animal world and the human world.

2. Symbol. In section 1, the speaker observes a "spear of summer grass"; the grass symbolizes the speaker's individuality and connectedness with the natural world and other living things. In section 6, a child asks, "What is the grass?" The speaker looks at the grass with the innocence of the child and introduces the idea that the grass is "the beautiful uncut hair of graves."

In section 31, the speaker says, "I believe a leaf of grass is no less than the journey-work of the stars," attempting to illustrate the perfection of the natural world.

In line 52, the speaker refers to his own death when he tells the reader, "I bequeath myself to the dirt to grow from the grass I love. . . ." In this instance he is returning to the idea expressed in part 6—that grass is "the beautiful uncut hair of graves."

3. Parallelism. As examples of parallelism, students might list the lines of section 31. The speaker begins by saying, "I believe a leaf of grass is no less than the journey-work of the stars,/And the pismire is equally perfect, and a grain of sand, and the egg of the wren. " The speaker then gives five lines with parallel structure, each stating the perfection of something in nature and beginning with the words "And the." The speaker ends section 32 with three long, parallel phrases, each beginning with the words "Not one." Here, the speaker is comparing the animal world with the human world.

(cont.)

ANALYTIC SCALES FOR RESPONDING IN WRITING

Grading scales appear on page 477.

ANSWERS FOR UNDERSTANDING LITERATURE (CONT.)

4. Catalog. In the poem, Whitman catalogs plants, animals, people, and general elements of nature. This cataloging is a way of illustrating his connectedness with the natural world and his belief in individuality. Students should be invited to list other elements of the natural world, particularly things that are symbolic to them in terms of expressing individuality, spirituality, and a connectedness with nature.

ADDITIONAL RESOURCES

READER'S GUIDE
- Selection Worksheet, 7.8

ASSESSMENT PORTFOLIO
- Selection Check Test, 4.7.15
- Selection Test, 4.7.16

ESSENTIAL SKILLS PRACTICE BOOKS
- *Language,* 2.147

ENRICHMENT ACTIVITIES

Some students might want to read more of Dunbar's work. Encourage them to go to a library and pick out a novel or a collection of poetry or prose by Dunbar. Ask each student to complete a short book review on the book he or she has chosen. How does it compare with the poem "We Wear the Mask"?

SUPPORT FOR LEP STUDENTS

The poem's syntax and formal language might be difficult for some students. You might read the poem aloud to these students. You should also encourage students to pay attention to the footnotes that explain some of the more difficult terms the poet uses.

ADDITIONAL VOCABULARY

subtleties—things not open or obvious

nay—not only that, but also; furthermore (used to reinforce what has just been said)

arise—move upward

PREREADING

POETRY

"We Wear the Mask"
by Paul Laurence Dunbar

ABOUT THE AUTHOR

Paul Laurence Dunbar (1872–1906) was born in Dayton, Ohio, the son of former slaves. His father, Joshua, was a United States Army soldier and plasterer, and his mother, Matilda, was a laundry worker. His mother had no formal education but taught Dunbar to read when he was four. He reported that both his parents were "fond of books" and read aloud to the family in the evenings as they sat around the fire. This poet, novelist, and short story writer said that he made his first attempt at rhyming when he was about six and found a poem by Wordsworth. He thought it had been written by a man in Dayton of the same name. The idea that someone he knew wrote poetry impressed his young mind and, "after that I rhymed continually," he said. He was encouraged in his writing aspirations by a high school teacher and by a classmate named Orville Wright who was later to become a pioneer of aviation. He was the only African American in his class, which served, he said, to spur his ambitions. After graduating with honors from high school, he held a series of manual labor jobs. He wrote in his free time, began submitting poems to local newspapers, and in 1893, printed *Oak and Ivy.* He gained national recognition in 1896 with the publication of *Lyrics of Lowly Life* and a full-page, enthusiastic review of *Majors and Minors (*1895) in *Harper's Weekly.* That launched him as a reader on the lecture circuit in the United States and in Europe and eventually landed him a series of jobs at the Library of Congress, where he worked until sickness forced him to leave. His works include *Majors and Minors* (1895), *The Uncalled* (novel, 1896), *Lyrics of the Hearthside* (1899), *The Love of Landry* (novel, 1900), *Uncle Eph's Christmas* (one-act musical, 1900), *The Fanatics* (novel, 1901), *The Sport of the Gods* (novel, 1902), *Lyrics of Love and Laughter* (1903), and *Lyrics of Sunshine and Shadow* (1905).

ABOUT THE SELECTION

While Dunbar's reputation rests on his poems and short stories written in African-American dialect, Dunbar himself considered his nondialectical work to be his best. At the time Dunbar wrote his poems, including **"We Wear the Mask,"** the use of dialect was very popular; consequently and regrettably, many of Dunbar's poems not written in dialect were neglected. In its formal language and use of rhyme, the selection shows the influence of poets Robert Burns and James Whitcomb Riley, both of whom Dunbar admired.

GOALS/OBJECTIVES

Studying this lesson will enable students to

- identify Paul Laurence Dunbar as an important poet, novelist, and short story writer of the late 1800s and early 1900s
- define *speaker* and *rhyme* using examples from the selection
- recognize formal and informal language
- create realistic dialogue to fit a particular scenario

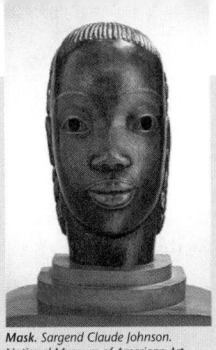

Mask. Sargend Claude Johnson. National Museum of American Art, Washington, DC/Art Resource

READER'S JOURNAL

Have you ever hidden your feelings from someone? Have you ever put on a "happy face" when you were feeling sadness or pain? Why did you wear an emotional mask? What did it feel like to wear such a mask? How did others respond to you? Write about the experience in your journal.

LANGUAGE SKILLS

Read the Language Arts Survey, 2.147, "Formal and Informal Language." Then identify some formal words in the selection and note what mood or tone they lend to the poem.

"We Wear the Mask"

PAUL LAURENCE DUNBAR

We wear the mask that grins and lies,
It hides our cheeks and shades our eyes—
This debt we pay to human guile;[1]
With torn and bleeding hearts we smile,
5 And mouth with myriad[2] subtleties.

Why should the world be otherwise,
In counting all our tears and sighs?
Nay, let them only see us, while
We wear the mask.

10 We smile, but, O great Christ, our cries
To thee from tortured souls arise.
We sing, but oh the clay is vile[3]
Beneath our feet, and long the mile;
But let the world dream otherwise,
15 We wear the mask! ■

1. **guile.** Secretiveness; sneakiness
2. **myriad.** Large number; of a varied nature
3. **vile.** Offensive

❶ *What does the mask show? What does it hide?*

❷ *What contradictions are apparent in stanza 3?*

Responding to the Selection

Imagine that you are the speaker in the poem. Write an entry in your journal explaining the kinds of emotions you hide when wearing the mask.

PREREADING NOTES

READER'S JOURNAL

Ask students to think about what emotions people are most likely to hide. Why are people afraid to show certain emotions? Why are people at times afraid to show their true selves to others? What might cause this fear?

LANGUAGE SKILLS

Ask students to compare the words they have chosen. Together, they should discuss the mood of the poem and how the poem's language affects this mood. Students might identify *myriad, nay, thee,* and the use of *O* as examples of formal language.

ANSWERS TO GUIDED READING QUESTIONS

❶ According to the poem, the mask shows a smiling mouth but hides cheeks, eyes, and "torn and bleeding hearts."

❷ The smiling and the singing are contradictory to the torture in the souls of the people who must wear masks and are unable to expose their true selves.

RESPONDING TO THE SELECTION

Encourage students to think of this poem as one that works on different levels. They can read it as a statement about the general human condition, but also encourage them to read it with a more specific, political interpretation. Explain that Dunbar was an African American in a world of racism. Ask students whether Dunbar might be addressing issues of racial discrimination in this poem.

ANSWERS FOR REVIEWING THE SELECTION (CONT.)

INTERPRETING

Responses will vary. Possible responses are given.

5. The "we" is people who must mask their true thoughts, wishes, and feelings. The "them" is people who judge, persecute, or impose the sort of control that causes others to feel they must hide behind a mask. If one reads the poem as a political statement about racism, "we" might be African Americans or any group of people who have suffered as a result of racism, and "them" might be those people in the world who have unjustly discriminated against and persecuted this group of people.

6. The speaker expresses a negative attitude about the human "guile," or duplicity, that causes people to hide their feelings.

7. The speaker suggests that "the world" is only interested in seeing the mask and is not interested in discovering the true feelings of others.

(cont.)

ANSWERS FOR REVIEWING THE SELECTION

RECALLING

1. A mask "grins and lies."
2. A debt is paid "to human guile."
3. All of the tears and sighs are not counted by the world.
4. The cries arise from tortured souls.

(cont.)

ANSWERS FOR REVIEWING THE SELECTION (CONT.)

8. The speaker, in the last stanza of the poem, addresses Christ.

SYNTHESIZING

Responses will vary. Possible responses are given.

9. People who are unable to be themselves or show their true feelings wear a mask. These people might be part of a specific group of people who have long suffered prejudice and discrimination. One might also say that human beings in general feel it necessary to hide behind some type of facade. The mask is a metaphor for the superficial personalities, interests, needs, and feelings people choose to show the world instead of showing their true selves.

10. The poem relates the fact that discrimination keeps people from being honest with one another. It also keeps people from truly understanding all the complexities and subtleties of one another. People who suffer persecution and discrimination must try to protect themselves in some way. Masking one's true feelings and needs is a way to protect oneself from further prosecution.

ANSWERS FOR UNDERSTANDING LITERATURE

▶ See the evaluation forms for discussion, active listening, and oral communication, *Assessment Portfolio,* 7.11–7.14.

Responses will vary. Possible responses are given.

1. Speaker. Some students might consider that Dunbar, being African American and probably having experienced discrimination, is speaking to other African Americans. In this case the "we" would be African Americans, and the "them" would be white society. Some students might feel the poem also speaks to humanity in general. If one is to interpret the poem as speaking to humanity in general, the "we" would be all people who feel they must hide behind a facade due to social standards. The "them" would be other people—to whom people feel they must not fully reveal themselves.

2. Rhyme. The end rhyme scheme of the poem is *aabbc aabd aabbad.* The most common repeated sounds are *lies/eyes* and *guile/smile.*

Reviewing the Selection

RECALLING

1. What "grins and lies"?
2. What is paid "to human guile"?
3. What does the speaker suggest is not counted by the world?
4. From what kind of souls do the cries mentioned in the poem arise?

INTERPRETING

5. Who is the "we" mentioned in the poem? Who is the "them"?
6. What attitudes toward human duplicity does the speaker express?
7. Why does the speaker suggest "Nay, let them only see us, while/We wear the mask"?
8. Whom is the speaker addressing in the poem?

SYNTHESIZING

9. Who wears the mask? For what is the mask a metaphor in the poem?
10. What terrible consequence of discrimination does this poem relate? Why can't people expect the people whom they are discriminating against to be guileless and open about their feelings?

Understanding Literature (Questions for Discussion)

1. **Speaker.** The **speaker** is the person who speaks in or narrates a poem—the voice assumed by the writer. The speaker in this poem uses the pronoun *we,* not *I.* For and to whom do you think the speaker is speaking? How might your interpretation of the poem change if you decided that the speaker were speaking for the entire human race? Who, then, would be the "we"? Who would be the "them"?

2. **Rhyme. Rhyme** is the repetition of sounds at the ends of words. One type of rhyme is *end rhyme,* the use of rhyming words at the ends of lines. What is the end rhyme scheme of the poem?

Responding in Writing

Dialogue. Imagine a situation in which a person is hiding his or her true feelings. Write a dialogue between two people in which the second person tries to convince the first person to drop his or her mask and be open about his or her true feelings.

ANALYTIC SCALES FOR RESPONDING IN WRITING

Assign a score from 1 to 25 for each grading criterion below. (For more detailed evaluation, see the evaluation forms for writing, revising, and proofreading, *Assessment Portfolio,* 7.1–7.10.)

Dialogue

- **Content/Unity.** The dialogue realistically addresses the issue of one person hiding his or her true feelings. Each speaker contributes to the conversation.
- **Organization/Coherence.** The dialogue is organized in a way that allows the reader to understand what the conversation is about. Each line reveals something about the speakers.
- **Language/Style.** The dialogue is realistic and sounds like natural speech.
- **Conventions.** The dialogue avoids errors in spelling, grammar, usage, and mechanics, except for errors that might be intentional to make the dialogue sound more realistic.

"I Am Alone"
by Cochise of the Apache

This for a very long time has been the home of my people; they came from the darkness, few in numbers and feeble. The country was held by a much stronger and more numerous people, and from their stone houses we were quickly driven. We were a hunting people, living on the animals that we could kill. We came to these mountains about us; no one lived here, and so we took them for our home and country. Here we grew from the first feeble band to be a great people, and covered the whole country as the clouds cover the mountains. Many people came to our country. First the Spanish, with their horses and their iron shirts, their long knives[1] and guns, great wonders to my simple people. We fought some, but they never tried to drive us from our homes in these mountains. After many years the Spanish soldiers were driven away and the Mexican ruled the land. With these little wars came, but we were now a strong people and we did not fear them. At last in my youth came the white man, your people. Under the counsels of my grandfather, who had for a very long time been the head of the Apaches, they were received with friendship. Soon their numbers increased and many passed through my country to the great waters of the setting sun.[2] Your soldiers came and their strong houses[3] were all through my country. I received favors from your people and did all that I could in return and we lived at peace. At last your soldiers did me a very great wrong, and I and my whole people went to war with them. At first we were successful and your soldiers were driven away and your people killed and we again possessed our land. Soon many soldiers came from the north and from the west, and my people were driven to the mountain hiding places; but these did not protect us, and soon my people were flying from one mountain to another, driven by the soldiers, even as the wind is now driving the clouds. I have fought long and as best I could against you. I have destroyed many of your people, but where I have destroyed one white man many have come in his place; but where an Indian has been killed, there has been none to come in his place, so that the great people that welcomed you with acts of kindness to this land are now but a feeble band that fly before your soldiers as the deer before the hunter, and must all perish if this war continues. I have come to you, not from any love for you or for your great father in Washington, or from any regard for his or your wishes, but as a conquered chief, to try to save alive the few people that still remain to me. I am the last of my family, a family that for very many years have been the leaders of this people, and on me depends their future, whether they shall utterly vanish from the land or that a small remnant remain for a few years to see the sun rise over these mountains, their home. I here pledge my word, a word that has never been broken, that if your great father will set aside a part of my own country, where I and my little band can live, we will remain at peace with your people forever. If from his abundance he will give food for my women and children, whose protectors his soldiers have killed, with blankets to cover their nakedness, I will receive them with gratitude. If not, I will do my best to feed and clothe them, in peace with the white man. I have spoken.

from *Life on the Mississippi*
by Mark Twain

When I was a boy, there was but one permanent ambition among my comrades in our village[4] on the west bank of the Mississippi River. That was, to be a steamboatman. We had transient ambitions of other sorts, but they were only transient.

When a circus came and went, it left us all burning to become clowns; the first Negro minstrel show that came to our section left us all suffering to try that kind of life; now and then we had a hope that if we lived and were good, God would permit us to be pirates. These ambitions faded out, each in its turn; but the ambition to be a steamboatman always remained.

Once a day a cheap, gaudy packet[5] arrived upward from St. Louis, and another downward form Keokuk.[6] Before these events, the day was glorious with expectancy; after them, the day was a dead and empty thing. Not only the boys, but the whole village, felt this. After all these years I can picture that old time to myself now, just as it was then: the white town drowsing in the sunshine of a summer's morning; the streets empty, or pretty nearly so; one or two clerks sitting in front of the Water Street stores, with their splint-bottomed chairs tilted back against the wall, chins on breasts, hats slouched over their faces, asleep—with shingle shavings enough around to show what broke them down; a sow and a litter of pigs loafing along the sidewalk, doing a good business in watermelon rinds and seeds; two or three lonely little freight piles scattered about the levee; a pile of skids[7] on the slope of the stone-paved wharf, and the

1. **horses . . . knives.** Spaniards introduced horses to the Americas. Metal armor and swords are referred to here.
2. **great . . . sun.** Pacific Ocean
3. **strong houses.** Forts
4. **our village.** Hannibal, Missouri
5. **packet.** Boat on a regular route
6. **Keokuk.** Town in southeastern Iowa
7. **skids.** Wooden platforms

"I AM ALONE"

About the Author. Cochise (*circa* 1812–1874) was a great chief and warrior of southern Arizona's Chiricahua Apaches. In 1861, Cochise and five other Native American leaders were arrested by the United States Army in connection with a cattle raid. Cochise managed to escape. Although he sustained injuries from the experience, he became a successful leader in fighting white settlers and soldiers in his own territory. He always managed to escape capture by hiding in the Dragoon Mountains. Cochise voluntarily surrendered himself in 1872 when the Chiricahua Apache Reservation was established.

QUOTABLES

"When I was young I walked all over this country, east and west, and saw no other people than the Apaches. After many Summers I walked again and found another race of people had come to take it. How is it? Why is it that the Apaches wait to die? . . . The Apaches were once a great nation; they are now but few."

—Cochise, 1866

FROM *LIFE ON THE MISSISSIPPI*

About the Author. A biography of **Mark Twain** appears on page 455.

Historical Note

Mark Twain moved into a large mansion in Hartford, Connecticut, in 1874, when he was about thirty-five years old. In 1974, the house was turned into a museum that is still in operation today. Next door to the Mark Twain House in Hartford is the final home of author Harriet Beecher Stowe (1811–1896). Stowe is known for her novel *Uncle Tom's Cabin* (1852), which is said to have ignited strong feelings of antislavery just before the start of the Civil War. Twain and Stowe were backyard neighbors for twenty years. Stowe's Hartford home is also open to the public as a museum.

Additional Questions and Activities

- Ask students to write about their own childhood ambitions. What sparked these ambitions? Were they encouraged when they shared these ambitions with other people? Which of these would they now consider realistic, and which of these do they now consider to be fanciful? Do they still have some of the same interests today?
- Ask students to freewrite about a special place, person, or event; something or someone that might have caused them to feel fascination. Have them carefully read over Twain's descriptions of the steamboat, the steamboat worker, and what he perceived to be the life of a steamboat worker. Encourage them to use vivid details in their descriptions.

fragrant town drunkard asleep in the shadow of them; two or three wood flats[1] at the head of the wharf, but nobody to listen to the peaceful lapping of the wavelets against them; the great Mississippi, the majestic, the magnificent Mississippi, rolling its mile-wide tide along, shining in the sun; the dense forest away on the other side; the point above the town, and the point below, bounding the river-glimpse and turning it into a sort of sea, and withal a very still and brilliant and lonely one. Presently a film of dark smoke appears above one of those remote points; instantly a Negro drayman,[2] famous for his quick eye and prodigious voice, lifts up the cry, "S-t-e-a-m-boat a-comin'!" and the scene changes! The town drunkard stirs, the clerks wake up, a furious clatter of drays follows, every house and store pours out a human contribution, and all in a twinkling the dead town is alive and moving. Drays, carts, men, boys, all go hurrying from many quarters to a common center, the wharf. Assembled there, the people fasten their eyes upon the coming boat as upon a wonder they are seeing for the first time. And the boat *is* rather a handsome sight, too. She is long and sharp and trim and pretty; she has two tall, fancy-topped chimneys, with a gilded device of some kind swung between them; a fanciful pilothouse, all glass and gingerbread, perched on top of the texas deck[3] behind them; the paddle-boxes are gorgeous with a picture or with gilded rays above the boat's name; the boiler, the hurricane deck, and the texas deck are fenced and ornamented with clean white railings; there is a flag gallantly flying from the jackstaff;[4] the furnace doors are open and the fires glaring bravely; the upper decks are black with passengers; the captain stands by the big bell, calm, imposing, the envy of all; great volumes of the blackest smoke are rolling and tumbling out of the chimneys—a husbanded grandeur created with a bit of pitch pine just before arriving at a town; the crew are grouped on the forecastle;[5] the broad stage is run far out over the port bow, and an envied deckhand stands picturesquely on the end of it with a coil of rope in his hand; the pent steam is screaming through the gauge cocks; the captain lifts his hand, a bell rings, the wheels stop; then they turn back, churning the water to foam, and the steamer is at rest. Then such a scramble as there is to get aboard, and to get ashore, and to take in freight and to discharge freight, all at one and the same time; and such a yelling and cursing as the mates facilitate it all with! Ten minutes later the steamer is under way again, with no flag on the jackstaff and no black smoke issuing from the chimneys. After ten more minutes the town is dead again, and the town drunkard asleep by the skids once more.

My father was a justice of the peace, and I supposed he possessed the power of life and death over all men and could hang anybody that offended him. This was distinction enough for me as a general thing; but the desire to be a steamboatman kept intruding, nevertheless. I first wanted to be a cabin boy, so that I could come out with a white apron on and shake a tablecloth over the side, where all my old comrades could see me; later I thought I would rather be the deckhand who stood on the end of the stage plank with the coil of rope in his hand, because he was particularly conspicuous. But these were only daydreams—they were too heavenly to be contemplated as real possibilities. By and by one of our boys went away. He was not heard of for a long time. At last he turned up as apprentice engineer or striker on a steamboat. This thing shook the bottom out of all my Sunday-school teachings. That boy had been notoriously worldly, and I just the reverse; yet he was exalted to this eminence, and I left in obscurity and misery. There was nothing generous about this fellow in his greatness. He would always manage to have a rusty bolt to scrub while his boat tarried at our town, and he would sit on the inside guard and scrub it, where we could all see him and envy him and loathe him. And whenever his boat was laid up he would come home and swell around the town in his blackest and greasiest clothes, so that nobody could help remembering that he was a steamboatman; and he used all sorts of steamboat technicalities in his talk, as if he were so used to them that he forgot common people could not understand them. He would speak of the labboard[6] side of a horse in an easy, natural way that would make one wish he was dead. And he was always talking about "St. Looey" like an old citizen; he would refer casually to occasions when he "was coming down Fourth Street," or when he was "passing by the Planter's House," or when there was a fire and he took a turn on the brakes of "the old Big Missouri"; and then he would go on and lie about how many towns the size of ours were burned down there that day. Two or three of the boys had long been persons of consideration among us because they had been to St. Louis once and had a vague general knowledge of its wonders, but the day of their glory was over now. They lapsed into a humble silence, and learned to disappear when the ruthless cub engineer approached. This fellow had money, too, and hair oil. Also an ignorant silver watch and a showy brass watch chain. He wore a leather belt and used no suspenders. If ever a youth was cordially admired and hated by his comrades, this one was. No girl could withstand his charms. He cut out every boy in the village. When his boat blew up at last, it diffused a tranquil contentment among us such as we had not known for months. But when he came home the next week, alive, renowned, and appeared in church all battered up and bandaged, a shining hero, stared at and wondered over by everybody, it seemed to us that the partiality of Providence for an undeserving reptile had reached a point where it was open to criticism.

1. **flats.** Flat-bottomed boats
2. **drayman.** Driver of a low cart called a dray
3. **texas deck.** Deck next to the officers' cabins
4. **jackstaff.** Rope running up and down a mast
5. **forecastle.** Front of the upper deck
6. **labboard.** Left side of a ship

This creature's career could produce but one result. and it speedily followed. Boy after boy managed to get on the river. The minister's son became an engineer. The doctor's and the postmaster's sons became mud clerks; the wholesale liquor dealer's son became a barkeeper on a boat; four sons of the chief merchant, and two sons of the county judge, became pilots. Pilot was the grandest position of all. The pilot, even in those days of trivial wages, had a princely salary—from a hundred and fifty to two hundred and fifty dollars a month, and no board to pay. Two months of his wages would pay a preacher's salary for a year. Now some of us were left disconsolate. We could not get on the river—at least our parents would not let us.

So by and by I ran away. I said I never would come home again till I was a pilot and could come in glory. But somehow I could not manage it. I went meekly aboard a few of the boats that lay packed together like sardines at the long St. Louis wharf, and very humbly inquired for the pilots, but got only a cold shoulder and short words from mates and clerks. I had to make the best of this sort of treatment for the time being, but I had comforting daydreams of a future when I should be a great and honored pilot, with plenty of money, and could kill some of these mates and clerks and pay for them.

"The Revolt of 'Mother'"
by Mary E. Wilkins Freeman

"Father!"

"What is it?"

"What are them men diggin' over there in the field for?"

There was a sudden dropping and enlarging of the lower part of the old man's face, as if some heavy weight had settled therein; he shut his mouth tight, and went on harnessing the great bay mare.[1] He hustled the collar on to her neck with a jerk.

"Father!"

The old man slapped the saddle upon the mare's back.

"Look here, father, I want to know what them men are diggin' over in the field for, an' I'm goin' to know."

"I wish you'd go into the house, mother, an' 'tend to your own affairs," the old man said then. He ran his words together, and his speech was almost as inarticulate as a growl.

But the woman understood; it was her most native tongue. "I ain't goin' into the house till you tell me what them men are doin' over there in the field," said she.

Then she stood waiting. She was a small woman, short and straight-waisted like a child in her brown cotton gown. Her forehead was mild and benevolent between the smooth curves of gray hair; there were meek downward lines about her nose and mouth; but her eyes, fixed upon the old man, looked as if the meekness had been the result of her own will, never of the will of another.

They were in the barn, standing before the wide open doors. The spring air, full of the smell of growing grass and unseen blossoms, came in their faces. The deep yard in front was littered with farm wagons and piles of wood; on the edges, close to the fence and the house, the grass was a vivid green, and there were some dandelions.

The old man glanced doggedly at his wife as he tightened the last buckles on the harness. She looked as immovable to him as one of the rocks in his pasture- land, bound to the earth with generations of blackberry vines. He slapped the reins over the horse, and started forth from the barn.

"*Father!*" said she.

The old man pulled up. "What is it?"

"I want to know what them men are diggin' over there in that field for."

"They're diggin' a cellar, I s'pose, if you've got to know."

"A cellar for what?"

"A barn."

"A barn? You ain't goin' to build a barn over there where we was goin' to have a house, father?"

The old man said not another word. He hurried the horse into the farm wagon, and clattered out of the yard, jouncing as sturdily on his seat as a boy.

The woman stood a moment looking after him, then she went out of the barn across a corner of the yard to the house. The house, standing at right angles with the great barn and a long reach of sheds and out-buildings, was infinitesimal compared with them. It was scarcely as commodious for people as the little boxes under the barn eaves were for doves.

A pretty girl's face, pink and delicate as aflower, was looking out of one of the house windows. She was watching three men who were digging over in the field which bounded the yard near the road line. She turned quietly when the woman entered.

"What are they digging for, mother?" said she. "Did he tell you?"

"They're diggin' for—a cellar for a new barn."

"Oh, mother, he ain't going to build another barn?"

"That's what he says."

A boy stood before the kitchen glass combing his hair. He combed slowly and painstakingly, arranging his brown hair in a smooth hillock over his forehead. He did not seem to pay any attention to the conversation.

"Sammy, did you know father was going to build a new barn?" asked the girl.

The boy combed assiduously.

"Sammy!"

He turned, and showed a face like his father's under his smooth crest of hair. "Yes, I s'pose I did," he said, reluctantly.

"How long have you known it?" asked his mother.

" 'Bout three months, I guess."

"Why didn't you tell of it?"

"Didn't think 'twould do no good."

"I don't see what father wants another barn for," said the

1. **bay mare.** Reddish-brown female horse

"THE REVOLT OF 'MOTHER'" (CONT.)

bands was expected. This is especially true of the people of New England about whom Mary Wilkins Freeman writes. They were the descendants of the Puritans of the Massachusetts Bay Colony. As the title of the story indicates, "The Revolt of 'Mother'" is the story of an apparently humble and obedient mother who revolts against these conditions.

"THE REVOLT OF 'MOTHER'"

About the Author. Mary E. Wilkins Freeman (1852–1930) was born in Randolph, Massachusetts, and moved to Brattleboro, Vermont, with her family in 1867. When her father's business failed in 1876, her mother found work as a housekeeper for a local minister, and the family moved into his house. For New Englanders whose faith taught poverty was punishment for sin, it was a painful psychological burden. After graduating from high school she spent one year at Mount Holyoke Female Seminary before returning to Vermont.

By the time she was thirty-one her parents and siblings had all died. She had only a tiny inheritance, but she had begun to achieve both economic independence and literary success by selling her poems and stories to magazines. In 1884, she returned to Massachusetts and lived in the home of a childhood friend until she married Dr. Charles Freeman in 1902. They moved to Metuchen, New Jersey, where she lived the remainder of her life.

Freeman was awarded the W. D. Howells Medal for Fiction in 1926. By the time she died she had published twenty volumes of adult fiction and six volumes of children's stories. Among her works are *A New England Nun and Other Stories* (1891), *A Humble Romance and Other Stories* (1887), *Pembroke* (1894), *The Heart's Highway* (1900), and *The Shoulders of Atlas* (1908).

About the Selection. "The Revolt of 'Mother'" is a fine example of women's writing in the nineteenth century, when the feminist movement was just beginning. Much fiction written by women at the time protests against their oppressive living conditions. Most women found it impossible to support themselves. Besides depending upon their parents, marriage was their only option. Once married, many women lived under the absolute and sometimes abusive power of their husbands. The communities in which they lived held them to strict standards of proper female behavior. Obedience to their hus-

(cont.)

Additional Questions and Activities

At one time or another all of us have had to live under the power of others—parents, teachers, bosses. Sometimes the frustration of living under someone else's power becomes unbearable, and we revolt. Think of a time when you revolted against an authority. Who was the authority? Why did you revolt? How did you revolt? What were the consequences of your revolt?

girl, in her sweet, slow voice. She turned again to the window, and stared out at the digging men in the field. Her tender, sweet face was full of a gentle distress. Her forehead was as bald and innocent as a baby's, with the light hair strained back from it in a row of curl-papers. She was quite large, but her soft curves did not look as if they covered muscles.

Her mother looked sternly at the boy. "Is he goin' to buy more cows?" said she.

The boy did not reply; he was tying his shoes.

"Sammy, I want you to tell me if he's goin' to buy more cows."

"I s'pose he is."

"How many?"

"Four, I guess."

His mother said nothing more. She went up into the pantry, and there was a clatter of dishes. The boy got his cap from a nail behind the door, took an old arithmetic from the shelf, and started for school. He was lightly built, but clumsy. He went out of the yard with a curious spring in his hips, that made his loose home-made jacket tilt up in the rear.

The girl went to the sink, and began to wash the dishes that were piled up there. Her mother came promptly out of the pantry, and shoved her aside. "You wipe 'em," said she; "I'll wash. There's a good many this mornin'."

The mother plunged her hands vigorously into the water, the girl wiped the plates slowly and dreamily. "Mother," said she, "don't you think it's too bad father's going to build that new barn, much as we need a decent house to live in?"

Her mother scrubbed a dish fiercely. "You ain't found out yet we're womenfolks, Nanny Penn," said she. "You ain't seen enough of men-folks yet to. One of these days you'll find it out, an' then you'll know that we know only what men-folks think we do, so far as any use of it goes, an' how we'd ought to reckon men-folks in with Providence, an' not complain of what they do any more than we do of the weather."

"I don't care; I don't believe George is anything like that, anyhow," said Nanny. Her delicate face flushed pink, her lips pouted softly, as if she were going to cry.

"You wait an' see. I guess George Eastman ain't no better than other men. You hadn't ought to judge father, though. He can't help it, 'cause he don't look at things jest the way we do. An' we've been pretty comfortable here, after all. The roof don't leak—ain't never but once—that's one thing. Father's kept it shingled right up."

"I do wish we had a parlor."

"I guess it won't hurt George Eastman any to come to see you in a nice clean kitchen. I guess a good many girls don't have as good a place as this. Nobody's ever heard me complain."

"I ain't complained either, mother."

"Well, I don't think you'd better, a good father an' a good home as you've got. S'pose your father made you go out an' work for your livin'? Lots of girls have to that ain't no stronger an' better able to than you be."

Sarah Penn washed the frying-pan with a conclusive air. She scrubbed the outside of it as faithfully as the inside. She was a masterly keeper of her box of a house. Her one living-room never seemed to have in it any of the dust which the friction of life with inanimate matter produces. She swept, and there seemed to be no dirt to go before the broom; she cleaned, and one could see no difference. She was like an artist so perfect that he has apparently no art. Today she got out a mixing bowl and a board, and rolled some pies, and there was no more flour upon her than upon her daughter who was doing finer work. Nanny was to be married in the fall, and she was sewing on some white cambric and embroidery. She sewed industriously while her mother cooked, her soft milk-white hands and wrists showed whiter than her delicate work.

"We must have the stove moved out in the shed before long," said Mrs. Penn. "Talk about not havin' things, it's been a real blessin' to be able to put a stove up in that shed in hot weather. Father did one good thing when he fixed that stove-pipe out there."

Sarah Penn's face as she rolled her pies had that expression of meek vigor which might have characterized one of the New Testament saints. She was making mince-pies. Her husband, Adoniram Penn, liked them better than any other kind. She baked twice a week. Adoniram often liked a piece of pie between meals. She hurried this morning. It had been later than usual when she began, and she wanted to have a pie baked for dinner. However deep a resentment she might be forced to hold against her husband, she would never fail in sedulous attention to his wants.

Nobility of character manifests itself at loop-holes when it is not provided with large doors. Sarah Penn's showed itself today in flaky dishes of pastry. So she made the pies faithfully, while across the table she could see, when she glanced up from her work, the sight that rankled in her patient and steadfast soul—the digging of the cellar of the new barn in the place where Adoniram forty years ago had promised her their new house should stand.

The pies were done for dinner. Adoniram and Sammy were home a few minutes after twelve o'clock. The dinner was eaten with serious haste. There was never much conversation at the table in the Penn family. Adoniram asked a blessing, and they ate promptly, then rose up and went about their work.

Sammy went back to school, taking soft sly lopes out of the yard like a rabbit. He wanted a game of marbles before school, and feared his father would give him some chores to do. Adoniram hastened to the door and called after him, but he was out of sight.

"I don't see what you let him go for, mother," said he. "I wanted him to help me unload that wood."

Adoniram went to work out in the yard unloading wood from the wagon. Sarah put away the dinner dishes, while Nanny took down her curl-papers and changed her dress. She was going down to the store to buy some more embroidery and thread.

When Nanny was gone, Mrs. Penn went to the door. "Father!" she called.

"Well, what is it!"

"I want to see you jest a minute, father."

"I can't leave this wood nohow. I've got to git it unloaded an' go for a load of gravel afore two o'clock. Sammy had ought to helped me. You hadn't ought to let him go to school so early."

"I want to see you jest a minute."

"I tell ye I can't, nohow, mother."

"Father, you come here." Sarah Penn stood in the door like a queen; she held her head as if it bore a crown; there was that patience which makes authority royal in her voice. Adoniram went.

Mrs. Penn led the way into the kitchen, and pointed to a chair. "Sit down, father," said she; "I've got somethin' I want to say to you."

He sat down heavily; his face was quite stolid, but he looked at her with restive eyes. "Well, what is it, mother?"

"I want to know what you're buildin' that new barn for, father?"

"I ain't got nothin' to say about it."

"It can't be you think you need another barn?"

"I tell ye I ain't got nothin' to say about it, mother; an' I ain't goin' to say nothin'."

"Be you goin' to buy more cows?"

Adoniram did not reply; he shut his mouth tight.

"I know you be, as well as I want to. Now, father, look here"—Sarah Penn had not sat down; she stood before her husband in the humble fashion of a Scripture woman[1]—"I'm goin' to talk real plain to you; I never have sence I married you, but I'm goin' to now. I ain't never complained, an' I ain't goin' to complain now, but I'm goin' to talk plain. You see this room here, father; you look at it well. You see there ain't no carpet on the floor, an' you see the paper is all dirty, an' droppin' off the walls. We ain't had no new paper on it for ten year, an' then I put it on myself, an' it didn't cost but ninepence a roll. You see this room, father; it's all the one I've had to work in an' eat in an' sit in sence we was married. There ain't another woman in the whole town whose husband ain't got half the means you have but what's got better. It's all the room Nanny's got to have her company in; an' there ain't one of her mates but what's got better, an' their fathers not so able as hers is. It's all the room she'll have to be married in. What would you have thought, father, if we had had our weddin' in a room no better than this? I was married in my mother's parlor, with a carpet on the floor, an' stuffed furniture, an' a mahogany cardtable. An' this is all the room my daughter will have to be married in. Look here, father!"

Sarah Penn went across the room as though it were a tragic stage. She flung open a door and disclosed a tiny bedroom, only large enough for a bed and bureau, with a path between. "There, father," said she—"there's all the room I've had to sleep in forty year. All my children were born there—the two that died, an' the two that's livin'. I was sick with a fever there."

She stepped to another door and opened it. It led into the small, ill-lighted pantry. "Here," said she, "is all the buttery[2] I've got—every place I've got for my dishes, to set away my victuals in, an' to keep my milk-pans in. Father, I've been takin' care of the milk of six cows in this place, an' now you're goin' to build a new barn, an' keep more cows, an' give me more to do in it."

She threw open another door. A narrow crooked flight of stairs wound upward from it. "There, father," said she, "I want you to look at the stairs that go up to them two unfinished chambers that are all the places our son an' daughter have had to sleep in all their lives. There ain't a prettier girl in town nor a more ladylike one than Nanny, an' that's the place she has to sleep in. It ain't so good as your horse's stall; it ain't so warm an' tight."

Sarah Penn went back and stood before her husband. "Now, father," said she, "I want to know if you think you're doin' right an' accordin' to what you profess. Here, when we was married, forty year ago, you promised me faithful that we should have a new house built in that lot over in the field before the year was out. You said you had money enough, an' you wouldn't ask me to live in no such place as this. It is forty year now, an' you've been makin' more money, an' I've been savin' of it for you ever since, an' you ain't built no house yet. You've built sheds an' cow-houses an' one new barn, an' now you're goin' to build another. Father, I want to know if you think it's right. You're lodgin' your dumb beasts better than you are your own flesh an' blood. I want to know if you think it's right."

"I ain't got nothin' to say."

"You can't say nothin' without ownin' it ain't right, father. An' there's another thing—I ain't complained; I've got along forty year, an' I s'pose I should forty more, if it wa'n't for that—if we don't have another house. Nanny she can't live with us after she's married. She'll have to go somewheres else to live away from us, an' it don't seem as if I could have it so, noways, father. She wa'n't ever strong. She's got considerable color, but there wa'n't never any backbone to her. I've always took the heft of everything off her, an' she ain't fit to keep house an' do everything herself. She'll be all worn out inside a year. Think of her doin' all the washin' an' ironin' an' bakin' with them soft white hands an' arms, an' sweepin'! I can't have it so, noways, father."

Mrs. Penn's face was burning; her mild eyes gleamed. She had pleaded her little cause like a Webster;[3] she had ranged from severity to pathos; but her opponent employed that obstinate silence which makes eloquence futile with mocking echoes. Adoniram arose clumsily.

"Father, ain't you got nothin' to say?" said Mrs. Penn.

"I've got to go off after that load of gravel. I can't stan' here talkin' all day."

---

1. **Scripture woman.** Biblical woman who is patient and obedient to her husband

2 **buttery.** Pantry

3. **Webster.** Daniel Webster (1782–1852), American diplomat and orator

LITERARY/HISTORICAL NOTE

Allusion. An **allusion** is a figure of speech in which a reference is made to a person, event, object, or work from history or literature. For example, the narrator says that Sarah Penn "pleaded her cause *like a Webster.*" The narrator is here describing the skill with which Mother argues against the new barn by comparing Mother to Daniel Webster, the celebrated American orator. Ask students to identify other allusions in the story.

"Father, won't you think it over, an' have a house built there instead of a barn?"

"I ain't got nothin' to say."

Adoniram shuffled out. Mrs. Penn went into her bedroom. When she came out, her eyes were red. She had a roll of unbleached cotton cloth. She spread it out on the kitchen table, and began cutting out some shirts for her husband. The men over in the field had a team to help them this afternoon; she could hear their halloos. She had a scanty pattern for the shirts; she had to plan and piece the sleeves.

Nanny came home with her embroidery, and sat down with her needlework. She had taken down her curl-papers, and there was a soft roll of fair hair like an aureole over her forehead; her face was as delicately fine and clear as porcelain. Suddenly she looked up, and the tender red flamed all over her face and neck. "Mother," said she.

"What say?"

"I've been thinking—I don't see how we're goin' to have any—wedding in this room. I'd be ashamed to have his folks come if we didn't have anybody else."

"Mebbe we can have some new paper before then; I can put it on. I guess you won't have no call to be ashamed of your belongin's."

"We might have the wedding in the new barn," said Nanny, with gentle pettishness. "Why, mother, what makes you look so?"

Mrs. Penn had started, and was staring at her with a curious expression. She turned again to her work, and spread out a pattern carefully on the cloth. "Nothin'," said she.

Presently Adoniram clattered out of the yard in his two-wheeled dump cart, standing as proudly upright as a Roman charioteer.[1] Mrs. Penn opened the door and stood there a minute looking out; the halloos of the men sounded louder.

It seemed to her all through the spring months that she heard nothing but the halloos and the noises of the saws and hammers. The new barn grew fast. It was a fine edifice for this little village. Men came on pleasant Sundays, in their meeting suits and clean shirt bosoms, and stood around it admiringly. Mrs. Penn did not speak of it, and Adoniram did not mention it to her, although sometimes, upon a return from inspecting it, he bore himself with injured dignity.

"It's a strange thing how your mother feels about the new barn," he said, confidentially, to Sammy one day.

Sammy only grunted after an odd fashion for a boy; he had learned it from his father.

The barn was all completed ready for use by the third week in July. Adoniram had planned to move his stock in on Wednesday; on Tuesday he received a letter which changed his plans. He came in with it early in the morning. "Sammy's been to the post-office," said he, "an' I've got a letter from Hiram." Hiram was Mrs. Penn's brother, who lived in Vermont.

"Well," said Mrs. Penn, "what does he say about the folks?"

"I guess they're all right. He says he thinks if I come up country right off there's a chance to buy jest the kind of horse I want." He stared reflectively out of the window at the new barn.

Mrs. Penn was making pies. She went on clapping the rolling-pin into the crust, although she was very pale, and her heart beat loudly.

"I dun' know but what I'd better go," said Adoniram. "I hate to go off jest now, right in the midst of hayin', but the ten-acre lot's cut, an' I guess Rufus an' the others can git along without me three or four days. I can't get a horse round here to suit me, nohow, an' I've got to have another for all the woodhaulin' in the fall. I told Hiram to watch out, an' if he got wind of a good horse to let me know. I guess I'd better go."

"I'll get out your clean shirt an' collar," said Mrs. Penn calmly.

She laid out Adoniram's Sunday suit and his clean clothes on the bed in the little bedroom. She got his shaving-water and razor ready. At last she buttoned on his collar and fastened his black cravat.[2]

Adoniram never wore his collar and cravat except on extra occasions. He held his head high, with a rasped dignity. When he was all ready, with his coat and hat brushed, and a lunch of pie and cheese in a paper bag, he hesitated on the threshold of the door. He looked at his wife, and his manner was defiantly apologetic. "*If* them cows come to-day, Sammy can drive 'em into the new barn," said he; "an' when they bring the hay up, they can pitch it in there."

"Well," replied Mrs. Penn.

Adoniram set his shaven face ahead and started. When he had cleared the door-step, he turned and looked back with a kind of nervous solemnity. "I shall be back by Saturday if nothin' happens," said he.

"Do be careful, father," returned his wife.

She stood in the door with Nanny at her elbow and watched him out of sight. Her eyes had a strange, doubtful expression in them; her peaceful forehead was contracted. She went in, and about her baking again. Nanny sat sewing. Her wedding-day was drawing nearer, and she was getting pale and thin with her steady sewing. Her mother kept glancing at her.

"Have you got that pain in your side this mornin'?" she asked.

"A little."

Mrs. Penn's face, as she worked, changed, her perplexed forehead smoothed, her eyes were steady, her lips firmly set. She formed a maxim for herself, although incoherently with her unlettered thoughts. "Unsolicited opportunities are the guide-posts of the Lord to the new roads of life," she repeated in effect, and she made up her mind to her course of action.

"S'posin' I *had* wrote to Hiram," she muttered once, when she was in the pantry—"s'posin' I had wrote, an' asked him if he knew of any horse? But I didn't, an' father's goin' wa'n't none of my doin'. It looks like a providence." Her voice rang out quite loud at the last.

"What you talkin' about, mother?" called Nanny.

---

1. **Roman charioteer.** Roman charioteers raced while standing on their vehicles.

2. **cravat.** Neckerchief or scarf; necktie

"Nothin'."

Mrs. Penn hurried her baking; at eleven o'clock it was all done. The load of hay from the west field came slowly down the cart track, and drew up at the new barn. Mrs. Penn ran out. "Stop!" she screamed—"stop!"

The men stopped and looked; Sammy upreared from the top of the load, and stared at his mother.

"Stop!" she cried out again. "Don't you put the hay in that barn; put it in the old one."

"Why, he said to put it in here," returned one of the haymakers, wonderingly. He was a young man, a neighbor's son, whom Adoniram hired by the year to help on the farm.

"Don't you put the hay in the new barn; there's room enough in the old one, ain't there?" said Mrs. Penn.

"Room enough," returned the hired man, in his thick, rustic tones. "Didn't need the new barn, nohow, far as room's concerned. Well, I s'pose he changed his mind." He took hold of the horses' bridles.

Mrs. Penn went back to the house. Soon the kitchen windows were darkened, and a fragrance like warm honey came into the room.

Nanny laid down her work. "I thought father wanted them to put the hay into the new barn?" she said, wonderingly.

"It's all right," replied her mother.

Sammy slid down from the load of hay, and came in to see if dinner was ready.

"I ain't goin' to get a regular dinner today, as long as father's gone," said his mother. "I've let the fire go out. You can have some bread an' milk an' pie. I thought we could get along." She set out some bowls of milk, some bread, and a pie on the kitchen table. "You'd better eat your dinner now," said she. "You might jest as well get through with it. I want you to help me afterward."

Nanny and Sammy stared at each other. There was something strange in their mother's manner. Mrs. Penn did not eat anything herself. She went into the pantry, and they heard her moving dishes while they ate. Presently she came out with a pile of plates. She got the clothes-basket out of the shed, and packed them in it. Nanny and Sammy watched. She brought out cups and saucers, and put them in with the plates.

"What you goin' to do, mother?" inquired Nanny, in a timid voice. A sense of something unusual made her tremble, as if it were a ghost. Sammy rolled his eyes over his pie.

"You'll see what I'm goin' to do," replied Mrs. Penn. "If you're through, Nanny, I want you to go up-stairs an' pack up your things; an' I want you, Sammy, to help me take down the bed in the bedroom."

"Oh, mother, what for?" gasped Nanny.

"You'll see."

During the next few hours a feat was performed by this simple, pious New England mother which was equal in its way to Wolfe's storming of the Heights of Abraham.[1] It took no more genius and audacity of bravery for Wolfe to cheer his wondering soldiers up those steep precipices, under the sleeping eyes of the enemy, than for Sarah Penn, at the head of her children, to move all their little household goods into the new barn while her husband was away.

Nanny and Sammy followed their mother's instructions without a murmur; indeed, they were overawed. There is a certain uncanny and superhuman quality about all such purely original undertakings as their mother's was to them. Nanny went back and forth with her light loads, and Sammy tugged with sober energy.

At five o'clock in the afternoon the little house in which the Penns had lived for forty years had emptied itself into the new barn.

Every builder builds somewhat for unknown purposes, and is in a measure a prophet. The architect of Adoniram Penn's barn, while he designed it for the comfort of four-footed animals, had planned better than he knew for the comfort of humans. Sarah Penn saw at a glance its possibilities. Those great boxstalls, with quilts hung before them, would make better bedrooms than the one she had occupied for forty years, and there was a tight carriage-room. The harness room, with its chimney and shelves, would make a kitchen of her dreams. The great middle space would make a parlor, by-and-by, fit for a palace. Up stairs there was as much room as down. With partitions and windows, what a house would there be! Sarah looked at the row of stanchions[2] before the allotted space for cows, and reflected that she would have her front entry there.

At six o'clock the stove was up in the harness-room, the kettle was boiling, and the table set for tea. It looked almost as homelike as the abandoned house across the yard had ever done. The young hired man milked, and Sarah directed him calmly to bring the milk to the new barn. He came gaping, dropping little blots of foam from the brimming pails on the grass. Before the next morning he had spread the story of Adoniram Penn's wife moving into the new barn all over the little village. Men assembled in the store and talked it over, women with shawls over their heads scuttled into each other's houses before their work was done. Any deviation from the ordinary course of life in this quiet town was enough to stop all progress in it. Everybody paused to look at the staid independent figure on the side track. There was a difference of opinion with regard to her. Some held her to be insane; some, of lawless and rebellious spirit.

Friday the minister went to see her. It was in the forenoon, and she was at the barn door shelling peas for dinner. She looked up and returned his salutation with dignity, then she went on with her work. She did not invite him in. The saintly expression of her face remained fixed, but there was an angry flush over it.

The minister stood awkwardly before her, and talked. She handled the peas as if they were bullets. At last she looked up, and her eyes showed the spirit that her meek front had covered for a lifetime.

---

1. **Wolfe's . . . Heights of Abraham.** James Wolfe (1727–1759) was a British general who led the British forces against the French in the capturing of Quebec and died shortly after his victory on the Plains of Abraham.

2. **stanchions.** Restraining devices fitted loosely around the necks of cows to confine them to their stalls

Additional Questions and Activities

Feminist criticism evaluates and interprets works of art according to their portrayal of men's and women's roles. Feminist literary critics often study women who wrote before the feminist movement. We can divide the characters in "The Revolt of 'Mother'" into three groups.

1. Mother, Sarah Penn, and her daughter Nanny
2. Father, Adoniram Penn, and his son Sammy
3. The village and its representative, the minister, Mr. Hersey

What kind of work do Mother and Nanny do at home? What kind of work do Father and Sammy do? How do the roles of the men and the women differ? How are they similar? What attitude does each of the groups take toward Mother's revolt?

Additional Questions and Activities

1. Why is Sarah, the mother, angry about Adoniram's plan to build a new barn in the field?
2. How does Sarah treat her husband after she has learned about his plan? Why does she treat him like this?
3. Why does Sarah want a new house instead of a new barn? What is wrong with her present house?
4. How would you describe Sarah's desire for a new house? Is it selfish or justified? Why?
5. Why does Adoniram decide to go to Vermont for a few days?
6. How does Sarah explain his sudden plan to go? What does she do in his absence?
7. How does the village respond to Sarah's action? Do the villagers approve of her actions? How does Sarah respond to the minister's visit?

(cont.)

Additional Questions and Activities (cont.)

8. How does Adoniram respond when he returns home to find the family living in the new barn?

9. Why does Sarah want a new home? Why does Adoniram desire a new barn when he does not need one? What do these desires reveal about each character's values?

10. Why is Mother's revolt so successful? What does Adoniram's final burst of tears tell us about the man? Who is stronger, Sarah, the mother, or Adoniram, the father?

Answers. 1. Sarah is angry because her husband promised to build her a house on that site.

2. She tends to his wants as she has always done. She bakes him a pie. She does so because she loves and respects him but also because she wants to put him in a good mood before she complains about his plan to build the new barn.

3. They do not need a new barn, and their present house is inadequate. There is no carpet, the wallpaper is falling off, the family room is too small for entertaining, the bedrooms are tiny, and the children's rooms are unfinished.

4. It is justified. She shows that she is not a selfish or greedy woman by her care for what she has and her patience in waiting for what she wants. She has waited forty years for a new house.

5. He receives a letter from Sarah's brother about the horses he can buy in Vermont, so he goes to buy a horse.

6. Sarah thinks it is the work of God or Providence. In his absence, she moves her household into the new barn.

7. The village gossips and argues about her action, and all the villagers disapprove of it. Some say she is crazy; others say she is bad. When the minister comes to visit her, she stands her ground.

8. At first he is stunned and then he weeps and gives in to his wife's desire.

9. Sarah wants a new home so that their daily lives can be more enjoyable and comfortable.

(cont.)

"There ain't no use talkin', Mr. Hersey," said she. "I've thought it all over an' over, an' I believe I'm doin' what's right. I've made it the subject of prayer, an' it's betwixt me an' the Lord an' Adoniram. There ain't no call for nobody else to worry about it."

"Well, of course, if you have brought it to the Lord in prayer, and feel satisfied that you are doing right, Mrs. Penn," said the minister, helplessly. His thin gray-bearded face was pathetic. He was a sickly man; his youthful confidence had cooled; he had to scourge himself up to some of his pastoral duties as relentlessly as a Catholic ascetic, and then he was prostrated by the smart.

"I think it's right jest as much as I think it was right for our forefathers to come over from the old country 'cause they didn't have what belonged to 'em," said Mrs. Penn. She arose. The barn threshold might have been Plymouth Rock from her bearing. "I don't doubt you mean well, Mr. Hersey," said she, "but there are things people hadn't ought to interfere with. I've been a member of the church for over forty year. I've got my own mind an' my own feet, an' I'm goin' to think my own thoughts an' go my own ways, an' nobody but the Lord is goin' to dictate to me unless I've a mind to have him. Won't you come in an' set down? How is Mis' Hersey?"

"She is well, I thank you," replied the minister. He added some more perplexed apologetic remarks; then he retreated.

He could expound the intricacies of every character study in the Scriptures, he was competent to grasp the Pilgrim Fathers and all historical innovators, but Sarah Penn was beyond him. He could deal with primal cases, but parallel ones worsted him. But, after all, although it was aside from his province, he wondered more how Adoniram Penn would deal with his wife than how the Lord would. Everybody shared the wonder. When Adoniram's four new cows arrived, Sarah ordered three to be put in the old barn, the other in the house shed where the cooking-stove had stood. That added to the excitement. It was whispered that all four cows were domiciled in the house.

Towards sunset on Saturday, when Adoniram was expected home, there was a knot of men in the road near the new barn. The hired man had milked, but he still hung around the premises. Sarah Penn had supper all ready. There was brown-bread and baked beans and a custard pie; it was the supper that Adoniram loved on a Saturday night. She had on a clean calico, and she bore herself imperturbably. Nanny and Sammy kept close at her heels. Their eyes were large, and Nanny was full of nervous tremors. Still there was to them more pleasant excitement than anything else. An inborn confidence in their mother over their father asserted itself.

Sammy looked out of the harness-room window. "There he is," he announced, in an awed whisper. He and Nanny peeped around the casing. Mrs. Penn kept on about her work. The children watched Adoniram leave the new horse standing in the drive while he went to the house door. It was fastened. Then he went around to the shed. That door was seldom locked, even when the family was away. The thought how her father would be confronted by the cow flashed upon Nanny. There was a hysterical sob in her throat. Adoniram emerged from the shed and stood looking about in a dazed fashion. His lips moved; he was saying something, but they could not hear what it was. The hired man was peeping around a corner of the old barn, but nobody saw him.

Adoniram took the new horse by the bridle and led him across the yard to the new barn. Nanny and Sammy slunk close to their mother. The barn doors rolled back, and there stood Adoniram, with the long mild face of the great Canadian farm horse looking over his shoulder.

Nanny kept behind her mother, but Sammy stepped suddenly forward, and stood in front of her.

Adoniram stared at the group. "What on airth you all down here for?" said he. "What's the matter over to the house?"

"We've come here to live, father," said Sammy. His shrill voice quavered out bravely.

"What"—Adoniram sniffed—"what is it smells like cookin?" said he. He stepped forward and looked in the open door of the harness-room. Then he turned to his wife. His old bristling face was pale and frightened. "What on airth does this mean, mother?" he gasped.

"You come in here, father," said Sarah. She led the way into the harness-room and shut the door. "Now, father," said she, "you needn't be scared. I ain't crazy. There ain't nothin' to be upset over. But we've come here to live, an' we're goin' to live here. We've got jest as good a right here as new horses an' cows. The house wa'n't fit for us to live in any longer, an' I made up my mind I wa'n't goin' to stay there. I've done my duty by you forty year, an' I'm goin' to do it now; but I'm goin' to live here. You've got to put in some windows and partitions; an' you'll have to buy some furniture."

"Why, mother!" the old man gasped.

"You'd better take your coat off an' get washed—there's the wash-basin—an' then we'll have supper."

"Why, mother!"

Sammy went past the window, leading the new horse to the old barn. The old man saw him, and shook his head speechlessly. He tried to take off his coat, but his arms seemed to lack the power. His wife helped him. She poured some water into the tin basin, and put in a piece of soap. She got the comb and brush, and smoothed his thin gray hair after he had washed. Then she put the beans, the hot bread, and tea on the table. Sammy came in, and the family drew up. Adoniram sat looking dazedly at his plate, and they waited.

"Ain't you goin' to ask a blessin', father?" said Sarah.

And the old man bent his head and mumbled.

All through the meal he stopped eating at intervals, and stared furtively at his wife; but he ate well. The home food tasted good to him, and his old frame was too sturdily healthy to be affected by his mind. But after supper he went out, and sat down on the step of the smaller door at the right of the barn, through which he had meant his Jerseys to pass in stately file, but which Sarah designed for her front house door, and he leaned his head on his hands.

Additional Questions and Activities (cont.)

Adoniram wants a new barn because he is obsessed with gaining more wealth in the form of livestock. Sarah cares more about family and domestic life. Adoniram cares more about the power and prestige that wealth brings.

10. Mother's revolt is successful because Adoniram genuinely loves his wife. Her active resistance shows him that he had misunderstood her wishes and unhappiness for many years. The story shows that Sarah, the one who appears meek and mild, is actually the stronger partner, though Adoniram's hard work and dedication to getting the family ahead also shows strength.

After the supper dishes were cleared away and the milk-pans washed, Sarah went out to him. The twilight was deepening. There was a clear green glow in the sky. Before them stretched the smooth level of field; in the distance was a cluster of hay-stacks like the huts of a village; the air was very cool and calm and sweet. The landscape might have been an ideal one of peace.

Sarah bent over and touched her husband on one of his thin, sinewy shouders. "Father!"

The old man's shoulders heaved; he was weeping.

"Why, don't do so, father," said Sarah.

"I'll—put up the—partitions, an'—everything you—want, mother."

Sarah put her apron up to her face; she was overcome by her own triumph.

Adoniram was like a fortress whose walls had no active resistance, and went down the instant the right besieging tools were used. "Why, mother," he said, hoarsely, "I hadn't no idee you was so set on't as all this comes to."

from *The Age of Innocence*
by Edith Wharton

The immense accretion of flesh which had descended on her in middle life like a flood of lava on a doomed city had changed her from a plump active little woman with a neatly-turned foot and ankle into something as vast and august as a natural phenomenon. She had accepted this submergence as philosophically as all her other trials, and now, in extreme old age, was rewarded by presenting to her mirror an almost unwrinkled expanse of firm pink and white flesh, in the center of which the traces of a small face survived as if awaiting excavation. A flight of smooth double chins led down to the dizzy depths of a still-snowy bosom veiled in snowy muslins that were held in place by a miniature portrait of the late Mr. Mingott; and around and below, wave after wave of black silk surged away over the edges of a capacious armchair, with two tiny white hands poised like gulls on the surface of the billows.

"When I Heard the Learn'd Astronomer"
by Walt Whitman

When I heard the learn'd astronomer,
When the proofs, the figures, were ranged in columns before me,
When I was shown the charts and diagrams, to add, divide, and measure them,
When I sitting heard the astronomer where he lectured with much applause in the lecture-room,
5 How soon unaccountable I became tired and sick,
Till rising and gliding out I wander'd off by myself,
In the mystical moist night-air, and from time to time,
Look'd up in perfect silence at the stars.

from *The Souls of Black Folk*
by W. E. B. Du Bois

Easily the most striking thing in the history of the American Negro since 1876[1] is the ascendancy of Mr. Booker T. Washington. It began at the time when war memories and ideals were rapidly passing; a day of astonishing commercial development was dawning; a sense of doubt and hesitation overtook the freedmen's sons,—then it was that his leading began. Mr. Washington came, with a simple definite program, at the psychological moment when the nation was a little ashamed of having bestowed so much sentiment on Negroes, and was concentrating its energies on Dollars. His program of industrial education, conciliation of the South, and submission and silence as to civil and political rights, was not wholly original; the Free Negroes from 1830 up to war-time had striven to build industrial schools, and the American Missionary Association had from the first taught various trades; and Price[2] and others had sought a way of honorable alliance with the best of the Southerners. But Mr. Washington first indissolubly linked these things; he put enthusiasm, unlimited energy, and perfect faith into this program, and changed it from a bypath into a veritable Way of Life. And the tale of the methods by which he did this is a fascinating study of human life.

It startled the nation to hear a Negro advocating such a program after many decades of bitter complaint; it startled and won the applause of the South, it interested and won the admiration of the North; and after a confused murmur of protest, it silenced if it did not convert the Negroes themselves.

To gain the sympathy and cooperation of the various elements comprising the white South was Mr. Washington's first task; and this, at the time Tuskegee[3] was founded, seemed, for a black man, well-nigh impossible. And yet ten years later it was done in the word spoken at Atlanta: "In all things purely social we can be as separate as the five fingers, and yet one as the hand in all things essential to mutual progress." This "Atlanta Compromise"[4] is by all odds the most notable thing in Mr. Washington's career. The South interpreted it in different ways: the radicals received it as a complete surrender of the demand for civil and political equality; the conservatives, as a generously conceived working basis for mutual understanding. So both approved it, and today its author is certainly the most distinguished Southerner since Jefferson Davis, and the one with the largest personal following.

1. **1876.** In 1876, Reconstruction ended, federal troops withdrew from the South, and African Americans lost political power.
2. **Price.** Thomas Frederick Price (1860–1919), editor, Roman Catholic priest, and founder of the American Missionary Association
3. **Tuskegee.** Tuskegee Institute, a vocational school for African Americans founded in 1881 by Booker T. Washington
4. **Atlanta Compromise.** Washington's speech at the Atlanta Exposition of 1895 essentially traded the political, civil, and social rights of African Americans for the promise of jobs and vocational-training schools.

FROM *THE AGE OF INNOCENCE*

About the Author. Edith Wharton (1862–1937) was born Edith Newbold Jones in New York City. Her family was wealthy and socially prominent. As a child, she was a voracious reader and later, remembering her adventures in her father's library, said, "I was enthralled by words. . . . Wherever I went, they sang to me like the birds in an enchanted forest." At sixteen her parents had published at their own expense a volume of poetry she had written.

Despite her own awareness of being caught between what appeared to be her social role by reason of birth and her intrinsic intellectual interests and creative aspirations, in 1885, at the age of twenty-three, she married Edward Wharton of Boston. He was thirteen years older than she but a social equal. They lived together for twenty-eight years, but it was an unhappy union, and she sought a divorce in 1913.

In the late 1880s, her stories and verses began to be published in major periodicals like *Scribner's, Harper's,* and *Century.* In 1898, she suffered a severe mental breakdown and sought treatment for "paralyzing melancholy." When she recovered, she committed herself to writing and from then on averaged about a book a year for the remainder of her life.

Her novel *The Age of Innocence* (1920) was awarded a Pulitzer Prize. In 1930, she won the Gold Medal of the National Institute of Arts and Letters. Among her other works are *Souls Belated* (1899), *The Other Two* (1904), *The House of Mirth* (1905), *Ethan Frome* (1911), and *The Custom of the Country* (1913).

"WHEN I HEARD THE LEARN'D ASTRONOMER"

About the Author. A biography of **Walt Whitman** appears on page 471.

FROM *THE SOULS OF BLACK FOLK*

About the Author. W. E. B. Du Bois (1868–1963), William Edward Burghardt Du Bois, was born in Great Barrington, Massachusetts, and educated at Fisk University, Harvard University, and the University of Berlin. His doctoral dissertation, *The Suppression of the African Slave Trade to the United States of America, 1638–1870,* was published as the first volume in the Harvard Historical Studies series.

Despite his education, racial prejudice prevented him from getting a faculty appointment at a major university, so he taught first at Wilberforce College in Ohio, then at the University of Pennsylvania before going to Atlanta University in 1897. There, during the next thirteen years, he wrote a steady stream of studies of African-American life.

A scholar by temperament, the particularly heinous

(cont.)

FROM *THE SOULS OF BLACK FOLK* (CONT.)

torture and murder, at the hands of a lynch mob, of a black man accused of a crime prompted Du Bois to a more active role in the struggle for civil rights. Publication in 1903 of *The Souls of Black Folk* reinforced his emerging activism and made him a leader in the Niagara Movement. He helped create the National Association for the Advancement of Colored People (NAACP) and was editor of *Crises,* its official publication, from 1910 to 1934. He was a Pan-African pioneer, and the year he died he became a citizen of Ghana. His other works include *John Brown* (1909), *The Negro* (1915), *Darkwater* (1920), *Black Reconstruction* (1935), *Dusk of Dawn* (1940), *Color and Democracy* (1945), and *The World and Africa* (1947).

About the Selection. W. E. B. Du Bois's essay "Of Mr. Booker T. Washington and Others" was first printed in the *Guardian* on July 27, 1902, and later published in Du Bois's collection of essays entitled ***The Souls of Black Folk.*** The essay was extremely controversial. At the time it was written, Booker T. Washington was the leading spokesperson for African Americans. Washington believed that African Americans should accept the fact that they were not allowed to vote, submit to the practice of segregation, and agree to receiving a low level of education. Washington founded Tuskegee Institute in Alabama, a school that taught black students farming and trades. Du Bois presents his opinions of Washington in a very calm and rational manner, but he completely rejects Washington's opinion.

Next to this achievement comes Mr. Washington's work in gaining place and consideration in the North. Others less shrewd and tactful had formerly essayed to sit on these two stools and had fallen between them, but as Mr. Washington knew the heart of the South from birth and training, so by singular insight he intuitively grasped the spirit of the age which was dominating the North. And so thoroughly did he learn the speech and thought of triumphant commercialism, and the ideals of material prosperity, that the picture of a lone black boy poring over a French grammar amid the weeds and dirt of a neglected home soon seemed to him the acme of absurdities.[1] One wonders what Socrates and St. Francis of Assisi[2] would say to this.

And yet this very singleness of vision and thorough oneness with his age is a mark of the successful man. It is as though Nature must needs make men narrow in order to give them force. So Mr. Washington's cult has gained unquestioning followers, his work has wonderfully prospered, his friends are legion, and his enemies are confounded. Today he stands as the one recognized spokesman of his ten million fellows, and one of the most notable figures in a nation of seventy millions. One hesitates, therefore, to criticize a life which, beginning with so little, has done so much. And yet the time is come when one may speak in all sincerity and utter courtesy of the mistakes and shortcomings of Mr. Washington's career, as well as of his triumphs, without being thought captious or envious, and without forgetting that it is easier to do ill than well in the world.

The criticism that has hitherto met Mr. Washington has not always been of this broad character. In the South especially has he had to walk warily to avoid the harshest judgments,—and naturally so, for he is dealing with the one subject of deepest sensitiveness to that section. Twice—once when at the Chicago celebration of the Spanish-American War he alluded to the color-prejudice that is "eating away the vitals of the South," and once when he dined with President Roosevelt[3]—has the resulting Southern criticism been violent enough to threaten seriously his popularity. In the North the feeling has several times forced itself into words, that Mr. Washington's counsels of submission overlooked certain elements of true manhood, and that his educational program was unnecessarily narrow. Usually, however, such criticism has not found open expression, although, too, the spiritual sons of the Abolitionists have not been prepared to acknowledge that the schools founded before Tuskegee, by men of broad ideals and self-sacrificing spirit, were wholly failures or worthy of ridicule. While, then, criticism has not failed to follow Mr. Washington, yet the prevailing public opinion of the land has been but too willing to deliver the solution of a wearisome problem into his hands, and say, "If that is all you and your race ask, take it."

Among his own people, however, Mr. Washington has encountered the strongest and most lasting opposition, amounting at times to bitterness, and even today continuing strong and insistent even though largely silenced in outward expression by the public opinion of the nation. Some of this opposition is, of course, mere envy; the disappointment of displaced demagogues and the spite of narrow minds. But aside from this, there is among educated and thoughtful colored men in all parts of the land a feeling of deep regret, sorrow, and apprehension at the wide currency and ascendancy which some of Mr. Washington's theories have gained. These same men admire his sincerity of purpose, and are willing to forgive much to honest endeavor which is doing something worth the doing. They cooperate with Mr. Washington as far as they conscientiously can; and, indeed, it is no ordinary tribute to this man's tact and power that, steering as he must between so many diverse interests and opinions, he so largely retains the respect of all.

But the hushing of the criticism of honest opponents is a dangerous thing. It leads some of the best of the critics to unfortunate silence and paralysis of effort, and others to burst into speech so passionately and intemperately as to lose listeners. Honest and earnest criticism from those whose interests are most nearly touched,—criticism of writers by readers, of government by those governed, of leaders by those led,—this is the soul of democracy and the safeguard of modern society. If the best of the American Negroes receive by outer pressure a leader whom they had not recognized before, manifestly there is here a certain palpable gain. Yet there is also irreparable loss,—a loss of that peculiarly valuable education which a group receives when by search and criticism it finds and commissions its own leaders. The way in which this is done is at once the most elementary and the nicest problem of social growth. History is but the record of such group leadership; and yet how infinitely changeful is its type and character! And of all types and kinds, what can be more instructive than the leadership of a group within a group?—that curious double movement where real progress may be negative and actual advance be relative retrogression. All this is the social student's inspiration and despair.

Now in the past the American Negro has had instructive experience in the choosing of group leaders, founding thus a peculiar dynasty which in the light of present conditions is worthwhile studying. When sticks and stones and beasts form the sole environment of a people, their attitude is largely one of determined opposition to and conquest of natural forces. But when to earth and brute is added an environment of men and ideas, then the attitude of the imprisoned group may take three main forms,—a feeling of revolt and revenge; an attempt to adjust all thought and action to the will of the greater group; or, finally, a determined effort at self-realization and self- development despite environing opinion. The influence of all of these attitudes at various times can be traced in

1. **acme of absurdities.** Refers to a passage in *Up From Slavery* in which Washington describes nonpractical knowledge as absurd

2. **Socrates and St. Francis of Assisi.** *Socrates*—(*circa* 470–399 BC), Greek philosopher; *St. Francis of Assisi*—(*circa* AD 1182–1226), founder of the Franciscan orders and leader of movements to reform the church

3. **he dined with President Roosevelt.** Theodore Roosevelt (1858–1919) asked Washington to dine with him in 1901, causing much controversy and criticism around the country.

the history of the American Negro, and in the evolution of his successive leaders.

Before 1750, while the fire of African freedom still burned in the veins of the slaves, there was in all leadership or attempted leadership but the one motive of revolt and revenge,—typified in the terrible Maroons, the Danish blacks, and Cato of Stono,[1] and veiling all the Americas in fear of insurrection. The liberalizing tendencies of the latter half of the eighteenth century brought, along with kindlier relations between black and white, thoughts of ultimate adjustment and assimilation. Such aspiration was especially voiced in the earnest songs of Phyllis, in the martyrdom of Attucks, the fighting of Salem and Poor, the intellectual accomplishments of Banneker and Derham, and the political demands of the Cuffes.[2]

Stern financial and social stress after the war cooled much of the previous humanitarian ardor. The disappointment and impatience of the Negroes at the persistence of slavery and serfdom voiced itself in two movements. The slaves in the South, aroused undoubtedly by vague rumors of the Haytian revolt, made three fierce attempts at insurrection,—in 1800 under Gabriel in Virginia, in 1822 under Vesey in Carolina, and in 1831 again in Virginia under the terrible Nat Turner.[3] In the Free States, on the other hand, a new and curious attempt at self-development was made. In Philadelphia and New York color prescription led to a withdrawal of Negro communicants from white churches and the formation of a peculiar socio-religious institution among the Negroes known as the African Church,—an organization still living and controlling in its various branches over a million of men.

Walker's[4] wild appeal against the trend of the times showed how the world was changing after the coming of the cotton-gin. By 1830, slavery seemed hopelessly fastened on the South, and the slaves thoroughly cowed into submission. The free Negroes of the North, inspired by the mulatto immigrants from the West Indies, began to change the basis of their demands; they recognized the slavery of slaves, but insisted that they themselves were freemen, and sought assimilation and amalgamation with the nation on the same terms with other men. Thus, Forten and Purvis of Philadelphia, Shad of Wilmington, Du Bois of New Haven, Barbadoes[5] of Boston, and others, strove singly and together as men, they said, not as slaves; as "people of color," not as "Negroes." The trend of the times, however, refused them recognition save in individual and exceptional cases, considered them as one with all the despised blacks, and they soon found themselves striving to keep even the rights they formerly had of voting and working and moving as freemen. Schemes of migration and colonization arose among them; but these they refused to entertain, and they eventually turned to the Abolition movement as a final refuge.

Here, led by Remond, Nell, Wells-Brown, and Douglass,[6] a new period of self-assertion and self-development dawned. To be sure, ultimate freedom and assimilation was the ideal before the leaders, but the assertion of the manhood rights of the Negro by himself was the main reliance, and John Brown's raid was the extreme of its logic. After the war and emancipation, the great form of Frederick Douglass, the greatest of American Negro leaders, still led the host. Self-assertion, especially in political lines, was the main program, and behind Douglass came Elliot, Bruce, and Langston, and the Reconstruction politicians, and, less conspicuous but of greater social significance Alexander Crummell and Bishop Daniel Payne.[7]

Then came the Revolution of 1876, the suppression of the Negro votes, the changing and shifting of ideals, and the seeking of new lights in the great night. Douglass, in his old age, still bravely stood for the ideals of his early manhood,—ultimate assimilation *through* self-assertion, and on no other terms. For a time Price arose as a new leader, destined, it

1. **Maroons . . . Stono.** *Maroons*—fugitive slaves or their descendants; *Danish blacks*—slaves in the Danish West Indies who revolted in 1733; *Cato of Stono*—leader of a slave revolt in South Carolina

2. **Phyllis . . . the Cuffes.** *Phillis Wheatley*—(*circa* 1753– 1784), African-American poet; *Crispus Attucks*—(*circa* 1723–1770), slain leader of the Boston Massacre; *Peter Salem*—(d. 1816), African-American patriot who was killed in the battle of Bunker Hill; *Benjamin Banneker*—(1731–1800), African-American mathematician; *James Derham*—(1762–?), first recognized African-American physician; *Paul Cuffe*—(1759–1817), organizer of a movement to resettle African Americans in African colonies

3. **Gabriel . . . Turner.** *Gabriel*—(*circa* 1775–1800) conspired to attack Richmond, Virginia; *Denmark Vesey*—(*circa* 1767–1822) led an unsuccessful uprising in 1822; *Nat Turner*—(1800–1831) led the Southampton insurrection in 1831, in which one hundred slaves and sixty-one whites were killed.

4. **Walker's.** *David Walker*—(1785–1830) wrote an inflammatory antislavery pamphlet.

5. **Forten . . . Barbadoes.** *James Forten*—(1766–1842), African-American philanthropist and civic leader; *Robert Purvis*—(1810–1898), founder of the American Anti-Slavery Society and president of the Underground Railroad; *Abraham Shadd*—African-American abolitionist and activist; *Alexander Du Bois*—(1803–1887), W. E. B. Du Bois's grandfather, helped form the Negro Episcopal Parish of St. Luke; *James G. Barbadoes*—attended the first National Negro Convention.

6. **Remond . . . Douglass.** *Charles Lenox Remond*— (1810–1873), African-American leader; *William Cooper Nell*—(1816–1874), first African American to acquire a governmental position (clerk in the post office), abolitionist, writer, and advocate for equal education; *William Wells Brown*—(*circa* 1816–1884), publisher of *Clotel*, the first novel and play by an African American; *Fredrick Douglass*—(1817–1895), African-American abolitionist and diplomat

7. **Elliot . . . Payne.** *Robert Brown Elliot*—(1842–1884), African-American South Carolina congressman in the United States House of Representatives; *Blanche K. Bruce*—(1841–1898), first African-American man to serve a full term in the United States Senate (1875–1881); *John Mercer Langston*—(1829–1897), African-American congressman, lawyer, diplomat, educator; *Alexander Crummell*—(1819–1898), clergyman of the protestant Episcopal Church, missionary in Liberia for twenty years and then in Washington, DC; *Daniel Alexander Payne*—(1811–1893), bishop of the African Methodist Episcopal Church and president of Wilberforce University (1863–1876)

Additional Questions and Activities

1. What were the three main points in Booker T. Washington's program for solving racial problems in the South?

2. According to Du Bois, what are the three attitudes that an imprisoned group like the African Americans can take toward their oppressors?

3. What is the main difference between Booker T. Washington and almost all past African-American leaders?

Answers. 1. Booker T. Washington's program urged African Americans to seek industrial education, to make peace with the South, and to abandon their desire for civil and political rights.

2. According to Du Bois, an imprisoned group can revolt and seek revenge, adjust their thoughts and action to the oppressors, or seek self-realization and self-development.

3. Past African-American leaders had become leaders at the request of their people. Booker T. Washington became a leader at the request of both African Americans and whites.

Additional Questions and Activities

1. What three things does Booker T. Washington ask the African Americans to give up?

2. Why does Du Bois disagree with Washington's program?

3. What three things does Du Bois desire for African Americans?

4. A paradox is a belief or statement that contradicts itself. According to Du Bois, what are the three great paradoxes of Booker T. Washington's career?

5. During what historical era did Booker T. Washington become the leading African-American spokesperson in the nation? What was the nation primarily concerned with at this time? What was the nation's response to Booker T. Washington's program for the South? Why do you think the nation approved of Washington's plan to develop industrial education for African Americans?

Answers. 1. Washington asks African Americans to give up political power, civil rights, and higher education.

2. Du Bois thinks that Washington's program puts too much emphasis on making a living and neglects the higher aims of life, and he thinks that Washington accepts the alleged inferiority of African Americans.

3. Du Bois wants African Americans to have the right to vote, civic equality, and the education of African-American youth according to their ability.

4. The three paradoxes are he wants to give African-American men the opportunity to be businessmen and property owners, but he does not support the African-American men's right to vote that would protect their rights as businessmen and property owners; he encourages African Americans to respect themselves and be thrifty so that they can improve their standard of living, but he advises them to submit to inequalities that make them despise themselves; and he supports basic education

(cont.)

seemed, not to give up, but to restate the old ideals in a form less repugnant to the white South. But he passed away in his prime. Then came the new leader. Nearly all the former ones had become leaders by the silent suffrage of their fellows, had sought to lead their own people alone, and were usually, save Douglass, little known outside their race. But Booker T. Washington arose as essentially the leader not of one race but of two,—a compromiser between the South, the North, and the Negro. Naturally the Negroes resented, at first bitterly, signs of compromise which surrendered their civil and political rights, even though this was to be exchanged for larger chances of economic development. The rich and dominating North, however, was not only weary of the race problem, but was investing largely in Southern enterprises, and welcomed any method of peaceful cooperation. Thus, by national opinion, the Negroes began to recognize Mr. Washington's leadership; and the voice of criticism was hushed.

Mr. Washington represents in Negro thought the old attitude of adjustment and submission; but adjustment at such a peculiar time as to make his program unique. This is an age of unusual economic development, and Mr. Washington's program naturally takes an economic cast, becoming a gospel of Work and Money to such an extent as apparently almost completely to overshadow the higher aims of life. Moreover, this is an age when the more advanced races are coming in closer contact with the less developed races, and the race-feeling is therefore intensified; and Mr. Washington's program practically accepts the alleged inferiority of the Negro races. Again, in our own land, the reaction from the sentiment of wartime has given impetus to race-prejudice against Negroes, and Mr. Washington withdraws many of the high demands of Negroes as men and American citizens. In other periods of intensified prejudice all the Negro's tendency to self-assertion has been called forth; at this period a policy of submission is advocated. In the history of nearly all other races and peoples the doctrine preached at such crises has been that manly self-respect is worth more than lands and houses, and that a people who voluntarily surrender such respect, or cease striving for it, are not worth civilizing.

In answer to this, it has been claimed that the Negro can survive only through submission. Mr. Washington distinctly asks that black people give up, at least for the present, three things,—

First, political power,

Second, insistence on civil rights,

Third, higher education of Negro youth,—

and concentrate all their energies on industrial education, the accumulation of wealth, and the conciliation of the South. This policy has been courageously and insistently advocated for over fifteen years, and has been triumphant for perhaps ten years. As a result of this tender of the palm-branch, what has been the return? In these years there have occurred:

1. The disfranchisement of the Negro.

2. The legal creation of a distinct status of civil inferiority for the Negro.

3. The steady withdrawal of aid from institutions for the higher training of the Negro.

These movements are not, to be sure, direct results of Mr. Washington's teachings; but his propaganda has, without a shadow of doubt, helped their speedier accomplishment. The question then comes: Is it possible, and probable, that nine millions of men can make effective progress in economic lines if they are deprived of political rights, made a servile caste, and allowed only the most meager chance for developing their exceptional men? If history and reason give any distinct answer to these questions, it is an emphatic *No.* And Mr. Washington thus faces the triple paradox of his career:

1. He is striving nobly to make Negro artisans businessmen and property-owners; but it is utterly impossible, under modern competitive methods, for workingmen and property-owners to defend their rights and exist without the right of suffrage.

2. He insists on thrift and self-respect, but at the same time counsels a silent submission to civic inferiority such as is bound to sap the manhood of any race in the long run.

3. He advocates common-school and industrial training, and depreciates institutions of higher learning; but neither the Negro common schools, nor Tuskegee itself, could remain open a day were it not for teachers trained in Negro colleges, or trained by their graduates.

This triple paradox in Mr. Washington's position is the object of criticism by two classes of colored Americans. One class is spiritually descended from Toussaint the Savior,[1] through Gabriel, Vesey, and Turner, and they represent the attitude of revolt and revenge; they hate the white South blindly and distrust the white race generally, and so far as they agree on definite action, think that the Negro's only hope lies in emigration beyond the borders of the United States. And yet, by the irony of fate, nothing has more effectually made this program seem hopeless than the recent course of the United States toward weaker and darker peoples in the West Indies, Hawaii, and the Philippines,—for where in the world may we go and be safe from lying and brute force?

The other class of Negroes who cannot agree with Mr. Washington has hitherto said little aloud. They deprecate the sight of scattered counsels, of internal disagreement; and especially they dislike making their just criticism of a useful and earnest man an excuse for a general discharge of venom from small-minded opponents. Nevertheless, the questions involved are so fundamental and serious that it is difficult to see how men like the Grimkes, Kelly Miller, J. W. E. Bowen,[2] and other representatives of this group, can much longer be silent. Such men feel in conscience bound to ask of this nation three things:

1. The right to vote.

2. Civic equality.

3. The education of youth according to ability.

---

1. **Toussaint the Savior.** Pierre-Dominique Toussaint (*circa* 1743–1803), Haitian general and liberator

2. **Grimkes . . . Bowen.** *Archibald Grimke*—(1849–1930) and *Francis Grimke*—(1850–1937), civic leaders concerned with African-American affairs; *Kelly Miller*—(1863–1939), dean of Howard University, lectured on African-American issues; *John Wesley Edward Bowen*—(1855–?), clergyman and educator

Additional Questions and Activities (cont.)

and industrial training for African Americans, but he does not support the higher education needed to train the African-American teachers who would work in such schools.

5. Washington became an African-American leader after 1876, at the end of Reconstruction of the South after the Civil War. At this time the nation was primarily concerned with making money. Both the North and the South approved and applauded his plan. Washington's program for industrial education for African Americans fit in with their efforts to make money.

They acknowledge Mr. Washington's invaluable service in counselling patience and courtesy in such demands; they do not ask that ignorant black men vote when ignorant whites are debarred, or that any reasonable restrictions in the suffrage should not be applied; they know that the low social level of the mass of the race is responsible for much discrimination against it, but they also know, and the nation knows, that relentless color-prejudice is more often a cause than a result of the Negro's degradation; they seek the abatement of this relic of barbarism, and not its systematic encouragement and pampering by all agencies of social power from the Associated Press to the Church of Christ. They advocate, with Mr. Washington, a broad system of Negro common schools supplemented by thorough industrial training; but they are surprised that a man of Mr. Washington's insight cannot see that no such educational system ever has rested or can rest on any other basis than that of the well-equipped college and university, and they insist that there is a demand for a few such institutions throughout the South to train the best of the Negro youth as teachers, professional men, and leaders.

This group of men honor Mr. Washington for his attitude of conciliation toward the white South; they accept the "Atlanta Compromise" in its broadest interpretation; they recognize, with him, many signs of promise, many men of high purpose and fair judgment, in this section; they know that no easy task has been laid upon a region already tottering under heavy burdens. But, nevertheless, they insist that the way to truth and right lies in straightforward honesty, not in indiscriminate flattery; in praising those of the South who do well and criticizing uncompromisingly those who do ill; in taking advantage of the opportunities at hand and urging their fellows to do the same, but at the same time in remembering that only a firm adherence to their higher ideals and aspirations will ever keep those ideals within the realm of possibility. They do not expect that the free right to vote, to enjoy civic rights, and to be educated will come in a moment; they do not expect to see the bias and prejudices of years disappear at the blast of a trumpet; but they are absolutely certain that the way for a people to gain their reasonable rights is not by voluntarily throwing them away and insisting that they do not want them; that the way for a people to gain respect is not by continually belittling and ridiculing themselves that, on the contrary, Negroes must insist continually, in season and out of season, that voting is necessary to modern manhood, that color discrimination is barbarism, and that black boys need education as well as white boys.

In failing thus to state plainly and unequivocally the legitimate demands of their people, even at the cost of opposing an honored leader, the thinking classes of American Negroes would shirk a heavy responsibility,—a responsibility to themselves, a responsibility to the struggling masses, a responsibility to the darker races of men whose future depends so largely on this American experiment, but especially a responsibility to this nation,—this common Fatherland. It is wrong to encourage a man or a people in evil-doing, it is wrong to aid and abet a national crime simply because it is unpopular not to do so. The growing spirit of kindliness and reconciliation between the North and South after the frightful differences of a generation ago ought to be a source of deep congratulation to all, and especially to those whose mistreatment caused the war; but if that reconciliation is to be marked by the industrial slavery and civic death of those same black men, with permanent legislation into a position of inferiority, then those black men, if they are really men, are called upon by every consideration of patriotism and loyalty to oppose such a course by all civilized methods, even though such opposition involves disagreement with Mr. Booker T. Washington. We have no right to sit silently by while the inevitable seeds are sown for a harvest of disaster to our children black and white.

First, it is the duty of black men to judge the South discriminatingly. The present generation of Southerners are not responsible for the past, and they should not be blindly hated or blamed for it. Furthermore, to no class is the indiscriminate endorsement of the recent course of the South toward Negroes more nauseating than to the best thought of the South. The South is not "solid"; it is a land in the ferment of social change, wherein forces of all kinds are fighting for supremacy; and to praise the ill the South is today perpetrating is just as wrong as to condemn the good. Discriminating and broad-minded criticism is what the South needs,—needs it for the sake of her own white sons and daughters, and for the insurance of robust, healthy mental and moral development.

Today even the attitude of the Southern whites toward the blacks is not, as so many assume, in all cases the same; the ignorant Southerner hates the Negro, the workingmen fear his competition, the money-makers wish to use him as a laborer, some of the educated see a menace in his upward development, while others—usually the sons of the masters—wish to help him to rise. National opinion has enabled this last class to maintain the Negro common schools, and to protect the Negro partially in property, life, and limb. Through the pressure of the money-makers, the Negro is in danger of being reduced to semi-slavery, especially in the country districts; the workingmen, and those of the educated who fear the Negro, have united to disfranchise him, and some have urged his deportation; while the passions of the ignorant are easily aroused to lynch and abuse any black man. To praise this intricate whirl of thought and prejudice is nonsense; to inveigh indiscriminately against "the South" is unjust; but to use the same breath in praising Governor Aycock, exposing Senator Morgan, arguing with Mr. Thomas Nelson Page, and denouncing Senator Ben Tillman,[1] is not only sane, but the imperative duty of thinking black men.

It would be unjust to Mr. Washington not to acknowledge that in several instances he has opposed movements in the South which were unjust to the Negro; he sent memorials to

1 **Governor Aycock . . . Ben Tillman.** *Charles Brantley Aycock*—(1859–1905), governor of North Carolina; *Edwin Denison Morgan*—governor of New York (1859–1863) and United States senator; *Thomas Nelson Page*—(1853–1922), novelist who glamorized the southern plantation; *Benjamin Ryan Tillman*—(1847–1918), United States senator who presented the views of southern extremists

FROM *THE ART OF FICTION*

About the Author. Henry James (1843–1916) was born in New York City. As an infant he was taken to Europe where his family would return when he was twelve years old. James spent much of his early life in the museums, libraries, and galleries of England, Switzerland, and France. He studied European literature and drew more on this tradition than on the rising tradition of American literature for the style of his own writing. James's works include *The Portrait of a Lady* (1881), *The American* (1877), *Daisy Miller* (1878), *The Bostonians* (1886), *The Tragic Muse* (1889), and *The Turn of the Screw* (1898).

About the Selection. Besides being a fiction writer, James often wrote essays or critiques of fiction. ***The Art of Fiction*** represents James's aesthetic ideals of fiction. In this selection from *The Art of Fiction* James offers an anecdote and advice to the writer.

the Louisiana and Alabama constitutional conventions, he has spoken against lynching, and in other ways has openly or silently set his influence against sinister schemes and unfortunate happenings. Notwithstanding this, it is equally true to assert that on the whole the distinct impression left by Mr. Washington's propaganda is, first, that the South is justified in its present attitude toward the Negro because of the Negro's degradation; secondly, that the prime cause of the Negro's failure to rise more quickly is his wrong education in the past; and, thirdly, that his future rise depends primarily on his own efforts. Each of these propositions is a dangerous half-truth. The supplementary truths must never be lost sight of: first, slavery and race-prejudice are potent if not sufficient causes of the Negro's position; second, industrial and common-school training were necessarily slow in planting because they had to await the black teachers trained by higher institutions,—it being extremely doubtful if any essentially different development was possible, and certainly a Tuskegee was unthinkable before 1880; and, third, while it is a great truth to say that the Negro must strive and strive mightily to help himself, it is equally true that unless his striving be not simply seconded, but rather aroused and encouraged, by the initiative of the richer and wiser environing group, he cannot hope for great success.

In his failure to realize and impress this last point, Mr. Washington is especially to be criticized. His doctrine has tended to make the whites, North and South, shift the burden of the Negro problem to the Negro's shoulders and stand aside as critical and rather pessimistic spectators; when in fact the burden belongs to the nation, and the hands of none of us are clean if we bend not our energies to righting these great wrongs.

The South ought to be led, by candid and honest criticism, to assert her better self and do her full duty to the race she has cruelly wronged and is still wronging. The North—her co-partner in guilt—cannot salve her conscience by plastering it with gold. We cannot settle this problem by diplomacy and suaveness, by "policy" alone. If worse come to worst, can the moral fiber of this country survive the slow throttling and murder of nine millions of men?

The black men of America have a duty to perform, a duty stern and delicate,—a forward movement to oppose a part of the work of their greatest leader. So far as Mr. Washington preaches Thrift, Patience, and Industrial Training for the masses, we must hold up his hands and strive with him, rejoicing in his honors and glorying in the strength of this Joshua called of God and of man to lead the headless host. But so far as Mr. Washington apologizes for injustice, North or South, does not rightly value the privilege and duty of voting, belittles the emasculating effects of caste distinctions, and opposes the higher training and ambition of our brighter minds,—so far as he, the South or the Nation, does this,—we must unceasingly and firmly oppose them. By every civilized and peaceful method we must strive for the rights which the world accords to men, clinging unwaveringly to those great words which the sons of the Fathers would fain forget: "We hold these truths to be self-evident: That all men are created equal; that they are endowed by their Creator with certain inalienable rights; that among these are life, liberty, and the pursuit of happiness."

from *The Art of Fiction*
by Henry James

I remember an English novelist, a woman of genius, telling me that she was much commended for the impression she had managed to give in one of her tales of the nature and way of life of the French Protestant youth. She had been asked where she learned so much about this recondite[1] being, she had been congratulated on her peculiar opportunities. These opportunities consisted in her having once, in Paris, as she ascended a staircase, passed an open door where, in the household of a *pasteur*,[2] some of the young Protestants were seated at table round a finished meal. The glimpse made a picture; it lasted only a moment, but that moment was experience. She had got her direct personal impression, and she turned out her type. She knew what youth was, and what Protestantism, she also had the advantage of having seen what it was to be French, so that she converted these ideas into a concrete image and produced a reality. Above all, however, she was blessed with the faculty which when you give it an inch takes an ell,[3] and which for the artist is a much greater source of strength than any accident of residence or of place in the social scale.

The power to guess the unseen from the seen, to trace the implication of things, to judge the whole piece by the pattern, the condition of feeling life in general so completely that you are well on your way to knowing any particular corner of it—this cluster of gifts may also be said to constitute experience, and they occur in country and in town, and in the most differing stages of education. If experience consists of impressions, it may be said that impressions *are* experience, just as (have we not seen it?) they are the very air we breathe.

Therefore, if I should certainly say to a novice, "Write from experience and experience only," I should feel that this was rather a tantalizing monition[4] if I were not careful immediately to add, "Try to be one of the people on whom nothing is lost!"

1. **recondite.** Profound, extraordinary
2. **pasteur.** Minister
3. **ell.** Former unit of measure in England, equal to forty-five inches
4. **monition.** Warning

UNIT REVIEW

Frontiers

VOCABULARY FROM THE SELECTIONS

abeyance, 472
afflicted, 460
anathema, 428
append, 456
barbaric, 477
bellicose, 429
cavalcade, 428
cavort, 458
conjecture, 427, 456
contender, 473
contortion, 430
coquetry, 428
course, 444
creed, 472
demure, 442
dilapidated, 456
dilatory, 439
disposition, 473
dissuade, 430
equanimity, 429
esculent, 476
exhorter, 457
expatriated, 428
extemporize, 431
felonious, 431
fissure, 477
gallantly, 441
garrulous, 456
gravity, 441
guileless, 429
harbor, 472
hermitage, 441
impalpable, 473
importunity, 452
inaudibly, 441
infelicitous, 428
infidel, 476
interminable, 457
jag, 477
jocular, 430
linguist, 473
loiter, 477
ominous, 427
ornery, 458
ornithologist, 442
ostentatiously, 432
pinion, 445
ponderous, 445
precipitous, 429
predisposing, 427
premonition, 443
proffer, 441
quadruped, 476
querulous, 434
rebuke, 446
remonstrance, 429
shoal, 440
squalor, 441
suffice, 472
tumultuously, 452
vagabond, 460
vex, 446
vituperative, 433
vociferation, 432
wretched, 440

LITERARY TERMS

catalog, 479
conflict, 448
dialect, 461
dialogue, 470
elaboration, 479
essay, 462
frame tale, 462
free verse, 471, 479
irony, 454, 470
motif, 448
Naturalism, 468
oral tradition, 467
parallelism, 479
parody, 437
personification, 470
protagonist, 448
Psychological Realism, 423
Realism, 423
reversal, 454
rhyme, 482
Romanticism, 471
sentimentality, 437
speaker, 482
stereotype character, 437
stock character, 437
symbol, 479
tall tale, 462

VOCABULARY DEVELOPMENT EXERCISES

► Give students the following exercise.

Choose twenty words from the list on page 497. For each word, write a sentence that relates to something you've read in this unit. The vocabulary word need not have appeared in the selection to which you refer.

Example. The outcasts were banished and left to lead a wretched existence outside of Poker Flat.

ADDITIONAL RESOURCES

ASSESSMENT PORTFOLIO

- Vocabulary Worksheet, 4.7.17
- Study Guide: Unit 7 Test, 4.7.18
- Unit 7 Test, 4.7.19

ESSENTIAL SKILLS PRACTICE BOOKS

Language

- Capitalization, 2.107–2.133
- Combining Sentences, 2.51–2.53
- Correcting Run-ons, 2.62
- Dialects of English, 2.150
- End Marks, 2.93
- Formal and Informal Language, 2.147
- Linking Verbs, 2.13
- Modifier Usage, 2.85–2.89
- Pronouns, 2.76–2.77
- Quotation Marks I and II, 2.104–2.105
- Varieties of English, 2.147–2.150

Speaking and Listening

- Elements of Verbal Communication, 3.2
- Oral Interpretation, 3.8
- Public Speaking, 3.7

These prompts are suitable as topics for research papers. Refer to the Language Arts Survey, 4.20–4.34, "Research Skills." (To evaluate research papers, see the evaluation forms for writing, revising, and proofreading, *Assessment Portfolio*, 7.1–7.10.)

These prompts can be adapted for use as topics for oral reports or debates. (To evaluate these projects, see the evaluation forms in the *Assessment Portfolio*, 7.17–7.19.)

SYNTHESIS: QUESTIONS FOR WRITING, RESEARCH, OR DISCUSSION

GENRE STUDIES

1. **Short Story.** Review the definition of *point of view* in the Handbook of Literary Terms. Examine the point of view used in the short stories in the unit. Do any authors combine two points of view? to what effect?

THEMATIC STUDIES

2. **Frontiers.** The name of this unit is "Frontiers." For every geographical frontier there is an interior psychological frontier. Choose characters from three separate works and explain how each character crosses an interior frontier.
3. **Connection and Indifference.** Contrast the views of the world expressed in the poems of Crane and Whitman.
4. **Rite of Passage.** A rite-of-passage story chronicles moving from childhood to adulthood. Examine Sylvia in "A White Heron" and Tom and Piney in "The Outcasts of Poker Flat." What events mark their maturation?

HISTORICAL/BIOGRAPHICAL STUDIES

5. **Dialect.** Note the use of dialect in both the Harte and Twain selections. What does it tell you about the expansion of America? What else might this tell you about the social strata of the country? What might the impact of the dialect be on readers in other countries?

LANGUAGE LAB PROOFREADING FOR COMMA ERRORS

When revising and proofreading, check for missing and misplaced commas.

COMMA USAGE	
MILD EXCLAMATION:	My, the prairie seems to stretch on forever.
PARTICIPIAL PHRASES:	Coming from the mountainous Northeast, I was quite surprised by the flatness of the land.
TWO PREPOSITIONAL PHRASES:	On the eve of our journey, I almost changed my mind.
ADVERB CLAUSE:	When I thought about the unknown dangers that lie ahead, I became uncertain about the journey.
PARENTHETICAL EXPRESSION:	I changed my mind, as you can see, when I thought about the lack of prospects in my hometown.
DIRECT ADDRESS:	Mother, I will write as soon as I am able.
WORDS IN A SERIES:	The heat, dust, and drudgery of the trail were sometimes unbearable.
PHRASES IN A SERIES:	We left Buffalo, reached Ohio a few days later, and arrived in Missouri by springtime.
CLAUSES IN A SERIES:	We had heard that the trip was long, that dangers were imminent, and that California was the land of promise.
TWO OR MORE ADJECTIVES:	The wagon train crawled like a long, white snake across the plain.
LONG INDEPENDENT CLAUSE:	The Oregon Trail opened the door to the "great migration," and thousands of people followed it to the Pacific.
SHORT CLAUSE:	The wagons rolled and the sky stretched endlessly.
RESTRICTIVE PHRASE OR CLAUSE:	The first thing that caught my eye was the buffalo.
NONRESTRICTIVE PHRASE OR CLAUSE:	The Oregon Trail, which opened in 1842, was eventually abandoned in 1870s.
APPOSITIVE OR APPOSITIVE PHRASE:	My father's ancestors, immigrants from Ireland, made the journey westward.

Exercise Avoiding Errors in Comma Usage

Rewrite the following sentences, adding commas as necessary.

1. First published in the *Overland Monthly* in 1869 "The Outcasts of Poker Flat" has become a classic of American literature.
2. Kate Chopin shocked turn-of-the-century critics with her depictions of women especially those in her novel *The Awakening.*
3. I sing a song of myself Walt Whitman.
4. Sarah Orne Jewett's father a doctor encouraged her to closely observe her environment.
5. In *The Souls of Black Folk* Du Bois proposes that a "veil" separates the races in America that education is crucial for young African Americans and that African Americans need to seek civil equality.

ANSWERS FOR LANGUAGE LAB

1. First published in the *Overland Monthly* in 1869, "The Outcasts of Poker Flat" has become a classic of American literature.

2. Kate Chopin shocked turn-of-the-century critics with her depictions of women, especially those in her novel *The Awakening.*

3. I sing a song of myself, Walt Whitman.

4. Sarah Orne Jewett's father, a doctor, encouraged her to closely observe her environment.

5. In *The Souls of Black Folk*, Du Bois proposes that a "veil" separates the races in America, that education is crucial for young African Americans, and that African Americans need to seek civil equality.

UNIT SKILLS OUTLINE

Literary Skills and Concepts
- Abstract, 544, 566
- Allusion, 520, 573, 590
- Anecdote, 538
- Character, 527
- Characterization, 526
- Concrete, 544, 566
- Diction, 532, 578
- Dramatic Monologue, 573
- Effect, 549, 596
- Free Verse, 573
- Iamb, 514
- Image, 544, 549, 562
- Inversion, 587
- Metaphor, 514, 532, 562
- Meter, 547, 593
- Paradox, 583
- Parallelism, 523
- Pathetic Fallacy, 536
- Personification, 523
- Pun, 527
- Refrain, 596
- Repetition, 551, 558, 587
- Rhyme, 558, 600, 593, 587, 578
- Rhythm, 547, 551
- Run-on Line, 551
- Simile, 514, 520, 583, 596
- Sonnet, 590
- Speaker, 547, 549, 600
- Stanza, 566
- Symbol, 527
- Syntax, 587
- Theme, 559
- Tone, 512, 532, 547, 593
- Understatement, 578

Writing Skills and Concepts
- Ballad, 515
- Caption, 544, 549
- Comparison-Contrast Essay, 549
- Critical Analysis, 533
- Critical Interpretation, 551
- Descriptive Paragraph, 551
- Dialogue and Debate, 527
- Elegy, 578
- Epitaph, 512
- Essay, 559
- Family History, 597
- Free Verse Poem, 523, 549
- Greeting Card, 593
- Haiku, 562
- Imagist Poem, 583
- Journal Entry, 544
- Love Letter, 587
- Lyric Poem, 596
- Myth, 538
- Parody, 574
- Personal Note, 547
- Poem, 547
- Slogan, 523
- Toast, 520

Grammar, Usage, and Mechanics Skills and Concepts
- Achieving Parallelism, 597
- Adding Prepositional Phrases, 559
- Cliches and Euphemisms, 515
- Colons, 585
- Commas I, 585
- Commas II, 585
- Commas III, 585
- Common Punctuation Errors, 610
- Complex Sentences, 595
- Compound Sentences, 595
- Compound-Complex Sentences, 595
- Concrete and Abstract Nouns, 580, 583
- Demonstrative Pronouns, 546
- End Marks, 585
- Expanding Sentences, 520
- The Form of a Personal Letter, 587
- Formal and Informal English, 576
- Functions of Sentences, 513, 533, 568
- Indefinite Pronouns, 525
- Linking Verbs, 535
- Personal Pronouns, 525, 537
- Place Names, 522
- Prepositions, 548, 554
- The Pronoun *I*, 522
- Replacing Linking Verbs with Action Verbs, 574
- Titles of Artworks, 552
- Tone and Voice, 576
- Using Colorful Modifiers, 592
- Using Context Clues I, 539, 588
- Using Context Clues II, 539, 588
- Using Precise Nouns, 561, 564
- Using the Parts of Speech in Writing, 583
- Verbals: Gerunds, 511, 550
- Verbals: Participles, 511, 550

Other Language Arts Skills and Concepts
- Bibliographies and Bibliography Cards, 552
- Comparing and Contrasting, 515, 559
- Elements of Nonverbal Communication, 533
- Generalizing, 574
- Interpersonal Communication, 528
- Observing, 583
- Oral Interpretation, 524
- Organizing Ideas, 517
- Recalling, 583
- Sensory Detail Charts, 583
- Using Reference Works, 597
- Using Searching Tools, 583
- Using the Active Voice, 599

UNIT 8 MODERN POETRY (1900–1960)

Can Fire in the Park. *Beauford Delaney, 1946. National Museum of American Art, Washington, DC/Art Resource, NY*

GOALS/OBJECTIVES

Studying this unit will enable students to

- have a positive experience reading modern poetry
- explain the characteristics of the Modernist movement in literature
- explain the characteristics of the politically charged works of the Harlem Renaissance
- identify twentieth-century forms of writing such as free verse, stream of consciousness, and imagist verse
- identify some of the major Modernist poets
- proofread for punctuation errors

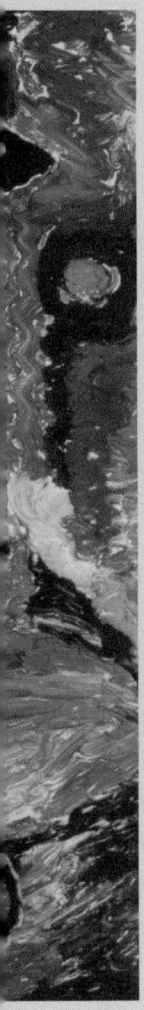

M ake it new.

—Ezra Pound

CONNECTIONS ACROSS THE CURRICULUM

Arts and Humanities
- Art History, 552
- Booklet of Poetic Images, 560
- Locating Allusions, 574
- Original Illustrations, 545
- Patterns and Forms, 559

Mathematics and Sciences
- Formation of Rivers, 595
- Researching Plants, 554

Social Studies
- Art History, 552
- The Lowell Family, 553
- Observing Crowds, 561
- Oral History, 597
- Researching Rivers, 595
- The War of Spanish Succession, 555
- West Indies, 591

Applied Arts
- Patterns and Forms, 559

TEACHING THE MULTIPLE INTELLIGENCES

Kinesthetic
- Dramatic Skit, 533

Interpersonal
- Art History, 552
- Circle Poetry Reading, 515
- Dramatic Skit, 533
- Observing Crowds, 561
- Oral History, 597
- Patterns and Forms, 559

Art Note

Beauford Delaney (1901–1979), the son of a Baptist minister, grew up in Knoxville, Tennessee, studied art in Boston, and lived in New York City before moving permanently to Paris in 1953. An Expressionist, Delaney used heavy strokes of paint and vivid colors reminiscent of Vincent van Gogh's works. Throughout his career, Delaney's work became increasingly abstract, and today he is considered one of the twentieth century's leading Abstract Expressionists.

Can Fire in the Park was painted while Delaney was living in Greenwich Village, then a bohemian artists' enclave on the Lower East Side of Manhattan. The work depicts an all-too-common scene in large cities in cold climates—street people gathered around a fire in a trash can or barrel. The grim subject of the painting contrasts dramatically with its vivid colors. The faces of the people are featureless, emphasizing the anonymity of the very poor.

THEMATIC CURRENTS

Use the following selections to explore these themes with your students.

DISAPPOINTMENT AND ALIENATION

- "Petit, the Poet," 513
- "Mr. Flood's Party," 516
- "Home Burial," 528
- "The Love Song of J. Alfred Prufrock," 567
- "An Old Man's Winter Night," 604
- "Disillusionment of Ten O'Clock," 604
- "The Geranium," 607

WAR

- "Grass," 521
- "Patterns," 553
- "For the Union Dead," 606
- "The Death of the Ball Turret Gunner," 607

LOVE

- "The Love Song of J. Alfred Prufrock," 567
- "somewhere i have never travelled, gladly beyond," 584
- "A Lover," 604
- "The River-Merchant's Wife: A Letter," 604

POETRY

- "Petit, the Poet," 513
- "Thirteen Ways of Looking at a Blackbird," 539
- "Poetry," 563
- "Ars Poetica," 579
- "Yet Do I Marvel," 588

WWI Troops in Gear. Courtesy of Archive/Welgos

THE MODERN ERA (1900–1960)

A CENTURY OF CHANGE

When William Faulkner delivered his Nobel Prize acceptance address in 1950, he asked his audience to remember "the old verities and truths of the heart." He wanted to make the point that however much the world might change, some things, such as the human capacity for courage, compassion, sacrifice, honor, and pride, remain the same.

Like other artists living in the twentieth century, Faulkner had to come to grips with change, for at no other time had the basic conditions of life changed so rapidly and so completely. Think, for example, of the effects on everyday life of electric lights, mass merchandising, mass media such as television and the movies, transportation by automobiles and airplanes, and instant communication by telephone anywhere in the world. Or consider the effects of antibiotics and anesthesia, weapons of mass destruction, suburban housing and skyscrapers, labor unions, women in the work force, the population explosion and the concentration of people in cities, and the development of such political ideologies as Communism and Fascism. Take these things away now, and our lives would be scarcely recognizable, yet all these developments took place in a few decades.[1]

THE FIRST WORLD WAR

One of the defining events of the first half of the twentieth century was **World War I.** Before the war, the United States was isolationist, involved in its own concerns. Writing before the war tended to be traditional and regional, providing portraits of life in the many different milieus to be found throughout the country. **Edgar Lee Masters's** *Spoon River Anthology,* with

1. Some developments, such as the telephone, the concentration of people in cities, and the appearance of women in the work force, had their origins in the nineteenth century but did not become truly significant until the twentieth century.

LITERARY EVENTS

►1905. Edith Wharton's *The House of Mirth* published
►1904. O. Henry's *Cabbages and Kings* published
►1903. Jack London publishes *The Call of the Wild*
►1902. Jack London's "To Build a Fire" published
►1901. Booker T. Washington's *Up from Slavery* published
1900. Sigmund Freud publishes *Interpretation of Dreams*
►1900. Theodore Dreiser's *Sister Carrie* published

►1913. William Carlos Williams's *The Tempers* published
►1912. James Weldon Johnson's *The Autobiography of an Ex-Colored Man* published
►1912. Amy Lowell's *A Dome of Many-Coloured Glass* published

1915. Franz Kafka pu *The Metamorphosis*
►1915. Carl Sandburg *Chicago Poems* and Masters's *Spoon Rive* published
►1914. Robert Frost's *North of Boston* published

► = American Events

1900 | 1905 | 1910 | 1915

HISTORICAL EVENTS

►1901. President McKinley assassinated; Theodore Roosevelt succeeds
►1904. President Roosevelt reelected
►1908. William Taft elected president
►1910. NAACP founded
►1912. Woodrow Wilson elected president
1912. The *Titanic* sinks

1914. World War I begins
1914. Mahatma Gandhi returns to India; begins nonviolent resistance
1915. German U-bo *Lusitania*

LITERARY NOTE

Ezra Pound (see the biography on page 560) was a talented poet, but it was as a critic that he had his major impact on twentieth-century writing. A leading Modernist, Pound championed a kind of lean, nonsentimental, impersonal, dramatic, allusive, and ironic free verse. His famous command to "Make it new" may be considered the rallying cry of the Modernist movement, summing up the desire of many early twentieth-century poets to break away from the sentimental, predictable verse popular during the Victorian Era.

its depictions of people from a small village in Illinois; **Edwin Arlington Robinson's** poems of life in New England; and **Jack London's** adventure tales of the great North country are examples of **regionalism.**

World War I began in 1914, but the United States delayed entering the conflict until 1917, primarily because Americans viewed the war as a European concern. The war changed the life and culture of the United States. The breakdown of traditional European society and the loss of ten million lives in Europe due to modern armaments led to a widespread belief among intellectuals and artists that the old order was passing away and that something altogether new would take its place.

Ernest Hemingway

The Lost Generation

To some of the writers who fought or participated in the war, such as **John Dos Passos, Ernest Hemingway,** and **E. E. Cummings,** the old rhetoric of heroic and glorious combat seemed hollow. Many writers saw the emerging society as chaotic, destructive, and increasingly meaningless. Particularly after the war, they felt that traditional expressions of order or meaning no longer applied; they felt, in some way, that the real America had been lost or distorted, and they came to feel a sense of dislocation, or "alienation," a sense of being cut off from the past. One American writer living in Paris, **Gertrude Stein,** would label this group of postwar writers the **"lost generation."**

This sense of dislocation and alienation led writers of the lost generation to question many fundamental tenets of the American dream, including the idea immortalized in Benjamin Franklin's *Autobiography* and in nineteenth-century Horatio Alger stories that through hard work, industry, and self-reliance any American could grasp a piece of the dream. In an age dominated by massive social forces, individuals seemed increasingly dominated by their environs, dehumanized by the numbing and squalid work conditions of modern industry and by the living conditions of modern cities, which swelled with the ranks of poor immigrants.

►1917. T. S. Eliot's *Prufrock and Other Observations* published and Edna St. Vincent Millay's *Renascence and Other Poems* published
►1919. Sherwood Anderson publishes *Winesburg, Ohio*
►1920. Sinclair Lewis's *Main Street* published
►1923. Wallace Stevens's *Harmonium* and William Carlos Williams's *Spring and All* published
1922. James Joyce publishes *Ulysses*
►1922. T. S. Eliot's *The Wasteland* published
►1925. Theodore Dreiser's *An American Tragedy,* F. Scott Fitzgerald's *The Great Gatsby,* and Ezra Pound's *The Cantos (I)* published
►1926. Ernest Hemingway's *The Sun Also Rises* and Langston Hughes's *Weary Blues* published
1930. Virginia Woolf's *A Room of One's Own*
►1930. Katherine Ann Porter's *Flowering Judas*
►1931. Henry Miller's *Tropic of Cancer* and Pearl Buck's *The Good Earth* published
►1932. William Faulkner's *Light in August*
►1933. Gertrude Stein's *The Autobiography of Alice B. Toklas*
►1934. F. Scott Fitzgerald's *Tender Is the Night* published

1920 **1925** **1930** **1935**

►1916. President Wilson reelected
►1917. U.S. declares war on Germany
1917. Bolshevik revolution in Russia
1918. Armistice signed
1919. Versailles Peace Conference
►1919. Prohibition begins
►1920. Warren G. Harding elected president
1921. Southern Ireland gains dominion status
1922. Benito Mussolini heads fascist Italy
►1923. President Harding dies; Calvin Coolidge succeeds
►1924. President Coolidge reelected
►1928. Herbert Hoover elected president
►1929. Stock market collapses; Great Depression begins
►1932. Franklin D. Roosevelt elected president
1933. Adolf Hitler becomes dictator of Germany
►1934. Prohibition ends

Literary Currents

Use the following selections to explore these techniques with your students.

Imagism
- "This Is Just to Say," 545
- "The Red Wheelbarrow," 548
- "In a Station of the Metro," 560
- "Wind and Silver," 604
- "A Lover," 604

Characterization
- "Lucinda Matlock," 510
- "Petit, the Poet," 513
- "Mr. Flood's Party," 516
- "The Love Song of J. Alfred Prufrock," 567
- "Miniver Cheevy," 601
- "Richard Cory," 601
- "The Death of the Hired Man," 602
- "An Old Man's Winter Night," 604
- "The River-Merchant's Wife: A Letter," 604
- "The Geranium," 607

Dramatic Monologues and Dialogues
- "Lucinda Matlock," 510
- "Petit, the Poet," 513
- "Mending Wall," 524
- "Home Burial," 528
- "The Love Song of J. Alfred Prufrock," 567
- "The Death of the Hired Man," 602
- "The River-Merchant's Wife: A Letter," 604
- "The Geranium," 607
- "The Death of the Ball Turret Gunner," 607

Literary Note

In order to grasp the impact of World War I upon the literary world, you might encourage students first to research Ernest Hemingway's involvement in the war and then to read his novel *A Farewell to Arms.* Many students will enjoy Hemingway's terse style of writing. Ask students to consider not only what Hemingway says but what he omits from his work as well. Point out that Hemingway omits descriptions of his narrator's feelings and instead focuses on mundane objects and activities. Suggest that the way in which the narrator deals with the horrors of World War I and his personal life is by focusing on mundane objects and activities. Hemingway's work is typical of much twentieth-century writing in that feelings must be inferred from dialogue and the description of exterior events and scenes.

Literary Note

The following is a list of suggested longer readings and collections by prose writers mentioned in this introductory essay.

Anderson, Sherwood
Winesburg, Ohio
Baldwin, James
Go Tell It on the Mountain
Notes of a Native Son
Tell Me How Long the Train's Been Gone
Bellow, Saul
The Adventures of Augie March
Henderson the Rain King
Benchley, Robert
Benchley Beside Himself
Love Conquers All
Boyle, Kay
Fifty Stories
Cather, Willa
My Antonia
O Pioneers!
Dos Passos, John
Manhattan Transfer
The U. S. A. Trilogy
Du Bois, W. E. B.
The Souls of Black Folk
Faulkner, William
As I Lay Dying
Go Down, Moses
Light in August
The Sound and the Fury
Fitzgerald, F. Scott
The Great Gatsby
Tales of the Jazz Age
Tender Is the Night
Hemingway, Ernest
A Farewell to Arms
The Nick Adams Stories
The Sun Also Rises
For Whom the Bell Tolls
Hurston, Zora Neale
Of Mules and Men
Their Eyes Were Watching God
Jackson, Shirley
The Haunting of Hill House
Jones, James
From Here to Eternity
Lewis, Sinclair
Babbitt
Elmer Gantry
London, Jack
The Call of the Wild
White Fang
Mailer, Norman
Armies of the Night
The Naked and the Dead
Malamud, Bernard
The Fixer
The Magic Barrel
The Natural

(cont.)

Edith Wharton

The Jazz Age and the New York Literary Scene

Increasingly during the 1920s, the so-called **Jazz Age,** conflicts developed between older, conservative people and a materially prosperous but alienated younger generation. Young people demonstrated their rebelliousness by flaunting Prohibition, the law passed in 1919 that prohibited the manufacture or sale of alcohol, and by frequenting "speak-easies" or "juke joints" and listening to jazz music. This was the era of the flapper, the Charleston, goldfish-swallowing college students in raccoon coats, and the gangster.

Rebelliousness among young people also affected the literary scene in New York City. New York was a literary center, the home of a number of publishing houses, newspapers, and magazines. **Edith Wharton** chronicled the breakdown of the traditional ways of life of the wealthy citizens of old New York in such novels as *The Age of Innocence,* written in 1920. In the 1920s and 1930s, New York became a center for avant-garde, bohemian writers, artists, and intellectuals, many of whom lived and worked in the area of lower Manhattan known as Greenwich Village. Here **Eugene O'Neill's** plays were produced by the Greenwich Village Theatre and **Thomas Wolfe** wrote his most famous novel, *Look Homeward, Angel.* During the twenties, thirties, and forties, a group of New York writers and artists, including the humorists **Dorothy Parker** and **Robert Benchley** and the playwright **George S. Kaufman,** met regularly in the dining room of the Algonquin Hotel, forming what has become known as the **Algonquin Round Table.**

The Great Depression and Thirties Radicalism

In 1925, the chief chronicler of the Jazz Age, **F. Scott Fitzgerald,** produced a novel, *The Great Gatsby,* replete with disillusionment and ambivalence about the morality of the ideal "self-made man" in American society. After the financial collapse of 1929, which initiated the period known as the **Great Depression,** many other writers would take such moral and ethi-

Literary Events

► = American Events

►1947. James Michener's *Tales of the South Pacific*
►1954. Wallace Stevens publishes *Collected Poems*
►1953. James Baldwin's *Go Tell It on the Mountain,* Karl Shapiro's *Poems, 1940–1953,* Theodore Roethke's *The Waking,* and Ralph Ellison's *Invisible Man* published
►1948. Truman Capote's *Other Voices, Other Rooms* published
►1949. Arthur Miller publishes *Death of a Salesman*
►1945. Tennessee Williams's *The Glass Menagerie* published
►1952. Ernest Hemingway publishes *The Old Man and the Sea*
►1951. J. D. Salinger's *The Catcher in the Rye* published

1940 **1945** **1950** **1955** **1960**

Historical Events

1936. World War II begins in Europe
►1941. Japanese attack Pearl Harbor; U.S. enters Word War II
►1942. Japanese Americans placed in internment camps
►1944. D-Day invasion; President Roosevelt reelected
►1945. President Roosevelt dies; Harry S Truman succeeds
1945. Atomic bombs dropped on Hiroshima and Nagasaki; World War II ends
►1948. President Truman elected
►1950. U.N. sends troops to South Korea
►1952. Dwight D. Eisenhower elected president
1953. Truce in Korea
►1954. Supreme Court rules racial segregation unconstitutional
►1955. Montgomery bus boycott
►1956. President Eisenhower reelected

cal questioning further, examining basic American ideals of individualism and free market capitalism. During the twenties and thirties, many American writers adopted socialist or communist ideals based on the theories of **Karl Marx**, the German political theorist who argued that the exploitation of workers would lead to the collapse of capitalism and to the establishment of states in which workers controlled the means of production. To many, the Great Depression, which put millions of Americans out of work, seemed proof that the unbridled capitalism of millionaire industrialists, such as **Andrew Carnegie, J. P. Morgan,** and **John D. Rockefeller,** offered little hope for the average worker. In the midst of the Great Depression, hunger, labor unrest in the cities, union organizing, and anarchist bombings seemed to indicate that the United States was headed toward a socialist revolution. That such a revolution did not occur can be attributed to later disillusionment with the totalitarian turn of the Russian communist state under Joseph Stalin, to cyclical economic recovery, and to President **Franklin D. Roosevelt's New Deal** policies, which provided Social Security, welfare, unemployment insurance, and federally funded jobs. In Oklahoma in the 1930s, severe droughts that caused the area to be known as the **Great Dust Bowl** added to the effects of the depression, leading to a great migration of workers to California. This story is eloquently told in **John Steinbeck's** novel *The Grapes of Wrath.* Other critics of American culture in the first half of the century included **Upton Sinclair**, whose book *The Jungle* offered a scathing exposé of the meatpacking industry; **Sinclair Lewis**, whose novels such as *Babbitt* and *Elmer Gantry* depicted the worst excesses of materialism—the hypocrisy and greed of small-town real estate dealers and showman preachers; and **Richard Wright**, whose *Native Son* told of discrimination against African Americans. Many American writers and intellectuals with socialist sympathies fought against fascism in the Spanish Civil War, in 1936–1937, only to turn from socialism on learning of Stalin's brutal purges of political opponents and his treaty with Germany's Adolph Hitler.

Some of the many migrants from the Great Dust Bowl.

The Expatriates

For some, like Fitzgerald, Hemingway, **Ezra Pound, Edna St. Vincent Millay, T. S. Eliot,** and Gertrude Stein, the effort to find more authentic beliefs and forms of expression went beyond the United States. In the teens and twenties, a large number of important American writers were living in Paris and London, comprising an identifiable group of **expatriates** that often gathered in salons and cafes to exchange ideas about art, literature, and society. Some of these writers, such as Pound and Eliot, believed the U. S. to be inhospitable to high culture, reflecting a division between popular culture, with its westerns, romances, and adventure stories, and highbrow culture of the kind now referred to as Modernism.

Modernism in American Literature

Modernism was an international literary and artistic movement characterized by a rejection of the artistic conventions of the past. As such, it was a response to the perceived

Literary Note (cont.)

Olsen, Tillie
Tell Me a Riddle
Parker, Dorothy
Here Lies
Porter, Katherine Anne
Flowering Judas
Ship of Fools
Sinclair, Upton
The Jungle
Stein, Gertrude
The Autobiography of Alice B. Toklas
Steinbeck, John
East of Eden
The Grapes of Wrath
Of Mice and Men
The Pearl
Tyler, Anne
The Accidental Tourist
Walker, Alice
The Color Purple
Warren, Robert Penn
All the King's Men
Understanding Poetry
Welty, Eudora
The Optimist's Daughter
The Robber Bridegroom
Wharton, Edith
The Age of Innocence
Ethan Frome
Williams, Tennessee
17 Wagon Loads of Cotton
Wolfe, Thomas
Look Homeward, Angel
Of Time and the River
You Can't Go Home Again
Wright, Richard
Native Son

LITERARY NOTE

In order to grasp the two very different directions prose took in the early twentieth century, read to students a passage from one of Hemingway's works and one from Faulkner's works. Ask students in what ways the styles of the passages differ. Which style do they prefer? Why? You also might compare the more traditional verse style Frost uses to the more experimental verse forms of a poet like E. E. Cummings.

T. S. Eliot

breakdown of modern culture. This breakdown was reflected graphically in the Cubist paintings of **Pablo Picasso, Georges Braque,** and others, who rendered people, places, and objects as stylized, abstract collections of forms such as cubes. In literature, Modernism found expression in many experiments in form, including **free verse,** such as that of T. S. Eliot and E. E. Cummings, and **stream-of-consciousness** prose, such as the novels of **William Faulkner** that presented the unedited thoughts and impressions passing through characters' minds.[2] Stream-of-consciousness writing was one example of the **subjectivism** of Modernist literature, its tendency to treat reality not as absolute and orderly but as depending upon the point of view of the observer. Modernist works tended to be written in the first person, revealing an individual's momentary thoughts, feelings, or perceptions. Paradoxically, this rendering of subjective experience was often done by omitting conventional commentary about the subjective states of characters. The **Imagist** poetry of Ezra Pound, **Amy Lowell, William Carlos Williams, H. D. (Hilda Doolittle),** and others sought to present single moments of sense perception without reference to the emotions or opinions of the author, narrator, or speaker. Williams formulated this aesthetic in a famous phrase, "no ideas but in things." Modernist writing, including the work of Pound, Eliot, and **Wallace Stevens,** tended to be alienated, understated, ironic, impersonal, lacking in transitions between ideas, and full of odd juxtapositions and sophisticated references, or allusions. If Modernism had a credo, it was probably Ezra Pound's "make it new."

Eliot and Pound saw art as a way to order and give coherence to the decay they saw, but most Modernist writers were tentative about the meanings they discovered. **Irony** became a signature technique of Modernist literature, indicating a retreat from a new social vision into the cold comfort of a purely literary or imaginative order. That comfort was usually limited, and much of the writing of this group conveyed a sense of hopelessness.

CHANGES IN THE ROLES OF WOMEN

Although the twenties and thirties were years of turmoil and disillusionment for many, one bright spot was the expanded role of women in American society. In 1920, women won the right to vote. Increasingly, they were able to attain higher education and entered the world of work outside the home. Some of the male writers of the period targeted women's participation in the literary and artistic world as alienating and disorienting and engaged in what some scholars have called a "war of words." A mild example of this is Eliot's narrator in "The Love Song of J. Alfred Prufrock" who mocks these "new women" in the line "In the room, the women come and go, talking of Michelangelo." The women are portrayed as overcasual in their approach to serious art, treating it as small talk.

The increased role of women in the arts and literature is one of the most dramatic changes to occur during the twentieth century. Of course, the United States had already produced some great women writers, from Anne Bradstreet and Phillis Wheatley in the eighteenth century to Emily Dickinson, Sarah Jewett, and Kate Chopin in the nineteenth. However, the twentieth century has been the golden age of American women writers, including Edith Wharton, **Eudora Welty, Kay Boyle, Willa Cather, Katherine Anne Porter, Zora Neale**

2. While Faulkner was a Modernist in his radical experiments in form, he was a traditionalist in his upholding of older values and in his concentration on regional subject matter.

Hurston, Amy Lowell, **Marianne Moore,** Edna St. Vincent Millay, **Shirley Jackson,** Dorothy Parker, **Lillian Hellman, Gina Berriault, Elizabeth Bishop, May Swenson, Denise Levertov, Gwendolyn Brooks, Anne Sexton, Sylvia Plath, Lucille Clifton, Nikki Giovanni, Adrienne Rich, Tillie Olsen, Alice Walker, Louise Erdrich, Maxine Kumin, Lorraine Hansberry, Li-Young Lee, Amy Bloom, Joyce Carol Oates, Anne Tyler, Marsha Norman,** and **Carol Henley,** to name but a few.

Edna St. Vincent Millay

Alternative Literary Responses: Regionalism and The Harlem Renaissance

During the twenties and thirties, some writers responded to feelings of discontent and hopelessness by probing for sources of renewal in the United States itself. Though often using ideas and techniques of Modernism, they are distinguished from the Modernists in their use of traditional forms and in their expression of traditional values. Prominent among these writers were various postwar **regionalists,** who wrote an "American" literature about the local, rural areas in which they had settled. Sometimes these writers found strength and hope in their works, other times only what poet **Robert Frost** called "a momentary stay against confusion." Such regional writers included Frost, who wrote deceptively simple verses set in rural New England; **Sherwood Anderson,** who lived in New Orleans and wrote of the people of a mythical *Winesburg, Ohio;* Zora Neal Hurston, who wrote novels about the African-American experience in the rural South; and **John Crow Ransom,** a poet and critic associated with a movement to recapture traditional Southern values. The novels of William Faulkner, though Modernist in their experimentation with plot structure and point of view, were nonetheless traditional in their use of a regional setting (Faulkner's mythical Yoknapatawpha County, Mississippi) and in their espousal of the lost values of an older time.

Another important alternative to the attitude and approach of the expatriate Modernists was the politically committed work of the **Harlem Renaissance** in upper Manhattan in the late teens and twenties. The Harlem Renaissance involved not only an explosion of diversely creative work by black artists, writers, and performers, but also a new direction for literature as a force for creating community. African-American writing at the time was sometimes supported financially by the National Association for the Advancement of Colored People (NAACP), formed earlier in the century, and was part of an organized movement to give expression to the oppression African Americans experienced and to the cultural heritage and traditions they shared. The alienation of the Harlem Renaissance writers differed from that of their white counterparts: they were forced into a "double consciousness," as **W. E. B. DuBois** had put it in 1903, of the self they knew and the "black" self-image society foisted on them. Alain Locke, in his 1925 book *The New Negro,* envisioned Harlem as a "race capital" where black culture, consciousness, and identity might find adequate social expression and stimulation and serve as a vital source for the future advancement of black people and "a new democracy in American culture." The social purpose behind this movement's literature influenced its choice of techniques and styles, as it sought to reach the entire community, not merely its most highly educated members. Important poets of the Harlem Renaissance include **Langston Hughes, Paul Laurence Dunbar, Countee Cullen, Claude McKay, Arna Bontemps,** and **Jean Toomer.**

Additional Questions and Activities

To impress upon your students the dramatic pace of change during the twentieth century, have them spend a day keeping a log in their journals of all the things that they encounter that did not exist before the twentieth century. Have students share their lists with one another in class.

QUOTABLES

"The horror of the Twentieth Century is the size of each event and the poverty of its reverberation."

—Norman Mailer

"An era can be said to end when its basic illusions are exhausted."

—Arthur Miller

Robert Lowell

World War II

World War I was supposed to be the war to end all wars. Events at mid-century would show how wrong that notion was. The Great Depression of the 1930s was a worldwide phenomenon, and citizens of several countries in Europe reacted by placing their hopes in the hands of ultranationalist leaders—Francisco Franco in Spain, Benito Mussolini in Italy, and Adolph Hitler in Germany. Expounding mystical, pseudoscientific theories of "racial purity" and a belief that the so-called "Aryan race" was destined to rule the world, Hitler initiated a campaign to conquer Europe, beginning with an invasion of Poland. The United States was reluctant to enter the war, doing so only after Germany's ally, Japan, attacked the American naval base at Pearl Harbor, Hawaii. **World War II** lasted until 1945, when the United States dropped atomic bombs on the Japanese cities of Hiroshima and Nagasaki, and the Allied Forces of the United States, Britain, and France captured the German capital of Berlin. Only after the war did the full extent of the atrocities committed by Hilter's Nazis become known, when it was revealed that Germany had conducted a systematic campaign to exterminate millions of Jews, Gypsies, and others in death camps such as Auschwitz and Buchenwald.

Postwar Literature: The Second American Renaissance

The period following World War II is sometimes referred to as the Second American Renaissance (the first being the New England Renaissance of the nineteenth century). This was a period of relative prosperity in the United States, punctuated by the beginnings of the Cold War and social and political conservatism in most of the population. It was also a time of great literary creativity. The war itself gave rise to many fine literary works, including Ernest Hemingway's *For Whom the Bell Tolls,* **Norman Mailer's** *The Naked and the Dead,* and **James Jones's** *From Here to Eternity.* Many of the finest American writers of the early to mid-century period were at the height of their powers during this time, including Faulkner, Frost, Eliot, and Stevens. Other great writers who continued to produce superb work in the forties and fifties included John Steinbeck, Katherine Anne Porter, Marianne Moore, E. E. Cummings, William Carlos Williams, Lillian Hellman, and Eugene O'Neill. The postwar period saw a flowering of American drama in work by new dramatists such as **Arthur Miller, Tennessee Williams,** and **William Inge,** as well as new work by established dramatists such as Eugene O'Neill and Lillian Hellman. The period also saw the emergence of important new voices, including those of fiction writers **Robert Penn Warren, James Baldwin, Saul Bellow,** and **Bernard Malamud,** and those of poets Gwendolyn Brooks, **Robert Lowell, Theodore Roethke,** and **Randall Jarrell.**

Echoes:
The Modern Age

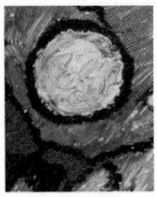

"Literature is news that STAYS news."
—Ezra Pound, from *The ABC of Reading*

"The critic . . . , if he is to justify his existence, should endeavor to discipline his personal prejudices and cranks . . . and compose his differences with as many of his fellows as possible, in the common pursuit of true judgment."
—T. S. Eliot, from "The Function of Criticism"

"She ran the whole gamut of emotions from A to B."
—Dorothy Parker, on a performance by an actress

"[L]ove and the imagination
are of a piece"
—William Carlos Williams,
coda to "Asphodel, That Greeny Flower"

". . . the old universal truths lacking which any story is ephemeral and doomed—love and honor and pity and pride and compassion and sacrifice."
—William Faulkner, from his Nobel Prize
Acceptance Speech

"Writing free verse is like playing tennis with the net down."
—Robert Frost, from his Speech to the Milton Academy

"My soul has grown deep like the rivers."
—Langston Hughes, from "The Negro Speaks of Rivers"

ADDITIONAL RESOURCES

READER'S GUIDE
- Selection Worksheets, 8.1, 8.2

ASSESSMENT PORTFOLIO
- Selection Check Tests, 4.8.1, 4.8.3
- Selection Tests, 4.8.2, 4.8.4

ESSENTIAL SKILLS PRACTICE BOOKS
- *Language,* 2.16, 2.17, 2.36

ENRICHMENT ACTIVITIES

Have students write epitaphs, written from the first-person point of view, describing the lives they imagine themselves living. Ask them to consider what events will be important to them. For what accomplishments, beliefs, and attitudes would they wish to be remembered?

SUPPORT FOR LEP STUDENTS

Share with students the following additional vocabulary.

ADDITIONAL VOCABULARY

discontent—restless desire for something more or different
degenerate—having sunk below a normal or former condition or character

PREREADING

from *Spoon River Anthology*
"Lucinda Matlock"
"Petit, the Poet"
by Edgar Lee Masters

ABOUT THE AUTHOR

Edgar Lee Masters (1868–1950) was born in Garnett, Kansas, but grew up in two small Illinois towns, Petersburg and Lewiston. Life in such small towns inspired his best-known work, *Spoon River Anthology* (1915). Masters briefly attended Knox College in Galesburg, Illinois; studied law in his father's office; and passed the bar. In 1891, he moved to Chicago, where he worked as a bill collector for the Edison Company until he was able to build a successful law practice. He later formed a law firm in which Clarence Darrow, the great criminal defense lawyer, was a partner. All the while, he was writing poems, having some published and many rejected. When an editor sent him a copy of *Selected Epigrams from the Greek Anthology,* Masters adapted the mode to his work. Harriet Monroe, editor of *Poetry: A Magazine of Verse,* discovered his work in this style and helped him get the work published as *Spoon River Anthology.* The book was an instant and undreamed of success. Masters gave up law and moved to New York City in the 1920s. His writing career included novels, plays, and biographies, but none of his other work ever achieved the recognition of *Spoon River Anthology.*

ABOUT THE SELECTIONS

"Lucinda Matlock" and **"Petit, the Poet"** are from *Spoon River Anthology,* a collection of **epitaphs** (verse written to be inscribed on a tomb or to be read in commemoration of someone who has died). The speakers in these poems all address the reader from beyond the grave, telling about the lives that they lived. First serialized in the St. Louis *Mirror* in 1914–1915 under Masters's pseudonym, Webster Ford, these epitaphs tell stories reminiscent of the life stories of people whom Masters knew in Petersburg and Lewiston, Illinois, near the Spoon River. Many of the names that Masters used in his anthology can be found on tombstones in the Lewiston cemetery.

GOALS/OBJECTIVES

Studying this lesson will enable students to

- appreciate poetic epitaphs
- understand the life and work of Edgar Lee Masters
- identify gerunds and participles
- write an epitaph and a ballad
- identify interrogative sentences
- define *metaphor* and *simile* and identify examples of them in their reading
- compare and contrast poets
- identify and replace clichés and euphemisms

READER'S JOURNAL

Have you ever known someone who lived to be quite old? What attitude toward life did that person express? What advice did that person have? Write about the person in your journal. If you have not known an elderly person well, write about the kind of person you would like to be when you are quite old.

LANGUAGE SKILLS

Read the Language Arts Survey, 2.16, "Verbals: Participles," and 2.17, "Verbals: Gerunds." Then identify some verbs ending in *–ing* in the selection, and note whether each verb is a participle or a gerund.

FROM *SPOON RIVER ANTHOLOGY*

"Lucinda Matlock"

EDGAR LEE MASTERS

I went to the dances at Chandlerville,
And played snap-out[1] at Winchester.
One time we changed partners,
Driving home in the moonlight of middle June,
5 And then I found Davis.
We were married and lived together for seventy years,
Enjoying, working, raising the twelve children,
Eight of whom we lost
Ere[2] I had reached the age of sixty.
10 I spun, I wove, I kept the house, I nursed the sick,
I made the garden, and for holiday
Rambled over the fields where sang the larks,
And by Spoon River gathering many a shell,
And many a flower and medicinal weed—
15 Shouting to the wooded hills, singing to the green valleys.
At ninety-six I had lived enough, that is all,
And passed to a sweet repose.[3]
What is this I hear of sorrow and weariness,
Anger, discontent and drooping hopes?
20 Degenerate sons and daughters,
Life is too strong for you—
It takes life to love Life. ■

1. **snap-out.** Parlor game
2. **Ere.** Before
3. **repose.** Rest

❶ *How many children did the speaker have? How many of her children were still living when the speaker turned sixty?*

PREREADING NOTES

READER'S JOURNAL

Ask students to think about the phrase "You're only as old as you think you are." In what ways might this be true? How can attitude affect age? What are students' attitudes toward aging? toward living a long life?

LANGUAGE SKILLS

Some examples are

Enjoying, working, raising—gerunds; *drooping*—participle (modifies *hope*)

▶Additional practice is provided in the *Essential Skills Practice Book: Language*, 2.16 and 2.17.

ANSWER TO GUIDED READING QUESTION

❶ The speaker had twelve children. When she turned sixty, four were still living.

ANSWERS TO SELECTION CHECK TEST 4.8.1

EX. What did the speaker do in Chandlerville?
The speaker went to the dances there.

1. When did the speaker find Davis?
The speaker found Davis in June.

2. How long was the speaker married?
The speaker was married seventy years.

3. How many children did the speaker have?
The speaker had twelve children.

4. Where did the speaker gather shells?
The speaker gathered shells by Spoon River.

5. What is needed to love Life?
Life is needed to love Life.

ANALYTIC SCALES FOR RESPONDING IN WRITING

Assign a score from 1 to 25 for each grading criterion below. (For more detailed evaluation, see the evaluation forms for writing, revising, and proofreading, *Assessment Portfolio*, 7.1–7.10.)

Epitaph

- **Content/Unity.** The epitaph relates the events or activities of the deceased person's life as well as the person's feelings and attitudes.
- **Organization/Coherence.** The epitaph is organized in a coherent, logical manner such as chronological order.
- **Language/Style.** The epitaph uses vivid and precise nouns, verbs, and modifiers.
- **Conventions.** The epitaph avoids errors in spelling, grammar, usage, mechanics, and manuscript form.

RESPONDING TO THE SELECTION

After experimenting with Lucinda Matlock's philosophy, students may wish to write their own philosophies. Students might wish to illustrate their philosophies with things that give them joy or reasons to see the world with wonder rather than with cynicism. Philosophies might then be displayed or shared with others.

ANSWERS FOR REVIEWING THE SELECTION

RECALLING

1. Lucinda marries Davis.
2. Lucinda collects shells near Spoon River.
3. At the age of ninety-six she decided she had lived long enough.
4. Lucinda calls her sons and daughters degenerate.

INTERPRETING

Responses will vary. Possible responses are given.

5. With her husband Lucinda enjoys life, works hard, and raises their children.
6. Lucinda collects medicinal herbs to treat the sick. Eight of Lucinda's children died before she was sixty.
7. "Sweet repose" is a euphemism for death.
8. Her sons and daughters do not embrace life the way that Lucinda did. They do not have the life it takes to love life.

SYNTHESIZING

Responses will vary. Possible responses are given.

9. Lucinda has a strong spirit. She enjoys the when and where of her life, finding pleasure where she is. She accepts that work and sorrow are part of life. She has not allowed herself to be bogged down in sorrow, weariness, anger, discontent, or drooping hopes.
10. Lucinda thinks that many people of the younger generation are

(cont.)

ANALYTIC SCALES FOR RESPONDING IN WRITING

Grading scales appear on page 511.

Responding to the Selection

Imagine that you are Lucinda Matlock. Write a letter to your "degenerate sons and daughters," explaining to them your philosophy of life.

Reviewing the Selection

RECALLING

1. Whom does Lucinda marry?
2. What does Lucinda collect near the Spoon River?
3. At what age does Lucinda decide that she "had lived enough"?
4. What does Lucinda call her sons and daughters?

INTERPRETING

5. What kind of life does Lucinda have with her husband?
6. Why does Lucinda have to collect medicinal herbs? What tragedies occurred in her life?
7. For what is "sweet repose" a euphemism?
8. Why is life "too strong" for her sons and daughters?

SYNTHESIZING

9. What qualities may have enabled Lucinda to live to be ninety-six?
10. What criticism does Lucinda have of the younger generation? Would she be sympathetic to what younger people consider to be the hardships in their lives? How would she react to people who complain all the time about how difficult their lives are? Why? Why does Lucinda believe that "It takes life to love Life"?

Understanding Literature (Questions for Discussion)

Tone. Tone is the emotional attitude toward the reader or toward the subject implied by a literary work. What tone, or emotional attitude, does Lucinda Matlock express toward weakness and sorrow? What attitude does she express toward life?

Responding in Writing

Epitaph. Think of someone who died within the last ten years. Gather some information about that person. Then write an epitaph to be inscribed on that person's grave. Have the speaker of the epitaph be the dead person, telling about his or her own life.

ANSWERS FOR REVIEWING THE SELECTION (CONT.)

not strong enough for life and that they let discontent and drooping hopes beat them down. Lucinda would have little sympathy for people who complain about life's hardships. Lucinda believes that you have to live the life you have rather than be unhappy that a different life is not yours.

ANSWERS FOR UNDERSTANDING LITERATURE

► See the evaluation forms for discussion, active listening, and oral communication, *Assessment Portfolio,* 7.11–7.14.

Responses will vary. Possible responses are given.

Tone. Lucinda Matlock looks on weakness and sorrow with scorn and contempt. "What is this I hear of sorrow and weariness,/Anger, discontent and drooping hopes?" she asks, suggesting that she has no patience for people who complain of these things. She believes that life should be loved but that one has to be strong and have life to love it.

READER'S JOURNAL

Who is your favorite poet? What attracts you to his or her poetry? Which poems written by this person do you find particularly moving or expressive? Write about your favorite poet and his or her poetry in your journal. (If you do not yet have a favorite poet, look through this anthology until you find a poem that you really like and write about that poem.)

LANGUAGE SKILLS

Read the Language Arts Survey, 2.36, "The Functions of Sentences." Then identify the interrogative sentences in the selection and note what tone the question marks lend to each sentence.

FROM *SPOON RIVER ANTHOLOGY*

"Petit, the Poet"

EDGAR LEE MASTERS

Seeds in a dry pod, tick, tick, tick,
Tick, tick, tick, like mites[1] in a quarrel—
Faint iambics that the full breeze wakens—
But the pine tree makes a symphony thereof.
5 Triolets, villanelles, rondels, rondeaus,
Ballades by the score with the same old thought:
The snows and the roses of yesterday are vanished,
And what is love but a rose that fades?
Life all around me here in the village:
10 Tragedy, comedy, valor[2] and truth,
Courage, constancy, heroism, failure—
All in the loom, and oh what patterns!
Woodlands, meadows, streams and rivers—
Blind to all of it all my life long.
15 Triolets, villanelles, rondels, rondeaus,
Seeds in a dry pod, tick, tick, tick,
Tick, tick, tick, what little iambics,
While Homer and Whitman[3] roared in the pines? ■

1 *To what does the speaker compare life in the village?*

1. **mites.** Small insects
2. **valor.** Courage
3. **Homer and Whitman.** *Homer*—Ancient Greek poet; *Whitman*—Walt Whitman (1819–1892), American poet, one of the first to write in free verse

PREREADING NOTES

READER'S JOURNAL

After writing in their journals students can discuss their favorite poems and poets and what they like or don't like about poetry.

LANGUAGE SKILLS

The interrogative sentences in the selection are "The snows and the roses of yesterday are vanished,/ And what is love but a rose that fades?" and "Tick, tick, tick, what little iambics,/While Homer and Whitman roared in the pines?"

ANSWER TO GUIDED READING QUESTION

1 The speaker compares life in the village to patterns woven on a loom.

ANSWERS TO SELECTION CHECK TEST 4.8.3

EX. What sound do seeds in a dry pod make?
They make the sound "tick, tick, tick."

1. What wakens the "faint iambics"?
The full breeze wakens the faint iambics.

2. What has vanished?
The snows and the roses of yesterday have vanished.

3. What question does the speaker ask about love?
The speaker asks, "And what is love but a rose that fades?"

4. To what was the speaker blind?
The speaker was blind to the life that surrounded him or her.

5. Who roared in the pines?
Homer and Whitman roared in the pines.

SUPPORT FOR LEP STUDENTS

Students may have difficulty understanding some of the literary terms used in the poem. Students need not be familiar with the exact nature of the verse forms described but should be aware that the speaker is referring to elaborate French verse forms. In addition to going over these literary terms with students, you should familiarize students with the additional vocabulary below.

ADDITIONAL VOCABULARY

constancy—firmness of mind or purpose
loom—machine for weaving thread or yarn into cloth

RESPONDING TO THE SELECTION

Samples of Whitman's poetry appear on pages 405, 406, 471, and 491. Students might wish to review these poems or others by Whitman as well as poetry by Homer before answering the question. Students might also write to other poets they admire.

ANSWERS FOR REVIEWING THE SELECTION

RECALLING

1. Petit compares his poetry to seeds in a dry pod, mites in a quarrel, and faint iambics woken by the breeze.

2. Petit wrote in triolets, villanelles, rondels, rondeaus, and ballades.

INTERPRETING

Responses will vary. Possible responses are given.

3. The image of dry seeds ticking in a pod suggests repetition, dryness, and a lack of vitality or life. Mites quarreling suggest a smallness of scope or pettiness. The faintness of the iambics reiterates this theme.

4. The tragedy, comedy, valor, truth, courage, constancy, heroism, and failure of life as well as the woodlands, meadows, streams, and rivers were ignored by Petit during his entire life. He regrets that his poetry does not celebrate these things.

SYNTHESIZING

Responses will vary. Possible responses are given.

5. Petit says that the poetry of Homer and Whitman roared in the pines, meaning it was full of life and vigor. Petit wishes he had written more powerful, vital poetry.

Responding to the Selection

Imagine that you are Petit, the poet. What do you admire about the poetry of Homer and Whitman? In your journal, write a letter to the two great poets, telling them what you think about their work.

Reviewing the Selection

RECALLING

1. To what three things does Petit compare his own poetry in lines 1–3?

2. In what different poetic forms did Petit write? What thoughts did his poems express?

INTERPRETING

3. Based on what Petit says about his poetry in lines 1–3, what characteristics would you say that it had?

4. What did Petit ignore as possible subjects for his poetry? What regrets does he have in this regard?

SYNTHESIZING

5. Petit compares the poetry that he wrote to seeds in a dry pod. Such seeds, of course, are not alive and will cause nothing to happen. To what does Petit compare the poetry of Homer and Whitman? In what ways does Petit wish that his verse had been different?

Understanding Literature (Questions for Discussion)

1. **Metaphor.** A **metaphor** is a figure of speech in which one thing is spoken or written about as if it were another. This figure of speech invites the reader to make a comparison between the two things, which can be analyzed into two parts: the *tenor* (or subject being described) and the *vehicle* (or object being used in the description). These two things can be compared because they share a particular quality. Consider the following metaphor from the selection: "While Homer and Whitman roared in the pines?" What is the tenor in this metaphor? What is the vehicle? What qualities do these two things share?
2. **Simile.** A type of metaphor, a **simile** is a comparison using *like* or *as*. Like any other metaphor, a simile can be analyzed into two parts, the *tenor* and the *vehicle*. Consider the following simile from the selection: "Seeds in a dry pod, tick, tick, tick,/Tick, tick, tick, like mites in a quarrel." What is the tenor of the simile? What is the vehicle? What quality do these two things share?
3. **Iamb and Iambic.** An **iamb** is a poetic foot made up of one weakly stressed syllable followed by one strongly stressed syllable, as in the word *afraid*. A line of poetry made up of iambs is said to be **iambic.** Petit describes his poetry as being made up of "faint iambics." With what should Petit have been concerned other than creating poems with regular rhythmical patterns?

ANSWERS FOR UNDERSTANDING LITERATURE

▶ See the evaluation forms for discussion, active listening, and oral communication, *Assessment Portfolio,* 7.11–7.14.

Responses will vary. Possible responses are given.

1. Metaphor. Homer and Whitman are the tenor. Wind that roars through the trees is the vehicle. The two things share power, vitality, and the force to move other things.

2. Simile. The tenor is seeds in a dry pod. The vehicle is mites in a quarrel. The two things make a small, almost unnoticeable sound that has little effect on people.

3. Iamb and Iambic. Petit should have been concerned with the emotion of his poetry—of choosing subjects from the rich life that surrounded him.

Responding in Writing

Ballad. Write a ballad, a simple narrative poem in four-line stanzas that rhyme *abcb,* about someone who has a particular skill or talent, such as a poet, cabinetmaker, gardener, or singer. To what will you compare the person's talent or ability? Use metaphors in your ballad to invite the reader to make comparisons. Refer to the entry on *metaphor* in the Handbook of Literary Terms.

Language Lab

Clichés and Euphemisms. Read the Language Arts Survey, 2.152, "Clichés and Euphemisms." Then rewrite the following sentences, replacing the clichés and euphemisms.

1. Martin whispered to Yolanda, "Love is like a red, red rose."
2. The minister told Sasha that time heals all wounds.
3. Paula looked out the window and saw that it was raining cats and dogs.
4. After chopping a cord of firewood, Jason felt dog tired.
5. Deidre's mother was determined to look on the bright side of the situation.

Thinking Skills

Comparing and Contrasting. Read the Language Arts Survey, 4.8, "Comparing and Contrasting." Then, make two columns on a piece of paper, one headed *Petit* and the other headed *Homer and Whitman.* To the left of the columns, write *Compare* and then under that, write *Contrast.* Draw lines across your page starting under each of these two words. List the characteristics of each poet within the boxes of the chart you have created with these four headings.

PROJECT

Circle Poetry Reading. Select a poem from *Spoon River Anthology* for each person in the class. Then sit in a circle and take turns reading aloud the epitaphs. As you read, try to imagine yourself as the speaker of the poem. As you listen, try to draw conclusions about the speaker's character from what he or she has to say. Ask yourself, each time, What lesson did this person learn from his or her life?

ANALYTIC SCALES FOR RESPONDING IN WRITING

Assign a score from 1 to 25 for each grading criterion below. (For more detailed evaluation, see the evaluation forms for writing, revising, and proofreading, *Assessment Portfolio,* 7.1–7.10.)

Ballad

- **Content/Unity.** The ballad describes the skill of a person with a specific talent and invites the reader to compare the talent to something else through the use of metaphor.
- **Organization/Coherence.** The ballad is organized in a coherent, logical manner in four-line stanzas.
- **Language/Style.** The ballad employs vivid, precise, and colorful nouns, verbs, and modifiers.
- **Conventions.** The ballad avoids errors in spelling, grammar, usage, mechanics, and manuscript form.

ANSWERS FOR THINKING SKILLS

Similarities include being deceased poets. Some differences are explored in Reviewing the Selection, question 5, and in the Understanding Literature questions. Students might refer to these questions to help them contrast the poets.

PROJECT NOTES

Circle Poetry Reading
Students may wish to read the poems a few times to allow them to understand better the people eulogized in the poems. Students might wish to make a book of life lessons based on lessons gathered from the poems.

ANSWERS FOR LANGUAGE LAB

1. Martin whispered to Yolanda, "Love is like a roller coaster ride in the rain."
2. The minister told Sasha that her pain and suffering would end one day.
3. Paula looked out the window and saw torrents of rain pouring from the sky.
4. After chopping a cord of firewood, Jason had no energy left.
5. Deidre's mother was determined not to be discouraged by the bad situation.

► Additional practice is provided in the *Essential Skills Practice Book: Language,* 2.152.

ADDITIONAL RESOURCES

READER'S GUIDE
- Selection Worksheet, 8.3

ASSESSMENT PORTFOLIO
- Selection Check Test, 4.8.5
- Selection Test, 4.8.6

ESSENTIAL SKILLS PRACTICE BOOKS
- *Writing,* 1.34

ENRICHMENT ACTIVITIES

Students can discuss Flood's tendency of talking aloud to himself. Remind students that the soliloquy has been used throughout English and American literature to reveal a lone character's thoughts and feelings. Students can debate whether Flood's conversations with himself are an essential part of his character, a literary technique used to reveal his feelings, or both.

SUPPORT FOR LEP STUDENTS

ADDITIONAL VOCABULARY

forsaken—abandoned; desolate; forlorn

warily—cautiously

huskily—in a manner that sounds deep and hoarse

valiant—full of or characterized by courage

salutation—act of greeting, addressing, or welcoming by gesture or words

PREREADING

"Mr. Flood's Party"
by Edwin Arlington Robinson

ABOUT THE AUTHOR

Edwin Arlington Robinson (1869–1935) was raised in the small town of Gardiner, Maine—a community he renamed "Tilbury Town" in some of his best poetry. A lonely child, Robinson's feelings of alienation followed him into maturity. He once wrote to a friend, "What strength I have is the result of tedious and almost intolerable isolation." Poor self-esteem plagued Robinson all of his life and was not eased when lack of funds forced him to drop out of Harvard. Then, depending on handouts to support himself as a poet, Robinson went into seclusion, feeling he had failed himself and his friends and family. In 1910, in spite of his pessimistic style, Robinson achieved critical acclaim with a fourth volume of poetry, *The Town Down the River.* His trilogy of long narrative poems based on the legends of King Arthur—*Merlin, Lancelot,* and *Tristram*—led to wider understanding of his work. During the 1920s, Robinson was a three-time winner of the Pulitzer Prize. Sometimes described as a "bridge" poet, Robinson's work reflects much of the traditional form of the nineteenth century, yet dwells on the problems of the inner self, which is more in keeping with twentieth-century styles.

ABOUT THE SELECTION

Psychological exploration of character is a central element in Robinson's longer narrative poems. In **"Mr. Flood's Party,"** the focus is on the character Eben Flood, an aging man who, in his loneliness, makes a party for one and engages in a dialogue with himself.

GOALS/OBJECTIVES

Studying this lesson will enable students to

- empathize with a speaker's feelings of loneliness
- describe Robinson's literary accomplishments and explain the historical significance of his writing
- define *simile* and *allusion* and recognize these techniques in literature they read
- identify different ways of organizing ideas
- expand sentences
- write a toast

READER'S JOURNAL

Have you ever felt alienated or lonely? What caused you to feel that way? What did you do to dispel that feeling? Write about the experience in your journal.

WRITING SKILLS

Read the Language Arts Survey, 1.34, "Organizing Ideas." Then identify the method of organization used in the poem and note why that method is appropriate for a narrative poem, one that tells a story.

"Mr. Flood's Party"

EDWIN ARLINGTON ROBINSON

Old Eben Flood, climbing alone one night
Over the hill between the town below
And the forsaken upland hermitage[1]
That held as much as he should ever know
On earth again of home, paused warily.
The road was his with not a native near;
And Eben, having leisure, said aloud,
For no man else in Tilbury Town to hear:

"Well, Mr. Flood, we have the harvest moon
Again, and we may not have many more;
The bird is on the wing, the poet says.[2]
And you and I have said it here before.
Drink to the bird." He raised up to the light
The jug that he had gone so far to fill,
And answered huskily: "Well, Mr. Flood,
Since you propose it, I believe I will."

❶ *What time of year is it? What two signs tell you?*

❷ *To whom is Eben Flood speaking?*

1. **upland hermitage.** Retreat house on a hill; monastery

2. **The bird . . . the poet says.** Flood may be thinking of these lines from *The Rubáiyát* by Omar Khayyám: "Come, fill the Cup . . . . The bird of Time has but a little way/To fly—and Lo! the Bird is on the Wing." He might also be thinking, ironically, of these lines from Robert Browning's verse play *Pippa Passes:* "The lark's on the wing;/The snail's on the thorn:/God's in his heaven—/All's right with the world!"

PREREADING NOTES

READER'S JOURNAL

Students should explain what strategies they have used or can use to cope with feelings of alienation or loneliness. What resources, both external and internal, do people draw upon to relieve these feelings? Do students believe that periods of loneliness can be valuable as well as being difficult? Why, or why not?

WRITING SKILLS

Students should have little difficulty recognizing that the narrative poem is written in chronological order, as indicated by its use of transitional words and phrases such as *then, and only when,* and *again.*

ANSWERS TO GUIDED READING QUESTIONS

❶ It is autumn. The harvest moon and the migrating birds indicate the season.

❷ Eben Flood is speaking to himself.

VOCABULARY FROM THE SELECTION

acquiescent
convivially

ADDITIONAL QUESTIONS AND ACTIVITIES

• Students might discuss the significance of the title of this poem. Ask students why the title is ironic. In what way does Mr. Flood's party differ from a conventional party? What does the solitary and lonely party reveal about Flood's character?

• Students might also be interested in discussing the significance of Eben Flood's name. You might tell them that the name *Eben* is suggestive of the word *ebb,* indicating a receding, or weakening and lessening, of water or of power and vitality. *Flood* may be suggestive of a temporary rush of feeling or emotion. Ask students to discuss the ways in which Eben Flood is experiencing both an ebbing of vitality and a flooding of emotion.

Answers to Guided Reading Questions

❶ Flood's friends have all died.

❷ The jug is compared to a sleeping child, or a fragile human life.

Answers to Selection Check Test 4.8.5

EX. With whom does Mr. Flood carry on a conversation?
Mr. Flood carries on a conversation with himself.

1. Where is Mr. Flood walking?
Mr. Flood is walking on a road between a town and a hermitage on a hill.

2. What does Mr. Flood carry with him?
Mr. Flood carries a jug "he had gone so far to fill."

3. What does Mr. Flood toast?
Mr. Flood toasts a bird in a poem.

4. Where are Mr. Flood's friends?
They are dead.

5. What does Mr. Flood sing?
Mr. Flood sings,"For auld lang syne."

What has happened to Flood's friends? ❶

To what is the jug compared? ❷

Alone, as if enduring to the end
A valiant armor of scarred hopes outworn,
He stood there in the middle of the road
Like Roland's ghost winding a silent horn.[3]
Below him, in the town among the trees,
Where friends of other days had honored him,
A phantom salutation of the dead
Rang thinly till old Eben's eyes were dim.

Then, as a mother lays her sleeping child
Down tenderly, fearing it may awake,
He set the jug down slowly at his feet
With trembling care, knowing that most things break;
And only when assured that on firm earth
It stood, as the uncertain lives of men
Assuredly did not, he paced away,
And with his hand extended paused again:

"Well, Mr. Flood, we have not met like this
In a long time; and many a change has come
To both of us, I fear, since last it was
We had a drop together. Welcome home!"
Convivially returning with himself,
Again he raised the jug up to the light;
And with an acquiescent quaver said:
"Well, Mr Flood, if you insist, I might.

"Only a very little, Mr. Flood—
For auld lang syne.[4] No more, sir; that will do."
So, for the time, apparently it did,
And Eben evidently thought so too;

3. **Roland's . . . horn.** The line is an allusion to the Christian martyr/soldier Roland, hero of the medieval French epic poem *The Song of Roland*, who failed to blow his horn to call Charlemagne and his troops to come to his aid in battle.

4. **auld lang syne.** In Scottish dialect, these words mean, literally, "old long since." The phrase is from a song about remembered friendship by Robert Burns, the national poet of Scotland. This song is traditionally sung in English-speaking countries on New Year's Day.

Words for Everyday Use:
con • viv • i • al • ly (kən viv´ē əl lē) *adv.,* festively
ac • qui • es • cent (ak´wē es´ənt) *adj.,* without protest

Vocabulary in Context

- Scrooge's nephew greeted him convivially, as he was filled with holiday spirit and both surprised and pleased to see his uncle.
- When I asked Lydia if she minded my using her computer, she gave an acquiescent shrug and said, "Go right ahead."

45 For soon amid the silver loneliness
Of night he lifted up his voice and sang,
Secure, with only two moons listening,
Until the whole harmonious landscape rang—

"For auld lang syne." The weary throat gave out;
50 The last word wavered, and the song was done.
He raised again the jug regretfully
And shook his head, and was again alone.
There was not much that was ahead of him,
And there was nothing in the town below—
55 Where strangers would have shut the many doors
That many friends had opened long ago. ■

❶ *What double meaning does this line have?*

Responding to the Selection

How did you feel toward Flood after reading the poem? What makes this poem both funny and sad?

Reviewing the Selection

Recalling

1. Where is Flood going and at what time? To whom does Flood speak?
2. What line from a poem does Flood quote in stanza 2?
3. What does Flood know about "most things"?
4. With whom does Flood hold a party? What song does he sing? Whom does he welcome home?

Interpreting

5. Why is he talking to himself? In what sense does he have leisure?
6. What does Flood not expect to have many more of? What, in addition to the bird, is on the wing? What is he toasting when he drinks "to the bird"?
7. How does Flood feel about life?
8. Under what circumstances do people normally sing "Auld Lang Syne"? What do the words *auld lang syne* mean? Why is this a sad situation?

Synthesizing

9. What circumstances in the poem cause the reader or listener to feel empathy for Flood?
10. Why does Flood engage in a dialogue with himself and sing "For auld lang syne"?

Answer to Guided Reading Question

❶ The line means both that there physically was nothing substantial or important in front of him and that he did not have much to look forward to before dying.

Responding to the Selection

You might ask students to discuss how they might have reacted had they been present to observe Flood. Would they have laughed at Flood or felt sympathy for him? Would they have ignored him or kept him company? Ask students if they believe that sometimes we laugh at people and situations to hide our discomfort. Why might a character like Flood evoke some uncomfortable feelings and emotions?

Answers for Reviewing the Selection

RECALLING

1. At night, Flood climbs over the hill between the town and the hermitage. Flood speaks to himself.
2. Flood quotes, "The bird is on the wing" from Omar Khayyám's *The Rubáiyát,* or perhaps he alludes to Robert Browning's *Pippa Passes.*
3. Flood knows that most things break.
4. Flood holds a party with himself. He sings the song "Auld Lang Syne." He welcomes himself home.

INTERPRETING

Responses will vary. Possible responses are given.

5. Flood is alone and lonely. He has leisure for there is no one to notice what he does or says.
6. Flood does not expect to have many more nights with the harvest moon. Time, or Flood's life, is swiftly passing.
7. Flood may be somewhat weary of life. He has scarred hopes, and he has learned that most things in life break.

(cont.)

Answers for Reviewing the Selection (cont.)

8. "Auld Lang Syne" is traditionally sung as part of the celebration of the new year. "Auld lang syne" literally means "old long since." The situation is sad because Flood is alone singing of friendship. He once had friends in the village, but now he does not.

SYNTHESIZING

Responses will vary. Possible responses are given.

9. Flood's loneliness, his scarred hopes, the tenderness he shows, and his knowledge that most things break cause the speaker to feel empathy for Flood. The conversation that he has with himself and his singing of "Auld Lang Syne" emphasize his loneliness.
10. Flood engages in dialogue with himself and sings "Auld Lang Syne" because he cannot bear his loneliness.

Understanding Literature (Questions for Discussion)

1. **Simile. A simile** is a comparison using *like* or *as.* A type of metaphor, a simile can be analyzed into two parts, the *tenor* (or subject being described) and the *vehicle* (or object being used in the description). The two parts of a simile can be compared because they share some particular quality. Consider the following lines from the poem: "Alone, as if enduring to the end/A valiant armor of scarred hopes outworn,/He stood there in the middle of the road,/Like Roland's ghost winding a silent horn." Identify and analyze the parts of each of the two similes contained within these lines. In the medieval French poem *The Song of Roland,* Roland is a warrior who has a horn for the purpose of summoning the aid of other warriors. What causes Flood to look like Roland? What makes the comparison of Flood with a young medieval warrior hero ironic?

2. **Allusion.** An **allusion** is a rhetorical technique in which reference is made to a person, event, object, or work from history or literature. This poem makes an allusion to Robert Burns's song "Auld Lang Syne," the opening lines of which read as follows:

   Should auld acquaintance be forgot
   And never brought to mind?
   Should auld acquaintance be forgot
   And days of auld lang syne.

   How do these lines from the song by Burns relate to Flood's experience on the hill?

Responding in Writing

Toast. Imagine that you are Flood standing on the hill, looking down at Tilbury Town. Write a toast, from Flood's point of view, in honor of the many friends who, long ago, had opened "the many doors" to you.

Language Lab

Expanding Sentences. Read the Language Arts Survey, 2.46–2.50, on expanding sentences. Then expand each of the following sentences by adding modifiers, prepositional phrases, appositives, predicates, or subordinate clauses.

1. Eben Flood walked to the top of the hill.
2. He looked down at Tilbury Town.
3. The harvest moon overhead symbolized not only the decline of the year but also the decline of Flood's life.
4. Flood drank a toast.
5. He remembered his friends.

Answers for Understanding Literature

▶ See the evaluation forms for discussion, active listening, and oral communication, *Assessment Portfolio,* 7.11–7.14.

1. Simile. The tenor of the first simile is Flood; the vehicle is a valiant armor of scarred hopes outworn, enduring to the end. Flood is forlorn and alone after once being with others, yet he endures or goes on with life. In the second simile, Flood is again the tenor. The vehicle is Roland's ghost winding a silent horn. Flood's song, like Roland's silent horn, does not summon others. Again, both figures are left alone. The comparison of Flood to a young medieval hero is ironic because Flood is a lonely, old man who does not seem to be heroic in any way.

2. Allusion. Burns's song refers to friendship and days of old, which is what Flood remembers as he has a lonely party for one on the hill.

Analytic Scales for Responding in Writing

Assign a score from 1 to 25 for each grading criterion below. (For more detailed evaluation, see the evaluation forms for writing, revising, and proofreading, *Assessment Portfolio,* 7.1–7.10.)

Toast

- **Content/Unity.** The toast honors friends from long ago for their kindness to you.
- **Organization/Coherence.** The toast should be organized in a logical order.
- **Language/Style.** The toast employs vivid, precise, and colorful nouns, verbs, and modifiers.
- **Conventions.** The toast avoids errors in spelling, grammar, usage, mechanics, and manuscript form.

Answers for Language Lab

Responses will vary. Possible responses are given.

1. Weary Eben Flood walked slowly to the top of the rocky hill upon a moonlit evening.

2. He, with lonely eyes, looked down the steep slopes at the twinkling lights of Tilbury Town.

3. The orange harvest moon high overhead symbolized not only the decline of the waning year but also the decline of Flood's long life.

4. Alone, Flood drank a touching toast to the friends who had once opened their doors to him.

5. With only himself to talk to, he fondly but sadly remembered his long-lost friends.

▶ **Teaching Note:** Additional practice is provided in the *Essential Skills Practice Book: Language,* 2.46–2.50.

PREREADING

"Grass"
by Carl Sandburg

About the Author

Carl Sandburg (1878–1967) was born in Galesburg, Illinois, the son of an immigrant Swedish blacksmith. He is often considered the poet of America's common people. During his life he was a populist, journalist, folk singer, poet, and biographer. Sandburg left school after the eighth grade and held a variety of jobs until he was twenty, when he enlisted as a volunteer in the Spanish-American War. When he came home, he attended Lombard College in Illinois but left in 1902 without graduating. His poems were first published in 1904, the year he began his journalism career at the Galesburg newspaper. In 1914, some of his poems were published in the magazine *Poetry*, and two years later, his first book of verse was published. During these years he held a variety of political jobs and wrote editorials for the *Milwaukee Leader* and other newspapers. He wrote for the *Chicago Daily News* from 1922 to 1930. Sandburg collected and wrote songs as well as poems and as a young man had traveled the United States reading his work and singing his songs to the accompaniment of a guitar. After World War II, he took his readings to the college campus circuit. He was awarded two Pulitzer Prizes, one for his *Complete Poems* (1950), and the other for his biography *Abraham Lincoln: The War Years* (1939). In later years, Sandburg enjoyed extraordinary acclaim. Several schools in Illinois were named for him, and he was awarded the Presidential Medal of Freedom in 1964. Sandburg wrote several children's stories. In addition to these and his books of biography, his works include *Chicago Poems* (1914), *Cornhuskers* (1918), *Smoke and Steel* (1920), *Slabs of the Sunburnt West* (1922), and *The People, Yes* (1936). Sandburg also compiled collections of folk songs, most notably *The American Songbag* (1927).

About the Selection

Although he participated in the Spanish-American War, Sandburg hated warfare. The following simple poem, **"Grass,"** is one of the most eloquent antiwar poems ever written, all the more so because of its simplicity. The poem **alludes**, or refers, to several battlefields—Austerlitz and Waterloo from the Napoleonic Wars, Gettysburg from the American Civil War, and Ypres and Verdun from World War I.

ADDITIONAL RESOURCES

Reader's Guide
- Selection Worksheet, 8.4

Assessment Portfolio
- Selection Check Test, 4.8.7
- Selection Test, 4.8.8

Essential Skills Practice Books
- *Language*, 2.121

ENRICHMENT ACTIVITIES

Students might research one of the battlefields mentioned in the poem, focusing on the significance the battle fought there had for a particular war. Students can then have a discussion about why Sandburg chose to focus on the massive loss of life rather than describing who was victorious, who was defeated, and why the battle was fought. What attitude does Sandburg take toward war? Do students agree or disagree with his attitude?

SUPPORT FOR LEP STUDENTS

Alert students to Sandburg's use of repetition and ask them to note the slight variations in repeated phrases or ideas. You might also inform students that the speaker envisions passengers on a train viewing the grass-covered battlefields in passing and asking questions of the train's conductor.

GOALS/OBJECTIVES

Studying this lesson will enable students to

- enjoy a poem that personifies a natural object
- recognize and understand the work of Carl Sandburg
- correctly capitalize place names
- understand personification
- identify parallelism in their reading
- write a free verse poem and a slogan

PREREADING NOTES

READER'S JOURNAL

You might ask students whether they have ever visited a battlefield and if so to describe their experience and feelings. If not, students should imagine that they have visited such a site or examine the photograph on this page and describe the feelings a grass-covered cemetery evokes.

LANGUAGE SKILLS

You might also have students read the Language Arts Survey, 2.127, "The Pronoun *I*." Inform students that both the personification of the grass and the use of a capitalized *And* to begin a sentence are poetic techniques.

READER'S JOURNAL

Why do people visit old battlefields? Why are battlefields often set aside for future generations to visit? What kinds of feelings do people have when they visit old battlefields? Write about these questions in your journal.

LANGUAGE SKILLS

Read the Language Arts Survey, 2.121, on the capitalization of place names. Then, as you read the poem, copy the capitalized place names that you find.

"Grass"

CARL SANDBURG

What work does the grass do? ❶

Pile the bodies high at Austerlitz and Waterloo.[1]
Shovel them under and let me work—
I am the grass; I cover all.

And pile them high at Gettysburg[2]
And pile them high at Ypres and Verdun.[3]
Shovel them under and let me work.
Two years, ten years; and passengers ask the conductor:
What place is this?
Where are we now?

I am the grass.
Let me work. ■

1. **Austerlitz and Waterloo.** Northern European battle sites in the Napoleonic Wars
2. **Gettysburg.** Civil War battlefield in southern Pennsylvania where Confederate soldiers fought and lost
3. **Ypres and Verdun.** World War I battle sites in northern France where French soldiers fought and lost

Responding to the Selection

In this poem the grass covers over places of death, hiding the horrors of war. Do you think the grass is hiding human atrocities or is it part of a healing process? Discuss your opinion with your classmates.

ANSWER TO GUIDED READING QUESTION

❶ The grass covers the buried bodies and heals the scars on the land caused by the battlefields and mass graves.

ANSWERS TO SELECTION CHECK TEST 4.8.7

EX. What is the speaker of the poem?
The speaker is grass.

1. What are the places the speaker says to pile bodies?
The speaker says to pile bodies at Austerlitz, Waterloo, Gettysburg, Ypres, and Verdun.

2. What does the speaker say should be done with the bodies?
The speaker says the bodies should be shoveled under in order to let the grass "work."

3. After how much time do the passengers ask questions?
The passengers ask questions after "two years, ten years."

4. Of whom do passengers ask questions?
Passengers ask questions of the conductor.

5. What questions do the passengers ask?
The passengers ask "What place is this? Where are we now?"

RESPONDING TO THE SELECTION

You might ask students whether or not they believe any good comes out of an experience as horrifying as war. If so, what? Ask students what ideals and beliefs are worth fighting for and what one might be able to learn from war.

Reviewing the Selection

RECALLING

1. Who is speaking in this poem? What is the speaker saying?
2. What do the passengers ask the conductor? When?

INTERPRETING

3. What work does the grass do?
4. What change occurs on the battlefields, over time, as a result of the work of the grass?

SYNTHESIZING

5. It is often said about soldiers and the battles in which they fight that they will be remembered forever. Does the speaker of this poem agree? Why, or why not? What indication does this poem give that soldiers' deaths are a terrible waste? Do you agree with the attitude toward soldiers and battles expressed by the speaker of this poem? Why, or why not?

Understanding Literature (Questions for Discussion)

1. **Personification. Personification** is a figure of speech in which an idea, animal, or thing is described as if it were a person. What is personified in this poem? What does that personified thing have to say? What is the work that it performs?
2. **Parallelism. Parallelism** is a rhetorical technique in which a writer emphasizes the equal value or weight of two or more ideas by expressing them in the same grammatical form. Identify instances of parallelism in this poem.

Responding in Writing

1. **Free Verse Poem. Free verse** is poetry that avoids use of regular rhyme, rhythm, meter, or division into stanzas. Write a free verse poem that expresses your feelings about an important issue facing people today.
2. **Slogan.** Many famous battles have been commemorated by slogans such as "Remember the Alamo." A slogan is simply a brief, catchy statement. Choose a cause that you feel strongly about and write a slogan to support that cause.

ANSWERS FOR REVIEWING THE SELECTION

RECALLING

1. Grass is speaking in this poem. The grass is saying that it will cover all the horrors of war. It asks people to let it do its work.

2. Two years or ten years after the bodies have been buried, people ask the conductor where they are and what place they are seeing.

INTERPRETING

Responses will vary. Possible responses are given.

3. The grass covers the bodies and removes the scars of battlefields from the land.

4. The battlefields become unrecognizable as the site of horrific killing. They are green and alive with grass.

SYNTHESIZING

Responses will vary. Possible responses are given.

5. The speaker does not think that soldiers and battles will be remembered forever. Instead the speaker wants to cover over or erase those things. The speaker suggests that the piles of bodies will be buried and later nobody will remember or know why.

ANALYTIC SCALES FOR RESPONDING IN WRITING

Assign a score from 1 to 25 for each grading criterion below. (For more detailed evaluation, see the evaluation forms for writing, revising, and proofreading, *Assessment Portfolio,* 7.1–7.10.)

1. Free Verse Poem

- **Content/Unity.** The poem expresses the feelings of the speaker about an issue of importance to the speaker.
- **Organization/Coherence.** The poem is organized in a coherent, logical manner. It is written in free verse, avoiding use of regular rhyme, rhythm, meter, or division into stanzas.
- **Language/Style.** The poem employs vivid, precise, and colorful nouns, verbs, and modifiers.
- **Conventions.** The poem avoids errors in spelling, grammar, usage, mechanics, and manuscript form.

(cont.)

ANSWERS FOR UNDERSTANDING LITERATURE

▶ See the evaluation forms for discussion, active listening, and oral communication, *Assessment Portfolio,* 7.11–7.14.

Responses will vary. Possible responses are given.

1. Personification. Grass is personified in this poem. Grass offers an appeal to be allowed to do the work of covering the sites of battles.

2. Parallelism. Lines 4 and 5 exhibit parallel structure "And pile them high at . . ." Following those two lines, line 6 is a repetition of line 2 and the combination of lines 5 and 6 parallels that of lines 1 and 2.

ANALYTIC SCALES FOR RESPONDING IN WRITING (CONT.)

2. Slogan

- **Content/Unity.** The slogan offers support for a cause.
- **Organization/Coherence.** The slogan is phrased in a concise, catchy way.
- **Language/Style.** The slogan employs vivid language.
- **Conventions.** The slogan avoids errors in spelling, grammar, usage, mechanics, and manuscript form.

ADDITIONAL RESOURCES

READER'S GUIDE
- Selection Worksheets, 8.5, 8.6

ASSESSMENT PORTFOLIO
- Selection Check Tests, 4.8.9, 4.8.11
- Selection Tests, 4.8.10, 4.8.12

ESSENTIAL SKILLS PRACTICE BOOKS
- *Language,* 2.6, 2.36
- *Speaking and Listening,* 3.3, 3.5

ENRICHMENT ACTIVITIES

Due to the beautiful musical qualities of Frost's poems, they are excellent for reading aloud. Have students read the Language Arts Survey, 3.8, "Oral Interpretation." Then students can read other poems by Robert Frost and, after they have carefully selected cuttings, perform an oral interpretation of some of Frost's work. Frost gave many creative readings of his poems during his lifetime, and recordings of some readings are available from Cædmon Records. Students might also include a poem read by Frost himself in their interpretation.

SUPPORT FOR LEP STUDENTS

You might have students read the Language Arts Survey, 2.64, "Inverting Sentences for Emphasis." Explain to students that Frost frequently inverts conventional sentence order in his poetry. Have students put sentences that are in inverted order into regular order. For example, "Something there is that doesn't love a wall" reads "There is something that doesn't love a wall" in regular order.

ADDITIONAL VOCABULARY

abreast—side by side

mischief—tendency to annoy with playful tricks

notion—general idea; vague thought

PREREADING

"Mending Wall"
"Home Burial"
by Robert Frost

ABOUT THE AUTHOR

Robert Frost (1874–1963) was without question the most popular American poet of the twentieth century. He was born in San Francisco and lived there until the age of eleven, when his father died. After that, Frost and his mother moved to New England. Frost graduated at the top of his high school class, sharing the position of valedictorian with Elinor White, whom he later married. At the age of seventeen, he published his first poem. After marrying Elinor, he continued to hold miscellaneous jobs and to write poetry, briefly going to Harvard as a special student before settling as a teacher at Pinkerton Academy in 1906. In 1912, Frost took his family to England, and it was there that his poetry first found a major audience with the publication of *A Boy's Will* (1913) and *North of Boston* (1914). Frost returned to the United States and began to achieve financial stability from the sale of his books. He taught and lectured at various colleges, including Dartmouth, Amherst, and Harvard. He was awarded Pulitzer Prizes in 1924, 1931, 1937, and 1943 and received honorary degrees from many universities. In 1961, he was invited to read a poem at the inauguration of John F. Kennedy, thirty-fifth president of the United States. Frost's many popular works, most of which deal with New England subject matter, include *Mountain Interval* (1916), *New Hampshire* (1923), *West-Running Brook* (1928), *A Way Out* (1929), *A Witness Tree* (1942), and *In the Clearing* (1962).

ABOUT THE SELECTIONS

Robert Frost had a rare talent that enabled him to produce poetry simple and clear enough to appeal to a large audience and yet intellectually rich enough to appeal to sophisticated literary critics. Frost wrote often of the nature and people of his adopted home of New England. He wrote in the language of ordinary speech and didn't care for modern free verse, which he likened to "playing tennis without a net." Instead, he wrote in conventional forms, including **blank verse** made up of unrhymed iambic pentameter lines, as in **"Mending Wall"** and **"Home Burial."** (An iambic pentameter line has ten alternating weakly stressed and strongly stressed syllables.) Many of Frost's finest poems such as "Home Burial," and "The Death of the Hired Man" in the Selections for Additional Reading on page 602, are **dramatic monologues** or **dramatic dialogues.** Such poems present a dramatic situation in which one or two people speak.

GOALS/OBJECTIVES

Studying this lesson will enable students to
- have a positive experience reading free verse and blank verse poems
- understand the life and work of Robert Frost
- identify personal pronouns
- understand symbols they encounter in their reading
- explain a pun
- write a dialogue and debate
- define *diction* and *tone*
- identify and understand metaphors they encounter in their reading

READER'S JOURNAL

What makes people afraid to reach out to others around them? What kinds of walls do people build around themselves to keep others from getting too close? Why might they do that? Freewrite about these questions in your journal.

LANGUAGE SKILLS

Read the Language Arts Survey, 2.6, "Personal Pronouns." Then identify some uses of the personal pronoun *it* in the selection and note to what noun the pronoun refers.

"Mending Wall"

ROBERT FROST

Something there is that doesn't love a wall,
That sends the frozen-ground-swell[1] under it,
And spills the upper boulders in the sun,
And makes gaps even two can pass abreast.
The work of hunters is another thing:
I have come after them and made repair
Where they have left not one stone on a stone,
But they would have the rabbit out of hiding,
To please the yelping dogs. The gaps I mean,
No one has seen them made or heard them made,
But spring mending-time we find them there.
I let my neighbor know beyond the hill;
And on a day we meet to walk the line
And set the wall between us once again.
We keep the wall between us as we go.
To each the boulders that have fallen to each.
And some are loaves and some so nearly balls
We have to use a spell to make them balance:
"Stay where you are until our backs are turned!"
We wear our fingers rough with handling them.
Oh, just another kind of outdoor game.
One on a side. It comes to little more;
There where it is we do not need the wall:
He is all pine and I am apple orchard.
My apple trees will never get across

1. **frozen-ground-swell.** Winter ground heaves

❶ *What do the speaker and his neighbor do together?*

PREREADING NOTES

READER'S JOURNAL

Ask students what emotional purpose a wall, either physical or psychological, serves. Which function do they believe is more important? Why? Also ask students to consider which type of wall, physical or psychological, is broken down more easily.

LANGUAGE SKILLS

You might also ask students to read the Language Arts Survey, 2.9, "Indefinite Pronouns," and have them identify where indefinite pronouns are used in the poem. Ask students to describe the effect of Frost's use of indefinite pronouns. Why does Frost maintain an atmosphere of ambiguity by refusing to state what, in fact, does not love a wall?

VOCABULARY FROM THE SELECTIONS

cower

ANSWER TO GUIDED READING QUESTION

❶ The speaker and his neighbor meet to mend the broken wall.

QUOTABLES

"Walls have tongues, and hedges ears."

—Jonathan Swift

LITERARY TECHNIQUE

Characterization is the use of literary techniques to create a character. Frost uses direct description and portrayal of behavior to create the character of the speaker's neighbor. Ask students what sort of person they believe the speaker's neighbor is. What do the following characteristics reveal about him: the neighbor's repetition of his father's aphorism, his carrying stones "like an old-stone savage armed," and his moving "in darkness"?

Answers for Understanding Literature

► See the evaluation forms for discussion, active listening, and oral communication, *Assessment Portfolio,* 7.11–7.14.

Responses will vary. Possible responses are given.

1. Symbol. The wall symbolizes separation between people both physically and spiritually. The speaker feels that walls are unnecessary and unnatural. It is ironic that the wall is the one thing that brings the speaker and his neighbor together.

2. Character. The neighbor is a reticent, private person. He looks like an old-stone savage. He says, "Good fences make good neighbors," revealing that he would like to keep his neighbors at a distance. The speaker might want to have a wall between himself and his neighbor because he feels that his neighbor moves in darkness.

3. Pun. The word *offense* could mean to cause somebody to be angry, hurt, or resentful. The pun lies in the similarity to *a fence.*

Answers to Selection Check Test 4.8.9

EX. What doesn't love a wall?
"Something" doesn't love a wall.

1. Who has damaged the wall while looking for a rabbit?
Hunters have damaged the wall.

2. What appears in the wall without anyone seeing or hearing?
Gaps appear without anyone seeing or hearing.

3. Whom does the speaker tell about the gaps?
The speaker tells his neighbor.

4. What does the speaker say is not needed?
The speaker says the wall is not needed.

5. What does the neighbor say about the wall?
The neighbor says, "Good fences make good neighbors."

And eat the cones under his pines, I tell him.
He only says, "Good fences make good neighbors."
Spring is the mischief in me, and I wonder
If I could put a notion in his head:
"*Why* do they make good neighbors? Isn't it
Where there are cows? But here there are no cows.
Before I built a wall I'd ask to know
What I was walling in or walling out,
And to whom I was like to give offense.
Something there is that doesn't love a wall,
That wants it down." I could say "Elves" to him,
But it's not elves exactly, and I'd rather
He said it for himself. I see him there
Bringing a stone grasped firmly by the top
In each hand, like an old-stone savage armed.
He moves in darkness as it seems to me,
Not of woods only and the shade of trees.
He will not go behind his father's saying,
And he likes having thought of it so well
He says again, "Good fences make good neighbors." ■

Responding to the Selection

Imagine that you are the speaker in the poem, mending the stone wall with your neighbor. Are you understanding of his position regarding the existence of the wall? Write an entry in your journal expressing your feelings about your neighbor and about the wall.

Analytic Scales for Responding in Writing

Assign a score from 1 to 25 for each grading criterion below. (For more detailed evaluation, see the evaluation forms for writing, revising, and proofreading, *Assessment Portfolio,* 7.1–7.10.)

Dialogue and Debate

- **Content/Unity.** The dialogue expresses the opinions held by two characters about tearing down a stone wall.
- **Organization/Coherence.** The dialogue presents the ideas of the speakers in a manner that echoes that of an actual dialogue.
- **Language/Style.** The dialogue is written in informal English and employs vivid, precise, and colorful nouns, verbs, and modifiers.
- **Conventions.** The dialogue uses the correct format for dialogue and avoids other errors in spelling, grammar, usage, mechanics, and form.

Reviewing the Selection

RECALLING

1. What is the wall like in the spring?
2. Why does the speaker contact his neighbor? What do they do together?
3. What does the speaker tell his neighbor as they repair the wall? What quote does the speaker's neighbor repeat?
4. What would the speaker like to know before he builds a wall?

INTERPRETING

5. What forces act to tear down the wall?
6. How does the neighbor look to the speaker? What reveals that the speaker doesn't totally trust his neighbor?
7. Why might the neighbor want to have a wall where one is not absolutely necessary? What does the neighbor's desire for a wall tell you about him?
8. Who is being "walled out" in this poem? by whom?

SYNTHESIZING

9. The speaker says, "Something there is that doesn't love a wall." What doesn't?
10. Which person in this poem is more thoughtful and reflective, the speaker or the neighbor? Explain.

Understanding Literature (Questions for Discussion)

1. **Symbol.** A **symbol** is a thing that stands for or represents both itself and something else. For example, a rose is a traditional symbol of love or beauty. What does the wall in this poem symbolize? Why does the speaker question the value of walls?
2. **Character.** A **character** is a figure who participates in the action of a literary work. What sort of person is the neighbor in this poem? What does he look like? How does he respond when the speaker suggests that perhaps a wall is not necessary here? What does this response reveal about the neighbor? Why might the speaker actually want to have a wall between himself and such a person?
3. **Pun.** A **pun** is a play on words. The speaker says, "Before I built a wall I'd ask to know . . . to whom I was like to give offense." What two meanings might be suggested by the word *offense?* What pun might be found in the sound of the word?

Responding in Writing

Dialogue and Debate. Create two characters, one who believes the stone wall should be torn down and one who doesn't. Write a dialogue between the two characters in which they debate the value of the wall.

RESPONDING TO THE SELECTION

Have students discuss their feelings about privacy and neighbors. Do they value their privacy greatly, or do they seek to have open and friendly relationships with their own neighbors? Are the two ideals, privacy and fellowship, incompatible?

ANSWERS FOR REVIEWING THE SELECTION

RECALLING

1. The wall needs to be mended in the spring.
2. The speaker contacts his neighbor so that they can set the wall again.
3. The speaker tells his neighbor that his apple trees will never get over and eat the cones under his neighbor's pine trees. The speaker's neighbor repeats, "Good fences make good neighbors."
4. Before the speaker builds a wall, he would like to know what he is fencing in or fencing out and to whom he is likely to give offense.

INTERPRETING

Responses will vary. Possible responses are given.

5. Frozen ground swells and hunters have torn down the wall.
6. The speaker says he looks like an armed savage. The speaker sees his neighbor moving in darkness.
7. The neighbor may want to mark off his place to have privacy or to indicate separateness from his neighbors. It tells you that the neighbor is not especially friendly or trusting of the people around him.
8. The speaker and other people are being walled out by the speaker's neighbor.

(cont.)

ANSWERS FOR REVIEWING THE SELECTION (CONT.)

SYNTHESIZING

Responses will vary. Possible responses are given.

9. Nature doesn't love a wall, nor do hunters or the speaker.
10. The speaker is more thoughtful and reflective as shown by his imaginative idea of the apple trees crossing to the pines. The speaker is also the one who initiates contact with his neighbor each spring. The neighbor on the other hand only says, "Good fences make good neighbors."

PREREADING NOTES

READER'S JOURNAL

You might ask students to describe the different ways people express grief. Why might people have a particularly difficult time understanding those who grieve in a different way?

SPEAKING AND LISTENING SKILLS

Students might also list the techniques, both positive and negative, that the couple in the poem use to communicate with each other. Ask students the following questions about the couple to generate ideas: When do they give each other feedback to show that they are listening? When do they fail to listen? Are they thinking before speaking? Are they keeping their emotions under control? What do their gestures and body language reveal?

SUPPORT FOR LEP STUDENTS

ADDITIONAL VOCABULARY

murmured—made a low, indistinct sound

inconsolably—brokenheartedly

sneering—expressing scorn or contempt

spade—heavy, flat-bladed, long-handled tool for digging

READER'S JOURNAL

What causes people sometimes to misunderstand one another? Freewrite in your journal about an experience in which you had a failure of communication with someone about whom you cared deeply.

SPEAKING AND LISTENING SKILLS

How can speaking with a family member or a dear friend help you in times of sorrow? Read the Language Arts Survey, 3.5, "Interpersonal Communication." Then list the important functions that interpersonal communication serves in every person's life.

"Home Burial"[1]

ROBERT FROST

He saw her from the bottom of the stairs
Before she saw him. She was starting down,
Looking back over her shoulder at some fear.
She took a doubtful step and then undid it
To raise herself and look again. He spoke
Advancing toward her: "What is it you see
From up there always—for I want to know."
She turned and sank upon her skirts at that,
And her face changed from terrified to dull.
He said to gain time: "What is it you see,"
Mounting[2] until she cowered under him.
"I will find out now—you must tell me, dear."
She, in her place, refused him any help
With the least stiffening of her neck and silence.
She let him look, sure that he wouldn't see,
Blind creature; and awhile he didn't see.
But at last he murmured, "Oh," and again, "Oh."

"What is it—what?" she said.

1. **Home Burial.** Reference to the custom of keeping a family cemetery on one's property
2. **Mounting.** Climbing

WORDS FOR EVERYDAY USE: **cow • er** (kou´ər) *vi.,* crouch or shrink back in fear

VOCABULARY IN CONTEXT

- The toy poodle cowered in fear before the snarling, wolflike mutt.

"Just that I see."

20 "You don't," she challenged. "Tell me what it is."

"The wonder is I didn't see at once.
I never noticed it from here before.
I must be wonted to it[3]—that's the reason.
The little graveyard where my people are!
25 So small the window frames the whole of it.
Not so much larger than a bedroom, is it?
There are three stones of slate and one of marble,
Broad-shouldered little slabs there in the sunlight
On the sidehill. We haven't to mind *those.*
30 But I understand: it is not the stones,
But the child's mound—"

❶ *What does the speaker see?*

"Don't, don't, don't, don't," she cried.

She withdrew shrinking from beneath his arm
That rested on the banister, and slid downstairs;
35 And turned on him with such a daunting[4] look,
He said twice over before he knew himself:
"Can't a man speak of his own child he's lost?"

"Not you!—Oh, where's my hat? Oh, I don't need it!
I must get out of here. I must get air.—
40 I don't know rightly whether any man can."

"Amy! Don't go to someone else this time.
Listen to me. I won't come down the stairs."
He sat and fixed his chin between his fists.
"There's something I should like to ask you, dear."

45 "You don't know how to ask it."
"Help me, then."

Her fingers moved the latch for all reply.

"My words are nearly always an offense.
I don't know how to speak of anything
50 So as to please you. But I might be taught
I should suppose. I can't say I see how.

3. **wonted to it.** Used to it
4. **daunting.** Challenging

ANSWER TO GUIDED READING QUESTION

❶ The speaker sees his family cemetery, which contains a child's grave.

Answer to Guided Reading Question

❶ The speaker is willing to agree not to speak about some things but does not believe it is right for a couple who love to have such restrictions.

Quotables

"Howl, howl, howl! O, you are men of stones!/Had I your tongues and eyes, I'd use them so/That heaven's vault should crack. She's gone for ever!"

—King Lear on the death of his daughter Cordelia in William Shakespeare's *The Tragedy of King Lear*

Answers to Selection Check Test 4.8.11

EX. Who is having a conversation in this poem?
A husband and wife are having a conversation.

1. What is the woman doing at the top of the stairs?
She is looking out a window "at some fear."

2. What does the man discover she has been looking at?
The man discovers she has been looking at the family cemetery.

3. Whose death upsets the couple?
The death of their child upsets the couple.

4. What does the husband ask his wife not to do?
He asks his wife not to bring her grief to someone else.

5. What made the woman angry with her husband?
The fact that her husband could dig his child's grave and then talk about "everyday concerns" made her angry.

Does the speaker think he and his wife should agree to not speak about some things? Why, or why not? ❶

A man must partly give up being a man
With womenfolk. We could have some arrangement
By which I'd bind myself to keep hands off
55 Anything special you're a-mind to name.
Though I don't like such things twixt those that love.
Two that don't love can't live together without them.
But two that do can't live together with them."
She moved the latch a little. "Don't—don't go.
60 Don't carry it to someone else this time.
Tell me about it if it's something human.
Let me into your grief. I'm not so much
Unlike other folks as your standing there
Apart would make me out. Give me my chance.
65 I do think, though, you overdo it a little.
What was it brought you up to think it the thing
To take your mother-loss of a first child
So inconsolably—in the face of love.
You'd think his memory might be satisfied—"

70 "There you go sneering now!"

"I'm not, I'm not!
You make me angry. I'll come down to you.
God, what a woman! And it's come to this,
A man can't speak of his own child that's dead."

75 "You can't because you don't know how to speak.
If you had any feelings, you that dug
With your own hand—how could you?—his little grave;
I saw you from that very window there,
Making the gravel leap and leap in air,
80 Leap up, like that, like that, and land so lightly
And roll back down the mound beside the hole.
I thought, Who is that man? I didn't know you.
And I crept down the stairs and up the stairs
To look again, and still your spade kept lifting.
85 Then you came in. I heard your rumbling voice
Out in the kitchen, and I don't know why,
But I went near to see with my own eyes.
You could sit there with the stains on your shoes
Of the fresh earth from your own baby's grave
90 And talk about your everyday concerns.
You had stood the spade up against the wall
Outside there in the entry, for I saw it."

"I shall laugh the worst laugh I ever laughed.
I'm cursed. God, if I don't believe I'm cursed."

95 "I can repeat the very words you were saying:
'Three foggy mornings and one rainy day
Will rot the best birch fence a man can build.'
Think of it, talk like that at such a time!
What had how long it takes a birch to rot
100 To do with what was in the darkened parlor?
You *couldn't* care! The nearest friends can go
With anyone to death, comes so far short
They might as well not try to go at all.
No, from the time when one is sick to death,
105 One is alone, and he dies more alone.
Friends make pretense of following to the grave,
But before one is in it, their minds are turned
And making the best of their way back to life
And living people, and things they understand.
110 But the world's evil. I won't have grief so
If I can change it. Oh, I won't, I won't!"

"There, you have said it all and you feel better.
You won't go now. You're crying. Close the door.
The heart's gone out of it: why keep it up?
115 Amy! There's someone coming down the road!"

"*You*—oh, you think the talk is all. I must go—
Somewhere out of this house. How can I make you—"

"If—you—do!" She was opening the door wider.
"Where do you mean to go? First tell me that.
120 I'll follow and bring you back by force. I *will!*—" ■

❶ *Why does the speaker feel bitter?*

❷ *Why does Amy think friends might as well not go?*

❸ *Where does the speaker think his wife is going? Why?*

Responding to the Selection

Imagine that you are either the wife or husband in this poem. Why would you be unable to understand your spouse's way of expressing his or her grief? What comfort or consolation would you seek from your spouse? Write an entry in your journal expressing your feelings about the death of your child.

Answers to Guided Reading Questions

❶ The speaker feels bitter because he cannot believe this misunderstanding is the root of his problems with his wife.

❷ Amy believes that friends might as well not go because in sickness and death people are alone and friends who pretend to follow the dying to the grave actually have their minds set on matters of life.

❸ The speaker believes that his wife is going to share her sorrow with another because she is unable to understand her husband's expression of grief and believes that he is hard-hearted.

Additional Questions and Activities

Have students discuss their feelings about the sentence that ruined this couple's relationship: "Three foggy mornings and one rainy day/Will rot the best birch fence a man can build." Ask students whether they believe that the speaker was just making idle small talk or expressing his grief metaphorically. Was the speaker talking about fences or about the human condition in general?

Responding to the Selection

Students may discuss which reaction to the child's death they most identify with. They might wish to debate whether a more stoical attitude signifies a lack of feeling.

Answers for Reviewing the Selection

RECALLING

1. The speaker sees his wife at the top of the stairs, staring at "some fear."
2. The wife thinks her husband is a "blind creature."
3. The husband's words to his wife are "nearly always an offense."
4. The wife carries her grief to someone else.

INTERPRETING

Responses will vary. Possible responses are given.

5. If the wife had seen her husband watching her, she probably would not have been as open about expressing her distress at seeing the grave through the window.
6. The wife challenges the husband to tell her what he sees because she doesn't believe that he is sensitive enough to see the same thing she sees through the window.
7. The husband asks the wife to help him learn how to communicate better with her.
8. Students might say the husband's defense against grief is to continue to fulfill his responsibilities as best he can without dwelling on his grief.

SYNTHESIZING

Responses will vary. Possible responses are given.

9. The husband is desperately trying to avoid a permanent rupture in the marriage and the departure of his wife.
10. The wife dwells on her grief, while the husband attempts to put it behind him. Neither understands the other's method of expressing grief, and their inability to communicate their grief to one another has damaged their marriage.

Reviewing the Selection

Recalling

1. What does he see "Before she saw him"?
2. What kind of "creature" does the wife think her husband is?
3. What are the husband's words "nearly always" to his wife?
4. What does the wife "carry to someone else"?

Interpreting

5. How might the wife's actions have been different if she had seen her husband watching her?
6. Why does the wife challenge the husband to tell her what he sees?
7. With what does the husband ask for his wife's help?
8. What is the husband's defense against his grief?

Synthesizing

9. What is the husband desperately trying to avoid?
10. What differences exist in how the husband and wife express their grief about the death of their infant son? How has the death of their child ruptured their marriage?

Understanding Literature (Questions for Discussion)

1. **Metaphor.** A **metaphor** is a figure of speech in which one thing is spoken or written about as if it were another. Consider the following lines in the poem: "I can repeat the very words you were saying:/'Three foggy mornings and one rainy day/Will rot the best birch fence a man can build.'" How are these lines an expression of the man's sense of loss? Does his wife understand that they are such an expression? What does she think that they mean? What has happened to the communication between this man and woman? If you were a therapist attempting to help this couple to deal with the death of their child, what advice would you give each person about communicating effectively with the other?
2. **Diction and Tone. Diction,** when applied to writing, refers to word choice. Much of a writer's style or voice is determined by his or her diction, the types of words that are chosen, whether formal or informal, simple or complex, contemporary or archaic, ordinary or unusual, standard or dialectical. **Tone** is the emotional attitude toward the reader or toward the subject implied by a literary work. Consider the following lines from the poem: "I saw you from that very window there,/Making the gravel leap and leap in air,/Leap up, like that, like that, and land so lightly/And roll back down the mound beside the hole." How would you describe the diction in these lines? How does the diction match with the character of the wife? What tone or emotional attitude toward the husband does the wife express in these lines? What effect do the repetitions within these lines have on the tone?

Answers for Understanding Literature

▶ See the evaluation forms for discussion, active listening, and oral communication, *Assessment Portfolio,* 7.11–7.14.

1. Metaphor. The lines the husband says after digging the child's

(cont.)

Answers for Understanding Literature (cont.)

grave can be read as a metaphoric expression of his grief. He is comparing his child to a sturdy birch fence and the unpredictability of life to the vagaries of weather that can destroy a fence. The wife cannot see the metaphoric meaning of his words; she believes he has already finished grieving for the child. Communication between the two people has broken down. Students' advice to the couple will vary but may include telling the husband to express himself more directly and telling the wife to listen to her husband with a more open mind.

2. Diction and Tone. The diction in the description of the husband digging is simple, informal, and contemporary. The wife is excited and upset, and the diction of these lines reflects that mood. The wife is impatient and upset with her husband, and the repetition in these lines intensifies the reader's experience of that attitude.

Responding in Writing

Critical Analysis. The two characters in this poem have very different ways of responding to grief and consequently fail to understand one another. Write a critical analysis contrasting the ways in which these characters deal with their grief and explaining why they do not understand one another.

Language Lab

Building Sentences. Read the Language Arts Survey, 2.36, "The Functions of Sentences." Then, decide what the function is of each of the following sentences from the selection. Write the classification of each sentence.

1. He saw her from the bottom of the stairs/Before she saw him.
2. "Tell me what it is."
3. "Can't a man speak of his own child he's lost?"
4. "I don't know how to speak of anything/So as to please you."
5. "There you go sneering now!"

Speaking and Listening Skills

Nonverbal Communication. Read the Language Arts Survey, 3.3, "Elements of Nonverbal Communication." Then, describe how each emotion listed below might be communicated through eye contact, facial expressions, gestures, body language, or proximity.

1. loneliness
2. grief
3. frustration
4. alienation

PROJECT

Dramatic Skit. Collaborate with one other student to write a dramatic scene based on this poem. In your scene, portray the characters of the husband and wife (and the failed communication between them) as they are portrayed in the poem. Write two parts and have one person play the husband and the other play the wife. Rehearse your skit and present it to the rest of the class.

ANALYTIC SCALES FOR RESPONDING IN WRITING

Assign a score from 1 to 25 for each grading criterion below. (For more detailed evaluation, see the evaluation forms for writing, revising, and proofreading, *Assessment Portfolio,* 7.1–7.10.)

Critical Analysis

- **Content/Unity.** The analysis contrasts the characters' methods and provides a clear explanation for their inability to understand one another.
- **Organization/Coherence.** The analysis is organized in a logical manner.
- **Language/Style.** The analysis uses an appropriate tone and precise noun, verbs, and modifiers.
- **Conventions.** The analysis avoids errors in spelling, grammar, usage, mechanics, and manuscript form.

ANSWERS FOR LANGUAGE LAB

1. declarative
2. imperative
3. interrogative
4. declarative
5. exclamatory

ANSWERS FOR SPEAKING AND LISTENING SKILLS

Responses will vary. Possible responses are given.

1. Students may respond that loneliness is communicated through hunched shoulders, a downturned head, downturned eyes and mouth, and a physical distancing from others.
2. Students may respond that grief is communicated by crying, by separating oneself from others or clinging to others, by a stoical expression, or by stiff and awkward movements.
3. Students may respond that frustration is communicated by glaring at others right in the eye, by sighs and rolling of the eyes, by flinging one's limbs and/or objects about, or by withdrawal from others' company.
4. Students may say that alienation is communicated by a placid or blank expression, by an inability to maintain eye contact, or by a physical withdrawal from others.

PROJECT NOTES

▶ See the worksheets and evaluation forms for projects, *Assessment Portfolio,* 7.20–7.23.

Dramatic Skit. Students should avoid repeating the dialogue presented in the poem verbatim. Students should imagine ways in which the conversation can be continued, discover other unresolved issues, or even pose a resolution of the conflict. Then students can improvise and express how they feel about the conflict in their performances.

ADDITIONAL RESOURCES

READER'S GUIDE

- Selection Worksheets, 8.7, 8.8, 8.9

ASSESSMENT PORTFOLIO

- Selection Check Tests, 4.8.13, 4.8.15, 4.8.17
- Selection Tests, 4.8.14, 4.8.16, 4.8.18

ESSENTIAL SKILLS PRACTICE BOOKS

- *Language,* 2.6, 2.13, 2.138, 2.139, 2.140

ENRICHMENT ACTIVITIES

Encourage students to write poems on the same object. The poems need not be long or complex in form; they can simply contain one vivid sensory detail or one metaphor that expresses their particular imaginative feelings about the object. Some possible objects include vegetables or fruits that are associated with particular seasons, worn articles of clothing, and artistic representations of animals or people. Once the object has been selected and the brief poems have been written, students should compare their artistic perceptions of the object. Have they looked at the same thing in similar or different ways? In what ways do their perceptions differ? What does a student's particular perception reveal about him or her?

PREREADING

"The Snow Man"
"Anecdote of the Jar"
"Thirteen Ways of Looking at a Blackbird"

by Wallace Stevens

ABOUT THE AUTHOR

Wallace Stevens (1879–1955) was born and raised in Reading, Pennsylvania. His day-to-day life was conventional to a fault. After spending three years at Harvard, he went to work for the *New York Herald Tribune,* but not liking this work, he left and went to the New York Law School. He was admitted to the bar in 1904 and maintained a private law practice until 1908, when he joined the legal staff of an insurance company. In 1916, he joined the Hartford Accident and Indemnity Company and moved to Hartford, Connecticut. In 1934, he was made a vice president of the company, a position he held until his death. Few of his colleagues knew that he wrote poetry. Five years before his death, he told a reporter, "It gives a man character as a poet to have this daily contact with a job." Stevens began writing poetry in high school and had some of his poetry published in the *Harvard Advocate.* His debut in a larger arena began, however, with the publication of some of his work in the magazine *Poetry* in 1914. *Harmonium,* his first volume, was published in 1923. While he lived in New York, Stevens was briefly involved in literary circles, but he dropped out of these after moving to Hartford. Unlike other poets of the time, he was not interested in political and social causes, so although he maintained an active correspondence with some literary figures like William Carlos Williams and Marianne Moore, his work as a poet did not drive the course of his life. His *Collected Poems* (1954) won a Pulitzer Prize and the National Book Award. Among his other works are *Ideas of Order* (1935), *The Man with the Blue Guitar* (1937), *Parts of a World* (1942), and *The Auroras of Autumn* (1950).

ABOUT THE SELECTIONS

These three selections were published in Stevens's first book of poems, *Harmonium,* which includes some of his finest work. The poems, while very different in subject matter, all treat a common theme, found in much of Stevens's poetry: the nature of perception and its relationship to the imagination. The first poem, **"The Snow Man,"** deals with what is known as the pathetic fallacy, the tendency of people to interpret nature in human ways and attribute to it human feelings and motivations. The second, **"Anecdote of the Jar,"** shows how even the simplest of human actions tends to bring order and form into the world. (The artist's job is, of course, to give order, shape, and meaning to things.) The third, **"Thirteen Ways of Looking at a Blackbird,"** shows how the same object of perception, in this case a blackbird, can yield different meanings, depending on the attitude and imagination of the perceiver.

GOALS/OBJECTIVES

Studying this lesson will enable students to

- enjoy poems that offer an imaginative perception
- describe Stevens's literary accomplishments and explain the historical significance of his writing
- define *pathetic fallacy* and recognize and interpret the use of a pathetic fallacy in a poem
- define *anecdote* and identify anecdotes
- define *image, abstract,* and *concrete,* and recognize and interpret images, abstract words, and concrete words in a poem
- write a myth, a journal entry, and a caption

READER'S JOURNAL

Nature can make people feel various emotions. A beautiful rose can cause elation. People may feel depressed on a gray, drizzly day. Often, when people respond to nature emotionally, they attribute emotions to nature: a "gloomy day." In your journal, make a list of different kinds of weather and phenomena in nature and the emotions that you associate with each. Then consider whether the feelings are in nature or in you.

LANGUAGE SKILLS

Read the Language Arts Survey, 2.13, "Linking Verbs." Identify a few linking verbs in the selection, and note what noun the linking verb connects with another noun, pronoun, or adjective.

"The Snow Man"

WALLACE STEVENS

One must have a mind of winter
To regard the frost and the boughs
Of the pine-trees crusted with snow;

And have been cold a long time
To behold the junipers shagged with ice,
The spruces rough in the distant glitter

Of the January sun; and not to think
Of any misery in the sound of the wind,
In the sound of a few leaves,

Which is the sound of the land
Full of the same wind
That is blowing in the same bare place

For the listener, who listens in the snow,
And, nothing himself, beholds
Nothing that is not there and the nothing that is. ■

❶ *What must one have in order to observe winter and not think of misery "in the sound of the wind"?*

❷ *What is the "sound of the land"?*

PREREADING NOTES

READER'S JOURNAL

Students might also consider why certain natural settings and seasons evoke different feelings and reactions in different people. For example, some people revel in the colors and the crisp air of fall, while others become depressed at the death of the summer season. Students might describe the feelings each season evokes in them.

LANGUAGE SKILLS

Students might also read the Language Arts Survey, 2.14, "Auxiliary Verbs," and identify the auxiliary verbs in the selection.

SUPPORT FOR LEP STUDENTS

Students might find following the construction of the sentence that comprises this poem difficult. On the board you might write out the poem and mark the parts of speech used in order to better students' understanding of the poem.

ADDITIONAL VOCABULARY

boughs—branches
shagged—made shaggy or rough

ANSWERS TO GUIDED READING QUESTIONS

❶ In order to observe winter and not think of misery, one must have "a mind of winter."

❷ The "sound of the land" is the sound of misery, or the sound of wind rustling the few remaining leaves.

VOCABULARY FROM THE SELECTIONS

euphony
indecipherable
inflection
lucid
pantomime

ANSWERS TO SELECTION CHECK TEST 4.8.13

EX. Who is the subject of the poem?
The subject is a snowman.

1. What are the pine-trees crusted with?
The pine-trees are crusted with snow.

2. What makes the ice-covered spruces glitter?
The January sun makes the spruces glitter.

3. What does winter make the speaker think of?
Winter makes the speaker think of misery.

4. What sound is the land "full of"?
The land is full of the sound of wind.

5. What is the listener?
The listener is "nothing himself."

RESPONDING TO THE SELECTION

Inform students that it is not the snowman but the speaker who hears misery in the sound of the wind. The snowman itself perceives and feels "nothing." Would students, like the speaker, feel misery in the scene depicted or would they feel another emotion?

ANSWERS FOR REVIEWING THE SELECTION

RECALLING

1. The poem describes winter. The details used are the snow-crusted pines, the cold, the ice-shagged junipers glittering in the sun, and the sound of the wind and the leaves.

2. The speaker says a person must have "a mind of winter."

INTERPRETING

Responses will vary. Possible responses are given.

3. Students may say they find the landscape either cold, bleak, and depressing or vibrant, sparkling, and exciting.

4. A "mind of winter" might be numb, unfeeling, and slow. A mind that is like winter might be unresponsive to others and its surroundings.

SYNTHESIZING

Responses will vary. Possible responses are given.

5. The poem says that the snowman is "nothing himself." The snowman observes the "nothing that is not there and the nothing that is." People differ from the snowman in that they can perceive and have feelings about what they have perceived. The speaker is saying that people have feelings and ascribe them to nature while objects in nature merely exist and are devoid of feeling.

Responding to the Selection

Imagine that you are experiencing the scene described in the opening lines of this poem: the frost, the boughs of pine trees crusted with snow, the junipers shagged with ice, the distant January sun, and the sounds of the wind and the few leaves. How would this scene make you feel? How do you differ from the snowman?

Reviewing the Selection

RECALLING

1. What time of year does this poem describe? What details are used in the description of the poem's setting?

2. What kind of mind does the speaker say a person must have not to think that there is misery in the sound of the wind and the leaves?

INTERPRETING

3. How do the details of the setting of this poem make you feel?

4. What characteristics would a "mind of winter" have? (Hint: Think about the characteristics of winter—the coldness, the numbness, the lack of life. What would a mind that is like winter be like?)

SYNTHESIZING

5. What does the poem say that the snowman is? What does the snowman behold? How do people differ from the snowman? What comment is the speaker making about the differences between people and objects in nature?

Understanding Literature (Questions for Discussion)

Pathetic Fallacy. The **pathetic fallacy** is the tendency of people to attribute human emotions and motivations to things in nature. Consider this small poem:

Other People's Sorrow

In its extremity,
on the farthest hill,
the willow weeps
alone.

—Robin Lamb

In this poem, a willow tree is imagined as being in some extremity, as weeping, and as being alone. The title of the poem invites the reader to compare the isolation of the willow to the isolation of a person who is feeling sorrow. How does Stevens's depiction of the snowman differ from Lamb's depiction of the willow? What do people sometimes see in nature that is not there, according to "The Snow Man"? In what sense is there "nothing" in nature until it is perceived by a human being?

ANSWERS FOR UNDERSTANDING LITERATURE

► See the evaluation forms for discussion, active listening, and oral communication, *Assessment Portfolio,* 7.11–7.14.

Responses will vary. Possible responses are given.

Pathetic Fallacy. Stevens depicts the snowman as feeling nothing, while Lamb depicts the willow as feeling sorrow. According to "The Snow Man," people see emotions and feelings in nature that are not there. There is "nothing" in nature until it is perceived by a human being because only humans react in an emotional way to nature and "make something" of their surroundings.

READER'S JOURNAL

Imagine what some place was like before humans ever set foot there. How do humans change places when they come onto the scene? Write about this question in your journal.

LANGUAGE SKILLS

Read the Language Arts Survey, 2.6, "Personal Pronouns." Then identify the personal pronoun that is used repeatedly in this poem. What is that personal pronoun, and to what does it refer?

"Anecdote of the Jar"

WALLACE STEVENS

I placed a jar in Tennessee,[1]
And round it was, upon a hill.
It made the slovenly wilderness
Surround that hill.

The wilderness rose up to it,
And sprawled around, no longer wild.
The jar was round upon the ground
And tall and of a port in air.

It took dominion everywhere.
The jar was gray and bare.
It did not give of bird or bush,
Like nothing else in Tennessee. ■

1. **Tennessee.** The speaker is not describing the real Tennessee but rather an imagined wilderness, what Tennessee was like before human beings came there. The actual Tennessee has not been a complete wilderness for a long, long time. Even the name *Tennessee* comes from that of a large Cherokee settlement, Tenasi, that existed before the coming of Europeans to North America.

❶ *What effect does the jar have on the wilderness?*

PREREADING NOTES

READER'S JOURNAL

You might also ask students to consider creation myths they may have heard and to write about the forces that create the natural world within these myths.

LANGUAGE SKILLS

Students should be able to recognize with very little prompting that *it* is used repeatedly in the poem and that the pronoun refers to the jar.

SUPPORT FOR LEP STUDENTS

Students may have some difficulty understanding the use of the word *port* in line 8. Inform students that aside from the meaning given in the additional vocabulary below, the word also implies a carriage or demeanor, a gateway, and the word *portly*, something large, round, heavy, and dignified.

ADDITIONAL VOCABULARY

slovenly—careless in appearance; untidy

sprawled—spread out in an awkward or uneven way

port—harbor; enclosed space

dominion—rule or power to rule

ANSWER TO GUIDED READING QUESTION

❶ The jar "tames" the wilderness.

ANSWERS TO SELECTION CHECK TEST 4.8.15

EX. In what way is this poem described in the title?
The poem is described as an anecdote.

1. Where did the speaker place the jar?
The speaker placed the jar on a hill in Tennessee.

2. What effect did the jar have on the hill?
The jar made the wilderness surround the hill.

3. What happened to the wilderness once it reached the hill and "sprawled around"?
The wilderness was no longer wild.

4. What did the jar look like?
The jar was round, tall, gray, and bare.

5. What else was the jar like in Tennessee?
The jar was like nothing else in Tennessee.

RESPONDING TO THE SELECTION

You might ask students to discuss why the narrator refers to the wilderness as "slovenly" and says it was "sprawled around," both descriptions that suggest that the wilderness is unkempt and lazy. In contrast, the jar is described as tall, upright, and powerful. What attitude toward nature is revealed in the speaker's description of the wilderness? Is this description meant ironically?

ANSWERS FOR REVIEWING THE SELECTION

RECALLING

1. The jar makes the "slovenly wilderness/Surround that hill."
2. The jar is tall and round and gray in color.

INTERPRETING

Responses will vary. Possible responses are given.

3. The jar makes the wilderness "no longer wild" because it is evidence of human occupation.
4. The jar is like "nothing else in Tennessee" because it is the only man-made object present in the imagined wilderness of Tennessee.

SYNTHESIZING

Responses will vary. Possible responses are given.

5. The jar has creative power and dominates the landscape. The speaker perceives that the jar "made the slovenly wilderness" and tames its wildness.

ANALYTIC SCALES FOR RESPONDING IN WRITING

Assign a score from 1 to 25 for each grading criterion below. (See the evaluation forms for writing, revising, and proofreading, *Assessment Portfolio,* 7.1–7.10.)

Myth

- **Content/Unity.** The myth presents an imaginative explanation for the presence of a jar in the wilderness.
- **Organization/Coherence.** The myth is written in a sensible order.
- **Language/Style.** The myth uses vivid and precise nouns, verbs, and modifiers.
- **Conventions.** The myth avoids errors in spelling, grammar, usage, mechanics, and manuscript form.

Responding to the Selection

How does the wild, natural place described in the poem differ after a jar is placed there? How does a completely untouched natural place differ from one that shows the impact of humans? What does this difference tell you about human beings?

Reviewing the Selection

RECALLING

1. What makes the "slovenly wilderness/Surround that hill"?
2. What shape and color is the jar?

INTERPRETING

3. How does the jar make the wilderness "no longer wild"?
4. In what way is the jar like "nothing else in Tennessee"?

SYNTHESIZING

5. What relationship between the jar and the landscape is described in the poem? What effect does the speaker perceive the jar to have upon the landscape?

Understanding Literature (Questions for Discussion)

Anecdote. An **anecdote** is a brief story, usually with a specific point or moral. The title of the selection identifies the subject of the poem as an anecdote about the jar. Does the selection contain a moral? What is the specific point of the selection? What does the poem tell us about the effects of human activity, about human nature, and about human perceptions?

Responding in Writing

Myth. Imagine that civilization has collapsed and that a few human beings are left. A couple hundred years later, one of the surviving human beings finds the jar placed on a hill in a wilderness area in Tennessee. Imagine that you are the human being who finds the jar. Write a brief myth that explains the presence of the jar and the purpose that it serves or once served. Let your imagination go to create a really fantastic story around this lowly object. Refer to the discussion of *myth* in the Handbook of Literary Terms.

ANSWERS FOR UNDERSTANDING LITERATURE

► See the evaluation forms for discussion, active listening, and oral communication, *Assessment Portfolio,* 7.11–7.14.

Responses will vary. Possible responses are given.

Anecdote. The moral of the anecdote of the jar is that humans have a civilizing effect on nature; they produce impressive and dominating physical objects but also destroy something of the magic of the wilderness, ruining its wildness. The point of the selection is that no true "wilderness" exists for man; once man perceives and sets his mark on an area of wilderness, it becomes a tame or civilized area. The poem tells us that human activity dominates the natural environment, human nature is creative and persevering but self-important, and humans perceive themselves as the creators of their own private worlds.

READER'S JOURNAL

What thoughts and feelings do you associate with blackbirds? Why do you think Alfred Hitchcock used blackbirds in his film about birds that turn malevolent and attack people? Freewrite about blackbirds in your journal. Share your freewriting with classmates, and discuss their thoughts and feelings.

LANGUAGE SKILLS

Read the Language Arts Survey, 2.138 and 2.139, "Using Context Clues I and II." Then identify some words in the selection that are unfamiliar to you and use context clues to decipher their meanings.

"Thirteen Ways of Looking at a Blackbird"

WALLACE STEVENS

I

Among twenty snowy mountains,
The only moving thing
Was the eye of the blackbird.

II

I was of three minds,
Like a tree
In which there are three blackbirds.

III

The blackbird whirled in the autumn winds.
It was a small part of the pantomime.

IV

A man and a woman
Are one.
A man and a woman and a blackbird
Are one.

V

I do not know which to prefer,
The beauty of inflections

❶ *What was the "only moving thing"?*

WORDS FOR EVERYDAY USE:
pan • to • mime (pan´tə mīm´) *n.,* gesture without speech
in • flec • tion (in flek´shən) *n.,* change in pitch or tone of voice

PREREADING NOTES

READER'S JOURNAL

Blackbirds are traditional subjects for literature, including many popular nursery rhymes. To spark students' remembrances of what they may have heard about blackbirds in their childhood, you might read them the following nursery rhyme. (There are others.)

Sing a song of sixpence
A pocket full of rye,
Four and twenty blackbirds,
Baked in a pie.

When the pie was opened,
The birds began to sing;
Was not that a dainty dish,
To set before the king?

The king was in the
counting-house,
Counting out his money;
The queen was in the parlor,
Eating bread and honey.

The maid was in the garden,
Hanging out the clothes,
There came a little blackbird,
And snapped off her nose.

LANGUAGE SKILLS

Students might write their own definitions of the unfamiliar words, derived from context clues, and then compare these definitions with the words' actual definitions in a dictionary.

ANSWER TO GUIDED READING QUESTION

❶ The eye of the blackbird was the "only moving thing."

VOCABULARY IN CONTEXT

- In the years before movies acquired sound, the action of a film was like a pantomime, more dependent on gestures because of the lack of speech.
- We could always tell when our mother was angry because of the sharp inflection in her usually sweet voice.

SUPPORT FOR LEP STUDENTS

ADDITIONAL VOCABULARY

accents—speech, words, utterances; emphasis; national or regional pronunciation

Answer to Guided Reading Question

❶ The speaker knows noble accents, easily understood rhythms, and that the blackbird is involved in everything the speaker knows.

Quotables

"I value my garden more for being full of blackbirds than of cherries, and very frankly give them fruit for their songs."

—Joseph Addison

Answers to Selection Check Test 4.8.17

EX. How many ways of looking at a blackbird are described in this poem?
Thirteen ways are described in this poem.

1. What does the speaker see among twenty snowy mountains?
The speaker sees the moving eye of the blackbird.

2. What three things are one?
A man, a woman, and a blackbird are one.

3. What do thin men of Haddam imagine?
They imagine golden birds.

4. What fear "pierced" the man in the glass coach?
He mistook the shadow of his equipage for blackbirds.

5. For how long was it evening?
It was evening all afternoon.

15 Or the beauty of innuendoes,[1]
The blackbird whistling
Or just after.

VI

Icicles filled the long window
With barbaric[2] glass.
20 The shadow of the blackbird
Crossed it, to and fro.
The mood
Traced in the shadow
An indecipherable cause.

VII

25 O thin men of Haddam,[3]
Why do you imagine golden birds?
Do you not see how the blackbird
Walks around the feet
Of the women about you?

VIII

30 I know noble accents
And lucid, inescapable rhythms;
But I know, too,
That the blackbird is involved
In what I know.

IX

35 When the blackbird flew out of sight,
It marked the edge
Of one of many circles.

X

At the sight of blackbirds
Flying in a green light,
40 Even the bawds of euphony
Would cry out sharply.

XI

He rode over Connecticut
In a glass coach.

1. **innuendoes.** Hints
2. **barbaric.** Wild
3. **Haddam.** Town in Connecticut

Words for Everyday Use:
in • de • ci • pher • a • ble (in´dē sī´fər ə bəl) *adj.,* illegible
lu • cid (lōō´sid) *adj.,* easily understood
eu • pho • ny (yōō´fə nē) *n.,* effect to the ear

Vocabulary in Context

- Most people have trouble reading my handwriting, but I find it hard to believe that it is as indecipherable as Egyptian hieroglyphs before the discovery of the Rosetta stone.
- Because of the professor's excellent explanation, the once-difficult material became lucid.
- I enjoy relaxing to classical music because the euphony of harmony soothes my frazzled nerves.

Once, a fear pierced him,
45 In that he mistook
The shadow of his equipage[4]
For blackbirds.

XII

The river is moving.
The blackbird must be flying.

XIII

50 It was evening all afternoon.
It was snowing
And it was going to snow.
The blackbird sat
In the cedar-limbs. ■

4. **equipage.** Refers to his coach

❶ *Why did it seem like "evening all afternoon"?*

ANSWER TO GUIDED READING QUESTION

❶ It seemed like "evening all afternoon" because the sky was darkened by clouds all afternoon.

RESPONDING TO THE SELECTION

You might also break students into small groups, one for each of the stanzas, and have them suggest interpretations for the stanzas. Each group could suggest what feelings are evoked by the particular perception in each stanza of a blackbird or blackbirds.

ANSWERS FOR REVIEWING THE SELECTION

RECALLING AND INTERPRETING

Responses will vary. Possible responses are given.

1. The speaker sees the moving eye of a blackbird "Among twenty snowy mountains." The perceptive power of the imagination is greater than the perceptive power of the senses in that only in the imagination can one see the startling contrast of a blackbird's eye moving in the white and otherwise still mountains; it is an image possible only in the mind's eye, not to the body's physical eye.

2. The speaker compares three blackbirds in a single tree to a single person being of three minds. A person might be of three minds when faced with a difficult decision.

3. The blackbird whirls in the autumn winds. The pantomime is the physical effects—the winds, the weather, and the falling leaves of autumn. Nature sometimes acts out in a stormy and gusty fashion in autumn.

4. A man and a woman and a blackbird are described as being "one." Men and women are sometimes described as being "one" when they are in love. The speaker might say this to emphasize that it is impossible for disparate creatures ever to be wholly united into one. A shared moment of experience can make two people feel connected both to that experience and to each other, in which case, a man, a woman, and a blackbird can indeed become "one"—part of one beautiful shared moment.

5. The speaker compares inflections and innuendoes to a blackbird whistling and "just

(cont.)

Responding to the Selection

Which of the "Thirteen Ways of Looking at a Blackbird" do you find most interesting? Why?

Reviewing the Selection

RECALLING AND INTERPRETING

1. In stanza 1, what does the speaker see "Among twenty snowy mountains"?
   ▶▶ What kind of eyesight would a person need to be able to see the eye of a blackbird move "Among twenty snowy mountains"? In what way is the perceptive power of the imagination greater than the perceptive power of the senses?

2. In stanza 2, to what does the speaker compare three blackbirds?
   ▶▶ In what circumstance might a person be "of three minds"?

3. In stanza 3, what does the blackbird do in the autumn winds?
   ▶▶ What is "the pantomime" referred to in stanza 3? In what way does nature sometimes seem to be acting out in the autumn?

4. In stanza 4, what groups of things are described as being "one"?
   ▶▶ In what circumstances are a man and a woman often spoken of as being "one"? Some critics have suggested that stanza 4 is a kind of joke in which the speaker demonstrates the absurdity of thinking of two people as one. If that reading of the stanza is accepted, why does the speaker say that "A man and a woman and a blackbird are one"? Suppose that the stanza is not a joke but is meant to be taken seriously, how might a man and a woman become one by sharing a moment of experiences, such as looking at a blackbird?

5. In stanza 5, what two aspects of human speech does the speaker of the poem compare to a blackbird whistling and "just after"?
   ▶▶ What is an inflection? What is an innuendo? What do these things have in common with a "blackbird whistling" and "just after"?

6. In stanza 6, what scene is described?
   ▶▶ What mood, or feeling, does that scene create? Why might the speaker consider a natural world that would create such a mood "indecipherable"?

7. In stanza 7, what do the men of Haddam look like? What do they imagine? What question does the speaker put to them?
   ▶▶ What might the "golden birds" represent? How do you feel when you think of blackbirds walking around people's feet? How does nature violate people's ambitions or wishes?

8. In stanza 8, what does the speaker know?
   ▶▶ A poet is someone who has command of "noble accents/And lucid, inescapable

ANSWERS FOR REVIEWING THE SELECTION (CONT.)

after." An inflection is a change in pitch or tone of voice. An innuendo is a hint or something implied. An inflection is like a whistle in that both involve sound, tone, and pitch or a change in one of these elements. An innuendo is like "just after" a blackbird sings because both involve a moment of speculation; after an innuendo is made, one wonders what was meant, while after a blackbird whistles, one wonders why it whistled, will it whistle again, and whether it has flown away. In both situations—when an innuendo is dropped and when a bird whistles—the cause of each is uncertain.

6. Stanza 6 describes a blackbird's shadow tracing a pattern across an icicle-covered window. The mood is eerie and mysterious. The speaker might consider such a natural world "indecipherable," as it offers no meaning or explanation for the events that have occurred.

(cont.)

rhythms." However, such a person does not come by these on his or her own. What role does nature play in teaching a poet his or her trade?

9. In stanza 9, what does the speaker think of when he sees the blackbird fly out of sight?
   ▶▶ The point at which the blackbird disappears from sight marks the limits of the speaker's physical perception. What might lie beyond those limits in other "circles"? What might one perceive through one's imagination or intuition that cannot be directly perceived by the senses? In what way is imagination or intuition dependent on the senses, so that in a sense the limits of imagination include, or encircle, the actual or concrete?

10. In stanza 10, what would cry out "At the sight of blackbirds/Flying in a green light"?
    ▶▶ Is green light natural? How would you feel if you saw a bunch of blackbirds flying in a green light? What is euphony? What is a bawd? Imagine a poet who normally writes only euphonious, pleasant-sounding verse. What kinds of subjects would force such a poet if he is to do justice to the subject, to "cry out sharply"?

11. In stanza 11, what does the man ride in? What causes him to feel fear?
    ▶▶ In the story of Cinderella, a fairy godmother creates for the central character a fancy coach and glass slippers. In what sense is being wealthy and privileged like magic? In what sense is wealth and privilege precarious, like riding in a glass coach? In what circumstance might the objects owned by a wealthy, privileged person, such as a fancy coach, take on a terrifying aspect to that person?

12. In stanza 12, what is moving? What must be flying?
    ▶▶ The ancient Greek philosopher Heraclitus wrote that "You can never step into the same river twice." What similar statement about the nature of the world is made by the speaker in stanza 12?

13. In stanza 13, what does the afternoon look like? What is happening? What is going to happen?
    ▶▶ What two things in this stanza are unchanging? How do you think the speaker feels? In what sense are both the speaker and the blackbird "waiting it out"? Picture the scene in the stanza in your mind. What would make the blackbird stand out in stark relief, thus intensifying the impression of the bird's stoic immobility?

SYNTHESIZING

14. Choose two stanzas from the poem that you especially like. What does the speaker think about as a result of observing the blackbird in these two stanzas?

15. With what is the number thirteen commonly associated? What sorts of feelings are associated in this poem with blackbirds? In which stanzas do blackbirds seem frightening? In which stanzas does the speaker seem to be attracted to or fascinated by blackbirds?

ANSWERS FOR REVIEWING THE SELECTION (CONT.)

7. The men of Haddam are thin. They imagine golden birds. The speaker asks the men why they do not see how blackbirds walk around the feet of the women about them. The golden birds might represent unrealizable ambitions. Students might say the image of blackbirds walking around feet is a more common, worldly image. Nature violates people's ambitions and wishes by offering them the physical realities of the world that are often less beautiful than people's hopes and dreams.

8. The speaker knows accents, rhythms, and that the blackbird is involved in what he or she knows. Nature can teach a poet the accents of music that occur in the wild and show a poet the rhythm of nature's creatures in motion.

9. The speaker thinks of the edge of one of many circles when the blackbird flies out of sight. Imagination lies beyond the limits of the circle of one's physical perception. One can perceive whatever one dreams or wishes beyond one's physical senses through one's imagination. The imagination is dependent upon the senses to provide the physical background from which fantastic images can be drawn.

10. Bawds of euphony would cry out at blackbirds flying in a green light. Green light is not natural. Students might say they would feel uneasy or disturbed if they witnessed this scene. Euphony is harmonious sound. Bawds are people who live riotously. Disturbing subjects might make a poet "cry out sharply."

11. The man rides in a glass coach. Mistaking his equipage for blackbirds makes him feel fear. Being wealthy and privileged is like magic because one has the ability to make one's fondest wishes come true. Just as a glass coach can be broken, wealth and privilege can be lost. The realization that things are not what they seem, that things can become lost (or fly away like blackbirds), or that physical possessions and life

(cont.)

ANSWERS FOR REVIEWING THE SELECTION (CONT.)

itself are transient might make a wealthy individual fear that his or her possessions will not continue to protect him or her from the realities of the natural world.

12. A river is moving. A blackbird must be flying. The speaker is stating that the imaginative perceptions that people make in their lives are subject to change so that when looking at a river again, the speaker may have an entirely different perception of what else must be occurring in the natural world.

13. The afternoon looks like evening. It is snowing. It will continue to snow. The snowfall is unchanging. The speaker may feel despondent. Both the speaker and the blackbird are waiting out storms—the speaker an emotional one, and the blackbird a physical one. The blackbird's dark color would make it stand out in stark relief to all the falling white.

(cont.)

ANSWERS FOR REVIEWING THE SELECTION (CONT.)

SYNTHESIZING

Responses will vary. Possible responses are given.

14. *Answers will vary.*

15. The number thirteen is associated with bad luck. Feelings of isolation, sadness, and despair are associated with blackbirds. Blackbirds seem frightening in stanzas 3, 6, 10, and 11. The speaker seem attracted to or fascinated by blackbirds in stanzas 1, 2, 4, 5, 7, 8, 9, 12, and 13.

ANALYTIC SCALES FOR RESPONDING IN WRITING

Assign a score from 1 to 25 for each grading criterion below. (For more detailed evaluation, see the evaluation forms for writing, revising, and proofreading, *Assessment Portfolio,* 7.1–7.10.)

1. Journal Entry

- **Content/Unity.** The entry describes a number of ways of thinking of or looking at a particular object.
- **Organization/Coherence.** Each way of perception described is written in a sensible order.
- **Language/Style.** The journal entry uses vivid and precise nouns, verbs, and modifiers.
- **Conventions.** The entry avoids errors in spelling, grammar, usage, mechanics, and manuscript form.

2. Caption

- **Content/Unity.** The captions represent five different ways of looking at the same photograph.
- **Organization/Coherence.** Each caption is written in a sensible order.
- **Language/Style.** The captions use vivid and precise nouns, verbs, and modifiers.
- **Conventions.** The captions avoid errors in spelling, grammar, usage, mechanics, and manuscript form.

ANSWERS FOR LANGUAGE LAB

1. inflections; change in pitch or tone
2. innuendoes; hints
3. indecipherable; illegible
4. inescapable; that cannot be escaped

Understanding Literature (Questions for Discussion)

1. **Image and Imagery.** An **image** is a word or phrase that names something that can be seen, heard, touched, tasted, or smelled. The images in a literary work are referred to, collectively, as the work's **imagery.** What primary image is used throughout the poem? How does the winter setting in many of the poem's parts contribute to the poem's imagery?

2. **Abstract and Concrete.** An **abstract** word or phrase is one that refers to something that cannot be directly perceived by the senses. *Freedom, power,* and *dignity* are examples of abstract terms. A **concrete** word or phrase is one that describes something that can be directly perceived by one or more of the five senses. Examples of concrete terms include *rainbow, lark,* and *scorpion.* Consider stanza 5 in the selection:

   I do not know which to prefer,
   The beauty of inflections
   Or the beauty of innuendoes,
   The blackbird whistling
   Or just after.

   What abstract terms are used in this stanza? What concrete terms are used to provide examples of the abstract terms?

Responding in Writing

1. **Journal Entry.** How many ways can you look at something? Choose a concrete thing, such as an oak tree, a tulip, a pumpkin, a crow, a snake, a cat, a beach, a motorcycle, an earthmover, the moon, a child's doll, or a pair of sneakers. Then, in your journal, brainstorm a list of different ways of thinking about or looking at that object.

2. **Caption.** Write five captions for a photograph you've selected from a newspaper or magazine. Have each caption represent a different perspective in which to look at and understand the photograph.

Language Lab

Base Words and Prefixes. Read the Language Arts Survey, 2.140, "Base Words and Prefixes." Then, on your own paper, underline the base word once and the prefix twice in each of the following words from "Thirteen Ways of Looking at a Blackbird." Next write the meaning of each word, consulting this text or a dictionary as necessary.

1. inflections 2. innuendoes 3. indecipherable 4. inescapable

ANSWERS FOR UNDERSTANDING LITERATURE

► See the evaluation forms for discussion, active listening, and oral communication, *Assessment Portfolio,* 7.11–7.14.

Responses will vary. Possible responses are given.

1. Image and Imagery. The image of the blackbird's darkness is used throughout the poem. The winter setting in which the world is covered in white stands in contrast to the blackbird's darkness.

2. Abstract and Concrete. The abstract terms are *beauty, inflections,* and *innuendoes.* The concrete terms are *blackbird* and *whistling.*

PREREADING

"This Is Just to Say"
"The Red Wheelbarrow"
"The Dance"
by William Carlos Williams

About the Author

William Carlos Williams (1883–1963) was born in Rutherford, New Jersey. After graduating from high school, he began studying to become a dentist, but he soon switched to medicine. In college he met and became friends with Ezra Pound, who would become one of the most influential American literary figures, and Hilda Doolittle, who later achieved fame as the poet and novelist, H. D. These relationships fed his interest in literature and poetry and changed his career plans even as he was completing his medical internship in New York City and doing postgraduate study in Leipzig, Germany. In 1912, Williams married and settled in Rutherford, where he began his medical practice. Specializing in pediatrics, Williams delivered thousands of babies, made house calls, and gained a reputation as a dedicated, old-fashioned doctor. He lived and practiced medicine in Rutherford for the rest of his life. It was an occupation that supported his poetry and his other writing. He was active in local politics and helped found several small magazines. In the 1930s and 1940s, he occasionally supported leftist causes, which later resulted in his not receiving the post of consultant in poetry at the Library of Congress. A heart attack in 1948 and a series of strokes later caused him to cede his medical practice to one of his two sons, and by 1961 he had stopped writing because of his health. Williams was awarded the Pulitzer Prize in 1962 for *Pictures from Breughel,* the Bollingen Prize in 1953, and the National Book Award in 1950, among other honors. His other works include *Spring and All* (1923), *The Edge of the Knife* (1932), *The Wedge* (1944), and an epic poem with a city as its hero, *Paterson* (1946–1958).

About the Selections

A map of Williams's lifelong journey in pursuit of the American idiom can be read in these three poems that span from 1923 to 1944. **"The Red Wheelbarrow,"** one of Williams's earlier poems, reflects the impact of **Imagism,** a movement that championed the use of free verse and concise images, or word pictures. In 1924, Williams rejected free verse and began his experimentation with controlled measure, eventually developing his signature "variable feet," or, as Williams called them, "loose verses." Williams said, "The iamb is not the normal measure of American speech. The foot has to be expanded or contracted in terms of actual speech. The key to modern poetry is measure, which must reflect the flux of modern life." The rhythm of speech that can be heard in **"This Is Just to Say,"** which Williams published in 1934, is further refined and experimented with in **"The Dance,"** which Williams published ten years later.

ADDITIONAL RESOURCES

Reader's Guide
- Selection Worksheets, 8.10, 8.11, 8.12

Assessment Portfolio
- Selection Check Tests, 4.8.19, 4.8.21, 4.8.23
- Selection Tests, 4.8.20, 4.8.22, 4.8.24

Essential Skills Practice Books
- *Language,* 2.8, 2.16, 2.17, 2.24

ENRICHMENT ACTIVITIES

- Have students read additional poetry by William Carlos Williams. Then ask them to compare and contrast these poems with the Williams poems featured in this book. Students might first get into small groups to discuss the poems. Then ask students to express ideas about the poetry in short essays.

- Ask students to create original illustrations or paintings based on one of the Williams poems in this book.

SUPPORT FOR LEP STUDENTS

Be sure that all students are able to visualize the pictures Williams presents in all three of his poems. Discuss with them the scenes being described.

Additional Vocabulary

sound—strong and in good condition

rollicking—lively

GOALS/OBJECTIVES

Studying this lesson will enable students to
- appreciate vivid and concise imagery presented in both free verse and structured verse
- recognize and understand work by William Carlos Williams
- understand the use of demonstrative pronouns, prepositions, and verbals
- create bibliographies and bibliography cards
- understand the terms *speaker, tone, rhythm, meter, image, effect, repetition,* and *run-on line*
- write a poem, a personal note, a caption, a critical interpretation, and a descriptive paragraph
- research art history

PREREADING NOTES

READER'S JOURNAL

Give students time to freewrite on this subject before they compose their final notes. After they have completed the assignment, you might suggest that they get into pairs and exchange notes. Students can judge how convincing and sympathetic their notes might be.

LANGUAGE SKILLS

Students should identify *this* in "this is just to say" and *they* in "they were delicious" as demonstrative pronouns. *This* refers to the note, and *they* refers to the plums.

ANSWERS TO GUIDED READING QUESTIONS

❶ The speaker has eaten the plums that were in the icebox.

❷ The speaker asks the owner of the plums for forgiveness.

ANSWERS TO SELECTION CHECK TEST 4.8.19

EX. Who wrote the poem "This Is Just to Say"?
William Carlos Williams wrote the poem "This Is Just to Say."

1. What has the speaker eaten?
The speaker has eaten plums.

2. Where were the plums?
The plums were in the icebox.

3. For what were the plums probably being saved?
The plums were probably being saved for breakfast.

4. What does the speaker want the owner of the plums to do?
The speaker wants the owner of the plums to forgive the mistake of eating the plums.

5. How does the speaker describe the plums?
The speaker says that the plums were delicious—sweet and cold.

READER'S JOURNAL

Have you ever written a brief note to tell someone that you borrowed something, that you will call later, or that you won't be home for dinner? What kinds of words and punctuation do you use in such a note? In your journal, write such a brief note, addressed to a friend.

LANGUAGE SKILLS

Read the Language Arts Survey, 2.8, "Demonstrative Pronouns." Then identify the demonstrative pronouns in the selection and note to what person, place, or thing they refer.

"This Is Just to Say"

WILLIAM CARLOS WILLIAMS

What has the speaker done? ❶

What does the speaker ask of the owner of the plums? ❷

I have eaten
the plums
that were in
the icebox[1]

and which
you were probably
saving
for breakfast

Forgive me
they were delicious
so sweet
and so cold ■

1. **icebox.** Refrigerator

ANSWERS FOR UNDERSTANDING LITERATURE

► See the evaluation forms for discussion, active listening, and oral communication, *Assessment Portfolio,* 7.11–7.14.

Responses will vary. Possible responses are given.

1. Speaker and Tone. One can infer that although the speaker is feeling humble and apologetic, he or she thoroughly enjoyed the experience of eating the plums. The speaker is afraid of angering or offending the owner of the plums and feels some guilt about eating the owner's breakfast. However, the speaker enjoyed eating the plums, and one gets the feeling that if the opportunity arose, the speaker would again be unable to control his or her actions and would eat the delicious plums.

2. Rhythm and Meter. "This Is Just to Say" is made up of measured feet that are varied throughout the poem.

Responding to the Selection

Imagine that you are the recipient of the poem, which you have found on the kitchen table, explaining why your plums are missing from the icebox. Would you forgive the speaker of the poem, as he asks? Why, or why not? Write an entry in your journal expressing your response to the poem.

Reviewing the Selection

RECALLING

1. What has the speaker eaten?
2. How does the speaker say that the plums tasted?

INTERPRETING

3. Why does the speaker ask for forgiveness?
4. Whom is the speaker addressing in the poem?

SYNTHESIZING

5. What connotation does the title, "This Is Just to Say," lend to the poem?

Understanding Literature (Questions for Discussion)

1. **Speaker and Tone.** The **speaker** is the character who speaks in a poem—the voice assumed by the writer. **Tone** is the emotional attitude toward the reader or toward the subject implied by a literary work. What can be inferred about the speaker from what he says and how he says it? What emotional attitude does the speaker have toward the person he is addressing? What emotional attitude does the speaker have toward the plums?
2. **Rhythm and Meter. Rhythm** is the pattern of beats or stresses in a line of verse or prose. The **meter** of a poem is its rhythmical pattern. Scan the poem, including the title, and identify the types of rhythmical units, or feet, that make up the poem.

Responding in Writing

1. **Poem.** Write a poem in which the speaker addresses someone he or she knows, telling that person about an ordinary event in the day. Use rhythm and meter to reflect the speech pattern appropriate to the speaker and what he or she is saying.
2. **Personal Note.** Write a personal note in response to the speaker in "This Is Just to Say." In your note, explain what you were saving the plums for and why you do or do not forgive the speaker.

RESPONDING TO THE SELECTION

Ask students to think about the feelings of the speaker in the poem. Why is the speaker sorry? Why, however, might the mistake be forgivable? Invite students to separate into pairs again and talk about the journal entries.

ANSWERS FOR REVIEWING THE SELECTION

RECALLING

1. The speaker has eaten plums.
2. The speaker says that the plums were delicious—"so sweet and so cold."

INTERPRETING

Responses will vary. Possible responses are given.

3. The speaker feels guilt at eating someone else's breakfast.
4. The speaker is addressing the owner of the plums.

SYNTHESIZING

Responses will vary. Possible responses are given.

5. The title "This Is Just to Say" connotes timidity and humility. The speaker seems to be making a conscious effort to sound humble as he or she delivers the apology.

ANALYTIC SCALES FOR RESPONDING IN WRITING

Assign a score from 1 to 25 for each grading criterion below. (For more detailed evaluation, see the evaluation forms for writing, revising, and proofreading, *Assessment Portfolio,* 7.1–7.10.)

1. Poem

- **Content/Unity.** The poem features a speaker addressing a person he or she knows and is centered around an interesting but ordinary, everyday event.
- **Organization/Coherence.** The poem is written clearly, with language appropriate to the speaker and the event.

(cont.)

ANALYTIC SCALES FOR RESPONDING IN WRITING (CONT.)

- **Language/Style.** The poem uses vivid details, concrete imagery, and rhythm and meter to reflect normal speech patterns.
- **Conventions.** The poem avoids errors in spelling, grammar, usage, and mechanics.

2. Personal Note

- **Content/Unity.** The personal note is a believable response to the speaker of "This Is Just to Say."
- **Organization/Coherence.** The personal note clearly states for what purpose the plums were being saved and why the speaker is or is not forgiven.
- **Language/Style.** The note is written in language appropriate to the speaker.
- **Conventions.** The note avoids errors in spelling, grammar, usage, and mechanics.

PREREADING NOTES

READER'S JOURNAL

Ask students first to freewrite striking images, writing down the first images that come to their minds. Then they should take time to analyze why the images are so striking to them. Invite students to share their images with the rest of the class.

LANGUAGE SKILLS

Students should identify *upon, with,* and *beside* as prepositions. *Upon* introduces the phrase "upon a red wheel barrow," *with* introduces "with rain water," and *beside* introduces "beside the white chickens."

ANSWERS TO SELECTION CHECK TEST 4.8.21

EX. Into how many parts is the poem divided?
The poem is divided into four parts.

1. What is the central image of the poem?
The central image of the poem is a red wheelbarrow.

2. Upon what item does so much depend?
So much depends upon a red wheelbarrow.

3. With what is the wheelbarrow glazed?
The wheelbarrow is glazed with rain water.

4. Beside what is the wheelbarrow?
The wheelbarrow is beside the white chickens.

5. Of how many complete sentences is the poem composed?
The poem is composed of one complete sentence.

READER'S JOURNAL

Think of an image from your personal experience that you find particularly striking, one that stuck with you after the original experience. What emotional impact did the image have upon you? Write about the experience in your journal.

LANGUAGE SKILLS

Read the Language Arts Survey, 2.24, "Prepositions." Then identify the prepositions in the poem and note what prepositional phrases they introduce.

"The Red Wheelbarrow"

WILLIAM CARLOS WILLIAMS

so much depends
upon

a red wheel
barrow

5 glazed with rain
water

beside the white
chickens ■

Responding to the Selection

Imagine that you are the speaker who sees the red wheelbarrow. Write an entry in your journal explaining why "so much depends upon" the image of the red wheelbarrow.

ANSWERS FOR UNDERSTANDING LITERATURE

► See the evaluation forms for discussion, active listening, and oral communication, *Assessment Portfolio,* 7.11–7.14.

Responses will vary. Possible responses are given.

1. Image and Imagery. One might see a red wheelbarrow and some chickens on a farm. The things mentioned in the poem are associated with a working farm scene. This association is part of the poem's meaning as a whole.

2. Speaker and Effect. The speaker focuses briefly on one small aspect of a world. The speaker sees the images with an eye for detail, and a sensitivity to how this world functions. The poem asks the reader to notice the items, and look at them with a new sensitivity to their importance.

Reviewing the Selection

RECALLING

1. With what is the red wheelbarrow glazed?

2. Beside what do the white chickens stand?

INTERPRETING

3. What colors are part of the image? What happens to your perception when those colors are placed beside each other?

4. How does the presence of the rainwater emphasize the momentariness of the image?

SYNTHESIZING

5. How does the phrase "so much depends/upon" intensify the image of the red wheelbarrow?

Understanding Literature (Questions for Discussion)

1. **Image and Imagery.** An **image** is a word or phrase that names something that can be seen, heard, touched, tasted, or smelled. The images in a literary work are referred to, collectively, as the work's **imagery.** Where might one see a red wheelbarrow and white chickens? To what kind of world does the imagery in the poem belong? Why does it matter to the speaker "how" the imagery is seen?

2. **Speaker and Effect.** The **speaker** is the character who speaks in a poem—the voice assumed by the writer. The **effect** of a literary work is the general impression or emotional impact that it achieves. With what kind of eye does the speaker see the image? What effect, or general impression, does the poem create upon the reader or listener?

Responding in Writing

1. **Free Verse Poem.** Write a very brief free verse poem in which the speaker describes, from his or her vantage point, an ordinary, yet momentary, image seen through a window of a house or of a moving vehicle.

2. **Caption.** Write a caption, in which context is established, to accompany a photograph of each of the following objects: a blue shoe, a yellow notebook, a green lamp, and a black telephone.

RESPONDING TO THE SELECTION

Ask students to think about what might depend upon a red wheelbarrow in certain situations. You might ask students to brainstorm this question as a class.

ANSWERS FOR REVIEWING THE SELECTION

RECALLING

1. The red wheelbarrow is glazed with rainwater.

2. The white chickens stand beside the red wheelbarrow.

INTERPRETING

Responses will vary. Possible responses are given.

3. The colors red and white are part of the image. The colors add clarity and authenticity to the images. They are no longer just a wheelbarrow and some chickens.

4. The rainwater would not stay glazed on the wheelbarrow for very long. The poem captures the moment right after a rain shower.

SYNTHESIZING

Responses will vary. Possible responses are given.

5. The phrase directs the reader's attention to the red wheelbarrow and makes it not simply one image in the whole picture, but the focus of the poem.

ANALYTIC SCALES FOR RESPONDING IN WRITING

Assign a score from 1 to 25 for each grading criterion below. (For more detailed evaluation, see the evaluation forms for writing, revising, and proofreading, *Assessment Portfolio,* 7.1–7.10.)

1. Free Verse Poem

- **Content/Unity.** The poem focuses on an ordinary image and shows this image through the vantage point of one speaker.

(cont.)

ANALYTIC SCALES FOR RESPONDING IN WRITING (CONT.)

- **Organization/Coherence.** The poem is organized so that the significance of the image is clear.
- **Language/Style.** The poem uses vivid details and concrete imagery.
- **Conventions.** The poem avoids errors in spelling, grammar, usage, and mechanics.

2. Caption

- **Content/Unity.** The caption establishes context for each of the four objects.
- **Organization/Coherence.** The context of the objects is clear to the reader.
- **Language/Style.** The caption is written in clear and concise language and uses vivid imagery.
- **Conventions.** The caption avoids errors in spelling, grammar, usage, and mechanics.

PREREADING NOTES

READER'S JOURNAL

Invite students to share their words with the rest of the class. You might also ask students to think about other words that sound or look like their meanings.

LANGUAGE SKILLS

Students should identify *tipping, kicking, rolling,* and *swinging* as gerunds and *rollicking* as a participle modifying *measures.*

ANSWERS TO SELECTION CHECK TEST 4.8.23

EX. To what painter does Williams refer in "The Dance"?
Pieter Brueghel the Elder is referred to in "The Dance."

1. What are the dancers in the poem celebrating?
The dancers are celebrating a wedding.

2. What do the dancers do in the painting?
The dancers go round and round and around.

3. What musical instruments are mentioned in the poem?
The poem mentions bagpipes, a bugle, and fiddles.

4. Where are the dancers dancing?
The dancers dance around the Fair Grounds.

5. What words describe the motion of the dancers?
The words *kicking, rolling, swinging,* and *prance* describe the motion of the dancers.

READER'S JOURNAL

How can words create a sense of movement? What is different about the rhythm of the words *careen* and *lollipop?* In your journal, write a word or phrase that creates a sense of each of the following rhythms: lumbering, dreamy, smooth, choppy, rapid, uneven, sudden, and soaring.

LANGUAGE SKILLS

Read the Language Arts Survey, 2.16, "Verbals: Participles" and 2.17, "Verbals: Gerunds." Then identify some verbals in the poem and note which are participles and which are gerunds.

"The Dance"

WILLIAM CARLOS WILLIAMS

In Brueghel's great picture, The Kermess,[1]
the dancers go round, they go round and
around, the squeal and the blare and the
tweedle of bagpipes, a bugle and fiddles
5 tipping their bellies (round as the thick-
sided glasses whose wash they impound)[2]
their hips and their bellies off balance
to turn them. Kicking and rolling about
the Fair Grounds, swinging their butts, those
10 shanks[3] must be sound to bear up under such
rollicking measures, prance as they dance
in Brueghel's great picture, The Kermess. ■

1. **Brueghel's . . . The Kermess.** Refers to *The Wedding Dance* by Flemish painter Pieter Brueghel the Elder (*circa* 1525–1569)
2. **wash they impound.** Beverage they drink
3. **shanks.** Upper legs.

Responding to the Selection

Imagine that you are one of the dancers going "round and around" in the poem. Write an entry in your journal describing what kind of music you were dancing to and what emotions you experienced while dancing.

ADDITIONAL QUESTIONS AND ACTIVITIES

You might have students read other poems that focus on particular paintings. Direct them to "The Starry Night" by Anne Sexton, which appears on page 810 of their text. This poem refers to the Vincent van Gogh painting *Starry Night on the Rhine.* You might also direct them to "Musée des Beaux Arts" by W. H. Auden, a poem which refers to another Brueghel painting, *Icarus.*

Reviewing the Selection

RECALLING

1. What do the dancers do "In Brueghel's great picture"?
2. What instruments are making the music?

INTERPRETING

3. What actions on the part of the dancers suggest celebration and enjoyment?
4. What sounds of the instruments support "the rollicking measures" they create?

SYNTHESIZING

5. As the dancers "go round" in the great picture, how does the poem "go round" on the page?

Understanding Literature (Questions for Discussion)

1. **Repetition. Repetition** is the use, again, of a sound, word, phrase, sentence, or other element. What sounds are repeated in the poem? What words and phrases are repeated? What is the purpose of the repetitions?
2. **Run-on Line and Rhythm.** A **run-on line** is a line of verse in which the sense or the grammatical structure does not end with the end of the line, but rather is continued on one or more subsequent lines. **Rhythm** is the pattern of beats or stresses in a line of verse or prose. What effect do the run-on lines have upon the rhythm of "The Dance"?

Responding in Writing

1. **Critical Interpretation.** Write a critical interpretation that analyzes how the content of "The Dance" is reflected in the meter, or rhythm, of the poem. Use examples of scanned lines from the poem to support your interpretation. Refer to *meter* in the Handbook of Literary Terms.
2. **Descriptive Paragraph.** Write a descriptive paragraph about a work of art that you find interesting. In the paragraph, tell what you see when you look at the work of art, describing as clearly as possible what is happening in that work.

RESPONDING TO THE SELECTION

Encourage students to use as much concrete detail as possible, and to use their imaginations to write as much as they can about the dance. They might try to gather ideas from their own personal experiences at dances or large friendly gatherings. What are the sights, sounds, and feelings they associate with these events?

ANSWERS FOR REVIEWING THE SELECTION

RECALLING

1. The dancers dance round and round and around.
2. Bagpipes, bugles, and fiddles are making the sounds.

INTERPRETING

Responses will vary. Possible responses are given.

3. The dancers are kicking, rolling about, "swinging their butts," and prancing.
4. The musical instruments are described as squealing, blaring, and tweedling.

SYNTHESIZING

Responses will vary. Possible responses are given.

5. The sentences run into one another, creating a sense of commotion, movement, and energy for the reader.

ANALYTIC SCALES FOR RESPONDING IN WRITING

Assign a score from 1 to 25 for each grading criterion below. (For more detailed evaluation, see the evaluation forms for writing, revising, and proofreading, *Assessment Portfolio,* 7.1–7.10.)

1. Critical Interpretation

- **Content/Unity.** The interpretation addresses meter and rhythm in the poem, and assertions are backed up with lines from the poem.

(cont.)

ANALYTIC SCALES FOR RESPONDING IN WRITING (CONT.)

- **Organization/Coherence.** The interpretation is clear and concise and includes supporting details.
- **Language/Style.** The interpretation is written with clear and precise language.
- **Conventions.** The interpretation avoids errors in spelling, grammar, usage, mechanics, and manuscript form.

2. Descriptive Paragraph

- **Content/Unity.** The paragraph focuses on a particular work of art and describes what is happening in the work of art.
- **Organization/Coherence.** The paragraph presents the work of art clearly to the reader. The paragraph maintains a clear focus.
- **Language/Style.** The paragraph includes colorful modifiers and careful detail.
- **Conventions.** The paragraph avoids errors in spelling, grammar, usage, mechanics, and manuscript form.

ANSWERS FOR UNDERSTANDING LITERATURE

► See the evaluation forms for discussion, active listening, and oral communication, *Assessment Portfolio,* 7.11–7.14.

Responses will vary. Possible responses are given.

1. Repetition. The phrase "In Brueghel's great picture" is repeated and the word *round* is repeated. References to bellies, hips, and shanks are scattered throughout the poem. The repetition of these words and phrases gives the poem focus and creates a sense of movement.

2. Run-on Line and Rhythm. The structure of the poem and the way in which the sentences run into one another create a fast-paced, rollicking rhythm. The rhythm of the poem matches the rhythm of the music and the event.

ANSWERS FOR LANGUAGE LAB

1. Dated 1565, *The Corn Harvester* is one of the five remaining panels representing months of the year.

2. Other paintings in Brueghel's cycle include *Hunters in the Snow, Return of the Herd, The Gloomy Day,* and *Haymaking.*

3. *Haymaking* is housed in the National Gallery in Prague.

4. In *The Return of the Herd,* cattle are shown leaving the pastures of summer.

5. *The Gloomy Day* depicts a cold, stormy day—probably in February.

ANSWERS FOR RESEARCH SKILLS

Students should go to the library or work with books that might be available at home or in the classroom to complete this assignment. Students should pay close attention to the models presented in the Language Arts Survey. Request that the cards be neat and thorough.

Language Lab

Titles of Artworks. Read the Language Arts Survey, 2.128, "Titles of Artworks." Then rewrite the following sentences, correcting the capitalization errors in each one.

1. Dated 1565, *the corn harvester* is one of five remaining panels representing months of the year.
2. Other paintings in Brueghel's cycle include *hunters in the snow, return of the herd, the gloomy day,* and *haymaking.*
3. *haymaking* is housed in the National Gallery in Prague.
4. In *the return of the herd,* cattle are shown leaving the pastures of summer.
5. *the gloomy day* depicts a cold, stormy day—probably in February.

Research Skills

Bibliography Cards. Read the Language Arts Survey, 4.29, "Bibliographies and Bibliography Cards." Then, on the topic of William Carlos Williams, write one bibliography card for each bibliography entry form listed below.

1. a book with one author
2. a book with an editor but no single author
3. a poem, short story, essay, or chapter in a collection of works by one author
4. an introduction, preface, foreword, or afterword written by someone other than the author(s) of a work
5. an article in an encyclopedia, dictionary, or other alphabetically organized reference work

PROJECT

Art History. Form small groups of three or four students to research the life and art of the sixteenth-century Flemish painter Pieter Brueghel the Elder. Assign to each group one of the following topics: biography, paintings, style, social and historical context, and works of other sixteenth-century Flemish painters. After completing the research, have each group present their findings to the rest of the class.

PROJECT NOTES

►See the worksheets and evaluation forms for projects, *Assessment Portfolio,* 7.20–7.23.

Art History
Give students ample time in which to organize the search and to assign tasks to one another. Suggest that they visit the school or local library as soon as possible. Encourage students to use pictures, maps, models, and any other visuals when they present their information to the class.

PREREADING

"Patterns"
by Amy Lowell

About the Author

Amy Lowell (1874–1925) was born in Brookline, Massachusetts, into one of the state's wealthiest families, whose members had played prominent roles in public life since the American Revolution. Their status was immortalized in the 1910 doggerel, "And this is good old Boston,/The home of the bean and the cod,/Where the Lowells talk to the Cabots,/And the Cabots talk only to God." The Lowell men attended Harvard and then went on to run or found businesses or major institutions. The Lowell women raised children and had roles in the social and philanthropic life of Boston. Amy Lowell understood the importance of being a Lowell, but temperamentally she was miscast for the role assigned her by gender. She wanted an independent life, which fortunately she had the money to achieve. Lowell's desire to contribute to public life found its outlet beginning at the age of thirty-eight, when she launched her public literary career with the publication of her poetry in *A Dome of Many-Coloured Glass.* She soon adopted the Imagist style, becoming its chief spokesperson. The Imagists sought to create poems free of "authorial intervention," that presented precisely observed sensory experiences and left to the reader the interpretation of those experiences. Lowell greatly admired the poet John Keats and wrote a massive two-volume biography of him during the 1920s. She was awarded the Pulitzer Prize in poetry posthumously in 1926 for *What's O'Clock* (1925). Her other works include *Sword Blades and Poppy Seed* (1914); *Men, Women, and Ghosts* (1916); *Can Grande's Castle* (1918); *Pictures of the Floating World* (1919); and *Legends* (1921).

About the Selection

"Patterns," from *The Collected Poems of Amy Lowell,* presents a poetic counterpoint, the news of death against a backdrop of beauty. Without preaching, the poem becomes a compelling antiwar statement. As an Imagist, Lowell sought to break from the tyranny of form; this poem portrays war as a devastating form.

ADDITIONAL RESOURCES

Reader's Guide
- Selection Worksheet, 8.13

Assessment Portfolio
- Selection Check Test, 4.8.25
- Selection Test, 4.8.26

Essential Skills Practice Books
- *Language,* 2.24, 2.47
- *Study and Research,* 4.8

ENRICHMENT ACTIVITIES

- Ask students to research other members of the Lowell family of Massachusetts and list the roles individual family members played in public life.
- Have students familiarize themselves with some of the work of John Keats, about whom Amy Lowell wrote a biography. Suggest that they compare and contrast the work of Keats and Lowell. Why might Lowell have admired him?
- Have students research the roles of women of all social classes during the time Lowell was writing. Did she live a life like that of other women during her time? How did her socioeconomic status affect her ability to launch a career?

SUPPORT FOR LEP STUDENTS

Some students might struggle with the length and subtleties of the poem. Discuss the theme before students read the piece.

Additional Vocabulary

squill—(also spelled *scilla*) plant of the lily family
rigid—stiff
whim—frivolous action
pillared—long and slender
asters—plants with purple, blue, pink, or white flowers resembling the flowers of a daisy
arrayed—displayed

GOALS/OBJECTIVES

Studying this lesson will enable students to

- empathize with a speaker sharing a tragic experience and with the speaker's ideas about war
- discuss the life and work of Amy Lowell
- understand the terms *rhyme* and *repetition*
- write an essay
- identify and understand prepositional phrases
- understand comparing and contrasting
- identify various patterns and forms

PREREADING NOTES

READER'S JOURNAL

Students should jot down specific thoughts and feelings. They should then recall the details of their surroundings when they heard the bad news. Students who might not have experienced something like this firthand may attempt to understand and write about another person's experience.

LANGUAGE SKILLS

Answers will vary. Students might identify *down* in "down the garden-paths." This phrase relates the speaker and the garden-path. The students might also identify *against* in "against the stiff brocade." This phrase relates the verb *wars* with the stiff brocade.

ANSWERS TO GUIDED READING QUESTIONS

❶ The speaker compares herself to a rare pattern, such as the pattern of the garden-paths and the pattern of her gown.

❷ The "current fashion" includes high-heeled, ribboned shoes; brocade; and whalebone corsets.

❸ The speaker feels a passion that is at odds with "the stiff brocade" of her fashionable, delicate clothing.

READER'S JOURNAL

Have you ever looked forward to a special event only to have it canceled? Have you ever received bad news on a beautiful day? In your journal, write about how you felt on these occasions.

LANGUAGE SKILLS

Read the Language Arts Survey, 2.24, "Prepositions." Then identify some prepositions in the selection and note how each preposition relates a noun or pronoun to some other word in the sentence in which it appears.

"Patterns"

AMY LOWELL

I walk down the garden-paths,
And all the daffodils
Are blowing, and the bright blue squills.
I walk down the patterned garden-paths
5 In my stiff, brocaded[1] gown.
With my powdered hair and jeweled fan,
I too am a rare
Pattern. As I wander down
The garden-paths.
10 My dress is richly figured,[2]
And the train[3]
Makes a pink and silver stain
On the gravel, and the thrift
Of the borders.
15 Just a plate of current fashion,
Tripping by in high-heeled, ribboned shoes.
Not a softness anywhere about me,
Only whalebone[4] and brocade.
And I sink on a seat in the shade
20 Of a lime-tree. For my passion
Wars against the stiff brocade.
The daffodils and squills
Flutter in the breeze
As they please.

❶ *To what does the speaker compare herself?*

❷ *What are some elements of the "current fashion"?*

❸ *What conflict is occurring?*

1. **brocaded.** Embroidered
2. **figured.** Patterned
3. **train.** Trailing fabric on a gown
4. **whalebone.** Used as base for corsets

ADDITIONAL QUESTIONS AND ACTIVITIES

• Ask students to research fashions and how fashions change and stay the same over time. Ask them to spend time looking for information about whalebone corsets. How were they made? Why were they worn? How might the tight-fitting garments be symbolic of certain social and gender constraints of the time? Are similar items used today? Invite students to write or discuss their ideas.

• Students might want to find information about the plants mentioned in this poem. What do they look like? Where might one find these flowers?

And I weep;
For the lime-tree is in blossom
And one small flower had dropped upon my bosom.

And the plashing of waterdrops
In the marble fountain
Comes down the garden-paths.
The dripping never stops.
Underneath my stiffened gown
Is the softness of a woman bathing in a marble basin,[5]
A basin in the midst of hedges grown
So thick, she cannot see her lover hiding,
But she guesses he is near,
And the sliding of the water
Seems the stroking of a dear
Hand upon her.
What is Summer in a fine brocaded gown!
I should like to see it lying in a heap upon the ground.
All the pink and silver crumpled up on the ground.

I would be the pink and silver as I ran along the paths,
And he would stumble after,
Bewildered by my laughter.
I should see the sun flashing from his sword hilt[6] and the buckles on his shoes.
I would choose
To lead him in a maze along the patterned paths,
A bright and laughing maze for my heavy-booted lover.
Till he caught me in the shade,
And the buttons of his waistcoat bruised my body as he clasped me
Aching, melting, unafraid.
With the shadows of the leaves and the sundrops,
And the plopping of the waterdrops,
All about us in the open afternoon—
I am very like to swoon
With the weight of this brocade,
For the sun sifts through the shade.
Underneath the fallen blossom
In my bosom,
Is a letter I have hid.
It was brought to me this morning by a rider from the Duke.[7]

❶ *What feeling does the speaker convey?*

❷ *What does the speaker have hidden?*

5. **basin.** Sink
6. **hilt.** Handle
7. **the Duke.** John Churchill, Duke of Marlborough (1650–1722), military commander in the War of Spanish Succession (1701–1714)

Answers to Guided Reading Questions

❶ The speaker expresses sadness and a feeling of wanting to break free from the constraints of the stiff gown.

❷ The speaker has a letter hidden in her gown.

Additional Questions and Activities

• How does the speaker imagine breaking away and escaping from the sadness and pain she is feeling? What are some other symbols students have seen used to demonstrate this feeling? What might they use if they were to create their own original symbols? Students might think back to the situation they wrote about in their journals. Ask them to focus on one detail that might be symbolic of the experience.

• Ask students to use the library to find more information about John Churchill, Duke of Marlborough, and the War of Spanish Succession. They should attempt to answer the following questions: Who was John Churchill? What was at stake during the War of Spanish Succession? Who was involved in this war? Students should consult the Language Arts Survey, 4.20–4.28, if they need help getting started.

Art Note

Samuel Palmer (1805–1881) was a British painter known for his landscapes, such as the painting shown on page 556. Palmer is also known for his etchings. An etching is an artistic print made from a plate of metal or glass. A design is carved into the plate with acid and from this plate a print is made.

Answer to Guided Reading Question

❶ The speaker has received a letter telling her that her fiancé has died in battle.

A Shoreham Garden. *Samuel Palmer, circa 1829. Courtesy of the Trustees of the Victoria & Albert Museum*

What news does the speaker receive? ❶

"Madam, we regret to inform you that Lord Hartwell
Died in action Thursday se'nnight."[8]
As I read it in the white, morning sunlight,
The letters squirmed like snakes.
"Any answer, Madam," said my footman.
"No," I told him.
"See that the messenger takes some refreshment.
No, no answer."
And I walked into the garden,
Up and down the patterned paths,
In my stiff, correct brocade.
The blue and yellow flowers stood up proudly in the sun,

8. **se'nnight.** Seven days and nights

Each one.
I stood upright too,
Held rigid to the pattern
By the stiffness of my gown.
Up and down I walked,
Up and down.

In a month he would have been my husband.
In a month, here, underneath this lime,
We would have broke the pattern;
He for me, and I for him,
He as Colonel, I as Lady,
On this shady seat.
He had a whim
That sunlight carried blessing.
And I answered, "It shall be as you have said."
Now he is dead.

In Summer and in Winter I shall walk
Up and down
The patterned garden-paths
In my stiff, brocaded gown.
The squills and daffodils
Will give place to pillared roses, and to asters, and to snow.
I shall go
Up and down,
In my gown.
Gorgeously arrayed,
Boned and stayed.
And the softness of my body will be guarded from embrace
By each button, hook, and lace.
For the man who should loose me is dead,
Fighting with the Duke in Flanders,
In a pattern called a war.
Christ! What are patterns for? ■

❶ *Who was Lord Hartwell?*

❷ *What happened to Lord Hartwell?*

Responding to the Selection

Imagine that you are the speaker, wearing a stiff, brocaded gown, walking along a garden path, and you receive bad news. What occasions were you anticipating? What memories leap to mind?

Answers to Guided Reading Questions

❶ Lord Hartwell was the man the speaker was to marry in a month.

❷ Lord Hartwell was killed in battle.

Answers to Selection Check Test 4.8.25

EX. Where does the speaker walk?
The speaker walks down garden-paths.

1. What does the speaker wear as she walks?
The speaker wears a brocaded gown.

2. How is the speaker feeling as she walks?
The speaker feels a great deal of sadness.

3. During what season does the poem take place?
The poem takes place in summer.

4. What does the speaker hide in her gown?
The speaker hides a letter in her gown.

5. What tragedy has occurred in the poem?
The speaker's fiancé has been killed in battle.

Responding to the Selection

Ask students to consider the possibility that the speaker had not seen her fiancé lately because he had been in battle. She probably missed him a great deal and anxiously anticipated his return. How might this fact have added to her despair? Ask students to think about what sort of life the speaker might have been expecting. Then ask the students to consider the attitude the speaker expresses about the pattern of war. How does she view war? Ask students to write about their own views of war. They may base their ideas on firsthand information from relatives and friends or on news reports about wars throughout the world.

Answers for Reviewing the Selection

RECALLING

1. The poem takes place during summer.

2. The speaker says that "not a softness" exists "anywhere about" her.

3. The speaker recalls the softness the speaker felt about her when her love was near.

4. The speaker carries a letter hidden in her bosom.

5. The speaker and Lord Hartwell were planning to be married in a month.

INTERPRETING

Responses will vary. Possible responses are given.

6. There is irony in the choice of season because summer is a season of growth and blossoming trees and flowers. It is a time during which nature is ripe and alive.

7. The flowers blossom and flutter in the breeze.

8. The speaker is recalling a time when she was free from the despair that binds her and feels heavy like the stiff dress.

9. The speaker is burying the pain of the message in her bosom.

10. Lord Hartwell would have returned from war, and the two would have lived peacefully and happily.

SYNTHESIZING

Responses will vary. Possible responses are given.

11. Examples of foreshadowing include: "For my passion/Wars against the stiff brocade"; "and I weep"; "And one small flower had dropped upon my bosom"; and the section that begins, "And the plashing of waterdrops. . . ."

Reviewing the Selection

Recalling

1. In what season does the poem take place?
2. What does not exist "anywhere about" the speaker?
3. What does the speaker recall about softness?
4. What does the speaker carry hidden in her bosom?
5. What were the speaker and Lord Hartwell planning?

Interpreting

6. What irony occurs because of the choice of season? What other ironies can you find?
7. What can the flowers in the garden do that the speaker cannot?
8. Why does the speaker wish to see her gown "lying in a heap upon the ground"?
9. In what figurative way is the message in the letter also hidden in the speaker's bosom?
10. What does the speaker mean when she says, "We would have broke the pattern"?

Synthesizing

11. Although many beautiful things are described in the poem, **foreshadowing**, or the act of presenting materials that hint at later events, of the crisis occurs. Find examples of this foreshadowing throughout the poem.

Understanding Literature (Questions for Discussion)

1. **Rhyme and Repetition. Rhyme** is the repetition of sounds at the ends of words. Types of rhyme include *end rhyme* (the use of rhyming words at the ends of lines), *internal rhyme* (the use of rhyming words within lines), *exact rhyme* (in which the rhyming words end with the same sound or sounds), and *slant rhyme* (in which the rhyming sounds are similar but not identical). **Repetition** is the use, again, of a sound, word, phrase, sentence, or other element. Consider the following line from the poem: "And the plopping of the waterdrops." What kinds of rhyme are used in that line? What repetition of that line occurs in the poem? What effect is created by the repetition and slight alteration of the internal rhymes?

Answers for Understanding Literature

► See the evaluation forms for discussion, active listening, and oral communication, *Assessment Portfolio,* 7.11–7.14.

Responses will vary. Possible responses are given.

1. Rhyme and Repetition. "And the plopping of the waterdrops" is an example of internal rhyme. Variations of this line in the poem include: "And the plashing of waterdrops," "The dripping never stops," "one small flower had dropped," and "With the shadows of the leaves and the sundrops." The repetition of dropping water and leaves emphasizes the idea of the sadness and weeping of the speaker.

2. Theme. One theme of this poem is the devastating pattern of war and the many ways in which it destroys life. The poem also addresses the theme of the life-giving and transforming power of love.

2. **Theme.** A **theme** is a central idea in a literary work. What themes are central to the selection? What is the speaker's attitude toward these ideas?

Responding in Writing

Essay. Write an essay that discusses in what ways war may be described as a pattern.

Language Lab

Prepositional Phrases. Read the Language Arts Survey, 2.47, "Adding Prepositional Phrases." Then expand each of the sentences below by adding a prepositional phrase.

1. The gardener knelt slowly.
2. Daffodils, tulips, and irises bloomed.
3. The rains washed the garden path.
4. The fountain had been carved from marble.
5. She enjoyed the sound of the water splashing.

Thinking Skills

Comparing and Contrasting. Read the Language Arts Survey, 4.8, "Comparing and Contrasting." Then, make two columns on a piece of paper, one headed "Patterns of Joy" and the other headed "Patterns of Sorrow." To the left of the columns, write *Comparison* and then under that *Contrast.* Draw lines across your page starting under each of these two words. List the characteristics of the patterns of joy and sorrow as described in the poem within the boxes of the chart that you have created with these four headings.

PROJECT

Patterns and Forms. Form small groups of three or four students. As a group, research various patterns and forms in different art media, such as textiles, ceramics, photographs, and so on, which have been inspired by or evoke a form or pattern in nature. For example, the form of a Japanese fan echoes the form of a gingko leaf. Have each group create three or four pairs of natural/artificial forms or patterns on a standard-size sheet of paper. Then, as a class, collect all of the pairs of patterns and forms in a book to display in your classroom.

ANALYTIC SCALES FOR RESPONDING IN WRITING

Assign a score from 1 to 25 for each grading criterion below. (For more detailed evaluation, see the evaluation forms for writing, revising, and proofreading, *Assessment Portfolio,* 7.1–7.10.)

Essay

- **Content/Unity.** The essay effectively addresses the theme of war being a pattern.
- **Organization/Coherence.** The essay is well organized and presents ideas that make sense and are convincing to the reader.
- **Language/Style.** The essay uses clear and concise language.
- **Conventions.** The poem avoids errors in spelling, grammar, usage, mechanics, and manuscript form.

ANSWERS FOR LANGUAGE LAB

Responses will vary. Possible responses are given.

1. The gardener knelt slowly beside the rose bushes.
2. Daffodils, tulips, and irises bloomed at the start of the warm weather.
3. The rain washed the garden path down the hill.
4. The fountain had been carved from marble found in the quarry.
5. She enjoyed the sound of the water splashing against the stone wall.

ANSWERS FOR THINKING SKILLS

Students might list the blooming of the flowers, the fluttering of flowers in the breeze, and the happy moments between the speaker and Lord Hartwell as patterns of joy. Students might list the weeping of the speaker, the walking through the garden in the stiff brocade gown, the hiding of the letter, and all references to war and death as patterns of sorrow.

PROJECT NOTES

▶See the worksheets and evaluation forms for projects, *Assessment Portfolio,* 7.20–7.23.

Patterns and Forms

Give students time to go to the library and research different art forms. You might want to ask them to take detailed notes as they conduct their research. Encourage students to organize and assign tasks required in order to complete the project. Students might want to display the finished book for other classes.

ADDITIONAL RESOURCES

READER'S GUIDE
- Selection Worksheet, 8.14

ASSESSMENT PORTFOLIO
- Selection Check Test, 4.8.27
- Selection Test, 4.8.28

ESSENTIAL SKILLS PRACTICE BOOKS
- *Language,* 2.32

ENRICHMENT ACTIVITIES

Ask students to create booklets of their favorite poetic images. They may choose lines from longer works or include brief poems similar to "In a Station of the Metro." Students might start by reading over selections studied in this text. They may also include favorite lines from pieces they find in the library or pieces they have read throughout their lives—including verses they enjoyed as children. Encourage students to provide illustrations and to create colorful covers for their booklets.

SUPPORT FOR LEP STUDENTS

Remind students of the significance of the title in understanding the image presented in the poem. You might want to spend time discussing the information presented in the About the Selection section on page 560.

ADDITIONAL VOCABULARY

bough—tree branch

VOCABULARY FROM THE SELECTION

apparition

PREREADING

"In a Station of the Metro"
by Ezra Pound

ABOUT THE AUTHOR

Ezra Pound (1885–1972) was born in Idaho but grew up in the East. The study of Latin in high school inspired him to become a poet. After graduating from Hamilton College in 1905 and receiving a master's degree from the University of Pennsylvania in 1906, he received a fellowship to go to France, Italy, and Spain to work on a dissertation. When he returned to the United States, he taught briefly at Wabash College in Indiana. He soon became an expatriate living in London, Paris, and Italy. He made his living teaching and reviewing. He also edited the magazines *Poetry* and *The Little Review.* Pound founded and defined Imagism, the literary movement that sought to present in poetry recreations of sensory experiences, without commentary about the emotional content or meaning of those experiences. Pound's influence on other writers was profound, especially in his call for a type of poetry that was harder, clearer, and nearer the bone and in his embracing of free verse.

Pound became obsessed with monetary reform and came to believe that Italian Fascist dictator Benito Mussolini embodied the ideal leader. By 1940, he had begun to give radio talks from Rome, denouncing American society, President Roosevelt, and the Jewish people. He continued the broadcasts when World War II began. He was indicted for treason, then arrested when United States soldiers entered Italy. After being held for weeks at a prison camp near Pisa, he was brought to trial but was declared insane and hospitalized. His winning of the Library of Congress's newly established Bollingen Prize for poetry in 1948 created a public furor. During his early years, Pound was generous with many other writers, including H. D. (Hilda Doolittle), T. S. Eliot, James Joyce, William Carlos Williams, Robert Frost, Ernest Hemingway, and Marianne Moore, helping them to refine their work and to find publication. Many of those writers rallied around him when he was charged with treason and imprisoned. The efforts of a committee of writers succeeded in winning Pound's release, and he returned to Italy, where he died at the age of eighty-seven. Pound began working on his long series of avant-garde poems, the *Cantos,* in 1915 and continued working on them throughout his imprisonment. He had produced more than one hundred by the time of his death. His other works include *Des Imagistes* (1915), *Hugh Selwyn Mauberly* (1920), *Make It New* (1934), *The ABC of Reading* (1934), *Polite Essays* (1937), and *Literary Essays* (1954).

ABOUT THE SELECTION

Pound said that one day, as he emerged from a train in the Paris subway, he suddenly saw "a beautiful face, and then another and another." He wrote the poem to convey that experience. Pound's original version of **"In a Station of the Metro"** was thirty lines long; his 1916 version of the poem, distilled into two lines, exemplifies the characteristic for which Pound's poetry is most noted, its imagery.

GOALS/OBJECTIVES

Studying this lesson will enable students to

- appreciate a brief and striking poetic image.
- understand aspects of the life and work of Ezra Pound
- recognize precise nouns
- define literary terms such as *image, imagery,* and *metaphor*
- write a haiku

READER'S JOURNAL

Have you ever been startled or dazzled by an image of something? What did you see? What kind of emotional response did the image evoke? Write in your journal about the image and the emotional impact it created.

LANGUAGE SKILLS

Read the Language Arts Survey, 2.32, "Using Precise Nouns." Then identify the precise nouns in the selection and note what effect they have on the poem.

"In a Station of the Metro"[1]

EZRA POUND

The apparition of these faces in the crowd;
Petals on a wet, black bough.

1. **In a Station of the Metro.** In a Paris subway station

WORDS FOR EVERYDAY USE: **ap • pa • ri • tion** (ap´ər rish´ən) *n.,* ghostly appearance of a person or thing

ANSWERS TO SELECTION CHECK TEST 4.8.27

EX. Who wrote "In a Station of the Metro"?
Ezra Pound wrote "In a Station of the Metro."

1. What is the setting of the Pound poem?
The setting is a metro station in Paris.

2. What appears in the crowd?
Apparitions of faces appear in the crowd.

3. What is on a wet bough?
Petals are on a wet bough.

4. How does the speaker describe the bough?
The speaker describes the bough as cold and wet.

5. What two things are being compared in the poem?
Faces and petal are being compared.

PREREADING NOTES

READER'S JOURNAL

You might want to ask students to keep observation notebooks and jot notes about images of people and places between classes and at home. If possible, you might send them to observe areas of the school during class time.

LANGUAGE SKILLS

Students should identify *apparition, faces, crowd, petals,* and *bough* as precise nouns. Precise nouns help the reader to visualize a scene and see an image through the eyes of the poet.

ADDITIONAL QUESTIONS AND ACTIVITIES

Ask students to be observant when in crowds of people—in the hallway between classes, on a bus going home, in a shopping mall, at a concert, and so on. How do people act in crowds? Encourage students to pay close attention to individuals in crowds. What facial expressions do they observe? What small incidents do they observe? Suggest that students spend time watching people and then record their observations in a journal. Ask students to gather in pairs to share their observations and form polished images from the rough notes gathered. Ask each pair to then create an original poem about people using their combined images.

VOCABULARY IN CONTEXT

- Thelma's faded reflection in the window resembled an eerie apparition, and it startled her.

RESPONDING TO THE SELECTION

Students should use their own observation experiences to try to understand the experience of the speaker.

ANSWERS FOR REVIEWING THE SELECTION

RECALLING

1. The speaker sees apparitions of faces in the crowd.
2. The speaker describes the bough as being wet and black.

INTERPRETING

Responses will vary. Possible responses are given.

3. *Apparition* connotes ghostly images, faces that are faded and that don't at first stand out when one glances over them.
4. The speaker is comparing "these faces" to petals on a bough.

SYNTHESIZING

Responses will vary. Possible responses are given.

5. The speaker expresses the idea that each ghostly face in the crowd has individual beauty.

ANSWERS FOR UNDERSTANDING LITERATURE

► See the evaluation forms for discussion, active listening, and oral communication, *Assessment Portfolio,* 7.11–7.14.

Responses will vary. Possible responses are given.

1. Image and Imagery. The "apparition" of the faces in the crowd and the petals on a wet, dark bough are the two central images of the poem. The reader can visualize the scene of a crowd in which faces do not stand out. Then the reader can visualize the speaker's idea of the beauty of the individual faces as petals.

2. Metaphor. The tenor of the metaphor is the group of faces in the crowd. The vehicle is the image of petals on the wet, dark bough. These things share a type of beauty.

Responding to the Selection

Imagine that you are the speaker of this poem, standing in a station of the Paris subway. Write in your journal about what you saw in the Metro, explaining what effect the image had on you.

Reviewing the Selection

RECALLING

1. What does the speaker see "in the crowd"?
2. How does the speaker describe the bough?

INTERPRETING

3. What connotation does the word *apparition* have?
4. To what is the speaker comparing "these faces"?

SYNTHESIZING

5. What attitude toward "The apparition of these faces" does the speaker express?

Understanding Literature (Questions for Discussion)

1. **Image and Imagery.** An **image** is a word or phrase that names something that can be seen, heard, touched, tasted, or smelled. The images in a literary work are referred to, collectively, as the work's **imagery.** What two images are central to the poem? What effect, or emotional impact, is created by the poem's imagery?
2. **Metaphor.** A **metaphor** is a figure of speech in which one thing is spoken or written about as if it were another. This figure of speech invites the reader to make a comparison between the two things, which can be analyzed into two parts: the tenor (or subject being described) and the vehicle (or object being used in the description). These two things can be compared because they share a particular quality. "In a Station of the Metro" is a metaphor. What is the tenor of the metaphor? the vehicle? What quality do these two things share?

Responding in Writing

Haiku. A **haiku** is a traditional Japanese three-line poem containing five syllables in the first line, seven in the second, and five again in the third. A haiku presents a picture, or image, in order to arouse in the reader a specific emotional response. Write a haiku that presents an image of something you have suddenly witnessed, such as a bird landing on a rooftop, a father bending down to pick up his child, or a cat stretching awake from a nap.

ANALYTIC SCALES FOR RESPONDING IN WRITING

Assign a score from 1 to 25 for each grading criterion below. (See the evaluation forms for writing, revising, and proofreading, *Assessment Portfolio,* 7.1–7.10.)

Haiku

- **Content/Unity.** The haiku focuses on a single moment and creates an emotional response in the reader.
- **Organization/Coherence.** The haiku is organized so that is creates a clear picture in the reader's mind. The image makes sense to the reader.
- **Language/Style.** The haiku uses precise nouns and language that form a picture in the reader's mind.
- **Conventions.** The haiku avoids errors in spelling, grammar, and usage and uses the proper number of syllables in each line.

PREREADING

"Poetry"
by Marianne Moore

About the Author

Marianne Moore (1887–1972) was born in Kirkwood, Missouri. Moore graduated from Bryn Mawr College in 1909, traveled with her mother in England and France in 1911, and taught at the U.S. Indian School in Carlisle from 1911 to 1915. Her poems were first published in England beginning in 1915, and in 1921, two of her friends conspired to have a collection of them, *Poems* (1921), published there. Moore and her mother moved to New York City in 1916 and lived together until her mother died. Her brother, a Presbyterian minister, had a parish in Brooklyn, New York, and she had a close relationship with him her entire life. In New York, she made her living as a teacher and as a librarian. The poet, who often made animals the subject of her musings, was a frequent visitor to the Bronx Zoo. She was also a lifelong Dodger fan and was once invited to throw out the first ball of the season. Her *Observations* won the Dial Award in 1924, and in 1925, she began work as an editor of *Dial* and continued to do so until it disbanded in 1929. During her career, Moore wrote many essays of poetry criticism. She received the Bollingen Award, the National Book Award, and the Pulitzer Prize. Her *Collected Poems* appeared in 1951.

About the Selection

Moore was often called a "poet's poet" because of her complex and subtle use of poetic technique. In using the entire stanza, rather than the word, line, image, or clause, as the unit of the poem, **"Poetry"** is characteristic of Moore's verse. The poem is also characteristic in its use of a catalog of particulars to define a general term, such as *poetry.*

ADDITIONAL RESOURCES

Reader's Guide
- Selection Worksheet, 8.15

Assessment Portfolio
- Selection Check Test, 4.8.29
- Selection Test, 4.8.30

Essential Skills Practice Books
- *Language,* 2.32

ENRICHMENT ACTIVITIES

- Ask students to consider how they might respond to someone who says, "I hate movies." One response would be to point out that movies differ from one another enormously. The chances are good that anyone could find some movie or genre of movies that he or she would enjoy. Point out that the same is true of poems. People who say that they dislike poetry probably simply haven't encountered poems that appeal to their tastes.
- Have each student look through the text and other sources to identify two poems, one that he or she dislikes and one that he or she likes. Have the student compare the two poems. Based on such a comparison, the student can formulate a tentative idea of what, in his or her estimation, constitutes a good poem.

SUPPORT FOR LEP STUDENTS

Additional Vocabulary

contempt—scorn, dislike

unintelligible—not understandable, confused, nonsensical

quest— journey or trial undertaken to accomplish some end

phenomena—things and occurrences

GOALS/OBJECTIVES

Studying this lesson will enable students to

- understand and appreciate a speaker's feelings about poetry
- describe Moore's literary accomplishments and explain the historical significance of her writing
- define *stanza* and recognize stanzas in their reading
- recognize concrete words and abstract words
- write a comparison-contrast paragraph

PREREADING NOTES

READER'S JOURNAL

Have students freewrite in their journals about their associations with the word *poetry* and then discuss in class whether they like reading poetry and why they do or do not. Do these things in preparation for attempting, as a class, to define poetry by listing its characteristics on the board. You may find that many students have fairly narrow notions about what poetry is (e.g., that it rhymes, that it is usually about love). Try to move your students toward a wider view of what poetry is, and explain that expanding people's ideas about what poetry can be or do was a central concern of the Modernist poets.

LANGUAGE SKILLS

Some precise nouns used in this poem include *fiddle,* which describes those aspects of poetry that are unnecessarily unnatural or artificial; *gardens,* which describes the imaginary context or world created by a poem; and *toads,* which refers to whatever is genuine, however unpleasant, in poetry.

ANSWERS TO GUIDED READING QUESTIONS

❶ The speaker makes the rather startling statement that she dislikes poetry, and she assumes that her reader shares this dislike. Reading the rest of the poem clarifies the opening statement. It is not poetry *per se* that the speaker dislikes but rather poetry as she perceives it.

❷ Poetry can describe real things that are useful and should describe things that are intelligible.

READERS' JOURNAL

Have you ever made lists of things you like or dislike? understand or do not understand? What particular things did you include on your lists? In your journal, write a list of characteristics that, for you, define the general term *poetry.*

LANGUAGE SKILLS

Read the Language Arts Survey, 2.32, "Using Precise Nouns." Then identify some precise nouns in the selection and note how they are used to define the abstract noun *poetry.*

"Poetry"

MARIANNE MOORE

What does the speaker dislike? ❶

What real things can poetry describe? ❷

I, too, dislike it: there are things that are important beyond all
this fiddle.[1]
Reading it, however, with a perfect contempt for it, one
discovers in
it after all, a place for the genuine
Hands that can grasp, eyes
that can dilate, hair that can rise
if it must, these things are important not because a

high-sounding interpretation can be put upon them but because
they are
useful. When they become so derivative[2] as to become
unintelligible,
the same thing may be said for all of us, that we
do not admire what
we cannot understand: the bat
holding on upside down or in quest of something to

eat, elephants pushing, a wild horse taking a roll, a tireless wolf
under

1. **fiddle.** Nonsense
2. **derivative.** Imitative

WORDS FOR EVERYDAY USE: **di • late** (dī´lāt) *vi.,* become larger or wider

VOCABULARY IN CONTEXT

- The cat's eyes dilated as it sought the mouse in the dark room.
- Mark's criticism of the play was valid; the acting was melodramatic.
- Martin Luther King, Jr., rose to national prominence when he led the successful boycott of buses in Montgomery, Alabama.
- The courtier criticized the queen's clothing and was punished for his insolence.
- Chandra hated the triviality of television news programs—the incessant "happy talk" and concentration on insignificant events.

a tree, the immovable[3] critic twitching his skin like a horse
20 that feels a flea, the base-
ball fan, the statistician[4]—
nor is it valid
to discriminate against "business documents and

school-books"; all these phenomena are important. One must make a distinction
25 however: when dragged into prominence by half poets the result is not poetry,
nor till the poets among us can be
"literalists of
the imagination"[5]—above
insolence and triviality and can present

30 for inspection, "imaginary gardens with real toads in them," shall we have
it. In the meantime, if you demand on the one hand,
the raw material[6] of poetry in
all its rawness and
35 that which is on the other hand
genuine, then you are interested in poetry. ■

3. **immovable.** Stubborn
4. **statistician.** Expert in statistics
5. **literalists of the imagination.** Term from W. B. Yeats's *Ideas of Good and Evil*
6. **raw material.** Basic ingredients

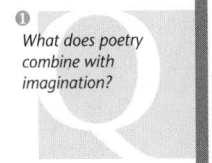

Responding to the Selection

Imagine that you are the reader or listener who is included as sharing the speaker's dislike of poetry: "I, too, dislike it." Why does the speaker assume that you, too, dislike it? Write a letter to the speaker, explaining why you do or do not dislike poetry.

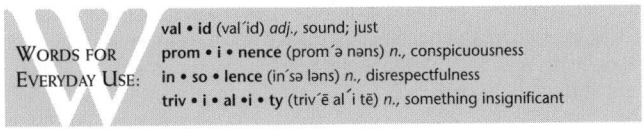

ANSWER TO GUIDED READING QUESTION

1 Poetry combines imagination with reality to present imaginary things literally.

ANSWERS TO SELECTION CHECK TEST 4.8.29

EX. Who claims to dislike poetry?
The speaker claims to dislike poetry.

1. What can one discover when reading poetry with "contempt"?
One can discover a "place for the genuine."

2. What don't we admire?
We don't admire what we cannot understand.

3. What is it not valid to discriminate against?
It is not valid to discriminate against "business documents and school-books."

4. What is the result of that which is dragged into prominence by half poets?
The result is not poetry.

5. What does the speaker hope to present for inspection?
The speaker hopes to present "imaginary gardens with real toads in them."

RESPONDING TO THE SELECTION

The speaker's inclusion of the reader in her opening statement emphasizes her certainty that most people would find poetry of the type written in her day exasperating.

ANALYTIC SCALES FOR RESPONDING IN WRITING

Assign a score from 1 to 25 for each grading criterion below. (For more detailed evaluation, see the evaluation forms for writing, revising, and proofreading, *Assessment Portfolio,* 7.1–7.10.)

Paragraph

- **Content/Unity.** The paragraph describes the differences between the two lines and the significance of those differences.
- **Organization/Coherence.** The paragraph has a clear topic sentence and uses transitions to connect ideas.
- **Language/Style.** The paragraph is written in formal language appropriate for a critical essay.
- **Conventions.** The paragraph avoids errors in spelling, grammar, usage, mechanics, and manuscript form.

Answers for Reviewing the Selection

RECALLING

1. The phrase "all this fiddle" refers to poetry, most likely to those aspects of the art that are unnatural, unrealistic, or artificial.

2. We do not admire what we do not understand. (Some early Modernist poets wrote verse that was difficult because it was highly elliptical, or contained lots of personal symbolism. Lesser poets wrote work that was derivatively elliptical and personal but often unintelligible, leading to a widespread feeling that modern poetry is obscure and not worth the effort. It is this tendency that Moore decries in her poem.)

3. We must make a distinction between those things that are proper subjects for poetry and those that are not.

4. The poets should be "literalists of the imagination."

INTERPRETING

Responses will vary. Possible responses are given.

5. They are useful. That is, they enable the organism to interact with and react to the environment.

6. "Elephants rolling" is an example of something that we cannot understand and therefore do not admire.

7. She has contempt for the work of half poets.

8. The listener or reader will prove that he or she shares Moore's view of poetry as a valuable undertaking.

SYNTHESIZING

Responses will vary. Possible responses are given.

9. A half poet simply drags whatever he or she considers important into prominence. A real poet, on the other hand, will rise above insolence and triviality, will be a "literalist of the imagination," and will "present for inspection 'imaginary gardens with real toads in them.'"

10. Readers or listeners should, while waiting for the appearance of the real poetry of which Moore speaks, demand "the raw material of poetry in all its rawness" and "that which is genuine."

Reviewing the Selection

RECALLING

1. To what does "all this fiddle" refer?
2. What do we not admire?
3. About what must one "make a distinction"?
4. According to the speaker, what should "the poets among us" be?

INTERPRETING

5. What quality do "hands that can grasp" and "eyes that can dilate" have in common?
6. Of what is the phrase "elephants rolling" an example?
7. What is the speaker's attitude toward what the half poets create?
8. What will the reader or listener prove by placing demands on poetry?

SYNTHESIZING

9. What is the difference between a half poet and a poet? What, according to the speaker, do the poets need to do?
10. According to the speaker, what demands should the reader or listener make on poetry?

Understanding Literature (Questions for Discussion)

1. **Stanza.** A **stanza** is a recurring pattern of grouped lines in a poem. Some types of stanzas include the couplet, triplet, quatrain, and quintain. What two types of stanza are used in the selection?

2. **Abstract and Concrete.** An **abstract** word or phrase is one that refers to something that cannot be directly perceived by the senses. *Truth, love, force, theory,* and *sadness* are examples of abstract terms. A **concrete** word or phrase is one that describes something that can be directly perceived by one or more of the five senses. *Book, pool, light,* and *car* are examples of concrete terms. Identify one abstract word used in the poem and the concrete words or phrases that describe it.

Responding in Writing

Comparison-Contrast Paragraph. In Moore's 1967 revision of "Poetry," she altered the first lines of the poem to read, "I, too, dislike it./Reading it, however, with a perfect contempt/for it, one discovers in/it, after all, a place for the genuine." Write a brief essay in which you compare and contrast the opening lines of the 1923 version of "Poetry," as it appears in this text, with the opening lines of the 1967 revision.

Answers for Understanding Literature

► See the evaluation forms for discussion, active listening, and oral communication, *Assessment Portfolio,* 7.11–7.14.

Responses will vary. Possible responses are given.

1. Stanza. This poem makes use of seven- and eight-line stanzas. A seven-line stanza is a heptastich. An eight-line stanza is an octave.

2. Abstract and Concrete. *Poetry* is an abstract term. Moore describes poems as presenting "imaginary gardens with real toads in them." *Gardens* and *toads* are concrete terms.

PREREADING

"The Love Song of J. Alfred Prufrock"
by T. S. Eliot

About the Author

T(homas) S(tearns) Eliot (1888–1965) was born in St. Louis, Missouri. He attended Milton Academy and Harvard University. In 1910, the year in which he earned his master's degree, he wrote one of his most famous poems, "The Love Song of J. Alfred Prufrock," a poem that was for its day radically experimental. During the pre-World War I period, Eliot attended the Sorbonne in Paris and studied Asian languages and religion. In 1915, following the outbreak of war, he moved to Oxford. A disappointment to his family, he supplemented his allowance by working as a bank teller. At the end of a difficult marriage to Vivian Haigh-Wood, Eliot received intensive psychiatric treatment for depression. Then, with the help of another expatriate poet, Ezra Pound, he published "Prufrock" and caught the attention of the literary world. In 1922, Eliot published an even more challenging poem, "The Waste Land"—a questioning of the moral bankruptcy of the interwar period poised against what Eliot saw as the superior values of the past. In 1928, shortly after embracing British citizenship, Eliot became a member of the Church of England. He married Valerie Fletcher in 1957. In addition to his invaluable poetic achievements, Eliot made successful contributions to other literary forms, including plays and literary criticism. In 1948, he was awarded the Nobel Prize for literature. *The Complete Poems and Plays of T. S. Eliot* was published in 1969.

About the Selection

Eliot wrote **"The Love Song of J. Alfred Prufrock"** in 1910–1911 while a graduate student at Harvard. The poem, a dramatic monologue, presents the "conversation with himself" of J. Alfred Prufrock, a middle-aged man who hesitates to speak directly to the woman he loves. First published in *Poetry* magazine in 1915, the poem was later collected in *Prufrock and Other Observations and Poems.* In many ways, this poem is typical of Eliot's work, which is **elliptical,** leaving out nonessential details, and highly **allusive,** making reference to people, events, objects, or works from history or literature.

GOALS/OBJECTIVES

Studying this lesson will enable students to

- empathize with the anxieties of a speaker
- describe Eliot's literary accomplishments and explain the historical significance of his writing
- define *dramatic monologue* and *free verse* and identify dramatic monologues and free verse in their reading
- recognize allusions in literature
- write a parody
- identify the functions of sentences
- replace linking verbs with action verbs

ADDITIONAL RESOURCES

Reader's Guide
- Selection Worksheet, 8.16

Assessment Portfolio
- Selection Check Test, 4.8.31
- Selection Test, 4.8.32

Essential Skills Practice Books
- *Language,* 2.34, 2.36
- *Study and Research,* 4.11

ENRICHMENT ACTIVITIES

Encourage students to locate as many allusions as they can in the poem and then find the original source. You might read students portions of *The Waste Land,* a longer verse form that is also rich in allusions. Students might then write their own short verses that use allusions to other works of literature. Students can come up with their own allusions, use one of Eliot's in a new way, or even allude to Eliot's work.

SUPPORT FOR LEP STUDENTS

Students will not recognize many of Eliot's allusions and thus have difficulty with the sense of the poem. You might have students work in groups to identify the meaning of some of Eliot's allusions. Encourage students to carefully read footnotes and the Words for Everyday Use. You might also review the additional vocabulary below with students before they read the selection.

Additional Vocabulary

mounting—climbing
fall—lowering of the voice in pitch or volume
scuttling—hurrying or scampering
snicker—laugh in a sly, derisive, partly stifled manner
politic—having practical wisdom
meticulous—extremely or excessively careful about details

PREREADING NOTES

READER'S JOURNAL

If students have not had this particular experience, they might write about any feelings they have held inside and why they did so.

LANGUAGE SKILLS

Some examples of interrogative sentences include the following: "Do I dare disturb the universe?"; "So how should I presume?"; "And how should I begin?"; "Should I, after tea and cakes and ices,/Have the strength to force the moment to its crisis?"; "Shall I part my hair behind?"; and "Do I dare to eat a peach?"

VOCABULARY FROM THE SELECTION

assert	linger
deferential	malinger
digress	obtuse
etherise	presume
formulated	tedious
insidious	

READER'S JOURNAL

Have you ever hesitated to tell someone how you feel about him or her? Why did you hesitate? What held you back? What would you have said if you had been able to speak frankly? Write about the experience in your journal.

LANGUAGE SKILLS

Read the Language Arts Survey, 2.36, "The Functions of Sentences." Then identify some interrogative sentences in the selection and note what the questions reveal about the speaker.

"The Love Song of J. Alfred Prufrock"

T. S. ELIOT

S'io credessi che mia risposta fosse
a persona che mai tornasse al mondo,
questa fiamma staria senza più scosse.
Ma per ciò che giammai di questo fondo
non tornò vivo alcun, s'i'odo il vero,
senza tema d'infamia ti rispondo.[1]

Let us go then, you and I,
When the evening is spread out against the sky
Like a patient etherised upon a table;
Let us go, through certain half-deserted streets,
The muttering retreats
Of restless nights in one-night cheap hotels
And sawdust restaurants with oyster-shells:
Streets that follow like a tedious argument
Of insidious intent
To lead you to an overwhelming question . . .

1. **S'io . . . rispondo.** Epigraph from Dante's *Inferno*, Canto XXVII, lines 61–66. The speaker is one of the damned telling of his torment: "If I believed that my response would be/to somebody who would ever return to the world,/this flame would be without more movement./But since nobody has returned from this depth alive,/if I hear the truth,/without fear of infamy, I answer you."

WORDS FOR EVERYDAY USE:
e • ther • ise (ē´thə rīz´) *vt.,* render groggy or numb
te • di • ous (tē´dē əs) *adj.,* long and tiresome
in • sid • i • ous (in sid´ē əs) *adj.,* deceitful

VOCABULARY IN CONTEXT

- Before modern anesthesia was developed, doctors etherised patients.
- We found the dry, lengthy speech to be tedious.
- We found it insidious that the salesperson took our money on Monday and still hadn't delivered the product by Friday.
- Summer lingered into autumn, and all were pleased with the sun-filled, balmy days.
- The puppy decided to assert her independence from her mother by venturing outdoors on her own.

Oh, do not ask, "What is it?"
Let us go and make our visit.
In the room the women come and go
Talking of Michelangelo.[2]

15 The yellow fog that rubs its back upon the window-panes,
The yellow smoke that rubs its muzzle on the window-panes,
Licked its tongue into the corners of the evening,
Lingered upon the pools that stand in drains,
Let fall upon its back the soot that falls from chimneys,
20 Slipped by the terrace, made a sudden leap,
And seeing that it was a soft October night,
Curled once about the house, and fell asleep.

❶ *What curls around the house and falls asleep? What does the color suggest?*

And indeed there will be time
For the yellow smoke that slides along the street
25 Rubbing its back upon the window-panes;
There will be time, there will be time
To prepare a face to meet the faces that you meet;
There will be time to murder and create,
And time for all the works and days of hands
30 That lift and drop a question on your plate;
Time for you and time for me,
And time yet for a hundred indecisions,
And for a hundred visions and revisions,
Before the taking of a toast and tea.

35 In the room the women come and go
Talking of Michelangelo.

And indeed there will be time
To wonder, "Do I dare?" and, "Do I dare?"
Time to turn back and descend the stair,
40 With a bald spot in the middle of my hair—
(They will say: "How his hair is growing thin!")
My morning coat, my collar mounting firmly to the chin,
My necktie rich and modest, but asserted by a simple pin—
(They will say: "But how his arms and legs are thin!")
45 Do I dare

❷ *Why might the speaker "turn back and descend the stair"?*

2. **Michelangelo.** (1475–1564) Italian sculptor, painter, architect, and poet

WORDS FOR EVERYDAY USE:
lin • ger (liŋ´gər) *vi.,* remain or stay longer than usual
as • sert (ə sûrt´) *vt.,* declare; affirm

ANSWERS TO GUIDED READING QUESTIONS

❶ The yellow fog curls around the house and falls asleep. Yellow suggests pollution, sickness, and fear.

❷ The speaker might "turn back and descend the stair" because he is nervous about progressing forward.

LITERARY TECHNIQUE

Characterization is the use of literary techniques to create a character. **Point of view** is the vantage point from which a story is told. In this poem, Prufrock, the speaker, is focusing on himself. Prufrock describes his own anxieties and feelings in the first-person point of view to reveal much about his character. Students should identify what Prufrock's hopes and fears are. Why does he keep emphasizing that "there will be time"?

Answers. Students might say that Prufrock is hoping for love and companionship and is fearful of rejection. Prufrock may emphasize that "there is time" so that he will not have to act and face rejection.

Answers to Guided Reading Questions

❶ No, the speaker believes that his life has been so timid and slow-paced that it could be measured in "coffee spoons."

❷ Prufrock describes himself as "pinned and wriggling on the wall."

Literary Technique

A **metaphor** is a figure of speech in which one thing is spoken or written about as if it were another. Ask students to consider the metaphor implied in the lines "And when I am formulated, sprawling on a pin,/When I am pinned and wriggling to the wall." To what does Prufrock compare himself? What is pinning him to the wall? Why is this metaphor appropriate, given the subject matter of the poem?

Answers. Prufrock compares himself to an insect pinned against a wall for examination. Students may say that Prufrock's own fears and obsessively introspective nature are pinning him to the wall. This metaphor is appropriate because, like a pinned insect, Prufrock is unable to act. Also, Prufrock is examining his own nature, or pinning himself to the wall.

Quotables

"A rat crept softly through
the vegetation
Dragging its slimy belly on the
bank
While I was fishing in the dull
canal
On a winter evening behind the
gashouse
Musing upon the king my
brother's wreck
And on the king my father's
death before him."

—T. S. Eliot, *The Waste Land*

Does the speaker believe his life has been bold or fast-paced? Explain. ❶

In what way does Prufrock describe himself? ❷

Disturb the universe?
In a minute there is time
For decisions and revisions which a minute will reverse.

For I have known them all already, known them all—
Have known the evenings, mornings, afternoons,
I have measured out my life with coffee spoons;
I know the voices dying with a dying fall
Beneath the music from a farther room.
So how should I presume?

And I have known the eyes already, known them all—
The eyes that fix you in a formulated phrase,
And when I am formulated, sprawling on a pin,
When I am pinned and wriggling on the wall,
Then how should I begin
To spit out all the butt-ends of my days and ways?
And how should I presume?

And I have known the arms already, known them all—
Arms that are braceleted and white and bare
(But in the lamplight, downed with light brown hair!)
Is it perfume from a dress
That makes me so digress?
Arms that lie along a table, or wrap about a shawl.
And should I then presume?
And how should I begin?

◆ ◆ ◆

Shall I say, I have gone at dusk through narrow streets
And watched the smoke that rises from the pipes
Of lonely men in shirt-sleeves, leaning out of windows? . . .

I should have been a pair of ragged claws
Scuttling across the floors of silent seas.

◆ ◆ ◆

And the afternoon, the evening, sleeps so peacefully!
Smoothed by long fingers,
Asleep . . . tired . . . or it malingers,

Words for Everyday Use:

pre • sume (pri zōōm´) *vi.,* dare; venture; take upon oneself

for • mu • lat • ed (fôr´myə lāt´əd) *part.,* systematical; precise

di • gress (di greś) *vi.,* deviate from the main topic in speaking or writing

ma • lin • ger (mə ling´gər) *vi.,* pretend illness

Vocabulary in Context

- "How dare you presume to approach the king without kneeling!" the courtier said.
- Her response to her brother's request sounded formulated, as she had planned her words precisely earlier that morning.
- It was hard to grasp the main ideas of the lecture because the speaker tended to digress.
- The employee was fired because he malingered about the office complaining of a head cold rather than doing his work.

Stretched on the floor, here beside you and me.
Should I, after tea and cakes and ices,
80 Have the strength to force the moment to its crisis?
But though I have wept and fasted, wept and prayed,
Though I have seen my head (grown slightly bald) brought in upon a platter,
I am no prophet[3]—and here's no great matter;
I have seen the moment of my greatness flicker,
85 And I have seen the eternal Footman hold my coat, and snicker,
And in short, I was afraid.

And would it have been worth it, after all,
After the cups, the marmalade, the tea,
Among the porcelain, among some talk of you and me,
90 Would it have been worth while,
To have bitten off the matter with a smile,
To have squeezed the universe into a ball
To roll it towards some overwhelming question,
To say: "I am Lazarus,[4] come from the dead,
95 Come back to tell you all, I shall tell you all"—
If one, settling a pillow by her head,
Should say: "That is not what I meant at all.
That is not it, at all."

And would it have been worth it, after all,
100 Would it have been worth while,
After the sunsets and the dooryards and the sprinkled streets,
After the novels, after the teacups, after the skirts that trail along the floor—
And this, and so much more?—
105 It is impossible to say just what I mean!
But as if a magic lantern threw the nerves in patterns on a screen:
Would it have been worth while
If one, settling a pillow or throwing off a shawl,
And turning toward the window, should say:
110 "That is not it at all,
That is not what I meant, at all."

♦ ♦ ♦

No! I am not Prince Hamlet, nor was meant to be;
Am an attendant lord, one that will do

❶ *What is the "crisis" to which the speaker refers? Of what is he afraid?*

❷ *What causes frustration? What patterns are projected?*

3. **I am no prophet.** The head of the prophet John the Baptist was brought to Princess Salome on a platter.
4. **Lazarus.** In John 11:1–44, Lazarus is resurrected.

Answers to Guided Reading Questions

❶ The "crisis" might be the speaker's confronting the woman about his feelings for her. He is afraid of others laughing at him.

❷ The fact that it is impossible for him to say exactly what he means causes the speaker's frustration. The pattern of the speaker's nerves might be projected on a screen.

Literary Note

In Shakespeare's *The Tragedy of Hamlet, Prince of Denmark,* the tragic hero's flaw is often seen as his inability to act upon his beliefs and feelings even when he knows that action is essential. Like Hamlet, Prufrock broods upon potential actions that he seems emotionally incapable of performing. Prufrock, however, denies this association, implying that his own inability to act does not make him a great figure as Hamlet was. Prufrock is examining his own life and finding it pathetic, not the tragic subject for a drama. Ask students whether or not they agree with Prufrock's self-assessment. Is his finding his own life a poor subject in itself a subject for literature? Why might Eliot have chosen such a self-effacing character to comment upon life in the early twentieth century?

Answer to Guided Reading Question

❶ The speaker believes he is a minor character, not Prince Hamlet, but his foolish advisor.

Answers to Selection Check Test 4.8.31

EX. What type of song does J. Alfred Prufrock sing?
J. Alfred Prufrock sings a love song.

1. What is the evening spread out against the sky like?
It is like "a patient etherised upon a table."

2. Of what do the women who come and go talk?
The women talk of Michelangelo.

3. What should the speaker have been?
He should have been "a pair of ragged claws/Scuttling across the floors of silent seas."

4. What does the "eternal Footman" do?
The "eternal Footman" holds the speaker's coat and snickers.

5. Who will not sing to the speaker?
The mermaids, "singing, each to each," will not sing to the speaker.

Responding to the Selection

Students might talk about fear of rejection and why it is sometimes difficult to share their feelings with others.

Vocabulary in Context

- Gene was a polite and respectful boy who always was deferential when in the company of adults.
- People who pollute the environment are acting as if they were obtuse.

Does the speaker believe he is a hero, a main character, or a minor character? Explain. ❶

To swell a progress,[5] start a scene or two,
Advise the prince; no doubt, an easy tool,
Deferential, glad to be of use,
Politic, cautious, and meticulous;
Full of high sentence,[6] but a bit obtuse;
At times, indeed, almost ridiculous—
Almost, at times, the Fool.

I grow old . . . I grow old . . .
I shall wear the bottoms of my trousers rolled.

Shall I part my hair behind? Do I dare to eat a peach?
I shall wear white flannel trousers, and walk upon the beach.
I have heard the mermaids singing, each to each.

I do not think that they will sing to me.

I have seen them riding seaward on the waves
Combing the white hair of the waves blown back
When the wind blows the water white and black.

We have lingered in the chambers of the sea
By sea-girls wreathed with seaweed red and brown
Till human voices wake us, and we drown. ■

5. **progress.** Procession
6. **sentence.** Opinions

Responding to the Selection

Imagine that you are J. Alfred Prufrock, the speaker who hesitates to declare his love. What causes you to hesitate? What would you say to the woman you love if you could speak freely?

Words for Everyday Use:
def • er • en • tial (def´ə ren´shəl) *adj.,* respectful
ob • tuse (əb tōōs´) *adj.,* slow to understand or perceive; insensitive

Answers for Reviewing the Selection

RECALLING

1. In stanza 1, the speaker requests that "you and I" go through twisting, half-deserted streets.
2. There will be time for a hundred indecisions, visions, and revisions.
3. The speaker has seen the moment of his greatness flicker.
4. It is impossible for the speaker to say what he means.

INTERPRETING

Responses will vary. Possible responses are given.

5. The speaker is self-effacing; he does not believe he is a hero, but rather a fool. He seems to dislike aspects of his own personality quite intensely.
6. Some details that reveal this difficulty are the speaker's constant assertion that "there will be time," the speaker's preparing "a face to meet the faces that you

(cont.)

Reviewing the Selection

RECALLING

1. What request does the speaker make in stanza 1 of the poem?
2. For how many indecisions, visions, and revisions will there be time "Before the taking of a toast and tea"?
3. What kind of moment has the speaker seen "flicker"?
4. What is impossible for the speaker to say?

INTERPRETING

5. What is the speaker's attitude toward himself?
6. What details in stanza 3 emphasize the difficulty the speaker has in committing himself to word or action?
7. Who is the "eternal Footman"? Of what is the speaker afraid?
8. Why does the speaker not think that the mermaids "will sing to me"? What happens when Prufrock begins to picture himself in a romantic scene? In what sense does reality intrude upon his daydreams? In what sense do human voices wake him, causing him to feel that he is drowning?

SYNTHESIZING

9. What are the causes of Prufrock's hesitation? What attitude does the speaker express toward himself and his hesitation?
10. What relationship between time and love is described in this poem?

Understanding Literature (Questions for Discussion)

1. **Dramatic Monologue.** A **dramatic monologue** is a poem that presents the speech of a single character in a dramatic situation. The speech is one side of an imagined conversation. In what dramatic situation is J. Alfred Prufrock? Does the reader have empathy for Prufrock's situation? Why, or why not?
2. **Allusion.** An **allusion** is a figure of speech in which a reference is made to a person, event, object, or work from history or literature. One of the allusions in the poem is to the poem "To His Coy Mistress," by Andrew Marvell, a seventeenth-century English writer. In Marvell's poem, the speaker appeals to the woman he loves for urgent action because there is not enough time to waste on pretenses such as coyness: "Had we but world enough, and time,/This coyness, Lady, were no crime." How do Prufrock's attitudes toward time and action differ from the attitudes of Marvell's speaker?
3. **Free Verse. Free verse** is poetry that avoids use of regular rhyme, rhythm, meter, or division into stanzas. Eliot controlled his free verse, however, with the precise use and variation of rhyme and meter. What rhyme pattern is used in stanza 1 of the poem? Of what poetic form is stanza 1 a variation?

ANSWERS FOR REVIEWING THE SELECTION (CONT.)

meet," and his belief that there is time "for a hundred indecisions . . . Before the taking of a toast and tea."

7. The "eternal Footman" might be a personification of death. The speaker is afraid of taking action, and he is also afraid of losing life and the chance to act.

8. The speaker thinks that the mermaids will not sing to him because he has a difficult time imagining anything wonderful or beautiful happening in his life. Prufrock searches for elaborate ways of describing his own unworthiness whenever he imagines himself in a romantic scene. Reality intrudes upon the speaker's romantic daydreams because he always realizes the unlikeliness of these dreams coming to pass. The real world and human voices remind Prufrock of how inadequate he feels in the world; in his despair and self-doubt, Prufrock feels that he is drowning.

SYNTHESIZING

Responses will vary. Possible responses are given.

9. The causes of Prufrock's hesitation are his lack of self-confidence and his tendency to overanalyze his situation. The speaker despises himself for his inability to act yet seems unable or unwilling to change.

10. In the poem, the speaker grows over time to think his love foolish; however, he still sustains this love even though he knows that it is fruitless.

ANSWERS FOR UNDERSTANDING LITERATURE

► See the evaluation forms for discussion, active listening, and oral communication, *Assessment Portfolio,* 7.11–7.14.

Responses will vary. Possible responses are given.

1. **Dramatic Monologue.** J. Alfred Prufrock is experiencing an emotional crisis—he is realizing he will never have the strength to declare his love. Students may or may not have empathy with Prufrock's situation, but they should provide reasons for their opinion.

2. **Allusion.** Prufrock believes that there is no need to act because there is time "for a hundred indecisions . . . visions and revisions," while Marlowe's speaker believes that action is necessary because little time is remaining.

3. **Free Verse.** The rhyme pattern of stanza 1 is *aabccdd.* Stanza 1 is a variation of a sonnet.

ANALYTIC SCALES FOR RESPONDING IN WRITING

Assign a score from 1 to 25 for each grading criterion below. (For more detailed evaluation, see the evaluation forms for writing, revising, and proofreading, *Assessment Portfolio,* 7.1–7.10.)

Parody

- **Content/Unity.** The parody is written on the topic of hesitation.
- **Organization/Coherence.** The parody follows the form of one of Eliot's stanzas.
- **Language/Style.** The parody uses vivid and precise nouns, verbs, and modifiers.
- **Conventions.** The parody avoids errors in spelling, grammar, usage, mechanics, and manuscript form.

ANSWERS FOR LANGUAGE LAB

Answers will vary. Possible responses are given.

1. Eliot's "The Love Song of J. Alfred Prufrock" dampens the reader's spirits.
2. Worries, including concerns about his baldness, plague Prufrock.
3. Prufrock's hesitations frustrate the reader.
4. Prufrock proves himself, at times, the Fool.

ANSWERS FOR THINKING SKILLS

1. supported
2. supported
3. not supported
4. not supported
5. not supported

Responding in Writing

Parody. A **parody** is a literary work that imitates another work for humorous, often satirical, purposes. Imitating one stanza from the poem, write a parody on the topic of hesitation.

Language Lab

Replacing Linking Verbs with Action Verbs. Read the Language Arts Survey, 2.34, "Replacing Linking Verbs with Action Verbs." Then, revise each of the following sentences, using action verbs in place of linking verbs.

1. Eliot's "The Love Song of J. Alfred Prufrock" is melancholy.
2. Prufrock is a man with many worries, including concerns about his baldness.
3. Prufrock's hesitations are sources of frustration for the reader.
4. Prufrock is, at times, the Fool.

Thinking Skills

Generalizing. Read the Language Arts Survey, 4.11, "Generalizing." Then, for each sentence below, decide whether the generalization is or is not supported by the poem.

1. Prufrock fears death.
2. Prufrock's youth is slipping away.
3. If Prufrock had been younger, he would not have hesitated to speak directly.
4. Prufrock is a man of action.
5. The mermaids will not sing to Prufrock because he is not intelligent.

PROJECT

Find the Allusion. In small groups, research the following allusions in the poem:

Epigram	Canto 27, lines 61–66, of the *Inferno,* book one of *The Divine Comedy,* by the Italian poet Dante Alighieri
Line 14	Michelangelo Buonoroti, Italian Renaissance painter
Line 23	Andrew Marvell's poem "To His Coy Mistress"
Line 29	"Works and Days," the title of a poem by the ancient Greek poet Hesiod
Line 52	Act I, scene i, line 4, of Shakespeare's play *Twelfth Night*
Line 82	The Bible, Mark 6:12–20 and Matthew 14:3–11
Line 94	The Bible, John 11:1–44

PROJECT NOTES

►See the worksheets and evaluation forms for projects, *Assessment Portfolio,* 7.20–7.23.

Find the Allusion. The class might break into seven groups; each group should research one of the allusions and perhaps share part of the original work with the class.

PREREADING

"Bells for John Whiteside's Daughter"
by John Crowe Ransom

About the Author

John Crowe Ransom (1888–1974) was born in Pulaski, Tennessee; received an A.B. from Vanderbilt University in 1909; and as a Rhodes Scholar took a B.A. at Christ Church, Oxford, in 1913. After serving as a lieutenant in the Army during World War I, Ransom returned to Vanderbilt and joined the English faculty. In 1937, to the surprise of many, he left to teach poetry at Kenyon College in Ohio, where he also founded the *Kenyon Review.* He served as its editor until retiring in 1959. His three books of poems were published between 1919 and 1927. After that, his interest shifted to criticism, until later in his life when he began rewriting some of his early poems. Ransom helped to found the school of literary thought known as the New Criticism, which emphasized close readings of texts themselves without reference to their authors' biographies or to the historical circumstances that produced them. Ransom believed that science, technology, industrialization, and urbanization were destructive forces that dominated culture in the North. That belief informed his poetry and criticism and was expressed in *I'll Take My Stand* (1930), a collection of essays by Southerners. He once described himself as "something like this: In manners, aristocratic; in religion, ritualistic; in art, traditional." The 1963 edition of his *Selected Poems* won the Library of Congress's Bollingen Prize for Poetry; the 1969 edition received the National Book Award. His other works include *Poems about God* (1919), *Chills and Fever* (1924), *Two Gentlemen in Bonds* (1927), *The World's Body* (1938), and *The New Criticism* (1941).

About the Selection

Ransom's small body of poems is characterized by irony, wit, and learning, but also by understatement, sincerity, and gracefulness of expression. These characteristics can all be found in **"Bells for John Whiteside's Daughter,"** about the death of a child.

ADDITIONAL RESOURCES

Reader's Guide
- Selection Worksheet, 8.17

Assessment Portfolio
- Selection Check Test, 4.8.33
- Selection Test, 4.8.34

Essential Skills Practice Books
- *Language,* 2.147, 2.149

ENRICHMENT ACTIVITIES

Have students read "Elegy in a Country Churchyard" by Thomas Gray and "To an Athlete Dying Young" by A. E. Housman. What ideas about death and coping with an individual's death are expressed in these poems? Ask students to write independently on this subject, and then invite students to share their views in a class discussion.

SUPPORT FOR LEP STUDENTS

Some student might experience difficulty because the poem is so understated. You might read the poem as a class and discuss some of the more challenging or unusual passages.

Additional Vocabulary

took arms—fought

Alas—an expression of pity or dismay

primly—properly, formally

GOALS/OBJECTIVES

Studying this lesson will enable students to
- empathize with a speaker's feelings about the death of a child
- become familiar with the life and work of John Crowe Ransom
- identify formal and informal English
- understand literary terms such as *diction, rhyme,* and *understatement*
- write an elegy

PREREADING NOTES

READER'S JOURNAL

Students who have not had the experience of attending a wake, funeral, or memorial service might imagine what the experience would be like or write about a fictional one they have read about or seen. They might also freewrite on the subject of death.

LANGUAGE SKILLS

Answers will vary. Students might identify *footfall, brown study, alas,* and *primly* as formal language, and *lazy, apple-dreams, scuttle,* and *goose-fashion* as informal language.

ANSWER TO GUIDED READING QUESTION

❶ The geese cry, "Alas."

RESPONDING TO THE SELECTION

Encourage students to use their imaginations as they write in their journals. How old do they imagine this child to have been, based on the words of the poem? What might she have looked like? What kind of voice might she have had? What games might she have enjoyed? Students should meet in small groups and share their ideas.

READER'S JOURNAL

Have you ever attended a wake, funeral, or memorial service for someone who has died? What was the person like when he or she was alive? What did he or she enjoy doing? Write about your memories of that person in your journal.

LANGUAGE SKILLS

Read the Language Arts Survey, 2.147, "Formal and Informal English," and 2.149, "Tone and Voice." Then identify some formal and informal words in the poem and note what tone the choice of words lends to each stanza.

"Bells for John Whiteside's Daughter"

JOHN CROWE RANSOM

There was such speed in her little body,
And such lightness in her footfall,
It is no wonder her brown study[1]
Astonishes us all.

Her wars were bruited[2] in our high window.
We looked among orchard trees and beyond,
Where she took arms against her shadow,
Or harried unto the pond

The lazy geese, like a snow cloud
Dripping their snow on the green grass,
Tricking and stopping, sleepy and proud,
Who cried in goose, Alas,

1. **study.** Serious thoughts
2. **bruited.** Rumored about

Q ❶ *Who cries "Alas"?*

WORDS FOR EVERYDAY USE: **har • ry** (har´ē´) *vt.,* push along; hurry forcefully

VOCABULARY IN CONTEXT

- The guards harried the crowd out of the auditorium when the fire alarm sounded.
- Mosquitoes continue to vex us when we eat lunch in the park.

For the tireless heart within the little
Lady with rod that made them rise
15 From their noon apple-dreams and scuttle
Goose-fashion under the skies!

But now go the bells, and we are ready,
In one house we are sternly stopped
To say we are vexed at her brown study,
20 Lying so primly propped. ■

❶ *What service do the bells announce?*

Responding to the Selection

Imagine that you are the speaker in the poem attending the funeral of John Whiteside's daughter. How do you remember her? What was the young girl like when she was alive? Write an entry in your journal expressing your feelings about the death of this girl.

Reviewing the Selection

Recalling

1. How does the speaker describe the footfall of John Whiteside's daughter?
2. Against what does the young girl take arms in stanza 2?
3. What are the lazy geese like?
4. What can be heard in the opening line of the last stanza? Where are the people? In what position is John Whiteside's daughter lying?

Interpreting

5. Why is the speaker astonished by the girl's "brown study"?
6. What actions on the part of the young girl showed her vitality and imagination?
7. With what feelings toward the dead girl does the speaker endow the geese?
8. Why are the bells ringing? For what are the people ready? What has "sternly stopped" them? Why are they "vexed"?

Words for Everyday Use: vex (veks) *vt.*, irritate; annoy

Answer to Guided Reading Question

❶ The bells announce a funeral service.

Answers for Reviewing the Selection

RECALLING

1. The speaker describes her footfall as light.
2. The young girl takes arms against her shadow in stanza 2.
3. The lazy geese are like snow clouds dripping snow on the grass.
4. Bells can be heard in the opening line of the last stanza. The people are in one house. John Whiteside's daughter is lying "primly propped."

INTERPRETING

Responses will vary. Possible responses are given.

5. The speaker is astonished because of the speed in her body and lightness in her footfall.
6. Her play—taking "arms" against her shadow in the orchard and running by the pond—showed her vitality and imagination.
7. The speaker endows the geese with feelings of sorrow over the loss of the girl.
8. The bells are ringing for the young girl's funeral. The people are ready for her funeral, but they are "sternly stopped" by her appearance. They are vexed at seeing her lie so "primly propped."

SYNTHESIZING

Responses will vary. Possible responses are given.

9. John Whiteside's daughter was energetic, imaginative, and full of life. The speaker characterizes her as being fast and light on her feet.
10. The speaker had positive feelings toward the little girl. The speaker feels sad and vexed by her death.

Answers to Selection Check Test 4.8.33

EX. For whom are the bells?
The bells are for John Whiteside's daughter.
1. How are the movements of the young girl described?
The girl is described as having speed and lightness in her footfall.
2. What astonishes the people who know her?
The girl's brown study, or death.
3. What are described as being lazy, "like a snow cloud"?
The geese are described as being lazy.
4. How do the geese feel about the child's death?
According to the poem, the geese are saddened by the child's death.
5. How is the child lying?
The child is lying "primly propped."

ANSWERS FOR UNDERSTANDING LITERATURE

► See the evaluation forms for discussion, active listening, and oral communication, *Assessment Portfolio,* 7.11–7.14.

Responses will vary. Possible responses are given.

1. Diction. Students might identify "apple-dreams" and "scuttle/Goose-fashion" as examples of unusual, childlike diction. The diction makes the child and her games endearing and realistic.

2. Rhyme. In stanza 1, "body/study" is an example of slant rhyme, and "footfall/all" is an example of exact rhyme; in stanza 2, "window/shadow" is an example of slant rhyme, and "beyond/pond" is an example of exact rhyme; in stanza 3, "cloud/proud" and "grass/alas" are examples of exact rhyme; in stanza 4, "little/scuttle" is an example of slant rhyme, and "rise/skies" is an example of exact rhyme; and in stanza 5, "ready/study" is an example of slant rhyme, and "stopped/propped" is an example of exact rhyme. "Stopped/propped" has a particularly strong exact rhyme; this word pair has an abrupt sound; this further emphasizes the astonishment people feel at seeing the child looking so "prim" in death.

3. Understatement. Understatements, when used on a subject such as this, make the feelings of the speaker seem more genuine and increase the significance and emotional impact of the piece. A poem that uses images and language specific to a particular incident is much more effective than a poem that is filled with "big" language, clichés, and generalities.

SYNTHESIZING

9. What kind of child was John Whiteside's daughter? How does the speaker characterize her?

10. What are the speaker's feelings toward John Whiteside's daughter? What are the speaker's feelings about her death?

Understanding Literature (Questions for Discussion)

1. **Diction. Diction,** when applied to writing, refers to word choice. Ransom's poetry is noted for its surprising and unusual mix of diction. For example, in the line "Who cried in goose, Alas," the phrase "in goose" is childlike and fun, even more so when placed next to the formal cry "Alas." Identify another example of surprising or unusual diction, or word choice, in the poem and analyze what effect the word choice creates.
2. **Rhyme. Rhyme** is the repetition of sounds at the ends of words. *End rhyme,* the use of rhyming words at the ends of lines, is one type of rhyme. Two other types of rhyme include *exact rhyme* (in which the rhyming words end with the same sound or sounds) and *slant rhyme* (in which the rhyming sounds are similar but not identical). Analyze the end rhymes in the poem, identifying each word pair as an exact or slant rhyme. Which of the word pairs has the strongest exact rhyme? What emotional impact is created by that word pair?
3. **Understatement. Understatement** is an ironic expression in which something of importance is spoken of as though it were not important. Treating an important, emotionally laden subject in an offhand manner serves, paradoxically, to underscore its importance. In this poem, the speaker does not wail or weep. Instead, he uses subdued, understated language, describing death as a "brown study"; the people gathered about the body as being "astonished," "ready," "stopped," and "vexed"; and the body of the girl as being "primly propped." What effect does such understatement have when used on a subject such as this?

Responding in Writing

Elegy. An elegy is a piece of writing that remembers and praises someone who has died. Consider the following lines from the poem:

> There was such speed in her little body,
> And such lightness in her footfall,
> It is no wonder her brown study
> Astonishes us all.

These lines express how alive the young girl was and how the vitality of her life, when seen in contrast to her death, causes astonishment. Write an elegy, in prose or in verse, about the death of a child or a pet. In your poem, portray the character of the child or pet through his or her behavior and actions.

ANALYTIC SCALES FOR RESPONDING IN WRITING

Assign a score from 1 to 25 for each grading criterion below. (For more detailed evaluation, see the evaluation forms for writing, revising, and proofreading, *Assessment Portfolio,* 7.1–7.10.)

Elegy

- **Content/Unity.** The elegy praises and remembers a child or a pet. It attempts to portray the character of the deceased by talking about his or her behavior and actions.
- **Organization/Coherence.** The elegy is organized and clear and presents important details about the subject.
- **Language/Style.** The subject of the elegy is described with vivid detail and understated, original language.
- **Conventions.** The elegy avoids errors in spelling, grammar, usage, and mechanics.

PREREADING

"Ars Poetica"
by Archibald MacLeish

About the Author

Archibald MacLeish (1892–1982), born in Glencoe, Illinois, graduated from Yale in 1915 and earned his LL.D. from Harvard in 1919. He practiced law in Boston from 1920 to 1923 and lived in France from 1923 to 1928. MacLeish's military experience in World War I and his return to the United States during the Great Depression shaped and forged his intellectual interests and work. As his social awareness grew, it was reflected in his writing. MacLeish was Librarian of Congress (1939–1944), Assistant Secretary of State (1944–1945), Boylston Professor at Harvard (1949–1962), and a lecturer at Amherst College (1963–1967). A prolific writer, he was awarded three Pulitzers, two for poetry (*Conquistador* in 1933 and *Collected Poems, 1917–1952* in 1953) and one for drama (*J. B.* in 1958). The play *J. B.* treated the biblical story of Job in a modern setting and idiom. MacLeish's other works include *New Found Land* (1930), *Public Speech* (1936), *The Fall of the City* (1937), *Songs for Eve* (1954), *The Wild Old Wicked Man* (1968), and *Herakles* (1967).

About the Selection

In a sense, a blade of grass or a cloud in the sky doesn't mean anything. It simply is. It exists. In **"Ars Poetica,"** the title of which means "The Art of Poetry" in Latin, MacLeish argues that a poem is like a blade of grass or a cloud in that respect. In his words, "A poem should not mean/But be." This idea was a central one to the New Criticism, which was a method of literary criticism that became popular in the 1930s and 1940s. This idea was also central to the Imagist movement of the early 1900s.

GOALS/OBJECTIVES

Studying this lesson will enable students to

- appreciate one point of view about poetry
- become familiar with the life and work of Archibald MacLeish
- identify and practice using concrete and abstract nouns
- understand the concepts simile and paradox
- write an imagist poem
- use searching tools at the library

ADDITIONAL RESOURCES

Reader's Guide
- Selection Worksheet, 8.18

Assessment Portfolio
- Selection Check Test, 4.8.35
- Selection Test, 4.8.36

Essential Skills Practice Books
- *Writing,* 1.10, 1.11, 1.18
- *Language,* 2.3, 2.4, 2.32–2.35
- *Study and Research,* 4.21

ENRICHMENT ACTIVITIES

As students learned in About the Selection, the idea about poetry expressed by MacLeish in "Ars Poetica" was central to the New Criticism movement of the 1930s and 1940s. Ask students to read the entry on *criticism* in The Handbook of Literary Terms. Then ask them to write a comparison-and-contrast essay comparing the New Criticism movement with biographical criticism and reader-response criticism. In their essays, students may express their own opinions about criticism and the reading of literature.

SUPPORT FOR LEP STUDENTS

Some students might experience difficulty with some of the imagery in the poem. Spend time discussing the ideas presented in About the Selection on page 579. After students have read the poem once, you might go through the poem line by line and discuss the images presented.

Additional Vocabulary

mute—silent

PREREADING NOTES

READER'S JOURNAL

Encourage students to write about specific poems and songs that they consider superb. Do students most enjoy poems and songs that speak directly to their own lives and experiences, or do they enjoy poems and songs that talk about different ideas and experiences?

LANGUAGE SKILLS

Students should identify words like *fruit, thumb, ledges, birds, moon, trees, leaves,* and *grass* as concrete nouns and words like *memory, history, grief,* and *love* as abstract nouns.

ANSWER TO GUIDED READING QUESTION

❶ The speaker compares a poem to globed fruit and old medallions.

READER'S JOURNAL

What makes one poem or song superb and another one not? What characteristics do good poems and song lyrics have in common that bad ones lack? Write about these questions in your journal.

LANGUAGE SKILLS

Read the Language Arts Survey, 2.4, "Concrete and Abstract Nouns." Then identify some concrete and abstract nouns in the selection and note what qualities they share.

"Ars Poetica"

ARCHIBALD MACLEISH

To what two items does the speaker compare a poem? ❶

A poem should be palpable and mute
As a globed fruit,

Dumb
As old medallions[1] to the thumb,

Silent as the sleeve-worn stone
Of casement ledges where the moss has grown—

A poem should be wordless
As the flight of birds.

A poem should be motionless in time
As the moon climbs,

Leaving, as the moon releases
Twig by twig the night-entangled trees,

Leaving, as the moon behind the winter leaves,
Memory by memory the mind—

1. **medallions.** Medals

WORDS FOR EVERYDAY USE: **pal • pa • ble** (pal´pə bəl) *adj.,* easily perceived; obvious; clear

VOCABULARY IN CONTEXT

• The ideas presented by the teacher at the seminar were interesting and palpable.

15 A poem should be motionless in time
As the moon climbs.

A poem should be equal to:
Not true.

For all the history of grief
20 An empty doorway and a maple leaf.

For love
The leaning grasses and two lights above the sea—

A poem should not mean
But be. ■

❶ *How might a poem depict love?*

Responding to the Selection

Imagine that you are a photographer who has been asked to provide a concrete image as a striking metaphor for the art of poetry. In your journal, brainstorm a list of possible images, noting your thoughts beside each one.

Answer to Guided Reading Question

❶ A poet might depict love by describing "the leaning grasses and two lights above the sea."

Responding to the Selection

Ask students to brainstorm their own images of poetry. Encourage them to express their ideas freely and refrain from editing themselves as they brainstorm. Hold a class discussion during which students are invited to share their ideas. If any students have cameras and would enjoy photographing an image, encourage them to do so.

Answers to Selection Check Test 4.8.35

EX. What is the meaning of the title "Ars Poetica"?
"Ars poetica" means "the art of poetry."
1. According to the speaker, what should be "palpable and mute/As a globed fruit"?
A poem should be "palpable and mute/As a globed fruit."
2. According to the speaker, what should be "wordless?"
A poem should be "wordless."
3. According to the speaker, how does the moon climb the sky at night?
According to the speaker, the moon is motionless.
4. To what abstract noun do the images of leaning grasses and lights above the sea refer?
The images refer to love.
5. According to the last line of the poem, is it more important for a poem to "mean" or simply "be"?
According to the last line of the poem, a poem should "not mean/But be."

Answers for Reviewing the Selection

RECALLING

1. To be palpable is to be clear and easily understood and appreciated. A poem should be "palpable and mute."
2. According to the speaker, a poem should be "dumb" and "wordless/As the flight of birds."
3. According to the speaker, a poem should be "motionless in time."
4. A poem might express a "history of grief" with "an empty doorway and a maple leaf" and love with "the leaning grasses and two lights above the sea."

INTERPRETING

Responses will vary. Possible responses are given.

5. Students might say that a poem should be palpable in the sense that it should use clear and concise imagery and present pictures in the reader's mind.
6. A poem that is so clear and vivid that one does not notice the words is a "dumb" or "wordless" poem.
7. The moon is not actually motionless in the sky; however, because it is so far away and because it moves so slowly, one does not notice any movement. A good poem might lead a reader or listener from part to part by keeping language clear, concise, and vivid. The language must be so subtle and careful that one does not notice it.
8. The speaker uses concrete images such as grass, lights above the sea, an empty doorway, or a maple leaf. Grasses and lights above the sea describe a possibly romantic setting; an empty doorway may signify a loss; and a maple leaf, when it has fallen, symbolizes endings.

SYNTHESIZING

Responses will vary. Possible responses are given.

9. The speaker of the poem most likely prefers poetry that is rich with vivid imagery and that creates vivid images in the reader's mind.

(cont.)

Reviewing the Selection

RECALLING

1. What does it mean to be palpable? What, according to the speaker, should be "palpable and mute"?
2. According to the speaker, what should be "dumb" and "wordless/As the flight of birds"?
3. According to the speaker, what should be "motionless in time"?
4. How might a poem express a "history of grief"? How might it express love?

INTERPRETING

5. Have you ever read or heard language that was so vivid that it made you feel as though you were actually experiencing the thing being described? In what sense should a poem be "palpable"?
6. When language is vivid and concrete, people forget that they are hearing or reading words and simply pay attention to the images that the words create in their minds. In what sense can a poem, which is made of words, be "dumb" and "wordless"?
7. Is the moon actually motionless in the sky? What gives it the appearance of stillness despite its movement? How might a really good poem lead a reader or listener from part to part without that person being aware of its progression?
8. Near the end of the poem, the speaker gives examples of how concrete images might be used in place of abstract concepts such as grief and love. What concrete images does the speaker suggest to communicate each meaning? What do these images have in common with grief and love?

SYNTHESIZING

9. What kind of poetry do you think the speaker of this poem might prefer? Why?
10. The speaker ends the poem with the line "A poem should not mean/But be." In what other lines of the poem does the word *be* occur? Consider the following phrases from the poem:

    "all the history of grief"

    "An empty doorway and a maple leaf"

    Which of these lines "means" in the speaker's sense? Which line, in the speaker's sense, simply is?

Answers for Reviewing the Selection (cont.)

10. The word *be* is repeated five other times, as part of the sentence "A poem should *be*. . . . " The line "all the history of grief" "means" in the speaker's sense. The line "An empty doorway and a maple leaf" simply "is."

Understanding Literature (Questions for Discussion)

1. **Simile.** A **simile** is a comparison using *like* or *as.* A simile can be analyzed into two parts, the *tenor* (or subject being described) and the *vehicle* (or object being used in the description). These two parts can be compared because they share some particular quality. Identify the tenor and the vehicle in the following simile in the first stanza of the poem: "A poem should be palpable and mute/As a globed fruit." What qualities do the tenor and vehicle share? Analyze another simile in the selection.
2. **Paradox.** A **paradox** is a contradictory statement, idea, or event. Consider the lines "A poem should be wordless/As the flight of birds." What paradox exists in that stanza? How can the paradox be resolved into a coherent, noncontradictory idea?

Responding in Writing

Imagist Poem. Choose a subject that is especially vivid in your imagination. Make a list of words that describe how the subject looks, sounds, tastes, feels, or smells. Then write a few lines that create a vivid picture of the subject. Keep all abstract statements of emotion out of your poem. For examples of Imagist poems, see Ezra Pound's "In a Station of the Metro," on page 561, and Amy Lowell's "Wind and Silver," on page 604 in Selections for Additional Reading. Refer to the Language Arts Survey, 1.10, "Recalling"; 1.11, "Observing"; 1.18, "Sensory Detail Charts"; and 2.4, "Concrete and Abstract Nouns." See also sections 2.32–2.35 on using precise, vivid, colorful nouns, verbs, and modifiers.

Language Lab

Concrete and Abstract Nouns. Read the Language Arts Survey, 2.4, "Concrete and Abstract Nouns." Then, for each of the abstract nouns listed below, write a definition using a simile that has as its vehicle a concrete noun.

EXAMPLE: fear Fear is the sudden trembling of a bough.

1. love 2. honor 3. cowardice 4. evil 5. purity

Research Skills

Using Searching Tools. Read the Language Arts Survey, 4.21, "Using Searching Tools." Then, use your library's computerized catalog to search for and provide a source of information about each of the following items.

1. *Poetry and the Age*
2. MacLeish, Archibald
3. modern American poetry
4. "Ars Poetica"
5. Marianne Moore
6. *The Well-Wrought Urn*
7. *The Verbal Icon*
8. Imagism
9. The New Criticism
10. *Seven Types of Ambiguity*

Answers for Understanding Literature

► See the evaluation forms for discussion, active listening, and oral communication, *Assessment Portfolio,* 7.11–7.14.

Responses will vary. Possible responses are given.

1. Simile. In the line "A poem should be palpable and mute/As a globed fruit," *palpable* is the tenor and *globed fruit* is the vehicle. In the line "A poem should be wordless/As the flight of birds," the tenor is *wordless* and the vehicle is *flight of birds.*

2. Paradox. The paradox in the statement is that because a poem is made of words, it seems strange to say that a poem should be "wordless." One might explain this and resolve the paradox by saying that a poem should present such clear and striking imagery that one does not notice words, only the image that has been created.

Analytic Scales for Responding in Writing

Assign a score from 1 to 25 for each grading criterion below. (For more detailed evaluation, see the evaluation forms for writing, revising, and proofreading, *Assessment Portfolio,* 7.1–7.10.)

Imagist Poem

- **Content/Unity.** The poem presents vivid images of its subject rather than abstract words and phrases.
- **Organization/Coherence.** The poem is organized in a way that allows the reader to experience the subject. Images are clear and concise.
- **Language/Style.** The language of the poem is clear, concrete, and vivid.
- **Conventions.** The paragraph avoids errors in spelling, grammar, usage, and mechanics.

Answers for Language Lab

Answers will vary

Students should be given time in which to freewrite on these subjects before they choose similes. Encourage students to choose a fresh image and to stay away from something that might be a cliché.

Answers for Research Skills

Give students time to visit the school library, or ask that they visit a local library in order to complete the assignment. Students who do not have a computerized catalog available to them should refer to the Language Arts Survey, 4.22, "Using the Card Catalog," and complete the assignment using a card catalog.

ADDITIONAL RESOURCES

READER'S GUIDE
- Selection Worksheet, 8.19

ASSESSMENT PORTFOLIO
- Selection Check Test, 4.8.37
- Selection Test, 4.8.38

ESSENTIAL SKILLS PRACTICE BOOKS
- *Language,* 2.93, 2.94–2.96, 2.98
- *Applied English,* 5.2

ENRICHMENT ACTIVITIES

Provide students with the following list of titles by E. E. Cummings: *The Enormous Room* (1922), *&* (1925), *is 5* (1926), *50 Poems* (1940), *I Times I* (1944), and *95 Poems* (1958). Ask each student to go to a library and find three other E. E. Cummings poems that they would like to read and compare to "somewhere i have never travelled,gladly beyond." Ask students to make notes about the poems they've chosen. Then ask them to meet in pairs to present the new poems to each other.

SUPPORT FOR LEP STUDENTS

Some students might struggle with the nonstandard syntax, punctuation, and grammar in this poem. You might want to assist these students in their first reading of the poem, helping them to find the meaning in the lines.

ADDITIONAL VOCABULARY

perceive—understand
compels—drives, forces
rendering—making, causing to be

PREREADING

"somewhere i have never travelled,gladly beyond"
by E. E. Cummings

ABOUT THE AUTHOR

E(dward) E(stlin) Cummings (1894–1962) was born in Cambridge, Massachusetts. His father was a Congregationalist minister and a Harvard faculty member. Cummings graduated from Harvard in 1915 and earned an M.A. in 1916. When the United States entered World War I, Cummings joined the ambulance corps in France but was imprisoned by the French for his outspoken letters home. *The Enormous Room* (1922) is his prose account of the experience. Intervention by his father in the form of a letter to President Woodrow Wilson freed him, and Cummings found the experience of being made a prisoner by one's own side outrageous, yet funny. After the war, he made a life primarily in Greenwich Village in New York City, working full time as a poet and painter. Prizes, royalties, commissions, and a small allowance from his mother supported his independence. Cummings's work is known for its radical innovations in punctuation, capitalization, spelling, and grammar. Some of his poems seem literally to explode into fragments across the page, for he often arranged letters, words, and phrases in unique ways to make a visual as well as a verbal impact. In keeping with his innovative style, Cummings often had his name printed in all lowercase letters: *e. e. cummings.* His works include four volumes of well-received poetry in the 1920s and a book of collected poems toward the end of the 1930s. During the 1950s, he lectured and read on the college campus circuit. He received a special citation from the National Book Award Committee in 1955 and the Bollingen Prize for poetry at Yale in 1957. In 1950, he was honored with a fellowship from the Academy of American Poets for "great achievement" over a period of years.

ABOUT THE SELECTION

Following the prolific first decade of his work, Cummings published in 1931 the volume of verse *w[viva]* which included **"somewhere i have never travelled,gladly beyond."** When Cummings wrote the selection, he was stretching to the limits his capacity for experimentation with poetic form. Seeking to catch the aliveness of the moment, Cummings manipulated typography, imagery, structure, diction, punctuation, grammar, syntax, rhyme, meter, and verse form.

GOALS/OBJECTIVES

Studying this lesson will enable students to
- have a positive experience reading a poem that is experimental in form
- become familiar with the life and work of E. E. Cummings
- identify standard placement of end marks, commas, and colons
- understand literary terms such as *syntax, inversion, repetition,* and *rhyme*
- write a love letter

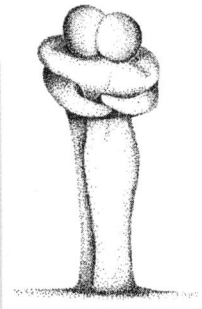

READER'S JOURNAL

Have you ever looked deeply into the eyes of someone else? What did you see? How did your feelings for the person affect what you saw at that moment? Write about the experience in your journal.

LANGUAGE SKILLS

Read the Language Arts Survey, 2.93, "End Marks"; 2.94–2.96, "Commas I, II, and III"; and 2.98, "Colons." Then identify some commas and colons in the selection and note how Cummings experiments with their use.

"somewhere i have never travelled,gladly beyond"

E. E. CUMMINGS

somewhere i have never travelled,gladly beyond
any experience,your eyes have their silence:
in your most frail gesture are things which enclose me,
or which i cannot touch because they are too near

5 your slightest look easily will unclose me
though i have closed myself as fingers,
you open always petal by petal myself as Spring opens
(touching skilfully,mysteriously)her first rose

or if your wish be to close me,i and
10 my life will shut very beautifully,suddenly,
as when the heart of this flower imagines
the snow carefully everywhere descending;

nothing which we are to perceive in this world equals
the power of your intense fragility:whose texture
15 compels me with the colour of its countries,
rendering death and forever with each breathing

(i do not know what it is about you that closes
and opens; only something in me understands
the voice of your eyes is deeper than all roses)
20 nobody,not even the rain,has such small hands ■

❶ *Where are things that enclose the speaker?*

❷ *What has so much power over the speaker?*

PREREADING NOTES

READER'S JOURNAL

Encourage students to write about both positive and negative feelings. Then ask them to write about the ways in which feelings can shape perceptions.

LANGUAGE SKILLS

Students should recognize that because Cummings has structured sentences in a nonstandard way, commas and colons fall in places they would not usually fall. Students might also notice that Cummings does not insert spaces after punctuation.

ANSWERS TO GUIDED READING QUESTIONS

❶ In the subject's most frail gesture are things that enclose the speaker.

❷ The subject's intense fragility has power over the speaker.

ANSWERS TO SELECTION CHECK TEST 4.8.37

EX. According to the speaker, what do "your eyes" have?
According to the speaker, "your eyes" have their silence.

1. Where are things that enclose the speaker?
There are things that enclose the speaker in the subject's most frail gesture.

2. To what season does the speaker compare the subject of the poem?
The speaker compares the subject of the poem to spring.

3. What weather change causes a flower to close?
Snowfall causes a flower to close.

4. What does "nothing we are to perceive in this world" equal?
The power of the subject's intense fragility.

5. What are the subject's eyes deeper than?
The subject's eyes are deeper than roses.

RESPONDING TO THE SELECTION

Some students might wish to keep this journal entry private or share the entry with only one or two students. Separate the class into small groups. Ask the groups to discuss why humans have the capacity for such feelings. What other movies, books, or stories have they read that express this theme?

ANSWERS FOR REVIEWING THE SELECTION

RECALLING

1. The speaker says that "your eyes" have silence.
2. The slightest look will easily "unclose" the speaker, even if he has closed himself like fingers.
3. According to the poem, nothing equals "the power of your intense fragility."
4. The speaker understands that "the voice of your eyes" is "deeper than all roses."

INTERPRETING

Responses will vary. Possible responses are given.

5. The speaker has never traveled to a place that is "gladly beyond any experience" the speaker sees in the beloved's eyes. Students might say that there are parts of the self that are always hidden, even in the most intimate of relationships.
6. The speaker compares the subject of the poem to spring. The speaker compares himself to a flower. When people speak of "opening up" to another person, they usually mean that they are sharing themselves and their intimate feelings with another person.
7. The "texture" of the subject's fragility "compels" the speaker "with the colour of its countries." By using the word *countries* the speaker is making reference to the vastness, diversity, and often unexplored nature of one person's personality.
8. The rain can open the rose. The person being addressed has the ability to open and close the

(cont.)

Responding to the Selection

How does the speaker feel about the person he or she is addressing? Have you ever felt this way about somebody? Explore these feelings in your journal and then discuss them with your classmates.

Reviewing the Selection

RECALLING

1. What does the speaker say "your eyes" have?
2. What will easily "unclose" the speaker, even if he has closed himself like fingers?
3. What equals "the power of your intense fragility"?
4. What does the speaker understand about "the voice of your eyes"?

INTERPRETING

5. Where has the speaker not traveled? What is gladly beyond any experience? What does it mean for eyes to "have their silence"? Is there a part of the self that others usually do not reach?
6. In the metaphor "you open always petal by petal," to what does the speaker compare the person addressed in the poem? To what does he compare himself? What does it usually mean when people speak of "opening up" to others?
7. What "compels" the speaker "with the colour of its countries"? What does the use of the word "countries" suggest about the vast, unexplored nature of the other person's personality?
8. What effect does rain have on roses? What effect does the person being addressed have on the speaker? What small gestures on the part of that person affect the speaker deeply?

SYNTHESIZING

9. Think of the various things to which the speaker compares the person being addressed: Spring opening a rose, snow descending and causing a rose to close, and the small hands of the rain. Then think of the descriptions of the person's frail gestures, slightest look, and intense fragility. What power does the person being addressed have over the speaker? What is ironic or paradoxical about this power?
10. What things mentioned in the poem are mysterious, not fully understandable or known, and thus "beyond experience"?

ANSWERS FOR REVIEWING THE SELECTION (CONT.)

speaker with small and delicate hands. The person's "slightest look" affects the speaker deeply.

SYNTHESIZING

Responses will vary. Possible responses are given.

9. It is ironic that the subject has "frail gestures," "intense fragility," and "small hands," yet makes such a powerful impression on the speaker.
10. The speaker does not completely understand the power that these feelings have over him. The speaker mentions the mysterious nature of the "silence" in the subject's eyes, how he opens and closes as a flower, and how nothing else in the world "equals/the power" of the beloved's "intense fragility." The other person, the beloved, is mysterious, not fully understandable or known, and thus "beyond experience."

Understanding Literature (Questions for Discussion)

1. **Syntax and Inversion. Syntax** is the pattern of arrangement of words in a statement. Cummings begins the poem with two modifying phrases, delaying until the middle of the second line the appearance of the noun that is modified—eyes. An **inversion** is a poetic technique in which the normal order of words is altered. How are the words in the first two lines inverted? How would the first two lines read if Cummings had followed the usual order of words in a sentence, placing the subject first?

2. **Repetition and Rhyme. Repetition** is the use, again, of a sound, word, phrase, sentence, or other element. **Rhyme** is the repetition of sounds at the ends of words. Types of rhyme include *end rhyme* (the use of rhyming words at the ends of lines), *internal rhyme* (the use of rhyming words within lines), *exact rhyme* (in which the rhyming words end with the same sound or sounds), and *slant rhyme* (in which the rhyming sounds are similar but not identical). What repetition of the words *open* and *close* occurs in this poem? What types of rhyme are used in the various repetitions of these words? What effect is enacted by the various repetitions and rhymes of the words *open* and *close?*

Responding in Writing

Love Letter. Imagine that you are the person whom the speaker addresses in this poem. Write him or her a letter expressing your feelings of love. Refer to the material in the Language Arts Survey, 5.2, "The Form of a Personal Letter."

Answers for Understanding Literature

► See the evaluation forms for discussion, active listening, and oral communication, *Assessment Portfolio,* 7.11–7.14.

Responses will vary. Possible responses are given.

1. Syntax and Inversion. The first two lines would read, "Your eyes have their silence: somewhere i have never travelled,gladly beyond any experience. . . ."

2. Repetition and Rhyme. The words *open* and *close* appear in the following places: in the first section, "enclose me"; in the second section, "unclose me," "closed myself as fingers," and "open always petal by petal myself as Spring opens"; in the third section, "If your wish be to close me,i . . . will shut very beautifully, suddenly"; in the fifth section, "i do not know what it is about you that closes and opens." The repetition of the words *open* and *close* demonstrates the forces that are at work in the relationship.

Analytic Scales for Responding in Writing

Assign a score from 1 to 25 for each grading criterion below. (For more detailed evaluation, see the evaluation forms for writing, revising, and proofreading, *Assessment Portfolio,* 7.1–7.10.)

Love Letter

- **Content/Unity.** The letter expresses feelings of love to the speaker of the Cummings poem.
- **Organization/Coherence.** The letter follows the standard form of a personal letter.
- **Language/Style.** The language of the letter is vivid, clear, and convincing.
- **Conventions.** The letter avoids errors in spelling, grammar, usage, and mechanics.

ADDITIONAL RESOURCES

READER'S GUIDE
- Selection Worksheet, 8.20

ASSESSMENT PORTFOLIO
- Selection Check Test, 8.39
- Selection Test, 8.40

ESSENTIAL SKILLS PRACTICE BOOKS
- *Language,* 2.138, 2.139

ENRICHMENT ACTIVITIES

Ask students to find and read the myths of Tantalus and Sisyphus, as well as other Greek myths that deal with punishment from the gods or unexplained tragedy. You might suggest reading the myth of Echo, Narcissus, or Icarus. Students should meet in small groups to discuss the ways in which people have tried to explain the ways of the world to one another through history.

SUPPORT FOR LEP STUDENTS

Some students might have trouble working through the section of the poem that talks about human struggles and hardships. Read this section with students, stopping after each line.

ADDITIONAL VOCABULARY

quibble—talking about a petty detail
fickle—unpredictable
immune—free

PREREADING

"Yet Do I Marvel"
by Countee Cullen

ABOUT THE AUTHOR

Countee Cullen (1903–1946) was born Countee Leroy Porter in New York City. In 1918, he was adopted by Reverend Frederick Cullen, a Methodist minister. He attended New York public schools, graduated Phi Beta Kappa with a B.A. from New York University in 1925, and took an M.A. at Harvard in 1926. He married twice. His first marriage to Yolande Du Bois, daughter of W. E. B. Du Bois, black educator and sociologist, lasted two years. Like many African Americans of his time, Cullen shaped the expression of his talents in reaction to racism in the society in which he lived. Recalling an incident in 1930 when he was barred from eating in a restaurant at the New York Central terminal in Buffalo, New York, he later said, "There may have been many things in my life that have hurt me, and I find that the surest relief from these hurts is in writing. Most things I write, I do for the sheer love of the music in them. Somehow or other, however, I find my poetry of itself treating of the Negro, of his joys and his sorrows, mostly of the latter, and of the heights and the depths of emotion which I feel as a Negro." From 1926 to 1928, Cullen was assistant editor of *Opportunity: Journal of Negro Life,* the magazine of the National Urban League, where he wrote "The Dark Tower," a column of reflections and literary criticism. He taught French at Frederick Douglass Junior High School in New York City from 1934 to 1945 and wrote and published children's stories. Cullen was proud of being African American, of his "ebony muse," but not surprisingly, he was bitter about the African-American experience in America. He is best known for his poems about racial issues, but was criticized by his contemporaries for the mildness of his attacks on racial injustice. Cullen was a middle-class New Yorker who wanted to be a traditional poet, and his ideas about poetry were counter to those of other writers of the Harlem Renaissance. Among other awards and honors, Cullen received a Guggenheim Fellowship in 1929 to complete *The Black Christ and Other Poems* (1929). His works include *Color* (poetry, 1925), *Caroling Dusk: An Anthology of Verse by Negro Poets* (1927), *Copper Sun* (1927), *The Ballad of the Brown Girl* (1928), *One Way to Heaven* (novel, 1932), and *On These I Stand* (1947).

ABOUT THE SELECTION

"Yet Do I Marvel" appeared in *On These I Stand,* the collection considered to include Cullen's best poetry. The final lines of the selection are among the most famous of all produced by the poets of the Harlem Renaissance.

GOALS/OBJECTIVES

Studying this lesson will enable students to

- appreciate reading a sonnet about the unexplained struggles of life
- become familiar with the life and work of Countee Cullen
- use context clues to learn unfamiliar words
- understand literary terms such as *sonnet* and *allusion*

READER'S JOURNAL

Have you ever marveled at a seemingly unexplainable event or occurrence? What was mysterious or inscrutable about the event? How did you try to understand it? Write about the experience in your journal.

LANGUAGE SKILLS

Read the Language Arts Survey, 2.138 and 2.139, "Using Context Clues I and II." Then identify some words in the selection that you cannot readily define and use context clues to find the meaning of each word.

"Yet Do I Marvel"

COUNTEE CULLEN

I doubt not God is good, well-meaning,
kind,
And did He stoop to quibble could tell why
The little buried mole continues blind,
Why flesh that mirrors Him must some day die,
5 Make plain the reason tortured Tantalus[1]
Is baited by the fickle fruit, declare
If merely brute caprice dooms Sisyphus[2]
To struggle up a never-ending stair.
Inscrutable[3] His ways are, and immune
10 To catechism[4] by a mind too strewn
With petty cares to slightly understand
What awful brain compels His awful hand.
Yet do I marvel at this curious thing:
To make a poet black, and bid him sing! ■

❶ *What kind of God does the speaker envision?*

❷ *What does the speaker say about understanding the motivations of God?*

1. **Tantalus.** King in Greek mythology who was doomed in Hades to stand in water that receded from him when he was thirsty and under branches of fruit that he could not reach when hungry
2. **Sisyphus.** King whose doom in Hades was to roll a heavy stone uphill only to have it always roll down again
3. **Inscrutable.** That cannot be easily understood
4. **catechism.** Close questioning; religious debate or discussion

WORDS FOR EVERYDAY USE: **ca • price** (kə prēs´) *n.,* whim, change in way of thinking

VOCABULARY IN CONTEXT

- On a caprice, my brother changed his plans and went to a special performance in the city.

PREREADING NOTES

READER'S JOURNAL

Encourage students to think about what their own personal philosophies of life are when things do not run smoothly. Ask them to think about why it is important to have ways to deal emotionally with struggle. You might invite students to discuss these ideas in class.

LANGUAGE SKILLS

Answers will vary. You might ask students to discuss how they were able to figure out difficult words.

ANSWERS TO GUIDED READING QUESTIONS

❶ The speaker envisions God to be good, well-meaning, and kind.

❷ The speaker believes that humans are not capable of truly understanding the motivations of God.

ANSWERS TO SELECTION CHECK TEST 4.8.39

EX. Who wrote the poem "Yet Do I Marvel?"
Countee Cullen wrote the poem.

1. What is the speaker's opinion of God?
The speaker believes God is good, well-meaning, and kind.

2. What does the speaker guess God would be able to explain?
The speaker guesses that God would be able to explain the reason for pain and suffering.

3. According to the speaker, what is "inscrutable"?
According to the speaker, God's ways are "inscrutable."

4. According to the speaker, with what is the human mind strewn?
According to the speaker, the human mind is strewn with petty cares.

5. At what does the speaker marvel?
The speaker marvels at the fact that God made a poet black, and "bid him sing."

RESPONDING TO THE SELECTION

Ask students to list in their journals what they believe are specific demonstrations of the world's cruelty, pain, and injustice. Then ask them to list what they see as specific demonstrations of love, generosity, and kindness in the world. They may list everyday things from their own lives or public incidents and events. Ask students to gather in small groups to share their ideas.

ANSWERS FOR REVIEWING THE SELECTION

RECALLING

1. The speaker mentions a mole's blindness, human mortality, the torturing of Tantalus, and the struggle of Sisyphus.

2. The speaker says that the minds of humans are too petty and small to understand the mind of God.

INTERPRETING

Responses will vary. Possible responses are given.

3. The speaker does not doubt that God is good, well-meaning, and kind, despite the existence of pain.

4. The speaker believes that God's ways are not easily understood, and that human minds cannot reason about God's motivation.

SYNTHESIZING

Responses will vary. Possible responses are given.

5. The speaker marvels at the fact that God made "a poet black, and bid him sing!" The speaker sees this as a paradox because of the struggles and indignities African Americans have faced in the world. The curiosity relates to the speaker's idea that God's work is not easily understood by humans. According to the speaker, pain and hardship, as well as God's gifts, are all mysteries to humans.

Responding to the Selection

Review lines 9–12 of the poem. What explanation does the speaker offer for the existence of cruelty, pain, death, and injustice in the world? Do you agree with this explanation? Why, or why not?

Reviewing the Selection

RECALLING

1. What negative aspects of the world does the speaker mention in lines 3–8?

2. What comparison does the speaker make between the mind of God and the mind of a human?

INTERPRETING

3. What does the speaker not doubt, despite the existence of pain?

4. How does the speaker respond to the old argument that a just God would not allow pain or injustice to continue?

SYNTHESIZING

5. At what does the speaker marvel? What paradox does the speaker seem to see in "this curious thing"? How does this curiosity relate to the speaker's comments about God?

Understanding Literature (Questions for Discussion)

1. **Sonnet.** A **sonnet** is a fourteen-line poem that follows one of a number of different rhyme schemes. Like the **English, Elizabethan,** or **Shakespearean sonnet,** the selection can be divided into four parts: three **quatrains,** or four-line stanzas, and a final **couplet,** or two-line stanza. A Shakespearean sonnet usually has the rhyme scheme *abab cdcd efef gg.* What is the rhyme scheme of the selection? How does the selection's rhyme scheme vary slightly from that of a Shakespearean sonnet? Another way of viewing the organization of this sonnet is as an **octave,** or group of eight lines, followed by a **sestet,** or group of six lines. What question is raised in the octave of this sonnet? How is that question answered in the sestet? What comment does the speaker make in the concluding couplet, or pair of rhymed lines?

2. **Allusion.** An **allusion** is a figure of speech in which a reference is made to a person, event, object, or work from history or literature. Cullen alludes, or refers, to the Greek myths of Tantalus and Sisyphus. In the former myth, the gods condemned Tantalus to spend eternity in the underworld, poised between water below him and food above him. Whenever he moved to get the food or water, it receded from him, leaving him eternally thirsty and hungry. In the latter myth, the gods condemned Sisyphus to spend eternity in the underworld pushing a rock to the top of a hill only to have it roll back down so that his task could never be complete. What purpose is served by the allusions to these two myths? Of what kinds of experiences are the myths examples?

ANSWERS FOR UNDERSTANDING LITERATURE

► See the evaluation forms for discussion, active listening, and oral communication, *Assessment Portfolio,* 7.11–7.14.

Responses will vary. Possible responses are given.

1. Sonnet. The rhyme scheme of the selection is *abab cdcd eeff gg.* The rhyme scheme differs from that of a Shakespearean sonnet in the third quatrain. In the octave of the sonnet, a question is raised about why God allows pain and suffering in the world. This question is addressed in the poem's sestet, when the speaker says that humans are simply incapable of understanding God's ways. In the final couplet, the speaker marvels at God's decision "to make a poet black, and bid him sing!"

2. Allusion. The myths illustrate pain, suffering, and struggle, particularly the struggles felt by African Americans. Both myths are examples of torture that is felt when one is unable to feel satisfied; when something seems just within one's grasp but is then taken away or destroyed.

PREREADING

"The Tropics in New York"
by Claude McKay

About the Author

Claude McKay (1890–1948), who also wrote under the pseudonym Eli Edwards, was born in Jamaica, in the West Indies, to poor farm workers. He was educated by his brother and by an Englishman who was a specialist in Jamaican folklore. His first two collections of poems, written in native dialect, were published in England in 1912. These collections earned him prize money that helped him to emigrate to the United States that year. He studied at Booker T. Washington's Tuskeegee Institute and at Kansas State College. He moved to Harlem in 1914, worked at odd jobs, and pursued his writing. He moved to England for a time, where his poems were published regularly, then returned to the United States in the early 1920s, where he took a job as editor of the radical newspapers *The Liberator* and *The Masses.* He was a prominent figure in the Harlem Renaissance, and the racial prejudice he witnessed and experienced helped to radicalize him. He left America to live in Europe but returned after the publication of his award-winning novel *Home to Harlem* (1928), one of the first bestsellers by an African-American writer. By the 1940s, he had repudiated his earlier radicalism and become a naturalized citizen. His poem "If We Must Die," written as a response to the Harlem race riots of 1919, was nevertheless embraced as a rallying cry by the majority white culture during World War II. Its stirring sentiments were admired by Winston Churchill, who read it to the British people. In the United States, the poem was entered into the Congressional Record. Some critics consider the poem to be a major impetus behind the Civil Rights movement that began after the war. One critic called it, "at once a shout of defiance and a proclamation of the unbreakable spirit and courage of the oppressed black American." In 1942, McKay joined the Catholic Church and for the last five years of his life lived in Chicago doing research for the National Catholic Youth Organization. His works include *Songs of Jamaica* (poetry, 1912), *Harlem Shadows* (poetry, 1922), *Banjo* (1929), *Banana Bottom* (1933), *Gingertown* (short stories, 1932), *A Long Way from Home* (autobiography, 1937), and *Harlem: Negro Metropolis* (sociological study, 1940).

About the Selection

After moving to the United States from Jamaica in 1912, McKay started again to write. Perhaps reflective of McKay's own experience, the speaker in **"The Tropics in New York,"** noting with realistic detail the fruits in a grocer's window, is reminded of his former life in the tropics and longs for its old and familiar ways.

ADDITIONAL RESOURCES

Reader's Guide
- Selection Worksheet, 8.21

Assessment Portfolio
- Selection Check Test, 4.8.41
- Selection Test, 4.8.42

Essential Skills Practice Books
- *Language,* 2.35

ENRICHMENT ACTIVITIES

- Have students learn more about the West Indies, the homeland of Claude McKay. Ask students to work in small groups or individually and pick a place in the West Indies on which to focus. Students should present their research to the class in the form of a creative presentation.
- Ask students to pick an artist from the Harlem Renaissance and learn more about that person's work. The subject can be a writer, a singer, or a musician. You might ask students to prepare either papers or oral presentations.

SUPPORT FOR LEP STUDENTS

Be sure students understand the two meanings of the word *hunger* before reading this poem.

Additional Vocabulary
rill—a small brook
laden—weighted down

GOALS/OBJECTIVES

Studying this lesson will enable students to

- empathize with a speaker who misses home
- become familiar with the life and work of Claude McKay
- identify colorful modifiers
- understand literary terms such as *meter, rhyme,* and *tone*
- write a greeting card

PREREADING NOTES

READER'S JOURNAL

Encourage students to be specific about the feelings and thoughts they associate with homesickness. When students are away from home, have there been certain sights, sounds, or smells that have triggered homesickness? How do they make themselves feel better?

LANGUAGE SKILLS

Students should identify "ripe and green," "low-singing," "dewy," "mystical," and "nun-like" as colorful modifiers. Students might say that the modifiers describing the fruit add to the lighter tone of stanza 1. The modifiers describing the place in the speaker's memory give stanza 2 a more somber, nostalgic tone.

ANSWERS TO GUIDED READING QUESTIONS

❶ The speaker sees bananas, ginger-root, cocoa, alligator pears, tangerines, mangoes, and grapefruit in the window. These things remind him of his homeland.

❷ The speaker grew hungry for "old, familiar ways." The fruit reminded him of the other place in which he lived.

RESPONDING TO THE SELECTION

Ask students to think about how the speaker's current setting might be different from the place for which he longs. Encourage them to incorporate specific details about his environment and feelings. You might want to ask students to share their letters in class.

READER'S JOURNAL

Have you ever felt homesick? Where were you when you felt this way? What did you miss most about home? Write about the experience in your journal.

LANGUAGE SKILLS

Read the Language Arts Survey, 2.35, "Using Colorful Modifiers." Then identify some modifiers in the poem and note what mood or tone the adjectives lend to each noun and to the overall selection.

"The Tropics in New York"

CLAUDE MCKAY

What does the speaker see in the window? What memories do these things bring? ❶

Bananas ripe and green, and ginger-root,
Cocoa in pods and alligator pears,
And tangerines and mangoes and grapefruit,
Fit for the highest prize at parish fairs,

Set in the window, bringing memories
Of fruit-trees laden by low-singing rills,
And dewy dawns, and mystical blue skies
In benediction[1] over nun-like hills.

For what did the speaker grow hungry? Why did the fruit have such an effect on him? ❷

My eyes grew dim, and I could no more gaze;
A wave of longing through my body swept,
And, hungry for the old, familiar ways,
I turned aside and bowed my head and wept. ■

1. **benediction.** Blessing

ANSWERS TO SELECTION CHECK TEST 4.8.41

EX. What is the setting of the poem?
According to the title, the poem is set in New York.

1. For what is the fruit in the window fit?
The fruit in the window is fit for the highest prize at parish fairs.

2. What does the sight of the fruit in the window do to the speaker?
The sight of the fruit in the window brings back memories for the speaker.

3. What sweeps through the speaker's body?
A wave of longing sweeps through the speaker's body.

4. For what is the speaker hungry?
The speaker is hungry for old, familiar ways.

5. What does the speaker do?
The speaker weeps.

Responding to the Selection

Imagine that you are the speaker standing outside the grocer's window, looking at the tropical fruits. Why does the image of those fruits suddenly fill you with longing? Write a letter to a friend in Jamaica, expressing to him or her your feelings of homesickness for the old and familiar ways.

Reviewing the Selection

RECALLING

1. What fruits are "fit for the highest prize at parish fairs"?
2. What sweeps through the speaker's body?

INTERPRETING

3. What images recall the past for the speaker? What effect, or emotional impact, do the images create?
4. How does the speaker feel toward "the old, familiar ways"?

SYNTHESIZING

5. What role does hunger have in the poem? What connotations and denotations of hunger are used in the poem?

Understanding Literature (Questions for Discussion)

1. **Meter and Rhyme.** The **meter** of a poem is its rhythmical pattern. A poem is made up of rhythmical units, called *feet.* Types of feet include iambic, trochaic, anapestic, dactylic, and spondaic. (For definitions of these terms, see the entry on *meter* in the Handbook of Literary Terms.) **Rhyme** is the repetition of sounds at the ends of words. One type of rhyme, **end rhyme,** is the use of rhyming words at the ends of lines. Scan the poem. What is the poem's meter? What is its rhyme scheme?

2. **Tone. Tone** is the emotional attitude toward the reader or toward the subject implied by a literary work. How do the different meanings of hunger cause the tone of the poem to shift in each stanza?

Responding in Writing

Greeting Card. Create a greeting card for the speaker of the poem, who is a long way from home. In your card, write a message that expresses your wishes and concerns for the speaker.

ANSWERS FOR REVIEWING THE SELECTION

RECALLING

1. Bananas, ginger-root, cocoa, alligator pears, tangerines, mangoes, and grapefruit are fit for the highest prize.
2. A wave of longing sweeps through the speaker's body.

INTERPRETING

Responses will vary. Possible responses are given.

3. Images of the fruit set in windows recall the past for the speaker. The images make the speaker long for the past.
4. The speaker longs for "the old, familiar ways."

SYNTHESIZING

5. The speaker describes the ripe fruit in a way that would lead the reader to believe the speaker is simply hungry for the taste of the fruit. However, the sight of the fruit also makes the speaker hunger for the past and for "old, familiar ways."

ANSWERS FOR UNDERSTANDING LITERATURE

► See the evaluation forms for discussion, active listening, and oral communication, *Assessment Portfolio,* 7.11–7.14.

Responses will vary. Possible responses are given.

1. Meter and Rhyme. The rhyme scheme of the poem is *abab cdcd efef.* The lines are written in iambic feet.

2. Tone. In stanza 1, the speaker appears to be gazing at the fruit because it is ripe, delicious, and inviting. In stanza 2, the speaker tells how the fruit brings back memories of another place, and the tone of the poem begins to change and become more somber. In stanza 3, the reader learns that the speaker hungers for much more than fruit; the speaker hungers for the "old, familiar ways" of the other land. The tone of stanza 3 is completely different from the tone of stanza 1.

ANALYTIC SCALES FOR RESPONDING IN WRITING

Assign a score from 1 to 25 for each grading criterion below. (For more detailed evaluation, see the evaluation forms for writing, revising, and proofreading, *Assessment Portfolio,* 7.1–7.10.)

Greeting Card

- **Content/Unity.** The greeting card is written for the speaker of the poem and expresses concerns for the speaker.
- **Organization/Coherence.** The ideas presented on the card are in a sensible order.
- **Language/Style.** The card sounds warm and interesting, like a personal message.
- **Conventions.** The writing avoids errors in spelling, grammar, usage, and mechanics.

ADDITIONAL RESOURCES

READER'S GUIDE
- Selection Worksheet, 8.22

ASSESSMENT PORTFOLIO
- Selection Check Test, 8.43
- Selection Test, 8.44

ESSENTIAL SKILLS PRACTICE BOOKS
- *Language,* 2.43–2.45, 2.57
- *Study and Research,* 4.23

ENRICHMENT ACTIVITIES

As mentioned in About the Selection on page 594, Hughes tried to unite elements of blues with elements of formal poetry. Explore with students the relationship between Langston Hughes's 1926 collection of poetry, *The Weary Blues*, and elements of blues music. Read selections from this collection with the class. Then try to bring into class musical pieces from blues artists of the period. Invite students to compare the music with the sounds and rhythms of the poetry. Ask them to make notes as they read and listen. Then hold a discussion about shared techniques in the two genres. You might ask students to conduct their own research into blues and Hughes's poetry.

SUPPORT FOR LEP STUDENTS

Some students might need assistance in understanding the central image of the poem. Spend time discussing the possible significance of rivers and other elements of nature in poetry.

ADDITIONAL VOCABULARY

Mississippi—Mississippi River

dusky—dark and cloudy

PREREADING

"The Negro Speaks of Rivers"
by Langston Hughes

ABOUT THE AUTHOR

Langston Hughes (1902–1967) was born in Joplin, Missouri, and lived for most of his childhood in Lawrence, Kansas, with his maternal grandmother, whose first husband had been one of the African-Americans killed in John Brown's raid on the arsenal at Harpers Ferry. Hughes was thirteen when she died, at which time he went to live with his mother. He graduated from high school in Cleveland, Ohio, and then spent more than a year with his father in Mexico. It was there that he wrote the poem "The Negro Speaks of Rivers," which would later gain him recognition as a writer. Hughes studied for a year at Columbia University, leaving in 1920. For the next several years, he traveled, taking whatever jobs he found, wherever he found himself. During this peripatetic period, he continued to write. His work began to be published in important African-American periodicals like *Opportunity* and *The Crises.* He accepted a scholarship from Lincoln University in Pennsylvania and graduated in 1929. While there, he wrote his first novel, *Not without Laughter* (1930). His political activism in the 1930s later resulted in his being called to testify before the House Un-American Activities Committee in 1953 and listed as a security risk by the FBI until 1959. Awards and honors recognizing his work include Rosenwald and Guggenheim fellowships and a grant from the American Academy of Arts and Letters. Hughes was a prolific, versatile writer and is especially well known for his famous fictional character Jesse B. Semple, or "Simple." His works include *The Weary Blues* (1926), *The Negro Artist and the Racial Mountain* (essay, 1926), *The Ways of White Folks* (stories, 1934), *Shakespeare in Harlem* (1942), *Simple Speaks His Mind* (1950), *First Book of Negroes* (anthology, 1952), *First Book of Jazz* (anthology, 1955), *Simple Stakes a Claim* (1957), *First Book of Negro Folklore* (anthology 1958).

ABOUT THE SELECTION

Before graduating from Lincoln University in Pennsylvania, Hughes had published his first collection of verse, *The Weary Blues.* Included in that 1926 collection was **"The Negro Speaks of Rivers."** During the 1920s, while writing these poems, Hughes worked to unite the elements of blues with formal poetry.

GOALS/OBJECTIVES

Studying this lesson will enable students to

- have a positive experience reading lyric poetry
- read and understand the work of poet Langston Hughes
- recognize compound, complex, and compound-complex sentences
- define literary terms such as *simile, refrain,* and *effect*
- write a lyric poem
- achieve parallelism in writing
- use reference works and conduct research

READER'S JOURNAL

With what object in the natural world do you most strongly identify? Choose one object and write about it in your journal, telling what you are attracted to it and what it means to you.

LANGUAGE SKILLS

Read the Language Arts Survey, 2.43-2.45, on compound, complex, and compound-complex sentences. Then identify two sentences in the selection that build on the simple sentence "I've known rivers." Note how the other sentences expand on the original simple sentence.

"The Negro Speaks of Rivers"

LANGSTON HUGHES

I've known rivers:
I've known rivers ancient as the world and older than the flow of human blood in human veins.

My soul has grown deep like the rivers.

I bathed in the Euphrates when dawns were young.
I built my hut near the Congo and it lulled me to sleep.
I looked upon the Nile[1] and raised the pyramids above it.
I heard the singing of the Mississippi when Abe Lincoln went down to New Orleans, and I've seen its muddy bosom turn all golden in the sunset.

I've known rivers:
Ancient, dusky rivers.

My soul has grown deep like the rivers. ■

1. **Euphrates ... Nile.** *Euphrates*—river that flows through Turkey, Syria, and Iraq; *Congo*—river in central Africa; *Nile*—river in north east Africa

❶ *What is significant about the rivers?*

❷ *To what aspect of the rivers does the speaker compare his soul?*

Responding to the Selection

Imagine that you are the speaker in the poem. For whom do you speak? What is the purpose of your message? Discuss what it means to grow deep like a river.

ANSWERS TO SELECTION CHECK TEST 4.8.43

EX. Who wrote "A Negro Speaks of Rivers"?
Langston Hughes wrote "A Negro Speaks of Rivers."

1. What has the speaker known?
The speaker has known rivers.

2. What does the speaker describe as ancient and "older than the flow of human blood in human veins"?
The speaker describes rivers as ancient and "older than the flow of human blood in human veins."

3. When Abe Lincoln went to New Orleans, of what did the speaker hear the singing?
The speaker heard the singing of the Mississippi River.

4. What color did one river turn in the sunset?
The Mississippi River turned golden in the sunset.

5. What has happened to the speaker's soul?
It has grown deep like the rivers.

PREREADING NOTES

READER'S JOURNAL

Give students time to freewrite about elements of the natural world. You might suggest the following things in helping them to get started: mountains, oceans, lakes, prairies, deserts, jungles, fields, forests, trees, flowers, fruit, and leaves.

LANGUAGE SKILLS

Students should identify "I've known rivers ancient as the world and older than the flow of human blood in human veins" and "I've known rivers: /Ancient, dusky rivers" as sentences that expand on the simple sentence "I've known rivers."

ANSWERS TO GUIDED READING QUESTIONS

❶ Rivers are ancient as the world, and they are older than human beings.

❷ The speaker compares the depth of his soul to the depth of rivers.

CROSS-CURRICULAR ACTIVITIES

Social Studies. Have students research the historical significance of the rivers mentioned in the poem—the Euphrates, the Congo, the Nile, and the Mississippi. Through what countries do each of these rivers flow? How have people who live near the rivers used the rivers as resources? What other historical and literary allusions might one find to each of these rivers? Have students work in groups, with each group focusing on a different river. Students can then share their findings with the class.

Mathematics and Sciences. Ask students to research the formation of rivers. How are rivers different from other bodies of water? Which are the longest rivers in the world?

RESPONDING TO THE SELECTION

Encourage students to think about the significance of the title when deciding for whom the poem speaks. Encourage students to discuss how certain experiences, particularly difficult experiences, can make a person stronger, more thoughtful, and more aware.

ANSWERS FOR REVIEWING THE SELECTION

RECALLING

1. The speaker has known rivers.
2. The speaker describes rivers as being "ancient as the world" and "older than the flow of human blood in human veins."
3. The speaker specifically mentions the Euphrates, the Congo, the Nile, and the Mississippi.
4. The speaker's soul has grown deep like the rivers.

INTERPRETING

5. The speaker is an African-American person speaking of the experiences of his race.
6. The speaker is saying the African race has been around for a long time and as a people has experienced a great deal.
7. The speaker says that he has bathed in the Euphrates, built a hut near the Congo, raised the pyramids above the Nile, and heard the singing of the Mississippi when Abe Lincoln went to New Orleans.
8. Experience has caused the speaker's soul to deepen.

SYNTHESIZING

Responses will vary. Possible responses are given.

9. This poem is about a group of people. The speaker is talking about the history and experiences of his race.
10. The speaker expresses pride and conviction. He is listing the accomplishments and experiences of his people and describing the ways in which they have made the collective soul of his people deeper.

Reviewing the Selection

RECALLING

1. What has the speaker known?
2. What phrases does the speaker use in lines 2 and 3 to describe the rivers?
3. What specific rivers does the speaker mention in the poem?
4. What has happened to the speaker's soul?

INTERPRETING

5. Who is the speaker in this poem?
6. The speaker associates himself with rivers "ancient as the world" and "older than the flow of human blood in human veins." What is the speaker saying about the age and experience of the Negro race?
7. What accomplishments and experiences are associated with each of the rivers in the poem?
8. What has caused the speaker's soul to deepen?

SYNTHESIZING

9. Is this a poem about an individual or about a group? Explain.
10. What overall emotion is expressed by this poem? Explain.

Understanding Literature (Questions for Discussion)

1. **Simile.** A **simile** is a comparison using *like* or *as.* A type of metaphor, a simile can be analyzed into two parts, the *tenor* (or subject being described), and the *vehicle* (or object being used in the description). The two parts can be compared because they share a particular quality. Consider the following simile in the selection: "My soul has grown deep like the rivers." What is the tenor? What is the vehicle? What quality do the two parts share? Identify and analyze another simile from the selection.

2. **Refrain and Effect.** A **refrain** is a line or group of lines repeated in a poem or song. The **effect** of a literary work is the general impression or emotional impact that it achieves. What refrains are used in the poem? What effect do these refrains lend to the overall emotional impact of the poem?

Responding in Writing

1. **Lyric Poem.** A **lyric poem** is a highly musical verse that expresses the emotions of a speaker. Write a lyric poem about a speaker's deep identity with a place. In your poem, use repetition and tone to express the feelings of the speaker.

ANSWERS FOR UNDERSTANDNG LITERATURE

► See the evaluation forms for discussion, active listening, and oral communication, *Assessment Portfolio,* 7.11–7.14.

1. Simile. In "My soul has grown deep like the rivers" the tenor is *soul* and the vehicle is *rivers.* The speaker is saying that his soul is as old and experienced as a river, and so his soul has grown deep like the rivers. Students should identify "ancient as the world" as another simile. In this case *ancient* is the tenor and *world* is the vehicle.

2. Refrain and Effect. The phrases "I've known rivers" and "My soul has grown deep like the rivers" are refrains. These refrains have a strong emotional impact on the reader by expressing the speaker's strong sense of pride and addressing the central theme of the piece.

2. **Family History.** Write a page of your family history. Begin by identifying a particular place where your family has lived for a long time, frequently visited, or gathered together.

Language Lab

Achieving Parallelism. Read the Language Arts Survey, 2.57, "Achieving Parallelism." Then revise the sentences below by correcting the faulty parallelism.

1. Langston Hughes attended high school in Cleveland and to publish fiction and poetry in his high school magazine.
2. For more than twenty years, Hughes wrote for the *Chicago Defender,* in which he introduced the character "Simple" and to make him the heart of his column.
3. Hughes said I've known rivers and his soul has grown deep like the rivers.
4. In 1932, the year Hughes lived and was working in the former Soviet Union, he wrote his most radical poetry.
5. Hughes published dozens of books of fiction, nonfiction, and poetry and to translate books by Lorca, Mistral, Guillen, and Roumain.

Research Skills

Using Reference Works. Read the Language Arts Survey, 4.23, "Using Reference Works." Then, for each subject in the following list, identify the type of reference work in which you can find out what you need to know.

1. location of the Congo River
2. history of the Nile River
3. news story about the most recent Mississippi River flood
4. quotations about rivers
5. name of the river with which the Euphrates unites

PROJECT

Oral History. Visit someone at a community for retired or elderly people, or seek out an elderly person in your own family. (Before visiting a facility, such as a retirement community, contact the administrative personnel to obtain permission for your visit.) Interview that person to prepare an oral history of his or her life in some specific place. If possible, tape record and transcribe the stories that the person tells you. If you do not have access to a tape recorder, take detailed notes during the interview, and then write up your notes in the form of a brief report. Share those stories in written form with your classmates.

ANALYTIC SCALES FOR RESPONDING IN WRITING

Assign a score from 1 to 25 for each grading criterion below. (For more detailed evaluation, see the evaluation forms for writing, revising, and proofreading, *Assessment Portfolio,* 7.1–7.10.)

1. Lyric Poem

- **Content/Unity.** The lyric poem is musical and expresses the emotions of the speaker concerning a special place.
- **Organization/Coherence.** The poem is organized in a clear way that allows the reader to appreciate the speaker's special place.
- **Language/Style.** The poem uses highly musical and rhythmic verse and contains vivid imagery.
- **Conventions.** The poem avoids errors in spelling, grammar, usage, and mechanics.

2. Family History

- **Content/Unity.** The page presents family history and focuses on a particular place.
- **Organization/Coherence.** The place is presented clearly, and the paper is well organized.
- **Language/Style.** The history is well written and makes good use of modifiers and precise nouns.
- **Conventions.** The paragraph avoids errors in spelling, grammar, usage, and mechanics.

ANSWERS FOR LANGUAGE LAB

1. Langston Hughes attended high school in Cleveland and published fiction and poetry in his high school magazine.
2. For more than twenty years, Hughes wrote for the *Chicago Defender,* in which he introduced the character "Simple" and made him the heart of his column.
3. Hughes said he's known rivers and his soul has grown deep like the rivers.
4. In 1932, the year Hughes lived and worked in the former Soviet Union, he wrote his most radical poetry.
5. Hughes published dozens of books of fiction, nonfiction, and poetry, and he translated books by Lorca, Mistral, Guillen, and Roumain.

PROJECT NOTES

▶See the worksheet and evaluation forms for projects, *Assessment Portfolio,* 7.20–7.23.

Encourage students to prepare ahead of time for the interview by writing out a list of questions. Remind them to have fun with the interview and to treat the interviewee with friendliness and respect.

ANSWERS FOR RESEARCH SKILLS

1. atlas
2. encyclopedia
3. almanacs and yearbooks
4. collections of quotations
5. atlas

▶**Teaching Note:** Students might use this exercise in combination with the cross-curricular activities provided on page 595.

ADDITIONAL RESOURCES

READER'S GUIDE
- Selection Worksheet, 8.23

ASSESSMENT PORTFOLIO
- Selection Check Test, 4.8.45
- Selection Test, 4.8.46

ESSENTIAL SKILLS PRACTICE BOOKS
- *Language*, 2.56

ENRICHMENT ACTIVITIES

Ask students to look for other work by Bontemps in their school or local library. Students might be especially interested in looking for *St. Louis Women* (1935), the dramatization he wrote with Countee Cullen, or *Popo and Fifina: Children of Haiti*, a book he wrote with Langston Hughes. Students might also be interested in sampling one of the books Bontemps wrote for children, such as *Sam Patch* or *Famous Negro Athletes*.

SUPPORT FOR LEP STUDENTS

Be sure that all students are clear on the important information packed into the last stanza of the poem. Spend time discussing what has happened to the fruits of the speaker's labor.

ADDITIONAL VOCABULARY

reaping—harvesting, gathering

yields—produces

PREREADING

"A Black Man Talks of Reaping"

by Arna Bontemps

ABOUT THE AUTHOR

Arna (Wendell) Bontemps (1902–1973) was born in Alexandria, Louisiana. His father was a brick mason and his mother a teacher. Arna was the nickname given him by his grandmother. He had a comfortable childhood, although his family relocated from Louisiana to Los Angeles after some racial harassment of his father. In 1923, Bontemps graduated from Pacific Union College. In 1943, he earned an M.A. from the University of Chicago. He married Alberta Johnson in 1926, and they had six children. A teacher, librarian, anthologist, poet, author of novels, plays, biographies, and children's fiction, Bontemps dealt in his work almost exclusively with black life and culture. Active in writers' organizations and in the American Library Association, he also served as a member of the Metropolitan Nashville Board of Education. He worked as a high school teacher and principal, as well as a freelance writer, before he was Librarian of Fisk University from 1943 to 1965. He also taught at the University of Chicago and Yale University. His writing identified him with the Harlem Renaissance. His correspondence with long-time friend and collaborator Langston Hughes was published in 1979. Much of his work, in all genres, reflects his attempts to reconcile his respect for the richness of African-American folk culture with his repudiation of negative ethnic stereotypes. His works for adults include *God Sends Sunday* (1931); *St. Louis Woman* (1946), a dramatization written with Countee Cullen; *Black Thunder* (1935); *Drums at Dusk* (1939); *Story of the Negro* (1948); *One Hundred Years of Negro Freedom* (1961); and *Popo and Fifina: Children of Haiti* (1932), written with Langston Hughes. His works for children include *Sam Patch* (1951), written with Jack Conroy, and *Famous Negro Athletes* (1964). Among the many awards and honors he received in recognition for his work were a Newbery Honor (for outstanding children's book, 1949), *The Crisis* magazine's poetry prize (1926), the Alexander Pushkin Poetry Prize (1926 and 1927), the short story prize of the journal *Opportunity* (1932), Julius Rosenwald fellowships (1938–1939, 1942–1943), a Guggenheim Fellowship for creative writing (1949–1950), and a Jane Addams Children's Book Award (1956).

ABOUT THE SELECTION

In his novels and poetry, Bontemps portrayed the lives and struggles of African Americans, a theme that can be seen in his poem **"A Black Man Talks of Reaping."** The speaker in the poem, in the process of telling about his experiences sowing and reaping, also reveals the disappointments, fears, and concerns of being human.

GOALS/OBJECTIVES

Studying this lesson will enable students to

- empathize with a speaker who has worked hard and experienced injustice
- become familiar with the life and work of Arna Bontemps
- understand the use of the active voice
- understand literary terms such as *rhyme* and *speaker*

READER'S JOURNAL

Have you ever worked hard at something only to see someone else reap the benefits of your efforts? How did you respond to the experience? What did you learn from it? Write about the experience in your journal.

LANGUAGE SKILLS

Read the Language Arts Survey, 2.56, "Using the Active Voice." Then identify verbs written in the active voice in the selection and note what effect the active voice creates in the poem.

"A Black Man Talks of Reaping"

ARNA BONTEMPS

I have sown[1] beside all waters in my day.
I planted deep, within my heart the fear
that wind or fowl would take the grain away.
I planted safe against this stark, lean year.

5 I scattered seed enough to plant the land
in rows from Canada to Mexico
but for my reaping only what the hand
can hold at once is all that I can show.

Yet what I sowed and what the orchard yields
10 my brother's sons are gathering stalk and root:
small wonder then my children glean[2] in fields
they have not sown, and feed on bitter fruit. ■

1. **sown.** Planted
2. **glean.** Pick up tiny pieces or crumbs.

❶ *How has the speaker done this year?*

❷ *How does the speaker estimate his labors?*

PREREADING NOTES

READER'S JOURNAL

Encourage students to be specific about the emotions one feels when this situation occurs. Ask them to consider what might happen to a person over time if this type of thing were to happen repeatedly. How would the constant anger and disappointment affect a person's view of the world and a person's view of his or her place in the world.

LANGUAGE SKILLS

Students should identify active voice in phrases such as "I planted . . .," "I scattered . . .," and "I sowed . . . ." Students might say that the active voice helps to make the speaker sound deliberate and sure of himself. He sounds firm and sure of all he has done.

ANSWERS TO GUIDED READING QUESTIONS

❶ It has been a stark, lean year for crops.

❷ The speaker estimates that he has scattered enough seed to plant the land from Canada to Mexico.

ANSWERS TO SELECTION CHECK TEST 4.8.45

EX. Who talks of reaping in the poem?
An African-American man talks of reaping.

1. What has the speaker feared as he planted crops?
The speaker has feared that wind or fowl would take away the crops.

2. What has the year been like?
It has been a stark, lean year.

3. How much seed has the speaker scattered?
The speaker estimates that he has scattered "seed enough to plant the land in rows from Canada to Mexico."

4. Who gathers what the orchard yields?
The speaker's "brother's children" gather what the orchard yields.

5. What do the speaker's own children get from the fields?
The speaker's children get the leftovers—the bitter fruit.

RESPONDING TO THE SELECTION

Ask students how it feels to have other people take credit or reap rewards for work they completed. How would it feel to spend your life working hard at something and then not be able to enjoy the rewards of the hard work or to share those rewards with family and friends. What specific emotions would students feel or have they felt in such situations?

Students might want to write their responses in the form of a letter from the speaker, written to the people who are reaping the rewards of the speaker's labor.

ANSWERS FOR REVIEWING THE SELECTION

RECALLING

1. It is a stark, lean year.
2. The speaker has sown enough seed to "plant the land in rows from Canada to Mexico."

INTERPRETING

Responses will vary. Possible responses are given.

3. The speaker plants the seeds "deep" for fear that "wind or fowl would take the grain away."
4. The speaker has not been able to reap the rewards of his efforts; other people take the best of the crops, leaving the speaker's own children to "feed on bitter fruit."

SYNTHESIZING

Responses will vary. Possible responses are given.

5. The speaker says that his "brother's sons" gather the best of the crops and leave the speaker's children with "bitter fruit." The speaker refers to the ways in which the fruits of African-American labor have often been reaped by others, particularly white people.

Responding to the Selection

Imagine that you are the speaker in the poem, who has seen his children "glean in fields/they have not sown, and feed on bitter fruit." What emotions would arise from watching your children eat what others have left behind in the fields? Write an entry in your journal expressing your feelings about the situation.

Reviewing the Selection

RECALLING

1. What kind of year is it?
2. How much seed has the speaker sown?

INTERPRETING

3. Why does the speaker plant the seeds "deep"?
4. Why do the speaker's children "feed on bitter fruit"?

SYNTHESIZING

5. Who reaps the benefits of the labor in this poem?

Understanding Literature (Questions for Discussion)

1. **Rhyme. Rhyme** is the repetition of sounds at the ends of words. One type of rhyme, *end rhyme,* is the use of rhyming words at the ends of lines. What is the end-rhyme scheme in this poem?
2. **Speaker.** The **speaker** is the character who speaks in a poem—the voice assumed by the writer. The speaker in this poem is identified in the title by his race. What is the speaker's view of reaping? How might his view of reaping be different from that of a white man?

ANSWERS FOR UNDERSTANDING LITERATURE

► See the evaluation forms for discussion, active listening, and oral communication, *Assessment Portfolio,* 7.11–7.14.

Responses will vary. Possible responses are given.

1. Rhyme. The end-rhyme scheme of the poem is *abab cdcd efef.*

2. Speaker. The speaker is not able to reap the rewards of his own work, so he feels he has nothing to show for his labor in the fields. A white man would most likely not have experienced this problem. In the past, white people have had more freedom and control, and they have more often been in the position to reap society's rewards. They have often reaped the fruits of African-American labor.

"Miniver Cheevy"
by Edwin Arlington Robinson

Miniver Cheevy, child of scorn,
Grew lean while he assailed the seasons;
He wept that he was ever born,
And he had reasons.

5 Miniver loved the days of old
When swords were bright and steeds
were prancing;
The vision of a warrior bold
Would set him dancing.

Miniver sighed for what was not,
10 And dreamed, and rested from his labors;
He dreamed of Thebes[1] and Camelot,[2]
And Priam's[3] neighbors.

Miniver mourned the ripe renown
That made so many a name so fragrant;
15 He mourned Romance, now on the town,
And Art, a vagrant.

Miniver loved the Medici,[4]
Albeit he had never seen one;
He would have sinned incessantly
20 Could he have been one.

Miniver cursed the commonplace
And eyed a khaki suit with loathing;
He missed the medieval[5] grace
Of iron clothing.

25 Miniver scorned the gold he sought,
But sore annoyed was he without it;
Miniver thought, and thought, and thought,
And thought about it.

Miniver Cheevy, born too late,
30 Scratched his head and kept on thinking;
Miniver coughed, and called it fate,
And kept on drinking.

1. **Thebes.** Ancient Greek city
2. **Camelot.** Mythical kingdom of Arthur and Guinevere (in southwestern England, Cornwall)
3. **Priam.** King of Troy (ancient Greek city)
4. **Medici.** Wealthy family in Renaissance Italy who supported artists, especially in the city of Florence

"Richard Cory"
by Edwin Arlington Robinson

Whenever Richard Cory went down town,
We people on the pavement looked at him:
He was a gentleman from sole to crown,
Clean favored, and imperially slim.

5 And he was always quietly arrayed,
And he was always human when he talked;
But still he fluttered pulses when he said,
"Good-morning," and he glittered when he walked.

And he was rich—yes, richer than a king—
10 And admirably schooled in every grace:
In fine, we thought that he was everything
To make us wish that we were in his place.

So on we worked, and waited for the light,
And went without the meat, and cursed the bread;
15 And Richard Cory, one calm summer night,
Went home and put a bullet through his head.

"The Flower-Fed Buffaloes"
by Vachel Lindsay

The flower-fed buffaloes of the spring
In the days of long ago,
Ranged[6] where the locomotives sing
And the prairie flowers lie low:—
5 The tossing, blooming, perfumed grass
Is swept away by the wheat,
Wheels and wheels and wheels spin by
In the spring that still is sweet.
But the flower-fed buffaloes of the spring
10 Left us, long ago.
They gore[7] no more, they bellow no more,
They trundle around the hills no more:—
With the Blackfeet, lying low,
With the Pawnees,[8] lying low,
15 Lying low.

5. **medieval.** Of the Middle Ages
6. **Ranged.** Roamed, feeding on the prairie grass
7. **gore.** Attack with their horns
8. **Blackfeet . . . Pawnees.** Refers to two Native American peoples of the western United States

"MINIVER CHEEVY"

"RICHARD CORY"

About the Author. A biography of **Edwin Arlington Robinson** appears on page 516.

About the Selections. Like many of Robinson's works, **"Miniver Cheevy"** and **"Richard Cory"** explore the modern themes of isolation and despair using traditional verse forms. Robinson may well have identified with the character described in "Miniver Cheevy," as Robinson felt alienated from his own time and longed for the glorious days of the past. Illusory longings are a prominent theme in much of twentieth-century writing. "Richard Cory" is one of Robinson's famous verses. Like "Miniver Cheevy," the sense and mood of the poem hinges upon the final line.

"THE FLOWER-FED BUFFALOES"

About the Author. Vachel Lindsay (1879–1931) was born in Springfield, Illinois. He spent three years at Hiram College (1897–1900), left to spend another three at the Art Institute in Chicago, and went to New York Art School for another year. His pursuit of art ended in New York when one day he took to the street to sell or give away some of his poems. He took in thirteen cents, but the experience led to his famous "tramps" across the United States reading and refining his poetry.

His work is best known for its vivid imagery, vigorous rhythm, and dramatic conception, and during his peak he was in great demand as a public reader of his own works.

Among his poetic broadsides and leaflets are *The Tree of Laughing Bells* (1905), *Rhymes To Be Traded for Bread* (1912), *General William Booth Enters into Heaven and Other Poems* (1913), *The Congo and Other Poems* (1914), and *The Chinese Nightingale and Other Poems* (1917).

(cont.)

"THE FLOWER-FED BUFFALOES" (CONT.)

At the time Lindsay was writing and publishing his poetry, Chicago was the new and vital center of American poetry. Poets of the Chicago school included Carl Sandburg, Edgar Lee Masters, Stephen Vincent Benét, Floyd Dell, and Lindsay. *Poetry* magazine, founded in Chicago in 1912 by Harriet Monroe, quickly became the principal periodical of modern poetry. Lindsay's verse, which was published in *Poetry* magazine, became highly popular. The variety of influences upon Lindsay's work include the poetry of Walt Whitman and Sidney Lanier, the addresses of Abraham Lincoln, revivalist sermons, hymns, Salvation Army music, and jazz.

"The Death of the Hired Man"

About the Author. A biography of **Robert Frost** appears on page 524.

About the Selection. **"The Death of the Hired Man"** is a narrative poem written in blank verse, which, like "Home Burial" on page 528, consists of dialogue between a husband and wife. However, while the husband and wife of "Home Burial" differ about how grief should be expressed for their dead child, the husband and wife of "The Death of the Hired Man" differ about how an older individual should be treated while still alive. In the last line of the poem, Frost makes brutally apparent the necessity of treating others with kindness during their lives. As an additional activity, students might give dramatic readings of the poem, one student playing the wife, one the husband, and one the narrator.

"The Death of the Hired Man"

by Robert Frost

Mary sat musing on the lamp-flame at the table,
Waiting for Warren. When she heard his step,
She ran on tiptoe down the darkened passage
To meet him in the doorway with the news
And put him on his guard. "Silas is back."
She pushed him outward with her through the door
And shut it after her. "Be kind," she said.
She took the market things from Warren's arms
And set them on the porch, them drew him down
To sit beside her on the wooden steps.

"When was I ever anything but kind to him?
But I'll not have the fellow back," he said.
"I told him so last haying,[1] didn't I?
If he left then, I said, that ended it.
What good is he? Who else will harbor him
At his age for the little he can do?
What help he is there's no depending on.
Off he goes always when I need him most.
He thinks he ought to earn a little pay,
Enough at least to buy tobacco with,
So he won't have to beg and be beholden.[2]
'All right,' I say, 'I can't afford to pay
Any fixed wages, though I wish I could.'
'Someone else can.' 'Then someone else will have to.'
I shouldn't mind his bettering himself
If that was what it was. You can be certain,
When he begins like that, there's someone at him
Trying to coax him off with pocket money—
In haying time, when any help is scarce.
In winter he comes back to us. I'm done."

"Sh! not so loud: he'll hear you," Mary said.

"I want him to: he'll have to soon or late."

"He's worn out. He's asleep beside the stove.
When I came up from Rowe's I found him here,
Huddled against the barn-door fast asleep,
A miserable sight, and frightening, too—
You needn't smile—I didn't recognize him—
I wasn't looking for him—and he's changed.
Wait till you see."

"Where did you say he'd been?"

"He didn't say. I dragged him to the house,
And gave him tea and tried to make him smoke.
I tried to make him talk about his travels.
Nothing would do: he just kept nodding off."

"What did he say? Did he say anything?"

"But little."

"Anything? Mary, confess
He said he'd come to ditch the meadow for me."

"Warren!"

"But did he? I just want to know."

"Of course he did. What would you have him say?
Surely you wouldn't grudge the poor old man
Some humble way to save his self-respect.
He added, if you really care to know,
He meant to clear the upper pasture, too.
That sounds like something you have heard before?
Warren, I wish you could have heard the way
He jumbled everything. I stopped to look
Two or three times—he made me feel so queer—
To see if he was talking in his sleep.
He ran on Harold Wilson—you remember—
The boy you had in haying four years since.
He's finished school, and teaching in his college.
Silas declares you'll have to get him back.
He says they two will make a team for work:
Between them they will lay this farm as smooth!
The way he mixed that in with other things.
He thinks young Wilson a likely lad, though daft
On education—you know how they fought
All through July under the blazing sun,
Silas up on the cart to build the load,
Harold along beside to pitch it on."

"Yes, I took care to keep well out of earshot."

"Well, those days trouble Silas like a dream.
You wouldn't think they would. How some things linger!
Harold's young college-boy's assurance piqued him.
After so many years he still keeps finding
Good arguments he sees he might have used.
I sympathize. I know just how it feels
To think of the right thing to say too late.
Harold's associated in his mind with Latin.
He asked me what I thought of Harold's saying
He studied Latin, like the violin,
Because he liked it—that an argument!

1. **haying.** Harvest, gathering of hay
2. **beholden.** Indebted to anyone

He said he couldn't make the boy believe
He could find water with a hazel prong—
Which showed how much good school had ever done him.
He wanted to go over that. But most of all
He thinks if he could have another chance
To teach him how to build a load of hay—"

"I know, that's Silas' one accomplishment.
He bundles every forkful in its place,
And tags and numbers it for future reference,
So he can find and easily dislodge it
In the unloading. Silas does that well.
He takes it out in bunches like big birds' nests.
You never see him standing on the hay
He's trying to lift, straining to lift himself."

"He thinks if he could teach him that he'd be
Some good perhaps to someone in the world.
He hates to see a boy the fool of books.
Poor Silas, so concerned for other folk,
And nothing to look backward to with pride,
And nothing to look forward to with hope,
So now and never any different."
Part of a moon was falling down the west,
Dragging the whole sky with it to the hills.
Its light poured softly in her lap. She saw it
And spread her apron to it. She put out her hand
Among the harplike morning-glory strings,
Taut with the dew from garden bed to eaves,
As if she played unheard some tenderness
That wrought on him beside her in the night.
"Warren," she said, "he has come home to die:
You needn't be afraid he'll leave you this time."

"Home," he mocked gently.

"Yes, what else but home?
It all depends on what you mean by home.
Of course he's nothing to us, any more
Than was the hound that came a stranger to us
Out of the woods, worn out upon the trail."
"Home is the place where, when you have to go there,
They have to take you in."

"I should have called it
Something you somehow haven't to deserve."

Warren leaned out and took a step or two,
Picked up a little stick, and brought it back
And broke it in his hand and tossed it by.
"Silas has better claim on us you think
Than on his brother? Thirteen little miles
As the road winds would bring him to his door.
Silas has walked that far no doubt today.
Why doesn't he go there? His brother's rich,
A somebody—director in the bank."

"He never told us that."

"We know it though."

"I think his brother ought to help, of course.
I'll see to that if there is need. He ought of right
To take him in, and might be willing to—
He may be better than appearances.
But have some pity on Silas. Do you think
If he had any pride in claiming kin
Or anything he looked for from his brother,
He'd keep so still about him all this time?"

"I wonder what's between them."

"I can tell you.
Silas is what he is—we wouldn't mind him—
But just the kind that kinsfolk can't abide.
He never did a thing so very bad.
He don't know why he isn't quite as good
As anybody. Worthless though he is,
He won't be made ashamed to please his brother."

"*I* can't think Si ever hurt anyone."

"No, but he hurt my heart the way he lay
And rolled his old head on that sharp-edged chair-back.
He wouldn't let me put him on the lounge.
You must go in and see what you can do.
I made the bed up for him there tonight.
You'll be surprised at him—how much he's broken.
His working days are done; I'm sure of it."

"I'd not be in a hurry to say that."

"I haven't been. Go, look, see for yourself.
But, Warren, please remember how it is:
He's come to help you ditch the meadow.
He has a plan. You mustn't laugh at him.
He may not speak of it, and then he may.
I'll sit and see if that small sailing cloud
Will hit or miss the moon."

It hit the moon.
Then there were three there, making a dim row,
The moon, the little silver cloud, and she.

"An Old Man's Winter Night"

About the Selection. Students might read **"An Old Man's Winter Night"** as a companion piece to "The Death of the Hired Man." "An Old Man's Winter Night" is written from the point of view of an older man, who, like the hired man, is essentially alone and facing death.

"Disillusionment of Ten O'Clock"

About the Author. A biography of **Wallace Stevens** appears on page 534.

About the Selection. In **"Disillusionment of Ten O'Clock,"** Stevens takes as his theme the lack of color in many people's lives and dreams. Stevens chooses to describe the house as "haunted," not only because of the ghostly appearance of the sleepers' white nightgowns but also because he believes that people who cannot dream vibrantly are not truly and fully alive.

"Wind and Silver"
"A Lover"

About the Author. A biography of **Amy Lowell** apears on page 553.

About the Selections. In **"Wind and Silver"** and **"A Lover,"** Lowell vividly portrays a sensory image in scant words. Stress to students that in poetry every word has meaning. The meaning of "A Lover," for example, is incomprehensible unless students pay close attention to the title.

"The River-Merchant's Wife: A Letter"

About the Author. A biography of **Ezra Pound** appears on page 560.

About the Selection. **"The River-Merchant's Wife: A Letter"** is one of Pound's most famous verses. Inform students that Chinese art tends to be minimalistic—what one leaves out is as important as what one includes. Pound called

(cont.)

Warren returned—too soon, it seemed to her,
Slipped to her side, caught up her hand and waited.

"Warren?" she questioned.

175 "Dead," was all he answered.

"An Old Man's Winter Night"
by Robert Frost

All out-of-doors looked darkly in at him
Through the thin frost, almost in separate stars,
That gathers on the pane in empty rooms.
What kept his eyes from giving back the gaze
5 Was the lamp tilted near them in his hand.
What kept him from remembering what it was
That brought him to that creaking room was age.
He stood with barrels round him—at a loss.
And having scared the cellar under him
10 In clomping here, he scared it once again
In clomping off—and scared the outer night,
Which has its sounds, familiar, like the roar
Of trees and crack of branches, common things,
But nothing so like beating on a box.
15 A light he was to no one but himself
Where now he sat, concerned with he knew what,
A quiet light, and then not even that.
He consigned[1] to the moon—such as she was,
So late-arising—to the broken moon,
20 As better than the sun in any case
For such a charge, his snow upon the roof,
His icicles along the wall to keep;
And slept. The log that shifted with a jolt
Once in the stove, disturbed him and he shifted,
25 And eased his heavy breathing, but still slept.
One aged man—one man—can't keep a house,
A farm, a countryside, or if he can,
It's thus he does it of a winter night.

"Disillusionment of Ten O'Clock"
by Wallace Stevens

The houses are haunted
By white night-gowns.
None are green,
Or purple with green rings,
5 Or green with yellow rings,
Or yellow with blue rings.
None of them are strange,
With socks of lace
And beaded ceintures.[2]
10 People are not going
To dream of baboons and periwinkles.[3]
Only, here and there, an old sailor,
Drunk and asleep in his boots,
Catches tigers
15 In red weather.

"Wind and Silver"
by Amy Lowell

Greatly shining,
The Autumn moon floats in the thin sky;
And the fish-ponds shake their backs and flash their dragon scales
As she passes over them.

"A Lover"
by Amy Lowell

If I could catch the green lantern of the firefly
I could see to write you a letter.

"The River-Merchant's Wife: A Letter"[4]
by Ezra Pound

While my hair was still cut straight across my forehead
I played about the front gate, pulling flowers.
You came by on bamboo stilts, playing horse,
You walked about my seat, playing with blue plums.
5 And we went on living in the village of Chōkan:
Two small people, without dislike or suspicion.

At fourteen I married My Lord you.
I never laughed, being bashful.
Lowering my head, I looked at the wall.
10 Called to, a thousand times, I never looked back.

At fifteen I stopped scowling,
I desired my dust to be mingled with yours
Forever and forever and forever.
Why should I climb the look out?

1. **consigned.** Put in care of
2. **ceintures.** Sashes; belts
3. **periwinkles.** Tiny, pale blue-violet sea snails

4. **"The River-Merchant's Wife: A Letter."** Pound's version of a translation of the eighth-century Chinese epic by poet Li Po (Rihaku in Japanese)

"The River-Merchant's Wife: A Letter" (cont.)

for the same minimalism in modern Western verse. Point out to students that Pound never specifically explicates his subject's situation; rather, Pound lets images convey the story of a woman who has married young and falls in love with her husband who then departs. The emotions of the narrator are never explicitly stated, but her despair is apparent in the way images are portrayed through her eyes—the early fall leaves and the paired butterflies become symbols of the speaker's loneliness and longing.

15 At sixteen you departed,
You went into far Ku-tō-en, by the river of swirling eddies,
And you have been gone five months.
The monkeys make sorrowful noise overhead.

You dragged your feet when you went out.
20 By the gate now, the moss is grown, the different mosses,
Too deep to clear them away!
The leaves fall early this autumn, in wind.
The paired butterflies are already yellow with August
Over the grass in the West garden;
25 They hurt me. I grow older.
If you are coming down through the narrows of the river Kiang,
Please let me know beforehand,
And I will come out to meet you
As far as Chō-fū-Sa.

By Rihaku

"Euclid Alone Has Looked on Beauty Bare"
by Edna St. Vincent Millay

Euclid alone has looked on Beauty bare.
Let all who prate of Beauty hold their peace,
And lay them prone upon the earth and cease
To ponder on themselves, the while they stare
5 At nothing, intricately drawn nowhere
In shapes of shifting lineage; let geese
Gabble and hiss, but heroes seek release
From dusty bondage into luminous air.
O blinding hour, O holy, terrible day,
10 When first the shaft into his vision shone
Of light anatomized! Euclid alone
Has looked on Beauty bare. Fortunate they
Who, though once only and then but far away,
Have heard her massive sandal set on stone.

"anyone lived in a pretty how town"
by E. E. Cummings

anyone lived in a pretty how town
(with up so floating many bells down)
spring summer autumn winter
he sang his didn't he danced his did

5 Women and men(both little and small)
cared for anyone not at all
they sowed their isn't they reaped their same
sun moon stars rain

children guessed(but only a few
10 and down they forgot as up they grew
autumn winter spring summer)
that noone loved him more by more

when by now and tree by leaf
she laughed his joy she cried his grief
15 bird by snow and stir by still
anyone's any was all to her

someones married their everyones
laughed their cryings and did their dance
(sleep wake hope and then)they
20 said their nevers they slept their dream

stars rain sun moon
(and only the snow can begin to explain
how children are apt to forget to remember
with up so floating many bells down)

25 one day anyone died i guess
(and noone stooped to kiss his face)
busy folk buried them side by side
little by little and was by was

all by all and deep by deep
30 and more by more they dream their sleep
noone and anyone earth by april
wish by spirit and if by yes.

Women and men(both dong and ding)
summer autumn winter spring
35 reaped their sowing and went their came
sun moon stars rain

"Any Human to Another"
by Countee Cullen

The ills I sorrow at
Not me alone
Like an arrow,
Pierce to the marrow,
5 Through the fat
And past the bone.

Your grief and mine
Must intertwine
Like sea and river,
10 Be fused and mingle,

"Euclid Alone Has Looked on Beauty Bare"

About the Author. A biography of **Edna St. Vincent Millay** appears on page 21.

About the Selection. Inform students that Euclid was an ancient Greek mathematician who founded a school at Alexandria and produced a work about geometry, the *Elements*. Geometry involves the study of abstract forms. In **"Euclid Alone Has Looked on Beauty Bare,"** Millay points out that Euclid, who founded the science of abstract forms, alone would have been able to see an abstract form such as Beauty.

"anyone lived in a pretty how town"

About the Author. A biography of **E. E. Cummings** appears on page 584.

About the Selection. "anyone lived in a pretty how town" follows the cycle of life of a character called "anyone." (This naming technique is reminsiscent of medieval morality plays, such as the famous *Everyman*.) Cummings describes how the events of a life, which seem so important at the time, are quickly forgotten, and in the end, the individual's memory itself is swallowed by death. Cummings points out that because life follows a circular pattern and people's lives are constantly growing and changing, it is difficult to single out a moment and make it have lasting meaning.

"Any Human to Another"

About the Author. A biography of **Countee Cullen** appears on page 588.

About the Selection. "Any Human to Another" is a lyric poem addressing the sorrow and pain that afflicts all humans and the need to share and alleviate one another's pain.

"Storm Ending"

About the Author. Jean Toomer (1894–1967) was born in Washington, DC, and grew up with his mother and his grandfather, who had served as acting governor of Louisiana during Reconstruction. He attended the University of Wisconsin, the Massachusetts College of Agriculture, the American College of Physical Training in Chicago, the University of Chicago, and the City College of New York but never earned a degree. He began to write in his mid-twenties and published his work in magazines such as *Broom, Little Review, Prairie, Liberator, Crisis,* and *Opportunity.* From 1918 to 1921, he taught school in Sparta, Georgia, and it was there that he started his best-known work, *Cane* (1923).

About the Selection. "Storm Ending" is rich in imagery and sensory details. Before reading the selection, ask students to freewrite their own images of a thunderstorm. As they read, they can compare and contrast their own images to the images Toomer uses.

"For the Union Dead"

About the Author. Robert Lowell, Jr. (1917–1977), born in Boston, was a descendent of the famous Lowell family of Massachusetts. Lowell made his living as an editor and teacher after graduating from Kenyon College and later taught writing and literature at Harvard.

Lowell tried to enlist in the army during World War II, was rejected, and then later refused to be drafted. He was tried as a conscientious objector and sentenced to a year in jail, of which he served six months. His interest in political and social issues continued, and during the Vietnam War, he was active in protests.

He received the Pulitzer Prize for poetry in 1947 for *Lord Weary's Castle* (1946) and in 1974 for *The Dolphin* (1973). Among his other works are *Life Studies* (1959), *For the Union Dead* (1964), *Near the Ocean* (1967), *Notebook 1967–1968* (1969), and *Notebook* (1970).

(cont.)

Diverse yet single,
Forever and forever.

Let no man be so proud
And confident,
To think he is allowed
A little tent
Pitched in a meadow
Of sun and shadow
All his little own.

Joy may be shy, unique,
Friendly to a few,
Sorrow never scorned to speak
To any who
Were false or true.

Your every grief
Like a blade
Shining and unsheathed
Must strike me down.
Of bitter aloes[1] wreathed,
My sorrow must be laid
On your head like a crown.

"Storm Ending"
by Jean Toomer

Thunder blossoms gorgeously above our heads,
Great, hollow, bell-like flowers,
Rumbling in the wind,
Stretching clappers to strike our ears . . .
Full-lipped flowers
Bitten by the sun
Bleeding rain
Dripping rain like golden honey—
And the sweet earth flying from the thunder.

"For the Union Dead"
by Robert Lowell

"Relinquunt Omnia Servare Rem Publicam."[2]

The old South Boston Aquarium stands
in a Sahara of snow now. Its broken windows are boarded.
The bronze weathervane cod has lost half its scales.
The airy tanks are dry.

Once my nose crawled like a snail on the glass;
my hand tingled
to burst the bubbles drifting from the noses of the cowed, compliant fish.

My hand draws back. I often sigh still
for the dark downward and vegetating kingdom
of the fish and reptile. One morning last March,
I pressed against the new barbed and galvanized

fence on the Boston Common. Behind their cage,
yellow dinosaur steamshovels were grunting
as they cropped up tons of mush and grass
to gouge their underworld garage.

Parking spaces luxuriate like civic
sandpiles in the heart of Boston.
A girdle of orange, Puritan-pumpkin colored girders
braces the tingling Statehouse,

shaking over the excavations, as it faces Colonel Shaw[3]
and his bell-cheeked Negro infantry
on St. Gauden's shaking Civil War relief,
propped by a plank splint against the garage's earthquake.

Two months after marching through Boston,
half the regiment was dead;
at the dedication
William James[4] could almost hear the bronze Negroes breathe.

Their monument sticks like a fishbone
in the city's throat.
Its Colonel is as lean
as a compass-needle.

He has an angry wrenlike vigilance,
a greyhound's gentle tautness;
he seems to wince at pleasure,
and suffocate for privacy.

He is out of bounds now. He rejoices in man's lovely,
peculiar power to choose life and die—
when he leads his black soldiers to death,
he cannot bend his back.

1. **aloes.** Succulent plant known for its medicinal quality
2. **Relinquunt . . . Publicam.** They leave all behind to serve the republic. (Latin)
3. **Colonel Shaw.** Commanding officer of the African-American regiment from Massachusetts in the Civil War
4. **William James.** Harvard philosopher (1842–1910)

"For the Union Dead" (cont.)

About the Selection. "For the Union Dead" is the last poem in a collection of the same title by Lowell. The poem was originally published as "Colonel Shaw and the Massachusetts' 54th" in a collection called *Life Studies.* The poem consists of seventeen unrhymed, meterless quatrains. Lowell uses irony to depict the degradation he saw as a part of modern life.

Lowell's epigraph is a slightly altered form of the inscription on a monument that stands on Boston Common to commemorate the death of Robert Gould Shaw and his regiment, the first all-African-American regiment during the Civil War.

On a thousand small town New England greens,
the old white churches hold their air
of sparse, sincere rebellion; frayed flags
quilt the graveyards of the Grand Army of the Republic.[1]

45 The stone statues of the abstract Union Soldier
grow slimmer and younger each year—
wasp-waisted, they doze over muskets
and muse through their sideburns . . .

Shaw's father wanted no monument
50 except the ditch,
where his son's body was thrown[2]
and lost with his "niggers."

The ditch is nearer.
There are no statues for the last war here;
55 on Boylston Street, a commercial photograph
shows Hiroshima boiling

over a Mosler Safe,[3] the "Rock of Ages"
that survived the blast. Space is nearer.
When I crouch to my television set,
60 the drained faces of Negro school-children rise like balloons.

Colonel Shaw
is riding on his bubble,
he waits
for the blessed break.

65 The Aquarium is gone. Everywhere,
giant finned cars nose forward like fish;
a savage servility
slides by on grease.

"The Geranium"
by Theodore Roethke

When I put her out, once, by the garbage pail,
She looked so limp and bedraggled,
So foolish and trusting, like a sick poodle,
Or a wizened aster[4] in late September,
5 I brought her back in again
For a new routine—
Vitamins, water, and whatever
Sustenance seemed sensible
At the time: she'd lived
10 So long on gin, bobbie pins, half-smoked cigars, dead beer,
Her shriveled petals falling
On the faded carpet, the stale
Steak grease stuck to her fuzzy leaves.
(Dried-out, she creaked like a tulip.)

15 The things she endured!—
The dumb dames shrieking half the night
Or the two of us, alone, both seedy,
Me breathing booze at her,
She leaning out of her pot toward the window.

20 Near the end, she seemed almost to hear me—
And that was scary—
So when that snuffling cretin[5] of a maid
Threw her, pot and all, into the trash-can,
I said nothing.

25 But I sacked the presumptuous hag the next week,
I was that lonely.

"The Death of the Ball Turret Gunner"
by Randall Jarrell

From my mother's sleep I fell into the State,
And I hunched in its belly till my wet fur froze.
Six miles from earth, loosed from its dream of life,
I woke to black flak[6] and the nightmare fighters.
When I died they washed me out of the turret with a hose.

---

1. **Grand Army of the Republic.** Union Army
2. **thrown.** Tossed after the battle of Fort Wagner
3. **Hiroshima . . . Safe.** The speaker is describing an advertisement for a safe that shows an atom bomb blowing up Hiroshima, Japan.
4. **wizened aster.** Aged flower
5. **cretin.** Speaker means someone lacking intelligence; brain damaged person
6. **black flak.** Antiaircraft bullet shells

"The Geranium"

About the Author. Theodore Roethke (1908–1963) was born in Saginaw, Michigan. His father and grandfather kept greenhouses for a living. Roethke once wrote that the greenhouse "is . . . my symbol for the whole of life, a womb, a heaven-on-earth." His first book of poetry, *Open House* (1941), was full of the imagery of plants and growth that would characterize much of his writing.

Roethke received a Pulitzer Prize for *The Waking* (1953); the National Book Award and Bollingen Prize for the collected poems, *Words for the Wind* (1958); and was honored posthumously with a National Book Award for *The Far Field* (1964). Among his other works are *The Lost Son* (1948) and *Praise to the End* (1951).

About the Selection. "The Geranium" appeared in *The Far Field.* Roethke's work often involves journeys of the soul through experience with actual objects of the natural world. In the selection, the speaker articulates his loneliness through his experience with a geranium.

"The Death of the Ball Turret Gunner"

About the Author. Randall Jarrell (1914–1965) was born in Nashville, Tennessee, but spent most of his childhood in Long Beach, California. He taught at several universities and was a gifted teacher who loved his work.

Jarrell's World War II experience influenced much of his early poetry. He was poetry editor of the *Nation* in 1946 and a valued reviewer and critic his entire life. His life ended tragically when he was struck by a car in October of 1965.

His works include *Blood for a Stranger* (poems, 1942); *Little Friend, Little Friend* (poems, 1945); *Losses* (poems, 1948); *Poetry and the Age* (essays and reviews, 1953); *Pictures from an Institution* (novel, 1954); and *The Woman at the*

(cont.)

"The Death of the Ball Turret Gunner" (cont.)

Washington Zoo (poems, 1960).

About the Selection. Jarrell's experiences in the air force during World War II provided material for the poems of *Little Friend, Little Friend.* Among the striking poems in that collection is **"The Death of the Ball Turret Gunner,"** a poem known for the grim image contained in its last line.

Vocabulary Development Exercises

▶ Give students the following exercise.

Make a crossword puzzle using twenty of the words from the list on page 608. First, set up the words in a crossword form. Try to make each word share a letter with two other words. Then, beginning at the top left and working your way across each row, number the words consecutively. Next, write definitions of the words to serve as clues. Be sure that your definition matches the form of the word you have used. Finally, number your definitions and label them across or down to match the words in the puzzle.

Teaching note: Bring in a crossword puzzle from a newspaper, magazine, or puzzle book as an example.

ADDITIONAL RESOURCES

Assessment Portfolio

- Vocabulary Worksheet, 4.8.47
- Study Guide: Unit 8 Test, 4.8.48
- Unit 8 Test, 4.8.49

Essential Skills Practice Books

Writing

- Observing, 1.11
- Organizing Ideas, 1.34
- Recalling, 1.10
- Sensory Detail Charts, 1.18

Language

- Achieving Parallelism, 2.57
- Adding Prepositional Phrases, 2.47
- Clichés and Euphemisms, 2.152
- Colons, 2.98
- Commas I, 2.94
- Commas II, 2.95
- Commas III, 2.96
- Common Punctuation Errors, 2.97–2.106
- Compound Sentences, 2.43
- Complex Sentences, 2.44
- Compound-Complex Sentences, 2.45
- Concrete and Abstract Nouns, 2.4
- Demonstrative Pronouns, 2.8
- End Marks, 2.93
- Expanding Sentences, 2.46–2.50
- Formal and Informal English, 2.147

(cont.)

Unit Review

Modern Poetry

VOCABULARY FROM THE SELECTIONS

acquiescent, 518
apparition, 561
assert, 569
caprice, 589
convivially, 518
cower, 528
deferential, 572
digress, 570
dilate, 564
etherise, 568
euphony, 540
formulated, 570
harry, 576
indecipherable, 540
inflection, 539
insidious, 568
insolence, 565
linger, 569
lucid, 540
malinger, 570
obtuse, 572
palpable, 580
pantomime, 539
presume, 570
prominence, 565
tedious, 568
triviality, 565
valid, 565
vex, 577

LITERARY TERMS

abstract, 544, 566
allusion, 520, 573, 590
anecdote, 538
blank verse, 524
character, 527
concrete, 544, 566
diction, 532, 578
dramatic monologue, 573
effect, 549, 596
epitaph, 510
free verse, 573
iamb, 514
iambic, 514
image, 544, 549, 562
imagery, 544, 549, 562
inversion, 587
metaphor, 514, 532, 562
meter, 547, 593
paradox, 583
parallelism, 523
pathetic fallacy, 536
personification, 523
pun, 527
refrain, 596
repetition, 551, 558, 587
rhyme, 558, 578, 587, 593, 600
rhythm, 547, 551
run-on line, 551
simile, 514, 520, 583, 596
sonnet, 590
speaker, 547, 549, 600
stanza, 566
symbol, 527
syntax, 587
theme, 559
tone, 512, 532, 547, 593
understatement, 578

ADDITIONAL RESOURCES (CONT.)

- The Functions of Sentences, 2.36
- Indefinite Pronouns, 2.9
- Linking Verbs, 2.13
- Personal Pronouns, 2.6
- Place Names, 2.121
- Prepositions, 2.24
- The Pronoun *I*, 2.127
- Replacing Linking Verbs with Action Verbs, 2.34
- Using Context Clues I, 2.138
- Using Context Clues II, 2.139
- Using the Active Voice, 2.56
- Using Colorful Modifiers, 2.35
- Using the Parts of Speech in Writing, 2.32–2.35
- Using Precise Nouns, 2.32
- Verbals: Gerunds, 2.17
- Verbals: Participles, 2.16

(cont.)

SYNTHESIS: QUESTIONS FOR WRITING, RESEARCH, OR DISCUSSION

GENRE STUDIES

1. **Imagist Poetry.** Poetry is a concentrated form of writing, and Imagist poetry is extremely concentrated, presenting single moments of sense perception without reference to the emotions or opinions of the author, narrator, or speaker. Select three Imagist poems from this unit and discuss the subject and message conveyed.

THEMATIC STUDIES

2. **Alienation.** Two world wars and a society rapidly changing yielded feelings of alienation and anxiety. Select three poems, one Imagist, one narrative, and one Modernist that deal with the theme of alienation. Explore the differences and similarities in the treatment of this theme in the poems you select.
3. **Poetry.** Three poems in this unit—"Petit, the Poet, " "Poetry," and " Ars Poetica" are about poetry. What statements do the poets make in these poems? In what ways do these poems themselves reveal the changing face of poetry?

HISTORICAL/BIOGRAPHICAL STUDIES

4. **Harlem Renaissance.** In much the same way words were important in the American Revolution, the art that flourished in Harlem in the 1920s and 1930s gave voice to the African-American struggle. Look at the selections in the unit from this period and discuss the statements of identity.

▶These prompts are suitable as topics for research papers. Refer to the Language Arts Survey, 4.20–4.34, "Research Skills." (To evaluate research papers, see the evaluation forms for writing, revising, and proofreading, *Assessment Portfolio,* 7.1–7.10.)

▶These prompts can be adapted for use as topics for oral reports or debates. (To evaluate these projects, see the evaluation forms in the *Assessment Portfolio,* 7.17–7.19.)

ADDITIONAL RESOURCES (CONT.)

Speaking and Listening
- Elements of Nonverbal Communication, 3.3
- Interpersonal Communication, 3.5
- Oral Interpretation, 3.8

Study and Research
- Bibliographies and Bibliography Cards, 4.29
- Comparing and Contrasting, 4.8
- Generalizing, 4.11
- Using Reference Works, 4.23
- Using Searching Tools, 4.21

Applied English
- The Form of a Personal Letter, 5.2

LANGUAGE LAB PROOFREADING FOR OTHER PUNCTUATION ERRORS

When proofreading your writing, check carefully for correct use of semicolons, colons, dashes, hyphens, apostrophes, quotation marks, parentheses, brackets, and ellipses.

LANGUAGE ARTS SURVEY

For additional help, see the Language Arts Survey, 2.97–2.106.

COMMON PUNCTUATION ERRORS

Semicolons. A **semicolon** is used in the following situations: between closely related independent clauses that are not joined by *and, but, for, nor, or, so,* or *yet;* between independent clauses joined by a conjunctive adverb or transitional expression that is followed by a comma; and between linked independent clauses or items in a list if the clauses or items already contain commas.

EXAMPLES: Sandburg depicts scenes from the Midwest; his verse duplicates the cadences of Midwestern speech.
Many people associate Sandburg with Chicago; however, the poet lived in several cities across the country during his lifetime.
"Chicago" immortalizes the city's noisy, bustling freight yards; hardworking, downtrodden citizens; and legendary spirit.

Colons. A **colon** introduces a long statement or quotation or a list of items.

EXAMPLE: Stock the icebox with the following: plums, milk, cheese, and grapes.

Dashes. A **dash** is used to show an abrupt break in thought or to replace an expression such as *in other words, that is,* or *namely.*

EXAMPLE: Do you remember who wrote "The Love Song"—oh, I remember now!

Hyphens. A **hyphen** is used to link words in a compound adjective, adverb, or noun.

EXAMPLES: flower-fed buffaloes, well-known book, self-knowledge

Apostrophes. An **apostrophe** is used to form the possessive of nouns and some pronouns. See the Language Arts Survey, 2.102, for complete rules about using apostrophes.

SINGULAR WITH ADDED *S:* Mr. Flood's party, Whiteside's daughter, winter's cold
SINGULAR WITHOUT ADDED *S:* goodness' sake
PLURAL ENDING WITH *S:* tropics' heat, bells' ringing, buffaloes' pelts
PLURAL ENDING WITHOUT *S:* women's conversation, geese's honking, mice's nests

Underlining and Italics. Italics are a type of slanted printing used to show emphasis. (**Underlining** is used when italics are not available.) Some words that receive italics are works of art, books, plays, films, television programs, periodicals, and long musical compositions. Words used as words, letters used as letters, and words from foreign languages also receive italics.

EXAMPLES: *Spoon River Anthology,* O'Keeffe's *New York Night, Consumer Reports, et tu Brute*

Quotation Marks. Quotation marks are used for a variety of purposes.

DIRECT QUOTATION: "Welcome home!" Mr. Flood cries.
DIRECT WITH PERIOD: Mr. Flood wears "valiant armor of scarred hopes outworn."
DIRECT WITH COMMA: "Drink to the bird," said Mr. Flood.
DIRECT WITH SEMICOLON: Mr. Flood drinks "for auld lang syne"; he seems weary of the world.
TITLES OF SHORT WORKS: "Mr. Flood's Party"

Ellipses. Ellipsis points indicate an omission in quoted material or a pause in a written passage.

EXAMPLE: "I don't think the professor knows what he's talking . . . oh, hello, Professor Alexander," the student finished sheepishly.

EXERCISE Proofreading Sentences for Punctuation Errors

Proofread the following sentences for correct punctuation.

EXAMPLE: Critics do not agree on which poet began the Harlem Renaissance both Langston Hughes and Claude McKay have been credited with starting the literary movement.

Critics do not agree on which poet began the Harlem Renaissance; both Langston Hughes and Claude McKay have been credited with starting the literary movement.

1. The peasants in Breughel's "Kermess" are enjoying a great celebration.
2. J. Alfred Prufrock asks the question Do I dare?
3. Langston Hughes The Negro Speaks of Rivers—dedicated to W. E. B. Du Bois—was one of the first poems of the Harlem Renaissance.
4. Many people associate lawyer poet Wallace Stevens with early twentieth century poetry.
5. Pound's In a Station of the Metro reminds me of Monet's Gare Saint-Lazare.
6. How many ways can one look at a black . . . oh, thirteen.
7. Please fill the wheelbarrow with the following items a bag of peat, seed packets, a trowel, and gardening gloves.
8. The owner of the apple orchard sees no need for the wall however he keeps his opinion from his neighbor.
9. Edgar Lee Masters "Spoon River Anthology" is based on the names taken from tombstones.
10. The note on the refrigerator reads Forgive me for eating the plums they were delicious.

LANGUAGE ARTS SURVEY

For additional help, see the Language Arts Survey, 2.97–2.106

ANSWERS FOR LANGUAGE LAB

1. The peasants in Brueghel's *Kermess* are enjoying a great celebration.
2. J. Alfred Prufrock asks the question, "Do I dare?"
3. Langston Hughes's "The Negro Speaks of Rivers"—dedicated to W. E. B. Du Bois—was one of the first poems of the Harlem Renaissance.
4. Many people associate lawyer-poet Wallace Stevens with early twentieth-century poetry.
5. Pound's "In a Station of the Metro" reminds me of Monet's *Gare Saint-Lazare.*
6. How many ways can one look at a black—oh, thirteen.
7. Please fill the wheelbarrow with the following items: a bag of peat, seed packets, a trowel, and gardening gloves.
8. The owner of the apple orchard sees no need for the wall; however, he keeps his opinion from his neighbor.
9. Edgar Lee Masters's *Spoon River Anthology* is based on the names taken from tombstones.
10. The note on the refrigerator reads, "Forgive me for eating the plums; they were delicious."

UNIT SKILLS OUTLINE

LITERARY SKILLS AND CONCEPTS
- Catastrophe, 628
- Characterization, 652, 655
- Conflict, 628
- Dialogue, 652, 655
- Internal Monologue, 655
- Irony, 648
- Minor Character, 636
- Motif, 651
- Narrator, 638
- Plot, 628
- Point of View, 638
- Setting, 628
- Simile, 638, 648

WRITING SKILLS AND CONCEPTS
- Character Sketch, 655
- Descriptive Paragraph, 628, 638
- Dialogue, 649, 655
- Documentation, 628
- Obituary, 649
- Personal Letter, 638

GRAMMAR, USAGE, AND MECHANICS SKILLS AND CONCEPTS
- Adding Modifiers, 631
- Base Words and Prefixes, 629, 639
- Capitalization, 678
- Dangling and Misplaced Modifiers, 639
- The Form of a Personal Letter, 638
- Suffixes, 629, 639
- Using Colorful Modifiers, 641
- Using Precise Nouns, 649
- Verbals: Infinitives, 615

OTHER LANGUAGE ARTS SKILLS AND CONCEPTS
- Active Listening, 651
- Nonverbal Communication, 649
- Synonym and Antonym Questions, 629

UNIT 9 MODERN FICTION (1900–1960)

Nighthawks. *Edward Hopper, 1942. American, 1882–1967. Oil on Canvas, 84.1 × 152.4 cm. The Art Institute of Chicago, Friends of American Art Collection, 1942.51*

GOALS/OBJECTIVES

Studying this unit will enable students to

- interpret and appreciate modern fiction
- read and compare the work of modern fiction writers
- complete writing activities related to chosen selections
- understand catastrophe, characterization, conflict, dialogue, internal monologue, irony, narrator, plot, point of view, setting, and simile

photograph ©1994, The Art Institute of Chicago, All rights reserved.

All good books are alike in that they are truer than if they had really happened.

—Ernest Hemingway

CONNECTIONS ACROSS THE CURRICULUM

Arts and Humanities

- Concert Scene, 634
- Connections to Music, 631
- Images of Death, 644
- Music History, 639
- Wagner Operas, 633

Mathematics and Sciences

- Frostbite and Hypothermia, 618
- Length of Day, 615
- Reacting to Trauma, 624
- Yukon Climate, 617

Social Studies

- Adapting to Lengthy Days, 615
- Attitudes toward Elderly, 643
- Dogs as Work Animals, 620
- Gold Rushes, 616
- Homesteading, 632
- Mapping Alaska, 616
- Near-death Experiences, 626
- Researching Modes of Travel, 631
- Rewording Prayers, 653

Applied Arts

- Firebuilding Techniques, 620

TEACHING THE MULTIPLE INTELLIGENCES

Spatial

- Mapping Alaska, 616

Musical

- Music History, 639
- Responding to Opera, 630

Kinesthetic

- Camping Trip, 629

THEMATIC CURRENTS

Use the following selections to explore these themes with your students.

Struggle and Survival

- "To Build a Fire," 614
- "The Jilting of Granny Weatherall," 640
- "A Clean, Well-Lighted Place," 650

Nature

- "To Build a Fire," 614

Choices

- "A Wagner Matinee," 630
- "The Jilting of Granny Weatherall," 640

ADDITIONAL RESOURCES

READER'S GUIDE
- Selection Worksheet, 9.1

ASSESSMENT PORTFOLIO
- Selection Check Test, 4.9.1
- Selection Test, 4.9.2

ESSENTIAL SKILLS PRACTICE BOOKS
- *Language,* 2.18, 2.140
- *Study and Research,* 4.44

ENRICHMENT ACTIVITIES

- Students may want to further research Jack London's life. Did London have any experiences similar to what happened to the main character in the story? How did he feel about dogs? Which of his works featured dogs?
- Interested students may choose to focus on the Yukon. What is the terrain and climate like? How is it different today than during the time of the gold rush?

SUPPORT FOR LEP STUDENTS

A discussion with students about nature imagery may be helpful in focusing on the story. Ask them to share words or images that describe nature in terms of its power or that express how human beings relate to it.

PREREADING

"To Build a Fire"
by Jack London

ABOUT THE AUTHOR

Jack London (1876–1916) was born in San Francisco. He supported himself and helped support his family from the time he was fourteen. By the time he was eighteen, he had worked in a cannery, as an oyster pirate, seaman, jute-mill worker, and coal shoveler. While still a teenager, he tramped halfway across the continent with the "army of the unemployed" in its "March on Washington," then struck out on his own for the Northeast. After spending thirty days in jail for vagrancy, London decided it was time to improve his life. He returned to California, entered the state university, and took English classes. He soon left, disenchanted with his fellow students, the professors, and the formal educational system. Within a few months, the twenty-one-year-old was on his way to the gold rush in the Klondike. The only nuggets he found, however, were the experiences he later wove into his stories.

London, who had been a voracious reader from about the age of ten, had been writing stories for some years. By the time he returned to Oakland from the Klondike, he was determined to make a living as a writer. He won a local writing contest, which was followed by numerous rejections and then a string of small sales. His break came when the *Atlantic Monthly* paid $120 for his story "The Odyssey of the North." London often said he disliked his profession and that he wrote to make money, but he was a master storyteller who turned out a prodigious amount of work during his career. His two most famous works, *The Call of the Wild* (1903) and *The Sea-Wolf* (1904), were written before he was thirty. Among his other works are *The People of the Abyss* (1903), *War of the Classes* (1905), *White Fang* (1906), *The Iron Heel* (1908), and *Martin Eden* (autobiographical novel, 1909).

ABOUT THE SELECTION

Published in 1908, **"To Build a Fire"** is one of the twenty-eight stories included in London's Northland Saga. In addition to the twenty-eight stories, the Northland Saga comprises four novels, one play, and six nonfiction pieces, all of which serve as examples of **Naturalistic** fiction, a style of fiction that viewed actions and events as resulting from biological or natural forces or from forces in the environment.

One of hundreds of thousands of people who joined the Klondike Gold Rush in 1887, Jack London had firsthand experience surviving a winter in the Yukon, a territory in northwest Canada and the setting of "To Build a Fire."

GOALS/OBJECTIVES

Studying this lesson will enable students to
- enjoy a Naturalistic short story
- describe Jack London's contributions to modern literature
- interpret and explain how London views nature and the place of humans within nature
- define *setting, conflict, plot,* and *catastrophe* and use them to analyze a short story
- write a descriptive paragraph about a real or imaginary setting and a documentation of a series of short, simple steps needed to complete a task

READER'S JOURNAL

Have you ever disregarded someone's advice? Did you later wish that you had taken that advice? Why did you disregard the advice in the first place? What might have been different about the outcome had you accepted the advice? Did you learn from your experience? Write about the experience in your journal.

LANGUAGE SKILLS

Read the Language Arts Survey, 2.18, "Verbals: Infinitives." Then identify some infinitives in the selection and note how each one is used—as a noun, an adjective, or an adverb.

"To Build a Fire"

JACK LONDON

Day had broken cold and gray, exceedingly cold and gray, when the man turned aside from the main Yukon[1] trail and climbed the high earth-bank, where a dim and little-traveled trail led eastward through the fat spruce timberland. It was a steep bank, and he paused for breath at the top, excusing the act to himself by looking at his watch. It was nine o'clock. There was no sun nor hint of sun, though there was not a cloud in the sky. It was a clear day, and yet there seemed an intangible pall over the face of things, a subtle gloom that made the day dark, and that was due to the absence of sun. This fact did not worry the man. He was used to the lack of sun. It had been days since he had seen the sun, and he knew that a few more days must pass before that cheerful orb, due south, would just peep above the skyline and dip immediately from view.

The man flung a look back along the way he had come. The Yukon lay a mile wide and hidden under three feet of ice. On top of this ice were as many feet of snow. It was all pure white, rolling in gentle undulations where the ice jams of the freeze-up had formed. North and south, as far as his eye could see, it was unbroken white, save for a dark hairline that curved and twisted from around the spruce-covered island to the south, and that curved and twisted away into the north, where it disappeared behind another spruce-covered island. This dark hairline was the trail—the main trail—that led south five hundred miles to the Chilcoot Pass, Dyea,[2] and salt water; and that led

❶ *What is the day like? Why does it have this atmosphere?*

1. **Yukon.** Territory and river in northwest Canada
2. **Chilcoot Pass, Dyea.** *Chilcoot Pass*—mountain pass leading to the Klondike; *Dyea*—once a town in Alaska that marked the beginning of the Yukon trail

WORDS FOR EVERYDAY USE: **pall** (pôl) *n.,* covering that obscures or cloaks gloomily
un • du • la • tion (un´dyōō lā´shən) *n.,* wave, curve

PREREADING NOTES

READER'S JOURNAL

Suggest that students think about a time when they gave someone advice. Was the advice heeded? If not, how did they feel when they realized the person had disregarded their advice? What did they learn about the person and about themselves?

LANGUAGE SKILLS

Suggest that students attempt to rewrite the sentences they find, using the infinitives in different ways, to better understand the usages.

ANSWER TO GUIDED READING QUESTION

❶ The day is clear but gloomy. The reason for this atmosphere is that there is no sun.

CROSS-CURRICULAR ACTIVITIES

Mathematics and Sciences. Although it is day, and there are no clouds, the man in the story never sees the sun because he is too far north in the middle of winter. Have students research the length of the day and of the night at extreme northerly or southerly latitudes. What natural phenomenon determines the length of the day at any given point on Earth?

Social Studies. Have students investigate the ways in which peoples native to extreme latitudes adapt to such lengthy summer days and winter nights. What effect does the environmental fact of lengthy days and nights have on these cultures? How does sunlight deprivation affect humans physiologically and emotionally?

VOCABULARY IN CONTEXT

- A gray pall hung over the town after the storm passed, making it seem dark and gloomy.
- We watched the undulation of the water as it curved and formed gentle waves that broke on the beach.

VOCABULARY FROM THE SELECTION

agitation	ebb	poignant
apathetically	imperative	reiterate
apprehension	nucleus	thresh
conflagration	pall	undulation
conjectural	peremptorily	

Answers to Guided Reading Questions

❶ The man's errand is to investigate the possibilities of getting out logs in the spring from the islands surrounding the Yukon.

❷ The man's limitation is that he is without imagination.

Cross-curricular Activities

Social Studies

• The protagonist of London's story is a gold prospector newly arrived in the Yukon during the Klondike Gold Rush. Have groups of students research different gold rushes, such as the California Gold Rush of 1849, the Klondike Gold Rush of 1887, and the Amazon Gold Rush of the 1980s. Ask students to consider how these events begin, the mob psychology that produces the "rush," and the lawlessness that characterizes mining communities during the rush. Have each group of students present its findings so that the class can discuss similarities and differences between various gold rushes.

• Ask a group of students to look at a map of the Yukon and Alaska and find the locations mentioned in the story. Have them locate the setting of the story as precisely as possible using the information provided by London. How accurate are London's geographical references? Does he exaggerate distances, or are they correct? How does this geographical information contribute to the story? In addition, have students list the population centers in the general vicinity of the story's setting. If this story were to take place today, would the protagonist have a greater chance of survival?

• The protagonist of the story has been looking "at the possibilities of getting out logs in the spring," suggesting that he intends to earn money in the future by logging. Ask another group of students to investigate the economic resources of the Yukon. What are the princi-

(cont.)

north seventy miles to Dawson, and still on to the north a thousand miles to Nulato,[3] and finally to St. Michael on Bering Sea, a thousand miles and half a thousand more.

What is the man's errand? ❶

What is the man's limitation? ❷

But all this—the mysterious, far-reaching hairline trail, the absence of sun from the sky, the tremendous cold, and the strangeness and weirdness of it all—made no impression on the man. It was not because he was long used to it. He was a newcomer in the land, a *chechaquo*,[4] and this was his first winter. The trouble with him was that he was without imagination. He was quick and alert in the things of life, but only in the things, and not in the significances. Fifty degrees below zero meant eighty-odd degrees of frost. Such fact impressed him as being cold and uncomfortable, and that was all. It did not lead him to meditate upon his frailty as a creature of temperature, and upon man's frailty in general, able only to live within certain narrow limits of heat and cold; and from there on it did not lead him to the conjectural field of immortality and man's place in the universe. Fifty degrees below zero stood for a bite of frost that hurt and that must be guarded against by the use of mittens, earflaps, warm moccasins, and thick socks. Fifty degrees below zero was to him just precisely fifty degrees below zero. That there should be anything more to it than that was a thought that never entered his head.

As he turned to go on, he spat speculatively. There was a sharp, explosive crackle that startled him. He spat again. And again, in the air, before it could fall to the snow, the spittle crackled. He knew that at fifty below spittle crackled on the snow, but this spittle had crackled in the air. Undoubtedly it was colder than fifty below—how much colder he did not know. But the temperature did not matter. He was bound for the old claim on the left fork of Henderson Creek, where the boys were already. They had come over across the divide from the Indian Creek country, while he had come the roundabout way to take a look at the possibilities of getting out logs in the spring from the islands in the Yukon. He would be in to camp by six o'clock: a bit after dark, it was true, but the boys would be there, a fire would be going, and a hot supper would be ready. As for lunch, he pressed his hand against the protruding bundle under his jacket. It was also under his shirt, wrapped up in a handkerchief and lying against the naked skin. It was the only way to keep the biscuits from freezing. He smiled agreeably to himself as he thought of those biscuits, each cut open and sopped in bacon grease, and each enclosing a generous slice of fried bacon.

He plunged in among the big spruce trees. The trail was faint. A foot of snow had fallen since the last sled had passed over, and he was glad he was without a sled, traveling light. In fact, he carried nothing but the lunch wrapped in the handkerchief. He was surprised, however, at the cold. It certainly was cold, he concluded, as he rubbed his numb nose and cheekbones with his mittened hand. He was a warm-whiskered man, but the hair on his face did not protect the high cheekbones

3. **Dawson . . . Nulato.** Gold-mining towns in the Yukon
4. **chechaquo.** Newcomer

Words for Everyday Use: **con • jec • tur • al** (kən jek´chər əl) *adj.,* based on guesses

Cross-curricular Activities (cont.)

pal sources of income for inhabitants of this region? What is the per capita income? If an ambitious, enterprising individual such as the protagonist wished to strike it rich in the Yukon, what would be his or her best opportunities?

Vocabulary in Context

- The study of the universe is highly conjectural; because so little is known, much of it is based on guesses and theories.
- He felt a strong sense of apprehension about the upcoming test; he was afraid he was going to fail.

and the eager nose that thrust itself aggressively into the frosty air.

At the man's heels trotted a dog, a big native husky, the proper wolf dog, gray-coated and without any visible or temperamental difference from its brother, the wild wolf. The animal was depressed by the tremendous cold. It knew that it was no time for traveling. Its instinct told it a truer tale than was told to the man by the man's judgment. In reality, it was not merely colder than fifty below zero: it was colder than sixty below, than seventy below. It was seventy-five below zero. Since the freezing point is thirty-two above zero, it meant that one hundred and seven degrees of frost obtained. The dog did not know anything about thermometers. Possibly in its brain there was no sharp consciousness of a condition of very cold such as was in the man's brain. But the brute had its instinct. It experienced a vague but menacing apprehension that subdued it and made it slink along at the man's heels, and that made it question eagerly every unwonted movement of the man as if expecting him to go into camp or to seek shelter somewhere and build a fire. The dog had learned fire, and it wanted fire, or else to burrow under the snow and cuddle its warmth away from the air.

The frozen moisture of its breathing had settled on its fur in a fine powder of frost, and especially were its jowls, muzzle, and eyelashes whitened by its crystalled breath. The man's red beard and mustache were likewise frosted, but more solidly, the deposit taking the form of ice and increasing with every warm, moist breath he exhaled. Also, the man was chewing tobacco, and the muzzle of ice held his lips so rigidly that he was unable to clear his chin when he expelled the juice. The result was that a crystal beard of the color and solidity of amber was increasing its length on his chin. If he fell down it would shatter itself, like glass, into brittle fragments. But he did not mind the appendage. It was the penalty all tobacco chewers paid in that country, and he had been out before in two cold snaps. They had not been so cold as this, he knew, but by the spirit thermometer[5] at Sixty Mile he knew they had been registered at fifty below and at fifty-five.

He held on through the level stretch of woods for several miles, crossed a wide flat, and dropped down a bank to the frozen bed of a small stream. This was Henderson Creek, and he knew he was ten miles from the forks. He looked at his watch. It was ten o'clock. He was making four miles an hour, and he calculated that he would arrive at the forks at half past twelve. He decided to celebrate that event by eating his lunch there.

The dog dropped in again at his heels, with a tail drooping discouragement, as the man swung along the creek bed. The furrow of the old sled trail was plainly visible, but a dozen inches of snow covered the marks of the last runners. In a month no man had come up or down that silent creek. The man held steadily on. He was not much given to thinking, and just then particularly he had nothing to think about save that he would eat lunch at the forks

❶ *In what way is the dog more advanced than the man?*

5. **spirit thermometer.** Thermometer that uses alcohol instead of mercury because of the lower freezing point of alcohol

WORDS FOR EVERYDAY USE: **ap • pre • hen • sion** (ap´rē hen´shən) *n.,* anxiety, dread

ANSWER TO GUIDED READING QUESTION

❶ The dog is more advanced in that it doesn't know anything about temperature and has no consciousness of cold the way humans do.

CROSS-CURRICULAR ACTIVITIES

Mathematics and Sciences

• According to London, the temperature experienced by the protagonist was seventy-five degrees below zero. Ask students to investigate the climate of the Yukon. What are the average temperatures in this region throughout the year? What extreme temperatures have been recorded? What is the average snowfall in the Yukon? What meteorological conditions mentioned by London cause such low temperatures? Have students present their data side-by-side with comparable meteorological information from their own region.

• Survival in the wilderness, even under favorable conditions, requires planning and prudence. Students may wish to research survival manuals that provide specific guidelines for people who intend to spend time in the wilderness (e.g., *How to Stay Alive in the Woods,* by Branford Angier, 1956; *Tom Brown's Field Guide to Wilderness Survival,* by Tom Brown, Jr., and Brandt Morgan, 1983). Have students decide which information is absolutely essential to wilderness survival and present their findings to the class. In addition, ask students to assess the protagonist's actions: What mistakes did he make? What could he have done at certain points to better ensure his survival?

ADDITIONAL QUESTIONS AND ACTIVITIES

Ask students to consider the role of the dog in the story. The author informs the reader that it is "a proper wolf dog," emphasizing its relation to "the wild wolf." Why does London provide his protagonist with a dog, and this kind of dog in particular?

Answer to Guided Reading Question

❶ The danger the man knows is about the hidden springs that run under the snow and on top of the ice, hiding pools of water that never freeze.

Cross-curricular Activities

Mathematics and Sciences. Ask students to research the symptoms of frostbite and hypothermia. What are the early warning signs of these conditions? What treatment is recommended at the early stages of these conditions? at advanced stages? Are the physiological symptoms mentioned in the story consistent with medical knowledge about these conditions? Have students present their findings in the form of a medical diagnosis of the protagonist's symptoms at different points in the story, with recommendations for treatment at each stage.

Additional Questions and Activities

The author writes that the protagonist "was keenly observant," and stresses his awareness of possible dangers. Have students discuss the importance of this aspect of the man's character. In what ways was the man not observant? How does this trait add to the dramatic tension of the story?

What danger does the man know? ❶

and that at six o'clock he would be in camp with the boys. There was nobody to talk to; and, had there been, speech would have been impossible because of the ice-muzzle on his mouth. So he continued monotonously to chew tobacco and to increase the length of his amber beard.

Once in a while the thought reiterated itself that it was very cold and that he had never experienced such cold. As he walked along he rubbed his cheekbones and nose with the back of his mittened hand. He did this automatically, now and again changing hands. But rub as he would, the instant he stopped his cheekbones went numb, and the following instant the end of his nose went numb. He was sure to frost his cheeks; he knew that, and experienced a pang of regret that he had not devised a nose strap of the sort Bud wore in cold snaps. Such a strap passed across the cheeks, as well, and saved them. But it didn't matter much, after all. What were frosted cheeks? A bit painful, that was all: they were never serious.

Empty as the man's mind was of thoughts, he was keenly observant, and he noticed the changes in the creek, the curves and bends and timber jams, and always he sharply noted where he placed his feet. Once, coming around a bend, he shied abruptly, like a startled horse, curved away from the place where he had been walking, and retreated several paces back along the trail. The creek he knew was frozen clear to the bottom—no creek could contain water in that arctic winter—but he knew also that there were springs that bubbled out from the hillsides and ran along under the snow and on top the ice of the creek. He knew that the coldest snaps never froze these springs, and he knew likewise their danger. They were traps. They hid pools of water under the snow that might be three inches deep, or three feet. Sometimes a skin of ice half an inch thick covered them, and in turn was covered by the snow. Sometimes there were alternate layers of water and ice skin, so that when one broke through he kept on breaking through for a while, sometimes wetting himself to the waist.

That was why he had shied in such panic. He had felt the give under his feet and heard the crackle of a snow-hidden ice skin. And to get his feet wet in such a temperature meant trouble and danger. At the very least it meant delay, for he would be forced to stop and build a fire, and under its protection to bare his feet while he dried his socks and moccasins. He stood and studied the creek bed and its banks, and decided that the flow of water came from the right. He reflected awhile, rubbing his nose and cheeks, then skirted to the left, stepping gingerly and testing the footing for each step. Once clear of the danger, he took a fresh chew of tobacco and swung along at his four-mile gait.

In the course of the next two hours he came upon several similar traps. Usually the snow above the hidden pools had a sunken, candied appearance that advertised the danger. Once again, however, he had a close call; and once, suspecting danger, he compelled the dog to go on in front. The dog did not want to go. It hung back until the man shoved it forward, and then it went quickly across the white, unbroken surface. Suddenly it broke through, floun-

Words for Everyday Use: **re • it • er • ate** (rē it´ ə rāt´) *vt.*, repeat

Vocabulary in Context

- The teacher felt the need to reiterate her argument to the principal about needing bigger classrooms when he admitted he hadn't been listening.
- The couple threshed wildly on the dance floor, amazing the crowd with their thrashing movements.

dered to one side, and got away to firmer footing. It had wet its forefeet and legs, and almost immediately the water that clung to it turned to ice. It made quick efforts to lick the ice off its legs, then dropped down in the snow and began to bite out the ice that had formed between the toes. This was a matter of instinct. To permit the ice to remain would mean sore feet. It did not know this. It merely obeyed the mysterious prompting that arose from the deep crypts of its being. But the man knew, having achieved a judgment on the subject, and he removed the mitten from his right hand and helped tear out the ice particles. He did not expose his fingers more than a minute, and was astonished at the swift numbness that smote them. It certainly was cold. He pulled on the mitten hastily, and beat the hand savagely across his chest.

At twelve o'clock the day was at its brightest. Yet the sun was too far south on its winter journey to clear the horizon. The bulge of the earth intervened between it and Henderson Creek, where the man walked under a clear sky at noon and cast no shadow. At half-past twelve, to the minute, he arrived at the forks of the creek. He was pleased at the speed he had made. If he kept it up, he would certainly be with the boys by six. He unbuttoned his jacket and shirt and drew forth his lunch. The action consumed no more than a quarter of a minute, yet in that brief moment the numbness laid hold of the exposed fingers. He did not put the mitten on, but, instead, struck the fingers a dozen sharp smashes against his leg. Then he sat down on a snowcovered log to eat. The sting that followed upon the striking of his fingers against his leg ceased so quickly that he was startled. He had had no chance to take a bite of biscuit. He struck the fingers repeatedly and returned them to the mitten, baring the other hand for the purpose of eating. He tried to take a mouthful. but the ice muzzle prevented. He had forgotten to build a fire and thaw out. He chuckled at his foolishness, and as he chuckled he noted the numbness creeping into the exposed fingers. Also, he noted that the stinging which had first come to his toes when he sat down was already passing away. He wondered whether the toes were warm or numb. He moved them inside the moccasins and decided that they were numb.

He pulled the mitten on hurriedly and stood up. He was a bit frightened. He stamped up and down until the stinging returned into the feet. It certainly was cold, was his thought. That man from Sulphur Creek had spoken the truth when telling how cold it sometimes got in the country. And he had laughed at him at the time! That showed one must not be too sure of things. There was no mistake about it, it was cold. He strode up and down, stamping his feet and threshing his arms, until reassured by the returning warmth. Then he got out matches and proceeded to make a fire. From the undergrowth, where high water of the previous spring had lodged a supply of seasoned twigs, he got his firewood. Working carefully from a small beginning, he soon had a roaring fire, over which he thawed the ice from his face and in the protection of which he ate his biscuits. For the moment the cold of space was

❶ *What is the man starting to feel? Whom had he met? What had he been told?*

Words for Everyday Use: **thresh** (thresh) *vt.*, thrash, toss about

Answer to Guided Reading Question

❶ The man is starting to feel a stinging sensation in his feet. He had met the man from Sulphur Creek, who had told him how cold it could sometimes get in the country.

Literary Technique

• **Hubris** (Greek for "wanton insolence") is a term often used to describe a character flaw in the protagonist of a Greek tragedy. Hubris is the fatal character defect that causes the hero to ignore the warnings of the gods and to transgress against their laws, a mistake that eventually leads to his downfall. Ask students how the man in London's story demonstrates hubris. What is his fatal flaw? What plays the role of the gods in this story? What lessons does the man learn before he dies?

• **Foreshadowing** is a technique by which an author arranges events or provides information that indicates in advance the eventual outcome of the story. One example of foreshadowing in "To Build a Fire" occurs on this page when the author writes that "the man . . . cast no shadow." The reader understands that a man who casts no shadow is metaphorically a dead man. Ask students to locate other instances of foreshadowing in this story. Discuss how this technique contributes to the rising tension of the story.

Answers to Guided Reading Questions

❶ The dog thinks that they should lie snug in a hole and wait for the weather to warm up.

❷ What unexpectedly happens is that the man falls through the ice.

Additional Questions and Activities

Prompt students to think about the man's character. What qualities do they admire in him the most? the least? If students could give him one piece of advice about his journey, what would it be?

▶**Teaching Note:** Students may write a short note addressed to the man in which they give their advice.

Cross-curricular Activities

Applied Arts. As the title indicates, the central event of this story revolves around the protagonist's attempts to build a fire. Ask students to research different techniques for building a fire without matches or a lighter. What materials can be used to ignite a fire in the woods? What materials are best for the different stages of a fire? Students may wish to present their findings and show sample firebuilding materials if possible.

outwitted. The dog took satisfaction in the fire, stretching out close enough for warmth and far enough away to escape being singed.

When the man had finished, he filled his pipe and took his comfortable time over a smoke. Then he pulled on his mittens, settled the earflaps of his cap firmly about his ears, and took the creek trail up the left fork. The dog was disappointed and yearned back toward the fire. This man did not know cold. Possibly all the generations of his ancestry had been ignorant of cold, of real cold, of cold one hundred and seven degrees below freezing point. But the dog knew; all its ancestry knew, and it had inherited the knowledge. And it knew that it was not good to walk abroad in such fearful cold. It was the time to lie snug in a hole in the snow and wait for a curtain of cloud to be drawn across the face of outer space whence this cold came. On the other hand, there was no keen intimacy between the dog and the man. The one was the toil slave of the other, and the only caresses it had ever received were the caresses of the whiplash and of harsh and menacing throat sounds that threatened the whiplash. So the dog made no effort to communicate its apprehension to the man. It was not concerned in the welfare of the man; it was for its own sake that it yearned back toward the fire. But the man whistled, and spoke to it with the sound of whiplashes, and the dog swung in at the man's heels and followed after.

The man took a chew of tobacco and proceeded to start a new amber beard. Also, his moist breath quickly powdered with white his mustache, eyebrows, and lashes. There did not seem to be so many springs on the left fork of the Henderson, and for half an hour the man saw no signs of any. And then it happened. At a place where there were no signs, where the soft, unbroken snow seemed to advertise solidity beneath, the man broke through. It was not deep. He wet himself halfway to the knees before he floundered out to the firm crust.

What does the dog think should happen? ❶

What happens unexpectedly? ❷

Cross-curricular Activities

Social Studies. The author refers to the dog as "the toil slave" of the man. While dogs are most commonly kept as pets nowadays in the United States, they continue to be employed as work animals in many regions. Students may wish to research the different uses to which humans have put dogs in the northern reaches of this continent as well as in other parts of the world. Which breeds of dogs are considered best suited for certain tasks? How does the local climate affect the use of dogs for various kinds of work?

He was angry, and cursed his luck aloud. He had hoped to get into camp with the boys at six o'clock, and this would delay him an hour, for he would have to build a fire and dry out his footgear. This was imperative at that low temperature—he knew that much; and he turned aside to the bank, which he climbed. On top, tangled in the underbrush about the trunks of several small spruce trees, was a high-water deposit of dry firewood—sticks and twigs, principally, but also larger portions of seasoned branches and fine, dry, last year's grasses. He threw down several large pieces on top of the snow. This served for a foundation and prevented the young flame from drowning itself in the snow it otherwise would melt. The flame he got by touching a match to a small shred of birch bark that he took from his pocket. This burned even more readily than paper. Placing it on the foundation. he fed the young flame with wisps of dry grass and with the tiniest dry twigs.

He worked slowly and carefully, keenly aware of his danger. Gradually, as the flame grew stronger, he increased the size of the twigs with which he fed it. He squatted in the snow, pulling the twigs out from their entanglement in the brush and feeding directly to the flame. He knew there must be no failure. When it is seventy-five below zero, a man must not fail in his first attempt to build a fire—that is, if his feet are wet. If his feet are dry, and he fails, he can run along the trail for half a mile and restore his circulation. But the circulation of wet and freezing feet cannot be restored by running when it is seventy-five below. No matter how fast one runs, the wet feet will freeze the harder.

All this the man knew. The old-timer on Sulphur Creek had told him about it the previous fall, and now he was appreciating the advice. Already all sensation had gone out of his feet. To build the fire he had been forced to remove his mittens, and the fingers had quickly gone numb. His pace of four miles an hour had kept his heart pumping blood to the surface of his body and to all the extremities. But the instant he stopped, the action of the pump eased down. The cold of space smote the unprotected tip of the planet, and he, being on that unprotected tip, received the full force of the blow. The blood of his body recoiled before it. The blood was alive, like the dog, and like the dog it wanted to hide away and cover itself up from the fearful cold. So long as he walked four miles an hour, he pumped that blood, willy-nilly, to the surface; but now it ebbed away and sank down into the recesses of his body. The extremities were the first to feel its absence. His wet feet froze the faster, and his exposed fingers numbed the faster, though they had not yet begun to freeze. Nose and cheeks were already freezing, while the skin of all his body chilled as it lost its blood.

But he was safe. Toes and nose and cheeks would be only touched by the frost, for the fire was beginning to burn with strength. He was feeding it with twigs the size of his finger. In another minute he would be able to feed it with branches the size of his wrist, and then he could remove his wet foot-gear, and, while it dried, he could keep his naked feet warm by the fire, rubbing them at first, of course, with snow. The fire was a success. He was safe. He remembered the

❶ *What does the man see as the negative consequences of his accident?*

❷ *To what is the man's blood compared? In what way are they similar?*

WORDS FOR EVERYDAY USE:

im • per • a • tive (im per´ə tiv) *adj.,* absolutely necessary

ebb (eb) *vi.,* flow back, recede

ANSWERS TO GUIDED READING QUESTIONS

❶ The man sees getting into camp late and having to build a fire to dry out his footgear as the negative consequences of his accident.

❷ The man's blood is compared to the dog. They are similar in that they both want to hide from the fearful cold.

ADDITIONAL QUESTIONS AND ACTIVITIES

The author writes that "the cold of space smote the unprotected tip of the planet, and he, being on that unprotected tip, received the full force of that blow." Ask students to discuss the importance of this image to the story as a whole. Why does the author make a point of situating the man in relation to the universe? How does this image contribute to the characterization of the protagonist? Students may also wish to discuss their own awareness of the universe. Do students ever dwell on the immensity of the universe? If so, how does it make them feel?

LITERARY TECHNIQUE

• **Repetition** of a word or a phrase is a device used for various purposes in poetry and prose. In the final paragraph on this page, the author repeats the phrase "he was safe" and calls further attention to it on the next page with the phrase "he had saved himself." Ask students to discuss the effect of this phrase. What thoughts and emotions does this phrase evoke? Does the reader believe that the man really is safe?

• **Dramatic irony** is a term applied to a situation in which a reader or audience possesses knowledge that a character in a story or play does not possess. In Sophocles's play, *Oedipus,* for example, the audience becomes aware of Oedipus's crime before he does. Ask students to discuss whether or not a phrase such as "he was safe" constitutes an example of dramatic irony. Does the reader know that the man is, in fact, not "safe"? If so, how?

VOCABULARY IN CONTEXT

- The lawyer knew it was imperative for his client to take the witness stand; otherwise, they would lose the trial.
- The tide ebbed gently on the beach, as the waves receded and the water flowed away from the shore.

Answers to Guided Reading Questions

❶ The fire symbolizes life in the midst of the cold.

❷ The mistake the man makes is building his fire under the spruce tree and then pulling twigs from the tree. The weight of snow in the tree is disturbed, and the snow falls on the fire, putting it out.

Literary Technique

Sentence Length. Prose writers vary the length of sentences for a variety of rhetorical effects. For example, a series of very short, declarative sentences can be used to quicken the pace of reading to coincide with the rapid actions in the text. On the other hand, long sentences with many qualifying phrases and subordinate clauses may be employed to slow down a reader's pace, to stress the complexity of an idea, or to convey a sense of paralysis experienced by a character. On this page and the previous one, London begins a number of paragraphs with very short sentences (e.g., "All this the man knew"; "But he was safe"; "The man was shocked"). Have students find other examples of short sentences and compare them with the length of adjacent sentences. Ask them to discuss the effect that these sentences have on the reader. Do they heighten the story's tension? Do they slow or quicken the reader's pace?

advice of the old-timer on Sulphur Creek, and smiled. The old-timer had been very serious in laying down the law that no man must travel alone in the Klondike after fifty below. Well, here he was; he had had the accident; he was alone; and he had saved himself. Those old-timers were rather womanish, some of them, he thought. All a man had to do was to keep his head, and he was all right. Any man who was a man could travel alone. But it was surprising, the rapidity with which his cheeks and nose were freezing. And he had not thought his fingers could go lifeless in so short a time. Lifeless they were, for he could scarcely make them move together to grip a twig, and they seemed remote from his body and from him. When he touched a twig, he had to look and see whether or not he had hold of it. The wires were pretty well down between him and his finger ends.

What does the fire symbolize in such cold? ❶

All of which counted for little. There was the fire, snapping and crackling and promising life with every dancing flame. He started to untie his moccasins. They were coated with ice; the thick German socks were like sheaths of iron halfway to the knees; and the moccasin strings were like rods of steel all twisted and knotted as by some conflagration. For a moment he tugged with his numb fingers, then, realizing the folly of it, he drew his sheath-knife.

What terrible mistake does the man make? ❷

But before he could cut the strings, it happened. It was his own fault or, rather, his mistake. He should not have built the fire under the spruce tree. He should have built it in the open. But it had been easier to pull the twigs from the brush and drop them directly on the fire. Now the tree under which he had done this carried a weight of snow on its boughs. No wind had blown for weeks, and each bough was fully freighted. Each time he had pulled a twig he had communicated a slight agitation to the tree—an imperceptible agitation, so far as he was concerned, but an agitation sufficient to bring about the disaster. High up in the tree one bough capsized its load of snow. This fell on the boughs beneath, capsizing them. This process continued, spreading out and involving the whole tree. It grew like an avalanche, and it descended without warning upon the man and the fire, and the fire was blotted out! Where it had burned was a mantle of fresh and disordered snow.

The man was shocked. It was as though he had just heard his own sentence of death. For a moment he sat and stared at the spot where the fire had been. Then he grew very calm. Perhaps the old-timer on Sulphur Creek was right. If he had only had a trail mate he would have been in no danger now. The trail mate could have built the fire. Well, it was up to him to build the fire over again, and this second time there must be no failure. Even if he succeeded, he would most likely lose some toes. His feet must be badly frozen by now, and there would be some time before the second fire was ready.

Such were his thoughts, but he did not sit and think them. He was busy all the time they were passing through his mind. He made a new foundation for a fire, this time in the open, where no treacherous tree could blot it out. Next, he gathered dry grasses and tiny twigs from the high-water flotsam.[6] He could not bring

6. **flotsam.** Odds and ends washed up by the water

Words for Everyday Use:
con • fla • gra • tion (kän´flə grā´shən) *n.,* destructive fire
ag • i • ta • tion (aj´ə tā´shən) *n.,* violent motion or disturbance

Vocabulary in Context

- The seven-alarm blaze was a conflagration of massive proportions; fire companies from ten towns were called out to fight it.
- The agitation of the washing machine caused the room to shake violently for almost an hour.

his fingers together to pull them out, but he was able to gather them by the handful. In this way he got many rotten twigs and bits of green moss that were undesirable, but it was the best he could do. He worked methodically, even collecting an armful of the larger branches to be used later when the fire gathered strength. And all the while the dog sat and watched him, a certain yearning wistfulness in its eyes, for it looked upon him as the fire provider, and the fire was slow in coming.

When all was ready, the man reached in his pocket for a second piece of birch bark. He knew the bark was there, and, though he could not feel it with his fingers, he could hear its crisp rustling as he fumbled for it. Try as he would, he could not clutch hold of it. And all the time, in his consciousness, was the knowledge that each instant his feet were freezing. This thought tended to put him in a panic, but he fought against it and kept calm. He pulled on his mittens with his teeth, and threshed his arms back and forth, beating his hands with all his might against his sides. He did this sitting down, and he stood up to do it; and all the while the dog sat in the snow, its wolf brush of a tail curled around warmly over its forefeet, its sharp wolf ears pricked forward intently as it watched the man. And the man, as he beat and threshed with his arms and hands, felt a great surge of envy as he regarded the creature that was warm and secure in its natural covering.

After a time he was aware of the first faraway signals of sensation in his beaten fingers. The faint tingling grew stronger till it evolved into a stinging ache that was excruciating, but which the man hailed with satisfaction. He stripped the mitten from his right hand and fetched forth the birch bark. The exposed fingers were quickly going numb again. Next he brought out his bunch of sulphur matches. But the tremendous cold had already driven the life out of his fingers. In his effort to separate one match from the others, the whole bunch fell in the snow. He tried to pick it out of the snow, but failed. The dead fingers could neither touch nor clutch. He was very careful. He drove the thought of his freezing feet, and nose, and cheeks, out of his mind, devoting his whole soul to the matches. He watched, using the sense of vision in place of that of touch, and when he saw his fingers on each side the bunch, he closed them—that is, he willed to close them, for the wires were down, and the fingers did not obey. He pulled the mitten on the right hand, and beat it fiercely against his knee. Then, with both mittened hands, he scooped the bunch of matches, along with much snow, into his lap. Yet he was no better off.

After some manipulation he managed to get the bunch between the heels of his mittened hands. In this fashion he carried it to his mouth. The ice crackled and snapped when by a violent effort he opened his mouth. He drew the lower jaw in, curled the upper lip out of the way, and scraped the bunch with his upper teeth in order to separate a match. He succeeded in getting one, which he dropped on his lap. He was no better off. He could not pick it up. Then he devised a way. He picked it up in his teeth and scratched it on his leg. Twenty times he scratched before he succeeded in lighting it. As it flamed he held it with his teeth to the birch bark. But the burning brimstone went up his nostrils and into his lungs, causing him to cough spasmodically. The match fell into the snow and went out.

The old-timer on Sulphur Creek was right, he thought in the moment of controlled despair that ensued: after fifty below, a man should travel with a partner. He beat his hands, but failed in exciting any sensation. Suddenly he bared both hands, removing the mittens with his

❶ *What does the man feel is happening? What is his reaction?*

❷ *What advice did the man fail to heed?*

Answers to Guided Reading Questions

❶ The man feels his feet freezing. His reaction is to panic, but he fights against it and tries to remain calm.

❷ The advice the man failed to heed was traveling with a partner when the temperature reached fifty below.

Additional Questions and Activities

One of the difficulties the man must deal with is the incredible cold. Prompt students to recall an experience during which they felt extremely cold. What kinds of thoughts did they experience? Would they respond differently now after reading the story? Why, or why not?

►**Teaching Note:** Students may freewrite on this topic before discussing it.

Literary Technique

Focus. On this page and the following, the narrative **focus** of the story is narrowed considerably, reduced primarily to a precise description of each movement made by the protagonist and to the notation of very small physical details. Discuss with students the reasons for this narrowing of focus. How does this reduced narrative focus imitate the man's experience at this moment of the story? What is the dramatic effect of this narrowed focus?

Answer to Guided Reading Question

❶ The man's plan is to kill the dog and bury his hands inside the body until they get warm.

Additional Questions and Activities

The author writes that the man "got on his hands and knees and crawled toward the dog." Ask students to discuss this image of the man crawling on his hands and knees. Why does the author portray the man in the posture of a dog at this point in the story? What similarities now exist between the man and the dog at this moment?

Cross-curricular Activities

Mathematics and Sciences. The protagonist of the story has been reduced to the level of a wild animal, obeying only a fundamental instinct to survive at any cost. Have students investigate the psychology of survival in different extreme situations. What happens to the psychology of an individual when he or she is in a life-threatening situation? What happens to an individual's ability to think rationally? What are the aftereffects of such traumas? Some students may wish to explore this issue further by reading accounts written by hostages, prisoners of war, and people who have been stranded in the wild. Have students present their findings to the class and discuss how they might react in different life-threatening situations.

teeth. He caught the whole bunch between the heels of his hands. His arm muscles not being frozen enabled him to press the hand heels tightly against the matches. Then he scratched the bunch along his leg. It flared into flame, seventy sulphur matches at once! There was no wind to blow them out. He kept his head to one side to escape the strangling fumes, and held the blazing bunch to the birch bark. As he so held it, he became aware of sensation in his hand. His flesh was burning. He could smell it. Deep down below the surface he could feel it. The sensation developed into pain that grew acute. And still he endured it, holding the flame of the matches clumsily to the bark that would not light readily because his own burning hands were in the way, absorbing most of the flame.

What plan does the man devise? ❶

At last, when he could endure no more, he jerked his hands apart. The blazing matches fell sizzling into the snow, but the birch bark was alight. He began laying dry grasses and the tiniest twigs on the flame. He could not pick and choose, for he had to lift the fuel between the heels of his hands. Small pieces of rotten wood and green moss clung to the twigs, and he bit them off as well as he could with his teeth. He cherished the flame carefully and awkwardly. It meant life, and it must not perish. The withdrawal of blood from the surface of his body now made him begin to shiver, and he grew more awkward. A large piece of green moss fell squarely on the little fire. He tried to poke it out with his fingers, but his shivering frame made him poke too far, and he disrupted the nucleus of the little fire, the burning grasses and tiny twigs separating and scattering. He tried to poke them together again, but in spite of the tenseness of the effort, his shivering got away with him, and the twigs were hopelessly scattered. Each twig gushed a puff of smoke and went out. The fire provider had failed. As he looked apathetically about him, his eyes chanced on the dog, sitting across the ruins of the fire from him, in the snow, making restless, hunching movements, slightly lifting one forefoot and then the other, shifting its weight back and forth on them with wistful eagerness.

The sight of the dog put a wild idea into his head. He remembered the tale of the man, caught in a blizzard, who killed a steer and crawled inside the carcass, and so was saved. He would kill the dog and bury his hands in the warm body until the numbness went out of them. Then he could build another fire. He spoke to the dog, calling it to him; but in his voice was a strange note of fear that frightened the animal, who had never known the man to speak in such way before. Something was the matter, and its suspicious nature sensed danger—it knew not what danger, but somewhere, somehow, in its brain arose an apprehension of the man. It flattened its ears down at the sound of the man's voice, and its restless, hunching movements and the liftings and shiftings of its forefeet became more pronounced; but it would not come to the man. He got on his hand and knees and crawled toward the dog. This unusual posture again excited suspicion, and the animal sidled mincingly away.

The man sat up in the snow for a moment and struggled for calmness. Then he pulled on his mittens, by means of his teeth, and got upon his feet. He glanced

Words for Everyday Use:
nu • cle • us (nōō´ klē əs) *n.*, core, central part
ap • a • thet • i • cal • ly (ap´ə thet´ə kə lē) *adv.*, without emotion

Vocabulary in Context

- The two aircraft carriers formed the nucleus of the fleet; all operations were centered around them.
- The crowd listened apathetically to the speaker, showing no emotion or interest in his words.
- The admiral spoke peremptorily to his crew, reminding them that he was in command.
- Poignant memories crowded sharply into Rachel's head, causing her to blink back sudden tears.

down at first in order to assure himself that he was really standing up, for the absence of sensation in his feet left him unrelated to the earth. His erect position in itself started to drive the webs of suspicion from the dog's mind; and when he spoke peremptorily, with the sound of whiplashes in his voice, the dog rendered its customary allegiance and came to him. As it came within reaching distance, the man lost his control. His arms flashed out to the dog, and he experienced genuine surprise when he discovered that his hands could not clutch, that there was neither bend nor feeling in the fingers. He had forgotten for the moment that they were frozen and that they were freezing more and more. All this happened quickly, and before the animal could get away, he encircled its body with his arms. He sat down in the snow, and in this fashion held the dog, while it snarled and whined and struggled.

But it was all he could do, hold its body encircled in his arms and sit there. He realized that he could not kill the dog. There was no way to do it. With his helpless hands he could neither draw nor hold his sheath-knife nor throttle the animal. He released it, and it plunged wildly away, with tail between its legs, and still snarling. It halted forty feet away and surveyed him curiously, with ears sharply pricked forward. The man looked down at his hands in order to locate them, and found them hanging on the ends of his arms. It struck him as curious that one should have to use his eyes in order to find out where his hands were. He began threshing his arms back and forth, beating the mittened hands against his sides. He did this for five minutes, violently, and his heart pumped enough blood up to the surface to put a stop to his shivering. But no sensation was aroused in the hands. He had an impression that they hung like weights on the ends of his arms, but when he tried to run the impression down, he could not find it.

A certain fear of death, dull and oppressive, came to him. This fear quickly became poignant as he realized that it was no longer a mere matter of freezing his fingers and toes, or of losing his hands and feet, but that it was a matter of life and death with the chances against him. This threw him into a panic, and he turned and ran up the creekbed along the old, dim trail. The dog joined in behind and kept up with him. He ran blindly, without intention, in fear such as he had never known in his life. Slowly, as he plowed and floundered through the snow, he began to see things again—the banks of the creek, the old timber jams, the leafless aspens, and the sky. The running made him feel better. He did not shiver. Maybe, if he ran on, his feet would thaw out: and, anyway, if he ran far enough, he would reach camp and the boys. Without doubt he would lose some fingers and toes and some of his face; but the boys would take care of him, and save the rest of him when he got there. And at the same time there was another thought in his mind that said he would never get to the camp and the boys; that it was too many miles away, that the freezing had too great a start on him, and that he would soon be stiff and dead. This thought he kept in the background and refused to consider. Sometimes it pushed itself forward and demanded to be heard,

❶ *What does the man begin to realize?*

❷ *How does the plan proceed?*

❸ *What thoughts fight in his mind?*

WORDS FOR EVERYDAY USE:

per • emp • to • ri • ly (pər emp´tə ri lē) *adv.,* commandingly

poign • ant (poin´yənt) *adj.,* sharp; painful

ANSWERS TO GUIDED READING QUESTIONS

❶ The man begins to realize that his situation is life and death, and chances are against him.

❷ The man proceeds by holding the dog in his arms. But he is unable to kill it given the poor condition of his hands.

❸ The thoughts fighting in his mind are that the camp is too far away, freezing has too great a start on him, and that he will soon be dead.

ADDITIONAL QUESTIONS AND ACTIVITIES

At no point in the story is the protagonist's name mentioned. Ask students to speculate on why the author did not give the protagonist a name. What does the protagonist symbolize as a result of this anonymity? How would the story have been different if the protagonist had had a name?

Answer to Guided Reading Question

❶ The man's final thought is that the old-timer at Sulphur Creek was right.

Additional Questions and Activities

Prompt students to recall a time when they relied on a pet such as a dog or cat for companionship, affection, or even survival. How is the man's feeling for the dog different from the kinds of feelings they experience about their pets?

▶**Teaching Note:** Students may bring pictures of their pets to class if they wish.

Cross-curricular Activities

Social Studies. In the penultimate paragraph on this page, the protagonist leaves his body ("he was outside of himself") in what would today be called a "near-death" experience (if the man had survived). In the early 1990s, numerous books were written by people claiming to have had "near-death" experiences, and a common element in these accounts is a description of the individual leaving his or her body. Ask one group of students to read some of these accounts and compare them with London's description. Another group of students can research medical studies that seek to explain the "near-death" phenomenon in scientific terms. Have students present their findings in class and discuss the plausibility of such experiences.

but he thrust it back and strove to think of other things.

It struck him as curious that he could run at all on feet so frozen that he could not feel them when they struck the earth and took the weight of his body. He seemed to himself to skim along above the surface, and to have no connection with the earth. Somewhere he had once seen a winged Mercury,[7] and he wondered if Mercury felt as he felt when skimming over the earth.

His theory of running until he reached camp and the boys had one flaw in it: he lacked the endurance. Several times he stumbled, and finally he tottered, crumpled up, and fell. When he tried to rise, he failed. He must sit and rest, he decided, and next time he would merely walk and keep on going. As he sat and regained his breath, he noted that he was feeling quite warm and comfortable. He was not shivering, and it even seemed that a warm glow had come to his chest and trunk. And yet, when he touched his nose or cheeks, there was no sensation. Running would not thaw them out. Nor would it thaw out his hands and feet. Then the thought came to him that the frozen portions of his body must be extending. He tried to keep this thought down, to forget it, to think of something else; he was aware of the panicky feeling that it caused, and he was afraid of the panic. But the thought asserted itself, and persisted, until it produced a vision of his body totally frozen. This was too much, and he made another wild run along the trail. Once he slowed down to a walk, but the thought of the freezing extending itself made him run again.

What are the man's final thoughts? ❶

And all the time the dog ran with him, at his heels. When he fell down a second time, it curled its tail over its forefeet and sat in front of him, facing him, curiously eager and intent. The warmth and security of the animal angered him, and he cursed it till it flattened down its ears appeasingly. This time the shivering came more quickly upon the man. He was losing in his battle with the frost. It was creeping into his body from all sides. The thought of it drove him on, but he ran no more than a hundred feet, when he staggered and pitched headlong. It was his last panic. When he had recovered his breath and control, he sat up and entertained in his mind the conception of meeting death with dignity. However, the conception did not come to him in such terms. His idea of it was that he had been making a fool of himself, running around like a chicken with its head cut off—such was the simile that occurred to him. Well, he was bound to freeze anyway, and he might as well take it decently. With this new-found peace of mind came the first glimmerings of drowsiness. A good idea, he thought, to sleep off to death. It was like taking an anaesthetic. Freezing was not so bad as people thought. There were lots worse ways to die.

He pictured the boys finding his body next day. Suddenly he found himself with them, coming along the trail and looking for himself. And, still with them, he came around a turn in the trail and found himself lying in the snow. He did not belong with himself any more, for even then he was out of himself; standing with the boys and looking at himself in the snow. It certainly was cold, was his thought. When he got back to the States he could tell the folks what real cold was. He drifted on from this to a vision of the old-timer on Sulphur Creek. He could see him quite clearly, warm and comfortable, and smoking a pipe.

"You were right, old hoss; you were right," the man mumbled to the old-timer of Sulphur Creek.

7. **Mercury.** In Roman mythology, Mercury, the messenger of the gods, is depicted with winged feet.

Answers to Selection Check Test 4.9.1

EX. Where does this story take place?
It takes place in the Yukon wilderness.

1. What is the man's destination?
The man is heading for his camp on Henderson Creek.

2. What is the temperature when the story takes place?
It is seventy-five degrees below zero.

3. What kinds of traps does the man attempt to avoid?
He attempts to avoid pools of water hidden under the snow.

4. Why does the man attempt to kill his dog?
He wants to warm his hands inside the dog's carcass.

5. Why is the man unable to run to his camp?
He lacks the necessary endurance.

Then the man drowsed off into what seemed to him the most comfortable and satisfying sleep he had ever known. The dog sat facing him and waiting. The brief day drew to a close in a long, slow twilight. There were no signs of a fire to be made, and, besides, never in the dog's experience had it known a man to sit like that in the snow and make no fire. As the twilight drew on, its eager yearning for the fire mastered it, and with a great lifting and shifting of forefeet, it whined softly, then flattened its ears down in anticipation of being chidden[8] by the man. But the man remained silent. Later, the dog whined loudly. And still later it crept close to the man and caught the scent of death. This made the animal bristle and back away. A little longer it delayed, howling under the stars that leaped and danced and shone brightly in the cold sky. Then it turned and trotted up the trail in the direction of the camp it knew, where were the other food providers and fire providers. ■

8. **chidden.** Scolded

Responding to the Selection

Imagine that you are one of the people waiting at camp for the return of the solitary traveler. What concerns do you have for his safety? Why do you think he is late in returning to camp? What is probably the greatest threat to his survival?

Reviewing the Selection

Recalling

1. What signals warn the man that it is much colder than he estimated?
2. What quality does the newcomer lack?
3. What advice, given by an old-timer on Sulphur Creek, does the newcomer ignore?
4. Against what does the man lose his battle?

Interpreting

5. What responses does the man have toward the cold? What does he think about to motivate himself to continue?
6. Why might the man's inexperience in this region make him slow to realize his own danger?
7. What would following the old-timer's advice have accomplished?
8. Why does the man think about the old-timer from Sulphur Creek? What is happening to the man's mind? What evidence do you have for your interpretation?

Responding to the Selection

Ask students to discuss Jack London's view of nature. Did the story end as they expected? If not, how was the ending different? How would the story have been different if the man had survived and the dog hadn't?

Answers for Reviewing the Selection

RECALLING

1. The signals that warn the man how cold it is are his spittle crackling in the air and the muzzle of ice that holds his lips so tightly that he is unable to clear his mouth of tobacco juice.
2. The newcomer lacks imagination and with it, fear of the cold.
3. The advice the newcomer ignores is to travel with a partner when the temperature dips under fifty below zero.
4. The man loses his battle against the cold, freezing to death.

INTERPRETING

Responses will vary. Possible responses are given.

5. The man's general responses toward the cold are that is it not particularly serious. He thinks about the camp he is trying to reach and the fire and hot supper that will be waiting for him.
6. The man's inexperience in the region might make him slow to realize the dangers that extreme cold presents. He has never been through a winter there before, and he falsely believes it to be like winters elsewhere.
7. Following the old-timer's advice would have saved the man's life, as a trail partner would have been able to build a fire for him.
8. The man thinks about the old-timer from Sulphur Creek because he realizes that he was right. The man's state of mind is deteriorating. Evidence includes trying to kill the dog, building his fire under the spruce tree, and running crazily even though his feet are completely frostbitten and numb.

(cont.)

Answers for Reviewing the Selection (cont.)

SYNTHESIZING

Responses will vary. Possible responses are given.

9. The man's conviction about cold temperatures tells you that he is extremely rugged but also unwise. It also tells you that he does not completely understand the full power of nature. His relationship with nature differs from the dog's in that the dog knows when not to challenge nature and the cold it presents, while the man stubbornly keeps going.

10. The author did not name the main character, most likely because he is meant simply to be a typical character from the region. The traits he possesses that are common to most human beings are the desire to conquer nature and the resistance to take advice when it is given by someone who is older or more experienced.

Answers for Understanding Literature

►See the evaluation forms for discussion, active listening, and oral communication, *Assessment Portfolio,* 7.11–7.14.

Responses will vary. Possible responses are given.

1. Setting. Some of the details that are particularly effective in creating the Yukon setting are the undulations of the snow where the ice jams have formed, "the mysterious, far-reaching hairline trail, the absence of sun from the sky, the tremendous cold and the strangeness and weirdness of it all." In terms of the cold temperature, the crackling of the man's spittle in the air and the muzzle of ice holding his lips together so that he cannot clear his chin of tobacco juice are effective.

2. Conflict, Plot, and Catastrophe. The external conflict that the main character struggles with is the forces of nature, which are represented by the extreme cold. His downfall is caused by falling through the ice, getting wet, and then having his fire go out. After the fire goes out, his death is inevitable, because there is really no way to keep from freezing to death in his situation.

►**Teaching Note:** Students might discuss how setting and plot relate to the story as a whole. How does the setting influence the events that take place in the story? How does the main character's feeling about the setting change as the plot unfolds?

Analytic Scales for Responding in Writing

Assign a score from 1 to 25 for each grading criterion below. (For more detailed evaluation, see the evaluation forms for writing, revising, and proofreading, *Assessment Portfolio,* 7.1–7.10.)

1. Descriptive Paragraph

- **Content/Unity.** The paragraph gives a clear impression of a real or imaginary setting by using sensory details.
- **Organization/Coherence.** The paragraph is clearly organized, with an opening sentence, a middle, and an end.

(cont.)

SYNTHESIZING

9. What does the man's conviction that "fifty degrees below zero was to him just precisely fifty degrees below zero" tell you about his personality? What does it tell you about his understanding of nature? How does the man's relationship with nature differ from the dog's?

10. What is probably the reason that the author does not name the main character? Is the character unique, or does he possess traits common to all human beings? If so, what are those traits?

Understanding Literature (Questions for Discussion)

1. **Setting.** The **setting** of a literary work is the time and place in which it occurs, together with all the details used to create a sense of a particular time and place. What details are particularly effective in creating the Yukon setting? What details are particularly effective in creating a vivid sense of the cold temperatures?

2. **Conflict, Plot, and Catastrophe.** A **conflict** is a struggle between two forces in a literary work. A **plot** involves the introduction, development, and eventual resolution of a conflict. One side of the central conflict in a story or drama is usually taken by the main character. That character may struggle against another character, against the forces of nature, against society, against fate, or against some element within himself or herself. What is the external conflict, or outside force, against which the main character struggles? One of the elements of plot is the **catastrophe**, the event that marks the ultimate tragic fall of the central character. Often this event is the character's death. What causes the main character's downfall? Is his death inevitable? Why, or why not?

Responding in Writing

1. **Descriptive Paragraph.** London's description of the Yukon is made vivid and real through its use of sensory detail. Write a descriptive paragraph that portrays a real or imaginary setting. In your paragraph, make use of sensory details—words and phrases that describe how things look, sound, smell, taste, and feel—to evoke a vivid setting. Reveal characteristics of the setting through the use of elements such as landscape, buildings, furniture, clothing, the weather, or the season.

2. **Documentation.** In the selection, London describes all the steps in the process of building a fire in the wilderness. Think of a skill or activity with which you are familiar and write a set of guidelines documenting the procedure. (You may wish to refer to the Language Arts Survey, 5.7, "Technical Writing.") To get started, familiarize yourself with the procedure you will be documenting. Then, break the task into a series of short, simple steps, listing each step in the proper sequence. In your documentation of the procedure, use simple and precise language, written in the form of second-person imperative.

Analytic Scales for Responding in Writing (cont.)

- **Language/Style.** The paragraph uses vivid and precise nouns, verbs, and modifiers.
- **Conventions.** The paragraph avoids errors in spelling, grammar, usage, mechanics, and manuscript form.

2. Documentation

- **Content/Unity.** The documentation uses second-person imperative to present a series of short, simple steps needed to complete a task.
- **Organization/Coherence.** The documentation lists the steps in a proper sequence.
- **Language/Style.** The documentation uses vivid and precise nouns, verbs, and modifiers.
- **Conventions.** The documentation avoids errors in spelling, grammar, usage, mechanics, and manuscript form.

Language Lab

Base Words and Suffixes. Read the Language Arts Survey, 2.140, "Base Words and Prefixes," and 2.141, "Suffixes." Then underline the base word once and the suffix twice in each of the following words from "To Build a Fire." Next look up each suffix in a dictionary and write two additional words that end with the same suffix.

1. uncomfortable
2. solidity
3. eastward
4. numbness
5. sensation

Test-taking Skills

Synonyms and Antonyms. Read the Language Arts Survey, 4.44, "Synonym and Antonym Questions." Then, write the letter of the word that is most nearly opposite in meaning to the word in capital letters.

1. IMAGINATION

a. invention b. improvisation c. unadorned d. foolishness e. whimsy

2. INSTINCT

a. intuition b. reason c. knowledge d. observation e. perception

3. FACT

a. falsehood b. certainty c. truth d. reality e. phenomenon

4. FRAILTY

a. weakness b. flaw c. vigor d. fault e. fit

5. ALLEGIANCE

a. devotion b. disobedience c. loyalty d. duty e. homage

PROJECT

Camping Trip. Plan an imaginary camping trip with your classmates. Working in small groups, choose an area of the world you would like to explore. Make lists of all the equipment and supplies you think you will need. Try to brainstorm difficulties you might encounter on your trip. Then, research your area of the world in an encyclopedia or in outdoor recreation magazines to see if there are any possible difficulties in this region you may have overlooked and for which you should be better prepared.

ANSWERS FOR LANGUAGE LAB

Responses will vary. Possible responses are given.

1. base: comfort; suffix: –able
   wearable, bearable
2. base: solid; suffix: –ity
   rigidity, frigidity
3. base: east; suffix: –ward
   toward, backward
4. base: numb; suffix: –ness
   dumbness, fullness
5. base: sense; suffix: –ation
   compilation, dilation

ANSWERS FOR TEST-TAKING SKILLS

1. a
2. b
3. a
4. c
5. b

PROJECT NOTES

▶See the worksheets and evaluation forms for projects, *Assessment Portfolio,* 7.20–7.23.

Camping Trip

- Students may want to find copies of topographical maps for certain areas and look at them when planning their trips.
- Remind students that when working in groups, all group members must participate and contribute ideas.

ADDITIONAL RESOURCES

READER'S GUIDE
- Selection Worksheet, 9.2

ASSESSMENT PORTFOLIO
- Selection Check Test, 4.9.3
- Selection Test, 4.9.4

ESSENTIAL SKILLS PRACTICE BOOKS
- *Language,* 2.46, 2.63, 2.140, 2.141
- *Applied English,* 5.2

ENRICHMENT ACTIVITIES

Play a recording of one of the operatic pieces mentioned in the story, if possible, or an excerpt from another opera (pieces mentioned in the story include the overture from *Tannhäuser* and the prelude to *Tristan und Isolde*). Most recordings of operas come with a copy of the libretto, and it may be helpful to give students a copy if the piece played includes singing. Ask students to freewrite about their responses to the piece, and then to share some of their responses with the class. (Two arias considered exceptionally beautiful are "Ebben? ne andrò lontana" from act 1 of *La Wally,* and "Casta Diva" from act 1 of *Norma.* Both of these arias are sung by Maria Callas and can be found on the album entitled "Callas: La Divina.")

SUPPORT FOR LEP STUDENTS

Students may benefit from a discussion about operatic terms such as *prelude* and *overture.* Discuss their significance in opera, as well as other meanings. Additionally, review with students the Words for Everyday Use listed on page 631.

PREREADING

"A Wagner Matinee"
by Willa Cather

ABOUT THE AUTHOR

Willa Cather (1873–1947) was born in Virginia. When she was ten her family moved to Nebraska, where her father was a frontier farmer and owner of a farm loan and mortgage business. Cather graduated from the University of Nebraska in 1895. She began writing in college, working for the *Nebraska Journal* reviewing books, plays, and music.

In the late 1890s and early 1900s, she lived in Pittsburgh, Pennsylvania, and worked as a newspaper and magazine writer and editor before teaching high school English and Latin. In 1906, she moved to New York City and joined *McClure's* magazine, first as a contributing editor from 1906 to 1908 and then as managing editor from 1908 to 1912.

Her early work about the Nebraska prairie and its pioneers made her famous. She is also remembered for her powerful female figures, who are often unconventional, like Cather herself.

Her first novel, *Alexander's Bridge* (1912), was published when she was thirty-nine. Her other works include the poetry of *April Twilights* (1903), the short stories in *The Troll Garden* (1912), and the novels *O Pioneers!* (1913), *The Song of the Lark* (1915), *My Antonia* (1918), *A Lost Lady* (1923), *The Professor's House* (1925), and *Death Comes for the Archbishop* (1926).

Cather was awarded the Pulitzer Prize for the novel *One of Ours* (1922) and the Howells Medal from the American Academy and Institute of Arts and Letters in 1930 for *Death Comes for the Archbishop.*

ABOUT THE SELECTION

In **"A Wagner Matinee,"** Cather juxtaposes the pioneer world of Red Willow, Nebraska, and the musical world of Boston. Cather's method of writing from firsthand experience, particularly about growing up in Red Cloud, Nebraska, is well known and typical of her work. Music was one of Cather's passionate interests. In "A Wagner Matinee," she created the character of Aunt Georgiana, a woman who studied music at the Boston Conservatory. A martyr in the eyes of her nephew, Aunt Georgiana "inexplicably" gives up her musical life for a life on the silent Nebraska frontier.

GOALS/OBJECTIVES

Studying this lesson will enable students to

- interpret and appreciate a short story
- describe the literary accomplishments of Willa Cather
- explain how the narrator's point of view is changed by his Aunt Georgiana
- define *narrator, point of view,* and *simile* and explain how Cather uses them in the story
- write a descriptive paragraph about a real or imaginary place
- write a personal letter from one character to another

READER'S JOURNAL

Have you ever had a strong emotional response to a piece of music? What was the music? What emotions did you experience while listening to the music? Why do you think you responded so strongly to that particular piece of music? Write about the experience in your journal.

LANGUAGE SKILLS

Read the Language Arts Survey, 2.46, "Adding Modifiers." Then identify some simple, compound, complex, and complex-compound sentences in the selection that have been expanded with modifiers.

"A Wagner Matinee"

WILLA CATHER

I received one morning a letter, written in pale ink on glassy, blue-lined note-paper, and bearing the postmark of a little Nebraska village. This communication, worn and rubbed, looking as if it had been carried for some days in a coat pocket that was none too clean, was from my Uncle Howard, and informed me that his wife had been left a small legacy[1] by a bachelor relative, and that it would be necessary for her to go to Boston to attend to the settling of the estate. He requested me to meet her at the station and render her whatever services might be necessary. On examining the date indicated as that of her arrival, I found it to be no later than tomorrow. He had characteristically delayed writing until, had I been away from home for a day, I must have missed my aunt altogether.

The name of my Aunt Georgiana opened before me a gulf of recollection so wide and deep that, as the letter dropped from my hand, I felt suddenly a stranger to all the present conditions of my existence, wholly ill at ease and out of place amid the familiar surroundings of my study. I became, in short, the gangling farmer-boy my aunt had known, scourged with chilblains[2] and bashfulness, my hands cracked and sore from the corn husking. I sat again before her parlor organ, fumbling the scale with my stiff, red fingers, while she, beside me, made canvas mittens for the huskers.

The next morning, after preparing my landlady for a visitor, I set out for the station. When the train arrived I had some difficulty in finding my aunt. She was the last of the passengers to alight, and it was not until I got her into the carriage that she seemed really to recognize me. She had come all the way in a day coach; her

❶ *Who wrote the letter to the narrator? Who is coming to visit? When is the visitor coming? What is the narrator asked to do?*

1. **legacy.** Inheritance
2. **scourged with chilblains.** Tormented by blisters on hands and feet

WORDS FOR EVERYDAY USE: **ren • der** (ren´dər) *vt.,* give, hand over, deliver, or present

PREREADING NOTES

READER'S JOURNAL

Students may begin by brainstorming pieces of music that they like or with which they feel a strong connection. What makes these pieces of music memorable? If students could listen to only one of them, which one would it be? Why?

LANGUAGE SKILLS

Students may choose to break up complex sentences into simple sentences or clauses to better understand the sentence structures.

ANSWER TO GUIDED READING QUESTION

❶ The letter to the narrator is written by his Uncle Howard. His wife is coming to visit him. She is coming tomorrow, and the narrator is asked to meet her at the station.

CROSS-CURRICULAR ACTIVITIES

Social Studies. The distance between Nebraska and Boston plays an important thematic role in this story, since it accounts in part for Aunt Georgiana's separation from music during her married life. While today such distances seem almost trivial due to the ease and speed of air travel, in the late nineteenth and early twentieth centuries, such a distance represented a formidable obstacle. Ask students to research modes of travel in this time period, in particular what a journey from Nebraska to Boston would have entailed. Students might consult firsthand accounts written by travelers to get a feel for the experience.

VOCABULARY IN CONTEXT

- The judge said she would render a verdict in the case on Monday, but she would not give out any other information before then.

VOCABULARY FROM THE SELECTION

excruciatingly	overture	reverential
immobility	prelude	revert
infatuation	render	tremulously
interminably	reproach	
jocularity	respective	

Answers to Guided Reading Questions

❶ Aunt Georgiana helped the narrator with his studies by keeping him awake late at night and listening to his recitations. She taught the narrator musical scales and exercises. The instrument they had was an organ.

❷ The land was measured by driving across the prairie in a wagon and counting the revolutions of one of its wheels. Howard and Georgiana built a cavelike dug-out in a hillside. They got their water from lagoons where buffalo drank.

Cross-curricular Activities

Social Studies. When Aunt Georgiana married Howard Carpenter, they went to Nebraska and "took up a homestead," most likely under the Homestead Act that Congress passed in 1862, which made public lands in the western United States available at no cost to settlers. Ask students to research the Homestead Act and the homesteading movement that resulted. What kind of life did the pioneers live on their homesteads? Did many of them live in the "dug-out" houses mentioned by Cather? What opportunities, if any, did settlers have for such cultural experiences as operas and concerts? Students could then write an essay entitled "Why I would/would not want to homestead."

Additional Questions and Activities

Ask students about trips that they have taken. What was the longest trip each student has ever taken? What was involved in the actual journey? How did he or she feel about making the trip? Was it exciting? frightening? disorienting? As an additional exercise, students might write the itinerary of a trip they have taken or an imaginary one from Omaha, Nebraska, to Boston, including time to and from airports as well as time waiting for a taxi and the plane.

linen duster[3] had become black with soot and her black bonnet grey with dust during the journey. When we arrived at my boarding-house the landlady put her to bed at once, and I did not see her again until the next morning.

Whatever shock Mrs. Springer experienced at my aunt's appearance, she considerately concealed. As for myself, I saw my aunt's battered figure with that feeling of awe and respect with which we behold explorers who have left their ears and fingers north of Franz-Joseph-Land, or their health somewhere along the Upper Congo.[4] My Aunt Georgiana had been a music teacher at the Boston Conservatory, somewhere back in the latter sixties.[5] One summer, while visiting in the little village among the Green Mountains where her ancestors had dwelt for generations, she had kindled the callow fancy of my uncle, Howard Carpenter, then an idle, shiftless boy of twenty-one. When she returned to her duties in Boston, Howard followed her, and the upshot of this infatuation was that she eloped with him, eluding the reproaches of her family and the criticism of her friends by going with him to the Nebraska frontier.[6] Carpenter, who, of course, had no money, took up a homestead in Red Willow County, fifty miles from the railroad. There they had measured off their land themselves, driving across the prairie in a wagon, to the wheel of which they had tied a red cotton handkerchief, and counting its revolutions. They built a dug-out in the red hillside, one of those cave dwellings whose inmates so often reverted to primitive conditions. Their water they got from the lagoons where the buffalo drank, and their slender stock of provisions[7] was always at the mercy of bands of roving Indians. For thirty years my aunt had not been farther than fifty miles from the homestead.

I owed to this woman most of the good that ever came my way in my boyhood, and had a reverential affection for her. During the years when I was riding herd for my uncle, my aunt, after cooking the three meals—the first of which was ready at six o'clock in the morning—and putting the six children to bed, would often stand until midnight at her ironing board, with me at the kitchen table beside her, hearing me recite Latin declensions and conjugations, gently shaking me when my drowsy head sank down over a page of irregular verbs. It was to her, at her ironing or mending, that I read my first Shakespeare, and her old textbook on mythology was the first that ever came into my empty hands. She taught me my scales and exercises[8] on the little parlor organ which her husband had bought her after fifteen years during which she had not so much as seen a musical instrument. She would sit beside me by the hour, darning and counting, while I struggled with the "Joyous Farmer." She seldom talked to me about music, and I understood why. Once when I had been doggedly beating out some easy

How did Aunt Georgiana help the narrator with his studies? What did she teach the narrator? What musical instrument did they have? ❶

How was the land measured? What did Georgiana and Howard build? Where did they get their water? ❷

3. **duster.** Lightweight coat
4. **north of Franz-Joseph-Land . . . Congo.** *Franz-Joseph-Land*—group of tiny islands in the Arctic Ocean; *Congo*—river in central Africa
5. **sixties.** 1860s
6. **Nebraska frontier.** Western border of Nebraska; uncharted territory
7. **provisions.** Supplies
8. **scales and exercises.** Musical scales and practice pieces

Words for Everyday Use:

in • fat • u • a • tion (in fach´ōō ā´shən) *n.,* foolish or shallow love or affection

re • vert (ri vurt´) *vi.,* return to a former practice, opinion, state, or subject

rev • er • en • tial (rev´ə ren´shal) *adj.,* showing a feeling of deep respect, love, and awe

Vocabulary in Context

- His infatuation with the movie star became serious after he sent her flowers and candy.
- Some young children revert to baby talk when they want attention.
- Her reverential feeling for her grandfather was based on deep respect, love, and a feeling of awe about his accomplishments.

passages from an old score of *Euryanthe* I had found among her music books, she came up to me and, putting her hands over my eyes, gently drew my head back upon her shoulder, saying tremulously, "Don't love it so well, Clark, or it may be taken from you."

When my aunt appeared on the morning after her arrival in Boston, she was still in a semi-somnambulant[9] state. She seemed not to realize that she was in the city where she had spent her youth, the place longed for hungrily half a lifetime. She had been so wretchedly train-sick throughout the journey that she had no recollection of anything but her discomfort, and, to all intents and purposes, there were but a few hours of nightmare between the farm in Red Willow County and my study on Newbury Street. I had planned a little pleasure for her that afternoon, to repay her for some of the glorious moments she had given me when we used to milk together in the straw-thatched cowshed and she, because I was more than usually tired, or because her husband had spoken sharply to me, would tell me of the splendid performance of the *Huguenots* she had seen in Paris, in her youth.

At two o'clock the Symphony Orchestra was to give a Wagner[10] program, and I intended to take my aunt; though, as I conversed with her, I grew doubtful about her enjoyment of it. I suggested our visiting the Conservatory and the Common[11] before lunch, but she seemed altogether too timid to wish to venture out. She questioned me absently about various changes in the city, but she was chiefly concerned that she had forgotten to leave instructions about feeding half-skimmed milk to a certain weakling calf, "old Maggie's calf, you know, Clark," she explained, evidently having forgotten how long I had been away. She was further troubled because she had neglected to tell her daughter about the freshly-opened kit of mackerel[12] in the cellar, which would spoil if it were not used directly.

I asked her whether she had ever heard any of the Wagnerian operas, and found that she had not, though she was perfectly familiar with their respective situations, and had once possessed the piano score of *The Flying Dutchman.* I began to think it would be best to get her back to Red Willow County without waking her, and regretted having suggested the concert.

From the time we entered the concert hall, however, she was a trifle less passive and inert, and for the first time seemed to perceive her surroundings. I had felt some trepidation lest she might become aware of her queer, country clothes, or might experience some painful embarrassment at stepping suddenly into the world to which she had been dead for a quarter of a century. But, again, I found how superficially I had judged her. She sat looking about her with eyes as impersonal, almost as stony, as those with which the granite Rameses[13] in a museum watches the froth and fret that ebbs and flows about his pedestal. I have seen this same aloofness in

❶ *Why did Aunt Georgiana tell the narrator not to love the music so well?*

❷ *How does Aunt Georgiana react to being in the concert hall? About what is the narrator concerned?*

❸ *What "little pleasure" does the narrator plan for the afternoon?*

9. **semi-somnambulant.** Like one who is sleepwalking
10. **Wagner.** Richard Wagner (1813–1883), German composer
11. **the Common.** Boston Common, park in a historic section of Boston
12. **kit of mackerel.** Container of pickled fish
13. **Rameses.** Name of a number of Egyptian kings who ruled from *circa* 1315 BC to *circa* 1090 BC

WORDS FOR EVERYDAY USE:

trem • u • lous • ly (trem´yōō ləs lē) *adv.,* in a trembling or quivering manner; fearfully, timidly

re • spec • tive (ri spek´tiv) *adj.,* as relates individually to each of two or more persons or things

ANSWERS TO GUIDED READING QUESTIONS

❶ Aunt Georgiana told the narrator not to love the music so well because it might be taken away from him.

❷ Aunt Georgiana reacts to being in the concert hall by becoming less passive and more aware of her surroundings. The narrator is concerned that she might feel out of place because of her country clothes.

❸ The "little pleasure" the narrator plans for the afternoon is taking his aunt to a symphony concert of Wagner.

ADDITIONAL QUESTIONS AND ACTIVITIES

The narrator of this story is Aunt Georgiana's nephew, Clark. Ask students why they think Cather, a woman, wrote this story using a male narrator. Would a woman at that time have had the same opportunities to leave Nebraska and go live in Boston alone? If Cather were writing the story today, do students think she would make the narrator a woman instead of a man? As an additional exercise, students might write an essay discussing how the story would be different if the narrator were female.

CROSS-CURRICULAR ACTIVITIES

Arts and Humanities. The narrator plans to take Aunt Georgiana to hear a concert of pieces from different operas by Richard Wagner, a nineteenth-century German composer who is best known for the romantic operas of *The Ring Cycle.* So that they might better understand the setting of this story as well as the character of Aunt Georgiana, ask students to research Wagner's operas. What kind of operas did he write? How were they received by the public at the end of the nineteenth century? Ask students to write an essay speculating on the reasons Cather had for making Wagnerian opera a central element in this story. What do these operas and Aunt Georgiana's reaction to them tell the reader about her character?

VOCABULARY IN CONTEXT

- Public speaking makes Lou nervous, and his voice wavers tremulously whenever he gives a speech.
- The boxers returned to their respective corners of the ring and waited with their trainers until the bell signaled the start of the second round.

Answers to Guided Reading Questions

❶ The matinee audience is made up mostly of women. They are dressed in shimmering fabrics of many different colors.

❷ Aunt Georgiana reacts to the music by clutching the narrator's coat sleeve. The narrator realizes that it is the first time his aunt has heard music of this sort in thirty years.

Cross-curricular Activities

Arts and Humanities. The narrator likens the scene at the concert to an Impressionist painting, declaring of the audience that "One lost the contour of faces and figures, indeed any effect of line whatever." Students with a special interest in art may wish to find reproductions of Impressionist paintings that they feel correspond to Cather's description of the concert audience. Have them show these paintings to the class as a whole so that the class might discuss this particular image. Why choose Impressionist painting instead of a Realist painting, or a Cubist work? How does this image contribute to the atmosphere of the story?

old miners who drift into the Brown hotel at Denver, their pockets full of bullion, their linen soiled, their haggard faces unshaven; standing in the thronged corridors as solitary as though they were still in a frozen camp on the Yukon.

Who comprises the matinee audience? How are they dressed? ❶

The matinee audience was made up chiefly of women. One lost the contour of faces and figures, indeed any effect of line whatever, and there was only the color of bodices past counting, the shimmer of fabrics soft and firm, silky and sheer; red, mauve, pink, blue, lilac, purple, ecru, rose, yellow, cream, and white, all the colors that an impressionist[14] finds in a sunlit landscape, with here and there the dead shadow of a frock coat. My Aunt Georgiana regarded them as though they had been so many daubs of tube-paint on a palette.

How does Aunt Georgiana react to the music? What awareness comes to the narrator? ❷

When the musicians came out and took their places, she gave a little stir of anticipation, and looked with quickening interest down over the rail at that invariable grouping, perhaps the first wholly familiar thing that had greeted her eye since she had left old Maggie and her weakling calf. I could feel how all those details sank into her soul, for I had not forgotten how they had sunk into mine when I came fresh from ploughing forever and forever between green aisles of corn, where, as in a treadmill, one might walk from daybreak to dusk without perceiving a shadow of change. The clean profiles of the musicians, the gloss of their linen, the dull black of their coats, the beloved shapes of the instruments, the patches of yellow light on the smooth, varnished bellies of the cellos and the bass viols in the rear, the restless, wind-tossed forest of fiddle necks and bows—I recalled how, in the first orchestra I ever heard, those long bow-strokes seemed to draw the heart out of me, as a conjurer's stick[15] reels out yards of paper ribbon from a hat.

The first number was the *Tannhauser* overture. When the horns drew out the first strain of the Pilgrim's chorus, Aunt Georgiana clutched my coat sleeve. Then it was I first realized that for her this broke a silence of thirty years. With the battle between the two motives, with the frenzy of the Venusberg theme and its ripping of strings, there came to me an overwhelming sense of the waste and wear we are so powerless to combat; and I saw again the tall, naked house on the prairie, black and grim as a wooden fortress; the black pond where I had learned to swim, its margin pitted with sun-dried cattle tracks; the rain gullied clay banks about the naked house, the four dwarf ash seedlings where the dishcloths were always hung to dry before the kitchen door. The world there was the flat world of the ancients; to the east, a cornfield that stretched to daybreak; to the west, a corral that reached to sunset; between, the conquests of peace, dearer-bought than those of war.

The overture closed, my aunt released my coat sleeve, but she said nothing. She sat staring dully at the orchestra. What, I wondered, did she get from it? She had been a good pianist in her day, I knew, and her musical education had been broader than that of most music teachers of a quarter of a century ago. She had often told me

14. **impressionist.** Painter, writer, or composer who seeks to render impressions and moods in which the chief aim is to capture a momentary glimpse of a subject
15. **conjurer's stick.** Magician's wand

Words for Everyday Use: **o • ver • ture** (o´vər chər) *n.,* musical introduction to an opera or other large musical work; independent orchestral composition of varying form

Vocabulary in Context

- The overture to the opera was powerful yet joyous and set a good tone for the production.
- The prelude of the opera moved along quickly, and before we knew it the first act was over and it was intermission.
- "Don't move," the robber said, and the immobility I displayed would have made a statue proud.

Photograph by Lee Stalsworth

First Row Orchestra. *Edward Hopper, 1951. Hirshhorn Museum and Sculpture Garden, Smithsonian Institution, Gift of the Joseph H. Hirshhorn Foundation, 1966*

of Mozart's operas and Meyerbeer's and I could remember hearing her sing, years ago, certain melodies of Verdi. When I had fallen ill with a fever in her house, she used to sit by my cot in the evening—when the cool, night wind blew in through the faded mosquito netting tacked over the window and I lay watching a certain bright star that burned red above the cornfield—and sing "Home to our mountains, O, let us return!" in a way fit to break the heart of a Vermont boy near dead of homesickness already.

I watched her closely through the prelude to *Tristan and Isolde*, trying vainly to conjecture what that seething turmoil of strings and winds might mean to her, but she sat mutely staring at the violin bows that drove obliquely downward, like the pelting streaks of rain in a summer shower. Had this music any message for her? Had she enough left to at all comprehend this power which had kindled the world since she had left it? I was in a fever of curiosity, but Aunt Georgiana sat silent upon her peak in Darien.[16] She preserved this utter immobility throughout the number from *The Flying Dutchman*, though her fingers worked mechanically upon her black dress, as if, of themselves,

❶ *What did Aunt Georgiana do when the narrator was sick? What effect did her action have on the narrator?*

16. **peak in Darien.** Mountain in Panama (formerly called the Isthmus of Darien) where Cortés was said to have looked westward at the Pacific Ocean, a new discovery for Europeans

WORDS FOR EVERYDAY USE:

pre • lude (prel´yōōd) *n.,* first movement of an opera; introduction

im • mo • bil • i • ty (im´mo bil´i tē) *n.,* state of being fixed or unmovable

ANSWER TO GUIDED READING QUESTION

❶ Aunt Georgiana used to sit by the narrator's cot when he was sick and sing to him. The effect on the narrator was to make him homesick for Vermont.

ADDITIONAL QUESTIONS AND ACTIVITIES

The narrator compares the movement of the violin bows in the orchestra to "the pelting streaks of rain in a summer shower." Ask students to think of other comparisons for the movement of the bows and write them on the board. Have the class discuss each suggested simile, as well as Cather's original, for the associations each one evokes.

Answers to Guided Reading Questions

❶ The tenor's solo makes Aunt Georgiana and the narrator cry. The insight the narrator has is that the soul can suffer a great deal but can be renewed if given the right experiences.

❷ Aunt Georgiana knows the "Prize Song" because of a young German boy who used to sing it on her farm. The singer disappeared under mysterious circumstances.

Literary Technique

Minor Character. A **minor character** is often introduced in a short piece of fiction to evoke a comparison with one of the major characters. Discuss the minor character of the "tramp cow-puncher." Why is he included in this story? What are the similarities and differences between his character and that of Aunt Georgiana? Ask the students to compare and contrast the responsibilities and freedoms exercised by each of these characters.

Answers to Selection Check Test 4.9.3

EX. Where does the narrator live?

He lives on Newbury Street in Boston.

1. Where did the narrator live as a child?

He lived in Red Willow County, Nebraska.

2. What was Aunt Georgiana's job before she was married?

She was a music teacher at the Boston Conservatory.

3. Which composer's works are played at the concert?

The orchestra plays pieces from the operas of Richard Wagner.

4. To what does the narrator compare Aunt Georgiana's hands?

He calls them "mere tentacles."

5. What was the mood of the audience at the end of the concert?

The audience was happy and relaxed as it left the hall.

they were recalling the piano score they had once played. Poor hands! They had been stretched and twisted into mere tentacles to hold and lift and knead with—on one of them a thin, worn band that had once been a wedding ring. As I pressed and gently quieted one of those groping hands, I remembered with quivering eyelids their services for me in other days.

How does the tenor's solo affect Aunt Georgiana? the narrator? What insight into the human soul does the narrator have? ❶

Soon after the tenor began the "Prize Song," I heard a quick drawn breath and turned to my aunt. Her eyes were closed, but the tears were glistening on her cheeks, and I think, in a moment more, they were in my eyes as well. It never really died, then—the soul which can suffer so excruciatingly and so interminably; it withers to the outward eye only; like that strange moss which can lie on a dusty shelf half a century and yet, if placed in water, grows green again. She wept so throughout the development and elaboration of the melody.

How does Aunt Georgiana know the "Prize Song"? Who used to sing it? What became of the singer? ❷

During the intermission before the second half, I questioned my aunt and found that the "Prize Song" was not new to her. Some years before there had drifted to the farm in Red Willow County a young German, a tramp cow-puncher, who had sung in the chorus at Bayreuth[17] when he was a boy, along with the other peasant boys and girls. Of a Sunday morning he used to sit on his gingham-sheeted bed in the hands' bedroom which opened off the kitchen, cleaning the leather of his boots and saddle, singing the "Prize Song," while my aunt went about her work in the kitchen. She had hovered over him until she had prevailed upon him to join the country church, though his sole fitness for this step, in so far as I could gather, lay in his boyish face and his possession of this divine melody. Shortly afterward, he had gone to town on the Fourth of July, been drunk for several days, lost his money at a faro[18] table, ridden a saddled Texas steer on a bet, and disappeared with a fractured collar-bone. All this my aunt told me huskily, wanderingly, as though she were talking in the weak lapses of illness.

"Well, we have come to better things than the old *Trovatore* at any rate, Aunt Georgie?" I queried, with a well meant effort at jocularity.

Her lip quivered and she hastily put her handkerchief up to her mouth. From behind it she murmured, "And you have been hearing this ever since you left me, Clark?" Her question was the gentlest and saddest of reproaches.

The second half of the program consisted of four numbers from the *Ring*, and closed with Siegfried's funeral march. My aunt wept quietly, but almost continuously, as a shallow vessel overflows in a rain-storm. From time to time her dim eyes looked up at the lights, burning softly under their dull glass globes.

The deluge of sound poured on and on; I never knew what she found in the shining current of it; I never knew how far it bore her, or past what happy islands. From the trembling of her face I could well believe

17. **Bayreuth.** Site of international music festivals in Germany
18. **faro.** Gambling game

Words for Everyday Use:

ex • cru • ci • at • ing • ly (eks krōō´shē āt´iŋ lē) *adv.,* in a painful or agonizing manner

in • ter • mi • na • bly (in tur´mi nə blē) *adv.,* endlessly; in a manner that seems to last forever

joc • u • lar • i • ty (jäk´yōō lar´ə tē) *n.,* humor, joking

re • proach (ri prōch´) *n.,* blaming or reproving; rebuke

Vocabulary in Context

- The operation was excruciatingly painful, and it took him months to recover fully.
- The concert went on interminably; we thought it was never going to end.
- Her jocularity was one of her best qualities; she was good at telling jokes and making people around her laugh.
- The president criticized Congress for blocking his legislation, saying that no member of either the House or Senate was above reproach and that they should all equally share the blame.

that before the last number she had been carried out where the myriad graves are, into the grey, nameless burying grounds of the sea; or into some world of death vaster yet, where, from the beginning of the world, hope has lain down with hope and dream with dream and, renouncing, slept.

The concert was over; the people filed out of the hall chattering and laughing, glad to relax and find the living level again, but my kinswoman made no effort to rise. The harpist slipped the green felt cover over his instrument; the flute-players shook the water from their mouthpieces; the men of the orchestra went out one by one, leaving the stage to the chairs and music stands, empty as a winter cornfield.

I spoke to my aunt. She burst into tears and sobbed pleadingly. "I don't want to go, Clark, I don't want to go!"

I understood. For her, just outside the concert hall, lay the black pond with the cattle-tracked bluffs; the tall, unpainted house, with weather-curled boards, naked as a tower; the crook-backed ash seedlings where the dishcloths hung to dry; the gaunt, moulting[19] turkeys picking up refuse about the kitchen door. ■

19. **moulting.** Shedding feathers

❶ *Where does the narrator believe the music transports Aunt Georgiana?*

❷ *Why does Aunt Georgiana want to stay in the concert hall?*

Responding to the Selection

Imagine that you are Aunt Georgiana listening to the music in the concert hall. How do you feel listening to music you have not heard in many years? Do you regret removing yourself from the world of music?

Reviewing the Selection

RECALLING

1. What is the reason for Aunt Georgiana's visit to Boston?
2. After eloping, how does Aunt Georgiana "elude the reproaches of her family"?
3. What job does the narrator perform for his uncle on the farm?
4. What pleasure does the narrator plan for his aunt?

INTERPRETING

5. Why does the name "Aunt Georgiana" open before the narrator's "feet a gulf of recollection so wide and deep"?
6. What facts emphasize the hardship of Aunt Georgiana's life on the Nebraska frontier?
7. What actions on the part of Aunt Georgiana emphasize that the narrator owes to her "most of the good" that came his way in boyhood?
8. Why doesn't Aunt Georgiana want to leave the concert hall?

Answers to Guided Reading Questions

❶ The narrator believes that the music transports his aunt into the world of the sea or a place where hope and dreams have been lain down since the beginning of time.

❷ Aunt Georgiana wants to stay in the concert hall because she does not want to go outside, back into the hard world from where she came.

Responding to the Selection

Ask students to think about the story's perspective on music, specifically opera. Do they feel as strongly as Aunt Georgina does about a type of music? How do they think an opera singer would respond to reading it?

Answers for Reviewing the Selection

RECALLING

1. Aunt Georgiana visits Boston in order to settle the estate of a bachelor relative.
2. Aunt Georgiana eluded the "reproaches of her family" by going with the narrator's uncle to live on the Nebraska frontier.
3. The narrator rides the herd for his uncle.
4. The narrator plans to take his aunt to hear a Wagner opera.

INTERPRETING

Responses will vary. Possible responses are given.

5. The name "Aunt Georgiana" opens up the narrator's memories because she did so much for him when he was growing up. He suddenly feels as if he is a farm boy again, sitting before her parlor organ.
6. The hardship of Aunt Georgiana's life on the frontier is emphasized by being fifty miles from the railroad, living in a cave dug-out, drinking water from buffalo lagoons, and not having been further than fifty miles from her homestead in thirty years.

(cont.)

Additional Questions and Activities

Why does Aunt Georgiana ask her nephew, "And you have been hearing this ever since you left me, Clark?" Why does the nephew describe this question as "the gentlest and saddest of reproaches"?

Answers for Reviewing the Selection (cont.)

7. The narrator owes Aunt Georgiana "most of the good" of his boyhood because she helped him stay awake to study at night and introduced him to the world of music by teaching him scales and exercises.
8. Aunt Georgiana does not want to leave the concert hall because the music has transported her to a different, magical place. She does not want the experience to end or to go back to the harsh realities of Boston and Nebraska.

(cont.)

Answers for Reviewing the Selection (cont.)

SYNTHESIZING

Responses will vary. Possible responses are given.

9. Aunt Georgiana tells the narrator not to love music because it had been taken away from her. She had been a music teacher and music lover, and when she moved to Nebraska, she was suddenly cut off from that important part of herself.

10. The relationship described between music and the human soul in the story is a powerful one. Music can transport the soul to different worlds while healing past losses and renewing hope and faith in the world. The evidence of this is Aunt Georgiana's response to hearing live opera for the first time in thirty years and the tears of joy that both she and the narrator shed.

Answers for Understanding Literature

► See the evaluation forms for discussion, active listening, and oral communication, *Assessment Portfolio,* 7.11–7.14.

Responses will vary. Possible responses are given.

1. Narrator and Point of View. The narrator misjudges his aunt by thinking that she might not enjoy going to the opera. He also thinks she might be embarrassed by her clothes and intimidated by the sophisticated atmosphere surrounding the opera. It affects his point of view by showing that he does not know his aunt very well, or at least does not remember her well. The narrator seems reliable in that he is not prone to exaggerations or outright lies. The narrator does not like his uncle. Evidence to support this includes the line, "I owed to this woman most of the good that ever came out of my boyhood," and his dislike for the way his uncle treated his aunt during the years he was growing up in Nebraska.

2. Simile. The tenor in the simile is the soul. The vehicle in the simile is the moss. The quality that the two parts of the simile share is that both suffer and wither but can be replenished under the right conditions.

SYNTHESIZING

9. Why does Aunt Georgiana warn the narrator "Don't love it so well, Clark, or it may be taken from you"? What relationship does the warning have to the aunt's own experience?

10. What kind of relationship between music and the human soul is described in this story? What evidence in the selection supports your analysis?

Understanding Literature (Questions for Discussion)

1. **Narrator and Point of View.** A **narrator** is one who tells a story. In this story, written in first-person **point of view,** the narrator is limited in his knowledge. As a character, however, the narrator is aware of his limitations and acknowledges his superficial judgment of Aunt Georgiana. In what ways does the narrator misjudge or underestimate his aunt? How does this affect the point of view of the narrator? Do you find him reliable? How does the narrator regard his uncle? What evidence supports your interpretation?

2. **Simile.** A **simile** is a comparison using *like* or *as.* A type of metaphor, a simile can be analyzed into two parts, the *tenor* (or subject being described) and the *vehicle* (or object being used in the description). Consider the simile in the following sentence from the selection: "It never really died, then—the soul that can suffer so excruciatingly and so interminably; it withers to the outward eye only; like that strange moss which can lie on a dusty shelf half a century and yet, if placed in water, grows green again." What is the tenor in the simile? the vehicle? What quality do the two parts of the simile share?

Responding in Writing

1. **Descriptive Paragraph.** In order to portray the vast and silent landscape of the prairie, Cather used sensory details—words and phrases that describe how things look, sound, smell, taste, and feel. For example, consider the following descriptive passage from the selection: ". . . and I saw again the tall, naked house on the prairie, black and grim as a wooden fortress; the black pond where I had learned to swim, its margin pitted with sun-dried cattle tracks. . . ." Write a descriptive paragraph that portrays a scene of a real or imaginary place. Use sensory details in your descriptive paragraph, emphasizing one of the senses, as Cather emphasized the sense of sight in her descriptive passages.

2. **Personal Letter.** Imagine that you are Aunt Georgiana in this story. Write a letter to your nephew, thanking him for taking you to the Wagner matinee, explaining what music used to mean in your life and why you sacrificed it. Try to explain to your nephew what two worlds battled for your heart. Refer to the Language Arts Survey, 5.2, "The Form of a Personal Letter."

Analytic Scales for Responding in Writing

Assign a score from 1 to 25 for each grading criterion below. (For more detailed evaluation, see the evaluation forms for writing, revising, and proofreading, *Assessment Portfolio,* 7.1–7.10.)

1. Descriptive Paragraph

- **Content/Unity.** The paragraph uses sensory details to portray a scene of a real or imaginary place.
- **Organization/Coherence.** The paragraph is clearly organized and connects several details to a central description.
- **Language/Style.** The paragraph uses vivid and precise nouns, verbs, and modifiers.
- **Conventions.** The paragraph avoids errors in spelling, grammar, usage, mechanics, and manuscript form.

(cont.)

Language Lab

Dangling and Misplaced Modifiers. Read the Language Arts Survey, 2.63, "Correcting Dangling or Misplaced Modifiers." Then, on your own paper, correct each of the following sentences so that its meaning is clear.

1. Carefully folded in half, he removed the rare and valuable letter from the envelope.
2. Searching for her lost necklace, the office was turned upside down.
3. To keep from feeling homesick, the cow herd occupied most of the young boy's time.
4. The young woman moved to the silent and faraway plains who wished to avoid her family's reproach.
5. Before moving to the Nebraska frontier, Boston had been Georgiana's home while studying music at the conservatory.

Vocabulary Skills

Base Words and Suffixes. Read the Language Arts Survey, 2.140, "Base Words and Prefixes," and 2.141, "Suffixes." On your own paper, underline the base word once and the suffix twice in each of the following words from "A Wagner Matinee." Next, look up each suffix in a dictionary and write two additional words that end with the same suffix.

1. reverential
2. mythology
3. martyrdom
4. glistening
5. immobility

Project

Music History. As a class, do research on some or all of the following composers mentioned in the selection: Carl Maria von Weber, Giacomo Meyerbeer, Wolfgang Amadeus Mozart, Giuseppi Verdi, and Wilhelm Richard Wagner. Divide the class into small groups and assign one composer to each group. Research the life and works of these composers. Then present the results of your research in class, combining oral reporting with pictures from books and musical recordings.

Analytic Scales for Responding in Writing (cont.)

2. Personal Letter

- **Content/Unity.** The letter uses information from the story to clearly expand on the themes expressed in the story.
- **Organization/Coherence.** The letter is clearly organized in a letter format, beginning with a statement of its intention and progressing to a clear ending.
- **Language/Style.** The letter uses vivid and precise nouns, verbs, and modifiers.
- **Conventions.** The letter avoids errors in spelling, grammar, usage, mechanics, and manuscript form.

Answers for Language Lab

Responses will vary. Possible responses are given.

1. He removed the rare and valuable letter, carefully folded in half, from the envelope.
2. She turned the office upside down searching for her lost necklace.
3. To keep from feeling homesick, the young boy occupied most of his time with the cow herd.
4. The young woman, who wished to avoid her family's reproach, moved to the silent and faraway plains.
5. Before moving to the Nebraska frontier, Georgiana lived in Boston while studying at the conservatory.

Answers for Vocabulary Skills

Responses will vary. Possible responses are given.

1. base: reverent; suffix: –ial
managerial, prejudicial
2. base: myth; suffix: –ology
psychology, methodology
3. base: martyr; suffix: –dom
kingdom, wisdom
4. base: glisten; suffix: –ing carpeting, washing
5. base: immobile; suffix: –ity
possibility, duplicity

Project Notes

▶See the worksheets and evaluation forms for projects, *Assessment Portfolio,* 7.20–7.23.

Music History. Students may want to look in their local library for information about classical composers and recordings of their works.

ADDITIONAL RESOURCES

READER'S GUIDE
- Selection Worksheet, 9.3

ASSESSMENT PORTFOLIO
- Selection Check Test, 4.9.5
- Selection Test, 4.9.6

ESSENTIAL SKILLS PRACTICE BOOKS
- *Language,* 2.32, 2.35
- *Speaking and Listening,* 3.3

ENRICHMENT ACTIVITIES

Students may wish to discuss times in their lives when they were jilted in some way, times when they had counted on others and those people let them down. How did they feel when they were jilted? Have they ever jilted other people? Is such rejection ever justified? necessary?

SUPPORT FOR LEP STUDENTS

Students may benefit from a discussion about the overall narrative and relationships between characters in the story. Because Porter implies information rather than stating it directly, the story is confusing to follow in some places. Make sure that students understand what has taken place in Granny Weatherall's past, as well as what is happening to her in the present. Additionally, discuss her relationship with John, George, and Hapsy, among other characters.

PREREADING

"The Jilting of Granny Weatherall"
by Katherine Anne Porter

ABOUT THE AUTHOR

Katherine Anne Porter (1890–1980) was born Callie Porter in Indian Creek, Texas. Her mother died when she was about two, and her father moved the family to live with his mother, where their grandmother raised them in a house that Porter recalled as "full of books" and extreme poverty. When Porter was eleven her grandmother died; when she was sixteen she married so she could leave home. It was a short union, and by 1916 she began her writing career as a reporter. She worked for newspapers in Dallas and Fort Worth, Texas, and Denver, Colorado.

She moved to Greenwich Village in New York City in 1918 and then spent the years between 1918 and 1924 living mainly in Mexico, freelancing and becoming involved in revolutionary politics. "Maria Conception," her first fiction story, was written while she was in Mexico. Published in *Century* magazine in 1922, it won her critical acclaim.

Porter lived a life filled with travel, activity, many jobs, and four marriages. She was a self-supporting woman with expensive tastes, so even though she considered herself a "serious writer" she didn't want to give up lucrative freelance offers, which had the effect of limiting her literary production. In 1931, Porter used a Guggenheim Fellowship to return to Mexico for several years. In the 1950s she lectured, and was a writer-in-residence at college campuses. *Collected Stories* (1965) received a National Book Award, the Pulitzer Prize, and the Gold Medal for fiction of the National Institute of Arts and Letters.

Among her other works are *Flowering Judas* (1929), *Noon Wine* (1937), *Pale Horse, Pale Rider* (1939), *The Leaning Tower* (1944), and her only novel, *Ship of Fools,* begun in 1931, but not published until 1962. *Ship of Fools* was made into a film and brought her a great deal of money.

ABOUT THE SELECTION

Like all of the other short stories published in the 1930 collection *Flowering Judas,* **"The Jilting of Granny Weatherall"** was first published in a magazine. While Porter's earliest audience was quite small, comprising mostly writers who read obscure magazines, it was nonetheless enthusiastic for her perfection of style and the short story form.

GOALS/OBJECTIVES

Studying this lesson will enable students to

- enjoy a short story
- describe the literary accomplishments of Katherine Anne Porter
- identify and interpret the story's theme
- explain what Granny Weatherall realizes at the end of the story
- define *irony, simile,* and *stream of consciousness* and explain how Porter uses them in the story
- write a dialogue between Granny Weatherall and the man who jilted her, and write an obituary for Granny Weatherall
- replace vague nouns with precise nouns

READER'S JOURNAL

Have you ever acted in a capricious manner toward someone? Did your impulsive act hurt his or her feelings? Why did you behave unpredictably? How would you feel if someone behaved in such a manner toward you? Write about these questions in your journal.

LANGUAGE SKILLS

Read the Language Arts Survey, 2.35, "Using Colorful Modifiers." Then identify some adjectives and adverbs that are particularly colorful in the selection and note how the modifiers add freshness and meaning to each sentence.

"The Jilting of Granny Weatherall"

KATHERINE ANNE PORTER

She flicked her wrist neatly out of Doctor Harry's pudgy careful fingers and pulled the sheet up to her chin. The brat ought to be in knee breeches. Doctoring around the country with spectacles on his nose! "Get along now, take your schoolbooks and go. There's nothing wrong with me."

Doctor Harry spread a warm paw like a cushion on her forehead where the forked green vein danced and made her eyelids twitch. "Now, now, be a good girl, and we'll have you up in no time."

"That's no way to speak to a woman nearly eighty years old just because she's down. I'd have you respect your elders, young man."

"Well, Missy, excuse me," Doctor Harry patted her cheek. "But I've got to warn you, haven't I? You're a marvel, but you must be careful or you're going to be good and sorry."

"Don't tell me what I'm going to be. I'm on my feet now, morally speaking. It's Cornelia. I had to go to bed to get rid of her."

Her bones felt loose, and floated around in her skin, and Doctor Harry floated like a balloon around the foot of the bed. He floated and pulled down his waistcoat and swung his glasses on a cord. "Well, stay where you are, it certainly can't hurt you."

"Get along and doctor your sick," said Granny Weatherall. "Leave a well woman alone. I'll call for you when I want you. . . . Where were you forty years ago when I pulled through milk leg[1] and double pneumonia? You weren't even born. Don't let Cornelia lead you on," she shouted, because Doctor Harry appeared to float up to the ceiling and out. "I pay my own bills, and I don't throw my money away on nonsense!"

She meant to wave good-bye, but it was too much trouble. Her eyes closed of themselves, it was like a dark curtain drawn around the bed. The pillow rose and floated under her, pleasant as a hammock in a light wind. She listened to the leaves rustling outside the window. No, somebody was swishing newspapers: no, Cornelia and Doctor Harry were whispering together. She leaped broad awake, thinking they whispered in her ear.

1. **milk leg.** Painful swelling of the leg

How old is Granny Weatherall? Approximately how old is Doctor Harry?

PREREADING NOTES

READER'S JOURNAL

Students may begin by brainstorming a list of experiences when they wanted to act capriciously but did not. The list may help them clarify their feelings about their behavior and how they would respond if somebody behaved in a cruel manner toward them. Ask students to consider positive and harmful results of impulsive actions.

LANGUAGE SKILLS

Some phrases that include colorful modifiers are "pudgy careful fingers," "forked green vein," and "death . . . felt clammy and unfamiliar." Students might also make a list of vivid verbs from the selection such as *flicked, danced, floated,* and *drowsed.*

▶ Additional practice is provided in *Essential Skills Practice Book: Language,* 2.35.

ANSWER TO GUIDED READING QUESTION

❶ Granny Weatherall is nearly eighty years old. Doctor Harry is approximately forty years old.

VOCABULARY FROM THE SELECTION

dwindle
jilt
rummage

LITERARY TECHNIQUE

Viewpoint. One of the hallmarks of Modernist fiction is its experimentation with different narrative **viewpoints**. The viewpoint can be understood generally as the perspective from which a narrative is written, the most common perspectives being those of a third-person omniscient

(cont.)

LITERARY TECHNIQUE (CONT.)

narrator and a first-person narrator. In this selection, Porter alters the narrative viewpoint frequently, and usually without signaling the shift to the reader. The opening sentence, for example, is written from a third-person viewpoint, while the second sentence shifts abruptly to Granny Weatherall's viewpoint. Ask students to identify other such shifts in viewpoint in this story and discuss with them the effects achieved by these changes in perspective. What do these shifts require the reader to do in his or her head? Does the first-person viewpoint make it easier for the reader to identify with Granny Weatherall? Have students rewrite some of their examples so that the viewpoint remains consistent (e.g., the second sentence might become: "She thought to herself that the brat ought to be in knee breeches"). How do the rewritten sentences change the meaning of the originals?

Answers to Guided Reading Questions

❶ Granny Weatherall needs to go through a box in the attic filled with letters tomorrow.

❷ Twenty years before, she had made farewell trips to see her children and grandchildren, thinking it would be the last time that she would see them.

Additional Questions and Activities

- Ask students why Granny Weatherall believes that Cornelia is whispering secrets. What do her reactions reveal about her character? Students may wish to discuss how they feel when they have the impression others are talking in secret about them.
- In planning for "tomorrow," Granny Weatherall thinks fondly of her daily habits, including straightening up and dusting off the lion on the bronze clock. Ask students to share some of their daily habits with the class. Why do they perform these habits? Do they take comfort from performing them? Why are habits an important part of daily life, as they are for Granny Weatherall?

"She was never like this, *never* like this!" "Well, what can we expect?" "Yes, eighty years old. . . ."

What does Granny Weatherall need to do tomorrow? ❶

Well, and what if she was? She still had ears. It was like Cornelia to whisper around doors. She always kept things secret in such a public way. She was always being tactful and kind. Cornelia was dutiful: that was the trouble with her. Dutiful and good: "So good and dutiful," said Granny, "that I'd like to spank her." She saw herself spanking Cornelia and making a fine job of it.

"What'd you say, Mother?"

Granny felt her face tying up in hard knots.

"Can't a body think, I'd like to know?"

"I thought you might want something."

"I do. I want a lot of things. First off, go away and don't whisper."

What had she done twenty years ago? ❷

She lay and drowsed, hoping in her sleep that the children would keep out and let her rest a minute. It had been a long day. Not that she was tired. It was always pleasant to snatch a minute now and then. There was always so much to be done, let me see: tomorrow.

Tomorrow was far away and there was nothing to trouble about. Things were finished somehow when the time came: thank God there was always a little margin over for peace: then a person could spread out the plan of life and tuck in the edges orderly. It was good to have everything clean and folded away, with the hair brushes and tonic bottles sitting straight on the white embroidered linen: the day started without fuss and the pantry shelves laid out with rows of jelly glasses and brown jugs and white stonechina jars with blue whirligigs and words painted on them: coffee, tea, sugar, ginger, cinnamon. allspice: and the bronze clock with the lion on top nicely dusted off. The dust that lion could collect in twenty-four hours! The box in the attic with all those letters tied up, well, she'd have to go through that tomorrow. All those letters George's letters and John's letters and her letters to them both—lying around for the children to find afterwards made her uneasy. Yes, that would be tomorrow's business. No use to let them know how silly she had been once.

While she was rummaging around she found death in her mind and it felt clammy and unfamiliar. She had spent so much time preparing for death there was no need for bringing it up again. Let it take care of itself now. When she was sixty she had felt very old, finished, and went around making farewell trips to see her children and grandchildren, with a secret in her mind: This is the very last of your mother, children! Then she made her will and came down with a long fever. That was all just a notion like a lot of other things, but it was lucky too, for she had once for all got over the idea of dying for a long time. Now she couldn't be worried. She hoped she had better sense now. Her father had lived to be one hundred and two years old and had drunk a noggin of strong hot toddy on his last birthday. He told the reporters it was his daily habit, and he owed his long life to that. He had made quite a scandal and was very pleased about it. She believed she'd just plague Cornelia a little.

"Cornelia! Cornelia!" No footsteps, but a sudden hand on her cheek. "Bless you, where have you been?"

Words for Everyday Use: **rum • mage** (rum´ij) *vt.,* search through thoroughly; ransack

Vocabulary in Context

- He knew he was going to have to rummage around in his garage in order to find what he had borrowed from his neighbor.

"Here, mother."

"Well, Cornelia, I want a noggin of hot toddy."

"Are you cold, darling?"

"I'm chilly, Cornelia. Lying in bed stops the circulation. I must have told you that a thousand times."

Well, she could just hear Cornelia telling her husband that Mother was getting a little childish and they'd have to humor her. The thing that most annoyed her was that Cornelia thought she was deaf, dumb, and blind. Little hasty glances and tiny gestures tossed around her and over her head saying, "Don't cross her, let her have her way, she's eighty years old," and she sitting there as if she lived in a thin glass cage. Sometimes Granny almost made up her mind to pack up and move back to her own house where nobody could remind her every minute that she was old. Wait, wait, Cornelia, till your own children whisper behind your back!

In her day she had kept a better house and had got more work done. She wasn't too old yet for Lydia to be driving eighty miles for advice when one of the children jumped the track, and Jimmy still dropped in and talked things over: "Now, Mammy, you've a good business head, I want to know what you think of this? . . ." Old. Cornelia couldn't change the furniture around without asking. Little things, little things! They had been so sweet when they were little. Granny wished the old days were back again with the children young and everything to be done over. It had been a hard pull, but not too much for her. When she thought of all the food she had cooked, and all the clothes she had cut and sewed, and all the gardens she had made—well, the children showed it. There they were, made out of her, and they couldn't get away from that. Sometimes she wanted to see John again and point to them and say, Well, I didn't do so badly, did I? But that would have to wait. That was for tomorrow. She used to think of him as a man, but now all the children were older than their father, and he would be a child beside her if she saw him now. It seemed strange and there was something wrong in the idea. Why, he couldn't possibly recognize her. She had fenced in a hundred acres once, digging the post holes herself and clamping the wires with just a negro boy to help. That changed a woman. John would be looking for a young woman with the peaked Spanish comb in her hair and the painted fan. Digging post holes changed a woman. Riding country roads in the winter when women had their babies was another thing: sitting up nights with sick horses and sick children and hardly ever losing one. John, I hardly ever lost one of them! John would see that in a

Photo courtesy of Digital Stock Corp.

❶ *What does Cornelia do that bothers her mother?*

❷ *Who is John? What does Granny Weatherall want him to know?*

❸ *What kinds of things has Granny done?*

Answers to Guided Reading Questions

❶ Cornelia bothers her mother by acting toward her as if she is deaf, dumb and blind.

❷ John is Granny Weatherall's dead husband. She wants him to know that she didn't do so badly in raising their children.

❸ Granny Weatherall has fenced in a hundred acres, dug post holes, ridden country roads, and sat up nights with sick horses and sick children, among other things.

Cross-curricular Activities

Social Studies. Cultural attitudes towards the elderly differ from country to country, and from era to era. For example, the United States is frequently criticized for being a country that prizes youth and has little respect for the elderly; while in Japan, the elderly traditionally command more respect than younger generations. Have students research different cultural attitudes towards the elderly and present their findings to the class. Ask them to discuss this question: How should society treat the elderly?

Additional Questions and Activities

The narrator writes of Granny Weatherall's life raising her children that "It had been a hard pull, but not too much for her." If students have read "A Wagner Matinee" by Willa Cather, ask them to compare the characters of Aunt Georgiana and Granny Weatherall. How were their lives similar? How were they different? How does each of them feel in reflecting back on their respective pasts? Students could write a comparison-and-contrast essay on this topic.

Literary Technique

Image. The author follows the phrase, "but she could not remember," with the image of "a fog" rising "over the valley." Ask students to discuss the symbolic meaning of this image. How does it function as a metaphorical representation of Granny Weatherall's state of mind?

Additional Questions and Activities

Granny Weatherall recalls some of the sayings she repeated to her children, such as "Don't let good things rot for want of using" and "You waste life when you waste good food." Ask students to offer examples of some of the maxims, or sayings, that they hear often in their families, and write these phrases on the board. Why do parents repeat these maxims? What role do they play in students' lives? Why does Granny Weatherall remember these sayings at this point in the story?

Cross-curricular Activities

Arts and Humanities. Porter portrays Granny Weatherall's encounter with death using the image of a cart with a man driving it. Have students compare this to the image of Death in Emily Dickinson's "Because I could not stop for Death." Ask them to research other ways in which death has been portrayed in art and literature in different countries in various time periods. Students should make a list of the images and metaphors they encounter and bring to class pictures with symbolic representations of death. What are the most common ways of portraying death? the most unusual? Why is Porter's image particularly effective for the character of Granny Weatherall?

minute, that would be something he could understand, she wouldn't have to explain anything!

It made her feel like rolling up her sleeves and putting the whole place to rights again. No matter if Cornelia was determined to be everywhere at once, there were a great many things left undone on this place. She would start tomorrow and do them. It was good to be strong enough for everything, even if all you made melted and changed and slipped under your hands, so that by the time you finished you almost forgot what you were working for. What was it I set out to do? she asked herself intently, but she could not remember. A fog rose over the valley, she saw it marching across the creek swallowing the trees and moving up the hill like an army of ghosts. Soon it would be at the near edge of the orchard, and then it was time to go in and light the lamps. Come in, children, don't stay out in the night air.

Lighting the lamps had been beautiful. The children huddled up to her and breathed like little calves waiting at the bars in the twilight. Their eyes followed the match and watched the flame rise and settle in a blue curve, then they moved away from her. The lamp was lit, they didn't have to be scared and hang on to mother any more. Never, never, never more. God, for all my life I thank Thee. Without Thee, my God, I could never have done it. Hail Mary, full of grace.

I want you to pick all the fruit this year and see that nothing is wasted. There's always someone who can use it. Don't let good things rot for want of using. You waste life when you waste good food. Don't let things get lost. It's bitter to lose things. Now, don't let me get to thinking, not when I am tired and taking a little nap before supper. . . .

The pillow rose about her shoulders and pressed against her heart and the memory was being squeezed out of it: oh, push down the pillow, somebody: it would smother her if she tried to hold it. Such a fresh breeze blowing and such a green day with no threats in it. But he had not come, just the same. What does a woman do when she has put on the white veil and set out the white cake for a man and he doesn't come? She tried to remember. No, I swear he never harmed me but in that. He never harmed me but in that . . . and what if he did? There was the day, the day, but a whirl of dark, smoke rose and covered it, crept up and over into the bright field where everything was planted so carefully in orderly rows. That was hell, she knew hell when she saw it. For sixty years she had prayed against remembering him and against losing her soul in the deep pit of hell, and now the two things were mingled in one and the thought of him was a smoky cloud from hell that moved and crept in her head when she had just got rid of Doctor Harry and was trying to rest a minute. Wounded vanity, Ellen, said a sharp voice in the top of her mind. Don't let your wounded vanity get the upper hand of you. Plenty of girls get jilted. You were jilted, weren't you? Then stand up to it. Her eyelids wavered and let in streamers of blue-gray light like tissue paper over her eyes. She must get up and pull the shades down or she'd never sleep.

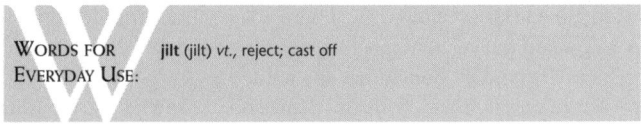

Words for Everyday Use: **jilt** (jilt) *vt.*, reject; cast off

Vocabulary in Context

- Carol jilted John at the altar because she realized she did not really love him.

She was in bed again and the shades were not down. How could that happen? Better turn over, hide from the light, sleeping in the light gave you nightmares. "Mother, how do you feel now?" and a stinging wetness on her forehead. But I don't like having my face washed in cold water!

Hapsy? George? Lydia? Jimmy? No, Cornelia, and her features were swollen and full of little puddles. "They're coming, darling, they'll all be here soon." Go wash your face, child, you look funny.

Instead of obeying, Cornelia knelt down and put her head on the pillow. She seemed to be talking but there was no sound. "Well, are you tongue-tied? Whose birthday is it? Are you going to give a party?"

Cornelia's mouth moved urgently in strange shapes. "Don't do that, you bother me, daughter."

"Oh, no, Mother. Oh, no. . . ."

Nonsense. It was strange about children. They disputed your every word. "No what, Cornelia?"

"Here's Doctor Harry."

"I won't see that boy again. He just left five minutes ago."

"That was this morning, Mother. It's night now. Here's the nurse."

"This is Doctor Harry, Mrs. Weatherall. I never saw you look so young and happy!"

"Ah, I'll never be young again—but I'd be happy if they'd let me lie in peace and get rested."

She thought she spoke up loudly, but no one answered. A warm weight on her forehead, a warm bracelet on her wrist, and a breeze went on whispering, trying to tell her something. A shuffle of leaves in the everlasting hand of God, He blew on them and they danced and rattled. "Mother, don't mind, we're going to give you a little hypodermic."[2] "Look here, daughter, how do ants get in this bed? I saw sugar ants yesterday." Did you send for Hapsy too?

It was Hapsy she really wanted. She had to go a long way back through a great many rooms to find Hapsy standing with a baby on her arm. She seemed to herself to be Hapsy also, and the baby on Hapsy's arm was Hapsy and himself and herself, all at once, and there was no surprise in the meeting. Then Hapsy melted from within and turned flimsy as gray gauze and the baby was a gauzy shadow, and Hapsy came up close and said. "I thought you'd never come," and looked at her very searchingly and said, "You haven't changed a bit!" They leaned forward to kiss, when Cornelia began whispering from a long way off. "Oh, is there anything you want to tell me? Is there anything I can do for you?"

❶ *Who is Hapsy? What are Granny Weatherall's feelings for her? What happened to her?*

Yes, she had changed her mind after sixty years and she would like to see George. I want you to find George. Find him and be sure to tell him I forgot him. I want him to know I had my husband just the same and my children and my house like any other woman. A good house too and a good husband that I loved and fine children out of him. Better than I hoped for even. Tell him I was given back everything he took away and more. Oh, no, oh, God, no, there was something else besides the house and the man and the children. Oh, surely they were not all? What was it? Something not given back. . . . Her breath crowded down under her ribs and grew into a monstrous frightening shape with cutting edges; it bored up into her head, and the agony was unbelievable: Yes, John, get the Doctor now, no more talk, my time has come.

❷ *Has Granny Weatherall's life been complete?*

When this one was born it should be the last. The last. It should have been born first, for it was the one she had truly wanted. Everything came in good time. Nothing left out, left over. She was

2. **hypodermic.** Injection

Answers to Guided Reading Questions

❶ Hapsy is Granny Weatherall's other daughter. Granny Weatherall wants to see her very much. Hapsy is dead.

❷ Granny Weatherall feels that her life has not been complete because George, the man who jilted her, took something from her that she has not been able to replace.

Literary Technique

Synaesthesia is a figure of speech or an expression that combines images related to two or more senses, such as "a heavy silence." On this page, the narrator employs synaesthesia when she writes that Granny Weatherall's "breath crowded under her ribs and grew into a monstrous frightening shape with cutting edges." Ask students to make a list of other instances of synaesthesia in this story.

Answer to Guided Reading Question

❶ On the day she was jilted, Father Connolly came to Granny Weatherall's aid.

Analytic Scales for Responding in Writing

Assign a score from 1 to 25 for each grading criterion below. (For more detailed evaluation, see the evaluation forms for writing, revising, and proofreading, *Assessment Portfolio,* 7.1–7.10.)

1. Dialogue

- **Content/Unity.** The dialogue relates an encounter between two significant characters in the story.
- **Organization/Coherence.** The dialogue is clearly organized and connects several ideas to a central theme.
- **Language/Style.** The dialogue uses vivid and precise nouns, verbs, and modifiers.
- **Conventions.** The dialogue avoids errors in spelling, grammar, usage, mechanics, and manuscript form.

2. Obituary

- **Content/Unity.** The obituary relates what was unique or characteristic about the story's main character.
- **Organization/Coherence.** The obituary is clearly organized and connects several ideas to a central theme.
- **Language/Style.** The obituary uses vivid and precise nouns, verbs, and modifiers.
- **Conventions.** The obituary avoids errors in spelling, grammar, usage, mechanics, and manuscript form.

strong, in three days she would be as well as ever. Better. A woman needed milk in her to have her full health.

"Mother, do you hear me?"

"I've been telling you—"

"Mother, Father Connolly's here."

"I went to Holy Communion only last week. Tell him I'm not so sinful as all that."

"Father just wants to speak to you."

He could speak as much as he pleased. It was like him to drop in and inquire about her soul as if it were a teething baby, and then stay on for a cup of tea and a round of cards and gossip. He always had a funny story of some sort, usually about an Irishman who made his little mistakes and confessed them, and the point lay in some absurd thing he would blurt out in the confessional showing his struggles between native piety and original sin. Granny felt easy about her soul. Cornelia, where are your manners? Give Father Connolly a chair. She had her secret comfortable understanding with a few favorite saints who cleared a straight road to God for her. All as surely signed and sealed as the papers for the new Forty Acres. Forever . . . heirs and assigns[3] forever. Since the day the wedding cake was not cut, but thrown out and wasted. The whole bottom dropped out of the world, and there she was blind and sweating with nothing under her feet and the walls falling away. His hand had caught her under the breast, she had not fallen, there was the freshly polished floor with the green rug on it, just as before. He had cursed like a sailor's parrot and said, "I'll kill him for you." Don't lay a hand on him, for my sake leave something to God. "Now, Ellen, you must believe what I tell you. . . ."

Who came to her aid on the day she was jilted? ❶

So there was nothing, nothing to worry about any more, except sometimes in the night one of the children screamed in a nightmare, and they both hustled out shaking and hunting for the matches and calling, "There, wait a minute, here we are!" John, get the doctor now. Hapsy's time has come. But there was Hapsy standing by the bed in a white cap. "Cornelia. tell Hapsy to take off her cap. I can't see her plain."

Her eyes opened very wide and the room stood out like a picture she had seen somewhere. Dark colors with the shadows rising towards the ceiling in long angles. The tall black dresser gleamed with nothing on it but John's picture, enlarged from a little one, with John's eyes very black when they should have been blue. You never saw him, so how do you know how he looked? But the man insisted the copy was perfect, it was very rich and handsome. For a picture, yes, but it's not my husband. The table by the bed had a linen cover and a candle and a crucifix. The light was blue from Cornelia's silk lampshades. No sort of light at all, just frippery. You had to live forty years with kerosene lamps to appreciate honest electricity. She felt very strong and she saw Doctor Harry with a rosy nimbus around him.

"You look like a saint, Doctor Harry, and I vow that's as near as you'll ever come to it."

"She's saying something."

"I heard you, Cornelia. What's all this carrying on?"

"Father Connolly's saying—"

Cornelia's voice staggered and bumped like a cart in a bad road. It rounded corners and turned back again and arrived nowhere. Granny stepped up in the cart very lightly and reached for the reins, but a man sat beside her and she knew him by his hands, driving the cart. She did not look in his face, for she knew without seeing, but looked instead down the road where the

3. **assigns.** People to whom property is transferred

trees leaned over and bowed to each other and a thousand birds were singing a Mass. She felt like singing too, but she put her hand in the bosom of her dress and pulled out a rosary, and Father Connolly murmured Latin in a very solemn voice and tickled her feet.[4] My God, will you stop that nonsense? I'm a married woman. What if he did run away and leave me to face the priest by myself? I found another a whole world better. I wouldn't have exchanged my husband for anybody except St. Michael himself, and you may tell him that for me with a thank you in the bargain.

Light flashed on her closed eyelids, and a deep roaring shook her. Cornelia, is that lightning? I hear thunder. There's going to be a storm. Close all the windows. Call the children in. "Mother, here we are, all of us." "Is that you, Hapsy?" "Oh, no, I'm Lydia. We drove as fast as we could." Their faces drifted above her, drifted away. The rosary fell out of her hands and Lydia put it back. Jimmy tried to help, their hands fumbled together, and Granny closed two fingers around Jimmy's thumb. Beads wouldn't do, it must be something alive. She was so amazed her thoughts ran round and round. So, my dear Lord, this is my death and I wasn't even thinking about it. My children have come to see me die. But I can't, it's not time. Oh, I always hated surprises. I wanted to give Cornelia the amethyst set—Cornelia, you're to have the amethyst set, but Hapsy's to wear it when she wants, and, Doctor Harry, do shut up. Nobody sent for you. Oh, my dear Lord, do wait a minute. I meant to do something about the Forty Acres, Jimmy doesn't need it and Lydia will later on, with that worthless husband of hers. I meant to finish the altar cloth and send six bottles of wine to Sister Borgia for her dyspepsia. I want to send six bottles of wine to Sister Borgia, Father Connolly, now don't let me forget .

Cornelia's voice made short turns and tilted over and crashed. "Oh, Mother, oh, Mother, oh Mother. . . ."

"I'm not going, Cornelia. I'm taken by surprise. I can't go."

You'll see Hapsy again. What about her? "I thought you'd never come." Granny made a long journey outward, looking for Hapsy. What if I don't find her? What then? Her heart sank down and down, there was no bottom to death, she couldn't come to the end of it. The blue light from Cornelia's lampshade drew into a tiny point in the center of her brain, it flickered and winked like an eye, quietly it fluttered and dwindled. Granny lay curled down within herself, amazed and watchful, staring at the point of light that was herself: her body was now only a deeper mass of shadow in an endless darkness and this darkness would curl around the light and swallow it up. God, give a sign!

For the second time there was no sign. Again no bridegroom and the priest in the house. She could not remember any other sorrow because this grief wiped them all away. Oh, no, there's nothing more cruel than this—I'll never forgive it. She stretched herself with a deep breath and blew out the light. ■

❶ *Is Granny Weatherall ready to die?*

❷ *Who jilts Granny Weatherall?*

4. **murmured . . . feet.** Administered the last rites, a sacrament for a person close to death

WORDS FOR EVERYDAY USE: **dwin •dle** (dwin´dəl) *vt.,* languish; fade

ANSWERS TO GUIDED READING QUESTIONS

❶ Granny Weatherall is not ready to die, because as her children come to her bedside, she realizes that there are things she still needs to do.

❷ Granny Weatherall is jilted by God at the end of the story.

ADDITIONAL QUESTIONS AND ACTIVITIES

In the final two paragraphs of this story, Porter describes the death of Granny Weatherall. Ask students to compare this scene with the scene from Jack London's "To Build a Fire" in which the man dies in the snow (pages 626–627). What similarities do these two descrip-tions share? In what ways is the act of dying described differently?

ANSWERS TO SELECTION CHECK TEST 4.9.5

EX. Who takes care of Granny Weatherall on her deathbed?
Her daughter Cornelia takes care of her.

1. What does Granny Weatherall tell the doctor about her health?
She tells him that there's nothing wrong with her.

2. Why does Granny Weatherall wish to get rid of her letters?
She does not want her children to see how silly she had once been.

3. Why would Granny Weatherall sometimes like to move back to her own house?
She would like to move back, so that she would not be reminded by her children that she was old.

4. What is Granny Weatherall's reaction when Doctor Harry reappears?
She thinks that he had left just five minutes before.

5. Why does Father Connolly visit Granny Weatherall?
He comes to administer her last rites.

VOCABULARY IN CONTEXT

- We noticed how the light dwindled at sunset until there was none left and we were standing in darkness.

RESPONDING TO THE SELECTION

Ask students to recall a time when they felt rejected by someone. What kinds of feelings did they experience? How are these feelings similar to or different from the feelings expressed by Granny Weatherall about George?

ANSWERS FOR REVIEWING THE SELECTION

RECALLING

1. Granny Weatherall says she has to go to bed to get rid of Cornelia, her daughter.

2. When Granny Weatherall was sixty, she prepared herself for death by paying farewell visits to all of her children and grandchildren.

3. What Granny Weatherall remembers most clearly about her wedding day is being jilted by George, her betrothed, at the altar.

4. At the end of the story, Granny Weatherall realizes that the experience of dying is similar to the experience of being left at the altar.

INTERPRETING

Responses will vary. Possible responses are given.

5. Granny Weatherall might have been described as strong, stubborn, hardworking, and able to do things that other women of her time did not attempt or want to do before she became ill.

6. Granny Weatherall does not worry about death because "she had a comfortable understanding with a few favorite saints who had cleared a straight road to God for her."

7. Granny Weatherall mingles the thought of the bridegroom with the thought of losing her soul in hell because of her illness. Her mind is weak, and she feels that to remember what George did to her will damn her soul to hell.

8. Granny Weatherall will never forgive being jilted a second time by God.

(cont.)

Responding to the Selection

Imagine that you are Granny Weatherall remembering George, the bridegroom who jilted her on their wedding day. After sixty years, how would you feel about him? Would you be able to forgive him? Why, or why not? What would you want him to know about your life? Write a letter to George in your journal expressing your feelings about his action years ago.

Reviewing the Selection

RECALLING

1. What explanation for being in bed does Granny Weatherall give to the doctor?
2. How had Granny Weatherall prepared herself for death when she was sixty years old?
3. What does Granny Weatherall remember most about her wedding day?
4. What does Granny Weatherall realize at the end of the story?

INTERPRETING

5. What traits might describe Granny Weatherall before she became ill?
6. Why doesn't Granny Weatherall worry now about death?
7. Why does Granny Weatherall mingle the thought of the bridegroom with the thought of losing her soul in hell?
8. What will Granny Weatherall never forgive?

SYNTHESIZING

9. How is Granny Weatherall's name appropriate for her character?
10. How is Granny Weatherall jilted a second time?

Understanding Literature (Questions for Discussion)

1. **Irony. Irony** is a difference between appearance and reality. In **irony of situation**, one of the types of irony, an event occurs that violates the expectations of the characters, the reader, or the audience. What are two major examples of irony of situation in this short story? How are the expectations of Granny Weatherall violated in each case?

2. **Simile.** A **simile** is a comparison using like or as. A type of metaphor, a simile can be analyzed into two parts, the *tenor* (or object being described) and the *vehicle* (or object being used in the description). In the simile from the selection "Her eyes closed of themselves, it was like a dark curtain drawn around the bed," the tenor is "eyes closed"

ANSWERS FOR REVIEWING THE SELECTION (CONT.)

SYNTHESIZING

Responses will vary. Possible responses are given.

9. Granny Weatherall's name is appropriate for the character in that she has weathered all of the difficult things that life has thrown at her, from tragedies to crushing disappointments, and survived for eighty years.

10. Granny Weatherall is jilted a second time by God. The circumstances are similar to the first time—no bridegroom and a priest in the house—but the sorrow is even greater, because there is no sign from him after her death. Because she believed that her religion had allowed her to clear a "straight path" to God after her death, she finds this jilting to be even more cruel than the first one.

and the vehicle is "dark curtain." They can be compared because they share some quality, in this case, darkness. Identify another simile from the selection, analyzing the two parts and noting what quality they share.

3. **Stream-of-Consciousness Writing. Stream-of-consciousness writing** is literary work that attempts to render the flow of feelings, thoughts, and impressions within the minds of characters. Identify a passage in the selection that uses stream-of-consciousness writing to reveal the feelings, thoughts, or impressions within Granny Weatherall's mind. What effect is created in the passage by this type of writing?

Responding in Writing

1. **Dialogue.** Write an imaginary dialogue between Granny Weatherall and George, the bridegroom who jilted her on their wedding day, who meet again after death. Have them discuss what happened on their wedding day, including an explanation from George for his behavior.

2. **Obituary.** Write an obituary for Granny Weatherall, including more than simply important facts noted about her life in the selection. Try to include details that will communicate to your readers what was unique or characteristic about Granny Weatherall.

Language Lab

Precise Nouns. Read the Language Arts Survey, 2.32, on "Using Precise Nouns." Then revise each of the sentences below by replacing the vague nouns with precise nouns.

1. The toys on the floor reminded her of the children.
2. Every fall, she lined the shelves with jars of food and spices.
3. Illnesses plagued the children throughout the horrible winter.
4. After finishing the evening chores, she came into the house and fixed dinner.
5. Years ago, the jilted bride was left behind with the promising vestiges of the day.

Speaking and Listening Skills

Nonverbal Communication. Read the Language Arts Survey, 3.3, "Elements of Nonverbal Communication." Then describe how each emotion listed below might be communicated through eye contact, facial expressions, gestures, body language, or proximity.

1. bewilderment
2. shock
3. determination
4. surprise
5. sorrow

Answers for Understanding Literature

► See the evaluation forms for discussion, active listening, and oral communication, *Assessment Portfolio,* 7.11–7.14.

Responses will vary. Possible responses are given.

1. Irony. Two major examples of irony of situation in the story are Granny Weatherall preparing for her death at age 60 but not being ready for it when it comes at age 80, and dying in a manner similar to the jilting she experienced 60 years before. In the first case, her expectations are violated because she thought she would never see her children again and then they all rush to her bedside, while in the second case, she feels violated because there is no sign from God that death has come.

2. Simile. Another simile would be, "A fog rose over the valley, she saw it marching across the creek and moving up the hill like an army of ghosts." The tenor is "fog" and the vehicle is "army of ghosts." The quality they share that is similar is whiteness.

3. Stream-of-Consciousness Writing. A stream of consciousness section of the story is when Granny Weatherall is thinking about Hapsy. The effect that is created is jarring. It allows the writer to move back and forth in time, mixing the past with the present, and to convince the reader that Granny Weatherall is close to dying and not thinking clearly.

Analytic Scales for Responding in Writing

Grading scales appear on page 646.

Answers for Speaking and Listening Skills

Responses will vary. Possible responses are given.

1. Bewilderment: puzzled face or hands thrown up in confusion
2. Shock: sudden stillness or an agape mouth
3. Determination: set jaw and an intensity of eye contact
4. Surprise: backward jump or wide eyes and an agape mouth
5. Sorrow: tears, lack of eye contact, and drooping shoulders

Answers for Language Lab

Responses will vary. Possible responses are given.

1. The pogo stick and the jump rope on the floor reminded her of the children.
2. Every fall, she lined the shelves with jars of applesauce, canned pumpkin, cinnamon, and cloves.
3. Colds and flus plagued the children throughout the horrible winter.
4. After finishing raking the yard, she came into the house and fixed a hearty stew.
5. Years ago, the jilted bride was left behind with her dress, sprays of flowers, and the three-tiered cake.

ADDITIONAL RESOURCES

READER'S GUIDE
- Selection Worksheet, 9.4

ASSESSMENT PORTFOLIO
- Selection Check Test, 4.9.7
- Selection Test, 4.9.8

ESSENTIAL SKILLS PRACTICE BOOKS
- *Speaking and Listening,* 3.4

ENRICHMENT ACTIVITIES

Students could find a coffee shop, a café, or a restaurant where they can sit for an hour alone. Suggest that they take their journals with them and write about what it is like to sit alone in such a locale. Does the presence of other people make them feel more or less alone? Do they enjoy the experience? Why, or why not?

SUPPORT FOR LEP STUDENTS

Students may have trouble with some of the Spanish words Hemingway uses. Point out that one of the reasons for using them is to give the setting and characters a more authentic feel. Encourage them to share phrases or images from their cultures that describe a café-style atmosphere.

PREREADING

"A Clean, Well-Lighted Place"
by Ernest Hemingway

ABOUT THE AUTHOR

Ernest Hemingway (1899–1961) was born and raised in Oak Park, Illinois, one of six children. His father was a successful doctor, his mother a music teacher. Hemingway began his writing career as a reporter at the *Kansas City Star* after high school. When World War I broke out and an eye problem prevented him from joining the United States army, he served as an ambulance driver and infantry soldier with the Italian army.

After the war he returned to Europe as a journalist and also began his serious writing career. There he was part of the large community of expatriate artists and writers—Gertrude Stein, Sherwood Anderson, Ezra Pound, and F. Scott Fitzgerald among others.

He was seriously injured in a 1953 plane crash in Africa and never fully recovered his mental health or productivity. He committed suicide in 1961 in Idaho after years of suffering from despair and paranoia.

Hemingway won a Pulitzer Prize in 1953 for *The Old Man and the Sea* (1952) and a Nobel Prize for literature in 1954. He was a prolific writer whose works include *The Sun Also Rises* (1926), *A Farewell to Arms* (1929), *The Snows of Kilimanjaro* (1936), *To Have and Have Not* (1937), *The Fifth Column* (play, 1938), *For Whom the Bell Tolls* (1940), *A Moveable Feast* (posthumously in 1964), and *Islands in the Stream* (posthumously in 1970).

ABOUT THE SELECTION

Between 1923 and 1933, Hemingway wrote all of his major short stories, including **"A Clean, Well-Lighted Place,"** which was published in the 1933 collection *Winner Take Nothing.* Five years later, *The Fifth Column* and the *First Forty-Nine Stories,* which compiled three collections—*In Our Time, Men Without Women,* and *Winner Take Nothing*—established Hemingway as one of the most admired writers of short fiction. Written with Hemingway's characteristic spare prose, "A Clean, Well-Lighted Place" unfolds primarily through dialogue. In the selection, two waiters at a Spanish café discuss one of their regular clients, an elderly man who likes to sit late at night at a table on the café terrace. A careful listener, Hemingway vitalized the writing of dialogue by stripping the verbal exchange to the essentials, producing the illusion of actual speech.

GOALS/OBJECTIVES

Studying this lesson will enable students to

- appreciate Hemingway's spare prose style
- describe the literary accomplishments of Ernest Hemingway
- define *characterization, dialogue,* and *internal monologue* and explain how they are used in the story
- identify what the old waiter reveals about himself in the story
- write a character sketch of an imaginary person and a dialogue between that character and a real or imagined person

READER'S JOURNAL

Have you ever felt lonely? Do you have a special place you like to go when you are feeling this way? What comfort does this special place offer you? Write about the place in your journal.

SPEAKING AND LISTENING SKILLS

Read the Language Arts Survey, 3.4, "Active Listening." Then identify some of the word repetitions in the dialogue between the two waiters that signal feedback or understanding. Identify those places in the dialogue where you think a statement is misunderstood.

"A Clean, Well-Lighted Place"

ERNEST HEMINGWAY

It was late and every one had left the café except an old man who sat in the shadow the leaves of the tree made against the electric light. In the day time the street was dusty, but at night the dew settled the dust and the old man liked to sit late because he was deaf and now at night it was quiet and he felt the difference. The two waiters inside the café knew that the old man was a little drunk, and while he was a good client they knew that if he became too drunk he would leave without paying, so they kept watch on him.

"Last week he tried to commit suicide," one waiter said.

"Why?"

"He was in despair."

"What about?"

"Nothing."

"How do you know it was nothing?"

"He has plenty of money."

They sat together at a table that was close against the wall near the door of the café and looked at the terrace where the tables were all empty except where the old man sat in the shadow of the leaves of the tree that moved slightly in the wind. A girl and a soldier went by in the street. The street light shone on the brass number on his collar. The girl wore no head covering and hurried beside him.

"The guard will pick him up," one waiter said.

"What does it matter if he gets what he's after?"

"He had better get off the street now. The guard will get him. They went by five minutes ago."

The old man sitting in the shadow rapped on his saucer with his glass. The younger waiter went over to him.

"What do you want?"

The old man looked at him. "Another brandy," he said.

"You'll be drunk," the waiter said. The old man looked at him. The waiter went away.

"He'll stay all night," he said to his colleague. "I'm sleepy now. I never get into bed before three o'clock. He should have killed himself last week."

The waiter took the brandy bottle and another saucer from the counter inside the

❶ *What does the waiter think is a valid reason for despair?*

PREREADING NOTES

READER'S JOURNAL

Students might also write about the differences between loneliness and solitude. Is loneliness necessarily a bad thing? Have students ever comforted someone who felt lonely? If so, what did they do? Their writing might give them ideas for their own stories later.

SPEAKING AND LISTENING SKILLS

Examples of repetition that signal feedback are "I have a wife waiting in bed for me." "He had a wife once too." "A wife would be no good to him now." "You can't tell. He might be better with a wife." The younger waiter thinks of himself and his wife. He does not understand the older waiter's point that the old man was once like him. "You have everything." "You have everything I have." The younger waiter does not understand the emptiness the older waiter feels.

ANSWER TO GUIDED READING QUESTION

❶ The waiter thinks that nothing is a valid reason for despair.

LITERARY TECHNIQUE

Motif. A **motif** is one of the dominant ideas or themes in a piece of literature, which may take the form of a character, a recurring image, or a particular verbal construction. Hemingway introduces two important motifs in the opening sentences, images of light versus shadow and cleanliness versus dirtiness. Ask students to identify other references to these motifs throughout the story. Have them discuss how Hemingway uses these motifs to enhance characterization. What do they inform the reader about the characters?

Answers to Guided Reading Questions

❶ The waiter tells the old man he should have killed himself last week. He says this because the man is deaf, and the waiter wants to go home.

❷ The man attempted suicide by hanging. His niece rescued him. The reason he tried to kill himself was fear for his soul.

❸ The waiters agree that drinking at home is not the same as drinking in a café.

Literary Technique

Characterization and Dialogue. One of the primary methods of characterization in this selection is the use of **dialogue.** Much of the dialogue is offered without indication of how the words are spoken or what kind of response they evoke. Ask students to examine closely the extended conversation on this page between the two waiters about the old man. What does the reader learn indirectly about each of the waiters?

Additional Questions and Activities

The young waiter says, "An old man is a nasty thing." Have students compare the portrayal of old age in Hemingway's story with that in "The Jilting of Granny Weatherall." Is old age viewed with compassion and respect? Do the two waiters have the same opinion of old age as Cornelia in Porter's story?

café and marched out to the old man's table. He put down the saucer and poured the glass full of brandy.

What does the waiter say to the old man? Why? ❶

"You should have killed yourself last week," he said to the deaf man. The old man motioned with his finger. "A little more," he said. The waiter poured on into the glass so that the brandy slopped over and ran down the stem into the top saucer of the pile. "Thank you," the old man said. The waiter took the bottle back inside the café. He sat down at the table with his colleague again.

"He's drunk now," he said.

"He's drunk every night."

"What did he want to kill himself for?"

"How should I know."

"How did he do it?"

How did the old man attempt suicide? Who rescued him? Why? ❷

"He hung himself with a rope."

"Who cut him down?"

"His niece."

"Why did they do it?"

"Fear for his soul."

"How much money has he got?"

"He's got plenty."

"He must be eighty years old."

"Anyway I should say he was eighty."

"I wish he would go home. I never get to bed before three o'clock. What kind of hour is that to go to bed?"

"He stays up because he likes it."

On what do the two waiters agree? ❸

"He's lonely. I'm not lonely. I have a wife waiting in bed for me."

"He had a wife once too."

"A wife would be no good to him now."

"You can't tell. He might be better with a wife."

"His niece looks after him."

"I know. You said she cut him down."

"I wouldn't want to be that old. An old man is a nasty thing."

"Not always. This old man is clean. He drinks without spilling. Even now, drunk. Look at him."

"I don't want to look at him. I wish he would go home. He has no regard for those who must work."

The old man looked from his glass across the square, then over at the waiters.

"Another brandy," he said, pointing to his glass. The waiter who was in a hurry came over.

"Finished," he said, speaking with that omission of syntax stupid people employ when talking to drunken people or foreigners. "No more tonight. Close now."

"Another," said the old man.

"No. Finished." The waiter wiped the edge of the table with a towel and shook his head.

The old man stood up, slowly counted the saucers, took a leather coin purse from his pocket and paid for the drinks, leaving half a peseta[1] tip.

The waiter watched him go down the street, a very old man walking unsteadily but with dignity.

"Why didn't you let him stay and drink?" the unhurried waiter asked. They were putting up the shutters. "It is not half past two."

"I want to go home to bed."

"What is an hour?"

"More to me than to him."

"An hour is the same."

"You talk like an old man yourself. He can buy a bottle and drink at home."

"It's not the same."

"No, it is not," agreed the waiter with a wife. He did not wish to be unjust. He was only in a hurry.

"And you? You have no fear of going home before your usual hour?"

"Are you trying to insult me?"

"No, hombre,[2] only to make a joke."

"No," the waiter who was in a hurry said, rising from pulling down the metal

1. **peseta.** Spanish currency
2. **hombre.** Man

Moulin de la Galette. *Pierre-Auguste Renoir*

shutters. "I have confidence. I am all confidence."

"You have youth, confidence, and a job," the older waiter said. "You have everything."

"And what do you lack?"

"Everything but work."

"You have everything I have."

"No. I have never had confidence and I am not young."

"Come on. Stop talking nonsense and lock up."

"I am of those who like to stay late at the café," the older waiter said. "With all those who do not want to go to bed. With all those who need a light for the night."

"I want to go home and into bed."

"We are of two different kinds," the older waiter said. He was now dressed to go home. "It is not only a question of youth and confidence although those things are very beautiful. Each night I am reluctant to close up because there may be some one who needs the café."

"Hombre, there are bodegas[3] open all night long."

"You do not understand. This is a clean and pleasant café. It is well lighted. The light is very good and also, now, there are shadows of the leaves."

"Good night," said the younger waiter.

"Good night," the other said. Turning off the electric light he continued the conversation with himself. It is the light of course but it is necessary that the place be clean and pleasant. You do not want music. Certainly you do not want music. Nor can you stand before a bar with dignity although that is all that is provided for these hours. What did he fear? It was not fear or dread. It was a nothing that he knew too well. It was all a nothing and a man was nothing too. It was only that and light was all it needed and a certain cleanness and order. Some lived in it and never felt it but he knew it all was nada[4] y pues nada y nada y pues nada. Our nada who art in nada, nada be thy name thy kingdom nada thy will be nada in nada as it is in nada. Give us this nada our daily nada

3. **bodegas.** Bars; taverns
4. **nada.** Nothing

❶ *How would you describe the older waiter's outlook on life?*

❷ *With whom does the older waiter sympathize?*

Answers to Guided Reading Questions

❶ The older waiter's outlook on life could be described as fearful, pessimistic, and nihilistic.

❷ The older waiter sympathizes with people who need to sit and drink in the café late at night.

Cross-curricular Activities

Social Studies. Have students find a copy of the Lord's Prayer and the Hail Mary, which the older waiter recites while substituting "nada" throughout both prayers. In addition, have them research the uses of these prayers. When are they normally spoken? Ask them to compare the original versions with the older waiter's versions. How does the waiter's use of "nada" alter the meaning of these prayers? What emotions does the waiter express by rewording these prayers as he does?

Answers to Selection Check Test 4.9.7

EX. What is the time and setting of this story?

It takes place in a café late at night.

1. Why are the waiters watching the old man?

They are afraid he might get drunk and leave without paying.

2. How does the waiter keep track of the number of drinks he has served?

He brings a new saucer every time he pours a drink.

3. Who takes care of the old man?

He has a niece who cares for him.

4. Why does the older waiter believe the old man likes the café?

It is a clean, well-lighted place.

5. Where does the older waiter go after closing the café?

He goes to a bar for a drink.

RESPONDING TO THE SELECTION

Ask students to recall a time when they had to wait for someone else. What kinds of feelings did they experience? Have they ever had somebody waiting for them? If so, how are both feelings similar? How are they different?

ANSWERS FOR REVIEWING THE SELECTION

RECALLING

1. One waiter tells the other that the old man tried to commit suicide the previous week.

2. The reason the waiter gives for not letting the old man stay in the café is that he is tired and wants to close so he can go home.

3. The older waiter thinks he lacks confidence and youth.

4. The older waiter thinks that the reason he cannot sleep is insomnia.

INTERPRETING

Responses will vary. Possible responses are given.

5. The attitudes the waiter expresses about the old man's despair have to do with money. He terms the despair to be over "nothing" because the old man has plenty of money, the attitude being that money can buy happiness and that the man has no reason to feel despair if he has enough money.

6. The waiter tells the older waiter that he talks like an old man because the older waiter criticizes the decision to close the café and kick the old man out. Like the old man, the older waiter does not want to leave and is not concerned about spending another hour there the way the younger waiter is.

7. The older waiter is reluctant to close the café because he cannot sleep.

8. The "nothing" that the older waiter knows too well is his life and human experience in general. It is why the light is so important to him.

SYNTHESIZING

Responses will vary. Possible responses are given.

(cont.)

and nada us our nada as we nada our nadas and nada us not into nada but deliver us from nada; pues nada. Hail nothing full of nothing, nothing is with thee.[5] He smiled and stood before a bar with a shining steam pressure coffee machine.

"What's yours?" asked the barman.

"Nada."

"Otro loco mas,"[6] said the barman and turned away.

"A little cup," said the waiter.

The barman poured it for him.

"The light is very bright and pleasant but the bar is unpolished," the waiter said.

The barman looked at him but did not answer. It was too late at night for conversation.

"You want another copita?"[7] the barman asked.

"No, thank you," said the waiter and went out. He disliked bars and bodegas. A clean, well-lighted café was a very different thing. Now, without thinking further, he would go home to his room. He would lie in the bed and finally, with daylight, he would go to sleep. After all, he said to himself, it is probably only insomnia. Many must have it. ■

5. **Our nada . . . thee.** The waiter is replacing words in two common prayers with *nada* or *nothing*.
6. **Otro loco mas.** Another crazy one
7. **copita.** Cup

Responding to the Selection

Imagine that you are one of the waiters watching the elderly man sit at the café table. Would you empathize with the man's loneliness? Would you patiently wait for him, or would you hurry him to leave in order to close the café?

Reviewing the Selection

RECALLING

1. What does one waiter tell the other the old man tried to do last week?
2. What reason does the waiter give for not letting the old man stay in the café?
3. What does the older waiter think he lacks?
4. What does the older waiter think is probably the reason he cannot sleep?

INTERPRETING

5. What attitudes toward the old man and his situation does the waiter express when stating the old man's despair was over "nothing"?
6. Why does the waiter tell the older waiter "You talk like an old man yourself"?
7. Why is the older waiter reluctant to close the café?
8. What is "a nothing" that the older waiter knows "too well"?

ANSWERS FOR REVIEWING THE SELECTION (CONT.)

9. The importance of the clean, well-lighted place to both older men is that light, cleanliness, and order are needed to balance out the tremendous nothingness of death and the mysteries of human existence that no one can answer.

10. The most likely reason the older waiter sympathizes with the elderly man is that he is also lonely. The two men have great despair in common.

ADDITIONAL QUESTIONS AND ACTIVITIES

Have students focus on the final sentence of the story ("Many must have it"), which the waiter says to himself. Ask them to discuss why the waiter says these words. Do students think that the waiter believes what he says? What fears does the waiter express in this short sentence? What is ironic about this sentence?

SYNTHESIZING

9. What is the importance of a "clean, well-lighted place" to the older waiter and the elderly client?

10. What is probably the reason that the older waiter empathizes with the elderly client? What do the two men have in common?

Understanding Literature (Questions for Discussion)

1. **Characterization and Dialogue. Characterization** is the use of literary techniques to create a character. In the selection, portrayal of a character's behavior, which presents the actions and speech of the character, is the technique primarily used. **Dialogue** is conversation involving two or more people or characters. In the selection, the older waiter states to the other waiter, "We are of two different kinds." How does the dialogue between the two men support the older waiter's assessment? What "two different kinds" are the two waiters?

2. **Internal Monologue.** An **internal monologue** presents the private sensations, thoughts, and emotions of a character. In the following passage from the selection, the reader is allowed to step inside the mind of the older waiter and overhear his private thoughts: "It is the light of course but it is necessary that the place be clean and pleasant. . . . What did he fear? It was not fear or dread. It was a nothing that he knew too well. It was all a nothing and a man was nothing too. It was only that and light was all it needed and a certain cleanness and order. . . . Our nada who art in nada, nada be thy name thy kingdom nada. . . ." What is revealed about the waiter's internal state? Why does the waiter substitute the Spanish word *nada,* which means "nothing," for words in the Lord's Prayer?

Responding in Writing

1. **Character Sketch.** Imagine you are sitting in a café people watching. Write a brief sketch about a person you see. What details do you notice about his or her appearance and dress? What is he or she doing? What do you hear the person say? Choose a few telling details about this character for your sketch.

2. **Dialogue.** Imagine that your character meets a person you know or another character you have invented. Write a dialogue between the two characters, portraying their attitudes, emotions, concerns, and so on, through their speech. After writing a first draft of the dialogue, listen carefully to how people speak and listen to each other. What kinds of words do they repeat? Do they speak in complete sentences? How do they indicate understanding or misunderstanding in their communication? Now revise your draft, working to make the dialogue seem like actual speech between the two characters.

ANSWERS FOR UNDERSTANDING LITERATURE

► See the evaluation forms for discussion, active listening, and oral communication, *Assessment Portfolio,* 7.11–7.14.

Responses will vary. Possible responses are given.

1. Characterization and Dialogue. The dialogue supports the older waiter's assessment by revealing how the men see the elderly customer in the café. They regard time differently, and the older waiter has more in common with the customer than he does with the other waiter. One has youth and confidence, while the older waiter is full of despair and fear.

2. Internal Monologue. The older waiter fears the nothingness and loneliness of human existence. His internal state reveals that he is in great disarray and may be suicidal. He substitutes the Spanish word *nada* because it somehow fits his state of mind more clearly than *nothing,* and it fits more cleanly into the phrases he recites.

ANALYTIC SCALES FOR RESPONDING IN WRITING

Assign a score from 1 to 25 for each grading criterion below. (For more detailed evaluation, see the evaluation forms for writing, revising, and proofreading, *Assessment Portfolio,* 7.1–7.10.)

1 Character Sketch

- **Content/Unity.** The sketch reveals telling details about the character being observed.
- **Organization/Coherence.** The sketch is clearly organized and unfolds its details in a logical order.
- **Language/Style.** The sketch uses vivid and precise nouns, verbs, and modifiers.
- **Conventions.** The sketch avoids errors in spelling, grammar, usage, mechanics, and manuscript form.

2. Dialogue

- **Content/Unity.** The dialogue portrays the attitudes, emotions, and concerns of two characters.

(cont.)

ANALYTIC SCALES FOR RESPONDING IN WRITING (CONT.)

- **Organization/Coherence.** The dialogue is clearly organized with a beginning, a middle, and an end.
- **Language/Style.** The dialogue uses vivid and precise nouns, verbs, and modifiers.
- **Conventions.** The dialogue avoids errors in spelling, grammar, usage, mechanics, and manuscript form.

"The Devil and Daniel Webster"

About the Author. Stephen Vincent Benét (1898–1943) was born in Bethlehem, Pennsylvania. His father was a soldier, and the family moved frequently from one army base to the next. His travels and an interest in history greatly affected his writing. Benét began writing at age fifteen and two years later published his first book of poetry. He continued to write poetry while a student at Yale. Later Benét received a Guggenheim Fellowship and went to Paris where he finished a narrative poem about the Civil War, *John Brown's Body* (1928), for which he won a Pulitzer Prize. Later in his career, Benét turned to writing stories and novels. His story "Sobbin Women" (1926) was made into the musical *Seven Brides for Seven Brothers,* and his work "The Devil and Daniel Webster" (1937) was made into an opera and a movie. In 1944, Benét was awarded a second Pulitzer Prize posthumously for his epic poem on the westward migration, *Western Star.*

About the Selection. In "**The Devil and Daniel Webster,**" Benét explores one of literature's popular themes in a distinctly New England setting. Like Christopher Marlowe's Doctor Faustus, Jabez Stone sells his soul in return for having his fondest wishes granted. (While Doctor Faustus as a true Renaissance man asks for knowledge, the more capitalistic New England farmer asks for prosperity.) Like Orpheus who sang Eurydice out of Hades in classical Greek mythology, Daniel Webster intercedes with an eloquent plea on Jabez Stone's behalf. Benét later adapted this short story into a one-act folk opera.

"The Devil and Daniel Webster"
by Stephen Vincent Benét

It's a story they tell in the border country, where Massachusetts joins Vermont and New Hampshire.

Yes, Dan'l Webster's dead—or, at least, they buried him. But every time there's a thunderstorm around Marshfield, they say you can hear his rolling voice in the hollows of the sky. And they say that if you go to his grave and speak loud and clear, "Dan'l Webster—Dan'l Webster!" the ground'll begin to shiver and the trees begin to shake. And after a while you'll hear a deep voice saying, "Neighbor, how stands the Union?" Then you better answer the Union stands as she stood, rock-bottomed and copper-sheathed, one and indivisible, or he's liable to rear right out of the ground. At least, that's what I was told when I was a youngster.

You see, for a while, he was the biggest man in the country. He never got to be President, but he was the biggest man. There were thousands that trusted in him right next to God Almighty, and they told stories about him and all the things that belonged to him that were the stories of patriarchs and such. They said, when he stood up to speak, stars and stripes came right out of the sky, and once he spoke against a river and made it sink into the ground. They said, when he walked the woods with his fishing rod, Killall, the trout would jump out of the streams right into his pockets, for they knew it was no use putting up a fight against him; and, when he argued a case, he could turn on the harps of the blessed and the shaking of the earth underground. That was the kind of man he was, and his big farm up at Marshfield was suitable to him. The chickens he raised were all white meat down through the drumsticks, the cows were tended like children, and the big ram he called Goliath had horns with a curl like a morning-glory vine and could butt through an iron door. But Dan'l wasn't one of your gentlemen farmers; he knew all the ways of the land, and he'd be up by candlelight to see that the chores got done. A man with a mouth like a mastiff, a brow like a mountain and eyes like burning anthracite—that was Dan'l Webster in his prime. And the biggest case he argued never got written down in the books, for he argued it against the devil, nip and tuck and no holds barred. And this is the way I used to hear it told.

There was a man named Jabez Stone, lived at Cross Corners, New Hampshire. He wasn't a bad man to start with, but he was an unlucky man. If he planted corn, he got borers; if he planted potatoes, he got blight. He had good-enough land, but it didn't prosper him; he had a decent wife and children, but the more children he had, the less there was to feed them. If stones cropped up in his neighbor's field, boulders boiled up in his; if he had a horse with the spavins, he'd trade it for one with the staggers and give something extra. There's some folks bound to be like that, apparently. But one day Jabez Stone got sick of the whole business.

He'd been plowing that morning and he'd just broke the plowshare on a rock that he could have sworn hadn't been there yesterday. And, as he stood looking at the plowshare, the off horse began to cough—that ropy kind of cough that means sickness and horse doctors. There were two children down with the measles, his wife was ailing, and he had a whitlow[1] on his thumb. It was about the last straw for Jabez Stone. "I vow," he said, and he looked around him kind of desperate, "I vow it's enough to make a man want to sell his soul to the devil! And I would, too, for two cents!"

Then he felt a kind of queerness come over him at having said what he'd said; though, naturally, being a New Hampshireman, he wouldn't take it back. But, all the same, when it got to be evening and, as far as he could see, no notice had been taken, he felt relieved in his mind, for he was a religious man. But notice is always taken, sooner or later, just like the Good Book says. And, sure enough, next day, about suppertime, a soft-spoken, dark-dressed stranger drove up in a handsome buggy and asked for Jabez Stone.

Well, Jabez told his family it was a lawyer, come to see him about a legacy. But he knew who it was. He didn't like the looks of the stranger, nor the way he smiled with his teeth. They were white teeth, and plentiful—some say they were filed to a point, but I wouldn't vouch for that. And he didn't like it when the dog took one look at the stranger and ran away howling, with his tail between his legs. But having passed the word, more or less, he stuck to it, and they went out behind the barn and made their bargain. Jabez Stone had to prick his finger to sign, and the stranger lent him a silver pin. The wound healed clean, but it left a little white scar.

After that, all of a sudden, things began to pick up and prosper for Jabez Stone. His cows got fat and his horses sleek, his crops were the envy of the neighborhood, and

1. **whitlow.** Painful abscess

Historical Note

Daniel Webster (1782–1852) was one of the greatest orators in the history of American politics. He argued many cases before the Supreme Court and served as a congressman, senator, and United States secretary of state. In his youth, Webster took strong states' rights stands, but later became a staunch supporter of the Union, ending one speech with the often-quoted line "Liberty *and* Union, now and forever, one and inseparable!" Many of Webster's pro-Union supporters, however, turned against him for supporting Henry Clay's Missouri Compromise and the Fugitive Slave Act. Whittier's "Ichabod!" on page 350 of this text was written in response to Webster's compromise position on slavery.

lightning might strike all over the valley, but it wouldn't strike his barn. Pretty soon he was one of the prosperous people of the county; they asked him to stand for selectman, and he stood for it; there began to be talk of running him for state senate. All in all, you might say the Stone family was as happy and contented as cats in a dairy. And so they were, except for Jabez Stone.

He'd been contented enough the first few years. It's a great thing when bad luck turns; it drives most other things out of your head. True, every now and then, especially in rainy weather, the little white scar on his finger would give him a twinge. And once a year, punctual as clockwork, the stranger with the handsome buggy would come driving by. But the sixth year the stranger lighted, and, after that, his peace was over for Jabez Stone.

The stranger came up through the lower field, switching his boots with a cane—they were handsome black boots, but Jabez Stone never liked the look of them, particularly the toes. And, after he'd passed the time of day, he said, "Well, Mr. Stone, you're a hummer! It's a very pretty property you've got here, Mr. Stone."

"Well, some might favor it and others might not," said Jabez Stone, for he was a New Hampshireman.

"Oh, no need to decry your industry!" said the stranger, very easy, showing his teeth in a smile. "After all, we know what's been done, and it's been according to contract and specifications. So when—ahem—the mortgage falls due next year, you shouldn't have any regrets."

"Speaking of that mortgage, mister," said Jabez Stone, and he looked around for help to the earth and the sky, "I'm beginning to have one or two doubts about it."

"Doubts?" said the stranger not quite so pleasantly.

"Why, yes," said Jabez Stone. "This being the U.S.A. and me always having been a religious man." He cleared his throat and got bolder. "Yes, sir," he said, "I'm beginning to have considerable doubts as to that mortgage holding in court."

"There's courts and courts," said the stranger, clicking his teeth. "Still, we might as well have a look at the original document." And he hauled out a big black pocketbook, full of papers. "Sherwin, Slater, Stevens, Stone," he muttered. "'I, Jabez Stone, for a term of seven years—' Oh, it's quite in order, I think."

But Jabez Stone wasn't listening, for he saw something else flutter out of the black pocketbook. It was something that looked like a moth, but it wasn't a moth. And as Jabez Stone stared at it, it seemed to speak to him in a small sort of piping voice, terrible small and thin, but terrible human. "Neighbor Stone!" It squeaked. "Neighbor Stone! Help me! For God's sake, help me!"

But before Jabez Stone could stir hand or foot, the stranger whipped out a big bandanna handkerchief, caught the creature in it, just like a butterfly, and started tying up the ends of the bandanna.

"Sorry for the interruption," he said. "As I was saying—"

But Jabez Stone was shaking all over like a scared horse.

"That's Miser Stevens' voice!" he said in a croak. "And you've got him in your handkerchief!"

The stranger looked a little embarrassed.

"Yes, I really should have transferred him to the collecting box," he said with a simper, "but there were some rather unusual specimens there and I don't want them crowded. Well, well, these little contretemps[1] will occur."

"I don't know what you mean by contertan," said Jabez Stone, "but that was Miser Stevens' voice! And he ain't dead! You can't tell me he is! He was just as spry and mean as a woodchuck Tuesday!"

"In the midst of life . . ." said the stranger, kind of pious. "Listen!" Then a bell began to toll in the valley and Jabez Stone listened, with the sweat running down his face. For he knew it was tolled for Miser Stevens and that he was dead.

"These long-standing accounts," said the stranger with a sigh; "one really hates to close them. But business is business."

He still had the bandanna in his hand, and Jabez Stone felt sick as he saw the cloth struggle and flutter.

"Are they all as small as that?" he asked hoarsely.

"Small?" said the stranger. "Oh, I see what you mean. Why, they vary." He measured Jabez Stone with his eyes, and his teeth showed. "Don't worry, Mr. Stone," he said. "You'll go with a very good grade. I wouldn't trust you outside the collecting box. Now, a man like Dan'l Webster, of course—well, we'd have to build a special box for him, and even at that, I imagine the wing spread would astonish you. He'd certainly be a prize. I wish we could see our way clear to him. But, in your case, as I was saying—"

"Put that handkerchief away!" said Jabez Stone, and he began to beg and to pray. But the best he could get at the end was a three years' extension, with conditions.

But till you make a bargain like that, you've got no idea of how fast four years can run. By the last months of those years Jabez Stone's known all over the state and there's talk of running him for governor—and it's dust and ashes in his mouth. For every day, when he gets up, he thinks, "There's one more night gone," and every night, when he lies down, he thinks of the black pocketbook and the soul of Miser Stevens, and it makes him sick at heart. Till, finally, he can't bear it any longer, and, in the last days of the last year, he hitches up his horse and drives off to seek Dan'l Webster. For Dan'l was born in New Hampshire,

1. **contretemps.** Awkward occurrence

LITERARY TECHNIQUE

- **Allusion.** An allusion is a reference in a literary work to a well-known item from literature, history, or culture. The stranger's interrupted statement, "In the midst of life . . .," comes from the Prayer for the Burial of the Dead, in the Book of Common Prayer: "In the midst of life we are in death."
- **Tall Tale.** A tall tale is a traditional story with highly exaggerated elements. Popular American tall tales include those concerning Paul Bunyan and Pecos Bill. Ask students to identify tall tale elements in the opening account of Daniel Webster: his voice rolling in the thunder, stars and stripes coming out in the sky when he spoke, and so on.

only a few miles from Cross Corners, and it's well known that he has a particular soft spot for old neighbors.

It was early in the morning when he got to Marshfield, but Dan'l was up already, talking Latin to the farm hands and wrestling with the ram, Goliath, and trying out a new trotter and working up speeches to make against John C. Calhoun. But when he heard a New Hampshireman had come to see him, he dropped everything else he was doing, for that was Dan'l's way. He gave Jabez Stone a breakfast that five men couldn't eat, went into the living history of every man and woman in Cross Corners, and finally asked him how he could serve him.

Jabez Stone allowed that it was a kind of mortgage case.

"Well, I haven't pleaded a mortgage case in a long time, and I don't generally plead now, except before the Supreme Court," said Dan'l, "but if I can, I'll help you."

"Then I've got hope for the first time in ten years," said Jabez Stone and told him the details.

Dan'l walked up and down as he listened, hands behind his back, now and then asking a question, now and then plunging his eyes at the floor, as if they'd bore through it like gimlets. When Jabez Stone had finished, Dan'l puffed out his cheeks and blew. Then he turned to Jabez Stone and a smile broke over his face like the sunrise over Monadnock.[1]

"You've certainly given yourself the devil's own row to hoe, Neighbor Stone," he said, "but I'll take your case."

"You'll take it?" said Jabez Stone, hardly daring to believe.

"Yes," said Dan'l Webster. "I've got about seventy-five other things to do and the Missouri Compromise[2] to straighten out, but I'll take your case. For if two New Hampshiremen aren't a match for the devil, we might as well give the country back to the Indians."

Then he shook Jabez Stone by the hand and said, "Did you come down here in a hurry?"

"Well, I admit I made time," said Jabez Stone.

"You'll go back faster," said Dan'l Webster, and he told 'em to hitch up Constitution and Constellation to the carriage. They were matched grays with one white forefoot, and they stepped like greased lightning.

Well, I won't describe how excited and pleased the whole Stone family was to have the great Dan'l Webster for a guest, when they finally got there. Jabez Stone had lost his hat on the way, blown off when they overtook a wind, but he didn't take much account of that. But after supper he sent the family off to bed, for he had most particular business with Mr. Webster. Mrs. Stone wanted him to sit in the front parlor, but Dan'l Webster knew front parlors and said he preferred the kitchen. So it was there they sat, waiting for the stranger, with a jug on the table between them and a bright fire on the hearth—the stranger being scheduled to show up on the stroke of midnight, according to specification.

Well, most men wouldn't have asked for better company than Dan'l Webster and a jug. But with every tick of the clock Jabez Stone got sadder and sadder. His eyes roved round, and though he sampled the jug you could see he couldn't taste it. Finally, on the stroke of 11:30 he reached over and grabbed Dan'l Webster by the arm.

"Mr. Webster, Mr. Webster!" he said, and his voice was shaking with fear and a desperate courage. "For God's sake, Mr. Webster, harness your horses and get away from this place while you can!"

"You've brought me a long way, neighbor, to tell me you don't like my company," said Dan'l Webster, quite peaceable, pulling at the jug.

"Miserable wretch that I am!" groaned Jabez Stone. "I've brought you a devilish way, and now I see my folly. Let him take me if he wills. I don't hanker after it, I must say, but I can stand it. But you're the Union's stay and New Hampshire's pride! He mustn't get you, Mr. Webster! He mustn't get you!"

Dan'l Webster looked at the distracted man, all gray and shaking in the firelight, and laid a hand on his shoulder.

"I'm obliged to you, Neighbor Stone," he said gently. "It's kindly thought of. But there's a jug on the table and a case in hand. And I never left a jug or a case half finished in my life."

And just at that moment there was a sharp rap on the door.

"Ah," said Dan'l Webster very coolly, "I thought your clock was a trifle slow, Neighbor Stone." He stepped to the door and opened it. "Come in!" he said.

The stranger came in—very dark and tall he looked in the firelight. He was carrying a box under his arm—a black japanned box with little air holes in the lid. At the sight of the box Jabez Stone gave a low cry and shrank into a corner of the room.

"Mr. Webster, I presume," said the stranger, very polite, but with his eyes glowing like a fox's deep in the woods.

"Attorney of record for Jabez Stone," said Dan'l Webster, but his eyes were glowing too. "Might I ask your name?"

---

1. **Monadnock.** Mountain in New Hampshire
2. **Missouri Compromise.** Bill passed in 1820 that allowed slavery in Missouri but not anywhere else west of the Mississippi

"I've gone by a good many," said the stranger carelessly. "Perhaps Scratch will do for the evening. I'm often called that in these regions."

Then he sat down at the table and poured himself a drink from the jug. The liquor was cold in the jug, but it came steaming into the glass.

"And now," said the stranger, smiling and showing his teeth, "I shall call upon you, as a law-abiding citizen, to assist me in taking possession of my property."

Well, with that the argument began—and it went hot and heavy. At first Jabez Stone had a flicker of hope, but when he saw Dan'l Webster being forced back at point after point, he just sat scrunched in his corner, with his eyes on that japanned box. For there wasn't any doubt as to the deed or the signature—that was the worst of it. Dan'l Webster twisted and turned and thumped his fist on the table, but he couldn't get away from that. He offered to compromise the case; the stranger wouldn't hear of it. He pointed out the property had increased in value, and state senators ought to be worth more; the stranger stuck to the letter of the law. He was a great lawyer, Dan'l Webster, but we know who's the King of Lawyers, as the Good Book tells us, and it seemed as if, for the first time, Dan'l Webster had met his match.

Finally, the stranger yawned a little. "Your spirited efforts on behalf of your client do you credit, Mr. Webster," he said, "but if you have no more arguments to adduce, I'm rather pressed for time . . ." and Jabez Stone shuddered.

Dan'l Webster's brow looked dark as a thundercloud.

"Pressed or not, you shall not have this man!" he thundered. "Mr. Stone is an American citizen, and no American citizen may be forced into the service of a foreign prince. We fought England for that in '12 and we'll fight all hell for it again!"

"Foreign?" said the stranger. "And who calls me a foreigner?"

"Well, I never yet heard of the dev—of your claiming American citizenship," said Dan'l Webster with surprise.

"And who with better right?" said the stranger with one of his terrible smiles. "When the first wrong was done to the first Indian, I was there. When the first slaver put out for the Congo, I stood on her deck. Am I not in your books and stories and beliefs, from the first settlements on? Am I not spoken of still in every church in New England? 'Tis true the North claims me for a Southerner and the South for a Northerner, but I am neither. I am merely an honest American like yourself—and of the best descent—for, to tell the truth, Mr. Webster, though I don't like to boast of it, my name is older in this country than yours."

"Aha!" said Dan'l Webster with the veins standing out in his forehead. "Then I stand on the Constitution! I demand a trial for my client!"

"The case is hardly one for an ordinary court," said the stranger, his eyes flickering. "And, indeed, the lateness of the hour—"

"Let it be any court you choose, so it is an American judge and an American jury!" said Dan'l Webster in his pride. "Let it be the quick or the dead; I'll abide the issue!"

"You have said it," said the stranger, and pointed his finger at the door. And with that, and all of a sudden, there was a rushing of wind outside and a noise of footsteps. They came, clear and distinct, through the night. And yet they were not like the footsteps of living men.

"In God's name, who comes by so late?" cried Jabez Stone in an ague of fear.

"The jury Mr. Webster demands," said the stranger, sipping at his boiling glass. "You must pardon the rough appearance of one or two; they will have come a long way."

And with that the fire burned blue and the door blew open and twelve men entered, one by one.

If Jabez Stone had been sick with terror before, he was blind with terror now. For there was Walter Butler, the loyalist, who spread fire and horror through the Mohawk Valley in the times of the Revolution; and there was Simon Girty, the renegade, who saw white men burned at the stake and whooped with the Indians to see them burn. His eyes were green, like a catamount's, and the stains on his hunting shirt did not come from the blood of the deer. King Philip was there, wild and proud as he had been in life, with the great gash in his head that gave him his death wound, and cruel Governor Dale, who broke men on the wheel. There was Morton of Merry Mount, who so vexed the Plymouth Colony, with his flushed, loose, handsome face and his hate of the godly. There was Teach, the bloody pirate, with his black beard curling on his breast. The Reverend John Smeet, with his strangler's hands and his Geneva gown, walked as daintily as he had to the gallows. The red print of the rope was still around his neck, but he carried a perfumed handkerchief in one hand. One and all, they came into the room with the fires of hell still upon them, and the stranger named their names and their deeds as they came, till the tale of twelve was told. Yet the stranger had told the truth—they had all played a part in America.

"Are you satisfied with the jury, Mr. Webster?" said the stranger mockingly, when they had taken their places.

The sweat stood upon Dan'l Webster's brow, but his voice was clear.

"Quite satisfied," he said. "Though I miss General Arnold[1] from the company."

"Benedict Arnold is engaged upon other business," said the stranger with a glower. "Ah, you asked for a justice, I believe."

He pointed his finger once more, and a tall man, soberly clad in Puritan garb, with the burning gaze of the fanatic, stalked into the room and took his judge's place.

"Justice Hathorne is a jurist of experience," said the stranger. "He presided at certain witch trials once held in Salem. There were others who repented of the business later, but not he."

"Repent of such notable wonders and undertakings?" said the stern old justice. "Nay, hang them—hang them all!" And he muttered to himself in a way that struck ice into the soul of Jabez Stone.

Then the trial began, and, as you might expect, it didn't look anyways good for the defense. And Jabez Stone didn't make much of a witness in his own behalf. He took one look at Simon Girty and screeched, and they had to put him back in his corner in a kind of swoon.

It didn't halt the trial though; the trial went on, as trials do. Dan'l Webster had faced some hard juries and hanging judges in his time, but this was the hardest he'd ever faced, and he knew it. They sat there with a kind of glitter in their eyes, and the stranger's smooth voice went on and on. Every time he'd raise an objection, it'd be "Objection sustained," but whenever Dan'l objected, it'd be "Objection denied." Well, you couldn't expect fair play from a fellow like this Mr. Scratch.

It got to Dan'l in the end, and he began to heat, like iron in the forge. When he got up to speak he was going to flay that stranger with every trick known to the law, and the judge and jury too. He didn't care if it was contempt of court or what would happen to him for it. He didn't care any more what happened to Jabez Stone. He just got madder and madder, thinking of what he'd say. And yet, curiously enough, the more he thought about it, the less he was able to arrange his speech in his mind.

Till, finally, it was time for him to get up on his feet, and he did so, all ready to bust out with lightnings and denunciations. But before he started he looked over the judge and jury for a moment, such being his custom. And he noticed the glitter in their eyes was twice as strong as before, and they all leaned forward. Like hounds just before they get the fox, they looked, and the blue mist of evil in the room thickened as he watched them. Then he saw what he'd been about to do, and he wiped his forehead, as a man might who's just escaped falling into a pit in the dark.

For it was him they'd come for, not only Jabez Stone. He read it in the glitter of their eyes and in the way the stranger hid his mouth with one hand. And if he fought them with their own weapons, he'd fall into their power; he knew that, though he couldn't have told you how. It was his own anger and horror that burned in their eyes; and he'd have to wipe that out or the case was lost. He stood there for a moment, his black eyes burning like anthracite. And then he began to speak.

He started off in a low voice, though you could hear every word. They say he could call on the harps of the blessed when he chose. And this was just as simple and easy as a man could talk. But he didn't start out by condemning or reviling. He was talking about the things that make a country a country and a man a man.

And he began with the simple things that everybody's known and felt—the freshness of a fine morning when you're young, and the taste of food when you're hungry, and the new day that's every day when you're a child. He took them up and he turned them in his hands. They were good things for any man. But without freedom they sickened. And when he talked of those enslaved, and the sorrows of slavery, his voice got like a big bell. He talked of the early days of America and the men who had made those days. It wasn't a spread-eagle speech, but he made you see it. He admitted all the wrong that had ever been done. But he showed how, out of the wrong and the right, the suffering and the starvations, something new had come. And everybody had played a part in it, even the traitors.

Then he turned to Jabez Stone and showed him as he was—an ordinary man who'd had hard luck and wanted to change it. And, because he'd wanted to change it, now he was going to be punished for all eternity. And yet there was good in Jabez Stone, and he showed that good. He was hard and mean, in some ways, but he was a man. There was sadness in being a man, but it was a proud thing too. And he showed what the pride of it was till you couldn't help feeling it. Yes, even in hell, if a man was a man, you'd know it. And he wasn't pleading for any one person any more, though his voice rang like an organ. He was telling the story and the failures and the endless journey of mankind. They got tricked and trapped and bamboozled, but it was a great journey. And no demon that was ever foaled could know the inwardness of it—it took a man to do that.

The fire began to die on the hearth and the wind before morning to blow. The light was getting gray in

1. **General Arnold.** Benedict Arnold, notorious American traitor

the room when Dan'l Webster finished. And his words came back at the end to New Hampshire ground, and the one spot of land that each man loves and clings to. He painted a picture of that, and to each one of that jury he spoke of things long forgotten. For his voice could search the heart, and that was his gift and his strength. And to one his voice was like the forest and its secrecy, and to another like the sea and the storms of the sea; and one heard the cry of his lost nation in it, and another saw a little harmless scene he hadn't remembered for years. But each saw something. And when Dan'l Webster finished he didn't know whether or not he'd saved Jabez Stone. But he knew he'd done a miracle. For the glitter was gone from the eyes of judge and jury, and, for the moment, they were men again, and knew they were men.

"The defense rests," said Dan'l Webster and stood there like a mountain. His ears were still ringing with his speech, and he didn't hear anything else till he heard Judge Hathorne say, "The jury will retire to consider its verdict."

Walter Butler rose in his place and his face had a dark, gay pride on it.

"The jury has considered its verdict," he said and looked the stranger full in the eye. "We find for the defendant, Jabez Stone."

With that, the smile left the stranger's face, but Walter Butler did not flinch.

"Perhaps 'tis not strictly in accordance with the evidence," he said, "but even the damned may salute the eloquence of Mr. Webster."

With that, the long crow of a rooster split the gray morning sky, and judge and jury were gone from the room like a puff of smoke and as if they had never been there. The stranger returned to Dan'l Webster, smiling wryly.

"Major Butler was always a bold man," he said. "I had not thought him quite so bold. Nevertheless, my congratulations, as between two gentlemen."

"I'll have that paper first, if you please," said Dan'l Webster, and he took it and tore it into four pieces. It was queerly warm to the touch. "And now," he said, "I'll have you!" and his hand came down like a bear trap on the stranger's arm. For he knew that once you bested anybody like Mr. Scratch in fair fight, his power on you was gone. And he could see that Mr. Scratch knew it too.

The stranger twisted and wriggled, but he couldn't get out of that grip. "Come, come, Mr. Webster," he said, smiling palely. "This sort of thing is ridic—ouch!—is ridiculous. If you're worried about the costs of the case, naturally, I'd be glad to pay—"

"And so you shall!" said Dan'l Webster, shaking him till his teeth rattled. "For you'll sit right down at that table and draw up a document, promising never to bother Jabez Stone nor his heirs or assigns nor any other New Hampshireman till doomsday! For any hades we want to raise in this state, we can raise ourselves, without assistance from strangers."

"Ouch!" said the stranger. "Ouch! Well, they never did run very big to the barrel, but—ouch!—I agree!"

So he sat down and drew up the document. But Dan'l Webster kept his hand on his coat collar all the time.

"And now may I go?" said the stranger, quite humble, when Dan'l'd seen the document's in proper and legal form.

"Go?" said Dan'l, giving him another shake. "I'm still trying to figure out what I'll do with you. For you've settled the costs of the case, but you haven't settled with me. I think I'll take you back to Marshfield," he said, kind of reflective. "I've got a ram there named Goliath that can butt through an iron door. I'd kind of like to turn you loose in his field and see what he'd do."

Well, with that the stranger began to beg and to plead. And he begged and he pled so humble that finally Dan'l, who was naturally kindhearted, agreed to let him go. The stranger seemed terrible grateful for that and said, just to show they were friends, he'd tell Dan'l's fortune before leaving. So Dan'l agreed to that, though he didn't take much stock in fortunetellers ordinarily. But, naturally, the stranger was a little different.

Well, he pried and he peered at the lines in Dan'l's hands. And he told him one thing and another that was quite remarkable. But they were all in the past.

"Yes, all that's true, and it happened," said Dan'l Webster. "But what's to come in the future?"

The stranger grinned, kind of happily, and shook his head.

"The future's not as you think it," he said. "It's dark. You have a great ambition, Mr. Webster."

"I have," said Dan'l firmly, for everybody knew he wanted to be President.

"It seems almost within your grasp," said the stranger, "but you will not attain it. Lesser men will be made President and you will be passed over."

"And, if I am, I'll still be Daniel Webster," said Dan'l. "Say on."

"You have two strong sons," said the stranger, shaking his head. "You look to found a line. But each will die in war and neither reach greatness."

"Live or die, they are still my sons," said Dan'l Webster. "Say on."

"You have made great speeches," said the stranger. "You will make more."

"Ah," said Dan'l Webster.

FROM *WINESBURG, OHIO*

About the Author. Sherwood Anderson (1876–1941) was born in Camden, Ohio, the third of seven children. When Anderson was sixteen, after a childhood punctuated by frequent moves and infrequent schooling, his family settled in Clyde, Ohio, which became the model for the fictious town made famous in his short story collection, *Winesburg, Ohio* (1919). In 1912, in his mid-thirties, he abruptly abandoned the middle-class life he'd made in Ohio, leaving his first wife and his business career and returning to Chicago where he'd lived several years earlier.

Although he had never finished high school, he had harbored an ambition to write. In Chicago he met the writers and artists who were creating the Chicago Renaissance and began his life's work. During the remainder of his life he lived in Chicago, New Orleans, and Paris. He wrote novels, short stories, essays, and an autobiography. Anderson died at sea on the way to South America while on a goodwill mission for the state department.

His first major publication was the novel *Windy McPherson's Son* (1916). His other works include *Marching Men* (1917), *The Triumph of the Egg* (1921, *Horses and Men* (1923), and *Death in the Woods and Other Stories* (1933).

About the Selection. *Winesburg, Ohio* is a collection of twenty-three short stories that gives psychological portraits of the residents of a small town. Sherwood was a Naturalist, and in "The Book of the Grotesque," the preface to the collection, he explains how his characters, and indeed all people, have become "grotesques," or caricatures, largely because of inner qualities or desires that are misunderstood or unappreciated by the rest of the world. Anderson believed that people embrace a truth, live by this truth, and in the process distort the truth, rendering themselves groteques and the truth a falsehood.

"But the last great speech you make will turn many of your own against you," said the stranger. "They will call you Ichabod; they will call you by other names. Even in New England some will say you have turned your coat and sold your country, and their voices will be loud against you till you die."

"So it is an honest speech, it does not matter what men say," said Dan'l Webster. Then he looked at the stranger and their glances locked.

"One question," he said. "I have fought for the Union all my life. Will I see that fight won against those who would tear it apart?"

"Not while you live," said the stranger grimly, "but it will be won. And after you are dead, there are thousands who will fight for your cause, because of words that you spoke."

"Why, then, you long-barreled, slab-sided, lantern-jawed, fortune-telling note shaver," said Dan'l Webster with a great roar of laughter, "be off with you to your own place before I put my mark on you! For, by the thirteen original colonies, I'd go to the Pit itself to save the Union!"

And with that he drew back his foot for a kick that would have stunned a horse. It was only the tip of his shoe that caught the stranger, but he went flying out of the door with his collecting box under his arm.

"And now," said Dan'l Webster, seeing Jabez Stone beginning to rouse from his swoon, "let's see what's left in the jug, for it's dry work talking all night. I hope there's pie for breakfast, Neighbor Stone."

But they say that whenever the devil comes near Marshfield, even now, he gives it a wide berth. And he hasn't been seen in the state of New Hampshire from that day to this.

I'm not talking about Massachusetts or Vermont.

from *Winesburg, Ohio*
by Sherwood Anderson

THE BOOK OF THE GROTESQUE

The writer, an old man with a white mustache, had some difficulty in getting into bed. The windows of the house in which he lived were high and he wanted to look at the trees when he awoke in the morning. A carpenter came to fix the bed so that it would be on a level with the window.

Quite a fuss was made about the matter. The carpenter, who had been a soldier in the Civil War, came into the writer's room and sat down to talk of building a platform for the purpose of raising the bed. The writer had cigars lying about and the carpenter smoked.

For a time the two men talked of the raising of the bed and then they talked of other things. The soldier got on the subject of the war. The writer, in fact, led him to that subject. The carpenter had once been a prisoner in Andersonville prison and had lost a brother. The brother had died of starvation, and whenever the carpenter got upon that subject he cried. He, like the old writer, had a white mustache, and when he cried he puckered up his lips and the mustache bobbed up and down. The weeping old man with the cigar in his mouth was ludicrous. The plan the writer had for the raising of his bed was forgotten and later the carpenter did it in his own way and the writer, who was past sixty, had to help himself with a chair when he went to bed at night.

In his bed the writer rolled over on his side and lay quite still. For years he had been beset with notions concerning his heart. He was a hard smoker and his heart fluttered. The idea had got into his mind that he would some time die unexpectedly and always when he got into bed he thought of that. It did not alarm him. The effect in fact was quite a special thing and not easily explained. It made him more alive, there in bed, than at any other time. Perfectly still he lay and his body was old and not of much use any more, but something inside him was altogether young. He was like a pregnant woman, only that the thing inside him was not a baby but a youth. No, it wasn't a youth, it was a woman, young, and wearing a coat of mail like a knight. It is absurd, you see, to try to tell what was inside the old writer as he lay on his high bed and listened to the fluttering of his heart. The thing to get at is what the writer, or the young thing within the writer, was thinking about.

The old writer, like all of the people in the world, had got, during his long life, a great many notions in his head. He had once been quite handsome and a number of women had been in love with him. And then, of course, he had known people, many people, known them in a peculiarly intimate way that was different from the way in which you and I know people. At least that is what the writer thought and the thought pleased him. Why quarrel with an old man concerning his thoughts?

In the bed the writer had a dream that was not a dream. As he grew somewhat sleepy but was still conscious, figures began to appear before his eyes. He imagined the young indescribable thing within himself was driving a long procession of figures before his eyes.

You see the interest in all this lies in the figures that went before the eyes of the writer. They were all grotesques. All of the men and women the writer had ever known had become grotesques.

The grotesques were not all horrible. Some were amusing, some almost beautiful, and one, a woman all drawn out of shape, hurt the old man by her grotesqueness. When she passed he made a noise like a small dog whimpering. Had you come into the room you might have supposed the old man had unpleasant dreams or perhaps indigestion.

For an hour the procession of grotesques passed before the eyes of the old man, and then, although it was a painful thing to do, he crept out of bed and began to write. Some one of the grotesques had made a deep impression on his mind and he wanted to describe it.

At his desk the writer worked for an hour. In the end he wrote a book which he called "The Book of the Grotesque." It was never published, but I saw it once and it made an indelible impression on my mind. The book had one central thought that is very strange and has always remained with me. By remembering it I have been able to understand many people and things that I was never able to understand before. The thought was involved but a simple statement of it would be something like this:

That in the beginning when the world was young there were a great many thoughts but no such thing as a truth. Man made the truths himself and each truth was a composite of a great many vague thoughts. All about in the world were the truths and they were all beautiful.

The old man had listed hundreds of the truths in his book. I will not try to tell you of all of them. There was the truth of virginity and the truth of passion, the truth of wealth and of poverty, of thrift and of profligacy, of carelessness and abandon. Hundreds and hundreds were the truths and they were all beautiful.

And then the people came along. Each as he appeared snatched up one of the truths and some who were quite strong snatched up a dozen of them.

It was the truths that made the people grotesques. The old man had quite an elaborate theory concerning the matter. It was his notion that the moment one of the people took one of the truths to himself, called it his truth, and tried to live his life by it, he became a grotesque and the truth he embraced became a falsehood.

You can see for yourself how the old man, who had spent all of his life writing and was filled with words, would write hundreds of pages concerning this matter. The subject would become so big in his mind that he himself would be in danger of becoming a grotesque. He didn't, I suppose, for the same reason that he never published the book. It was the young thing inside him that saved the old man.

Concerning the old carpenter who fixed the bed for the writer, I only mentioned him because he, like many of what are called very common people, became the nearest thing to what is understandable and lovable of all the grotesques in the writer's book.

from *The Grapes of Wrath*[1]
by John Steinbeck

The spring is beautiful in California. Valleys in which the fruit blossoms are fragrant pink and white waters in a shallow sea. Then the first tendrils of the grapes, swelling from the old gnarled vines, cascade down to cover the trunks. The full green hills are round and soft as breasts. And on the level vegetable lands are the mile-long rows of pale green lettuce and the spindly little cauliflowers, the gray-green unearthly artichoke plants.

And then the leaves break out on the trees, and the petals drop from the fruit trees and carpet the earth with pink and white. The centers of the blossoms swell and grow and color: cherries and apples, peaches and pears, figs which close the flower in the fruit. All California quickens with produce, and the fruit grows heavy, and the limbs bend gradually under the fruit so that little crutches must be placed under them to support the weight.

Behind the fruitfulness are men of understanding and knowledge and skill, men who experiment with seed, endlessly developing the techniques for greater crops of plants whose roots will resist the million enemies of the earth: the molds, the insects, the rusts, the blights. These men work carefully and endlessly to perfect the seed, the roots. And there are the men of chemistry who spray the trees against pests, who sulphur the grapes, who cut out disease and rots, mildews and sicknesses. Doctors of preventive medicine, men at the borders who look for fruit

1. **Grapes of Wrath.** From the first stanza of Julia Ward Howe's "Battle Hymn of the Republic:"

> Mine eyes have seen the glory of the coming of the Lord;
> He is trampling out the vintage where the grapes of wrath are stored. . . .

Howe's battle hymn refers to the Civil War. The battle in Steinbeck's *The Grapes of Wrath* is being fought by poverty-stricken migrant workers during the Great Depression of the United States. Another source for the title is the Bible, where it is written in the Revelation of St. John that the "wine of wrath" is forced upon people by a "Babylon." In the Bible, Babylon is an ancient city-state that is described as being wicked. In *The Grapes of Wrath,* Steinbeck is comparing the mistreatment of the migrant workers to the mistreatment of the citizens of ancient Babylon. He seems to suggest that the wrath of the migrant workers will cause the fall of their own wicked Babylon.

FROM *THE GRAPES OF WRATH*

About the Author. John Steinbeck (1902–1968) was born in California, and many of his novels, including *The Grapes of Wrath,* are set in his home state. Some of his other major novels include *Of Mice and Men* and *East of Eden.* His works combine elements of Romance and Realism and often focus upon agriculturalists, farm hands, and migrant workers in rural areas. Steinbeck won a Nobel Prize for literature in 1962.

About the Selection. The selection describes Steinbeck's distaste with the economic situation of the United States in which a bounty existed and was not distributed among the needy. Steinbeck indicates that it was not only fruit that was rotting, but people's morals and concern with each other as well.

LITERARY TECHNIQUE

Mood, or **atmosphere,** is the emotion created in the reader by part or all of a literary work. Encourage students to note where and how the mood changes in the selection. Point out that while the mood is one of beautiful serenity and rejoicing in the natural bounty at the beginning of the piece, it changes immediately to a bitter mood once the speaker contemplates the waste of nature's bounty.

flies, for Japanese beetle, men who quarantine the sick trees and root them out and burn them, men of knowledge. The men who graft the young trees, the little vines, are the cleverest of all, for theirs is a surgeon's job, as tender and delicate; and these men must have surgeons' hands and surgeons' hearts to slit the bark, to place the grafts, to bind the wounds and cover them from the air. These are great men.

Along the rows, the cultivators move, tearing the spring grass and turning it under to make a fertile earth, breaking the ground to hold the water up near the surface, ridging the ground in little pools for the irrigation, destroying the weed roots that may drink the water away from the trees.

And all the time the fruit swells and the flowers break out in long clusters on the vines. And in the growing year the warmth grows and the leaves turn dark green. The prunes lengthen like little green bird's eggs, and the limbs sag down against the crutches under the weight. And the hard little pears take shape, and the beginning of the fuzz comes out on the peaches. Grape blossoms shed their tiny petals and the hard little beads become green buttons, and the buttons grow heavy. The men who work in the fields, the owners of the little orchards, watch and calculate. The year is heavy with produce. And men are proud, for of their knowledge they can make the year heavy. They have transformed the world with their knowledge. The short, lean wheat has been made big and productive. Little sour apples have grown large and sweet, and that old grape that grew among the trees and fed the birds its tiny fruit has mothered a thousand varieties, red and black, green and pale pink, purple and yellow; and each variety with its own flavor. The men who work in the experimental farms have made new fruits: nectarines and forty kinds of plums, walnuts with paper shells. And always they work, selecting, grafting, changing, driving themselves, driving the earth to produce.

And first the cherries ripen. Cent and a half a pound. Hell, we can't pick 'em for that. Black cherries and red cherries, full and sweet, and the birds eat half of each cherry and the yellowjackets buzz into the holes the birds made. And on the ground the seeds drop and dry with black shreds hanging from them.

The purple prunes soften and sweeten. My God, we can't pick them and dry and sulphur them. We can't pay wages, no matter what wages. And the purple prunes carpet the ground. And first the skins wrinkle a little and swarms of flies come to feast, and the valley is filled with the odor of sweet decay. The meat turns dark and the crop shrivels on the ground.

And the pears grow yellow and soft. Five dollars a ton. Five dollars for forty fifty-pound boxes; trees pruned and sprayed, orchards cultivated—pick the fruit, put it in boxes, load the trucks, deliver the fruit to the cannery—forty boxes for five dollars. We can't do it. And the yellow fruit falls heavily to the ground and splashes on the ground. The yellowjackets dig into the soft meat, and there is a smell of ferment and rot.

Then the grapes—we can't make good wine. People can't buy good wine. Rip the grapes from the vines, good grapes, rotten grapes, wasp-stung grapes. Press stems, press dirt and rot.

But there's mildew and formic acid in the vats.

Add sulphur and tannic acid.

The smell from the ferment is not the rich odor of wine, but the smell of decay and chemicals.

Oh, well. It has alcohol in it, anyway. They can get drunk.

The little farmers watched debt creep up on them like the tide. They sprayed the trees and sold no crop, they pruned and grafted and could not pick the crop. And the men of knowledge have worked, have considered, and the fruit is rotting on the ground, and the decaying mash in the wine vats is poisoning the air. And taste the wine—no grape flavor at all, just sulphur and tannic acid and alcohol.

This little orchard will be a part of a great holding next year, for the debt will have choked the owner.

This vineyard will belong to the bank. Only the great owners can survive, for they own the canneries too. And four pears peeled and cut in half, cooked and canned, still cost fifteen cents. And the canned pears do not spoil. They will last for years.

The decay spreads over the State, and the sweet smell is a great sorrow on the land. Men who can graft the trees and make the seed fertile and big can find no way to let the hungry people eat their produce. Men who have created new fruits in the world cannot create a system whereby their fruits may be eaten. And the failure hangs over the State like a great sorrow.

The works of the roots of the vines, of the trees, must be destroyed to keep up the price, and this is the saddest, bitterest thing of all. Carloads of oranges dumped on the ground. The people came for miles to take the fruit, but this could not be. How would they buy oranges at twenty cents a dozen if they could drive out and pick them up? And men with hoses squirt kerosene on the oranges, and they are angry at the crime, angry at the people who have come to take the fruit. A million people hungry, needing the fruit—and kerosene sprayed over the golden mountains.

And the smell of rot fills the country.

Burn coffee for fuel in the ships. Burn corn to keep warm, it makes a hot fire. Dump potatoes in the rivers and place guards along the banks to keep the hungry people from fishing them out. Slaughter the pigs and bury them, and let the putrescence drip down into the earth.

There is a crime here that goes beyond denunciation. There is a sorrow here that weeping cannot symbolize. There is a failure here that topples all our success. The fertile earth, the straight tree rows, the sturdy trunks, and the ripe fruit. And children dying of pellagra must die because a profit cannot be taken from an orange. And coroners must fill in the certificates—died of malnutrition—because the food must rot, must be forced to rot.

The people come with nets to fish for potatoes in the river, and the guards hold them back; they come in rattling cars to get the dumped oranges, but the kerosene is sprayed. And they stand still and watch the potatoes float by, listen to the screaming pigs being killed in a ditch and covered with quicklime, watch the mountains of oranges slop down to a putrefying ooze; and in the eyes of the hungry there is a growing wrath. In the souls of the people the grapes of wrath are filling and growing heavy, growing heavy for the vintage.

from *Invisible Man*
by Ralph Ellison

When I reached the door of Mr. Emerson's office it occurred to me that perhaps I should have waited until the business of the day was under way, but I disregarded the idea and went ahead. My being early would be, I hoped, an indication of both how badly I wanted work, and how promptly I would perform any assignment given me. Besides, wasn't there a saying that the first person of the day to enter a business would get a bargain? Or was that said only of Jewish business? I removed the letter from my brief case. Was Emerson a Christian or a Jewish name?

Beyond the door it was like a museum. I had entered a large reception room decorated with cool tropical colors. One wall was almost covered by a huge colored map, from which narrow red silk ribbons stretched tautly from each division of the map to a series of ebony pedestals, upon which sat glass specimen jars containing natural products of the various countries. It was an importing firm. I looked around the room, amazed. There were paintings, bronzes, tapestries, all beautifully arranged. I was dazzled and so taken aback that I almost dropped my brief case when I heard a voice say, "And what would your business be?"

I saw the figure out of a collar ad: ruddy face with blond hair faultlessly in place, a tropical weave suit draped handsomely from his broad shoulders, his eyes gray and nervous behind clear-framed glasses.

I explained my appointment. "Oh, yes," he said. "May I see the letter, please?"

I handed it over, noticing the gold links in the soft white cuffs as he extended his hand. Glancing at the envelope he looked back at me with a strange interest in his eyes and said, "Have a seat, please. I'll be with you in a moment."

I watched him leave noiselessly, moving with a long hip-swinging stride that caused me to frown. I went over and took a teakwood chair with cushions of emerald-green silk, sitting stiffly with my brief case across my knees. He must have been sitting there when I came in, for on a table that held a beautiful dwarf tree I saw smoke rising from a cigarette in a jade ash tray. An open book, something called *Totem and Taboo*, lay beside it. I looked across to a lighted case of Chinese design which held delicate-looking statues of horses and birds, small vases and bowls, each set upon a carved wooden base. The room was quiet as a tomb—until suddenly there was a savage beating of wings and I looked toward the window to see an eruption of color, as though a gale had whipped up a bundle of brightly colored rags. It was an aviary of tropical birds set near one of the broad windows, through which, as the clapping of wings settled down, I could see two ships plying[1] far out upon the greenish bay below. A large bird began a song, drawing my eyes to the throbbing of its bright blue, red and yellow throat. It was startling and I watched the surge and flutter of the birds as their colors flared for an instant like an unfurled oriental fan. I wanted to go and stand near the cage for a better view, but decided against it. It might seem unbusinesslike. I observed the room from the chair.

These folks are the Kings of the Earth! I thought, hearing the bird make an ugly noise. There was nothing like this at the college museum—or anywhere else that I had ever been. I recalled only a few cracked relics from slavery times: an iron pot, an ancient bell, a set of ankle-irons and links of chain, a primitive loom, a spinning wheel, a gourd for drinking, an ugly ebony African god that seemed to sneer (presented to the school by some traveling millionaire), a leather whip with copper brads,[2] a branding iron with the double letter . . . Though I had seen them very seldom, they were vivid in my

1. **plying.** Sailing regularly back and forth
2. **brads.** Wire nails of uniform thickness with small heads

FROM *INVISIBLE MAN*

About the Author. Ralph Ellison (1914–) was born in Oklahoma and gained fame for his novel, *Invisible Man,* which is a Naturalistic exploration of growing up African American in modern American society. Ellison has taught creative writing at several universities and has written essays as well.

About the Selection. *Invisible Man* is written from a first-person point of view from the perspective of a young, nameless African American. The selection is taken from the narrator's experiences on his own in the city. The narrator has just been asked to leave his college for accidentally exposing one of the college's white benefactors to an element of rural life that the college president, Dr. Bledsoe, wished to keep hidden. Dr. Bledsoe has provided the narrator with "letters of recommendation" to take to the city and present to men who might help him find a job.

mind. They had not been pleasant and whenever I had visited the room I avoided the glass case in which they rested, preferring instead to look at photographs of the early days after the Civil War, the times close to those blind Barbee[1] had described. And I had not looked even at these too often.

I tried to relax; the chair was beautiful but hard. Where had the man gone? Had he shown any antagonism when he saw me? I was annoyed that I had failed to see him first. One had to watch such details. Suddenly there came a harsh cry from the cage, and once more I saw a mad flashing as though the birds had burst into spontaneous flame, fluttering and beating their wings maliciously against the bamboo bars, only to settle down just as suddenly when the door opened and the blond man stood beckoning, his hand upon the knob. I went over, tense inside me. Had I been accepted or rejected?

There was a question in his eyes. "Come in, please," he said.

"Thank you," I said, waiting to follow him.

"*Please*," he said with a slight smile.

I moved ahead of him, sounding the tone of his words for a sign.

"I want to ask you a few questions," he said, waving my letter at two chairs.

"Yes, sir?" I said.

"Tell me, what is it that you're trying to accomplish?" he said.

"I want a job, sir, so that I can earn enough money to return to college in the fall."

"To your old school?"

"Yes, sir."

"I see." For a moment he studied me silently. "When do you expect to graduate?"

"Next year, sir. I've completed my junior classes . . ."

"Oh, you have? That's very good. And how old are you?"

"Almost twenty, sir."

"A junior at nineteen? You *are* a good student."

"Thank you, sir," I said, beginning to enjoy the interview.

"Were you an athlete?" he asked.

"No, sir . . ."

"You have the build," he said, looking me up and down. "You'd probably make an excellent runner, a sprinter."

"I've never tried, sir."

"And I suppose it's silly even to ask what you think of your Alma Mater?"[2] he said.

"I think it's one of the best in the world," I said, hearing my voice surge with deep feeling.

"I know, I know," he said, with a swift displeasure that surprised me.

I became alert again as he mumbled something incomprehensible about "nostalgia for Harvard yard."

"But what if you were offered an opportunity to finish your work at some other college," he said, his eyes widening behind his glasses. His smile had returned.

"*Another* college?" I asked, my mind beginning to whirl.

"Why, yes, say some school in New England . . ."

I looked at him speechlessly. Did he mean Harvard? Was this good or bad. Where was it leading? "I don't know, sir," I said cautiously. "I've never thought about it. I've only a year more, and, well, I know everyone at my old school and they know me . . ."

I came to a confused halt, seeing him look at me with a sigh of resignation. What was on his mind? Perhaps I had been too frank about returning to the college, maybe he was against our having a higher education . . . But hell, he's only a secretary . . . Or *is* he?

"I understand," he said calmly. "It was presumptuous of me to even suggest another school. I guess one's college is really a kind of mother and father . . . a sacred matter."

"Yes, sir. That's it," I said in hurried agreement.

His eyes narrowed. "But now I must ask you an embarrassing question. Do you mind?"

"Why, no, sir," I said nervously.

"I don't like to ask this, but it's quite necessary . . ." He leaned forward with a pained frown. "Tell me, did you *read* the letter which you brought to Mr. Emerson? This," he said, taking the letter from the table.

"Why, no, sir! It wasn't addressed to me, so naturally I wouldn't think of opening it . . ."

"Of course not, I know you wouldn't," he said, fluttering his hand and sitting erect. "I'm sorry and you must dismiss it, like one of those annoying personal questions you find so often nowadays on supposedly impersonal forms."

I didn't believe him. "But was it opened, sir? Someone might have gone into my things . . ."

"Oh, no, nothing like that. Please forget the question . . . And tell me, please, what are your plans after graduation?"

"I'm not sure, sir. I'd like to be asked to remain at the college as a teacher, or as a member of the administrative staff. And . . . Well . . ."

"Yes? And what else?"

---

1. **Barbee.** The character Homer A. Barbee appeared earlier in the novel and gave a speech at the narrator's college about the period after the Emancipation during which the narrator's college was founded.
2. **Alma Mater.** College or school that one attended

"Well—er, I guess I'd really like to become Dr. Bledsoe's[1] assistant . . ."

"Oh, I see," he said, sitting back and forming his mouth into a thin-lipped circle. "You're very ambitious."

"I guess I am, sir. But I'm willing to work hard."

"Ambition is a wonderful force," he said, "but sometimes it can be blinding . . . On the other hand, it can make you successful—like my father . . ." A new edge came into his voice and he frowned and looked down at his hands, which were trembling. "The only trouble with ambition is that it sometimes blinds one to realities . . . Tell me, how many of these letters do you have?"

"I had about seven, sir," I replied, confused by his new turn. "They're—"

"*Seven!*" He was suddenly angry.

"Yes, sir, that was all he gave me . . ."

"And how many of these gentlemen have you succeeded in seeing, may I ask?"

A sinking feeling came over me. "I haven't seen any of them personally, sir."

"And this is your last letter?"

"Yes, sir, it is, but I expect to hear from the others . . . They said—"

"Of course you will, and from all seven. They're all loyal Americans."

There was unmistakable irony in his voice now, and I didn't know what to say.

"Seven," he repeated mysteriously. "Oh, don't let me upset you," he said with an elegant gesture of self-disgust. "I had a difficult session with my analyst last evening and the slightest thing is apt to set me off. Like an alarm clock without control— Say!" he said, slapping his palms against his thighs. "What on earth does that mean?" Suddenly he was in a state. One side of his face had begun to twitch and swell.

I watched him light a cigarette, thinking, What on earth is this all about?

"Some things are just too unjust for words," he said, expelling a plume of smoke, "and too ambiguous for either speech or ideas. By the way, have you ever been to the Club Calamus?"

"I don't think I've ever heard of it, sir," I said.

"You haven't? It's very well known. Many of my Harlem friends go there. It's a rendezvous for writers, artists and all kinds of celebrities. There's nothing like it in the city, and by some strange twist it has a truly continental flavor."

"I've never been to a night club, sir. I'll have to go there to see what it's like after I've started earning some money," I said, hoping to bring the conversation back to the problem of jobs.

He looked at me with a jerk of his head, his face beginning to twitch again.

"I suppose I've been evading the issue again—as always. Look," he burst out impulsively. "Do you believe that two people, two strangers who have never seen one another before can speak with utter frankness and sincerity?"

"Sir?"

"Oh, damn! What I mean is, do you believe it possible for us, the two of us, to throw off the mask of custom and manners that insulate man from man, and converse in naked honesty and frankness?"

"I don't know what you mean exactly, sir," I said.

"Are you sure?"

"I . . ."

"Of course, of course. If I could only speak plainly! I'm confusing you. Such frankness just isn't possible because all our motives are impure. Forget what I just said. I'll try to put it this way—and remember this, please . . ."

My head spun. He was addressing me, leaning forward confidentially, as though he'd known me for years, and I remembered something my grandfather had said long ago: *Don't let no white man tell you his business, 'cause after he tells you he's liable to git shame he tole it to you and then he'll hate you. Fact is, he was hating you all the time . . .*

". . . I want to try to reveal a part of reality that is most important to you—but I warn you, it's going to hurt. No, let me finish," he said, touching my knee lightly and quickly removing his hand as I shifted my position.

"What I want to do is done very seldom, and, to be honest, it wouldn't happen now if I hadn't sustained a series of impossible frustrations. You see—well, I'm a thwarted . . . Oh, damn, there I go again, thinking only of myself . . . We're both frustrated, understand? Both of us, and I want to help you . . ."

"You mean you'll let me see Mr. Emerson?"

He frowned. "Please don't seem so happy about it, and don't leap to conclusions. I want to help, but there is a tyranny involved . . ."

"A *tyranny?*" My lungs tightened.

"Yes. That's a way of putting it. Because to help you I must disillusion you . . ."

"Oh, I don't think I mind, sir. Once I see Mr. Emerson, it'll be up to me. All I want to do is speak to him."

"*Speak* to him," he said, getting quickly to his feet and mashing his cigarette into the tray with shaking fingers. "No one speaks *to* him. *He* does the speaking—" Suddenly he broke off. "On second thought, perhaps you'd better leave me your address and I'll mail you Mr. Emerson's reply in the morning. He's really a very busy man."

---

1. **Dr. Bledsoe.** President of the college which the narrator has been asked to leave. Bledsoe has, however, provided the narrator with letters of "introduction" to help him find a job.

His whole manner had changed.

"But you said . . ." I stood up, completely confused. Was he having fun with me? "Couldn't you let me talk to him for just five minutes?" I pleaded. "I'm sure I can convince him that I'm worthy of a job. And if there's someone who has tampered with my letter, I'll prove my identity . . . Dr. Bledsoe would—"

"Identity! My God! Who has any identity any more anyway? It isn't so perfectly simple. Look," he said with an anguished gesture. "Will you trust me?"

"Why, yes, sir, I trust you."

He leaned forward. "Look," he said, his face working violently, "I was trying to tell you that I know many things about you—not you personally, but fellows like you. Not much, either, but still more than the average. With us it's still Jim and Huck Finn.[1] A number of my friends are jazz musicians, and I've been around. I know the conditions under which you live— Why go back, fellow? There is so much you could do here where there is more freedom. You won't find what you're looking for when you return anyway; because so much is involved that you can't possibly know. Please don't misunderstand me; I don't say all this to impress you. Or to give myself some kind of sadistic catharsis. Truly, I don't. But I do know this world you're trying to contact—all its virtues and all its unspeakables— Ha, yes, unspeakables. I'm afraid my father considers me one of the unspeakables . . . I'm Huckleberry, you see . . ."

He laughed drily as I tried to make sense of his ramblings. *Huckleberry?* Why did he keep talking about that kid's story? I was puzzled and annoyed that he could talk to me this way because he stood between me and a job, the campus . . .

"But I only want a job, sir," I said. "I only want to make enough money to return to my studies."

"Of course, but surely you suspect there is more to it than that. Aren't you curious about what lies behind the face of things?"

"Yes, sir, but I'm mainly interested in a job."

"Of course," he said, "but life isn't that simple . . ."

"But I'm not bothered about all the other things, whatever they are, sir. They're not for me to interfere with and I'll be satisfied to go back to college and remain there as long as they'll allow me to."

"But I want to help you do what is best," he said. "What's *best*, mind you. Do you wish to do what's best for yourself?"

"Why, yes, sir. I suppose I do . . ."

"Then forget about returning to the college. Go somewhere else . . ."

"You mean leave?"

"Yes, forget it . . ."

"But you said that you would help me!"

"I did and I am—"

"But what about seeing Mr. Emerson?"

"Oh, God! Don't you see that it's best that you do *not* see him?"

Suddenly I could not breathe. Then I was standing, gripping my brief case. "What have you got against me?" I blurted. "What did I ever do to you? You never intended to let me see him. Even though I presented my letter of introduction. Why? Why? I'd never endanger *your* job—"

"No, no, no! Of course not," he cried, getting to his feet. "You've misunderstood me. You mustn't do that! God, there's too much misunderstanding. Please don't think I'm trying to prevent you from seeing my—from seeing Mr. Emerson out of prejudice . . ."

"Yes, sir, I do," I said angrily. "I was sent here by a friend of his. You read the letter, but still you refuse to let me see him, and now you're trying to get me to leave college. What kind of man are you, anyway? What have you got against me? You, a northern white man!"

He looked pained. "I've done it badly," he said, "but you must believe that I am trying to advise you what is best for you." He snatched off his glasses.

"But *I* know what's best for me," I said. "Or at least Dr. Bledsoe does, and if I can't see Mr. Emerson today, just tell me when I can and I'll be here . . ."

He bit his lips and shut his eyes, shaking his head from side to side as though fighting back a scream. "I'm sorry, really sorry that I started all of this," he said, suddenly calm. "It was foolish of me to try to advise you, but please, you mustn't believe that I'm against you . . . or your race. I'm your friend. Some of the finest people I know are Neg—Well, you see, Mr. Emerson is my father."

"Your father!"

"My father, yes, though I would have preferred it otherwise. But he is, and I could arrange for you to see him. But to be utterly frank, I'm incapable of such cynicism. It would do you no good."

"But I'd like to take my chances, Mr. Emerson, sir . . . This is very important to me. My whole career depends upon it."

"But you *have* no chance," he said.

"But Dr. Bledsoe sent me here," I said, growing more excited. "I must have a chance . . ."

"Dr. Bledsoe," he said with distaste. "He's like my . . . he ought to be horsewhipped! Here," he said, sweeping up the letter and thrusting it crackling toward me. I took it, looking into his eyes that burned back at me.

---

1. **Jim and Huck Finn.** Characters in the novel *The Adventures of Huckleberry Finn*, by Mark Twain

"Go on, read it," he cried excitedly. "Go on!"

"But I wasn't asking for this," I said.

"Read it!"

My dear Mr. Emerson:

The bearer of this letter is a former student of ours (I say *former* because he shall never, under any circumstances, be enrolled as a student here again) who has been expelled for a most serious defection from our strictest rules of deportment.

Due, however, to circumstances the nature of which I shall explain to you in person on the occasion of the next meeting of the board, it is to the best interests of the college that this young man have no knowledge of the finality of his expulsion. For it is indeed his hope to return here to his classes in the fall. However, it is to the best interests of the great work which we are dedicated to perform, that he continue undisturbed in these vain hopes while remaining as far as possible from our midst.

This case represents, my dear Mr. Emerson, one of the rare, delicate instances in which one for whom we held great expectations has gone grievously astray, and who in his fall threatens to upset certain delicate relationships between certain interested individuals and the school. Thus, while the bearer is no longer a member of our scholastic family, it is highly important that his severance with the college be executed as painlessly as possible. I beg of you, sir, to help him continue in the direction of that promise which, like the horizon, recedes ever brightly and distantly beyond the hopeful traveler.

Respectfully, I am your
humble servant,

A. Hebert Bledsoe

I raised my head. Twenty-five years seemed to have lapsed between his handing me the letter and my grasping its message. I could not believe it, tried to read it again. I could not believe it, yet I had a feeling that it all had happened before. I rubbed my eyes, and they felt sandy as though all the fluids had suddenly dried.

"I'm sorry," he said. "I'm terribly sorry."

"What did I do? I always tried to do the right thing . . ."

"*That* you must tell me," he said. "To what does he refer?"

"I don't know, I don't know . . ."

"But you must have done *something*."

"I took a man for a drive, showed him into the Golden Day[1] to help him when he became ill . . . I don't know . . ."

I told him falteringly of the visit to Trueblood's[2] and the trip to the Golden Day and of my expulsion, watching his mobile face reflecting his reaction to each detail.

"It's little enough," he said when I had finished. "I don't understand the man. He is very complicated."

"I only wanted to return and help," I said.

"You'll never return. You can't return now," he said. "Don't you see? I'm terribly sorry and yet I'm glad that I gave in to the impulse to speak to you. Forget it; though that's advice which I've been unable to accept myself, it's still good advice. There is no point in blinding yourself to the truth. Don't blind yourself . . ."

I got up, dazed, and started toward the door. He came behind me into the reception room where the birds flamed in the cage, their squawks like screams in a nightmare.

He stammered guiltily, "Please, I must ask you never to mention this conversation to anyone."

"No," I said.

"I wouldn't mind, but my father would consider my revelation the most extreme treason . . . You're free of him now. I'm still his prisoner. You have been freed, don't you understand? I've still my battle." He seemed near tears.

"I won't," I said. "No one would believe me. I can't myself. There must be some mistake. There must be . . ."

I opened the door.

"Look, fellow," he said. "This evening I'm having a party at the Calamus. Would you like to join my guests? It might help you—"

"No, thank you, sir. I'll be all right."

"Perhaps you'd like to be my valet?"

I looked at him. "No, thank you, sir," I said.

"Please," he said. "I really want to help. Look, I happen to know of a possible job at Liberty Paints. My father has sent several fellows there . . . You should try—"

I shut the door.

The elevator dropped me like a shot and I went out and walked along the street. The sun was very bright now and the people along the walk seemed far away. I stopped before a gray wall where high above me the headstones of a church graveyard arose like the tops of buildings. Across the street in the shade of an awning a shoeshine boy was dancing for pennies. I went on to the corner and got on a bus and went automatically to the rear. In the seat in front of me a dark man in a panama hat kept whistling a tune between his teeth.

1. **Golden Day.** Tavern
2. **Trueblood's.** Farm of a local African American near the narrator's college

FROM *THEIR EYES WERE WATCHING GOD*

About the Author. Zora Neale Hurston (1891–1960) was born in Eatonville, Florida. Her Eatonville years laid the foundation for the self-confident, high-spirited woman she would become. Her mother's death when Hurston was a young girl and her father's subsequent remarriage left Hurston feeling alienated. By the time she was fourteen, she had left home and was working as a wardrobe girl in a traveling Gilbert and Sullivan troupe. Hurston, however, wanted an education. Through her dedication and hard work she received one, first at Howard University in Washington, DC, and later as a scholarship student in anthropology at Barnard College, from which she graduated in 1927. Most of her important writings were published during the 1930s. In that decade she also held a graduate fellowship in anthropology at Columbia University, taught college courses, did research in the Caribbean on a Guggenheim Fellowship, and worked as an editor for the Federal Writers' Project in Florida. A complex personality, Hurston was attacked by African-American male intellectual leaders in the 1940s and 1950s because of the conservative cast of her essays. During the last decade of her life, she was plagued by poverty, poor health, and obscurity. When she died in 1960, her work had long been neglected. However, her fine artistry has received renewed interest in recent years.

My mind flew in circles, to Bledsoe, Emerson and back again. There was no sense to be made of it. It was a joke. Hell, it couldn't be a joke. Yes, it is a joke . . . Suddenly the bus jerked to a stop and I heard myself humming the same tune that the man ahead was whistling, and the words came back:

O well they picked poor Robin clean
O well they picked poor Robin clean
Well they tied poor Robin to a stump
Lawd, they picked all the feathers round
from Robin's rump
Well they picked poor Robin clean.

Then I was on my feet, hurrying to the door, hearing the thin, tissue-paper-against-the-teeth-of-a-comb whistle following me outside at the next stop. I stood trembling at the curb, watching and half expecting to see the man leap from the door to follow me, whistling the old forgotten jingle about a bare-rumped robin. My mind seized upon the tune. I took the subway and it still droned through my mind after I had reached my room at Men's House and lay across the bed. What was the who-what-when-why-where of poor old Robin? What had he done and who had tied him and why had they plucked him and why had we sung of his fate? It was for a laugh, for a laugh, all the kids had laughed and laughed, and the droll tuba player of the old Elk's band had rendered it solo on his helical horn; with comical flourishes and doleful phrasing, "*Boo boo boo booooo*, Poor Robin clean"—a mock funeral dirge . . . But who was Robin and for what had he been hurt and humiliated?

Suddenly I lay shaking with anger. It was no good. I thought of young Emerson. What if he'd lied out of some ulterior motive of his own? Everyone seemed to have some plan for me, and beneath that some more secret plan. What was young Emerson's plan—and why should it have included me? Who was I anyway? I tossed fitfully. Perhaps it was a test of my good will and faith—But that's a lie, I thought. It's a lie and you know it's a lie. I had seen the letter and it had practically ordered me killed. By slow degrees . . .

"My dear Mr. Emerson," I said aloud. "The Robin bearing this letter is a former student. Please hope him to death, and keep him running. Your most humble and obedient servant, A. H. Bledsoe . . ."

Sure, that's the way it was, I thought, a short, concise verbal *coup de grace*,[1] straight to the nape of the neck. And Emerson would write in reply? Sure: "Dear Bled, have met Robin and shaved tail. Signed, Emerson."

I sat on the bed and laughed. They'd sent me to the rookery, all right. I laughed and felt numb and weak, knowing that soon the pain would come and that no matter what happened to me I'd never be the same. I felt numb and I was laughing. When I stopped, gasping for breath, I decided that I would go back and kill Bledsoe. Yes, I thought, I owe it to the race and to myself. I'll kill him.

And the boldness of the idea and the anger behind it made me move with decision. I had to have a job and I took what I hoped was the quickest means. I called the plant young Emerson had mentioned, and it worked. I was told to report the following morning. It happened so quickly and with such ease that for a moment I felt turned around. Had they planned it this way? But no, they wouldn't catch me again. This time *I* had made the move.

I could hardly get to sleep for dreaming of revenge.

from *Their Eyes Were Watching God* by Zora Neale Hurston

It was a spring afternoon in West Florida. Janie had spent most of the day under a blossoming pear tree in the back-yard. She had been spending every minute that she could steal from her chores under that tree for the last three days. That was to say, ever since the first tiny bloom had opened. It had called her to come and gaze on a mystery. From barren brown stems to glistening leaf-buds; from the leaf-buds to snowy virginity of bloom. It stirred her tremendously. How? Why? It was like a flute song forgotten in another existence and remembered again. What? How? Why? This singing she heard that had nothing to do with her ears. The rose of the world was breathing out smell. It followed her through all her waking moments and caressed her in her sleep. It connected itself with other vaguely felt matters that had struck her outside observation and buried themselves in her flesh. Now they emerged and quested about her consciousness.

She was stretched on her back beneath the pear tree soaking in the alto chant of the visiting bees, the gold of the sun and the panting breath of the breeze when the inaudible voice of it all came to her. She saw a dust-bearing bee sink into the sanctum of a bloom; the thousand sister-calyxes arch to meet the love embrace and the ecstatic shiver of the tree from root to tiniest branch creaming in every blossom and frothing with delight. So this was a marriage! She had been summoned to behold a revelation. Then Janie felt a pain remorseless sweet that left her limp and languid.

1. **coup de grace.** Death blow

After a while she got up from where she was and went over the little garden field entire. She was seeking confirmation of the voice and vision, and everywhere she found and acknowledged answers. A personal answer for all other creations except herself. She felt an answer seeking her, but where? When? How? She found herself at the kitchen door and stumbled inside. In the air of the room were flies tumbling and singing, marrying and giving in marriage. When she reached the narrow hallway she was reminded that her grandmother was home with a sick headache. She was lying across the bed asleep so Janie tipped on out of the front door. Oh to be a pear tree—*any* tree in bloom! With kissing bees singing of the beginning of the world! She was sixteen. She had glossy leaves and bursting buds and she wanted to struggle with life but it seemed to elude her. Where were the singing bees for her? Nothing on the place nor in her grandma's house answered her. She searched as much of the world as she could from the top of the front steps and then went on down to the front gate and leaned over to gaze up and down the road. Looking, waiting, breathing short with impatience. Waiting for the world to be made.

Through pollinated air she saw a glorious being coming up the road. In her former blindness she had known him as shiftless Johnny Taylor, tall and lean. That was before the golden dust of pollen had beglamored his rags and her eyes.

In the last stages of Nanny's sleep, she dreamed of voices. Voices far-off but persistent, and gradually coming nearer. Janie's voice. Janie talking in whispery snatches with a male voice she couldn't quite place. That brought her wide awake. She bolted upright and peered out of the window and saw Johnny Taylor lacerating her Janie with a kiss.

"Janie!"

The old woman's voice was so lacking in command and reproof, so full of crumbling dissolution,—that Janie half believed that Nanny had not seen her. So she extended herself outside of her dream and went inside of the house. That was the end of her childhood.

from *The Great Gatsby*
by F. Scott Fitzgerald

About half way between West Egg and New York the motor-road hastily joins the railroad and runs beside it for a quarter of a mile so as to shrink away from a certain desolate area of land. This is a valley of ashes—a fantastic farm where ashes grow like wheat into ridges and hills and grotesque gardens, where ashes take the form of houses and chimneys and rising smoke and finally, with a transcendent effort, of men who move dimly and already crumbling through the powdery air. Occasionally a line of grey cars crawls along an invisible track, gives out a ghastly creak and comes to rest, and immediately the ash-grey men swarm up with leaden spades and stir up an impenetrable cloud which screens their obscure operations from your sight.

But above the grey land and the spasms of bleak dust which drift endlessly over it, you perceive, after a moment, the eyes of Doctor T. J. Eckleburg. The eyes of Doctor T. J. Eckleburg are blue and gigantic—their retinas[1] are one yard high. They look out of no face but, instead, from a pair of enormous yellow spectacles which pass over a nonexistent nose. Evidently some wild wag[2] of an oculist[3] set them there to fatten his practice in the borough of Queens and then sank down himself into eternal blindness or forgot them and moved away. But his eyes, dimmed a little by many paintless days under sun and rain, brood on over the solemn dumping ground.

The valley of ashes is bounded on one side by a small foul river, and when the drawbridge is up to let barges through, the passengers on waiting trains can stare at the dismal scene for as long as half an hour. There is always a halt there of at least a minute and it was because of this that I first met Tom Buchanan's mistress.

from *Tell Me How Long the Train's Been Gone*
by James Baldwin

My brother, Caleb, was seventeen when I was ten. We were very good friends. In fact, he was my best friend and, for a very long time, my only friend.

I do not mean to say that he was always nice to me. I got on his nerves a lot, and he resented having to take me around with him and be responsible for me when there were so many other things he wanted to be doing. Therefore, his hand was often up against the side of my head, and my tears caused him to be punished many times. But I knew, somehow, anyway, that when he was being punished for my tears, he was not being punished for anything he had done to me; he was being punished because that was the way we lived; and his punishment, oddly, helped unite us. More oddly still, even as his great hand caused my head to stammer and dropped a

1. **retinas.** Innermost coat lining the interior of the eyeballs
2. **wag.** Comical or humorous person
3. **oculist.** Early term for ophthalmologist or eye doctor

FROM *TELL ME HOW LONG THE TRAIN'S BEEN GONE*

About the Author. James Baldwin (1924–1987) was born in Harlem, a section of New York City. His love of books and his talent for writing emerged at an early age, and his teachers encouraged him. At age fourteen he joined a church and became a minister, preaching in different churches in Harlem. Eventually Baldwin moved to Greenwich Village where he produced his first work to gain recognition, some of which is collected in *Notes of a Native Son.* Like many twentieth-century American writers, Baldwin moved to Paris to continue his work and joined the rank of expatriate authors such as T. S. Eliot, Ezra Pound, F. Scott Fitzgerald, and Henry Miller. It was in Europe that Baldwin completed his first semiautobiographical novel, *Go Tell It on the Mountain* (1953), which explored his life as a young minister. In 1957, Baldwin returned to the New York that had so influenced his work and became an active figure in the Civil Rights movement. After traveling throughout the United States, Baldwin produced a collection of essays, *Nobody Knows My Name* (1961), exploring race relations. Although his early work received more critical acclaim, Baldwin continued writing while he divided his time between the United States and abroad. He wrote a Broadway play, *Blues for Mr. Charlie* (1964); essays, such as *The Fire Next Time* (1963), which was another powerful civil rights piece; and novels, including *Tell Me How Long the Train's Been Gone* (1968) and *Just Above My Head* (1979).

FROM *THE GREAT GATSBY*

About the Author. F. Scott Fitzgerald (1896–1940) captures the spirit of the Jazz Age in many of his works including *This Side of Paradise* and *Tender Is the Night.* His works are often semi-autobiographical in nature and deal with the glamorous but sometimes empty lives of the upper classes.

About the Selection. ***The Great Gatsby*** is considered Fitzgerald's finest work. In this novel, Fitzgerald ironically explores the hollowness of any purely materialistic conception of the "American Dream." This excerpt, Fitzgerald's famous description of the "valley of ashes," describes in intensely symbolic language the lives and circumstances of the underclass, those for whom the dream is a nightmare.

flame-colored curtain before my eyes, I understood that he was not striking *me*. His hand leapt out because he could not help it, and I received the blow because I was there. And it happened, sometimes, before I could even catch my breath to howl, that the hand that had struck me grabbed me and held me, and it was difficult indeed to know which of us was weeping. He was striking, striking out, striking out, striking out; the hand asked me to forgive him. I felt his bewilderment through the membrane of my own. I also felt that he was trying to teach me something. And I had, God knows, no other teachers.

For our father—how shall I describe our father?—was a ruined Barbados[1] peasant, exiled in a Harlem[2] which he loathed, where he never saw the sun or sky he remembered, where life took place neither indoors nor without, and where there was no joy. By which I mean no joy that he remembered. Had he been able to bring with him any of the joy he had felt on that far-off island, then the air of the sea and the impulse to dancing would sometimes have transfigured our dreadful rooms. Our lives might have been very different.

But no, he brought with him from Barbados only black rum and blacker pride and magic incantations, which neither healed nor saved.

He did not understand the people among whom he found himself; they had no coherence, no stature and no pride. He came from a race which had been flourishing at the very dawn of the world—a race greater and nobler than Rome or Judea, mightier than Egypt—he came from a race of kings, kings who had never been taken in battle, kings who had never been slaves. He spoke to us of tribes and empires, battles, victories, and monarchs of whom we had never heard—they were not mentioned in our textbooks—and invested us with glories in which we felt more awkward than in the secondhand shoes we wore. In the stifling room of his pretensions and expectations, we stumbled wretchedly about, stubbing our toes, as it were, on rubies, scraping our shins on golden caskets, bringing down, with a childish cry, the splendid purple tapestry on which, in pounding gold and scarlet, our destinies and our inheritance were figured. It could scarcely have been other-wise, since a child's major attention has to be concentrated on how to fit into a world which, with every passing hour, reveals itself as merciless.

If our father was of royal blood and we were royal children, our father was certainly the only person in the world who knew it. The landlord did not know it; our father never mentioned royal blood to *him*. When we were late with our rent, which was often, the landlord threatened, in terms no commoner had ever used before a king, to put us in the streets. He complained that our shiftlessness, which he did not hesitate to consider an attribute of the race, had forced him, an old man with a weak heart, to climb all these stairs to plead with us to give him the money we owed him. And this was the last time; he wanted to make sure we understood that this was the last time.

Our father was younger than the landlord, leaner, stronger, and bigger. With one blow, he could have brought the landlord to his knees. And we knew how much he hated the man. For days on end, in the wintertime, we huddled around the gas stove in the kitchen, because the landlord gave us no heat. When windows were broken, the landlord took his time about fixing them; the wind made the cardboard we stuffed in the windows rattle all night long; and when snow came, the weight of the snow forced the cardboard inward and onto the floor. Whenever the apartment received a fresh coat of paint, we bought the paint and did the painting ourselves; we killed the rats. A great chunk of the kitchen ceiling fell one winter, narrowly missing our mother.

We all hated the landlord with a perfectly exquisite hatred, and we would have been happy to see our proud father kill him. We would have been glad to help. But our father did nothing of the sort. He stood before the landlord, looking unutterably weary. He made excuses. He apologized. He swore that it would never happen again. (We knew that it *would* happen again.) He begged for time. The landlord would finally go down the stairs, letting us and all the neighbors know how good-hearted he was, and our father would walk into the kitchen and pour himself a glass of rum.

But we knew that our father would never have allowed any black man to speak to him as the landlord did, as policemen did, as storekeepers and welfare workers and pawnbrokers did. No, not for a moment. He would have thrown him out of the house. He would certainly have made a black man know that he was not the descendant of slaves! He had made them know it so often that he had almost no friends among them, and if we had followed his impossible lead, we would have had no friends, either. It was scarcely worthwhile being the descendant of kings if the kings were black and no one had ever heard of them.

And it was because of our father, perhaps, that Caleb and I clung to each other, in spite of the great difference in our ages; or, in another way, it may have been

1. **Barbados.** Island in the British West Indies
2. **Harlem.** Section of New York City

precisely the difference in our ages that made the clinging possible. I don't know. It is really not the kind of thing anyone can ever know. I think it may be easier to love the really helpless younger brother, because he cannot enter into competition with one on one's own ground, or on any ground at all, and can never question one's role or jeopardize one's authority. In my own case, certainly, it did not occur to me to compete with Caleb, and I could not have questioned his role or his authority, because I needed both. He was my touchstone,[1] my model and my only guide.

Anyway, our father, dreaming bitterly of Barbados, despised and mocked by his neighbors and all but ignored by his sons, held down his unspeakable factory job, spread his black gospel in bars on the weekends, and drank his rum. I do not know if he loved our mother. I think he did.

They had had five children—only Caleb and I, the first and the last, were left. We were both dark, like our father; but two of the three dead girls had been fair, like our mother.

She came from New Orleans. Her hair was not like ours. It was black, but softer and finer. The color of her skin reminded me of the color of bananas. Her skin was as bright as that, and contained that kind of promise, and she had tiny freckles around her nose and a small black mole just above her upper lip. It was the mole, I don't know why, which made her beautiful. Without it, her face might have been merely sweet, merely pretty. But the mole was funny. It had the effect of making one realize that our mother liked funny things, liked to laugh. The mole made one look at her eyes—large, extraordinary dark eyes, eyes which seemed always to be amused by something, eyes which looked straight out, seeming to see everything, seeming to be afraid of nothing. She was a soft, round, plump woman. She liked nice clothes and dangling jewelry, which she mostly didn't have, and she liked to cook for large numbers of people, and she loved our father.

She knew him—knew him through and through. I am not being coy or colloquial but bluntly and sadly matter-of-fact when I say that I will now never know what she saw in him. What she saw was certainly not for many eyes; what she saw got him through his working week and his Sunday rest; what she saw saved him. She saw that he was a man. For her, perhaps, he was a great man. I think, though, that for our mother any man was great who aspired to become a man: this meant that our father was very rare and precious. I used to wonder how she took it, how she bore it—his rages, his tears, his cowardice.

On Saturday nights he was almost always evil, drunk, and maudlin. He came home from work in the early afternoon and gave our mother some money. It was never enough, of course, but she never protested, at least not as far as I know. Then she would go out shopping. I would usually go with her, for Caleb would almost always be out somewhere, and our mother didn't like the idea of leaving me alone in the house. And this was probably, after all, the best possible arrangement. People who disliked our father were sure (for that very reason) to like our mother; and people who felt that Caleb was growing to be too much like his father could feel that I, after all, might turn out like my mother. Besides, it is not, as a general rule, easy to hate a small child. One runs the risk of looking ridiculous, especially if the child is with his mother.

And especially if that mother is Mrs. Proudhammer. Mrs. Proudhammer knew very well what people thought of Mr. Proudhammer. She knew, too, exactly how much she owed in each store she entered, how much she was going to be able to pay, and what she had to buy. She entered with a smile, ready.

"Evening. Let me have some of them red beans there."

"Evening. You know you folks been running up quite a little bill here."

"I'm going to give you something on it right now. I need some cornmeal and flour and some rice."

"You know, I got my bills to meet, too, Mrs. Proudhammer."

"Didn't I just tell you I was going to pay? I want some cornflakes, too, and some milk." Such merchandise as she could reach, she had already placed on the counter.

"When do you think you're going to be able to pay this bill? All of it, I mean."

"You know I'm going to pay it just as soon as I can. How much does it all come to? Give me that end you got there of that chocolate cake." The chocolate cake was for Caleb and me. "Well, now you put this against the bill." Imperiously, as though it were the most natural thing in the world, she put two or three dollars on the counter.

"You lucky I'm softhearted, Mrs. Proudhammer. "

"Things sure don't cost this much downtown—you think I don't know it? Here." And she paid him for what she had bought. "Thank you. You been mighty kind."

And we left the store. I often felt that in order to help her, I should have filled my pockets with merchandise while she was talking. But I never did, not only because the store was often crowded or because I was afraid of being caught by the storekeeper, but because I was afraid of humiliating her.

1. **touchstone.** Test of genuineness or value

When we had to do "heavy" shopping, we went marketing under the bridge at Park Avenue—Caleb, our mother, and I; and sometimes, but rarely, our father came with us. The most usual reason for heavy shopping was that some relatives of our mother's, or old friends of both our mother's and our father's, were coming to visit. We were certainly not going to let them go away hungry—not even if it meant, as it often did mean, spending more than we had. In spite of what I have been suggesting about our father's temperament, and no matter how difficult he may sometimes have been with us, he was much too proud to offend any guest of his; on the contrary, his impulse was to make them feel that his home was theirs; and besides, he was lonely, lonely for his past, lonely for those faces which had borne witness to that past. Therefore, he would sometimes pretend that our mother did not know how to shop, and our father would come with us under the bridge, in order to teach her.

There he would be then, uncharacteristically, in shirt sleeves, which made him look rather boyish; and as our mother showed no desire to take shopping lessons from him, he turned his attention to Caleb and me. He would pick up a fish, opening the gills and holding it close to his nose. "You see that? That fish looks fresh, don't it? Well, that fish ain't as fresh as I am, and I *been* out of the water. They done doctored that fish. Come on." And we would walk away, a little embarrassed but, on the whole, rather pleased that our father was so smart.

Meantime, our mother was getting the marketing done. She was very happy on days like this, because our father was happy. He was happy, odd as his expression of it may sound, to be out with his wife and his two sons. If we had been on the island that had been witness to his birth, instead of the unspeakable island of Manhattan, he felt that it would not have been so hard for us all to trust and love each other. He sensed, and I think he was right, that on that other, never to be recovered island, his sons would have looked on him very differently, and he would have looked very differently on his sons. Life would have been hard there, too; we would have fought there, too, and more or less blindly suffered and more or less blindly died. But we would not have been (or so it was to seem to all of us forever) so wickedly menaced by the mere fact of our relationship, would not have been so frightened of entering into the central, most beautiful and valuable facts of our lives. We would have been laughing and cursing and tussling in the water, instead of stammering under the bridge; we would have known less about vanished African kingdoms and more about each other. Or, not at all impossibly, more about both.

If it was summer, we bought a watermelon, which either Caleb or our father carried home, fighting with each other for this privilege. They looked very like each other on those days—both big, both black, both laughing.

Caleb always looked absolutely helpless when he laughed. He laughed with all his body, perhaps touching his shoulder against yours, or putting his head on your chest for a moment, and then careening off you, halfway across the room or down the block. I will always hear his laughter. He was always happy on such days, too. Caleb certainly needed his father. Such days, however, were rare—one of the reasons, probably, that I remember them now.

Eventually, we all climbed the stairs into that hovel which, at such moments, was our castle. One very nearly felt the drawbridge rising behind us as our father locked the door.

The bathtub could not yet be filled with cold water and the melon placed in the tub, because this was Saturday, and, come evening, we all had to bathe. The melon was covered with a blanket and placed on the fire escape. Then we unloaded what we had bought, rather impressed by our opulence, though our father was always, by this time, appalled by the money we had spent. I was always sadly aware that there would be nothing left of all this once tomorrow had come and gone and that most of it, after all, was not for us, but for others.

Our mother was calculating the pennies she would need all week—carfare for our father and for Caleb, who went to a high school out of our neighborhood; money for the life insurance; money for milk for me at school; money for light and gas; money put away, if possible, toward the rent. She knew just about what our father had left in *his* pockets and was counting on him to give me the money I would shortly be demanding to go to the movies. Caleb had a part-time job after school and already had his movie money. Anyway, unless he was in a very good mood or needed me for something, he would not be anxious to go to the movies with me.

Our mother never insisted that Caleb tell her where he was going, nor did she question him as to how he spent the money he made. She was afraid of hearing him lie, and she did not want to risk forcing him to lie. She was operating on the assumption that he was sensible and had been raised to be honorable and that he, now more than ever, needed his privacy.

But she was very firm with him, nevertheless. "I do not want to see you rolling in here at three in the morning, Caleb. I want you here in time to eat, and you know you got to take your bath."

"Yes, indeed, ma'am. Why can't I take my bath in the morning?"

"Don't you start being funny. You know you ain't going to get up in time to take no bath in the morning."

"Don't nobody want you messing around in that bathroom all morning long, man," said our father. "You just git back in the house like your ma's telling you."

"Besides," I said, "you never wash out the tub. "

Caleb looked at me in mock surprise and from a great height, allowing his chin and his lids simultaneously to drop and swiveling his head away from me.

"I see," he said, "that everyone in this family is ganging up on me. All right, Leo. I was planning to take you to the show with me, but now I've changed my mind."

"I'm sorry," I said quickly. "I take it back."

"You take *what* back?"

"What I said—about you not washing out the tub."

"Ain't no need to take it back," our father said stubbornly. "It's true. A man don't take back nothing that's true."

"So *you* say," Caleb said, with a hint of a sneer. But before anyone could possibly react to this, he picked me up, scowling into my face, which he held just above his own. "You take it back?"

"Leo ain't going to take it back," our father said.

Now I was in trouble. Caleb watched me, a small grin on his face. "You take it back?"

"Stop teasing that child, and put him down," our mother said. "The trouble ain't that Caleb don't wash out the tub—he just don't wash it out very clean."

"I never knew him to wash it out," our father said, "unless I was standing behind him."

"Well, ain't neither one of you much good around the house," our mother said.

Caleb laughed and set me down. "You didn't take it back," he said.

I said nothing.

"I guess I'm just going to have to go on without you."

Still, I said nothing.

"You going to have that child to crying in a minute," our mother said. "If you going to take him, go on and take him. Don't do him like that."

Caleb laughed again. "I'm going to take him. The way he got them eyes all ready to water, I'd better take him somewhere." We walked toward the door. "But you got to make up *your* mind," he said to me, "to say what *you* think is right. . . ."

VOCABULARY DEVELOPMENT EXERCISES

►Give students the following exercise.

Write a dialogue for two people that incorporates fifteen words from the list on page 676. Then, with a partner, practice both dialogues aloud, paying attention to the correct pronunciation of the new vocabulary words.

ADDITIONAL RESOURCES

ASSESSMENT PORTFOLIO

- Vocabulary Worksheet, 4.9.9
- Study Guide: Unit 9 Test, 4.9.10
- Unit 9 Test, 4.9.11

ESSENTIAL SKILLS PRACTRICE BOOKS

Language

- Adding Modifiers, 2.46
- Base Words and Prefixes, 2.140
- Capitalization, 2.107–2.133
- Dangling and Misplaced Modifiers, 2.63
- Suffixes, 2.141
- Using Colorful Modifiers, 2.35
- Using Precise Nouns, 2.32
- Verbals: Infinitives, 2.18

Speaking and Listening

- Nonverbal Communication, 3.3

Study and Research

- Synonym and Antonym Questions, 4.44

Applied English

- The Form of a Personal Letter, 5.2

UNIT REVIEW

Modern Fiction

VOCABULARY FROM THE SELECTIONS

agitation, 622
apathetically, 624
apprehension, 617
conflagration, 622
conjectural, 616
dwindle, 647
ebb, 621
excruciatingly, 636
immobility, 635
imperative, 621
infatuation, 632
interminably, 636
jilt, 644
jocularity, 636
nucleus, 624
overture, 634
pall, 615
peremptorily, 625
poignant, 625
prelude, 635
reiterate, 618
render, 631
reproach, 636
respective, 633
reverential, 632
revert, 632
rummage, 642
thresh, 619
tremulously, 633
undulation, 615

LITERARY TERMS

catastrophe, 628
characterization, 655
conflict, 628
dialogue, 655
internal monologue, 655
irony, 648
narrator, 638
plot, 628
point of view, 638
setting, 628
simile, 638, 648
stream-of-consciousness writing, 649

SYNTHESIS: QUESTIONS FOR WRITING, RESEARCH, OR DISCUSSION

GENRE STUDIES

1. **Short Story.** According to Poe's definition, the short story must achieve creation of one dominant impression. How does portrayal of the cold in London's "To Build a Fire" and of the night in Hemingway's "A Clean Well-Lighted Place" meet this requirement?

THEMATIC STUDIES

2. **Loss.** Both Ellen Weatherall and Georgiana Carpenter feel a "shock of recognition." They have both led lives filled with hard work and caring for family but acknowledge emptiness. What do both regret?

HISTORICAL/BIOGRAPHICAL STUDIES

3. **Roles of Women.** Review the comments in the introduction on page 502 about changes in the roles of women. In some ways the two female characters in the Porter and Cather stories bridge two eras. What eras are they? What do the authors seem to be saying about women?

▶These prompts are suitable as topics for research papers. Refer to the Language Arts Survey, 4.20–4.34, "Research Skills." (To evaluate research papers, see the evaluation forms for writing, revising, and proofreading, *Assessment Portfolio,* 7.1–7.10.)

▶These prompts can be adapted for use as topics for oral reports or debates. (To evaluate these projects, see the evaluation forms in the *Assessment Portfolio,* 7.17–7.19.)

ANSWERS FOR LANGUAGE LAB

Exercise A

1. South (regions), Flannery O'Connor (personal names), William Faulkner (personal names)
2. *Their Eyes Were Watching God* (titles of literary works), Florida (place names)
3. Pulitzer Prize (awards)
4. reporter (occupations), Spain (place names), Spanish Civil War (events)
5. Zippo (brand and trade names)
6. Jazz Age (periods), Depression (periods)
7. Unless (first word), I (pronoun *I*), story (type of literary work)
8. Brother Jack (family relationships), Brotherhood (organizations)
9. Sunday (days), Chicago Public Library (buildings)
10. twentieth-century (centuries)

LANGUAGE LAB PROOFREADING FOR CAPITALIZATION ERRORS

Proper nouns are always capitalized. The following chart shows other cases when capitalization is required.

CAPITALIZE	EXAMPLES
Awards	Pulitzer Prize, Nobel Prize in literature
Brand and Trade Names	Rollerblade skates, Band-Aid bandages
Buildings and Structures	Tate Gallery, Great Pyramid of Khufu
Days, Months, Years, and Holidays	Monday, September, Labor Day
Directions and Regions	The West, Pacific Rim
Events and Periods	Civil War, Gilded Age
Family Relationships (unmodified)	Mother, Aunt June
First Words	Read the story for tomorrow's class.
Letters	from A to Z, middle C
Personal Names	Jack London, Willa Cather
Place Names	Harlem, New York City, U.S.A.
Pronoun *I*	I wish I had read "The Bear."
Titles of Art, Literary, and Musical Works	"To Build a Fire," Copland's *Billy the Kid*

LANGUAGE ARTS SURVEY

For additional help, see the Language Arts Survey, 2.107–2.133.

Exercise A Correcting Capitalization Errors

In each of the following sentences decide if the underlined words should be capitalized or not. Write each word correctly along with the rule it follows.

1. The south has produced many great writers, such as flannery o'Connor and william faulkner.
2. Hurston's *their eyes were watching god* takes place in florida.
3. Katherine Anne Porter won a pulitzer prize in 1965.
4. Ernest Hemingway worked as a Reporter in spain during the spanish civil war.
5. You can use my zippo lighter to light the fire.
6. F. Scott Fitzgerald, a celebrated writer of the jazz age, experienced severe financial problems during the depression.
7. unless someone explains it to me, there's no way i will understand this Faulkner Story.

8. In *Invisible Man,* brother jack leads a revolutionary group called the brotherhood.
9. Next sunday the chicago public library will host a reading of Willa Cather's writing.
10. Eudora Welty is one of my favorite Twentieth-Century writers.

Exercise B Proofreading for Capitalization Errors
In the paragraph that follows correct any errors in capitalization.

Although she was born in virginia, Willa cather is most often associated with nebraska, which became her home when she was Nine. The young Cather was graduated from the university of nebraska, worked as a Magazine Editor and english teacher in pittsburgh, and then moved to new york city to work as an editor for *mcClure's* magazine. However, when she began writing, her thoughts turned to her childhood in the midwest. many of Cather's most memorable novels, including *O pioneers!* and *My Antonia,* are set during Nebraska's frontier days. In these Novels, cather explores the myths of pioneer life in Nineteenth-Century America. The central characters of *O Pioneers!* are an immigrant family from sweden, and the title character of *My Antonia* is an immigrant woman from czechoslovakia. In *One of ours,* which was awarded the pulitzer prize, Cather intermingles scenes of Nebraska with world war I battle scenes. After her mother's death in 1931, Cather returned to her Home State for a brief family visit; it was to be her last one. Cather worked and lived out the rest of her life in her park avenue apartment in new york and in an Autumn retreat in new hampshire.

LANGUAGE ARTS SURVEY

For additional help, see the Language Arts Survey, 2.107–2.133.

ANSWERS FOR LANGUAGE LAB

Exercise B

Although she was born in **Virginia,** Willa **Cather** is most often associated with **Nebraska,** which became her home when she was **nine.** The young Cather was graduated from the **University** of **Nebraska,** worked as a **magazine editor** and **English** teacher in **Pittsburgh,** and then moved to **New York City** to work as an editor for ***McClure's*** magazine. However, when she began writing, her thoughts turned to her childhood in the **Midwest. Many** of Cather's most memorable novels, including *O **Pioneers!*** and *My Antonia,* are set during Nebraska's frontier days. In these **novels, Cather** explores the myths of pioneer life in **nineteenth-century** America. The central characters of *O Pioneers!* are an immigrant family from **Sweden,** and the title character of *My Antonia* is an immigrant woman from **Czechoslovakia.** In *One of **Ours,*** which was awarded the **Pulitzer Prize,** Cather intermingles scenes of Nebraska with **World War** I battle scenes. After her mother's death in 1931, Cather returned to her **home state** for a brief family visit; it was to be her last one. Cather worked and lived out the rest of her life in her **Park Avenue** apartment in **New York** and in an **autumn** retreat in **New Hampshire.**

UNIT SKILLS OUTLINE

LITERARY SKILLS AND CONCEPTS
- Archetype, 699
- Character, 690, 714
- Cliché, 707
- Conflict, 699
- Expressionism, 682, 690
- Irony, 694
- Metaphor, 686, 690
- Setting, 715
- Southern Gothic, 682
- Stage Directions, 689
- Symbol, 699, 701, 714, 739
- Theme, 738

WRITING SKILLS AND CONCEPTS
- Critical Analysis, 739
- Diary Entry, 739
- Dream Analysis, 715

GRAMMAR, USAGE, AND MECHANICS SKILLS AND CONCEPTS
- Correcting Sentence Fragments, 684
- Proofreading for Spelling Errors, 742

OTHER LANGUAGE ARTS SKILLS AND CONCEPTS
- Reading Actively, 716

UNIT 10 MODERN DRAMA (1900–1960)

New York Movie. *Edward Hopper, 1939. The Museum of Modern Art, New York, Given anonymously.*

GOALS/OBJECTIVES

Studying this unit will enable students to

- interpret and appreciate an Expressionist drama
- describe Tennessee Williams's literary accomplishments and explain the historical significance of *The Glass Menagerie*
- describe the structure of a drama
- identify, define, and give examples of archetypes, irony, metaphors, and symbols in literature
- write a critical essay
- proofread for spelling errors

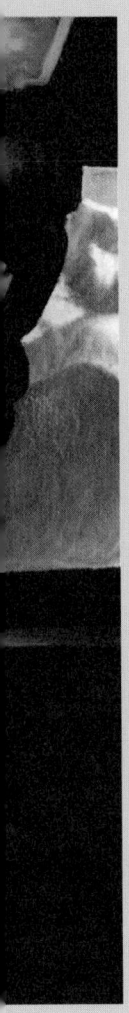

Photograph © 1995. The Museum of Modern Art, New York.

I am the opposite of the stage musician. He gives you illusion that has the appearance of truth. I give you truth in the pleasant disguise of illusion.

—Tennessee Williams

CONNECTIONS ACROSS THE CURRICULUM

Arts and Humanities

- Acting, 740
- Expressionism, 683
- Film Critism, 740

Mathematics and Sciences

- Temperament, 685

Social Studies

- Cultural and Social Background of the 1920s and 1930s, 682

Applied Arts

- Making a Model Stage Set, 685

TEACHING THE MULTIPLE INTELLIGENCES

Musical

- Expressionism, 683

Spatial

- Expressionism, 683

Interpersonal

- Cultural and Social Background of the 1920s and 1930s, 682
- Expressionism, 683
- Film Criticism, 740
- Making a Model Stage Set, 685

Kinesthetic

- Acting, 740

ADDITIONAL RESOURCES

READER'S GUIDE
- Selection Worksheets, 10.1, 10.2

ASSESSMENT PORTFOLIO
- Selection Check Tests, 4.10.1, 4.10.3
- Selection Tests, 4.10.2, 4.10.4

ESSENTIAL SKILLS PRACTICE BOOKS
- *Language,* 2.16

ENRICHMENT ACTIVITIES

Students might research the cultural and social background in which *The Glass Menagerie* is set. Topics from the 1920s and1930s that students might research include the Great Depression; the Sacco and Vanzetti trial; the Scopes "Monkey Trial"; the women's suffrage movement; the rise of dance halls; jazz, swing, and/or big band music; or gangsters. Students could then prepare oral reports and share what they have learned about the 1920s and 1930s. Such a project should help students recognize the social and cultural atmosphere that is such a distinctive part of *The Glass Menagerie.*

SUPPORT FOR LEP STUDENTS

Students will find Williams's vocabulary challenging, especially in his stage directions. Explain to students that since so much of this play is about mood and feeling, it is less important that they understand every diffcult term than that they are able to enter into the dreamlike atmosphere Williams creates. In addition to having students refer to the Words for Everyday Use and the footnotes as they read, you might familiarize them with the additional vocabulary below.

ADDITIONAL VOCABULARY

impulse—tendency coming from within

(cont.)

PREREADING

The Glass Menagerie
by Tennessee Williams

ABOUT THE AUTHOR

Tennessee Williams (1911–1983) was the pen name of one of America's finest dramatists. Born Thomas Lanier Williams, he grew up in Mississippi and St. Louis. Williams began writing early, publishing his first short story at the age of fourteen. He attended the University of Washington and the University of Iowa and then worked at various jobs in Chicago, St. Louis, New Orleans, and California. In 1939, his *American Blues,* a collection of short plays, was produced in New York to enthusiastic reviews. However, his next play, *Battle of Angels,* later rewritten and retitled *Orpheus Descending,* failed when it was produced in Boston. *The Glass Menagerie,* produced in 1944 and a tremendous success, was followed by *A Streetcar Named Desire* (1947), *Summer and Smoke* (1948), *Camino Real* (1953), *Cat on a Hot Tin Roof* (1955), *Suddenly Last Summer* (1958), *Sweet Bird of Youth* (1959), and *The Night of the Iguana* (1962). Williams also wrote the novella *The Roman Spring of Mrs. Stone* (1950) and his *Memoirs* (1975). Williams's plays often deal with troubled, emotionally intense social misfits and are often set in the post-Civil War, or antebellum, South. Because of the intensity of emotion in these plays and because of their powerfully evocative settings, they are often referred to as examples of **Southern Gothic**. Williams was also a pioneering American Expressionist. **Expressionism** was an artistic movement of the early and mid-twentieth century that sought to express emotions by exaggerating the artistic medium itself. Expressionist painters tended to use heavy strokes of the brush or palette knife and vivid, intense colors. Expressionist dramatists often exaggerated the elements of spectacle and the literary techniques in their works, using lighting, sound, properties, and elements of the stage set for symbolic purposes.

ABOUT THE SELECTION

The closest companion of Williams's youth, his sister Rose, provided the model for the central character in the play that was to be his first major success, ***The Glass Menagerie.*** This largely autobiographical play, originally called *The Gentleman Caller,* deals with a socially isolated young woman, Laura, whose intense fragility is symbolized by her collection of glass

SUPPORT FOR LEP STUDENTS (CONT.)

automatism—automatic action
lattice-work—open-work door, gate, shutter, or trellis
gallantly—in a brave or noble manner
ascend—move upward
secretion—substance released
temperament—one's frame of mind or natural disposition
nimble—quick; agile
absurd—ridiculous; silly; nonsensical
inaudibly—in a manner unable to be heard clearly
humility—state or quality of being humble
vivacity—liveliness
allusion—indirect reference; casual mention
martyr—person who suffers great pain or misery for a long time
debutante—girl or woman making debut into society
confiscate—take away from

(cont.)

figurines. Laura's nickname, "Blue Roses," recalls the name of Williams's sister, Rose, and evokes numerous connotations: oddness and rarity (because blue roses do not actually occur in nature), fragility and weakness (because of the association of the color blue with the blue veins that show so clearly against the white skin of a sickly, anemic person), and sadness (because of the use of the word *blues* to describe a melancholic or depressed state). Such strong symbolism is characteristic of Williams's work and that of other Expressionist writers. The character Tom in the play, a young writer, is something of a self-portrait, and critics have often expressed the idea that Williams wrote the play because of the guilt that he felt for abandoning his sister Rose, who ended up in a mental institution. Williams's sister, like Laura, collected glass figures, and this remembered detail became an evocative image in his work. Williams wrote of his fascination with his sister's glass collection, "They were mostly little glass animals. By poetic association they came to represent, in my memory, all the softest emotions that belong to recollection of things past. They stood for all the small and tender things that relieve the austere pattern of life and make it endurable to the sensitive."

First staged in Chicago in 1944, *The Glass Menagerie* was an immediate success, opening in New York the following year. Since that time the play has been produced many times on Broadway and by theater companies throughout the world. Several film versions of the play have been produced, one in 1950 starring Jane Wyman and Arthur Kennedy, one in 1973 starring Katherine Hepburn and Sam Waterston, and one in 1987 starring Joanne Woodward and John Malkovich. The last of these versions was directed by Paul Newman.

SUPPORT FOR LEP STUDENTS (CONT.)

impudence—quality of being bold or disrespectful
jeopardize—endanger, put in risk
vice—bad or harmful habit
solemn—serious; somber
avert—turn away, look away from
bower—person or thing with great strength
compensation—amends for a loss or damage
pathetic—pitifully unsuccessful

CROSS-CURRICULAR ACTIVITIES

Arts and Humanities. Students might enjoy experiencing other forms of Expressionist art. Encourage students to work in small groups to research different Expressionist art forms and to share their findings with the class. One group might focus on Expressionist painters, such as Vincent van Gogh, Edvard Munch, or the Die Brücke artists who gained prominence right after the turn of the century and remained important in post-World War I Europe. Another group of students might focus on other works of Expressionist literature, in the form of the short story, novel, drama, or poetry. (The plays of Eugene O'Neill would be an excellent starting point.) Robert Wiene and Fritz Lang were two important directors of the Expressionist films that appeared in the 1920s, and some students might enjoy studying their work. Musically inclined students might research the influence of Expressionism upon opera. All students should share their findings with the class. Students who have focused on the visual arts should bring in books of prints, while students who have focused on literature might give readings. Students who have researched films could describe a particular film's plot or even show brief portions of a videotape to the class, and students who have researched opera might play a recording for the class.

PREREADING NOTES

READER'S JOURNAL

You might inform students that many psychologists believe extroversion and introversion are inherited traits. Being extroverted, introverted, or falling somewhere in the middle of this range does not make an individual better or worse than another; rather, this temperamental characteristic adds to the unique richness of an individual's personality.

LANGUAGE SKILLS

Students might also correct these sentence fragments by making them into complete sentences.

ANSWER TO GUIDED READING QUESTION

❶ The author says that memory exaggerates details because it is "seated predominantly in the heart."

VOCABULARY FROM THE SELECTION: ACT I

aghast	interfused
bombardment	listlessly
cater	mastication
conglomeration	matriculate
cultivate	menagerie
czar	motley
discreet	pinion
dismal	premature
emissary	prominent
endowment	querulous
fiasco	resume
imminent	sheepishly
implacable	Spartan
imploringly	sublimation
importunately	supercilious
induct	symptomatic
ineluctably	ulterior
inquisition	

READER'S JOURNAL

Psychologists often speak of extroverts and introverts. An extrovert is someone who takes naturally to social situations. An introvert has a more introspective personality. Are you an extrovert, an introvert, or somewhere in between? Write about this question in your journal.

LANGUAGE SKILLS

Read the Language Arts Survey, 2.61, "Correcting Sentence Fragments." Plays consist of dialogue and stage directions. In dialogue, as in ordinary speech, people often use sentence fragments. As you read this play, copy onto a sheet of paper five examples of sentence fragments spoken by the characters.

The Glass Menagerie

TENNESSEE WILLIAMS

CAST OF CHARACTERS

AMANDA WINGFIELD
LAURA WINGFIELD
TOM WINGFIELD
JIM O'CONNOR

ACT ONE, SCENE 1

The Wingfield apartment is in the rear of the building, one of those vast hive-like conglomerations of cellular living-units that flower as warty growths in overcrowded urban centers of lower middle-class population and are symptomatic of the impulse of this largest and fundamentally enslaved section of American society to avoid fluidity and differentiation and to exist and function as one interfused mass of automatism. The apartment faces an alley and is entered by a fire-escape, a structure whose name is a touch of accidental poetic truth, for all of these huge buildings are always burning with the slow and implacable fires of human desperation. The fire-escape is included in the set—that is, the landing of it and steps descending from it. (Note that the stage L. *alley may be entirely omitted, since it is never used except for* TOM'*s first entrance, which can take place stage* R.*) The scene is memory and is therefore nonrealistic. Memory takes a lot of poetic license. It omits some details, others are exaggerated, according to the emotional value of the articles it touches, for memory is seated predominantly in the heart. The interior is therefore rather dim and poetic.* (CUE #1. *As soon as the house lights dim, dance-hall music*

What does the author say about memory? ❶

WORDS FOR EVERYDAY USE:

con • glom • er • a • tion (kən gläm´ər ā´shən) *n.*, collection or mixture

symp • to • mat • ic (simp´tə mat´ik) *adj.*, indicative; that constitutes a condition

in • ter • fused (in tər fyōōzd´) *part.*, combined, blended

im • pla • ca • ble (im plā´kə bəl) *adj.*, that cannot be appeased or pacified

VOCABULARY IN CONTEXT

- During the Elizabethan period, the theater entertained a conglomeration of classes; everyone from the king to the average commoner went occasionally.
- Sneezing and watery eyes are symptomatic of allergies.
- Snorkeling among the coral reefs, we were awed by the color of the water interfused with light.
- The two year old was implacable; unless he was constantly appeased he would throw a tantrum.
- Greek playwrights often portrayed fate ineluctably, as something that could not be escaped.
- The class that recently matriculated in the school were reputed to be some of the hardest working students in years.

heard on-stage R. *Old popular music of, say 1915–1920 period. This continues until* TOM *is at fire-escape landing, having lighted cigarette, and begins speaking.)*

AT RISE: *At the rise of the house curtain, the audience is faced with the dark, grim rear wall of the Wingfield tenement. (The stage set proper is screened out by a gauze curtain, which suggests the front part, outside, of the building.) This building, which runs parallel to the footlights, is flanked on both sides by dark, narrow alleys which run into murky canyons of tangled clotheslines, garbage cans and the sinister lattice-work of neighboring fire-escapes. (The alleys are actually in darkness, and the objects just mentioned are not visible.) It is up and down these side alleys that exterior entrances and exits are made, during the play. At the end of* TOM*'s opening commentary, the dark tenement wall slowly reveals (by means of a transparency) the interior of the ground-floor Wingfield apartment. (Gauze curtain, which suggests front part of building, rises on the interior set.) Downstage is the living-room, which also serves as a sleeping room for* LAURA, *the day-bed unfolding to make her bed. Just above this is a small stool or table on which is a telephone. Up-stage,* C., *and divided by a wide arch or second proscenium*[1] *with transparent faded portieres (or second curtain, "second curtain" is actually the inner gauze curtain between the living-room and the dining-room, which is up-stage of it), is the dining-room. In an old-fashioned whatnot in the living-room are seen scores of transparent glass animals. A blown-up photograph of the father hangs on the wall of the living-room, facing the audience, to the* L. *of the archway. It is the face of a very handsome young man in a doughboy's*[2] *First World War cap. He is gallantly smiling, ineluctably smiling, as if to say, "I will be smiling forever." (Note that all that is essential in connection with dance-hall is that the window be shown lighting lower part of alley. It is not necessary to show any considerable part of dance-hall.) The audience hears and sees the opening scene in the dining-room through both the transparent fourth wall (this is the gauze curtain which suggests outside of building) of the building and the transparent gauze portieres of the dining-room arch. It is during this revealing scene that the fourth wall slowly ascends, out of sight. This transparent exterior wall is not brought down again until the very end of the play, during* TOM*'s final speech. The narrator is an undisguised convention of the play. He takes whatever license with dramatic convention as is convenient to his purposes.*

TOM *enters, dressed as a merchant sailor, from alley, stage* L. *(i.e., stage* R. *if* L. *alley is omitted), and strolls across the front of the stage to the fire-escape. (*TOM *may lean against grillwork of this as he lights cigarette.) There he stops and lights a cigarette. He addresses the audience.*

TOM. I have tricks in my pocket—I have things up my sleeve—but I am the opposite of the stage magician. He gives you illusion that has the appearance of truth. I give you truth in the pleasant disguise of illusion. I take you back to an alley in St. Louis. The time that quaint period when the huge middle class of America was matriculating from a school for the blind. Their eyes had failed them,

❶ *What does Tom, the narrator, say about the nature of truth and illusion in this play?*

1. **proscenium.** Plane, including the arch and the curtain, separating the stage proper from the audience
2. **doughboy's.** Belonging to a World War I United States infantryman

WORDS FOR EVERYDAY USE: **in • e • luc • ta • bly** (in´ē luk´tə blē) *adv.,* in an inescapable or unavoidable manner
ma • tric • u • late (mə trik´yōō lāt´) *vt.,* enroll

CROSS-CURRICULAR ACTIVITIES

Mathematics and Sciences. Students might research extroverted and introverted personalities. Psychiatric journals are good sources of information on this subject. You might also wish to refer students to an excellent work by one of the foremost researchers in developmental psychology, Jerome Kagan's *Unstable Ideas: Temperament, Cognition, and Self* (Cambridge, MA: Harvard University Press, 1989).

As they read the play, students can make a case study of Laura. Encourage them to consider the following questions: What type of temperament does she have? Do you think she inherited this temperament? Is she able to change? Most people who possess either an extroverted or an introverted temperament live perfectly full and functional lives. Might there be another reason that Laura is dysfunctional? What might this reason be?

Applied Arts. Students might enjoy working in groups to build models of the set for *The Glass Menagerie* as described on pages 684–685. Models may be as sophisticated as skills will allow, from simple cardboard constructions to elaborate scale replicas. Students who have access to computers might try designing a set using computer aided design, or CAD. Encourage students to use their imaginations, as well as Williams's stage directions, to create a model that captures the mood of *The Glass Menagerie.*

ANSWER TO GUIDED READING QUESTION

❶ Tom says that the play is truth disguised as illusion.

Answers to Guided Reading Questions

❶ The play is about people's memories. Memory is associated with music.

❷ The gentleman caller is a symbol of "the long-delayed but always expected something that we live for."

❸ Tom and Laura's father has left town; his last postcard was sent from the Pacific coast of Mexico.

Literary Technique

A **metaphor** is a figure of speech in which one thing is spoken or written about as if it were another. Ask students the following questions: To what is the speaker comparing the economic situation of many Americans? What was the economic situation of the United States in the period in which the play is set? Why might the economic situation be compared to this thing?

Answers. The speaker compares the economic situations of many Americans to "having their fingers pressed forcibly on the fiery Braille alphabet of a dissolving economy." The play is set during the Great Depression, a period in which many people lost their livelihoods, their homes, their hopes, and their dreams. The economic situation might be compared to having Americans' fingers pressed on fiery Braille because in both situations people are forced to face unpleasant and painful realities. There is also the implication that Americans were deluding themselves (or blinding themselves to reality) and so are forced now to "feel" reality in a painful manner.

or they had failed their eyes, and so they were having their fingers pressed forcibly down on the fiery Braille alphabet of a dissolving economy.—In Spain there was revolution.—Here there was only shouting and confusion and labor disturbances, sometimes violent, in otherwise peaceful cities such as Cleveland—Chicago—Detroit. . . . That is the social background of this play. . . . The play is memory. (MUSIC CUE #2.) Being a memory play, it is dimly lighted, it is sentimental, it is not realistic.—In memory everything seems to happen to music.—That explains the fiddle in the wings. I am the narrator of the play, and also a character in it. The other characters in the play are my mother, Amanda, my sister, Laura, and a gentleman caller who appears in the final scenes. He is the most realistic character in the play, being an emissary from a world that we were somehow set apart from.—But having a poet's weakness for symbols, I am using this character as a symbol—as the long-delayed but always expected something that we live for.—There is a fifth character who doesn't appear other than in a photograph hanging on the wall. When you see the picture of this grinning gentleman, please remember this is our father who left us a long time ago. He was a telephone man who fell in love with long distance—so he gave up his job with the telephone company and skipped the light fantastic out of town. . . . The last we heard of him was a picture postcard from the Pacific coast of Mexico, containing a message of two words—"Hello—Good-bye!" and no address.

❶ *What do you think is meant by "a memory play"? What is memory associated with in this play?*

❷ *Of what is the gentleman caller a symbol?*

❸ *Where is Tom and Amanda's father?*

(LIGHTS UP IN DINING-ROOM. TOM *exits* R. *He goes off downstage, takes off his sailor overcoat and skull-fitting knitted cap and remains off-stage by dining-room* R. *door for his entrance cue.* AMANDA'*s voice becomes audible through the portieres—i.e., gauze curtains separating dining-room and living-room.* AMANDA *and* LAURA *are seated at a drop-leaf table.* AMANDA *is sitting in* C. *chair and* LAURA *in* L. *chair. Eating is indicated by gestures without food or utensils.* AMANDA *faces the audience. The interior of the dining-room has lit up softly and through the scrim*[3]*—gauze curtains—we see* AMANDA *and* LAURA *seated at the table in the upstage area.)*

AMANDA. You know, Laura, I had the funniest experience in church last Sunday. The church was crowded except for one pew way down front and in that was just one little woman. I smiled very sweetly at her and said, "Excuse me, would you mind if I shared this pew?" "I certainly would," she said, "this space is rented." Do you know that is the first time that I ever knew that the Lord rented space. *(Dining-room gauze curtains open automatically.)* These Northern Episcopalians! I can understand the Southern Episcopalians, but these Northern ones, no. *(*TOM *enters dining-room* R., *slips over to table and sits in chair* R.*)* Honey, don't push your food with your fingers. If you have to push your food with something, the thing to use is a crust of bread. You must chew your food. Animals have secretions in their stomachs which enable them to digest their food without mastication, but human beings must chew their food before they swallow it down, and chew, chew. Oh, eat leisurely. Eat leisurely.

3. **scrim.** Hanging of light cloth as a semitransparent curtain in a theatrical production

Words for Everyday Use:
em • is • sar • y (em´i ser´ē) *n.,* person or agent sent on a mission
mas • ti • ca • tion (mas´ti kā´shən) *n.,* chewing

Vocabulary in Context

- The emissary to the foreign prince succeeded in her mission to establish friendly foreign relations.
- "Brush your teeth," the dentist warned. "You will need them for mastication all of your life."
- Just when we thought the shriek of the car alarm had ceased, the horrible noise resumed.

A well-cooked meal has many delicate flavors that have to be held in the mouth for appreciation, not just gulped down. Oh, chew, chew—chew! *(At this point the scrim curtain—if the director decides to use it—the one suggesting exterior wall, rises here and does not come down again until just before the end of the play.)* Don't you want to give your salivary glands a chance to function?

TOM. Mother, I haven't enjoyed one bite of my dinner because of your constant directions on how to eat it. It's you that makes me hurry through my meals with your hawk-like attention to every bite I take. It's disgusting—all this discussion of animal's secretion—salivary glands—mastication! *(Comes down to armchair in living-room* R., *lights cigarette.)*

AMANDA. Temperament like a Metropolitan star! You're not excused from this table.

TOM. I'm getting a cigarette.

AMANDA. You smoke too much.

LAURA *(Rising).* Mother, I'll bring in the coffee.

AMANDA. No, no, no, no. You sit down. I'm going to be the servant today and you're going to be the lady.

LAURA. I'm already up.

AMANDA. Resume your seat. Resume your seat. You keep yourself fresh and pretty for the gentlemen callers. (LAURA *sits.)*

LAURA. I'm not expecting any gentlemen callers.

AMANDA *(Who has been gathering dishes from table and loading them on tray).* Well, the nice thing about them is they come when they're least expected. Why, I remember one Sunday afternoon in Blue Mountain when your mother was a girl . . .

(Goes out for coffee, U. R.*)*

TOM. I know what's coming now! (LAURA *rises.)*

LAURA. Yes. But let her tell it. *(Crosses to* L. *of day-bed, sits.)*

TOM. Again?

LAURA. She loves to tell it.

AMANDA *(Entering from* R. *in dining-room and coming down into living-room with tray and coffee).* I remember one Sunday afternoon in Blue Mountain when your mother was a girl she received—seventeen—gentlemen callers! (AMANDA *crosses to* TOM *at armchair* R., *gives him coffee, and crosses* C. LAURA *comes to her, takes cup, resumes her place on* L. *of day-bed.* AMANDA *puts tray on small table* R. *of day-bed, sits* R. *on day-bed. Inner curtain closes, light dims out.)* Why sometimes there weren't chairs enough to accommodate them all and we had to send the servant over to the parish house to fetch the folding chairs.

TOM. How did you entertain all those gentlemen callers? (TOM *finally sits in armchair* R.*)*

AMANDA. I happened to understand the art of conversation!

TOM. I bet you could talk!

AMANDA. Well, I could. All the girls in my day could, I tell you.

TOM. Yes?

❶ *What event in her life does Amanda enjoy remembering?*

❷ *Why does Amanda tell Laura to remain seated? How does Laura feel about her mother's expectations?*

WORDS FOR EVERYDAY USE: **re • sume** (ri zōōm´) *vt.,* take, get, or occupy again

ANSWERS TO GUIDED READING QUESTIONS

❶ She enjoys remembering an afternoon in her youth in the Blue Mountains when she received seventeen gentleman callers.

❷ Amanda tells Laura to remain seated so she will keep herself pretty for gentleman callers. Laura feels that her mother's expectations are unrealistic.

LITERARY NOTE

Tom says that he is using the gentleman caller as a symbol "of the long-delayed but always expected something that we live for" because he has "a poet's weakness for symbols." Tennessee Williams might well have been describing his own weakness for symbols. While many writers use symbols subtly to enhance meaning, Williams's symbols are often overt and are further emphasized by the stage set and stage directions. Because this play is rich in easily decodable symbols, it provides an excellent opportunity for students to explore the deeper levels of meaning symbolism brings to a literary work. As students read, have them examine the following symbolic elements: the glass menagerie, the name "Blue Roses," the father's picture, and the glass unicorn.

Answers to Guided Reading Questions

❶ Amanda regrets marrying Laura and Tom's father instead of J. Duncan Fitzhugh.

❷ Amanda says there must have been a flood or a tornado. Laura says that there are no gentlemen callers because she is not popular. Laura might feel that her mother is being insensitive.

Amanda. They knew how to entertain their gentlemen callers. It wasn't enough for a girl to be possessed of a pretty face and a graceful figure—although I wasn't slighted in either respect. She also needed to have a nimble wit and a tongue to meet all occasions.

Tom. What did you talk about?

Amanda. Why, we'd talk about things of importance going on in the world! Never anything common or coarse or vulgar. My callers were gentlemen—all! Some of the most prominent men on the Mississippi Delta—planters and sons of planters! There was young Champ Laughlin. (MUSIC CUE #3.) He later became Vice-President of the Delta Planters' Bank. And Hadley Stevenson; he was drowned in Moon Lake.—My goodness, he certainly left his widow well provided for—a hundred and fifty thousand dollars in government bonds. And the Cutrere Brothers—Wesley and Bates. Bates was one of my own bright particular beaus! But he got in a quarrel with that wild Wainwright boy and they shot it out on the floor of Moon Lake Casino. Bates was shot through the stomach. He died in the ambulance on his way to Memphis. He certainly left his widow well provided for, too—eight or ten thousand acres, no less. He never loved that woman; she just caught him on the rebound. My picture was found on him the night he died. Oh and that boy, that boy that every girl in the Delta was setting her cap for! That beautiful (MUSIC FADES OUT.) brilliant young Fitzhugh boy from Greene County!

❶ *What does Amanda regret?*

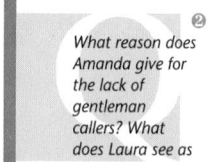

❷ *What reason does Amanda give for the lack of gentleman callers? What does Laura see as the reason? How do you think her mother's joking and prodding might make Laura feel?*

Tom. What did he leave his widow?

Amanda. He never married! What's the matter with you—you talk as though all my old admirers had turned up their toes to the daisies!

Tom. Isn't this the first you've mentioned that still survives?

Amanda. He made an awful lot of money. He went North to Wall Street and made a fortune. He had the Midas touch—everything that boy touched just turned to gold! *(Gets up.)* And I could have been Mrs. J. Duncan Fitzhugh—mind you! *(Crosses* L. C.*)* But—what did I do?—I just went out of my way and picked your father! *(Looks at picture on* L. *wall. Goes to small table* R. *of day-bed for tray.)*

Laura *(Rises from day-bed).* Mother, let me clear the table.

Amanda *(Crossing* L. *for* LAURA*'s cup, then crossing* R. *for* TOM*'s).* No, dear, you go in front and study your typewriter chart. Or practice your shorthand a little. Stay fresh and pretty! It's almost time for our gentlemen callers to start arriving. How many do you suppose we're going to entertain this afternoon? *(*TOM *opens curtains between dining-room and living-room for her. These close behind her, and she exits into kitchen* R. TOM *stands* U. C. *in living-room.)*

Laura *(To* AMANDA, *off-stage).* I don't believe we're going to receive any, Mother.

Amanda *(Off-stage).* Not any? Not one? Why, you must be joking! Not one gentleman caller? What's the matter? Has there been a flood or a tornado?

Laura *(Crossing to typing table).* It isn't a flood. It's not a tornado, Mother. I'm just

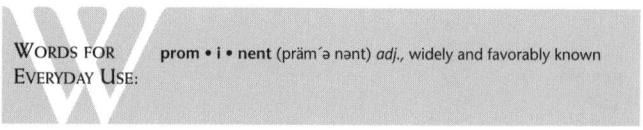

Words for Everyday Use: **prom • i • nent** (präm´ə nənt) *adj.,* widely and favorably known

Vocabulary in Context

- Mr. McGregor was one of the most prominent men in the community until people lost respect for him because he treated his produce with pesticides.
- The heiress was wealthy enough to support a private menagerie that rivaled the local zoo.

not popular like you were in Blue Mountain. Mother's afraid that I'm going to be an old maid. (MUSIC CUE #4.) *(Lights dim out.* TOM *exits* U. C. *in blackout.* LAURA *crosses to* <u>*menagerie*</u> R.*)*

Responding to the Selection

How do you feel about Amanda Wingfield after reading the first scene of the play? In what sense does she live in a dream world? Why might her children sometimes find her talk irritating?

Reviewing the Selection

RECALLING

1. What does the narrator, Tom, say a stage magician does?
2. What memory from her past does Amanda relate? What question does she pose to Laura?

INTERPRETING

3. How does Tom differ from a stage magician?
4. About what is Amanda nostalgic? What does she want for her daughter?

SYNTHESIZING

5. Whom does Amanda expect to be calling? Why does she ask Laura to study her typewriter chart and to practice her shorthand? What does Amanda want for her daughter?

Understanding Literature (Questions for Discussion)

1. **Stage Directions. Stage directions** are notes included in a play in addition to the dialogue for the purpose of describing how something should be performed on stage. Sometimes writers also include information about the economic, political, or cultural background of the play. Reread the stage directions at the opening of this play, before the entrance of the narrator. What is the social class of the people who live in the "overcrowded urban centers" described in those stage directions? What "poetic truth" is expressed by the term *fire-escape?*

WORDS FOR EVERYDAY USE: **me • nag • er • ie** (mə naj´ər ē) *n.,* collection of wild or strange animals kept in enclosures for exhibition

RESPONDING TO THE SELECTION

Ask students why it might be foolish to live entirely in the past. On what does a person like Amanda Wingfield miss out?

ANSWERS FOR REVIEWING THE SELECTION

RECALLING

1. Tom says a stage magician presents illusion as truth.
2. Amanda relates the story about receiving seventeen gentleman callers. She asks Laura how many gentleman callers she will be receiving this afternoon.

INTERPRETING

Responses will vary. Possible responses are given.

3. Tom does just the opposite of a stage magician; he presents truth in the form of illusion.
4. Amanda is nostalgic for her youth in the Blue Mountains. She wants her daughter to be as happy and popular as she was when she was young.

SYNTHESIZING

Responses will vary. Possible responses are given.

5. Amanda expects gentlemen callers. She asks Laura to study her typewriter chart so she will stay "fresh and pretty." Amanda wants her daughter to be happy and feel good about herself.

ANSWERS FOR UNDERSTANDING LITERATURE

► See the evaluation form for discussion, active listening, and oral communication, *Assessment Portfolio,* 7.11–7.14.

Responses will vary. Possible responses are given.

1. Stage Directions. The people are lower middle-class. The term *fire-escape* expresses the truth that the buildings in which these people live are burning with "human desperation."

2. Expressionism. Tom's memory will be viewed by the audience. The unrealistic elements of setting are the apart- ment's being entered via a fire-escape, the gauze curtain, the "sinister" network of alleys,

(cont.)

ANSWERS FOR UNDERSTANDING LITERATURE (CONT.)

clotheslines, and fire-escapes, the inside of the house being revealed through a transparent wall, and the huge photograph of the father.

3. Character. Amanda's statements about the decorous South include "we had to send the servant over," "I happened to understand the art of conversation . . . All the girls in my day could, I tell you," and "Never anything common or coarse or vulgar. My callers were gentlemen—all!" Her repeated questioning about when the gentlemen callers are coming to visit Laura reveals that she wants the same kind of life for her children. The commentary between her children ("I know what's coming now!" and "Yes. But let her tell it.") indicate that the world has changed and her children cannot relate to her memories and are merely humoring her by letting her recount them.

4. Metaphor. Tom is saying that because people of this

(cont.)

ANSWERS FOR UNDERSTANDING LITERATURE (CONT.)

period did not wish to see or understand the world around them, they were being forced to face reality by the economic hardships brought on by the Great Depression. People might be beginning to question the American dream or ideal of material success.

2. **Expressionism. Expressionism** is the name given to a twentieth-century movement in literature and art that reacted against Realism in favor of an exaggeration of the elements of the artistic medium itself. In the stage directions at the beginning of this play, we are told that the "scene is memory." Whose emotional recollections will be viewed by the audience? What elements of the setting, as described in the opening stage directions, are unrealistic and calculated to create emotional responses in the audience? What is special about the play's lighting and use of sound effects?

3. **Character.** A **character** is someone who figures in the action of a literary work. Amanda, the mother of Laura and Tom, is nostalgic about her Southern upbringing. What statements made by her show that she remembers the South as a special, cultivated, refined place where life was more decorous and elegant? What statements and actions on her part show that she wants the same kind of life for her children? What suggestions are there in scene 1 that Amanda's ideas are unrealistic, that she is clinging to a past that has disappeared?

4. **Metaphor.** A **metaphor** is a figure of speech in which something is spoken or written about as if it were another. The figure of speech invites the reader to make a comparison between the two things. Tom, the narrator, says that at the time in which the play is set, "the huge middle class of America was matriculating from a school for the blind. Their eyes had failed them, or they had failed their eyes, and so they were having their fingers pressed forcibly down on the fiery Braille alphabet of a dissolving economy." What is Tom saying about life just before the Great Depression? What does Tom compare to the Braille alphabet? What might people be reading or learning as a result of the economic depression?

ACT ONE, SCENE 2

Scene is the same. Lights dim up on living-room.

LAURA *discovered by menagerie, polishing glass. Crosses to phonograph, plays record. She times this business so as to put needle on record as* MUSIC CUE #4 *ends. Enter* AMANDA *down alley* R. *Rattles key in lock.* LAURA *crosses guiltily to typewriter and types. (Small typewriter table with typewriter on it is still on stage in living-room* L.*)* AMANDA *comes into room* R. *closing door. Crosses to armchair, putting hat, purse and gloves on it. Something has happened to* AMANDA. *It is written in her face: a look that is grim and hopeless and a little absurd. She has on one of those cheap or imitation velvety-looking cloth coats with imitation fur collar. Her hat is five or six years old, one of those dreadful cloche*[4] *hats that were worn in the late twenties and she is clasping an enormous black patent-leather pocketbook with nickel clasps and initials. This is her full-dress outfit, the one she usually wears to the* D.A.R.[5] *She purses her lips, opens her eyes very wide, rolls them upward and shakes her head. Seeing her mother's expression,* LAURA *touches her lips with a nervous gesture.*

LAURA. Hello, Mother, I was just . . .

4. **cloche.** Close-fitting, bell-shaped hat
5. **D.A.R.** Daughters of the American Revolution, a civic organization

AMANDA. I know. You were just practicing your typing, I suppose. *(Behind chair* R.*)*

LAURA. Yes.

AMANDA. Deception, deception, deception!

LAURA *(Shakily).* How was the D.A.R. meeting, Mother?

AMANDA *(Crosses to* LAURA*).* D.A.R. meeting!

LAURA. Didn't you go to the D.A.R. meeting, Mother?

AMANDA *(Faintly, almost inaudibly).* No, I didn't go to any D.A.R. meeting. *(Then more forcibly.)* I didn't have the strength—I didn't have the courage. I just wanted to find a hole in the ground and crawl in it and stay there the rest of my entire life.

(Tears type charts, throws them on floor.)

LAURA *(Faintly).* Why did you do that, Mother?

AMANDA *(Sits on* R. *end of day-bed).* Why? Why? How old are you, Laura?

LAURA. Mother, you know my age.

AMANDA. I was under the impression that you were an adult, but evidently I was very much mistaken.

(She stares at LAURA.*)*

LAURA. Please don't stare at me, Mother! *(*AMANDA *closes her eyes and lowers her head. Pause.)*

AMANDA. What are we going to do? What is going to become of us? What is the future? *(Pause.)*

LAURA. Has something happened, Mother? Mother, has something happened?

AMANDA. I'll be all right in a minute. I'm just bewildered—by life . . .

LAURA. Mother, I wish that you would tell me what's happened!

AMANDA. I went to the D.A.R. this afternoon, as you know; I was to be inducted as an officer. I stopped off at Rubicam's Business College to tell them about your cold and to ask how you were progressing down there.

LAURA. Oh . . .

AMANDA. Yes, oh—oh—oh. I went straight to your typing instructor and introduced myself as your mother. She didn't even know who you were. Wingfield, she said? We don't have any such scholar enrolled in this school. I assured her she did. I said my daughter Laura's been coming to classes since early January. "Well, I don't know," she said, "unless you mean that terribly shy little girl who dropped out of school after a few days' attendance?" "No," I said, "I don't mean that one. I mean my daughter, Laura, who's been coming here every single day for the past six weeks!" "Excuse me," she said. And she took down the attendance book and there was your name, unmistakable, printed, and all the dates you'd been absent. I still told her she was wrong. I still said, "No, there must have been some mistake! There must have been some mix-up in the records!" "No," she said, "I remember her perfectly now. She was so shy and her hands trembled so that her fingers couldn't touch the right keys! When we gave a speed-test—she just broke down completely—was sick at the stomach and had to be carried to the washroom! After that she never came back. We telephoned the house every single day and never got any answer." *(Rises*

❶ *How does Amanda say she feels? What effect does she hope to produce in Laura?*

❷ *Why is Amanda angry with her daughter?*

❸ *In what way does Laura's former teacher describe her?*

WORDS FOR EVERYDAY USE: **in • duct** (in dukt´) *vt.,* place in official position

ANSWERS TO GUIDED READING QUESTIONS

❶ She says it faintly, as if she had been drained of vitality. Amanda is hoping to make Laura feel guilty.

❶ Amanda is angry with Laura because she dropped out of business school.

❸ Laura's former teacher describes her as being so painfully shy that she got physically ill.

VOCABULARY IN CONTEXT

- Before you were inducted into the club, you had to receive a secret name and learn how to greet fellow club members.

Answers to Guided Reading Questions

❶ Laura has been spending her time at the zoo and in a glass house where they raise tropical flowers.

❷ Amanda says they cannot spend the rest of their lives watching parades, playing with the glass menagerie, and playing worn-out records.

❸ Amanda envisions them as worn-out spinsters depending on relatives.

How has Laura been spending her time? ❶

from day-bed, crosses R. C.*)* That was while I was working all day long down at that department store, I suppose, demonstrating those—*(With hands indicates brassiere.)* Oh! I felt so weak I couldn't stand up! *(Sits in armchair.)* I had to sit down while they got me a glass of water! *(*LAURA *crosses up to phonograph.)* Fifty dollars' tuition. I don't care about the money so much, but all my hopes for any kind of future for you—gone up the spout, just gone up the spout like that. *(*LAURA *winds phonograph up.)* Oh, don't do that, Laura!—Don't play that victrola![6]

LAURA. Oh! *(Stops phonograph, crosses to typing table, sits.)*

AMANDA. What have you been doing every day when you've gone out of the house pretending that you were going to business college?

LAURA. I've just been going out walking.

What does Amanda say they can't do now that Laura has failed at business school? ❷

AMANDA. That's not true!

LAURA. Yes, it is, Mother, I just went walking.

AMANDA. Walking? Walking? In winter? Deliberately courting pneumonia in that light coat? Where did you walk to, Laura?

LAURA. All sorts of places—mostly in the park.

AMANDA. Even after you'd started catching that cold?

LAURA. It was the lesser of two evils, Mother. I couldn't go back. I threw up on the floor!

What sort of future does Amanda envision? ❸

AMANDA. From half-past seven till after five every day you mean to tell me you walked around in the park, because you wanted to make me think that you were still going to Rubicam's Business College?

LAURA. Oh, Mother, it wasn't as bad as it sounds. I went inside places to get warmed up.

AMANDA. Inside where?

LAURA. I went in the art museum and the bird-houses at the Zoo. I visited the penguins every day! Sometimes I did without lunch and went to the movies. Lately I've been spending most of my afternoons in the Jewelbox, that big glass house where they raise the tropical flowers.

AMANDA. You did all that to deceive me, just for deception! Why? Why? Why? Why?

LAURA. Mother, when you're disappointed, you get that awful suffering look on your face, like the picture of Jesus' mother in the Museum! *(Rises.)*

AMANDA. Hush!

LAURA *(Crosses* R. *to menagerie).* I couldn't face it. I couldn't. (MUSIC CUE #5.)

AMANDA *(Rising from day-bed).* So what are we going to do now, honey, the rest of our lives? Just sit down in this house and watch the parades go by? Amuse ourselves with the glass menagerie? Eternally play those worn-out records your father left us as a painful reminder of him? *(Slams phonograph lid.)* We can't have a business career. (END MUSIC CUE #5.) No, we can't do that—that just gives us indigestion. *(Around* R. *day-bed.)* What is there left for us now but dependency all our lives? I tell you, Laura, I know so well what happens to unmarried women who aren't prepared to occupy a position in life. *(Crosses* L., *sits on day-bed.)* I've seen such pitiful cases in the South—barely tolerated spinsters living on some brother's wife or a sister's husband—tucked away in some mousetrap of a room—encouraged by one in-law to go on and visit the next in-law—little birdlike women—without any nest—eating the crust of humility all their lives! Is

6. **victrola.** Record player

that the future that we've mapped out for ourselves? I swear I don't see any other alternative. And I don't think that's a very pleasant alternative. Of course—some girls *do* marry. My goodness, Laura, haven't you ever liked some boy?

LAURA. Yes, Mother, I liked one once.

AMANDA. You did?

LAURA. I came across his picture a while ago.

AMANDA. He gave you his picture too? *(Rises from day-bed, crosses to chair* R.*)*

LAURA. No, it's in the year-book.

AMANDA *(Sits in armchair).* Oh—a high-school boy.

LAURA. Yes. His name was Jim. *(Kneeling on floor, gets year-book from under menagerie.)* Here he is in "The Pirates of Penzance."

AMANDA *(Absently).* The what?

LAURA. The operetta the senior class put on. He had a wonderful voice. We sat across the aisle from each other Mondays, Wednesdays and Fridays in the auditorium. Here he is with a silver cup for debating! See his grin?

AMANDA. So he had a grin, too! *(Looks at picture of father on wall behind phonograph. Hands year-book back.)*

LAURA. He used to call me—Blue Roses.

AMANDA. Blue Roses? What did he call you a silly name like that for?

LAURA *(Still kneeling).* When I had that attack of pleurosis[7]—he asked me what was the matter when I came back. I said pleurosis—he thought that I said "Blue Roses." So that's what he always called me after that. Whenever he saw me, he'd holler, "Hello, Blue Roses!" I didn't care for the girl that he went out with. Emily Meisenbach. Oh, Emily was the best-dressed girl at Soldan. But she never struck me as being sincere . . . I read in a newspaper once that they were engaged. *(Puts year-book back on a shelf of glass menagerie.)* That's a long time ago—they're probably married by now.

AMANDA. That's all right, honey, that's all right. It doesn't matter. Little girls who aren't cut out for business careers sometimes end up married to very nice young men. And I'm just going to see that you do that, too!

LAURA. But, Mother—

AMANDA. What is it now?

LAURA. I'm—crippled!

AMANDA. Don't say that word! *(Rises, crosses to* C. *Turns to* LAURA.*)* How many times have I told you never to say that word! You're not crippled, you've just got a slight defect. *(*LAURA *rises.)* If you lived in the days when I was a girl and they had long graceful skirts sweeping the ground, it might have been considered an asset. When you've got a slight disadvantage like that, you've just got to cultivate something else to take its place. You have to cultivate charm—or vivacity—or *charm*! *(Spotlight on photograph. Then dim out.)* That's the only thing your father had plenty of—charm! *(*AMANDA *sits on day-bed.* LAURA *crosses to armchair and sits.)* (MUSIC CUE #6.) *(Blackout.)*

7. **pleurosis.** Inflammation of the lungs

❶ *What does Amanda ask Laura? Why does she ask her this?*

❷ *What does Amanda set as her goal?*

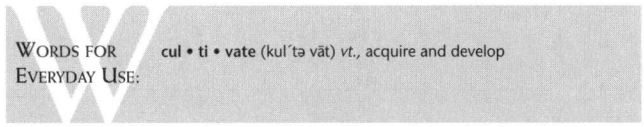

WORDS FOR EVERYDAY USE: **cul • ti • vate** (kul´tə vāt) *vt.,* acquire and develop

ANSWERS TO GUIDED READING QUESTIONS

❶ Amanda asks Laura if she has ever liked a boy because marriage would be one solution to Laura's predicament.

❷ Amanda sets as her goal getting Laura married to a nice young man.

VOCABULARY IN CONTEXT

- Bob tried to cultivate a 1920s feel at his party by encouraging dancing to old swing music.

RESPONDING TO THE SELECTION

You might ask students to recall Laura's former teacher's description of her behavior.

ANSWERS FOR REVIEWING THE SELECTION

RECALLING

1. Amanda discovers that Laura has dropped out of business school. She is distraught because Laura has no other future or career plans.

2. Amanda says the only other alternative is to marry.

INTERPRETING

3. Laura was so frightened that she could not type because of her trembling. She dropped out because when asked to take a speed test she broke down, got sick, and had to be carried to the bathroom. She spends her days at the zoo and in the glass house where tropical flowers are grown. Jim called her "Blue Roses," because that is what he thought she said when she told him she had pleurosis. These details reveal that Laura has been sickly throughout her life and so painfully shy that being misunderstood by a stranger has stuck out in her memory as a wonderful moment in her life.

4. Amanda fears that they will become spinsters and a burden on others. Because of the departure of her husband, Amanda is in a desperate financial situation. She immediately decides she will get Laura a husband.

SYNTHESIZING

Responses will vary. Possible responses are given.

5. Laura doesn't embrace the plan both because she is skeptical and because she is shy and insecure. Laura's physical condition is that she is sickly and has a slight limp but is under no dire physical threat. Psychologically she is very frail. The latter is more significant because it is her psychological condition that prevents her from interacting with others and becoming part of the world of reality rather than the world of dreams.

Responding to the Selection

What is the difference between nervousness and fear? Which do you think Laura experienced when at the business college? Why might some people be prone to strong emotions in situations that would not upset another individual? In what way can sensitivity be both a special gift and a painful affliction?

Reviewing the Selection

RECALLING

1. What does Amanda discover when she stops by the business school? Why is she distraught?

2. According to Amanda, what alternative to going to business college does a young woman have?

INTERPRETING

3. What happened to Laura when she went to the business college? Why did she drop out? What does she spend her days doing? What did Jim call her, and how did he come up with this name? What do all of these details tell you about Laura's personality and character?

4. What does Amanda fear? What circumstance is she in because of the departure of her husband? What does she want for Laura? When she realizes that Laura will not attend business school, what alternative plan does she immediately devise?

SYNTHESIZING

5. Why doesn't Laura enthusiastically embrace Amanda's plan for her? How would you describe Laura's physical condition? her psychological condition? Why is the latter more significant than the former?

Understanding Literature (Questions for Discussion)

Irony. Irony is a difference between appearance and reality. At the end of this scene, Amanda mentions the portrait of the father that hangs in the room. What became of this man? What makes it ironic that Amanda should pin her hopes on Laura's having a gentleman caller and then immediately think of her husband's picture? What does this sequence of events suggest about the fulfillment of Amanda's hopes?

ANSWERS FOR UNDERSTANDING LITERATURE

▶ See the evaluation form for discussion, active listening, and oral commnication, *Assessment Portfolio,* 7.11–7.14.

Irony. Amanda's husband has left her and her children. The scene is ironic because it contrast the illusory hopes of marriage with the grim reality of abandonment. The sequence of events suggests that Amanda's hopes will not be realized.

SCENE: *The same. Lights up again but only on* R. *alley and fire-escape landing, rest of the stage dark. (Typewriter table and typewriter have been taken offstage.) Enter* TOM, *again wearing merchant sailor overcoat and knitted-cap, in alley* R. *As* MUSIC CUE #6 *ends,* TOM *begins to speak.*

TOM *(Leans against grill of fire-escape, smoking).* After the fiasco at Rubicam's Business College, the idea of getting a gentleman caller for my sister Laura began to play a more and more important part in my mother's calculations. It became an obsession. Like some archetype[8] of the universal unconscious, the image of the gentleman caller haunted our small apartment. An evening at home rarely passed without some allusion to this image, this spectre, this hope. . . . And even when he wasn't mentioned, his presence hung in my mother's preoccupied look and in my sister's frightened, apologetic manner. It hung like a sentence passed upon the Wingfields! But my mother was a woman of action as well as words. (MUSIC CUE #7.) She began to take logical steps in the planned direction. Late that winter and in the early spring—realizing that extra money would be needed to properly feather the nest and plume the bird—she began a vigorous campaign on the telephone, roping in subscribers to one of those magazines for matrons called "The Homemaker's Companion," the type of journal that features the serialized sublimations of ladies of letters who think in terms of delicate cup-like breasts, slim, tapering waists, rich creamy thighs, eyes like wood-smoke in autumn, fingers that soothe and caress like soft, soft strains of music. Bodies as powerful as Etruscan[9] sculpture. *(He exits down* R. *into wings. Light in alley* R. *is blacked out, and a head-spot falls on* AMANDA, *at phone in living-room.* MUSIC CUE #7 *ends as* TOM *stops speaking.)*

AMANDA. Ida Scott? *(During this speech* TOM *enters dining-room* U. R. *unseen by audience, not wearing overcoat or hat. There is an unlighted reading lamp on table. Sits* C. *of dining-room table with writing materials.)* This is Amanda Wingfield. We missed you at the D.A.R. last Monday. Oh, first I want to know how's your sinus condition? You're just a Christian martyr. That's what you are. You're just a Christian martyr. Well, I was just going through my little red book, and I saw that your subscription to the "Companion" is about to expire just when that wonderful new serial by Bessie Mae Harper is starting. It's the first thing she's written since "Honeymoon for Three." Now, that was unusual, wasn't it? Why, Ida, this one is even lovelier. It's all about the horsey set on Long Island and a debutante is thrown from her horse while taking him over the jumps at the—regatta. Her spine—her spine is injured. That's what the horse did—he stepped on her. Now, there is only one surgeon in the entire world that can keep her from being completely paralyzed, and that's the man she's engaged to be married to and he's tall and he's blond and he's handsome. That's unusual, too, huh? Oh, he's not perfect. Of course he has a weakness. He has the

❶ *What does Tom say about his mother's plan? How does it change his mother and sister? Does he see this plan as realistic?*

8. **archetype.** Original pattern; prototype
9. **Etruscan.** Of a culture that flourished on the Italian peninsula before the Romans

WORDS FOR EVERYDAY USE:
fi • as • co (fē as´ko) *n.,* complete failure
sub • li • ma • tion (sub´lə ma´shən) *n.,* expression of socially or personally unacceptable impulses in constructive, acceptable forms

ANSWER TO GUIDED READING QUESTION

❶ Tom says his mother's hope to find a gentleman caller haunted them like a "spectre." His mother becomes preoccupied; his sister becomes frightened and apologetic. He does not see this plan as realistic.

VOCABULARY IN CONTEXT

- Once we cut open the birthday cake and found it spoiled, we knew the party was a fiasco.
- Paul's painting of a table laden with food was a sublimation of his desire to eat food while on his diet.

ANSWER TO GUIDED READING QUESTION

❶ Tom enjoys reading and writing. His mother's talkative personality conflicts with an activity that requires silence.

most terrible weakness in the entire world. He just drinks too much. What? Oh, no, Honey, don't let them burn. You go take a look in the oven and I'll hold on . . . Why, that woman! Do you know what she did? She hung up on me. *(Dining-room and living-room lights dim in. Reading lamp lights up at same time.)*

What does Tom enjoy doing? In what way does this activity and his mother's personality conflict? ❶

LAURA. Oh, Mother, Mother, Tom's trying to write. *(Rises from armchair where she was left at curtain of previous scene, goes to curtain between dining-room and living-room, which is already open.)*

AMANDA. Oh! So he is. So he is. *(Crosses from phone, goes to dining-room and up to* TOM.*)*

TOM *(At table).* Now what are you up to?

AMANDA. I'm trying to save your eyesight. *(Business with lamp.)* You've only got one pair of eyes and you've got to take care of them. Oh, I know that Milton was blind, but that's not what made him a genius.

TOM. Mother, will you please go away and let me finish my writing?

AMANDA *(Squares his shoulders).* Why can't you sit up straight? So your shoulders don't stick through like sparrows' wings?

TOM. Mother, please go busy yourself with something else. I'm trying to write.

AMANDA *(Business with* TOM*).* Now, I've seen a medical chart, and I know what that position does to your internal organs. You sit up and I'll show you. Your stomach presses against your lungs, and your lungs press against your heart, and that poor little heart gets discouraged because it hasn't got any room left to go on beating for you.

TOM. What in hell! . . . *(Inner curtains between living-room and dining-room close. Lights dim down in dining-room.* LAURA *crosses, stands* C. *of curtains in living-room listening to following scene between* TOM *and* AMANDA.*)*

AMANDA. Don't you talk to me like that—

TOM. —am I supposed to do?

AMANDA. What's the matter with you? Have you gone out of your senses?

TOM. Yes, I have. You've driven me out of them.

AMANDA. What is the matter with you lately, you big—big—idiot?

TOM. Look, Mother—I haven't got a thing, not a single thing left in this house that I can call my own.

AMANDA. Lower your voice!

TOM. Yesterday you confiscated my books! You had the nerve to——

AMANDA. I did. I took that horrible novel back to the library—that awful book by that insane Mr. Lawrence.[10] I cannot control the output of a diseased mind or people who cater to them, but I won't allow such filth in my house. No, no, no, no, no!

TOM. House, house! Who pays the rent on the house, who makes a slave of himself to—!

AMANDA. Don't you dare talk to me like

10. **Mr. Lawrence.** D. H. Lawrence (1858–1930) was a poet and novelist whose writings were considered outrageous by some of his contemporaries.

WORDS FOR EVERYDAY USE: **ca • ter** (kāt´ər) *vi.,* take special pains in seeking to gratify another's needs or desires

VOCABULARY IN CONTEXT

- We decided not to cater to Raymond's wishes; we would no longer do only the things he liked to do.

that! *(*LAURA *crosses* D. L. *to back of armchair.)*

TOM. No, *I* mustn't say anything! I've just got to keep quiet and let you do all the talking.

AMANDA. Let me tell you something!

TOM. I don't want to hear any more.

AMANDA. You will hear more—*(*LAURA *crosses to phonograph.)*

TOM *(Crossing through curtains between dining-room and living-room. Goes up stage of door* R. *where, in a dark spot, there is supposedly a closet).* Well, I'm not going to listen. I'm going out. *(Gets out coat.)*

AMANDA *(Coming through curtains into living-room, stands* C.*).* You are going to listen to me, Tom Wingfield. I'm tired of your impudence.—And another thing—I'm right at the end of my patience!

TOM *(Putting overcoat on back of armchair and crossing back to* AMANDA*).* What do you think I'm at the end of, Mother? Aren't I supposed to have any patience to reach the end of? I know, I know. It seems unimportant to you, what I'm *doing*—what I'm trying to do—having a difference between them! You don't think that.

AMANDA. I think you're doing things that you're ashamed of, and that's why you act like this. *(*TOM *crosses to day-bed and sits.)* I don't believe that you go every night to the movies. Nobody goes to the movies night after night. Nobody in their right minds goes to the movies as often as you pretend to. People don't go to the movies at nearly midnight and movies don't let out at two A.M. Come in stumbling, muttering to yourself like a maniac. You get three hours' sleep and then go to work. Oh, I can picture the way you're doing down there. Moping, doping, because you're in no condition.

TOM. That's true—that's very, very true. I'm in no condition!

AMANDA. How dare you jeopardize your job? Jeopardize our security? How do you think we'd manage—? *(Sits armchair* R.*)*

TOM. Look, Mother, do you think I'm *crazy* about the *warehouse?* You think I'm in love with the Continental Shoemakers? You think I want to spend fifty-five years of my life down there in that—*celotex interior!* with *fluorescent tubes?!* Honest to God, I'd rather somebody picked up a crow-bar and battered out my brains—than go back mornings! But I *go!* Sure, every time you come in yelling that bloody *Rise and Shine!* Rise and shine!! I think how lucky dead people are. But I get up. *(Rises from day-bed.)* I *go!* For sixty-five dollars a month I give up all that I dream of doing and being *ever*! And you say that is all I think of. Oh, God! Why, Mother, if self is all I ever thought of, Mother, *I'd* be where *he* is—*GONE! (Crosses to get overcoat on back of armchair.)* As far as the system of transportation reaches! *(*AMANDA *rises, crosses to him and grabs his arm.)* Please don't grab at me, Mother!

AMANDA *(Following him).* I'm not grabbing at you. I want to know where you're going now.

TOM *(Taking overcoat and starts crossing to door* R.*)* I'm going to the movies!

AMANDA *(Crosses* C.*).* I don't believe that lie!

TOM *(Crosses back to* AMANDA*).* No? Well, you're right. For once in your life you're right. I'm not going to the movies. I'm going to opium dens! Yes, Mother, opium dens, dens of vice and criminals' hang-outs, Mother. I've joined the Hogan gang. I'm a hired assassin, I carry a tommy-gun in a violin case! I run a string of cathouses in the valley! They call me

❶ *How does Tom feel about his job? Why does he continue doing it? What has "doing the right thing" made him give up?*

ANSWER TO GUIDED READING QUESTION

❶ Tom loathes his job. He continues doing his job to support his mother and his sister. "Doing the right thing" has made him give up his personal hopes and dreams.

Answers to Guided Reading Questions

❶ The glass menagerie is overturned.

❷ Tom's actions reveal that he cares very much for his sister and dislikes seeing her hurt.

Responding to the Selection

Ask students how they feel about Tom's outburst when the menagerie overturns. Do they feel more sympathetic when he collects the fallen glass?

What happens to the glass menagerie? ❶

Killer, Killer Wingfield, I'm really leading a double life. By day I'm a simple, honest warehouse worker, but at night I'm a dynamic czar of the underworld. Why, I go to gambling casinos and spin away a fortune on the roulette table! I wear a patch over one eye and a false moustache, sometimes I wear green whiskers. On those occasions they call me—El Diablo![11] Oh, I could tell you things to make you sleepless! My enemies plan to dynamite this place some night! Some night they're going to blow us all sky-high. And will I be glad! Will I be happy! And so will you be. You'll go up—up—over Blue Mountain on a broomstick! With seventeen gentlemen callers. You ugly babbling old witch! *(He goes through a series of violent, clumsy movements, seizing his overcoat, lunging to* R. *door, pulling it fiercely open. The women watch him, aghast. His arm catches in the sleeve of the coat as he struggles to pull it on. For a moment he is pinioned by the bulky garment. With an outraged groan he tears the coat off again, splitting the shoulder of it, and hurls it across the room. It strikes against the shelf of* LAURA*'s glass collection, there is a tinkle of shattering glass.* LAURA *cries out as if wounded.)*

What feelings for his sister are revealed by Tom's actions? ❷

LAURA. My glass!—menagerie . . . *(She covers her face and turns away.* MUSIC CUE #8 *through to end of scene.)*

AMANDA *(In an awful voice).* I'll never speak to you again as long as you live unless you apologize to me! *(*AMANDA *exits through living-room curtains.* TOM *is left with* LAURA. *He stares at her stupidly for a moment. Then he crosses to shelf holding glass menagerie. Drops awkwardly on his knees to collect fallen glass, glancing at* LAURA *as if he would speak, but couldn't. Blackout.* TOM, AMANDA, *and* LAURA *exit in blackout.)*

11. **El Diablo.** Spanish for "the devil"

Responding to the Selection

How do you feel about Tom's outburst? Do you sympathize with him? What is difficult about conflict between one's personal desires and one's duties?

Words for Everyday Use:

czar (zar) *n.*, emperor
a • ghast (ə gast´) *adj.*, feeling great horror or dismay
pin • ion (pin´yən) *vt.*, disable or impede

Vocabulary in Context

- The Russian czar was an absolute monarch who crushed any rebellion by his people.
- When Simon dropped the beautiful lemon meringue pie I had made, I looked at him, aghast.
- They pinioned the prize parrot's wings so that it could not fly away.

Reviewing the Selection

RECALLING

1. What does Tom do for a living? What is his role in the financial stability of the family? About what do Tom and Amanda argue?
2. What happens at the end of the scene to Laura's menagerie?

INTERPRETING

3. What does Tom want to do with himself? What does he fear will happen if he continues working at Continental Shoemakers?
4. As a result of his argument with his mother, Tom acts in a way that hurts Laura. What does Tom want to do with his life? How would doing that also harm Laura?

SYNTHESIZING

5. Tom and his mother want very different things in life, but in a sense they are quite similar, for they both are passionate dreamers. Of what does each person dream? In what ways do their dreams conflict with one another?

Understanding Literature (Questions for Discussion)

1. **Archetype.** An **archetype** is an inherited, often unconscious ancestral memory or motif that recurs throughout history and literature. The notion of the archetype derives from the psychology of Carl Jung, who wrote of archetypes as making up humanity's "collective unconscious." Tom says that "like some archetype of the universal unconscious, the image of the gentleman caller haunted our small apartment." Why is Amanda so insistent on Laura's having gentlemen callers? How does Laura respond to the idea? How is the idea of the gentleman caller related to the picture of the absent father, the one that is always smiling?
2. **Conflict.** A **conflict** is a struggle between two forces in a literary work. What struggle does Tom face? What family circumstances make it very difficult for him to pursue his own dreams? What options does Tom have? Why do none of these options seem particularly attractive?
3. **Symbol.** A **symbol** is a thing that stands for or represents both itself and something else. Of what is the glass menagerie in this play a symbol? With whom is the menagerie associated? What similarities do the menagerie and this person have? How might Tom's actions affect his sister, Laura? What symbolic significance does the breaking of the menagerie have?

ANSWERS FOR REVIEWING THE SELECTION

RECALLING

1. Tom works in a shoe warehouse. He is the primary supporter of his family. Tom and Amanda argue about whether Tom has been endangering his job.

2. Laura's menagerie is overturned and the sound of shattering glass suggests that some pieces may have been broken.

INTERPRETING

Responses will vary. Possible responses are given.

3. Tom wants to travel and experience the world. He fears that he will never be able to realize this dream if he continues to work at Continental Shoemakers.

4. Tom wants to leave his family and explore the world. Doing so might ruin his sister as she would have no means of financial support and she would also suffer emotionally.

SYNTHESIZING

Responses will vary. Possible responses are given.

5. Tom dreams of seeing the world and Amanda dreams of returning to her period of glory as a young woman in the South. Their dreams conflict as Tom dreams of the future and Amanda dreams of the past.

ANSWERS FOR UNDERSTANDING LITERATURE

► See the evaluation form for discussion, active listening, and oral communication, *Assessment Portfolio,* 7.11–7.14.

Responses will vary. Possible responses are given.

1. Archetype. Amanda is insistent on Laura having gentlemen callers because she had them herself. Laura responds weakly to the idea. The gentleman caller, like the father, is an unreachable, intangible image, not a reality.

2. Conflict. Tom faces the struggle between family duty and personal desire. His dependent mother and sister make it difficult for him to

(cont.)

ANSWERS FOR UNDERSTANDING LITERATURE (CONT.)

pursue his own dreams. Tom can either abandon his family or continue to slave away in the shoe warehouse. Both options involve difficult choices and a form of sacrifice.

3. Symbol. The glass menagerie is symbolic of Laura's beauty and fragility. The menagerie is associated with Laura. Both are easily damaged by the ordinary happenings of the real world. Tom's actions—his leaving—might destroy Laura. The breaking of the menagerie signifies that Laura may be destroyed by Tom.

Answers to Guided Reading Questions

❶ Tom gives Laura a magician's magic scarf. He gives this to her to try to make up for breaking her menagerie.

❷ Tom compares his desire to get out of his situation to getting out of a coffin without removing one nail.

ACT ONE, SCENE 4

The interior is dark. Faint light in alley R. *A deep-voiced bell in a church is tolling the hour of five as the scene commences.*

TOM *appears at the top of* R. *alley. After each solemn boom of the bell in the tower he shakes a little toy noisemaker or rattle as if to express the tiny spasm of man in contrast to the sustained power and dignity of the Almighty. This and the unsteadiness of his advance make it evident that he has been drinking. As he climbs the few steps to the fire-escape landing light steals up inside.* LAURA *appears in night-dress, entering living-room from* L. *door of dining-room, observing* TOM'*s empty bed (day-bed) in the living-room.* TOM *fishes in his pockets for door-key, removing a* motley *assortment of articles in the search, including a perfect shower of movie-ticket stubs and an empty bottle. At last he finds the key, but just as he is about to insert it, it slips from his fingers. He strikes a match and crouches below the door.*

❶ *What does Tom give Laura? Why does he give this to her?*

❷ *To what trick does Tom compare his desire to get out of his situation?*

TOM *(Bitterly).* One crack—and it falls through! (LAURA *opens door* R.)

LAURA. Tom! Tom, what are you doing?

TOM. Looking for a door-key.

LAURA. Where have you been all this time?

TOM. I have been to the movies.

LAURA. All this time at the movies?

TOM. There was a very long program. There was a Garbo picture and a Mickey Mouse and a travelogue and a newsreel[12] and a preview of coming attractions. And there was an organ solo and a collection for the milk-fund—simultaneously—which ended up in a terrible fight between a fat lady and an usher!

LAURA *(Innocently).* Did you have to stay through everything?

TOM. Of course! And, oh, I forgot! There was a big stage show! The headliner on this stage show was Malvolio the Magician. He performed wonderful tricks, many of them, such as pouring water back and forth between pitchers. First it turned to wine and then it turned to beer and then it turned to whiskey. I know it was whiskey it finally turned into because he needed somebody to come up out of the audience to help him, and I came up—both shows! It was Kentucky Straight Bourbon. A very generous fellow, he gave souvenirs. *(He pulls from his back pocket a shimmering rainbow-colored scarf.)* He gave me this. This is his magic scarf. You can have it, Laura. You wave it over a canary cage and you get a bowl of gold-fish. You wave it over the gold-fish bowl and they fly away canaries. . . . But the wonderfullest trick of all was the coffin trick. We nailed him into a coffin and he got out of the coffin without removing one nail. *(They enter.)* There is a trick that would come in handy for me—get me out of this 2 by 4 situation! *(Flops onto day-bed and starts removing shoes.)*

LAURA. Tom—shhh!

TOM. What're you shushing me for?

LAURA. You'll wake up Mother.

12. **travelogue and a newsreel.** *Travelogue*—film about a foreign place; *newsreel*—short motion picture of recent news events; both were formerly shown as part of the program in movie theaters.

WORDS FOR EVERYDAY USE: **mot • ley** (mät´lē) *adj.,* composed of many different elements

Vocabulary in Context

- The junk drawer held a motley collection of broken gadgets, rubber bands, bills, and chewing gum wrappers.

TOM. Goody goody! Pay'er back for all those "Rise an' Shines." *(Lies down groaning.)* You know it don't take much intelligence to get yourself into a nailed-up coffin, Laura. But who in hell ever got himself out of one without removing one nail? *(As if in answer, the father's grinning photograph lights up.* LAURA *exits up* L. *Lights fade except for blue glow in dining-room. Pause after lights fade, then clock chimes six times. This is followed by the alarm clock. Dim in fore-stage.)*

Responding to the Selection

How do you think Laura was affected by her brother's strange behavior in this scene?

Reviewing the Selection

RECALLING

1. According to Tom, what was "the wonderfullest trick of all" performed by Malvolio the Magician?
2. What lights up at the end of this scene?

INTERPRETING

3. Why is Tom so impressed by the magic trick of escaping from a coffin without removing a nail? What similarities are there between the trick and what Tom would have to do to get himself out of his current situation?
4. What is Tom thinking about doing? How would doing that make him like his father?

SYNTHESIZING

5. In what ways is Tom already preparing to escape in this scene? In what ways is he distancing himself from his present life?

Understanding Literature (Questions for Discussion)

Symbol. A **symbol** is a thing that stands for or represents both itself and something else. Writers use two types of symbols—conventional, and personal or idiosyncratic. What does the coffin of which Tom speaks symbolize for him? What "trick" does Tom want to be able to perform? What "nails" would he have to remove in order to perform this trick? Why does Tom think that it would take magic for him to be able to do that?

RESPONDING TO THE SELECTION

Ask students how they feel about the fact that Tom treats Laura as a child and does not reveal his intentions to her. Would it be kinder of him to prepare her in advance of his possible leaving?

ANSWERS FOR REVIEWING THE SELECTION

RECALLING

1. The most wonderful trick was the magician's escaping from a nailed coffin without removing one nail.
2. The "grinning photograph" of the father lights up.

INTERPRETING

Responses will vary. Possible responses are given.

3. Tom is impressed because it is impossible to escape from a nailed coffin without removing one nail. Tom must somehow, like the magician, escape from an impossible situation and make as little commotion and leave the least damage behind as possible.
4. Tom is thinking about leaving his job and his family. He would be like his father because he would be abandoning two people who are unable to support themselves.

SYNTHESIZING

Responses will vary. Possible responses are given.

5. Tom is already preparing to escape by his goodbye gift to his sister, his strange and reckless behavior, and his inability to explain his feelings to his sister. He is attempting to divert himself from his difficult situation by behaving in a thoughtless and reckless manner.

ANSWERS FOR UNDERSTANDING LITERATURE

► See the evaluation form for discussion, active listening, and oral communication, *Assessment Portfolio,* 7.11–7.14.

Responses will vary. Possible responses are given.

Symbol. The trick of the coffin symbolizes a way of escaping from a life that leaves him feeling half-dead. He wants to be able to escape his tedious job and his financial obligation to his family. He would have to remove the nails of his mother and his sister's emotional and financial dependence. He thinks that such a feat would be "magic" because he can think of no way for his sister and his mother to continue without his support.

ANSWER TO GUIDED READING QUESTION

❶ When Laura falls, Tom rushes to the door, and Amanda rushes in from the dining room. Their actions express concern and anxiety for Laura's well-being.

Scene is the same. Immediately following. The churchbell is heard striking six. At the sixth stroke the alarm clock goes off in AMANDA'S *room off* R. *of dining-room and after a few moments we hear her calling, "Rise and shine! Rise and shine!* LAURA, *go tell your brother to rise and shine!"*

TOM *(Sitting up slowly in day-bed).* I'll rise—but I won't shine. *(The light increases.)*

AMANDA *(Offstage).* Laura, tell your brother his coffee is ready. *(*LAURA, *fully dressed, a cape over her shoulders, slips into living-room.* TOM *is still in bed, covered with blanket, having taken off only shoes and coat.)*

What do Tom and Amanda do when Laura falls? What feelings are revealed by their actions? ❶

LAURA. Tom!—It's nearly seven. Don't make Mother nervous. *(He stares at her stupidly. Beseechingly.)* Tom, speak to Mother this morning. Make up with her, apologize, speak to her!

TOM *(Putting on shoes).* She won't to me. It's her that started not speaking.

LAURA. If you just say you're sorry she'll start speaking.

TOM. Her not speaking—is that such a tragedy?

LAURA. Please—please!

AMANDA *(Calling offstage* R. *from kitchen).* Laura, are you going to do what I asked you to do, or do I have to get dressed and go out myself?

LAURA. Going, going—soon as I get on my coat! *(She rises and crosses to door* R.*)* Butter and what else?

(To AMANDA.*)*

AMANDA *(Offstage).* Just butter. Tell them to charge it.

LAURA. Mother, they make such faces when I do that.

AMANDA *(Offstage).* Sticks and stones can break our bones, but the expression on Mr. Garfinkel's face won't harm us! Tell your brother his coffee is getting cold.

LAURA *(At door* R.*).* Do what I asked you, will you, will you, Tom? *(He looks sullenly away.)*

AMANDA. Laura, go now or just don't go at all!

LAURA *(Rushing out* R.*)* Going—going! *(A second later she cries out. Falls on fire-escape landing.* TOM *springs up and crosses to door* R. AMANDA *rushes anxiously in from dining-room, puts dishes on dining-room table.* TOM *opens door* R.*)*

TOM. Laura?

LAURA. I'm all right. I slipped, but I'm all right. *(Goes up* R. *alley, out of sight.)*

AMANDA *(On fire-escape).* I tell you if anybody falls down and breaks a leg on those fire-escape steps, the landlord ought to be sued for every cent he——*(Sees* TOM.*)* Who are you? *(Leaves fire-escape landing, crosses to dining-room and returns with bowls, coffee cup, cream, etc. Puts them on small table* R. *of day-bed, crosses to arm-chair, sits. Counts 3.* MUSIC CUE #9. *As* TOM *reenters* R., *listlessly for his coffee, she turns her back to him, as she sits in armchair. The light on her face with its aged but childish*

WORDS FOR EVERYDAY USE: **list • less • ly** (list´lis lē) *adv.,* in a disinterested manner

VOCABULARY IN CONTEXT

- It was such a hot day that I lay listlessly in a hammock, drained of all energy.
- Steve looked at us sheepishly when we pointed out that he was wearing one black and one brown sock.
- Wit and writing skill were only two of Samuel Johnson's natural endowments.

features is cruelly sharp, satirical as a Daumier print.[13] TOM *glances sheepishly but sullenly at her averted figure and sits on day-bed next to the food. The coffee is scalding hot, he sips it and gasps and spits it back in the cup. At his gasp,* AMANDA *catches her breath and half turns. Then catches herself and turns away.* TOM *blows on his coffee, glancing side-wise at his mother. She clears her throat.* TOM *clears his. He starts to rise. Sinks back down again, scratches his head, clears his throat again.* AMANDA *coughs.* TOM *raises his cup in both hands to blow on it, his eyes staring over the rim of it at his mother for several moments. Then he slowly sets the cup down and awkwardly and hesitantly rises from day-bed.)*

TOM *(Hoarsely).* I'm sorry, Mother. I'm sorry for all those things I said. I didn't mean it. I apologize.

AMANDA *(Sobbingly).* My devotion has made me a witch and so I make myself hateful to my children!

TOM. No, you don't.

AMANDA. I worry so much, I don't sleep, it makes me nervous!

TOM *(Gently).* I understand that.

AMANDA. You know I've had to put up a solitary battle all these years. But you're my right hand bower! Now don't fail me. Don't fall down.

TOM *(Gently).* I try, Mother.

AMANDA *(With great enthusiasm).* That's all right! You just keep on trying and you're bound to succeed. Why, you're—you're just full of natural endowments! Both my children are—they're very precious children and I've got an awful lot to be thankful for; you just must promise me one thing.

(MUSIC CUE #9 *stops.)*

TOM. What is it, Mother?

AMANDA. Promise me you're never going to become a drunkard!

TOM. I promise, Mother. I won't ever become a drunkard!

AMANDA. That's what frightened me so, that you'd be drinking! Eat a bowl of Purina.

TOM. Just coffee, Mother.

AMANDA. Shredded Wheat Biscuit?

TOM. No, no, Mother, just coffee.

AMANDA. You can't put in a day's work on an empty stomach. You've got ten minutes—don't gulp! Drinking too-hot liquids makes cancer of the stomach. . . . Put cream in.

TOM. No, thank you.

AMANDA. To cool it.

TOM. No! No, thank you, I want it black.

AMANDA. I know, but it's not good for you. We have to do all that we can to build ourselves up. In these trying times we live in, all that we have to cling to is—each other. . . . That's why it's so important to—Tom, I—I sent out your sister so I could discuss something with you. If you hadn't spoken I would have spoken to you. *(Sits down.)*

❶ *What has Amanda's life been like? Why does she depend on her son?*

13. **Daumier print.** Lithograph by Honoré Daumier (1808–1879), artist famed for his caricatures and satires

ANSWER TO GUIDED READING QUESTION

❶ Amanda's life has been "a solitary battle." She depends on her son to be her "right hand bower," or support.

WORDS FOR EVERYDAY USE:

sheep • ish • ly (shēp ish lē) *adv.,* in an embarrassed manner

en • dow • ment (en dow´mənt) *n.,* gift of nature; inherent talent

Answers to Guided Reading Questions

❶ Laura is upset because she senses that Tom hates the apartment and wants to get away from it (and them).

❷ It is hard for Amanda to admit that she loved her husband.

Why is Laura upset?

❶ **Tom** *(Gently).* What is it, Mother, that you want to discuss?

Amanda. Laura! *(Tom puts his cup down slowly.* MUSIC CUE #10.*)*

Tom. Oh.—Laura . . .

Amanda *(Touching his sleeve).* You know how Laura is. So quiet but—still water runs deep! She notices things and I think she—broods about them. *(Tom looks up.)* A few days ago I came in and she was crying.

Tom. What about?

Amanda. You.

Tom. Me?

Amanda. She has an idea that you're not happy here.

*(*MUSIC CUE #10 *stops.)*

Tom. What gave her that idea?

Amanda. What gives her any idea? However, you do act strangely. *(Tom slaps cup down on small table.)* I—I'm not criticizing, understand that! I know your ambitions do not lie in the warehouse, that like everybody in the whole wide world—you've had to—make sacrifices, but—Tom—Tom—life's not easy, it calls for—Spartan endurance! There's so many things in my heart that I cannot describe to you! I've never told you but I—loved your father . . .

What is hard for Amanda to admit?

❷

Tom *(Gently).* I know that, Mother.

Amanda. And you—when I see you taking after his ways! Staying out late—and—well, you had been drinking the night you were in that—terrifying condition! Laura says that you hate the apartment and that you go out nights to get away from it! Is that true, Tom?

Tom. No. You say there's so much in your heart that you can't describe to me. That's true of me, too. There's so much in my heart that I can't describe to you! So let's respect each other's—

Amanda. But why—why, Tom—are you always so restless? Where do you go to, nights?

Tom. I—go to the movies.

Amanda. Why do you go to the movies so much, Tom?

Tom. I go to the movies because—I like adventure. Adventure is something I don't have much of at work, so I go to the movies.

Amanda. But, Tom, you go to the movies entirely too much!

Tom. I like a lot of adventure. *(Amanda looks baffled, then hurt. As the familiar inquisition resumes he becomes hard and impatient again.* Amanda *slips back into her querulous attitude toward him.)*

Amanda. Most young men find adventure in their careers.

Tom. Then most young men are not employed in a warehouse.

Amanda. The world is full of young men employed in warehouses and offices and factories.

Tom. Do all of them find adventure in their careers?

Amanda. They do or they do without it!

Words for Everyday Use:

Spar • tan (spärt´n) *adj.,* like the Spartans; warlike, stoical, or disciplined

in • qui • si • tion (in´kwə zish´ən) *n.,* severe or intensive questioning

quer • u • lous (kwer´yōō ləs) *adj.,* full of complaint; peevish

Vocabulary in Context

- Without sleep, without food, and without a moment's respite, Charles trudged on; truly, he was a man of Spartan endurance.
- When the employer found that some money was missing from the register, he immediately began an intensive inquisition of all employees.
- There is nothing so annoying as a querulous child on a long, hot car ride.
- The abandoned old house was not spooky, but it did have a dismal atmosphere of gloom.

Not everybody has a craze for adventure.

TOM. Man is by instinct a lover, a hunter, a fighter, and none of those instincts are given much play at the warehouse!

AMANDA. Man is by instinct! Don't quote instinct to me! Instinct is something that people have got away from! It belongs to animals! Christian adults don't want it!

TOM. What do Christian adults want, then, Mother?

AMANDA. Superior things! Things of the mind and the spirit! Only animals have to satisfy instincts! Surely your aims are somewhat higher than theirs! Than monkeys—pigs——

TOM. I reckon they're not.

AMANDA. You're joking. However, that isn't what I wanted to discuss.

TOM *(Rising).* I haven't much time.

AMANDA *(Pushing his shoulders).* Sit down.

TOM. You want me to punch in red at the warehouse, Mother?

AMANDA. You have five minutes. I want to talk about Laura.

TOM. All right! What about Laura?

AMANDA. We have to be making some plans and provisions for her. She's older than you, two years, and nothing has happened. She just drifts along doing nothing. It frightens me terribly how she just drifts along.

TOM. I guess she's the type that people call home girls.

AMANDA. There's no such type, and if there is, it's a pity! That is unless the home is hers, with a husband!

TOM. What?

AMANDA *(Crossing* D. R. *to armchair).* Oh, I can see the handwriting on the wall as plain as I see the nose in front of my face! It's terrifying! More and more you remind me of your father! He was out all *(Sits in armchair)* hours without explanation!—Then left! Good-bye! And me with the bag to hold. I saw that letter you got from the Merchant Marine. I know what you're dreaming of. I'm not standing here blindfolded. Very well, then. Then do it! But not till there's somebody to take your place.

TOM. What do you mean?

AMANDA. I mean that as soon as Laura has got somebody to take care of her, married, a home of her own, independent—why, then you'll be free to go wherever you please, *(Rises, crosses to* TOM.*)* on land, on sea, whichever way the wind blows you! But until that time you've got to look out for your sister. *(Crosses* R. *behind armchair.)* I don't say me because I'm old and don't matter! I say for your sister because she's young and dependent. I put her in business college—a dismal failure! Frightened her so it made her sick at the stomach! I took her over to the Young People's League at the church. Another fiasco. She spoke to nobody, nobody spoke to her. *(Sits armchair.)* Now all she does is fool with those pieces of glass and play those worn-out records. What kind of a life is that for a girl to lead?

TOM. What can I do about it?

❶ *Under what circumstances does Amanda say Tom can free himself from the responsibility of supporting his family?*

ANSWER TO GUIDED READING QUESTION

❶ Amanda says Tom can free himself once a husband is found for Laura.

WORDS FOR EVERYDAY USE: **dis • mal** (diz´ məl) *adj.,* causing gloom or misery

ANSWER TO GUIDED READING QUESTION

❶ Amanda asks Tom to find a nice young man and ask him out for Laura.

RESPONDING TO THE SELECTION

You might ask students whether they believe that Amanda's talkativeness is caused by her essential loneliness.

AMANDA. Overcome selfishness! Self, self, self is all that you ever think of! *(TOM springs up and crosses* R. *to get his coat and put it on. It is ugly and bulky. He pulls on a cap with earmuffs.)* Where is your muffler? Put your wool muffler on! *(He snatches it angrily from the hook and tosses it around his neck and pulls both ends tight.)* Tom! I haven't said what I had in mind to ask you.

TOM. I'm too late to——

AMANDA *(Catching his arm—very importunately. Then shyly).* Down at the warehouse, aren't there some—nice young men?

TOM. No!

AMANDA. There must be—some . . .

TOM. Mother——*(Gesture.)*

What does Amanda ask Tom to do?

❶ **AMANDA.** Find out one that's clean-living—doesn't drink and—ask him out for sister!

TOM. What?

AMANDA. For sister! To meet! Get acquainted!

TOM *(Stamping to door* R.*).* Oh, my go-osh!

AMANDA. Will you? *(He opens door. Imploringly.)* Will you? *(He starts out.)* Will you? Will you, dear? *(TOM exits up alley* R. AMANDA *is on fire-escape landing.)*

TOM *(Calling back).* Yes!

AMANDA *(Re-entering* R. *and crossing to phone.* MUSIC CUE #11*).* Ella Cartwright? Ella, this is Amanda Wingfield. First, first, how's that kidney trouble? Oh, it has? It has come back? Well, you're just a Christian martyr, you're just a Christian martyr. I was noticing in my little red book that your subscription to the "Companion" has run out just when that wonderful new serial by Bessie Mae Harper was starting. It's all about the horsey set on Long Island. Oh, you have? You have read it? Well, how do you think it turns out? Oh, no. Bessie Mae Harper never lets you down. Oh, of course, we have to have complications. You have to have complications—oh, you can't have a story without them—but Bessie Mae Harper always leaves you with such an uplift——What's the matter, Ella? You sound so mad. Oh, because it's seven o'clock in the morning. Oh, Ella, I forgot that you never got up until nine. I forgot that anybody in the world was allowed to sleep as late as that. I can't say any more than I'm sorry, can I? Oh, you will? You're going to take that subscription from me anyhow? Well, bless you, Ella, bless you, bless you, bless you. *(*MUSIC CUE #11 faces into MUSIC CUE #11-A, *dance music, and continues into next scene. Dim out lights.* MUSIC CUE #11-A.*)*

Responding to the Selection

Have you ever known someone as talkative and persistent as Amanda? Why do such people tend to get their way? Why is it frustrating to talk to such a person?

WORDS FOR EVERYDAY USE:

im • por • tu • nate • ly (im pôr´chōō nit lē) *adv.,* in an annoyingly urgent or persistent manner

im • plor • ing • ly (im pôr´iŋ le) *adv.,* in a beseeching manner

VOCABULARY IN CONTEXT

- Alicia finally got the bicycle she had been eyeing because she had importunately begged her parents for it for months.
- I could not resist granting the child his every whim when he looked at me so imploringly.

Reviewing the Selection

RECALLING

1. What does Tom's mother say when she wakes him up in the morning?
2. How is Amanda acting toward Tom at the beginning of this scene? Why?
3. Amanda is afraid that Tom is becoming like someone else. Who is that person?
4. What does Amanda want Tom to delay doing? What specific request does she make of him at the end of the scene?

INTERPRETING

5. How does Tom feel about getting up in the morning and going to work at the warehouse? Why might Tom find his mother's way of waking him up particularly annoying, given the feelings that he has?
6. At the beginning of the scene, we learn that Amanda has decided not to speak to Tom. What happens in the rest of the scene? In what way is such behavior typical of Amanda?
7. What similarities does Amanda see between Tom and her husband? Of what is she afraid?
8. What is Amanda's plan for her family? Why does she need Tom in order to carry out that plan?

SYNTHESIZING

9. Why does Tom go to the movies? What does he want out of life? Where does Amanda suggest that he might find that? Why doesn't Tom agree?
10. What philosophical differences do Amanda and Tom have in their views of human beings? Why is Amanda horrified at Tom's discussion of instincts?

Understanding Literature (Questions for Discussion)

Cliché. A **cliché** is a tired or hackneyed expression such as *quiet as a mouse* or *couch potato.* Identify some of the many clichés with which Amanda's speech is peppered. What does Amanda's use of clichés reveal about her? How does her language differ from that of Tom? of Laura?

ANSWERS FOR REVIEWING THE SELECTION

RECALLING

1. Tom's mother says, "Rise and shine!"
2. Amanda is acting cold and distant because Tom said he wished they would all be blown up and called his mother a "babbling witch."
3. Amanda is afraid that Tom is becoming like his father.
4. Amanda wants Tom to delay joining the Merchant Marines. She asks him to find a nice, young man for his sister.

INTERPRETING

Responses will vary. Possible responses are given.

5. Tom thinks how lucky dead people are when he gets up in the morning to go to work in the warehouse. Yelling "Rise and shine!" is a cheerful greeting and Tom feels anything but cheerful in the mornings.
6. Amanda keeps talking but not to Tom directly, and when she sees him she says, "Who are you?" Such prattling and childish behavior is typical of Amanda because even when determined not to speak her garrulousness is unstoppable.
7. Like his father, Tom wishes to leave Amanda and Laura and stays out "all hours without explanation."
8. Amanda's plan is to find a husband to support Laura, allow Tom to leave, and then remain dependent upon her daughter and son-in-law for support.

SYNTHESIZING

Responses will vary. Possible responses are given.

9. Tom goes to the movies because he likes adventure and wishes to escape the depressing realities of his life. He wants more adventure and excitement from life. Amanda suggests that he might find adventure in his career. Tom doesn't believe there is much adventure to be had in a warehouse.
10. Tom believes that humans are creatures of instinct. Amanda believes that Christian adults should focus on the mind and spirit, not the body. Amanda believes instinct to be a base motivation shared by pigs and monkeys.

ANSWERS FOR UNDERSTANDING LITERATURE

► See the evaluation form for discussion, active listening, and oral communication, *Assessment Portfolio,* 7.11–7.14.

Cliché. Some of Amanda's clichés include "Rise and shine," "sticks and stones can break our bones," "sued for every cent," "my right hand bower," "just keep on trying and you're bound to succeed," "I can see the handwriting on the wall as plain as I see the nose in front of my face," and "whichever way the wind blows you." Amanda's use of clichés reveals that she is given to speaking without thinking. Her language is less original, lyrical, and metaphorical than Tom's. Laura barely speaks except in an embarrassed phrase or two that is most unlike Amanda's constant prattle.

ACT ONE, SCENE 6

SCENE: *The same.—Only* R. *alley lighted, with dim light.*

TOM *(Enters down* R. *and stands as before, leaning against grillwork, with cigarette, wearing merchant sailor coat and cap).* Across the alley was the Paradise Dance Hall. Evenings in spring they'd open all the doors and windows and the music would come outside. Sometimes they'd turn out all the lights except for a large glass sphere that hung from the ceiling. It would turn slowly about and filter the dusk with delicate rainbow colors. Then the orchestra would play a waltz or a tango, something that had a slow and sensuous rhythm. The young couples would come outside, to the relative privacy of the alley. You could see them kissing behind ashpits and telephone poles. This was the compensation for lives that passed like mine, without change or adventure. Changes and adventure, however, were imminent this year. They were waiting around the corner for all these dancing kids. Suspended in the mist over Berchtesgaden,[14] caught in the folds of Chamberlain's umbrella. In Spain there was Guernica![15] Here there was only hot swing music and liquor, dance halls, bars, and movies, and sex that hung in the gloom like a chandelier and flooded the world with brief, deceptive rainbows. . . . While these unsuspecting kids danced to "Dear One, The World Is Waiting for the Sunrise." All the world was really waiting for bombardments. *(*MUSIC #11-A *stops. Dim in dining-room: faint glow.* AMANDA *is seen in dining-room.)*

AMANDA. Tom, where are you?

TOM *(Standing as before).* I came out to smoke. *(Exit* R. *into the wings, where he again changes coats and leaves hat.)*

AMANDA *(*TOM *re-enters and stands on fire-escape landing, smoking. He opens door for* AMANDA, *who sits on hassock on landing).* Oh, you smoke too much. A pack a day at fifteen cents a pack. How much would that be in a month? Thirty times fifteen? It wouldn't be very much. Well, it would be enough to help towards a night-school course in accounting at the Washington U! Wouldn't that be lovely?

TOM. I'd rather smoke.

AMANDA. I know! That's the tragedy of you. This fire-escape landing is a poor excuse for the porch we used to have. What are you looking at?

TOM. The moon.

AMANDA. Is there a moon this evening?

TOM. It's rising over Garfinkel's Delicatessen.

AMANDA. Oh! So it is! Such a little silver slipper of a moon. Have you made a wish on it?

TOM. Um-mm.

AMANDA. What did you wish?

TOM. That's a secret.

AMANDA. All right, I won't tell you what I wished, either. I can keep a secret, too. I can be just as mysterious as you.

TOM. I bet I can guess what you wished.

AMANDA. Why, is my head transparent?

14. **Berchtesgaden.** Town in southern Germany that was destroyed by an Allied air attack in 1945
15. **Guernica.** City in northern Spain that was heavily bombed by the Germans in 1937

WORDS FOR EVERYDAY USE:
im • mi • nent (im´ə nənt) *adj.,* likely to happen without delay
bom • bard • ment (bäm bard´mənt) *n.,* attack by bombs

VOCABULARY IN CONTEXT

- When the clouds become a dark bluish gray and the air feels thick and oppressive, rain is imminent.
- Citizens took refuge in bomb shelters during the bombardment.

TOM. You're not a sphinx.

AMANDA. No, I don't have secrets. I'll tell you what I wished for on the moon. Success and happiness for my precious children. I wish for that whenever there's a moon, and when there isn't a moon, I wish for it, too.

TOM. I thought perhaps you wished for a gentleman caller.

AMANDA. Why do you say that?

TOM. Don't you remember asking me to fetch one?

AMANDA. I remember suggesting that it would be nice for your sister if you brought home some nice young man from the warehouse. I think that I've made that suggestion more than once.

TOM. Yes, you have made it repeatedly.

AMANDA. Well?

TOM. We are going to have one.

AMANDA. *What?*

TOM. A gentleman caller!

AMANDA. You mean you have asked some nice young man to come over? *(Rising from stool, facing* TOM.*)*

TOM. I've asked him to dinner.

AMANDA. You really did?

TOM. I did.

AMANDA. And did he accept?

TOM. He did!

AMANDA. He did?

TOM. He did.

AMANDA. Well, isn't that lovely!

TOM. I thought that you would be pleased.

AMANDA. It's definite, then?

TOM. Oh, very definite.

AMANDA. How soon?

TOM. Pretty soon.

AMANDA. How soon?

TOM. Quite soon.

AMANDA. How soon?

TOM. Very, very soon.

AMANDA. Every time I want to know anything you start going on like that.

TOM. What do you want to know?

AMANDA. Go ahead and guess. Go ahead and guess.

TOM. All right, I'll guess. You want to know when the gentleman caller's coming—he's coming tomorrow.

AMANDA. Tomorrow? Oh, no, I can't do anything about tomorrow. I can't do anything about tomorrow.

TOM. Why not?

AMANDA. That doesn't give me any time.

TOM. Time for what?

AMANDA. Time for preparations. Oh, you should have phoned me the minute you asked him—the minute he accepted!

TOM. You don't have to make any fuss.

AMANDA. Of course I have to make a fuss! I can't have a man coming into a place that's all sloppy. It's got to be thrown together properly. I certainly have to do some fast thinking by tomorrow night, too.

TOM. I don't see why you have to think at all.

AMANDA. That's because you just don't know. *(Enter living-room, crosses to* C. *Dim in living-room.)* You just don't know, that's all. We can't have a gentleman caller coming into a pig-sty ! Now, let's see. Oh, I've got those three pieces of wedding silver left. I'll polish that up. I wonder how that

❶ *What does Amanda wish for her children?*

❷ *How does Amanda feel about Tom's news? In what way does her speech betray this emotion?*

ANSWERS TO GUIDED READING QUESTIONS

❶ Amanda wishes for success and happiness for her children.

❷ Amanda is overwhelmed and surprised. This is revealed because for once she has little to say and can only repeat Tom's words.

ANSWER TO GUIDED READING QUESTION

❶ Amanda is excited because this is the first gentleman caller that Laura has ever had.

old lace tablecloth is holding up all these years? We can't wear anything. We haven't got it. We haven't got anything to wear. We haven't got it. *(Goes back to door* R.*)*

TOM. Mother! This boy is no one to make a fuss over.

Why is Amanda so excited about this gentleman caller? ❶

AMANDA *(Crossing to* C.*).* I don't know how you can say that when this is the first gentleman caller your little sister's ever had! I think it's pathetic that that little girl has never had a single gentleman caller! Come on inside! Come on inside!

TOM. What for?

AMANDA. I want to ask you a few things.

TOM *(From doorway* R.*).* If you're going to make a fuss, I'll call the whole thing off. I'll call the boy up and tell him not to come.

AMANDA. No! You mustn't ever do that. People hate broken engagements. They have no place to go. Come on inside. Come on inside. Will you come inside when I ask you to come inside? Sit down. *(*TOM *comes into living-room.)*

TOM. Any particular place you want me to sit?

AMANDA. Oh! Sit anywhere. *(*TOM *sits armchair* R.*)* Look! What am I going to do about that? *(Looking at day-bed.)* Did you ever see anything look so sad? I know, I'll get a bright piece of cretonne.[16] That won't cost much. And I made payments on a floor lamp. So I'll have that sent out! And I can put a bright cover on the chair. I wish I had time to paper the walls. What's his name?

TOM. His name is O'Connor.

AMANDA. O'Connor—he's Irish and tomorrow's Friday—that means fish. Well, that's all right, I'll make a salmon loaf and some mayonnaise dressing for it. Where did you meet him? *(Crosses to day-bed and sits.)*

TOM. At the warehouse, of course. Where else would I meet him?

AMANDA. Well, I don't know. Does he drink?

TOM. What made you ask me that?

AMANDA. Because your father did.

TOM. Now, don't get started on that!

AMANDA. He drinks, then.

TOM. No, not that I know of.

AMANDA. You have to find out. There's nothing I want less for my daughter than a man who drinks.

TOM. Aren't you being a little bit premature? After all, poor Mr. O'Connor hasn't even appeared on the scene yet.

AMANDA. But he will tomorrow. To meet your sister. And what do I know about his character? *(Rises and crosses to* TOM *who is still in armchair, smooths his hair.)*

TOM *(Submitting grimly).* Now what are you up to?

AMANDA. I always did hate that cowlick. I never could understand why it won't sit down by itself.

16. **cretonne.** Heavy, printed cotton used for slipcovers

WORDS FOR EVERYDAY USE: **pre • ma • ture** (prē´mə tōōr´) *adj.,* too early

VOCABULARY IN CONTEXT

- Until we can gather more data, it is premature to state whether our experiment has been a success.
- Rumor had it the queen adopted a supercilious attitude toward anyone who held a title less than that of an archduke.
- Because we didn't want Susan to find out about her surprise party we had to be discreet.

TOM. Mother, I want to tell you something and I mean it sincerely right straight from my heart. There's a lot of boys who meet girls which they don't marry!

AMANDA. You know you always had me worried because you could never stick to a subject. *(Crosses to day-bed.)* What I want to know is what's his position at the warehouse?

TOM. He's a shipping clerk.

AMANDA. Oh! Shipping clerk! Well, that's fairly important. That's where you'd be if you had more get-up. How much does he earn? *(Sits on day-bed.)*

TOM. I have no way of knowing that for sure. I judge his salary to be approximately eighty-five dollars a month.

AMANDA. Eighty-five dollars? Well, that's not princely.

TOM. It's twenty dollars more than I make.

AMANDA. I know that. Oh, how well I know that! How well I know that! Eighty-five dollars a month. No. It can't be done. A family man can never get by on eighty-five dollars a month.

TOM. Mother, Mr. O'Connor is not a family man.

AMANDA. Well, he might be some time in the future, mightn't he?

TOM. Oh, I see . . . Plans and provisions.

AMANDA. You are the only young man that I know of who ignores the fact that the future becomes the present, the present the past, and the past turns into everlasting regret if you don't plan for it.

TOM. I will think that over and see what I can make of it!

AMANDA. Don't be supercilious with your mother! Tell me some more about this—What do you call him? Mr. O'Connor, Mr. O'Connor. He must have another name besides Mr.——?

TOM. His full name is James D. O'Connor. The D. is for Delaney.

AMANDA. Delaney? Irish on both sides and he doesn't drink?

TOM *(Rises from armchair).* Shall I call him up and ask him? *(Starts toward phone.)*

AMANDA *(Crossing to phone).* No!

TOM. I'll call him up and tell him you want to know if he drinks. *(Picks up phone.)*

AMANDA *(Taking phone away from him).* No, you can't do that. You have to be discreet about that subject. When I was a girl in Blue Mountain if it was (TOM *sits on* R. *of day-bed*) suspected that a young man was drinking and any girl was receiving his attentions—if any girl *was* receiving his attentions, she'd go to the minister of his church and ask about his character—or her father, if her father was living, then it was his duty to go to the minister of his church and ask about his character, and that's how young girls in Blue Mountain were kept from making tragic mistakes. *(Picture dims in and out.)*

TOM. How come you made such a tragic one?

AMANDA. Oh, I don't know how he did it, but that face fooled everybody. All he had to do was grin and the world was bewitched. *(Behind day-bed, crosses to arm-*

❶ *What does Tom try to tell his mother?*

❷ *Does Amanda listen? What does she do instead?*

❸ *Why does Amanda say you have to plan for the future?*

WORDS FOR EVERYDAY USE:

su • per • cil • i • ous (sōō´pər sil´ē əs) *adj.*, disdainful, contemptuous

dis • creet (di skrēt´) *adj.*, careful about what one says and does

ANSWERS TO GUIDED READING QUESTIONS

❶ Tom tries to tell his mother that there are a lot of boys who meet girls they do not marry.

❷ Amanda does not listen but immediately inquires how much Mr. O'Connor makes, planning for him to become "a family man."

❸ Amanda says you have to plan for the future because "the future becomes the present, the present the past, and the past turns into everlasting regret if you don't plan for it."

ANSWER TO GUIDED READING QUESTION

❶ Tom warns his mother not to expect too much of Laura.

chair.) I don't know of anything more tragic than a young girl just putting herself at the mercy of a handsome appearance, and I hope Mr. O'Connor is not too good-looking.

TOM. As a matter of fact he isn't. His face is covered with freckles and he has a very large nose.

AMANDA. He's not right-down homely?

TOM. No. I wouldn't say right-down—homely—medium homely, I'd say.

AMANDA. Well, if a girl had any sense she'd look for character in a man anyhow.

TOM. That's what I've always said, Mother.

AMANDA. You've always said it—you've always said it! How could you've always said it when you never even thought about it?

What warning does Tom give about Laura?

❶ **TOM.** Aw, don't be so suspicious of me.

AMANDA. I am. I'm suspicious of every word that comes out of your mouth, when you talk to me, but I want to know about this young man. Is he up and coming?

TOM. Yes. I really do think he goes in for self-improvement.

AMANDA. What makes you think it?

TOM. He goes to night school.

AMANDA. Well, what does he do there at night school?

TOM. He's studying radio engineering and public speaking.

AMANDA. Oh! Public speaking! Oh, that shows, that shows that he intends to be an executive some day—and radio engineering. Well, that's coming . . . huh?

TOM. I think it's here.

AMANDA. Well, those are all very illuminating facts. *(Crosses to back of armchair.)* Facts that every mother should know about any young man calling on her daughter, seriously or not.

TOM. Just one little warning, Mother. I didn't tell him anything about Laura. I didn't let on we had dark ulterior motives. I just said, "How about coming home to dinner some time?" and he said, "Fine," and that was the whole conversation.

AMANDA. I bet it was, too. I tell you, sometimes you can be as eloquent as an oyster. However, when he sees how pretty and sweet that child is, he's going to be, well, he's going to be very glad he was asked over here to have some dinner. *(Sits in armchair.)*

TOM. Mother, just one thing. You won't expect too much of Laura, will you?

AMANDA. I don't know what you mean. *(*TOM *crosses slowly to* AMANDA. *He stands for a moment, looking at her. Then—)*

TOM. Well, Laura seems all those things to you and me because she's ours and we love her. We don't even notice she's crippled any more.

AMANDA. Don't use that word.

TOM. Mother, you have to face the facts; she is, and that's not all.

AMANDA. What do you mean "that's not all"? *(*TOM *kneels by her chair.)*

WORDS FOR EVERYDAY USE: **ul • te • ri • or** (ul tir´ē ər) *adj.,* further; more remote; undisclosed; concealed

VOCABULARY IN CONTEXT

- Although the salesman said he was giving us a free birdcage just because he liked us, we suspected he had ulterior motives.

TOM. Mother—you know that Laura is very different from other girls.

AMANDA. Yes, I do know that, and I think that difference is all in her favor, too.

TOM. Not quite all—in the eyes of others—strangers—she's terribly shy. She lives in a world of her own and those things make her seem a little peculiar to people outside the house.

AMANDA. Don't use that word peculiar.

TOM. You have to face the facts.—She is.

AMANDA. I don't know in what way she's peculiar. (MUSIC CUE #12, *till curtain.* TOM *pauses a moment for music, then—)*

TOM. Mother, Laura lives in a world of little glass animals. She plays old phonograph records—and—that's about all——*(*TOM *rises slowly, goes quietly out the door* R., *leaving it open, and exits slowly up the alley.* AMANDA *rises, goes on to fire-escape landing* R., *looks at moon.)*

AMANDA. Laura! Laura! *(*LAURA *answers from kitchen* R.*)*

LAURA. Yes, Mother.

AMANDA. Let those dishes go and come in front! *(*LAURA *appears with dish towel. Gaily.)* Laura, come here and make a wish on the moon!

LAURA *(Entering from kitchen* R. *and comes down to fire-escape landing).* Moon—moon?

AMANDA. A little silver slipper of a moon. Look over your left shoulder, Laura, and make a wish! *(*LAURA *looks faintly puzzled as if called out of sleep.* AMANDA *seizes her shoulders and turns her at an angle on the fire-escape landing.)* Now! Now, darling, wish!

LAURA. What shall I wish for, Mother?

AMANDA *(Her voice trembling and her eyes suddenly filling with tears).* Happiness! And just a little bit of good fortune! *(The stage dims out.)*

CURTAIN

End of Act One

❶ *Who views Laura's predicament and character more honestly? Who views her with blind devotion?*

Responding to the Selection

What emotions is Amanda feeling at the end of the scene? Is anticipating the success of one's endeavors sometimes more exciting than the success itself? Do you find it strange that Amanda is more excited than Laura?

ANSWER TO GUIDED READING QUESTION

❶ Tom views Laura's predicament more honestly. Amanda views Laura with blind devotion.

ANSWERS TO SELECTION CHECK TEST 4.10.1

EX. What does Laura collect?
Laura collects glass animals.

1. Where is Tom and Laura's father?
Their father has left.

2. What has Laura done to disappoint her mother?
She has dropped out of business school.

3. Where does Tom work?
Tom works in the warehouse of Continental Shoemakers.

4. What does Amanda ask Tom to do?
She asks him to seek out a nice young man for his sister.

5. What warning does Tom give his mother before the gentleman caller comes for dinner?
Tom warns her not to expect too much from Laura.

RESPONDING TO THE SELECTION

You might ask students to predict what will happen in the next act. Will Amanda's hopes be realized or are they just dreams? How can you tell?

Reviewing the Selection

RECALLING

1. What news does Tom give his mother at the beginning of the scene?
2. What questions does Amanda ask about Jim O'Connor?

INTERPRETING

3. Why is Amanda excited about Tom's news?
4. What do Amanda's questions about Jim O'Connor reveal about her plans for him? What makes it funny that she is making such plans at this time?

SYNTHESIZING

5. Amanda accuses Tom of ignoring "the fact that the future becomes the present, the present the past, and the past . . . everlasting regret if you don't plan for it." In your own words, what is the warning that Amanda gives Tom here?

Understanding Literature (Questions for Discussion)

1. **Symbol.** A **symbol** is a thing that stands for or represents both itself and something else. Explain the symbolic significance of the following elements of act one:
   a. the fire-escape
   b. the gauze curtains
   c. the gentleman caller
   d. the glass menagerie
   e. the name "Blue Roses"
   f. the father's picture
   g. Tom's breaking the glass menagerie
   h. the difficulty that Tom has in getting on his coat
   i. Laura's tripping and falling on her way out to Garfinkle's Delicatessen
   j. Tom's trying unsuccessfully to use a key to open the door
   k. the coffin trick performed by Malvolio the Magician

2. **Character.** A **character** is a person who figures in the action of a literary work. Amanda, Tom, and Laura are all dreamers. Amanda and Tom are alike in that they have dreams for the future. What are those dreams? What does Laura spend all of her time doing? How does Laura's dreaminess differ from Amanda's and Tom's?

Answers for Reviewing the Selection

RECALLING

1. Tom tells his mother that he invited a gentleman caller to dinner.

2. Amanda asks what his name is, where Tom met him, whether he drinks, what his position is in the warehouse, how much he earns, what his first name is, whether he is too good looking, whether he is downright homely, and whether he is up and coming.

INTERPRETING

Responses will vary. Possible responses are given.

3. Amanda is excited because Laura is about to receive her first gentleman caller and she hopes that her plans are about to be realized.

4. Amanda's questions reveal that she is planning on the gentleman caller marrying Laura. It is funny that she is making such plans because (as far as Amanda knows) Laura and Jim O'Connor have not even met yet.

SYNTHESIZING

Responses will vary. Possible responses are given.

5. Amanda is warning Tom that time moves rapidly and unless you make plans for the future you will end up spending your life regretting the choices and decisions you have made in the past.

Answers for Understanding Literature

▶ See the evaluation form for discussion, active listening, and oral communication, *Assessment Portfolio,* 7.11–7.14.

1. Symbol. a. The fire-escape symbolizes a way out of the human desperation that burns within the apartment building.
b. The gauze curtains soften the play and give it the ethereal quality of memory; the material gauze also suggests medical bandages indicating that this is a painful memory.
c. The gentleman caller represents "the long-delayed but always expected something that we live for."

(cont.)

Answers for Understanding Literature (cont.)

d. The glass menagerie symbolizes Laura's strangeness and fragility.
e. The name "Blue Roses" symbolizes oddness and rarity, fragility and weakness, and sadness.
f. The father's picture symbolizes adventure and freedom from responsibility.
g. Tom's breaking the glass menagerie symbolizes that his actions over the course of the play will destroy Laura.
h. The difficulty Tom has getting on his coat symbolizes the difficulty of picking himself up and leaving.
i. Laura's tripping and falling symbolizes her inability to operate on the most minimal level in the real world; she is unable to secure even the most basic of her needs.
j. Tom's difficulty opening the door symbolizes both his desire never to reenter the apartment and his inability to escape, or open the door to a new stage of his life.

(cont.)

3. **Setting.** The **setting** of a literary work is the time and place in which it occurs, together with all the details used to create a sense of a particular time and place. Writers create a setting by various means. In drama, the setting is often revealed by the stage set and the costumes, though it may be revealed through what the characters say about their environs. In its widest sense, setting includes the general social, political, moral, and psychological conditions in which characters find themselves. In part, *The Glass Menagerie* is a play about people's dreams for the future. In keeping with the play's subject, the play takes place in Tom's memory, and the setting itself has a dreamlike quality. What aspects of the setting are dreamlike? Laura herself may be read as a symbol of people's wishes or dreams. She is entirely out of touch with reality, incapable of acting in the world, and extremely fragile. In what sense are dreams also fragile? From what realities are the characters in the play escaping? What must Tom do if he is to confront reality and realize his dreams, rather than simply continuing to escape by going to the movies?

Responding in Writing

Dream Analysis. Throughout the centuries, people have been fascinated by dreams and their interpretation. In the past, many people believed that dreams provided clues about what was going to happen in the future. The father of psychoanalysis, Sigmund Freud, believed that dreams were wish fulfillments in which people's unexpressed desires were expressed symbolically. For example, a person who wanted to change his or her life might dream of rising out of a pool of water, a symbolic rebirth. Today, one popular theory or explanation of dreams is that they are an attempt of the sleeping person's mind to sort out, store, and catalog recent events. Another popular theory is that when a person dreams, stored memories, feelings, and thoughts simply appear at random, and some executive part of the mind tries to piece these random impressions together in a logical way by connecting them and giving them a narrative structure. This theory explains why dreams often seem so sensible when a person is dreaming and yet seem illogical when one is awake and thinking back on the dream.

Choose a dream you have had and write a paragraph interpreting it. Report the dream in detail and then explain what you think the dream might mean, using any combination of the theories about dreaming discussed above.

Answers for Understanding Literature (cont.)

k. The coffin trick symbolizes Tom's difficulty in leaving his family.

2. Character. Amanda's dream is that Laura will marry; Tom's dream is to join the Merchant Marines and live a life of adventure. Laura spends all her time thinking about the past—playing her father's old records, leafing through her yearbook, and playing with the glass menagerie. Laura's dreaminess is centered on the past while Amanda and Tom also dream of the future.

3. Setting. The gauze curtain; the tangle of alleys, clotheslines, garbage cans, and fire-escapes; the use of unusual lighting effects; and the music all are dreamlike. Dreams are also fragile because they easily dissipate upon the sleeper's awakening. The characters in this play are trying to escape from their grim financial situation and their apparently bleak futures. Tom must act if he is to confront reality and realize his dreams.

Analytic Scales for Responding in Writing

Assign a score from 1 to 25 for each grading criterion below. (For more detailed evaluation, see the evaluation forms for writing, revising, and proofreading, *Assessment Portfolio,* 7.1–7.10.)

Dream Analysis

- **Content/Unity.** The analysis reports and interprets the meaning of a dream.
- **Organization/Coherence.** The analysis first presents the dream and then interprets this dream in a logical and sensible order.
- **Language/Style.** The analysis uses vivid and precise nouns, verbs, and modifiers.
- **Conventions.** The analysis avoids errors in spelling, grammar, usage, mechanics, and manuscript form.

PREREADING NOTES

READER'S JOURNAL

Many writers have expressed different notions of success. You might read students some of the aphorisms below to stimulate their thinking about what the word *success* means to them. You could then have students try to formulate their own aphorism about success.

- "Success is counted sweetest/By those who ne'er succeed."
—Emily Dickinson
- "They never fail who die/ In a great cause."—Lord Byron
- "The common idea that success spoils people by making them vain, egoistic, and self-complacent is erroneous; on the contrary, it makes them, for the most part, humble, tolerant, and kind. Failure makes people cruel and bitter."—Somerset Maugham
- "Everything yields to success, even grammar."—Victor Hugo
- "All you need in this life is ignorance and confidence, and then success is sure."—Mark Twain
- "Whenever a friend succeeds a little something in me dies."
—Gore Vidal
- "The moral flabbiness born of . . . *success*. That—with the squalid cash interpretation put on the word success—is our national disease."—William James
- "Yes, my love, whosoever lives loses, but he also wins."—Johann Wolfgang von Goethe
- "To burn always with this hard, gemlike flame, to maintain this ecstasy, is success in life."
—Walter Pater

READING SKILLS

Students might also predict what they think the gentleman caller will be like and how he will react to Laura and Amanda.

READER'S JOURNAL

What does being successful mean to you? Does it mean finding a good job and making a great deal of money? Does it mean finding fulfillment in work? in a creative life? in friends and family? Freewrite in your journal about the meaning of success.

READING SKILLS

Read the Language Arts Survey, 4.18, "Reading Actively." Then, based on what you have read in act one, predict what will happen in act two of the play when Laura's gentleman caller comes.

ACT TWO, SCENE 7

What happened to Jim after high school? ❶

SCENE: *The same.*

Inner curtains closed between dining-room and living-room. Interiors of both rooms are dark as at beginning of play. TOM *has on the same jacket and cap as at first. Same dance-hall music as* CUE #1, *fading as* TOM *begins.*

TOM *(Discovered leaning against grill on fire-escape landing, as before, and smoking).* And so the following evening I brought Jim home to dinner. I had known Jim slightly in high school. In high school, Jim was a hero. He had tremendous Irish good nature and vitality with the scrubbed and polished look of white chinaware. He seemed to move in a continual spotlight. He was a star in basketball, captain of the debating club, president of the senior class and the glee club, and he sang the male lead in the annual light opera. He was forever running or bounding, never just walking. He seemed always just at the point of defeating the law of gravity. He was shooting with such velocity through his adolescence that you would just logically expect him to arrive at nothing short of the White House by the time he was thirty. But Jim apparently ran into more interference after his graduation from high school because his speed had definitely slowed. And so, at this particular time in our lives he was holding a job that wasn't much better than mine. He was the only one at the warehouse with whom I was on friendly terms. I was valuable to Jim as someone who could remember his former glory, who had seen him win basketball games and the silver cup in debating. He knew of my secret practice of retiring to a cabinet of the washroom to work on poems whenever business was slack in the warehouse. He called me Shakespeare. And while the other boys in the warehouse regarded me with suspicious hostility, Jim took a humorous attitude toward me. Gradually his attitude began to affect the other boys and their hostility wore off. And so, after a time they began to smile at me too, as people smile at some oddly fashioned dog that

What was Jim like in high school? What did people expect of him? ❷

WORDS FOR EVERYDAY USE:

ve • loc • i • ty (və läs´ə tē) *n.,* quickness or rapidity of motion or action

in • ter • fer • ence (in´ter fir´ens) *n.,* something that comes into collision or opposition

ANSWERS TO GUIDED READING QUESTIONS

❶ Jim's rise to the top has slowed down and he has not reached the success his high school classmates expected of him.

❷ In high school Jim was an energetic hero. He was good natured and good looking. It was expected he would become president.

VOCABULARY IN CONTEXT

- The bay mare ran with such velocity that there was no doubt she would be the winner of the race.
- Allan hoped to finish his project by midafternoon and he would have, if it had not been for his insistent young son's interference.
- He always wore plain clothing and sat toward the back of any lecture hall to be unobtrusive.
- In ancient Canaan civilization, many people were devout and faithful followers of the storm god Ba'al.

trots across their path at some distance. I knew that Jim and Laura had known each other in high school because I had heard my sister Laura speak admiringly of Jim's voice. I didn't know if Jim would remember her or not. Because in high school Laura had been as unobtrusive as Jim had been astonishing. And, if he did remember Laura, it was not as my sister, for when I asked him home to dinner, he smiled and said, "You know, a funny thing, Shakespeare, I never thought of you as having folks!" Well, he was about to discover that I did . . . *(*MUSIC CUE #13. TOM *exits* R. *Interior living-room lights dim in.* AMANDA *is sitting on small table* R. *of day-bed sewing on hem on* LAURA*'s dress.* LAURA *stands facing the door* R. AMANDA *has worked like a Turk in preparation for the gentleman caller. The results are astonishing. The new floor lamp with its rose-silk shade is in place,* R. *of living-room next to wall, a colored paper lantern conceals the broken light fixture in the ceiling, chintz*[1] *covers are on chairs and sofa, a pair of new sofa pillows make their initial appearance.* LAURA *stands in the middle of room with lifted arms while* AMANDA *crouches before her, adjusting the hem of the new dress, devout and ritualistic. The dress is colored and designed by memory. The arrangement of* LAURA*'s hair is changed; it is softer and more becoming. A fragile, unearthly prettiness has come out in* LAURA; *she is like a piece of translucent glass touched by light, given a momentary radiance, not actual, not lasting.* AMANDA, *still seated, is sewing* LAURA*'s dress.* LAURA *is standing* R. *of* AMANDA.*)*

AMANDA. Why are you trembling so, Laura?

LAURA. Mother, you've made me so nervous!

AMANDA. Why, how have I made you nervous?

LAURA. By all this fuss! You make it seem so important.

AMANDA. I don't understand you at all, honey. Every time I try to do anything for you that's the least bit different you just seem to set yourself against it. Now take a look at yourself. *(*LAURA *starts for door* R.*)* No, wait! Wait just a minute—I forgot something. *(Picks two powder puffs from day-bed.)*

LAURA. What is it?

AMANDA. A couple of improvements. *(Business with powder puffs.)* When I was a girl we had round little lacy things like that and we called them "Gay Deceivers."

LAURA. I won't wear them!

AMANDA. Of course you'll wear them.

LAURA. Why should I?

AMANDA. Well, to tell you the truth, honey, you're just a little bit flat-chested.

LAURA. You make it seem like we were setting a trap.

AMANDA. We are. All pretty girls are a trap and men expect them to be traps. Now look at yourself in that glass. *(*LAURA *crosses* R. *Looks at mirror, invisible to audience, which is in darkness up* R. *of* R. *door.)* See? You look just like an angel on a postcard. Isn't that lovely? Now you just wait. I'm going to dress myself up. You're going

1. **chintz.** Cotton cloth printed in color with flower designs or other patterns

❶ *What does Laura object to? What does her mother say in response about the relationship between men and women? Do you agree with Amanda's statement? Why, or why not?*

WORDS FOR EVERYDAY USE:
un • ob • tru • sive (un əb tro̅o̅´siv) *adj.,* not calling attention to itself
de • vout (di vout´) *adj.,* showing reverence

SUPPORT FOR LEP STUDENTS

Review with students the additional vocabulary below before they read the selection.

ADDITIONAL VOCABULARY

vitality—power to go on living
hostility—feeling of ill will; unfriendliness
ritualistic—characaterized by having a set form or system of rites
translucent—able to be seen through
compose—pull together; settle
domestic—of the home
illumination—light
negligence—carelessness
revival—coming back into life or use
decanter—decorative glass bottle
indulgence—giving way to one's desires
inferiority complex—any feeling of being inferior to, or not as good as, others
aggravate—make worse; annoy
partial—favoring one more than another
extinct—no longer in existence
rejuvenate—make feel or seem

ANSWER TO GUIDED READING QUESTION

❶ Laura objects to the fact that it seems as if they are setting a trap for Jim. Amanda says that men expect pretty women to be traps.

VOCABULARY FROM THE SELECTION: ACT 2

acutely	pantomime
aptitude	paragon
beleaguer	poise
devout	relish
exposition	sashay
incredulously	tribulation
indolently	unobtrusive
interference	velocity
intolerable	vestige
jauntily	vivacity
limelight	wince
ornamentation	

Answers to Guided Reading Questions

❶ Malaria fever, jonquils, and Laura and Tom's father are united in her memory. The juxtaposition of three such diverse elements is both startling and bitterly humorous. The reference is humorous because the father, who probably once evoked beautiful memories, such as Amanda's love for jonquils, is now most likely associated with malaria, or sickness and disease.

❷ Amanda's dress reminds her of her youth as a debutante in the Blue Mountains. She constantly thinks back to this time because it was the pinnacle of her existence or the happiest time in her life.

to be astonished at your mother's appearance. (END OF MUSIC CUE. *End of music cue leads into dance music, which then leads in* MUSIC CUE #14, *a few lines below, at stage direction.* AMANDA *exits through curtains upstage off* L. *in dining-room.* LAURA *looks in mirror for a moment. Removes "Gay Deceivers," hides them under mattress of day-bed. Sits on small table* R. *of day-bed for a moment, goes out to fire-escape landing, listens to dance music, until* AMANDA'*s entrance.* AMANDA, *off.)* I found an old dress in the trunk. But what do you know? I had to do a lot to it but it broke my heart when I had to let it out. Now, Laura, just look at your mother. Oh, no! Laura, come look at me now! *(Enters dining-room* L. *door. Comes down through living-room curtain to living-room* C. MUSIC CUE. #14.*)*

❶ *What three things are united in Amanda's memory? In what way are her associations bitterly humorous?*

LAURA *(Re-enters from fire-escape landing. Sits on* L. *arm of armchair).* Oh, Mother, how lovely! *(AMANDA wears a girlish frock. She carries a bunch of jonquils.)*

❷ *Of what does Amanda's dress remind her? Why might she always think back to this time?*

AMANDA *(Standing* C., *holding flowers).* It used to be. It used to be. It had a lot of flowers on it, but they got awful tired so I had to take them all off. I led the cotillion[2] in this dress years ago. I won the cakewalk[3] twice at Sunset Hill, and I wore it to the Governor's ball in Jackson. You should have seen your mother. You should have seen your mother how she just sashayed around *(Crossing around* L. *of day-bed back to* C.*)* the ballroom, just like that. I had it on the day I met your father. I had malaria fever, too. The change of climate from East Tennessee to the Delta—weakened my resistance. Not enough to be dangerous, just enough to make me restless and giddy. Oh, it was lovely. Invitations poured in from all over. My mother said, "You can't go any place because you have a fever. You have to stay in bed." I said I wouldn't and I took quinine[4] and kept on going and going. Dances every evening and long rides in the country in the afternoon and picnics. That country—that country—so lovely—so lovely in May, all lacy with dogwood and simply flooded with jonquils. My mother said, "You can't bring any more jonquils in this house." I said, "I will," and I kept on bringing them in anyhow. Whenever I saw them I said, "Wait a minute, I see jonquils," and I'd make my gentlemen callers get out of the carriage and help me gather some. To tell you the truth, Laura, it got to be a kind of a joke. "Look out," they'd say, "here comes that girl and we'll have to spend the afternoon picking jonquils." My mother said, "You can't bring any more jonquils in the house, there aren't any more vases to hold them." "That's quite all right," I said, "I can hold some myself." Malaria fever, your father and jonquils. (AMANDA *puts jonquils in* LAURA'*s lap and goes out on to fire-escape landing.* MUSIC CUE #14 *stops. Thunder heard.)* I hope they get here before it starts to rain. I gave your brother a little extra change so he and Mr. O'Connor could take the service car home. (LAURA *puts flowers on armchair* R., *and crosses to door* R.*)*

LAURA. Mother!

AMANDA. What's the matter now? *(Re-entering room.)*

---

2. **cotillion.** Formal ball, especially one at which debutants are presented
3. **cakewalk.** Elaborate, strutting dance
4. **quinine.** Bitter medicine used to treat malaria

WORDS FOR EVERYDAY USE: **sa • shay** (sa shā´) *vi.,* move or walk in such a way as to attract attention

Vocabulary in Context

- The little girl put on her mother's dress, shoes, and jewelry and sashayed around the table.

LAURA. What did you say his name was?

AMANDA. O'Connor. Why?

LAURA. What is his first name?

AMANDA *(Crosses to armchair* R.*).* I don't remember—Oh, yes, I do too—it was—Jim! *(Picks up flowers.)*

LAURA. Oh, Mother, not Jim O'Connor!

AMANDA. Yes, that was it, it was Jim! I've never known a Jim that wasn't nice. *(Crosses* L.*, behind day-bed, puts flowers in vase.)*

LAURA. Are you sure his name was Jim O'Connor?

AMANDA. Why, sure I'm sure. Why?

LAURA. Is he the one that Tom used to know in high school?

AMANDA. He didn't say so. I think he just got to know him—*(Sits on day-bed.)* at the warehouse.

LAURA. There was a Jim O'Connor we both knew in high school. If that is the one that Tom is bringing home to dinner——Oh, Mother, you'd have to excuse me, I wouldn't come to the table!

AMANDA. What's this now? What sort of silly talk is this?

LAURA. You asked me once if I'd ever liked a boy. Don't you remember I showed you this boy's picture?

AMANDA. You mean the boy in the year-book?

LAURA. Yes, that boy.

AMANDA. Laura, Laura, were you in love with that boy?

LAURA *(Crosses to* R. *of armchair).* I don't know, Mother. All I know is that I couldn't sit at the table if it was him.

AMANDA *(Rises, crosses* L. *and works up* L. *of day-bed).* It won't be him! It isn't the least bit likely. But whether it is or not, you will come to the table—you will not be excused.

LAURA. I'll have to be, Mother.

AMANDA *(Behind day-bed).* I don't intend to humor your silliness, Laura, I've had too much from you and your brother, both. So just sit down and compose yourself till they come. Tom has forgotten his key, so you'll *have* to let them in when they arrive.

LAURA. Oh, Mother—*you* answer the door! *(Sits chair* R.*)*

AMANDA. How can I when I haven't even finished making the mayonnaise dressing for the salmon?

LAURA. Oh, Mother, please answer the door, don't make me do it! *(Thunder heard off-stage.)*

AMANDA. Honey, do be reasonable! What's all this fuss about—just one gentleman caller—that's all—just one! *(Exits through living-room curtains.* TOM *and* JIM *enter alley* R.*, climb fire-escape steps to landing and wait outside of closed door. Hearing them approach,* LAURA *rises with a panicky gesture. She retreats to living-room curtains. The doorbell rings.* LAURA *catches her breath and touches her throat. More thunder heard off-stage.)*

❶ *Why can't Laura sit at the table with Jim O'Connor?*

AMANDA *(Off-stage).* Laura, sweetheart, the door!

LAURA. Mother, please, you go to the door! *(Starts for door* R.*, then back.)*

AMANDA *(Off-stage, in a fierce whisper).* What is the matter with you, you silly thing? *(Enters through living-room curtains, and stands by day-bed.)*

LAURA. Please you answer it, please.

AMANDA. Why have you chosen this moment to lose your mind? You go to that door.

❷ *Does Amanda understand why Laura is afraid? What words does she use to describe her daughter's behavior?*

ANSWERS TO GUIDED READING QUESTIONS

❶ Laura cannot sit at the table because she is terrified when she realizes the gentleman caller is the same boy she had a crush on in high school.

❷ Amanda does not understand why Laura is afraid. She calls her a "silly thing" and says that she is losing her mind.

ANSWERS TO GUIDED READING QUESTIONS

❶ Amanda says she is putting courage in Laura "for living."

❷ Tom seems unwilling to have much to do with the matchmaking and seems embarrassed and uncomfortable.

LAURA. I can't.

AMANDA. Why can't you?

LAURA. Because I'm sick. *(Crosses to* L. *end of day-bed and sits.)*

AMANDA. You're sick! Am I sick? You and your brother have me puzzled to death. You can never act like normal children. Will you give me one good reason why you should be afraid to open a door? You go to that door. Laura Wingfield, you march straight to that door!

What reason does Amanda say she has for forcing Laura to open the door? ❶

LAURA *(Crosses to door* R.*).* Yes, Mother.

AMANDA *(Stopping* LAURA*).* I've got to put courage in you, honey, for living. *(Exits through living-room curtains, and exits* R. *into kitchen.* LAURA *opens door.* TOM *and* JIM *enter.* LAURA *remains hidden in hall behind door.)*

TOM. Laura—*(*LAURA *crosses* C.*)* this is Jim. Jim, this is my sister Laura.

JIM. I didn't know that Shakespeare had a sister! How are you, Laura?

LAURA *(Retreating stiff and trembling. Shakes hands).* How—how do you do?

JIM. Well, I'm okay! Your hand's *cold,* Laura! *(*TOM *puts hats on phone table.)*

LAURA. Yes, well—I've been playing the victrola. . . .

JIM. Must have been playing classical music on it. You ought to play a little hot swing music to warm you up. *(*LAURA *crosses to phonograph.* TOM *crosses up to* LAURA. LAURA *starts phonograph—looks at* JIM. *Exits through living-room curtains and goes off* L.*)*

JIM. What's the matter?

TOM. Oh—Laura? Laura is—is terribly shy. *(Crosses and sits on day-bed.)*

Does Tom seem willing to take part in bringing Jim together with his sister? ❷

JIM *(Crosses down* C.*).* Shy, huh? Do you know it's unusual to meet a shy girl nowadays? I don't believe you ever mentioned you had a sister?

TOM. Well, now you know I have one. You want a piece of the paper?

JIM *(Crosses to* TOM*).* Uh-huh.

TOM. Comics?

JIM. Comics? Sports! *(Takes paper. Crosses, sits chair* R.*)* I see that Dizzy Dean is on his bad behavior.

TOM *(Starts to door* R. *Goes out).* Really?

JIM. Yeah. Where are *you* going? *(As* TOM *reaches steps* R. *of fire-escape landing.)*

TOM *(Calling from fire-escape landing).* Out on the terrace to smoke.

JIM *(Rises, leaving newspaper in armchair, goes over to turn off victrola. Crosses* R. *Exits to fire-escape landing).* You know, Shakespeare—I'm going to sell you a bill of goods!

TOM. What goods?

JIM. A course I'm taking.

TOM. What course?

JIM. A course in public speaking! You know you and me, we're not the warehouse type.

TOM. Thanks—that's good news. What has public speaking got to do with it?

JIM. It fits you for—executive positions!

TOM. Oh.

JIM. I tell you it's done a helluva lot for me.

TOM. In what respect?

JIM. In all respects. Ask yourself: what's the difference between you and me and the guys in the office down front? Brains?—No!—Ability?—No! Then what? Primarily, it amounts to just one single thing——

TOM. What is that one thing?

JIM. Social poise! The ability to square up to somebody and hold your own on any social level!

AMANDA *(Off-stage)*. Tom?

TOM. Yes, Mother?

AMANDA. Is that you and Mr. O'Connor?

TOM. Yes, Mother.

AMANDA. Make yourselves comfortable.

TOM. We will.

AMANDA. Ask Mr. O'Connor if he would like to wash his hands?

JIM. No, thanks, ma'am—I took care of that down at the warehouse. Tom?

TOM. Huh?

JIM. Mr. Mendoza was speaking to me about you.

TOM. Favorably?

JIM. What do you think?

TOM. Well——

JIM. You're going to be out of a job if you don't wake up.

TOM. I'm waking up——

JIM. Yeah, but you show no signs.

TOM. The signs are interior. I'm just about to make a change. I'm right at the point of committing myself to a future that doesn't include the warehouse or Mr. Mendoza, or even a night school course in public speaking.

JIM. Now what are you gassing[5] about?

TOM. I'm tired of the movies.

JIM. The movies!

TOM. Yes, movies! Look at them. *(He waves his hands.)* All of those glamorous people—having adventures—hogging it all, gobbling the whole thing up! You know what happens? People go to the *movies* instead of *moving*. Hollywood characters are supposed to have all the adventures for everybody in America, while everybody in America sits in a dark room and watches them having it! Yes, until there's a war. That's when adventure becomes available to the masses! Everyone's dish, not only Gable's![6] Then the people in the dark room come out of the dark room to have some adventures themselves—goody—goody! It's our turn now to go to the South Sea Island—to make a safari—to be exotic, far off! . . . But I'm not patient. I don't want to wait till then. I'm tired of the movies and I'm about to move!

JIM *(Incredulously)*. Move?

TOM. Yes.

JIM. When?

TOM. Soon!

JIM. Where? Where?

TOM. I'm starting to boil inside. I know I seem dreamy, but inside—well, I'm boiling! Whenever I pick up a shoe I shudder a little, thinking how short life is and what I am doing!—Whatever that means, I know it doesn't mean shoes—except as something to wear on a traveler's feet! *(Gets card from inside coat pocket.)* Look!

JIM. What?

TOM. I'm a member.

5. **gassing.** Talking in an idle or boastful way
6. **Gable's.** Clark Gable (1901–1960), leading star in Hollywood films who often played a rough, adventurous, romantic hero

❶ *What quality does Jim value? Which characters have this quality? Which characters lack it?*

❷ *What does Tom see as the problem with movies?*

WORDS FOR EVERYDAY USE:
poise (poiz) *n.*, ease and dignity of manner
in • cred • u • lous • ly (in krej´oo ləs lē) *adv.*, in a doubting or skeptical manner

ANSWERS TO GUIDED READING QUESTIONS

❶ Jim admires social poise. Amanda and Jim have this characteristic; Laura and Tom lack this characteristic.

❷ Tom believes that movies keep people from moving or acting on their own.

VOCABULARY IN CONTEXT

- The speaker did not seem nervous at all; on the contrary, he seemed relaxed, dignified, and perfectly poised.
- "What! You found the leprechaun's pot of gold! You must be joking," she said incredulously.

Answers to Guided Reading Questions

❶ Tom has joined the Union of Merchant Seamen. He acquired the money by not paying the electric bill.

❷ Tone feels that he is like his father. His desire to leave responsibility behind makes him like his father.

❸ Amanda appears as a Southern girl full of vivacity and exuding social charm. Tom is embarrassed by his mother. Jim, more at ease in social situations, responds warmly.

What has Tom joined? Where has he acquired the money? ❶

Jim *(Reading).* The Union of Merchant Seamen.

Tom. I paid my dues this month, instead of the electric light bill.

Jim. You'll regret it when they turn off the lights.

Tom. I won't be here.

Jim. Yeah, but how about your mother?

To whom does Tom feel that he is similar? What desire makes the two similar? ❷

Tom. I'm like my father. See how he grins? And he's been absent going on sixteen years.

Jim. You're just talking, you drip. How does your mother feel about it?

Tom. Sh! Here comes Mother! Mother's not acquainted with my plans!

Amanda *(Off-stage).* Tom!

Tom. Yes, Mother?

Amanda *(Off-stage).* Where are you all?

Tom. On the terrace, Mother.

Amanda *(Enters through living-room curtain and stands* C.*).* Why don't you come in? *(They start inside. She advances to them.* Tom *is distinctly shocked at her appearance. Even* Jim *blinks a little. He is making his first contact with girlish Southern vivacity and in spite of the night-school course in public speaking is somewhat thrown off the beam*[7] *by the unexpected outlay of social charm. Certain responses are attempted by* Jim *but are swept aside by* Amanda's *gay laughter and chatter.* Tom *is embarrassed but after the first shock* Jim *reacts very warmly. Grins and chuckles, is altogether won over.* Tom *and* Jim *come in, leaving door open.)*

In what way does Amanda appear before Jim and Tom? Why do the two men react differently to her presence? ❸

Tom. Mother, you look so pretty.

Amanda. You know, that's the first compliment you ever paid me. I wish you'd look pleasant when you're about to say something pleasant, so I could expect it. Mr. O'Connor? *(*Jim *crosses to* Amanda.*)*

Jim. How do you do?

Amanda. Well, well, well, so this is Mr. O'Connor? Introduction's entirely unnecessary. I've heard so much about you from my boy. I finally said to him, "Tom, good gracious, why don't you bring this paragon to supper finally? I'd like to meet this nice young man at the warehouse! Instead of just hearing you sing his praises so much?" I don't know why my son is so standoffish—that's not Southern behavior. Let's sit down. *(*Tom *closes door, crosses* U. R., *stands.* Jim *and* Amanda *sit on day-bed,* Jim, R., Amanda L.*)* Let's sit down, and I think we could stand a little more air in here. Tom, leave the door open. I felt a nice fresh breeze a moment ago. Where has it gone to? Mmmm, so warm already! And not quite summer, even. We're going to burn up when summer really gets started. However, we're having—we're having a very light supper. I think light things are better fo'—for this time of year. The same as light clothes are. Light clothes and light food are what warm weather calls fo'. You know our blood get so thick during th' winter—it takes a while fo' us to adjust ourselves—when the season changes. . . . It's come so quick this year. I wasn't prepared. All of a sudden—Heavens! Already summer!—I ran to the trunk an'—pulled out this light dress—terribly old!

7. **off the beam.** Off-balance or in the wrong direction

Words for Everyday Use: **vi • vac • i • ty** (vī vas´ə tē) *n.,* liveliness of spirit; animation **par • a • gon** (par´ ə gän´) *n.,* model or pattern of perfection or excellence

Vocabulary in Context

- Everyone liked Lana because she was so energetic and filled with vivacity.
- Because Arnie was such a talented calculus student, his teacher described him to others as a paragon of mathematical genius.
- Nadine was so hungry that she ate the entire roast chicken, not leaving a vestige of the meal.
- Cloe was a fine dramatist who induced us to empathize with her tribulations and suffering until we discovered she had only been asked to babysit her brother for an hour or two.

Historical almost! But feels so good—so good and cool, why, y' know——

TOM. Mother, how about our supper?

AMANDA *(Rises, crosses* R. *to* TOM*).* Honey, you go ask sister if supper is ready! You know that sister is in full charge of supper. Tell her you hungry boys are waiting for it. *(*TOM *exits through curtains and off* L. AMANDA *turns to* JIM.*)* Have you met Laura?

JIM. Well, she came to the door.

AMANDA. She let you in?

JIM. Yes, ma'am.

AMANDA *(Crossing to armchair and sitting).* She's very pretty.

JIM. Oh, yes ma'am.

AMANDA. It's rare for a girl as sweet an' pretty as Laura to be domestic! But Laura is, thank heavens, not only pretty but also very domestic. I'm not at all. I never was a bit. I never could make a thing but angel-food cake. Well, in the South we had so many servants. Gone, gone, gone. All vestige of gracious living! Gone completely! I wasn't prepared for what the future brought me. All of my gentlemen callers were sons of planters and so of course I assumed that I would be married to one and raise my family on a large piece of land with plenty of servants. But man proposes—and woman accepts the proposal!—To vary that old, old saying a little bit—I married no planter! I married a man who worked for the telephone company!—That gallantly smiling gentleman over there! *(Points to picture.)* A telephone man who—fell in love with long-distance!—Now he travels and I don't even know where!—But what am I going on for about my—tribulations? Tell me yours—I hope you don't have any! Tom?

TOM *(Re-enters through living-room curtains from off* L.*).* Yes, Mother.

AMANDA. What about that supper?

TOM. Why, supper is on the table. *(Inner curtains between living-room and dining-room open. Lights dim up in dining-room, dim out in living-room.)*

AMANDA. Oh, so it is. *(Rises, crosses up to table* C. *in dining-room and chair* C.*)* How lovely. Where is Laura?

TOM *(Going to chair* L. *and standing).* Laura is not feeling too well and thinks maybe she'd better not come to the table.

AMANDA. Laura!

LAURA *(Off-stage. Faintly).* Yes, Mother? *(*TOM *gestures re:* JIM.*)*

AMANDA. Mr. O'Connor. *(*JIM *crosses up* L. *to table and to chair* L. *and stands.)*

JIM. Thank you, ma'am.

AMANDA. Laura, we can't say grace till you come to the table.

LAURA *(Enters* U. L., *obviously quite faint, lips trembling, eyes wide and staring. Moves unsteadily toward dining-room table).* Oh, Mother, I'm so sorry. *(*TOM *catches her as she feels faint. He takes her to day-bed in living-room.)*

AMANDA *(As* LAURA *lies down).* Why, Laura, you are sick, darling! Laura—rest on the sofa. Well! *(To* JIM.*)* Standing over the hot stove made her ill!—I told her that it was just too warm this evening, but—— *(To* TOM.*)* Is Laura all right now?

❶ *What happens when Laura comes to the table? Why might she apologize to her mother and not the others?*

WORDS FOR EVERYDAY USE:

ves • tige (ves´tij) *n.,* trace, mark, or sign of something that once existed but has passed away

trib • u • la • tion (trib´yoo lā´shən) *n.,* great misery or distress

ANSWER TO GUIDED READING QUESTION

❶ Laura feels faint when she comes to the table. She apologizes to her mother because she knows that her mother had high hopes for her and is the person most affected by her failure.

TOM. She's better, Mother. *(Sits chair* L. *in dining-room. Thunder off-stage.)*

AMANDA *(Returning to dining-room and sitting at table, as* JIM *does).* My goodness, I suppose we're going to have a little rain! Tom, you say grace.

TOM. What?

AMANDA. What do we generally do before we have something to eat? We say grace, don't we?

TOM. For these and all Thy mercies—God's Holy Name be praised. *(Lights dim out.* MUSIC CUE #15.*)*

Responding to the Selection

How do Tom and Jim differ in their goals, their dreams for the future? Which believes in the "American Dream" of material success? Which has a different sort of dream, and what is it? Consider the philosophies of the two young men. Which is more attractive to you? With which do you most agree? Why?

Reviewing the Selection

RECALLING

1. Why doesn't Laura want to come to the table when she learns who the gentleman caller will be?
2. What is Jim's nickname for Tom?
3. What course is Jim taking in night school? Why?
4. What plan does Tom have? What did he pay instead of the electric bill?

INTERPRETING

5. How does Laura feel toward Jim? How do you know?
6. What attitude does Jim have toward Tom's writing? What comment is the playwright making about the role of the artist in a society driven by material success?
7. Why is Jim studying public speaking? What does he hope to do? Why is Tom not interested in taking such a course?
8. According to Tom, what do people in America do instead of living their own lives and having their own adventures? What has Tom decided to do?

SYNTHESIZING

9. Is Jim O'Connor the sort of person whom Amanda would want to have as a suitor for Laura? Why, or why not?
10. Do you believe that Amanda's hopes for Jim and Laura are realistic? Why, or why not? In what ways are Jim and Laura different? Explain.

RESPONDING TO THE SELECTION

You might have students make a pro and con chart for the different philosophies of the two men. Draw the two charts up on the board with the heads *Jim: Materialism* and *Tom: Artistry* and have students suggest the benefits and drawbacks of each philosophy.

ANSWERS FOR REVIEWING THE SELECTION

RECALLING

1. Laura is overawed and terrified when she learns that Jim O'Connor is the same boy who once paid attention to her by calling her "Blue Roses."
2. Jim gives Tom the nickname Shakespeare.
3. Jim is taking a public speaking course so that he may one day hold an executive position.
4. Tom has planned to join the Merchant Marines and has paid his dues instead of paying the light bill.

INTERPRETING

Responses will vary. Possible responses are given.

5. Laura is in love with Jim. Her love is apparent in her extremely overwhelmed reaction when she discovers he is coming to dinner.
6. Jim thinks the fact that Tom enjoys writing is humorous and calls him Shakespeare in fun. The playwright is saying that the artist is misunderstood and is treated as an eccentric object of fun in a material society.
7. Jim is studying public speaking to improve his social poise. He hopes to assume an executive position. Tom is not interested in taking such a course because he is interested neither in social poise nor in assuming an executive position.
8. Tom says that people live vicariously through the lives and adventures of movie stars unless a war occurs, in which case adventure becomes available to the masses. Tom has decided to seek adventure on his own rather than watching other people's adventures.

(cont.)

ANSWERS FOR REVIEWING THE SELECTION (CONT.)

SYNTHESIZING

Responses will vary. Possible responses are given.

9. Jim is exactly the sort of person Amanda would like to have as Laura's suitor because he has social poise and is determined to advance himself financially.
10. Laura's hopes are unrealistic because while Jim is outgoing and happiest in a social situation, Laura is painfully shy and is happiest when she is alone and listening to old records or playing with her glass collection.

ACT TWO, SCENE 8

SCENE: *The same. A half-hour later. Dinner is coming to an end in dining-room.*

AMANDA, TOM *and* JIM *sitting at table as at end of last scene. Lights dim up in both rooms, and* MUSIC CUE #15 *ends.*

AMANDA *(Laughing, as* JIM *laughs too).* You know, Mr. O'Connor, I haven't had such a pleasant evening in a very long time.

JIM *(Rises).* Well, Mrs. Wingfield, let me give you a toast. Here's to the old South.

AMANDA. The old South. *(Blackout in both rooms.)*

JIM. Hey, Mr. Light Bulb!

AMANDA. Where was Moses when the lights went out? Do you know the answer to that one, Mr. O'Connor?

JIM. No, ma'am, what's the answer to that one?

AMANDA. Well, I heard one answer, but it wasn't very nice. I thought you might know another one.

JIM. No, ma'am.

AMANDA. It's lucky I put those candles on the table. I just put them on for ornamentation, but it's nice when they prove useful, too.

JIM. Yes, ma'am.

AMANDA. Now, if one of you gentlemen can provide me with a match we can have some illumination.

JIM *(Lighting candles. Dim in glow for candles).* I can, ma'am.

AMANDA. Thank you.

JIM *(Crosses back to* R. *of dining-room table).* Not at all, ma'am.

AMANDA. I guess it must be a burnt-out fuse. Mr. O'Connor, do you know anything about a burnt-out fuse?

JIM. I know a little about them, ma'am, but where's the fuse box?

AMANDA. Must you know that, too? Well it's in the kitchen. *(*JIM *exits* R. *into kitchen.)* Be careful. It's dark. Don't stumble over anything. *(Sound of crash off-stage.)* Oh, my goodness, wouldn't it be awful if we lost him! Are you all right, Mr. O'Connor?

JIM *(Off-stage).* Yes, ma'am, I'm all right.

AMANDA. You know, electricity is a very mysterious thing. The whole universe is mysterious to me. Wasn't it Benjamin Franklin who tied a key to a kite? I'd like to have seen that—he might have looked mighty silly. Some people say that science clears up all the mysteries for us. In my opinion they just keep on adding more. Haven't you found it yet?

JIM *(Re-enters* R.*).* Yes, ma'am. I found it all right, but them fuses look okay to me. *(Sits as before.)*

AMANDA. Tom.

TOM. Yes, Mother?

AMANDA. That light bill I gave you several days ago. The one I got the notice about?

TOM. Oh—yeah. You mean last month's bill?

AMANDA. You didn't neglect it by any chance?

❶ *By the end of the dinner, how do Amanda and Jim get along? Why might they get along so well?*

❷ *What happens to the lights? Why?*

ANSWERS TO GUIDED READING QUESTIONS

❶ Jim and Amanda are getting along like old friends. They get along well because they are both talkative and love social situations.

❷ The lights go out because Tom did not pay the electric bill.

WORDS FOR EVERYDAY USE: **or • na • men • ta • tion** (or´na men ta´shen) *n.,* decoration

VOCABULARY IN CONTEXT

- The crystal goblets were lovely, but they were more for ornamentation than for use.

ANSWER TO GUIDED READING QUESTION

❶ Amanda suggests that Jim keep Laura company.

TOM. Well, I——

AMANDA. You did! I might have known it!

JIM. Oh, maybe Shakespeare wrote a poem on that light bill, Mrs. Wingfield?

AMANDA. Maybe he did, too. I might have known better than to trust him with it! There's such a high price for negligence in this world today.

JIM. Maybe the poem will win a ten-dollar prize.

AMANDA. We'll just have to spend the rest of the evening in the nineteenth century, before Mr. Edison[8] found that Mazda lamp!

JIM. Candle-light is my favorite kind of light.

AMANDA. That shows you're romantic! But that's no excuse for Tom. However, I think it was very nice of them to let us finish our dinner before they plunged us into everlasting darkness. Tom, as a penalty for your carelessness you can help me with the dishes.

JIM *(Rising.* TOM *rises).* Can I be of some help, ma'am?

AMANDA *(Rising).* Oh, no, I couldn't allow that.

JIM. Well, I ought to be good for *something.*

AMANDA. What did I hear?

JIM. I just said, "I ought to be good for something."

AMANDA. That's what I thought you said. Well, Laura's all by her lonesome out front. Maybe you'd like to keep her company. I can give you this lovely old candelabrum[9] for light. *(*JIM *takes candles.)* It used to be on the altar at the Church of the Heavenly Rest, but it was melted a little out of shape when the church burnt down. The church was struck by lightning one spring, and Gypsy Jones who was holding a revival meeting in the village, said that the church was struck by lightning because the Episcopalians had started to have card parties right in the church.

JIM. Is that so, ma'am?

AMANDA. I never say anything that isn't so.

JIM. I beg your pardon.

AMANDA *(Pouring wine into glass—hands it to* JIM*).* I'd like Laura to have a little dandelion wine. Do you think you can hold them both?

JIM. I can try, ma'am.

AMANDA *(Exits* U. R. *into kitchen).* Now, Tom, you get into your apron.

TOM. Yes, Mother. *(Follows* AMANDA. JIM *looks around, puts wine-glass down, takes swig from wine decanter, replaces it with thud, takes wine-glass—enters living-room. Inner curtains close as dining-room dims out.* LAURA *sits up nervously as* JIM *enters. Her speech at first is low and breathless from the almost intolerable strain of being alone with a stranger. In her speeches in this scene, before* JIM*'s warmth overcomes her paralyzing shyness,* LAURA*'s voice is thin and breathless as though she has just run up a steep flight of stairs.)*

8. **Mr. Edison.** American inventor of the incandescent lamp
9. **candelabrum.** Large, branched candleholder

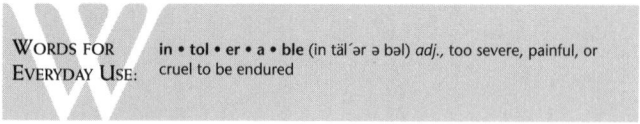

VOCABULARY IN CONTEXT

- Oliver found the loud, pounding music to be intolerable, so he left the concert.
- Jessica wanted to become an actress because she loved being in the limelight.
- The Crystal Palace was one of the first grand expositions, or world's fairs.

JIM *(Entering holding candelabra with lighted candles in one hand and glass of wine in other, and stands).* How are you feeling now? Any better? *(JIM's attitude is gently humorous. In playing this scene it should be stressed that while the incident is apparently unimportant, it is to* LAURA *the climax of her secret life.)*

LAURA. Yes, thank you.

JIM *(Gives her glass of wine).* Oh, here, this is for you. It's a little dandelion wine.

LAURA. Thank you.

JIM *(Crosses* C.*).* Well, drink it—but don't get drunk. *(He laughs heartily.)* Say, where'll I put the candles?

LAURA. Oh, anywhere . . .

JIM. Oh, how about right here on the floor? You got any objections?

LAURA. No.

JIM. I'll spread a newspaper under it to catch the drippings. *(Gets newspaper from armchair. Puts candelabra down on floor* C.*)* I like to sit on the floor. *(Sits on floor.)* Mind if I do?

LAURA. Oh, no.

JIM. Would you give me a pillow?

LAURA. What?

JIM. A pillow!

LAURA. Oh . . . *(Puts wine-glass on telephone table, hands him pillow, sits* L. *on day-bed.)*

JIM. How about you? Don't you like to sit on the floor?

LAURA. Oh, yes.

JIM. Well, why don't you?

LAURA. I—will.

JIM. Take a pillow! *(Throws pillow as she sits on floor.)* I can't see you sitting way over there. *(Sits on floor again.)*

LAURA. I can—see you.

JIM. Yeah, but that's not fair. I'm right here in the limelight. *(LAURA moves a little closer to him.)* Good! Now I can see you! Are you comfortable?

LAURA. Yes. Thank you.

JIM. So am I. I'm comfortable as a cow! Say, would you care for a piece of chewing-gum? *(Offers gum.)*

LAURA. No, thank you.

JIM. I think that I will indulge. *(Musingly unwraps it and holds it up.)* Gee, think of the fortune made by the guy that invented the first piece of chewing gum! It's amazing, huh? Do you know that the Wrigley Building is one of the sights of Chicago?—I saw it summer before last at the Century of Progress.[10] Did you take in the Century of Progress?

LAURA. No, I didn't.

JIM. Well, it was a wonderful exposition, believe me. You know what impressed me most? The Hall of Science. Gives you an idea of what the future will be like in America. Oh, it's more wonderful than the present time is! Say, your brother tells me you're shy. Is that right, Laura?

LAURA. I—don't know.

JIM. I judge you to be an old-fashioned type of girl. Oh, I think that's a wonderful type to be. I hope you don't think I'm being too personal—do you?

10. **Century of Progress.** World's Fair held in Chicago in 1933

❶ *What do Laura's brief responses reveal about her feelings? Is she comfortable? overwhelmed? nervous? annoyed?*

❷ *What description of Laura does Jim suggest? How does he feel about such a girl?*

WORDS FOR EVERYDAY USE:

lime • light (līm līt´) *n.,* prominent or conspicuous position, as if under a spotlight

ex • po • si • tion (eks´pə zish´ən) *n.,* large, public exhibition or show, often international in scope

ANSWERS TO GUIDED READING QUESTIONS

❶ Laura's response reveals that she is overwhelmed, nervous, and at a loss for words.

❷ Jim says that Laura is "an old-fashioned type of girl." He says that's a wonderful kind of girl to be.

ANSWERS TO GUIDED READING QUESTIONS

❶ The brace on her leg made high school embarrassing and difficult for Laura. Other people did not notice her difficulty.

❷ The memory of Jim calling her "Blue Roses" establishes a connection.

LAURA. Mr. O'Connor?

JIM. Huh?

LAURA. I believe I *will* take a piece of gum, if you don't mind. *(JIM peels gum—gets on knees, hands it to LAURA. She breaks off a tiny piece. JIM looks at what remains, puts it in his mouth, and sits again.)* Mr. O'Connor, have you—kept up with your singing?

JIM. Singing? Me?

LAURA. Yes. I remember what a beautiful voice you had.

What made high school hard for Laura? Did other people notice this difficulty? ❶

JIM. You heard me sing?

LAURA. Oh, yes! Very often. . . . I—don't suppose—you remember me—at all?

JIM *(Smiling doubtfully).* You know, as a matter of fact I did have an idea I'd seen you before. Do you know it seemed almost like I was about to remember your name. But the name I was about to remember—wasn't a name! So I stopped myself before I said it.

What shared memory establishes a connection between Laura and Jim? ❷

LAURA. Wasn't it—Blue Roses?

JIM *(Grinning).* Blue Roses! Oh, my gosh, yes—Blue Roses! You know, I didn't connect you with high school somehow or other. But that's where it was, it was high school. Gosh, I didn't even know you were Shakespeare's sister! Gee, I'm sorry.

LAURA. I didn't expect you to.—You barely knew me!

JIM. But, we did have a speaking acquaintance.

LAURA. Yes, we—spoke to each other.

JIM. Say, didn't we have a class in something together?

LAURA. Yes, we did.

JIM. What class was that?

LAURA. It was—singing—chorus!

JIM. Aw!

LAURA. I sat across the aisle from you in the auditorium Mondays, Wednesdays, and Fridays.

JIM. Oh, yeah! I remember now—you're the one who always came in late.

LAURA. Yes, it was so hard for me, getting upstairs. I had that brace on my leg then—it clumped so loud!

JIM. I never heard any clumping.

LAURA *(Wincing at recollection).* To me it sounded like—thunder!

JIM. I never even noticed.

LAURA. Everybody was seated before I came in. I had to walk in front of all those people. My seat was in the back row. I had to go clumping up the aisle with everyone watching!

JIM. Oh, gee, you shouldn't have been self conscious.

LAURA. I know, but I was. It was always such a relief when the singing started.

JIM. I remember now. And I used to call you Blue Roses. How did I ever get started calling you a name like that?

LAURA. I was out of school a little while with pleurosis. When I came back you asked me what was the matter. I said I had pleurosis and you thought I said Blue Roses. So that's what you always called me after that!

JIM. I hope you didn't mind?

WORDS FOR EVERYDAY USE: **wince** (wins) *vi.,* Shrink or draw back slightly, usually with a grimace, as in pain, embarrassment, or alarm

VOCABULARY IN CONTEXT

- Although Don said his ankle wasn't hurting him, his wince at every step revealed that he was in a good deal of pain.
- I look forward with relish to a vacation at the beach.
- The Vikings beleaguered the castle, and, once they had surrounded it entirely, they waited to starve out the Saxons.

LAURA. Oh, no—I liked it. You see, I wasn't acquainted with many—people . . .

JIM. Yeah. I remember you sort of stuck by yourself.

LAURA. I never did have much luck at making friends.

JIM. Well, I don't see why you wouldn't.

LAURA. Well, I started out badly.

JIM. You mean being——?

LAURA. Well, yes, it—sort of—stood between me . . .

JIM. You shouldn't have let it!

LAURA. I know, but it did, and I——

JIM. You mean you were shy with people!

LAURA. I tried not to be but never could——

JIM. Overcome it?

LAURA. No, I—never could!

JIM. Yeah. I guess being shy is something you have to work out of kind of gradually.

LAURA. Yes—I guess it——

JIM. Takes time!

LAURA. Yes . . .

JIM. Say, you know something, Laura? *(Rises to sit on day-bed* R.*)* People are not so dreadful when you know them. That's what you have to remember! And everybody has problems, not just you but practically everybody has problems. You think of yourself as being the only one who is disappointed. But just look around you and what do you see—a lot of people just as disappointed as you are. You take me, for instance. Boy, when I left high school I thought I'd be a lot further along at this time than I am now. Say, you remember that wonderful write-up I had in "The Torch"?

LAURA. Yes, I do! *(She gets year-book from under pillow* L. *of day-bed.)*

JIM. Said I was bound to succeed in anything I went into! Holy Jeez! "The Torch"! *(She opens book, shows it to him and sits next to him on day-bed.)*

LAURA. Here you are in "The Pirates of Penzance"!

JIM. "The Pirates"! "Oh, better far to live and die under the brave black flag I fly!" I sang the lead in that operetta.

LAURA. So beautifully!

JIM. Aw . . .

LAURA. Yes, yes—beautifully—beautifully!

JIM. You heard me then, huh?

LAURA. I heard you all three times!

JIM. No!

LAURA. Yes.

JIM. You mean all three performances?

LAURA. Yes!

JIM. What for?

LAURA. I—wanted to ask you to—autograph my program. *(Takes program from book.)*

JIM. Why didn't you ask me?

LAURA. You were always surrounded by your own friends so much that I never had a chance.

JIM. Aw, you should have just come right up and said, "Here is my——"

LAURA. Well, I—thought you might think I was——

JIM. Thought I might think you was—what?

LAURA. Oh——

JIM *(With reflective relish)*. Oh! Yeah, I was beleaguered by females in those days.

❶ *On what period in their lives—past, present, or future—do Laura and Jim seem to be focused? Do they have the same feelings about this period? Why might Jim be focused on it? Laura?*

❷ *In what way is Jim disappointed?*

WORDS FOR EVERYDAY USE:

rel • ish (rel´ish) *n.*, pleasure; enjoyment

be • lea • guer (bē lē´gər) *vt.*, besiege by encircling

ANSWERS TO GUIDED READING QUESTIONS

❶ Laura and Jim seem to be focused on the past. Jim looks back to his high school days as his period of glory. Laura looks back with regret and longing, fondly remembering Jim paying attention to her. Jim and Laura both look back to the past because they find their present lives unsatisfying.

❷ Jim is disappointed because in high school he thought he would have been farther along that he is now.

LAURA. You were terribly popular!

JIM. Yeah . . .

LAURA. You had such a—friendly way——

JIM. Oh, I was spoiled in high school.

LAURA. Everybody liked you!

JIM. Including you?

LAURA. I—why, yes, I—I did, too. . . .

JIM. Give me that program, Laura. *(She does so, and he signs it.)* There you are—better later than never!

LAURA. My—what a—surprise!

JIM. My signature's not worth very much right now. But maybe some day—it will increase in value! You know, being disappointed is one thing and being discouraged is something else. Well, I may be disappointed but I am not discouraged. Say, you finished high school?

LAURA. I made bad grades in my final examinations.

JIM. You mean you dropped out?

LAURA *(Rises)*. I didn't go back. *(Crosses* R. *to menagerie.* JIM *lights cigarette still sitting on day-bed.* LAURA *puts year-book under menagerie. Rises, picks up unicorn*[11]*—small glass object—her back to* JIM. *When she touches unicorn,* MUSIC CUE #16-A.*)* How is Emily Meisenbach getting along?

JIM. That kraut-head!

LAURA. Why do you call her that?

JIM. Because that's what she was.

LAURA. You're not still—going with her?

JIM. Oh, I never even see her.

LAURA. It said in the Personal section that you were—engaged!

JIM. Uh-huh. I know, but I wasn't impressed by that—propaganda!

LAURA. It wasn't the truth?

JIM. It was only true in Emily's optimistic opinion!

LAURA. Oh . . . *(Turns* R. *of* JIM. JIM *lights a cigarette and leans indolently back on his elbows, smiling at* LAURA *with a warmth and charm which lights her inwardly with altar candles. She remains by the glass menagerie table and turns in her hands a piece of glass to cover her tumult.* CUT MUSIC CUE #16-A.*)*

JIM. What have you done since high school? Huh?

LAURA. What?

JIM. I said what have you done since high school?

LAURA. Nothing much.

JIM. You must have been doing something all this time.

LAURA. Yes.

JIM. Well, then, such as what?

LAURA. I took a business course at business college . . .

JIM. You did? How did that work out?

LAURA *(Turns back to* JIM*)*. Well, not very—well . . . I had to drop out, it gave me—indigestion. . . .

JIM *(Laughs gently)*. What are you doing now?

LAURA. I don't do anything—much. . . . Oh, please don't think I sit around doing nothing! My glass collection takes a good

11. **unicorn.** According to legend, the mythical unicorn could only be tamed by a young, unmarried woman.

WORDS FOR EVERYDAY USE: **in • do • lent • ly** (in´də lənt lē) *adv.,* lazily

VOCABULARY IN CONTEXT

- While George is always working, Sean spends his time lying indolently on the couch.
- Kim and Sara felt the results of their lack of sleep acutely.
- Louis, my pet hamster, displayed quite an aptitude for climbing the bars of his cage.

deal of time. Glass is something you have to take good care of.

JIM. What did you say—about glass?

LAURA *(She clears her throat and turns away again, acutely shy).* Collection, I said—I have one.

JIM *(Puts out cigarette. Abruptly).* Say! You know what I judge to be the trouble with you? *(Rises from day-bed and crosses* R.*)* Inferiority complex! You know what that is? That's what they call it when a fellow low-rates himself! Oh, I understand it because I had it, too. Uh-huh! Only my case was not as aggravated as yours seems to be. I had it until I took up public speaking and developed my voice, and learned that I had an aptitude for science. Do you know that until that time I never thought of myself as being outstanding in any way whatsoever!

LAURA. Oh, my!

JIM. Now I've never made a regular study of it—*(Sits armchair* R.*)* mind you, but I have a friend who says I can analyze people better than doctors that make a profession of it. I don't claim that's necessarily true, but I can sure guess a person's psychology. Excuse me, Laura. *(Takes out gum.)* I always take it out when the flavor is gone. I'll just wrap it in a piece of paper. *(Tears a piece of paper off the newspaper under candelabrum, wraps gum in it, crosses to day-bed, looks to see if* LAURA *is watching. She isn't. Crosses around day-bed.)* I know how it is when you get it stuck on a shoe. *(Throws gum under day-bed, crosses around* L. *of day-bed. Crosses* R. *to* LAURA.*)* Yep—that's what I judge to be your principal trouble. A lack of confidence in yourself as a person. Now I'm basing that fact on a number of your remarks and on certain observations I've made. For instance, that clumping you thought was so awful in high school. You say that you dreaded to go upstairs? You see what you did? You dropped out of school, you gave up an education all because of a little clump, which as far as I can see is practically non-existent! Oh, a little physical defect is all you have. It's hardly noticeable even! Magnified a thousand times by your imagination! You know what my strong advice to you is? You've got to think of yourself as *superior* in some way! *(Crosses* L. *to small table* R. *of day-bed. Sits.* LAURA *sits in armchair.)*

LAURA. In what way would I think?

JIM. Why, man alive, Laura! Look around you a little and what do you see? A world full of common people! All of 'em born and all of 'em going to die! Now, which of them has one-tenth of your strong points! Or mine! Or anybody else's for that matter? You see, everybody excels in some one thing. Well—some in many! You take me, for instance. My interest happens to lie in electrodynamics.[12] I'm taking a course in radio engineering at night school, on top of a fairly responsible job at the warehouse. I'm taking that course *and* studying public speaking.

LAURA. Ohhhh. My!

JIM. Because I believe in the future of television! I want to be ready to go right up along with it. *(Rises, crosses* R.*)* I'm planning to get in on the ground floor. Oh, I've already made the right connections.

12. **electrodynamics.** Branch of physics dealing with electric currents and magnetic forces

❶ *What problem does Jim say that he and Laura share? Do you believe his assessment of Laura? of himself?*

❷ *What does Jim really think about himself?*

❸ *What does Jim do with his gum? What does this action reveal about him?*

WORDS FOR EVERYDAY USE:

a • cute • ly (ə kyoot´lē) *adv.,* sharply, painfully, or severely

ap • ti • tude (ap´tə tōōd´) *n.,* natural tendency or inclination

ANSWERS TO GUIDED READING QUESTIONS

❶ Jim says that both Laura and he suffer from an inferiority complex. His assessment of Laura is probably accurate; however, Jim has too high an opinion of himself to be suffering from an inferiority complex.

❷ Jim thinks he is unique and wonderful as illustrated by his saying, "You see, everybody excels in some one thing. Well—some in many! You take me, for instance."

❸ Jim throws his gum under the day-bed. The action reveals that he is inconsiderate, self-centered, and boorish.

ANSWERS TO GUIDED READING QUESTIONS

❶ Laura talks about her glass animals as if they were companions.

❷ She gives Jim the unicorn to hold because she likes and trusts him. The unicorn is her favorite glass piece.

All that remains now is for the industry itself to get under way—full steam! You know, *knowledge*—ZSZZppp! *Money*—Zzzzzzpp! *POWER*! Wham! That's the cycle democracy is built on! *(Pause.)* I guess you think I think a lot of myself!

LAURA. No—o-o-o, I don't.

JIM *(Kneels at armchair* R.*)*. Well, now how about you? Isn't there some one thing that you take more interest in than anything else?

❶ *Does Laura talk about her glass animals as if they were objects or companions?*

LAURA. Oh—yes . . .

JIM. Well, then, such as what?

LAURA. Well, I do—as I said—have my—glass collection . . . *(*MUSIC CUE #16-A.*)*

JIM. Oh, you do. What kind of glass is it?

LAURA *(Takes glass ornament off shelf.)*. Little articles of it, ornaments mostly. Most of them are little animals made out of glass, the tiniest little animals in the world. Mother calls them the glass menagerie! Here's an example of one, if you'd like to see it! This is one of the oldest, it's nearly thirteen. *(Hands it to* JIM.*)* Oh, be careful—if you breathe, it breaks! *(*THE BELL SOLO SHOULD BEGIN HERE. *This is last part of* CUE #16-A *and should play to end of record.)*

JIM. I'd better not take it. I'm pretty clumsy with things.

❷ *Why does Laura give Jim the glass unicorn to hold? How does she feel about the unicorn?*

LAURA. Go on, I trust you with him! *(*JIM *takes horse.)* There—you're holding him gently! Hold him over the light, he loves the light! *(*JIM *holds horse up to light.)* See how the light shines through him?

JIM. It sure does shine!

LAURA. I shouldn't be partial, but he is my favorite one.

JIM. Say, what kind of a thing is this one supposed to be?

LAURA. Haven't you noticed the single horn on his forehead?

JIM. Oh, a unicorn, huh?

LAURA. Mmmm-hmmmmm!

JIM. Unicorns, aren't they extinct in the modern world?

LAURA. I know!

JIM. Poor little fellow must feel kind of lonesome.

LAURA. Well, if he does he doesn't complain about it. He stays on a shelf with some horses that don't have horns and they all seem to get along nicely together.

JIM. They do. Say, where will I put him?

LAURA. Put him on the table. *(*JIM *crosses to small table* R. *of day-bed, puts unicorn on it.)* They all like a change of scenery once in a while!

JIM *(*C., *facing upstage, stretching arms)*. They do. *(*MUSIC CUE #16-B: *Dance Music.)* Hey! Look how big my shadow is when I stretch.

LAURA *(Crossing to* L. *of day-bed)*. Oh, oh, yes—it stretched across the ceiling!

JIM *(Crosses to door* R., *exits, leaving door open, and stands on fire-escape landing. Sings to music. [Popular record of day for dance-hall.] When* JIM *opens door, music swells)*. It's stopped raining. Where does the music come from?

LAURA. From the Paradise Dance Hall across the alley.

JIM *(Re-entering room, closing door* R., *crosses to* LAURA*)*. How about cutting the rug[13] a little, Miss Wingfield? Or is your program filled up? Let me take a look at it. *(Crosses back* C. *Music, in dance hall, goes into a waltz. Business here with imaginary*

13. **cutting the rug.** Dancing

dance-program card.) Oh, say! Every dance is taken! I'll just scratch some of them out. Ahhhh, a waltz! *(Crosses to* LAURA.*)*

LAURA. I—can't dance!

JIM. There you go with that inferiority stuff!

LAURA. I've never danced in my life!

JIM. Come on, try!

LAURA. Oh, but I'd step on you!

JIM. Well, I'm not made out of glass.

LAURA. How—how do we start?

JIM. You hold your arms out a little.

LAURA. Like this?

JIM. A little bit higher. *(Takes* LAURA *in arms.)* That's right. Now don't tighten up, that's the principal thing about it—just relax.

LAURA. It's hard not to.

JIM. Okay.

LAURA. I'm afraid you can't budge me.

JIM *(Dances around* L. *of day-bed slowly).* What do you bet I can't?

LAURA. Goodness, yes, you can!

JIM. Let yourself go, now, Laura, just let yourself go.

LAURA. I'm——

JIM. Come on!

LAURA. Trying!

JIM. Not so stiff now—easy does it!

LAURA. I know, but I'm——!

JIM. Come on! Loosen your backbone a little! *(When they get to up-stage corner of day-bed—so that the audience will not see him lift her—*JIM*'s arm tightens around her waist and he swings her around* C. *with her feet off floor about 3 complete turns before they hit the small table* R. *of day-bed. Music swells as* JIM *lifts her.)* There we go! *(*JIM *knocks glass horse off table.* MUSIC FADES.*)*

LAURA. Oh, it doesn't matter——

JIM *(Picks horse up).* We knocked the little glass horse over.

LAURA. Yes.

JIM *(Hands unicorn to* LAURA*).* Is he broken?

LAURA. Now he's just like all the other horses.

JIM. You mean he lost his——?

LAURA. He's lost his horn. It doesn't matter. Maybe it's a blessing in disguise.

JIM. Gee, I bet you'll never forgive me. I bet that was your favorite piece of glass.

LAURA. Oh, I don't have favorites—*(Pause)* much. It's no tragedy. Glass breaks so easily. No matter how careful you are. The traffic jars the shelves and things fall off them.

JIM. Still I'm awfully sorry that I was the cause of it.

LAURA. I'll just imagine he had an operation. The horn was removed to make him feel less—freakish! *(Crosses* L., *sits on small table.)* Now he will feel more at home with the other horses, the ones who don't have horns. . . .

JIM *(Sits on arm of armchair* R., *faces* LAURA*).* I'm glad to see that you have a sense of humor. You know—you're—different than anybody else I know? *(*MUSIC CUE #17.*)* Do you mind me telling you that? I mean it. You make me feel sort of—I don't know how to say it! I'm usually pretty good at expressing things, but—this is something I don't know how to say! Did anybody ever tell you that you were pretty? *(Rises, crosses to* LAURA.*)* Well, you are! And in a different way from anyone else. And all the nicer because of the difference. Oh, boy, I wish that you were my sister. I'd teach you to have confidence in yourself. Being different is nothing to

❶ *What happens to the unicorn? What does Laura say about her favorite piece being broken? How do you think she really feels?*

❷ *What does Laura imagine the horn made the unicorn feel? Is this a feeling with which she is familiar?*

ANSWERS TO GUIDED READING QUESTIONS

❶ Jim drops the unicorn and its horn breaks off. Laura says it doesn't matter because she didn't have "favorites . . . much." In actuality she is probably very upset.

❷ Laura imagines that the horn made the unicorn feel "freakish." Laura feels freakish also because of her limp.

Answers to Guided Reading Questions

❶ Jim says Laura is special because she stays where she is and is unique because she is like blue roses.

❷ Jim says that he won't call again because he is engaged. He has misled her by flattering and kissing her.

❸ Laura gives Jim the broken unicorn. She gives it to him as a reminder of her. Symbolically, it is an appropriate gesture that reveals Laura's broken dreams and heart.

❹ Amanda's song is ironic because she mentions old maids, not knowing that Laura has discovered that Jim will never marry her. Amanda has unknowingly described Laura's future.

What does Jim say about Laura? Why is she special? ❶

What does Jim say that hurts Laura? Has he misled her in any way? ❷

What does Laura give Jim? Why does she give this to him? Is this an appropriate gesture? Why, or why not? ❸

Given what has occurred, in what way is Amanda's song ironic? ❹

be ashamed of. Because other people aren't such wonderful people. They're a hundred times one thousand. You're one times one! They walk all over the earth. You just stay here. They're as common as—weeds, but—you, well you're—*Blue Roses!*

Laura. But blue is—wrong for—roses . . .

Jim. It's right for you!—You're pretty!

Laura. In what respect am I pretty?

Jim. In all respects—your eyes—your hair. Your hands are pretty! You think I'm saying this because I'm invited to dinner and have to be nice. Oh, I could do that! I could say lots of things without being sincere. But I'm talking to you sincerely. I happened to notice you had this inferiority complex that keeps you from feeling comfortable with people. Somebody ought to build your confidence up—way up! and make you proud instead of shy and turning away and—blushing——*(*Jim *lifts* Laura *up on small table on "way up.")* Somebody ought to—*(Lifts her down.)* somebody ought to kiss you, Laura! *(They kiss.* Jim *releases her and turns slowly away, crossing a little* D. R. *Then, quietly, to himself: As* Jim *turns away,* MUSIC ENDS.*)* Gee, I shouldn't have done that—that was way off the beam. *(Gives way* D. R. *Turns to* Laura. Laura *sits on small table.)* Would you care for a cigarette? You don't smoke, do you? How about a mint? Peppermint—Life-Saver? My pocket's a regular drug-store. . . . Laura, you know, if I had a sister like you, I'd do the same thing as Tom. I'd bring fellows home to meet you. Maybe I shouldn't be saying this. That may not have been the idea in having me over. But what if it was? There's nothing wrong with that.—The only trouble is that in my case—I'm not in a position to——I can't ask for your number and say I'll phone. I can't call up next week end—ask for a date. I thought I had better explain the situation in case you—misunderstood and I hurt your feelings . . .

Laura *(Faintly).* You—won't—call again?

Jim *(Crossing to* R. *of day-bed, and sitting).* No, I can't. You see, I've—got strings on me. Laura, I've—been going steady! I go out all the time with a girl named Betty. Oh, she's a nice quiet home girl like you, and Catholic and Irish, and in a great many ways we—get along fine. I met her last summer on a moonlight boat trip up the river to Alton, on the *Majestic.* Well—right away from the start it was—love! Oh, boy, being in love has made a new man of me! The power of love is pretty tremendous! Love is something that—changes the whole world. It happened that Betty's aunt took sick and she got a wire and had to go to Centralia. So naturally when Tom asked me to dinner—naturally I accepted the invitation, not knowing—I mean—not knowing. I wish that you would—say something. *(*Laura *gives* Jim *unicorn.)* What are you doing that for? You mean you want me to have him? What for?

Laura. A—souvenir. *(She crosses* R. *to menagerie.* Jim *rises.)*

Amanda *(Off-stage).* I'm coming, children. *(She enters into dining-room from kitchen* R.*)* I thought you'd like some liquid refreshment. *(Puts tray on small table. Lifts a glass.)* Mr. O'Connor, have you heard that song about lemonade? It's "Lemonade, lemonade, Made in the shade and stirred with a spade—And then it's good enough for any old maid!"

Jim. No, ma'am, I never heard it.

Amanda. Why are you so serious, honey? *(To* Laura.*)*

JIM. Well, we were having a serious conversation.

AMANDA. I don't understand modern young people. When I was a girl I was gay about everything.

JIM. You haven't changed a bit, Mrs. Wingfield.

AMANDA. I suppose it's the gaiety of the occasion that has rejuvenated me. Well, here's to the gaiety of the occasion! *(Spills lemonade on dress.)* Oooo! I baptized myself. *(Puts glass on small table* R. *of day-bed.)* I found some cherries in the kitchen, and I put one in each glass.

JIM. You shouldn't have gone to all that trouble, ma'am.

AMANDA. It was no trouble at all. Didn't you hear us cutting up[14] in the kitchen? I was so outdone with Tom for not bringing you over sooner, but now you've found your way I want you to come all the time—not just once in a while—but all the time. Oh, I think I'll go back in that kitchen. *(Starts to exit* U. C.*)*

JIM. Oh, no, ma'am, please don't go, ma'am. As a matter of fact, I've got to be going.

AMANDA. Oh, Mr. O'Connor, it's only the shank of the evening![15] *(*JIM *and* AMANDA *stand* U. C.*)*

JIM. Well, you know how it is.

AMANDA. You mean you're a young working man and have to keep working-men's hours?

JIM. Yes, ma'am.

AMANDA. Well, we'll let you off early this time, but only on the condition that you stay later next time, much later—— What's the best night for you? Saturday?

JIM. Well, as a matter of fact, I have a couple of time-clocks to punch, Mrs. Wingfield, one in the morning and another one at night!

AMANDA. Oh, isn't that nice, you're so ambitious! You work at night, too?

JIM. No, ma'am, not work but—Betty!

AMANDA *(Crosses* L. *below day-bed).* Betty? Who's Betty?

JIM. Oh, just a girl. The girl I go steady with!

AMANDA. You mean it's serious? *(Crosses* D. L.*)*

JIM. Oh, yes, ma'am. We're going to be married the second Sunday in June.

AMANDA *(Sits on day-bed).* Tom didn't say anything at all about your going to be married?

JIM. Well, the cat's not out of the bag at the warehouse yet. *(Picks up hat from telephone table.)* You know how they are. They call you Romeo and stuff like that.—It's been a wonderful evening, Mrs. Wingfield. I guess this is what they mean by Southern hospitality.

AMANDA. It was nothing. Nothing at all.

JIM. I hope it don't seem like I'm rushing off. But I promised Betty I'd pick her up at the Wabash depot an' by the time I get my jalopy[16] down there her train'll be in. Some women are pretty upset if you keep them waiting.

AMANDA. Yes, I know all about the tyranny of women! Well, good-bye, Mr. O'Connor. *(*AMANDA *puts out hand.* JIM *takes it.)* I wish you happiness—and good fortune. You wish him that, too, don't you, Laura?

LAURA. Yes, I do, Mother.

---

14. **cutting up.** Clowning, joking
15. **shank of the evening.** Early part of the evening
16. **jalopy.** Old, ramshackle car

❶ *What is Amanda's response when Jim thanks her for her hospitality? Why is this comment appropriate given the evening's outcome?*

ANSWER TO GUIDED READING QUESTION

❶ Amanda says "It was nothing at all." The comment is appropriate because, like the evening, her hopes have come to nothing.

Answers to Guided Reading Questions

❶ Amanda says that Tom lives in a dream and manufactures illusions.

❷ Amanda is angry with Tom because she feels that he purposely led them to make fools of themselves. She is more angry with the sad situation than the expense incurred.

What does Amanda say about Tom? ❶

Why is Amanda angry with Tom? Is she more angry with the expense incurred or in the sad situation of both mother and daughter? ❷

JIM *(Crosses* L. *to* LAURA*).* Good-bye, Laura. I'll always treasure that souvenir. And don't you forget the good advice I gave you. So long, Shakespeare! *(Up* C.*)* Thanks, again, ladies.—Good night! *(He grins and ducks jauntily out* R.*)*

AMANDA *(Faintly).* Well, well, well. Things have a way of turning out so badly——*(*LAURA *crosses to phonograph, puts on record.)* I don't believe that I would play the victrola. Well, well—well, our gentleman caller was engaged to be married! Tom!

TOM *(Off).* Yes, Mother?

AMANDA. Come out here. I want to tell you something very funny.

TOM *(Entering through* R. *kitchen door to dining-room and into living-room, through curtains,* D. C.*).* Has the gentleman caller gotten away already?

AMANDA. The gentleman caller made a very early departure. That was a nice joke you played on us, too!

TOM. How do you mean?

AMANDA. You didn't mention that he was engaged to be married.

TOM. Jim? Engaged?

AMANDA. That's what he just informed us.

TOM. I'll be jiggered! I didn't know.

AMANDA. That seems very peculiar.

TOM. What's peculiar about it?

AMANDA. Didn't you tell me he was your best friend down at the warehouse?

TOM. He is, but how did I know?

AMANDA. It seems very peculiar you didn't know your best friend was engaged to be married!

TOM. The warehouse is the place where I work, not where I know things about people!

AMANDA. You don't know things anywhere! You live in a dream; you manufacture illusions! *(*TOM *starts for* R. *door.)* Where are you going? Where are you going? Where are you going?

TOM. I'm going to the movies.

AMANDA *(Rises, crosses up to* TOM*).* That's right, now that you've had us make such fools of ourselves. The effort, the preparations, all the expense! The new floor lamp, the rug, the clothes for Laura! All for what? To entertain some other girl's fiancé! Go to the movies, go! Don't think about us, a mother deserted, an unmarried sister who's crippled and has no job! Don't let anything interfere with your selfish pleasure! Just go, go, go—to the movies!

TOM. All right, I will, and the more you shout at me about my selfish pleasures, the quicker I'll go, and I won't go to the movies either. *(Gets hat from phone table, slams door* R.*, and exits up alley* R.*)*

AMANDA *(Crosses up to fire-escape landing, yelling).* Go, then! Then go to the moon—you selfish dreamer! *(*MUSIC CUE #18. INTERIOR LIGHT *dims out. Re-enters living-room, slamming* R. *door.* TOM*'s closing speech is timed with the interior pantomime. The interior scene is played as though viewed through soundproof glass, behind outer scrim curtain.* AMANDA*, standing, appears to be making a comforting speech to* LAURA *who is huddled on* R. *side of day-bed. Now that we cannot hear the mother's speech, her silliness is gone and she has dignity and tragic beauty.* LAURA*'s hair*

Words for Everyday Use:
jaun • ti • ly (jôntˈə lē) *adv.,* in a confident, carefree manner
pan • to • mime (panˈtə mīm) *n.,* dramatic presentation without words

Vocabulary in Context

- Drew tipped his hat to a rakish ankle and jauntily stepped behind the wheel of his convertible.
- Because we sat so far back in the theater and the actors did not project their voices, it was almost as if we had seen a pantomime rather than a conventional play.

hides her face until at the end of the speech she lifts it to smile at her mother. AMANDA*'s gestures are slow and graceful, almost dance-like, as she comforts her daughter.* TOM, *who has meantime put on, as before, the jacket and cap, enters down* R. *from off-stage, and again comes to fire-escape landing, stands as he speaks. Meantime lights are upon* AMANDA *and* LAURA, *but are dim.)*

TOM. I didn't go to the moon. I went much farther. For time is the longest distance between two places. . . . I left Saint Louis. I descended these steps of this fire-escape for the last time and followed, from then on, in my father's footsteps, attempting to find in motion what was lost in space. . . . I travelled around a great deal. The cities swept about me like dead leaves, leaves that were brightly colored but torn away from the branches. I would have stopped, but I was pursued by something. It always came upon me unawares, taking me altogether by surprise. Perhaps it was a familiar bit of music. Perhaps it was only a piece of transparent glass. . . . Perhaps I am walking along a street at night, in some strange city, before I have found companions, and I pass the lighted window of a shop where perfume is sold. The window is filled with pieces of colored glass, tiny transparent bottles in delicate colors, like bits of a shattered rainbow. Then all at once my sister touches my shoulder. I turn around and look into her eyes. . . . Oh, Laura, Laura, I tried to leave you behind me, but I am more faithful than I intended to be! I reach for a cigarette, I cross the street, I run into a movie or a bar. I buy a drink, I speak to the nearest stranger—anything that can blow your candles out!—for nowadays the world is lit by lightning! Blow out your candles, Laura . . . *(*LAURA *blows out candles still burning in candelabrum and the whole interior is blacked out.)* And so—good-bye! *(Exits up alley* R. *Music continues to the end.)* ■

CURTAIN

END OF PLAY

❶ *What does Tom say about his sister? What image does he use to describe her?*

Responding to the Selection

If you had been Tom, would you have left? Why, or why not?

ANSWER TO GUIDED READING QUESTION

❶ Tom says he can never completely leave his sister behind. He describes her as possessing the glow of candles rather than the lightning that lights the modern world.

ANSWERS TO SELECTION CHECK TEST 4.10.3

EX. Who does Tom bring home?
Tom brings Jim O'Connor home.

1. What does Jim call Tom?
Jim calls Tom "Shakespeare."

2. What happens when Laura comes to the table?
Laura faints when she comes to the table.

3. Why do the lights go out?
The lights go out because Tom did not pay the electric bill.

4. What does Jim do with Laura's unicorn?
Jim breaks Laura's unicorn.

5. Why will Jim never call again?
Jim will never call again because he is engaged.

RESPONDING TO THE SELECTION

Students may wish to consider how they would have felt if they had been in either Amanda's or Laura's position as well.

Answers for Reviewing the Selection

RECALLING

1. The lights go out because Tom has not paid the electric bill.
2. Amanda asks Jim to keep Laura company.
3. Jim and Laura use a candelabrum for light.
4. Laura shows Jim a glass unicorn. The unicorn is Laura's favorite piece. Jim reveals that he is engaged to another woman. The unicorn is broken.

INTERPRETING

Responses will vary. Possible responses are given.

5. Being plunged into darkness makes the final scene more intimate. The darkness creates a situation in which Laura and Jim get to know each other in an intimate setting. The darkness may represent Laura's dreamlike state and confusion about whether life offers her any possibilities, or, since it is Tom who plunges Amanda and Laura into darkness, it may represent the bleak situation in which he is leaving them.
6. Amanda wants to leave Jim and Laura alone together in hopes that Jim will develop a liking for Laura. This event is the climax of her life because she is sitting in an intimate setting with the person who has been the inspiration of her private hopes and fantasies.
7. The candelabrum is special because it is symbolic of Laura. Tom thinks of candlelight in association with his sister, as both are old-fashioned, faint, and easily quenched in life. The blowing out of the candles at the play's end is symbolic of the end of Tom's memory, the end of the memory play, and of Laura's destruction.
8. The figurine is associated with Laura. Both the figurine and Laura are fragile, rare, and feel "freakish." Jim's breaking of the unicorn corresponds to his breaking of her heart and dreams—both were acts he committed carelessly and thoughtlessly.

(cont.)

Reviewing the Selection

RECALLING

1. What happens to the lights in the apartment? Why?
2. What does Amanda ask Jim to do while she and Tom take care of the dishes?
3. What source of illumination is used by Jim and Laura during their scene together?
4. What figurine does Laura show to Jim? What is special about this figurine? What does Jim reveal about himself after kissing Laura and dancing with her? What happens to the figurine?

INTERPRETING

5. How does being plunged into darkness affect the final scene of the play? What situation is thereby created for Jim and Laura? What might this darkness represent?
6. Why does Amanda want to leave Jim and Laura alone together? In what sense is this "apparently unimportant" event the climax of Laura's "secret life"?
7. What is special about the candelabrum? With whom is the candelabrum associated? How is this candelabrum related to Tom's comments at the very end of the play?
8. With whom is the figurine associated? What do this person and the figurine have in common? How is the breaking of the figurine related to the breaking of Laura's heart and of her dreams?

SYNTHESIZING

9. What is an inferiority complex? Who, according to Jim, has one? What advice does Jim give about overcoming an inferiority complex? Does his advice seem realistic to you? Why, or why not?
10. Why does Tom leave? Years afterward, how does he feel about leaving? What continues to haunt him?

Understanding Literature (Questions for Discussion)

1. **Theme.** A **theme** is a central idea in a literary work. Jim, who is taking night classes and who wishes to become an executive, epitomizes those people who aspire to a dream of material success. What sort of person is Jim? Would you describe him as optimistic or pessimistic? What indications does the play give that Jim is shallow and egotistical? Jim says, "You know, *knowledge*—ZSZZppp! *Money*—Zzzzzzpp! *POWER!* Wham! That's the cycle democracy is built on!" Do you agree with him? Why, or why not? What has happened to the old, gracious way of life that Amanda remembers? At

Answers for Reviewing the Selection (cont.)

SYNTHESIZING

Responses will vary. Possible responses are given.

9. An inferiority complex is a condition in which one feels that one is not as good as others. Jim says Laura has one. His advice is to think of yourself as superior in some way. While attempting to feel superior to others is not beneficial for anyone, trying to develop one's unique abilities is a good method for combating feelings of inferiority.
10. Tom leaves because he cannot develop into the person he wants to become in his present environment. Years later, he still feels guilty about leaving, and images of Laura continue to haunt him.

the end of the play, Tom says, "I speak to the nearest stranger—anything that can blow your [Laura's] candles out!—for nowadays the world is lit by lightning!" How is Tom's phrase "lit by lightning" related to Jim's statements about television and electricity? Is someone like Laura suited to life in the modern world? Why not? What commentary is Williams making about modern urban life by drawing this comparison?

2. A **symbol** is a thing that stands for or represents both itself and something else. Explain the symbolic significance of the following elements of act two:

   a. Amanda's jonquils

   b. the movies

   c. the partially melted candelabrum

   d. the glass unicorn

   d. the breaking of the unicorn's horn

   e. Jim's giant shadow

   f. the bits of colored glass that Tom sees in shop windows

   g. the candles referred to by Tom at the end of the play

   h. the lightning that now lights the world, referred to by Tom at the end of the play

Responding in Writing

1. **Diary Entry.** According to the sociologist Erik Erickson, young people go through a stage that can be called an identity crisis in which they attempt to break away from childhood and establish their own adult identities. This period in a person's life is often characterized by turmoil and uncertainty and sometimes involves conflicts with parents. In this play, Tom experiences an identity crisis and decides to break away for good. Write a diary entry from the point of view of Tom explaining how he views himself and why he feels he must break away in order to be the person that he wants to be.

2. **Critical Analysis.** Write a critical analysis on one of the following topics related to the play:

   a. What view of artists and their relationship to the culture around them is presented in *The Glass Menagerie?* What aspects of the character Tom are in direct conflict with the values of the society in which he lives? Why might a person who has the values and experiences that Tom has be driven to write?

   b. How do the dreams of the various characters in this play differ? What dreams do Tom, Amanda, and Jim have? Which of these dreams is presented most sympathetically in the play? Which are treated unsympathetically?

   c. How does Williams use symbolism in the play to characterize Laura? What symbols are related to her, and what do these symbols mean?

Answers for Understanding Literature

► See the evaluation form for discussion, active listening, and oral communication, *Assessment Portfolio,* 7.11–7.14.

Responses will vary. Possible responses are given.

1. Theme. Jim is a shallow, thoughtless, and egotistical person. He is an optimist. His throwing the gum beneath the day-bed, his constant chatter about his abilities, his misleading of Laura, and his cruel indifference to the hurt he has caused Laura all indicate that he is shallow and egotistical. Students may say that Jim's interpretation of democracy is both false and simplistic. Amanda's way of life has disappeared. Both Tom and Jim realize they are situated in a modern world. Laura is not suited to life in the modern world because she is unable to be self-sufficient and strong. Williams is saying that urban life is filled with cold, insensitive, but strong individuals, like Jim.

2. Symbol. a. Amanda's jonquils symbolize her youth when she collected as many gentleman callers as she did jonquils.

b. The movies symbolize the mindlessness and inactivity of life for most individuals.

c. The partially melted candles symbolize both the dying of Amanda's past and Laura's future.

d. The glass unicorn symbolizes Laura's difference and fragility.

e. Jim's giant shadow is symbolic of Jim's giant ego.

f. The bits of colored glass are symbolic of the menagerie and, hence, Laura.

g. The candles are symbolic of Laura's unsuitableness for the modern world.

h. The lightning is symbolic of the stronger, less fragile forces that dominate the modern world.

Analytic Scales for Responding in Writing

Assign a score from 1 to 25 for each grading criterion below. (For more detailed evaluation, see the evaluation forms for writing, revising, and proofreading, *Assessment Portfolio,* 7.1–7.10.)

1. Diary Entry

- **Content/Unity.** The diary entry is written from Tom's point of view and explains how he feels about himself and why he leaves.
- **Organization/Coherence.** The diary entry is written in a clear and sensible order.
- **Language/Style.** The diary entry uses vivid and precise nouns, verbs, and modifiers.
- **Conventions.** The diary entry avoids errors in spelling, grammar, usage, mechanics, and manuscript form.

(cont.)

ANALYTIC SCALES FOR RESPONDING IN WRITING (CONT.)

2. Critical Analysis

- **Content/Unity.** The critical analysis takes a position on a topic and supports this position with evidence from the text.
- **Organization/Coherence.** The critical analysis is written in a clear and sensible order.
- **Language/Style.** The critical analysis uses vivid and precise nouns, verbs, and modifiers.
- **Conventions.** The critical analysis avoids errors in spelling, grammar, usage, mechanics, and manuscript form.

PROJECT NOTES

1. Acting. The class could divide into groups, each group performing a critical scene from the play. Allow students ample time to prepare for their scene. Time and interest permitting, students might perform the play as a whole for an audience of other students, parents, or members of the community.

2. Film Criticism. Students might state what they would change in the film version. Then, students might describe their ideal rendition of the play.

d. What commentary on modern urban life is made by this play? How is the modern world contrasted with the world that Amanda remembers? What role does the artist, Tom, play in offering a critique of that world?

e. What is Expressionism? What elements of *The Glass Menagerie* make it an Expressionist play?

f. What is the central conflict in *The Glass Menagerie?* How is that conflict introduced, developed, and resolved? What remains unresolved at the end of the play?

PROJECTS

1. **Acting.** With other students in your class, stage a scene from *The Glass Menagerie* for other students in the class.

2. **Film Criticism.** Find a film version of *The Glass Menagerie* at a video store or at a library and view it with your class. After the viewing, discuss the film. Consider these questions:

   a. Is the film version true to the play? What differences, if any, exist in the film version and in the script that you have read? Do these differences make the play better or worse? Why?

   b. Which are the best performances in the film? Which are the worst? Why?

   c. What aspects of the play are emphasized in the film?

   d. Does the film live up to the playwright's expressed intention of creating a "memory play"? Do its scenes have the dreamlike quality described in the playwright's stage directions? If so, how are these effects achieved? If not, what might the director and set designers have done to give the film such a quality?

UNIT REVIEW

Modern Drama

VOCABULARY FROM THE SELECTIONS

acutely, 731
aghast, 698
aptitude, 731
beleaguer, 729
bombardment, 708
cater, 696
conglomeration, 684
cultivate, 693
czar, 698
devout, 717
discreet, 711
dismal, 705
emissary, 686
endowment, 703
exposition, 727
fiasco, 695
imminent, 708
implacable, 684
imploringly, 706
importunately, 706
incredulously, 721
indolently, 730
induct, 691
ineluctably, 685
inquisition, 704
interference, 716
interfused, 684
intolerable, 726
jauntily, 736
limelight, 727
listlessly, 702
mastication, 686
matriculate, 685
menagerie, 689
motley, 700
ornamentation, 725
pantomime, 736
paragon, 722
pinion, 698
poise, 721
premature, 710
prominent, 688
querulous, 704
relish, 729
resume, 687
sashay, 718
sheepishly, 703
Spartan, 704
sublimation, 695
supercilious, 711
symptomatic, 684
tribulation, 723
ulterior, 712
unobtrusive, 717
velocity, 716
vestige, 723
vivacity, 722
wince, 728

LITERARY TERMS

archetype, 699
character, 690, 714
cliché, 707
conflict, 699
Expressionism, 682, 690
irony, 694
metaphor, 690
setting, 715
Southern Gothic, 682
stage directions, 689
symbol, 699, 701, 714, 739
theme, 738

SYNTHESIS: QUESTIONS FOR WRITING, RESEARCH, OR DISCUSSION

1. In *The Glass Menagerie,* each character in the Wingfield family faces a struggle. Identify each character's conflict and whether it is primarily internal or external. In what ways does each character face the challenge of balancing personal desires with familial responsibilities?
2. *The Glass Menagerie* is an example of Expressionist drama. In such drama, literary and dramatic elements such as the set design and symbolism are often heightened or exaggerated. What elements of this setting are exaggerated and unrealistic? Why? What symbolism does Williams use and for what purposes?

VOCABULARY DEVELOPMENT EXERCISES

►Give students the following exercise.

Choose twenty words from the list on page 741. Make a crossword puzzle with these words. Write a clue for each word. Then fit the words together in a crossword format. Exchange puzzles with another student and try to fill in his or her puzzle.

ADDITIONAL RESOURCES

ASSESSMENT PORTFOLIO

- Vocabulary Worksheet, 4.10.5
- Study Guide: Unit 10 Test, 4.10.6
- Unit 10 Test, 4.10.7

ESSENTIAL SKILLS PRACTICE BOOKS

Language

- Correcting Sentence Fragments, 2.61
- Proofreading for Spelling Errors, 2.134

Study and Research

- Reading Actively, 4.18

►These prompts are suitable as topics for research papers. Refer to the Language Arts Survey, 4.20–4.34, "Research Skills." (To evaluate research papers, see the evaluation forms for writing, revising, and proofreading in the *Assessment Portfolio,* 7.1–7.10.)

►These prompts can be adapted for use as topics for oral reports or debates. (To evaluate these projects, see the evaluation forms in the *Assessment Portfolio,* 7.17–7.19.)

LANGUAGE LAB PROOFREADING FOR SPELLING ERRORS

After checking for other errors in your writing, you should read it carefully for errors in spelling. If you come across any words that you are not completely sure about, check them in a dictionary.

LANGUAGE ARTS SURVEY

For additional help, see the Language Arts Survey, 2.134–2.136.

COMMON SPELLING ERRORS

Forming Plurals

Add *es* to nouns ending in *o* preceded by a consonant and to nouns ending in *s, x, z, ch,* or *sh.*

EXAMPLES: *potatoes, vetoes, tomatoes, dresses, boxes, splashes*

Add *s* to most musical terms ending in *o.*

EXAMPLES: *solos, concertos, pianos*

Add *s* to nouns ending in *y* preceded by a vowel.

EXAMPLES: *Mondays, keys, boys, turkeys*

In nouns ending in *y* preceded by a consonant, change the *y* to *i* and add *es.*

EXAMPLES: *theories, stories, flies*

Remember irregular plurals of certain words.

EXAMPLES: *oxen, feet, men, mice*

Form the plural of a compound noun consisting of a noun and a modifier by making the noun component plural.

EXAMPLES: *mothers-in-law, attorneys-at-law*

Adding Prefixes

A **prefix** is a letter or a group of letters added to the beginning of a word to change its meaning. When adding a prefix to a word, do not change the word itself.

EXAMPLES: super + highway = superhighway
re + crystallize = recrystallize
un + founded = unfounded

Adding Suffixes

A **suffix** is a letter or group of letters added to the end of a word to change its meaning. The spelling of most words is not changed when the suffix *-ness* or *-ly* is added.

EXAMPLES: high + ness = highness
high + ly = highly

If a word has more than one syllable and ends in *y,* change the *y* to *i* before adding *-ly* or *-ness.*

EXAMPLES: easy + ly = easily
easy + ness = easiness

In most cases of words ending in a final silent *e,* drop the *e* when adding a suffix beginning with a vowel, and keep the *e* when adding a suffix beginning with a consonant.

EXAMPLES: live + able = liva**ble**
strange + er = strang**er**
hate + ful = hat**eful**
taste + less = tast**eless**

Exercise A Using Spelling Rules

In the following sentences, make all the italicized words plural, and add prefixes or suffixes to the underlined words. Use the spelling rules and refer to a dictionary if you are unsure of the correct spelling.

1. Of the many wonder (ful) *play* that Thornton Wilder wrote, he is most fame (ous) for one.
2. Wilder won great (ly) deserved Pulitzer *Prize* for imagine (ative) writing.
3. The stage *direction* indicate that the set should be decorated sparing (ly), without any scene (ry).
4. The play offers a lighting designer many *opportunity* to use experiment (al) lighting methods.
5. Emily speaks moving (ly) of her *memory* of the man and woman whom she knew in the town.

Exercise B Proofreading for Spelling Errors

Read the following paragraph carefully and correct any spelling errors you find. If you are uncertain about any words, refer to a dictionary.

Thornton Wilder had an inter-national education, experiencing the dramatickally different societys of China and the United States during his youth. He had many literary success' during his lifetime; one of his noveles and two of his playes won Pulitzer Prizes'. He also enjoyed remarkble success as a createtive writing instructer at the University of Chicago, engaging his students' with his fascinateing lecturs. As he did with *Our Town,* Wilder structured his play *The Skin of Our Teeth* loosly, allowing the characters to speak directlee to the audience. The play addresses morality through satireic and humorrous elements, using many of the unnusual theatriccal technique's that made *Our Town* so succesful.

Answers for Language Lab

Exercise A

1. wonderful, plays, famous
2. greatly, Prizes, imaginative
3. directions, sparingly, scenery
4. opportunities, experimental
5. movingly, memories

Exercise B

Thornton Wilder had an **international** education, experiencing the **dramatically** different **societies** of China and the United States during his youth. He had many literary **successes** during his lifetime; one of his **novels** and two of his **plays** won Pulitzer **Prizes.** He also enjoyed **remarkable** success as a **creative** writing **instructor** at the University of Chicago, engaging his **students** with his **fascinating lectures.** As he did with *Our Town,* Wilder structured his play *The Skin of Our Teeth* **loosely,** allowing the characters to speak **directly** to the audience. The play addresses morality through **satiric** and **humorous** elements, using many of the **unusual theatrical techniques** that made *Our Town* so **successful.**

UNIT SKILLS OUTLINE

LITERARY SKILLS AND CONCEPTS

- Aim, 767, 777
- Alliteration, 767
- Anecdote, 757
- Antithesis, 768
- Collage, 751
- Essay, 763
- Farce, 757
- Interior Monologue, 764
- Modernism, 763
- Onomatopoeia, 768
- Parallelism, 768
- Point of View, 764
- Simile, 776
- Stream of Consciousness, 764
- Tone, 776

WRITING SKILLS AND CONCEPTS

- Biographical Sketch, 768
- Comparison-and-Contrast Essay, 763
- Family History, 758
- A Moment in Your Life, 751
- Press Release, 758

GRAMMAR, USAGE, AND MECHANICS SKILLS AND CONCEPTS

- Adjectives and Articles, 768
- Apostrophes, 751
- Base Words and Prefixes, 778
- Concrete and Abstract Nouns, 765
- Parentheses and Brackets, 758
- Suffixes, 778
- Tone and Voice, 753
- Using Colorful Modifiers, 768
- Using Context Clues I, 778
- Using Context Clues II, 778

OTHER LANGUAGE ARTS SKILLS AND CONCEPTS

- Avoiding Faulty Arguments, 760
- Comparing and Contrasting, 770
- Generalizing, 760
- Reading Actively, 747
- Reading Rates, 747
- Remembering and Visualizing, 758

UNIT 11 MODERN NONFICTION (1900–1960)

Incantation. *Charles Sheeler, 1946. Oil on canvas, 61.0 x 50.8 (24 x 20). The Brooklyn Museum, 49.67. John B. and Ella C. Woodward Memorial Funds*

GOALS/OBJECTIVES

Studying this unit will enable students to

- enjoy a variety of modern nonfictional works
- define *essay* and give examples of various types of essays—personal, humorous, satirical, and analytical
- explain how nonfictional writing has been used by various modern writers as a vehicle for reaction to modern problems
- explain the ways in which particular nonfictional works embrace or reject aspects of Modernism
- understand the meanings of many prefixes and suffixes
- use context clues to decipher the meanings of words

An essayist is a lucky person who has found a way to discourse without being interrupted.

—Charles Poore

CONNECTIONS ACROSS THE CURRICULUM

Arts and Humanities

- Artistic Movements of the Twentieth Century, 763
- Golden Age, 760
- Pastoral Poetry, 773
- Themes in Literature, 768

Mathematics and Sciences

- Cost of a Journey, 775
- Environmental Preservation, 774
- Flora and Fauna, 772

Social Studies

- Artistic Movements of the Twentieth Century, 763
- Cultural Beliefs about Sleep, 754
- Dreams, 755
- Freedom of Speech, 766
- The Great Depression, 748
- Hometown History, 771
- Transcendentalism, 770

TEACHING THE MULTIPLE INTELLIGENCES

Logical/Mathematical

- Cost of a Journey, 775

Spatial

- Artistic Movements of the Twentieth Century, 763
- Photograph of the Depression, 746

Kinesthetic

- Role Play, 759

Interpersonal

- Themes in Literature, 768

LITERARY CURRENTS

List for Literary Currents appears on page 777.

THEMATIC CURRENTS

Use the following selections to explore these themes with your students.

Economic Hardship

- "Newsreel LXVII," 746

Family Matters

- "The Night the Bed Fell," 752

Reacting to Modernity

- "Newsreel LXVII," 746
- Letter to *The Amherst Student*, 759
- Nobel Prize Acceptance Speech, 764
- "Walden," 769

ADDITIONAL RESOURCES

READER'S GUIDE
- Selection Worksheet, 11.1

ASSESSMENT PORTFOLIO
- Selection Check Test, 4.11.1
- Selection Test, 4.11.2

ESSENTIAL SKILLS PRACTICE BOOKS
- *Language,* 2.102
- *Study and Research,* 4.16, 4.18, 4.20–4.28

ENRICHMENT ACTIVITIES

Irony plays an important role in "Newsreel LXVIII"; Dos Passos is constantly juxtaposing disparate elements in an attempt to urge the reader to look beneath the surface of words and statements, especially those spoken by politicians and other government officials. Encourage students to locate a copy of Margaret Bourke-White's famous photograph from the Depression era that shows a large group of unemployed people standing in line at a relief center with a billboard depicting the American dream of middle-class prosperity in the background. Ask students to explain why the photograph is ironic. Then challenge them to draw, photograph, describe in words, or make a collage of an example of irony in the world around them.

SUPPORT FOR LEP STUDENTS

Many students will find this selection especially challenging because of its nontraditional style. Students may find it helpful for you to point out in advance the excerpts from songs that are woven throughout the piece. For example, the excerpt that begins, "This is not Thirtyeight," on page 747, is continued later on the same page with "He looked 'round and said." Some students may need support in understanding the abbreviated style of newspaper headlines throughout the selection.

ADDITIONAL VOCABULARY

sympathizer—one who supports a particular cause

mustachioed—having a mustache

PREREADING

"Newsreel LXVIII" from *The Big Money,* the third volume in the trilogy *U.S.A.*

by John Dos Passos

ABOUT THE AUTHOR

John Dos Passos (1896–1970) was born in Chicago and educated at Harvard University. After graduating from college, he went to Europe and served in World War I as an ambulance driver and a medic. His wartime experiences provided the basis of *One Man's Initiation: 1917* (1919) and *Three Soldiers* (1921). His first great novel, *Manhattan Transfer* (1925), was written using the technique that would become Dos Passos's trademark and his major contribution to the form of the novel. In *Manhattan Transfer* and in his three-volume *U.S.A.* (1938), Dos Passos attempted to create epic portraits of American life by telling many interrelated or parallel stories. *U.S.A.,* which consisted of *The 42nd Parallel, 1919,* and *The Big Money,* was Dos Passos's major contribution to Modernism, the twentieth-century artistic movement characterized by experiments in form, impersonality, and extensive use of allusion. In the three *U.S.A.* volumes, Dos Passos included not only stories of many characters' lives but also biographies of famous Americans such as Andrew Carnegie, personal commentaries called "The Camera Eye," and collages of materials from popular culture that he called "newsreels." The total effect was to create an overall portrait of the country in the early part of this century. In addition to his novels, Dos Passos wrote poetry, history, biographies of famous Americans, and autobiographical works.

ABOUT THE SELECTION

The Big Money is the third volume in John Dos Passos's *U.S.A.* trilogy. As an experiment in providing context for the stories in the volume, Dos Passos created a new fictional form, the newsreel, modeled on the newsreels that, prior to the introduction of television, were shown before films in movie houses. Dos Passos's newsreels were collages, reminiscent of the work of such Modernist painters as Picasso and Braque. They contained bits and pieces of the popular culture of the day, including headlines, advertising slogans, jingles, bits of popular song, common sayings of the time, and excerpts from conversations and speeches. **"Newsreel LXVIII"** focuses on issues related to the Great Depression of the 1930s, a time when millions of Americans were without work and facing severe economic hardship. At the time, strong and sometimes violent conflicts arose between those who felt that government should help and those who felt that it should not.

GOALS/OBJECTIVES

Studying this lesson will enable students to

- have a positive experience reading an unconventional work of nonfiction
- describe John Dos Passos's literary accomplishments and explain the historical significance of his writings
- apply appropriate reading skills to a nontraditional style of text
- define *collage,* analyze the use of this technique in the selection, and apply it in their own writing
- recognize and correct errors in the use of apostrophes

READER'S JOURNAL

People today are deluged with information, much of it trivial. Carry a notebook with you for a day. Jot down an assortment of words that you encounter—headlines, lyrics of songs, phrases from cereal boxes, announcements over the school P. A. system, slogans from billboards, phrases from television or the movies, and so on. Then, compare your list with lists made by your classmates. What do these lists tell you about the culture in which you live? What are its preoccupations? its values? its goals? Write about these questions in your journal.

READING SKILLS

"Newsreel LXVIII" is a challenging text without traditional narrative structure. As such, it may require careful and repeated readings. Refer to the Language Arts Survey, 4.16, "Reading Rates," and 4.18, "Reading Actively," for suggestions on how to approach the text.

FROM *THE BIG MONEY*

"Newsreel LXVIII"

JOHN DOS PASSOS

WALL STREET STUNNED

This is not Thirtyeight, but it's old
Ninetyseven
You must put her in Center on time[1]

MARKET SURE TO RECOVER FROM SLUMP

DECLINE IN CONTRACTS

POLICE TURN MACHINE GUNS ON
COLORADO MINE STRIKERS KILL 5 WOUND 40

sympathizers appeared on the scene just as thousands of office workers were pouring out of the buildings at the lunch hour. As they raised their placard high and started an indefinite march from one side to the other, they were jeered and hooted not only by the office workers but also by workmen on a building under construction

NEW METHODS OF SELLING SEEN

RESCUE CREWS TRY TO UPEND
ILL-FATED CRAFT
WHILE WAITING FOR PONTOONS

He looked 'round an' said to his black greasy
fireman
Jus' shovel in a little more coal
And when we cross that White Oak Mountain
You can watch your Ninety-seven roll

I find your column interesting and need advice. I have saved four thousand dollars

1. **This is not . . . on time.** The allusion is to the "old Ninetyseven" train, which was wrecked and became a subject for popular railroad ballads. One recording of such a railroad ballad sold over a million copies in the 1920s and was one of the earliest pop singles.

❶ *Who jeers and hoots at the sympathizers?*

WORDS FOR EVERYDAY USE:

plac • ard (plak´ärd) *n.,* notice for display in a public place; sign

in • def • i • nite (in def´ə nit) *adj.,* having no exact limits

pon • toon (pän tōōn´) *n.,* flat-bottomed boat; floating object used for support

PREREADING NOTES

READER'S JOURNAL

You might encourage students to look for ideas or messages in popular culture that are contradictory, either because the ideas contradict reality or because they contradict each other. Ask students to think about how these mixed messages come about. Who is sending each message, and to whom? What motivates the senders? Do students share or approve of these motives? In what way can popular culture change or shape people's perceptions of reality? What positive and negative effects might the messages of popular culture have on a society?

READING SKILLS

After students have read the text, they might discuss which of the strategies suggested in the Language Arts Survey were the most (and least) helpful for this particular selection. Then they could develop their own list of strategies that would be useful for approaching other texts written in Dos Passos's collage style.

▶Additional practice is provided in the *Essential Skills Practice Book: Study and Research,* 4.16 and 4.18.

ANSWER TO GUIDED READING QUESTION

❶ Office and construction workers jeer at the sympathizers.

VOCABULARY FROM THE SELECTION

disbar	pontoon
hem	propagandist
ideology	rickety
indefinite	solidarity
meddling	tallowy
placard	

VOCABULARY IN CONTEXT

- Did you read the placard posted at the entrance, which told us which way to go to reach the festival?
- George prepared food for an indefinite number of guests, since he wasn't sure how many people would show up.
- The airplane was able to land on the water by floating on its pontoons.

Answer to Guided Reading Question

❶ The capitalist and socialist schools of economics are juxtaposed.

Additional Questions and Activities

- What might the "rescue of men" have referred to in the actual newspaper headline? What other meaning might it have in the context of Dos Passos's work?
- What is ironic in the headline "Radicals Fight with Chairs at Unity Meeting"?

Answers. "Rescue of men" probably meant a physical rescue effort of some men caught in a disaster. Dos Passos seems to suggest that the next generation of Americans needs to be rescued from economic and social problems. The headline about the "unity meeting" is ironic because the meeting apparently broke into factions who attacked each other violently.

Answers to Selection Check Test 4.11.1

EX. What does "Wall Street" refer to in the opening line?
It refers to the financial center of New York City.

1. To what event do the excerpts from the first song in the passage refer?
They refer to a well-known train wreck.

2. What did rescue crews do while waiting for pontoons?
They attempted to turn over a capsized boat.

3. To what period in history does the headline "President Sees Prosperity Near" refer?
It refers to the Great Depression of the 1930s.

4. Why was the President on "a tiny island"?
He was there to dedicate a wildlife refuge and a carillon.

5. Why do the prisoners have "tallowy" faces?
They are miners who work all day underground.

which I want to invest for a better income. Do you think I might buy stocks?

POLICE KILLER FLICKS CIGARETTE AS HE GOES TREMBLING TO DOOM

PLAY AGENCIES IN RING OF SLAVE GIRL MARTS

MAKER OF LOVE DISBARRED AS LAWYER

Oh the right wing clothesmakers
And the Socialist fakers
They make by the workers . . .
Double cross

They preach Social-ism
But practice Fasc-ism
To keep capitalism
By the boss[2]

What two opinions of economics are juxtaposed? ❶

MOSCOW CONGRESS OUSTS OPPOSITION

It's a mighty rough road from Lynchburg to Danville
An' a line on a three mile grade
It was on that grade he lost his average
An' you see what a jump he made

MILL THUGS IN MURDER RAID

here is the most dangerous example of how at the decisive moment the bourgeois ideology liquidates class solidarity and turns a friend of the workingclass of yesterday into a most miserable propagandist for imperialism[3] today

RED[4] PICKETS FINED FOR PROTEST HERE

We leave our home in the morning
We kiss our children goodbye

OFFICIALS STILL HOPE FOR RESCUE OF MEN

He was goin' downgrade makin' ninety miles an hour
When his whistle broke into a scream
He was found in the wreck with his hand on the throttle
An' was scalded to death with the steam

RADICALS FIGHT WITH CHAIRS AT UNITY MEETING

PATROLMEN PROTECT REDS

U.S. CHAMBER OF COMMERCE URGES CONFIDENCE

REAL VALUES UNHARMED

While we slave for the bosses
Our children scream an' cry
But when we draw our money
Our grocery bills to pay

PRESIDENT SEES PROSPERITY NEAR

Not a cent to spend for clothing
Not a cent to lay away

STEAMROLLER IN ACTION AGAINST MILITANTS

MINERS BATTLE SCABS[5]

But we cannot buy for our children
Our wages are too low
Now listen to me you workers
Both you women and men
Let us win for them the victory
I'm sure it ain't no sin

2. **Oh the . . . By the boss.** Socialist labor-union protest song that is interspersed throughout the work
3. **imperialism.** Policy or practice of seeking to dominate the economic or political affairs of underdeveloped areas or weaker countries
4. **red.** Political radical or reactionary, especially a communist
5. **scab.** Derogatory term for a worker who refuses to join a union, or who works for lower wages or under different conditions than those accepted by the union; worker who refuses to strike, or who takes the place of a striking worker

Words for Everyday Use:
dis • bar (dis bär´) *vt.*, deprive (a lawyer) of the right to practice law
i • de • ol • o • gy (ī´dē äl´ə gē) *n.*, doctrine, opinion, or way of thinking
sol • i • dar • i • ty (säl´ə dar´ə tē) *n.*, combination or agreement of all elements or individuals
prop • a • gan • dist (präp´ə gan´dist) *n.*, one who spreads ideas for a particular cause

Vocabulary in Context

- The lawyer debated whether bending the rules was worth the risk of being disbarred and never practicing law again.
- Communism and capitalism are economic ideologies that propose very different ways of distributing wealth.
- Although there had been many disagreements among members of the union, the group maintained solidarity during the strike.
- The speaker did not make a balanced presentation but instead acted as a propagandist for one particular ideology.

CARILLON PEALS IN SINGING TOWER[6]

the President declared it was impossible to view the increased advantages for the many without smiling at those who a short time ago expressed so much fear lest our country might come under the control of a few individuals of great wealth.

HAPPY CROWDS THRONG CEREMONY

on a tiny island nestling like a green jewel in the lake that mirrors the singing tower, the President today participated in the dedication of a bird sanctuary and its pealing carillon, fulfilling the dream of an immigrant boy

The Camera Eye (51)

at the head of the valley in the dark of the hills on the broken floor of a lurched-over[7] cabin a man halfsits halflies propped up by an old woman two wrinkled girls that might be young chunks of coal flare in the hearth flicker in his face white and sagging as dough blacken the cavedin mouth the taut throat the belly swelled enormous with the wound he got working on the minetipple[8]

the barefoot girl brings him a tincup of water the woman wipes sweat off his streaming face with a dirty denim sleeve the firelight flares in his eyes stretched big with fever in the women's scared eyes and in the blanched faces of the foreigners

without help in the valley hemmed by dark strike-silent hills the man will die (my father died we know what it is like to see a man die) the women will lay him out on the rickety cot the miners will bury him

in the jail it's light too hot the steamheat hisses we talk through the greenpainted iron bars to a tall white mustachioed old man some smiling miners in shirtsleeves a boy faces white from mining have already the tallowy look of jailfaces

foreigners what can we say to the dead? foreigners what can we say to the jailed? the representative of the political party talks fast through the bars join up with us and no other union we'll send you tobacco candy solidarity our lawyers will write briefs speakers will shout your names at meetings they'll carry your names on cardboard on picketlines the men in jail shrug their shoulders smile thinly our eyes look in their eyes through the bars what can I say? (in another continent I have seen the faces looking out through the barred basement windows behind the ragged sentry's boots I have seen before day the straggling footsore prisoners herded through the streets limping between bayonets heard the volley

I have seen the dead lying out in those distant deeper valleys) what can we say to the jailed?

in the law's office we stand against the wall the law is a big man with eyes angry in a big pumpkinface who sits and stares at us meddling foreigners through the door the deputies crane with their guns they stand guard at the mines

❶ *What does the party representative say the party will do for the prisoners?*

❷ *How does the imagery in this passage, or "clip," compare with the imagery in the rest of the newsreel? Explain.*

❸ *Who is "the law"?*

6. **carillon . . . singing tower.** *Carillon*—set of stationary bells, each producing one tone of the chromatic scale; *singing tower*—the Spring Tower erected in Florida; President Calvin Coolidge spoke at the dedication of the tower in 1929.

7. **lurchedover.** Dos Passos has run the words *lurched* and *over* together. The selection contains several more run-together words.

8. **minetipple.** Equipment that tips cars in a coal mine to unload the coal

WORDS FOR EVERYDAY USE:

hem (hem) *vt.*, encircle; surround

rick • e • ty (rik´it ē) *adj.*, weak in the joints; shaky

tal • low • y (tal´ō ē) *adj.*, fatty and pale

med • dling (med´liŋ) *part.*, interfering; concerning oneself with other people's affairs without being asked

ANSWERS TO GUIDED READING QUESTIONS

❶ The party representative says the union will give them candy and will provide solidarity both by having the union's lawyers defend them with briefs and by having union leaders speak and picket on their behalf.

❷ This clip offers images of a peaceful natural paradise, a hopeful place of great beauty and tranquility. Much of the imagery in the rest of the newsreel is concerned with economic decline, poverty, strife, violence, and death, presenting a world in chaos with little to hope for in the future.

❸ The law is represented by a powerful man with a "big pumpkinface" who hates "meddling foreigners."

ADDITIONAL QUESTIONS AND ACTIVITIES

- What attitude does the author seem to have toward the president and his words? Do you think Dos Passos would say the president is in touch with reality? Explain.
- What has happened to the man in the "lurchedover cabin"? Who is taking care of him? What will happen to him when he dies? What point do you think Dos Passos is trying to make by telling this story?

Answers. Dos Passos contrasts the president's confident statements that the nation's economic troubles are over and that fears about capitalism giving too much power to a few individuals have been proven misinformed, with images of suffering working people. The image of the president dedicating the bird sanctuary makes him seem very removed from the real lives of these people. The man in the cabin has been badly injured in a mining accident and has only his family to take care of him. When he dies, he will be buried by his family and friends, without fanfare. Dos Passos may be trying to show that American society places little value on the working-class people who live and die anonymously while keeping society functioning.

VOCABULARY IN CONTEXT

- Sheryl was hemmed in by the crowd and could not reach the train's doors before they closed.
- "I'd rather face the fire than climb down that rickety fire escape!" Aunt Martha declared.
- Tallowy clumps of congealed fat floated on the surface of last night's dishwater.
- Christopher's meddling personality would not allow him to stay out of other people's business.

ANSWER TO GUIDED READING QUESTION

❶ The "law" has firearms at its disposal and is supported by numerous public officials and private individuals who occupy positions of considerable authority.

RESPONDING TO THE SELECTION

Because some students will enjoy this selection more than others, you may wish to have students debate the merits of the piece. Encourage students on both sides to clearly articulate their reasons for liking or disliking the work. Remind them that there is no right or wrong answer, since people's responses to literature are highly subjective. Each student should keep an open mind, however, to their classmates' observations.

ANSWERS FOR REVIEWING THE SELECTION

RECALLING

1. Sympathizers were jeered by people working in offices and construction sites in the neighborhood.
2. The operator wanted to get the train into the station on time, so he let the train reach ninety miles an hour going down a hill and the train crashed.
3. They want to be able to spend more time with their families and to have enough money to buy them new clothes and save for the future.
4. The effects of the Great Depression on the working class, prejudice against foreigners and "communists," and the cooperation among powerful people to oppress the poor are consistent themes.

INTERPRETING

Responses will vary. Possible responses are given.

5. The office and construction workers probably wanted to protect their jobs and the economic system that had provided them, and they perceived the protesters as threatening that system.

(cont.)

they blockade the miners' soupkitchens they've cut off the road up the valley the hiredmen with guns stand ready to shoot (they have made us foreigners in the land where we were born they are the conquering army that has filtered into the country unnoticed they have taken the hilltops by stealth they levy toll they stand at the minehead they stand at the polls they stand by when the bailiffs carry the furniture of the family evicted from the city tenement out on the sidewalk they are there when the bankers foreclose[9] on a farm they are ambushed and ready to shoot down the strikers marching behind the flag up the switchback road to the mine those that the guns spare they jail)

the law stares across the desk out of angry eyes his face reddens in splotches like a gobbler's neck with the strut of the power of submachine guns sawedoffshotguns teargas and vomitinggas the power that can feed you or leave you to starve

sits easy at his desk his back is covered he feels strong behind him he feels the prosecutingattorney the judge an owner himself the political boss the minesuperintendent the board of directors the president of the utility the manipulator of the holdingcompany

he lifts his hand towards the telephone
the deputies crowd in the door
we have only words against ■

What powers does "the law" have? Who supports "the law"? ❶

9. **foreclose.** Deprive a mortgagor of the right to redeem a mortgage through a legal procedure in which satisfaction may be obtained from the proceeds of a forced sale of the property

Responding to the Selection

Do you enjoy literary works that employ nontraditional structures? Did you find "Newsreel LXVIII" interesting? Why, or why not? Which parts were easy to understand? Which were not so easy? Why?

Reviewing the Selection

RECALLING

1. How were sympathizers greeted as they started a march outside an office building?
2. What events led to the death of the train operator?
3. What did the workers say they wanted for their families?
4. What issues are raised throughout "Newsreel LXVIII"?

INTERPRETING

5. Why was there tension between people who were protesting conditions and others who tolerated them?
6. How did the train operator's death symbolize what was happening at the time to other American workers?
7. Why couldn't workers buy what their families needed?
8. What conflict in American society did Dos Passos present in "Newsreel LXVIII"?

ANSWERS FOR REVIEWING THE SELECTION (CONT.)

6. American workers were also on a "runaway train" in the sense that they were part of a system that was growing unchecked and that was pursuing a goal without taking their well-being into account.
7. The workers' wages were too low for them to buy what their families needed.
8. The piece explores the debate over what kind of economic system the United States should have and the role the government should play in that system.

SYNTHESIZING

Responses will vary. Possible responses are given.

9. By combining news headlines, story excerpts, song lyrics, and images of people in various situations, Dos Passos captures a broad picture of what was happening in the 1930s and makes links between events that might otherwise seem unrelated. He uses this technique to show

(cont.)

SYNTHESIZING

9. How do the many elements in "Newsreel LXVIII" contribute to the selection's overall point?

10. What makes the newsreel structure suitable for presenting a portrait of life at a particular time and in a particular place?

Understanding Literature (Questions for Discussion)

Collage. In literature, a **collage** is a work that incorporates or brings together an odd assortment of materials, such as allusions, quotations, bits of song, dialogue, foreign words, mythical or folkloric elements, headlines, and pictures or other graphic devices. John Dos Passos used collage as a way to capture a moment of history. List the kinds of materials that make up the collage that is "Newsreel LXVIII."

Responding in Writing

A Moment in Your Life. Using the collage approach, create an impression of a particular time in your life. Pick any time you like and incorporate as many different types of materials as you wish. Try to follow the approach used in "Newsreel LXVIII." Do research in the library to gather materials for your collage. Try to use as wide a variety of materials as possible. Refer to the Language Arts Survey, 4.20–4.28, for information on possible sources of information.

Language Lab

Apostrophes. Read the Language Arts Survey, 2.102, "Apostrophes." Then rewrite the sentences below to correct errors in the use of apostrophes.

1. John Dos Passos *U.S.A.* depicts a moment in Americas history.
2. In each of his newsreel's, Dos Passos was able to capture a moment, including it's vivid contradictions.
3. Dos Passoss vision was molded by his wartime experiences and by the Great Depression.
4. Were fortunate to have been born after the Great Depression, arent we?
5. Todays society is no less troubled, despite it's many advances.

ANSWERS FOR REVIEWING THE SELECTION (CONT.)

the far-reaching effects of allowing a few people to control the wealth of a large society.

10. This structure allows an author to touch on many themes and events without having to weave them into a narrative. By flashing a series of "snippets" before the reader, the author can give a quick but very rich impression of the setting he or she is describing.

ANSWERS FOR UNDERSTANDING LITERATURE

►See the evaluation forms for discussion, active listening, and oral communication, *Assessment Portfolio,* 7.11–7.14.

Responses will vary. Possible responses are given.

Collage. Newspaper headlines, song lyrics, excerpts from news stories, letters to newspaper columnists, excerpts from editorial pieces, and impressionistic descriptions of scenes involving symbolic characters are some of the elements that compose "Newsreel LXVIII."

ANALYTIC SCALES FOR RESPONDING IN WRITING

Assign a score from 1 to 25 for each grading criterion below. (For more detailed evaluation, see the evaluation forms for writing, revising, and proofreading, *Assessment Portfolio,* 7.1–7.10.)

A Moment in Your Life

- **Content/Unity.** The collage includes materials that relate to a particular time and place.
- **Organization/Coherence.** The collage is arranged so that elements are juxtaposed in a thoughtful and thought-provoking way.
- **Language/Style.** Narrative portions of the collage use vivid and precise nouns, verbs, and modifiers.
- **Conventions.** Narrative portions of the collage avoid errors in spelling, grammar, usage, mechanics, and manuscript form.

ANSWERS FOR LANGUAGE LAB

1. John Dos Passos's *U.S.A.* depicts a moment in America's history.

2. In each of his newsreels, Dos Passos was able to capture a moment, including its vivid contradictions.

3. Dos Passos's vision was molded by his wartime experiences and by the Great Depression.

4. We're fortunate to have been born after the Great Depression, aren't we?

5. Today's society is no less troubled, despite its many advances.

►Additional practice is provided in the *Essential Skills Practice Books: Language,* 2.102.

ADDITIONAL RESOURCES

READER'S GUIDE
- Selection Worksheet, 11.2

ASSESSMENT PORTFOLIO
- Selection Check Test, 4.11.3
- Selection Test, 4.11.4

ESSENTIAL SKILLS PRACTICE BOOKS
- *Language,* 2.101, 2.149
- *Study and Research,* 4.5

ENRICHMENT ACTIVITIES

Have students listen to a recording of a comedian telling an anecdote in order to compare oral humor with written humor. What techniques does the comedian use to generate humor? How does he or she use language differently than a writer of humorous works? What are the different difficulties faced by a comedian and a humor writer?

SUPPORT FOR LEP STUDENTS

Review with students the additional vocabulary below before they read the selection.

ADDITIONAL VOCABULARY

recitation—saying aloud in public
calamity—disaster
phobia—irrational or excessive fear

PREREADING

"The Night the Bed Fell"
by James Thurber

ABOUT THE AUTHOR

James Thurber (1894–1961), born in Columbus, Ohio, lost an eye in a childhood accident and had impaired vision in his other eye. He attended Ohio State University from 1913 to 1918 but never graduated. He then spent sixteen months in Paris writing and deciphering coded messages for the army. Returning to Columbus, he became a reporter, and in 1922 began his first marriage, which lasted twelve years. In 1925, Thurber went to France as a freelance writer for English-language papers in Paris and Nice, but returned to the United States a year later and moved to New York City. He soon joined *New Yorker* magazine, where he was managing editor from 1927 to 1933. He shared an office with E. B. White, who had an enormous influence on his writing style, helping to make it direct and clear. White also discovered Thurber's ability to draw; soon his cartoons became as well known and loved as his essays. His story "The Secret Life of Walter Mitty," which first appeared in *New Yorker* in 1939, is considered an American classic. Thurber had a happy second marriage, but the last twenty years of his life were filled with serious health problems, including a series of small strokes and failing vision. Toward the end of his life, he wrote stories for children. Collections of his works include *The Owl in the Attic* (1931), *The Seal in the Bedroom* (1932), *My Life and Hard Times* (1933), *The Middle-aged Man on the Flying Trapeze* (1935), *Fables of Our Time* (1940), *The Thurber Carnival* (1945), and *The Thurber Album* (1952).

ABOUT THE SELECTION

"The Night the Bed Fell" is a fine example of a personal essay, using an informal, first-person voice to recount a particular experience in the writer's life. A comedy of errors, the essay describes a night in James Thurber's childhood when confusion and chaos overtook the household. Thurber's father, asleep in the attic, is believed to be trapped under his fallen bed. In the scramble to rescue him, no one notices Thurber, the narrator, who actually is trapped under his overturned bed. A collection of odd relatives people the story, from Briggs Beall, who must be awakened every hour for fear that he will stop breathing while he sleeps, to Aunt Gracie Shoaf, who every night throws shoes at imaginary burglars. While Thurber is said to have based his story on a real event, he did embellish it significantly. A matter-of-fact tone mixed with exaggeration lends the piece its humor. "The Night the Bed Fell" is just one of many personal reminiscences James Thurber captured in his writing.

GOALS/OBJECTIVES

Studying this lesson will enable students to

- enjoy a humorous personal essay
- describe Thurber's literary accomplishments and explain the historical significance of his writing
- define *anecdote* and recognize anecdotes in their reading
- define and give examples of *farce*
- write a press release and a family history
- use parentheses and brackets correctly

READER'S JOURNAL

Have you ever been involved in a situation in which everything went wrong all at once? What happened? Did the situation seem funny at the time? Did it seem funnier when you looked back on it later? How does laughter help people cope? Write about these questions in your journal.

LANGUAGE SKILLS

Read the Language Arts Survey, 2.149, "Tone and Voice." Then write a short paragraph about the experience you described in your reader's journal. What tone and voice did you use for your paragraph? Why?

"The Night the Bed Fell"

JAMES THURBER

I suppose that the high-water mark[1] of my youth in Columbus, Ohio, was the night the bed fell on my father. It makes a better recitation (unless, as some friends of mine have said, one has heard it five or six times) than it does a piece of writing, for it is almost necessary to throw furniture around, shake doors, and bark like a dog, to lend the proper atmosphere and verisimilitude to what is admittedly a somewhat incredible tale. Still, it did take place.

It happened, then, that my father had decided to sleep in the attic one night, to be away where he could think. My mother opposed the notion strongly because, she said, the old wooden bed up there was unsafe; it was wobbly and the heavy headboard would crash down on father's head in case the bed fell, and kill him. There was no dissuading him, however, and at a quarter past ten he closed the attic door behind him and went up the narrow twisting stairs. We later heard ominous creakings as he crawled into bed. Grandfather, who usually slept in the attic bed when he was with us, had disappeared some days before. (On these occasions he was usually gone six or eight days and returned growling and out of temper, with the news that the federal Union was run by a passel[2] of blockheads and that the Army of the Potomac[3] didn't have any more chance than a fiddler's bitch.)

We had visiting us at this time a nervous first cousin of mine named Briggs Beall, who believed that he was likely to cease breathing when he was asleep. It was his feeling that if he were not awakened every

❶ *Why did Thurber's father sleep in the attic?*

❷ *Who is Briggs Beall? Of what is he afraid?*

1. **high-water mark.** Culminating point, highest point
2. **passel.** Group or collection, especially a fairly large one
3. **Army of the Potomac.** One of the main armies of the Union Forces in the Civil War; led by General George B. McClellan

WORDS FOR EVERYDAY USE:

ver • i • si • mil • i • tude (vər´ si mil´ ə tōōd´) *n.,* appearance of being true or real

dis • suade (di swād´) *vt.,* turn (someone) aside by persuasion or advice

om • i • nous (äm´ ə nəs) *adj.,* threatening, sinister

PREREADING NOTES

READER'S JOURNAL

Students might consider numerous events in their lives that have provoked laughter to see if there are common themes among these events.

LANGUAGE SKILLS

Students can read their paragraphs to each other in small groups, offering each other suggestions on how to improve the tone and voice of their passages or use tone and voice more consistently.

ANSWERS TO GUIDED READING QUESTIONS

❶ He went to sleep in the attic so that he could be alone and reflect.

❷ Briggs Beall is Thurber's first cousin; Beall is terrified he will stop breathing while he is asleep.

VOCABULARY FROM THE SELECTION

allay	juncture
culprit	ominous
deluge	perilous
dissuade	premonition
extricate	racket
fortitude	verisimilitude

VOCABULARY IN CONTEXT

- Ellen dislikes novels written in the fantasy genre because their plots lack verisimilitude.
- Nothing she could say would dissuade him from quitting his job.
- Thunderclouds gathering in the western sky were an ominous indication of the severe weather lying in the ship's path.

Answers to Guided Reading Questions

❶ Once he thought Thurber was asleep, Beall held his breath to see if Thurber would wake up.

❷ Aunt Sarah left her most valuable possessions outside her bedroom door with a note telling burglars to take the goods and asking them not to chloroform her.

Cross-curricular Activities

Social Studies. Throughout history, humankind has generated a variety of theories and beliefs regarding sleep, from the ancient idea that spirits visited sleepers during the night to the contem-porary notion that alien beings abduct sleepers in order to conduct medical experiments. Have students research various cultural beliefs concerning sleep and present their findings to the class. Ask them to discuss why the act of sleeping evokes such a wide range of fantastic beliefs.

Additional Questions and Activities

Ask students why the author includes character sketches of his three aunts, Melissa Beall, Sarah Shoaf, and Gracie Shoaf, even though these characters do not play roles in the story's central event. What do these character sketches add to the story? Would the story be as amusing without these sketches?

hour during the night, he might die of suffocation. He had been accustomed to setting an alarm clock to ring at intervals until morning, but I persuaded him to abandon this. He slept in my room and I told him that I was such a light sleeper that if anybody quit breathing in the same room with me, I would wake instantly. He tested me the first night—which I had suspected he would—by holding his breath after my regular breathing had convinced him I was asleep. I was not asleep, however, and called to him. This seemed to allay his fears a little, but he took the precaution of putting a glass of spirits of camphor[4] on a little table at the head of his bed. In case I didn't arouse him until he was almost gone, he said, he would sniff the camphor, a powerful reviver. Briggs was not the only member of his family who had his crotchets.[5] Old Aunt Melissa Beall (who could whistle like a man, with two fingers in her mouth) suffered under the premonition that she was destined to die on South High Street, because she had been born on South High Street and married on South High Street. Then there was Aunt Sarah Shoaf, who never went to bed at night without the fear that a burglar was going to get in and blow chloroform[6] under her door through a tube. To avert this calamity—for she was in greater dread of anesthetics than of losing her household goods—she always piled her money, silverware, and other valuables in a neat stack just outside her bedroom, with a note reading: "This is all I have. Please take it and do not use your chloroform, as this is all I have." Aunt Gracie Shoaf also had a burglar phobia, but she met it with more fortitude. She was confident that burglars had been getting into her house every night for forty years. The fact that she never missed anything was to her no proof to the contrary. She always claimed that she scared them off before they could take anything, by throwing shoes down the hallway. When she went to bed she piled, where she could get at them handily, all the shoes there were about her house. Five minutes after she had turned off the light, she would sit up in bed and say "Hark!" Her husband, who had learned to ignore the whole situation as long ago as 1903, would either be sound asleep or pretend to be sound asleep. In either case he would not respond to her tugging and pulling, so that presently she would arise, tiptoe to the door, open it slightly and heave a shoe down the hall in one direction, and its mate down the hall in the other direction. Some nights she threw them all, some nights only a couple of pair.

❶ *How did Beall test Thurber?*

❷ *What did Aunt Sarah do to avoid being chloroformed?*

But I am straying from the remarkable incidents that took place during the night that the bed fell on father. By midnight we were all in bed. The layout of the rooms and the disposition of their occupants is important to an understanding of what later occurred. In the front room upstairs (just under father's attic bedroom) were my mother and my brother Herman, who sometimes sang in his sleep, usually

4. **spirits of camphor.** Solution with a strong characteristic odor, derived from the wood of the camphor tree; in medicine used as an irritant and stimulant

5. **crotchets.** Peculiar whims or stubborn notions

6. **chloroform.** Toxic, carcinogenic, colorless liquid used as a solvent, fumigant, and formerly, as a general anesthetic

Words for Everyday Use: **al • lay** (a lā´) *vt.,* put to rest; quiet, calm **prem • o • ni • tion** (prēm´ə nish ən) *n.,* warning; feeling that something bad will happen **for • ti • tude** (fort´ə tōōd) *n.,* strength to bear misfortune or pain

Vocabulary in Context

- Our fears about the weather were only allayed once the plane had landed safely.
- Some people believe that a premonition is nothing more than the product of an overly active imagination.
- The documentary was an homage to the great fortitude of the human spirit when confronted with a boundless, oppressive evil.

"Marching Through Georgia" or "Onward, Christian Soldiers." Briggs Beall and myself were in a room adjoining this one. My brother Roy was in a room across the hall from ours. Our bull terrier, Rex, slept in the hall.

My bed was an army cot, one of those affairs which are made wide enough to sleep on comfortably only by putting up, flat with the middle section, the two sides which ordinarily hang down like the sideboards of a drop-leaf table. When these sides are up, it is perilous to roll too far toward the edge, for then the cot is likely to tip completely over, bringing the whole bed down on top of one, with a tremendous banging crash. This, in fact, is precisely what happened, about two o'clock in the morning. (It was my mother who, in recalling the scene later, first referred to it as "the night the bed fell on your father.")

Always a deep sleeper, slow to arouse (I had lied to Briggs), I was at first unconscious of what had happened when the iron cot rolled me onto the floor and toppled over on me. It left me still warmly bundled up and unhurt, for the bed rested above me like a canopy. Hence I did not wake up, only reached the edge of consciousness and went back. The racket, however, instantly awakened my mother, in the next room, who came to the immediate conclusion that her worst dread was realized: the big wooden bed upstairs had fallen on father. She therefore screamed, "Let's go to your poor father!" It was this shout, rather than the noise of my cot falling, that awakened Herman, in the same room with her. He thought that mother had become, for no apparent reason, hysterical. "You're all right, Mamma!" he shouted, trying to calm her. They exchanged shout for shout for perhaps ten seconds: "Let's go to your poor father!" and "You're all right!" That woke up Briggs. By this time I was conscious of what was going on, in a vague way, but did not yet realize that I was under my bed instead of on it. Briggs, awakening in the midst of loud shouts of fear and apprehension, came to the quick conclusion that he was suffocating and that we were all trying to "bring him out." With a low moan, he grasped the glass of camphor at the head of his bed and instead of sniffing it poured it over himself. The room reeked of camphor. "Ugf, ahfg," choked Briggs, like a drowning man, for he had almost succeeded in stopping his breath under the deluge of pungent spirits. He leaped out of bed and groped toward the open window, but he came up against one that was closed. With his hand, he beat out the glass, and I could hear it crash and tinkle on the alleyway below. It was at this juncture that I, in trying to get up, had the uncanny sensation of feeling my bed above me! Foggy with sleep, I now suspected, in my turn, that the whole uproar was being made in a frantic endeavor to extricate me from what must be an unheard-of and perilous situation. "Get me out of this!" I bawled. "Get me out!" I think I had the nightmarish belief that I was entombed in a mine. "Gugh," gasped Briggs, floundering in his camphor.

By this time my mother, still shouting, pursued by Herman, still shouting, was trying to open the door to the attic, in

❶ *On what kind of bed did the author sleep? What happened to it?*

❷ *What happened when the author tried to stand up? What did he think had happened?*

Words for Everyday Use:

per • il • ous (per´ə ləs) *adj.*, dangerous
rack • et (rak´it) *n.*, noisy confusion; uproar
del • uge (del´yōōj) *n.*, overwhelming floodlike rush
junc • ture (junk´chər) *n.*, point in time
ex • tri • cate (eks´tri kāt) *vt.*, release or disentangle

Answers to Guided Reading Questions

❶ He slept on an army cot that flipped over on top of him during the night.

❷ He felt the bed on top of him and in his sleepy confusion thought that he had been trapped in a mine.

Cross-curricular Activities

Social Studies. The act of dreaming has inspired numerous explanations of its purpose; some Buddhists believe that the physical world is a dream, and that dreams during sleep provide access to true reality; Sigmund Freud famously interpreted dreams as symbolic representations of the individual's subconscious emotions; and Carl Jung argued that dreams serve as a gateway into the "collective unconscious" of the human species. Students may wish to investigate both ancient and modern explanations of dreams. Students should research the subject of dreams from a variety of perspectives, including the biological, psychological, and literary.

Additional Questions and Activities

Ask students to name habits and rituals that are associated with going to sleep and make a list of them on the chalkboard. What different themes emerge from this list (e.g., taking safety precautions or preparing for a kind of journey)? Does this list reveal certain unconscious beliefs about the act of sleeping? Which habits or rituals seem humorous out of context, and why?

Vocabulary in Context

- The ascent up Mt. McKinley can be extremely perilous and should only be attempted by experts.
- The racket from the party next door kept her from getting a good night's sleep.
- The audience was so intrigued with the speaker's talk that they responded with a deluge of questions.
- "We have no comment at this juncture" was the only reply the defense attorney would give the press on leaving the trial.
- Rarely can an insect extricate itself once it has been caught in a spider's web.

Answer to Guided Reading Question

❶ She mistakenly believed that he was calling to God when he said, "I'm coming!"

Answers to Selection Check Test 4.11.3

EX. What event is central to Thurber's story?
The central event is the collapsing of a bed.

1. When in Thurber's life did this story take place?
The story occurred during Thurber's youth.

2. What did the family hear when Thurber's father went upstairs?
They heard "ominous creakings" from the bed in the attic.

3. Who usually slept in the attic?
Thurber's grandfather usually slept in the attic.

4. Who slept in the room just beneath the attic?
Thurber's mother and his brother Herman slept in the room beneath the attic.

5. Why did Thurber not wake up when his bed turned over?
He was a very deep sleeper.

Responding to the Selection

Suggest that students compare this selection, or other personal memoirs, with fictional writing. What are the similarities and differences between these two kinds of writing?

Vocabulary in Context

• The police were astonished to discover that the true culprit was not their original suspect.

order to go up and get my father's body out of the wreckage. The door was stuck, however, and wouldn't yield. Her frantic pulls on it only added to the general banging and confusion. Roy and the dog were now up, the one shouting questions, the other barking.

Father, farthest away and soundest sleeper of all, had by this time been awakened by the battering on the attic door. He decided that the house was on fire. "I'm coming, I'm coming!" he wailed in a slow, sleepy voice—it took him many minutes to regain full consciousness. My mother, still believing he was caught under the bed, detected in his "I'm coming!" the mournful, resigned note of one who is preparing to meet his Maker. "He's dying!" she shouted.

Why did Thurber's mother think his father was dying? ❶

"I'm all right!" Briggs yelled to reassure her. "I'm all right!" He still believed that it was his own closeness to death that was worrying mother. I found at last the light switch in my room, unlocked the door, and Briggs and I joined the others at the attic door. The dog, who never did like Briggs, jumped for him—assuming that he was the culprit in whatever was going on—and Roy had to throw Rex and hold him. We could hear father crawling out of bed upstairs. Roy pulled the attic door open, with a mighty jerk, and father came down the stairs, sleepy and irritable but safe and sound. My mother began to weep when she saw him. Rex began to howl. "What in the name of God is going on here?" asked father.

The situation was finally put together like a gigantic jig-saw puzzle. Father caught a cold from prowling around in his bare feet but there were no other bad results. "I'm glad," said mother, who always looked on the bright side of things, "that your grandfather wasn't here." ■

Responding to the Selection

Do you enjoy reading personal memoirs? How do they offer insight into people's emotions, behavior, and motivations? Did you find "The Night the Bed Fell" funny? Why, or why not?

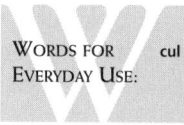

Words for Everyday Use: **cul • prit** (kul´prit) *n.*, guilty person

Answers for Reviewing the Selection

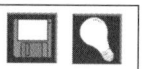

RECALLING

1. Thurber's father was sleeping in the attic. Thurber's mother is nervous about his location because the bed is very old, and she fears the headboard may fall on his head and kill him.

2. Cousin Briggs Beall is visiting. He is afraid he will stop breathing during the night, so he wants to be awakened every hour.

3. Thurber's mother and brother are in a room adjacent to his and Briggs's; his brother Roy is in a room across the hall; and Rex the dog sleeps in the hallway.

4. The family can't reach Thurber's father because the door to the attic is stuck.

(cont.)

Reviewing the Selection

RECALLING

1. Where was Thurber's father on the night the bed fell? How does Thurber's mother feel about his location?
2. Who is visiting at Thurber's house on the night in question? What odd behavior has he displayed during the earlier part of his visit?
3. Who and where are the other members of the household?
4. Why can't the family reach Thurber's father to insure his safety?

INTERPRETING

5. How does his location contribute to the confusion of the night?
6. What does Thurber think of his roommate's behavior? How does he respond to it?
7. What event first triggered the confusion of the night? Which family member initiated it? What events followed?
8. How does Thurber's father react to the chaos? How does the description of his behavior suggest Thurber's own view of his family?

SYNTHESIZING

9. What do you think is suggested by the stories about Thurber's odd relatives?
10. Why do you think Thurber chose to poke fun at his own family?

Understanding Literature (Questions for Discussion)

1. **Anecdote.** An **anecdote** is a brief story, usually with a specific point or moral. With an anecdote, a writer can support a persuasive argument or, as in the case of "The Night the Bed Fell," show a character's behavior. Find one or two anecdotes within the selection. How do they contribute to James Thurber's description of his family and the characters it contains?

2. **Farce.** A **farce** is a type of comedy that depends heavily on so-called low humor and on improbable, exaggerated, extreme situations or characters. "The Night the Bed Fell" contains many elements of farce. What elements of farce can you identify in the selection?

ANSWERS FOR REVIEWING THE SELECTION (CONT.)

INTERPRETING

Responses will vary. Possible responses are given.

5. Since Thurber's father is behind the closed door of the attic, it is difficult for people to rouse him and find out that he is not hurt.

6. Thurber thinks his cousin's fears are ridiculous. Thurber talks Briggs out of setting an alarm clock to go off every hour by trying to make him believe that Thurber is such a light sleeper he can hear his cousin stop breathing.

7. Thurber's bed flips over on him, his mother hears the noise and assumes that her husband's bed has collapsed on and possibly killed him, and the screaming that follows wakes up everyone else.

8. Thurber's father slowly rouses himself and comes down to see what is the matter. When he arrives, he cannot imagine why everyone is making such an uproar. Like Thurber himself, he seems to find the quirks of his various family members incomprehensible and rather ridiculous.

SYNTHESIZING

Responses will vary. Possible responses are given.

9. Thurber's childhood may have been full of interesting characters and bizarre events, which influenced his later writings.

10. His own family seems to have provided Thurber with ample material for amusing stories. He may have chosen to write about his family so that their personalities and lives would be recorded and they would live on in his work.

ANSWERS FOR UNDERSTANDING LITERATURE

▶See the evaluation forms for discussion, active listening, and oral communication, *Assessment Portfolio,* 7.11–7.14.

Responses will vary. Possible responses are given.

1. Anecdote. Thurber tells an anecdote about the way Briggs Beall tests him to see if he will notice when Briggs stops breathing, and another about his Aunt

(cont.)

ANSWERS FOR UNDERSTANDING LITERATURE (CONT.)

Gracie Shoaf who throws shoes down the hallway every night to scare off imaginary burglars. These and other anecdotes contribute to the impression that Thurber has a family full of strange characters who are always getting into funny situations.

▶**Teaching Note:** If they feel comfortable doing so, students may share their own anecdotes, either in a class discussion or in a writing assignment. They may use exaggeration to make their stories funnier, as Thurber has done.

2. Farce. Thurber exaggerates the behavior of his relatives and the pandemonium of the night the bed fell. An example of exaggeration is his statement that his mother "came to the immediate conclusion that her worst dread was realized: the big wooden bed upstairs had fallen on father." Her fears about the bed were

(cont.)

ANSWERS FOR UNDERSTANDING LITERATURE (CONT.)

probably not really her "worst dread," but Thurber's exaggeration has a humorous effect and makes her extreme reaction to the situation seem more believable. The way that all of the characters have completely different and self-centered interpretations of what the screaming is about is also farcical.

ANALYTIC SCALES FOR RESPONDING IN WRITING

Assign a score from 1 to 25 for each grading criterion below. (For more detailed evaluation, see the evaluation forms for writing, revising, and proofreading, *Assessment Portfolio,* 7.1–7.10.)

1. Press Release

• **Content/Unity.** The press release contains only the most important facts about the story.

• **Organization/Coherence.** The press release is organized in chronological order and clearly conveys the events in the story.

• **Language/Style.** The press release uses vivid and precise nouns, verbs, and modifiers.

• **Conventions.** The press release avoids errors in spelling, grammar, usage, mechanics, and manuscript form.

2. Family History

• **Content/Unity.** The family history contains enough information about the characters and events to bring the family to life.

• **Organization/Coherence.** The information in the family history is organized around one incident, which is described with a satisfying conclusion.

• **Language/Style.** The family history uses vivid and precise nouns, verbs, and modifiers.

• **Conventions.** The family history avoids errors in spelling, grammar, usage, mechanics, and manuscript form.

Responding in Writing

1. **Press Release.** In a press release, the important facts or points related to an event are presented to the media in a brief form. Suppose you had to tell a newspaper or television reporter about the events in "The Night the Bed Fell." Try your hand at writing a press release that includes only the most essential information while still capturing the humorous tone of the night.

2. **Family History.** "The Night the Bed Fell" is based on an actual event, and presumably real people, from James Thurber's family history. Think about your family. Identify some eccentric or interesting characters. Write a brief family history portraying an incident involving these characters.

Language Lab

Editing for Correct Use of Parentheses. Read the Language Arts Survey, 2.101, "Parentheses and Brackets." Then rewrite the sentences below using parentheses correctly.

1. James Thurber was affiliated for many years with *New Yorker* (a literary magazine based in New York.
2. He became skilled at writing casuals (,brief works that appear to have been very quickly, or casually, written.)
3. E. B. White (Who also worked for *New Yorker*), became Thurber's friend during this period.
4. Thurber's classic short story "The Secret Life of Walter Mitty"—which now appears as an entry in many dictionaries) first appeared in *New Yorker.*
5. His cartoons (,for White had earlier discovered this additional Thurber talent,) became popular as well.

Thinking Skills

Remembering and Visualizing. One way to experience a work of literature is to visualize its events and characters. Seeing them in your mind, as if through a camera's eye, makes these people and events more immediate. Recall and visualize a favorite section of "The Night the Bed Fell." Describe what you see and how you respond to it. Before beginning, you may want to read the Language Arts Survey, 4.5, "Remembering and Visualizing."

ANSWERS FOR LANGUAGE LAB

1. James Thurber was affiliated for many years with *New Yorker* (a literary magazine based in New York).

2. He became skilled at writing casuals (brief works that appear to have been very quickly, or casually, written).

(cont.)

ANSWERS FOR LANGUAGE LAB (CONT.)

3. E. B. White (who also worked for *New Yorker*) became Thurber's friend during this period.

4. Thurber's classic short story "The Secret Life of Walter Mitty" (which now appears as an entry in many dictionaries) first appeared in *New Yorker.*

5. His cartoons (for White had earlier discovered this additional Thurber talent) became popular as well.

ANSWERS FOR THINKING SKILLS

Students may recall certain specific details from Thurber's description, or they might remember mainly the humorous tone and mood of the story. Invite them to discuss which aspects of Thurber's writing make it most memorable for them.

PREREADING

Letter to *The Amherst Student*
by Robert Frost

About the Author

See the biography of **Robert Frost** on page 524.

About the Selection

After the success of his first few volumes of poetry, Robert Frost became a renowned public figure, one of the few poets in this century to make a living writing verse. He taught at several colleges, including Amherst College, in Massachusetts, and was much in demand as a visiting teacher, lecturer, and artist in residence. The following letter from Frost appeared in *The Amherst Student,* a college newspaper, on March 25, 1935, and was written in response to the paper's congratulating him on reaching his sixtieth birthday. Frost took the occasion of this response to provide some words of wisdom, his message to the young people of the Modern Age.

ADDITIONAL RESOURCES

Reader's Guide
- Selection Worksheet, 11.3

Assessment Portfolio
- Selection Check Test, 4.11.5
- Selection Test, 4.11.6

Essential Skills Practice Books
- *Study and Research,* 4.11, 4.14

ENRICHMENT ACTIVITIES

A small group of students can role play a panel of writers or other celebrated figures they admire and field questions from the rest of the class. Questions and answers should focus on the lessons the panel would like to pass on to the younger generation.

SUPPORT FOR LEP STUDENTS

Review with students the additional vocabulary below before they read the selection.

Additional Vocabulary

immodest—not shy or humble

gape—stare with the mouth open as in surprise or wonder

engrossing—very interesting, absorbing

GOALS/OBJECTIVES

Studying this lesson will enable students to

- have a positive experience reading the advice of an older author to a younger generation
- describe Robert Frost's literary accomplishments and the context of his letter to *The Amherst Student*
- recognize overgeneralizations and explain why such statements are faulty arguments
- define *essay* and recognize the elements that make a particular selection fit into this genre
- define *Modernism* and formulate an opinion of this artistic movement
- write a comparison-and-contrast essay

PREREADING NOTES

READER'S JOURNAL

Students should note their basic criteria for assessing the human condition. Why do they feel the way they do about the human condition?

THINKING SKILLS

Students can brainstorm common generalizations as a class and discuss the truth and fallacy of these phrases.

ANSWER TO GUIDED READING QUESTION

❶ He is impatient with the idea that the past represents a happier time than the present.

CROSS-CURRICULAR ACTIVITIES

Arts and Humanities. The myth of the "golden age" of the past and of the subsequent decline of human society is ancient, as Frost suggests, and can be found in such diverse sources as the "Theogony" of Hesiod (*circa* 8th century BC), the book of Genesis in the Old Testament, and John Milton's *Paradise Lost* (1667). Ask one group of students to research the myth of the "golden age" of humankind and its various manifestations in literature and art. Have another group of students investigate the contradictory myth concerning the ideas of "enlightenment" and "progress," in which education, science, and technology are viewed as the instruments by which humankind will attain a kind of golden age. Students can present their findings and discuss possible reasons why these myths remain powerful social influences.

VOCABULARY FROM THE SELECTION

dilation	integrity
engorge	mobilize
excruciation	vortex

READER'S JOURNAL

Do you think that life today is better or worse than it was in the past? Read the Language Arts Survey, 1.22, "Pro and Con Charts." Then write one of these sentences at the top of a piece of paper: "Life is better today than it was in the past" or "Life is worse today than it was in the past." Draw a line down the middle of the page and label the columns thus created *Pro* and *Con*. Then list reasons for and against the position listed at the top of the page.

THINKING SKILLS

Read the Language Arts Survey, 4.11, "Generalizing," and 4.14, "Avoiding Faulty Arguments." Then, as you read the selection, think about why it is an overgeneralization to say that "These are terrible times" or "This is the most difficult age so far in the history of humankind."

Letter to The Amherst Student

ROBERT FROST

It is very, very kind of the *Student* to be showing sympathy with me for my age. But sixty is only a pretty good age. It is not advanced enough. The great thing is to be advanced. Now ninety would be really well along and something to be given credit for.

Of what talk is Frost impatient? ❶

But speaking of ages, you will often hear it said that the age of the world we live in is particularly bad. I am impatient of such talk. We have no way of knowing that this age is one of the worst in the world's history. Arnold[1] claimed the honor for the age before this. Wordsworth[2] claimed it for the last but one. And so on back through literature. I say they claimed the honor for their ages. They claimed it rather for themselves. It is immodest of a man to think of himself as going down before the worst forces ever mobilized by God.

All ages of the world are bad—a great deal worse anyway than Heaven. If they weren't the world might just as well be Heaven at once and have it over with. One can safely say after from six to thirty thousand years of experience that the evident design is a situation here in which it will always be about equally hard to save your soul. Whatever progress may be taken to mean, it can't mean making the world any easier a place in which to save your soul—or if you dislike hearing your soul mentioned in open meeting, say your decency, your integrity.

1. **Arnold.** Matthew Arnold (1822–1888) was one of the foremost poets and critics of the Victorian Age in England.
2. **Wordsworth.** William Wordsworth (1770–1850) was one of the leading poets of the Romantic Movement in England.

WORDS FOR EVERYDAY USE:

mo • bi • lize (mō´bə līz´) *vi.*, become organized and ready, as for war

in • teg • ri • ty (in teg´rə tē) *n.*, uprightness, honesty, and sincerity

VOCABULARY IN CONTEXT

- The success of a charity event depends upon the ability of its coordinator to mobilize large numbers of volunteers.
- In a political world known for its schemers and hypocrites, the senator stood apart as an individual of high integrity.

Ages may vary a little. One may be a little worse than another. But it is not possible to get outside the age you are in to judge it exactly. Indeed it is as dangerous to try to get outside of anything as large as an age as it would be to engorge a donkey. Witness the many who in the attempt have suffered a dilation from which the tissues and the muscles of the mind have never been able to recover natural shape. They can't pick up anything delicate or small any more. They can't use a pen. They have to use a typewriter. And they gape in agony. They can write huge shapeless novels, huge gobs of raw sincerity bellowing with pain and that's all that they can write.

Fortunately we don't need to know how bad the age is. There is something we can always be doing without reference to how good or bad the age is. There is at least so much good in the world that it admits of form and the making of form. And not only admits of it, but calls for it. We people are thrust forward out of the suggestions of form in the rolling clouds of nature. In us nature reaches its height of form and through us exceeds itself. When in doubt there is always form for us to go on with. Anyone who has achieved the least form to be sure of it, is lost to the larger excruciations. I think it must stroke faith the right way. The artist [,] the poet [,] might be expected to be the most aware of such assurance. But it is really everybody's sanity to feel it and live by it. Fortunately, too, no forms are more engrossing [,] gratifying, comforting, staying than those lesser ones we throw off, like vortex rings of smoke, all our individual enterprise and needing nobody's co-operation; a basket, a letter, a garden, a room, an idea, a picture, a poem. For these we haven't to get a team together before we can play.

The background in hugeness and confusion shading away from where we stand into black and utter chaos; and against the background any small man-made figure of order and concentration. What pleasanter than that this should be so? Unless we are novelists or economists we don't worry about this confusion; we look out on [it] with an instrument or tackle it to reduce it. It is partly because we are afraid it might prove too much for us and our blend of democratic-republican-socialist-communist-anarchist party. But it is more because we like it, we were born to it, born used to it and have practical reasons for wanting it there. To me any little form I assert upon it is velvet,[3] as the saying is, and to be considered for how much more it is than nothing. If I were a Platonist[4] I should have to consider it, I suppose, for how much less it is than everything. ■

❶ *According to Frost, is it possible to judge the age one is in?*

❷ *What are the results of trying to judge something as large as an age?*

❸ *According to Frost, why do most people not worry about the confusion in the world?*

❹ *In what ways might nature reach its height through humanity? exceed itself through humanity?*

3. **is velvet.** Literally, like velvet cloth, soft and comfortable; figuratively, a luxury, something that brings comfort

4. **Platonist.** A follower of Plato, the ancient Greek philosopher who believed that things in the world were but reflections or imitations of pure forms that existed in the transcendent realm of ideas. Plato didn't think much of art, which he considered an imitation of nature and thus, to him, an imitation of an imitation of ideal form.

WORDS FOR EVERYDAY USE: **en • gorge** (en gôrj´) *vt.*, devour greedily; **di • la • tion** (dī lā´shən) *n.*, widening, expansion; **ex • cru • ci • a • tion** (ex cru´cī ā´shən) *n.*, torment; **vor • tex** (vôr´ teks) *n. pl.* swirling mass

ANSWERS TO GUIDED READING QUESTIONS

❶ No, one cannot get outside the current age in order to assess it accurately.

❷ Writers who attempt to judge an age lose the ability to focus on important details of the human condition.

❸ People ignore confusion in the world either because it is too overwhelming to fit into their belief systems or because they are used to it and actually prefer its presence.

❹ Frost suggests that it is through any and all acts of individual human creation that nature achieves and even exceeds its potential.

ANSWERS TO SELECTION CHECK TEST 4.11.5

EX. What is *The Amherst Student*?

It is the student newspaper published at Amherst College.

1. How old was Robert Frost when he wrote this letter?

He was sixty years old.

2. What past writers have proclaimed their eras the worst in history?

Among others, Matthew Arnold and William Wordsworth made this claim.

3. According to Frost, what does *progress* not mean?

***Progress* does not mean making the world an easier place to save one's soul.**

4. Who is "lost to the larger excrutiations" that plague humankind?

Everybody who produces creations of any kind is free from these torments.

5. What two professions are preoccupied with confusion?

Novelists and economists worry about the confusion of the world.

VOCABULARY IN CONTEXT

- People often remember the film "Cool Hand Luke" for the scene in which Paul Newman engorges over two dozen hard-boiled eggs.
- The dilation of the pupil is directly proportionate to the amount of ambient light.
- A true fan, Max took three days to recover from the excruciation of watching his favorite team lose in the playoffs.
- The vortex of a tornado fascinates some people, for despite its deadly force, it is a beautiful natural phenomenon.

RESPONDING TO THE SELECTION

Encourage students to expand their conception of the act of creation by defining the verb "to create" as broadly as possible.

ANSWERS FOR REVIEWING THE SELECTION

RECALLING

1. The paper had made a point of congratulating him on his sixtieth birthday.

2. Frost was impatient with talk about how the 1930s was a more difficult time to be alive than any other era in human history.

3. Frost thought that such writers could create only "huge shapeless novels, huge gobs of raw sincerity bellowing with pain."

4. Frost says that "people are thrust forward out of the suggestions of form in the rolling clouds of nature." In other words, people are one of the forms created by nature, as opposed to the shapeless chaos of the universe as a whole. Therefore, humans take comfort in form and order.

INTERPRETING

Responses will vary. Possible responses are given.

5. Frost himself did not think sixty was such a venerable age; he would be proud to be reaching ninety.

6. He believed that all ages were approximately the same in terms of the hardships they imposed on people.

7. The mental stretching needed to consider something so large as an entire era would destroy the artist's mind, rendering him or her incapable of appreciating subtle or beautiful things.

8. Each of these items is a form made by an individual human being. Creating such things is important because it is a way to bring order to a chaotic world.

(cont.)

Responding to the Selection

Frost says that "no forms are more engrossing, gratifying, comforting, staying than those lesser ones we throw off, like vortex rings of smoke, all our individual enterprise and needing nobody's co-operation: a basket, a letter, a garden, a room, an idea, a picture, a poem." What individual activities, like these, do you enjoy? Why is it fulfilling to bring a little form, a little order into the world by creating something on one's own? What did Frost want his readers, the students at Amherst, to do instead of worrying about how good or bad the age they lived in was?

Reviewing the Selection

RECALLING

1. What was the occasion that prompted Frost to write this letter to *The Amherst Student*?

2. With what sort of talk was Frost impatient?

3. What did Frost think of novelists who try in their works to capture a picture of the entire age?

4. According to Frost, where do people come from, and what do they find gratifying, comforting, and staying?

INTERPRETING

5. What did Frost think of turning sixty years old?

6. Why was Frost impatient with talk about how bad the age was?

7. What are the consequences, according to Frost, of an artist's trying to step outside his or her age and consider it as a whole?

8. What do baskets, letters, gardens, rooms, ideas, pictures, and poems have in common? Why is creating such things important?

SYNTHESIZING

9. What advice would Frost give to people for dealing with the "hugeness and confusion" of life?

10. Of what larger human propensity or inclination does Frost consider writing poetry to be one example? In an essay, Frost once described the writing of poetry as "a momentary stay against confusion." How can writing a poem, weaving a basket, planting a garden, or decorating a room help to make the world more sensible, comprehensible, meaningful? What does Frost think people should do instead of worry about large questions about the nature of the age in which they live?

ANSWERS FOR REVIEWING THE SELECTION (CONT.)

SYNTHESIZING

Responses will vary. Possible responses are given.

9. He would probably advise people not to try to comprehend or remedy the large-scale confusion in the world, but instead to create small pockets of order against the backdrop of chaos. He would probably also say that appreciating beauty and order in small things is important.

10. Writing a poem is one example of the human inclination to create form, or order. By drawing on one's reservoir of creativity, a person sees that confusion and disorder can be overcome. Bringing such order to one's individual world makes life seem more sensible and meaningful. In short, Frost believes that people should focus their attention on their own creative activities rather than trying to solve problems that are too large even to be understood.

Understanding Literature (Questions for Discussion)

1. **Essay.** An essay is a brief piece of nonfictional prose that treats a single subject and advances a single thesis, or main idea. What is the main idea of Frost's Letter to *The Amherst Student*?

2. **Modernism. Modernism** was a twentieth-century artistic movement characterized by a rejection of traditional forms and much experimentation. Some poets and other writers of the twentieth century rejected Modernism as a retreat from the central purpose of art, which they believed to be giving clear, sensible form to experience. Robert Frost was one such poet. He claimed, for example, that "Writing free verse is like playing tennis with the net down." Do you agree with Frost? Do you prefer traditional, representational art or the abstract, experimental work characteristic of much of the twentieth century? Do you prefer traditional verse that employs regular patterns of meter, rhyme, and stanza form, or do you prefer free verse, which rejects all these elements of form as too limiting or constraining? Why?

Responding in Writing

Comparison-and-Contrast Essay on Representational and Abstract Art. Choose one piece of traditional, representational art from this text, such as the Grant Wood painting on page 416, and one piece of modern abstract art, such as the Jackson Pollock on page 744. Write a brief essay in which you define representational and abstract art and discuss the two pieces you have chosen as examples of the two styles. Compare and contrast the two pieces and explain which you prefer and why.

PROJECT

Artistic Movements of the Twentieth Century. Using art history books, encyclopedias, dictionaries of art, and other reference works, identify and provide examples of the following movements and styles in twentieth-century art. Work with other students to prepare a poster describing each movement or style and providing an example of it. Examples can be photocopied from art books or found on postcards or posters available in art supply shops, frame shops, museum stores, and bookstores.

Abstract Expressionism	Impressionism
Dada, or Dadaism	Minimalism
Expressionism	Proletarian Art
Fauvism	Surrealism
Futurism	Trompe d'Oeil

ANSWERS FOR UNDERSTANDING LITERATURE

►See the evaluation forms for discussion, active listening, and oral communication, *Assessment Portfolio,* 7.11–7.14.

1. Essay. Frost's main idea is that people who try to understand the confusion of an entire era are wasting their lives; instead, they should bring meaning to their own individual lives with smaller creative acts that give rise to form or order in a small part of the world.

►**Teaching Note:** Students may wish to discuss or debate Frost's thesis. Is his description of human nature accurate? Is focusing on one's own creativity a worthwhile way to spend one's life? What problems are really too large to be solved through human effort, and what problems need to be addressed even though they may seem overwhelmingly large and complex?

2. Modernism. Students' answers will be highly subjective, but they should be encouraged to formulate articulate reasons to support their opinions.

►**Teaching Note:** Students might organize into teams to conduct a formal debate of this issue. They should keep in mind that the central question is "What is art?"

ANALYTIC SCALES FOR RESPONDING IN WRITING

Assign a score from 1 to 25 for each grading criterion below. (For more detailed evaluation, see the evaluation forms for writing, revising, and proofreading, *Assessment Portfolio,* 7.1–7.10.)

Comparison-and-Contrast Essay

- **Content/Unity.** The essay contains clear definitions of both types of art and offers a sensible explanation for why the student prefers one type over the other.
- **Organization/Coherence.** The essay has a clear introduction, body, and conclusion, with reasons to support each argument.
- **Language/Style.** The essay uses vivid and precise nouns, verbs, and modifiers.
- **Conventions.** The essay avoids errors in spelling, grammar, usage, mechanics, and manuscript form.

PROJECT NOTES

►See the worksheets and evaluation forms for projects, *Assessment Portfolio,* 7.20–7.23.

Artistic Movements of the Twentieth Century

- Some students may wish to prepare biographical sketches of artists who specialized in certain styles. They should include information about why the artist chose that style or how the artist would have defined *art.*

- Other students may wish to create their own artworks in the styles they have researched.

ADDITIONAL RESOURCES

READER'S GUIDE
- Selection Worksheet, 11.4

ASSESSMENT PORTFOLIO
- Selection Check Test, 4.11.7
- Selection Test, 4.11.8

ESSENTIAL SKILLS PRACTICE BOOKS
- *Language,* 2.4, 2.19

ENRICHMENT ACTIVITIES

Have students take turns reading sections of this speech aloud. Encourage them to be creative in the ways the use intonation, volume, and pace to convey meaning. Afterward, discussion should focus on the differences between hearing a speech given and reading it silently.

SUPPORT FOR LEP STUDENTS

While Faulkner's language is simpler in this speech than in many of his novels, students may still have difficulty with his sentence structure and vocabulary. Review with students the additional vocabulary below before they read the selection.

ADDITIONAL VOCABULARY

pinnacle—highest point
inexhaustible—tireless

VOCABULARY FROM THE SELECTION

commensurate	prevail
ephemeral	travail
endure	verity

PREREADING

Nobel Prize Acceptance Speech
by William Faulkner

ABOUT THE AUTHOR

William Faulkner (1897–1962) was born in New Albany, Mississippi, to a prominent Southern family and spent most of his life in Oxford, Mississippi. He dropped out of high school and, except for one year as a student at the University of Mississippi, had no further formal education. His first novel, *Soldier's Pay* (1926), published through the help of Sherwood Anderson, earned him an advance of two hundred dollars each on his next two novels. Recalling those events, he is reported to have said, "I liked that money," and to have noted that Anderson "worked only in the morning," which seemed to him "a mighty easy way to earn money." Whether or not it was easy, Faulkner spent most of his adult life earning his living as a writer. Most of his many novels are set in a mythical Yoknapatawpha County, Mississippi, and tell stories related to the decline of traditional Southern ways of life. Long, sonorous sentences with abundant details are one of the hallmarks of Faulkner's style. He also experimented considerably with **point of view**, telling the stories in some of his novels from the points of view of several different characters, including that of a mentally handicapped man in *The Sound and the Fury* (1929) and those of a mentally deficient poor white family in *As I Lay Dying* (1930). Much of Faulkner's fiction employed a **stream-of-consciousness** mode, presenting characters' random thoughts, feelings, and impressions in **interior monologues**. In addition to his novels, Faulkner wrote screenplays, the most notable of which are his adaptations of Ernest Hemingway's *To Have and Have Not* and Raymond Chandler's *The Big Sleep.* Faulkner's work was recognized with a Nobel Prize for literature and two Pulitzer Prizes, among other awards and honors. Other works by Faulkner include *The Marble Faun* (poetry, 1924), *Mosquitoes* (1927), *Sartoris* (1929), *Sanctuary* (1931), *Light in August* (1932), *Absalom, Absalom*! (1936), *Go Down, Moses* (1942), and *Intruder in the Dust* (1948).

ABOUT THE SELECTION

Faulkner received the Nobel Prize for literature in 1950 for his novel *As I Lay Dying.* The brief address that he delivered on accepting the prize presents a noble view of the role to be played by imaginative literature in the modern age.

GOALS/OBJECTIVES

Studying this lesson will enable students to

- appreciate a speech exploring the role of literature in the modern era
- describe Faulkner's literary accomplishments and explain the historical context of this speech
- recognize the aim of a speech or writing
- define *antithesis* and *parallelism* and explain how these rhetorical techniques contribute to a speech
- define *onomatopoeia* and recognize this technique in their reading
- identify adjectives and use colorful modifiers

READER'S JOURNAL

What roles can literature play in people's lives, besides simply providing entertainment? Write about this question in your journal.

LANGUAGE SKILLS

Read the Language Arts Survey, 2.4, "Concrete and Abstract Nouns." Then, as you read the selection, make a list of the abstract nouns that Faulkner uses to describe human qualities or characteristics.

Nobel Prize Acceptance Speech

WILLIAM FAULKNER

I feel that this award was not made to me as a man, but to my work—a life's work in the agony and sweat of the human spirit, not for glory and least of all for profit, but to create out of the materials of the human spirit something which did not exist before. So this award is only mine in trust.[1] It will not be difficult to find a dedication for the money part of it commensurate with the purpose and significance of its origin. But I would like to do the same with the acclaim too, by using this moment as a pinnacle from which I might be listened to by the young men and women already dedicated to the same anguish and travail, among whom is already that one who will some day stand here where I am standing.

Our tragedy today is a general and universal physical fear so long sustained by now that we can even bear it. There are no longer problems of the spirit. There is only the question: When will I be blown up? Because of this, the young man or woman writing today has forgotten the problems of the human heart in conflict with itself which alone can make good writing because only that is worth writing about, worth the agony and the sweat.

He must learn them again. He must teach himself that the basest of all things is to be afraid; and, teaching himself that, forget it forever, leaving no room in his workshop for anything but the old verities and truths of the heart, the old universal truths lacking which any story is ephemeral and doomed—love and honor and pity and pride and compassion and sacrifice. Until he does so, he labors under a curse. He writes not of love but of lust, of defeats in which nobody loses anything of value, of victories without hope and,

1. **in trust.** In another's care

❶ *What have young writers forgotten today?*

❷ *What is the basest of all things?*

WORDS FOR EVERYDAY USE:

com • men • su • rate (kə men´shoor it) *adj.,* equal in measure or size, proportionate

trav • ail (trə vāl) *n.,* very hard work, toil

ver • i • ty (vər´ə tē) *n.,* principle or belief taken to be fundamentally and permanently true

e • phem • er • al (e fem´ər əl) *adj.,* short-lived, transitory

PREREADING NOTES

READER'S JOURNAL

Students can begin by writing about the different ways in which literature has affected their own lives.

LANGUAGE SKILLS

Students should list some of the following abstract nouns: love, honor, pity, pride, compassion, sacrifice, and endurance.

ANSWERS TO GUIDED READING QUESTIONS

❶ They forget that the only good writing is writing that has as its subject the internal struggles of human beings.

❷ Fear is the basest of all things.

ANSWERS TO SELECTION CHECK TEST 11.7

EX. What was the occasion of Faulkner's speech?

He gave this speech upon accepting the Nobel Prize for literature.

1. What did Faulkner "create out of the materials of the human spirit"?

He created something that had not previously existed.

2. Who does Faulkner hope will listen to his speech?

He hopes young writers will hear his words.

3. What must a person do when he has learned that fear is base?

He or she must forget this fact immediately.

4. What is the fate of humankind in Faulkner's opinion?

Humankind will not only endure, but prevail.

5. Who can play a central role in ensuring the survival of humankind?

Poets and writers can be invaluable supports in helping humankind to survive.

VOCABULARY IN CONTEXT

- Alicia decided to quit her job because the pay was not commensurate with the amount of work required of her.
- The image of a struggling artist suffering many travails to produce great art is a relatively recent popular myth.
- Ancient Greek tragedies continue to be produced today because they contain timeless verities regarding the human condition.
- Japanese haiku poetry is renowned for capturing ephemeral emotions in very few words.

worst of all, without pity or compassion. His griefs grieve on no universal bones, leaving no scars. He writes not of the heart but of the glands.

Until he relearns these things, he will write as though he stood among and watched the end of man. I decline to accept the end of man. It is easy enough to say that man is immortal simply because he will endure: that when the last ding-dong of doom has clanged and faded from the last worthless rock hanging tideless in the last red and dying evening, that even then there will still be one more sound: that of his puny inexhaustible voice, still talking. I refuse to accept this. I believe that man will not merely endure: he will prevail. He is immortal, not because he alone among creatures has an inexhaustible voice, but because he has a soul, a spirit capable of compassion and sacrifice and endurance. The poet's, the writer's, duty is to write about these things. It is his privilege to help man endure by lifting his heart, by reminding him of the courage and honor and hope and pride and compassion and pity and sacrifice which have been the glory of his past. The poet's voice need not merely be the record of man, it can be one of the props, the pillars to help him endure and prevail. ■

Responding to the Selection

Speaking at the height of the cold war, a few years after the end of World War II and the dropping of atomic bombs on Hiroshima and Nagasaki, Faulkner said, "There are no longer problems of the spirit. There is only the question: When will I be blown up?" Do you feel that the world is more or less dangerous today than it was when Faulkner gave his address in 1950? Why do you think Faulkner wanted his listeners not to live in fear but rather to remember the "old verities and truths of the heart"?

Words for Everyday Use:

en • dure (en door´) *vi.* continue in existence, last, remain

pre • vail (prē vāl) *vi.* gain advantage or mastery, be victorious, triumph

Cross-curricular Activities

Social Studies. Faulkner's ideas about the role that a writer can play in his or her society are strongly predicated upon the individual's right to freedom of speech. Ask students to investigate the issues of freedom of speech and of censorship in different societies at different points in time. Topics might include the following: the First Amendment of the United States Constitution; legal trials involving censorship of books; the authority of the English Home Secretary to ban controversial works; and the rating system used by the movie industry to warn viewers of potentially offensive content matter. Students can present their findings in class and discuss their ideas on what limits, if any, should be placed on the guarantees of freedom of speech. Is there ever a time in which certain types of speech should be curtailed? If so, when? If not, why not?

Additional Questions and Activities

Ask students to use Faulkner's conception of a writer's "duty" to evaluate contemporary art, including painting, music, and film as well as literature. Which works of art do students believe meet Faulkner's dictum that art must concern itself with "the old verities and truths of the heart"? What contemporary writers do the students admire? Why do they admire these writers? Would students define the role of the writer or artist differently than Faulkner did? If so, how would they redefine this role?

Responding to the Selection

You might ask students to consider how the ideas expressed by Robert Frost in his letter to *The Amherst Student* either support or contradict Faulkner's views about the value of literature.

Vocabulary in Context

- Even before they left the island, they knew their memory of the time spent in such a paradise would endure for years to come.
- George's opinions often prevailed simply because he spoke louder and longer than anyone else.

Reviewing the Selection

RECALLING

1. Faulkner said that he felt that the Nobel Prize was given not to him as a man but to what?
2. According to the first sentence of the address, what did Faulkner attempt to do in his fiction?
3. According to Faulkner, what is the "general and universal physical fear" with which people in the modern age live?
4. According to Faulkner, what elements must any story have if it is not to be ephemeral and doomed?

INTERPRETING

5. A carpenter works in wood. A blacksmith works in metal. In what, according to the first sentence of Faulkner's address, does a writer work? What human characteristic, according to Faulkner, gives rise to writing and to the immortality of humankind?
6. Why did Faulkner say that the award was "only [his] in trust"? To whom does he address his comments? What does he want to communicate to these people?
7. According to Faulkner, what have young writers today forgotten? Why?
8. According to Faulkner, why must a story deal with "the old verities and truths of the heart"?

SYNTHESIZING

9. Despite the possibility of universal annihilation created by the advent of nuclear weapons, Faulkner remained optimistic about the human capacity not only to endure but to prevail. Why? What reason does he give for his optimism?
10. What, according to Faulkner, is a writer's duty? What can writers do to be "the props, the pillars to help [human beings] endure and prevail"?

Understanding Literature (Questions for Discussion)

1. **Aim.** A writer's **aim** is the primary purpose that his or her work is meant to achieve. What do you think Faulkner wanted to achieve in his Nobel Prize acceptance speech? What was his purpose, or aim?
2. **Alliteration. Alliteration** is the repetition of initial consonant sounds. Faulkner's writing makes frequent use of alliteration. Find three examples in the selection.

ANSWERS FOR REVIEWING THE SELECTION

RECALLING

1. He felt that the prize was awarded to his life's work rather than to him personally.
2. He attempted to "create out of the materials of the human spirit something which did not exist before."
3. They live in fear that they will be blown up in a nuclear war.
4. To be of lasting value, a story must involve "love and honor and pity and pride and compassion and sacrifice."

INTERPRETING

Responses will vary. Possible responses are given.

5. Faulkner believes that the material of writing is "the agony and sweat of the human spirit." He says that humankind is immortal because people have souls and are capable of love, honor, pity, and compassion; these characteristics are also the appropriate subjects for writing.
6. He is only holding the award until it is passed on to the next generation of writers. He wants these young writers to remember that writing should deal with the great questions of the human soul, rather than on the fear of physical annihilation in the atomic age.
7. In their obsession with the threat of nuclear war, they have forgotten "the problems of the human heart in conflict with itself."
8. These "old verities" are the only subjects with any depth or enduring value; without them, a story deals only with fear, lust, or other petty emotions.

SYNTHESIZING

Responses will vary. Possible responses are given.

9. Faulkner is optimistic because human beings have souls—they are capable of noble feelings and actions.
10. A writer's duty is to help the human spirit to prevail by exploring the aspects of the soul that make it immortal, such as love and compassion.

ANSWERS FOR UNDERSTANDING LITERATURE

► See the evaluation forms for discussion, active listening, and oral communication, *Assessment Portfolio,* 7.11–7.14.

Responses will vary. Possible responses are given.

1. Aim. Faulkner wanted to remind young writers that the purpose of writing is to explore the depths of the human soul, not superficial topics such as the fear of nuclear war or hopeless and compassionless victories.

► **Teaching Note:** Students may work in pairs or small groups to discuss their opinions of Faulkner's definition of worthwhile writing.

2. Alliteration. Examples include "not **m**ade to **m**e as a **m**an," "Our **t**ragedy **t**oday," "**f**orget it **f**orever," "**p**ity and **p**ride," "not of **l**ove but of **l**ust," "last **d**ing**d**ong of **d**oom," "**c**apable of **c**ompassion," and "the **p**rops, the **p**illars to help him endure and **p**revail."

(cont.)

ANSWERS FOR UNDERSTANDING LITERATURE (CONT.)

3. Antithesis. Examples include "There are no longer problems of the spirit. There is only the question: When will I be blown up?"; "not of love but of lust"; and "not of the heart but of the glands."
4. Onomatopoeia. Examples include the words *dingdong* and *clanged.*
5. Parallelism. Examples include "love and honor and pity and pride and compassion and sacrifice"; "of defeats in which nobody loses anything of value, of victories without hope"; and "easy enough to say that man is immortal simply because he will endure: that when the last dingdong of doom has clanged . . . that even then there will be one more sound."

ANALYTIC SCALES FOR RESPONDING IN WRITING

Assign a score from 1 to 25 for each grading criterion below. (For more detailed evaluation, see the evaluation forms for writing, revising, and proofreading, *Assessment Portfolio,* 7.1–7.10.)

Biographical Sketch

- **Content/Unity.** The sketch includes a complete description of the person's actions and gives sensible reasons why the student interprets these actions as virtuous.
- **Organization/Coherence.** The sketch is well organized and builds to a logical conclusion.
- **Language/Style.** The sketch uses vivid and precise nouns, verbs, and modifiers.
- **Conventions.** The sketch avoids errors in spelling, grammar, usage, mechanics, and manuscript form.

ANSWERS FOR LANGUAGE LAB

Adjectives are underlined in each phrase. The words the adjectives modify are in brackets.

[It] is easy enough
[man] is immortal
last [dingdong]
last worthless [rock]
last red and dying [evening]
one more [sound]
puny inexhaustible [voice]

3. **Antithesis. Antithesis** is a rhetorical technique in which opposing ideas are presented in balanced grammatical forms, as in the sentence "To err is human, to forgive divine." Find three examples of antithesis in the selection.

4. **Onomatopoeia. Onomatopoeia** is the use of words that sound like what they name or describe. Examples of onomatopoeia include the words *murmur* and *buzz.* What examples of onomatopoeia can you find in the selection?

5. **Parallelism. Parallelism** is a rhetorical technique in which a writer emphasizes the equal value or weight of two or more ideas by expressing them in the same grammatical form. Find examples of parallelism in Faulkner's speech that involve using the coordinating conjunction *and* and the relative pronoun *that.*

Responding in Writing

Biographical Sketch. According to Faulkner, "the glory" of our past has been our capacity for "courage and honor and hope and pride and compassion and pity and sacrifice." Think of someone you know who has at some time demonstrated one of these virtues. Write a brief narrative in which you describe what that person did and why you consider his or her actions virtuous.

Language Lab

Colorful Adjectives. Read the Language Arts Survey, 2.19, "Adjectives and Articles," and 2.35, "Using Colorful Modifiers." Then identify all the adjectives, along with the nouns that they modify, in the following sentence from Faulkner's speech:

> "It is easy enough to say that man is immortal simply because he will endure: that when the last dingdong of doom has clanged and faded from the last worthless rock hanging tideless in the last red and dying evening, that even then there will still be one more sound: that of his inexhaustible voice, still talking."

PROJECT

Themes in Literature. Faulkner said that it was the poet's and writer's duty to write about the human spirit's capacity for compassion, sacrifice, endurance, courage, honor, hope, pride, and pity. Work with other students to find short works of literature that illustrate each of these themes. Hold a reading of these works, following each reading with a discussion of the virtue that the work illustrates.

PROJECT NOTES

▶ See the worksheets and evaluation forms for projects, *Assessment Portfolio,* 7.20–7.23.

Themes in Literature

- Some students may wish to locate art that illustrates these virtues, or to create their own artwork to illustrate literature selections.
- Remind students that good oral reading requires practice, and that they should become thoroughly familiar with the works they intend to read aloud before sharing them with an audience.

PREREADING

"Walden"
by E. B. White

About the Author

E. B. White (1899–1985) was born in Mount Vernon, New York and as he explained, ". . . was a busy writer long before [he] went into long pants." He studied English at Cornell University and was editor-in-chief of the *Cornell Daily Sun.* After graduating in 1921, White worked for newspapers and an advertising agency before becoming a regular contributor to *The New Yorker* in 1927. His witty essays in the "Notes and Comment" column helped shape the magazine's early success. In 1929 he published a book of poetry, *The Lady is Cold,* and *Is Sex Necessary?,* a collection of humorous essays by White and his colleague, James Thurber. In 1938 White and his wife, Katharine Angell, an editor for *The New Yorker,* moved to a farm in Maine where White later received his inspiration to write the children's stories, *Stuart Little, Charlotte's Web,* and *The Trumpet of the Swan.* He wrote the "One Man's Meat" column for *Harper's* and contributed often to *The New Yorker.* White also continued to publish essay and poetry collections as well as a revision of William Strunk, Jr.'s *The Elements of Style.* In 1978, E. B. White received a Pulitzer Prize Committee special citation in recognition of his life's work.

About the Selection

In this satirical essay, E. B. White responds to Henry David Thoreau's important Transcendental work, *Walden,* which was written by Thoreau from the journals he kept during his stay on Walden Pond between 1845 and 1847. Thoreau's work focused on many ideas, but a central point was that people need considerably fewer material comforts than they think they do to live a full life. Thoreau also felt that he, and others, could learn and experience the truly essential realities and requirements of life by observing nature. As E. B. White visits Concord, Massachusetts, site of Walden Pond, he questions the validity of Thoreau's ideas in today's world.

ADDITIONAL RESOURCES

Reader's Guide
- Selection Worksheet, 11.5

Assessment Portfolio
- Selection Check Test, 4.11.9
- Selection Test, 4.11.10

Essential Skills Practice Books
- *Study and Research,* 4.8

ENRICHMENT ACTIVITIES

Students might read parts of Thoreau's *Walden* in order to understand all of the allusions to this work that White makes in his satirical essay.

SUPPORT FOR LEP STUDENTS

Review with students the additional vocabulary below before they read the selection.

Additional Vocabulary

imbibe—drink
wayside—roadside
degenerate—lose former normal or higher qualities
wicket—small wire arch
proprietor—owner

VOCABULARY FROM THE SELECTION

accumulate
congeniality
cryptic
distillation
game
immemorial
impetuous
implement
inauspicious
intervening
nimble
pertinence
sheer
sojourn
steadfastness
stupefaction
undulate

GOALS/OBJECTIVES

Studying this lesson will enable students to

- enjoy a satirical essay
- describe White's literary accomplishments and explain the historical significance of his writing
- define *simile* and recognize similes in literature
- define *tone* and identify the tone of works they read

PREREADING NOTES

READER'S JOURNAL

Students might write about their original ideas and expectations in a serious tone, and then describe their reactions upon arrival in a satiric tone or vice versa.

THINKING SKILLS

Similarities: The evening sky White sees on arriving in Concord had the "same everlasting great look" as Thoreau described (page 771). The robins White hears "still love the elms of New England villages at sundown" (page 772).

Differences: White describes the sound of cars as "wholly unlike that of a train," which was a sound familiar to Thoreau (page 772). In place of a house, White finds "four small granite posts" on the site of Thoreau's home (page 774).

▶**Teaching Note:** Note that White also describes apparent similarities ironically, in order to illustrate differences between his Walden and Thoreau's, as, for example, when White remarks that "Concord hasn't changed much . . . the farm implements still have the upper hand" (page 770).

READER'S JOURNAL

Think about a recent visit you made to a place you knew through literature or another source. Describe the ideas and expectations you had before reaching your destination. How did the visit confirm or unseat your initial assumptions?

THINKING SKILLS

"Walden" contains many elements of a comparison-contrast essay. Read the Language Arts Survey, 4.8, "Comparing and Contrasting." Then list two similarities and two differences between E. B. White's experience of Walden today and his view of Thoreau's Walden.

"Walden"

E. B. WHITE

June 1939

Miss Nims, take a letter[1] to Henry David Thoreau. Dear Henry: I thought of you the other afternoon as I was approaching Concord doing fifty on Route 62. That is a high speed at which to hold a philosopher in one's mind, but in this century we are a nimble bunch.

Why was White journeying to Concord? What does he say to Thoreau about Walden? ❶

On one of the lawns in the outskirts of the village a woman was cutting the grass with a motorized lawn mower. What made me think of you was that the machine had rather got away from her, although she was game enough, and in the brief glimpse I had of the scene it appeared to me that the lawn was mowing the lady. She kept a tight grip on the handles, which throbbed violently with every explosion of the one-cylinder motor, and as she sheered around bushes and lurched along at a reluctant trot behind her impetuous servant, she looked like a puppy who had grabbed something that was too much for him. Concord hasn't changed much, Henry: the farm implements and the animals still have the upper hand.

I may as well admit that I was journeying to Concord with the deliberate intention of visiting your woods; for although I have never knelt at the grave of a philosopher nor placed wreaths on moldy poets, and have often gone a mile out of my way to avoid some place of historical interest, I have always wanted to see Walden Pond. The account which you left of your sojourn there is, you will be amused to learn, a document of increasing pertinence; each year it seems to gain a little headway, as the world loses ground. We may all be transcendental[2] yet,

1. **take a letter.** Write down the letter dictated
2. **transcendental.** Refers to the Transcendental movement in New England in the nineteenth century. The philosophical ideas of Ralph Waldo Emerson and Henry David Thoreau were based on a search for reality through spiritual intuition.

WORDS FOR EVERYDAY USE:

nim • ble (nim´ bəl) *adj.,* mentally quick
game (gām) *adj.,* having spirit or enthusiasm
sheer (shir) *vi.,* turn sharply aside from a course
im • pet • u • ous (im pech´ ōō əs) *adj.,* rushing with force or violence
im • ple • ment (im´plə mənt) *n.,* tool
so • journ (sō´ jurn) *n.,* brief visit
per • ti • nence (pur´tə nəns) *n.,* relevance

ANSWER TO GUIDED READING QUESTION

❶ White is going to Concord to visit Walden Pond, and he says that the ideas expressed in *Walden* are becoming more relevant as time goes on.

CROSS-CURRICULAR ACTIVITIES

Social Studies. Have students investigate the Transcendental movement in America during the first half of the nineteenth century. In addition to reading selections of Thoreau's *Walden,* students may wish to consult Ralph Waldo Emerson's treatise, *Nature,* or research the Brook Farm Institute, a self-supporting community which attempted to put Transcendental philosophy into practice. Students might debate whether or not Transcendentalism continues to play an important, if invisible, role in American life today.

VOCABULARY IN CONTEXT

- By successfully acting out situations suggested by the audience, the improvisational actors demonstrated how nimble they were.
- Although he had never parachuted before, Jim said he was game to give it a try.
- We only avoided the renegade ship by sheering quickly away from the dock.
- His choice of colleges was an impetuous one, and he regretted it once he realized his options.
- Chimpanzees use long blades of grass as effective implements to draw ants out of anthills.
- Our unplanned sojourn in Chicago ended once the airport reopened.
- Amy dismissed Sheila's comments as having no pertinence to the discussion at hand.

whether we like it or not. As our common complexities increase, any tale of individual simplicity (and yours is the best written and the cockiest) acquires a new fascination; as our goods accumulate, but not our well-being, your report of an existence without material adornment takes on a certain awkward credibility.

My purpose in going to Walden Pond, like yours, was not to live cheaply or to live dearly there, but to transact some private business with the fewest obstacles. Approaching Concord, doing forty, doing forty-five, doing fifty, the steering wheel held snug in my palms, the highway held grimly in my vision, the crown of the road now serving me (on the righthand curves), now defeating me (on the lefthand curves), I began to rouse myself from the stupefaction which a day's motor journey induces. It was a delicious evening, Henry, when the whole body is one sense, and imbibes delight through every pore, if I may coin a phrase. Fields were richly brown where the harrow,[3] drawn by the stripped Ford, had lately sunk its teeth; pastures were green; and overhead the sky had that same everlasting great look which you will find on page 144 of the Oxford pocket edition:[4] I could feel the road entering me, through tire, wheel, spring, and cushion: shall I not have intelligence with earth too? Am I not partly leaves and vegetable mold myself?—a man of infinite horsepower, yet partly leaves.

Stay with me on 62 and it will take you into Concord. As I say, it was a delicious evening. The snake had come forth to die in a bloody S on the highway, the wheel upon its head, its bowels flat now and exposed. The turtle had come up too to cross the road and die in the attempt, its hard shell smashed under the rubber blow, its intestinal yearning (for the other side of the road) forever squashed. There was a sign by the wayside which announced that the road had a "cotton surface." You wouldn't know what that is, but neither, for that matter, did I. There is a cryptic ingredient in many of our modern improvements—we are awed and pleased without knowing quite what we are enjoying. It is something to be traveling on a road with a cotton surface.

❶ *What is cryptic about modern improvements? What point is White making about modern improvements?*

The civilization round Concord today is an odd distillation of city, village, farm, and manor. The houses, yards, fields look not quite suburban, not quite rural. Under the bronze beech and the blue spruce of the departed baron grazes the milch[5] goat of the heirs. Under the porte-cochère[6] stands the reconditioned station wagon; under the grape arbor sit the puppies for sale. But why do men degenerate ever? What makes families run out?

It was June and everywhere June was publishing her immemorial stanza; in the lilacs, in the syringa,[7] in the freshly edged paths and the sweetness of moist beloved gardens, and the little wire wickets that preserve the tulips' front. Farmers were already moving the fruits of their toil into their yards, arranging the rhubarb, the

3. **harrow.** Frame with spikes drawn by a horse or tractor and used for breaking up and leveling plowed ground
4. **Page 144 of the Oxford pocket edition.** Edition of Thoreau's *Walden* published by the Oxford University Press
5. **milch.** Milk-giving
6. **porte-cochère.** Covered driveway
7. **syringa.** Shrub or tree with large clusters of small white flowers

WORDS FOR EVERYDAY USE:

ac • cu • mu • late (ə kyōōm´ yōō lāt´) *vi.*, pile up over time
stu • pe • fac • tion (stōō´pə fak´shən) *n.*, state of dullness or lethargy
cryp • tic (krip´tik) *adj.*, having a hidden meaning; baffling
dis • til • la • tion (dis´tə lā´shən) *n.*, something separated out into parts
im • me • mo • ri • al (im´me môr´ē əl) *adj.*, something too old to be remembered

ANSWER TO GUIDED READING QUESTION

❶ The improvements are cryptic because most people don't fully understand what they mean. White is suggesting that these improvements are happening to us whether we want them to or not; people do not decide to make their lives more complex with modern technology but are carried along with the tide.

LITERARY TECHNIQUE

Irony. Irony is a difference between appearance and reality. The literary critic Wayne Booth has called irony an "aggressively intellectual exercise that . . . accuses other men not only of wrong beliefs but of being wrong at their very foundations and blind to what these foundations imply." Ask students to discuss whether White's essay requires the reader to find fault with Thoreau's ideas and beliefs in order to side with White. Is White satirizing modern society or Thoreau's Transcendental vision of the world? After reading this essay, do students have the impression that White likes and respects Thoreau's work?

CROSS-CURRICULAR ACTIVITIES

Social Studies. White's essay presents a contrast between the Concord of his day and the Concord of Thoreau's time. Ask students to research the history of the town or city in which they live in order to discover what it was like in 1845, when Thoreau lived at Walden Pond. Have them consider the physical size and layout of the town, its major sources of income, the number and backgrounds of its inhabitants, as well as its social and political life. Students might formulate their information in a comparision-contrast essay format, juxtaposing the past and the present.

VOCABULARY IN CONTEXT

- When Mr. Sanchez moved, he discovered how many things he had accumulated over the years.
- Ellis had to work late so often that he could only gaze in stupefaction when his boss said to go home early.
- Egyptian hieroglyphics remained cryptic until a key to their interpretation was discovered.
- The movie was so vacuous that a distillation of its plot and message would take no more than a single sentence to express.
- Family stories often have immemorial origins and are repeated so frequently that people accept them without questioning their truth.

Answers to Guided Reading Questions

❶ White says that the philosophical spirit is still alive as he observes some boys in a vacant lot constructing a rude shelter that reminds him of Thoreau's cabin at Walden Pond. White is being satiric; he knows that the boys are not engaging in the activity for any philosophical purpose.

❷ White contrasts the simple and soothing sound of a train, which "whistles once or twice sadly and is gone," with the cacophonous sounds of automobiles, which "buzz, cease, pause, start, shift, stop, halt, brake."

Cross-curricular Activities

Mathematics and Sciences. White makes reference to the flora and fauna of Concord often in this essay, in part to draw similarities with Thoreau's descriptions of nature, and in part to suggest that a person can live among other people and still remain aware of his or her environment. Have students make a list of the different kinds of flora and fauna which live in their immediate surroundings. Ask them to be specific in naming animals and vegetation. Which types of flora and fauna are found in abundance? Which are rareties? Which are native to the area and which have been introduced by humans? When students have compiled their lists, have them comment on which plants or creatures were unfamiliar to them. Did compiling this list make them more conscious of the natural world around them?

Literary Note

White uses onomatopoeia, a literary technique in which words are chosen because they sound like what they mean, in the phrases "they buzz, cease, pause, start, shift, stop, halt, brake" and "the toc toc of ping pong balls."

asparagus, the strictly fresh eggs on the painted stands under the little shed roofs with the patent shingles. And though it was almost a hundred years since you had taken your ax and started cutting out your home on Walden Pond, I was interested to observe that the philosophical spirit was still alive in Massachusetts: in the center of a vacant lot some boys were assembling the framework of a rude shelter, their whole mind and skill concentrated in the rather inauspicious helter-skeleton of studs and rafters. They too were escaping from town, to live naturally, in a rich blend of savagery and philosophy.

What does White say is still alive? What observation causes him to say this? Is White serious or satiric here? ❶

That evening, after supper at the inn, I strolled out into the twilight to dream my shapeless transcendental dreams and see that the car was locked up for the night (first open the right front door, then reach over, straining, and pull up the handles of the left rear and the left front till you hear the click, then the handle of the right rear, then shut the right front but open it again, remembering that the key is still in the ignition switch, remove the key, shut the right front again with a bang, push the tiny keyhole cover to one side, insert key, turn, and withdraw). It is what we all do, Henry. It is called locking the car. It is said to confuse thieves and keep them from making off with the laprobe. Four doors to lock behind one robe. The driver himself never uses a laprobe, the free movement of his legs being vital to the operation of the vehicle; so that when he locks the car it is a pure and unselfish act. I have in my life gained very little essential heat from laprobes, yet I have ever been at pains to lock them up.

What sounds does White describe? In what way do the two sounds differ? ❷

The evening was full of sounds, some of which would have stirred your memory. The robins still love the elms of New England villages at sundown. There is enough of the thrush in them to make song inevitable at the end of day, and enough of the tramp to make them hang round the dwelling of men. A robin, like many another American, dearly loves a white house with green blinds. Concord is still full of them.

Your fellow-townsmen were stirring abroad—not many afoot, most of them in their cars; and the sound which they made in Concord at evening was a rustling and a whispering. The sound lacks steadfastness and is wholly unlike that of a train. A train, as you know who lived so near the Fitchburg line, whistles once or twice sadly and is gone, trailing a memory in smoke, soothing to ear and mind. Automobiles, skirting a village green, are like flies that have gained the inner ear—they buzz, cease, pause, start, shift, stop, halt, brake, and the whole effect is a nervous polytone[8] curiously disturbing.

As I wandered along, the toc toc of ping pong balls drifted from an attic window. In front of the Reuben Brown house a Buick was drawn up. At the wheel, motionless, his hat upon his head, a man sat, listening to Amos and Andy[9] on the radio (it is a drama of many scenes and without an end). The deep voice of Andrew Brown, emerging from the car, although it originated more than two hundred miles away, was unstrained by

8. **polytone.** Variety of sounds
9. **Amos and Andy.** Radio show popular in the 1930's and 1940's

Words for Everyday Use: **in • aus • pi • cious** (in´ô spish´əs) *adj.,* unfavorable, unlucky **stead • fast • ness** (sted´fast´nes) *n.,* quality of being firm, fixed, or settled

Vocabulary in Context

- The team came back to win the game after an inauspicious start.
- In giving the award, the speaker praised the recipient for her steadfastness in the face of daunting obstacles.

Walden Pond

distance. When you used to sit on the shore of your pond on Sunday morning, listening to the church bells of Acton and Concord, you were aware of the excellent filter of the intervening atmosphere. Science has attended to that, and sound now maintains its intensity without regard for distance. Properly sponsored, it goes on forever.

A fire engine, out for a trial spin, roared past Emerson's house, hot with readiness for public duty. Over the barn roofs the martins dipped and chittered. A swarthy daughter of an asparagus grower, in culottes,[10] shirt, and bandanna, pedaled past on her bicycle. It was indeed a delicious evening, and I returned to the inn (I believe it was your house once) to rock with the old ladies on the concrete veranda.

Next morning early I started afoot for Walden, out Main Street and down Thoreau, past the depot and the Minuteman Chevrolet Company. The morning was fresh, and in a bean field along the way I flushed an agriculturalist, quietly studying his beans. Thoreau Street soon joined Number 126, an artery of the State. We number our highways nowadays, our speed being so great we can remember little of their quality or character and are lucky to remember their number. (Men have an indistinct notion that if they keep up this activity long enough all will at length ride somewhere, in next to no time.) Your pond is on 126.

I knew I must be nearing your woodland retreat when the Golden Pheasant lunchroom came into view—Sealtest ice cream, toasted sandwiches, hot frankfurters, waffles, tonics, and lunches. Were I the proprietor, I should add rice, Indian meal, and molasses—just for old time's sake. The Pheasant, incidentally, is for sale: a chance for some nature lover who wishes to set himself up beside a pond in the

10. **culottes.** Trousers that resemble a skirt

Additional Questions and Activities

- What does White mean when he says of sound in the modern era, "Properly sponsored, it goes on forever"?
- What is humorous about White's statement that he "flushed an agriculturalist"?

Answers. White is referring to radio technology; a radio program that is financially supported by corporate sponsors can potentially be heard all around the world. The statement about the agriculturalist is humorous because the word *flushed* is usually used to describe birds being scared out of hiding.

Cross-curricular Activities

Arts and Humanities. Thoreau's *Walden* is closely related to the literary tradition of pastoral poetry and prose, the earliest examples of which include the "Idylls" of Theocritus and the "Eclogues" of Virgil. Pastoral literature portrays an escape from city life into country pleasures and, especially in its later form, served as a vehicle for social commentary. Ask students to research the pastoral tradition in literature, keeping in mind the question: Why did authors use country life to comment on urban civilization? Students may wish to read some of the "Idylls" and the "Eclogues" as a basis for discussing White's essay and Thoreau's book.

Additional Questions and Activities

Why does White go into such detail in describing how he locks his car each night? In what way does this description relate to his theme of the complexity of modern life? Is locking the car a serious example of modern complexity? Why, or why not?

Answers. He describes locking his car in excruciating detail in order to show how many individual steps are involved and how "complex" the activity is when thus broken down. Since Thoreau lived before cars were invented, White is making the point that locking a car is something Thoreau would not have experienced, and that it might seem to him a symptom of modern complexity. The example is not a serious one; there were many everyday activities in Thoreau's day that involved just as many steps and were therefore just as "complex" as locking a car in White's day.

Answers to Guided Reading Questions

❶ White compares the life of the trailer people—including the solitude and escape from city life—to Thoreau's self-imposed exile from modern life. White says that instead of finding philosophical satisfaction in solitude, these trailer people simply "get bogged deeper in the mud."

❷ The natural things White sees include dried oak leaves, a violet, flies, and a frog. Signs of the human presence include old newspapers, a popcorn wrapper, a man's shirt, and a No Bathing sign.

Literary Note

White's statement about "some nature lover who wishes to set himself up beside a pond in the Concord atmosphere and live deliberately" is an allusion to Thoreau's stated purpose in going to live in a cabin on the shores of Walden Pond, "I went to the woods because I wished to live deliberately."

Cross-curricular Activities

Mathematics and Sciences. Ask groups of students to investigate issues related to environmental preservation. Topics might include the rise of the environmental movement in the 1970s; congressional legislation designed to protect the environment, such as the Clean Air Act; local recycling programs; the effects of ecological disasters, such as Chernobyl or the Exxon *Valdez;* the management of national parks; and radical environmental protest groups such as Greenpeace. Have students present their findings in groups to the rest of the class and discuss the following question: What can one individual do to help preserve the environment?

Concord atmosphere and live deliberately, fronting only the essential facts of life on Number 126. Beyond the Pheasant was a place called Walden Breezes, an oasis whose porch pillars were made of old green shutters sawed into lengths. On the porch was a distorting mirror, to give the traveler a comical image of himself, who had miraculously learned to gaze in an ordinary glass without smiling. Behind the Breezes, in a sun-parched clearing, dwelt your philosophical descendants in their trailers, each trailer the size of your hut, but all grouped together for the sake of congeniality. Trailer people leave the city, as you did, to discover solitude and in any weather, at any hour of the day or night, to improve the nick of time; but they soon collect in villages and get bogged deeper in the mud than ever. The camp behind Walden Breezes was just rousing itself to the morning. The ground was packed hard under the heel, and the sun came through the clearing to bake the soil and enlarge the wry smell of cramped housekeeping. Cushman's bakery truck had stopped to deliver an early basket of rolls. A camp dog, seeing me in the road, barked petulantly. A man emerged from one of the trailers and set forth with a bucket to draw water, from some forest tap.

❶ *What comparison is made between trailer people and Thoreau? What is the experience of the trailer people actually like?*

Leaving the highway I turned off into the woods toward the pond, which was apparent through the foliage. The floor of the forest was strewn with dried old oak leaves and *Transcripts.*[11] From beneath the flattened popcorn wrapper (*granum explosum*) peeped the frail violet. I followed a footpath and descended to the water's edge. The pond lay clear and blue in the morning light, as you have seen it so many times. In the shallows, a man's waterlogged shirt undulated gently. A few flies came out to greet me and convoy me to your cove, past the No Bathing signs on which the fellows and the girls had scrawled their names. I felt strangely excited suddenly to be snooping around your premises, tiptoeing along watchfully, as though not to tread by mistake upon the intervening century. Before I got to the cove I heard something which seemed to me quite wonderful: I heard your frog, a full, clear *troonk*, guiding me, still hoarse and solemn, bridging the years as the robins had bridged them in the sweetness of the village evening. But he soon quit, and I came on a couple of young boys throwing stones at him.

❷ *Thoreau believed that he could learn a lot about life by observing nature. What natural items does White observe? What signs of humans does he observe?*

Your front yard is marked by a bronze tablet set in a stone. Four small granite posts, a few feet away, show where the house was. On top of the tablet was a pair of faded blue bathing trunks with a white stripe. Back of it is a pile of stones, a sort of cairn, left by your visitors as a tribute I suppose. It is a rather ugly little heap of stones, Henry. In fact the hillside itself seems faded, browbeaten; a few tall skinny pines, bare of lower limbs, a smattering of young maples in suitable green, some birches and oaks, and a number of trees felled by the last big wind. It was from the bole of one of these fallen pines, torn up by the roots, that I extracted the stone which I added to the cairn—a sentimental act in which I was interrupted by a small terrier from a nearby picnic group, who confronted me and wanted to know about the stone.

11. **Transcripts.** *The Evening Transcripts,* a Boston newspaper that is no longer published

Words for Everyday Use:
con • ge • ni • al • i • ty (kən jē´nē al´ə tē) *n.,* friendliness
un • du • late (un´dyōō lāt) *vi.,* move in waves
in • ter • ven • ing (in tər vēn´ing) *part.,* coming or lying between

Vocabulary in Context

- Steve's congeniality makes him everyone's favorite employer.
- The crowd at the concert undulated back and forth and gave the impression of being one gigantic entity.
- In the intervening years since E. B. White wrote his essay, Walden Pond has become even more of a tourist mecca.

I sat down for a while on one of the posts of your house to listen to the bluebottles and the dragonflies. The invaded glade sprawled shabby and mean at my feet, but the flies were tuned to the old vibration. There were the remains of a fire in your ruins, but I doubt that it was yours; also two beer bottles trodden in the soil and become part of the earth. A young oak had taken root in your house, and two or three ferns, unrolling like the ticklers at a banquet. The only other furnishings were a DuBarry pattern sheet, a page torn from a picture magazine, and some crusts in wax paper.

Before I quit I walked clear round the pond and found the place where you used to sit on the northeast side to get the sun in the fall, and the beach where you got sand for scrubbing your floor. On the eastern side of the pond, where the highway borders it, the State has built dressing rooms for swimmers, a float with diving towers, drinking fountains of porcelain, and rowboats for hire. The pond is in fact a State Preserve, and carries a twenty-dollar fine for picking wild flowers, a decree signed in all solemnity by your fellow citizens Walter C. Wardwell, Erson B. Barlow, and Nathaniel I. Bowditch. There was a smell of creosote where they had been building a wide wooden stairway to the road and the parking area. Swimmers and boaters were arriving; bodies plunged vigorously into the water and emerged wet and beautiful in the bright air. As I left, a boatload of town boys were splashing about in mid-pond, kidding and fooling, the young fellows singing at the tops of their lungs in a chorus:

Amer-ica, Amer-ica, God shed his grace on thee,
And crown thy good with brotherhood
From sea to shi-ning sea!

I walked back to town along the railroad, following your custom. The rails were expanding noisily in the hot sun, and on the slope of the roadbed the wild grape and the blackberry sent up their creepers to the track.

The expense of my brief sojourn in Concord was:

Canvas shoes	$1.95	
Baseball bat	.25	gifts to take back to a boy
Left-handed fielder's glove	1.25	gifts to take back to a boy
Hotel and meals	4.25	
In all	$7.70	

As you see, this amount was almost what you spent for food and eight months. I cannot defend the shoes or the expenditure for shelter and food: they reveal a meanness and grossness in my nature, which you would find contemptible. The baseball equipment, however, is the kind of impediment with which you were never on even terms. You must remember that the house where you practiced the sort of economy which I respect was haunted only by mice and squirrels. You never had to cope with a shortstop. ■

❶ *What changes have taken place at Walden Pond? What do you think Thoreau would think of these changes?*

Responding to the Selection

Do you enjoy reading literary criticism, in which one writer analyzes or responds to another writer's work? Why, or why not? What emotions do you feel when you read satire? How does it make the writer's ideas harder or easier to understand?

Answer to Guided Reading Question

❶ Walden Pond has become a state park, with changing rooms and a float for swimmers, drinking fountains, and rowboats for rent. It is noisy and crowded with vacationers. Thoreau would probably have been sad to see these changes but not completely surprised.

Answers to Selection Check Test 4.11.9

EX. From what book does E. B. White take the title of his essay?

The title of his essay is the title of a book by Henry David Thoreau.

1. When did E. B. White visit Walden Pond?

He visited there in June of 1939.

2. What does White see farmers doing on his arrival in Concord?

They are setting produce out for sale.

3. Where does White spend the night?

He stays in an inn that used to be Thoreau's house.

4. How does White get to Walden Pond?

He goes on foot down Main Street, Thoreau Street, and Route 126.

5. What has Walden Pond become by White's time?

It has become a state preserve.

Cross-curricular Activities

Mathematics and Science. Have students research and calculate what it would cost a person living in their city or town to make a two-day journey to Concord, Massachusetts, similar to White's. Expenses they may need to consider include the cost of airfare to Boston, a rental car, gas, lodging in Concord, three meals a day, and souvenirs for close relatives or friends. Students could present their travel budgets in the form of a satirical letter addressed either to E. B. White or to Thoreau.

Responding to the Selection

Students may wish to respond to the selection by writing an essay that satirizes White's experience.

Reviewing the Selection

RECALLING

1. To whom is E. B. White's essay addressed? To what journey does the writer refer?
2. What description of the civilization around Concord does White give?
3. What does White enjoy about Concord? What elements does he enthusiastically describe?
4. When White finally reaches Walden Pond, what does he find? What natural element links him briefly to Thoreau's Walden?

INTERPRETING

5. Why is the location relevant to White's essay?
6. In what ways does White suggest the town has changed since Thoreau's time?
7. How do machines work throughout "Walden" to symbolize the contrast between White's Walden and Thoreau's Walden?
8. How have the sounds of Walden Pond changed and stayed the same since Thoreau's time?

SYNTHESIZING

9. Why do you think E. B. White traveled to Concord? How do his reasons compare to Thoreau's long-ago quest for what he called the "essential facts of life"?
10. How do White's descriptions of Concord and Walden suggest his feelings about Thoreau's ideas?

Understanding Literature (Questions for Discussion)

1. **Simile.** A **simile** is a comparison using *like* or *as,* as in "she blossomed like a rose." Find at least one example of a simile in "Walden." In what ways are the things being compared similar?
2. **Tone. Tone** is emotional attitude toward the reader or toward the subject implied by a literary work. Tone ranges from humor, sadness, and anger to sarcasm, seriousness, and friendlines. Describe the tone of E. B. White's "Walden."

Answers for Reviewing the Selection

RECALLING

1. The essay is addressed to Henry David Thoreau, author of *Walden.* The writer refers to his car trip to Walden Pond.
2. He describes it as "an odd distillation of city, village, farm, and manor."
3. White enjoys the natural beauty around Concord, such as the freshly turned fields, the green pastures, the sky, the lilacs and syringa, and the sound of robins.
4. When White reaches Walden Pond, he finds a tourist site. White hears a frog croaking, which reminds him of a description in Thoreau's account.

INTERPRETING

Responses will vary. Possible responses are given.

5. Since he is responding to Thoreau's description of his life at Walden Pond, White's travels through Concord and around the pond allow him to compare Thoreau's experiences with his own.
6. Concord retains vestiges of the homes and scenery with which Thoreau would have been familiar, but there are now modern additions, such as lawn mowers and station wagons.
7. The presence of lawn mowers and cars, especially, show that Concord and Walden Pond have entered the modern age.
8. The sound of the frog is the same, but the sound of the rowdy boys singing "God Bless America" would have been jarring to Thoreau's ears.

SYNTHESIZING

Responses will vary. Possible responses are given.

9. White probably went to Concord expecting things there to be very different from Thoreau's description. He was looking not for the "essential facts of life" but for signs that people are no more in touch with these essential facts in Concord than anywhere else.
10. The fact that White has read *Walden* carefully and can make many points of comparison between Thoreau's Walden Pond and that of the present day suggests that he values Thoreau's ideas. On the other hand, he observes that these ideas are mostly irrelevant to people's everyday lives.

Answers for Understanding Literature

►See the evaluation forms for discussion, active listening, and oral communication, *Assessment Portfolio,* 7.11–7.14.

Responses will vary. Possible responses are given.

1. Simile. Examples of similes include "she looked like a puppy who had grabbed something that was too much for him" (page 770) and "Automobiles, skirting the village green, are like flies that have gained the inner ear" (page 772). The woman is like the puppy because both have innocently grabbed onto something that is too strong for them to control. The cars are like flies in that they make irritating and inescapable noises.

2. Tone. The tone of "Walden" is humorous, irreverent, and satirical.

UNIT REVIEW

Modern Nonfiction

VOCABULARY FROM THE SELECTIONS

accumulate, 771
allay, 754
commensurate, 765
congeniality, 774
cryptic, 771
culprit, 756
deluge, 755
dilation, 761
disbar, 748
dissuade, 753
distillation, 771
endure, 766
engorge, 761
ephemeral, 765
excruciation, 761
extricate, 755
fortitude, 754
game, 770
hem, 749
ideology, 748
immemorial, 771
impetuous, 770
implement, 770
inauspicious, 772
indefinite, 747
integrity, 760
intervening, 774
juncture, 755
meddling, 749
mobilize, 760
nimble, 770
ominous, 753
perilous, 755
pertinence, 770
placard, 747
pontoon, 747
premonition, 754
prevail, 766
propagandist, 748
racket, 755
rickety, 749
sheer, 770
sojurn, 770
solidarity, 748
steadfastness, 772
stupefaction, 771
tallowy, 749
travail, 765
undulate, 774
verisimilitude, 753
verity, 765
vortex, 761

LITERARY TERMS

aim, 767
alliteration, 767
anecdote, 757
antithesis, 768
collage, 751
essay, 763
farce, 757
modernism, 763
onomatopoeia, 768
parallelism, 768
simile, 775
tonel, 776

SYNTHESIS: QUESTIONS FOR WRITING, RESEARCH, OR DISCUSSION

1. **Mass Media.** Modern mass media have made it possible for people to reach enormous audiences. What elements of mass media are reflected in John Dos Passos's "Newsreel LXVII"?
2. **Purpose or aim.** A writer's purpose, or aim, is the goal that he or she wishes to accomplish. What is the major purpose of each of the selections in this unit? How does each writer achieve his purpose?

VOCABULARY DEVELOPMENT EXERCISE

►Give students the following exercise.

Choose twenty words from the list on page 777. For each word, write a sentence that relates to something you've read in this unit. The vocabulary word need not have appeared in the selection to which you refer.

Example.

Thurber's mother took the crash of Thurber's bed as an ominous sign that Thurber's father had been severely injured.

ADDITIONAL RESOURCES

ASSESSMENT PORTFOLIO

- Vocabulary Worksheet: Unit 11, 4.11.11
- Study Guide: Unit 11 Test, 4.11.12
- Unit 11 Test, 4.11.13

ESSENTIAL SKILLS PRACTICE BOOKS

Language

- Adjectives and Articles, 2.19
- Apostrophes, 2.102
- Base Words and Prefixes, 2.140
- Concrete and Abstract Nouns, 2.4
- Parentheses and Brackets, 2.101
- Suffixes, 2.141
- Tone and Voice, 2.149
- Using Colorful Modifiers, 2.35
- Using Context Clues I, 2.138
- Using Context Clues II, 2.139

Study and Research

- Avoiding Faulty Arguments, 4.14
- Comparing and Contrasting, 4.8
- Generalizing, 4.11
- Reading Actively, 4.18
- Reading Rates, 4.16
- Remembering and Visualizing, 4.5

LITERARY CURRENTS

Use the following selections to explore these techniques with your students.

IRONY

- "Newsreel LXVII," 746
- "The Night the Bed Fell," 752
- "Walden," 769

ANECDOTE

- "The Night the Bed Fell," 752

ADVICE LETTER

- Letter to *The Amherst Student,* 759

SPEECH

- Nobel Prize Acceptance Speech, 764

PERSONAL ESSAY

- "The Night the Bed Fell," 752
- Letter to *The Amherst Student,* 759
- "Walden," 769

LANGUAGE LAB VOCABULARY DEVELOPMENT

Most times when you encounter a new word, you can check the meaning in a dictionary. However, when a dictionary is not available, you can use the following strategies to help you deduce the meaning.

LANGUAGE ARTS SURVEY

For additional help, see the Language Arts Survey, 2.138–2.139.

USING CONTEXT CLUES

Restatement. In a **restatement** the author reveals the meaning of a word by using different words to express the same idea in another sentence.

EXAMPLE: Dos Passos's newsreels were *collages* of news headlines, song lyrics, and catch phrases. He used these *pieced-together fragments of diverse ideas* to comment on society.

Apposition. Apposition is the use of a word or phrase that is specifically intended to clarify or modify an unknown word.

EXAMPLE: Thurber uses *hyperbole,* or *extreme exaggeration,* when he says he's such a light sleeper that he will wake up if someone in the room stops breathing.

Examples. Sometimes **examples** are included within the sentence to reveal a word's meaning.

EXAMPLE: Black Elk speaks of such *mystical* experiences as *visions* and *prophecies.*

Comparison. Comparison allows a reader to deduce a word's meaning by comparing it to familiar meanings.

EXAMPLE: There was no way to *dissuade* my father. Once he made up his mind, my mother couldn't *talk him out of* his decision. No amount of *reasoning or pleading* could make him reverse himself.

Contrast. Contrast allows a reader to deduce a word's meaning by contrasting it to familiar meanings.

EXAMPLE: Lewis Thomas's *lucid* prose makes his scientific essays intriguing and enjoyable. His essays are a refreshing change from the *difficult* and sometimes *incomprehensible* writings of most scientists.

PREFIXES AND SUFFIXES

Prefixes and Base Words. Some words are formed by adding a **prefix** to a **base word.** If the word is unfamiliar, you can deduce its meaning by looking at the meaning of these parts. The following are some common prefixes and their meanings.

Prefix	Meaning
il–	"not"
pre–	"before"
post–	"after"
un–	"not"

Suffixes. Suffixes are added to the end of words. The following are some common suffixes and their meanings.

Suffix	Meaning
–ible, –ic	"capable of, able to be"
–ly	"having nature of"
–ness	"in the manner of"

Exercise A Using Context Clues

Write the meaning of the italicized word in each sentence that follows. Then write the type of context clue you used to deduce the meaning.

LANGUAGE ARTS SURVEY

For additional help, see the Language Arts Survey, 2.138–2.139.

1. Faulkner is known for his *monolithic* sentences. A reader might read for several pages before encountering a period.
2. E. B. White declared that essayists must always be *veracious* because readers can instantly detect deceit or half-truths.
3. I would describe my literary tastes as *eclectic.* Rather than limit myself to nonfiction, I enjoy various types of literature.
4. Some feminist scholars have criticized the *patriarchal,* or male-centered, elements of Faulkner's writing.
5. *Black Elk Speaks* is not the only *ethnographic* autobiography. In *Black Hawk, An Autobiography* (1833), Black Hawk's recollections of his Sauk culture are systematically recorded.

Exercise B Using Prefixes and Suffixes

Identify the prefixes and suffixes in the italicized words in the following sentences. Then write a definition for each word. If necessary, use a dictionary to check the meaning of a particular prefix or suffix.

LANGUAGE ARTS SURVEY

For additional help, see the Language Arts Survey, 2.140–2.141.

1. After the cot turned over, Thurber appeared to be in a state of *unconsciousness.*
2. Lewis Thomas has an *optimistic* attitude toward science.
3. The disturbing events leading to World War II prompted Dos Passos to adopt a *utopian* viewpoint in his writing.
4. Some scientific writing is nearly *unintelligible* to the layperson.
5. Thousands listened *raptly* to Kennedy's speech.

ANSWERS FOR LANGUAGE LAB

Responses will vary. Possible responses are given.

Exercise A

1. *Monolithic* means "of a large, single entity." (example)
2. *Veracious* means "honest" or "truthful." (contrast)
3. *Eclectic* means "drawn from various sources." (restatement)
4. *Patriarchal* means "male-centered." (appositive)
5. *Ethnographic* means "related to the systematic recording of culture." (comparison)

Exercise B

1. un-, -ness; *Unconsciousness* means "not having a conscious state."
2. -ic; *Optimistic* means "having the quality of optimism."
3. -an; Utopian means "of a utopia."
4. un-, -ible; *Unintelligible* means "not able to be known."
5. -ly; *Raptly* means "in a rapt manner."

UNIT SKILLS OUTLINE

Literary Skills and Concepts

- Alliteration, 796, 823
- Allusion, 805, 812
- Anaphora, 833
- Assonance, 795
- Confessional Poetry, 813
- Consonance, 796
- Epigraph, 813
- Existentialism, 792
- Free Verse, 809
- Internal Rhyme, 828
- Irony, 800
- Metaphor, 792, 823
- Modernism, 823
- Objective Correlative, 823
- Parallelism, 828, 833
- Personification, 816
- Plot, 843
- Point of View, 843
- Pun, 805
- Repetition, 796
- Rhyme, 813
- Symbol, 816
- Theme, 853
- Tone, 805, 853

Writing Skills and Concepts

- Allusion Piece, 813
- Dialogue Poem, 817
- Family History, 843
- Lyric Poem, 796
- Professional Letter, 853
- Story That Could Be True, 800

Grammar, Usage, and Mechanics Skills and Concepts

- Adding Predicates, 825
- Adjectives and Articles, 789
- Base Words and Prefixes, 828
- Capitalization, 817
- Connotation and Denotation, 819
- Formal and Informal English, 817
- Greek and Latin Roots, 828
- Interjections, 807
- Linking Verbs, 825
- Register, 817
- Tone and Voice, 817
- Using Colorful Modifiers, 789
- Using Vivid Verbs, 811
- Verbals: Participles, 789

Other Language Arts Skills and Concepts

- Comparing and Contrasting, 845
- Computer-Assisted Research, 830
- Elements of Nonverbal Communication, 802, 835
- Generalizing, 794
- Making Hypotheses, 798
- Remembering and Visualizing, 815

Unit 12 Contemporary Literature

(1960–Present)

Photograph by Lee Stalsworth

Number 3, 1949: TIGER. *Jackson Pollock, 1949. Hirshhorn Museum and Sculpture Garden, Smithsonian Institution. Gift of Joseph H. Hirshhorn, 1972*

GOALS/OBJECTIVES

Studying this unit will enable students to

- name the impact on literature of some of the major historic events of the period
- discuss some of the major themes of 1960s literature, including individual freedom, community, and the search for spiritual enlightenment
- describe the literary themes of the period as they relate to the selections in this unit, including individual freedom, sensory awareness, psychology of personality, mysticism, roots/heritage
- explain characteristic elements of the literature of the 1960s and 1970s, including collage, confessional poetry, and the use of the first-person narrator in short fiction

write of one life only. My own. If my story is true, I trust it will resonate with significance for other lives.

—Richard Rodriguez

CONNECTIONS ACROSS THE CURRICULUM

ARTS AND HUMANITIES

- Art Commentary, 790
- Group Poem, 808
- Existentialism, 807
- Celebration of African-American Women Poets, 828
- Season Poem, 814
- Praising Nonfamous People, 800

MATHEMATICS AND SCIENCES

- Conditions for Snow, 815
- Siblings' Personalities, 836

SOCIAL STUDIES

- History of Pets, 819
- Life in the 1920s, 794
- Play of Children, 817
- Research on 1960s, 784

APPLIED ARTS

- Interviewing an EMT, 789

TEACHING THE MULTIPLE INTELLIGENCES

INTERPERSONAL

- Group Poem, 808
- Play of Children, 817
- Praising Nonfamous People, 800

ART NOTE

Jackson Pollock (1912–1956) was a leader of the Abstract Expressionism movement and well known for his distinctive spattering technique. In the late 1960s, authority figures in business, education, and government glanced up in bewildered consternation from their desks to see a social revolution advancing upon them. A popular poster of the seventies shows a middle-aged businessman peering up into the spinning center of a Jackson Pollack mural. The meek folded hands, pale gray-suited back, and uptilted balding head of the businessman seem to be pleading for a sensible explanation. The mural does not reply.

QUOTABLES

"When written in Chinese the word *crisis* is composed of two characters. One represents danger and the other represents opportunity."

—John F. Kennedy

"What is objectionable, what is dangerous about extremists is not that they are extreme, but that they are intolerant. The evil is not what they say about their cause, but what they say about their opponents."

—Robert Kennedy

BIOGRAPHICAL NOTE

Richard Rodriguez was born in 1946 and grew up in Sacramento, California. He is the author of a highly acclaimed autobiography, ***Hunger of Memory: The Education of Richard Rodriguez.*** Rodriguez's first language was Spanish, but he became a master of English prose style. Today, he is a scholar and teacher of English. You may wish to share with your students the following excerpt from his autobiography:

"In spite of my earnestness, I found reading a pleasurable activity. I came to enjoy the lonely good company of books. Early on weekday mornings, I'd read in my bed. I'd feel a mysterious comfort then, reading in the dawn quiet—the blue-gray silence interrupted by the occasional churning of the refrigerator motor a few rooms away or the more distant sounds of a city bus beginning its run. On weekends I'd go to the public library to read, surrounded by old men and women. Or, if the weather was fine, I would take my books to the park and read in the shade of a tree. A warm summer evening was my favorite reading time. Neighbors would leave for vacation and I would water their lawns. I would sit through the twilight on the front porches or in backyards, reading to the cool, whirling sounds of the sprinklers."

Robert and John Kennedy

CONTEMPORARY LITERATURE (1960–PRESENT)

PRELUDE TO THE SIXTIES

The events that would shake the United States in the 1960s had their roots in the Cold War Era of the 1940s and 1950s. The Korean War, fought against North Korea and its ally Communist China, led the United States to commit itself to defense against Communism in other parts of Southeast Asia, thus laying the groundwork for war in Vietnam. Throughout the late forties and the fifties, tensions escalated between the United States and the Communist "Eastern Bloc," especially after such events as the detonation of an atomic bomb by the Soviet Union in 1949 and the Soviet repression of an uprising in Hungary in 1956. In 1957, the Soviet Union launched the first orbital satellite, Sputnik, raising fears that the United States was falling behind technologically and initiating the Space Race that would result in the landing of United States astronauts on the moon in 1969.

Domestically, the 1950s were a time of prosperity characterized by rising employment, movement of workers into suburban housing developments, the building of an unprecedented system of interstate highways, the growth of the television industry, political and social conservatism, and rapidly rising birth rates (the so-called "baby boom" of the late fifties and early sixties).

THE TURBULENT SIXTIES

When **John F. Kennedy** defeated **Richard Nixon** in 1960, becoming the youngest man ever to hold the office of president, it seemed to many that a new age had dawned. Kennedy, a committed cold warrior, supported a covert operation to invade **Fidel Castro's**

LITERARY EVENTS

► = American Events

►1964. Saul Bellow's *The Zog* published

►1963. Sylvia Plath's *The Bell Jar* published

►1962. Rachel Carson's *Silent Spring* published

►1961. Joseph Heller's *Catch 22* published

►1960. John Updike's *Rabbit, Run* and Anne Sexton's *To Bedlam and Half Way Back* published

1970. John Fowles's *The French Lieutenant's Woman* published

1967. Gabriel García Márquez's *One Hundred Years of Solitude* published

►1966. Katherine Anne Porter's *Collected Short Stories* published

►1965. *The Autobiography of Malcolm X* published

1960 **1965** **1970**

HISTORICAL EVENTS

►1960. John F. Kennedy elected president

►1961. United States severs relations with Cuba; Bay of Pigs invasion fails; Berlin wall erected

►1962. Cuban missile crisis

►1963. President Kennedy assassinated; Lyndon B. Johnson sworn in as president; Martin Luther King, Jr., delivers his "I have a dream" speech

►1964. President Johnson reelected

►1965. Vietnam War begins; Malcolm X is killed

►1967. Thurgood Marshall becomes first African-American Supreme Court justice

►1968. Robert F. Kennedy assassinated

►1968. Martin Luther King, Jr. assassinated

►1969. Neil Armstrong walks on the moon

THEMATIC CURRENTS

Use the following selections to explore these themes with your students.

STANDING TOGETHER IN ADVERSITY
- "Auto Wreck," 789
- "Those Winter Sundays," 794
- "House Guest," 802
- "Adlai Stevenson," 821
- "Everyday Use," 834
- "I Stand Here Ironing," 845

WISDOM
- "The Secret," 807
- "The Starry Night," 811
- "Winter Poem," 815
- "At Vespers," 821

INDIVIDUAL FREEDOM
- "A Story That Could Be True," 798
- "To Black Women," 825
- "Inaugural Address," 830

Cuba, the Bay of Pigs Invasion. The invasion failed and further increased tensions with the Soviets, leading in 1962 to the Cuban Missile Crisis, in which Kennedy warned the Soviets to remove newly installed nuclear missiles from Cuba or face war. The threat of nuclear war seemed, for a few days, all too real. Thereafter, the Soviet Union, Great Britain, and the United States negotiated the first of many treaties related to limitations on the testing and use of nuclear arms. However, the arms race continued unabated, with each side following a policy of "mutually assured destruction" to prevent the other from making a first strike.

The Reverend Martin Luther King, Jr.

In the 1950s, race relations had become a central issue in the United States following the 1954 decision in which the Supreme Court ruled separate but unequal schools unconstitutional. This ruling was followed in 1955 by a successful boycott, led by the **Reverend Martin Luther King, Jr.**, of segregated buses in Montgomery, Alabama. Kennedy supported the Civil Rights movement, sending federal troops in 1962 and 1963 to ensure enrollment of African-American students in two Southern universities. Late in 1963, the popular President Kennedy was assassinated in Dallas, Texas. This act and the subsequent assassinations of Martin Luther King, Jr. and Robert Kennedy left the United States reeling.

Kennedy's successor, Lyndon Johnson, carried on his predecessor's civil rights policies, pressing for the passage of the Civil Rights Act of 1964, which protected against discrimination in accommodations and employment and tied federal funding of education to desegregation of schools. The Voting Rights Act of 1965, followed protecting against discrimination at the polls. In spite of these measures, major race riots occurred in several American cities in 1965, 1967, and 1968.

After defeating Barry Goldwater in the presidential election of 1964, Johnson initiated a legislative program designed to build what he called the "Great Society," using his considerable political skills to push through a series of social welfare measures, including bills related to housing, health care for the elderly, and education. The political life of the United States since the Johnson Era has been dominated by debates over such legislation, with conservatives supporting greater defense spending and less spending on domestic programs and liberals supporting less spending on defense and greater spending on domestic programs.

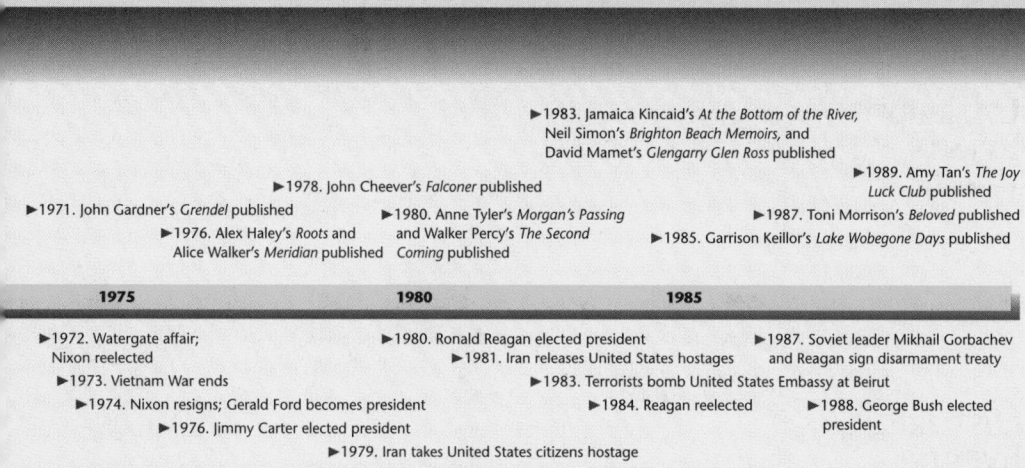

QUOTABLES

"We will meet your physical force with soul force. We will not hate you, but we will not obey your evil laws. We will soon wear you down by pure capacity to suffer."

—Martin Luther King, Jr.

BIOGRAPHICAL NOTE

The Reverend Martin Luther King, Jr., was perhaps the single most important figure in the Civil Rights movement of the 1960s. Born in 1929, King was ordained a minister in the Baptist Church and later became president of the Southern Christian Leadership Conference. Strongly influenced by the teachings of Jesus and of the Indian political leader Mohandas Gandhi, King followed a policy of nonviolent, passive resistance to racisim and segregation and was instrumental in mobilizing the political forces that led to the 1964 Civil Rights Act. Important events of his career include the organization of a successful boycott of segregated buses in Montgomery, Alabama, and the leadership of the 1963 Civil Rights March on Washington, where he delivered his famous "I Have a Dream" speech in front of the Lincoln Memorial. In 1964, King received the Nobel Peace Prize. In 1968, he was assassinated by a lone lunatic.

LITERARY CURRENTS

Use the following selections to explore these techniques with your students.

CONFESSIONAL POETRY

- "Those Winter Sundays," 794
- "House Guest," 802
- "The Starry Night," 810

REVELATION

- "A Story That Could Be True," 798
- "The Secret," 807

FAMILY HERITAGE/FIRST-PERSON NARRATOR

- "Everyday Use," 834
- "I Stand Here Ironing," 835

Historical Note

The 1960s saw a blossoming of radicalism in the United States even more intense than than the Socialist agitation of the 1920s and 1930s. Many trends of the 1960s—"back-to-nature" experiments in communal living, antiwar protests and demonstrations, the Civil Rights movement, feminism, Black Power and African-American militarism, the gay rights movement, drug experimentation, the environmental movement, relaxed sexual mores, and belief in the existence of an insuperable "generation gap"—generate considerable controversy even today.

Additional Questions and Activities

The following are some possible topics for research reports on the 1960s:

1963 Civil Rights March on Washington
1968 Democratic National Convention in Chicago
The assassination of John F. Kennedy
The Black Panther Party
The British Invasion (popular music)
The Cuban Missile Crisis
Earth Day
The Feminine Mystique, by Betty Friedan
The Great Society Programs
The Gulf of Tonkin Resolution
Hippie dress, gestures, habits, and slang
Malcolm X
Marshall McLuhan and the Global Village
The Montgomery Boycott
The Peace Corps
The rhetoric of peace in popular music of the 1960s
The "Summer of Love"
The trial of the Chicago Seven

Despite his political accomplishments, Johnson was to have a troubled administration because of involvement in a widely unpopular war in the Southeast Asian country of Vietnam. In 1964, an attack on United States ships led to the Gulf of Tonkin Resolution, committing the country to a "police action," commonly referred to as the Vietnam War, that proved to be extremely divisive, fomenting antiwar demonstrations throughout the United States. These demonstrations were part of a larger "counterculture" rebellion among American youth who, relatively prosperous themselves due to their parents' material gains during the fifties, challenged the war and traditional "materialistic" values. The extreme styles of dress and speech that characterized the so-called "Hippie Movement" soon passed into oblivion, along with the more radical politics of the period. However, the resurgence of feminism that occurred as part of the youth movement had a more lasting influence, leading to an expanded role for women in American society.

The Seventies and Eighties

Following the turbulent Democratic National Convention in Chicago in 1968, Richard Nixon, a Republican from California, was elected by a landslide. The Nixon Administration pursued a policy of détente, or improved relations, with the Soviet Union, negotiating the first of a series of Strategic Arms Limitation Treaties (SALT) with the Soviets. Relations with China also improved following President Nixon's visit there in 1972. In 1973, after the signing of a peace treaty, the United States withdrew from Vietnam. Then, in 1974, following charges of a coverup of improprieties during the 1972 election campaign, including a break-in at the Watergate hotel in Washington, DC, President Nixon resigned, to be succeeded by Gerald Ford.

The Ford Administration faced difficult economic problems, not the least of which was an oil embargo during the Yom Kippur War that caused fuel prices to soar. Ford lost the 1976 election campaign to Jimmy Carter of Georgia. The Carter Administration followed a policy of promoting human rights around the world and succeeded in bringing Israel and Egypt, traditional enemies in the Middle East, to the negotiating table. However, domestic economic troubles, coupled with the administration's inability to deal with the Iran Hostage Crisis, in which Islamic fundamentalists in Tehran, Iran, took over the American Embassy and held its

Literary Events

► = American Events

Historical Events

1990 — **1995**

1990. Germany reunited; Iraq invades Kuwait; and Nelson Mandela released from South African prison

►1992. Bill Clinton elected president

1991. Serbo-Croatian war begins in Yugoslavia

►1991. United States Desert Storm attack on Iraq

Space Shuttle Challenger. National Aeronautics and Space Administration. (NASA)

occupants hostage, led to Carter's defeat by Ronald Reagan in 1980. During his two terms in office, Reagan, an extremely popular president, increased defense spending considerably, which greatly boosted the country's budget deficit but helped to hasten the collapse of the Soviet Union. That collapse occurred during the administration of George Bush, Reagan's vice-president and successor. Despite fairly high standings in the polls at the end of the Gulf War with Iraq, Bush was defeated for reelection by Bill Clinton of Arkansas.

American Literature and the Contemporary Era

The end of the 1950s and beginning of the 1960s saw the emergence in California of the Beatnik Movement. Centered in San Francisco, this avant-garde literary movement, whose leading lights included the novelist Jack Kerouac and the poets Lawrence Ferlinghetti and Allen Ginsberg, drew heavily on Existentialist thought. **Existentialism** was a twentieth-century philosophical movement that posited the absurd freedom of the individual to create meaning in a world that was itself devoid of meaning. Ridiculed in the popular media, the beatniks nonetheless represented another variation on the theme of American individualism.

The 1960s were a time of radical experimentation in all the arts in the United States, including literature. Boundaries between literature, painting, sculpture, music, and dance broke down in the development of "Happenings," spontaneous expressions of creative freedom that were precursors of the performance art of the 1970s and 1980s. Emerging during this period were a number of experimental literary forms, including found poems, made up primarily or exclusively of bits of language collected from the culture at large, from billboards,

Literary Note

Existentialism was a twentieth-century philosophical movement that had tremendous influence on literature produced during the middle part of the century. There are many varieties of Existentialism, but the basic premises of this philosophy may be stated quite simply: People come into this world undefined and unknown even to themselves. Life and the universe are both arbitrary, without an underlying purpose or unifying moral direction. Any defining choices that a person makes once he or she reaches the stage of adult, conscious decision making will necessarily be, because of the lack of moral order in the universe, absurd or irrational. Thus existence precedes essence, and essence is a consequence of absurd choices. This absurdity is experienced as oppressive by the individual who, being nothing, longs to establish an identity or essence and feels that there should be, but isn't, a rational procedure for doing so. Much of the literature of the mid to late twentieth century can be read as reflecting or reacting against such a view of life. Students interested in learning more about Existentialism might read Albert Camus's magnificent essay "The Myth of Sisyphus." In this essay, the ancient Greek character Sisyphus is viewed in Hades, pushing a boulder up a hill. While engaged in his task, he is too intent on what he is doing to be fully conscious. It is only when he has reached the top of the hill and the boulder has rolled back down that he can, for a brief moment, pause and choose to feel joy. Thus Camus shows that Existentialism needn't necessarily lead to despair.

Literary Note

Recommended works by the authors mentioned on this page include the following:

Ackerman, Diane. *The Moon by Whale Light.*
Barth, John. *The Floating Opera.*
Berryman, John. *The Dream Songs.*
Bloom, Amy. *Come to Me.*
Bly, Robert. *The Light around the Body.*
Brautigan, Richard. *Trout Fishing in America.*
Brooks, Gwendolyn. *The Bean Eaters.*
Didion, Joan. *Slouching Toward Bethlehem.*
Dillard, Annie. *Pilgrim at Tinker Creek.*
Doctorow, E. L. *Ragtime.*
Durang, Christopher. *An Actor's Nightmare.*
Fowles, John. *The French Lieutenant's Woman.*
Gilchrist, Ellen. *Starcarbon.*
Giovanni, Nikki (with Alice Walker). *A Poetic Equation.*
Gould, Stephen Jay. *Wonderful Life.*
Hansberry, Lorainne. *A Raisin in the Sun.*
Henley, Beth. *Crimes of the Heart.*
Hoffman, Alice. *Seventh Heaven.*
Irving, John. *The World According to Garp.*
Jones, LeRoi. *Blues People.*
Le Guin, Ursula K. *Searoad: Chronicles of Klatsand.*
Levertov, Denise. *The Sorrow Dance.*
Lowell, Robert. *For the Union Dead.*
Mamet, David. *Glengarry, Glen Ross.*
Norman, Marsha. *'Night, Mother.*
Oates, Joyce Carol. *them.*
Percy, Walker. *The Moviegoer.*
Plath, Sylvia. *The Bell Jar.*
Pynchon, Thomas. *Gravity's Rainbow.*
Roth, Philip. *Goodbye, Columbus.*
Salinger, J. D. *Catcher in the Rye.*
Sexton, Anne. *All My Pretty Ones.*
Shepard, Sam. *True West.*
Thomas, Lewis. *Lives of a Cell.*
Tyler, Anne. *The Accidental Tourist.*
Updike, John. *The Music School and Other Stories.*
Vonnegut, Kurt. *Slaughterhouse Five.*
Walker, Alice. *The Color Purple.*
Wilson, August. *Joe Turner's Come and Gone.*
Wilson, Lanford. *Talley's Folly.*

Nikki Giovanni

graffiti, subway posters, and other such materials. Concrete poems, designed to appeal to the eye, also enjoyed a vogue during this time. Many poets of the period, notably **Robert Lowell, Anne Sexton, Sylvia Plath,** and **John Berryman,** wrote what is known as confessional poetry, extremely personal verse that described intimate, often troubled or troubling experiences. During the political agitation of the sixties and early seventies, a number of antiwar poets emerged, including **Robert Bly** and **Denise Levertov,** and many African-American poets, such as **LeRoi Jones, Nikki Giovanni, Gwendolyn Brooks,** and **Mari Evans,** produced compelling work related to problems of race and discrimination. The sixties and seventies were also times of experimentation in fictional forms, which reached new heights of zaniness and dark comic invention in the works of **John Barth, J. D. Salinger, Kurt Vonnegut, Thomas Pynchon, Richard Brautigan, Philip Roth, John Updike, John Fowles, Ursula K. Le Guin, E. L. Doctorow, John Irving, Walker Percy,** and **Joyce Carol Oates.**

In the period from the mid-seventies to the nineties, the audience for poetry and short stories in the United States dwindled considerably, while nonfiction and novels in many genres—romances, science fiction, detective stories, mysteries, and the like—remained extremely popular. Despite this trend, the United States continued to produce many fine young poets and writers of short fiction who found their chief outlets in small literary magazines. Perhaps the most significant of all developments in recent years in American literature has been the appearance of a large number of superb women writers of novels and short fiction, including **Alice Walker, Anne Tyler, Alice Hoffman, Amy Bloom,** and **Ellen Gilchrist.** Excellent dramatists of the contemporary era include **Beth Henley, August Wilson, Lanford Wilson, Lorainne Hansberry, Marsha Norman, David Mamet, Sam Shepard,** and **Christopher Durang.** Recent nonfiction writers of note include the essayists **Joan Didion, Stephen Jay Gould, Lewis Thomas, Annie Dillard,** and **Diane Ackerman.**

Echoes:

The Contemporary Era

"I have a dream . . . that my four little children will one day live in a nation where they will not be judged by the color of their skin but by the content of their character."

—Martin Luther King, Jr.

"The first problem for all of us, men and women, is not to learn, but to unlearn."

—Gloria Steinem, "A New Egalitarian Life Style"
The New York Times
August 26, 1971

"And so, my fellow Americans, ask not what your country can do for you; ask what you can do for your country."

—John F. Kennedy

"Yes Celie, she say. Everything want to be loved. Us sing and dance, make faces and give flower bouquets, trying to be loved. You ever notice that trees do everything to git attention we do, except walk?"

—Alice Walker, from *The Color Purple*

ADDITIONAL RESOURCES

READER'S GUIDE
- Selection Worksheet, 12.1

ASSESSMENT PORTFOLIO
- Selection Check Test, 4.12.1
- Selection Test, 4.12.2

ESSENTIAL SKILLS PRACTICE BOOKS
- *Language,* 2.16, 2.19, 2.35

ENRICHMENT ACTIVITIES

- Ask students to list descriptive modifiers for the following nouns from the first seven lines of the selection: *bell, flare, light, ambulance, beacons, clocks, brakes, crowd.*
- Ask students to think of a scene of confusion or trauma. Ask them to describe the sights, sounds, smells, tastes, and feelings associated with this scene. What is the most vivid detail about the scene? What effect does this detail have on the viewer? Students can write a short description of the scene from the point of view of an uninvolved spectator.

SUPPORT FOR LEP STUDENTS

Ask students to share stories of accidents they have seen or experienced. Write precise adjectives and participles on the board or on a flip chart as they call them out.

ADDITIONAL VOCABULARY

flare—warning light used to mark road hazards
artery—blood vessel that carries oxygen away from the heart
stowed—stored safely
douches—rinses as with a hose
physics—medicines or treatments

PREREADING

POETRY

"Auto Wreck"
by Karl Shapiro

ABOUT THE AUTHOR

Karl Shapiro (1913–) was born in Baltimore, Maryland, the grandson of Russian Jewish immigrants. He attended the University of Virginia and Johns Hopkins University. During World War II, while serving in the United States Army in the South Pacific, he wrote and published his first successful poetry collection, *V-Letter and Other Poems* (1944), for which he received a Pulitzer Prize. As a poet, editor of poetry journals, and critic, Shapiro developed strong ideas about what poetry should be. He embodied his opinions in his own poems, which were raw expressions of sensations. Shapiro believed in using common, everyday language in poetry and was highly critical of the intellectual poetry of the Modernists Ezra Pound and T. S. Eliot, praising instead poets of the people such as Walt Whitman and William Carlos Williams. His later poetry, which included *Poems of a Jew* (1957) and *The Bourgeois Poet* (1964), explores his own past. Critical works by Shapiro include his *Essay on Rime* (1945); a verse commentary on modern poetry, *Beyond Criticism* (1953); and *In Defense of Ignorance* (1960). Shapiro has served as editor of the influential literary magazines *Poetry* and *Prairie Schooner* and has taught at many universities around the United States, including the University of Nebraska, the University of Illinois, and the University of California at Davis.

ABOUT THE SELECTION

The automobile has been a major force in shaping twentieth-century life. Cars have changed the American landscape, given people unprecedented mobility, created millions of jobs, and threatened environmental quality. The poet T. S. Eliot even claimed that the rhythms of the internal combustion engine affected the rhythms of modern poetry. In **"Auto Wreck,"** Karl Shapiro details an all too frequent experience made commonplace by the presence of the automobile in the modern world.

GOALS/OBJECTIVES

Studying this lesson will enable students to

- empathize with the feelings of the speaker
- define *Existentialism* and explain how this philosophy is related to the poem
- explain a metaphor and identify metaphors they encounter in their reading
- identify adjectives and participles

READER'S JOURNAL

Why do automobile accidents draw onlookers? What do people find so fascinating about such tragedies? What questions are raised by the seemingly arbitrary and absurd nature of such accidents? Freewrite about these questions in your journal.

LANGUAGE SKILLS

Read the Language Arts Survey, 2.19, "Adjectives and Articles"; 2.16, "Verbals: Participles"; and 2.35, "Using Colorful Modifiers." Then, as you read the selection, make a list of the precise adjectives and participles used by the author to make his poem vivid and memorable.

"Auto Wreck"

KARL SHAPIRO

Its quick soft silver bell beating, beating,
And down the dark one ruby flare
Pulsing out red light like an artery,
The ambulance at top speed floating down
5 Past beacons and illuminated clocks
Wings in a heavy curve, dips down,
And brakes speed, entering the crowd.
The doors leap open, emptying light;
Stretchers are laid out, the mangled lifted
10 And stowed into the little hospital.
Then the bell, breaking the hush, tolls once,
And the ambulance with its terrible cargo
Rocking, slightly rocking, moves away,
As the doors, an afterthought, are closed.

15 We are deranged, walking among the cops
Who sweep glass and are large and composed.
One is still making notes under the light.
One with a bucket douches ponds of blood
Into the street and gutter.

❶ *How do the spectators feel? the police?*

WORDS FOR EVERYDAY USE:
de • ranged (dē rānj´d) *adj.,* disordered; upset; insane
com • posed (kəm pōzd´) *adj.,* calm, tranquil

PREREADING NOTES

READER'S JOURNAL

Students may wish to consider the differences between idle onlookers and people who help in times of crisis. Ask students to discuss their responses to the following questions: What events, other than car accidents, prompt a similar response? Why might people be so fascinated with tragedy? Be sensitive to students who may have difficultly discussing this topic because of personal experience with an accident.

LANGUAGE SKILLS

Ask students which images they find most memorable in the poem. Which colorful modifiers are used to create these images? Students might also identify vivid verbs and precise nouns in the poem. Refer them to the Language Arts Survey, 2.32, "Using Precise Nouns," and 2.33, "Using Vivid Verbs."

CROSS-CURRICULAR ACTIVITIES

Applied Arts. Have students prepare a list of questions for an interview with an emergency medical technician from their local ambulance corps. Questions should include requests for information about ambulance protocol for auto accidents. What equipment do they carry? What other support people do they expect to assist them at the accident scene? How do they determine which victim to treat first? (This emergency medical procedure is called triage.)

ANSWER TO GUIDED READING QUESTION

❶ The spectators feel shocked, helpless, and confused. The police appear composed.

VOCABULARY IN CONTEXT

- In Alec's deranged state, he was confused and appeared slightly menacing.
- In the midst of the hubbub, Corrine remained composed and unruffled.

VOCABULARY FROM THE SELECTION

banal
composed
convalescent
deranged
expedient
gauche
occult

Additional Questions and Activities

Ask students to comment on "Steering Wheel." How is the disjointed image fitting for the mood and scene depicted in the poem? Have students create their own illustrations for the poem. Students might choose to represent a particular image that they find striking, create a series of illustrations that demonstrates the action of the poem, or simply capture the mood of the poem. Other students might create a representation in sound, capturing the sirens, bells, and general confusion and horror of the scene.

Steering Wheel. *David Hockney, October 1982. Photographic Collage, 30 × 36. © David Hockney*

One hangs lanterns on the wrecks that cling,
Empty husks of locusts,[1] to iron poles.

Our throats were tight as tourniquets,[2]
Our feet were bound with splints, but now,
Like convalescents intimate and gauche,
We speak through sickly smiles and warn
With the stubborn saw of common sense,
The grim joke and the banal resolution.
The traffic moves around with care,

1. **locusts.** Large grasshoppers
2. **tourniquets.** Devices used to stop the flow of blood

Words for Everyday Use:

con • va • les • cent (kän´ və les´ ənt) *n.,* person recovering from an illness
gauche (gōsh) *adj.,* tactless; lacking social grace
ba • nal (bā´nəl) *adj.,* commonplace; trite

Vocabulary in Context

- Most convalescents need plenty of rest as they recover their health.
- Paul's comment about the overcooked vegetables seemed gauche to everyone else at the table.
- Priya refused to discuss her feelings and instead offered banal comments about the weather.
- Alchemy was one of many occult studies popular during the Middle Ages.
- An expedient solution is not always a wise one.

But we remain, touching a wound
30 That opens to our richest horror.
Already old, the question Who shall die?
Becomes unspoken Who is innocent?

For death in war is done by hands;
Suicide has cause and stillbirth, logic;
35 And cancer, simple as a flower, blooms.
But this invites the occult mind,
Cancels our physics with a sneer,
And spatters all we knew of dénouement[3]
Across the expedient and wicked stones. ■

3. **dénouement.** Revelation or outcome

What do the onlookers who remain feel they are doing? What questions are asked?

Responding to the Selection

What details in the poem are particularly striking emotionally? How do the people viewing the scene respond? What questions does the accident raise in their minds? Discuss these questions with your classmates.

WORDS FOR EVERYDAY USE:

oc • cult (ə kult´) *adj.*, mysterious; hidden

ex • pe • di • ent (ek spē´dē ənt) *adj.*, convenient

ANSWER TO GUIDED READING QUESTION

❶ The remaining onlookers feel that they are looking for answers to the questions "Who shall die?"and "Who is innocent?"

RESPONDING TO THE SELECTION

If students have ever viewed a scene similar to the one described in the poem, they might discuss the feelings the scene evoked in them. Students could discuss vivid details of the scene, but the focus should be on their emotional response to these details and the accident as a whole. Thoughts about life, sudden death, grief, shock, and condolence might be addressed.

ANSWERS TO SELECTION CHECK TEST 4.12.1

EX. What is the "quick soft silver bell" doing?
The "quick soft silver bell" is "beating, beating."

1. Like what does the ambulance pulse out red light?
The ambulance pulses out red light like an artery.

2. Who are laid on the stretchers?
The "mangled" are laid on the stretchers.

3. What does the speaker call the injured people carried by the ambulance?
The speaker calls the injured people a "terrible cargo."

4. What are the police doing after the accident?
The police are making notes and washing up blood in a "composed" manner.

5. What does the speaker say the accident invites?
The speaker says the accident invites "the occult mind."

ANSWERS FOR REVIEWING THE SELECTION

RECALLING

1. He compares the red light to the blood from an artery.
2. The words used are "terrible cargo."
3. The police sweep glass, make notes, and wash blood into the gutter.
4. The onlookers' statements might be characterized as warnings, dark humor, and advice.

INTERPRETING

Responses will vary. Possible responses are given.

5. They foreshadow human tragedy.
6. The mood is foreboding and fearful. The onlookers are paralyzed with fear.
7. The police seem calm; the onlookers seem hysterical. The police are experienced in confronting tragedy unexpectedly.
8. They are trying to convince themselves that they are not like the victims. The onlookers face these questions: What can protect them? Who decides each individual's fate?

SYNTHESIZING

Responses will vary. Possible responses are given.

9. Death in an auto accident is sudden and unexpected, and it could happen to anyone. Some other deaths are more predictable and happen to people who live risky lives, are elderly, or are physically debilitated. Auto accidents are inexplicable and defy our technical knowledge.
10. The accident seems meaningless; its significance is impossible to determine.

Reviewing the Selection

RECALLING

1. To what does the speaker compare the red light of the ambulance?
2. What words does the speaker use to describe the contents of the ambulance?
3. What do the police do after the ambulance speeds away?
4. What words characterize the statements made by the onlookers after the ambulance leaves?

INTERPRETING

5. What do the ambulance and its red light foreshadow?
6. What mood is created by the descriptions in stanzas 1 and 2? In what sense are the onlookers' throats "tight as tourniquets" and their feet "bound with splints"?
7. How do the descriptions of the police and of the onlookers differ? Why might these people react differently to the scene?
8. What might be the reason for the types of statements the onlookers make? What difficult questions are the onlookers confronting?

SYNTHESIZING

9. According to the speaker, how does death in an auto accident differ from death by other causes?
10. People generally expect the events in their lives to be significant or meaningful. In what sense does an auto accident violate this expectation?

Understanding Literature (Questions for Discussion)

1. **Existentialism. Existentialism** is a twentieth-century philosophy that postulates the absurdity and meaninglessness of life. Existentialist philosophers such as Albert Camus and Jean-Paul Sartre argued that existence, or being, emerges out of nothingness without any essential, or defining, nature. As described in the poem, what is absurd or meaningless about an auto accident? What decides who will die and who will not? In what sense do auto accidents defy attempts to explain them, to make sense of them, to describe them in terms of purpose or cause?
2. **Metaphor.** A **metaphor** is a figure of speech in which one thing is spoken or written about as if it were another. This figure of speech invites the reader to make a comparison between the two things. What in the poem is compared to a bird? to the pulsing of blood from an artery? to the empty husks of locusts? to being bound with tourniquets or splints? to convalescents? to a wound?

ANSWERS FOR UNDERSTANDING LITERATURE

▶ See the evaluation forms for discussion, active listening, and oral communication, *Assessment Portfolio,* 7.11–7.14.

Responses will vary. Possible responses are given.

1. Existentialism. An auto accident is meaningless in the sense that it does not follow a plan or purpose. Chance decides who will die and who will not. Because accidents are random, they defy attempts to make sense of them, to ascribe purpose or cause to their results.

2. Metaphor. The ambulance is compared to a bird. The ambulance light is compared to blood pulsing from an artery. The auto wrecks on the poles are compared to the empty husks of locusts. The onlookers' throats seem bound by tourniquets; the onlookers' feet seem encumbered by splints. The onlookers are like convalescents. The tragedy and its meaninglessness are like a wound that the onlookers keep probing.

PREREADING

POETRY

"Those Winter Sundays"
by Robert Hayden

ABOUT THE AUTHOR

Robert Hayden (1913–1980) grew up in a poor neighborhood of Detroit, Michigan, a place to which he would return in poems collected in *Elegies for Paradise Valley* (1978). He attended Wayne State University and received a master's degree from the University of Michigan, where he was professor of English from 1968 until his death in 1980. From 1946 to 1968, he taught at Fisk University in Tennessee. Hayden built upon his experiences and on the heritage of African Americans to write poetry that spoke for different groups of people throughout history. He made connections to the universal from the experiences and voice of the individual, be it the gypsy, the slave, or the slave trader. His poem "Middle Passage" uses the technique of collage, pioneered by writers such as John Dos Passos, T. S. Eliot, and William Carlos Williams, to evoke the many voices associated with the slave ships that brought African Americans to the New World. Hayden was a versatile writer, trying various poetic forms and styles to express universal emotions. His collections include *Heart-Shape in the Dust* (1940), *The Lion and the Archer* (1948), and *A Ballad of Remembrance* (1962), which contains the poem "Those Winter Sundays." He received the Grand Prize for Poetry at the First World Festival for Negro Arts in 1966 for *A Ballad of Remembrance.* In 1976, Hayden was appointed poetry consultant to the Library of Congress in Washington, DC.

ABOUT THE SELECTION

"Those Winter Sundays" recalls a single, recurring event from the speaker's childhood and draws from it a moving generalization about the nature of love. The poem thus demonstrates how writers can arrive at and justify conclusions by presenting even minor events in concrete detail. The poem is remarkable for its simplicity, beauty, and precision of language.

ADDITIONAL RESOURCES

READER'S GUIDE
- Selection Worksheet, 12.2

ASSESSMENT PORTFOLIO
- Selection Check Test, 4.12.3
- Selection Test, 4.12.4

ESSENTIAL SKILLS PRACTICE BOOKS
- *Study and Research,* 4.11

ENRICHMENT ACTIVITIES

Ask students to make a list of images that they associate with love. Students might consider conventional symbols or images such as hearts, but they should also consider personal images based on special experiences. Students should work individually to create their lists, but they may wish to discuss and explain their images to others. Students might use these images in a personal essay on love.

SUPPORT FOR LEP STUDENTS

Students may list examples from the selection of figurative language that include a noun and a modifier, such as "blueblack cold." For each example, students should attempt to define the poet's language in their own words. For example, "blueblack cold" might mean dark, frozen night air.

ADDITIONAL VOCABULARY
indifferently—carelessly

GOALS/OBJECTIVES

Studying this lesson will enable students to

- empathize with the feelings of the speaker
- define *assonance* and *consonance* and identify examples of these techniques
- identify examples of alliteration in a poem
- explain the purpose of repetition
- write a lyric poem
- draw conclusions about the nature of love from a poem

PREREADING NOTES

READER'S JOURNAL

Student responses should include a description of a gift of help they have received from someone who expected no thanks. The journal entry should address the student's interpretation of the giver's motivation for acting in the student's behalf. Does the giver feel unselfish love for the student? Does the student understand the reason for the giver's generosity?

THINKING SKILLS

Students might conclude that love is sacrificing, thankless, and selfless. Acts of love may be simple, everyday acts that often go unnoticed.

ANSWERS TO GUIDED READING QUESTIONS

❶ He got no thanks for his painful task.

❷ He also polished his son's shoes. The speaker did not realize that his father's actions were acts of love.

CROSS-CURRICULAR ACTIVITIES

Social Studies. Hayden spent his childhood in Detroit, Michigan, during the second and third decades of this century. His family was not wealthy, and their opportunities were limited. How might the young Hayden have worked to help support his family during the 1920s, when he was an adolescent and a teenager? Students may want to research African-American life in the urban North during the 1920s. For example, many families at that time traveled from the rural South to get factory jobs in Detroit and Chicago. The workers and their families often had to build their own temporary housing near the factories.

READER'S JOURNAL

Think of some small service that someone once did for you that demonstrated their love or concern. Write about this person and what he or she did for you in your journal.

THINKING SKILLS

Read the Language Arts Survey, 4.11, "Generalizing." Then, as you read the poem, think about what conclusions you can draw from it about the speaker's father and about the nature of love.

"Those Winter Sundays"

ROBERT HAYDEN

Sundays too my father got up early
and put his clothes on in the blueblack cold,
then with cracked hands that ached
from labor in the weekday weather made
5 banked fires blaze. No one ever thanked him.

What reaction did the father get for making the fire? ❶

I'd wake and hear the cold splintering, breaking.
When the rooms were warm, he'd call,
and slowly I would rise and dress,
fearing the chronic angers of that house,

10 Speaking indifferently to him,
who had driven out the cold
and polished my good shoes as well.
What did I know, what did I know
of love's austere and lonely offices? ■

What other task did the father do for the speaker? What didn't the speaker realize about the father's actions? ❷

WORDS FOR EVERYDAY USE:

banked (baŋkd) *part.*, arranged to continue burning slowly

chron • ic (krän´ ik) *adj.*, constant; perpetual

aus • tere (o stir´) *adj.*, plain; without luxury or ornamentation

VOCABULARY IN CONTEXT

- If the small sticks, wadded newspaper, and dry logs are not banked in the fireplace, the fire will burn out quickly.
- Sasha's tardiness was chronic; her friends had never known her to arrive anywhere at the appointed time.
- At one time the Murphys' lives had centered around material wealth; now, they prefer to rent a simply furnished, austere cottage in the woods.

Responding to the Selection

What makes the father's actions especially admirable? How did the speaker feel about those actions when he was a child? How does the speaker feel as an adult looking back on those actions? In what ways has the speaker changed since his childhood? Discuss these questions with your classmates.

Reviewing the Selection

Recalling

1. What did the speaker's father do on Sunday mornings?
2. How did the hands of the speaker's father look?
3. When would the speaker's father call him to get up?
4. What did the speaker fear, and how did he speak to his father?

Interpreting

5. What did the speaker's father do on weekdays? Why does the speaker use the word *too* in line 1 of the poem?
6. What changed the appearance of the speaker's father's hands?
7. What did the speaker's father want to spare his child?
8. Was the speaker's household always happy? Was his relationship with his father always a warm one? How do you know?

Synthesizing

9. What other deed did the speaker's father do for him on those winter mornings? Why did the father do these deeds, even though he did not receive thanks for them?
10. What has the speaker learned about love since his childhood? What does he now recognize that he did not recognize before? What makes love's offices, or duties, sometimes austere and lonely?

Understanding Literature (Questions for Discussion)

1. **Assonance. Assonance** is the repetition of vowel sounds in stressed syllables that end with different consonant sounds. An example is the repetition of the long *o* sound in the words *clothes* and *cold* in line 2 of the poem. Find two other examples of assonance in the poem.

Responding to the Selection

Students should discuss with each other the father's humility and selflessness and the son's lack of understanding for his father's gifts. Students should recognize that the adult speaker feels grateful and remorseful about his boyhood ingratitude toward his father. The speaker has perhaps experienced indifference and neglect from people he has tried to help.

Answers for Reviewing the Selection

RECALLING

1. He makes a fire for the family.
2. His hands are cracked and sore.
3. The speaker's father would call him to get up when the rooms were warm enough.
4. The speaker fears the anger he seems to have experienced repeatedly in the house. He spoke indifferently to his father.

INTERPRETING

Responses will vary. Possible responses are given.

5. The speaker rose early and did hard labor away from the house every weekday; on Sunday, he had to rise early to do hard physical labor at home.
6. The father's hands were probably changed by the cold and trauma without protection.
7. The father probably wanted to spare his son physical discomfort in his future work and in his present home by hard work and by building the fire; he tried to spare his son humiliation by polishing the boy's shoes.
8. The speaker's household was not always happy; his relationship with his father seems strained, but it is unclear whether the "chronic anger" in the house is expressed by the father or by someone else in the family.

(cont.)

Answers for Reviewing the Selection (cont.)

SYNTHESIZING

Responses will vary. Possible responses are given.

9. He polished his son's shoes. He may have done these deeds because he wished his son to have a better life than he himself had.
10. The speaker has learned that love shows itself in unselfish actions, not in words. When someone gives an unselfish gift to someone else, the receiver may or may not recognize the gift or the love behind it. Thus, love's duties can be lonely.

Answers for Understanding Literature

1. **Assonance.** Two other examples of assonance are the repetition of the long *a* sound in the words *labor, weekday,* and *made* in line 4 and the *o* sound in the words *austere* and *offices* in line 14.

2. **Consonance.** Another example of consonance appears on line 7 in which the *m* sound is repeated in the words *rooms* and *warm.*

3. **Alliteration.** Examples of alliteration in the poem include **c**lothes/**c**old (line 2), **bl**ue**bl**ack (line 2), **th**en/**th**at (line 3), **w**eekday **w**eather (line 4), **b**anked/**b**laze (line 5), **l**ove's/**l**onely (line 14).

4. **Repetition.** The question "What did I know?" is repeated in line 13. The repetition indicates the speaker's feeling of remorse for his lack of understanding of his father's love and his own unresponsiveness to that love.

Analytic Scales for Responding in Writing

Assign a score from 1 to 25 for each grading criterion below. (For more detailed evaluation, see the evaluation forms for writing, revising, and proofreading, *Assessment Portfolio,* 7.1–7.10.)

Lyric Poem

- **Content/Unity.** The lyric poem expresses feelings of love or concern.
- **Organization/Coherence.** The lyric poem uses a central image to explore the theme of love.
- **Language/Style.** The lyric poem uses vivid and precise nouns, verbs, and modifiers.
- **Conventions.** The lyric poem avoids errors in spelling, grammar, usage, mechanics, and manuscript form.

2. **Consonance. Consonance** is the repetition of a consonant sound preceded by a different vowel sound. An example in the poem is the repetition of the final consonant sounds in the words *cracked* and *ached.* Find one other example of consonance in the poem.

3. **Alliteration. Alliteration** is the repetition of initial consonant sounds, as in the words *babbling brook.* Identify six examples of alliteration in this poem.

4. **Repetition. Repetition** is the use, again, of a word, phrase, or other element in a work. Find one example of repetition in the poem. What does this repetition indicate about the emotion with which the line is spoken?

Responding in Writing

Lyric Poem. Review your Reader's Journal entry on the small service performed because of someone's love or concern for you. Write a list of images or sensory details connected with this event. Think about what physical details best characterize the person who performed the service. Did you understand what this act meant at the time? Has it developed a richer meaning for you now? After you have jotted down your ideas, select the most powerful phrases and images as building blocks for your poem. You may either select a rhyme scheme and meter that you feel comfortable using or you may write free verse.

Answers to Selection Check Test 4.12.3

EX. To what day of the week does the poem refer?
The poem refers to Sundays.

1. What was the weather like on winter Sundays?
It was "blueblack cold."

2. With what did the father's hands ache?
They ached with "labor in the weekday weather."

3. What two actions does the father perform for the speaker?
He lights the fire and polishes his son's shoes.

4. In what way did the speaker speak to his father?
The speaker spoke to his father indifferently.

5. What did the speaker not understand as a child?
The speaker did not understand "love's austere and lonely offices."

PREREADING

POETRY

"A Story That Could Be True"
by William Stafford

ABOUT THE AUTHOR

William Stafford (1914–1993) was born in Hutchinson, Kansas. He attended the University of Kansas and began a long-term teaching position at Oregon's Lewis and Clark College in 1948. Stafford's poetry explores the difficult choices faced by people all over the world. For example, how can the delicate relationship between nature and humanity be preserved? His simple, poignant verses reflect his reverence for nature and the need to protect the outdoors from urban expansion and technological greed. Like Robert Lowell and Anne Sexton, Stafford often writes what can be called confessional poetry, laying bare private, deep, intimate experiences. Stafford's lifelong horror of war led him to register as a conscientious objector during World War II. His personal account of that experience, *Down In My Heart,* was published in 1947. Although he submitted poems to literary journals as a young man, his first collection of poetry, *West of Your City,* was not published until 1960. His poetry collection *Traveling Through the Dark* won the National Book Award in 1962. Other collections of Stafford's sensitive, moving verse include *The Rescued Year* (1966); *Allegiances* (1970); *Someday, Maybe* (1973); and *Stories That Could Be True* (1977).

ABOUT THE SELECTION

As its title indicates, **"A Story That Could Be True"** invites the reader to consider something that could be true of any reader of the poem, something that is nonetheless exotic and wonderful. Like much imaginative literature, the poem begins by posing a "What if" question and ends with an intriguing answer.

GOALS/OBJECTIVES

Studying this lesson will enable students to

- enjoy an imaginative poem
- define *irony* and explain irony in a poem
- write a story based on something improbable
- identify and celebrate the qualities of a nonfamous person
- understand hypotheses and conclusions

ADDITIONAL RESOURCES

READER'S GUIDE
- Selection Worksheet, 12.3

ASSESSMENT PORTFOLIO
- Selection Check Test, 4.12.5
- Selection Test, 4.12.6

ESSENTIAL SKILLS PRACTICE BOOKS
- *Study and Research,* 4.13

ENRICHMENT ACTIVITIES

Suggest that students research the biography of a famous hero, past or present, who went through childhood without a mother or a father. Then ask them the following questions: What did the fatherless or motherless child do to become a hero? What was his or her contribution to humanity? How did he or she benefit other people? How do you think this person's generosity toward humanity, the ability to give with no expectation of personal gain, was influenced by his or her childhood?

SUPPORT FOR LEP STUDENTS

Ask students to make a pro-and-con chart to show the advantages and disadvantages of knowing or not knowing your family history. One advantage could be a feeling of confidence and security based on the family identity. A corresponding disadvantage could be a feeling of being trapped by a family identity with which you do not feel comfortable.

ADDITIONAL VOCABULARY

exchanged—transferred to take the place of another

PREREADING NOTES

READER'S JOURNAL

Encourage students to be imaginative in their question writing. Improbable ideas can lead to wonderfully imaginative writing. After students have made their lists, they may wish to share some of their questions to spark further ideas.

THINKING SKILLS

Wording may vary. A possible response is given.

The hypothesis is that a child was switched at birth and never learned anything about his or her family. The conclusion to the hypothesis is that a child who has no knowledge of his or her family history cannot imagine any possible heritage for himself or herself.

► Additional practice is provided in the *Essential Skills Practice Book: Study and Research,* 4.13.

ANSWER TO GUIDED READING QUESTION

❶ The baby's name at birth would have been given by the mother had she not died. As a preverbal infant, the baby could not know his or her birth mother's or birth father's last names. Without written documentation, no one else could know those names either.

READER'S JOURNAL

In your journal, write ten interesting questions beginning with the words *What if.* Save these questions as possible ideas for future writing.

THINKING SKILLS

Read the Language Arts Survey, 4.13, "Making Hypotheses." Then, as you read the selection, pose these questions to yourself: With what hypothesis does the selection begin? What conclusions does the speaker draw based on this hypothesis?

"A Story That Could Be True"

WILLIAM STAFFORD

Why might no one know your name? ❶

If you were exchanged in the cradle and
your real mother died
without ever telling the story
then no one knows your name,
and somewhere in the world
your father is lost and needs you
but you are far away.

He can never find
how true you are, how ready.
When the great wind comes
and the robberies of the rain
you stand on the corner shivering.
The people who go by—
you wonder at their calm.

They miss the whisper that runs
any day in your mind,
"Who are you really, wanderer?"—
and the answer you have to give
no matter how dark and cold
the world around you is:
"Maybe I'm a king." ■

ADDITIONAL QUESTIONS AND ACTIVITIES

Students might research their family history. Ask students to write a short essay about a part of their family history they find interesting. If students know little about their family history or prefer to be inventive, they might write about part of their family history that could be true. Instead of an essay, students might write diary entries from the point of view of an ancestor or a series of letters between two relatives.

Responding to the Selection

What parts of the poem indicate that the "you" referred to by the speaker is not a famous, well-known person? What other parts of the poem show that the speaker recognizes himself to be someone special? Discuss with your classmates what really determines who a person is and what he or she might become.

Reviewing the Selection

Recalling

1. To whom is this poem addressed?
2. What hypothetical situation does the speaker ask the reader to consider in lines 1–3? What would be true, given that situation, of your name?
3. What would be true of your father?
4. Given that situation, what would you wonder at, and what would other people miss?

Interpreting

5. About whom was this poem written?
6. What does the phrase "no one knows your name" suggest about how well people know one another's true, inner selves?
7. What does the father in the poem not know about "you"? What does the speaker of the poem suggest is true about "you"?
8. Do you ever feel like a wanderer, like someone out of place whose true qualities are not recognized? Explain.

Synthesizing

9. What parts of the poem suggest that "you" sometimes do not find the world to be a warm, hospitable place?
10. What can "you" reasonably believe even if the world is sometimes dark and cold?

Responding to the Selection

The lines that show that "you" may not be famous are 2–6, 19, and 20. The lines that show that the speaker believes something special about himself or herself are 17 and 21. Students might discuss the qualities they think make a person special and what qualities they possess that will shape what they will become.

Answers for Reviewing the Selection

RECALLING

1. The poem addresses a child of unknown parentage and history.
2. The child lost its mother and father, was switched at birth, and comes to the world with no known history or parentage.
3. If you were this child, your father would have lost you, too, with no means of finding you.
4. You would wonder at the calm of other people. They would miss the whisper that you hear constantly saying, "Who are you really, wanderer?"

INTERPRETING

Responses will vary. Possible responses are given.

5. The poem could be written about anybody.
6. The phrase suggests that anyone can be a stranger no matter how long he or she has lived or what they have created or accomplished.
7. The father does not know your loyalty; the speaker suggests you are innocent and full of possibility and greatness.
8. *Most students will answer yes; explanations will vary.*

SYNTHESIZING

Responses will vary. Possible responses are given.

9. This sense of the world is suggested by the image of "you" standing in the wind and the rain shivering as people pass by you.
10. You can reasonably believe that you were born a king.

Answers to Selection Check Test 4.12.5

EX. What does no one know?
No one knows "your" name.

1. Who is lost?
"Your" father is lost.

2. What will your father never know?
He will never know how true and ready you are.

3. At what do "you" wonder?
"You" wonder at the calm of other people.

4. What do other people miss?
They miss the constant whisper in your head.

5. With what conslusion does the poem end?
It ends with the conclusion, "Maybe I'm a king."

ANSWERS FOR UNDERSTANDING LITERATURE

► See the evaluation forms for discussion, active listening, and oral communication, *Assessment Portfolio,* 7.11–7.14

Responses will vary. Possible responses are given.

Irony. The poem is doubly ironic because it appears that "you" are an unknown outsider when you may be royalty and the people who appear so calm have, in reality, no way of knowing who they are any more than "you" do.

ANALYTIC SCALES FOR RESPONDING IN WRITING

Assign a score from 1 to 25 for each grading criterion below. (For more detailed evaluation, see the evaluation forms for writing, revising, and proofreading, *Assessment Portfolio,* 7.1–7.10.)

A Story That Could Be True

- **Content/Unity.** The story presents an improbable occurrence as if it were true.
- **Organization/Coherence.** The story is presented in a logical order such as chronologically.
- **Language/Style.** The story uses vivid and precise nouns, verbs, and modifiers.
- **Conventions.** The story avoids errors in spelling, grammar, usage, mechanics, and manuscript form.

Understanding Literature (Questions for Discussion)

Irony. Irony is a difference between appearance and reality. This poem makes the ironic point that even when people feel out of place and different, even when they experience the world as cold and dark, they remain unique, they have unrecognized potentials, in fact, they could be royalty. Note that what is true of the "you" in the poem is also true of all those other people, the ones that go by and cause "you" to "wonder at their calm." Given this observation, what makes the poem doubly ironic?

Responding in Writing

A Story That Could Be True. Think of something wildly improbable that could, nonetheless, be true. Some famous examples of such "stories that could be true" include the idea that someone was switched at birth, the idea that some famous person from the past didn't really die but is still living an obscure life somewhere on the planet, and the idea that the last hour didn't really happen but was really part of a dream that you are having while lying in bed at night. With a group of classmates, brainstorm a list of such "stories that could be true" but probably aren't. Choose one of these ideas and develop it into a paragraph, an essay, a poem, or a story of your own.

PROJECT

Let Us Now Praise Nonfamous People. Long ago, the poet Thomas Gray, in his "Elegy Written in a Country Churchyard," pointed out that fame isn't all it is cracked up to be, for "the paths of glory lead but to the grave." In "A Story That Could Be True," William Stafford reminds us that everyone, whether famous or not, has greatness inside. Choose someone you know well but who is not well known in the outside world and prepare some work to celebrate his or her greatness. Your work can be a thank-you letter, a poem, or song of praise, an illustration or drawing, an interpretive dance, or any other work that demonstrates or celebrates the special qualities of the person you have chosen.

PROJECT NOTES

► See the worksheets and evaluation forms for projects, *Assessment Portfolio,* 7.20–7.23.

Let Us Now Praise Nonfamous People. Students might begin by freewriting about the person they have chosen considering the following questions: What qualities of this person would I like to share? What has this person done that I admire? What is unique about this person's spirit? How would this person like to be remembered? The ideas generated in this freewrite might help students to choose an appropriate medium for their celebration of the person. If the person chosen is still living, students may wish to share their creation with the person whose greatness they celebrate.

PREREADING

POETRY

"House Guest"
by Elizabeth Bishop

ABOUT THE AUTHOR

Elizabeth Bishop (1911–1979) was born in Worcester, Massachusetts, but, on the death of her father just eight months after her birth, Bishop's mother took her to live with her maternal grandparents in Nova Scotia, Canada. When she was five years old, her mother was permanently institutionalized, and Bishop became the pawn of warring family members, eventually being returned to Worcester by her paternal grandparents. Those early traumatic experiences left Bishop with a series of stress-related illnesses and an emotionally restrained personality that was later to characterize her poetry. While attending Vassar College in the early 1930s, Bishop became an ardent admirer of poet Marianne Moore and abandoned thoughts of medical school for the greater attraction of travel. She finally settled in Brazil for sixteen years. On her return to the United States, Bishop taught at Harvard from 1970 to 1977. Inspired by such events as the exile of her youth and her life as an expatriate in Brazil, Bishop's poetry is known for its meticulous detail and understated style. Her many honors include the 1956 Pulitzer Prize for the combined collection *Poems: North and South—A Cold Spring* and the 1969 National Book Award for *Complete Poems.*

ABOUT THE SELECTION

Some people's personalities challenge us, raising basic, uncomfortable questions. Elizabeth Bishop's **"House Guest"** presents a portrait of such a person. Bishop creates this portrait through precise description, vivid images, and bits of dialogue.

GOALS/OBJECTIVES

Studying this lesson will enable students to

- appreciate the self-revelation in a poem that is ostensibly a character portrait
- identify and explain allusions in a poem
- define *tone* and *pun* and apply these terms to the understanding of a poem
- identify examples of nonverbal communication

ADDITIONAL RESOURCES

READER'S GUIDE
- Selection Worksheet, 12.4

ASSESSMENT PORTFOLIO
- Selection Check Test, 4.12.7
- Selection Test, 4.12.8

ESSENTIAL SKILLS PRACTICE BOOKS
- *Speaking and Listening,* 3.3

ENRICHMENT ACTIVITIES

Ask students to imagine a personal history for the subject of the poem and then to write the history in a brief essay. Students should give a description of the personal history they imagine for the seamstress. The description can include her childhood family, hometown, and particular experiences from her childhood that could have led to her present situation in life.

SUPPORT FOR LEP STUDENTS

Students should make a list of sensory images from the poem, such as "roast chicken," "zigzags," and "bony." Ask students to write the sense to which each image appeals. Possible responses are the following: roast chicken (taste); zigzags (sight); bony (touch).

ADDITIONAL VOCABULARY

bitter—full of mistrust and hopelessness
confides—reveals one's secret to another
fates—imaginary forces of destiny or fate
knife grinder—tool for sharpening a kitchen knife blade
zigzags—repeated horizontal pattern of connected *Zs*

PREREADING NOTES

READER'S JOURNAL

You may wish to have students consider the differences between disappointments that are remediable and those that are not. In the latter case, one must simply go on, chart a different course, and find an alternative. This needn't be a negative experience; in fact, such a time in one's life can be quite creative and interesting.

SPEAKING AND LISTENING SKILLS

Examples of nonverbal communication from the poem include the following: Watching static on the television for long periods of time; wearing shabby clothes; continued disinterest despite the family's offers to include her in their fun; and her closed expression.

LITERARY TECHNIQUE

Sentence Variety. Point out to students how Bishop maintains interest through sentence variety. Some sentences are quite long, running to several lines. Others are short, elliptical fragments ("No hope"). Some connect ideas with conjunctions ("small and thin and bitter"), others with commas ("a dress, a drink, roast chicken, or fried fish"). The use of dialogue in some sentences adds to the variety.

ANSWER TO GUIDED READING QUESTION

❶ A seamstress is visiting the speaker's home; she is sad and uncommunicative.

READER'S JOURNAL

What are your dreams and goals for the future? What would you do if one of your dreams or goals became impossible to fulfill? Would you retreat into disappointment, or would you seek another dream or goal to take its place? Write about these questions in your journal.

SPEAKING AND LISTENING SKILLS

Read the Language Arts Survey, 3.3, "Elements of Nonverbal Communication." Then, as you read the selection, look for examples of the nonverbal ways in which the seamstress communicates her attitude toward life.

"House Guest"

ELIZABETH BISHOP

Who is visiting the speaker? What is the visitor like? ❶

The sad seamstress
who stays with us this month
is small and thin and bitter.
No one can cheer her up.
Give her a dress, a drink,
roast chicken, or fried fish—
it's all the same to her.

She sits and watches TV.
No, she watches zigzags.
"Can you adjust the TV?"
"No," she says. No hope.
She watches on and on,
without hope, without air.[1]

Her own clothes give us pause,
but she's not a poor orphan.
She has a father, a mother,
and all that, and she's earning
quite well, and we're stuffing
her with fattening foods.

We invite her to use the binoculars.
We say, "Come see the jets!"

1. **without air.** Without spirit

We say, "Come see the baby!"
Or the knife grinder who cleverly
plays the National Anthem[2]
25 on his wheel so shrilly.
Nothing helps.

She speaks: "I need a little
money to buy buttons."
She seems to think it's useless
30 to ask. Heavens, buy buttons,
if they'll do any good,
the biggest in the world—
by the dozen, by the gross![3]
Buy yourself an ice cream,
35 a comic book, a car!

Her face is closed as a nut,
closed as a careful snail
or a thousand-year-old seed.
Does she dream of marriage?
40 Of getting rich? Her sewing
is decidedly mediocre.

Please! Take our money! Smile!
What on earth have we done?
What has everyone done
45 and when did it all begin?
Then one day she confides
that she wanted to be a nun[4]
and her family opposed her.

Perhaps we should let her go,
50 or deliver her straight off
to the nearest convent—and wasn't
her month up last week, anyway?

❶ *What does the visitor ask for? What is her attitude toward her request? What is the speaker's response?*

❷ *What personal secret does the visitor share? What light does this shed on her life?*

2. **National Anthem.** "The Star Spangled Banner" by Francis Scott Key (1779–1843)
3. **gross.** Twelve dozen
4. **nun.** Religious woman who takes vows of obedience to the Roman Catholic Church

WORDS FOR EVERYDAY USE: **me • di • o • cre** (mē´dē ō´ kər) *adj.,* average; not very good

ANSWERS TO GUIDED READING QUESTIONS

❶ She asks for buttons; she asks without expectation of receiving the buttons; the speaker is frustrated with the meagerness of the request and wishes the seamstress would ask for more.

❷ She reveals that she once wanted to be a nun, but that her family would not allow it. Perhaps the loss of her dream is the reason for her disinterest and hopelessness.

LITERARY TECHNIQUE

Characterization. Characterization is the act of revealing the nature of a character. In this poem, Bishop reveals both through descriptions of what the seamstress is like ("She sits and watches . . . zigzags") and what she is not like (she is not interested in "the binoculars," "the jets," "the baby," "the knife grinder who cleverly/plays the National Anthem/on his wheel"). The seamstress's lack of affect or interest in the world, her monosyllabic replies, her willingness to stare off into space for hours—all are signs of depression. The poem is entitled "House Guest" and much of it is given to a description of this guest; however, the real interest of the poem lies not in this guest but in the speaker's response to the guest. Such a guest is unnerving. The last lines of the poem suggest why the speaker might be so unnerved: the speaker, despite his or her interest in the world, fears becoming like the seamstress. The very presence of the seamstress seems to be proof that such a fate is possible, and the speaker doesn't want to think about that possibility.

VOCABULARY IN CONTEXT

- The owner of the restaurant, famous for its excellent food, was only a mediocre cook himself.

ANSWER TO GUIDED READING QUESTION

❶ The speaker raises the fear that his or her fate, and the fate of everyone around the seamstress, will be like her fate.

RESPONDING TO THE SELECTION

Students may answer that they would feel frustrated, confused, hopeless, angry, or perhaps bewildered or amused. Students' advice for the seamstress should relate to her attitude and to ways she could achieve a higher quality of life.

ANSWERS FOR REVIEWING THE SELECTION

RECALLING

1. A temporary, live-in, seamstress has arrived; adjectives used are *sad, small, thin,* and *bitter.*

2. She watches a television screen with a zigzag pattern on it.

3. They ask her if they can adjust the television; they feed her; they offer her the use of binoculars, to show her the baby and the musical knife grinder; they offer more money.

4. The speaker asks: "What on earth have we done?"; "What has everyone done/and when did it all begin?"; "Can it be that we nourish one of the Fates . . . and our fates will be like hers,/and our hems crooked forever.

INTERPRETING

Responses will vary. Possible responses are given.

5. She is indifferent and without hope or confidence.

6. She shows no interest in what she is watching. She is a seamstress, yet her clothes are shabby. She asks for buttons as if she assumes she will not receive them, but she doesn't care. She has no hope that she can change her life.

7. She gives no response to attempts to cheer her.

8. The lines that indicate this attitude toward the seamstress are 49–52.

(cont.)

Can it be that we nourish
one of the Fates[5] in our bosoms?
55 Clotho,[6] sewing our lives
with a bony little foot
on a borrowed sewing machine,
and our fates will be like hers,
and our hems crooked forever? ■

What fear does the speaker raise at the end of the poem? ❶

5. **Fates.** In Greek and Roman mythology, Clotho, Lachesis, and Atropos, the three goddesses who control human destiny and life

6. **Clotho.** Spinner of the thread of human life

Responding to the Selection

How would being around someone like the seamstress make you feel? What advice might you have for her? Discuss these questions with your classmates.

Reviewing the Selection

RECALLING

1. Who has come to stay at the speaker's house, and what adjectives are used in the first three lines to describe her?

2. How does the seamstress spend her spare time?

3. In what ways do the people in the house try to cheer up the seamstress?

4. What questions does the seamstress raise in the mind of the speaker?

INTERPRETING

5. How would you describe the seamstress's attitude toward life?

6. What is unusual about the way in which the seamstress watches television? about her clothing? about the way in which she asks for money for buttons? What do these things reveal about her?

7. How does the seamstress respond to attempts to cheer her up?

8. What lines in the poem indicate that the speaker is uncomfortable about the presence of the seamstress and would like to see her out of the house?

ANSWERS FOR REVIEWING THE SELECTION (CONT.)

SYNTHESIZING

Responses will vary. Possible responses are given.

9. She may be unhappy because she is isolated and has no hope of fulfilling her dreams.

10. This uncomfortable question is raised: If your fate is beyond your control, why have dreams?

SYNTHESIZING

9. Why is the seamstress so unhappy?

10. What uncomfortable questions does the seamstress raise for the speaker about dreams in general?

Understanding Literature (Questions for Discussion)

1. **Tone. Tone** is the emotional attitude toward the reader or toward the subject implied by a literary work. What is the tone of the speaker's comments in stanza 5? Why does the speaker take this tone?

2. **Allusion.** An **allusion** is a rhetorical technique in which reference is made to a person, event, object, or work from history or literature. In Greek mythology, the Fates were three goddesses, often pictured as extremely ancient sisters, who controlled the destinies of human beings. Clotho, the spinner, spun the thread of human fate; Lachesis, the allotter, spooled it out; and Atropos cut it, thus deciding when a person would die. To which of these sisters does the speaker allude in the final stanza of the poem? Why is this choice of allusions particularly appropriate? What fears about her own fate does the seamstress raise in the speaker? Why does the seamstress make the speaker think of Clotho?

3. **Pun.** A **pun** is a play on words, one that wittily exploits a double meaning. What pun exists in the name *Clotho,* applied to the seamstress?

ANSWERS FOR UNDERSTANDING LITERATURE

▶ See the evaluation form for discussion, active listening, and oral communication, *Assessment Portfolio,* 7.11–7.14.

Responses will vary. Possible responses are given.

1. Tone. The speaker seems frustrated with the seamstress; the speaker wonders why the seamstress does not act for herself, using the resources she has available to her.

2. Allusion. The speaker alludes to Clotho, the spinner of human destiny. This allusion is relevant because like Clotho, the seamstress works with thread; and like the goddess, the seamstress seems to be working outside the realm of everyday human life focused only on one task. The speaker has fears about fate, realizing that the seamstress's fate could be anyone's fate.

3. Pun. Clotho contains the word "cloth." Cloth is the seamstress's medium.

ANSWERS TO SELECTION CHECK TEST 4.12.7

EX. Who is staying with the speaker's family?
A sad seamstress is staying with the speaker's family.

1. What does the speaker say the seamstress is like?
The speaker says she is "small and thin and bitter."

2. In what manner does the seamstress watch TV?
The seamstress watches zigzags on the TV "without hope, without air."

3. For what does the speaker ask?
The speaker asks for money to buy buttons.

4. What is the seamstress's sewing like?
Her sewing is "decidedly mediocre."

5. What does the seamstress confess?
The seamstress confesses that she wanted to be a nun and her family opposed her.

ADDITIONAL RESOURCES

READER'S GUIDE
- Selection Worksheet, 12.5

ASSESSMENT PORTFOLIO
- Selection Check Test, 4.12.9
- Selection Test, 4.12.10

ESSENTIAL SKILLS PRACTICE BOOKS
- *Language,* 2.29

ENRICHMENT ACTIVITIES

Interested students might chose to write the dialogue between the two girls who discover the secret in the poem and the third person who delivers the girls' response to the poet.

SUPPORT FOR LEP STUDENTS

To aid comprehension, remind students that they should read the poem sentence by sentence, not line by line.

Students may want to do a group writing activity. The object will be to write a poem that answers the question, "What is the secret of life?" The activity is as follows:

Each student in turn writes one or more lines about the secret of life at the top of a piece of paper and folds back the paper with his or her writing on it before passing it to the next student. When all the students in the group have written one line, the resulting poem can be read aloud. Refer students to the Reader's Journal activity on page 807.

PREREADING

POETRY

"The Secret"
by Denise Levertov

ABOUT THE AUTHOR

Denise Levertov (1923–) draws from many rich traditions to create her unique, visionary poetry, including the Welsh mysticism of her mother's ancestry and the Russian Hasidic Judaism of her father's. Born in Essex, England, Levertov was schooled at home. During the London blitz of World War II, she served as a nurse. She became a poet at a very early age, publishing her first collection, *The Double Image,* in 1946. In 1947, she moved to the United States. There she developed her distinctive voice, finding, in poem after poem, the magic and mystery just behind the banal and ordinary. Influences on Levertov's style include the poet H. D. (Hilda Doolittle) and, later, William Carlos Williams, whom she credits with helping her to find a voice as an American poet. During the 1960s, she translated, with Edward Dimock, Jr., *In Praise of Krishna: Songs from the Bengali* and became involved in the antiwar movement. *Relearning the Alphabet* appeared in 1970 and contains some of her best verse, including the magnificent "A Tree Telling of Orpheus." Other collections of her poetry include *Here and Now* (1957), *Overland to the Islands* (1958), *Candles in Babylon* (1982), and *Breathing the Water* (1987). Levertov has taught at Drew University, Vassar College, and Stanford University.

ABOUT THE SELECTION

"The Secret" is from Levertov's collection *O Taste and See,* published in 1964. The title poem of that collection encourages people to taste and see "all that lives/to the imagination's tongue." Levertov wants us not simply to exist from day to day but to live our lives fully, intensely, engaged with the wonders of the world around us. Such enthusiasm for life, active engagement in the world coupled with imagination, constitutes a secret worth remembering.

GOALS/OBJECTIVES

Studying this lesson will enable students to

- appreciate a lyric poem about innocence and wonder
- identify interjections and explain their purpose in a poem
- define *free verse* and explore the use of line breaks for emphasis in a free verse poem

READER'S JOURNAL

What do you think is "the secret of life"? Can you even begin to answer such a question? If so, write about your answer in your journal. If not, write in your journal about why you find the question difficult to answer.

LANGUAGE SKILLS

Read the Language Arts Survey, 2.29, "Interjections." Then, as you read the poem, find one interjection and explain how it is used to emphasize the poem's main idea.

"The Secret"

DENISE LEVERTOV

Two girls discover
the secret of life
in a sudden line of
poetry.

I who don't know the
secret wrote
the line. They
told me

(through a third person)
they had found it
but not what it was,
not even

what line it was. No doubt
by now, more than a week
later, they have forgotten
the secret,

❶ *What does the word* sudden *suggest here?*

PREREADING NOTES

READER'S JOURNAL

Students should attempt to answer the question, giving support from their own learning or experience.

LANGUAGE SKILLS

The interjection is the word *yes* in line 34. The interjection serves the dual purpose of introducing the final statement and of expressing a positive attitude. The main idea of the poem is the speaker's approval of an attitude toward life that assumes that there are "secrets to life" to be discovered—the opposite of a cynical belief that life is uninteresting, meaningless, or banal.

ANSWER TO GUIDED READING QUESTION

❶ The word *sudden* means "startling" or "unexpected."

LITERARY TECHNIQUE

Existentialism. Existentialism is a philosophy of life that rejects the idea that existence has an ultimate purpose. An Existentialist believes that now is the only moment we have in life, so it is pointless to analyze the past or plan the future. Debate the following question with your classmates: Is focusing only on the present beneficial or harmful to society?

ANSWER TO GUIDED READING QUESTION

❶ The qualities they have are hope and innocence.

RESPONDING TO THE SELECTION

Student responses should include recognition of Levertov's theme about the power of individual hope, innocence, and spontaneity. A single expression of hope by one individual can generate hope in many other people who receive that expression directly or indirectly.

ANSWERS TO SELECTION CHECK TEST 4.12.9

EX. Who discovers something in one of the speaker's poems?
Two girls discover something in a line from one of the speaker's poems.

1. What do they discover?
They discover "the secret of life."

2. Ironically, who does not "know the/secret"?
The person who wrote the line does not know the secret contained in the line.

3. Who tells the speaker about the discovery?
A "third person" tells the speaker.

4. What will happen "a thousand times, till death/finds them"?
The girls will discover the secret of life in other lines.

5. For what, most of all, does the speaker love the people who made the discovery?
She loves them, most of all, for assuming that there is a secret of life.

the line, the name of
the poem. I love them
for finding what
20 I can't find,

and for loving me
for the line I wrote,
and for forgetting it
so that

25 a thousand times, till death
finds them, they may
discover it again, in other
lines,

in other
30 happenings. And for
wanting to know it,
for

assuming there is
such a secret, yes,
35 for that
most of all. ■

What qualities do the two girls have? ❶

Responding to the Selection

What is the secret to which the title of this poem refers? How can having lots of little enthusiasms that change from day to day or from week to week help a person to live a happy, healthy, productive life?

Reviewing the Selection

RECALLING

1. What do the two girls discover in a line of poetry? Who wrote the line? What does the speaker think most likely happened "more than a week/later"?
2. Why does the speaker love these girls?

INTERPRETING

3. Does the speaker of this poem think that she knows the secret of life? Why is she so sure that, a week later, the girls have forgotten the line?
4. Why does the speaker love the fact that the girls have forgotten the line? What does the speaker's loving this fact reveal about her?

SYNTHESIZING

5. Why might it be important for people to assume that "there is/such a secret"? Why is it also important for people to "discover it again, in other/lines,/in other happenings"?

Understanding Literature (Questions for Discussion)

Free Verse. Free verse, or **vers libre,** is poetry that avoids use of regular rhyme, rhythm, meter, or division into stanzas. Notice that this poem is written in complete sentences. How many sentences make up the poem? Notice also that the breaks between lines and stanzas often occur in the middles of sentences. A poet writing free verse can decide where to break a line or stanza not based on the number of beats, or stresses, in the line but rather based on what he or she wants to emphasize. The materials before and after breaks receive the greatest emphasis. Consider, for example, the breaks between stanzas 7 and 8. What two points are emphasized by breaking the sentence in this particular place?

ANSWERS FOR REVIEWING THE SELECTION

RECALLING

1. They discover the "secret of life" in a line written by the speaker. The speaker thinks the two girls shared the line with others and forgot the line but remembered the message they received from it.

2. She loves them because they assume there is a secret of life.

INTERPRETING

Responses will vary. Possible responses are given.

3. No, she does not. She is sure the girls have forgotten the words of the line because she believes they will continue to search for the secret elsewhere.

4. The speaker loves that the girls have forgotten the words of the line but will continue to look for the secret; this reveals the unselfish nature of the speaker's creativity and her belief in the hope and joy of life.

SYNTHESIZING

Responses will vary. Possible responses are given.

5. People need hope. Hope needs to be refueled by ideas and experiences that appear in daily existence.

ANSWERS FOR UNDERSTANDING LITERATURE

► See the evaluation forms for discussion, active listening, and oral communication, *Assessment Portfolio,* 7.11–7.14.

Responses will vary. Possible responses are given.

Free Verse. There are six sentences in the poem. Stanza 7 is broken after the word *happenings* and before the words "And for wanting to know"; this reveals the importance to the speaker of the girls "wanting to know." Stanza 8 is broken with the interjection *Yes* in the second line and then after the last phrase in the poem, "for that most of all." This reveals the most important idea of the poem that the belief in a secret of life is more important than anything else.

ADDITIONAL RESOURCES

READER'S GUIDE
- Selection Worksheet, 12.6

ASSESSMENT PORTFOLIO
- Selection Check Test, 4.12.11
- Selection Test, 4.12.12

ESSENTIAL SKILLS PRACTICE BOOKS
- *Language,* 2.33
- *Study and Research,* 4.25

ENRICHMENT ACTIVITIES

Interested students might read other works by Anne Sexton and works by other confessional poets such as Robert Lowell, Sylvia Plath, and John Berryman. Students might read biographies of these writers as well. Ask student to discuss the difference between learning about a life from a biography and through deeply personal poetry.

SUPPORT FOR LEP STUDENTS

Have students look at van Gogh's *The Starry Night* on page 813 before they read the poem. Students may find it helpful to listen to the poem being read as they look at the painting. Share the art note found on page 813 of the teacher's edition and discuss the feelings evoked by the painting.

PREREADING

POETRY

"The Starry Night"
by Anne Sexton

ABOUT THE AUTHOR

Anne Sexton (1928–1974) made a significant contribution to American poetry though she did not begin writing until she was twenty-eight years old. Sexton was born in Newton, Massachusetts, and attended boarding school and Garland Junior College before marrying Alfred Sexton II in 1948. Sexton gave birth to two daughters, Linda and Joyce. Sexton began writing in 1956 after attending a class taught by Robert Lowell at Boston University. In her work, Sexton presented painful memories and experiences in extremely personal poetry of a kind referred to by critics as confessional. Sexton's first collection, *To Bedlam and Part Way Back* (1959), described her stay in a mental institution and her recovery from an emotional breakdown. In 1967, Sexton received the Pulitzer Prize for her collection *Live or Die.* Sexton's shockingly personal poems brought her literary fame but received mixed reactions from critics. Her *Transformations* (1971) is a collection of frightening, macabre retellings of fairy tales by the Brothers Grimm. Unfortunately, she was plagued by depression and tragically ended her life on October 4, 1974. Two volumes of her poetry and a collection of her personal letters were published after her death by her daughter Linda.

ABOUT THE SELECTION

"The Starry Night" comes from Sexton's collection *All My Pretty Ones* (1962). The title of the collection comes from a statement made by MacDuff, in Shakespeare's tragedy *Macbeth,* after hearing of the deaths of his wife and children. The title of the poem refers to a famous painting by Vincent Van Gogh. Van Gogh, like Sexton, suffered from depression, which was intensified by a crisis of religious faith. The epigraph at the beginning of Sexton's poem comes from one of the remarkable letters that Van Gogh wrote to his brother Theo.

GOALS/OBJECTIVES

Studying this lesson will enable students to

- experience an intense moment of personal revelation in a confessional poem
- appreciate one artist's highly personal view of a work by another artist
- define the terms *allusion, epigraph, rhyme,* and *confessional poetry* and apply these terms to the analysis of a poem
- write a brief work that attempts to capture the essence of some work of art

READER'S JOURNAL

What things in nature inspire you with awe because of their power or drama? Choose one of these things and freewrite about it in your journal.

LANGUAGE SKILLS

Read the Language Arts Survey, 2.33, "Using Vivid Verbs." Then, as you read the poem, make a list in your journal of verbs in it that are particularly colorful or interesting. Choose one of these verbs and make a list of related verbs. Use a thesaurus, if necessary. Refer to the Language Arts Survey, 4.25, "Using Thesauruses."

"The Starry Night"

ANNE SEXTON

That does not keep me from having a terrible
need of—shall I say the word—religion.
Then I go out at night to paint the stars.
—Vincent Van Gogh[1]
in a letter to his brother

The town does not exist
except where one black-haired tree slips
up like a drowned woman into the hot sky.
The town is silent. The night boils with eleven stars.
Oh starry starry night! This is how
I want to die.

It moves. They are all alive.
Even the moon bulges in its orange irons
to push children, like a god, from its eye.
The old unseen serpent swallows up the stars.
Oh starry starry night! This is how
I want to die:

into that rushing beast of the night,
sucked up by that great dragon, to split
from my life with no flag,
no belly,
no cry. ■

1. **Vincent Van Gogh.** (1853–1890) Dutch artist, first of the great modern Expressionist painters. This letter was written while he was painting "Starry Night on the Rhône."

❶ *To what is the tree compared?*

❷ *What is the "rushing beast"?*

PREREADING NOTES

READER'S JOURNAL

Students can freewrite about a dramatic image from nature, using sensory details that make the image concrete for the reader.

LANGUAGE SKILLS

Vivid verbs that should appear in the students' list include *slips up, boils, bulges, swallows, sucked up,* and *split.* Whichever verb the student chooses, the related verbs should be plausible alternates for that verb.

▶ Additional practice for using thesauruses is provided in the *Essential Skills Practice Book: Study and Research,* 4.25.

ANSWERS TO GUIDED READING QUESTIONS

❶ The tree is compared to a drowned woman.

❷ The rushing beast is death or eternity.

BIOGRAPHICAL/ART NOTE

Vincent van Gogh ended his own life in 1890 shortly after writing a letter to his brother expressing his emotional pain and crisis of religious faith. In van Gogh's time, chronic sadness and disinterest in life was called "melancholia." Long journeys and rest cures away from home were the recommended treatment for melancholia in the late 1800s. In 1889, when van Gogh painted *The Starry Night,* the Dutch artist was away from Holland and living along the Rhone River in France.

QUOTABLES

"It's as interesting and difficult to say a thing well as to paint it, isn't it?"

—Vincent van Gogh, in a letter to Emile Bernard

RESPONDING TO THE SELECTION

Answers will vary. Students might begin by describing the feelings the painting evokes in them and then comparing the painting to the poem.

ANSWERS FOR REVIEWING THE SELECTION

RECALLING

1. The town under the starry night does not exist.

2. The tree is the only individual in a ghost town. It is like a drowned woman.

3. The speaker sees eleven stars. The moon seems to be swelling out of its boundaries, pushing out children from within it. The stars are being swallowed by a serpent.

4. The speaker addresses the starry sky. She says that she wants to die by being pulled up into the darkness of the starry night.

INTERPRETING

Responses will vary. Possible responses are given.

5. The view of the eleven stars and the tall, dark tree blot out the town.

6. The town is silent, perhaps uncaring, about the tree/woman.

7. The speaker feels awe, longing, and perhaps despair. The sky is hot and powerful, engulfing the stars.

8. The serpent is death/eternity. Lives are being consumed. New lives are being born. Eventually, every creature will die.

SYNTHESIZING

Responses will vary. Possible responses are given.

9. The speaker wants to leave life with no trace that she has gone or has ever lived.

10. Thomas was telling his father to express as much passion as he could about life before its end. Sexton's speaker is saying that she has no passion for life, only for death and darkness; she wants to pass from her life unnoticed.

Responding to the Selection

Look at the reproduction of Van Gogh's painting "The Starry Night" on page 813. Do you feel that Sexton captured the feeling of the painting in her poem? Why, or why not?

Reviewing the Selection

RECALLING

1. What "does not exist"?
2. What is the "one black-haired tree" like?
3. What does the speaker see in the sky? What is the moon like? What is it doing? What is happening to the stars?
4. What does the speaker address directly in the last two lines of stanza 2? What does she say to this thing?

INTERPRETING

5. What view overpowers and blots out the town?
6. What is the town's response to the "drowned woman" who "slips . . . into the hot sky"? What might the speaker be suggesting about the relationship between the woman and the town?
7. What emotion do you think the speaker feels looking at this sky? What is the sky like?
8. What is "the old unseen serpent"? What is being swallowed up? What is being born? How does the second stanza portray birth and death? In what sense are all things eventually swallowed up by night?

SYNTHESIZING

9. Assuming that the flag mentioned in the last lines of the poem is a flag of surrender, with what attitude does the speaker want to go into her death? What does she want that death to be like?
10. The poet Dylan Thomas wrote to his dying father, "Do not go gentle into that good night." In what ways is the sentiment expressed in Sexton's poem similar? In what ways is it different?

Understanding Literature (Questions for Discussion)

1. **Allusion.** An **allusion** is a figure of speech in which reference is made to a person, event, object, or work from history or literature. To what work is this entire poem an allusion? What thoughts and emotions does this work create in the speaker? Do you feel that the speaker caught the essence of the painting in her interpretation of it?

ANSWERS FOR UNDERSTANDING LITERATURE

► See the evaluation forms for discussion, active listening, and oral communication, *Assessment Portfolio,* 7.11–7.14.

Responses will vary. Possible responses are given.

1. Allusion. The work is an allusion to van Gogh's painting The Starry Night. The speaker seems to respond to the hypnotic pull of the swirling moon and stars in the picture and to identify with the stars as points of life, and the moon as the evil machine that creates mortal life and death.

2. Epigraph. The mythic elements are the tree woman, the moon god, the serpent of death, the night beast, and the dragon.

3. Rhyme. The end rhyme is the following:

sky (line 3) *die* (line 6)
eye (line 9) *die* (line 12)
cry (line 17)

(cont.)

2. **Epigraph.** An **epigraph** is a quotation placed at the beginning of a literary work to help establish the work's theme. In the epigraph to this poem, Van Gogh implies that painting the stars is for him a religious experience. What mythic elements are found in Sexton's poem?

3. **Rhyme. Rhyme** is the repetition of sounds at the ends of words. What end rhyme ties together the stanzas of the poem? What lines contain end rhymes? What are the rhyming words at the ends of these lines?

4. **Confessional Poetry. Confessional poetry** is verse that presents extremely personal ideas, feelings, or experiences. Often confessional poetry has the quality of a diary entry or of an overheard interior monologue, but equally often it is highly artificial, employing much personal symbolism. What personal experience does this poem relate? With what extremely personal subject does it deal?

Responding in Writing

Allusion Piece. Try to capture the essence of a particular painting, photograph, sculpture, or song in a poem or short essay of your own. What about your chosen piece do you find fascinating? Freewrite about your subject before you begin.

The Starry Night. *Vincent van Gogh, 1889. Oil on canvas, 29" x 36 1/4" (73.7 x 92.1 cm). The Museum of Modern Art, NY. Acquired through the Lillie P. Bliss Bequest*

Answers for Understanding Literature (cont.)

4. Confessional Poetry. The personal experience that the poem relates is van Gogh's (and the poet's) spiritual struggle with life. The extremely personal subject is the overwhelming despair and bouts of depression that van Gogh and Sexton both experienced.

Analytic Scales for Responding in Writing

Assign a score from 1 to 25 for each grading criterion below. (For more detailed evaluation, see the evaluation forms for writing, revising, and proofreading, *Assessment Portfolio,* 7.1–7.10.)

Allusion Piece

- **Content/Unity.** The piece presents a workable allusion.
- **Organization/Coherence.** The piece uses vivid and precise nouns, verbs, and modifiers.
- **Language/Style.** The piece uses vivid and precise nouns, verbs, and modifiers.
- **Conventions.** The piece of writing avoids errors in spelling, grammar, usage, mechanics, and manuscript form.

Art Note

Vincent van Gogh (1853–1890) was one of the greatest of the Expressionist painters. Expressionism is an artistic style in which the artist makes exaggerated use of his or her medium to express a unique personal vision. Expressionist painters tend to use a lot of paint, heavy brush strokes, and vivid lines. *The Starry Night* is an excellent example of Expressionism, for it is not at all a realistic portrayal of the night sky above a village. It is, rather, a portrayal of the artist's feelings about his subject. The emotional intensity of the work is perfectly captured in Sexton's poem.

Answers to Selection Check Test 4.12.11

EX. To what work of art does this poem allude?
It alludes to Vincent van Gogh's *The Starry Night.*

1. What slips into the hot sky?
The black-haired tree slips into the hot sky.

2. How many stars are there in the sky?
There are eleven stars.

3. What bulges in "orange irons"?
The moon bulges in "orange irons."

4. What swallows up the stars?
The "old unseen serpent" swallows the stars.

5. By what does the speaker wish to be sucked up?
The speaker wishes to be sucked up by the "great dragon."

ADDITIONAL RESOURCES

READER'S GUIDE
- Selection Worksheet, 12.7

ASSESSMENT PORTFOLIO
- Selection Check Test, 4.12.13
- Selection Test, 4.12.14

ESSENTIAL SKILLS PRACTICE BOOKS
- *Writing,* 1.17
- *Language,* 2.107–2.133, 2.147, 2.148, 2.149
- *Study and Research,* 4.5

ENRICHMENT ACTIVITIES

Interested students should choose a season and brainstorm a list of everyday, ordinary events that could be considered miraculous elements of that season.

Students might then write a brief poem celebrating one of those events and share it with the class.

SUPPORT FOR LEP STUDENTS

Point out to students that Giovanni does not use punctuation in this selection. Suggest that students read the poem once quickly to get a feel for the rhythm and beauty of the language and then read it carefully for sense.

PREREADING

POETRY

"Winter Poem"
by Nikki Giovanni

ABOUT THE AUTHOR

Nikki (Yolande Cornelia) Giovanni (1943–) grew up in Cincinnati, Ohio, but returned often to her birthplace in Knoxville, Tennessee, to visit her grandmother. She attended Nashville's Fisk University in the mid-1960s. Entering college as a self-described conservative, Giovanni soon switched to activism in the African-American Civil Rights movement and was a college organizer for the Student Non-Violent Coordinating Committee (SNCC). By 1970, Giovanni had a son, was teaching at Rutgers University, and had already published three books of poetry—*Black Feeling, Black Talk; Black Judgment;* and *Re: Creation.* Though hailed as a leading figure of the new African-American poetry between 1968 and 1971, motherhood shifted her priorities. In 1975 she said, "To protect [my son] Tommy there is no question I would give my life. I just cannot imagine living without him. But I can live without the revolution." Her later publications are more personal and more concentrated on the African-American family. Some of her most popular poems, including *Spin a Soft Black Song* (1971) and *Ego Tripping* (1973), were written for children. Giovanni has received dozens of honorary degrees and literary awards and is much sought after as a lecturer and reader of her own works. *A Dialogue* (1972) and *A Poetic Equation* (1974) are transcripts of talks between Giovanni and her fellow authors James Baldwin and Alice Walker.

ABOUT THE SELECTION

"Winter Poem" demonstrates why Nikki Giovanni has become such a widely read, beloved poet. It shows her ability to transform an ordinary event, through imagination, into a miracle.

GOALS/OBJECTIVES

Studying this lesson will enable students to

- appreciate a lyric poem about a magical transformation
- define the terms *personification* and *symbol* and apply them to an analysis of a lyric poem
- write a poem employing dialogue
- analyze the breaking of capitalization rules in a contemporary free verse poem
- understand the importance and functions of play among children

READER'S JOURNAL

The American poet E. E. Cummings once wrote that "children guessed (but only a few/and down they forgot as up they grew/autumn winter spring summer)." Have your attitudes toward play changed since your childhood? How might retaining playful, childlike qualities help people to be happier and more productive as adults? Write about these questions in your journal.

THINKING SKILLS

Read the Language Arts Survey, 4.5, "Remembering and Visualizing." Then, as you read the following poem, visualize the scene remembered by the speaker in the poem, part by part. Outline the sequence of events of the poem in your journal.

"Winter Poem"

NIKKI GIOVANNI

once a snowflake fell
on my brow and i loved
it so much and i kissed
it and it was happy and called its cousins
5 and brothers and a web
of snow engulfed me then
i reached to love them all
and i squeezed them and they became
a spring rain and i stood perfectly
10 still and was a flower ■

WORDS FOR EVERYDAY USE: **en • gulf** (en gulf´) *vt.,* swallow up; overwhelm

PREREADING NOTES

READER'S JOURNAL

Journal entries might include references to the child's freedom from worry about practical concerns—status, economic security, family relationships. Responses to the productivity question could raise the qualities of spontaneity, humor, and freedom from inhibition as necessary for enhancing the adult's sense of freedom to generate new ideas and creations.

THINKING SKILLS

The sequence of events described could be outlined as follows:

- Snowflake fell
- Snowflake landed on speaker's brow
- Speaker kissed the snowflake
- Web of snow engulfed the speaker
- Speaker reached for all the snowflakes
- Speaker squeezed handfuls of snow
- Snowflakes became rain
- Speaker became a flower

CROSS-CURRICULAR ACTIVITIES

Earth Science. Ask students to make a graph showing temperature and air pressure conditions necessary for snow formation. The labels on the graph's two axes can be "temperature" and "barometric pressure."

VOCABULARY IN CONTEXT

- The thirty-foot wave engulfed the windsurfer.

RESPONDING TO THE SELECTION

The feelings created could be exhilaration, peace, and warm appreciation of life. Students' experiences will vary.

ANSWERS FOR REVIEWING THE SELECTION

RECALLING

1. A snowflake fell on the speaker's brow, and the speaker kissed the snowflake.

2. The speaker was engulfed in snow; when she squeezed the snowflakes, they became raindrops.

INTERPRETING

Responses will vary. Possible responses are given.

3. The emotion created was joy.

4. Students might imagine the speaker grabbing handfuls of falling snow. The speaker squeezes the snow to show her love.

SYNTHESIZING

Responses will vary. Possible responses are given.

5. The speaker is rejuvenated by the sensation of being covered in snowflakes. She stands still to receive the full impact of the snow.

ANSWERS FOR UNDERSTANDING LITERATURE

▶ See the evaluation form for discussion, active listening, and oral communication, *Assessment Portfolio,* 7.11–7.14.

Responses will vary. Possible responses are given.

1. Personification. The snowflakes are personified by the speaker's reaction to them as fellow beings. At the end of the poem, the speaker becomes "unpersonified." She becomes a flower, a part of the plant kingdom. The speaker feels connection to the natural world outside humanity.

2. Symbol. Flowers and spring rain traditionally symbolize the renewal of life.

Responding to the Selection

What feelings does this poem create in you? Describe an experience you have had that created a similar feeling.

Reviewing the Selection

RECALLING

1. What fell and where? What did the speaker do in response?

2. In what was the speaker engulfed? What happened when the speaker squeezed the flakes?

INTERPRETING

▶▶ 3. What emotion was created in the speaker by the event that occurs in the first line?

▶▶ 4. What action do you imagine the speaker performing when she says, "i squeezed them"? Why does the speaker squeeze the flakes?

SYNTHESIZING

5. Spring is a time of beginnings, when the world blossoms. In what sense do the events described in this poem cause the speaker to blossom? What emotion is conveyed by the speaker's standing "perfectly still"?

Understanding Literature (Questions for Discussion)

1. **Personification. Personification** is a figure of speech in which an idea, animal, or thing is described as if it were a person. What things are personified in this poem? In what sense is the event described at the end of the poem the opposite of personification? What does the event at the end of the poem tell you about the speaker's feelings about her connection to the natural world?

2. **Symbol.** A **symbol** is a thing that stands for or represents both itself and something else. For example, a rose is a traditional symbol of beauty. What do flowers and spring rain traditionally symbolize?

ANSWERS TO SELECTION CHECK TEST 4.12.13

EX. What season is the subject of this poem?
The poem is about winter.

1. Where did the snowflake land?
The snowflake landed on the speaker's brow.

2. Whom did the snowflake call?
It called its cousins and brothers.

3. Why did the speaker reach out to the snowflakes?
The speaker reached out to love the snowflakes.

4. What did the snowflakes become?
The snowflakes became spring rain.

5. What does the speaker say she is in the last line?
The speaker says she is a flower.

Responding in Writing

Dialogue Poem. Think of an imaginative game that is often played by children, and create a cluster chart to come up with details related to the game. Refer to the Language Arts Survey, 1.17, "Clustering." Then create two children to be characters in a dialogue. Write a brief free verse poem that captures the dialogue of your two characters playing an imaginative game. Try to capture in your characters' voices the actual sound of the speech of children. Refer to the Language Arts Survey, 2.147, "Formal and Informal English"; 2.148, "Register"; and 2.149, "Tone and Voice."

Language Lab

Capitalization. Review the Language Arts Survey, 2.107–2.133, on capitalization rules. What capitalization rules are broken in Nikki Giovanni's "Winter Poem"? Why might poets choose to bend the rules of capitalization? Discuss this question with your classmates.

PROJECT

Social Science/Psychology: The Play of Children. With other students in your class, research current thought about the nature and function of play in children. Refer to child development textbooks, books on parenting, and encyclopedias. Then hold a full-class discussion of the following topic: "Play Is Children's Work." Consider such issues as the role that play performs in socialization with peers, in learning to talk, and in learning about the adult world.

ANALYTIC SCALES FOR RESPONDING IN WRITING

Assign a score from 1 to 25 for each grading criterion below. (For more detailed evaluation, see the evaluation forms for writing, revising, and proofreading, *Assessment Portfolio,* 7.1–7.10.)

Dialogue Poem

- **Content/Unity.** The dialogue poem contains a conversation between two children playing an imaginative game.
- **Organization/Coherence.** The poem has coherence and the rhythm or natural speech.
- **Language/Style.** The poem uses vivid and precise nouns, verbs, and modifiers.
- **Conventions.** The dialogue poem avoids errors in spelling, grammar, usage, mechanics, and manuscript form.

ANSWERS FOR LANGUAGE LAB

Responses will vary. Students might note that this poem deals with a quiet, lovely event, and the lack of capitalization reinforces the reader's impression of the delicacy of the moment.

PROJECT NOTES

▶See the worksheets and evaluation forms for projects, *Assessment Portfolio,* 7.20–7.23.

The Play of Children

- Excellent sources of information about the functions and value of play are the parenting books by Benjamin Spock, Penelope Leach, and T. Berry Brazelton.
- Discussion should be orderly and deal expressly with the topics raised.

ADDITIONAL RESOURCES

READER'S GUIDE
- Selection Worksheet, 12.8

ASSESSMENT PORTFOLIO
- Selection Check Test, 4.12.15
- Selection Test, 4.12.16

ESSENTIAL SKILLS PRACTICE BOOKS
- *Language,* 2.153

SUPPORT FOR LEP STUDENTS

ADDITIONAL VOCABULARY

soldered—Joined with melted metal

evaded—avoided; tried to escape from

etched—scratched a pattern on a surface

unwitting—unknowing

VOCABULARY FROM THE SELECTIONS

cadenced	quell
crucify	spurn
mitigate	surrogate

PREREADING

POETRY

Selected Poems
by James Worley

ABOUT THE AUTHOR

James Worley (1921–) was born in the Miner's Hospital in Welch, West Virginia, in the heart of coal-mining country. He attended Emory University and Atlanta University, then served in the United States Army in World War II, spending nineteen months in combat. He was among the United States soldiers who liberated the Nazi concentration camp at Dachau. After the war, he attended Columbia University on the G.I. Bill. There he was privileged to have as teachers some of the leading thinkers of his day, including Mark Van Doran, Lionel Trilling, Margaret Mead, and W. Y. Tyndall. After receiving his M.A. from Columbia, Worley taught high school English in Virginia, Tennessee, and New York. For twenty-four years he served on the English Department staff of Columbus East High School, in Columbus, Indiana. Throughout this time, he published his poetry widely in newspapers and magazines, including *The Christian Science Monitor,* the *Western Humanities Review,* the *New York Herald Tribune,* and *Prairie Schooner.* His poetry, similar to Emily Dickinson's in its wonderful economy of language and flashes of insight, appears in two collections, *Cold Comfort* and *Colder Comfort.* Worley lives in Columbus, Indiana, with his wife and his many cats.

ABOUT THE SELECTIONS

The poet and critic Randall Jarrell once wrote that when taking up the collected works of a fine poet, one has the sense of being in the presence not of a book but of a life. This is especially true of the poems of James Worley. In these poems one finds hundreds of moments captured as if in a snapshot, exquisitely rendered in precise, often playfully punning language. In "The Figure a Poem Makes," Robert Frost wrote that "it is but a trick poem and no poem at all if the best of it was thought of first and saved for the last." Worley's poems meet Frost's criteria: they begin with delight in some small observation and then skate through imagination and reflection into wisdom.

GOALS/OBJECTIVES

Studying this lesson will enable students to

- enjoy several contemporary poems by a master of epigrammatic free verse
- identify recurring themes in several works by one author
- define the terms *Modernism, alliteration, objective correlative,* and *metaphor* and use these terms in the analysis of poems

READER'S JOURNAL

Why do people keep pets? What functions do pets serve in people's lives? What do pets teach their owners? What do different kinds of pets reveal about those owners? Freewrite about these questions in your journal.

LANGUAGE SKILLS

Read the Language Arts Survey, 2.153, "Connotation and Denotation." Then, as you read the following poems, pick three words that are particularly rich in connotations, or associations, and describe the connotations of these words in your journal.

Selected Poems

JAMES WORLEY

"PETS"

Living, they are surrogates for our sadness,
but at their times of sudden ice,
when dawn doesn't and noon nevers and night is,
they go without apology or regret
and leave all grief to us.

"TO WALDEN WHEREVER"

My eyes mist
as I remember Walden the tomcat
who leapt upon the small dog's back
and off again—whist!—
just because it was spring.
Walden wherever, leap and leap and
leap!

"SWANS TRAPPED IN A WINTER STREAM"

Betrayed by water, then crucified by ice,
their beaks now soldered shut with frozen blood,
they suffer silent the foxes gliding out.

WORDS FOR EVERYDAY USE:

sur • ro • gate (sʉr´ə git) *n.,* substitute
cru • ci • fy (krōō´sə fī´) *vt.,* torment; be cruel to

PREREADING NOTES

READER'S JOURNAL

Student responses should include answers such as the following: pets give their owners affection and companionship, teach their owners appreciation for simple joys, and reveal their owners' inner nature.

LANGUAGE SKILLS

Student word choices will vary. The following are examples from the selection of words with their connotations:

apology—connotes feelings of guilt, shame, or weakness
betrayed—connotes cowardly retreat from a pledge; wickedness
sails—connotes flying free with nature supporting motion

CROSS-CURRICULAR ACTIVITIES

Social Studies. Ask students to write their findings about the history of pets as companions over the past hundred years in the United States. Students should answer the following questions: How did dogs contribute to the settlement of the West? How were cats useful as household pets in waterfront settlements? What was the contribution of the horse to work on the frontier and to cross-continental communication?

LITERARY TECHNIQUE

Rhyme. Rhyme is the repetition of sounds at the ends of words. Writers of free verse sometimes use rhyme, as in the rhyme *mist/whist* in lines 1 and 4 of "To Walden Wherever."

VOCABULARY IN CONTEXT

- I'm not the dog's real owner; I'm just a surrogate who's keeping the dog for a couple of days.
- The audience crucified the mediocre actor.

Literary Technique

• **Symbol.** A **symbol** is something that represents both itself and something beyond itself. Because of the changes in appearance throughout its monthly cycle, the moon has long been a traditional symbol of mutability and inconstancy. See, for example, Juliet's lines in act II, scene ii of *Romeo and Juliet*: "O, swear not by the moon, th' inconstant moon./That monthly changes in her circled orb,/Lest that thy love prove likewise variable." Thus the association of the moon with love and love poetry has a venerable history, playfully suggested in "The Readiness is All" by the phrase "an insistent twig was spurned."

• **Allusion.** An **allusion** is a reference in a literary work to some well-known part of another work, of history, or of culture. The title of this poem is an allusion to the following lines from act V, scene ii of *Hamlet:*

> There is a special providence in the fall of a sparrow. If it be now, 'tis not to come; if it be not to come, it will be now; if it be not now, yet it will come. The readiness is all.

In this poem, it is the speaker's readiness that is all—his or her willingness to watch the moon until the perfect poetic moment occurs.

"The Readiness is All"

That moon there quite above the woods
botched its first attempts at verse tonight
(a branch evaded, an insistent twig was spurned,
a trunk hid what another might have etched)
but wait—there's cadenced foliage to come—
and go—and come most delicately again:
see the cirrus?[1] quick! a sonnet sails.

1. **cirrus.** Wispy clouds

Words for Everyday Use: **spurn** (spŭrn) *vt.,* reject
ca • denced (kăd′nst) *adj.,* measured; rhythmic

Vocabulary in Context

- The board members spurned the vice president's reorganization strategy.
- The cadenced ticking of a clock will help a puppy sleep.
- The senator's apologies did not quell the demands for his resignation.
- Wearing a seatbelt will mitigate the damage that a person receives from an auto accident.

"AT VESPERS"

Its bells a-meow, a dusk-cuff round its neck,
the church crouched like a great iron-throated cat
godawful in the plangent[2] gloom,
where belfry bats, black beyond confession,
wove a net of night,
and cattle at their evening gate lowed long their discontent.

"IN RE: NOTIFICATION OF WIVES AND MOTHERS"

If first she sits, so much the better;
but do not touch the woman
even if she trembles terribly:
what she is hearing no touch can quell,
no presence mitigate:
leave the letter and go away.

"ADLAI STEVENSON"[3]

(JULY, 14, 1965)

On a day when Mars first had its mystery forced
and the Bastille[4] fell again in the few freed minds,
by an exercise of taste (on Grosvenor Street)
a man of grace graced England with his death.
At home both man and grace went still ungrasped:
a president cocked his head from side to side
to find the cameras he'd been told would watch
and said some "right" things at the unwitting land. ■

2. **plangent.** Loud, mournful sounding
3. **Adlai Stevenson.** (1900–1965) Delegate to the United Nations, governor of Illinois, and presidential candidate
4. **Bastille.** State prison in Paris, France, that was destroyed on July 14, 1789, during the French Revolution

Responding to the Selection

Choose one of these poems that you particularly like and write a letter to the poet explaining what you like about it.

WORDS FOR EVERYDAY USE:

quell (kwel) *vt.,* end
mit • i • gate (mit´ə gāt´) *vt.,* make less severe or painful

HISTORICAL NOTE

In the Roman Catholic Church, there are seven canonical hours, or times for public prayers that are recited or sung. Matins were originally said at night in the early morning hours. Lauds are morning prayers. Terce, Sext, and None are midmorning, noon, and midafternoon prayers. Vespers are evening prayers, and Complines are night prayers.

HISTORICAL NOTE

The first line of "Adlai Stevenson" refers to pictures taken of the planet Mars by a space probe. The second line refers to the storming of the Bastille prison, which set off the French Revolution. Adlai Stevenson, the poem's subject, helped found the United Nations. He was a diplomat, governor of Illinois, chief United States representative to the United Nations, and an unsuccessful candidate for president. The president referred to in line 6 is Lyndon B. Johnson, who in 1965 was escalating the war in Vietnam.

ANSWERS TO SELECTION CHECK TEST 4.12.15

EX. What kind of animal was Walden?
Walden was a tomcat.

1. What kinds of animals were trapped in ice?
Swans were trapped in ice.

2. What natural element botched an attempt at poetry?
The moon botched an attempt at poetry.

3. What wove a "web of night"?
Belfry bats wove a "web of night."

4. What should the bearer of bad news to a wife or mother do?
The bearer should leave the letter and go away.

5. What two historical events occured on the day Adlai Stevenson died?
Pictures were taken of Mars and the Bastille was stormed on the date of Stevenson's death.

Reviewing the Selection

RECALLING

1. According to the speaker in "Pets," what function is served by pets while they are alive?
2. What did the tomcat Walden do?
3. What "betrayed" and "crucified" the swans?
4. In "The Readiness Is All," what is compared to the moon? What does the speaker want the person being addressed to see?
5. What is compared to a cat in "At Vespers"? How are the bats described, and what do they do?
6. Who is being addressed by the speaker in "In Re: Notification of Wives and Mothers"? What advice does the speaker give?
7. Who was the "man of grace" who died on July 14, 1965? What else happened on that day? What was the response, at home, to this man's death?

INTERPRETING

8. What ends with the death of a pet? What can people no longer do with their emotions?
9. Why do you think the speaker's "eyes mist" when he remembers Walden? What characteristic in humans and in animals does the speaker admire?
10. Why do the swans "suffer silent"? An old myth has it that the swan, silent throughout its life, trumpets at the time of its death. What happens, instead, in "Swans Trapped in a Winter Stream"? In what sense does the poem speak for those creatures that cannot speak for themselves? What aspect of nature does this poem describe?
11. Why are the twigs and the cirrus clouds necessary to make the view of the moon really interesting in "The Readiness Is All"? Why is some sort of complication, conflict, or tension necessary to the production of a great work of literature?
12. What details in "At Vespers" create an ominous mood?
13. Why does the speaker in "In Re: Notification of Wives and Mothers" advise the person being addressed to "leave the letter and go away"? Why would any words that were said be hollow at such a time?
14. Of what does the cocking of the head from side to side in "Adlai Stevenson" remind you? What is literally being described? What aspects of the description show that the remarks made to the cameras are insincere?

Answers for Reviewing the Selection

RECALLING

1. People visualize their sadness inhabiting their pets.
2. Walden attacked a small dog and then leapt off.
3. Water betrayed them; ice crucified them.
4. The poet's perception is compared to the moon. Sometimes moonlight catches a tiny piece of beauty unexpectedly; the moon also misses many delicate images when shadows fall in front of them.
5. The church is compared to a cat; bats described as "black beyond confession" weave "a net of night."
6. The one who delivers the message of death is being addressed and is advised not to stay and try to comfort the woman.
7. Adlai Stevenson was the man who died on the day when astronomers first examined Mars closely, which was also the day the Bastille was stormed, for the second time in history, by French revolutionaries. The response at home was generally indifference.

INTERPRETING

Responses will vary. Possible responses are given.

8. Surrogacy ends with the death of a pet. Owners are forced to face grief.
9. The speaker misses Walden; the speaker admires the cat's exuberance and free spirit.
10. The swans are frozen in the water. Since they have no premonition of their death, they do not cry out. The poem expresses the swan's sense of betrayal; the poem describes the cruel aspect of nature.
11. The twigs and clouds add detail and depth to the scene lit by moonlight; conflict, tension, and the varied viewpoints of the characters in a piece of literature add interest and depth to what would otherwise be a boring list of people, places, or events.
12. Some details that create an ominous mood are the meowing bells, the church crouching, the black bats, and the night gloom.

(cont.)

Answers for Reviewing the Selection (cont.)

13. Any words would be hollow because someone hearing of death of a loved one is in shock and grief too intense to be assuaged by words.
14. It could remind the student of a plump bird looking for seed. What is being described is a politician displaying mannerisms that don't reflect true feelings. The politican is looking for the cameras to make sure his appearance of grief is visible to the public, so his attention is upon himself and his image.

SYNTHESIZING

Responses will vary. Possible responses are given.

15. The response to loss in "Pets" is the speaker's realization that the living animal had carried the owner's psychic burden of sadness. The theme is the pet's sharing the owner's identity. In "To Walden Wherever," the response to loss is admiration for a separate independent

(cont.)

SYNTHESIZING

15. Several of these poems deal with death or with responses to death. What differing responses to death are treated in these poems? What recurring themes can you find in them?

Understanding Literature (Questions for Discussion)

1. **Modernism. Modernism** was a twentieth-century artistic movement characterized by a rejection of traditional forms and much experimentation. One common device in Modernist poetry that can be found in the poetry of Walt Whitman, who strongly influenced the Modernists, is the intentional use of words in ways that violate traditional grammatical expectations. The word *never,* for example, is usually an adverb, a word that modifies a verb, an adjective, or another adverb. As what part of speech is the word *never* used in "Pets"? What state is described by the line "when dawn doesn't and noon nevers and night is"? What does it mean to say that "dawn doesn't and noon nevers"?

2. **Alliteration. Alliteration** is the repetition of initial consonant sounds. Find two examples of alliteration in "Swans Trapped in a Winter Stream." Find five examples in "At Vespers." Find two examples in "In Re: Notification of Wives and Mothers." Find three examples in "Adlai Stevenson."

3. **Objective Correlative.** An **objective correlative** is a group of images that together create a particular emotion in a reader. What emotion, or mood, is created by the images in "At Vespers"? What details in the poem contribute to the creation of this mood?

4. **Metaphor.** A **metaphor** is a figure of speech in which one thing is spoken or written about as if it were another. The figure of speech invites the reader to make a comparison between two things. Explain the metaphors in the following lines from these poems:

"their beaks now soldered shut"
"cadenced foliage"
"a sonnet sails"
"its bells a-meow"
"a dusk-cuff round its neck"
"belfry bats, black beyond confession"
"a net of night"
"the Bastille fell again in a few freed minds"
"cocked his head from side to side"

ANSWERS FOR REVIEWING THE SELECTION (CONT.)

being with a life apart from the owner's. Similarly, in "Adlai Stevenson," the theme and response to death is great admiration for a separate and heroic individual and also a wish to protect that person's memory. In "Swans Trapped in a Winter Stream," the response is empathy toward the swans who were betrayed by their former protector, the stream. The theme is avenging the lost dignity of swans who had no chance to cry out their last song. "In Re: Notification of Wives and Mothers" is also a poem about protecting someone's dignity; here the speaker tells how one should protect another person by leaving him or her alone in a time of grief.

ANSWERS FOR UNDERSTANDING LITERATURE

►See the evaluation forms for discussion, active listening, and oral communication, *Assessment Portfolio,* 7.11–7.14.

Responses will vary. Possible responses are given.

1. Modernism. In "Pets," the word never is used as a verb. Students may answer that "dawn doesn't" means that the sun doesn't rise, that "noon nevers" means that it is never daytime, and that "night is" means that night will last forever.

2. Alliteration. Examples of alliteration are "Betrayed/beaks" and "suffer/silent" in "Swans Trapped in a Winter Stream"; "belfry/bats," "net/night," "lowed/long," "where/wove," "confession/cattle" in "At Vespers"; "better/but" and "trembles/terribly" in "In Re: Notification of Wives and Mothers"; and "Mars/mystery" and "few/free" in "Adlai Stevenson."

3. Objective Correlative. The mood is gloom and foreboding. Some details that contribute to the mood are the dark, dusky church crouching; the black bats; and the discontented lowing of the cattle.

4. Metaphor

• "their beaks now soldered shut"—The beaks are compared to pieces of metal being burned together.

(cont.)

ANSWERS FOR UNDERSTANDING LITERATURE (CONT.)

• "cadenced foliage"—The foliage is compared to a musical composition.
• "a sonnet sails"—The sonnet is compared to a sailboat.
• "its bells a-meow"—The church is compared to a cat.
• "a dusk-cuff round its neck"—The darkness around the church steeple is compared to a collar.
• "belfry bats, black beyond confession"—The bats are compared to sinners.
• "a net of night"—The darkness is compared to a woven net.
• "the Bastille fell again in a few free minds"—The Bastille is compared to a set of societal laws that toppled, because people could no longer respect them.
• "cocked his head from side to side"—The politician is compared to a bird looking in a mirror.

ADDITIONAL RESOURCES

READER'S GUIDE
- Selection Worksheet, 12.9

ASSESSMENT PORTFOLIO
- Selection Check Test, 4.12.17
- Selection Test, 4.12.18

ESSENTIAL SKILLS PRACTICE BOOKS
- *Writing,* 1.23
- *Language,* 2.13, 2.49, 2.140, 2.142

ENRICHMENT ACTIVITIES

Ask students to discuss civil rights issues related to their school or community. Have them review the rights given to American citizens by the Constitution,especially in the Bill of Rights. What groups seem to face the most resistance in their attempts to control their individual lives? What groups are not included in decision-making for the community? What groups do not seem to have a fair share in the economic, educational, and natural resources of the community? What might be done to remedy this situation?

SUPPORT FOR LEP STUDENTS

Have students review the Constitution and the Bill of Rights. Ask them to write in their own words the basic rights that are guaranteed to each American under the Constitution.

ADDITIONAL VOCABULARY

trudge—weary walk
shrewd—clever

PREREADING

POETRY

"To Black Women"
by Gwendolyn Brooks

ABOUT THE AUTHOR

Gwendolyn Brooks (1917–) was born in Topeka, Kansas, and raised in the "Bronzeville" section of Chicago, Illinois. She attended Englewood High School and Wilson Junior College. Brooks began writing poetry at age seven and published her earliest work in the *Chicago Defender.* Her first book of poetry, *A Street in Bronzeville,* appeared in 1945. In 1950, Brooks received the Pulitzer Prize for her second book of poetry, *Annie Allen* (1949), becoming the first African American to receive this prestigious award. Brooks's first two books of poetry and her novel *Maude Martha* (1953) all draw upon her experiences growing up in the Chicago inner city. Other works by Brooks include *The Bean Eaters* (1960), a collection of poetry; *Bronzeville Boys and Girls* (1956), a children's book; and *Report from Part One* (1972), an autobiographical work. In 1969, Brooks was named poet laureate of the State of Illinois. In 1985, she was appointed Poetry Consultant to the Library of Congress, the first African-American woman to hold that position. Her *Winnie* (1988) is a book of poetry inspired by the South African leader Winnie Mandela, wife of Nelson Mandela, the anti-apartheid activist who became president of South Africa's first black majority government.

ABOUT THE SELECTION

The Civil Rights Movement of the late 1950s and 1960s made enormous strides toward achieving equality of rights for African Americans in the United States. An important part of that movement was the call by activists such as Eldridge Cleaver, Malcolm X, and others for Black Pride—pride in the traditions, history, and culture of the African-American people. Gwendolyn Brooks has for many years been an important voice for Black Pride, and especially for pride among African-American women, reminding the world of her sisters' struggles, triumphs, and potential in poems such as **"To Black Women."**

GOALS/OBJECTIVES

Studying this lesson will enable students to

- enjoy a lyric poem about struggle
- describe Brooks's literary accomplishments and explain the historical significance of her writing
- define *parallelism* and *internal rhyme*
- recognize the use of these techniques in their reading
- understand the use of linking verbs and predicates
- understand the use of base words and prefixes

READER'S JOURNAL

Have you ever felt unrecognized for some quality or potential that you have? In your journal, make a list of those qualities or characteristics of yourself of which you are particularly proud.

LANGUAGE SKILLS

Read the Language Arts Survey, 2.13, "Linking Verbs," and 2.49, "Adding Predicates." Then, identify the linking verb in the third stanza of this poem and the four predicates that follow it. (Note that only the first of these predicates is actually included in the sentence with the linking verb.)

"To Black Women"

GWENDOLYN BROOKS

Sisters,
where there is cold silence—
no hallelujahs, no hurrahs at all, no handshakes,
no neon red or blue, no smiling faces—
5 prevail.
Prevail across the editors[1] of the world!
who are obsessed, self-honeying and self-crowned
in the seduced arena.

It has been a
10 hard trudge, with fainting, bandaging and death.
There have been startling confrontations.
There have been tramplings. Tramplings
of monarchs[2] and of other men.

❶ *What do "sisters" face? What does the speaker tell them to do?*

❷ *Why has it been a hard trudge?*

1. **editors.** Those who revise and make corrections in written statements of thought
2. **monarchs.** Kings, queens; rulers of nations, who have absolute authority

WORDS FOR EVERYDAY USE:
pre • vail (prē vāl´) *vi.,* triumph; be common
ob • sessed (əb sest´) *part.,* greatly preoccupied or troubled

PREREADING NOTES

READER'S JOURNAL

Students should list the qualities and characteristics of which they feel most proud. Their journal entries might also give examples of incidents when their strengths were not recognized. Students could write about the response they would like to have received and feel they deserved.

LANGUAGE SKILLS

The linking verb is *remain;* the four predicates are *large countries in your eyes, shrewd sun, the civil balance,* and *the listening secrets.*

ANSWERS TO GUIDED READING QUESTIONS

❶ "Sisters" face lack of recognition for their struggle. The speaker tells them to "prevail across the editors of the world," who decide what will be publicized based on their own desire for fame.

❷ The trudge has been hard because the women are tired from the long battle for respect and independence; some have been injured and killed in the struggle.

VOCABULARY IN CONTEXT

- Despite all the setbacks, we prevailed and held firm to our ideals.
- Leroy was obsessed with his own appearance and constantly preened in front of the mirror.

Answer to Guided Reading Question

❶ In the people addressed, there remains their unique perception, their wisdom and sense, their ability to create social harmony, and their understanding. The people continue to "create and train" flowers. The speaker may feel going onward, creating new things, is important when faced with oppression.

Literary Technique

Alliteration is the repetition of initial consonant sounds. In free verse, techniques such as alliteration help give poetry the musical quality that is provided in more standard verse by meter and rhyme. Encourage students to note the places where alliteration is used in the poem. Students should readily recognize the use of alliteration in stanza 1 in the following lines: "**S**isters,/where there is cold **s**ilence—"; "no **h**allelujahs, no **h**urrahs . . . no **h**andshakes"; and "**o**bsessed, **s**elf-honeying and **s**elf-crowned/in the **s**educed arena." An example of alliteration in stanza 2 is "**m**onarchs and of other **m**en." An example of alliteration in stanza 3 is "**s**hrewd **s**un . . . **c**ivil . . . **s**ecrets."

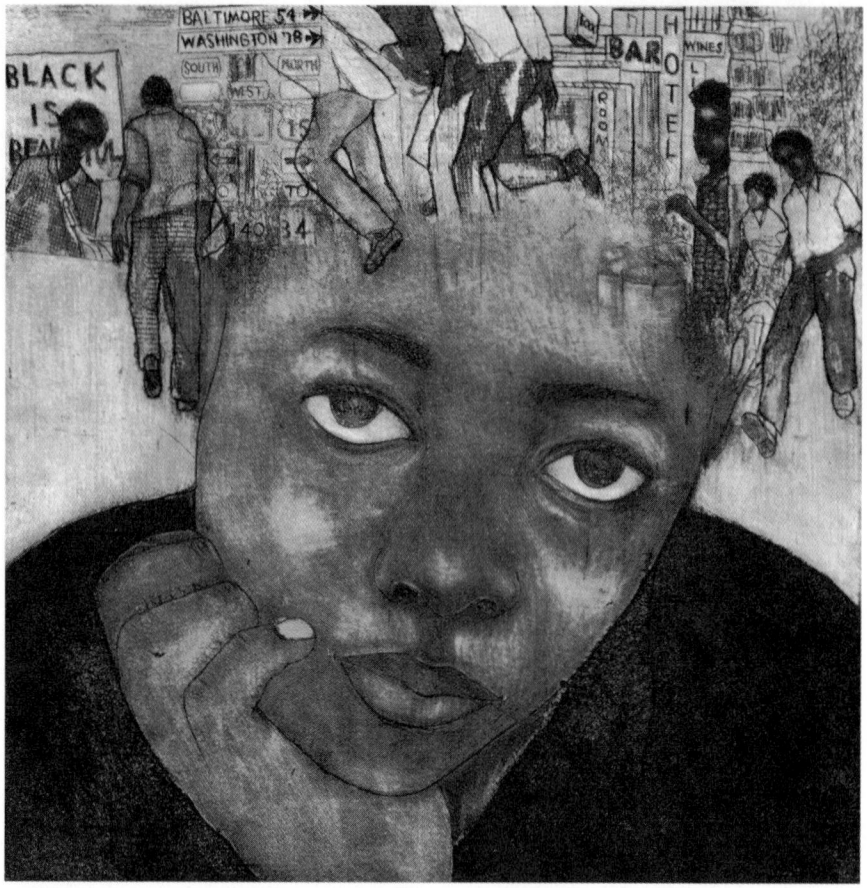

Gemini Etching. *Lout Mills, 1969.*
Evans-Tibbs collection Washington, DC.

What remains in the people addressed in the poem? What do they continue to do? Why does the speaker feel these things are important? ❶

But there remain large countries in your eyes.
15 Shrewd sun.
The civil balance.
The listening secrets.

And you create and train your flowers still. ■

Answers to Selection Check Test 4.12.17

EX. Whom does the speaker address in the first line of the poem?
The speaker addresses "sisters."

1. What does not exist in cold silence?
Hallelujahs, hurrahs, handshakes, neon red or blue, and smiling faces do not exist.

2. Across whom should "sisters" prevail?
Sisters should prevail across editors of the world.

3. Who has trampled the people the speaker addresses?
Monarchs and other men have trampled these people.

4. What remains in the eyes of the people addressed?
Large countries remain in their eyes.

5. What do the people addressed continue to do?
They continue to create and train flowers.

Responding to the Selection

Read the Language Arts Survey, 1.23, "Analysis Charts." Then, make an analysis chart with four heads, one for each of the four stanzas of this poem. (The last stanza consists of a single line.) On your chart, list the topic and main idea of each stanza.

Reviewing the Selection

Recalling

1. To whom is this poem addressed? What does the speaker tell these people to do in line 5?
2. What adjectives does the speaker use to describe "the editors of the world"?
3. What sorts of trials or struggles are mentioned in stanza 3?
4. What can be found in the "sisters'" eyes?

Interpreting

5. What conditions listed in stanza 1 would make life difficult for the people mentioned in line 1?
6. Editors are people who make decisions about what ideas and writings will be published or broadcast. Does the speaker believe that the "editors of the world" pay proper attention to the voices of her "sisters"? Why, or why not?
7. To what might the "It" at the beginning of line 9 refer?
8. Which line in stanza 3 suggests that the "sisters" have large, unexplored potentials? that they are intelligent and warm? that they help others to achieve harmony and community? that they pay attention to other people and therefore know many things that others do not know?

Synthesizing

9. If the statements made in stanza 3 are true, why should "the editors of the world" pay more attention to what the "sisters" have to say?
10. The verb train means "to drag or follow behind." What might be the "flowers" that the "sisters" create and train?

Responding to the Selection

Students might list the following main ideas: the topic of stanza 1 is the speaker's sisters; the main idea of stanza 1 is the lack of recognition of the struggles and triumphs of the speaker's sisters. The topic of stanza 2 is the "hard trudge"; the main idea of stanza 2 is that "monarchs" and "other men" have trampled the speaker's sisters. The topic of stanza 3 is the speaker's sisters' eyes; the main idea of stanza 3 is all that remains in these eyes. The topic of stanza 4 is the act of creation performed by the sisters; the main idea of stanza 4 is that despite all adversity the sisters addressed in the poem still create and train flowers.

Answers for Reviewing the Selection

RECALLING

1. The poem is addressed to African-American women. The speaker tells them to prevail.
2. The speaker calls "the editors of the world" obsessed, self-honeying, and self-crowned.
3. The struggles are physical and emotional tests of endurance.
4. The "sisters" eyes hold large countries, the sun, civil balance, and secrets.

INTERPRETING

Responses will vary. Possible responses are given.

5. Being ignored by the press would make life difficult for them.
6. No. The speaker says the "editors" are self-interested and obsessed only with fame.
7. "It" could be the struggle for recognition and equality.
8. Line 14 suggests that the "sisters" have large, unexplored potentials; line 15 suggests that they are intelligent and warm; line 16 suggests that they help others to achieve harmony and community; line 17 suggests that they pay attention to other people and therefore know many things that others do not know.

(cont.)

Answers for Reviewing the Selection (cont.)

SYNTHESIZING

Responses will vary. Possible responses are given.

9. They should pay attention because the "sisters" understand and know the truth of the struggle for freedom. They are intelligent and in tune with both themselves and others.
10. The flowers might be the woman's children, or the flowers might symbolize any creative endeavor.

Answers for Language Lab

1. **monopoly**—exclusive control of a commodity or service in a given market
2. **monotone**—uninterrupted repetition of the same tone
3. **monochromatic**—of or having one color
4. **monogamy**—practice of being married to only one person at a time
5. **monologue**—long speech by one speaker
6. **monotheism**—belief or doctrine that there is only one God
7. **archangel**—chief angel
8. **archbishop**—bishop of the highest rank
9. **archenemy**—chief enemy
10. **matriarch**—woman who rules her family or people

Answers for Understanding Literature

► See the evaluation forms for discussion, active listening, and oral communication, *Assessment Portfolio,* 7.11–7.14.

Responses will vary. Possible responses are given.

1. Parallelism. Four examples are the following: lines 3 and 4 "no hallelujahs, no hurrahs . . . no handshakes, no neon . . . no smiling faces"; lines 11 and 12 "There have been . . . There have been"; line 12 "tramplings. Tramplings"; and line 13 "of monarchs . . . of other men."

2. Internal Rhyme. The rhyming words in stanza 3 are *remain* and *train.*

Language Lab

Base Words and Prefixes. Read the Language Arts Survey, 2.140, "Base Words and Prefixes," and 2.142, "Greek and Latin Roots." The word *monarch* comes from *mono,* meaning "one," and *arch,* meaning "to rule." Use a dictionary to find the meanings of the following words that use the prefix *mono* and the root *arch.*

1. monopoly
2. monotone
3. monochromatic
4. monogamy
5. monologue
6. monotheism
7. archangel
8. archbishop
9. archenemy
10. matriarch

Understanding Literature (Questions for Discussion)

1. **Parallelism. Parallelism** is a rhetorical technique in which a writer emphasizes the equal value or weight of two or more ideas by expressing them in the same grammatical form, as in Abraham Lincoln's reference in the Gettysburg Address to "government of the people, by the people, for the people." Find four examples of parallelism in this poem.
2. **Internal Rhyme. Internal rhyme** is the use of rhyming words within lines. What word at the beginning of stanza 3 rhymes with what word in the final line?

Project

A Celebration of African-American Women Poets. Work with students in your class to plan a celebration of the work of the many great women poets of African descent in the American literary tradition. Divide into small groups and assign one poet from the following list to each group.

Brooks, Gwendolyn
Clifton, Lucille
Dove, Rita
Evans, Mari
Giovanni, Nikki
Harper, Frances
Sanchez, Sonia
Shange, Ntozake
Walker, Alice
Walker, Margaret
Wheatley, Phillis

Project Notes

►See the worksheets and evaluation forms for projects, *Assessment Portfolio,* 7.20–7.23.

A Celebration of African-American Women Poets. Students might wish to give an oral interpretation of works by these poets. Refer students to the Language Arts Survey, 3.8, "Oral Interpretation."

PREREADING

NONFICTION

Inaugural Address
by John F. Kennedy

ABOUT THE AUTHOR

John F. Kennedy (1917–1963), thirty-fifth president of the United States, was born in Brookline, Massachusetts, to a family already very familiar with politics. Kennedy earned his undergraduate degree at Harvard University in 1940. That same year, his senior thesis, *Why England Slept,* was published. It examined Britain's reaction to the rise of the Nazi Party in Germany. From 1941 to 1945, Kennedy served in World War II as a torpedo boat commander and was honored for his bravery. His political career began when he returned home to Massachusetts. In 1946, he was elected to the United States House of Representatives and, in 1952, to the United States Senate. During his eight years as a senator, Kennedy married Jacqueline Bouvier and wrote the 1956 Pulitzer Prize winner *Profiles in Courage,* a book that examined the brave and moral actions of eight politicians. In 1960, he was elected president of the United States, the youngest person and the first Catholic to achieve that office. In 1962, President Kennedy faced a serious nuclear confrontation with what was then the Soviet Union in an episode known as the Cuban Missile Crisis. He also created the Peace Corps and was a supporter of civil rights legislation. Kennedy was assassinated on November 22, 1963, in Dallas, Texas.

ABOUT THE SELECTION

When John F. Kennedy was elected president of the United States, he took over the office from Dwight Eisenhower, who had been a much-decorated general in World War II. At the time of Kennedy's election, the nation was essentially peaceful and prosperous. Tensions existed, however, between the United States and the Communist-run Soviet Union—allies during World War II but later competitors for global influence.

In his **Inaugural Address**, Kennedy spoke of this turning point for his country and set the goals of his presidency. He also sought to establish himself as a forceful leader, a special challenge for him as the youngest man ever elected president. This speech is considered one of Kennedy's most inspiring, incorporating both literary techniques such as repetition and unifying cultural references.

GOALS/OBJECTIVES

Studying this lesson will enable students to

- appreciate a famous work of American political oratory
- understand the political situation to which Kennedy's Inaugural Address was a response
- define the terms *anaphora* and *parallelism* and find examples of these techniques in a nonfiction work

ADDITIONAL RESOURCES

READER'S GUIDE
- Selection Worksheet, 12.10

ASSESSMENT PORTFOLIO
- Selection Check Test, 4.12.19
- Selection Test, 4.12.20

ESSENTIAL SKILLS PRACTICE BOOKS
- *Study and Research,* 4.26

ENRICHMENT ACTIVITIES

Have students research the Kennedy administration. Students might wish to focus on feelings in the country about this young president, issues such as the Cuban Missile Crisis, or the assassination of Kennedy and its effects on the nation.

SUPPORT FOR LEP STUDENTS

Ask students to list the main ideas and topics of each paragraph in the selection.

ADDITIONAL VOCABULARY

signifying—meaning
mortal—human, subject to death
republics—independent nations with democratic government
invective—verbal attack
endeavor—try
testimony—supportive speech

VOCABULARY FROM THE SELECTION

asunder	sovereign
belabor	subversion
civility	temper
invoke	venture

PREREADING NOTES

READER'S JOURNAL

Student responses should include references to Kennedy's legacy—responsibility of citizens, responsibility to the developing world, commitment to world unity, and commitment to universal freedom.

RESEARCH SKILLS

Students should share their methodology and sources for the recordings they locate.

ANSWER TO GUIDED READING QUESTION

❶ The new generation has the power to end all human poverty; it also has the power to end all human life.

READER'S JOURNAL

Think about your image of John F. Kennedy. In your journal, describe what you know about him and the role he played in shaping recent American history.

RESEARCH SKILLS

Find a recording of Kennedy's inaugural address. Check your school and community libraries for recordings on records, CDs, audiocassettes, videotape, or other media, and listen to it with other students in your class. If you have access to electronic reference sources or on-line information services, use these to gather additional information about Kennedy and his presidency. Refer to the Language Arts Survey, 4.26, "Computer-Assisted Research."

Inaugural Address

JOHN F. KENNEDY

What are the characteristics of the new American generation? ❶

We observe today not a victory of party but a celebration of freedom—symbolizing an end as well as a beginning—signifying renewal as well as change. For I have sworn before you and Almighty God the same solemn oath our forebears[1] prescribed nearly a century and three-quarters ago.

The world is very different now. For man holds in his mortal hands the power to abolish all forms of human poverty and all forms of human life. And yet the same revolutionary beliefs for which our forebears fought are still at issue around the globe—the belief that the rights of man come not from the generosity of the state but from the hands of God.

We dare not forget today that we are the heirs of that first revolution. Let the word go forth from this time and place, to friend and foe alike, that the torch has been passed to a new generation of Americans—born in this century, tempered by war, disciplined by a hard and bitter peace, proud of our ancient heritage—and unwilling to witness or permit the slow undoing of those human rights to which this nation has always been committed, and to which we are committed today at home and around the world.

Let every nation know, whether it wishes us well or ill, that we shall pay any price, bear any burden, meet any hardship, support any friend, oppose any foe to assure the survival and the success of liberty.

This much we pledge—and more.

To those old allies whose cultural and spiritual origins we share, we pledge the loyalty of faithful friends. United, there is little we cannot do in a host of cooperative ventures. Divided, there is little we can do—for we dare not meet a powerful challenge at odds and split asunder.

1. **forebears.** Ancestors

WORDS FOR EVERYDAY USE:

tem • per (tem´pər) *vt.,* toughen, as by rigors or trying experiences

ven • ture (ven´chər) *n.,* risky or dangerous undertaking

a • sun • der (ə sun´dər) *adv.,* apart or separate in direction or position

VOCABULARY IN CONTEXT

- The blacksmith held the blade of the sword in the fire to temper it so that it would not break.
- The cross-country cycling trip was a courageous venture for the two disabled Vietnam veterans.
- The house was torn asunder by the tornado's whirling fury.

To those new states whom we welcome to the ranks of the free, we pledge our word that one form of colonial control shall not have passed away merely to be replaced by a far more iron tyranny. We shall not always expect to find them supporting our view. But we shall always hope to find them strongly supporting their own freedom—and to remember that, in the past, those who foolishly sought power by riding the back of the tiger ended up inside.

To those people in the huts and villages of half the globe struggling to break the bonds of mass misery, we pledge our best efforts to help them help themselves, for whatever period is required—not because the Communists may be doing it, not because we seek their votes, but because it is right. If a free society cannot help the many who are poor, it cannot save the few who are rich.

To our sister republics south of our border, we offer a special pledge—to convert our good words into good deeds—in a new alliance for progress—to assist free men and free governments in casting off the chains of poverty. But this peaceful revolution of hope cannot become the prey of hostile powers. Let all our neighbors know that we shall join with them to oppose aggression or subversion anywhere in the Americas. And let every other power know that this hemisphere intends to remain the master of its own house.

To that world assembly of sovereign states, the United Nations, our last best hope in an age where the instruments of war have far outpaced the instruments of peace, we renew our pledge of support—to prevent it from becoming merely a forum for invective—to strengthen its shield of the new and the weak—and to enlarge the area in which its writ may run.

Finally, to those nations who would make themselves our adversary, we offer not a pledge but a request—that both sides begin anew the quest for peace before the dark powers of destruction unleashed by science engulf all humanity in planned or accidental self-destruction. We dare not tempt them with weakness. For only when our arms are sufficient beyond doubt can we be certain beyond doubt that they will never be employed.

But neither can two great and powerful groups of nations take comfort from our present course—both sides overburdened by the cost of modern weapons, both rightly alarmed by the steady spread of the deadly atom, yet both racing to alter that uncertain balance of terror that stays the hand of mankind's final war.

So let us begin anew—remembering on both sides that civility is not a sign of weakness, and sincerity is always subject to proof. Let us never negotiate out of fear. But let us never fear to negotiate.

Let both sides explore what problems unite us instead of belaboring those problems which divide us.

Let both sides, for the first time, formulate serious and precise proposals for the inspection and control of arms—and bring the absolute power to destroy other nations under the absolute control of all nations.

Let both sides seek to invoke the wonders of science instead of its terrors. Together let us explore the stars, conquer the deserts, eradicate disease, tap the

❶ *Who is invited to join an "alliance for progress"?*

❷ *What must be controlled?*

WORDS FOR EVERYDAY USE:

sub • ver • sion (səb ver´zhən) *n.,* systematic attempt to overthrow a government
sov • er • eign (säv´ərn) *adj.,* independent
ci • vil • i • ty (sə vil´ə tē) *n.* politeness
be • la • bor (bē lā´bər) *vt.,* spend too much time or effort on
in • voke (in vōk´) *vt.,* call on for blessing, help, or inspiration
e • rad • i • cate (ē rad´i kāt´) *vt.,* get rid of; wipe out; destroy

ANSWERS TO GUIDED READING QUESTIONS

❶ The nations of the western hemisphere are invited to join an "alliance for progress."

❷ Arms and atomic weapons must be controlled.

VOCABULARY IN CONTEXT

- No subversion can defeat the individual who is self-reliant.
- Sovereign powers must treat one another with diplomacy.
- With unexpected civility the wrestler shook hands with his opponent.
- Don't belabor the point; simply make it and go on to the next item.
- At the beginning of the powwow, the chief spoke briefly to invoke the memory of the ancestors.
- We must eradicate our own weaknesses before judging the weaknesses of others.

Answer to Guided Reading Question

❶ This generation faces the challenge of defeating tyranny, poverty, disease, and war.

Answers to Selection Check Test 4.12.19

EX. What does Kennedy say is being observed on his inauguration day?
He says a celebration of freedom is being observed.

1. What power does Kennedy say humans now have?
He says humans have the power to abolish both poverty and human life.

2. For what purpose will Americans "pay any price"?
Americans will pay any price to "assure the survival and the success of liberty."

3. What special pledge is offered to "our sister republics south of the border"?
A pledge is given to turn our good words into good deeds.

4. What, according to Kennedy, is not a sign of weakness?
Civility is not a sign of weakness.

5. What can the energy, faith, and devotion to defending freedom do?
These forces can "light the world."

Responding to the Selection

Students may respond that Kennedy was full of hope and optimism about taking the presidency. Their view on taking political office may include optimism, pessimism, self-doubt, or confidence.

ocean depths, and encourage the arts and commerce.

Let both sides unite to heed in all corners of the earth the command of Isaiah—to "undo the heavy burdens . . . [and] let the oppressed go free."[2]

And if a beachhead[3] of cooperation may push back the jungle of suspicion, let both sides join in creating a new endeavor, not a new balance of power but a new world of law, where the strong are just and the weak secure and the peace preserved.

What challenge does this generation face? ❶

All this will not be finished in the first 100 days. Nor will it be finished in the first 1,000 days, nor in the life of this administration, nor even perhaps in our lifetime on this planet. But let us begin.

In your hands, my fellow citizens, more than mine, will rest the final success or failure of our course. Since this country was founded, each generation of Americans has been summoned to give testimony to its national loyalty. The graves of young Americans who answered the call to service surround the globe.

Now the trumpet summons us again—not as a call to bear arms, though arms we need—not as a call to battle, though embattled we are—but a call to bear the burden of a long twilight struggle, year in and year out, "rejoicing in hope, patient in tribulation"[4]—a struggle against the common enemies of man: tyranny, poverty, disease, and war itself.

Can we forge against these enemies a grand and global alliance, North and South, East and West, that can assure a more fruitful life for all mankind? Will you join in that historic effort?

In the long history of the world, only a few generations have been granted the role of defending freedom in its hour of maximum danger. I do not shrink from this responsibility—I welcome it. I do not believe that any of us would exchange places with any other people or any other generation. The energy, the faith, the devotion which we bring to this endeavor will light our country and all who serve it—and the glow from that fire can truly light the world. ■

2. **undo . . . free.** Isaiah 58:6
3. **beachhead.** Position gained as a secure starting point for an action
4. **rejoicing . . . tribulation.** Romans 12:12

Responding to the Selection

How do you think Kennedy felt about becoming president? How would you feel about undertaking such an important job, on which the lives of millions depended? Can you imagine ever seeking such a position? Why, or why not?

Reviewing the Selection

RECALLING

1. How does Kennedy compare the world at the time of his address to the world facing the founders of the United States?
2. What does Kennedy pledge to the nations of South and Central America? To whom is he also speaking?
3. To what emotion does Kennedy link negotiation? What issue is at highest stake in the negotiations he discusses?
4. In what way does Kennedy feel his generation is uniquely situated?

INTERPRETING

5. To what important change does Kennedy refer?
6. Why might Kennedy's pledge be particularly important?
7. How does Kennedy suggest the two sides approach negotiation? What benefits for humanity might arise from his plans?
8. What challenges and privileges does the unique situation of Kennedy's generation create?

SYNTHESIZING

9. Why do you think Kennedy included several references to God and the Bible? How might these references engage listeners?
10. What unifying concept runs through Kennedy's speech? How does he build his ideas around this concept?

Understanding Literature (Questions for Discussion)

1. **Anaphora. Anaphora** is any word or phrase that repeats or refers to something that precedes or follows it. For example, the phrase "let both sides" is repeated at the beginning of several paragraphs in Kennedy's speech. How does this anaphora emphasize Kennedy's ideas? Find two other examples of anaphora in the inaugural address.
2. **Parallelism. Parallelism** is a rhetorical technique in which a writer emphasizes the equal weight of two or more ideas by presenting them in the same grammatical form. Look at the opening phrase of Kennedy's speech. What is similar about the grammatical structure of the phrases "victory of party" and "celebration of freedom"? What does Kennedy suggest about the two ideas? How does he link them?

ANSWERS FOR REVIEWING THE SELECTION

RECALLING

1. Kennedy says the world at the time of his address and the world facing the Founding Fathers are similar because the same inequities and oppression exist for many people throughout the world and here in this country; they are different because the United States is more powerful and also because more Americans are committed to the struggle against inequity and oppression.
2. He pledges the support of the United States in helping them to achieve independence and democracy in their nations. He is also speaking to the rest of the impoverished peoples of the world.
3. He links negotiation to hope; the issue at highest stake is the survival of humanity.
4. He feels his generation of Americans has a unique opportunity in history to create peace and freedom throughout the world.

INTERPRETING

Responses will vary. Possible responses are given.

5. He refers to the change from a postwar focus inward, to a peacetime focus outward in a spirit of negotiation.
6. His pledge is important because the western hemisphere is in danger of annihilation by atomic warfare, and the nations in poverty will support whichever military power (East or West) feeds their people.
7. He suggests the two sides approach negotiation with strength but be willing to compromise; the benefits for humanity are peace and security.
8. The challenge is to remain united and focused on the goal of world peace and freedom from oppression; the privilege is to be a generation like no other in history with the power to change the world.

SYNTHESIZING

Responses will vary. Possible responses are given.

9. He included biblical references because many of his ideals are rooted in Christianity; most of his listeners at that time were familiar with the ideals of Christianity and with the Bible.
10. Students might say that triumphing over hardship and enduring difficulties is a unifying concept.

ANSWERS FOR UNDERSTANDING LITERATURE

▶ See the evaluation form for discussion, active listening, and oral communication, *Assessment Portfolio,* 7.11–7.14.

Responses will vary. Possible responses are given.

1. Anaphora. The anaphora gives coherence to the speech—the restatement reminds the listener of the first statement and also emphasizes the present statement. Two other examples of anaphora are in the phrases "a new generation of Americans" and "we dare not."

2. Parallelism. Kennedy subordinates the idea of "victory of party" to the idea of "celebration of freedom" with the negatives *not* and *but.*

ADDITIONAL RESOURCES

READER'S GUIDE
- Selection Worksheet, 12.11

ASSESSMENT PORTFOLIO
- Selection Check Test, 4.12.21
- Selection Test, 4.12.22

ESSENTIAL SKILLS PRACTICE BOOKS
- *Speaking and Listening,* 3.3

ENRICHMENT ACTIVITIES

Students might write about an heirloom or family tradition that is important to them. Students should try to describe the heirloom or tradition using vivid sensory details, whether it is their grandmother's afghan or an annual family feast. Students should explain why this object or event is special to them. What is the history of the heirloom or tradition? Was the value of this object or event explained to them when they were young? Do they plan to pass on the heirloom or carry on the family tradition? Why, or why not? Students might then discuss family heirlooms and traditions as a class. Do these objects or events have symbolic meaning? Why might something as mundane as an object or a gathering speak volumes about love to certain people?

SUPPORT FOR LEP STUDENTS

Review with students the additional vocabulary below before they read the selection.

IDIOMS

talk a blue streak—talk too much

fair weather—good weather

ADDITIONAL VOCABULARY

kinky—tightly curled

churn—container in which milk or cream is beaten or stirred into butter

PREREADING

FICTION

"Everyday Use"
by Alice Walker

ABOUT THE AUTHOR

Alice Walker (1944–) was raised in a sharecropping family in Eatonton, Georgia, and educated at Atlanta's Spelman College and then at Sarah Lawrence. In 1964, Walker visited Africa, and then took part in the voter registration drive in Mississippi in 1966. She tapped these experiences for her first book of poetry, *Once,* which explores her roots and the African-American struggle for civil rights. Her first novel, *Meridian,* also dealt with civil rights and was later hailed as a sensitive portrayal of the movement. Walker was married to civil rights lawyer Mel Leventhal from 1967 to 1976 and has one daughter. Her works reached a wider audience when her 1983 novel *The Color Purple* won the Pulitzer Prize for fiction and was turned into a successful movie. A central theme in Walker's writing is her belief that "not enough credit has been given to the black woman who has been oppressed beyond recognition."

ABOUT THE SELECTION

Like many of Alice Walker's writings, the story "**Everyday Use**" explores the idea of African-American heritage. In a conflict between a woman and her sister and mother, two different interpretations of heritage are explored.

GOALS/OBJECTIVES

Studying this lesson will enable students to

- enjoy a contemporary short story about cultural heritage
- describe Walker's literary accomplishments and explain the historical significance of her writing
- understand and assess elements of nonverbal communication
- define *point of view* and identify the point of view of literature they read
- define and identify the elements of plot
- write a family history

READER'S JOURNAL

Did you ever value something that had little monetary value? Why was this thing important to you? Did others value this thing as you did? Write in your journal about the item's importance to you.

SPEAKING AND LISTENING SKILLS

Read the Language Arts Survey, 3.3, "Elements of Nonverbal Communication." Then, as you read the story, note ways that Maggie communicates nonverbally. What are her actions? What do these actions communicate?

"Everyday Use"

ALICE WALKER

for your grandmama

I will wait for her in the yard that Maggie and I made so clean and wavy yesterday afternoon. A yard like this is more comfortable than most people know. It is not just a yard. It is like an extended living room. When the hard clay is swept clean as a floor and the fine sand around the edges lined with tiny, irregular grooves, anyone can come and sit and look up into the elm tree and wait for the breezes that never come inside the house.

Maggie will be nervous until after her sister goes: she will stand hopelessly in corners, homely and ashamed of the burn scars down her arms and legs, eying her sister with a mixture of envy and awe. She thinks her sister has held life always in the palm of one hand, that "no" is a word the world never learned to say to her.

You've no doubt seen those TV shows where the child who has "made it" is confronted, as a surprise, by her own mother and father, tottering in weakly from backstage.[1] (A pleasant surprise, of course: What would they do if parent and child came on the show only to curse out and insult each other?) On TV mother and child embrace and smile into each other's faces. Sometimes the mother and father weep, the child wraps them in her arms and leans across the table to tell how she would not have made it without their help. I have seen these programs.

Sometimes I dream a dream in which Dee and I are suddenly brought together on a TV program of this sort. Out of a dark and soft-seated limousine I am ushered into a bright room filled with many people. There I meet a smiling, gray, sporty man like Johnny Carson[2] who

1. **TV shows . . . backstage.** Refers to *This Is Your Life*, a television show in which celebrities were surprised by a group of family and friends.
2. **Johnny Carson.** Host of a television show

❶ *How does Maggie feel toward her sister?*

WORDS FOR EVERYDAY USE: **home • ly** (hōm´lē) *adj.*, simple, plain; **ush • er** (ush´ər) *vt.*, escort, conduct

PREREADING NOTES

READER'S JOURNAL

You should stress to students that often the most priceless objects are those that are imbued with a history that money could never replace. Encourage students to think about objects that have special importance only to them or other family members but that might go unnoticed and unappreciated by the rest of the world.

SPEAKING AND LISTENING SKILLS

Students may mention Maggie's shyness and self-protection that emerge in nervous gestures such as scraping her feet, hiding her scarred hands, and looking to her mother for approval.

ANSWER TO GUIDED READING QUESTION

❶ Maggie feels in awe of her sister because she feels her sister has the world in control; Maggie will be nervous until her sister leaves.

VOCABULARY FROM THE SELECTION

alcove	homely
doctrine	recompose
furtive	rifle
hangdog	scalding
heritage	usher

VOCABULARY IN CONTEXT

- A bald baby is never thought homely.
- The soldier will usher you to your tent.

Answers to Guided Reading Questions

❶ The speaker compares Maggie to a lame animal.

❷ She says she is a large-boned woman with calloused hands who dresses in overalls and can slaughter livestock with her bare hands. She says that on television she would need to have glistening hair, be a hundred pounds lighter, and be quick-witted and charming.

❸ The other house burned; Maggie was burned. Dee appeared to be happy that the house was destroyed.

Cross-curricular Activities

Mathematics and Sciences. Psychologists have long been interested in the reasons why siblings, who have similar genetic information and have been raised in the same environment, often grow up to be very different individuals with disparate temperaments, goals, and ambitions. Some psychologists believe that one's personality is shaped by one's ordinal birth number, and whether one is the oldest, youngest, or middle child will produce a lasting impression that forever affects the individual. You might wish to conduct a class poll. Have students make a list of ten qualities that they believe define them as individuals. On the top of each list, students should write whether they are the oldest, youngest, or middle child (or whether they are an only child). You should then encourage students to research what traits psychologists believe are associated with a child's ordinal birth number. (Psychology journals might be a good source of information.) Tabulate the results of the class poll. What qualities did oldest children, youngest children, and middle children claim to have? Were there any similarities by birth position, or were the answers widely varied? Do the class's findings support or refute the hypothesis supported by psychologists?

❶ *To what does the speaker compare Maggie?*

❷ *How does the speaker describe herself in real life? How does she visualize herself appearing on TV?*

❸ *What happened to the other house? What happened to Maggie? How did Dee appear to feel about the house?*

shakes my hand and tells me what a fine girl I have. Then we are on the stage and Dee is embracing me with tears in her eyes. She pins on my dress a large orchid, even though she has told me once that she thinks orchids are tacky flowers.

In real life I am a large, big-boned woman with rough, man-working hands. In the winter I wear flannel nightgowns to bed and overalls during the day. I can kill and clean a hog as mercilessly as a man. My fat keeps me hot in zero weather. I can work outside all day, breaking ice to get water for washing; I can eat pork liver cooked over the open fire minutes after it comes steaming from the hog. One winter I knocked a bull calf straight in the brain between the eyes with a sledge hammer and had the meat hung up to chill before nightfall. But of course all this does not show on television. I am the way my daughter would want me to be: a hundred pounds lighter, my skin like an uncooked barley pancake. My hair glistens in the hot bright lights. Johnny Carson has much to do to keep up with my quick and witty tongue.

But that is a mistake. I know even before I wake up. Who ever knew a Johnson with a quick tongue? Who can even imagine me looking a strange white man in the eye? It seems to me I have talked to them always with one foot raised in flight, with my head turned in whichever way is farthest from them. Dee, though. She would always look anyone in the eye. Hesitation was no part of her nature.

"How do I look, Mama?" Maggie says, showing just enough of her thin body enveloped in pink skirt and red blouse for me to know she's there, almost hidden by the door.

"Come out into the yard," I say.

Have you ever seen a lame animal, perhaps a dog run over by some careless person rich enough to own a car, sidle up to someone who is ignorant enough to be kind to him? That is the way my Maggie walks. She has been like this, chin on chest, eyes on ground, feet in shuffle, ever since the fire that burned the other house to the ground.

Dee is lighter than Maggie, with nicer hair and a fuller figure. She's a woman now, though sometimes I forget. How long ago was it that the other house burned? Ten, twelve years? Sometimes I can still hear the flames and feel Maggie's arms sticking to me, her hair smoking and her dress falling off her in little black papery flakes. Her eyes seemed stretched open, blazed open by the flames reflected in them. And Dee. I see her standing off under the sweet gum tree she used to dig gum out of; a look of concentration on her face as she watched the last dingy gray board of the house fall in toward the red-hot brick chimney. Why don't you do a dance around the ashes? I'd wanted to ask her. She had hated the house that much.

I used to think she hated Maggie, too. But that was before we raised the money, the church and me, to send her to Augusta[3] to school. She used to read to us without pity; forcing words, lies, other folks' habits, whole lives upon us two, sitting trapped and ignorant underneath her voice. She washed us in a river of make-believe, burned us with a lot of knowledge we didn't necessarily need to know. Pressed us to her with the serious way she read, to shove us away at just the moment, like dimwits, we seemed about to understand.

Dee wanted nice things. A yellow organdy[4] dress to wear to her graduation from high school; black pumps to match a green suit she'd made from an old suit

3. **Augusta.** City in Georgia where Paine College is located

4. **organdy.** Sheer cotton fabric

somebody gave me. She was determined to stare down any disaster in her efforts. Her eyelids would not flicker for minutes at a time. Often I fought off the temptation to shake her. At sixteen she had a style of her own: and knew what style was.

I never had an education myself. After second grade the school was closed down. Don't ask me why: in 1927 colored asked fewer questions than they do now. Sometimes Maggie reads to me. She stumbles along good-naturedly but can't see well. She knows she is not bright. Like good looks and money, quickness passed her by. She will marry John Thomas (who has mossy teeth in an earnest face) and then I'll be free to sit here and I guess just sing church songs to myself. Although I never was a good singer. Never could carry a tune. I was always better at a man's job. I used to love to milk till I was hooked in the side[5] in '49. Cows are soothing and slow and don't bother you, unless you try to milk them the wrong way.

I have deliberately turned my back on the house. It is three rooms, just like the one that burned, except the roof is tin; they don't make shingle roofs any more. There are no real windows, just some holes cut in the sides, like the portholes in a ship, but not round and not square, with rawhide holding the shutters up on the outside. This house is in a pasture, too, like the other one. No doubt when Dee sees it she will want to tear it down. She wrote me once that no matter where we "choose" to live, she will manage to come see us. But she will never bring her friends. Maggie and I thought about this and Maggie asked me, "Mama, when did Dee ever *have* any friends?"

She had a few. Furtive boys in pink shirts hanging about on washday after school. Nervous girls who never laughed. Impressed with her they worshiped the well-turned phrase, the cute shape, the scalding humor that erupted like bubbles in lye.[6] She read to them.

When she was courting Jimmy T she didn't have much time to pay to us, but turned all her faultfinding power on him. He *flew* to marry a cheap city girl from a family of ignorant flashy people. She hardly had time to recompose herself.

When she comes I will meet—but there they are!

Maggie attempts to make a dash for the house, in her shuffling way, but I stay her with my hand. "Come back here," I say. And she stops and tries to dig a well in the sand with her toe.

It is hard to see them clearly through the strong sun. But even the first glimpse of leg out of the car tells me it is Dee. Her feet were always neat-looking, as if God himself had shaped them with a certain style. From the other side of the car comes a short, stocky man. Hair is all over his head a foot long and hanging from his chin like a kinky mule tail. I hear Maggie suck in her breath. "Uhnnnh," is what it sounds like. Like when you see the wriggling end of a snake just in front of your foot on the road. "Uhnnnh."

Dee next. A dress down to the ground, in this hot weather. A dress so loud it hurts

❶ *In what way does the speaker characterize Dee's humor?*

5. **hooked in the side.** Kicked by a cow
6. **lye.** Alkaline substance used to make soap

WORDS FOR EVERYDAY USE:
fur • tive (fʊr´tiv) *adj.,* sneaky; stealthy
scald • ing (skôld´iŋ) *part.,* burning; injuring
re • com • pose (rē´kəm pōz´) *vt.,* restore calmness of mind

ANSWER TO GUIDED READING QUESTION

❶ The speaker implies that Dee's humor is hurtful and vicious.

ADDITIONAL QUESTIONS AND ACTIVITIES

How does Dee feel about her home and her family? In what way do her feelings affect her personality? How does the speaker seem to feel about her daughter Dee and her attitude?

Answers. Dee is embarrassed by her home and family, as she is described as wanting her home to burn down and as saying she will never bring her friends home. Students might say that such negative feelings are the reason why Dee has such a caustic, bitterly humorous personality. The speaker seems a little hurt by Dee's attitude but is forgiving and still loves her daughter.

VOCABULARY IN CONTEXT

- With furtive whispers, the girls took their seats.
- Scalding hot water turned the shellfish from brown to pink.
- Let me take a moment to recompose myself after the match.

Answers to Guided Reading Questions

❶ Dee says that *Dee* is a name given by her oppressors and that Dee is dead now.

❷ Dee might want to use the pictures of the house to show that she is in touch with her heritage and background.

Quotables

"What's in a name? that
which we call a rose
By any other name would
smell as sweet."

—William Shakespeare
The Tragedy of Romeo and Juliet

Additional Questions and Activities

Ask students to discuss whether or not they agree with the above quotation from *Romeo and Juliet*. Why are names important? What is significant about Dee choosing a new name for herself? How do students think the speaker feels about her daughter choosing a new name?

Answers. Students may suggest that Dee might be separating herself from her oppressors by choosing a new name, but she is separating herself from her family as well. "Dee" is a family name, and by rejecting the name, Dee is rejecting part of her family history. Students might say that the speaker feels hurt by her daughter's decision to change her given name.

my eyes. There are yellows and oranges enough to throw back the light of the sun. I feel my whole face warming from the heat waves it throws out. Earrings gold, too, and hanging down to her shoulders. Bracelets dangling and making noises when she moves her arm up to shake the folds of the dress out of her armpits. The dress is loose and flows, and as she walks closer, I like it. I hear Maggie go "Uhnnnh" again. It is her sister's hair. It stands straight up like the wool on a sheep. It is black as night and around the edges are two long pigtails that rope about like small lizards disappearing behind her ears.

❶ *What reason does Dee cite for changing her name to Wangero?*

"Wa-su-zo-Tean-o!"[7] she says, coming on in that gliding way the dress makes her move. The short stocky fellow with the hair to his navel is all grinning and he follows up with "Asalamalakim,[8] my mother and sister!" He moves to hug Maggie but she falls back, right up against the back of my chair. I feel her trembling there and when I look up I see the perspiration falling off her chin.

"Don't get up," says Dee. Since I am stout it takes something of a push. You can see me trying to move a second or two before I make it. She turns, showing white heels through her sandals, and goes back to the car. Out she peeks next with a Polaroid. She stoops down quickly and lines up picture after picture of me sitting there in front of the house with Maggie cowering behind me. She never takes a shot without making sure the house is included. When a cow comes nibbling around the edge of the yard she snaps it and me and Maggie *and* the house. Then she puts the Polaroid in the back seat of the car, and comes up and kisses me on the forehead.

❷ *Why might Dee want to include the house in all the photographs?*

Meanwhile Asalamalakim is going through motions with Maggie's hand. Maggie's hand is as limp as a fish, and probably as cold, despite the sweat, and she keeps trying to pull it back. It looks like Asalamalakim wants to shake hands but wants to do it fancy. Or maybe he don't know how people shake hands. Anyhow, he soon gives up on Maggie.

"Well," I say. "Dee."

"No, Mama," she says. "Not 'Dee,' Wangero Leewanika Kemanjo!"

"What happened to 'Dee'?" I wanted to know.

"She's dead," Wangero said. "I couldn't bear it any longer, being named after the people who oppress me."

"You know as well as me you was named after your aunt Dicie," I said. Dicie is my sister. She named Dee. We called her "Big Dee" after Dee was born.

"But who was she named after?" asked Wangero.

"I guess after Grandma Dee," I said.

"And who was *she* named after?" asked Wangero.

"Her mother," I said, and saw Wangero was getting tired. "That's about as far back as I can trace it," I said. Though, in fact, I probably could have carried it back beyond the Civil War through the branches.

"Well," said Asalamalakim, "there you are."

"Uhnnnh," I heard Maggie say.

"There I was not," I said, "before 'Dicie' cropped up in our family, so why should I try to trace it that far back?"

He just stood there grinning, looking down on me like somebody inspecting a Model A car.[9] Every once in a while he and Wangero sent eye signals over my head.

"How do you pronounce this name?" I asked.

7. **Wa-su-zo-Tean-o.** African dialect greeting
8. **Asalamalakim.** Muslim greeting
9. **Model A car.** Very old type of car

"You don't have to call me by it if you don't want to," said Wangero.

"Why shouldn't I?" I asked. "If that's what you want us to call you, we'll call you."

"I know it might sound awkward at first," said Wangero.

"I'll get used to it," I said. "Ream it out again."

Well, soon we got the name out of the way. Asalamalakim had a name twice as long and three times as hard. After I tripped over it two or three times he told me to just call him Hakim-a-barber. I wanted to ask him was he a barber, but I didn't really think he was so I didn't ask.

"You must belong to those beef-cattle peoples down the road," I said. They said "Asalamalakim" when they met you, too, but they didn't shake hands. Always too busy: feeding the cattle, fixing the fences, putting up salt-lick shelters,[10] throwing down hay. When the white folks poisoned some of the herd the men stayed up all night with rifles in their hands. I walked a mile and a half just to see the sight.

Hakim-a-barber said, "I accept some of their doctrines, but farming and raising cattle is not my style." (They didn't tell me, and I didn't ask, whether Wangero (Dee) had really gone and married him.)

We sat down to eat and right away he said he didn't eat collards[11] and pork was unclean. Wangero, though, went on through the chitlins and corn bread, the greens and everything else. She talked a blue streak over the sweet potatoes. Everything delighted her. Even the fact

10. **salt-lick shelters.** Places where cows are kept out of the heat by being given salt to lick
11. **collards.** Leafy vegetable

WORDS FOR EVERYDAY USE: **doc • trine** (däk´trin) *n.,* teachings; beliefs

ADDITIONAL QUESTIONS AND ACTIVITIES

Students might make a sensory detail chart of the images they associate with their childhood home. Refer students to the Language Arts Survey, 1.18, "Sensory Detail Charts." Students should capture as vividly as possible the sights, sounds, feelings, smells, and tastes that made each person's childhood unique. Students should also try to capture something of the region in which they grew up in their charts. Dee, for example, is ecstatic about the sweet potatoes and butter churn that were part of growing up in the rural South. Ask students to consider what was special about childhood in their part of the country. Students should save their sensory detail charts as they would be an excellent starting point for a personal essay or a short story about childhood with a local flair.

QUOTABLES

"Childhood is not from birth to
a certain age and at a certain age
The child is grown, and puts
away childish things,
Childhood is the kingdom
where nobody dies.
Nobody that matters, that
is."

—Edna St. Vincent Millay

VOCABULARY IN CONTEXT

- A doctrine of fairness is hypocritical if it applies only to the group present when it is formulated.

Answer to Guided Reading Question

❶ Dee is going to use the churn top and dasher as a centerpiece and a handicraft or piece of art; the speaker and Maggie were using them to make butter.

Additional Questions and Activities

What items does Dee wish to take from her mother and her sister's home? What do these objects mean to Dee? What do these objects mean to Dee's mother and to Maggie? Why might these objects mean different things to them? What attitude does Dee express toward her family?

Answers. Dee wishes to take the butter churn and some quilts. These objects are artistic cultural curios to Dee. These objects are useful parts of everyday life and are important parts of family history to the speaker and Maggie; the speaker dwells on all the fingerprints worn by hard labor into the churn, and Maggie drops something in the kitchen and slams the door when Dee suggests taking the quilts. To Maggie and her mother the objects have personal, sentimental value, while to Dee they are curiosities. The objects mean something more on a personal sentimental level to Maggie and her mother because they have lived with and used the objects; they know the history of these heirlooms. Dee wants to acquire these objects to display that she is aware of her heritage, but she distances herself from these objects and sees them as collectibles. Students might say that Dee has a patronizing attitude toward her family.

that we still used the benches her daddy made for the table when we couldn't afford to buy chairs.

"Oh, Mama!" she cried. Then turned to Hakim-a-barber. "I never knew how lovely these benches are. You can feel the rump prints," she said, running her hands underneath her and along the bench. Then she gave a sigh and her hand closed over Grandma Dee's butter dish. "That's it!" she said. "I knew there was something I wanted to ask you if I could have." She jumped up from the table and went over in the corner where the churn stood, the milk in it clabber[12] by now. She looked at the churn and looked at it.

"This churn top is what I need," she said. "Didn't Uncle Buddy whittle it out of a tree you all used to have?"

"Yes," I said.

"Uh huh," she said happily. "And I want the dasher, too."

"Uncle Buddy whittle that, too?" asked the barber.

Dee (Wangero) looked up at me.

"Aunt Dee's first husband whittled the dash," said Maggie so low you almost couldn't hear her. "His name was Henry, but they called him Stash."

For what is Dee going to use the churn top? the dasher? For what were the speaker and Maggie using them? ❶

"Maggie's brain is like an elephant's," Wangero said, laughing. "I can use the churn top as a centerpiece for the alcove table," she said, sliding a plate over the churn, "and I'll think of something artistic to do with the dasher."

When she finished wrapping the dasher the handle stuck out. I took it for a moment in my hands. You didn't even have to look close to see where hands pushing the dasher up and down to make butter had left a kind of sink in the wood. In fact, there were a lot of small sinks; you could see where thumbs and fingers had sunk into the wood. It was beautiful light yellow wood, from a tree that grew in the yard where Big Dee and Stash had lived.

After dinner Dee (Wangero) went to the trunk at the foot of my bed and started rifling through it. Maggie hung back in the kitchen over the dishpan. Out came Wangero with two quilts. They had been pieced by Grandma Dee and then Big Dee and me had hung them on the quilt frames on the front porch and quilted them. One was in the Lone Star pattern. The other was Walk Around the Mountain. In both of them were scraps of dresses Grandma Dee had worn fifty and more years ago. Bits and pieces of Grandpa Jarrell's Paisley shirts. And one teeny faded blue piece, about the size of a penny matchbox, that was from Great Grandpa Ezra's uniform that he wore in the Civil War.

"Mama," Wangero said sweet as a bird. "Can I have these old quilts?"

I heard something fall in the kitchen, and a minute later the kitchen door slammed.

"Why don't you take one or two of the others?" I asked. "These old things was just done by me and Big Dee from some tops your grandma pieced before she died."

"No," said Wangero. "I don't want those. They are stitched around the borders by machine."

"That'll make them last better," I said.

12. **clabber.** Sour milk

Words for Everyday Use: **al • cove** (al´ kōv´) *n.,* recessed section, nook; **ri • fle** (rī´f´əl) *vt.,* shuffle, move quickly through

Vocabulary in Context

- Marny fed the baby in a dark alcove off the kitchen.
- The detective had to rifle through the file quickly while the secretary was on the telephone.
- With a hangdog expression, the young hiker walked into the campsite without his knapsack.

"That's not the point," said Wangero. "These are all pieces of dresses Grandma used to wear. She did all this stitching by hand. Imagine!" She held the quilts securely in her arms, stroking them.

"Some of the pieces, like those lavender ones, come from old clothes her mother handed down to her," I said, moving up to touch the quilts. Dee (Wangero) moved back just enough so that I couldn't reach the quilts. They already belonged to her.

"Imagine!" she breathed again, clutching them closely to her bosom.

"The truth is," I said, "I promised to give them quilts to Maggie, for when she marries John Thomas."

She gasped like a bee had stung her.

"Maggie can't appreciate these quilts!" she said. "She'd probably be backward enough to put them to everyday use."

"I reckon she would," I said. "God knows I been saving 'em for long enough with nobody using 'em. I hope she will!" I didn't want to bring up how I had offered Dee (Wangero) a quilt when she went away to college. Then she had told me they were old-fashioned, out of style.

"But they're *priceless!*" she was saying now, furiously; for she has a temper. "Maggie would put them on the bed and in five years they'd be in rags. Less than that!"

"She can always make some more," I said. "Maggie knows how to quilt."

Dee (Wangero) looked at me with hatred. "You just will not understand. The point is these quilts, *these* quilts!"

"Well," I said, stumped. "What would *you* do with them?"

"Hang them," she said. As if that was the only thing you *could* do with quilts.

Maggie by now was standing in the door. I could almost hear the sound her feet made as they scraped over each other.

"She can have them, Mama," she said, like somebody used to never winning anything, or having anything reserved for her. "I can 'member Grandma Dee without the quilts."

I looked at her hard. She had filled her bottom lip with checkerberry snuff and it gave her face a kind of dopey, hangdog look. It was Grandma Dee and Big Dee who taught her how to quilt herself. She stood there with her scarred hands hidden in the folds of her skirt. She looked at her sister with something like fear but she wasn't mad at her. This was Maggie's portion. This was the way she knew God to work.

When I looked at her like that something hit me in the top of my head and ran down to the soles of my feet. Just like when I'm in church and the spirit of God touches me and I get happy and shout. I did something I never had done before: hugged Maggie to me, then dragged her on into the room, snatched the quilts out of Miss Wangero's hands and dumped them into Maggie's lap. Maggie just sat there on my bed with her mouth open.

"Take one or two of the others," I said to Dee.

But she turned without a word and went out to Hakim-a-barber.

"You just don't understand," she said, as Maggie and I came out to the car.

"What don't I understand?" I wanted to know.

❶ *What does the speaker do? To whom does she give the quilts?*

WORDS FOR EVERYDAY USE: **hang • dog** (haŋ´ dôg´) *adj.,* ashamed and cringing

ANSWER TO GUIDED READING QUESTION

❶ The speaker takes the quilts from Dee and gives them to Maggie.

QUOTABLES

"What thou lovest well
remains,
the rest is dross
What thou lov'st well shall
not be reft from thee
What thou lov'st well is thy
true heritage."

—Ezra Pound

ADDITIONAL QUESTIONS AND ACTIVITIES

Why does Maggie say that Dee can have the quilts? What does Maggie's body language convey in this scene? Why does the speaker give the quilts to Maggie instead? Why does Dee say, "You just don't understand"? What doesn't Dee herself understand?

Answers. Maggie says that Dee can have the quilts because she has heard Dee say that she "can't appreciate them" and that she is "backward"; Maggie is feeling embarrassed, and because she is self-sacrificing, she is willing to give to her more "cultured" sister something that means much to her. Maggie's scraping feet, "hangdog" expression, and hidden hands suggest that she is feeling hurt, worthless, and inferior to her sister who is claiming the right to take the quilts from her. The speaker gives the quilts to Maggie because Maggie's self-sacrificing nature has moved her as much as Dee's patronizing attitude has angered her. Dee says, "You just don't understand" because she thinks her mother and her sister are too ignorant to appreciate the quilts. Dee herself doesn't understand that her mother and Maggie love the quilts as a part of family history and would prefer to see such items used as a part of everyday life than displayed as quaint, useless, and old-fashioned curios.

ANSWERS TO SELECTION CHECK TEST 4.12.21

EX. Of what television show does the narrator dream?
The narrator dreams of *This Is Your Life.*

1. What nice things did Dee want?
Dee wanted an organdy dress and black pumps.

2. To what has Dee changed her name?
She now calls herself Wangero.

3. Who whittled the churn top Dee wants?
Uncle Buddy whittled it.

4. What does Dee say Maggie would do with the quilts?
She says Maggie would put the quilts to everyday use and ruin them.

5. What does Dee say her mother doesn't understand?
She says her mother does not understand their heritage.

RESPONDING TO THE SELECTION

Students will respond that Maggie valued the quilts more; students may agree or disagree with the speaker about how the quilts should be used. They should support their opinions about whether or not family heirlooms should be put to everyday use.

ANSWERS FOR REVIEWING THE SELECTION

RECALLING

1. The speaker dreams that she and Dee are brought together on a television program.
2. The mother compares Maggie to a hopeful but downtrodden dog.
3. Dee is wearing a full-length colorful robe. She gives a greeting in Swahili. She has changed her name to Wangero.
4. She asks her mother for the top of the butter churn, the dasher, and the quilts.

INTERPRETING

Responses will vary. Possible responses are given.

5. The dream reveals that the mother would like to have fame, glory, and adventure like her daughter Dee. The reality of her life is that it is, for the most part, physically grueling and ordinary.
6. They are different in appearance because Maggie is less glamorous, less confident, more shy, and more generous.
7. Dee thought life with them was pointless and boring. She made changes because she wanted adventure and material wealth for herself.
8. She wants the items as art pieces to entertain and amuse her friends; Maggie and her mother want the items as members of their household, to use and to help sustain themselves from day to day.

(cont.)

"Your heritage," she said. And then she turned to Maggie, kissed her, and said, "You ought to try to make something of yourself, too, Maggie. It's really a new day for us. But from the way you and Mama still live you'd never know it."

She put on some sunglasses that hid everything above the tip of her nose and her chin.

Maggie smiled; maybe at the sunglasses. But a real smile, not scared. After we watched the car dust settle I asked Maggie to bring me a dip of snuff. And then the two of us sat there just enjoying, until it was time to go in the house and go to bed. ■

Responding to the Selection

Who valued the quilts more, Dee or Maggie? With whom do you agree about the use of the quilts? Do you think it is important to preserve historic and family heirlooms, or do you think they are better honored by being put to "everyday use"?

Reviewing the Selection

RECALLING

1. What does the mother dream?
2. To what does the mother compare Maggie?
3. What is Dee wearing? What greeting does she give? To what has she changed her name?
4. What things does Dee ask her mother to give her while she is at the house?

INTERPRETING

5. What does the mother's dream reveal about how she would like her life to be like? What does it reveal about the reality of her life?
6. In what ways are Maggie and Dee different in both personality and appearance?
7. What did Dee think of life with her mother and Maggie? For what reasons did she make changes in her life?
8. Why does Dee want several items from the house? Why does she think they are significant? What meaning do the items have for Maggie and her mother?

WORDS FOR EVERYDAY USE: **her • it • age** (her´ i tij´) *n.,* cultural traditions handed down by ancestors

ANSWERS FOR REVIEWING THE SELECTION (CONT.)

SYNTHESIZING

Responses will vary. Possible responses are given.

9. Dee does not understand the inner meaning of her heritage—to live simply and to be self-sufficient. Maggie and her mother do understand their heritage. They still live as their ancestors lived.
10. She says Maggie ought to make something of herself away from the family home. She thinks they should live as she does, traveling from place to place, building an identity based on outward appearance of status. Maggie and her mother want to stay at home and live the lives they know and understand, finding peace and comfort in their place of origin.

SYNTHESIZING

9. Dee says that her mother does not understand her heritage. Does Dee understand her heritage? Do Maggie and the mother understand? Explain.

10. What does Dee suggest Maggie and their mother do with their lives? What kind of life does she think they should lead? What kind of life do you think Maggie and the mother want? What do they think of Dee's life?

Understanding Literature (Questions for Discussion)

1. **Point of View. Point of view** is the vantage point from which a story is told. This story is told from a first-person point of view, in which the narrator uses words such as *I* and *we*. What information do we learn from the narrator? What information is she unable to tell us? What might we know if the story were told by an omniscient narrator, one who knows all things including the minds of others, or from the point of view of Dee?

2. **Plot.** A **plot** is a series of events related to a central conflict, or struggle. Review the parts of a plot in the Handbook of Literary Terms. Then identify the inciting incident, climax, crisis, and resolution of the plot of "Everyday Use."

Responding in Writing

Family History. Maggie knows many family stories and the histories of many items created by her family. Write about a story from your own family. It may be one that has been told to you, or it may be something that has happened during your lifetime that you wish to share with future generations of your family. Try to write the story as you would orally tell it. You may wish to share the story with a classmate or another person in your family to get a feel for telling it.

ANSWERS FOR UNDERSTANDING LITERATURE

▶ See the evaluation forms for discussion, active listening, and oral communication, *Assessment Portfolio,* 7.11–7.14.

Responses will vary. Possible responses are given.

1. Point of View. The narrator can tell the reader her own point of view and part of Maggie's point of view because she identifies with Maggie. She cannot tell the reader Dee's point of view except by reporting things that Dee says. With an omniscient narrator, we would understand Dee's motivation to leave the farm and to make a new life for herself elsewhere.

2. Plot

Inciting Incident. Dee returns home and decides to take the quilt regardless of her mother or Maggie's wishes.

Climax. Maggie retreats, saying that Dee can have the quilt.

Crisis. The mother must choose what to do with the quilt.

Resolution. The mother takes the quilt from Dee by force and gives it to Maggie.

ANALYTIC SCALES FOR RESPONDING IN WRITING

Assign a score from 1 to 25 for each grading criterion below. (For more detailed evaluation, see the evaluation forms for writing, revising, and proofreading, *Assessment Portfolio,* 7.1–7.10.)

Family History

- **Content/Unity.** The family history presents a sensible representation of events in the life of a family.
- **Organization/Coherence.** The descriptions of events and individuals are discussed within a logical framework and connected with logical transitions.
- **Language/Style.** The family history uses vivid and precise nouns, verbs, and modifiers.
- **Conventions.** The family history avoids errors in spelling, grammar, usage, mechanics, and manuscript form.

VOCABULARY IN CONTEXT

- Our heritage is the same as yours; many Americans are refugees from oppressive governments.

ADDITIONAL RESOURCES

READER'S GUIDE
- Selection Worksheet, 12.12

ASSESSMENT PORTFOLIO
- Selection Check Test, 4.12.23
- Selection Test, 4.12.24

ESSENTIAL SKILLS PRACTICE BOOKS
- *Study and Research,* 4.8
- *Applied English,* 5.3

ENRICHMENT ACTIVITIES

Develop a strategy for Emily's mother that would help to raise this child and the child's four siblings so that they would have self-confidence and dignity as a family unit. Be specific about sources of financial and emotional support that could help this mother and her children. Make your plan include both short-term and long-term solutions to the problems this mother faces with an infant daughter and limited financial resources.

SUPPORT FOR LEP STUDENTS

Review with students the additional vocabulary below before they read the selection.

ADDITIONAL VOCABULARY

endure—withstand

assured—self-confident

PREREADING

FICTION

"I Stand Here Ironing"
by Tillie Olsen

ABOUT THE AUTHOR

Tillie Olsen (1913–) was born in Nebraska to parents who escaped from Russia during the political repression of 1905. Olsen dropped out of high school and worked at various jobs while raising her children. "My great colleges were the worlds of work, motherhood, struggle, and literature," she says of herself. When still in her teens, she began writing a novel, *Yonnondio,* a chapter of which was published in the prestigious *Partisan Review* in 1934. Work, union activities, and, above all, duties as a mother consumed her time for many years; however, when her youngest child enrolled in school, she began writing again in earnest, assisted by a writing fellowship received in 1956 and a Ford grant received in 1959. The title story of her collection *Tell Me a Riddle* won the O. Henry Award in 1961, one of many awards she has received for her works. *Yonnondio: From the Thirties,* the story of a family struggling through the Great Depression, was finally completed for publication in 1974. Her collection of essays and lectures, *Silences* (1978), champions writers whose voices have been silenced because of their class or gender.

ABOUT THE SELECTION

"I Stand Here Ironing" shows characteristics common to much of the great short fiction produced in the United States in the past few decades. This fiction is often written in the first person, employing a narrator who tells his or her own story, and often deals with significant issues involving relationships with others. The first-person narrators so common in contemporary fiction tend to relate intense, private experiences, but they do so in what has come to be known as a **Minimalist** style marked by concreteness, compression of language, the inclusion of no more details than are absolutely necessary to advance the story, and avoidance of direct statements of the narrator's feelings. As you read this story, notice how the details speak for themselves, revealing clearly the narrator's pain, pride, defensiveness, and other emotions by letting the narrator's tone and the details of the story speak for themselves. Also note that the basic situation to which the narrator responds is given only in the barest of outlines, providing just enough background information to let the reader infer what is going on.

GOALS/OBJECTIVES

Studying this lesson will enable students to

- appreciate a contemporary short story written in the Minimalist style
- describe Tillie Olsen's literary accomplishments
- discuss the theme of the story
- identify the tone of the story
- write a business letter
- compare and contrast actions toward two people

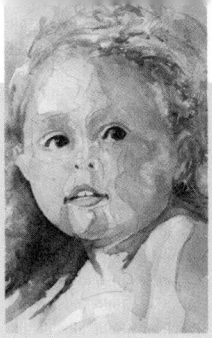

READER'S JOURNAL

Would you like to be a parent? Why, or why not? What are some of the difficulties and worries that parents face? How can parents help their children to grow up happy, confident, and secure? What factors in their children's lives are out of parents' control, and how do you think parents feel about these factors? Write about these questions in your journal.

THINKING SKILLS

Read the Language Arts Survey, 4.8, "Comparing and Contrasting." Then, as you read the selection, compare and contrast the mother's actions toward her first child, Emily, and her actions toward her other children.

"I Stand Here Ironing"

TILLIE OLSEN

I stand here ironing, and what you asked me moves tormented back and forth with the iron.

"I wish you could manage the time to come in and talk with me about your daughter. I'm sure you can help me understand her. She's a youngster who needs help and whom I'm deeply interested in helping."

"Who needs help." Even if I came, what good would it do? You think because I am her mother I have a key, or that in some way you could use me as a key? She has lived for nineteen years. There is all that life that has happened outside of me, beyond me.

And when is there time to remember, to sift, to weigh, to estimate, to total? I will start and there will be an interruption and I will have to gather it all together again. Or I will become engulfed with all I did or did not do, with what should have been and what cannot be helped.

She was a beautiful baby. The first and only one of our five that was beautiful at birth. You do not guess how new and uneasy her tenancy in her now-loveliness. You did not know her all those years she was thought homely, or see her poring over her baby pictures, making me tell her over and over how beautiful she had been—and would be, I would tell her—and was now, to the seeing eye. But the seeing eyes were few or nonexistent. Including mine.

I nursed her. They feel that's important nowadays. I nursed all the children, but with her, with all the fierce rigidity of first motherhood, I did like the books then said. Though her cries battered me to trembling and my breasts ached with swollenness, I waited till the clock decreed.

Why do I put that first? I do not even know if it matters, or if it explains anything.

❶ *What does the speaker believe will happen if she tries to remember her daughter's life?*

WORDS FOR EVERYDAY USE:

en • gulf (en gulf´) *vt.*, overwhelm
ten • an • cy (ten´ən sē) *n.*, occupation of something by right
ri • gid • i • ty (ri jid´ə tē) *n.*, state of being inflexible
de • cree (dē krē´) *vt.*, order

PREREADING NOTES

READER'S JOURNAL

Students might consider the things they have learned from their parents, the differences in parenting styles of parents they know, and what qualities they think are important to instill in children.

THINKING SKILLS

Students might make a Venn diagram to organize the similarities and differences they notice in the mother's treatment of Emily and her other children. Refer students to the Language Arts Survey, 1.24, "Venn Diagrams."

ANSWER TO GUIDED READING QUESTION

❶ The speaker believes she will be interrupted or that she will be overwhelmed with guilt.

VOCABULARY FROM THE SELECTION

anonymity	glib
articulate	implore
coherent	laceration
corroding	preen
communicative	prestige
decree	ravaged
delirious	replica
denunciation	rigidity
dredge	shoddy
eddy	tenancy
engulf	

VOCABULARY IN CONTEXT

- The next wave will engulf our sand castle.
- Our tenancy in this home will end on Saturday when the new family moves in.
- The retired colonel's unwavering ideas about household management showed his stubborn rigidity.
- The queen decreed that her birthday would be celebrated with festivities throughout the land.

ANSWER TO GUIDED READING QUESTION

❶ Emily's spirit is broken, and she has lost her childhood loveliness.

She was a beautiful baby. She blew shining bubbles of sound. She loved motion, loved light, loved color and music and textures. She would lie on the floor in her blue overalls, patting the surface so hard in ecstasy her hands and feet would blur. She was a miracle to me, but when she was eight months old, I had to leave her daytimes with the woman downstairs, to whom she was no miracle at all, for I worked or looked for work and for Emily's father, who "could no longer endure" (he wrote in his goodbye note) "sharing want with us."

I was nineteen. It was the pre-relief, pre-WPA world of the depression.[1] I would start running as soon as I got off the streetcar, running up the stairs, the place smelling sour, and awake or asleep to startle awake, when she saw me, she would break into a clogged weeping that could not be comforted, a weeping I can yet hear.

After a while I found a job hashing[2] at night so I could be with her days, and it was better. But it came to where I had to bring her to his family and leave her.

It took a long time to raise the money for her fare back. Then she got chicken pox, and I had to wait longer. When she finally came, I hardly knew her, walking quick and nervous like her father, looking like her father, thin, and dressed in a shoddy red that yellowed her skin and glared at the pockmarks. All the baby loveliness gone.

What changes have occurred in Emily when she returns? ❶

She was two. Old enough for nursery school they said, and I did not know then what I know now—the fatigue of the long day, and the lacerations of group life in the nurseries that are only parking places for children.

Except that it would have made no difference if I had known. It was the only place there was. It was the only way we could be together, the only way I could hold a job.

And even without knowing, I knew. I knew the teacher was evil because all these years it has curdled into my memory, the little boy hunched in the corner, her rasp, "Why aren't you outside, because Alvin hits you? That's no reason, go out, scaredy." I knew Emily hated it even if she did not clutch and implore "Don't go, Mommy" like the other children, mornings.

She always had a reason why we should stay home. Momma, you look sick. Momma, I feel sick. Momma, the teachers aren't there today, they're sick. Momma, there was a fire there last night. Momma, it's a holiday today, no school, they told me.

But never a direct protest, never rebellion. I think of our others in their three-, four-year-oldness—the explosions, the tempers, the denunciations, the demands—and I feel suddenly ill. I put the iron down. What in me demanded that goodness in her? And what was the cost, the cost to her of such goodness?

The old man living in the back once said in his gentle way: "You should smile at Emily more when you look at her." What

1. **pre-relief . . . depression.** The WPA (Works Progress Administration) was one of several relief programs instituted by the government during the Great Depression to help the poor and unemployed.
2. **hashing.** Serving hash (chopped mixture of meat and vegetables) in a diner

WORDS FOR EVERYDAY USE:

shod • dy (shäd´ē) *adj.*, poorly made; cheap, inferior
lac • er • a • tion (las´ər ā´shən) *n.*, wound; distress
im • plore (im plôr´) *vt.*, beg
de • nun • ci • a • tion (dē nun´sē ā´shən) *n.*, criticism; speaking against

VOCABULARY IN CONTEXT

- The porch construction was shoddy, and it did not weather the storm.
- The nurse bandaged the laceration on the child's heel.
- I implore you not to miss an opportunity to exercise your right to vote.
- No denunciation will change the behavior of an adult committed to serving himself above others.
- The night before the performance, we were delirious with excitement and nervousness.

was in my face when I looked at her? I loved her. There were all the acts of love.

It was only with the others I remembered what he said, and it was the face of joy, and not of care or tightness or worry I turned to them—too late for Emily. She does not smile easily, let alone almost always as her brothers and sisters do. Her face is closed and somber, but when she wants, how fluid. You must have seen it in her pantomimes;[3] you spoke of her rare gift for comedy on the stage that rouses a laughter out of the audience so dear they applaud and applaud and do not want to let her go.

Where does it come from, that comedy? There was none of it in her when she came back to me that second time, after I had had to send her away again. She had a new daddy now to learn to love, and I think perhaps it was a better time.

Except when we left her alone nights, telling ourselves she was old enough.

"Can't you go some other time, Mommy, like tomorrow?" she would ask. "Will it be just a little while you'll be gone? Do you promise?"

The time we came back, the front door open, the clock on the floor in the hall. She rigid awake. "It wasn't just a little while. I didn't cry. Three times I called you, just three times, and then I ran downstairs to open the door so you could come faster. The clock talked loud. I threw it away; it scared me when it talked."

She said the clock talked loud again that night when I went to the hospital to have Susan. She was delirious with the fever that comes before red measles, but she was fully conscious all the week I was gone and the week after we were home, when she could not come near the new baby or me.

She did not get well. She stayed skeleton thin, not wanting to eat, and night after night she had nightmares. She would call for me, and I would rouse from exhaustion to sleepily call back, "You're all right, darling—go to sleep—it's just a dream," and if she still called, in a sterner voice, "now go to sleep Emily, there's nothing to hurt you." Twice, only twice, when I had to get up for Susan anyhow, I went in to sit with her.

Now, when it is too late (as if she would let me hold and comfort her like I do the others), I get up and go to her at once at her moan or restless stirring. "Are you awake, Emily? Can I get you something?" And the answer is always the same: "No, I'm all right, go back to sleep, Mother."

They persuaded me at the clinic to send her away to a convalescent home[4] in the country where "she can have the kind of food and care you can't manage for her, and you'll be free to concentrate on the new baby." They still send children to that place. I see pictures on the society page of sleek young women planning affairs to raise money for it, or dancing at the affairs, or decorating Easter eggs or filling Christmas stockings for the children.

They never have a picture of the children, so I do not know if the girls still wear those gigantic red bows and the

❶ *What does Emily not do easily?*

3. **pantomimes.** Acting without words, using only actions and gestures
4. **convalescent home.** Place where one can recover from illness and regain strength and health

WORDS FOR EVERYDAY USE: **de • lir • i • ous** (di lir´ē əs) *adj.,* hallucinating; restless and confused

ANSWER TO GUIDED READING QUESTION

❶ Emily does not smile easily.

ADDITIONAL QUESTIONS AND ACTIVITIES

If students have not read Robert Hayden's "Those Winter Sundays," have them do so. The father in that poem performs certain tasks that the son later realizes were signs of love. Have students compare the father in the poem with the mother in "I Stand Here Ironing." What acts of love does she perform for her daughter? Does her daughter understand the meaning of her mother's actions? What attitudes do the children in these two selections seem to have toward their parents? What hopes and dreams do the parents have for their children?

Answers. The father in "Those Winter Sundays" makes the fire in the mornings and polishes his son's shoes. The mother in "I Stand Here Ironing" works at several jobs and then rushes home to be with her child. Emily does not seem to understand why her mother left her often as a child. The son in "Those Winter Sundays" is respectful and appreciative of his father though regretful that he did not reach his conclusions about his father earlier. Emily seems somewhat aloof and disconnected from her mother. The father in the poem wanted a better life for his son as demonstrated by the efforts he made to make his son's life more pleasant. The mother in the story has lost hope. She does not hope that her child will reach her full potential and find happiness; it is enough to just watch her child survive and get by.

Answer to Guided Reading Question

❶ The home looks beautiful and well-cared for on the outside, but the children are treated like diseased animals and kept apart from any love or family support.

Illustration © Rodney Busch

ravaged looks on the every other Sunday when parents can come to visit "unless otherwise notified"— as we were notified the first six weeks.

Oh, it is a handsome place, green lawns and tall trees and fluted flower beds. High up on the balconies of each cottage the children stand, the girls in their red bows and white dresses, the boys in white suits and giant red ties. The parents stand below shrieking up to be heard and the children shriek down to be heard, and between them the invisible wall "Not to Be Contaminated by Parental Germs or Physical Affection."

How does the description of the surroundings of the convalescent home differ from the description of the childrens' lives there? ❶

There was a tiny girl who always stood hand in hand with Emily. Her parents never came. One visit she was gone. "They moved her to Rose Cottage," Emily shouted in explanation. "They don't like you to love anybody here."

She wrote once a week, the labored writing of a seven-year-old. "I am fine. How is the baby. If I write my leter nicly I will have a star. Love." There never was a star. We wrote every other day, letters she could never hold or keep but only hear read—once. "We simply do not have room for children to keep any personal possessions," they patiently explained when we pieced one Sunday's shrieking together to plead how much it would mean to Emily, who loved so to keep things, to be allowed to keep her letters and cards.

Each visit she looked frailer. "She isn't eating," they told us. (They had runny eggs for breakfast or mush with lumps, Emily said later; I'd hold it in my mouth and not swallow. Nothing ever tasted good, just when they had chicken.)

It took us eight months to get her

Words for Everyday Use: **rav • aged** (rav´ijd) *part.,* ruined; devastated

Vocabulary in Context

- After making her way through the crowd of excited fans, the rock star had a ravaged appearance.

released home, and only the fact that she gained back so little of her seven lost pounds convinced the social worker.

I used to try to hold and love her after she came back, but her body would stay stiff, and after a while she'd push away. She ate little. Food sickened her, and I think much of life too. Oh, she had physical lightness and brightness, twinkling by on skates, bouncing like a ball up and down, up and down, over the jump rope, skimming over the hill; but these were momentary.

She fretted about her appearance, thin and dark and foreign-looking at a time when every little girl was supposed to look or thought she should look a chubby blonde replica of Shirley Temple.[5] The doorbell sometimes rang for her, but no one seemed to come and play in the house or be a best friend. Maybe because we moved so much.

There was a boy she loved painfully through two school semesters. Months later she told me how she had taken pennies from my purse to buy him candy. "Licorice was his favorite and I brought him some every day, but he still liked Jennifer better'n me. Why, Mommy?" The kind of question for which there is no answer.

School was a worry to her. She was not glib or quick in a world where glibness and quickness were easily confused with ability to learn. To her overworked and exasperated teachers she was an overconscientious "slow learner" who kept trying to catch up and was absent entirely too often.

I let her be absent, though sometimes the illness was imaginary. How different from my now-strictness about attendance with the others. I wasn't working. We had a new baby, I was home anyhow. Sometimes, after Susan grew old enough, I would keep her home from school, too, to have them all together.

Mostly Emily had asthma, and her breathing, harsh and labored, would fill the house with a curiously tranquil sound. I would bring the two old dresser mirrors and her boxes of collections to her bed. She would select beads and single earrings, bottle tops and shells, dried flowers and pebbles, old postcards and scraps, all sorts of oddments; then she and Susan would play Kingdom, setting up landscapes and furniture, peopling them with action.

Those were the only times of peaceful companionship between her and Susan. I have edged away from it, that poisonous feeling between them, that terrible balancing of hurts and needs I had to do between the two, and did so badly, those earlier years.

Oh, there are conflicts between the others too, each one human, needing, demanding, hurting, taking—but only between Emily and Susan, no, Emily toward Susan, that corroding resentment. It seems so obvious on the surface, yet it is not obvious. Susan, the second child, Susan, golden- and curly-haired and chubby, quick and articulate and assured, everything in appearance and manner Emily was not. Susan, not able to resist Emily's precious things, losing or sometimes clumsily breaking them; Susan

5. **Shirley Temple.** (1928–), famous child actress of the 1930s

❶ *What sickened Emily? What words are used to describe her actions?*

❷ *How did Emily feel toward Susan? In what ways were they different?*

WORDS FOR EVERYDAY USE:

rep • li • ca (rep´li kə) *n.,* copy
glib (glib) *adj.,* able to speak in a smooth, easy manner
cor • rod • ing (kə rōd´iŋ) *part.,* wearing away; causing deterioration
ar • tic • u • late (är tik´yōō lit) *adj.,* able to express oneself easily and clearly

ANSWERS TO GUIDED READING QUESTIONS

❶ Food sickened Emily. She twinkled on skates, bounced like a ball, and skimmed over a hill.

❷ Emily felt resentful toward Susan, who was cheerful, pretty, and careless. Emily was somber, serious, and unconventional in appearance.

VOCABULARY IN CONTEXT

- Even an expert can be fooled by a good replica of a piece of fine art.
- The governor's glib remarks about every cloud having a silver lining were not at all comforting to the flood victims.
- The car's corroding fender was replaced by the body shop.
- If you articulate your needs clearly and repeatedly, they will eventually be met.

Answers to Guided Reading Questions

❶ The speaker is relieved that Emily will not have to compete in the adolescent beauty pageant.

❷ Emily invented the word *shoogily,* which means "comfort."

❸ She suggests that Emily try her talent for imitation in the school amateur shows. Emily competes and wins first prize.

Answers to Selection Check Test 4.12.23

EX. What is the speaker doing when she begins her story?
The speaker is ironing.

1. What was Emily like as a baby?
The speaker says Emily was beautiful and happy as a baby.

2. Where happened to Emily's father?
Emily's father left her and her mother.

3. Where did the speaker send Emily when she was sick?
The speaker sent Emily to a convalescent home.

4. How does Emily feel toward her sister Susan?
Emily has corrosive resentment toward her sister Susan.

5. What is Emily's outstanding skill?
She is skilled at imitating others.

telling jokes and riddles to company for applause, while Emily sat silent (to say to me later: that was *my* riddle, Mother, I told it to Susan); Susan, who for all the five years' difference of age was just a year behind Emily in developing physically.

Why is the speaker glad for Emily's slow physical development? ❶

I am glad for that slow physical development that widened the difference between her and her contemporaries, though she suffered over it. She was too vulnerable for that terrible world of youthful competition, of preening and parading, of constant measuring of yourself against every other, of envy, "If I had that copper hair," "If I had that skin . . . ." She tormented herself enough about not looking like the others, there was enough of the unsureness, the having to be conscious of words before you speak, the constant caring—what are they thinking of me?—without having it all magnified by the merciless physical drives.

Ronnie is calling. He is wet and I change him. It is rare there is such a cry now. That time of motherhood is almost behind me when the ear is not one's own but must always be racked and listening for the child cry, the child call. We sit for a while and I hold him, looking out over the city spread in charcoal with its soft aisles of light. "*Shoogily,*" he breathes and curls closer. I carry him back to bed, asleep. *Shoogily.* A funny word, a family word, inherited from Emily, invented by her to say: *comfort.*

What special family word did Emily invent? What does it mean? ❷

In this and other ways she leaves her seal, I say aloud. And startle at my saying it. What do I mean? What did I start to gather together, to try and make coherent? I was at the terrible, growing years. War years. I do not remember them well. I was working, there were four smaller ones now, there was not time for her. She had to help be a mother, and housekeeper, and shopper. She had to set her seal. Mornings of crisis and near hysteria trying to get lunches packed, hair combed, coats and shoes found, everyone to school or child care on time, the baby ready for transportation. And always the paper scribbled on by a smaller one, the book looked at by Susan then mislaid, the homework not done. Running out to that huge school where she was one, she was lost, she was a drop; suffering over her unpreparedness, stammering and unsure in her classes.

What does the speaker suggest Emily do? What does Emily do? ❸

There was so little time left at night after the kids were bedded down. She would struggle over books, always eating (it was in those years she developed her enormous appetite that is legendary in our family), and I would be ironing, or preparing food for the next day, or writing V-mail[6] to Bill, or tending the baby. Sometimes, to make me laugh, or out of her despair, she would imitate happenings or types at school.

I think I said once: "Why don't you do something like this in the school amateur shows?" One morning she phoned me at work, hardly understandable through the weeping: "Mother, I did it. I won, I won; they gave me first prize; they clapped and clapped and wouldn't let me go."

6. **V-Mail.** Mail to or from the armed forces in World War II, reduced to microfilm to save shipping space

Words for Everyday Use:
preen (prēn´) vi., dress up in a fussy, vain way
co • her • ent (kō hir´ənt) *adj.,* logically connected; making sense

Vocabulary in Context

- The canary would preen itself in the mirror every morning.
- The boy's alibi was coherent, and the judge believed him.

Now suddenly she was Somebody, and as imprisoned in her difference as she had been in her anonymity.

She began to be asked to perform at other high schools, even in colleges, then at city and statewide affairs. The first one we went to, I only recognized her that first moment when thin, shy, she almost drowned herself into the curtains. Then: Was this Emily? the control, the command, the convulsing and deadly clowning, the spell, then the roaring, stamping audience, unwilling to let this rare and precious laughter out of their lives.

Afterward: You ought to do something about her with a gift like that—but without money or knowing how, what does one do? We have left it all to her, and the gift has as often eddied inside, clogged and clotted, as been used and growing.

She is coming. She runs up the stairs two at a time with her light, graceful step, and I know she is happy tonight. Whatever it was that occasioned your call did not happen today.

"Aren't you ever going to finish the ironing, Mother? Whistler[7] painted his mother in a rocker. I'd have to paint mine standing over an ironing board." This is one of her communicative nights, and she tells me everything and nothing as she fixes herself a plate of food out of the icebox.

She is so lovely. Why did you want me to come in at all? Why were you concerned? She will find her way.

She starts up the stairs to bed. "Don't get *me* up with the rest in the morning," "But I thought you were having midterms." "Oh, those," she comes back in, kisses me, and says quite lightly, "in a couple of years when we'll be atom-dead, they won't matter a bit."

She has said it before. She *believes it.* But because I have been dredging the past, and all that compounds a human being is so heavy and meaningful in me, I cannot endure it tonight.

I will never total it all. I will never come in to say: She was a child seldom smiled at. Her father left me before she was a year old. I had to work away from her her first six years when there was work, or I sent her home and to his relatives. There were years she had care she hated. She was dark and thin and foreign-looking in a world where the prestige went to blondness and curly hair and dimples; she was slow where glibness was prized. She was a child of anxious, not proud, love. We were poor and could not afford for her the soil of easy growth. I was a young mother, I was a distracted mother. There were the other children pushing up, demanding. Her younger sister seemed all that she was not. There were years she did not let me touch her. She kept too much in herself; her life has been such she had to keep too much in herself. My wisdom came too late. She has much to her and probably little will come of it. She is a child of her age, of depression, of war, of fear.

Let her be. So all that is in her will not bloom—but in how many does it? There is still enough left to live by. Only help her to know—help make it so there is cause for her to know—that she is more than this dress on the ironing board, helpless before the iron. ■

7. **Whistler.** James Abbot McNeil Whistler (1834–1903), American painter in England, best known for the portrait of his mother in a rocking chair

❶ *How might being "Somebody" imprison a person? being anonymous?*

❷ *What does Emily believe about the future?*

❸ *How does the speaker know Emily is happy?*

❹ *What does the speaker seem to be saying about people fulfilling their potential?*

WORDS FOR EVERYDAY USE:

an • o • nym • i • ty (an´ə nim´ə tē) *n.,* condition of having no special or distinguishing qualities

ed • dy (ed´ē) *n.,* move with a circular motion against the main current

com • mu • ni • ca • tive (kə myōō´ni kāt´iv) *adj.,* talkative; giving information readily

dredge (drej) *vt.,* dig up (in search of something)

pres • tige (pres tēzh´) *n.,* reputation; power to impress

ANSWERS TO GUIDED READING QUESTIONS

❶ Being "Somebody" makes one prisoner to other people's expectations; being anonymous gives one freedom to answer only to one's own expectations.

❷ Emily believes that everyone will be killed in atomic warfare.

❸ The speaker knows Emily is happy because of her light, graceful step up the stairs.

❹ She is saying that few people reach their full potential. Thus, the fact that Emily won't reach her full potential is less important than that she understands that she is not helpless like the cloth on the ironing board; she is responsible for shaping her own identity and her own dreams.

VOCABULARY IN CONTEXT

- Many people prefer anonymity to fame.
- The leaf fell into the water, eddied a moment behind a rock, then slipped free and rapidly disappeared downstream.
- A good attorney knows when to be communicative and when to be silent.
- We shall have to dredge the pond to find the missing boat.
- The mayor's prestige had been hard-earned, but after six years in office, she was almost universally respected.

RESPONDING TO THE SELECTION

Emily did not have her mother with her most of the time, even when she was ill. Students should respond with the lesson that Emily's mother has learned—that self-hood is enough. What Emily's mother has not learned is confidence in her child and ability to believe in her success.

ANSWERS FOR REVIEWING THE SELECTION

RECALLING

1. She is ironing and thinking about her daughter's life; a request from the school for a meeting sets her thinking about her daughter.

2. Her response is to say that a meeting would do no good.

3. The mother was abandoned by Emily's father and had to earn a living while caring for Emily's needs. Emily was isolated by her serious nature and emotional pain.

4. She had a talent for mimicry, for pantomime.

INTERPRETING

Responses will vary. Possible responses are given.

5. Emily's drama coach or a teacher might have made the request. Emily might have a lack of self-confidence and inability to trust adults.

6. Emily's mother has surrendered her own creativity and freedom for her children; she herself has no confidence that individual freedom is possible for her children. The mother's sense of defeat has probably had a strong effect on Emily and continues to effect her sense of the possibilities in life.

7. With no financial support from her father, Emily had to be cared for by strangers for long hours while her mother worked for wages. Emily was also often ill when she was young.

8. Emily could not identify with other people, but she could watch them and spend long hours trying to emulate their behaviors, perhaps so she could someday be accepted by them.

(cont.)

Responding to the Selection

What parts of Emily's childhood were painful? In what way has Emily managed to become successful despite the pain of her childhood? Emily's mother says, "My wisdom came too late. She has much to her and probably little will come of it." To what wisdom is she referring? What has she learned? Given the second half of her statement, what has she not learned?

Reviewing the Selection

RECALLING

1. What is the mother doing throughout the story? What request sets her to thinking about her daughter?
2. What is the mother's initial response to the request made of her?
3. What circumstances in the mother's life made Emily's young life difficult? What circumstances isolated Emily from others?
4. What talent did Emily discover that she had?

INTERPRETING

5. Who do you think might have made the request to Emily's mother? What kind of problem do you think Emily might have?
6. Why does the mother feel incapable of helping her daughter? How do you feel about the mother's attitude in this respect? Do you agree with her, or do you think that the mother's attitude is a continuation of the problem that the daughter has? Explain.
7. What economic conditions contributed to making young Emily's life difficult, and in what ways?
8. Why might Emily have developed this particular talent? What perspective does isolation give that a comedic actor might exploit?

SYNTHESIZING

9. The mother says of Emily, "So all that is in her will not bloom—but in how many does it? There is still enough left to live by." To what has the mother resigned herself? What do you think of this philosophy of life? Why might it be important that people around Emily want to see all that is in her bloom? How might they help to make that happen?
10. The mother in this story asks the unnamed person who has contacted her to "help [Emily] to know . . . that she is more than this dress on the ironing board, helpless before the iron." In what sense is the mother like the dress on the ironing board? In what ways does she feel helpless? What circumstances have contributed to making her feel that way?

ANSWERS FOR REVIEWING THE SELECTION (CONT.)

SYNTHESIZING

Responses will vary. Possible responses are given.

9. Emily's mother believes that most people don't do what they want to do with their lives and that Emily probably won't either. Emily needs people to have confidence and faith in her ability to bloom.

10. The mother feels flattened by circumstances beyond her control. She has given up her individual happiness and has sacrificed herself for her children, but she is unable to provide her children with what they need most: their mother's confidence in a world of possibilities.

Understanding Literature (Questions for Discussion)

1. **Theme.** A **theme** is a central idea in a literary work. What attitude does the mother in this story have about helping her daughter? What circumstances in the mother's life have led her to develop this attitude? What points do you think the author of the story wanted to make about the effects of poverty, youth, and abandonment on poor, young, single mothers?
2. **Tone. Tone** is the emotional attitude toward the reader or the subject implied by a literary work. What is the mother's tone throughout this story? How does that tone differ from the tone of the daughter in the concluding scene? The narrator in this story talks about her daughter, but the story is really not about the daughter; it is about the narrator herself. Why does this narrator feel so burdened, so helpless, so unable to take control and effect change in the world around her? In what sense does the mother herself feel "helpless before the iron"?

Responding in Writing

Professional Letter. Imagine that you are a school counselor and that you have received a letter from Emily's mother that reads as follows:

> *Let her be. So all that is in her will not bloom—but in how many does it? There is still enough left to live by. Only help her to know—help make it so there is cause for her to know—that she is more than this dress on the ironing board, helpless before the iron.*

How would you respond to the mother? Write a letter addressed to the mother, stating your response. Follow proper business letter form as described in the Language Arts Survey, 5.3, "The Form of a Business Letter."

Language Lab

Writing Grammatical Sentences. "I Stand Here Ironing" is told from a first-person point of view. It presents an interior monologue—the thoughts, associations, and impressions that float through the mind of the central character. To render the narrator's stream-of-consciousness realistically, Tillie Olsen has occasionally scrambled the grammar of her sentences. Rewrite each of the following sentences from the story using more conventional grammar.

Answers for Understanding Literature

► See the evaluation forms for discussion, active listening, and oral communication, *Assessment Portfolio,* 7.11–7.14.

Responses will vary. Possible responses are given.

1. Theme. The mother's attitude is that she cannot help any more. The mother believes she is a failure. The author wants to illustrate that abandoning the adult poor means abandoning people that they could otherwise nurture, creating a cycle that condemns the children to the fate of their mothers.

2. Tone. The mother's tone is hopeless. The daughter's tone in the final paragraphs of the story is almost reckless and carefree. She also believes in the ultimate doom of everything, but she believes that impending doom gives her freedom to live as she wants to live today.

Analytic Scales for Responding in Writing

Assign a score from 1 to 25 for each grading criterion below. (For more detailed evaluation, see the evaluation forms for writing, revising, and proofreading, *Assessment Portfolio,* 7.1–7.10.)

Professional Letter

- **Content/Unity.** The letter presents a logical response to the mother's views.
- **Organization/Coherence.** The ideas within the letter are organized within a logical framework and connected with logical transitions.
- **Language/Style.** The writer uses vivid and precise nouns, verbs, and modifiers.
- **Conventions.** The letter avoids errors in spelling, grammar, usage, mechanics, and business letter form.

► Additional practice is provided in the *Essential Skills Practice Book: Applied English,* 5.3.

ANSWERS FOR LANGUAGE LAB

Responses will vary. Possible responses are given.

1. You have no idea how new and uneasy was her emerging loveliness.

2. I would start running as soon as I got off the streetcar, running up the stairs. The place would smell sour, and she would be awake already, or I would startle her awake. When she saw me, she would break into a supressed weeping that could not be comforted, a weeping that I can still hear.

3. But eventually I had to leave her with his family.

4. "Are you not outside because you want to avoid being hit by Alvin? That's no reason. Go out, scaredy."

5. Being human, being creatures with demands who could hurt and take, the others experienced conflict, but only from Emily toward Susan could I see that corroding resentment.

1. You do not guess how new and uneasy her tenancy in her now-loveliness.
2. I would start running as soon as I got off the streetcar, running up the stairs, the place smelling sour, and awake or asleep to startle awake, when she saw me, she would break into a clogged weeping that could not be comforted, a weeping I can yet hear.
3. But it came to where I had to bring her to his family and leave her.
4. "Why aren't you outside, because Alvin hits you? That's no reason, go out, scaredy."
5. Oh, there are conflicts between the others too, each one human, needing, demanding, hurting, taking—but only between Emily and Susan, no, Emily toward Susan, that corroding resentment.

"For the Last Wolverine"[1]
by James Dickey

They will soon be down

To one, but he still will be
For a little while still will be stopping

The flakes in the air with a look,
5 Surrounding himself with the silence
Of whitening snarls. Let him eat
The last red meal of the condemned

To extinction, tearing the guts

From an elk. Yet that is not enough
10 For me. I would have him eat

The heart, and, from it, have an idea
Stream into his gnawing head
That he no longer has a thing
To lose, and so can walk

15 Out into the open, in the full

Pale of the sub-Arctic sun
Where a single spruce tree is dying

Higher and higher. Let him climb it
With all his meanness and strength.
20 Lord, we have come to the end
Of this kind of vision of heaven,

As the sky breaks open

Its fans around him and shimmers
And into its northern gates he rises

25 Snarling complete in the joy of a weasel
With an elk's horned heart in his stomach
Looking straight into the eternal

Blue, where he hauls his kind. I would have it all

My way: at the top of that tree I place

30 The New World's last eagle

Hunched in mangy feathers giving

Up on the theory of flight.
Dear God of the wildness of poetry, let them mate
To the death in the rotten branches,
35 Let the tree sway and burst into flame

And mingle them, crackling with feathers,

In crownfire. Let something come
Of it something gigantic legendary

Rise beyond reason over hills
40 Of ice SCREAMING that it cannot die,
That it has come back, this time
On wings, and will spare no earthly thing:

That it will hover, made purely of northern

Lights, at dusk and fall
45 On men building roads: will perch

On the moose's horn like a falcon
Riding into battle into holy war against
Screaming railroad crews: will pull
Whole traplines like fibres from the snow

50 In the long-jawed night of fur trappers.

But, small, filthy, unwinged,
You will soon be crouching

Alone, with maybe some dim racial notion
Of being the last, but none of how much
55 Your unnoticed going will mean:

How much the timid poem needs

The mindless explosion of your rage,

The glutton's internal fire the elk's
Heart in the belly, sprouting wings,

60 The pact of the "blind swallowing
Thing," with himself, to eat

1. **Wolverine.** Fur-bearing animal related to the weasel and mink

"FOR THE LAST WOLVERINE"

About the Author. James Dickey (1928–) has had a variety of careers as a poet, an advertising executive, a teacher, a training officer, a novelist, and a film writer. He adapted his novel *Deliverance* into a popular film. Dickey's work often deals with crises and frequently features animals.

About the Selection. In **"For the Last Wolverine,"** the speaker expresses his rage at the destruction of a unique form of life.

"A Story"

About the Author. Li-Young Lee (1957–) was born in Jakarta, Indonesia, and later immigrated with his family to Pennsylvania. Much of his work is filled with vivid sensory details.

About the Selection. In "A Story," Lee explores the difficulty of creating an original work.

"The Lesson of Walls"

About the Author. Alberto Ríos (1952–) was born and educated in Arizona. In addition to writing poems, Ríos writes short stories. Ríos's work owes much to the school of Magical Realism.

"Traveling Through the Dark"

About the Author. A biography of **William Stafford** appears on page 797.

About the Selection. Much of Stafford's work is confessional poetry; this selection takes as its subject the choices people make when they hold the power of life and death in their hands.

The world, and not to be driven off it
Until it is gone, even if it takes

Forever. I take you as you are

And make of you what I will,
Skunk-bear, carcajou,[1] bloodthirsty

Non-survivor.
Lord, let me die but not die
Out.

"A Story"
by Li-Young Lee

Sad is the man who is asked for a story
and can't come up with one.

His five-year-old son waits in his lap.
Not the same story, Baba. A new one.
The man rubs his chin, scratches his ear.

In a room full of books in a world
of stories, he can recall
not one, and soon, he thinks, the boy
will give up on his father.

Already the man lives far ahead, he sees
the day this boy will go. Don't go!
Hear the alligator story! The angel story once more!
You love the spider story. You laugh at the spider.
Let me tell it!

But the boy is packing his shirts,
he is looking for his keys. *Are you a god,*
the man screams, *that I sit mute before you?*
Am I a god that I should never disappoint?

But the boy is here. *Please, Baba, a story?*
It is an emotional rather than logical equation,
an earthly rather than heavenly one,
which posits that a boy's supplications
and a father's love add up to silence.

"The Lesson of Walls"
by Alberto Ríos

Florencio built a wall and told no one why.
He was stubborn this way about things.
Too beautiful to be described by the ill-educated
tax assessor in this small but honorable town,
it was entered in no book and so did not exist
in that way that other walls are known.
Florencio stood behind his invisible wall
and so quite reasonably was invisible himself
and could do for the first time whatever he chose.
People came from the big cities on Sunday noons
to see this thing that did not by its nature exist
and Florencio, Florencio as he had always wanted
since the early days of his troublesome schooling,
made his five ugly faces at the faces of the people,
inverting his eyelids and pushing to the side his nose
so as to look like the devil that children imagine,
and he made sounds with his mouth to his pleasure.
But through the years finally he grew
bored of his invisible fame, and his mouth, or entirely
his face, became tired, so that it rested,
let its weight fall, and it rolled over onto itself
in its leisure making Florencio wrinkled and heavy.
One morning he took a workman's hammer to his wall.
People saw him again, and he found himself
drawing up his face, as one might pull up
a stomach in front of a favorite aunt.
He was young again, and unhappy, and happy.
This business of the invisible,
of a thing too beautiful for the weak
recreations of words and of penmanship,
had taught Florencio who was a young fine horse of a boy
again, why a man builds a common wall
ugly, two bricks uneven, why he lets the paint chip.

"Traveling Through the Dark"
by William Stafford

Traveling through the dark I found a deer
dead on the edge of the Wilson River road.
It is usually best to roll them into the canyon:
that road is narrow; to swerve might make more dead.

By glow of the tail-light I stumbled back of the car
and stood by the heap, a doe, a recent killing;
she had stiffened already, almost cold.
I dragged her off; she was large in the belly.

1. **Skunk-bear, carcajou.** Other names for the wolverine

My fingers touching her side brought me the
reason—
her side was warm; her fawn lay there waiting,
alive, still, never to be born.
Beside that mountain road I hesitated.

The car aimed ahead its lowered parking lights;
under the hood purred the steady engine.
I stood in the glare of the warm exhaust turning red;
around our group I could hear the wilderness listen.

I thought hard for all of us—my only swerving—,
then pushed her over the edge into the river.

"Song of Solomon"
by Amy Bloom

Kate stood in front of the mirror trying on dresses. She could almost get into her black suit, but that couldn't be right for the New Year and it was almost eighty outside. She put on a yellow sleeveless dress with a white linen blazer and white sandals. Too summery but not bizarre. Do they wear hats? In church, women wear hats. Do Jewish women wear hats? Kate stared into the mirror, sweating in her slip, milk starting to come through her nursing pads.

Not now, she thought. If I nurse the baby, I'll be late for the ceremony—no, the services. Be calm, you must nurse the baby, Dr. Sheldon would want you to nurse the baby, you can tell him that you were almost late because you had to nurse Sarah and he'll smile. Kate relaxed, thinking of his smile, like a cool cloth on her cheek.

Okay, we're all right. Kate took off her yellow dress, laid it out, and called to Sarah, who was just starting to make her little sucking noises, "It's okay, Mommy's coming, everything's okay." On her way to the baby's room, she grabbed a towel and looked on the top shelf of the closet for her white cartwheel straw hat. God did love her. He knew she had to get to the temple. The hat was there, and it was unblemished and unbent.

Kate looked at Sarah and felt the milk slide under her bra, down her rib cage. "Here we are, little duck. Mommy's baby. Dr. Sheldon's perfect girl." She picked Sarah up and changed her, watching herself move smoothly and competently, like a Pampers commercial. Sarah didn't wiggle, just knotted her toes in Kate's long blond hair. She plunked down in the rocking chair with Sarah and nursed her, wincing for a second as that ruthless, sweet mouth clamped down on her nipple. She watched Sarah and she watched the clock.

"Okay, Sarah beans, ten on one, ten on the other, and then we're out of here. Going to temple. Going out today, Miss Sarah." While Sarah took a short break between breasts, Kate grabbed a clean blue dress from the laundry basket and put Sarah into it.

We're almost there, Kate thought. Come on, plan ahead. Plan it so you don't screw up. Okay, she finishes nursing, I burp her, on the towel. I put her in her crib while I get dressed, my shoes are not in my closet, they're still in the hall closet. Okay, we're walking down the hall—no, the diaper bag. The diaper bag is in Sarah's room and it's already packed, with another dress. Good girl, Kate. Okay, we have a fed baby, a diaper bag, a dressed mother. The hat, the hat is still in the closet, you don't put it on until you get there and you can see what they wear.

Make-up. You put your make-up in your purse, your white purse sitting on the hall bench, ready to roll. All you need is a little lip gloss and some cover-up for your raccoon eyes. You're all right. He doesn't care for make-up. Remember, in the hospital, sitting on your bed, he said that he didn't care for makeup and that you didn't need it anyway.

Kate closed her eyes, to remember better what he said, his saying it, to feel the weight of his body at the end of the bed, her bare feet almost touching his hip.

The whole seventy-two hours in the hospital Kate's body was never dry. She was damp and awake for every sunrise, her wet nightgown twisted up around her waist. Blood, milk, and sweat streamed over and through her. The night nurse had told her to get up and walk, but she was terrified that when she stood up her organs would just fall out, the cut muscles and tissue crumbling away like rotted newspaper.

"I promise you, you start walking now, when all the other ladies are home taking Percoset you'll be pushing Miss Sarah around the block. I'll take that catheter out now, too."

She saw the nurse's smooth, thick hands flick back the heavy hem of her nightgown, and she shut her eyes when she felt the slight emptying tug.

"All right, let's roll."

Let's roll, Kate thought, and stood up, wanting her voice to match the nurse's light bounce. Let's roll on out of here. She could hear the crowds cheering in her head as she walked down the hall; the i.v. rack skittering alongside her, the nurse's hand gently pulling on her good arm. She felt the shimmery heat of his presence before she really saw him, his back to her, talking to the nurses at the coffee station. They were barricaded

"Song of Solomon"

About the Author. Amy Bloom lives in Connecticut. In addition to writing, she also works as a psychotherapist.

About the Selection. **"Song of Solomon"** is taken from Bloom's collection of short stories *Come to Me.* The stories focus upon individuals who are searching for love, acceptance, and understanding from others.

behind twin coffeepots, personalized mugs, wide open doughnut boxes.

Kate shook off her nurse and strolled, with great effort, toward the coffee station.

"Wonderful. You're walking already, isn't that wonderful?" Dr. Sheldon turned to the nurses, who smiled politely; they didn't care if she walked or not, and Kate didn't care about them either. If she didn't say something, he'd be gone, and she was too tired to stand around waiting for the right moment.

"Could I speak to you?" The sweat slid from her underarms right down to her feet, wetting the paper slippers they'd given her.

"Of course. I'll save your nurse a trip, even if your quality of care suffers a little."

The nurses all smiled; he was a corny old guy, but nice. He practically lived in the maternity ward. His patient, the new mother, looked like she was about to pass out, and Kate's nurse went to grab a cup of coffee before the inevitable call.

He put his hand around her bicep, and Kate could feel the blood rushing from her arm to her cheeks.

"The nurses like you," she said, looking at the passing room numbers so he couldn't see her face.

"Yes? I like them. It's hard work, they're terribly understaffed. First there weren't enough nurses because they were paid so badly. Now there aren't enough nurses because it costs the hospitals too much to keep a full shift."

Kate smiled. Even though her back ached and she could picture each of her twenty stitches clearly, lighting a hot, narrow torch across her belly, she beamed. He gripped her arm a little tighter, and as her face went white and the walls around Dr. Sheldon began to spin, she smiled again and he smiled back before he called the nurse.

Sarah had stopped sucking a little sooner than usual, and Kate was so grateful she sang to her all the way through burping. Everything went smoothly; little Sarah, stoned from nursing, was completely content to lie in her crib and murmur to the world. Kate dressed like a surgeon prepping, precise and careful in every movement. She checked her watch again. Twenty-five minutes to get to the temple. She had driven there yesterday and timed it; it was only fifteen minutes away. Five minutes to find a parking space, five minutes to get Sarah out of her NASA-designed carseat and into her Snugli. Forget the Snugli, in a summer dress and a blazer you can't carry a baby in a blue corduroy Snugli. Okay, no Snugli. I carry her in my arms, wrapped in a yellow and blue blanket, to show off her eyes and her hair. Fine.

Kate moved through all of her steps, locked the front door, and got into the car, strapping Sarah in with the blanket tucked around her, supporting her soft boneless neck.

"We're rolling now. Off we go, into the wild blue yonder, flying high into the sky . . . " Sarah had fallen into one of her instant naps, from which she would emerge charming and alert but not yet hungry. Perfect for seeing Dr. Sheldon.

Kate didn't even look pregnant until her sixth month. The other women in the library began to talk to her a little, to tell her things. They had left her alone all summer, feeling that whether her silence was due to a bad attitude, problems at home, or painful shyness, she was too much trouble. Pregnant and single and willing to take anyone's advice, Kate was not too much trouble. "Go to Dr. Sheldon," they said over lunch in the back room. "He's the best." Especially for the weird, the dispossessed, the single mothers, the ones who wished they were, the ones who needed to talk at two in the morning, not just about their babies. And when Kate met Dr. Sheldon and he didn't purse his lips when she said she had only met the father once and hoped she never would again, she knew that she and the baby were in the right place. When he helped her out of her chair, she felt ethereally beautiful and as delicate as baby's breath, her ankles and heartburn forgotten.

She drove up to the synagogue and was appalled to see millions of cars. It looked like an airport terminal, women and children piling out of backseats, all the women wearing hats. Kate laid her hand happily on the white hat next to her, perfect for her blond hair. He'd like it. She could tell he liked her hair from the way he commented on Sarah's duck fuzz. "Not much now," he said the night he sat so close to her, "but she'll have your curls by the time she's one." The men were pulling away from the entrance, craning their necks to find parking spaces. They weren't wearing hats, of course, just those little beanies—what were they called? She could ask Dr. Sheldon. Unless he'd be offended by her ignorance, rather than charmed by her interest? Please let him find me charming, and my daughter irresistible.

She was damp and rumpled by the time she found a spot behind the A&P. She scooped up Sarah like she was going for a touchdown and trotted toward the temple, hugely domed and out of scale between a sandwich shop and a dry cleaners. A block away, Kate slowed down, licked her lips, and smoothed the front of her dress with her free hand. Please.

He was standing on the sidewalk talking to some other men, but alone. No wife. She would put one of those St.

Jude ads in the paper, the kind that said, "Thank you for helping me. Now I need you more than ever." She shifted Sarah to her left shoulder, lined up her purse and the diaper bag on her right shoulder, and smiled the way her mother had always wanted her to.

"Why, Dr. Sheldon."

"Ms. Tillinghast. What a surprise, what a pleasure. I didn't know we belonged to the same shul."

Kate thought quickly, circling the strange word. "I've never been here before, actually, but I've wanted to come for a long time. I hope nobody will mind the baby, my regular sitter couldn't make it." Kate smiled self-deprecatingly, showing that she knew some people didn't like babies and would consider her careless for having brought Sarah. But Dr. Sheldon wouldn't think so, which was why she had told Joan not to come today.

"No, of course not. Who could object to this angel, this proof of God's goodness?"

As he bent his head toward Sarah to kiss the back of her round moist head, Kate felt so happy she thought her heart would break through her chest and fly around the temple, like a dove released.

They squinted at each other in the September light, smiling and wondering what the other person saw. Dr. Sheldon thought Kate saw a pallid, overweight man sweating in an old navy blue suit, black-rimmed glasses sliding halfway down his big nose and wild gray curls floating around his bald spot. She didn't; she saw God. Kate thought he saw a slightly crazy woman, wild with exhaustion and loneliness, but he didn't see that. He saw that her dark blue eyes lit up when they rested on his face and that her hand lay tenderly, unconsciously, on his sleeve, like a lily. He saw that their house would have white flowers and bright plastic toys on the floor. He would not be alone.

"People are starting to go in," he said.

"Oh." She sounded wounded, which alarmed him. Had he offended her? Maybe she didn't want to sit with him.

Dr. Sheldon shuffled backward, to show that he hadn't meant to intrude, and Kate's eyes filled with tears. How could he be leaving now, now that they were together?

Sarah thrust one pink foot through her blanket, and they both looked at it, flexing in the air. Dr. Sheldon reached out for her, and she pressed his hand to her hip as they carried Sarah up the temple stairs.

VOCABULARY DEVELOPMENT EXERCISES

▶Give students the following exercise.

Read the Language Arts Survey, 4.4, "Memorizing." Then devise mnemonics to help you remember the meanings of the vocabulary words on page 860. You may represent mnemonics in prose, pictures, or charts. Try to rehearse the entire set of mnemonics three times a day for two days.

ADDITIONAL RESOURCES

ASSESSMENT PORTFOLIO

- Vocabulary Worksheet, 4.12.25
- Study Guide: Unit 12 Test, 4.12.26
- Unit 12 Test, 4.12.27

ESSENTIAL SKILLS PRACTICE BOOKS

Language

- Adding Predicates, 2.49
- Adjectives and Articles, 2.19
- Base Words and Prefixes, 2.140
- Capitalization, 2.107–2.133
- Connotation and Denotation, 2.153
- Formal and Informal English, 2.147
- Interjections, 2.29
- Linking Verbs, 2.13
- Tone and Voice, 2.149
- Using Colorful Modifiers, 2.35
- Using Vivid Verbs, 2.33
- Verbals: Participles, 2.16

Speaking and Listening

- Elements of Nonverbal Communication, 3.3

Study and Research

- Comparing and Contrasting, 4.8
- Computer-assisted Research, 4.26
- Generalizing, 4.11
- Making Hypotheses, 4.13
- Remembering and Visualizing, 4.5

UNIT REVIEW

Contemporary Literature

VOCABULARY FROM THE SELECTIONS

alcove, 840
anonymity, 851
articulate, 849
asunder, 830
austere, 794
banal, 790
banked, 794
belabor, 831
cadenced, 820
chronic, 794
civility, 831
coherent, 850
communicative, 851
composed, 789
convalescent, 790
corroding, 849
crucify, 819
decree, 845
delirious, 847
denunciation, 846
deranged, 789
doctrine, 839
dredge, 851
eddy, 851
engulf, 815, 845
eradicate, 831
expedient, 791
furtive, 837
gauche, 790
glib, 849
hangdog, 841
heritage, 842
homely, 835
invoke, 831
implore, 846
laceration, 846
mediocre, 803
mitigate, 821
obsessed, 825
occult, 791
preen, 850
prestige, 851
prevail, 825
quell, 821
ravaged, 848
recompose, 837
replica, 849
rifle, 840
rigidity, 845
scalding, 837
shoddy, 846
sovereign, 831
spurn, 820
subversion, 831
surrogate, 819
temper, 830
tenancy, 845
usher, 835
venture, 830

LITERARY TERMS

alliteration, 796, 823
allusion, 805, 812
anaphora, 833
assonance, 795
confessional poetry, 813
consonance, 796
epigraph, 813
Existentialism, 792
free verse, 809
internal rhyme, 828
irony, 800
metaphor, 792, 823
Modernism, 823
objective correlative, 823
parallelism, 828, 833
personification, 816
plot, 843
point of view, 843
pun, 805
repetition, 796
rhyme, 813
symbol, 816
theme, 853
tone, 805, 853

SYNTHESIS: QUESTIONS FOR WRITING, RESEARCH, OR DISCUSSION

GENRE STUDIES

1. **Poetry.** Figures of speech, especially simile and metaphor, are the tools of the poet. Refer to the Handbook of Literary Terms for definitions of figures of speech. Then, select two poems and analyze the figures of speech.

THEMATIC STUDIES

2. **Symbols.** In "Everyday Use" and "I Stand Here Ironing" domestic items represent abstract ideas. What are the items and what do they represent? In "Everyday Use," for Dee the concept changes. Discuss both concepts and what Walker tells us about this character.
3. **Despair.** Select two poems that present views of despair. Compare their treatment of the theme and the ultimate effect on the reader.
4. **Advice Column.** Tillie Olsen, Gwendolyn Brooks, and to some extent, William Stafford and Elizabeth Bishop offer advice in their work. Analyze the message they send. Do they present views of those who succeed or fail to follow good advice?
5. **Love.** Several poems in this unit are about love, though not romantic love. Discuss the theme of love and the relationships in three poems from this unit.
6. **Artistic Expression.** Select one of the illustrations in the unit. Discuss how the theme and mood of the art are related to the theme and mood of the writing. Create or describe your artistic expression of this piece of writing.

HISTORICAL/BIOGRAPHICAL STUDIES

7. **Anti-Cultural Poetry.** Karl Shapiro advocated a move away from the complex, demanding style of T. S. Eliot and Ezra Pound toward the simple, straightforward style of Walt Whitman and Carl Sandburg. Which poems in the unit are most like the "poetry for the common person" of Whitman and Sandburg? in what ways?

▶These prompts are suitable as topics for research papers. Refer to the Language Arts Survey, 4.20–4.34, "Research Skills." (To evaluate research papers, see the evaluation forms for writing, revising, and proofreading, *Assessment Portfolio,* 7.1–7.10.)

▶These prompts can be adapted for use as topics for oral reports or debates. To evaluate these projects, see the evaluation forms, *Assessment Portfolio,* 7.17–7.19.

LANGUAGE LAB VARIETIES OF ENGLISH

Formal English is used in writing papers, some magazine articles and nonfiction books, and some literary works. It is spoken at public ceremonies and in official speeches. Check your writing to be sure it is free of informal English, clichés, euphemisms, and connotations that might make your writing unclear or inappropriate. The following chart describes these varieties of English.

VARIETIES OF ENGLISH
Informal English. Informal English allows grammatical constructions that would not be acceptable in formal English. Informal English also includes **colloquialisms**, which are words and phrases that speakers of a language use naturally in conversation, and **slang**, a form of speech made up of coined words, words whose meanings have been changed for no known reason, and words used facetiously. EXAMPLES: Where are you going *to?* I'm going to *catch* that new *flick.* *Hey,* can I *tag* along?
Clichés and Euphemisms. A **cliché** is an expression that has been used so often it has become colorless and uninteresting. A **euphemism** is an inoffensive term that substitutes for one considered offensive. CLICHÉS: green with envy, stick out like a sore thumb EUPHEMISM: passed away (for "died")
Denotations and Connotations. A **denotation** of a word is its dictionary definition. A **connotation** of a word is all the associations that it has in addition to its literal meaning. EXAMPLES: disease, pestilence, plague conversation, talk, discussion, chat

LANGUAGE ARTS SURVEY

For additional help, see the Language Arts Survey, 2.147 and 2.152–2.153.

Exercise A Recognizing Varieties of English

Rewrite the following sentences, eliminating any instances of informal English, clichés, euphemisms, or inappropriate connotations.

EXAMPLE: The two cars slammed into each other.
The two cars hit each other with great force.

1. The traveler finds a deer taking an eternal rest at the roadside.
2. Hey, did you check out Alice Walker's lastest book?
3. Dee was mad as a wet hen when her mother gave the quilts to Maggie.

4. The host is sick and tired of the seamstress hanging around the house all the time.
5. Gwendolyn Brooks's poetry really knocks my socks off.
6. Although the pressure was on, she stayed cool as a cucumber.
7. Where is the powder room?
8. In July even a shady place gets hot as an oven.
9. Emily found that being in the spotlight was just her cup of tea.
10. The speaker doesn't realize what a swell guy his old man is in "Those Winter Sundays."

Exercise B Using Formal English

Rewrite the following paragraph, eliminating any instances of informal English, clichés, euphemisms, or inappropriate connotations.

LANGUAGE ARTS SURVEY

For additional help, see the Language Arts Survey, 2.147 and 2.152–2.153.

American poetry since 1960 comes in lots of different forms and is mostly a response to Modernism. Most contemporary poets have a much more autobiographical focus than their predecessors, drawing from really strong personal feelings of being cut off from people and not being sure about things. Although some poets, such as Donald Hall, still use old-fashioned poetic forms, most poets scribble away in free verse. The Black Mountain Poets, a movement that lists Denise Levertov on its roll call, attempt to escape suffocating poetic forms. Confessional poets, most notably Sylvia Plath and Anne Sexton, spill their guts about such problems as the generation gap and feeling blue. Of course, few of the greatest contemporary poets can be pigeonholed into a single category.

ANSWERS FOR LANGUAGE LAB

Responses will vary. Possible responses are given.

Exercise A

1. The traveler finds a dead deer at the roadside.
2. Have you read Alice Walker's latest book?
3. Dee was angry when her mother gave the quilts to Maggie.
4. The host resented the seamstress's presence in the house.
5. Gwendolyn Brooks's poetry impresses me.
6. Despite the unnerving circumstances, she kept her composure.
7. Where is the bathroom?
8. In July, even a shady place becomes stifling hot.
9. Emily found that she enjoyed being the center of attention.
10. The speaker dosn't appreciate his father in "Those Winter Sundays."

Exercise B

American poetry since 1960 comes in **many** different forms and is mostly a response to Modernism. Most contemporary poets have a more autobiographical focus than their predecessors, drawing from strong personal feelings of being **isolated** and **uncertain**. Although some poets, such as Donald Hall, still use **traditional** poetic forms, most poets **write** in free verse. The Black Mountain Poets, a movement that lists Denise Levertov **among its members**, attempt to escape **rigid** poetic forms. Confessional poets, most notably Sylvia Plath and Anne Sexton, **reveal their feelings** about such problems as the generation gap and **depression.** Of course, few of the greatest contemporary poets can be **classified** in a single category.

LANGUAGE ARTS SURVEY

1. *Essential Skills: Writing*

Introduction to Writing
Prewriting: Developing a Plan for Writing
Prewriting: Exploring Ideas on Your Own
Prewriting: Using Outside Sources
Prewriting: Organizing Your Ideas
Drafting: Approaches to Writing a Draft
Drafting: Paragraphs
Drafting: Compositions
Revising: Approaches to Revision
Proofreading and Publishing

2. *Essential Skills: Language*

Grammar Handbook
Usage Handbook
Mechanics Handbook
Spelling Handbook
Vocabulary Development
Varieties of English

3. *Essential Skills: Speaking and Listening*

4. *Essential Skills: Study and Research*

Thinking Skills
Reading Skills
Research Skills
Test-taking Skills

5. *Essential Skills: Applied English/Tech Prep*

Letters and Forms
Writing on the Job

ESSENTIAL SKILLS: *Writing*

INTRODUCTION TO WRITING

For writers of all ages and abilities, writing can sometimes seem a daunting task. The key to writing with confidence and pleasure, though, is simple: just keep writing as much as you can, as often as you can. Like any other skill, writing will improve with practice. Reading will also improve your writing, for reading can expose you to the full range and power of the written word.

1.1 THE PROCESS OF WRITING

Any writing task is much more manageable if you think of it as a process. Each person's writing process is a little different. Some people prefer to get everything down on paper quickly in rough form. Then they rewrite many times to "boil down" and refine what they have written. Other people work slowly and carefully, refining their thoughts and words as they go. For the purpose of instruction, the writing process is often divided into six stages:

SIX STAGES IN THE PROCESS OF WRITING	
1. **Prewriting**	Choose a topic, audience, purpose, and form. Then gather ideas and organize these in a reasonable way.
2. **Drafting**	Get your ideas down on paper in rough form without worrying about perfecting spelling, grammar, usage, and mechanics.
3. **Peer and Self-Evaluation**	Study your draft by yourself or with one or more of your peers to find ways to improve it.
4. **Revising**	Revise your draft to improve its content, organization, and style.
5. **Proofreading**	Check your revised draft for errors in spelling, grammar, usage, and mechanics (including punctuation and capitalization). Then prepare a final copy in an appropriate manuscript form and proofread again.
6. **Publishing and Presenting**	Share your work with an audience.

▸▸▸ ACTIVITY 1.1

Take a few moments to reflect on your past experiences as a writer. In your journal or on a sheet of paper, answer the following questions.

1. Do you usually enjoy writing? What positive and negative experiences have you had as a writer? What do you think are your strengths and weaknesses as a writer?
2. Is there a certain kind of writing that you most enjoy doing? (Consult the list of Forms of Writing on pages 876–878.) Do you like to write stories, persuasive essays, reports, or poems? What do you enjoy about this kind of writing? At what kind of writing would you like to improve?
3. Many writers find they can work more easily when they use certain tools. What sort of writing materials do you prefer? Do you generally use a pencil or a pen? Does it have to be a particular kind? Do you prefer to write on lined or unlined paper? in a notebook or on loose sheets? on a typewriter or a computer?
4. In your previous writing experiences, how much time did you generally spend on prewriting? What types of prewriting activities did you do? Which activities were generally most helpful to you?
5. Describe your approach to writing. Do you like to produce a very rough draft and then revise it heavily, or do you like to work slowly, refining the material as you go?
6. Which of the six stages of the writing process gives you the most trouble?
7. When other people read or listen to your writing, how do you feel? How might other people, such as your classmates and teacher, help you become a better writer?

1.2 KEEPING A WRITER'S JOURNAL

Keeping a **writer's journal** can help you capture ideas that you may want to use later in your writing. You can keep your journal in a spiral notebook, a loose-leaf binder, a composition book, a scrapbook, or a bound "blank book" of the kind sold in bookstores and stationery stores. Keeping your journal separate from your other notebooks will help you remember its special purpose. No matter where you store your ideas, you'll get more out of your journal if you write an entry in it every day. The following ideas will help get you started.

IDEAS FOR JOURNAL ENTRIES	
The Journal as Diary	Record the observations and experiences from your daily life. Explore your feelings about people and events.
The Journal as Commonplace Book	Record interesting phrases or ideas that you hear from others or that you encounter in your reading.
The Journal as Writer's Lab	Record your ideas for pieces of writing to do in the future. Do freewriting on subjects of interest to you. Try out different kinds of writing, such as monologues, dialogues, song lyrics, concrete poetry, and riddles.

CONTINUED

The Journal as Planner	Write about what you want to do over the next week, month, year, or ten years. Explore your goals and dreams. Think on paper about how to meet your goals. Make lists of activities to help yourself grow.
The Journal as Reader Response Forum	Record your reactions to works that you read for class and on your own. Talk back to the authors, take issue with them, expand on what they say, and explore their ideas

▶▶▶ ACTIVITY 1.2

Start a journal. During the first week, write at least one daily entry of each type described. Add a date to each entry. Be sure to write your name and address somewhere on your journal in case it gets lost.

1.3 Keeping a Writer's Portfolio

Your teacher may ask you to keep a **writer's portfolio** in which you store your drafts and finished pieces of writing. A portfolio allows you and your teacher to review past work and evaluate your progress.

The portfolio you keep may be a comprehensive or a selected portfolio. A **comprehensive portfolio** contains all the writing that you do for your class along with evaluation forms for that writing. A **selected portfolio** contains the pieces of writing that you think are your best. The pieces that you choose for a selected portfolio should demonstrate the various skills you have developed in your class as well as the various types of writing you have done (such as informative, persuasive, and creative writing).

For each piece of writing you place in your portfolio, attach any earlier notes or drafts. Your teacher can then refer to these to see how each piece of writing developed. Also include any completed evaluation forms that your teacher requests.

If you are keeping a selected portfolio, hang on to the pieces that you decide not to include. Store them in a safe place, so they will be available for you or your teacher to review later.

At different times, you and your teacher will evaluate your portfolio. You will probably each evaluate the portfolio separately and then have a meeting, or **student-teacher conference**, to discuss your work and to set goals for your writing in the future.

▶▶▶ ACTIVITY 1.3

Following your teacher's instructions, start a writer's portfolio. You can include in this portfolio past pieces of writing that you felt were especially successful. You could also include your answers to the Activity questions that follow Language Arts Survey, 1.1, "The Process of Writing."

1.4 Using Computers for Writing

A computer cannot make you a good writer, but it can make some of the mechanical tasks of writing much easier. A computer is especially helpful during the revising and proofreading stages of the writing process.

Computer Hardware

Hardware refers to the physical components, or machinery, of the computer. The most important part of this machinery is the **central processing unit**, or **CPU**. The CPU carries out the instructions given by the computer user. Connected to the CPU, or sometimes in the same case with it, are various **peripherals**, devices for storing, inputting, and outputting information, or **data**.

COMMON COMPUTER PERIPHERALS	
Storage Devices	• **Floppy diskettes**, or **floppies**, are small, flat media used to store and to transport limited amounts of data, such as individual computer files and programs. • **Hard drives** store large amounts of data on revolving disks. A hard drive can be **internal** (located inside the case with the CPU) or **external** (housed in a separate case and connected to the CPU by a cable). • **Removable media**, like hard drives, store large amounts of data. However, unlike hard drives, they can be inserted and ejected, like floppy disks. Common removable media include CD/ROMs, optical disks, and DAT tapes.
Input Devices	• **Keyboards**, the most common of all input devices, allow you to type numbers, alphabetic characters, and special computer commands. • **Mice** and **trackballs** are devices that are used to point to and select items on a computer monitor. • **Digitizing tablets** allow you to write in longhand and to draw directly onto the computer screen. • **Scanners** allow you to turn pictures or words into computer files that can then be edited or otherwise manipulated. • **Voice recognition devices** allow you to speak commands to the computer. Some will even transcribe, or write, your speech into a computer file that can then be edited.
Output Devices	• **Monitors** are the most common output devices. A monitor is a screen, similar to the ones on televisions, that shows you the work that you are doing on the computer. • **Printers** are machines that create **hard copies**, or printed paper, of the work that you have done on the computer. • **Modems** are devices for communicating, over telephone lines, with other computers.

Computer Software

Software is the set of instructions for making a computer do particular tasks. A specific piece of software is called a program, and the people who create software are called **programmers**. The chart below describes common software used by writers.

SOFTWARE FOR WRITERS	
Operating System	An **operating system,** or **OS,** is a program that tells the computer how to do general tasks—how to create, save, and store files; what to do when specific commands are given; how to print files, and so on.
Application Software	An **application program** enables the user to accomplish a particular kind of task. Common application programs include the following: • **Word-processing programs** allow you to key in words. Most such programs also allow you to revise your writing, to check its spelling, to add special formatting such as boldface or italic letters, and to save and print your work. Many of these programs also allow you to consult a built-in dictionary and/or thesaurus and to check your grammar, usage, capitalization, and punctuation. • **Page-layout programs** allow you to put your writing into columns and boxes and to add graphic elements such as lines, borders, photographs, and illustrations. Such programs are used to produce newsletters, posters, flyers, newspapers, magazines, and books. • **Graphics programs** allow you to create illustrations and to edit photographs. • **Telecommunications programs** allow you to use a **modem** to connect over telephone lines to other computers, to **on-line information services,** or to **computer networks** such as the **Internet.** Other types of programs often used by writers include ones for creating outlines, graphs, charts, indexes, and bibliographies.

Applications of Computers to Writing

A computer, like a typewriter, enables you to put words down on a page, but a computer has other capabilities as well. Equipped with the appropriate applications software, a computer allows you to

- revise your writing easily, simply by moving words, sentences, or paragraphs;
- format your writing in special ways (by adding bold or italic, by specifying a particular style of lettering, by automating functions such as paragraph, page, and line breaks, and so on);
- perform editing functions (such as checking spelling, punctuation, and grammar) automatically;
- look up definitions, synonyms, and antonyms;
- print multiple copies of your work;
- add photographs and illustrations to your work;
- use computer-accessed information sources such as on-line information services and CD/ROM encyclopedias.

Although the computer offers numerous advantages over the typewriter, many writers prefer to use a typewriter or to write with a pen or pencil. The choice of writing tool is a personal one. Of course, it also depends on the availability of machines and instruction on how to use them. Many schools have **writing labs** where computers are available to students. In addition, computers are sometimes available in school and public libraries.

▶▶▶ ACTIVITY 1.4a

Interview a writer who uses a computer regularly. Ask the person to demonstrate the word processing program he or she uses. Also, ask what the person especially likes or dislikes about the program and about using a computer for writing. Does the person prefer to handle certain steps of the writing process away from the computer?

PREWRITING: DEVELOPING A PLAN FOR WRITING

Experienced writers spend some time prewriting, or planning, what they will write. Prewriting is something like drawing a map before you set off on a trip; the plan you develop becomes your guide when you begin to write. By collecting your thoughts on paper in some form, you have a chance to "see" your ideas. Then you can react to them, manipulate them, and build on them before you settle down to write.

Good writing sometimes does occur spontaneously. However, if you make a plan before you write, your writing is likely to go more smoothly and be more enjoyable. The elements of a good writing plan are described in the following chart.

ELEMENTS OF A WRITING PLAN	
Topic	The specific subject that you will be writing about
Purpose	The aim, or goal, that you want the piece of writing to accomplish: to express yourself, to create a literary work, to inform, or to persuade
Audience	The person or persons who will read or hear your work
Form	The specific type of writing that you will be doing (for example, a press release or a short story)
Mode	The method of presentation of the ideas in a piece of writing. Common modes, often combined in actual pieces of writing, include narration, dialogue, description, and various kinds of exposition, such as analysis or comparison and contrast.

▶▶▶ ACTIVITY 1.4b

On a page of your journal, develop a plan for a piece of writing that you would like to do sometime in the future. Briefly describe the topic, purpose, audience, form, and mode of the piece. Refer to sections 1.5–1.8 of the Language Arts Survey for information to help you complete this activity.

1.5 CHOOSING AND FOCUSING A TOPIC

Choosing a Topic

Ideas for writing can come from anywhere—from memories, research, conversations, observations. They come simply from your awareness of the world around you. Even so, most writers find it difficult to come up with good ideas for writing. The following suggestions can help you find an interesting and engaging topic.

TIPS FOR DISCOVERING WRITING TOPICS	
Mine Your Journal	Make a habit of jotting down ideas for writing in your journal. Pretty soon, you will have a store of good ideas to draw from.
Draw on Your Experience	Think about experiences that you have had in the past, from early childhood on. People, places, and events from personal experience make excellent topics for writing. Making a time line of your life might help to jog your memory.
Consult Reference Works and Other Media	Browsing through reference works, looking through the shelves in a library, paging through magazines or newspapers, exploring the contents of informational CD/ROMs—all can help you to find topics worth writing about.
Do Some Freewriting	One interesting way to come up with a writing idea is simply to put your pen to paper and start writing about whatever pops into your mind, without stopping to think about spelling, grammar, usage, and mechanics. Don't force yourself to stick to one subject. Freewriting is one situation in which it's actually good to let your mind wander! Write for five to ten minutes. Then look over your freewriting for topic ideas.
Talk to People	Other people can be excellent resources for writing ideas. Draw on the experiences of the people around you. Ask them about subjects of interest to you and to them.

▶▶▶ ACTIVITY

Select a separate part of your journal to list possible writing topics. Using the techniques described, come up with a list of at least ten topics. Continue to add to your list as other ideas occur to you. Then, when you have writing assignments in the future, refer to your list for possible ideas.

Focusing a Topic

One technique for coming up with topics is to start with a general topic and then think about more specific, or narrower, topics that are related it. Here is an example:

General topic: the American Revolution

Focused topic 1: what a soldier's life was like

Focused topic 2: Thomas Jefferson's role

Focused topic 3: popular patriotic tunes

During prewriting, check the focus of your topic to make sure that you can cover it in sufficient detail. Generally the shorter the piece of writing that you plan to do, the more focused the topic should be. For example, in a few paragraphs you would not be able to provide much detail about a topic as broad as the American Revolution. However, if you were writing about just one aspect of it, such as the life of a typical soldier, you could include more detail. By the same token, you might begin with the idea of writing about several patriotic tunes but decide during prewriting to focus on just one tune so you can treat that topic in greater depth.

TECHNIQUES FOR FOCUSING TOPICS	
Analyze the Topic	Break the topic down into its parts. Then think about how the parts relate to one another.
Do a Tree Diagram	Write the topic at the top of a page. Then break it into parts, and break those parts into parts.
Ask Questions	Write questions about the topic beginning with the words *who, what, where, when, why,* and *how.* Decide which answers to these questions are most important for your piece.

Other techniques for focusing topics include freewriting and clustering (see the Language Arts Survey, 1.12, "Freewriting," and 1.17, "Clustering").

▶▶▶ ACTIVITY 1.5

Choose a general topic from the list below. Using one of the techniques described, come up with three specific, focused topics that are related to it:

General topics:	freedom	singing	astronomy
	religion	boredom	being a teenager

1.6 Choosing a Purpose or Aim

Although a topic is a starting point for writing, you really can't move forward until you know your purpose in writing about that topic. The **purpose,** or **aim,** of a piece of writing is the goal that the writer wants to achieve. It is the writer's reason for writing. The study of purpose in writing and speaking is called **rhetoric.**

Teachers of rhetoric, going back to the ancient Greeks, have worked out various systems for classifying types of writing and speech. One useful classification scheme, described in the chart that follows, is based on the writer's purpose.

THE CLASSIFICATION OF WRITING AND SPEECH BY PURPOSE OR AIM			
Type	**Focus is on . . .**	**Purpose is to . . .**	**Examples**
Expressive Writing	the sender (the writer or speaker)	express the feelings of the writer or speaker	journal entry, credo
Informative Writing	the subject	provide information about the subject	accident reports, book report

CONTINUED

Persuasive Writing	the recipient (the reader or listener)	move the reader or listener to adopt a point of view or to act in a particular way	campaign speech, public service ad
Literary Writing	the signs or symbols used to communicate the message	create a work of art	lyric poem, short story

This classification scheme also takes into account the fact that writing is a form of communication. **Communication** is the act of sending and receiving **messages.** Each time a message is sent, four elements are involved: the **sender** of the message, the **recipient** of the message, the **subject** of the message, and the **code** (the signs or symbols) used to communicate the message. This model of communication is often pictured as a **communication triangle.** Notice that each classification, or type of writing, in this scheme stresses one part of the communication triangle.

The Communication Triangle

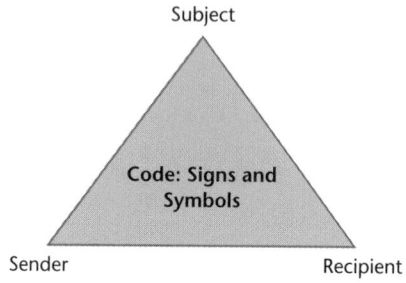

Limitations of Classification Systems

A classification scheme is helpful for thinking about and discussing writing and speech. In reality, however, a single piece of writing often has more than one purpose. Take, for example, the *Declaration of Independence,* which was drafted by Thomas Jefferson (see page 172). The primary purpose of this document is to *inform* its readers that the thirteen American colonies have decided to separate from England and become a sovereign nation. It describes recent events that led Americans to claim their independence, and it gives reasons for the decision. The document, however, is also *persuasive.* It seeks to persuade readers of the validity of the American claim to independence. The writing is also *literary* in that the language is elegant and memorable and was carefully selected for its effect upon the reader.

Purpose and the Writing Process

Thinking about purpose can help you decide what tasks to focus on. If you have decided that your main purpose is to persuade the reader to take a certain action—for example, to use negotiation rather than violence to resolve disputes—you will need to find arguments to support your position. You might also make lists of words and phrases that will appeal to your readers emotionally. If your purpose is to inform, you will probably need to gather facts.

Purpose is also an important consideration during revision. As you reread your draft to evaluate it, ask yourself, "Have I accomplished my purpose?" If the answer is no, think about how you could change the piece to accomplish your goal.

▸▸▸ ACTIVITIES 1.6

A. Identify the primary purpose of each of type of writing in the following list.

1. a statement on an anti-littering poster
2. instructions for playing a board game
3. a poem about the first day of spring
4. a magazine article about surfing

B. For each of the following communications situations, identify the sender, the recipient, the subject, and the code (signs or symbols) used.

1. A mayor addresses a local community group to inform them about construction plans for a new water-treatment plant.
2. A student describes her personal goals in a written statement on a college application.
3. A hiker on a mountaintop uses a small mirror that reflects the sunlight to signal to another hiker below that he has arrived at the summit.
4. A computer sends a document that has been converted into digital code to another computer via a modem, which transmits information over regular telephone lines.

1.7 CHOOSING AND ANALYZING AN AUDIENCE

All those who read or hear what a writer has written, the receivers of the message, are collectively known as the **audience.** Experienced writers write with a specific audience in mind. They tailor their text so it is appropriate and interesting to those they expect to read it. Often you may not know exactly who your audience will be, but thinking about a specific audience can assist the writing process. Knowing your audience can help you

- focus your writing;
- select details, examples, or arguments that your reader will find interesting or convincing;
- decide what information to include or to leave out;
- determine how formal or informal and how complex or simple your language should be.

QUESTIONS TO ASK ABOUT YOUR AUDIENCE

How much does my audience already know about the subject? How much background information do I have to provide to make my writing understandable to this audience? Does the audience know enough about the subject to make it possible for me to write technically or to use jargon?

What interests, wishes, or goals does my audience have? How can I relate what I am writing to those interests, wishes, and goals?

How old and how well educated is my audience? How complex or sophisticated should my writing be?

Which would be more effective and appropriate for my audience, formal or informal language?

▸▸▸ ACTIVITY 1.7

Rewrite each of the following passages for the audience indicated in parentheses. Discuss with your classmates the kinds of changes you introduced to make the piece appropriate for its new audience.

1. From a science text: "To ward off 'predatory' herbivores, many plants produce chemicals that render them unpalatable." (Rewrite as an explanation for fourth graders.)
2. From a sports story in a magazine: The score was 30-love when underdog Regina McIntyre aced three serves in a row to tie the score at 30-all. (Rewrite for someone from another country who knows nothing about tennis.)
3. From a newspaper article: Cleanup teams working along the Scioto River gathered 654 pounds of trash including paper and plastic, cans and bottles, thirty-four old tires, and a dilapidated couch. (Rewrite as part of a paragraph designed to persuade people to volunteer in a riverbank cleanup project.)
4. From a television weather report: The sun set today at 7:49, and the sunset was quite beautiful, I might add. (Rewrite as a description in a letter to a friend; assume that you viewed the sunset.)

1.8 CHOOSING A FORM

The form you choose for your writing will be influenced by the nature of your topic, your purpose, and your audience, as well as your personal and creative inclinations. The following chart lists some forms you can use in the writing you do for class and on your own.

Obviously, a single topic can be treated in many different forms, but some forms are more suited to certain topics than others. A good way to become familiar with the possibilities and limitations of forms of writing is to try your hand at transforming one form into another.

FORMS OF WRITING

Abstract	Biography	Cinquain
Acceptance speech	Birth announcement	Classified ad
Ad copy	Blank verse	Comeback speech
Address to a jury	Book review	Comedy
Adventure	Brief	Comic strip
Advice column	Brochure	Community calendar
Afterword	Bulletin board	Concrete poem
Agenda	Business letter	Constitution
Allegory	Business proposal	Constructive speech
Annals	Bylaws	Consumer report
Annotation	Campaign speech	Contract
Annual report	Captions	Court decision
Apology	Cartoon	Credo
Appeal	Cause-and-effect essay	Critical analysis
Autobiography	Chant	Curriculum
Ballad	Character sketch	Daydream
Ballet	Charter	Debate
Bibliography	Cheer	Detective story
Billboard	Children's story	Dialogue

CONTINUED

Diary
Diatribe
Dictionary entry
Directions
Docudrama
Dramatic narrative
Dream analysis
Dream report
Editorial
Elegy
Encyclopedia article
Epic
Epic poem
Epilogue
Epistolary fiction
Epitaph
Essay
Eulogy
Experiment
Explication
Exposé
Fable
Fabliaux
Family history
Fantasy
Filmstrip
Flyer
Foreword
Fortune cookie insert
Found poem
Free verse
Gothic tale
Graduation speech
Graffiti
Grant application
Greeting card
Haiku
Headline
History
Horoscope
Human interest story
Informative essay
Instructions
Insult
Interview questions
Introduction
Invitation
Itinerary
Jingle
Joke
Journal entry
Keynote address
Lament
Law (statute)
Learning log
Letter of complaint
Letter to the editor
Libretto
Limerick
Love letter
Lyric poem
Magazine article
Manifesto
Manual
Memorandum
Memorial plaque
Menu
Minutes
Monologue
Monument inscription
Movie review
Mystery
Myth
Narrative poem
Nature guide
News story
Nomination speech
Nonsense rhyme
Novel
Novella
Nursery rhyme
Obituary
One-act play
Oracle
Ottava rima
Packaging copy
Parable
Paragraph
Paraphrase
Parody
Party platform
Pastoral
Persuasive essay
Petition
Play
Police/Accident report
Political advertisement
Prediction
Preface
Press release
Proclamation
Profile
Prologue
Proposal
Prose poem
Protocol
Public service announcement
Quatrain
Radio play
Radio spot
Rap
Reader's theater production
Rebuttal
Recipes
Recommendation
Referendum question
Research report
Resignation
Restaurant review
Résumé
Riddle
Roast
Romance
Sales letter
Schedule
Science fiction
Screenplay
Sermon
Short short story
Short story
Sign
Situation comedy
Slide show
Slogan
Song lyric
Sonnet (Petrarchan, Elizabethan, or Spenserian)
Specifications
Spell
Sports story
Storyboard
Stream-of-consciousness fiction
Summary
Summation
Survey
Sutra
Tall tale
Tanka
Technical writing
Terza rima

CONTINUED

Test	Tragedy	Vows
Thank-you note	Translation	Want ad
Theater review	Treaty	Wanted poster
Toast	TV spot	Warrant
Tour guide	Villanelle	Wish list

▸▸▸ ACTIVITY 1.8

Choose one of the rewriting exercises that follow and experiment with it in your journal. Refer to the Handbook of Literary Terms if you need more information about a particular form of writing.

1. Choose a short or long passage from a science textbook. Rewrite the passage as a poem.
2. Rewrite the lyrics to a popular song about relationships as an advice column.
3. Convert a scene from a play into a narrative passage; that is, describe what takes place in the scene and omit all the dialogue.
4. Choose a paragraph or two from an encyclopedia article about an interesting, faraway place. Rewrite the passage as an excerpt from a travel guide.

1.9 MODES OF WRITING

A piece of writing can also be classified by **mode.** A mode is a way of presenting ideas, information, and details. The following chart lists some of the most common modes.

COMMON MODES OF WRITING

Mode	*Explanation*	*Forms in Which This Mode Dominates*
Narration	Presents events, usually in chronological order	Short story News report Process/How-to writing
Dialogue	Presents the speech of characters	Drama Dramatic poem Docudrama
Description	Uses images to present a portrait in words	Imagist poem Tour guide
Exposition	Presents information	(See below)

Most forms of writing combine several different modes, but one is usually dominant. For example, in drama the primary mode is dialogue. In a news report, narration is the primary mode. Short stories and novels usually use several modes. The writer will use narration to present events in sequence, description to flesh out the setting and characters, dialogue to show characters interacting, and exposition to comment on what is happening in the story.

Exposition is the mode writers use when they want to clarify or explain something. There are many, many types of exposition. Among the most common types of exposition are analysis, comparison and contrast, classification, and cause-and-effect analysis.

In an **analysis,** the writer breaks a subject down into parts and then shows how the parts are related to each other and to the whole. An analysis of a speech might break it down into the introduction, body, and conclusion. An analysis of a short story might break it down into setting, characters, plot, and theme.

A writer using **comparison and contrast** points out similarities and differences between one or more subjects. For example, a writer might compare and contrast the careers of two early-American patriots or two poems about the same subject.

An exposition based on **classification** divides some group of things into smaller groups of things that have one or more features in common. An author discussing modern American fiction might group writers from different regions of the country, such as the South, the Northeast, and the Great Plains.

In a **cause-and-effect** analysis the writer describes events that led to or resulted from certain other events. For instance, a writer might use this form of exposition to explain how the westward movement of settlers affected the lives of Indians in North America, or how social reformers of the late 1800s influenced labor laws and practices.

▸▸▸ ACTIVITY 1.9

Write a short passage about each topic in the mode indicated.

1. an activity in physical education class (narration)
2. a minor car accident (dialogue)
3. a day outdoors in March (description)
4. friendship (exposition)

PREWRITING: EXPLORING IDEAS ON YOUR OWN

Once you have settled on a particular topic, purpose, and form for a piece of writing, you are ready to begin exploring ideas and gathering information. This stage may involve reading and research, holding conversations, making notes to yourself, drawing charts, asking questions, and any other kind of activity that helps you collect your thoughts and gather useful details for writing. Some of the most common activities that writers use to explore ideas and prepare for writing are described in the following sections.

1.10 RECALLING

Students sometimes think that they must be experts before they can write about a topic in a serious or meaningful way. The fact is, you *are* an expert—on the subject of your own life. Experiences from your life, past and present, can be turned into excellent writing. The key is **recalling,** or remembering, these experiences vividly. The suggestions in the chart that follows can help you use recalling to generate topics and ideas for writing:

USING RECALL TO GATHER WRITING IDEAS

1. Choose some time in your life that you want to think about. It might be early childhood, for example, when you were first learning about the world around you. It might be the time when you started going to a new school or working at a new part-time job.

CONTINUED

2. Make a time line of events that occurred during that period. (See the Language Arts Survey, 1.19, for more information on making time lines.)
3. Make a list of questions, problems, opinions, wishes, dreams, or goals that you had during that time.
4. List important things that you learned during that time. How did you grow or change? What brought about this growth or change?
5. Make a list of the important people in your life at that time. What was interesting or engaging or unusual about each of these people? How did they look , dress, talk, and behave? What ideas, opinions, attitudes, and habits did they have? What did you learn from them? How did they act toward you and you toward them? Why?
6. Make a list of specific places that you associate with that time in your life. Close your eyes and try to imagine one of these places. Think about what it looked like. What sights, sounds, smells, or tastes come to mind when you think of this place? How did the place make you feel?
7. If you wish to do a piece of imaginative writing, think of past experiences as raw materials to be reshaped and transformed. Choose aspects of your past experience and ask yourself questions about them. Begin your questions with the words "What if . . ."

   What if my family had moved to a foreign country when I was young?

   What if I discovered that I had a twin whom I had never met before?

   What if someone like my mother or father had lived during the Civil War?

When you have decided on a particular person, place, thing, or event from your past to write about, try to recall as many details about it as you can. Use a graphic device such as a cluster diagram, sensory detail chart, or time line to generate specific details to use in your writing. For information about these devices, see the Language Arts Survey, 1.18–1.24.

▸▸▸ ACTIVITIES 1.10

A. In your journal, make a chart with three columns, one for each year you've spent in high school. In each column, list two or three experiences that stand out in your mind. Consider experiences related to school, family, work, or other aspects of your life.

B Choose one experience from your chart and do a cluster diagram or freewrite about this experience.

C. Write two or three "what if" questions based on past experiences that you might use in a piece of imaginative writing. (See the examples in item 7 of the chart above.)

1.11 OBSERVING

Good writers are people who look closely at life. They notice details in everyday events—the way passengers sway on a city bus, the shape of clouds and autumn leaves, the sound of a basketball whamping the spring pavement. They also record interesting observations in their journals so they won't forget them. Later, they can browse and study these, like snapshots in a scrapbook, for possible use in their writing. Writers are especially alert for the **telling detail**, one that implies a great deal. For example, in a newsroom the nonstop clatter of keys at dozens of computers could suggest the industry and determination of the reporters to meet their deadlines.

One way to make sure that your observations of an event or situation are thorough is to use the questions that news reporters use when they gather information: *who? what? where? when? why?* and *how?* These questions are especially helpful when you are gathering information at a live event, such as a meeting or performance. Jot down answers to these questions in brief form as you view the event. Also record details of sight, sound, touch, taste, and smell (see Section 1.18, "Sensory Details Charts").

▸▸▸ ACTIVITIES 1.11

A. Take a seat in a place where plenty of activity is going on, such as a restaurant, shopping mall, or city park. Closely observe the scene, using all of your senses, and make notes of your observations. Afterward, use your details to make a sensory details chart.

B. Describe the physical appearance of a friend or relative you know well. Include in your description details about the person's features, facial expressions, clothing, posture, movements, voice, way of talking, and so on. Try to choose details that tell your readers something about the person's personality.

C. Make observations at a live event, such as a track meet, pep rally, concert, or play rehearsal. Before observing, jot down the headings *who? what? where? when? why?* and *how?* on a sheet of paper, leaving space for notes. Then take notes under each heading while observing the event.

1.12 FREEWRITING

Another way to come up with ideas and details for writing is freewriting. When you freewrite, you write quickly and freely, about a particular subject or about no subject at all. The point is to keep writing, letting your mind roam where it will. Don't stop to organize or judge or revise what you have already written; just try to generate as much material as you can. Generally, you should attempt to write for several minutes without stopping. If you find yourself getting stuck, try repeating the last few words you wrote until something else comes into your head. Here's a portion of what one student wrote during a three-minute freewriting session:

> Hmmmm. What in the world should I write about? write about. write about. Well, there's always the weather. It's a really nice April day today. Sunny, warm enough to take off your sweater. The daffodils are still around. Looking kind of tired though. Some of the blossoms look like soggy bits of crepe paper. Lots of rain the last two days. Now you can smell the earth warming up again. warming up. warming up. Warming up for track is a lot more fun now. Wonder if I'll break my personal record in the 200-meter this year. Or maybe I'll try the 400-meter. Coach thinks I have the staying power for a longer race. My best friend Jill runs in the 400-meter. She's really good. Might feel funny, though, to compete against your best friend. What if I did better? Or what if I did worse? Hey, that might even make a good story idea, only I would use two other people as the characters. I mean, how do you balance friendship and competition? There's got to be a way to blend them. There would have to be a race, of course, in the story. Funny to be thinking about a story now—maybe this freewriting actually works . . .
>
> —Keiko Weber

You can use freewriting to come up with topics for writing, as in the preceding example. You can also use it to explore a particular topic. A focused freewrite is like a regular freewrite, except that you begin with a topic and keep bringing yourself back to that topic whenever your mind wanders somewhere else.

▸▸▸ ACTIVITIES 1.12

A. Do a ten-minute freewrite. Write about anything that comes into your mind, and try to keep your pen or pencil moving throughout the period. At the end of ten minutes, look over what you have written and circle two or three ideas that might serve as writing topics in the future.

B. Choose one of the following topics. Do a five-minute focused freewrite about the topic in your journal.

competition	using computers	Saturdays
homework	popular music	language
preparing for college	clothing	abstract art
swimming	neighborhood safety	things that fly

1.13 QUESTIONING

An excellent way to gather ideas or focus a writing topic is to ask questions. Many writers approach questioning by asking the so-called **reporting questions:** *who? what? where? when? why?* and *how?* This approach is especially useful when collecting information about an event for a news story or review or planning a narrative such as a short story or narrative poem.

When you're doing expressive or literary writing, questions that begin with *what if* can be useful. Asking *what if* questions can get your creative juices flowing and lead you down some surprising and interesting paths. Here are a few examples:

EXAMPLES

What if you were designing a city from scratch? How would it be organized? Where would people live and work? Where would businesses, shops, and recreational facilities be located? What transportation systems would be used?

What if Thomas Paine were somehow transported into the present? How would he react to current politics? What causes would he support? How would he be regarded by the public? by the media? by politicians?

What if the next president was a woman or an African American?

What if the United States officially became a bilingual nation?

▸▸▸ ACTIVITIES 1.13

A. Choose one of the following topics. In your journal, write questions about the topic beginning with *who, what, where, when, why,* and *how.*

B. Choose three topics from the list above and write *"What if . . . ?"* questions about them.

baseball	job training	pets	space travel
elections	Africa	television	the American Civil War
tourism	English	the ocean	car racing
fashion	tornadoes	pollution	elephants

1.14 Analyzing

Analyzing is a technique you can use to gather and sort information about a topic. In analyzing, you break down a thing into its parts and then think about how the parts are related. An **analysis chart** lists and describes the parts and explains how each part is related to the whole.

ANALYSIS OF EMERSON'S "CONCORD HYMN" (PAGE 318)

Part	Description	Relationship of Part to Whole
Stanza 1 (lines 1–4)	The speaker describes where he is and what happened there (in battle, farmers "fired the shot" that sparked the American Revolutionary War)	Establishes the setting of the poem and states the significant event that took place there.
Stanza 2 (lines 5–8)	The speaker notes that those who fought are long gone, as is the bridge they fought by.	Gives additional information about the site and the people who made it significant.
Stanza 3 (lines 9–12)	The speaker states that a memorial to those who fought is being raised today, and he explains the purpose of the memorial (to restore the memory of the event in people's minds, now and in the future).	Describes the present occasion and its connection to the past and the future.
Stanza 4 (lines 13–16)	The speaker remembers why the heroic soldiers fought (to "leave their children free") and asks the spirit that guided them to preserve the memorial through time.	Restates the significance of the past event and underscores the connection between the past, the present, and the future.

▸▸▸ Activities 1.14

A. Choose a poem from Unit 5, 6, 7, or 8. Do an analysis chart for the poem, following the preceding model.

B. Analyze a work of art created by you or another student. First, decide how you will break the work down into parts (for example, subject matter, style, materials used, and impact on the viewer). Then describe and explain each part in an analysis chart.

C. Choose an activity that you are familiar with, such as practicing a musical instrument, cleaning your bedroom, tuning an engine, or preparing a certain food. Create an analysis chart to describe that process.

1.15 Imagining

When you think about things not as they actually are but as they might be, you are **imagining.** The faculty of imagination is what enables writers to create new settings, themes, characters, and plots.

The sources of the imagination have long been regarded as a mystery. The ancient Greeks pointed to the **Muses** as the source of creative inspiration. The Muses were the nine daughters of Memory and the king of the gods, Zeus. An artist engaged in creative work, the Greeks believed, was filled by the spirit of one of the Muses. Each Muse was the guiding light for a different art form such as lyric poetry, tragedy, comedy, history, and dance.

The creative process remains quite mysterious. Inspiration doesn't always occur when you need it most. However, some simple techniques, called **heuristics**, can help a writer come up with new, creative ideas. Some examples are given in the following chart.

HEURISTICS FOR IMAGINING

1. Ask questions beginning with the words *what if.* (Example: What if humans evolved in such a way that either a man or a woman could bear children?)
2. Combine previously existing things in a new way. (Example: Create a plot for a story that involves the Internet, a world-wide computer network, and two characters from hostile families who are similar to Romeo and Juliet.)
3. Magnify something, making it bigger or more significant than it is now. (Example: Coyotes, which have spread to the fringes of many urban areas, move into cities in large numbers and cause new problems.)
4. Simplify something to make it more manageable to write about. (Example: In a story, name two related minor characters after human qualities, such as Charity and Mercy, and let the single quality define each character.)
5. Make a drawing, sketch, or diagram of the thing. (Example: Draw a diagram that shows the different social classes of a society on another planet where a story takes place.)
6. Start with something as it is and change it systematically. (Example: Write a children's story about a family that is like your family except that they live in the 1880s instead of the 1990s, in a sod house instead of an apartment, in Nebraska instead of Indiana, and so on.)
7. Project a trend into the future. (Example: Write a poem about a "colorblind" society—that is, one where full racial equality has been achieved.)
8. Work against type. (Example: Write a poem about a seventy-year-old person who loves skydiving.)

▶▶▶ Activity 1.15

Select a heuristics technique from the chart and use it to come up with an idea for a piece of imaginative writing.

1.16 Role Playing

Role playing is acting out an imagined situation with others. Each person takes the role of a different character. Role playing can help you generate ideas for writing and is especially useful when you are developing characters for a story or exploring different points of view for a piece of persuasive writing. You might consider tape recording or videotaping the role-playing session for closer study later. Alternatively, you might have someone watch the role playing and take notes on it.

▸▸▸ Activities 1.16

A. Work with a partner to role play one of the following situations, or one you come up with on your own:

- a guidance counselor and a student talking about the student's plans after high school
- two teachers sharing positive or negative classroom experiences with each other
- two friends talking about plagiarizing: one is astonished to discover that the other has plagiarized material for a report
- a discussion between two neighbors about the damage that one neighbor's dog did to the other neighbor's garden

B. Use the preceding role plays as source material to write a scene for a play.

1.17 Clustering

A **cluster chart** is one way to gather and relate ideas and details for a piece of writing. To begin a cluster chart, write your topic in the middle of a sheet of paper and circle it. Then, in the space around the circle, jot down ideas that are related to your topic, circling each item and connecting related items with lines. Continue in this manner until you have a web of associated ideas. This technique can help you group related details and also discover connections between ideas that you may not have noticed before.

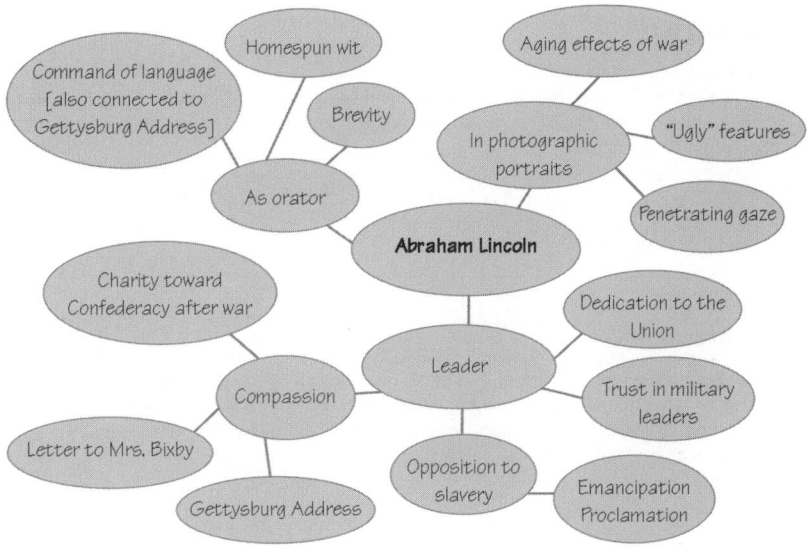

▶▶▶ ACTIVITY 1.17

Draw a cluster chart for one of the topics in Activity 1.13.

1.18 SENSORY DETAIL CHARTS

When you are planning a piece of descriptive writing, a **sensory detail chart** is a useful tool for gathering details. Begin by listing your subject at the top of a page. Beneath the subject, make five columns with headings for the five senses: sight, hearing, touch, taste, and smell. Then, under each heading, list details about your subject.

Sample Sensory Detail Chart

OWLING HIKE				
Sight	Hearing	Touch	Taste	Smell
crescent moon beams from flashlights owl taking off from oak tree dim outlines of trees	guide whispering horselike whinny (screech owl) hoo-hoo, hoo-hoo (barred owl)	cold hands without gloves	lip balm	dry leaves

▶▶▶ ACTIVITY 1.18

Create a sensory detail chart for one of the topics in Activity 1.13.

1.19 TIME LINES

A **time line** is often useful when you are planning a piece of narrative writing. Draw a straight line on a piece of paper and divide it into equal units of time. Then add key events at the appropriate points on the time line. Examples of time lines can be found in the unit introductions throughout this textbook.

▶▶▶ ACTIVITY 1.19

Create a time line for your life.

1.20 FLOWCHARTS

A **flowchart** shows a series of events. If you are writing an expository piece that deals with a process or sequence of events, making a flowchart can help you gather and organize information. In this type of chart, a circle around a step means "continue to the next step," a triangle means "make a decision," and a square means stop.

Sample Flowchart

❶ Pour water on suction cups of rack
❷ Center rack on top of car
❸ Does car have gutters above windows?
❹ If yes, attach and tighten gutter straps
❺ Strap kayak to rack
❻ Stop
❼ If no, strap kayak to rack
❽ Tie ends of kayak to front and rear bumpers with rope
❾ Stop

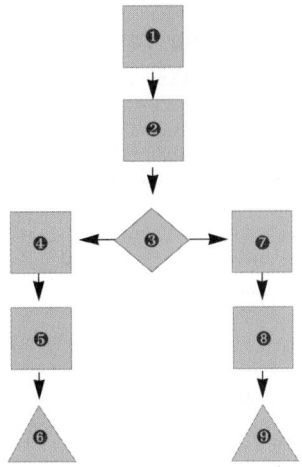

▶▶▶ **ACTIVITY 1.20**

Create a flow chart to describe a process that you go through often.

1.21 Story Maps

A **story map** is a chart that shows the elements of a short story. You can use a story map to lay out the basic elements of a story you are planning. While story maps take different forms, most include notes about the mood, conflict, plot, major characters, and theme.

Sample Story Map

Setting and Mood

Time 1990s

Place a large city

Mood optimistic

Major characters

Phil Whisner (a middle-class teenager)

Jerry Spate (a middle-aged homeless man)

Conflict ✓ internal ____ external

Teenager must confront his ignorance and wariness of homeless persons.

Plot

Inciting incident Phil begins a conversation with Jerry, who has approached him seeking a handout.

Climax Jerry invites Phil to visit his "home" in a subway tunnel.

Resolution Phil discovers that he shares a common interest in art with Jerry, who makes sculptures with found objects.

Themes Each person is an individual worthy of respect.

This story map gives only a brief description of the major elements. Some story maps go into great detail, describing elements of the setting, traits of the characters, and the specific events in the plot.

▶▶▶ **ACTIVITY 1.21**

Create a story map for a story that you have read.

1.22 Pro and Con Charts

A **pro and con chart** lists arguments or evidence for and against a particular point of view or course of action. This type of chart is helpful when you are planning a piece of persuasive writing or trying to make a decision. List the proposition at the top of the chart. This could be a statement of fact, a policy, or a personal value. Under the proposition, create two columns, one labeled *Pro* and the other *Con*. Then list the appropriate arguments in each column.

Sample Pro and Con Chart

Proposition: A new outerbelt should be built around our town.	
Pro	**Con**
—will help solve traffic problems in the center of town	—will draw business away from downtown area, leaving empty storefronts
—will draw new companies (that need good transportation network) to the area, improving employment	—will require sacrifice of farmland and other private property

▶▶▶ **Activity 1.22**

Create a pro and con chart about an important decision faced by students.

1.23 Analysis Charts

An **analysis chart** breaks down a thing into its parts and then shows how the parts are related to the whole and to each other. See the sample chart in the Language Arts Survey, 1.14, "Analyzing."

▶▶▶ **Activity 1.23**

Create an analysis chart to show the elements of a city.

1.24 Venn Diagrams

A **Venn diagram** allows you to show the similarities and differences between two things. Use this type of diagram when you plan a piece of writing that involves comparison and contrast. To create a Venn diagram, draw two overlapping circles. Label each with the name of one of your subjects. Note the similarities of the two subjects in the space where the circles overlap. Note differences outside the overlapping space.

Sample Venn Diagram

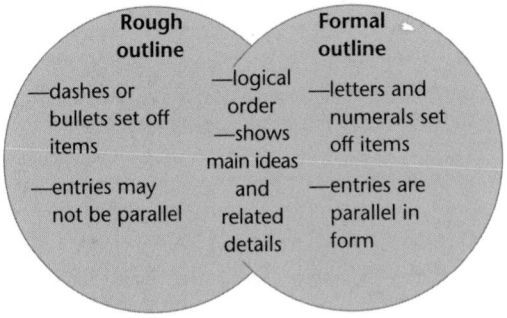

▶▶▶ ACTIVITY 1.24

Choose a graphic device from sections 1.17 to 1.24. Use it to develop an idea for a piece of writing.

PREWRITING: USING OUTSIDE SOURCES

1.25 BRAINSTORMING

Brainstorming is the process of thinking of as many different ideas as you can within a limited period of time. The process is akin to freewriting or to improvisation in acting. You can brainstorm alone, but the process works best in a group. Brainstorming can be used to solve a problem or plan a creative project. Keep things loose and spontaneous, and do not reject or judge any idea that is offered. Encourage everyone to contribute ideas. The more different the ideas are, the better. Once you have generated a large number of ideas, you can go back and evaluate them.

▶▶▶ ACTIVITY 1.25

In a small group, pick a subject about which you can brainstorm for ten minutes. For example, you might brainstorm ideas for a story about a main character who has a physical disability. Have one person record ideas on a chalkboard or flip chart. Be sure to give everyone a chance to speak.

1.26 DISCUSSION

Discussion is another idea-generating technique that involves other people. In a discussion, participants often have specific roles as they focus their conversation on a specific topic. The **group leader** introduces the topic, asks questions, encourages responses, mediates between group members, and generally keeps the discussion on track. The **participants** in the discussion share their thoughts, listen attentively to others, and build on others' comments. All discussion members should speak calmly and politely. Sometimes the group appoints a **secretary** to record the ideas that are discussed.

> ▸▸▸ ACTIVITY 1.26
>
> Get together with four other students to hold a discussion about planning a literary celebration for Martin Luther King, Jr., Day. Choose names out of a hat to designate a group leader and a secretary.

1.27 INTERVIEWING

Conducting an **interview** is another way to gather information and ideas for writing. The person you interview will probably be someone who has an extensive understanding of your subject. Newspaper articles, for example, frequently include information obtained from experts through interviews. When you interview, remember these tips:

- Get permission from the interviewee to print his or her statements.
- Ask questions that start with the words *who, what, when, where, why,* and *how.*
- Write down the interviewee's most important statements word-for-word, so you can quote some of them in your writing.
- Get the correct spelling of the interviewee's name, so that you can properly attribute the information you gather to its source.

> ▸▸▸ ACTIVITY 1.27
>
> Think of a person you know who is well informed about a subject that interests you, and conduct an interview with that person. For example, if you are interested in horseback riding and know someone who has taken riding lessons for several years, you could interview that person. Use a notepad or tape recorder to record your interview. Then write a brief article that includes a quotation from your expert.

1.28 USING PRINT SOURCES

For certain kinds of writing projects, you will need to gather information about your subject from print sources. These are likely to include books, magazines, newspapers, brochures, and reference works. To locate books, use your library's card catalog or online catalog. For magazines, consult the *Readers' Guide to Periodical Literature.* To find newspaper articles, use the print, microfilm, or microfiche indexes to newspapers.

> ▸▸▸ ACTIVITY 1.28
>
> Choose a subject that interests you and that has been covered in magazines and newspapers in the past few years. At the library, find three different kinds of print sources of information about your subject. Briefly identify each source by author and title. In addition, for books list the publisher and date; for magazines and newspapers list the publication name and date.

1.29 Using Nonprint Sources

The number of nonprint sources of information is growing rapidly. Explore these sources as well as you gather ideas and information for writing. Nonprint sources include radio and television programs, films, videos, slides, photographic prints, filmstrips, audiocassette tapes, and CD/ROM discs as well as computer services, networks, and bulletin boards. Many nonprint sources are available in libraries. For specific information about accessing information via computer, talk to a resource person at your school or library.

> ▸▸▸ **Activity 1.29**
>
> Locate at least three nonprint sources offering information about one of the subjects that follow or another that you would like to explore. List the sources that you found and write a brief description of the content of each source.
>
> the Olympics birdwatching acid rain folk music

PREWRITING: ORGANIZING YOUR IDEAS

1.30 Revising Your Writing Plan

After you have collected information for a piece of writing, review your writing plan. Are you still satisfied with the topic, purpose, audience, and form you have chosen? Do you know what mode or modes of writing you will be using? You may decide to change certain parts of your plan as a result of your research and other preparation. For example, while doing research for an informative piece about state fair livestock competitions, you might become interested in the debate about whether huge cash prizes encourage cheating in the show ring. You might then decide to focus on this narrower topic. This change in topic, in turn, might lead you to change your purpose, from informative to persuasive.

> ▸▸▸ **Activity 1.30**
>
> Choose a subject that you find interesting and make plans for two very different pieces of writing related to that subject. For each piece of writing, list a topic, purpose, audience, form, and primary mode.

1.31 Identifying Main Ideas and Supporting Details

Once you have gathered information for a piece of writing, read through your notes to select the main ideas that you will present. Then look for details to support these main ideas. For a short piece of writing, such as a paragraph, you will need to identify one main idea and several supporting details. For a longer piece of writing, you might begin by writing a **thesis statement** that presents the major idea that you want to express. Then select several main ideas related to the thesis statement and details to support them.

▶▶▶ ACTIVITY 1.31

Choose one of the following subjects for a persuasive paragraph.

- How television influences young people
- All-boy or all-girl high schools
- Conflict-resolution programs that use peer mediators

Write a topic sentence to express a main idea about the subject. Then write three sentences that support the main idea.

1.32 MAKING A ROUGH OUTLINE

Outlines are useful for sorting and organizing main ideas and details. In a **rough outline**, or **informal outline**, main ideas are listed in some logical order and supporting details are grouped under each main idea. Dashes or bullets precede each supporting detail. Here is a rough outline for a composition about nineteenth-century whaling in New England:

Importance of whale oil

—Source of illumination in lamps
—Used in soap-making and lubrication
—Whalebone used in corsets

Hunting the whale

—Lookout on mast spots whales
—Six-man crews in small boats pursue whale
—Harpooned whale drags boat along until it tires
—Boat tows dead animal back to ship

Processing the whale

—Whale is lashed to side of ship
—Crew carves hulk into pieces
—Pieces are boiled to yield oil
—Oil is stored in barrels below deck

▶▶▶ ACTIVITY 1.32

Make a rough outline for a composition on a topic from American history.

1.33 MAKING A FORMAL OUTLINE

In a **formal outline**, the writer uses Roman numerals, letters, and numbers to identify headings and subheadings. The entries at each level should be parallel in grammatical structure and begin with capital letters. A formal outline may be one of two types. A **topic outline** uses words, phrases, or clauses in the entries. A **sentence outline** uses complete sentences. The following sample is from a topic outline:

Plantations in the Old South

I. Cotton
  A. Entire South
  B. Labor-intensive harvesting
    1. Picking from August to January

2. Slave labor
3. Long sacks tied to waist

C. Horse-powered gins

II. Sugar

A. Mainly southeastern Louisiana

B. Sugar cane stalks slashed with machete-type knives

C. Mills for grinding and boiling cane

▶▶▶ ACTIVITY 1.33

Choose a subject related to wildlife or the environment. Create a sentence outline for a paper on that subject.

1.34 ORGANIZING IDEAS

Outlines provide a way to put ideas and information into some logical order before writing. The chart that follows shows some common methods for organizing ideas for writing.

METHODS FOR ORGANIZING IDEAS	
Chronological Order	Events are organized in order of their occurrence, often from first to last. Ideas are connected by transitional words and phrases that indicate time or sequence, such as *first, second, finally, next, then, afterward,* and *before.*
Spatial Order	Subjects are organized according to their their positions or locations, often from top to bottom, left to right, front to back, clockwise, or the reverse of any of these. Ideas are connected by transitional words and phrases that indicate position or location, such as *beside, in the middle, next, to the right, on top,* and *in front.*
Degree Order	Ideas are presented in order of degree from most to least or vice versa. For example, they might be presented from most important to least important. Ideas are connected by transitional words and phrases that indicate degree, such as *more, less, most, least, most important,* and *least promising.*
Comparison and Contrast Order	Details about two subjects are presented, in one of two ways. In the first method, the characteristics of one subject are presented, followed by the characteristics of a second subject. In the second method, both subjects are compared and contrasted with regard to one characteristic, then with regard to a second characteristic, and so on. Ideas are connected by transitional words and phrases that indicate similarities or differences, such as *likewise, similarly, in contrast, a different kind,* and *another difference.*
Cause-and-Effect Order	One or more causes are presented followed by one or more effects, or one or more effects are presented followed by one or more causes. Ideas are connected by transitional words and phrases that indicate cause and effect, such as *one cause, another effect, as a result, consequently,* and *therefore.*

CONTINUED

Classification Order	Subjects are divided into groups, or classes. These groups are then presented, one-by-one, in some reasonable order. Ideas are connected by transitional words and phrases that indicate class membership or the method by which the writer has organized the classes, such as *another group, the first type, one kind,* and *other sorts.*
Part-by-Part Order	Ideas are presented according to no *overall* organizational pattern. However, each idea is connected logically to the one that precedes it and/or to the one that follows it. After chronological order, this is the most common method for organizing ideas in writing. Ideas are connected by any transitional word or phrase that indicates the relationship or connection between the ideas.

▶▶▶ ACTIVITY 1.34

Choose an appropriate method for organizing ideas for each piece of writing listed. Then briefly explain why you think the method you chose is appropriate.

1. a composition about the works of two humorous writers
2. a paper about life in a Puritan colony in New England
3. a description of a flower garden
4. a composition explaining Lincoln's reasons for issuing the Emancipation Proclamation
5. a paragraph analyzing the wildlife in a particular forest

DRAFTING: APPROACHES TO WRITING A DRAFT

1.35 WRITING A DISCOVERY DRAFT

Drafting is the stage where you begin to impose a particular form on your prewriting material. There are several approaches you can take to drafting. Some writers begin by writing a **discovery draft**. In a discovery draft, the writer tries to get all of his or her ideas down on paper quickly, without worrying much about matters such as organization, style, grammar, spelling, and mechanics. This type of draft is generally quite rough. It furnishes raw material that the writer then shapes and polishes in extensive revisions.

▶▶▶ ACTIVITY 1.35

Choose one of the following topics and take a few minutes to think about what you want to say on the subject. Then write a discovery draft for a paragraph about the topic. As you write, strive to put all of your ideas on paper without going back to revise and polish those ideas.

- a movie that had a strong effect on you
- a place where you feel comfortable
- a celebration or holiday that you enjoy

1.36 WRITING A CAREFUL DRAFT

Some writers prefer to work slowly and carefully through the first draft. As they write, they reread sentences and paragraphs, revising and polishing them before continuing. Such a **careful**

draft usually unfolds more easily when it is based on a thorough outline. The choice of whether to create a careful draft, by writing slowly and revising as you go, or a discovery, which is written quickly and then revised in subsequent drafts, is up to the writer. Either approach can produce excellent writing.

▸▸▸ ACTIVITY 1.36

Select a topic from the list in the Activity for section 1.35, and write a careful draft of a paragraph on that subject. To begin, outline your paragraph, listing the main idea and three or four supporting details. Next, draft the topic sentence and revise it until it reads just the way you want it to. Draft the next sentence; reread it and revise it as needed. Continue in this manner until you have completed your paragraph.

1.37 The Prewriting, Drafting, and Revising Cycle

Writing sometimes occurs in neat stages—first prewriting, then drafting, and then revising. More frequently, however, writers shift back and forth between these activities. For example, in the middle of writing your draft, you might realize that you haven't really thought through one of the arguments you want to present. You might need to return to a prewriting activity such as role playing to clarify your position. Then you would go back and revise the new material before continuing with the rest of the draft. The steps in the writing process are flexible and can be adapted to meet specific problems that arise as you write.

DRAFTING: PARAGRAPHS

1.38 Paragraphs with Topic Sentences

A paragraph frequently contains a **topic sentence**, which presents the main idea of the paragraph. This topic sentence can occur at the beginning, in the middle, or at the end of the paragraph. Most paragraphs also contain two or more sentences that illustrate, give examples of, or elaborate on the topic sentence. The **supporting sentences** often begin with transitions that relate them to the other sentences or to the topic sentence. The paragraph may also end with a **clincher sentence**, which restates the main idea of the paragraph. These parts of a paragraph are identified in the following sample.

Topic Sentence

John Muir was a key figure in the national parks movement. The son of a Wisconsin farmer, he studied natural science and philosophy and read the great naturalists. From a young age, Muir felt a sense of fulfillment and exhilaration in the presence of nature. In the 1860s, he traveled throughout the majestic Sierra Nevada, becoming intimately familiar with it. He urged others to experience the power and splendor of wilderness, which he saw as a precious resource of the human spirit. Wilderness, however, needed protection from those who would plunder it, especially lumberers, who had been eating away at centuries-old redwood groves in California. Muir believed that federal government control was needed to preserve California's forests. In the early 1890s, he organized the Sierra Club, wrote articles, and personally lobbied President Theodore Roosevelt to help preserve the Sierra Nevada. The persuasive Muir was successful. The state-controlled redwood forests came under federal protection as a national park. Muir's efforts fueled the conservation movement which helped to create sixteen national parks by 1916.

Supporting Sentences

Clincher Sentence

►►► ACTIVITY 1.38

Write a paragraph about one of the following topics or one of your own. Lead off your paragraph with a topic sentence. Then write three sentences that present details related to the topic sentence. Close with a clincher sentence that wraps up the paragraph.

- a person who has contributed to your school or community
- a book, story, or poem you would recommend to others

1.39 PARAGRAPHS WITHOUT TOPIC SENTENCES

Not every paragraph contains a topic sentence. In some cases, the main idea of the paragraph is not stated directly but implied. In other cases, the paragraph serves simply as a transition between sections of a composition. Probably the most common kind of paragraph with a topic sentence is a narrative paragraph that presents a sequence of events but does not include a sentence summarizing the events. The following paragraph is an example:

> The sign at the top of the trail read "Steep Descent." Miranda plunged both ski poles into the snow as she took off. The wooded trail was straight at first, and she picked up speed. Luckily the first turn was wide and well banked. Miranda made a slight snowplow to slow her speed as she rounded it. Then came a twisty section. She leaned inward slightly ahead of each turn. Finally, the trail flattened out, and she coasted to a stop to catch her breath.

►►► ACTIVITY 1.39

Write a narrative paragraph about a procedure or activity, such as performing a lab experiment, demonstrating a skill in sports, or preparing a certain food. Organize your paragraph in chronological order, and do not include a topic sentence.

1.40 ELABORATION: TYPES OF SUPPORTING DETAILS

In a typical paragraph, the main idea is stated in a topic sentence. Other sentences in the paragraph elaborate on the main idea. The kinds of supporting details used to **elaboration** include **sensory details, facts and statistics, illustrations and examples, anecdotes,** and **quotations**. In the sample paragraph in section 1.38, the author uses illustrations and examples to expand on the main topic.

►►► ACTIVITY 1.40

For each topic sentence, write at least two supporting sentences that contain details of the type specified.

1. The weekly farmer's market is always a delight to the senses. (sensory details)
2. Cramming for a test has several drawbacks. (examples)
3. Even when you fail at something, you can learn a valuable lesson. (anecdote)
4. Smoking is hazardous to your health in a number of ways. (facts and statistics)

DRAFTING: COMPOSITIONS

1.41 Writing a Thesis Statement and Topic Sentences

A **thesis statement** expresses the main idea of a composition and usually occurs in the first paragraph. The remainder of the paragraph introduces the composition as a whole, using one of many techniques for writing introductions (see section 1.42, "Organizing a Composition"). Your thesis statement should be brief and to the point. Readers should be able to tell from your thesis statement whether the composition is primarily expressive, informative, or persuasive.

Once you have written a thesis statement, you may wish to write the **topic sentences** for each paragraph. These sentences should express the major ideas that support your thesis. Approaching drafting in this way will help to ensure the unity and coherence of your composition (see section 1.43, "Self-Evaluation"). Once you have the basic framework of a thesis statement and related topic sentences, you can write the rest of your introduction, supporting sentences for the body paragraphs, and your conclusion.

▶▶▶ Activity 1.41

Develop a focused topic from one of the general topics in the following list. Write a thesis statement for an informative or persuasive composition about the focused topic. Then write three topic sentences for body paragraphs to support the thesis statement.

an organization in your community
graduating from high school
cultural traditions
the effects of technology

1.42 Organizing a Composition

Every composition should have three parts: an introduction, a body, and a conclusion.

Introduction. The purpose of the introduction is to capture the reader's attention and present the main idea of the composition. To draw readers in to your composition, you can do the following:

- Describe a scene
- State an opinion
- Pose a question
- Present a fascinating fact
- Offer a quotation
- Tell an anecdote
- Give a summary
- Use an allusion
- Provide background information
- Paraphrase a statement or idea

Body. The body of the composition includes several paragraphs that support the thesis statement. Generally, each paragraph has a topic sentence that expresses one main idea related to the thesis. The rest of the sentences in each paragraph elaborate on the main idea.

Conclusion. The conclusion should wrap up the composition and give the reader a sense that your presentation is complete. In writing your conclusion, you might want to use any of the following techniques:

- Make a generalization
- Pose a question
- Restate the thesis
- Make a prediction
- Issue a call to action
- Summarize the main ideas
- Imagine the future
- Present a resolution
- Present the last event

▶▶▶ ACTIVITIES 1.42

A. Find an essay in a magazine, textbook, or essay collection that has an introduction that you especially like. Bring the selection to class and read the introduction aloud in a small group of students. Before or after your reading, explain what technique the writer used to interest the reader and what the piece is about.

B. Repeat the preceding activity, but this time look for an interesting conclusion. Before reading each conclusion, briefly describe the content and purpose of the piece as background for your listeners.

REVISING: APPROACHES TO REVISION

1.43 SELF-EVALUATION

When your draft is finished, read it through to **evaluate**, or judge, the effectiveness of the piece at this point. Many writers recommend waiting a couple of days before reading it for **self-evaluation**. Waiting allows you to look at your work more objectively. The purpose of the self-evaluation is to make any needed changes that will improve the content, organization, and style of the piece.

A good method for doing a self-evaluation is to read the composition three times. On the first reading, look particularly at the content of the piece. Second, read for organization and coherence. Third, check the voice and style. You can use the questions in the checklists that follow to guide you in evaluating your draft.

REVISION CHECKLIST: CONTENT AND UNITY

1. Does the writing achieve its purpose?
2. Are the main ideas related to the thesis statement?
3. Are the main ideas clearly stated and supported by details?

REVISION CHECKLIST: ORGANIZATION AND COHERENCE

1. Are the ideas arranged in a logical order?
2. Do transitions connect ideas to one another both within and between paragraphs?

REVISION CHECKLIST: VOICE AND STYLE

1. Is the voice—the tone, word choice, and perspective of the writing—authentic? Is it consistent?
2. Is the level of language appropriate to the audience and purpose?
3. Is the mood appropriate to the purpose and form of the writing?

Making improvements in a draft usually involves adding, deleting, replacing, and moving material (see section 1.45, "Four Types of Revision"). When you have made your revisions, read through the piece aloud to spot and adjust any awkward passages.

▶▶▶ ACTIVITY 1.43

Choose a piece of writing that you have already done. Revise your work using the three checklists provided.

1.44 PEER EVALUATION

Peer evaluation is a type of evaluation in which another person reads your writing and gives you suggestions for improving it. Both the writer and the evaluator have specific roles in this process. The guidelines that follow will help you get the most out of a peer evaluation.

For the evaluator

- Focus on matters of revision. Evaluate content, organization, and style. Ignore proofreading matters, such as spelling, punctuation, and mechanics, which can be dealt with later.
- Be positive. Let the writer know what he or she has done right. Discuss weak spots by pointing out what the writer would gain by making a certain change.
- Be specific. Give the writer concrete ideas for improving the piece. For example, if you think that organizing the piece in chronological order rather than in spatial order makes more sense, suggest how the writer could rearrange the content of the piece to fit this pattern.
- Be tactful. Use constructive language and a pleasant tone of voice. Word your comments so the writer knows you are critiquing the writing, not the writer.

For the writer

- Tell your evaluator what aspect of the composition worries you. Here are some examples:
  - —Should I move the quotation in the conclusion to the introduction? (organization)
  - —Do you think my vocabulary level is suited to this audience? (style)
  - —Did you find my arguments persuasive? (content)
- Accept the evaluator's comments politely. If you are confused by a particular comment, ask the evaluator to clarify it. Avoid taking criticism of your writing personally.

▶▶▶ ACTIVITY 1.44

Choose a writing assignment that all members of the class have done. Trade drafts with another student, then take turns offering comments on each other's work.

1.45 FOUR TYPES OF REVISION

The four basic processes used in revising what you have written are **adding, deleting, replacing**, and **moving**. These processes can be applied to words, phrases, sentences, and entire paragraphs. For example, as you revise a paragraph, you might add transition words to help the sentences flow more smoothly. You might delete a detail that does not relate to the main idea. You might replace a paraphrase with a quotation, and you might move a passage that is out of sequence to its correct place.

▶▶▶ ACTIVITY 1.45

Revise the following paragraph to improve its unity, organization, and style. Add, delete, replace, or move material as needed.

There is nothing wrong with having a litter of kittens or puppies in the house as long as each of these pets finds a home and proper care. Too many of these animals become unwanted pets. They are discarded. They may end up abandoned along a country road or some such thing. All pet owners should know about the importance of spaying or neutering their pets. Spaying and neutering is part of responsible pet ownership. According to the American Society for the Prevention of Cruelty to Animals, out of every 100 dogs and cats born, only 10 find permanent, loving homes. Some folks think spaying and neutering is too darned expensive, but consider the cost of not doing it. One unspayed female dog and her descendants can produce over 4,000 puppies in just seven generations! This creates a terrible overpopulation problem. It creates starving and unhealthy animals roaming everywhere. An unspayed female cat and her offspring can produce even more individuals.

1.46 MARKING A MANUSCRIPT

To mark revisions on a draft, use the standard proofreading symbols shown in the following chart. Using these symbols saves space on your draft and makes it easier to read when you are ready to make a clean copy.

SYMBOL AND EXAMPLE	MEANING OF SYMBOL
The very first time	Delete this material.
≡ french toast	Capitalize this letter.
the vice-President	Lowercase this letter.
cat cradle	Insert something that is missing. Write the missing letter(s) or punctuation above the line.
Georze	Replace this letter or word.
housse	Take out this letter and close up space.
book keeper	Close up space.
gebril	Change the order of these letters.
All the horses king's	Move this word to where the arrow points.
¶ end. "Watch out," she yelled.	Begin a new paragraph.
Love conquers all.	Put a period here.
Welcome friends.	Put a comma here.
Get the stopwatch	Put a space here.
Dear Madam:	Put a colon here.
She walked he rode.	Put a semicolon here.

CONTINUED

name=brand	Put a hyphen here.
products	Put an apostrophe here.
cats meow (stet)	Ignore the correction.

PROOFREADING AND PUBLISHING

1.47 Proofreading Checklist

After making a clean copy of your revised draft, proofread it for errors in spelling, grammar, usage, and mechanics. Use the following proofreading checklist.

PROOFREADING CHECKLIST	
Spelling	• Are all words, including names, spelled correctly?
Grammar	• Does each verb agree in number with its subject? • Are verb tenses consistent and correct? • Are irregular verbs formed correctly? • Is the referent of each pronoun clear? • Does every pronoun agree with its antecedent? • Are subject and object forms of pronouns used correctly? • Are there any sentence fragments or run-on sentences? • Have double negatives been avoided?
Usage	• Have frequently confused words, such as *affect* and *effect*, been used correctly?
Mechanics	• Does every sentence end with an end mark? • Are commas, semicolons, hyphens, and dashes used correctly? • Do all proper nouns and proper adjectives begin with capital letters? • Has proper manuscript form been used?

▶▶▶ Activity 1.47

Using the Proofreading Checklist, correct the following paragraph for spelling, grammar, usage, and mechanics errors. Use a dictionary as needed to check spelling.

The gutenberg elegies, by Sven Birkerts, is a very interesting book. His topic is "the fate of reading in an electronic age." Birkerts believes, that the world of reading will be transformed as much by computers as it was by Gutenberg's invention of the printing press. His view somewhat is bleak, however. He fears that people will be preoccupied with organizing data rather than discovering truth. He also points out that books have a Magical influence on our lives. They provide a placce for escape and dreaming.They teach us about what it means to be human. All bok lovers will share the authors concerns.

1.48 Preparing Your Manuscript

When you have proofread your draft, you are ready to prepare the final manuscript. Follow the guidelines given by your teacher. The following guidelines, however, are typical:

Guidelines for preparing your manuscript:

1. Type, word process, or write neatly in blue or black ink.
2. Double-space your paper. In other words, leave one blank line between every line of type.
3. Use one side of the paper.
4. Leave one-inch margins on all sides of the text.
5. Indent the first line of each paragraph.
6. In the upper right-hand corner, put your name, class, and date. On every page after the first, include the page number in this heading as follows:

   Gloria Ramirez
   English 12
   May 6, 1999
   p. 2

7. Make a cover sheet containing the title of the work, your name, the date, and the class.

After preparing a final manuscript based on these guidelines, proofread it one last time for errors introduced in the typing, word processing, or handwriting.

1.49 Publishing or Presenting Your Work

Some writing is done just for oneself. Journal writing usually falls into that category. However, most writing is meant to be shared with others. There are many, many ways in which to share your work. Here are several ways in which you can publish your writing or present it to others:

- Find a local publication that will accept such work (a school literary magazine, a school newspaper, or a community newspaper are possibilities).
- Submit the work to a regional or national publication. Check a reference work such as *Writer's Market* to find information on types of manuscripts accepted, manuscript form, methods and amounts of payment, and so on.
- Enter the work in a contest. Your teacher may be able to tell you about writing contests for students. You can also find out about such contests by looking for announcements in writer's magazines and literary magazines.
- Read your work aloud to classmates, friends, or family members.
- Obtain permission to read your work aloud over the school's public address system.
- Work with other students to prepare a publication—a brochure, literary magazine, anthology, or newspaper.
- Prepare a poster or bulletin board, perhaps in collaboration with other students, to display your writing.
- Make your own book by typing or word processing the pages and binding them together in some way. Another possibility is to copy your work into a blank book.
- Hold a recital of student writing as a class or school-wide project.

- Share your writing with other students in a small writer's group that meets periodically to discuss one or two students' recent work. (Members of the group should receive the work to be discussed beforehand so they can read it and make notes on it.)
- If the work is dramatic in nature, work with other students to present a performance of it, either as straight drama or as reader's theater. If the work is poetry, fiction, or nonfiction, work with others to present it as an oral interpretation. (One possibility is to pair with another student, exchange pieces, and then coach one another in oral interpretations of the pieces.)

ESSENTIAL SKILLS: *Language*

GRAMMAR HANDBOOK

INTRODUCTION TO GRAMMAR

2.1 THE GRAMMAR YOU ALREADY KNOW

Grammar is something you know, even if you have never studied it. Inside the head of every person is a sophisticated device that works, all by itself, to learn how to put words and phrases together grammatically. Even if you don't know an adverb from an aardvark, you know, if you are a speaker of English, that

the little leaf-eating bug

is grammatical and that

the bug little leaf-eating

is not. You can tell that one string of words is grammatical and the other isn't because you have learned, unconsciously, many thousands of rules governing how words can be put together and how they can't.

When you study a grammar textbook, therefore, what you are really learning is not the grammar of the language—for the most part, that's something you already know. What you are learning is terminology for describing what you know so that you can use that terminology when discussing language. Incidentally, as you study textbook grammar, you will also learn a few rules that you never quite learned unconsciously. Remember, however, that most of the grammar is already inside your head. Learning to describe that grammar can therefore be viewed as learning more about yourself and your amazing unconscious abilities.

2.2 THE USES OF GRAMMAR

Why study grammar? After all, no amount of grammar study can match the value of hands-on reading and writing. Grammar is useful, however. It gives you a way to speak about and understand your own writing and that of others. Contrast the following examples:

> He had been contemptuous of those who wrecked. You did not have to like it because you understood it. He could beat anything, he thought, because no thing could hurt him if he did not care.
>
> —Ernest Hemingway, "The Snows of Kilimanjaro"

He seemed to see it entire with a child's complete divination before he ever laid eyes on either—the doomed wilderness whose edges were being constantly and punily gnawed at by men with axes and plows who feared it because it was wilderness, men myriad and nameless even to one another in the land where the old bear had earned a name, through which ran not even a mortal animal but an anachronism, indomitable and invincible, out of an old dead time, a phantom, epitome and apotheosis of the old wild life at which the puny humans swarmed and hacked in a fury of abhorrence and fear, like pygmies about the ankles of a drowsing elephant: the old bear solitary, indomitable and alone, widowered, childless, and absolved of mortality—old Priam reft of his old wife and having outlived all his sons.

—William Falkner, "The Bear"

If you had to describe the difference between these two passages, you would find it useful to have precise grammatical terms at your command. The first passage by Faulkner is one long, complex sentence containing many parts—numerous prepositional phrases, appositions, clauses, and Faulkner's characteristic vivid modifiers (*myriad, nameless, indomitable, invincible, wild, puny, drowsing, solitary,* and so on). In contrast, the second passage is characterized by short sentences containing few modifiers or embedded clauses or phrases. You may *sense* the differences in these two styles of writing instinctively, but grammar gives you a way to *understand* and *communicate* those differences.

THE PARTS OF SPEECH

2.3 Common and Proper Nouns

A **noun** is a word used to refer to a person, place, thing, or idea.

NOUNS David Robinson, Mexico, tree, honesty

A **common noun** is a name that belongs to (is *common* to) all the persons, places, or things in a group. A **proper noun** refers to a *particular* person, place, or thing and begins with a capital letter.

COMMON NOUNS star, beach, river
PROPER NOUNS Malibu Beach, Spoon River

2.4 Concrete and Abstract Nouns

A **concrete noun** refers to an object that you can perceive by hearing, seeing, smelling, tasting, or touching. An **abstract noun** names a quality, characteristic, or idea.

CONCRETE scream, onions, chocolate, asphalt
ABSTRACT meanness, sincerity, patience

2.5 Compound and Collective Nouns

A **compound noun** is made up of two or more words used together as a single noun. A **collective noun** refers to a group of similar things.

COMPOUND NOUNS basketball, houseboat, stoplight, torchbearer
COLLECTIVE NOUNS litter, Celtics, senators, faculty, cast

2.6 Personal Pronouns

A **pronoun** is a word used as a substitute for a noun. The word a pronoun stands for is called an **antecedent** or **referent.** In the following example, *student* is the antecedent of the pronoun *he.*

PRONOUN AND ANTECEDENT	Was the **student** bored? **He** may just have been tired.

A **personal pronoun** is a pronoun that substitutes for a person's name. The personal pronouns are *I, me, my, mine, we, us, our, ours, you, your, yours, he, him, his, she, her, hers, it, its, they, them, their,* and *theirs.*

PERSONAL PRONOUNS	**They** were convinced it would not be on the test. **Our** only hope was a multiple-choice test.

2.7 Reflexive and Intensive Pronouns

A **reflexive pronoun** is a pronoun used to show that an action is done to or reflects upon someone or something. An **intensive pronoun** is a pronoun used to emphasize a noun or pronoun already given. The reflexive and intensive pronouns are *myself, ourselves, yourself, yourselves, himself, herself, itself,* and *themselves.*

REFLEXIVE PRONOUN	After final exams, he rewarded **himself** with a new CD player.
INTENSIVE PRONOUN	I **myself** would never have agreed to it in the first place.

2.8 Demonstrative Pronouns

A **demonstrative pronoun** is a pronoun used to point out a particular person, place, or thing. The demonstrative pronouns are *this, that, these,* and *those.*

DEMONSTRATIVE PRONOUNS	**This** too shall pass. **That** was the last time we saw each other.

2.9 Indefinite Pronouns

An **indefinite** pronoun is a pronoun that points out a person, place, or thing, but not a particular one. Some of the most common indefinite pronouns are *some, someone, somebody, something, any, anyone, anybody, anything, everyone, everybody, everything, other, another, either, neither, all, many, few, each, both, one, none, nobody,* and *nothing.*

INDEFINITE PRONOUNS	**Nothing** she can say will change my mind. **Someone** had better explain this to me right now.

2.10 Interrogative Pronouns

An **interrogative pronoun** is a pronoun used in asking a question. The interrogative questions are *who, whose, what, whom,* and *which.*

INTERROGATIVE PRONOUNS	**Whose** magazine is this? **Which** one of you is responsible for this mess?

2.11 Relative Pronouns

A **relative pronoun** is a pronoun that connects a group of words with an antecedent. The relative pronouns are *that, which, who, whom,* and *whose.*

RELATIVE PRONOUNS	The mansion **that** Gatsby owned was on Long Island. The uncle **who** left them the money had been a stockbroker.

2.12 Action Verbs

A **verb** is a word that expresses action or a state of being. An **action verb** expresses physical or mental activity.

ACTION VERBS	skate, worry, scream, fly, lurch

2.13 Linking Verbs

A **linking verb** connects a noun with another noun, pronoun, or adjective that describes it or identifies it. Most linking verbs are forms of the verb *to be.* They include *am, are, is, was,* and *been.* Other words that can be used as linking verbs include *seem, sound, look, stay, feel, remain* and *become.*

LINKING VERBS	The Caribbean **is** the vacationer's paradise. Their latest song **will become** a hit.

2.14 Auxiliary Verbs

An **auxiliary verb** is a verb that helps to make some form of another verb. Common auxiliary verbs are *can, could, may, might, must, shall, should, will, would,* and forms of the verbs *to be, to have,* and *to do.*

AUXILIARY VERBS	**must** persist, **shall** fight, **will** become, **may** leave We **would** win more games if we played less selfishly.

2.15 Transitive and Intransitive Verbs

The **direct object** of a verb is a noun or pronoun that names the person or thing upon which the verb acts. Verbs that must have direct objects are **transitive verbs**. Verbs that do not need direct objects are **intransitive verbs**. Some verbs are both transitive and intransitive.

TRANSITIVE VERB	He **named** the band after his favorite city.
INTRANSITIVE VERB	The storm **ended** abruptly, and we resumed our picnic.

2.16 Verbals: Participles

A **participle** is a form of a verb that can be used as an adjective. (See the Language Arts Survey, 2.19, for the definition of an adjective.)

PARTICIPLES	The **broken** glass was everywhere. **Seeing** an opening in the traffic, he stepped on the gas.

2.17 Verbals: Gerunds

A **gerund** is a form of a verb ending in *–ing* that is used as a noun. Be careful not to confuse gerunds with participles, verbal adjectives that end in *–ing*.

GERUNDS	The German philosopher Martin Heidegger stressed **becoming** over **being**.

2.18 Verbals: Infinitives

An **infinitive** is a form of a verb that can be used as a noun, an adjective, or an adverb. Most infinitives begin with *to*. (See the Language Arts Survey, 2.19 and 2.22, for more information about adjectives and adverbs.)

INFINITIVES	I have taken pains **to show** you how this works. I did not intend **to offend** anyone. **To offend** intentionally is unacceptable in this school.

2.19 Adjectives and Articles

An **adjective** is a word used to modify a noun or pronoun. *To modify* means to change the meaning of something. Adjectives change the meaning of nouns or pronouns by answering the questions *What kind? Which one?* or *How many?*

ADJECTIVES	**inferior** writer, **last** resort, **third** loss

The adjectives *a, an,* and *the* are called **articles.** *A* and *an* are **indefinite articles** because they refer indefinitely to any one of a group. *The* is the **definite article** because it refers to a definite person, place, thing, or idea.

ARTICLES **a** disappointment, **an** orange, **the** films of Scorsese

2.20 Proper Adjectives

A **proper adjective** is an adjective formed from a proper noun.

PROPER ADJECTIVES **American** humor, **British** invasion, **Nirvanaesque** sound

2.21 Predicate Adjectives

Every sentence is made up of two parts, a **subject** and a **predicate.** The subject is what or whom the sentence is about. The predicate tells something about the subject's actions or condition.

SUBJECT **Eddie Vedder** may soon retire.
PREDICATE Michael Stipe is **environmentally conscious.**

A **predicate adjective** is an adjective that follows a linking verb and modifies the subject of a verb.

PREDICATE ADJECTIVES That play was **humorless.**
In his prime, Michael Jordan was **unstoppable.**

2.22 Adverbs

An **adverb** is a word used to modify a verb, an adjective, or another adverb.

ADVERBS She **briskly** reviewed the novel before the test.
He closed the door **quietly**, but they still heard him come in.
There is nothing left for me to do, he thought **despairingly.**

2.23 Adjective or Adverb?

If you know a word is either an adjective or adverb but are not sure which it is, look at the word it modifies. Adjectives modify nouns and pronouns. Adverbs modify verbs, adjectives, and adverbs.

ADJECTIVES **bald** eagle, **lame** excuse, **awesome** performance
ADVERBS Her fingers ran up and down the frets **effortlessly.**

Many, but not all words with *–ly* endings are adverbs. Generally speaking, if you take the *–ly* ending off a word and are left with a noun, the *–ly* word is an adjective. If you are left with an adjective, the *–ly* word is an adverb.

ADJECTIVES quarterly, neighborly, deathly, stately
ADVERBS lamely, hopelessly, anxiously, maniacally, senselessly, brilliantly

2.24 Prepositions

A **preposition** is used to show how a noun or a pronoun, its **object**, is related to some other word in the sentence. Common prepositions are *after, among, at, behind, beside, off, through, until, upon,* and *with.* A preposition introduces a **prepositional phrase**. The following examples show prepositional phrases in sentences.

PREPOSITIONAL PHRASES

They had hoped to stay on the camping trip **until** the day before school started.
He had been seen **in** the audience.
She had hidden the book **behind** the planter.

2.25 Coordinating Conjunctions

A **conjunction** is a word used to join words or groups of words. A **coordinating conjunction** connects words or groups of words that are used in the same way—nouns with nouns, verbs with verbs, and so on. Thus a coordinating conjunction *coordinates,* or orders the relationship between, two words or groups of words. The main coordinating conjunctions are *and, but, for, nor, or, so,* and *yet.*

COORDINATING CONJUNCTIONS

Stevens **and** Williams were poets.
We drove into town **but** the shops were all closed.
You can have the compact disc **or** the laserdisc, but not both.

2.26 Correlative Conjunctions

A **correlative conjunction** is a pair of conjunctions that joins words or groups of words that are used in the same way. Some common correlative conjunctions are *both . . . and; either . . . or; neither . . . nor; not only . . . but also;* and *whether . . . or.*

CORRELATIVE CONJUNCTIONS

William Carlos Williams was **both** a poet **and** a physician.
I was **neither** prepared **nor** motivated.

2.27 Subordinating Conjunctions

A **clause** is a group of words with its own subject and verb.

CLAUSES

The world is a very small place.
Life is a long song.
Ernest Hemingway, **who went to high school in Oak Park, Illinois,** won the Nobel Prize for literature.

A **subordinate clause** is a clause that cannot stand by itself as a complete sentence. It depends on another clause and adds information about that clause. A **subordinating conjunction** connects a subordinate clause to another clause. Some common subordinating conjunctions are *after, as, as well as, because, if, in order that, provided, since, so that, than, that, though, unless, when,* and *why.*

SUBORDINATING CONJUNCTIONS	**Since** I joined the team, I have not had much time to study. **Although** he had been saving for a long time, he still could not afford a new car.

2.28 Conjunctive Adverbs

A **conjunctive adverb** is a conjunction that both introduces and modifies a clause. Some conjunctive adverbs are *accordingly, furthermore,* and *moreover.*

CONJUNCTIVE ADVERBS	They were not good musicians; **moreover,** they did not have good equipment or a sellable image. In the last year, he had caused two car accidents; **accordingly,** his parents revoked his driving privileges indefinitely.

2.29 Interjections

An **interjection** is a word used to express emotion. It stands apart from the rest of a sentence. Common interjections are *ah, oh, say, well,* and *wow.*

INTERJECTIONS	**Gee,** do you think Mom and Dad will be mad at me, Wally? **Well,** do the best you can.

2.30 Words as Other Parts of Speech I

Words often serve as more than one part of speech. A noun, for instance, can become an adjective when it is used to modify another noun.

NOUNS AS ADJECTIVES	**speed** trap, **speech** therapy, **performance** artist

Sometimes pronouns can be used as adjectives. Such pronouns show who possesses something and are called *possessive pronouns.*

PRONOUNS AS ADJECTIVES	**my** genius, **your** ignorance, **their** stupidity

2.31 Words as Other Parts of Speech II

A word that is commonly used as a preposition may also be used as an adverb. In such cases, you can tell that such a word is being used as an adverb because it will not have a **prepositional object.** A prepositional object is the noun or pronoun that ends the prepositional phrase.

PREPOSITION	He had never seen a grunge band **before** the Nirvana concert.
ADVERB	He had never seen a grunge band **before.**

Not only can other parts of speech serve as adjectives and adverbs, but nearly any word can serve as a noun or verb if necessary.

INTERJECTION AS NOUN	He was pleased by the number of **okays** he heard after his speech.
INTERJECTION AS VERB	We were **wowed** by the originality of her lyrics.

USING THE PARTS OF SPEECH IN WRITING

2.32 Using Precise Nouns

When you are writing, choose nouns that tell your reader precisely what you mean. If you use precise nouns, rather than nouns with a vague or general meaning, your writing will be more effective. Avoid using an adjective and a noun, as in *expensive house,* when using a single precise noun, such as *mansion,* will do.

VAGUE	The landscape was stunning.
PRECISE	The green, sunny hills and broad, towering oak trees were stunning.

Note the use of precise nouns in this passage from Whitman's "There Was a Child Went Forth":

PRECISE NOUNS

Shadows, aureola and **mist**, the light falling on the roofs and **gables** of white or brown two miles off,
The **schooner** near by sleepily dropping down the tide, the little boat slack-towed astern,
The hurrying tumbling **waves**, quick-broken **crests**, slapping,
The **strata** of colored clouds, the long bar of **maroon-tint** away solitary by itself, the spread of **purity** it lies motionless in,
The horizon's **edge**, the flying **sea-crow**, the fragrance of salt **marsh** and shore **mud**

2.33 Using Vivid Verbs

Like precise nouns, vivid verbs create a picture in the reader's mind. Instead of using a vague, general verb like *walk,* a writer can produce a concrete picture by using a vivid verb such as *hobble, stroll, meander, saunter, march, tramp, pace, stride, trudge, trek, hoof,* or *hike.* Instead of using an adverb and a verb, as in *ran quickly,* a writer can use a single precise verb such as *sprinted.*

DULL	He **left** the party without saying any goodbyes.
VIVID	He **slipped out** of the party without saying any goodbyes.

Note the vivid verbs Emily Dickinson uses to describe children's activity:

They storm the Earth and stun the Air
A Mob of solid Bliss

2.34 Replacing Linking Verbs with Action Verbs

To give color to your writing, avoid using linking verbs, especially forms of the verb *to be* (*am, are, is, was,* and so on). Instead, use action verbs. Using action verbs will force you to restructure your sentences for greater impact.

LINKING Jodie Foster **gave** an overwhelming performance.
ACTION Jodie Foster's performance **overwhelmed** us.

Note how Dickinson uses the action verb "beheads" instead of the more common "covers" or "wilts":

> Apparently with no surprise
> To any happy Flower
> The Frost **beheads** it at its play—
> In accidental power—

2.35 Using Colorful Modifiers

A **modifier** is a word that modifies—that is, changes or explains—the meaning of another word. Adjectives and adverbs are modifiers. Rather than use trite or vague modifiers in your writing, search out adjectives and adverbs that add freshness and meaning. Notice the modifiers Wallace Stevens chose for his poem "Sunday Morning":

COLORFUL MODIFIERS

> . . . Neither the **golden** underground, nor isle
> **melodious**, where spirits gat them home,
> Nor **visionary** south, nor **cloudy** palm . . .
>
> . . . The **silken** weavings of our afternoons
> And pick the strings of our **insipid** lutes!

By using precise nouns, vivid action verbs, and colorful modifiers, you can turn bland prose into dynamic reading.

DULL We went to the park to look at the flowers.
COLORFUL We strolled to Wilson Park to enjoy the blooming tulips.

BUILDING SENTENCES

2.36 The Functions of Sentences

Sentences are classified according to their functions. They may be **declarative, imperative, interrogative,** or **exclamatory.** A **declarative sentence** makes a statement and is followed by a period.

DECLARATIVE SENTENCES

> David Letterman is losing his hair.
> John Lennon once allegedly did a guest recording appearance under the pseudonym Winston O. Boogie.

An **imperative sentence** gives a command or makes a request. It usually ends with a period but may end with an exclamation point.

IMPERATIVE SENTENCES

> Take out the garbage!
> Get a life!

An **interrogative sentence** asks a question. It ends with a question mark.

INTERROGATIVE SENTENCES	Why don't you take out the garbage? May I have the car Saturday night?

An **exclamatory sentence** expresses a strong feeling about something. It ends with an exclamation point.

EXCLAMATORY SENTENCES	I'm not taking the garbage out! She started dating his best friend the next day! There was a car accident right on our front lawn!

2.37 Substantives

A **substantive** is a noun or any other word or group of words that is used as a noun. If a word is used as a subject, direct object, indirect object, object of a preposition, predicate nominative, or objective complement, then it is a substantive. The following are some examples of substantives used as **subjects**, words that name the thing that does the action of the verb.

	SUBSTANTIVES
NOUN	**Shakespeare** wrote *King Lear.*
PRONOUN	**He** made the whole team do an extra ten laps.
INFINITIVE	**To teach** us discipline was his motive.
GERUND	**Coaching** was his life's passion.
CLAUSE	**That he loved coaching** was obvious.

2.38 Simple Sentences: SUB + V

The most basic sentence is one that combines a **substantive** and a verb in the form SUB + V. A substantive is anything used as a noun—a noun, pronoun, gerund, infinitive, or noun clause.

NOUN	The **convict** escaped.
PRONOUN	**We** lost the game.
GERUND	**Dieting** is popular.
INFINITIVE	**To worry** would be a waste of time.
NOUN CLAUSE	**What to do after school lets out** is never a problem.

2.39 Simple Sentences: SUB + AV + SUB

You can build the next kind of basic sentence by adding another substantive as the direct object of an action verb, producing a sentence with the form SUB + AV + SUB. In the following examples, the direct object is boldfaced.

EXAMPLES The fireworks impressed **everyone**.
To study exhausts **me**.
Thinking generates **results**.
They motivated the **school**.

2.40 Simple Sentences: SUB + LV + SUB or ADJ

Imagine you had a linking verb in your simple sentence instead of an action verb. Your sentence would then follow the pattern SUB + LV + SUB. The second substantive would be a **predicate nominative**, which is a word or group of words that follows a linking verb and refers to the same person or thing as the subject of the verb. In the following examples, the predicate nominative is boldfaced.

EXAMPLES Clinton is a consummate **politician**.
We are **members**.
Studying is **suffering**.
To work is **to sacrifice**.

Now imagine you made the element after the verb a predicate adjective. (See the Language Arts Survey, 2.21, for the definition of a predicate adjective.) Then the sentence pattern would be SUB + LV + ADJ. In the following examples, the predicate adjective is boldfaced.

EXAMPLES Kennedy was **charismatic**.
They felt **fortunate**.
Writing seems **difficult**.
To argue would be **ridiculous**.

2.41 Simple Sentences: SUB + AV + SUB + SUB

Another type of simple sentence can be formed by following the pattern substantive + action verb + substantive + substantive (SUB + AV + SUB + SUB). One of the substantives after the action verb will be a direct object. The other may be an **indirect object**. An indirect object is a noun or pronoun that comes between an action verb and a direct object. It shows *to whom* or *to what* or *for whom* or *for what* the action of the verb is done. In the following examples, the indirect object is boldfaced.

EXAMPLES The student offered **the teacher** his excuse.
He gave **the president** his regards.
Exercise gave **them** a new attitude.
To wait earns **you** nothing.

Instead of an indirect object, however, one of the elements may be an **objective complement.** An objective complement is a word or group of words that helps complete the meaning of an action verb by identifying or modifying the direct object. The words *to be* may be inferred as appearing before the objective complement. In the following examples, the objective complement is boldfaced.

EXAMPLES The team elected Scottie **captain.**
Clinton made Reich his **labor secretary.**

2.42 Independent Clauses

An **independent clause** expresses a complete thought and can stand by itself as a sentence. All the examples in the Language Arts Survey, 2.38 through 2.41, are also examples of independent clauses.

2.43 Compound Sentences

You can expand on a sentence that has only one independent clause by adding another independent clause. You will then have a **compound sentence**—one formed of two or more independent clauses but no subordinate clauses. (See the Language Arts Survey, 2.27, for the definition of a subordinate clause.) Related independent clauses can be joined by a semicolon; by a coordinating conjunction such as *and, or, for, nor, but, so,* or *yet* and a comma; or by a semicolon followed by a conjunctive adverb such as *however* or *therefore* and a comma.

COMPOUND SENTENCES The tree shook; the birds chirped.
I failed the math test; however, the teacher will be giving a make-up exam.
Home improvements can be costly, but in the long run they pay off.

2.44 Complex Sentences

You can also expand a sentence that has only one independent clause by adding a subordinate clause. You will then have a **complex sentence**—one formed of an independent clause and at least one subordinate clause. In the following examples, the subordinate clauses are boldfaced.

COMPLEX SENTENCES She finally finished the paper, **which was on Mark Twain.**
Dickens wrote novels **that deal with social issues.**

2.45 Compound-Complex Sentences

If you combine a compound sentence and a complex sentence, you will have a **compound-complex** sentence. This kind of sentence must have two or more independent clauses and at least one subordinate clause. In the following examples the subordinate clauses are boldfaced.

COMPOUND-COMPLEX SENTENCES **Although they are extremely long,** Dickens's novels are often humorous, and I enjoy reading them.
The movie ended abruptly, and people left the theater confused **when they realized it was really over.**

EXPANDING SENTENCES

2.46 Adding Modifiers

Simple, compound, complex, and compound-complex sentences can be expanded by adding modifiers such as adjectives and adverbs.

BASIC SENTENCE	The class ended.
SENTENCE WITH ADDED MODIFIERS	The **literature** class ended **suddenly**.
BASIC SENTENCE	The tree shook, which made it brush against the house.
SENTENCE WITH ADDED MODIFIERS	The tree shook **violently**, which made it brush against the house **threateningly**.
BASIC SENTENCE	The rock star retired and applied to law school when his money ran out.
SENTENCE WITH ADDED MODIFIERS	The **teenage** rock star retired and applied **reluctantly** to law school when his money ran out.

2.47 Adding Prepositional Phrases

Adding a prepositional phrase is another way to expand sentences. The prepositional phrase you add can be an **adjectival phrase** or an **adverbial phrase.** An adjectival phrase modifies a noun or pronoun. An adverbial phrase modifies a verb, an adjective, or an adverb. The following examples are from the Language Arts Survey, 2.46, with added prepositional phrases.

WITH ADDED PREPOSITIONAL PHRASES	The literature class **for advanced students** ended suddenly.
	The tree **with the hanging limb** shook violently in the storm, which made it brush against the house threateningly.
	The teenage rock star **with the solar system tattoos** retired and applied reluctantly to law school **in his hometown** when his money ran out.

Note that expanding sentences can cause problems instead of adding interest and variety. The third sentence above is bloated and should be trimmed down.

2.48 Adding Appositives and Appositive Phrases

Still another way to expand sentences is to add an **appositive** or an **appositive phrase.** An appositive is a noun or pronoun placed beside another noun or pronoun to identify or explain it. An appositive phrase is the appositive and its modifiers. The modifiers can be adjectives or adverbs.

BASIC SENTENCE	William Butler Yeats wrote poetry.
WITH APPOSITIVES	William Butler Yeats, a **playwright** and **essayist,** wrote poetry.
WITH APPOSITIVE PHRASES	William Butler Yeats, a **symbolist playwright** and **visionary essayist,** wrote poetry.

2.49 Adding Predicates

A **predicate** is a main verb and any auxiliary verbs, together with any words, phrases, or clauses that modify or complement the verb. You can expand sentences by adding predicates.

BASIC SENTENCE	Orson Welles directed movies.
WITH ADDED PREDICATE	Orson Welles directed movies **and performed in television commercials.**

2.50 Adding Subordinate Clauses

Subordinate clauses may also be used to expand the meaning of a sentence.

BASIC SENTENCE	*Raging Bull* and *Goodfellas* are Martin Scorsese's best films.
WITH SUBORDINATE CLAUSES	*Raging Bull*, **which chronicles the violent life of a boxer**, and *Goodfellas*, **which demythologizes organized crime**, are Martin Scorsese's best films.

COMBINING SENTENCES

2.51 Combining Sentences Using Single Words

Often you can combine two sentences that deal with the same topic to make your writing briefer and more effective. Rather than repeat information, you take the vital information from one sentence and insert it in the other, either in its original form or slightly altered.

GIVEN SENTENCES	Tom left the play. He did it noisily.
COMBINED SENTENCE	Tom left the play **noisily**.
GIVEN SENTENCES	Angela called Rayanne on the phone. She called her repeatedly.
COMBINED SENTENCE	Angela called Rayanne on the phone **repeatedly**.
GIVEN SENTENCES	The school punished the students. They were tardy.
COMBINED SENTENCE	The school punished the **tardy** students.

2.52 Combining Sentences Using Phrases

A second way to combine two sentences that deal with the same topic is to take a prepositional phrase or a participial phrase from one sentence and move it into the other.

GIVEN SENTENCES	He wanted a retest. He wanted it on the second part.
COMBINED SENTENCE	He wanted a retest **on the second part**.
GIVEN SENTENCES	Anthony was arguing for gun control. He said it would reduce violent crime.
COMBINED SENTENCE	Anthony, **arguing for gun control,** said it would reduce violent crime.

Sometimes you may need to change a part of the sentence into a prepositional phrase or change a verb into a participle before you can insert the idea into another sentence.

GIVEN SENTENCES Bishop sometimes created an abstract poetry. She used unusual images.
COMBINED SENTENCE Bishop sometimes created a highly abstract poetry **with unusual images**.

GIVEN SENTENCES He ran around the track energetically. He tried to decide what his next paper would be about.
COMBINED SENTENCE **Running around the track energetically,** he tried to decide what his next paper would be about.

2.53 Combining Sentences Using Clauses

A third way to combine two sentences that have the same topic is to make one the independent clause and the other the subordinate clause in a combined sentence.

GIVEN SENTENCES That movie was exciting. That movie was too long.
COMBINED SENTENCE **Though it was exciting,** that movie was too long.

GIVEN SENTENCES I love English class. We often watch movies or plays.
COMBINED SENTENCE I love English class **when we watch movies or plays**.

EDITING SENTENCES

2.54 Varying Sentence Openings

Many of the examples in this handbook begin with a subject for the sake of simplicity. When you are writing, however, you will find that *always* beginning with a subject makes for a dull style. You can make your writing more varied and interesting by beginning sentences with adjectives, adverbs, participles—just about any part of speech—as well as with phrases and clauses. You may have to reword your sentences slightly as you vary the sentence openings.

GIVEN SENTENCE Life is easy for those with money.
EDITED SENTENCE **For those with money,** life is easy.

GIVEN SENTENCE The newsanchor excused herself, coughing heavily.
EDITED SENTENCE **Coughing heavily,** the newsanchor excused herself.

GIVEN SENTENCE The parents agreed that summer was a time for their children to learn the value of work.
EDITED SENTENCE **Summer,** the parents agreed, was a time for their children to learn the value of work.

2.55 Varying Sentence Length and Structure

Repeated sentences of the same length and structure soon become monotonous. Use a variety of simple, compound, complex, and compound-complex sentences in your writing.

PASSAGE WITH SIMPLE SENTENCES

There was music from my neighbor's house through the summer nights. In his blue gardens men and girls came and went. They were like moths among the whisperings and the champagne and the stars. At high tide in the afternoon I watched his guests diving from the tower of his raft. I watched them taking the sun on the hot sand of his beach. Meanwhile, his two motor-boats slit the waters of the Sound, drawing aquaplanes over the cataracts of foam. On week-ends, his Rolls-Royce became an omnibus. It bore parties to and from the city between nine in the morning and long past midnight. His station wagon scampered like a brisk yellow bug to meet all trains.

PASSAGE WITH VARIED SENTENCE LENGTH AND STRUCTURE

There was music from my neighbor's house through the summer nights. In his blue gardens men and girls came and went like moths among the whisperings and the champagne and the stars. At high tide in the afternoon I watched his guests diving from the tower of his raft, or taking the sun on the hot sand of his beach while his two motorboats slit the waters of the Sound, drawing aquaplanes over the cataracts of foam. On week-ends, his Rolls-Royce became an omnibus, bearing parties to and from the city between nine in the morning and long past midnight, while his station wagon scampered like a brisk yellow bug to meet all trains.

—F. Scott Fitzgerald, *The Great Gatsby*, chapter 3

2.56 Using the Active Voice

A verb is in the **active voice** when the subject of the verb performs the action. It is in the **passive voice** when the subject of the verb receives the action.

ACTIVE Students **flooded** the school with requests.
PASSIVE The school **was flooded** with requests.

A common characteristic of poor writing is overuse of the passive voice. Keep your verbs in the active voice unless you have a good reason for using the passive voice. In the examples that follow, note how the active verbs make the writing more natural, interesting, and concise.

WITH PASSIVE VERBS One week after graduation, Anthony was accosted by his younger brother. He was given a letter by his brother. It was a notice to appear in court. The request was from the Clerk of the Court. A jury summons was enclosed; Anthony had been ordered by the court to appear in one month. He was upset by the letter because he knew his summer vacation in Canada might be interrupted by jury duty.

WITH ACTIVE VERBS One week after graduation, Anthony's brother accosted him and gave him a letter. It was a notice from the Clerk of the Court summoning Anthony to appear for jury duty in one month. Anthony found this upsetting, since he knew it might interrupt his vacation in Canada.

2.57 Achieving Parallelism

A sentence has **parallelism** when it uses the same grammatical forms to express ideas of equal, or parallel, importance. When you edit your sentences during revision, check to be sure that your parallelism is not faulty.

FAULTY The teacher told me to think better and having more focus.
PARALLEL The teacher told me to think better and **to have more focus**.

FAULTY Being too late for the bus and to get something to eat, I decided to walk through the mall.
PARALLEL Being too late for the bus and **wanting to get something to eat**, I decided to walk through the mall.

FAULTY Clinton said, "I will not run for public office again, so he will have more time to spend with his family."
PARALLEL Clinton said, "I will not run for public office again, so **I** will have more time to spend with my family."

2.58 Deleting Repeated or Unnecessary Ideas

When you edit your writing, check carefully for repeated or unnecessary ideas.

SENTENCE WITH REPETITION They moved the boat **down the river** and began fishing **down the river.**
CORRECTED SENTENCE They moved the boat down the river and began fishing.
SENTENCE WITH UNNECESSARY IDEA She was always happiest on **Christmas Day, the twenty-fifth of December.**
CORRECTED SENTENCE She was always happiest on Christmas Day.

2.59 Reducing Wordiness

When you write, use only as many words as you need to express your meaning. While editing, remove words that do not contribute to your meaning and replace complicated or unclear words with ones that are simple and clear.

WORDY With regard to summer employment, I have not been successful in securing a position that will provide a source of income.
DIRECT I haven't found a paying job for the summer.

WORDY With respect to house refuse materials, he has not yet executed the plan to fully collect and consolidate all transferable disposables into one location outside.
DIRECT He hasn't taken the garbage out.

Look for ways to reduce the length of your sentences by replacing a clause with a phrase that conveys the same meaning. In some cases, you can even replace a lengthy phrase with a single word.

WORDY Elizabeth, **who was a three-time champion**, was favored to win.
DIRECT Elizabeth, **a three-time champion**, was favored to win.

WORDY Most young people believe they are **going to live forever.**
DIRECT Most young people believe they are **immortal.**

2.60 Correcting Sentence Strings

Sentence strings are formed of several sentences strung together with conjunctions. Edit sentence strings by breaking them up into separate sentences and subordinate clauses. In the examples that follow, the first passage is a sentence string; the second is a passage broken up into separate sentences and clauses.

STRINGY All night there were coaches in my broken sleep, going to wrong places instead of to London, and having in the traces, now dogs, now cats, now pigs, now men—never horses, and fantastic failures of journeys occupied me until the day dawned and the birds were singing, and then, I got up and partly dressed, and sat at the window to take a last look out, and in taking it fell asleep.

REVISED All night there were coaches in my broken sleep, going to wrong places instead of to London, and having in the traces, now dogs, now cats, now pigs, now men—never horses. Fantastic failures of journeys occupied me until the day dawned and the birds were singing. Then, I got up and partly dressed, and sat at the window to take a last look out, and in taking it fell asleep.

—Charles Dickens, *Great Expectations,* chapter 19

2.61 Correcting Sentence Fragments

A **sentence** should express a complete thought and contain both a subject and a verb. A **sentence fragment** is a phrase or clause that does not express a complete thought but has been punctuated as though it did. You can correct a sentence fragment by changing its punctuation or structure so that it expresses a complete thought.

FRAGMENTED I was confident of success. **Being a master of deception.**
CORRECTED I was confident of success, being a master of deception.

FRAGMENTED Each of them was given three detentions. **Which they deserved.**
CORRECTED Each of them was given three detentions, which they deserved.

In sentences in which the subject will be understood by the reader, the subject can be left unexpressed. Such sentences are not sentence fragments.

SENTENCE WITH IMPLIED, UNEXPRESSED SUBJECT [You] Remember to bring an umbrella.

2.62 Correcting Run-ons

A **run-on** is formed of two or more sentences that have been run together as if they were one complete thought. Edit a run-on by making it into two sentences, by adding a comma and a coordinating conjunction, or by adding a semicolon.

RUN-ONS	I drove the car to the garage my sister picked it up later.
TWO SENTENCES	I drove the car to the garage. My sister picked it up later.
COORDINATED CLAUSES	I drove the car to the garage, and my sister picked it up later.

2.63 Correcting Dangling or Misplaced Modifiers

A **dangling modifier** is a modifying phrase or clause that seems to modify a word it is not intended to modify. Sometimes this error occurs because the modifier is too far from the word it is supposed to modify. It is then called a **misplaced modifier**. You can edit dangling and misplaced modifiers by adding a word for the phrase or clause to modify or by rewording the sentence.

DANGLING	Reading Foucault, the purpose of prisons became clear.
WORDS ADDED	Reading Foucault, I came to understand the purpose of prisons.
DANGLING	Waiting for the light to change, the car she drove was revving.
REWORDED	Waiting for the light to change, she revved the car she was driving.
MISPLACED	The principal questioned my motives at the end of the meeting.
REWORDED	At the end of the meeting, the principal questioned my motives.
MISPLACED	The owner of the building had the student who was tired of the noise from the stereo evicted.
REWORDED	The owner of the building, who was tired of the noise from the stereo, had the student evicted.

2.64 Inverting Sentences for Emphasis

When editing your writing, look for opportunities to add emphasis and clarify your meaning. One way to add emphasis is to **invert** a sentence—to change the usual order of its parts.

REGULAR ORDER	I cannot take all the credit for the ghastly performance.
INVERTED ORDER	For this ghastly performance I cannot take all the credit.
REGULAR ORDER	Shakespeare's play ends with dead bodies strewn all over the stage.
INVERTED ORDER	With dead bodies strewn all over the stage, Shakespeare's play ends.

EDITING FOR ERRORS IN VERB TENSE

2.65 Improper Shifts in Verb Tense

When the verbs in a sentence or group of sentences shift from past to present or from present to past without reason, the reader may not be able to follow the intended meaning. Correct the shift by using consistent tenses for all verbs.

WITH TENSE SHIFT	We were all tired from the drive but **are** still looking forward to dinner.
CORRECTED	We were all tired from the drive but **were** still looking forward to dinner.

2.66 Irregular Verbs I

Every verb has four **principal parts**: the **base form**, the **present participle**, the **past**, and the **past participle**. All the other verb forms can be made from these parts. As you can see from the table below, the present participle is formed by adding *–ing* to the base form (sometimes dropping an *e*), and the past and past participle are formed by adding *–d* or *–ed* (or sometimes *–t*) to the base form.

BASE FORM	PRESENT PARTICIPLE	PAST	PAST PARTICIPLE
believe	[is] believing	believed	[have] believed
obey	[is] obeying	obeyed	[have] obeyed
serve	[is] serving	served	[have] served

Some verbs, however, form the past and past participle in some other way than by adding *–d* or *–ed* (or sometimes *–t*) to the base form. These verbs are called *irregular verbs*. English has dozens of them. The table below shows just a few examples. If you are in doubt about whether a verb is irregular, look it up in the dictionary; if it is irregular, you will find its principal parts listed.

BASE FORM	PRESENT PARTICIPLE	PAST	PAST PARTICIPLE
do	[is] doing	did	[have] done
fly	[is] flying	flew	[have] flown
know	[is] knowing	knew	[have] known
eat	[is] eating	ate	[have] eaten
break	[is] breaking	broke	[have] broken

2.67 Irregular Verbs II

When using irregular verbs in the so-called perfect tenses (with *has* or *have*), make sure you do not use the past form instead of the past participle.

NONSTANDARD PARTICIPLE	**I have knew** him since I was in junior high.
STANDARD PARTICIPLE	**I have known** him since I was in junior high.

Another error to watch for is using the past participle form without a helping verb or mistaking the past participle for the past.

NONSTANDARD PARTICIPLE	**I flown** this plane dozens of times.
STANDARD PARTICIPLE	**I have flown** this plane dozens of times.
NONSTANDARD PARTICIPLE	**I done** all I could with that bike.
STANDARD PARTICIPLE	**I did** all I could with that bike.

Finally, do not add *–d* or *–ed* or *–t* to the past form of an irregular verb.

NONSTANDARD	I ated an apple.
STANDARD	I ate an apple.

2.68 Split Infinitives

In English, the infinitive often takes the form of two words, *to* and the base. In their discussion of this form, the first English grammarians—influenced by their knowledge of Latin in which the infinitive is a single word—decreed that the infinitive should never be "split" in English. Under this rule, adverbs and other sentence components should not stand between *to* and the base form. However, the normal sentence rhythms of English, and the demands of sense, often call for an infinitive to be split.

STRAINED WORD ORDER	Finally, I would like **to discuss briefly** my proposal for a shorter school year.
NATURAL WORD ORDER	Finally, I would like **to briefly discuss** my proposal for a shorter school year.
STRAINED WORD ORDER	They hoped to find a way **to refute quickly** their opponents' claims.
NATURAL WORD ORDER	They hoped to find a way **to quickly refute** their opponents' claims.
EXAMPLES	**To freely express** themselves without fear of government reprisals . . . **To truly believe** in themselves they . . .

In using the infinitive, keep *to* and the base form together where possible, but do not hesitate to separate them where the rhythm or sense of the sentence requires it. (Note that a phrase such as *to be proudly aware* is not a split infinitive; it is an infinitive of the verb *to be* followed by a predicate nominative modified by an adverb.)

Although the rule that infinitives should not be split was based on Latin rather than English, it has been widely accepted. You should be aware that some people may find fault with the use of a split infinitive even in cases where such a use is required by sound and sense. (For more information on the use of split infinitives, see the entry on split infinitives in Fowler's *Modern English Usage.*)

2.69 Voice and Mood

Shifts in **voice** from active to passive can be as confusing as shifts in tense. Check your sentences to be sure voice is consistent. Rewrite and change subjects as necessary.

WITH VOICE SHIFT	Although **she admitted** leaving early, **a reason was not given** by her.
CORRECTED	Although she admitted leaving early, she gave no reason.

In addition to watching for voice shifts, check to be sure your verbs are in the appropriate **mood.** Mood is a characteristic that shows the way in which a verb is used. Each verb has three moods: **indicative, imperative,** and **subjunctive.**

Use a verb in the *indicative mood* to express a fact, an opinion, or a question.

INDICATIVE MOOD	For long bike rides, most professionals **carry** two water bottles. Roosevelt **believed** that the country was at a crossroads. Didn't Shakespeare **own** shares in the Globe Theater?

Use the *imperative mood* to express a direct command or request.

IMPERATIVE MOOD	**Get** a clue! Please **leave** this room.

Use the *subjunctive mood* in the present to express a suggestion or a necessity.

SUBJUNCTIVE MOOD	Shakespeare suggests through one of his characters that we **be** neither borrowers nor lenders. It is essential that we **conserve** resources.

Use the *past subjunctive* to express a wish or a condition that is not true (contrary to fact).

PAST SUBJUNCTIVE	He wished they **were** young again. If the responsible parties **were** here, I would give them a piece of my mind.

Notice that the singular of most verbs in the subjunctive looks like a plural of a verb in the indicative.

INDICATIVE PLURAL	They **were** upset at the decision.
SUBJUNCTIVE SINGULAR	If I **were** really mad, I would cancel my membership.

EDITING FOR ERRORS IN SUBJECT/VERB AGREEMENT

2.70 Agreement of Subject and Verb

A word that refers to one person or thing is said to be **singular in number.** A word that refers to more than one person or thing is said to be **plural in number.** Most nouns that end in *s* are plural, but most verbs that refer to the present and end in *s* are singular.

SINGULAR NOUNS	book, faucet, car, scone
PLURAL NOUNS	books, faucets, cars, scones
SINGULAR VERBS	entangles, aggravates, extinguishes, heightens
PLURAL VERBS	entangle, aggravate, extinguish, heighten

Each verb in a sentence should be singular if its subject is singular and plural if its subject is plural. In other words, a verb must **agree in number** with its subject.

EXAMPLES **It bothers** me all the time.
The **poems heighten** our awareness of time.

The pronouns *I* and *you,* though singular, almost always take forms that look plural. The only exceptions are the forms *I am* and *I was.*

EXAMPLES **I believe** the car industry will continue to rebound.
You sense my uneasiness.

2.71 Agreement with Compound Subjects

A **compound subject** is formed of two or more nouns or pronouns that are joined by a conjunction and have the same verb. A compound subject joined by the conjunction *and* usually takes a plural verb.

EXAMPLE **Salt** and **acid rain are** hard on a car's body.

A compound subject in which the subjects are joined by the conjunction *and* takes a singular verb if the compound subject really names only one person or thing.

EXAMPLE His **work** and **love is** writing

A compound subject formed of two singular subjects joined by the conjunctions *or* or *nor* takes a singular verb.

EXAMPLES Neither **Streep** nor **Foster is** usually guilty of underpreparing.
Either **poetry** or **drama is** appropriate for public performance.

A compound subject formed of a singular subject and a plural subject joined by the conjunctions *or* or *nor* takes a verb that agrees in number with the subject nearer the verb.

EXAMPLES Either **Kim** or the backup **vocalists are** responsible for the recording.
Either the backup **vocalists** or **Kim is** responsible for the recording.

2.72 Agreement with Indefinite Pronouns

These indefinite pronouns are singular and take a singular verb: *anybody, anyone, anything, each, either, everybody, everyone, everything, neither, nobody, no one, nothing, one, somebody, someone,* and *something.*

EXAMPLES **Nobody wants** to take the exam on Friday.
Everybody enjoys some kind of music.

These indefinite pronouns are plural and take a plural verb: *both, few, many,* and *several.*

EXAMPLES **Both** of these choices **are** unacceptable.
Several new students **are** on the honor roll.

The following indefinite pronouns can be singular or plural: *all, any, most, none,* and *some.*

EXAMPLES **All** of the cookies **were saved.** (*All* is plural.)
All of the pie **was eaten.** (*All* is singular.)

2.73 Agreement in Inverted Sentences

When you invert sentences for emphasis, make sure you maintain agreement in number between subject and verb.

EXAMPLES For those ghastly performances **he takes** full credit.
The last straw **she took.**

2.74 Agreement with *Doesn't* and *Don't*

The contraction *doesn't* (from *does not*) is third-person singular and should be used only with a third-person singular subject. The contraction *don't* (from *do not*) should be used with all other subjects.

EXAMPLES **She doesn't** want material things.
They don't understand the procedure.
I don't find the subject boring.

2.75 Other Problems in Subject/Verb Agreement

When a sentence begins with *here, there, when,* or *where,* often the subject follows the verb. In editing your writing, use extra care to check that the subject and verb of such sentences agree in number. Remember that the contractions *here's, there's, when's,* and *where's* contain a singular verb (*is*) and should only be used with a singular subject.

EXAMPLES Here's the team.
There is one more exam being given.
When's the test?
When are the band members joining us?
Where's the rub?

Also check to be sure a verb in a sentence with a predicate nominative agrees in number with the subject and not with the predicate nominative.

EXAMPLES Essays are the hardest part of school.
The hardest part of school is essays.

A collective noun takes a singular verb when the noun refers to the group as a unit, and it takes a plural verb when it refers to the members of the group as individuals.

AS SINGULAR The team runs laps every day.
AS PLURAL The team joke among themselves behind the coach's back.

While editing your work, check for nouns that are plural in form but singular in meaning. They should take singular verbs.

EXAMPLES cryogenics, slacks, measles

The title of a creative work such as a book or song takes a singular verb, as does a group of words used as a unit.

EXAMPLES *Aphorisms* **has** been on the bestseller list for two weeks.
Sidney and Austen **is** the smallest firm in Chicago.

An expression stating an amount is singular and takes a singular verb when the amount is considered as one unit. It is plural and takes a plural verb when the amount is considered as something with many parts.

AS SINGULAR Three eggs is a high-cholesterol breakfast.
AS PLURAL Three eggs were found splattered across the windshield.

A fraction or a percentage is singular when it refers to a singular word and plural when it refers to a plural word.

AS SINGULAR One-fourth of the text was footnotes.
AS PLURAL One-fourth of all the pages were footnotes.

AS SINGULAR Over 60 percent of the nation is hopeful about the economy.
AS PLURAL Over 60 percent of all citizens are hopeful about the economy.

Expressions of measurement, such as area, length, volume, and weight, are usually singular.

EXAMPLE **Two quarts** is a lot of milk to drink in one sitting.

EDITING FOR ERRORS IN PRONOUN USAGE

2.76 Pronoun Case I

Case is the form that a noun or a pronoun takes to indicate its use in a sentence. English nouns and pronouns have three cases: **nominative, objective,** and **possessive.** The nominative case is used for the subject of a verb or for a predicate nominative. The objective case is used for a direct object, an indirect object, or the object of a preposition. The possessive case is used to show possession. The form of the nominative and objective cases of nouns is the same, and most nouns form possessives by adding an apostrophe and an *s* to the singular and an apostrophe only to the plural. But many pronouns have different forms to show nominative, objective, and possessive cases.

PERSONAL PRONOUNS		
SINGULAR		
Nominative Case (for subjects or predicate nominatives)	**Objective Case** (for direct objects, indirect objects, and objects of prepositions)	**Possessive Case** (to show possession)
I	me	my, mine
you	you	your, yours
he, she, it	him, her, it	his, her, hers, its
PLURAL		
we	us	our, ours
you	you	your, yours
they	them	their, theirs

To determine which form of the pronoun to use when writing a sentence, first decide whether the pronoun is used as a subject, predicate nominative, as some kind of object, or as a possessive. Doing so will tell you what case the pronoun should be.

SUBJECT	**He** is no longer working for that company.
PREDICATE NOMINATIVE	It is **she** you should be blaming.
DIRECT OBJECT	The cold weather depressed **her.**
INDIRECT OBJECT	The nurse brought **me** the book.
OBJECT OF PREPOSITION	I brought three boxes for **you** and **me**.

Remember that in standard English, prepositions *always* take an object in the objective case. The phrase *between you and I* is nonstandard English.

2.77 Pronoun Case II

Use the possessive pronouns *mine, yours, his, hers, its, ours,* and *theirs* just as you use the pronouns in the nominative and objective cases.

AS SUBJECT	**Theirs** is a complicated relationship
AS PREDICATE NOMINATIVE	This book is **yours**.
DIRECT OBJECT	He ticketed **ours**.
INDIRECT OBJECT	The officer gave **ours** the ticket.
OBJECT OF PREPOSITION	The most-improved-house award went to **theirs**.

Use the possessive pronouns *my, your, his, her, its, our,* and *their* as adjectives before nouns.

EXAMPLE **His** indignation allowed him to escape criticisms.

As you edit your writing, check the case of nouns and pronouns before a gerund. They should always be in the possessive case.

WITH GERUND	**Her calling for help** saved his life.

Do not confuse the gerund and the present participle (see the Language Arts Survey, 2.17). Compare the example above with the following example, in which no possessive is required before the participle:

WITH PARTICIPLE	We watched her **painting** the ceiling.

2.78 *Who* and *Whom*

The pronoun *who* is referred to as an **interrogative pronoun** when it is used to form a question. When it is used to introduce a **subordinate clause,** it is referred to as a **relative pronoun.** In both cases, the nominative is *who,* the objective is *whom,* and the possessive is *whose.* As you edit your writing, check these pronouns to see if the form of the pronoun you have used is appropriate for its use in the sentence or subordinate clause in which it appears.

In spoken English, *whom* is gradually being replaced by *who.* In some formal speech, however,

SUBJECT	**Who** asked that question?
SUBJECT	The student **who** came in late had no admit slip.
DIRECT OBJECT	**Whom** did you say you were calling?
DIRECT OBJECT	The teacher **whom** you saw driving toward the mall has recently retired.
OBJECT OF PREPOSITION	**To whom** did you wish to address your complaint?
OBJECT OF PREPOSITION	We do not care **from whom** you were sent; you are not welcome here.

and in all writing of standard English except dialogue, the form *whom* should still be used where grammatically correct.

2.79 Pronouns with Appositives

When a pronoun is used with an appositive, its form matches its use in the sentence.

SUBJECT	**I, Claudius,** am emperor of Rome.
PREDICATE NOMINATIVE	The burned-out wrecks in this photo are **we students** after exam week.
INDIRECT OBJECT	Give **us expert hostage negotiators** a chance.
OBJECT OF PREPOSITION	The blame for the revolt fell upon **us peasants.**

2.80 Pronouns as Appositives

When a pronoun is itself used as an appositive, it should be in the same case as the word to which it refers.

PRONOUN IN APPOSITION TO SUBJECT	Two consummate rhymers, Skelton and **he**, wrote about the death of a sparrow.
PRONOUN IN APPOSITION TO THE OBJECT OF A PREPOSITION	Praising Yeats, T. S. Eliot gave the title of great poet only to Dante, Shakespeare, and **him**.

2.81 Pronouns in Comparisons

The ends of sentences that compare people or things are often left unexpressed. Pronouns in such sentences should be in the same case as they would have been if the sentence had been completed.

EXAMPLES	Sting knew that there were pop stars wealthier than **he** [was]. His success as a performer meant as much to his father as [it did to] **him**.

2.82 Agreement of Pronouns and Antecedents

Check the pronouns in your writing to be sure they agree in **number**, **person**, and **gender** with their antecedents. (For a discussion of number, see the Language Arts Survey, 2.70.) Person is the form a word takes to indicate the person speaking (the *first person,* corresponding to *I* or *we*), the person spoken to (the *second person,* corresponding to *you*), or the person spoken of or about (the *third person,* corresponding to *he, she, it,* or *they*). Gender is the form a word takes to indicate whether it is *masculine, feminine,* or *neuter* (neither masculine nor feminine).

INCORRECT NUMBER	The **individual** who is cautious and reserved should know **they** cannot avoid all risk in life.
CORRECT NUMBER	**Individuals** who are cautious and reserved should know **they** cannot avoid all risk in life.
INCORRECT GENDER	Elizabeth Bishop lived much of her adult life in South America, though **he** had been born in the United States.
CORRECT GENDER	Elizabeth Bishop lived much of her adult life in South America, though **she** had been born in the United States.

2.83 Reference of Pronouns to Antecedents I

As you edit, check each pronoun to be sure that it refers clearly to its antecedent.

CLEAR REFERENCE	**Emily** could not stop for death; **she** had appointments through the end of the month.
CLEAR REFERENCES	The **leaves** were scattered across **the lawn; they** gave **it** a new look.

Weak reference occurs when a pronoun refers to an antecedent that has not been expressed. If you find a weak reference while editing your writing, either change the pronoun into a noun or give the pronoun a clear antecedent.

WEAK REFERENCE	In the postgame locker-room meeting, **it** was discussed very briefly.
PRONOUN CHANGED TO NOUN	In the postgame locker-room meeting, **the game** was discussed very briefly.
WEAK REFERENCE	The teacher had a reputation for coming to a room full of students and mispronouncing **them** all.
PRONOUN GIVEN CLEAR ANTECEDENT	The teacher had a reputation for coming to a room full of students and mispronouncing **the names** of **them** all.

Ambiguous reference occurs when a pronoun can refer to either of two antecedents. Clarify ambiguous references by rewording the sentence or by replacing the pronouns with a noun.

AMBIGUOUS	Tom suggested his father supplement **his** income.
CLEAR	Tom suggested his father supplement **Tom's** income.

2.84 Reference of Pronouns to Antecedents II

An **indefinite reference** occurs when the pronouns *you, it,* or *they* have no reference to a specific person or thing. Edit out an indefinite reference by rewording the sentence to explain to whom or what the pronoun refers, or by eliminating the pronoun altogether.

INDEFINITE REFERENCE	In convenience stores **they** don't allow skating.
PRONOUN ELIMINATED	**Convenience stores** don't allow skating.
INDEFINITE REFERENCE	In some rural areas **they** depend on government price supports for grain and soybeans.
PRONOUN ELIMINATED	In some rural areas **farmers** depend on government price supports for grain and soybeans.

A **general reference** occurs when a pronoun refers to a general idea implied in the previous clause, rather than to a specific antecedent. Edit general references by replacing the pronoun with a noun or by rewording the sentence.

GENERAL REFERENCE	He clearly stated his opposition to gun control during his announcement he would run for the Senate, **which** worried some voters.
SENTENCE REWORDED	**His clear opposition to gun control,** stated during his announcement he would run for the Senate, worried some voters.
GENERAL REFERENCE	The team had lost six in a row, **which** angered some of the players.
PRONOUN REPLACED AND SENTENCES REWORDED	**The team's six-game losing streak** angered some of the players.

EDITING FOR ERRORS IN MODIFIER USAGE

2.85 Modifiers with Action and Linking Verbs

When you wish to modify the subject of a linking verb, use an adjective. When you wish to modify an action verb, use an adverb.

LINKING VERB AND ADJECTIVE	It **is cold** outside, and some people are staying indoors.
ACTION VERB AND ADVERB	He **drove carefully** after hearing of the accident.

Check whether your use of an adjective or adverb is correct by temporarily replacing the verb you have written with the verb *seem.* If the sentence still makes some kind of sense, the original verb is a linking verb and should take an adjective. If the substitution of *seem* produces nonsense, the original verb is an action verb and should take an adverb. You can see how this works by substituting *seem* in each of the examples given above.

SUBSTITUTION MAKES SENSE	It **seems cold** outside, and some people are staying indoors.
SUBSTITUTION MAKES NO SENSE	He **seemed carefully** after hearing of the accident.

2.86 Comparison of Adjectives and Adverbs

Comparison refers to the change in the form of a modifier to show an increase or a decrease in the quality expressed by the modifier. Each modifier has three forms of comparison: **positive, comparative,** and **superlative**. Most one-syllable modifiers and some two-syllable modifiers form the comparative and superlative degrees by adding *–er* and *–est.* Other two-syllable modifiers, and all modifiers of more than two syllables, use *more* and *most* to form these degrees.

	POSITIVE	COMPARATIVE	SUPERLATIVE
ADJECTIVES	dumb	dumber	dumbest
	tall	taller	tallest
	perilous	more perilous	most perilous
	enigmatic	more enigmatic	most enigmatic
ADVERBS	easily	more easily	most easily
	happily	more happily	most happily
	sonorously	more sonorously	most sonorously

To show a decrease in the quality of any modifier, form the comparative and superlative degrees by using *less* and *least.*

EXAMPLES	angry, less angry, least angry frivolously, less frivolously, least frivolous

Some modifiers form their comparative and superlative degrees irregularly. Check the dictionary if you are unsure about the comparison of a modifier.

EXAMPLES	some, more, most	bad, worse, worst

Use the comparative degree when comparing two things. Use the superlative degree when comparing more than two things.

COMPARATIVE	Of the novels *Bleak House* and *Little Dorrit,* there has been much debate over which is the **more important** contribution to English literature.
SUPERLATIVE	China is the **most populous** of the world's nations.

2.87 Illogical and Double Comparisons

As you edit your writing, check sentences for **illogical comparison.** Such comparison occurs when one member of a group is compared with the group of which it is a part. Clarify illogical comparison by including the word *other* or *else* in the sentence.

ILLOGICAL Eliot wrote poems more than bankers in England.
LOGICAL Eliot wrote poems more than other bankers in England.

Another problem to check for is **double comparison.** This occurs when two comparative forms or two superlative forms are used to modify the same word. Correct double comparison by editing out one of the comparative or superlative forms.

DOUBLE COMPARISON Let's not put language into the contract that is even **more redundanter** than what we have already.
SINGLE COMPARISON Let's not put language into the contract that is even **more redundant** than what we have already.

2.88 Double Negatives

In English a **double negative** is a nonstandard construction in which two negative words are used instead of one. Check your writing to be sure you have not used a negative word such as *no, none, not* (and its contraction, *–n't*), *nothing, barely, hardly,* or *scarcely* with any other negative word. If you find a double negative, change it by deleting one of the negative words.

DOUBLE NEGATIVE He who does not know himself **cannot hardly** know the world.
SINGLE NEGATIVE He who does not know himself **cannot** know the world.
SINGLE NEGATIVE He who does not know himself **can hardly** know the world.

DOUBLE NEGATIVE Like most writers, Coleridge did**n't** make **no** money.
SINGLE NEGATIVE Like most writers, Coleridge made **no** money.

2.89 Other Problems with Modifiers

The demonstrative pronouns *this* and *these* are used to refer to things near the speaker. The pronouns *that* and *those* refer to objects at some distance. Thus you might say, "This apple in my hand is poisonous" if you were referring to an apple you were actually holding, but if you were pointing at an apple in a picture of yourself, you might say, "That apple in my hand is poisonous." The two pairs of pronouns are often used to distinguish between objects or sets of objects.

EXAMPLE This scar is almost invisible; that one is unsightly.

Check your writing to see that your use of *this* and *these,* and *that* and *those* makes sense.

NONSENSICAL Those blisters on my face are worse than these blisters on your face.
SENSIBLE These blisters on my face are worse than those blisters on your face.

The pronoun *them* is a personal pronoun in standard English and should not be substituted for the demonstrative pronoun *those.*

NONSTANDARD **Them** mice are annoying.
STANDARD **Those** mice are annoying.

Modifiers that often give writers trouble are *bad* and *badly.* Check instances of these words in your writing to make sure you have used *bad* as an adjective and *badly* as an adverb. Only the adjective should follow a linking verb such as *feel, hear, see, smell,* or *taste.*

NONSTANDARD The food tasted **badly,** and I had to excuse myself from the table.
STANDARD The food tasted **bad,** and I had to excuse myself from the table.

Similarly distinguish between *good* and *well. Good* is an adjective and should not be used to modify an action verb. *Well,* however, can be used either as an adverb meaning "capably" or "in a satisfactory way," or as an adjective meaning "healthy" or "of a satisfactory condition."

NONSTANDARD Henry James wrote complex sentences **good.**
STANDARD Henry James wrote complex sentences **well.**
STANDARD Henry James wrote **good** complex sentences.
STANDARD His aging car did not run **well.**
STANDARD Though they had been through surgery, his knees worked **well.**

USAGE HANDBOOK

2.90 Usage Problems I

Sections 2.90–2.92 explain some common problems to watch for as you edit your writing.

adapt, adopt. *Adapt* means "to make something fit a specific use or situation by modifying"; *adopt* means to "take something and make it in some sense one's own."

EXAMPLES He was a great one-on-one player, but he **adapted** to the team concept.
After already having three children, they **adopted** three more.

affect, effect. If you wish to use a verb meaning "have an effect on," use *affect.* If you wish to use a noun meaning "the result of an action," use *effect.*

VERB In one of Chopin's short stories, the news of her husband's death **affects** a woman strangely.
NOUN The news of her husband's death had a strange **effect** on her.

As a verb, *effect* means to bring something about despite obstacles.

EXAMPLE They **effected** an agreement between the two nations.

2.91 Usage Problems II

imply, infer. Most writers accept the following meanings for these words: *imply* means "to express indirectly rather than openly"; *infer* means "to arrive at a conclusion by reasoning from evidence." Although this distinction between *imply* and *infer* has not always been observed, it is a useful one.

EXAMPLES Her absence **implied** that she did not think it was a very important event.
He **inferred** from her absence that she had better things to do.

like, as, as if. Although *like* is frequently used to introduce subordinate clauses in informal English, it is considered a preposition, not a conjunction. Do not use it in place of *as* or *as if* in your writing.

INFORMAL It looks **like** it might rain
FORMAL It looks **as if** it might rain
FORMAL Houses look **like** snow from a distance.

literally. Most writers limit their use of *literally* to the sense "actually" and avoid using it in the sense "not actually, but in effect, or for all practical purposes." This distinction, though sometimes ignored, is worth observing.

CLEAR She **literally** fell to the floor when I told her what I had won.
CONFUSING She **literally** went off the deep end when I came home late.

2.92 Usage Problems III

of. The preposition *of* should not be used in place of *have* after verbs such as *could, should, would, might, must,* and *ought.*

NONSTANDARD They should **of** at least called to say they could not come.
STANDARD They should **have** at least called to say they could not come.
STANDARD They should**'ve** at least called to say they could not come.

Avoid *off of.*

NONSTANDARD The apple fell **off of** William's head.
STANDARD The apple fell **off** William's head.

then, than. Use *than* as a conjunction in comparisons. Use *then* as an adverb that tells when something occurred.

EXAMPLES Symbols are more important **than** images.
First find the symbols, **then** the images.

PROOFREADING FOR ERRORS IN END MARKS AND COMMAS

2.93 End Marks

An **end mark** signals the end of a sentence. It also shows the purpose of the sentence.

A declarative sentence ends with a **period.** If a declarative sentence already has a period at the end because an abbreviation occurs there, no other end mark is needed. If a declarative sentence ends with a quotation, place the period inside the quotation marks.

DECLARATIVE	His most interesting worker was Bartleby.
WITH ABBREVIATION AT END	He had worked for three years at Winston and Barnes, Inc.
WITH QUOTATION AT END	One day Bartleby responded to a job request by saying "I prefer not to."

A question ends with a **question mark.** Indirect questions, however, do not require a question mark. If a question ends with an abbreviation, add a question mark after the final period. If a question is quoted, the question mark appears inside the closing quotation marks; if a question contains a quotation, the question mark appears outside the closing quotation marks. Polite questions often end with a period instead of a question mark.

DIRECT QUESTION	Who took my collection of poems?
ENDING IN ABBREVIATION	Who expected him to end up with a Ph.D.?
INDIRECT QUESTION	They asked where we lived.
QUOTED QUESTION	They asked, "Where do you live?"
QUESTION INCLUDING QUOTATION	Did she say "I like Ezra Pound's poetry"?
POLITE QUESTION	Will you please take out a blank sheet of paper.

An exclamation ends with an **exclamation point.** If an exclamation is quoted, the exclamation point appears inside the closing quotation marks; if an exclamation contains a quotation, the exclamation point appears outside the closing quotation marks. An imperative sentence may end with a period instead of an exclamation point.

EXCLAMATION	Now! Take out a sheet of paper now!
QUOTED EXCLAMATION	Edward reflected, "Pound's Cantos are impenetrable!"
EXCLAMATION CONTAINING QUOTE	I can't believe Edward said "I am dropping this course"!
IMPERATIVE SENTENCE	Let us all recite the Pisan Cantos together.

2.94 Commas I

As you proofread your writing, check to see that you have used commas after certain introductory elements. Such elements include mild exclamations such as *yes, no, oh,* and *well;* participial phrases; two or more prepositional phrases; and adverb clauses.

MILD EXCLAMATION	**Well,** take your time while you're at it.
PARTICIPIAL PHRASE	**Believing the library to be closed,** he decided to stop and visit a friend.
TWO PREPOSITIONAL PHRASES	**Out of the game for a fairly short time,** Jordan hoped to easily regain his old form.
ADVERB CLAUSE	**While waiting for his friends at the mall,** he suddenly remembered his term paper was due the next day.

A comma is also used to set off an element that interrupts a sentence, such as a parenthetical expression or a word used in direct address.

PARENTHETICAL EXPRESSION	Rebecca planned, **despite her misgivings,** to go with Cody to the dance.
DIRECT ADDRESS	**Hilary,** have you seen our health insurance policy anywhere?

2.95 Commas II

A **serial comma** is a comma used to separate items in a series, whether the items are words, phrases, or clauses. Some writers omit the last comma when *and, or,* or *nor* joins the last two items in a series, but this construction sometimes makes a sentence unclear.

WORDS	**Fans, players, and owners** all had their share of frustration during the baseball strike.
PHRASES	He has constrained our fellow citizens taken captive on the high seas, **to bear arms against their country, to become the executioners of their friends and brethren, or to fall themselves by their hands.** —Thomas Jefferson, "Declaration of Independence"
OR	He has **plundered our seas, ravaged our coasts, burnt our towns, and destroyed the lives of our people.** —Thomas Jefferson, "Declaration of Independence"
CLAUSES	Twain's novel is proof **that humor can be used for quite serious purposes, that race and politics can be part of good literature, and that first-person narration can be effective with younger characters.**

Some paired words may be considered a single item.

PAIRED WORDS	Recognizing that we had lost our luggage, they offered us dry clothes, **food and drink,** and shelter.

If all the items in a series are joined by *and, or,* or *nor,* do not separate them with commas.

EXAMPLE	The team **attacked and defended and contested relentlessly,** until their opponents were exhausted.

Two or more adjectives preceding a noun are separated by commas.

EXAMPLE He had a **cold, weary, humorless expression** on his face that made us all very uncomfortable.

Use a comma before *and, but, for, nor, or, so,* and *yet* when they join two independent clauses. The comma may be omitted before *and, but, nor,* and *or* if the clauses are very short and the resulting sentence is still clear in meaning.

LONG CLAUSE My eyes were the greenest of things blue, and hers were the bluest of things gray.
SHORT CLAUSE Clarissa sighed but Franz did not hear.

Do not use a comma between two parts of a compound verb or compound predicate.

EXAMPLE Alvin bought a burger and ate it.

2.96 Commas III

A **nonrestrictive** participial phrase or clause is one that does not restrict or limit the meaning of the substantive to which it refers. You can test a phrase or clause when proofreading your writing by seeing if the main meaning of the sentence is lost if you omit the phrase or clause. If the phrase or clause is indeed nonrestrictive, make sure it is set off by commas.

RESTRICTIVE The play we attended is the one **that has been sold out for the last two months.**
NONRESTRICTIVE I have tickets for *Fences,* **which has been sold out for the last two months.**

Appositives and appositive phrases can be either restrictive or nonrestrictive.

RESTRICTIVE The movie directed by Quentin Tarantino was criticized for having too much violence.
NONRESTRICTIVE *Pulp Fiction,* **a movie directed by Quentin Tarantino,** was criticized for having too much violence.

PROOFREADING FOR OTHER PUNCTUATION ERRORS

2.97 Semicolons

A **semicolon** is used as punctuation between clauses in several situations. Use a semicolon between closely related independent clauses that are not joined by *and, but, for, nor, or, so,* or *yet.*

EXAMPLE Mr. Heard, the chair of the Chemistry Department, refused to hear the petition; he sent the students out of his office without further discussion.

Use a semicolon between independent clauses joined by a conjunctive adverb or transitional expression that is followed by a comma.

EXAMPLE Mr. Heard, the chair of the Chemistry Department, refused to postpone the test; however, he invited the students to stay and discuss the material covered on it.

Use a semicolon between linked independent clauses or items in a list if the clauses or items already contain commas.

EXAMPLES He entered the mayoral race, though his family was against it; he invested his own money in advertising for it, though he had little to spare; and he campaigned around the clock, though he was in poor health.

The car was loaded: it had the latest audio system, with six speakers and a CD player; it had advanced handling features, including double-wishbone suspension; and it had many luxury features, including power door locks and windows.

2.98 Colons

A **colon** introduces a long statement or quotation or a list of items.

QUOTATION Faulkner had simple advice for those who would be writers: read everything you can get your hands on to see how other writers do it.

LIST In the last twenty years, three state governors have gone on to become president: Jimmy Carter, Ronald Reagan, and Bill Clinton.

2.99 Dashes

A **dash** is used to show an abrupt break in thought.

EXAMPLE Everyone had been late for the rehearsal—again.

Sometimes the dash serves in place of an expression such as *in other words, that is,* or *namely.*

EXAMPLE He had been given clear instructions—to take no prisoners.

2.100 Hyphens

A **hyphen** is used to link words in a compound adjective, adverb, or noun.

EXAMPLES cross-reference, lily-livered, full-blown war, ill-conceived prank, self-absorbed junior, self-congratulatory senior, pseudo-intellectual, card-carrying member

If you have questions about whether you should hyphenate a particular compound word, look it up in the dictionary. If the dictionary offers no information, consider whether the hyphen is needed to make the meaning of the sentence clear.

UNCLEAR The new homeowners decided to use plants as living room dividers.
CLEAR The new homeowners decided to use plants as living-room dividers.

2.101 Parentheses and Brackets

Parentheses are used to enclose an aside or information that is less important than the main information offered in a sentence.

EXAMPLES If you happen to be near the Art Institute **(which some think is the best of its kind)**, you should stop in to see the Hockney exhibit.
When I get the inclination to memorize **(and that's not often)**, I usually reach for a book of poetry.

Brackets are used to enclose a writer's corrections or comments in someone else's quoted material, and as parentheses within parentheses.

QUOTED MATERIAL Stevens writes, "The squirming facts exceed squamous **[scaly]** mind."
PARENTHESES WITHIN PARENTHESES The story "Carried Away" (in Alice Munro, *Open Secrets* **[New York: Knopf, 1994]**) uses flashback and an epistolary format to create one of the great short stories of the decade.

2.102 Apostrophes

An **apostrophe** is used to form the possessive of nouns and some—but not all—pronouns. To form the possessive of a singular noun, add an apostrophe and an *s*. If the noun already ends in an *s* sound, has two or more syllables, and would be hard to pronounce with an additional *s*, add only an apostrophe. These rules apply also to hyphenated words, names of organizations, and indefinite pronouns.

WITH ADDED *S* Hamlet's ghost, Harvard's Business School, sister-in-law's family, Emily's privacy, Keats's odes, everyone's business
WITHOUT ADDED *S* fairness' sake, Summersons', Aeschelus' play

To form the possessive of a plural noun, add only an apostrophe if the plural form ends in *s*. If the plural form ends in some other letter, add an apostrophe and an *s*.

ENDING WITH *S* three weeks' vacation, twenty dollars' worth
ENDING WITHOUT *S* men's hairstyles, children's habits

While proofreading, check to see that you have not used an apostrophe to form the plural of a noun. Note also that the possessive pronouns, including *yours, ours, hers,* and *its,* do not have an apostrophe.

INCORRECT PLURAL	The state will ticket all **vehicle's** without license plates.
CORRECT PLURAL	The state will ticket all **vehicles** without license plates.
INCORRECT POSSESSIVE	The novel's greatest strength was **it's** brevity.
CORRECT POSSESSIVE	The novel's greatest strength was **its** brevity.

To show joint possession by all people in a group, add *'s* (or an apostrophe only) to the last word. To show individual possession of similar items by each member of a group, add *'s* (or an apostrophe only) to each noun in the group.

JOINT POSSESSION	They revoked Whitman, Thoreau, and **Hawthorne's** lease.
INDIVIDUAL POSSESSION	They removed **Whitman's, Thoreau's,** and **Hawthorne's** manuscripts.

Use an apostrophe to form the possessive of words that refer to time or that indicate amounts in dollars or cents.

EXAMPLES a week's reprieve on the exam, a long night's journey into day, a dollar's worth of gas for free

2.103 Underlining and Italics

Italics are a type of slanted printing used to show emphasis. (**Underlining** is used instead of italics in handwritten documents or in forms of printing in which italics are not available.) The following examples show the categories of words that should receive italics (underlining) for emphasis.

WORKS OF ART	Hopper's *Nighthawks at the Diner,* Picasso's *The Three Musicians,* Brueghel's *The Fall of Icarus*
BOOKS, PLAYS	O'Neill's *Mourning Becomes Electra,* Hemingway's *A Farewell to Arms*
FILMS, TELEVISION PROGRAMS, PERIODICALS	*Critical Inquiry, The New England Journal of Medicine, Forrest Gump, 60 Minutes*
AIRCRAFT, SHIPS, SPACECRAFT, TRAINS	*Commodore, Robert E. Lee, Apollo, Discovery*

Italicize the titles of long musical compositions unless they are merely the names of musical forms such as *fantasy, symphony, concerto, sonata,* and *nocturne.* The titles of short pieces such as songs should be placed in quotation marks.

SHORT MUSICAL COMPOSITION	"You're So Vain"
LONG MUSICAL COMPOSITION	Gorecki's Symphony no. 3

As you proofread your writing, check for words used as words, letters used as letters, and words from foreign languages. These should all be in italics (or underlined).

EXAMPLES The letter *x* is sometimes pronounced as a *z.*
The word *friend* is often used loosely.
I enjoyed being thought of as a *bête noire* until I learned it referred to someone who is especially disliked.

2.104 Quotation Marks I

Quotation marks are used to enclose a **direct quotation,** or a person's exact words. They are not used to enclose an **indirect quotation,** which is a reworded version of a person's words. Commas and periods that follow a quotation should be placed inside closing quotation marks; colons and semicolons should be placed outside. Do not, however, use a period to separate a direct quotation from the rest of a sentence.

When writing **dialogue,** a conversation between speakers, begin a new paragraph each time the speaker changes and enclose each speaker's words in quotation marks. When an indication of the speaker, such as *she said,* divides a sentence into two parts, the second part begins with a small letter.

2.105 Quotation Marks II

Quotation marks are also used to enclose titles of short works.

PARTS OF BOOKS	"The Colonial Period"
SONGS	"Corduroy"
SHORT POEMS	"The Love Song of J. Alfred Prufrock"
STORIES	"Hills Like White Elephants"
ESSAYS, ARTICLES	Hawthorne's "Concept of Evil"

Single quotation marks are used to enclose a quotation within a quotation.

EXAMPLE The boy's father said, "When that coach says 'be more aggressive,' do what he tells you."

2.106 Ellipsis

Ellipsis points are used to indicate an omission in quoted material. Use three ellipsis points (with a space before the first point) if the quoted material that precedes the omission is not a complete sentence; if it is a complete sentence, keep the end mark and add the ellipsis points.

INCOMPLETE SENTENCE BEFORE OMISSION	Franklin admits his failings openly: "In truth I found . . . I never arrived at the Perfection I had been so ambitious of obtaining, but fell far short of it."
COMPLETE SENTENCE BEFORE OMISSION	"Life is a series of surprises. . . . I can know that truth is divine and helpful, but how it shall help me, I can have no guess."

Ellipsis points are also used in much the same way to show a pause in a written passage.

EXAMPLE "Take this reward . . . oh never mind," said the aging miser.

2.107 Astronomical Terms

Capitalize the names of astronomical bodies.

PLANETS	**Neptune, Jupiter, Venus**
STARS	**Elnath, North Star (Polaris)**
CONSTELLATIONS	**Taurus, Little Dipper, Centaurus**

2.108 Awards

Capitalize the names of awards and prizes. Some words that go with prize names are not capitalized, however.

EXAMPLES **National Book Award, O. Henry Prize, Grammy Award, Nobel Prize in literature**

2.109 Brand and Trade Names

Capitalize the brand names and trademarks of products made by businesses. The dictionary may indicate if a name is trademarked. Do not capitalize the noun following a trade name that indicates what type of product it is.

EXAMPLES Guess shirts, Kleenex facial tissues, Gatorade

2.110 Buildings and Structures

Capitalize the names of important or widely recognized buildings and other structures or monuments. Capitalize the noun following a building, structure, or monument name that indicates its type.

EXAMPLES the Lincoln Memorial, Fenway Park, Sears Tower, the Roman Coliseum, Westminster Abbey

Contrast the absence of capitalization in the following example of a building that is not widely known:

EXAMPLE The covered bridge is very shaky.

2.111 Days, Months, Years, and Holidays

Capitalize the names of days, months, and holidays.

DAYS OF THE WEEK	Wednesday, Friday
MONTHS	August, March, June
HOLIDAYS	Christmas, Independence Day

Do not capitalize references to decades or centuries.

EXAMPLES	the twenties, the twelfth century

2.112 Directions and Regions

Capitalize the names of commonly recognized geographical regions.

EXAMPLES	the Mississippi Delta, the Caribbean, the Great Plains

Do not capitalize words such as *east, west, north,* and *south* when they are used only to indicate direction.

EXAMPLES	Move that sensor two miles west of the riverbed. She flew east every fall.

The adjectives *eastern, western, northern,* and *southern* are not capitalized when they are used as temporary designations.

TEMPORARY	south central Los Angeles, upper east side
STANDARD	Eastern cultures, Southern Hemisphere

2.113 Events and Periods

Capitalize historical events, special events, and recognized periods of time.

HISTORICAL EVENTS	Haymarket Riots, Cuban Missile Crisis, March on Washington
HISTORICAL PERIODS	Progressive Era, Renaissance
SPECIAL EVENTS	World Series, Canadian Shakespeare Festival

2.114 Family Relationships

Capitalize the names of family relationships used as titles unless they are preceded by a modifier.

MODIFIED	your great aunt, my youngest sister, Tom's father
NOT MODIFIED	Say, Mom, do you need any help with those groceries?

If the name of a family relationship precedes a proper name, capitalize it even if it is modified.

EXAMPLES boisterous **A**untie **M**ame, belligerent **U**ncle **H**enry

2.115 First Words

Capitalize the first word in a sentence.

EXAMPLES **U**nder the bridge lies a long lost poem of mine.
Her explanation was completely unacceptable.

2.116 Interjections

Do not capitalize an interjection such as *oh* unless it begins a sentence or stands alone. Do, however, capitalize the word *O*, which is technically not an interjection but a **vocative**—a word used to call someone.

EXAMPLES **O**h, why not try again?
This deserves a celebration . . . **o**h, never mind.
O Stella, why won't you come to the window?
Tell me, **O** great one, the secret of eternal life.

2.117 Letters

Capitalize letters used as grades, as musical tones, or as a designation for a person, thing, or location.

EXAMPLES Krakow always gets an **A** in English.
We just bought a new recording of Mozart's Serenade in **D** major.
If **A** is greater than **B**, and **B** is less than **C**, is **A** greater than **C**?
How much force will be required to move this one-pound weight from point **A** to point **B**?

2.118 Organizations and Institutions

Capitalize the names of organizations and institutions, whether they are public, private, athletic, business, or government bodies.

PUBLIC **S**tate **U**niversity of **N**ew **Y**ork, **M**ajor **L**eague **P**layers **A**ssociation
PRIVATE **C**hicago **L**yric **O**pera
ATHLETIC **O**rlando **M**agic, **B**oston **R**ed **S**ox
BUSINESS **A**pple **C**omputer, **S**un **M**icrosystems
GOVERNMENT **C**ircuit **C**ourt, **F**ederal **A**viation **A**dministration

2.119 Outlines

Capitalize the first word of each entry in an outline. Most of the index letters that identify parts of the outline are also capitalized. The following example is the first part of an outline for a report on Matthew Arnold; observe that lowercase letters are used as index letters after the Arabic numeral level.

Title: Matthew Arnold as Poet

Thesis statement: Matthew Arnold found less and less impetus to write poetry as he grew older.

I. Background and early life
  A. Family
    1. Mother
    2. Father
    3. Siblings
  B. Education
    1. Rugby School
    2. Oxford University
      a. Newdigate Prize
      b. Second-class honors

II. Employment
  A. Private secretary
  B. School inspector

2.120 Personal Names

Capitalize the names of persons and titles of address such as *Mr., Mrs., Ms., Miss, Madame,* or *Monsieur* when used in addressing a person or before a name.

EXAMPLES **Elizabeth Bishop, Georgia Yeats, Dr. Shorthair, Mr. Potter**

Check a reference book if you are unsure about the capitalization of *de la, du, van, von,* and other parts of names. Sometimes the part of a name that follows *Mc–* or *Mac–* is capitalized and sometimes it is not.

EXAMPLES Charles **de** Gaulle, William **McKinley**, Douglas **MacArthur**, Alexander **Mackenzie**

2.121 Place Names

Capitalize the names of places, including terms such as *lake, mountain, river,* or *valley,* if it is used as part of a name.

BODIES OF WATER	**Lake Michigan, Mississippi River, Yangtze River**
CITIES AND TOWNS	**Leeds, Austen, Durham, Seattle**
COUNTIES	**Fulton County, Dupage County**

CONTINUED

COUNTRIES	Paraguay, Guatemala, Canada
ISLANDS	Grenada, St. Thomas
MOUNTAINS	Mount Everest, Pikes Peak, Mount Whitney
STATES	Rhode Island, Oregon
STREETS AND HIGHWAYS	Fifth Avenue, State Street, Highway 61

Do not capitalize generic terms for places without specific modifiers.

EXAMPLES We drove to **the park** for a walk.
The cat stared at us for a moment and then darted into **the forest.**

2.122 Poetry

The first word in each line of a poem was capitalized in English until recent times.

EXAMPLE A noiseless patient spider,
I mark'd where on a little promontory it stood isolated,
Mark'd how to explore the vacant vast surrounding,
It launched forth filament, filament, filament, out of itself,
Ever unreeling them, ever tirelessly speeding them.
—Walt Whitman

Most writers in this century, however, have broken with this tradition.

EXAMPLE so much depends
upon

a red wheel
barrow

glazed with rain
water

beside the white
chickens
—William Carlos Williams

2.123 Proper Nouns and Adjectives

Capitalize proper nouns and adjectives.

EXAMPLES Francis, Franciscan priest
Canada, Canadian water

2.124 Quotations

Capitalize the first word of a sentence in a direct quotation even if it begins within the sentence where it is quoted.

EXAMPLE Thoreau wrote, "At a certain season of our life we are accustomed to consider every spot as the possible site of a house."

Do not capitalize a quoted fragment that completes the sense of part of the sentence outside the quotation marks.

EXAMPLE Poe claimed that to be effective a story must not "exceed in length what might be perused in an hour."

2.125 Sacred Beings and Writings

Capitalize references to sacred beings or persons, including God, gods, prophets, apostles, and saints. Some adjectives traditionally linked to such beings and persons are sometimes capitalized as well.

EXAMPLE Son of God, the Prophet, Allah, Jesus, Buddha, Mohammed

Capitalize the names of sacred writings and parts of such writings.

EXAMPLES Book of Psalms, Quran, Old Testament, the Talmud, the Bible

2.126 School Subjects, Courses, Grades, and Years

Capitalize a school subject when it is also the name of a language or when it is followed by a number indicating that it is the name of a specific course.

EXAMPLES Calculus II, Chinese, computer studies, English

Expressions such as *tenth grade, twelfth grade, sophomore, junior,* or expressions such as *freshman year, junior year,* are not capitalized unless they are part of the title of an official program.

EXAMPLES Senior Honors Program, sophomore English

2.127 The Pronoun *I*

Capitalize the pronoun *I* wherever it appears, except in quoted material where the pronoun is lowercased in the original.

EXAMPLE for life's not a paragraph
And death **i** think is no parenthesis
—e. e. cummings

2.128 Titles of Artworks

Apply **title capitalization** to titles of works of art. In title capitalization, the following are capitalized: the first word, the last word, all nouns, pronouns, adjectives, verbs, adverbs, and subordinating conjunctions. Articles *(a, an, the)* are written lowercased unless they are the first or last word. Some writers also capitalize any preposition over five letters long.

EXAMPLES Hopper's *Nighthawks at the Diner,* Vermeer's *Young Woman with a Jug,* Van Gogh's *The Public Gardens in Arles*

2.129 Titles of Literary Works

Apply title capitalization to titles of literary works.

EXAMPLES Yeats's "Sailing to Byzantium," Thoreau's *Civil Disobedience,* Fitzgerald's *The Beautiful and the Damned*

2.130 Titles of Musical Works

Apply title capitalization to titles of musical works.

EXAMPLES "All Apologies," Mozart's Serenade in D Major, "The Man Who Fell to Earth"

2.131 Titles of Persons and Occupations

Capitalize official titles of persons when they immediately precede a person's name or when they are used instead of a name in direct address.

EXAMPLES President Dwight Eisenhower, Prince Philip, Sir Laurence Olivier, Reverend King; Captain, the enemy vessels have surrounded us!

Do not capitalize references to occupations.

EXAMPLES the banker, the broker, the lawyer, the doctor, the teacher

2.132 Units of Time

Do not capitalize units of time such as the words *second, minute, hour, day, year, decade, century,* or the names of the seasons.

EXAMPLES We missed the flight by ten **m**inutes, and our weekend was ruined.
In the **s**ummer we travel north; in the **w**inter we don't travel.

2.133 Vehicles

Capitalize the names of vehicles only if they are trade names.

EXAMPLES **A**cura, **T**riumph, **V**olvo, **H**yundai, **v**an, **w**agon, **s**ports, **c**oupe, **r**ickshaw

SPELLING HANDBOOK

2.134 Proofreading for Spelling Errors

After you have checked your writing for other problems, read it through for spelling errors. Even if you have confidence in your spelling, you may make a mistake in keyboarding your work or writing it out by hand. Of course, the difficulty in detecting errors is that you will tend to see the words as you meant to write them, rather than as they really stand on the page. Professional proofreaders have a helpful technique: they read the text backward word by word. If you come across a word that causes the slightest doubt, check it in the dictionary.

2.135 Using Spelling Rules I

Many spelling problems arise from a common operation: forming plurals. Form the plurals of most nouns by simply adding *s*.

EXAMPLES fool**s**, tree**s**, friend**s**, fee**s**

Some nouns ending in *o* preceded by a consonant have plurals ending in *es,* as do nouns ending in *s, x, z, ch,* or *sh.*

EXAMPLES hero**es**, tomato**es**
crash**es**, mix**es**, bush**es**, fox**es**

Form the plurals of most musical terms ending in *o* by adding *s*.

EXAMPLES The du**os** on the pian**os** were not coordinated in those concert**os**.

Form the plurals of nouns ending in *y* preceded by a vowel by adding *s*. (The **vowels** are the letters *a, e, i, o, u*. Sometimes the letter *y* also represents a vowel sound.)

EXAMPLES The candidate's pl**oys** to distract us with dec**oys** were orchestrated by attorn**eys**.

Form the plurals of nouns ending in *y* preceded by a consonant by changing the *y* to *i* and adding *es*. (The **consonants** are all the letters that are not vowels.)

EXAMPLES Several new theor**ies** about government were tested in the eight**ies**.

The plurals of some nouns are irregular.

EXAMPLES Do more **women** than **men** have problems with their **teeth**?

Form the plural of a compound noun consisting of a noun and a modifier by making the main noun component plural.

EXAMPLES The brother**s**-in-law showed interest in becoming sergeant**s**-at-arms for the organization.

2.136 Using Spelling Rules II

Another operation that causes spelling errors is adding **prefixes** or **suffixes** to a word. A prefix is a letter or a group of letters added to the beginning of a word to change its meaning. When adding a prefix to a word, do not change the word itself.

EXAMPLES pre + amble = **pre**amble
dis + concert = **dis**concert
un + reliable = **un**reliable

A **suffix** is a letter or group of letters added to the end of a word to change its meaning. The spelling of most words is not changed when the suffix *–ness* or *–ly* is added.

EXAMPLES sad + ness = sad**ness**
sad + ly = sad**ly**

In the case of many words of more than one syllable ending in *y*, however, change the *y* to *i* before adding *–ly* or *ness*.

EXAMPLES happy + ly = happ**ily**
happy + ness = happ**iness**

In most cases of words ending in a final silent *e*, drop the *e* when adding a suffix beginning with a vowel, and keep the *e* when adding a suffix beginning with a consonant.

EXAMPLES desire + able = desir**able**
believe + er = believ**er**
peace + ful = peace**ful**
shame + less = shame**less**

VOCABULARY DEVELOPMENT

2.137 Making a Plan for Vocabulary Development

You can increase your **vocabulary**—the words you have at your command that empower you in communicating with others—by taking a few simple steps. When you encounter a new word, whether in reading, in speaking with others, in class, or outside school altogether, write it down in a list in your journal. Check the meaning in a dictionary and jot that down, too. Then review your vocabulary list from time to time. This procedure will vastly increase the chances that you will recall the new words you encounter.

2.138 Using Context Clues I

Although a dictionary is the best resource to check when you encounter a new word, sometimes a dictionary is not at hand. Even if a dictionary is available, you may prefer not to break the stream of your thought by consulting it. At times like these, you can often deduce the meaning of a word from context clues.

One type of context clue to look for is **restatement.** The author may tell you the meaning of a word you do not know by using different words to express the same idea in another sentence. Consider the following example.

EXAMPLE During political campaigns, candidates often offer **nostrums** for our most serious problems. Special interest groups weigh in with donations to insure that their causes will not be singled out for reform, and the politicians respond by offering vague but **popular solutions that have no track record.**

The reader will notice here from the restatement that *nostrum* means "a favored but untested remedy for problems or evils."

A second and related type of context clue is **apposition.** Look for a word or phrase that is specifically intended to clarify or modify the word you do not know.

EXAMPLE The book was really a **melange, or mixture,** of styles.

A third related type of context clue is the use of **examples.**

EXAMPLE The Nixon presidency, **despite its accomplishments,** had its **nadir** during the Watergate scandal; the Reagan presidency had its during the Iran-Contra affair.

Here the context shows that *nadir* is a "low point."

2.139 Using Context Clues II

Another context clue is the use of **comparison.** Imagine a reader does not know the meaning of the word *kumquat.* The comparison in the following passage will allow him or her to deduce the meaning from the context.

EXAMPLE Two kumquats sat on the counter. I couldn't decide whether to have one. I thought first about having an apple, but we had none. Then I decided to have a pear, but the only one left was rotten. I was saving the bananas for baking. Finally, I decided to eat something sweeter—a large slice of watermelon.

Comparison indicates that a *kumquat* is some kind of fruit.

Contrast is a similar type of context clue. Contrast here suggests that watermelon is sweeter than a kumquat.

2.140 Base Words and Prefixes

Building vocabulary is easier if you know the building blocks of words. Many words are formed by adding **prefixes** to a **base.** For example, imagine you come across the word *counter-revolution* and are unfamiliar with it. You do, however, recognize the **base word,** *revolution.* And you know from words such as *counterclockwise* and *countermeasure* that the prefix *counter–* means "against" or "contrary to." You can then quickly deduce that a counterrevolution is a movement in opposition to a revolution. The following table gives further examples.

PREFIX	MEANING	EXAMPLE	MEANING
anti–	"against"	antiformalist	against formalism
bi–	"two"	bipolar	having two poles
re–	"again"	reassign	assign again
co–	"together, joint"	coauthor	joint author

2.141 Suffixes

Like prefixes, **suffixes** can provide valuable clues to words you do not know. The following table lists a few examples.

SUFFIX	MEANING	EXAMPLE	MEANING
–ment	"action"	atonement	act of atoning
–al	"act or process"	retrieval	act of retrieving
–y	"quality"	honesty	quality of being honest
–ship	"office, rank"	professorship	rank of professor

2.142 Greek and Latin Roots

Although English is primarily a Germanic language, its vocabulary is in large part based on ancient Greek and Latin. Some Greek and Latin words came to English by way of other languages such as French; others were borrowed directly from Greek and Latin sources by scientists, researchers, and writers, who have always looked to Greek and Latin for components to build new words. The word *telephone,* for instance, comes from the Greek root *tele–*, meaning "far away," and *phone,* meaning "voice."

The following table shows some words with **Greek and Latin roots.** Notice that the words formed from Latin roots are more common, though the words formed from Greek roots are nearly identical in meaning.

FROM GREEK	FROM LATIN	MEANING OF GREEK AND LATIN ROOTS
dys-trophy	mal-nutrition	"bad-nourishment"
hypo-thesis	sup-position	"under-put"
peri-phrasis	circum-locution	"around-say"
sym-pathy	com-passion	"with-feel"
dia-phanous	trans-parent	"through-show"
mono-morphic	uni-form	"one-form"
poly-glottal	multi-lingual	"many-tongued"

2.143 Word Origins I

Knowing how speakers of English form words can help you recognize new words when you see them. **Names of people and places** are a common source of new words. The following table gives several examples.

WORD	ORIGIN
Spartan	From Sparta, Greece, a city-state known for its "austerity" and "frugality" in the service of military prowess. Today the word means "rigorously self-disciplined or self-restrained."
Machiavellian	From the name of an Italian political writer who wrote a famous book, *The Prince,* in 1513 that described the maneuvers of a calculating and morally unscrupulous ruler. The word now means "characterized by expediency, deceit, and cunning."

Another source of new words are **acronyms,** or words formed from the first letter or letters of each of the major parts of a compound term.

EXAMPLES radar, from "**ra**dio **d**etecting **a**nd **r**anging"; pixel, from "**pi**cture **el**ement"; smog, from **sm**oke and **fog**

Many words are simply **borrowed** from other languages.

EXAMPLES **ensemble** (French), **sonata** (Italian), **arroyo** (Spanish), **delicatessen** (German), **sauna** (Finnish), **honcho** (Japanese), **yacht** (Dutch), **luau** (Hawaiian), **tomato** (Nahuatl), **potato** (Taino)

2.144 Word Origins II

New words are also formed by shortening longer words. The word *phone,* short for *telephone,* is one such **clipped form.**

EXAMPLES **memo** (from *memorandum,* "something that should be remembered"), **limo** (from *limousine*), **cab** (from *cabriolet,* "light carriage"), **bus** (from *omnibus*), **piano** (from *pianoforte*), **stereo** (from *stereophonic receiver*)

New words are often **coined,** or deliberately created to fill a need.

EXAMPLES **spin doctor,** from the expression "to put a positive spin on something." The term now means an official whose job it is to interpret news in a way that furthers the ends of the group with which he or she is associated.
boom box, a term applied to a portable stereo because of its shape and its ability to project a high volume of sound

Brand names are often taken into the language, even though their owners may struggle to protect their exclusive status.

EXAMPLES Kleenex, Band-Aid, Xerox

2.145 Words from Other Curricular Areas I

As you study other subjects besides English, be alert for colorful words that have extended meanings that might be of use in your writing. Keep a list of these words in your journal. The table below gives a few examples of words of this type, as well as sample sentences showing how these words might be used in the study of English.

SUBJECT	WORDS
Arts and Humanities	Many contemporary novels have a **metaphysical** component. Some of the fiction of the Vietnam War is **surrealistic** in its portrayal of events. Ginsberg calls to Whitman in the supermarket in a kind of **hortatory.**
Mathematics	The critic remains **obtuse** about Stevens's "Sunday Morning." It is true that Stevens makes his point **obliquely;** but that is part of his point about perception in the poem. Stevens **divides** our attention between the woman and the poet.

2.146 Words from Other Curricular Areas II

More examples of words from other curricular areas are shown in the table below.

SUBJECT	WORDS
Social Studies	Eliot was **at war** with himself when he wrote *The Wasteland.* Some critics have an **impoverished** view of modern poetry.
Science	The poem's contrary tendencies reach an **equilibrium** by the end. Near the end of the play, Laertes **explodes** in anger. Until that point in the play, she had been living in an emotional **vacuum,** without any way to grow.
Technical Preparatory	In the first staging of the play, the audience was **charged** with enthusiasm by the final curtain. Yeats's poetry was sometimes **fueled** by political concerns.

VARIETIES OF ENGLISH

2.147 Formal and Informal English

Formal English is the kind of English used in writing papers, some magazine articles and nonfiction books, and some literary works. It is spoken at public ceremonies and in official speeches. **Informal English** is the kind of English used in personal notes and letters, in most newspaper and magazine articles, in some nonfiction and fiction books, and in some short stories and plays. It is spoken in everyday conversation.

How do you decide whether to use formal or informal English? You will naturally tend to use informal English, so all you need to bear in mind are those situations (just described) in which formal English may be expected instead.

How do you distinguish formal from informal English? First, informal English allows grammatical constructions that would not be acceptable in formal English. Many of these constructions are described in the Grammar Handbook (where they are labeled "nonstandard"). Second, informal English is enlivened by **colloquialisms.** These are the words and phrases that speakers of a language use naturally in conversation.

EXAMPLES
That test just **blew me away!**
He **went off on me** for being late.
She asked me if I wanted to **hang out with** them.

Third, informal English is often salted with **slang,** a form of speech made up of coined words, words whose meaning has been changed for no known reason, and words used facetiously.

EXAMPLES
That's a nice new **ride** you're driving. (car)
That coach must hate me because he never gives me any **clock.** (playing time)

Informal grammatical constructions, colloquialisms, and slang sometimes have a place even in writing that is otherwise formal. Literary works, for example, may rely on these devices to make dialogue colorful and realistic.

2.148 Register

To understand the concept of **register,** imagine that all the different kinds of usage in a language—both formal and informal—form one large set. A register is a subset of language usage that is used in a particular relationship between people. In talking to a friend, for example, you speak in a register that is casual, warm, and open. In speaking to a little child, you speak in a register that is nonthreatening and simple to understand. In speaking to an official such as a police officer or a government clerk, you speak in a register that is polite but firm—the same register they should use with you. The words you choose, the grammar you employ to say those words, and your tone of voice will change depending on the register in which you are speaking.

Another way to understand register is to think of the meaning of the musical term. In music, *register* means the range of notes a singer or instrument is capable of producing. Your speaking and writing, however, are not limited to one range of usage. You can use any part of a broad scale of usage from a grunt to a complex and formal declaration of your thought.

One hallmark of people who adapt to society is their ability to choose and use the appropriate register for whatever situation they are in. They do not offend strangers by being too familiar or puzzle their friends by being too formal. The same is true of written language. When you write, use language that is appropriate for the context and for your intended reader. Your personal journal will be in a different register from a term paper, and a story you write for a child will be in a different register from a short story you write for your English class.

2.149 Tone and Voice

Tone is the quality of a work that shows the attitude of the person writing or supposedly writing it. Compare the dark and foreboding tone of "The Raven" introduced in the first line, "Once upon a midnight dreary, while I pondered weak and weary," and continued throughout the poem to the joyous celebratory tone of "The Rhodora."

In any writing you do, you can adopt a tone appropriate for the message you wish to convey. Your **diction,** or choice of words, determines much of your tone. For instance, when writing a letter to a government official protesting a new regulation, do you want to say, "Your new regulation is utterly unacceptable to the honest citizens of this state," or "The new regulation is unpopular among many of your constituents"? The tone you convey will depend on your choice.

Voice is the quality of a work that tells you that one person in particular wrote it—not several, and not just anyone. Voice is one feature that makes a work unique. The voice of a work can be difficult to define; it may have to do with the way a writer views people, events, objects, ideas, the passage of time, even life itself. If this treatment of the subject is consistent throughout, despite variations in tone, register, point of view, and so forth, then the writer has **established a voice,** a sense of individuality, in the work.

In your own writing, you should strive to develop your own voice, not to imitate the voices of others. What that voice is, and how it compares to those of others, are matters no one can decide for you. "To thine own self be true," says Polonius in Shakespeare's *Hamlet,* "and thou canst not then be false to any man." He might well have been speaking about literary voice. Be true to your own voice, and your experience will speak directly to the experience of others.

2.150 Dialects of English

Dialects are varieties of a language. Dialects fall into one of two main classes: dialects based on **social differences** (for example, upper class, middle class, and lower class) and dialects based on **regional differences** (in the United States the major regional dialects are northern, southern, midland, and western).

All dialects are equally capable of expressing thought, which is what language is for. Therefore, no dialect is *better* than any other dialect. Some dialects are accepted by social classes that hold power; their dialect is generally considered the **standard** form of a language, and other dialects are considered **nonstandard.** But *standard* does not mean "correct" or "better than others." Knowledge of the standard dialect is useful because it is widely understood, and because in many situations, speaking or writing in the standard dialect will ensure that people focus on *what* you say rather than *how* you say it. They will understand your meaning, without being distracted by your use of an unfamiliar dialect.

2.151 Jargon and Gobbledygook

Jargon is the specialized vocabulary used by members of a profession. It tends to be incomprehensible to people outside the profession. A plumber may speak of a "hubless fitting" or a "street elbow" (kinds of pipe). A computer programmer may talk of "ram cache" (part of computer memory) or a "shell" (a type of operating software for computers).

Jargon is useful to writers who want to lend authenticity to their description of situations in which jargon would naturally be used. For instance, a novel about fighter pilots on an aircraft carrier would probably be full of aviation jargon. A scriptwriter developing a science fiction film would be sure to work in futuristic jargon about warps in space, energy shields, and tractor beams.

Gobbledygook is unclear, wordy jargon used by bureaucrats or government officials. For instance, instead of saying, "raise taxes," a bureaucrat might say "proactively maximize voluntary revenue income." In requesting six billion dollars for a kind of paper handkerchief for the armed services, a military planner might call the product a "disposable fiber wipeage utensil."

The most famous literary examples of gobbledygook occur in the novel *Nineteen Eighty-four,* by the English writer George Orwell. Gobbledygook is there raised to a standard of its own; called *doublespeak,* it is the officially approved form of communication between the government and the people.

2.152 Clichés and Euphemisms

A **cliché** is an expression that has been used so often it has become colorless and uninteresting. The use of clichés makes writing dull.

EXAMPLES tried and true
happy as a clam
busy as a bee
white as a ghost
ax to grind

A **euphemism** (from the Greek verb meaning "to speak with good words") is an inoffensive term that substitutes for one considered offensive.

EXAMPLES the company let her go (for "the company fired her")
conflict (for "war")

2.153 Connotation and Denotation

A **denotation** of a word is its dictionary definition. A **connotation** of a word is all the associations that it has in addition to its literal meaning. For example, the denotations of *mud* and *muck* are identical; but *muck* carries a connotation of moral filthiness that makes it a much stronger word than *mud*. Contrast the denotations and connotations of the following examples.

EXAMPLES bald-headed, hairless, tonsured, smooth-topped
fat, hefty, corpulent, rotund, overweight, wide-bodied

Writers should be aware of the connotations as well as the denotations of the words they use. You would be remiss to say, "The honcho jabbered for eons about his pet proposition," when what you meant was "The president spoke for a long time about the proposal he favored."

ESSENTIAL SKILLS: *Speaking and Listening*

3.1 A COMMUNICATION MODEL

Sometimes when we communicate with others, our message is conveyed just as we intended. Other times, communication breaks down or becomes unclear. To see how communication works, or doesn't work, it is helpful to consider a model.

In any act of communication, there is a **sender** and a **recipient** of a **message.** The sender **encodes** the message using **symbols,** and the recipient **decodes** the message and provides **feedback.** The message is sent along a particular **channel.** Among humans the channel of communication is often speech, but people use many different channels to communicate, such as hand gestures, facial expressions, body movement, and music. The following chart shows an application of this model.

COMMUNICATION MODEL	
Sender	You
Message	"Do you want to go to the game Saturday night?"
Symbols Used	Words in the English language
Channel	Speech
Recipient	Your friend
Feedback	"Sure, I haven't missed a game yet."

For communication to be successful, the encoding must be correct, the channel must be clear, and the decoding must be correct. For example, if your friend couldn't hear you because a large truck was passing by, the communication would be incomplete. You might adjust to this situation by repeating your question in a louder voice. This basic communication system is one you use every day and modify frequently when communication problems arise.

▸▸▸ ACTIVITY 3.1

1. Identify the sender, the message, the channel, and the recipient in each communication situation.
   a. Two drivers have had a minor car accident. While they wait for the police, one person uses hand signals to direct traffic around the two cars.
   b. A blind student gets on an elevator and places her fingertips on the braille "numbers" next to the elevator buttons. She pushes the button for her floor.

CONTINUED

2. Explain what adjustment you would make to successfully communicate in each of the following situations.
   a. You have just had two wisdom teeth taken out. Your mouth is swollen and the anesthetic has not yet worn off. You say to a friend, "Ah con tah ery ell." Your friend gives you a puzzled look.
   b. From across a crowded room Angie asks, "Where's Tyrone?" You answer, "He's in the doorway." Angie responds, "He's in Norway?"
3. What feedback might you give in each communication example? In each case, what does the feedback tell the sender of the message?
   a. You are at a rock concert and really enjoying the music.
   b. A friend is telling you about a problem.
   c. Someone pays you a compliment.
   d. A newspaper publishes an editorial with which you strongly disagree.

3.2 Elements of Verbal Communication

In **verbal communication**, also called oral communication, messages are conveyed using words and other sounds uttered by speakers. In **nonverbal communication**, channels other than spoken words or sounds are used. The following chart describes the most important elements of verbal communication:

ELEMENTS OF VERBAL COMMUNICATION

ELEMENT	DESCRIPTION	GUIDELINES FOR SPEAKERS
Volume	The loudness or softness of the voice	Speak loudly enough to be heard, but not so loudly as to make your audience uncomfortable.
Pitch, or Intonation	The highness or lowness of the voice	Vary your pitch to give your expressions a musical quality and to communicate meaning (for example, a rising pitch at the end of a sentence indicates a question). Avoid using a single pitch, or **monotone.**
Enunciation	The clearness with which syllables are spoken	Slightly exaggerate the clearness of your syllables to ensure that you are understood. Do not drop or clip the ends of words or sentences.
Pace	The speed with which something is said	Do not speak too slowly or too quickly.
Stress	The emphasis given to syllables, words, or phrases	Use stress to emphasize important ideas. Vary stress along with pitch to avoid monotony.
Tone	The emotional quality of the speech	Suit the tone to the message. Vary the tone appropriately throughout the communication.

In everyday speech, people use the elements of verbal communication without thinking much about them. In more formal situations, such as speaking to an audience, controlling how you use these elements can greatly enhance your communication. When speaking in front of a group, follow these guidelines:

USING ELEMENTS OF VERBAL COMMUNICATION IN PUBLIC SPEAKING

1. Make sure that you can be heard and understood by using an appropriate volume and pace.
2. Suit your volume, pitch, pace, stress, and tone to your message.
3. Vary all the verbal elements of your speech to make the presentation more lively, colorful, and interesting.
4. Slightly heighten or exaggerate each of the verbal elements of your speech over the level that you would use in ordinary conversation.

ACTIVITY 3.2

Choose a poem from this textbook to read aloud to your classmates. Make a copy of the poem and mark it to show the following:

- Places where you will increase or decrease your volume
- Places where you will increase or decrease your pace
- Words or phrases you will emphasize using volume, pitch, or stress
- Words or phrases that you might have trouble enunciating and will want to give special attention to when practicing
- Changes in tone or emotion through the piece

Take time to practice reading the selection aloud following the notes that you have made.

3.3 Elements of Nonverbal Communication

Nearly every face-to-face message is accompanied by nonverbal communication. When you ask a question, you may raise your eyebrows. When you listen to someone, you may nod your head. When a friend tells you something in confidence, you may lean closer. Much nonverbal communication is unconscious. When speaking in public, however, you will want to consciously use nonverbal communication to enhance your message. The following chart offers some guidelines for using the elements of nonverbal communication.

ELEMENTS OF NONVERBAL COMMUNICATION		
ELEMENT	**DESCRIPTION**	**GUIDELINES FOR SPEAKERS**
Eye contact	Looking your audience in the eye	Maintain eye contact to keep your audience engaged in what you are saying.
Facial expressions	Displays of emotion using the face (e.g., smiles, scowls, frowns, etc.)	Match your facial expressions to your message.
Body language	Positions of the body that have meaning to an audience	Match your body language to your message. Maintain good posture.
Gestures	Meaningful motions of the hands and arms	Use gestures sparingly to emphasize points. Match gestures to your message.
Proximity	Distance from the audience	Maintain a comfortable distance, not too close for comfort, but not so far away as to hamper communication.

►►► ACTIVITY 3.3

Go back to the poem that you selected for Section 3.2. Mark the poem to show how you will use appropriate facial expressions, gestures, and body language to make your reading more interesting to the audience.

3.4 ACTIVE LISTENING

Think about a pitcher and a catcher in baseball. One sends the ball and the other receives it, but both are active participants in the exchange. It's the same with a speaker and a listener. For complete communication to occur, the listener must participate fully in the process. Here are some suggestions for listening actively:

- **Mentally process what you hear.** Listen for main ideas and supporting details. Summarize, predict, question, and interpret as you listen.
- **Take notes.** Jot down especially interesting ideas or details. If you are listening to a lecture, you may want to take notes in outline form.
- **Ask questions and give other feedback.** Maintain eye contact. Use gestures, facial expression, and body language to give feedback to the speaker. In conversation, you might show that you have understood the speaker by saying "uh-huh" or "I see." If you are confused by something the speaker said, pause and rephrase it to check your understanding. Ask questions if you need to, but wait till the speaker has finished a whole thought.

►►► ACTIVITY 3.4

With a classmate role play a listening situation. First, think of something relatively complex that you would like to explain to the other person. It might be a theory or idea from one of your classes or an issue that involves getting along with other people. Take a few moments to outline what you want to say. Then take turns listening to each other using the techniques for active listening.

3.5 INTERPERSONAL COMMUNICATION

Communication between individuals is called **interpersonal communication.** This type of communication can be quite formal, as in a job interview, or very informal, as in a telephone chat with a friend. Individuals use interpersonal communication to:

- **Transmit information**
- **Establish relationships**
- **Maintain relationships**
- **Confirm their identity**
- **Form personal bonds**

You can use both verbal and nonverbal techniques to improve your interpersonal communication. Here are some examples:

- Make eye contact and stand in a relaxed way.
- Provide feedback by asking questions or reflecting back what the speaker said. For example:

SPEAKER Whew! We met the deadline, but I'm so tired I can barely move.
LISTENER Sounds like you've been working really hard. Maybe you should give yourself a reward.

- Think before you speak. Thinking first makes communication clearer and more efficient. It also shows respect for your listener.
- Keep strong emotions under control. If you begin to feel angry, for example, pause and take a deep breath before continuing the conversation. If you don't think you can get your anger under control, ask to resume the conversation later.

►►► ACTIVITY 3.5

With a partner, role play a conversation about a difficult decision you need to make. (This decision could be real or imaginary.) As you speak or listen, apply the techniques for improving interpersonal communication given in the previous section. Then reverse roles.

3.6 Discussion

A discussion is an exchange of ideas and information among a group of people. Discussions range widely in their degree of formality, from congressional committee meetings to after-school conversations with friends. In formal and semiformal discussions, the participants often assume roles and the discussion is structured in some way.

DISCUSSION	
Roles	• **Group leader or chairperson.** Keeps the discussion on track when people begin to digress or veer away from the subject, asks questions when the discussion starts to flag, makes sure everyone participates • **Secretary.** Takes notes or records what is said and later prepares a description (**minutes**) of the discussion • **Participants.** Take part in the discussion, listen attentively to others, provide feedback
Process	• **Discussion question.** States the goal or main idea of the discussion and is usually put forward by the group leader. In a formal discussion, the discussion question is called a **proposition**. • **Agenda.** A step-by-step plan for the discussion, usually written and distributed at the beginning of the discussion by the group leader or secretary

▸▸▸ Activity 3.6

Assume that a committee from the junior class is meeting to discuss what to do with the money that is in its treasury at the end of the year. Write an agenda for a meeting at which you will discuss possible plans for the money.

3.7 Public Speaking

The prospect of speaking in public makes many people nervous. Even famous people have this common fear. Speaking in public, however, need not be a grueling experience. Preparation can help you to feel more comfortable about speaking. Remember that nervousness is a form of energy. If you can convert this energy into enthusiasm about your subject, speaking in front of others will seem much easier.

Types of Speeches. There are three main types of speeches. An **impromptu speech** is spontaneous; it is given without any preparation. A **memorized speech** is one that is written out before the occasion and then recited almost word for word to the audience. An impromptu speech can seem unfocused; on the other hand, a memorized speech may not engage the audience completely. For these reasons, most professional speakers prefer to deliver an **extemporaneous speech.** In this type of speech, the speaker refers to concise, carefully organized notes while giving the speech. The extemporaneous speech thus combines the liveliness of the impromptu speech with the careful preparation of the memorized speech.

Writing a Speech. A well-prepared speech has a beginning, a middle, and an end. The **beginning,** or **introduction,** should spark the audience's interest and present your main topic or idea. The **middle,** or **body,** should elaborate on the main idea. The **end,** or **conclusion,** should cap off the speech in a memorable way and give the audience a sense of completion. For more information on writing introductions and conclusions, see the Language Arts Survey, 1.42, "Organizing a Composition."

Preparing an Extemporaneous Speech. The chart below gives the basic procedure for preparing an extemporaneous speech:

STEPS IN PREPARING AN EXTEMPORANEOUS SPEECH

1. Do prewriting.
2. Do research.
3. Prepare note cards.
4. Make a plan for using verbal and nonverbal elements of communication in your speech.
5. Rehearse with your note cards, using a tape recorder, a video recorder, a mirror, or a practice audience.
6. Deliver your speech, attending to both verbal and nonverbal elements of the delivery.

ACTIVITY 3.7

Prepare an extemporaneous speech for one of the following situations of for an occasion of your choice. Complete steps 1 through 5 in the foregoing list.

- A thank-you speech to a local community group that awarded you a $500 college scholarship, in which you discuss your plans for college and after
- A speech at a school Earth Day celebration about one way in which people can care for the environment
- A speech to accompany a slide presentation about your neighborhood to a group of friends

3.8 ORAL INTERPRETATION

An **oral interpretation** is a dramatic reading of a literary work or group of works. In this type of presentation, the speaker vividly conveys the particular feeling or sense of the work. The art of oral presentation is an ancient one. Before the dawn of writing, stories and poems were presented orally in front of other people and transmitted from generation to generation in this way.

To prepare an oral presentation, follow these steps:

1. **Choose a cutting.** The cutting may be a single piece, a selection from a single piece, or several short, related pieces on a single topic.

2. **Write the introduction and any needed transitions.** The introduction should present the overall topic or theme of the presentation. The transitions should introduce and connect the different readings. Be sure to include the author and title of each selection.

3. **Plan your use of verbal and nonverbal elements.** Decide how you will use volume, pitch, stress, tone, gestures, facial expressions, and body language to present the work effectively. However, avoid movement. Movement is a characteristic of drama rather than oral interpretation. If there are different voices (for different characters), be sure to distinguish them.

4. **Rehearse.** Practice in front of an audience or a mirror. Alternatively, you can make an audiotape or videotape of your presentation to review and critique.

▶▶▶ ACTIVITY 3.8

Select three short pieces or portions of pieces in this text for an oral interpretation. All cuttings should be from a particular period of American literature (Units 2–8). Copy the cuttings onto notebook paper. Then write an introduction and transitions. In the introduction, present your topic or theme in a way that will capture the attention of your listeners. In each transition, state the title and author of the selection and briefly relate the selection to the overall topic or theme. Combine the introduction, the cuttings, and the transitions to make a script. Mark the script to show variations in volume, pitch, pace, stress, tone, gestures, facial expressions, and body language. Memorize your script and rehearse your presentation. Then present it to your classmates.

ESSENTIAL SKILLS: *Study and Research*

THINKING SKILLS

Although every human being is capable of thinking, most people do not take time to cultivate and improve their thinking skills. The effort, however, can be rewarding. By learning how to use a number of essential thinking strategies, you can learn more, solve problems more easily, and make decisions more effectively.

4.1 STRATEGIES FOR PROBLEM SOLVING I

All problem solving involves four steps.

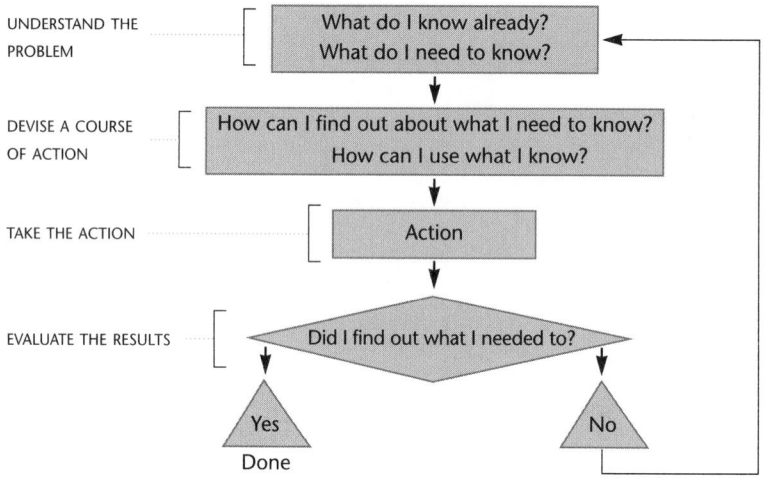

You can use many strategies within this **general problem-solving framework**. An **algorithm** is a step-by-step procedure that leads to a definite solution. A math formula is an example of an algorithm. Other strategies, called **heuristics**, do not lead to a specific solution but help you explore a problem: for example, asking "what if" questions to explore the problem of homelessness or using feedback from a listener to improve your oral presentation skills. A **rule of thumb** is a guideline or principle that is roughly accurate and based on common sense. To solve a complex problem, you will need to use more than one strategy. Try to stay flexible, and remember that using a good strategy does not guarantee that you will solve a specific problem.

Trial and error. In this problem-solving strategy, you make a guess and see if it works. Trial and error can be useful when only a few possible solutions seem likely. You can also use this strategy when there are many possibilities and you need to become familiar with the problem in order to find a more systematic strategy. Generally, though, other problem-solving methods will be more fruitful and efficient.

Representing the situation. When you are working on a complex or confusing problem, making a visual or physical **representation** of the problem may help. You might draw a diagram or a picture or construct a model. This technique often helps you to see how different parts of a problem are related. The communications triangle in the Language Arts Survey, 1.6, "Choosing a Purpose or Aim," on page 874 is an example of a visual representation. Try to be creative and flexible: using even a good strategy does not guarantee that you will solve a given problem.

4.2 Strategies for Problem Solving II

Means-end analysis. An **end** is a goal, and **means** are the tools and methods used to achieve the goal. To use means-end analysis, you compare what you know about the current situation and what you know about the situation that will exist when the goal has been reached. Then you think of ways to reduce the differences between the two situations.

Divide and conquer. Sometimes the best way to tackle a complex problem is to divide it into parts and then solve each part in a logical sequence. If a particular part is still difficult to solve, you can divide it into still parts.

PROBLEM	You want to ensure passage of the school tax levy so your high school will not have to switch to a "pay to play" policy for school athletics and other extracurricular activities.
SOLUTION STRATEGY	Break the goal down into parts: the levy needs the support of voters who are (1) parents, (2) nonparents, and (3) senior citizens. Then for each group, such as parents, decide (1a) what message will work best, and (1b) what techniques will work best to get the message across.

Work backward. This strategy involves thinking about a cause-and-effect chain of events, only backward. Describe in detail the final situation you want to achieve. Then think about what would have to happen to have that situation come about. Continue working backward until you get to a situation that you know how to create.

4.3 Strategies for Decision Making

When making a decision, you must often compare outcomes or weigh several factors. Making a chart like one of those that follow can help you evaluate your options.

Pros and cons. Make a list of your options. For each option, list the reasons for choosing it (the *pros)* and the drawbacks of choosing it (the *cons)*. Then compare the lists.

PROS AND CONS OF PLANTING DIFFERENT TREES

	White Pine	Apple	Maple
Pros	green year round no leaf cleanup in fall	spring blossoms fruit for eating and cooking	shade beautiful fall color
Cons	no bright fall color	picking up rotten apples extra maintenance (pruning, spraying)	raking leaves in fall

Criteria analysis. On the left side of the chart, list the results you want to achieve. Across the top, list your options. Assign points from 1 to 5 to each option based on how well it will achieve each result you have listed. Then add up the points in each column and choose the option with the highest total.

CRITERIA ANALYSIS: CHOOSING A ROUTE FOR BICYCLE TRIP

	Route A	Route B	Route C
1. Interesting sights	4	3	3
2. Good-quality roads	2	3	1
3. Terrain not too hilly	3	2	1
4. Plenty of camping places	2	3	3
	11	11	8

4.4 Memorizing

Remembering involves two steps: storing the information in your mind and being able to retrieve it when you need it. Because the memory function has these two aspects, it has sometimes been compared to a filing system. For example, if you want to save an important document, such as a letter of recommendation from a teacher, you wouldn't just toss it into a large drawer with other papers. To be sure you can find it later, you might put it in a folder labeled "Recommendations" or "Letters: Recommendations," and then place the folder in alphabetical order with other folders. By thinking about why you are saving the letter, you can save it in a way that makes it easier to find later. Your mind works in a similar way. If you take time to understand an idea or a piece of information and relate it to things you already know, you will be able to "file" it in a logical place in your mind and to retrieve it more easily later.

Mnemonics. An association that aids memorizing is called a **mnemonic.** To use a mnemonic, you combine new information that you need to remember with information you already know very well or can remember very easily. For example, many children learn the alphabet by associating it with an easy-to-remember tune. Mnemonics are commonly based on either words or images.

MNEMONICS			
Name of Strategy	**Strategy**	**Information to be Learned**	**Information Easy to Remember**
Embellished Letter	Form an acronym using the first letters of the information to be remembered.	Items in a series, e.g., the colors of the spectrum (red, orange, yellow, green, blue, indigo, violet)	Roy G. Biv
Method of Loci	Imagine a place you know well (a baseball diamond, etc.). Form an image of each object to be remembered in a particular spot in that place.	Items in a series, e.g., the first ten presidents (Washington, Adams, Jefferson, Adams, Madison, Monroe, Jackson, Van Buren, Harrison, Tyler)	Washington is pitcher, Adams is catcher, Jefferson at first base, etc.
Key Word	Form an image of the items doing something to or with each other.	Associations, e.g., a server at a restaurant must remember that the man in the blue shirt ordered chicken with baked potato.	Bizarre images, e.g., a man is terrified (chicken) of a potato.

Repetition. Generally, simply repeating information over and over is not a good way to remember it. A better approach is to become familiar with the information in a variety of ways. However, repetition, has an effect on remembering. The more often you use a piece of information or work with an idea, the more likely you are to remember it. For example, to remember the content of the Gettysburg Address, you might write a paraphrase of the address, present it as an oral interpretation, and discuss its importance in American history with other students.

4.5 Remembering and Visualizing

Think back to your last birthday. Can you see and feel the event in your mind? Close your eyes and try.

Visualizing a place, person, event, or object can help you write about it and describe it accurately and vividly. As you visualize, you can use various thinking skills to help you remember details. If you are trying to remember your birthday, you might think about the events of the day in the order in which they occurred. If you are trying to visualize your twin cousins, you might think about the ways in which they are different and similar.

4.6 Observing

Both purpose and point of view can affect how you observe a situation. Consider two observers of a high school basketball game. One is a college coach prospecting for new talent. Another is a sociologist studying the behavior of crowds. The two observers will come away from the game with very different information. Before you observe any situation, think about what kinds of details you need to accomplish your purpose. Then, when you are observing, focus your attention on the relevant details.

Sometimes when you observe, you will be gathering evidence to test a hypothesis (see the Language Arts Survey, 4.13, "Making Hypotheses"). In such situations, you need to avoid making prejudgments. If you have a bias or strong expectation about what you will see, you may be blind to evidence that goes against your expectation.

4.7 Classifying

When you put items or ideas into categories, you are **classifying.** Items in the same category share one or more characteristics. For example, Ralph Waldo Emerson and Henry David Thoreau are classified as Transcendentalists because their writings express ideas characteristic of Transcendentalism (e.g., nature as a source of eternal truths, the presence of spirit in nature).

Developing a classification scheme is an excellent way to organize a piece of informative or persuasive writing. Remember that categories often overlap. Some items may have features that allow them to be classified in more than one of the categories you have selected. The following chart gives some guidelines for using categories when you think about literature.

GUIDELINES FOR USING CLASSIFICATION

Guideline	Example
Define categories precisely.	When classifying poems based on use of rhyme, you might define a rhymed poem as one that "has a distinct pattern of rhyme throughout" (rather than one that "has some rhyme").
Choose categories that fit your purpose.	If your purpose is to analyze an author's style, you might classify his or her works using the categories *essays, letters, speeches,* and *poems,* and then show how style is related to the form of writing.
Ignore characteristics unrelated to the categories chosen.	When classifying short stories based on theme, you would ignore characteristics related to setting, mood, plot, and so on.
Use parallel (nonoverlapping) categories.	When classifying poems from the Harlem Renaissance, you might use the categories "poems about childhood" and "poems about work" (rather than "poems about childhood" and "poems about the black experience").

4.8 Comparing and Contrasting

Both comparing and contrasting involve analyzing two things at the same time. When **comparing,** you describe similarities between two things. When **contrasting,** you describe their differences. When you compare two things, you place them in the same category. When you contrast them, you place them in separate categories.

When you compare and contrast, you will often be contrasting items that are similar in some important way. For example, in the novel *Huckleberry Finn,* Huck and Jim are both runaways, but they are different in that Huck is a runaway child and Jim is a runaway slave. Thus, while they possess a common characteristic, they possess it in different ways. As characters, they belong in the same category but in different **subcategories.** In literature, characters, often exhibit shared features, but they exhibit these features in different ways. Such differences are often well worth exploring.

In your literature class, you will probably be asked to compare and contrast the subject matter, techniques, and themes used in different works and by different authors. Remember to discuss both points of similarity and points of difference. (See also the Language Arts Survey, 1.18, "Sensory Detail Charts;" and 1.34, "Organizing Ideas," for tips on organizing a "compare and contrast" essay.)

4.9 Estimating and Quantifying

In a persuasive essay or speech, you need to support your points with facts. Frequently, the facts you need are numbers, or **quantities.** For example, if you claim that smoking is a significant cause of lung cancer, you ought to **quantify** your claim by stating **how many** smokers develop lung cancer. The number you need may be available in reference works (see the Language Arts Survey, 4.23, "Using Reference Works"). If not, you may be able to come up with an **estimate,** or approximate quantity, based on a combination of research, general knowledge, and common-sense reasoning. Sometimes you may only be able to estimate a **range** within which the actual number probably falls.

UNQUANTIFIED:	Cigarette smoking causes lung cancer.
QUANTIFIED:	Cigarette smoking is responsible for 87 percent of lung cancer cases and accounts for 30 percent of all cancer deaths.
ESTIMATED:	Almost a third of all lung cancer deaths can be attributed to cigarette smoking.

4.10 Analyzing

Analyzing is the process of breaking something down into logical parts and then examining the parts individually to see how they are related. Since the idea of "parts" can be understood in many different ways, there are many ways to analyze a particular thing. For instance, if you were to analyze a city, you might analyze it in terms of population groups (by age, sex, ethnic background, and so on), infrastructure systems (roads, bridges, sewage and water lines), sources of employment (businesses, industries, government offices, schools and colleges), government departments (administration, taxation, development, and so on), or individual neighborhoods.

You can analyze a work of literature in many ways. With a play, you might analyze different acts or different scenes within an act. With an essay, you might analyze the introduction, the body, and the conclusion, or the individual arguments presented. With a poem, you might analyze such figures of speech as metaphor, simile, and personification. (For other ideas on analyzing written works, see the Language Arts Survey 1.14, "Analyzing;" and 1.34, "Organizing Ideas.")

4.11 Generalizing

Generalizing is making a broad claim based on some particular observations. Generalizations are frequently false because they make a claim that is not justified by the available information. Perhaps you have observed squirrels in a city park nearly every day on your way to school and have seen only gray squirrels there. From this experience, you might make the generalization "All squirrels are gray." However, there are red and albino squirrels. Thus, a broad generalization based on a limited number of observations may be very flimsy. A generalization that is qualified, or more restricted in scope, however, is less likely to be false. For example, you could truthfully generalize from your observations, "All the squirrels I have ever seen in the park are gray."

A generalization based on reasoning, not merely observation, is likely to be true. Say that at the zoo you observe an unfamiliar animal that has fur and is suckling its young and you conclude that the animal is a mammal. Your conclusion is not based on numerous observations of these animals; you have seen only one. It is based on knowing the scientific concept of *mammal*—an animal that has skin covered with hair and that nourishes its young with milk from its own body. Making a generalization about a particular situation based on reasoning, rather than mere observation, is called **induction.**

4.12 Deducing

Deducing, or inferring, is the process of drawing a logical conclusion from certain facts, which are called **premises.** When the conclusion follows from, or is forced by, the premises, the deduction is **valid,** as in the following:

PREMISES: (1) The members of the 1787 Constitutional Convention are called the Founding Fathers of the United States.
(2) Thomas Jefferson was a member of the 1787 Convention.
CONCLUSION: Thomas Jefferson was a Founding Father of the United States.

If, from the same premises, you had concluded "Thomas Jefferson was a man of many talents," that conclusion would be **invalid.** Although this statement is true, it is not true *because* the premises stated above are true. Valid deductions are said to preserve truth; if the premises are true, then the conclusion is always true.

A deduction is commonly expressed in the form of a **conditional,** or "If . . . , then . . ." statement. A conditional says that *if* something is true, *then* something else must be true: If a person was a member of the 1787 Constitutional Convention, then that person was a Founding Father of the United States. In a conditional, the part of the statement following the *if* is called the **antecedent,** and the part following *then* is called the **consequent.**

You can draw certain kinds of conclusions, or inferences, from conditional statements. First, if the antecedent in a conditional is true, you can conclude that the consequent is true:

EXAMPLE If it rains today, I cannot play softball.
It rained today. (antecedent is true)
Therefore, I did not play softball today. (consequent is also true)

Second, you can draw a conclusion when the consequent is false: if the consequent is false, then the antecedent is also false.

EXAMPLE If it rains today, I cannot play softball.
I played softball today. (consequent is false)
Therefore, it did not rain. (antecedent is also false)

You cannot make a valid inference, however, when the antecedent is false or the consequent is true (see the Language Arts Survey 4.14, "Avoiding Faulty Arguments").

4.13 Making Hypotheses

A **hypothesis** is an educated guess about a cause or an effect. When you observe something and then suggest an explanation for it, your explanation is a hypothesis. A prediction based on a theory is also a hypothesis. A hypothesis must always be tested against experience. You can test a hypothesis by performing actual experiments, by examining numerous relevant examples, or by conducting a **thought experiment**, asking "What if" questions (see the Language Arts Survey 1.13, "Questioning: 'What if' Questions").

Remember that a single counterexample is enough to disprove a hypothesis, and you cannot prove a hypothesis by gathering a large number of examples (see the Language Arts Survey, 4.11, "Generalizing"). The examples lend support for the hypothesis but they do not guarantee its truthfulness. Thus, hypotheses are continually modified as new evidence is discovered.

4.14 Avoiding Faulty Arguments

When you are writing a persuasive piece of writing or evaluating the writing of others, be alert for faulty arguments or errors in logical reasoning. Many of these errors are based on **logical fallacies.** A writer commits a fallacy when he or she makes an **invalid** inference, one that is not justified by the facts at hand.

Errors in reasoning can result from incorrect information, lack of information, carelessness, or other problems. It is often hard to tell when a mistake in thinking is due to faulty logic or some other factor.

False analogy. An argument by analogy claims that if two things are alike in some way, then they must be alike in another way.

EXAMPLE "The president is the captain of the ship of state. People in government should obey his orders."

ANALYSIS This analogy creates a striking image, but there are many ways in which the president is not like the captain of a ship. For example, the power of the president is checked and balanced by the powers of the legislative and judicial branches of government.

Although analogies are useful for stimulating discussion and help us see things in new and interesting ways, arguments based on analogy do not prove what they state.

Circularity. A circular argument assumes the truth of what it is trying to prove. This type of argument is sometimes called **question-begging.** In a circular argument, the premises and the conclusion often state the same thing, only in different words.

EXAMPLE "Joe Montana was king among football players because he was the greatest and he excelled beyond all other players."

ANALYSIS The "reasons" the speaker gives for the proposition are other ways of stating that Montana was the best.

Post hoc (ergo) propter hoc. In a cause-and-effect sequence, the effect always follows the cause. A speaker who commits the *post hoc* fallacy assumes that because one event followed another it must have been caused by that event. However, not every sequence of events involves cause and effect.

EXAMPLE "Under Mayor Lashutka's administration, the streets are in much better condition. This winter there were hardly any potholes."

ANALYSIS This argument confuses sequence with consequence. The streets might be in better condition, not because of the mayor's actions, but because the winter was unusually mild and dry, without the freezing and thawing that damages road surfaces. Many politicians are fond of the *post hoc* argument.

Fallacies of denying the antecedent and of affirming the consequent. A conditional states that *if* something (the antecedent) is true, *then* something else (the consequent) must be true. As shown in the Language Arts Survey, 4.12, "Deducing," you can draw a valid conclusion from a conditional when the antecedent is true or when the consequent is false. If the antecedent is false, however, nothing is implied about the consequent.

EXAMPLE "If it rains today, then I cannot play softball. It did not rain today. Did I play softball?"

ANALYSIS Maybe yes, maybe no. The proposition makes "raining" a condition of "not playing softball"; it does not establish a conditional for "not raining." You cannot draw a conclusion when the antecedent is denied.

In addition, if the consequent is true, nothing is implied about the antecedent.

EXAMPLE "If it rains today, then I will not play softball. I did not play softball. Did it rain today or not?"

ANALYSIS Again, you cannot draw a conclusion because raining is not the only possible cause of not playing softball. Too much homework, a sprained ankle, or a lack of other players could also prevent you from playing softball.

Fallacies of composition and decomposition. If a whole has a certain quality, it does not follow that each part of that whole has that quality on its own. To assume that it does is to commit the fallacy of decomposition.

EXAMPLE "Switzerland is a pacifist country; it does not take arms against other countries. Therefore, each person in Switzerland is a pacifist."

ANALYSIS Many people in Switzerland may agree with the country's pacifist stance, but others may not. The characteristic of the whole does not necessarily apply to each person who makes up the whole.

Likewise, it is fallacious to argue that because some parts have a certain quality, then the whole must also have that quality. This is the fallacy of composition.

EXAMPLE "The first chapter of this book is very exciting. Therefore, the whole book must be very exciting."

ANALYSIS Generally, some parts of a book are more exciting than others. The author may have made the first chapter especially exciting as a way to draw readers into the story.

Non sequitur. A *non sequitur* is a conclusion that simply does not follow from the reasons given and may have nothing to do with them.

EXAMPLE "Abraham Lincoln was a master of rhetoric because he came from a very humble background."

ANALYSIS To support the claim that Lincoln was a master of rhetoric, the writer would have to furnish evidence relating to the use of language in writing or speaking. The fact that Lincoln grew up in a small log cabin of the American frontier is not relevant to the writer's claim.

Ad hominem. The phrase *ad hominem* means "to the person." An ad hominem argument attacks or defends a person instead of the point under discussion. The truth of what people say, however, is not determined by their background, political affiliation, or social ties. It is determined by the validity of their arguments.

EXAMPLE "There's no reason to support this new welfare reform law. Only Democrats are in favor of it, and we all know that Democrats can't solve social problems."

ANALYSIS This statement does not address the merits or deficiencies of the new law. It simply attacks those who support it.

False dichotomy. To set up a false dichotomy is to assume that there are only two sides to an issue. This type of argument is also known as an "either/or" argument.

EXAMPLE "If you're not a Christian, then you must be an atheist."

ANALYSIS A Christian is a person who believes in the teachings of Jesus. An atheist is someone who does not believe in the existence of a deity. There are, however, many examples of non-Christians who believe in a deity, such as Muslims, Buddhists, and Jews.

Hasty generalization. A generalization, or universal claim, that is based on only a few examples or unrepresentative samples is faulty (see Language Arts Survey, 4.11, "Generalizing").

EXAMPLE "Three Canadian men were recently charged with planting a bomb at the metropolitan airport. Therefore, all Canadians should be considered dangerous."

ANALYSIS This claim is based on a sample that is infinitesimally small (Canada has some 28 million people). Furthermore, the men have only been charged with, not convicted of, a crime.

Equivocation. To equivocate is to shift the meaning of an ambiguous term in the middle of an argument. Equivocation creates the appearance of a logical connection between the reasons and the conclusion where, in fact, there is no logical connection. Like other logical fallacies, equivocation may be intentional or unintentional.

EXAMPLE "By his many past actions Senator Samuelson has shown his patriotism, his affection and high regard for his own country. Now, however, he is criticizing our country's foreign policy. This lack of patriotism makes him unworthy of reelection."

ANALYSIS The passage equivocates on the word *patriotism.* In the first sentence, it is defined as "affection and high regard for one's country." In the second passage, the term includes the idea of never criticizing one's country. Because of this shift of meaning, it is difficult to accept the speaker's conclusion as logical.

Vague terms. In all kinds of speaking situations, from everyday conversation to public debates, people often do not use precise language. They may not clarify what they mean by terms such as *good, large, harmful,* or *morally wrong.* Such imprecise language hinders communication and can lead to misunderstandings. It can also slow decision making and keep people from getting to the heart of difficult issues.

EXAMPLE "I believe in family values."

ANALYSIS What does this speaker believe in? It's hard to say. The term "family values" is extremely vague. It can mean many different things to different people, in part because families are so different. Would the "family values" of a Buddhist be the same as those of a Catholic? What specific values, or principles, does the speaker have in mind—obedience to one's parents? reverence for one's ancestors? equal sharing of childcare responsibilities by both parents? To be clear, the speaker should be more specific about what he or she means.

4.15 Understanding Propaganda Techniques

Messages and materials created with the aim of stirring up support for (or opposition to) a particular cause are known as **propaganda.** Writers of propaganda materials frequently employ faulty arguments, such as those described in the preceding section. In addition, they try to influence readers and listeners by appealing to the emotions rather than logic. Becoming aware of the common techniques used in these materials can help you avoid being manipulated by propaganda appeals.

Bandwagon. Human beings have a basic need to feel included. **Bandwagon appeals** exploit this need by trying to make people worry about being different from others or being left out of the crowd.

EXAMPLE "If you don't take a cruise of the Caribbean on the *Grand Regina,* you'll be missing out on the time of your life. Don't be left out of the fun!"

ANALYSIS Is this statement really true? Are you being left out of the fun by not taking the cruise? Are there other ways you could have fun?

Transfer. The propaganda technique of **transfer** works on the principle of association. Two different things are linked together to make a positive (or negative) impression on the receiver of the message. For example, a television commercial for a particular cat food may show a cat doing amusing tricks. A billboard may show an attractive model wearing a certain brand of jeans. A political poster may show the candidate in front of a large American flag. In each example, the message-maker's intention is for the good qualities of one thing (the cat, the model, the flag) to "rub off on," or transfer to, another thing (the cat food, the jeans, the politician). Messages based on transfer, of course, do not appeal to your powers of reasoning.

False testimonial. A testimonial is a statement endorsing a person, product, or idea. Advertisers and politicians often solicit testimonials from experts as well as celebrities. Unpaid testimonials may be worth listening to, provided the person giving the testimonial has the appropriate expertise.

EXAMPLE A veterinarian, whose real name is given, appears on a television commercial to recommend a particular dog food.

ANALYSIS Although a veterinarian may be knowledgeable enough about dog nutrition to make a trustworthy endorsement, the vet was almost surely paid to take part in the commercial. Thus, his opinion may not be objective.

Loaded words. Different words can refer to the same thing but carry radically different connotations (see the Language Arts Survey, 2.153, "Connotation and Denotation"). A word may have strongly positive, strongly negative, or relatively neutral connotation. Using words with strong connotations can be a way to sway opinion without offering reasons.

EXAMPLE "It's time to transfer responsibility for welfare from the federal government to the states."
"Congress is dumping the welfare program on the states without channeling funds to the states to carry out the programs."

ANALYSIS The word choices in each statement reflect different points of view. The first speaker views the shifting of welfare programs to the states positively and thus uses the phrase *transfer responsibility.* The second speaker describes the same action using the word *dumping,* a word with a negative connotation.

Character assassination. This is a form of *ad hominem* argument that tries to persuade by attacking the character of one's opponent.

EXAMPLE "Ms. Velasquez, a mother of three children, was divorced after five years of marriage. Anyone who can't keep a family together doesn't belong on the school board."

ANALYSIS Ms. Velasquez may be very well qualified to serve on the school board. The speaker, however, has not addressed her relevant qualifications but only attacked her character.

Bias charges. The charge of bias is a form of *ad hominem* argument that attacks a speaker's neutrality on an issue. A person who has something to gain from the outcome of a decision has a motive for distorting information in his or her favor. However, a person may have a personal stake in an issue and still be objective. If you suspect that a person is biased, use extra care in examining his or her arguments to make sure they are logical.

EXAMPLE "Congressman Doody of Texas is only in favor of this legislation because it will give a big tax break to Texas ranchers."

ANALYSIS The congressman represents a state that will benefit significantly from the legislation, so he may indeed be biased. The possibility of bias does not mean his arguments on the issue should be ignored, but they should be scrutinized.

READING SKILLS

4.16 Reading Rates

The purpose you have for reading something affects how you read it. You may read slowly and carefully in many situations and use skimming or scanning in others.

READING RATES

Technique	Purpose	Tips
Scanning	Finding specific information quickly	Look for key words; look at chapter and part headings.
Skimming	Getting a general idea of the content of a piece	Ask questions; look at introductions; look at chapter and part headings.
Slow and careful reading	Learning and enjoyment	Read actively.

Scanning

When you are looking through written material to locate some particular piece of information, you use the quick-reading technique of **scanning.** For example, you might scan the newspaper to find out whether your city council voted to approve a curbside recycling program at a recent meeting. You would turn to the section on city news, and then glance quickly over the headlines on each page until you saw the words "city council" or "recycling." Once you located the article, you would then begin reading carefully to gather the information.

You use scanning frequently during research, whenever you consult a reference work or look up something in the index of a book. In your classes, you have probably also scanned reading selections to find answers to questions or quotations and other support for your opinions. When you scan, you should pick out just a few key words to look for; this will help you find the desired information faster.

Skimming

When you read by **skimming,** you glance quickly through a piece of writing to get a general idea of it. When doing research, skimming can help you determine which books and articles will be most useful or interesting. Skimming is also a good way to preview assigned reading selections or review them before taking a test or writing an essay.

Your skimming will be more effective if you keep the following questions in mind:

- What is this piece of writing about?
- What does the author say about it?
- What evidence or support is given?

When you skim, read the title and any headings and subheadings within the piece first. This step should answer the first question. Then, read the first few paragraphs until you have a satisfactory answer to the second question. To find an answer to the third question, read the first and last paragraphs of each section. Also, glance at any material that is set off from the main text, such as boxed paragraphs or other special features.

Slow and Careful Reading

When you read for learning or for pleasure, you will read slowly and carefully to get the most out of what you are reading. When reading in this thorough way, you will read every word and look up any words you do not know in a dictionary. You will also take time to reread sentences or passages that you found especially striking or that seemed unclear the first time through.

Slow and careful reading allows you to reflect on your reading as you go. You may pose questions, evaluate evidence, or imagine yourself in the place of a character or the author. In these ways and many more, you become engaged in what you are reading (see the Language Arts Survey, 4.18, "Reading Actively").

4.17 Previewing Your Reading

If you take a few moments to preview your reading, you will read more efficiently. The previewing steps described can help get you thinking about what you are about to read.

PREVIEWING ACTIVITIES	
1. **Read** the title.	**Ask:** What is the piece about? What seems to be the author's attitude toward it?
2. **Skim** the first paragraph(s).	**Ask:** What is the main point of the piece?
3. **Skim** the last paragraph(s) (but not if the piece to be read is work of literature).	**Ask:** What is the author's conclusion?
4. **Read** the headings.	**Ask:** What are the main points?
5. **Summarize** and **plan** your reading.	**Ask:** Do all the parts seem to fit together? Do I have any unresolved questions?

4.18 Reading Actively

When you read actively, you respond mentally to what you are reading. Thinking about what you are reading can increase your enjoyment of reading as well as your comprehension.

Responding to Your Reading

One good active-reading technique is to keep your journal close by and record your reactions to what you are reading (see the Language Arts Survey, 1.2, "Keeping a Writer's Journal"). After a section or paragraph you might pause to ask yourself questions like these:

- "Do I agree with what the author (or character) just said?"
- "This last section makes me feel especially happy (or sad). What in particular makes me feel this way?"

You can note and evaluate your responses as you read, or you might prefer to wait until after you finish reading to record your thoughts and feelings.

Questioning

Questions have a way of commanding a listener's attention more than statements. If you pose questions to yourself as you read, your mind will be more alert to the content and meaning of what you are reading. You can use *who, what, where, when, why,* and *how* questions, as shown in the chart that follows. In this book, you can also use the Guided Reading questions and the Responding to the Selection questions to assist your reading.

TYPES OF READER RESPONSE QUESTIONS	
Who?	• Questions about characters or persons in the text • Questions about the author
What?	• Questions about objects and events
Where?	• Questions about location
When?	• Questions about sequence • Questions about time period

CONTINUED

Why?	• Questions about motivation • Questions about reasoning and evidence
How?	• Questions about possibilities • Questions about actions

Predicting

Trying to guess what will happen next, and why, is an excellent way to become involved in your reading. The impulse to predict is a natural part of reading, and predictions can be a useful starting point for a discussion when you are reading a selection with others.

Summarizing

To **summarize** is to simplify a piece of writing into a briefer statement of main points. Summarizing can help you understand what you have read by forcing you to focus on the most important points. When you summarize ideas in your own words, you are more likely to remember and understand them. Just remember not to go beyond the ideas that are actually in the piece.

Identifying Main Ideas

You can often locate the main idea in a piece of nonfiction writing in the introduction; look for a thesis statement. In a single paragraph, the main idea will frequently be stated in a topic sentence. Sometimes, though, you will have to infer the main idea because it is not stated directly. When you are reading difficult material, pausing briefly after each paragraph to restate the main idea in your own words can increase your understanding.

Identifying Relationships

Another technique that can improve your understanding of what you read is to notice words and phrases that reveal how the piece is organized. For example, words such as *first, second,* and *finally* are clues that the ideas are being presented in chronological or degree order. In addition, writers often use phrases or explicit statements to call attention to relationships between people, things, or ideas.

Making Inferences

When you **make an inference,** you put together pieces of information to draw a conclusion that is not explicitly stated. In a work of fiction, an author may describe a character's personality directly. More often, though, the author shows what the character is like through the character's actions and words. The reader must then infer the character's traits from these details.

Making inferences is an essential skill in reading nonfiction. An author may present certain evidence but leave the intended conclusion unstated. In other cases, such as a persuasive piece, an author may be unaware of certain inferences that can be drawn from the evidence given. As a critical reader, you might spot such overlooked inferences and use them to show flaws in the author's reasoning.

4.19 Reading Charts and Graphs

Charts and graphs are handy ways to present ideas and information in a compact, visual form. Readers use the title, headings, labels, and notes on the chart or graph to understand the information it contains.

Pie charts. A **pie chart** is a circle divided into pie-shaped sections that represent portions of some whole thing. It shows how different amounts compare to each other and to the whole.

EXAMPLE: The whole pie represents the crop production in a particular state. The pie is divided into four sections. Each section represents a different crop harvested: corn, soybeans, wheat, and all others. Each section is also labeled, in thousands of bushels as well as the percentage of the whole represented by that amount. The pie chart quickly shows that corn represents more than half the total crop production of the state, and that more than twice as much corn as soybeans was produced.

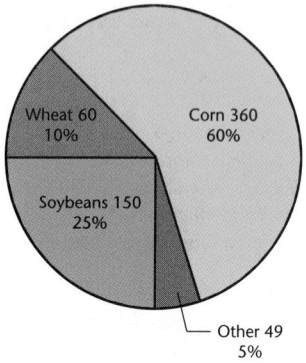

Bar graphs. A **bar graph** shows absolute amounts of something by representing the amounts as parallel bars of different lengths. A bar graph allows you to quickly compare relative quantities. However, you cannot tell from a bar graph how those quantities are related to some whole amount. Be sure to read all the labels on a bar graph carefully so you know exactly what quantities are represented.

EXAMPLE: The following graph shows the number of fiction and nonfiction books read by students in four different English classes in one year. Each class's totals are grouped together, so you can readily make comparisons within and between classes.

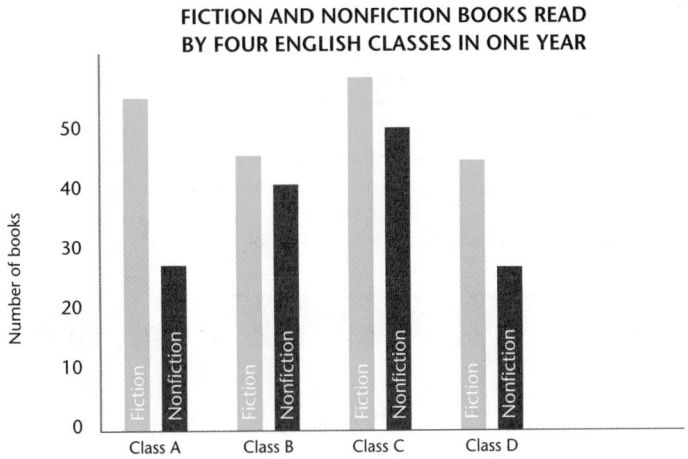

Sometimes designers use unusual "bars" to make bar graphs more interesting visually. These design changes can misrepresent the relative sizes of the bars and give a misleading impression. Be sure to read the graph labels and related text carefully before drawing a conclusion.

Line graphs. A **line graph** shows how the amount of one thing changes in relation to some other thing over time. The line connecting the amounts shows that the change is a continuous process.

RESEARCH SKILLS

When you conduct **research,** you are looking for ideas and information. The spark for your research could be a question you want to answer, a hypothesis you want to test, or a certain subject or idea you want to better understand. As you explore various sources of information, you will find not only part of the answer to your question but also leads to additional sources of information that will assist your investigation.

Different kinds of library materials require slightly different researching techniques. The ones you will use most frequently are described in the following sections.

4.20 The Classification of Library Materials

Each book in a library has a unique identification number, or **call number,** that is printed on the **spine,** or edge of the book. This number is used to classify the book; it also helps the library keep track of the book as it is used.

There are two common systems for classifying library books. The **Dewey Decimal System** is used in most school and public libraries. The **Library of Congress Classification System** (known as the LC system) is used in most college libraries.

In either system, the first part of the call number categorizes the book by its subject. Books on the same subject are conveniently grouped together on the library shelves in call number order. As you can see from the following charts, the subjects used in each system are very general. Each classification system has a way to narrow down the book's subject by using a specific number for each different subtopic. For example, in the Dewey Decimal System the book *Arctic Dreams* by Barry Lopez might have the call number 508.98 / Lo. This book is in the 500s, the general category that includes science. Within that class the number 508 shows that the book is a work of literature about natural history. The additional numbers after the decimal indicate that the book is about the natural history of the Arctic region.

THE DEWEY DECIMAL SYSTEM

Call Numbers	Subjects[1]
000–099	Reference and General Works
100–199	Philosophy, Psychology
200–299	Religion
300–399	Social Studies
400–499	Language
500–599	Science, Mathematics
600–699	Technology
700–799	Arts
800–899	Literature
900–999	History, Geography, Biography[2]

1. The Dewey system does not number fiction. Works of fiction are arranged alphabetically by author.
2. Biographies (920s) are arranged alphabetically by subject.

In the LC system, the call number begins with one or two letters that identify the general subject area. The numbers after the letters identify the more precise topic within the overall area. For example, the Lopez book might have the call number QH84.1 / L67 /1986. The Q shows that the book is in the general category that includes science. The letter pair QH identifies the subject more specifically as natural history, and the number after QH specifies the geographic area that the author is writing about.

The second part of the call number distinguishes individual books on the same subject. In the Dewey system, the first one to three letters of the author's last name may be added on a second line; notice the *Lo* in the Dewey number above. In the LC system, the second part of the number usually includes a letter (the author's last initial) and number that uniquely identifies the author. This second element falls after a decimal point. An LC call number may also include a date of publication.

THE LIBRARY OF CONGRESS SYSTEM	
Call Letters	**Subjects**
A	Reference and General Works
B–BJ	Philosophy, Psychology
BK–BX	Religion
C–DF	History
G	Geography, Autobiography, Recreation
H	Social Sciences
J	Political Science
K	Law
L	Education
M	Music
N	Fine Arts
P	Language, Literature
Q	Science, Mathematics
R	Medicine
S	Agriculture
T	Technology
U	Military Science
V	Naval Science
Z	Bibliography, Library Science

Locating materials in the library. In addition to books, library collections contain many other types of materials including magazines, newspapers, audio and video recordings, microfilm and microfiche, and government documents. Each type of material is typically stored in a separate part of the library and has its own classification system. For example, back issues of newspapers stored on microfilm have their own index and numbering system, and the microfilm materials and equipment may be located in the periodicals department or a separate microfilm section. Government documents are shelved in one location and also have their own numbering system.

If you know the call number of a book or the subject classification number you want, you can generally go directly to the bookshelves, or **stacks,** to obtain the book. Use the signs at the ends of the rows to locate the section of call numbers that you need. Then scan the call numbers on the spines of the books to find the right shelf. In a large library you may need to consult a map or sign showing where different call number areas are located. Look for these signs at assistance desks or near elevators and room entrances.

Some libraries, such as large city libraries or historical societies, have closed rather than open stacks. If you want to obtain a book, you write its call number on a request slip and give it to a librarian, who will retrieve the book for you.

4.21 Using Searching Tools

The library's **catalog** lists of all the books in the library. If your library has a computerized catalog, you will need to learn how to use your library's particular system. Usually you will find a sign or flyer near the computer that explains how to use the system. In addition, the computer keys may be labeled to assist you.

Author info.	Lopez, Barry Holstun, 1945-
Title	Arctic dreams: Imagination and Desire in a Northern Landscape
Date of pub.	1986
Publisher	Charles Scribner's Sons
LC Call no.	QH84.1 L67 1986
ISBN no.	ISBN 0-684-18578-4
No. of pages	xxix, 464 p.
Page size, cover material	23 cm., pap
Copyright info.	c1986 Barry Lopez
Index info.	Includes index
Supplementary sections	xvi, 222 p.: maps: 24 cm.
Subject	Natural history—Arctic regions

With most computerized catalogs, you have a choice of searching by author, title, subject, or key words. The following chart gives you some hints for doing each type of search. Capitalization does not matter when you type your entry. You should, however, double-check your spelling, because the computer cannot compensate for spelling errors.

COMPUTERIZED CATALOG SEARCHES

Search by . . .	Example	Hints
author	gould, stephen j	Type last name first. Type as much of the name as you know.
title	mismeasure of man	Omit articles such as *a, an,* or *the* at the beginning of titles.
subject	intelligence tests; ability—testing	Use the list of subjects provided by the library.
key words	darwin; intelligence; craniology	Use related topics if you can't find anything in your subject.

Author and title searches are generally straightforward. Subject searches, on the other hand, require extra thought. It is important to make sure that the subject heading you use is one that the computer recognizes. For example, if you look up "South Sea Islands" and find nothing, it is likely that the library uses different wording for this subject, such as "Pacific Islands." Sometimes the system will respond with a message telling you how to reword your heading or with a list of related subject headings.

Many libraries use the list of subjects published by the Library of Congress, but others use different lists. Your best bet is to look up a particular subject before doing your search to see what wording the library uses. **Cross-references** in the list will help you find the right subject headings to use. For example, after typing in the search heading: "South Sea Islands," you might find "*See* Pacific Islands."

Once you locate a list of books that match your subject search, you can "page" through the list of titles and call up a screen of detailed information for each title that interests you. This screen provides such information as the number of pages in the book and the subject headings that are used to classify the book. This screen may also tell you if the book is checked out. If you find books that seem to be exactly what you are looking for, jot down the subject headings listed on the screen and use those in new searches. For each book you want, write down the call number and then head for the stacks (see the Language Arts Survey, 4.20, "The Classification of Library Materials: Locating Materials in the Library").

Interlibrary Loan. Many libraries are part of a larger library network. In these libraries, the computerized catalog lists all the books owned by several libraries. The catalog will tell you which library has the volume you want. If the book is in a different library, you can request it. In some libraries, you do this by typing a particular command on the computer and entering your library card number; in other libraries, you fill out a request slip and give it to a librarian. The book is then shipped to your library. Depending on whether the book is checked out by someone else, you may wait a few days or several weeks for the book.

4.22 Using the Card Catalog

A **card catalog,** like a computerized catalog, contains brief information about each book in the library. In this type of catalog, the information is typed on paper cards, and the cards are arranged alphabetically in drawers. For each book there is a **title card,** one **author card** for each author, and at least one **subject card.** All of these cards show the book's title, author, and call number. Thus, you can search for a book by author, title, or subject (see the Language Arts Survey, 4.21, "Using Searching Tools").

Once you have located the books you want, write down the call number of each book and then go to the shelves (see the Language Arts Survey, 4.20, "The Classification of Library Materials: Locating Materials in the Library). If you cannot find a particular book you need in the card catalog, ask the librarian if your library can obtain books from another library through an interlibrary loan.

Some libraries are in the process of changing from card catalogs to computerized catalogs. To be thorough in your search, you may need to search in the computer system for newer books and in the card catalog for older books.

AN AUTHOR CARD

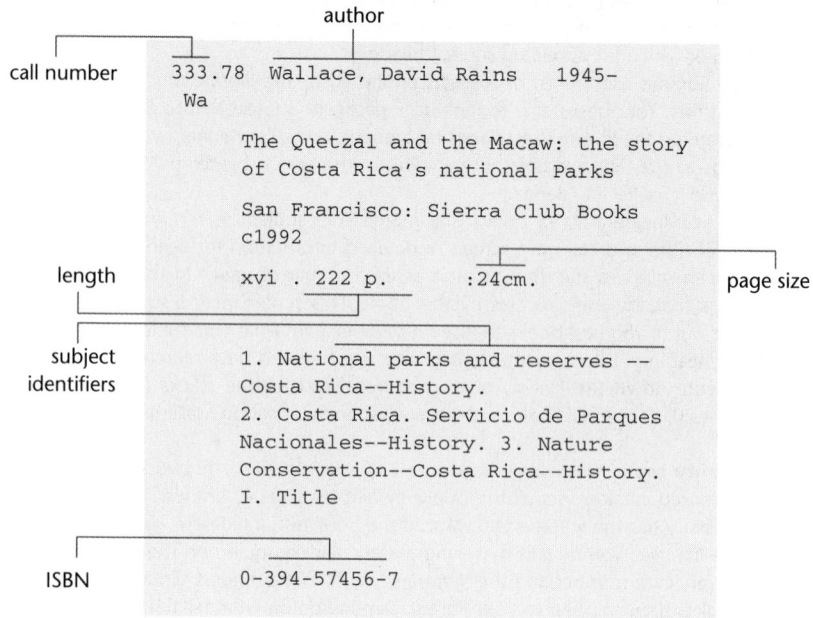

A TITLE CARD

```
333.78  The Quetzal and the Macaw: the story
Wa      of Costa Rica's national parks

        Wallace, David Rains, 1945-.

        The Quetzal and the Macaw: the story
        of Costa Rica's national parks.

        San Francisco: Sierra Club Books,
        1992

        xvi. 222 p: maps:24cm.


        1. National Parks and reserves--
        Costa Rica--History.
        2. Costa Rica. Servicio de Parques
        Nacionales--History. 3. Nature
        conservation--Costa Rica--History.
        I. Title


        0-394-57456-7
```

A SUBJECT CARD

```
NATIONAL PARKS AND RESERVES--COSTA RICA--
                HISTORY

333.78  Wallace, David Rains, 1945-
  Wa.

        The Quetzal and the Macaw: the story
        of Costa Rica's national parks

        San Francisco: Sierra Club Books,1992

        xvi. 222 p.: maps: 24cm.


        1. National parks and reserves--Costa
        Rica--History.  2.  Costa  Rica.
        Servicio de Parques Nacionales--
        History. 3. Nature conservation--
        Costa Rica--History. I. Title.


        0-394-57456-7
```

4.23 Using Reference Works

If you've ever browsed through the reference section of a library, you have some idea of the fabulous array of reference books that are published. **Reference works** are compilations of knowledge organized for easy access. No matter what question you have, the chances are good that a reference book can help satisfy your curiosity. Some reference works, such as the library catalog and **indexes,** list sources of information. Other reference works, such as encyclopedias, atlases, and almanacs, contain the actual information that may answer your question. In most libraries, current reference works cannot be checked out.

Almanacs and **Yearbooks.** An **almanac** is a densely packed collection of facts and statistics of all sorts, often presented in list form. The information in an almanac covers many different fields such as economics, education, crime, postal information, elections, natural disasters, and sports. Do you want to find out the year when President Woodrow Wilson was born? the Oscar-winning pictures for last year? the capital of Bosnia Herzgovina? An almanac is often the quickest way to answer such factual questions. Use the index to locate information in an almanac.

Most almanacs are published annually and include a summary of major events from the previous year. A more detailed overview of the year's events can be found in a **yearbook,** which is published separately. Some encyclopedia publishers produce yearbooks, which are shelved with the encyclopedias.

Atlases. An **atlas** is a collection of maps, but every atlas has a specific focus and typically includes other information as well. The maps in some atlases show natural features, such as rivers, lakes, and mountain ranges. Others show political features, such as countries and cities. Still others show more specialized kinds of geographic information, such as climate, population, natural resources, or transportation routes. A **historical atlas** features maps of places as they were in the past; such maps can help you locate and trace historical events. To locate a specific item on a map, use the **gazetteer,** an index that lists every feature on each map.

Encyclopedias. An encyclopedia is intended to be a survey of knowledge. **General encyclopedias,** such as *Grolier's, Britannica,* and *World Book,* contain information on topics from all branches of knowledge. **Specialized encyclopedias,** such as *The Encyclopedia of World War II,* contain articles about a particular branch of knowledge.

The different topics in an encyclopedia are treated in **articles,** which are arranged alphabetically by topic. Sometimes you will look up a topic in an encyclopedia and not find an article about it. In such cases, a different word or phrase was probably used to identify the topic. Look in the index to determine which headings to use for your topic. The index of a multivolume encyclopedia is found in one or two separate volumes.

When you begin to research a topic, the relevant article in the encyclopedia will give you a concise overview of the subject. However, since an encyclopedia article is a survey, it may not contain the specific information you need. For more detailed information, you will need to delve into books, magazine articles, and other sources. The sources of information listed at the end of the encyclopedia article can be a good starting point.

Indexes. An **index** lists articles or other published works according to their subject. Indexes help you locate possible sources of information about your topic.

An index covers a limited number of publications, usually of a certain type. For example, *The Reader's Guide to Periodic Literature* is a comprehensive index to articles in a large number of popular weekly, monthly, and quarterly magazines and journals. Other indexes list only newspapers. Some periodicals, such as the *New York Times* and *National Geographic,* publish their own indexes, listing articles in past issues. Most indexes are published in sequential volumes that are issued yearly, monthly, or every few months. Some indexes, including the *New York Times Index,* are available on microfilm.

Periodicals. A **periodical** is a publication that is issued at regular intervals, such as weekly, monthly, or quarterly. Magazines, newspapers, and professional journals are all examples of periodicals. Because they are published frequently, periodicals are excellent sources of up-to-date information. However, they are also published quickly; therefore, the information in periodicals is sometimes less reliable than similar information found in books.

You can usually find current issues of periodicals in a library reading room. Recent issues may be stored beneath or behind the current issues or on shelves in the periodicals section. Older issues may be stored as bound volumes in open or closed stacks, or copied onto microfilm or microfiche. Generally, older issues will be kept only for periodicals containing information of lasting interest.

Other reference works. In addition to the works previously described, most libraries have a range of basic reference works, including collections of biographies (for example, *Dictionary of American Biography, Contemporary Authors, Who's Who),* quotations (for example, *Bartlett's Familiar Quotations),* and book reviews (for example, *Book Review Digest).* Your library may also have specialized dictionaries, telephone and business directories, law books, college catalogs, and many other kinds of materials.

4.24 Using Dictionaries

Dictionaries provide the spelling and definition of words, but they also provide other kinds of information about each word.

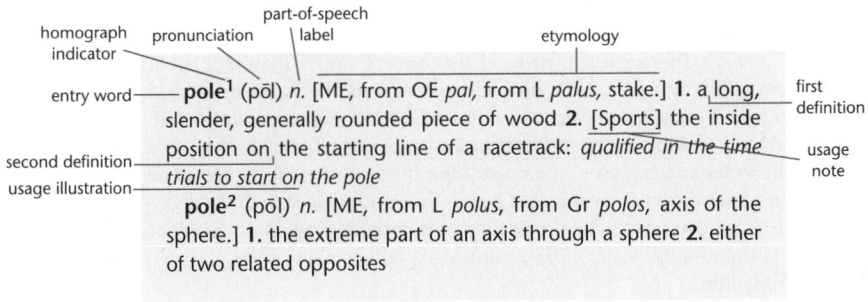

Directly after the entry word the **pronunciation** is given, usually in parentheses. A complete key to pronunciation symbols is given in the Table of Contents. In some dictionaries, a simplified key is also provided at the bottom of each page.

The abbreviation of the **part of speech** commonly follows the pronunciation (see the Language Arts Survey, 2.3–2.31, "The Parts of Speech"). In the example, the letter *n* shows that the word is used as a noun. If a word can be used as more than one part of speech, the definitions will be grouped by part of speech; for example, all noun meanings might precede all verb meanings.

The **etymology** is the history of a word. In the first entry, the word *pole* can be traced back through Middle English (ME) and Old English (OE) to the Latin word *palus* which means "stake." Sometimes two words that are spelled exactly alike have different etymologies. Such words are called **homographs** and are always listed as separate entries. A number superscript before or after the word indicates that the word is a homograph.

Each **definition,** or meaning of the word, is numbered. The first definition is the most common meaning.

Usage notes, such as "slang" or "colloquial," describe any nonstandard usages. Sometimes an entry includes an illustration of how the word is used. In the second definition of *pole*[1], the **usage note** is in square brackets and the **usage illustration** appears in italics after the colon.

4.25 Using Thesauruses

When writers find themselves at a loss for the right word, they often turn to a thesaurus. A **thesaurus** is a reference book that groups words with similar meanings. The entries lists synonyms and related words, as well as antonyms. You can use a thesaurus to find fresh words and more precise words to use in your writing. If you become a frequent user of a thesaurus, as well as the dictionary, you will become more aware of the different shades of meaning that similar words can have. This knowledge will add richness to your writing.

Thesauruses are of two types. A dictionary-type thesaurus is organized alphabetically. However, it does not contain as many entries as a dictionary. If a particular word is not listed, try looking up a word with a similar meaning. In lengthy entries, words that share a particular shade of meaning may be grouped together under a subheading. Antonyms are listed at the end of the entry. You may also find cross-references to entries for related words.

Roget's Thesaurus is organized by concept rather than alphabetically. Pierre Roget invented a system to categorize all existence and ideas. He used his categories as headings and grouped words with similar or related meanings under each heading. He also created an index of related words. To use *Roget's Thesaurus,* you look up your word in the index at the back of the book. Under the word are listed a number of related words and their essential meanings. Choose the related word with the meaning that is closest to what you want. Then look up the numbered section or subsection given after the word. Although *Roget's Thesaurus* takes a little while to master, many writers prefer this thesaurus.

4.26 Computer-Assisted Research

On-line Research

Many different sources of information are available via computer. Users access these on-line sources by subscribing to individual services such as CompuServe, Nexis, America Online, and Eworld. Through such services you can obtain current news, refer to on-line encyclopedias, look at government documents, receive homework and study assistance, and use various research databases. You may also be able to use the service to connect to the Internet, an electronic network that links you to universities, libraries, businesses, government agencies, and individuals around the world. Your school may also be connected to a special education network, such as TENET (Texas Education Network). If your school and library have access to some on-line services, take some time to find out what resources are available to students.

CD/ROM and Other Computer Media

A large and growing number of databases, indexes, reference works, and other educational materials are available on CD/ROM. For example, many public libraries have a comprehensive periodicals index on CD/ROM, similar to the *Reader's Guide,* that is updated regularly. In some cases the CDs are changed only by the librarians; in other situations, you may be able to select from a collection of CDs and insert them in the computer yourself.

4.27 Other Sources of Information

Vertical files. Many libraries collect and store useful information of various kinds in vertical file cabinets. The folders in these files contain miscellaneous materials such as brochures, local newspaper clippings, maps, posters, and photographs. The files are usually arranged alphabetically, but the materials are uncataloged. Depending on your topic, you may want to check these files for relevant materials.

Organizations and associations. For some research projects you may need to obtain information from organized groups. Local businesses and business associations; religious, political, and community organizations; and professional societies are usually eager to provide information on topics of interest to them. Keep in mind, though, that such groups often take a particular stand on an issue or have a particular point of view. Since their materials may be biased, you will need to read them carefully (see the Language Arts Survey, 4.15, "Understanding Propaganda Techniques").

Community institutions such as colleges, museums, historical societies, art galleries, orchestras, and other performing arts groups can also be good sources of ideas and information on certain topics.

You can find information about many kinds of organizations in the *Encyclopedia of Associations.* If you need to contact local groups, check the telephone book for names and addresses.

Experts. You may be able to find someone in your own community who is knowledgeable about your topic. This person might be a working professional with a specialized education—such as a college professor, doctor, engineer, or lawyer—or someone who has acquired their expertise simply through experience, such as a business owner, weekend woodworker, or Little League coach. Many of these people are eager to share their knowledge and experience with others.

If you don't know anyone who is an expert on your topic, ask your teachers, parents, friends, and relatives if they know of anyone who might help you. You can either ask your contact to arrange an interview, or arrange one yourself by calling the person directly (see the Language Arts Survey, 1.27, "Interviewing"). You can also check the phone book or library resources to locate experts.

Before speaking to your expert for the first time, remember that you are asking a favor. When you call, be specific about why you are contacting the person and how you would like the person to help you. Then prepare for the interview, so you can obtain the information you need without wasting the interviewee's time. A maximum time limit on the interview of fifteen to twenty minutes is a good guideline.

4.28 Evaluating Sources

When researching a project, you won't be able to read everything that has been written on your topic. Because you must be selective about your sources, you will need to evaluate each one carefully. A source must not only contain the information you need, but also be accurate. Ideally, a source will be

- **Unbiased.** An author who has something to gain personally from what people think about a subject may distort or omit certain facts. Possible signs of author bias are using loaded words, overlooking obvious counterarguments, and being associated with a particular organization, especially one that is politically active.

- **Authoritative.** When a source is reliable and trustworthy, it is considered authoritative. An authoritative author is one who is highly respected by others in the same field. An authoritative publication is one that has a reputation for being responsible and precise in presenting information.
- **Timely.** Depending on the subject, a current source or a less-than-current source may be reliable. In fields such as medicine or computer science, knowledge is expanding rapidly, and books can go out of date very fast. In a field such as mythology or art, however, a book that is ten years old may be acceptable. If you are doing historical research, you might seek out older works deliberately. Your teacher or librarian can help you decide how current your sources need to be.
- **Available.** If a source seems excellent but will not be available in the time you need it, you may have to rely on other sources instead. If you want to use a book that is not immediately available, find out from your librarian how long you can expect to wait.
- **At the appropriate level.** A source must present the information you need at a level you can understand. Materials written for much younger readers may be uninformative or even misleading. On the other hand, books written for an expert audience may presume knowledge that you do not have, and thus be too difficult to use.

4.29 Bibliographies and Bibliography Cards

Bibliographies. A **bibliography** is a list of sources on a particular topic. When you write a research paper, your teacher will ask you to include one of the following types of bibliography.

TYPES OF BIBLIOGRAPHY	
Complete Bibliography	A comprehensive list of works on your topic
Works Cited *or* References	A list of all the works referred to or quoted in your paper
Works Consulted	A list of every work you learned from in your research, even if you did not directly use or cite these works in your paper

The chart on pages 999–1002 gives examples of proper bibliographic form for many different types of materials.

When you are preparing your bibliography, first arrange your bibliography cards (see page 1003) in alphabetical order. Type or copy the information from each card onto your paper. Follow the correct form for each type of entry, as shown in the chart. Set up your pages and type the bibliography as described in the chart on page 1003.

FORMS FOR BIBLIOGRAPHY ENTRIES

A. A book with one author

Freidel, Frank. Franklin D. Roosevelt: A Rendezvous with Destiny. Boston: Little, Brown, 1990.

B. A book with two authors

Note that only the first author's name is inverted.

Laycock, George, and Ellen Laycock. The Ohio Valley: Your Guide to America's Heartland. Garden City, NY: Doubleday, 1983.

C. A book with three authors

Note that only the first author's name is inverted.

Alred, Gerald, Walter Oliu, and Charles Brusaw. The Professional Writer: A Guide for Advanced Technical Writing. New York: St. Martin's, 1992.

D. A book with four or more authors

The abbreviation *et al.* means "and others." Use *et al.* (and others) instead of listing all the authors.

Carlson, Arthur E., et al. Essentials of Accounting. 6th ed. Cincinnati, OH: South-Western, 1991.

E. A book with no author given

Pictures of Ideas: Learning Through Visual Comparison and Analogy. Dickson, Australia: Curriculum Development Centre, 1980.

F. A book with an editor, but no single author

Wiggington, Eliot ed. The Foxfire Books. Garden City, NY: Anchor/Doubleday, 1972.

G. A book with two or three editors

Driscoll, Mark, and Jere Confrey, eds. Teaching Mathematics: Strategies That Work. Portsmouth, NH: Heinemann, 1986.

H. A book with four or more editors

The abbreviation *et al.* means "and others." Use *et al.* instead of listing all the editors.

Covington, Paula H., et al. Latin America and the Caribbean: A Critical Guide to Research Sources. New York: Greenwood Press, 1992.

I. A book with an author and a translator

Dostoevsky, Fyodor. The Brothers Karamazov. Trans. Constance Garnett. New York: Modern Library, 1950.

J. A second or later edition of a book

Kennedy, X. J. An Introduction to Poetry. 2nd ed. Boston: Little, Brown, 1971.

K. A book or monograph that is part of a series

McNeil, W. K., ed. Southern Folk Ballads. American Folklore Series. Little Rock, AR: August House, 1987.

L. A multivolume work

If you use only one volume of a multivolume work, cite only that volume; otherwise cite only the entire work.

James, D. Clayton. The Years of MacArthur. Vol. 3. Boston: Houghton Mifflin, 1985.

James, D. Clayton. The Years of MacArthur. 3 vols. Boston: Houghton Mifflin, 1970-1985.

M. A titled volume with its own title that is part of a multivolume work with a different title

Smith, Page. A New Age Begins. Vol. 1, A People's History of the American Revolution. New York: Penguin Books, 1976.

N. A republished book or literary work available in several editions

Give the original publication date after the title. Then give complete information, for the edition that you have used.

Austen, Jane. Sense and Sensibility. 1811. New York: Oxford University Press, 1990.

O. A government publication

U.S. Commission on Civil Rights. Accommodating the Spectrum of Individual Abilities. Washington, DC: GPO, 1983.

Parts of Books

A. A poem, short story, essay, or chapter in a collection of works by one author

Helprin, Mark. "A Vermont Tale." Ellis Island and Other Stories. New York: Laurel, 1981. 84-104.

B. A poem, short story, essay, or chapter in a collection of works by several authors

Dickinson, Emily. "There's a certain slant of light." Master Poems of the English Language. Ed. Oscar Williams. New York: Washington Square Press, 1967. 783.

C. A novel or play in a collection under one cover

Shakespeare, William. Henry VIII. King John and Henry VIII. Ed. David Bevington. New York: Bantam Books, 1988. 179-295.

D. An introduction, preface, foreword, or afterword written by the author(s) of a work

Altick, Richard. Introduction. The Scholar Adventurers. New York: Free Press, 1966.

E. An introduction, preface, foreword, or afterword written by someone other than the author(s) of a work

Keillor, Garrison. Foreword. The Sheep Book. By Ron Parker. New York: Ballantine Books, 1983.

F. A reprint of a previously published article or essay
Give complete information for the original publication, followed by "Rpt. in" and complete information for the collection.
Toth, Susan Allen. "Free to Just Be." Family Life (Mar./Apr.) 1994. Rpt. in Utne Reader (July/Aug. 1994): 128-130.

Magazines, Encyclopedias, Reports, Newspapers, and Newsletters

A. An article in a quarterly or monthly magazine
Hill, Mary. "Medieval Dyeing." Spin-Off. Fall 1989: 66-69.

B. An article in a weekly magazine
Lodge, Sally. "The School Book Club Wars." Publishers Weekly, 27 July 1990: 118-126.

C. A magazine article with no author given
"Cameras." Consumers Digest, Nov./Dec. 1993:90+.

D. An article in a daily newspaper
Hong, Sun. "China Spurs German Trade." China Daily, 25 April 1995:5.

E. An editorial in a newspaper
"Talking Straight about Taxes." Editorial. Plain Dealer, 26 April 1995: 10B.

F. An article or story in a journal
Give the volume number, the year, and the page number(s) after the title of the journal.
Miller, Allan, and Dorita Coen. "The Case for Music in the Schools." Choral Journal, 35.7 (1995): 9-11.

G. An article in an encyclopedia, dictionary, or other alphabetically organized reference work
Give the title of the article, the title of the work, and the year.
"Ida Bell Wells-Barnett." Black Women in America: An Historical Encyclopedia. Ed. Darlene Clark Hine. Brooklyn, NY: Carlson, 1993.

H. A review
Slung, Michele. "Hairballs and Havoc." Rev. of James Herriot's Cat Stories. By James Herriot. New York: St. Martin's Press, 1994. New York Times Book Review, 11 Sept. 1994: 12.

I. A report for a pamphlet
Same as for a book.

Media and Other Sources

A. An interview that you have conducted

Jacques, Brian. Personal interview. 3 March 1995.

B. A letter that you have received

Giovanni, Nikki. Letter to the author. 10 November 1994.

C. A fax or e-mail communication

Same as for a letter.

D. A thesis or dissertation

Debois, Hayward. "Archaeological Remains in Mammoth Cave, Kentucky." Thesis. University of Kentucky, 1991.

E. A film

The Conversation. Writ., prod., dir. Francis Ford Coppola. 113 min. Paramount Pictures, 1974.

F. A work of visual art

Klee, Paul. The Idea of Firs. Solomon R. Guggenheim Museum, New York.

G. A television or radio program

Give the episode name; the names of the episode's writer, director, producer, or actors; the series or program title; and any information that you wish to include about the series's writer, director, or producer. Then give the network, station call letters, city, and date.

"Ambos Nogales." Writ. Marty Rochlin. SoundPrint. PBS. WOSU-AM News 820, Columbus, 6 May 1995.

H. A musical composition

Weill, Kurt. The Three-Penny Opera.

I. An audio recording (LP, compact disc, audio-cassette tape)

O'Brien, Tim and Molly. Remember Me(CD). Dunham, NC: Sugar Hill Records, 1992.

J. A lecture, speech, or address

Give the name of the speaker and the name of the speech. If there is no title, give the kind of speech—e.g. lecture, introduction, address. Then give the event, place, and date.

Abraham, Ronald. Keynote address. Tree-planting ceremony. Mount Vernon, OH. 30 April 1995.

MANUSCRIPT FORM FOR BIBLIOGRAPHIES

1. Begin on a new page.
2. Indent one inch from both side margins, one and one-half inches on the left side and one inch on the right side if the report is to be bound.
3. Place your last name and the page number, flush right, half-an-inch from the top of the paper.
4. Drop down another one-half-inch and insert the title "Works Consulted" or "Works Cited." Use uppercase and lowercase letters, and do not underscore.
5. Begin each entry at the left margin. Single space within each entry. Indent run-over lines five spaces from the left margin.
6. Double space between the title and the first entry and between each entry.

Bibliography cards. For each source that you might use, you should prepare a 3" x 5" card giving complete bibliographical information. Having each source on an individual card will make it easy to organize and prepare your list of sources when you are done writing (see the Language Arts Survey, 4.33, "Documenting Sources in a Report"). The cards can also help you find the source again later if you need it. Follow the proper form for the type of material when preparing your cards. A sample bibliography card is shown following the chart.

INFORMATION TO INCLUDE ON A BIBLIOGRAPHY CARD

Author(s)	Write the complete name(s) of all author(s), editor(s), and translator(s).
Title	Write the complete title, including any subtitle and any series title. If the piece is an article or chapter in a periodical or book, write • the title of the particular piece; • the beginning and ending page numbers; and • the title of the larger work.
Edition	Note "2nd edition," "revised edition," etc.
Publisher	Write exactly as it appears on the title page.
Place and date of publication	For periodicals, write the date as well as the issue and volume numbers. For republished works, write both the original publication date and the date of your edition.
Location and call number	Note where you found the book. If it is in a library collection, write the call number.
Card number	Give each bibliography card that you prepare a number. Write that number in the top right-hand corner of the card and circle it. When you take notes from the source, include this number on each note card so that you will be able to identify the source of the note later on.

SAMPLE BIBLIOGRAPHY CARD

①

Lopez, Barry. Arctic Dreams: Imagination and Desire in a Northern Landscape. New York: Charles Scribner's Sons, 1986.

QH Ferguson Public Library
84.1
L67

4.30 Paraphrasing and Summarizing

Quoting. A **quotation** is a phrase, statement, or passage borrowed word for word from someone else. To show that the words are not your own, place quotation marks before and after the quoted sentences or words (see the Language Arts Survey, 2.104 and 2.105, "Quotation Marks I and II," and 2.124, "Quotations"). Generally, you should use quotations in your writing when you need to prove that someone made a specific statement or when the unique wording of the quotation is essential to a point you are trying to make. Do not use quotations simply as a replacement for writing about a topic in your own words. Whenever you quote someone else, be sure to check the accuracy of the quote and provide an appropriate citation (see the Language Arts Survey, 4.33, "Documenting Sources in a Report").

Paraphrasing. A **paraphrase** is a restatement of someone else's ideas in your own words. Many of the notes you take may be paraphrases. However, it is generally safer to quote directly in your notes and then paraphrase as you draft your piece. This practice can help you avoid quoting a source without realizing it.

Remember that if you paraphrase someone else's ideas, you are still obliged to give credit to the source of those ideas (see the language Arts Survey, 4.33, "Documenting Sources in a Report"). In this way, you acknowledge that you are borrowing the ideas.

Summarizing. When you summarize a piece of writing, you condense and simplify it into a brief statement of the main points. Most details are omitted. A one-sentence summary of a

Gettysburg Address

President Lincoln mourns the Union and Confederate soldiers who died at Gettysburg and places their sacrifice in the larger context of preserving the Union.

piece of writing will include very few details, as in the following example:

A summary should be written entirely in your own words and should present only what the author said. Be careful not to incorporate your own ideas or opinions when you write a summary.

Outlining. Outlining is a good way to summarize nonfiction reading (see the Language Arts Survey, 1.32 and 1.33, on outlining). An **outline** includes the main points of a piece of writing and the most important details about each main point. Minor or trivial details are omitted. When making an outline, you may wish to paraphrase the headings in the piece and to use your paraphrases as headings in your outline. After each heading, you can note the main points made in the section.

4.31 Informal Note-taking

When you are gathering information for personal use only, you can take **informal notes.** Informal note-taking is appropriate during class, when reading homework, or taking reporter's notes at a live event. Informal note-taking is similar to outlining (see the Language Arts Survey, 1.32, "Making a Rough Outline"). The main ideas become headings in your notes, and related details are written under each heading. If you are taking notes at a live event, you will also want to record the date, time, place, speaker or performer, and so on. Using phrases and abbreviations in your notes will allow you to take notes more efficiently.

EXAMPLE OF INFORMAL NOTES

SOURCE MATERIAL "Immigrants to the United States came for many reasons: to escape poverty, unemployment, and crowded living conditions and to escape religious and political persecution."

NOTE Reasons for immig. to U.S.
—poverty, unemploy., overpop.
—relig., and polit. persecution

When you are through taking notes, it's a good idea to read over them. If you spot any illegible or confusing phrases or abbreviations, write them out so they will make sense when you review your notes later.

4.32 Formal Note-taking

When you may need to quote or document your sources, you will need to take **formal notes.** Research for a paper or debate, for example, requires formal note-taking. Use 4" x 6" index cards and record a single quotation, paraphrase, or summary on each card, as shown in the following:

SAMPLE NOTE CARD

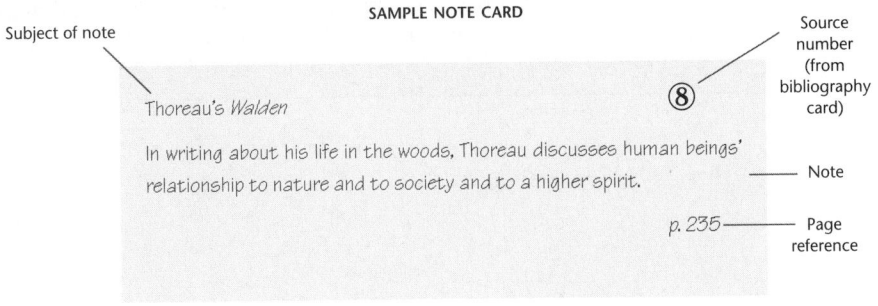

PREPARING NOTE CARDS

1. Identify the source at the top right corner of the card. (Use the source numbers from your bibliography cards.)
2. Identify the subject or topic of the note on the top line of the card. (This will make it easier to organize the cards later.)
3. Use a separate card for each fact or quotation. (This will make it easier to organize the cards later.)
4. Write the page number or numbers after the note.

Observe the guidelines that follow when making each type of formal note.

FORMAL NOTE-TAKING

Type of Note	When to Use	What to Watch for
Quotation	When the exact wording of a primary source is important to your topic; or When you are providing a definition; or When the wording of a secondary source is particularly elegant, pithy, concise, amusing, etc.	Be sure you exactly copy spelling, capitalization, punctuation, and numbers. Place quotation marks around all direct quotations. Record, when appropriate, explanatory background information about the speaker or the context of a quotation.
Paraphrase	Most of the time	Bear in mind your main purpose, and note only points that are related to your topic. Place quotation marks around any quoted words or phrases.
Summary	When the point in which you are interested does not require the detail of a paraphrase	Reread the source after writing your summary to be sure that you have not altered the meaning.

4.33 Documenting Sources in a Report

Documentation. Always let your readers know when you are using the words or ideas of others by **documenting** your sources. A note that tells the source of an idea or statement is called a **citation** or a **reference.**

Any writer who presents the words or ideas of someone else as if they were the writer's own is guilty of **plagiarism.** Plagiarizing may be intentional or unintentional; in either case, the writer has used others' words or ideas without giving them credit. Plagiarism is a form of stealing. This offense is seriously punished in most schools, often with a failing grade for the project, or worse. Outside of school, those who plagiarize may be charged with violating copyright law and sued by those from whom they have stolen.

Documenting your sources helps to prevent plagiarizing, but it is important for other reasons as well.

- **Accuracy.** Properly documenting facts and opinions helps readers to judge their accuracy and reliability. Your writing will be more convincing and authoritative if you tell readers the exact source of your information.
- **Courtesy to Reader.** Knowing the source for an idea or fact allows readers to go to the source on their own for further information.
- **Scholarship.** Furnishing documentation shows honesty as well as respect for the contributions to knowledge made by others.

Parenthetical documentation. The most widely used method for citing sources is **parenthetical documentation.** In this method, the writer places a brief note identifying the source immediately after the borrowed material. This type of note is called a **parenthetical citation,** and the act of placing such a note is called **citing a source.**

A parenthetical citation has two parts. The first part briefly identifies the source. This identification should clearly correspond to the entry as it appears in your list of "Works Cited" or "Works Consulted" (see the following examples). For example, if the entry begins with a title, the citation often includes the first word or two of the title. The second part of the citation gives the specific page number or place in the source where the information can be found. If the source is named in the text, omit the source in the citation and give only the page number.

SAMPLE PARENTHETICAL CITATIONS

A. For works listed by title, use an abbreviated title.

Sample bibliographic entry

"Ida Bell Wells-Barnett." Black Women in America: An Historical Encyclopedia. Ed. Darlene Clark Hine. Brooklyn, NY: Carlson, 1983.

Sample citation

. . . Wells, orphaned at the age of sixteen, became the caretaker of her younger brothers and sisters . . .("Ida" 1242)

B. For works listed by author or editor, use the author's or editor's last name.

Sample bibliographic entry

Mettger, Zak. Reconstruction: American After the Civil War. New York: Lodestar, 1994.

CONTINUED

Sample citation

. . . Many female teachers who set up schools for freed slaves were persecuted by white vigilantes (Mettger 32-33). . .

C. When the listed name or title is stated in the text, cite only the page number.

. . . Mettger notes that Southern churches acted as schoolhouses (34). . . .

D. For works of multiple volumes, use a colon after the volume number.

Sample bibliographic entry

"Man in the Moon." Funk and Wagnalls Standard Dictionary of Folklore, Mythology and Legend, 2 vols. Ed. Maria Leach. New York: Funk and Wagnalls, 1950.

Sample citation

"Probably all North American Indians . . .have some explanation for the dark patches of the moon." ("Man" 2:672).

E. For works quoted in secondary sources, use the abbreviation "qtd. in."

Sample bibliographic entry

Lloyd, Pamela. How Writers Write. Portsmouth, NH: Heinemann, 1987.

Sample citation

. . . Sue Townsend notes, "My characters are all the people I've ever observed or met." (qtd. in Lloyd 73). . . .

F. For classic works that are available in various editions, give the page number from the edition you are using, followed by a semicolon; then identify the section of the work to help people with other editions find the reference.

Sample citation

. . . At the opening of Hardy's Tess of the D'Urbervilles, Tess's father learns that his ancestors were once nobility (18:ch.1). . . .

G. For classic works of poetry or drama you may omit the page reference completely and cite the section and line numbers.

Sample citation

. . . Wordsworth describes the soothing effects of solitude in nature (Prelude 4.354-369). . . .

ABBREVIATIONS FOR CITATIONS	
pt.	part
bk.	book
ch.	chapter
sec.	section
sc.	scene
par.	paragraph

4.34 Footnotes and Endnotes

Footnoting and endnoting are less widely used than parenthetical documentation. You may encounter these two systems of documentation in your research.

Footnotes. Citations that are placed at the bottom of the page rather than within the text in parentheses are called **footnotes.** With this system, a superscript number or other symbol is placed in the text at the appropriate point, and a matching number or symbol identifies the footnote. Footnotes may be used for purposes other than documentation. They may supply additional information that is useful or interesting but not important enough to be placed in the text. For example, the numbered footnotes in the literature selections of this book define obscure words and provide background information.

Endnotes. Many books have **endnotes** instead of footnotes. Endnotes are exactly like footnotes, but they are gathered at the end of a book, chapter, or article. Some authors or publishers prefer endnotes because they are less distracting to the reader than footnotes and they make it easier to lay out the pages of the book.

TEST-TAKING SKILLS

OBJECTIVE TESTS

4.35 Strategies for Taking Objective Tests

The tests you take in your classes, like other tests that life offers, challenge you to do and be your best. Most athletes, for example, willingly enter into challenging situations. These situations test their skills and allow them to excel to new levels. In the same way, when you prepare for and take a classroom test, you can actually increase your knowledge and understanding. Tests not only assess learning; they stimulate it.

To do your very best on a classroom test, you need to study and get involved with the material presented by your teacher. When you read your text or other books, read carefully. During class discussions, listen actively and take thorough notes. It's also important to stay healthy, so you will be alert to the information and ideas you encounter.

Many of the tests you take will be objective tests containing multiple-choice, true/false, and short-answer questions. The suggestions in the following chart and the subsequent sections can help you do your best when taking objective tests.

STRATEGIES FOR TAKING OBJECTIVE TESTS

Before the Test

- Get ample sleep the night before the test.
- Eat a nutritious breakfast.
- Study over as long a period of time as possible.
- Review frequently.
- Try to predict questions that may be on the test, and make sure you can answer them.
- Bring *extra* pencils, erasers, and any other required materials.

During the Test

- Determine how much time is allowed for each question. If a question takes too long, guess and/or come back to it if you have time.
- *Read each question carefully.*
- Work quickly but do not rush.
- Write legibly.
- Review all your work before submitting it.

4.36 True/False Questions

A true/false question is really a statement; your task is to decide whether the statement is true or false. If you do not know the answer to a true/false question, guess.

Because true/false tests are strongly influenced by guessing, you have a 50/50 chance of guessing correctly on each question. Their results may not accurately reflect a person's knowledge. If you are given a true/false test, keep an eye out for these possible traps:

Negatives and double negatives. The word *not* completely changes the meaning of a sentence. To evaluate a sentence that contains a negative, see if its opposite makes sense or is plausible. If it does, the original must be false.

Quantifiers and qualifiers. Look for words such as *all, sometimes, never, many, some,* and *few.* Since few statements are true without exception, statements containing absolute words such as *all* or *never* are more likely to be false. Statements with qualifiers such as *some* or *few* are more likely to be true.

Excess information. In a true/false question, the more information a statement contains, the more likely it is to be false. Only one part of the statement needs to be false to make the entire statement false.

4.37 Multiple-choice Questions

In a multiple-choice item, a question is presented and you must select the correct or best answer from a list of choices. Sometimes the "question" is an incomplete statement and you must complete the statement correctly from the list of choices. If you read a question and know the answer immediately, look for it in the choices. Otherwise, read through each answer to rule out incorrect or inappropriate choices.

EXAMPLE The "Gettysburg Address" and "Concord Hymn" are two works that pay honor to

a. the foresight of the founding fathers.
b. the sacrifice of soldiers killed in battle.
c. the contributions of African Americans.
d. the ideals of the transcendentalists.

4.38 Short-answer Questions

Short-answer questions are answered with a word, a phrase, or a sentence. They frequently occur in quizzes and in class discussions. Your teachers may require that responses to short-answer questions be complete sentences.

EXAMPLE What incident gave rise to Walt Whitman's poem, "When Lilacs Last in the Dooryard Bloom'd"?

The poem was a response to the assassination of President Abraham Lincoln.

STANDARDIZED TESTS

4.39 Strategies for Taking Standardized Tests

As a high school student, you may encounter standardized tests at several points in your school career. States and school districts use such tests to assess achievement. In addition, students planning to go to college take standardized tests in order to apply for admission and scholarships.

SOME STANDARDIZED TESTS

Common Abbreviation	Test
PSAT/NMSQT	Pre-Scholastic Aptitude Test/National Merit Scholarship Qualifying Test
ACT	American College Testing Program
MAT	Miller Analogies Test
SAT	Scholastic Aptitude Test
ACH	College Board Achievement Tests

Standardized tests are made up of multiple-choice questions. You answer the questions on special sheets that can then be read and graded by a computer. To show your answer, you fill in a bubble. Be sure to use the type of pencil or pen specified by the test monitor and to fill in the bubble *completely* and *neatly.*

As you choose answers on a standardized test, keep these points in mind. If you don't know the answer, try to rule out some choices and then guess from the ones that remain. If you are worried about time, you can skip a difficult question and come back to it later (look for a blank space on your answer sheet). You should, however, try to fill in a bubble for each question, since an unanswered question is automatically incorrect. Remember, too, that you can only go back to questions within the current section of the test. Always follow the instructions of the test monitor.

4.40 Analogy Questions

An analogy question asks you to detect the relationship between a given pair of words and then recognize a similar relationship between another pair of words.

EXAMPLE WIND : AIR
(A) sound : instrument
(B) current : water
(C) sky : atmosphere
(D) breath : lungs
(E) heat : furnace

Before answering an analogy question, read and evaluate *all* of the answers. If two or more answers seem correct, choose the *best* answer. Make sure you focus on the *relationship* between the two words in the example. Do not be thrown off by irrelevant connections between individual words in the example and words in the choices.

4.41 Sentence-completion Questions

A sentence-completion question presents a sentence in which one or two words are missing. You must discover the relationship between the parts of the sentence, and then choose the word or words that best complete the sentence.

To answer a sentence-completion question you must try *all* of the choices to see which pair of words work *best* in the sentence. You can usually rule out one or two answers right away because they do not fit the structure or the context of the sentence.

EXAMPLE The senator_____ the new bill; he said it would have _____ effects on the environment.
(A) praised . . . mixed
(B) denounced . . . unfavorable
(C) invented . . . interesting
(D) rejected . . . positive
(E) ignored . . . incredible

4.42 Grammar, Usage, and Mechanics Questions

Grammar, usage, and mechanics questions present a sentence or paragraph with underlined and labeled words or passages for you to evaluate.

An **error-identification question** asks you to identify the part of the sentence that contains an error. You do not have to identify the type of error.

> Choose the letter that corresponds to any error in the sentence.
>
> "The Notorious Jumping Frog of Calaveras County" is among
> A
> Twain's most famous short storys. No error.
> B C D E
>
> (A) (B) (C) (D) (E)

An **error-correction question** asks you to choose a word or passage to replace the erroneous part of the sentence.

> Select the letter of the word or words that should replace the underlined word.
>
> By the time people arrive for the picnic, Marcus mows the lawn.
>
> (A) had mowed
> (B) will have mowed
> (C) has mowed
> (D) will mow
> (E) had been mowing

ANSWERING ERROR-IDENTIFICATION AND ERROR-CORRECTION QUESTIONS

1. Ignore the underlining and proofread the sentence or paragraph carefully.
   - Proofread for errors in grammar, usage, and mechanics.
   - Look especially for agreement—in tense, person, number, and mood.
2. If you do not find the error, look specifically at the underlined passages.
3. Read the whole sentence through before settling on your answer.

For information about grammar, usage, and mechanics refer to the Language Arts Survey, 2.1–2.153, "Essential Skills: Language." Completing your reading and writing assignments conscientiously will also help you prepare for these kinds of questions.

4.43 Reading Comprehension Questions

Reading comprehension questions require you to read a short piece of writing and then answer several questions about it. Some questions may address the content of the passage. Others may ask you to make an inference or draw a conclusion from the text. To select the correct answer, try all the choices. Make your selection based on the passage itself, rather than other knowledge or opinions.

STEPS IN ANSWERING READING COMPREHENSION QUESTIONS

1. Read all the questions quickly.
2. Read the passage.
3. Reread the first question carefully.
4. Reread the passage while bearing in mind the first question.
5. Answer the first question.
6. Continue with each subsequent question in the same manner.

4.44 Synonym and Antonym Questions

A synonym and antonym question presents a word and asks you to select a word that has the same meaning (for a synonym) or the opposite meaning (for an antonym). If none of the answers seem exactly correct, select the *best* answer.

EXAMPLE Write the letter of the word that is most nearly the *same* in meaning to the word in capital letters.

1. SVELT

(A) sour (B) soft (C) swollen (D) sleek (E) severe

To answer this type of question, try all of the choices to see which one works best. Often both synonyms and antonyms are included among the answers, so you should have the instructions clearly in mind to avoid accidentally choosing the wrong type of word. Also, don't choose an answer just because it (1) looks like or sounds like the given word, (2) has the same root, prefix, or suffix as the given word, or (3) is a long or unfamiliar word.

STRATEGIES FOR TAKING ESSAY TESTS

4.45 Analyzing an Essay Question

The first step in writing a good answer to an essay question is to make sure you understand the question. Read through the entire question. Then underline the key words that show what type of response is expected; if this is not possible, jot down the key words on your own paper. Many questions have more than one part, so check to see if more than one type of response is requested. By taking a few moments to analyze the question, you will know what tasks you must accomplish in the time available. The following chart identifies several common types of essay questions. The numbers in parentheses refer to the related sections of the Language Arts Survey.

UNDERSTANDING AN ESSAY QUESTION	
Type of Essay Question	**Tasks of Essay**
analyze (1.14, 1.33, 4.11)	break into parts and describe the parts and their relationships
compare; compare and contrast (1.33, 4.8)	identify and describe similarities and differences
describe; explain (1.33, 4.6)	tell the steps in a process; identify causes and effects
define; describe; identify (4.7)	classify and tell the features of
interpret (4.13)	tell the meaning and significance of
summarize (4.30)	retell very briefly, stating only the main points
argue; prove; show (4.12)	tell and evaluate reasons for believing a statement

4.46 Organizing an Answer to an Essay Question

Although you will probably not have time to go through the entire writing process, you should allow time for planning, drafting, and reviewing. If you take a moment to sketch out a plan and then pace yourself as you write, you should be able to complete your essay in the time available.

The planning stage is critical to your success. Begin by making a brief outline of the main points you want to make. Keep the tasks of the question in mind as you plan. Then add notes to support each point, such as examples and any quotations that fit your purpose.

When you begin drafting, work carefully to write a clear introduction that states your main points and leads logically into the body of your essay. Refer to the introduction as you write the body of the essay to help yourself stay on track.

If you find yourself running out of time, try to state your remaining main points, even if you cannot elaborate on them, and add a conclusion. Rounding out your essay in this way gives your reader a better idea of what you know and understand than if you abruptly break off before the end.

4.47 Reviewing an Answer to an Essay Question

Take as much time as you can to review and polish your essay. If you revise as you go, make sure you don't use up all your time editing an incomplete essay. The following chart offers some guidelines for reviewing essay questions.

QUESTIONS FOR REVIEWING AN ANSWER TO AN ESSAY QUESTION

- Does the essay answer all parts of the question?
- Does the introduction state clearly the main point of the essay?
- Is the conclusion consistent with the main point?
- Does the essay cover all the points in your outline?
- Are there any points that could be made more strongly or clearly?
- Is every word in the essay easily legible?
- Is the essay free of errors in grammar, usage, and mechanics?

ESSENTIAL SKILLS: *Applied English/Tech Prep*

LETTERS AND FORMS

Writing letters is one of the most practical kinds of writing you will ever do. You can use letters to develop and maintain friendships, to obtain information, to solve problems with individuals or businesses, to express appreciation, to speak out on social issues, and to impress future employers. Whenever you write a letter, you'll want to make sure that your writing reflects your purpose, has a voice and style appropriate for your reader, and conveys your message clearly.

Becoming familiar with the conventions of letter writing will help you achieve positive results with your letters. Following these conventions is especially important when writing letters to individuals or groups who don't know you personally.

5.1 FILLING OUT FORMS AND APPLICATIONS

Because forms are such an efficient tool for obtaining information, you can expect to encounter them in many day-to-day situations, such as registering for courses, visiting the doctor or dentist, doing business at the bank, and, of course, applying for employment. When you fill out a form or application, you should provide all of the information requested. At the same time, you should strive to make a positive impression on those who will read and evaluate the information you give.

Guidelines for completing forms:

- If possible, obtain an extra copy of the form or application.
- Gather any information you will need to complete the form.
- Read all the directions before you begin to enter your data.
- Be neat. Type or print your responses legibly, in pencil or ink, as directed. Avoid smudges or cross-outs.
- Write "N.A." or "not applicable," rather than leave a space blank, if a section of the form or application does not apply to you.
- Proofread. When you've completed the form, check your spelling, grammar, and punctuation, and review the information you've provided.
- If the form is messy or inaccurate, discard it and complete the extra form or application if you have one.
- When you've completed the form to your satisfaction, submit it to the appropriate person, or mail it to the correct address.

Application for Employment
City Services Department

Position Desired: Groundskeeping Assistant

Personal Data

Applicant's Name: Alvarez (*Last name*) Hector (*First Name*) M. (*Middle Initial*)

Address: 9818 Pontius Avenue (*Street*) Santee (*City*) CA (*State*) 92071 (*Zip*)

Phone: (619) 555-7643

Previous Work Experience

(List last two positions held, beginning with the most recent.)

Employer: Santee Public Library (*Name*) 200 James St. (*Address*)

Phone: (619) 555-9818

Employment Period: 1/95–present

Job Title: Library Assistant

Hours Worked: 4:00–6:00, Monday–Friday

Salary: $5.50/hr.

Description: Shelve books; assist at book return desk

Reason for Leaving: N.A.

Employer: Shawn's Lawn Care Service (*Name*) 927 West High Street (*Address*)

Phone: (619) 555-1918

Employment Period: June–August 1995

Job Title: Mower/trimmer

Hours Worked: Flexible, about 20 hrs./wk.

Salary: $5.00/hr.

Description: Mowed and trimmed lawns of all sizes; cleaned and maintained equip.

Reason for Leaving: Returned to school after summer vacation

CONTINUED

Education

(List last school attended.)

Santee High School	Santee CA 92071	9/93–	College Prep	N.A.
School Name	*Address*	*Dates Attended*	*Field of Study*	*Date Graduated*

References

Name: Mr. Shawn Dudgeon

Relationship to Job Applicant: Owner, Shawn's Lawn Care Service Years Acquainted: 1

Address: 22096 Montgomery Rd., Santee CA Phone: (619) 555-1177

Name: Mrs. Nadia Nijinski

Relationship to Job Applicant: Director, Milton Public Library Years Acquainted: 1

Address: 200 James St., Santee CA Phone: (619) 555-1918

Signature: Hector M Alvarez **Date:** 4/30/96

5.2 The Form of a Personal Letter

In an age when phones can follow us anywhere, communicating with distant friends and family by letter is far less common than it once was. Still, most people are delighted when a personal letter appears in the mail box. Unlike a phone call, a letter can be saved and enjoyed more than once. In addition, comments made in a letter tend to carry more weight than spontaneous comments. The reader knows that the writer sat down to compose the letter and took time to express his or her thoughts with care.

You can use personal letters to stay in touch with friends and relatives. You can also use them to say thank you for a gift or kindness, to congratulate others on their achievements, and to extend invitations. A personal letter may be semiformal or quite informal depending on the writer's relationship with the person who will receive the letter. It will typically include the following parts:

1. a **return address**, including the writer's address and the date the letter was composed;
2. a **salutation**, or greeting, followed by a comma;
3. the **body**, or text, of the letter;
4. an appropriate **closing**, followed by a comma;
5. a **signature**; and
6. an optional **postscript**, preceded by the abbreviation "P.S."

SAMPLE THANK-YOU LETTER

❶ 35889 Blanchard Road
Indianapolis, IN 46240
May 12, 1996

❷ Dear Grandad,

❸ I just want to thank you for the wonderful week at your cabin. I can't seem to keep myself from daydreaming about the Smokies—the popsicle-colored rhododendrons, the sunsets over the peaks, the soaring hawks—and your blueberry pancakes!

I especially enjoyed our early morning hike up Bald Mountain. The views in all directions were amazing. It would be fun to make the same trip in the fall or winter (hint, hint). Hope to see you soon.

❹ Love,

❺ *Lyonel*

❻ P.S.—In a separate package I'm sending you one of the sketches I made from the front porch of the cabin.

5.3 The Form of a Business Letter

When you write a personal letter, you can usually expect the recipient to respond positively to the letter and to you. A business letter, however, is frequently addressed to someone who has never met you or does not know you very well. The recipient often has only the letter on which to form an impression of you. Therefore, a more formal tone is appropriate. Following the widely accepted format for a business letter will also help to ensure that your letter makes a positive impression.

A business letter includes a **heading, salutation, body, closing,** and **signature,** just as in a personal letter. In addition, an **inside address** is used. The inside address is placed below the heading and above the salutation. It includes the name and title of the person to whom you are writing, the name of the company or organization, and its address (see the letter on page 1022). If you do not know the name of a person at an organization, you can use a department name instead. Occasionally, a business letter will include a **postscript.**

Make sure the salutation and closing of a business letter are respectful and formal. The most common salutation begins with the word "Dear" followed by the courtesy or professional title used in the inside address, such as "Ms.," "Mr.," "Dr.," "Miss," or "Mrs." If you are not writing to a specific person, use a salutation such as "Ladies and Gentlemen" or "Dear Sir or Madam." Complete the salutation with a colon.

In a business letter, you should avoid using creative closings. There are a number of acceptable closings, such as "Sincerely," "Yours truly," "Very truly yours," or "Respectfully yours." Capitalize only the first word of the closing and end the closing with a comma. Add your signature below the closing, in either blue or black ink. Your full name should be typed below your signature.

Business letters commonly take one of two forms. In **block form** (see page 1022), all the elements of the letter—the heading, inside address, salutation, body, closing, and signature—are aligned at the left margin. Paragraphs are not indented. In **modified block form** (see page 1022), the heading and closing appear on the right side of the page, just left of center and aligned with each other. Paragraphs are indented, usually five spaces in from the left margin.

In the body of your letter, word your message in a way that is clear and courteous. Use standard English, and avoid using slang or pet expressions, as you might in a personal letter. To make sure your letter is well organized, outline your main points before you begin to write. Then when you draft, strive to get your message across without wasting any words. Finally, proofread your letter carefully. Using correct grammar, punctuation, and spelling is essential if you want your reader to respond favorably to your letter.

Guidelines for Writing a Business Letter

- Outline your letter's main points before you begin the writing process.
- Type your letter, if at all possible, and use clean $8^1/_2$" × 11" white or off-white paper. Type on one side of the paper only.
- Select a standard business-letter format, either block form or modified block form.
- Use single-spacing, leaving a blank line between paragraphs.
- Select a standard salutation and closing.
- Stick to the subject, keeping the letter brief and informative.
- Be neat. A sloppy appearance may make your letter less effective.
- Check your grammar, usage, punctuation, capitalization, and spelling.
- Reread your letter. Have you conveyed your main points clearly and effectively? Don't make your reader guess at your intentions.

5.4 Types of Business Letters I

You will have many opportunities to compose business letters. For example, you might want to obtain information from a college or organization, request a refund from a company for a faulty product, tell an author why you admire a certain book, or state an opinion to your representative in Congress.

In any of these situations, you make a phone call, but a letter is often more effective. People generally pay more attention to written communications than they do to verbal ones. In addition, writing a letter allows you to save a copy of it as a record of your action. The copy could be an electronic one (if you typed your letter on a computer) or a photocopy. For example, if you are sending letters to several colleges to obtain admissions information, having copies of the letters allows you to keep track of your correspondence.

SAMPLE LETTER OF REQUEST

850 Bethel Road
Racine, WI 53404
November 30, 1996

Kenyon College
Office of Admissions
Gambier, OH 43022

Ladies and Gentlemen:

At a recent college fair at James Madison High School, I met Charlie Otting, an alumnus of Kenyon College who lives in the Racine area. His glowing comments about Kenyon made me think that this is a school I would like to know more about.

I think I would like the small-college atmosphere at Kenyon as well as the rural setting, since I come from a small town. Kenyon's high academic standards are also attractive to me, as is its commitment to high-quality teaching. I might be interested in studying biology or English.

I would appreciate receiving an information packet from you as well as information about how to apply for financial aid. I look forward to hearing from you soon.

Sincerely,

Rohini Pragasam

Rohini Pragasam

5.5 Types of Business Letters II

Some of the most important business letters you will write are those you address to potential employers. These letters will strongly influence which jobs you are hired for and thus the course of your career.

When you apply for a position, you will typically submit both a **résumé** and a letter of application, also called a **cover letter.** Your résumé presents a summary of your work experience and education. Your cover letter highlights specific accomplishments from your résumé and suggests how your unique mix of skills and abilities qualifies you for the position.

The information in your résumé and cover letter must be truthful and accurate, but you should shed a positive light on your experience. Don't be shy about emphasizing your strengths. Your résumé should be fairly specific in describing your background, but it's best to word it in a way that allows you to use it in various situations. You can use your cover letter to address specific qualifications for a particular job.

Guidelines for composing a cover letter:

- Limit your cover letter to a single page.
- State your interest in obtaining a position within the organization, indicating the type of position (or specific job opening) for which you'd like to be considered.
- If you are applying for a specific position, describe how you learned of the job's availability.
- Briefly describe your qualifications.
- Refer to your résumé, enclosed with your letter.
- Mention your interest in scheduling an interview and where and when you may be reached (typically by telephone) to make arrangements.
- Thank the reader for considering your application.

SAMPLE COVER LETTER

212 Hart Road
Centralia, IA 52009
May 15, 1996

Mr. Lynn Brannon
Director
Agriculture Broadcasting Network
4656 Lane Avenue
Dubuque, IA 52001

Dear Mr. Brannon:

Recently I spoke with an officer of the Dubuque County Farm Bureau, Ced Clinton, who told me that you may be looking for a summer intern to work as an office assistant at ABN. I am very eager to get involved with an agriculture-related organization and would like to be considered for the position, if it becomes available.

I have been a member of Future Farmers of America at Centralia High School for the past two years and have just been elected president of the local chapter. This summer I will be attending a National FFA Leadership Conference in Washington, DC. My plans after graduation in 1996 are to attend a four-year college and eventually join an agricultural business or organization.

I also have a strong interest in journalism. As a junior, I edit news articles for the school paper, *The Bee,* and contribute a monthly column about farm subjects of interest to teenagers. As a writer and editor, I have strong word skills and am familiar with word processing software.

If you would be interested in talking to me about my background and qualifications, please call me at 555–6636 any weekday after 4 p.m. Thank you for your interest.

Sincerely,

Donna McCreary

Donna McCreary
Enclosure: résumé

The information in a résumé may be organized in many different ways. Before you select an arrangement and style, take a look at some sample résumés in books at the library. Your guidance counselor also may have samples that you can study. Choose a style that looks neat and businesslike. Most résumés list the applicant's **objective,**or career goal, **work experience, education, extracurricular activities, skills,** and **references.**

The information in your résumé should fit on a single page and be typed on high-quality paper. Printed copies should also be on high-quality paper, preferably of the same type that you used for your cover letter. Make sure the printed copies are clean and easy to read.

SAMPLE RÉSUMÉ

Donna McCreary
212 Hart Road
Centralia, IA 52009
(319) 555–6636

Objective:

To obtain an entry-level job related to agriculture.

Work Experience:

10/95–present Check-out clerk, Quality Farm and Fleet, Dubuque, IA 52001

Handle customer purchases at check-out including returns and discounts. Named "Employee of the Month," March 1995

Summer 1995 Member, Junior Fair Board, Dubuque County Fair
Assist in planning and scheduling fair activities for youth, including livestock competitions, equine events, and 4-H displays

Education:

Centralia High School, Class of '97, College Preparatory program
Grade-point average: 3.4

Extracurricular Activities:
President, Future Farmers of America, Centralia Chapter
Secretary, Students Against Drunk Driving
Statistician for the varsity wrestling team

References:

Mr. Ced Clinton
President, Dubuque County Farm Bureau
3468 Amity Road, Dubuque, IA
(319) 555–9571

Ms. Debbie Armfeldt
Supervisor, Quality Farm and Fleet
460 Rockton Avenue, Dubuque, IA
(319) 555–8398

WRITING ON THE JOB

The ability to communicate clearly in writing is essential not just in the communications professions, such as journalism and publishing, but in almost every job. At work, you might use your writing skills to prepare instructions for others to use, evaluate a procedure, or summarize a conference with a coworker or client. If you know how to organize your thoughts and communicate them clearly on paper, you will have a big advantage in the workplace.

5.6 WRITING MEMORANDA

Employees within organizations frequently communicate using the interoffice **memorandum,** or **memo.** A memo may be sent to just one person, to a group of people, or to everyone working for an organization. The type of information communicated by memo varies. For example, a personnel officer might send a memo to all employees explaining a new benefit. A department manager might outline an assignment for someone in a memo. A secretary might send the boss a memo requesting a certain vacation time.

Memos are generally short, just a few sentences or paragraphs, but in some cases a longer memo is appropriate. A memo should be clear and to the point. It should also be free of errors, both factual and grammatical. Therefore, it's a good idea to review and proofread all memos before sending them.

In many organizations employees compose and type memos at computer workstations at their desks. Then, instead of distributing paper copies of the memo, they send the message over a computer network via electronic mail, or e-mail, to the desired recipients. In organizations that do not use computers extensively, employees may type their memos on standard forms. In the top area of a standard memo, after the letter "c:" (for "copies to") the sender usually lists the names of all recipients of the memo.

Memos range in tone from formal to informal. If you are conveying work-related information, the tone will be formal to semiformal. If the recipient knows you well or the purpose of the memo is social (such as announcing an office party), the tone will probably be more informal.

SAMPLE MEMO

MEMORANDUM

TO: Marketing Staff
FROM: Maria Kelly
DATE: June 30, 1995
SUBJECT: Tricia's going-away party
c: Ann Leonardo, president

As we all sadly know, Tricia Martin's last day will be Friday, July 3. However, we won't let her go without a proper send-off. At 4:00 on Friday, we will cut a cake and enjoy some punch in Tricia's honor and wish her well in her new job. The festivities will be in the large conference room on the second floor.

—Maria

5.7 Technical Writing

Technical writing is writing that tells the reader how to use certain equipment or execute certain tasks. Companies that produce complex equipment, such as computers or machines used in medical analysis, hire technical writers to produce the documentation that accompanies these products. This documentation is essential for using the equipment successfully. Consumers, as well as specialists such as automotive mechanics, engineers, pilots, and lab workers, rely on technical materials for instruction and training.

Regardless of what job you may have in the future, knowing the basic principles of technical writing can help you in your work. For example, most employees are at some time asked to explain a procedure or complex process in writing so that others can learn it. Understanding the characteristics of good technical writing can help you prepare clear and useful instructions.

Guidelines for documenting technical procedures:

- First, make sure you are very familiar with the procedure you'll be documenting.
- Break the task into a series of short, simple steps.
- Warn the reader of any potentially hazardous steps or materials.
- List any tools or equipment needed to complete the process.
- List each step in the proper sequence.
- Use the second person imperative. Write "Press the enter key," not "The user should press the enter key."
- Keep your vocabulary simple, avoiding unexplained technical jargon.
- If appropriate, incorporate pictures and diagrams.
- Don't leave out any steps or include unnecessary steps.
- Proofread your instructions to make sure they are easy to follow and unambiguous.
- Ask someone who isn't familiar with the operation to follow the directions you have written. If necessary, adjust your instructions based on his or her experience.

Writing about a technical procedure is a good test of how well you understand what you are trying to explain. Indeed, after you have written about the process, you will probably understand it much better. The ultimate test of your documentation, however, is to give it to someone else and see if your instructions lead to successful results.

5.8 Writing Promotional and Public Relations Copy

Like technical writing, public relations (PR) writing is a profession unto itself. The job of PR writers is to promote a particular product, organization, or cause through the messages they compose. They must know how to seize readers' attention and persuade them to feel positive about the thing they are promoting. PR writers must have excellent writing skills, but they must also have an in-depth understanding of both the product and the audience they are trying to appeal to. This understanding allows them to predict how people will respond to their messages. By studying the basic principles of good promotional writing, you can make your own persuasive writing more effective.

Promotional writers produce many kinds of materials including ads for radio, television, and newspapers; news and feature articles; press releases; scripts for audiovisual presentations; direct-mail materials; speeches for political candidates; and copy for annual reports. They work for private companies as well as government and community organizations.

Research and planning are essential for good public relations writing. Although the purpose of promotional writing is to persuade, the content of the writing must reflect the actual merits of the product. Messages that distort the truth can backfire, creating negative rather than positive feelings in the audience. At the top of a press release, you list the date on which the information can be released to the public, the name and phone number of the person to contact with questions about the release, and the name of the city in which the announcement is being made. At the bottom of a press release, write the word *end* surrounded by dashes.

SAMPLE PRESS RELEASE

For immediate release
June 1, 1996

Contact:
Trish Howley
(614) 555-1032

Columbus:

The Thurber House summer picnic series, a regular program of outdoor readings by authors, begins June 19. This year's lineup includes five distinguished writers of poetry and fiction: Peter Meindl (June 19), Sue Miller (July 3), P. F. Kluge (July 17), Julia Kastner (July 31), and David Citino (August 14).

The Wednesday-evening readings are held on the west lawn of the Thurber House, 77 Jefferson Avenue (indoors in inclement weather), just off the Broad Street exit from Interstate 71. Admission is $3. Box picnic dinners, catered by Moveable Feast, may be reserved in advance for $7. Doors open at 6:30. Readings begin at 7:30.

The Thurber House is a boyhood home of writer and cartoonist James Thurber. As a nonprofit learning center, Thurber House sponsors public readings, writing workshops, and literary conferences, as well as the Thurber House writer-in-residence program.

—END—

HANDBOOK OF *Literary Terms*

abridgment An **abridgment** is a shortened version of a work. When doing an abridgment, an editor attempts to preserve the most significant elements of the original. See also *abstract, bowdlerize,* and *paraphrase.*

abstract 1. *n.* An **abstract, *précis,*** or **summary** is a brief account of the main ideas or arguments presented in a work. A well-made abstract presents those ideas or arguments in the same order as in the original. Writing an abstract is an excellent way to commit to memory the major ideas of a nonfiction work such as an essay or a chapter in a textbook. See *paraphrase.* 2. *adj.* An **abstract** word or phrase is one that refers to something that cannot be directly perceived by the senses. *Liberty, justice, hope, courage,* and *loyalty* are examples of abstract terms. The opposite of *abstract* in this sense is *concrete.* See *concrete.*

absurd See *literature of the absurd.*

accent See *stress.*

acronym An **acronym** is a word created from the first, or initial, letters of a series of words. Examples of acronyms include *scuba,* from the words *self-contained underwater breathing apparatus,* and *SADD,* from the phrase students against drunk driving.

acrostic An **acrostic** is a poem organized so that the first or last letters of each line form a word, a phrase, or a regular sequence of letters of the alphabet.

act An **act** is a major division of a drama. The dramas of ancient Rome were generally divided into five acts, as were the plays of Shakespeare and other dramatists of the Elizabethan Age. In modern times, plays are most often divided into three acts, and short plays called "one-acts" are quite common. Tennessee Williams's "The Glass Menagerie" is a two-act play.

action The **action** is the sequence of events that actually occur in a literary work, as opposed to those that occur off-scene or that precede or follow the events in the work itself. A common literary technique, inherited from the classical *epic,* is to begin a work *in medias res,* in the middle of the action, and to fill in the background details later through flashbacks. This technique is often used in modern fiction, as in Ambrose Bierce's "Occurrence at Owl Creek Bridge." See *flashback.*

actor An **actor** is one who performs the role of a character in a play. The term is now used both for male and female performers.

adage See *proverb.*

adaptation An **adaptation** is a rewriting of a literary work in another form. A film adaptation of Edith Wharton's *The Age of Innocence,* directed by Martin Scorsese, appeared in 1993.

aesthetics **Aesthetics** is the philosophical study of beauty. *Aesthetic principles* are guidelines established for the making and judging of works of art. From age to age, accepted aesthetic principles have differed, and these differences have dramatically influenced the nature of works of art produced in those ages.

The ancient Greek philosopher Aristotle propounded an aesthetic of *mimesis,* or *imitation,* believing that the proper function of art was to provide an accurate portrayal of life, an idea perhaps best expressed in Shakespeare's description of dramatic art as "a mirror held up to nature." In sharp contrast to such an aesthetic is the idea, derived from the Greek philosopher Plato, that the function of art is to rise above ordinary nature and to embody ideal, or *sublime,* forms of a kind not found in this material world of the ordinary and transient.

In England and the United States, the dominant aesthetics have been the Neoclassical, dating from the eighteenth century; the Romantic, dating from the nineteenth century; and the Realistic and Naturalistic, dating from the late nineteenth and early twentieth centuries.

The Neoclassical aesthetic, typified by the works of Phillis Wheatley and Benjamin Franklin, values order, rationality, and artifice. The Romantic aesthetic, typified by the works of Edgar Allan Poe, values wildness, emotion, imagination, and nature. The Realistic aesthetic, typified by the works of Edith Wharton, Ernest Hemingway, and John Steinbeck, harkens back to Aristotle and values imitation, but imitation of a modern kind—of the depths as well as the heights of human experience. The Naturalistic aesthetic, like the Realistic, views the purpose of art as the accurate imitation of life, but it also attempts to show how all things, including human actions, thoughts, and feelings, are caused, or determined, by circumstances. Superb Naturalist writers include Stephen Crane and Theodore Dreiser.

The critic I. A. Richards claimed that a radical shift away from an aesthetic based on beauty to one based on interest occurred in the twentieth century. While beauty, however defined, remains the guiding principle of artistic judgment in lowbrow circles—as for example, in popular judgments made about sentimental novels and verses—interest has emerged as the primary standard by which professional critics today judge works of art. See *Naturalism, Neoclassicism, Realism,* and *Romanticism.*

affective fallacy The **affective fallacy** is the evaluation of works of art based not on their artistic merit but rather on their emotional effects on the reader, viewer, or listener. A person who holds a didactic or utilitarian view of the function of art would not consider this approach a fallacy. See *didacticism* and *Utilitarianism.*

afterword An **afterword** is a statement made at the end of a work, often an analysis, a summary, or a celebration of the preceding work. See *epilogue.*

Age of Reason See *Enlightenment* and *Neoclassicism.*

aim A writer's **aim** is the primary purpose that his or her work is meant to achieve. One commonly used method of classifying writing by aim, proposed by James Kinneavey in *A Theory of Discourse,* describes four major aims: to express oneself (expressive writing), to persuade (persuasive writing), to inform (informative writing), and to create a work of literary art (literary writing).

alexandrine An **alexandrine,** or **iambic hexameter,** is a verse with six iambic feet. See *meter.*

allegory An **allegory** is a work in which each element *symbolizes,* or represents, something else. Spirituals such as "Go Down, Moses" are often allegorical. "Go Down, Moses" is on one level about the captivity of the Israelites in Egypt but on another level can be read as being about the captivity of African Americans during the era of slavery. The fiction of Nathaniel Hawthorne, in which characters, objects, and events often represent moral qualities or circumstances, is highly allegorical. In one sense, all literature can be viewed as allegorical in that individual characters, objects, places, and actions are types representing others of their kind. See *concrete universal* and *extended metaphor.*

alliteration **Alliteration** is the repetition of initial consonant sounds. Some writers use the term as well to describe repeated initial vowel sounds. The following line from Henry Wadsworth Longfellow's "The Village Blacksmith" contains two examples of alliteration:

the repetition of the *h* sound in *He* and *hears* and the repetition of the *p* sound in *parson, pray,* and *preach:* "**He h**ears the **p**arson **p**ray and **p**reach."

allusion An **allusion** is a rhetorical technique in which reference is made to a person, event, object, or work from history or literature. In *Walden,* Henry David Thoreau makes allusions to many sources, including the *New England Primer*, the Bible, and Virgil's *Aeneid*. The alphabet rhymes in the *New England Primer* make many allusions to the Bible.

ambiguity An **ambiguity** is a statement that has a double meaning or a meaning that cannot be clearly resolved. In English, the word *cleave* is oddly ambiguous, for it can mean either "to cling together" or "to cut apart." Many literary *figures of speech,* including *metaphors, similes, personifications,* and *symbols,* are examples of intentional ambiguity, speaking of one thing when another is intended. In Poe's "The Pit and the Pendulum," after several struggles and victories with his "shackles," the prisoner exclaims "Free!—and in the grasp of the Inquisition!" He has staved off immediate doom but is still held prisoner. Poe thus examines the ambiguity or shades of meaning of a state like freedom.

amplification See *elaboration.*

anagram An **anagram** is a word or a phrase created by rearranging the letters of another word or phrase.

analogy An **analogy** is a comparison of two things that are alike in some respects but different in others. In an analogy, the comparison is direct, not implied. A *simile* is a type of analogy. See *simile.*

analysis **Analysis** is a thinking strategy in which one divides a subject into parts and then examines the relationships among the parts and between individual parts and the whole. An analysis of a short story, for example, might consist of a division of the work into such parts as the exposition, the rising action, the climax, the resolution, and the dénouement, along with an examination of the role played by each of these parts in advancing the plot. An analysis of a line of poetry might consist of a careful examination of its rhythm, its figures of speech, its images, and its meaning or meanings.

anapest An **anapest** is a poetic foot containing two weakly stressed syllables followed by one strongly stressed syllable, as in the word *wolverine.* A line of poetry made up of anapests is said to be *anapestic.*

anaphora An **anaphora**, as that term is used by linguists, is any word or phrase that repeats or refers to something that precedes or follows it. Consider, for example, the opening line of the Tewa "Song of Sky Loom":

> O our Mother the Earth, O our Father
> the Sky,

In this line, *the Earth* and *the Sky* are both examples of anaphora because they refer back to, or rename, the Mother and Father. The simplest form of anaphora is repetition of a word or phrase, as in the repetition of the word *nevermore* in Poe's "The Raven."

anecdote An **anecdote** is a brief story, usually with a specific point or moral. See *exemplum.*

antagonist See *character.*

antihero An **antihero** is a central character who lacks all the qualities traditionally associated with heroes. An antihero may be lacking in beauty, courage, grace, intelligence, or moral scruples. Antiheroes are common figures in modern fiction and drama.

antithesis **Antithesis** is a rhetorical technique in which words, phrases, or ideas are strongly contrasted, often by means of a repetition of grammatical structure.

aphorism An **aphorism** is a short saying or pointed statement. Examples of aphorisms include "Little strokes fell great oaks" and "Don't count your chickens before they hatch," both from Franklin's *Poor Richard's Almanac.* An aphorism that gains currency and is passed from generation to generation is called a *proverb* or *adage.* See *proverb.*

apology An **apology** is a literary defense. Emily Dickinson's "This is my letter the World" can be read as an apology.

apostrophe An **apostrophe** is a rhetorical technique in which an object or person is directly addressed. In "Song of the Sky Loom," the earth and the sky are addressed in the opening line.

apposition An **apposition** is a grammatical form in which a thing is renamed, in different words, in a word, phrase, or clause. The title of Frederick Douglass's autobiography contains an example: *Frederick Douglass, an American Slave.*

archaic language **Archaic language** consists of old or obsolete words or phrases such as *smote* for *hit.*

archetype An **archetype** is an inherited, often unconscious ancestral memory or motif that recurs throughout history and literature. The notion of the archetype derives from the psychology of Carl Jung, who wrote of archetypes as making up humanity's "collective unconscious." The term is often used, more generally, to refer to any element that recurs throughout the literature of the world. Thus the story of the journey, in which someone sets out on a path, experiences adventures, and emerges wiser, may be considered archetypal, for it is found in all cultures and in all times. See *motif.*

argument 1. An **argument** is a summary, in prose, of the plot or meaning of a poem or drama. 2. In nonfiction writing, an **argument** is the case for accepting or rejecting a proposition or course of action.

argumentation **Argumentation,** one of the modes of writing, presents reasons or arguments for accepting a position or for adopting a course of action. See *mode.*

art for art's sake **Art for art's sake** was the rallying cry of a group of nineteenth-century writers who believed that art should serve the ends of beauty and beauty alone, rather than some political, social, religious, or moral purpose. Champions of art for art's sake included Edgar Allan Poe and British writers Walter Pater, Oscar Wilde, and Andrew Lang.

article An **article** is a brief work of nonfiction on a specific topic. The term *article* is typically used of encyclopedia entries and short nonfiction works that appear in newspapers and popular magazines. The term is sometimes used as a synonym of *essay,* though the latter term often connotes a more serious, important, or lasting work. See *essay.*

aside An **aside** is a statement made by a character in a play, intended to be heard by the audience but not by other characters on the stage.

assonance **Assonance** is the repetition of vowel sounds in stressed syllables that end with different consonant sounds. An example is the repetition of the short *i* sound in this line from Robert Frost's "Birches":

> I like to think some boy's been swinging them.

atmosphere See *mood.*

autobiography An **autobiography** is the story of a person's life, written by that person. *The Autobiography of Benjamin Franklin* is a famous American autobiography. *Narrative of the Life of Frederick Douglass* is another well-known autobiography. Some editors and critics distinguish between *autobiographies,* which focus on personal experiences, and *memoirs,* which focus on public events, though the terms are often used interchangeably.

background information See *flashback, plot,* and *setting.*

ballad A **ballad** is a simple narrative poem in four-line stanzas, usually meant to be sung and usually rhyming *abcb. Folk ballads,* composed orally and passed by word of mouth from generation to generation, have enjoyed enormous popularity throughout history, from the Middle Ages to the present. Examples of popular American ballads include "The Ballad of Casey Jones" and "Bonny Barbara Allan." *Literary ballads* are ones written in imitation of folk ballads. The folk ballad stanza usually alternates between lines of four and three feet. Common techniques used in ballads include repeated lines, or *refrains,* and *incremental repetition,* the repetition of lines with slight, often cumulative, changes throughout the poem. See *refrain.*

bibliography A **bibliography** is a list of works on a given subject or of works consulted by an author. See *List of Works Cited.*

Bildungsroman A ***Bildungsroman*** is a novel that tells the story of the growth or development of a person from youth to adulthood. A fine American example is Betty Smith's *A Tree Grows in Brooklyn.*

biographical criticism See *criticism.*

biography A **biography** is the story of a person's life, told by someone other than that person. Carl Sandburg wrote a famous six-volume biography of Abraham Lincoln.

blank verse **Blank verse** is unrhymed poetry written in iambic pentameter. An *iambic pentameter* line consists of five *feet,* each containing two syllables, the first weakly stressed and the second strongly stressed.

blend A **blend,** or **portmanteau,** is a word created by joining together two previously existing words, such as *walrus,* from *whale* and *horse,* or *pixel,* from *picture* and *element.*

bowdlerize To **bowdlerize** a piece of writing is to censor it by deleting material considered offensive. The term comes from the name of Thomas Bowdler, who published a "bowdlerized" edition of Shakespeare's works in the nineteenth century.

bucolic A **bucolic** is a fanciful pastoral poem. See *pastoral poem.*

cacophony **Cacophony** is harsh or unpleasant sound. Writers sometimes intentionally use cacophony for effect, as Randall Jarrell does to describe an airplane dogfight: "I woke to blackflak and the nightmare fighters."

cæsura A **cæsura** is a major pause in a line of poetry, as in the following line from T. S. Eliot's "The Love Song of J. Alfred Prufrock":

Let us go then, || you and I,

Calvinism **Calvinism** is a Protestant theology, based on the teachings of John Calvin, that stresses original sin, the inability of people to exercise free will, the preordination of events by God, and the choice (or election) by God of those who will be saved (the elect) and those who will be condemned. Puritanism was a Calvinist movement. See *Puritanism.*

canon A **canon** is a group of literary works considered to be authentic or worthy. The term was originally used for Biblical books believed to be divinely inspired. It was later adapted to describe works that can be definitely assigned to a given author (as in *the canonical works of Mark Twain).* The term is also used to describe those works in a given literary tradition considered to be classics and thus worthy of inclusion in textbooks, in anthologies, and on the reading lists of courses in schools and universities. In the eighteenth century, there was much debate in France and England concerning whether the canon should include primarily modern or ancient works. In the twentieth century, debates over the canon often centered on the extent to which it should include works by non-male, non-European writers. Feminist critics, in particular, noted the tendency of editors and anthologists to include in their collections works by writers and to exclude works by female writers. See *feminist criticism* under the entry for *criticism.*

canto A **canto** is a section or part of a long poem. The word comes from the Latin *cantus,* meaning "song." Ezra Pound's masterwork was a collection of poems called *The Cantos.*

caricature In literature, a **caricature** is a piece of writing that exaggerates certain qualities of a character in order to satirize or ridicule that character or type. Washington Irving's Ichabod Crane in "The Legend of Sleepy Hollow" is an example of a caricature. See *satire.*

carmen figuratum See *concrete poem.*

carpe diem ***Carpe diem*** is a Latin term meaning "seize the day." The *carpe diem* theme urges people not to waste time but rather to enjoy themselves while they have a chance.

catalog A **catalog** is a list of people or things. Many examples of catalogs can be found in Walt Whitman's "Song of Myself."

catastrophe The **catastrophe** is a conclusion of a play, particularly of a tragedy, marked by the fall of the central character. In the catastrophe, the central conflict of the play is ended, or resolved. See *plot.*

catharsis The ancient Greek philosopher Aristotle described tragedy as bringing about a

catharsis, or purging, of the emotions of fear and pity. Debate has raged around the proper interpretation of Aristotle's statement. Some critics take it to mean, simply, that at the end of a tragedy, in the catastrophe or resolution, the emotional equilibrium of the characters is restored. Others take it to mean that viewing a tragedy causes the audience to feel emotions of fear and pity, which are then released at the end of the play, leaving the viewer calm, wiser, and perhaps more thoughtful. This idea of the purgative or cathartic effect of viewing enacted displays of strong emotion is contradicted by psychological studies that suggest that people tend to imitate enacted feelings and behaviors that they witness. Much of the current debate over violence on television and in films centers on this question of whether enacted violence has a cathartic or an arousing effect on the viewer.

censorship **Censorship** is the act of examining works to see if they meet predetermined standards of political, social, or moral acceptability. Official censorship is aimed at works that will undermine authority or morals and has often in the past resulted in the suppression of works considered dangerous or licentious. Famous American novels that have been frequent targets of censorship include *The Adventures of Huckleberry Finn,* by Mark Twain, and *Catcher in the Rye,* by J. D. Salinger.

central conflict A **central conflict** is the primary struggle dealt with in the plot of a story or drama. See *conflict* and *plot.*

character A **character** is a person (or sometimes an animal) who figures in the action of a literary work. A *protagonist,* or *main character,* is the central figure in a literary work. An *antagonist* is a character who is pitted against a protagonist. *Major characters* are ones who play significant roles in a work. *Minor characters* are ones who play lesser roles. A *one-dimensional character, flat character,* or *caricature* is one who exhibits a single dominant quality, or *character trait.* A *three-dimensional, full,* or *rounded character* is one who exhibits the complexity of traits associated with actual human beings. A *static character* is one who does not change during the course of the action. A *dynamic character* is one who does change. A *stock character* is one found again and again in different literary works. Examples of stock characters include the gunslinging outlaw of western fiction and the mad scientist of science fiction.

characterization **Characterization** is the use of literary techniques to create a character. Writers use three major techniques to create characters: direct description, portrayal of characters' behavior, and representations of characters' internal states. When using direct description, the writer, through a speaker, a narrator, or another character, simply comments on the character, telling the reader about such matters as the character's appearance, habits, dress, background, personality, motivations, and so on. When using portrayal of a character's behavior, the writer presents the actions and speech of the character, allowing the reader to draw his or her own conclusions from what the character says or does. When using representations of internal states, the writer reveals directly the character's private thoughts and emotions, often by means of an *internal monologue.* See *character* and *internal monologue.*

chiasmus A **chiasmus** is a rhetorical technique in which the order of occurrence of words or phrases is reversed, as in the line "We can weather changes, but we can't change the weather." Benjamin Franklin uses a chiasmus in "Remarks Concerning the Natives of North America" when he writes, "we should find no people so rude, as to be without any rules of politeness; nor any so polite, as not to have some remains of rudeness."

chronicle A **chronicle** is a record of historical events. *The General History of Virginia,* by John Smith, is a chronicle of the early years of the Virginia colony from 1607 through 1609.

chronological order **Chronological order** is the arrangement of details in order of their occurrence. It is the primary method of organization used in narrative writing. It is also common in nonfiction writing that describes processes, events, and cause-and-effect relationships.

classic A **classic** is a work of literature that is widely believed to be one of the greatest creations within a given literary tradition. (Mark Twain defined a classic as "something that everybody wants to have read and nobody wants to read.") The question of just what works may be considered classic, and thus the question of what constitutes the *canon,* is a much-debated one. See *canon.*

Classical Era The **Classical Era** is the period in European history that saw the flowering of the ancient Greek and Roman cultures. *Classical literature* is the literature of ancient Greece and Rome from the time of Homer and Hesiod to the fall of the Roman Empire in AD 410.

Classicism **Classicism** is a collection of ideas about literature and art derived from study of works by Greeks and Romans of the *Classical Era.* Definitions of what constitutes the Classical style differ, but most would agree that the Classical aesthetic emphasizes authority, austerity, clarity, conservatism, decorum, imitation, moderation, order, reason, restraint, self-control, simplicity, tradition, and unity. Classicism is most often contrasted with *Romanticism.* See *Classical Era* and *Neoclassicism.*

cliché A **cliché** is a tired or hackneyed expression such as *old as the hills* or *slow as molasses.* Most clichés originate as vivid, colorful expressions but lose their interest because of overuse. Careful writers and speakers avoid clichés, which are dull and signify lack of originality.

climax The **climax** is the point of highest interest and suspense in a literary work. The term also is sometimes used to describe the *turning point* of the action in a story or play, the point at which the rising action ends and the falling action begins. See *crisis* and *plot.*

closed couplet A **closed couplet** is a pair of rhyming lines that present a complete statement. The alphabet rhymes in the *New England Primer* are written in closed couplets, for example:

My *Book* and *Heart*
Shall never part.

closet drama A **closet drama** is one that is meant to be read rather than acted. Tennessee Williams wrote two versions of *The Glass Menagerie,* one of them a closet drama and the other an acting version of the play.

coherence **Coherence** is the logical arrangement and progression of ideas in a speech or piece of writing. Writers achieve coherence by presenting their ideas in a logical sequence and by using transitions to show how their ideas are connected to one another. See *transition.*

coined words **Coined words** are ones that are intentionally created, often from the raw materials provided by already existing words and word parts. Examples of recently coined words include *yuppie* and *e-mail.*

collage In literature, a **collage** is a work that incorporates or brings together an odd assortment of materials, such as allusions, quotations, bits of song, dialogue, foreign words, mythical or folkloric elements, headlines, and pictures or other graphic materials. Collage is an interesting way to present a portrait of a particular time. The "Newsreels" in John Dos Passos's *U. S. A.* trilogy of novels are collages. The technique is also used in much modern poetry, including Ezra Pound's *The Cantos.*

colloquialism **Colloquialism** is the use of informal language. Modern poetry often makes use of colloquialism, as in Robert Frost's "The Death of the Hired Man" and "Home Burial."

comedy Originally a literary work with a happy ending, a **comedy** is any lighthearted or humorous work, especially one prepared for the stage or the screen. Comedy is often contrasted with tragedy, in which the hero meets an unhappy fate. (It is perhaps only a slight exaggeration to say that comedies end with wedding bells and tragedies with funeral bells.) Comedies typically present less-than-exalted characters who display all-too-human limitations, foibles, faults, and misunderstandings. The typical progression of the action in a comedy is from initial order to a humorous misunderstanding or confusion and back to order again. Stock elements of comedy include mistaken identities, word play, satire, and exaggerated characters and events. See *tragedy.*

comic relief Writers sometimes insert into a serious work of fiction or drama a humorous scene that is said to provide **comic relief** because it relieves the seriousness or emotional intensity felt by the audience. Paradoxically, a scene introduced for comic relief can sometimes, because of the contrast it provides, increase the perceived intensity or seriousness of the action around it.

commonplace book A **commonplace book** is a collection of quotations gleaned from various sources.

comparative literature **Comparative literature** is the study of relationships among works of literature written at different times, in different places, or in different languages. A study that showed influences of English *Romanticism* on American *Transcendentalism* would be an example.

complication The **complication** is the part of a plot in which the conflict is developed or built to its high point of intensity. See *plot.*

conceit A **conceit** is an elaborate or extremely fanciful analogy or metaphor. Oliver Wendell Holmes's comparison in "The Chambered Nautilus" of the development of the soul to the building of a nautilus shell is an example of a conceit.

concrete A **concrete** word or phrase is one that names or describes something that can be directly perceived by one or more of the five senses. *Buffalo, geranium, storm,* and *heron* are examples of concrete terms. See *abstract* and *concrete universal.*

concrete poem A **concrete poem** is one printed or written in a shape that suggests its subject matter. A concrete poem is also known as a *shape poem* or *carmen figuratum.*

concrete universal A **concrete universal** is a particular object, person, action, or event that provides an instance or example of a general type. Thus in writing about one lonely, isolated man in "Mr. Flood's Party," Edwin Arlington Robinson in a sense writes about all such men. In our time, literary taste tends toward the particular and concrete. In the *minimalist style* championed by writers such as Ezra Pound, T. S. Eliot, and Hilda Doolittle, direct statement of abstract ideas and emotions is avoided. Instead, images are presented as concrete examples meant to arouse abstract ideas and emotions in readers. So, for example, instead of saying, abstractly, "My life has not amounted to much; I'm cultured but have not been creative," Eliot writes, "I have measured out my life with coffee spoons." See *abstract, concrete, Neoclassicism,* and *objective correlative.*

confessional poetry **Confessional poetry** is verse that describes, sometimes with painful explicitness, the private or personal experiences of the writer. Contemporary American confessional poets include Sylvia Plath, Anne Sexton, Robert Lowell, and Allen Ginsberg.

conflict A **conflict** is a struggle between two forces in a literary work. A *plot* involves the introduction, development, and eventual resolution of a conflict. One side of the *central conflict* in a story or drama is usually taken by the *main character.* That character may struggle against another character, against the forces of nature, against society or social norms, against fate, or against some element within himself or herself. A struggle that takes place between a character and some outside force is called an *external conflict.* A struggle that takes place within a character is called an *internal conflict.* Melville's Captain Ahab experiences an external conflict with the white whale Moby-Dick and an internal conflict against the limits placed on human power. See *central conflict* and *plot.*

connotation A **connotation** is an emotional association or implication attached to an expression. For example, the word *inexpensive* has positive emotional associations, whereas the word *cheap* has negative ones, even though the two words both *denote,* or refer to, low cost. Good writers choose their words carefully in order to express appropriate connotations. See *denotation.*

consonance **Consonance** is the repetition of a consonant sound preceded by a different vowel sound, as in the words *roads* and *wood* in Robert Frost's line "Two roads diverged in a yellow wood."

convention A **convention,** in a literary work, is an unrealistic element that is accepted by readers or viewers because the element is traditional. One of the conventions of fiction, for example, is that it uses the past tense to describe current or present action. Rhyme schemes and organization into stanzas are among the many commonly employed conventions of poetry. Violation of accepted conventions is one of the hallmarks of *avant garde* or *Modernist* literature. See *dramatic convention.*

conventional symbol See *symbol.*

couplet A **couplet** is a pair of rhyming lines that expresses a complete thought. These lines from Phillis Wheatley's "To S. M., a Young African Painter, on Seeing His Works" are an example:

> Cease, gentle muse! the solemn gloom
> of night
> Now seals the fair creation from my
> sight.

A pair of rhyming iambic pentameter lines, like these, is also known as a *heroic couplet.*

crisis In the plot of a story or a drama, the **crisis** is that point in the development of the conflict at which a decisive event occurs that causes the main character's situation to become better or worse. See *plot.*

critic A literary **critic** is a person who evaluates or interprets a work of literature. See *criticism.*

critical essay A **critical essay** is a type of informative or persuasive writing that presents an argument in support of a particular interpretation or evaluation of a work of literature. A well-constructed critical essay presents a clear *thesis,* or main idea, supported by ample evidence from the work or works being considered.

criticism **Criticism** is the act of evaluating or interpreting a work of art or the act of developing general guidelines or principles for such evaluation or interpretation. Over the centuries, many schools, or philosophies, of criticism have been developed. However, most readers and teachers are eclectic critics, drawing consciously or unconsciously upon various schools of critical thought. Common schools of criticism include the following:

Biographical criticism attempts to account for elements of literary works by relating them to events in the lives of their authors. A reading of Anne Bradstreet's poem "To My Dear and Loving Husband" as a reflection on her real-life relationship with Simon Bradstreet would be an example of biographical criticism.

Deconstructionist criticism calls into question the idea that a literary work has a particular interpretation by inviting the reader to reverse the binary, or two-part, relations that structure meaning in the work. For example, a deconstructionist analysis of *The Glass Menagerie* might invite the reader to reconsider the play's opposition of the artistic temperament as embodied in the character Tom and the materialistic temperament as embodied in the character Jim, arguing that the artist produces illusions and believes them to be truths, a process leading inevitably to subjectivism and isolation, whereas the materialist successfully operates in the world, finding or creating purpose and connection. Such a reading deconstructs the conventional reading of the play, which insists that Williams intended a critique of materialistic values. See *structuralist criticism.*

Didactic criticism evaluates works of art in terms of the moral, ethical, or political messages that they convey. Dismissal of a book as dangerous or obscene would be an example of didactic criticism.

Feminist criticism evaluates and interprets works of art with regard to their portrayal of or influence upon gender roles. Many feminist critics and scholars have been particularly concerned to rescue women writers from obscurity. Other critics have been concerned with pointing out gender bias in literary works, with analyzing variations in literary depictions of males and females, and with understanding the effects of literary works, activities, and movements on cultural norms related to gender. An example of feminist criticism would be an analysis of the determination and self-reliance of women characters in literature of the American frontier.

Formal criticism analyzes a work of literature in terms of its genre or type. An explanation of those characteristics of "Swing Low, Sweet Chariot" that make it a spiritual would be an example of formal criticism.

Freudian criticism draws upon the works of the founder of psychoanalysis, Sigmund

Freud, and generally views literary works or the parts thereof as expressions of unconscious desires, as wish fulfillments, or as neurotic sublimations of unresolved conflicts from childhood. An example of Freudian criticism would be the interpretation of the ancient Greek Œdipus myth, in which Œdipus unwittingly marries his mother, as an expression of the young male child's competition with his father for his mother's affection.

Historical criticism views the work of art as a product of the period in which it was produced. An example of historical criticism would be an analysis of the Puritan influence on Nathaniel Hawthorne's "Rappaccini's Daughter."

Jungian criticism explores the presence in works of art of *archetypes*—unconscious images, symbols, associations, or concepts presumed to be a common inheritance of all human beings. An analysis of symbols of rebirth in a number of myths or folk tales would be an example of Jungian criticism.

Marxist criticism, based upon the work of the German-born political philosopher Karl Marx, evaluates and interprets works of art with regard to the material economic forces that shape them or with regard to their origins in or depictions of struggle between the social classes. An example of Marxist criticism would be an explanation of the emergence of Realism in the novels of early twentieth-century American writers such as Theodore Dreiser and Sinclair Lewis in terms of increased awareness of the disparity between the classes, poor labor conditions, and urban discontent.

Mimetic criticism, which derives from the teachings of Aristotle, views works of art as imitations of nature or of the real world and evaluates them according to the accuracy of those portrayals. Insisting that a character is poorly drawn because he or she is unrealistic is an example of mimetic criticism.

The ***New Criticism*** championed in the early to mid-twentieth century by such critics as I. A. Richards and Cleanth Brooks insisted upon the interpretation and evaluation of literary works based on details found in the works themselves rather than on information gathered from outside the works. It disregarded such matters as the life of the author, the period in which the work was written, the literary movement that led to its production, and the emotional effect of the work upon the reader. The New Critics insisted on the importance of close analysis of literary texts and the irreducibility of those texts to generalizations or paraphrases.

Pragmatic or ***rhetorical criticism*** interprets or evaluates a work of art in terms of its effects on an audience. An example of rhetorical criticism would be a reading of Poe's "The Raven" that describes the various techniques used in the poem to evoke feelings of mystery, sorrow, and horror.

Reader-response criticism views the meaning of a text as resulting from a relationship between the text itself and the subjective experiences or consciousness of a reader. According to reader-response theory, a literary text has no meaning *per se.* It is, instead, an occasion for a participatory experience that the reader has. That experience may be meaningful or significant to the reader, but the meaning and significance of the experience will depend, in part, on what the reader brings to the text.

Romantic or ***expressivist criticism*** views a work of art as primarily an expression of the spirit, ideas, beliefs, values, or emotions of its creator. A reading of *Invisible Man* as expressive of the beliefs and emotions of Ralph Ellison would be an example of expressivist criticism.

Structuralist criticism analyzes works of literature and art in terms of binary, or two-part, relationships or structures. A structuralist analysis of Williams's *The Glass Menagerie,* for example, might view the characters as caught between dreams and realities, a rural Southern past and an urban Northern present, and so on.

Textual criticism analyzes the various existing manuscript and printed versions of a work to construct an original or definitive text for use by readers.

dactyl A **dactyl** is a poetic foot made up of a strongly stressed syllable followed by two weakly stressed syllables, as in the word *feverish.* A line of poetry made up of dactyls is said to be *dactylic.*

dead metaphor A **dead metaphor** is one that is so familiar that its original metaphorical meaning is rarely thought of when the expression is used. An example would be the word *nightfall,* which describes the coming of darkness as a falling object.

deconstructionist criticism See *criticism.*

definition A **definition** is an explanation of the meaning of a word or phrase. A dictionary definition typically consists of two parts: the *genus,* or class to which the thing belongs, and the *differentia,* or differences between the thing and other things of its class. Consider, for example, Ambrose Bierce's tongue-in-cheek definition of *love:* "A temporary insanity, curable by marriage." In this definition, "insanity" is the genus. The rest of the definition presents the differentia.

denotation The **denotation** is the basic meaning or reference of an expression, excluding its emotional associations, or *connotations.* For example, the words *dirt* and *soil* share a single common denotation. However, *dirt* has negative connotations of uncleanliness, whereas *soil* does not. See *connotation.*

dénouement See *plot.*

description A **description,** one of the modes of writing, portrays a character, an object, or a scene. Descriptions make use of *sensory details*—words and phrases that describe how things look, sound, smell, taste, or feel. See *mode.*

dialect A **dialect** is a version of a language spoken by the people of a particular place, time, or social group. Writers often use dialect, as in Mark Twain's "The Notorious Jumping Frog of Calaveras County," to give their works a realistic flavor. A *regional dialect* is one spoken in a particular place. A *social dialect* is one spoken by members of a particular social group or class.

dialogue 1. **Dialogue** is conversation involving two or more people or characters. Plays are made up of dialogue and stage directions. Fictional works are made up of dialogue, narration, and description. 2. **Dialogue** is also used to describe a type of literary composition in which characters debate or discuss an idea. Many of Plato's philosophical works were presented in the form of dialogues.

diary A **diary** is a day-to-day record of a person's activities, experiences, thoughts, and feelings. Both Ralph Waldo Emerson and Henry David Thoreau kept diaries in which they experimented with thoughts and feelings they later reworked into speeches and essays.

diction **Diction,** when applied to writing, refers to word choice. Much of a writer's *style* is determined by his or her diction, the types of words that he or she chooses. Diction can be formal or informal, simple or complex, contemporary or archaic, ordinary or unusual, foreign or native, standard or dialectical, euphemistic or blunt. See *style.*

didactic criticism See *criticism.*

didactic poem A **didactic poem** is a verse that has a primary purpose of teaching one or more lessons. James Russell Lowell's "Stanzas on Freedom" is an example. See *didacticism.*

didacticism **Didacticism** is the use of works of art to convey moral, social, educational, or political messages. A didactic work is one in which the artistic values of the work are subordinated to the message or meaning. Henry Wadsworth Longfellow's "A Psalm of Life" is an example of a didactic poem.

dimeter See *meter.*

dominant impression See *effect.*

drama A **drama** is a story told through characters played by actors. The script of a drama typically consists of characters' names, *dialogue* spoken by the characters, and *stage directions.* Because it is meant to be performed before an audience, drama can be distinguished from other forms of non-performance-based literary works by the central role played in it by the *spectacle*—the sensory presentation to the audience, which includes such elements as lighting, costumes, make-up, properties, set pieces, music, sound effects, and the movements and expressions of actors. Another important distinguishing feature of drama is that it is *collaborative.* The interpretation of the work depends not only upon the author and his or her audience but also upon the director, the actors, and others involved in mounting a production. Two major types of drama are *comedy* and *tragedy*. See *comedy, dialogue, spectacle, stage directions,* and *tragedy*.

dramatic convention A **dramatic convention** is an unreal element in a drama that is accepted as realistic by the audience because it is traditional. Such conventions include the impersonation of characters by actors, the use of a curtain to open or close an act or a scene, the revelation of a character's thoughts through *asides* and *soliloquies*, and the removal of the so-called *fourth wall* at the front of the stage that allows the audience to see action taking place in an imagined interior. See *convention* and *suspension of disbelief*.

dramatic irony See *irony*.

dramatic monologue A **dramatic monologue** is a poem that presents the speech of a single character in a dramatic situation. The speech is one side of an imagined conversation. The British poet Robert Browning is often credited with the creation of the dramatic monologue. A modern example of a dramatic monologue is Edwin Arlington Robinson's "Mr. Flood's Party." See *soliloquy*.

dramatic poem A **dramatic poem** is a verse that relies heavily on dramatic elements such as monologue or dialogue. Types of dramatic poetry include the *dramatic monologue* and the *soliloquy*.

dramatis personæ ***Dramatis personæ*** are the characters in a literary work. The term is most often used for the characters in a drama.

dream record A **dream record** is a *diary* or *journal* in which a writer records his or her dreams. See *diary* and *journal*.

dynamic character See *character*.

dystopia A **dystopia** is an imaginary horrible world, the opposite of a *utopia*. Dystopias are common in science fiction. Famous examples of dystopias include the societies described in Aldous Huxley's *Brave New World*, H. G. Wells's *The Time Machine*, George Orwell's *1984*, and Ray Bradbury's *Fahrenheit 451*. See *utopia*.

eclogue An **eclogue** is a pastoral poem written in imitation of Greek works by Theocritus and Virgil. See *pastoral poem*.

editorial An **editorial** is a short persuasive piece that appears in a newspaper, magazine, or other periodical.

effect The **effect** of a literary work is the general impression or emotional impact that it achieves. Some writers and critics, notably Edgar Allan Poe, have insisted that a successful short story or poem is one in which each detail contributes to the overall effect, or *dominant impression*, produced by the piece.

elaboration **Elaboration**, or **amplification**, is a writing technique in which a subject is introduced and then expanded upon by means of repetition with slight changes, the addition of details, or similar devices.

elegiac lyric An **elegiac lyric** is a poem that expresses a speaker's feelings of loss. Emily Dickinson's "After great pain, a formal feeling comes—" and Edgar Allan Poe's "Annabel Lee" are examples.

elegy An **elegy** is a long formal poem about death or loss. Walt Whitman's "When Lilacs Last in the Dooryard Bloom'd" and John Crowe Ransom's "Bells for John Whiteside's Daughter" are examples.

Elizabethan sonnet See *sonnet*.

emphasis **Emphasis** is importance placed on an element in a literary work. Writers achieve emphasis by various means, including repetition, elaboration, stress, restatement in other words, and placement in a strategic position at the beginning or end of a line or a sentence.

end rhyme **End rhyme** is rhyme that occurs at the ends of lines of verse. See *rhyme*.

end-stopped line An **end-stopped line** is a line of verse in which both the sense and the grammar are complete at the end of the line. The opposite of an end-stopped line is a *run-on line*. The following lines are end-stopped:

> Make me, O Lord, Thy Spinning Wheel
> complete.
> Thy Holy Word my Distaff make for me.
> —Edward Taylor, "Huswifery"

Excessive use of end-stopped lines gives verse an unnatural, halting quality. See *run-on line*.

English sonnet See *sonnet.*

enjambment See *run-on line.*

Enlightenment The **Enlightenment** was an eighteenth-century philosophical movement characterized by belief in reason, the scientific method, and the perfectibility of people and society. Thinkers of the Enlightenment Era, or Age of Reason, believed that the universe was governed by discoverable, rational principles like the laws of physics discovered by Sir Isaac Newton. By extension, they believed that people could, through application of reason, discover truths relating to the conduct of life or of society. Leading thinkers of the Enlightenment included Diderot, Franklin, Gibbon, Hume, Jefferson, Kant, Montesquieu, Pope, Swift, and Voltaire. See *Neoclassicism.*

epic An **epic** is a long story, often told in verse, involving heroes and gods. Grand in length and scope, an epic provides a portrait of an entire culture, of the legends, beliefs, values, laws, arts, and ways of life of a people. Famous epic poems include Homer's *Iliad* and *Odyssey,* Virgil's *Aeneid,* Dante's *The Divine Comedy,* the anonymous Old English *Beowulf,* and Milton's *Paradise Lost.*

epigram An **epigram** is a short, often witty, saying. An example of an epigram is Benjamin Franklin's "Three may keep a secret, if two of them are dead."

epigraph An **epigraph** is a quotation or motto used at the beginning of the whole or part of a literary work to help establish the work's theme. T. S. Eliot uses an epigraph from Dante's *Inferno* at the beginning of "The Love Song of J. Alfred Prufrock."

epilogue An **epilogue** is a concluding section or statement, often one that comments on or draws conclusions from the work as a whole.

epiphany When applied to literature, the term *epiphany* refers to a moment of sudden insight in which the essence, or nature, of a person, thing, or situation is revealed. The use of the term in this sense was introduced by James Joyce.

episode An **episode** is a complete action within a literary work.

episodic structure **Episodic structure** is the stringing together of loosely related incidents, or episodes. Mark Twain's *The Adventures of Huckleberry Finn* has an episodic structure.

epistle An **epistle** is a letter, especially one that is highly formal. Letters in verse are sometimes called epistles.

epistolary fiction **Epistolary fiction** is imaginative prose that tells a story through letters, or epistles. Samuel Richardson pioneered this form in his novels *Pamela* and *Clarissa,* written in the mid-1700s. Despite a slight decline in popularity, epistolary fiction is still written today. Richard Brautigan's *Trout Fishing in America* is a contemporary example of epistolary fiction.

epitaph An **epitaph** is an inscription or verse written to be used on a tomb or written in commemoration of someone who has died. The epitaph on the grave of Benjamin Franklin, written by Franklin himself, reads as follows:

The body of
Benjamin Franklin, printer,
(Like the cover of an old book,
Its contents worn out,
And stript of its lettering and gilding)
Lies here, food for worms!
Yet the work itself shall not be lost,
For it will, as he believed, appear once more
In a new
And more beautiful edition,
Corrected and amended
By its Author!

epithet An **epithet** is a word or phrase used to describe a characteristic of a person, place, or thing. Eliot's description of sea-girls as "wreathed with seaweed red and brown" is an example.

eponym An **eponym** is a person or character from whose name a word or title is derived, or a name that has become synonymous with some general characteristic or idea. Julius Cæsar is the eponym of the medical term *Cesarean section.* England's Queen Victoria is the eponym of Victoria Falls. A reference to *Helen of Troy,* used in place of the more general term *beauty,* or a reference to *an Einstein,* in place of a more general term such as *a smart person,* would be an eponym.

essay An **essay** is a brief work of prose nonfiction. The original meaning of essay was "a trial or attempt," and the word retains some of this original force. An essay need not be a complete or exhaustive treatment of a subject but rather a tentative exploration of it. A good essay develops a single idea and is characterized by *unity* and *coherence*. See *coherence* and *unity*.

euphemism A **euphemism** is an indirect word or phrase used in place of a direct statement that might be considered too offensive. The phrase *the dearly departed,* used instead of *the dead person,* is a euphemism.

euphony **Euphony** is pleasing sound. Writers achieve euphony by various means, including repetitions of vowel and consonant sounds, rhyme, and parallelism. See *cacophony*.

Existentialism **Existentialism** is a twentieth-century philosophical school that postulates the essential absurdity and meaninglessness of life. Existentialist philosophers such as Albert Camus and Jean-Paul Sartre argued that existence, or being, emerges out of nothingness without any essential, or defining, nature. A human being simply finds himself or herself alive and aware without having any essential defining direction. Any choices that a person makes in order to define himself or herself are made freely and therefore absurdly—one may as well make one choice as another. Freedom of the will is therefore seen by the Existentialist as a terrific burden, one causing anguish to the thinking person, who longs for meaningfulness, not absurd choices. Another significant aspect of Existentialism is its insistence on the essential isolation of each individual consciousness and the consequent anguish of people looking for meaningful connection to others. Though many of the essential tenets of Existentialism have been discredited by contemporary philosophers, the school nonetheless exerted tremendous influence on mid-twentieth-century literature in Europe, Great Britain, and the United States. See *literature of the absurd* and *theater of the absurd*.

exposition **1. Exposition,** one of the modes of writing, presents factual information. See *mode*. **2.** In a plot, the **exposition** is that part of a narrative that provides background information, often about the characters, setting, or conflict. See *plot*.

Expressionism **Expressionism** is the name given to a twentieth-century movement in literature and art that reacted against Realism in favor of an exaggeration of the elements of the artistic medium itself in an attempt to express ideas or feelings. Tennessee Williams's *The Glass Menagerie,* with its unrealistic setting and its generous use of symbolism, is an example of Expressionism.

extended metaphor An **extended metaphor** is a point-by-point presentation of one thing as though it were another. The description is meant as an implied comparison, inviting the reader to associate the thing being described with something that is quite different from it. Dickinson's "Because I could not stop for Death—" is an extended metaphor, where Death is characterized as a carriage driver and the speaker of the poem as his passenger.

external conflict See *conflict*.

eye rhyme See *sight rhyme*.

fable A **fable** is a brief story with animal characters told to express a moral. Famous fables include those of Æsop and La Fontaine.

fairy tale A **fairy tale** is a story that deals with mischievous spirits and other supernatural occurrences, often in medieval settings. The name is generally applied to stories of the kinds collected by Charles Perrault in France and the Brothers Grimm in Germany or told by Hans Christian Andersen of Denmark. "Cinderella" and "The Little Mermaid" are famous examples.

falling action See *plot*.

fantasy A **fantasy** is a literary work that contains highly unrealistic elements. Stephen Vincent Benét's "The Devil and Daniel Webster" is a fantasy. Fantasy is often contrasted with *science fiction,* in which the unreal elements are given a scientific or pseudoscientific basis. See *science fiction*.

farce A **farce** is a type of comedy that depends heavily on so-called low humor and on improbable, exaggerated, extreme situations or characters.

feminist criticism See *criticism.*

fiction **Fiction** is prose writing about imagined events or characters. The primary forms of fiction are the *novel* and the *short story.*

figurative language **Figurative language** is language that suggests something more than the literal meanings of the words might be taken to suggest. See *figures of speech.*

figures of speech **Figures of speech,** or **tropes,** are expressions that have more than a literal meaning. Hyperbole, metaphor, metonymy, personification, simile, synaesthesia, synecdoche, and understatement are all figures of speech. See *hyperbole, metaphor, metonymy, personification, simile, synaesthesia, synecdoche,* and *understatement.*

first-person point of view See *point of view.*

flashback A **flashback** is a section of a literary work that presents an event or series of events that occurred earlier than the current time in the work. Writers use flashbacks for many purposes, but most notably to provide *background information,* or exposition. In popular melodramatic works, including modern romance fiction and detective stories, flashbacks are often used to end suspense by revealing key elements of the plot such as a character's true identity or the actual perpetrator of a crime. One common technique is to begin a work with a final event and then to tell the rest of the story as a flashback that explains how that event came about. Another common technique is to begin a story *in medias res* (in the middle of the action) and then to use a flashback to fill in the events that occurred before the opening of the story.

flash fiction See *short short.*

flat character See *character.*

foil A **foil** is a character whose attributes, or characteristics, contrast with and therefore throw into relief the attributes of another character. In "The Legend of Sleepy Hollow," Brom Bones, "a burley, roaring, roystering blade," provides a foil for Ichabod Crane, who is characterized as a coward and described as "tall, but exceedingly lank."

folk ballad See *ballad.*

folk song A **folk song** is an anonymous song that is transmitted orally. Examples include the ballad "Bonny Barbara Allan," the sea chantey "Blow the Man Down," the children's song "Row, Row, Row Your Boat," the spiritual "Go Down, Moses," the railroad song "Casey Jones," and the cowboy song "The Streets of Laredo." The term *folk song* is sometimes used for works composed in imitation of true folk songs. Contemporary composers of songs in the folk tradition include Bob Dylan, Paul Simon, Joan Baez, and the Indigo Girls. See *ballad.*

folk tale A **folk tale** is a brief story passed by word of mouth from generation to generation. Writers often make use of materials from folk tales, such as the little people who appear in Washington Irving's "The Legend of Rip Van Winkle." Famous collections of folk tales include the German *Märchen,* or fairy tales, collected by the Brothers Grimm; Yeats's collection of Irish stories, *Mythologies;* and Zora Neale Hurston's collection of African-American folk tales and other folklore materials, *Their Eyes Were Watching God.* See *fairy tale, folklore,* and *oral tradition.*

folklore **Folklore** is a body of orally transmitted beliefs, customs, rituals, traditions, songs, verses, or stories. Folk tales, fables, fairy tales, tall tales, nursery rhymes, proverbs, legends, myths, parables, riddles, charms, spells, and ballads are all common kinds of folklore, though each of these can be found, as well, in literary forms made in imitation of works from the *oral tradition.*

foot In a poem, a **foot** is a unit of rhythm consisting of strongly and weakly stressed syllables. See *meter* and *scansion.* Also see the specific types of feet: *anapest, dactyl, iamb, spondee,* and *trochee.*

foreshadowing **Foreshadowing** is the act of presenting materials that hint at events to occur later in a story. In "Rappaccini's Daughter," when Guasconti first sees the figure of Rappaccini, the latter man's "demeanor was that of one walking among malignant influences, . . . which . . . would wreak upon him some terrible fatality." The events of the tale lead inexorably to the grim conclusion foreshadowed in that line.

foreword See *preface.*

formal criticism See *criticism.*

fourteener See *meter.*

fourth wall See *dramatic convention.*

frame tale A **frame tale** is a story that itself provides a vehicle for the telling of other stories. The *Thousand and One Nights,* Boccaccio's *Decameron,* Chaucer's *The Canterbury Tales,* and Sherwood Anderson's *Winesburg, Ohio,* are frame tales.

free verse **Free verse,** or ***vers libre,*** is poetry that avoids use of regular rhyme, rhythm, meter, or division into stanzas. Denise Levertov's "The Secret" and James Dickey's "For the Last Wolverine" are examples, though both poems make use of numerous regularities of rhythm. Much of the English and American poetry written in the twentieth century is in free verse.

Freudian criticism See *criticism.*

full character See *character.*

genre A **genre** (zhän´rə) is one of the types or categories into which literary works are divided. Some terms used to name literary genres include *autobiography, biography, comedy, drama, epic, essay, lyric, narrative, novel, pastoral, poetry, short story,* and *tragedy.* Literary works are sometimes classified into genres based on subject matter. Such a classification might describe *detective stories, mysteries, adventure stories, romances, westerns,* and *science fiction* as different genres of fiction.

Gothic novel A **Gothic novel,** or **Gothic romance,** is a long story containing elements of horror, suspense, mystery, and magic. Gothic novels often contain dark, brooding descriptions of settings and characters. Mary Shelley's *Frankenstein* and Daphne du Maurier's *Rebecca* are examples of the form. Gothic elements can also be found in the short stories of Nathaniel Hawthorne and Edgar Allan Poe. See *Southern Gothic.*

Gothic romance See *Gothic novel.*

haiku A **haiku** is a traditional Japanese three-line poem containing five syllables in the first line, seven in the second, and five again in the third. A haiku presents a picture, or image, in order to arouse in the reader a specific emotional and/or spiritual state.

half rhyme See *slant rhyme.*

heptameter See *meter.*

Harlem Renaissance The Harlem Renaissance was a period of intense creative activity among African-American writers and other artists living in Harlem in New York City during the 1920s. Major writers of the Harlem Renaissance included Arna Bontemps, Countee Cullen, Langston Hughes, Claude McKay, and Jean Toomer.

heroic couplet See *couplet.*

heroic epic A **heroic epic** is an epic that has a main purpose of telling the life story of a great hero. Examples of the heroic epic include Homer's *Iliad* and *Odyssey,* Virgil's *Aeneid,* and the Old English poem *Beowulf.* See *epic.*

hexameter See *meter.*

high style See *style.*

historical criticism See *criticism.*

hymn A **hymn** is a song or verse of praise, often religious. "Just a Closer Walk with Thee," by Red Foley, is a contemporary hymn.

hyperbole A **hyperbole** (hī pur´bə lē) is an exaggeration made for rhetorical effect. Anne Bradstreet uses hyperbole when she writes,

> My love is such that rivers cannot quench,
> Nor ought but love from thee, give recompense.

iamb An **iamb** is a poetic foot containing one weakly stressed syllable followed by one strongly stressed syllable, as in the words *afraid* and *release.* A line of poetry made up of iambs is said to be *iambic.*

iambic See *iamb.*

image An **image** is a word or phrase that names something that can be seen, heard, touched, tasted, or smelled. The images in a literary work are referred to, collectively, as the work's *imagery.*

imagery See *image.*

Imagism **Imagism** was a twentieth-century literary movement that championed short verse free of anything except images. Important Imagist writers included Amy Lowell, Ezra Pound, H. D. and William Carlos Williams.

inciting incident See *plot.*

incremental repetition See *ballad.*

in medias res See *action* and *flashback.*

internal conflict See *conflict.*

internal monologue An **internal monologue** presents the private sensations, thoughts, and emotions of a character. The reader is allowed to step inside the character's mind and overhear what is going on there. Which characters' internal states can be revealed in a work of fiction depends on the *point of view* from which the work is told. See *point of view.*

introduction See *preface.*

inversion An **inversion** is a poetic technique in which the normal order of words in an utterance is altered. Robert Frost's "Whose woods these are, I think I know" is an inversion of the usual order of expression: "I think I know whose woods these are."

irony **Irony** is a difference between appearance and reality. Types of irony include the following: *dramatic irony,* in which something is known by the reader or audience but unknown to the characters; *verbal irony,* in which a statement is made that implies its opposite; and *irony of situation,* in which an event occurs that violates the expectations of the characters, the reader, or the audience.

irony of situation See *irony.*

journal A **journal,** like a *diary,* is a day-to-day record of a person's activities, experiences, thoughts, and feelings. In contrast to *diary,* the word *journal* connotes an outward rather than an inward focus. However, the two terms are often used interchangeably. See *diary.*

limited point of view See *narrator* and *point of view.*

List of Works Cited A **List of Works Cited** is a type of bibliography that lists works used or referred to by an author. A standard feature of a research paper, the List of Works Cited appears at the end of the paper and is arranged in alphabetical order.

literature of the absurd **Literature of the absurd** is literature influenced by Existentialist philosophy, which represents human life as meaningless or absurd because of the supposed lack of essential connection between human beings and the world around them. In brief, the existentialist philosophers, such as Albert Camus and Jean-Paul Sarte, believed that a person's conscious existence precedes, or comes before, any essential self-definition and that self-definition can occur only as a result of making an absurd, completely free choice to act, think, or believe in certain ways. The literature of the absurd emphasizes the meaninglessness of life and the isolation, or alienation, of individuals. Much of the literature of the absurd is filled with horrors, anguish, random events, and illogical or improbable occurrences. Modern practitioners of the literature of the absurd include the novelists Franz Kafka, Thomas Pynchon, and Kurt Vonnegut, Jr., and the playwrights Eugène Ionesco, Samuel Beckett, Edward Albee, and Harold Pinter. See *Existentialism* and *theater of the absurd.*

lyric poem A **lyric poem** is a highly musical verse that expresses the emotions of a speaker. Edna St. Vincent Millay's "Sonnet XXX" and Ralph Waldo Emerson's "Brahma" are examples. Lyric poems are often contrasted with narrative poems, which have telling a story as their main purpose.

Magical Realism **Magical Realism** is a kind of fiction that is for the most part realistic but that contains elements of fantasy. Bernard Malamud's "The Magic Barrel" is an example of Magical Realism.

main character See *character.*

major character See *character.*

Marxist criticism See *criticism.*

metaphor A **metaphor** is a figure of speech in which one thing is spoken or written about as if it were another. This figure of speech invites the reader to make a comparison between the two things. The two "things" involved are the writer's actual subject, the *tenor* of the metaphor, and another thing to which the subject is likened, the *vehicle* of the metaphor. When, in "'Hope' is the thing with feathers," Emily Dickinson writes that "'Hope' is the thing with feathers—/that perches in the soul—," she is using a metaphor.

Personifications and similes are types of metaphor. See *dead metaphor, mixed metaphor, personification,* and *simile.*

meter The **meter** of a poem is its rhythmical pattern. English verse is generally described as being made up of rhythmical units called *feet,* as follows:

TYPE OF FOOT	STRESS PATTERN	EXAMPLE
iambic	⏑ /	insist
trochaic	/ ⏑	freedom
anapestic	⏑ ⏑ /	unimpressed
dactylic	/ ⏑ ⏑	feverish
spondaic	/ /	baseball

Some scholars also use the term *pyrrhic* to describe a foot with two weak stresses. Using this term, the word *unbelievable* might be described as consisting of two feet, an anapest followed by a pyrrhic:

⏑ ⏑ / | ⏑ ⏑
un be liev | a ble

Terms used to describe the number of feet in a line include the following:

monometer for a one-foot line
dimeter for a two-foot line
trimeter for a three-foot line
tetrameter for a four-foot line
pentameter for a five-foot line
hexameter, or *Alexandrine,* for a six-foot line
heptameter for a seven-foot line
octameter for an eight-foot line

A seven-foot line of iambic feet is called a *fourteener.*

A complete description of the meter of a line includes both the term for the type of foot that predominates in the line and the term for the number of feet in the line. The most common English meters are iambic tetrameter and iambic pentameter. The following are examples of each:

IAMBIC TETRAMETER:
⏑ / ⏑ / ⏑ / ⏑ /
I would | your bloom | of youth | re pair

IAMBIC PENTAMETER:
⏑ / ⏑ / ⏑ / ⏑ /
Now seals | the fair | cre a | tion from |
⏑ /
my sight.

metonymy **Metonymy** is the naming of an object associated with a thing in place of the name of the thing itself. Speaking of *the White House* when one means *the administrative or executive branch of the United States government* is an example of metonymy.

middle style See *style.*

mimetic criticism See *criticism.*

minor character See *character.*

mixed metaphor A **mixed metaphor** is an expression or passage that conflates, or garbles together, two or more metaphors. An example of mixed metaphor would be the sentence "The chariot of the sun screamed across the sky," in which the sun is described, inconsistently, as both a chariot and as something that screams. See *metaphor.*

mode A **mode** is a form of writing. One common classification system, based on content, divides types of writing into four modes: argumentation, description, exposition, and narration. See *argumentation, description, exposition,* and *narration.*

Modernism **Modernism** was an artistic and literary movement of the early twentieth century that championed experimentation, technicality, primitivism, impersonalism, aestheticism, and intellectualism. Important Modernists included the poets Ezra Pound and T. S. Eliot, the painters

Pablo Picasso and Paul Klee, and the musicians Arnold Schönberg and Anton Webern.

monometer See *meter.*

mood **Mood,** or **atmosphere,** is the emotion created in the reader by part or all of a literary work. A writer creates a mood through judicious use of concrete details.

motif A **motif** is any element that recurs in one or more works of literature or art. Examples of common folk tale motifs found in oral traditions throughout the world include grateful animals or the grateful dead, three wishes, the trial or quest, and the magical metamorphosis, or transformation of one thing into another. Much can be revealed about a literary work by studying the motifs within it. In "Rappaccini's Daughter," Nathaniel Hawthorne uses the recurring motifs of deadliness and of beauty, both natural and unnatural, to explore Giovanni's attraction to Beatrice.

motivation A **motivation** is a force that moves a character to think, feel, or behave in a certain way. In Ambrose Bierce's "An Occurrence at Owl Creek Bridge," the main character is motivated by a desire to save his own life by escaping from his captors.

Muse In ancient Greek and Roman myth, the **Muses**—the nine daughters of Zeus and Mnemosyne, or Memory—were believed to provide the inspiration for the arts and sciences. Calliope was the Muse of epic poetry; Clio, the Muse of history; Erato, the Muse of lyrical poetry; Euterpe, the Muse of music; Melpomene, the Muse of tragedy; Polyhymnia, the Muse of sacred choral poetry; Terpischore, the Muse of choral dance and song; Thalia, the Muse of comedy; and Urania, the Muse of astronomy. The idea of the Muse has often been used by later writers to explain the vagaries and mysteries of literary inspiration. For example, Phillis Wheatley writes, "And may the muse inspire each future song!" in "To S. M., a Young African Painter, on Seeing His Works." The connection of the Muses with entertainments and the arts survives in our words *amusing* and *amusement.*

myth A **myth** is a story that explains objects or events in the natural world as resulting from the action of some supernatural force or entity, most often a god. Every early culture around the globe has produced its own myths. An example of a myth is the explanation of the sky as a piece of weaving in "Song of the Sky Loom."

narration **Narration,** one of the modes of writing, tells a story. The story is made up of occurrences, or events. See *mode.*

narrative poem A **narrative poem** is a verse that tells a story. Edwin Arlington Robinson's "Mr. Flood's Party" and Robert Frost's "Home Burial" are examples of narrative poems. See *ballad* and *epic.*

narrator A **narrator** is one who tells a story. In a drama, the narrator may be a character who introduces, concludes, or comments upon the action of the play. However, dramas typically do not have narrators. Works of fiction, on the other hand, always do, unless they consist entirely of dialogue without *tag lines,* in which case they become no longer fictions but *closet dramas,* ones meant to be read but not performed. The narrator in a work of fiction may be a central or minor character or simply someone who witnessed or heard about the events being related. Writers achieve a wide variety of ends by varying the characteristics of the narrator chosen for a particular work. Of primary importance is the choice of the narrator's *point of view.* Will the narrator be *omniscient,* knowing all things, including the internal workings of the minds of the characters in the story, or will the narrator be *limited* in his or her knowledge? Will the narrator participate in the action of the story or stand outside that action and comment on it? Will the narrator be reliable or unreliable? That is, will the reader be able to trust the narrator's statements? These are all questions that a writer must answer when developing a narrator. See *point of view* and *speaker.*

Naturalism **Naturalism** was a literary movement of the late nineteenth and early twentieth centuries that saw actions and events as resulting inevitably from biological or natural forces or from forces in the environment. Often these forces were beyond the comprehension or control of the characters subjected to them. Taken to its extreme, Naturalism views all events as mechanically determined by external forces, including the decisions made by people. Much of modern fiction, with its emphasis on social conditions leading to particular consequences for characters, is naturalistic in this sense. Great writers of fiction informed by the philosophy of Naturalism include Émile Zola, Stephen Crane, Jack London, and Theodore Dreiser.

near rhyme See *slant rhyme.*

Neoclassicism **Neoclassicism** is the term used to describe the revival during the English Enlightenment or Restoration Era of ideals of art and literature derived from the Greek and Roman classics. These ideals included respect for authority and tradition, austerity, clarity, conservatism, decorum, economy, grace, imitation of the natural order, harmony, moderation, proportion, reason, restraint, self-control, simplicity, tradition, wit, and unity. Neoclassical literature was witty and socially astute but tended toward excessive *didacticism* and an excessive distrust of invention and imagination. Popular forms of Neoclassical writing included the essay, the epistle, the satire, the parody, poems in rhymed couplets, and the earliest novels. As if in response to Pope's dictum that "The proper study of man is man," Neoclassical writers wrote primarily about social life and social interactions. Of all American writers, Benjamin Franklin perhaps best reflects the Neoclassical spirit of urbane rationality. Romanticism can be seen as a reaction against Neoclassical restraint. See *Classicism, didacticism,* and *Romanticism.*

New Criticism See *criticism.*

nonfiction Nonfiction is writing about real events. Essays, autobiographies, biographies, and news stories are all types of nonfiction. See *prose.*

nonsense verse A **nonsense verse** is a kind of light verse that contains elements that are silly, absurd, or meaningless. Sometimes, as is the case with Lewis Carroll's "Jabberwocky," the apparent nonsense of the verse gives way to sense upon closer analysis. Carroll's poem turns out not to be nonsense at all, but rather an ingenious retelling, in a mock heroic ballad, of a stock folk tale story, that of a young person who sets off on a quest, slays a terrible beast, and returns home victorious. A purer example of nonsense can be found in the following lines of a famous nursery rhyme:

As I was going up the stair,
I met a man who wasn't there.
He wasn't there again today.
I wish, I wish he'd go away.

novel A **novel** is a long work of prose fiction. Often novels have involved plots; many characters, both major and minor; and numerous settings. Among the first extended works of prose fiction in English were Aphra Behn's *Oroonoko,* written in 1688; John Bunyan's *Pilgrim's Progress,* completed in 1684; and Swift's *Gulliver's Travels,* written in 1726. Early novels of note include Defoe's *Robinson Crusoe,* Richardson's *Pamela* and *Clarissa,* Fielding's *Tom Jones,* and Sterne's *Tristram Shandy.* Nineteenth-century American novelists include Herman Melville, Mark Twain, and Stephen Crane. Some outstanding modern American novelists include Edith Wharton, Henry James, Ernest Hemingway, William Faulkner, Ralph Ellison, Alice Walker, and Anne Tyler.

novella A **novella** is a short novel.

objective correlative An **objective correlative** is a group of images that together create a particular emotion in the reader. The term was coined by T. S. Eliot. See *image.*

occasional verse An **occasional verse** is one written to celebrate or commemorate some particular event. Ralph Waldo Emerson's "Concord Hymn," for example, was written for the dedication of a monument to soldiers who fought in the first battle of the Revolutionary War.

octameter See *meter.*

octave An **octave** is an eight-line stanza. A Petrarchan sonnet begins with an octave. See *meter* and *sonnet.*

off rhyme See *slant rhyme.*

omniscient point of view See *narrator* and *point of view.*

one-act See *act.*

one-dimensional character See *character.*

onomatopoeia **Onomatopoeia** is the use of words or phrases that sound like the things to which they refer. Examples of onomatopoeia include words such as *buzz, click,* and *pop.* Poets and other writers often make use of onomatopoeia, as in Edgar Lee Masters's description of flat poetry in "Petit, the Poet":

> Seeds in a dry pod, tick, tick, tick,
> Tick, tick, tick, what little iambics

oral tradition An **oral tradition** is a work, a motif, an idea, or a custom that is passed by word-of-mouth from generation to generation. Materials transmitted orally may be simplified in the retelling. They also may be sensationalized because of the tendency of retellers to add to or elaborate upon the materials that come down to them. Often, works in an oral tradition contain miraculous or magical elements. Common works found in the oral traditions of peoples around the world include *folk tales, fables, fairy tales, tall tales, nursery rhymes, proverbs, legends, myths, parables, riddles, charms, spells,* and *ballads.* The spiritual "Follow the Drinking Gourd" belongs to the African-American oral tradition. See *folklore.*

ottava rima ***Ottava rima*** is a stanza form made up of eight iambic pentameter lines rhyming *abababcc.*

oxymoron An **oxymoron** is a statement that contradicts itself. Words like *bittersweet, tragicomedy,* and *pianoforte* (literally, "soft-loud") are oxymorons that develop complex meanings from seemingly contradictory elements.

palindrome A **palindrome** is a word, a phrase, or a sentence that reads the same backward as forward. Examples include the word *radar* and the sentence *Able was I ere I saw Elba,* which describes Napoleon's condition prior to his exile to the island of Elba.

parable A **parable** is a very brief story told to teach a moral lesson. The most famous parables are those such as "The Parable of the Prodigal Son" told by Jesus in the Bible.

paradox A **paradox** is a seemingly contradictory statement, idea, or event. All forms of *irony* involve paradox. An *oxymoron* is a paradoxical statement. Anne Bradstreet's line "That when we live no more, we may live ever" is paradoxical. Some paradoxes present unresolvable contradictory ideas. An example of such a paradox is the statement, "This sentence is a lie." If the sentence is true, then it is false; if it is false, then it is true. See *irony* and *oxymoron.*

parallelism **Parallelism** is a rhetorical technique in which a writer emphasizes the equal value or weight of two or more ideas by expressing them in the same grammatical form. Thomas Jefferson used parallelism in the Declaration of Independence in his list of grievances against King George, starting each grievance with "He has . . . ."

paraphrase A **paraphrase** is a rewriting of a passage in different words. A paraphrase is often distinguished from an *abstract* or *summary* as follows: a summary is shorter than the original, whereas a paraphrase may be as long as or longer than the original. One of the central ideas of the so-called New Criticism was that it is impossible to paraphrase a literary work precisely. Much of the content or meaning of a literary work lies in how it is expressed. Changing the expression therefore inevitably changes the meaning. See *abstract.*

parody A **parody** is a literary work that imitates another work for humorous, often satirical, purposes. In the indented stanzas of "Do Not Weep, Maiden, for War is Kind," Stephen Crane subtly parodies hortatory patriotic speech.

pathetic fallacy The **pathetic fallacy** is the tendency to attribute human emotions to nonhuman things, particularly to things in the natural world. The term was coined by the Victorian critic John Ruskin and has often been used to describe the excesses of sentimental verse.

pentameter See *meter.*

periodical A **periodical** is a newspaper, magazine, journal, newsletter, or other publication that is produced on a regular basis. *The Dial,* a periodical, was the chief organ of American Transcendentalism. *Poetry* magazine has been a leading force in shaping the course of modern American poetry.

persona A **persona** consists of the qualities of a person or character that are shown through speech or actions.

personal essay A **personal essay** is a short work of nonfictional prose on a single topic related to the life or interests of the writer. Personal essays are characterized by an intimate and informal style and tone. They often, but not always, are written in the first person. See *essay*.

personal symbol See *symbol*.

personification **Personification** is a figure of speech in which an idea, animal, or thing is described as if it were a person. The speaker in Edgar Allan Poe's "The Raven" uses personification when he addresses and questions the raven:

> " . . . Tell this soul with sorrow laden if,
> within the distant Aidenn,
> It shall clasp a sainted maiden whom the
> angels name Lenore—
> Clasp a rare and radiant maiden whom the
> angels name Lenore.
> Quoth the raven, 'Nevermore.'"

Petrarchan sonnet See *sonnet*.

plagiarism **Plagiarism** is the act of using material gathered from another person or work without crediting the source of the material.

plot A **plot** is a series of events related to a central *conflict*, or struggle. A typical plot involves the introduction of a conflict, its development, and its eventual resolution. Terms used to describe elements of plot include the following:

- The **exposition**, or **introduction**, sets the tone or mood, introduces the characters and the setting, and provides necessary background information.
- The **inciting incident** is the event that introduces the central conflict.
- The **rising action**, or **complication**, develops the conflict to a high point of intensity.
- The **climax** is the high point of interest or suspense in the plot.
- The **crisis**, or **turning point**, often the same event as the climax, is the point in the plot where something decisive happens to determine the future course of events and the eventual working out of the conflict.
- The **falling action** is all of the events that follow the climax.
- The **resolution** is the point at which the central conflict is ended, or resolved.
- The **dénouement** is any material that follows the resolution and that ties up loose ends.
- The **catastrophe**, in tragedy, is the event that marks the ultimate tragic fall of the central character. Often this event is the character's death.

Plots rarely contain all these elements in precisely this order. Elements of exposition may be introduced at any time in the course of a work. A work may begin with a catastrophe and then use flashback to explain it. The exposition or dénouement or even the resolution may be missing. The inciting incident may occur before the beginning of the action actually described in the work. These are but a few of the many possible variations that plots can exhibit. See *conflict*.

poetic license **Poetic license** is the right claimed by writers to change elements of reality to suit the purposes of particular works that they create. Edgar Lee Master's use in his *Spoon River Anthology* of characters who rise from their graves and talk is an example of poetic license. Such things do not happen in reality, but they are accepted by readers willing to suspend disbelief in order to have imaginary experiences. See *suspension of disbelief*.

point of view **Point of view** is the vantage point from which a story is told. Stories are typically written from a *first-person point of view*, in which the narrator uses words such as *I* and *we*, or from a *third-person point of view*, in which the narrator uses words such as *he*, *she*, *it*, and *they* and avoids the use of *I* and *we*. In stories written from a first-person point of view, the narrator may be a participant or witness of the action. In stories told from a third-person point of view, the narrator generally stands outside the action. In some stories, the narrator's point of view is *limited*. In such stories, the narrator can reveal the private, internal thoughts of himself or herself or of a single character. In other stories, the narrator's point of view is *omniscient.* In such stories the narrator can reveal the private, internal thoughts of any character.

portmanteau See *blend.*

poulter's measure **Poulter's measure** is a metrical form that makes use of couplets containing alternating iambic hexameter and iambic heptameter lines.

pragmatic criticism See *criticism.*

précis See *abstract.*

preface A **preface** is a statement made at the beginning of a literary work, often by way of introduction. The terms *foreword, preface,* and *introduction* are often used interchangeably.

prologue A **prologue** is an introduction to a literary work, often one that sets the scene and introduces the conflict or the main characters. *The Glass Menagerie,* by Tennessee Williams, begins with a prologue by Tom Wingfield, the protagonist and narrator of the play.

proscenium stage See *stage.*

prose **Prose** is the broad term used to describe all writing that is not drama or poetry, including fiction and nonfiction. Types of prose writing include novels, short stories, essays, and news stories. Most biographies, autobiographies, and letters are written in prose. See *fiction.*

prose poem A **prose poem** is a work of prose, usually a short work, that makes such extensive use of poetic language, such as figures of speech and words that echo their sense, that the line between prose and poetry, never a clear one, becomes blurred. Many passages from the work of William Faulkner have the quality of prose poetry.

prosody **Prosody,** or **versification,** is the study of the structure of poetry. In particular, prosodists study meter, rhyme, rhythm, and stanza form. See *meter, rhyme, rhythm,* and *stanza.*

protagonist See *character.*

proverb A **proverb,** or **adage,** is a traditional saying, such as "You can lead a horse to water, but you can't make it drink" or the title of Shakespeare's play "All's Well That Ends Well."

psalm A **psalm** is a lyrical hymn of praise, supplication, or thanksgiving. The Biblical hymn, attributed to David, that begins with the line "The Lord is my shepherd," is an example.

pseudonym A **pseudonym** is a name assumed by a writer. For example, *Mark Twain* was the pseudonym of Samuel Clemens.

psychological fiction **Psychological fiction** is fiction that emphasizes the interior, subjective experiences of its characters, and especially such fiction when it deals with emotional or mental disturbance or anguish. Kate Chopin's "The Story of an Hour" is an example.

pun A **pun** is a play on words, one that wittily exploits a double meaning. In "Mending Wall," Frost uses a pun in the sentence "Before I built a wall I'd ask to know . . . to whom I was like to give offense." The sentence can also be read (or heard) as "to whom I was like to give a fence."

Puritanism **Puritanism** was a Protestant religious movement that emerged in England in the 1500s and later spread to the colonies of New England. The Puritans objected to the wealth, power, authority, and elaborate ritual of the Catholic Church. They professed a desire to "purify" the Church of England by ridding it of Catholic practices. The Puritans are known for their austerity and acceptance of the basic principles of Calvinism, including the ideas of preordination and original sin. The Plymouth Colony in Massachusetts was founded by Separatist Puritans who came from England via Holland. Important British Puritan writers include John Bunyan and John Milton. Important American Puritan writers include Cotton Mather and Jonathan Edwards. See *Calvinism.*

purpose See *aim.*

pyrrhic See *meter.*

quatrain A **quatrain** is a stanza containing four lines.

quintain A **quintain,** or **quintet,** is a stanza containing five lines.

quintet See *quintain.*

rap A **rap** is an improvised rhymed verse that is chanted or sung, often to a musical accompaniment.

reader-response criticism See *criticism.*

Realism **Realism** is the attempt to render in art an accurate portrayal of reality. The theory that the purpose of art is to imitate life is at least as old as Aristotle. The eighteenth-century development of the novel, with its attention to details of character, setting, and social life, can be thought of as a step toward increased Realism in writing. However, the term *Realism* is generally applied to literature of the late nineteenth century written in reaction to Romanticism and emphasizing details of ordinary life.

redundancy **Redundancy** is needless repetition. The phrase *firmly determined* is redundant because the word *determined* already implies firmness.

refrain A **refrain** is a line or group of lines repeated in a poem or song. Many ballads contain refrains.

regional dialect See *dialect.*

Renaissance The **Renaissance** was the period from the fourteenth to the early seventeenth century when Europe was making the transition from the medieval to the modern world. The word *renaissance* means "rebirth." The term refers to the rebirth of interest in ancient Greek and Latin writing that occurred during the period, a rebirth that is known as Humanism. The Renaissance was characterized by a lessening of reliance on authority, by a decline in feudalism and in the universal authority of the church, by increased nationalism, by increasingly active university and city life, by increased opportunities for individual economic attainment and freedom, and by increased belief in the value of this life in and of itself.

repetition **Repetition** is the use, again, of a sound, word, phrase, sentence, or other element.

resolution See *plot.*

reversal A **reversal** is a dramatic change in the direction of events in a drama or narrative, especially a change in the fortunes of the protagonist. See *plot.*

review A **review** is a written evaluation of a work of art, a performance, or a literary work, especially one that appears in a periodical or on a broadcast news program. Common subjects of reviews include books, films, art exhibitions, restaurants, and performances of all kinds, from rock concerts to ballets.

rhetoric **Rhetoric** is the study of ways in which speech and writing affect or influence audiences.

rhetorical criticism See *criticism.*

rhetorical question A **rhetorical question** is one asked for effect but not meant to be answered because the answer is clear from context. The questions "Are ye then truly free and brave?" and "are ye fit to be/mothers of the brave and free?" in Lowell's "Stanzas on Freedom" are rhetorical questions.

rhetorical technique A **rhetorical technique** is an extraordinary but literal use of language to achieve a particular effect on an audience. Common rhetorical techniques include *antithesis, apostrophe, catalog, chiasmus, parallelism, repetition,* and the *rhetorical question.*

rhyme **Rhyme** is the repetition of sounds at the ends of words. Types of rhyme include *end rhyme* (the use of rhyming words at the ends of lines), *internal rhyme* (the use of rhyming words within lines), *exact rhyme* (in which the rhyming words end with the same sound or sounds), and *slant rhyme* (in which the rhyming sounds are similar but not identical). An example of exact rhyme is the word pair *moon/June.* Examples of slant rhyme are the word pairs *rave/rove* and *rot/rock.* See *slant rhyme.*

rhythm **Rhythm** is the pattern of beats or stresses in a line of verse or prose. See *meter.*

riddle A **riddle** is a word game in which something is described in an unusual way and the reader or listener must figure out what that something is. Riddles are common in folklore and myth throughout the world.

rising action See *plot.*

romance **Romance** is a term used to refer to four types of literature: 1. medieval stories about the adventures and loves of knights; 2. novels and other fictions involving exotic locales and extraordinary or mysterious events and characters; 3. nonrealistic fictions in general; and 4. in popular modern usage, love stories of all kinds. The term originated in the Middle Ages. It was first used to describe stories believed to be based upon Latin originals (stories told by the Romans). It came to be used in Europe and England for stories in prose or poetry about knightly exploits. Because the later medieval romances were for the most part told in prose, the term came to be applied to prose fictions in general, and especially to those that were highly imaginative. In the nineteenth century, the term was commonly used to describe fictional works, such as the novels of Sir Walter Scott, that dealt with adventure in exotic locales. It was used by Nathaniel Hawthorne to describe stories like his *Blithedale Romance* and *House of the Seven Gables* because of their deviations from Realism. Today, the term is quite widely used to refer to love stories, especially popular, sentimental stories of the sort often turned into television movies.

Romantic criticism See *criticism.*

Romanticism **Romanticism** was a literary and artistic movement of the eighteenth and nineteenth centuries that placed value on emotion or imagination over reason, the individual over society, nature and wildness over human works, the country over the town, common people over aristocrats, and freedom over control or authority. Whittier's *Snow-Bound: A Winter Idyl* is Romantic in its celebration of the connection between people and nature. Much of Poe's poetry is Romantic in its intensity of emotion. Transcendentalism was a particularly American form of Romanticism. See *Transcendentalism.*

rounded character See *character.*

run-on line A **run-on line** is a line of verse in which the sense or the grammatical structure does not end with the end of the line but rather is continued on one or more subsequent lines. The following lines from Whittier's "Telling the Bees" form a single sentence:

> Then I said to myself, "My Mary weeps
> For the dead today:
> Haply her blind old grandsire sleeps
> The fret and the pain of his age away."

The act of continuing a statement beyond the end of a line is called *enjambment.* See *end-stopped line.*

satire **Satire** is humorous writing or speech intended to point out errors, falsehoods, foibles, or failings. It is written for the purpose of reforming human behavior or human institutions. Edwin Arlington Robinson's "Miniver Cheevy," for example, satirizes those who reject modern times as debased.

scansion **Scansion** is the art of analyzing poetry to determine its meter. See *meter.*

scene A **scene** is a short section of a literary work that presents action that occurs in a single place or at a single time. Long divisions of dramas are often divided into scenes.

science fiction **Science fiction** is highly imaginative fiction containing fantastic elements based on scientific principles, discoveries, or laws. It is similar to *fantasy* in that it deals with imaginary worlds but differs from fantasy in having a scientific basis. Often science fiction deals with the future, the distant past, or with worlds other than our own such as distant planets, parallel universes, and worlds under the ground or the sea. The genre allows writers to suspend or alter certain elements of reality in order to create fascinating and sometimes instructive alternatives. Important writers of science fiction include H. G. Wells, Jules Verne, Ray Bradbury, Arthur C. Clarke, Isaac Asimov, Ursula K. Le Guin, Robert Heinlein, and Kurt Vonnegut, Jr. See *fantasy.*

sensory detail See *description.*

sentimentality **Sentimentality** is an excessive expression of emotion. Much popular literature of the nineteenth and twentieth centuries is characterized by sentimentality.

septet A **septet** is a stanza with seven lines.

sestet A **sestet** is a stanza with six lines, such as the second part of a Petrarchan sonnet. See *meter* and *sonnet*.

set A **set** is a collection of objects on a stage arranged in such a way as to create a scene.

setting The **setting** of a literary work is the time and place in which it occurs, together with all the details used to create a sense of a particular time and place. Writers create setting by various means. In drama, the setting is often revealed by the stage *set* and the costumes, though it may be revealed through what the characters say about their environs. In fiction, setting is most often revealed by means of description of such elements as landscape, scenery, buildings, furniture, clothing, the weather, and the season. It can also be revealed by how characters talk and behave. In its widest sense, setting includes the general social, political, moral, and psychological conditions in which characters find themselves. See *set*.

Shakespearean sonnet See *sonnet*.

shape poem See *concrete poem*.

short short A **short short**, or **flash fiction**, is an extremely brief short story. This recently recognized genre of the short story is currently enjoying considerable popularity among readers of literary magazines and short story collections published in the United States. Short shorts sometimes take the form of *anecdotes*, or retellings of single incidents. Alternatively, they may attempt to develop an entire plot within the compass of a few paragraphs. Many short shorts are highly poetic and may be considered prose poems. See *anecdote* and *prose poem*.

sight rhyme A **sight rhyme**, or **eye rhyme**, is a pair of words, generally at the ends of lines of verse, that are spelled similarly but pronounced differently. These lines from Phillis Wheatley's "To S. M., a Young African Painter, on Seeing His Works" provide an example.

> On what seraphic pinions shall we *move*,
> And view the landscape in the realms *above?*

simile A **simile** is a comparison using *like* or *as*. Henry Wadsworth Longfellow uses a simile when he describes a blacksmith, saying, "And the muscles of his brawny arms/Are strong as iron bands."

A simile is a type of *metaphor*, and like any other metaphor, can be analyzed into two parts, the *tenor* (or subject being described), and the *vehicle* (or object being used in the description). In Longfellow's simile, the tenor is *brawny arms* and the vehicle is *iron bands*. They can be compared because they share some quality, in this case, strength. See *metaphor*.

slang **Slang** is extremely colloquial speech not suitable for formal occasions and usually associated with a particular group of people. An example of slang current among young people in the United States in the 1920s is "the bee's knees," for something uniquely attractive or wonderful. Among young people in the northeastern United States, the word *wicked* is now sometimes used as a slang term meaning "extremely," as in "That song is *wicked* good." Writers sometimes use slang in an attempt to render characters and setting vividly.

slant rhyme A **slant rhyme, half rhyme, near rhyme,** or **off rhyme** is substitution of assonance or consonance for true rhyme. The pairs *world/boiled* and *bear/bore* are examples. See *assonance, consonance,* and *rhyme*.

social dialect See *dialect*.

soliloquy A **soliloquy** is a speech delivered by a lone character that reveals the speaker's thoughts and feelings. Tom's opening and closing speeches in *The Glass Menagerie* are soliloquies.

sonnet A **sonnet** is a fourteen-line poem that follows one of a number of different rhyme schemes. The *English, Elizabethan,* or *Shakespearean sonnet* is divided into four parts: three *quatrains* and a final *couplet*. The rhyme scheme of such a sonnet is *abab cdcd efef gg*. "Sonnet XXX" by Edna St. Vincent Millay is an example of an English sonnet. The *Italian* or *Petrarchan sonnet* is divided into two parts: an *octave* and a *sestet*. The rhyme scheme of the octave is *abbaabba*. The rhyme scheme of the sestet can be *cdecde, cdcdcd,* or *cdedce*. Millay's sonnet "Euclid Alone Has Looked on Beauty Bare" is an Italian sonnet.

sonnet cycle See *sonnet sequence.*

sonnet sequence A **sonnet sequence** is a group of related sonnets. See *sonnet.*

source A **source** is a work from which an author takes his or her materials.

Southern Gothic **Southern Gothic** is writing containing elements of horror, suspense, mystery, or magic, produced in or set in the southern States. Tennessee Williams's work is often described as Southern Gothic.

speaker The **speaker** is the character who speaks in, or narrates, a poem—the voice assumed by the writer. The speaker and the writer of a poem are not necessarily the same person. For example, T. S. Eliot takes on the voice of J. Alfred Prufrock in "The Love Song of J. Alfred Prufrock." In Carl Sandburg's "Grass," the grass is the speaker.

spectacle In drama, the **spectacle** is all the elements that are presented to the senses of the audience, including the lights, setting, costumes, makeup, music, sound effects, and movements of the actors.

spondee A **spondee** is a poetic foot containing two strongly stressed syllables, as in the words *compound* and *roughhouse*. Such a foot is said to be *spondaic*.

stage A **stage** is any arena on which the action of a drama is performed. In the Middle Ages, stages often consisted of the beds of wagons, which were wheeled from place to place for performances. From the use of such wagons in innyards, the *thrust stage* developed. This was a platform that extended out into the audience and that was closed at the back. In front of the platform in the first English theaters, such as Shakespeare's Globe Theatre, was an open area, the pit, where common people stood. Around the pit were balconies in imitation of the balconies of inns. The modern *proscenium stage* typically is closed on three sides and open at the front, as though the fourth wall had been removed. Sometimes contemporary plays are performed as *theater in the round,* with the audience seated on all sides of the playing area.

stage directions **Stage directions** are notes included in a play in addition to the dialogue for the purpose of describing how something should be performed on stage. Stage directions describe setting, lighting, music, sound effects, entrances and exits, properties, and the movements of characters. They are usually printed in italics and enclosed in brackets or parentheses.

stanza A **stanza** is a recurring pattern of grouped lines in a poem. The following are some types of stanza:

two-line stanza	couplet
three-line stanza	tercet or triplet
four-line stanza	quatrain
five-line stanza	quintain
six-line stanza	sestet
seven-line stanza	heptastich
eight-line stanza	octave

static character See *character.*

stereotype A **stereotype** is an uncritically accepted fixed or conventional idea, particularly such an idea held about whole groups of people. A *stereotypical,* or *stock,* character is one who does not deviate from conventional expectations of such a character. Examples of stereotypical characters include the merciless villain, the mad scientist, and the hard-boiled private eye. In his autobiography, Frederick Douglass disputes the stereotype of the contented singing slave because, in his experience, slave songs were a release of sorrow. See *character.*

stock character See *character* and *stereotype.*

story A **story,** or **narrative,** is writing or speech that relates a series of events. When these events are causally connected and related to a conflict, they make up a *plot.* See *plot.*

stream-of-consciousness writing **Stream-of-consciousness writing** is literary work that attempts to render the flow of feelings, thoughts, and impressions within the minds of characters. Modern masters of stream-of-consciousness writing include Virginia Woolf, James Joyce, and William Faulkner. An example of stream-of-consciousness writing is the work of Katherine Anne Porter in "The Jilting of Granny Weatherall."

stress **Stress,** or **accent,** is the level of emphasis given to a syllable. In English *metrics,* the art of rhythm in written and spoken expression, syllables are generally described as being *strongly* or *weakly stressed,* in other words, *accented* or *unaccented.* A strongly stressed or accented syllable receives a strong emphasis. A weakly stressed or unaccented syllable receives a weak one. In the following line from Walt Whitman's "When Lilacs Last in the Dooryard Bloom'd," the strongly stressed or accented syllables are marked with a slash mark (/).

/ / / /
When lilacs last in the dooryard bloom'd

structuralist criticism See *criticism.*

style **Style** is the manner in which something is said or written. Traditionally, critics and scholars have referred to three levels of style: *high style,* for formal occasions or lofty subjects; *middle style,* for ordinary occasions or subjects; and *low style,* for extremely informal occasions or subjects. A writer's style depends upon many things, including his or her *diction* (the words that the writer chooses), selection of grammatical structures (simple versus complex sentences, for example), and preference for abstract or concrete words. Any recurring feature that distinguishes one writer's work from another can be said to be part of that writer's style. See *abstract* and *fiction.*

subplot A **subplot** is a subordinate story told in addition to the major story in a work of fiction. Often a subplot mirrors or provides a foil for the primary plot. See *plot* and *story.*

summary See *abstract.*

suspense **Suspense** is a feeling of expectation, anxiousness, or curiosity created by questions raised in the mind of a reader or viewer.

suspension of disbelief **Suspension of disbelief** is the phrase used by Coleridge in his *Biographia Literaria* to describe the act by which the reader willingly sets aside his or her skepticism in order to participate imaginatively in the work being read. In Stephen Vincent Bénet's "The Devil and Daniel Webster" the dead and damned return to earth to pass judgment on Jabez Stone. To enjoy the story, readers must suspend their disbelief in people rising from the dead. The willingness to suspend disbelief, to participate imaginatively in a story being read, is the most important attribute, beyond literacy, that a person can bring to the act of reading.

symbol A **symbol** is a thing that stands for or represents both itself and something else. Writers use two types of symbols—conventional, and personal or idiosyncratic. A *conventional symbol* is one with traditional, widely recognized associations. Such symbols include doves for peace; laurel wreaths for heroism or poetic excellence; the color green for jealousy; the color purple for royalty; the color red for anger; morning or spring for youth; winter, evening, or night for old age; wind for change or inspiration; rainbows for hope; roses for beauty; the moon for fickleness or inconstancy; roads or paths for the journey through life; woods or darkness for moral or spiritual confusion; thorns for troubles or pain; stars for unchangeableness or constancy; mirrors for vanity or introspection; snakes for evil or duplicity; and owls for wisdom. A *personal* or *idiosyncratic symbol* is one that assumes its secondary meaning because of the special use to which it is put by a writer. In "Song of Myself" Walt Whitman uses grass as a personal symbol for the beauty and value of simple, lowly things.

synaesthesia **Synaesthesia** is a figure of speech that combines in a single expression images related to two or more different senses. In Emily Dickinson's "I heard a Fly buzz—when I died—", the line "With Blue—uncertain stumbling Buzz—" contains an example of synaesthesia because "stumbling Buzz" is an image that appeals both to the senses of sight and of sound.

synecdoche A **synecdoche** is a figure of speech in which the name of part of something is used in place of the name of the whole or *vice versa*. In the command *"All hands on deck!" hands* is a synecdoche in which a part (hands) is used to refer to a whole (people, sailors). Addressing a representative of the country of France as *France* would be a synecdoche in which a whole (France) is used to refer to a part (one French person).

syntax **Syntax** is the pattern of arrangement of words in a statement. Abraham Lincoln's Gettysburg Address is often noted for its unusual syntax. Poets often vary the syntax of ordinary speech or experiment with unusual syntactic arrangements as in "anyone lived in a pretty how town/(with up so floating many bells down)," from E. E. Cummings's, "anyone lived in a pretty how town." See *inversion.*

tag line A **tag line** is an expression in a work of fiction that indicates who is speaking and sometimes indicates the manner of speaking. Examples include the familiar *she said* as well as more elaborate expressions such as *Bernard muttered moodily.*

tall tale A **tall tale** is a story, often light-hearted or humorous, that contains highly exaggerated, unrealistic elements. Mark Twain's "The Notorious Jumping Frog of Calaveras County" is an example.

tenor See *metaphor.*

tercet See *triplet.*

terza rima ***Terza rima*** is a three-line stanza of the kind used in Dante's *Divine Comedy,* rhyming *aba, bcb, cdc, ded,* and so on.

tetrameter See *meter.*

textual criticism See *criticism.*

theater (playing area) See *stage.*

theater in the round See *stage.*

theater of the absurd The **theater of the absurd** is a kind of twentieth-century drama that presents illogical, absurd, or unrealistic scenes, characters, events, or juxtapositions in an attempt to convey the essential meaninglessness of human life, although playwrights have often used the form to convey significant moral messages. Practitioners of the theater of the absurd, which grew out of the philosophy of *Existentialism,* include Eugène Ionesco, Samuel Becket, Edward Albee, and Harold Pinter. See *Existentialism* and *literature of the absurd.*

theme A **theme** is a central idea in a literary work. The value of each individual is the theme of Ralph Waldo Emerson's "The Rhodora."

thesis A **thesis** is a main idea that is supported in a work of nonfictional prose.

third-person point of view See *point of view.*

three-dimensional character See *character.*

thrust stage See *stage.*

tone **Tone** is the emotional attitude toward the reader or toward the subject implied by a literary work. Examples of the different tones that a work may have include familiar, ironic, playful, sarcastic, serious, and sincere.

tragedy A **tragedy** is a drama (or by extension any work of literature) that relates the fall of a person of high status. Tragedy tends to be serious. It celebrates the courage and dignity of a tragic hero in the face of inevitable doom. Sometimes that doom is made inevitable by a *tragic flaw* in the hero. In the twentieth century, writers have extended the definition of *tragedy* to cover works that deal with the fall of any sympathetic character, despite his or her status. Willie Loman in Arthur Miller's play *The Death of a Salesman* is such a character. His downfall is precipitated by his adherence to the mistaken belief that success in life is gained by being "well liked" by people of importance.

tragic flaw A **tragic flaw** is a personal weakness that brings about the fall of a character in a tragedy. See *tragedy.*

Transcendentalism As a variation of European Romanticism, Transcendentalism advocated a belief in spiritual, or transcendent, truths beyond sense perception and material existence. Placing oneself in natural environs would increase one's ability to attain transcendent thought. In contrast to the materialism valued by the Puritans and Benjamin Franklin, Transcendentalists exalted the spiritual and the individual. The group of Transcendental thinkers and writers gathered in Boston and Concord, Massachusetts, in the middle of the nineteenth century included Henry David Thoreau, Ralph Waldo Emerson, Bronson Alcott, Margaret Fuller, and W. H. Channing.

transition A **transition** is a word, phrase, sentence, or paragraph used to connect ideas and to show relationships between them. *However, therefore, in addition,* and *in contrast* are common transitions. Repeated nouns, synonyms, and pronouns can also serve as transitions. For more information on transitions, see the Language Arts Survey, 1.34, "Organizing Ideas"; 1.38, "Paragraphs with Topic Sentences"; and 1.39, "Paragraphs without Topic Sentences." See *coherence.*

translation **Translation** is the art of rendering speech or writing into another language.

trimeter See *meter.*

triplet A **triplet,** or **tercet,** is a stanza of three lines.

trochee A **trochee** is a poetic foot consisting of a strongly stressed syllable followed by a weakly stressed syllable, as in the word *winter.* A line of poetry made up of trochees is said to be *trochaic.*

trope See *figure of speech.*

turning point See *plot.*

understatement An **understatement** is an ironic expression in which something of importance is emphasized by being spoken of as though it were not important, as in the opening lines of "Sonnet XXX" by Edna St. Vincent Millay:

> Love is not all: it is not meat nor drink
> Nor slumber nor a roof against the rain

unity A work has **unity** when its various parts all contribute to creating an integrated whole. An essay with unity, for example, is one in which all the parts help to support the thesis statement, or main idea. See *essay.*

Utilitarianism **Utilitarianism** was a philosophical movement of the nineteenth century associated with Jeremy Bentham and John Stuart Mill in England and with Charles Peirce and William James in the United States. The primary guiding principle of Utilitarianism was that the truth of an idea or the rightness of an action should be judged not according to some abstract or ideal principle but rather according to its practical consequences. Another tenet of Utilitarianism was that moral and political decisions should be made as a result of considering what course of action would bring about "the greatest good [or happiness] for the greatest number" of people.

utopia A **utopia** is an imaginary, idealized world. The term comes from the title of Sir Thomas More's *Utopia,* which described what More believed to be an ideal society. More took the word from the Greek roots meaning "no-place." See *dystopia.*

vehicle See *metaphor.*

verbal irony See *irony.*

vernacular The **vernacular** is the speech of the common people. The term *vernacular* is often used to refer to dialogue or to writing in general that uses colloquial, dialectical, or slang expressions.

versification See *prosody.*

vers libre See *free verse.*

villanelle A **villanelle** is a complex and intricate nineteen-line French verse form. The rhyme scheme is *aba aba aba aba abaa.* The first line is repeated as lines 6, 12, and 18. The third line is repeated as lines 9, 15, and 19. The first and third lines appear as a rhymed couplet at the end of the poem.

Glossary

OF WORDS FOR EVERYDAY USE

Pronunciation Key

Vowel Sounds

a	hat	i	sit	ōō	blue, stew	ə	extra
ā	play	ī	my	oi	boy		under
ä	star	ō	go	ou	wow		civil
e	then	ô	paw, born	u	up		honor
ē	me	oo	book, put	ʉ	burn		bogus

Consonant Sounds

b	but	j	jump	p	pop	th	the
ch	watch	k	brick	r	rod	v	valley
d	do	l	lip	s	see	w	work
f	fudge	m	money	sh	she	y	yell
g	go	n	on	t	sit	z	pleasure
h	hot	ŋ	song, sink	th	with		

ab • di • cate (ab´di kāt´) *vt.*, give up a right or a responsibility

a • bey • ance (ə bā´əns) *n.*, temporary suspension, as of an activity or function

ab • hor (ab hôr´) *vt.*, shrink from in disgust

ab • ject • ly (ab´jekt´lē) *adv.*, *miserably;* in a manner that suggests a lack of self-respect

ab • strac • tion (ab strak´shən) *n.*, mental withdrawal; absent-mindedness

a • byss (ə bis´) *n.*, bottomless hole

ac • cen • tu • a • tion (ak sen´chōō ā´shən) *n.*, emphasis; clear pronunciation

ac • cliv • i • ty (ə kliv´ə tē) *n.*, upward slope

ac • cu • mu • late (ə kyōōm´yōō lāt´) *vi.*, pile up over time

ac • qui • esce (ak´wē es´) *vi.*, agree without protest

ac • qui • es • cent (ak´wē es´ənt) *adj.*, without protest

a • cute • ly (ə kyoot´lē) *adv.*, sharply, painfully, or severely

ad • jure (ə jer´) *vt.*, urge; beg

ad • mon • ish (ad män´ish) *vt.*, caution against specific faults

af • fin • i • ty (ə fin´i tē) *n.*, close relationship; connection

af • flic • ted (ə flikt´əd) *part.*, having a physical condition, usually painful or distressing

a • ghast (ə gast´) *adj.*, feeling great horror or dismay

ag • i • ta • tion (aj´ə tā´shən) *n.*, violent motion or disturbance

a • gue (a´gyōō) *n.*, fever with chills

al • cove (al´kōv´) *n.*, recessed section, nook

al • lay (a lā´) *vt.*, put to rest; quiet, calm

a • nal • o • gy (ə nal´ə jē) *n.*, similarity in some respects between things otherwise unlike

a • nath • e • ma (ə nath´ə mə) *n.*, curse

a • noint • ed (ə noint´əd) *part.*, rubbed with the oil from the meat

an • o • nym • i • ty (an´ə nim´ə tē) *n.*, condition of having no special or distinguishing qualities

ap • a • thet • i • cal • ly (ap´ə thet´ə kə lē) *adv.*, without emotion

ap • er • ture (ap´ər cher) *n.*, opening; hole

ap • pa • ra • tus (ap´ə rat´əs) *n.*, materials and tools needed for a specific purpose

ap • pa • ri • tion (ap´ər rish´ən) *n.*, ghostly appearance of a person or thing

ap • pend (ə pend´) *vt.*, attach or affix

ap • pre • hen • sion (ap´rē hen´shən) *n.*, anxiety, dread

ap • ti • tude (ap´tə tōōd´) *n.*, natural tendency or inclination

ar • dent (ärd´ ´nt) *adj.*, intensely enthusiastic or devoted

ar • du • ous (är´jōō əs) *adj.*, difficult

ar • tic • u • late (är tik´yōō lit) *adj.*, able to express oneself easily and clearly

ar • tic • u • lat • ed (ar tik´yōō lāt´əd) *adj.*, made up of distinct syllables or words, as human speech

as • cet • ic (ə set´ik) *adj.*, self-denying; austere

as • cribe (ə skrīb´) *vt.*, assign; attribute

as • pect (as´pekt´) *n.*, appearance

as • pi • rat • ed (as´pə rāt´əd) *adj.*, articulated with a puff of breath before or after

as • pi • ra • tion (as´pə rā´shən) *n.*, strong ambition

as • sent (ə sent´) *n.*, agreement

as • sert (ə sûrt´) *vt.*, declare; affirm

as • suage (ə swāj´) *vt.*, lessen; calm; pacify

a • sun • der (ə sun´der´) *adv.*, apart or separate in direction or position

au • gust (ô gust´) *adj.*, magnificent; worthy of respect

aus • tere (o stir´) *adj.*, plain; without luxury or ornamentation

a • vail (ə vāl´) *vi.*, be of use or advantage

a • ver • sion (ə vur´zhən) *n.*, definite dislike

a • vert (ə vurt´) *vt.*, prevent

a • vid • i • ty (ə vid´ə tē) *n.*, eagerness; enthusiasm

a • vow (ə vou´) *vt.*, admit frankly

balm (bäm) *n.*, anything healing or soothing

balm • y (bäm´ē) *adj.*, soothing, mild, or pleasant

ba • nal (bā´nəl) *adj.*, commonplace; trite

bane • ful (bān´fəl) *adj.*, causing distress, death, or ruin

banked (baŋkd) *part.*, arranged to continue burning slowly

bar • bar • ic (bär ber´ik) *adj.*, wild, crude, and unrestrained

be • guil • ing (bē gīl´iŋ) *part.*, charming; leading by deception

be • la • bor (bē lā´bər) *vt.*, spend too much time or effort on

be • lea • guer (bē lē´gər) *vt.*, besiege by encircling

bel • li • cose (bel´i kōs) *adj.*, hostile, eager to fight

be • nig • ni • ty (bi nig´nə tē) *n.*, kindliness

blight (blīt) *n.*, anything that destroys or prevents growth

bom • bard • ment (bäm bard´mənt) *n.*, attack by bombs

brink (briŋk) *n.*, edge, especially at the top of a steep place

buf • fet (buf´it) *n.*, blow with the hand or fist

bur • nish (bur´nish) *vt.*, make shiny by rubbing

ca • dence (kād´´ns) *n.*, rhythmic flow of sound or tone

ca • denced (kād´´nst) *adj.*, measured; rhythmic

ca • lam • i • ty (kə lam´ə tē) *n.*, deep trouble or misery

can • on • ize (kan´ən īz´) *vt.*, declare a deceased person a saint in formal church procedure

ca • price (kə prēs´) *n.*, whim, change in way of thinking

cat • a • lyst (kat´ə list´) *n.*, something that stimulates or hastens a result

ca • ter (kāt´ər) *vi.*, take special pains in seeking to gratify another's needs or desires

cav • al • cade (kav´əl kād´) *n.*, procession (of horses)

ca • vort (kə vôrt´) *vi.*, leap about, prance

cen • ser (sen´sər) *n.*, container for burning incense

ces • sa • tion (se sā´shən) *n.*, ceasing or stopping

chron • ic (krän´ik) *adj.*, constant; perpetual

ci • vil • i • ty (sə vil´ə tē) *n.*, gentleness; a civilized manner

clod (kläd) *n.*, lump, such as lump of earth or clay

cog • ni • zance (käg´nə zəns) *n.*, knowledge

co • her • ent (kō hir´ənt) *adj.*, logically connected; making sense

com • men • da • tion (käm´ən dā´shən) *n.*, praise

com • men • su • rate (kə men´shoor it) *adj.*, equal in measure or size, proportionate

com • mu • ni • ca • tive (kə myōō´ni kāt´iv) *adj.*, talkative; giving information readily

com • mun • ion (kə myōōn´yən) *n.*, act of sharing thoughts and actions

com • pli • ance (kəm plī´əns) *n.*, act of giving in to wishes or demands

com • port (kəm pôrt´) *vi.*, agree; go along

com • posed (kəm pōzd´) *adj.*, calm, tranquil

con • ceit (kən sēt´) *n.*, idea, thought; personal opinion

con • ceiv • a • bly (kən sēv´ə blē) *adv.*, in a manner that can be understood or imagined

con • fed • er • a • cy (kən fed´ər ə sē) *n.*, people or groups united for common purpose

con • fla • gra • tion (kän´flə grā´shən) *n.*, destructive fire

con • found (kən found´) *vt.*, confuse, bewilder

con • ge • ni • al • i • ty (kən jē´nē al´ə tē) *n.*, friendliness

con • glom • er • a • tion (kən gläm´ər ā´shən) *n.*, collection or mixture

con • jec • tur • al (kən jek´chər əl) *adj.*, based on guesses

con • jec • ture (kən jek´chər) *n.*, speculation; *vi.*, guess

con • junc • tion (kən juŋk´shən) *n.*, association; combination

con • jur • a • tion (kän´joo rā´shən) *n.*, magic; sorcery

con • jure (kun´jər) *vt.*, call

con • nois • seur (kän´ə sur´) *n.*, person who has expert knowledge in some field

con • se • crate (kan´si krāt´) *vt.*, make or declare sacred

con • so • la • tion (kän´sə lā´shən) *n.*, comfort

con • ster • na • tion (kän´stər nā´shən) *n.*, dismay; great fear

con • sti • tu • tion (kän´stə tōō´shən) *n.*, physical makeup of a person

con • sul • ta • tion (kän´səl tā´shən) *n.*, meeting to discuss, decide, or plan something

con • tem • pla • tion (kän´ təm plā´shən) *n.*, thoughtful inspection, study, or meditation

con • tend • er (kən ten´dər) *n.*, one who strives or fights in competition

con • tor • tion (kən tôr´shən) *n.*, twisting out of shape

con • triv • ance (kən trī´vəns) *n.*, invention; ingenious plan

con • va • les • cent (kän´ və les´ ənt) *n.*, person recovering from an illness

con • viv • i • al • ly (kən viv´ē əl lē) *adv.*, festively

con • vo • lu • tion (kän´və lōō´ shən) *n.*, twist, coil, fold

con • vul • sion (kən vul´ shən) *n.*, sudden, violent disturbance

con • vul • sive (kən vul´siv) *adj.*, marked by violent contractions or spasms

co • quet • ry (kō´kə trē) *n.*, flirting

cor • di • al • i • ty (kôr´jē al´ə tē) *n.*, warm, friendly act or remark

cor • rod • ing (kə rōd´iŋ) *part.*, wearing away; causing deterioration

course (kôrs) *vi.*, move swiftly; flow through

cow • er (kou´ər) *vi.*, crouch or shrink back in fear

cra • ven (krā´vən) *adj.*, very cowardly; *n.*, coward

creed (krēd) *n.*, statement of belief, principles, or opinions on any subject

cru • ci • fy (krōō´sə fī´) *vt.*, torment; be cruel to

cryp • tic (krip´tik) *adj.*, having a hidden meaning; baffling

cul • prit (kul´prit) *n.*, guilty person

cul • ti • vate (kul´tə vāt) *vt.*, acquire and develop

czar (zar) *n.*, emperor

dal • ly (dal´ē) *vi.*, waste time

de • cree (dē krē´) *vt.*, order

def • er • en • tial (def´ə ren´shəl) *adj.*, respectful

del • e • te • ri • ous (del´ə tir´ ē əs) *adj.*, harmful to health or well-being

de • lib • er • a • tion (di lib´ər ā´shən) *n.*, discussion; consideration of alternatives

de • lir • i • ous (di lir´ē əs) *adj.*, hallucinating; restless and confused

del • uge (del´yōōj) *n.*, overwhelming floodlike rush

de • lu • so • ry (di lōō´sə rē) *adj.*, quality of seeming unreal

de • mean • or (di mēn´ər) *n.*, way of behaving; manner

de • mure (di myoor´) *adj.*, modest; shy

de • nun • ci • a • tion (dē nun´sē ā´shən) *n.*, criticism; speaking against

de • pop • u • late (dē päp´yə lāt´) *vt.*, reduce the population of, especially by violence or disease

de • port • ment (dē pôrt´mənt) *n.*, manner of conducting or bearing oneself

de • praved (dē prāvd´) *adj.*, morally bad; corrupt

de • ranged (dē rānjd´) *adj.*; disordered; upset; insane

de • vout (di vout´) *adj.*, showing reverence

dif • fuse (di fyōōs´) *vt.*, spread out; pour out

di • gress (di greś) *vi.*, deviate from the main topic in speaking or writing

di • lap • i • dat • ed (də lap´ə dāt´ id) *adj.*, falling to pieces or into disrepair

di • late (dī´lāt) *vi.*, become larger or wider

di • la • tion (dī lā´shən) *n.*, widening, expansion

dil • a • to • ry (dil´ə tôr´ē) *adj.*, causing delay

dil • i • gent • ly (dil´ə jənt lē) *adv.* painstakingly, industriously

dis • bar (dis bär´) *vt.*, deprive (a lawyer) of the right to practice law

dis • cord • ant (dis kôrd´´nt) *adj.*, disagreeing; conflicting

dis • creet (di skrēt´) *adj.*, careful about what one says and does

dis • mal (diz´məl) *adj.*, causing gloom or misery

dis • po • si • tion (dis´ pə zish´ ən) *n.*, state of mind; general nature

dis • suade (di swād´) *vt.*, talk out of

dis • til • la • tion (dis´tə lā´shən) *n.*, something separated out into parts

di • ver • si • ty (də vur´sə tē) *n.*, variety

doc • trine (däk´trin) *n.*, teachings; beliefs

dole • ful (dōl´fəl) *adj.*, full of or causing sorrow or sadness

dredge (drej) *vt.*, dig up (in search of something)

du • ra • tion (dōō rā´shən) *n.*, continuance in time

dwin •dle (dwin´dəl) *vt.*, languish; fade

ear • nest (ur´nist) *adj.*, serious; intense

ebb (eb) *vi.*, flow back, recede

eb • ul • li • tion (eb´ə lish´ən) *n.*, boiling or bubbling up

ed • dy (ed´ē) *n.*, move with a circular motion against the main current

ee • rie (ir´ē) *adj.*, mysterious; weird

ef • face (ə fās´) *vt.*, erase, wipe out

ef • fec • tu • al (e fek´chōō əl) *adj.*, effective

ef • fi • ca • cious (ef´i kā´shəs) *adj.*, producing or capable of producing the desired effect

e • late (ē lāt´) *vt.*, raise the spirits of

e • lu • ci • date (ə lōō´sə dāt´) *vt.*, make clear

e • ma • ci • at • ed (ē mā´shē āt əd) *part.*, abnormally thin

em • bra • sure (em brā´zhər) *n.*, slanted opening in a wall that increases the firing angle of a gun

em • is • sar • y (em´i ser´ē) *n.*, person or agent sent on a mission

en • com • pass (en kum´pəs) *vt.*, surround

en • cum • brance (en kum´brəns) *n.*, hindrance

en • deav • or (en dev´ər) *n.*, effort, attempt

en • dow • ment (en dow´mənt) *n.*, gift of nature; inherent talent

en • dure (en door´) *vi.* continue in existence, last, remain

en • gorge (en gôrj´) *vt.*, devour greedily

en • gulf (en gulf´) *vt.*, overwhelm

en • sue (en sōō´) *vi.*, come afterward; follow immediately

en • treat (en trēt´) *vt.*, beg; implore; ask earnestly

en • treat • y (en trēt´ē) *n.*, earnest request

en • voy (än´voi) *n.*, messenger; agent

e • phem • er • al (e fem´ər əl) *adj.*, short-lived, transitory

e • qua • nim • i • ty (ek´wə nim´ə tē) *n.*, evenness of mind or temper

e • rad • i • cate (ē rad´i kāt´) *vt.*, get rid of; wipe out; destroy

er • ro • ne • ous (ər rō´nē əs) *adj.*, mistaken, wrong

es • cu • lent (es´kyōō lənt) *adj.*, fit for food, edible

es • ti • ma • tion (es´tə mā´shən) *n.*, respect; value

e • the • re • al (ē thir´ē əl) *adj.*, not earthly; heavenly, celestial

e • ther • ise (ē´thə rīz´) *vt.*, render groggy or numb

eu • pho • ny (yōō´fə nē) *n.*, pleasing effect to the ear

e • vade (ē vād´) *vt.*, avoid or escape from by deceit or cleverness

ev • a • nes • cent (ev´ə nes´ənt) *adj.*, tending to fade; vanishing

e • vince (ē vins´) *vt.*, show plainly; indicate

ex • as • per • a • ting (eg zas´pər āt iŋ) *part.*, irritating, annoying

ex • cru • ci • at • ing • ly (eks krōō´shē āt´iŋ lē) *adv.*, in a painful or agonizing manner

ex • cru • ci • a • tion (ex kru´shē ā´shən) *n.*, torment

ex • hor • ter (eg zôrt´ər) *n.*, one who urges earnestly, by advice or warning

ex • pa • tri • at • ed (eks pā´trē āt´id) *part.*, driven from one's land

ex • pe • di • ent (ek spē´dē ənt) *adj.*, convenient

ex • po • si • tion (eks´pə zish´ən) *n.*, large, public exhibition or show, often international in scope

ex • tem • po • rize (eks tem´pə rīz´) *vt.*, contrive in a makeshift way to meet a pressing need

ex • trem • i • ty (ek strem´ə tē) *n.*, state of extreme necessity, danger, etc.

ex • tri • cate (eks´tri kāt) *vt.*, release or disentangle

feign (fān) *vt.*, make up, invent

fe • lo • ni • ous (fə lō´nē əs) *adj.*, of a criminal

fer • vor (fur´vər) *n.*, great warmth or emotion

fes • tooned (fes tōōnd´) *part.*, adorned with curving decorations

fet • ter (fet´ər) *n.*, shackle or chain for the feet

fi • as • co (fē as´ko) *n.*, complete failure

fis • sure (fish´ər) *n.*, deep crack

flour • ish (flur´ish) *vi.*, grow vigorously; thrive; prosper

fluc • tu • ate (fluk´chōō āt´) *vi.*, change or vary continuously

for • mal • ize (fôr´mə līz´) *vt.*, give definite form to

for • mi • da • ble (fôr´mə də bəl) *adj.*, strikingly impressive

for • mu • lat • ed (fôr´myə lāt´əd) *part.*, systematical; precise

for • ti • tude (fort´ə tōōd) *n.*, strength to bear misfortune or pain

fur • nish (fur´nish) *vt.*, supply or provide

fur • tive (fur´tiv) *adj.*, secretive, stealthy

gal • lant • ly (gal´ənt lē) *adv.*, politely, nobly

game (gām) *adj.*, having spirit or enthusiasm

gar • ru • lous (gar´ə ləs) *adj.*, talking much or too much

gauche (gōsh) *adj.*, tactless; lacking social grace

gaud • i • est (gôd´ē əst) *adj.*, brightest and showiest, but lacking good taste

gaunt • let • ed (gônt´lit id) *adj.*, wearing a gauntlet, or glove; figuratively, combative

ges • tic • u • late (jes tik´yōō lat´) *vi.*, make gestures with hands or arms

ges • tic • u • lat • ing (jes tik´yōō lāt´iŋ) *part.*, making gestures

glib (glib) *adj.*, able to speak in a smooth, easy manner

glut • ton • y (glut´'n ē) *n.*, habit or act of eating too much

grav • i • ty (grav´i tē) *n.*, seriousness

guile • less (gīl´lis) *adj.*, without deceit

gulf (gulf) *n.*, wide, deep gap or separation

gull (gul) *vt.*, trick; dupe

hag • gard (hag´ərd) *adj.*, having a wasted or exhausted look

hang • dog (haŋ´dôg´) *adj.*, ashamed and cringing

har • bor (här´bər) *vt.*, serve as, or provide, a place of protection

har • ry (har´ē´) *vt.*, push along; hurry forcefully

heart • i • ly (härt´'l ē) *adv.*, in a friendly, sincere, way

hem (hem) *vt.*, encircle; surround

her • it • age (her´i tij´) *n.*, cultural traditions handed down by ancestors

her • mi • tage (hur´mi tij) *n.*, place where a person can live away from others

hoar • y (hôr´ē) *adj.*, having white or gray hair

home • ly (hōm´lē) *adj.*, simple, plain

hy • poc • ri • sy (hi päk´rə sē) *n.*, pretending to be what one is not, or to feel what one does not feel

i • de • ol • o • gy (ī´dē äl´ə gē) *n.*, doctrine, opinion, or way of thinking

il • lu • mi • nate (i lōō´mə nāt´) *vt.*, light up

im • bue (im byōō´) *vt.*, fill; saturate

im • me • mo • ri • al (im´me môr´ē əl) *adj.*, something too old to be remembered

im • mi • nent (im´ə nənt) *adj.*, likely to happen without delay

im • mo • bil • i • ty (im´mo bil´i tē) *n.*, state of being fixed or unmovable

im • pal • pa • ble (im pal´pə bəl) *adj.*, that which cannot be felt by touching

im • par • ti • al • i • ty (im pär´shē al´ i tē) *n.*, free of bias

im • pede (im pēd´) *vt.*, obstruct; hinder

im • pend (im pend´) *vi.*, be about to happen

im • per • a • tive (im per´ə tiv) *adj.*, absolutely necessary

im • per • cep • ti • ble (im´ pər sep´ tə bəl) *adj.*, not able to be detected by the senses or the mind

im • per • turb • a • ble (im´pər tur´ bə bəl) *adj.*, that cannot be disconnected or disturbed

im • pet • u • ous (im pech´ōō əs) *adj.*, rushing with force or violence

im • pe • tus (im´pə təs) *n.*, driving force behind an activity

im • pi • ous (im´pē əs) *adj.*, lacking reverence for God

im • pla • ca • ble (im plā´kə bəl) *adj.*, that cannot be appeased or pacified

im • ple • ment (im´plə mənt) *n.*, tool

im • plore (im plôr´) *vt.*, beg

im • plor • ing • ly (im plôr´iŋ lē) *adv.*, in a beseeching manner

im • por • tu • nate • ly (im pôr´chōō nit lē) *adv.*, in an annoyingly urgent or persistent manner

im • por • tu • ni • ty (im´por tōōn´ i tē) *n.*, persistent demand

im • pre • ca • tion (im´pri kā´shən) *n.*, curse

in • a • ni • tion (in´ə nish´ən) *n.*, lack of strength due to lack of food

in • au • di • bly (in ô´də blē) *adv.*, not loudly enough to be heard

in • aus • pi • cious (in´ô spish´əs) *adj.*, unfavorable, unlucky

in • can • ta • tion (in´kan tā´shən) *n.*, chanting of magical words; spell

in • cense (in sens´) *vt.*, make very angry

in • ces • sant (in ses´ənt) *adj.*, not ceasing or stopping

in • cred • u • lous • ly (in krej´oo ləs lē) *adv.*, in a doubting or skeptical manner

in • de • ci • pher • a • ble (in´dē sī´fər ə bəl) *adj.*, illegible

in • def • i • nite (in def´ə nit) *adj.*, having no exact limits

in • de • ter • mi • nate (in´dē tur´mi' nit) *adj.*, unspecific; unsettled

in • do • lent (in´də lənt) *adj.*, lazy or inactive

in • do • lent • ly (in´də lənt lē) *adv.*, lazily

in • duce (in dōōs) *vt.*, persuade; prevail on

in • duct (in dukt´) *vt.*, place in official position

in • dul • gence (in dul´jəns) *n.*, favor or privilege

in • ef • fa • ble (in ef´ə bəl) *adj.*, too overwhelming to be expressed in words; awesome

in • e • luc • ta • bly (in´ē luk´tə blē) *adv.*, in an inescapable or unavoidable manner

in • es • ti • ma • ble (in es´tə mə bəl) *adj.*, too great to be measured

in • ev • i • ta • ble (in ev´ i tə bəl) *adj.*, that cannot be avoided or evaded

in • fat • u • a • tion (in fach´ōō ā´shən) *n.*, foolish or shallow love or affection

in • fe • lic • i • tous (in fə lis´ə təs) *adj.*, unfortunate, unsuitable

in • fest (in fest´) *vt.*, overrun or inhabit in large numbers

in • fi • del (in´fə del´) *n.*, person who does not believe in a particular religion

in • flec • tion (in flek´shən) *n.*, change in pitch or tone of voice

in • fring • ing (in frinj´ iŋ) *part.*, violating; trespassing

in • gen • ious (in jēn´yəs) *adj.*, having great mental ability

in • ge • nu • i • ty (in´jə nōō´ə tē) *n.*, cleverness

in • her • ent • ly (in hir´ ənt lē) *adv.*, characteristically; naturally

in • hu • man (in hyōō´mən) *adj.*, unfeeling; cruel; barbarous

in • qui • si • tion (in´qwə zish´ən) *n.*, severe or intensive questioning

in • quis • i • to • ri • al (in kwiz´ə tôr´ē əl) *adj.*, prying

in • sen • si • ble (in sen´sə bəl) *adj.*, lacking sensation; unaware

in • sid • i • ous (in sid´ē əs) *adj.*, deceitful; sly; crafty

in • sin • u • ate (in sin´yōō āt´) *vt.*, introduce or work into gradually

in • so • lence (in´sə ləns) *n.*, disrespectfulness

in • su • per• a • ble (in sōō´pər ə bəl) *adj.*, insurmountable

in • sur • rec • tion (in´sə rek´shən) *n.*, uprising

in • teg • ri • ty (in teg´rə tē) *n.*, uprightness, honesty, and sincerity

in • ter • fer • ence (in´ter fir´ens) *n.*, something that comes into collision or opposition

in • ter • fused (in tər fyōōzd´) *part.*, combined, blended

in • ter • mi • na • ble (in tur´mi nə bəl) *adj.*, without, or seemingly without, end

in • ter • mi • na • bly (in tər´mi nə blē) *adv.*, endlessly; in a manner that seems to last forever

in • ter • ven • ing (in tər vēn´ing) *part.*, coming or lying between

in • tol • er • a • ble (in täl´ər ə bəl) *adj.*, too severe, painful, or cruel to be endured

in • vi • o • late (in vī´ə lit) *adj.*, sacred

in • voke (in vōk´) *vt.*, call on for blessing, help, or inspiration

ir • re • spec • tive (ir´ri spek´tiv) *adj.*, regardless

jag (jag) *n.*, sharp, toothlike projection

jaun • ti • ly (jôn´tə lē) *adv.*, in a confident, carefree manner

jilt (jilt) *vt.*, reject; cast off

joc • u • lar (jäk´yoo lər) *adj.*, humorous

joc • u • lar • i • ty (jäk´yōō lar´ə tē) *n.*, humor, joking

junc • ture (junk´chər) *n.*, point in time

lac • er • a • tion (las´ər ā´shən) *n.*, wound; distress

lapse (laps) *n.*, gliding or passing away

lat • tice (lat´is) *n.*, shutter; openwork structure used as a screen

lax • ly (laks´lē) *adv.*, loosely, not strictly

light (līt) *vi.*, fall or strike suddenly

lime • light (līm līt´) *n.*, prominent or conspicuous position, as if under a spotlight

lin • ger (liŋ´gər) *vi.*, remain or stay longer than usual

lin • guist (liŋ´gwist) *n.*, specialist in the science of language

list • less • ly (list´lis lē) *adv.*, in a disinterested manner

loath (lōth) *adj.*, unwilling, reluctant

loath • some (lōth´səm) *adj.*, disgusting

lo • cu • tion (lō kyōō´shən) *n.*, word; phrase

loi • ter (loi´tər) *vi.*, linger in an aimless way

loz • enge (läz´ənj) *n.*, diamond shape

lu • cid (lōō´sid) *adj.*, easily understood

lu • di • crous (lōō´di krəs) *adj.*, absurd, ridiculous

lu • rid (loor´id) *adj.*, vivid in a harsh or shocking way

mach • i • na • tion (mak ə nā´ shən) *n.*, clever plot or scheme

mag • na • nim • i • ty (mag´nə nim´ə tē) *n.*, state of being above pettiness

ma • lign (mə līn´) *adj.*, malicious, evil

ma • lig • nant (mə lig´nənt) *adj.*, wishing evil

ma • lin • ger (mə liŋ´gər) *vi.*, pretend illness

man • i • fold (man´ə fōld´) *adv.*, in many forms or ways

mar • tial (mär´shəl) *adj.*, warlike; of the military

mas • ti • ca • tion (mas´ti kā´shən) *n.*, chewing

ma • tric • u • late (mə trik´yōō lāt´) *vt.*, enroll

mea • ger (mē´ gər) *adj.*, not rich or bountiful; inadequate

med • dling (med´liŋ) *part.*, interfering; concerning oneself with other people's affairs without being asked

me • di • o • cre (mē´dē ō´ kər) *adj.*, average; not very good

me • nag • er • ie (mə naj´ ər ē) *n.*, collection of wild or exotic animals

met • ri • cal (me´ tri kəl) *adj.*, related to the number of beats in each line of a verse or song

mien (mēn) *n.*, manner; appearance

mit • i • gate (mit´ə gāt´) *vt.*, make less severe or painful

mo • bi • lize (mō´bə līz´) *vi.*, become organized and ready, as for war

moi • e • ty (moi ə tē) *n.*, half

mol • li • fy (mäl´ə fī´) *vt.*, soothe the temper of

mor • row (mär´ō) *n.*, next day

mot • ley (mät´lē) *adj.*, composed of many different elements

mu • ti • nous (myōōt´´n əs) *adj.*, inclined to revolt against authority

nat • u • ral • i • za • tion (nach´ər əl iz´ā shən) *n.*, bestowal of the rights of citizenship

nim • ble (nim´ bəl) *adj.*, mentally quick

nu • cle • us (nōō´klē əs) *n.*, core, central part

nup • tial (nup´ shəl) *adj.*, concerning marriage or a wedding

ob • dur • ate (äb´door it) *adj.*, unsympathetic; hardened

o • bei • sance (ō bā´səns) *n.*, gesture of respect

ob • lit • er • ate (ə blit´ər āt´) *vt.*, do away with entirely, leaving no trace

ob • sessed (əb sest´) *part.*, greatly preoccupied or troubled

ob • tuse (əb tōōs´) *adj.*, slow to understand or perceive; insensitive

oc • cult (ə kult´) *adj.*, mysterious; hidden

of • fen • sive (ə fen´siv) *adj.*, attacking; aggressive

om • i • nous (äm´ə nəs) *adj.*, threatening, sinister

op • pres • sion (ə prəsh´ən) *n.*, keeping down by cruel or unjust use of authority

op • u • lent (äp´yōō lənt) *adj.*, very wealthy or rich

or • a • to • ry (ôr´ə tôr´ē) *n.*, art of public speaking

or • dain (ôr dān´) *vt.*, officially give someone the authority and duties of a minister, priest, or rabbi

or • di • nance (ôrd´´n əns) *n.*, regulation; direction, command

or • na • men • ta • tion (or´na men tā´shən) *n.*, decoration

or • ner • y (ôr´nər ē) *adj.*, having an ugly or mean disposition

or • ni • thol • o • gist (ôr´nə thäl´ə jist) *n.*, one who studies birds

os • cil • la • tion (äs´ə lā´shən) *n.*, act of swinging back and forth

os • ten • ta • tious • ly (äs ten tā´shəs lē) *adv.*, so as to attract attention

o • ver • ture (o´vər chər) *n.*, musical introduction to an opera or other large musical work; independent orchestral composition of varying form

pall (pôl) *n.*, covering that obscures or cloaks gloomily

pal • pa • ble (pal´pə bəl) *adj.*, easily perceived; obvious; clear

pal • sied (pôl´ zēd) *part.*, paralyzed

pal • try (pôl´trē) *adj.*, insignificant

pan • to • mime (pan´tə mīm) *n.*, dramatic presentation without words

par • a • gon (par´ə gän´) *n.*, model or pattern of perfection or excellence

pa • tri • arch (pā´trē ärk´) *n.*, father, ruler; founder

pen • i • ten • tial • ly (pen´i ten´shəl lē) *adv.*, in a manner suggesting regret for wrongdoing

pen • sive (pen´siv) *adj.*, expressing deep thoughtfulness, often with some sadness

per • emp • to • ri • ly (pər emp´tə ri lē) *adv.*, commandingly

per • en • ni • al (pər en´ē əl) *adj.*, throughout the year; perpetual

per • il • ous (per´ə ləs) *adj.*, dangerous

per • se • vere (pur´sə vīr´) *vi.*, continue in spite of difficulty; persist

per • ti • nac • i • ty (pur´tə nas´ə tē) *n.*, stubborn persistence; obstinacy

per • ti • nence (pur´tə nəns) *n.*, relevance

phe • nom • e • non (fə näm´ə nən´) *n.*, extremely unusual or extraordinary thing or occurrence

pil • fer (pil´fər) *vt.*, steal

pin • ion (pin´yən) *n.*, part of a bird's wing; *vt.*, disable or impede

plac • ard (plak´ärd) *n.*, notice for display in a public place; sign

plume (plüm) *n.*, feather

poign • ant (poin´yənt) *adj.*, sharp; painful

poise (poiz) *n.*, ease and dignity of manner

pon • der • ous (pän´dər əs) *adj.*, very heavy

pon • toon (pän tōōn´) *n.*, flat-bottomed boat; floating object used for support

por • tal (pôrt´'l) *n.*, doorway, gate, or entrance

por • ten • tous (pôr ten´təs) *adj.*, ominous; warning of evil

pos • ter • i • ty (päs ter´ə tē) *n.*, succeeding generations

pre • cip • i • tous (prē sip´ə təs) *adj.*, steep

pre • dis • pos • ing (prē dis pō´ziŋ) *part.*, giving previous tendency

pre • dom • i • nant • ly (prē däm´ə nənt lē) *adv.*, mostly; prevailingly

pre • dom • i • nate (prē däm´ə nāt´) *vi.*, have authority or influence over others

preen (prēn´) vi., dress up in a fussy, vain way

pre • lude (prel´yōōd) *n.*, first movement of an opera; introduction

pre • ma • ture (prē´mə tōōr´) *adj.*, too early

prem • o • ni • tion (prēm´ə nish ən) *n.*, warning; feeling that something bad will happen

pres • tige (pres tēzh´) *n.*, reputation; power to impress

pre • sume (pri zōōm´) *vi.*, dare; venture; take upon oneself

pre • sump • tion (prē zump´shən) *n.*, overstepping of proper bounds or the taking of something for granted

pre • vail (prē vāl´) *vi.* gain advantage or mastery, be victorious, triumph

pri • me • val (prī mē´ vəl) *adj.*, of the earliest times or ages

pro • fane (prō fān´) *adj.*, showing disrespect for sacred things

prof • fer (präf´ər) *vt.*, offer

pro • fu • sion (prō fyōō´ zhən) *n.*, large number; abundance

prom • i • nence (prom´ə nəns) *n.*, conspicuousness

prom • i • nent (präm´ə nənt) *adj.*, widely and favorably known

prop • a • gan • dist (präp´ə gan´dist) *n.*, one who spreads ideas for a particular cause

pros • per • ous (präs´pər əs) *adj.*, conducive to success; favorable

pros • trate (präs´trāt´) *vt.*, bow down

pro • vi • sion • al (prō vizh´ə nəl) *adj.*, lasting for a short while, not permanent

pro • voke (prō vōk´) *vt.*, anger, irritate, annoy

pun • gent • ly (pun´jənt lē) *adv.*, sharply, strongly

quad • ru • ped (kwä´drōō ped´) *n.*, animal, especially a mammal, with four feet

quaff (kwäf) *vi.*, drink deeply

quell (kwel) *vt.*, end

quer • u • lous (kwer´yōō ləs) *adj.*, full of complaint; peevish

rack • et (rak´it) *n.*, noisy confusion; uproar

rap • tur • ous (rap´ chər əs) *adj.* full of joy or pleasure

rav • aged (rav´ijd) *part.*, ruined; devastated

rav • e • nous • ly (rav´ ə nəs lē) *adv.*, in a greedy or wildly hungry manner

re • buke (ri byōōk´) *vt.*, blame or scold in a sharp way

rec • om • pense (rek´əm pens´) *vt.*, repay; reward; *n.*, payment or reward

re • com • pose (rē´kəm pōz´) *vt.*, restore calmness of mind

rec • ti • tude (rek´tə tōōd´) *n.*, correctness

re • dress (rē´dres´) *n.*, compensation

re • flec • tion (ri flek´shən) *n.*, serious thought; contemplation

re • frain (ri frān´) *vi.*, hold back; keep oneself from doing something

re • it • er • ate (rē it´ə rāt´) *vt.*, repeat

re • lent • less (ri lent´lis) *adj.*, harsh; pitiless

rel • ish (rel´ish) *n.*, pleasure; enjoyment

rem • i • nis • cence (rəm´ə nis´əns) *n.*, memory or something remembered

re • mon • strance (ri män´strəns) *n.*, protest, objection

re • mon • strate (ri män´strāt´) *vt.*, demonstrate

ren • der (ren´dər) *vt.*, give, hand over, deliver, or present

rep • li • ca (rep´li kə) *n.*, copy

re • proach (ri prōch´) *n.*, blaming or reproving; rebuke

re • prove (ri prōōv´) *vt.*, speak to in disapproval

re • pulse (ri puls´) *vt.*, drive back

res • ig • na • tion (rez´ig nā´shən) *n.*, submission, patient acceptance

res • o • lu • tion (rez´ə lōō´shən) *n.*, determined state of mind; faithfulness to some person or idea

re • spec • tive (ri spek´tiv) *adj.*, as relates individually to each of two or more persons or things

re • splend • ent (ri splen´dənt) *adj.*, shining brightly

re • sume (ri zōōm´) *vt.*, take, get, or occupy again

rev • er • en • tial (rev´ə ren´shəl) *adj.*, showing a feeling of deep respect, love, and awe

rev • er • ie (rev´ər ē) *n.*, dreamy thinking

re • vert (ri vʉrt´) *vi.*, return to a former practice, opinion, state, or subject

rib • and (rib´ənd) *n.*, ribbon

rick • e • ty (rik´it ē) *adj.*, weak in the joints; shaky

ri • fle (rīf´əl) *vt.*, shuffle, move quickly through

ri • gid • i • ty (ri jid´ə tē) *n.*, state of being inflexible

ruf • fi • an (ruf´ē an) *adj.*, brutal; violent; lawless

ru • mi • nate (rōō´mə nāt´) *vt.*, turn over in one's mind

rum • mage (rum´ij) *vt.*, search through thoroughly; ransack

sa • shay (sa shā´) *vi.*, move or walk in such a way as to attract attention

sat • u • rat • ed (sach´ə rāt´əd) *adj.*, thoroughly soaked

scald • ing (skôld´iŋ) *part.*, burning; injuring

score (skôr) *n.*, set of twenty

sen • ti • nel (sen´ti nəl) *n.*, person acting as a guard

sep • ul • cher (sep´əl kər) *n.*, vault for burial

sheep • ish • ly (shēp´ish lē) *adv.*, in an embarrassed manner

sheer (shir) *vi.*, turn sharply aside from a course

shoal (shōl) *adj.*, shallow

shod • dy (shäd´ē) *adj.*, poorly made; cheap, inferior

sin • ew • y (sin´yōō ē) *adj.*, muscular; strong

so • journ (sō´ jʉrn) *n.*, brief visit

so • lace (säl´is) *vt.*, comfort, relieve

sol • i • dar • i • ty (säl´ə dar´ə tē) *n.*, combination or agreement of all elements or individuals

soph • ist • ry (säf´is trē) *n.*, unsound or misleading but clever, plausible, and subtle argument or reasoning

sot • tish (sät´ish) *adj.*, foolish

sov • er • eign (säv´ərn) *adj.*, independent; above or superior to all others

Spar • tan (spart´´n) *adj.*, like the Spartans; warlike, stoical, or disciplined

spec • u • la • tive (spek´yōō lāt´iv) *adj.*, theoretical

spurn (spʉrn) *vt.*, reject

squal • id (skwäl´id) *adj.*, wretched, miserable

squal • or (skwäl´ər) *n.*, filth and misery

stead • fast • ness (sted´fast´nes) *n.*, quality of being firm, fixed, or settled

sto • lid • i • ty (stə lid´ə tē´) *n.*, display of little or no emotion

stu • pe • fac • tion (stōō´pə fak´shən) *n.*, state of dullness or lethargy

sub • jec • tion (sub jek´shən) *n.*, bringing under control or dominion

sub • ju • ga • tion (sub´jə gā´shen) *n.*, takeover; enslavement

sub • li • ma • tion (sub´lə ma´shən) *n.*, expression of socially or personally unacceptable impulses in constructive, acceptable forms

sub • lime (sə blīm´) *adj.*, noble; majestic

sub • mis • sion (sub mish´ən) *n.*, act of yielding; surrendering

sub • serve (səb sʉrv´) *vt.*, be useful or helpful; serve

sub • ver • sion (səb ver´zhən) *n.*, systematic attempt to overthrow a government

suf • fer • ance (suf´ər əns) *n.*, power to tolerate pain

suf • fice (sə fīs´) *vi.*, be enough

sun • dry (sun´drē) *adj.*, various; miscellaneous

su • per • cil • i • ous (sōō´pər sil´ē əs) *adj.*, disdainful, contemptuous

su • per • flu • ous (sə pʉr´flōō əs) *adj.*, excessive

su • per • vene (sōō´pər vēn´) *vi.*, happen unexpectedly

su • pine • ly (sōō´pīn´lē) *adv.*, passively

sur • cease (sʉr sēs´) *n.*, respite; end

sur • mise (sər mīz´) *n.*, conjecture; guess

sur • ro • gate (sʉr´ə git) *n.*, substitute

symp • to • mat • ic (simp´tə mat´ik) *adj.*, indicative; that constitutes a condition

tal • low • y (tal´ō ē) *adj.*, fatty and pale

te • di • ous (tē´dē əs) *adj.*, long and tiresome

tem • per (tem´pər) *vt.*, toughen, as by rigors or trying experiences

tem • pest (tem´pəst) *n.*, violent storm

tem • po • ral (tem´pə rəl) *adj.*, lasting only for a time; temporary

ten • an • cy (ten´ən sē) *n.*, occupation of something by right

ten • ure (ten´yər) *n.*, right to hold a position permanently

ter • mi • nate (tur´mə nāt´) *vi.*, end, stop, cease

tes • ti • ly (tes´tə lē) *adv.*, in an irritable manner

thresh (thresh) *vt.*, thrash, toss about

tran • scend • ent (tran sen´dənt) *adj.*, beyond the limits of knowledge or experience

tran • si • ent (tran´ sē ənt) *adj.*, not permanent; temporary

trans • mute (trans myōōt´) *vt.*, change from one form, species, or condition into another

trans • port (trans´ pôrt) *n.*, strong emotion; rapture

trav • ail (trə väl) *n.*, very hard work, toil

trem • u • lous • ly (trem´yōō ləs lē) *adv.*, in a trembling or quivering manner; fearfully, timidly

trep • i • da • tion (trep´ ə dā´ shən) *n.*, anxiety; nervousness

trib • u • la • tion (trib´yoo lā´shən) *n.*, great misery or distress

triv • i • al • i • ty (triv´ē al´i tē) *n.*, something insignificant

tu • mul • tu • ous • ly (tōō mul´ chōō əs lē) *adv.*, wildly

ul • te • ri • or (ul tir´ē ər) *adj.*, further; more remote; undisclosed; concealed

un • al • ien • a • ble (un āl´ yən ə bəl) *adj.*, that which may not be taken away

un • daunt • ed (ən dônt´əd) *adj.*, resolute in the face of danger

un • du • late (un´dyōō lāt) *vi.*, move in waves

un • du • la • tion (un´dyōō lā´shən) *n.*, act of moving in waves

un • in • tel • li • gi • ble (un in tel´i jə bəl) *adj.*, that cannot be understood

un • ob • tru • sive (un əb trōō´siv) *adj.*, not calling attention to itself

un • to • ward (un tō´ərd) *adj.*, improper, unseemly; not favorable

un • wield • y (un wēl´dē) *adj.*, hard to manage

ush • er (ush´ər) *vt.*, escort, conduct

u • sur • pa • tion (yōō zər pā´ shən) *n.*, unlawful or violent taking of power

va • cu • i • ty (va kyōō´ə tē) *n.*, empty space, void, or vacuum

vag • a • bond (vag´ə bänd´) *n.*, wandering, idle, disreputable, or shiftless person

va • ga • ry (və ger´ ē) *n.*, odd, whimsical, or freakish idea or notion

val • id (val´id) *adj.*, sound; just

ve • loc • i • ty (və läs´ə tē) *n.*, quickness or rapidity of motion or action

ven • er • a • ble (ven´ər ə bəl) *adj.*, worthy of respect by reason of age and dignity

venge • ance (ven´jəns) *n.*, revenge

ven • ture (ven´chər) *n.*, risky or dangerous undertaking; undertake the risk of

ver • dure (vur´jər) *n.*, green growing plants and trees

ver • i • si • mil • i • tude (vər´ si mil´ə tōōd´) *n.*, appearance of being true or real

ver • i • ty (vər´ə tē) *n.*, principle or belief taken to be fundamentally and permanently true

ver • min (vur´mən) *n.*, small animals regarded as pests

ves • ti • bule (ves´tə byōōl´) *n.*, hallway or small room at the entrance of a building

ves • tige (ves´tij) *n.*, trace, mark, or sign of something that once existed but has passed away

vex (veks) *vt.*, irritate; annoy

vi • and (vī´ənd) *n.*, article of food

vi • tu • per • a • tive (vī tōō´ pə rā´tiv) *adj.*, abusive; viciously fault-finding

vi • vac • i • ty (vī vas´ə tē) *n.*, liveliness of spirit; animation

vo • cif • er • a • tion (vō sif´ər ā´shən) *n.*, shouting

vol • a • tile (väl´ə təl) *adj.*, unstable; fleeting

vo • rac • i • ty (vô ras´ə tē) *n.*, greediness

vor • tex (vôr´ teks´) *n. pl.* swirling mass

wince (wins) *vi.*, shrink or draw back slightly, usually with a grimace, as in pain, embarrassment, or alarm

wretch • ed (rech´id) *adj.*, miserable

writhe (rīth) *vt.*, make twisting movements

wrought (rôt) *alt. pp. of* work, worked; made

Index of Titles and Authors

Adams, Abigail, 179
"Adlai Stevenson," 821
"After great pain a formal feeling comes," 348
Age of Innocence, 491
"Alone," 348
Anderson, Sherwood, 507
"Anecdote of the Jar," 534, 537
"Annabel Lee," 348
"Any Human to Another," 605
"anyone lived in a pretty how town," 605
An Appeal in Favor of That Class of Americans Called Africans, 410
"Appeal to the Christian Women of the Southern States," 411
Argument before the Supreme Court in the Case of Wharton Jones v. John Vanzandt, 1846, 411
"Arsenal at Springfield, The," 349
Art of Fiction, The, 496
"At Vespers," 821
"Auto Wreck," 788, 789
Autobiography of Benjamin Franklin, The, 141
Baldwin, James, 671
Baraka, Imamu Amiri, 56
"Because I could not stop for Death—," 332
Benét, Stephen Vincent, 656
Berryman, John, 786
Bierce, Ambrose, 362, 380, 422
Big Money, The, 746
Bill of Rights, The, 137, 178
Bishop, Elizabeth, 801
"Black Man Talks of Reaping, A," 598, 599
Bloom, Amy, 857
Blues People, 56
Bly, Robert, 786
Bontemps, Arna, 598
"Boyhood Days," 406
Bradford, William, 71, 101
Bradstreet, Anne, 73, 75, 114, 125
"Brahma," 346
Brooks, Gwendolyn, 786, 824
Bryant, William Cullen, 290
Cable, George Washington, 422
Calvin, John, 72
Casas, Bartolomé de las, 70, 88
Cather, Willa, 630
"Chambered Nautilus, The," 297
Channing, William Ellery, 411
Chase, Salmon P., 411
Child, Lydia Marie, 410
Chopin, Kate, 422, 450
"Clean, Well-Lighted Place, A," 650, 651
Clemens, Samuel. *See* Mark Twain
Cochise of the Apache, 483
Common Sense, 136, 185
"Concord Hymn," 318
Constitution, preamble to the, 138
Cooper, James Fenimore, 196
Cornish, Samuel, 359
Crane, Stephen, 362, 391, 422, 468
Crèvecœur, J. Hector St. Jean de, 67, 139, 184
Crisis, No. 1, 160
Crucible, The , 46
Cullen, Countee, 588, 605
Cummings, E. E., 503, 605
"Dance, The," 545, 550
"Death of the Ball Turret Gunner, The," 605
"Death of the Hired Man, The," 601
Declaration of Independence, 136, 172
"Devil and Daniel Webster, The," 656
Dickey, James, 855
Dickinson, Emily, 196, 324, 347, 348
"Disillusionment of Ten O'Clock," 604
"Do not weep, maiden, for war is kind," 402
Dos Passos, John, 503, 746
Douglass, Frederick, 357, 363, 364
Dreiser, Theodore, 424
Du Bois, W. E. B., 491, 507

Dunbar, Paul Laurence, 480
"Each and All," 346
Editorial in *The Liberator,* January 1, 1831, 410
Edwards, Jonathan, 74, 118
Eggleston, Edward, 422
Eliot, T. S., 505, 509, 567
Ellison, Ralph, 665
Emerson, Ralph Waldo, 197, 252, 317, 346
"Euclid Alone Has Looked on Beauty Bare," 605
Evans, Mari, 786
"Everyday Use," 834, 835
"Fall of the House of Usher, The," 283
"Farewell to His Army," 405
Faulkner, William, 502, 506, 509, 764
Fireside Poets, 196
Fitzgerald, F. Scott, 504, 671, 920
"Flower-Fed Buffaloes, The," 601
"Follow the Drinking Gourd," 6
"For the Last Wolverine," 855
"For the Union Dead," 605
Franklin, Benjamin, 134, 136, 139, 140
Freedom Journal March 16, 1827, 410
Freeman, Mary E. Wilkins, 422, 485
Frost, Robert, 507, 509, 524, 601, 604, 759
Garrison, William Lloyd, 359, 411
General History of Virginia, New England, and the Summer Isles, The, 95
"Geranium, The," 605
Gettysburg Address, The, 375, 376
Gilman, Charlotte Perkins, 424
Giovanni, Nikki, 786, 814
Glass Menagerie, The, 682, 1028
Grapes of Wrath, The, 663
"Grass," 521, 522
Great Gatsby, The, 671, 920
Grimké, Angelina, 411
Harris, Joel Chandler, 422
Harte, Bret, 422, 426
Hawthorne, Nathaniel, 195, 198
Hayden, Robert, 793
Hemingway, Ernest, 503, 650
Henry, Patrick, 152
Holmes, Oliver Wendell, 196, 296, 346
"Home Burial," 524, 528
" 'Hope' is the thing with feathers," 347
"House Divided, A," 404
"House Guest," 801, 802
Howells, William Dean, 423
Hughes, Langston, 509, 594
Hurston, Zora Neale, 670
"Huswifery," 125
Hutchinson, Anne, 72
"I Am Alone," 483
"I heard a Fly buzz—when I died—," 335
"I never saw a Moor," 347
"I Stand Here Ironing," 844, 845
"I Will Fight No More Forever," 465
"Ichabod!," 350
"If you were coming in the Fall," 347
"In a Station of the Metro," 560, 561
In Re: Notification of Wives and Mothers," 821
Inaugural Address (Kennedy), 829, 830
Invisible Man, 665
Iroquois Constitution, 76
Irving, Washington, 193, 272
James, Henry, 422, 424, 496
Jarrell, Randall, 605
Jefferson, Thomas, 133, 136, 139, 171
Jewett, Sarah Orne, 422, 438
"Jilting of Granny Weatherall, The," 640, 641
Jones, LeRoi, 56, 786
Joseph, Chief of the Nez Percé, 421, 464
Kennedy, John F., 782, 787, 829
King, Martin Luther, Jr., 783, 787
Kinneavey, James, 1029
Lamb, Robin, 536
Lee, Li-Young, 855
Lee, Robert E., 360, 363, 405
"Legend of Sleepy Hollow, The," 272
"Lesson of Walls, The," 855
Letter to *The Amherst Student,* 759, 760
Letter to John Adams, May 7, 1776, 180
Letter to Mrs. Bixby, 404
"Letters from an American Farmer," 184
Levertov, Denise, 786, 806
Liberator, The, January 1, 1831, 411
Life on the Mississippi, 483
Lincoln, Abraham, 357, 363, 374, 375, 404
Lindsay, Vachel, 601

London, Jack, 424, 503, 614
Longfellow, Henry Wadsworth, 196, 306, 349
"Love Song of J. Alfred Prufrock, The ," 567, 568
"Lover, A," 604
Lowell, Amy, 505, 604
Lowell, James Russell, 196, 301
Lowell, Robert, 605, 786
"Lucinda Matlock," 510, 511
Madison, James, 139
"Magic Barrel, The," 27
Malamud, Bernard, 27
"Man Said to the Universe, A" 469
Mann, Horace, 192
Masters, Edgar Lee, 502, 510
Mather, Cotton, 74, 126
Melville, Herman, 191, 195, 241
"Mending Wall," 524, 525
Millay, Edna St. Vincent, 18, 505, 605
Miller, Arthur, 46
"Miniver Cheevy," 601
Moby-Dick, 242
Model of Christian Charity, A, 72
Moore, Marianne, 563
"Mr. Flood's Party," 516, 517
"Much Madness is divinest Sense," 347
"Mystery of Heroism, A" 392
Narrative of the Life of Frederick Douglass, an American Slave, Written by Himself," 365
"Negro Speaks of Rivers, The," 594, 595
New England Primer, The, 75, 109
"Newsreel LXVII," 746, 747
"Night the Bed Fell, The ," 752, 753
Nobel Prize Acceptance Speech, 764
Norris, Frank, 424
"Notorious Jumping Frog of Calaveras County, The," 456
"O Captain! My Captain!" 405
"Occurrence at Owl Creek Bridge, An," 381
Of Plymouth Plantation, 102
"Old Ironsides," 346
"Old Man's Winter Night, An," 604
Olsen, Tillie, 844
"Other People's Sorrow," 536
"Outcasts of Poker Flat, The," 427
Paine, Thomas, 136, 139, 159, 185
Parker, Dorothy, 504, 509
"Petit, the Poet," 510, 513
"Pets," 819
"Pit and the Pendulum, The," 226
Plath, Sylvia, 786
Poe, Edgar Allan, 195, 196, 225, 283, 338, 348
"Poetry," 563, 564
Porter, Katherine Anne, 640
Pound, Ezra, 501, 505, 509, 560
"Psalm of Life, A," 350
Ransom, John Crowe, 507
"Rappaccini's Daughter," 199
"Raven, The," 338, 339
"Readiness is All, The," 820
"Red Wheelbarrow, The," 545, 548
"Remarks Concerning the Natives of North America," 147
"Revolt of 'Mother', The," 485
"Rhodora, The," 321
"Richard Cory," 601
Riley, James Whitcomb, 422
Ríos, Alberto, 855
"River-Merchant's Wife: A Letter, The," 604
Robinson, Edwin Arlington, 503, 516, 601
Rodriguez, Richard, 781
Roethke, Theodore, 605
Russwurm, John B., 359, 410
Sandburg, Carl, 521
Schoolroom Poets, 196
Seattle, Chief of the Suquamish and Duwamish, 417
Second Inaugural Address (Lincoln), 404
"Secret, The," 806, 807
Self-Reliance, 253
Sexton, Anne, 786, 810
Shapiro, Karl, 788
"Sinners in the Hands of an Angry God," 119
Slavery, 411
Smith, John, 70, 94
Snow-Bound: A Winter Idyl, 351
"Snow Man, The," 534, 535
"Some Verses upon the Burning of Our House," 125

"somewhere i have never travelled,gladly beyond," 503
"Song of Myself," 472
"Song of the Sky Loom," 84
"Song of Solomon," 857
"Sonnet XXX," 18
"Soul selects her own Society, The," 329
Souls of Black Folk, The, 491
Speech in the Virginia Convention, 153
Spoon River Anthology, 502, 510
Stafford, William, 797, 855
"Stanzas on Freedom," 302
"Starry Night, The," 810, 811
Stein, Gertrude, 503, 505
Steinbeck, John, 663
Steinem, Gloria, 787
Stevens, Wallace, 505, 534, 604
"Storm Ending," 605
"Story, A," 855
"Story of an Hour, The," 451
"A Story That Could Be True," 797, 798
Stowe, Harriet Beecher, 360
"Swing Low, Sweet Chariot," 370
Taylor, Edward, 75, 125
Tecumseh, 75
Tell Me How Long the Train's Been Gone, 671
"Telling the Bees," 312
Tewa, 83
"Thanatopsis," 291
Their Eyes Were Watching God, 670
Theory of Discourse, A, 1029
"There's a certain Slant of light," 347
"There Was a Child Went Forth," 912
"Thirteen Ways of Looking at a Blackbird," 534, 539
"This Is Just to Say," 545, 546
"This is my letter to the World," 326
Thoreau, Henry David, 194, 197, 258, 360
"Those Winter Sundays," 793, 794
Thurber, James, 752
"To Black Women," 824, 825
"To Build a Fire," 614, 615
"To Helen," 348
"To My Dear and Loving Husband," 115
"To S. M., a Young African Painter, on Seeing His Works," 166
"To the Right Honorable William, Earl of Dartmouth," 185
"To Walden Wherever," 819
Toomer, Jean, 605
"Traveling Through the Dark," 855
Tubman, Harriet, 359
Twain, Mark, 422, 425, 455, 483
Up From Slavery, 406
"Upon the Burning of Our House," 125
Very Brief Relation of the Devastation of the Indies, The, 89
"Village Blacksmith, The," 307
"Wagner Matinee, A," 630, 631
Walden, 194, 259
"Walden," 769, 770
Walker, Alice, 786, 787, 834
Washington, Booker T., 406
"We Wear the Mask," 480
Wharton, Edith, 491, 504
Wheatley, Phillis, 138, 165, 185
"When I Heard the Learn'd Astronomer," 491
"When Lilacs Last in the Dooryard Bloom'd," 406
White, E. B., 769
"White Heron, A," 439
"Whiteness of the Whale, The," 242
Whitman, Walt, 405, 406, 471, 491, 912
Whittier, John Greenleaf, 196, 311, 350, 351
Williams, Roger, 72
Williams, Tennessee, 682, 1028
Williams, William Carlos, 505, 509, 545
"Wind and Silver," 604
"Winter Poem," 814, 815
Winthrop, John, 72, 75
Wonders of the Invisible World, The, 126
Worley, James, 818
"Yet do I Marvel," 588, 589

Index of Skills

Reading and Literature

abstract, 544, 566, 1028
aim, 112, 183, 767, 1029
alliteration, 177, 310, 320, 344, 403, 767, 796, 823, 1029
allusion, 112, 169, 222, 250, 270, 373, 520, 567, 573, 590, 805, 812, 1030
ambiguity, 1030
amplification, 250, 295, 1030
anaphora, 833, 1030
anecdote, 59, 538, 757, 1030
annotations, 112
antithesis, 378, 768, 1030
aphorism, 145, 256, 270, 1030
apology, 327, 1030
apostrophe, 300, 305, 320, 1030
archetype, 699, 1031
argumentation, 164, 1031
assonance, 164, 334, 795, 1031
atmosphere, 239
autobiographies, 52, 145, 1031
background information, 41, 1031
ballads, 4, 1031
biographies, 52, 1032
blank verse, 295, 524, 1032
blocking, 50
catalog, 479, 1032
catastrophe, 628, 1032
character, 50, 527, 690, 714, 1033
characterization, 41, 655, 1033
chiasmus, 150, 1033
chronological order, 108, 1033
cliché, 707, 1034
climax, 390, 1034
collage, 751, 1034
concrete, 544, 566, 1035
confessional poetry, 786, 813, 1035
conflict, 448, 628, 699, 1035
consonance, 796, 1035
couplet, 112, 169, 305, 590, 1036
curriculum, 112
dialect, 41, 461, 1038
dialogue, 50, 470, 655, 1038
diary, 52, 1038
diction, 532, 1038
didacticism, 353, 1038
dramatic monologue, 524, 573, 1039
dramatic dialogue, 524
effect, 123, 549, 596
elaboration, 250, 295, 479, 1039
elliptical, 567
emphasis, 123, 1039
Enlightenment, 157, 1040
epigraph, 813, 1040
essay, 256, 763, 1041
euphony, 300, 1041
Existentialism, 785, 792, 1041
Expressionism, 682, 690, 1041
extended metaphor, 334, 1041
eye rhyme, 117, 331, 1041
fantasy, 222, 1041
farce, 757, 1041
figurative language, 41, 1042
flashback, 389, 1042
frame tale, 462, 1043
free verse, 403, 471, 573, 809, 1043
heroic couplet, 169, 1043
histories, 52
hymn, 86, 1043
hyperbole, 117, 1043
iamb, 514, 1043
image, 310, 544, 549, 562, 1044
imagery, 544, 549, 562, 1044
Imagism, 545, 1044
internal conflict, 448, 1044
internal monologue, 655, 1044
internal rhyme, 828
irony, 108, 334, 403, 454, 470, 648, 694, 800, 1044
journals, 52, 1044

legends, 4
letters, 52
metaphor, 85, 256, 334, 400, 514, 532, 562, 690, 792, 823, 1045
meter, 319, 327, 547, 1045
Minimalist style, 844
Modernism, 763, 823, 1045
mood, 93, 239, 315, 1046
motif, 448, 1046
motivation, 41, 1046
myth, 4, 85, 538, 1046
narrator, 638, 1046
narrative poem, 310, 1046
Naturalism, 389, 400, 468, 614, 1046
Neoclassicism, 150, 1047
nonfiction, 52, 1047
objective correlative, 823, 1047
occasional verse, 353, 1047
octave, 590, 1047
onomatopoeia, 250, 337, 768, 1048
oral tradition, 4, 467, 1048
oxymoron, 117, 1048
parallelism, 20, 85, 157, 177, 378, 403, 479, 523, 768, 828, 833, 1048
pathetic fallacy, 536, 1048
persona, 144, 1049
personification, 20, 327, 470, 523, 816, 1049
plot, 628, 843, 1049
point of view, 93, 238, 315, 334, 638, 843, 1049
properties, 50
protagonist, 448, 1050
proverb, 145, 1050
psychological fiction, 389, 400, 1050
pun, 527, 805, 1050
quatrain, 590, 1050
refrain, 8, 373, 596, 1051
repetition, 8, 331, 551, 796, 1051
reversal, 454, 1051
rhetoric, 873, 1051
rhetorical question, 156, 164, 305, 1051
rhyme, 323, 344, 599, 813, 1051
rhyme scheme, 20
rhythm, 547, 551,1051
romance, 239, 1052
Romantic poetry, 353
Romanticism, 323, 471, 1052
run-on line, 344, 551, 1052
sentimentality, 437, 1052
sestet, 590, 1053
set, 50, 1053
setting, 628, 715, 1053
sight rhyme, 117, 331, 1053
simile, 400, 514, 520, 596, 638, 648, 776, 1053
slant rhyme, 331, 1053
sonnet, 19, 590, 1053
Southern Gothic, 682, 1054
speaker, 547, 549, 599, *1054
special vocabulary, 59
spiritual, 4, 8, 361, 373
stage directions, 50, 689, 1054
stanza, 300, 305, 334, 566, 1054
stereotype, 150, 369, 437, 1054
stock character, 437, 1054
stream-of-consciousness writing, 649, 1054
style, 144, 1055
symbol, 20, 80, 222, 337, 479, 527, 699, 701, 714, 739, 816, 1055
synaesthesia, 336, 1055
syntax, 378, 1056
tall tales, 4, 1056
theme, 8, 20, 50, 256, 373, 400, 738, 853, 1056
thesis, 369, 1056
tone, 86, 270, 315, 369, 512, 532, 547, 776, 805, 853, 1056

Writing

abstract, 170
adding, 899
advice column, 256
agenda, 150
aim, 54, 873
allusion piece, 813
analysis, 55, 879
analysis charts, 888
analyzing, 883
annotations, 112
audience, 871, 875

ballad, 515
billboard ad, 256
biographical sketch, 768
biography, 256
blues, 280
body, 897
brainstorming, 889
captions, 170, 544, 549
careful draft, 894–895
cartoon, 150
cause-and-effect, 879, 893
character sketch, 310, 448, 655
choosing a topic, 871
chronological order, 893
citation, 401
classification, 55, 873–874, 879, 893
clincher sentence, 895
clustering, 885
collage approach, 751
comic strip, 344
communication triangle, 874
comparison and contrast, 55, 123, 467, 566, 763, 879, 893
compositions, 897
computer hardware, 869
computer software, 869
computers, and writing, 868–871
conclusion, 897
credo, 177
critical analysis, 533, 739
critical interpretation, 551
daydream, 390
debate, 527
degree order, 893
deleting, 899
description, 55, 335, 878
descriptive paragraph, 250, 551, 628, 638
dialogue, 55, 470, 527, 649, 655, 878
dialogue poem, 817
diary entries, 223, 316, 454, 739
directions, 390
discovery draft, 894
discussion, 889–890
documentation, 628
drafting, 866, 894–898
dream analysis, 715
editorial, 323
elaboration, 896
epitaph, 270, 512
essay, 462
evaluation and revision, 41, 866
exposition, 54, 55, 878
expressive writing, 54, 873
family history, 597, 758, 843
fantasy, 344
flowcharts, 886
focusing a topic, 872–873
forms of writing, 871, 876–878
free verse, 479, 523, 549
freewriting, 881
Gothic tale, 239
haiku, 562
heuristics for imagining, 884
hymn, 86
imagining, 884
informative writing, 54, 873
interviewing, 890
introduction, 897
journal entries, 544, 867
lesson story, 112
letter, 183
literary writing, 54, 874
lyric poem, 328, 596, 796
main ideas, identification of, 891
manuscript marking, 900–901
manuscript preparation, 902
minutes, 157
modes of writing, 55, 871, 878–879
moving, 899
narration, 55, 878
narrative message, 9
news story, 223, 378
nomination speech, 157
nonprint sources, 891
obituary, 250, 316, 649
observing, 880
organizing compositions, 897
organizing ideas, 893
outlining, 892
paragraphs, 454, 895–896
parody, 437, 574
part-by-part order, 894

peer evaluation, 866, 899
personal note, 547, 638
persuasive writing, 54, 874
petition, 157
poem, 547
portfolio, 868
press release, 239, 758
prewriting, 9, 866
prewriting: developing a writing plan, 871–879
prewriting, drafting, revising cycle, 895
prewriting: exploring ideas, 879–889
prewriting: organizing your ideas, 891–894
prewriting: using outside sources, 889–891
print sources, 890
pro and con charts, 888
process, how to, 55
process of writing, 9, 866
professional letter, 853
proofreading, 51, 866
proofreading checklist, 901
proofreading symbols, 900–901
publishing and presenting, 866, 902–903
purpose, 54, 871, 873, 874
questioning, 882
real estate ad, 270
recalling, 879
recommendations, 222
replacing, 899
revising, 866, 891, 898–901
revision checklist, 898
revision, types of, 899–900
role playing, 885
self-evaluation, 866, 898
sensory detail charts, 886
slogan, 250, 523
software. *See* computer software
spatial order, 893
speech, 81
story map, 887
story that could be true, 800
storyboard, 239
stream of consciousness, 323
supporting details, 896
supporting sentence, 895
tall tale, 462
thesis statement, 897
time lines, 886
toast, 520
topic, 871–873
topic sentence, 895, 897
Venn diagrams, 81, 888
wanted poster, 479
writer's journal, 867
writer's portfolio, 868
writing plan, elements, 871

Language

abstract nouns, 124, 905
achieving parallelism, 597, 921
action verbs, 574, 907, 912, 914, 937
active voice, 921
adding prepositional phrases, 310
adjectival phrase, 917
adjectives, 62, 250, 354, 768, 908–909, 937
adverbial phrase, 917
adverbs, 62, 250, 354, 909, 911, 937
agreement in inverted sentences, 930
agreement of pronouns and antecedents, 164, 286, 300, 935–936
agreement of subject and verb, 926–929, 930
agreement with compound subjects, 929
agreement with *doesn't* and *don't,* 930
agreement with indefinite pronouns, 929
antecedents, 164, 286, 300
apostrophes, 610, 751, 947–948
apposition, 778
appositives, 369, 917, 934
articles, 908
astronomical terms, 951
auxiliary verbs, 390, 907
awards, 951
base form of verbs, 925
base words, 544, 628, 639, 779, 828, 960
brackets, 947
brand names, 951
building sentences, 533
buildings, names of, 951
capitalization, 817

clause, 910
clichés, 515, 862
colons, 610, 946
combining sentences, 454
common nouns, 170, 905
comparison of adjectives and adverbs, 937
comparisons with pronouns, 935
collective nouns, 905
combining sentences, 918–919
commas, 943–944
comparative, 354
comparison, 778
comparison of adjectives and adverbs, 250, 354
complex sentences, 916
compound nouns, 905
compound sentences, 916
compound-complex sentences, 916
compound subjects, 929
concrete nouns, 124, 905
conjunctions, 62, 910
conjunctive adverbs, 911
connotations, 862
consonants, 959
context clues, 239, 960
contractions, 930, 931
contrast, 778
coordinating conjunctions, 910
correcting modifiers, 323
correcting run-ons, 257
correlative conjunctions, 910
dangling modifiers, 639, 924
dashes, 328, 610, 946
days of the week, 951
declarative sentences, 913
demonstrative pronouns, 906, 938
denotations, 862
direct quotation, 949
directions, capitalization, 951
double comparison, 354, 938
double negatives, 305, 354, 938
editing for correct use of parentheses, 758
editing for errors in modifiers, 354, 937–943
editing for errors in pronouns, 286, 932–936
editing for errors in subject/verb agreement, 928–932
editing for errors in usage, 414
editing sentences, 271
ellipses, 610, 950
end marks, 943
euphemisms, 515, 862
events, capitalization, 951
examples, 778
exclamation point, 943
exclamatory sentences, 914
expanding sentences, 520, 916–917
family relationships, 951
formal English, 87, 862, 961
functions of sentences, 158
gerunds, 146, 908
grammar, 86, 904
Greek word roots, 960
historical periods, 951
hyphens, 610, 946
I, 955
illogical comparison, 354, 938
imperative mood, 927, 928
imperative sentences, 913
indefinite pronouns, 906, 929
independent clauses, 916
indicative mood, 927, 928
indirect object, 915
indirect quotation, 949
infinitives, 908, 926
informal English, 87, 862, 961
institutions, 951
intensive pronouns, 906
interjections, 62, 911, 951
interrogative pronouns, 906, 934
interrogative sentences, 914
intransitive verbs, 908
inverting sentences, 117, 924, 930
irregular verbs, 925
italics, 610, 948
Latin word roots, 960
letters, 951
linking verbs, 113, 574, 907, 912, 937
misplaced modifiers, 639, 924
modifiers, 323, 354, 639, 913, 917, 924, 937
months, capitalization, 951

mood, 331, 927
nouns, 62, 124, 649, 905, 912
number, 929
objective complement, 915
organizations, 951
outlines, capitalization in, 951
parallelism, 379, 597, 921
parentheses, 758, 947
participles, 146, 908
parts of speech, 51, 62, 905–912
past, 925
past participle, 925
past subjunctive, 928
periods, 943
personal names, 951
personal pronouns, 906, 930
place names, 951
plurals, 742, 928, 958
poetry, 951
possessive pronouns, 911
precise nouns, 649
predicates, 917
predicate adjectives, 909
predicate nominative, 915
prefixes, 544, 779, 828, 959, 960
prepositional object, 911
prepositional phrases, 310, 917
prepositions, 62, 295, 910
present participle, 925
pronouns, 62, 164, 286, 300, 906–907, 911, 929, 932–934, 955
proofreading for capitalization errors, 951–957
proofreading for punctuation errors, 610, 943–950
proofreading for spelling errors, 742, 958
proper adjectives, 909, 954
proper nouns, 170, 905, 954
punctuation errors, 610
question mark, 943
quotation marks, 345, 610, 949–950
quotations, 955
reducing wordiness, 922
reflexive pronouns, 906
regions, capitalization, 951
register, 87, 962
relative pronouns, 906, 934
remembering, 758
repetition, deletion of, 922
replacing linking verbs with action verbs, 574, 912
restatement, 778
run-ons, 257, 449, 924
sacred beings and writings, 955
school subjects, courses, grades, and years, 951
semicolons, 320, 328, 610, 945–946
sentence fragments, 923
sentence strings, 922–923
sentences, 158, 853, 913–924
shifts in verb tense, 316
singular, 928
spelling, 742, 958–959
split infinitives, 926–927
structures, names of, 951
subjunctive, 331, 927, 928
subordinate clauses, 223, 918, 934
subordinating conjunctions, 910
substantives, 914
suffixes, 628, 639, 742, 779, 959, 960
superlative, 354
titles of art, literary, and musical works, 552, 956
titles of persons and occupations, 956
trade names, 951
transitive verbs, 908
underlining, 610, 948–949
units of time, 957
usage errors, 414, 941–943
varieties of English, 463, 862, 961–962
varying sentence openings, 919
vehicles, 957
verb tense errors, 925–928
verbs, 62, 316, 390, 907–908
verbals, 146, 908, 912
visualizing, 758
vocabulary development, 778, 959–961
voice, 331, 927
vowels, 959
who and *whom,* 286, 934
word origins, 960–961
wordiness, reducing, 922

words as other parts of speech, 151, 911
writing grammatical sentences, 853
years, 951

Speaking and Listening

active listening, 965
body language, 965
channel, 962
communication model, 962
discussion, 251, 967
encoding, 962
enunciation, 963
extemporaneous speech, 967, 968
eye contact, 965
facial expressions, 965
feedback, 962
gestures, 965
impromptu speech, 967
interpersonal communication, 966
intonation, 963
listening, 965
memorized speech, 967
message, 962
nonverbal communication 533, 649, 963, 964–965
oral interpretation, 968–969
pace, 963
pitch, 963
proximity, 965
public speaking, 158, 964, 967
receiver, 962
sender, 962
speeches, 967, 968
stress, 963
symbols, 962
tone, 963
verbal communication, elements, 963–964
volume, 963

Study and Research

abbreviations for citations, 1009
ad hominem, 979
algorithm, 971
almanacs, 993
analogy questions, 1012
analyzing, 975
antecedent, 976
antonym questions, 1014
atlases, 993
author card, 991
bandwagon, 981
bar graphs, 986
bias charges, 982
bibliographies, 998–1003, 1031
bibliography cards, 552, 998, 1003, 1004
card catalog, use of, 991–992
character assassination, 982
charts, 986
circularity, 978
citation of sources, 1007, 1008
classifying, 113, 974
computer-assisted research, 996
comparing and contrasting, 515, 975
conditional, 976
contrasting. *See* comparing and contrasting
criteria analysis, 972
cross-references, 990
decision making, 224, 972
deducing, 976
definition, 995
Dewey decimal system, 987
dictionaries, 995
divide the problem, 971
documentation of sources, 1007
embellished letter, 973
encyclopedias, 993
endnotes, 1009
equivocation, 980
error correction questions, 1013
error identification questions, 1013
essay tests, strategies for, 1015–1016
estimating, 975
etymology, 331, 995
experts, use in research, 997
fallacies of composition and decomposition, 978–979
fallacies of denying the antecedent and affirming the consequent, 978
false analogy, 977

false dichotomy, 979
false testimonial, 981
faulty arguments, how to avoid, 977–978
footnotes, 1009
formal note-taking, 117, 1005–1006
generalizing, 574, 976
grammar, usage and mechanics questions, 1013
graphs, 986
hasty generalization, 980
heuristics, 971
homographs, 995
hypotheses, 977
identifying main ideas, 985
identifying relationships, 985
indexes, 993, 994
induction, 976
inferring, 985
informal note-taking, 240, 1005
interlibrary loan, 991
journal, use of, 984
key word, 973
library materials, 987–1004
Library of Congress classification system, 988
line graphs, 987
loaded words, 981
logical fallacies, 977
making hypotheses, 316
making inferences, 985
means-end analysis, 971
memorizing, 379, 972
method of loci, 973
mnemonics, 972
multiple-choice questions, 1010
non sequitur, 979
note-taking, 1005–1006
objective tests, strategies for 1009–1011
observing, 974
organizations and associations, use in research, 997
outlining, 1005
paraphrasing, 183, 257, 1004, 1006
parenthetical citation, 1007
parenthetical documentation, 1007
periodicals, 994
pie charts, 986
plagiarism, 1007
post hoc (ergo) propter hoc, 978
predicting, 985
premises, 976
previewing your reading, 982, 983, 984
problem solving, 271, 970
propaganda techniques, 980–982
pros and cons, 972
propaganda, 164
quantifying, 975
question-begging, 978
questioning, 984
quoting, 1004, 1006
Reader's Guide to Periodical Literature, 994
reading actively, 984
reading comprehension questions, 1014
reading rates, 982
reading skills, 982–987
reference to sources, 1007
reference works, 300, 345, 597, 993
remembering, 390, 973
repetition, 973
representation of the problem, 971
research skills, 987–1009
responding to reading, 984
rule of thumb, 971
scanning, 982, 983
searching tools, 305, 989
sentence-completion questions, 1012
short-answer questions, 1011
skimming, 982, 983
slow and careful reading, 982, 983
source evaluation criteria, 997–998
standardized tests, strategies for, 1011–1015
subject card, 992
summarizing, 257, 985, 1004, 1006
synonym questions, 1014
test-taking skills, 1009–1016
thesauruses, 996
thought experiment, 977
title card, 992
transfer, 981
trial and error, 971
true-false questions, 1010
usage illustration, 995

usage notes, 995
vague terms, 980
vertical files, 997
visualizing, 390, 973
work backward, 971
yearbooks, 993

Applied English/Tech Prep

body of letter, 1019
business letter, 1020–1024
closing of letter, 1019
cover letter, 1022, 1023
documenting technical procedures, 1026
forms, guidelines for completing, 1017
letter of request, 1022
letters and forms, 1017–1024
memoranda, 170, 1025
personal letters, 328, 1019
postscript, 1019
press release, 1027
promotional writing, 1026–1027
public relations writing, 1026–1027
résumé, 1022, 1024
return address, 1019
salutation, 1019
technical writing, 1026

Index of Fine Art

American Gothic. *Grant Wood, 416, 425*
Among the Sierra Nevada Mountains, California. *Albert Bierstadt, 291, 292*
The Beginning of New England: after the painting by Clyde O. Deland. *102, 103, 106*
Breezing Up (a Fair Wind). *Winslow Homer, cover*
Buffalo Bull's Back Fat, head chief, Blood Tribe (Blackfoot). *George Catlin, 68*
Carnival Evening. *Henri Rousseau, 199, 207*
Elizabeth Freake and Baby Mary. *Artist unknown, 115, 116*
Elk Foot of the Taos Tribe. *Eanger Irving Course, 83*
Folksinger. *Charles White, 57*
The Hilltop. *Frank Weston Benson, 10, 11*
Horace Mann. *193*
Illustration to Edgar Allan Poe's Le Corbeau (The Raven). *Edouard Manet, 339, 341*
In the Morning. *Winslow Homer, 2*
The Janitor Who Paints. *Palmer Hayden, 166, 168*
John Adams. *Gilbert Stuart, 181*
The Lord Is My Shepherd. *Eastman Johnson, 4, 5*
Last Sale of Slaves on Courthouse Steps. *T. Satterwhite Noble, 302, 303*
Louisiana Heron. *Rodney Busch, 439, 443*
Midnight Ride of Paul Revere. *Grant Wood, 132, 139*
Mother Moon, Sister Crow. *Jillian Gatto 541*
Nathaniel Hawthorne. *195, 198*
Original wagon wheel from Oregon Trail carriage. *423*
Pat Lyon at the Forge. *John Neagle, 308*
Patrick Henry speaking against the Stamp Act in the Virginia House of Burgesses in 1765. *153, 154*
Paul Revere. *John Singleton Copley, 137*
The Poor Man's Store. *John Frederick Peto, 22, 23*
Portrait of Benjamin Franklin. *Robert Feke, 134*
Quaker Meeting. *66, 75*
Rainy Day in Camp. *Winslow Homer, 356, 363*
Share Croppers. *Robert Gwathmey, 52, 53*
Still Life with Copper Tankard. *William M. Harnett, 288*
Stone City Iowa. *Grant Wood, 312, 313*
The Sermon. *Gari Melchers, 119, 121*
The trial of two "witches" at Salem, Massachusetts, in 1692. *Illustration by Howard Pyle, 42, 43*
The Twin, Wife of Bloody Hand. *George Catlin, 147, 148*
Watson and the Shark. *John Singleton Copley, 190, 197*
The Whale Fishery, The Sperm Whale in a Flurry. *Currier & Ives, 242, 246*
Winter Sunday in Norway, Maine. *Artist unknown, 329, 332, 333, 335*
A witch trial at Salem, Massachusetts, in 1692. *73*
Young Soldier. *Winslow Homer, 381, 387*

Art Acknowledgments

Breezing Up (a Fair Wind). Winslow Homer, 1876. National Gallery of Art, Washington, DC (1943.13.1). Gift of the W. L. and May T. Mellon Foundation **cover;** In the Morning. Winslow Homer. Courtesy Corel Professional Photos. **2;** The Lord Is My Shepherd. Eastman Johnson. National Museum of American Art, Washington DC/Art Resource, NY **4, 5;** The Hilltop. Frank Weston Benson, Malden Public Library **11;** The Poor Man's Store. John Frederick Peto, 1885. Courtesy of Museum of Fine Arts, Boston. Gift of Maxim Karolik to the M. and M. Karolik Collection of American Paintings, 1815–1865 **22, 23;** The trial of two "witches" at Salem, Massachusetts, in 1692. Illustration by Howard Pyle. The Granger Collection, NY **42, 43;** Share Croppers. Robert Gwathmey, 1941. Courtesy of San Diego Museum of Art. Museum purchase with funds provided by Mrs. Leon D. Bonnet **53;** Folksinger. Charles White. Collection of Harry Belafonte. Courtesy Heritage Gallery, Los Angeles, CA **57;** Quaker Meeting. Courtesy of Museum of Fine Arts, Boston. Bequest of Maxim Karolik **66;** Buffalo Bull's Back Fat, head chief, Blood Tribe (Blackfoot). George Catlin, 1832. National Museum of American Art, Washington DC/Art Resource, NY **68;** A witch trial at Salem, Massachusetts, in 1692. The Granger Collection, NY **73;** Elk Foot of the Taos Tribe. Eanger Irving Course, *circa* 1909. National Museum of American Art, Washington, DC/Art Resource, NY **83;** The Beginning of New England: after the painting by Clyde O. Deland. The Granger Collection, NY **103;** Elizabeth Freake and Baby Mary. Artist unknown, *circa* 1671–74. Worcester Art Museum, Worcester, MA. Gift of Mr. and Mrs. Albert W. Rice **115;** The Sermon. Gari Melchers, 1886. National Museum of American Art, Washington, DC/Art Resource, NY **119, 121;** Midnight Ride of Paul Revere. Grant Wood, 1931. The Metropolitan Museum of Art. Arthur Hoppock Hearn Fund, 1950. (50.117) **132, 139;** Portrait of Benjamin Franklin. Robert Feke, *circa* 1746. Harvard University, Portrait Collection. Bequest of Dr. John Collins Warren, 1856 **134;** Phillis Wheatley, Courtesy, Library of Congress Photo Duplication Service **138, 165;** The Twin, Wife of Bloody Hand. George Catlin, 1832. National Museum of American Art, Washington, DC/Art Resource, NY **147, 148;** Patrick Henry speaking against the Stamp Act in the Virginia House of Burgesses in 1765. Nineteenth-century colored engraving. The Granger Collection, NY **153, 154;** The Janitor Who Paints. Palmer Hayden, *circa* 1937. National Museum of American Art, Washington, DC/Art Resource **166, 168;** John Adams. Gilbert Stuart, 1826. National Museum of American Art, Washington DC/Art Resource, NY **181;** Watson and the Shark. John Singleton Copley. Courtesy of Museum of Fine Arts, Boston. Gift of Mr. George von Lengerke Meyer **190, 197;** Washington Irving, Courtesy, Library of Congress Photo Duplication Service **194;** Nathaniel Hawthorne. Peabody Essex Museum **195, 198;** Carnival Evening. Henri Rousseau, 1886. Philadelphia Museum of Art, Louis E. Stern Collection **199, 207;** The Whale Fishery, The Sperm Whale in a Flurry. Lithograph by Currier & Ives. The Granger Collection, NY **242, 246;** Still Life with Copper Tankard. William M. Harnett, Courtesy Corel Professional Photos **288;** Among the Sierra Nevada Mountains, California. Albert Bierstadt, 1868. National Museum of American Art, Washington, DC/Art Resource, NY **291, 292;** Last Sale of Slaves on Courthouse Steps. T. Satterwhite Noble, 1860. Missouri Historical Society **302, 303;** Pat Lyon at the Forge. John Neagle, 1826–7. Courtesy of the Museum of Fine Arts, Boston. Herman and Zoe Oliver Sherman Fund, 1975 **308;** Stone City Iowa. Grant Wood. Joslyn Art Museum, Omaha, NE **312, 313;** Winter Sunday in Norway, Maine. Artist unknown, *circa* 1860. New York State Historical Association, Cooperstown, NY **332;** Illustration to Edgar Allan Poe's Le Corbeau (The Raven). Edouard Manet, 1875. Courtesy, Museum of Fine Arts, Boston **339, 341;** Rainy Day in Camp. Winslow Homer, 1871. The Metropolitan Museum of Art. Gift of Mrs. William F. Milton, 1923 (23.77.1) **356, 363;** Robert E. Lee, Courtesy, Library of Congress Photo Duplication Service **360;** Ulysses S. Grant, Courtesy, Library of Congress Photo Duplication Service **360, 361;** Young Soldier. Separate study of a soldier giving water to a wounded companion. Winslow Homer, 1861. Cooper-Hewitt, National Design Museum, Smithsonian Inst./Art Resource, NY. Photograph: Ken Pelka **381, 387;** American Gothic. Grant Wood, American, 1891–1942. Oil on beaverboard, 1930, 74.3 × 62.4 cm. Friends of the American Art Collection, 1930.934 **416;** Jesse James. Courtesy, Library of Congress Photo Duplication Service **419;** Four Young Ilte Indians. Popper photo/Archive photo **420;** Jack London. Courtesy, Library of Congress Photo Duplication Service **424;** Sarah Orne Jewett. Courtesy, Library of Congress Photo Duplication Service **438;** Louisiana Heron. Rodney Busch. Private collection **439, 443;** Walt Whitman. Courtesy, Library of Congress Photo Duplication Service **471;** Paul Laurence Dunbar. Courtesy, Library of Congress Photo Duplication Service **480;** Mask. Sargeant Claude Johnson. National Museum of American Art, Washington, DC/Art Resource **481;** Can Fire in the Park. Beauford Delaney, 1946. National Museum of American Art, Washington, DC/Art Resource, NY **500** WWI Troops in Gear. Courtesy of

Archive/Welgos **502;** Ernest Hemingway. Courtesy, Library of Congress Photo Duplication Service **503, 650;** Edith Wharton. Courtesy, Library of Congress Photo Duplication Service **504;** Courtesy, Library of Congress Photo Duplication Service **505;** Edna St. Vincent Millay. Courtesy, Library of Congress Photo Duplication Service **507;** Carl Sandburg. Courtesy, Library of Congress Photo Duplication Service **521;** Robert Frost. Courtesy, Library of Congress Photo Duplication Service **524;** Mother Moon, Sister Crow, 1981. Jillian Gatto **541;** A Shoreham Garden. Samuel Palmer, *circa* 1829. Courtesy of the Trustees of the Victoria & Albert Museum **556;** Langston Hughes. Courtesy, Library of Congress Photo Duplication Service **594;** Nighthawks. Edward Hopper, 1942. American, 1882–1967. Oil on Canvas, 84.1 x 152.4 cm. The Art Institute of Chicago, Friends of American Art Collection, 1942.51 **612;** Jack London. Courtesy, Library of Congress Photo Duplication Service **614;** First Row Orchestra. Edward Hopper, 1951. Hirshhorn Museum and Sculpture Garden, Smithsonian Institution, Gift of the Joseph H. Hirshhorn Foundation, 1966 **635;** Moulin de la Galette. Pierre-Auguste Renoir. Courtesy Corel Professional Photos **653;** New York Movie. Edward Hopper, 1939. The Museum of Modern Art, New York, Given anonymously **680;** Incantation. Charles Sheeler, 1946. Oil on canvas, 61.0 x 50.8 (24 x 20).The Brooklyn Museum, 49.67. John B. and Ella C. Woodward Memorial Funds **744;** Courtesy, Library of Congress Photo Duplication Service **747;** Number 3, 1949: TIGER. Jackson Pollock, 1949. Hirshhorn Museum and Sculpture Garden, Smithsonian Institution. Gift of Joseph H. Hirshhorn, 1972. **780;** John and Robert Kennedy. Courtesy, Library of Congress Photo Duplication Service **782;** Reverend Martin Luther King, Jr. Courtesy, Library of Congress Photo Duplication Service **783;** Space Shuttle Challenger. National Aeronautics and Space Administration. (NASA) **785;** Steering Wheel. David Hockney, October 1982. Photographic Collage, 30 x 36. © David Hockney. **790;** The Starry Night. Vincent van Gogh, 1889. Oil on canvas, 29" x 36$^{1}/_{4}$" (73.7 x 92.1 cm). The Museum of Modern Art, NY. Acquired through the Lillie P. Bliss Bequest **813;** Gemini Etching. Lout Mills, 1969. Evans-Tibbs collection Washington, DC **826;** John F. Kennedy. Courtesy, Library of Congress Photo Duplication Service **829**

Additional Photo and Illustration Credits

Courtesy Digital Stock Corp.: 472, 476, 511, 535, 537, 564, 576, 580, 581, 589, 595, 599, 760, 864, 866, 904, 970, 1017 **Courtesy Corel Professional Photos:** 69, 71, 136, 137, 358, 418, 421, 423, 451, 517, 522, 528, 550, 568, 592, 615, 620, 641, 643, 684, 716, 753, 765, 794, 798, 802, 807, 815, 820, 830, 962 **Jena Busch:** 513, 546 **Rodney Busch:** 456, 561, 819, 845, 848, 854 **David Benoit:** 265, 770, 773 **Ed Parker:** 506, 567 **Helen Abraham:** 585 **Heath P. O'Leary:** 835, 839

Literary Acknowledgments (*continued from copyright page*)

Elizabeth Barnett
"Euclid Alone Has Looked On Beauty Bare" and Sonnet XXX of FATAL INTERVIEW by Edna St. Vincent Millay. From COLLECTED POEMS, HarperCollins. Copyright © 1923, 1931, 1951, 1958 by Edna St. Vincent Millay and Norma Millay Ellis. Reprinted by permission of Elizabeth Barnett, literary executor.

BOA Editions, Ltd.
LI-YOUNG LEE. "A Story" copyright © 1990, by Li-Young Lee. Reprinted from THE CITY IN WHICH I LOVE YOU, by Li-Young Lee, with the permission of BOA Editions, Ltd., 92 Park Ave., Brockport, NY 14420

Brandt & Brandt Literary Agents, Inc.
"The Devil and Daniel Webster" by Stephen Vincent Benet. From THE SELECTED WORKS OF STEPHEN VINCENT BENET. Copyright 1936 by The Curtis Publishing Company. Copyright renewed © 1964 by Thomas C. Benet, Stephanie B. Mahin, and Rachel Lewis Benet. Reprinted by permission of Brandt & Brandt Literary Agents, Inc.

Gwendolyn Brooks
"To Black Women," © 1991 by Gwendolyn Brooks. From BLACKS, 1991. Published by Third World Press, Chicago. Reprinted by permission of the author.

The Continuum Publishing Company
from *The Very Brief Relation of the Devastation of the Indies* by Bartolome de las Casas. Copyright © 1974.

David Campbell Publishers Ltd.
from "Letters from an American Farmer" by J. Hector St. Jean de Crèvecoeur. By permission of Everyman's Library, Campbell Publishers Ltd.

Elizabeth H. Dos Passos
"Newsreel LXVII," by John Dos Passos. From *The Big Money,* copyright by Elizabeth H. Dos Passos. Reprinted by permission of Elizabeth H. Dos Passos.

Farrar, Straus & Giroux, Inc.
"House Guest" from THE COMPLETE POEMS 1927–1979 by Elizabeth Bishop. Copyright ©1979, 1983 by Alice Helen Methfessel. Reprinted by permission of Farrar, Straus & Giroux, Inc. "The Death of the Ball Turret Gunner" from THE COMPLETE POEMS by Randall Jarrell. Copyright © 1969 by Mrs. Randall Jarrell. Reprinted by permission of Farrar, Straus & Giroux, Inc. "For the Union Dead" from FOR THE UNION DEAD by Robert Lowell. Copyright © 1960 by Robert Lowell. Copyright renewed ©1992 by Harriet Lowell, Sheridan Lowell, and Caroline Lowell. Reprinted by permission of Farrar, Straus & Giroux, Inc. "The Magic Barrel" from THE MAGIC BARREL by Bernard Malamud. Copyright © 1958 and renewed © 1986 by Bernard Malamud. Reprinted by permission of Farrar, Straus & Giroux, Inc.

Harcourt Brace & Company
"The Jilting of Granny Weatherall" from FLOWERING JUDAS AND OTHER STORIES, copyright 1930 and renewed 1958 by Katherine Anne Porter, reprinted by permission of Harcourt Brace & Company. "Grass" from CORNHUSKERS by Carl Sandburg, copyright 1918 by Holt, Rinehart and Winston, Inc. and renewed 1946 by Carl Sandburg, reprinted by permission of Harcourt Brace & Company. "Everyday Use" from IN LOVE AND TROUBLE: STORIES OF BLACK WOMEN © 1973 by Alice Walker. Reprinted by permission of Harcourt Brace and Company. Booker T. Washington, "Boyhood Days," from *Up from Slavery.* Used by permission of Harcourt Brace & Company.

Harold Ober Associates
"A Black Man Talks of Reaping" by Arna Bontemps. Reprinted by permission of Harold Ober Associates Incorporated. Copyright © 1963 by Arna Bontemps.

HarperCollins Publishers, Inc.
"SONG OF SOLOMON" from COME TO ME by AMY BLOOM. Copyright © 1993 by Amy Bloom. Reprinted by permission of HarperCollins Publishers, Inc. EXCERPT from THEIR EYES WERE WATCHING GOD by ZORA NEALE HURSTON. Copyright 1937 by Harper & Row, Publishers, Inc. Renewed 1965 by John C. Hurston and Joel Hurston. Reprinted by permission of HarperCollins Publishers, Inc. ALL PAGES from "WALDEN" FROM ONE MAN'S MEAT by E. B. WHITE. Copyright 1939 by E. B. White. Copyright renewed 1967 by E. B. White. Reprinted by permission of HarperCollins Publishers, Inc.

Harvard University Press
Letter from Abigail Adams to John Adams. Reprinted by permission of the publishers from THE ADAMS FAMILY CORRESPONDENCE edited by L.H. Butterfield et al, Cambridge, Mass.: The Belknap Press of Harvard University Press, Copyright © 1963 by the Massachusetts Historical Society. "Some Verses Upon the Burning of Our House" and "To My Dear and Loving Husband." Reprinted by permission of the publishers from THE WORKS OF ANNE BRADSTREET edited by Jeannine Hensley, Cambridge, Mass.: The Belknap Press of Harvard University Press, Copyright © 1967 by the President and Fellows of Harvard College. From THE POEMS OF EMILY DICKINSON: "After great pain a formal feeling comes," "Because I could not stop for Death," "'Hope' is the thing with feathers," "I heard a Fly buzz—when I died—," "I never saw a Moor," "The Soul selects her own Society," "If you were coming in the fall," "Much Madness is divinest Sense," "There's a certain Slant of light," and "This is my letter to the World," Reprinted by permission of the publishers and

the Trustees of Amherst College from THE POEMS OF EMILY DICKINSON, Thomas H. Johnson, ed., Cambridge, Mass.: The Belknap Press of Harvard University Press, Copyright © 1951, 1955, 1983 by the President and Fellows of Harvard College. "Concord Hymn" and "Rhodora." Reprinted by permission of the publishers from THE JOURNALS AND MISCELLANEOUS NOTEBOOKS OF RALPH WALDO EMERSON edited by William H. Gilman et al, Cambridge, Mass.: The Belknap Press of Harvard University Press, Copyright © 1960, 1961, 1963, 1964, 1965, 1966, 1969, 1970, 1971, 1973, 1975, 1976, 1977, 1978, 1982 by the President and Fellows of Harvard College. From "The Wonders of the Invisible World." Reprinted by permission of the publishers from BONIFACIUS: AN ESSAY UPON THE GOOD by Cotton Mather, edited by David Levin, Cambridge, Mass.: The Belknap Press of Harvard University Press, Copyright © 1966 by the President and Fellows of Harvard College.

Henry Holt and Co., Inc.
"The Death of the Hired Man," "Home Burial," "Mending Wall," and "An Old Man's Winter Night" from THE POETRY OF ROBERT FROST edited by Edward Connery Lathem. Copyright 1936, 1944 © 1958 by Robert Frost. Copyright © 1964, 1967 by Lesley Frost Ballantine. Copyright 1916, 1930, 1939 © 1969 by Henry Holt and Co., Inc. Reprinted by permission of Henry Holt and Co., Inc. "Letter to *The Amherst Student*" by Robert Frost, from SELECTED PROSE OF ROBERT FROST edited by Hyde Cox and Edward Connery Lathem. Copyright 1949, 1954 © 1966 by Henry Holt and Co., Inc. Copyright 1946 © 1959 by Robert Frost. Copyright © 1956 by The Estate of Robert Frost. Reprinted by permission of Henry Holt and Co., Inc.

Houghton Mifflin Company
"Wind and Silver", *What's O'Clock,* THE COMPLETE POETICAL WORKS OF AMY LOWELL. Copyright © 1955 by Houghton Mifflin Company, © renewed 1983 by Houghton Mifflin Company, Brinton P. Roberts, and G. D'Andelot Belin, Esquire. Reprinted by permission of Houghton Mifflin Co. All rights reserved. "Ars Poetica", COLLECTED POEMS 1917–1982 by Archibald MacLeish. Copyright © 1985 by The Estate of Archibald MacLeish. Reprinted by permission of Houghton Mifflin Co. All rights reserved. "The Starry Night" from ALL MY PRETTY ONES by Anne Sexton. Copyright © 1962 by Anne Sexton, © renewed 1990 by Linda G. Sexton. Reprinted by permission of Houghton Mifflin Co. All rights reserved.

James Thurber Literary Properties
"The Night the Bed Fell" by James Thurber. Copyright © 1933, 1961 James Thurber. From *My Life and Hard Times,* published by HarperCollins. By permission of Rosemary A. Thurber.

JJKR Associates
"Any Human to Another" and "Yet Do I Marvel" by Countee Cullen. Copyrights held by the Amistad Research Center, Tulane University, New Orleans, Louisiana. Administered by JJKR Associates, New York, New York.

Liveright Publishing Corporation
"anyone lived in a pretty how town" and "somewhere I have never travelled, gladly beyond" are reprinted from COMPLETE POEMS: 1904–1962 by E. E. Cummings, Edited by George J. Firmage, by permission of Liveright Publishing Corporation. Copyright © 1926, 1931, 1940, 1954, 1959, 1968, 1991 by the Trustees for the E. E. Cummings Trust. Copyright © 1979, 1985 by George Firmage. "Those Winter Sundays" Reprinted from ANGLE OF ASCENT New and Selected Poems by Robert Hayden, with the permission of Liveright Publishing Corporation. Copyright © 1966 by Robert Hayden. "Storm Ending" Reprinted from CANE by Jean Toomer, with the permission of Liveright Publishing Corporation. Copyright 1923 by Boni & Liveright, renewed 1951 by Jean Toomer.

Ellen C. Masters
The poems "Lucinda Matlock" and "Petit, the Poet" are from *Spoon River Anthology* by Edgar Lee Masters. Originally published by the Macmillan Company. Permission granted by Ellen C. Masters.

New Directions Publishing Corporation
"The Secret" Denise Levertov: POEMS 1960–1967. Copyright © 1966 by Denise Levertov. Reprinted by permission of New Directions Publishing Corp. "In a Station of the Metro" and "The River-Merchant's Wife: A Letter." Ezra Pound: PERSONAE. Copyright ©1926 by Ezra Pound. Reprinted by permission of New Directions Publishing Corp. "The Dance," "The Red Wheelbarrow," and "This Is Just to Say." William Carlos Williams: COLLECTED POEMS: 1909–1939, Volume I.. Copyright ©1938 by New Directions Publishing Corp. Reprinted by permission of New Directions Publishing Corp.

Penguin Books USA, Inc.
"The Book of the Grotesque," from *Winesburg, Ohio,* by Sherwood Anderson. Copyright 1919 by B.W. Huebsch; © 1947 by Eleanor Copenhaver Anderson. Used by permission of Viking Penguin, a division of Penguin Books USA, Inc. "The Flower-Fed Buffaloes", from GOING TO THE STARS by Vachel Lindsay. Copyright 1926 by D. Appleton & Co., renewed 1954 by Elizabeth C. Lindsay. A Hawthorn Book. Used by permission of Dutton Children's Books, a division of Penguin Books USA, Inc. Excerpt from *The Crucible* by Arthur Miller. Copyright

1952, 1953, 1954, renewed © 1980 by Arthur Miller. Used by permission of Viking Penguin, a division of Penguin Books USA, Inc. Excerpt from *The Grapes of Wrath* by John Steinbeck. Copyright 1939 by John Steinbeck, renewed © 1969 by John Steinbeck. Used by permission of Viking Penguin, a division of Penguin Books USA, Inc.

Princeton University Press
Taylor, Edward; HUSWIFERY. © 1943 by Princeton University Press. Reprinted by permission of Princeton University Press.

Random House, Inc.
From INVISIBLE MAN by Ralph Ellison. Copyright 1947, 1948, 1952 by Ralph Ellison. Reprinted by permission of Random House, Inc. "Address upon Receiving the Nobel Prize for Literature" From ESSAYS SPEECHES & PUBLIC LETTERS by William Faulkner, edited by James B. Meriwether. Copyright © 1950 by William Faulkner. Copyright © 1965 by Random House, Inc. Reprinted by permission of Random House, Inc. From THE GLASS MENAGERIE by Tennessee Williams. Copyright © 1945 by Tennessee Williams and Edwina D. Williams. Reprinted by permission of Random House, Inc.

Alberto Ríos
"The Lesson of Walls" from *Five Indiscretions* (Sheep Meadow Press), © 1985 by Alberto Ríos. Reprinted by permission of author. All rights reserved.

Simon and Schuster, Inc.
"Miniver Cheevy" from THE TOWN DOWN THE RIVER by Edwin Arlington Robinson (New York: Charles Scribner's Sons, 1910) "Mr. Flood's Party" Reprinted with permission of Simon & Schuster, Inc. from COLLECTED POEMS OF EDWIN ARLINGTON ROBINSON. Copyright 1921 by Edwin Arlington Robinson, renewed 1949 by Ruth Nivison. "Richard Cory" from THE CHILDREN OF THE NIGHT by Edwin Arlington Robinson (New York: Charles Scribner's Sons, 1987) Reprinted with permission of Scribner, Division of Simon & Schuster, Inc., from THE GREAT GATSBY ("Authorized Text") by F. Scott Fitzgerald. Copyright 1925 Charles Scribner's Sons. Copyright renewed 1953 by Frances Scott Fitzgerald Lanahan. Copyright © 1991, 1992 by Eleanor Lanahan, Matthew J. Bruccoli, and Samuel J. Lanahan as Trustees u/a dated 7/3/75, Created by Frances Scott Fitzgerald Smith. "A Clean, Well-Lighted Place." Reprinted with permission of Scribner, an imprint of Simon & Schuster, Inc., from WINNER TAKE NOTHING by Ernest Hemingway. Copyright 1933 Charles Scribner's Sons. Copyright renewed © 1961 by Mary Hemingway. "Poetry" Reprinted with permission of Simon & Schuster, Inc. from COLLECTED POEMS OF MARIANNE MOORE. Copyright 1935 by Marianne Moore, renewed 1963 by Marianne Moore and T. S. Eliot.
Reprinted with the permission of Scribner, an imprint of Simon & Schuster, Inc. from THE AGE OF INNOCENCE by Edith Wharton. Copyright 1920 D. Appleton and Company; copyright renewed 1948 William R. Tyler.

Sterling Lord Literistic, Inc.
Crisis, No.1, by Thomas Paine. From THE SELECTED WORK OF TOM PAINE, edited by Howard Fast. Reprinted by permission of Sterling Lord Literistic, Inc. Copyright © 1945 by Howard Fast.

Sunstone Press
"Song of the Sky Loom" This poem from SONGS OF THE TEWA by Joseph Spinden appears courtesy of Sunstone Press, Box 2321, Santa Fe, NM 87504-2321, USA.

Syracuse University Press
From "The Iroquois Constitution" from Arthur C. Parker, "The Constitution of the Five Nations" in *Parker on the Iroquois,* edited with an introduction by William N. Fenton. Syracuse, N.Y.: Syracuse University Press, 1968. By permission of the publisher.

University of North Carolina Press
"To S. M., a Young African Painter, on Seeing His Works" and "To the Right Honorable William, Earl of Dartmouth." Reprinted from THE POEMS OF PHILLIS WHEATLEY. Revised and enlarged edition. Edited by Julian D. Mason, Jr. Copyright © 1989 by the University of North Carolina Press. Used by permission of the publisher.

University Press of New England
James Dickey, "For the last Wolverine" from *Poems 1957–1967* © 1978 by James Dickey, Wesleyan University Press by permission of University Press of New England.

University Press of Virginia
"A Mystery of Heroism" from *The Complete Works of Stephen Crane, Volume 60,* edited by Fredson Bowers (Charlottesville: Virginia 1969) Used by permission of the University Press of Virginia.

Wieser and Wieser, Inc.
"Auto Wreck" by Karl Shapiro. Copyright © 1968 by Karl Shapiro and appears by arrangement with Weiser and Weiser, Inc. 118 East 25th Street, New York, NY 10010.

William Morrow & Company, Inc.
Text of "Winter Poem" from MY HOUSE by Nikki Giovanni. Copyright © 1972 by Nikki Giovanni. By permission of William Morrow and Company, Inc. Text pgs. 66–70 from BLUES PEOPLE by LeRoi Jones. Copyright © 1963 by LeRoi Jones. By permission of William Morrow and Company, Inc.

The Estate of William Stafford
"A Story That Could Be True" and "Traveling Though the Dark," by William Stafford. Copyright © 1978 William Stafford, from *Stories That Could Be True* (Harper & Row). Reprinted by permission of The Estate of William Stafford.

James Worley
Selected poems by James Worley reprinted by permission of the author.

Yale University Press
"Sinners in the Hands of an Angry God" by Jonathan Edwards from *Images Or Shadows of Divine Things* (The Works of Jonathan Edwards). By permission of Yale University Press.

Every effort has been made to trace the ownership of all copyrighted selections found in this book. Omissions brought to our attention will be corrected in subsequent editions.